THE GUINNESS BOOK OF

answers

the complete reference handbook

tenth *edition*

GUINNESS

Editor: Clive Carpenter
Editorial assistants: Kathy Milligan, Hal Norman and Kim Chesher
Design: Amanda Ward
Layout: Amanda Ward and Amanda Sedge
Cover design: D.H. Publicity
Index: Marijka Skipp
Production manager: Chris Lingard
Information systems manager: Alex Reid
Artwork, maps and diagrams: Ad Vantage Studios, Rhoda and Robert Burns, Pat Gibbons, Peter Harper, The Maltings Partnership

10th Edition

First published 1995

Reprint 10 9 8 7 6 5 4 3 2 1 0

Published in Great Britain by Guinness Publishing Ltd,
33 London Road, Enfield, Middlesex

Printed and bound in Great Britain by the Bath Press, Bath

British Library Cataloguing in Publication Data
The Guinness Book of Answers
1. Miscellaneous facts
1. The Book of Answers
032.02

ISBN 0-85112-659-6

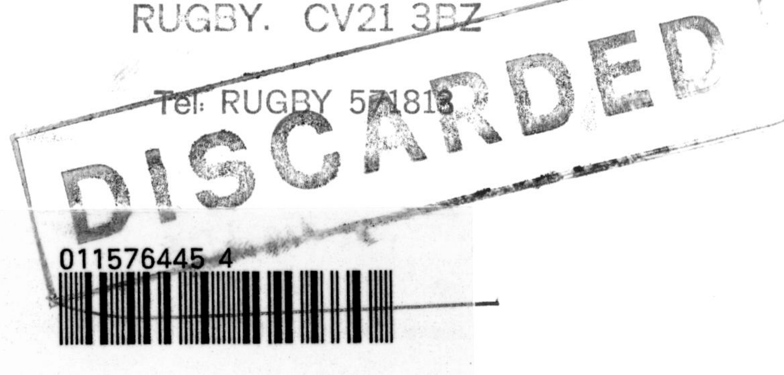
DISCARDED
011576445 4

Contributors

John Arblaster
Art Sales Index
Ephraim Borowski, University of Glasgow
Antonia Boström
Martin Caiger-Smith, Hayward Gallery, London
Clive Carpenter
Gill Carpenter, University of Sussex
Kim Chesher
Andrew Clifford
Robert Dearling
Beryl Dixon
Ben Dupré
Di Ellis
Dr David Evans, University of Exeter
John Foley
Dr Trevor Ford, formerly of the University of Leicester
Beatrice Frei
Tim Furniss
Professor Brian Gardiner, King's College, London
Professor Frank Glockling, University of Oxford
Dr Martin Godfrey, GP Magazine
The late Dr Beverley Halstead
John Harding
Nigel Hawkes of The Times
Nick Heath-Brown
Dr Peter Hobson, Brunel the University of West London
Ingrid Holford
Will Hutchings
ICOREC (International Consultancy on Religion, Education and Culture, Manchester Metropolitan University)
Dr Gareth Jones, University of Strathclyde
Colin Juneman
Dr Kim Knott, University of Leeds
Howard Loxton
Norris McWhirter
Anne Marshall
John Marshall
Peter Matthews
Richard Milbank
Dr D.M.P. Mingos, Imperial College, London
David J. Nash, University of Brighton
Stewart Newport
Dr Chris Pass, University of Bradford
Tina Persaud
Dr John Pimlott, The Royal Military Academy Sandhurst
Rev. Will Pratt
Dr Jonathon Ree, Middlesex University
Aileen Reid
Alex Reid
Andrew Scott, University College, London
Paola Simoneschi
Ian Sinclair
Dr Elizabeth Sirreyeh, University of Leeds
Dr Peter J. Smith, The Open University
Dr John Sommerville, MRCP, MRCGP
David Sweet
Michael J.H. Taylor
Mona Taylor
Dr David Thomas, University of Sheffield
Dr Francis Toase, The Royal Military Academy Sandhurst
Dr John Walton, University College of Wales, Aberystwyth
David Wells
Dr Richard Weston
Andrew Wood
Douglas Wyn, University of Strathclyde

Grateful thanks for additional help is made to:
The (Catholic) Bishop's Conferences of England and Wales, of Ireland, and of Scotland
The Church of Scotland
The Department of the Environment
Barbara Edwards
The Foreign and Commonwealth Office
General Synod of the Church of England
The Information Office of the European Union
The Kennel Club
The Local Government Commission
The Northern Ireland Office
The Novosti News Agency
Phobias Confidential
The Royal Automobile Club
The Scottish Office
The United Nations Information Centre
The Welsh Office

Contents

Contents

CONTENTS

Contents

SPACE AND TIME

The Nature of the Universe

UNITS OF ASTRONOMY

The large-scale units used in astronomy are based on the properties of the Earth's orbit.

The astronomical unit is the average distance from the Earth to the Sun as defined in 1938. The current value is 149,597,871 km (92,955,807 mi).

The light year is a unit used to measure great distance. In 1888, the light year was first defined as the equivalent of the distance travelled by light in one mean solar year. It is more accurately defined as the distance travelled by light – velocity 299,792·458 km/s (186,282·397 mi/sec) in vacuo – in a tropical year of 365·24219878 mean solar days; that is, 9,460,528,405,000 km (5,878,499,814,000 mi).

The parsec is the unit by which distance to the nearest stars is measured using the parallax method. By the parallax method, the position of a star is viewed from the Earth at intervals of six months during which time the Earth has moved from one side of its orbit to the other and the star will appear to have moved against a background of more distant or 'fixed' stars. The parallax angle – given in seconds of arc – is one half of the angle subtended by the star across the orbit baseline. Using the parallax angle and the Earth's diameter, the distance to the star can be calculated. The parsec – short for parallax in seconds of arc – is therefore the distance at which an object would exhibit a parallax of one second of arc (i.e. one thirty-six thousandth of a degree) and is equal to 206,264·806 astronomical units or 3·2616 light years (30,856,776,000,000 km or 19,173,511,000,000 mi). With the exception of the Sun, no stars are at present closer than one parsec.

COSMOLOGY

The *universe* is the sum total of all that exists, or has existed, both in space and time. *Cosmology* is the science of the cosmos or universe. Theoretical cosmology became possible in the 20th century when Albert Einstein's special (1905) and general (1915) theories (see Physical Sciences, Quantum Theory and Relativity) combined space and time into an indivisible four-dimensional space-time continuum. However, theoretical views as to how the universe began are based on 20th-century advances in observational astronomy and high energy physics.

The expansion of the universe

In 1868, the English astronomer Sir William Huggins (1824–1910) noted that the spectra of some stars were displaced towards the red end of the spectrum (red-shifted), but others were shifted towards the violet end (blue-shifted). This was interpreted as a Doppler effect, the change in the frequency of sound waves, light and electromagnetic radiation when the source and the observer become closer or more distant. This was first described in 1842 by the Austrian physicist Christian Doppler to explain why the noise from a moving vehicle appears to change pitch as it passes. The French physicist Armand Fizeau extended the principle to light waves in 1848.

Stars that are moving away from us are red-shifted; stars that are approaching us are blue-shifted. Red shift on a cosmological scale was discovered in 1912 by the American astronomer Vesto Melvin Slipher (1875–1969), who noted that nearly all nebulae – clouds of dust or gas – were highly red-shifted and only a few, including the Andromeda nebula, were blue-shifted. In 1924, the American astronomer Edwin Powell Hubble (1889–1953) was able to show that these nebulae were, in fact, galaxies in their own right.

Extensive measurements of galactic red-shifts (z) and magnitudes – and estimates of distance – led Hubble in 1929 to propose that the speed of recession of a galaxy (v) was related to its distance (r) by the relationship $v = z.c = H.r$, where c is the velocity of light and H is a constant known as the *Hubble Constant.* This formula is flawed when the red-shift exceeds 1 since it implies that v exceeds c but this problem was solved by modifying the formula to take into account Einstein's Special Relativity Doppler Formula:

$$z = \left[\frac{c+v}{c-v}\right]^{\frac{1}{2}} - 1$$

Hubble's Law states that the distance to a distant galaxy is in direct proportion to its observed velocity of recession. This indicates a uniformly expanding universe and implies that the age of the universe is in inverse proportion to c – the constant of proportionality – in the formula above. Current determinations of Hubble's Constant vary between 50 and 90 km/s/Mpc (kilometres per second per megaparsec). The median value of 70 km/s/Mpc agrees with the current estimated age of the universe of 14,000 million years, which has been calculated by *cosmochronology* (a measure of the relative abundance of radioactive nuclei used to determine the timescale for the nucleosynthesis of these nuclei). The median value also accords with estimates of the ages of the stars in the oldest globular clusters.

The big bang theory

The realization that the universe was expanding, and also appeared to have a definable age, led to the suggestion that it may have initially existed as a point-like source or *singularity.* The theory of the expansion of the universe from a cataclysmic event known as the '*big bang*' was originally developed by the Russian mathematician and astronomer Aleksandr Friedmann (1888–1925) and the Belgian astronomer Georges Le Maître (1894–1966). The so-called 'standard model' – based upon their work – could not explain either the present large-scale uniformity of the universe or the smaller scale non-uniformity (i.e. the 'clumping' of matter into galaxies).

These problems were largely overcome by the introduction of the 'inflationary model' by Alan Guth in 1979 and the subsequent suggestion that all parts of the universe were in contact with each other during the initial critical period, but, when it was between 10^{-35} and 10^{-32} seconds old, it underwent a 10^{50} expansion. Subsequent, virtually linear, expansion has occurred until the universe has reached its present size. However, the sudden formation of the universe, which may have resulted from a quantum fluctuation, may only be explicable with the development of a quantum theory for gravity.

It is thought that the initial period lasted from 10^{-45} to 10^{-43} seconds (the Planck Era) when the temperature was 10^{32} K and the radius 10^{-54} cm. At the end of this time, gravity assumed its unique characteristics. After 10^{-35} seconds – when the temperature had dropped to 10^{27} K and the universe had expanded to 10^{-49} cm – the strong force may have separated from the electroweak force and triggered a 10^{50} expansion to a diameter of 10 cm (4 in). However, during the initial expansion period – which lasted until 10^{-32} seconds, the universe supercooled to 10^{22} K, causing the nucleation of matter (quarks and leptons, and an equal number of anti-particles), before returning to 10^{27} K. Particles and anti-particles began to annihilate each other to form photons of radiation. At the end of this period, all of the anti-particles had been destroyed and only one particle of matter per 1000 million present at the beginning remained. (The predominance of matter over anti-matter remains to be explained.)

Protons and neutrons began to form from quarks between 10^{-9} and 0.1 seconds as the temperature fell from 10^{14} K to 10^{10} K, and in the next 1000 seconds surviving neutrons combined with protons to form nuclei of the light elements deuterium, helium and lithium. Beyond this time, free neutrons spontaneously decayed and free protons (hydrogen nuclei) became dominant in the universe. After 100,000 years, the temperature had fallen to 4000 K, and ions and electrons combined together to form atoms. Proto-galaxies began to form when the temperature had fallen to 400 K. The formation of coherent galaxies is calculated to have begun 1000 million years after the big bang.

The 3K microwave background

If the big bang model of the universe is correct, the universe should be filled with a uniform 'sea' of cosmic background radiation that was produced in the very early stages of the creation of the universe and cooled by its expansion. This cosmic background radiation was predicted by George Gamow (1904–68) in 1948 and discovered in the microwave region by Arno Penzias (1933–) and Robert W. Wilson (1936–) in 1965. Relating data for microwave radiation to an energy curve suggests a temperature of 2·73K (–270·42 °C or –454·76 °F), which is virtually the temperature that would be expected if the universe had cooled from the primordial fireball proposed in the big bang theory.

The microwave background radiation appears to be *isotropic*; that is, it has the same physical properties in all directions. However, in April 1992 the COBE satellite detected differences in temperature of the order of parts per million. These have been interpreted as detection of the infinitesimal density fluctuations that caused local gravity instability in the expanding fireball and led to the formation of the proto-galaxies.

The future of the universe

Cosmological models developed by Friedmann (see above), H.P. Robinson and A.G. Walker between 1922 and 1936 suggested that the universe could only have one of three endings.

The first suggestion was that there is insufficient matter in the universe to overcome the expansion. The universe was said to be 'open' and will therefore expand until all the hydrogen has been used up, after which the universe will become 'dead'.

The second possibility envisaged a 'closed' universe in which the amount of matter was sufficient to overcome the expansion of the universe and would eventually cause the universe to collapse back into the singularity from which it came. In this thesis, the possible creation of another universe from the singularity was suggested.

The third suggestion was that the universe is 'flat' – that is, the universe has just enough matter to overcome the expansion and will eventually reach a definite optimum size. However, such a universe will eventually die. Which of these theories is correct will not be known until we are able to determine both the deceleration rate of the expansion of the universe and the exact amount of matter present in it.

The edge of the observable universe

Hubble's Law (see above) states that the speed of a galaxy is proportional to its distance and that when the speed becomes equal to the velocity of light the galaxy is no longer detectable. Such a galaxy is then said to be at the 'edge of the observable universe'. For a Hubble Constant of 70 km/s/Mpc, this is equivalent to a distance of 14,000 million light years. However, for a number of reasons, Hubble's Law breaks down at these large distances – for example, it does not take into account the fact that the universe is decelerating. Many models for assumed values of the deceleration parameter and density parameter would place the furthest galaxies well beyond the distance of 14,000 million light years obtained from Hubble's Law. This limit is in reality only the scale factor, or yardstick, by which the universe is measured. The true size of the universe is unknown because both the deceleration parameter and the density parameter are unknown.

Distances within the universe

The time taken for light to travel to Earth from heavenly bodies may be used as a guide to the size of the universe. In the following list, the times given are surface to surface in the case of nearby objects.

Heavenly body from which light is travelling	*Time taken by light to travel from the heavenly body*
From the Moon (at mean distance)	1.26 sec
From the Sun (at mean distance)	8 min 17 sec
From Pluto (at mean distance)	5 hr 20 min
From the nearest star (Proxima Centauri)	4.22 years
From the centre of our galaxy	26,100 years
From the most distant star in our galaxy (present distance)	63,600 years
From the nearest extra-galactic body (Sagittarius Dwarf galaxy)	82,000 years
From the limit of naked eye vision (Andromeda galaxy)	2,309,000 years
From the most distant quasar known (QSO PC 1247 + 3406)	13,200,000,000 years
From the 'edge of the observable universe'	14,000,000,000 years

GALAXIES

A galaxy is a system of many thousands of millions of stars, together with interstellar gas and dust.

The galaxies resulted from the accumulation of gas on the proto-galaxies that were formed by density fluctuations and gravity instabilities in the expanding primordial fireball. It is thought that they originally consisted only of those elements formed in the big bang (mainly hydrogen and helium).

Most of the first stars formed were probably very large and are thought to have lasted for about one million years. Their destruction in supernova explosions led to the formation of the heavier elements in the form of cosmic dust. (Today, cosmic dust is thought to compose no more than 2% of all matter.)

The number of galaxies in the universe is estimated to be between 100 billion and a trillion (10^{11} to 10^{12}). Each galaxy contains about 100 billion stars.

The total number of stars is calculated to be between 10^{22} and 10^{23}. Recent observations of the large-scale structure of the universe suggest that the galaxies may have been formed on the 'surfaces' of 'bubbles', each about 100 million light years in diameter. In the process, the centres of the bubbles became virtually devoid of matter.

The classification of galaxies

In 1924, Hubble compared the magnitude changes of variable stars in our own galaxy (*Cepheid variables*) with similar stars in the Andromeda nebula. By so doing, he established that the distance to Andromeda is so great that it must be an independent galaxy. Having established the existence of other galaxies, Hubble formulated a classification of galaxies based upon their appearance. Hubble distinguished three types – elliptical, spiral and irregular galaxies.

Elliptical galaxies (E) appear as luminous elliptical discs with a smooth distribution of light. Their surface brightness decreases outwards from the centre. Elliptical galaxies are further divided into types E0–7, according to their aspect in the sky. For example, E0 types are seen face on as circular discs, while E7 types are seen almost edge on.

Spiral galaxies are either normal (S), in which spiral-shaped arms emerge directly from the nucleus, or barred (SB), in which the arms originate from a 'bar' that appears through the centre of the galaxy. Spiral galaxies are further divided into types a, b and c, depending on the extent of the 'unwinding' of the arms and on the relative clarity of the arms and the nucleus. Lenticular (lens-shaped) galaxies (SO) appear to be intermediate between the elliptical and spiral types.

Irregular galaxies do not appear to have a definite structure. However, two types are distinguished – Irr I, which appears to be an extension of the spiral type Sc and includes the nearby Magellanic Clouds, and Irr II, which includes all galaxies that are peculiarly shaped.

Cold dark matter

The dynamics of galaxies suggests that the mass of any galaxy, determined from the amount of light that it emits, is only about one-tenth of its true mass. This 'missing mass' – or more correctly 'missing light' – is called Cold Dark Matter. There is speculation as to whether Cold Dark Matter is an exotic form of matter unknown on Earth or ordinary matter (such as very cool stars) that are too dim to be detected by current astronomical instruments.

Quasars

There is increasing evidence that the centres of regularly-shaped galaxies are powered by massive *black holes*, although our own galaxy does not appear to contain such an object.

Quasars, (short for *quasi-stellar sources*) are very luminous distant objects characterized by having extremely red-shifted spectra.

Originally considered to be active nuclei of distant galaxies, Hubble Space Telescope observations have now shown that many of these quasars are just naked cores without surrounding material so the energetic nature of quasars remains unresolved. The most luminous object in the sky – quasar HS 1946 + 7658 – is at least 1.5×10^{15} times more luminous than the Sun.

Over 7200 quasars are now known. The most remote object currently known is quasar PC 1247 + 3406, which is at a distance of 13,200 million light years.

The Milky Way Galaxy

Although only seen edge-on, our own Milky Way galaxy is considered to be a typical spiral galaxy. It is about 75,000 light years in diameter and is a member of the ellipsoidal so-called 'Local Group' of about 20 galaxies.

The Local Group has a maximum extent of about six million light years. Its two dominant members are our own Milky Way galaxy and the Andromeda galaxy, which are at either end of its diameter. These two galaxies are approaching each other, with the stronger pull being exerted by the Andromeda galaxy. (Although these two galaxies will be closer within several thousand million years, they will not collide.)

The Local Group is part of the 'Local Supercluster', whose centre of gravity is close to the most prominent member of the group, the Virgo cluster. However, the centre of gravity is being drawn towards the even more massive Hydra-Centaurus supercluster, and both are being drawn towards a vast concentration of galaxies known as the 'Great Attractor'.

The Sun is located in the Orion spiral arm in the outer regions of the Milky Way at a distance of 26,100 light years from the centre of the galaxy.

The orbital velocity of the Sun and a large number of nearby stars have been averaged to a *local standard of rest* of 220 km/s (137 mi/sec) which leads to a *cosmic year* (the time to orbit the galaxy) of about 220 million years. The Sun's current motion is actually 17 km/s (11 mi/sec) faster than the local standard of rest. The principal galaxies, stars and constellations visible in the Northern sky and the Southern sky are shown on the star charts on p. 12 and p. 13 respectively.

The Sky at Night
The Northern Hemisphere

POPULAR NAMES OF CONSTELLATIONS

Aquarius the Water-carrier, **Aquila** the Eagle, **Aries** the Ram, **Auriga** the Charioteer or Waggoner, **Boötes** the Herdsman, **Cancer** the Crab, **Capricorn** the Goat, **Centaurus** the Centaur, **Cygnus** the Swan, **Gemini** the Twins (Castor and Pollux), **Leo** the Lion, **Libra** the Scales, **Lyra** the Lyre, **Orion** the Hunter, **Pisces** the Fishes, **Sagittarius** the Archer, **Scorpio** the Scorpion, **Taurus** the Bull, **Ursa Major** the Great Bear; also known as the Plough (UK) or the Big Dipper (USA), **Ursa Minor** the Little Bear; also known as the Little Dipper (USA), **Virgo** the Virgin

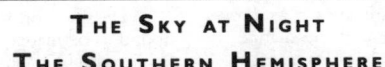

POPULAR NAMES OF STARS
Pleiades the Seven Sisters, **Praesepe** (part of Cancer) the Beehive, **Sirius** the Dog Star

STARS

Stars – of which our Sun is an example – are accretions of gas that radiate energy produced by nuclear-fusion reactions. Stars may be up to 200 times more massive than the Sun but below 0·08 solar masses either fusion cannot occur or if it does then only sporadically and such failed stars are known as *brown dwarfs*. The properties of a star and the manner in which it evolves depend principally on its mass.

The magnitude scale

Magnitude is a measure of stellar brightness. On the scale of magnitude, a first magnitude star is exactly 100 (or 2·5118865) times brighter than a sixth magnitude star. Therefore, the light of a star of any magnitude has a ratio of 2·511886 to that of a star of the next magnitude on the scale.

Nearby bodies that are exceptionally bright have a magnitude that is expressed as a negative quantity. The Sun – the brightest object in our sky - has a magnitude of –26·75, while the magnitudes of the Moon and Venus are respectively –12·74 and –4·40. At the other extreme, the faintest stars that can be seen on a clear night have a magnitude of +6. However, all of these values are the 'apparent magnitude' (mV) as viewed from Earth. For purposes of comparison, the intrinsic brightness – *the absolute magnitude* – must be known. The absolute magnitude is defined as the magnitude that a star would have if it were to be viewed at a distance of 10 parsecs (32·6 light years). On this basis, the Sun's absolute magnitude would be +4·82, or a four billionfold reduction in observed brightness. The absolute magnitude is related to the apparent magnitude and distance in parsecs (d) by means of the equation:

$$M_V = m_V + 5 - 5 \times \log(d)$$

Stellar classification

The colour of a star gives an indication of its temperature. Stars are classed according to their spectra in a sequence of decreasing temperature. Hot stars (known as type O) are blue, while cool stars (type M) are red. Stars closest to type O are called 'early'; those closest to type M are called 'late'. Each spectral type is subdivided into ten grades, from 0 (early) to 9 (late). On this basis, the Sun is classified as a type G2 star. The types of star according to the *Henry Draper stellar classification* are:

Type O the hottest blue stars with surface temperatures between 25,000 and 40,000 °C (45,000 and 72,000 °F) and spectra dominated by ionized helium.

Type B hot blue stars with temperatures between 11,000 and 25,000 °C (20,000 and 45,000 °F) and spectra dominated by neutral helium.

Type A blue-white stars with temperatures between 7500 and 11,000 °C (13,500 and 20,000 °F) and spectra dominated by hydrogen, with some ionized metal lines present.

Type F white stars with temperatures between 6000 and 7500 °C (10,800 and 13,500 °F) and spectra dominated by neutral metal lines.

Type G yellow stars with temperatures between 5000 and 6000 °C (9000 and 10,800 °F) and spectra dominated by many metal lines.

Type K orange stars with temperatures between 3500 and 5000 °C (6300 and 9000 °F) and spectra dominated by neutral metal lines and some molecular bands.

Type M red stars with temperatures between 3000 and 3500 °C (5400 and 6300 °F) and spectra dominated by molecular bands.

This classification was introduced in 1920, but it was found to be inadequate as it assumes that all the stars in a particular class share identical characteristics. Therefore, in 1937, an extra dimension was added, based on stellar luminosity. This extra element classifies stars in groups ranging from type I (the 'supergiant' stars) to type VI (the 'sub-dwarfs'). Type V comprises dwarf stars, a certain size of star that is undergoing normal stellar evolution – this is known as a *main sequence* star. The full classification of the Sun – a yellow dwarf star type – is G2 V.

Stellar evolution

Stars form from the gravitational contraction of a gas and dust cloud. A central core forms rapidly and the remainder of the surrounding cloud falls on to the core to form a star. In the case of a star the size of the Sun, the whole process is thought to take less than one million years. The continuing gravitational collapse of the star is accompanied by an increase in temperature of the core, which eventually becomes hot enough and dense enough to initiate the nuclear fusion of hydrogen to helium. The vast amount of energy produced counteracts the gravitational collapse and the star achieves a state of equilibrium that can last up to 10,000 million years in the case of a star of the size of the Sun or perhaps only one million years in the case of a much more massive star.

Eventually, a critical amount of hydrogen will have been used up and fusion reactions will stop in the helium-rich core. However, energy is still radiated from the surface, draining energy from the star. In an attempt to re-establish equilibrium, the core contracts, releasing gravitational energy. This results in fusion reactions in the hydrogen envelope that surrounds the core. The 'shell' of the star swells and, because of the reduced temperature, glows red rather than white, and the star becomes a *red giant*. The red giant stage lasts up to 100 million years in the case of a solar mass star such as the Sun, but for much less time in the case of a more massive star. During this stage, the core continues to contract and heat until it reaches a temperature at which the fusion of helium to carbon is triggered. Subsequent developments largely depend upon the mass of the star

White dwarfs may eventually be formed from stars whose mass is similar to that of the Sun. In these stars, the temperatures are not high enough to trigger the fusion of carbon. The core continues to contract until prevented from doing so further when the electron fields surrounding the nuclei of the atoms becomes compressed. The surrounding envelope continues to expand and cool, and eventually separates from the core to form a transparent shell known as a *planetary nebula*, revealing the core as a small white star – a white dwarf. White dwarfs may be as small as the Earth but they possess a mass equivalent to that of the Sun. Therefore, the density of a white dwarf may be up to 100,000 times that of the Earth. White dwarfs continue to shine for several thousand million years, simply by using up the thermal energy that was stored up after the core collapsed. In time, however, they cool completely.

Neutron stars and pulsars may eventually be formed from stars of between eight and 50 solar masses. In these large stars, the contraction of the core leads to temperatures in excess of 1000 million °C (1800 million °F). This causes carbon and other elements to undergo fusion reactions until iron is formed and the core collapses. The outer layers of the envelope also collapse on to the core leading to the formation of very heavy elements. The energy involved is so great that the outer layers are blown back into space, leaving a very bright star known as a *supernova*. The ejection of this material is accompanied by radiation so intense that a supernova can briefly outshine a galaxy. The remaining core, which weighs 1–3 solar masses, is only 10–30 km (6–20 mi) in diameter. Its density is 10^{14} times that of the Earth. Such a density is possible because the electrons in the atoms collapse on to the nuclei and react with the protons to form neutrons. The whole star can be considered to be one gigantic nucleus and is known as a *neutron star*.

Some neutron stars – known as *pulsars* – spin. Their rotation can be detected as a pulse caused by an interaction between a star's emission of radiation and its magnetic field. Pulsars were first detected in 1967. A group of very fast rotating pulsars – known as *millisecond pulsars* – were discovered in 1982. The faster rotating pulsars are expected to be stable for several thousand million years. The spin rates of millisecond pulsars are so stable that it has been proposed that they could be used as 'stellar clocks'.

Black holes and quark stars may eventually be formed from stars in excess of 50 solar masses. In these very large stars, the collapse of the core is so extreme that the whole mass collapses into a single point or singularity. The intense gravitational field of such a star extends a 'sphere of influence' into space and prevents radiation (i.e. light) from escaping. In the case of a singularity of ten solar masses, the sphere of influence extends to a radius of 29·5 km (18·3 mi). Such a singularity would appear as a *black hole*, with a diameter of 59 km (37 mi).

Black holes can only be detected indirectly, by the X-rays given off when matter from a companion star is dragged into a black hole. Currently, the only black hole for which strong evidence exists is the central star of the binary system V404, which is 500 light years distant in the constellation Cygnus. This star appears to have a mass at least 12 times greater than the Sun and is therefore above the maximum value that has been calculated for a neutron star. Related to this inconsistency, there is increasing evidence that core collapse may have to overcome one further quantum barrier – the *quark barrier* – before a singularity can be formed. It is thought that the core collapses into a 'quark soup' of immense density, but, because detection methods are so indirect, it may not be possible to distinguish between these quark stars and black holes. It may be that only supermassive stars can collapse into black holes.

Multiple and variable stars

At least 75% of all stars are members of a binary or multiple star system, in which physically-related stars orbit one another under the influence of their mutual gravitational attraction. *Binary stars* consist of two stars each orbiting around their common centre of gravity. *Visual binaries* can be identified as two stars by means of a telescope. In the case of *astrometric binaries*, only one star is revealed by telescope, but the peculiar motion of that star indicates that it is accompanied by an unseen companion. *Unresolved binaries* may be detected spectroscopically either as periodic oscillations in the lines of the spectra or as two superimposed spectra. They may also be detected by regular changes in the apparent brightness of the system when the stars periodically eclipse one another.

The variations observed in multiple star systems mimic true *variable stars*, which experience changes in brightness. In the case of young stars, such changes are irregular and may occur because these stars are still trying to achieve thermal equilibrium. In the case of old stars, irregular changes represent the final stages of the process of decay. *Pulsating stars* experience regular variations in brightness caused by the periodic expansion and contraction of their atmospheres. The Cepheid variables, examples of this type, undergo periodic changes in brightness that can be directly related to their absolute magnitudes. Based on this fact, observations of the pulsation periods are apparent magnitudes of similar stars in other galaxies can be used to estimate their absolute magnitudes and hence their distances.

METEORITES

When a meteoroid – consisting of broken fragments originating from either comets or asteroids, and ranging in size from fine dust to bodies several km in diameter – becomes visible from Earth it is referred to as a meteor. When it penetrates to the Earth's surface it is known as a meteorite. Up to 150 meteorites – which may be either stony (aerolite) or metallic (siderite) – fall to the land surface of the Earth each year. A 'shooting star' is a tiny meteorite that burns up as it penetrates the atmosphere.

A meteorite shower is a 'swarm' of separate meteorites that arrive on the surface of the Earth at the same time. Such an occurrence is probably produced by the disintegration of a large meteorite at considerable altitude. Meteorite showers may contain many separate bodies – the record is held by an estimated 100,000 bodies falling at Pulutsk, Poland, in 1868.

Largest known meteorites

Location	Found	Weight
Hoba West[1] (Namibia)	1920	59 tonnes
Cape York[2] (Greenland)	1897	30.9 tonnes
Bacubirito (Mexico)	1863	27 tonnes
Mbosi (Tanzania)	1930	25 tonnes
Armanty (Mongolia)	not known	20 tonnes

[1] The meteorite found at Hoba West is a block 2·75 m (9 ft) long by 2·43m (8 ft) broad.

[2] Known as the 'Tent' meteorite – and to the Eskimos as Abnighito – this is the largest meteorite exhibited in any museum. Discovered by the expedition of Commander (later Rear Admiral) Peary on the west coast of Greenland, this meteorite is now displayed at the Hayden Planetarium in New York City, USA.

THE NEAREST STARS

Over the next 100,000 years the nearest approach to the Sun by any stars will be to within 2·84 light years by the binary system Alpha Centauri in AD 29700 (N.B. present distance 4·35 light years).

Name	*Distance in light years*	*Visual magnitude Apparent*	*Absolute*	*Brightness on scale Sun = 1*
Proxima Centauri	4·22	11·05	15·49	0·000 056
Alpha Centauri	4·35	*A* –0·01 B 1·33	*A* 4·37 B 5·71	*A* 1·6 B 0·5
Barnard's Star	5·98	9·54	13·22	0·000 46
Wolf 359	7·75	13·53	16·65	0·000 019
Lalande 21185	8·22	7.50	10.49	0·0056
Luyten 726-8*	8·43	*A* 12·52 *B* 13·02	*A* 15·46 *B* 15·96	*A* 0·000 058 *B* 0·000 037
Sirius	8·65	*A* –1·46 *B* 8·68	*A* 1.42 *B* 11.56	*A* 24·0 *B* 0·0021
Ross 154	9·45	10·6	13·3	0·000 42
Ross 248	10·4	12·29	14·77	0·000 11
Epsilon Eridani	10·8	3·73	6·13	0·31
Ross 128	10·9	11·10	13·47	0·000 36
61 Cygni	11·1	*A* 5·22 *B* 6·03	*A* 7·56 *B* 8·37	*A* 0·084 *B* 0·040
Epsilon Indi	11·2	4·68	7·00	0·14
Luyten 789-6	11·2	*A* 12·7 *B* 13·4	*A* 15·0 *B* 15·7	*A* 0·000 089 *B* 0·000 047
Groombridge 34	11·2	*A* 8·08 *B* 11·06	*A* 10·39 *B* 13·37	*A* 0·0062 *B* 0·000 40
Procyon	11·4	*A* 0·38 *B* 10·7	*A* 2·65 *B* 13·0	*A* 7·7 *B* 0·000 56
Sigma 2398	11·6	*A* 8·90 *B* 9·69	*A* 11·15 *B* 11·94	*A* 0·0031 *B* 0·0015
Lacaille 9352	11·7	7·36	9·59	0·013
Giglas 51–15	11·7	14·81	17·03	0·000 014
Tau Ceti	11·8	3·50	5·71	0·46
Luyten's Star	12·3	9·82	11·94	0·0015
Luyten 725–32	12·5	12·04	14·12	0·000 20
Lacaille 8760	12·5	6·67	8·74	0·028
Kapteyn's Star	12·7	8·81	10·85	0·0041
Kruger 60	12·9	*A* 9·85 *B* 11·3	*A* 11·87 *B* 13·3	*A* 0·000 16 *B* 0·000 42

* The B star companion is known as UV Ceti.

THE BRIGHTEST STARS

Rank	Name	Bayer designations	Visual magnitude Apparent	Absolute	Brightness on scale (Sun = 1)	Distance in light years
1	Sirius	α Canis Majoris	–1·46*	+1·4	24	8·7
2	Canopus[1]	α Carinae	–0·72	–8·5	220,000	1200
3	Rigel Kentaurus[1]	α Centauri	–0·27**	+4·1**	A 1.6 B 0.5	4·2
4	Arcturus	α Bootis	–0·04	–0·1	98	34
5	Vega	α Lyrae	+0·03	+0·5	56	26
6	Capella	α Aurigae	+0·08**	–0·6**	A 87 B 69	45
7	Rigel	β Orionis	+0·12	–7·1	60,000	900
8	Procyon	α Canis Minoris	+0·38	+2·7	7·7	11·4
9	Achernar[1]	α Eridani	+0·46	–1·6	390	85
10	Betelgeuse	α Orionis	+0·50 v	–5·6 v, s	15,000	310
11	Hadar (Agena)[1]	β Centauri	+0·61	–5·1	9900	460
12	Altair	α Aquilae	+0·77	+2·3	11	16
13	Aldebaran	α Tauri	+0·85 v	–0·8 v	180	68
14	Acrux	α Crucis	+0·87**	–4·3**	A 2900 B1900	360
15	Antares	α Scorpii	+0·96 v	–4·7 v, s	6700	330
16	Spica	α Virginis	+0·98	–3·5	2200	260
17	Pollux	β Geminorum	+1·14	+1·0	35	35
18	Fomalhaut	α Piscis Austrini	+1·16	+2·0	14	22
19	Deneb	α Cygni	+1·25	–7·5	88,000	1800
20	Mimosa	β Crucis	+1·25	–5·0 s	8900	425
21	Regulus	α Leonis	+1·35	–0·7	170	85
22	Adhara	ε Canaris Majoris	+1·50	–4·4	5000	490

* The apparent visual magnitude of Sirius will reach a maximum of –1·67 by AD 61000.
[1] Not visible from the British Isles.
** Combined magnitude for a double star system.
v Average value for very variable magnitude.
s Absolute magnitude estimated from spectroscopic data alone.

The Solar System

THE AGE AND FORMATION OF THE SOLAR SYSTEM

Meteoric evidence suggests that the solar system is 4540 million years old. It is believed to have been formed in less than 25 million years from a globe of gas and dust that consisted mainly of hydrogen, but also included helium (about 25% of the total) and heavier elements (2%).

During coalescence, the globe started to rotate and flatten. The central core rotated faster and therefore became denser than the outer regions.

In the outer regions, grains of dust and ice, and methane and ammonia, began to collide and coagulate into larger and larger bodies. It is thought that the initial larger bodies so formed were meteroids (see above), followed by small bodies known as planetismals and, finally, by protoplanets. The latter acquired large atmospheres from the reservoir of surrounding gases.

When the central core became dense enough and hot enough to trigger the fusion of hydrogen to helium, the resulting protostar – which was to become the Sun – emitted large amounts of matter and radiant energy in order to establish equilibrium. This emission blew away not only the remnants of the original globe of gas and dust, but also the primordial atmospheres of the inner planets. Most of the large atmospheres of the outer planets remained.

The death of the solar system

In about 5000 million years time the Sun will enter its red giant stage (see above). It will swell up to about 40 million km (25 million mi) in diameter and its luminosity will be so great that the inner planets will be roasted.

The outer layers of the red giant's atmosphere will separate from the core to form a planetary nebula – a diffuse cloud of dust and gases. This separation will leave an exposed core that will contract to a white dwarf with about half of the mass of the present Sun and a diameter about one and half times that of the present planet Earth. The white dwarf star will continue shining for several thousand million years by using the thermal energy that was stored up in the collapse of the core, but eventually it will become a burnt-out cinder.

THE SUN

Our nearest star, the Sun, is at a true distance of 1·00000102 astronomical units or 149,598,023 km (92,955,902 mi) from the Earth. The minimum distance between the Sun and the Earth – the *perihelion* – is 147,098,200 km (91,402,600 mi) – and the maximum distance – the *aphelion* – is 152,097,900 km (94,092,200 mi).

The Sun is classified as a 'yellow dwarf' star of spectral type G2 V. It has a diameter of 1,392,140 km (865,040 mi) – that is 109·13 times greater than that of the Earth – and a mass of $1{\cdot}9889 \times 10^{27}$ tonnes ($1{\cdot}9575 \times 10^{27}$ tons) – that is equivalent to 332,946·04 times the mass of the Earth.

The low density of the Sun, 1·408 g/cm^3, is consistent with its overall composition by mass of 73% hydrogen, 25% helium, and 2% of other elements. Its internal structure consists of a helium-rich core with a central temperature of 15,400,000 °C (27,720,032 °F). The core is surrounded by a radiative layer several hundred thousand kilometres thick, a convective layer several tens of thousands of kilometres thick – in which heat is transported by convection in the form of cells – and a 300 km (200 mi) outer layer - or *photosphere* – which represents the maximum depth of visibility within the Sun and reveals the convective layer cells as a patchwork of granules. The observed overall temperature of the photosphere is 5504 °C (9939 °F).

The photosphere rotates at a rate of 25·38 days (27·28 days as viewed from Earth). This value is determined from observations of *sunspots*, which occur in this layer. The production of sunspots is due to magnetic anomalies. The darkness of the sunspots is actually a contrast effect since they are still very bright, but at a temperature about 2000 °C (3600 °F) less than the overall photosphere temperature.

The Sun's atmosphere consists of a *chromosphere*, which extends about 10,000 km (6000 mi) above the photosphere. It has a low density but a sufficiently high temperature that all elements are in an ionized state – its pinkish hue is due to the presence of ionized hydrogen. The outer atmosphere – or *corona* – appears as a white halo and is an extremely thin gas at a very high temperature (1,000,000 °C/1,800,000 °F).

The most spectacular features – extending from the top of the chromosphere and into the corona – are huge jets of gas flung many thousands of kilometres into space and then looped back into the chromosphere by intense magnetic fields. The extremely high temperature of the corona continuously disperses the Sun's outer atmosphere into space in the form of a plasma of protons and electrons – the 'solar wind' – which permeates the whole of the solar system.

At the centre of the Sun, hydrogen undergoes nuclear fusion. In stars the size of the Sun this occurs mainly by direct proton–proton reaction, i.e. two protons react together to form a deuteron, a positron and a neutrino, then the deuteron reacts with another proton to form helium 3 and a photon, and the cycle is complete when two helium 3 nuclei react together to form helium 4 and two protons.

The net result is that an extremely small amount of matter is converted to energy per cycle but the overall result for the Sun is that four million tonnes/tons of matter is lost per second. However, the high temperature and luminosity of the Sun are not due directly to the nuclear reaction but to the energy generated by the extremely high internal gas pressures required to counteract the intense gravitational contraction pressure that acts on such a large mass.

Acting alone, this source of energy could only supply the Sun's needs for several tens of millions of years, but this effect is extended to 10,000 million years since the nuclear fusion reaction replaces the energy lost through radiation.

The Titius-Bode Rule

A theory by Titius of Wittenberg (Germany) in 1766 – publicized by Johan Bode in 1772 – suggested that the orbital distances adopted by the planets around the Sun may not be arbitrary. Titius noted that the simple series 4, 4 + (3×2^0), 4 + (3×2^1), 4 + (3×2^2) etc, when divided by ten, reproduced the orbital distances in astronomical units of the six known planets. The discovery of Uranus in 1781 also led to a satisfactory agreement. The gap at 2·8 astronomical units (AU) was solved by the discovery of the asteroid Ceres in 1801 and the subsequent discovery of several thousand more asteroids orbiting between 2·3 and 3·3 AU.

However, the total mass of the asteroids is only two-thousandths of the Earth's mass and therefore hardly planet size, but attempts to form a planet in this region may have been disrupted by nearby Jupiter when it may have been an even more massive protoplanet.

Beyond Uranus, the Titius-Bode prediction is that the next two planets would be at 38·8 and 77·2 AU respectively, but giant Neptune is actually at 30·1 AU and small Pluto at 39·5 AU.

Whilst Pluto's orbit would appear to approximate to the Titius-Bode Rule, it is actually very eccentric and highly inclined and therefore the agreement is almost coincidental. However, the fact that the two planets do not obey the prediction has been interpreted as an indication of a catastrophe that may have befallen them during the early history of the solar system.

MEAN ELEMENTS OF THE PLANETARY ORBITS

Planet	*Mean distance from Sun*		*Orbital*	*Orbital*	*Sidereal period*	*Mean orbital velocity*	
	km	*mile*	*eccentricity*	*inclination*	*days*	*km/s*	*mps*
Mercury	57,909,100	35,983,000	0·205631	7° 00′ 18″	87·9693	47·87	29·75
Venus	108,208,600	67,237,700	0·006774	3° 23′ 41″	224·7008	35·02	21·76
Earth	149,598,000	92,955,900	0·016710	–	365·2564	29·78	18·51
Mars	227,939,200	141,634,800	0·093397	1° 50′ 59″	686·9799	24·13	14·99
Jupiter	778,298,400	483,612,200	0·048491	1° 18′ 13″	4332·59	13·06	8·12
Saturn	1,429,394,000	888,184,000	0·055562	2° 29′ 20″	10759·2	9·66	6·00
Uranus	2,875,039,000	1,786,466,000	0·046382	0° 46′ 23″	30688·5	6·81	4·23
Neptune	4,504,450,000	2,798,935,000	0·009456	1° 46′ 13″	60182·3	5·44	3·38
Pluto	5,913,514,000	3,674,490,000	0·248596	17° 09′ 01″	90777·6	4·74	2·94

The minimum (perihelion) and maximum (aphelion) distances from the Sun can be calculated from the mean distance (a) and eccentricity (e) through the formulae: Perihelion = $a(1 - e)$ and Aphelion = $a(1 + e)$.

The mean elements of the seven largest minor planets, or asteroids, are given under individual entries for Ceres, Pallas, Vesta, Hygeia, Davida, Interamnia, and Europa (see below)

PHYSICAL PARAMETERS OF THE PLANETS

Planet		*Diameter*		*Equatorial sidereal rotation period*				*Equatorial inclination*	*Mass**	*Density*
		km	*miles*	*d*	*h*	*m*	*s*		*kg*	*g/cm³*
Mercury		4880	*3032*	58	15	30	33·9	0°	$3·302 \times 10^{23}$	5·428
Venus		12,104	*7521*	R 243	00	26	38	177° 22′	$4·869 \times 10^{24}$	5·244
Earth	Equ.	12,756	*7926*		23	56	04·1	23° 26′	$5·974 \times 10^{24}$	5·515
	Polar	12,714	*7900*							
Mars	Equ.	6794	*4221*	1	00	37	22·7	25° 11′	$6·419 \times 10^{23}$	3·934
	Polar	6752	*4196*							
Jupiter	Equ.	142,984	*88,846*		9	50	30·0	3° 08′	$1·899 \times 10^{27}$	1·325
	Polar	133,708	*83,082*							
Saturn	Equ.	120,536	*74,898*		10	39	22·1	26° 43′	$5·685 \times 10^{26}$	0·685
	Polar	108,718	*67,560*							
Uranus	Equ.	51,118	*31,763*		R 17	14	24	97° 52′	$8·683 \times 10^{25}$	1·271
	Polar	49,946	*31,035*							
Neptune	Equ.	49,532	*30,778*		16	07		28° 19′	$1·024 \times 10^{26}$	1·638
	Polar	48,684	*30,251*							
Pluto		2320	*1442*	R 6	09	17	38	122° 31′	$1·27 \times 10^{22}$	1·95

R = Retrograde motion.
* Mass excluding satellites.

The physical parameters of the seven largest minor planets, or asteroids, are given under individual entries for Ceres, Pallas, Vesta, Hygeia, Davida, Interamnia, and Europa – see below.

PHYSICAL PARAMETERS OF THE PLANETS ON THE SCALE EARTH = 1

Planet	*Equatorial diameter*	*Volume*	*Mass excluding satellites*	*Surface gravity*
Mercury	0·3825	0·0562	0·055 27	0·3769
Venus	0·9488	0·8571	0·815 00	0·9032
Earth	1·0000	1·0000	1·000 00*	1·0000
Mars	0·5326	0·1507	0·107 45	0·3795
Jupiter	11·209	1323·3	317·828	**
Saturn	9·449	766·3	95·161	**
Uranus	4·007	63·09	14·536	**
Neptune	3·883	57·74	17·148	**
Pluto	0·182	0·0060	0·0021	0·064

* The mass of the combined Earth-Moon system is 1·0123 Earth masses. ** Not comparable for the giant gas planets as they do not have a solid surface. The equatorial diameters of the seven largest minor planets on the same scale are: Ceres 0·0712, Pallas 0·0378, Vesta 0·367, Hygeia 0·0359, Davida 0·0270, Interamnia 0·0261, and Europa 0·0245.

THE INNER PLANETS

The four inner planets – Mercury, Venus, Earth and Mars – are small and rocky. Because the Earth is a member of the group of inner planets, they are often referred to as the *terrestrial planets*.

MERCURY

Because of its proximity to the Sun, Mercury is difficult to see with the naked eye and only appears low in the west after sunset, or low in the east before sunrise. The first telescopic observation was made by the Polish astronomer Hevelius (1611–87), who saw that the planet has phases like the Moon. Radar observations in the 1960s established that Mercury's rotational period is exactly two-thirds of the planet's orbital period. However, most of what we know about the planet derives from visits by the *Mariner 10* spacecraft in 1974 and 1975. Data returned by *Mariner 10* revealed that Mercury looks remarkably like the Moon, with similar craters and highlands, but it lacks the large frozen lava 'seas' or *maria*. The surface appears to be dominated by large basins representing epochs in the formation of the crust. The largest of these features is Caloris, which has a major diameter of 1340 km (830 mi) and appears to have six associated ring-like structures ranging in diameter from 630 km (390 mi) to 3700 km (2300 mi). The surface of Mercury is covered with a large number of impact craters, the largest of which is Boccaccio with a diameter of 160 km (100 mi). The deepest Mercurian crater is Ictinus, which is 4800 m (15,570 ft) from floor to rim.

Because the surface pressure is only one trillionth (10^{-12}) of that of Earth, Mercury has virtually no atmosphere. Therefore, temperatures on Mercury vary between 420 °C (790 °F) in the day and –180 °C (–290 °F) at night, with an average sunlit side temperature of 170 °C (340 °F). Because of the peculiar relationship between Mercury's rotation period and orbital period, a 'day' (sunrise to sunset) on the planet is equivalent to two Mercurian years or 176 Earth days.

Mercury has an iron-rich core – 3600 km (2200 mi) in diameter – containing 65% of the planet's mass. This accounts for the planet's extraordinarily high density compared with its size. A recent theory has associated Mercury's relatively thin surface layers with the same type of 'giant impact' that is thought to have formed the Moon (see below). However, in Mercury's case the debris could not be retained to form a satellite.

VENUS

Apart from the Moon, Venus is often the brightest object in the sky. However, like Mercury, Venus can only be seen with the naked eye in the morning or the evening. The planet has been the object of many space probes, starting with the *Mariner II* flyby in 1962. The most recent probe is the *Magellan* orbitor, which between 1990 and 1994 carried out precision mapping of the whole surface of Venus. There have also been a number of landings on the planet including the Soviet *Venera* series (1967–82) and *Vega I* and *2* (1985), and the four US *Pioneer* Venus probes (1978). Although similar in size to the Earth, Venus is an intensely hostile planet. Its atmosphere consists almost entirely of carbon dioxide at a pressure 94 times that of the Earth. Its average temperature of 464 °C (867 °F) – with little difference between the equator and the poles – is maintained by a runaway 'greenhouse effect' in which heat received from the Sun is trapped within the atmosphere. A thick planet-wide cloud cover between 50 and 75 km (30 and 45 mi) above the surface contains a high concentration of aerosol droplets of sulphuric acid – the source of the sulphur may be due to emanations from active volcanoes. The upper clouds sweep around the planet in about four to five days, which is equivalent to wind speeds of up to 360 km/h (220 mph).

Although the surface of Venus cannot be seen from the Earth, pictures sent back by the Venera probes 7, 9, 10, 13 and 14 indicate that the sunlight filtering through the clouds turns the grey rocks a pinkish-orange hue. Radar mapping indicates that the surface is essentially flat – with 80% of the surface being within 1 km (0.6 mi) of the planet's average radius – and covered by a vast network of faults and cracks. However, Venus has a number of notable highlands including Aphrodite Terra close to the equator, which is 9700 km (6000 mi) long and up to 3000 km (1900 mi) wide, and Ishtar Terra in the north, which is 2900 km (1800 mi) in diameter and contains the Maxwell Montes mountain chain, which rises up to 8 km (5 mi) above the surrounding plateau. The Magellan mission suggested that the whole of the planet had been resurfaced in the last 500 million years and that large volcanoes such as Maat Mons are almost certainly still active. Although the rotation period of Venus is longer than its year, a Venusian 'day' (sunrise-to-sunrise) is equivalent to 116 Earth days.

NOTABLE ASTEROIDS

Nysa (Number 44). *Discovered:* 1857. *Diameter:* 70 km (43 mi). Most asteroids are very dark. However, Nysa is one of a small number of very bright asteroids that reflect back nearly one half of the light that they receive from Sun.

Eros (Number 433). *Discovered:* 1898. *Average diameter:* 20 km (12 mi). An irregularly shaped asteroid whose orbit takes it far away from the main swarm of asteroids. In 1975 it came within 24 million km (15 million mi) of the Earth.

Hektor (Number 624). *Discovered:* 1907. *Dimensions:* about 440 km (273 mi) long, with cross-sectional diameters of 180 ¥ 140 km (112 ¥ 87 mi). Hektor is an extraordinary very dark, elongated asteroid. It is dumbbell shaped and probably represents the crashing together of two or more regularly shaped asteroids. It is a member of the Trojan group of asteroids that is trapped in Jupiter's orbit.

Icarus (Number 1566). *Discovered:* 1949. *Diameter:* 900 m (2950 ft). Icarus has the shortest known rotation period of only 2.273 hours. It has a highly irregular orbit that takes it to halfway between Mercury and the Sun at perihelion.

Chiron (Number 2060). *Discovered:* 1977. *Diameter:* under 182 km (under 113 mi). One of the remotest asteroids, Chiron orbits mainly between Saturn and Uranus. Observations have revealed a large, faint surrounding coma – luminous cloud – formed principally by the degassing of carbon dioxide from small areas of the asteroid's surface. This activity is characteristic of comets and has led to suggestions that Chiron is, in fact, the largest comet but because of its distance from the sun it does not show spectacular cometary behaviour. It is one of the four known 'Centaurs' whose orbits cross those of Saturn, Uranus and Neptune, the other three being Pholus (number 5145) (disc. 1992), 1993 HA2 (disc 1993) and 1994 TA (disc 1994).

Phaethon (Number 3200). *Discovered:* 1983. *Diameter:* 5 km (3 mi). Phaethon displays a large orbital eccentricity that brings it closer to the Sun than any other asteroid. It is only 21 million km (13 million mi) from the Sun at perihelion, when the surface temperature on the sunlit side rises to 450°C (842°F).

Ida (Number 243). *Discovered:* 1884. This 30 km (19 mi) diameter asteroid is the only one definitely known to have a moon, the 1·4 km (0·9 mi) diameter Dactyl discovered with the Galileo spacecraft in August 1993.

1993 KA2 – the smallest known asteroid with a diameter of only 5m (16 ft) discovered in May 1993 when it approached the Earth to within 150,000 km (93,000 mi).

1994 XM1 – this 10m (33 ft) diameter asteroid approached the Earth to within 100,000 km (62,000 mi) in December 1994 – a record close approach.

THE OUTER PLANETS

The outer planets are very different from the inner planets. They are very much further away from the Sun and, with the exception of Pluto, they are much larger than the inner planets. Jupiter, Saturn, Uranus and Neptune are giant 'gas' planets with no discernible solid surfaces. The outermost planet, Pluto, has a solid surface but is tiny in comparison.

JUPITER

Jupiter is the largest planet in the solar system. When it is closest to the Earth, it is often the brightest object in the sky – apart from the Moon, Venus and Mars. Jupiter has been investigated by four space probes – *Pioneer 10* and *11* in 1973 and 1974 respectively, and *Voyager 1* and *2* in 1979. These probes led to the discovery of three new moons and Jupiter's ring system.

A model of the structure of Jupiter suggests that it has a rock-iron-ice core about 15,000 km (9,000 mi) thick, weighing about 15 Earth masses. The core is surrounded by shell of metallic hydrogen, containing a small amount of helium, which extends up to 55,000 km (34,000 mi) from the centre of the planet. An outer envelope consists mainly of liquid molecular hydrogen. Jupiter has a gaseous hydrogen atmosphere, about 18% of which comprises helium and small quantities of compounds such as water, ammonia ices and ammonium hydrosulphide. These compounds impart the light and dark bands to the planet's atmosphere that can be observed by telescope from Earth.

The 'Great Red Spot' – which may have been observed as early as 1664 – appears to be a long-lived whirling storm in the planet's atmosphere. This 'Great Red Spot' may rise up to 8 km (5 mi) above the surrounding cloud. Its red colour may be due to the presence of phosphorus, derived from decomposition of the minor atmospheric constituent phosphine. The squashed appearance of Jupiter is entirely consistent with the rapid rotation of a gas sphere.

Jupiter radiates 67% more heat than it receives from the Sun. This is mainly due to dissipation of the primordial heat of the planet. A secondary source of heat is gravitational energy released as a result of the precipitation of helium in Jupiter's metallic core.

Between the 16 and 22 July 1994 the planet was struck by 19 fragments of the comet *Shoemaker-Levy 9*, leading to massive plumes rising up to 3000 km (1860 mi) above the cloud tops and spectacular fireballs as the debris cascaded back in to the atmosphere. Black *bruises* larger than the Earth were formed on the planet's surface and although they have now been stretched into belts they will take many years to fade.

The rings of Jupiter

The ring system of Jupiter was discovered in March 1979. A bright central ring – 7000 km (4300 mi) in width and less than 30 km (20 mi) in thickness – has a maximum brightness at 126,100 km (78,400 mi) from the centre of Jupiter and an abrupt outer boundary at 129,130 km (80,240 mi) from the centre of the planet. A faint inner halo – 20,000 km (12,400 mi) in thickness – extends down to the top of the clouds that surround Jupiter. A very tenuous 'gossamer ring' extends out to 214,000 km (133,000 mi), beyond the main ring.

Satellites of Jupiter

The 16 satellites, or moons, of Jupiter can be considered in four distinct clusters – four inner satellites, the four massive Galilean satellites, four satellites in a prograde orbit (orbiting in the same direction as Jupiter's rotation) at 163 Jupiter radii, and four satellites in a retrograde orbit at 314 Jupiter radii.

The Inner Satellites

Metis (Number XVI) *Discovered*: 1980. *Distance from Jupiter*: 127,960 km (79,520 mi). *Diameter*: 40 km (25 mi). Metis is embedded in the main ring of Jupiter.

Adrastea (Number XV) *Discovered*: 1980. *Distance from Jupiter*: 128,980 km (80,140 mi). *Diameter*: 26 × 20 × 16 km (16 × 12 × 10 mi), giving an average of 20 km (12 mi). Adrastea orbits just inside the edge of the main ring and may control it.

Amalthea (Number V) *Discovered*: 1892. *Distance from Jupiter*: 181,370 km (112,700 mi). *Diameter*: 262 × 146 × 134 km (163 × 91 × 83 mi), giving an average of 172 km (107 mi). The dark red colour of Amalthea's surface may be due to the capture of sulphur from the nearby volcanic satellite Io.

Thebe (Number XIV) *Discovered*: 1980. *Distance from Jupiter*: 221,890 km (137,880 mi). *Diameter*: 110 × 90 km (68 × 56 mi), giving an average of 100 km (62 mi).

The Galilean satellites

The Galilean Satellites were named after Galileo Galilei (1564–1642), who independently observed them at the same time as Simon Marius (Simon Mayr; 1573–1624) in 1610. They have proved to be unique 'worlds', entirely different to Jupiter's other satellites.

Io (Number I). *Discovered*: 1610. *Distance from Jupiter*: 421,800 km (262,100 mi). *Diameter*: 3660 × 3637 × 3631 km (2274 × 2260 × 2256 mi), giving an average of 3643 km (2264 mi). Io is continuously subject to volcanic eruptions due to gravitational interactions with Jupiter. This has resulted in a vividly coloured surface that is covered with various forms of sulphur and its compounds.

Europa (Number II). *Discovered*: 1610. *Distance from Jupiter*: 671,000 km (417,000 mi). *Diameter*: 3130 km (1945 mi). Europa has a 'billiard ball' smooth surface that is covered with numerous thin dark lines. Its structure may comprise a 100 km (60 mi) thick water ice layer overlying a rocky core, but with an intermediate layer of liquid water. The detection of an oxygen atmosphere with a pressure ten trillionths (10^{-11}) that of the Earth's atmosphere was reported in 1995.

Ganymede (Number III). *Discovered*: 1610. *Distance from Jupiter*: 1,070,400 km (665,100 mi). *Diameter*: 5268 km (3237 mi). The largest and heaviest satellite in the solar system, Ganymede has a mass 2·017 times greater than our own Moon. Its water ice surface has a strange darkened mottled appearance.

Callisto (Number IV). *Discovered*: 1610. *Distance from Jupiter*: 1,882,600 km (1,169,800 mi). *Diameter*: 4806 km (2986 mi). Callisto – the outermost Galilean satellite – has the most heavily cratered surface of any body in the solar system. It is dominated by two large multi-ringed basins – Valhalla, which shows ring structures up to 4000 km (2500 mi) in diameter, and Asgard, which shows ring structures up to 1600 km (1000 mi) in diameter.

The outer satellites

These small satellites – in two distinct orbits (see above) – may represent the disruption of two (groups of) captured asteroids, a theory given strength by the fact that their surface composition appears to be similar to the carbonaceous chrodites found on asteroids.

Leda (Number XIII) *Discovered*: 1974. *Distance from Jupiter*: 11,094,000 km (6,893,000 mi). *Diameter*: 18 km (11 mi).

Himalia (Number VI) *Discovered*: 1904. *Distance from Jupiter*: 11,480,000 km (7,133,000 mi). *Diameter*: 156 km (97 mi).

Lysithea (Number X) *Discovered*: 1938. *Distance from Jupiter*: 11,720,000 km (7,282,000 mi). *Diameter*: 34 km (21 mi).

Elara (Number VII) *Discovered*: 1905. *Distance from Jupiter*: 11,737,000 km (7,293,000 mi). *Diameter*: 70 km (43 mi).

Ananke (Number XII) *Discovered*: 1951. *Distance from Jupiter*: 21,200,000 km (13,200,000 mi). *Diameter*: 25 km (16 mi).

Carme (Number XI) *Discovered*: 1938. *Distance from Jupiter*: 22,600,000 km (14,000,000 mi). *Diameter*: 40 km (25 mi).

Pasiphae (Number VIII) *Discovered*: 1908. *Distance from Jupiter*: 23,500,000 km (14,600,000 mi). *Diameter*: 56 km (35 mi).

Sinope (Number IX) *Discovered*: 1914. *Distance from Jupiter*: 23,700,000 km (14,700,000 mi). *Diameter*: 34 km (21 mi).

SATURN

The next planet out from the Sun is Saturn, with its magnificent system of rings. In 1610 Galileo became the first person to look at Saturn through a telescope. His low powered telescope did not reveal the rings distinctly, and Galileo thought he was looking at a 'triple planet'. It was not until 1659 that the Dutch physicist Christiaan Huygens (1629–95) realized Saturn's true nature. The planet has been investigated by three space probes – *Pioneer 11* in 1979 and *Voyager 1* and *2* in 1980 and 1981 respectively. These probes led to the discovery of three new satellites and the F and G rings.

Saturn is generally considered to be similar to Jupiter but on a smaller scale. Saturn has a similar rock-iron-ice core to Jupiter, but the metallic hydrogen layer is much smaller, extending only 26,000 km (16,000 mi) from the centre of the planet. It is also rich in helium but the outer molecular hydrogen envelope is depleted in this element because of the presence of an intermediate zone 3000 km (1900 mi) thick in which helium is precipitating out and falling into the metallic zone. The gravitational energy released from this 'precipitation' is the source of heat – Saturn radiates 76% more heat than it receives from the Sun.

The rings of Saturn

The distinct ring system surrounding Saturn's equator is composed of water ice or ice-covered material. Although the main ring system is 273,550 km (169,980 mi) in diameter, the overall thickness is only 10m (33 ft), giving a total mass of only about 5×10^{-8} of that of Saturn. Although the main rings appear to consist of many thousands of individual ringlets, it is now thought that this is an optical effect caused by variations in reflectivity.

For details of the main features of the rings of Saturn, see the table on p. 24.

Satellites of Saturn

The 18 known satellites of Saturn appear to be either small misshapen water ice moons or medium-sized water ice satellites with rocky cores. The largest satellite, Titan, is big enough to have its own atmosphere.

Pan *Discovered*: 1990. *Distance from Saturn*: 133,580 km (83,000 mi). *Diameter*: 20 km (12 mi). Pan orbits at the centre of the 322 km (200 mi) wide Encke Gap in the A Ring.

Atlas (Number XV) *Discovered*: 1980. *Distance from Saturn*: 137,670 km (85,540 mi). *Diameter*: 37 × 34 × 27 km (23 × 21 × 17 mi), giving an average of 32 km (20 mi). Atlas controls the outer edge of the A Ring.

Prometheus (Number XVI) *Discovered*: 1980. *Distance from Saturn*: 139,380 km (86,610 mi). *Diameter*: 145 × 85 × 65 km (90 × 53 × 40 mi), giving an average of 93 km (58 mi). Prometheus is a highly irregularly shaped satellite, which controls the inner edge of the F Ring.

THE RINGS OF SATURN

Feature	Distance from centre km	miles	Notes
Saturn radius	60,367	37,510	Radius at the 100 millibar level
D Ring inner edge	66,970	41,610	Tenuous dusty ring that may extend down to Saturn's surface
C Ring inner edge outer edge	74,491 91,983	46,287 57,156	The 270 km(168 mi) wide Maxwell Gap is located at 87,500 km (54,400mi)
B Ring inner edge outer edge	91,983 117,516	57,156 73,021	The eccentric Huygens Gap, which is 285–440 km (174–273 mi) wide, islocated just beyond the edge of B Ring
Cassini Division			This 4533 km (2817 mi) wide gap contains many ringlet features, most notably the Huygens Ringlet, which is located 308 km (191 mi) from the edge of the B Ring
A Ring inner edge	122,049	75,838	The 322 km (200 mi) wide Encke Gap, centred at 133,585 km(83,006 mi), contains the satellite Pan
outer edge	136,774	84,988	The 34 km (21 mi) wide Keeler Gap is located 270 km (168 mi) from the outer edge
F Ring centre	140,460	87,280	A multiple-stranded eccentric ring varying in width from 30 to 500 km (19–311mi), shepherded either side by the satellites Prometheus and Pandora
G Ring centre	170,100	105,700	This ring optically appears thin, although it is approximately 1000 km (600 mi) wide and possibly up to 1000 km thick
E Ring inner edges outer edge	181,000 483,000	112,500 300,100	Diffuse ring with maximum brightness near the orbit of the satellite Enceladus

Pandora (Number XVII) *Discovered*: 1980. *Distance from Saturn*: 141,710 km (88,050 mi). *Diameter*: 114 × 84 × 62 km (71 × 52 × 39 mi), giving an average of 84 km (52 mi). Pandora is a highly irregularly shaped satellite, which – with Prometheus – controls the outer edge of the F Ring.

Epimetheus (Number XI) *Discovered*: 1980 (preliminary identification 1977). *Distance from Saturn*: 151,410 km (94,110 mi) – see below. *Diameter*: 144 × 108 × 98 km (89 × 67 × 61 mi), giving an average of 115 km (71 mi). Epimetheus is a highly irregularly shaped satellite with very low density. It may be made totally of porous water ice. Epimetheus interchanges orbit with Janus every four years with an average orbit for the two satellites of 151,450 km (94,110 mi).

Janus (Number X) *Discovered*: 1980 (preliminary identification 1966). *Distance from Saturn*: 151,460 km (94,110 mi) – see also Epimetheus, above. *Diameter*: 196 × 191 × 153 km (122 × 119 × 95 mi), giving an average of 179 km (111 mi). Janus is a highly irregularly shaped satellite with a very low density. It interchanges orbit with Epimetheus – see above.

Mimas (Number I) *Discovered*: 1789. *Distance from Saturn*: 185,530 km (115,280 mi). *Diameter*: 418 × 392 × 383 km (260 × 244 × 238 mi), giving an average of 398 km (247 mi). The surface features of Mimas are dominated by the 130 km (81 mi) diameter crater Herschel, with walls 5 km (3 mi) high and a central peak rising 6 km (4 mi) from the crater floor.

Enceladus (Number II) *Discovered*: 1789. *Distance from Saturn*: 238,030 km (147,900 mi). *Diameter*: 513 × 495 × 489 km (319 × 308 × 304 mi), giving an average of 499 km (310 mi). Enceladus is characterized by an extremely bright surface that reflects back all of the light it receives.

Tethys (Number III) *Discovered*: 1684. *Distance from Saturn*: 294,670 km (183,100 mi). *Diameter*: 1,071 × 1,056 × 1,052 km (665 × 656 × 654 mi), giving an average of 1060 km (659 mi). Tethys is a large moon with an icy cratered surface, which is dominated by the 400 km (250 mi) diameter crater Odysseus and the huge valley Ithaca Chasma, which stretches at least two-thirds of the way around the satellite's circumference.

Telesto (Number XIII) *Discovered*: 1980. *Distance from Saturn*: 294,670 km (183,100 mi). *Diameter*: 30 × 25 × 15 km (19 × 16 × 9 mi), giving an average of 22 km (14 mi). Telesto – a highly irregularly shaped satellite – is trapped in the orbit of Tethys at a null gravity (Lagrangian) point in the Tethys-Saturn-Sun system.

Calypso (Number XIV) *Discovered*: 1980. *Distance from Saturn*: 294,670 km (183,100 mi). *Diameter*: 30 × 16 × 16 km (19 × 10 × 10 mi), giving an average of 19 km (12 mi). Like Telesto, Calypso is trapped at a Lagrangian point in the orbit of Tethys.

Dione (Number IV) *Discovered*: 1684. *Distance from Saturn*: 377,410 km (234,510 mi). *Diameter*: 1120 km (696 mi). Dione is a large icy satellite whose surface is pockmarked with craters, the largest of which – Aeneas – is 160 km (100 mi) in diameter.

Helene (Number XII) *Discovered*: 1980. *Distance from Saturn*: 377,410 km (234,510 mi). *Diameter*: 32 km (20 mi), but Helene is probably irregularly shaped. Helene accompanies Dione because it is trapped in a Lagrangian point in Dione's orbit (see above).

Rhea (Number V) *Discovered*: 1672. *Distance from Saturn*: 527,070 km (327,510 mi). *Diameter*: 1,528 km (949 mi). Rhea is a large icy satellite, which is heavily cratered. Izanagi – the main crater – is 300 km (186 mi) in diameter.

Titan (Number VI) *Discovered*: 1655. *Distance from Saturn*: 1,221,860 km (759,230 mi). *Diameter*: 5150 km

(3200 mi). After Ganymede, Titan is the second largest satellite in the solar system and is the only one to have an extensive atmosphere, which comprises mainly nitrogen with small amounts of methane and argon. The surface pressure is one and a half times that of Earth, but the surface is obscured from view by an orange haze that is the result of the formation of complex organic molecules in the upper atmosphere.

Hyperion (Number VII) *Discovered*: 1848. *Distance from Saturn*: 1,481,090 km (920,310 mi). *Diameter*: 360 × 280 × 225 km (224 × 174 × 140 mi), giving an average of 283 km (176 mi). Hyperion – a highly irregularly shaped satellite – is spinning chaotically with no fixed rotation period. It is possibly the remnant of a larger satellite (known as proto-Hyperion) that was struck by a stray comet.

Iapetus (Number VIII) *Discovered*: 1671. *Distance from Saturn*: 3,561,670 km (2,213,120 mi). *Diameter*: 1436 km (892 mi). Iapetus is a bright cratered icy satellite. About 40% of its surface – Cassini Regio – is covered by very dark dust, possibly the result of debris flung into Iapetus's orbit when proto-Hyperion (see above) was struck by a comet. The result is that one hemisphere of Iapetus reflects light efficiently while the other hemisphere appears dull.

Phoebe (Number IX) *Discovered*: 1898. *Distance from Saturn*: 12,954,000 km (8,049,000 mi). *Diameter*: 230 × 220 × 210 km (143 × 137 × 130 mi), giving an average of 220 km (137 mi). Phoebe is a small dark remote satellite spining in 9·282 hours in a retrograde orbit (opposite to the sense of rotation of Saturn). Its surface composition appears to be identical to that of the most common type of asteroid and it is possible that Phoebe may be a captured asteroid.

URANUS

When the sky is very dark and very clear, Uranus can just be seen with the naked eye. The planet was discovered by William Herschel (1732–1822) in March 1781. Herschel was making a routine survey of the sky when he came across an object that did not look like a star. At first he thought he had found a comet, but subsequent calculation of the orbit showed it to be in remarkable agreement with the Titus-Bode Rule for planetary distances (see p. 17). The Uranian system was explored by the *Voyager 2* space probe in 1986. This led to the discovery of ten new moons and two new rings.

Because of its smaller size and higher density, the internal structure of Uranus may be different to that of Jupiter and Saturn. Models for Uranus suggest that the planet possesses a similar central rocky core, although it is surrounded by a 'sea' of water, methane and ammonia. The planet has an outer hydrogen atmosphere containing about 26% helium and a smaller amount of methane. (Methane gives Uranus its greenish colour.)

Unlike the other giant planets, Uranus does not radiate more heat than it receives from the Sun. (This may be because its various internal layers form a stable stratification.) The lack of energy radiation may also explain the bland appearance of the planet, which displays little evidence of clouds.

The large tilt of Uranus (98°) means that day and night on some parts of the planet may last up to 21 years, but the present sunlit 'south' pole – which points towards the Sun – and dark opposite pole show little difference in temperature. This suggests that there is a strong temperature equilibrium within the atmosphere of Uranus. The magnetic axis of Uranus is offset 7000 km (4300 mi) from the centre of the planet and is also inclined at an angle of 59° to the axis of rotation. This difference has been used to suggest that the large tilt of the equator may be due to a catastrophic collision between Uranus and one or more planetesimals early in its history.

The rings of Uranus

In 1977–78 it was discovered that Uranus had nine narrow rings orbiting the equator. Two further rings – a diffuse ring (1986 U2R) and a narrow ring (1986 U1R or Lambda) – were discovered by the *Voyager 2* imaging team in January 1986. The rings are very dark and probably rich in carbon, and the outermost ring, Epsilon, is shepherded by the satellites Cordelia and Ophelia.

Satellites of Uranus

The five major satellites identified telescopically from Earth are all composed of water ice overlaying rocky cores. The ten small satellites orbiting inside the orbit of Miranda were discovered by the *Voyager 2* imaging team. They may have been formed by the fragmentation of a larger satellite 3500 million years ago. In 1992, scientists at the University of Colorado, USA, suggested that many additional small moons – 1–10 km (0.6–5.6 mi) in diameter – may orbit Uranus.

THE RINGS OF URANUS

Features	*Distance from centre km*	*miles*
Uranus radius	25,559	15,882
1986 U2R inner edge	37,000	23,000
1986 U2R outer edge	39,500	24,500
6 centres	41,837	25,996
5 centres	42,235	26,244
4 centres	42,571	26,452
Alpha centres	44,718	27,786
Beta centres	45,661	28,372
Eta centres	47,176	29,314
Gamma centres	47,627	29,594
Delta centres	48,300	30,012
Lambda centres	50,024	31,083
Epsilon centres	51,149	31,783

With the exceptions of the very diffuse 1986 U2R ring and the dominant Epsilon ring, all the other rings are less than 12 km (7 mi) wide. The Epsilon ring width varies between 22 and 93 km (14 and 58 mi) and its orbit has the highest eccentricity at 0.00794.

Cordelia (Number VI) *Discovered*: 1986. *Distance from Uranus*: 49,750 km (30,910 mi). *Diameter*: 26 km (16 mi). Cordelia and Ophelia act as shepherding satellites for the major ring (epsilon) of Uranus.

Ophelia (Number VII) *Discovered*: 1986. *Distance from Uranus*: 53,760 km (33,410 mi). *Diameter*: 32 km (20 mi). (See Cordelia, above.)

Bianca (Number VIII) *Discovered*: 1986. *Distance from Uranus*: 59,170 km (36,760 mi). *Diameter*: 44 km (27 mi).

Cressida (Number IX) *Discovered*: 1986. *Distance from Uranus*: 61,770 km (38,380 mi). *Diameter*: 66 km (41 mi).

Desdemona (Number X) *Discovered*: 1986. *Distance from Uranus*: 62,660 km (38,930 mi). *Diameter*: 58 km (36 mi).

Juliet (Number XI) *Discovered*: 1986. *Distance from Uranus*: 64,360 km (39,990 mi). *Diameter*: 84 km (52 mi).
Portia (Number XII) *Discovered*: 1986. *Distance from Uranus*: 66,100 km (41,070 mi). *Diameter*: 110 km (68 mi).
Rosalind (Number XIII) *Discovered*: 1986. *Distance from Uranus*: 69,930 km (43,450 mi). *Diameter*: 58 km (36 mi).
Belinda (Number XIV) *Discovered*: 1986. *Distance from Uranus*: 75,260 km (46,760 mi). *Diameter*: 68 km (42 mi).
Puck (Number XV) *Discovered*: 1985. *Distance from Uranus*: 86,000 km (53,440 mi). *Diameter*: 154 km (96 mi).
Miranda (Number V) *Discovered*: 1948. *Distance from Uranus*: 129,850 km (80,680 mi). *Diameter*: 481 × 468 × 466 km (299 × 291 × 290 mi), giving an average of 472 km (293 mi). Miranda – the smallest of the five outer satellites that are identifiable from Earth – has a most bizarre surface structure that is thought to be the result of being disrupted and reformed several times during its existence.
Ariel (Number I) *Discovered*: 1851. *Distance from Uranus*: 190,930 km (118,640 mi). *Diameter*: 1162 × 1156 × 1155 km (722 × 718 × 718 mi), giving an average of 1158 km (720 mi). The long grooves that cover the surface of Ariel may have resulted from the satellite being disrupted and reformed at least once.
Umbriel (Number II) *Discovered*: 1851. *Distance from Uranus*: 265,980 km (165,270 mi). *Diameter*: 1169 km (727 mi). The surface of Umbriel – which is much darker than the other major Uranian satellites – is pockmarked with craters.
Titania (Number III) *Discovered*: 1787. *Distance from Uranus*: 436,280 km (271,090 mi). *Diameter*: 1578 km (980 mi). Titania is densely pockmarked with craters and a few deep chasms, which may have been formed during the final solidification of the surface.
Oberon (Number IV) *Discovered*: 1787. *Distance from Uranus*: 583,430 km (362,530 mi). *Diameter*: 1523 km (946 mi). The main surface feature of Oberon is thought to be a crater several hundred km in diameter, but it was on the far side of the satellite during the *Voyager 2* encounter and only revealed itself as a central mountain peak rising 20 km (12 mi) above the surface of the planet.

NEPTUNE

Neptune is not visible to the naked eye, but can be observed by telecope. It was discovered in September 1846 by the German astronomers Johann Galle (1812–1910) and Heinrich d'Arrest (1822–75), based on mathematical predictions by calculations by Urbain Le Verrier (1811–77) and John Couch Adams (1819–92). Le Verrier and Adams independently deduced that Uranus was being pulled by the gravity of another 'hidden' planet.

In 1989, the Neptune system was explored by the *Voyager 2* space probe, which led to the discovery of six new moons and confirmed the nature of Neptune's ring system. *Voyager* revealed what is – compared with Uranus – an extremely dynamic world with many discernible cloud features and wind speeds exceeding 2160 km/h (1340 mph) in the case of the equatorial easterlies and 1080 km/h (670 mph) in the case of the polar westerlies. A notable atmospheric feature is the 'Great Dark Spot', which is the smaller equivalent of the 'Great Red Spot' on Jupiter but still a larger feature than the planet Earth. This swirling storm rolls in a counterclockwise direction around the planet in 16 days. However by the time of observations with the Hubble space Telescope in 1994 this large feature appeared to have disappeared, indicating the true dynamic nature of the atmosphere.

Neptune owes its turbulent nature to the fact that the planet radiates back into space 161% more heat than it receives from the Sun. The reason for this amount of radiation is not known as the internal structure of Neptune is thought likely to be similar to that of docile Uranus. However, there may be some significance in the fact that the outer hydrogen atmosphere of Neptune contains more helium – 32% – than that of any of the other gas planets. Small amounts of methane in the atmosphere give Neptune its bluish appearance when observed from a distance.

Like Uranus, Neptune has a magnetic axis that is displaced from the axis of rotation – it is offset by 13,600 km (8500 mi) from the centre – that is, over one half of the planet's radius – and tilted at an angle of 47°. It is thought that this large difference may be the result of catastrophic events during the formation of the planet.

The rings of Neptune

Although partial evidence for the existence of rings around Neptune was obtained prior to the *Voyager* observations, it was not until the space probe passed the planet that it was established that there are three distinct complete rings and a diffuse ring of material between 38,000 km (23,600 mi) and 59,000 km (36,700 mi) from the centre of the planet.

Galle Ring is a broad dusty ring about 1700 km (1060 mi) wide, centred at 41,900 km (26,000 mi) from the planet.
Leverrier Ring is a narrow dusty ring, 30 km (19 mi) wide, centred at 53,200 km (33,060 mi) from the planet.
Adams Ring is a narrow ring, 15 km (9 mi) wide, centred at 62,930 km (39,100 mi). The ring contains four dusty arcs – Courage, Liberté, Egalité and Fraternité – whose movements are controlled by the nearby satellite Galatea.

Satellites of Neptune

In 1989, the *Voyager 2* imaging team reported the discovery of six new satellites in addition to the two already known, but almost certainly one of these, Larissa, was detected in 1981. The five innermost satellites of Neptune are either close to or inside the *Roche Limit* of Neptune – the point at which the gravitational force of the planet should totally destroy such moons. It is thought that these inner moons may represent the break-up of larger bodies in the past. In 1992, scientists at the University of Colorado, USA, suggested that many additional small moons – 1–10 km (0.6–5.6 mi) in diameter – may orbit Neptune.

Naiad (Number III) *Discovered*: 1989. *Distance from Neptune*: 48,230 km (29,970 mi). *Diameter*: 58 km (36 mi).
Thalassa (Number IV) *Discovered*: 1989. *Distance from Neptune*: 50,070 km (31,110 mi). *Diameter*: 80 km (50 mi).
Despina (Number V) *Discovered*: 1989. *Distance from Neptune*: 52,530 km (32,640 mi). *Diameter*: 148 km (92 mi).

Galatea (Number VI) *Discovered*: 1989. *Distance from Neptune*: 61,950 km (38,490 mi). *Diameter*: 158 km (98 mi). Galatea controls the dust arcs in the Adams Ring.
Larissa (Number VII) *Discovered*: 1989 (probable preliminary identification 1981) *Distance from Neptune*: 73,550 km (45,700 mi). *Diameter*: 208 × 192 × 178 km (129 × 119 × 111 mi), giving an average of 192 km (119 mi).
Proteus (Number VIII) *Discovered*: 1989. *Distance from Neptune*: 117,650 km (73,100 mi). *Diameter*: 424 × 396 × 390 km (263 × 246 × 242 mi), giving an average of 403 km (250 mi). The most prominent feature on Proteus is the impact crater Bogle.
Triton (Number I) *Discovered*: 1846. *Distance from Neptune*: 354,760 km (220,440 mi). *Diameter*: 2705 km (1681 mi). The biggest of Neptune's satellites, Triton has a large orbital inclination (157°) and a retrograde orbit – opposite to the direction of rotation of Neptune. This suggests that Triton is a captured satellite that may have wreaked havoc in the early Neptunian system. *Voyager 2* showed the surface to be very colourful, with a 150–200 km (90–120 mi) thick water ice crust overlain by a brilliant coating of a mixture of nitrogen and methane ices. The slightly darkened reddish colour of the surface may be due to contamination with organic polymer materials. Triton's surface ices are at a temperature of −235°C (−391°F), which is the coldest measured surface in the solar system. The surface has a strange mottled appearance known as a *cantaloupe* terrain because of its ressemblance to the fruit. Triton has a large bright polar cap in which vents or geysers eject nitrogen and dust 8 km (5 mi) up into the satellite's thin atmosphere.
Nereid (Number II) *Discovered*: 1948. *Distance from Neptune*: 5,513,410 km (3,425,870 mi). Diameter: 340 km (211 mi). The large eccentricity of its orbit suggests that this satellite may have been captured by Neptune's gravitational field.

PLUTO

The discovery of the outermost planet by Clyde Tombaugh was announced on 13 March 1930, but little was known about the planet until after the discovery of its moon Charon on 22 June 1978.

The planet has a diameter only two-thirds of our own Moon and is a little over twice the size of the minor planet Ceres. Pluto appears to be the twin of Neptune's moon Triton, with a similar density and a similar surface covering consisting of a mixture of nitrogen and methane ices (together with carbon monoxide).The planet's thin atmosphere is probably predominantly nitrogen with small amounts of methane and carbon monoxide. Its surface temperature must be at least as low as that on Triton, −235 °C (−391 °F) although darker areas on the surface may be up to 20° C (36° F) warmer.

A model of the interior of Pluto suggests a core of partially hydrated rock, surrounded by a water ice layer up to 320 km (200 mi) thick and an outer layer 10 km (6 mi) thick consisting mainly of methane ice. The orbit of Pluto is so eccentric that at perihelion it is closer to the Sun than Neptune is. This situation exists between 23 January 1979 and 15 March 1999. The two planets are locked in a resonance that prevents them from coming together.

Satellite of Pluto

Charon (Number I) *Discovered*: 1978. *Distance from Pluto*: 19,550 km (12,150 mi). *Diameter*: 1240 km (771 mi). Charon is large compared with its parent planet, having 7% of Pluto's mass – compared with the Moon, which has only 1·2% of the Earth's mass. It is in captive rotation with one face of Pluto and one face of Charon always opposite one another. Observations in 1992 indicate that Charon appears to consist mainly of water ice but with a small rocky core.

KUIPER BELT OBJECTS

In 1951 the US astronomer Gerard P. Kuiper (1905–1973) proposed that comets with periods less than 200 years originated in a belt just beyond the outer planets. The discovery in September 1992 of an object, temporary designated 1992 QB_1 by David Jewitt (UK) and Jane Luu (US) and the realization that it orbited beyond Pluto was considered as the discovery of the first such object. Although only about 20 objects have been discovered it is speculated that altogether there may be 35,000 with diameters in the range 100 to 400 km (60 to 250 mi). The nature of these dark objects is believed to be somewhere between asteroids and comets.

COMETS

Comets have long been known as apparitions in the sky and they have entered the folklore and literature of many societies. However, their structure is mundane – they consist mainly of a central nucleus that can be regarded as a 'dirty snowball'. On approaching the Sun, the ice in a comet starts to evaporate, producing a coma around the nucleus and a tail or tails behind. The tail is the streaming of ions and dust from the coma – the ions being repelled by sunlight and the dust by the solar wind. Thus, when moving away from the Sun, the tail of the comet leads.

Comets either orbit within the solar system or adopt parabolic orbits that sweep them outside the system. The source of comets is unknown. Jan Oort (1900–92) suggested that there is a reservoir or 'cloud' of comets in the outer solar system as a residue from the original accretion disc from which the solar system was formed. A recent study suggests that there is an outer 'Oort Cloud', which has been described as a 'halo' of comets, orbiting between 20,000 and 50,000 astronomical units from the Sun. A denser inner concentration of comets, between 3000 and 20,000 astronomical units, is thought to contain about a million million (1012) comets. It is suggested that periodic perturbations by giant interstellar molecular clouds, or close encounters with other stars, triggers the release of the comets into the inner solar system.

Halley's comet is the most famous and was named after Edmond Halley (1656–1742), who correctly predicted its return in 1758, 16 years after his death. In 1986 the space probe Giotto photographed the comet's nucleus and showed it to be an elongated, blackened iceball about 15 km (9 mi) long and 8 km (5 mi) in cross-section. Most comets are in very eccentric orbits with periods of several hundred years. Several new comets are discovered every year. The brightest comets tend to be those with very long periods and it is therefore impossible to predict when the next bright comet will appear.

COMPARATIVE TABLE OF CELESTIAL BODIES IN THE SOLAR SYSTEM

Name	Diameter km*	Diameter miles*
Sun	1,392,140	865,040
Jupiter	139,892	86,925
Saturn	116,600	72,452
Uranus	50,724	31,518
Neptune	49,248	30,601
Earth	12,742	7918
Venus	12,104	7521
Mars	6780	4213
Ganymede (Jupiter III)	5268	3273
Titan (Saturn VI)	5150	3200
Mercury	4880	3032
Callisto (Jupiter IV)	4806	2986
Io (Jupiter I	3643	2264
Moon	3475	2159
Europa (Jupiter II)	3130	1945
Triton (Neptune I)	2705	1681
Pluto	2320	1442
Titania (Uranus III)	1578	981
Rhea (Saturn V)	1528	949
Oberon (Uranus IV)	1523	946
Iapetus (Saturn VIII)	1436	892
Chiron (Pluto I)	1240	771
Umbriel (Uranus II)	1169	726
Ariel (Uranus I)	1158	720
Dione (Saturn IV)	1120	696
Tethys (Saturn III)	1060	659
Ceres (Asteroid I)	941	585
Pallas (Asteroid 2)	524	326
Vesta (Asteroid 4)	512	318
Enceladus (Saturn II)	499	310
Miranda (Uranus V)	472	293
Hygeia (Asteroid 10)	457	284
Proteus (Neptune VIII)	403	250
Mimas (Saturn I)	398	247
Davida (Asteroid 511)	344	214
Nereid (Neptune II)	340	211
Interamnia (Asteroid 704)	333	207
Europa (Asteroid 52)	312	194
Hyperion (Saturn VII)	283	176
Sylvia (Asteroid 87)	277	172
Eunomia (Asteroid 15)	272	169
Cybele (Asteroid 65)	269	167
Psyche (Asteroid 16)	249	155
Euphrosyne (Asteroid 31)	248	154
Juno (Asteroid 3)	244	152
Bamberga (Asteroid 324)	242	150
Themis (Asteroid 24)	237	147
Patienta (Asteroid 451)	230	143
Doris (Asteroid 48)	225	140
Eugenia (Asteroid 45)	223	139
Hektor (Asteroid 624)	222	138
Phoebe (Saturn IX)	220	137
Camilla (Asteroid 107)	220	137
Herculina (Asteroid 532)	220	137
Amphitrite (Asteroid 29)	219	136
Hermione (Asteroid 121)	217	135
Diotima (Asteroid 423)	217	135
Ursula (Asteroid 375)	216	134

*Average diameter. In addition there are ten satellites with diameters between 100 and 200 km (60 and 120 mi), about 220 asteroids within the same range, and there is the possibility of 35,000 Kuiper Belt objects with diameters between 100 and 400 km (60 and 250 mi).

EARLY ASTRONOMY

1223 BC Oldest known record of a total solar eclipse, on a clay tablet in ruins of Ugarit(Syria).

1059 BC Possible sighting of Halley's comet by Chinese astronomers.

585 BC Thales of Miletus correctly predicted the occurrence of a solar eclipse.

c. 500 BC Pythagoras realized that the bright morning star and the bright evening star were Venus.

c. 440 BC Philolaus suggested that the Earth is not the centre of the universe and that the Earth, Sun, Moon and the planets revolve around a central 'fire'.

c. 350 BC Chinese observers recorded earliest known reference to a supernova. Aristotle surmised that the Earth is not flat.

c. 300 BC Chinese astronomers compiled star maps that were in use for several centuries.

c. 280 BC Aristarchus estimated the distance to and size of the Sun.

c. 240 BC Eratosthenes of Cyrene calculated the circumference of the Earth.

c. 150 BC Hipparchus produced an accurate map of 1000 stars.

130 BC Hipparchus calculated the distance to and size of the Moon.

AD 140 Ptolemy assumed that the universe was Earth-centred. His mathematical model for the movements of the planets was in use for 14 centuries.

1054 Chinese astronomers observed a new very bright star in the constellation Taurus, the remnants of which are now observed as the Crab Nebula.

1252 Commencement of a 32-year task to produce a new set of planetary tables – the Alphonsine Tables – to replace those of Ptolemy.

1472 Johann Müller made the first accurate observations of the path of a comet across the sky.

1543 Copernicus established that the solar system is Sun-centred and not Earth-centred.

1596 Tycho Brahe published his 'pre-telescope' star catalogue, the result of 20 years' observations.

1608 Invention of the telescope by Hans Lippershey.

1609 Johannes Kepler published his first two laws of planetary motion - the third was published in 1619.

1610 Galileo Galilei and Simon Marius independently discovered the major moons of Jupiter.

1631 First observation of a transit of Mercury across the Sun by Gassendi.

1638 The first identification of a variable star (Mira Ceti) by P. Holwarda.

1655 Christiaan Huygens discovered Titan, the major moon of Saturn, and described Saturn's ring system.

1668 The first reflector telescope was built by Isaac Newton.

1687 Publication of Newton's mathematical theories of celestial mechanics. These explained the orbital motions of the planets and why the solar system is Sun-centred.

1705 Edmond Halley accurately predicted the return of Halley's comet in 1758.

1781 William Herschel discovered the planet Uranus.

1801 Giuseppe Piazzi discovered the first and largest of the minor planets, Ceres.

1838 The first measurement of the distance of a star (61 Cygni) by Friedrich Bessel.

1846 Johann Galle discovered Neptune.

1862 The construction of the first great refractor telescopes.

Space Travel

SPACEFLIGHT

Manned spaceflights (to January 1995)

1 Vostok 1 (USSR 1): 12 Apr 1961, Yuri Gagarin, 1 hr 58 min; landed separately from craft after ejecting at 1 hr 48 min in a procedure followed by all Vostok pilots.

2 Freedom 7 (USA 1): 5 May 1961, Alan Shepard, 15 min 28 sec; suborbital; splashdown.

3 Liberty Bell 7 (USA 2): 21 Jul 1961, Gus Grissom,15 min 37 sec; spacecraft sank.

4 Vostok 2 (USSR 2): 6 Aug 1961, Gherman Titov, 1 day 1 hr 18 min; at 25, youngest person ever in space.

5 Friendship 7 (USA 3): 20 Feb 1962, John Glenn, 4 hr 55 min 23 sec; first American to orbit.

6 Aurora 7 (USA 4): 24 May 1962, Scott Carpenter, 4 hr 56 min 5 sec; landing overshoot of 250 miles.

7 Vostok 3 (USSR 3): 11 Aug 1962, Andrian Nikolyev, 3 day 22 hr 25 min.

8 Vostok 4 (USSR 4): 12 Aug 1962 Pavel Popovich, 2 day 22 hr 59 min; came to within 6.4 km (4 miles) of Vostok 3.

9 Sigma 7 (USA 5): 3 Oct 1962, Wally Schirra, 9 hr 13 min 11 sec; Pacific splashdown.

10 Faith 7 (USA 6): 15 May 1963, Gordon Cooper, 1 day 10 hr 19 min 49 sec; final US one-man flight.

11 Vostok 5 (USSR 5): 14 Jun 1963, Valeri Bykovsky, 4 day 23 hr 7 min 2 sec; solo flight record-holder.

12 Vostok 6 (USSR 6): 16 Jun 1963, Valentina Tereshkova, 2 day 22 hr 50 min 8 sec; first woman in space.

13 Voskhod 1 (USSR 7): 12 Oct 1964, Vladimir Komarov, Konstantin Feoktistov, Boris Yegerov, 1 day 0 hr 17 min 3 sec: riskiest flight, no spacesuits, no ejection seats, inside a 'Vostok'.

14 Voskhod 2 (USSR 8): 18 Mar 1965, Pavel Belyayev, Alexei Leonov, 1 day 2 hr 2 min 17 sec; Leonov made first walk in space.

15 Gemini 3 (USA 7): 25 Mar 1965, Gus Grissom, John Young, 4 hr 52 min 51 sec; Grissom first man in space twice.

16 Gemini 4 (USA 8): 3 Jun 1965, James McDivitt, Edward White, 4 day 1 hr 56 min 12 sec; White walked in space.

17 Gemini 5 (USA 9): 21 Aug 1965, Gordon Cooper, Charles Conrad, 7 day 22 hr 55 min 14 sec; broke endurance record.

18 Gemini 7 (USA 10): 4 Dec 1965, Frank Borman, James Lovell, 13 day 18 hr 35 min 1 sec; acted as rendezvous target; broke endurance record.

19 Gemini 6 (USA 11): 15 Dec 1965, Wally Schirra, Tom Stafford, 1 day 1 hr 51 min 54 sec; first rendezvous in space; launch pad abort 12 Dec.

20 Gemini 8 (USA 12): 16 Mar 1966, Neil Armstrong, David Scott, 10 hr 41 min 26 sec; emergency landing after first space docking.

21 Gemini 9 (USA 13): 3 Jun 1966, Tom Stafford, Eugene Cernan, 3 day 20 min 50 sec; rendezvous; spacewalk; bull's-eye splashdown.

22 Gemini 10 (USA 14): 18 Jul 1966, John Young,, Michael Collins, 2 day 22 hr 46 min 39 sec; docking; spacewalk; record altitude of 763 km (474 miles).

23 Gemini 11 (USA 15): 12 Sept 1966, Charles Conrad, Richard Gordon, 2 day 23 hr 17 min 8 sec; docking; spacewalk; altitude of 1368 km (850 miles); automatic landing.

24 Gemini 12 (USA 16): 11 Nov 1966, James Lovell, Edwin Aldrin, 3 day 22 hr 34 min 31 sec; docking; record spacewalk of over 2 hr.

Apollo 1 (USA): 27 Jan 1967, Gus Grissom, Edward White, Roger Chaffee; killed in spacecraft fire.

25 Soyuz 1 (USSR 9): 23 Apr 1967, Vladimir Komarov, 1 day 2 hr 47 min 52 sec; Komarov killed when parachute failed; intended to dock with Soyuz 2.

Soyuz 2 (USSR): 24 Apr 1967, Valeri Bykovsky, Alexei Yeliseyev, Yevgeny Khrunov; flight cancelled; was to have docked with Soyuz 1.

26 Apollo 7 (USA 17): 11 Oct 1968, Wally Schirra, Donn Eisele, Walt Cunningham, 10 day 20 hr 9 min 3 sec; Earth orbit shakedown of Command and Service Module.

27 Soyuz 3 (USSR 10): 26 Oct 1968, Georgi Beregovoi, 3 day 22 hr 50 min 45 sec; failed to dock with unmanned Soyuz 2.

USSR: Dec 1968, Alexei Leonov, Oleg Makarov; circumlunar flight cancelled.

28 Apollo 8 (USA 18): 21 Dec 1968, Frank Borman, James Lovell, William Anders, 6 day 3 hr 42 sec; ten lunar orbits over Christmas.

29 Soyuz 4 (USSR 11): 14 Jan 1969, Vladimir Shatalov, 2 day 23 hr 20 min 47 sec; launched with one man, returned with three.

30 Soyuz 5 (USSR 12): 15 Jan 1969, Boris Volynov, Alexei Yeleseyev, Yevgeny Khrunov, 3 day 0 hr 54 min 15 sec; Yeliseyev and Khrunov spacewalk to Soyuz 4 after docking.

31 Apollo 9 (USA 19): 3 Mar 1969, James McDivitt, David Scott, Russell Schweickart, 10 day 1 hr 54 sec; test of Lunar Module in Earth orbit; spacewalk.

32 Apollo 10 (USA 20): 18 May 1969, Tom Stafford, John Young, Eugene Cernan, 8 day 3 min 23 sec; Lunar Module tested in lunar orbit; came to 14.5 km (9 miles) of surface of Moon.

33 Apollo 11 (USA 21): 17 Jul 1969, Neil Armstrong, Michael Collins, Edwin Aldrin, 8 day 3 hr 18 min 35 sec; Armstrong and Aldrin walked on Moon for over 2 hours.

34 Soyuz 6 (USSR 13): 11 Oct 1969, Georgi Shonin, Valeri Kubasov, 4 day 22 hr 42 min 47 sec, welding tests.

35 Soyuz 7 (USSR 14): 12 Oct 1969, Anatoli Filipchenko, Vladislav Volkov, Viktor Gorbatko, 4 day 22 hr 40 min 23 sec; rendezvous to within 488 m (1600 ft) of Soyuz 8, but failed to dock.

36 Soyuz 8 (USSR 15): 13 Oct 1969, Vladimir

Shatalov, Alexei Yeliseyev, 4 day 22 hr 51 min 49 sec; third flight in strange troika mission by Soviets.

37 Apollo 12 (USA 22): 14 Nov 1969, Charles Conrad, Richard Gordon, Alan Bean, 10 day 4 hr 36 min 25 sec; pinpoint landing near Surveyor 3.

38 Apollo 13 (USA 23): 11 Apr 1970, James Lovell, Jack Swigert, Fred Haise, 5 day 22 hr 54 min 41 sec; service module exploded 55 hours into mission; crew limped home using Lunar Module as lifeboat.

39 Soyuz 9 (USSR 16): 1 Jun 1970, Andiran Nikolyev, Vitali Sevastyanov, 17 day 16 hr 58 min 50 sec; crew carried from craft on stretchers suffering acute stress of readapting to gravity after longest flight.

40 Apollo 14 (USA 24): 31 Jan 1971, Alan Shepard, Stuart Roosa, Edgar Mitchell, 9 day 2 min 57 sec; Shepard only Mercury astronaut to walk on Moon.

41 Soyuz 10 (USSR 17): 23 Apr 1971, Vladimir Shatalov, Alexei Yeliseyev, Nikolai Ruckavishnikov, 1 day 23 hr 45 min 54 sec; failed to enter Salyut 1 space station after soft docking.

42 Soyuz 11 (USSR 18): 6 Jun 1971, Georgi Dobrovolsky, Vladislav Volkov, Viktor Patsayev, 23 day 18 hr 21 min 43 sec; crew died as craft depressurized before re-entry; not wearing spacesuits.

43 Apollo 15 (USA 25): 26 Jul 1971, David Scott, Alfred Worden, James Irwin, 12 day 7 hr 11 min 53 sec; first lunar rover.

44 Apollo 16 (USA 26): 16 Apr 1972, John Young, Ken Mattingly, Charles Duke, 11 day 1 hr 51 min 5 sec; Space Shuttle approved during Moon landing mission; Mattingly in lunar orbit made longest solo US flight.

45 Apollo 17 (USA 27): 7 Dec 1972, Eugene Cernan, Ron, Evans, Jack Schmitt, 12 day 13 hr 51 min 59 sec; last manned expedition to Moon this century.

46 Skylab 2 (USA 28): 25 May 1973, Charles Conrad, Joe Kerwin, Paul Weitz, 28 day 49 min 49 sec; spacewalk to repair severely disabled Skylab 1 space station.

47 Skylab 3 (USA 29): 28 Jul 1973, Alan Bean, Owen Garriott, Jack Lousma, 59 day 11 hr 9 min 4 sec; stranded in space temporarily as Command Module malfunctioned.

48 Soyuz 12 (USSR 19), 27 Sept 1973, Vasili Lazarev, Oleg Makarov, 1 day 23 hr 15 min 32 sec; test of space-station ferry.

49 Skylab 4 (USA 30): 16 Nov 1973, Gerry Carr, Edward Gibson, Bill Pogue, 84 day 1 hr 15 min 31 sec; longest US manned spaceflight.

50 Soyuz 13 (USSR 20): 18 Dec 1973, Pyotr Klimuk, Valetin Lebedev, 7 day 20 hr 55 min 35 sec; Soviets and Americans in space together for first time, although they did not meet.

51 Soyuz 14 (USSR 21): 3 Jul 1974, Pavel Popvich, Yuri Artyukhin, 15 day 17 hr 30 min 28 sec; first space spies, on Salyut 3.

52 Soyuz 15 (USSR 22): 26 Aug 1974, Gennadi Serafanov, Lev Demin, 2 day 0 hr 12 min 11 sec; failed to dock with Salyut 3.

53 Soyuz 16 (USSR 23): 2 Dec 1974, Anatoli Filipchenko, Nikolai Ruckavishnikov, 5 day 22 hr 23 min 35 sec; rehearsal for US-USSR joint flight, ASTP.

54 Soyuz 17 (USSR 24): 11 Jan 1975, Alexei Gubarev, Georgi Grechko, 29 day 13 hr 19 min 45 sec; aboard Salyut 4.

55 Soyuz 18-1 (USSR 25): 5 Apr 1975, Vasili Lazarev, Oleg Makarov, 21 min 27 sec; second stage failed; flight aborted.

56 Soyuz 18 (USSR 26): 24 May 1975, Pyotr Klimuk, Vitali Sevastyanov, 62 day 23 hr 20 min 8 sec; aboard Salyut 4.

57 Soyuz 19 (USSR 27): 15 Jul 1975, Alexei Leonov, Valeri Kubasov, 5 day 22 hr 30 min 51 sec; docked with Apollo 18 in joint ASTP mission.

58 Apollo 18 (USA 31): 15 Jul 1975, Tom Stafford, Vance Brand, Deke Slayton, 9 day 1 hr 28 min 24 sec; docked with Soyuz 19; crew gassed during landing, recovered.

59 Soyuz 21 (USSR 28): 6 Jul 1976, Boris Volynov, Vitali Zholobov, 49 day 6 hr 23 min 32 sec, evacuated Salyut 5. (Soyuz 20 was unmanned.)

60 Soyuz 22 (USSR 29): 22 Sept 1976, Valeri Bykovsky, Vladimir Aksyonov, 7 day 21 hr 52 min 17 sec; independent Earth survey flight.

61 Soyuz 23 (USSR 30): 14 Oct 1976, Vyacheslav Zudov, Valeri Rozhdestvensky, 2 day 0 hr 6 min 35 sec; failed to dock with Salyut 5; splashed down in lake.

62 Soyuz 24 (USSR 31), 7 Feb 1977, Viktor Gorbatko, Yuri Glazkov, 17 day 17 hr 25 min 50 sec; aboard Salyut 5.

63 Soyuz 25 (USSR 32): 9 Oct 1977, Vladimir Kovalyonok, Valeri Ryumin, 2 day 0 hr 44 min 45 sec; failed to dock with Salyut 6.

64 Soyuz 26 (USSR 33): 10 Dec 1977, Yuri Romanenko, Georgi Grechko, 96 day 10 hr 0 min 7 sec; aboard Salyut 6; broke endurance record; spacewalk.

65 Soyuz 27 (USSR 34): 10 Jan 1978, Vladimir Dzhanibekov, Oleg Makarov, 5 day 22 hr 58 min 58 sec; visitors to Salyut 6.

66 Soyuz 28 (USSR 35): 2 Mar 1978, Alexei Gubarev, Vladimir Remek, 7 day 22 hr 16 min; Remek was from Czechoslovakia, first non-American, non-Soviet in space; visit to Salyut 6.

67 Soyuz 29 (USSR 36): 15 Jun 1978, Vladimir Kovalyonok, Alexander Ivanchenkov, 139 day 14 hr 47 min 32 sec; aboard Salyut 6; landed in Soyuz 31.

68 Soyuz 30 (USSR 37): 27 Jun 1978, Pyotr Klimuk, Miroslaw Hermaszewski, 7 day 22 hr 2 min 59 sec; visit to Salyut 6; Hermaszewski from Poland.

69 Soyuz 31 (USSR 38): 26 Aug 1978, Valeri Bykovsky, Sigmund Jahn, 7 day 29 hr 49 min 4 sec; visit to Salyut 6; Jahn from East Germany; landed in Soyuz 29.

70 Soyuz 32 (USSR 39): 25 Feb 1979, Vladimir Lyakhov, Valeri Ryumin, 175 day 0 hr 35 min 37 sec; visit to Salyut 6; landed in Soyuz 34, which was launched unmanned.

71 Soyuz 33 (USSR 40): 10 Apr 1979, Nikolai

Ruckavishnikov, Georgi Ivanov; 1 day 23 hr 1 min 6 sec; failed to dock with Salyut 6; Bulgarian Ivanov only Intercosmos visitor not to reach space station.

72 Soyuz 35 (USSR 41): 9 Apr 1980, Leonid Popov, Valeri Ryumin, 184 day 20 hr 11 min 35 sec; Salyut 6 mission took Ryumin to 361 days' space experience.

73 Soyuz 36 (USSR 42): 26 May 1980, Valeri Kubasov, Bertalan Farkas, 7 day 20 hr 45 min 44 sec; visit to Salyut 6; Farkas from Hungary; landed in Soyuz 35.

74 Soyuz T2 (USSR 43): 5 Jun 1980, Yuri Malyshev, Vladimir Aksyonov, 3 day 22 hr 19 min 30 sec, test of new Soyuz model to Salyut 6. (Soyuz T1 was unmanned.)

75 Soyuz 37 (USSR 44): 23 Jul 1980, Viktor Gorbatko, Pham Tuan, 7 day 20 hr 42 min; Visit to Salyut 6; Tuan from Vietnam; landed in Soyuz 36.

76 Soyuz 38 (USSR 45): 18 Sept 1980, Yuri Romanenko, Arnaldo Mendez, 7 day 20 hr 43 min

24 sec; visit to Salyut 6; Mendez from Cuba.

77 Soyuz T3 (USSR 46): 27 Nov 1980, Leonid Kizim, Oleg Makarov, Gennadi Strekalov, 12 day 19 hr 7 min 42 sec; maintenance crew to Salyut 5; first three-man Soyuz since Soyuz 11 accident.

78 Soyuz T4 (USSR 47): 12 Mar 1981, Vladimir Kovalyonok, Viktor Savinykh, 74 day 17 hr 37 min 23 sec; final Salyut 6 long-stay crew; Savinykh 100th person in space.

79 Soyuz 39 (USSR 48): 22 Mar 1981, Vladimir Dzhanibvekov, Jugderdemidyin Gurragcha, 7 day 20 hr 42 min 3 sec; Salyut 6 visit; Gurragcha from Mongolia.

80 Columbia STS 1 (USA 32): 12 Apr 1981, John Young, Bob Crippen, 2 day 6 hr 20 min 52 sec; maiden flight of Space Shuttle.

81 Soyuz 40 (USSR 49): 15 May 1981, Leonid Popov, Dumitru Prunariu, 7 day 20 hr 41 min 52 sec; final visiting crew to Salyut 6; Prunariu from Romania.

82 Columbia STS 2 (USA 33): 12 Nov 1981, Joe Engle, Dick Truly, 2 day 6 hr 13 min 11 sec; first manned flight of used vehicle.

83 Columbia STS 3 (USA 34): 22 Mar 1982, Jack Lousma, Gordon Fullerton, 8 day 0 hr 4 min 46 sec; third test flight.

84 Soyuz T5 (USSR 50): 13 May 1982, Anatoli Berezevoi, Valentin Lebedev, 211 day 9 hr 4 min 32 sec; first, record-breaking, visit to Salyut 7; landed in T7; spacewalk.

85 Soyuz T6 (USSR 51): 24 Jun 1982, Vladimir Dzhanibekov, Alexander Ivanchenkov, Jean-Loup Chrétien, 7 day 21 hr 50 min 52 sec; visit to Salyut 7; Chrétien from France, first West European in space.

86 Columbia STS 4 (USA 35): 27 Jun 1982, Ken Mattingly, Hank Hartsfield, 7 day 1 hr 9 min 31 sec, military flight; final test flight.

87 Soyuz T7 (USSR 52): 19 Aug 1982, Leonid Popov, Alexander Serebrov, Svetlana Savitskaya, 7 day 21 hr 52 min 24 sec; Savitskaya second woman in space after 20 years; landed in T5.

88 Columbia STS 5 (USA 36): 11 Nov 1982, Vance Brand, Robert Overmyer, Joe Allen, William Lenoir, 5 day 2 hr 14 min 26 sec, first commercial mission of Shuttle; deployed two communications satellites; first four-person flight.

89 Challenger STS 6 (USA 37): 4 Apr 1983, Paul Weitz, Karol Bobko, Don Peterson, Story Musgrave, 5 day 0 hr 23 min 42 sec; deployed TDRS 1; limped into orbit after upper stage failure; performed spacewalk.

90 Soyuz T8 (USSR 53): 20 Apr 1983, Vladimir Titov, Gennadi Strekalov, Alexander Serebrov, 2 day 0 hr 17 min 48 sec; failed to dock with Salyut 7; Serebrov first person to fly consecutive missions.

91 Challenger STS 7 (USA 38): 18 Jun 1983, Bob Crippen, Rick Hauck, John Fabian, Sally Ride, Norman Thagard, 6 day 2 hr 24 min 10 sec; satellite deployment mission; first by five people; included first US woman in space.

92 Soyuz T9 (USSR 54): 27 Jun 1983, Vladimir Lyakhov, Alexander Alexandrov, 149 day 10 hr 46 min; trouble with space station, Salyut 7, halted flight; spacewalk.

93 Challenger STS 8 (USA 39): 30 Aug 1983, Richard Truly, Dan Brandenstein, Guoin Bluford, Dale Gardner, William Thornton, 6 day 1 hr 8 min 40 sec; night launch and landing.

Soyuz T10-1 (USSR): 27 Sept 1983, Vladimir Titov, Gennadi Strekalov, 5 min 30 sec; launcher exploded on pad; crew saved by launch escape system.

94 Columbia STS 9 (USA 40): 28 Nov 1983, John Young, Brewster Shaw, Owen Garriott, Robert Parker, Byron Lichtenberg, Ulf Merbold, 10 day 7 hr 47 min 23 sec; flight of European Spacelab 1; Merbold from West Germany; first six-up flight.

95 Challenger STS 41B (USA 41): 3 Feb 1984, Vance Brand, Robert Gibson, Bruce McCandless, Robert Stewart, Ronald McNair, 7 day 23 hr 15 min 54 sec; first independent spacewalk using MMU by McCandless; first space mission to end at launch site (Kennedy/ Canaveral).

96 Soyuz T10 (USSR 55): 8 Feb 1984, Leonid Kizim, Vladimir Solovyov, Oleg Atkov, 236 day 22 hr 49 min 4 sec; longest manned space mission to date; Kizim and Solovyov made record six spacewalks, landed in T11.

97 Soyuz T11 (USSR 56): 3 Apr 1984, Yuri Malyshev, Gennadi Strekalov, Rakesh Sharma, 7 day 21 hr 40 min; visit to Salyut 7; Sharma from India, landed in T10.

98 Challenger STS 41C (USA 42): 6 Apr 1984, Bob Crippen, Dick Scobee, George Nelson, Terry Hart, James van Hoften, 6 day 23 hr 40 min 5 sec; repaired Solar Max; with Soyuz T10 and T11 crews in space, 11 people were up at once.

99 Soyuz T12 (USSR 57): 17 Jul 1984, Vladimir Dhzanibekov, Svetlana Savitskaya, Oleg Volk, 11 day 19 hr 14 min 36 sec; Savitskaya became first woman spacewalker, outside Salyut 7.

100 Discovery STS 41D (USA 43): 30 Aug 1984, Hank Hartsfield, Michael Coats, Judy Resnik, Steven Hawley, Michael Mullane, Charlie Walker, 6 day 0 hr 56 min 4 sec; launch pad abort 27 June; three satellites deployed; Walker first industry-engineer astronaut.

101 Challenger STS 41G (USA 44): 5 Oct 1984, Bob Crippen, Jon McBride, Sally Ride, Kathy Sullivan, David Leestma, Marc Garneau, Paul Scully Power, 8 day 5 hr 23 min 33 sec; first seven-up flight; first carrying two women; Ride first US woman in space twice; Sullivan first US woman to spacewalk; Garneau from Canada.

102 Discovery STS 51A (USA 45): 8 Nov 1984, Rick Hauck, Dave Walker, Joe Allen, Dale Gardner, Anna Fisher, 7 day 23 hr 45 min 54 sec; two spacewalks to retrieve lost communications satellites and return them to Earth.

103 Discovery STS 51C (USA 46): 24 Jan 1985, Ken Mattingly, Loren Shriver, Ellison Onizuka, James Buchli, Gary Payton, 3 day 1 hr 33 min 13 sec; military mission; Payton first USAF Manned Space Flight Engineer.

104 Discovery STS 51D (USA 47): 12 Apr 1985, Karol Bobko, Don Williams, Rhea Seddon, Jeff Hoffman, David Griggs, Charlie Walker, JakeGarn, 6 day 23 hr 55 min 23 sec; deployed three communications satellites; unscheduled EVA (extra-vehicular activity) to attempt repair of one; Senator Jake Garn first passenger observer in space.

105 Challenger STS 51B (USA 48): 29 Apr 1985, Bob Overmyer, Fred Gregory, Don Lind, William Thornton, Norman Thagard, Lodewijk van den Berg, Taylor Wang, 7 day 8 min 50 sec; Spacelab 3 research mission.

106 Soyuz T13 (USSR 58): 6 Jun 1985, Vladimir Dzhanibekov, Viktor Savinykh, 112 day 3 hr 12 min, complete overhaul of Salyut 7 after systems failures; Savinykh came home in Soyuz T14 and Georgi Grechko of T14 in Soyuz T13; spacewalk.

107 Discovery STS 51G (USA 49): 17 Jun 1985, Dan Brandenstein, John Creighton, Shannon Lucid, Steve Nagel, John Fabian, Patrick Baudry, Abdul Aziz Al-Saud, 7 day 1 hr 38 min 58 sec; satellite deployment and research mission; first with three nations represented, Baudry from France (first non-US, non-USSR nation to make two flights), Abdul Aziz Al-Saud, a Prince from Saudi Arabia.

108 Challenger STS 51F (USA 50): 20 Jul 1985, Gordon Fullerton, Roy Bridges, Karl Henize, Anthony England, Story Musgrave, John-David Bartoe, Loren Acton, 7 day 22 hr 45 min 27 sec; launch pad abort on July 12; one engine shutdown during launch, causing abort-to-orbit; Henize oldest man in space at 58; Spacelab 2 research mission.

109 Discovery STS 51I (USA 51): 27 Aug 1985, Joe Engle, Dick Covey, William Fisher, James van Hoften, Mike Lounge, 7 day 2 hr 14 min 42 sec; three satellites deployed; Leasat 3 captured, repaired and redeployed; spacewalks.

110 Soyuz T14 (USSR 59): 17 Sept 1985, Vladimir Vasyutin, Georgi Grechko, Alexander Volkov, 64 day 21 hr 52 min; mission cut short after Vasyutin becomes ill; Grechko returned in Soyuz T13; Savinykh stayed with Soyuz T14 and clocked up mission time of 168 days.

111 Atlantis STS 51J (USA 52): 3 Oct 1985, Karol Bobko, Ron Grabe, Dale Hilmers, Bob Stewart, William Pailes, 4 day 1 hr 45 min 30 sec; military mission.

112 Challenger STS 61A (USA 53): 30 Oct 1985, Hank Hartsfield, Steve Nagel, Bonnie Dunbar, Guion Gluford, James Buchli, Ernst Messerschmitt, Reinhard Furrer, Wubbo Ockels, 7 day 44 min 51 sec; West German-funded Spacelab D1 mission; Messerschmitt and Furrer from West Germany; Ockels from Netherlands; first eight-up mission.

113 Atlantis STS 61B (USA 54): 27 Nov 1985, Brewster Shaw, Bryan O'Connor, Mary Cleave, Jerry Ross, Sherwood Spring, Rudolpho Neri Vela, Charlie Walker, 6 day 21 hr 4 min 50 sec; Neri Vela from Mexico; Walker's third flight as Shuttle payload specialist; Ross and Spring assembled structures during EVAs.

114 Columbia STS 61C (USA 55): 12 Jan 1986, Robert Gibson, Charles Bolden, Franklin Chang-Diaz, George Nelson, Steve Hawley, Robert Cenker, Bill Nelson, 6 day 2 hr 4 min 9 sec; much-delayed flight; Bill Nelson, a Congressman, second 'political' passenger.

Challenger STS 51L (USA): 28 Jan 1986, Dick Scobee, Mike Smith, Judith Resnik, Ronald McNair, Ellison Onizuka, Christa McAuliffe, Gregory Jarvis, 73 sec; disintegrated at 14,330 m (47,000 ft); crew killed; first flight to take off but not to reach space; first US in-flight fatalities.

115 Soyuz T15 (USSR 60): 13 Mar 1986, Leonid Kizim, Vladimir Solovyov, 125 day 0 hr 1 min; first mission to new space station Mir 1; also docked with Salyut 7; Kizim clocked up over a year in space experience; spacewalks.

116 Soyuz TM2 (USSR 61): 5 Feb 1987, Yuri Romanenko, Alexander Laveikin, 326 day 11 hr 38 min; record duration mission by Romanenko aboard Mir 1; landed in Soyuz TM3 (Soyuz TM1 was unmanned). Laveikin, 200th person in space, returned in TM 3 after 174 days. Spacewalks.

117 Soyuz TM3 (USSR 62): 22 Jul 1987, Alexander Viktorenko, Alexander Alexandrov, Muhammed Faris, 7 day 23 hr 4 min 5 sec; Faris from Syria. Alexandrov remained on Mir for 160 days. Viktorenko and Faris landed in Soyuz TM2 with Laveikin.

118 Soyuz TM4 (USSR 63): 21 Dec 1987, Vladimir Titov, Musa Manarov, Anatoli Levchenko, 365 day 22 hr 39 min; Levchenko returned in Soyuz TM3 with Romanenko and Alexandrov after flight of 7 days. Titov and Manarov returned in Soyuz TM6. Spacewalks.

119 Soyuz TM5 (USSR 64): 7 Jun 1988, Anatoli Solovyov, Viktor Savinykh, Alexander Alexandrov, 9 day 20 hr 10 min; Alexandrov second Bulgarian in space. Crew returned in Soyuz TM4.

120 Soyuz TM6 (USSR 65): 31 Aug 1988, Vladimir Lyakhov, Valeri Polyakov, Abdol Mohmand, 8 day 20 hr 27 min; Mohmand from Afghanistan. Polyakov remained on Mir. Lyakhov and Mohmand landed in Soyuz TM5 after 'stranded in space' scare.

121 Discovery STS 26 (USA 56): 29 Sept 1988, Rick Hauck, Dick Covey, Mike Lounge, David Hilmers, George Nelson, 4 day 1 hr 0 min 11 sec; America's return to space 32 months after Challenger disaster. Nelson first American to make successive national spaceflights.

122 Soyuz TM7 (USSR 66): 26 Nov 1988, Alexander Volkov, Sergei Krikalev, Jean-Loup Chrétien. 151 day

11 hr 10 min; visit to Mir. Chrétien. (French) was first non-US, non-USSR to make two spaceflights and to make a spacewalk. Chrétien returned after 25 days.

123 Atlantis STS 27 (USA 57): 2 Dec 1988, Robert Gibson, Guy Gardner, Jerry Ross, Mike Mullane, William Shepherd, 4 day 9 hr 5 min 35 sec, military mission to deploy Lacrosse spy satellite. With six cosmonauts on Mir, 11 people were in space.

124 Discovery STS 29 (USA 58): 13 Mar 1989, Michael Coats, John Blaha, James Buchli, James Bagian, Robert Springer, 4 day 23 hr 38 min 52 sec; deployed TDRS satellite. STS 28 delayed.

125 Atlantis STS 30 (USA 59): 4 May 1989, David Walker, Ron Grabe, Norman Thagard, Mary Cleave, Mark Lee, 4 day 0 hr 57 min 31 sec; deployed *Magellan* for its journey to orbit the planet Venus. First deployment of a planetary spacecraft from a manned spacecraft.

126 Columbia STS 28 (USA 60): 8 Aug 1989, Brewster Shaw, Richard Richards, David Leestma, James Adamson, Mark Brown, 5 day 1 hr 0 min 9 sec; military mission to deploy KH-12 reconnaissance satellite.

127 Soyuz TM8 (USSR 67): 6 Sept 1989, Alexander Viktorenko, Alexander Serebrov, 166 day 6 hr 58 min; occupied Mir space station. First Soviet manned flight to operate commercial US experiments. First Soviet test of tethered MMU.

128 Atlantis STS 34 (USA 61): 18 Oct 1989, Donald Williams, Michael McCulley, Shannon Lucid, Franklin Chang-Diaz, Ellen Baker, 4 day 23 hr 39 min 24 sec; deployed Jupiter orbiter *Galileo.*

129 Discovery STS 33 (USA 62): 22 Nov 1989, Frederick Gregory, John Blaha, Story Musgrave, Manley Carter, Kathryn Thornton, 5 day 0 hr 6 min 46 sec; military mission to deploy Magnum elite spacecraft. First military manned spaceflight with civilian and female crew.

130 Columbia STS 32 (USA 63): 9 Jan 1990, Dan Brandenstein, James Wetherbee, Bonnie Dunbar, Marsha Ivins, David Low, 10 day 21 hr 0 min 37 sec; retrieved LDEF from orbit.

131 Soyuz TM9 (USSR 68): 11 Feb 1990, Anatoli Solovyov, Alexander Balandin, 179 day 2 hr 19 min; occupation of Mir space station. Included Soviet record 7 hr spacewalk

132 Atlantis STS 36 (USA 64): 28 Feb 1990, John Creighton, John Caspar, Mike Mullane, David Hilmers, Pierre Thuot, 4 day 10 hr 18 min 22 sec; military mission to deploy KH-12 reconnaissance satellite, which broke up in orbit later.

133 Discovery STS 31 (USA 65): 24 Apr 1990, Loren Shriver, Charles Bolden, Steven Hawley, Bruce McCandless, Kathryn Sullivan, 5 day 1 hr 16 min 6 sec; deployed Hubble Space Telescope. Reached record 532 km Shuttle altitude.

134 Soyuz TM10 (USSR 69): 1 Aug 1990, Gennadi Manakov, Gennadi Strekalov, 130 day 19 hr 36 min; occupation of Mir space station. Spacewalk.

135 Discovery STS 41 (USA 66): 6 Oct 1990, Richard Richards, Robert Canbana, Thomas Akers, Bruce Melnick, William Shepherd, 4 day 2 hr 10 min 12 sec; deployed *Ulysses* solar polar orbiter.

136 Atlantis STS 38 (USA 67): 15 Nov 1990, Richard Covey, Frank Culbertson, Robert Springer, Carl Meade, Sam Gemar, 4 day 21 hr 54 min 27 sec; military mission.

137 Columbia STS 35 (USA 68): 2 Dec 1990, Vance Brand, Guy Gardner, Jeff Hoffman, Mike Lounge, Robert Parker, Ronald Parise, Samual Durrance, 8 day 23 hr 5 min 7 sec; launch of Astro-1 observatory.

138 Soyuz TM11 (USSR 70): 2 Dec 1990, Viktor Afanasyef, Musa Manarov, Toyohiro Akiyama, 175 day 1 hr 51 min 18 sec; new occupation of Mir space station with spacewalks. Akiyama –a Japanese journalist – returned to Earth withSoyuz TM10 after 7 days. With two people already aboard Mir, and STS 35 in orbit a record 12 people were in space at once.

139 Atlantis STS 37 (USA 69): 5 Apr 1991, Steven Nagel, Ken Cameron, Jay Apt, Linda Godwin, Jerry Ross, 5 day 23 hr 33 min 44 sec; development of Gamma Ray Observatory and two spacewalks by Ross and Apt.

140 Discovery STS 39 (USA 70): 28 Apr 1991, Michael Coats, Blaine Hammond, Guion Bluford, Gregory Harbaugh, Richard Heib, DonaldMcMonagle, Charles Veach, 8 day 7 hr 22 min 2 sec; Star Wars research mission, first unclassified military flight, first with seven NASA astronauts.

141 Soyuz TM12 (USSR 71): 18 May 1991, Anatoli Artsebarski, Sergei Krikalyov, Helen Sharman, 144 day 15 hr 22 min; Sharman first Briton in space; returned in TM12. Krikalev stayed aboard Mir and returned after 311 days (during which time the USSR had ceased to exist). Artsebarski and Krikalyov made six spacewalks in record 33 days.

142 Columbia STS 40 (USA 71): 5 Jun 1991, Bryan O'Connor, Sidney Gutierrez, JamesBagian, Tamara Jerni gan, Rhea Seddon, Drew Gaffney, Millie Hughes-Fulford, 9 day 2 hr 14 min 20 sec; Spacelab Life Sciences 1 mission. First mission with three women aboard.

143 Atlantis STS43 (USA 72): 2 Aug 1991, John Blaha, Michael Baker, James Adamson,David Low, Shannon Lucid, 8 day 21 hr 21 min 25 sec, deployed TDRS satellite. Lucid first woman to make three flights and also oldest woman in space (48)

144 Discovery STS 48 (USA 73): 12 Sept 1991, John Creighton, Kenneth Reightler, Mark Brown, James Buchli, Sam Gemar, 5 day 8 hr 27 min 34 sec; deployment of Upper Atmosphere Researchsatellite (UARS). Manoeuvred to avoid space debris.

145 Soyuz TM13 (USSR 72): 2 Oct 1991, Alexander Volkov, Taktar Aubakirov, Franz Viebock, 175 day 2 hr 52 min; Aubakirov, first Kazakh and Viebock first Austrian in space, flying commercial missions.Both returned in TM12 after 7 day flight. Volkov remained on Mir. This was the last Soviet spaceflight before the USSR was dissolved.

146 Atlantis STS 44 (USA 74): 24 Nov 1991, Frederick Gregory, Terence Henricks, StoryMusgrave, Mario Runco, James Voss, Thomas Hennen, 6 day 22 hr 50 min 42 sec; deployed DSP early warning satellite and conducted reconnaissance mission, with first 'space spy' Hennen. Flight cut short.

147 Discovery STS 42 (USA 75): 22 Jan 1992, Ronald Grabe, Stephen Oswald, Norman Thagard, David Hilmers, William Readdy, Roberta Bondar, Ulf Merbold, 8 day 1 hr 14 min 45 sec; International Microgravity Laboratory mission.Bondar from Canada and Merbold from Germany.

148 Soyuz TM14 (Russia 1): 17 Mar 1992, Alexander Viktorenko, Alexander Kaleri, Klaus Dietrich Flade, 145 day 14 hr 10 min; new residents for Mir, while the German commercial passenger Flade returned in TM13 after 7-day mission. Spacewalk. This was the first Soyuz launched by Russia rather than the former USSR.

149 Atlantis STS 45 (USA 76): 24 Mar 1992, Charles Bolden, Brian Duffy, Kathryn Sullivan, Michael Foale, David Leestma, Byron Lichtenberg, Dirk Frimout, 8 day 22 hr 9 min 25 sec; Atlas science mission Frimout first Belgian in space.

150 Endeavour STS 49 (USA 77): 7 May 1992, Dan Brandenstein, Kevin Chilton, Rick Heib, Bruce Melnick, Pierre Thuot, Kathryn Thornton, Tom Akers, 8 day 21 hr 17 min 38 sec; retrieved Intelsat 6 and reboosted it into geo-stationary orbit. Record-breaking 8 hr 29 minEVA by Thuot, Hieb and Akers, the third of four EVAs during the mission and the first by three crew.

151 Columbia STS 50 (USA 78): 25 Jun 1992, Richard Richards, Kenneth Bowersox, BonnieDunbar, Ellen Baker, Carl Meade, Lawrence De Lucas, Eugene Trinh, 13 day 19 hr 30 min 4 sec; longest space shuttle mission to date and first to fly extended duration orbiter (EDO) cryogenic pallet. US Microgravity Laboratory mission 1.

152 Soyuz TM15 (Russia 2): 27 Jul 1992, Anatoli Solovyov, Sergei Avdeyev, Michel Tognini, 188 day 21 hr 40 min; new occupation of Mir. French visiting mission.Tognini returns in TM14 after 14-day flight. Space walks.

153 Atlantis STS 46 (USA 79): 31 Jul 1992, Loren Shriver, Andrew Allen, Claude Nicollier, Marsha Ivins, Jeff Hoffman, Franklin-Chang Diaz, Franco Malerba, 7 day 23 hr 15 min 5 sec; deployed Eureca and Tethered satellites. Nicollier first Swiss astronaut and first non-US NASA mission specialist. Malerba first Italian in space. Record five space nations being represented with Tognini on Mir at the same time and 12 persons in space.

154 Endeavour STS 47 (USA 80): 12 Sept 1992, Robert Gibson, Curtis Brown, Mark Lee, Jay Apt, Jan Davis, Mae Jemison, Mamoru Mohri, 7 day 22 hr 31 min 11 sec; Japan's Spacelab J mission. Mohri second Japanese in space. Lee and Davis first marriedcouple. Jemison first coloured female.

155 Columbia STS 52 (USA 81): 22 Oct 1992, James Wetherbee, Michael Baker, Charles Veach, William Shepherd, Tamara Jernigan, Steven MacLean, 9 day 20 hr 56 min 13 sec; science research mission, also deployed Italian Lageos satellite. Maclean from Canada.

156 Discovery STS 53 (USA 82): 2 Dec 1992, David Walker, Robert Cabana, Guion Bluford, James Voss, Michael Clifford, 7 day 7 hr 19 min 17 sec; final US Dept. of Defense Shuttle mission.

157 Endeavour STS 54 (USA 83): 13 Jan 1993, John Casper, Donald McMonagle, GregoryHarbaugh, Mario Runco, Susan Helms, 5 day 23 hr 38 min 17 sec; satellite deployment, science and EVA mission. Helms first female military officer in space.

158 Soyuz TM16 (Russia 3): 24 Jan 1993, Gennadi Manakov, Alexander Polishchuk, 19 day 0 hr 44 min; crew rotation flight to Mir space station; spacewalks.

159 Discovery STS 56 (USA 84): 8 Apr 1993, Kenneth Cameron, Stephen Oswald, Michael Foale, Kenneth Cockrell, Ellen Ochoa, 9 day 6 hr 8 min 19 sec; Atlas 2 laboratory mission.

160 Columbia STS 55 (USA 85): 26 Apr 1993, Steven Nagel, Tom Henricks, Jerry Ross, Charles Precourt, Bernard Harris, Ulrich Walter, Hans W. Schlegel, 9 day 23 hr 39 min 59 sec; German-funded Spacelab D2 mission; Walter and Schlegel from Germany. Launch pad abort on 22 March.

161 Endeavour STS 57 (USA 86): 21 June 1993, Ronald Grabe, Brian Duffy, David Low, Nancy Sherlock, Jeff Wisoff, Janice Voss, 9 day 23 hr 46 min 1 sec; Eureca retrieval,EVA.

162 Soyuz TM17 (Russia 4): 1 July 1993, Vasili Tsiblyev, Alexander Serebrov, Jean-Pierre Haignere, 196 days 17 hr 45 min; crew rotation to Mir 1 space station lus commercial visiting mission by French cosmonaut Hagnere. The landing of Endeavour 1 on 1 July marked another record: a manned launch and landing on the same day. Haignere landed after 20 days in Soyuz TM16. Serebrov made five mission spacewalks, bringing his total to 10, a record.

163 Discovery STS 51 (USA 87): 12 September 1993, Frank Culbertson, William Readdy, James Newman, Daniel Bursch, Carl Walz, 9 day 20 hr 11 min 7 sec; deployed ACTS communications, deployed and retrieved German satellite; performed 6 hr spacewalk. Launch pad abort on 12 Aug.

164 Columbia STS 58 (USA 88): 18 October 1993, John Blaha, Richard Searfoss, Rhea Seddon, William McArthur, David Wolf, Shannon Lucid, Martin Fettmann, 14 day 0 hr 13 min 32 sec; Spacelab Life Sciences 2 mission brought Lucid's flight time on Shuttle to woman's record 34 days in four flights.

165 Endeavour STS 61 (USA 89): 2 December 1993, Richard Covey, Ken Bowersox, Claude Nicollier, Story Musgrave, Jeff Hoffman, Tom Akers, Kathryn Thornton, 10 day 19 hr 58 min 33 sec; Hubble space telescope servicing and repair mission. US record of five EVAs. Musgrave, first to fly five Shuttle missions, clocked up record 35 days Shuttle flight time. Nicollier, Swiss, made second flight.

166 Soyuz TM18 (Russia 5): 8 January 1994, Viktor Afanasyev, Yuri Usachev, Valeri Poliakov, 182 day 0 hr 27 min; new residency aboard Mir 1 space station; Poliakov remained on Mir.

167 Discovery STS 60 (USA 90): 3 February 1994, Charles Bolden, Kenneth Reightler, Franklin-Chang Diaz, Jan Davis, Ron Sega, Sergei Krikalev, 8 day 7 hr 9 min 22 sec; Krikalev first Russian on a US mission.

168 Columbia STS 62 (USA 91): 4 March 1994, John Casper, Andrew Allen, Pierre Thuot, Sam Gemar, Marsha Ivins, 13 day 23 hr 16 min 33 sec; third

RECORDS IN MANNED SPACEFLIGHT

(to January 1995)

First in space: Yuri Gagarin (USSR) 12 April 1961.

First American in orbit: John Glenn 20 February 1962.

First woman in space: Valentina Tereshkova (USSR) 16 June 1963.

First non-US, non-Soviet spaceman: Vladimir Remek (Czech) 2 March 1978.

First to make two flights: Gus Grissom USA 25 March 1965.

First to walk in space: Alexei Leonov (USSR) 18 March 1965.

First to walk in space independently: Bruce McCandless USA 3 February 1984.

First woman spacewalker: Svetlana Savitskaya USSR 17 July 1984.

First military mission: Soyuz 14 (USSR) 3 July 1974.

First flight to the Moon: Apollo 8 (USA) 21 December 1968.

First landing on the Moon: Apollo 8 (USA) 16 July 1969.

First men on the Moon: Neil Armstrong and Buzz Aldrin (USA) 16 July 1969.

First mother in space: Anna Fisher (USA) 8 November 1984.

First passenger-observer: Jake Garn (USA) on 12 April 1985.

First rendezvous in space: Gemini 6 and 7 (USA) 16 December 1965.

First to fly solo in lunar orbit: John Young (USA) 18 May 1969.

First woman spacewalker: Svetlana Savitskaya (USSR) 17 July 1984.

First Briton in space: Helen Sharman 18 May 1991.

First person to be launched on both Russian and US rockets: Sergei Krikalev (Russia) who flew Soyuz TM7, TM 12 and STS 60.

Oldest person in space: Vance Brand (USA) 59 years old on a spaceflight on 2 December 1990.

Youngest person in space: Gherman Stepanovich (USSR) 25 years old on a spaceflight on 6 Aug 1961.

Longest manned spaceflight: on 9 January 1995 Valeri Poliakov (Russia) achieved 366 days in space. He is due to return in March 1995.

Greatest altitude: the crew of the Apollo 13 attained a distance of 400 187 km (248 655 mi) above the Earth's surface on 15 April 1970.

Greatest speed: the fastest speed at which humans have travelled is 39 897 km/h (24 791 mph) during the Apollo 10 mission on 26 May 1969.

Greatest fatalities: the largest number of fatalities in a single spaceflight was suffered aboard the American Challenger 51L on 28 January 1986 when seven crew (five men and two women) died.

First spacecraft manoeuvres: Gemini 3 USA 25 March 1965.

First docking: Gemini 8 USA 16 March 1966.

First dual flight: Vostok 3 and 4 USSR 12 August 1961.

First military mission: Soyuz 14 USSR 3 July 1974.

First night launch: Soyuz 1 USSR 23 April 1967.

First night landing: Soyuz 10 USSR 23 April 1971.

Extended Duration Orbiter mission, dedicated to science and engineering.

169 Endeavour STS 59 (USA 92): 9 Apr 1994, Sidney Gutierrez, Kevin Chilton, Linda Godwin, Jay Apt, Michael Clifford, Thomas Johns, 11 day 5 hr 49 min 30 sec, Space Radar Laboratory mission.

170 Soyuz TM19 (Russia 6): 1 July 1994, Yuri Malenchencko, Talgat Musabayev, 125 day 22 hr 53 min; new Mir crew; first all-rookie Russian crew since 1977; landed with Merbold from TM20.

171 Columbia STS 65 (USA 93): 8 July 1994, Robert Cabana, James Halsell, Richard Hieb, Carl Walz, Leroy Chiao, Donald Thomas, Chiaki Naito-Mukai, 14 day 17 hr 55 min 1 sec; International Microgravity Laboratory 2 mission; Mukai first Japanese woman in space.

172 Discovery STS 64 (USA 94): 9 Sept 1994, Dick Richards, Blaine Hammond, Carl Meade, Mark Lee, Susan Helms, Jerry Linenger, 10 day 22 hr 49 min 57 sec; Earth observation, science and spacewalk mission. Lee and Meade made untethered EVAs to test space rescue back pack.

173 Endeavour STS 68 (USA 95): 30 Sept 1994, Mike Baker, Terry Wilcutt, Tom Jones, Steve Smith, Jeff Wisoff, Dan Bursch, 11 day 5 hr 46 min 9 sec; Space Radar Laboratory 2 mission for Earth observation. Launch pad abort on 18 Aug.

174 Soyuz TM20 (Russia 7): 3 October 1994, Alexander Viktorenko, Yelena Kondakova, Ulf Merbold, in flight at time of going to press; Kondakova, first woman to make a long duration space flight. Merbold (German), a European Space Agency visitor, first non-US, non-Soviet/Russian spaceperson to make three flights and first West European to fly in both US and Russian flights. With Shuttle in space, 12 people were in space at the same time. Merbold landed in TM19 after 31 days.

175 Atlantis STS 66 (USA 96): 3 Nov 1994, Donald McMonagle, Curtis Brown, Ellen Ochoa, Scott Parazynsky, Joseph Tanner, Jean-Francois Clervoy, 10 day 22 hr 34 min 2 sec; Atlas 3 Earth atmosphere research mission; Clervoy European Space Agency astronaut from France.

Planned flights for 1995

Despite the large budget cuts resulting from the economic problems faced by Russia, the Russian space programme continues. The flights planned for 1995 are characterized by increased cooperation between Russia and the USA. One of the major projects for the year is the planned docking of Shuttle and Mir 1. Canadian, French, Japanese and Swedish astronauts are scheduled to make flights during 1995.

February

Discovery STS 63 (USA): James Wetherbee, Eileen Collins, Michael Foale, Janice Ford, Bernard Harris, Vladimir Titov; Mir rendezvous; Titov from Russia; Collins first female Shuttle pilot.

Endeavour STS 67 (USA): Stephen Oswald, William Gregory, Tamara Jernigan, John Grunsfield, Wendy Lawrence, Ronald Parice, Sam Durrance; Astro 2 laboratory.

March

Soyuz TM21 (Russia): Vladimir Dezhurov, Gennadi Strekalov, Norman Thagard; Mir 1 flight; Thagard first US astonaut to fly on Russian mission.

June

Atlantis STS 71 (USA): Robert Gibson, Charles Precourt, Ellen Baker, Greg Harbaugh, Bonnnie Dunbar, Anatoli Solovyov, Nikolai Budarin; Mir 1 docking; Solovyov and Budarin to remain on Mir 1.

Discovery STS 70 (USA): Terrence Henricks, Kevin Kregal, Nancy Sherlock, Donald Thomas, Mary Ellen Webber; TDRS deploy.

July

Endeavour STS 69 (USA): Davod Walker, Ken Cockrell, James Voss, James Newman, Michael Gernhardt; Wake Shield deploy.

August

Soyuz TM22 (Russia): Yuri Gidzenko, Sergei Avdeyev, Christa Fuglesang; Mir 1 flight; Fuglesang (Swedish) of European Space Agency will make spacewalk.

September

Columbia STS 73 (USA): Ken Bowersox, Kent Rominger, Kathryn Thornton, Catherine Coleman, Micheal Lopez-Alegria, Fred Leslie, Albert Sacco; US Microgravity Laboratory 2.

October

Atlantis STS 74 (USA): Kenneth Cameron, James Halsell, Jerry Ross, William McArthur, Chris Hadfield; Mir 1 docking; may carry Russians Yuri Onufrienko and Alexander Polishchuk and return Gidzenko and Avdeyev of Soyuz TM22. Hadfield from Canada.

November

Endeavour STS 72 (USA): Brian Duffy, Brent Jett, Leroy Chiao, Daniel Brady, Winston Scott, Koichi Wakata; SFU retrieval.

December

Soyuz TM23 (Russia): Vasili Tsiblyev, Sergei Treshev, Claudie Andre-Deshays; Mir 1 flight; crew to be confirmed; Andre-Deshays from France.

MAJOR NATIONAL CIVILIAN SPACE AGENCIES

Canada The Canadian Space Agency is playing a major role in the USA's NASA Space Shuttle and Freedom space station programmes, providing remote manipulator systems.

China The Ministry of Astronautics manages the national space programme through several organizations. China launches its own applications satellites, using a range of boosters that are marketed commercially worldwide.

Europe The European Space Agency is one of the world's leading space organizations, managing a diverse programme on behalf of members: Austria, Belgium, Denmark, Finland, France, Germany, Ireland, Italy, the Netherlands, Norway, Spain, Sweden, Switzerland and the UK. Current major programmes are the development of the Ariane 5 launcher; a manned space laboratory, Columbus, to be attached to the Freedom space station; and a series of environmental monitoring spacecraft.

France Centre National d'Etudes Spatiales (CNES) is Europe's busiest and largest national agency, organizing several manned flights to the Mir space station and planning to launch Europe's first military spy satellite, Helios.

Germany The German space agency is involved in manned spaceflights to the Russian Mir 1 and aboard the US Space Shuttle.

India The Indian Space Research Organization (ISRO) has developed its own satellite launcher and has ambitious plans for an autonomous communications satellite system.

Italy The Italian Space Agency is playing a role in the USA's Freedom space station, supplying a logistics module.

Japan The National Space Development Agency (NASDA) and Institute of Space and Astronautical Science manage a programme that includes a range of satellite launch vehicles, communications and science satellites and a module to be operated at the US Freedom space station.

Russia Since the break up of the USSR, the Russian Space Agency manages about 80% of the former Soviet programme which has, however, been hit by drastic budget cuts. The RSA is trying to offset this lack of funding by commercializing as much of its programme as possible.

UK The British National Space Centre may have a modest budget but has become the European leader in remote sensing and Earth observation work within the European Space Agency.

USA The National Aeronautics and Space Administration (NASA) is the world's leading space organization, managing major manned, science and applications programmes. It operates a Space Shuttle Fleet and plans to operate a permanently manned space station, Freedom in Orbit by the year 2000.

NATIONAL MANNED SPACE-FLIGHT TOTALS (to 9 January 1995)

Nationality	*Time*	*No. of flights*
Soviet	3835 day 8 hr 16 min 44 sec	72
Russian[1]	1125 day (Soyuz TM20 still in flight)	7
Russian	8 day 7 hr 9 min 22 sec	1 (US)
Soviet & Russian	4960 day 1 hr 59 min 44 sec	96
American	804 day 19 hr 9 min 19 sec	96

Other nations which have flown with the USSR/Russia and USA:

Nationality	Time	No. of flights
French (2 US; 4 Soviet; 2 Russian)	85 day 3 hr 16 min 46 sec	8
German (4 US, 1 Soviet, 2 Russian)	82 day 18 hr 49 min 2 sec	7
Japanese (2 US, 1 Soviet)	30 day 14 hr 21 min 12 sec	3
Canadian	26 day 3 hr 34 min 31 sec	3 (US)
Swiss	18 day 19 hr 13 min 38 sec	2 (US)
Bulgarian	11 day 19 hr 11 min 6 sec	2 (Soviet)
Belgian	8 day 22 hr 9 min 25 sec	1 (US)
Afghan	8 hr 20 hr 27 min	1 (Soviet)
Italian	7 day 23 hr 15 min 5 sec	1 (US)
Syrian	7 day 23 hr 4 min 5 sec	1 (Soviet)
Czech	7 day 22 hr 16 min	1 (Soviet)
Austrian	7 day 22 hr 13 min	1 (Soviet)
Polish	7 day 22 hr 2 min 59 sec	1 (Soviet)
Indian	7 day 21 hr 40 min	1 (Soviet)
British	7 day 21 hr 14 min 28 sec	1 (Soviet)
Hungarian	7 day 20 hr 45 min 44 sec	1 (Soviet)
Cuban	7 day 20 hr 43 min 24 sec	1 (Soviet)
Mongolian	7 day 20 hr 42 min 3 sec	1 (Soviet)
Vietnamese	7 day 20 hr 42 min	1 (Soviet)
Romanian	7 day 20 hr 41 min 52 sec	1 (Soviet)
Saudi	7 day 1 hr 38 min 58 sec	1 (US)
Dutch	7 day 0 hr 44 min 51 sec	1 (US)
Mexican	6 day 21 hr 4 min 50 sec	1 (US)

[1] *Russia became a separate independent state on 25 December 1991. The figures for Russia do not include figures from the Soyuz TM20 flight nor the Russian flight on a US mission. Some Soviet missions flew with cosmonauts born in what are now independent states (Kazakhstan, Ukraine and Latvia).*

One German cosmonaut was from the former East Germany.

MOST EXPERIENCED PERSONS IN SPACE (to 9 Jan 1995)

Name and (no. of flights)	**Country**	**Time**
MEN		
Valeri Poliakov (2) (in flight on 9 Jan 1995)	USSR/Russia	606 day
Musa Manarov (2)	USSR	541 day 0 hr 31 min 18 sec
Sergei Krikalev (3)	USSR/Russia	471 day 14 hr 20 min 22 sec
Yuri Romanenko (3)	USSR	430 day 18 hr 21 min 30 sec
Alexander Viktorenko (4)	USSR/Russia (in flight on 9 Jan 1995)	417 day
Alexander Volkov (3)	USSR/Russia	391 day 11 hr 54 min
Anatoli Solovyov (3)	USSR/Russia	377 day 20 hr 9 min
Leonid Kizim (3)	USSR	374 day 17 hr 57 min 42 sec
Alexander Serebrov (4)	USSR/Russia	373 day 2 hr 53 min 12 sec
Vladimir Titov (2)	USSR	367 day 22 hr 56 min 48 sec
Vladimir Solovyov (2)	USSR	361 day 22 hr 50 min
Valeri Ryumin (3)	USSR	361 day 21 hr 31 min 57 sec
Viktor Afanasyev (3)	USSR/Russia	357 day 2 hr 19 min 18 sec
Vladimir Lyakhov (3	USSR	333 day 7 hr 48 min 37 sec
Gennadi Manakov (2)	USSR/Russia	309 day 20 hr 20 min
WOMEN		
Yelena Kondakova (1) (in flight on 5 January 1995)	Russia	98 day
Shannon Lucid (4)	USA	34 day 22 hr 52 min 13 sec
Marsha Ivins (3)	USA	32 day 21 hr 32 min 15 sec
Bonnie Dunbar (3)	USA	31 day 17 hr 15 min 32 sec
Rhea Seddon (3)	USA	30 day 2 hr 22 min 15 sec
Kathryn Thornton (3)	USA	24 day 17 hr 22 min 57 sec
Kathryn Sullivan (3)	USA	22 day 4 hr 48 min 39 sec
Ellen Ochoa (2)	USA	20 day 4hr 43 min 5 sec

Time

TIME SYSTEMS

Time forms the basis of many scientific laws, but time itself is very difficult to define. Time, like distance, separates objects and events, and for this reason can be regarded as the fourth dimension. However, time cannot be measured directly. We must make do with measuring the way in which the passage of time affects things.

The Earth's orbit is not circular but elliptical, so the Sun does not appear to move against the stars at a constant speed. Most everyday time systems are therefore based on a hypothetical 'mean Sun', which is taken to travel at a constant speed equal to the average speed of the actual Sun.

A *day* is the time taken for the Earth to turn once on its axis. A *sidereal day* is reckoned with reference to the stars and is the time taken between successive passes of the observer's meridian by the same star. One sidereal day is 23 hours 56 minutes 4 seconds. A solar day is calculated with respect to the mean Sun. The mean solar day is 24 hours long. A *year* is the time taken for the Earth to complete one orbit of the Sun. The Earth's true revolution period is 365 days 6 hours 9 minutes 10 seconds, and this is known as a *sidereal year*. However, the direction in which the Earth's axis points is changing due to an effect known as precession. The north celestial pole now lies near the star Polaris in the constellation Ursa Minor, thus Polaris is also known as the Pole Star. By the year AD 14,000, the Earth's axis will point in a different direction and the bright star Vega in Lyra will be near the pole. This effect also means that the position of the Sun's apparent path across the sky is changing with respect to the stars. A tropical year compensates for the effects of precession and is 365 days 5 hours 48 minutes 45 seconds long. It is the tropical year that is used as the basis for developing a calendar.

MEASURING TIME

The earliest device for measuring time was the *sundial*, which can be traced back to the Middle East c. 3500 BC. A sundial comprises a rod or plate called a *gnomon* that casts a shadow on a disc; where the shadow points indicates the position of the Sun and hence the time of day. Mechanical clocks, driven by falling weights, appeared in the 14th century, and the first *mechanical watches*, driven by a coiled mainspring, in the 16th century.

The first pendulum clock was invented by Christiaan Huygens (1629–95), a Dutch physicist, in the middle of the 17th century. Pendulum clocks could not be used on board ships owing to the vessel's motion. In 1714 the British Longitude Board offered a prize for the development of a marine chronometer. The English clockmaker John Harrison (1693–1776) produced his first *marine chronometer* in 1735 after seven years' work.

The first *quartz clock*, operated by the vibrations of a quartz crystal when an electrical voltage is applied, appeared in 1929. The quartz clock is accurate to within one second in ten years. This was followed in 1948 by the atomic clock, which depends on the natural vibrations of atoms. The most accurate modern atomic clocks are accurate to one second in 1·7 million years.

The SI unit of time is the *second*, which was originally defined as $^1/_{86400}$ of the mean solar day. However, as we have seen, the Earth is not a very good timekeeper, so scientists no longer use it to define the fundamental unit of time. The second is now defined as the duration of 9,192,631,770 periods of the radiation corresponding to the transition between the two hyperfine levels of the ground state of a caesium-133 atom.

Greenwich Mean Time (GMT) is the local time at Greenwich, England. The *Greenwich Meridian* is the line of 0° longtitude, which passes through Greenwich Observatory. The mean Sun crosses the Greenwich Meridian at midday GMT. Also known as *Universal Time* (UT), GMT is used as a standard reference time throughout the world. *Sidereal time* literally means 'star time'. It is reckoned with reference to the stars and not the Sun.

THE JULIAN AND GREGORIAN CALENDARS

By 46 BC the Roman calendar had become confused and in need of reform. On the advice of the Egyptian astronomer Sosigenes, Julius Caesar therefore introduced what became known as the Julian calendar. The year 46 BC – known as the 'Year of Confusion' – was lengthened to 445 days to bring it in line with the solar year. Under the Julian calendar the solar year was calculated at 365 days and divided into 12 months. Each month contained 30 or 31 days except for February, which contained 28 days (or 29 days in a leap year). However, by 1582 an overestimation by Sosigenes of about 11 minutes a year had accumulated into a 10-day difference between the Julian calendar and the astronomical year. Pope Gregory XIII therefore ordered that 5 October 1582 should become 15 October, and that century years would only be leap years if divisible by 400 (i.e. 1600, 2000). In error by 0·0005 days per year, the present Gregorian calendar will not need to be revised for many years.

Seasons

The four seasons in the northern hemisphere are astronomically speaking:

Spring from the vernal equinox (about 21 March) to the summer solstice (21 or 22 June);

Summer from the summer solstice (21 or 22 June) to the autumnal equinox (about 21 September);

Autumn (or Fall in the USA) from the autumnal equinox (about 21 September) to the winter solstice (21 December or 22 December);

Winter from the winter solstice (21 or 22 December) to the vernal equinox (about 21 March).

In the southern hemisphere, of course, autumn corresponds to spring, winter to summer, spring to autumn and summer to winter.

The solstices (from Latin *sol*, sun; *sistere*, to stand still) are the two times in the year when the sun is farthest from the Equator and appears to be still. The equinoxes (from Latin *aequalis*, equal; *nox*, night) are the two times in the year when day and night are of equal length when the Sun crosses the equator. The longest day has the longest interval between sunrise and sunset. It is the day on which the summer solstice falls and in the northern hemisphere occurs on 21 June, or more rarely on 22 June.

MONTHS OF THE YEAR

January 31 days; from the Roman republican calendar month Januarius, named after Janus, god of doorways and of beginnings.

February 28 days (29 in a leap year); from from the Roman republican calendar month Februarius, named after Februa, the festival of purification held on the 15th.

March 31 days; from the Roman republican calendar month Martius, named after the god Mars.

April 30 days; from the Roman republican calendar month Aprilis. The Romans considered the month sacred to Venus and may have named it after her Greek equivalent Aphrodite. It may also have derived from the Latin *aperire*, 'to open', in reference to the spring blossoming.

May 31 days; from the Roman republican calendar month Maius, named after the goddess Maia.

June 30 days; from the Roman republican calendar month Junius, named after the goddess Juno.

July 31 days; from the Roman republican calendar month Julius, named after Julius Caesar in 44 BC.

August 31 days; from the Roman republican calendar month Augustus named after the emperor Augustus in 8 BC.

September 30 days; 7th month of the early Roman republican calendar, from Latin *septem*, 'seven'.

October 31 days; 8th month of the early Roman republican calendar, from the Latin *octo*, 'eight'.

November 30 days; 9th month of the early Roman republican calendar, from the Latin *novem*, 'nine'.

December 31 days; 10th month of the early Roman republican calendar, from Latin *decem*, 'ten'.

Leap year

The use of leap years – years with an extra intercalary period – is common to most calendars. In the Gregorian calendar it is an extra day (29 February) that compensates for the quarter-day difference between a calendar year of 365 days and the astronomical year of 365·24219878 days. Every centennial year divisible by 400 and every other year divisible by four is a leap year. The date when it will be necessary to suppress a further leap year, sometimes assumed to be AD 4000, AD 8000, etc., is not yet clearly definable, owing to minute variations in the Earth-Sun relationship. The word 'leap' derives from the Old Norse *hlaupar*, indicating a leap in the sense of jump. The origin of the term probably derives from the observation that in a leap year any fixed-day festival falls on the next day of the week but one to that on which it fell in the preceding year, and not on the next day of the week as happens in common years.

The New Year

In early medieval times Christian Europe regarded March 25 (Annunciation Day) as New Year's Day. Anglo-Saxon England, however, used December 25 to mark the year's beginning until William I decreed that the year should begin on January 1. England later fell into line with the rest of Christendom, recognizing March 25. The introduction of the Gregorian Calendar in 1582 confirmed 1 January as New Year's Day. The adoption of 1 January as New Year's Day in various European countries took place in the following years: *1522* Venice and some other Italian states; *1544* Catholic states and some Protestant states of Germany; *1556* Spain, Portugal, Catholic Netherlands; *1559* Denmark, Prussia, Sweden; *1564* France; *1583* Protestant Netherlands; *1600* Scotland; *1725* Russia; *1751* England.

DAYS OF THE WEEK

Sunday is named after the Sun

Monday is named after the Moon

Tuesday is named after Tiw, the Anglo-Saxon counterpart of the Nordic god Tyr, son of Odin

Wednesday is named after Woden, the Ango-Saxon counterpart of Odin, the Nordic god of war

Thursday is named after Thor, the Nordic god of thunder, eldest son of Odin

Friday is named after Frigg, the Nordic goddess of love, wife of Odin

Saturday is named after Saturn, Roman god of agriculture and vegetation

THE PERPETUAL CALENDAR

There is a formula that works out the days of the week in any month in any year of the 20th century. The method for working out the day of the week, using the table of values below, is as follows.

Using 14 June 1947 as an example, add together

a) the date (14) = 14

b) the value of the month (June) = 4

c) the year = 47

d) the leap years already experienced that century (divide the previous line by 4 and ignore the remainder; 47 divided by 4) = 11

Total **76**

Divide the total by 7 = 10

remainder 6

The remainder is the value of the day of the week in the table below. 6 = Saturday, thus 14 June 1947 was a Saturday.

Month	Value
January	0 (Leap year 6)
February	3 (Leap year 2)
March	3
April	6
May	1
June	4
July	6
August	2
September	5
October	0
November	3
December	5

Day	Value
Monday	1
Tuesday	2
Wednesday	3
Thursday	4
Friday	5
Saturday	6
Sunday	0

THE JEWISH CALENDAR

It is thought that the Jewish Calendar, as used today, was popularly in use from the 9th century BCE. It is based on the biblical calculations that place the creation in 3761 BCE.

The abbreviation BCE means Before the Common Era, while CE stands for Common Era; they correspond to BC and AD, respectively.

The complicated rules of the Jewish Calendar with regard to festivals and fasts have resulted in a calendar scheme in which a Jewish year may be one of the following six types:

Minimal Common (353 days);
Regular Common (354 days);
Full Common (355 days);
Minimal Leap (383 days);
Regular Leap (384 days);
Full Leap (385 days).

Months of the Jewish Calendar

1. Nisan	30 days
2. Iyar	29 days
3. Sivan	30 days
4. Tammuz	29 days
5. Ab	30 days
6. Elul	29 days
7. Tishri	30 days
8. Cheshvan (Marcheshvan)	29/30 days*
9. Kislev	29/30 days*
10. Tebet	29 days
11. Shebat	30 days
12. Adar	29 days (30 in a leap year)
Ve-Adar †	29 days

* can have either 29 or 30 days depending on the year.

† a 13th month is intercalated into the calendar every 3rd, 6th, 8th, 11th, 14th, 17th and 19th year of a 19-year cycle. It contains all the religious observances that usually occur in Adar.

COMPARATIVE JEWISH CALENDAR 1996–1997

Jan 1996	1 2 3 4 5 6 7 8 9 10 11 12 13 14 15 16 17 18 19 20 21		22 23 24 25 26 27 28 29 30 31
Tebet 5756 (cont'd)	9 10 11 12 13 14 15 16 17 18 19 20 21 22 23 24 25 26 27 28 29	**Shebat**	1 2 3 4 5 6 7 8 9 10
Feb 1996	1 2 3 4 5 6 7 8 9 10 11 12 13 14 15 16 17 18 19 20		21 22 23 24 25 26 27 28 29
Shebat (cont'd)	11 12 13 14 15 16 17 18 19 20 21 22 23 24 25 26 27 28 29 30	**Adar**	1 2 3 4 5 6 7 8 9
Mar 1996	1 2 3 4 5 6 7 8 9 10 11 12 13 14 15 16 17 18 19 20		21 22 23 24 25 26 27 28 29 30 31
Adar (cont'd)	10 11 12 13 14 15 16 17 18 19 20 21 22 23 24 25 26 27 28 29	**Nisan**	1 2 3 4 5 6 7 8 9 10 11
April 1996	1 2 3 4 5 6 7 8 9 10 11 12 13 14 15 16 17 18 19		20 21 22 23 24 25 26 27 28 29 30
Nisan (cont'd)	12 13 14 15 16 17 18 19 20 21 22 23 24 25 26 27 28 29 30	**Iyar**	1 2 3 4 5 6 7 8 9 10 11
May 1996	1 2 3 4 5 6 7 8 9 10 11 12 13 14 15 16 17 18		19 20 21 22 23 24 25 26 27 28 29 30 31
Iyar (cont'd)	12 13 14 15 16 17 18 19 20 21 22 23 24 25 26 27 28 29	**Sivan**	1 2 3 4 5 6 7 8 9 10 11 12 13
June 1996	1 2 3 4 5 6 7 8 9 10 11 12 13 14 15 16 17		18 19 20 21 22 23 24 25 26 27 28 29 30
Sivan (cont'd)	14 15 16 17 18 19 20 21 22 23 24 25 26 27 28 29 30	**Tammuz**	1 2 3 4 5 6 7 8 9 10 11 12 13
July 1996	1 2 3 4 5 6 7 8 9 10 11 12 13 14 15 16		17 18 19 20 21 22 23 24 25 26 27 28 29 30 31
Tammuz (cont'd)	14 15 16 17 18 19 20 21 22 23 24 25 26 27 28 29	**Ab**	1 2 3 4 5 6 7 8 9 10 11 12 13 14 15
Aug 1996	1 2 3 4 5 6 7 8 9 10 11 12 13 14 15		16 17 18 19 20 21 22 23 24 25 26 27 28 29 30 31
Ab (cont'd)	16 17 18 19 20 21 22 23 24 25 26 27 28 29 30	**Elul**	1 2 3 4 5 6 7 8 9 10 11 12 13 14 15 16
Sept 1996	1 2 3 4 5 6 7 8 9 10 11 12 13		14 15 16 17 18 19 20 21 22 23 24 25 26 27 28 29 30
Elul 5757 (cont'd)	17 18 19 20 21 22 23 24 25 26 *27 28 29*	**Tishri***	1 2 3 4 5 6 7 8 9 10 11 12 13 14 15 16 17

* Jewish New Year 5757

Oct 1996 1 2 3 4 5 6 7 8 9 10 11 12 13 14 15 16 17 18 19 20 21 22 23 24 25 26 27 28 29 30 31
Tishri 5757 (cont'd) 18 19 20 21 22 23 24 25 26 27 28 29 30 **Cheshvan** 1 2 3 4 5 6 7 8 9 10 11 12 13 14 15 16 17 18

Nov 1996 1 2 3 4 5 6 7 8 9 10 11 12 13 14 15 16 17 18 19 20 21 22 23 24 25 26 27 28 29 30
Cheshvan (cont'd) 19 20 21 22 23 24 25 26 27 28 29 **Kislev** 1 2 3 4 5 6 7 8 9 10 11 12 13 14 15 16 17 18 19

Dec 1996 1 2 3 4 5 6 7 8 9 10 11 12 13 14 15 16 17 18 19 20 21 22 23 24 25 26 27 28 29 30 31
Kislev (cont'd) 20 21 22 23 24 25 26 27 28 29 **Tebet** 1 2 3 4 5 6 7 8 9 10 11 12 13 14 15 16 17 18 19 20 21

Jan 1997 1 2 3 4 5 6 7 8 9 10 11 12 13 14 15 16 17 18 19 20 21 22 23 24 25 26 27 28 29 30 31
Tebet (cont'd) 22 23 24 25 26 27 28 29 **Shebat** 1 2 3 4 5 6 7 8 9 10 11 12 13 14 15 16 17 18 19 20 21 22 23

Feb 1997 1 2 3 4 5 6 7 8 9 10 11 12 13 14 15 16 17 18 19 20 21 22 23 24 25 26 27 28
Shebat (cont'd) 24 25 26 27 28 29 30 **Adar** 1 2 3 4 5 6 7 8 9 10 11 12 13 14 15 16 17 18 19 20 21

Mar 1997 1 2 3 4 5 6 7 8 9 10 11 12 13 14 15 16 17 18 19 20 21 22 23 24 25 26 27 28 29 30 31
Adar (cont'd) 22 23 24 25 26 27 28 29 30 **Ve-Adar** 1 2 3 4 5 6 7 8 9 10 11 12 13 14 15 16 17 18 19 20 21 22

April 1997 1 2 3 4 5 6 7 8 9 10 11 12 13 14 15 16 17 18 19 20 21 22 23 24 25 26 27 28 29 30
Ve-Adar (cont'd) 23 24 25 26 27 28 29 **Nisan** 1 2 3 4 5 6 7 8 9 10 11 12 13 14 15 16 17 18 19 20 21 22 23

May 1997 1 2 3 4 5 6 7 8 9 10 11 12 13 14 15 16 17 18 19 20 21 22 23 24 25 26 27 28 29 30 31
Nisan (cont'd) 24 25 26 27 28 29 30 **Iyar** 1 2 3 4 5 6 7 8 9 10 11 12 13 14 15 16 17 18 19 20 21 22 23 24

June 1997 1 2 3 4 5 6 7 8 9 10 11 12 13 14 15 16 17 18 19 20 21 22 23 24 25 26 27 28 29 30
Iyar (cont'd) 25 26 27 28 29 **Sivan** 1 2 3 4 5 6 7 8 9 10 11 12 13 14 15 16 17 18 19 20 21 22 23 24 25

July 1997 1 2 3 4 5 6 7 8 9 10 11 12 13 14 15 16 17 18 19 20 21 22 23 24 25 26 27 28 29 30 31
Sivan (cont'd) 26 27 28 29 30 **Tammuz** 1 2 3 4 5 6 7 8 9 10 11 12 13 14 15 16 17 18 19 20 21 22 23 24 25 26

Aug 1997 1 2 3 4 5 6 7 8 9 10 11 12 13 14 15 16 17 18 19 20 21 22 23 24 25 26 27 28 29 30 31
Tammuz (cont'd) 27 28 29 **Ab** 1 2 3 4 5 6 7 8 9 10 11 12 13 14 15 16 17 18 19 20 21 22 23 24 25 26 27 28

Sept 1997 1 2 3 4 5 6 7 8 9 10 11 12 13 14 15 16 17 18 19 20 21 22 23 24 25 26 27 28 29 30
Ab 5758 (cont'd) 29 30 **Elul** 1 2 3 4 5 6 7 8 9 10 11 12 13 14 15 16 17 18 19 20 21 22 23 24 25 26 27 28

Oct 1997 1 2 3 4 5 6 7 8 9 10 11 12 13 14 15 16 17 18 19 20 21 22 23 24 25 26 27 28 29 30 31
Elul (cont'd) 29 **Tishri*** 1 2 3 4 5 6 7 8 9 10 11 12 13 14 15 16 17 18 19 20 21 22 23 24 25 26 27 28 29 30

* Jewish New Year 5758

Nov 1997 1 2 3 4 5 6 7 8 9 10 11 12 13 14 15 16 17 18 19 20 21 22 23 24 25 26 27 28 29 30
Cheshvan 1 2 3 4 5 6 7 8 9 10 11 12 13 14 15 16 17 18 19 20 21 22 23 24 25 26 27 28 29 **Kislev** 1

Dec 1997 1 2 3 4 5 6 7 8 9 10 11 12 13 14 15 16 17 18 19 20 21 22 23 24 25 26 27 28 29 30 31
Kislev (cont'd) 2 3 4 5 6 7 8 9 10 11 12 13 14 15 16 17 18 19 20 21 22 23 24 25 26 27 28 29 30 **Tebet** 1 2

THE ISLAMIC CALENDAR

The Islamic calendar is based on lunar years beginning with the year of the Hejirah (AD 622 of the Julian calendar), when Muhammad travelled from Mecca to Medina. It runs in cycles of 30 years, of which the 2nd, 5th, 7th, 10th, 13th, 16th, 18th, 21st, 24th, 26th and 29th are leap years.

A year consists of 12 months containing alternately 30 days and 29 days, with the intercalation of one day at the end of the 12th month – Dhû'l Hijja – in a leap year. Common years have 354 days, leap years 355. The extra day is intercalated in order to reconcile the date of the first of the month with the date of the actual New Moon. Some Muslims register the first of the month on the evening that the crescent becomes visible.

Hejirah years are used principally in Iran, Turkey, Saudi Arabia and other states of the Arabian peninsula, Egypt, certain parts of India, and Malaysia.

Months of the Muslim Calendar

1. Muharram — 30 days
2. Safar — 29 days
3. Rabîa I — 30 days
4. Rabîa II — 29 days
5. Jumâda I — 30 days
6. Jumâda II — 29 days
7. Rajab — 30 days
8. Shaabân — 29 days
9. Ramadan — 30 days
10. Shawwâl — 29 days
11. Dhû'l-Qa'da — 30 days
12. Dhû'l Hijja — 29 days (30 days in a leap year)

COMPARATIVE ISLAMIC CALENDAR 1996–1997

Jan 1996 1 2 3 4 5 6 7 8 9 10 11 12 13 14 15 16 17 18 19 20 21 22 23 24 25 26 27 28 29 30 31
Shaabân 1416 (cont'd) 9 10 11 12 13 14 15 16 17 18 19 20 21 22 23 24 25 26 27 28 29 **Ramadan** 1 2 3 4 5 6 7 8 9 10

Feb 1996 1 2 3 4 5 6 7 8 9 10 11 12 13 14 15 16 17 18 19 20 21 22 23 24 25 26 27 28 29
Ramadan (cont'd) 11 12 13 14 15 16 17 18 19 20 21 22 23 24 25 26 27 28 29 30 **Shawwâl** 1 2 3 4 5 6 7 8 9

Mar 1996 1 2 3 4 5 6 7 8 9 10 11 12 13 14 15 16 17 18 19 20 21 22 23 24 25 26 27 28 29 30 31
Shawwâl (cont'd) 10 11 12 13 14 15 16 17 18 19 20 21 22 23 24 25 26 27 28 29 **Dhû'l-Qa'da** 1 2 3 4 5 6 7 8 9 10 11

April 1996 1 2 3 4 5 6 7 8 9 10 11 12 13 14 15 16 17 18 19 20 21 22 23 24 25 26 27 28 29 30
Dhû'l-Qa'da (cont'd) 12 13 14 15 16 17 18 19 20 21 22 23 24 25 26 27 28 29 30 **Dhû'l Hijja** 1 2 3 4 5 6 7 8 9 10 11

May 1996 1 2 3 4 5 6 7 8 9 10 11 12 13 14 15 16 17 18 19 20 21 22 23 24 25 26 27 28 29 30 31
Dhû'l Hijja (cont'd) 12 13 14 15 16 17 18 19 20 21 22 23 24 25 26 27 28 29 **Muharram***1 2 3 4 5 6 7 8 9 10 11 12 13

* Islamic New Year 1417

June 1996 1 2 3 4 5 6 7 8 9 10 11 12 13 14 15 16 17 18 19 20 21 22 23 24 25 26 27 28 29 30
Muharram (cont'd) 14 15 16 17 18 19 20 21 22 23 24 25 26 27 28 29 30 **Safar** 1 2 3 4 5 6 7 8 9 10 11 12 13

July 1996 1 2 3 4 5 6 7 8 9 10 11 12 13 14 15 16 17 18 19 20 21 22 23 24 25 26 27 28 29 30 31
Safar (cont'd) 14 15 16 17 18 19 20 21 22 23 24 25 26 27 28 29 **Rabîa I** 1 2 3 4 5 6 7 8 9 10 11 12 13 14 15

Aug 1996 1 2 3 4 5 6 7 8 9 10 11 12 13 14 15 16 17 18 19 20 21 22 23 24 25 26 27 28 29 30 31
Rabîa I (cont'd) 16 17 18 19 20 21 22 23 24 25 26 27 28 29 30 **Rabîa II** 1 2 3 4 5 6 7 8 9 10 11 12 13 14 15 16

Sept 1996 1 2 3 4 5 6 7 8 9 10 11 12 13 14 15 16 17 18 19 20 21 22 23 24 25 26 27 28 29 30
Rabîa II (cont'd) 17 18 19 20 21 22 23 24 25 26 27 28 29 **Jumâda I** 1 2 3 4 5 6 7 8 9 10 11 12 13 14 15 16 17

Oct 1996 1 2 3 4 5 6 7 8 9 10 11 12 13 14 15 16 17 18 19 20 21 22 23 24 25 26 27 28 29 30 31
Jumâda I (cont'd) 18 19 20 21 22 23 24 25 26 27 28 29 30 **Jumâda II** 1 2 3 4 5 6 7 8 9 10 11 12 13 14 15 16 17 18

Nov 1996 1 2 3 4 5 6 7 8 9 10 11 12 13 14 15 16 17 18 19 20 21 22 23 24 25 26 27 28 29 30
Jumâda II 19 20 21 22 23 24 25 26 27 28 29 **Rajab** 1 2 3 4 5 6 7 8 9 10 11 12 13 14 15 16 17 18 19
(cont'd)

Dec 1996 1 2 3 4 5 6 7 8 9 10 11 12 13 14 15 16 17 18 19 20 21 22 23 24 25 26 27 28 29 30 31
Rajab 20 21 22 23 24 25 26 27 28 29 30 **Shaabân** 1 2 3 4 5 6 7 8 9 10 11 12 13 14 15 16 17 18 19 20
(cont'd)

Jan 1997 1 2 3 4 5 6 7 8 9 10 11 12 13 14 15 16 17 18 19 20 21 22 23 24 25 26 27 28 29 30 31
Shaabân 21 22 23 24 25 26 27 28 29 **Ramadan** 1 2 3 4 5 6 7 8 9 10 11 12 13 14 15 16 17 18 19 20 21 22
(cont'd)

Feb 1997 1 2 3 4 5 6 7 8 9 10 11 12 13 14 15 16 17 18 19 20 21 22 23 24 25 26 27 28
Ramadan 23 24 25 26 27 28 29 30 **Shawwâl** 1 2 3 4 5 6 7 8 9 10 11 12 13 14 15 16 17 18 19 20
(cont'd)

Mar 1997 1 2 3 4 5 6 7 8 9 10 11 12 13 14 15 16 17 18 19 20 21 22 23 24 25 26 27 28 29 30 31
Sawwal 21 22 23 24 25 26 27 28 29 **Dhû'l-Qa'da** 1 2 3 4 5 6 7 8 9 10 11 12 13 14 15 16 17 18 19 20 21 22
(cont'd)

April 1997 1 2 3 4 5 6 7 8 9 10 11 12 13 14 15 16 17 18 19 20 21 22 23 24 25 26 27 28 29 30
Dhû'l-Qa'da 23 24 25 26 27 28 29 30 **Dhû'l Hijja** 1 2 3 4 5 6 7 8 9 10 11 12 13 14 15 16 17 18 19 20 21 22
(cont'd)

May 1997 1 2 3 4 5 6 7 8 9 10 11 12 13 14 15 16 17 18 19 20 21 22 23 24 25 26 27 28 29 30 31
Dhû'l Hijja 23 24 25 26 27 28 29 30 **Muharram*** 1 2 3 4 5 6 7 8 9 10 11 12 13 14 15 16 17 18 19 20 21 22 23
(cont'd)

* Islamic New Year 1418

June 1997 1 2 3 4 5 6 7 8 9 10 11 12 13 14 15 16 17 18 19 20 21 22 23 24 25 26 27 28 29 30
Muharram 24 25 26 27 28 29 30 **Safar** 1 2 3 4 5 6 7 8 9 10 11 12 13 14 15 16 17 18 19 20 21 22 23
(cont'd)

July 1997 1 2 3 4 5 6 7 8 9 10 11 12 13 14 15 16 17 18 19 20 21 22 23 24 25 26 27 28 29 30 31
Safar 24 25 26 27 28 29 **Rabîa I** 1 2 3 4 5 6 7 8 9 10 11 12 13 14 15 16 17 18 19 20 21 22 23 24 25
(cont'd)

Aug 1997 1 2 3 4 5 6 7 8 9 10 11 12 13 14 15 16 17 18 19 20 21 22 23 24 25 26 27 28 29 30 31
Rabîa I 26 27 28 29 30 **Rabîa II** 1 2 3 4 5 6 7 8 9 10 11 12 13 14 15 16 17 18 19 20 21 22 23 24 25 26
(cont'd)

Sept 1997 1 2 3 4 5 6 7 8 9 10 11 12 13 14 15 16 17 18 19 20 21 22 23 24 25 26 27 28 29 30
Rabîa II 27 28 29 **Jumâda I** 1 2 3 4 5 6 7 8 9 10 11 12 13 14 15 16 17 18 19 20 21 22 23 24 25 26 27
(cont'd)

Oct 1997 1 2 3 4 5 6 7 8 9 10 11 12 13 14 15 16 17 18 19 20 21 22 23 24 25 26 27 28 29 30 31
Jumâda I 28 29 30 **Jumâda II** 1 2 3 4 5 6 7 8 9 10 11 12 13 14 15 16 17 18 19 20 21 22 23 24 25 26 27 28
(cont'd)

Nov 1997 1 2 3 4 5 6 7 8 9 10 11 12 13 14 15 16 17 18 19 20 21 22 23 24 25 26 27 28 29 30
Jumâda II 29 **Rajab** 1 2 3 4 5 6 7 8 9 10 11 12 13 14 15 16 17 18 19 20 21 22 23 24 25 26 27 28 29
(cont'd)

Dec 1997 1 2 3 4 5 6 7 8 9 10 11 12 13 14 15 16 17 18 19 20 21 22 23 24 25 26 27 28 29 30 31
Rajab 30 **Shaabân** 1 2 3 4 5 6 7 8 9 10 11 12 13 14 15 16 17 18 19 20 21 22 23 24 25 26 27 28 29 **Ramadan** 1
(cont'd)

THE CHINESE CALENDAR

The ancient Chinese calendar is based on a lunar year and consists of 12 months of alternately 29 and 30 days, making 354 days in total. To keep the calendar in step with the solar year intercalary months are inserted. The months are numbered and sometimes given one of the 12 animal names that are usually attached to years and hours in the Chinese calendar:

Years of the rat (include): 1900, 1912, 1924, 1936, 1948, 1960, 1972, 1984, 1996, 2008.

Years of the ox: 1901, 1913, 1925, 1937, 1949, 1961, 1973, 1985, 199, 2009.

Years of the tiger: 1902, 1914, 1926, 1938, 1950, 1962, 1974, 1986, 1998, 2010.

Years of the rabbit: 1903, 1915, 1927, 1939, 1951, 1963, 1975, 1987, 1999, 2111.

Years of the dragon: 1904, 1916, 1928, 1940, 1952, 1964, 1976, 1988, 2000.

Years of the snake: 1905, 1917, 1929, 1941, 1953, 1965, 1977, 1989, 2001.

Years of the horse: 1906, 1918, 1930, 1942, 1954, 1966, 1978, 1990, 2002.

Years of the sheep (or goat): 1907, 1919, 1931, 1943, 1955, 1967, 1979, 1991, 2003.

Years of the monkey: 1908, 1920, 1932, 1944, 1956, 1968, 1980, 1992, 2004.

Years of the chicken: 1909, 1921, 1933, 1945, 1957, 1969, 1981, 1993, 2005.

Years of the dog: 1910, 1922, 1934, 1946, 1958, 1970, 1982, 1994, 2006.

Years of the pig: 1911, 1923, 1935, 1947, 1959, 1971, 1983, 1995, 2007.

The calendar was in use until the establishment of the republic (1911) when the Gregorian calendar was introduced, and was formally banned in China in 1930. The calendar is, however, still widely used unofficially in China, and the New Year festival remains a national holiday. It is also used in Hong Kong, Singapore, and Malaysia, and by Chinese communities elsewhere.

The Chinese New Year begins at the first new moon after the Sun enters Aquarius, and therefore falls between 21 January and 19 February in the Gregorian calendar.

THE JAPANESE CALENDAR

The Japanese calendar has the same structure – in terms of years, months and weeks – as the Gregorian calendar. The difference lies in the numeration of the years as the Japanese chronology is based on a series of imperial epochs. As the Gregorian calendar calculates the years from one religious date, the Japanese calendar calculates each epoch from the accession of an emperor.

The four most recent epochs are based on the reigns of the last four emperors, who are referred to by their epoch names – their personal names are never used.

Epoch Meiji (Emperor Mutsuhito)	13 Oct 1868–31 July 1912
Epoch Taisho (Emperor Yoshihito)	1 Aug 1912–25 Dec 1926
Epoch Showa (Emperor Hirohito)	26 Dec 1926–7 Jan 1989
Epoch Heisei (Emperor Akihito)	8 Jan 1989–

The months are unnamed, simply numbered. The days of the week, however, do have names:

Nichiyobi	Sun-day (Sunday)
Getsuyobi	Moon-day (Monday)
Kayobi	Fire-day (Tuesday)
Suiyobi	Water-day (Wednesday)
Mokuyobi	Wood-day (Thursday)
Kinyobi	Metal-day (Friday)
Doyobi	Earth-day (Saturday)

INDIAN CALENDARS

The principal Indian calendars reckon their epochs from historical events such as the accession or death of a ruler or a religious founder.

The Vikrama era

The Vikrama era originated in northern India and is still used in western India. It dates from 23 February 57 BC in the Gregorian calendar.

The Saka era

The Saka era dates from 3 March AD78 in the Gregorian calendar. It is based on the solar year – beginning with the spring equinox. The 365 days (366 in a leap year) are divided into 12 months. The first five months are of 31 days and the remaining seven of 30 – in a leap year the first six months are of 31 days and the last six of 30. In 1957 the Saka era was declared the national calendar of India, to run concurrently with the Gregorian calendar.

The Buddhist era

The Buddhist era dates from 543 BC, the believed date of Buddha's death (Nirvana), although many Buddhist sects adopt different dates for his death. The actual date of his death was 487 BC.

The Jain era

The Jain era dates from the death of the founder of the Jainist religion, Vardhamana, in 527 BC.

The Parsee (Zoroastrian) era

The Parsee era dates from 16 June AD 632 in the Gregorian calendar.

THE COPTIC CALENDAR

The Coptic calendar – which is still used in areas of Egypt and Ethiopia for religious purposes – dates from 29 August AD 284 of the Gregorian calendar.

The Coptic year is made up of 12 months of 30 days, followed by five complementary days. In a leap year – which immediately precedes the leap year of the Julian calendar – the last month is followed by six days.

THE ANCIENT GREEK CALENDAR

The chronology of Ancient Greece was based on cycles of four years – Olympiads – corresponding with the periodic Olympic Games held on the plain of Olympia in Elis. The intervening years were simply numbered, 1st, 2nd, etc., and each Olympiad was named after the victor of the Games. The first recorded Olympiad is Choroebus, 776 BC.

A lunar year of 12 months and (usually) 354 days was aligned with the solar year by the addition of an extra month every other year. However, this extra month was not always added in the same position within the year. The names of the months varied in the Hellenistic world. The Athenian months were called: Hecatombaion (midsummer), Metageitnion, Boedromion, Pyanopsion, Maimacterion, Poseideion, Gamelion, Anthesterion, Elaphebolion, Mounychion, Thargelion, and Scirophorion.

THE FRENCH REPUBLICAN CALENDAR

The French republican calendar was adopted in 1793, replacing the Gregorian calendar with a secular and more regular alternative. The year was divided into 12 months of 30 days with five (in leap years, six) supplementary days at the end of the year. Weeks were replaced by decades of ten days, which were named primidi, duodi, tridi, quartidi, quintidi, sextidi, septidi, octidi, nonidi and décadi. Each month comprised three decades. The era dated from 22 September 1792 of the Gregorian calendar. The republican calendar was abolished by Napoleon I on 1 January 1806.

The months of the calendar were:

Vendémiaire (meaning 'the month of the grape harvest'). Gregorian equivalent: 23 September to 22 October.

Brumaire (meaning 'the month of mist'). Gregorian equivalent: 23 October to 21 November.

Frimaire (meaning 'the month of frost'). Gregorian equivalent: 22 November to 21 December.

Nivôse (meaning 'the month of snow'). Gregorian equivalent: 22 December to 20 January.

Pluviôse (meaning 'the month of rain'). Gregorian equivalent: 21 January to 19 February.

Ventôse (meaning 'the month of wind'). Gregorian equivalent: 20 February to 21 March.

Germinal (meaning 'the month of buds'). Gregorian equivalent: 22 March to 20 April.

Floréal (meaning 'the month of flowers'). Gregorian equivalent: 21 April to 20 May.

Prairial (meaning 'the month of meadows'). Gregorian equivalent: 21 May to 19 June.

Messidor (meaning 'the month of harvest'). Gregorian equivalent: 20 June to 19 July.

Thermidor (meaning 'the month of heat'). Gregorian equivalent: 20 July to 18 August.

Fructidor (meaning 'the month of fruit'). Gregorian equivalent: 19 August to 22 September, including the supplementary days.

SIGNS OF THE ZODIAC

The zodiac – in astronomy – is an imaginary belt that extends eight degrees on either side of the annual path or eliptic of the Sun. The concept was devised in Mesopotamia c. 3000 BC. The orbits of the Moon and of the major planets of the solar system (except Pluto) lie entirely within the zodiac. It is divided into 12 equal areas – the signs of the zodiac – each of 30 degrees.

In astrology the zodiac is a diagram depicting the zodiac belt with symbols representing each of the 12 sections of the zodiac. The zodiac – from the Greek *zoidiakos,* circle of animals – is used by astrologers to predict the future.

Although the original periods during which the Sun appears to be in each of the constellations of the zodiac no longer apply, astrology nonetheless adheres to the original dates.

Astrology is the interpretation of the influence of planets and stars upon human lives. It is based upon the concept that if an event occurred while the planets were in a particular configuration, a similar event would be likely to happen when those planetary circumstances were repeated.

Astrology originated in Mesopotamia and was developed in ancient Greece, before being absorbed into the Indian, Islamic and West European cultures. In ancient times astrology was regarded as a science.

Although it has been condemned by various Christian councils, astrology retains great popularity through daily predictions in newspapers and specialist almanacs.

The signs of the zodiac are:

Aries (symbol: the Ram) The Sun is in the first sign of the zodiac from about March 21 to April 19.

Taurus (symbol: the Bull) The Sun is in Taurus from about April 20 to May 20.

Gemini (symbol: the Twins) The Sun is in Gemini from about May 21 to June 21.

Cancer (symbol: the Crab) The Sun is in Cancer from about June 22 to July 22.

Leo (symbol: the Lion) The Sun is in Leo from about July 23 to August 22.

Virgo (symbol: the Virgin) The Sun is in Virgo from about August 23 to September 22.

Libra (symbol: the Balance) The Sun is in Libra from about September 23 to October 23.

Scorpio (symbol: the Scorpion) The Sun is in Scorpio from about October 24 to November 21.

(The second half of Scorpio is sometimes referred to as Ophiuchus – symbol: the Serpent-Bearer – by some European astrologers.)

Sagittarius (symbol: the Archer) The Sun is in Sagittarius from about November 22 to December 21.

Capricorn (symbol: the Goat) The Sun is in Capricorn from about December 22 to January 19.

Aquarius (symbol: the Water Carrier) The Sun is in Aquarius from about January 20 to February 18.

Pisces (symbol: the Fishes) The Sun is in Pisces from about February 19 to March 20.

Time Zones

In 1880 Greenwich Mean Time (GMT) became the legal time in the British Isles and by 1884 international time zones had been established over much of the world. The world is divided into 24 zones, or segments, each of 15° of longitude. Twelve zones are to the east of the Greenwich meridian (0°) and are therefore in advance of GMT. Twelve are to the west of the Greenwich meridian and are behind GMT. Each zone extends 7½° on either side of its central meridian. The *International Date Line* runs down the 180° meridian – with some variations to include certain Pacific island nations entirely within one zone. Travelling eastward across the date line Sunday becomes Saturday; travelling westward across the date line Sunday becomes Monday.

Some large countries extend over several segments and are thus obliged to have several time zones.

The USA

The 48 contiguous states of the USA are divided between the Eastern, Central, Mountain and Pacific time zones (respectively five, six, seven and eight hours behind GMT), while the addition of Alaska and Hawaii adds a further four time zones.

Eastern time is kept by: Connecticut, Florida (except far west), Georgia, Indiana, Kentucky (eastern part), Maine, Maryland, Massachusetts, Michigan, New Hampshire, New Jersey, New York State, North Carolina, Ohio, Pennsylvania, Rhode Island, South Carolina, Tennessee (eastern part), Vermont, Virginia, Washington DC and West Virginia.

Central time is kept in: Alabama, Arkansas, Florida (far west), Illinois, Iowa, Kansas (except far west), Kentucky (western part), Louisiana, Minnesota, Mississippi, Missouri, Nebraska (except far west), North Dakota (eastern part), Oklahoma, South Dakota (eastern part), Tennessee (western part), Texas (except far west) and Wisconsin.

Mountain time is kept in: Arizona, Colorado, Idaho (except far north), Kansas (far west), Montana, Nebraska (far west), New Mexico, North Dakota (western part), Oregon (far east), South Dakota (western part), Texas (far west), Utah and Wyoming.

Pacific time is kept in: California, Idaho (far north), Nevada, Oregon (except far east) and Washington State.

Canada

Canada is divided into Atlantic, Eastern, Central, Mountain and Pacific zones (respectively four, five, six, seven and eight hours behind GMT).

Atlantic time is kept in: New Brunswick, Newfoundland, Nova Scotia, Prince Edward Island, Quebec (far east), and part of the Northwest Territories.

Canadian Eastern time is kept in: Ontario (except far west), Quebec (except far east), and part of the Northwest Territories.

Canadian Central time is kept in: Manitoba, Ontario (far west), Saskatchewan (far east), and part of the Northwest Territories.

Canadian Mountain time is kept in: Alberta, Saskatchewan (except far east), and part of the Northwest Territories.

Canadian Pacific time is kept in: British Columbia and Yukon.

Australia

Australia has three zones (see map). However, owing to daylight saving schemes, for most of the year Australia has five time zones: Western Australia is eight hours ahead of GMT, South Australia is ten and a half hours, Northern Territory is nine and a half hours, Queensland is ten hours, and the rest of the country eleven hours ahead.

Russia

Russia is divided into 11 time zones with all of European Russia four hours ahead of GMT. Crossing the border from Poland to the Kaliningrad enclave of Russia, watches are advanced by two hours.

Europe

Europe has three time zones: GMT, mid-European time (one hour in advance of GMT), and east European time (two hours in advance of GMT).

GMT in Europe is kept by: Iceland, Ireland, Portugal, and the UK.

Mid-European time is kept by: Albania, Andorra, Austria, Belgium, Bosnia, Croatia, Czech Republic, Denmark, France, Germany, Gibraltar, Hungary, Italy, Liechtenstein, Luxembourg, Macedonia, Monaco, Netherlands, Norway, San Marino, Slovakia, Slovenia, Spain, Sweden, Switzerland, the Vatican, and Yugoslavia (Serbia and Montenegro).

East European time is kept by: Belarus, Bulgaria, Cyprus, Estonia, Finland, Greece, Latvia, Lithuania, Moldova, Romania, and Ukraine.

A very few countries, or divisions of countries, do not adhere to the Greenwich system at all. Certain other countries, such as China, do not use a zoning system, and the whole nation – despite spanning more than one of the 24 segments – elects to keep the same time. Yet a third group – including Suriname, Iran, Afghanistan and India – use differences of half an hour.

SUMMER TIME

In 1916 legal time in the UK was advanced one hour ahead of GMT as a means of extending daylight in the evening. Between 1941 and 1945 and again in 1947, 'double summer time' was introduced in the UK. Since then Summer Time has been in force during most years, although between 1968 and 1971 British Standard Time, in which the legal time was one hour head of GMT throughout the year, was in force. British Summer Time is defined as 'the period beginning at two o'clock, GMT, in the morning of the day after the third Saturday in March or, if that day is Easter Day, the day after the second Saturday in March, and ending at two o'clock, GMT, in the morning of the day after the fourth Saturday in October'. This has been amended to bring the UK closer to the beginning and ending of daylight-saving time in neighbouring EU countries. In 1996 Summer Time begins on 31 March and ends on 27 October.

Time Zones of the World

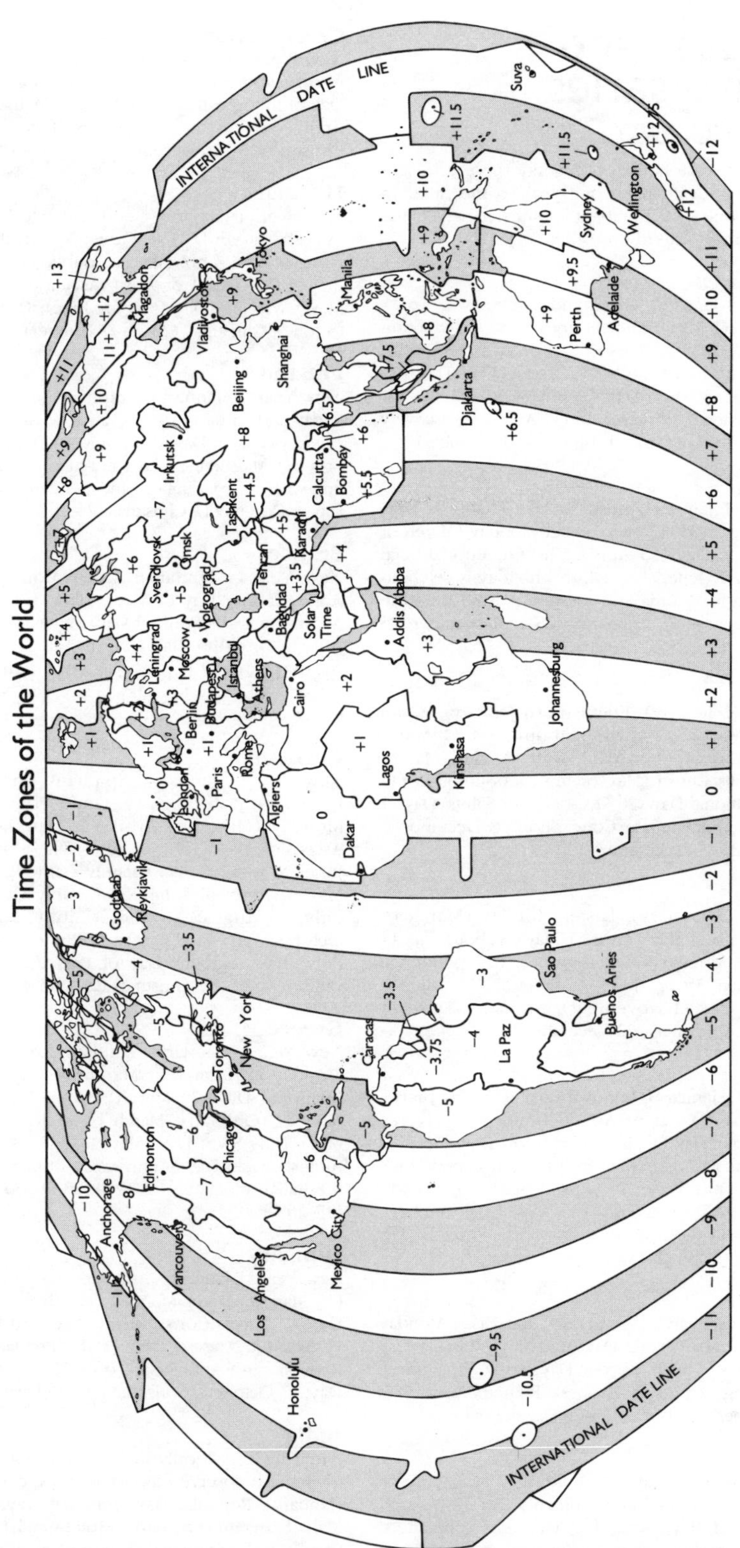

Holidays and Anniversaries

PUBLIC HOLIDAYS

The dates of some holidays – mainly those of a religious nature – vary from one year to the next. In such cases only the month or months in which the holiday normally falls are recorded.

Argentina
New Year (1 January), Good Friday (March or April), Labour Day (1 May), Anniversary of 1810 Revolution (National Day; 25 May), Occupation of Islas Malvinas/Falkland Islands (10 June), Flag Day (21 June), Independence Day (9 July), Anniversary of Death of General de San Martín (17 August), Discovery of America (12 October), Christmas (25 December).

Australia
New Year (1 January), Australia Day (National Day; 26 January), Good Friday to Easter Monday (March or April), Anzac Day (25 April), The Queen's Official Birthday (early June, although this holiday is celebrated in March in Victoria and Western Australia, and in May in Queensland), Christmas (25–26 December; 25 December only in South Australia).

Austria
New Year (1 January), Epiphany (6 January), Easter Monday (March or April), Labour Day (1 May), Ascension Day (April or May), Whit Monday (May or June), Corpus Christi (May or June), Assumption (15 August), National Day (26 October), All Saints' Day (1 November), Immaculate Conception (8 December), Christmas (25–26 December).

Belgium
New Year (1 January), Easter Monday (March or April), Ascension Day (April or May), Labour Day (1 May), Whit Monday (May or June), Independence Day (National Day; 21 July), Assumption (15 August), All Saints' Day (1 November), Armistice Day (11 November), Christmas (25 December).

Brazil
New Year (1 January), Carnival (2 days in February), Good Friday (March or April), Tiradentes Day (21 April), Labour Day (1 May), Ascension Day (April or May), Corpus Christi (May or June), Independence Day (National Day; 7 September), Our Lady Aparecida (12 October), All Souls' Day (2 November), Anniversary of the Proclamation of the Republic (15 November), Christmas (25 December).

Canada
New Year (1 January), Good Friday and Easter Monday (March or April), Victoria Day (mid-May), Canada Day (National Day; 1 July), Labour Day (early September), Thanksgiving Day (mid-October), Remembrance Day (11 November), Christmas (25–26 December).

China
Solar New Year (1 January), Lunar New Year (January or February), International Women's Day (8 March), Labour Day (1 May), Army Day (1 August), Teachers' Day (9 September), National Days (October 1–2).

Czech Republic
New Year (1 January), Easter Monday (March or April), Labour Day (1 May), Liberation Day (8 May), Day of the Apostles St Cyril and St Methodius (5 July), Anniversary of the Martyrdom of Jan Hus (6 July), Christmas (24–26 December).

Denmark
New Year (1 January), Good Friday to Easter Monday (March or April), The Queen's Birthday (National Day; 19 April – not taken as public holiday), General Prayer Day (April or May), Ascension Day (April or May), Whit Monday (May or June), Constitution Day (5 June), Christmas (25–26 December).

Finland
New Year (1 January), Epiphany (6 January), Good Friday and Easter Monday (March or April), May Day (1 May), Ascension Day (April or May), Whit Monday (May or June), Midsummer Day (mid-June), All Saints' Day (in first week of November), Independence Day (National Day; 6 December), Christmas (24–26 December).

France
New Year (1 January), Easter Monday (March or April), Labour Day (1 May), Liberation Day (8 May), Ascension Day (April or May), Whit Monday (May or June), Bastille Day (National Day; 14 July), Assumption (15 August), All Saints' Day (1 November), Armistice Day (11 November), Christmas (25 December).

Germany
New Year (1 January), Epiphany (mainly Catholic Länder only; 6 January), Good Friday and Easter Monday (March or April), Labour Day (1 May), Ascension Day (April or May), Whit Monday (May or June), Corpus Christi (mainly Catholic Länder only; May or June), Assumption (mainly Catholic Länder only; 15 August), Day of Unity (National Day; 3 October), All Saints' Day (mainly Catholic Länder only; 1 November), Day of Prayer and Repentance (mid-November), Christmas (25–26 December).

Greece
New Year (1 January), Epiphany (6 January), Clean Monday (February or March), Independence Day (National Day; 25 March), Good Friday to Easter Monday (Orthodox; March or April), Labour Day (1 May), Holy Spirit Day (May or June), Assumption (15 August), Ochi Day (Anniversary of Greek defiance to the Italian ultimatum of 1940; 28 October), Christmas (25–26 December).

Hungary
New Year (1 January), Anniversary of 1848 Revolution (15 March), Easter Monday (March or April), Labour Day (1 May), Constitution Day and St Stephen's Festival (20 August), Day of the Proclamation of the Republic and Anniversary of 1956 Uprising (National Day; 23 October), Christmas (25–26 December).

India
(Holidays vary locally in India and not all of the following are observed throughout the country.) Pongal (January), Republic Day (National Day; 26 January), Maha Shrivratri (February), Holi (March), Ram Navami (April), Mahabir Jayanti (March or April), Good Friday

(March or April), End of Ramadan (March, April or May), Buddha Purnima (May), Id-uz-Zuha, Feast of the Sacrifice (June, July or August), Islamic New Year (July or August), Janmashtami (August), Onam (August or September), Birth of the Prophet (August, September or October), Mahatma Gandhi's Birthday (2 October), Maha Ashtami (October), Diwali (October), Durga Puja (October or November), Guru Nanak Jayanti (November), Christmas (25–26 December).

Ireland
New Year (1 January), St Patrick's Day (National Day; 17 March), Good Friday and Easter Monday (March or April), June Bank Holiday Monday (early June), August Bank Holiday Monday (early August), October Bank Holiday Monday (late October), Christmas (25–26 December).

Italy
New Year (1 January), Epiphany (6 January), Easter Monday (March or April), Liberation Day (25 April), Labour Day (1 May), National Day (2 June – not taken as a public holiday), Assumption (15 August), All Saints' Day (1 November), National Unity Day (5 November), Immaculate Conception (8 December), Christmas (25–26 December).

Japan
New Year (1 January), Coming of Age Day (15 January), National Foundation Day (11 February), Vernal Equinox Day (21 March), Greenery Day (29 April), Constitution Day (3 May), Children's Day (5 May), Respect for the Aged Day (15 September), Autumnal Equinox Day (23 September), Sports Day (10 October), Culture Day (3 November), Labour Thanksgiving Day (23 November), The Emperor's Birthday (National Day; 23 December).

Luxembourg
New Year (1 January), Easter Monday (March or April), Ascension Day (April or May), Whit Monday (May or June), National Day (23 June), Assumption (15 August), All Saints' Day (1 November), Christmas (25–26 December).

Mexico
New Year (1 January), Constitution Day (5 February), Birthday of Benito Juárez (21 March), Good Friday to Easter Monday (March or April), Labour Day (1 May), Anniversary of the Battle of Puebla (5 May), President's Annual Message Day (1 September), Independence Day (National Day; 16 September), Discovery of America Day (12 October), All Souls' Day (unofficial; 2 November), Anniversary of the Revolution (20 November), Our Lady of Guadeloupe (unofficial; 12 December), Christmas (24–25 December).

Netherlands
New Year (1 January), Good Friday and Easter Monday (March or April), Queen's Day (National Day; 30 April), National Liberation Day (5 May), Ascension Day (April or May), Whit Monday (May or June), Christmas (25–26 December).

New Zealand
New Year (1 January), Waitangi Day (National Day; 6 February), Good Friday to Easter Monday (March or April), Anzac Day (25 April), The Queen's Official Birthday (early June), Labour Day (late October), Christmas (25–26 December).

Nigeria
New Year (1 January), Id al-Fitr (date varies), Good Friday to Easter Monday (March or April), End of Ramadan (March, April or May), Id al-Kabir (Feast of the Sacrifice; June, July or August), Mouloud (Birthday of the Prophet Muhammad; August, September or October), National Day (1 October), Christmas (25–26 December).

Pakistan
Beginning of Ramadan (February, March or April), Pakistan Day (National Day; 23 March), Id al-Fitr End of Ramadan (March, April or May), Id al-Adha (July or August), Independence Day (National Day; 14 August), Ashoura (June, July or August), Birthday of the Prophet (August, September or October), Defence of Pakistan Day (6 September), Anniversary of death of Quaid-i-Azam (11 September), Allama Iqbal Day (9 November), Birthday of Quaid-i-Azam and Christmas (25 December). Good Friday, Easter Monday (March or April), and Boxing Day (26 December) are optional holidays for Christians only.

Poland
New Year (1 January), Easter Monday (March or April), Labour Day (1 May), National Day (3 May), Victory Day (9 May), Corpus Christi (May or June), Assumption (15 August), All Saints' Day (1 November), Anniversary of the Proclamation of the Polish Republic (Independence Day; 11 November), Christmas (25–26 December).

Portugal
New Year (1 January), Carnival Day (February or March), Good Friday (March or April), Liberty Day (25 April), Labour Day (1 May), Corpus Christi (May or June), Portugal Day (National Day; 10 June), St Anthony's Day (Lisbon and south only; 13 June), St John the Baptist's Day (Oporto and north only; 24 June), Assumption (15 August), Anniversary of the Proclamation of the Republic (5 October), All Saints' Day (1 November), Anniversary of the Restoration of Independence (1 December), Immaculate Conception (8 December), Christmas (25 December).

Russia
New Year (1–2 January), Christmas (Orthodox; 7 January), International Women's Day (8 March), May Day (1–2 May), Victory Day (9 May), Day of the Sovereignty of the Russian Federation (12 June), Anniversary of the 1917 Revolution (7 November), Constitution Day (12 December).

South Africa
New Year (1 January), Human Rights Day (March 21), Good Friday and Family Day (Easter Monday) (March or April), Freedom Day (April 27), Youth Day (June 16), National Women's Day (August 9), Heritage Day (September 29), Reconciliation Day (December 16), Christmas (25–26 December).

Spain
New Year (1 January), Epiphany (6 January), Maundy Thursday (not a public holiday in Catalonia; March or

April), Good Friday (March or April), Easter Monday (Catalonia and Balearic Islands only; March or April), St Joseph the Worker (1 May), Corpus Christi (May or June), King Juan Carlos's Saint's Day (24 June), St James (25 July), Assumption (15 August), Day of the Hispanidad (National Day – although not celebrated in Catalonia; 12 October), All Saints' Day (1 November), Constitution Day (6 December), Immaculate Conception (not a public holiday in Catalonia; 8 December), Christmas (25 December, plus 26 December in Catalonia and the Balearic Islands). (Additional local holidays are celebrated.)

Sweden

New Year (1 January), Epiphany (6 January), Good Friday and Easter Monday (March or April), May Day (1 May), Ascension Day (April or May), Whit Monday (May or June), Day of the Swedish Flag (National Day – although not celebrated as a public holiday; 6 June), Midsummer Day (24 or 25 June), All Saints' Day (1 November), Christmas (25–26 December).

Switzerland

New Year (1–2 January), Good Friday and Easter Monday (March or April), Labour Day (not in all cantons; 1 May), Ascension Day (April or May), Whit Monday (May or June), National Day (not celebrated as a public holiday in all cantons; 1 August), Christmas (25–26 December). (Additional holidays are celebrated in individual cantons.)

Turkey

New Year (1 January), End of Ramadan (March, April or May), National Sovereignty and Children's Day (23 April), Spring Day (1 May), Youth and Sports Day (19 May), Feast of the Sacrifice (June, July or August), Victory Day (30 August), Republic Day (National Day; 29 October).

United Kingdom

New Year (1 January; 2 January Scotland only), St Patrick's Day (Northern Ireland only; 17 March), Good Friday (March or April), Easter Monday (March or April; not Scotland), May Day (early May; not Scotland), Liberation Day (Channel Islands only; 9 May), Spring Bank Holiday (late May in England, Wales and Northern Ireland; early May in Scotland); May Bank Holiday (Scotland only; late May), Anniversary of the Battle of the Boyne (Northern Ireland only; mid-July), Summer Bank Holiday (early August in Scotland; late August in England, Wales and Northern Ireland); Christmas (25–26 December).

NB In Scotland holidays that coincide with religious festivals are universal. Other Bank holidays are specific to individual cities or districts (although most districts follow the public holidays of Glasgow or Edinburgh).

USA

New Year (1 January), Martin Luther King Day (mid-January), Washington-Lincoln Day (mid-February), Good Friday (March or April), Memorial Day (end of May), Independence Day (National Day; 4 July), Labor Day (early September), Columbus Day (12 October), Veterans' Day (11 November), Thanksgiving Day (end of November), Christmas (25 December).

NATIONAL DAYS

Afghanistan 18 August, Independence Day (international recognition of independence, 1919).

Albania 28 November, Declaration of Independence (1912).

Algeria 1 November, the anniversary of the beginning of the Revolution (1954).

Andorra 8 September, National Day, the festival of the coronation of the Virgin of Meritxell, the patron of Andorra.

Angola 11 November, Independence Day (1975).

Antigua and Barbuda 1 November, Independence Day (1981).

Argentina 25 May, the anniversary of the 1810 Revolution.

Armenia 23 September, Independence Day (1991).

Australia 26 January, Australia Day, the anniversary of the raising of the British flag at Port Jackson by Captain Cook (1788).

Austria 26 October, National Day, the anniversary of the referendum establishing perpetual neutrality (1955).

Azerbaijan 18 October, Day of Statehood (1991).

Bahamas 10 July, Independence Day (1973).

Bahrain 16 December, the anniversary of the accession of the Emir, Shaikh Isa (1961).

Bangladesh 16 December, National Day, the anniversary of the 1972 constitution.

Barbados 30 November, Independence Day (1966).

Belarus 27 July. Independence Day (1991).

Belgium 21 July, Independence Day, the anniversary of the presentation of the constitutional document of King Leopold I (1831).

Belize 21 September, Independence Day (1981).

Benin 30 November, National Day, the anniversary of the proclamation of the 1975 constitution.

Bhutan 17 December, National Day, the anniversary of the installation of the first king (1907).

Bolivia 6 August, Independence Day (1825).

Bosnia-Herzegovina does not have a recognized national day.

Botswana 30 September, Botswana Day, the anniversary of independence (1966).

Brazil 7 September, Independence Day, the anniversary of the proclamation of the independence of the Empire of Brazil by Dom Pedro I (1822).

Brunei 23 February, National Day, commemorates the anniversary of independent statehood, which was celebrated in Brunei on 23 February 1984, although Brunei effectively became a fully sovereign state on 31 December 1983.

Bulgaria 3 March, National Day, the anniversary of the Treaty of San Stefano (1877), which established an autonomous principality of Bulgaria.

Burkina Faso 4 August, National Day, the anniversary of the eve of independence (1960).

Burundi 1 July, Independence Day (1962).

Cambodia 9 November, Independence Day (1953).

Cameroon 20 May, Cameroon Day, the anniversary of the referendum that established the unitary state (1972).

Canada 1 July, Canada Day, the anniversary of the creation of the Confederation of Canada (1867).

Cape Verde 5 July, Independence Day (1975).

Central African Republic 1 December, National Day, the anniversary of the adoption of the name Central African Republic (1958).

Chad 11 August, Independence Day (1960).

Chile 18 September, National Day, the anniversary of the first proclamation of independence (1810).

China 1–2 October, National Days, the anniversary of the proclamation of the People's Republic of China (1949).

China (Taiwan) 10 October, Double Tenth Day, the anniversary of the end of Japanese occupation (1945).

Colombia 20 July, Independence Day (1819).

Comoros 6 July, Independence Day (1975).

Congo 15 August, Independence Day (1960).

Costa Rica 15 September, Independence Day (1821).

Côte d'Ivoire (Ivory Coast) 7 December, National Day, a combined celebration of the proclamation of the republic (4 December 1958) and independence (7 August 1960).

Croatia 30 May, National Day, commemorating the declaration of independence of Croatia (1991).

Cuba 1 January, Day of Liberation, the anniversary of the revolution led by Fidel Castro (1959).

Cyprus 1 October, Independence Day – although independence was achieved on 16 August 1960.

Czech Republic has four co-equal National Days: 8 May (Liberation Day, 1945), 5 July (the feast day of the Apostles St Cyril and St Methodius), 6 July (the anniversary of the martyrdom of Jan Hus, 1415), and 28 October (the anniversary of the proclamation of the Republic, 1918).

Denmark 19 April, The Queen's Birthday – not taken as a public holiday.

Djibouti 27 June, Independence Day (1977).

Dominica 3 November, Independence Day (1978).

Dominican Republic 27 February, Independence Day (1844).

Ecuador 10 August, Independence (1830).

Egypt 23 July, Revolution Day, the anniversary of the revolution of 1952.

El Salvador 15 September, Independence Day (1821).

Equatorial Guinea 5 March, Independence Day – although independence was achieved on 12 October 1968.

Eritrea 24 May, Independence Day (1993).

Estonia 24 February, National Day, the anniversary of the proclamation of independence (1918).

Ethiopia 2 March, Battle of Adowa Day, the anniversary of the defeat of the Italians at Adowa (1896).

Fiji 10 October, Fiji Day, the anniversary of independence (1970).

Finland 6 December, Independence Day (1917).

France 14 July, National Day, the anniversary of the storming of the Bastille (1789).

Gabon 17 August, Independence Day (1960).

Gambia 18 February, Independence Day (1965).

Georgia 26 May, Independence Day, the anniversary of the proclamation of independence (1918).

Germany 3 October, Unity Day, the anniversary of the unification of the German Democratic Republic and the Federal Republic of Germany (1990).

Ghana 6 March, Independence Day (1957).

Greece 25 March, Independence Day, the anniversary of the start of the rising against Turkey (1821).

Grenada 7 February, Independence Day (1974).

Guatemala 15 September, Independence Day (1821).

Guinea 2 October, Republic Day (1958).

Guinea-Bissau 24 September, National Day – the commemoration of independence – although independence was achieved on 10 September, 1974.

Guyana 26 May, Independence Day (1966) and Republic Day, the anniversary of the proclamation of the republic (1970).

Haiti 1 January, Independence Day, the anniversary of the declaration of independence by Jean-Jacques Dessalines (1804).

Honduras 15 September, Independence Day (1821).

Hungary 23 October, National Day, the anniversary of the Hungarian Uprising (1956) and of the proclamation of the Republic of Hungary (1989).

Iceland 17 June, National Day, the anniversary of complete independence from Denmark (1944).

India 26 January, Republic Day, the anniversary of the declaration of the republic (1950).

Indonesia 17 August, National Day, the anniversary of the initial declaration of independence (1945).

Iran 11 February, National Day, the anniversary of the overthrow of the Shah (1979).

Iraq 14 July, Republic Day, the anniversary of the revolution that overthrew the monarchy (1958) and of the accession to power of the Arab Socialist Renaissance (Ba'ath) Party (1968).

Ireland 17 March, St Patrick's Day.

Israel 5 Iyyar (in Jewish calendar, see p. 40), Independence Day (1948). (In the Gregorian calendar the Israeli declaration of independence took place on 14 May, 1948. The celebration of the anniversary occurs in April or May.)

Italy 2 June, National Day, the anniversary of the foundation of the republic (1946) – not taken as a public holiday.

Jamaica First Monday in August, Independence Day (6 August 1962).

Japan 23 December, The Emperor's Birthday.

Jordan 25 May, Independence Day, the anniversary of the coronation of King Abdullah (1946).

Kazakstan 16 December, Independence Day (1991).

Kenya 12 December, Independence Day (1963).

Kiribati 12 July, Independence Day (1979).

Korea (North) 9 September, Independence Day, the anniversary of the foundation of the People's Democratic Republic of Korea (1948).

Korea (South) 15 August, Liberation Day, the anniversary of the end of Japanese occupation (1945).

Kuwait 25 February, National Day – the official anniversary of independence (1961), although Kuwait's independence was formally recognized on 19 June 1961.

Kyrgyzstan 31 August, Independence Day (1991).

Laos 2 December, National Day, the anniversary of the proclamation of the republic (1975).

Latvia 18 November, National Day, proclamation of the republic (1917).

Lebanon 22 November, Independence Day (1943).

Lesotho 4 October, Independence Day (1966).

Liberia 26 July, Independence Day (1847).

Libya 1 September, Revolution Day, the anniversary of the overthrow of the monarchy (1969).

Liechtenstein 15 August, the Assumption (see Christian Festivals) and the eve of the birthday of Prince Franz Joseph II (reigned 1938-89).

Lithuania 16 February, National Day, the anniversary of the restoration of the state (1918).

Luxembourg 23 June, National Day, the official birthday of the sovereign.

Macedonia 8 September, the anniversary of the vote to secede from Yugoslavia (1991).

Madagascar 26 June, Independence Day (1960).

Malawi 6 July, Republic Day, the anniversary of independence (1964) and of the proclamation of a republic (1966).

Malaysia 31 August, National Day, the anniversary of the independence of Malaya (1957).

Maldives 26 July, Independence Day (1965).

Mali 22 September, National Day, the anniversary of the adoption of the name Mali (1960).

Malta 21 September, Independence Day (1964).

Marshall Islands 1 May, National Day, the anniversary of the present constitution of the Marshall Islands (1979).

Mauritania 28 November, National Day, the anniversary of the establishment of the republic (1958).

Mauritius 12 March, Independence Day (1968).

Mexico 16 September, Independence Day (1821).

Micronesia 10 May, National Day (Constitution Day), the anniversary of the present constitution of the Federated States of Micronesia (1979).

Moldova 27 August, Independence Day (1991).

Monaco 19 November, National Day, the feast of St Devote, patron saint of Monaco.

Mongolia 11 July, National Day, the anniversary of the recovery of independence (1921).

Morocco 3 March, the Festival of the Throne, the anniversary of the coronation of King Hassan II.

Mozambique 25 June, Independence Day (1975).

Myanmar (Burma) 4 January, Independence Day (1948).

Namibia 21 March, Independence Day (1990).

Nauru 31 January, Independence Day (1968).

Nepal 18 February, National Democracy Day, the birthday of King Tribhuvana (reigned 1911–55).

Netherlands 30 April, Queen's Day, the birthday of Queen Juliana (reigned 1948–80).

New Zealand 6 February, Waitangi Day, the anniversary of the signing of the Treaty of Waitangi between Britain and the Maori chiefs (1840).

Nicaragua 15 September, Independence Day (1821).

Niger 18 December, Republic Day, the anniversary of the proclamation of the republic (1958).

Nigeria 1 October, National Day, the anniversary of independence (1960) and the establishment of the republic (1963).

Norway 17 May, Independence Day, the anniversary of the adoption of the 1814 constitution.

Oman 18 November, National Day, associated with the birthday of the Sultan (19 November).

Pakistan 23 March, Pakistan Day, the anniversary of the adoption of the resolution by the Muslim League to establish a Muslim state in the Indian subcontinent (1940) and of the proclamation of a republic (1956).

Palau 1 October, Independence Day (1994).

Panama 3 November, Independence Day (1903).

Papua New Guinea 16 September, Independence Day and Constitution Day (1975).

Paraguay 14–15 May, Independence Day (1811).

Peru 28–29 July, National Days, the anniversary of independence (1826).

The Philippines 12 June, Independence Day, the anniversary of the declaration of independence during the 1898 revolution.

Poland 3 May, National Day, the anniversary of the proclamation of the constitution of 1791.

Portugal 10 June, Portugal Day, the anniversary of the death of the 'national poet' Camoes (1580).

Qatar 3 September, National Day, in commemoration of independence (1 September 1971).

Romania 1 December, National Day, the anniversary of the reunion of Walachia, Moldavia and Transylvania (1918).

Russia 12 June, Day of State Sovereignty of the Russian Federation (1991).

Rwanda 1 July, Independence Day (1962).

St Christopher and Nevis 19 September, Independence Day (1983).

St Lucia 22 February, Independence Day (1979).

St Vincent and the Grenadines 27 October, Independence Day (1979).

San Marino 3 September, Republic Day, the feast of St Marino, patron saint of the republic.

São Tomé e Príncipe 12 July, Independence Day (1975).

Saudi Arabia 23 September, the anniversary of the creation of the unified kingdom (1932) – not celebrated as a public holiday.

Senegal 4 April, National Day, the anniversary of the signature of the Accords of Paris (1960) that brought independence to Senegal on 20 August 1960.

Seychelles 29 June, Independence Day (1976).

Sierra Leone 27 April, Independence Day (1961).

Singapore 9 August, National Day, the anniversary of the declaration of independence (1965).

Slovakia 1 September, Constitution Day, the anniversary of the pasage of the Slovak constitution (1992).

Slovenia 25 June, National Statehood Day, the anniversary of the proclamation of sovereignty (1991).

Solomon Islands 7 July, Independence Day (1978).

Somalia 26 June, National Day, the anniversary of independence (1960).

South Africa 27 April, Freedom Day, the anniversary of the first multi-racial elections in South Africa (1994).

Spain 12 October, the Day of the Hispanidad; honours Columbus' discovery of the Western hemisphere.

Sri Lanka 4 February, National Day, the anniversary of the attainment of independence as Ceylon (1948).

Sudan 1 January, Independence Day (1956).

Suriname 25 November, Independence Day (1975).

Swaziland 6 September, Independence Day (1968).

Sweden 6 June, the Day of the Swedish Flag – although not celebrated as a public holiday.

Switzerland 1 August, National Day, the anniversary of the alliance of the 'Forest Cantons' (1291). National Day is not celebrated as a public holiday in all cantons.

Syria 16 November, National Day, the anniversary of the accession to power of President Assad (1970).

Tajikistan 9 September, Independence Day, (1991).

Tanzania 26 April, Union Day, the anniversary of the union of Tanganyika and Zanzibar (1964).

Thailand 5 December, The King's Birthday.

Togo 13 January, Liberation Day, the anniversary of the revolution of 1963.

Tonga 4 June, Independence Day (1970).

Trinidad and Tobago 31 August, Independence Day (1962).

Tunisia 20 March, Independence Day (1956).

Turkey 29 October, Republic Day, the anniversary of the election of Kemal Atatürk as the first president of Turkey (1924).

Turkmenistan 27 October, Independence Day (1991).

Tuvalu 1 October, Independence Day (1978).

Uganda 9 October, Independence Day (1962).

Ukraine 24 August, Independence Day (1991).

United Arab Emirates 2 December, National Day, the anniversary of the establishment of the federation as an independent state (1971).

United Kingdom has no national day. The national day of England is 23 April (St George's Day), of Wales 1 March (St David's Day), of Scotland 30 November (St Andrew's Day) and of Northern Ireland 17 March (St Patrick's Day).

USA 4 July, Independence Day, the anniversary of the declaration of independence (1776).

Uruguay 25 August, Declaration of Independence Day (1825).

Uzbekistan 31 August, Independence Day (1991).

Vanuatu 30 July, Independence Day (1980).

Vatican City has no national day.

Venezuela 5 July, Independence Day (1811).

Vietnam 1–2 September, National Day, the anniversary of the original proclamation of independence (1945).

Western Samoa 1 January, Independence Day (1962).

Yemen 22 May, National Day, the anniversary of the reunification of Yemen (1990) – although not taken as a public holiday.

Yugoslavia (Serbia and Montenegro) 29–30 November, Republic Days, the anniversary of the establishment of the Partisan government (1943).

Zaïre 24 November, National Day, the anniversary of the establishment of the Second Republic (1965).

Zambia 24 October, Independence Day (1964).

Zimbabwe 18 April, Independence Day (1980).

CHRISTIAN FESTIVALS

Sunday
Christian Sabbath is observed on Sunday, in accordance with the Fourth Commandment, which forbids work on the holy day.

Epiphany
(6 January.) The Festival of the Epiphany commemorates the manifestation of the infant Christ to the Magi or 'wise men'. The festival was of great importance in the (Eastern) Orthodox Churches because it marked the proclamation, by the Patriarch of Alexandria, of the date of the next Easter.

In western Europe, the Epiphany was a significant landmark in the Church and lay calendars, determining the dates of other festivals and activities later in the year, for example, ploughing in England began on the Monday of the first complete week after the Festival of the Epiphany. It is a public holiday in several European countries.

Shrove Tuesday
(Any Tuesday between 3 February and 9 March.) Shrove Tuesday is the last day before the beginning of Lent – see Ash Wednesday, below. Shrovetide (the Sunday, Monday and Tuesday before Lent) were set aside as days for the confession of sins ('shrove' is the past tense of 'shrive', meaning 'to hear confession'). Shrove Tuesday was traditionally marked by festivities before the rigours of Lent and is commemorated by carnivals in, for example, Portugal, Brazil and parts of Germany.

In England, Shrove Tuesday is also known as *Pancake Day*, the day on which fats that could not be consumed during Lent were used to make pancakes.

Ash Wednesday
(Any Wednesday between 4 February and 10 March.) The first day of Lent, Ash Wednesday takes its name from the custom of scattering ashes on the heads of penitents (in its modern form, marking the forehead with ashes in the sign of the Cross).

Lent
(February to March or March to April.) Lent is a period of 40 days beginning on Ash Wednesday and ending at midnight on Holy Saturday, the day before Easter Day. A reminder of the time spent by Christ in the wilderness, Lent is observed as a period of reflection, repentance and preparation for Easter. It used to be thought that the observance of Lent dated from the time of the first disciples, but it is now usually accepted that the practice probably began in the 4th century and may, originally, have been a fast of 40 hours. Lent begins on the following days between 1996 and 2000.

1996 21 February

1997 12 February

1998 25 February

1999 17 February

2000 8 March

Palm Sunday
(Any Sunday between 15 March and 18 April.) Palm Sunday – the last Sunday of Lent – commemorates Christ's triumphal entry into Jerusalem when His way was lined by palm branches.

Maundy Thursday
(Any Thursday between 19 March and 22 April.) Maundy Thursday – the last Thursday of Lent – takes its name from the Latin *dies mandati,* meaning 'the day of the mandate', referring to the mandate given by Christ to His disciples to love one another. It is marked in the Roman Catholic Church by the symbolic washing of feet by the priest, in commemoration of Christ washing the feet of the disciples. In England, Maundy money – specially minted coins – is distributed by the sovereign to as many elderly men and women as the sovereign's age.

Good Friday
(Any Friday between 20 March and 23 April.) Good Friday is the commemoration of the Crucifixion. It is a public holiday in most Christian countries.

Holy Saturday (or Easter Eve)
(Any Saturday between 21 March and 24 April.) Holy Saturday (the usual Roman Catholic designation) or Easter Eve (the usual Anglican designation) is often wrongly called 'Easter Saturday' in secular usage in English-speaking countries. Holy Saturday is the last day of Lent. NB. Easter does not begin until the stroke of midnight at the end of Holy Saturday.

Easter Day
(Any Sunday between 22 March and 25 April.) Easter Day is the celebration of the Resurrection of Christ. There is no historical basis for celebrating Easter in the spring as it is not known at what time of the year these events took place.

Easter is celebrated on the first Sunday after the Full Moon that happens on or following 21 March. If the Full Moon falls upon a Sunday, Easter is celebrated upon the following Sunday. The 'Moon' used in these calculations is not the celestial Moon but a hypothetical 'calendar Moon' whose cycles alternate in periods of 30 and 29 days. Although the Orthodox Churches calculate Easter in the same manner as other Christian Churches, their festivities take place later because Eastern Christendom still uses the Julian calendar.

Easter falls on the following days between 1996 and 2000.

1996 7 April

1997 30 March

1998 12 April

1999 4 April

2000 23 April

The day following Easter Sunday is a public holiday in most Christian countries.

Ascension Day
(Any Thursday between 30 April and 3 June.) Ascension Day - which falls 40 days after Easter Day – is when the Ascension of Christ into Heaven is

celebrated. It is a public holiday in many Christian countries. Ascension Day falls on the following days between 1996 and 2000.

1996 16 May

1997 8 May

1998 21 May

1999 13 May

2000 1 June

Pentecost (Whit Sunday)

(Any Sunday between 10 May and 13 June.) Pentecost – which falls seven weeks after Easter Day – commemorates the descent of the Holy Spirit upon the apostles. It marks the beginning of the activities of the Church on Earth. Its English name 'Whit' Sunday is said to come from 'White' Sunday in a reference to the white robes worn by the newly baptized. Whit Monday is a public holiday in some Christian countries. Pentecost falls on the following days between 1996 and 2000.

1996 26 May

1997 18 May

1998 31 May

1999 23 May

2000 11 June

Trinity Sunday

(Any Sunday between 17 May and 20 June.) Trinity Sunday is a celebration of the Holy Trinity. In Churches of the Anglican Communion the remaining Sundays of the year are numbered 'after Trinity'.

Corpus Christi

(Any Thursday between 21 May and 24 June.) Corpus Christi – celebrated on the Thursday following Trinity Sunday – is a major festival of the Roman Catholic Church held in devotion to the Eucharist. Corpus Christi is a public holiday in some Roman Catholic countries.

The Assumption

(15 August). The Feast of the Assumption of the Blessed Virgin Mary is a Roman Catholic and (Eastern) Orthodox festival commemorating the doctrine of the assumption of Mary – in both body and soul – into Heaven at the end of her earthly life. It is a public holiday in most Roman Catholic countries and in Greece.

All Saints' Day

(1 November.) All Saints' Day – a public holiday in some Christian (mainly Roman Catholic) countries – is a celebration of the lives of all the saints of the Church, including those who are remembered on individual named saints' days.

All Souls' Day

(2 November.) All Souls' Day – a public holiday in some Latin American countries – is a major Roman Catholic festival. It is a day of prayer for the souls of the departed now in Purgatory.

Advent Sunday

(The Sunday nearest to 30 November, that is any Sunday between 27 November and 3 December.) Advent Sunday (Latin *adventus* meaning 'coming') is the beginning of the season of preparation for Christmas. There are usually three, and occasionally four, Sundays of Advent. Advent begins on the following days between 1996 and 2000.

1996 1 December

1997 30 November

1998 29 November

1999 28 November

2000 3 December

Immaculate Conception

(8 December.) The festival of the Immaculate Conception commemorates the (Roman Catholic) doctrine that Mary was conceived without sin. It is a public holiday in some Roman Catholic countries.

Christmas Eve

(24 December.) The day before the celebration of Christmas. It is a public holiday in a few Christian countries.

Christmas Day

(25 December.) The celebration of the birth of Christ to Mary at Bethlehem, probably in c. 4 BC. Christmas (literally 'Christ mass') has been celebrated by Christians from the earliest times. There is, however, no reason to assume that this historical event took place on 25 December. There is some evidence to suggest that Christ was born in September.

The early Church in the East celebrated both Christmas and the Epiphany on 6 January. In the West the Feast of the Nativity has been celebrated on 25 December since AD 336 in order to take the place of the pagan Sun festival held on or near the same date.

By the end of the 4th century Christmas was celebrated on 25 December throughout Christendom, except in Armenia, which still commemorates 6 January. Although the Orthodox Churches celebrate Christmas on 25 December, their festivities take place in January in the Gregorian calendar because Eastern Christendom still uses the Julian calendar.

St Stephen's Day

The day following Christmas Day is usually known as St Stephen's Day, although in England and some other English-speaking countries it is known as Boxing Day, from the custom of exchanging Christmas 'boxes' or presents upon that day. St Stephen's Day is a public holiday in many Christian countries.

ORTHODOX EASTER

The Easter festivals in the Greek Orthodox Church will occur on the following dates in 1996:

Holy Friday (Good Friday)

April 12

Orthodox Easter

April 14

JEWISH FESTIVALS

Shabat a weekly festival (the sabbath) observed on the seventh day of the week, Saturday, in commemoration of the day of rest taken by God after the completion of the creation. It is the covenant between God and the Jewish people.

On the sabbath, Jews are obliged to engage in worship and prayer at home or in the synagogue and to avoid work.

Rosh Hodesh a monthly festival, the celebration of the new moon.

Other festivals are celebrated according to the Jewish calendar (see pp. 40–41). The equivalent date in the Gregorian calendar varies from one year to another. Jewish festivals commence on the evening of the dates shown and last until sunset on the following day.

15 Shebat – Tu B'shevat (Festival for New Trees). In modern times this festival is associated with the planting of trees in Israel.

13 Adar – Taanit Ester (Fast of Ester).

14 Adar – Purim (Festival of Lots). Purim commemorates the deliverance of Persian Jews from persecution in the 5th century BCE (see Jewish calendar).

14 Nisan – Taanit Behorim (Fast of the First-born).

15 Nisan – Pesah (Passover). The Passover commemorates the Israelites' servitude in Egypt and the subsequent exodus from Egypt. It is called 'Passover' because on the eve of the Jewish flight from Egypt the last of the 10 plagues 'passed over' the homes of the Israelites.

27 Nisan – Yom Ha-Shoah (Holocaust Day). A modern commemoration of the victims of the Holocaust but not marked by a public holiday in Israel.

4 Iyar – Yom H'zikharon (Remembrance Day). A modern commemoration but not marked by a public holiday in Israel.

5 Iyar – Yom Ha'Atzmaut (Independence Day), an Israeli public holiday.

18 Iyar – the 33rd Day of 'Counting the Omer'.

28 Iyar – Yom Yerushalayim (Jerusalem Day).

6–7 Sivan – Shavuot (the Festival of Weeks, or Pentecost). This festival commemorates the revelation of the Torah (Law) at Sinai.

20 Sivan – the Fast of 20 Sivan.

17 Tammuz – the Fast of 17 Tammuz.

9 Ab – Tisha B'Av (the Fast of 9 Ab).

15 Ab – Tu B'Av (the Festival of 15 Ab).

1 Elul – Festival of 1 Elul.

1–2 Tishri – Rosh Hashanah (New Year). This festival celebrates the New Year of the Jewish Calendar but also begins the Ten Days of Penitence that ends on Yom Kippur (see below). These days are considered the Days of Judgement for all mankind. Many rabbinic laws govern behaviour during this time – they include the strict prohibition of work – but celebrations are also enjoyed.

3 Tishri – Tsom Gedaliah (the Fast of Gedaliah).

10 Tishri – Yom Kippur (the Day of Atonement) is the most solemn and holy day in the Jewish Calendar. The festival is spent in prayer and fasting. Sins are confessed in acts of reconciliation.

15 or 16–22 or 23 Tishri – Sukkot (the Festival of Tabernacles). Commemorated in Israel by a series of half-day public holidays, Sukkot is a remembrance of the Israelites' wanderings after the Exodus. Sukkot is named after the booths *(sukkot,* 'booth') that the Israelites lived in during this time.

22 or 23 Tishri – Shemini Atzeret (the Eighth Day of Conclusion). This is the final day of the Festival of Tabernacles and it is celebrated independently.

23 Tishri – Simhat Torah (Rejoicing in the Torah). This festival is celebrated on the completion of the cycle of readings from the Torah.

25 Kislev – 2 Tebet – Hanukah (the Festival of the Dedication of the Temple, otherwise known as the Festival of Lights). Celebrated for eight days, the festival commemorates the revolt against the Seleucid ruler Antiochus IV Epiphanes and the rededication of the Temple in 164 BCE (see Jewish calendar). The festival is characterized by songs, candles, feasting and giving gifts to children.

10 Tebet – the Feast of 10 Tebet

See also Judaism, pp. 343–44.

ISLAMIC FESTIVALS

Many of the following festivals are public holidays in Islamic countries. As these holidays are celebrated according to the Islamic lunar calendar (see pp. 42–43), the equivalent date in the Gregorian calendar varies from one year to another.

Day of Assembly a weekly festival on Friday.

Other festivals

1 Muharram New Year's Day

1–10 Muharram Muharram (New Year Festival)

12 Rabîa I Eid Milad-un-Nabi (Festival of the Prophet's Birthday)

26 Rajab Shab-i-Maraj (Festival of the Prophet's Night Journey and Ascension)

15 Shaabân Night of Forgiveness

1–29/30 Ramadan Ramadan; the annual fast lasting a month. Ramadan is observed by abstention from food, drink and sexual intercourse from dawn to dusk.

1 Shawwâl Eid-ul-Fitr; the Festival of Fast Breaking (the end of Ramadan), which is celebrated by feasting and visiting graves.

9 Dhû'l Hijja Day of Arafat

Dhû'l Hijja Haj (Pilgrimage to Mecca)

10 Dhû'l Hijja Eid-ul-Adha (Festival of Sacrifice, marking the end of the Pilgrimage to Mecca).

See also Islam, pp. 339–40.

HINDU FESTIVALS

January *Makar Sankranti*, Winter solstice festival.

Pongal, harvest festival in southern India.

Kumbha Mela, festival held every 12 years; worshippers bathe in the waters at the confluence of the Ganges and Jumna rivers.

January–February *Vasanta Panchami*, held in honour of goddess Saraswati.

Mahashivratri, 'Great Night of Shiva', celebrated by vigils, vows, fasting and worship of goddess Shiva.

February–March *Ramakrishna utsav* (20 Feb), festival for Hindu saint Ramakrishna.

Holi, a boisterous festival characterized by the throwing of red powder and by bonfires (possible origins in the celebration of the god of sexual desire, Kama).

Shivrati, main festival in honour of Shiva; spent in meditation.

March–April *Ramanavami*, celebrates the birth of Shi Rama observed in sanctity and fasting.

Hanuman Jayanti, in honour of the god Hanuman.

April–May *Baisakhi*, New Year festival celebrated by gift-giving, feasting, praying and bathing in sacred waters.

May–June *Ganga Dussehra*, in honour of goddess Ganga; devotees bathe in the sacred waters of the River Ganges.

June–July *Jagannatha (Ratha-yatra)*, celebrates Krishna as the Lord of the Universe.

July–August *Naga Panchami*, celebrates the birth of serpents. Worshippers empty pots of milk over snakes from the temple of Shiva.

Raksha Bandhan, an old festival in which sisters give wrist decorations to their brothers to ward off evil spirits.

August–September *Ganesh Chaturthi*, in honour of the elephant-headed god, Ganesh.

Janmashtani, celebrates the birth of Krishna.

September–October *Dussehra (Durja Puja)*, celebrates the goddess Durga during the period of Navratri ('Nine Nights').

Gandhi Jayanti (2 October), celebrates the birth of Mahatma Gandhi.

Diwali (October), a major festival honouring Laksmi, goddess of wealth. During this time merchants open fresh accounts. Festivities include visiting, exchanging gifts, decorating houses, feasting and wearing new clothes.

BUDDHIST FESTIVALS

Different festivals and, in some cases, different dates for the same festivals, are observed in the various countries where Buddhism is practised.

Uposatha Days are fortnightly meetings of the Buddhist monastic assembly – at times of full moon and new moon – to reaffirm the rules of discipline. These meetings exclude novices and laymen. The Uposatha Day is also the name given to the more modern weekly visit to a monastery by laymen.

Other festivals

New Year is celebrated in Burma/Myanmar (16–17 April), Sri Lanka (13 April), Thailand (between 13–16 April), Tibet (in February)

The Buddha's Birth, Enlightenment and Death is celebrated in Burma/Myanmar, Sri Lanka, and Thailand (as The Buddha's Cremation) in May or June, and in Tibet in May.

The Buddha's First Sermon is celebrated in June or July in Burma/Myanmar (in conjunction with the Beginnings of the Rains Retreat Festival), and in Sri Lanka and Tibet.

The Rains Retreat is celebrated in Thailand (between July and October.

Summer Retreat is celebrated in China between June and October.

The establishment of Buddhism in Sri Lanka is celebrated in Sri Lanka in June or July.

The Procession of the Month of Asala is celebrated in Sri Lanka in July or August.

Festival of Hungry Ghosts is celebrated in China in August.

The Buddha's Birth is celebrated in China in August.

Kuan-Yin is celebrated in China in August.

The Buddha's first visit to Sri Lanka is celebrated in Sri Lanka in September.

The Buddha's Descent from Tushita is celebrated in Tibet in October.

Kathina Ceremony is celebrated in Burma/Myanmar and Thailand in November.

Festival of Lights is celebrated in Sri Lanka and Thailand in November.

The Death of Tsongkhapa is celebrated in Tibet in November.

The Arrival of Sanghamitta is celebrated in Sri Lanka in December or January.

The Conjunction of Nine Evils and the *Conjunction of the Ten Virtues* is celebrated in Tibet in January.

Saints' Day is celebrated in Thailand in February.

SHINTO FESTIVALS

Several major festivals are celebrated at Shinto temples in Japan during the year. The most important of these include:

Haru Matsuri, also known as Toshigoi Matsuri – the Spring Festival, which is traditionally the Prayer for a Good Harvest Festival in the religious calendar. In modern times, this festival has come to be associated with the civil Japanese public holiday, Vernal Equinox Day, which is observed on 21 March.

Aki Matsuri or Niiname-sai – the Autumn Festival, which is traditionally the Harvest Festival in the religious calendar. This holiday has come to be associated with the civil Japanese public holiday, Autumnal Equinox Day, which is observed on 23 September.

Rei-sai, which is an annual festival celebrated at each Shinto temple – not necessarily on the same day. The Annual Festival is the occasion of the temple's Divine Procession – Shinko-sai – when miniature shrines (mikoshi) are carried in procession throughout the area that is served by the temple in question.

The date of accession of the emperor is also of significance in Shinto belief. The present Heisei imperial epoch is dated from 8 January (Emperor Akihito succeeded to the throne on 8 January 1989).

EARTH SCIENCES

The Earth

THE EARTH'S STRUCTURE

There has been little penetration into the Earth's interior. The deepest mine (in South Africa) is only 3·8 km (2·4 mi) deep, and the deepest drilling (in Russia) is only 12·3 km (7·6 mi) deep – or 0·19% of the Earth's radius, which has an average value of 6371 km (3959 mi). The only other direct access to the internal nature of Earth is the study of lava flows from volcanic eruptions.

Unable to visit the Earth's deep interior or place instruments within it, scientists must explore in more subtle ways. One method is to measure natural phenomena, in particular the magnetic and gravitational fields, which are measured at the Earth's surface and from satellites. These observations are interpreted in terms of the planet's internal properties. A second approach is to study the Earth with non-material probes, the most important of which are the seismic waves emitted by earthquakes. As seismic waves pass through the Earth, they undergo sudden changes in direction and velocity at certain depths. These depths mark the major boundaries, or *discontinuities*, that divide the Earth into crust, mantle and core.

The crust

The thin outermost layer of the Earth, the crust, has an average depth of 24 km (15 mi). The crust accounts for only 1·05% of the planet's volume and 0·5% of its mass. The sharp boundary between the crust and the mantle is called the *Mohorovicic discontinuity* (or *Moho* for short) after the Croatian seismologist Andrija Mohorovicic (1857–1936) who discovered it in 1909.

There is a wide variation in the thickness of the crust and three main crustal types – continental, oceanic and transitional – have been identified. The *continental crust* averages between 30 and 50 km (19–31 mi) thick, although beneath the central valley of California, for example, the crust is only about 20 km (12 mi) thick, and beneath parts of major mountain ranges such as the Himalaya it can exceed 80 km (50 mi). By contrast, the *oceanic crust* is only 5 to 15 km (3–9 mi) thick and can be as little as 3 km (2 mi) under ocean fracture zones (see below). The *transitional zone* – of islands, island arcs and continental margins – averages 15 to 30 km (9–19 mi) in thickness.

The elements oxygen, silicon and aluminium dominate the crustal composition. The major mineral type – the feldspars – are alumino-silicates of the alkali and alkaline-earth metals. The second most common group – quartz – is silicon dioxide. The major rock types reflect this basic composition with differences mainly being due to small amounts of other minerals. By contrast, the oceanic crust is mainly basalt, which contains both feldspars and quartz, but has also notable amounts of olivine and pyroxene, which are magnesium iron silicates. The basalt is underlain by gabbro, which is a coarser grained rock of similar composition.

The mantle

The mantle extends from the base of the crust to the core and is about 2865 km (1780 mi) thick. It occupies about 82·5% of the Earth's volume and 66·0% of its mass. The upper mantle is rich in olivine and pyroxenes, present in the rock type peridotite. Discontinuities revealed by seismic data show several distinct layers in the mantle. The outermost – the *lithosphere* – is generally 50 to 100 km (31–62 mi) thick under the oceans and 100 to 200 km (62–124 mi) thick under the continents. The strong rigid lithosphere overlays a weak thick layer known as the *athenosphere*. The athenosphere – which is 320 km (199 mi) thick – has an average temperature of about 1300 °C (2372 °F), which approaches the melting points of its constituent rocks. It is probable that *magma* – molten or semi-molten rock – is formed in this region.

A major discontinuity at a depth of 670 km (416 mi) from the surface separates the upper and lower mantles. Below this discontinuity there appears to be a change in mineral types brought about by the increasing pressure. There is also a 10% jump in density and a rise in temperature from about 1560 °C (1840 °F) to 1710 °C (3110 °F). The major mineral type in the lower mantle appears to be pyroxenes, especially magnesium silicate.

In the *D layer* – the lowest 200 km (124 mi) of the mantle – temperatures reach up to 2660 °C (4820 °F). It is thought that the D layer is richer in aluminium and calcium than the higher layers of the mantle.

The core

The core extends from the base of the mantle to the Earth's centre and is 6964 km (4327 mi) in diameter. It accounts for only 16·3% of the Earth's volume but 33·5% of its mass. The discontinuity between the mantle and core is called the *core-mantle boundary* or, sometimes, the *Gutenberg discontinuity*, after its discoverer the German-American seismologist Beno Gutenberg. The core comprises two distinct parts – a liquid *outer core*, which is 2260 km (1404 mi) thick, and a solid *inner core*, which has a radius of 1222 km (759 mi). The core is chemically distinct from the mantle and comprises about 89% iron and 6% nickel. The remaining 5% comprises a lighter element, which is possibly sulphur but the presence of oxygen and silicon cannot be ruled out. There is a 78% increase in density at the mantle-core boundary and a 700 °C (1260 °F) jump in temperature to about 3360 °C (6080 °F). There is a smooth increase in temperature to a maximum of about 4530 °C (8190 °F) at the centre of the core.

The magnetic field

The Earth has a magnetic field, which is why a compass needle points approximately north at most places on the Earth's surface. The magnetic field has two parts. Most of it is that of a simple dipole; it is as if a giant bar magnet were placed at the centre of the Earth (although the magnet slopes at 11° to the Earth's axis of rotation). But a small proportion of it is much more complicated and changes very rapidly. This is why a compass needle points in a slightly different direction each year.

The rapid changing indicates that the magnetic field must be produced in a part of the Earth that is fluid, for no solid region could reorganize itself rapidly enough without shaking the planet to pieces. The only liquid zone inside the Earth is the outer core. This fits in with something else. The only conceivable way in which a magnetic field could be generated within the Earth is by the flow of very large electric currents, and electric currents need a conductor. The Earth's core is the most conductive zone in the whole planet, because it consists largely of iron. The silicates of the mantle simply would not conduct well enough.

CONTINENTAL DRIFT

There is ever-increasing evidence that the Earth's land surface once comprised a single primeval land mass, now called Pangaea, and that this land mass split during the Upper Cretaceous period (100,000,000 to 65,000,000 years ago) into two super-continents, the northern one called Laurasia and the southern one called Gondwanaland (see p. 60). Throughout the whole of human history, most people have imagined the continents to be fixed in their present positions and the ocean floors to be the oldest and most primitive parts of the planet. In the space of a few years during the 1960s, however, both of these assumptions were overthrown in an intellectual revolution. It suddenly became possible to prove that the continents are drifting across the Earth's surface, that the ocean floors are spreading, and that none of the oceanic crust is more than about 200,000,000 years old, less than 5% of the age of the Earth. The Earth's *lithosphere*, the rigid layer that comprises the crust and the uppermost mantle, is divided into 15 *plates* of various sizes. The plates 'float' on the partially molten layer (the *asthenosphere*) below, and it is because they are floating that they have the freedom to move horizontally. A few of the plates (for example, the Pacific) are almost completely oceanic, but most include both oceanic and continental lithosphere. There are no completely continental plates. The plate boundaries are the most tectonically active parts of the Earth: they are where most mountain building, earthquakes and volcanoes occur.

How continental drift was proved

Many rocks contain minute magnetic particles, usually oxides of iron and titanium. When a rock forms, these particles become magnetized in the direction of the Earth's magnetic field at the particular site. Using higly sensitive instruments, it is possible to measure this weak magnetism and, from it, determine the position of the north pole at the time the rock was formed. Scientists were surprised to discover that for rocks older than a few million years the north poles determined in this way did not lie at the present north pole, and that the older the rocks the greater was the discrepancy. They were even more surprised to find that rocks of the same age from different continents gave ancient north poles in quite different positions. There can be only one north pole at any given time, however, and that must lie close to the north end of the Earth's rotational axis. The only way of explaining the rock magnetic data, therefore, was to assume that the continents have drifted with respect to both the present north pole and each other.

MASS AND DENSITY

The Earth, including its atmosphere, has a mass of 5·974 × 10^{21} tonnes (5,879,000,000,000,000,000,000 tons), the average density is 5.515 times that of water. The density of the Earth, in g/cm^3, and the percentage mass of each layer (in terms of the total Earth mass) are given in the following table.

Layer	*Density in g/cm^3*	*% of mass*
Ocean	1·020	0·03
Upper crust	2·600	0·27
Lower crust	2·900	0·23
Mantle	*	65·99
Outer core	11·238	31·82
Inner core	12·980	1·66

* Mantle: the percentage of the mass is calculated as a remainder.

The atmosphere of the Earth weighs 5.24 x 1015 tonnes (5,160,000,000,000,000 tons) or 0·000088% of the total mass. The mass of the Earth is being added to as the planet picks up about 40,000 tonnes of cosmic dust per annum.

VOLUME

The volumes of the individual layers of the Earth are calculated using an average Earth radius of 6371 km (3957 mi):

Layer	*Outer radius*	*Inner radius*	*% of volume*
Ocean	6371 km *3959 mi*	6368 km *3957 mi*	0·14
Crust	6368 km *3957 mi*	6347 km *3944 mi*	1·00
Mantle	6347 km *3944 mi*	3482 km *2163 mi*	82·53
Outer core	3482 km *2163 mi*	1222 km *759 mi*	15·62
Inner core	1222 km *759 mi*		0·70

COMPOSITION

The overall composition of the Earth (including crust, mantle and core) in terms of major elements has been estimated as follows:

Element		*%*
Iron	(Fe)	35·9%
Oxygen	(O)	28·5%
Silicon	(Si)	14·3%
Magnesium	(Mg)	13·2%
Nickel	(Ni	2·0%
Calcium	(Ca)	1·9%
Sulphur	(S)	1·8%
Aluminium	(Al)	1·8%

DIMENSIONS

The Earth is not a true sphere but an ellipsoid. Its equatorial diameter is 12,756·2726 (7926·3803 mi) and its polar diameter 12,713·5032 (7899·8046 mi). The Earth's equatorial circumference is 40,075·012 km (24,901·458 mi) and its polar meridianal circumference is 40,007·858 km (24,859·731 mi). The volume of the Earth is 1,083,207,000 km^3 (259,875,300,000 cu mi). The Earth has a pear-shaped asymmetry with the north polar radius being 44m (144 ft) longer than the south polar radius, and there is also a slight ellipticity of the Equator since its long axis (about latitude 14·95°W) is 139m (456 ft) greater than the short axis.

CONTINENTAL DRIFT

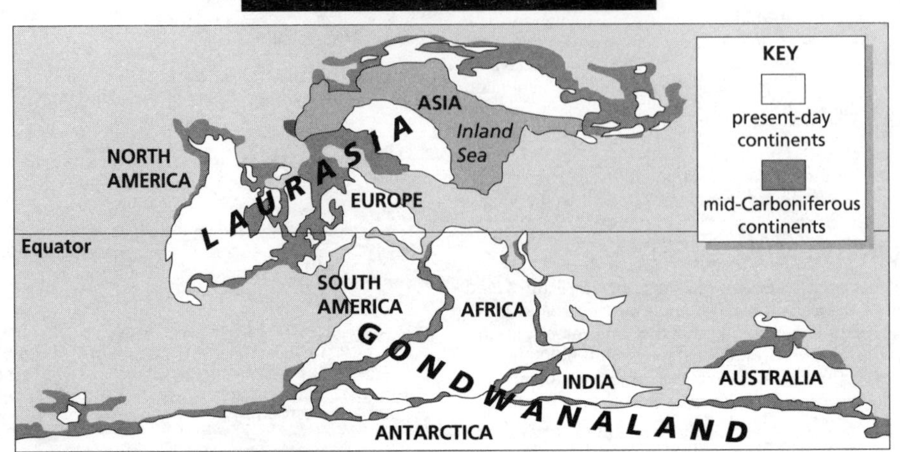

MID-CARBONIFEROUS PERIOD 355–300 million years ago

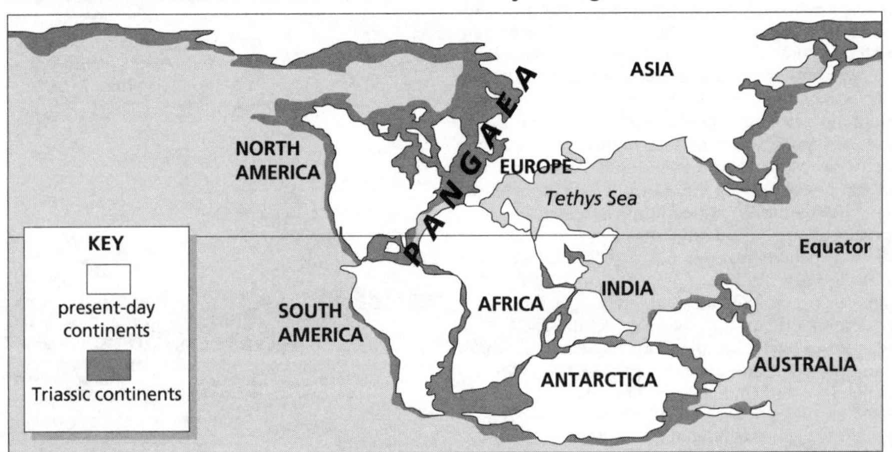

LATE TRIASSIC PERIOD 250–205 million years ago

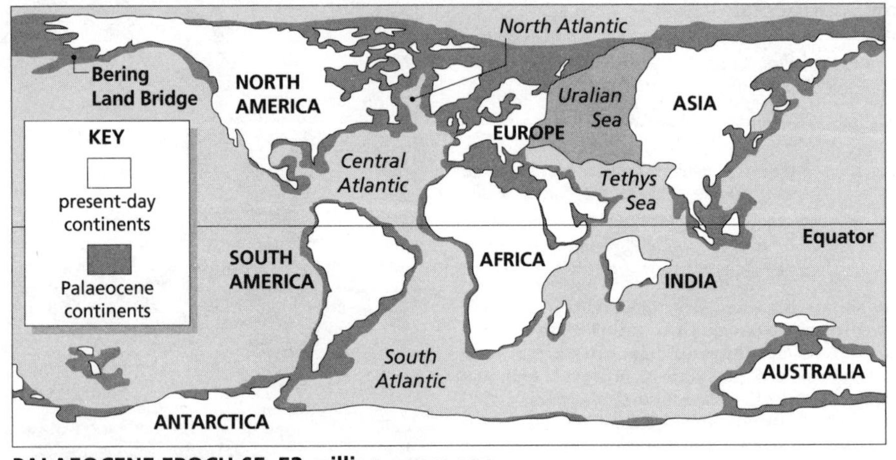

PALAEOCENE EPOCH 65–53 million years ago

THE CONTINENTS

The Earth's land surface comprises seven continents, each with attendant islands.

Europe, Africa and Asia, though politically distinct, physically form one land mass known as Afro-Eurasia, which covers 57·2% of the Earth's land mass. Central America (which includes Mexico) is often included in North America (Canada, the USA and Greenland), with South America being regarded as a separate continent. Europe includes all of Russia west of the Urals. Oceania embraces Australasia (Australia and New Zealand) and the non-Asian Pacific islands. The seventh continent is Antarctica.

The seven continents defined, in order of size, are:

Asia

Area: 44,614,000 km² (17,226,000 sq mi).

Greatest extremity north to south:* 6435 km (4000 mi).

Greatest extremity east to west:* 7560 km (4700 mi).

Russia, which straddles the divide between Asia and Europe, does not recognize a dividing line between the continents. However, a boundary running along the eastern foot of the Ural Mountains and then following the boundary of Kazakhstan to the Caspian Sea is generally recognized internationally. The boundary between Asia and Europe in the Caucasus is disputed. Some authorities recognize the crest of the Caucasus Mountains between the Black Sea and the Caspian as the dividing line, while others prefer a boundary following the valley of the River Manych to the estuary of the River Don. However, the former Soviet republics of Armenia and Georgia, which are south of the crest of the Caucasus Mountains, regard themselves as being European. Together with Azerbaijan, which straddles the crest of the Caucasus Mountains, all three Transcaucasian states are often included within Europe.

The island of Cyprus, which is physically an attendant island to Asia, is often regarded as part of Europe. Turkey is physically divided between Europe and Asia, and is often all included in Europe for many purposes (see Europe).

In the east, the boundary between Asia and Oceania is also disputed. Western New Guinea (Irian Jaya) is politically part of Indonesia but is generally regarded as part of Oceania rather than part of Asia. The rest of Indonesia is regarded as Asian.

Africa

Area: 30,216,000 km² (11,667,000 sq mi).

Greatest extremity north to south:* 7080 km (4400 mi).

Greatest extremity east to west:* 6035 km (3750 mi).

The boundary between Africa and Asia is usually regarded as the Suez Canal rather than the political boundary between Egypt and Israel/Gaza. Africa includes a number of attendant islands, the largest of which are Madagascar, Mauritius, Réunion, Zanzibar and Bioko. The islands of Madeira, the Azores and the Canaries, which are all strictly attendant islands to Africa, are almost always included within Europe as they are integral parts of either Portugal or Spain. The island of Socotra, which is politically part of Yemen, is almost always included in Asia although it is strictly an attendant island to Africa.

North America

Area: 24,230,000 km² (9,355,000 sq mi).

Greatest extremity north to south:* 7885 km (5000 mi).

Greatest extremity east to west:* 6035 km (3750 mi).

North America includes Central America (up to the Panama-Colombia border) as well as Greenland and the Caribbean islands of the Greater Antilles, and the Windward and Leeward Islands. Hawaii is often included as part of North America because it is politically part of the USA, although it is physically part of Oceania.

South America

Area: 17,814,000 km² (6,878,000 sq mi).

Greatest extremity north to south:* 7240 km (4500 mi).

Greatest extremity* east to west: 5150 km (3200 mi).

South America includes the Caribbean islands of Trinidad and Tobago, Aruba, Bonaire, Curaçao, and the Venezuelan Antilles. The northern boundary of the continent is usually taken as the Panama-Colombia boundary rather than the Panama Canal. (Until the 20th century, what is now Panama was considered to be part of South America.)

Antarctica

Area: 14,245,000 km² (5,500,000 sq mi).

Greatest extremity:* 4340 km (2700 mi).

Antarctica includes an relatively small number of attendant islands.

Europe

Area: 10,505,000 km² (4,056,000 sq mi).

Greatest extremity north to south:* 2900 km (180 mi).

Greatest extremity east to west:* 4000 km (2500 mi).

Physically, Europe excludes Asiatic Turkey, thus dividing the city of Istanbul between two continents However, for economic and political purposes Turkey is usually regarded as being part of Europe. The boundary between Europe and Asia is described above (see Asia).

The islands of Madeira, the Azores and the Canaries, although strictly attendant islands to Africa, are almost always included in Europe. The island of Cyprus, an attendant island to Asia, is also almost always included in Europe.

Oceania

Area: 8,503,000 km² (3,283,000 sq mi).

*Greatest extremity** north to south:* 3000 km (1870 mi).

*Greatest extremity** east to west:* 3700 km (2300 mi).

Oceania comprises Australia, New Zealand, and the entire island of New Guinea, as well as the Melanesian, Micronesian and Polynesian islands. Hawaii, although physically part of Oceania, is often included in North America because it is politically part of the USA.

* excluding attendant islands; ** Australia.

Geology

THE FORMATION OF ROCKS

Rock can be one of three types: igneous, sedimentary or metamorphic.

The Earth is perpetually recycling its rocks. Material brought to the surface is eroded, transported and ultimately returned to the Earth's interior, where it becomes available to begin the cycle all over again. This series of processes is known as the rock cycle or geological cycle. The energy to maintain it comes partly from the Sun (to fuel the erosion processes) and partly from the Earth's interior (to generate volcanic activity and uplift).

Igneous rock

Igneous rock starts deep in the Earth as molten magma, which then forces its way up through the crust to cool and solidify.

Magma, which comes to the Earth's surface via volcanic activity, comprises a mixture of oxides (compounds with oxygen) and silicates (compounds with silica and oxygen). When it cools and solidifies, the oxides and silicates produce a complex mixture of mineral crystals. The nature and properties of the crystals in any particular igneous rock depend partly on the composition of the original magma and partly upon the physical conditions under which the magma crystallized. As compositions and conditions vary greatly, there are thousands of different igneous rock types.

Igneous rocks that form on the Earth's surface are known as *extrusive*. Those that form within the crust from magma that never reached the surface are known as *intrusive*. Intrusive rocks cool more slowly because, being surrounded by other rock rather than being open to the air, the heat cannot escape so readily. As a result, the crystals have longer to grow, and the mineral grains are larger (coarser).

Despite the many varieties of igneous rock, just six account for most of the igneous components of the crust. These are *granite, diorite* and *gabbro,* which are coarse-grained intrusive rocks, and *rhyolite, andesite* and *basalt,* which are fine-grained extrusive rocks.

Sedimentary rock

Sedimentary rock is mostly formed when rock of any type is weathered down into fine particles that are then re-deposited under water and later compressed.

At least 75% of all sedimentary rock is known as *clastic sedimentary rock*, which means that it is derived from the erosion products of other rocks. All rocks, even those in the most massive mountain ranges, are ultimately broken down into smaller and smaller fragments. When the particles become small enough they are then transported by water, wind or ice, usually ending up in the ocean. There they fall as sediment to the ocean floor where, under the pressure of subsequent deposits, they are compacted into hard rock. The most common sedimentary rock is *sandstone*.

The remaining 25% of sediment is either chemical or organic. Rivers dissolve minerals out of the rocks through which they pass, and the mineral solutions end up in the oceans. When the oceans reach their saturation limit for the particular mineral concerned, the excess mineral is precipitated out chemically as solid particles, which fall to the ocean floor. The most common chemical sedimentary rock is *limestone* (calcium carbonate). Not all limestone is precipitated chemically, however. Many ocean organisms extract calcium carbonate from water to build their shells and when they die the shells sink to the ocean floor to form sediment in their own right. The most common organic sedimentary rock is again limestone, but there are other organisms that in a similar way generate silica sediments.

Most sedimentary rocks are a mixture of clastic, chemical and organic, although one type usually predominates.

Metamorphic rock

Metamorphic rock is igneous or sedimentary rock that has been subjected to high pressure and/or temperature, thereby changing its nature.

When igneous or sedimentary rocks are subjected to high temperatures and pressures, especially in the presence of percolating fluids, their internal structures, and sometimes even their mineralogical compositions, may be changed. The processes involved are collectively known as *metamorphism*. The sort of temperatures and pressures required are, respectively, 300 °C (572 °F) and 100 megapascals (equivalent to almost 100 atmospheres).

The most extreme conditions in the Earth's crust occur at plate boundaries where continents collide. Most metamorphic rocks are thus generated in the roots of mountains, Depending upon temperature and pressure, there are various grades of metamorphis; but in the most intense (high-grade) metamorphism, rock structures, holes and even fossils are so completely obliterated that the original rock type can no longer be identified.

As a result of the realignment of minerals under pressure, many metamorphic rocks are layered, or banded. Sometimes the layering is visible; but even when it is not, it can often be detected by the way that the rock breaks. A common example is slate, which easily breaks into thin sheets along the layering. Not all metamorphic rock is layered, however. Common examples of non-layered metamorphics are marble, formed by the metamorphism of limestone, and quartzite, which is derived from sandstone.

GEOCHRONOLOGY

The four eras into which geological time is usually divided are: the Cenozoic (Greek *kainos* 'new'), the most recent; the Mesozoic (Greek *mesos* 'middle), the Palaeozoic (Greek *palaios* 'ancient), and the Proterozoic (Greek *protos* 'first') or Precambrian, the most ancient.

The Hadean and Archaen periods, usually regarded as divisions of the Proterozoic, are sometimes added before the Proterozoic as distinct eras.

The eras and periods of geological time are shown on the chart on the following page.

GEOLOGICAL TIMECHART				
ERA	**PERIOD**	**EPOCH**	**BEGAN** MILLIONS OF YEARS AGO	**GEOGRAPHY**
CENOZOIC	**QUATERNARY**	**HOLOCENE**	**0.01**	Retreat of glaciers leaves continents, seas and landscapes in more or less their present forms.
		PLEISTOCENE	**1.6**	The thickest continental glaciers depressed the Earth's crust to such an extent that large areas of northwestern Europe and North America are still rising at a considerable rate today (30 mm a year around Hudson Bay).
	TERTIARY	**PLIOCENE**	**5.3**	Time of marked, often rapid change. Uplift of the Isthmus of Panama results in the connection of North and South America.
		MIOCENE	**23**	Africa moves northwards into Eurasia. The Himalaya are raised as the Indian plate collides with Asia. The Red Sea opens and the Mediterranean has its origin.
		OLIGOCENE	**34**	The main phase of Alpine mountain-building begins, followed soon afterwards by East Africa and Red Sea rifting. South America separates from Antarctica.
		EOCENE	**53**	The Indian plate begins to collide with Eurasia (leading to the formation of the Himalaya in the Miocene). The Eurasian Basin opens as the final fragmentation of the Eurasian continent occurs. Pyrenean mountains form in the late Eocene. Australia separates from South America and Antarctica.
		PALAEOCENE	**65**	Iberia converges on Europe. The Atlantic and Pacific Oceans are linked through the straits of Panama.
MESOZOIC	**CRETACEOUS**		**135**	India separates from Antarctica, while Atlantic rifting brings about the separation of South America from Africa. Further opening of the Atlantic and the separation of Greenland.
	JURASSIC		**205**	At the start of the Jurassic, rifting occurs between Gondwanaland and Laurasia, initially separating southern Europe from Africa and eventually tearing Pangaea in two. Central Atlantic opens.
	TRIASSIC		**250**	The start of the Mesozoic era sees all the major continents joined together. Consequently almost all of the Earth's land surface is concentrated on one side of the globe, with the result that large areas lie far from the oceans and become very arid.
PALAEOZOIC	**PERMIAN**		**300**	Pangaea is formed and in the late Permian Siberia collides with northern Pangaea to form the Ural mountains.
	CARBONIFEROUS Divided in USA into Mississippian (early part) and Pennsylvanian (later part)		**355**	The major continents move closer and closer together, until, early in the next period, Laurasia collides with Gondwanaland to form the supercontinent Pangaea.
	DEVONIAN		**410**	The gap between Laurasia and Gondwanaland has narrowed, but ocean levels remain high.
	SILURIAN		**438**	Laurasia forms as Laurentia and Baltica become welded together. Ocean levels are high, probably from melting of the ice cap.
	ORDOVICIAN		**510**	Baltica moves from South Polar region towards the Equator and closer to Laurentia. Meanwhile Gondwanaland moves towards the South Pole, and increased glaciation causes lowering of the sea level.
	CAMBRIAN		**570**	Near the end of the Precambrian most landmasses fused into a giant supercontinent, but by the late Cambrian Gondwanaland, Siberia and Laurentia are separate continents and more or less sit astride the Equator.
PRECAMBRIAN ERA			**4600**	North America, Greenland and Scotland united as Laurentia, equatorial in position. Gondwanaland in the southern hemisphere.

MODERN DATING METHODS

At the beginning of the 20th century radioactive decay was used as a measurement of geochronology. In 1907 the US chemist and physicist B.B. Boltwood showed that a sample of Precambrian rock dated from 1640 million years before the present (BP), measured by the uranium-lead method. Geological time now extends back about 4600 million years ago to the beginning of the Proterozoic era. Modern dating methods, using the duration of radio-isotopic half-lives, include also the contrasts obtained from thorium-lead, potassium-argon, rubidium-strontium, rhenium-osmium, helium-uranium and, in the recent range up to 40,000 BP, carbon-14. Modern developments, using accelerator equipment, allow carbon-14 dating to extend back beyond 100,000 years. Other methods include thermoluminescence (used since 1968) and racemization (used since 1972): the latter method is dependent upon the rate of change from optically active to inactive forms over a long-term period of time.

FOSSILS

A fossil may be defined as an impression or remnant of a long-dead organism in a deposit of sedimentary rock. By studying rocks and the fossils preserved within them, scientists have been able to trace the momentous changes that the Earth has undergone since its formation. Sedimentary rocks are usually arranged in a succession of horizontal bands or *strata,* with the oldest strata lying at the bottom. Each band will often contain the fossilized remains of plants and animals that died at the time at which the sediment was laid down. The strata of sedimentary rock are therefore like the pages of a book, each with a record of contemporary life etched upon it. Unfortunately, however, the record is far from complete. The process of sedimentation in any one place is invariably interrupted by periods in which new sediment is not laid down or existing sediment is eroded away. The succession of layers is further obscured by folding or faulting, and by mountain building. However patchy the record may be, any interpretation of it depends on first establishing a chronology. Relative dating is usually achieved by correlating strata on the basis of their fossil content, since a specific assemblage of fossils willl be characteristic of a stratum of a particular age. The discovery and study of fossils of extinct animals in the 18th and 19th centuries began to stimulate evolutionary speculation.

Fossilization

In order for an organism to be preserved as a fossil, it must include hard parts capable of preservation and it must be covered rapidly after death to slow decomposition and safeguard it from destruction. The hard parts of some organisms are preserved unaltered, for example the shells of clams. However, most fossilized remains are altered; for example, bones and shells may be *permineralized;* that is, they are made denser by the addition of calcium carbonate, iron and other minerals. Alternatively, the crystal structure of a shell may be *recrystallized,* although its outer appearance remains unaltered. *Replacement* of the hard parts of an organism is a common form of fossilization. This involves the dissolution of the existing hard structure and its replacement by another substance such as silica or hematite.

MILESTONES OF THE FOSSIL RECORD

Precambrian era: Many microfossils dating back 3·25 million years were perhaps produced by bacteria and blue-green algae. Fossilized impressions of the first multicellular animals date back some 590 million years.

Cambrian period: Fossil record of the start of the period is characterized by the emergence of many larger marine animals, including gastropods, trilobites, lamp shells, and graptolites. Nautiloids appeared at the end of the period.

Ordovician period: Typical fossils include highly diversified trilobites, lamp shells and tree-like graptolites, as well as new groups of gastropods and the first sea urchins, ammonites and jawless fish (the first vertebrate remains).

Silurian period: Mass extinction at the end of the Ordovician was followed by a rediversification of marine life. The fossil record includes the first true jawed fish.

Devonian period: The record shows a progressive colonization of the land by plants, including large vascular plants such as club mosses as large as trees as well as the first ferns. The first land animals included scorpions, wingless insects and the earliest tetrapod (a primitive amphibian).

Carboniferous period: Typical fossils include sharks and bony fish, and more diverse amphibians. The first conifers, the first reptiles and the earliest flying insects appeared. Graptolites became extinct.

Permian period: The record includes more diverse reptiles and conifers. Trilobites became extinct.

Triassic period: Gymnosperm flora predominate in the fossil record, although ferns remain important. Many new groups emerged: teleosts (the dominant fish group today), enormous marine reptiles, thecodonts (which evolved into flying reptiles), dinosuars and the first mammals. The Triassic ended with the greatest mass extinction of all time, eliminating many marine invertebrates.

Jurassic period: Flora includes cycads, gingkos and conifers. Animals include turtles, many types of dinosaur, crocodiles and the first undisputed bird.

Cretaceous period: The record includes spectacular marine pleisiosaurs and giant turtles. The end of the period saw mass extinction of ammonites, dinosaurs, ichthyosaurs and pterosaurs. Angiosperms and the first grasses emerged.

Palaeocene epoch: Many mammals, including primates, emerged. Modern plant families evolved.

Eocene epoch: Forests were of a distinctly modern appearance. Typical mammalian fossils include artiodactyls, elephants, edentates, whales, rodents, carnivores, and early higher primates. All bird orders appeared before the end of the epoch.

Oligocene epoch: The earliest monkeys appeared and the largest land mammal of all time, the rhinoceros-like titanotheres, became extinct.

Miocene epoch: The epoch was characterized by the spread of grasslands and the retreat of forests, accompanied by the radiation of apes and horses.

Pliocene epoch: Although the plants were largely similar to today, distinct animals emerged, including mammoths and the first hominids.

MAJOR ROCKS AND ROCK TYPES

Other common rocks are recorded in the geology glossary (below).

Rock	*Main constituents and formation*
andesite (igneous)	Formed from surface lava, volcanic plugs and dikes as well as volcanic ash and mud flows. Fine-grained rocks containing andesine (a feldspar) and pyroxene or biotite.
basalt (igneous)	Formed by cooling of extrusive (i.e. on land surface or under water) lava flows. Contains about 50% silica and high quantities of feldspar, pyroxene and olivine minerals.
breccia (sedimentary)	Formed from angular fragments of material (larger than 2mm/0.08 in across) from pre-existing rocks.
chalk	Fine-grained white limestone (see below).
clay (sedimentary)	Generic term for a wide range of sedimentary rocks formed of tiny clay mineral particles, organic and detrital materials (including quartz). Includes soils, clay shales, mudstones, glacial clays, etc.
diorite (igneous)	Formed from the crystallization of magma or from a reaction between magma and a foreign rock. Medium- or coarse-grained containing about 60% feldspar.
dolomite (sedimentary)	Limestone (see below) that is formed when calcite is replaced after deposition by calcium magnesium carbonate either through contact with sea water or by solution.
gabbro (igneous)	Formed by cooling of intrusive molten rock. Medium- or coarse-grained with variable composition. Contains mainly feldspar and pyroxene.
gneiss (metamorphic)	Formed from granite where the mineral content and structure has been changed through heating caused by intrusion of a new molten mass.
granite (igneous)	Formed by slow cooling of intrusive molten material (i.e. within the Earth's body). Has large crystals (quartz, feldspar, mica).
hornfels (metamorphic)	Fine-grained granular rock formed by thermal metamorphosis.
limestone (sedimentary)	Pure forms are totally calcium carbonate. Comprises the remains of microscopic organisms and always deposited in water. Fine-grained.
marble (metamorphic)	Thermal changes to limestone result in the formation of marble, which is a granular crystalline rock.
marl (sedimentary)	Generic term for a variety of fine-grained mudstones (see below). Calcareous and greensand types are common.
mudstone (sedimentary)	Generic term for a variety of sedimentary rocks formed of tiny clay and silt particles. Characterized by a lack of lamination.
nevadite (igneous)	A rhyolite (see below) with large crystals in which the glassy components are so small that the rock is often mistaken for granite.
obsidian	A glassy black rhyolite (see below)
pitchstone	A glassy rhyolite (see below)
pumice (igneous)	Formed from material thrown from a volcano. Contains a high proportion of air space.
quartzite (metamorphic)	Formed from sandstone by recrystallization under high temperatures or by precipitation of silica. Solid quartz rock with no pores.
rhyolite (igneous)	Formed from volcanic lava in which crystallization began prior to extrusion on the surface. Contains either large, single crystals or, when crystallization is rapid, forms a glassy microcrystalline matrix.
sandstone (sedimentary)	Predominantly quartz grains with other minor components. May preserve bedding structures from original deposition, e.g. dune bedding, ripples, etc.
shale (sedimentary)	Formed by deposition of silt and clay particles in deep water. Contains clay minerals, quartz, feldspars, organic material and iron oxides. (See also clay, above.)
silt	Unconsolidated aggregate of tiny sedimentary particles. (See siltstone, below.)
siltstone (sedimentary)	Consolidated tiny silt particles deposited by water. Typically occurs in thin layers. (See silt, above.)
slate (metamorphic)	Formed from sedimentary rocks that have been metamorphosed. Slates all show cleavage. New minerals may show up as marks or even crystals.

MAJOR METALLURGICAL MINERALS

Some minerals, for example iron and copper, occur in a number of ores; others are naturally occurring.

Mineral	*Element*	*Abundance in crust, parts per million*	*Major uses include*	*Major deposits are worked in the following countries*
bauxite	aluminium	81,000	conductors, aircraft, ships, cars, foil	Australia, Guinea, Jamaica, Brazil, Russia
cassiterite	tin	1.5	tin-plating, alloys (bronze and pewter)	Brazil, China, Malaysia, Indonesia, Bolivia
chalconite, chalcopyrite, bornite, cuprite, etc	copper	100	conductors, alloys (brass, bronze), coinage, plumbing	Chile, USA, Russia, Canada, Zambia
chromite	chromium	under 700	chromium-plating, stainless steel	South Africa, Russia, India, Albania, Turkey
cinnabar	mercury	under 1	explosives, scientific instruments, dentistry	Russia, China, Spain, Algeria, Mexico
galena	lead	20	batteries, roofing, radiological protection	Russia, Australia, USA, China, Canada
garnierite, pentlandite	nickel	under 80	nickel-plating, steel alloys, gas-turbine engines, coinage	Russia, Canada, New Caledonia, Australia
gold	gold	under 0·005	source of value, jewellery some electronic uses	South Africa, Russia USA, China, Australia, Canada
hematite, magnetite	iron	50,000	structures, machines, cars, foil	Russia, Brazil, China, Australia, USA, Ukraine
magnesite	magnesium	25,000	low-density alloys for aircraft, machinery, etc.	Russia, China, North Korea, Slovakia, Turkey
pitchblende	uranium	under 7	nuclear power stations	Russia, Canada, Australia, USA, Namibia
platinum, sperrylite	platinum	under 0·0005	catalyst in chemical processes and in car exhausts	Russia, Finland, USA, Australia, Brazil
silver, sylvanite	silver	under 1	jewellery, silverware, photographic emulsions	Mexico, USA, Peru, Russia, Canada
sphalerite	zinc	under 80	alloys (brass), galvanizing steel	Canada, Russia, Australia, China, Peru
wolframite, scheelite	tungsten	1·5	lamp filaments, electronics steel alloys, cutting tools	China, Russia, Mongolia, Austria, Portugal

The quantities of most metals in the crust are small: only iron, aluminium and magnesium are really plentiful. We are able to extract them only because they are not evenly distributed but occur in local concentrations where mining is economically possible. There are far greater concentrations of some metals, such as iron and nickel, but for the moment they are beyond our reach. The first metals to be used by humanity were those that occurred in their natural state and appeared in outcrops on the surface: gold, silver, iron (in the form of fallen meteorites) and copper. However, supplies of elemental iron and copper soon ran out, and during the Bronze and Iron Ages it was discovered how to extract metals from their ores, in which they are chemically combined with other elements, most often oxygen and sulphur.

Today, the consumption of all metals and minerals is rising fast. Will there be enough to go round? A number of studies carried out since the early 1960s have cast doubt on this. While iron and aluminium are abundant, there are many important metals (lead, zinc, tin, silver, platinum and mercury), the supplies of which seem less certain. In many cases, as one metal ore becomes scarcer, it can be replaced with another, or with plastic or composite material, but this is not always possible.

GEOLOGY GLOSSARY

acid rock igneous rock with over 10% free quartz.

adobe a type of clay.

aeolian deposits particles carried and deposited by the wind.

alluvium sands and gravels carried by rivers and deposited along the course of the river.

amber a type of resin.

amorphous material having no regular arrangement.

anhedral having no crystalline structure.

anticline a fold system in the form of an arch.

aquifer a stratum of rock containing water.

arenaceous rocks sedimentary sandstones, deposited by wind or water.

argillaceous rocks sedimentary rocks deposited by water; usually marls, silts, shales, muds and clays.

ash fine material formed by volcanic explosions.

asphalt hydrocarbon, either solid or just fluid at normal temperatures.

asthenosphere a part of the Earth's mantle.

automorphic grains having a crystal structure.

ball clay reworked china clay.

banket a conglomerate of quartz.

basalt fine-grained basic igneous rock, sometimes with a glassy characteristic look.

basic rock igneous rock containing little or no quartz.

batholith an intrusive mass of igneous rock.

bauxite an aluminium ore of aluminium oxide, out of which the easily leached ions have been removed.

bedding plane a surface parallel to the surface of deposition. Some rocks split along bedding planes; others have less obvious physical characteristics such as changes of particle size.

biolith rock of organic material, formed by organic processes.

bitumen a hydrocarbon mineral with a tarry texture, ranging from a viscous liquid to a solid.

black-band ironstone a sedimentary rock, formed principally from a form of coal and iron carbonate (siderite).

boghead coal coal formed from algal and fungal material.

bort anhedral diamonds in a granular mass.

boss a mass of igneous rock with steep contact surfaces with the surrounding rock.

boudinage the stretching of a rock layer to give a sausage-shaped structure.

boulder bed sedimentary rock consisting of boulders together with fine-grained material.

breccia a sedimentary rock consisting of angular material of more than 2 mm (0·08 in) diameter.

brown coal another name for lignite; a coal containing a low carbon content.

carbonate a large group of minerals, all having the carbonate group bond – CO_3 in common. They can be divided into sedimentary and non-sedimentary carbonates, limestone being the most common form of sedimentary carbonate.

carbonatite a magmatic rock consisting of calcium carbonate and occasionally other carbonates.

carstone a form of sandstone with a high proportion of limonite.

cassiterite tin oxide ore.

cataclasis the mechanical break-up of rock.

caulk barytes (barium sulphate).

celestite a strontium mineral found mainly in sedimentary rock.

ceylonite a spinel mineral.

chalcedony a silica-based mineral, found in many forms, some of which are semi-precious stones, e.g. agate, onyx, carnelian, jasper.

chalcocite copper sulphide ore.

chalcopyrite one of the principal copper ores.

chalk a fine-grained white limestone, calcium carbonate.

charnockite a granular rock, mainly consisting of quartz, feldspar and hypersthene.

chert a form of silica, found as bands and nodules in sedimentary rocks.

chiastolite a form of aluminium silicate.

china clay kaolin, formed by decomposition of feldspar in granite.

chlorite a green mineral consisting of talc units.

chondrites stony meteorites.

chromite a chromium ore, containing iron.

chrysocolla a copper ore mineral, copper silicate.

chrysoprase a green chalcedony.

chrysotile a form of asbestos.

cinnabar mercury sulphide, associated with volcanic activity.

citrine a yellow quartz.

clastic rock fragments of rock, transported to a site of deposition and built up into a conglomerate.

clay a sedimentary rock with a fine particle structure and a soft plastic texture when wet.

cleat jointing found in coal.

cleavage a flat plane of breakage, perhaps parallel to a crystal face.

cleavage plane the plane of fracture in a rock.

clint a ridge in a limestone rock surface.

coal stratified deposits of carbonaceous material, originally derived from decayed vegetable matter.

cobble a rock particle, between 125 mm (5 in) and 250 mm (10 in) in diameter.

columnar structure vertical columns or prisms, formed, for example, in lava and basalt, caused by the cooling of the rock.

competent the flow or flexion of a rock layer, in which it is not broken.

composite igneous bodies that have more than one material in them, e.g. due to intrusion.

concretion accumulations of sedimentary constituents in certain defined areas of rock, often around a nucleus.

conglomerate rounded pebbles cemented together in one mass.

convergence the metamorphosis of two dissimilar rocks so that they become similar.

corundum aluminium oxide, used as an abrasive and also found as gemstones, e.g. sapphire, ruby.

country rock the body of rock that encloses an intrusion by another rock, e.g. an igneous rock.

creep the gradual deformation of a rock by stress applied over a long time.

crystal a three-dimensional structure arising from the atomic structure of the substance. The symmetrical arrangement for a given substance means that the angles within the structure are constant for that substance.

culm Carboniferous rocks found in Devon and Cornwall (England).

cuprite copper oxide, an important copper ore.

deflation surface debris transported by the wind.

deformation any change in a bed or stratum after it has been formed.

dendritic branching into a many-fingered appearance.

denudation any process that results in a lowering of the land surface.

detritus particles of minerals and rocks formed by weathering and corrosion.

diamond a crystalline form of carbon. It has a cubic structure, distinguishing it from graphite.

diatomite the remains of unicellular organisms called diatoms. It is highly-absorbent powdery material.

diorite a coarse-grained igneous rock consisting of feldspar plus ferromagnesium minerals.

dog-tooth spar calcite, crystallized into tooth-like forms.

dolerite an igneous rock similar to basalt.

dolomite calcium magnesium carbonate, or limestone with a substantial proportion of magnesium carbonate.

dyke a sheet of igneous rock that cuts across the bedding or structural planes of the host rock.

elaterite an elastic or rubbery form of bitumen.

elvan a dyke of granite.

emerald a green form of beryl.

emery fine granules of corundum and magnetite.

epidiorite a metamorphic granular rock derived from igneous rock and containing the minerals of diorite.

epidotes a group of rock-forming silicate minerals.

evaporite sediment left by the evaporation of salt water.

extrusive igneous rock that has flowed out at the Earth's surface.

fault a fracture plane in rock, along which displacement occurs.

feldspar silicate minerals, in which the silicon ions are in part replaced with aluminium ions. Calcium, sodium and potassium feldspars exist, as do the rare barium feldspars.

feldspathoid rock-forming silicates with sodium and/or potassium in the lattice structure. They never occur with quartz.

festoon bedding a type of cross-bedding.

fire clay argillaceous fossil soil found in some coal seams.

flint a type of chert.

flowage irreversible deformation, i.e. deforming a material beyond its elastic limit.

fluorite calcium fluoride, found as veins in rocks.

fold a flexing of a rock stratum.

fool's gold iron pyrites.

fossil the impression of an animal or plant, or its skeletal remains, buried by natural processes and then preserved.

fracture a break in a direction that is not a cleavage plane.

fuchsite a mica mineral containing chromium.

fulgurite a branching tube of fused silica, caused by lightning striking sandy soil.

gabbro a coarse-grained igneous rock, equivalent to basalt and dolerite. It contains feldspar, pyroxene and olivine as the major constituents.

galena lead sulphide, the most important lead ore.

gangue the material in which an ore deposit from the metal is not extracted.

gannister an arenaceous stratum found beneath coal seams.

gas cap a collection of gas above an oil deposit.

gems hard minerals, free from cleavages. Fragments are artificially cut and polished for decorative use.

garnet a semi-precious mineral with a wide range of colours, although red is the most commonly found.

geode a rock cavity containing crystals pointing inwards.

geosyncline an elongated basin, filled with sedimentary deposits. These deposits can then be deformed by orogenic forces.

gneiss banded coarse-grained rocks formed during metamorphosis.

granite a coarse-grained igneous rock, consisting essentially of quartz and feldspar and occurring as intrusive bodies in a variety of forms.

granule a rock particle of about 2–4 mm (0·08–0·16 in).

graphite a soft black form of carbon.

grike a cleft in a limestone pavement.

grit a rock in which the particle shape is angular.

gull a fissure which tapers downwards and is then filled with material from above.

gumbo a soil which, when wet, gives a sticky mud.

gypsum an evaporite calcium sulphate mineral found in clays and limestone.

hade a fault plane's angle to the vertical.

haematite an iron-oxide iron ore.

halite common salt, left as an evaporite.

hardness the mineral property propounded by Mohs. It measures the ability of one mineral to scratch another. Corundum – number 9 – can scratch topaz – number 8 – but not diamond – number 10.

10	Diamond	5	Apatite
9	Corundum	4	Fluorite
8	Topaz	3	Calcite
7	Quartz	2	Gypsum
6	Orthoclase	1	Talc

hard-pan strongly cemented material occurring below the surface of some sediments as a result of groundwater action.

hemicrystalline rocks containing both crystalline and glassy material.

hornfels a fine-grained granular rock formed by thermal metamorphosis.

hornstone a fine-grained volcanic ash.

horst an area thrown up between two parallel faults.

humus organic material in soil.

Iceland spar a variety of calcite.

igneous one of the three major divisions of rocks. Generally they are crystalline, although glassy forms can be found. They are either extrusive, i.e. produced on the Earth's surface as a result of volcanic action, or intrusive into other rocks, in which case they only appear on the Earth's surface if the surrounding rock is eroded.

impervious (a rock) not allowing the passage of water.

impregnation the in-filling of pores by mineral material, e.g. oil.

inclusion a portion of one material totally enclosed within another.

incretion a cylindrical hollow concretion.

inlier an area of older rock surrounded by younger rock.

interbedded (a layer of rock) situated between two other layers.

intermediate rock rock containing no more than 10% quartz plus a feldspar.

intrusion an igneous rock structure that has forced its way into pre-existing rock.

jade a gemstone of a hard compact aggregate.

jasper a red chert-like variety of chalcedony.

jet a homogeneous form of cannel coal or black lignite.

joint a fracture in a rock structure along which no movement can be observed.

kaolin the main constituent of china clay.

kieselguhr diatomite.

kimberlite a brecciated peridotite containing mica and other minerals.

kyanite an aluminium silicate.

labradorite a type of feldspar.

landscape marble a type of limestone that, when sliced at right angles to the bedding plane, reveals patterns reminiscent of a landscape scene.

laterite an iron-oxide ore, out of which the easily leached ions have been removed.

lava molten silicates that flow out of volcanoes. In general they are basic, although acidic lava flows are known. Acidic lavas flow readily and tend to cover much larger areas, while basic lavas are more viscous.

leaching the removal of ions from a soil or rock by the through-flow of water.

lepidolite a type of mica.

lignite brown coal, low in carbon content.

limestone a group of sedimentary rocks consisting of carbonates, principally calcium carbonate. Calcite and dolomite are the most important limestone rocks.

limonite a group of iron oxides and hydroxides.

lithifaction the formation of a large rock from small fragments.

loam sand, silt and clay in equal proportions in a soil.

loess deposits of wind-blown fine particles.

lustre the ability of minerals to reflect light.

magma the molten fluid within the Earth's interior. Igneous rocks are formed from the magma, although various constituents of the magma will be lost during this process of consolidation.

magnesite magnesium carbonate.

magnetite an iron ore consisting of ferric oxide.

malachite a carbonate ore of copper.

marble metamorphosed limestone, usually with other compounds giving marble its recognizable appearance.

marl a mudstone with a high calcium content.

metamorphism the process of heating, pressure and chemical action that causes rocks to change from one form to another in the Earth's crust.

mica a large group of silica-based minerals, characterized by the fact that the crystal structure gives cleavage into flat flexible sheets.

migmatite a form of gneiss.

mobile belt a part of the Earth's crust in which metamorphosis, igneous activity and deformation occur.

monzonite coarse igneous rock with a high feldspar content.

mud wet clay soil in a near-liquid state.

mudstone a type of argillaceous rock, similar to shale, but without the property of splitting along bedding planes.

muscovite a type of mica.

natural gas gaseous hydrocarbons found together with oil deposits.

neck a volcanic plug.

nodule a round concretion.

obsidian a type of rhyolite with a black glassy sheen to it.

oceanite a type of basalt.

oil often called petroleum, oil is naturally occurring liquid hydrocarbon. It is invariably found in association with saline water and natural gas, and often with solid hydrocarbons.

oil shale a dark argillaceous rock. It does not contain liquid oil, but a solid organic material called kerogen, which gives oil on distillation.

olivine a group of silicates, containing ferrous iron and magnesium. They largely occur in igneous rocks.

onyx a type of banded chalcedony.

oolith a rounded lump of rock formed by accretion round a nucleus. Ooliths usually contain calcium minerals.

opal an amorphous type of silica, believed to have been derived from silica gel.

ore an aggregate of minerals from which a valued mineral is extracted.

orogeny the process or period of mountain building.

outlier a relatively small area of young rock, surrounded by older rock.

overburden soil found on top of a bed of useful mineral.

peat an early, earth-like form of coal. It is a dark-brown to black mass of partially decomposed vegetation.

pebble a rock fragment of 5–60 mm (0·2–2·3 in) diameter.

pedalfer leached soil in a region with high rainfall.

pegmatite a coarse-grained igneous rock, usually granitic. Very long crystals may be apparent.

peridot gem-quality olivine.

permeability the ability of water to percolate through a rock.

pervious rock rock through which water may pass via cracks, fissures, etc.

pitchblende uranium oxide ore.

plug the solidified lava and other material left in the neck of a volcano. Often the surrounding material is subsequently eroded away.

plutonic rock igneous material of a deep-seated origin, i.e. originating from the magma.

pudding stone a conglomerate.

pumice one of the pyroclastic rocks thrown out of a volcano. It contains a high proportion of air space.

pyrite iron sulphide.

pyroclastic rock a rock formed either by liquid lava thrown out of a volcano or solid lumps of surrounding rock broken up by volcanic action.

quartz a silica mineral with three different forms. Sand is the most common. Low quartz is a crystalline form, occurring in a variety of colours. At 573 °C (1063 °F) low quartz gives rise to high quartz, but its natural occurrence is rare.

red bed sedimentary rocks containing a high proportion of ferric minerals, giving them a reddish colour.

residual deposit minerals left when part of a rock is dissolved or leached away.

rhyolite a fine-grained or glassy volcanic rock, rich in quartz.

rock a mass of mineral material, usually consisting of more than one mineral type.

rock crystal a clear form of quartz.

ruby a red transparent form of corundum.

rudaceous rock sedimentary rock deposited as detritus by water or air, and divided into conglomerates and breccias.

rutile titanium oxide ore.

salt dome salt forced up through an overlying sediment as a dome. Under pressure salt behaves like a magma.

sand a type of quartz, formed of fine particles. It can also be taken to mean any fine particles of 0·0625–2 mm (0·0025–0·08 in).

sandstone arenaceous rocks, consisting of fine grains cemented together by a variety of minerals.

sapphire a blue transparent form of corundum.

schist a metamorphosed rock with the constituent minerals arranged in parallel.

scree fragments formed by the weathering of rocks.

sedimentary rock rock formed out of the material resulting from erosion and weathering, along with organic material. The principal sedimentary rocks are sandstone, limestone and shale.

shale a sedimentary rock composed of clay particles.

shingle gravel or pebbles found on beaches.

silica silicon dioxide, which can take a variety of forms, e.g. quartz, chalcedony, opal.

silicates the most prolific mineral group in the Earth's crust. They are based on a silicon-oxide structure, but a variety of other elements and ions can be substituted in this structure, particularly aluminium. The group includes the clays, the feldspars, the garnets, the micas, the silicas.

sill a sheet of igneous rock, lying along a bedding plane.

silt a type of argillaceous rock.

slate argillaceous rock that has been metamorphosed. The slates all show cleavage, and may have new minerals showing up as marks or even crystals.

soapstone any greasy rock, although usually applied to talc rocks.

soil the loose weathered material covering most of the Earth's land surface. It contains humus – a partially decomposed matter – which improves the fertility and water retention of the soil and so encourages plant growth.

spinels a group of minerals including magnetite and chromite.

stalactite calcium carbonate formed as a spike hanging down from the ceiling in a limestone cave.

stalagmite calcium carbonate formed as a spike pointing up from the floor in a limestone cave.

stock an intrusive mass of igneous rock, smaller than a batholith.

streak a mineral's colour when in a powdered state, e.g. formed by scratching it.

subsoil partly weathered rock lying between the soil and the bedrock.

syenites a group of coarse-grained igneous rocks containing feldspars and feldspathoids.

talc magnesium silicate, the softest common mineral.

tar pit areas where asphalt or bitumen rises to the surface from an underground hydrocarbon source.

terra rossa red clayey soil formed as a result of carbonates being leached out of limestone.

topaz a clear semi-precious form of aluminium silicate.

tor piles of granite blocks, left by differential weathering of the rock around them.

touchstone a very hard fine-grained black form of basalt or chert.

tripoli a type of diatomite.

ultrabasic rock igneous ferromagnesian rock, with little or no feldspar, quartz or feldspathoid in it.

ultramarine a type of feldspathoid.

valley fill loose material filling or partly filling a valley.

vein a sheet of mineral that has intruded into a fissure or joint of a rock.

water table the upper limit of the groundwater saturation.

weathering the breaking down of stationary rocks by mechanical means, e.g. by the action of ice and the sun, and by chemical means.

wind erosion the abrasive action of wind-driven particles of sand against stationary rocks.

wolframite a tungsten ore.

xenolith an inclusion of pre-existing rock in an igneous rock.

zeolites a group of silicates containing water of crystallization, and capable of reversible dehydration. They can act as powerful base exchangers.

zircon zirconium silicate.

Physical Geography

THE OCEANS

The oceans cover a greater area of the Earth than does the land – 71% or almost three quarters of the Earth's surface. The three major oceans are the Pacific, Atlantic and Indian Oceans. The Pacific is the largest ocean, and covers more than a third of the surface of the Earth. The Arctic Ocean is smaller than the other three and is covered almost entirely by ice. Seas are smaller than the four oceans.

The depth of the oceans is very small compared with their area. The deepest part – in the Western Pacific – is only about 11,000m (36,000 ft) deep. However this is greater than the height of the highest mountain on land, Mount Everest.

Sea water

Sea water has solid substances dissolved in it. Sodium and chlorine (which together in their solid form make up sodium chloride – common salt) are the most abundant of these, and together with magnesium, calcium and potassium they make up over 90% of the elements dissolved in sea water. Other elements are present only in very small amounts.

The saltiness, or *salinity*, of sea water depends on the amount of these substances dissolved in it. An average of about 3·5% of the volume of sea water consists of dissolved substances. High evaporation removes more of the pure water, leaving behind the dissolved substances, so the salinity is higher where evaporation is high, particularly if the sea water is also enclosed and cannot mix easily with the sea water in a larger ocean. This occurs, for example, in the Mediterranean and Red Seas. Low values of salinity occur in polar regions, particularly in the summer months when melting ice dilutes the sea water. Low salinity also occurs in seas such as the Baltic, which is linked to the Atlantic Ocean only by a narrow channel and which is fed by a larger number of freshwater rivers.

Most of the water on the Earth, about 94% of it, is in the oceans. More pure water is evaporated from the oceans than is returned as precipitation (rain, snow, etc), but the volume of water in the oceans remains the same because water is also returned to the oceans from the land by rivers.

Waves

Sea water is rarely still: it is usually moving in waves, tides or currents. Waves are caused by wind blowing across the surface of the ocean. The height of a wave is determined by the wind speed, the time the wind has been blowing, and the distance the wave has travelled over the ocean. The highest wave ever recorded had a height of 34m (116 ft), although usually they are much smaller. Waves play a very important role in the shaping of coastlines.

Water does not move along with waves. Instead the water changes shape as a wave passes, moving in a roughly circular motion, rising towards a wave crest as it arrives and falling as it passes. This motion can be seen by watching a boat: the boat bobs up and down as the waves move past it but does not move along with the waves.

There is another type of wave in the ocean, which is not generated by the winds. These are *tsunami*. They are also popularly called *tidal waves*, but this name is quite wrong because they are not caused by tides. Tsunami are due to earthquakes or the eruption of undersea volcanoes, which move a large amount of water rapidly, disturbing the sea surface and creating waves that travel away from the area of the earthquake or volcano. Tsunami travel at very high speeds, around 750 km/h (470 mph). However, in the open ocean they cause little damage because their wave height is very low, usually less than 1m (3 ft), but in shallow water they slow down and their height increases to 10m (33 ft) or more, and they can cause extensive damage when they hit a shore.

Tides

Tides are caused by the gravitational pull of the Moon and the Sun on the Earth, causing the level of the oceans to change. The pull is greatest on the side of the Earth facing the Moon, and this produces a high tide. The pull is weakest on the side away from the Moon, where the sea water rises away from the Moon, and this also gives a high tide. The Sun is much further away than the Moon and although it is much larger its effect on tides is less than half that of the Moon. When both the Moon and the Sun are on the same or opposite sides of the Earth, the pull is greatest, producing very high tides called *spring tides*. Weaker tides, called *neap tides*, occur when the Moon and the Sun form a right angle with the Earth, because the pulls of the two are in different directions. Spring tides occur every 14 days and neap tides half-way between each spring tide. There are two high tides and two low tides every day in most parts of the Earth, but a few areas have only one high tide and one low tide, or a mixture, with one high tide being much higher than the other. The *tidal range* (the difference between the high and the low water levels) varies from place to place, from less than a metre (3 ft) in the Mediterranean Sea and Gulf of Mexico to 14·5m (47 ft) in the Bay of Fundy on the coast of Canada.

Currents

Currents near the surface of the oceans, like waves, are driven by the winds. The wind drags the water along with the wind. Currents move much more slowly than the wind, with speeds of less than 8 km/h (5 mph). They do not flow exactly in the same direction as the wind, but are deflected to one side by the Earth's spin.

Features of the sea bed

The region of the sea bed closest to land is the *continental margin*, which is divided into the *continental shelf*, *slope* and (sometimes) the *continental rise*.

Continental shelf The continental shelf is the shallowest – around 130m (430 ft) deep – and is relatively flat. It is about 100 km (60 mi) wide. The sea over continental shelves usually has abundant marine life and most fishing is done here. Some 25% of the world's oil and gas comes from the continental shelves.

Oceanic ridges These are vast, rugged, undersea mountain chains often, at the centre of oceans. On average they are some 1000 km (620 mi) wide and stand up to 3000m (10,000 ft) above the adjacent ocean basins. They form a more or less linked system about 80,000 km (50,000 mi) long, and this system enters all the major oceans.

Different parts of it have different names: in the centre and south Atlantic, for example, it is called the Mid-Atlantic Ridge; in the north Atlantic to the southwest of Iceland it is the Reykjanes Ridge; in the Pacific it is known as the East Pacific Rise.

On average, ridge crests lie some 2500m (8200 ft) below the ocean surface, but there are a few places, such as Iceland, where the rocks have risen above the water surface, forming an island.

Abyssal plains Between the ocean ridges and the continental margins there are abyssal plains. These are very flat and featureless parts of the sea floor, around 4000m (13,000 ft) deep. Abyssal plains are broken in some places by seamounts, underwater volcanoes that have erupted from the sea floor. Seamounts may rise above the sea surface to form islands, such as Hawaii.

Ocean trenches The deepest parts of the oceans are the ocean trenches. These are on average about 100 km (62 mi) wide and 7000–8000m (23,000–26,000 ft) deep, and may be thousands of kilometres long.

COASTAL FRONTIERS

Countries with the longest coastlines

Canada*	244,800 km (152,110 mi)
Russia**	103,000 km (64,000 mi)
Indonesia**	40,000 km (25,000 mi)
Australia*	36,735 km (22,826 mi)
Japan*	33,287 km (20,684 mi)
Norway*	21,347 km (13,264 mi)
USA*	19,924 km (12,380 mi)
China**	18,500 km (11,500 mi)

* including islands ** estimate; including islands

Countries with the shortest coastlines

Monaco	5.6 km (3.5 mi)
Nauru	19 km (12 mi)
Bosnia	20 km (13 mi)
Jordan	25 km (16 mi)
Slovenia	30 km (19 mi)
Zaïre	39 km (24 mi)
Iraq	45 km (28 mi)
Togo	50 km (31 mi)
Belgium	66 km (41 mi)

Coasts On coastlines, new land can be created by the deposition of sediment, and existing land can be lost through marine erosion. What happens where on coasts depends on factors such as climate, coastal geology, the orientation of the coast to wind and waves, and human activities.

DEEP-SEA TRENCHES

Length (km)	*Length (mi)*	*Name*	*Deepest point*	*Depth (m)*	*Depth (ft)*
2250	1400	Mariana Trench* (western Pacific)	Challenge Deep**	11,022	36,160
2575	1600	Tonga-Kermadec Trench*** (southern Pacific)	Vityaz 11 (Tonga)	10,882	35,702
2250	1400	Kuril-Kamchatka Trench* (western Pacific)		10,542	34,587
1325	825	Philippine Trench (western Pacific)	Galathea Deep	10,497	34,439
		Idzu-Bonin Trench (sometimes included in the Japan Trench, see below)		9810	32,196
800	500	Puerto Rico Trench (western Atlantic)	Milwaukee Deep	9220	30,249
320+	200+	New Hebrides Trench (southern Pacific)	North Trench	9165	30,080
640	400	Solomon or New Britain Trench (southern Pacific)		9140	29,988
560	350	Yap Trench* (western Pacific)		8527	27,976
1600	1000	Japan Trench* (western Pacific)		8412	27,591
965	600	South Sandwich Trench (southern Atlantic)	Meteor Deep	8263	27,112
3200	2000	Aleutian Trench (northern Pacific)		8100	26,574
3540	2200	Peru-Chile (Atacama) Trench (eastern Pacific)	Bartholomew Deep	8064	26,454
		Palau Trench (sometimes included in the Yap Trench)		8050	26,420
965	600	Romanche Trench (north-south Atlantic)		7864	25,800
2250	1400	Java (Sunda) Trench (Indian Ocean)	Planet Deep	7725	25,344
965	600	Cayman Trench (Caribbean)		7535	24,720
1040	650	Nansei Shoto (Ryukyu) Trench (western Pacific)		7505	24,630
240	150	Banda Trench (Banda Sea)		7360	24,155

* These four trenches are sometimes regarded as a single 7400 km (4600 mi) long system.
** In 1969, the Soviet research ship *Vityaz* claimed 11,022m (36,198 ft), using echo-sounding only.
*** Kermadec Trench is sometimes considered to be a separate feature; depth 10,047m (32,974 ft).

OCEANS

Size of the world's oceans

Oceans with adjacent seas	*Area (sq. kilometres)*	*Area (sq. mi)*	*Percentage of the world's area*
Pacific	181,200,000	69,960,000	35·52%
Atlantic	106,480,000	41,110,000	20·88%
Indian	74,060,000	28,590,000	14·52%
Total	**361,740,000**	**139,660,000**	**70·92%**

If the adjacent seas are detached and the Arctic is regarded as as a separate ocean, the oceanic areas may be given as:

Oceans without adjacent seas	*Area (sq. kilometres)*	*Area (sq. mi)*	*Percentage of the world's area*
Pacific	166,240,000	64,190,000	46·0%
Atlantic	86,560,000	33,420,000	23·9%
Indian	73,430,000	28,350,000	20·3%
Arctic	13,230,000	5,110,000	3·7%
Other seas	22,280,000	8,600,000	6·1%

Depth of the world's oceans

Oceans with adjacent seas	*Greatest depth (m)*	*Greatest depth (ft)*	*Greatest depth location*	*Average depth (m)*	*Average depth (ft)*
Pacific	11,022	36,160	Mariana Trench	4188	13,740
Atlantic	9460	31,037	Puerto Rico Trench	3736	12,257
Indian	7542	24,744	Java Trench	3872	12,703

SEAS

Principal seas	*Area (sq. kilometres)*	*Area (sq. mi)*	*depth (m)*	*depth (ft)*
South China*	2,974,600	1,148,500	1200	4000
Caribbean Sea	2,753,000	1,063,000	2400	8000
Mediterranean Sea	2,503,000	966,750	1485	4875
Bering Sea	2,268,180	875,750	1400	4700
Gulf of Mexico	1,542,985	595,750	1500	5000
Sea of Okhotsk	1,527,570	589,800	840	2750
East China Sea	1,249,150	482,300	180	600
Hudson Bay	1,232,300	475,800	120	400
Sea of Japan	1,007,500	389,000	1370	4500
Andaman Sea	797,700	308,000	865	2850
North Sea	575,300	222,125	90	300
Black Sea	461,980	178,375	1100	3600
Red Sea	437,700	169,000	490	1610
Baltic Sea	422,160	163,000	55	190
Persian Gulf**	238,790	92,200	24	80
Gulf of St Lawrence	237,760	91,800	120	400
Gulf of California	162,000	62,530	810	2660
English Channel	89,900	34,700	54	177
Irish Sea	88,550	34,200	60	197
Bass Strait	75,000	28,950	70	230

* The Malayan Sea, which embraces the South China Sea and the Straits of Malacca (8,142,000 sq kilometres or 3,144,000 sq mi), is not now an entity accepted by the International Hydrographic Bureau.

** Also referred to as the Arabian Gulf or, popularly, 'the Gulf'.

MOUNTAINS

Mountains and mountain ranges are largely formed by the interaction of mountain-building processes (*orogeny*) and the subsequent erosional processes that destroy them. The distribution of the world's major mountain ranges generally follows those belts of the Earth's landmasses where earthquakes and volcanoes are common. These phenomena are, in turn, caused by the collision of the moving plates that make up the Earth's lithosphere. Such collisions often result in the margin of one plate being forced upwards, and this process has resulted in the formation of many mountain ranges, although other processes may also play a part in mountain building. The Earth's largest mountain ranges today, the Alps, Himalaya, Rockies and Andes, are all relatively young, resulting from plate collisions in the last 25 million years or so. Much older ranges include the Scottish Highlands, the Scandinavian mountains and the Appalachians in the USA, which are all around 300-400 million years old. Deeply eroded remnants of older ranges, up to 3000 million years old, occur in many parts of Africa and Australia.

Folded mountains

The largest and most complex continental mountain ranges are the result of the collision of tectonic plates. Mountains formed directly by plate collisions are known as *fold mountains*, because they are conspicuously folded, faulted and otherwise deformed by the hugh collision pressures. In some cases the collision is between landmasses. Thus India is pressing into the rest of Asia to form the Himalaya, and Africa is being forced into Europe, producing the Alps. In other cases the collision is between an oceanic plate and a continent. Thus the Pacific plate is spreading towards South America, forcing up the Andes. The Himalaya, Alps and Andes are still being formed. Other ranges, for example the Urals of Russia, are products of older, long-ceased plate collisions.

Fault-block and upwarped mountains

Other types of mountain exist that have not been formed by plate collisions. In *fault-block mountains* a central block of the Earth's crust has sunk and the adjacent blocks have been forced upwards. Mountains of this type define the Basin and Range Province of the western USA (Nevada and parts of Utah, New Mexico, Arizona and California) and form the Sierra Nevada of California and the Teton Range of Wyoming. In *upwarped mountains*, on the other hand, a central block has been forced upwards. Examples are the Black Hills of Dakota and the Adirondacks of New York state.

Volcanic mountains

Spectacular mountains may also be built by volcanic action. Mauna Loa in Hawaii, for example, is, at 10,203m (33,476 ft), the world's highest mountain if measured from the Pacific Ocean floor, although less than half is above sea level. Much more important than such isolated volcanoes, however, are the oceanic ridges, the undersea mountain ranges along which the bulk of the Earth's volcanism takes place. Intense volcanism also occurs where oceanic and continental plates collide. The Andes, for example, owe not a little of their mass to volcanic activity.

WORLD'S HIGHEST MOUNTAINS

Key to Ranges: H = Himalaya; K = Karakoram. Subsidiary peaks or tops in the same mountain massif are italicized.

Mountain	*Height (m)*	*Height (ft)*	*Range*	*Date of first ascent*
1.Mount Everest*	8863	29,078	H	29 May 1953
Everest South Summit	8750	28,707	H	26 May 1953
2.K2 (Chogori)	8610	28,250	K	31 July 1954
3.Kangchenjunga	8598	28,208	H	25 May 1955
Yalung Kang (Kangchenjunga West)	8502	27,894	H	14 May 1973
Kangchenjunga South Peak	8488	27,848	H	19 May 1978
Kangchenjunga Middle Peak	8475	27,806	H	22 May 1978
4.Lhotse	8511	27,923	H	18 May 1956
Subsidiary Peak	8410	27,591	H	unclimbed
Lhotse Shar	8383	27,504	H	12 May 1970
5.Makalu I	8481	27,824	H	15 May 1955
Makalu South-East	8010	26,280	H	unclimbed
6.Dhaulagiri I	8167	26,795	H	13 May 1960
7.Manaslu I (Kutang I)	8156	26,760	H	9 May 1956
8.Cho Oyu	8153	26,750	H	19 Oct 1954
9.Nanga Parbat (Diamir)	8124	26,660	H	3 July 1953
10. Annapurna I	8091	26,546	H	3 June 1950
Annapurna East	8010	26,280	H	29 Apr 1974
11. Gasherbrum I (Hidden Peak)	8068	26,470	K	5 July 1958
12. Broad Peak I	8047	26,400	K	9 June 1957
Broad Peak Middle	8016	26,300	K	28 July 1975
Broad Peak Central	8000	26,246	K	28 July 1975
13. Shisham Pangma (Gosainthan)	8046	26,398	H	2 May 1964
14. Gasherbrum II	8034	26,360	K	7 July 1956

THE WORLD'S GREATEST MOUNTAIN RANGES

Length	*Name*	*Location*	*Culminating Peak*	*Height*
7200 km (4500 mi)	**Andes**	western South America	Cerro Aconcagua	6960m (22,834 ft)
4800 km (3000 mi)	**Rocky Mountains**	western North America	Mount Elbert	4400m (14,433 ft)
3800 km (2400 mi)	**Himalaya-Karakorum-Hindu Kush**	southern Central Asia	Everest	8863m (29,078 ft)
3600 km (2250 mi)	**Great Dividing Range**	eastern Australia	Kosciusko	2230m (7316 ft)
3500 km (2200 mi)	**Trans Antarctic Range**	Antarctica	Mt Vinson	5140m (16,863 ft)
3000 km (1900 mi)	**Brazilian Atlantic Coast Range**	eastern Brazil	Pico de Bandeira	2890m (9482 ft)
2900 km (1800 mi)	**West Sumatran-Java Range**	west Sumatra and Java	Kerintji	3805m (12,484 ft)
2650 km (1650 mi)*	**Aleutian Range**	Alaska and NW Pacific	Shishaldin	2861m (9387 ft)
2250 km (1400 mi)	**Tien Shan**	Kyrgyzstan/China	Pik Pobedy	7439m (24,406 ft)
2000 km (1250 mi)	**Central New Guinea Range**	Irian Jaya/Papua New Guinea	Ngga Pulu	5030m (16,503 ft)
2000 km (1250 mi)	**Altai Mountains**	Russia/Mongolia	Gora Belukha	4505m (14,783 ft)
2000 km (1250 mi)	**Ural Mountains**	Russia	Gora Narodnaya	1894m (6214 ft)
1930 km (1200 mi)	**Kamchatka Mountains**	eastern Russia	Klyuchevskaya Sopka	4850m (15,910 ft)
1930 km (1200 mi)	**Atlas Mountains**	northwest Africa	Jebel Toubkal	4165m (13,665 ft)
1610 km (1000 mi)	**Verkhoyanskiy Mountains**	Russia	Gora Mas Khaya	2959m (9708 ft)
1610 km (1000 mi)	**Western Ghats**	India	Anai Madi	2694m (8841 ft)
1530 km (950 mi)	**Sierra Madre Oriental**	Mexico	Volcan Citlaltépetl (Pico de Orizaba)	5610m (18,405 ft)
1530 km (950 mi)	**Zagros Mountains**	Iran	Zard Kuh	4547m (14,921 ft)
1530 km (950 mi)	**Scandinavian Range**	Norway/Sweden	Galdhopiggen	2469m (8098 ft)
1450 km (900 mi)	**Ethiopian Highlands**	Ethiopia	Ras Dashan	4620m (15,157 ft)
1450 km (900 mi)	**Sierra Madre Occidental**	Mexico	Nevado de Colima	4265m (13,993 ft)
1370 km (850 mi)	**Malagasy Range**	Madagascar	Tsaratanana peak	2876m (9436 ft)
1290 km (800 mi)	**Drakensberg**	southern Africa	Thabana Ntlenyana	3482m (11,425 ft)
1290 km (800 mi)	**Chersky Range**	Russia	Gora Pobeda	3147m (10,325 ft)
1200 km (750 mi)	**Caucasus**	Georgia/Russia/Azerbaijan	Elbrus	5642m (18,510 ft)
1130 km (700 mi)	**Alaska Range**	Alaska, USA	Mt McKInley	6194m (20,320 ft)
1130 km (700 mi)	**Assam Burma Range**	Assam (India)-W Burma	Hkakado Razi	5881m (19,296 ft)
1130 km (700 mi)	**Cascade Range**	NW USA/Canada	Mt Rainier	4392m (14,410 ft)
1130 km (700 mi)	**Central Borneo Range**	Borneo (Indonesia)/ Malaysia	KInabalu	4101m (13,455 ft)
1130 km (700 mi)	**Apennines**	Italy	Corno Grande	2931m (9617 ft)
1130 km (700 mi)	**Appalachians**	eastern USA	Mt Mitchell	2037m (6684 ft)
1050 km (650 mi)	**Alps**	Central Europe	Mt Blanc	4807m (15,771 ft)

* Continuous mainland length (excluding islands) 720 km (450 mi).

HIGHEST MOUNTAINS OF NORTH AND CENTRAL AMERICA

Mt McKinley (known to local Indians as Denali) is the only peak in excess of 6100m (20,000 ft) in North and Central America. It was first climbed on 7 June 1913.

Peak	*Height*	*Location*
Mt McKinley, South Peak*	6194m (20,320 ft)	USA
Mt Logan	5951m (19,524 ft)	Canada
Volcan Citlaltépetl (Pico de Orizaba)	5610m (18,405 ft)	Mexico
Mt St Elias	5489m (18,008 ft)	USA/ Canada
Popocatépetl	5452m (17,887 ft)	Mexico
Mt Foraker	5304m (17,400 ft)	USA
Ixtaccihuatl	5286m (17,342 ft)	Mexico
Mt Lucania	5227m (17,150 ft)	Canada
King Peak	5221m (17,130 ft)	USA
Mt Blackburn	5036m (16,522 ft)	USA
Mt Steele	5011m (16,440 ft)	USA
Mt Bona	5005m (16,420 ft)	USA

* Mt McKinley, North Peak, is 5934m (19,470 ft)

HIGHEST MOUNTAINS OF SOUTH AMERICA

The mountains of the Andes are headed by Aconcagua at 6960m (22,834 ft) – first climbed on 14 January 1897. Aconcagua is the highest mountain in the world outside the great ranges of Central Asia.

Peak	*Height*	*Location*
Cerro Aconcagua	6960m (22,834 ft)	Argentina
Ojos de Salado	6895m (22,588 ft)	Argentina/ Chile
Nevado de Pissis	6780m (22,244 ft)	Argentina/ Chile
Huascarán Sur	6768m (22,205 ft)	Peru
Llullaillaco	6723m (22,057 ft)	Argentina/ Chile
Mercadario	6670m (21,884 ft)	Argentina/ Chile
Huascarán Norte	6655m (21,834 ft)	Peru
Yerupajá	6634m (21,765 ft)	Peru
Nevados de Tres Crucées	6620m (21,720 ft)	Argentina/ Chile
Coropuna	6613m (21,696 ft)	Peru
Nevado Incahuasi	6601m (21,657 ft)	Argentina/ Chile
Tupungato	6550m (21,490 ft)	Argentina/ Chile
Sajama	6542m (21,463 ft)	Bolivia
Nevado Gonzalez	6500m (21,326 ft)	Argentina

HIGHEST MOUNTAINS OF AFRICA

All the peaks listed in Zaïre and Uganda are in the Ruwenzori Mountains.

Peak	*Height*	*Location*
Kilimanjaro*	5894m (19,340 ft) *Hans Meyer Peak, Mawenzi 5148m (16,890 ft) Shira Peak 4005m (13,139 ft)*	Tanzania
Mt Kenya (Batian)	5199m (17,058 ft)	Kenya
Mt Ngaliema**	5109m (16,763 ft)	Zaïre/Uganda
Duwoni***	4896m (16,062 ft)	Uganda
Mount Baker (Edward Peak)	4843m (15,889 ft)	Uganda
Mount Emin§	4798m (15,741 ft)	Zaïre
Mount Gessi	4715m (15,470 ft)	Uganda
Sella Peak	4626m (15,179 ft)	Uganda
Ras Dashen (Rasdajan)	4620m (15,158 ft)	Ethiopia
Humphreys Peak	4578m (15,021 ft)	Uganda

* Uhuru Point (also called Kibo and formerly called Kaiser Wilhelm Spitze).
** Formerly called Mt Stanley and Margherita Peak.
*** Formerly called Mt Speke and Vittorio Emanuele Peak.
§ Formerly called Umberto Peak.

HIGHEST MOUNTAINS OF OCEANIA

Several of the mountains of West Irian (Indonesia) are known by more than one name. Some have changed their name since Dutch colonial days, and more than one mountain was (temporarily) renamed Sukarno or Peak Sukarno. The two highest mountains in Polynesia are Mauna Kea – 4205m (13,796 ft) – and Mauna Loa – 4170m (13,680 ft). The former is an extinct volcano; the latter is an active volcano. Both are in Hawaii, which has been politically part of the USA since Aug 1959. The highest mountain in Australia is Mt Kosciusko – 2230 m (7316 ft) – in the Snowy Mountains, New South Wales. The highest mountain in New Zealand is Mt Cook in Taranaki, North Island. Mt Cook – which is called Aorangi by the Maoris – is now 3754 m (12,315 ft) high. Before a major rock slide from the summit in December 1991, the mountain was 3764m (12,349 ft).

Peak	*Height*	*Location*
Ngga Pulu (Jayakusumu)*	5030m (16,503 ft)	W. Irian
Daam	4922m (16,250 ft)	W. Irian
Jayakusumu Timur	4840m (15,879 ft)	W. Irian
Trikora	4730m (15,518 ft)	W. Irian
Enggea	4717m (15,475 ft)	W. Irian
Mandala	4640m (15,223 ft)	W. Irian
Mt Wilhelm	4509m (14,493 ft)	Papua New Guinea

* Also known as Jaya. In Dutch colonial days, Jayakusumu was known as Carstensz Pyramid.

HIGHEST MOUNTAINS OF ALPINE EUROPE

Subsidiary peaks or tops on the same massif have been omitted except in the case of Mont Blanc and Monte Rosa, where they have been indented in italic type.

Name		*Height*	*Country*	*First ascent*
Mont Blanc		4807m (15,771 ft)	France	1786
	Monte Bianco di Courmayeur	4748m (15,577 ft)	Italy*-France	1877
	Le Mont Maudits	4465m (14,649 ft)	Italy*-France	1878
	Picco Luigi Amedeo	4460m (14,632 ft)	Italy*	1878
	Dôme du Goûters	4304m (14,120 ft)	France	1784
Monte Rosa				
	Dufourspitze	4634m (15,203 ft)	Switzerland	1855
	Nordend	4609m (15,121 ft)	Swiss-Italian border	1861
	Ostspitze	4596m (15,078 ft)	Swiss-Italian border	1854
	Zumstein Spitze	4563m (14,970 ft)	Swiss-Italian border	1820
	Signal Kuppe	4556m (14,947 ft)	Swiss-Italian border	1842
Dom		4545m (14,911 ft)	Switzerland	1858
Lyskamm (Liskamm)		4527m (14,853 ft)	Swiss-Italian border	1861
Weisshorn		4506m (14,780 ft)	Switzerland	1861
Täschhorn		4491m (14,733 ft)	Switzerland	1862
Matterhorn		4476m (14,683 ft)	Swiss-Italian border	1865
Dent Blanche		4357m (14,293 ft)	Switzerland	1862
Nadelhorn		4327m (14,196 ft)	Switzerland	1858
Grand Combin		4314m (14,153 ft)	Switzerland	1859
Lenzspitze		4294m (14,087 ft)	Switzerland	1870
Finsteraarhorn		4274m (14,021ft)	Switzerland	1829**

* The highest point in Italian territory is a shoulder of the main summit of Mont Blanc (Monte Bianco) through which a 4760m (15,616 ft) contour passes. The highest top exclusively in Italian territory is Picco Luigi Amedeo (see above) to the south of the main Mont Blanc peak, which is itself exclusively in French territory.

** Also reported climbed in 1812 but evidence lacking.

HIGHEST MOUNTAINS OF CAUCASIA

The spine of the Caucasus Mountains, forming the boundaries between Russia and Georgia, and Russia and Azerbaijan, includes the following peaks higher than Mont Blanc – 4807m (15,771 ft).

Peak	*Height*
Elbrus, West Peak	5642m (18,510 ft)
Elbrus, East Peak	*5595m (18,356 ft)*
Dykh Tau	5203m (17,070 ft)
Shkhara	5201m (17,063 ft)
Pik Shota Rustaveli	5190m (17,028 ft)
Koshtantau	5144m (16,876 ft)
Pik Pushkin	5100m (16,732 ft)
Jangi Tau, West Peak	5051m (16,572 ft)
Janga, East Peak	*5038m (16,529 ft)*
Dzhangi Tau	5049m (16,565 ft)
Kazbek	5047m (16,558 ft)
Katyn Tau (Adish)	4985m (16,355 ft)
Pik Rustaveli	4960m (16,272 ft)
Mishirgi, West Peak	4922m (16,148 ft)
Mishirgitau, East Peak	*4917m (16,135 ft)*
Kunjum Mishirgi	4880m (16,011 ft)
Gestola	4860m (15,944 ft)
Tetnuld	4853m (15,921 ft)

HIGHEST MOUNTAINS OF ANTARCTICA

The following mountains are the highest peaks surveyed in Antarctica. Large areas of Greater Antarctica remain unsurveyed, particularly the regions inland of Wilkes Land, Enderby Land and Queen Maud Land.

Peak	*Height*
Mt Vinson	5140m (16,863 ft)
Mt Tyree	4965m (16,289 ft)
Mt Shinn*	4800m (15,750 ft)
Mt Gardner	4690m (15,387 ft)
Mt Epperley	4602m (15,098 ft)
Mt Kirkpatrick	4511m (14,799 ft)

LOWEST POINTS

The lowest-lying countries, in terms of the highest point above sea-level, are as follows:

Maldives	unnamed spot	3m (10 ft)
Marshall Islands	unnamed spot	6m (20 ft)
Tuvalu	unnamed spot	6m (20 ft)
Gambia	unnamed spot	43m (141 ft)

VOLCANOES

A volcano is a mountain, often conical in shape, which has been built up above an opening in the Earth's crust during violent and spectacular events called *eruptions*. When these occur, molten rock, or *magma*, wells up from deep below ground and is thrown out through the opening, frequently with other rock debris.

Few spectacles in nature are more awesome or more terrifying than volcanic eruptions. In the most violent ones, tremendous explosions inside the volcano hurl large rocks, cinders and great clouds of ash, steam and gas high into the sky from the *crater*, at the top. Streams of molten rock known as *lava*, and sometimes boiling mud, pour down the surrounding slopes destroying everything in their path.

Although above 800 volcanoes have been recorded as active in historic times, 500 to 350 million years ago there were very violent periods of volcanic activity. Many thousands of volcanoes erupted constantly, and many mountain ranges today consist of the remains of long dead volcanoes. Even now, thousands of volcanoes may be erupting unseen beneath the oceans. Many volcanoes soar to great heights amid the Earth's major mountain ranges. The highest is Cerro Aconcagua, a snow-clad peak 6960m (22,834 ft) high in the Andes of Argentina.

Because Aconcagua no longer erupts, it is said to be *extinct*. Other volcanoes that have been quiet for a very long time but may erupt again are described as *dormant*. Volcanoes that are known to have erupted in historic times are referred to as *active*, and these are always dangerous. The highest volcano regarded as active is Ojos del Salado, which rises to a height of 6895m (22,588 ft) on the frontier between Chile and Argentina. The mountain has recently produced vents emitting hot gases and steam known as *fumaroles*.

In modern times, scientists have been able to observe and record the dramatic birth and growth of new volcanoes. A famous example is Paricutín, Mexico, which began as a plume of smoke in a farmer's field in 1943 and by 1952 had grown more than 430m (1400 ft). Another appeared 20 years later, when the volcanic island of Surtsey emerged from the sea off southern Iceland amid loud explosions and billowing clouds of ash and steam. The new island now occupies 2·5 km² (1 sq mi).

What causes volcanic eruptions?

Volcanoes are like gigantic safety valves that release the tremendous pressures that build up inside the Earth. These pressures are affected by the constant movement of the plates that make up the surface crust. As a result of this movement, molten magma in the mantle is sometimes forced upward under pressure through any breaks it can find in the surface rocks. As it rises, gases dissolved in it are released by the fall in pressure, and the magma shoots out of the volcano in explosive eruptions.

The Earth's volcanic zones

Volcanoes are found where the Earth's crust is weakest, especially along the edges of the crustal plates and most notably in the 'Ring of Fire' around the Pacific Ocean plate. Large numbers of volcanoes, known as *abyssal volcanoes*, are also scattered over the ocean floors away from the plate margins. Here the crust is only about 5 km (3 mi) thick and is easily breached by molten magma rising from the mantle below. Localized hot spots in the mantle also cause the formation of volcanoes, such as those in the Hawaiian Islands and those found on land away from the plate margins.

SOME MAJOR VOLCANIC ERUPTIONS

Santorini (Thera) *Height:* 584m (1960 ft). *Location:* Cyclades, Greece. *Date:* c. 1550 BC.

A massive explosion virtually destroyed the island, and is thought by some to have contributed to the demise of Minoan civilization on nearby Crete. The disaster may also have given rise to the legend of the lost city of Atlantis.

Vesuvius *Height:* 1280m (4198 ft). *Location:* Bay of Naples, Italy. *Date:* AD 79.

The towns of Pompeii, Herculaneum and Stabiae were completely buried, and thousands died. In 1631, 3000 people were killed, since when there have been around 20 major eruptions, the last in 1944.

Unnamed *Height:* unknown. *Location:* North Island, New Zealand. *Date:* c. AD 130.

Around 30 million tonnes (tons) of pumice were ejected, creating the vast caldera now filled by Lake Taupo. An area of c. 16 000 km² (6180 sq mi) was devastated - the most violent of all documented volcanic events.

Etna *Height:* 3311m (10 855 ft). *Location:* Sicily, Italy. *Date:* 1669.

20,000 people were killed, and lava overran the west part of the city of Catania, 28 km (17 mi) from the summit.

Kelud *Height:* 1731m (5679 ft). *Location:* Java, Indonesia. *Date:* 1586

10,000 people killed. Another eruption in 1919 killed 5000 people.

Tambora *Height:* 2850m (9350 ft). *Location:* Jumbawa, Indonesia. *Date:* 1815.

An estimated 150–180 km³ (36–43 cu mi) were blasted from the cone, which dropped in height from 4100m (13,450 ft) to 2850m (9350 ft) in minutes. About 90,000 people were killed in the explosion and subsequent giant wave, or died later of famine.

Krakatau *Height*: 813m (2667 ft) *Location:* Krakatau, Indonesia. *Date:* 1883.

163 villages were wiped out and 36,380 people killed by the giant wave caused by this, the greatest volcanic explosion recorded – although possibly only one fifth of the Santorini explosion. Rocks were thrown 55 km (34 mi) into the air, and dust fell 5330 km (3313 mi) away 10 days later. The explosion was heard over one thirteenth of the Earth's surface.

Mont Pelée *Height:* 1397m (4582 ft) *Location:* Martinique, West Indies *Date:* 1902

Within three minutes a nuée ardente destroyed the town of St Pierre, killing all 26,000 inhabitants - except for one, a prisoner who survived in the thick-walled prison.

Mount St Helens *Height:* 2549m (8360 ft.). *Location:* Washington State, USA. *Date:* 1980.

66 people were presumed dead and 260 km² (100 sq mi) of forest destroyed. Smoke and ash rose to a height of 6000m (20,000 ft), depositing ash 800 km (440 mi) away.

MAJOR VOLCANOES

Among the principal volcanoes active in recent times are:

Name	Height	Range/location (and country)	Date of last notified eruption
Ojos del Salado	6895m (22,588 ft)	Andes (Argentina/Chile)	1981; steams
Llullaillaco	6723m (22,057 ft)	Andes (Argentina/Chile)	1877
San Pedro	6199m (20,325 ft)	Andes (Chile)	1960
Guallatiri	6060m (19,882 ft)	Andes (Chile)	1993
San José	5919m (19,405 ft)	Andes (Chile)	1931
Cotopaxi	5897m (19,347 ft)	Andes (Ecuador)	1975
El Misti	5862m (19,220 ft)	Andes (Ecuador)	1878
Tutupaca	5844m (19,160 ft)	Andes (Ecuador)	1902
Antisana	5793m (18,995 ft)	Andes (Ecuador)	1801; subglacial
Ubinas	5710m (18,720 ft)	Andes (Peru)	1969
Lascar	5641m (18,507 ft)	Andes (Chile)	1991
Tupungatito	5640m (18,504 ft)	Andes (Chile)	1986
Volcán Citlaltepetl (Pico de Orizaba)	5610m (18,405 ft)	Altiplano de Mexico (Mexico)	1687
Isluga	5566m (18,250 ft)	Andes (Chile)	1960
Popocatépetl	5451m (17,887 ft)	Altiplano de Mexico (Mexico)	1920; steams
Ruiz	5435m (17,820 ft)	Andes (Colombia)	1992
Tolima	5249m (17,210 ft)	Andes (Colombia)	1943
Sangay	5230m (17,159 ft)	Andes (Ecuador)	1989; rumbles
Tungurahua	5048m (16,550 ft)	Andes (Ecuador)	1944
Guagua Pichincha	4880m (16,000 ft)	Andes (Ecuador)	1988; rumbles
Klyuchevskaya Sopka (Kamchatka Peninsula)	4850m (15,910 ft)	Khrebet Mountains (Russia)	1992; plumes
Cumbal	4795m (15,720 ft)	Andes (Colombia)	1926
Purace	4590m (15,059 ft)	Andes (Colombia)	1977
Cerro Negro de Mayasquer	4499m (14,750 ft)	Andes (Colombia)	1936
Mt Rainier	4392m (14,410 ft)	Cascade Range (USA)	1882
Mt Shasta	4317m (14,159 ft)	Cascade Range (USA)	1855
El Galeras	4294m (14,080 ft)	Andes (Colombia)	1993
Doña Juana	4277m (14,025 ft)	Andes (Colombia)	1906
Tajumulco	4220m (13,845 ft)	Sierra Madre (Guatemala)	rumbles
Mauna Loa	4170m (13,680 ft)	Hawaii (USA)	1988; rumbles
Tacanáa	4078m (13,379 ft)	Sierra Madre (Guatemala)	rumbles
Mt Cameroon	4069m (13,353 ft)	isolated mountain (Cameroon)	1986
Erebus	3795m (12,450 ft)	Ross Island (Antarctica)	1991
Fujiyama	3776m (12,388 ft)	Kanto (Japan)	steams
Rindjani	3726m (12,224 ft)	Lombok (Indonesia)	1966
Pico de Teide	3718m (12 198 ft)	Tenerife, Canary Is (Spain)	1909
Semeru	3676m (12,060 ft)	Java (Indonesia)	1994
Nyiragongo	3470m (11,385 ft)	Virunga (Zaïre)	1982
Koryakskaya	3456m (11,339 ft)	Kamchatka Peninsula (Russia)	1957

EUROPEAN VOLCANOES (active in historical times)

Name	Height	Notes	Number of eruptions since 1700	Last eruption
Iceland (18 volcanoes)				
Eldeyjar	na	ephemeral island	4	1926
Trölladyngja	381m (1250 ft)	central Iceland	0	1390
Hekla	1501m (4920 ft)	southern Iceland	67	1991
Krakatindur	na	eruption from a fissure	2	1913
Surtsey	174m (570m)	island formed	1	1967
Eyjafallajökull	1678m (5500m)	subglacial eruption	1	1821
Katla	1449m (4750ft)	southern Iceland	6	1955
Laki	824m (2700ft)	southern Iceland	1	1783
Grimsvötn	na	subglacial eruption	33	1954
Oraefajökull	c.2356m (c.6900 ft)	subglacial eruption	1	1727
Kverkfjöll	c.1861m (c.6100)	subglacial eruption	3	1729
Askja	1520m (4983 ft)	central Iceland	2	1961
Sveinagja	946m (3100 ft)	eruption from a fissure	1	1875
Myvatn	na	major lava flow from a fissure	1	1729
Krafla	824m (2700 ft)	northern Iceland	1	1984
Leirhafnarskörd	244m (800 ft)	northern Iceland	1	1823
Mánáreyar		submarine	1	1867
Heimaey	na	Vestmann Islands	1	1973
Norway (1 volcano)				
Beerenberg	2546m (8347 ft)	Jan Mayen Island	2	1970
Italy (7 volcanoes)				
Monte Nuovo	140m (460 ft)	Flegrean Islands	1	1538
Vesuvius	1290m (4230 ft)	Campania	many	1944
Ischia	793m (2600 ft)	Flegrean Islands	0	1301
Stromboli	932m (3055 ft)	Eolian Islands	many	1992
Vulcano	503m (1650 ft)	Eolian Islands	6	1988; rumbles
Etna	3311m (10,855 ft)	Sicily	many	1992
Giulia Ferdinandeo	na	ephemeral island	3	1863
Mediterranean Sea (2 volcanoes)				
Pinne		submarine	2	1911
Foerstner		submarine	1	1891
Greece (1 volcano)				
Santoríni (Thera)	1316m (4316 ft)	Santoríni, Cyclades	6	1950
Portugal - Azores (9 volcanoes)				
Faial	1049m (3440 ft)	Faial Island	1	1958
Pico	2315m (7713 ft)	Pico Island	3	1963
San Jorge Island	1060m (3475 ft)		2	1964 ?
(unnamed) lat 38°30′N, long 27°25′W		submarine	2	1902
Santa Barbara	1029m (3375 ft)	Terceira Island	2	1867
Castro Bank	na	submarine	1	1720
Sete Cidades	862m (2825 ft)	San Miguel Island	4	1811
Agua de Pau	955m (3130 ft)	San Miguel Island	0	1652
Furnas	810m (2655 ft)	San Miguel Island	0	1630
Spain – Canaries (3 volcanoes)				
Caldera de Taburiente	1861m (6100 ft)	La Palma	2	1971
Pico de Teide	3716m (12,192 ft)	Tenerife	5	1909
Timanfaua	566m (1855 ft)	Lanzarote	2	1824

RIVERS AND LAKES

Rivers and lakes are the most important bodies of surface water on land masses. A river is a freshwater body confined in a channel which flows down a slope into another river, a lake or the sea, or sometimes into an inland desert. Small, narrow rivers may be called brooks, streams or creeks.

A lake is an inland body of water occupying a depression in the Earth's surface. Usually, lakes receive water from rivers, but sometimes only directly from springs. Lakes normally lose water into an outlet or river, but some, called *closed lakes*, have no outlet and lose water only by evaporation - for example, Lake Eyre in Australia and Great Salt Lake in Utah, USA.

Where do rivers get their water from?

Rivers may receive their water from several sources, but all of these are indirectly or directly related to *precipitation* - a collective term for the fall of moisture onto the Earth's surface from the atmosphere. Rain falling on the ground may immediately run down slopes as *overland flow*, becoming concentrated and eventually forming a stream. This tends to occur when the ground surface is *impermeable* (i.e. water cannot pass through it, as is the case with some kinds of rock). It may also occur when the ground is already saturated with water, or when rainfall is very heavy.

Often, however, rivers receive their water from *springs*. This is because rainfall will commonly soak into the ground, to accumulate in the soil or to pass into permeable and porous rocks as *groundwater*. In *permeable* rock, water can pass right through the rock itself, whereas in *porous* rock there are holes and fissures through which water can pass. Springs occur where the top of the *aquifer* – a layer of rock containing water – intersects with the ground surface. Groundwater is important as a source for rivers in that it can supply water even when precipitation is not occurring, thereby constantly maintaining river flow.

A third source of water for rivers is the melting of solid precipitation (snow) or snow which has been turned to ice to form a glacier or ice sheet. This is particularly important in high-latitude and mountainous areas.

Perennial, seasonal and ephemeral rivers

Rivers occur in all the world's major environments, even in polar areas and deserts. In temperate areas, such as Western Europe, northeastern USA and New Zealand, and in the wet tropics, enough precipitation tends to fall, fairly evenly throughout the year, to replenish groundwater constantly and therefore to allow rivers to flow all year round. These *perennial rivers* do, however, experience seasonal and day-to-day variations in the volume of water they carry (the *flow regime*), owing to seasonal fluctuations in precipitation and additional inputs from individual storms.

Some rivers may only flow seasonally, particularly in environments with Mediterranean-type climates, which have a very distinct wet, winter season and a dry summer. Rivers in glaciated areas may also have very seasonal flow regimes. *Glacial meltwater streams*, which receive their water directly from glaciers, usually only flow during the few months in the summer when the ice melts.

In dry desert climates, rivers may not flow for years on end, because of the infrequency of desert storms, and then only for a few days, or even hours. However, when storms do occur these *ephemeral rivers* may flow at great rates, because desert rainfall is often very heavy. This gives them considerable power and the ability to erode and transport large quantities of sediment.

Some deserts do possess perennial rivers. The Nile, for example, despite experiencing a distinctly seasonal flow regime, flows all year round through the Egyptian Desert; likewise, the Colorado River passes through desert areas of the southwestern USA. The reason that these and other rivers can successfully exist in deserts is that their *catchments* (source areas) lie in areas with wetter climates.

River basins

Only some very short rivers are able to flow from a source to the sea without either being joined by others or becoming a *tributary* of a large river. Most rivers therefore form part of a *drainage network*, occupying a *drainage basin*. In fact, the whole of the Earth's land surface can be divided up into drainage basins, and these basins are separated by areas of relatively high ground called *watersheds*. Some drainage basins occupy only a few square kilometres, but others are enormous – the largest, the Amazon Basin, covers over 7 million sq km (2·7 million sq mi).

ARTIFICIAL LAKES

Artificial lakes (reservoirs) are either constructed as sources of water supply for an area and/or as sources to generate electricity by water power.

Largest reservoirs by capacity:

Reservoir	*Country*	*Capacity (million cubic m)*
* Owen Falls, R. Nile.	Uganda	2,700,000
Kakhovskaya Res., R. Dnepr	Russia	182,000
Kariba, R. Zambezi	Zimbabwe/Zambia	180,600
Bratskoye Res., R. Angara	Russia	169,270
Lake Nasser, R. Nile	Egypt	168,900
Lake Volta, R. Volta	Ghana	153,000

* The completion of the Owen Falls Dam in 1954 marginally raised the level of the *natural* Lake Victoria, technically turning it into a reservoir.

Largest reservoirs by area:

Reservoir	*Country*	*Area (km^2)*
Lake Volta, R. Volta	Ghana	8482 (3275 sq mi)
Kuybyshev Res, R. Volga	Russia	2490 (961 sq mi)
Rybin Res, R. Volga	Russia	1768 (683 sq mi)

WORLD'S GREATEST RIVERS

Length	*Name*	*Source*	*Course*	*Notes*
6670 km (4145 mi)	**Nile** (Bahr-el-Nil)-White Nile (Bahr el-Jabel)-Albert Nile-Victoria Nile-Victoria Nyanza-Kagera-Luvironza	Burundi: Luvironza branch of the Kagera,a feeder of the Victoria Nyanza	Through Tanzania (Kagera) Uganda (Victoria Nile and Albert Nile), Sudan (White Nile), Egypt to the eastern Mediterranean	Navigable length to first cataract (Aswan 1545 km/960 mi). Egyptian Irrigation Dept. states a length of 6700 km (4164 mi).
6448 km (4007 mi)	**Amazon** (Amazonas)	Peru: Lago Villafro, head of the Apurimac branch of the Ucayali, which joins the Marañon to form the Amazon	Through Colombia to equatorial Brazil (Solimoes) to South Atlantic (Canal do Sul)	Total of 15,000 tributaries, ten over 1600 km (1000 mi). Navigable 3700 km (2300 mi) upstream. Delta extends 400 km (250 mi) inland.
6300 km (3915 mi)	**Yangtze** (Chang Jiang)	Western China: Kunlun Shan Mountains, (as Tuotuo and Tongtian)	Begins W of Tuotuohe in Qinghai, through Yunnan, Sichaun, Hubei, Anhui, Jiangsu to Yellow Sea	Estuary 190 km (120 mi long)
6020 km (3741 mi)	**Mississippi-Missouri**-Jefferson-Beverhead-Red Rock	Beverhead County, southern Montana USA	Through N. and S. Dakota, Nebraska, Iowa, Missouri, Kansas, Illinois, Kentucky, Tennessee, Arkansas, Mississippi, Louisiana, SouthWest Pass into Gulf of Mexico	Missouri is 3725 km (2315 mi) long; the Jefferson-Beaverhead-Red Rock is 349 km (217 mi) long. Total Mississippi from Lake Itasca (Minn) is 3778 km (2348 mi).
5540 km (3442 mi)	**Yenisey-Angara** Selenge	Mongolia: Ideriin branch of Selenge (Selenga)	Through Buryatia (Russia): Selenge branch into Lake Baikal, thence via Angara to Yenisey	Estuary 386 km (240 mi) long. Yenisey is 3540 km (2200 mi) long; the Angara is 1850 km (1150 mi)
5464 km (3395 mi)	**Hwang He** (Yellow River)	China: West of Bayan, Qinghai Province	Through Gansu, Inner Mongolia, Henan, Shandongto Gulf of China, Yellow Sea	Changed mouths by 400 km (250 mi) in 1852. Only last 40 km (25 mi) is navigable.
5409 km (3361 mi)	**Ob-Irtysh**	Mongolia: Kara (Black) Irtysh via northern China (Xinjiang) feeder	Through Kazakhstan into Russia to Ob confluence at Khanty Mansiysk, thence as the Ob to Kara Sea	Estuary is 725 km (450 long. Ob is 3679 km (2286 mi) long; Irtysh is 2960 km (1840 mi) long
4880 km (3032 mi)	**Paraná-Rio de la Plata**	Brazil: as Paranáiba. Flows south to east Paraguay border and into eastern Argentina	Emerges into confluence with R. Uruguay to form Rio de la Plata	After the 120 km (75 mi) long delta estuary, the river shares the 340 km (210 mi) long estuary of the Uruguay called the Rio de la Plata
4700 km (2920 mi)	**Zaire** (Congo)	Zambia-Zaïre border as Lualaba	Through Zaire as Lualaba, along Zaire/Congo border to NW Angola	Navigable for 1730 km mi) from Kisangani to KInshasa. Estuary 96 km (60 mi).
4400 km (2734 mi)	**Lena-** Kirenga	Russia: hinterland of west central shores of Lake Baikal as Kirenga	Northwards through eastern Russia to Leptev Sea, Arctic Ocean	Lena delta extends 177 km (110 mi) inland. Estuary frozen Oct. to July.
4350 km (2702 mi)	**Mekong** (Me Nam Kong)	Central Tibet: as Lants'ang on slopes of Dza-Nag-Lung-Mong	Flows into China, thence south to form Burmese-Laotian, and most of Thai-Laotian-borders, thence via Cambodia and Vietnam to South China Sea	Source discovered 1995
4345 km (2700 mi)	**Amur-Argun** (Heilongjiang)	Northern China in Khingan Ranges as Heilongjiang	North along Inner Mongolian-Russian and and Chinese-Russian-border for 3743 km (2326 mi) to Tatar Strait, Sea of Okhotsk	Amur is 2824 km (1755 mi) long. China Handbook claims total length of 4670 km (2903 mi).

Length	Name	Source	Course	Notes
4241 km (2635 mi)	**Mackenzie-** Peace River – Slave	Tatlatui Lake, Skeena Mts, Rockies, British Columbia, Canada	Flows as Finlay for 400 km (250 mi) to confluence with Peace, then 1690 km (1050 mi) to join Slave (415 km/ 258 mi), which feeds Great Slave Lake, from which Mackenzie flows to Beaufort Sea	Peace River is 1923 km (1195 mi) long; Mackenzie is 1733 km (1077 mi) long
4181 km (2600 mi)	**Niger**	Guinea: Loma Mts. near Sierra Leone border	Flows through Mali, Niger and along Benin border into Nigeria and the Atlantic	Delta extends 128 km 80 mi) inland and 200 km (130 mi) in coastal length
3750 km (2330 mi)	**Murray-Darling** Condamine	Queensland (Australia): as the Condamine, a tributary of the Culgoa, which is a tributary of the Balonne branch of the Darling	Balonne (intermittent flow) crosses into New South Wales to join Darling, which itself joins the Murray on the NSW-Victoria border, and-flows west into Lake Alexandrine (South Australia)	Darling is c. 2740 km (1700 mi) long; Murray 2590 km (1609 mi) or 1870 km (1160 mi) if only permanent streams are considered.
3540 km (2200 mi)	**Zambezi** (Zambeze)	Zambia; NW extremity as Zambezi	Flows after 72 km (45 mi) mi) across E Angola for 354 km (220 mi) and back into Zimbabwe, later forming border with Namibia. After Victoria Falls, it forms the Zambia-Zimbabwe border before entering Mozambique and reaching the Indian Ocean	Navigable 610 km (380 mi) up to Quebrabasa Rapids
3530 km (2193 mi)	**Volga**	Russia: in Valdai Hills, northwest of Moscow	Flows south and east in great curve and empties in a delta into the north of the Caspian Sea	Delta exceeds 280 km (175 mi) inland and arguably 450 km (280 mi) inland.
3380 km (2100 mi)	**Madeira-Mamoré-** Guapay	Bolivia: rises on the Beni near Illimani	Flows north and east into Brazil to join the Amazon at the Ilha Tupinambaram	World's longest tributary. Navigable for 1070 km (663 mi)
3283 km (2040 mi)	**Jurua**	Peru: south of Puerto Portillo	Flows east and north into into Brazil to join Amazon below Fonte Boa	Navigable for 965 km (600 mi). Most pronounced meanders in Amazon Basin
3211 km (1995 mi)	**Purus**	Peru: as Alto Purus	Flows north and east into Brazil to join Amazon below Beruri	Navigable for 2575 km (1600 mi). Purus was formerly called the Coxiuara
3185 km	**Yukon-Teslin**	Northwest British Columbia	Flows north into Yukon Territory and into west Alaska (USA) and thence to Bering Sea	Delta 136 km (85 mi) inland. Navigable for shallow draft boats for 2855 km (1775 mi)
3130 km (1945 mi)	**St Lawrence**	Head of St Louis River, Minn (USA)	Flows into Lake Superior, thence Lakes Huron, Erie, Ontario, to Gulf of St Lawrence and N. Atlantic	Estuary 407 km (253 mi) long or 616 km (383 mi) to Anticosti Island
3035 km	**Rio Grande-** Rio Bravo	SW Colorado (USA): in San Juan Mts.	Flows south through New Mexico and along Texas-Mexico border to Gulf of Mexico	
3019 km (1876 mi)	**Syrdarya-Naryn**	Kyrgyzstan: in Tien Shan Mts.	Flows west through Kyrgyzstan and Tajikistan, then north and west through Kazakhstan to the Aral Sea	Known to the ancient Greeks as the Jaxartes

Length	Name	Source	Course	Notes
2989 km (1857 mi)	**Nizhnaya Tunguska**	In central Siberia, Russia	Flows east then west and north to theYenisey	
2914 km (1811 mi)	**São Francisco**	Brazil: in Serra Canastra	Flows north and east into South Atlantic	Navigable 238 km (148
2900 km (1800 mi)	**Brahmaputra**	Southwest Tibet as Matsang (Tsangpo)	Flows east 1240 km (770 mi) south, then west through Assam (India). Joins Ganges (as Jumuna) to flow into Bay of Bengal	Joint delta with Ganges extends 360 km (225 mi) across and 330 km (205 mi) inland; world's largest delta. Navigable 1290 km (800 mi).
2880 km (1790 mi)	**Indus**	Tibet: as Sengge	Flows west through Kashmir, into Pakistan and into Arabian Sea	Delta extends 120 km (75 mi) inland
2850 km (1770 mi)	**Danube**	SW Germany: in Black Forest as Breg	Flows east into Austria then along Czech-Hungarian-border, into Hungary, Yugoslavia (Serbia), along Romania-Bulgaria border, into Romania, along Romania-Ukraine border into Black Sea	Delta extends 96 km (60 mi) inland
2810 km (1750 mi)	**Salween** (Nu Chiang)	Tibet: in Tanglha Range	Flows (as Nu) E and S into W China, and E Burma, along Thai border to Andaman Sea	
2800 km (1740 mi)	**Euphrates-Tigris-**	Eastern Turkey (as Murat)	Flows west to join Firat, thence south and east into Syria and Iraq joining Tigris to flow into Persian Gulf	
2740 km (1700 mi)	**Tocantins**	Brazil: near Brasilia	Flows north to join Pará in in the Marajó estuary bay	Not usually regarded as a tributary of the Amazon.
2740 km (1700 mi)	**Orinoco**	SE Venezuela	Flows north and west to Colombian border, thence northeast across Venezuela to the Atlantic	
2650 km (1650 mi)	**Vilyuy**	Evenky region of central Siberia (Russia)	Flows east and south to join Lena	
2650 km (1650 mi)	**Xi Jiang** (Si Kiang)	China: in Yunnan plateau as Nanp'an	Flows as east as Hungshui and Hsun to emerge as the Hsi in South China Sea	Delta exceeds 145 km (90 mi) inland
2627 km (1632 mi)	**Araguaia**	In Mato Grosso (Brazil)	Flows north and east to join Tocantins	
2600 km (1615 mi)	**Kolyma**	Russia: in Khrebet Suntarkhayata (as Kulu)	Flows north across Arctic Circle to the east Siberian Sea	
2575 km (1600 mi)	**Amu Dar'ya**	In Wakhan (Afghanistan) near Chinese border	Flows west to form Afghan-Tajik border, through Turkmenistan, west and north to Aral Sea	Known formerly as the Oxus
2575 km (1600 mi)	**Nelson-Saskatchewan**	Canada: Bow Lake, British Columbia	Flows NE across Canada to Cedar Lake and Lake Winnipeg, then (as Nelson) to Hudson Bay	Saskatchewan is 1940 km (1205 mi) long
2540 km (1575 mi)	**Ural**	Russia: south central Urals	Flows south and west into the Caspian Sea in Kazakhstan	
2510 km (1553 mi)	**Ganges** (Ganga)	In southern Himalaya (India)	Flows southeast to join Brahmaputra delta	
2410 km (1500 mi)	**Paraguay**	Brazil: in the Mato Grosso as Paraguai	Flows south to touch Bolivian and Paraguayan borders, thence across Paraguay and Argentina to join Paraná.	

LONGEST RIVERS IN EUROPE

Name	Length	Countries	Notes
Volga	3530 km (2193 mi)	Russia	After (nameless) headwaters of 160 km (99 mi) the Volga flows into the Rybinskoye reservoir in the Valdai Hills north of Moscow and becomes known as the Volga. It then flows south and east to the Caspian Sea.
Danube	2850 km (1770 mi)	Germany, Austria, Slovakia Hungary, Yugoslavia (Serbia), Romania, Bulgaria, Ukraine	Rises as the Rivers Breg and Brisach in the Black Forest in Germany, and flows east through Central and Southeast Europe into the Black Sea
Ural	2540 km (1770 mi)	Russia and Kazakhstan	The Ural is sometimes quoted as the third longest river in Europe, but much of its path to the Caspian Sea is through Asiatic Kazakhstan.
Dnepr	2285 km (1420 mi)	Russia, Belarus and Ukraine	Rises west of Moscow and flows south through Russia, Belarus and Ukraine to the Black Sea.
Don	1969 km (1224 mi)	Russia	Rises in southwest Russia and flows south to the Sea of Azov.
Pechora	1809 km (1124 mi)	Russia	Rises in the Ural Mountains and flows north to the Barents Sea.
Kama	1805 km (1122 mi)	Russia	Rises north of Perm and flows south through Russia to join the Volga through the Kuybyshevskoye reservoir.
Oka	1500 km (930 mi)	Russia	Rises southwest of Moscow and flows east through Russia to join the Volga near Nizhny Novgorod.
Belaya	1430 km (889 mi)	Russia	Rises in the south of the Ural Mountains and flows north to join the River Kama.
Dnestr	1352 km (840 mi)	Ukraine, Moldova,	Rises near the Polish border in western Ukraine and flows east through Ukraine and Moldova to reach the Black Sea in Ukraine.
Rhine	1320 km (820 mi)	Switzerland, Liechtenstein, Austria, Germany, France, Germany, and the Netherlands.	Rises in the Swiss Alps and flows east, then north, across Northern Europe, to the Norh Sea.
Northern Dvina	1302 km (809 mi)	Russia	Rises in northern Russia as the Sukhona and flows north to the White Sea.
Elbe	1165 km (724 mi)	Czech Republic and Germany.	Rises in Bohemia and flows north to the North Sea.
Vistula	1069 km (664 mi)	Poland	Rises near the Polish-Czech border and flows north to the Baltic Sea.
Loire north	1020 km (634 mi)	France	Rises in the Massif Central of France and flows and then west to the Atlantic Ocean.
Western Dvina (Daugava)	1020 km (634 mi)	Russia, Belarus and Latvia	Rises in the Valdai Hills, west of Moscow, and flows in a great arc south and west to the Gulf of Riga on the Baltic Sea.
Tagus	1007 km (626 mi)	Spain and Portugal	Rises on the border of Aragon and Castile and flows west to the Atlantic Ocean.
Tisza	996 km (619 mi)	Ukraine, Romania, Hungary, Yugoslavia (Serbia)	Rises in the Carpathian Mountains and flows west and then south to join the Danube north of Belgrade.

RIVERS WITH THE GREATEST MEAN DISCHARGE RATE

River	*Continent*	*Mean discjarge rate (cubic metres per second)*	*Mean discharge rate (cubic feet per second)*	
Amazon	South America	180,000	6,350,000	(see p.82)
Zaire (Congo)	Africa	41,000	1,450,000	(see p.82)
Brahmaputra	Asia	38,500	1,360,000	(see p.84)
Paraná-Rio de la Plata	South America	27,500	970,000	(see p.82)
Hwang He	Asia	22,650*	800,000	(see p.82)
Yangtze	Asia	21,800	770,000	(see p.82)
Yenisey-Angara	Asia	19,000	670,000	(see p.82)
Mississippi-Missouri	North America	18,400	650,000	(see p.82)

* varies; has been recorded as low as 2,800 (100,000).

THE WORLD'S LARGEST RIVER BASINS BY AREA

Name	*Continent*	*Area in square km*	*Area in square miles*	*Notes*
Amazon-Madeira-Mamoré-Grande-Purus-Jurua-Negro-Putumayo-Japura-Madre - Ucayali-de Dios Maranon-Xingu-Tapajós	South America	7,050,000	2,722,000	See p.82
Paraná-Rio de la Plata	South America	4,145,000	1,600,000	See p.82
Zaire (Congo)-Lualaba-Oubangui-Uele-Kasai-Cuango	Africa	3,400,000	1,314,000	See p.82
Nile-Blue Nile-White Nile-Bahr al Ghazal	Africa	3,350,000	1,293,000	See p.82
Mississippi-Missouri Arkansas-Platte-Ohio-Red River-Tennessee	North America	3,224,000	1,245,000	See p.82
Ob-Irtysh	Asia	2,978,000	1,150,000	See p.82
Yenisey-Angara-Selenge	Asia	2,580,000	996,000	See p.82
Lena-Kirenga-Aldan	Asia	2,490,000	960,0000	See p.82
Amur-Argun-Kerulen	Asia	2,038,000	787,000	See p.82
Yangtze (Chang Jiang)	Asia	1,960,000	756,000	See p.82
Niger-Benue	Africa	1,890,000	730,000	See p.83
Mackenzie-Peace River-Slave-Athabasca	North America	1,841,000	711,000	See p.83
Brahmaputra*	Asia	1,620,000	626,000	See p.84
St Lawrence	North America	1,378,000	532,000	See p.83
Volga	Europe	1,360,000	525,000	See p.83
Zambezi	Africa	1,330,000	514,000	See p.83
Indus-Sutlej-Chenab	Asia	1,166,000	450,000	See p.84
Paraguay	South America	1,150,000	440,000	See p.84
Tigris-Euphrates	Asia	1.115,000	430,000	See p.84
Nelson-Saskatchewan	North America	1,072,000	414,000	See p.84
Murray-Darling-Murrumbidgeee-Lachlan-Barwon	Oceania	1,059,000	408,000	See p.83
Orinoco	South America	1,036,000	400,000	See p.84
Hwang He (Yellow River)	Asia	979,000	378,000	See p.82
Mekong	Asia	987,000	381,000	See p.82
Ganges*	Asia	976,000	377,000	See p.84
Tocantins-Araguaia	South America	905,000	350,000	See p.84
Yukon-Teslin	North America	855,000	330,000	See p.83
Danube	Europe	815,000	315,000	See p.84
São Francisco	South America	700,000	270,000	See p.84
Xi Jiang (or Si Kiang)	Asia	602,000	232,300	See p.84
Kolyma	Asia	534,000	206,000	See p.84
Vilyuy	Asia	491,000	190,0000	See p.84
Nizhnaya Tunguska	Asia	471,000	188,000	See p 84
Amu'Darya (or Oxus)	Asia	465,000	179,500	See p.84
Syrdarya-Naryn	Asia	462,000	178,000	See p.83
Salween (or Nu Chiang)	Asia	325,000	125,000	See p.84
Ural	Europe/Asia	220,000	84,900	See p.84

* The Ganges and Brahmaputra are sometimes regarded as having a combined basin of 2,596,000 square kilometres (or 1,033,000 square miles).

WATERFALLS

World's greatest waterfalls – by height

Name	*Height*	*River*	*Location*	*Notes*
Angel*	979m (3212 ft)	Carrao, an upper tributary of the Caroni	Venezuela	highest fall 807m (2648 ft)
Tugela	947m (3110 ft)	Tugela	KwaZulu Natal, South Africa	5 falls (highest 410m/1350 ft)
Utigård	800m (2625 ft)	Jostedal Glacier	Nesdale, Norway	highest fall 600m (1970 ft)
Mongefossen	774m (2540 ft)	Monge	Mongebekk, Norway	
Yosemite	739m (2425 ft)	Yosemite Creek, a tributary of the Merced	Yosemite Valley, Yosemite National Park, Cal., USA 97m (320 ft)	Upper Yosemite 435m (1430 ft), Cascades in middle section 205m (675 ft), Lower Yosemite
Ostre Mardola Foss	656m (2154 ft)	Mardals	Eikisdal, W. Norway	highest fall 296m (974 ft)
Tyssestrengane	646m (2120 ft)	Tysso	Hardanger, Norway	highest fall 289m (948 ft)
Kukenaam (or **Cuquenán**)	610m (2000 ft)	Arabopó, upper tributary of Caroni	Venezuela	
Sutherland	580m (1904 ft)	Arthur	nr, Milford Sound, Otago, New Zealand	highest fall 248m (815 ft)
Kile (or **Kjellfossen**)	561m (1841 ft)	Naerö Fjord feeder	nr. Gudvangen, Norway	highest fall 149m (490 ft)§
Takkakaw	502m (1650 ft)	a tributary of the Yoho	Daly Glacier, British Columbia, Canada	highest fall 365m (1200 ft)
Ribbon	491m (1612 ft)	Ribbon Fall Stream	5km (3 mi) west of Yosemite Falls (see above)	
King George VI	487m (1600 ft)	Utshi, upper tributary of Mazaruni	Guyana	
Roraima	457m (1500 ft)	an upper tributary of the Mazaruni	Guyana	

* There are other very high but seemingly unnamed waterfalls in this area.

World's greatest waterfalls – by volume of water

Name	*Maximum height*	*Mean annual flow* cubic m per sec	*Mean annual flow* cubic ft per sec	*Location*
Buyoma (formerly Stanley)	60m (200 ft)	17,000	600,000	Zaire R., nr Kisangani (Zaire)
Khône	21m (70 ft)	11,500	410,000	Mekong R., Laos
Niagara				Niagara R., Lake Erie to Lake Ontario (Canada/USA)
Horseshoe/Canadian	48m (160 ft)	5640	199,300	
American	50m (167 ft)	360	12,700	
Paolo Afonso	58m (192 ft)	2800	100,000	São Francisco R., Brazil
Iguazú	93m (308 ft)	1700	61,660	Iguazú R., Brazil/ Argentina
Patos-Maribondo	35m (115 ft)	1500	53,000	Rio Grande, Brazil
Victoria (Mosi-oa-tunya)	108m (355 ft)	1100§	38,430	Zambezi R., Zambia/ Zimbabwe

§ This figure applies to the Main Fall only, omitting Leaping Water and Rainbow Falls.

NB. Two of the world's largest waterfalls - in terms of the volume of water passing over them - are being, or have been, inundated by the rising water behind the Itaipu Dam (Paraguay/Brazil). These falls were, respectivey, the second and sixth greatest in the world by volume. They were:

Guaíra (or Salto dos Sete Quedras)	114m (374 ft)	13,000*	470,000	Alto Paraná, Paraguay/Brazil
Urubu-punga	12m (40 ft)	2700	97,000	Alto Paraná, Brazil

* The flow of water over Guaíra peaked at 50,000 cubic m per sec.

The World's Largest Lakes

1. Caspian Sea
(Russia, Kazakhstan, Turkmenistan, Azerbaijan and Iran)
Area: 371 800 km²
(143 550 sq mi)
Length: 1225 km
(760 mi)

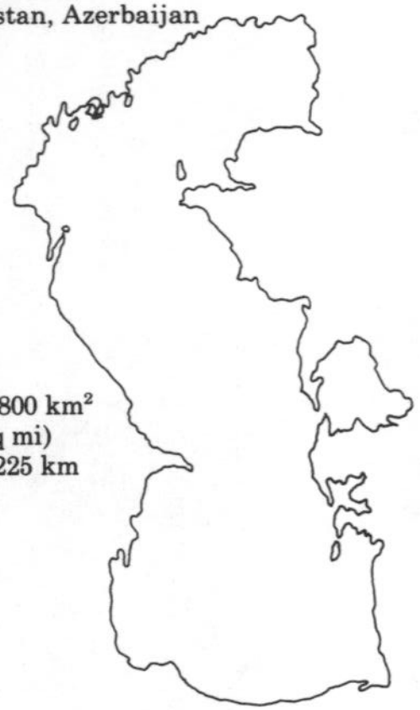

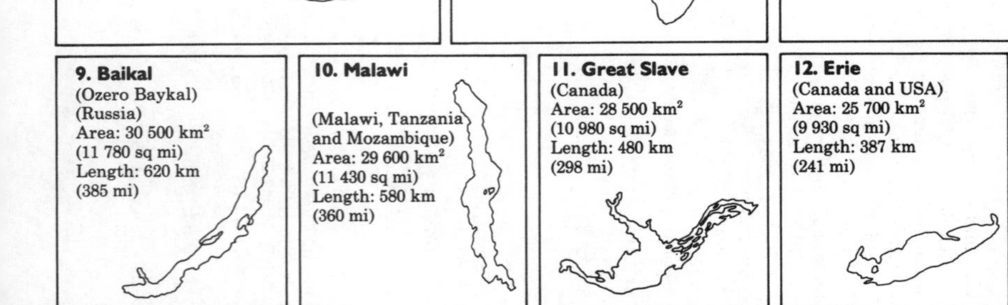

2. Superior
(Canada and USA)
Area: 82 350 km²
(31 800 sq mi)
Length: 560 km
(350 mi)

3. Victoria Nyanza
(Uganda, Tanzania and Kenya)
Area: 69 500 km²
(26 828 sq mi)
Length: 360 km
(225 mi)

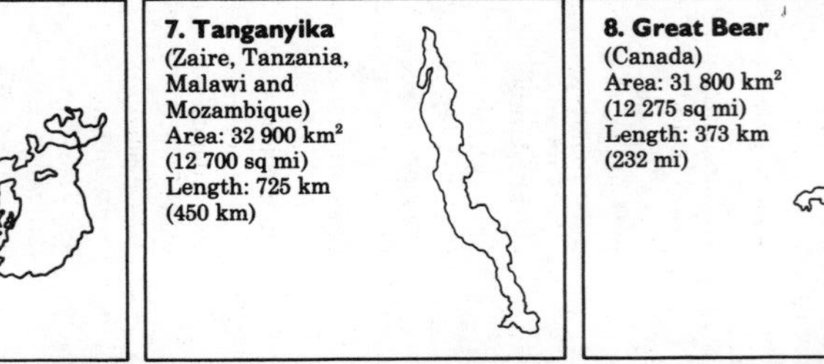

4. Huron
(Canada and USA)
Area: 59 600 km²
(23 010 sq mi)
Length: 330 km
(206 mi)

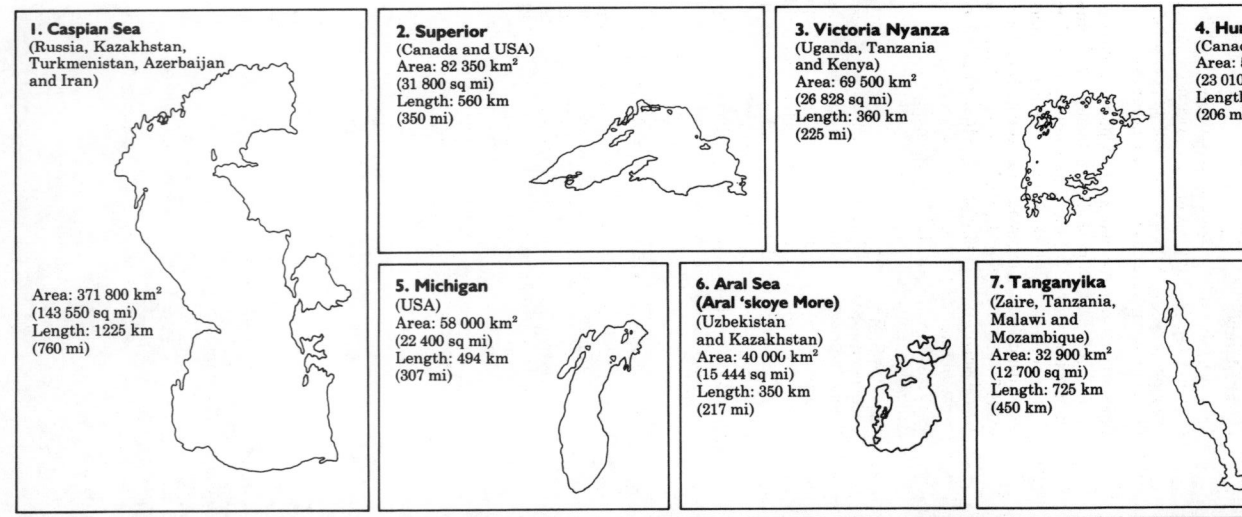

5. Michigan
(USA)
Area: 58 000 km²
(22 400 sq mi)
Length: 494 km
(307 mi)

6. Aral Sea (Aral 'skoye More)
(Uzbekistan and Kazakhstan)
Area: 40 000 km²
(15 444 sq mi)
Length: 350 km
(217 mi)

7. Tanganyika
(Zaire, Tanzania, Malawi and Mozambique)
Area: 32 900 km²
(12 700 sq mi)
Length: 725 km
(450 km)

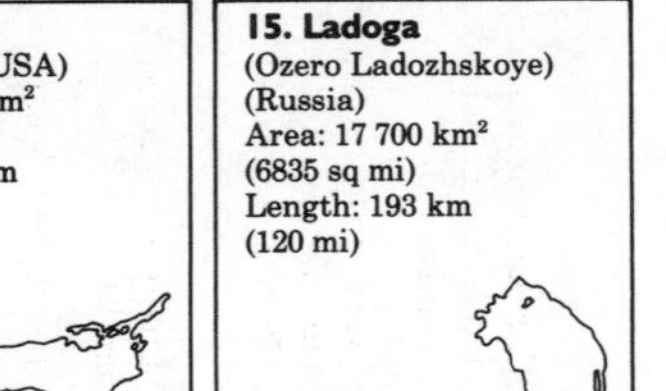

8. Great Bear
(Canada)
Area: 31 800 km²
(12 275 sq mi)
Length: 373 km
(232 mi)

9. Baikal
(Ozero Baykal)
(Russia)
Area: 30 500 km²
(11 780 sq mi)
Length: 620 km
(385 mi)

10. Malawi
(Malawi, Tanzania and Mozambique)
Area: 29 600 km²
(11 430 sq mi)
Length: 580 km
(360 mi)

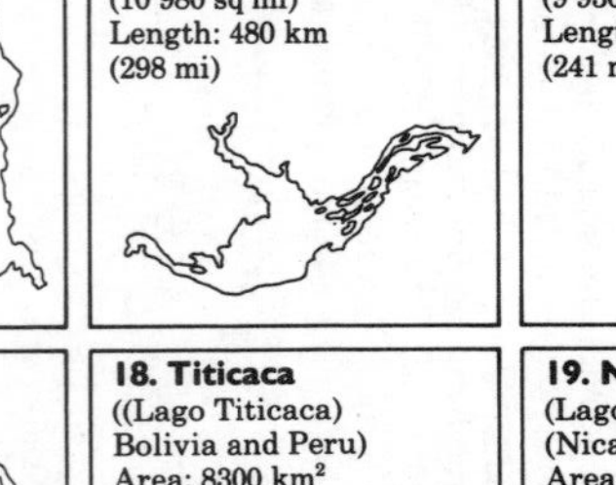

11. Great Slave
(Canada)
Area: 28 500 km²
(10 980 sq mi)
Length: 480 km
(298 mi)

12. Erie
(Canada and USA)
Area: 25 700 km²
(9 930 sq mi)
Length: 387 km
(241 mi)

13. Winnipeg
(Canada)
Area: 24 500 km²
(9464 sq mi)
Length: 428 km
(266 mi)

14. Ontario
(Canada and USA)
Area: 19 500 km²
(7520 sq mi)
Length: 310 km
(193 mi)

15. Ladoga
(Ozero Ladozhskoye)
(Russia)
Area: 17 700 km²
(6835 sq mi)
Length: 193 km
(120 mi)

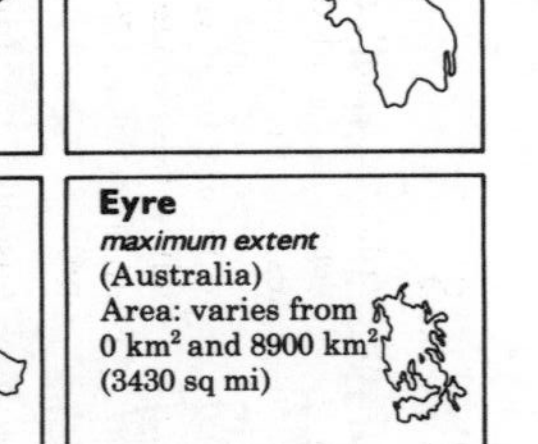

16. Balkhash
(Ozero Balkhas) (Kazakh)
Area: 17 400 km²
(6720 sq mi)
Length: 482 km
(300 sq mi)

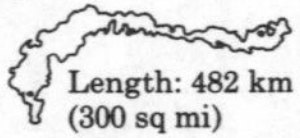

17. Onega
(Ozero Onezhskoye)
(Russia)
Area: 9600 km²
(3710 sq mi)
Length: 233 m
(145 ft)

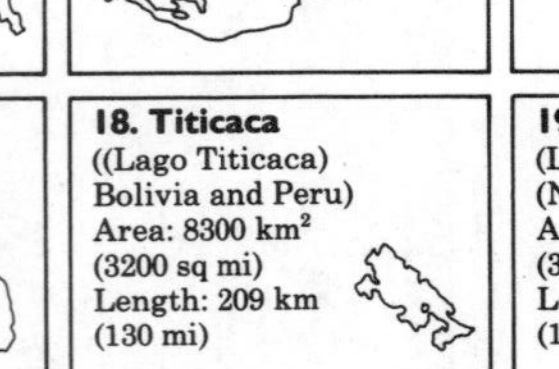

18. Titicaca
((Lago Titicaca)
Bolivia and Peru)
Area: 8300 km²
(3200 sq mi)
Length: 209 km
(130 mi)

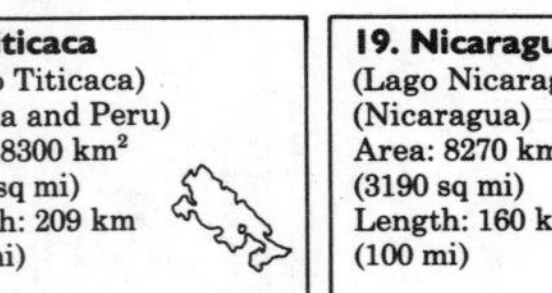

19. Nicaragua
(Lago Nicaragua)
(Nicaragua)
Area: 8270 km²
(3190 sq mi)
Length: 160 km
(100 mi)

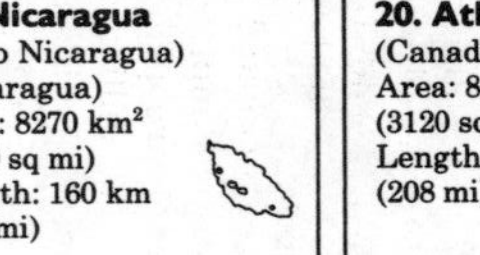

20. Athabasca
(Canada)
Area: 8100 km²
(3120 sq mi)
Length: 334 km
(208 mi)

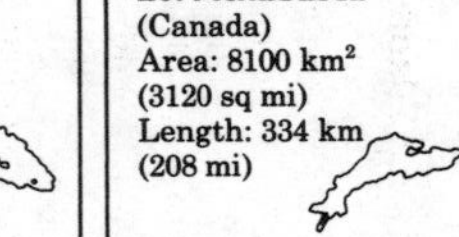
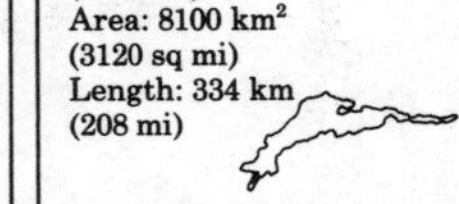
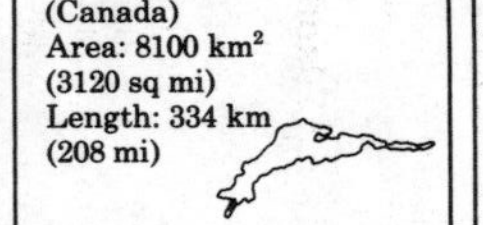
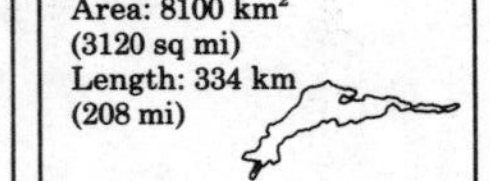
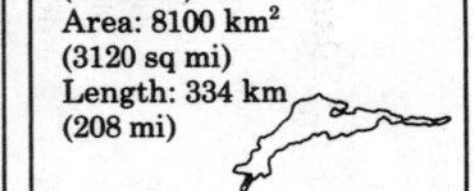
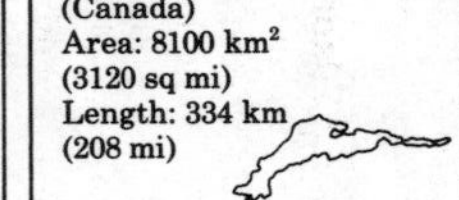
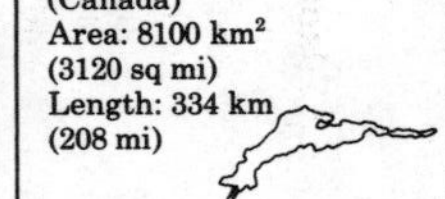
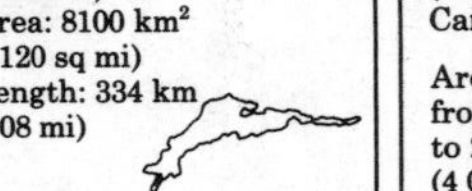

Chad (Lac Tchad)
(Nigeria, Chad, and Cameroon)
Area: varies from 10 000 km² to 26 000 km²
(4 000 and 10 000 sq mi)

Eyre
maximum extent
(Australia)
Area: varies from 0 km² and 8900 km²
(3430 sq mi)

ISLANDS

An island is a body of land, smaller than a continent, that is completely surrounded by water. Islands occur in rivers, lakes, and the seas and oceans.

Islands range in size from very small mud and sand islands of only a few square metres, to Greenland, which has an area of 2,175,600 square kilometres (840,000 sq mi).

(Note that Australia is normally considered to be a continent rather than an island.)

Islands, especially those in seas and oceans, have a range of origins. Islands can develop through constructional processes. They may also be formed by erosional processes that cause an area of land to become separated from the mainland.

Rising sea levels can also lead to the development of islands, by drowning low-lying areas of land and separating higher areas from the main land mass.

Volcanic islands

When volcanic activity occurs beneath the oceans, it can lead to the growth of islands. This is often closely linked to the movement of the Earth's crustal plates, with island-building (e.g. Iceland) occurring both at constructive plate margins and at destructive margins. Volcanic islands (e.g. Hawaii) can also form far from any plate boundary.

Iceland, situated on the mid-Atlantic ridge, is the largest example of a volcanic island formed at a constructive plate margin. Iceland started forming about 20 million years ago – the age of the oldest rocks on the island. It is still growing in size today, as new material is periodically added, along a line of volcanic activity running from the southwest to the northeast of the island. Much of the volcanic activity responsible for Iceland's growth has not been in the form of spectacular eruptions, but rather as quiet extrusive fissure eruptions, involving the outpouring of large quantities of lava from cracks in the Earth's surface, giving rise to basaltic rocks.

Spectacular eruptions, have, however, also played their part. For example, in 1963, eruptions occurred off the south coast of Iceland. In the space of a few weeks, ash and lava built up on the sea floor and a new, small island named Surtsey was born.

Island archipelagos

The collision of crustal plates at destructive margins can generate significant volcanic activity. If this occurs at the edge of a land mass it can cause mountain building, but when the collision zone lies beneath an ocean, island development can result. Islands which are born in this way do not occur singly, but in chains or archipelagos ('arcs') that parallel the plate boundary.

This is well illustrated on the western side of the Pacific Ocean. Here thousands of islands – most of them volcanic but some formed by the folding up of the ocean floor – mark the western edge of the Pacific Plate. These islands start in the south at New Zealand, run north to the Tongan chain before heading west to New Guinea, and north again through the Philippines, Japan, the Kurile island chain and finally the Aleutian Islands, which continue to the mainland of North America.

The Indonesian archipelago, which extends westwards into the Indian Ocean from the island chains of the west Pacific, is the world's largest, its 13,000 islands stretching over a distance of 5600 km (3500 mi).

The archipelago of Micronesia, which includes the island nations of the Federated States of Micronesia, Palau, Tuvalu, the Marshall Islands and Kiribati, comprises over 2000 main islands. However, only 90 of these islands are inhabited.

Coral islands

Coral islands and reefs are an important component of warm tropical and subtropical oceans and seas. They are formed from the skeletons of the group of primitive marine organisms known as corals.

Coral islands develop where coral grows up towards the ocean surface from shallow submarine platforms - often volcanic cones. If the cone is totally submerged, then a coral atoll will develop - a circular or horseshoe-shaped coral ring which encloses a body of sea water called a lagoon. Upward growth of the coral ceases once sea level has been reached. Coral islands are therefore flat and low, unless a change in sea level has caused their elevation to change.

Sea level and islands

Changes in sea level can cause new islands to appear or existing ones to disappear. During the last Ice Age eastern Britain was joined to mainland Europe, because sea levels were lower as much of the world's water was frozen in the ice caps and glaciers. As the ice melted, and the sea level rose, the North Sea and the Straits of Dover were re-established. By about 8500 years ago Britain was again an island.

FRESHWATER ISLANDS

Islands also occur in freshwater lakes and in the (freshwater) estuarine mouths of rivers. Such islands are often the result of depositions of eroded material, although they may also owe their origin to a number of other causes including glaciation. The largest freshwater islands are:

Name	*Area*	*Notes*
Marajó	48,000 km^2 (18,5900 sq mi)	In the mouth of the River Amazon (Pará state; Brazil);Marajó is larger in area than Switzerland.
Bananal	18,130 km^2 (7000 sq mi)	In the mouth of the River Amazon (Tocantins state, Brazil); Bananal is the world's largest inland island (that is land surrounded by rivers).
Caviana	5000 km^2 (1930 sq mi)	In the mouth of the River Amazon (Pará state, Brazil).
Gurupá	4864 km^2 (1878 sq mi)	In the mouth of the River Amazon (Pará state, Brazil).
Manitoulin	2766 km^2 (1068 sq mi)	In Lake Huron,Canada.

The World's Largest Islands

1. Greenland
Area: 2 175 600 km^2
(840 000 sq mi)
Location:
Arctic Ocean
Status: an internally self-governing part of the Kingdom of Denmark.

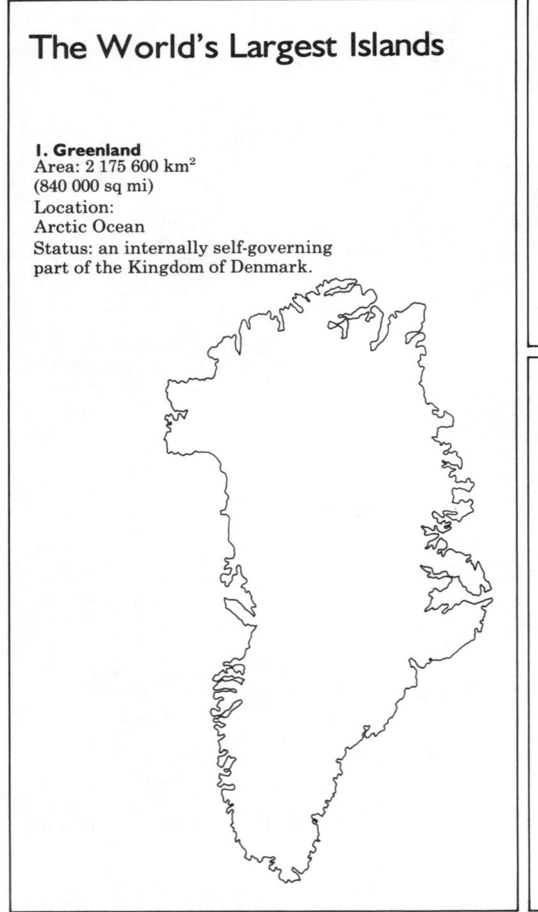

2. New Guinea
Area: 821 030 km^2
(317 000 sq mi)
Location:
western Pacific

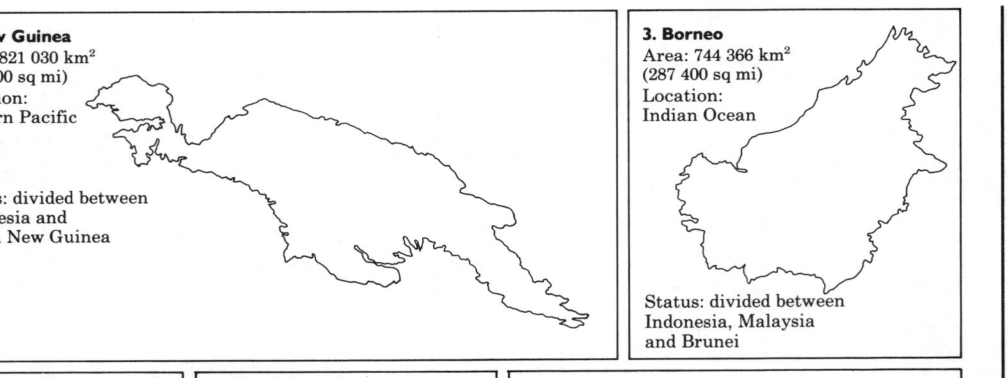

Status: divided between Indonesia and Papua New Guinea

3. Borneo
Area: 744 366 km^2
(287 400 sq mi)
Location:
Indian Ocean
Status: divided between Indonesia, Malaysia and Brunei

4. Madagascar
Area: 587 041 km^2
(226 658 sq mi)
Location:
Indian Ocean
Status: republic

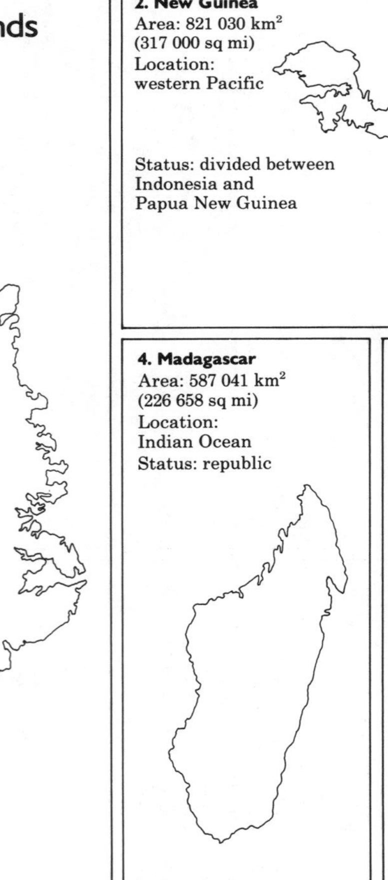

5. Baffin Island
Area: 476 068 km^2
(183 810 sq mi)
Location:
Arctic Ocean
Status: part of Nunavut Territory, Canada

6. Sumatra (Sumatera)
Area: 473 607 km^2
(182 860 sq mi)
Location:
Indian Ocean
Status: part of Indonesia

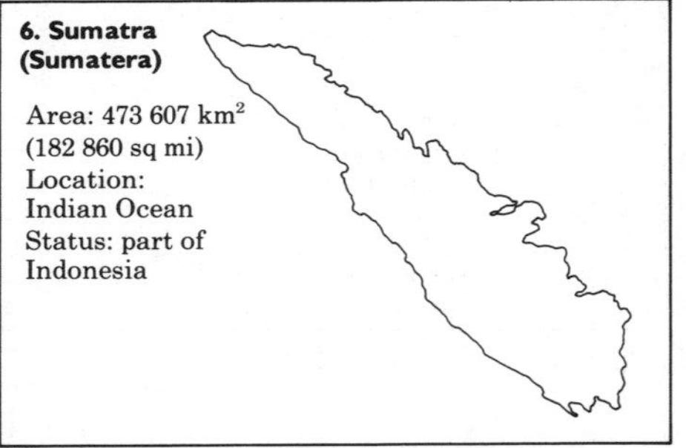

7. Honshu
Area: 230 448 km^2
(88 976 sq mi)
Location:
NW Pacific
Status: part of Japan

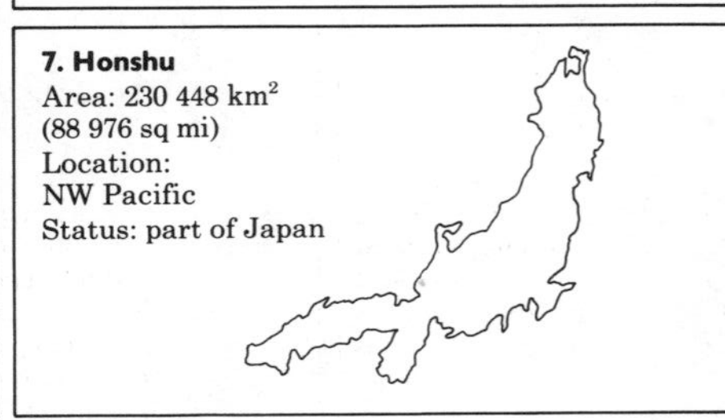

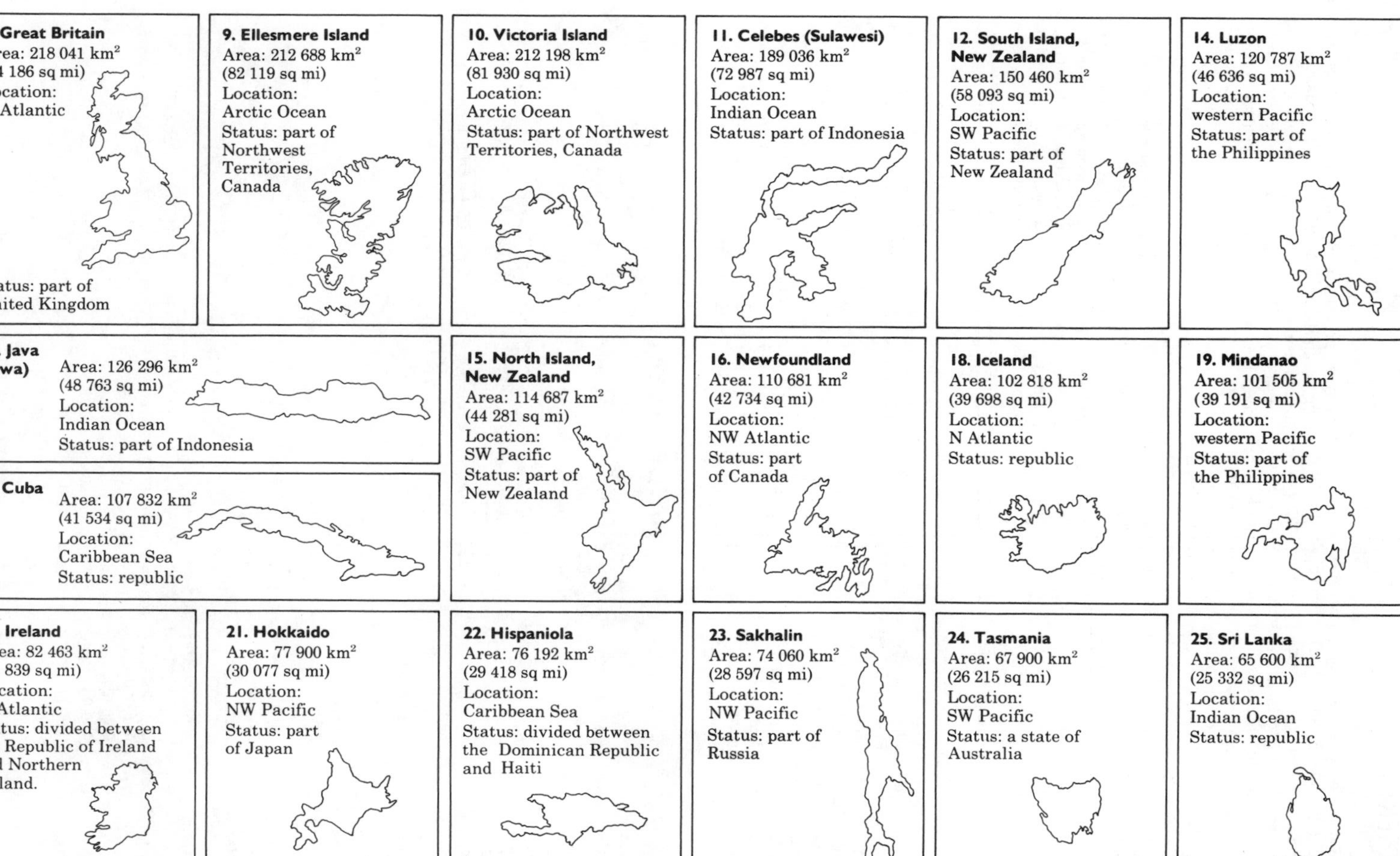
8. Great Britain
Area: 218 041 km²
(84 186 sq mi)
Location:
N Atlantic
Status: part of
United Kingdom
9. Ellesmere Island
Area: 212 688 km²
(82 119 sq mi)
Location:
Arctic Ocean
Status: part of
Northwest
Territories,
Canada
10. Victoria Island
Area: 212 198 km²
(81 930 sq mi)
Location:
Arctic Ocean
Status: part of Northwest
Territories, Canada
11. Celebes (Sulawesi)
Area: 189 036 km²
(72 987 sq mi)
Location:
Indian Ocean
Status: part of Indonesia
12. South Island,
New Zealand
Area: 150 460 km²
(58 093 sq mi)
Location:
SW Pacific
Status: part of
New Zealand
14. Luzon
Area: 120 787 km²
(46 636 sq mi)
Location:
western Pacific
Status: part of
the Philippines
13. Java
(Jawa)
Area: 126 296 km²
(48 763 sq mi)
Location:
Indian Ocean
Status: part of Indonesia
17. Cuba
Area: 107 832 km²
(41 534 sq mi)
Location:
Caribbean Sea
Status: republic
15. North Island,
New Zealand
Area: 114 687 km²
(44 281 sq mi)
Location:
SW Pacific
Status: part of
New Zealand
16. Newfoundland
Area: 110 681 km²
(42 734 sq mi)
Location:
NW Atlantic
Status: part
of Canada
18. Iceland
Area: 102 818 km²
(39 698 sq mi)
Location:
N Atlantic
Status: republic
19. Mindanao
Area: 101 505 km²
(39 191 sq mi)
Location:
western Pacific
Status: part of
the Philippines
20. Ireland
Area: 82 463 km²
(31 839 sq mi)
Location:
N Atlantic
Status: divided between
the Republic of Ireland
and Northern
Ireland.
21. Hokkaido
Area: 77 900 km²
(30 077 sq mi)
Location:
NW Pacific
Status: part
of Japan
22. Hispaniola
Area: 76 192 km²
(29 418 sq mi)
Location:
Caribbean Sea
Status: divided between
the Dominican Republic
and Haiti
23. Sakhalin
Area: 74 060 km²
(28 597 sq mi)
Location:
NW Pacific
Status: part of
Russia
24. Tasmania
Area: 67 900 km²
(26 215 sq mi)
Location:
SW Pacific
Status: a state of
Australia
25. Sri Lanka
Area: 65 600 km²
(25 332 sq mi)
Location:
Indian Ocean
Status: republic

DESERTS

Desert areas are defined in terms of aridity or the availability of water. Semi-arid areas receive on average 200–500 mm (8–20 in) of precipitation per annum, arid areas 25–200 mm (1–8 in) and hyper arid areas are those in which a continuous period of 12 months without any rainfall has been recorded. A desert may fall in any of these categories of aridity or may contain areas experiencing each of these conditions. The definitions and delineations of the desert areas listed are very approximate because deserts are advancing on many fronts and, in some places, are being reclaimed. Globally, 13.3% of the world's land area is semi-arid, 13.7% is arid and 5.8% is hyper arid.

What causes deserts?

Many of the world's deserts coincide with areas characterized by stable atmospheric high pressure, conditions that do not favour rainfall. The sub-tropical high pressure belts are responsible for deserts such as the Sahara and Kalahari in Africa and the deserts of Arabia and Australia. Other deserts, for example, the Gobi Desert in Central Asia, exist because of their *continentality*, that is their distance from the sea. This prevents them being reached by moisture-bearing winds from the oceans. This effect may be enhanced by the shape of the landscape; for example, moist air coming in from the sea will precipitate on mountains as rain or snow, and by the time the air has reached the far side of the mountains it will be dry, so forming a *rain-shadow* desert. Such deserts occur, for example, to the north of the Himalaya. The deserts of the west coast of southern Africa and South America (the Namib and Atacama Deserts) are affected by the presence of cold ocean currents running along the coast. These cool the air that they come into contact with, so preventing the evaporation of moisture from the ocean surface and the formation of rain. At some places in the Atacama Desert, no rain was recorded for 400 years prior to 1971. The cold ocean water does, however, cause a high frequency of fog, which is the major source of moisture in these extremely dry, or *hyper-arid*, deserts.

Desertification

In 1949, the French explorer André Aubreville discovered in the Sahel of Africa that the savannah grasslands and tropical rain forest were being damaged by farming. The land was deteriorating, the trees were being cleared and the desert was advancing. He coined the word 'desertification' to describe what was happening. There is an assumption in the very word 'desert' that it has changed, that it was once a better environment. The Latin *desertus* means 'abandoned', which implies that it was formerly inhabited and adequately watered for agriculture. This, in turn, implies that deserts are the result of human activity and can be reclaimed by planting wadis in and around the fringes. Underlying such theories is a misconception about the very nature of the desert and the climate that created it. Most derserts are natural features. The desert landscape, its soils and what little flora there is are a perfect adaptation to that climate. By assuming that deserts are man-made rather than being a response to climate, we are in danger of assuming that it is possible to reclaim deserts on a large scale.

MAJOR DESERTS

Name	*Area*	*Location*
The Sahara	8,400,000 km^2 (3,250,000 sq mi)	Algeria, Chad, Libya, Mali, Mauritania, Niger, Sudan, Tunisia, Egypt, Morocco, W. Sahara. Includes Libyan Desert (1,550,000 km^2/ 600 000 sq mi) and Nubian Desert (260,000 km^2/ 100,000 sq mi).
Australian Desert	1,550,000 km^2 (600,000 sq mi)	Australia. Embraces the Great Sandy (or Warburton) Desert (420,000km^2/ 160,000 sq mi), Great Victoria (325,000 km^2/125,000 sq mi), Simpson (Arunta) (310 000 km^2/120,000 sq mi), Gibson (220,000 km^2/ 85,000 sq mi), and Sturt Desert.
Arabian Desert	1,300,000 km^2 (500,000 sq mi)	Saudi Arabia, Jordan, Oman, Yemen, UAE. Includes the Rub' al Khali or 'Empty Quarter' (647,500 km^2/250,000 sq mi), Syrian (325,000 km^2/125,000 sq mi), and An Nafud (129,500 km^2/50,000 sq mi) Deserts.
The Gobi	1,040,000 km^2 (400,000 sq mi)	Mongolia and China (Inner Mongolia)
Kalahari Desert	520,000 km^2 (200,000 sq mi)	Botswana
Takla Makan	320,000 km^2 (125,000 sq mi)	Xinjiang, China
Sonoran Desert	310 000 km^2 (120,000 sq mi)	Arizona and California, USA and Mexico
Namib Desert	310,000 km^2 (120,000 sq mi)	Namibia
Kara Kum*	270,000 km^2 (105,000 sq mi)	Turkmenistan * With the Kyzyl Kum known as the Turkestan Desert.
Thar Desert	260,000 km^2 (100,000 sq mi)	North-western India and Pakistan
Somali Desert	260,000 km^2 (100,000 sq mi)	Somalia
Atacama Desert	180,000 km^2 (70,000 sq mi)	Northern Chile
Kyzyl Kum*	180,000 km^2 (70,000 sq mi)	Uzbekistan, Kazakhstan * With the Kara Kum known as the Turkestan Desert.

EARTHQUAKES

An earthquake is a sudden release of energy in the Earth's crust or upper mantle. As the planet's tectonic plates jostle against each other and become distorted, tremendous strain builds up – and from time to time the strain energy is discharged in zones where the rocks are weakest. The result is a sudden violent shock that can have highly destructive effects on the Earth's surface nearby.

The damaging effects of an earthquake are due to the vibrations (*seismic waves*) emitted by the shock. For a brief moment the waves shake the ground close to the earthquake, frequently producing permanent effects. Few people are ever killed or injured directly by an earthquake; death and injury are more likely to result from the collapse of buildings caused by the earthquake.

Whether or not there are people or buildings present, earthquakes may cause fissures to appear in the ground, produce changes in the level and tilt of the ground surface, divert rivers and streams, and trigger landslides and avalanches. Undersea earthquakes may also give rise to *tsunami* – huge amounts of sea water that can travel across the oceans for thousands of kilometres, causing devastation when they hit land.

Where earthquakes occur

Most earthquakes take place along the boundaries of the tectonic plates – along oceanic ridges, transform faults and subduction zones – because this is where the plates interact most intensely, and hence where distortion and strain build-up are greatest.

However, not all earthquakes occur along plate margins. In North America, for example, the most damaging earthquakes of historic times have taken place not in California, through which runs a transform fault (the San Andreas fault), but in South Carolina and Missouri, both of which are far from plate margins. The reasons for this are unclear, but earthquakes within the interiors of plates may be due to deep, still active faults remaining from a much earlier phase of plate tectonics. California is still America's most notorious seismic area, however, because it is there that earthquakes are most frequent.

The point at which an earthquake occurs is called the *focus*, or *hypocentre*. The point on the Earth's surface directly above the focus is called the *epicentre*. A world map of epicentres is largely a map of the Earth's plate boundaries.

All earthquake foci lie within about the upper 700 km (435 mi) of the Earth. Within this range, earthquakes are classified as *shallow* (focal depths of 0–70 km / 0–43 mi), *intermediate* (70–300 km / 43–186 mi), or *deep* (below 300 km / 186 mi). There are about three times as many intermediate earthquakes as there are deep ones, and about ten times as many shallow ones.

It is the shallow shocks that produce most of the damage at the Earth's surface, for the obvious reason that they are closer to it. Collectively, the shallow earthquakes also release the most energy – about 75% of the total, compared to 3% for deep earthquakes.

Measuring earthquakes

The size of an earthquake is specified by its magnitude, sometimes called the Richter magnitude after the American seismologist, Charles Richter, who devised the scale in the 1930s (see p. 95).

Magnitude is actually a measure of the size (*amplitude*) of the waves emitted by the earthquake. However, the magnitude scale is logarithmic. This means that each step up the scale represents a ten-fold increase in the amplitude of the emitted waves. Thus the waves from a magnitude-7 earthquake are 10 times bigger than those from a magnitude-6 shock, 100 times bigger than those from a magnitude-5 event, and so on.

Magnitude can also be regarded as a measure of the energy released by an earthquake, because energy is related to wave size. The relationship is such that each division on the magnitude scale represents an approximately thirty-fold difference in energy. Thus a magnitude-7 earthquake releases about 30 times more energy than a magnitude-6 shock and about 30 × 30 = 900 times more energy than a magnitude-5 event. This explains why most of the energy released by earthquakes comes from the very few big shocks that occur each year rather than from the million or so smaller earthquakes.

To specify the size of an earthquake in terms of its effects, an intensity scale, the Richter Scale (see p. 95), is used. In Japan and Russia, a slightly different system, the *Modified Mercalli Scale*, is used.

The destructive effect of an earthquake depends not only on its size but also on the human population of the area affected, the nature of buildings and any other natural events that may be triggered. This is well indicated by the data below, which considers recent major earthquakes.

HISTORIC EARTHQUAKES

Eastern Mediterranean

In the eastern Mediterranean about 1,100,000 people were killed in an earthquake c. July 1201.

Shanxi Province, China

On 2 February 1556, 830,000 people were killed in an earthquake.

Calcutta, India

On 11 October 1737, 300,000 died in an earthquake.

Tangshan, China

An earthquake of 8.2 on the Richter Scale killed 242,000 at Tangshan on 27 July 1976. The original death toll of 655,237 was unaccountably reduced in January 1977.

Gansu Province, China

On 16 December 1920, 180,000 died in landslides accompanying an earthquake which registered 8.6 on the Richter Scale.

Kanto Plain, Japan

An earthquake registering 8.3 on the Richter Scale killed 142,807 on the Kanto Plain, Honshu, Japan, on 1 September 1923. The material damage done in the Kanto Plain, which includes Tokyo, was estimated at £1,000,000,000.

TWENTIETH-CENTURY EARTHQUAKES

1906 (31 Jan): Colombian coast; 8.6 on the Richter Scale.

1906 (18 Apr): San Francisco, USA; 8.3 on the Richter Scale; 452 fatalities.

1908 (28 Dec): Messina, Italy; 7.5 on the Richter Scale; 80,000 fatalities.

1915 (13 Jan): Avezzano, Italy; 29,970 fatalities.

1920: Gansu, China (see box, p.93).

1923: Kanto Plain, Japan (see box, p.93).

1932 (26 Dec): Gansu Province, China; 7.6 on the Richter Scale; 70,000 fatalities.

1935 (31 May): Quetta (now Pakistan), 7.5 on the Richter Scale; 25,000 fatalities.

1939 (27 Dec): Erzincan, Turkey; 7.9 on the Richter Scale; 30,000 fatalities.

1950 (15 Aug): Assam, India; 8.6 on the Richter Scale; 1500 deaths.

1952 (4 Nov): Kamchatka, Russia; 8.5 on the Richter Scale.

1957 (9 Mar): Aleutian Islands, Alaska, USA; 8.3 on the Richter Scale.

1960 (29 Feb): Agadir, Morocco; 5.8 on the Richter Scale; 12,000 fatalities.

1960 (22 May): Lebu, Chile; 8.3 on the Richter Scale.

1964 (28 Mar): Anchorage, Alaska, USA; 8.5 on the Richter Scale; 131 fatalities.

1970 (31 May): Northern Peru; 7.7 on the Richter Scale; 66,800 fatalities.

1971 (9 Feb): Los Angeles, USA; 6.5 on the Richter Scale; 64 fatalities.

1972 (23 Dec): Nicaragua; 6.2 on the Richter Scale; 5000 fatalities.

1976 (4 Feb): Guatemala; 7.5 on the Richter Scale; 22,700 deaths.

1976: Tangshan, China (see box, p. 93).

1977 (4 Mar): Bucharest, Romania; 7.5 on the Richter Scale; 1541 fatalities.

1978 (16 Sep): Tabas, Northeast Iran; 7.7 on the Richter Scale; 25,000 fatalities.

1980 (10 Oct): El Asnam, Algeria; 7.5 on the Richter Scale; 2327 fatalities.

1980 (23 Nov): Potenza, Italy; 6.8 on the Richter Scale; c. 3000 fatalities.

1982 (13 Dec): Yemen; 6.0 on the Richter Scale; 2800 fatalities.

1983 (31 Mar): Papayan, Colombia; 5.5 on the Richter Scale; 264 dead; 150 000 homeless.

1983 (26 May): North Honshu, Japan; 7.7 on the Richter Scale; 58 deaths, mostly due to the effects of a tsunami.

1983 (30 Oct): Eastern Turkey; 7.1 on the Richter Scale, 1233 deaths.

1985 (3 Mar): Algarroba, Chile; 7.8 Richter Scale; 177 fatalities and 150,000 homeless.

1985 (19 and 20 Sep): Mexico City; 8.1 Richter Scale; 20,000 fatalities, 31,000 homeless; 40,000 injured.

1987 (5 Mar): Northeastern Ecuador; 7.0 on the Richter Scale; 2000 fatalities; 75,000 injuries.

1988 (6 Nov): Southwest China; 7.6 on the Richter Scale; over 1000 fatalities and 500,000 homeless.

1988 (7 Dec): Armenia; 6.9 on the Richter Scale; 25,000 fatalities. Six cities devastated; 500,000 made homeless.

1989 (22 Jan): Tajikistan; 5.3 on the Richter Scale; 574 deaths, all owing to a mud slide on the village of Sharora.

1989 (17 Oct): San Francisco Bay, USA: 7.1 on the Richter Scale; 67 deaths.Oakland section of raised highway collapsed. Billons of dollars of damage.

1989 (29 Oct): Algiers, Algeria; 6.0 on the Richter Scale; 24 deaths and 746 injured.

1989 (27 Dec): Newcastle, NSW, Australia; 5.5 on the Richter Scale; 40 deaths and 120 injuries

1990 (27 Apr): Qinghai Province, China; 6.9 on the Richter Scale; 115 fatalities, 160 injured, many homeless.

1990 (21 Jun): Roudhon, NW Iran; 7.3 on the Richter Scale; at least 36,000 killed; many towns and villages destroyed.

1990 (17 Jul): Luzon, Philippines; 7.7 on the Richter Scale; over 1000 fatalities in area north of Manila.

1990 (6 Nov): Southern Iran; 6.8 on the Richter Scale; 22 deaths and over 12,000 made homeless.

1990 (13 Dec): Sicily, Italy: 4.7 on the Richter Scale; 12 deaths.

1991 (1 Feb): Northwest Frontier, Pakistan; 6.7 on the Richter Scale; over 1000 deaths; many made homeless.

1991 (22 Apr): Costa Rica/Panama; 7.5 on the Richter Scale; over 80 fatalities and 800 injured.

1991 (29 Apr): Georgia; 7.2 on the Richter Scale; 100 deaths.

1992 (14 Mar): Eastern Turkey; 6.2 on the Richter Scale; over 1000 deaths; town of Erzinka devastated.

1992 (28 Jun): Landers, Cal., USA; 7.4 on the Richter Scale; 1 killed; 100 injured.

1992 (12 Oct): Cairo, Egypt; 5.9 on the Richter Scale; at least 540 deaths and 4000 injured. Fatalities largely caused by collpase of poorly-constructed tenements.

1993 (12 Jul): Hokkaido, Japan; 7.8 on the Richter Scale; 192 killed, with most deaths on island of Okushiri.

1993 (30 Sep): Latur, India; 6.5 on the Richter Scale; 9748 deaths.

1993 (13 and 16 Oct): Papua New Guinea; max. of 6.8 on Richter Scale; 60 dead in four quakes.

1994 (17 Jan): Los Angeles; 6.6 on the Richter Scale; 57 dead, 25,000 made homeless.

1994 (16 Feb): Sumatra, Indonesia; 6.5 on the Richter Scale; 131 dead, 2700 injured, mainly in town of Liwa.

1994 (7 Jun):SW Colombia; 401 dead in avalanches following a minor quake.

1994 (18 Aug): Mascara, Algeria; 5.6 on the Richter Scale; 149 fatalities.

1994 (4 Oct): Japan; 8.2 on the Richter Scale; 16 killed in Russian Kuril Islands as a result of submarine earthquake off Hokkaido.

1994 (28 Dec): Northern Japan; 7.5 on the Richter Scale; 3 deaths, 267 injuries.

1995 (17 Jan): Kobe, Japan; 7.2 on the Richter Scale; over 5000 fatalities; over 275,000 made homeless; centre of Kobe was devastated.

SCALES OF MEASUREMENT OF EARTHQUAKES

Richter Scale

The Richter Scale is the scale of measurement of earthquakes that is most widely used.

It is a measurement of an earthquake's magnitude, and, as such, would mean little to the layperson. However, it is possible to convert these readings to a scale of intensity:

Magnitude	*Characteristics*
Magnitude 1	Detectable only by instruments.
Magnitude 2	Barely detectable, even near epicentre.
Magnitude 4-5	Detectable within 32 km (20 mi) of the epicentre; possible slight damage within a small area.
Magnitude 6	Moderately destructive.
Magnitude 7	A major earthquake.
Magnitude 8	A great earthquake.

Modified Mercalli Scale

This scale is mainly used in Japan and most of the former Soviet republics. However, as Japan (and Georgia and Armenia) are among the areas of the world that are most prone to earthquakes, the Modified Mercalli Scale is often quoted with regard to earthquakes in those countries.

The readings on this scale have been converted into a scale of intensity that may be summarized as follows:

I **Not felt** except by a few

II **Felt by a few people at rest.** Delicately suspended objects swing.

III **Felt noticeably indoors.** Standing cars may rock.

IV **Felt generally indoors.** Sleeping people are woken.

V **Felt generally**. Some plaster falls and dishes and windows are broken. Pendulum clocks stop.

VI **Felt by all.** Many are frightened. Chimneys and plaster damaged. Furniture moved and objects are upset.

VII **Everyone runs outdoors.** Felt in moving cars. Moderate structural damage.

VIII **General alarm**. Weak structures badly damaged. Walls and furniture fall over. Water level changes in wells.

IX **Panic.** Weak structures totally destroyed. Extensive damage to well-built structures, foundations, and underground pipes. Ground fissured and cracked.

X **Panic.** Only the strongest buildings survive the earthquake. Ground badly cracked. Rails bent. Water slopped over river banks.

XI **Panic.** Few buildings survive the earthquake. Broad fissures open up in the ground. Fault scarps are formed. Underground pipes are put out of service.

XII **Total destruction.** Waves are seen on the ground, and lines of sight and level are distorted. Objects are thrown up into the air.

EARTHQUAKES IN GREAT BRITAIN

It may come as a surprise that Northern Europe experiences so many earthquakes. British earthquakes of an intensity sufficient to move the chair of an observer have been recorded on the following dates:

Date	Year	Location and notes
25 Apr	1180	Nottinghamshire
15 Apr	1185	Lincoln
1 Jun	1246	Canterbury, Kent
21 Dec	1246	Wells, Somerset
19 Feb	1249	South Wales
11 Sep	1275	Somerset
21 May	1382	Southern North Sea
28 Dec	1480	Norfolk
26 Feb	1575	from York to Bristol
6 Apr	1580	Southern North Sea/ Dover Straits
30 Apr	1736	Menstrie, Clackmannan
1 May	1736	Menstrie, Clackmannan
14 Nov	1769	Inverness; resulted in several fatalities
18 Nov	1795	Derbyshire
13 Aug	1816	Inverness
23 Oct	1839	Comrie, Perthshire and Kinross
30 July	1841	Comrie, Perthsire and Kinross
6 Oct	1863	Hereford
22 Apr	1884	Colchester, Essex; Although it did not result directly in loss of life, it was perhaps the most damaging earthquake in the UK historical record.
17 Dec	1896	Hereford
18 Sep	1901	Inverness
27 Jun	1906	Swansea
30 Jul	1926	Jersey
15 Aug	1926	Hereford
7 Jun	1931	Dogger Bank; force 5.6 on the Richter Scale
11 Feb	1957	English Midlands
26 Dec	1979	Longtown, Cumbria
19 Jul	1984	widespread in western Britain; also felt in Ireland; 5.5 on the Richter Scale
2 Apr	1990	5.1 on the Richter Scale
5 Feb	1994	East Anglia; 3.5 on the Richter Scale
10 Feb	1994	Bangor, North Wales; 3 on the Richter Scale
26 Nov	1994	Mansfield, Nottinghamshire; 1.5 on the Richter Scale

GLACIATION

It has been estimated that over a tenth of the Earth's land surface – about 15,600,000 km² (6,020,000 sq mi) – is permanently covered with ice. Ice is in fact the world's biggest reservoir of fresh water, with over three quarters of the global total contained in ice sheets, ice caps and glaciers. These range in size from the huge Antarctic and Greenland ice sheets, to the small glaciers found in high-latitude and high-altitude mountain ranges.

Ice bodies develop where winter snowfall is able to accumulate and persist through the summer. Over time this snow is compressed into an ice body, and such ice bodies may grow to blanket the landscape as an ice sheet or ice cap. Alternatively, the ice body may grow to form a mass that flows down a slope – a glacier – often cutting a valley and eroding rock material that is eventually deposited at a lower altitude as the ice melts.

The formation of ice bodies

Ice bodies develop mainly through the accumulation of snow, or sometimes by the freezing of rain as it hits an ice surface.

Obviously, not all the snow that falls is turned into ice – during the northern-hemisphere winter over half the world's land surface and up to one third of the surfaces of the oceans may be blanketed by snow and ice. Most of this snow and ice is only temporary, as the Sun's warmth and energy are able to melt the cover during warm winter days or as winter passes into spring and summer.

In some places, however, the summer warmth is unable to melt all the snowfall of the previous winter. This may be because summer temperatures are rather low, or summer is very short, or because winter snowfall is very high. Where this occurs, snow lies all year round (this snow is sometimes called *firn* or *névé*) and becomes covered by the snow of the next winter.

As this process continues from year to year, the snow that is buried becomes compressed and transformed into *glacier ice*.

Latitude and altitude both determine where permanent snow can accumulate. The level that separates permanent snow cover from places where the snow melts in the summer is called the *snowline* or *firnline*. The snowline increases in altitude towards the Equator: in polar regions it lies at sea level, in Norway at 1200–1500m (4000–5000 ft) above sea level, and in the Alps at about 2700m (9000 ft). Permanent snow and ice can even occur in the tropics close to the equator: in East Africa, for example, the snowline lies at about 4900m (16,000 ft), so that glaciers are found on Mount Kenya, Kilimanjaro, and the Ruwenzori Mountains.

Ice sheets and ice caps

Ice sheets and ice caps are ice bodies that have grown into domes that blanket an area of land, submerging valleys, hills and mountains. Occasionally, 'islands' of land, called *nunataks*, protrude through the 'sea' of ice. Ice sheets are defined as having an area over 50,000 km² (19,000 sq mi); ice caps are smaller.

Sea ice

There is no ice sheet over the North Pole because there is no land there – however, the Arctic Ocean is always frozen and, during the winter, Arctic *sea ice* covers about 12 million km² (4.6 million sq mi).

An area of sea ice that is joined to a coast is called an *ice shelf*. Ice shelves occur in the Arctic, joined to the coasts of northern Canada and Greenland, and in the Antarctic – notably the Ross Ice Shelf, which has an area greater than France.

Ocean currents and seasonal melting can cause ice sheets to break up, creating areas of *pack ice* or smaller *ice floes*.

Ice movements

Ice bodies move and flow under the influence of gravity. The movement of frozen water is obviously much slower than when it is in its liquid form.

Most glaciers flow at a velocity between 3 and 300m (10 and 1000 ft) per year. Glaciers on steep slopes may move much faster, and the Quarayaq Glacier, which is supplied with ice from the Greenland Ice Sheet, averages 20-24m (65-80 ft) per day.

Many glaciers experience *surges* — which may last a few days or several years – when flow is extremely rapid, often equivalent to rates of up to 10 km (6 mi) a year.

Glaciers and landscape

Glacier ice is a very powerful erosional agent, smoothing rock surfaces and cutting deep valleys. *Fjords* (for example, along the coasts of Norway and Alaska) are U-shaped glacial valleys that become submerged by the sea after the melting of the ice that produced them.

U-shaped valleys are classically regarded as glacial features, but they can be formed by other processes - for example, by rivers in their middle and lower reaches.

A sliding glacier erodes by *plucking* blocks of rock from its bed and by *abrading* rock surfaces, i.e. breaking off small particles and rock fragments. The rock that is eroded is transported by the ice and deposited as the glacier travels down slope and melts.

Glacial deposits can form distinct landforms such as *moraines* (ridges) and *drumlins* (small hills), or they may simply be deposited as *glacial till*, a blanket of sediment covering the landscape.

RECENT GLACIAL PERIODS

The last six glacial periods (identified from ocean core evidence) have been dated as follows:

	began	*ended*
1.	72,000 years ago	10,000 years ago
2.	188,000 years ago	128,000 years ago
3.	280,000 years ago	244,000 years ago
4.	347,000 years ago	334,000 years ago
5.	475,000 years ago	421,000 years ago
6.	650,000 years ago	579,000 years ago

ICE AGES

Ice ages, more correctly called glacial periods, have been a major phenomenon of the last 2 millon years. Geological evidence, however, demonstrates that glacial periods have affected the Earth periodically over 2300 million years. It is not known why the Earth's atmosphere and surface change substantially, although it is generally thought that the causes of major ice ages relate to cyclic changes in the pattern and character of the Earth's orbit around the Sun. Evidence for glacial periods comes from a range of sources, including studies of sediments accumulated in deep oceans and lake basins, and investigations of long cores of ice extracted from Antarctic and Greenland ice sheets. Ocean sediments are particularly valuable with their long, undisturbed sequences that can be dated using modern radiometric and palaeomagnetic methods. It is thought that there have been between 15 and 22 glacials during the last 2 million years - they become harder to determine further back in time. At its height the most recent glacial period saw Canada and Scandinavia covered by great ice sheets. Ice caps centered on Highland Scotland, Snowdonia, the English Lake District and the Alps, with outlet and valley glaciers extending out over the lowlands.

GLACIATED AREAS OF THE WORLD

It is estimated that 15,600,000 km^2 (6,020,000 miles^2) or about 10.4 per cent of the world's land surface is permanently covered with ice.

Location	*Area (sq kilometres)*	*(sq mi)*
South polar region	12,588,000	5,250,000
Antarctic icesheet	*12,535,000*	*4,839,000*
other Antarctic glaciers	*53,000*	*20,500*
North Polar regions	2,070,000	799,000
Greenland ice sheets	*1,726,000*	*666,400*
other Greenland glaciers	*76,200*	*29,400*
Canadian archipelago	*153,200*	*59,100*
Svalbard (Spitzbergen)	*58,000*	*22,400*
other Arctic islands	*55,700*	*21,500*
Asia	115,800	44,400
Alaska/Rockies	76,900	29,700
South America	26,500	10,200
Iceland	12,170	4699
Alpine Europe	9280	3580
New Zealand	1015	391
Africa	12	7

WORLD'S LONGEST GLACIERS

km	*miles*	*Name*
515	320	Lambert-Fisher Ice Passage, Antarctica
418	260	Novaya Zemlya, North Island, Russia
362	225	Arctic Institute Ice Passage, Victoria Land, E Antarctica
289	180	Nimrod-Lennox-King Ice Passage, E Antarctica
241	150	Denman Glacier, E Antarctica
225	140	Beardmore Glacier, E Antarctica
225	140	Recovery Glacier, W Antarctica
200	124	*Petermanns Gletscher, Knud Rasmussen Land, Greenland

* Petermanns Gletscher is the largest in the northern hemisphere: it extends 40 km (24.8 miles) out to sea.

The largest glacier in Europe is the Aletsch Glacier (Bernese Oberland, Switzerland), which is 35 km (22 miles) long.

CAVES

Caves are naturally occurring holes in the ground that can be penetrated by humans. They are often linked into complex systems of chambers and passageways, which can extend many kilometres in length, and penetrate deep into the Earth.

The entrances to many caves have provided shelter for both animals and humans in the past, and their accumulated remains can tell us much about extinct animal forms and the life of prehistoric man. Some caves are also noted for their animal life today; as well as numerous invertebrates, bats, birds, snakes and even crocodiles may make their homes in caves.

Formation of caves

By far the majority of caves occur in limestone areas. This is because of the solubility of limestone in rainwater (H_2O) containing carbon dioxide (CO_2) in solution. This solution is carbonic acid (H_2CO_3), a weak acid that can attack limestone on its own, but its effects are much greater if it is augmented by acids from soil and vegetation.

Not all limestones have caves as some, such as chalk, are mechanically weak and will not support cave roofs. Others have few caves owing to their high porosity.

Karst landscape

Limestone landscapes with cave systems are known as *karst landscapes*, named after an area of Croatia and Slovenia. Karst landscapes are typified by a lack of surface streams, the presence of swallets (stream sinks) and collapse potholes, dry valleys (which once had streams now flowing underground), resurgences, and of bare rock pavements. These *limestone pavements* are intersected into areas known as *clints* by fissures about 50 cm (20 in) wide known as *grikes*, this process being caused by the etching out of joints and subsequent glacial smoothing. Karst landscapes may also have numerous *dolines* (funnel-shaped hollows at joint intersections) and *poljes* (enclosed valleys with internal drainage through caves).

Caves in rocks other than limestone include a variety of *sea caves* where erosion has etched out weaknesses in sea cliffs.

Lava and other caves

Lava caves occur in many basalt volcanic areas, such as Iceland, Hawaii, Kenya and Australia. They are generally tubes within lava flows where molten material has flowed out from beneath the solidified crust. *Fissure caves* occur in a few hard-rock areas where fault zones have been widened by erosion.

Ice caves are of two sorts. First, there are *englacial tubes* through which streams of melt water run beneath glaciers. Though entirely in ice, they show many of the features of limestone caves, although rapid changes may take place owing to glacier movement. Second, there are caves in high mountain regions where the air within the cave rarely if ever rises above freezing point, so that water percolating in from the surface during the summer freezes into icicles, often very large, and sometimes joining into ice masses underground.

WORLD'S DEEPEST CAVES

Name	Depth
Réseau Jean Bernard, Haute-Savoie, Frances	1602m (5256 ft)
Shakta Pantjukhina, Georgia	1508m (4947ft)
Sistema del Trave, Asturias, Spain	1441m (4728ft)
Aminakoateak, Navarre, Spain	1408m (4630ft)
Snezhnaya, Abkhazia, Georgia	1370m (4495ft)
Sistema Huautla, Oaxaca, Mexico	1353m (4439ft)
Réseau de la Pierre-Saint-Martin, Pyrenees, France	1342m (4403ft)
Boj-Bulok, Pamir, Tajikistan	1315m (4313ft)
Sisterna Cuicateca, Mexico	1243m (4077ft)
Réseau Rhododendrons-Gouffre Berger, Isère, France	1242m (4072ft)
V.V. Iljukhina, Georgia	1240m (4068 ft)
Scwersystem, Salzburg, Austria	1219m (3999 ft)
Gouffre Mirolda, Haute-Savoie, France	1211m (3973 ft)
Abisso Ulivefer, Apennines, Italy	1210m (3969 ft)
Veliko Fbrego, Croatia	1198m (3930 ft)

WORLD'S LONGEST CAVE SYSTEMS

Name	Length
Mammoth Cave, Kentucky, USA	560 km/348 mi
Optimisticeskaya, Ukraine	165 km/103 mi
Hölloch, Schwyz, Switzerland	133 km/83 mi
Jewel Cave, South Dakota, USA	127 km/79 mi
Siebenhengste-Hohganthöhlen, Berne, Switzerland	110 km/68 mi
Ozernaya, Ukraine	107 km/66 mi
La Coume d'Hyouernede, Haute--Garonne, France	90 km/56 mi
Ojo Guareña, Castile-Leon, Spain	89 km/55 mi
Wind Cave, South Dakota, USA	82 km/51 mi
Zoluska, Ukraine	82 km/51 mi
Fisher Ridge Cave, Kentucky, USA	77 km/49 mi
Gua Airjernih, Sarawak, Malaysia	75 km/47 mi
Sistema Purificacion, Mexico	72 km/45 mi
Friars Hole Cave, West Virginia, USA	69 km/43 mi
Lechuguilla Cave, New Mexico, USA	67 km/42 mi
Ease Gill, West Yorkshire, England	66 km/41 mi

WORLD'S LARGEST CAVE CHAMBERS

Sarawak Chamber, Lubang Nasib Bagus, Gunung Mulu National Park, Sarawak, Malaysia, has an area of 162,700 cubic metres (1,751,287 cubic feet). The chamber is 700m (2300 ft) long, with an average width of 300m (980 ft). The chamber is nowhere less than 70m (230 ft) high).

Torca del Carlista, Spain, is the second largest known cave chamber. It has an area of 76,600 cubic metres (824,515 cubic feet).

Majlis al Jinn (in Oman) is known to have an area of 58,000 cubic metres (624,306 cubic feet).

DEPRESSIONS

Depressions (see below) are sunken hollows in the surface of the ground. These may be caused by a number of natural processes including water erosion, glaciation, wind erosion, changes in sea level, and faulting.

Immense areas of western Antarctica would be below sea level if they were to be stripped of their ice sheet. The deepest estimated Antarctic crypto-depression is the bed rock on the Hollick-Kenyon plateau beneath the Marie Byrd Land ice cap (84° 3' S 110° W) which is at – 2468m (–8100 ft).

The bed of Lake Baykal (Russia) is 1484m (4872 ft) below sea level, and the bed of the Dead Sea (Israel/West Bank/Jordan) is 792m (2600 ft) below sea level.

The ground surface of large areas of Central Greenland under the overburden of ice up to 3410m (11,190 ft) thick are depressed to 365m (1200 ft) below sea level.

THE WORLD'S LARGEST EXPOSED DEPRESSIONS

The world's largest exposed depression is the Prikaspiyskaya Nizmennost', which includes the northern third of the Caspian Sea, which itself is 28m (92 ft) below sea level, and stretches up to 400 km (250 mi) inland.

The Qattara Depression (in Egypt) extends for 547 km (340 mi) and is up to 128 km (80 mi) wide.

THE WORLD'S DEEPEST EXPOSED DEPRESSIONS

Name	Maximum depth below sea level
Dead Sea, Jordan-Israel-West Bank	395m (1296 ft)
Turfan Depression, Xinjiang, China	153m (505 ft)
Munkhafad el Qattâra (Qattâra Depression), Egypt	132m (436ft)
Poluostrov Mangyshlak, Kazakhstan	131m (433 ft)
Danakil Depression, Ethiopia	116m (383 ft)
Death Valley, California, USA	86m (282 ft)
Salton Sink, California, USA	71m (235 ft)
Zapadnyy Chink Ustyurta, Kazakhstan	70m (230ft)
Prikaspiyskaya Nizmennost', Russia/Kazakhstan	67m (220ft)
Ozera Sarykamysh, Uzbekistan/ Turkmenistan.	45m (148 ft)
El Faiyûm, Egypt	44m (147 ft)
Peninsula Valdiés Lago , Enriquillo, Dominican Republic	40m (131 ft)

Note: Over one quarter of the Netherlands lies below sea level. The only other significant areas in Western Europe below sea level are in Cambridgeshire and Norfolk, England, and in northern Belgium. These areas below sea level comprise areas of geologically recent marine and river sediments, commonly reclaimed from tidal marshland and the sea by draining and the construction of protective barriers.

PHYSICAL GEOGRAPHY GLOSSARY

abyssal pertaining to the depths of the oceans.

affluent a tributary stream flowing into a larger stream or river.

aiguille (French, 'needle') a sharp point or pinnacle of rock.

alluvial fan a fan-shaped area of sediment deposited where the gradient of a stream or river is reduced and flow is slowed.

alluvium the fine sediment (sand, silt, clay) deposited by a river.

altitude height above sea level.

archipelago a group of islands.

arête a sharp ridge between two cirques.

artesian well a well that taps water held in a permeable layer of rock, sandwiched between two impermeable layers of rock in a basin. The rim of the permeable section of the basin is higher than the level of the well, so the water contained in the permeable layer pushes the water up out of the well.

atoll a ring of coral islands or coral reefs.

avalanche a mass of snow and/or ice that slides down a mountainside under its own weight.

bar shingle and sand deposited in a line or ridge across a bay or mouth of a river, or offshore, parallel to a beach.

barchan a crescent-shaped sand dune. Its shape is due to the effect of the wind from a constant direction.

bayou a swampy creek leading off a river, found in flat land.

bergschrund a gap between the upper edge of a glacier and the rock or ice wall in the back of a cirque. Also called a rimage.

bight a large bay.

bill a small peninsula.

bluff a vertical cliff, standing out prominently from the surrounding countryside.

bog an area of wet spongy ground consisting of waterlogged and partly decaying moss and other plants.

bore a tidal wave running up a river estuary.

boulder clay sediment consisting of a mix of clay and boulders deposited by a glacier. Also called till.

bourne a stream that only flows intermittently.

bund (in the Indian subcontinent) an artificial embankment.

bush scrubland not cleared for cultivation.

butte a flat-topped hill, often with steep sides, formed in horizontal strata. A mesa is a large butte.

cairn a man-made heap of stones.

caldera a crater flanked by steep cliffs. It is usually formed when the top of a volcano has been eroded.

canal a man-made waterway, either for transport or irrigation.

canyon a river-cut gorge with steep sides, often of great depth.

cape a piece of land projecting into the sea.

cascade a small waterfall.

cataract a large waterfall.

cave an underground opening reached from the surface or from the sea.

cavern a cave.

chaparral dry scrubland, particularly in the south-eastern USA.

chimney a wide vertical crack in a rock face.

cirque a rounded basin in a mountainside, formed by the action of a glacier. Also called a corrie or cwm.

cliff a steep face of rock.

col a pass or saddle between higher mountains.

coombe a short valley into the side of a hill.

confluence the point at which two rivers converge.

continent a single large landmass.

continental drift the movement of crustal plates on the molten rock that makes up the Earth's interior.

continental shelf the offshore seabed, down to a depth of 200 m (600 ft).

contour a line joining all points at the same height.

coral the exoskeleton of small marine animals of the same name, which live in colonies. When each animal dies the calcium-rich exoskeleton remains. As generation succeeds generation, masses of coral build up into reefs, atolls, etc.

coral reef a line of coral at or just below the surface of the sea.

cordillera parallel lines of mountains.

corrasion the mechanical erosion of rocks by the action of other rocks, gravel, etc., in a river or by wind-borne sand.

corrie a cirque.

corrosion the chemical erosion of rocks.

cove a small bay.

crater the hollow at the top of a volcanic cone, or the depression caused by the impact of a meteorite.

crevasse a vertical crack in a glacier or ice sheet.

cuesta a ridge or hill formed by sloping rock strata.

cwm a cirque.

dale an open valley, especially in northern England.

deep a marine valley or trench, considerably deeper than the surrounding seabed.

delta deposits of alluvium in a fan shape, formed where a river flows into the sea or a lake.

desert an area of arid and semi-arid climates where rainfall is low and moisture availability is scarce.

drowned valley a valley that has been submerged by a rise in sea level or by the land sinking.

drumlin a small hump-backed hill formed by the action of a glacier. Composed of boulder clay and sometimes with a rock core, swarms of drumlins are exposed as ice-sheets recede.

dune a wind-formed accumulation of sand.

dust bowl a dry region that has been badly managed agriculturally to such a degree that the topsoil has been removed by wind erosion.

dyke a vertical sheet of rock that cuts across the bedding or structural planes of the host rock.

earthquake a series of shock waves generated from a single point within the Earth's mantle or crust.

epicentre the point on the Earth's surface above the point at which the shock waves of an earthquake are generated.

Equator an imaginary circle around the Earth's circumference, midway between the poles.

equinox the time when the Sun appears vertically overhead at noon at the Equator – 21 March and 21 September.

erg a desert area composed of wind-blown sand and dunes.

erosion the removal or wearing away of the land surface by natural means.

estuary the mouth of a river, and the tidal stretch of that river immediately up-river of the mouth.

étang a shallow lake among coastal sand dunes.

fall line the line showing where a number of rivers leave an upland area for a lowland area, in each case passing over a waterfall or series of waterfalls.

fathom a unit of depth at sea: 1·83 m (6 ft).

fell bare hill or exposed upland area, especially in northern England.

fen marshy land in which peat is formed, especially in eastern England.

fjord a glaciated steep-sided valley that runs into the sea and is subsequently flooded. They are characterized by a great depth of water in the main body of the fjord, with a shallower bar across the mouth.

firth (known as a sea loch in Scotland) a narrow inlet in the sea coast; either an estuary or a fjord.

flood plain the plain on either side of a river formed by alluvial deposits left when the river floods and then recedes again.

fold a vertical bend in the rock strata, formed by compression within the Earth's crust.

forest a large area of land, extensively covered with trees.

frost hollow a hollow into which cold air sinks from the surrounding slopes. The hollow is therefore more liable to suffer frost than the surrounding land.

garrigue a form of scrub found in dry limestone areas around the Mediterranean.

geyser a hot spring of such depth that steam periodically forms, erupting from the mouth of the spring in a fountain of steam and hot water.

glacier a mass of ice, formed through the accumulation of snow and its transformation to ice under pressure. Glaciers slowly move down a valley towards the sea.

glen a long narrow steep-sided valley in Scotland.

gorge a deep, narrow, rugged valley with near-vertical walls.

grassland a large area where the rainfall is greater than that of a desert but not enough to support a forest.

great circle a circle on the Earth's surface whose centre is the Earth's centre, and hence the shortest route between two places follows the great circle on which both are situated.

gulf a large bay.

gully a narrow steep-sided channel formed by water erosion.

hammada a bare rocky desert.

hanging valley a glaciated valley entering a main valley part-way up the valley side.

headland an isolated cliff projecting into the sea.

hot spring a spring whose water is heated by hot volcanic rocks.

iceberg a massive lump of ice that has broken off the end of a glacier or ice sheet and floats in the sea or a lake.

ice floe a floating sheet of ice that has detached from an ice shelf.

ice sheet a great sheet of ice and snow covering a land mass.

ice shelf a mass of ice and snow floating on the sea.

inlet an opening into the sea or lake coast.

inselberg an isolated hill in a relatively flat area.

irrigation an artificial supply of water to a crop-producing area.

island a mass of land surrounded by water. It may occur in a river, a lake, a sea or an ocean.

islet a small island.

isthmus a narrow neck of land connecting two land masses.

jebel (in Arabic countries) a mountain range.

jungle a popular name for tropical rain forest.

karst a type of limestone scenery produced by water erosion of limestone rock. It is characterized by sinks, underground rivers and caves, and other erosion features.

kettle hole a hollow in the outwash plain of a glacier, formed where an ice block melts.

key or **cay** a small island or sandbank in the Caribbean.

knick point a point at which the slope of a river changes.

knoll a small rounded hill.

kyle (in Scotland) a channel of water or strait.

lagoon an expanse of water that has been separated from the sea by a narrow strip of land.

lake an expanse of water entirely surrounded by land.

landslide a mass of soil, mud and rock that slides down a mountainside or cliff-slope because of its own weight.

latitude a degree of latitude (°) is the angular distance of a point on the surface of the Earth, north or south of the Equator, taken from the centre of the Earth. A line of latitude is the line joining all point with the same degree of latitude, i.e. it is a circle with the axis of the Earth between the two poles at its centre. (Compare longitude.)

lava see Geology Glossary.

lava fountain a fountain of molten lava ejected from a volcano.

lava plateau a plateau formed from a flat sheet of volcanic rock.

levée a river-bank formed during flooding of the river. As the river water spreads out, alluvium is deposited, the greatest quantity being along the line of the river bank.

littoral that part of the seashore between high and low tide.

load solid material carried by a river, ranging from boulders to fine silt.

loch (in Scotland) an inlet of the sea, a fjord, or a lake.

longitude the angular distance between one of the Earth's meridians and the standard or Greenwich meridian.

longshore drift the movement of sand and shingle along the shore due to the action of the waves as they advance and retreat obliquely along the shore.

lough (in Ireland) an inlet of the sea, a fjord, or a lake.

lunar day the time between successive crossings of a meridian by the Moon - about 24 hours 50 minutes.

lunar month the time between two successive new Moons, i.e. the time the Moon takes to travel around the Earth once – 29½ days.

maelstrom a large whirlpool.

magnetic pole the point at which the Earth's magnetic flux is strongest. The magnetic poles do not coincide with the true poles. They also move slightly with time.

mangrove swamp a tropical coastal swamp characterized by the extensive growth of mangroves, whose long tangled roots drop from the trunks and branches of the mangroves, trapping sediment.

maquis a low scrub growing on rocky soil in the Mediterranean area.

marsh low-lying soft wet land.

massif a block of mountains that only breaks up into separate peaks towards the various summits.

meander a wide curve or loop in a river. These often link up in a series of meanders.

meridian half a great circle on the Earth's surface, finishing at each pole and cutting the Equator at right-angles, i.e. a line of longitude.

mesa a tableland with steep sides. Buttes are small mesas.

meteorite a solid lump of rock that enters the atmosphere from space and is large enough not to burn up in the atmosphere but to reach the Earth's surface.

midnight sun the appearance of the sun throughout the day and night. This occurs in latitudes close to the poles at times around the solstices.

monadnock an isolated hill or rock, left when the surrounding rock has been eroded more rapidly.

monsoon forest tropical forest found where a monsoon climate is prevalent. Because of the dry season between monsoons, it is not so dense as tropical equatorial forest.

moor an area of high rolling land covered in grass, heather and bracken, often with marshy areas.

moraine rock and other debris transported by a glacier. Terminal moraines are formed at the ends of glaciers; lateral moraines are formed at the sides of glaciers; median moraines are formed in the middle of glaciers where two glaciers meet and unite.

mountain a mass of high land projecting well above the level of the surrounding land.

muskeg (in northern Canada) a mossy swamp.

neap tide the small tidal difference between high and low tide, caused when the Sun and Moon are out of phase.

névé granular snow, formed as snow is gradually impacted. Eventually névé forms the ice of a glacier.

nunatak a mountain peak projecting through an ice sheet.

oasis an area in a desert in which water occurs, giving rise to fertile land and allowing cultivation.

ocean a very large area of seawater, divided off by or surrounding the continents.

outwash alluvium carried from the end of a glacier by the melting ice.

outwash plain a plain formed by the outwash of a glacier.

oxbow lake a lake formed when a river cuts off one of its meanders, leaving a crescent-shaped or horseshoe-shaped lake.

pack ice ice floes that have been forced together to form an almost continuous sheet.

pampas grasslands between the Andes and the Atlantic in South America.

pass a gap through a mountain range that is relatively easy to traverse.

pediment a sloping plain that leads up to a mountain range.

percolation the descent of water through porous rock.

permafrost ground that is always frozen solid.

piedmont pertaining to the foot of a mountain or mountain range.

plain an extensive area of flat or gently rolling land.

plateau an extensive area of flat or gently rolling land that is raised above the level of the surrounding land.

playa a lake in an area that experiences a dry climate. It is often dry seasonally or for many years and has a saline surface.

plug a vertical core of solidified lava at the centre of a volcanic cone.

polder (in the Netherlands) an area that has been reclaimed from the sea.

pole one end of the Earth's axis; it remains stationary while all other points on Earth rotate round the axis.

pothole a hole worn down through solid rock by the swirling action of water, or water and accompanying debris.

prairie flat or rolling plains, largely grasslands, that occupy the central areas of North America east of the Rockies.

profile the profile of a river is a cross-section of its total length, showing the various slopes and changes of slope.

promontory a headland.

puy (in France) an isolated cone of a long-extinct volcano.

quagmire soft wet ground that shakes when walked on. Known as a 'shoog-bog' in some parts of Scotland.

quicksand loose sand in a dense suspension in water. Although it may look solid, its properties are those of a liquid.

race a rapid marine current caused by the tides.

ravine a small steep-sided valley, usually caused by water erosion.

reef a line of rocks just below the surface of the sea.

reg an area of the desert consisting of gravel and small rocks, but no sand.

ria an inlet of the sea, formed from a submerged river valley.

rift a valley formed by the sinking of a section of land between two parallel faults.

river capture the process by which one river erodes a larger and larger valley, eventually cutting into the valley of another river and 'capturing' its waters.

river terrace flat land on either side of a river, left when a river erodes a channel well below the level of its flood plain.

roads or **roadstead** a large area of deepwater anchorage for ships, usually well protected from bad weather.

rognon (French, 'kidney') an isolated island of rock in a glacier.

run-off rainfall that pours over the ground surface and into streams and rivers.

salt dome a mass of salt that has been forced up through layers of rock until it lies relatively close to the Earth's surface.

salt lake a lake that has only a limited outlet or no outlet at all, occurring in an area experiencing a hot dry climate. As water evaporates, the concentration of salt in the water increases.

salt marsh an area of marsh that is flooded by seawater at high tides.

salt pan an area in which salt water has evaporated completely, leaving behind a deposit of salt.

sandbank a line or bank of sand just below the surface of the sea or of a river.

savanna or **savannah** an area of grassland with few trees, found to the north and south of the equatorial areas. There is a wet and a dry season each year, limiting the growth of trees.

scarp or **escarpment** a steep slope, often forming the steeper slope of a cuesta.

scree broken rocks at the foot of a rocky slope. They are broken off by the action of weathering and tumble down the slope. Also known as talus.

sea level the mean level between high and low tides.

sea loch sea fjord.

seif a linear sand dune with a sinuous crest.

serac a tower or band of very steep ice formed when the part of the glacier below it has fallen away.

shoal an area of sandbanks.

sidereal day the interval of time for a star to describe a circle around the pole star.

sierra a long mountain range, usually very jagged.

sill a slab of igneous rock, forced when molten between two layers of sedimentary rock and subsequently exposed by erosion.

snowfield a permanent mass of snow.

snowline the level above which snow is permanently present.

solar day the interval of time between successive appearances of the Sun in the meridian of any one place.

solstice the time when the Sun appears vertically overhead at its most northerly or southerly point – 21 June and 22 December.

sound a narrow inlet of the sea.

source the point at which a river begins – a spring, lake, etc.

spit a long narrow strip of shingle or sand, attached at one end to a land mass, projecting into the sea or across an estuary.

spring a flow of water up through the ground at a particular point. It can be permanent or intermittent.

spring tide the greatest tidal difference between high and low tide, caused when the Sun and Moon are in phase.

stack an isolated pillar of rock off the coast, caused by erosion.

steppes flat grasslands stretching from central Europe to eastern Russia and on into Central Asia.

strait a narrow stretch of sea connecting two large expanses of sea or ocean.

subtropical the region between the tropics and temperate regions.

swamp low marshland that is permanently wet.

swash a flow of water up a beach after a wave has broken.

taiga a vast belt of coniferous forests in the northern hemisphere, particularly Siberia.

talus another word for scree.

tarn a mountain lake, often occupying a cirque.

temperate the region experiencing cool summers and mild winters. It lies between subtropical regions and polar circles, excluding the continental and eastern coastal regions of the northern hemisphere.

tide the rise and fall of the surface of the sea, caused by the gravitational pull of the sun.

tombolo a bar joining an island to the mainland.

trench a long deep submarine valley.

tributary a river that flows into another river rather than into a lake or the sea.

Tropic of Cancer latitude 23°27' N. The position at which the Sun appears vertically overhead at midday on the 21 June solstice.

Tropic of Capricorn latitude 23°27' S. The position at which the Sun appears vertically overhead at midday on the 22 December solstice.

tropics the region between the Tropics of Cancer and Capricorn.

truncated spur a spur that has at some time been foreshortened by the action of a glacier.

tsunami a tidal wave caused by an earthquake under the sea's surface.

tundra the area in the northern hemisphere, north of the coniferous forest belt, characterized by the absence of trees. The ground is covered by mosses, lichens and a few other plants that can survive the long harsh winters and short cool summers.

undertow the undercurrent after a wave has broken on a beach.

volcanic ash particles of lava ejected by a volcano and often falling over a wide area.

volcano a vent or fissure in the Earth's crust through which molten magma can force its way to the surface.

wadi a watercourse in the desert. It is usually dry but can contain water after the occasional rainstorms.

waterfall an abrupt fall of water in the course of a river.

water gap a gap in a ridge or line of hills, cut by a river.

watershed the dividing line, running along high land, between the tributaries feeding into two separate river systems.

water table the surface of a water-saturated part of the ground.

weir an artificial structure across a river, constructed to regulate flow.

well a hole dug from ground level to below the surface of the water table to gain access to water.

whirlpool a circular eddy of water, formed by the interaction of two or more currents.

year the time taken for the Earth to complete one revolution about the Sun.

zenith a point vertically above the ground.

Weather and Climate

Meteorology is the science of the atmosphere, from the Greek word '*meteorologica*', meaning 'matters of the atmosphere', and first used in a treatise by Aristotle.

Weather is the condition of the atmosphere at any one place and time, as described by air temperature and humidity, wind speed and direction, cloud amount and precipitation from cloud (drizzle, rain, snow, hail), together with atmospheric pressure, sunshine and visibility.

Climate is the normal weather condition for an area during a season or year. The climate of an area is described by means of an average of the statistics of the various weather factors over a period of time, normally 30 years. At any one time the weather may be quite different from the accepted climate.

CONSTITUENTS OF AIR

Atmospheric air consists of gases in fixed proportion, and gases in variable quantities. The most important of the fixed proportion gases are:

nitrogen which constitutes 78% of atmospheric air.

oxygen which constitutes 21% of atmospheric air.

The most important of the variable gases are:

ozone which occurs at high altitudes. It provides some protection against the ultraviolet rays from the sun.

carbon dioxide which acts like glass in a greenhouse to retain heat in the lower atmosphere.

water vapour which is acquired by evaporation from oceans, rivers, and even puddles. All precipitation is produced from water vapour by condensation.

Water in the atmosphere

There is one basic supply of water in the world which is continually recycled. Water evaporates from oceans; vapour condenses again as dew, fog or cloud; rain or snow falls from clouds and percolates through soil back to the oceans, or is absorbed by plants and transpired as vapour from foliage. The warmer the air, the more vapour it can hold, although there is a maximum capacity for every temperature. The path followed by an air mass determines its moisture content. Wind, which is moving air, is moist after a long sea track and relatively dry after a long land track.

Relative humidity

Relative humidity is the actual vapour content of air, expressed as a percentage of the maximum possible at that temperature. If air is saturated its relative humidity (RH) is 100% and the air temperature is called *dew point*. No more water can then be evaporated into the air until air temperature rises above dew point, when its capacity for vapour increases.

If air is not saturated, for instance has an RH of only 80%, then its temperature can only fall as far as dew point before some vapour has to be discarded as visible water drops. This is called *condensation*.

INTRODUCTION TO WEATHER

All wet weather phenomena are the result of air cooling to dew point or below. The higher the RH when such cooling begins, the quicker condensation will occur.

Air temperature falls when in contact with colder surfaces of land or sea, in which case dew, hoar frost or fog will result when dew point is reached. Air also cools because of expansion when lifted into regions of lower atmospheric pressure. Air may have to rise over high ground, rise in thermal upcurrents, or be carried upwards on meeting air of different density. Cloud forms once air has cooled to dew point or below, and rain or snow may fall from cloud. Therefore, topography has a considerable effect upon weather. It is generally colder at the top of mountains, wetter on their windward side and drier on the leeward side because of rain lost over the top. In extreme cases, where the rain-bearing winds come mainly from one direction, the opposite side of a mountain range may develop into a rain-shadow desert.

Air temperature rises when in contact with warming surfaces of land and sea. The Earth's chief heat source is the Sun, which is a radiant globe of gases that whirl in a vortex around an axis and transmit energy by electromagnetic waves of various wavelengths. The Earth moves in an elliptical path around the Sun so that the distance between the two varies but is on average 150 million km (93 million mi).

Seasons exist because the Earth's axis is tilted at 66½° to the plane in which it travels around the Sun, and each hemisphere alternately leans towards or away from the Sun.

Day and night occur because the Earth rotates about its own axis once in 24 hours, so that everywhere alternately faces towards or away from the Sun.

Equinox means equality of day and night and happens when the Sun is vertical over the Equator on 21 March and 22 September.

Solstices are the two occasions occurring about 21 June and 21 December when the Earth's Equator is furthest from the Sun, so that there is maximum and minimum daylight in the two hemispheres.

The Tropics of Cancer and Capricorn, 23°27' north and south of the Equator respectively, encompass the only regions of the Earth on which the Sun shines directly overhead at some time of the year.

All these different variations of the Sun's altitude over places on Earth means that air temperature is always higher at the Equator than at the Poles, always higher in summer than in winter, and mostly higher in the day than at night. However, temperature does not fall evenly from equatorial latitudes to polar regions, because of geographical complications. Sea temperature varies hardly at all from one day to another and only gradually over a whole season, so that the weather near the oceans is generally more equable and milder than inland. Inland, where soil responds well to the rise of the Sun, temperatures can soar each day but fall equally rapidly under clear skies at night. Air temperatures, either on the coast or inland, are often modified because of cloud cover.

CLOUD CLASSIFICATION

Clouds comprise water drops or ice crystals suspended in air. The water is condensed from air which rises into levels of lower atmospheric pressure, expands and cools to dew point. Air may be lifted in this manner over high ground, in thermals or at the convergence of air masses of different temperature, when cold air undercuts warm air. Water drops can remain liquid when supercooled to temperatures of –30 °C (–22 °F) but below this temperature an increasing number of water drops freeze to ice crystals. At temperatures lower than –40 °C (–40 °F), clouds consist of ice crystals alone. Water drops and crystals are transparent, but take on shades between white and grey, depending upon how thick the clouds are and how light is bent travelling through. Clouds may also be coloured when illuminated by the Sun. Clouds are classified according to the height of their base above the ground and whether they are rounded (*cumulus*) or flat (*stratus*).

CLOUD TYPES

High Cloud

cirrus (Latin 'lock of hair') contain ice crystals in air colder than –30 °C (–22 °F), and are usually higher than about 5000m (16,500 ft); detached clouds forming delicate white filaments, or white, or mostly white, patches or narrow bands; have a fibrous (hair-like) appearance or a silky sheen, or both; the highest of the standard cloud forms.

cirrocumulus rounded small clouds, rather than feathery or hair-like; appear in the form of grains or ripples; often more or less regularly arranged.

cirrostratus a white veil of smooth fibrous ice crystal; often seen making a halo around the Sun or Moon.

Medium-level cloud

Medium-level clouds are composed of water drops, either warm or supercooled. Their bases can be anywhere between 2000m (6500 ft) and 7000m (23,000 ft).

altocumulus grey or white clouds having rounded shapes, sometimes touching.

altostratus flat, thick sheet cloud, often obscuring the Sun and totally hiding it when about to rain or snow; all shades of grey.

Low cloud

Low cloud is defined as any which has its base at or below 2000m (6500 ft).

cumulus detached clouds with sharp billowing upper contours, which develop upwards in thermals; vary in appearance from small fleeces to giant cauliflowers.

cumulonimbus tallest of the cumulus clouds; sometimes have an ice-crystal anvil-shaped top at the limit of convection; give showers or rain, snow or hail, often with thunder and lightning.

nimbostratus flat, relatively shapeless clouds; often seen below altostratus; grey clouds, which often merge, they give rain or snow.

stratus patches or sheets of shapeless low grey cloud; often thin enough to see the Sun through, especially when about to disperse; often start as fog and later lifted by strenghthening wind; give drizzle and (in winter) snow grains.

stratocumulus patches of cloud, or whole sheets, with discernible rounded shapes; often formed by cumulus clouds spreading out under an inversion of temperature.

CLIMATIC ZONES

Climate is merely average weather, and climatic patterns are complicated but logical results of meteorological and geographical factors. Temperature roughly follows the bands of latitude, warm near the Equator, cold in the Polar regions, and often modified because of cloud cover created by the physical processes of the atmosphere. Low pressure generally breeds clouds and precipitation; high pressure areas have little cloud. There are four major pressure belts:

Tropical low pressure an area between 10 °N or S of the Equator, where there is frequent and regular rain mainly from convection clouds. The large equatorial forests lie within this band.

Subtropical high pressure an area approximately 10–40 °N or S, where there is little cloud or rain. High pressure extends across to the interior of continents in middle latitudes during the winter, but retreats into smaller cells over the relatively cold oceans during summer. The major hot deserts of the world lie within this subtropical belt.

Mid-latitude low pressure an area of mainly low pressure in the mid-latitudes 40–70 °N or S, where there is frequent but irregular rain from depressions and convection clouds, interspersed with occasional spells of high pressure. The interiors of continents in this zone are very cold in winter (when there is high pressure) but hot in summer with some rain (low pressure). Regions bordering the oceans have a more equable climate, with much less fluctuation in temperature.

Polar high pressure belts of mainly high pressure between the poles and 70 °N or S, because the air is too cold to contain much water vapour.

The middle latitudes are called *temperate,* having cool summers and mild winters in maritime climates, and hot summers with cold winters in continental climates. There is very little change in temperature in equatorial regions because of season, but a great difference between winter and summer temperatures in polar regions.

NOTES ON CLIMATOLOGICAL STATISTICS

The statistics given opposite enable you to confirm the differences in climate due to physical factors of geography and topology.

Rainfall increases when air is forced over high ground. Compare the precipitation figures for Bergen, which lies in the path of westerly moist air masses, and Stockholm, in the rain shadow to the east of the Scandinavian Mountains. Rainfall increases with proximity to the most frequent paths of depressions (areas of low pressure). Compare the precipitation totals of Dublin, with those of London.

Rainfall is often markedly seasonal. Monsoon rain is particularly heavy over India and Pakistan when accentuated by the summer low pressure area over the Thar Desert. Rainfall may also be seasonal because of the shift of the subtropical high-pressure belt. Beijing (Peking), for instance, has little rain in winter, but plenty in summer. Madrid has little rain in summer, but experiences appreciably more in the winter.

AVERAGE RAINFALL IN SELECTED CITIES (to the nearest 5 mm)

	J	F	M	A	M	J	J	A	S	O	N	D
In Europe												
Amsterdam, Neths	70	50	50	50	50	65	80	95	80	80	85	85
Athens, Greece	45	35	40	25	15	5	5	5	15	15	55	65
Bergen, Norway	190	145	140	110	100	115	140	180	235	245	205	195
Berlin,Germany	30	30	40	40	60	70	80	70	50	40	40	40
Bucharest, Romania	40	30	35	45	70	85	70	55	40	40	45	40
Budapest, Hungary	40	40	35	45	60	75	60	55	40	40	65	50
Copenhagen, Dk	50	40	30	40	40	45	70	65	60	60	50	50
Dublin, Ireland	70	50	50	45	60	55	60	75	75	70	70	80
Geneva, Switz	65	60	70	65	70	80	75	100	100	85	90	80
London, UK	40	30	40	40	45	50	40	50	55	45	55	50
Madrid, Spain	40	40	45	45	40	30	10	10	30	50	50	45
Moscow, Russia	40	35	30	50	55	75	75	75	50	70	45	40
Paris, France	55	45	30	40	50	50	55	60	50	50	50	50
Prague, Czech Rep	25	25	25	30	60	65	80	65	35	40	25	25
Rome, Italy	80	75	75	50	35	20	5	35	75	85	125	110
Stockholm, Sweden	45	30	25	30	35	45	60	75	60	50	55	50
Vienna, Austria	40	45	45	45	70	65	85	70	40	55	55	45
Other Continents												
Bombay, India	5	0	5	5	15	520	710	440	300	90	20	0
Casablanca. Morocco	65	55	55	40	20	5	0	0	5	40	60	85
Dakar, Senegal	0	0	0	0	0	15	90	250	160	50	5	5
Darwin, Australia	385	310	250	95	15	5	5	5	15	50	120	240
Douala, Cameroon	20	65	145	180	205	150	55	75	200	300	125	120
Jeddah, S. Arabia	30	0	0	0	0	0	0	0	0	0	40	10
New York, USA	85	80	105	90	90	85	95	130	100	80	90	85
Montréal, Canada	25	15	35	65	65	80	90	90	90	75	60	35
Beijing, China	5	5	5	15	30	75	250	125	60	10	10	5
Tehran, Iran	40	25	30	25	15	0	5	0	0	5	25	25

AVERAGE TEMPERATURES IN SELECTED CITIES (°C)

	J	F	M	A	M	J	J	A	S	O	N	D
In Europe												
Amsterdam, Neths	2	2	5	8	12	15	17	17	14	11	6	4
Athens, Greece	9	10	12	15	20	25	27	26	23	18	14	11
Bergen, Norway	1	1	3	6	10	13	14	14	12	9	4	2
Berlin,Germany	–1	1	4	8	13	17	18	17	14	8	4	1
Bucharest, Romania	–3	–1	5	11	16	20	22	22	18	11	5	0
Budapest, Hungary	–1	2	6	12	16	20	21	21	17	11	6	2
Copenhagen, Dk	1	0	2	7	12	16	18	17	14	9	5	1
Dublin, Ireland	5	5	6	8	11	14	15	15	13	10	7	4
Geneva, Switz	0	1	5	9	13	16	18	18	16	13	9	6
London, UK	5	6	7	10	13	16	18	18	16	13	9	6
Madrid, Spain	5	7	10	13	16	21	24	24	20	15	9	6
Moscow, Russia	–9	–9	–4	4	12	17	18	17	11	4	-3	-8
Paris, France	3	4	7	10	14	17	19	18	16	11	7	4
Prague, Czech Rep	1	2	3	8	13	16	19	17	14	8	3	1
Rome, Italy	8	9	11	14	17	22	24	24	21	17	13	9
Stockholm, Sweden	–3	–3	–1	4	10	15	18	17	12	7	3	0
Vienna, Austria	–1	0	4	9	14	17	19	19	15	10	4	0
Other Continents												
Bombay, India	24	25	27	28	31	29	28	28	27	28	27	26
Casablanca. Morocco	12	13	15	16	18	20	22	23	22	19	16	13
Dakar, Senegal	21	20	21	22	23	26	27	27	27	27	26	23
Darwin, Australia	28	28	29	29	28	26	25	26	28	29	30	29
Douala, Cameroon	24	25	24	24	24	23	22	22	23	23	22	24
Jeddah, S. Arabia	23	25	27	29	30	32	33	31	30	28	27	25
New York, USA	0	0	5	11	16	22	25	24	20	15	8	2
Montréal, Canada	–10	–9	–3	6	13	18	21	20	15	9	2	-7
Beijing, China	–5	–4	4	15	27	31	31	30	26	20	10	-5
Tehran, Iran	4	4	8	15	20	27	29	28	25	18	10	7

VEGETATION ZONES

Any attempt to define the world's vegetation regions is complicated by the fact that the *natural vegetation*, that is the vegetation as it was originally, has been greatly changed by human interference such as deforestation and agriculture. Elevation, slope, drainage, soil type, soil depth and climate all influence the vegetation distribution.

Climate is a major factor in determining the type and number of plants (and to a lesser extent animals) that can live in an area. Three main terrestrial ecosystems can be recognized: deserts, grasslands and forests. Precipitation is the element that determines which vegetation type will occur in an area. If the annual precipitation is less than 250 mm (10 in) then deserts usually occur. Grasslands can be found when precipitation is between 250 and 750 mm (10 and 30 in) per annum, while areas that receive more than 750 mm (30 in) of rainfall a year are usually covered by forests.

The average temperature and the nature of the seasons in a region are important in that they can determine the type of desert, grassland or forest. Wherever the monthly average temperature exceeds 21 °C (70 °F) then hot deserts, savannah grasslands or tropical forests occur.

In the middle latitudes, the winter temperatures are low enough (one month or more below 5 °C/41 °F) to cause vegetation to become dormant. In autumn, growth stops, leaves are often shed and the plant survives the unfavourable winter months in a resting or dormant phase. In spring, when temperatures rise, new growth begins. In high latitudes, the winter conditions are such that between four or six months are dark and average temperatures fall well below 0 °C (32 °F). The evergreen conifers can survive these conditions but growth is very slow and confined to the short, cool summers. In the highest latitudes, trees disappear and only small low-growing plants can survive the low temperatures.

BEAUFORT SCALE

A scale of numbers, designated Force 0 to Force 12, was originally devised by Commander Francis Beaufort in 1805. (Force 13 to 17 were added in 1955 by the US Weather Bureau, but are not in international use.)

Force	Description	Wind speed
0	Calm	0–1 km/h 0–1 mph 0–1 knots
1	Light air	1–5 km/h 1–3 mph 1–3 knots
2	Light breeze	6–11 km/h 4–7 mph 4–6 knots
3	Gentle breeze	12–19 km/h 8–12 mph 7–10 knots
4	Moderate breeze	20–29 km/h 13–18 mph 11–16 knots
5	Fresh breeze	30–39 km/h 19–24 mph 17–21 knots
6	Strong breeze	40–50 km/h 25–31 mph 22–27 knots
7	Near gale	51–61 km/h 32–38 mph 28–33 knots
8	Gale	62–74 km/h 39–46 mph 34–40 knots
9	Strong gale	75–87 km/h 47–54 mph 41–47 knots
10	Storm	88–101 km/h 55–63 mph 48–55 knots

WEATHER MAPS

Weather forecasting is based upon upper-air data and surface weather observations made all over the world. The material is collected and retransmitted after processing, on an international telecommunications network organized by the World Meteorological Organization.

Information is relayed in numerical code, with five or six numerals in each group, and each observation is plotted in symbol form on a map at the position it was made.

One of the items plotted on the map is atmospheric pressure. Forecasters draw in isobars, which are lines joining places that have equal pressure, corrected to Mean Sea Level, at the same hour. These isobars form concentric patterns around low and high pressure centres and indicate wind direction at 600m (2000 ft) above ground, where it is deemed unaffected by the drag of surface friction.

Wind blows parallel to the isobars so that low pressure is on the left hand when the wind is on the back in the northern hemisphere. (Low pressure is on the right hand in the southern hemisphere.) In other words, wind blows anticlockwise around low pressure areas (depressions, cyclones, hurricanes) in the northern hemisphere and clockwise around high pressure areas (anticyclones). Wind directions are reversed in the southern hemisphere. Wind speed is inversely proportional to the distance between the isobars (the stronger the wind, the closer the isobars) and can be measured by a specially graduated scale placed across the isobars.

From the other plotted data, forecasters can detect the boundaries between air masses having different temperatures and humidity characteristics. A *warm front* is the surface boundary of approaching warm air with existing cool air. Warm air slides upwards over the cooler air ahead, to form sheet cloud several hundred kilometres ahead of the warm front, giving rain (or snow in winter). A *cold front* is the surface boundary between vigorous cold air which undercuts warmer air ahead, giving a line of huge shower clouds, often with torrential but short-lived rain or snow. A cold front usually travels faster than a warm front, eventually catching up with it and lifting the warm air off the ground into the upper atmosphere. The fronts are then said to be *occluded*. The *warm sector* lies between the warm front ands the cold front. Fronts are usually associated with low pressure circulations, as in the accompanying diagram.

On a black-on-white chart in the newspapers, a warm front is drawn as a thick line with semicircles on the side of the advance; a cold front has triangles along the leading edge of the line; and an occlusion has both symbols. Diagrams of well-defined fronts on weather charts (also called *isobaric* or *pressure charts*) show up clearly on satellite photographs as spiral or comma shaped cloud bands. Weather charts for the general public are broadcast on a regular basis, both on radio and TV. Most countries that border the oceans make special forecasts for shipping, dividing the sea areas into convenient sections. (For the UK, shipping areas and land areas used in the official forecasts are shown on p. 108.)

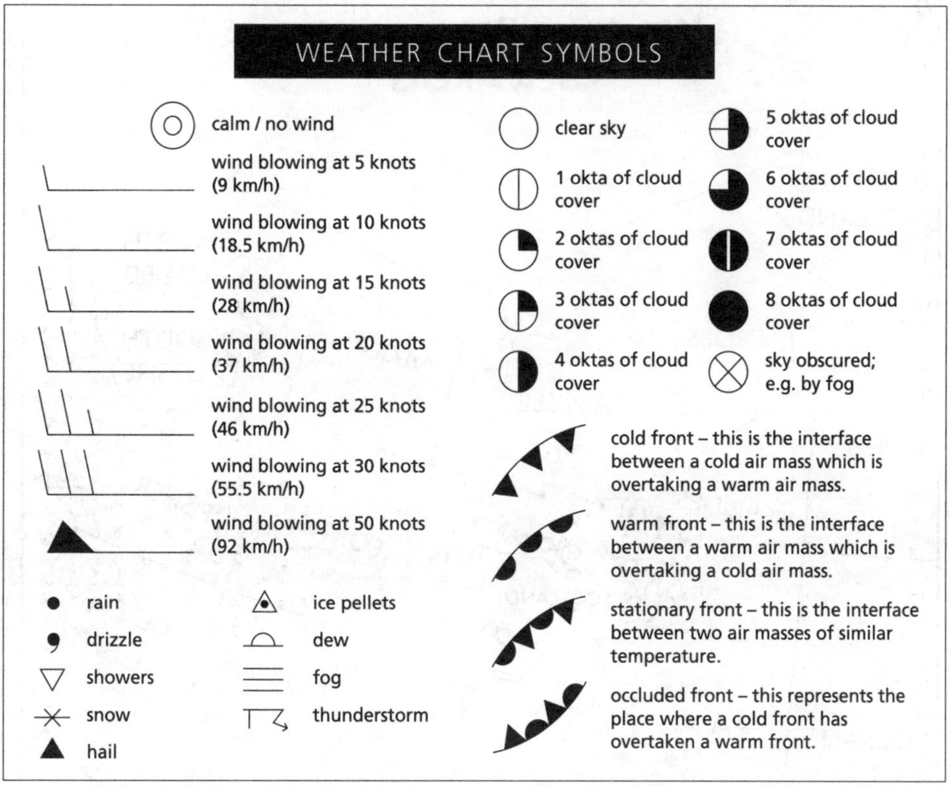
WEATHER CHART SYMBOLS
calm / no wind
wind blowing at 5 knots (9 km/h)
wind blowing at 10 knots (18.5 km/h)
wind blowing at 15 knots (28 km/h)
wind blowing at 20 knots (37 km/h)
wind blowing at 25 knots (46 km/h)
wind blowing at 30 knots (55.5 km/h)
wind blowing at 50 knots (92 km/h)
rain
drizzle
showers
snow
hail
ice pellets
dew
fog
thunderstorm
clear sky
1 okta of cloud cover
2 oktas of cloud cover
3 oktas of cloud cover
4 oktas of cloud cover
5 oktas of cloud cover
6 oktas of cloud cover
7 oktas of cloud cover
8 oktas of cloud cover
sky obscured; e.g. by fog
cold front – this is the interface between a cold air mass which is overtaking a warm air mass.
warm front – this is the interface between a warm air mass which is overtaking a cold air mass.
stationary front – this is the interface between two air masses of similar temperature.
occluded front – this represents the place where a cold front has overtaken a warm front.

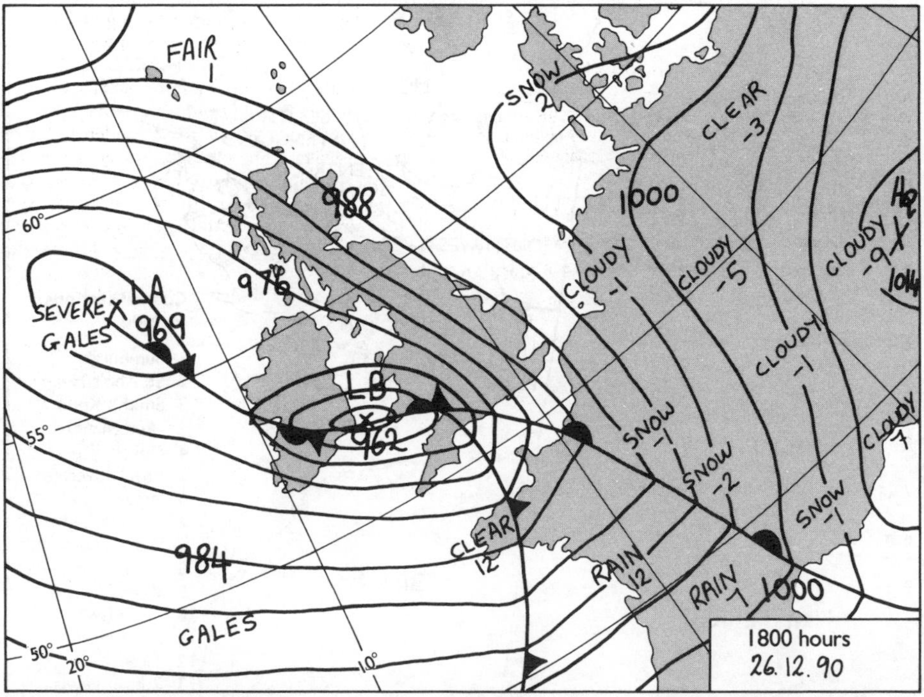
FAIR 1
SNOW 2
CLEAR -3
1000
988
976
CLOUDY -1
CLOUDY -5
CLOUDY -9
SEVERE GALES
LA
969
LB
962
CLOUDY -1
SNOW -1
SNOW -2
SNOW -1
CLOUDY 7
CLEAR 12
984
RAIN 12
RAIN 7
1000
GALES
60°
55°
50°
20°
10°
1800 hours
26.12.90

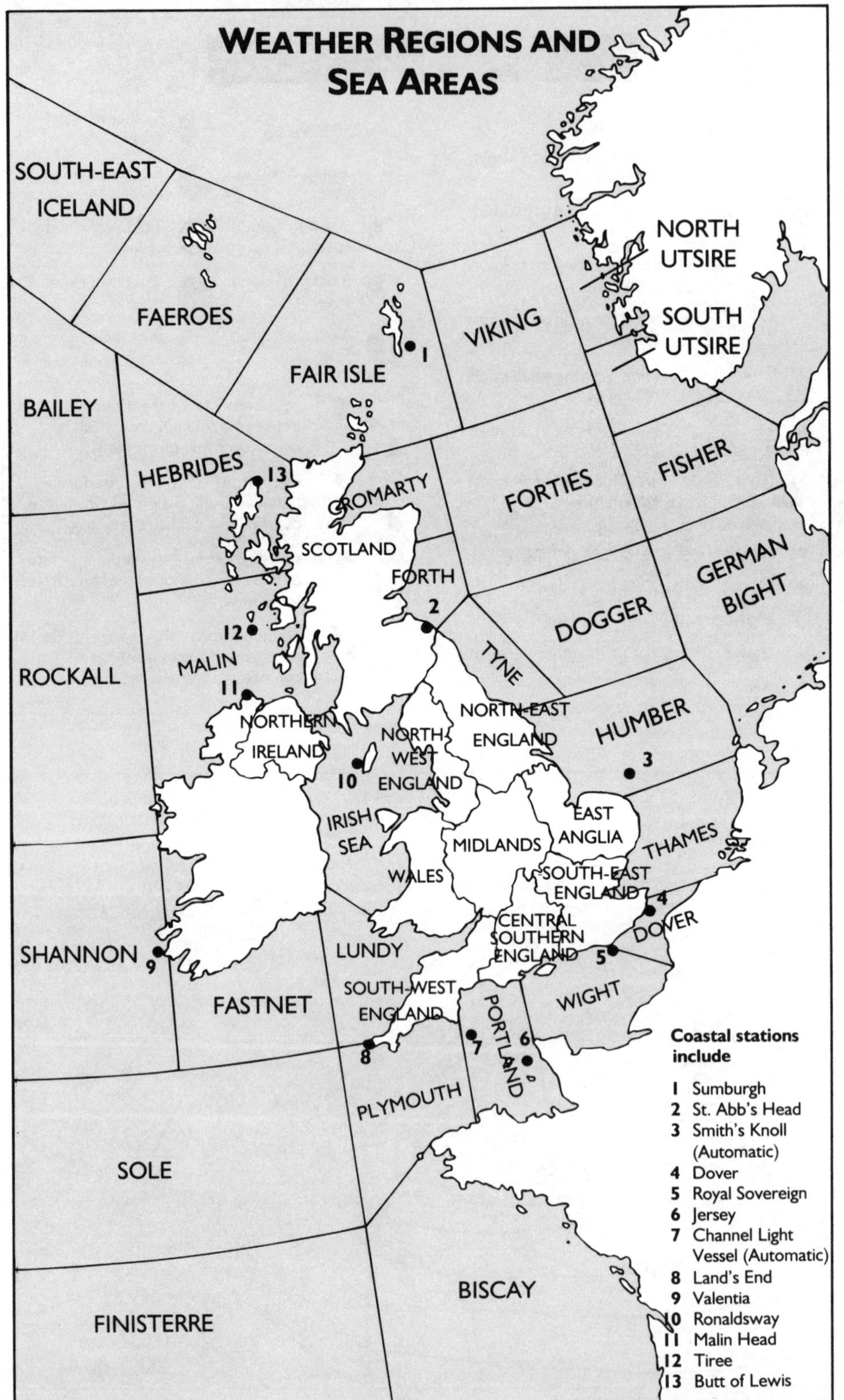
WEATHER REGIONS AND SEA AREAS
SOUTH-EAST ICELAND
FAEROES
FAIR ISLE
VIKING
NORTH UTSIRE
SOUTH UTSIRE
BAILEY
HEBRIDES
CROMARTY
FORTIES
FISHER
SCOTLAND
FORTH
GERMAN BIGHT
DOGGER
MALIN
ROCKALL
TYNE
NORTHERN IRELAND
NORTH-EAST ENGLAND
HUMBER
NORTH WEST ENGLAND
IRISH SEA
EAST ANGLIA
THAMES
MIDLANDS
WALES
SOUTH-EAST ENGLAND
DOVER
CENTRAL SOUTHERN ENGLAND
SHANNON
LUNDY
FASTNET
SOUTH-WEST ENGLAND
PORTLAND
WIGHT
PLYMOUTH
SOLE
FINISTERRE
BISCAY
Coastal stations include
1 Sumburgh
2 St. Abb's Head
3 Smith's Knoll (Automatic)
4 Dover
5 Royal Sovereign
6 Jersey
7 Channel Light Vessel (Automatic)
8 Land's End
9 Valentia
10 Ronaldsway
11 Malin Head
12 Tiree
13 Butt of Lewis

CLIMATOLOGY AND METEOROLOGY GLOSSARY

adiabatic lapse rate the rate at which air cools because of expansion when rising into regions of lower atmospheric pressure: 1 °C per 100 m (5·4 °F per 1000 ft) in clear air, less in cloud. Similar rates apply when air subsides into higher pressure and warms.

advection fog fog that forms when air cools to dew point by travelling across a surface that is already colder, such as sea or snow.

air frost air having a temperature of 0 °C (32 °F) or less.

air mass a huge volume of air that has acquired temperature and humidity characteristics from its region of origin.

anabatic wind an upslope wind created when air rises from a warming hillside and is replaced by cooler air from the valley.

anemometer an instrument for measuring wind speed.

anticyclone an area of high pressure, having a clockwise wind circulation in the northern hemisphere (anticlockwise in the southern).

aurora spectacular displays of light, mostly seen in latitudes higher than 70°. Caused by electrical solar discharges, they sometimes appear like waving curtains.

atmospheric pressure pressure due to the weight of the atmosphere. The pressure is less at higher altitudes than at sea level.

backing a change of wind direction in an anticlockwise manner, e.g. from W back to SW.

ball lightning a spherical glowing ball of electrically charged air.

banner cloud a cloud that streams downwind from a mountain peak, formed in the rising eddy behind the peak.

barometer an instrument for measuring atmospheric pressure.

barograph a barometer connected to a pen and rotating drum, so as to make a trace of changing pressure on a chart.

Beaufort scale numerals indicating the force and speed of the wind.

Berg wind a hot, dry wind from the interior of South Africa, blowing down the mountains and offshore.

black ice a transparent film of ice, taking the colour of the surface (e.g. a road) on which it forms.

blizzard a strong wind carrying falling snow. It gives bad visibility and causes drifting.

blood rain rain coloured with dust particles carried on upper winds; in Europe it is often reddish-brown with dust from the Sahara.

blue moon the moon appears blue when excessive dust in the atmosphere (e.g. after a volcanic eruption) scatters more red light than blue.

Bora a cold, usually dry, NE wind blowing from the mountains in Slovenia, Croatia and NE Italy.

Brickfielder a very hot NE wind in SE Australia. It blows in summer, carrying dust and sand.

brockenspectre the magnified shadow of an observer cast on to cloud or fog from high ground.

buoyancy an air current is buoyant if it is warmer and therefore lighter than its surroundings.

Buys Ballot's law a convention used to locate areas of low pressure. When an observer has his back to the wind, low pressure is on the left hand in the northern hemisphere and on the right hand in the southern.

Buran a strong NE wind in Russia and Central Asia, most frequent in winter. Known as Purga when carrying snow.

calm conditions in which there is no perceptible movement of air.

capcloud a cloud that sits above the summit of high ground, apparently stationary but in reality constantly forming on the windward edge and dispersing to leeward.

castellanus a cloud with a 'turretted' appearance, taller than it is wide. It often occurs at medium level, giving thunderstorms.

Celsius scale of temperature the temperature scale on which 0 °C denotes freezing level and 100 °C the boiling point of water. It is sometimes called Centigrade. See conversion tables p. 190.

Chinook a warm and dry wind that blows down the eastern side of the Rocky Mountains, USA.

climate a distinct pattern of weather found in a particular geographical zone.

cloud water drops or ice crytals held in suspension above the ground.

cloudburst a very heavy but short lived downpour of rain.

col an area of light variable wind, between two anticyclones and two depressions.

condensation the change of state of water vapour (an invisible gas) into water drops.

conduction the transference of heat from one substance to another with which it is in contact. The transfer is always from the warmer surface to the colder.

contrail short for 'condensation trail'. A contrail is produced by an aircraft flying at heights above about 6000 m (20,000 ft). It may be persistent if the atmosphere is already moist.

convection the transmission of heat by movement of fluid particles, like air or water. Air which warms near the ground becomes less dense and rises, and cold air takes its place, to warm in turn.

convection rain rain that falls from convection (cumulus) clouds.

cyclone a (roughly circular) pressure pattern in which pressure is lower at the centre than on the periphery. Wind circulation around the centre is anticlockwise in the northern hemisphere and clockwise in the southern. The name 'cyclone' is more specifically used for intense storms in the Indian Ocean, Arabian Sea and Bay of Bengal. Cyclones in middle and high latitudes are called depressions or lows.

deepening a low-pressure circulation is said to deepen if the atmospheric pressure at its centre continues to fall.

depression a low-pressure circulation in middle or high latitudes. See cyclone.

deposition the change of vapour directly to ice crystals when air becomes saturated and dew point is below 0 °C (32 °F). Hoar frost results.

dew water drops condensed directly from air when the air temperature falls below a dew point that is warmer than 0 °C (32 °F).

dew point the temperature at which air becomes saturated, holding the maximum amount of vapour possible. Further cooling results in condensation.

desert an area in which rainfall is insufficient to support vegetation.

diffraction the bending of light rays around particles or water drops having the same diameter as the wavelength of light.

doldrums a belt of light variable winds near the Equator, outside the range of the trade winds. They give frequent rain storms and squalls.

drizzle precipitation consisting of very small water drops, less than 0 ·5 mm (0 ·02 in) diameter.

drought a long period of dry weather.

equatorial climate the tropical rainy climate experienced in a belt on and on either side of the Equator.

evaporation the change of state of water into invisible vapour.

eye of the storm the centre of a hurricane or cyclone. It is characterized by well-broken cloud, no rain, light wind, and wild seas.

false cirrus ice-crystal cloud at the top of a cumulonimbus cloud, which is drawn along by the wind into the shape of an anvil.

Fata Morgana a complicated mirage. It usually occurs over water, and is most frequently seen over the Strait of Messina, Italy.

Fahrenheit scale of temperature the scale of temperature in which 32 °F denotes freezing level and 212 °F the boiling point of water. See conversion tables p. 190.

filling a depression is said to fill when the pressure at its centre starts to rise.

flaschenblitz an unusual form of lightning that strikes upwards from the top of a cumulonimbus.

fog a layer of very small waterdrops forming upwards from the surface of the sea or ground and restricting visibility. See also advection fog, radiation fog.

fog bow a bow formed – in the same way as a rainbow – when the Sun shines on to smaller fog drops. The coloured rays overlap to form a white bow with only the faintest tinge of colour.

Föhn wind a dry, warm wind blowing down a mountain under certain conditions, and warming by compression on descent.

freezing rain rain which falls into air whose temperature is below freezing, and then freezes to ice. Also called glazed frost.

freezing the change of state of water into ice, starting at a temperature of 0 °C (32 °F).

front the surface boundary between air masses of different temperature and humidity, which confront each other from different directions.

frost see air frost, hoar frost.

funnel cloud a whirling, tapering cloud that descends from the main base of a storm cloud.

gale a wind in excess of force 7 on the Beaufort Scale.

geostrophic wind a wind that blows horizontally, because of pressure differences, parallel to the isobars and according to Buys Ballot's Law.

glaciation (in meteorology) the sudden change of supercooled water drops into ice crystals within a cloud.

glazed frost the coating of ice over subfreezing surfaces from freezing rain.

graupel soft, partly melted hail.

glory a ring of light, like a corona, seen around a brockenspectre.

greenhouse effect the accumulation of heat in a greenhouse because glass is more transparent to incoming solar radiation than it is to outgoing radiation from the surface beneath the glass. In the atmosphere, carbon dioxide and various other gases perform the same function as glass, trapping heat near the Earth.

Gregale a strong NE wind blowing in the Mediterranean in the cooler months of the year.

gust a momentary increase in wind speed.

haboob any wind strong enough to raise sand into a sand storm, particularly in the Sudan.

hail ice pellets, created in strong vertical currents within cumulonimbus. Snow flakes or water drops are tossed up and down, alternately freezing and melting, until they are heavy enough to fall to the ground.

halo a ring of light around the Sun or Moon, caused by the refraction of light through ice-crystal cloud. A halo is reddish on the inside, bluish on the outside – the reverse order of corona colours.

Harmattan a dry and cool wind, blowing from the E or NE across NW Africa. It is often dust-laden and dry enough to wither vegetation.

hectopascal a unit of pressure – the equivalent to 1 millibar of pressure.

helm wind a strong, cold, often violent wind from the NE blowing down western slopes of Cumbria (England), mainly in late winter and spring.

high an area of high pressure or anticyclone. It brings fine weather in summer, but often frost or fog in winter. Winds blow clockwise in the northern hemisphere, anticlockwise in the southern.

hill fog low cloud covering high ground.

hoar frost the deposition of ice crystals directly out of the air when dew point is at or below 0 °C (32 °F) and the air is saturated with vapour.

humidity see relative humidity.

hurricane an intense low-pressure storm, affecting the West Indies and Gulf of Mexico. Similar storms in the Pacific are called typhoons. Circular winds around the centre follow Buys Ballot's Law and attain wind speeds in excess of 119 km/hr (64 knots or 74 mph).

hygrometer an instrument used for measuring the humidity of air.

inversion of temperature the conditions in which temperature increases with height in the atmosphere. This is a reverse of the normal situation in which temperature decreases with height.

isobar a line on a map joining places having equal atmospheric pressure (corrected to mean sea level) at a particular time.

isohyet a line on a map joining places having equal rainfall over a given period.

isotherm a line on a map joining places having equal temperature at the same time.

jet stream a strong but narrow belt of wind near the tropopause, blowing from west to east.

Karaburan a hot dusty NE wind in central Asia.

katabatic wind a downslope wind, created on otherwise calm nights with no cloud. The air nearest to the slope cools and flows downhill, to be replaced by warmer air from above the valley.

Khamsin a hot oppressive wind over Eygpt in early summer, often laden with desert sand.

knot a unit of speed used by sailors and aviators who have no fixed points of reference with which to measure distance against time. One knot denotes a speed of one nautical mile per hour – a nautical mile is the length of a minute of latitude, standardized as 1852m (6080 ft).

land breeze a wind blowing during the night from cooling land onto warmer sea.

latent heat heat emitted, without a change in temperature, when vapour condenses to water drops or water freezes to ice.

lenticular cloud a cloud shaped like a lens.

leeward the side opposite from the direction of the wind; the sheltered side.

Levanter a moist E wind in the eastern Mediterranean. Often strong, it is most frequent from June to October.

lightning a discharge of an electric field within a cloud, usually cumulonimbus. It may occur within the cloud, from one cloud to another, or between the cloud and the ground.

low the circulation around a centre of low pressure. (See cyclone.)

lull a momentary fall in wind speed.

mackerel sky a sky featuring cirrocumulus or altocumulus, arranged as a regular pattern resembling the scales of a mackerel.

mare's tails wispy cirrus clouds.

mean sea-level pressure the atmospheric pressure corrected for the height of a barometer above sea level, by adding an imaginary column of air as high as the level at which the barometer is situated.

melting the change of state from ice to water.

microclimate a climate found in a very restricted area such as a valley, garden or even a room.

millibar an international unit by which atmospheric pressure is measured. Recently it was replaced by the hectopascal. 1 millibar (mb) = 1 hectopascal (hPa) where 1000 mb is the pressure exerted by 750·06 mm/29·53 in of mercury at 0 °C.

mirage an optical illusion, caused by the bending of light when passing through adjacent layers of air that have different density. An inferior mirage is seen below the real object when light passes through very hot air, shimmering like water because of convection. A superior image is seen above the real object when light bends downwards through very cold dense air.

mist very small water drops suspended in air near the ground, reducing visibilty.

Mistral a cold dry NW or N wind, funnelling down the Rhône Valley before reaching the south coast of France.

monsoon a wind that changes direction markedly according to season, akin to a sea breeze – for example the seasonal winds of south Asia that blow from the SW in summer bringing heavy rainfall. The term 'monsoon' is also applied to the rainy season during which these winds blow.

nacreous clouds clouds having the appearance of mother-of-pearl. They form in the stratosphere, often in mountainous areas, and are seen after sunset.

noctilucent clouds wispy, bluish clouds, resembling cirrus, very high in the atmosphere - usually at an altitude of 80–85 km (50–55 miles). They are probably dust or ice particles.

occlusion the surface boundary between fresh cold air and modified cool air ahead. In effect, it is a cold front that has overtaken a warm front and lifted the warm air off the ground.

orographic rain rain that is caused entirely by forced lifting of moist air over high ground.

Pampero a very cold wind which blows over the Andes across from Argentina and Uruguay to the Atlantic.

parhelion a mock sun, sometimes called a sun dog, caused by refraction of light through ice crystals that have their axes aligned vertically. There may be two parhelia, one either side of the sun and at the same elevation as the sun.

precipitation a composite term that includes rain, drizzle, snow, sleet or hail, all of which fall from clouds.

permafrost that part of the soil which remains permanently frozen in cold climates.

pressure tendency the rate of change of atmospheric pressure. A rapid fall indicates deteriorating weather, a rapid rise indicates a temporary improvement, and a slow persistent rise a developing anticyclone.

prevailing wind the most frequent wind direction to affect a particular area.

Purga a strong NE wind in parts of Russia and Central Asia, often raising snow from the ground to give a blizzard.

radiation fog condensation within a layer of air near the ground that is cooling because of radiation heat loss from the Earth under clear skies. Light wind stirs saturated air into fog.

rain precipitation of water drops larger than 0·5 mm (0·02 in) in diameter.

rainbow a coloured arc of light in the sky, caused by refraction and internal reflection of light in raindrops. A rainbow can only be seen by an observer with his back to the Sun and facing distant rain. A primary rainbow has violet on the inside and red outside; a secondary rainbow, outside the primary, has colours in the reverse order.

rainfall the depth of all forms of precipitation for a given period as measured in a rain gauge.

rain shadow an area where rainfall is reduced because of protection by high ground from the prevailing, rain-bearing wind.

refraction the change of direction of light rays when passing through transparent media (water drops, ice crystals, air) that have different densities.

regelation the refreezing of water that has been temporarily melted because of pressure exerted on it.

relative humidity a measure of the actual vapour in air, as a percentage of the total amount that is required to saturate the air at that temperature.

ridge of high pressure isobars with exaggerated curvature extending from an anticyclone.

rime a crust of ice crystals that forms when supercooled water drops in fog make contact with solid objects whose temperature is less than 0 °C (32 °F). In calm air, rime builds up all around objects; in a light wind, mainly on the windward side.

Roaring Forties the region between latitudes 40° and 50 °S where strong westerly winds prevail.

St Elmo's fire a discharge of static electricity from the masts of ships, wings of aircraft, etc, when the electrical field is strong. It is characterized by a bluish glow, often accompanied by a crackling noise.

scud shreds of low stratus below the main base of cloud. They appear to move very fast because they are so close to the ground.

sea breeze a daytime wind that blows from the sea to the shore, to replace air rising in thermals over the land.

sea fog an advection fog formed when warm air travels and condenses over colder sea.

secondary depression a depression that forms within the circulation of another depression, usually in a trough. It often develops at the expense of the original depression.

Seistan a strong N wind in summer in eastern Iran and Afghanistan, carrying dust and sand.

Shamal a hot, dry, dusty NW wind that blows in summer in Iraq and the Persian Gulf.

shower precipitation from a convection cloud, often heavy but usually short-lived.

Sirocco or **Scirocco** a hot dry S wind on the north coast of Africa, blowing from the Sahara.

sleet a mixture of snow and rain.

snow precipitation of ice crystals, latched together as feathery flakes.

smog (short for 'smoke-fog') fog that is heavily polluted.

Southerly Buster a sudden cold and strong S wind in southeast Australia.

squall a sudden strong wind, lasting only a few minutes. It often comes from a different direction from that which has just been experienced.

stable atmosphere the atmospheric condition in which a rising current of air soon becomes non-buoyant (i.e. colder than its surroundings) and ceases to rise. In such conditions, cumulus clouds remain small or do not form.

surface wind a wind that blows within 10 m (30 ft) of the surface of ground or sea.

sunshine the visible light received from the Sun.

sunshine recorder a glass sphere used to record hours of sunshine. It is mounted so as to focus the rays from the Sun and burn a trace upon a paper chart.

sun pillar a column of light, above or below the sun when it is low on the horizon, caused by reflection of light from the base of big storms. The intense vertical current at the centre is capable of much damage. See also funnel cloud.

trade winds are so named because as a belt of regular winds they were of benefit to sailing trading vessels. They blow on the equatorial side of the subtropical high-pressure belts, NE winds in the northern hemisphere, SE winds in the southern.

Tramontana a cool, dry N wind blowing across the Mediterranean coast of Spain.

tropopause the upper boundary of the troposphere.

tropical cyclone an intense low-pressure storm originating over tropical seas. It is called a hurricane in the Atlantic, and a typhoon in the Pacific.

trough of low pressure isobars with exaggerated curvature extending from a depression. It often brings cloud and rain.

turbulence the fluctuation of wind speed and direction. At ground level, turbulence is mainly due to surface friction.

typhoon the name given to a hurricane in the Pacific.

unstable atmosphere atmospheric conditions in which a rising current of air can remain buoyant (i.e. warmer than its surroundings) to great heights. It is characterized by the development of tall cumulonimbus.

veering a change of wind direction in a clockwise manner, e.g. from N to NE.

virga trails of precipitation falling from a cloud base but evaporating before reaching ground.

visibility the greatest distance at which an object can be seen with the naked eye.

warm front the surface boundary between a mass of warm air and cooler air ahead, over which the warm air slides.

waterspout a tornado that occurs over the sea, sucking up water from the sea.

wet-and-dry bulb thermometer a thermometer used for measuring relative humidity. Two identical thermometers are mounted alongside, one with its bulb wrapped in muslin kept moist by a wick dipping into water. Evaporation from the muslin uses up heat, so that the wet bulb thermometer reads lower than the dry, except when air is saturated and they read the same. Mathematical tables enable humidity and dew point to be obtained from the two readings.

whirlwind a local column of rotating and rising air, originating at ground level. They usually occur in hot weather when there is no cloud.

whiteout a visibility condition, in a snow storm or over extensive snow surfaces, where natural contours or landmarks are indistinguishable from each other or from cloud.

Williwaw a cold and strong downslope wind in Alaska.

wind air that is moving owing to pressure differences between places. Wind direction is desribed by the direction from which it blows, e.g. NW or 315° blows from the northwest towards the southeast.

wind vane a device for registering wind direction. The shorter arm, usually an arrow, points to the wind direction, while the broader fin blows downwind.

The Environment

GLOBAL WARMING

The greenhouse effect
The planet Earth is showing signs of gradually becoming warmer, a process known as the greenhouse effect.

Scientists have discovered that the average temperature of the Earth's atmosphere has increased by 0.5°C (0.9 °F) since accurate records began in about 1860.

Global warming
This may seem to be a very small increase in absolute terms, but the *rate* of temperature change - which is now faster than at any time in the past - is significant. This trend is called *global warming.*

Greenhouse gases
The main reason for the greenhouse effect is a substantial increase in the so-called *greenhouse gases* such as carbon dioxide, methane, nitrous oxide, chlorofluorocarbons (CFCs) and, most recently, of benzine in the atmosphere.

To understand how the greenhouse gases cause the rise in temperature we must understand the vertical structure of the atmosphere.

Each of the layers of the atmosphere has its own distinct chemical and physical properties. For example, in the troposphere the temperature cools rapidly. It is in the troposphere that most of our daily weather is formed and it is here too that most of the pollutants released into the atmosphere by human activities accumulate. The stratosphere is important as it is the layer in which atmospheric ozone is found.

The gaseous composition of the atmosphere allows approximately one half of the total energy from the Sun (solar radiation) to pass into the lower atmosphere, thus warming the planet.

Eventually, the incoming energy - which has arrived as short-wave, intensive radiation - is reflected back into space as long-wave dissipated energy. In this way, the average temperature of the Earth remains relatively constant at +14 °C.

Greenhouse gases restrict the loss of the long-wave radiation and, as a result, the Earth's atmosphere is warming.

The atmosphere comprises a complex mixture of gases and water vapour.

Component gases of the lower atmosphere

Gas	*Volume of the lower atmosphere*
nitrogen	78.084%
oxygen	20.946%
argon	0.934%
carbon dioxide	0.033%
neon	0.00182%
helium	0.00053%
krypton	0.00012%
xenon	0.00009%
hydrogen	0.00005%
nitrous oxide	0.00005%
methane	0.00002%

Since the beginning of the Industrial Revolution (from c. 1750), the composition of the atmosphere has been gradually changing. Most significantly, carbon dioxide has increased by 28%, from 265 parts per million (p.p.m.) in 1850 to 354 p.p.m. in 1989, and is predicted to rise to 600 p.p.m. by 2050.

Carbon dioxide is currently responsible for 57% of the global warming trend, with 80% of the gas originating from the burning of fossil fuels (coal, petroleum, etc.).

Carbon dioxide production
The per capita carbon dioxide output for the 15 top producing carbon dioxide countries (1991 figures) is given in the following table.

Country	*Tonnes of carbon dioxide per capita*
Iraq	28
USA	19
Canada	15.5
Russia/plus former Soviet republics*	12
Germany	11.5
UK	10
Japan	8
Poland	7.5
South Africa	7
Italy	7
France	6.5
South Korea	6
Mexico	4
China	3
India	1.5

THE RIO DE JANEIRO CONFERENCE

The environmental consequences of events such as ozone depletion, climatic change, deforestation, species extinction and soil erosion prompted the UN to convene a UN Conference on Environment and Development (UNCED) in Rio de Janeiro, Brazil, in June 1992.

The conference attracted a larger number of heads of state and of government, and other senior politicians, than any other conference. A large number of declarations and action plans were presented. These can be summarized as follows:

1. Climatic Change Convention
2. Biological Diversity Convention
3. Statement of Forest Principles
4. The Rio Declaration
5. Agenda 21
6. Mechanism for Financial Assistance for Developing Countries
7. Establishment of a Sustainable Development Commission

A principle outcome of the Rio Conference has been Agenda 21, best described as an action plan for the remaining years of the 1990s and the first decades of the 21st century. It attempts to halt and reverse the effects of environmental degradation and to encourage environmentally sound and sustainable development in all countries.

Relative contributions to the greenhouse effect
It has been calculated that the relative contributions to the greenhouse effect in the 1980s were as follows:

carbon monoxide	57%
methane	17%
CFCs	10%
surface ozone	11%
nitrous oxide	5%

The effects of industry
From about 1950, the chemical composition of the atmosphere has changed more rapidly. Industry has been responsible for the release of huge quantities of sulphur dioxide, hydrogen sulphide and nitrous oxides, all the result of burning fossil fuels.

The effects of agriculture
Agriculture has contributed large amounts of methane gas. Rice (paddy) fields contribute 115 million tonnes of methane every year, and 1.2 billion domesticated farm animals (particularly cattle), through the expulsion of intestinal gas, add a further 73 million tonnes. Methane comprises only 2 p.p.m. of the atmosphere, but its effectiveness as a greenhouse gas is about 30 times that of carbon dioxide, and its volume has increased by more than 400% over the last century.

The effects of transport systems
The transportation systems of the world, especially aviation and motor vehicles, are responsible for the release of vast quantities of nitrous oxides, carbon dioxide, lead and benzine into the atmosphere. In the USA, all forms of transport consume 63% of all petroleum used each year. In Western Europe, this figure is 44%. In many countries, efforts are being made to increase the energy efficiency of transportation systems, and some progress has been made to reduce the reliance on the private motor car. In California, for example, legislation is being prepared to reduce the use of private cars by 1% per annum for the next 20 years.

The extent of global warming
The Intergovernmental Panel on Climatic Change (IPCC) has concluded that, based on a 'business-as-usual' scenario (no change), mean global temperatures will rise by 0.3°C per decade. By 2030 an increase of more than 1°C will have occurred and by 2100 the increase will exceed 3°C.

The prediction of future planetary warming is a highly controversial subject. Some experts claim that the rise in average temperature is nothing more than a natural fluctuation in the long-term history of our planet. To support this view, they claim that the existence of the Ice Age which ended about 10,000 years ago is evidence of a cooling process, whereas the current increase in temperature is merely the reverse of this trend. However, most scientists now recognize the current rate of temperature increase to be beyond the normal range and ascribe the increase to human factors rather than to natural causes. Supporters of the global-warming theory would argue that it has been the pollution produced by domestic, agricultural and industrial activities that has caused major changes to the atmosphere. They state that unless action is taken to reduce the release of the greenhouse gases then further warming of the atmosphere will occur.

CFCs
To combat the threat of global warming an agreement, known as the Montréal Protocol, was reached by representatives of the main industrialized nations meeting in Montréal, Canada, in 1987. Under the terms of the Protocol, the use of CFCs was to be halved by 1998. However, by June 1990 evidence had shown that even more stringent targets were required and a total ban on their use in the developed world by the year 2000 was agreed. World consumption of certain CFCs, notably CFC 11, 12 and 113, is now 40% lower than in 1986, achieved by the development of alternatives to CFCs.

The alternatives, such as HCFCs and HFCs, contain hydrogen in their structure and, unlike CFCs, have a short atmospheric life and are destroyed in the lower atmosphere by natural processes. HFCs contain no chlorine and therefore do not contribute to stratospheric ozone depletion. The ozone depletion potential (ODP) of CFCs is classified as 1.0, whereas the ODP for various HCFCs ranges from 0.02 to 0.11 and for HFCs is zero. The CFC replacements are approximately four times as expensive as the substances they replace.

The impact of global warming
It is thought that the impact of global warming on the planet would be unevenly distributed. The southern hemisphere, with its extensive oceans, would suffer less increase in temperature, as the seas would be able to absorb more heat than the land masses of the northern hemisphere. The Arctic region may become, on average, 8°C (13.4°F) warmer than at present by 2100. As a result, some of the polar ice sheet would melt, causing a rise in sea levels of 20-30 cm (8-12 in) by the middle of the 21st century, with predictions of a 60-100 cm (24-40 in) rise by 2100. This would threaten many low-lying areas with inundation, including the island nations of Kiribati, Tuvalu and the Maldives, as well as much of Bangladesh and parts of some important cities including New York, London, St Petersburg, Alexandria, Rotterdam and Venice.

Climatic change
Profound climatic changes could also result. According to some meteorologists, the climatic belts of the northern hemisphere would be likely to move north, bringing a desert climate to the Mediterranean region and to California, Texas and Florida, and a Mediterranean-type climate to much of north-western Europe. Storminess could also increase and rainfall totals could rise by as much as 15%, particularly in the high latitudes.

The ozone layer
The ozone layer is a naturally occurring zone found in the stratosphere, situated between 10-15 km (6-9 mi) above the Earth's surface. Ozone (O_3) is a natural component of the atmosphere. It is classified as a trace gas with a concentration of about 0.2 parts per billion (p.p.b.). A highly reactive and unstable gas, it is formed by the recombination of pairs of oxygen (O_2) atoms in the presence of intense solar radiation (mainly ultraviolet energy).

The main function of the ozone layer is to act as a shield against ultraviolet (UV) radiation from the Sun. In 1977, the British Antarctic Survey reported a thinning of the ozone layer over Antarctica. Measurements in the spring of 1991 showed a reduction of almost 50% in the ozone level.

The depletion is caused by certain highly stable synthetic chemicals, which are the product of the petrochemical industry. These include chlorofluorocarbons (CFCs) used as propellants in aerosol spray cans, as refrigerant gases, solvent cleaners and in the manufacture of foam-blown plastics, and halons, used in fire-fighting equipment. These gases rise into the atmosphere, where they become partly decomposed into methyl chloroform and carbon tetrachloride. These gases become concentrated above the polar areas in the stratosphere and actively destroy the ozone molecules, thus allowing increased levels of ultraviolet light to reach the ground.

Exposure to UV light causes damage to crops, kills plankton and fish larvae, and can cause burning of the skin (sunburn) in humans. Severe sunburn produces temporary soreness, dehydration and sickness. In the longer term it can result in skin cancers, and is estimated to cause 100,000 additional eye cataracts worldwide. Epidemiologists in many hospitals in northern Europe have recorded a doubling in the incidence of skin cancers in recent years, while in Australia, doctors have claimed that a 1% decrease in the ozone layer results in a 3% increase in non-melanoma skin cancers in humans. As a result of the Montréal Protocol, CFCs and halons will be phased out by the year 2000, but so many CFCs already exist in the atmosphere that the concentration will continue to rise to 6 p.p.b. by 2000 before declining.

Photo-chemical smog

A second, and quite separate, environmental problem associated with ozone is the build-up of ground-level ozone to produce photo-chemical smog. This hazard - first recorded in Los Angeles, California - now occurs worldwide in industrial cities. The amount of ground level ozone has doubled over Europe this century. A combination of oxides of nitrogen and volatile organic compounds in the presence of sunlight causes the formation of ground level ozone. These substances are almost entirely the result of human activity, for example motor-vehicle exhausts, and the chemical paint and ceramics industries.

The problem becomes most serious in summer, when stationary air masses allow the build-up of high concentrations of oxides of nitrogen and volatile organic compounds. The World Health Organization has set a safety limit of 120 p.p.b., though this figure is regularly exceeded and has reached a peak of 600 p.p.b. in California. (In Britain a maximum of 250 p.p.b. was reached in southern England in 1976.) Concentrations of 300 p.p.b. are sufficient to cause irritation to respiratory tissue and the eyes of humans, while even lower concentrations severely damage citrus fruits. It is estimated that agricultural output in Europe and North America is 5-10% lower than expected owing to exposure to ozone.

The problem of oxides of nitrogen and volatile organic compounds is a serious one, but it is at present overshadowed by the international concern with the depletion of the ozone layer.

DROUGHT AND DESERTIFICATION

Nearly one half of the countries of the world face problems of drought. A drought occurs when an area of land does not receive enough water to sustain life at the existing levels. Droughts may be due to lower than normal amounts of precipitation, to higher evaporation as a result of warmer temperatures than normal, or to a combination of these two factors.

Drought years appear to occur in cycles. From records of the Nile floods over the last 2000 years, a cycle of varying length is apparent. In the well-known Biblical story, the pharaoh of Egypt dreamed of seven ears of grain, fat and healthy, followed by seven ears of shrivelled and thin grain. This symbolized a cycle of seven damp years followed by seven years of drought. In recent decades, the years between 1968 and 1973 were drought years, from 1973 until 1979 adequate moisture occurred, while in 1980 another cycle of drought began.

Between 1982 and 1986 much of Africa was devastated by severe drought, which resulted in widespread human deprivation. Some 10 million people were forced to leave their homes in search of food and water. China, India and North America all suffered major droughts in the 1980s. In the summer of 1988 about 43% of the central states of the USA suffered a drought of intensity equal to that of the 'Dust Bowl' years (1926-34). The grain harvest in 1988 was 31%

WATER MANAGEMENT APPROACHES

Input Approaches

Increase the usable supply by:

1. Building dams and creating lake reservoirs.
2. Diverting water from one region to another; draining swamps; and diverting rivers.
3. Tapping ground water.
4. Desalting seawater and purifying degraded water.
5. Towing icebergs from the Antarctic.
6. Controlling' the weather, for example by seeding clouds.

Control the pollution of existing supplies by preventing or limiting the addition of certain chemicals.

Redistribute population by:

1. Encouraging people to live in areas with adequate water.
2. Restricting population levels in areas with water problems (deserts or flood plains).
3. Decrease population growth.

Output Approaches

Decrease evaporation and plant transpiration.

Use better drainage for irrigated agriculture to minimize the salt build-up in soils.

Treat polluted waters before returning them to their sources.

Dispose of wastes by burial on land or sea or by injection into deep wells.

Reclaim waste water to allow multiple re-use.

WORLD WATER REQUIREMENTS BY AD 2000

Human consumption of water has increased 35 times in the last 300 years. The rate of consumption is increasing by some 4-8% p.a.

The figures in the following table are given in cubic kilometres.

Water use	Total required	Amount returned as waste (%)	Amount required by 2000 (% increase)
agricultural	2236	559 (25%)	2261 (19%)
domestic	259	155 (60%)	unknown
industry	745	640 (86%)	1000 (34%)

CONTAMINATED DRINKING WATER

A number of common diseases are transmitted to humans through the use of contaminated drinking water.

Type of organism	Diseases
bacteria	typhoid fever cholera bacterial dysentery enteritis
viruses	infectious hepatitis polio
parasitic protozoa	amoebic dysentery giardia
parasitic worms	schistosomiasis

See also pp. 163-70 (Diseases).

AVERAGE DAILY USE OF WATER IN THE UNITED STATES (litres)

Direct personal use

Shower (5 minutes)	100
Shaving/washing hands	14
Washing clothes	75
Cooking	30
Washing dishes	38
Toilet (4 flushes)	48
House cleaning	30
Sprinkling lawn (800 m^2)	300

Daily average: 635 litres

Indirect agricultural use

One egg	150
One ear of corn	300
One of loaf of bread	570
One kilo of flour	625
One kilo beef	20,800

Daily average: 2300 litres

Indirect industrial use

Cooling water for electric power plants (per person per day)	2700
Sunday paper	1060
One kilo synthetic rubber	2500
One kilo aluminium	8340
One kilo steel	300
One litre petrol	7-2
One motor car	380,000

Daily average: 4 000 litres

Total daily average: 6 935 litres per person

down on that of the previous year and financial losses reached $15 billion, making the drought the costliest natural disaster in US history.

The occurrence of major droughts appears to be linked to weather changes which affect up to 66% of the globe. Changes in atmospheric pressure-patterns combine at irregular intervals of between two and seven years to produce modifications to the flow of ocean currents in the southern hemisphere.

The Pacific Ocean heats up between Papua New Guinea and Micronesia, resulting in the easterly flow of a powerful warm current called *El Niño* ('the boy child'). It combines with other climatic changes over the southeastern Pacific to bring about the irregularity in ocean currents called the Southern Oscillation, which causes major weather disturbances lasting up to two years. On these occasions, serious droughts have occurred in India, Australia, Africa and Indonesia.

Prolonged drought in much of Western Europe in 1989-90 increased awareness of the need for proper water management. The options most frequently proposed are summarized on page 115.

Desertification

About 35% of the planet is classified as arid or semi-arid. True deserts - which have less than 250 mm (about 10 in) of rain a year - can be divided into cold deserts near the Earth's poles and hot deserts between about 20° and 30° latitude north and south of the Equator. Hot deserts cover about 20% of the land between the Tropics. Semi-arid areas receive up to 500 mm (about 20 in) a year. See also p.92.

CHEMICAL CONTAMINATION OF DRINKING WATER AND RELATED HEALTH HAZARDS

Inorganic material

Contaminant	*Effects*
arsenic	cancer of the liver, of the kidneys and of the blood, and also cancer of the nervous system
cadmium	kidney damage, anaemia, high blood pressure
lead	headaches, anaemia, nervous disorders, birth abnormalities, mental retardation especially in the case of children
mercury	damage to the central nervous system and to the kidneys
nitrates	respiratory problems particularly to the new born and to the chronically sick

Synthetic organic substances

benzine	anaemia, leukemia, chromosome damage
carbon	cancer of the liver, the tetrachloride kidneys, and the lungs, damage to the central nervous system
dionysian	skin disorders, cancer and genetic malfunction
ethylene	cancer and male sterility
PCBs	liver, kidney and lung damage

WATER POLLUTION

Rivers and seas have been used for the dumping of wastes since earliest times. The constant flow of rivers and the tidal movements of seas have been used as a natural sink to disperse all forms of wastes. Clean, fresh water is vital for the survival of humans. The assessment of water quality depends upon its intended use. The main forms of pollution are:

1. Disease-carrying agents (bacteria, viruses, parasitic worms). These kill an estimated 25,000 people each day, mainly in the less developed countries.

2. Sediment and suspended matter (soil, silt and partially treated sewage).

3. Radioactive substances (from the nuclear power industry).

4. Organic chemicals (oil, plastics, pesticides, cleaning solvents, detergents).

5. Inorganic plant nutrients (nitrates and phosphates washed from agricultural land).

6. Waste heat (in the form of cooling water from power stations and industry).

River pollution

Rivers can normally dilute small amounts of pollution quickly and safely. When overloaded with pollutants, or when the volume of water is reduced during summer drought, dilution becomes impossible and pollution occurs.

In Britain, the National Rivers Authority (NRA) is responsible for the prevention of water pollution. It uses a five-point classification scheme to monitor pollution (see box). Even slightly polluted water is damaging for human health, especially so if consumed over a long time span (see the accompanying table).

Because of the health risk, most developed countries have comprehensive laws and regulations concerning water quality. Fines are imposed on persons or industries found guilty of polluting water courses. Much pollution occurs accidentally from leaching of nitrates, phosphates and pesticides from agricultural land, or from leaks in underground storage tanks (petrol and oil).

NRA RIVER AND CANAL WATER CLASSIFICATION

Class		*Current potential use*
1A	Good	Water of high quality suitable for potable supply and with high amenity value
1B		Of lower quality than 1A but usable for substantially the same purposes.
2	Fair	Waters suitable for potable supply after advanced treatment. Medium amenity quality.
3	Poor	Waters polluted to an extent that fish are absent. Usable for low-grade industrial abstraction. Of considerable use if cleaned up.
4	Bad	Grossly polluted waters which cause nuisance value

In less developed countries and in Eastern Europe most rivers are severely polluted. Over 66% of India's rivers are polluted and 90% of child deaths are attributable to water-borne disease. In Poland, almost 50% of the nation's water is unfit even for industrial use - 90% of Poland's river water is too polluted to drink and it has been forecast that by the year 2000 this figure will be almost 100%.

Pollution of the seas

The oceans receive not only pollution carried in by rivers, but also direct inputs of sewage, oil spills from tankers and offshore drilling platforms, and industrial waste deliberately dumped at sea. During the 1980s ocean dumping around the world amounted to more than 172 million tonnes of solid waste each year. About 80% of this was dredged materials, taken from rivers to maintain shipping channels. EU legislation bans the dumping of this material into European waters after 1995.

About 20% of the solid waste dumped at sea is sewage sludge, a lethal mixture of toxic chemicals, infectious materials and settled solids from sewage treatment plants.

In Britain, 16% of the sewage output is still discharged, untreated, to the sea. In Europe, as a whole, 28% of all sewage is released in its untreated form to rivers and seas. New stricter standards were introduced in 1992 resulting in only 17 British beaches gaining the (EC) Blue Flag, compared to 35 in 1991. Water samples must contain fewer than 100 faecal coliforms/100 ml of water compared wih the 2000 previously permitted.

An estimated 2 million sea birds and over 100,000 marine mammals die each year by poisoning or by becoming entangled in plastic netting.

Prevention of water pollution as well as cleaning up past pollution will be expensive. Britain spent £13.7 billion between 1989 and 1992 on new sewage plants. The UN has calculated that it would cost $5 billion to provide treatment plants for Mediterranean sewage output. In the USA, greater use of technology is seen as the way to reduce water pollution. This method is called MACT (Maximum Available Control Technology). Many ecologists believe that reliance on this approach, the so-called 'technological fix', will become too expensive and has no guarantee of success.

As an alternative, low cost treatment methods have been developed for use in developing countries. These include filtering sewage through marshes and land fill sites and, in Calcutta, settled sewage is used as a feedstock for fish (mainly carp), which can be used as a source of human food.

NUCLEAR DUMPING AT SEA

Between 1946 and 1982, 46 petabecquerels of dumped, packaged and liquid nuclear waste was dumped in more than 50 sites, mainly in the northern Atlantic and Pacific Oceans. Most waste came from civil and military power stations and reprocessing plants. In the 1980s, a moratorium on dumping nuclear wastes at sea was established by trade unions and by diplomatic concern.

LAND POLLUTION

Since earliest times humans have been responsible for polluting the planet. As the population grew and industrial growth became greater, then so too did the amount and complexity of pollution.

Many old industrial areas bear the scars of extractive industries (coal mining, brick works, china clay quarries). Land left standing without a present use as a result of past activity and which has been physically despoiled or disfigured is called *derelict land*. Often, in the past, lower standards of pollution control were exercised. Formal land-use planning was largely unknown in Europe and North America until 1945, and industrial land use was intermingled with residential and agricultural landscapes. As a result many degraded landscapes could be found, especially in old industrial areas.

Now, derelict sites have become the focal point of rehabilitation projects in which wastes are made safe by burial or by detoxification, and the land reused for a new purpose.

Governments of the developed world now recognize that the rehabilitation of polluted land areas requires a completely integrated approach. It involves preventing further pollution at source, minimizing the risk of harm to human health, applying the most appropriate and technologically advanced solutions to restoring degraded areas, and managing them by means of sustainable land-use policies. The principle of *integrated pollution control*, in which air, water and land pollution become the total responsibility of one environmental management body, has been adopted in many developed countries.

Waste disposal

A major problem facing developed countries throughout the world is the disposal of domestic and industrial rubbish. In the UK, industry produces about 100 million tonnes of waste each year, of which about 27 million tonnes are recycled and valued at over £2 billion. British domestic sources produce a further 20 million tonnes, of which only 1 million tonnes is recycled. Modern waste contains a high proportion of non-degradable products - plastics, metals and chemicals. These items can cause long-term contamination if disposed of incorrectly.

Packaging and packaging waste presents a special problem. In the EC, some 50 million tonnes of package waste were generated in 1991, of which only 19% was recycled. By 2002, EU regulations will ensure that 60% of packaging materials must be made of recycled materials, and 90% of all packaging waste must be recycled.

Traditionally, rubbish has been burned, dumped into disused quarries, or dumped at sea. None of these methods is wholly acceptable today. Burning can generate highly toxic gases, few old quarries remain to be filled in, and dumping at sea has created major pollution of bathing waters.

National and local authorities in many countries are encouraging the recycling of materials, the prevention of waste and the conservation of new resources. Waste minimization is being achieved by better design, longer design life and improved potential for re-use. The public is also becoming more educated in environmental issues.

AIR POLLUTION

Any particulate matter or gaseous material which accumulates in the atmosphere to such proportions that it causes harm to humans, other animals, vegetation, or damage to building materials can be described as an *air pollutant*.

Nowadays, air pollution is primarily the result of human activity, but it is often overlooked that natural sources of air pollution can sometimes exceed the quantity of human-produced pollutants. In June 1991, Mount Pinatubo, in the Philippines, emitted about 18

A CLASSIFICATION OF AIR-POLLUTION TYPES

Particulate matter

Human derived	*Naturally derived*
smoke	volcanic dust, smoke and ash
ash	sea-salt particles
grit	
soot	
dust	
liquid droplets (acid deposition)	
particles of tramac and rubber	

Gaseous pollution

Human derived	*Naturally derived*
gases from combustion	volcanic gases and water vapour
	gases from organic decomposition

COMPARISONS OF SOURCES OF SELECTED POLLUTANTS, EMISSIONS AND EXPOSURES

Pollutant	Major emission source	Major exposure sources
benzine	industry; automobiles	smoking
tetrachloroethylene	dry-cleaning shops	dry-cleaned clothes
chloroform	sewage treatment plants	showers
p-dichlorobenzene	chemical manufacturing	air deodorizers
particulates	industry; automobiles; home heating	smoking
carbon monoxide	automobiles	driving; gas stoves
nitrogen dioxide	industry; automobiles	gas stoves

million tonnes of sulphur dioxide, equivalent to all the sulphur dioxide produced in the USA during the course of a single year.

Pollutants from human activitity have attracted notoriety because of their chemical complexity, their reactivity once released to the atmosphere and their intercation with all other living components of the biosphere.

Particles

Particulate matter (comprising smoke, soot, dust and liquid droplets) is normally considered to be the simpler form of air pollution as it can be removed from the atmosphere more easily than gaseous material. All particulate matter, even the finest aerosols, have a mass greater than air, and thus in still air will gravitate out of the atmosphere.

Large particles, over 10 micrometers in size, normally fall out of the atmosphere within five or six hours of their release from source.

The finest particles, smaller than 1 micrometer, can remain in the air for several months, or even years. They are also the most damaging as they can enter the lungs of animals and cause illness. Soot, rubber and tarmac particles are known to be carcinogenic to human lung tissue.

Vegetation surfaces can become coated with fine dusts, thus reducing their ability to photosynthesis.

Gaseous pollution

Gaseous pollution (comprising mainly sulphur dioxide, nitrogen dioxides and carbon dioxide) presents a major problem for modern societies and exacts enormous health and environmental costs. Gases are usually invisible but, once released, can be transported hundreds of kilometres and react with many other atmospheric components to produce secondary pollutants. It is these products rather than the primary pollutants that are usually responsible for vegetation damage and respiratory illness in humans.

Damage caused by air pollution

So severe is the damage caused by air pollution that stringent legislation has been introduced by many governments, particularly in the developed world. Overall, urban air quality has improved during the 1980s and early 1990s, especially for the traditional pollutants such as sulphur dioxide, which has fallen by up to 64% throughout Europe and North America.

The UN estimated in 1987 that 70% of the world's population lived in cities where the level of suspended particles exceeded the World Health Organization guidelines, and 66% of the world's urban population are subjected to sulphur dioxide levels above WHO guidelines.

New air pollutants

New air pollutants are continually emerging, and for these emission-control measures must be found. For example, the increasing use of unleaded petrol, while resulting in a reduction of air-borne lead of up to 50%, has been accompanied by an increase in the amount of benzine accumulating in the atmosphere. It has increased with an alarming rapidity, especially as it is a greater hazard to the atmosphere than CFCs.

ACID PRECIPITATION (ACID RAIN)

Both 'wet' and 'dry' forms of acidic fallout can occur as a result of the combustion of large quantities of fossil fuels.

Coal-fired power stations and other industrial processes emit sulphur dioxide and nitrogen oxides, which, when combined with atmospheric moisture, create acid precipitation (dilute sulphuric acid or nitric acid).

Acid rain (or snow) is the main atmospheric fallout of industrial pollutants, although these may also occur as dry deposits (such as ash). Acid rain damages forests, plants and agriculture, raises the acid level in lakes and ground water, killing fish and other waterbound life, and contaminating drinking water.

Temperate forests have been seriously damaged by acid rain. The Black Forest in Germany has been steadily losing its trees through *Waldsterben* ('tree death'). The problem is also very acute in the north of Bohemia (Czech Republic). But Britain has the highest percentage of damaged trees in Europe: 67%. In Europe, it has been estimated that in 1987 the value of the timber harvest was reduced by 82 million cubic metres, worth $23 billion.

In southern Norway 80% of the lakes are devoid of fish life, and Sweden has 20,000 acidified lakes.

Acid rain upsets the fine chemical balance in lakes that are home to numerous species of fish. Salmon, roach and trout are very sensitive to pH (i.e.acid) levels in their habitat.

Even a slight dip in pH levels causes heavy metals such as aluminium, mercury, lead, zinc and cadmium to become more concentrated, decreasing the amount of oxygen the fish can absorb and eventually causing their death. The absence of large fish destabilizes the ecosystem and the effects are felt throughout the food chain. The ecosystem is seriously depleted, and only some smaller creatures, such as water beetles, seem to be able to survive.

Acid rain also causes damage to the soil. High levels of acid rain in the soil cause lead and other heavy metals to become concentrated and interrupt the lifecycles of microorganisms. The bacteria and fungi that help break down organic matter into nutrients are disturbed and soils can lose their ability to support forests or agriculture.

Not only ecosystems are damaged by acid precipitation. Corrosion of metals and rapid weathering of building materials has become a serious problem for the older buildings of Europe. Cathedrals and castles are suffering substantial damage.

There is increasing evidence to suggest that acid aerosols may enter the respiratory system of human beings and animals, causing an intensification of respiratory illnesses such as bronchitis and asthma.

There are various methods of reducing the amount of pollutants reaching the atmosphere, such as lead-free petrol, catalytic converters attached to car exhausts (which destroy some of the harmful gases), and filter systems that reduce dangerous emissions from power stations and industry.

DEFORESTATION

The tropical rain forests cover over 30,000,000 square kilometres (12,000,000 square miles), that is over 20% of the Earth's land surface.

The vast sea of green leaves of these forests play a vital role in the climatic regime of the Earth. Chlorophylls in leaves drive the chemical reaction *photosynthesis* in which carbon dioxide enters the leaves through microscopic pores to be converted into sugar glucose. At the end of the reaction, oxygen is released by leaves. In this way, the tropical rain forests provide much of the oxygen upon which we rely for life itself, and the destruction of considerable areas of these forests for logging and farming is of considerable concern.

In photosynthesis, quantities of carbon dioxide are used up. Thus, in a situation where plants and animals live together, the ratio is maintained in the existing levels of oxygen and carbon dioxide. This fine balance is in danger of being upset by the felling and burning of large areas of tropical forest.

The imbalance caused through the increased emission of carbon dioxide that would result from the destruction of much of the rain forest through clearing and burning would gradually increase the amount of greenhouse gases in the atmosphere and could produce global warming.

An immense amount of water is held in the ecosystem of the tropical forests, which are both a result and a determinant of climate. The destruction of the forest not only increases erosion and the rate of runoff, but also greatly reduces the humidity and, in turn, the precipitation of the area.

Erosion is a major problem. Equatorial soils tend to be poor and lateritic. The forest cover affords them some protection, but, once cleared, the earth is exposed to severe erosion and leaching. The new farmland created by deforestation can support agriculture for only a couple of years. It is exhausted quickly and the topsoil is soon washed away.

This is dramatically illustrated in Madagascar where the greater part of the tropical rain forest has been cleared for farming. Gullying has occurred within two or three years as deep-sided small valleys have been carved out and the soil has been eroded.

The rain forests are the 'lungs' of the planet. Once the rich and varied forests of the tropics covered virtually all of the Amazon Basin of South America, the West African coasts, the basin of the River Zaire (Congo) and its tributaries in central Africa, the islands of Indonesia and most of Malaysia and Papua New Guinea. Now, because of agricultural and other human pressure upon the land, vast swathes of equatorial forest have been cleared. Clearing and burning is destroying a resource that cannot be replaced.

How quickly are the forests being lost?
Accurate data on deforestation awaited the availability of satellite images.

Preliminary work has shown that deforestation in the Amazon Basin in 1989 was approximately 30,000 square kilometres, some 17.5% more than earlier ground surveys had suggested. The most recent figures available from the Food and Agriculture Organization in 1993 showed that deforestation in tropical Africa is now less than half that which occurs in tropical America and tropical Asia. Major deforestation had occurred ten or even 20 years earlier in Africa.

Brazil is gradually invading its great natural reserve, the Amazonian rain forest. In most years in the 1980s and early 1990s, an area the size of Belgium was cleared and burned in the Amazon Basin to create new pastures or farming land, or to allow for the construction of HEP dams. In Southeast Asia too there is much pressure on the rain forests, but Thailand, which has seen very considerable reduction of its forests, has banned logging altogether and both Indonesia and the Philippines have enacted restrictions on the amount of timber that can be taken.

Deforestation has been most evident in Malaysia where the extent of forest had decreased from nearly 320,000 square kilometres (125,000 sq mi) in 1900 to 70,000 square kilometres (27,000 sq mi) by 1992.

DEFORESTATION IN THE TROPICS

The following table gives estimates of natural forest deforestation rates in the tropics.

Country	*annual % deforested 1981-90*
Jamaica	7.0%
Haiti	4.75%
Bangladesh	3.9%
Pakistan	3.5%
Thailand	3.25%
Philippines	3.25%
Costa Rica	3.0%
Paraguay	2.75%
Dominican Republic	2.75%
El Salvador	2.25%
Honduras	2.0%
Malaysia	2.0%
Trinidad and Tobago	2.0%
Nicaragua	1.9%
Panama	1.9%
Ecuador	1.8%
Guatemala	1.7%
Mexico	1.5%
Vietnam	1.5%
Venezuela	1.5%
Bolivia	1.5%
Togo	1.5%
Malawi	1.5%
Cuba	1.25%
Burma (Myanmar)	1.25%
Ghana	1.25%
Benin	1.25%
Sri Lanka	1.25%
Tanzania	1.2%
Zambia	1.2%
Guinea	1.2%

LIFE SCIENCES

Living World

EVOLUTION

In 1831 Charles Darwin became the naturalist on *HMS Beagle* on her five-year voyage of discovery. The extensive observations he made on this voyage led him to the conception of evolution by natural selection. Darwin's ideas were published in 1859 in his *On the Origin of the Species by Means of Natural Selection.*

adaptive evolution is a speeding up of the normal process of evolutionary divergence of species.

coevolution is where two or more species evolve in continuous adaptation to each other.

convergent evolution is where different organisms have evolved similar solutions to similar problems, even though they have different ancestors.

evidence for evolution has been identified in embryonic development, in vestigial structures (e.g. vestigial limbs in whales), homologous structures (resemblances in anatomy resulting from shared ancestry), the fossil record, adaptive radiation, and biochemical similarities.

gene see p. 122. Genes that make bodies that are better at surviving and reproducing will perpetuate themselves and will have a high frequency in the gene pool; genes that are not so good in these respects will be rarer. As the make-up of the gene pool changes over time, so will the characteristics of the individuals of the species.

genetic drift random shuffling of parental genes that may purely by chance perpetuate mutations.

Mendelism the theory formulated by Gregor Mendel in 1865 that a particular trait is either passed on or not – there is no blending.

natural selection (theory of) was outlined by Darwin in his *Origin of the Species.* He showed how the adaptation of organisms to their environment, and hence of evolution, was due to the blind operation of everyday laws of nature, by means of 'natural selection'. Darwin concluded that, in the 'struggle for existence' resulting from competition among individuals, variations in attributes (some due to heredity) will affect success in survival and reproduction. In other words, a fitter individual – one that is better adapted to its surroundings – will be more likely to survive and leave descendants than a less fit one, and hence will tend to perpetuate within the population those inherited differences to which it owed its success. In this way natural selection can act over time to change the characteristics of a population. In other words there is what Darwin called 'descent with modification', dubbed by Herbert Spencer 'the survival of the fittest'.

parallel evolution is where unrelated plants and animals will adapt in similar ways to fill ecological niches in similar but geographically separated ecosystems.

speciation the development of one or more species from an existing species.

uniformitarianism the theory that stated that all geological change is slow, gradual and continuous. It was one of the bases upon which Darwin based his theory of natural selection.

CELLS

Cells are the basic biological units of all living things. A single cell is the smallest component of an organism that is able to function independently. Virtually every cell in an organism carries a complete genetic blueprint for the formation and development of that organism. Bacteria and protoctists are unicellular. All higher animals and plants are multicellular. In multicellular organisms, groups of cells have different functions, e.g. nerve cells, blood cells, etc. All cells are constructed from four groups of organic molecules: nucleic acids (DNA and RNA), proteins, carbohydrates (including sugars) and lipids. There are two basic types of cell: prokaryote and eukaryote.

centrioles self-replicating organelles in animal cells, but rare in plants; the focal point of production of part of the cytoskeleton.

chromosome a coiled structure in the nucleus of cells.

cytoplasm the solution surrounding the nucleus and organelles.

endoplasmic reticulum an organelle which provides an intracellular transportation system.

eukaryote cells are generally larger than prokaryotes. They exist as single cells, colonies of cells, or constructs (multicellular organisms).

Golgi apparatus an organelle; an assembly of vesicles and folded membranes which manipulate material for secretion.

lysosome an organelle containing enzymes for controlled digestion of molecules, bacteria, red blood cells and worn-out organelles.

membrane sheet-like tissue covering, connecting or lining cells and their organelles and structures. The membrane of all living cells has a similar configuration. The basic membrane (the plasmamembrane) separates the inside of the cell from its environment and provides a variety of compartments in eukaryote cells (the organelles). The membrane provides a large surface inside the cell on which chemical reactions occur, permits specialized transport systems within the cell, and separates the different activities of the cell.

mitochondria organelles which are important in cell respiration for the release of energy.

nucleus the central part of a cell. It is surrounded by a membrane and contains genetic material in the form of chromosomes. It makes m-RNA, t-RNA and r-RNA and regulates cell division.

organelles miniature organs found in prokaryote cells. They have specialized functions.

plastids organelles which form chloroplasts in plants, colourless leucoplasts, and chromoplasts.

prokaryote cells the most primitive form of cell, consist of an outer membrane with some rudimentary membrane systems within it. The DNA of prokaryote cells resides in a special area, the nucleoid. Prokaryotes contain no organelles.

protoplasm the material of the cell within the membrane of a prokaryote cell.

vesicle any small, usually fluid-filled, membrane-bound sac within the cytoplasm.

GENETICS

The Austrian monk Gregor Mendel (1822–84) observed specific features of the pea plant and counted the number of individuals in which each characteristic appeared through several generations. By concentrating on a few features and determining what proportion of each generation received them, he was able to demonstrate specific patterns of inheritance. The discrete nature and independent segregation of genetic characteristics that he observed became known as Mendel's laws of inheritance, and have been shown to apply to most genetic systems.

adenine (A) one of the four bases found in the central region of the double helix of DNA.

allele one of a pair of genes which together determine which of a pair of characteristics will appear in the offspring.

chromosome a coiled structure in the nucleus of cells. It consists of several different types of protein wrapped tightly associated with a single DNA molecule. Each chromosome carries a large number of genes. Most eukaryote organisms have several chromosomes, but bacteria have only one.

codon (or **triplet**) a combination of three bases within a DNA molecule.

cytosine (C) one of the four bases found in the central region of the double helix of DNA.

DNA (short for deoxyribonucleic acid). In 1944 the American microbiologist Oswald T. Avery demonstrated that the inherited characteristics of a certain bacterium could be altered by deoxyribonucleic acid (DNA) taken up from outside the cell. In 1953 the American James Watson and the Englishman Francis Crick established that DNA is a large molecule in the shape of a double helix. DNA is the basic genetic material of most living organisms. A single DNA molecule consists of two single strands wound around each other to form a double-helical (spiral) structure. Each strand is made up of just four chemical components (nucleotides). The central region of the helix comprises four bases – adenine, cytosine, guanine and thymine.

gene the basic unit of inheritance, consisting of a linear section of a DNA molecule. Mendel discovered that characteristics are passed from generation to generation in discrete units. Once the structure of DNA was established, these units (genes) could be understood at the molecular level.

guanine (G) one of the four bases found in the central region of the double helix of DNA.

mutation occurs when there is a change in the sequence of nucleotide bases in a piece of DNA.

nucleotide any of the four components that make up a single strand of DNA.

RNA short for ribonucleic acid. RNA occurs in different forms – m-RNA (messenger RNA), t-RNA (transfer RNA), and r-RNA (ribosomal RNA) – all of which are involved in the processes by which DNA leads to the construction of proteins.

thymine (T) one of the four bases found in the central region of the double helix of DNA.

TAXONOMY

The study of the classification of life – or taxonomy – aims to provide a rational framework in which to organize our knowledge of the great diversity of living and extinct organisms. The first well-authenticated system of classification goes back to Aristotle (384–322 BC), but it was not until the 17th century that the Englishman John Ray (1628–1705) proposed the first natural classification rather than an artificial scheme aiming merely to facilitate identification. In the 18th century the Swedish naturalist Carl Linnaeus (1707–78), produced a rational system of classification based on patterns of similarity between different organisms. Linnaeus developed one of the first comprehensive subordinated schemes of taxonomy.

class a classificatory group between phylum (or division) and order. For example all mammals belong to the class Mammalia.

division 1) any of several high-ranking classificatory groups into which the plant kingdom is divided. The equivalent of phylum in the animal kingdom. 2) a classificatory group between phylum and class in the animal kingdom.

family a classificatory group between order and genus.

genus a classificatory group between family and species. Generic names are always written in italics.

kingdom the highest classificatory group. Most authorities today recognize five kingdoms: Animalia (animals), Plantae (plants), Fungi (fungi), Protoctista and Prokaryotae.

Linnaean system a scheme of classification that places each organism in a group that is itself part of a larger group. The essential feature of Linnaeus's scheme is that it is binomial. He gave every distinct type or species of organism (e.g. the lion) a two-part (binomial) name (e.g. *Felis leo*) in which the second element of the name identified the individual species, while the first element placed the species in a particular genus. Having subordinated each species to a particular genus, he went on to place groups of genera in a higher rank or category he called a family, then families in orders, and so on through classes, phyla (or divisions for plants), and finally kingdoms. Within this hierarchy each division is more embracing than the last, each containing a greater number of organisms with fewer characteristics in common.

monophyletic group a group consisting of species descending from a single ancestor and including all the most recent common ancestors of all its members.

order a classificatory group between class and family. For example, the order Primates in the class Mammalia contains all the primates.

phylum (plur. **phyla**) any of several high-ranking classificatory groups into which the animal kingdom is divided. The equivalent of phylum in the plant kingdom is division.

species in general, the smallest classificatory group (although there are some subspecies). The members of a species are able to breed among themselves to produce fertile offspring: this defines the term.

SIMPLE LIFE FORMS – Bacteria, Viruses and Protoctists

Of the five kingdoms of living organisms, the most primitive is the kingdom Prokaryota (formerly Monera), which includes the archaebacteria, bacteria and mycoplasms. The kingdom Protoctista (formerly Protista) consists of the protozoa, the slime moulds and the Oomycota.

algae an important and diverse group of Protoctista which are oxygen producing, photosynthetic, and are mostly inhabitants of aquatic environments. They no longer include the blue-green bacteria (formerly known as blue-green algae) and are *not* plants.

amoeba any member of the rhizopod genus *Amoeba*. Members of this genus are characterized by pseudopodia which are used for locomotion and feeding and result in a constantly changing body shape. Most species are free-living in water or soil, but some are parasitic.

autotrophic protoctists protoctist organisms that are able to convert simple inorganic molecules into complex organic molecules.

bacillus rod-like bacteria.

bacteria (sing. **bacterium**) a diverse group of prokaryote single-celled organisms. Bacteria form the majority of prokaryote species of unicellular organisms. They vary in shape from almost spherical (coccus) to comma-shaped (vibrio) to rod-like (bacillus) to corkscrew-shaped (spirochaete) and spiral (spirillium). Some bacteria, such as *Salmonella*, are motile. Bacteria, which vary in size from 0.0003mm to more than 0.02mm, cause a wide range of diseases. Although we think of bacteria as disease-causing parasites, they are very diverse in both their habitat and biology. Although many are parasites, there are also saprophytes, free-living organisms, and bacteria that have developed a symbiotic relationship with plants.

chloroxybacteria green-coloured prokaryote organisms that are structurally similar to cyanobacteria.

cilia specialized structures used in the movement of some protoctists.

coccus spherical bacteria.

contractile vacuole a miniature organ (or organelle) found in some protoctists, especially those living in fresh water. They are primarily used to remove excess water.

cyanobacteria (formerly **blue-green algae**) a group of bacteria capable of photosynthesis in the same way as green plants. Blue-green algae, which occur either as small rounded cells or mobile filaments or cells, can be free-living or present in symbiotic relationships either together with fungi to form lichens or inside the cells of higher plants.

eukaryote any organism whose cells are eukaryotic, i.e. in which the genetic material is contained in a distinct nucleus. Protoctists and all higher animals are eukaryotes.

flagella specialized structures used in the movement of some protoctists.

heterotrophic protoctists protoctist organisms that are dependent upon the consumption of other organic matter as a source of complex molecules.

mesosome an area of infolded plasma membrane in a prokaryote cell.

motile organism any organism that is capable of spontaneous and independent movement.

mycoplasm any of a group of minute prokaryote organisms. Mycoplasms are the smallest known free-living organisms (0.0001 mm), differing from true bacteria by the absence of a cell wall and mesosomes.

Prokaryota one of the five kingdoms of living things, including archaebacteria, bacteria and mycoplasms. (Formerly known as Monera.)

prokaryote any unicellular organism whose cells are prokaryotic, i.e. in which there is no nucleus.

protoctist any member of the kingdom Protoctista. The protoctists include the algae and protozoa, slime moulds and nets, all of which have developed incredible degrees of complexity and sophistication. Although remaining as single cells, some of them form the first approach to multicellular organisms through the construction of colonies. Algal forms include the major forms green, red and brown algae, also diatoms and dinoflagellates. Protoctists are ubiquitous on land and in water (where they form a major component of plankton), as well as inside other organisms as parasites or symbionts. Free-living forms can live in the soil; slime moulds live on decaying leaves and rotting logs; other protoctists live as parasites.

Protoctista one of the five kingdoms of living things.

protozoa obsolete name, still in common use, for any animal-like unicellular organism amongst the Protoctista.

pseudopodium a 'false foot'; a temporary projection of an amoebic protozoan used in movement.

slime mould any of the myxomycetes, a group of protoctists that are formed either by individual small amoeboid cells or by the fusion of such cells.

spirillium spiral-shaped bacteria.

spirochaete corkscrew-shaped bacteria.

vibrio comma-shaped bacteria.

viral replication occurs when a virus infects a host cell. On infecting such a cell, a virus can use the mechanisms of the host cell in order to make viral nucleic acids and proteins from which new virus particles can be constructed. A virus can also enter a cell, insert itself into the host chromosome, remain dormant, leave the chromosome, replicate and then leave the cell.

viroid a particle that is even smaller than a virus; they are small infectious single-stranded RNA molecules.

virus any of a group of minute organisms that lack a cell structure. Viruses are even simpler forms of life than bacteria and are very much a grey area between living and non-living things. They are completely dependent upon living cells as vehicles. A large range of viruses is known to exist. Many cause diseases – from AIDS to the common cold. Viruses have also been implicated in evolution as transmitters of blocks of genetic material from one organism to another. Viruses consist simply of a single nucleic acid – either DNA or RNA – surrounded by a protein layer.

FUNGI

The fungi are not, as is popularly supposed, plants. They constitute an entirely separate kingdom, the Fungi. Unlike the plants, the fungi lack chlorophyll and hence cannot photosynthesize. They therefore have to obtain the carbon and energy necessary for life from other sources. In most fungi groups there are examples of parasites, which grow on living animals, plants or other fungi, and also of saprotrophs – the function of the latter as decomposers is a very important one, assisting in the recycling of materials needed for life. Some parasitic fungi continue to live as saprotrophs on the dead remains of their hosts. Other fungi have developed a symbiotic relationship with other organisms; for example some are mycorrhizal, while others associate with algae to form lichens (see box).

Although some fungi, such as yeasts, are unicellular, most fungi consist of a mass of filaments. Aggregates of these filaments may give rise to quite large fruiting bodies – the obvious visible parts of fungi such as toadstools. Although in some fungi the cell walls – like those of plants – contain cellulose, in most fungi the cell walls contain chitin (also the principal material in the exoskeletons of insects and other arthropods). Reproduction is by spores, which may be produced sexually or asexually. The spores are usually dispersed by the wind, but sometimes by water or insects. There are five Phyla, of which the largest are the Ascomycota and Basidiomycota. (The names and relationships given here conform to the most recent classification.)

agaric any species of basidiomycote fungus of the orders Agaricales or Russulales. They are mushroom-shaped fungi with gills. Several are grown commercially for food.

Ascomycota the phylum consisting of both unicellular and filamentous species. In most species the ascus contains eight spores, which may be explosively discharged several cm into the air. Microscopic forms include the unicellular yeast *Saccharomyces* and the filamentous *Ceratocystis ulmi*, the cause of Dutch elm disease.

ascus a sac containing spores.

basidia characteristic special cells found in the fruiting bodies of basidiomycote fungi.

Basidiomycota the phylum containing most of the fungi generally thought of as mushrooms and toadstools – though it also includes microscopic plant parasites, the rusts and smuts. Many members of this class are important as decomposers, being wood-rotting or leaf-litter fungi. Others are parasitic and yet others are mycorrhizal.

basidiospore a characteristic swelling found on the basidia of basidiomycote fungi.

bolete any species of the order Boletales of basidiomycote fungi. They are mushroom-shaped fungi with spores.

budding fragmentation of the mycelium.

Ceratocystis ulmi a filamentous member of the phylum Ascomycota. It is the cause of Dutch elm disease.

LICHENS

Lichens are often linked in popular imagination with mosses although they are, in fact, not even remotely related.

Lichens are composite organisms formed by the symbiotic relationship of a fungus and an alga or a cyanobacterium. The fungus provides a protective environment for the 'green partner', which provides the fungus with the products of photosynthesis. The metabolism of lichens is suspended when they become dry or are exposed to the heat of the Sun, but they soon become active again when conditions are moist. This intermittent activity results in a very slow growth rate but enables them to colonize some relatively inhospitable habitats.

Asexual reproduction is achieved by the production of soredia, clumps of algal cells surrounded by fungus. Thus fungus and alga are disseminated together.

Deuteromycota a 'dustbin' group of fungi, whose true classification cannot yet be decided as they have no sexual stage, which forms the basis of classification into Ascomycota and Basidiomycota.

Fungi imperfecti another name for the Deuteromycota.

hypha (plur. **hyphae**) an individual filament of fungi.

lichen a symbiotic relationship between an alga and a fungus. (See box).

meiois the process by which sex cells are produced from body cells.

motile organism any organism that is capable of spontaneous and independent movement.

mushroom any species of agaric or bolete fungus. Some people would confine the term to the common mushroom and its relatives.

mycelium a mass of hyphae.

mycorrhizal living in a symbiotic relationship with the roots of a plant.

rust a plant disease in which plant leaves appear rusty, caused by the microscopic species of basidiomycote fungus.

Saccharomyces a genus of the phylum Ascomycota – unicellular yeast, which is important in making bread and alcoholic beverages.

saprotroph an organism that grows on dead remains.

sporangium a body in which spores are produced.

symbiosis a close association between two different species from which both derive benefit.

toadstool a non-technical term for the visible fruiting body of certain basiodiomycote fungi. The term is sometimes restricted to poisonous varieties.

yeast see *Saccharomyces*.

Zygomycetes one of two classes of the Zygomycota. They produce asexual spores, while in sexual reproduction two special hyphae fuse to form a zygospore.

zygospore a 'resting stage' in the life cycle of zygomycete fungi. A zygospore eventually germinates to produce a sporangium containing many spores.

Plant World

PLANTS

The hundreds of thousands of species of plants comprise the kingdom Plantae, one of the five kingdoms of living things. Plant species have colonized a very wide range of habitats, showing tolerance of extremes of temperature and other climatic variations. In so doing, plants have evolved an astonishing variety of adaptations, resulting in one of the most diverse groups of living organisms.

The Plant kingdom has six phyla or divisions: Bryophyta (liverworts and mosses), Lycopodophyta (club mosses), Sphenophyta (horsetails), Filicinophyta (ferns), Coniferophyta (conifers) and Angiospermatophyta (flowering plants). All are eukaryotic and autotrophic.

The same basic functions occur in plants as in all other living organisms. They grow and, therefore, they assimilate materials from the environment, and this material provides the chemicals of which they are made. To maintain life they require energy; and they need water, which like the substances for growth and energy is taken up from their surroundings and transported around the plant body. Plants, like animals, perceive their environment and react towards it. They also reproduce. But there are unique properties of green plants – principally their structure and the fact that they are fixed in one location – that determine the way they carry out these functions.

In general, the material for energy and growth is not obtained from organic material as it is in animals. Green plants – together with the algae and some bacteria – are the only autotrophic organisms on Earth.

amino acid a building block of protein, consisting of one or more carboxyl groups and one or more amino groups attached to a carbon atom. There are over 80 naturally occurring amino acids, 20 of which occur in proteins.

angiosperm a flowering plant; any member of the phylum or division Angiospermatophyta.

Angiospermatophyta a plant division; flowering plants. See pp. 129–32.

Antarctic a floral region lying south of the Antarctic Circle (66° 33´S) plus the extreme southern tip of South America.

Australian a floral region that covers not only Australia but also New Zealand, New Guinea and adjacent islands.

autotrophic organism any organism that can make organic materials from simple inorganic sources of carbon, nitrogen, hydrogen, oxygen and other elements that are found in living things. To do this they need energy, and they derive this energy from sunlight. In so doing, they are converting simple inorganic chemicals into forms upon which the whole animal, fungal and some bacterial life depends.

bacteroid modified bacteria; for example, modified *Rhizobium* bacteria living in a nodule on leguminous roots.

bark tissue in woody stems and roots external to the cambium.

blade another name for the lamina.

Boreal a floral region covering all of Europe, most of North America, part of North Africa and that part of Asia to the north of the Himalaya.

Bryophyta a plant division; liverworts and mosses. See p. 128.

cambium a secondary meristem extending down the length of a root or stem. It is responsible for producing new cells, which differentiate into xylem and phloem.

carbohydrate any of a large number of organic compounds such as sugars and polysaccharides.

cellulose a polysaccharide carbohydrate made up of unbranched chains of many glucose molecules (i.e. a polymer). Its fibrils form the framework of plant cell walls. Cellulose is generally an important component in the diets of herbivorous animals.

chlorophyll the chemicals in plants that give them their green colour. The chlorophylls are particularly abundant in leaves and are contained in chloroplasts. Chlorophyll strongly absorbs the blue and red regions of the light spectrum, and this ability is used to drive the most important single chemical reaction on Earth. This reaction, which maintains both plant and animal life, is photosynthesis.

chloroplast a miniature organ (organelle) within cells in plants.

club mosses plants of the phylum or division Lycopodophyta.

conifer a member of the phylum or division Coniferophyta.

Coniferophyta a plant division; conifers. See p. 128.

Fabaceae the legume family; see legume and nitrogen fixation.

Filicinophyta a plant division; ferns. See p. 128.

floral region (or **phytogeographic region**) a distinct region that can be defined principally on the basis of the similarity of the flowering plant inhabitants that it contains.

flowers see Flowering plants, pp. 129–132.

glucose a simple sugar, an essential source of energy produced by plants via photosynthesis and obtained by animals from plants.

'guard cells' see stomata.

horsetails plants of the phylum or division Sphenophyta.

lamina the blade of a leaf.

leaf a lateral organ on a plant stem, in higher plants often consisting of a petiole and lamina. Leaves play a crucial role in transpiration, respiration and photosynthesis.

leghaemoglobin a red pigment in legumes that carries oxygen; see nitrogen fixation.

legume any member of the plant family Fabaceae, including peas, beans, clover, gorse, etc., nearly all of which are symbiotic with nitrogen-fixing bacteria.

lignin an important strengthening component of cell walls in the woody tissues of plants. It is a polymer of sugars, phenols, amino acids and alcohols.

liverworts plants of the phylum or division Bryophyta.

Lycopodophyta a plant division; club mosses. See p. 128.

malic acid an acid produced by starch breakdown.

meristem a group of cells in plants that divide by mitosis and thereby contribute to plant growth and organ formation. Meristematic activity may be generalized (as in the developing embryo) or localized (as in the apices of stems or roots). Primary meristems are those that have always been meristematic; secondary meristems develop from differentiated cells.

mitosis the mechanism by which body cells divide.

mosses plants of the phylum or division Bryophyta.

Neotropical a floral region that covers Central and South America (except for the extreme southern tip).

nitrogen fixation a means of obtaining nitrogen that has been developed by the legumes.

Almost all plant species in the legume family that have been examined have entered into symbiotic relationships with certain bacteria living in their roots. These bacteria, which invade the roots from the soil, can fix gaseous or molecular nitrogen. The legume family includes many important crop plants (beans, soybeans, etc.) that produce high protein seeds, and it has been estimated that up to 50% of the nitrogen in the protein comes from the activity of the bacteria. Several species in other families also have nitrogen-fixing bacteria; these are generally plants such as bog myrtle and alder, that typically colonize soils poor in nitrates.

The bacteria infecting the leguminous plants belong to the genus *Rhizobium*, and each species of leguminous plant has a particular species of *Rhizobium* that will infect no other legume. Infection occurs on a damaged root hair, from where the bacteria will spread into the centre of the root. There, root cells are stimulated to divide to produce a nodule, inside whose cells the modified *Rhizobium* bacteria (now called bacteroids) live. The bacteroids require oxygen, and this is carried to the bacteria in leghaemoglobin, which confers a pinkish colour to the interior of the nodule. Using carbohydrate (in the form of sucrose) provided by the host plant, the bacteroids convert the nitrogen that has diffused into the nodule into ammonia, which is then changed by the nodule cells into amino acids and other nitrogenous compounds. These compounds pass into the xylem of the vascular tissue to be carried up the shoot where they are used for protein synthesis.

Nitrogen fixation in legume crops plays an extremely important part in the nitrogen economy: these plants need far less nitrogen fertilizer than other crops, and do not deplete the soil of this essential element. In addition, when ploughed in, legumes enrich the soil, and are commonly used in four-crop rotation.

osmosis the movement or diffusion of water (or another solvent) from a less concentrated solution to a more concentrated solution.

Palaeotropical a floral region that covers Africa (except the northern coastal regions and the extreme south).

petiole the stalk of a leaf.

phloem the part of the vascular tissue system of plants responsible for conducting substances manufactured by the plant, e.g. sugars and amino acids. The conducting cells are sieve elements, and other 'general purpose' cells are also present. Primary phloem is formed in the region of the apex of roots and shoots; secondary phloem develops from the secondary cambium, and in some cases forms part of the bark.

photoperiodism the ability of plants to judge the seasonal changes in daylight hours and, thus, to regulate the time of the year when they flower.

photosynthesis the process by which plants, algae and various bacteria convert simple inorganic molecules into complex compounds necessary for life.

Life is based upon the element carbon. Green plants obtain this from the air in the form of carbon dioxide, which they change (synthesize) into more elaborate chemicals – various carbohydrates such as sugars (glucose and sucrose) and starch. (Water is also essential as a source of hydrogen atoms in the sugars, and, as a by-product, molecules of oxygen are given off. This oxygen is essential to virtually all life on Earth.)

Chloroplasts from individual cells acquire carbon dioxide through the intercellular spaces after it has entered the leaf through the stomata. In photosynthesis, the carbon dioxide is then transformed into carbohydrates, initially the sugar glucose, and eventually sucrose and starch. This transformation is powered by the energy from sunlight absorbed by the chlorophylls. This is how the plant obtains carbon needed for the synthesis of materials of which it is composed. As vegetation is the primary food of all animal food chains, it is by photosynthesis that almost all of the carbon enters the living world.

Photosynthesis comprises a set of reactions involved with the absorption of light (the light reactions) and a set that do not require light. The essential feature of the light reactions is that the light energy absorbed by chlorophyll is used to split water molecules into hydrogen and oxygen. The oxygen ultimately released by plants is the source of all oxygen in the atmosphere of this planet.

In the remaining reactions carbon dioxide is converted into glucose by a complex cycle of chemical transformations, some of which use the hydrogen generated from water, and the chemical energy that has been produced from light energy.

As plants acquire their carbon dioxide, they also give off water vapour through the open stomata. As this water loss is potentially a problem in arid climates, many plants living in such environments have evolved physiological adaptations to overcome the danger. Many succulent plants, for example, keep their stomata closed during the day but open them at night when there is no drying effect of the Sun. The carbon dioxide is assimilated (or 'fixed') at night not into sugars but into certain organic acids, which later, during daylight hours, release the carbon dioxide within the leaf when the stomata are closed; the carbon dioxide then participates in photosynthesis in the normal way. In other types of plant adapted to semi-arid climates (such as maize) the carbon dioxide is again fixed very efficiently into organic acids during the day, even by leaves with partially closed stomata;

these organic acids then move across to the inner cells of the leaf where the carbon dioxide is liberated and used in photosynthesis.

Because in photosynthesis carbon dioxide is used up and oxygen is given out as a waste product – the reverse of plant and animal respiration – the overall effect of plants and animals living together is to keep the atmospheric levels of these gases more or less constant.

The carbohydrates from photosynthesis provide the carbon from which nearly all the constituents of the plant body are made. Especially important among these is protein. Protein contains nitrogen, an element that is taken up by plants from the soil or water, generally in the form of nitrates. In the majority of higher plants nitrates are converted to ammonium in the leaves; the ammonium is then combined with the carbon coming from the photosynthetic products to produce amino acids, the molecules from which proteins are produced.

phototropism the ability of plant stems to grow towards light. Stem extension is regulated by the brightness and quality of light, which are perceived by light-absorbing molecules (pigments). One of these pigments, phytochrome, is sensitive to the different parts of the red region of the spectrum and can tell the plant if it is shaded by the green leaves of its neighbours. If it is, the plant increases its stem growth to carry it out of the shade. This same property of phytochrome enables seeds (which also contain the pigment) to detect how deeply they are buried in the soil, or if they are in vegetational shade.

phytogeographical region another name for a floral region.

polymer any natural or synthetic compound that is made up of repeated units; e.g. starch.

polypeptide any polymer made up of amino acids.

polysaccharide any of a class of large carbohydrate molecules, including cellulose, glycogen and starch.

primary meristem see meristem.

primary phloem see phloem.

primary xylem see xylem.

protein any of a large number of polymers made up of polypeptide chains of amino acids.

respiration (in plants) the use of oxygen to oxidize various compounds, releasing energy from them. This oxidation occurs in all living cells in plants; partly in the cytoplasm and partly in the mitochondria. Respiration is used to support the synthesis of various chemical compounds, growth and the uptake and accumulation of various mineral elements.

Rhizobium a genus of bacteria found on the roots of leguminous plants; see nitrogen fixation.

South African a floral region covering the extreme southern tip of the African continent.

Sphenophyta a plant division; horsetails. See p. 128.

spore-bearing plants see p. 128.

stalk see petiole.

starch a polysaccharide carbohydrate into which glucose is converted for storage in plants.

stem the part of a plant bearing leaves, buds and flowers.

stomata (sing. **stoma**) the microscopic pores in the surface of leaves. They are located mostly on the lower surface of the leaf at a frequency ranging from 20 to over 1000 per square mm depending upon the species. The stomata allow carbon dioxide for photosynthesis into the leaf, and water vapour to escape during transpiration.

Each pore is bordered by two 'guard cells', which are typically about 0.045 mm long and about 0.012 mm wide. The guard cells can open and close the stomatal pore, so regulating the entry and exit of gases. They do this by taking up or losing water. When the water enters the guard cell it swells up into a crescent shape, so that when both guard cells are swollen, the pore that they border becomes bigger. Conversely, when water is lost, the cells collapse and block off the pore.

These water movements are regulated as follows. Water enters and leaves by osmosis, passing from a solution that is less concentrated to one that is stronger. Changes in potassium ion concentration occur in the guard cells: when the concentration increases, water is subsequently drawn in and the guard cell swells into its unique shape. As potassium ions enter, hydrogen ions (protons) leave: the hydrogen ions come from certain organic acids (malic acid), produced by starch breakdown.

sucrose a type of sugar into which glucose is converted in plants for transport.

sugar any of a group of carbohydrates of low molecular weight. They are a source of cellular energy, and also act as structural molecules (e.g. for plant cell walls).

symbiont a species living in symbiosis.

symbiosis a close association between two different species from which both derive benefit.

tracheid the conducting cells in xylem.

tracheophyte a vascular plant.

transpiration the evaporation of water from plants through the stomata in leaves.

vascular plant (or **tracheophyte**) any plant with a vascular system, characteristic of all higher plants.

vascular system (in plants) the system of tissues comprising the xylem (for conducting dissolved mineral salts and water) and the phloem (for transporting chemicals synthesized within the plant), together with various other specialized cells (e.g. for strengthening).

vernalization the process by which a period of cold induces many plant species – such as winter wheat and barley – to form flowers.

xylem the part of the vascular tissue of plants responsible for conducting water and dissolved mineral salts. Characteristically, the cells are elongated, with relatively thick walls strengthened by lignin. The conducting cells are the vessels and tracheids. The xylem formed just below the apex is the primary xylem; that formed from the lateral secondary meristem is the secondary xylem, making up the principal component of wood in trees and shrubs.

SPORE-BEARING PLANTS

These plants – which are characterized by the use of spores rather than seeds as their dispersal unit – belong to four of the six phyla or divisions of the Plant kingdom: Bryophyta (the liverworts and mosses), Lycopodophyta (the club mosses), Sphenophyta (the horsetails) and Filicinophyta (the ferns). Some spore-bearing plants, for example the bryophytes, become dry and are able to remain dormant during adverse conditions, but virtually all spore-bearing plants have the additional protection of a resistant outer layer – the cuticle – during adverse conditions.

alternation of generations (in spore-bearing plants) a reproductive process by which a sexually produced generation (gametophyte) is followed by one (or more) asexual generations (sporophyte). In bryophytes, it is the gametophyte stage that is the obvious plant; the sporophyte plant consists only of a 'foot', stalk and capsule. Spores are produced in the capsule. The sporophyte obtains nutrients from its gametophyte parent and is therefore never entirely independent. In the other spore-bearing plants (the ferns, liverworts, club mosses, horsetails, etc.), it is the sporophyte stage that is the obvious plant, with the sporangia usually borne on the leaves. The gametophytes of these plants are independent and mostly capable of photosynthesis, but they are very small and lack cuticle and conducting tissues. They are restricted to moist sites and can easily be overwhelmed by leaf litter and other plants.

bryophyte any member of the division Bryophyta, which contains three classes: Musci (the mosses), Hepaticae (the liverworts) and Anthocerotae (the hornworts). Although rather diminutive plants, they show remarkable diversity of form and habit. The majority are leafy, with leaves for the most part one-cell thick, so that they very easily dry out. Bryophytes have no roots and attach themselves by means of rhizoids.

club moss any member of the division Lycopodophyta. The club mosses are widespread and diverse, generally small, vascular, herbaceous and possess roots. Their leaves are microphyllous and some bear spores.

fern any of some 9000 species in the Filicinophyta division. Ferns are distinguished from other spore-bearing plants by their large leaves known as fronds. These leaves have an extensive network of conducting strands and are often intricately subdivided. Sporangia are borne on leaves in groups called sori. In some species, the sporangial wall is modified, enabling spores to be thrown into the air.

horsetail any of about 15 species belonging to the division Sphenophyta. They are temperate plants that are characterized by hollow segmented stems, round which diminutive leaves and branches are borne in whorls.

liverwort any member of the bryophyte class Hepaticae. Some liverworts are flat and have no leaves; most, however, have leaves like mosses.

moss any member of the bryophyte class Musci. All mosses are leafy and their growth habit may be either erect, often forming tufts or cushions, or creeping, forming a weft over the surface. Their leaves characteristically form a spiral.

CONIFERS AND THEIR ALLIES

Conifers – members of the division or phyla Coniferophyta – share with the flowering plants the distinction of bearing seeds rather than spores. Seed-bearing has a number of advantages over spore-bearing in successfully spreading and increasing the species, and in ensuring survival if the parents are short-lived or suffer some catastrophe. The conifers and their allies are gymnosperms.

cone a structure containing the reproductive organs of a conifer. The mature female cone has pairs of papery or woody scales, comprising a sterile outer or bract scale and an inner ovule-carrying or ovuliferous scale. In the male cones, pollen sacs are borne on the underside of cone scales.

conifers are widespread and diverse with over 500 modern species. Most are tall forest trees. Their leaves are usually needle-like, usually with a single vascular strand. Most conifers secrete resin. The reproductive structures are grouped in cones. Most conifers have a long life cycle with several static periods – the period between pollination and fertilization often exceeds a year and seedlings are very slow to establish. They are a major element in the high-latitude Boreal forests of North America and Eurasia. Members of the Pinaceae family dominate, including larch, pines, spruces, firs, Douglas fir, and western hemlock. Conifers are adapted to withstand harsh conditions: the conical shape encourages shedding of snow and optimizes interception of low-angled light; needle-like leaves are xeromorphic (drought resistant) with a low ratio of surface area to volume and a thick outer layer to cope with the drying effects of frost and high winds; most leaves are evergreen, enabling rapid establishment of productivity as soon as conditions are suitable.

cycad any member of 11 modern genera of cycadophyte, most with restricted tropical distributions. Cycads emerged about 250 million years ago and for 100 million years dominated land vegetation. They resemble small palms with a short trunk, covered with the bases of old leaves. A few species reach up to 18m (60 ft) high.

fir any species of conifer of the genera *Abies* (firs) and *Pseudotsuga* (Douglas firs).

ginkgo (or **maidenhair tree**) a single species of ginkgophyte, which formerly had a very broad distribution. A large, much branched tree, it is distinguished from conifers by its fan-shaped leaf.

gymnosperm any plant that bears a 'naked' seed, i.e. a seed that is not enclosed in an ovary.

larch any of about 10 species of conifer of the genus *Laris*.

pine any of 96 species of conifer of the northern hemisphere genus *Pinus*.

spruce any of around 50 species of conifer of the northern temperate genus *Picea*.

western hemlock (or **hemlock spruce**) any of around 10 species of conifer of the North American and Asian genus *Tsuga*.

FLOWERING PLANTS

The flowering plants belong to the phylum or division Angiospermatophyta. They are the most diverse, widespread and abundant group of multicellular plants with at least 250,000 to 300,000 species.

acacia 800 species of spiny trees and shrubs (genus *Acacia*).

Aceraceae a dicotyledonous plant family; maples and sycamore.

Agave a genus of 300 species of New World plants characterized by large, fleshy, tough leaves.

alder 35 species of deciduous trees (genus *Alnus*).

Alismataceae a monocotyledonous family; water plantains.

Alismatidae a subclass of monocotyledons; water plantains and pondweed.

Alliaceae a family of the subclass Liliidae; onions and garlic.

Amaryllidaceae a monocotyledonous family; daffodils and snowdrops.

anemone 80 species of perennial temperate herb (genus *Anemone*).

angiosperm any seed-bearing plant in which the seed is enclosed in an ovary, i.e. a flowering plant.

annual any flowering plant that completes its life cycle from seed germination to death in less than one year.

anther a pollen-containing sac found on a stamen.

Apiaceae a dicotyledonous plant family; carrot, parsley, hogweeds, celery, hemlock.

apple 35 species of temperate trees and shrubs (genus *Malus*).

Aquifoliaceae a dicotyledonous plant family; hollies.

Araliaceae a dicotyledonous plant family; ivies and ginseng.

Arecaceae a monocotyledonous plant family; palm trees.

Arencidae a subclass of monocotyledons; palm trees.

ash 60 species of temperate trees (genus *Fraxinus*).

asparagus 300 species of perennial herbs, shrubs and climbers (genus *Asparagus*).

Asteraceae a dicotyledonous plant family (formerly Compositae) in which the flowers are arranged in multiple flower heads; thistles, daisies, chrysanthemums, lettuce.

Asteridae a dicotyledonous subclass.

bamboo 1000 species of mainly tropical perennial woody grasses (the family Poaceae).

bean any of various leguminous plant (family Fabaceae).

beech 10 species of deciduous tree (genus *Fagus*).

begonia 350 species of tropical and subtropical herbs (genus *Begonia*).

berry a fruit that usually contains a large number of small seeds.

Betulaceae a dicotyledonous family; birches, alders and hazels.

biennial any flowering plant that completes its life cycle in more than one year but less than two years. Flowering and seed production usually occur in the second year.

birch 60 species of the genus *Betula*.

bluebell a member of the family Liliaceae.

borage a medical and culinary herb (family Boraginaceae).

Brassicaceae a dicotyledonous plant family (formerly Cruciferae); broccoli, cabbage, calabrese, cauliflower, kale, mustard, rape, swede, turnip.

bromeliad 40 species of tropical New World herbs (genus *Bromelia*). Most have stiff spiny rosettes of leaves.

broom any shrub in the three leguminous genera *Cytisus*, *Genista* and *Spartium*.

bud a very compact stem with densely packed young leaves or flower parts.

bulb a perennating organ; a compact underground stem bearing fleshy leaves.

buttercup 400 members of the genus *Ranunculus*.

cabbage a cultivar of the Brassicaeae family.

cactus 800 species of plant of the family Cactaceae. They are strongly adapted to arid conditions having succulent photosynthetic stems (rather than photosynthetic leaves), which are often spiny.

calyx the collective term for the sepals, the outer whorl of leaf-like organs of a flower.

cambium a secondary meristem extending down the length of a root or stem. It is responsible for producing new cells, which differentiate into xylem and phloem or the periderm of the bark.

camellia 84 species of trees (genus *Camellia*).

campanula (or **bellflower**) 300 species of usually perennial herbs (genus *Campanula*).

campion any of several species of the genus *Dianthus*.

Caprifoliaceae a dicotyledonous family; honeysuckle and elder.

carpel one of a series of four organs in a flower. Carpels consist of an ovary surmounted by a style and a stigma.

carrot a biennial herb (family Apiaceae).

Caryophyllaceae a dicotyledonous family; pinks, campion and carnations.

Caryophyllidae a dicotyledonous subclass containing pinks, beets, spinach, cacti, dock, knotgrass and buckwheat.

catkin an inflorescence (usually hanging) in which small, reduced, unisexual flowers are borne on a central stem, as in willow and birch.

cereals members of the family Poaceae.

Chenopodiaceae a dicotyledonous family of plants; beet and spinach.

cherry any of a number of species of genus *Prunus* .

chrysanthemum some 200 herbaceous plants (family Asteridae).

citrus fruit the juicy fruit of two genera in the family Rutaceae; they include orange, lemon, lime, grapefruit.

clematis 250 species of woody climbers (genus *Clematis*).

clover a number of annual perennial leguminous herbs (genus *Trifolium*).

Commeliniceae a monocotyledonous family; tradescantias.

Commelinidae a monocotyledon subclass containing the grasses, bromeliads and tradescantias.

convolvulus a number of species of the family Convolvulaceae.

corm a perennating organ; a swollen stem base.

cotyledon the 'leaf' on seed embryos, sometimes modified for food storage (e.g. in peas). The number of seed leaves provides one of the principal distinctions between the two classes of flowering plants: the Liliopsida (the monocotyledons) and the Magnoliopsida (the dicotyledons).

crocus 75 species belonging to the genus *Crocus*.

cultivar a variety of a cultivated plant species that has been bred for agricultural or horticultural purposes.

daffodil (or **narcissus**) 60 species of bulbous herbs (family Amaryllidaceae).

daisy 15 species of the genus *Bellis* and other genera of the family Asteridacae.

dandelion a large number of weeds (genus *Taraxacum*).

deciduous plants characterized by the seasonal shedding of leaves. Many broadleaved trees of the higher latitudes shed their leaves in winter, entering a dormant phase. In lower-latitude temperate zones related species may be evergreen.

dicotyledon any member of the flowering-plant class Magnoliopsida. The main distinguishing feature is a double-seed leaf (cotyledon). The dicotyledons comprise about 70% of the flowering plant species. Distinguishing features include: two seed leaves (cotyledons); leaves with branching main veins connected by a net-like venation; floral organs in fours or fives; a persistent primary root system.

Dillenidae a dicotyledonous plant subclass.

dock a number of species of perennial herb (genus *Rumex*).

drupe an indehiscent fruit consisting of an outer layer (skin), a fleshy middle layer and a stony inner layer, within which there is a single seed.

elder a European and North American shrub (family Caprifoliaceae).

elm 20 species of large tree (genus *Ulmus*).

epiphyte any plant that grows on other plants without damage to them.

Ericaceae a dicotyledonous plant family; heathers, rhododendrons and cranberry.

eucalyptus 175 species of mainly Australian tree or shrub (genus *Eucalyptus*).

Euphorbiaceae a dicotyledonous plant family; spurges.

evergreen plants characterized by the tendency of the leaves not to fall in unison. In tropical rainforests the leaves of most trees are evergreen.

Fabaceae (or **Papilionaceae**) a dicotyledonous plant family (the legumes); peas, beans, clovers, brooms, lupins, peanuts, etc.

Fagaceae a dicotyledonous plant family; oaks and beeches.

flower the part of a plant containing the sexual organs. In true flowering plants the complete flower contains a series of four organs arranged in succession on the receptacle. From base to apex these are sepals, petals, stamens and carpels. They may occur in a continuous spiral, sometimes with a series of gradual changes between organs. Alternatively, each organ occurs in a discrete, distinct whorl, often with fusion between the elements of the whorl.

forget-me-not 50 species of the temperate genus *Myosotis*.

fruit the seed-containing structure that develops from the ovary of a flower, usually after fertilization. A great variety of fruits have developed to attract different types of dispersers.

funicle the small stalk that emerges from an almost mature seed.

garlic a herb of the family Alliaceae.

gentian 400 mainly alpine species of perennial herbs (family Gentianaceae).

geranium 400 mainly temperate species of herbs (family Geraniaceae).

ginger a tropical perennial herb (family Zingiberaceae).

gladiolus 300 species of Old World bulbous herb (family Iridaceae).

gorse 15 species of spiny temperate shrub (family Fabaceae).

grapefruit an evergreen citrus tree (family Rutaceae).

grape vine several vines of the genus *Vitis*.

grasses constitute the monocotyledonous family Poaceae. This group – of which there about 9000 species – includes the cereal or grain crops that provide staple foods for much of the world's population: rice, wheat, maize, barley, rye, oats, etc. The group also includes sugar cane. In grasses typical of grassland habitats the growing points of the stems are below ground and are protected by encircling leaves.

Grossulariaceae a dicotyledonous plant family; currants and gooseberries.

Hamamelidaceae a dicotyledonous plant family; witch hazel.

Hamamelidae a dicotyledonous subclass containing witch hazels, elms, nettles, walnuts, plane trees, birches, alders, hazels, oaks and beeches.

hazel 15 species of shrubs and trees (genus *Corylus*).

heather a mainly European low evergreen shrub (family Ericaceae).

herbaceous perennial (**herb**) any flowering plant that lacks woody cells and therefore dies back to the roots (or to other perennating organs) at the outset of frost or drought, and which produces new growth above ground upon the return of spring or rain.

Hippocastanaceae a dicotyledonous plant family; horse chestnuts.

holly 400 species of trees and shrubs (genus *Ilex*).

honeysuckle 200 temperate shrubs and woody climbers (genus *Lonicera*).

hydrangea 25 species of New World shrub (family Hydrangeaceae).

indehiscent (of plant structures) not opening of their own accord.

inflorescence a mass of small flowers clustered together.

Iridaceae a monocotyledonous plant family; irises.

iris 300 bulbous herbs with rhizomes, belonging to the family Iridaceae.

ivy 15 temperate species of climbers and woody shrubs (genus *Hedera*).

Juglandaceae a dicotyledonous plant family; walnut trees.

Lamiaeae a dicotyledonous plant family; mints, thyme and basil.

Lauraceae a dicotyledonous plant family; laurel, bay and avocado.

laurel a number of small trees and bushes (family Lauraceae).

legumes members of the family Fabaceae; see pp. 125–26.

lemon a citrus fruit (family Rutaceae).

lettuce a number of species of herb of the temperate genus *Lactuca.*
Liliaceae a monocotyledonous family; lilies, tulips and bluebells.
Liliidae a monocotyledonous subclass containing the lilies, onions, daffodils, irises, agaves, asparagus and orchids.
Liliopsida a plant class – the monocotyledons.
lily 90 species of bulbous herb (family Liliaceae).
lime (or **linden**) 1) 30 species of tree (genus *Tilia*). 2) a lemon-like citrus fruit (family Rutaceae).
lupin 200 species of leguminous annual and perennial herbs (genus *Lupinus*).
magnolia 85 species of trees and bushes of the Old World genus *Magnolia.*
Magnolidiidae a dicotyledonous subclass including magnolias, water lilies, laurels, buttercups and poppies.
Magnoliopsida a plant class – the dicotyledons.
maple 200 temperate species of evergreen and deciduous trees and shrubs (genus *Acer*).
marigold an annual herb (family Asteraceae).
marjoram a number of aromatic herbs (genus *Origanum*).
mimosa 400 leguminous species of trees, shrubs and herbs (genus *Mimosa*).
mint 25 temperate species of aromatic perennial herbs (genus *Mentha*).
monocotyledon any member of the flowering-plant class Liliopsida. The main distinguishing feature is a single-seed leaf (cotyledon). The monocotyledons comprise about 30% of flowering-plant species.
Most monocotyledons are herbaceous. Those that are trees lack wood and therefore cannot support a branching canopy. Distinguishing features include: a single-seed leaf (cotyledon) in the embryo and young plant; parallel veins in leaves (which are usually long, narrow and pointed); floral organs arranged in threes; fibrous root systems.
mustard several herbs of the family Brassicaceae.
Myrtaceae a dicotyledonous plant family; eucalyptuses.
nectar a sugary liquid that serves to attract the interest of pollinators.
nectary that part of the flower which produces nectar to attract pollinators.
nettles 50 species of temperate plants (genus *Urtica*).
nightshade a number of species of the genus *Solanum.*
Nymphaeaceae a dicotyledonous family; water lilies.
oak 450 species of deciduous tree (genus *Quercus*).
Oleaceae a dicotyledonous plant family; olive and ash.
olive a Mediterranean tree (family Oleaceae).
onion a biennial herb (family Alliaceae).
orange a citrus tree (family Rutaceae).
orchid 18,000 members of the family Orchidaceae.
ovary (of flowering plants) a protective structure surrounding the ovule. The ovary contains one or more ovules, within each of which is a female gamete (the ovum or egg).
Paeoniaceae a dicotyledonous plant family; peonies.
palm any member of the family Arecaceae. Most are trees.
pansy a number of annual and perennial herbs (genus *Viola*).
Papaveraceae a dicotyledonous plant family; poppies.
parsley a temperate biennial herb (family Apiaceae).
pea a number of leguminous plants (family Fabaceae).
peanut an annual tropical herb (family Fabaceae).
pear 30 species of temperate trees and shrubs (genus *Pyrus*).
peony 33 species of temperate perennial herbs (genus *Paeonia*).
perennating organ an underground organ for storing food. Perennating organs – which allow biennials and herbaceous perennials to survive frost and drought – occur in a variety of forms: taproots, bulbs, corms, and tubers. In many cases these perennating organs are used for reproductive purposes.
petal one of a series of four organs in a flower. Petals are usually large, delicate and colourful. Their function is one of advertisement and attraction of pollinators.
phloem the parts of vascular tissue in plants responsible for conducting substances manufactured by the plant. See also p. 126.
phlox 65 species of annual and perennial shrubs and herbs of the North American genus *Phlox.*
pink several species of the genus *Dianthus.*
Platanaceae a family of the subclass Hamamelidae. It contains the plane tree.
plane 10 species of the genus *Platanus.*
plum several species of the genus *Prunus.*
plumule the shoot from which the rest of the plant grows.
Poaceae a monocotyledonous family (formerly known as Graminae); grasses, cereals and reeds.
Polemoniaceae a monocotyledonous plant family; the phloxes.
pollen male gametes (male sex cells) in flowers. The pollen grain consists of only two gametes and one vegetative nucleus.
pollination the process by which pollen is brought from the male organs to the female organs of seed-bearing plants. Most flowers are hermaphrodite and although some flowers are naturally self-pollinated, there is a genetic bonus to be gained from cross-pollination, which can maintain or increase the vigour of the population. A flower that depends upon an animal to carry pollen to another plant needs to advertise its wares. To this end many flowers are conspicuous and may also be scented. Flowers frequently have nectar guides. As well as acting as an advertisement, a flower must also provide – or seem to provide – a reward to the pollinator. The most common rewards are a share in the pollen itself and nectar. Flowers that rely on the wind for pollination do not need to expend energy on attracting pollinators. However, they must produce vast quantities of pollen to saturate the air and ensure that any sticky stigma exposed to air currents will pick up pollen of the same species.
pollinator any animal (usually an insect) that is an agent of pollination.
Polygonaceae a monocotyledonous plant family; dock, knotgrass and buckwheat.
pondweed 100 species of aquatic herbs.
poplar 35 species of trees of the northern temperate genus *Populus.*

poppy a large number of members of two genera of the family Papaveraceae.
Potamogetonaceae a dicotyledonous plant family; pondweeds.
potato a South American herb (family Solanaceae).
primula 600 species of temperate perennial herbs (genus *Primula*).
Ranunculaceae a dicotyledonous plant family; buttercups, anemones, clematis and delphiniums.
raspberry several species of the genus *Rubus*).
receptacle the reproductive axis of a flowering plant.
reed any of a number of grasses of wet places (family Poaceae).
rhizome a perennating organ; an underground horizontal stem.
rhododendron 500 species of shrubs (family Ericaceae).
root any of a number of (usually underground) leafless outgrowths of a plant, used for anchorage and the absorption of water and mineral nutrients. Variations of the basic root form include: the tubers of dahlias, taproots of carrots and dandelions, buttress roots of some tropical trees, aerial roots in epiphytes.
Rosaceae a dicotyledonous plant family; roses, strawberry, apple, hawthorn, cherry, etc.
rose 250 species of usually prickly temperate shrub (genus *Rosa*).
Rosidae a large dicotyledonous subclass.
Rutaceae a dicotyledonous plant family; citrus fruit.
Salicaceae a dicotyledonous plant family; willows, poplars and aspen.
saxifrage 370 species of perennial herbs (family Saxafragaceae).
seed the unit of dispersal containing the embryo of seed-bearing plants.
seed dispersal the distribution of seeds from the parent plant. This is achieved by wind, water or animals.
sepal one of a series of four organs in a flower. Sepals are usually small, tough and green. Their function is one of protection, especially in the bud stage, when they enclose the unopened flower.
shrub (or **bush**) a small or medium-sized woody plant with numerous main stems.
snowdrop 12 species of bulbous herb (genus *Galanthus*).
spinach several species of plant of the family Chenopodiaceae.
stalk the main stem of a plant.
stamen one of a series of four organs in a flower. Stamens consist of a stalk or filament that carries anthers. Their function is pollen production and release at the appropriate time and place.
stem the part of a plant bearing leaves, buds or flowers.
stigma the specialized surface of a carpel at which pollen is received and recognized.
strawberry 15 species of perennial herbs (genus *Fragaria*).
style that part of the carpel that serves to position the stigma within the flower at an appropriate place to receive pollen from wind or animal pollination.
sycamore a large maple native to Europe.
taproot a perennating organ; a large single root growing vertically downwards, and from which smaller lateral roots extend (e.g. the carrot).
tendril a specially modified leaf or stem.
testa the seed coat.
Theaceae a dicotyledonous plant family; camellias and the tea plant.
thistle any prickly perennial herb of the genera *Carduus* and *Cirsium*.
thyme 300 species of small aromatic temperate shrubs (genus *Thymus*).
Tiliaceae a dicotyledonous plant family; lime trees.
tobacco several species of herbs (genus *Nicotiana*).
tomato a perennial herb (family Solanaceae).
tradescantia 40 New World herbs (family Commelinaceae).
tree a large, woody plant having one or more main stems; distinguished from a shrub or bush by its greater size and by having fewer stems. Most forest and woodland communities are dominated by flowering-plant trees – the only exceptions being the great coniferous forests of the northern hemisphere and high altitudes. Most of these trees – such as beeches, oaks, figs, mahoganies and eucalyptuses – are dicotyledons and are often referred to as broadleaved or hardwood trees. Some are evergreen, while others are deciduous. All broadleaved trees possess an extensive growth of wood and bark. The major group of monocotyledonous trees are the palms, which do not possess wood or bark.
tuber a perennating organ; a much-swollen underground stem (e.g. the potato).
tulip 100 bulbous herbs (genus *Tulipa*).
turnip a cultivar of the Brassicaceae family.
Ulmaceae a dicotyledonous plant family; elm.
Urticaceae a dicotyledonous plant family; nettles.
vegetable any part of a plant that is used in salads or savoury dishes; note that 'vegetable' is not used as a botanical definition.
vetch 140 species of annual or perennial temperate leguminous herbs (genus *Vicia*).
violet 500 species of temperate herbs (genus *Viola*).
Vitaceae a dicotyledonous plant family; grape vine and virginia creeper.
wallflower 10 species of annual perennial herbs and shrubs (genus *Cheiranthus*).
walnut 15 species of deciduous trees (genus *Juglans*).
water lily 75 species of perennial herb (family Nymphaeaceae).
water plantain several species of marsh or swamp plants (genus *Alisma*).
willow 500 species of trees and shrubs (genus *Salix*).
wind pollination see pollination.
wood the hard fibrous tissues of the stems and roots of woody plants (shrubs, bushes, many climbers and trees). Wood is composed mainly of secondary xylem produced by the cambium.
woody perennial any flowering plant that takes longer than two years to complete its life cycle and does not die back to the roots.
xylem the part of the vascular tissue of plants responsible for conducting water and dissolved mineral salts. Characteristically, the cells are elongated, with relatively thick walls strengthened by lignin. The secondary xylem makes up the principal part of wood in trees.
Zingiberaceae a monocotyledonous plant family; ginger.

FRUITS

Common name	Scientific name	Geographical origin	Date first described or known
apple	*Malus pumila*	Southwestern Asia	c. 450 BC
apricot	*Prunus armeniaca*	Central and western China	BC (Piling and Dioscorides)
avocado (pear)	*Persea americana*	Mexico and Central America	Early Spanish explorers, Clusius 1601
banana	*Musa sapientum*	Southern Asia	Intro: Africa 1st century AD, Canary Is 15th century
blackcurrants	*Ribes nigrum*	Northern Europe	First recorded in Britain in 17th-century herbals
cherry	*Prunus avium*	Europe (near Dardanelles)	Prehistoric times
coconut	*Cocus nucifera*	Pacific	Active planting since 12th century
cranberry	*Oxycccus macrocarpus*	America	–
custard apple	*Annona squamosa*	Peru and Ecuador	–
date	*Phoenix dactylifera*	Unknown	Prehistoric times
fig	*Ficus carica*	Syria westward to the Canary Is	c. 4000 BC (Egypt)
gooseberry	*Ribes grossularia*	Europe	Fruiterer's bills from France (1276–92) of Edward I
grape	*Vitis vinifera*	Around Caspian and Black Seas	c. 4000 BC
grapefruit	*Citrus grandis*	Malay Archipelago and neighbouring islands	12th or 13th century
kiwi fruit	*Actinidia chinensis*	China	–
lemon	*Citrus limon*	SE Asia	11th–13th centuries
lime	*Citrus aurantifolia*	Northern Burma	11th–13th centuries
lychee	*Litchi chinensis*	Southern China	–
mandarin	*Citrus reticulata*	China	220 BC in China; Europe 1805
mango	*Mangifera indica*	Southeastern Asia	c. 16th century; Cult. India 4th–5th century BC
olive	*Olea europaea*	Syria to Greece	Prehistoric times
orange	*Citrus sinensis*	China	2200 BC (Europe 15th century)
papaya	*Carica papaya*	West Indian Islands or Mexican mainland	14th–15th centuries
passion fruit	*Passiflora edulis*	South America	–
peach	*Prunus persica*	China?	300 BC (Greece)
pear	*Pyrus communis*	Western Asia	Prehistoric times
persimmon	*Diospyros kaki*	China/Japan	–
pineapple	*Ananas comosus*	Guadeloupe	c. time of Columbus
plum	*Prunus domestica*	Western Asia	Possibly AD 100
pomegranate	*Punica granatum*	Iran	–
quince	*Cydonia oblonga*	Northern Iran	BC
raspberry	*Rubus idaeus*	Europe	Turner's Herbal of 1548
redcurrants	*Ribes species*	Europe/Northern Asia	First description in German 17th-century herbals
rhubarb	*Rheum rhaponticum*	Eastern Mediterranean lands and Asia Minor	2700 BC (China)
strawberry	*Fragaria species*	Europe	Rome 200 BC
ugli	*Citrus reticulata*	Jamaica	–
water melon	*Citrullus laratus*	Central Africa	c. 2000 BC (Egypt)

NATIONAL PARKS

Many countries have set aside areas for the conservation of the landscape and as a protected habitat for flora and fauna.

Abruzzi (Italy) Part of the Apennine mountains. Area: 392 km^2 (151 sq mi). Fauna includes brown bear, chamois, golden eagle, lynx, polecat, wolf.

Amazonia (Brazil) Area of tropical rain forest along the Amazon river basin. Area: 10,000 km^2 (4000 sq mi). Fauna includes armadillo, capybara, tapir, great anteater, manatee, many species of monkey, and numerous species of bird (hummingbird, toucan, parrots and macaws).

Angkor (Cambodia) Tropical forest surrounding the Angkor temple ruins. Area: 107 km^2 (41 sq mi). Primarily designated to preserve the historic site.

Arusha (Tanzania) A region of mountains, swamps, forest and lakes. Area: 137 km^2 (53 sq mi). Fauna includes hippopotamus, elephants, various species of antelope and flamingos.

Banff (Alberta, Canada) Mountainous terrain in the central Canadian Rockies. Area: 6641 km^2 (2564 sq mi). Fauna includes mule deer, caribou, elk, bear (grizzly and black) and golden eagle.

Bialowieski (Poland) and Belovezhskaya (Belarus) (contiguous) The best-preserved primeval lowland forest in Europe. Combined area: 928 km^2 (358 sq mi). Fauna includes European bison, tarpan, lynx, brown bear.

Canaima (Venezuela) The large mountainous La Gran Sabana basin. Area: 30,000 km^2 (11,583 sq mi). Fauna includes jaguar, tiger cat, tapir, peccary, armadillo, agouti, capybara, opossums, spider monkeys, jacamars, harpy eagle and puffbirds.

Carlsbad Caverns (New Mexico, USA) A system of 35 limestone caverns in the Guadelupe Mountains. Area: 189 km^2 (73 sq mi). Fauna includes bats and surface mammals.

Cévennes (France) In the south of the Massif Central. Area: 844 km^2 (326 sq mi). Fauna includes genet, golden eagle, mountain sheep, wild boar.

Daisetsuzan (Japan) Part of the Ishikari volcanic mountain range in Hokkaido. Area: 2309 km^2 (892 sq mi). Fauna includes Asiatic black bear, northern pika, chipmunk, Japanese macaque, black woodpecker and three-toed woodpecker.

Dartmoor (England, UK) Moorland in central Devon. Area: 945 km^2 (365 sq mi). Fauna includes fallow, red and roe deer, wild pony.

Death Valley (California-Nevada, USA) A large low-lying desert, surrounded by mountains. Area: 8368 km^2 (3231 sq mi). Fauna includes desert bighorn sheep, cougar and fishes descended from fish of the Pleistocene Age. It is the lowest point in the Western Hemisphere.

Denali (Alaska, USA) A mountainous area on the northern flank of the Alaska Range, including North America's highest mountain, Mt McKinley. Area: 24,419 km^2 (9428 sq mi). Fauna includes moose, grizzly bear, Arctic ground squirrel, golden eagle.

Etosha (Namibia) Semiarid plains around the Etosha Pan. Area: 22,270 km^2 (8598 sq mi). Fauna includes elephants, rhinoceros, lion, leopard, lynx, Burchell's zebra, and various species of antelope.

Everglades (Florida, USA) A large flat area of swamps and islands, plus Florida Bay. Area: 5661 km^2 (2186 sq mi). Fauna includes manatee, saltwater crocodile, matamata and other turtles, cougar, ibis, bald eagle and kites.

Fiordland (New Zealand) A rugged area on the southwestern coast of South Island. Area: 12,116 km^2 (4678 sq mi). Fauna includes seals and many birds (mountain parrot, bush hawk, kiwi), and land mammals introduced by man. The park is a refuge for the takahe and kakapo.

Fuji-Hakone-Izu (Japan) Comprises Mount Fuji, the Izu peninsula and the seven active volcanic islands of Izu. Area: 1232 km^2 (476 sq mi). Fauna includes skia deer, wild boar, Japanese macaque monkeys, Japanese dormouse, Japanese auk and many other birds.

Galápagos (Ecuador) Santa Cruz Island on the Galápagos archipelago. Area: 6790 km^2 (2621 sq mi). Fauna includes the giant tortoise, giant iguana, flamingo, pelican and Darwin's finches.

Gemsbok (Botswana) A region of desert, plains and grasslands in southeast Botswana. Area: 24,305 km^2 (9384 sq mi). Fauna includes eland, gemsbok, hartebeest, springbok, wildebeest and kuku.

Gir Lion (Gujarat, India) A hilly region on the Kathiawar Peninsula. Area: 1412 km^2 (545 sq mi). Fauna includes lion, leopard, hyena, antelope, deer, wild pig, sloth bear and monkey.

Grand Canyon (Arizona, USA) Gorge of the Colorado River. Area: 4931 km^2 (1904 sq mi). Fauna includes 100 species of mammals, 100 varieties of birds and 25 kinds of reptiles and amphibians. The gorge's rocks represent a vast stretch of geological time.

Gran Paradiso (Italy) In the Alps on the Piedmont-Valle d'Aosta border. Area: 700 km^2 (270 sq mi). Fauna includes chamois, golden eagle, otter, ibex, marten, ptarmigan, white grouse.

Hohe Tauern (Austria) In the eastern Alps – the park includes the Grossglockner. Area: 2589 km^2 (1000 sq mi). Fauna includes chamois, marmot.

Hortobágyi (Hungary) Steppe and marshes in central Hungary. Area: 520 km^2 (201 sq mi). Fauna includes many species of geese.

Hwange (Zimbabwe) Expanse of the Kalahari Desert, including Nyamandhlovu Pan. Area: 14,651 km^2 (5657 sq mi). Fauna includes black rhinoceros (for which it is a refuge), buffalo, brindled gnu, roan antelope, impala and sassaby.

Jasper (Alberta, Canada) Part of the eastern Canadian Rockies. Area: 10,878 km^2 (4200 sq mi). Fauna includes elk, moose, mountain caribou, cougar, osprey, golden eagle, and blue grouse.

Kafue (Zambia) A pleateau area including some of the Kalahari Desert in the south, and bordered by the Kafue river. Area: 22,400 km^2 (8650 sq mi). Fauna includes hippopotamus, black rhinoceros (for which the park is a refuge), crocodile, many species of antelope, and numerous birds.

Katmai (Alaska, USA) Area of dying volcanoes in the Aleutian Range. Area: 16,550 km^2 (6390 sq mi). Fauna includes the Alaskan brown bear (the largest land carnivore), caribou, moose, and many small mammals, birds and fish.

Khao Yai (Thailand) An area of mountains and plateaus in southwest Thailand. Area: 2168 km^2 (837 sq mi). Fauna includes elephant, tiger, wild boar, mongoose, civet, langur, gibbon and numerous birds (silver pheasant, red-billed blue magpie).

Kosciusko (New South Wales, Australia) An area of alpine peaks and plateaus in the Great Dividing Range. Area: 6297 km^2 (2431 sq mi). Fauna includes grey forester kangaroo, brush-tailed rock wallaby, wombats, marsupial and pouched mice, koala, duck-billed platypus, and many birds (emu, currawongs).

Kruger (Transvaal, South Africa) An area of hills and plains. Area: 19,485 km^2 (7523 sq mi). Fauna includes white rhinoceros (for which the park is a refuge), African buffalo and red jackal.

Lake District (England, UK) The mountains of Cumbria. Area: 2243 km^2 (866 sq mi). Fauna includes fell ponies, mountain sheep, red deer.

Lake Mead (Arizona-Nevada, USA) An area of canyons of the Colorado River. Area: 6057 km^2 (2309 sq mi). Fauna includes desert bighorn sheep, wild burro, cougar, bobcat and many small animals. The canyons contain fossils of prehistoric animals.

Manovo-Gounda-Saint Floris (Central African Republic) Part of the upper basin of the Chari River. Area: 17,400 km^2 (6718 sq mi). Fauna includes buffalo, large antelope, many species of birds including egret.

Manu (Peru) Comprises a rugged Andean area, part of the Amazon River system and tropical forest. Area: 15,328 km^2 (5918 sq mi). Fauna includes various birds and small mammals.

Mount Aspiring (New Zealand) A mountainous region that includes the slopes of the Southern Alps on South Island. Area: 2873 km^2 (1109 sq mi). Fauna includes many varieties of birds (parakeets, owl parrot), red deer and opossum.

Namib Desert/Naukluft (Namibia) The park stretches from the Atlantic coast to the Namib Desert and the Naufkluft Mountains. Area: 23,400 km^2 (9035 sq mi). Fauna includes elephant shrew, the desert golden mole, black-backed jackal, bat-eared fox, sand grouse, egret and lark.

Ngorongoro (Tanzania) Several extinct volcanic craters, some including lakes. Area: 8292 km^2 (3202 sq mi). Fauna includes a cross-section of wildlife typical of African savannah.

Pallas-Ounastunturi (Finland) On a plateau in Lapland. Area: 500 km^2 (193 sq mi). Fauna includes brown bear, crane, elk, lemming, reindeer, whooper swan.

Pembrokeshire Coast (Wales, UK) Coastal region of Pembrokeshire. Area: 583 km^2 (225 sq mi). Fauna includes many varieties of bird, including buzzard, chough, merlin and sea birds as well as grey seal, otter, polecat.

Pfälzerwald (Germany) The Palatinate plateau. Area: 1793 km^2 (692 sq mi). Fauna includes European bison, mountain sheep, mountain goat.

Redwood (California, USA) On the Pacific coast. Area: 442 km^2 (171 sq mi). Fauna includes Roosevelt elk, fox, squirrel, rabbit, salmon, trout, and numerous birds.

Rocky Mountain (Colorado, USA) A region in the Front Range of the Rocky Mountains. Area: 1068 km^2 (412 sq mi). Fauna includes bighorn sheep, elk, beaver, deer, cougar, golden eagle and hawks.

Rondane (Norway) A mountainous region on the borders of Hedmark and Oppland. Area: 572 km^2 (221 sq mi). Fauna includes brown bear, elk, golden eagle, lemming, lynx, reindeer, wolf.

Sarek (Sweden) A mountainous area in Lapland. Area: 1940 km^2 (749 sq mi). Fauna includes similar species to those found in Rondane, see above.

Serengeti (Tanzania) A large plain with hilly ranges and rocky kopjes. Area: 14,763 km^2 (5700 sq mi). Fauna includes elephant, black rhinoceros (for which the park is a refuge), lion, leopard, cheetah, hyena, buffalo, zebra, giraffe and various species of antelope.

Skaftafell (Iceland) In the south of Iceland. Area: 500 km^2 (193 sq mi). Fauna includes bear, grey seal, many species of sea bird.

Snowdonia (Wales, UK) The mountainous area around Snowdon. Area: 2171 km^2 (838 sq mi). Fauna includes otter, polecat, pine marten.

Tsavo (Kenya) An area stretching from the semiarid plains in the southeast to the Chyulu Hills and the foothills of Mt Kilimanjaro in the West. Area: 20,821 km^2 (8039 sq mi). Fauna includes black rhinoceros (for which the park is a refuge), various species of antelope (lesser kudu, fringe-eared oryx, gerenuk, hartebeest), and numerous birds.

Uluru (Northern Territory, Australia) An area of rocky terrain, including Ayers Rock, the monolith cluster of Mt Olga, and aboriginal rock paintings. Area: 1261 km^2 (487 sq mi). Fauna includes kangaroo, wallaby, euro, dingo, bandicoot rat, emu, and various snakes and lizards.

Vanoise (France) Along the Italian border in Savoy. Area: 528 km^2 (204 sq mi). Fauna includes chamois, golden eagle, otter, ibex, marten, ptarmigan, white grouse.

Wood Buffalo (Alberta-Northwest Territories, Canada) Area of open plains between Lake Athabasca and Great Slave Lake. Area: 44,800 km^2 (17,300 sq mi). Fauna includes bison (wood buffalo and plains buffalo), elk, moose, woodland caribou, bear (black and grizzly), lynx, whooping crane and grouse. The park is a refuge for bison and whooping cranes.

Yellowstone (Wyoming-Montana-Idaho, USA) Part of the Rocky Mountains. Area: 8984 km^2 (3469 sq mi). Fauna includes wapiti, bison and over 200 species of birds (trumpeter swan, tanager, Canada goose). The largest thermal area in the world, the park contains mud volcanoes, hot springs, sulfur pools and geysers.

Yosemite (California, USA) A region of canyons, gorges and peaks in the Sierra Nevada. It contains the highest waterfall in America, Yosemite Falls. Area: 3079 km^2 (1189 sq mi). Fauna includes bear, deer, ground squirrel, chipmunk, Steller's jay, Clark's nutcracker and mountain quail.

The Animal World

ANIMALS – an introduction

In spite of the pre-eminent importance of the animal kingdom, there is surprisingly little agreement about the precise features that characterize animals and consequently about the exact boundaries of the kingdom itself. The kingdom Animalia is conventionally restricted to multicellular forms, but there is a multitude of single-celled protozoans, generally classed with other unicellular life in the kingdom Protoctista, that show all or most of the features normally regarded as defining animals and that might reasonably be classed with them. Even with this restriction, the animal kingdom is unsurpassed in size and diversity. It ranges from simple sponges and corals, through a host of more complex invertebrates such as insects and squid, to vertebrates, which include the most advanced animals of all, the birds and mammals. We can only guess at the number of species contained in this enormous kingdom. One and half million species have been scientifically described, but this must still represent only a fraction of the animals that actually exist. The majority of animals described – over one million – are insects.

Acoelomata a subdivision of the division Bilateralia. The members of the four phyla comprising this subdivision do not possess a coelom. The best known are members of the phylum Platyhelminthes, which includes the flatworms, flukes and tapeworms.

Annelida a phylum of the subdivision Coelomata, the annelids or true worms.

Arthropoda a phylum of the subdivision Coelomata, the arthropods.

Bilateralia the division of the subkingdom Eumetazoa. It includes animals that may only be divided by one plane to yield mirror images. They possess an extra embryonic cell layer – the mesoderm – which forms most of the body. In most animals, there is a body cavity – the coelom – containing the digestive tract and other visceral organs.

Chordata a phylum of the subdivision Coelomata. It contains all those animals (chordates) that have a stiffening rod that provides a flexible support along the back. The phylum contains four subphyla – the largest, the subphylum Craniata, includes birds, fish, reptiles and mammals.

Cnidaria a phylum of the division Radiata. It includes jellyfish, sea anemones and the corals.

coelom see Bilateralia.

Coelomata a subdivision of the division Bilateralia. It contains all the animals in possession of a true coelom.

distinguishing features (of animals) include:

1) Animals lack the cell walls that are characteristic of plants.

2) Animals obtain their food in a quite different manner to plants. While virtually all plants are able to harness the energy of the Sun to synthesize the complex organic compounds they require from simple inorganic molecules (photosynthesis), animals rely on ready-made sources of such compounds – in other words they are dependent on plants, either by eating them directly or by feeding on the body tissues of animals that have done so.

3) Although some aquatic animals, such as sea anemones and corals, are more or less immobile and can rely upon their food coming to them, the majority of animals must actively find it or seize it. Unlike plants, therefore, animals generally require at least some degree of mobility.

4) Movement in multicellular animals requires a great deal of coordination between different body parts; in all but the simplest animals, such as jellyfish, this entails a reasonably sophisticated system of nervous controls.

5) Furthermore, an animal needs to move not only in a coordinated fashion but also in a particular direction; thus it requires some form of sensory apparatus tied in with its nervous system. Although plants can detect various environmental stimuli and react accordingly, animals have evolved an astonishing range of systems by which they can perceive what is going on around them.

6) Most animals have a digestive tract or cavity.

7) Most animals have a central coordinating point of the nervous system – a 'brain'.

Echinodermata a phylum of the subdivision Coelomata, the echinoderms.

Ectoprocta a phylum of the subdivision Coelomata, the bryozoans or moss animals.

Eumetazoa the subkingdom that includes all those animals not found in the subkingdom Parazoa. They are characterized by discrete tissues and organs that develop from early embryonic cell layers. The subkingdom is divided into two divisions – Radiata and Bilateralia.

faunal regions the distinct regions into which the world can be divided, each of which is characterized by a distinct range of animal species.

Mollusca a phylum of the subdivision Coelomata, the molluscs.

Nematoda a phylum of the subdivision Pseudocoelomata, the roundworms.

Parazoa the subkingdom that includes animals in which different cell types perform different functions – feeding, defence, reproduction, etc. – although they are not grouped into tissues or organs. It includes the sponges.

Pseudocoelomata a subdivision of the division Bilateralia. The animals assigned to this subdivision possess a body cavity that is not developed as a true coelom. The two most important phyla are the nematodes and the rotifers.

Radiata one of the two divisions of the animal subkingdom Eumetazoa. The animals of this division all show radial symmetry – the animal may be divided along more than one plane through the centre to give mirror-image halves. The body is organized as two layers of cells separated by a jelly-like middle layer, while the nervous system forms a diffuse net. The Cnidaria is the larger of its two phyla.

Rotifera a phylum of the subdivision Pseudocoelomata, the rotifers.

SPONGES

Sponges are among the simplest and most primitive of multicellular animals. Although not animal-like in appearance, they have all the properties associated with animals. They feed on other organic matter and reproduce sexually by means of an ovum (egg) and a spermatozoon. Movement in mature sponges is limited to slight contraction of muscle-like cells, but the larval forms are free-swimming. There is also some degree of coordination of activity, even though there is no real nervous system. Sponges are widespread in marine habitats, ranging from the intertidal zone to the greatest depths, and also in freshwater. Some sponges are only 1 cm long, but various tropical and Antarctic species can reach more than 1m (39 in) in height and breadth. A single sponge may have thousands of other tiny animals living in it.

Calcarea the class of sponges that contains small, exclusively marine sponges with a skeleton of calcite. The simplest sponges, they are usually purse- or vase-shaped.

Demospongia the largest class of sponges and also the only one with both freshwater and marine species.

feeding (in sponges) is by extracting small particles from the surrounding water.

flagellum (plur. **flagella**) a whip-like projection of special cells in chambers of the canals; the beating of the flagella draws water (containing food particles) into the sponge through pore cells.

Hexactinellida the glass sponges – deep-water species that have complex silica skeletons.

incurrent pore pore cells in the external surface of a sponge through which water is drawn by the beating of the flagella.

osculum the single excurrent opening at the top of a sponge through which filtered water and waste products are discharged.

Porifera the phylum to which all sponges belong.

reproduction (of sponges) is sexual. The eggs of a female sponge are fertilized by sperm drawn in with the feeding currents. Free-swimming larvae develop and are released into the sea. These disperse, settle on suitable surfaces, and metamorphose into young sponges.

Sclerospongia the coralline sponges – thought to be extinct until found in the 1960s.

skeleton (of sponges) may be a complex and highly specific structure. The skeleton makes sponges unattractive as food. Some species have no skeleton at all.

spicules the pin-like or complex star-shaped rods of silica or calcite that form the skeleton of some sponges.

spongin a meshwork of fibrous protein that entirely or almost entirely makes up the body of a sponge or which occurs in combination with spicules.

structure (of sponges) is typically a honeycomb-like structure of canals separated by cells and a hard skeleton.

ECHINODERMS

The animals of this group are characterized by five-part radial symmetry. Other common features of the group are an internal skeleton based on calcite and tube feet. Frequently echinoderms are very spiny. There are some 5000 species in the phylum Echinodermata. They are found in every marine habitat, from intertidal zones to ocean depths.

Asteroidea an echinoderm class that includes starfish.

brittlestar any member of the class Ophiuroidea. They have long, thin, spiny, flexible arms that are linked to a compact central disc. They are very mobile and found in huge numbers in all marine habitats.

Crinoidea an echinoderm class that includes sea lilies.

Echinoidea an echinoderm class that includes sea urchins.

Holothuroidea an echinoderm class that includes sea cucumbers.

Ophiuroidea an echinoderm class that includes brittlestars.

pedicellarium small pincer-like defensive organs found on echinoderms.

reproduction (of echinoderms) is mainly sexual. Echinoderms disperse through the free-swimming larvae, but are also able to multiply their numbers asexually. Individuals that split in half or are damaged can replace missing parts without difficulty.

sea cucumber any member of the class Holothuroidea. Worm- or sausage-like sea cucumbers have little internal skeleton and lack spines. Soft and flexible, some can swim actively; others are sedentary. They live on the sea bottom, feeding by means of tentacles surrounding the mouth.

sea lily any member of the class Crinoidea. Two groups of sea lilies exist: stalked, sedentary forms found exclusively in deep water and mobile, stalkless forms occurring mainly in shallow water. Both feed by sieving small particles from surrounding water. Sea lilies have up to 10, 20 or 40 branched arms.

sea urchin any member of the class Echinoidea. They may be globular, oval or disc-shaped. They have a complete skeleton (or test) of strong linked plates and are densely covered with mobile spines (used in locomotion and defence) and small pedicellaria, both of which may be poisonous. Their tube feet – in five rows around the test – are used in movement, food collection, attachment and sensory perception.

starfish any member of the class Asteroidea. Starfish usually have five hollow arms linked to a central disc. Some have six or more arms; sunstars can have up to 40. A few reach 1m (39 in) in diameter; most are much smaller. Small spines and pedicellaria cover the upper surface. On the underside are five rows of tube feet stretching from the central mouth to the arm tips. Starfish are mostly scavengers or predators and are capable of prising open clams. The gut may be turned inside out over the prey.

tube feet small, hollow walking and feeding organs that are characteristic of all echinoderms.

WORMS

The many invertebrate animals known as 'worms' are of diverse origins; what they share is a typically slender elongated body form, not a common ancestry. Many are parasitic, but there are also free-living forms in the soil and aquatic habitats. The digestive system of most worms is a continuous tube with a mouth and an anus.

annelid any member of the phylum Annelida, the segmented worms. Annelids have long, thin bodies with distinct front and hind ends. The body comprises a series of separate segments, each of which usually bears parapodia (limb-like protrusions) and/or chaetae (hair-like protrusions).

cilia tiny hair-like projections on the sides of worms.

earthworm any member of the annelid class Oligochaeta. Earthworms burrow through earth or detritus, feeding on decaying vegetable matter. They are long, thin worms without external structures except retractable chaetae (used in burrowing) and a reproductive organ (the clitellum). Earthworms are important because they recycle nutrients in the soil.

flatworm any member of the phylum Platyhelminthes. Flatworms are simple, bilaterally symmetrical animals with an upper and a lower surface. They have a distinct head with a simple brain and simple organ systems. Food is taken in and waste is expelled through a single opening.

leech any member of the annelid class Hirudinea. Predatory or parasitic, they are common in aquatic and in moist terrestrial habitats. Suckers at each end of the body grasp prey. Parasitic leeches have saliva that contains an anaesthetic to prevent detection and an anticoagulant so that blood remains fluid in the gut.

nematode any member of the phylum Nematoda, which includes eelworms, threadworms and hookworms. They have long, thin bodies that are sharply-pointed at one or both ends and a thick, resistant cuticle ('skin'). They range from the microscopic to 1 m (39 in) long and have a second opening to the gut (an anus). Many are parasitic to plants or animals.

polychaetes (or **bristleworms**) members of the annelid class Polychaeta which includes paddle-worms, lugworms, ragworms and fan worms. They are characterized by a pair of parapodia on each segment. Most live on the sea bed.

tapeworm any member of the flatworm class Cestoda. Tapeworms are ribbon-like worms living a parasitic life in the guts of vertebrates. Their bodies are made up of many repeated, egg-producing segments. Some worms reach several metres long. They have no gut, all food being absorbed through the body wall.

trematode (or **fluke**) any member of the flatworm class Trematoda. Similar in shape to turbellarians, trematodes live as external and internal parasites. They have complex life cycles, usually involving an aquatic snail and at least one other species.

turbellarian any member of the flatworm class Turbellaria. They are free-living, small, flattened, leaf-like worms found in aquatic and damp terrestrial habitats.

MOLLUSCS

The phylum Mollusca contains over 50,000 species. Common characteristics, some or all of which are found in all molluscs, include a broad locomotory foot, a protective shell, a radula (tongue-like feeding organ), and a ctenidia (gills).

bivalve any member of the class Bivalvia, which comprises molluscs whose shell is made of two parts (valves) connected by an elastic hinge. They include clams, mussels, oysters and cockles. Most live permanently attached to rocks. They have no distinct head. Water is drawn into the shell through a siphon by the rhythmic beating of thousands of tiny projections (cilia) on the gills. Small floating particles are sieved off as water passes over the gills.

cephalopod any member of the predatory gastropod class Cephalopoda, which includes squid, cuttlefish and octopuses. They are fast-moving, alert and more intelligent than other invertebrates. All cephalopods can change colour.

clam any burrowing marine or freshwater bivalve of the genus *Venus*.

cockle some 250 species of bivalve estuarine mollusc.

cuttlefish any marine cephalopod mollusc of the genus *Sepia*. Predatory, they occur in shallow inshore waters. They have an internal shell, which is a flotation device.

gastropod any marine, freshwater or terrestrial member of the class Gastropoda. They include slugs, snails, periwinkles, and limpets. Among the 35,000 species are herbivores, carnivores, parasites and particle-feeders, ranging in size from tiny forms to giant conchs up to 70 cm (28 in) long. All gastropods have a muscular foot for walking or swimming, and most have a radula, which in carnivorous species has sharp pointed teeth. Most gastropods have strong external shells – some simple cones, but most complex spirals. Most gastropods reproduce sexually, producing free-swimming larvae, but some lay eggs. Land gastropods have a closeable lung in place of gills.

mussel any bivalve mollusc of the family Mytilidae. They attach themselves to rocks by byssi (threads).

octopus any marine cephalopod mollusc of the order Octopoda. Mainly bottom-living predators, octopuses have eight tentacles. Most are relatively small; some reach up to 1·8 m (6 ft) in length. They have extraordinarily sophisticated nervous systems.

oyster a number of sedentary bivalve molluscs especially those of the family Ostreidae. They live attached to hard surfaces such as rocks.

sea slug any predatory marine shell-less gastropod of the order Nudibranchia.

slug any terrestrial gastropod mollusc in which the shell is absent or greatly reduced.

snail any of the numerous gastropod molluscs. Most belong to the subclass Pulmonata.

squid a marine cephalopod mollusc with long, streamlined bodies and no shell. The head bears two large eyes and ten tentacles. Squid – which have well-developed sensory systems – are fast-moving predators.

ARTHROPODS

Arthropods are characterized by having external skeletons and pairs of jointed limbs. Judged by the number and variety of species, they are the most successful of all living creatures. Crustaceans are the dominant arthropods in the sea, while insects can be found in most available habitats on land.

abdomen the hindmost section of the body behind the thorax. The digestive and reproductive systems occupy the abdomen. In many insects the abdomen is clearly segmented.

amphipods small shrimp-like crustaceans found in enormous numbers in aquatic habitats.

antenna one of a pair of appendages projecting from the head of insects. They are generally highly mobile and have a sensory function.

apterygote any insect of the group Apterygota, the 'wingless insects'.

arachnids any member of the class Arachnida, the largest group of arthropods after the insects. Scorpions, spiders and ticks are the most important members of this group. Several members of the group have colonized marine habitats.

barnacle any marine crustacean of the class Cirripedia. Most live as sedentary filter-feeders. Some are parasitic.

blood system (of arthropods) a relatively simple system whereby nutrients, waste products, etc. are dissolved and circulated around the body. The blood (or haemolymph) is stirred by a tubular heart.

carapace a protective crustacean shell plate.

caterpillar the larva of a butterfly or moth.

centipede any of some 2800 predatory myriapods, characterized by a body comprising 15 or so segments, each bearing a pair of legs.

cephalothorax the head/thorax region of a crustacean. It is often protected by a carapace. The head segments bear sensory antennae, compound eyes and mouthparts.

chitin a complex sugar molecule, the principal component of arthropod exoskeletons.

copepod any minute marine or freshwater crustacean of the class Coperoda.

crab any of more than 4500 decapod crustaceans of the genus *Cancer*. They have a reduced abdomen that is concealed beneath a short broad cephalothorax, and the first pair of limbs is modified as pincers.

crayfish any freshwater decapod crustacean of the genera *Astacus* and *Cambarus*.

crustaceans any member of the subphylum Crustacea. There are some 42,000 species. The most important are the fairy shrimps, copepods, crabs, shrimps and prawns, and woodlice. Crustaceans are the major component of the marine zooplankton. The far fewer freshwater species, though numerous, suffer competition from insects. A very few – land crabs and woodlice – have successfully adapted to life on land. Crustaceans are typically elongated animals with segmented bodies clearly divided into a cephalothorax and a tail or abdomen. Each segment bears a pair of limbs.

cuticle a protective hard layer covering the epidermis of arthropods. It is also known as the epidermis.

decapod any member of the class Decapoda, including crabs, spider crabs, shrimps, lobsters, prawns and crayfish.

endopterygote any pterygote insect of the group Endopterygota, comprising over 85% of all known insect species. Familiar endopterygotes include beetles, butterflies and moths, flies, and bees, ants and wasps. The group is characterized by complete metamorphosis, i.e. juveniles bear no similarity to adults, and the adult form is attained via larval and pupal stages.

exopterygote any pterygote insect of the group Exopterygota, including grasshoppers, dragonflies, earwigs and aphids. They are characterized by incomplete metamorphosis, i.e. juveniles resemble adults and there is no pupal stage.

exoskeleton the external skeleton of all arthropods. It both supports and protects the animal, and is formed by the cuticle. The arthropod skeleton shows remarkable versatility, varying from the soft elastic bag that surrounds a caterpillar to the immensely hard claws of a crab. The exoskeleton is further strengthened by tanning. The hard, external skeleton limits the size of the animal.

fairy shrimp (brine shrimp) any small, primitive crustacean of the class Branchiopoda, found in abundance in temporary pools.

growth (of arthropods) can only take place if the old hard exoskeleton is discarded and a new larger one is grown in its place. This process is known as moulting. Moulting has to occur a number of times in all arthropods as they grow to full adult size. At each moult the animal is vulnerable to attack by predators, parasites or disease and – in the case of terrestrial species – the danger of dehydration. Much of the old exoskeleton is absorbed and re-used in the new one, but even so, at each moult there is a loss of old cast 'skin'.

head (of insects) the front section of the body of an insect. It usually has a pair of compound eyes for vision and often two or three small single eyes (ocelli), which respond to varying light levels. Two antennae and two pairs of palps at the mouth provide information on both touch and taste. The mouthparts are typically adapted for biting, but in many species they are modified for other functions.

imago an insect in its final mature winged state.

insect any arthropod of the class Insecta, an enormously successful group comprising several million species. Conventionally, the class is divided into wingless insects (apterygotes) and winged insects (pterygotes), but this is not universally accepted. They have colonized almost every habitat except the sea where crustaceans are the dominant arthropods. The success of insects stems from the light, strong, wax-covered cuticle, which is highly protective, especially against dehydration. In general, adult insects are easily recognizable by their three body sections – head, thorax and abdomen.

krill any small shrimp-like crustacean of the order Euphausiacea.

larva an insect in an immature but active state, often markedly different in structure and life style from the adult.

legs (of insects) occur in three pairs which are attached to the lower part of the thorax. Insects' legs are highly varied, ranging from the strong digging forelegs of the mole cricket to the long hindlegs of grasshoppers, which are adapted for jumping. Aquatic insects have legs adapted for swimming – diving beetles and water boatmen, for instance, have flattened hindlegs fringed with long hairs, which are used as oars.

limbs (of crustaceans) occur in primitive forms as a series of similar jointed structures behind the cephalothorax. In more advanced crustaceans the limbs have different functions and are structurally modified. The limbs on the thorax are generally used for walking, digging or swimming, while the abdominal limbs are usually adapted for respiratory or reproductive functions. The front limbs of crustaceans often take the form of claws for food capture and defence.

lobster any large decapod crustacean of the genus *Homarus*. All lobsters have the first pair of limbs modified into pincers.

Malpighian tubes the excretory organs of insects.

metamorphosis a radical structural transformation in an animal. In insects two kinds of metamorphosis are recognized, endopterygotes and exopterygotes. In insects the adult form is not reached by progressive growth (as it is, for example, in mammals). Instead, intermediate larval stages occur, which differ radically from the adult in both structure and life style. In such cases the adult stage is attained by means of a major transformation of structure (metamorphosis). A number of larval stages may follow each other before the adult stage is reached. A caterpillar is a larva that metamorphoses during the pupal stage to a butterfly.

millipede any of some 8000 herbivorous myriapods, characterized by a body comprising numerous segments, each bearing a pair of legs.

mite any tiny parasitic arachnid of the order Acari.

myriapod name given to several groups of arthropods characterized by a long segmented body and many legs. They include centipedes and millipedes.

ocellus (plur. **ocelli**) a simple eye found in some insects.

ovipositor the egg-laying structure of female insects, at the tip of the abdomen. In some insects (bees, wasps, etc.) it is modified into a sting.

palp a segmented sense organ of touch and taste, paired and comprising some of the mouth parts of insects.

prawn the name given to numerous decapod crustaceans, especially those of the genus *Palaemon*. They typically have flattened bodies and two pairs of pincers.

pterygote any insect of the group Pterygota, the 'winged insects', accounting for the vast majority of living insect species. The group is subdivided into the exopterygotes (such as grasshoppers, dragonflies and aphids) and the endopterygotes (such as butterflies and bees).

pupa the intermediate, usually inactive, form of an insect between the larval and imago (adult) stages.

scorpion any of about 800 predatory arachnids of the order Xiphosura, characterized by large pincers, a squat eight-legged body, and a long abdomen with a prominent pointed sting.

shrimp the common name given to numerous small decapod crustaceans, especially those of the genus *Crangon*. Shrimps typically have flattened transparent bodies and a fan-like tail. The difference between shrimps and prawns is imprecise.

spider any predatory arachnid of the order Araneae, characterized by eight legs, a large abdomen, and a combined head and thorax (cephalothorax). Of the 30,000 described species most are terrestrial. As well as bearing the four pairs of legs the cephalothorax has two other pairs of appendages – one is a pair of hollow fangs used to inject venom into prey; the other is leg-like in females, and a complicated reproductive structure in males. At the tip of the abdomen there are a number of glands (developed only in females) that are used to produce silks. Fluids secreted by these glands dry as threads as they are forced out through three pairs of nozzles called spinnerets. Spiders have evolved many techniques to trap prey.

spider crab any decapod crustacean of the family Maiidae, with a small triangular body and extremely long legs.

spider mite any herbivorous mite of the family Tetranychidae.

spiracle any of a series of small, paired openings in the cuticle of an insect or arachnid by which air enters and leaves the tracheae.

sting a sharp organ in insects such as bees and wasps that is adapted to wound a predator or prey by piercing and injecting poison.

tanning a process that hardens the exoskeleton of arthropods.

thorax the section of an insect's body between the head and the abdomen. It consists of a rigid box containing the muscles that operate the two pairs of wings. Three pairs of legs are attached to the lower part of the thorax.

tick any tiny parasitic arachnid of the families Ixodidae (hard ticks) and Argasidae (soft ticks) in the order Acari.

trachea any of the numerous tiny tubes by which air is conveyed from the spiracles.

velvet worm any arthropod of the class Onchychopora, small, worm-like animals with short joint-less limbs.

water fleas a group of tiny freshwater crustaceans.

wings (of insects) the flight structure of insects. The wings are usually thin yet strong, with the wing membrane stiffened by a network of veins. Some insects move their wings by contraction of muscles attached directly to them, while others use an indirect 'click' mechanism. Wings may have other functions besides flight. In some insects, such as beetles and grasshoppers, the forewings are hardened, covering and protecting the large hindwings underneath. Crickets use their wings to produce sound, while in many insects the wings are coloured or patterned and used in courtship display, or as camouflage.

winged insects see pterygote.

woodlouse any crustacean of the class Isopoda, the principal group of terrestrial crustaceans. They have flattened bodies, simple antennae and seven pairs of similar legs.

FISHES

Fishes are cold-blooded vertebrates that belong to the classes Chondrichthyes and Osteichthyes. An elongated, streamlined body, a well-muscled hind end of the body and a powerful tail fin are all adaptations to propulsion through water, while the gills absorb oxygen with great efficiency.

actinopterygians the ray-finned fishes (see below).

agnathans the jawless fish. All the earliest fossil fishes were jawless. The group is now represented only by the hagfish and lampreys.

anal fin the single fin that in most fishes is on the underside of a fish and in front of the tail.

bony fish (or **osteichthyans**) any fish of the class Osteichthyes. Bony fishes are distinguished by the possession of an internal skeleton of endochondrial bones, that is bone that replaces cartilage during the course of development. There are two principal subclasses: the fleshy-finned fishes (lungfishes and coelacanths) and the ray-finned fishes (the great majority of living species).

cartilaginous fish (or **chondrichthyans**) any fish belonging to the class Chondrichthyes, which includes sharks, rays and chimaeras. Their entire skeleton is made from cartilage, in contrast to bony fishes. Most are predators. Fertilization is internal; some species lay eggs, but many give birth to live young.

caudal fin the tail fin.

Chondrichthyes the class comprising cartilaginous fishes.

cod common name given to many members of the family Gadidae.

dorsal fin the fin that runs down the centre of the back.

fin any of the projecting structures by which fishes swim, steer, maintain balance, etc. Fins are supported by rays, which may be soft or hard. The dorsal, caudal (tail) and anal fins are single; the pectoral and pelvic fins are in pairs.

flatfish any fish of the order Pleuronectiformes, mainly occurring in relatively shallow marine waters. Young flatfishes are symmetrical, but during development one eye migrates over the head to lie next to the one on the other side; the flattened adult then swims with its eyeless side facing downwards. Most flatfishes lie on the bottom; many are able to change colour to merge with their background.

gill cavity a cavity which in most teleosts produces a sucking motion. Combined with compression of the water by the mouth, this sucking motion ensures a pressurized flow of water to the gills, so increasing the oxygen supply.

gills the respiratory organs used for gas exchange in water by fish. Although a number of shark species have six or seven pairs of gills and some hagfishes have 16, most fishes have four gills on each side of the head, which look like a row of V-shaped bars. Red filaments on the hind edge of the bars extract oxygen from the water flowing over them. Blood passes through the gill filaments in the opposite direction to the flow of water, thus meeting successively 'fresher' water (containing more and more oxygen) as it does so. Gills are able to absorb up to 80% of the oxygen passing over them. Water for respiration is generally taken in through the mouth.

gill slit one or more openings in the pharynx region of fish, containing the gills.

herring either of two species of the genus *Clupea.*

lateral-line system a sensory system in fish involved in the detection of pressure, vibration, etc.

Osteichthyes the class that comprises bony fish.

pectoral fin in most fishes, the pair of fins just behind the head. When turned to face the water, pectoral fins and pelvic fins are used in 'braking'.

pelvic fin in most fishes, the pair of fins centrally-placed on either side of the underside.

Pleuronectiformes the order that comprises flatfish.

poikilothermic (or **ectothermic**) relating to an animal whose body temperature varies with and is largely dependent on the environmental temperature. Fishes are poikilothermic, that is 'cold-blooded'.

ray any of 250 members of the subclass Selachii.

ray-finned fishes (or **actinopterygians**) any bony fish of the subclass Actinopterygii, the dominant group of living fishes.

scales disc-like protective overlapping plates that form a covering in the majority of bony fishes. The forward edge of each scale is embedded in the dermis (the inner layer of skin) and all the scales are covered by a continuous layer of epidermis (the outermost layer). Although this is the most common type of scale, highly modified forms are found. Some groups, including lampreys, some catfishes and very deep-sea fishes, have no scales.

shark any of 250 cartilaginous fish of the subclass Selachii.

swim bladder (or **air bladder**) a gas-filled sac in the upper part of the body cavity of teleost fish. The bladder is either filled with air taken in at the surface of the water via the mouth or charged with gases from the blood by means of a special gas gland. The swim bladder enables fish to achieve buoyancy in the water.

swimming (in fish) movement through water principally by means of segmental muscle contractions. In most fishes forward propulsion is produced by a series of contractions that cause undulations of the lateral curvature of the body. As these waves pass backwards down the body, the effect is to present a series of moving inclined planes pushing outwards and backwards against the water. These waves are of very small amplitude at the head end, which oscillates only slightly from side to side as a fish swims, but they become more pronounced towards the tail. The tail fin may contribute up to 90% of the total thrust, but some fishes, such as eels, have very small tails and it is the undulations of the body alone that provide the propulsive force. Flatfishes undulate the whole body and/or the vertical fins (which are in the horizontal plane) to produce the waves that generate thrust.

teleost any ray-finned fish belonging to the subdivision Teleostei, comprising about 95% of living fish species. Teleosts typically have swim bladders, and tails in which the upper and lower halves are equal.

AMPHIBIANS

The amphibians played a central role in the evolution of life on Earth, since they were the first of the vertebrates to leave the water to live part of their lives on land. The amphibians belong to three orders: frogs and toads to the order Anura, newts and salamanders to the order Urodela, and caecilians to the order Gymnophiona. The basic body plan of amphibians reflects their adaptation to life on land and in water. In order to spend at least part of their lives on land, amphibians must minimize the danger of drying out when exposed to air. At the same time, they must be able to obtain and use gaseous oxygen from the air for respiration. Finally, they have had to develop means of moving on land under the full force of gravity, without the buoyancy provided by water. Amphibians are a diverse group, but most share several common features.

anuran any amphibian of the order Anura, comprising approximately 3500 species of frog and toad (the 'tailless amphibians'). Anurans exhibit great diversity of habitat, and terrestrial, arboreal, burrowing and totally aquatic forms are known. Most anurans have a free-swimming tadpole stage.

axolotl a species of Mexican salamander that reproduces by neoteny.

caecilian any amphibian of the order Gymnophiona, comprising some 150 species. They are limbless tropical amphibians; most are burrowing, but one group is aquatic. Caecilians have streamlined heads; their eyes have become reduced in size and in function.

eggs (of amphibians) are relatively large and yolky. They have gelatinous outer capsules but lack the protective membranes seen in higher animals.

frog the common name of many Anuran amphibians (the group also includes toads). The term is often used to distinguish smooth-skinned, short-legged jumping species from warty-skinned, short-legged forms, which are generally called 'toads', but the distinction is imprecise and has no taxonomical significance. In a restricted sense, the name 'frog' may be used for the 'true' frogs of the family Ranidae. Typical frogs and toads live on or near the ground and take fast-moving prey such as insects and spiders. The large keen eyes, long hind legs to assist the forward thrust of the body, and a large head with a broad mouth and a wide gape all increase the likelihood of capturing prey.

locomotion (of amphibians) is by swimming in the larval stage and again in the adult stage when amphibians return to the water to breed. Tadpoles swim by lashing their tails from side to side. Aquatic caecilians, newts and salamanders swim in a fish-like manner. Most frogs and toads swim by thrusting the hind legs against the water. This is assisted by webbing between the toes. Most frogs and toads have well-developed hind limbs that can be used to leap.

lungless salamander any salamander of the family Plethodontidae.

lungs (of amphibians) are simple sac-like organs, which are well supplied with blood vessels, permitting gas exchange while limiting water loss. Some lungless salamanders breathe through the skin and mouth.

metamorphosis the change from the larval to adult stage. The change is far more dramatic in frogs than in salamanders and caecilians. The spawn of a typical frog initially has a spherical yolk, which assumes an oval shape after about a week. After about two weeks the tadpole hatches out from the egg mass and attaches itself to waterweed. After a few days, the mouth and external gills are formed. At about five weeks hind-limb buds appear, and by ten weeks proper feet are formed. By 12 weeks, the major changes of metamorphosis commence: the tail is reabsorbed, a true mouth forms, the eyes grow, and the forelimbs are released.

migration (of amphibians) occurs because frogs, toads and newts show great fidelity to certain breeding sites. They often migrate some kilometres, passing other 'suitable' sites to reach their 'home' pond.

neoteny the ability of some newts and salamanders (for example, the axolotl) to breed while still in the tadpole stage.

newt any of 22 species of highly aquatic salamander, included in the 'true' salamander family Salamandridae. Newts are notable for their highly ritualistic courtship behaviour.

nictitating membrane a third eyelid present in all amphibians except caecilians. It keeps the corneal surface clean and moist.

pelvic patch (or **pelvic seat**) an area of baggy skin on the underside of the thighs of toads. Through this patch – which is in contact with the ground when the toad is sitting – a toad may take up to 70% of the water that passes through its skin.

salamander (or **urodele**) any of 350 species of tailed amphibians of the order Urodela (or Caudata). They are lizard-like in appearance, but do not have a scaly skin. They live on or near the ground and take slow-moving invertebrates such as worms, slugs and snails. The term 'salamander' is sometimes used in a restricted sense to refer to members of the family Salamandridae ('true' salamanders and newts).

siren any eel-like salamander of the family Sirenidae, from southern USA and Mexico. They have tiny fore limbs but no hind limbs.

skin (of amphibians) is hairless and kept moist by mucus secreted from special glands embedded in the skin; it is permeable and capable of some control over water uptake and loss.

spawn the fertilized eggs of amphibians.

tadpole the aquatic larva of amphibians.

tails (of amphibians) are universal in the tadpole stage. However, adult frogs and toads lack tails, having lost the s-shaped movement of the larval stage.

toad the common name given to many of the anuran amphibians, generally to warty-skinned species. In a restricted sense, the name 'toad' may be used for the 'true' toads of the family Bufonidae.

tongue (of amphibians) is generally long and can be extended in capturing and controlling prey.

urodele another name for a salamander.

REPTILES

Of the once mighty reptiles there are now only four orders: Chelonia (turtles, tortoises and terrapins), Crocodilia (crocodiles), Squamata (snakes, lizards and amphisbaenians), and Rhynchocephalia (tuatara). Reptiles have made a complete break from living in water by developing two features lacking in living amphibians – scaled waterproof skins and shelled yolk-bearing eggs. These developments have allowed reptiles to adapt to a wide range of habitats.

agamid any of some 300 species of Old World lizard of the family Agamidae.

alligator the American and the Chinese alligators.

amphisbaenian any of about 100 small, virtually blind, limbless, burrowing lizards belonging to the suborder Amphisbaenia. They feed principally on worms and other invertebrates.

basilisk any small American iguanid of the genus *Basiliscus.*

chameleon any of around 85 species of mainly tree-dwelling lizard of the family Chamaeleontidae, famous for their capacity to change colour rapidly.

cobra any highly venomous elapid snake of the genus *Naja* or *Ophiophagus.* When alarmed, they give a threat display by expanding the ribs in the neck region (the 'hood').

constrictor any of around 80 species of non-venomous snake in the family Boidae that kill their prey by constriction.

cranial kinesis a modification of the skull. In snakes and lizards the skull is an extremely loose structure, with numerous joints that allow the animal to dislocate its skull in order to swallow prey that may be several times the normal diameter of the mouth.

crocodile any large predatory reptile of the family Crocodilidae. They have a body armoured with bony plates set in the skin of the back, a long deep-sided tail and a long-snouted skull. Crocodiles and alligators have a large pair of teeth near the front of the lower jaw, which in crocodiles are visible when the mouth is closed.

dinosaur any reptile of the orders Saurischia and Ornithischia that dominated life on earth for over 160 million years.

egg (reptilian) is well protected by a chalky or leathery shell. The egg is retained by many species of lizard and snake during the development of the young, which hatch as the eggs are laid. However, most reptiles abandon their eggs.

elapid any of some 200 species of venomous snake belonging to the family Elapidae. They include cobras, coral snakes, mambas and kraits.

gecko any of over 600 small, mainly insectivorous, lizards belonging to the family Gekkonidae.

iguanid any of around 600 species of lizard of the mainly New World family Iguanidae. Most are agile tree- or ground-dwellers. They include iguanas and basilisks.

lizard any reptile of the suborder Sauria, containing some 3000 species. Major families include agamids, chameleons, geckos, iguanids, lacertids, monitors, skinks, and teiids.

locomotion (of snakes) lacking limbs, snakes have developed a number of characteristic modes of movement: serpentine (the most characteristic), concertina, straight line (by stretching and contracting), and sidewinding.

mamba any tropical elapid snake. They are notoriously venomous and aggressive.

monitor (or **vanarid**) any of about 30 species of lizard of the family Vanaridae. All are large predatory carnivores. They include the Komodo dragon, the largest of all lizards.

poikilothermic (or **cold-blooded**) relating to an animal whose body temperature varies with and is largely dependent upon the environmental temperature. Reptiles are poikilothermic.

skink any lizard of the family Scincidae, the largest family of lizards with around 800 species.

sloughing the process of shedding the skin.

snake any limbless reptile of the suborder Serpentes (or Ophidia), containing over 2000 species. The major families include (mostly harmless) colubrids, constrictors (pythons and boas), (venomous) elapids (cobras, coral snakes, mambas and kraits) and pit vipers, (highly venomous) sea snakes, and vipers. Snakes kill their prey by suffocation, by biting or by venom. The smallest snakes are 20 cm (8 in) long and feed on termites; the longest constrictors are 10 m (33 ft) long.

terrapin name given to a number of freshwater turtles of the family Emydidae. They have flattened, webbed limbs.

tortoise any of several slow-moving terrestrial chelonian reptiles, especially of the family Testudinidae. They are typically herbivorous, with a high-domed shell and clawed feet.

tuatara the only surviving species of the reptilian order Rhynchocephalia; a medium-sized lizard-like animal with a primitive non-kinetic skull.

turtle any of several aquatic chelonian reptiles, especially of the marine family Chelonidae. In US and scientific usage, the term may apply to any chelonian reptile, including tortoises and terrapins. Turtles have no teeth; instead the bony edges of the jaws are lined with a horny beak, with which they can handle most food. Their limbs are short and strong, and may be adapted for walking on land or (if expanded into a broad paddle) for swimming. All chelonians can retract their limbs, short tail and head, if in danger.

venom snake poison, produced by the salivary glands of many snakes. In front-fanged snakes, two very large teeth swing down as the mouth opens wide, and the snake stabs its prey and injects venom.

vertebral column (of reptiles) is well developed, with snakes having up to 450 vertebrae, each with a pair of ribs.

viper any venomous snake of the Old World family Viperidae, containing some 40 species.

BIRDS

The three features that conspicuously distinguish birds from other animals are a beak, a pair of wings, and feathers.

albatross large gliding bird (family Procellariidae).

beak (or **bill**) the projecting jaws of a bird. The beak is covered in hardened keratin. Beaks are highly adapted to meet the needs of particular species.

bee-eaters slender birds (family Meropidae).

claws solid hooked nails at the end of the hind limbs of birds. Ground birds use their claws to dig and gather food; perching birds use them to grip branches.

contour feathers feathers which serve to streamline the bird's body and act as an outer insulating layer by trapping warm air.

cormorants large water birds (family Phalacrocoracidae).

cranes any of about 15 species of large water birds with long, slender necks (family Gruidae).

crop a small storage compartment for food preceding the gizzard.

cuckoos any of about 100 birds of the order Cuculiformes, about one half of which are characterized by laying their eggs in the nests of other birds.

doves smaller, more slender species of the order Columbiformes.

down a layer of soft, fine feathers which form the principal insulating covering.

duck any of about 130 waterfowl belonging to the family Anatidae.

eagles any of about 30 large birds of prey (family Accipitridae).

feather any of the keratin-based epidermal structures of a bird that together make up its plumage. Closest to the skin is the down; beyond this are the contour feathers. Tail feathers and flight feathers on the wings have the strongest shafts (quills), in order to withstand the tremendous stresses of flight and steering.

finch name given to a variety of small, seed-eating passerine birds.

flamingo long-legged slender bird (family Phoenicopteridae).

flight the great power needed for flight is provided by two pairs of massive pectoral muscles anchored to the large, keeled sternum. These muscles work in the same direction, but one set pulls directly on the wings to bring them down and in, while the other is carried over the shoulder by a tendon-pulley arrangement to pull the wings up and back. A bird's wing has a characteristic profile with a convex upper surface and a concave lower surface. Air moving over the wing has to travel further, and thus faster, over the upper surface than the lower; this causes a reduction in air pressure above the wing, and hence creates lift.

furcula the wishbone, by which wings are attached to the skeleton.

gannets large sea birds (family Sulidae).

gizzard a special compartment early in the digestive tract. As birds have no teeth they often swallow small stones to assist the grinding process.

goose the name given to various birds of the family Anatidae. The distinction between geese and ducks is not clear-cut.

grebes swimming and diving birds (family Podicipedidae).

grouse gamebirds (family Phasianidae).

gulls web-footed sea birds (family Laridae).

hawk common name for many smaller birds of prey.

herons long-legged wading birds (family Ardeidae).

hornbills members of the order Bucerotiformes, characterized by large curved bills.

hummingbirds tiny birds (family Trochilidae), characterized by long bills and hovering flight.

ibis wading birds of the family Treshkiornithidae.

kingfishers compact-bodied birds (order Coraciiformes).

kites birds of prey (family Accipitridae).

nightjars cryptically coloured birds (family Caprimulgidae).

ostrich the world's largest bird (family Struthionidae).

owls any of about 175 birds of prey (order Strigiformes), characterized by flattened faces that allow the large eyes to point forwards.

parrots (usually) brightly coloured species of the order Psittaciformes.

partridges any of about 60 gamebirds (family Phasianidae).

passerine birds the order Passeriformes, the songbirds and 'perching birds' – over 5500 species.

pelicans any of seven large, heavily built water birds (family Pelecanidae).

penguins any of 17 species of the family Spheniscidae, characterized by short stubby wings used as underwater flippers.

pheasants large gamebirds (family Phasianidae).

pigeons any of approximately 140 of the larger species of the order Columbiformes.

quill the shaft of a feather.

rhea large flightless birds (family Rheidae).

storks any of 17 species of long-legged wading birds (family Ciconiidae).

swans heavily built birds (family Anatidae).

swifts any of about 100 small birds (order Apodiformes), characterized by spending much of their time flying fast.

syrinx the singing organ of birds.

thrush any of about 180 species of passerine birds.

vultures any of 18 large scavenging birds (families Ciconiidae and Accipitridae).

wing the flight structure of birds. Birds' wings are highly modified fore limbs: the digits are reduced in size, and the wrist bones are elongated and fused, to protect the supporting structure for the flight feathers.

woodpeckers species of the family Picidae, characterized by long strong bills and the ability to chisel trees.

MAMMALS

The class Mammalia has fewer than 5000 species, of an extraordinary variety of size and form. Characteristics of mammals include the following (although not all are found in all mammals):

1) The production of milk from mammary glands in the female. (Although monotremes produce milk, they do not have teats with which to suckle the young.)

2) Mammals are homoiothermic – they maintain a constant internal temperature by means of a high metabolic rate. Birds are also homoiothermic but their external 'lagging' is feathers rather than the hair or fur that is unique to mammals.

3) Only mammals have three sound-conducting bones (ossicles) in the middle ear.

4) Mammals have larger and far fewer teeth than reptiles. Mammalian teeth are specialized in different parts of the jaw for different functions.

5) Only mammals have milk teeth, which are replaced by permanent adult teeth.

6) The roof of the mammalian mouth is arched; most mammals also have a secondary palate.

7) The way in which the head articulates with the rest of the body is unique to mammals.

8) Intelligence is a most significant characteristic of mammals – although the most difficult to quantify.

9) The chest and abdominal cavities of mammals are separated by a muscular diaphragm.

aardvark ant- and termite-feeding African mammal with a long tubular snout, long ears and stocky body.

agouti 10 species of large cavy-like South American rodents.

alpaca domesticated South American camelid.

anteaters four species of toothless edentates (family Myrmecophagidae) of Central and South America.

antelope common name given to many bovids, typically graceful, long-legged grazers and browsers – they include oryxes, gazelles, impala, waterbuck and wildebeest.

apes higher primates of the superfamily Hominoidea.

armadillos 20 species of edentates (family Dasypodidae), found in Central and South America. Distinguished by body armour of plates, armadillos are omnivorous.

artiodactyls members of the order Artiodactyla – the even-toed ungulates. Some 200 species include pigs, sheep, cattle, deer and antelope. They are typically big mammals with large bellies to carry their bulky food of grasses and leaves. They have large heads with long jaws and a battery of grinding teeth. The third and fourth toes form the typical semicircular cloven hoof. Except for the pigs, peccaries and hippopotamuses, all artiodactyls are ruminants. Artiodactyls have a four-chambered stomach (but see camelid) incorporating a large fermentation chamber (the rumen) containing bacteria to help break down the food. Food is swallowed with little chewing, passes to the rumen where it is softened and is then regurgitated to the mouth and chewed as cud. Swallowed for a second time, it bypasses the rumen and passes to the other chambers of the stomach.

asses two perissodactyls of the family Equidae.

aye-aye a lemur.

baboons large, often brightly coloured, Old World monkeys.

badgers several stockily built mustelids, typically with black and white head markings.

bandicoots 15 species of marsupial of the Australasian family Peramelidae.

bats mammals of the order Chiroptera, one of the largest groups of mammals and the only one to have achieved true flight. There are two suborders: Megachiroptera (fruit bats) and Microchiroptera (about 800 other species of bat), most of which are capable of echolocation. The flying membrane of bats consists of skin stretched between the four extremely elongated fingers of each hand; only the thumb remains free.

bears eight species of the omnivorous mammalian family Ursidae. Grizzly and polar bears are the largest of all carnivores. They are characterized by large heads with relatively small rounded ears, dog-like faces with long snouts and heavily built bodies with small tails.

beavers two large swimming rodents of the Castoridae, characterized by building dams to form ponds.

bison two massively built cattle-like bovids (genus *Bison*) – North American bison (buffalo) and European bison or wisent.

bobcat a stocky, reddish-brown North American cat.

bovids ruminating artiodactyl mammals of the family Bovidae, which includes cattle, sheep, goats, antelopes and duikers. Bovids vary considerably in size and form, but all are characterized by unbranched horns in the adult male (and in the females of some species).

browser any animal that forages leaves, shoots and other vegetation raised above the ground.

buffaloes two massively built species of cattle – the herd-dwelling African buffalo and larger, black Asiatic water buffalo.

camelids six species of the family Camelidae, including the Old World camels and the New World llamas, guanacos, etc. Camelids differ from other ruminants in that their stomachs have three not four chambers. They have characteristic long thin necks, small heads, and two toes on each foot.

camels two large ruminating camelids, adapted to arid desert conditions: the domesticated one-humped African camel (dromedary) and two-humped (Central Asian) Bactrian camel.

canids members of the mammalian family Canidae, including wolves, foxes, jackals, dogs and the coyote. They are remarkably similar in appearance with slim, muscular, deep-chested bodies. The sense of smell is particularly strongly developed.

capuchins lively New World monkeys of the genus *Cebus*, whose members have a 'hood' of thick hair on the back of the head.

capybara the largest living rodent; a stocky semi-aquatic South American mammal.

caribou (or **reindeer**) a large deer with branched antlers in both sexes. It is native to the tundra of Eurasia (the reindeer) and of North America (the caribou).

carnivore a carnivorous animal, i.e. one that feeds primarily or solely on other animals. Carnivores are distinguished by their canine teeth, which are usually large, curved and dagger-like (for stabbing and tearing flesh).

cats 34 species of carnivore (family Felidae). They have shorter skulls and jaws than the other carnivores.

cattle common name given to large bovid mammals of the genus *Bos* and related genera in the subfamily Bovinae, such as gaur, banteng, yak, kouprey, bison and buffalo.

cavy several small, stockily built South American rodents of the genus *Cavia.*

cetaceans aquatic mammals of the order Cetacea, which is divided into two main groups: the toothed whales, which include dolphins, porpoises and most of the smaller whales, and the baleen whales, which include the large to very large filter-feeding whales.

cheetah a slim, lithe African cat – reputedly the fastest land animal.

chimpanzees two species of ape of the genus *Pan* (superfamily Hominoidea).

chinchillas two soft-furred, agile Andean rodents with large ears and a long floppy tail.

civets cat-like viverrids, typically omnivorous, solitary and nocturnal.

coyote a North American canid resembling a small wolf with a grey coat.

dasurids 50 species of carnivorous marsupial (family Dasuridae).

deer 38 species of the family Cervidae, which includes red, roe, sika, and fallow deer, wapiti, moose, and caribou (or reindeer). Compared with other hoofed mammals, deer are finely built with long legs and slim bodies. Their most distinctive feature is branched antlers. Except for reindeer, these are borne only by the males and are shed annually.

dog the common name given to many canids.

dolphins small marine toothed cetaceans (family Delphinidae). They are known for their intelligence.

dugong a herbivorous marine mammal (family Dugongidae), found in tropical and subtropical coastal waters in the Indian and Pacific Oceans.

echidna (or **spiny anteater**) two species of mainly insectivorous, Australasian monotremes which are covered in long protective spines.

echolocation non-visual orientation and detection involving the emission of high-frequency sounds and monitoring their echoes from intervening objects. The system is used by bats and toothed whales.

edentates mammals belonging to the order Edentata that includes the anteaters, armadillos and sloths. They are distinguished by the strange and unique additional articulations (bony projections) between the vertebrae at the base of the spine.

eland a large stocky grey or brown African antelope.

elephants two trunked herbivorous mammals of the family Elephantidae, the largest living land animals: the African and the Indian elephant. The most characteristic feature is the long, flexible, muscular trunk, which is an elongation of the nose and the upper lip, with nostrils at the end. The tusks are much enlarged upper incisors.

fox common name given to many canids, especially the smaller, more solitary ones.

gazelle 18 species of small, elegant, agile antelopes of the genus *Gazella.*

genet any small cat-like viverrid, typically striped or spotted.

gerbil some 81 species of mouse-like, burrowing rodents (family Muridae).

gibbons nine species of Southeast Asian ape (family Hylobatidae).

giraffe a sub-Saharan artiodactyl (family Giraffidae), characterized by its long neck (which contains the normal mammalian seven vertebrae).

goat common name for various sure-footed, agile bovid mammals of the genus *Capra,* such as the ibex.

gorilla a herbivorous great ape (superfamily Hominoidea) of central Africa.

grazer any animal that crops grass and other ground vegetation.

hare any lagomorph mammal of the genus *Lepus.* In contrast to rabbits, hares are typically solitary, produce fully furred young and live in shallow scrapes rather than burrows.

hedgehogs 12 species of the mammalian family Erinaceidae. Distinguished by their covering of spines, hedgehogs are insectivorous.

herbivore a herbivorous animal, i.e. one that feeds primarily or solely on plants.

hippopotamus two non-ruminating artiodactyl mammals (family Hippopotamidae): the massively built common hippopotamus of sub-Saharan Africa and the pygmy hippopotamus of West Africa.

homoiothermic 'warm-blooded', i.e. able to maintain a steady body temperature above that of the surroundings.

horses two perissodactyls of the family Equidae: the domesticated horse, probably descended from the now extinct tarpan, and Przewalski's horse, the only true surviving wild horse.

howlers large New World monkeys (genus *Alouatta*), characterized by a booming call.

hyenas three species of carnivore (family Hyaenidae), which also includes the unusual aardwolf (which feeds on termites).

ibex a nimble, large goat with massive horns. It inhabits alpine Eurasia.

impala a common gregarious African antelope, known for its leaps when frightened.

insectivore any member of the order Insectivora, a diverse group that is divided into three major groups: the hedgehog types, the shrew types and the tenrec types.

insectivorous animal one that feeds primarily or solely on insects.

jackals four small fox-like canids (genus *Canis*).

kangaroos Australian herbivorous marsupials of the genus *Macropodus* and related genera in the family Macropodidae (smaller wallabies, etc.). Kangaroos typically have powerful hind limbs adapted for jumping.

koala a marsupial of Australia, a highly specialized tree-dweller.

lagomorphs members of the order Lagomorpha including rabbits, hares and pikas. They have long, exceptionally soft, fur, furred feet, eyes high set on the sides of the head and narrow nostrils.

lemming several species of small vole-like rodents (genus *Lemmus*).

lemurs 21 species of lower primate, found mainly in Madagascar.

leopard a solitary, versatile African and Asian big cat, noted for its spotted coat. The black leopard is called the panther.

lion a large, social big cat now largely confined to sub-Saharan Africa.

llama a domesticated South American camelid.

loris several slow-moving, nocturnal primates (family Lorisidae).

lynx a pale brown, spotted cat distinguished by its short tail and found in Eurasia and North America.

macaques Old World monkeys (genus *Macaca*).

manatees three species of herbivorous marine mammal (family Trichechidae) are found in tropical and subtropical coastal waters of the Atlantic Ocean.

marine mammals cetaceans (whales and dolphins), sirenians (the dugong) – both of which live their entire lives in water, and have lost the hind limbs and the ability to move on land – and the pinnipeds (seals and walruses) – which have come ashore to breed and retain their hind limbs, but move awkwardly on land.

marmosets tree-dwelling New World monkeys.

marmots large, squirrel-like, burrowing, colonial, alpine rodents (genus *Marmota*).

marsupials 266 species of the Australasian and New World mammalian order Marsupiala including possums and opossums, bandicoots, wombats, kangaroos and wallabies, the numbat and the koala. Marsupials are distinguished from other mammals by their reproduction. In its form and development, the marsupial egg more closely resembles that of birds and reptiles than that of mammals. Marsupial young are born in an undeveloped state, tiny and blind, and make their own way unassisted from the birth canal to the mother's teats which – in most cases – are situated in a pouch.

moles 27 species of insectivores (family Talpidae). Moles are highly adapted as burrowers, feeding mainly on earthworms.

mongoose small, agile viverrid (genus *Herpestes*), widespread in Africa and Asia.

monkey common name given to all the higher primates except the tarsiers, apes and man. Two major groups are recognized: New World monkeys (marmosets, tamarinds, capuchins and howlers) and Old World monkeys (macaques, baboons, langurs, colobus, etc.).

monotremes members of the Australasian mammalian order Monotremata – the duck-billed platypus and the echidnas. Even though they are furry and feed their young on milk, they lay eggs that are structurally very similar to those of birds, and – like birds – they incubate them in a nest or burrow. Monotremes do not have breasts or teats but have special glands that ooze milk.

moose (or **elk**) a stocky forest-dwelling deer with a broad muzzle and shoulder hump. In North America it is called the moose, in Eurasia the elk.

mouse common name of many species of small rodents (family Muridae).

musk deer three species of small deer-like artiodactyls lacking antlers. The males have long pointed protruding upper canines.

mustelids 67 species of mammalian carnivore (family Mustelidae), including weasels, badgers, otters and skunks. They are distinguished by strong carnassial teeth (long cutting teeth) and by anal scent glands.

ocelot a yellowish cat with black markings found in Central and South America.

okapi a shy artiodactyl native to central Africa (family Giraffidae).

omnivore an omnivorous animal; any animal that has unspecified feeding habits, i.e. it feeds both on plants and other animals.

opossum about 70 species of marsupial mammal (family Dedelphidae), widely distributed in North, Central and South America.

orang-utan a hominoid great ape; a large primate restricted to Sumatra and Borneo.

oryx three species of elegant, long-horned antelope of arid Africa and Arabia.

otters several aquatic mustelids, typically with streamlined bodies and webbed feet.

panda (giant) a large black and white mammal usually placed in the bear family, inhabiting bamboo forests in China.

pangolins (or **scaly anteater**) seven species of the Old World family Manidae. Their bodies are covered in overlapping horny scales.

perissodactyl any herbivorous hoofed mammal of the order Perissodactyla (the odd-toed ungulates), comprising 16 species: Equidae (horses, asses and zebras), Rhinocerotidae (rhinoceroses) and Tapiridae (tapirs). The weight of the body is borne on the central toes, with the main axis of the limb passing through the third (central) toe, which is the longest. In horses only the single central toe is functional; in rhinoceroses three hoofed toes are present and in tapirs four. All other toes are absent or present only as vestiges.

pigs eight stockily built, non-ruminating, Old World artiodactyl mammals (family Suidae). Pigs are distinguished by their flexible, muscular snouts, and males by their curved tusks.

pinnipeds carnivorous marine mammals (order Pinnipedia) – two families of seals and the walrus.

platypus a small, semi-aquatic Australian monotreme that forages underwater for freshwater invertebrates.

porcupines large, mainly nocturnal, cavy-like rodents, typically covered in stiff spines.

porpoises small, toothed cetaceans (family Phocoenidae), inhabiting coastal waters, mainly in the northern hemisphere.

possum common name for a large number of small, arboreal, nocturnal marsupials from Australia – they include phalangers and gliders.

primates 180 species of mammal including lemurs, lorises, monkeys, apes and *Homo sapiens.* Primates are characterized by having five digits on each hand and foot, with (except for the aye-aye) the claws of other mammals being replaced by flattened nails. Hands and feet are highly modified to allow these animals to grasp and manipulate objects with a greater dexterity than any other mammals. They are also distinguished by their relatively poor sense of smell and by their relatively large brain size.

primitive ungulates comprise four distinct orders: the proboscides, the hyraxes, the sirens and the order Tubulidentata (the aardvark). They differ dramatically in form, but they share certain anatomical and biochemical features – elephants and hydraxes, for example, both have toes bearing short, flattened nails rather than well-developed hooves, and both have grinding cheek teeth.

proboscideans trunked mammals of the order Proboscidea (elephants).

prototherians members of the small subclass Prototheria distinguished by the fact that its members lay eggs – the monotremes.

rabbit common name given to those lagomorphs of the family Leporidae that live socially in burrows and give birth to very immature young.

racoons small New World mammals (genus *Procyon*).

rat common name given to numerous larger species of the rodent family Muridae; see mouse.

rhinoceros massively built, horned perissodactyl mammals (family Rhinocerotidae) of sub-Saharan Africa and Southeast Asia.

rodents almost 1700 species of the family Rodentia, which represents 40% of all living mammalian species. Rodents are characterized by two pairs of chisel-like incisors that continue to grow through the animal's life.

seals carnivorous marine mammals of the families Phocidae ('true seals', 18 species) and Otariidae (eared seals, including fur seals and sea lions, 14 species).

sheep common name given to various bovid mammals of the genus *Ovis* and related genera.

shrews over 200 species of insectivores (family Soricidae). They are small, agile predators with characteristic long snouts.

sirenians (or **sea cow**) herbivorous marine mammals (order Sirenia).

skunks several New World mustelids, typically with black and white markings. They eject a foul-smelling liquid at attackers.

sloths slow-moving, herbivorous New World edentate mammals (families Megalonychidae and Bradypodidae). Adapted for life in the trees – they rarely come to the ground.

squirrels some 270 species of rodents (family Sciuridae). Many are arboreal; others are ground-dwelling including the chipmunk and prairie dog.

stoat a weasel-like mustelid with an elongated body.

tapirs sturdily-built, forest-dwelling perissodactyls of Central and South America and Southeast Asia, with a distinctive, short, flexible trunk.

tenrec any of 31 species of shrew-like insectivores of the mainly Madagascan family Tenrecidae.

therian a mammal that bears live young, i.e. all mammals except the monotremes.

tiger the largest of the cats; a solitary predator now largely confined to southern Asia.

tree shrews 18 species of the family Tupalidae, which comprises small squirrel-like animals whose status as rodents or primates is debatable.

ungulate any mammal that has hooves. The group of mammals so defined is divided into two sub-groups (orders): the perissodactyls and the artiodactyls.

vicuna a South American camelid.

viverrids carnivores of the Old World order Viverridae, comprising 66 species of civets, mongooses, genets, etc. They are typically small, lithe and long-bodied, with long bushy tails.

voles small, burrowing, herbivorous rodents (genus *Microtus*).

wallaby a herbivorous marsupial (genus *Petrogale*). Wallabies are similar to kangaroos but smaller.

walrus a large carnivorous pinniped found in Arctic coastal waters, the sole species of the family Odobenidae.

wapiti a large deer resembling the red deer, found in Eurasia and North America (where it is called the elk).

waterbuck a large stocky, shaggy antelope of the African savannah.

weasel common name given to many small Eurasian mustelids.

whale common name for most of the larger cetaceans.

wildebeest (or **gnu**) two stocky, gregarious antelopes (genus *Connochaetes*), both inhabiting the African savannah.

wolves two dog-like canids (genus *Canis*) – the grey or timber wolf and the red wolf.

wombats three short-legged, stocky, burrowing Australian marsupials (family Vombatidae). They are nocturnal and herbivorous.

yak a massively built dark-brown species of cattle with shaggy fur. It inhabits mountainous Central Asia.

zebras three species of distinctively striped African perissodactyls (family Equidae).

ENDANGERED SPECIES

Many species, particularly invertebrates, are becoming extinct every year, some of them undescribed by science. By 1993 the International Union for Conservation of Nature and Natural Resources (IUCN) had identified over 5000 threatened species. Of these, 698 were mammals, 1047 birds, 191 reptiles, 63 amphibians, 762 fishes and over 2250 invertebrates. Threats to these animals include hunting, trapping, fishing, pollution, destruction of their natural habitat and competition from introduced species. The following list features some of the better known endangered vertebrates.

Animal	Location	Notes
aye-aye	Madagascar	About 20 individuals of these lemur-like animals remain.
California condor	USA	Close to extinction in the wild.
crocodile (American)	USA	Endangered by threats to its habitat.
European bison (wisent)	Poland, Belarus, Russia	Under 2000 individuals remain in Bialowieza Forest and the Caucasus.
giant panda	China	The symbol of the World Wildlife Fund for Nature. Confined to the Sichuan mountains. Fewer than 700 individuals remain.
golden marmoset	Brazil	Threatened by destruction of the rain forest.
hooded crane	Japan, Russia	Threatened by destruction of its breeding grounds.
howler monkey	Central and South America	Endangered by destruction of its habitat.
indigo macaw	Brazil	Threatened by destruction of the rain forest.
Japanese ibis	Japan	Under 20 individuals have survived destruction of their breeding grounds.
kakapo (parrot owl)	New Zealand	Hunted almost to extinction. Fewer than 10 individuals remain.
Komodo dragon	Indonesia	The largest living lizard. Although protected, its numbers have fallen to a dangerous level because of poaching.
lemur	Madagascar	Some 14 species of these very small to medium primates existed 50 years ago. Some are already extinct; the remainder are under threat owing to drought and deforestation.
lion (Asiatic)	India	Under 200 individuals remain in Gir Forest National Park (Gujarat).
Mediterranean monk seal	Mediterranean	Under 500 individuals remain. Numbers reduced by hunting and pollution.
mountain gorilla	Rwanda, Zaïre	Threatened by poachers. Habitat under threat because of civil war, disorder and population pressure.
mountain zebra	South Africa	Being pushed into more marginal areas by farming.
nene (Hawaiian goose)	Hawaii (USA)	Became extinct in the wild. Successfully reintroduced from Slimbridge Wildfowl and Wetlands Trust (UK) to Hawaii where some 500 individuals now live in the wild.
orang-utan	Indonesia and Malaysia	Threatened by destruction of the rain forest.
oryx (Arabian)	Jordan, Oman, Saudi Arabia	Hunted almost to extinction. Numbers now increasing as animals bred in captivity are released.
Père David's deer	China	Was extinct in the wild; reintroduced from captivity.
rhinoceros	India, Nepal and sub-Saharan Africa, Indonesia	All species – African black, white, Indian, Sumatran, Javan – under threat, largely owing to poaching (the horn is regarded as an aphrodisiac). Under 60 Javan and 700 Sumatran remain.
tiger	India, Indonesia, Russia	Fewer than 4000 individuals remain. Of the four species – Indian, Sumatran, Javanese and Russian – the latter is under the greatest threat.
whale (blue, fin and humpback)	all oceans	Hunted close to extinction.
Yangtze River dolphin	China	Fewer than 150 individuals remain in the Yangtze River.

PREHISTORIC ANIMALS

Dinosaurs

The dinosaurs, the most advanced reptiles of all time, dominated the Earth for 140 millon years – compared with the 2 million years that man has been on the planet. Unlike living reptiles – which either crawl or walk with their limbs extended out to their sides – dinosaurs walked with their limbs directly under their bodies, just like modern mammals and birds. However, like modern reptiles, most dinosaurs were probably cold-blooded. Many dinosaurs were of gigantic size, some weighing up to 100 tonnes. Nearly 1000 species have been identified, and although the word 'dinosaur' is from the Greek for 'terrible lizard', there were herbivores as well as carnivores.

There were two orders of dinosaur, the Saurischia ('lizard-hipped') – and the ('bird-hipped') Ornithischia. Saurischians – whose pelvic girdle was like that of modern lizards – included exclusively two-legged carnivores such as *Tyrannosaurus* and enormous four-legged, predominately plant-eating semi-aquatic sauropods such as *Diplodocus*. Ornithischians – whose pelvic girdle was like that of birds – included ankylosaurs, ceratopsians, hadrosaurs, stegosaurs, and *Iguanodon*. Species included:

ankylosaurus ('fused lizard'), a dinosaur whose body was covered in a thick armour of fused bony plates.

apatosaurus the original brontosaur; weighed 30 tonnes. It lived for 120 years, equally at home swimming in lakes and walking on land.

baryonyx ('heavy claw'), named 'claws' after the massive claw on its hand, thought to have been for disembowelling dinosaurs or catching fish.

brachiosaurus ('arm lizard'), 12 m (39 ft) tall and 23 m (75 ft) long; a dinosaur that weighed 80 tonnes and had long front legs.

compsognathus a chicken-sized dinosaur that fed on lizards. It was related to birds.

deinonychus ('terrible claw'), 3 m (10 ft) long; a leaping dinosaur with a sickle-like claw on its hind feet for killing prey.

diplodocus total length 23 m (75 ft); a brontosaur with the longest known tail of all dinosaurs – 11 m (36 ft) long.

gallimimus ('chicken-mimic'), 4 m (13 ft) long; an ostrich-like dinosaur, with a large beak and no teeth.

iguanodon ('iguana tooth'), a plant-eating dinosaur with a pronounced bony spike on its 'thumb'.

kentrosaurus ('centre lizard'), a dinosaur with long sharp spikes running along the back and the tail.

maiasaurus ('mother lizard'), a duck-billed dinosaur which built nests and cared for its young in 'dinosaur nurseries'.

mamenchisaurus total length 23 m (75 ft); a brontosaur with the longest known neck of all dinosaurs – 11 m (36 ft).

megalosaurus ('giant lizard'), 9 m (30 ft) long; a flesh-eater, the first dinosaur ever discovered.

mussaurus ('mouse lizard'), 200 mm (8 in) long; the smallest known relative of the brontosaurs.

pachycephalosaurus ('thick-head lizard'), a bone-headed dinosaur with a distinctive massive bony thickening on the top of its head forming a 'battering ram'.

parasaurolophus ('near ridged lizard'), a duckbilled dinosaur with a 2 m (7 ft) long hollow crest – containing nasal passages – projecting behind its head.

plateosaurus ('flat lizard'), 6 m (20 m) long; a plant-eating ancestor of the brontosaurs. It had a strong claw on each hand and small serrated teeth.

polacanthus ('many spines'), 4 m (13 ft) long; a dinosaur with a large square bony 'blanket' over its hips and triangular plates along its back and tail.

protoceratops ('first horned'), 2 m (7 ft) long; the ancestor of triceratops. It possessed a similar bony frill over the neck but had no horns.

pterodactyl a flying reptile, whose membranous wings had spans of up to 11–12 m (36–39 ft).

saltasaurus ('lizard from Salta, Argentina'), a brontosaur with bony plates – each 12 cm (5 in) in diameter – embedded in the skin.

seismosaurus ('earthquake lizard'), 33 m (108 ft) long; probably the largest land animal that has ever lived.

shantungosaurus ('Shantung lizard'), 12 m (39 ft) long; the largest of the duck-billed dinosaurs.

stegosaurus ('roof lizard'), 9 m (30 ft) long, a dinosaur with two pairs of spikes on its tail, and a row of large triangular plates – 1 m high – running along its back.

supersaurus 15 m (49 ft) tall and 30 m (98 ft) long; a large dinosaur that may have weighed up to 100 tonnes.

torosaurus ('bull lizard'), a dinosaur with a bony frill extending over its shoulders. Its skull – 2·6 m (8·5 ft) long – was the largest known of any land animal.

triceratops ('three horned'), 9 m (30 ft) long; a dinosaur with a bony frill over its neck and three long horns on its forehead.

tyrannosaurus ('tyrant lizard'), 12 m (39 ft) long; a slow moving flesh-eating scavenger with relatively small two-fingered hands.

Birds

Birds share a common ancestry with reptiles. The first bird – archaeopteryx – had many characteristics in common with dinosaurs.

aepyornis a giant ostrich-like bird – the largest ever known. Its remains found in Mauritius gave rise to the 'Roc' of Sinbad and its fossilized eggs – the largest known eggs – were used to hold sailors' rum.

archaeopteryx ('ancient wing') the first bird, it appeared about 175 million years ago. In many respects it was indistinguishable from small carniverous dinosaurs, but the fact that it was covered in perfect feathers indicates that it was warm-blooded and that it could fly. It had a long bony tail and teeth in its jaws.

diatryma a tall – 2 m (7 ft) – flightless bird. This flesh-eater lived at the beginning of the age of mammals, 60 million years ago.

gigantornis a bird – with an 8 m (26 ft) wingspan – dating from c. 50 million years ago.

hesperornis ('western bird'), a flightless diving bird with teeth.

ichthyornis ('fish bird'), a tern-like bird with teeth in its jaws.

Mammals

The first reptiles that conquered the land about 295 million years ago were the mammal-like reptiles or paramammals. From detailed study of their skulls, it is presumed that the mammals originated from them. The first true mammals appeared during the later Triassic period about 220 million years ago.

arsinoitherium a rhinoceros-like animal with horns side by side on its snout; c. 35 million years old.

basilosaurus a 20 m (66 ft) long small-headed whale with the appearance of a 'sea serpent'. It lived c. 50 million years ago.

brontotherium a large rhinoceros-like animal, 2·5 m (8 ft) at the shoulder. It had double-curved horns at the tip of the snout, and lived c. 30 million years ago.

coelodonta a thick-haired woolly rhinoceros, which lived during the last Ice Age.

diprotodon a giant rhinoceros-sized wombat; 4 m (13 ft) long.

enteledon a giant pig-like animal; 2 m (7 ft) long. With bony projections on its lower jaws and sides of its skull, it has been called the ugliest mammal ever.

glyptodon a heavily armoured relative of the armadillo – 3.3 m (11 ft) long and 1·5 m (5 ft) high.

icaronycteris first known insect-eating bat; c. 50 million years old.

indricotherium a giant hornless rhinoceros, weighing 30 tonnes, and standing 5·5 m (18 ft) at the shoulder; c. 30 million years old.

kuehneotherium, the first true mammal, about the size of a shrew, dating from 220 million years ago.

mammuthus the woolly mammoth, a thick-haired elephant with spirally curved tusks inhabiting the tundra during the last Ice Age.

megaloceros a giant deer whose antlers had a 3·7 m (12 ft) span and weighed 45 kg (99 lb). It lived during the last Ice Age.

megatherium a giant ground sloth – 5·5 m (18 ft) tall – with huge clawed feet.

pakicetus the first toothed whale, c. 53 million years old. It had four paddle-like legs.

procoptodon a giant short-faced kangaroo standing 3 m (10 ft) tall.

propalaeotherium a 40 cm (16 in) high four-toed horse; c. 50 million years old.

purgatorius named after Purgatory Hill, Montana, USA, where remains of this first primate were found alongside dinosaur remains.

smilodon a sabre-tooth cat with long stabbing canine teeth.

thoatherium a one-toed horse-like litoptern, not related to true horses.

thylacoleo a marsupial lion with incisor 'stabbing' teeth at front of jaws.

thylacosmilus a pouched (marsupial) sabre-tooth cat, unrelated to true sabre-tooths; c. 15 million years old.

VELOCITY OF ANIMAL MOVEMENT

The data on this topic are notoriously unreliable because of the many inherent difficulties of timing the movement of most animals – whether running, flying, or swimming – and because of the absence of any standardization of the method of timing, of the distance over which the performance is measured, or of allowance for wind conditions.

The most that can be said is that a specimen of the species below has been timed to have attained as a maximum the speed given.

kph	mp	Species
362	*225*	(a) Peregrine falcon (*Falcoperegrinus*)
240+	*150+*	(b) Golden eagle (*Aquilachrysaetos*)
109	*68*	Sailfish (*Istiophorusplatypterus*)
96·5	*60*	Cheetah (*Acinonyx jubatus*)
88·5+	*55+*	Pronghorn antelope (*Antilocapra americana*)
75·5	*47*	Grant's gazelle (*Gazella granti*)
75	*46·61*	Yellowfin tuna (*Thunnus albacares*)
72	*45*	Ostrich (*Struthio camelus*)
69·62	*43·26*	(c) Race horse (*Equuscaballus*) (mounted)
67·14	*41·72*	(d) Greyhound (*Canis familiaris*)
64	*40*	(e) Eastern grey kangaroo (*Macropus giganteus*)
56–64	*35–40*	American free-tailed bat (*Tadarida brasiliensis*)
59·5	*37*	Blue wildebeest (*Connochaetes taurinus*)
58	*36*	Dragonfly (*Austro-phlebia costalis*)
55·5	*34·5*	Killer whale (*Orcinus* orca)
51·5	*32*	Giraffe (*Giraffa camelopardalis*)
45	*28*	Black rhinoceros (*Diceros bicornis*)
44·88	*27·89*	(f) Man (*Homo sapiens*)
44·4	*27·6*	Common dolphin(*Delphinus delphis*)
39	*24·5*	African elephant (*Loxodonta africana*)
32	*20*	Arabian camel (*Camelus dromedarius*)
c. 29	*c.18*	Pacific leatherback turtle (*Dermochelys coriacea schlegeli*)
11·5	*7·26*	Honey-bee (*Apismellifera*)
9·5	*6*	House rat (*Rattus rattus*)
7·24	*4·5*	Common flea (*Pulex irritans*) (jumping)
1·80	*1·12*	Centipede (*Scutiger coleoptrata*)
0·37	*0·23*	Giant tortoise
0·00062	*0·00039*	(g) Neptune crab (*Neptunus pelagines*)

(a) *45-deg angle of stoop in courtship display. Cannot exceed 100·5 kph* (62·5 mph) *in level flight.*
(b) *Vertical dive.*
(c) *Average over 402 m* (440 yd).
(d) *Average over 375 m* (410 yd).
(e) *Young mature females.*
(f) *Over 13·7 m* (15 yd) (*flying start*)
(g) *Travelled 163·3 km* (101·5 miles) *in 29 years.*

DOGS

There are 35 species and about 400 modern domestic breeds, which are classed as working dogs, gundogs, hounds, terriers, special, or toy dogs. The most popular breeds include:

Afghan hound large, slender, graceful dog; originally bred for hunting in Afghanistan; very long, silky coat; different colours.

Airedale terrier (or **Old English terrier**) medium-sized terrier, bred for badger and otter hunting; rough-haired; dark coat with tan head and legs; named after a Yorkshire district.

Alsatian see German shepherd dog.

American cocker spaniel gundog derived from English spaniel; a popular pet; flat or wavy silky coat; different colours.

Australian terrier small, wire-haired guard dog, imported into Australia by early British settlers; dark and tan coat.

Basset hound extremely good scent dog, originally from France; long body; short legs, front legs bow; smooth, short coat, white, black and tan.

beagle medium-sized hound; bred for hunting hare; sturdy body; short coat, white, tan and black.

bearded collie (or **Highland collie**) friendly, medium-sized working dog; bred as a sheepdog in Scotland; mainly black, grey and sandy coat.

Bernese mountain dog hardy Swiss working dog; brought to Switzerland by the Romans – it was used to pull carts; long, silky black coat with brown patches on legs and over eyes.

bichon frisé small, affectionate pet, originally from France; silky, white coat.

bloodhound large hound with keen sense of smell, used for tracking and police work; long neck; loose wrinkled skin on its head; short coat, tan, black and tan, or liver and tan.

Border collie intelligent working dog, bred in Scottish border area as a sheepdog; medium size; silky coat, generally black and white.

Border terrier small, tough, dense-coated dog, bred in Scottish border hills to hunt foxes; fawn and tan coat.

borzoi (or **Russian wolfhound**) fast, tall, slender dog; originally bred in Russia for hunting wolves; long, wavy or flat coat.

Boston terrier small, affectionate pet; developed in Massachusetts by crossing bulldogs and terriers.

boxer large dog; smooth-haired reddish brown coat; short nose; docked tail; developed in Germany; used as police and watch-dog.

Brittany spaniel developed in France; a working dog that points and puts up quarry for the guns; wavy or flat coat, dark orange and white or brown and white.

bulldog good pet and watch-dog; originally bred for bull-baiting; sturdy, heavy body with bowed front legs; short, soft, brown or brown and white coat.

bull terrier developed for dog fighting; short flat coat, usually white; any size.

cairn terrier lively, small dog bred in Scotland to drive foxes out of their holes; shaggy, thick, grey or sandy coat.

Cardigan Welsh corgi dog bred to work with cattle; small, short-legged breed with long body; many colours, usually with white markings.

cavalier King Charles spaniel attractive pet, larger than the King Charles spaniel; long, slightly wavy coat, generally brown or black and white.

Chihuahua the smallest breed of dog, originally from Mexico; short coat; eyes spaced wide apart.

chow chow a spitz type, originally bred in China 3000 years ago as a hunting dog; solid body, stiff gait; thick coat, various colours; blue tongue.

cocker spaniel popular pet, originally a gundog; flat, silky coat with some feathering; originally black but now different colours.

collie bearded (q.v.), border (q.v.), rough (q.v.), smooth.

corgi Cardigan Welsh (q.v.), Pembroke Welsh (q.v.).

dachshund (or **sausage dog**) long-bodied, short-legged dog originally bred from small terriers in Germany; dense and smooth coat, various colours; also wire- and long-haired varieties.

Dalmatian origin unclear, but not from Dalmatia (Croatia); large, lively dog, good pet; short, white coat with black or brown spots.

Dandie Dinmont terrier originally bred for fox, badger and otter hunting; now a popular pet; soft, long-haired coat, black-grey or light brown; short front legs.

Doberman pinscher large dog, bred in Germany as a guard dog and tracker; glossy black or brown with tan markings.

German shepherd dog (or **Alsatian**) popular guard dog, developed in 19th-century Germany; flat coat, many colours.

golden retriever popular pet; long, silky cream or gold coat.

Great Dane (or **German mastiff**) one of the largest breeds; originally developed in Germany as a hunting and guard dog; short, pale brown or greyish coat with black markings.

greyhound originally bred in the Middle East for hunting; tall, slender, extremely fast dog; track, coursing and show dog; close, silky coat.

hound Afghan (q.v.), basset (q.v.), blood (q.v.), English fox, Fox, grey (q.v.), harrier, Ibizan, Irish wolf (q.v.), Italian grey, otter, pharaoh, and Scottish deer.

Irish red setter (or **red setter**) gundog trained to freeze and set (drop to ground when it scents game); long, flat, chestnut coat. Also English setter.

Irish wolfhound tall, ancient breed, used by Celts for hunting; thick, rough coat; different colours.

Jack Russell intelligent, lively, small terrier, originally bred for fox hunting; usually white with dark markings.

Labrador retriever gundog originally from Newfoundland; excellent family pet, used as a guide-dog; short, black or golden brown coat.

Lhasa apso small, friendly dog, originally from Tibet; thick golden, brown or white coat.

Maltese affectionate, small terrier originally from Malta or Sicily; very long, silky white coat.

mastiff large, gentle, working dog; short, flat, usually fawn coat. Also bull mastiff.

miniature schnauzer small friendly dog developed in Germany as a rat-catcher; wiry, black or greyish coat.

Newfoundland large, gentle working dog, originally from Canada; flat, thick, water-resistant coat, usually black.

Norfolk terrier small, lively breed, similar to Norwich terrier but drop-eared; wiry, flat, tan coat.

Norwich terrier small terrier bred for hunting; good guard dog; wiry, tan coat.

Old English sheepdog developed in southwest England to protect cattle and sheep; long, shaggy coat, usually grey with white patches.

papillon an intelligent toy dog developed in France and Belgium; long, silky coat, white with dark markings.

Pekingese (or **Pekinese**) small breed of pet and watchdog from China; very long, straight coat, different colours.

Pembroke Welsh corgi intelligent, outgoing working dog; similar to the Cardigan Welsh corgi; thick coat, fawn, black and tan.

pointer hunting dog of Spanish origin; short, smooth coat, different colours; when scenting game, it freezes and 'points'.

Pomeranian developed from the spitz in Germany; good watchdog; thick, long, straight coat; different colours.

poodle developed in Germany for hunting and retrieval of game from water; now a very popular pet; thick, curly coat, generally clipped for effect; many colours.

pug affectionate, small, toy breed developed in China; smooth, short coat, different colours.

Pyrenean mountain dog large, very strong, loyal dog, bred in the Pyrenees to protect sheep; thick, pale-coloured coat.

retriever flat-coat, curly-coat, Chesapeake Bay, golden (q.v.), and Labrador (q.v.).

Rottweiler used as a police and guard dog; originally bred in Germany to protect cattle; short, black and tan coat.

rough collie (or **Scotch collie**) very intelligent and beautiful breed; originally a Scottish herding dog; long, yellowish brown and white coat, or black, white and tan.

St Bernard along with the English mastiff, the heaviest breed of domestic dog; bred at the Hospice of St Bernard, Switzerland, as a rescue dog to track people buried in avalanches; dense, red and white coat.

saluki (or **gazelle hound**) originally developed in the Middle East to hunt gazelle; soft coat, different colours; long hair on ears and legs.

Samoyed a good-natured spitz developed in Siberia by Samoyed people to herd reindeer; long, white or cream coat.

schnauzer giant, miniature (q.v.), and standard.

Scottish terrier (or **Scottie**) small, long-haired pet with very short legs; usually black coat.

setter English, Gordon, and Irish red (q.v.).

sheepdog Belgian, Old English (q.v.), Shetland (q.v.).

Shetland sheepdog (or **Sheltie**) small sheepdog, originally bred in the Shetlands, Scotland; long, thick coat, tan, black and white.

shih tzu small breed of Chinese origin, 'similar to Pekingese; thick, very long coat; many colours.

Siberian husky gentle Arctic spitz, developed in Siberia as a sledge-dog; thick coat, white with grey or tan.

silky terrier spirited breed, developed in Australia; long, silky, straight coat, blue-grey or brown.

Skye terrier short-legged breed from Scotland; originally bred to hunt foxes and badgers; long, straight coat, mainly grey; long hair covers the ears.

spaniel American cocker (q.v.), American water, Brittany, Blenheim and Prince Charles, cavalier King Charles (q.v.), Clumber, cocker (q.v.), English cocker, English springer, English toy, field, King Charles, Irish water, springer (q.v.), Sussex, Tibetan, and Welsh springer.

spitz Akita, keeshond, and Samoyed (q.v.).

springer spaniel medium-sized gundog, bred to 'spring' game; brown and white or black and white coat. Also Welsh springer spaniel.

Staffordshire bull terrier (or **pit bull**) originally bred as a fighting dog; smooth coated, muscular body; many colours. Also American Staffordshire.

terrier Airedale (q.v.), American Staffordshire, Australian (q.v.), Bedlington, Border (q.v.), Boston (q.v.), bull (q.v.), cairn (q.v.), Dandie Dinmont (q.v.), English, English toy, fox, Irish, Jack Russell (q.v.), Kerry blue, Lakeland, Manchester, Norfolk (q.v.), Norwich (q.v.), pit bull, rough, Scottish (q.v.), Sealyham, silky (q.v.), Skye (q.v.), soft-coated wheaten, Staffordshire bull (q.v.), Tibetan, Welsh, West Highland white (q.v.), wire fox (q.v.), and Yorkshire (q.v.).

Weimaraner old breed of gundog from Germany; grey coat; short- and long-haired breeds.

West Highland white terrier small, affectionate breed, developed in Scotland as a watchdog; thick, white coat.

whippet small, slender, fast hound whose history goes back to ancient Egypt; resembles the greyhound; short, fine coat, various colours.

wire fox terrier lively, small, popular pet; usually white with black and white markings.

Yorkshire terrier very small breed, originally from northern England; long, fine, straight and glossy coat; various colours.

COLLECTIVE NOUNS

Angel fish	Host
Animals	Menagerie, Tribe
Antelope	Herd, Troop
Ants	Army, Column, State, Swarm
Apes	Shrewdness
Asses	Herd, Pace
Baboons	Troop
Badger	Cete, Colony
Barracuda	Battery
Bass	Fleet
Bears	Sloth
Beavers	Colony
Bees	Cluster, Erst, Hive, Swarm
Birds	Congregation, Dissimulation (young), Flight, Flock, Volery, Volley
Bison	Herd
Bitterns	Sedge, Siege
Bloodhounds	Sute
Boars	Herd, Singular, Sounder
Budgerigars	Chatter
Buffalo	Herd
Bustard	Flock
Camels	Caravan, Flock
Capercaillie	Tok
Caterpillars	Army
Cats	Chowder, Clowder, Cluster
Cats, wild	Dout
Cattle	Drove, Herd
Chamois	Herd
Chickens	Brood, Clutch, Peep
Choughs	Chattering
Clams	Bed
Cockles	Bed
Colts	Race, Rag, Rake
Coots	Covert, Raft
Cormorants	Flight
Cranes	Herd, Siege
Crows	Clan, Hover, Murder
Curlews	Herd
Deer	Herd, Leash
Dogfish	Brood, Troop
Dogs	Cowardice, Kennel, Pack
Dogs (hunting)	Cry
Dolphins	Pod, School
Donkeys	Herd, Drove
Dottrel	Trip
Doves	Dole, Flight, Prettying
Ducklings in nest	Clutch
Ducklings off nest	Clatch
Ducks (diving)	Dopping, Dropping
Ducks (flying)	Flush, Plump, Team
Ducks (on land)	Flight, Flock, Leash, Mob Sail
Ducks (on water)	Badeling, Paddling, Sail
Eagles	Convocation
Eels	Swarm
Elephants	Herd
Elk (Europe)	Gang
Falcons	Cast
Ferrets	Business, Cast, Fesynes
Finches	Charm, Flight
Fish	Haul, Run, School, Shoal
Flamingos	Flurry, Regiment, Skein
Flies	Business, Cloud, Scraw, Swarm
Foxes	Earth, Lead, Skulk
Foxhounds	Pack
Frogs	Army, Colony
Geese (flying)	Flock, Gaggle, Skein
Geese (on land)	Gaggle
Geese (on water)	Gaggle, Plump
Giraffes	Corps, Herd, Troop
Gnats	Cloud, Horde, Swarm
Goats	Flock, Herd, Tribe, Trippe
Goldfinch	Charm, Chattering, Chirp, Drum
Goldfish	Troubling
Goshawks	Flight
Grasshoppers	Cloud
Greyhounds	Brace, Leash, Pack
Grouse	Brood, Covey, Pack
Guillemots	Bazaar
Gulls	Colony
Hares	Down, Drove, Husk, Lie, Trip
Hart	Herd, Stud
Hawks	Cast
Hedgehogs	Array
Hens	Brood, Flock
Heron	Scattering, Sedge, Siege
Herring	Army, Gleam, Shoal
Hippopotamuses	Herd, School
Hogs	Herd, Drove, Sounder
Horses	Harass, Herd, Stable, Stud, Troop
Horses (race)	Stable, String
Hounds	Brace, Couple, Cry, Mute, Pack, Stable
Ibis	Crowd
Insects	Swarm
Jays	Band, Party
Jellyfish	Brood, Smuck
Kangaroos	Herd, Mob, Troop
Kittens	Brood, Kindle, Litter
Lapwings	Deceit, Desert
Larks	Exultation
Lemurs	Troop
Leopards	Leap
Lice	Flock
Lions	Flock, Pride, Sawt, Souse, Troop
Locusts	Cloud, Horde, Plague, Swarm
Mackerel	School, Shoal
Magpies	Tiding, Tittering
Mallards (on land)	Bord, Flock, Flush, Suite, Sute
Mallards (on water)	Sord
Mares	Flock, Stud
Martens	Raches, Richesse
Mice	Nest
Minnows	Shoal, Steam, Swarm
Moles	Company, Labour, Movement, Mumble
Monkeys	Troop
Moose	Gang, Herd
Mules	Barren, Cartload, Pack, Span
Mussels	Bed
Nightingale	Match, Puddling, Watch
Ostrich	Flock, Troop
Otters	Bevy, Family
Owls	Parliament, Stare
Oxbirds	Fling
Oxen (domestic)	Drove, Rake, Team, Yoke
Oxen (wild)	Drove, Herd
Oyster	Bed
Parrots	Flock
Partridges	Covey
Passenger pigeons	Roost
Peacocks	Muster
Peafowl	Muster, Ostentation, Pride
Penguins	Colony, Rookery
Perch	Pack, Shoal

Pheasants	Brook, Ostentation, Pride, Nye
Pigeons	Flight, Flock
Piglets	Farrow
Pigs	Litter, Herd, Sounder
Pilchards	Shoal
Plover	Congregation, Flight, Stand, Wing
Polecats	Chine
Ponies	Herd
Porpoises	Gam, Pod, School
Poultry	Flock
Poultry (domestic)	Run
Ptarmigan	Covey
Pups	Litter
Quail	Bevy, Covey
Rabbits	Bury, Colony, Nest, Warren
Raccoons	Nursery
Racehorses	Field, String
Rats	Colony
Ravens	Unkindness
Redwings	Crowd
Rhinoceros	Crash
Roach	Shoal
Roe deer	Bevy
Rooks	Building, Clamour, Parliament
Ruffs	Hill
Sandpipers	Fling
Sardines	Family
Seals, elephant	Rookery, Team, Troop
Seals	Harem, Herd, Pod, Rookery
Sheep	Down, Drove, Flock, Hurtle, Trip
Sheldrakes	Dapping, Dropping
Smelt	Quantity
Snakes	Den, Pit
Snakes (young)	Bed
Snipe	Walk, Whisper, Wish, Wisp
Spaniels	Couple
Sparrows	Host, Surration, Quarrel
Spiders	Cluster, Clutter
Squirrels	Drey
Starlings	Chattering, Crowd, Murmuration
Sticklebacks	Shoal
Stoats	Pack
Storks	Herd, Mustering
Swallows	Flight
Swans	Bank, Bevy, Game, Herd, Squadron, Teeme, Wedge, Whiteness
Swifts	Flock
Swine	Doyet, Dryft
Swine (wild)	Sounder
Teal (on land)	Bunch, Coil, Knab, Raft
Teal (on water)	Spring (rising from water)
Thrush	Mutation
Tigers	Ambush
Toads	Knab, Knot
Trout	Hover
Turkeys	Dule, Raffle, Rafter
Turtle Doves	Pitying
Turtles	Bale, Dole
Vipers	Den, Nest
Walrus	Herd, Pod
Wasps	Herd, Nest, Pladge
Weasels	Pack, Pop
Whales	Colony, Gam, Herd, Pod, School
Whiting	Pod
Widgeon	Coil, Company, Flight, Knob
Wildfowl	Plump, Sord, Sute, Trip
Wolves	Pack, Rout
Woodcocks	Covey, Fall, Flight, Plump
Woodpeckers	Descent
Wrens	Herd
Zebras	Herd

MAJOR ZOOS

Amsterdam (Netherlands) Founded in 1836, the zoo exhibits nearly 1400 species and contains a famous animal behaviour laboratory.

Antwerp (Belgium) Antwerp Zoo houses over 1100 species, including important exhibits of black rhinoceros and Père David's deer. The zoo is famous for the innovative nature of its animal enclosures, especially in the reptile house.

Beijing/Peking (China) Beijing Zoo – established in 1906 – is known for its collection of rare Asian species, and its success in breeding the giant panda.

Berlin (Germany) One of the largest zoos in the world, Berlin Zoo was opened in 1841. The best known collections include the birds of prey, wild cattle and the aquarium.

Bronx Zoo (New York, USA) Founded in 1899, the Bronx Zoo includes several threatened species such as Père David's deer, the European bison and the okapi. Its other attractions include the collection of Asian mammals and birds.

Chicago Brookfield Zoo (USA) Opened in 1934, the Brookfield Zoo is known for its open-air, unbarred enclosures. It houses over 400 species of animal, especially those of the tropical rain forests.

Cologne (Germany) Cologne Zoo – which houses over 700 species – specializes in primates and is known for its aquarium.

Copenhagen (Denmark) The 2500 species in Copenhagen Zoo include a particularly comprehensive collection of birds. The zoo, founded in 1859, has bred a number of rare species, including the musk ox.

Frankfurt (Germany) Founded in 1858, the zoo exhibits over 600 species. This major collection is known for breeding endangered species, including the lowland gorilla, okapi and black rhinoceros.

London (UK) The Regent's Park Zoo (established 1828) has approaching 1000 species. London Zoo – which has the world's largest zoological library – has a separate collection of 250 species in spacious enclosures in a country setting at Whipsnade in Bedfordshire.

Moscow (Russia) The Moscow Zoo, founded in 1864, houses a formidable collection of northern animals and exotic species. Its collection has recently diminished from a 1990 total of over 3000 specimens of 550 species, but it remains one of the world's most important zoos.

Paris (France) The Paris Zoo dates back to 1793. Its spacious natural enclosures include the famous Rocher, an artifical mountain for wild sheep. The zoo has about 300 species and is noted for breeding especially rare deer, wild horses and giraffes.

San Diego (USA) Founded in 1922, the San Diego Zoo is now the largest in the world. It uses barless, mixed-species enclosures, with exotic plants providing the natural diet for some of the animals. Among the 800 species, koalas and pygmy chimpanzees have bred successfully.

Toronto (Canada) Opened in 1974, Metro Toronto Zoo is one of the largest zoos in the world. The 280 species of animal are grouped by continent in mixed-species enclosures. Indigenous plants are used to create natural settings.

The Human Anatomy

THE HUMAN SKELETON

The human skeleton is a hard structure that supports the body, protects the soft inner organs, and provides anchorage for muscles. As in all vertebrates the human skeleton is internal. (In insects and other arthropods the skeleton is external, an exoskeleton.) The human skeleton comprises 206 bones.

ankle see tarsus.

anvil see incus.

arm either of the human forelimbs. Each arm comprises 30 bones:

humerus 1 bone; *radius* 1 bone; *ulna* 1 bone; *carpus* (comprising scaphoid 1 bone, lunate 1 bone, triquetral 1 bone, pisiform 1 bone, trapezium 1 bone, trapezoid 1 bone, capitate 1 bone, hamate 1 bone); *metacarpals* 5 bones; *phalanges* (comprising first digit or thumb 2 bones, second digit 3 bones, third digit 3 bones, fourth digit 3 bones, fifth digit 3 bones).

breastbone see sternum.

carpals the bones that make up the carpus or wrist.

carpus the wrist comprising a number of smaller bones (carpals).

cervical vertebrae the vertebrae of the neck supporting the head. Two of these provide articulating surfaces against which the head can move in relation to the backbone.

clavicle either of the collar bones attached to the sternum.

coccyx the lowermost element of the backbone; a vestigial human tail.

collarbone see clavicle.

digit a finger or toe.

ear the sense organ of vertebrates that is specialized to detect sound and to help maintain balance. The two human ears each contain three bones: the malleus, the incus and the stapes.

femur the thigh bone; it articulates at one end with the pelvis and at the other with the tibia.

fibula the smaller of two bones in the lower leg.

finger any of the five digits of the hand.

foot see metatarsus.

hammer another name for the malleus.

hip see pelvic girdle.

humerus the long bone of the upper arm.

hyoid a single bone in the throat supporting the tongue.

ilium the largest of the three bones that combine to make up one half of the pelvic girdle. The ilium has a flattened 'wing' attached by ligaments to the sacrum.

incus (or **'anvil'**) one of the three auditory ossicles in the mammalian inner ear.

ischium the most posterior of the three bones that combine to make up one half of the pelvic girdle.

joint a point or junction between two body parts at which movement is possible. Various types occur. A ball-and-socket joint, as in the hip and shoulder, allows movement in all directions, including rotation, but is susceptible to dislocation. A saddle joint allows versatile movement in several directions, and very significantly – in the case of the primitive thumb joint – the 'opposition' of the thumb to the fingers that is characteristic of precise movements such as grasping. A hinge joint, as in the elbow and knee, allows swinging movement, mostly in a single plane. A pivotal joint is mainly restricted to rotational movement – movement of the head from side to side is primarily due to a pivotal joint between the first and second neck vertebrae. A condyloid joint, such as the wrist joint, allows both rotation and backward and forward movement. A plane joint, such as that between the pelvis and the base of the spine, allows only very limited movement, except in pregnancy when the pelvis expands to accommodate the growing foetus.

leg either of the human hind or lower limbs. Each leg contains 29 bones:

femur 1 bone; *tibia* 1 bone; *fibula* 1 bone; *tarsus* (comprising talus 1 bone, calcaneus 1 bone, navicular 1 bone, medial cuneiform 1 bone, intermediate cuneiform 1 bone, lateral cuneiform 1 bone, cuboid 1 bone); *metatarsals* 5 bones; *phalanges* (comprising first digit or big toe 2 bones, second digit 3 bones, third digit 3 bones, fourth digit 3 bones, fifth digit 3 bones).

malleus (or **'hammer'**) one of the three auditory ossicles in the mammalian inner ear.

mandible the lower jaw of vertebrates.

metatarsus the foot, comprising a series of small rod-shaped bones (metatarsals).

occiput the back part of the skull.

ossicle a small bone, especially (in mammals) any one of the three ossicles of the ear.

parietal bone either of two bones forming part of the top and sides of the skull.

patella either of the two kneecaps.

pectoral girdle (or **shoulder girdle**) the structure to which the arms are attached. The human pelvic girdle comprises 4 bones: *clavicle* (a pair) 2 bones; *scapula* (including the coracoid; a pair) 2 bones.

pelvic girdle (or **pelvis**) the structure to which the legs are attached. Also known as the hip girdle, it articulates dorsally with the backbone. The human pelvic girdle comprises two bones – a pair of hip bones that represent the fusion of the ilium, ischium and pubis.

phalanx any of the bones that make up the digits of either the hand or the foot.

pubis the foremost of the three bones that combine to make up one half of the pelvic girdle.

radius the smaller of the two bones in the lower section of the arm.

ribs see vertebral ribs.

sacral vertebrae five vertebrae fused together to form the sacrum. They articulate securely with the pelvic girdle and, as they are fused to form a single bone, they provide firm support.

sacrum see sacral vertebrae.

scapula either of the shoulder blades attached to the backbone.

shoulder blade see scapula.

shoulder girdle see pectoral girdle.

skull the part of the skeleton enclosing the brain. The human skull comprises 22 bones:

occipital 1 bone; *parietal* (a pair) 2 bones; *sphenoid* 1 bone; *ethmoid* 1 bone; *inferior nasal conchae* (a pair) 2 bones; *frontal* (a pair – fused) 1 bone; *nasal*

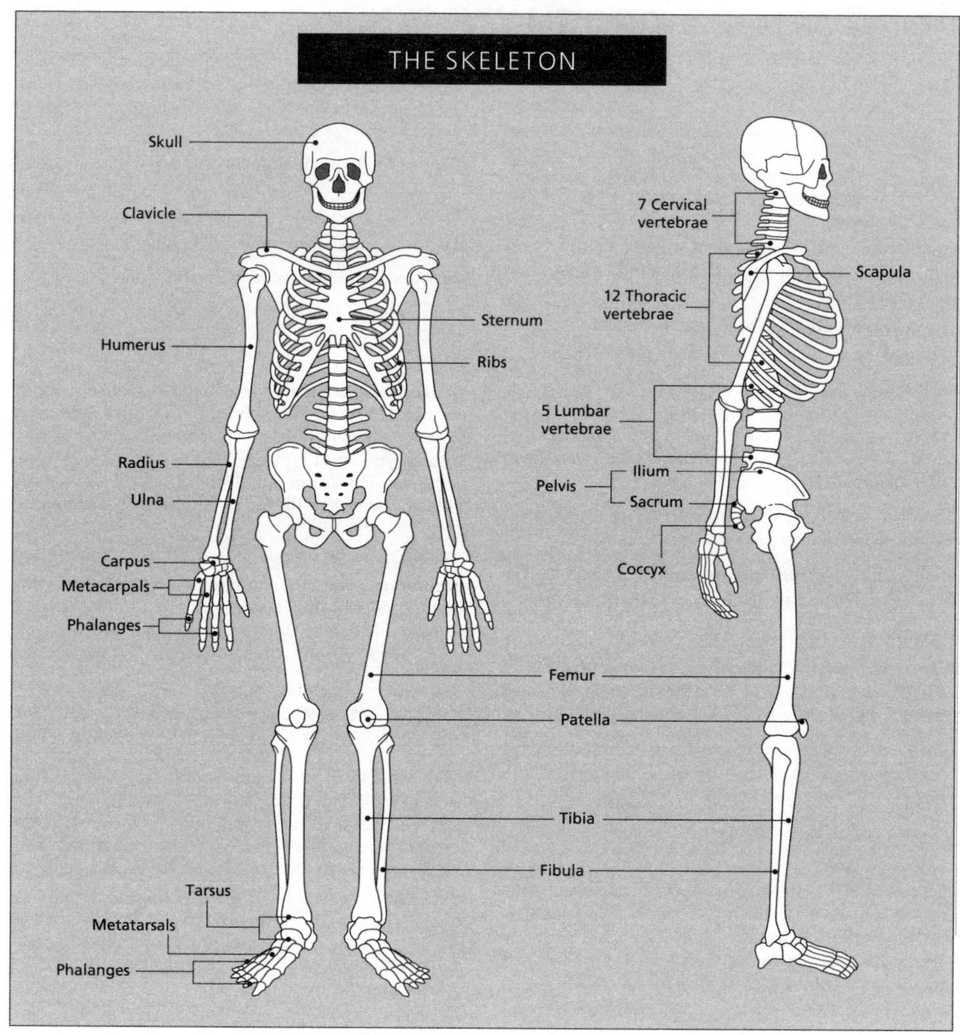

(a pair) 2 bones; *lacrimal* (a pair) 2 bones; *temporal* (a pair) 2 bones; *maxilla* (a pair) 2 bones; *zygomatic* (a pair) 2 bones; *vomer* 1 bone; *palatine* (a pair) 2 bones; *mandible* (a pair – fused) 1 bone.

spinal column see vertebra.

stapes (or '**stirrup**') one of three auditory ossicles in the mammalian inner ear.

sternum (or **breastbone**) the breastbone in vertebrates. The human sternum comprises three bones: manubrium, sternebrae, and xiphisternum.

stirrup see stapes.

tarsals see tarsus.

tarsus the ankle comprising a number of small bones (called tarsals).

temporal bone either of a pair of compound bones that form the sides of the skull.

thoracic vertebrae the vertebrae of the upper back. They articulate with the ribs and are characterized by a number of articulating facets for the attachment of ribs.

thumb the first digit of the human hand.

tibia the larger of two bones in the lower leg.

toe any of the five digits of the foot.

ulna the larger of the two bones in the lower section of the arm.

vertebra (plur. **vertebrae**) any of the independent bony segments that form the spinal column, through which the spinal cord passes. The human body has 26 vertebrae:

cervical 7 bones; *thoracic* 12 bones; *lumbar* 5 bones; *sacral* (five vertebrae fused together to form the sacrum) 1 bone; *coccyx* 1 bone.

vertebral rib any of a series of slender curved bones forming a cage that encloses, supports and protects the lungs and heart. Pairs of ribs articulate with the thoracic vertebrae at the back and the sternum at the front. The human body has 24 vertebral ribs:

ribs 'true' (7 pairs) 14 bones, which articulate directly with the sternum; *ribs 'false'* (5 pairs, of which 2 pairs are 'floating' and 3 pairs articulate with the sternum via elastic cartilage) 10 bones.

wrist see carpus.

THE HUMAN DIGESTIVE SYSTEM

Digestion is the process in which the energy and nutrients contained in food are broken down into a suitable form to be absorbed by the body and utilized as a source of energy, or to synthesize substances such as proteins, enzymes and hormones that are required for the normal functioning of the body. The nutrients required by the body are proteins, carbohydrates, fats, mineral salts and vitamins. Water is not a nutrient but an adequate intake is essential to replace the water that is lost each day through the skin and lungs, and in urine and faeces.

alimentary canal another name for the gastro-intestinal tract.

amino acid an organic compound containing one or more amino groups. Eight amino acids must be provided by the diet – these are called the essential amino acids. The others can be synthesized from other amino acids.

anus the opening at the end of the digestive tract through which waste products are discharged.

appendix (or **vermiform appendix**) a small narrow pouch extending from the lower part of the caecum.

ascorbic acid see vitamin C.

bile a secretion of the liver formed by the breakdown of haemoglobin. It helps break down fats in the small intestine. Bile ducts conduct bile to the duodenum.

biotin a B vitamin essential for metabolism of fat; found in egg yolks, liver, tomatoes, raspberries, artichokes.

caecum a pouch that forms the first part of the colon.

carbohydrate any of a large number of organic compounds. They contain carbon, hydrogen and oxygen and provide energy. The most important is starch, a polysaccharide obtainable mainly from cereals. The simple carbohydrates are the monosaccharides (glucose, fructose and galactose) and the disaccharides (sucrose, lactose and maltose). A disaccharide consists of two molecules of monosaccharide. Good sources of simple carbohydrates are fruits, honey, milk and table sugar.

cellulose a polysaccharide carbohydrate made up of unbranched chains of many glucose molecules.

chyme the semi-liquid state into which food is reduced in the human stomach.

colon the large intestine.

cyanocobalamin see vitamin B12.

digestive tract see gastrointestinal tract.

duodenum the first part of the small intestine extending from the stomach to the jejunum. On average the duodenum is about 25 cm long.

enzyme any protein that acts as a catalyst in certain biochemical reactions.

essential amino acids see amino acid.

faeces the waste residue of food, dead and live bacteria, and water, expelled through the rectum.

fats provide twice the amount of energy as carbohydrates and protein. Fatty acids may be either saturated or unsaturated. A diet high in fat, particularly 'saturated fat' (found, for example, in red meat and dairy products), has been linked to the development of heart disease.

folic acid a B vitamin essential for maturing red blood cells in bone marrow; found in spinach, liver, broccoli, peanuts.

fructose a monosaccharide carbohydrate.

galactose a monosaccharide carbohydrate.

gall bladder a membranous muscular sac associated with the liver and in which bile, made in the liver, is stored.

gastrointestinal tract a long tube about 9 m long through the human body from the mouth to the anus. Here the complex structures present in food are mixed with enzymes and broken down into their simple constituents. These are small enough to be absorbed through the wall of the intestine into the bloodstream.

Food is chewed in the mouth and mixed with saliva that begins starch digestion. It passes through the oesophagus into the stomach which produces the enzyme pepsin and hydrochloric acid to start protein digestion, and mixes the food until it is in a semi-liquid state called chyme. This is then released slowly into the duodenum.

Most digestion takes place in the duodenum. Enzymes, secreted by the pancreas and the duodenum lining, convert fats into fatty acids and glycerol, and polysaccharides into glucose and fructose. These are then absorbed through the wall of the ileum. Glucose, fructose and amino acids are absorbed into the bloodstream and carried to the liver. Fatty acids and glycerol are absorbed into the lymphatic system and enter the bloodstream.

Substances that cannot be digested pass into the colon. Some compounds are fermented by the bacteria there and others are egested as waste products in the faeces via the rectum.

glucose a monosaccharide carbohydrate.

glycogen the form in which carbohydrates are stored in the liver and muscles. It is a polysaccharide carbohydrate consisting of glucose units and is readily converted to glucose.

gullet see oesophagus.

ileum the lower part of the small intestine, on average about 4 m long.

intestine the part of the alimentary canal between the stomach and the rectum.

jejunum the middle part of the small intestine, on average about 2·5 m long.

lactose a disaccharide carbohydrate.

large intestine (or **colon**) the latter part of the intestine between the small intestine and the rectum. Its main function is to reabsorb water from food wastes into the bloodstream. See gastrointestinal tract.

liver a large organ well-supplied with blood vessels. It has four functions, two of which are associated

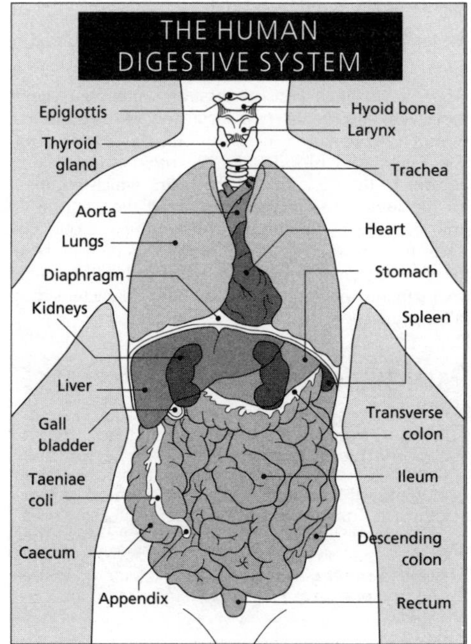

with the digestive system: the production of bile; and the reception of all the products of food absorption. The other two functions of the liver are to manufacture and destroy proteins (producing urea, a major nitrogenous excretory product), and to remove many toxins from blood.

maltose a disaccharide carbohydrate.

mineral salts soluble ions essential in the diet, such as calcium, iron, phosphate, sodium and chloride.

mouth the first part of the digestive tract.

niacin see nicotinic acid.

nicotinic acid (niacin) a B vitamin essential for metabolism of carbohydrates and the functioning of the digestive tract and nervous system; found in yeast, fish, meat, cereals, peas and beans.

oesophagus (or **gullet**) a 23 cm muscular tube by which food passes from the mouth to the gastro-intestinal tract.

pancreas a large compound gland near the stomach. One of its functions is to secrete digestive enzymes.

pepsin an enzyme produced in the stomach. When activated by acid it starts the digestion of polypeptide chains (proteins).

peptide the bond linking the amino acids in a polypeptide.

polysaccharide any of a large number of polymers made of peptide chains of amino acids.

proteins are made up of large numbers of amino acids. There are about 20 different amino acids and they can be arranged in any order to produce a larger number of different proteins. Proteins provide cell structure, help fight infections, transport substances around the body and form enzymes and hormones. Milk, eggs, meat, fish and pulses are rich in proteins.

pyloric sphincter the small circular opening at the base of the stomach through which partly digested food passes to the duodenum.

pyridoxine see vitamin B6.

rectum the last section of the gastrointestinal tract.

retinol see vitamin A.

riboflavin see vitamin B2.

small intestine the longest part of the gastrointestinal tract. It comprises the duodenum, jejunum and ileum.

starch a polysaccharide carbohydrate into which glucose is converted for storage in plants, and which forms the main source of carbohydrate for humans.

stomach a muscular bag between the oesophagus and duodenum.

sucrose a disaccharide carbohydrate. Sucrose (table sugar) is formed from a molecule of glucose and a molecule of fructose.

thiamin see vitamin B1.

vitamins complex chemical compounds that are essential in small quantities for many chemical reactions. If a vitamin is lacking in the diet a deficiency disease arises.

vitamin A (retinol) a vitamin essential for growth, vision of poor light, health of the cornea and resistance to infection; found in dairy products, fish-liver oils, egg yolks.

vitamin B1 (thiamin) a vitamin essential for carbohydrate metabolism and nervous system functioning; found in yeast, egg yolks, liver, wheatgerm, peas, beans.

vitamin B2 (riboflavin) a vitamin essential for tissue respiration; found in yeast, meat extracts, milk, liver, kidneys, cheese, eggs, green vegetables.

vitamin B6 (pyridoxine) a vitamin essential for metabolism of fat and protein; found in liver, eggs, meat, peas, beans.

vitamin B12 (cyanocobalamin) a vitamin essential for maturing of red blood cells in bone marrow; found in liver, fish, eggs, meat.

vitamin C (ascorbic acid) a vitamin essential for formation of red blood cells, antibodies and connective tissue, the formation and maintenance of bones, maintenance of blood capillaries; found in blackcurrants, citrus fruits, green vegetables, potatoes.

vitamin D a vitamin essential for absorption of calcium and phosphorus; found in fish liver oil, eggs, butter, cheese. Humans can synthesize vitamin D by exposing the skin to sunlight.

vitamin E is thought to prevent oxidation of unsaturated fatty acids in cells; found in vegetable oils, cereals, green vegetables, eggs, butter.

vitamin K is associated with the clotting mechanism of blood; found in green vegetables, liver; can be synthesized in the human gut.

THE HUMAN CIRCULATORY SYSTEM

The circulatory system is responsible for bringing oxygen and nutrients to cells and carrying away carbon dioxide and other waste products. Each animal cell requires an uninterrupted supply of oxygen and nutrients, and waste products must be continuously removed. The circulatory system consists of three components:

1) a fluid transport medium (blood) in which nutrients, gases and waste products are dissolved.

2) a mechanism by which the blood is pumped around the body (the heart).

3) a system of spaces through which blood circulates.

artery a blood vessel by which blood is carried away from the heart.

atrium (plur. **atria**) a chamber in the heart in which blood is collected from the veins and passed to a ventricle.

blood the fluid in which nutrients, oxygen and waste products (including carbon dioxide) are dissolved and carried around the body. The human blood consists of a fluid medium (plasma) in which cells are suspended. The white blood cells (leucocytes) are important in combating invading organisms, while the red blood cells (erythrocytes) carry the respiratory pigment.

capillary a minute, thin-walled blood vessel.

closed circulatory system the circulatory system found in vertebrates including humans. In closed circulatory systems the blood passes through a continuous network of flexible blood vessels, and can be pumped more quickly. Arteries branch into smaller and smaller vessels, carrying blood away from the heart to all parts of the body. The smallest vessels (capillaries) are quite permeable and allow fluid to leak out to form the tissue fluid (interstitial fluid) that surrounds all cells. The exchange of gases, nutrients and waste materials between cells and the blood takes place by diffusion through the interstitial fluid. Humans and other vertebrates have a separate system of small vessels, the lymphatic system, by which excess interstitial fluid is collected and returned to the blood. After passing through the capillaries, blood returns to the heart through a network of veins. Pressure is necessary to force blood through vessels and around circulatory systems. This pressure may simply be generated by movements of the surrounding muscles in the body. Return of blood through the veins in the human leg is assisted by contractions of the leg muscles during walking. Valves are used in the heart and veins to ensure that the flow of blood proceeds in the right direction.

OPEN CIRCULATORY SYSTEMS

Open circulatory systems are found in arthropods and many molluscs. In such a system the heart pumps blood into vessels that are open-ended. Blood flows out of the open vessels to bathe all the cells directly. The blood-filled spaces are called haemocoels. Blood returns to the heart via other open-ended vessels or through holes in the heart. Blood flow in such open systems is relatively slow.

erythrocyte a red blood cell.

heart the specialized structure by which blood is pumped around the body.

The human heart consists of strong, muscular chambers. The heart has two atria and two ventricles, which serve as a double circulatory system. Deoxygenated blood from the organs and tissues returns to the right side of the heart, which pumps it to the lungs. The oxygenated blood then returns to the left side of the heart, which pumps it out with great force to the rest of the body. This high-pressure flow of oxygenated blood to active cells allows them to maintain the high metabolic rate characteristic of all mammals.

SINGLE CIRCULATORY SYSTEMS

Lower vertebrates, such as fish, have a single circulatory system. In a fish such as a shark, deoxygenated blood from the veins is collected in a thin-walled chamber (atrium) and then passed to a muscular, thick-walled chamber (ventricle), which contracts forcibly to send it to the gills, where it gains oxygen, and then straight to the rest of the body. Because the passage of blood from the heart to the organs and tissues takes place via the gills, the pressure in such a system is rather low.

interstitial fluid see closed circulatory system and the lymphatic system.

leucocyte a white blood cell.

lymphatic system a network of small vessels by which the interstitial fluid that surrounds cells and through which gas exchange takes place is collected and returned to the blood.

peristalsis rhythmical contractions of the muscles in the arterial walls that force the blood along.

plasma (of blood) the fluid portion of blood.

red blood cell an erythrocyte.

respiratory pigment a special molecule in blood that has a high oxygen-carrying capacity and which combines with oxygen at the respiratory surfaces and releases it to tissues in the body.

valve a structure (especially in the heart and veins) that closes temporarily to prevent the back-flow of blood.

vein a blood vessel by which deoxygenated blood is carried to the heart.

ventricle a chamber in the heart that receives blood from an atrium and pumps it through the arteries.

white blood cell a leucocyte.

ANIMALS WITHOUT CIRCULATORY SYSTEMS

Small, simple animals that live in a watery environment, such as sponges (all of which belong to the order Porifera) and flatworms (belonging to the phylum Platyhelminthes), have no special circulatory systems. Their bodies are only a few cells thick and diffusion alone is sufficient.

THE HUMAN RESPIRATORY SYSTEM

All animal cells require a constant supply of oxygen, so that food can be oxidized ('burnt') to release energy. At the same time, nutrients must be carried to each cell, and the various waste products of cellular activity – including carbon dioxide, the by-product of respiration – must be transported away.

In active, multicellular animals, special systems have developed to meet these needs. Respiratory systems allow sufficient oxygen to be obtained from the environment and carbon dioxide to be removed.

The way an animal obtains oxygen from the environment is dictated by its basic body plan, its life style, and whether it lives in water or in air. The amount of oxygen entering an animal and the amount of carbon dioxide lost depends upon the surface area available for gas exchange.

The human respiratory system allows sufficient oxygen to be obtained from the environment and carbon dioxide to be removed.

air sac see alveoli.

alveoli (sing. **alveolus**; or **air sac**) numerous tiny swellings at the termini of the bronchioles in the lungs that increase the surface area for gas exchange with the blood.

bronchi (sing. **bronchus**) two large branches by which air is conveyed from the trachea to the two lungs.

bronchiole any of numerous tiny branching tubes in the lungs.

diaphragm a muscular partition that separates the chest from the abdomen.

haemoglobin the respiratory pigment in vertebrate blood.

lung a large respiratory structure used for exchange of gases with air.

In mammals (including humans), which have very high metabolic rates, the lungs are complex and efficiently ventilated. Regular ventilation is achieved by contractions of the diaphragm. The enormous surface area of mammalian lungs is due to millions of tiny air sacs known as alveoli. Air is drawn through the nose and down the trachea and passes into the lungs through a system of ever-narrowing, branching tubes (bronchi and bronchioles), which finally terminate in millions of alveoli. The wall of each alveolus is lined with a network of minute, thin-walled blood vessels called capillaries. As deoxygenated blood from the heart passes through the capillaries, it loses the carbon dioxide it is carrying, which diffuses into the alveoli to be breathed out from the lungs, and picks up oxygen; the oxygenated blood is then returned to the heart, to be pumped around the body once again.

oxygen a highly reactive element (symbol O), and the most abundant in the Earth's crust. In its molecular form it is a gas which comprises 21% of the atmosphere. In this form it is essential to the respiration of plants and animals – as described here, and in the energy-producing processes (cell respiration) of virtually all cells apart from certain bacteria. It is also crucial to all life as a constituent of water and many organic compounds.

Oxygen does not diffuse very far in tissues, penetrating only about 1 mm (1/25 in) into tissues in sufficient amounts to maintain life. To ensure that sufficient oxygen reaches all cells, the respiratory surfaces are usually well supplied with blood. They are also very thin, to allow oxygen to diffuse quickly.

Only small amounts of oxygen can be carried in simple solution, so many animals have special molecules called respiratory pigments in their blood. These molecules are able to combine with oxygen, picking it up at respiratory surfaces and liberating it to the cells inside the body. Haemoglobin – the respiratory pigment in vertebrates – contains iron atoms and is responsible for its red colour. It increases the capacity of the blood to carry oxygen by about 75 times. (Although haemoglobin is also present in many invertebrates, some molluscs and arthropods have a blue, copper-containing pigment called haemocyanin.) The metal atoms in both these molecules are important in binding oxygen. In vertebrates the respiratory pigment is contained within blood cells, but in many invertebrates the pigments are free in the blood fluid or plasma.

pharynx the cavity formed by the upper part of the alimentary canal, lying behind the mouth and in front of the larynx and oesophagus.

respiration in air is the method of obtaining oxygen for all land animals.

Air contains far more oxygen than water – about 30 times as much for a given volume. Getting oxygen from air is therefore much easier than from water. Another advantage of air breathing is that air has a low heat capacity and relatively little heat is lost despite the continuous ventilation of large respiratory surfaces. It is no coincidence that the only truly warm-blooded animals – birds and mammals – are air-breathers.

Breathing air does have some disadvantages, however. The large respiratory surfaces have to be kept moist, so that gases can dissolve in the surface layers before they diffuse across. Evaporation of water from these moist surfaces can be an important cause of water loss in terrestrial animals. (Water lost in this way can easily be seen on cold days, when water vapour in the breath condenses in the cold air.)

respiratory pigment a special molecule in blood that has a high oxygen-carrying capacity and which combines with oxygen at the respiratory surfaces and releases it to tissues within the body. The respiratory pigment in vertebrates is haemoglobin.

trachea the windpipe; in air-breathing vertebrates, the tube by which air is conveyed from the throat to the lungs.

ventilation (in respiration) the means by which oxygen-carrying air or water is brought into contact with the respiratory surfaces; see introduction (above).

windpipe see trachea.

NERVOUS AND ENDOCRINE SYSTEMS

The coordination system of animal cells – which may be widely separated in the body – depends upon two basic mechanisms. Nervous systems based upon vast networks of intercellular connections provide a means of extremely rapid communication between cells, while endocrine systems allow communication between cells in different tissues by means of chemicals (hormones) in the blood. Some nerves produce hormones, so providing the link between the neural and endocrine systems – these neurones are neurosecretory cells. In humans, the main link between the nervous and endocrine systems is provided by the pituitary gland.

afferent nerves carry information from sensory receptors in the outer regions of the body to the central nervous system.

brain a concentration of nerve cells acting as the central coordinating point of a nervous system, progressively complex in more complex animals. Different regions of the brain specialize to perform different functions. In mammals, two cerebral hemispheres (together forming the cerebrum) develop from the forebrain, and in more advanced species (such as humans), the surface area of the brain is increased by numerous folds or convolutions. In humans, this area of the brain is associated with intelligent behaviour, language, memory and consciousness.

central nervous system (or **CNS**) comprises the brain and spinal cord. Within the central nervous system, linking the afferent and efferent nerves, are large numbers of special nerves known as interneurones. These form a complex but highly organized network of interconnecting nerve cells and are responsible for integrating the information coming from all sources. All the patterns of movement and behaviour are the result of the way interneurones process and pass on the incoming signals. The brain – large concentrations of nerve cells – integrates all the incoming information.

cerebellum the part of the brain associated with voluntary movement and balance.

dopamine see neurotransmitters.

efferent nerves carry signals from the central nervous system to outlying systems: stimulation of muscle systems, by means of motor nerves, causes contraction, while stimulation of glandular systems causes secretion.

endocrine cell any cell that has been modified to produce secretions that act as chemical signals over much greater distances.

endocrine system a system of glands that produce chemicals (hormones) that are transported in the blood and carried to distant tissues, whose activity they modify. The system is principally involved in the control and regulation of growth, reproduction, the internal environment, and energy production. Chemical signals are used by all multicellular animals. Different hormones affect almost every part of the body.

ganglion (plur. **ganglia**) an encapsulated group of nerve-ending cells.

gland any organ producing a secretion that is either carried by the blood or passed via a duct to where it is needed.

growth hormone a hormone produced by the pituitary gland. It controls general body growth and metabolism.

hormone a chemical signal produced by a particular type of cell and carried in the blood. The structure of each hormone is highly specific, and the 'target cells' that respond to it have special receptor molecules that recognize and bind with the hormone concerned. The binding of the hormone to the receptor causes changes in the metabolic or genetic machinery of the target cell in such a way as to alter its activity.

hypothalamus part of the brain, controlling the pituitary gland and an integrating centre for many autonomic functions.

insulin a hormone produced from the pancreas. It controls the levels of blood sugar.

medulla oblongata part of the brain associated with involuntary actions such as breathing and heart beat.

nerve cell (or **neurone**) the functional unit of the nervous system. Many millions of these work together to form an intricate network. Neurones typically consist of a cell body from which there are a variable number of very thin, branching projections (dendrites) and a single much longer extension (the axon). Communication along nerves depends upon tiny electrical signals. Axons normally terminate at synapses, where they link up with the cell bodies or dendrites of other neurones, or with secretory cells or muscles. At the synapse, the electrical impulses passing along the axon cause the release of tiny amounts of neurotransmitters, which diffuse across to the next cell.

nervous system a network of cells adapted for very rapid communication over long distances within an animal body.

neuromodulator any chemical substance that acts beyond the vicinity from which it is released. Neuromodulators produce much more diffuse effects and change the levels of excitability in whole groups of neurones.

neurosecretory cell a hormone-secreting nerve cell. The hormones produced pass down the axons to be stored at the nerve terminals and are released during neural activity.

neurotransmitters tiny amounts of chemicals which are released at the synapse when electrical impulses pass along the axon. Many different chemicals are known to act as neurotransmitters: acetylocholine, noradrenaline, dopamine, glycine and serotonin are common examples. The neurotransmitters bind to specific receptors and cause new electrical or chemical signals to be initiated in the neighbouring cell.

noradrenaline see neurotransmitters.

oestradiol in females, a hormone produced from the ovaries. It influences sexual characteristics.

pancreas an endocrine gland; see insulin.

peripheral nervous system (or **PNS**) the combination of nerves, ganglia and the brain monitoring the involuntary functions of the body.

pituitary gland an endocrine gland; see growth hormone.

synapse a specialized junction between nerve cells.

testosterone in males, a hormone produced by the testes. It influences sexual characteristics.

thyroid gland an endocrine gland; see thyroxine.

thyroxine a hormone associated with body growth and metabolism. It is produced by the thyroid gland.

Medicine

MAJOR COMMUNICABLE DISEASES

Transmission of diseases

An infectious disease is one in which one living organism inhabits and multiplies on or within another, harming it in the process, either by the production of toxic substances or by damaging, digesting or destroying part or all of its cellular structure. Such harmful organisms are mostly microscopic – viruses, bacteria and protozoans – but also include various kinds of fungus, worms and arthropods.

Infections can be transmitted in the following ways:

Airborne transmission infection through infected droplets in the air from the nose, throat/lungs or saliva, or from dust particles from fallen skin.

Contamination infection through food or water supplies containing infected material such as faeces or urine.

Direct contact (contagion) infection from close contact with an infected person.

Sexual transmission infection through vaginal or anal intercourse, or oral sex. The use of condoms may reduce the risk of infection.

Blood-borne transmission infection through the injection of contaminated blood or blood products, or by improperly sterilized instruments. Blood-borne transmission is most common among haemophiliacs and intravenous drug users, and is occasionally the result of tattooing or acupuncture.

Animal-borne transmission infection through the injection of contaminated saliva; e.g. malaria (carried by the mosquito) and bubonic plague (transmitted by flea bites).

AIDS

AIDS – acquired immune deficiency syndrome – was first identified in Los Angeles, USA, in 1981. The virus responsible for causing AIDS was isolated in 1983 and is now known as HIV (human immunodeficiency virus). The disease is spreading rapidly throughout the Western world, and has reached epidemic proportions in the countries of eastern and central Africa.

The virus attacks one particular type of white blood cell in the body (the helper/inducer lymphocytes) and this causes immunosuppression (reduced ability to combat infection). It may also attack the nervous system and cause dementia. Acute infection with HIV after exposure leads to the production of antibodies (sero-conversion). These antibodies are detected by blood tests which become positive on average within three months of the virus being acquired, but may take up to 12 months or longer to appear. In some cases there may be no symptoms during the period of sero-conversion; in other cases a transient flu-like illness with gland swelling and muscle aches may occur.

Not all patients who sero-convert go on to experience chronic infection. In those patients who do, the infection may be without symptoms, or may give rise to illnesses of varying degrees of severity – known as PGL, ARC or AIDS itself. Current knowledge suggests that between 10% and 30% of HIV-antibody-positive patients progress to AIDS within five years.

PGL – persistent generalized lymphodenopathy – is the mildest illness caused by HIV infection. It is characterized by the swelling of lymph glands at various sites of the body, but there are no other symptoms. Many patients with PGL remain well for several years.

ARC – AIDS-related complex – is the second stage of the disease, during which there is some impairment of the immune system as well as lymph gland enlargement. Symptoms may include episodes of fever, weight loss, night sweats, diarrhoea, coughing, skin rashes and profound fatigue. Blood tests may show reduced numbers of white blood cells, anaemia, or changes in blood proteins. ARC is usually only diagnosed if such symptoms or blood-test abnormalities persist over a three-month period.

AIDS itself is diagnosed once certain specific infections or types of tumour begin to appear. The most common infection is an unusual form of pneumonia (*Pneumocystis carinii*); the most common tumour is Kaposi's sarcoma – a form of skin cancer that may spread to the internal organs. The course of the disease usually involves increasingly serious episodes of infection and it is often fatal within two years. Approximately 30% of subjects suffer dementia by the later stages of their disease. Advances in treatment have included better treatments for the episodes of infection, and the development of the drug AZT, which shows some promise in retarding the disease itself. The use of AZT has also been shown to reduce the risk of pregnant women infecting their babies.

In July 1994 the United Nations World Health Organization (WHO) announced that the number of persons infected by HIV worldwide was 17,000,000, an increase of 3,000,000 from the previous year. WHO predicted that by the year 2000 the number of people who were HIV positive would be between 30,000,000 and 40,000,000. An estimated 4,000,000 people have developed full-blown AIDS, including those who have died. In Europe and North America AIDS is at present more common in homosexual men and intravenous drug users, but the AIDS virus is spreading more rapidly among heterosexuals. In Africa heterosexual infection is much more frequent.

The only ways of acquiring HIV infection or AIDS are: by having oral sex or sexual intercourse (particularly anal intercourse) with someone who carries the virus;

by sharing needles or other instruments contaminated with the blood of someone carrying the virus;

by receiving blood or blood products from someone with the virus – in the past some haemophiliacs have acquired the AIDS virus from treatment with blood products, but all blood products and blood transfusions in countries of the developed world are now thoroughly tested before use;

by mothers, who have the virus, passing it on to their babies.

Anthrax

Anthrax is a form of blood poisoning in cattle, sheep and horses that is normally fatal. It can upon rare occasions be passed to vets or butchers disposing of infected carcases or to those handling infected animal hides, wool or bone meal. The initial lesion is usually on the hand – a painful swollen boil with a black crust and surrounding redness. If untreated, blood poisoning (septicaemia) may result. It can be cured by penicillin, and a vaccine exists for those in high-risk occupations.

Chickenpox (Varicella)

Chickenpox is caused by the same virus as shingles (*Herpes zoster*). It is a mild disease, common in childhood and infectious from four days before the rash appears until seven days after the rash appears. The incubation period is usually 14 days. The rash – which may be preceded by mild headache or fever – begins as red spots, which over a few hours become raised and topped by a clear blister. Over two to three days these small blisters become opalescent and then scab over, with several crops of blisters appearing over a perod of five to seven days. The rash can occur on any part of the body – including the mouth and scalp – but tends to be most profuse on the trunk. No specific treatment is needed, except to relieve itch and prevent scratching with dirty finger nails. Complications are rare and there is no vaccine.

Cholera

Cholera is an acute infection of the intestine that causes profuse watery diarrhoea, vomiting and dehydration. It is caused by consuming water or food contaminated by the bacterium *Vibrio comma*, which is found in faeces. In 1854 the Englishman John Snow proved that cholera is transmitted in contaminated water when he stopped an epidemic by removing the pump handle from a well that he suspected was the source of infection. The last epidemic in Britain was in Cleethorpes in 1879. Today the disease is largely restricted to the tropics. Prevention is achieved by the availability of a clean water supply. Vaccination – two injections at an interval of two to four months – is effective for six to nine months, after which booster doses are needed.

Common cold (Coryzal)

At least 40 different viruses – either airborne or transmitted by direct contact – can cause sneezing, coughing, sore throat, running eyes and nose, headache and mild fever. Aspirin may help reduce the symptoms.

Creutzfeld-Jakob disease

See p. 171.

Diphtheria

Diphtheria is an infection of the pharynx caused by airborne bacteria. The symptoms are an initial sore throat, obstructed breathing and inflammation of the heart. The condition is complicated by the formation of a membrane of dead tissue that can totally obstruct the airway and necessitate a tracheotomy – a surgical opening in the neck over the windpipe to allow breathing. Immunization programmes have eradicated diphtheria in the UK, where as recently as 1941 the disease caused 1622 deaths. Immunization is achieved by a series of three injections in infancy – combined with injections against tetanus and, usually, whooping cough – and booster doses at school age.

Dysentery

Two types of dysentery occur – *bacillary dysentery*, which is caused by the bacterium *Shigella*, and *amoebic dysentery*, caused by the amoeba *Entamoeba hystolytica*. Both types cause profuse diarrhoea (often containing blood), abdominal pain, weight loss and dehydration. Complications include liver abscesses. Amoebic dysentery is confined to the tropics. Bacillary dysentery occurs worldwide as a result of contamination of food by faecal bacteria, usually carried by water. The disease can be mild, but even after complete recovery the organism can still be excreted for several weeks. Prevention is through high standards of hygiene and the provision of a clean water supply. No immunization exists.

Food poisoning (Gastroenteritis)

Most short-lasting cases of sickness or diarrhoea are due to *viral gastroenteritis*. The most common cause is human rotavirus, to which children under the age of three are particularly susceptible. The treatment is to stop all solid-food intake, and to concentrate instead on fluid intake to prevent dehydration. In babies, feeds of boiled water are given instead of milk. Breast-fed babies are less likely to get gastroenteritis.

Bacterial gastroenteritis may be caused by a number of bacteria, including *Salmonella*, *Listeria* and, more rarely, *Clostridium botulinum* (which causes the often fatal disease called *botulism*). Raw meat, poultry or eggs can be contaminated by the *Salmonella* bacterium, which is able to survive deep freezing. If thawing is not complete, or if the cooking time or temperature is inadequate, the cooked food remains infected. Symptoms of diarrhoea, fever and vomiting usually begin 12 to 48 hours after the food has been consumed. If complications such as septicaemia (blood poisoning) occur, the patient is treated with antibiotics. Without treatment, an infected person may become a carrier, although showing no symptoms.

Other forms of food poisoning are due to the release of a toxic chemical from the contaminating organism, rather than infection by the organism itself. Such infection usually begins within one to six hours of ingestion. Examples include *staphylococcal toxin* (often from infected cream, sometimes from meat or poultry) and the toxin of *Bacillus cereus* (from fried rice). All forms of gastroenteritis may be prevented by high standards of hygiene in food preparation and by the provision of a clean water supply.

German measles (Rubella)

The first symptoms of German measles – a headache and sore throat – are followed by mild fever, a pink blotchy rash (first on the face, then on the body) and swelling of the lymph glands at the back of the neck. Cases are mildly infectious from five days before until five days after the rash appears. The incubation period is usually 17 to 18 days. There may be transient joint soreness, particularly in adults, but serious complications are very rare. However, German measles in a woman in the first three months of pregnancy can cause foetal damage – in the first month the risk of congenital abnormalities of eyes, ears or heart is 50%. This falls to about 4% by the fourth month.

Transmission is by direct contact with an infected person. In the UK immunization programmes were once aimed mainly at teenage girls. However, vaccination is now usual from the age of 14 months since the introduction in 1988 of the measles, mumps and rubella vaccine, which has been used for some years in North America.

Glandular fever

Glandular fever – or infectious mononucleosis – is caused by the Epstein-Barr virus. Transmission is by direct contact and, because it mainly affects young adults (aged 15 to 25), a popular theory was that it was contracted by kissing. The initial symptom is a particularly sore throat, often producing a thick white coating over the area of the tonsils. Other characteristics include fever and enlargement of the lymph glands of the neck and sometimes also of the liver and spleen. This enlargement can last ten or more days and is often followed by a period of severe fatigue and mild depression before complete recovery. No treatment other than rest is available. Diagnosis can be confirmed by blood tests. No immunization is available.

Gonorrhoea

Gonorrhoea is a sexually transmitted (venereal) disease caused by the bacterium *Neisseria gonorrhoea.* It has an average incubation period of four days. In men it almost always causes a purulent discharge at the tip of the penis. Complications include infection of the epididymis (the tube behind the testicle) and of the prostate gland, or, in later stages, a narrowing of the urethra (urine tube). One half of the women infected by the disease may initially have no symptoms; others may suffer vaginal discharge, urinary symptoms and/or abdominal pain. The pain is due to infection spreading to the pelvic organs, including the Fallopian tubes, which may become scarred and blocked, sometimes leading to infertility. Penicillin is usually an effective cure. No immunization exists.

Hepatitis

Hepatitis is inflammation of the liver, usually caused by a virus. It can also be caused by excessive alcohol or drug consumption. Viral hepatitis is classified as A, B, and Non A, Non B. There is no effective antiviral drug.

Hepatitis A – also called infectious hepatitis – is transmitted by close contact or faecal contamination of food or water. Following an incubation period of two to six weeks, initial symptoms include fever, nausea, weakness, discomfort and tenderness over the liver area. After about the first four days of the illness, jaundice (yellow skin) develops and the patient passes dark urine and pale faeces. Jaundice lasts one or two weeks and then appetite returns. A complete recovery is usual. An injection of human immunoglobulin gives temporary protection to travellers to those areas of the Third World where the disease is endemic.

Hepatitis B – also called serum hepatitis – is bloodborne, usually transmitted by sharing contaminated needles or through sexual contact. The incubation period varies between one and five months. Symptoms identical to Hepatitis A may develop, but a high percentage of cases are 'sub-clinical', i.e. the illness is mild without evidence of jaundice. In about 19 out of 20 cases the patient becomes free of the virus within four to six months. One case in 20 becomes a chronic carrier, liable to pass on infection by blood or sexual contact, and liable to develop liver complications such as cirrhosis. Only one in 1000 cases dies of acute hepatitis. Immunization by a series of three injections is now available for those at high risk, e.g. nurses, doctors and dentists.

Herpes simplex

There are two common types of herpes simplex, a viral infection transmitted by direct contact.

The most common lesion produced by *Type I* of this virus is the 'cold sore' – a small crop of painful blisters that usually develop around the lips or nose and last for several days before fading. The virus may then be latent and flare up again in response to such events as another infection, trauma, emotional upset or exposure to sunlight. Other infections include blisters of the fingers (whitlow), ulceration of the cornea of the eye, and, rarely, a serious encephalitis (brain infection) to which infants are vulnerable. Those suffering from 'cold sores' should therefore avoid close contact with infants.

A variety of *Type II* of this virus causes genital herpes, a painful recurrent blistering eruption of the genitalia similar in appearance to a 'cold sore' but transmitted through sexual contact. Treatment with idoxuridine limits attacks, but does not prevent recurrence. No immunization exists.

Herpes zoster

see Chickenpox and Shingles.

Influenza

Influenza is an airborne viral infection. Symptoms include fever, muscle pain, sore throat, coughing, loss of appetite and general weakness. Complications include viral pneumonia, which can lead to a rapidly progressive pneumonia owing to further bacterial infection by staphylococci. Influenza may be fatal in elderly people. Pandemics can occur, such as in April-November 1918, when 21,600,000 people are thought to have died. Various types of influenza virus exist. The virus has the capacity to change through time. Immunity from previous exposure or from vaccination is therefore never complete, and second or further attacks in the one individual can occur.

Legionnaire's disease

Legionnaire's disease is an uncommon form of pneumonia identified in 1976 and caused by the bacterium *Legionella pneumophilia.* It is transmitted airborne in water droplets from contaminated supplies, often through air-conditioning systems or showers. Symptoms include fever, coughing, chest pain and breathlessness, and the disease is sometimes fatal.

Leprosy

Leprosy is a chronic inflammatory disease caused by the bacterium *Mycobacterium leprae,* which is transmitted by prolonged or close contact. The characteristics are very variable. Mild cases may show only a small area of altered skin pigmentation, which may heal spontaneously. Other cases progress to a thickening of superficial nerves, areas of skin without feeling, and muscle paralysis. In extreme forms there is distortion of the skin by nodule formation, thickening, fissuring and ulceration, resulting in the deformity and disfigurement that are traditionally feared. Control with sulphone drugs is possible, and some use has been made of plastic surgery.

Malaria

Malaria is caused by a protozoa of one of four types – *Plasmodium ovale, P. malaria, P. vivax* and *P. falciparum* – and is transmitted to the bloodstream of man by the female anopheles mosquito. This mode of transmission was first proved in 1895 by the English bacteriologist Sir Ronald Ross, who discovered the protozoa in the gastrointestinal tract of the mosquito. Infection results in the destruction of red blood cells, causing intermittent fever and anaemia. The incubation period and the severity of the disease depends on the infecting species. *P. falciparum* – the most dangerous infection – causes malignant tertian malaria, in which the brain can be affected, and fits or coma – and even sudden death – may occur.

Every year in the tropics more than 1,000,000 people still die of malaria and 2,000,000 new cases appear, despite worldwide efforts to control the disease. All efforts at controlling malaria focus on the mosquito – the carrier – and include the destruction of the mosquito's breeding grounds, treating water with chemicals to destroy mosquito larvae, and the use of insecticides to kill adult mosquitoes. Drugs can be used to treat infected people, and measures – such as the use of nets, repellents and suitable clothing – can be taken to prevent the mosquito biting. Throughout the 1950s and 1960s the WHO had considerable success in malaria eradication, particularly in the USA and Europe. The programme also led to a 500-fold decrease in malaria in India. Unfortunately, resistance of mosquitoes to DDT then developed, and in many areas in the 1970s eradication began to falter. The drugs used to prevent malaria are becoming more complex because in certain areas of the world malaria has become resistant to drugs that were previously effective. Whatever drug is used must be started one week before travel into the endemic area and should be continued for four to six weeks after leaving the area. In North Africa and the Middle East chloroquine taken once per week or proguanil taken daily are the usual preventative. For the Indian sub-continent, China, Africa and South America both drugs are advised in combination. For some parts of Southeast Asia pyrimethamine and chloroquine are advised.

Measles (Rubeola)

Measles is a viral airborne infection. An incubation period of between eight and 14 days precedes the onset of fever and catarrhal symptoms, which last for three days before the rash appears. The rash is red and blotchy, usually starting behind the ears and spreading to the face and trunk. The inside of the cheeks may be red and Koplik's spots (little white spots – like grains of salt – in the area behind the lower back teeth) confirm the diagnosis. Other characteristics include running eyes and nose. The rash fades after three or four days. Cases are highly infectious from the onset of the fever and the catarrhal phase until the rash fades. Bacterial infections of the ears, sinuses and chest are the most immediate complications. A rare but serious progressive brain disease known as subacute sclerosing panencephalitis can occur four or more years after infection.

Immunization is recommended from the age of 14 months and, since 1988 in the UK, is combined with a vaccine for mumps and rubella (German measles). The intensive use of this vaccine has made measles an extremely rare condition in North America.

Meningitis

Meningitis is a viral or bacterial infection, causing inflammation of membranes surrounding the brain.

Bacterial meningitis can be caused by a number of organisms – the most common are mengingococcal meningitis, pneumococcal meningitis and haemophilus meningitis. *E. coli* meningitis occurs mainly in new-born infants. The symptoms of bacterial meningitis are fever, severe headache, neck stiffness, intolerance of bright lights and vomiting. The speed of onset depends on the infecting organism – tubercular meningitis has a gradual onset. Meningococcal meningitis is particularly rapid and can cause sudden collapse and the rapid appearance of a rash looking like small bruises or blood blisters. Antibiotic therapy must be started with the utmost urgency.

Viral meningitis can be caused by a great number of viruses. The symptoms are similar but less severe than those of bacterial meningitis. Spontaneous recovery can be expected without specific treatment.

Mumps

Mumps is caused by an airborne paramyxovirus. Its incubation period is usually 21 days. Initial symptoms are three to five days of mild fever and vague malaise followed by tender swelling of the parotid glands (the salivary glands on the side of the face, in front of and below the ears). Usually both sides are affected, but one side may become swollen one or two days before the other. The swelling lasts several days, and cases are infectious for one week before the swelling and until the swelling subsides. Possible complications include inflammation of the testicles (orchitis) in adult males, inflammation of the pancreas, and a mild viral meningitis. In North America, Britain and some European countries, immunization is available by means of a single injection combined with vaccination against measles and rubella (German measles).

Myalgic encephalomyelitis (ME)

Myalgic encephalomyelitis is a condition probably developing as a sequel to various viral infections, most notably to Coxsackie virus infection. The symptoms are diverse, but include muscle fatigue and muscle pain provoked by minimal exercise and relieved or prevented by adequate rest. The condition is similar to the fatigue encountered after glandular fever, but may last for months or even years. The condition is also known as post-viral syndrome and Royal Free disease, so called because of an apparent epidemic in the Royal Free Hospital, London, in the 1950s. No treatment is available.

Plague

Plague is a disease of rodents that can be transmitted to man by flea bites or by airborne infection. It is caused by the bacterium *Yersinia pestis*. Symptoms include fever, weakness, delirium and painful buboes (swelling of lymph nodes). The condition is often fatal. During the 14th century – when the condition was known as the Black Death – one quarter of the population of Europe died because of plague. The Great Plague of London (1664–65) caused the death of one person in seven in the city.

Pneumonia

Pneumonia is a bacterial or viral infection transmitted by direct contact or by airborne infection. The principal characteristic is the inflammation of one or both lungs, in which the air sacs become filled with liquid. This causes pain and difficulty in breathing. Pneumonia can be fatal, particularly in the elderly.

Poliomyelitis
Polio is a viral infection of the nervous system transmitted by direct contact. It is no longer endemic in Western Europe – as recently as 1948 polio caused 241 deaths in England and Wales. The majority of cases are characterized by mild fever, headache, stiffness of the neck and gastrointestinal symptoms lasting only a few days. However, other cases develop meningitis or paralysis of muscles. Paralysis may affect the breathing muscles – causing respiratory failure – or the limb muscles – resulting in permanent muscle thinning and weakness. Polio has been eradicated by immunization in the majority of developed countries. The oral vaccine Sabin is given from infancy with later booster doses. The earlier Salk vaccine was given by injection.

Rabies
Rabies is an acute viral infection endemic in warm-blooded animals in Africa and Eurasia as far west as central Europe. (Rabies reached central France in the 1980s, but the advance has now been controlled and it is thought that France, the Low Countries and most of Germany no longer have infected wild animals.) Ordinarily fatal in man, rabies is transmitted in the saliva of warm-blooded animals through broken skin as a result of a bite (e.g. from dogs, foxes). The symptoms include spasm of the throat muscles when swallowing is attempted, aversion to water (hence the alternative name 'hydrophobia'), maniacal behaviour, and finally involvement of other muscles to cause paralysis and death. Vaccine is available for those in high-risk occupations.

Rheumatic fever
Rheumatic fever is caused by streptococcal bacteria and can, like scarlet fever, occur as a sequel to tonsillitis. The symptoms are fever and an arthritis that seems to move from one joint to another, causing swelling and pain. Rheumatic fever may cause damage to the heart valves, damage which only becomes apparent in later years. Occasionally it can cause chorea (St Vitus's dance), a type of involuntary movement. The disease can recur, but is today very much less common than 50 years ago. No immunization exists.

Rubella
See German measles.

Scarlet fever (Scarlatina)
Scarlet fever is a throat infection caused by an airborne bacterium *Streptococcus pyogenus.* Symptoms include fever and a sore throat, complicated by the appearance of a uniform pink blush of the skin, which on close inspection appears as many fine red points. The cheeks are usually flushed and the area round the lips is white (circumoral pallor). The tongue has a strawberry-like colour. About a week after the rash appears there is often peeling of the skin, especially on the hands and feet. The condition is sometimes accompanied by ear and kidney infections. The incubation period is between two and five days and cases are infectious for up to ten days unless treated with penicillin. In recent years this disease seems to have become much milder in developed countries, in part because of the use of antibiotics and in part because of improved social conditions. Complications are now accordingly rare.

Schistosomiasis (Bilharzia)
Bilharzia is a tropical disease caused by infestation of the body with larvae of the parasitic flatworm *Schistosoma.* Eggs excreted in the faeces or urine of infected people undergo part of the larval development in freshwater snails. Larvae released by the snails penetrate the skin of people bathing in infected water and colonize blood vessels in the intestine. Symptoms include diarrhoea, and an enlargement of the spleen and liver. The condition can be fatal.

Shingles (Herpes zoster)
Shingles is caused by a reactivation of the *Herpes zoster* virus which causes chickenpox. The virus may be present and dormant in the nerve root for years before reactivation. This painful condition is therefore not truly infectious, but it is possible to pass it on as chickenpox by close physical contact. Symptoms include groups of small blisters on a red base that appear in the skin area supplied by a particular nerve root, for example in a narrow band round one side of the chest or abdomen. The groups of blisters commonly occur in a band on one side of the face, or on one limb. Pain may precede the rash by two to three days, and may endure at the site for an average of six weeks. Sensitivity (post-herpetic neuralgia) may last for months.

Smallpox
The World Health Organization declared the world free of smallpox from 1 January 1980. Vaccination is only needed for certain research scientists.

Syphilis
Syphilis is a sexually transmitted (venereal) disease caused by the bacterium *Treponema pallidum.* The disease has three stages. The primary stage begins after an incubation phase of (usually) two to four weeks and is characterized by a firm ulcer on the site of infection, usually the genitalia, accompanied by swelling in the nearest lymph glands (e.g. the groin). The secondary stage – six weeks later – has varying characteristics, including skin rashes, mouth ulcers, glandular swelling, and fever with muscle aches. The tertiary stage follows after a long dormant period (up to 25 years) and can affect any organ of the body but particularly the brain and nerves, possibly causing insanity, blindness and loss of balance. Syphilis may also cause localized swellings (gumma) in the skin, bones or heart. Diagnosis is by blood tests, and treatment by penicillin.

Tetanus (Lockjaw)
The bacterium *Clostridium tetani* is widespread in nature, commonly occurring in the topsoil. Tetanus spores can gain access to the body through cuts, resulting in intense muscle spasm ('lockjaw'). Prevention is by immunization with tetanus toxoid, given as three doses in infancy with booster doses at school age and then every five years. If immunity has waned the initial three doses are repeated.

Thrush
Thrush is a fungal disease caused by the fungus *Candida albicans,* which lives in the alimentary canal and the vagina. Thrush arises when the growth of fungus increases, in some cases following a course of broad-spectrum antibiotics. It can be passed to a baby at birth. Thrush is characterized by white patches in the mouth (particularly in infants) and by irritation of the vagina.

Tuberculosis (TB)

Tuberculosis is caused by the bacterium *Mycobacterium tuberculosis,* first discovered in 1882 by the German scientist Robert Koch (1843–1910). Evidence of this disease has been found in an Egyptian mummy from the 10th century BC. The mortality rate in England and Wales in the 1850s was 60,000 per year, both adults and children dying of what was known as 'consumption'. Two strains of organism exist – human and bovine. The main source of bovine tuberculosis was infected milk, but this has been eliminated in the developed world by pasteurization. The source of the human strain is the respiratory tract of an 'open' case of pulmonary tuberculosis, i.e. the organism is coughed up or breathed out by the sufferer.

The initial infection is in the lungs and the lymph glands in the middle of the chest cavity. In the majority of cases there are no symptoms and the infection heals without treatment, but may leave a scar on the lung. During this primary infection the body develops an immunity that can be detected by means of the Mantoux test. In this test a tiny amount of dead tubercle is injected just under the skin surface and if immunity is present, a raised red lump develops. In a minority of primary infections, insufficient immunity develops and the infection spreads either all through the lungs (consumption or miliary pulmonary tuberculosis) or to other organs, leading to meningitis or kidney or bone infection. In cases where the primary illness has disappeared, the infection can flare up again years later, particularly if there is undernourishment or general debility. This is known as chronic tuberculosis and most commonly affects the lungs, but can affect any organ.

Modern drug treatment is very effective for all forms of the disease, but 'open' cases are still kept in isolation until their sputum becomes free of the infecting organism. Immunization is achieved by BCG (*Bacille Calmette-Guérin*), a live attenuated vaccine (i.e. a very mild form of TB) first used in 1906. It is given by injection into the skin and results in a small ulcer that heals after several weeks, leaving a scar.

Typhoid

Typhoid is an infection of the digestive system caused by the bacterium *Salmonella typhi,* transmitted to the body by faecally contaminated food or water. Symptoms begin with fever and progress to a rash and profuse diarrhoea with blood loss. Untreated, the mortality rate is 10% to 15%, the remainder of cases recover after about three weeks, although some 3% become chronic carriers without symptoms. The last major epidemic in the UK was in Aberdeen in 1964, when 414 cases occurred. Immunization is achieved with two injections at an interval of one month, and immunity lasts for five years.

Typhus

Typhus is the name given to a group of closely related acute infectious diseases caused by *Rickettsia* parasites, which are transmitted by lice, fleas or ticks. Typhus is characterized by severe headaches, rash, high fever and delirium, and can be fatal. Typhus has been eliminated from the developed world but remains a threat to undernourished people living in unhygienic conditions in developing countries.

Varicella

See Chickenpox.

Whooping cough (Pertussis)

Whooping cough is an acute respiratory infection caused by the bacterium *Bordetella pertussis.* It is transmitted by direct contact or by airborne infection. In developing countries, where poor nutrition exists, whooping cough has a considerable death rate. It can affect any age group, but is most common in children and is most severe in young babies. The illness begins with what seems to be an ordinary cold, but, instead of improving after a few days, the cough becomes progressively worse and is most severe at night. There are spasms of coughing, with one cough after another, until the child is forced to take in breath rapidly with a loud whooping sound. During an attack the child becomes red (or even blue) in the face, with streaming eyes. A severe coughing spasm usually ends with a bout of vomiting. These symptoms may persist for several weeks before easing, but often a cough at night may persist for several months after the infection. Complications include middle ear infection, pneumonia, and encephalitis (brain infection).

The incubation period is seven to ten days. The disease is highly infectious from seven days after exposure to three weeks after the symptoms develop. Before the introduction of vaccine in 1957 there were on average some 100,000 cases per year in the UK. By 1973, when vaccine acceptance was 80%, cases had fallen to 2400. In the mid-1970s levels of vaccination fell to about 30% and major epidemics followed in 1977, 1979, 1981 and 1983. Mortality from whooping cough in the UK in the 1970s remained about 1 per 1000 notified cases, with a higher death rate for infants under one year. Three vaccinations are usually given in combination with diphtheria and tetanus vaccine. Complications of vaccination are very rare, and are considerably less likely than a child dying of the disease.

PHYSICIANS

In the following countries citizens have, in theory, the greatest chance of receiving treatment from a physician. These countries have the smallest number of inhabitants per physician.

Country	*Year of figure*	*Population per physician*
Italy	(1989)	228
Latvia	(1991)	246
Spain	(1991)	257
Estonia	(1991)	262
Lithuania	(1992)	274
Hungary	(1991)	295
Belgium	(1991)	296
Cuba	(1989)	303
Greece	(1989)	303
Norway	(1993)	305
Switzerland	(1990)	311
Bulgaria	(1992)	312
Germany	(1992)	313
Czech Republic	(1991)	319
Austria	(1992)	327

NON-INFECTIOUS DISEASES

Diseases that are not transmitted have – in the developed world – replaced infections as the primary health problem. Infectious diseases such as smallpox, tuberculosis and diphtheria have been ousted from their positions as major killers by cancer, heart disease and strokes.

While factors such as an inappropriate diet, lack of exercise, excessive intake of alcohol and tobacco smoking have to take the blame for many of the diseases that afflict people today, they are not the only culprits. The genes that each of us inherit from our parents may also put us at risk from developing heart disease, schizophrenia, rheumatoid arthritis or certain types of cancer. More than 4000 genetic diseases result from the inheritance of a mutant gene. A number of the most common single-gene disorders are X-linked – that is, they affect, in general, only males and are carried by females. The X-linked genetic disorders include haemophilia, Alport's syndrome, Ehlers-Danlos syndrome, Lesch-Nyhan syndrome and testicular feminization syndrome.

Major genetic diseases and disorders

Major genetic diseases and disorders include:

Cystic fibrosis a hereditary mutation resulting in abnormally thick mucous secretions in the lungs and intestine. This disorder affects about one person in 1500. Treatment for digestive problems and lung infections can help to prolong the lives of people with cystic fibrosis, many of whom survive into their mid-twenties.

Dementia see p. 171.

Diabetes mellitus a common and – as yet – incurable metabolic disease. In many cases the disease is genetically determined but it can also be precipitated by certain viral infections, toxins, chronic disease or pregnancy (usually temporary). In all cases, the primary defect is an absolute or relative deficiency of pancreatic insulin. Insulin deficiency results in profound metabolic derangements, the most common of which is hyperglycaemia (blood glucose levels above the normal range of 50 to 120 mg per 100 millilitres).

As blood sugar rises, glucose appears in the urine, carrying water with it and giving rise to the increased urine output and thirst that characterizes the disorder. Fat metabolism may also be enhanced, leading to the accumulation of acidic by-products which, if unchecked, can result in coma or death. Diabetics can become susceptible to degenerative complications involving the nerves, eyes, kidneys and blood vessels, and it is these secondary problems that make diabetes such a devastating disease. Many diabetics are treated by dietary restrictions and the use of drugs, but some are dependent upon daily administration of insulin to control their symptoms.

Down's syndrome a chromosomal abnormality in which the affected child has an extra copy of chromosome number 21. The condition is characterized by a flat face and nose, a vertical fold of skin at the inner edge of the eye, short fingers, and mental retardation. Formerly known as mongolism, the syndrome is named after the English physician John Langdon-Down (1828–96).

Haemophilia a single gene disorder causing a lifelong tendency to excessive bleeding owing to a deficiency of a substance necessary for blood clotting. The missing substance is most commonly factor VIII (AHG). Haemophilia may be of variable severity and features (often) severe spontaneous external bleeding from the slightest wound and painful internal bleeding, particularly in the joints, without any apparent cause. Damaged joints may become deformed. The transmission of the condition is sex-linked – it is suffered almost exclusively by males. There is a 50% chance of a mother, who is a carrier, transmitting haemophilia to her son and a 50% chance of her daughter, in turn, becoming a carrier. The disease thus tends to be familial – the incidence of haemophilia in the royal families of Britain, Russia, Spain and Hesse is well-known. The condition is treated by means of repeated injections of blood-clotting factors, obtained from donated blood. In the late 1970s and in the 1980s (up until 1986), many sufferers from haemophilia who received transfusions of blood or of coagulation factor VIII became infected with HIV (see p. 163).

Huntington's chorea a particularly distressing hereditary disease, affecting one person in 20,000. Dementia (a disorder of the mental processes) and uncontrolled movements occur, but the symptoms fail to become apparent until the affected person has reached middle age. By this time, he or she has often had children who risk suffering the same fate.

Retinitis pigmentosa affects about one person in 4000. There is a progressive degeneration of the retinas, leading to poor night vision and sometimes eventual blindness.

Sickle-cell disease a hereditary blood disease that mainly affects people with malarial immunity – usually people from Africa and their descendants – although it was common in malarial parts of Europe. Large numbers of red blood cells in sufferers become sickle-shaped and can cause obstructions in the blood vessels, with possible damage to organs such as the kidneys and the brain. No satisfactory treatment has yet been developed.

Steroid sulfatase deficiency is a sex-linked recessive disorder that affects about one male in 6000, causing severe scaliness of the skin (*ichthyosis* or 'fish-skin'). It also affects vision by causing opacities in the corneas. It is due to partial or total deletion of the gene that codes for the enzyme steroid sulfatase, the absence of which can be detected by hair root analysis.

Thalassaemia a hereditary disease caused by a haemoglobin deficiency. Affected red blood cells cannot function normally, resulting in anaemia, enlargement of the spleen, and bone-marrow disorders. Thalassaemia – which is common in Mediterranean countries, Asia and Africa – can be treated by repeated blood transfusions.

Major environmental diseases

Environmental hazards such as radiation and pollutants account for some types of disease. People normally encounter only small doses of radiation, from diagnostic X-rays or perhaps as a treatment for cancer. In addition, everyone is exposed to low background levels of natural radiation from the Sun and from some types of rock. However, excessive doses of radiation may follow accidents, for example at nuclear reactors. Chemical hazards are probably more often encountered at work than at home. The list of industrial diseases is long and includes poisoning by lead, mercury and other heavy metals.

Asbestosis an industrial disease caused by inhaling fibres of asbestos. The lungs become fibrous and the affected person not only experiences increasing breathlessness, with failure of the heart and lungs, but also has an increased risk of developing lung cancer.

Lead poisoning a debilitating condition resulting from an accumulation of lead in the body, usually from water pipes or lead-based paint. Symptoms are variable and include digestive problems, irritability, severe abdominal pain, constipation, anaemia and paralysis. The illness can be acute in children, and may result in brain damage, blindness, deafness and death.

Radiation sickness a disease caused by high exposures of radiation. It is characterized by loss of cells from the bone marrow and the lining of the stomach. The person loses appetite and suffers diarrhoea, sickness, chills, fever and extreme tiredness. Death may follow because of the damage to the bowel and bone marrow, the latter resulting in loss of resistance to infection and severe anaemia. Long-term sufferers are at risk of developing cancers.

HOSPITAL BEDS

In the following countries citizens have, in theory, the greatest chance of receiving treatment in a hospital bed. These countries have the greatest number of hospital beds per inhabitant.

Country	*Year of figure*	*Hospital beds per 10,000 people*
Nauru	(1980)	250
Monaco	(1987)	180
Iceland	(1988)	172
Japan	(1990)	136
Kazakhstan	(1991)	136
Latvia	(1991)	135
North Korea	(1982)	135
Russia	(1991)	135
Ukraine	(1991)	135
Moldova	(1991)	131
France	(1988)	126
Finland	(1990)	125
Uzbekistan	(1991)	123
Kyrgyzstan	(1991)	122
Mongolia	(1981)	121

Cancer

Cancer occurs when cells grow out of control. A single cell can accumulate changes in its genes that allow it to replicate in an uncontrolled way. Such a cell can give rise to a tumour, which may manifest itself as a palpable lump or mass. Once cells become cancerous they lose the function that they once had; they simply reproduce themselves indefinitely.

A tumour is said to be *benign* if it remains localized in the place where it originated. Nevertheless, benign tumours can be life-threatening if they jeopardize normal structures, e.g. benign tumours of the brain. *Malignant* tumours have the capacity to spread around the body. Individual cells, or groups of cells, can detach themselves from the primary tumour, migrate via the blood or the lymph and become deposited on other organs. There they form secondary tumours.

In many cases the cause of the cancer is unknown. Treatment for cancer varies according to the type of tumour, the site of the primary tumour, and the extent of the spread of cancerous cells. Chemotherapy – drug therapy – can produce long remissions in some forms of cancer, but side effects occur as normal cells are damaged and white blood cells become depleted. Radiation therapy uses ionizing radiation – including X-rays and gamma rays – to destroy cancer cells. Surgery is used to remove malignant growths but is only effective if cancer cells have not migrated into other parts of the body.

Carcinoma a cancer of the skin (*melanoma*) or of the inner tissues that cover the internal cavity structures of the breast, the respiratory tracts (including lung cancer), the gastrointestinal tract (including cancers of the stomach, colon and rectum), the endocrine glands and the genitourinary tract (including cancers of the prostate, testes, fallopian tubes, ovaries, bladder and kidneys).

Leukaemia a cancer of the blood-forming tissues, related to sarcoma.

Lymphoma a cancer of the lymphoid cells; either Hodgkin's disease or non-Hodgkin's disease.

Sarcoma a cancer of the connective tissues, including bones, muscles, blood vessels and fibrous tissues.

Heart diseases

Heart disease is the leading cause of death in developed countries. Diseases of the heart may be genetic or caused by infection or environmental factors. There are four principal types:

Congenital cardiovascular disease a heart disease affecting one person in 200. The most common conditions include abnormalities of valves, narrowing of the aorta, shunt lesions (a malformation that allows oxygen-rich blood to be pumped back to the lungs) or the tetralogy of Fallot (a defect that commonly causes 'blue babies'). Some of these conditions may be hereditary, but often the reason for a defect is unknown. In many cases surgery to correct such defects is possible.

Coronary heart disease is the most common heart disease in developed countries and the most common cause of sudden death. The coronary arteries supply blood to the heart muscle. If the lining of these arteries becomes gradually thickened by fatty tissue (atheroma), the blood supply decreases. This causes episodes of chest pain (angina) often brought on by exercise. If a blood clot then develops at one such thickened area (coronary thrombosis), the artery becomes completely blocked causing a heart attack (myocardial infarction) or even sudden death. The main factors which put an individual at risk of coronary disease are cigarette smoking, high blood pressure and high levels of cholesterol in the blood. Other risk factors include obesity, lack of exercise, diabetes, stress and genetic factors such as a family history of coronary disease. Many drug treatments are now available and surgery can bypass a narrowed artery.

Hypertensive heart disease a condition resulting from prolonged, untreated high blood pressure (hypertension). The high pressure within the arteries forces the heart to pump against a greater resistance. This strain initially causes an increase in the thickness of the heart muscle, and then an enlargement of the heart itself. If left untreated, the heart becomes unable to cope and heart failure results.

Rheumatic heart disease is becoming less common in developed countries, but remains a major problem in the Third World. It is a delayed complication of rheumatic fever which has usually occurred in childhood. Over the years, scarring of the heart valves causes increased narrowing of the valve (sterosis), or failure of the valve to close completely, thus allowing a back-flow of blood in the wrong direction (regurgitation or incompetence). By middle age breathlessness or heart failure may result. Surgical splitting of the valve (valvotomy) or valve replacement can be dramatically beneficial.

Allergies

An allergy is a hypersensitivity or an abnormal response in the body to contact with a particular substance. The term was first used in 1906 by the German paediatrician Baron Clemens von Pirquet to describe an abnormal reaction to tuberculin. The reaction may provoke illnesses such as asthma, or may be mild, producing slight discomfort and inconvenience. Many individuals have only one specific allergy (for example to a particular food or drug), but some have an inherited susceptibility to allergy in general (atopy). Examples of allergy include:

Hay fever (allergic rhinitis) is a seasonal allergy characterized by sneezing, nasal congestion and itching of the eyes, and is caused by sensitivity to pollen from grass or trees in the spring and summer months.

Hives (urticaria) an intensely itchy skin reaction characterized by raised smooth red or pale weals. In severe cases there may be swelling of the lips or the skin around the eyes. The causal allergy may be to food (e.g. fish, eggs, berries), to drugs (e.g. penicillin), or to contact with chemicals, feathers or fur. Allergy to drugs may also take the form of a red blotchy rash rather like measles.

Asthma is a respiratory disorder characterized by wheezing owing to narrowing of the airways (bronchi), partly because of spasm in the muscle of the bronchi, and partly because of swelling and congestion of the lining (mucosa) of the bronchi. Childhood asthma, unlike asthma in later life, often occurs in those who are atopic (prone to allergy), and allergy to such things as house dust, feathers, pollen, and animal fur or hair can trigger asthma attacks. There is often a family history of allergy; boys are more often affected than girls, and childhood asthma may disappear at puberty. Attacks can also be triggered by infections, by irritants such as cold air or cigarette smoke, or by stress. Many drug treatments are now available, many in the form of inhalers.

Arthritis

Arthritis is a term applied to a variety of conditions which cause pain in the joints. There are two main categories.

Osteoarthritis the most common form of arthritis. It is a degeneration caused by 'wear and tear'. The cartilage covering the bone ends becomes eroded and this eventually leads to roughening and swelling of the bone itself, especially at the edges of the joint. Surgery to replace hip and knee joints which have been badly affected by osteoarthritis is now commonly performed.

Inflammatory arthritis takes many different forms but is in general due to inflammation of the tissues lining the joints (synovium). The milder forms are popularly known as *rheumatism*; more severe forms can be due to rheumatoid arthritis, gout, or bacterial infection. In rheumatoid arthritis, the body's immune system starts to react against its own synovial tissue, damaging it, and in the process causing pain, stiffness and swelling of the joints. Any joint may be affected, but the fingers are often an obvious site. In its severe forms, progressive deformity of joints occurs. In gout, tiny crystals of the chemical uric acid are deposited within the joint (characteristically the joint at the base of the big toe) causing intense pain and tenderness. Bacterial infection causing arthritis is uncommon and results from an open wound, or spread of infection from another area in the body (e.g. pneumonia or venereal disease).

Dementia

Dementia simply means 'loss of memory'. It can result from any of the causes of the organic syndrome, known pathological changes (disease) in the brain or from known brain malfunction caused by poisons or deprivation of essential materials. Some common diseases of dementia are:

Alzheimer's disease the commonest reason for dementia in people over the age of about 60 years. The cause remains unclear although we do know that there are specific brain changes, such as tangles of fibres within the nerve cells and severe loss of nerve tissue.

Senile dementia is caused in most cases by progressive loss of brain function from multiple areas of brain death. This is a result of reduced blood flow from the brain.

Creutzfeld-Jakob disease is an infectious disease caused by, or associated with, an agent simpler than a virus, known as a prion protein. This 'organism' can reproduce, resist normal sterilization methods and can be transmitted during surgery.

Huntington's chorea see p. 169.

Pick's disease a rare genetic disorder causing atrophy of the frontal and temporal lobes of the brain and mainly featuring loss of speech function.

Parkinson's disease a disease of the central nervous system. Parkinson's disease is a brain disorder that mainly affects men. It involves a progressive loss of muscular coordination and often severe tremor. The onset of the disease usually begins in late adult life and its course is slowly progressive over ten to 20 years. Early symptoms include the scuffing of one foot when walking, a 'heavy' feeling in one limb or a gentle tremor in one hand. As the disease progresses, manual skills are gradually lost and speech becomes slurred. Sufferers have a characteristic fixed expression, stooped posture, slow movement, short-stepped gait, and tremor of the hands. Some 40% of sufferers develop dementia, and this often starts with hallucinations. The outlook varies greatly. The later the onset the less severe it is likely to become. Sufferers have a marked decrease in the amount of the neurotransmitter dopamine present in the cells in the midbrain. The symptoms of Parkinson's disease can be alleviated by administering L-dopa, the metabolic precursor of dopamine. This treatment can, however, have unpleasant side-effects. Attempts have been made to treat the disorder by implanting cells from the fetal mid-brain in the hope of replacing missing dopamine-forming tissue. It is still too early to judge the results.

PSYCHOLOGY

Psychology is the study of the mind, of behaviour and of thinking.

In the 1950s and 1960s psychology was dominated by behaviourism (behavioural psychology) and, even today, many psychologists call themselves behaviourists, insisting that they are not interested in any data purporting to be a report on consciousness.

Modern psychology is essentially concerned with mental function. Given the present state of science, this is primarily assessed by the observation of behaviour. In this context, the word 'behaviour' is used in a very wide sense, and includes all responses that are detectable.

The rapid growth in the knowledge of brain structure (neuroanatomy) and brain function (neurophysiology) – together with the new sciences of information theory, digital computing and artificial intelligence – has placed psychology in a new and ever-widening perspective calling for more sophisticated techniques of research. At the same time the practical applications of psychology have expanded in many directions, and applied psychology now has a part to play in almost every area of life.

Brief biographical details of leading psychologists are to be found on pp. 257–66. See also Philosophy, pp. 320–24.

PUBLIC HEALTH EXPENDITURE

In the following countries the provision of public health care is, in theory, the greatest. The following countries have the highest public health expenditure per capita. Figures are 1989–1993.

Country	*Public health expenditure per capita (US$)*
Japan	1540
Greenland	1510
Iceland	1500
Faeroes	1310
Netherlands	1260
Jersey	1240
Norway	1160
France	1100
Austria	1070
Guernsey	1020
Germany	1010
United Kingdom	860
Finland	830
USA	780
Italy	770

Schools of psychology

Adlerian psychology see individual psychology.

analytical psychology a branch of psychology developed by Carl Gustav Jung as a result of disagreements with Sigmund Freud. See Jungian theory.

applied psychology see clinical psychology, educational psychology and occupational psychology (below).

behavioural psychology a school of psychology largely based on the work of B.F. Skinner. Its central tenet is that human behaviour can be modified by reinforcement, i.e. the provision of a 'reward' – either physical or social – or the avoidance of punishment. It assumes that the symptom is the illness and that the patient can be 'cured' by deconditioning and reconditioning.

body-centred psychology a loose grouping of therapies and ideas – rather than a school of psychology – in which work on the physical body results in an alteration in the personality or the image of self. It includes such diverse philosophies and therapies as yoga, the Alexander technique (p. 178), rolfing (p. 179) and T'ai Chi.

clinical psychology is not to be confused with psychiatry (see below). Clinical psychology is a practically based area of psychology (that is, applied psychology) in which research findings and methods are applied to human behaviour, both normal and abnormal. It is a broadly based discipline, encompassing experimental psychology, social psychology, environmental psychology, and ethology. Clinical psychologists are often concerned with the assessment of learning difficulties, whether present from birth or the result of later brain damage, and with the progress of functional recovery from brain injury.

developmental psychobiology the study of biological processes and systems that affect the development of behaviour. In particular, interest focuses on the behavioural characteristics enabling species to cope with environmental challenges, and the behaviour and development of the young as they relate to their environment.

educational psychology is an area of applied psychology. Educational psychology is concerned with the practical problems of teaching and learning, and is directed both to the production of improved teaching methods and to the assistance of people with learning difficulties.

ego psychology a branch of psychoanalytical theory that has developed from Sigmund Freud's book *The Ego and the Id*. It is now associated with Freud's daughter, Anna Freud, who developed the thinking in *The Ego and the Mechanisms of Defence*. Ego psychology concentrates on the manner in which the individual develops and acquires functions that enable him to control his impulses and his environment and to act independently.

existential analysis an area of psychology heavily influenced by existential philosophers such as Jean-Paul Sartre and Martin Heidegger. Essentially it lays emphasis on the here and now, expecting the patient to take responsibility for his or her actions through which his life will take on meaning. There is little emphasis on the unconscious mental processes dwelt on by other schools of psychology.

Freudian psychoanalysis the classical psychoanalysis that can be traced back directly to teachings and writings of Sigmund Freud, particularly to his *An Outline of Psychoanalysis*.

humanistic psychology a branch of psychology in which the self-image of the patient (client) is paramount. The therapist is honest with the patient, but does not seek to change the patient by any approval or disapproval. This school was developed by the American psychologist Carl Ransom Rogers.

individual psychology a branch of psychoanalysis founded by Alfred Adler, who regarded the individual as responsible for his own actions and able to work towards his own goals.

Jungian theory a branch of psychology contained within the ideas of Carl Gustav Jung and covering a very wide spectrum of psychology.

Kleinian theory a branch of psychology contained in the ideas of Melanie Klein, who laid emphasis on the first years of a child's life as being a time rich in fantasy and a time during which the origins of neurosis occur.

learning theory a group of psychological theories that aim to explain individual behaviour and personality arising as a result of learned reactions and responses to the environment. This is in contrast to psychoanalysis, which sees behaviour and personality arising as a result of developmental processes.

neo-Freudian theory a variety of psychological thought united by the common thread that those who formulated its ideas initially espoused Sigmund Freud's ideas on psychoanalysis, but subsequently broke away from, or modified, or added to, Freud's thinking. In general neo-Freudian theory emphasizes the social needs of individuals to a greater extent than Freud did.

neurolinguistics a combination of psychology, linguistics and neurology that looks at the acquisition of language, its production and processing, and its disruption or disturbances, especially those disturbances related to organic brain disease.

neuropsychiatry the study of organic brain disorders and the effects they have on behaviour and personality.

occupational psychology is an area of applied psychology. It is the application of psychology to the problems of industry, management, business and the workplace. It is a large subject, encompassing such matters as personnel selection and placement, training, career planning, and working conditions.

phenomenology literally, the study of phenomena, i.e. of the experiences that we have and the effect they have on personality and behaviour.

psychiatry is not so much a school of psychology as a medical speciality. Psychiatry is the treatment and study of mental, emotional, personality and behavioural disorders.

psychoanalysis a method of treating mental illness, originated by Sigmund Freud. Psychoanalysis aims to bring to the surface those fears and conflicts between instinct and conscience that have been pushed into the unconscious.

psychometrics literally means 'measuring the mind'. It is concerned with assessing intelligence, aptitudes, talents, skills, potential in various fields, personality traits and predisposition towards psychological breakdown. Psychometrics is an applied psychology.

psychopathology the study of the abnormal workings of the mind and of abnormal behaviour.

psychosynthesis a branch of psychological thinking that aims to bring together those elements of personality that are at odds with each other.

psychotherapy the treatment of mental disturbance, personality problems, behavioural difficulties, etc., by psychological means. Invariably a strong link is forged between the therapist and the patient, who often meet on a one-to-one basis.

radical therapy a relatively recent movement in psychology that calls into question society's definitions of such words as 'sane' and 'insane'. In radical therapy, 'insanity' – if there is such a thing – is seen as a social problem needing social solutions. Radical therapy – which undermines the medical model of psychology – was developed by R.D. Laing, and derives much from existentialism and humanism.

social psychiatry the examination of mental disorder as a part of society. Both the social causes of such disorders and the social methods of prevention are looked at.

PSYCHIATRIC CONDITIONS

alienation a state of feeling in which the patient feels set apart from or removed from either himself or others.

anxiety an irrational fear, often in response to an unrecognized stimulus.

behaviour disorders a group of conditions in which the behaviour of the patient is unacceptable to society.

catatonia a schizophrenic condition in which the patient suffers periods of excitement and/or stupor, during which he seems out of touch with his environment.

delusion a fixed idea, held by a patient, that is at variance with the beliefs and ideas held by normal people.

depression a disorder of mood in which the patient suffers from low spirits (the traditional 'melancholy'), an impairment of some mental processes, and often a lack of sleep and appetite.

extraversion an outgoing behaviour pattern. This is a component, to a greater or lesser extent, of most people's behaviour; it only becomes a problem when taken to extremes. Compare introversion.

hypochondriasis an imagined belief on the patient's part that he is ill, often with an incurable complaint.

inferiority complex a feeling of inadequacy.

introversion an introspective behaviour pattern. This is a component, to a greater or lesser extent, of most people's behaviour; it only becomes a problem when taken to extremes.

neurosis a mental disorder of the personality in which there is no organic damage to the nervous system.

paranoia a psychosis in which the patient suffers from delusions of persecution.

phobia an unrealistic and excessive fear of an object or situation; a form of anxiety. See pp. 174–75.

schizophrenia a functional psychosis characterized by disturbances of thinking, motivation and mood, coupled with hallucinations and delusions.

PHOBIAS

A phobia is an intense or irrational or inappropriate fear of an object, person, organism or situation, of a degree that interferes with normal living.

Phobias may take many forms but most commonly involve fear of enclosed spaces (claustrophobia) or fear of public places (agoraphobia). Phobias are most effectively treated by behaviour therapy.

Terms have been coined for a wide range of phobias, including the following:

Animal and plant phobias

animals	zoophobia
bacteria	bacteriophobia, microphobia
bees	apiphobia, melissophobia
birds	ornithophobia
cats	ailurophobia, gatophobia
chickens	alektorophobia
dogs	cynophobia
feathers	pteronophobia
fish	ichthyophobia
flowers	anthophobia
fur	doraphobia
horses	hippophobia
insects	entomophobia
leaves	phyllophobia
lice	pediculophobia
mice	musophobia
microbes	bacilliphobia
parasites	parasitophobia
reptiles	batrachophobia
snakes	ophidiophobia, ophiophobia
spiders	arachnophobia
trees	dendrophobia
wasps	spheksophobia
worms	helminthophobia

Environmental phobias

auroral lights	auroraphobia
clouds	nephophobia
dampness, moisture	hygrophobia
flood	antlophobia
fog	homichlophobia
ice, frost	cryophobia
lakes	imnophobia
lightning	astraphobia
meteors	meteorophobia
precipices	cremnophobia
rain	ombrophobia
rivers	potamophobia
sea	thalassophobia
snow	chionophobia
stars	siderophobia
sun	heliophobia
thunder	brontophobia, keraunophobia
water	hydrophobia
wind	ancraophobia

Food and drink phobias

drink, alcohol	potophobia
drinking	dipsophobia
eating	phagophobia
food	sitophobia
meat	carnophobia

Health and anatomical phobias

beards	pogonophobia
blood	haematophobia
cancer	cancerophobia, carcinophobia
childbirth	tocophobia
cholera	choleraphobia
death or corpses	necrophobia, thanatophobia
deformity	dysmorphophobia
disease	nosophobia, pathophobia
drugs	pharmacophobia
eyes	ommatophobia
faeces	coprophobia
germs	spermophobia
hair	chaetophobia
heart conditions	cardiophobia
heredity	patroiophobia
illness	nosemaphobia
infection	mysophobia
inoculations, injections	trypanophobia
insanity	lyssophobia, maniaphobia
knees	genuphobia
leprosy	leprophobia
mind	psychophobia
physical love	erotophobia
poison	toxiphobia
pregnancy	maieusiophobia
semen	spermatophobia
sex	genophobia
sexual intercourse	coitophobia
skin	dermatophobia
skin disease	dermatosiophobia
soiling	rypophobia
surgical operations	ergasiophobia
syphilis	syphilophobia
teeth	odontophobia
tuberculosis	phthisiophobia
venereal disease	cypridophobia
vomiting	emetophobia
wounds, injury	traumatophobia

Inanimate object phobias

books	bibliophobia
crystals, glass	crystallophobia
glass	nelophobia
machinery	mechanophobia
metals	metallophobia
mirrors	eisoptrophobia
missiles	ballistophobia
money	chrometophobia
needles	belonophobia
pins	enetephobia
points	aichurophobia
slime	blennophobia, myxophobia
string	linonophobia

Miscellaneous phobias

certain names	onomatophobia
darkness	nyctophobia
dawn	eosophobia
daylight	phengophobia
depth	bathophobia
dirt	mysophobia
disorder	ataxiophobia
draughts	anemophobia
dreams	oneirophobia
duration	chronophobia
dust	amathophobia, koniphobia

electricity	electrophobia
everything	pantophobia
failure	kakorraphiaphobia
fall of man-made satellites	keraunothnetophobia
fears	phobophobia
fire	pyrophobia
flashes	selaphobia
flogging	mastigophobia
freedom	eleutherophobia
ghosts	phasmophobia
graves	taphophobia
gravity	barophobia
ideas	ideophobia
imperfection	atelophobia
jealousy	zelophobia
justice	dikephobia
marriage	gamophobia
monsters, monstrosities	teratophobia
music	musicophobia
names	nomatophobia
narrowness	anginaphobia
neglect of duty	paralipophobia
new things	neophobia
night, darkness	achluophobia
novelty	cainophobia
nudity	gymnophobia
number 13	triskaidekaphobia, terdekaphobia
one thing	monophobia
poverty	peniaphobia
punishment	poinephobia
responsibility	hypegiaphobia
ridicule	katagelophobia
ruin	atephobia
rust	iophobia
shock	hormephobia
stealing	kleptophobia
stillness	eremophobia
strong light	photophobia
void	kenophobia
weakness	asthenophobia
words	logophobia
work	ergophobia
writing	graphophobia

Phobias concerning groups

black people	negrophobia
children	paediphobia
human beings	anthropophobia
men	androphobia
robbers	harpaxophobia
women	gynophobia
young girls	parthenophobia

Phobias concerning religion

churches	ecclesiaphobia
demons	demonophobia
God	theophobia
heaven	ouranophobia
hell	hadephobia, stygiophobia
sacred things	hierophobia
Satan	Satanophobia
sinning	peccatophobia

Sensory phobias

being cold	frigophobia
being dirty	automysophobia
being scratched	amychophobia
being touched	haphephobia
blushing	ereuthophobia, eyrythrophobia
cold	cheimatophobia
colour	chromatophobia, chromophobia, psychrophobia
fatigue	kopophobia, ponophobia
heat	thermophobia
itching	acarophobia, scabiophobia
noise	phonophobia
odours	osmophobia
odours (body)	osphresiophobia
pain	algophobia, odynophobia
pleasure	hedonophobia
sleep	hypnophobia
smell	olfactophobia
smothering, choking	pnigerophobia
sound	akousticophobia
speaking	halophobia
speaking aloud	phonophobia
speech	alophobia
sourness	acerophobia
stings	cnidophobia
stooping	kyphophobia
taste	geumatophobia
thinking	phronemophobia
touch	haptophobia
touching	haphephobia, thixophobia
trembling	tremophobia

Situation phobias

being alone	monophobia, autophobia
being beaten	rhabdophobia
being bound	merinthophobia
being buried alive	taphophobia
being looked at	scopophobia
crowds	demophobia, ochlophobia
enclosed spaces	claustrophobia
going to bed	clinophobia
heights	acrophobia, altophobia
high places	hypsophobia
home	domatophobia, oikophobia
home surroundings	ecophobia
infinity	apeirophobia
passing high objects	batophobia
places	topophobia
public places	agoraphobia
school	scholionophobia
shadows	sciophobia
sitting idle	thaasophobia
solitude	eremitophobia, eremophobia
standing	stasophobia
standing upright	stasiphobia

Travel phobias

crossing a bridge	gephyrophobia
crossing streets	dromophobia
flying, the air	aerophobia
motion	kinesophobia, kinetophobia
sea swell	cymophobia
speed	tachophobia
travel	hodophobia
travelling by train	siderodromophobia
vehicles	amaxophobia, ochophobia
walking	basiphobia

NOBEL PRIZEWINNERS IN PHYSIOLOGY OR MEDICINE

The Nobel Prize for achievement in physiology or medicine is awarded annually under the terms of the will of Alfred Nobel by the Royal Caroline Medico-Chirurgical Institute in Stockholm (Sweden).

Winners of the Prize, their nationality and a summary of the citation are as follows:

1901 Emil von Behring, German: for his work in serum therapy.

1902 Sir Ronald Ross, English: for the discovery of how malaria enters an organism.

1903 Niels R. Finsen, Danish: for his work on light radiation treatment of skin diseases.

1904 Ivan Pavlov, Russian: for work on the physiology of digestion.

1905 Robert Koch, German: for tuberculosis research.

1906 Camillo Golgi, Italian, and S. Ramón y Cajal, Spanish: for studies of the structure of the nervous system.

1907 Alphonse Laveran, French: for his discovery of the role of protozoa in diseases.

1908 Paul Ehrlich, German, and Ilya Mechnikov (Elie Metchnikoff), Russian: for immunity systems research.

1909 Emil Kocher, Swiss: for work on the physiology, pathology and surgery of the thyroid gland.

1910 Albrecht Kossel, German: for cellular chemistry research.

1911 Allvar Gullstrand, Swedish: for his work on the dioptics of the eye.

1912 Alexis Carrel, French: for studies of vascular suture and transplantation of organs.

1913 Charles Richet, French: for anaphylaxis research.

1914 Robert Bárány, Austrian: for studies on the vestibular apparatus of the inner ear.

1915 No award.

1916 No award.

1917 No award.

1918 No award.

1919 Jules Bordet, Belgian: for his studies of the immunity system.

1920 August Krogh, Danish: for the discovery of the capillary motor-regulating mechanism.

1921 No award.

1922 Archibald Hill, English: for studies of heat production in muscles;

and Otto Meyerhof, German-born US citizen: for work on the metabolism of lactic acid in muscles.

1923 Sir Frederick Banting, Canadian, and John James R. Macleod, Scottish: for the discovery of insulin.

1924 Willem Einthoven, Dutch: for the discovery of electrocardiogram mechanism.

1925 No award.

1926 Johannes Fibiger, Danish: for cancer research.

1927 Julius Wagner-Jauregg, Austrian: for malaria inoculation in dementia paralytica.

1928 Charles Nicolle, French: for typhus research.

1929 Christiaan Eijkman, Dutch: for his discovery of antineuritic vitamin;

and Sir Frederick Hopkins, English: for his discovery of growth stimulating vitamins.

1930 Karl Landsteiner, Austrian-born US citizen: for his work in the grouping of human blood.

1931 Otto Warburg, German: for the discovery of the nature and action of a respiratory enzyme.

1932 Edgar D. Adrian (Lord Adrian) and Sir Charles Sherrington, English: for their studies on the function of neurons.

1933 Thomas Hunt Morgan, US: for his work on the role of chromosomes in transmission of heredity.

1934 George R. Minot, William P. Murphy and George H. Whipple, all US: for work on liver therapy to treat anaemia.

1935 Hans Spemann, German: for work on organization in embryos.

1936 Sir Henry Dale, English, and Otto Loewi, German-born US citizen: for work on the chemical transmission of nerve impulses.

1937 Albert Szent-Györgyi, Hungarian-born US citizen: for his studies on biological combustion.

1938 Corneille Heymans, Belgian: for research on the role of sinus and aortic mechanisms in respiration regulation.

1939 Gerhard Domagk, German (who declined the award as Hitler refused to allow Germans to accept Nobel Prizes): for work on the antibacterial effect of prontosil.

1940 No award.

1941 No award.

1942 No award.

1943 Henrik Dam, Danish: for the discovery of Vitamin K;

and Edward A. Doisy, US: for the discovery of the chemical nature of vitamin K.

1944 Joseph Erlanger, and Herbert S. Gasser, both US: for their studies of the differentiated functions of nerve fibres.

1945 Sir Alexander Fleming, Scottish, Ernst Boris Chain, German-born British citizen, and Howard Florey (Lord Florey), Australian: for the discovery of penicillin and its curative value.

1946 Hermann J. Muller, US: for the production of mutations by X-ray irradiation.

1947 Carl F. Cori and Gerty Cori, both Czech-born US citizens: for their discovery of the catalytic conversion of glycogen;

and Bernardo Houssay, Argentinian: for research on pituitary hormone function in sugar metabolism.

1948 Paul Müller, Swiss: for work on the properties of DDT.

1949 Walter Rudolf Hess, Swiss: for the discovery of function of the midbrain;

and António Egas Moniz, Portuguese: for work on the therapeutic value of leucotomy in psychoses.

1950 Philip S. Hench and Edward Kendall, both US, and Tadeusz Reichstein, Polish-born Swiss citizen: for adrenal cortex hormones research.

1951 Max Theiler, South African-born US citizen: for his research on yellow fever.

1952 Selman A. Waksman, Ukrainian-born US citizen: for the discovery of streptomycin.

1953 Fritz A. Lipman, German-born US citizen, and Sir Hans Krebs, German-born British citizen: for the discovery of coenzyme, a citric acid cycle in the metabolism of carbohydrates.

1954 John F. Enders, Thomas H. Weller and Frederick Robbins, all US: for their work on the tissue culture of poliomyelitis viruses.

1955 Axel Hugo Theorell, Swedish: for his work on the nature and mode of action of oxidation enzymes.

1956 Werner Forssmann, German, Dickinson Richards, US, and André F. Cournand, French-born US citizen: for their work on heart catheterization and circulatory changes.

1957 Daniel Bovet, Swiss-born Italian citizen: for the production of synthetic curare.

1958 George W. Beadle and Edward L. Tatum, both US: for their work on genetic regulation of chemical processes;

and Joshua Lederberg, US: for work on genetic recombination.

1959 Severo Ochoa, Spanish-born US citizen, and Arthur Kornberg, US: for the production of artificial nucleic acids.

1960 Sir MacFarlane Burnet, Australian, and Sir Peter B. Medawar, English: for research into acquired immunity in tissue transplants.

1961 Georg von Békésy, Hungarian-born US citizen: for research on functions of the inner ear.

1962 Francis Crick, English, James D. Watson, US, and Maurice Wilkins, New Zealand-born British citizen: for the discovery of molecular structure of DNA.

1963 Sir John Eccles, Australian, Sir Alan Lloyd Hodgkin, English, and Sir Andrew Huxley, English: for work on transmission of nerve impulses along a nerve fibre.

1964 Konrad Bloch, Swiss-born US citizen, and Feodor Lynen, German: for research into cholesterol and fatty acid metabolism.

1965 François Jacob, Jacques Monod and André Lwoff, all French: for research into regulatory activities of body cells.

1966 Charles B. Huggins, Canadian-born US citizen, and Francis Peyton Rous, US: for cancer research.

1967 Haldan Keffer Hartline and George Wald, both US, and Ragner A. Granit, Finnish-born Swedish citizen: for research on the chemical and physiological visual processes in the eye.

1968 Robert W. Holley, US, H. Gobind Khorana, Indian-born US citizen, and Marshall W. Nirenberg, US: for research into deciphering the genetic code.

1969 Max Delbrück, German-born US citizen, Alfred D. Hershey, US, and Salvador E. Luria, Italian-born US citizen: for research into viruses and viral diseases.

1970 Julius Axelrod, US, Sir Bernard Katz, German-born British citizen, and Ulf von Euler, Swedish: for work on the chemistry of nerve transmission.

1971 Earl W. Sutherland, US: for studies of the action of hormones.

1972 Gerald M. Edelman, US, and Rodney Porter, English: for research into the chemical structure of antibodies.

1973 Karl von Frisch and Konrad Lorenz, both Austrian, and Nikolaas Tinbergen, Dutch: for research on animal behaviour patterns.

1974 Albert Claude, Luxembourg-born US citizen, Christian R. de Duve, Belgian, and George E. Palade, Romanian-born US citizen: for work on the structural and functional organization of cells.

1975 Renato Dulbecco, Italian-born US citizen, Howard M. Temin and David Baltimore, both US: for work on the interactions between tumour viruses and the genetic material of the cell.

1976 Baruch S. Blumberg and Daniel Carleton Gajdusek, both US: for studies on the origin and spread of infectious diseases.

1977 Rosalyn S. Yalow, US, Roger Guillemin, French-born US citizen, and Andrew Schally, Polish-born US citizen: for the development of radio-immuno-assay and research on pituitary hormones.

1978 Werner Arber, Swiss, Daniel Nathans and Hamilton O. Smith, both US: for the discovery and application of enzymes that fragment DNA.

1979 Allan M. Cormack, South African-born US citizen, and Sir Godfrey N. Hounsfield, English: for the development of computerized axial tomography scanning.

1980 Baruj Benacerraf, Venezuelan-born US citizen, George D. Snell, US, and Jean Dausset, French: for work on genetic control of the immune response to foreign substances.

1981 Roger W. Sperry, US: for studies of the functions of the cerebral hemispheres;

and Torsten N. Wiesel, Swedish, and David H. Hubel, Canadian-born US citizen: for work on visual information processing by the brain.

1982 Sune K. Bergström and Bengt I. Samuelsson, both Swedish, and Sir John R. Vane, English: for work on the biochemistry and physiology of prostaglandins.

1983 Barbara McClintock, US: for the discovery of mobile plant genes which affect heredity.

1984 Niels K. Jerne, British/Danish, Georges J. F. Köhler, German, and César Milstein, Argentinian-born British citizen: for the technique for producing monoclonal antibodies.

1985 Michael S. Brown and Joseph L. Goldstein, both US: for the discovery of cell receptors involved in cholesterol metabolism.

1986 Stanley Cohen, US, and Rita Levi-Montalcini, Italian: for the discovery of chemical agents that help regulate cell growth.

1987 Tonegawa Susumu, Japanese: for research into genetic aspects of antibodies.

1988 Sir James W. Black, Scottish, Gertrude B. Ellison and George H. Hitchings, both US: for the development of new classes of drugs.

1989 Harold Varmus and Michael Bishop, both US: for cancer research.

1990 Joseph Murray and E. Donnall Thomas, both US: for transplant surgery.

1991 Erwin Neher and Bert Sakmann, both German: for research in cell biology, particularly the understanding of disease mechanisms.

1992 Edmond Fischer and Edwin Krebs, both US: for the discovery of a cellular regulatory mechanism used to control a variety of metabolic processes.

1993 Richard Roberts, English, and Phillip Sharp, US: for their discovery of split genes.

1994 Martin Rodbell, and Alfred G. Gilman, both US: for the discovery of G-proteins, and their role, in cells.

Complementary Medicine

Complementary medicine encompasses all the forms of healing that lie outside the sort of medicine people normally receive from a GP or hospital. It includes a wide variety of different therapies used by millions of people worldwide to treat every ill imaginable. That they appear to work in some cases is beyond doubt. How they work, however, is still to a large extent a mystery. Medical science has made great advances and has long seemed to promise a 'pill for every ill'. Virtually every drug, however, has been shown to have some side-effects and many patients have become dissatisfied with the inability of orthodox treatments to cure certain conditions – particularly chronic diseases such as arthritis. The common feature that seems to run through every one of the alternative treatments is the importance placed on the whole person, not just on specific symptoms – this is known as the *holistic* approach. The terms *'alternative medicine'* and *'complementary medicine'* are both used. Alternative' is perceived to imply that the treatment is an alternative to conventional medicine; 'complementary' is perceived to imply that the treatment is received to complement conventional medicine. The most common forms of complementary medicine are:

Acupuncture

Acupuncture originated in China thousands of years ago. The technique uses fine needles inserted at specific points on the body in order to restore the balance of an inner 'life force' known as *chi* energy and believed to flow along a number of *meridians* or channels in the body. Each of the 12 main meridians is believed to have its own pulse – six in each wrist – and the acupuncturist checks these carefully in order to decide which points to stimulate. The technique has been shown to be remarkably successful at stopping pain, and in China major operations have been carried out using only acupuncture for pain relief. Scientists have discovered that the needles appear to make the body produce its own natural painkillers, *endorphins.* Acupuncture is also claimed to be effective in treating a very wide range of diseases, including respiratory, digestive, bone and muscle disorders.

Alexander technique

The Alexander technique is a method of producing postural changes, which are claimed to relieve a number of physical disorders. The technique was developed in the 19th century by an Australian actor, Matthias Alexander (1869–1955). He realized that the position of his head and neck were the cause of his frequent loss of voice during performances, and found that by altering his posture he could cure himself. During a series of lessons – 12 or more – the person 'relearns' how to use the body, breaking harmful postural habits. The technique is claimed to be beneficial for everyone, but in particular for those who have suffered long spells of general ill health – lethargy and poor sleeping, for example.

Aromatherapy

Aromatherapy is principally a massage technique in which essential oils derived from herbs, flowers and spices are rubbed into the skin and eventually inhaled. The natural fragrances these oils produce are said to be particularly effective for psychological complaints such as anxiety or depression, but are used to treat a range of conditions including skin disorders and burns.

Biofeedback

Biofeedback is used to help people learn to control physical phenomena governed by the autonomic nervous system, such as blood pressure, heartbeat and temperature. Electrodes placed on the body pick up electrical impulses produced by physical changes. The impulses are transformed by the biofeedback machine into an electronic sound, or shown by the rise and fall of a needle on a dial. The person concentrates on changing the tone of the sound or on causing the needle to move and in doing so learns, for instance, to lower blood pressure or slow down the heartbeat.

Chiropractic

Chiropractic was founded by the Canadian osteopath D. D. Palmer. The central philosophy of chiropractic is that malalignments or 'subluxations' of the bones in the spine cause disturbances of the nervous and vascular systems, leading to disease not only in the bones and muscles themselves, but in any organ of the body. Chiropractitioners work with the help of X-rays to discover where the malalignments are and to identify 'intersegmental dysrelationships'. They then manipulate the bones using short, but very forceful, thrusts to the 'subfluxed' joint, thus relieving the root cause of the problem. However, chiropractic should not be used in any case of bone malignancy or where the spinal chord is compressed. Unlike osteopathy, often regarded as complementary to orthodox medicine, chiropractors regard their philosophy as a completely alternative system of medicine.

Herbalism

Herbalism is an ancient form of medicine. From the dawn of humanity, people have been using plants to cure their illnesses. From the Middle Ages, herbals – manuals listing the names of plants and what they could be used for – were widely used. In the 17th century Nicholas Culpeper (1616–54) combined herbalism with astrology in his *Herbal.* Herbalists today use the roots, leaves, stems, flowers and seeds of plants to produce medicines. A large number of orthodox modern medicines are also derived from plants – the heart drug *digoxin* is produced from the foxglove, and the group of painkillers known as *opiates* are derived from the opium poppy. Once a diagnosis has been made, the herbalist will dilute a concentrated extract of a certain herb in water or mix it into a paste to form a cream or ointment. Conditions such as arthritis, colds and coughs, skin problems, digestive disorders and minor injuries are regarded as the most likely to benefit from herbalism.

Homoeopathy

Homoeopathy was invented by a German doctor, Samuel Hahnemann (1755–1843). He reasoned that since many of the symptoms people suffer during illness – fever or pain, for example – are actually visible signs of the body's own defences working against the disease, it would make sense to try to boost these defences. He based his therapy on the principle that 'like cures like', giving patients tiny quantities of substances known to produce exactly these symptoms in healthy people. One homoeopathic remedy for fever, for instance, is sulphur, which produces a feeling of heat and promotes sweating if taken by mouth in larger doses. Homoeopathy offers remedies for virtually every medical complaint, but it is less frequently used in acute or life-threatening illness. Homoeopathic remedies are prescribed by some GPs as well as by homoeopaths.

In order to produce the tiny quantities that are needed for homoeopathic remedies, the active substance must be diluted. This process is known as potentizing. The active substance is diluted in proportions of 1 to 10, usually in distilled water, and this dilution is carried out six or more times in succession – the homoeopathic 'potency 6' is one million times diluted. Theoretically, with sufficient dilution, there can be none of the active substance left. So how is it that these remedies can still work? The secret is claimed to lie in the rapid shaking or succussion that must be performed after each dilution. If the succussion is not carried out, the remedy is ineffective. The explanation for this phenomenon is best given by comparing each molecule of the homoeopathic remedy, suspended in the dilution, to a person walking across a snow-field. Once the person has passed by, nothing physical remains, and only the footprints are left in the snow. Although there are few, if any, molecules of the active ingredient left, its 'footprints', thought to be produced by succussion, remain to do their work in the body.

Iridology

Iridology is the study of the iris as a tool for diagnosing illness. It is used by a range of alternative therapists including osteopaths, acupuncturists, herbalists and homeopaths. The left side of the body is reflected in the left eye and vice versa. The head is revealed at the top, the feet at the bottom of the eye. There are three zones: the inner zone represents the functions of digestion and absorption; the middle zone transport, utilization and elimination by the kidneys; and the outer zone, structure, skeleton and skin.

Osteopathy

Osteopathy is a manipulative technique founded by the American doctor Andrew Taylor Still (1828-1917). Joints are pushed and occasionally pulled so as to restore them to their natural positions, thus relieving tensions on surrounding muscles, tendons and ligaments. Osteopaths tend to concentrate their work on the spine since this contains the spinal chord and all the nerves that control the body. Back pain is the disorder most commonly treated by an osteopath.

Reflexology

Like acupuncture, reflexology is based on the idea that the body contains channels of 'life force'. Reflexologists believe that this force exists in 10 'zones' of energy that each begin in the toes and end in the fingers. By touching and feeling the toes and feet, reflexologists claim to be able to feel blocks in these channels of energy (they say these feel like crystals below the skin surface), and by manipulating and massaging the foot in a specific way they try to move the blockage, thus curing the illness. Like acupuncture, reflexology is used to treat most conditions.

Other alternative therapies

Anthroposophical medicine Formulated by the Austrian scientist Rudolph Steiner (1861–1925), anthroposophy is based on the premise that the human intellect can contact spirit worlds. Anthroposophical medicine is not, strictly speaking, a therapy but rather an attitude to health. Using homeopathic remedies, it stresses the need for a doctor to attain a spiritual understanding of both the patient and the plants used in treatment.

Applied kinesiology (or **touch for healing**) is a therapy that is often used in conjunction with chiropractic. Its practitioners use a system of 'muscle testing' to identify weaknesses in individual organs of the body and in muscles. The aim is to balance these weak elements by touch.

Bach flower remedies Dr Edward Bach (1880–1936) used plants to impregnate spring water and dew to produce 38 flower herbal remedies. These are used by practitioners in the treatment of conditions such as anxiety and depression.

Biochemics The German chemist Dr W.H. Schuessler recognized 12 inorganic salts and oxides in the human body. He maintained that – for the body to be healthy – these salts and oxides should be kept in a natural balance. By using homeopathic methods, practitioners of biochemics seek to redress any imbalance in these and in any of an additional 30 trace elements since identified.

Colour therapy Colour therapists use different colours – in the form of light – as a treatment for various conditions, including stress. They claim that specific energies possessed by each colour have a restorative effect upon patients.

Hydrotherapy Water is used in a number of therapies, for example to stimulate circulation or in colonic irrigation. Various elimination treatments – including sweating, the drinking of mineral waters, etc. – are also employed.

Megavitamin therapy (or **orthomolecular medicine**) is treatment by large measured doses of Vitamin C. This therapy was developed by the chemistry Nobel Prize winner Dr Linus Pauling in the 1960s and 1970s. It now embraces treatment with other vitamins.

Naturopathy Naturopaths treat themselves using the healing forces that they claim are present within them.

Rolfing is a system of deep massage developed by Dr Ida Rolf in the 1920s and 1930s to break down connective tissues that have become thickened.

Shiatsu is a Japanese system of deep massage used to stimulate acupuncture points (see above). Claimed to be preventative as well as a cure, Shiatsu is widely practised within Japanese families. When a practitioner treats him- or herself, the therapy is referred to as *Do-in.*

Nutrition

Nutrition as a science is said to have been founded by the chemist Antoine Lavoisier (1743–94) towards the end of the 18th century. It is the study of all the processes of growth, maintenance and repair of the living body that are dependent upon the digestion of food. The term 'food' is used to cover any solid or liquid matter that provides materials that can be used for growth, repair, energy, maintenance or protection.The term 'nutrient' refers to the components of foods that can perform these functions. All nutrients are present in the correct proportions in the diets of healthy people. A lack of the necessary minimum amount of any nutrient leads to a state of malnutrition. A general deficiency of all nutrients produces undernutrition or, in extreme cases, starvation.

Other essential nutrients

Although not strictly nutrients, water and fibre are essential for a healthy diet. Water is essential to life. It helps digestion and the elimination of waste products, and lubricates all the body joints and tissues.

Fibre – non starch polysaccharide (NSP) – together with water increases the bulk of food and so aids digestion of food and the elimination of waste products. Minerals are essential to a number of body processes.

Calcium works with phosphorus to give teeth and bones their hardness and strength. It helps blood to clot after an injury, and ensures muscles and nerves work properly. Calcium is found in milk, cheese, bread, green vegetables, pulses and canned fish.

Sodium, Potassium and Chloride help to maintain the correct salt concentration of body fluids. The minerals are found in milk, meat, vegetables, cheese, fruit, fish, nuts and table salt.

NUTRIENTS

Nutrient	Function	Sources of nutrient	Result of excess/deficiency
Protein	Growth; repairs and replaces damaged cells; energy	Meat, fish, eggs, cheese, milk, peas, beans, bread, rice, wheat, maize, nuts	Excess animal protein leads to too much saturated fat. Severe deficiency leads to kwashiorkor
Fat (Saturated, monounsaturated, polyunsaturated)	Energy store, body insulation, forms part of cell membranes	Saturated: butter, margarine, lard, cream, cheese. Polyunsaturated: sunflower and corn oil, fish, soft margarine	Correlation between heart disease and high fat intake. Too little fat means deficiency of fatty acids and fat soluble vitamins
Carbohydrates	Quick energy store; often source of dietary fibre	Sugar, sweets, cakes, jams, cereal, bread, biscuits, potatoes, pasta, some fruit, vegetables	Excess sugar causes obesity, dental caries and contributes towards diabetes. A deficiency can result in a diet too high in fat, and lacking in dietary fibre.
Vitamin A	Essential for growth; vision in poor light; the body's immune system	Dairy products, fish-liver oils, egg yolks, carrots and green vegetables	Deficiency causes stunted growth, night blindness, and susceptibility to infection.
Vitamin B group*	Important for metabolism, growth, and healthy nerves, muscles and blood	Meat, yeast, wholemeal bread, cereals, pulses, milk, eggs, fish	Deficiency of vitamin B can cause beriberi, pellagra, skin problems, anaemia.
Vitamin C	Helps absorb iron, keeps skin healthy, helps form blood cells, helps form body tissue	Citrus fruit (oranges, lemons), potatoes, cabbage, peppers, peas, tomatoes, apples	Deficiency causes scurvy (weakened capillaries, internal haemorrhaging, anaemia, general debility)
Vitamin D	Helps form healthy bones and teeth; helps body absorb calcium and phosphorus	Produced within body when exposed to sunlight. Also available in cream, margarine, butter, milk, cheese, egg yolk, vegetable oils	Deficiency causes rickets (in children), softening of bones (in adults)
Vitamin E	The actual function of vitamin unknown, thought to help in reproduction	Vegetable oils, cream, butter, cheese, egg yolk	Unknown
Vitamin K	Essential to blood clotting	Spinach, caulifower, cabbage, peas, cereal	Deficiency causes lengthy blood clotting

*B1 Thiamine; Folic Acid; B_2 Riboflavin; B_3 Niacin; B6 Pyridoxine; $B1_2$ (Cyanocobalamin)

Iodine is essential for the formation of thyroid gland hormones, which help to control the chemical processes in the body. Iodine is present in water, green vegetables and fish.

Phosphorus works with calcium to give teeth and bones their strength and hardness. It also helps liberate energy from food. It is present in yeast extracts, cheese, eggs, wholemeal bread, fish, nuts and meat.

Iron is used for transporting oxygen in red blood cells. It is present in meat, kidney, liver, heart, treacle, bread, chocolate and cocoa.

Magnesium helps in the formation of healthy bones. It aids the maintenance of healthy muscles and nerves. It is present in tea, nuts, spices, cereals and wholegrain breads.

Zinc is involved in producing several enzymes. Zinc also forms part of the structure of cell membranes.

Copper helps in the production of various enzymes. It is present in liver, fish and green vegetables.

Selenium is involved in the production of various enzymes. It is present in cereals and meat.

Fluoride helps in the formation of healthy teeth and bones. It is present in drinking water, tea and fish.

A BALANCED DIET

An individual's personal dietary requirements depend on many factors such as age, sex and size. It is impossible to know how much of a particular nutrient an individual requires without doing complicated biochemical tests. It is possible, however, to estimate the amount of each nutrient needed by virtually everybody in the population. These 'Recommended Daily amounts' are defined for different ages and different states – for example requirements are greater in pregnancy. A person's energy requirements also depend on their level of activity. Any excess energy taken in is stored in the form of fat. It is therefore important to ensure that the energy taken in is not greater than the amount expended. The proportion of energy derived from fat, carbohydrate and protein is important, and current dietary guidelines suggest that no more than 35% of energy should come from fat, 10% from protein and 50% from carbohydrates. A diet high in fat, particularly 'saturated fat' (as found in red meat and dairy products), has been linked to the development of coronary heart disease. Most people would benefit from reducing their total fat intake, particularly if it contains a lot of saturated fatty acids. To ensure the right balance of nutrients in a diet it is important to base one's eating on a wide range of foods. This should also ensure that adequate amounts of vitamins and minerals are consumed.

FIBRE CONTENT IN SELECTED FOODS

Food	gms of fibre per 100 gms
All Bran	27.0
Wheat bran	44.0
Lentils	12.0
Figs	19.0
White flour	4.0
Wholemeal flour	10.0
Butter beans	22.0
Cornflakes	11.0
Sponge cake	1.0
Bread: granary	7.0
wholemeal	9.0
white	4.0
Prunes	16.0
Peanuts	8.0
Chickpeas	15.0
Spaghetti	6.0
Oatmeal	8.0
Apples	2.0
Lettuce	1.5

HIDDEN SUGARS

In the UK, the average person eats approximately 38 kg (84 lb) of sugar a year, plus more in the form of glucose and honey. Much of that sugar is hidden in foods, so it is not always obvious how much is being eaten. The sugar content of some common foods are given below.

	Sugar content as %	Approx content as (tsp)
Small tube of boiled sweets	98	10
Drinking chocolate (3 tsp)	75	2½
Jam (1 tbp)	68	3
Milk chocolate (50 gms)	45	6
Dried tomato soup (1 pkt)	40	8
Instant custard (1 pkt)	38	6¾
Chocolate biscuit (1)	33	2
Slice of chocolate cake (med)	26	2
Sweet pickle (3 tsp)	25	¾
Slice of lemon meringue pie (med)	22	3
Carton of fruit yoghurt (small)	15	4½
Ice cream (small brick)	15	2
Salad cream	13	½
Dried chicken soup	10	2
Can of cola	10	7
Cornflakes (6 tbp)	8	¼
Peanut butter (1 tbp)	3	1

AVERAGE DAILY ENERGY REQUIREMENTS (Kcal/kJoule)

	Heavy activity		Moderate activity		Light activity	
	Kcal	*kJoule*	*Kcal*	*kJoule*	*Kcal*	*kJoule*
Women	2730	11,430	2314	9688	2015	8436
Men	2912	12,192	2624	10,986	2496	10,450

ADDITIVES

Additives are artificial or natural chemicals that are added to food to prolong their shelf life, alter colour, enhance flavour and improve nutritional value. Acceptable, established additives are now classified as 'Generally Regarded as Safe' (GRAS); new ones must undergo years of testing to ensure freedom from harmful effects. The EC assesses additives and grants permitted ones *E numbers*, which must appear on food labels. Many of these E-number additives are natural (or identical to natural) substances, such as

Vitamin C (ascorbic acid, an anti-oxidant and acidulant). Others are artificial, such as tartrazine, a yellow-orange dye currently implicated in food allergies. The categories of additives include:

Acidulants add or control acidity or sourness.

Anticaking agents stop powdered products from coagulating into lumps.

Antioxidants prevent fatty foods from going rancid by retarding their natural oxidation.

Bleaching agents whiten flours.

Clarifying agents – the most common of which is gelatin – are used in vinegars and fruit juices.

Colourings enhance the appearance of foods.

Emulsifiers alter the texture and consistency of food, and stop the ingredients from separating out. **Stabilizers** do the same thing.

Enhancers heighten smell or flavour. Monosodium glutamate (MSG) is a flavour enhancer.

Firming agents restore the shape and texture of vegetables damaged during processing.

Flavours alter or intensify taste. They may be artificial or natural and include artificial sweetners.

Leavening agents lighten the texture of baked food. They include sodium bicarbonate but not yeast.

Preservatives, by controlling the growth of bacteria and fungi, slow down the rate of spoilage.

FAT CONTENT IN SELECTED FOODS

Food	gms fat per 100 gms
Almonds	54.0
Bacon	29.0
Baked Beans	0.5
Beef	20.0
Bread: white	1.7
brown	2.2
Butter	82.0
Cod	0.7
Cheddar cheese	34.0
Chicken	4.0
Chocolate biscuit	27.0
Cottage cheese	0.5
Cream, double	48.0
Flavoured yoghurt	1.0
Lamb	36.0
Mackerel	16.0
Mars bar	19.0
Mayonnaise	79.0
Milk: whole	3.8
skimmed	0.1
Potatoes	0.0
Pork	30.0
Salad cream	27.0

E NUMBERS: Common Additives

Antioxidants

	Name	Use
E310	propyl gallate	vegetable oils, chewing gum
E311	octyl gallate	
E312	dodecyl gallate	
E320	butylated hydroxynisole (BHA)	beef stockcubes; cheese spread
E321	butylated hydroxytoluene (BHT)	chewing gum

Colouring agents

	Name	Use
E102	tartrazine	soft drinks
E104	quinoline yellow	
E110	sunset yellow	biscuits
E120	cochineal	alcoholic drinks
E122	carmoisine	jams and preserves
E123	amaranth	
E124	ponceau 4R	dessert mixes
E127	erythrosine	glacé cherries
E131	patent blue V	
E132	indigo carmine	
E142	green S	pastilles
E150	caramel	beers, soft drinks, sauces, gravy browning
E151		
E160(b)	annatto; bixin; norbixin	crisps
E180	pigment rubine (lithol rubine BK)	

Emulsifiers and stabilizers

	Name	Use
E407	carageenan	jelly mixes; milk shakes
E413	tragacanth	salad dressings; processed cheese

Preservatives

	Name
E210	benzoic acid
E211*	sodium benzoate
E212*	potassium benzoate
E213*	calcium benzoate
E214*	ethyl para-hydroxy-benzoate
E215*	sodium ethyl para-hydroxy-pbenzoate
E216*	propyl para-hydroxy-benzoate
E217*	sodium propyl para-hydroxy-pbenzoate
E218*	methyl para-hydroxy-benzoate
E220	sulphur dioxide
E221†	sodium sulphate
E222†	sodium bisulphite
E223†	sodium metabisulphite
E224†	potassium metabisulphite
E226†	calcium sulphite
E227†	calcium bisulphite
E249π	potassium nitrite
E250π	sodium nitrite
E251π	sodium nitrite
E252π	potassium nitrate

* beer, jam, salad cream, soft drinks, fruit pulp, fruit pie filling, marinated herring and mackerel.

† dried fruit, dehydrated vegetables, fruit juices, syrups, sausages, fruit-based dairy desserts, cider, beer, wine.

π bacon, ham, cured meats, corned beef, some cheeses.

FOOD PRESERVATION

Food preservation is the treatment of food to enable it to maintain its quality and prevent it from deteriorating. Many food stuffs are seasonal, although fruits and vegetables that were traditionally only available after their harvest are now generally available all year round as imports from abroad. Bacterial growth may be prevented by canning, drying, deep-freezing, salting, pickling and irradiation. There are, however, time limits beyond which food should not be used. Many products carry a 'best before' date after which they become unpleasant and then unsafe to consume. *The following lists are a guide to the time beyond which a food product is no longer at its best and, in many cases, unsafe.*

Packet foods

biscuits (plain) keep for five months unopened, ten days opened.
biscuits (with 'cream' fillings) three months unopened; seven days opened.
coffee (beans) nine months unopened, seven days opened.
coffee (ground) up to 18 months unopened, seven days opened.
custard powder nine months.
dried beans nine months – they will last for much longer but are past their best by nine months.
dried fruit (most) nine months unopened, six months opened.
flour (plain) 13 months.
flour (self-raising) 10 months.
flour (wholemeal) up to six months.
muesli up to six months.
pasta nine months.
porridge oats up to a year.
rice nine months.
sugar up to 18 months.
tea up to 18 months unopened, one month opened.

Food in bottles and jars

coffee (instant) up to 18 months unopened, one month opened.
honey up to two years unopened, several days opened.
jam up to two years unopened, several days opened.
lemonade up to a year unopened, two days opened.
meat and fish pastes up to six months unopened, several days opened.

Food in a refrigerator

bacon (loose) 10 days.
bacon (vacuum packed) two weeks.
beef and veal up to five days.
butter two months.
cheese (hard) three weeks (unopened), one week opened.
cheese (soft) up to five days.
eggs one month.
fish two days.
ham two days.
lamb up to five days.
milk three days.
mince (any variety) one day.
pork (cooked) two days.
pork (uncooked) one day.
poultry (uncooked) one day.

Tinned food

fish two years.
fruit (except prunes and rhubarb) 18 months.
meat five years – although pasteurized meat in tins weighing over 1 kilo (2 lb 2 oz) keep for only less than one year and should be stored in the refrigerator.
potatoes 18 months.
prunes and rhubarb one year.
vegetables two years.

Food in a freezer

bacon joints (vacuum packed) three months.
bacon rashers (vacuum packed) six months.
beef joints and cuts one year.
bread about five months.
cakes (decorated or filled) three months.
cakes (dry) up to nine months.
casseroles (cooked) three months.
chicken up to one year – freeze giblets for no longer than three months.
chipped potatoes (raw) up to six months.
cream (whipped or whipping) one month – other creams will not freeze without separating.
egg whites one year.
egg yolks six months – will only keep if one pinch of salt per egg is added.
fish (herring, mackerel and salmon) up to three months.
fish (white) five months.
fruit (cooked or in sugar) up to one year.
fruit (plain) nine months.
fruit juice five months.
fruit pies (cooked) up to four months.
game about six months.
ice cream up to two months.
meat pies (cooked) about three months.
mince up to three months.
pastry (uncooked) nine months.
pâté one month.
pork joints and cuts nine months.
sandwiches one month.
sausages three months.
veal nine months.
vegetables (blanched) about nine months.
venison no longer than eight months.

The limits given above are a guide to the average keeping times and assume that the product is fresh and in perfect condition, and that it is stored in ideal conditions. Any 'best before' date on the product should be used rather than those listed here. If you are in any doubt about the freshness or safety of a product do not use it.

NATURAL REFRIGERATION

Before mechanical refrigeration was introduced in the 19th century, people transported snow and ice and used snow cellars (cavities dug in the ground and insulated with boards and thick layers of straw). In the 18th and early 19th centuries many large houses in Europe and North America had ice houses in which large blocks of ice from frozen lakes and ponds were stored for use during the summer. Nature provides natural refrigeration in a number of ways. Meat from the bodies of mammoths, frozen in Siberian ice for up to 30,000 years, has been fed to sled dogs, and tinned food, lost or left by Antarctic expeditions more than half a century ago, has been found to be palatable.

PHYSICAL SCIENCES

Weights and Measures

MEASUREMENT

Measurement – in terms of length, weight or capacity involves *comparison*. The measurement of any physical quantity entails comparing it with an agreed and clearly defined *standard*. The result is expressed in terms of agreed *units*. Each measurement is expressed in terms of the appropriate unit preceded by a number which is the *ratio* of the measured quantity of that unit. The science of measurement is called *metrology*.

Crude measurements probably date back to prehistory. The first – units of weight and length – were based upon parts of the human body. The average pace of a man was a common unit in many ancient civilizations. The length of the human thumb was another widely used measure – in England, it was the precursor of the inch. The length of ploughs and of other agricultural implements were also frequently used as early units of measurement. As civilization and trade developed the need for standardization grew. Units were fixed by local tradition or by national rulers, and many different (though sometimes related) systems developed.

THE METRIC SYSTEM

The metric system was adopted in Revolutionary France in 1799 to replace the existing traditional illogical units. It was based upon a natural physical unit to ensure that it should be unchanging. The unit selected was 1/10 000 000 of a quadrant of a great circle of the Earth, measured around the poles of the meridian that passed through Paris. This unit – equivalent to 39·37003 inches in the British Imperial system – was called the metre (from Greek *metron*, 'measure').

Several other metric units are derived from the metre. The gram – the unit of weight – is one cubic centimetre of water at its maximum density, while the litre – the unit of capacity – is one cubic decimetre. Prefixes – from Danish, Latin and Greek – are used for multiples of ten from *atto* ($\times 10^{-18}$) to *exa* ($\times 10^{18}$) – see below.

In 1875 an international conference established the International Bureau of Weights and Measures and founded a permanent laboratory at Sèvres, near Paris, where international standards of the metric units are kept and metrological research is undertaken.

The prototype metre was an archive standard rather than an actual measurement upon the ground. In 1983 the metre was redefined as the length of the path travelled by light in vacuum during a time interval of 1/299 792 458 of a second.

Base units

The metric system is centred on a small number of *base units*, see SI units (below). These relate to the fundamental standards of length, mass and time, together with a few others to extend the system to a wider range of physical measurements, e.g. to electrical and optical quantities.

These few base units can be combined to form a large number of derived units. For example, units of area, velocity and acceleration are formed from units of length and time. Thus very many different kinds of measurement can be made and recorded employing very few base units.

Supplementary units

There are also two geometrical units that are sometimes referred to as *supplementary units*. See the table below.

SI Units

A number of systems of units based upon the metric system have been in use. Initially the *cgs system* – based upon the centimetre for length, the gram for mass and the second for time – was widespread. It has, however, largely been replaced by the *mks system* in which the fundamental units are the metre for length, the kilogram for mass and the second for time. The mks system is central to the *Système International d'Unités*, which was adopted by the 11th General Conference on Weights and Measures in 1960. The SI units are now employed for all scientific and most technical purposes, and are in general use for most other purposes in the majority of countries. The SI base units are:

metre the unit of length;

kilogram the unit of mass;

second the unit of time;

ampere the unit of electric current;

kelvin degree of temperature measured on the Kelvin scale;

candela the unit of luminous intensity;

mole the unit of substance.

Details of these and supplementary and derived SI units are given in the tables below.

METRIC UNITS

Units of Length

10 ångström	=	1 nanometre
1000 nanometres	=	1 micrometre
1000 micrometres	=	1 millimetre
10 millimetres	=	1 centimetre
10 centimetres	=	1 decimetre
1000 millimetres	=	1 metre
100 centimetres	=	1 metre
10 decimetres	=	1 metre
10 metres	=	1 dekametre
10 dekametres	=	1 hectometre
10 hectometres	=	1 kilometre
1000 metres	=	1 kilometre
1000 kilometres	=	1 megametre
Nautical		
1852 metres	=	1 int. nautical mile

Units of Area

100 sq millimetres	=	1 sq centimetre
100 sq centimetres	=	1 sq decimetre
100 sq decimetres	=	1 sq metre
100 sq metres	=	1 are
100 ares	=	1 hectare
10,000 sq metres	=	1 hectare
100 hectares	=	1 sq kilometre

Units of Weight (mass)

1000 milligrams	=	1 gram
10 grams	=	1 dekagram
10 dekagrams	=	1 hectogram
10 hectograms	=	1 kilogram
100 kilograms	=	1 quintal
1000 kilograms	=	1 tonne

Units of Volume

1000 cu millimetres	=	1 cu centimetre
1000 cu centimetres	=	1 cu decimetre
1000 cu decimetres	=	1 cu metre
1000 cu metres	=	1 cu dekametre

Units of Capacity

10 millilitres	=	1 centilitre
10 centilitres	=	1 decilitre
10 decilitres	=	1 litre
1000 millilitres	=	1 litre
1 litre	=	1 cu decimetre
10 litres	=	1 dekalitre
10 dekalitres	=	1 hectolitre
10 hectolitres	=	1 kilolitre
1 kilolitre	=	1 cu metre

THE SI UNITS

Base Units

Quantity	Unit	Symbol	Definitions
length	metre	m	the length of a path travelled by light in a vacuum during a time interval of 1/299 792 458 of a second.
mass	kilogram	kg	the mass of the international prototype of the kilogram, which is in the custody of the Bureau International des Poids et Mésures (BIPM) at Sèvres near Paris, France.
time	second	s	the duration of 9,192,631,770 periods of the radiation corresponding to the transition between the two hyperfine levels of the ground state of the caesium-133 atom.
electric current	ampere	A	that constant current which, if maintained in two straight parallel conductors of infinite length of negligible circular cross-section, and placed 1 metre apart in a vacuum, would produce between these conductors a force equal to 2×10^{-7} newtons per metre of length.
thermodynamic temperature	kelvin	K	the fraction 1/273·15 of the thermodynamic temperature of the triple point of water. The triple point of water is the point where water, ice and water vapour are in equilibrium.
luminous intensity	candela	cd	the luminous intensity, in a given direction, of a source that emits monochromatic radiation of frequency 540×10^{12} Hz and has a radiant intensity in that direction of (1/683) watts per steradian.
amount of substance	mole	mol	the amount of substance of a system that contains as many elementary entities as there are atoms in 0.012 kilogram of carbon-12.

Supplementary units

plane angle	radian	rad	the plane angle between two radii of a circle that cut off on the circumference an arc equal in length to the radius.
solid angle	steradian	sr	the solid angle that, having its vertex in the centre of a sphere, cuts off an area of the surface of the sphere equal to that of a square having sides of length equal to the radius of the sphere.

Derived Units

Quantity	Unit	Symbol	Other SI units
area	square metre	m^2	–
volume	cubic metre	m^3	–
velocity	metre per second	$m{\cdot}s^{-1}$	–
angular velocity	radian per second	rad s^{-1}	–
acceleration	metre per second squared	$m{\cdot}s^{-2}$	–
angular acceleration	radian per second squared	rad s^{-2}	–

frequency	hertz	Hz	s^{-1}
density	kilogram per cubic metre	$kg{\cdot}m^{-3}$	–
momentum	kilogram metre per second	$kg{\cdot}m{\cdot}s^{-1}$	–
angular momentum	kilogram metre squared per sec.	$kg{\cdot}m^{2}{\cdot}s^{-1}$	–
moment of inertia	kilogram metre squared	$kg{\cdot}m^{2}$	–
force	newton	N	$kg{\cdot}m{\cdot}s^{-2}$
pressure, stress	pascal	Pa	$N{\cdot}m^{-2} = kg{\cdot}m^{-1}{\cdot}s^{-2}$
work, energy, quantity of heat	joule	J	$N{\cdot}m = kg{\cdot}m^{2}{\cdot}s^{-2}$
power	watt	W	$J{\cdot}s^{-1} = kg{\cdot}m^{2}{\cdot}s^{-3}$
surface tension	newton per metre	$N{\cdot}m^{-1}$	$kg{\cdot}s^{-2}$
dynamic viscosity	newton second per metre squared	$N{\cdot}s{\cdot}m^{-2}$	$kg{\cdot}m^{-1}{\cdot}s^{-1}$
kinematic viscosity	metre squared per second	$m^{2}{\cdot}s^{-1}$	–
temperature	degree Celsius	°C	–
thermal coefficient of linear expansion	per degree Celsius, or per kelvin	$°C^{-1}$, K^{-1}	–
thermal conductivity	watt per metre degree C	$W{\cdot}m^{-1}{\cdot}°C^{-1}$	$kg{\cdot}m{\cdot}s^{-3}{\cdot}°C^{-1}$
heat capacity	joule per kelvin	$J{\cdot}K^{-1}$	$kg{\cdot}m^{2}{\cdot}s^{-2}{\cdot}K^{-1}$
specific heat capacity	joule per kilogram kelvin	$J{\cdot}kg^{-1}{\cdot}K^{-1}$	$m^{2}{\cdot}s^{-2}{\cdot}K^{-1}$
specific latent heat	joule per kilogram	$J\ kg^{-1}$	$m^{2}{\cdot}s^{-2}$
electric charge	coulomb	C	A·s
electromotive force, potential difference	volt	V	$W{\cdot}A^{-1} = kg{\cdot}m^{2}{\cdot}s^{-3}{\cdot}A^{-1}$
electric resistance	ohm	Ω	$V{\cdot}A^{-1} = kg{\cdot}m^{2}{\cdot}s^{-3}{\cdot}A^{-2}$
electric conductance	siemens	S	$A{\cdot}V^{-1} = kg^{-1}{\cdot}m^{-2}{\cdot}s^{3}{\cdot}A^{2}$
electric capacitance	farad	F	$A{\cdot}s{\cdot}V^{-1} = kg^{-1}{\cdot}m^{-2}{\cdot}s^{4}{\cdot}A^{2}$
inductance	henry	H	$V{\cdot}s{\cdot}A^{-1} = kg{\cdot}m^{2}{\cdot}s^{-2}{\cdot}A^{-2}$
magnetic flux	weber	Wb	$V{\cdot}s = kg{\cdot}m^{2}{\cdot}s^{-2}{\cdot}A^{-1}$
magnetic flux density	tesla	T	$Wb{\cdot}m^{-2} = kg{\cdot}s^{-2}{\cdot}A^{-1}$
magnetomotive force	ampere	A	–
luminous flux	lumen	lm	cd·sr
illumination	lux	lx	$lm{\cdot}m^{-2} = cd{\cdot}sr{\cdot}m^{-2}$
radiation activity	becquerel		Bq s^{-1}
radiation absorbed dose	gray	Gy	$J{\cdot}kg^{-1} = m^{2}{\cdot}s^{-2}$

Multiples and Submultiples

In the metric system the following decimal multiples and sub-multiples are used:

Prefix	**Symbol**	**Value**	**Factor**
yocto- (Latin *octo* = eight)	y	septillionth	$\times 10^{-24}$
zepto- (Latin *septo* = seven)	z	sextillionth	$\times 10^{-21}$
atto- (Danish *atten* = eighteen)	a	squintillionth	$\times 10^{-18}$
femto- (Danish *femtem* = fifteen)	f	quadrillionth	$\times 10^{-15}$
pico- (L. *pico* = minuscule)	p	trillionth	$\times 10^{-12}$
nano- (L. *nanus* = dwarf)	n	thousand millionth part or billionth[1]	$\times 10^{-9}$
micro- (Gk. *mikros* = small)	m	millionth part	$\times 10^{-6}$
milli- (L. *mille* = thousand	m	thousandth part	$\times 10^{-3}$
centi- (L. *centum* = hundred)	c	hundredth part	$\times 10^{-2}$
deci- (L. *decimus* = tenth)	d	tenth part	$\times 10^{-1}$
deka- (Gk. *deka* = ten)	da	tenfold	$\times 10$
hecto- (Gk. *hekaton* = hundred)	h	hundredfold	$\times 10^{2}$
kilo- (Gk. *chilioi* = thousand)	k	thousandfold	$\times 10^{3}$
mega- (Gk. *megas* = large)	M	millionfold	$\times 10^{6}$
giga- (Gk. *gigas* = mighty)	G	thousand millionfold or billionfold	$\times 10^{9}$
tera- (Gk. *teras* = monster)	T	trillion	$\times 10^{12}$
peta- (Gk. *penta* = five)	P	quadrillion	$\times 10^{15}$
exa- (Gk. *hexa* = six)	E	quintillion	$\times 10^{18}$
zetta- (Latin *septo* = seven)	Z	sextillion	$\times 10^{-21}$
yotta- (Latin *octo* = eight)	Y	septillion	$\times 10^{-24}$

[1] *In the UK and Germany it has been customary to advance by increments of one million, and in France and the USA in increments of a thousand. Thus in the UK, one billion was originally defined as one million million; a billion is now increasingly used in the sense of one thousand million in the UK.*

OTHER SYSTEMS

The most widely used remaining systems of units are the related (British) Imperial System and the US Customary Units. Although the names of most of the units of both systems are the same, the sizes of some of the units differ.

Imperial System

The two basic units are the yard (the unit of length) and the pound (the unit of mass). Subdivisions and multiples of these units are traditional in origin and do not follow the logical tenfold stages of the metric system.

The Imperial System is complicated by the existence of three different systems of measurement of weight. The *avoirdupois system* is the most widely used.

The *troy system* is used to measure precious metals, while the *apothecaries' system* uses the same units as the troy system but with certain differences of name.

The use of the metric system was legalized in the United Kingdom in 1897. The intention to switch to the metric system 'within ten years' was declared in May 1965 by the President of the Board of Trade, although in March 1976 the Government decided not to proceed with the second reading of the Weights and Measures (Metrication) Act.

However, since 1965 the metric system has replaced the Imperial System for many purposes,although loose fruit and vegetables continue to be sold by the pound, the pint and the dram will remain as the unit of capacity for alcohol, and the mile will not be replaced as the standard unit of length over long distances.

US Customary Units

Some units of the Imperial system have fallen into disuse in North America. The yard, for example, is only encountered in sport. The differences between English and American units make conversion difficult; for example, a ton in Britain is a unit of mass equivalent to 2240 pounds (or 1016·046 909 kg), while a ton in the USA and Canada is equivalent to 2000 pounds (or 907·184 kg).

There are also considerable differences between the English and American gallon, and the English and American bushel.

Imperial Units

Definition of Units is by the (British) Weights and Measures Act, 1963.

yard (yd) is equal to 0·9144 metre.

pound (lb) is equal to 0·453 592 37 kilogram.

gallon (gal) is the space occupied by 10 pounds weight of distilled water of density 0·998 859 gram per millilitre weighed in air of density 0·001 217 gram per millilitre against weights of density 8·136 gram per millilitre.

Units of length

12 inches	=	1 foot
3 feet	=	1 yard
5½ yards	=	1 rod, pole or perch
4 rods	=	1 chain
10 chains	=	1 furlong
5280 feet	=	1 mile
1760 yards	=	1 mile
8 furlongs	=	1 mile

Nautical

6 feet	=	1 fathom
100 fathoms	=	1 cable length
6080 feet	=	1 nautical mile

Units of area

144 sq inches	=	1 sq foot
9 sq feet	=	1 sq yard
30¼ sq yards	=	1 sq rod, pole or perch
40 sq rods	=	1 rood
4 roods	=	1 acre
4840 sq yards	=	1 acre
640 acres	=	1 sq mile

Units of weight

avoirdupois

437½ grains	=	1 ounce
16 drams	=	1 ounce
16 ounces	=	1 pound
14 pounds	=	1 stone
28 pounds	=	1 quarter
4 quarters	=	1 hundredweight
20 hundredweights	=	1 ton

Units of volume

1728 cu inches	=	1 cu foot
27 cu feet	=	1 cu yard
5·8 cu feet	=	1 bulk barrel

Units of capacity

8 fluid drams	=	1 fluid ounce
5 fluid ounces	=	1 gill
4 gills	=	1 pint
2 pints	=	1 quart
4 quarts	=	1 gallon
2 gallons	=	1 peck
4 pecks	=	1 bushel
8 bushels	=	1 quarter
36 gallons	=	1 bulk barrel

OTHER UNITS OF LENGTH EMPLOYED

animal stature	the hand = 4 in. A horse of, for example, 14 hands 3 in to the withers is often written 14·3 hands.
surveying	the link = 7·92 in or one hundredth part of a chain.
approximate	the span = 9 in (from the span of the hand).
biblical	the cubit = 18 in. approximate the pace = 30 in. (from the stride).
navigation	the International nautical mile (adopted also by the USA on 1 July 1954) = 6076·1 ft (0.99936 of a UK nautical mile).

MISCELLANEOUS UNITS

Water

1 litre	weighs 1 kilogram
1 cubic metre	weighs 1 tonne
1 UK gallon	weighs 10·022 lb
1 UK gallon salt water	weighs 10·3 lb

Speed

1 knot = 1 nautical mph

Beer, Wines and Spirits

Proof spirit contains 57·03% pure alcohol by volume (at 50 °F).
Proof strength in degrees = % of alcohol by volume (at 50 °F) multiplied by 1·7535.

Beer

nip	=	¼ pint
small	=	½ pint
large	=	1 pint
flagon	=	1 quart
anker	=	10 gallons
tun	=	216 gallons

Wines and spirits

tot (whisky)	=	⅙, ⅕, ¼, or ⅓ gill
noggin (rum)	=	1 gill
bottle	=	1⅓ pints

Champagne

2 bottles	=	1 magnum
4 bottles	=	1 jeroboam
20 bottles	=	1 nebuchadnezzar

Type Sizes

Depth

72¼ points (approx)	=	1 inch
1 didot point	=	0·376 mm

Width

1 pica em	=	12 points
1 pica en	=	6 points

Book Sizes

Crown Quarto	=	246 × 189 mms (7½ × 10 ins)
Crown Octavo	=	186 × 123 mm (5 × 7½ ins)
Demy Quarto	=	276 × 219 mm (8¾ × 11¼in)
Demy Octavo	=	216 × 138 mm (5⅝ × 8¾ in)
Royal Quarto	=	312 × 237 mm (10 × 12½ in)
Royal Octavo	=	234 × 156 mm (6¼ × 10 in)
A4	=	297 × 210 mm (8¾ × 11¼ in)
A5	=	210 × 148 mm (5¾ × 9 in)

Crops

UK (Imperial) bushels

of wheat	=	60 lb
barley	=	50 lb
oats	=	39 lb
rye	=	56 lb
rice	=	45 lb
maize	=	56 lb
linseed	=	52 lb
potatoes	=	60 lb

US bushel:

as above except

barley	=	48 lb
linseed	=	56 lb
oats	=	32 lb

bale (cotton):

US (net) = 480 lb

Units of Energy

1000 British thermal unit (Btu)	=	0·293 kW h
100,000 Btu	=	1 therm
1 UK horsepower	=	0·7457 kilowatt

Paper Sizes

Large post	=	419·1 × 533·4 mm (16½ × 21 in)
Demy	=	444·5 × 571·5 mm (17½ × 22½ in)
Medium	=	457·2 × 584·2 mm (18 × 23 in)
Royal	=	508 × 635 mm (20 × 25 in)
Double crown	=	508 × 762 mm (20 × 30 in)

'A' Series (metric sizes)

A0	=	841 × 1189 mm (33⅛ × 46¾ in)
A1	=	594 × 841 mm (23⅜ × 33⅛in)
A2	=	420 × 594 mm (16½ × 23⅜ in)
A3	=	297 × 420 mm (11¾ × 16½ in)
A4	=	210 × 297 mm (8¼ × 11¾ in)
A5	=	148 × 210 mm (5⅞ × 8¼ in)

Petroleum

1 barrel	=	42 US gallon
	=	34·97 UK gallons
	=	0·159 cubic metres

Precious Metals

24 carat implies pure metal

1 metric carat	=	200 milligrams
1 troy (fine) ounce	=	480 grains

Paper Quantities

In the UK, paper is traditionally bought in the following measures:

Writing paper

480 sheets = 1 ream
24 sheets = 1 quire
20 quires = 1 ream

Printing paper

516 sheets = 1 ream
2 reams = 1 bundle
5 bundles = 1 bale

International clothing sizes

The tables below should be used as approximate guides as actual sizes may vary according to manufacturers. It is wise to check all measurements in centimetres.

Ladies' coats and jackets

UK	8/30	10/32	12/34	14/36	16/38	18/40
USA	6	8	10	12	14	16
Germany & Netherlands	34	36	38	40	42	44
Italy & Scandinavia	36	38	40	42	44	46
Spain	40	42	44	46	48	50
France & Belgium	38/	40/	42/	44/	46/	48/
Japan	7	9	11	13	15	17

Men's suits and overcoats use the same sizes (46 to 56) in the above countries (except Japan).

Men's shirts

EC	36	37	38	39	40	41
UK & USA	14	14½	15	15½	16	16½

Ladies' shoes

UK	3	4	5	6	7
USA	6½	7½	8½	9½	10½
EC	36	37	38	39	40
Japan	22	23	24	25	25½

Men's shoes

UK	6	7	8	9	10
USA	6½	7½	8½	9½	10½
Europe except Scandinavia	39	40	41	42	43
Scandinavia	40	41	42	43	44

METRIC AND IMPERIAL CONVERSIONS

(* = exact)

Column One	*Equivalent*	*Column Two*	*To convert Col.2 to Col.1 multiply by*	*To convert Col.1 to Col.2 multiply by*
Length				
inch (in)	–	centimetre (cm)	0·393 700 78	2·54*
foot (ft)	12 in	metre	3·280 840	0·3048*
yard (yd)	3 ft	metre	1·093 61	0·9144*
mile	1760 yd	kilometre (km)	0·621 3711	1·609 344*
fathom	6 ft	metre	0·546 80	1·8288*
chain	22 yd	metre	0·049 70	20·1168*
UK nautical mile	6080 ft	kilometre	0·539 6118	1·853 184*
International nautical mile	6076·1 ft	kilometre	0·539 9568	1·852*
ångström unit (Å)	10^{-10} m	nanometre	10	10^{-1}
Area				
square inch	–	square centimetre	0·155 00	6·4516*
square foot	144 sq in	square metre	10·7639	0·092 903*
square yard	9 sq ft	square metre	1·195 99	0·836 127*
acre	4840 sq yd	hectare (ha) (10^4 m^2)	2·471 05	0·404 686*
square mile	640 acres	square kilometre	0·386 10	2·589 988*
Volume				
cubic inch	–	cubic centimetre	0·061 024	16·3871*
cubic foot	1728 cu in	cubic metre	35·314 67	0·028 317*
cubic yard	27 cu ft	cubic metre	1·307 95	0·764 555*
Capacity				
litre	100 centilitres	cubic centimetre or millilitre	0·001*	1000*
pint	4 gills	litre	1·759 753	0·568 261
UK gallon	8 pints or 277.4 in^3	litre	0·219 969	4·546 092
barrel (for beer)	36 gallons	hectolitre	0·611 026	1·636 59
US gallon	0·832 675 UK gallons	litre or dm^3	0·264 172	3·785 412
US barrel (for petroleum)	42 US gallons	hectolitre	0·628 998	1·589 83
fluid ounce	0·05 pint	millilitre	0·035 195	28·413 074
Velocity				
feet per second (ft/s)	–	metres per second	3·280 840	0·3048
miles per hour (mph)	–	kilometres per hour	0·621 371	1·609 344
UK knot (1.00064 Int knots)	nautical mile/hour	kilometres per hour	0·539 6118	1·853 184
Acceleration				
foot per second per second (ft/s^2)	–	metres per second per second ($m\ s^{-2}$)	3·280 840	0·3048*
Mass				
grain (gr)	1/480th of an oz troy	milligram (mg)	0·015 4324	64·798 91
dram (dr)	27·3438 gr	gram	0·564 383	1·771 85
ounce (avoirdupois)	16 drams	gram	0·035 2740	28·349 523 125
pound (avoirdupois)	16 ounces	kilogram	2·204 62*	0·453 592 37*
stone	14 pounds	kilogram	0·157 473 04	6·350 293 18*
quarter	28 pounds	kilogram	0·078 7375	12·700 586 36*
hundredweight (cwt)	112 pounds	kilogram	0·019 6841	50·802 345 44*
ton (long)	2240 pounds	tonne (= 1000 kg)	0·984 2065	1·016 046 9088
Note: A pound troy consists of 12 ounces troy each of 480 grains				
Density				
pounds per cubic inch	–	grams per cubic centimetre	0·036 1272	27·6799
pounds per cubic foot	–	kilograms per cubic metre	0·062 342 80	16·0185
Force				
dyne (dyn)	10^{-5}newton	newton	10^5	10^{-5}
poundal (pdl)	–	newton	7·233 01	0·138 255
pound-force (lbf)	–	newton	0·224 809	4·448 22
tons-force	–	kilonewton (kN)	0·100 361	9·964 02
kilogram-force (kgf) (or kilopond)	–	newton	0·101 972	9·806 65
Energy (Work, Heat)				
erg	10^{-7} joule	joule	10^7	10^{-7}
horse-power (hp) (550 ft/lbf/s)	–	kilowatt (kW)	1·341 02	0·745 700
therm	–	mega joule (MJ)	0·009 478 17	105·506
kilowatt hour (kWh)	–	mega Joule (MJ)	0·277 778	3·6
calorie (international)	–	joule	0·238 846*	4·1868*
British thermal unit (Btu)	–	kilo-joule (kJ)	0·947 817	1·055 06
Pressure, Stress				
millibar (mbar or mb)	1000 dynes/cm^2	Pa	0·01*	100*
standard atmosphere (atm)	760 torrs	kPa	0·009 8692	101·325
pounds per square inch (psi)	–	Pa	0·000 145 038	6894·76
pounds per square inch (psi)	–	kilogram-force per cm^2	14·2233	0·070 3070

CELSIUS AND FAHRENHEIT COMPARED

The two principal temperature scales are Celsius and Fahrenheit. Temperatures in a meteorological context are given in both in this and other chapters. The Celsius scale was devised in 1743 by J. P. Christen (1683–1755) but is referred to by its present name because of the erroneous belief that it was invented by the Swedish astronomer Anders Celsius (1701–44). The Fahrenheit scale is named after Gabriel Daniel Fahrenheit (1686–1736), a German physicist.

Quick conversion

To convert ° C to ° F, multiply the ° C reading by 9, divide by 5 and add 32.

To convert ° F to ° C, subtract 32 from the ° F reading and multiply by 5, divide by 9.

Kelvin Scale

Scientists in a non-meteorological context most frequently employ the Kelvin Scale in which one degree kelvin (K) = 1/273·16 of the triple point of water (where ice, water and water vapour are in equilibrium).

Temperature Comparisons

The following tables compare points on the Celsius and Fahrenheit scales.

(1) Absolute zero	=	−273·15 °C	=	−459·67 °F	=	0K
(2) Zero Fahrenheit	=	−17·8 °C	=	0·0 °F	=	255·35K
(3) Freezing point of water	=	0·0 °C	=	32·0 °F	=	273·15K
(4) Triple point of water	=	0·01 °C	=	32·02 °F	=	273·16K
(5) Normal human bloods temperature	=	36·9 °C	=	98·4 °F	=	310·05K
(6) Boiling point of waters (at standard pressure)	=	100·0 °C	=	212·0 °F	=	373·15K

°C		°F	°C		°F	°C		°F
−40 °C	=	−40 °F	1 °C	=	34 °F	42 °C	=	108 °F
−39 °C	=	−38 °F	2 °C	=	36 °F	43 °C	=	109 °F
−38 °C	=	−36 °F	3 °C	=	37 °F	44 °C	=	111 °F
−37 °C	=	−35 °F	4 °C	=	39 °F	45 °C	=	113 °F
−36 °C	=	−33 °F	5 °C	=	41 °F	46 °C	=	115 °F
−35 °C	=	−31 °F	6 °C	=	43 °F	47 °C	=	117 °F
−34 °C	=	−29 °F	7 °C	=	45 °F	48 °C	=	118 °F
−33 °C	=	−27 °F	8 °C	=	46 °F	49 °C	=	120 °F
−32 °C	=	−26 °F	9 °C	=	48 °F	50 °C	=	122 °F
−31 °C	=	−24 °F	10 °C	=	50 °F	51 °C	=	124 °F
−30 °C	=	−22 °F	11 °C	=	52 °F	52 °C	=	126 °F
−29 °C	=	−20 °F	12 °C	=	54 °F	53 °C	=	127 °F
−28 °C	=	−18 °F	13 °C	=	55 °F	54 °C	=	129 °F
−27 °C	=	−17 °F	14 °C	=	57 °F	55 °C	=	131 °F
−26 °C	=	−15 °F	15 °C	=	59 °F	56 °C	=	133 °F
−25 °C	=	−13 °F	16 °C	=	61 °F	57 °C	=	135 °F
−24 °C	=	−11 °F	17 °C	=	63 °F	58 °C	=	136 °F
−23 °C	=	−9 °F	18 °C	=	64 °F	59 °C	=	138 °F
−22 °C	=	−8 °F	19 °C	=	66 °F	60 °C	=	140 °F
−21 °C	=	−6 °F	20 °C	=	68 °F	61 °C	=	142 °F
−20 °C	=	−4 °F	21 °C	=	70 °F	62 °C	=	144 °F
−19 °C	=	−2 °F	22 °C	=	72 °F	63 °C	=	147 °F
−18 °C	=	0 °F	23 °C	=	73 °F	64 °C	=	147 °F
−17 °C	=	1 °F	24 °C	=	75 °F	65 °C	=	149 °F
−16 °C	=	3 °F	25 °C	=	77 °F	66 °C	=	151 °F
−15 °C	=	5 °F	26 °C	=	79 °F	67 °C	=	153 °F
−14 °C	=	7 °F	27 °C	=	81 °F	68 °C	=	154 °F
−13 °C	=	9 °F	28 °C	=	82 °F	69 °C	=	156 °F
−12 °C	=	10 °F	29 °C	=	84 °F	70 °C	=	158 °F
−11 °C	=	12 °F	30 °C	=	86 °F	71 °C	=	160 °F
−10 °C	=	14 °F	31 °C	=	88 °F	72 °C	=	162 °F
−9 °C	=	16 °F	32 °C	=	90 °F	73 °C	=	163 °F
−8 °C	=	18 °F	33 °C	=	91 °F	74 °C	=	165 °F
−7 °C	=	19 °F	34 °C	=	93 °F	75 °C	=	167 °F
−6 °C	=	21 °F	35 °C	=	95 °F	76 °C	=	169 °F
−5 °C	=	23 °F	36 °C	=	97 °F	77 °C	=	171 °F
−4 °C	=	25 °F	37 °C	=	99 °F	78 °C	=	172 °F
−3 °C	=	27 °F	38 °C	=	100 °F	79 °C	=	174 °F
−2 °C	=	28 °F	39 °C	=	102 °F	80 °C	=	176 °F
−1 °C	=	30 °F	40 °C	=	104 °F	81 °C	=	178 °F
0 °C	=	32 °F	41 °C	=	106 °F	82 °C	=	180 °F

Physics

Physics is the study of the basic laws that govern matter. The following section explores these laws through a series of themes – Mechanics, Optics, Atoms, etc. A check list of the major laws of physics follows.

THE LAWS OF PHYSICS

Archimedes' principle	states that an object placed in a fluid is buoyed up by a force equal to the weight of the fluid displaced by the body.	See p. 197.
Boyle's law	states that the volume of a fixed mass of gas is inversely proportional to the pressure, provided the temperature remains constant.	See p. 199.
Charles' law	states that the volume of a fixed mass of gas is directly proportional to its absolute temperature, provided the pressure remains constant.	See p. 199.
conservation of energy, principle of	states that the total magnitude of a certain physical property of a system will remain unchanged even though there may be exchanges of that property between the various components of that system.	See p. 198.
Coulomb's law	describes the electric force.	See p. 208.
dual nature of light,	states that light behaves as a wave during interference experiments but as a stream of particles during the photoelectric effect.	See p. 201.
general relativity theory		See p. 201.
Hooke's law	states that, for small forces, the extension is proportional to the applied force.	See p. 196.
Huygens' principle	states that every point on a wavefront may itself be regarded as a source of secondary waves.	See pp. 204–05.
ideal gas law	combines the equations derived from Boyle's law, Charles' law and the pressure law.	See pp. 198–99.
indeterminism, principle of	see uncertainty principle (below).	See p. 201.
laws of uniformly accelerated motion	are equations that describe the relationships of displacement, velocity and acceleration.	See pp. 192–93.
Maxwell's theory	unites the separate concepts of electricity and magnetism in terms of electromagnetism.	See p. 209.
Newton's first law of motion	states that a body will remain at rest or travelling in a straight line at constant speed unless it is acted upon by an external force.	See p. 194.
Newton's second law of motion	states that the resultant force exerted on a body is directly proportional to the acceleration produced by the force.	See p. 194.
Newton's third law of motion	states that a single isolated force cannot exist on its own; there is always a resulting 'mirror-image' force. In Newton's words: 'To every action there is always an equal reaction'.	See p. 194.
Newton's law of gravitation	states that every particle in the universe attracts every other particle with a force that is directly proportional to the product of their masses and inversely proportional to the square of the distance between them.	See p. 193.
Ohm's law	states that the current through a metallic conductor is directly proportional to the potential difference between its ends if the temperature and other physical conditions are constant.	See p. 211.
pressure law of gas	states that the pressure of a fixed mass of gas is directly proportional to its absolute temperature, provided its volume remains constant.	See p. 199.
quantum theory	states that nothing can be measured or observed without disturbing it.	See pp. 192 & 201.
Snell's law		See p. 203.
special relativity theory		See p. 201.
thermodynamics, first law of	states that if, during an interaction, a quantity of heat is absorbed by a body, it is equal to the sum of the increase in internal energy of the body and any external work done by the body.	See p. 198.
thermodynamics, second law of	states that heat cannot itself flow from a cold object to a hot object. Certain processes may operate only in one direction.	See pp. 198–99.
uncertainty principle (or Heisenberg uncertainty principle)	states that it is not possible to know with unlimited accuracy both the position and momentum of a particle.	See pp. 192 & 201.

MECHANICS – Motion and force

Mechanics is the branch of physics that describes the movement or motion of objects, ranging in scale from a planet to the smallest particle within an atom. Sir Isaac Newton developed a theory of mechanics that has proved highly successful in describing most types of motion, and his work has been acclaimed as one of the greatest advances in the history of science.

The Newtonian approach, although valid for velocities and dimensions within normal experience, has been shown to fail for velocities approaching the speed of light and for dimensions on a subatomic scale. Newton's discoveries are considered to be a special case within a more general theory.

Newtonian mechanics were so successful that a mechanistic belief developed in which it was thought that with the knowledge of Newton's laws (and later those of electromagnetism) it would be possible to predict the future of the universe if the positions, velocities and accelerations of all particles at any one instant were known. Later the quantum theory and the Heisenberg Uncertainty Principle confounded the belief by predicting the fundamental impossibility of making simultaneous measurements of the position and velocity of a particle with infinite accuracy.

acceleration the rate of change of the velocity, if a body moves with a changing velocity.

Acceleration may be defined as the change in velocity in a given time interval. Its dimensions are velocity divided by time, and are (usually) given in metres per second (ms^{-2}).

At its simplest, the equation may be given as:

$$\text{Acceleration} = \frac{\text{change in velocity}}{\text{time taken for this change}}$$

Note that since velocity is speed in a given direction a change in velocity may involve a change in direction rather than speed or perhaps a combination of speed and direction.

See circular motion (below) and centripetal acceleration (below).

When a body moves with uniform acceleration, the displacement, velocity and acceleration are related – these relationships are described in the kinematic equations.

acceleration due to gravity see gravitational acceleration.

acceleration of free fall see gravitational acceleration.

centrifugal force a 'centre-fleeing' force.

In an accelerating or non-inertial frame of reference, Newton's second law of motion (see below) will not work unless some fictitious force is introduced. For example, passengers on a fair ground merry-go-round feel as if they are being forced outward when the machine is operating. This is ascribed to a 'centre-fleeing' or centrifugal force.

The passengers experience this 'centre-fleeing' force because they are moving within the system; they are within an accelerating frame of reference (see circular motion, below). To an observer on the ground it appears that the passengers on the merry-go-round should fly off at a tangent to the circular motion unless there were a force keeping them aboard. This is the centripetal force and is experienced as the friction between each passenger and the seat. If a passenger were to fall off, it would be because the centripetal force was not strong enough, not because the centrifugal force was too great.

centripetal acceleration literally means 'centre-seeking' acceleration. It is the acceleration of a body moving in a circular path. See circular motion (below). Centripetal acceleration is directed inward, towards the centre of the circle.

centripetal force a force acting on a body which causes it to move in a circular path. See centrifugal force, above.

circular motion occurs when a body moves in a circular path at constant speed – in this case its direction of motion (and therefore its velocity) will be changing continuously. Since the velocity is changing, the body must have acceleration, which is also changing continuously. Thus the laws of uniformly accelerated motion do not apply. The acceleration that occurs in this case is centripetal acceleration.

conservation of momentum, principle of states that, when two bodies interact, the total momentum before impact is the same as the total momentum after impact. Thus the total of the components of momentum in any direction before and after the interaction are equal.

This can be stated as:
$m_1 u_1 + m_2 u_2 = m_1 v_1 + m_2 v_2$
where
m_1 m_2 are the masses
u_1 u_2 are the initial velocities
v_1 v_2 are the resultant velocities of the bodies.

decreasing velocity means that the velocity has different values at different times; it is decreasing with time. See velocity (below).

displacement see motion (below).

electro-weak force see fundamental forces.

force (in physics) something that causes a change in the velocity of an object.

fundamental forces (in physics) are the four forces that occur in nature – they are:
– gravitational force,
– the electromagnetic force, and
– the strong and weak nuclear forces.

The electromagnetic and weak forces have recently been shown to be part of an electro-weak force.

gravitation see gravitational force (below).

gravitational acceleration (or **acceleration due to gravity** or **acceleration of free fall**) the downward acceleration of objects falling towards the Earth.

The 16th century Italian physicist and astronomer Galileo Galilei investigated the motion of objects falling freely in air. He believed that all objects falling freely towards the Earth have the same downward acceleration. This is gravitational acceleration. Near the surface of the Earth it is $9{\cdot}80ms^2$, but there are small variations in its value depending upon latitude and elevation.

In the idealized situation, air resistance is neglected, although in a practical experiment it would have to be considered. In a demonstration on the Moon in August 1971, an American astronaut showed that, under conditions where air resistance is negligible, a feather and a hammer, released at the same moment from the same height, would fall side by side. They landed on the lunar surface together.

gravitational constant (symbol ***G***) is the constant of proportionality implicit in Newton's law of gravitation (q.v.).

gravitational force or **gravity** is one of the four fundamental forces (q.v.) that occur in nature.

Gravitational force is the mutual force of attraction between masses. The gravitational force is much weaker than the other three fundamental forces. However, this long-range force should not be thought of as weak force.

An object resting on a table is acted on by the gravitational force of the whole Earth – a significant force. The almost equal force exerted by the table on that object is the result of short-range forces exerted by molecules on its surface.

Newton's law of gravitation was first described in his *Philosophiae Naturalis Principia Mathematica* (The Mathematical Principles of Natural Philosophy), which he wrote in 1687. Newton used the notion of a particle, by which he meant a body so small that its dimensions are negligible compared to other distances.

Newton's law of gravitation states that every particle in the universe attracts every other particle with a force that is directly proportional to the product of their masses and inversely proportional to the square of the distance between them.

This may be given as

$$F = \frac{Gm_1m_2}{x^2}$$

where
G is the gravitational constant,
F is the force,
$m_1 m_2$ are the masses,
x is the distance between the particles.
The law is an 'inverse-square law', since the magnitude of the force is inversely proportional to the square of the distance between the masses. (A similar inverse-square law applies for the force between two electric charges – Coulomb's law.)

If Newton's law of gravitation is combined with his second law of motion (q.v.) it follows that:

$$g = \frac{GM}{d^2}$$

where
g is the acceleration due to gravity,
G is the gravitational constant,
M is the mass of the Earth, and
d is the distance of the body from the centre of the Earth.
(For a body on the surface of the Earth g (that is gravity) = 9·806 65ms^{-2})

Gravity also exists on other planets and their satellites (their moons), but because gravity depends upon the mass of those bodies and their diameters, the strength of the gravitational force is not the same as it is on Earth.

increasing velocity means that the velocity has a different value at different times; it is increasing with time. See velocity (below).

inertia see Newton's first law of motion (below).

instantaneous velocity the velocity of any instant. When real motion is considered, both the magnitude and the direction of the velocity have to be investigated. A golf ball, hit upwards, will return to the ground. During flight its velocity will change in both magnitude and direction. In this case, instead of average velocity, the instantaneous velocities have to be evaluated. The velocity can, at any instant, be considered to be acting in two directions, vertical and horizontal. Then the velocity at that instant can be split into a vertical component and a horizontal component.

Each component can be considered as being uniformly accelerated rectilinear motion, so the kinetic equations can be applied in each direction. Then the instantaneous velocity and position at any point of the flight can be calculated.

kinematic equations (or **laws of uniformly accelerated motion**) equations that describe the relationships of displacement, velocity and acceleration.

For a body moving in a straight line with uniformly accelerated motion:

1. $v = u + at$
2. $s = ½\ at^2$
3. $v^2 = u^2 + 2as$
4. $s = ½\ t(u+v)$

where
s = displacement
t = time
u = initial or starting velocity
v = velocity after time t
a = acceleration.

To use the kinematic equations to solve a problem in kinematics it is necessary to identify the information given in the problem, then to identify which of the four equations can be manipulated to give the answer required.

kinematics the study of bodies in motion, ignoring masses and forces.

linear motion see motion.

mass (of a body) is often confused with its weight. The mass is the amount of matter in the body, and is a measure of its inertia (see Newton's first law of motion). See also weight (below).

mechanics see introduction.

momentum (of a body) is defined as the product of its mass and velocity. Newton called momentum the 'quantity of motion'.

motion (of a body) occurs when a body is moving in time and space. If the body moves from one position to another, the straight line joining its starting point to its finishing point is its displacement. Displacement has both magnitude and direction, and is therefore said to be a vector quantity. The motion is linear.

newton (symbol **N**) the SI unit of force. The newton is defined as the resultant force that, acting on a mass of 1 kg, produces an acceleration of 1ms^{-2}.

Newton's laws of motion state relationships between the acceleration of a body and the forces acting on it.

Newton's first law of motion states that a body will remain at rest or travelling in a straight line at constant speed unless it is acted upon by an external force.

Notice that the force has to be an external one. In general, a body does not exert a force upon itself.

The tendency of a body to remain at rest or moving with constant velocity is called the inertia of the body. The inertia is related to the mass, which is the amount of substance in the body. The unit of mass is the kilogram (kg).

Newton's second law of motion states that the resultant force exerted on a body is directly proportional to the acceleration produced by the force. (See weight and force.)

The unit of force is known as the newton (N) – see above.

Newton expressed his second law by stating that the force acting on a body is equal to the rate of change in its 'quantity of motion', which is now called momentum.

$F = ma$

or

$$F = \frac{mv_2 - mv_1}{t}$$

where
F is the force exerted,
m is the mass of the body,
a is the acceleration,
v_1 is the initial velocity,
v_2 is the final velocity, and
t is the time for which the force acts.

Newton's third law of motion states that a single isolated force cannot exist on its own; there is always a resulting 'mirror-image' force. In Newton's words: 'To every action there is always opposed an equal reaction'.

(It is important that the equal and opposite forces do not act on the same body.)

This means that, because any two masses exert on each other a mutual gravitational attraction, the Earth is always attracted towards a ball as much as the ball is attracted towards the Earth. Because of the huge difference in their sizes, however, the observable result is the downward acceleration of the ball.

The principle of the conservation of momentum (q.v.) follows from the third law.

Newton's law of gravitation see gravitational force (above).

particle (Newtonian) was defined by Newton as being a body so small that its dimensions are negligible compared to other distances. See gravitational force (above).

principle of the conservation of momentum see conservation of momentum, principle of.

quantity of motion see momentum (above) and Newton's second law of motion.

scalar quantity a quantity in which direction is either not applicable or not specified.

speed the ratio of a distance covered by a body in a given amount of time to that time.

At its simplest, the equation may be given as:

$$\text{Average speed} = \frac{\text{distance moved}}{\text{time taken}}$$

Speed – compare with velocity – has magnitude, but is not considered to be in any particular direction. Speed is a scalar quantity rather than a vector quantity.

static equilibrium see zero net force.

uniform acceleration uniformly accelerated motion.

uniformly accelerated motion, laws of see kinematic equations.

uniform velocity means that the speed and the direction taken remain the same.

velocity the rate at which a body moves in a straight line or rectilinearly.

At its simplest the equation may be given as:

$$\text{Velocity} = \frac{\text{distance moved in a particular direction}}{\text{time taken}}$$

Like displacement, velocity has both magnitude and direction and is a vector quantity. (See also speed.)

The average velocity during this rectilinear motion is defined as the change in displacement divided by the total time taken. Its dimensions are therefore length divided by time, and are given in metres per second (ms^{-1}). The instantaneous velocity at any point is the rate of change of velocity at that point.

vector a quantity in which both the magnitude and the direction must be stated.

vertical component of velocity see instantaneous velocity.

weight the gravitational force acting on the body. Weight, therefore, varies with location. Thus a body can have the same mass on the Moon as on Earth, but its weight on the Moon will be less than on Earth since the gravitational force on the Moon is approximately one sixth of that on Earth.

The same person, stepping on a set of compression scales at the bottom of a mountain and then at the top, would weigh less at the top because of the slight decrease in the gravitational force, which results from the slight increase in distance from the centre of Earth.

Weight is sometimes confused with mass (q.v.).

The unit of weight is the newton (q.v.).

zero net force the condition when the total or resultant of all the forces acting on a body are zero – i.e. all the forces cancel each other out. If the body is at rest it is in static equilibrium. (Studies of such conditions are important in the design of bridges, dams and buildings.)

STATICS AND FORCES INVOLVED IN ROTATION

In addition to the fundamental forces, other forces may be encountered. Because of their different natures, solids and fluids appear in some ways to react differently to similar applied forces. When forces are applied to solids they tend to resist.

Newton's first law of motion, stated for a single particle, can also apply to real bodies that have definite shapes and sizes and consist of many particles. Such a body may be at equilibrium. This means that it is acted on by net zero force, and that it has no tendency to rotate.

In the simple action of opening a door, or using a spanner, a turning force is exerted. The size of the turning effect depends upon two factors: firstly, the magnitude of the force and, secondly, the distance of the line of action of the force from the pivot. A large turning effect can be produced even if only a small force is exerted if the distance from the pivot is large – this is, for example, the effect that can be produced with certain spanners.

centre of mass (of a body) is a point, normally within the body itself, such that the net resultant force produces an acceleration at this point, as though all the mass of the body were concentrated at that point.

The weight of a body is the force with which the Earth attracts it. The many particles that go to make up the body are each attracted to the Earth with the same force. Thus, the Earth's pull on a body comprises a very large number of equal parallel forces. These parallel forces can be replaced by the concept of a single force that acts through the point known as the centre of mass.

The centre of gravity of a body is the point of application of the resultant force due to the attraction of the Earth on the body. If a uniform gravitational field is present, the centre of gravity coincides with the centre of mass. Thus all the weight can be considered to act at this single point. The stability of an object is helped by keeping the centre of gravity as low as possible. A racing car is low-slung to improve stability.

The centre of mass of a body may be located by means of a simple experiment. If a thin sheet of material is balanced on a straight edge in a number of positions the centre of mass may be determined. The centre of mass of an irregular sheet may be determined by making three holes near to the edge of the sheet and then, in turn, suspending the sheet along with a plumbline from each hole. If the position of the plumbline is marked on the sheet, the point of intersection of the three lines so drawn may be determined. This point of intersection is the centre of mass.

couple two equal and opposite forces applied to the same body where the two forces do not act in the same line; see moment (below) and diagram.

equilibrium the state in which a body is at rest or moving with constant velocity.

moment (or **torque**) the size of the turning effect. The moment (or torque) of a force about a point is the product of the force acting on a body and the perpendicular distance from the axis of the rotation of the body to the line of action of the force – see diagram. Torque measures the tendency of a force to cause the body to rotate. In this case torque causes angular acceleration, which is the rate of change of angular velocity of the body. Torque has units of force × distance, usually expressed as newton metres (N m).

Torque is increased if either the force or the perpendicular distance is increased. If a wedge is used to keep a door open, it has maximum effect if it is placed on the floor as far away from the hinge as possible. When a body is acted upon by two equal and opposite forces, not in the same line, then the result is a couple, which has a constant turning moment about any axis perpendicular to the plane in which they act – see diagram.

Moments can be observed in a simple experiment using a ruler, a fulcrum and several small weights. A weight is tied to one end of the ruler and a second weight is tied to the other end of the ruler. The ruler is then placed on a fulcrum and is adjusted so that a balance is achieved. When the body is in equilibrium, the sum of the anti-clockwise moments about the fulcrum is equal to the sum of the anti-clockwise moments about the same point – thus the sum of the clockwise moments by the weighted ruler on one side of the fulcrum is equal to the sum of the anti-clockwise moments by the other end of the weighted ruler on the side of the fulcrum.

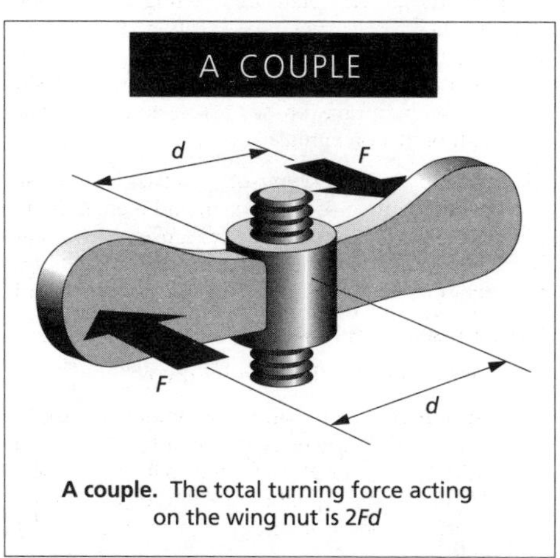

A couple. The total turning force acting on the wing nut is $2Fd$

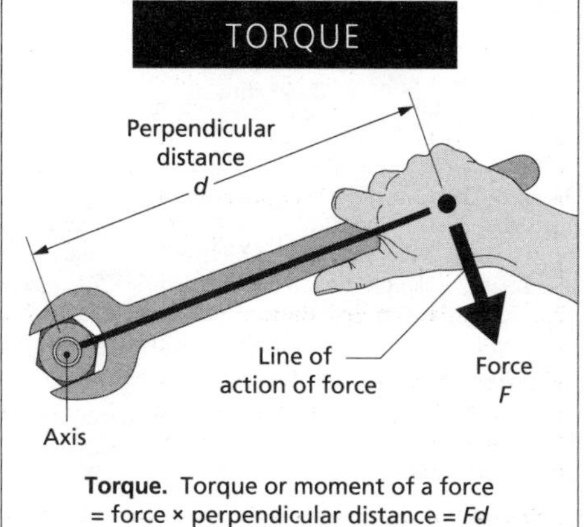

Torque. Torque or moment of a force = force × perpendicular distance = Fd

FRICTION AND ELASTICITY

In addition to the fundamental forces, other forces, such as friction and elasticity, may be encountered. Because of their different natures, solids and fluids appear in some ways to react differently to similar applied forces. When forces are applied to solids they tend to resist. Friction inhibits displacement, but is overcome after a certain limit. Bodies may be deformed by tensions.

bulk modulus of elasticity one of the three types of elastic modulus. This modulus characterizes the behaviour of a substance subject to a uniform volume comparison. The bulk modulus is the ratio of the pressure on a body to its fractional decrease in volume. See also Young's modulus and shear modulus.

coefficient of friction (symbol μ) is the ratio of the frictional force (F) to the normal reaction (N) hence

$$\mu = \frac{F}{N}$$

The coefficients are different for limiting and sliding friction.

deformation (in physics) the act of impairing the form or shape of a body.

elasticity deals with deformations that disappear when the external applied forces are removed. Most bodies may be deformed by the action of external forces and behave elastically for small deformations.

elastic modulus the constant of proportionality in stress and strain; in other words, the ratio of the stress applied to a body to the strain produced. The elastic modulus varies according to the material and the type of deformation. See also Young's modulus, shear modulus, bulk modulus and Hooke's law.

friction the force that resists the motion of one surface relative to another with which it is in contact. See sliding friction, static friction, and rolling friction.

Friction is caused because any and every body, no matter how smooth it may look, has bumps, lumps and cracks on it that can be seen microscopically. Because of this the number of points of contact between two surfaces are few; they are represented by these irregularities and not by the entire area of the adjoining surfaces. Consequently, very high pressure results in local pressure welding of the two surfaces. When one, or both, of these surfaces move, the welds are broken and are remade time after time and, thus, friction occurs.

Hooke's law applies to a special example of deformation – the extension or elongation of a spring by an applied force. Hooke's law, which was formulated by the English scientist Robert Hooke (1635–1703), states that, for small forces, the extension is proportional to the applied force. Thus a spring balance will have a uniform scale for the measurement of various weights.

imperfect elasticity occurs when a substance does not readily regain its initial state. It can also be demonstrated in the case of a soft rubber ball which – when dropped on hard ground – bounces to only about one half of its initial height.

perfect elasticity the state where a substance returns to its initial state readily. This is found, for instance, in the case of spring steel, which in scientific terms, is almost perfectly elastic.

perfect plasticity is the opposite of perfect elasticity: the material shows *no* tendency to return to its original size and shape.

plastic flow occurs when a substance behaves in a viscous manner. Some bodies behave elastically for low values of stress, but above a critical level they behave in a perfectly viscous manner and 'flow' like thick treacle with irreversible deformation.

rolling friction occurs when a wheel rolls. Energy is dissipated through the system, because of imperfect elasticity. This effect does not depend upon surfaces and is unaffected by lubrication.

shear modulus of elasticity (or **rigidity modulus of elasticity**) one of the three types of elastic modulus. The shear modulus relates to the type of deformation where planes in a solid slide past each other. The shear modulus of elasticity is the tangential force per unit area which is divided by the angular deformation of radians. See also Young's modulus and bulk modulus.

sliding friction occurs when a solid body slides on a rough surface. Its progress is hindered by an interaction of the surface of the solid with the surface it is moving on. This is called the *kinetic frictional force*. See also static friction.

static friction occurs as described in the following situation. Before an object moves, the resultant force acting on it must be zero. The frictional force acting between the object and the surface on which it rests cannot exceed its limiting value. Thus, when the other forces acting on the object, against friction, exceed this value the object is caused to accelerate. The limiting or maximum value of the frictional force occurs when the stationary object acted on by the resultant force is just about to slip. Both sliding friction and static friction involve interaction with a solid surface. The frictional forces depend on the two contacting surfaces and in particular on the presence of any surface contaminants. The friction between metal surfaces is largely due to adhesion, shearing and deformation within and around the regions of real contact. Energy is dissipated in sliding friction and appears as internal energy, which can be observed as heat. Thus car brakes heat up when used to slow a vehicle. The results of friction may be reduced by the use of lubricants between the surfaces of contact. This is one function of the oil used in car engines.

strain is a measure of the amount of deformation expressed as a fraction of the original length or volume.

stress is a quantity proportional to the force causing the deformation. (See elasticity.) Its value at any point is given by the magnitude of the force acting at that point divided by the area over which it acts. It is found that for small stresses the stress is proportional to the strain. The constant of proportionality is called the elastic modulus.

Young's modulus of elasticity one of the three types of elastic modulus. Young's modulus refers to longitudinal stress and strain. It refers to changes in the length of a material under the action of an applied force. See also shear modulus and bulk modulus.

FLUIDS AND PRESSURE

Various forces affecting solids are described on p. 195 and p. 196. Here forces, including pressure, affecting fluids are dealt with.

Fluids, although lacking definite shape, are held together by internal forces. They exert pressure on the walls of the containing vessel. Fluids – by definition – have a tendency to flow; this may be greater in some substances than in others and is governed by the viscosity of the fluid.

aneroid barometer a barometer containing no liquid (see barometer). This device is a flat cylindrical metal box that has been partially evacuated of air and then sealed.

Archimedes' principle see buoyancy force (below).

atmospheric pressure results from the 'weight' of the large volume of air that surrounds the planet Earth. As a result of this weight, air exerts a pressure on the Earth and everything upon Earth. This atmospheric pressure – which is measured in newtons per square metre – may be measured using a barometer. At sea level, it is equivalent to the weight of a column of mercury about 0·76m high, which is about $1{\cdot}01 \times 10^6$. It varies by up to about 5%, depending on the weather systems overhead.

barometer a devise used for measuring atmospheric pressure. A simple barometer comprises a thick-walled glass tube about a metre long, closed one end and filled almost to the top with mercury – it is necessary to have a vacuum at the top of the tube as atmospheric pressure is to be measured. The tube is inverted several times and a large air bubble will form; this bubble will collect any smaller bubbles as it goes up and down the tube upon each inversion. More mercury is gradually added so that the tube eventually becomes full. The open end is then covered as the tube is inserted – open end down – into mercury contained in a reservoir. When this end is opened again, the level of the mercury in the tube will fall until the vertical difference between the level of the mercury in the two containers is about 76 cm. Daily small rises and falls in the level of the mercury will chart changes in atmospheric pressure.

buoyancy force was described by the Greek mathematician and physicist Archimedes (287–212 BC). Archimedes' principle states that an object placed in a fluid is buoyed up by a force equal to the weight of fluid displaced by the body. A body with density greater than that of the fluid will sink, because the fluid it displaces weighs less than it does itself. A body with density less than that of the fluid will float. The following equation can be given:

$$\text{density} \times \text{volume} = \text{mass}.$$

A submarine varies its density by flooding ballast tanks with sea water or emptying them; this enables it to dive or rise to the surface.

density is sometimes described as the 'lightness' or 'heaviness' of a material. More precisely, density is the mass of a substance per unit of volume. In SI units density is measured in kgm^{-3}.

$$\text{Density} = \text{mass} \div \text{volume}.$$

Equal volumes of different substances clearly have very considerably different masses. The aluminium alloys that are used in the manufacture of airliners, for example, have a very different density from the steel that is used in the manufacture of a railway locomotive.

hydrostatics the study of fluids at rest.

laminar flow the steady state when adjacent layers of a fluid flow smoothly past each other.

manometer an instrument used for measuring the pressure of a gas. It is basically a U-shaped tube that contains water.

newtonian fluid see viscosity.

pascal the SI unit of pressure. It is equivalent to 1 newton per square metre Mn^{-2}.

pressure is defined as the perpendicular or normal force per unit area of a plane surface in, for example, a fluid. Its unit is the pascal (symbol Pa). At all points in the fluid at the same depth the pressure is the same. The pressure depends only upon depth in an enclosed fluid and, is independent of cross-sectional area. (In the hydraulic brakes of a car a force is applied by the foot pedal to a small piston. The pressure is transmitted via the hydraulic fluid to a larger piston connected to the brake. In this way the force applied to the brake is magnified by comparison with the force applied to the pedal.)

Reynold's number see turbulence.

turbulence the state when – if the flow velocity of a fluid is increased – the flow becomes disordered with irregular and random motions. Turbulence may also be seen in the smoke rising from a cigarette. When smoke rises from a cigarette it starts with smooth laminar flow but soon breaks into turbulent flow with the formation of eddies.

Reynold's number is used to predict the onset of turbulence. It is defined as:

$$\text{Re} = (\text{speed} \times \text{density} \times \text{dimension}) \div \text{viscosity}$$

or, alternatively, as a ratio of the inertial force to the viscous force:

$$\text{Re} = \text{inertial force} \div \text{viscous force}.$$

This is a pure ratio so has no units. It is a characteristic of the system and the dimension may be the diameter of a pipe or the radius of a ballbearing. Viscosity is relevant for small values of Reynold's number. Above certain values turbulence is likely to break out. Thus, for the fall of a very small raindrop, resistance is viscous and is proportional to the product of the viscosity of air, the radius of the raindrop and its speed. For a large raindrop, the resistance is proportional to the density of air, the square of the radius of the raindrop and the square of its speed. Sometimes when special smooth surfaces are involved the onset of turbulence is delayed.

viscosity a measure of the resistance to flow that a fluid offers when it is subjected to shear stress (see p. 196). Viscosity relates to the internal friction in the flow of a fluid – how adjacent layers in the fluid exert retarding forces on each other. This arises from cohesion of the molecules in the fluid. In a solid, deformation of adjacent layers is usually elastic. In a fluid, however, there is no permanent resistance to change of shape; the layers can slide past each other, with continuous displacement of these layers. Fluids are described as newtonian if they obey Newton's law that the ratio of the applied rate of shearing has a constant value.

THERMODYNAMICS

Thermodynamics is the study of heat and temperature.

absolute zero see thermodynamic temperature scale.

calorie a former unit of internal energy (see below and kelvin).

A calorie is equivalent to 4·2 joules and is defined as the heat required to raise the temperature of 1 gram of water from 14·5 °C (58·1 °F) to 15·5 °C (58·9 °F). (The unit used by nutritionists is actually the kilocalorie – which is commonly written Calorie but is equal to 1000 calories.)

Carnot engine see second law of thermodynamics.

closed system a system in which no external forces are experienced.

conservation of energy a fundamental principle of thermodynamics that states that the total magnitude of a certain physical property of a system – its mass, its charge or its energy – will remain unchanged even though there may be exchanges of that property between the various components of that system. This may be more simply expressed that energy is neither created nor destroyed.

This theory was developed in the late 19th century by about a dozen scientists including James Joule and Baron Herman von Helmholtz. Although there seemed to be plenty of evidence that energy was not conserved, this important principle was eventually established.

Much of the energy that seems to be lost in typical interactions – such as a box sliding across a floor – is converted into internal energy; in the case of the sliding box, this the kinetic energy (see below) gained by the atoms and molecules within the box and the floor as they interact and are pulled from their equilibrium position. This 'hidden energy' is thermal energy. Strictly speaking, heat is transferred between two bodies as a result of a change in temperature, although the term 'heat' is commonly used for the thermal energy as well.

Processes that turn kinetic energy into thermal energy include viscosity and friction. In a steam engine heat is turned into work.

energy is the capacity of a body to do work.

The total energy stored in a closed system (see above) remains constant, however it may be transformed. This is the principle of conservation of energy (see above). It may take the form of mechanical energy (kinetic or potential), electrical energy, chemical energy, or heat energy.

There are other forms of energy including gravitational energy, magnetic energy, the energy of electromagnetic radiation, and the energy of matter.

first law of thermodynamics states that if, during an interaction, a quantity of heat is absorbed by a body, it is equal to the sum of the increase in internal energy of the body and any external work done by the body.

This law is a development of the law of conservation of energy.

The increase in internal energy will be made up of an increase in the kinetic energy of the molecules in the body and an increase in their potential energy, since work will have to be done against intermolecular forces as the body expands.

The change in internal energy of a body thus depends only on its initial and final states. The change may be the result of an increase in energy in any form – thermal, mechanical, gravitational, etc. Another statement of this law is that is possible to convert work totally into heat.

flow of heat a transfer of energy resulting from differences in temperature.

heat a form of energy; the term 'heat' is commonly used for thermal energy as well.

internal energy the molecular energy (kinetic and potential) within a body. When this energy is transferred from a place of high energy to one of lower energy, it is described as a flow of heat.

If two bodies of different temperatures are placed in thermal contact with each other, after a time they are found both to be at the same temperature. Energy is transferred from the warmer to the colder body, until both are at a new equilibrium temperature.

joule (J) the SI unit of work or internal energy. A joule is defined as the work done on a body when it is displaced 1 metre as the result of the action of a force of 1 newton acting in the direction of motion. This is given by the following equation: 1J = 1Nm.

Units of internal energy used previously include the calorie, see above.

kelvin (K) the SI unit of thermodynamic temperature equal to the fraction

$$\frac{1}{273 \cdot 15}$$

of the thermodynamic temperature of the triple point of water. The kelvin is named after the Scottish physicist William Thompson, later Lord Kelvin, who did important work in thermodynamics and electricity.

kelvin scale see thermodynamic temperature scale.

kinetic energy the organized energy of a moving body. The kinetic energy of a body is the energy that it has because it is moving. It is equal to half the product of the mass and the square of the velocity.

laws of thermodynamics see first law of thermodynamics and second law of thermodynamics.

potential energy acts as a store of energy. It can be converted into kinetic energy or it can be used to do work. In contrast to kinetic energy, which is dependent upon velocity, potential energy is dependent upon position.

The gravitational potential energy of a body of mass m at height h above the ground is mgh, where g is the acceleration due to gravity. This gravitational potential energy is equal to the work that the Earth's gravitational field will do on the body as it moves to ground level.

If a body moves upward against the gravitational force, work is done on it and there is an increase in gravitational potential energy.

second law of thermodynamics states the converse to the situation described above under the entry for the first law of thermodynamics. There are several ways in

GASES

Three important laws – Boyle's law, Charles' law and the pressure law – relate to the behaviour of gases.

The relation between volume and pressure at a constant temperature is expressed in Boyle's law.

The relation between volume and temperature at a constant pressure is expressed in Charles' law.

The relation between pressure and temperature at a constant volume is expressed in the pressure law.

The three quantities of a gas – volume, temperature and pressure – are thus related and can be further related in the equations of the ideal or universal gas law.

Boyle's law states that the volume of a fixed mass of gas is inversely proportional to the pressure, provided the temperature remains constant. Thus, the pressure multiplied by the volume is constant. This may be given as:

$$pV = \text{constant.}$$

Charles' law states that the volume of a fixed mass of gas is directly proportional to its absolute temperature, provided the pressure remains constant. Thus, the volume divided by the absolute temperature is a constant. This may be give as:

$$V \div T = \text{constant.}$$

ideal gas is one that would obey the ideal gas law perfectly. In fact, no gas is ideal but most behave sufficiently closely that the ideal gas law can be used in calculation providing the pressures are low and temperatures well above those at which they liquefy. At ordinary temperatures, dry air can be considered as a very good approximation to an ideal gas.

ideal gas law combines the equations derived from Boyle's law, Charles' law and the pressure law. The more general equation may be given – for a fixed mass of gas – as:

$$\frac{pV}{T} = \text{constant} \quad \text{or} \quad \frac{p_1V_1}{T_1} = \frac{p_2V_2}{T_2}$$

where
P = pressure of the gas,
T = temperature of the gas on the Kelvin scale, and
V = volume the gas occupies.
If one mole of gas is used the equation is given as:

$$PV = RT$$

where R= the universal gas constant.

internal energy (of a gas) see kinetic theory of gases.

kinetic the result of movement.

kinetic theory of gases takes Newton's laws and applies them to a group of molecules. It treats a gas as if it were made up of extremely small – dimensionless – particles, all in constant random motion. It is based on an ideal gas.

One conclusion is that the pressure and the volume of that gas are related to the average kinetic energy for each molecule. The kinetic theory explains that pressure in a gas is due to the impact and elastic rebound of the molecules on the containing walls around the gas. The equation that relates the pressure, temperature and volume of an ideal gas is given above.

The temperature of an ideal gas is a measure of the average molecular kinetic energies. At a higher temperature the mean speed of the molecules is increased. For air at room temperature and atmospheric pressure the mean speed is about 500ms^{-1} (about 1800 km/h or 1100 mph, the velocity of a bullet).

The internal energy of a gas is associated with the motion of its molecules and their potential energy. For a gas that is more complex than one with monatomic molecules, account has to be taken of the energies associated with the rotation and vibration of its molecules as well as their speed.

pressure law (of gas) states that the pressure of a fixed mass of gas is directly proportional to its absolute temperature provided its volume remains constant. Thus, the pressure divided by the temperature is a constant. This may be given as:

$$P \div T = \text{constant.}$$

universal gas law see ideal gas law.

---

which the second law may be stated but, essentially, it means that heat cannot itself flow from a cold object to a hot object. Thus the law shows that certain processes may only operate in one direction. It implies heat cannot be completely converted into work.

The second law was established after work by a French engineer Sadi Carnot, who was trying to build the most efficient engine. His ideal engine – the Carnot engine – established an upper limit for the efficiency with which thermal energy could be converted into mechanical energy. Real engines fall short of this ideal efficiency because of losses due to friction and heat conduction. As the temperature of the sink in a working engine is near room temperature, the amount of work that can be done is restricted by the relatively small temperature difference. This limits the efficiency of most steam engines to about 30–40%. Thus it makes sense to use the vast amounts of waste heat from electrical power stations for heating purposes rather than allow it to be lost in cooling towers.

sink (of an engine) the place where energy is removed from the system.

temperature (of a substance) a measure of its internal energy or 'hotness' of a body, *not* the heat of the body. Thermometers are used to measure temperature. They may be based on the change in volume of a liquid (as in a mercury thermometer), the change in length of a strip of metal (as used in many thermometers), or the change in electrical resistance of a conductor. Other parameters may also be involved in measuring temperature.

thermal energy disorganized energy due to the motion of atoms and molecules.

thermodynamic temperature scale (or **kelvin scale** or **ideal gas scale**) is based on the kelvin. The thermodynamic temperature scale is used in both practical and theoretical physics. On the thermodynamic temperature or kelvin scale the freezing point of water is 273·15K (0 °C or 32 °F) and its boiling point is 373·15K (100 °C or 212 °F): thus one degree kelvin is equal in magnitude to one degree in the Celsius scale. The temperature of 0 (zero) K is known as absolute zero. At this temperature, for an ideal gas, the volume would be infinitely large and the molecular kinetic energy zero.

triple point the temperature at which the vapour, liquid and solid phases of a substance are at equilibrium.

work (done on a body by a constant force) is defined as the product of the magnitude of the force and the consequent displacement of the body in the direction of the force. (When a force acts on a body, causing acceleration in the direction of the force, work is done.) The unit of work is the joule, sometimes referred to as the newton metre.

SPECIFIC HEAT AND LATENT HEAT

Heat is a form of energy (see Thermodynamics; pp. 198–99). Like any other form of energy, heat is measured in joules.

conduction (of heat) occurs when kinetic and molecular energy is passed from one molecule to another. Metals are good conductors of heat because of electrons that transport energy through the material. Air is a poor conductor in comparison.

convection (of heat) results from the motion of the heated substance. Warm air is less dense than cold air and so, according to Archimedes' principle, it rises. Convection is the main mechanism for mixing the atmosphere and diluting pollutants emitted into the air.

fusion (in physics) melting. In the same way that latent heat is taken in when water changes to steam at the same temperature, so the same thing happens when ice melts to form water.

The specific latent heat of fusion of a substance is the quantity of heat that is required to convert unit mass of that substance from a solid state into a liquid state without a change of temperature. The value of specific latent heat of fusion for water ice at 0 °C is $3{\cdot}34 \times 10^5$J/kg.

Thus if *m* kilograms of a particular substance, whose specific heat is *L*, undergo a phase change from one state to another without any change in temperature, then the heat that is either absorbed or given out (depending upon the nature of the phase change) will be *mL* joules. Thus

energy change = *mL* joules.

joule (symbol J) the SI unit of work and energy equal to the work done when the point of application of a force of one newton moves – in the direction of the force – a distance of one metre. 1 joule = 0·2388 calorie.

latent heat literally means 'hidden' or 'concealed' heat.

When heat flows between a body and its surroundings there is usually a change in the temperature of the body, as well as changes in internal energies. This is not so when a change of state occurs, as from solid to liquid or from liquid to gas (a phase change). Such a change involves a change in the internal energy of the body only.

The amount of heat needed to make the change of phase is called the hidden heat or latent heat. To change water at 100 °C (212 °F) to water vapour requires nearly seven times as much heat (latent heat of vaporization) as to change ice to water (latent heat of fusion; see fusion below). This varies for water at different temperatures – more heat is required to change it to water vapour at 80 °C (176 °F), less at 110 °C (230 °F). In each case the attractive forces binding the water molecules together must be loosened or broken.

phase change a change of form or state, for example from solid to liquid or from liquid to gas. A phase change involves a change only in the internal energy of the body.

radiation (of heat) is the third process of heat transfer.

All bodies radiate energy in the form of electromagnetic waves. This radiation may pass across a vacuum, and thus the Earth receives energy radiated from the Sun. A body remains at a constant temperature when it both radiates and receives energy at the same rate.

specific heat heat expressed per unit mass. The specific heat capacity of a substance may be defined as the quantity of heat that is required to raise the temperature of one kilogram of that substance by 1 K. It is thus expressed in units of joules per kilogram per kelvin.

If equal masses of two substances – water and oil – were to be heated in separate containers for the same period of time and in identical conditions, the temperature of one of those substances – water – would rise more rapidly than the other substance – oil. These two substances thus have different specific heat capacities.

If *m* kilograms of a substance, of specific heat capacity *c*, are raised in temperature (*T*) by K, then the heat required would be *mc T* joules.

Heat required = *mc T* joules.

Water requires 4200 joules of heat to raise the temperature of one kilogram by 1 K. The specific heat capacity of water is thus 4200 J/kg K. (This is considerably higher than the figure for many other substances. Thus a much greater amount of energy is needed to raise the temperature of water by a particular amount than would be required to raise the same mass of certain other substances to the same temperature. For this reason, water is very suitable substance to be used in radiators.)

The temperature of a substance can be raised by supplying energy to the substance. This can be done in a number of ways: by obtaining the energy from another hot body; by supplying energy by means of an electric current; by allowing the object to fall by the necessary amount (this supplies mechanical energy).

When two substances at different temperatures are mixed – and then come to a common temperature – the heat that is lost by cooling in one substance will be equal to the heat that is gained by the other substance.

The specific heat of the block may be worked out according to the following equation:

energy supplied = heat gained by the block

$$VIt = mc\,(\theta_2 - \theta_1)$$

where V is the potential difference, I is the electric current, *t* is the time in seconds, *m* is the mass, *c* is the specific heat capacity, and $\theta_2 - \theta_1$ is the temperature rise K. (θ_1 is the first temperature taken of the block; θ_2 is the final temperature of the block.)

vaporization the conversion of water, or any solution, to a vapour state.

If water is heated it begins to boil at 100 °C (212 °F) at atmospheric pressure. Once the water reaches boiling point its temperature will remain at 100 °C even if heating continues. In heating, the water steadily absorbs energy but the temperature does not rise further. The energy is used instead to convert the water from its liquid state into the vapour state. This involves 'freeing' the molecules from the influence of other molecules and thus allowing them to move more independently. This energy is latent heat.

The specific latent heat of vaporization of a substance is the quantity of heat required to change unit mass of the substance from the liquid state into the vapour state without additional change in temperature. Its value for water is at 100 °C is $2{\cdot}26 \times 10^6$J/kg.

QUANTUM THEORY AND RELATIVITY

Three of the most important theories of the 20th century are the quantum theory and the theories of special and general relativity.

dual nature of light (theory of) states that light behaves as a wave during interference experiments but as a stream of particles during the photoelectric effect.

general relativity theory is an extension of special relativity to include gravitational fields and accelerating reference frames. Space-time, mass and gravity are interdependent. The concept of curved space-time was proposed by Einstein in his general theory of relativity. The motion of astronomical bodies is controlled by this curvature of space and time close to large masses.

particles (behaviour of) cannot be described by the theories of classical physics, since there is no equivalence to subatomic particles in everyday mechanics. Thus it is not helpful to discuss the behaviour of electrons in atoms in terms of tiny 'planets' orbiting a 'sun'. The French physicist de Broglie (1892–1987) suggested that if light waves can behave like particles, then particles might in certain circumstances behave like waves. Later experiments confirmed that under appropriate conditions particles can exhibit wave phenomena. The de Broglie equation is given as:

$$\lambda = \frac{h}{p}$$

where
λ is the wavelength of the particle of momentum p,
h is a constant called Planck's constant (value $6{\cdot}626 \times 10^{-34}$Js).

photoelectric effect the effect when – if light (usually visible or ultraviolet) is directed onto a piece of metal in a vacuum – electrons are knocked from the surface of the metal. For light of a given wavelength, the number of electrons emitted per second increases with the intensity of the light, although the energies of the electrons are independent of the intensity. Increasing the frequency of the incident radiation increases the energies of the emitted electrons, providing the frequency is above a certain 'threshold frequency' that depends on the metal. The discovery of the photoelectric effect led Einstein to deduce that the energy in a light beam exists in small discrete packets called photons or quanta.

photons the name given to light quanta, or 'packets' of energy. They have both particle and wave behaviour. Photons can be detected in experiments in which light is allowed to fall on a detector, usually photographic film. This has led to the theory of the dual nature of light.

quantum (plur. **quanta**) a separate packet of electromagnetic energy. The energy E of a quantum is given by: $E = hf$ where h is Planck's constant (see particles, above), f is the frequency of radiation.

quantum mechanics is the study of the observable behaviour of particles. This includes electromagnetic radiation in all its details (see pp. 212–13). In particular, it is the only appropriate theory for describing the effects that occur on an atomic scale. Quantum mechanics deals exclusively with what can be observed, and does not attempt to describe what is happening in between measurements. This is not true of classical theories, which are essentially complete descriptions of what is occurring whether or not attempts are made to measure it. In quantum mechanics the experimenter is directly included within the theory. Quantum mechanics predicts all the possible results of making a measurement, but it does not say which one will occur when an experiment is actually carried out. All that can be known is the probability of something being seen.

quantum theory states that nothing can be measured or observed without disturbing it: the observer can affect the outcome of the effect of being measured. Quantum theory is the only correct description of effects on an atomic scale, and special relativity must be used when speeds approaching the speed of light, with respect to the observer, is involved.

special relativity theory was proposed by Einstein in 1905. Einstein stated that all inertial frames are equally good for carrying out experiments. This assumption, coupled with the evidence that the speed of light is the same in all frames, led Einstein to develop this theory which has been extensively tested using particles accelerators, where electrons or protons travel at speeds within a fraction of 1% of the speed of light. The masses of such particles measured by an observer in the laboratory in which particles are travelling are higher than the masses measured by an observer at rest with respect to the particles.

The classical view of time is that if two events take place simultaneously with reference to one frame then they must also occur simultaneously within another frame. In terms of special relativity, however, two events that occur simultaneously in one frame may not be seen as simultaneous in another frame moving relative to the first. The sequence of cause and effect in related events is not, however, affected. Also, in special relativity each observer has an individual time scale. In special relativity time and space have to be considered as unified and not as two separate things. This means that time is related to the frame of reference in which it is being measured. The equations of special relativity lead to the very simple prediction that the length of a moving body in the direction of its motion measured in another frame is reduced by a factor dependent on its velocity with respect to the observer.

uncertainty principle (or **Heisenberg uncertainty principle** or **principle of indeterminism**) states that it is not possible to know with unlimited accuracy both the position and the momentum of a particle. The German physicist Heisenberg interpreted wave-particle duality differently to Einstein. He proposed that when a beam of light is directed at a screen with two slits, the interference pattern formed exists only if we do not know which slit the photon passed through. If we make an additional measurement and determine which slit was traversed, we destroy the interference pattern. Heisenberg showed that it is impossible to measure position and momentum simultaneously with infinite accuracy; he expressed his findings in the uncertainty principle named after him. This changed the thinking about the precision with which simultaneous measurement of two physical quantities can be made.

WAVE TYPES

Water waves are phenomena that can be seen, and the effects of sound waves are sensed directly by the ear. Some of the waves in the electromagnetic spectrum can also be sensed by the body: light waves by the eye, and the heating effect of infrared waves. However, other electromagnetic waves cannot be experienced directly through any of the human senses, and even infrared can generally only be observed using specialized detectors.

Wave phenomena are found in all areas of physics, and similar mathematical equations may be used in each application. Some of the general principles of wave types are explored here.

amplitude the maximum displacement from the equilibrium position.

angle of incidence see reflection.

angle of reflection see reflection.

angle of refraction see refraction.

beat frequency see interference.

constructive interference see interference.

destructive interference see interference.

frequency (symbol f) the rate of repetition of a regular event. The frequency of wave motion is defined as the number of complete oscillations or cycles per second; see diagram. The unit of frequency is the hertz (Hz).

hertz (symbol Hz) the SI unit of frequency. It is equivalent to one cycle per second. The hertz is named after the German physicist Heinrich Hertz (1857–94).

interference the phenomenon that occurs when two or more waves combine together in the manner described in the superposition principle (see below). If the resultant wave amplitude is greater than that of the individual waves then constructive interference is taking place.

If the resultant wave is smaller, then destructive interference is taking place. If two sound waves of slightly different frequencies and similar amplitudes are played together (for example two tuning forks), then the resulting sound has varying amplitude. The varying amplitudes are called beats and their frequency is the beat frequency. This frequency is equal to the difference between the frequencies of the two original notes. (Listening for beats is an aid to tuning musical instruments; the fewer the beats, the more nearly in tune is the instrument.)

longitudinal waves periodic oscillations in which the vibrations are parallel to the direction of travel; see diagram.

mechanical waves travelling waves that propagate through a material – as, for example, happens when a metal rod is tapped at one end with a hammer. An initial disturbance at a particular place in a material will cause a force to be exerted on adjacent parts of the material.

An elastic force then acts to restore the material to its equilibrium position. In doing so, it compresses the adjacent particles and so the disturbance moves outward from the source. In attempting to return to their original positions, the particles overshoot, so that at a particular point a rarefaction follows a compression (or squeezing). The passage of the wave is observed as variations in the pressure about the equilibrium position or by the speed of oscillations. The change is described as oscillatory (like a pendulum) or periodic.

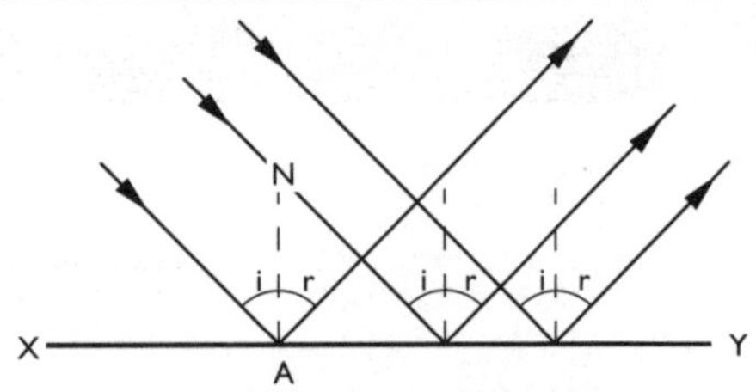

Reflection of plane waves at a plane surface. The waves are parallel as they approach XY and after they are reflected. AN is the normal to XY at A. i is the angle of incidence of the wave as it meets XY. The angle of reflection is r, and $i = r$.

Wave motions transfer energy – for example, sound waves, seismic waves and water waves transfer mechanical energy. However, energy is lost as the wave passes through a medium. The amplitude (see diagram) diminishes and the wave is said to be attenuated.

There are two distinct processes – spreading and absorption. In many cases there is little or no absorption – electromagnetic radiation from the Sun travels through space without any absorption at all, but planets that are more distant than the Earth receive less radiation because it is spreading over a larger area and so the intensity (the ratio of power to area) decreases according to an inverse-square law.

The same applies to sound in the atmosphere. In some cases, however, energy is absorbed in a medium as, for example, when light enters and exposes a photographic film or when X-rays enter flesh.

oscillatory change see mechanical waves.

period (symbol T) the time taken for the wave to undergo one complete oscillation or cycle; also the time taken for the wave to travel one wavelength. See diagram.

periodic oscillation a travelling wave propagates by periodic oscillations either perpendicular or parallel to the direction of travel. There are two main types of periodic oscillation – longitudinal waves and transverse waves (see above and below). (See also mechanical waves.)

phase speed (of a wave) see speed of propagation.

rarefaction a stretching.

reflection of waves is the return of part or all of the waves when they encounter the boundary between two materials or media. Reflection and refraction of waves are two different and distinct phenomena.

In the reflection of plane waves at a plane surface the angle between the direction of the wavefront and the normal – i.e. a line perpendicular to the plane surface – is the angle of incidence (i). The angle between the reflected wave and the normal to the plane surface is the angle of reflection (r), and these angles i and r are equal.

AMPLITUDE

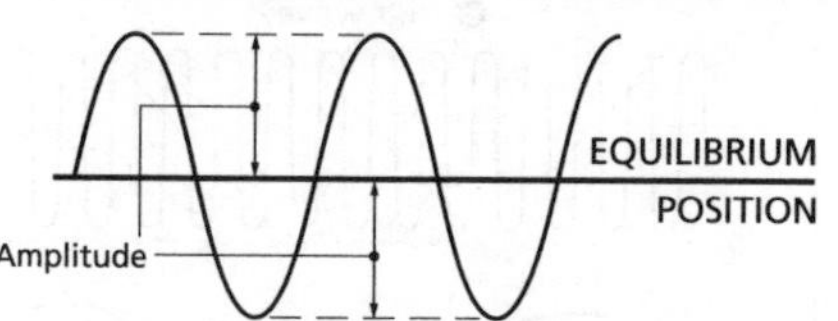

Amplitude is the maximum displacement from the equilibrium position.

PERIOD

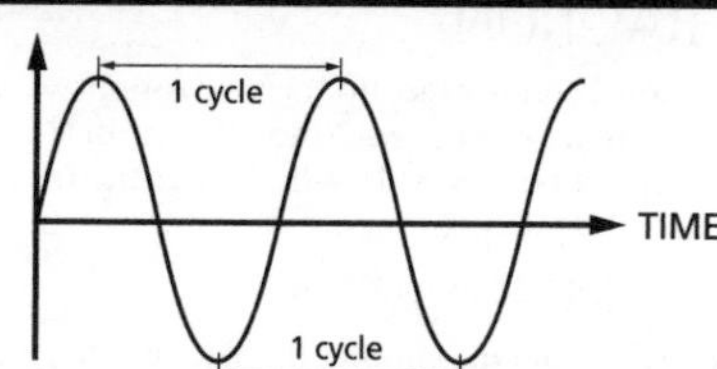

Frequency. Frequency = cycles per second
1 cycle per second = 1 hertz (Hz).

WAVE ATTENUATION

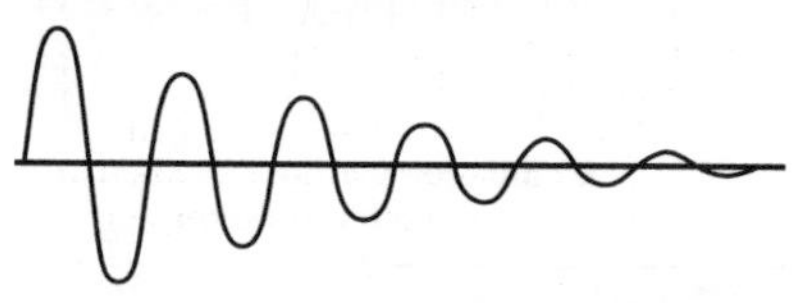

Wave attenuation. Energy is lost as a wave travels through a medium - the amplitude is reduced, and the wave is said to be attenuated.

WAVELENGTH

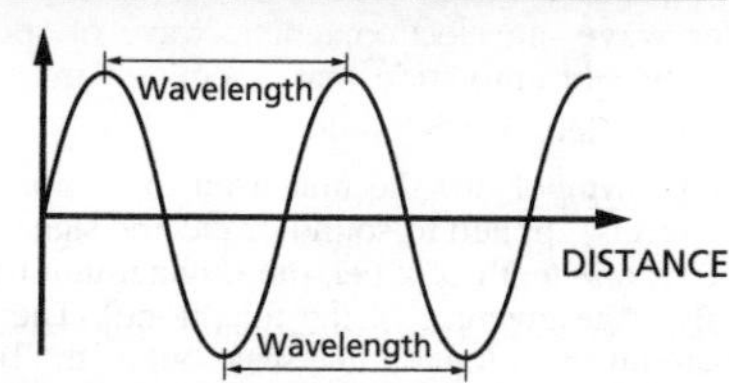

Wavelength. Wavelength is the distance between two successive points along a wave with similar amplitudes.

LONGITUDINAL WAVE

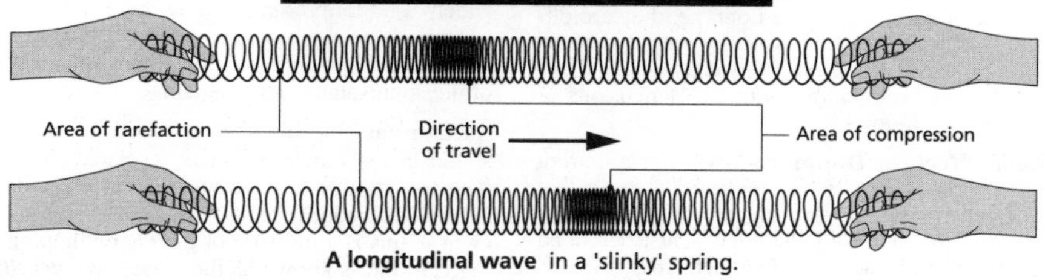

A longitudinal wave in a 'slinky' spring.

refraction of waves is the change of direction of a wavefront as it passes obliquely from one medium to another in which its speed is altered. Reflection and refraction of waves are two different and distinct phenomena.

If a wave travels from one medium to another, the direction of propagation is changed or 'bent'; the wave is said to be refracted. The wave will travel in the first medium (medium 1) with velocity v_1, and come upon the surface of the second medium (medium 2) with angle of incidence *i*. Then the wave will be refracted, and *r* is the angle of refraction. The velocity will be v_2, which will be less than v_1 if medium 2 is more dense than medium 1, but greater than v_2 if medium 2 is less dense. The velocities are related by:

$$\frac{v_1}{v_2} = \frac{\sin i}{\sin r}$$

and the ratio of sin i/sin r is a constant. This constant is the refractive index of medium 2 with respect to medium 1. This relationship was formulated by the Dutch astronomer Willebrord Snell (1591–1626) and is known as Snell's Law.

refractive index see refraction.

Snell's Law see refraction.

speed of propagation (of the compressions of waves) or **phase speed** (of a wave) (symbol v) is equal to the product of the frequency and the wavelength.

sound waves see acoustics (p. 204).

superposition principle the state when several waves are travelling through a medium. The resultant at any point and time is the vector sum of the amplitudes of the individual waves. See also interference.

transverse waves periodic oscillations in which the vibrations are perpendicular to the direction of travel; see diagram.

travelling wave a disturbance that moves or propagates from one point to another.

varying amplitude see interference.

wavelength (symbol λ) the distance between two successive peaks or troughs in the wave (or two successive compressions or rarefactions); see diagram.

water waves vibrations produced in water by the wind or some other disturbance. The particles move in vertical circles so there are both transverse and longitudinal displacements. The motion causes the familiar wave profile with narrow peaks and broad troughs. Water waves transfer mechanical energy.

wave attenuation occurs when energy is lost as a wave travels through a medium – the amplitude is reduced and the wave is said to be attenuated. See diagram.

ACOUSTICS, MODULATION, STANDING WAVES AND DIFFRACTION

The range of frequencies for which sound waves are audible to humans is from 20 to 20,000 Hz (i.e. vibrations or cycles per second) – the higher the frequency, the higher the pitch.

AM see amplitude modulation.

amplitude the maximum displacement from the equilibrium position.

amplitude modulation or **AM** the most widely used form of modulating radio waves. The amplitude of the radio carrier wave is made to vary with the amplitude of the sound signal.

carrier wave an electromagnetic wave of specified frequency and amplitude that is emitted by a radio transmitter.

decibel (symbol db) the unit used to compare two power levels, applied to sound or electric signals. The decibel is one tenth of a bel, the original unit (named after Bell, the inventor of the telephone). The bel is graduated using a logarithmic scale but as the bel is a rather large unit, the decibel is more normally used.

diffraction the bending or spreading of waves when they pass through a slit or aperture or round the edge of a structure. Waves will usually proceed in a straight line through a uniform medium. However, when they pass though a slit with width comparable to their wavelength, they spread out, i.e. they are diffracted. Thus waves are able to bend round corners. For a sound wave of 256 Hz the wavelength is about 1·3m (4 ft 3 in), comparable with the dimensions of open doors or windows.

Doppler effect (or **Doppler shift**) the apparent change in the observed frequency of a wave that results from motion between the source of the wave and the observer. The Doppler effect – first described by the Austrian physicist C.J. Doppler (1803–53) – is valid for all waves. It is more often noticed in acoustics and is particularly noticeable in the sirens used for emergency-service vehicles. The intensity and pitch of the siren seems to rise as the vehicle is approaching, then diminishes as it moves away. This is explained by the fact that, as an observer moves towards a sound source, the pressure oscillations are encountered more frequently than if the observer were stationary. Thus the source seems to be emitting at a higher frequency. Conversely, if the observer is moving away from the source, the frequency seems to decrease. It also applies if the source is moving and the observer is stationary.

The Doppler effect is also observed in optics.

echo is produced by the reflection of sound. Sound is reflected off a hard surface such as a high wall of the sides of a ravine.

FM see frequency modulation.

frequency (symbol f) the rate of repetition of a regular event. The number of waves or vibrations per second is expressed in hertz (Hz), cycles per second. Frequencies that are lower than the human audible range are referred to as infrasonic and those above as ultrasonic. Many mammals such as dolphins and bats have sensitive hearing in the ultrasonic range and they use high-pitched squeaks for echolocation. Large animals such as whales and elephants use frequencies in the infrasonic range to communicate over long distances. It is thought that migrating birds can use infrasonic sounds produced by various natural features.

FREQUENCY MODULATION (FM)

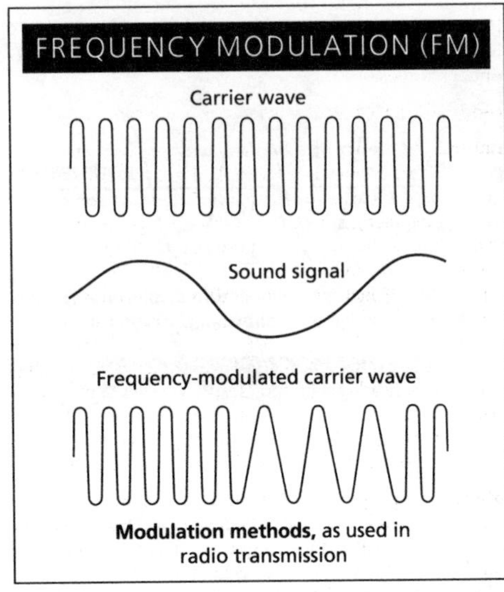

Modulation methods, as used in radio transmission

frequency modulation or **FM** the second and less widely used form of modulating radio waves. The frequency of the carrier wave is made to vary so that the variations are in step with the changes in amplitude of the sound signal; see diagram.

human ear the organ of the body that perceives sound in the human being is an extremely sensitive detector. Its threshold of hearing corresponds to an intensity of sound of 10^{-12} watts per square metre (Wm^{-2}): this is a measure of the energy impinging on the ear, and is known as the *threshold intensity.* The range is enormous, so a logarithmic scale, to the base 10, is used.

The ear canal resonates slightly to sounds with frequencies of about 3200 Hz. The human ear is most sensitive in the range 2500–4000 Hz. The response of the ear is not linear, i.e. there is no direct relationship with the intensity of the sound it detects. Sensitivity is related to frequency: it decreases strongly at the lowest audible frequencies, but less so at the highest. The audible range of the normal human ear varies with age – the upper limit is about 20,000 Hz in the mid-teens, but more likely to be 12,000–14,000 Hz for someone 40 years old.

Huygens' principle (also known as **Huygens' construction**) a law proposed in 1676 by the Dutch physicist Christiaan Huygens (1629–95) to explain the laws of reflection and refraction (see pp. 202–03). He postulated that light was a wave motion. Each point on a wavefront becomes a new or secondary source. The new wavefront is the surface that touches all the wavefronts from the secondary sources. Diffraction describes the interference effects observed between light derived from a continuous portion of a wavefront, such as that at a narrow slit; see diffraction (above). The work of the British physicist and physician Thomas

Young (1773–1829) and others eventually supported Huygens' theory, which states that every point on a wavefront may itself be regarded as a source of secondary waves.

modulation see radio waves.

natural frequency the frequency of free oscillation in a system. If a periodic force is applied to a system with frequency at or near to the natural frequency of the system, then the resulting amplitude of vibration is much greater than for other frequencies. These natural frequencies are called resonant frequencies. When a driving frequency equals the resonant frequency then maximum amplitude is obtained. (The natural frequency of objects can be used destructively. High winds can cause suspension bridges to reach their natural frequency and vibrate, sometimes resulting in the destruction of the bridge. Soldiers marching in formation need to break step when crossing bridges in case they achieve the natural frequency of the structure and cause it to disintegrate.)

pitch the property of a sound that characterizes its highness or its lowness to a hearer. It is related to – but it is not identical with – frequency. Pitch is closely related to frequency. In music (see tones), if frequency of vibration is doubled the pitch rises by one octave. In general, the higher the frequency the higher the pitch.

radio waves can be used to carry sound waves by superimposing the pattern of the sound wave onto the radio waves. This is called *modulation* and is one of the basic forms of radio transmission. There are two forms of modulating radio waves – amplitude modulation and frequency modulation.

refraction of sound the change of direction by a wavefront as it passes obliquely from one medium to another in which its speed its altered.

At night the air near the ground is often colder than the air which is higher up, as the Earth cools after sunset. Thus a sound wave moving upwards will be slowly bent back towards the horizontal as it meets warmer layers of air. Eventually it will be reflected back downwards. Under these circumstances sound can be heard over long distances. This phenomenon is explained by Snell's law of refraction (see p. 203); layers of air at different temperatures act as different media through which sound travels at different velocities. (During World War I the guns at the front line in northern France could sometimes be heard in southern England, although not in the intervening area.)

AMPLITUDE MODULATION (AM)

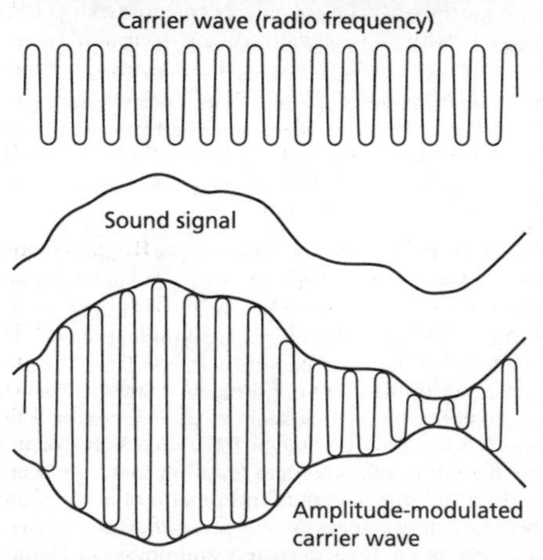

sonic booms a loud bang and large pressure variations caused by a supersonic plane. If the velocity of the source of the sound wave is greater than the velocity of sound – $300ms^{-1}$ (1080 km/h or 670 mph) in the upper troposphere (up to 10 km/6 mi above the Earth's surface) – then the wavefront produced is not spherical but conical. Different wave crests bunch together, forming a shock wave. A supersonic plane (travelling faster than the speed of sound) produces such a shockfront, causing the characteristic double loud bang.

sound waves are longitudinal compressions (squeezings) and rarefactions (stretchings) of the medium through which they are travelling, and are produced by a vibrating object. If a sound wave is travelling in any medium then the pressure variations formed along its path cause strains as a result of the applied stresses.

standing waves (or **stationary waves**) are the result of confining waves in a specific region. When a travelling wave, such as a wave propagating along a guitar string towards the bridge, reaches the support, the string must be almost at rest. A force is exerted on the support that then reacts by setting up a reflected wave travelling back along the string. This wave has the same frequency and wavelength as the source wave. At certain frequencies the two waves, travelling in opposite directions, interfere to produce a stationary- or standing-wave pattern. Each pattern or mode of vibration corresponds to a particular frequency. The standing wave may be transverse, as on a plucked violin string, or longitudinal, as in the air in an organ pipe. The positions of maximum and minimum amplitude are called *antinodes* and *nodes* respectively.

tones (characteristics of notes played by musical instruments) include loudness, pitch and timbre or tone quality. (The concept of loudness is not dependent just on the energy reaching the ear, but also on frequency.) Sounds created by musical instruments are not simple waveforms, but are the result of several waves combining. This complexity results in the tone quality, or timbre, of a note played by a particular stringed musical instrument. Even a 'pure' note may contain many waves of different frequencies.

These frequencies are harmonics or multiples of the fundamental or lowest frequency, which has 2 nodes and 1 antinode, and is called the first harmonic. The second harmonic has 3 nodes and 2 antinodes. The wavelength is one third of the original wavelength, and the frequency has tripled. Different instruments emphasize different harmonics.

velocity of sound is given by the square root of the appropriate elastic modulus (see p. 196) divided by the density. The velocity of sound – as with other types of wave – differs in different media. In still air at 0 °C, the velocity of sound is about $331ms^{-1}$ (1191·6 km/h, or 740 mph). If the air temperature rises by 1 °C, then the velocity of sound increases by about $0{\cdot}6ms^{-1}$. The velocity of sound in a metal such as steel is about $5060ms^{-1}$.

OPTICS

Optics is the branch of physics that deals with high-frequency electromagnetic waves that we call light. Optics is concerned with the way in which light propagates from sources to detectors via intermediate lenses, mirrors and other modifying elements. The electromagnetic spectrum includes a wide range of waves in addition to light. The region with wavelengths from 700 nanometres in the red region to 400 nm in the violet is extended for practical optical systems into the ultraviolet and the mid-infrared regions.

A beam of light may be considered to be made up of many rays, all travelling outwards from the source. This approach is used in ray diagrams. The wavelength and amplitude of light are very short compared to the other dimensions of the system. The basic concept is a very simple one: light travels in straight lines unless it is refracted by a lens or a prism. A point source of light emits rays in all directions. Light is reflected and refracted (i.e. bent) in the same way as other waves.

angle of incidence the angle between an incoming beam of light and a line at 90° to the surface of the medium which that beam is coming into contact with.

deviation (of light) the turning away from the normal, or perpendicular, of light when it travels from a medium to a less dense medium.

dispersion the effect of a prism on light whereby white light is separated into its component colours. This effect has been known for centuries. Newton used dispersion to produce and study the spectrum of sunlight.

fibre optics the use of flexible glass fibres with which light can be transmitted over great distances. (See Digital Communications, pp. 316–19.)

focal length (of lens) the distance between the optical centre of the lens and the principal focus. The focal length is usually designated as *f*.

hologram a 'three-dimensional' or stereoscopic image formed by beams of light. Holography differs from conventional photography in that both the amplitude of the light and its phase are recorded on the film. It has many scientific uses as well as the more familiar display holograms that are, for instance, being used on credit cards.

incident ray an incoming ray of light.

intensity (in light) the ratio of power to area.

interference the interaction of two or more wave motions.

laser a term derived from the technical name for the process Light Amplification by Stimulated Emission of Radiation. When an amplifying material, such as a gas, crystal or liquid, is placed between appropriate mirrors, photons from a light beam repeatedly pass through it stimulating more photons and thus increasing their number with each pass. The additional photons all have the same frequency, phase and direction. One of the mirrors is made so that a small amount of light passes through it; this is the external laser beam, which can be continuous or pulsed. This beam can be focused onto very small areas and the intensity can be very great, enabling some lasers to burn through thick metal plates. Lasers have a wide variety of applications, for example in surveying, communications and eye surgery.

lens a piece of transparent material made in a simple geometric shape. Usually at least one surface is spheric, and often both are. Under appropriate conditions a lens will produce an image of an object by refraction of light. It does this bending rays of light from an object. Some rays are refracted more than others, depending on how they arrive at the surface of the lens. The lens affects the velocity of the rays, since light travels more slowly in a dense medium such as the lens than in a less dense medium such as air. In this way, the expanding geometric wavefront that is generated by an object beyond the focal point is changed into a wavefront which, for a convex or converging lens, converges to a point behind the lens. If the object is located a long distance from the lens – strictly an infinite distance but a star is an excellent approximation for practical purposes – this point is known as the *rear focal point* or *principal focus*.

A lens has two principal foci – one on each side. For objects closer than the focal point the lens is unable to converge the waves – no 'real' image can be formed; instead a 'virtual' image is seen on the same side of the lens as the object. The lens is now being used as a 'magnifying glass'. If a point source of light is placed at the principal focus of the convex lens, the rays of light will be refracted to form a parallel beam.

Because of the effects of dispersion, the distance from the lens at which red light and blue light from an object will be focused will be different. This can be demonstrated in the colour fringes that can be seen in simple hand magnifiers (small magnifying glasses). Such fringes are unacceptable, for instance, in camera lens. A lens made from two different types of glass can be made to bring two colours to exactly the same focus. Such a lens is called *achromatic*. Lenses for cameras, binoculars, telescopes and microscopes are made with many elements, with different curvatures.

light that small part of the spectrum that can be detected by the human eye.

microscope a device for making very small objects visible. It was probably invented by a Dutch spectacle-maker Zacharias Janssen (1580–1638) in 1609. Essentially it is an elaboration of the simple magnifying glass. The objective is used to form a highly magnified image of a small object placed close to its focal point. This can be viewed directly, by means of another lens called the eyepiece. It can also be recorded directly on film or viewed via a video camera.

mirrors are reflecting optical elements. Plane mirrors are used to deviate light beams without dispersion or to reverse or invert images. Curved mirrors, which usually have spherical or parabolic surfaces, can form images, and are often used in illumination systems such as car headlamps. Properties of mirrors vary according to their form and manufacture. Mirrors can be coated with metals such as aluminium or silver, which have high resistance for visible light (or gold for the infrared). Alternatively, they may be coated with many thin layers of non-metallic materials for very high reflectances over a more restricted range of frequencies. A freshly coated aluminium mirror will

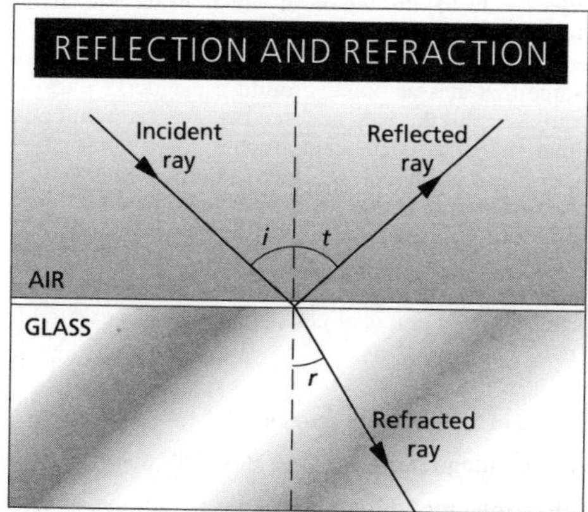

reflect about 90% of visible light. Mirrors such as those used in lasers can reflect over 99·7% of the light at one frequency.

objective a lens with a short focus for a microscope but long for a telescope.

optical activity the property of some substances to rotate the plane of plane-polarized light as it passes through, for example, a crystal, a solution or a liquid. This happens because the molecules of the substance are asymmetric – they can occur in different structures that are exact mirror images of each other. There are two forms – one will rotate the light in one direction; the other will rotate the light by an equal amount in the opposite direction.

phase (of light) a measure of the relative distance that light has travelled from an object.

photon a particle of light; a particle consisting of quantum electromagnetic radiation.

point of incidence the point at which an incident ray is reflected.

prism a block of glass, or any other transparent material, usually with a triangular base and always with a triangular cross-section. The refractive index of optical glass is not constant for light of all frequencies. It is greater at the violet end and less at the red end of the spectrum. This means that a beam of light containing a mixture of different frequencies, for example, sunlight, will leave a prism with the different frequencies bent by different amounts. A prism is used to deviate a beam of light by refraction. A beam of white light will be split into its component monochromatic coloured lights – from red to violet – which will form the familiar rainbow effect. Any light can be split up in this way; the display of separated wavelengths is called the spectrum of the original beam. Under the right conditions dispersion occurring in spherical raindrops in the atmosphere produces a *rainbow*.

real image is one through which rays of light actually pass, hence it can be formed on a screen.

reflection (of light) one of the three results that can happen when one medium meets the surface of another medium – see also refraction and absorption. In reflection of light the rays of light are 'thrown back'. In the accompanying figure, a monochromatic (single colour) beam of light falls or is incident upon a transparent material such as a block of glass. Angle *i* is the angle of incidence of the beam. Part of the beam is reflected at an angle *t*, the angle of reflection, and part is transmitted according to the law of refraction.

The two laws of reflection allow a prediction to be made as to where an incident ray will go after it has been reflected from the point of incidence. These laws state: that the reflected ray is in the same plane as the incident ray; and that the angle of reflection, *r*, equals the angle of incidence, *i*.

refraction one of the three results that can happen when one medium comes into contact with the surface of another medium; see also reflection and absorption. In refraction, the ray travels on through the second medium almost always taking a different direction. (See Snell's law of refraction; pp. 202–03.)

refractive index is often expressed relative to another material. If no other material is quoted, the refractive index of a medium is assumed to be relative to air. The refractive index of a medium can also be derived as the ratio of the speed of light in a vacuum to the speed of light in the medium. The refractive index for a typical optical glass is 1.6, whereas the refractive index of diamond is about 2.4 in visible light. The refractive index of a material determines how much it will refract light.

spectrum a range of electromagnetic energies arranged in order of increasing, or decreasing, wavelength or frequency. This is often assumed to mean the visible spectrum which is, however, only a small part of the electromagnetic spectrum which ranges from X-rays to radio waves.

speed of light varies in different materials – the speed of light (as of other electromagnetic waves) in a vacuum is $3 \times 10^8 ms^{-1}$ (300,000 km or 186,000 mi per second), but it travels more slowly through other media.

telescope a device used to form an enlarged image of an infinitely distant object. The enlarged object is viewed by the observer by means of an eyepiece. The term 'infinite' is used relatively in this context: compared with the length of the telescope, the distance of the object can be considered as infinite. Telescopes are often made with reflecting mirrors instead of glass lenses, as large lenses sag under their own weight, introducing distortions into the image. The primary mirror is often a large concave paraboloid.

total internal reflection exceeds a certain angle, which depends on the refractive index. When light travels from one medium to another less dense medium it is deviated or turned away from the normal – perpendicular to the interface at the point of incidence. This means the angle of refraction (*r*) is greater than the angle of incidence (*i*).

When the angle of refraction is less than 90°, some of the incident light will be refracted and some will be reflected. If the angle of incidence increases, the angle of refraction will increase more. It is possible to increase the angle of incidence to such a value that eventually the reflected ray disappears and all the light is refracted. This is total internal reflection.

virtual image is one from which rays of light cannot be formed on a screen. Both convex and concave lenses can produce both types of image, depending on the position of the object.

wavelength the distance in metres between the successive points of equal phase in a wave; see pp. 202–03.

MAGNETS AND ELECTRICITY

Certain materials have the ability to attract iron. This property – known as magnetism – has been used since about 500 BC when metallic ores with magnetic properties were being used as compasses. These materials include lodestone (or magnetite), an iron ore, as well as iron, steel, nickel, cobalt and a host of various alloys. If a bar magnet is placed on a cork that is floating on water, in such a way that the magnet is able to swing in a horizontal plane, it will come to rest with its axis in a north-south direction. It will lie in the magnetic meridian. A lasting magnet can be created by electricity – see solenoid (below). The interaction between magnetism and electricity – which were initially observed separately – was first noticed in the 19th century. It was discovered that electricity and magnetism were both manifestations of a single force, the electromagnetic force. Magnetic effects are now known to be caused by moving electric charges.

attraction occurs between the N and S poles of two magnets; compare with repulsion (below). This may be summed up in the saying 'Like poles repel, unlike poles attract'.

coulomb the unit of charge; the quantity of electric charge carried past a given point in one second by a current of one ampere.

Coulomb's law the law that describes the electric force. This is an inverse-square law that is similar to the law for gravitational force. Coulomb's law states that the attraction or repulsive force (*F*) between two point (or spherically symmetrical) charges is given by:

$$F = K\frac{Q_1Q_2}{r^2}$$

where *k* is a constant, Q_1 and Q_2 are the magnitudes of the charges, and *r* is the distance between them. The force acts along the direction of *r*.

electric charge a flow of charged particles, especially electrons, that constitutes an electric current. In dry weather, a nylon sweater being pulled off over the hair of the wearer may crackle; sparks may even be seen. This is caused by an electric charge, the result of electrons being pulled from one surface to the other. Objects can gain an electric charge by being rubbed against another material. There are two types of charge. These are now associated with the negative and positive charges on electrons and protons respectively. Similar electric charges (i.e. two positives or two negatives) repel each other and unlike charges (i.e. a positive and a negative) attract. (Note that positive and negative are just conventional terms for opposite properties.) The force of repulsion or attraction is known as the electric force. It is described by Coulomb's law.

electric current consists of a flow of electrons, usually through a material but also through a vacuum, as in a cathode-ray tube in a TV set. Current flows where there is a potential difference or voltage between two ends of a conductor. Conventional current flows from the positive terminal to the negative terminal. However, electron flow is in fact from negative to positive.

For measurement purposes, an electric current is defined as the rate of flow of charge. The unit of electric current is the *ampere* (A), often abbreviated to amp: one ampere = one coulomb per second.

electric field the region in which an electric charge experiences a force. Just as arrows can be plotted to show the magnitude and direction of the magnetic force that acts at points around a magnet, so arrows can also plot the electric force that acts on a unit positive charge at each point. Such a chart would show the distribution of the electric field intensity. It is measured in terms of a force per unit charge, or newtons per coulomb. In the same way that mass may have gravitational potential energy because of its position, so a charge can have electrical potential energy. This potential per unit charge is measured in *volts* (V) – named after the Italian physicist Alessandro Volta (1745–1827).

electric force see electric field.

electromagnetic force see Maxwell's theory.

electromagnetic induction began with the advance in 1831 when the English physicist Michael Faraday (1791–1867) found that an electric current could be induced in a wire by another, changing current in a second wire. Faraday published his findings before the US physicist Joseph Henry (1797–1878), who had first made the same discovery. Faraday showed that the magnetic field at the wire had to be changing for an electric current to be produced. This may be done by changing the current in a second wire, by moving a magnet relative to the wire, or by moving the wire relative to a magnet. This last technique is that employed in a dynamo generator, which maintains an electric current when it is driven mechanically. An electric motor uses the reverse process, being driven by electricity to provide a mechanical result.

electromagnetic spectrum the range of wavelengths over which electromagnetic radiation extends. Prior to Maxwell's discoveries it had been known that light was a wave motion, although the type of wave motion had not been identified. Maxwell was able to show that the oscillations were of electric and magnetic field. Hertz's waves had a wavelength of about 60cm; thus they were of much longer wavelength than light waves. Nowadays, we recognize a spectrum of electromagnetic radiation that extends from about 10^{-15}m to 10^{9}m. It is subdivided into smaller, sometimes overlapping ranges.

electromagnetic waves were demonstrated experimentally in 1887 by the German physicist Heinrich Hertz (1857–94) – who also gave his name to the unit of frequency. In his laboratory, Hertz transmitted and detected electromagnetic waves, and he was able to verify that their velocity was close to the speed of light. The electric and magnetic field components in electromagnetic waves are perpendicular to each other and to the direction of propagation.

electromagnetism is the study of the effects caused by stationary and moving electric charges. Electricity and magnetism were originally observed separately but, in the 19th century, scientists began to investigate their interaction. This work resulted in a theory that electricity and magnetism were both manifestations of a single force, the electromagnetic force. This force is one of the fundamental forces of nature, the others being the gravitational force and the weak and strong nuclear forces. Recently the electromagnetic and weak forces have been shown to be manifestations of an electro-weak force.

In 1820 the Danish physicist Hans Christiaan Oersted (1777–1851) discovered that a copper wire bearing an electric current caused a pivoted magnetic needle to be deflected until it was tangential to a circle drawn around the wire. This was the first connection to be established between electrical and magnetic forces. Oersted's work was developed by the Frenchmen Jean-Baptiste Biot (1774–1862) and Félix Savart (1791–1841), who showed that the field strength of a current flowing in a straight wire varied with the distance from the wire. Biot and Savart were able to find a law relating the current in a small part of the conductor to the magnetic field. Ampère, at about the same time, found a more fundamental relationship between the current in a wire and the magnetic field about it.

Gamma rays have wavelengths less than 10^{-11}m. They are emitted by certain radioactive nuclei and in the course of some nuclear reactions.

infrared waves of different wavelengths are radiated by bodies at different temperatures. (Bodies at higher temperatures radiate either visible or ultraviolet waves.) The Earth and its atmosphere, at a mean temperature of 250K (–23 °C or –9.4 °F), radiates infrared waves with wavelengths centred at about 10 micrometres (μm) or 10^{-5}.

magnetic field the region around a magnet in which a force is exerted. These lines of force can be demonstrated by means of small plotting compasses or iron filings. Its direction at any point, shown by the lines of force, is that of the force that acts on the north pole. From Newton's third law and Oersted's observations it might be expected that a magnetic force can exert a force on a moving charge. This is observed if a magnet is brought up close to a cathode-ray tube in a TV set. The beam of electrons moving from the cathode to the screen is deflected. The force acts in a direction perpendicular to both the magnetic field and the direction of electron flow. If the magnetic field is perpendicular to the direction of the electrons, then the force has its maximum value. This is the second way in which electric and magnetic properties are linked.

magnetic meridian the north-south vertical plane in which a magnet lies.

magnetism a group of physical phenomena associated with magnetic fields.

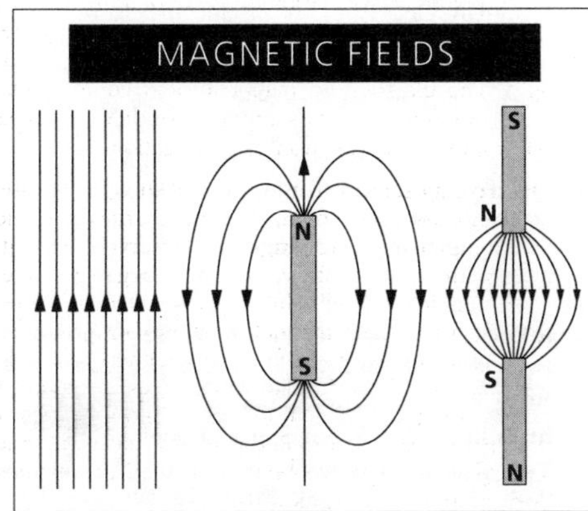

Maxwell's theory was developed as a result of the work of the Scottish physicist James Clerk Maxwell (1831–79) in electromagnetism. Of immense importance to physics, it united the separate concepts of electricity and magnetism in terms of a new electromagnetic force. Maxwell extended the ideas of Ampère, then in 1864 he proposed that a magnetic field could also be caused by a changing electric field. Thus, when either an electric or magnetic field is changing, a field of the other type is induced. Maxwell predicted that electrical oscillations would generate electromagnetic waves, and he derived a formula giving the speed in terms of electric and magnetic quantities. When these quantities were measured he calculated the speed and found that is was equal to the speed of light in a vacuum. This suggested that light might be electromagnetic in nature – a theory that was later confirmed in various ways. Thus, when an electric current in a wire changes, electromagnetic waves are generated, which will be propagated with a velocity equal to that of light.

microwaves are radio waves with shorter wavelengths, between 1mm and 30cm. They are used in radar and microwave ovens.

negative charge see electric charge.

neutral point the place where two magnetic fields are equal and opposite such that the total field is zero.

north-seeking pole (or **N pole**) the end of a magnet which points towards north.

positive charge see electric charge.

repulsion occurs when the N pole of a second magnet is brought near to the N pole of a magnet which is placed on a floating cork. The cork and magnet will swing round. Repulsion will also take place between two S poles in a similar fashion.

solenoid is a long cylindrical coil. Solenoids are used in magnetization by electrical methods – a form of magnetization which is quick and efficient. A cylindrical coil is wound with a couple of hundred turns of insulated copper wire and is then connected to a direct current supply. A steel bar is then inserted into the coil and when the current is switched it creates a strong magnetic field within the coil. The steel, thus, becomes a magnet and retains its magnetism even when the power is switched off.

south-seeking pole (or **S pole**) the end of a magnet which points towards south.

ultraviolet waves have wavelengths from about 380 nanometres down to 60nm. The radiation from hotter stars (above 25,000K/25,000 °C/45,000 °F) is shifted towards the violet and ultraviolet parts of the spectrum.

visible waves have wavelengths of 400–700 nanometres. The peak of the solar radiation (temperature about 6000K/6270 °C/11,323 °F) is at a wavelength of about 550nm, where the human eye is not at its most sensitive.

volt (V) the unit of electric potential. The volt may be defined as follows: if one joule is required to move one coulomb of electric charge between two points, then the potential difference between the two points is one joule per coulomb = one volt.

X-rays have wavelengths from about 10 nanometres down to 10^{-4} nm.

BATTERIES, CELLS, CIRCUITS AND CURRENTS

The first source of a steady electric current was demonstrated by the Italian physicist Alessandro Volta (1745–1827) in 1800 – the voltaic pile, the first battery which used chemical energy to produce an electric current. The pile consisted of a series of pairs of metal plates (one of silver and one of zinc) piled on top of each other, each pair sandwiching a piece of cloth soaked in a dilute acid solution. The same principle is still used.

accumulator a battery designed so that it can be 'recharged' by the passage of an electric charge back through it; a 12-volt car battery consists of six lead-acid cells in series.

alternating current (AC) the type of current used in most electrical appliances. In AC the direction of the drift velocity reverses, usually many times a second. The frequency of AC can vary over an enormous range. The electric mains operate at 50 Hz (cycles per second) in Europe and at 60 Hz in North America. AC generators are more common than DC generators.

alternator a type of generator. Large alternators are used in power stations; small alternators, used to charge car batteries, produce AC that is then rectified to DC using semiconductor diodes.

anode a positive electrode; the electrode from which power normally flows in a cell.

battery a series of cells connected positive to negative.

cathode a negative electrode; the electrode to which power normally flows in a cell.

cell (simple) a source of electric current. A single cell can normally produce only a small voltage, but a number of them connected in a series (positive to negative) will give a higher voltage. A series of cells connected in this way is a battery.

charge carrier the entity that transports electric charge in an electric current. The type of carrier depends upon the type of conductor: in metals the carriers are electrons; in semiconductors the carriers are either electrons (n-type) or positive holes (p-type).

circuit a complete conductive path between positive and negative terminals; conventionally power flows from positive to negative, although the direction of electron flow is actually from negative to positive.

conduction (electrical) the process by which a charge is transferred through a medium. It is usually accompanied by a transfer of energy.

conductivity (electrical) the reciprocal of the resistivity of a material. Conductivity is measured in siemens per metre.

conductor any material that is able to pass an electric charge with ease. (The only materials able to do this are carbon and metals.)

diode (thermionic) a device in which electrons are emitted by a heated cathode and flow through a vacuum to the anode. A diode allows the passage of electricity in one direction only.

direct current (DC) the type of electric current in which the drift velocity of the charge carriers is in one direction only. A battery produces a steady DC whereas rectified AC changes continually.

drift velocity the typical velocity of electrons moving along a conductor.

dynamo an electrical current generator, consisting of a coil that is rotated in a magnetic field by some external means. The source of the rotation may be a turbine in which blades are moved by the passage through them of water, as in a hydroelectric plant, or steam, produced by a boiler heated by nuclear fission or by burning fossil fuels. Wind turbines spin as a result of the passage of air through the large rotors. Different types of generators produce either AC or DC, while alternators produce AC. In a large generator the armature is fixed and the magnetic field is rotated.

electric motor a device similar to a dynamo or generator. However, it works in reverse. An electric current is applied to the coil windings, causing rotation of the armature.

electrodes the plates in a cell. They must be made of dissimilar materials, for example copper and zinc. Alternatively, one may be made of carbon.

electrolyte the solution used in a cell. In a dry cell it is a paste of ammonium chloride.

electromotive force (EMF) of a source (battery, generator, etc.) is the energy converted into electrical energy when unit charge passes through it. Its unit is the volt.

electron emission the escape of electrons when, for example, the filament of a light bulb is heated and the energy of some of the electrons in the filament is greatly increased by thermal motion, although the average increase for all the electrons is very small. If their energy reaches an adequate level, many are able to escape. This process of electron emission is called thermionic emission. If another electrode is put in the evacuated bulb and placed at a higher potential than the filament, this will act as an anode and will attract electrons towards it. A current will then flow in an external circuit; the device so formed is called a thermionic diode.

filament (light bulb) a fine coiled tungsten wire of high resistance.

fuse a small resistance consisting of wire with a low melting point usually tinned copper. The *maximum* amount of current that can flow will be determined by its presence. If too much current flows, the fuse will overheat and melt, breaking the circuit.

heating (by electricity) is produced because when electrons pass through a wire they cause the atoms in it to vibrate and transfer kinetic energy thus generating heat – the greater the resistance, the greater the heat generated. This effect is used in electric heating devices. An electric radiant heater glows red hot. The temperature reached by using a special tough resistance wire is 900 °C (1650 °F). The connecting wires are of low resistance and stay cool.

hole a vacant electron position.

insulator any material in which the numbers of unoccupied states and of electrons free to move into them are small.

light bulb a device consisting of a glass envelope containing an inert (noble) gas, usually argon, at low pressure. The bulb has two electrodes connected by a filament. The passage of a suitable electric current through the filament will raise its temperature sufficiently to make it glow white hot (2500 °C/4500 °F). The inert gas prevents the filament from evaporating.

light-emitting diode a device made from material such as gallium arsenide in which the p-n junction will emit light whenever an electric current passes through it. Light-emitting diodes are used in digital displays in clocks and radios. The light is emitted when an electron and a hole meet at the junction and cancel each other out.

negative electrode the electrode towards which power flows in a cell; the cathode.

n-type semiconductor a semiconductor in which the doping results in the charge carriers being negative electrons.

ohm (symbol Ω) the unit of resistance; the resistance of a conductor in which the current is 1 ampere when a potential difference of 1 volt is applied across it. It is named after the German physicist Georg Ohm (1787–1854), who discovered a relationship between the current (I) and the voltage (V) in a conductor – $V = IR$. Ohm's Law states that the current through a metallic conductor is directly proportional to the potential difference between its ends if the temperature and other physical conditions are constant.

parallel connection the arrangement when electrical components such as bulbs and switches are connected side to side.

photodiode a semiconducting device whose resistance decreases as the incident light increases owing to the production of more electron-hole pairs.

photoelectric effect occurs when electromagnetic radiation of a sufficiently high frequency shines onto a metal, causing electrons to be emitted from its surface.

photovoltaic effect an effect which occurs when light is absorbed by a p-n or n-p junction. Electrons are liberated at the junction by an incident photon and diffuse through the n-type region. The hole drifts through the p-type layer until it recombines with an electron flowing round the external circuit.

p-n junction the boundary between p-type and n-type materials in a semiconductor. In some materials, such as gallium arsenide, a p-n junction will emit light whenever an electric current passes through it. Such a device is called a light-emitting diode.

positive electrode the electrode from which power flows inside a cell; the anode.

power the rate at which a body or system does work. The power in an electric conductor is measured in watts.

p-type semiconductor a semiconductor in which the doping results in the charge carriers being electron deficiencies or holes.

rectifier a device used to convert AC to DC.

resistance the force that acts to reduce or resist the flow of an electric current passing through a conductor as well as the temperature. Resistance depends upon the nature of the conductor and its dimensions. The unit of resistance is the ohm.

resistivity (symbol p) the measure of the ability of a material in opposing the flow of electric current. Resistivity is measured in ohm-metres.

semiconductor any material in which there are more free electrons and unoccupied states than in an insulator. Semiconductors have a charge-carrier density that lies between those of conductors and insulators. Two metal-like elements, silicon and germanium, are the two semiconductors used most frequently. These may be *'doped'* with an impurity to modify their conduction behaviour – n-type doping increases the number of free electrons, p-type doping increases the number of unoccupied states.

Most semiconductor devices are made from materials that are partly n-type and partly p-type. The boundary between them is known as a *p-n junction*. Such a device is known as a *semiconductor diode* and acts as a rectifier.

solar cell in essence, a light-emitting diode acting in reverse. It converts light into electric current, which is the basis of solar power.

superconductivity the absence of measurable electrical current in materials at critical low temperatures. This was discovered by the Dutch physicist Kamerlingh Onnes (1853–1926) in 1911.

Below a certain critical temperature, various metals show zero resistance to current flow. Once a current is started in a closed circuit, it keeps flowing as long as the circuit is kept cold. The critical temperature for aluminium is 1.19K (–272 °C/–457 °F), and similar values hold for other metals. Some alloys have higher critical temperatures. A new class of copper oxide and other materials have shown superconductivity at up to at least 125K (–148 °C/–234 °F).

transformer a device used to transfer electrical energy from AC circuit to another with a change of voltage or a change of current or phase. If, for example, two insulated coils of wire are wound on the same soft iron core and an AC is passed through one of the coils, a current will be induced in the other coil. In this way transformers can either step voltage up or step it down. Note that transformers have the reverse effect on current. This principle is used for efficient long-distance power transmission at very high tension.

triode a device in which a third electrode in the shape of a grid is placed in a tube between a filament and an anode.

volt (symbol V) the unit of electric potential or potential difference; defined as the potential difference (p.d.) between two points in a circuit it is the amount of electrical energy changed to other forms of energy when unit charge passes from one point to the other. That is, 1 volt = 1 joule per coulomb (equivalent to 1 watt per ampere).

watt (symbol W) the unit for measuring the power in an electric conductor. One watt is one joule per second, or the energy used per second by a current of one amp flowing between two points with a potential difference of one volt. In an electric conductor the power (W) is the product of the current (I) and the voltage (V).

ATOMIC AND SUBATOMIC PARTICLES

Of the fundamental forces that are the most important in the natural world, the gravitational force is the dominant long-range force when the motion of planets and other celestial bodies is considered. When the smallest entities are considered, the other fundamental forces – the electromagnetic force, the strong force (which holds together the atomic nuclei) and the weak force (which is involved in nuclear decay) – become important.

In his atomic theory of 1803, the British chemist John Dalton (1766–1844) defined the atom as the smallest particle of an element that retained its chemical properties. Various phenomena could be explained using this hypothesis. However, no physical description of the atom was available until after the discovery of the electron.

alpha decay produces nuclei of helium that each contain two neutrons and two protons. They are called *alpha-particles* and are formed in spontaneous decay of the parent nucleus. Thus uranium-238 decays to thorium-234 with emission of an alpha particle.

antiparticle a particle with the same mass but opposite in some other characteristic such as charge. Thus the positron with positive charge is the antiparticle of the negatively charged electron. Some particles such as the photon may be their own antiparticle.

baryon a hadron resulting from the combination of three quarks.

beta decay is characterized by the emission of particles that are either electrons or positrons. The parent nucleus retains the same number of nucleons but its charge varies by plus or minus 1. In these processes another kind of particle is produced – a neutrino or an antineutrino.

boson (or **Bose-Einstein particle**) a particle that can be produced and destroyed freely, provided the laws of conservation of charge and of mechanics are obeyed.

colour charge a type of charge of quarks. The force associated with the colour charge binds the quarks together and is thought to be the source of the strong force binding the hadrons together. Thus the colour force is the most fundamental force.

critical mass the level above which a chain reaction will be set in nuclear fission.

electron a small subatomic particle. Electrons carry a negative charge and move around the nuclei of an atom. When an atom gains or loses an electron, ions are formed. Electrons have an electric charge of −1, and a mass (MeV) of 0·511.

The discovery of the electron was in 1897 by J.J. Thompson. The nuclear model was proposed by Ernest Rutherford (1871–1937) in 1911. His model consists of a small but dense central nucleus, which is positively charged, orbited by negatively charged electrons. The electron was recognized by its behaviour as a particle.

electronic configuration the way in which electrons are located in an atom.

electronvolt (symbol eV) the increase in energy of an electron when it undergoes a rise in potential of 1 volt.

fermion (or **Fermi-Dirac particle**) a particle that has a permanent existence. Leptons are fermions.

fission a nuclear reaction from which nuclear power comes. In the fission process, a large nucleus, such as uranium-235, splits to form two smaller nuclei that have greater binding energies than the original uranium. Thus energy is given out in the process. Fission is used in nuclear reactors and in atomic weapons. There are other isotopes in addition to uranium-235, such as plutonium-239, that give rise to fission.

fusion a nuclear reaction from which nuclear power comes. In the fusion process, two light nuclei fuse together to form two particles, one smaller and one larger than the original nuclei. Usually one of them is sufficiently strongly bound to give a great release of energy. The fusion of hydrogen to form helium is a power source in stars such as the Sun, although solar fusion processes differ in detail from the simple process described here. Nuclear fusion is the basis of the hydrogen bomb.

gamma decay a type of radiation. In gamma decay, high-energy photons may be produced in a process of radioactive decay if the resultant nucleus jumps from an excited energy state to a low energy state. The rate at which radioactive decay takes place depends only on the number of radioactive nuclei that are present. Thus the half-life is characteristic for that type of nucleus. Decay can result in a series of new elements being produced, each of which may in its turn decay until a stable state is achieved.

hadron a heavy particle (for example, a proton or a neutron) that is affected by the strong force. Hadrons – unlike leptons which are thought to be fundamental particles – are thought to be made up of quarks.

half-life the time taken for half a given number of radioactive nuclei to decay. The isotope carbon-14 has a half-life of 5730 years, and measurement of its decay is used in *carbon-dating* of organic material.

isotopes different atoms of the same element containing equal numbers of protons but different numbers of neutrons in their nuclei hence having different atomic mass.

Isotopes of an element contain the same nuclear charge, and their chemical properties are identical, but they display different physical properties. An isotope may be represented in a number of ways, such as uranium-235 or U-235 – the 235 refers to the total number of protons and neutrons in a nucleus.

lepton a (generally) light particle – such as an electron or a neutrino – that is not subject to the strong force. Leptons are fermions. Leptons are thought to be fundamental particles, while the hadrons are thought to be made up of quarks.

mass defect the difference between the masses of the nucleus and its component parts.

meson a subatomic particle resulting from the combination of a quark and an antiquark. A meson is a boson; it is a short-lived particle that jumps between protons and neutrons, thus holding them together.

neutrino a particle produced in beta decay. The neutrino has no charge and a mass that – if it could be measured at rest – would probably be zero.

neutron a subatomic particle of similar size to a proton but electrically neutral. Protons and neutrons in the atomic nucleus are held tightly together by the strong nuclear force.

nuclear accelerator a large machine that can accelerate particle beams to a very high speed, so enabling research into particle physics. Electric fields are used to accelerate the particles, either in a straight line (linear accelerator) or in a circle (cyclotron, synchrotron or synchro-cyclotron). Powerful magnetic fields are used to guide the beams. Nuclear accelerators have provided experimental evidence for the existence of numerous subatomic particles predicted in theory.

nuclear particle any of over 200 elementary particles that are now known. They may be divided into two types: hadrons and leptons. A further very important distinction is that between fermions and bosons. Every type of particle is thought to have a companion antiparticle.

nuclear reaction see fission and fusion.

nucleons collectively, protons and neutrons.

nucleus the central part of an atom where mass is concentrated – the nucleus contains over 99·9% of the mass but its diameter is in the order of 10^{-15}m (compared with the much larger size – about 10^{-10}m – of the atom). The nucleus has a positive charge – in the neutral atom the positive nucleus is balanced by the negatively charged electrons which orbit around it. The nucleus comprises protons and neutrons. (NB. The isotope hydrogen-1 comprises atoms that contain no neutrons.) Protons and neutrons are known collectively as nucleons.

positron a particle that is identical to an electron but with a positive charge.

proton a subatomic particle carrying a positive charge, equal in magnitude to that of the negatively charged electron.

quantum (plur. **quanta**) an elemental unit; a discrete amount.

quark a subatomic particle that is thought to be the 'building blocks' for hadrons. Quarks may have fractional electrical charge. It is probable that free quarks do not exist. If three quarks combine the resulting hadron is called a baryon. In the same way that Mendeleyev's table of chemical elements predicted new elements that were subsequently discovered, so a pattern of hadrons may be drawn up based on combinations of the different types of quark. This pattern is called the *eight-fold way.* It predicted the existence of the omega-particle, the discovery of which in 1963 helped to validate the theory.

There are believed to be six types or flavours of quark – up, down, charmed, strange, top and bottom. Evidence for the existence of all except the top quark is now available. Quarks carry electrical charge and another type of charge that is called colour.

radiation radiant energy. Radiation is either the result of spontaneous emission of particles or is an electromagnetic wave. There are three types of radiation – from alpha decay, from beta decay and from gamma decay.

radioactivity giving off radiant energy in particles or rays as a result of the disintegration of atomic nuclei.

shell the outer layer or layers of an atom.

The Danish physicist Niels Bohr (1885–1962) had suggested that electrons were allowed to move in circular orbits or shells around the nucleus, but that only certain orbits were allowable. This theory was able to explain many of the features of the spectrum of light emitted by excited hydrogen atoms. The wavelengths of the spectral lines are related to the energy levels of the allowed orbits. These would be those whose circumference was a multiple of the electron's wavelength. When Rutherford showed experimentally that an atom must consist of a small nucleus surrounded by electrons, there was a fundamental problem. To avoid collapsing into the nucleus, the electrons would have to move in orbits – as Bohr had proposed. This means that they must have continuous acceleration towards the nucleus. But according to the electromagnetic theory, an accelerated charge must radiate energy, so no permanent orbit could exist. Bohr, therefore, argued that energy could not be lost continuously but only in quanta (discrete amounts) equivalent to the difference in energies between allowed orbits. Thus light would be emitted when an electron jumps from one allowed level to another level of energy.

strong nuclear force the force that holds together protons and neutrons in the atomic nucleus. The strong nuclear force overcomes the weaker electromagnetic force of repulsion between positively charged protons. The mass of a nucleus is always less than the sum of the masses of its constituent nucleons. This is explained using the relationship derived by Einstein. If the nucleus is to be separated into protons and neutrons then the strong nuclear force needs to be overcome and energy has to be supplied to the nucleus from an external source to break it up. This energy is equal in value but opposite in sign to the binding energy and is related to the mass defect. Those nuclei with large binding energies per nucleon are most stable; these have about 50–75 nucleons in the nucleus.

In fission, unstable U-235 splits into two more stable nuclei; in fusion H-2 or H-3 join to make more stable nuclei. In both cases energy is released equal to the charge in binding energies.

wave-particle duality a concept proposed by de Broglie to describe the movement of particles.

The wavelength of a particle would be equal to the Planck constant divided by its momentum. As the wavelength is dependent upon momentum it can take any value. For an electron the wavelength can be of the order of the atomic diameter. At suitable energy levels the wavelength of electrons and neutrons can be equivalent to the atomic spacing in solids.

weak force is associated with the radioactive beta-decay of some nuclei. It has been shown – in the theory of the electroweak force – that the electromagnetic and weak forces are linked.

NOBEL PRIZEWINNERS IN PHYSICS

1901 Wilhelm Röntgen, German: discovery of X-rays.

1902 Hendrik Antoon Lorentz and Pieter Zeeman, Dutch: investigation of influences of magnetism on radiation.

1903 Antoine-Henri Becquerel, French: discovery of spontaneous radioactivity;

Pierre Curie, French, and Marie Curie, Polish-born French citizen: investigating radiation phenomena.

1904 Lord Rayleigh (John William Strutt), English: discovery of argon.

1905 Philipp von Lenard, Austro-Slovak-born German: research on cathode rays.

1906 Sir Joseph J. Thomson, English: investigation of electrical conductivity of gases.

1907 A. A. Michelson, German-born US: established speed of light as a constant, and other spectroscopic and metrological investigations.

1908 Gabriel Lippmann, Luxembourg-born French: photographic reproduction of colours.

1909 Guglielmo Marconi, Italian, and Karl Braun, German: development of wireless telegraphy.

1910 Johannes van der Waals, Dutch: investigating the relationships between states of gases and liquids.

1911 Wilhelm Wien, German: investigating the laws governing heat radiation.

1912 Nils Gustav Dalén, Swedish: invention of automatic regulators for lighting buoys and beacons.

1913 Helke Kamerlingh Onnes, Dutch: studies into the properties of matter at low temperatures and producing liquid helium.

1914 Max von Laue, German: achieving diffraction of X-rays using crystals.

1915 Sir William Bragg and Sir Lawrence Bragg, both English: analysis of crystal structure using X-rays.

1916 No award.

1917 Charles Barkla, English: discovery of characteristics of X-radiation of elements

1918 Max Plank, German: for the formulation of the first quantum theory.

1919 Johannes Stark, German: discovered Doppler effect in positive ion rays and division of spectral lines when source of light is subjected to strong electric force fields.

1920 Charles Guillaume, Swiss: discovering anomalies in alloys.

1921 Albert Einstein, German-born US: elucidating theories fundamental to theoretical physics.

1922 Niels Bohr, Danish: investigations into atomic structure and radiation.

1923 Robert Millikan, US: work on elementary electric charge and the photoelectric effect.

1924 Karl Siegbahn, Swedish: work on X-ray spectroscopy.

1925 James Franck and Gustav Hertz, German: definition of the laws governing the impact of an electron upon an atom.

1926 Jean-Baptiste Perrin, French: work on the discontinuous structure of matter.

1927 Arthur Holly Compton, US: discovery of wavelength change in diffused X-rays;

Charles Wilson, Scottish: invention of cloud chamber.

1928 Sir Owen Richardson, English: discovery of Richardson's Law, concerning the electron emissions by hot metals.

1929 Prince Louis de Broglie, French: discovery of the wave nature of electrons.

1930 Sir Chandrasekhra Raman, Indian: for work on light diffusion and discovery of the Raman effect.

1931 No award.

1932 Werner Heisenberg, German: formulating the indeterminacy principle of quantum mechanics.

1933 Paul Dirac, English, and Erwin Schrödinger, Austrian: introduction of wave-equations in quantum mechanics.

1934 No award.

1935 Sir James Chadwick, English: discovery of the neutron.

1936 Victor Hess, Austrian: discovered cosmic radiation.

1937 Clinton Davisson, US, and Sir George Thomson, English: demonstrated interference phenomenon in crystals irradiated by electrons.

1938 Enrico Fermi, Italian-born US: discovery of radioactive elements produced by neutron irradiation.

1939 Ernest Lawrence, US: invention of the cyclotron.

1940–42 No awards.

1943 Otto Stern, German-born US: discovery of the magentic moment of the proton.

1944 Isodor Rabi, Austrian-born US: resonance method for observing the magnetic properties of atomic nuclei.

1945 Wolfgang Pauli, Austrian-born US-Swiss: discovery of the exclusion principle.

1946 Percy Bridgman, US: discoveries in high-pressure physics.

1947 Sir Edward Appleton, English: discovery of the Appleton Layer in the upper atmosphere.

1948 Patrick Blackett, English: discoveries in nuclear physics and cosmic radiation.

1949 Hudeki Yukawa, Japanese: predicted existence of mesons.

1950 Cecil Powell, English: developed photographic method of studying nuclear processes and for discoveries about mesons.

1951 Sir John Cockcroft, English, and Ernest Walton, Irish: pioneered use of accelerated particles to study atomic nuclei.

1952 Felix Bloch, Swiss-born US, and Edward Purcell, US: discovered nuclear magnetic resonance in solids.

1953 Frits Zernike, Dutch: phase-contrast microscopy method.

1954 Max Born, German-born British: statistical studies on wave functions;

Walther Bothe, German: invented coincidence method.

1955 Willis Lamb, Jr., US: discoveries in the hydrogen spectrum;

Polykarp Kusch, German-born US: measuring the magnetic moment of the electron.

1956 William Shockley, English-born US, John Bardeen, US, and Walther Brattain, US: investigating semi-conductors and discovering the transistor effect.

1957 Tsung-Dao Lee and Chen Ning Yang, Chinese-born US: discovery of violations of principle of parity.

1958 Pavel A. Cherenkov, Ilya M. Frank, and Igor Y. Tamm, Russian: investigating the effects produced by high-energy particles (the Cherenkov effect).

1959 Emilio Segrè, Italian-born US, and Owen Chamberlain, US: confirmed existence of the antiproton.

1960 Donald Glaser, US: development of the bubble chamber.

1961 Robert Hofstadter, US: determining the shape and size of atomic nucleons;

Rudolf Mössbauer, German: discovery of the Mössbauer effect (emission of gamma rays from certain crystal substances).

1962 Lev D. Landau, Azeri: contributions to the understanding of condensed states of matter.

1963 Johannes H. D. Jensen, German, and Maria Goeppert-Mayer, Polish-German-born US: shell model theory of the structure of atomic nuclei;

Eugene Paul Wigner, Hungarian-born US: work on principles governing interaction of protons and neutrons in the nucleus.

1964 Charles H. Townes, US, Nikolay G. Basov, Russian and Aleksandr M. Prokhorov, Russian: studies in quantum electronics leading to construction of instruments based on maser-laser principles.

1965 Julian S. Schwinger, US, Richard P.Feynman, US, Tomonaga Shin'ichiro, Japanese: work on basic principles of quantum electrodynamics.

1966 Alfred Kastler, French: work on optical methods for studying Hertzian resonances in atoms.

1967 Hans A. Bethe, German-born US: discoveries concerning the energy production of stars.

1968 Luis W. Alvarez, US: discovery of resonance states as part of work with elementary particles.

1969 Murray Gell-Mann, US: classification of elementary particles and their interactions.

1970 Hannes Alfvén, Swedish, and Louis Néel, French: work on magneto-hydrodynamics and antiferromagnetism and ferrimagnetism.

1971 Dennis Gabor, Hungarian-born British: invention of holography.

1972 John Bardeen, Leon N. Cooper and John R. Schrieffer, US: developed theory of superconductivity.

1973 Leo Esaki, Japanese, Ivar Giaever, Norwegian-born US, and Brian Josephson,Welsh: tunnelling in semiconductors and superconductors.

1974 Sir Martin Ryle and Antony Hewish, English: work in radio astronomy.

1975 Aage Bohr, Danish, Ben R. Mottelson, US-born Danish, and L. James Rainwater, US: contributions to the understanding of the atomic nucleus.

1976 Burton Richter and Samuel C. C. Ting, US: discovering a new class of elementary particles (psi).

1977 Philip W. Anderson, US, Sir Neville Mott, English, and John H. Van Vleck, US: contributions to understanding the behaviour of electrons in magnetic, non-crystalline solids.

1978 Pyotr L. Kapitsa, Russian: invented helium liquefier, and its applications;

Arno A. Penzias, German-born US, and Robert W. Wilson, US: discovered cosmic microwave background radiation.

1979 Sheldon Glashow, US, Abdus Salam, Pakistani, and Steven Weinberg, US: established analogy between electromagnetism and the 'weak' interactions of subatomic particles.

1980 James W. Cronin and Val L. Fitch, US: work on the simultaneous violation of both charge-conjugation and parity-inversion.

1981 Kai M. Siegbahn, Swedish, and Nicolaas Bloembergen, Dutch-born US: work on electron spectroscopy for chemical analysis;

Arthur L. Schalow, US: applications of lasers in spectroscopy.

1982 Kenneth G. Wilson, US: analysis of continuous phase transitions.

1983 Subrahmanyan Chandrasekhar, Indian-born US, and William A. Fowler, US: contributions to understanding the evolution and devolution of stars.

1984 Carlo Rubbia, Italian and Simon van der Meer, Dutch: discovery of subatomic particles (W;Z), supporting the electro-weak theory.

1985 Klaus von Klitzing, German: discovery of Hall effect, permitting exact measurements of electrical resistance.

1986 Ernst Ruska, German, Gerd Binnig, German, and Heinrich Rohrer, Swiss: development of special electron microscopes.

1987 J. Georg Bednorz, German and K. Alex Müller, Swiss: discovery of new superconducting materials.

1988 Lwon Lederman, Melvin Schwartz, and Jack Steinberger, US: research into subatomic particles.

1989 Norman Harvey, US: development of the separated field method;

Hans Dehmelt, German-born US, and Wolfgang Paul, German: developed and exploited the ion trap.

1990 Richard E. Taylor, Canadian, Jerome Friedman, US, and Henry Kendall, US: proved the existence of the quark.

1991 Pierre-Gilles de Gennes, French: for studies in changes in liquid crystals.

1992 George Charpak, Polish-born French: devised an electronic detector that reads trajectories of subatomic particles.

1993 Russell A. Hulse and Joseph H. Taylor, US: discovery of a new type of quasar.

1994 Clifford Shull, US, and Bertram Brockhouse, Canadian: for neutron-scattering techniques.

Chemistry

PRINCIPLES OF CHEMISTRY

The core of modern chemistry is a fundamental belief in the importance of understanding the physical laws that govern the behaviour of atoms and molecules. Elements (see pp. 217–24) have been called the building blocks of matter. They may occur singly or in compounds and mixtures.

compound a substance formed by combination of two or more elements. In a compound of oxygen and hydrogen, the two elements are made to react or combine with one another. The reaction yields the liquid water, hydrogen oxide, which is a compound of hydrogen and oxygen. If equal volumes of hydrogen and oxygen had been present in the reaction vessel not all of the oxygen would be combined into the compound, water, but some oxygen would still be left unreacted. Some oxygen would be left because water is formed by the reaction of exactly twice as much hydrogen by volume as oxygen. The 'recipe' – or formula – for hydrogen oxide (water) is unique: two 'parts' hydrogen to one 'part' oxygen.

concentration the strength or density of a solution. The concentration of a solution is a measure of the quantity of solute dissolved in the solution. This is expressed in terms of mass or the number of particles per unit volume of the solution.

fraction a part separated – for example by distillation – from a mixture.

mixture is composed of two or more different substances not chemically combined. Air, for instance, is a mixture of elements (nitrogen, oxygen, argon, etc.) and compounds (carbon dioxide, water vapour, etc.). The substances in the mixture do not affect one another. Each substance behaves in exactly the same way that it would if the other substances in the mixture were absent. The properties of a mixture are the sum of the properties of all the components of that mixture. The proportions of the substances that occur in a mixture can vary and these substances can be separated by physical means. No energy is either absorbed or released when a mixture is made.

molecule the smallest particle of either an element or a compound that can exist independently. Apart from the noble gases whose molecules consist of single atoms, a molecule contains two or more atoms that are bonded together in small whole numbers, for example O_2, a molecule of oxygen.

reaction (chemical) the action of one substance with another to produce a chemical change. The speed or rate of reaction depends upon several factors: temperature, particle size of a solid, concentration of a solution and catalysts, for instance.

Temperature: the higher the temperature the faster the reaction will be because at a high temperature the particles will move at greater speed, with the result that they collide more frequently and more energetically.

Particle size: the smaller the particles of a solid reactant the greater will be the total surface area that is available for chemical reactions to take place and, therefore, the reaction will be faster.

Concentration: the more concentrated the closer together the particles of solute and, hence, the more frequently they collide with particles of the other reactant(s).

Catalysts: the presence of catalysts will change the rate as they provide an alternative means by which a reaction may take place.

reaction techniques the different techniques used to carry out different chemical reactions. They include: heating solids or liquids; reacting solids with a solution in order to collect a gas; precipitation; passing a gas or a vapour over a heated solid; combustion – burning a solid or a liquid in a gas.

solute the substance that is dissolved in a solvent to produce a solution.

solvent the substance that dissolves a solute to produce a solution.

solution the dispersion of one or more solutes in a solvent. A solution is a homogenous mixture not a compound. The substances in a solution can be separated by physical processes.

METHODS OF SEPARATING MIXTURES

To separate the elements of a compound a chemical reaction is required because the elements are bonded together. However to separate components in a mixture various physical processes may be used.

centrifugation a physical method of separating a solid from a liquid in which it does not dissolve. Centrifugation requires the use of a piece of specialist machinery, a centrifuge, which uses centrifugal force to separate particles of varying density by spinning.

chromatography a physical method of separating several components from a mixture in solution. This is done by running the solution through an adsorbent material on which the different substances are separated out as spots or bands.

crystallization a physical method of separating a solid from its solution in a solvent. Crystallization initially involves evaporation of solvent up to the point at which a saturated solution is formed.

decantation a physical method of separating a solid from a liquid in which it does not dissolve. The liquid (usually a solution) is carefully poured from one beaker into another.

distillation a physical method of separating a liquid from a solution. In simple distillation heat is applied to the solution, the liquid rises as water vapour and is condensed. Fractional distillation is used to separate several liquids from a mixture.

evaporation a physical method of separating a solid from its solution in a solvent.

filtration a physical method of separating a solid from a liquid in which it does not dissolve. This is achieved by straining out solid particles from a liquid.

HPLC high performance liquid chromatography, which is partition column chromatography under high pressure in which there is distribution between two liquids in a column.

reflux a process in which liquid is obtained from partial condensation of vapour.

sublimation a physical method of separating one solid from another solid. Sublimation is similar to distillation but is used for purifying solids rather than liquids.

ELEMENTS AND THE PERIODIC TABLE

The world is made up of a limited number of chemical elements. In the Earth's crust there are 82 stable elements and a few unstable (radioactive) ones. Among the stable elements, there are some, such as oxygen and silicon, that are very abundant, while others – the metals ruthenium and rhodium, for example – are extremely rare. Indeed 98% of the Earth's crust is made up of just eight elements – oxygen, silicon, aluminium, iron, calcium, sodium, magnesium, and potassium. Each element is associated with a unique number, called its atomic number.

atom the smallest particle of an element that can exist. Atoms are the 'building blocks' of everything. They are, in turn, made up of subatomic particles – protons, neutrons and electrons.

atomic number the figure that represents the number of protons (positively charged particles) in the nucleus of each atom of an element. Each hydrogen atom has one proton, so hydrogen is the first and lightest of the elements and is placed first in the Periodic Table; each helium atom has two protons and helium is thus the second lightest element and is placed second in the Periodic Table; and so one can continue through each of the elements, establishing their place on the Periodic Table according to their atomic numbers. The atomic number of bismuth is 83, and this number of protons represents the upper limit for a stable nucleus. Beyond 83 all elements are unstable. The largest atomic number observed so far is 111, but only three atoms of this element, unununium, have been made artificially, so little is known about it.

d sub-level one of the sub-levels (see electron). The d sub-level identifies one of the main blocks or groups of the Periodic Table containing the elements of atomic number 21 to 30, 39 to 48, 71 to 80 and 103 to 111.

electron a subatomic negatively charged particle that moves around the nucleus of an atom. The number of electrons always equals the number of protons in an atom when that atom is electrically neutral. Thus, for example, an electrically neutral atom of calcium contains 20 protons and 20 electrons. Electrons can be thought of as moving around the nucleus in certain fixed orbits or 'shells', the electrons in a particular shell being associated with a particular energy level.

With regard to an atom's chemical behaviour, it is the electrons in the outer shell that are most important and it is these that fix the group position of the atom in the Periodic Table. The shells and the major energy levels of electrons are numbered 1, 2, 3, etc., counting outwards from the nucleus. This number is called the principal quantum number and is given the symbol **n**.

Each shell/energy level can hold only a certain number of electrons; the further out it is, the more it can accommodate. This capacity is related to the value of **n**. The nearest shell to the nucleus can hold only 2 electrons, the next 8, then 18, then 32, and so on. Each energy level is divided into sub-levels, called **s, p**, **d** and **f,** which hold a maximum of 2, 6, 10 and 14 electrons respectively.

f sub-level one of the sub-levels (see electron). The f sub-level identifies one of the main blocks of the Periodic Table containing the elements of atomic numbers 57 to 70, and 89 to 102.

group position the position of an element in a group of similar elements on the Periodic Table.

The groups of the Periodic Table are numbered 1 to 18 with the **f**-block not included. Members of the same group have the same number of electrons in the outer shell of the atom and consequently behave in a similar manner chemically. This fact is reflected in the composition of their chemical compounds (which in turn can be explained in terms of their oxidation states).

As we go from left to right across the table we can see particular properties change in a regular fashion. It was this periodic rise and fall in such properties as density and melting point that led to the term 'Periodic Table'.

noble gases (or **inert gases**) monatomic gases whose configurations are very stable because of their electron arrangement. A hydrogen atom has one electron in the first principal energy level, while a helium atom has two – the maximum capacity for this level.

The possession of one extra electron may seem a trivial difference, but a world of difference separates hydrogen and helium. Hydrogen is very reactive and forms compounds with many other elements; helium combines with nothing. These two elements are rather exceptional in all their chemical behaviour and are usually either given a small section of their own on the table or are placed apart at either end of the table with hydrogen above group 1 and helium in group 18. Helium is placed in the same group as the other chemically unreactive gases – the noble gases – even though it does not have the eight outer electrons that they do.

To the left of neon is fluorine (configuration 2·7), a reactive element. Fluorine (like the other elements in group 17 – the halogens) is one electron short of a noble gas electron arrangement. Fluorine's tendency to combine with other elements in order to achieve a noble gas electron arrangement makes it one of the most reactive of all elements – so reactive that it will even combine with the noble gases krypton and xenon.

The noble gases with their stable electron arrangement make a natural break in the arrangement of the Periodic Table. After the **p** sub-shell has been filled, the next electron starts another shell further out from the nucleus. This lone electron makes the elements of group 1 – the alkali metals – highly reactive, because they tend to lose the extra electron in order to achieve a noble gas electron arrangement. They are indeed so reactive that some of them, such as caesium, explode when dropped into water.

neutron a subatomic particle found at the centre of the nucleus of most atoms. It has the same mass as a proton but carries no electric charge.

oxidation to become oxidized by losing an electron (or by gaining oxygen or losing hydrogen).

Periodic Table a table that represents all of the elements in such a manner as to show similarities and differences in their chemical properties.

The elements are arranged in increasing number of atomic number as one reads from left to right across the table.

The discovery of the Periodic Table was made possible by an Italian chemist, Stanislao Cannizzaro (1826–1910), who in 1858 published a list of fixed atomic weights (now known as relative atomic masses) for the 60 elements that were then known. By arranging the elements in order of increasing atomic weight, a curious repetition of chemical properties at regular intervals was revealed. This was noticed in 1864 by the English chemist John Newlands (1838–98), but his 'law of octaves' brought him nothing but ridicule. It was left to the Russian chemist Dmitri Ivanovich Mendeleyev (1834–1907) to make essentially the same discovery five years later. What Mendeleyev did, however, was so much more impressive that he is rightly credited as the true discoverer of the Periodic Table.

While working on his *Principles of Chemistry* (1869), Mendeleyev wrote the names and some of the main features of the elements on individual cards, to help establish a suitable order in which to discuss their chemistry. It was while he was arranging this pack of cards that he stumbled upon the pattern we now recognize as the Periodic Table. Mendeleyev laid out his cards in order of atomic weights of the elements, placing together elements that formed similar oxides. By arranging similar elements in columns, he established the arrangement of the table that has been followed ever since.

Mendeleyev's genius lay in he recognized that there was an underlying order to the elements – he did not design the Periodic Table, he discovered it. If he was right, he knew that there were places in his table for new elements. He was so confident in his discovery that he predicted the properties of these missing elements – and his predictions were subsequently shown to be accurate. In some cases, Mendeleyev also swapped the order of the atomic weights, so that similar elements appeared in the same group.

Since 1869 when Mendeleyev published his table, over 40 elements have been found or produced by nuclear reactions, and the Periodic Table has been redesigned to accommodate them. Mendeleyev lived long enough to learn of the discovery of the electron, but not long enough to know how the arrangement of electrons about the nucleus of the atom explains the structure of the Table.

p sub-level one of the sub-levels (see electron). The p sub-level identifies one of the main blocks of the Periodic Table containing the elements of atomic number 5 to 10, 13 to 18, 21 to 36, 49 to 54 and 81 to 86 (or the elements of groups 13 to 18).

proton a positively charged subatomic particle found in the nucleus of an atom. The number of protons in an atom is its atomic number and the atomic number of each element is unique.

s sub-level one of the sub-levels (see electron). The s sub-level identifies one of the main blocks of the Periodic Table containing the elements of groups 1 and 2.

THE ELEMENTS

The following notes refer to the tables of 111 elements on pp. 219–24.

1. The spelling 'sulfur' is that recommended by the International Union of Pure and Applied Chemistry (IUPAC) but the former spelling 'sulphur' is still widely used throughout the UK and in many other English-speaking countries.

2. A value in brackets is the relative atomic mass of the isotope with the longest known half-life.

3. For the highly radioactive elements the density value has been calculated for the isotope with the longest known half-life.

4. The value given for the melting point of helium is the minimum pressure under which helium can be liquified.

5. The melting and boiling points given are based on the International Temperature Scale of 1990 (ITS–90).

Elements 104 to 109
The names of the elements 104 to 109 given here are those recommended by IUPAC in September 1994:

104 dubnium (Db)
105 joliotium (Jl)
106 rutherfordium (Rf)
107 bohrium (Bh)
108 hahnium (Hn)
109 meitnerium (Mt)

The American Chemical Society is currently using a different set of names:

104 rutherfordium (Rf)
105 hahnium (Ha)
106 seaborgium (Sg), after Glenn T. Seaborg (1912–)
107 nielsbohrium (Ns)
108 hassium (Hs), after the Latin name for the German state of Hesse
109 meitnerium (Mt)

Elements 110 and 111
The names for elements 110 and 111 are those provisionally recommended by the IUPAC:

110 ununnilium (Uun)
111 unununium (Uuu)

Elements 110 and 111 were discovered late in 1994 at the GSI heavy-ion cyclotron at Darmstadt, Hesse (Germany) by a team led by Peter Armbruster and Sigurd Hofmann. The two elements each existed for about a millisecond before decaying. GSI was also responsible for the discovery of elements 107, 108 and 109 in 1981, 1984 and 1982 respectively. Recent innovations concerning the GSI apparatus at Darmstadt have helped the discovery of the two newest elements. It is not thought impossible that a further one or two new elements will be detected at Darmstadt before the end of 1995. In November 1994, two isotopes of element 110 were found with an atomic mass of 269 and 271. These isotopes were identified after bombarding atoms of lead with atoms of nickel-64.

In December 1994, the same team detected three atoms of element 111 after bismuth-209 was bombarded with billions of atoms of nickel. These three atoms had an atomic mass of 272. They decayed into previously unknown isotopes of elements 109 and 107.

THE PERIODIC TABLE OF ELEMENTS

13 — Group number
Atomic Number — 5
B — Symbol
Boron — Name
10.811 — 1994 Standard Atomic Weight Abridged to Five Significant Figures (where available) [or Relative Atomic Mass of Longest - Living Isotope]
2 — Period Number

Gas at Room Temperature
Liquid at Room Temperature
Radioactive

	1	2	3	4	5	6	7	8	9	10	11	12	13	14	15	16	17	18	
1	1 H Hydrogen 1.0079																	2 He Helium 4.0026	1
2	3 Li Lithium 6.941	4 Be Beryllium 9.0122											5 B Boron 10.811	6 C Carbon 12.011	7 N Nitrogen 14.007	8 O Oxygen 15.999	9 F Fluorine 18.998	10 Ne Neon 20.180	2
3	11 Na Sodium 22.990	12 Mg Magnesium 24.305											13 Al Aluminium 26.982	14 Si Silicon 28.086	15 P Phosphorous 30.974	16 S Sulphur 32.066	17 Cl Chlorine 35.453	18 Ar Argon 39.948	3
4	19 K Potassium 39.098	20 Ca Calcium 40.078	21 Sc Scandium 44.956	22 Ti Titanium 47.867	23 V Vanadium 50.942	24 Cr Chromium 51.996	25 Mn Manganese 54.938	26 Fe Iron 55.845	27 Co Cobalt 58.933	28 Ni Nickel 58.693	29 Cu Copper 63.546	30 Zn Zinc 65.39	31 Ga Gallium 69.723	32 Ge Germanium 72.61	33 As Arsenic 74.922	34 Se Selenium 78.96	35 Br Bromine 79.904	36 Kr Krypton 83.80	4
5	37 Rb Rubidium 85.468	38 Sr Strontium 87.62	39 Y Yttrium 88.906	40 Zr Zirconium 91.224	41 Nb Niobium 92.906	42 Mo Molybdenum 95.94	43 Tc Technetium [97.907]	44 Ru Ruthenium 101.07	45 Rh Rhodium 102.91	46 Pd Palladium 106.42	47 Ag Silver 107.87	48 Cd Cadmium 112.41	49 In Indium 114.82	50 Sn Tin 118.71	51 Sb Antimony 121.760	52 Te Tellurium 127.60	53 I Iodine 126.90	36 Xe Xenon 131.29	5
6	55 Cs Caesium 132.91	56 Ba Barium 137.33	57 - 71 LANTHANIDES	72 Hf Hafnium 178.49	73 Ta Tantalum 180.95	74 W Tungsten 183.84	75 Re Rhenium 186.21	76 Os Osmium 190.23	77 Ir Iridium 192.217	78 Pt Platinum 195.08	79 Au Gold 196.97	80 Hg Mercury 200.59	81 Ti Thallium 204.38	82 Pb Lead 207.2	83 Bi Bismuth 208.98	84 Po Polonium [208.98]	85 At Astatine [209.99]	86 Rn Radon [222.02]	6
7	87 Fr Francium [223.02]	88 Ra Radium [226.03]	89 - 103 ACTINIDES	104 Db Dubnium [261.11]	105 Jl Joliotium [262.11]	106 Rf Rutherfordium [266.12]	107 Bh Bohrium [264.12]	108 Hn Hahnium [265.13]	109 Mt Meitnerium [268]	110 Uun Ununnilium [271]	111 Uuu Unununium [272]								7

6	LANTHANIDES	57 La Lanthanum 138.91	58 Ce Cerium 140.12	59 Pr Praseodymium 140.91	60 Nd Neodymium 144.24	61 Pm Promethium [144.91]	62 Sm Samarium 150.36	63 Eu Europium 151.96	64 Gd Gadolinium 157.25	65 Tb Terbium 158.93	66 Dy Dysprosium 162.50	67 Ho Holmium 164.93	68 Er Erbium 167.26	69 Tm Thulium 168.93	70 Yb Ytterbium 173.04	71 Lu Lutetium 174.97	6
7	ACTINIDES	89 Ac Actinium [227.03]	90 Th Thorium 232.04	91 Pa Protactinium 231.04	92 U Uranium 238.03	93 Np Neptunium [237.05]	94 Pu Plutonium [244.06]	95 Am Americium [243.06]	96 Cm Curium [247.07]	97 Bk Brekelium [247.07]	98 Cf Californium [251.08]	99 Es Einsteinium [252.08]	100 Fm Fermium [257.10]	101 Md Mendelevium [258.10]	102 No Nobelium [259.10]	103 Lr Lawrencium [262.1098]	7

THE 109 ELEMENTS (see also notes p. 218)

Atomic Number	Symbol	Element Name	Derived From	Discoverers	Year	Atomic Weight (Note 2)	Density At 20°C (Unless Otherwise State) (g/cm3) (Note 3)	Melting Point (°C)	Boiling Point (°C)	Number of Nuclides
1	H	Hydrogen	Greek 'hydro genes' = water producer	H. Cavendish (UK)	1766	1·007 94	0·0871 (solid at mp) 0·000 089 89 (gas at 0°C)	–259·198	–252·762	3
2	He	Helium	Greek 'helios' = sun	J. N. Lockyer (UK) and P. J. C. Jannsen (France)	1868	4·002 602	0·190 8 (solid at mp) 0·000 1785 (gas at 0°C)	–272·375 24·985 atm (Note 4)	–268·928	8
3	Li	Lithium	Greek 'lithos' = stone	J. A. Arfwedson (Sweden)	1817	6·941	0·5334	180·54	1339	8
4	Be	Beryllium	Greek 'beryllion' = beryl	N. L. Vauquelin (France)	1798	9·012 182	1·846	1287	2471	9
5	B	Boron	Persian 'burah' = borax	L. J. Gay Lussac and L. J. Thenard (France) and H. Davy (UK)	1808	10·811	2·333 (b Rhombahedral)	2130	3910	13
6	C	Carbon	Latin 'carbo' = charcoal	Prehistoric		12·011	2·266 (Graphite) 3·515 (Diamond)	3530	3870	15
7	N	Nitrogen	Greek 'nitron genes' = saltpetre producer	D. Rutherford (UK)	1772	14·006 74	0·9426 (solid at mp) 0·001 250 (gas at 0°C)	–210·000	–195·798	13
8	O	Oxygen	Greek 'oxys genes' = acid producer	C. W. Scheele (Sweden) and J. Priestley (UK)	1772–1774	15·9994	1·359 (solid at mp) 0·001 429 (gas at 0°C)	–218·792	–182·954	15
9	F	Fluorine	Latin 'fluo' = flow	H. Moissan (France)	1886	18·998 403	1·780 (solid at mp) 0·001 696 (gas at 0°C)	–219·673	–188·191	14
10	Ne	Neon	Greek 'neos' = new	W. Ramsay and M. W. Travers (UK)	1898	20·1797	1·434 (solid at mp) 0·000,899 9 (gas at 0°C)	–248·594	–246·053	17
11	Na	Sodium	English 'soda'	H. Davy (UK)	1807	22·989 768	0·9688	97·82	882	17
12	Mg	Magnesium	Magnesia, a district of Thessaly	H. Davy (UK)	1808	24·3050	1·737	650	1095	17
13	Al	Aluminium	Latin 'alumen' = alum	H. C. Oerstedt (Denmark) and F. Wöhler (Germany)	1825–1827	726·981 539	2·699	660·323	251	18
14	Si	Silicon	Latin 'silex' = flint	J. J. Berzelius (Sweden)	1824	28·0855	2·329	1414	3190	21
15	P	Phosphorus	Greek 'phosphorus' = light bringing	H. Brand (Germany)	1669	30·973 762	1·825 (White) 2·361 (Violet)	44·13 597 at 45 atm	277 431 sublimes	21
16	S	Sulphur (Note 1)	Sanskrit 'solvere'; Latin 'sufrum'	Prehistoric		32·066	2·070 (Rhombic)	115·18	444·614	22
17	Cl	Chlorine	Greek 'chloros' = green	C. W. Scheele (Sweden)	1774	35·4527	2·038 (solid at mp) 0·003 214 (gas at 0°C)	–100·97	–33·97	20
18	Ar	Argon	Greek 'argos' = inactive	W. Ramsay and Lord Rayleigh (UK)	1894	39·948	1·622 (solid at mp) 0·001 784 (gas at 0°C)	–189 ·344	–185·848	20
19	K	Potassium (Kalium)	English 'potash'	H. Davy (UK)	1807	39·0983	0·8591	63·58	758	20
20	Ca	Calcium	Latin 'calx' = lime	H. Davy (UK)	1808	40·078	1·526	842	1495	19
21	Sc	Scandium	Scandinavia	L. F. Nilson (Sweden)	1879	44 ·955 910	2 ·989	1541	2830	16
22	Ti	Titanium	Latin 'Titanes' = sons of the earth	M. H. Klaproth (Germany)	1795	47 ·867	4 ·504	1672	3360	20
23	V	Vanadium	Vanadis, a name given to	N. G. Sefström (Sweden) Freyja, the Norse goddess	1830	50·9415	6·099	1928	3410	19

24	Cr	Chromium	Greek 'chromos' = colour	N. L. Vauquelin (France)	1798	51·9961	7·193	1860	2680	21
25	Mn	Manganese	Latin 'magnes' = magnet	J. G. Gahn (Sweden)	1774	54·938 05	7·472	1246	2051	21
26	Fe	Iron (Ferrum)	Anglo-Saxon 'iren'	Earliest smelting	c. 4000 BC	55·845	7·874	1538	2840	22
27	Co	Cobalt	German 'kobold' = goblin	G. Brandt (Sweden)	1737	58·933 20	8·834	1495	2940	22
28	Ni	Nickel	German abbreviation of 'Kupfernickel' (devil's 'copper') or niccolite	A. F. Cronstedt (Sweden)	1751	58·6934	8·905	1455	2890	24
29	Cu	Copper	Cyprus (Cuprum)	Prehistoric (earliest known use)	c. 8000 BC	63 ·546	8·934	1084·62	2570	25
30	Zn	Zinc	German 'zink'	A. S. Marggraf (Germany)	1746	65·39	7·140	419·527	908	25
31	Ga	Gallium	Latin 'Gallia' = France	L. de Boisbaudran (France)	1875	69·723	5·912	29·765	2203	24
32	Ge	Germanium	Latin 'Germania' = Germany	C. A. Winkler (Germany)	1886	72·61	5·327	938·2	2770	25
33	As	Arsenic	Latin 'arsenicum'	Albertus Magnus (Germany)	c. 1220	74·921 59	5·781	817 at 38 atm	603 sublimes	23
34	Se	Selenium	Greek 'selene' = moon	J. J. Berzelius (Sweden)	1818	78·96	4·810 (Trigonal)	221·14	685	23
35	Br	Bromine	Greek 'bromos' = stench	A. J. Balard (France)	1826	79·904	3·937 (solid at mp) 3·119 (liquid at 20°C)	−7·25	59·74	26
36	Kr	Krypton	Greek 'kryptos' = hidden	W. Ramsay and M. W. Travers (GB)	1898	83·80	2·801 (solid at mp) 0·003 749 (gas at 0°C)	−157·374	−153·340	25
37	Rb	Rubidium	Latin 'rubidus' = red	R. W. Bunsen and G. R. Kirchhoff (Germany)	1861	85·4678	1·534	39·29	687	28
38	Sr	Strontium	Strontian, a village in Highland region, Scotland	W. Cruikshank (UK)	1787	87·62	2·582	769	1388	28
39	Y	Yttrium	Ytterby, in Sweden	J. Gadolin (Finland)	1794	88·905 85	4·468	1522	3300	24
40	Zr	Zirconium	Persian 'zargun' = gold coloured	M. H. Klaproth (Germany)	1789	91·224	6·506	1854	4360	24
41	Nb	Niobium	Latin 'Niobe' daughter of Tantalus	C. Hatchett (UK)	1801	92·906 38	8·595	2472	4860	25
42	Mo	Molybdenum	Greek 'molybdos' = lead	P. J. Hjelm (Sweden)	1781	95·94	10·22	2623	4710	24
43	Tc	Technetium	Greek 'technetos' = artificial	C. Perrier (France) and E. Segré (Italy/USA)	1937	(97·9072)	11·40	2180	4860	23
44	Ru	Ruthenium	Ruthenia (in Ukraine)	K. K. Klaus (Estonia)	1844	101·07	12·37	2333	4310	25
45	Rh	Rhodium	Greek 'rhodon' = rose	W. H. Wollaston (UK)	1804	102·905 50	12·42	1962	3700	24
46	Pd	Palladium	The asteroid Pallas (discovered 1802)	W. H. Wollaston (UK)	1803	106·42	12·01	1554·7	2970	27
47	Ag	Silver (Argentum)	Anglo-Saxon 'seolfor'	Prehistoric (earliest silversmithery)	c. 4000 BC	107·8682	10·50	961·78	2167	29
48	Cd	Cadmium	Greek 'kadmeia' = calamine	F. Stromeyer (Germany)	1817	112·411	8·648	321·068	768	33
49	In	Indium	indigo spectrum	F. Reich and H. T. Richter (Germany)	1863	114·818	7·289	156·599	2019	32

Atomic Number	Symbol	Element Name	Derived From	Discoverers	Year	Atomic Weight (Note 2)	Density At 20°C (Unless Otherwise State) (g/cm3) (Note 3)	Melting Point (°C)	Boiling Point (°C)	Number of Nuclides
50	Sn	Tin (Stannum)	Anglo-Saxon 'tin'	Prehistoric (intentionally alloyed with copper to make bronze)	c. 3500 BC	118·710	7·288	231·928	2590	33
51	Sb	Antimony (Stibium)	Lower latin 'antimonium'	Near historic	c. 1000 BC	121·760	6·693	630·636	1635	29
52	Te	Tellurium	Latin 'tellus' = earth	F. J. Muller (Baron von Reichenstein) (Austria)	1783	127·60	6·237	449·81	989	33
53	I	Iodine	Greek 'iodes' = violet	B. Courtois (France)	1811	126·904 47	4·947	113·6	185·1	33
54	Xe	Xenon	Greek 'xenos' = stranger	W. Ramsay and M. W. Travers (UK)	1898	131·29	3·410 (solid at mp) 0·005897 (gas at 0°C)	–111·774	–108·083	36
55	Cs	Caesium	Latin 'caesius' = bluish-grey	R. W. von Bunsen and G. R.Kirchoff (Germany)	1860	132·905 43	1·896	28·46	668	36
56	Ba	Barium	Greek 'barys' = heavy	H. Davy (UK)	1808	137·327	3·595	729	1740	31
57	La	Lanthanum	Greek 'lanthano' = conceal	C. G. Mosander (Sweden)	1839	138·9055	6·145	921	3410	30
58	Ce	Cerium	The asteroid Ceres (discovered 1801)	J. J. Berzelius and W. Hisinger (Sweden) and M. H. Klaproth (Germany)	1803	140·115	6·688 (beta) 6·770 (gamma)	799	3470	30
59	Pr	Praseodymium	Greek 'prasios didymos' = green twin	C. Auer von Welsbach (Austria)	1885	140·907 65	6·772	934	3480	29
60	Nd	Neodymium	Greek 'neos didymos' = new twin	C. Auer von Welsbach (Austria)	1885	144·24	7·006	1021	3020	30
61	Pm	Promethium	Greek demi-god 'Prometheus' – the fire stealer	J. Marinsky, L. E.Glendenin, and C. D. Coryell (USA)	1945	(144·9127)	7·141	1042	3000	28
62	Sm	Samarium	The mineral Samarskite (named after Col. M. Samarski, a Russian engineer)	L. de Boisbaudran (France)	1879	150·36	7·517	1077	1794	30
63	Eu	Europium	Europe	E. A. Demarçay (France)	1901	151·965	5·243	822	1556	29
64	Gd	Gadolinium	Johan Gadolin (1760–1852)	J. C. G. de Marignac (Switzerland)	1880	157·25	7·899	1313	3270	27
65	Tb	Terbium	Ytterby, in Sweden	C. G. Mosander (Sweden)	1843	158·925 34	8·228	1356	3230	26
66	Dy	Dysprosium	Greek 'dysprositos' = hard to get at	L. de Boisbaudran (France)	1886	162·50	8·549	1412	2570	29
67	Ho	Holmium	Holmia, a Latinized form of Stockholm	J. L. Soret (France) and P. T. Cleve (Sweden)	1878–1879	164·930 32	8·794	1474	2700	29
68	Er	Erbium	Ytterby, in Sweden	C. G. Mosander (Sweden)	1843	167·26	9·064	1529	2810	29
69	Tm	Thulium	Latin and Greek 'Thule' = Northland	P. T. Cleve (Sweden)	1879	168·934 21	9·319	1545	1950	31
70	Yb	Ytterbium	Ytterby, in Sweden	J. C. G. de Marignac (France)	1878	173·04	6·967	817	1227	30

71	Lu	Lutetium	Lutetia, Roman name for the city of Paris	G. Urbain (France)	1907	174·967	9·839	1665	3400	35
72	Hf	Hafnium	Hafnia = Copenhagen	D. Coster (Netherlands) and G. C. de Hevesy (Hungary/Sweden)	1923	178·49	13·28	2230	4700	31
73	Ta	Tantalum	'Tantalus' - a mythical Greek king	A. G. Ekeberg (Sweden)	1802	180·9479	16·67	3020	5490	31
74	w	Tungsten (Wolfram)	Swedish 'tung sten' = heavy stone	J. J. de Elhuyar and F. de Elhuyar (Spain)	1783	183·84	19·26	3420	5860	33
75	Re	Rhenium	Latin 'Rhenus' = the river Rhine	W. Noddack, Fr. I. Tacke and O. Berg (Germany)	1925	186·207	21·01	3185	5610	33
76	Os	Osmium	Greek 'osme' = odour	S. Tennant (UK)	1804	190·23	22·59	3127	5020	35
77	Ir	Iridium	Latin 'iris' = a rainbow	S. Tennant (UK)	1804	192·217	22·56	2446	4730	33
78	Pt	Platinum	Spanish 'platina' = small silver	A. de Ulloa (Spain)	1748	195·08	21·45	1768·1	3870	35
79	Au	Gold (aurum)	Anglo-Saxon 'gold'	prehistoric	-	196·966 54	19·29	1064·18	2870	32
80	Hg	Mercury (Hydrargyrum)	'Hermes' (Latin 'Mercurius'), the divine patron of the occult sciences	Near historic	*c.* 1600 bc	200·59	14·17 (solid at mp) 13·55 (liquid at 20°c)	–38·829	356·661	33
81	Tl	Thallium	Greek 'thallos' = a budding twig	W. Crookes (UK)	1861	204·3833	11·87	303	1468	29
82	Pb	Lead (Plumbum)	Anglo-Saxon 'lead'	Prehistoric	-	207·2	11·35	327·462	1748	34
83	Bi	Bismuth	German 'weissmuth' = white matter	C. F. Geoffroy (France)	1753	208·980 37	9·807	271·402	1566	30
84	Po	Polonium	Poland	Mme. M. S. Curie (Poland/France)	1898	(208·9824)	9·155	254	948	27
85	At	Astatine	Greek 'astos' = unstable	D. R. Corson and K. R. Mackenzie (USA) and E. Segré (Italy/USA)	1940	(209·9871)	7·0	302	377	28
86	Rn	Radon	Latin 'radius' = ray	F. E. Dorn (Germany)	1900	(222·0176)	4·7 (solid at mp) 0·010 04 (gas at 0°C)	–64·9	–61·2	31
87	Fr	Francium	France	Mlle. M. Perey (France)	1939	(223·0197)	2·8	23	650	31
88	Ra	Radium	Latin 'radius' = ray	P. Curie (France), Mme. M. S. Curie (Poland/France), and M. G. Bemont (France)	1898	(226·0254)	5·50	707	1530	28
89	Ac	Actinium	Greek 'aktinos', genetive of 'aktis' = a ray	A. Debierne (France)	1899	(227·0278)	10·04	1230	3600	26
90	Th	Thorium	'Thor', the Norse god of thunder	J. J. Berzelius (Sweden)	1829	232·0381	11·72	1760	4660	25
91	Pa	Protactinium	Greek 'protos' = first, plus actinium	O. Hahn (Germany) and Fr. L. Meitner (Austria); F. Soddy and J. A. Cranston (UK)	1917	231·035 88	15·41	1570	4490	24
92	U	Uranium	The planet Uranus (discovered 1781)	M. H. Klaproth (Germany)	1789	238·0289	19·05	1134	4160	20
93	Np	Neptunium	The planet Neptune	E. M. McMillan and P. H. Abelson (USA)	1940	(237·0482)	20·47	637	4090	18

Atomic Number	Symbol	Element Name	Derived From	Discoverers	Year	Atomic Weight (Note 2)	Density At 20°C (Unless Otherwise State) (g/cm3) (Note 3)	Melting Point (°C)	Boiling Point (°C)	Number of Nuclides
94	Pu	Plutonium	The planet Pluto	G. T. Seaborg, E. M. McMillan J. W. Kennedy and A. C. Wahl (USA)	1940–1941	(244·0642)	20·26	640	3270	17
95	Am	Americium	America	G. T. Seaborg, R. A. James, L. O. Morgan and A. Ghiorso (USA)	1944–1945	(243·0614)	13·76	1176	2023	13
96	Cm	Curium	Pierre Curie (1859–1906) (France) and Marie Curie (1867–1934) (Poland/France)	G. T. Seaborg, R. A. James and A. Ghiorso (USA)	1944	(247·0703)	13·68	1340	3180	14
97	Bk	Berkelium	Berkeley, a town in California, USA	S. G. Thompson, A. Ghiorso and G. T. Seaborg (USA)	1949	(247·0703)	14·65	1050	2710	11
98	Cf	Californium	California	S. G. Thompson, A. Ghiorso K. Street Jr., and G. T. Seaborg (USA)	1950	(251·0796)	15·20	900	1612	18
99	Es	Einsteinium	Dr Albert Einstein (1879–1955) (USA, b. Germany)	A. Ghiorso et al (USA)	1952	(252·0830)	9·05	860	996	14
100	Fm	Fermium	Dr Enrico Fermi (1901–1954) (Italy)	A. Ghiorso et al (USA)	1953	(257·0951)	9.42	852	1077	18
101	Md	Mendelevium	Dmitriy I. Mendeleyev (1834–1907) (Russia)	A. Ghiorso, B. G. Harvey, G. R. Choppin, S. G. Thompson and G. T. Seaborg (USA)	1955	(258·0984)	–	–	–	13
102	No	Nobelium	Alfred B. Nobel (1833–1896) (Sweden)	E.D. Donets, A. Shchegolev, V.E. Ermakov (Russia)	1958	(259·1011)	–	–	–	11
103	Lr	Lawrencium	Dr Ernest O. Lawrence (1901–1958) (USA)	E.D. Donets, A. Shchegolev, V.E. Ermakov (Russia)	1961	(262·1098)	–	–	–	10
104	Db	Dubnium	Moscow location of chemical research	A. Ghiorso, M. Nurmia, K. Eskola, J. Harris and P. Eskola (USA/Finland)	1969	(261·1089)	–	–	–	10
105	Jl	Joliotium	Frédéric and Irène Joliot Curie (1900–58 and 1896–58) (France)	A. Ghiorso, M. Nurmia, K. Eskola, J. Harris and P. Eskola (USA/Finland)	1970	(262·1144)	–	–	–	8
106	Rf	Rutherfordium	Ernest Rutherford (1871–1937) (NZ)	A. Ghiorso et al (USA)	1974	(266·12)	–	–	–	4
107	Bh	Bohrium	Niels Bohr (1885–1962) (Denmark)	G. Münzenberg (Germany)	1981	(264·1249)	–	–	–	3
108	Hn	Hahnium	Otto Hahn (1879–1968) (Germ)	G. Münzenberg (Germany)	1984	(265·1306)	–	–	–	2
109	Mt	Meitnerium	Lise Meitner (1878–1968) (Sweden; b. Austria)	G. Münzenberg (Germany)	1982	(268)	–	–	–	2
110	Uun	Ununnilium	Un-un-nil (1-1-0)	P. Armbruster (Germany)	1994	(271)	–	–	–	
111	Uuu	Unununium	Un-un-un (1-1-1)	P. Armbruster (Germany)	1995	(272)	–	–	–	

STATES OF MATTER

Solid, liquid and gas (or vapour) are the three states in which substances can exist. The state in which any particular substance exists depends upon the temperature and upon the pressure being exerted upon it. Virtually all substances are able to exist in more than one of these states. At normal temperature or pressure water is a liquid but can exist as a vapour (steam) or as a solid (ice) at different temperatures and pressures.

In chemical equations, initials are sometimes used to indicate the state of a particular substance: (g) = gas; (l) = liquid; (s) = solid. (aq) = aqueous solution is also used but this is not a state.

The particles in a gas move very quickly, are not close together and consequently have relatively little attraction for one another. If the temperature of that gas is reduced, the particles in it will move more slowly. The slower particles take up less space and, because they are closer, there will be a stronger attraction between them. If the temperature is reduced enough, the particles adhere to one another and the gas becomes a liquid. In the liquid, particles move randomly and more slowly than in the gas. If the temperature is decreased further, the particles may cease to move randomly and may then vibrate in fixed positions. The liquid becomes a solid. The reverse situation occurs when the temperature of a solid is raised. The solid will be turned to a liquid and, with a further increase in temperature, the liquid will be turned into a gas.

bond the chemical link which holds atoms together.

gas (or **vapour**) the normal state of a substance whose particles have very high energy. When heat is applied to a liquid, the kinetic energy of the atoms, ions and molecules within that liquid is increased. The increased energy may be enough to weaken the forces of attraction that bond these atoms, ions and molecules together as a liquid. If this happens, the liquid will boil and it turns into a gas. In a container, collisions of gas particles with the container's walls exert a pressure. Gas particles move very quickly – usually at a rate of hundreds of metres a second; they also move in random directions and, in so doing, fill all the available spaces.

The density of gases is much less – averaging about 1/1000th – than that of a solid or of a liquid.

liquid a state of matter in which particles are held together, but not in a rigid lattice, which is the case in a solid. During evaporation and boiling the particles acquire enough energy to overcome the forces that hold them together and become a gas.

solid a state of matter in which ions or molecules are fixed in position and do not have the freedom to move that atoms, ions and molecules do in a liquid or a gas. The particles vibrate about fixed positions. The atoms, ions and molecules are held together in a lattice of bonds. Movement of atoms, ions and molecules in a solid is only possible when these bonds are partly broken, for example, by the application of heat to such an extent that the solid melts.

vapour see gas.

DIFFUSION

Diffusion is the movement of particles to achieve an even distribution of concentration. Particles collide with one another thus slowing down their progress. Diffusion only takes place very rapidly when a substance is present in a vacuum.

diffusion in gases may be demonstrated in the following experiment. A piece of cotton wool is placed at either end of a tube – one piece of cotton wool is soaked in concentrated ammonia solution; the other is soaked in concentrated hydrochloric acid. The tube is corked to prevent draughts from moving the gases and is maintained in a level position so that the effect of gravity is avoided. Gases are given off from each piece of cotton wool and a white compound – ammonium chloride – is formed in the tube at the point at which the ammonia and hydrogen chloride meet. The compound forms nearer the hydrogen chloride concentration. It can thus be deduced that the ammonia molecules have moved further, and therefore faster, than the hydrogen chloride molecules over the same period of time.

diffusion in liquids may be demonstrated as follows. If a crystal of potassium manganate (VII) is placed in a beaker of water diffusion will slowly occur. After 15 minutes a purple colour will begin to spread from the crystal as it starts to dissolve. After a day, a solution with a uniform purple colour will have resulted. Because the particles in a liquid are closer together than the particles in a gas, the rate of diffusion in the liquid is, therefore, much slower than in a gas.

diffusion in solids occurs but is a very slow process indeed although it can be speeded up by the introduction of heat.

kinetic energy energy that a moving object processes. The amount of energy depends upon the object's mass and its speed and can be given in the following equation:

$$\text{kinetic energy} = \tfrac{1}{2}\,\text{mass} \times \text{speed}^2$$

When considering a single substance, the kinetic energy decreases gas → liquid → solid because these states exist at different temperatures. When comparing different substances, the kinetic energy of their particles depends only on their temperature. Thus a solid, a liquid and a gas, *all at the same temperature*, will contain particles with the *same* average kinetic energy. Kinetic energy can be converted into heat energy.

rate of diffusion depends upon the speed at which particles move and the closeness of the particles. The quicker particles move, the faster diffusion occurs. Thus, the collision of particles slows down the rate of diffusion. The rate of diffusion depends upon three factors: the concentration of the particles, the speed of the particles and the mass of the particles. The concentration of particles has an important effect upon the rate of diffusion – the fewer particles present, the greater the rate of diffusion. This is because the particles do not collide with one another so often. The speed of particles depends upon the temperature of the substance. The higher the temperature, the greater the rate at which diffusion occurs. The mass of particles also has an effect upon the rate of diffusion, particularly in a gas. Thus, the lighter the particles, will be and the faster the rate of diffusion.

CHEMICAL BONDS

Although there are only 111 known elements, there are millions of chemical substances found in nature or made artificially. These substances are not simply mixtures of two or more elements: they are chemical compounds, formed or combining two or more elements together in a chemical reaction. The chemical 'glue' that holds these compounds together is chemical bonding. The properties of a compound are very different from those of its constituent elements. To understand how and why these differences arise, we need to understand the different types of chemical bond.

allotrope an allotropic form; allotropy is the property that certain chemical elements have of existing in two or more different forms.

anion a negatively charged ion, e.g. F^-.

buckminsterfullerene an allotropic form of carbon. *Fullerenes* are hollow clusters of carbon atoms that are joined into geometrical shapes.

carbon a non-metallic element, which is found in group 4 of the Periodic Table. Atomic number: 6. Symbol: C. Carbon is found in three different forms or allotropes – diamond, graphite and fullerene. All living tissue contains carbon compounds – organic compounds – such as carbohydrates, proteins and fats, without which life would not be possible.

cation a positively charged ion, e.g. Na^+.

colloid a substance composed of insoluble, non-diffusable particles that remain in suspension in a medium of different matter. When a colloid does diffuse it does so slowly.

compound a substance that is made of atoms of two or more elements bonded together. The properties of compounds are quite different from the properties of the elements from which they are made. For example, sodium chloride is a solid and is better known as common salt. Sodium, by contrast, is a corrosive metal which reacts violently with water, while chlorine is a poisonous gas which has a characteristic choking smell. The atoms in a compound may be held together by either ionic bonds or covalent bonds.

covalent bonding the type of bond that is formed when two atoms share electrons. If we bring together two fluorine atoms, each having seven outer electrons (one less than neon), the formation of two ions with the noble-gas configuration is not possible. If, however, they share a pair of electrons – one from each atom – then both achieve the noble-gas configuration and a stable molecule results. There is a force of attraction between the shared pair of electrons and both positive nuclei, and this is what is known as a covalent bond. The stronger the attraction of the nuclei for the shared pair, the stronger the bond.

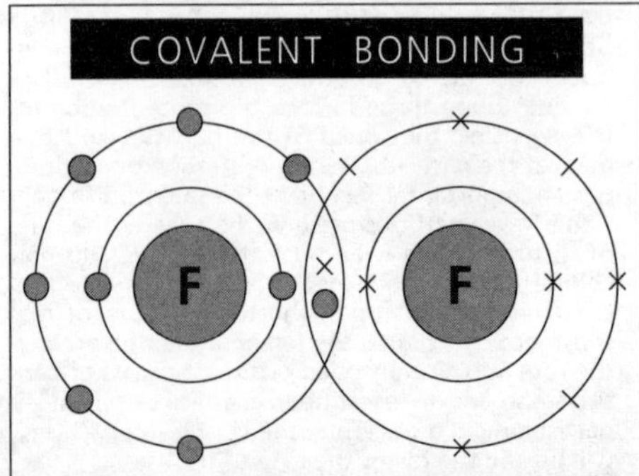

An atom of oxygen, having two electrons less than neon, must form two covalent bonds to attain a share in eight outer electrons. A molecule of water, consisting of two hydrogen atoms (H) and one oxygen atom (O), has two covalent O-H bonds. Another way for oxygen to achieve the stable noble-gas configuration is to form two bonds with the same atom. Thus two oxygen atoms bond covalently to one another by sharing two pairs of electrons. This is known as *double bonding*.

Like oxygen, sulphur has six outer electrons and again needs to form two bonds to attain a share in eight electrons. There are two ways in which sulphur atoms join together – either in rings of eight atoms or in long chains of many atoms bonded together. The different forms in which elemental sulphur exists are known as allotropes. Other elements found in allotropic forms include carbon (graphite, diamond and fullerene) and oxygen (oxygen and ozone).

Atoms of nitrogen (N), containing five outer electrons, need to form three covalent bonds to attain a share in eight outer electrons. This may be done, for example, by forming one bond to each of three hydrogen atoms to give ammonia. Another possibility is to form all three bonds to a second nitrogen atom, which produces a nitrogen molecule, containing a *triple covalent bond*.

The carbon atom (C), which has four outer electrons, needs to form four bonds to attain the noble-gas configuration. Thus a carbon atom forms one bond to each of four hydrogen atoms to give methane.

crystalloid a substance – usually crystallizable – which, when in solution, readily passes through membranes. Crystalloids diffuse quickly.

diamond an allotropic mineral that consists of nearly pure carbon in a tetrahedral crystalline form.

giant molecule a structure in which a large and indefinite number of atoms are present. These particles may form a crystal lattice in which each particle has a strong attraction for the particles around it, but other structures are also possible. Although two carbon atoms do not form a *quadruple bond* (see covalent bond) to one another, carbon atoms can combine to form a giant crystal lattice if each atom is bonded to four others by single covalent bonds. This is the structure of diamond. Many other elements and compounds exist as giant covalent crystal lattices, including quartz. Crystals of these substances contain many millions of atoms held together by strong covalent bonds, so that a large amount of energy is needed to break them. Thus these substances all have high melting points and are hard solids.

giant structure a structure in which a very large number of atoms or ions are present in a regular arrangement, known as a lattice. Ionic compounds, metals and giant molecular elements and compounds have giant structures.

graphite an allotropic soft black hexagonal form of carbon.

hydrogen bond a force of attraction between hydrogen and oxygen, nitrogen or fluorine atoms in neighbouring molecules. Some small molecules have much higher melting points and boiling points than would be expected on the basis of their size. One such example is water, which has about the same mass as a neon atom but has a much higher melting point. There must therefore be unusually strong intermolecular forces between the water molecules. Although the oxygen and hydrogen atoms share a pair of electrons in a covalent bond, the oxygen atom exerts a stronger 'pull' on these electrons and so becomes electron-rich, leaving the hydrogen atom electron-poor. As a result, there is a force of attraction between hydrogen and oxygen atoms on neighbouring molecules.

Although hydrogen bonds are stronger than van der Waals forces, they are still much weaker than covalent bonds.

ion an atom or group of atoms that has become electrically charged by either gaining or losing one or more electrons. Atoms tend to lose or to gain electrons to produce an ion with the same stable configuration as a noble gas.

ionic bonding (or **electrovalent bonding**) a chemical bond that occurs because of electrostatic attractive forces between positively and negatively charged ions. The atoms of the element neon have eight electrons in their outer shell, with the electron arrangement 2·8. This arrangement is very stable and neon is not known to form a chemical bond with any other element. An atom of the element sodium (Na) has one more electron than neon (configuration 2·8·1), while an atom of the element fluorine (F) has one electron less than neon (configuration 2·7). If an electron is transferred from a sodium atom to a fluorine atom, two species are produced with the same stable electron configuration as neon. Unlike neon, however, the species are charged and are known as ions. The sodium atom, having lost a (negative) electron, has a net positive charge and is known as a cation (q.v.; written Na^+), while the fluorine atom, having gained an electron, has a net negative charge and is called a fluoride anion (q.v.; written F^-).

When oppositely charged ions such as Na^+ and F^- approach one another, there is a strong attraction between them; a large amount of energy is released – the same amount of energy as would have to be supplied in order to separate the ions again. This force of attraction is called an ionic (or electrovalent) bond. The energy released more than compensates for the energy input required to transfer the electron from the sodium atom to the fluorine atom. Overall there is a net release of energy and a solid crystalline compound – sodium fluoride (NaF) – is formed.

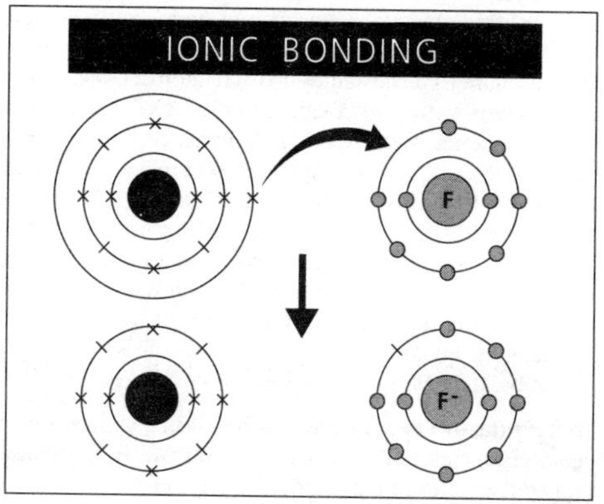

Atoms that have two more electrons than the nearest noble gas (such as magnesium, configuration 2·8·2) or two less (such as oxygen, configuration 2·6) also form ions having the noble-gas configuration by transfer of electrons. The ionic compound magnesium oxide (MgO) has the same arrangement of ions as NaF, but since the ions in MgO have a greater charge, there is a stronger force between them. Thus more energy must be supplied to overcome this force of attraction, and the melting point of MgO is higher than that of NaF.

Although the ions are fixed in position in the crystal, they become free to move when the solid is melted. As a liquid, therefore, the compound becomes electrolytic and is able to conduct electricity.

large molecule a type of macromolecule which is characterized by the very great number of atoms contained. Large molecules have thousands rather than billions of atoms per molecule. Polymers (proteins, starches and plastics) are large molecules. Large molecules have lower melting points than giant molecular structures, but they have higher melting points than simple molecules. Large molecules do not conduct electricity (because they lack ions). They are not particularly soluble in water.

macromolecule a molecule containing up to billions of atoms.

radical a group of atoms that acts as a single atom. A radical goes through a chemical reaction unchanged.

valency the number of bonds which an atom forms with another atom. The valency of an element is the number of electrons that it needs to form a compound or a radical. These electrons may be lost, or gained, or shared with another atom. Some elements always have the same valency; for example, the valency of sodium is always 1. This means that – in compounds such as sodium chloride – it gives one electron away when it forms the sodium ion Na^+. Oxygen, on the other hand, always has a valency of 2. Thus oxygen accepts two electrons when it forms the oxide ion or shares two of carbon's electrons in a covalent compound such as carbon dioxide.

van der Waals forces a weak intermolecular force whose strength depends upon the number of electrons in the molecule involved. Two neon atoms do not form covalent bonds with one another because of their stable configuration of electrons. There are, however, weak forces of attraction between two neon atoms. This can be shown because, when neon gas is compressed or cooled, it eventually turns into a liquid in which the atoms are weakly attracted to one another. These weak forces are called van der Waals forces.

CHEMICAL REACTIONS

Chemical reactions are the means by which new substances are formed from old ones. Among the chemical reactions occurring everywhere around us are the changes that take place when fuels are burnt, the industrial means by which metals are extracted from their ores, and the processes controlling life itself. Since chemistry is centrally concerned with the means by which substances change, the study of reactions lies at the heart of the subject. An essential characteristic of all chemical reactions is that there is an exchange of energy between the reacting system and the surroundings.

acid a substance that tends to donate protons (H^+s) (the Brønsted-Lowry definition).

Example: Hydrogen chloride (HCl) readily dissolves in water. The HCl donates its proton to water in a reversible reaction:

$$HCl(aq) + H_2O(l) \rightleftharpoons H_3O^+(aq) + Cl^-(aq)$$

The products of the forward reaction are ions:

H_3O (the oxonium ion) and Cl^- (the chloride ion).

Many non-metal oxides form acids when added to water.

Example: Sulphur trioxide gas (SO_3) reacts with water to form sulphuric acid (H_2SO_4) – the reaction that occurs in the formation of acid rain.

alkali a soluble base.

balanced chemical equation an equation that gives information concerning a reaction. By convention the reactants appear on the left-hand side and the products appear on the right-hand side. A balanced equation is a quantitative statement about the chemical reaction concerned. Such an equation – combined with the mole concept – enables us to predict how much of a product will be formed from a given mass of reactants. This provides valuable information that can be put to use, for example, in industrial production processes and in the analysis of chemical samples of unknown composition.

base a proton acceptor. Bases are capable of accepting protons of oxonium ions present in a solution. A good example of a Brønsted-Lowry base is the hydroxide ion OH^-, which reacts reversibly with the oxonium ion to produce two molecules of water:

$$H_3O^+(aq) + OH^-(aq) \rightleftharpoons 2H_2O(l)$$

Examples of bases include sodium and potassium hydroxides (NaOH and KOH), which liberate aqueous hydroxide ions in solution. Many metal oxides, such as calcium oxide (CaO; 'lime'), are also basic. CaO reacts violently with water to form calcium hydroxide; 'slaked lime'. Soluble bases are known as alkalis.

basic pertaining to a base.

catalyst a substance that is chemically unchanged at the end of a reaction or at equilibrium but whose presence serves to alter its rate. (NB. Catalysts *do* change during the course of a chemical reaction, but go back to their original composition at the end of the reaction or at equilibrium.)

cation a positive ion.

chemical equation see balanced chemical equation.

disproportionation reaction a reaction in which a single chemical species is simultaneously oxidized and reduced.

Example: Copper (I) sulphate (Cu_2SO_4) dissolves in water to produce copper metal and copper (II) sulphate:

$$Cu_2SO_4\,(aq) \rightarrow Cu(s) + CuSO_4\,(aq)$$

Here one Cu^+ ion is oxidized to Cu^{2+}, while the second is reduced to Cu metal.

indicator a dye upon which the effects of acids and alkalis can be observed. Indicators are used as detectors of acids and alkalis. The best-known is litmus.

ion electrically charged species.

law of constant composition states that matter cannot be created or destroyed during a chemical reaction. Thus in the reaction of potassium with water (see reactants; below), the number of atoms of potassium, hydrogen and oxygen (calculated by multiplying each symbol in the equation by the number placed before the chemical formula and the number immediately after the symbol) is the same before and after the reaction, and the equation is said to be balanced.

litmus an indicator; a dye derived from lichen, which is turned into red by acids and blue by alkalis.

molar quantity the number of moles.

mole a measure of the amount of substance, based on the atomic theory of matter. A mole is defined as the amount of substance that contains as many entities as there are carbon atoms in 12 grams of the isotope carbon-12. The mass of 1 mole of an entity (atom, molecule, ion, etc.) is the relative mass of that entity, expressed in grams. Every chemical compound has a fixed relative molecular mass, which is determined by the relative atomic masses of its constituent elements, so that molar quantities of any substance can be found using simple arithmetic.

oxidation a class of reactions that includes all combustion processes such as those occurring when fuels burn in air, as well as the reactions that cause metals to corrode in air.

Example: Magnesium metal burns with an incandescent white flame in air because of a vigorous reaction with oxygen, forming magnesium oxide. The product in this case is an ionic solid, which we could write more specifically as $Mg^{2+}O^{2-}$. During the reaction, magnesium losses two electrons to form the cation Mg^{2+}; the electrons are accepted by oxygen. The transfer of electrons between chemical entities is a common process in many chemical reactions, so the term oxidation has come to possess a wider meaning than that implying solely the addition of oxygen atoms to an element or compound. As in the case of the formation of magnesium oxide, oxidation means the loss of electrons by an entity; the opposite process is reduction.

precipitation reactions involve the formation of an insoluble material from the reaction of two soluble substances on mixing their two solutions.

Example: Silver nitrate ($AgNO_3$) dissolves readily in water, producing a colourless solution of aqueous silver (Ag^+) and nitrate (NO_3^-) ions. If solutions of silver nitrate and sodium chloride are mixed, a white turbidity (cloudiness) instantly forms; this is due to the precipitation of fine particles of highly insoluble silver chloride. The precipitate gradually accumulates at the bottom of the vessel, leaving colourless sodium nitrate in solution:

$$NaC1\ (aq) + AgNO_3(aq) \rightarrow AgC1(s) + NaNO_3(aq)$$

The overall reaction is one in which ions are exchanged between partners. It is possible to predict the outcome of such precipitation reactions from our knowledge of the solubilities of the various species involved.

products the substances that result from the rearrangement of atomic constituents during a chemical reaction.

proton a positively-ionized hydrogen atom.

reactants substances that react together during a chemical reaction. The atomic constituents of reactants are rearranged to produce other substances (products). Thus, for example, during the reaction of potassium (K) with water (H_2O), potassium hydroxide (KOH) and hydrogen gas (H_2) are formed. This information can be represented by a chemical equation:

$$2K(s) + 2H_2O(1 + aq) \rightarrow 2KOH\ (aq) + H_2(g)$$

So much heat is liberated during the reaction of water and potassium that the highly flammable hydrogen gas frequently ignites.

reaction equilibrium the end of a reaction. The point at which there is no further change in the amount of products formed or reactants destroyed. At equilibrium, there may still be appreciable amounts of reactants present. At equilibrium, the rate of the forward reaction equals the rate of the backward reaction, and the quantities of all the substances become constant.

redox reaction a reaction in which oxidation and reduction take place. Thus in the equation:

$$2Na(s) + C1_2(g) \rightarrow 2NaC1(s)$$

the sodiums are oxidized once they each lose an electron to the chlorines, which are thereby reduced. If an electric current is passed through an electrolyte such as an aqueous solution of copper (II) chloride ($CuC1_2$), a redox process known as *electrolysis* occurs. Positively charged ions are attracted to the negative electrode (cathode), where they take up two electrons each and are thereby reduced to copper metal, which is deposited at the cathode. The negative chloride ions are attracted to the positive electrode (anode) where they each lose an electron and are thereby oxidized to atoms before pairing off to give chlorine gas.

reduction the process of losing oxygen or gaining electrons.

salt a compound formed by the replacement of some or all of the hydrogens in an acid by a metal or ammonium ion. Thus the reactions between the base sodium hydroxide and sulphuric acid yield two salts, sodium hydrogen sulphate and sodium sulphate.

stoichiometry the numerical proportions in which substances combine to form the products of a chemical reaction.

strong acid/base an acid/base that is ionized to a large extent in aqueous solutions. Thus hydrochloric acid and sodium hydroxide are both strong.

weak acid/base an acid/base that is ionized to a small extent in aqueous solution. Thus ethanic acid and ammonia are weak.

METALS

Metals are usually defined by their physical properties, such as strength, hardness, lustre, conduction of heat and electricity, malleability and high melting point. They can also be characterized chemically as elements that react with (or whose oxides react with) acids, usually to free positively charged metal ions. More than 75% of the elements are metals. They occupy all but the right-hand top corner of the Periodic Table.

alkali metals and alkaline earth metals see p. 230.

conduction of heat and electricity characterizes metals. This property is due to their unique type of bonding. The solid metals behave as though they were composed of arrays of positively charged ions, with electrons free to move throughout the crystalline structure of the metal. This results in high electrical conductivity. The conduction of heat can also be seen in terms of the motion of electrons, which becomes faster as temperature rises. Since the electrons are mobile, the heat can be conducted readily through the solid. The majority of metals are good conductors of electricity, but germanium and tin (in the form stable below 19 °C/64 °F) are semiconductors.

mechanical strength is the reason why many metals are used for purposes such as construction. However, most pure metals are actually quite soft. In order to obtain a tough hard metal, something else has to be added. For instance, the earliest useful metal was not copper but bronze, which is copper alloyed to tin. Similarly, iron is never used in the pure form but as some form of steel. (The softness of a metal results from a lack of perfection in the crystal framework formed by its ions.)

metalloids the borderline elements – for instance, germanium, arsenic and antimony – that are not true metals.

natural occurrence (of metals) is mostly as oxides. Some metals – mostly the heavier ones such as mercury and lead – occur as sulphides, and the more reactive ones as chlorides and carbonates. Only a few – the noble and coinage metals – are found in the metallic state.

tarnishing (and **corrosion**) occur in nearly all metals, which are prone to surface oxidation, i.e. the surface reacts with oxygen or other components of the atmosphere.

transition metals are not a group of the Periodic Table – they do not all have the same number of electrons in the outer shell of their atoms. They rather a 'family' of metals – a block of metals in the middle of the Periodic Table which share certain properties in common. They have special properties (coloured compounds, variable oxidation state, etc.).

ALKALINITY

The alkali metals are the most reactive metals in the Periodic Table. They are the elements of group 1 of the Periodic Table. These elements – lithium, sodium, potassium, rubidium, caesium and francium – are soft metals. Their softness and low melting point are both the result of the weakness of the metallic bonding in these elements. Their low melting point is a characteristic which – along with their low density – makes them quite distinct from other metals. The alkali metals can be cut easily with a knife to reveal a shiny surface which quickly tarnishes. The elements of group 1 are called alkali metals because of the alkalis that are formed when they are in reaction with either air or water. The pure metals themselves are not alkalis.

The alkaline earth metals are the elements of group 2 – beryllium, magnesium, calcium, strontium, barium and radium. Of these elements, calcium and magnesium are the most common. The alkaline earth metals are not so reactive as the alkali metals. They are harder than the alkali metals – they are not so easy to cut with a knife – and also have higher melting points than the elements in group 1. As with all groups of metals, the melting points of the metals in group 2 decrease going down on the Periodic Table. By contrast, their density increases down the group.

acidity see pH (below).

alkali a base that is soluble in water. They are usually metal hydroxides, such as sodium hydroxide.

Properties of alkalis:
Alkalis are corrosive.
Alkalis turn red litmus blue.
In solution, they have a pH of over 7; see pH (below).
Alkalis neutralize acids.
Alkalis react with acids and, in so doing, produce only water and a salt.

barium an alkaline earth metal. Atomic number: 56. Symbol: Ba.

beryllium an alkaline earth metal. Atomic number: 4. Symbol: Be.

caesium an alkali metal. Atomic number: 55. Symbol: Cs.

calcium an alkaline earth metal. Atomic number: 20. Symbol: Ca.

compounds of alkali metals are formed when alkali metals react strongly with halogens or with oxygen. As a result, the compounds alkali metal halides or alkali metal oxides are formed. In these reactions the alkali metal atoms lose their single outer shell electron.

The chloride compounds – for example, LiCl (lithium chloride), NaCl (sodium chloride), KCl (potassium chloride) – are all ionic salts. These can be electrolysed when in the molten state, the alkali metal being given at the cathode and the chlorine being given at the anode. (Electrolysis initiates the decomposition.)

The hydroxide compounds – for example, LiOH (lithium hydroxide), NaOH (sodium hydroxide), KOH (potassium hydroxide) – are all strong alkalis.

compounds of alkaline earth metals are formed when alkaline earth metals react with halogens or oxygen. However, they react less vigorously than the alkali metals do with halogens or oxygen.

francium the most reactive of the alkali metals. Atomic number: 87. Symbol: Fr. Francium is a synthetic element and has only been made in very small quantities. Its reactions, however, have been just as those predicted from an observation of the properties of the other elements within the group.

ionic salt a salt containing ionic bonds.

kalium an alternative name for potassium.

lithium the least reactive of the alkali metals. Atomic number: 3. Symbol: Li.

magnesium a light silvery-coloured alkaline earth metal. Atomic number: 12. Symbol: Mg.

pH scale is a measure of acidity or alkalinity. The lower the value on the pH scale, the more acidic the solution, i.e. the greater the concentration of hydrogen ions in it. By contrast, the higher the value on the pH scale, the more alkaline the solution. A neutral solution has equal concentrations of hydrogen and hydroxide ions and has a pH of 7.

potassium (or **kalium**) an alkali metal. Atomic number: 19. Symbol: K.

radium an alkaline earth metal. Atomic number: 88. Symbol: Ra.

reactions of the alkali metals The alkali metals are so reactive that – in laboratory conditions – they must not be allowed to contact other elements with which they react. They are, therefore, normally stored under a liquid hydrocarbon – for example, paraffin oil – to prevent them from making contact with water, carbon dioxide and oxygen. Alkali metals react with all non-metals (except for the noble gases) and with most compounds that contain these non-metals.

The reactivity of the alkali metals increases down the group – thus lithium is the least reactive of the alkali metals and francium is the most reactive of the group.

The reaction of alkali metals with water is distinctive. Sodium, lithium and potassium float on water because they are less dense than water.

reactions of the alkaline earth metals In reaction, the group 2 metals lose two electrons from their outer shell and, in so doing, gain a double positive charge. Compared with the elements of group 1 (the alkali metals), the alkaline earth metals all tarnish more slowly.

Their reactions with water are also much slower than those of the elements in group 1. In reaction with water, group 2 elements produce hydrogen and a metal oxide or hydroxide. Alkaline earth metals are, nevertheless, reactive and – except for magnesium and beryllium – have to be kept under, for example, paraffin, to avoid reactions with water vapour, oxygen or carbon dioxide.

rubidium an alkali metal. Atomic number: 37. Symbol: Rb.

salt a compound formed when the hydrogen of an acid is either totally or partially replaced by a metal.

sodium an alkali metal. Atomic number: 11. Symbol: Na.

strontium an alkaline earth metal. Atomic number: 38. Symbol: Sr.

NOBLE (INERT) GASES

The noble gases form a group of almost totally inert gases. They are the elements helium, neon, argon, krypton, xenon and radon – the elements of group 18 of the Periodic Table. The noble gases are all monatomic. They do not need to combine with any other atom in order to obtain stable electronic configuration because they already have that configuration. (From shell 3 onwards, eight is the maximum number of electrons that an electron can accommodate.) The noble gases all occur in the air, but, with the exception of argon, they are all relatively rare. Helium is sometimes found in natural gas and so may be obtained from it; the other noble gases are obtained by fractional distillation of liquid air.

argon a noble or inert gas. Argon – which is odourless – forms nearly 1% of the atmosphere. Atomic number: 18. Symbol: Ar. Argon is the principal gas to be used to fill electric light bulbs where it prevents the tungsten filament from burning. As argon is readily available in the atmosphere it is a relatively cheap gas to produce commercially. It is, therefore, commonly used where a non-reactive atmosphere is needed – it is used, for example, in welding.

helium a noble or inert gas. Helium is light and colourless. Because it is so light, helium is used as a non-flammable substitute for inflating balloons. (It is not, however, used in so-called 'hot air' balloons.) Helium mixed with oxygen is given to deep-sea divers in order to prevent the 'bends'. Helium has the smallest molecule of the noble gases – this means that its molecules attract one another least. Consequently, helium has the lowest melting and boiling points of any group 18 element. Atomic number: 2. Symbol: He.

krypton a rare noble or inert gas. Atomic number: 36. Symbol: Kr. Krypton is used as a filling for light bulbs to prevent the filament of the bulb from burning.

lack of reactivity (of noble gases) is due to the inability of the atoms of these elements to transfer or to share electrons. This is because each of the noble gas elements has atoms with a stable electronic configuration. Noble gases, thus, do not need to react with other atoms – not even their own – in order to obtain a stable configuration. They are, therefore, inert with other substances.

monatomic molecule molecules that contain a single atom.

neon a rare noble or inert gas. Neon is colourless. Atomic number: 10. Symbol: Ne. Neon is used in the familiar red illuminated signs and is also employed as a 'starter gas' in sodium street lamps – the characteristic red glow of neon is seen when these lamps are first turned on. Electric current is conducted by the neon and sodium is vaporized as the lamp warms up. When the sodium is fully vaporized it conducts the current.

radon a noble or inert gas. This radioactive gas is formed in the atomic disintegration of radium. Radon has the largest molecules of any of the noble gases. It has the highest boiling and melting points in the group. Atomic number: 86. Symbol: Rn.

xenon a noble or inert gas. Xenon – which is heavy and colourless – is present in the atmosphere in minute quantities. Atomic number: 54. Symbol: Xe. Xenon is used to fill light bulbs to prevent the filament from burning. It is particularly used in the bulbs found in lighthouses. Xenon allows the filament to be run at a very high temperature and, therefore, to produce a much more intense light.

HALOGENS

Halogens are reactive non-metals of group 17 – fluorine, chlorine, bromine and iodine (plus astatine). As a group they share certain characteristics. To achieve a noble gas electron structure of eight electrons in its outer shell, each halogen atom must accept an electron. This is accomplished by either accepting an electron by transfer from a metal atom or by accepting a share of an electron from another non-metal atom. An electron that is being accepted by a halogen will be most strongly held if it becomes part of an electron shell that is close to the nucleus, which strongly attracts electrons. The halogen with an outer electron shell nearest to the nucleus is fluorine, which is the most reactive halogen and will readily form compounds. Reactivity decreases down the group as the outer electron shells get further away from the nucleus. Halogens react vigorously with metals and hydrogen to form halides (see below).

astatine a synthetic halogen which is placed below iodine in the Periodic Table. It is the least reactive of the halogens. Atomic number: 85. Symbol: At.

bromine a halogen that is a liquid at room temperature. Atomic number: 35. Symbol: Br.

characteristics of halogens include:

– they are all diatomic; that is, they have two atoms for each molecule;

– they are coloured (chlorine and fluorine are green gases, bromine is a brown liquid, and iodine is grey as a solid and purple as a vapour);

– reactivity decreases down the group (this a reversal of the situation with the metals).

chlorine a halogen that is a gas at room temperature. Atomic number: 17. Symbol: Cl. The usual chemical test for chlorine relies upon the formation of acid and bleach upon the reaction of chlorine and water. With chlorine, a piece of damp litmus paper will first turn red and then will be become colourless. A similar reaction will occur with bromine and iodine but the reaction will be very much slower.

fluorine a halogen that is a gas at room temperature. Atomic number: 9. Symbol: F. Fluorine is a dangerous highly reactive substance, the most reactive member of the group. It displaces chlorine, bromine and iodine from their ionic compounds.

halides compounds of a halogen and one other element. Thus, hydrogen bromide, phosphorus pentachloride and chromium (III) fluoride are all halides.

iodine a halogen that is a solid when at room temperature. Atomic number: 53. Symbol: I.

melting point (of halogens) increases down the group. Thus fluorine has the lowest melting point and astatine the highest.

reactions of the halogens The halogen that is most commonly used for study in experimentation is chlorine. Fluorine, the most reactive, would not be studied in a college laboratory. *Chlorine reacts with water in the following manner:* There is no vigorous reaction when chlorine comes into contact with water. A similar result is experienced in the cases of iodine and bromine. Chlorine, bromine and iodine react to decreasing extents to form an acidic solution. These solutions have bleaching powers that increase as the reactivity of the halogen decreases.

SMALL MOLECULES

Although the Earth's atmosphere consists almost entirely of two gases – nitrogen and oxygen – a number of other gases are also present at low concentration, together with varying amounts of water vapour. Not only are these gases of major importance in relation to industrial processes that dominate economies throughout the world, but cyclical processes involving water, oxygen, carbon dioxide and nitrogen – together with solar radiation – are essential to plant and animal life. Although small molecules are simple in that they are composed of few atoms, their structures and their shapes vary. In most cases, their atoms are held together in the molecule by two, four or six electrons, resulting in single, double or triple covalent bonds.

ammonia a colourless gas with a penetrating odour. It is less dense than air. Ammonia is highly soluble in water, giving an alkaline solution. World production is in the order of 100 million tonnes – 80% of which is turned into fertilizers. *Concentration in unpolluted air (parts per million):* variable.

carbon dioxide a colourless gas with slight odour and an acid taste. It is available as a gas, as liquid and as the white solid known as 'dry ice'. Its cycle in nature is tied to that of oxygen, the relative levels of the two gases in the atmosphere (apart from human activity) being regulated by the photosynthetic activity of plants. It is produced on a vast scale, mostly as a by-product of other processes. With the ever-increasing input of carbon dioxide to the atmosphere, due largely to the burning of fossil fuels and forests, and the manufacture of cement, the natural 'sinks' for carbon dioxide (photosynthesis and transfer to the oceans) can no longer keep pace with the total input. If this imbalance continues, it is thought that the infrared-absorbing properties of carbon dioxide will result in a progressive warming of the Earth's atmosphere – the so-called *greenhouse effect. Concentration in unpolluted air (parts per million):* c. 315.

carbon monoxide is a colourless, odourless, toxic gas. The input to the atmosphere due to human activity is about 360 million tonnes per year, mostly from the incomplete combustion of fossil fuels. The natural input is about 10 times this figure and results from the partial oxidation of biologically produced methane. The background level of 0·1 parts per million can rise to 20ppm at a busy road junction, and a five-minute cigarette gives an intake of 400ppm. Since the atmospheric level of carbon monoxide is not rising significantly, there must be effective sink processes, one being its oxidation in air to carbon dioxide. In addition, there are soil micro-organisms that utilize carbon monoxide in photosynthesis. *Concentration in unpolluted air (parts per million):* 0·1.

dinitrogen monoxide a colourless, odourless gas. *Concentration in unpolluted air (parts per million):* 0·5.

hydrogen the simplest of all stable molecules, consisting of two protons and two electrons. It is a colourless, odourless gas and is lighter than air. The last of these properties led to its use in lifting airships. Most hydrogen is used on site where it is produced, but it is also transported as compressed gas in steel cylinders and in liquid form at very low temperatures. *Concentration in unpolluted air (parts per million):* 0·5.

methane a colourless, odourless, flammable gas. *Concentration in unpolluted air (parts per million):* 1–1·6.

nitrogen monoxide occurs at high levels in the atmosphere. This is closely connected with the internal combustion engine. At the high temperature reached when petroleum and air ignite, nitrogen and oxygen combine to form nitrogen monoxide, which slowly reacts with more oxygen to form nitrogen dioxide. *Concentration in unpolluted air (parts per million):* variable.

nitrogen is a colourless, odourless gas. Although it is very stable and chemically unreactive, it cycles both naturally and as a result of its use in the chemical industry. The natural cycle results from the ability of some types of bacteria (in sunlight) to 'fix' nitrogen. Since 1900, human activity has increasingly contributed to the cycling of nitrogen, because of the catalytic production of ammonia, which ultimately reverts to nitrogen gas. *Concentration in unpolluted air (parts per million):* 780,900.

nitrogen dioxide is present at a high level in the atmosphere. This is closely connected to the internal combustion engine, which produces nitric acid. This, in turn, reacts with oxygen to produce nitrogen dioxide. Most internal combustion engines produce some unburnt or partially burnt fuel. In the presence of sunlight, this reacts with nitrogen dioxide by a sequence of fast reactions, forming organic peroxides, which are harmful constituents of photochemical smog. *Concentration in unpolluted air (parts per million):* 0·02.

oxygen a highly reactive colourless, odourless and tasteless gas. At low temperature, it condenses to a pale blue liquid, slightly denser than water. Oxygen supports burning, causes rusting and is vital to both plant and animal respiration. *Concentration in unpolluted air (parts per million):* 209,400.

ozone is a highly toxic, unstable colourless gas. Its primary importance stems from its formation in the stratosphere. In this layer of the atmosphere, temperature increases with height, principally because of the reaction of high-energy ultraviolet solar radiation with oxygen. Ozone in the stratosphere functions as a very effective filter for high-energy ultraviolet solar radiation. Radiation in this energy range is sufficiently high to break bonds between carbon and other atoms, making it lethal to all forms of life. It is currently thought that the introduction of CFCs (used in sprays and refrigerants) and the related 'halons' (used in fire extinguishers) may contribute to the partial destruction of the ozone layer. *Concentration in unpolluted air (parts per million):* c. 0·01.

sulphur dioxide (modern chemical usage sulfur dioxide) a pungent-smelling acidic gas, which is produced through volcanic eruptions and – to a small extent – through the burning of fossil fuels. *Concentration in unpolluted air (parts per million):* 0·0002.

sulphur trioxide (modern chemical usage sulfur trioxide) a pungent-smelling acidic gas, which is produced by volcanic action. In the atmosphere sulphur dioxide is slowly oxidized to sulphur trioxide, reactions that are catalysed by sunlight, water droplets and particulate matter in the air. Ultimately, sulphur trioxide is deposited as dilute sulphuric acid – acid rain. *Concentration in unpolluted air (parts per million):* variable.

water a covalent molecule consisting of two atoms of hydrogen and one atom of oxygen. The total amount of water on Earth is fixed: most is recycled and re-used. *Concentration in unpolluted air (parts per million):* variable.

ORGANIC CHEMISTRY – Natural Compounds

The molecular basis for life processes, which have evolved with such remarkable elegance around carbon as the key element, is beginning to be understood, thanks to the combined triumphs of biological, chemical and physical scientists during the last hundred years. Chemistry can now make synthetically almost any chemical compound that nature produces.

acyclic skeleton an open-chain skeleton of atoms when, for example, carbon combines with other atoms.

alanine an amino acid. Many organic compounds, such as alanine (2-aminopropanoic acid) and limonene are built up asymmetrically around a central carbon atom and can exist in two mirror-image forms, known as enantiomers. In the case of naturally-occurring amino acids such as alanine, one enantiomer predominates greatly over the other, the latter having a small role in nature.

alcohols an homologous series. Alcohols are colourless volatile liquids. e.g. methanol and ethanol.

aldehydes an homologous series; colourless volatile fluids that are obtained from alcohol by distillation. An important example is methanal.

aliphatic compound a compound with an open chain of carbon atoms. The chain may be branched or unbranched and may contain single, double or triple bonds or combinations of these.

alkanes an homologous series. Alkanes, which are hydrocarbons, include methane and ethane. They are referred to as saturated hydrocarbons – they contain no double bonds. Alkanes are used as fuels and to make alkenes by a process known as cracking. Alkanes react with chlorine and bromine in the presence of sunlight. The differences between alkanes and alkenes include:

– alkanes are characterized by a C-C bond; alkenes are characterized by a C=C bond;

– alkanes do not react with bromine solution, although they make bromine lose colour very slowly; alkenes make bromine lose colour rapidly.

alkenes an homologous series. Alkenes are hydrocarbons that contain one or more carbon-carbon double bonds. Alkenes with just one double bond form a series including ethene, propene and butene.

amides an homologous series. The most important type of amide group is that formed in protein synthesis, when the carbooxyl group of one amino acid condenses with the amine group of another to give what, in this context, is known as a peptide link.

amines an homologous series. Amines are derivatives of ammonia in which hydrogen atoms are replaced by groups that contain hydrogen and carbon atoms. Amines occur in all amino acids.

amino acid a building block of protein, consisting of one or more carboxyl groups (-COOH) and one or more amino groups ($-NH_2$) attached to a carbon atom. There are over 80 naturally occurring amino acids, 20 of which occur in proteins. Each amino acid is distinguished by a different side chain (an 'R' group). Organisms can sythesize many amino acids, but there are some that have to be obtained from the diet.

aromatic compounds compounds containing at least one benzene ring.

benzene ring a ring of six carbons in which the fourth electron in one outer shell of each carbon shell is delocalized.

bivalent having two valences.

butane an alkane; $CH_3CH_2CH_3$. A hydrocarbon in the methane series. It is used as a fuel, for example as camping gas and as lighter fuel.

butanol 4-carbon, straight-chain alcohols; $CH_3CH_2CH_2CH_2\,OH$ is butan-1-ol, $CH_3CH_2CH(OH)CH_3$ is butan-2-ol. It is used as a fuel, for example, as camping gas and as lighter fuel.

butene 4-carbon straight-chain alkenes; $CH_3CH_2CH{=}CH_2$ is but-1-ene, $CH_3CH = CHCH_3$ is but-2-ene.

carbon (Atomic number: 6) is unique in the readiness with which it forms bonds both with other carbon atoms and with the atoms of other elements. Having four electrons in its outer shell, a carbon atom requires four more electrons to achieve a stable noble-gas configuration. It therefore forms four covalent bonds with other atoms, each of which donates a single electron to each bond. In this way electronic requirements are satisfied and a 'tetracovalent' environment is built up around the carbon atom. Carbon bonds are found both in pure forms (diamond, graphite and buckminsterfullerene) and in association with other atoms in a vast array of compounds. Carbon bonds readily with hydrogen, oxygen, nitrogen, sulphur, phosphorus and the halogens (such as chlorine and bromine). Often the covalent bonds between carbon and other atoms are stable enough for us to handle the resulting compounds at room temperature; yet these compounds are not so strongly bonded that they cannot be manipulated by means of well-known chemical reactions. Carbon combines with itself and other atoms to produce acyclic and cyclic skeletons.

carboxylic acids an homologous series. As well as occurring in organic acids, such as ethanoic acid (vinegar), the functional group (-COOH) of this homologous series is also found in all the amino acids, including alanine.

compound a substance that is made of atoms of two or more elements bonded together. In organic chemistry, the first part of the name of compounds indicates the number of carbon atoms that are in that compound:

meth- indicates 1 carbon atom (e.g. methane);

eth- indicates 2 carbon atoms (e.g. ethene);

prop- indicates 3 carbon atoms (e.g. propane);

but- indicates 4 carbon atoms (e.g. but-2-ene);

pent- indicates 5 carbon atoms.

configuration (chemical) the spatial arrangement of groups bonded to a central carbon atom in such a way as to define a tetrahedron in three dimensions. If four different atoms or groups are attached to the central carbon, this spatial arrangement can exist in two forms – enantiomers – which are non-superimposable mirror images.

covalent bond the type of bond that is formed when two atoms share electrons; see also p. 226.

cracking the process of breaking long-chain molecules into small molecules. The reaction needs a high temperature and a catalyst.

cyclic skeleton a ring-shaped skeleton formed by atoms when, for example, carbon combines with other atoms.

electrophilic electron-pair seeking.

empirical formula the simplest possible formula showing stoichiometric proportions only. *Example*: 2-hyrdoxypropanoic acid ($CH_3CH(OH)COOH$) has the empirical formula CH_2O.

enantiomer either of the two non-superimposable mirror-images that a configuration can take. The spatial arrangement, or configuration, of four different groups bonded to a central carbon atom, can take two forms (enantiomers), one the non-superimposable image of the other.

ethanol an alcohol. Ethanol is a colourless liquid which is completely miscible with water. In an excess of air, it burns to give carbon dioxide and water. Ethanol, which can be manufactured by reacting ethene with steam in the presence of a catalyst, is used as a solvent.

ethane an alkane. It contains a pair of electrons between the carbon atoms. The molecule contains a single bond: carbon-carbon.

ethanethiol a thiol, which is added to aid the detection of North Sea gas from open taps and gas leaks.

ethene an alkene. An ethene molecule consists of two pairs of shared electrons between carbon atoms. The molecule contains a carbon-carbon double bond. Ethene is a flammable gas which is used as a fuel and an anaesthetic. Ethene is used to manufacture ethanol and to make a number of polymers including poly(ethene) (also known as polythene), poly(phenylethene) (also known as polystyrene) and poly(chloroethene) (also known as P.V.C.).

functional group an atom or group of atoms that give a compound its particular chemical properties. Thus ethanol (CH_3CH_2OH), ethanal (CH_3CHO), ethanoic acid (CH_3COOH), and ethene ($CH_2 = CH_2$) behave differently because they have different functional groups (–OH, –CHO, –COOH and C=C respectively).

The diverse but predictable chemical behaviour of the different functional groups is a consequence of their ability either to attract or to repel electrons compared. with the rest of the carbon skeleton. The overall effect of the resulting charge distribution is to create a molecule in which some regions are nucleophilic and others are electrophilic.

Most organic reactions involve the electrophilic and nucleophilic centres of different molecules coming together as a prelude to the formation of new covalent bonds. An appreciation of how particular compounds behave towards others and of the various mechanisms by which such reactions occur forms the basis of classical organic synthesis.

homologous series a family of compounds containing the same functional group. Homologous series include alkenes, alcohols, ketones, aldehydes, carboxylic acids, amines, amides, and thiols.

hydrocarbon any compound consisting of hydrogen and carbon only. Hydrocarbons are extremely important, notably as the principal components of fossil fuels and the starting materials in the synthesis of most man-made organic compounds.

isomers compounds with the same molecular formula. Thus ethanol (CH_3CH_2OH) and methoxymethane (CH_3OCH_3) are isomers since they have the molecular formula (C_2H_6O).

ketones an homologous series. Ketones are organic chemical compounds containing the functional group CO in combination with two hydrocarbon radicals. Examples include propanone and MVK.

limonene an organic compound which, like alanine, is built up asymmetrically around a central carbon atom and can exist in two non-superimposable mirror-image forms, known as enantiomers.

methanal an aldehyde also known as formaldehyde; HCHO. It is used in the production of formalin (a disinfectant) and of synthetic resins.

methane an alkane. Methane is a colourless, odourless gas, which is less dense than air. It is neutral and is insoluble in water.

methanol an alcohol. A poisonous liquid, which is obtained by the destructive distillation of wood. It is used as a fuel.

methylated spirit see ethanol.

methylvinylketone see MVK.

miscible mixable; usually applied to liquids, e.g. water and ethanol are completely miscible.

molecular formula the formula showing the molecular composition, but not the sequence of atoms.

Example: 2-hydroxypropanoic acid (CH_3OH) has the molecular formula HCHO.

MVK the abbreviation for methylvinylketone, more correctly known as but-3-en-2-one ($CH_3COCH = CH_2$); a ketone.

nucleophilic electron-pair donating.

octane an alkane; a hydrocarbon present in petrol.

organic chemistry the branch of chemistry dealing with carbon compounds, excluding the oxides of carbon and the carbonates. There is something very special about the chemistry of carbon that has singled it out as the atomic building block from which all naturally occurring compounds in living systems are constructed. The subject that deals with this important area of science, nestling between biology and physics, has become so vast and significant that it has earned recognition as a separate field of scientific investigation. As it was originally thought that such carbon-based compounds could be obtained only from natural sources (e.g. organisms), this field of study became known as organic chemistry.

propane an alkane; C_3H_8.

propan-1-ol and **propan-2-ol** alcohols with the molecular formula C_3H_8O and with the structure $CH_3CH_2CH_2OH$ and $CH_3CH(OH)CH_3$ respectively.

propanone (acetone) a ketone; CH_3COCH_3.

propene an alkene (q.v.); C_3H_6. Propene polymerizes to form poly(propene).

radical a group of atoms that operates as a single atom and either goes through a reaction unchanged or is replaced by another atom.

structural formulae a formula which shows the sequence and arrangement of the atoms in a molecule, for example, CH_3COCH_3 for propanone.

substitution reaction a reaction in which an atom or group of atoms is replaced by another atom or group of atoms.

thiols an homologous series. The functional group is characterized by a strong disagreeable odour. An example is ethanethiol.

POLYMERS

Polymers are chemicals composed of large molecules in which a group of atoms is repeated. They include naturally occurring substances such as starch and cellulose and synthetic substances such as nylon and poly(ethene). The structure of many polymers is complicated. They can be made up of very many molecules arranged in a chain of monomers. The way in which these chains interact with one another depends upon the monomers from which the polymers are composed, and can differ greatly. This accounts for the wide range of properties that polymers can possess, including flexibility, strength and heat resistance. Polymerization is the process in which many small molecules of monomers combine together to form large molecules of polymers. *Note that the term polymer refers to the chemical and not the polymer molecule.*

addition polymerization polymerization that involves one type of molecule containing a carbon-carbon double bond. The carbon-carbon double bond in, for example, ethene is very reactive. Electrons are transferred from these double bonds, allowing ethene molecules to link together, a process that allows the formation of a long chain of single carbon-carbon bonds in the polymer poly(ethene), which is also known as polythene. The requirements for this reaction to occur are an initiator, a temperature of 200°C and high pressure. In any such reaction the number of monomer molecules is variable and for this reason the exact molecular formula may not always be known. By convention the number of monomer units in a polymer is shown by the number *n*, which represents the number of times that the unit is repeated. This is usually a large number. As an example, poly(ethene) may be represented as:

$$[CH_2 - CH_2]_n$$

Poly(ethene) molecules have very large relative molecular masses which are in excess of 100,000. The polymer that is formed in this manner has none of the properties of ethene and the double carbon bond is, in fact, absent from the product. The monomer is an unsaturated hydrocarbon while the resulting polymer is a saturated hydrocarbon. Any other molecule that has the carbon-carbon double bond will also polymerize in exactly the same manner. The polymers that are derived from such monomers are simply chains of monomer units that are linked together, but in that process they lose the carbon-carbon double bond. The monomer from which a polymer is made can be discovered by identifying the repeating unit, by inserting a double bond between the carbon atoms and eliminating the unused bonds at the end of the unit in the polymer.

amino acid a building block of protein, consisting of one or more carboxyl groups and one or more amino groups attached to a carbon atom. See p. 233.

cellulose a polysaccharide carbohydrate made up of unbranched chains of many glucose molecules. Its fibrils form the framework of plant cell walls and it is the main constituent in the shells of certain protoctists. Cellulose is generally important in the diets of herbivorous animals.

chloroethene monomer molecules combine to give the polymer poly(chloroethene) (P.V.C).

condensation polymerization the type of polymerization that occurs with monomers with reactive groups at each end of the molecule. This is a quite different type of polymerization to that involving the carbon-carbon double bond. It involves two kinds of molecule that condense together to form long chains in a process that involves the loss of a small molecule by the monomers during linking. The molecule that is lost as each link is formed is usually either a water molecule or a hydrogen chloride molecule. Monomers must be capable of reacting together in order for condensation polymerization to occur – there must be a reactive group at each end. In the reaction, these groups link together to form polymer molecules and the polymer molecules can continue to grow at either end at reactive points. The compounds thus formed tend to be more complex than those formed by addition polymerization. Nylon and terylene are examples of condensation polymers.

ethene a monomer whose molecules combine to give the polymer poly(ethene) (polythene).

fat (or **lipid**) any polymer formed from the reaction of fatty acids and glycerol. Fats are organic compounds formed from carbon, hydrogen and oxygen. They normally comprise one glycerol molecule linked to three different fatty acid molecules. Fat molecules are large. The linkages between the glycerol and fatty acid molecules of which fat molecules are composed are ester linkages.

glycerol (or **glycerin,** or more correctly **propane-1,2,3-triol**) is the alcohol to which three carboxylic acid molecules are attached by ester linkages in fats.

hydrolysis the breaking down of a substance into other substances by reaction with water.

initiator a catalyst used in the reaction of polymerization.

insulin a natural polymer; a hormone secreted by the pancreas in vertebrates. Insulin – which regulates blood-sugar levels – is regarded as a relatively simple protein although it is composed of no fewer than 51 molecules and 14 different amino acids.

low-density polythene or **LD polythene** see poly(ethene).

melamine a thermosetting plastic polymer. Because thermosets like melamine cannot be softened by heat once set, it is used for heat-proof containers and heat-resisting surfaces.

methyl methacrylate a monomer whose molecules combine to give poly(methyl methacrylate) (perspex).

monomer a chemical whose molecules react to make up the chain of a polymer molecule.

natural polymers natural compounds that are made up of a large number of repeated units. Natural polymers differ from synthetic polymers in their constituents. Whereas synthetic polymers can be formed from a variety elements, natural polymers are formed principally from just four elements: carbon, hydrogen, nitrogen and oxygen. Chlorine, which is an element commonly used in the formation of synthetic polymers, is not found in any known natural polymer. Natural polymers may be divided into three main types: starches, proteins, and fats.

nylon a synthetic condensation polymer. The advent of synthetic fibre nylons in the 1930s caused a major revolution in the fashion industry. Nylon can be synthesized by polymerizing hexane-1,6-diamine (hexamethylenediamine) with hexanedioyl dichloride (adipyl chloride). Nylon is a polyamide.

perspex see poly(methyl methacrylate).

phenylethene a monomer whose molecules combine to give the polymer poly(phenylethene) (which is also known as polystyrene).

plastic any synthetic polymer that can be formed into a desired form or shape. Plastics are either thermosetting plastics or thermosoftening plastics. Plastics are easy to make, cheap, lightweight, resistant to chemicals, waterproof and tough. Many plastics are, however, flammable and the disposal of such resistant substances is a major pollution problem.

polyamide a polymer containing many amide linkages.

poly(chloroethene) (better known as **P.V.C.**) a synthetic addition polymer. It is formed from the combination of chloroethene monomer molecules. P.V.C. is tough, rubbery and strong, and yet remarkably flexible. It is flame resistant and resists solvents. P.V.C. is also an electrical insulator.

polyester a polymer with many ester linkages.

poly(ethene) (also known as **polythene**) a synthetic addition polymer which is formed from the combination of ethene monomer molecules in addition polymerization. The polymer poly(ethene) is waterproof and is a cheap, strong substance that resists acids found in most foods and also resists solvents. There are two types of polythene – high-density polythene (HD polythene) and low-density polythene (LD polythene). In HD polythene the molecules lie closely parallel to each other which increases the force of attraction between them. HD polythene is, therefore, stronger and more rigid than LD polythene and also has a higher softening temperature than LD polythene. HD polythene is, therefore, used in situations where strength is important.

poly(methyl methacrylate) (also known as **perspex**) a synthetic addition polymer which is formed from the combination of methyl methacrylate monomer molecules. Perspex is a tough, glass-like substance that is shatterproof.

polypeptide any natural polymer made up of amino acids.

poly(phenylethene) (also known as **polystyrene**) a synthetic addition polymer which is formed from the combination of phenylethene monomer molecules. The polymer polystyrene is flexible and strong and retains its strength at low temperatures. It is, however, somewhat brittle.

poly(propene) a synthetic addition polymer which is formed by the combination of propene monomer molecules. The polymer poly(propene) is both harder and more rigid than poly(ethene). One of its most useful properties is a high softening point which is >100 °C (212 °F).

polysaccharide any of a class of large carbohydrate molecules, including cellulose, glycogen and starch.

polystyrene see poly(phenylethene).

poly(tetrafluoroethene) (also known as **PTFE**) a synthetic addition polymer which forms from the combination of tetrafluoroethene monomer molecules.

PTFE is heat-resistant and solvent-resistant. It has low friction and is generally 'non-stick'.

polythene see poly(ethene).

propene a monomer whose molecules combine to give molecules of the polymer poly(propene).

protein any of a number of natural polymers – found in plants and animals. Proteins contain nitrogen, hydrogen, carbon, and oxygen (and sometimes sulphur). The structure of proteins is complex and protein molecules are large. These polymers are made up of long chains of different amino acids. Chains may be folded and are joined to other chains in several different ways. No part of a protein polymer repeats itself. The linkage in a protein polymer is known as either an amide or a peptide linkage.

P.V.C. see poly(chloroethene).

radical a group of atoms that acts as a single atom and goes through a chemical reaction unchanged.

starch a natural polymer which is a compound of carbon, hydrogen and oxygen – the hydrogen and oxygen elements are present in the same ratio as in water. The reaction to form the linkage involves the –OH group at each end of the monomer. Starch is a polysaccharide carbohydrate into which glucose is converted for storage in plants. (Starch is formed in all plants by photosynthesis.) Glucose is the repeating monomer in chains of starch.

sugar any of a group of carbohydrates of low molecular weight, including mono-, di- and some oligosaccharides. Sugars include glucose, maltose and lactose, which act as monomers.

synthesize to form a complex compound by the combination of two or more simpler compounds, elements or radicals.

terylene a synthetic condensation polymer. Terylene is made by the polymerization of benzene-1,4-dicarboxylic acid (terephthalic acid) and ethane-1,2-diol (ethylene glycol). Terylene is a thermosoftening polymer.

tetrafluorethene monomer molecules combine to form poly(tetrafluoroethene) (which is also known as PTFE).

thermosetting plastics thermosets; plastics that cannot be melted by heat once they have set. This useful property is possessed by Araldite resin, Bakelite and melamine. In the case of thermosets the polymer is more rigid as molecules are built up from polymer molecules by a series of 'cross-links' rather than the 'end-to-end' links that characterize thermoplastics.

thermosoftening plastics thermoplastics; plastics that have the property of thermoplasticity, that is they soften when heated. When softened by heat, these polymers can be shaped. Thermoplastics are made up of long polymer molecules which are in constant motion and are attracted to one another by the weak force.

NOBEL PRIZEWINNERS IN CHEMISTRY

1901 Jacobus van't Hoff, Dutch: for laws of chemical dynamics and osmotic pressure.

1902 Emil Fischer, German: for work on sugar and purine syntheses.

1903 Svante Arrhenius, Swedish: for his theory of electrolytic dissociation.

1904 Sir William Ramsay, Scottish: for discovery and periodic system classification of inert gas elements.

1905 Adolf von Baeyer, German: for work on organic dyes and hydroaromatic compounds.

1906 Henri Moissan, French: for the Moissan furnace, and isolation of fluorine.

1907 Eduard Buchner, German: for the discovery of non-cellular fermentation.

1908 Ernest Rutherford, New Zealand: for his description of atomic structure and the chemistry of radioactive substance.

1909 Wilhelm Ostwald, Latvian-born German: for pioneering catalysis, chemical equilibrium and reaction velocity work.

1910 Otto Wallach, German: for pioneering work on alicyclic combinations.

1911 Marie Curie, Polish-born French: for the discovery of radium and polonium, and isolation of radium.

1912 Victor Grignard, French: for Grignard reagents; and Paul Sabatier, French: for his method of hydrogenating compounds.

1913 Alfred Werner, French-born Swiss: for work on the linkage of atoms in molecules.

1914 Theodore Richards, US: for the precise determination of atomic weights of many elements.

1915 Richard Willstätter, German: for pioneering research on plant pigments, especially chlorophyll.

1916-17 No award

1918 Fritz Haber, German: for synthesis of ammonia.

1919 No award.

1920 Walther Nernst, German: for work in thermochemistry.

1921 Frederick Soddy, English: for studies of radio-active materials, and the occurrence and nature of isotopes.

1922 Francis Aston, English: for work on mass spectrography, and on whole number rule.

1923 Fritz Pregl, Austrian: for his method of microanalysis of organic substances.

1924 No award.

1925 Richard Zsigmondy, German: for the elucidation of the heterogeneous nature of colloidal solutions.

1926 Theodor Svedberg, Swedish: for work on disperse systems.

1927 Heinrich Wieland, German: for research into the constitution of bile acids.

1928 Adolf Windaus, German: for work on the constitution of sterols and their connection with vitamins.

1929 Sir Arthur Harden, English, and Hans von Euler-Chelpin, German-born Swedish: for studies of sugar fermentation and the enzymes involved in the process.

1930 Hans Fischer, German: for chlorophyll research, and the discovery of haemoglobin in the blood.

1931 Karl Bosch, German, and Friedrich Bergius, German: for the invention and development of high-pressure methods.

1932 Irving Langmuir, US: for furthering understanding of surface chemistry.

1933 No award.

1934 Harold Urey, US: for the discovery of heavy hydrogen.

1935 Frédéric Joliot-Curie, French, and Irène Joliot-Curie, French: for the synthesis of new radioactive elements.

1936 Peter Debye, Dutch: for work on dipole moments and the diffraction of X-rays and electrons in gases.

1937 Sir Walter Haworth, English: for research into carbohydrates and vitamin C; and Paul Karrer, Swiss: for research into carotenoid, flavin, and vitamins.

1938 Richard Kuhn, German: for carotenoid and vitamin research (award declined as Hitler forbade Germans to accept Nobel prizes).

1939 Adolf Butenandt, German: for work on sex hormones (award declined as Hitler forbade Germans to accept Nobel prizes); and Leopold Ruicka, Croat-born Swiss: for research on steroid hormones.

1940-42 No awards.

1943 George von Hevesy, Hungarian: for the use of isotopes as tracers in research.

1944 Otto Hahn, German: for the discovery of the fusion of heavy nuclei.

1945 Arturri Virtanen, Finnish: for the invention of fodder preservation method.

1946 James Sumner, US: for the discovery of enzyme crystallization; and John Northrop, US, and Wendell Stanley, US: for the preparation of pure enzymes and virus proteins.

1947 Sir Robert Robinson, English: for research on alkaloids and plant biology.

1948 Arne Tiselius, Swedish: for research on electrophoretic and adsorption analysis, and serum proteins.

1949 William Giauque, US: for work on the behaviour of substances at very low temperatures.

1950 Otto Diels, German, and Kurt Alder, German: for the discovery and development of diene synthesis.

1951 Edwin McMillan, US, and Glenn Seaborg, US: for the discovery of and research on trans-uranium elements.

1952 Archer Martin and Richard Synge, both English: for the development of partition chromatography.

1953 Hermann Staudinger, German: for work on macromolecules.

1954 Linus Pauling, US: for studies on the nature of the chemical bond.

1955 Vincent Du Vigneaud, US: for pioneer work on the synthesis of a polypeptide hormone.

1956 Nikolay Semyonov, Russian, and Cyril Hinshelwood, English: for work on the kinetics of chemical reactions.

1957 Alexander Todd, Scottish: for work on nucleotides and nucleotide coenzymes.

1958 Frederick Sanger, English: for determining the structure of the insulin molecule.

1959 Jaroslav Heyrovsky, Czech: for the discovery and development of polarography.

1960 Willard Libby, US: for the development of radio-carbon dating.

1961 Melvin Calvin, US: for studies of the chemical stages that occur in photosynthesis.

1962 John C. Kendrew, English, and Max F. Perutz, Austrian-born British: for determining the structure of haemoproteins.

1963 Giulio Natta, Italian, and Karl Ziegler, German: for research into the structure and synthesis of plastics polymers.

1964 Dorothy Hodgkin, English: for determining the structure of compounds essential in combating pernicious anaemia.

1965 Robert B. Woodward, US: for synthesizing sterols, chlorophyll, etc. (previously produced only by living things).

1966 Robert S. Mulliken, US: for investigations into chemical bonds and electronic structure of molecules.

1967 Manfred Eigen, German, Ronald G. W. Norrish, English, and George Porter, English: for studies of extremely fast chemical reactions.

1968 Lars Onsager, Norwegian-born US: for his theory of the thermodynamics of irreversible processes.

1969 Derek H. R. Barton, English, and Odd Hasell, Norwegian: for determining the actual 3-dimensional shape of certain organic compounds.

1970 Luis F. Leloir, French-born Argentinian: for his discovery of sugar nucleotides and their role in carbohydrate biosynthesis.

1971 Gerhard Herzberg, German-born Canadian: for research on the structure of molecules.

1972 Christian B. Anfinsen, Stanford Moore, and William H. Stein, all US: for contributions to the fundamentals of enzyme chemistry.

1973 Ernst Fischer, German, and Geoffrey Wilkinson, English: for work in organometallic chemistry.

1974 Paul J. Flory, US: for studies of long-chain molecules.

1975 John Cornforth, Australian-born British, and Vladimir Prelog, Bosnian-born Swiss: for work on stereochemistry.

1976 William N. Lipscomb, US: for work on the structure of boranes.

1977 Ilya Prigogine, Russian-born Belgian: for work in advanced thermodynamics.

1978 Peter D. Mitchell, English: for his theory of energy transfer processes in biological systems.

1979 Herbert C. Brown, English-born US, and Georg Wittig, German: for introducing boron and phosphorus compounds in the synthesis of organic compounds.

1980 Paul Berg, US: for the first preparation of a hybrid DNA; and Walter Gilbert, US, and Frederick Sanger, English: for chemical and biological analysis of the structure of DNA.

1981 Fukui Kenichi, Japanese, and Roald Hoffmann, Polish-born US: for orbital symmetry interpretation of chemical reactions.

1982 Aaron Klug, Lithuanian-born South African (a British naturalized citizen): for determining the structure of some biologically active substances.

1983 Henry Taube, Canadian: for studies into electron transfer reactions.

1984 Bruce Merrifield, US: for formulating a method of polypeptide synthesis.

1985 Herbert A. Hauptman and Jerome Karle, both US: for developing a means of mapping the chemical structure of small molecules.

1986 Dudley R. Herschbach, US, Yuan T. Lee, Taiwanese-born US, and John C. Polanyi, Canadian: for introducing methods for analysing basic chemical reactions.

1987 Donald J. Cram, US, Charles J. Pedersen, Norwegian-born US, and Jean-Marie Lehn, French: for developing molecules that could link with other molecules.

1988 Johann Deisenhofer, Robert Huber, and Hartmut Michel, all German: for studies into the structure of the proteins needed in photosynthesis.

1989 Tom Cech, US, and Sidney Altman, Canadian-born US: for establishing that RNA catalyses biochemical reactions.

1990 Elias Corey, US: for work on synthesizing chemical compounds based on natural substances.

1991 Richard R. Ernst, Swiss: for refining the technology of nuclear magnetice resonance imaging (NMR and MRI).

1992 Rudolph A. Marcus, US: for mathematical analysis of the cause and effect of electrons jumping from one molecule to another.

1993 Kary B. Mullis, US: for the invention of his PCR method; and Michael Smith, English-born Canadian: for contributions to oligonucleotide-based, site-directed mutagenisis.

1994 George Olah, US: for pioneering work in controlling hydrocarbon reactions.

Mathematics

NUMBERS

Natural numbers or whole numbers are those that we use in counting. Natural numbers – one, two, three, four and so on – are learned at an early age. Important features of our number system, these numbers can be used to count sets of objects, and form a naturally ordered progression that has a first member, the number 1, but no last number. No matter how big a number you come up with, it can always be capped with a bigger one – simply by adding 1.

addition a mathematical operation by which the sum of two numbers is calculated. The operation is normally indicated by the symbol +.

Example: 3 + 4 = 7.

cubic number any number that has been formed by multiplying a whole number by itself and then multiplying the result by that whole number.

Example: 4 x 4 x 4 = 64, thus 64 is a cubic number. 4 x 4 x 4 may be written 4^3, that is to say 'four cubed'.

difference (of numbers) the result when the smaller of two numbers is taken away from the larger.

division a mathematical operation in which the quotient of two numbers is calculated. The operation is normally indicated by the symbol ÷.

Example: 20 ÷ 5 = 4. Note that this is the inverse operation of multiplication.

even number any number that will divide by 2 exactly.

Examples: 2, 4, 6, 8, 10, 12, 14, 16, 18, 20, ...

exponent another name for an index.

factor any number that divides exactly into another number.

Examples: 6 divides into 48 exactly (that is, without leaving a remainder) 8 times. Thus both 6 and 8 are factors of 48.

Similarly 2 divides into 6 exactly 3 times – thus both 2 and 3 are factors of 6 – and 2 divides into 8 exactly 4 times – thus 2 and 4 are factors of 8.

HCF the abbreviation for highest common factor.

highest common factor (or **HCF**) the largest number that will divide into two or more numbers exactly (that is, without leaving a remainder).

Examples: 78 = 3 x 26. 182 = 7 x 26.

Thus 26 is the highest common factor of 78 and 182.

index (or **exponent**) a number placed above the line after another number to show how many times the number is to be multiplied by itself. The number of times that the number occurs in the operation is called the power.

Example: 7 x 7 x 7 x 7 x 7 is the fifth power of 7. In index form, this is shown as 7^5.

integer any negative or positive whole number.

Examples: -3, -2, -1, 0, +1, +2, +3, +4, ...

Note that 0 is an integer, but it is neither a positive nor a negative integer.

irrational number any number that cannot be expressed as a fraction or ratio.

Examples: √3.
π (*pi*), which to seven decimal places is 3·141 5926. π has been calculated to 1,073,740,000 decimal places, but the decimal (probably) has no end.

LCM the abbreviation for lowest common multiple.

lowest common multiple (or **LCM**) the lowest common multiple of two or more numbers is the smallest number that is exactly divisible by them without leaving a remainder.

Example: to find the lowest common multiple of 4, 8 and 20.
Factors of 4 = 2 x 2, that is (2^2).
Factors of 8 = 2 x 2 x 2, that is (2^3).
Factors of 20 = 2 x 2 x 5, that is ($2^2 \times 5$).
Thus the lowest common multiple of 4, 8 and 20 = $2^3 \times 5$ = 40.

multiple any number that is the product of a given number and any other whole number.

Examples: 14 is a multiple of 2, 14 is also a multiple of 7.
15 is a multiple of 3. 15 is also a multiple of 5.

multiplication a mathematical operation by which the product of two or more numbers is calculated. This operation is the inverse operation to division. The operation is normally indicated by the symbol x.

Example: 5 x 4 = 20.

natural number (or **whole number**) any number that is a positive integer.

Examples: 1, 2, 3, 4, 5, 6, 7, 8, 9, 10, 11, 12, 13, ...
Note that 0 is not a natural number.

odd number any integer that will not divide by 2 exactly.

Examples: 1, 3, 5, 7, 9, 11, 13, ...

perfect number any number that is equal to the sum of its factors, excluding the number itself.

The first perfect number is 6 whose factors (excluding 6 itself) are 1, 2 and 3. As 1 + 2 + 3 = 6, 6 is a perfect number.

The next perfect number is 28. The factors of 28 are 1, 2, 4, 7 and 14. 1 + 2 + 4 + 7 + 14 = 28.

Pythagoras knew these first two perfect numbers in the 6th century BC. In the 3rd century BC Nicomachus of Alexandria discovered the next two perfect numbers – 496 and 8128. The fifth perfect number – 33,550,336 – was not discovered until over 1000 years later. Until the 1950s only seven perfect numbers were known. Today, even with the help of computers, only 30 perfect numbers have been discovered.

power see index.

prime number any natural number that can only be divided by itself and 1. The number 1 is not considered to be a prime number.

Prime numbers can be found by taking a sequence of numbers such as

1, 2, 3, 4, 5, 6, 7, 8, 9, 10, 11, 12, 13, 14, 15, 16, 17, 18, ...

and first deleting all the numbers divisible by 2 (excluding 2 itself, which is only divisible by itself and 1), then all those divisible by 3, then (since anything divisible by 4 has already been deleted) all those numbers divisible by 5, and so on.

All non-prime numbers must by definition be divisible by other numbers apart from themselves and 1; these other numbers can be repeatedly divided until you are left with a series of prime numbers. All non-prime numbers can be expressed as the product of a series of primes – in fact, for each number the series is unique. See below.

Prime numbers between 1 and 1000

2	3	5	7	11	13	17
19	23	29	31	37	41	43
47	53	59	61	67	71	73
79	83	89	97	101	103	107
109	113	127	131	137	139	149
151	157	163	167	173	179	181
191	193	197	199	211	223	227
229	233	239	241	251	257	263
269	271	277	281	283	293	307
311	313	317	331	337	347	349
353	359	367	373	379	383	389
397	401	409	419	421	431	433
439	443	449	457	461	463	467
479	487	491	499	503	509	521
523	541	547	557	563	569	571
577	587	593	599	601	607	613
617	619	631	641	643	647	653
659	661	673	677	683	691	701
709	719	727	733	739	743	751
757	761	769	773	787	797	809
811	821	823	827	829	839	853
857	859	863	877	881	883	887
907	911	919	929	937	941	947
953	967	971	977	983	991	997

product (of numbers) the result of multiplying numbers together.

quotient (of numbers) the result of dividing one number by another number.

rational number any number that can be expressed as a fraction or a ratio.

Examples: 0·5 = ½. 8:5 = $^8/_5$

remainder the amount left over when one number cannot be exactly divided by another.

square number any number that has been formed by multiplying a whole number by itself.

Examples: 4 x 4 = 16 thus 16 is a square number. 4 x 4 may be written as 4^2, that is to say 'four squared'.

square root any number which, when multiplied by itself, gives a specified number. The symbol for square root is √.

Examples: √36 = 6 √81 = 9

subtraction a mathematical operation in which one number is taken from another. The operation is normally indicated by the symbol – .

Example: 7 – 3 = 4.

sum (of numbers) the added total of given numbers.

whole number see natural number.

OTHER NUMBER SYSTEMS

Binary system

The binary system uses only the digits 0 and 1; so it has base 2. This is used in the representation of numbers within computers, since the two numerals correspond to the on and the off positions of an electronic switch. In the binary system, we count as follows: 1, 10 (=2+0), 11 (=2+1), 100 (=4+0+0), 1001 (=8+0+0+1), etc.

Binary numbers from 1 to 20:

Decimal	Binary				
1	1	7	111	14	1110
2	10	8	1000	15	1111
3	11	9	1001	16	10000
4	100	10	1010	17	10001
5	101	11	1011	18	10010
6	110	12	1100	19	10011
		13	1101	20	10100

This appears difficult at first sight, but is relatively easy to decipher if the following rules are remembered:

- ignore all noughts in calculation;
- count the right columns as 1;
- count the second column on the right as 2;
- count the third column on the right as 4;
- count the fourth column on the right as 8;
- count the fifth column on the right as 16; and so on. Thus 1101001 in the binary system would be the equivalent of 105 in the decimal system.

The Roman number system

Of all the early grouping systems, the Roman system is the one that has remained in regular use. The system uses seven of the Roman letters of the alphabet, used in isolation or in various combinations to represent numbers. The Romans incorporated a subtractive system in which a lesser symbol appearing before a greater one altered the value of the latter, thus LX represents 60 while XL represents 40.

Thus 1995 in Roman numerals would be MCMXCV.

Arabic numeral	Roman numeral		
1	I	16	XVI
2	II	17	XVII
3	III	18	XVIII
4	IV	19	XIX
5	V	20	XX
6	VI	25	XXV
7	VII	30	XXX
8	VIII	40	XL
9	IX	50	L
10	X	60	LX
11	XI	70	LXX
12	XII	80	LXXX
13	XIII	90	XC
14	XIV	100	C
15	XV	200	CC
		500	D
		1000	M

The Chinese number system

The Chinese number system is an example of multiplicative grouping systems. In multiplicative systems, specific digits (such as the conventional 1, 2, 3, 4, 5, 6, 7, 8, 9) are combined with basic symbols to avoid the repetition involved in a simple grouping system such as the Roman number system. In the Chinese system, the number 4624 would be represented by the character for four followed by the character for 1000, the character for six followed by the character for 100, the character for two followed by ten, and finally, the character for four.

FRACTIONS, DECIMALS AND PERCENTAGES

Fractions, decimals and percentages are three ways of showing the same information: ½, 0·5 and 50% are, for example, recording the same part of a larger amount.

A fraction is any quantity that is defined in terms of a numerator (the term above the line in a fraction which indicates how many parts of a specified number of parts of a unit are being taken) and a denominator (the term below the line in a fraction which indicates the number of equal parts into which the whole is divided).

A decimal is a fraction with an unwritten denominator of some power of ten. This is shown by the decimal point which is placed before the numerator (see above).

A percentage (shown by the symbol %) can also be regarded as a fraction. It shows a quantity as a part of 100.

decimal see introduction (above).

decimal point separates the whole numbers from the fractions in a decimal.

Examples: 17·3 represents 17 whole units and 3 tenths.

(0·3 is another way of saying 3⁄10).

5·25 represents 5 whole units, 2 tenths and 5 hundredths.

(0·25 is another way of saying 25⁄100, or ¼.)

9·837 represents 9 whole units, 8 tenths, 3 hundredths and 7 thousandths; and so on.

By convention a space is left after every three units following a decimal point, for example 3·677 245 21.

denominator see introduction (above).

equivalent fractions two fractions that express the same relationship of quantities.

Example: ¾, 6⁄8, 9⁄12 and 12⁄16 are equivalent fractions.

Of these equivalent fractions ¾ is any of 6⁄8, 9⁄12 and 12⁄16 in its lowest terms – the numerator and the denominator cannot be further divided by the whole numbers.

fraction see introduction (above).

improper fraction a fraction in which the numerator is larger than the denominator, for example 3⁄2, 7⁄5 and 18⁄11.

See also vulgar fraction (below).

irrational number a number which cannot be expressed as a fraction; such numbers have decimals which neither stop nor recur.

Examples: π and √2.

LCM lowest common multiple. For two or more integers, their LCM is the smallest integer into which all can be divided exactly.

lowest common denominator the LCM of the integers forming the denominators of the separate fractions.

Example: To compare ½, 3⁄5 and 7⁄10 we need to express all three fractions in terms of the same denominator.

½ = 5⁄10
3⁄5 = 6⁄10
7⁄10 = 7⁄10

Thus 10 is the lowest common denominator and all three fractions can be converted into tenths.

lowest terms see equivalent fraction (see above).

mixed number a number that comprises an integer and a fraction, for example 3¾ (in other words 3+¾).

numerator see introduction (above).

percentage see introduction (above).

proper fraction an alternative name for a vulgar fraction.

rational number any number which can be expressed as a fraction (or 'ratio').

recurring (of fractions, decimals and percentages) a pattern which repeats indefinitely.

vulgar fraction (or **proper fraction**) a fraction in which the numerator is smaller than the denominator, for example in 3⁄7, 6⁄12 and 5⁄14.

See also improper fraction (above).

Corresponding fractions, decimals and percentages

These are three ways of showing the same information.

Fraction	*Decimal*	*Percentage*
1⁄20	0·05	5%
1⁄10	0·10	10%
1⁄9	0·111 11*	11 1⁄9%
1⁄8	0·125	12·5%
1⁄7	0·142 86	14 1⁄7%
1⁄6	0·166 67*	16⅔%
1⁄5	0·20	20%
¼	0·25	25%
⅓	0·333 33*	33⅓%
3⁄8	0·375	37·5%
2⁄5	0·40	40%
½	0·50	50%
3⁄5	0·60	60%
5⁄8	0·625	62.5%
⅔	0·666 67*	66⅔%
¾	0·75	75%
4⁄5	0·80	80%
5⁄6	0·833 33*	83⅓%
7⁄8	0·875	87·5%
8⁄9	0.888·89*	88 8⁄9%
9⁄10	0·90	90%

* = recurring; by convention a recurring digit over 5 is rounded up.

ALGEBRA

In simple algebra, we generalize arithmetic by using letters to stand for unknown numbers whose value is to be discovered, or to stand for numbers in general. Certain conventions are followed.

Usually letters from the beginning of the alphabet are used to stand for numbers in general – for example, to stand for a general truth about numbers, such as

$$a + b = b + a.$$

The letters at the end of the alphabet are generally used to represent unknown numbers.

Example: A farmer has 42 cows and goes to market and purchases an unknown number of cows. When these additional cows are added to the herd the farmer has a total of 53 cows. This may be expressed as:

$$42 + x = 53,$$

where x is the unknown number of additional cows.

The operations of addition, subtraction, multiplication and division – that are used in normal arithmetic – can also be used in algebra, with certain basic restrictions. In addition and subtraction in algebra it is only possible to collect like terms (that is, terms that are expressed as parts or multiples of the same unknown quantity).

Examples: $3b + 2b + b + 7b = 13b$.
$3x + 2y + 5x + y + 2y + 6x = 14x + 5y$.
$2a + 7b - 3c + 3a + 2b + 6c - 8a + 2b - 2c = -3a + 11b + c$.

Multiplication and division in algebra also follow certain simple rules – the multiplication and division signs may be omitted and the numbers placed in juxtaposition to indicate multiplication.

Examples: $7 \times a = 7a$; $-b \times c = -bc$; $12y \div 4 = 3y$.

brackets (in algebra) are used to enclose a classified grouping within specified limits.

Examples: $(-2) + (-3)$; $(4x + 5x)^2$

In the removal of brackets in an expression each term inside the bracket has to be multiplied by the number or term outside the bracket.

Example: $7(z + 2) = 7$ multiplied by $z + 7$ multiplied by $2 = 7z + 14$.

change of subject see transformation of formulae (below).

equation a statement of equality between two quantities (expressed as numbers and/or letters). The equality of the two parts of the equation is shown by the equal sign (=).

Working out the answer to an equation is said to be 'solving' it. In solving a simple equation, the aim is to group the letters on one side of the equation and the numbers on the side.

Example: $9y - 3 = 7y + 3$ becomes $2y = 6$ giving $y = 3$.

Note that when terms are moved from one side of an equation to the other the addition and subtraction signs change. Thus in the example:

$9y - 7y = 3 + 3$ giving $2y = 6$.

expression a symbol or symbols that express some mathematical fact – for example, $3a + 3b$. (Note that when an equal sign is introduced it becomes an equation.)

factorization of an expression is basically the reverse operation of removing brackets from an expression – see brackets (above).

Examples: $4x + 4y$ becomes $4(x + y)$
$6a - 3b$ becomes $3(2a - b)$ – note that in this example 3 is the common factor.

formula a set of symbols that express a mathematical rule.

Example: Simple interest is calculated using the formula

$$I = \frac{PRT}{100}$$

where
I = simple interest,
P = principal (the amount borrowed),
R = the rate of interest, and
T = the time for which the amount is borrowed (in years).

index (plur. **indices**) another word for power.

inequality the use of one or other of the symbols < and >. The statement $x < y$ means that x is less than y; the statement $x > y$ means that x is greater than y.

inequation the use of one or other of the symbols ≤ and ≥. The symbol ≤ means less than or equal to; the symbol ≥ means greater than or equal to.

negative index (plur. **negative indices**) are common features in many equations.

$$b^2 = b \times b$$

$$\text{but } b^2 = \frac{1}{b^2}$$

like terms see the introduction (above).

power (multiplication and division) in equations and expressions the powers of the same number are added together in multiplication and subtracted in division.

Examples: $6^n \times 6^q = 6^{(n+q)}$
$p^9 \div p^3$ can be given as $p^{(9-3)} = p^6$

transformation of formulae (or **change of subject**) is a simple rearrangement of a formula.

Example: The simple interest formula – see formula (above) – can be transformed in the following manner.

$$\text{As } I = \frac{PRT}{100,}$$

I is the subject, but this can be transformed to make T the subject.

If both sides of the formula are multiplied by 100 it gives

$$100I = PRT.$$

T is then isolated to become the subject of the formula by dividing both sides of the formula by PR. This gives

$$\frac{100I}{PR} = T$$

RATIO AND PROPORTION

A ratio is the relation between quantities – two or more – of the same kind. Ratios are another way of expressing the same relationship that can seen in a fraction.

Proportion is the comparative relation between things – their price, size or amount, etc.

direct proportion the relationship between two quantities whereby an increase in one quantity is matched by an increase in a second quantity. Two quantities are also in direct proportion if a decrease in one quantity is matched by a decrease in the second quantity.

Example: 5 plastic card index boxes cost £14. How much will 12 boxes cost?

If 5 boxes cost £14, one box will cost £14 divided by 5 = £2.80.

Therefore 12 boxes will cost £2.80 times 12 = £33.60.

inverse proportion the relationship whereby an increase in one quantity produces a decrease in a second quantity in the same ratio. Two quantities are also in indirect proportion where a decrease in one quantity results in an increase in a second quantity in the same ratio.

Example: If it takes 9 days for 3 council workers to prune all the trees in a park, how long will it take 6 workers? As it is reasonable to assume that a greater number of council workers will complete the task in a shorter period of time, the two quantities are related in inverse proportion. In the example above it is reasonable to assume that 6 workers will complete the task in half the time taken by 3 workers, i.e. 4.5 days.

ratio the relation between two (or more) quantities of the same kind. A ratio is a comparison of sizes (of, for example, masses, prices of items, lengths or heights, etc.) and therefore no units are needed in this comparison.

Example: The ratio of a journey of 5 km to a journey of 25 km = 5 km:25 km, or – as in this comparison of units of the same kind no units are required 5:25. This ratio cancels down to 1:5 in its most simple form as both 5 and 25 can be divided by 5.

Ratios and fractions are linked.
Examples: the ratio 2:10 may also be expressed as the fraction $\frac{2}{10}$;
the ratio 3:15 may also be expressed as the fraction $\frac{3}{15}$;
likewise, the ratio 7:35 may also be expressed as the fraction $\frac{7}{35}$.
All of these fractions cancel down to $\frac{1}{5}$; therefore the ratios 2:10, 3:15 and 7:35 may be expressed in the simplest form as 1:5.
NB: Only units of the same kind can be compared in a ratio.

Example: The ratio of 1 sq metre to 1 hectare is not 1:1 as the two quantities are not of the same kind. It is 1 sq metre:1000 sq metres (1 hectare = 1000 sq metres) or 1:1000.

Ratios may be used to solve problems.

Example: 120 tonnes may be divided in the ratio 1:5.

The ratio 1:5 means that altogether 6 parts (1 plus 5) are involved in the division of the 120 tonnes. Each share is therefore worth 20 tonnes (that is, 120 divided by six); one share is 20 tonnes and five shares is 100 tonnes. Therefore 120 tonnes divided in the ratio of 1:5 is 20 tonnes:100 tonnes.

NUMBER PATTERNS

Some numbers are said to be rectangular, square or triangular. A number pattern may be either a representation of a particular number in the form of dots or some other symbol arranged in a pattern or a diagram in which different numbers are related (see Pascal's triangle, below).

Pascal's Triangle is one of the most famous and most important of all number patterns. Although it was long known before Pascal – who died in 1626 – he was the first to make ingenious and wide use of its properties. The numbers in Pascal's triangle appear in the binomial theorem, in problems about the selection of combinations of objects, and therefore in the theory of probability and statistics. Each number is formed by adding the two numbers diagonally above it, e.g. 10 = 6 + 4, as ringed in the table. The numbers in the rows so formed are then the coefficients of the terms in the binomial theorem. Thus the numbers in the fourth row (1 3 3 1) are the coefficients of the terms in the expansion of $(a + x)^3$, while those in the sixth row would be the expansion of $(a + x)^5$, i.e. 1 5 10 10 5 1.

1
1 1
1 2 1
1 3 3 1
1 4 6 4 1
1 5 10 10 5 1

rectangular numbers are composite numbers, that is any number that is not prime. Any composite number may be represented in the form of a rectangle of dots, Thus 6 =

2 x 3 = 6

square numbers are numbers with a pair of equal factors, and may therefore be represented as a square. Thus 4 =

$2 \times 2 = 2^2 = 4$

and 9=

$3 \times 3 = 3^2 = 9$

triangular numbers are numbers that can be formed into a series of equilateral triangles. Triangular numbers – such as 3, 6, 10 and 15 – can be represented by a triangular pattern of dots. Thus 6=

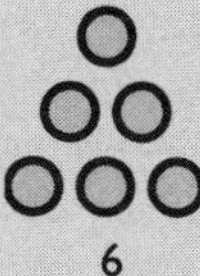

6

The differences between successive triangular numbers are the natural numbers.

PROBABILITY

At its most basic, probability may be described as the study of chance and choice. Not all actions and happenings have completely predictable results. Often we know that there is only a limited range of possible outcomes, but we do not know with certainty which of these to expect. Probability theory enables us to describe with mathematical rigour the chance of an action or happening having a particular outcome. We may not, even then, make the right choice, but at least we shall have made a justifiable choice.

empirical probability is based on observation and experiment. Here the probability of a particular outcome is calculated from the proportion of times it has been observed to have happened before under the same conditions – that is its relative frequency. Thus, if you tossed a coin ten times and the coin came up heads three times, the empirical probability that one of these throws comes up heads is $\frac{3}{10}$.

frequency (mathematical) the number of times that any event, value, etc., is repeated in a given period or group. When we toss a coin, we cannot predict which side will land facing upwards – this, after all, is the point of tossing coins. Assuming we accept the fairness of the coin and the way it is tossed, we know it is just as likely to come up heads or tails, and there is no other possible outcome. The outcomes are said to be equiprobable. The *a priori* probability of a coin coming up heads is 1 in 2 – or in the case of throwing a 6 on a single die the *a priori* probability is 1 in 6 or $\frac{1}{6}$. See also empirical probability.

law of large numbers states that as the number of trials increases, the observed empirical probability comes closer and closer to the theoretical value. There is no law of averages. Suppose we toss a coin ten times and the outcome is only three heads. The probability of a head is $\frac{1}{2}$, so why do we not get five heads? We try a total of 100 tosses of the coin, and the outcome is now, say, 40 heads, the last six being all heads. A gambler might back the chance of the 101st toss of the coin being tails, because, previously, there had been more tails than heads. Another gambler might back heads because there seemed to be 'a run' of heads, which would conform with the so-called 'law of averages'. However, we know that the probability of a head or a tail at any one toss of the coin is $\frac{1}{2}$ and a coin cannot remember – it cannot be influenced by what has gone before. In this example it means that only in a very long run will the relative frequency settle down towards $\frac{1}{2}$.

likelihood ratio (or **'odds'**) means the proportion of favourable to unfavourable possibilities or outcomes, and is a different way of expressing probability. As we can see in the entry on frequency, the probability of throwing, say, a 4 with a die is $\frac{1}{6}$. Therefore, the probability of not throwing a 4 is $\frac{5}{6}$. The 'odds' are thus expressed as 1 to 5 on throwing a 4 (or 5 to 1 against throwing a 4).

odds a scale of measuring chance. Odds are more formally known as likelihood ratio.

probability scale When an outcome is certain, it occurs every time: 1 in 1, 2 in 2, etc. Expressing this as a fraction, we say the probability is $\frac{1}{1}$, that is, one. When an outcome is impossible, it occurs no times in any number of tests, so we say the probability is zero.

SETS

Sets can be considered simply as collections of objects. A set can be specified by stipulating some property for an object as a condition of membership of a set, or by listing the members of a set in any order. Conventionally this is written within braces i.e. curly sets of brackets { }.

disjoint sets sets that have no members in common.

intersection the set of members that is common to one or more sets, denoted by $\cap$.

member an object belonging to a set. $x \in A$ denotes that x is a member of set A.

null set a set containing no members, denoted by $\emptyset$.

relative complement those items in a universal set that are not part of a particular set. The complement of set A is denoted by A'.

subset a set in which all of the members are also members of another set. Thus a set may be said to be a subset of another set where one set is contained within another. If the larger set is X and the smaller set – the subset – is Y, the equation $Y \subset X$ means that Y is a subset of X. The equation $Y \supset X$ means that X is a subset of Y.

union the total of all of the members in one or more sets, denoted by $\cup$.

universal set a set containing all of the items under consideration in a particular situation. It is denoted by the symbol ξ.

Example: Consider the Smith family which has a bicycle, a motor cycle, a van, a family car and a sports car. We could represent the vehicles ridden or driven by Mrs Smith as

{motor cycle, van, family car}.

The number of elements in a set are indicated by the notation n(s) where s is the set. In this case n(s) = 3.

Sets are often shown by drawing a circle around representations of their members. We can use circles to represent the relationship between two or more sets.

If Mr Smith drives the sports car and the motor cycle but also shares the use of the van with Mrs Smith the set of vehicles used by him is

{motor cycle, van, sports car}

If R is the set of vehicles used by Mr Smith and S is the set of vehicles used by Mrs Smith R and S can be shown as two intersecting circles.

The set of all the vehicles used by the Smiths is

$R \cup S$ = {bicycle, motor cycle, van, family car, sports car}

The two sets have one member in common, the van.

The set of members that belong to both sets is known as their intersection. In the example given here it is the set whose only member is the van. This is written $R \cap S$ = {van}.

In this example, among the Smiths' vehicles {van} is a subset of {bicycle, motor cycle, van, family car, sports car}. All of the vehicles used by the Smith family constitute a universal set.

COORDINATES AND GRAPHS

A graph is a diagram that shows the relationship between sets of numbers. It may be thought of as a picture that shows the values taken by a function.

A function can be represented by a curve, or by a straight line, so allowing us to picture how a process changes and develops.

Graphs can be used for many purposes: for showing rates of change, for example in temperature in a scientific experiment, or for rates of exchange of currencies to convert one currency to another.

A common use of graphs is the time/distance graph which shows how far a traveller, or a particular form of transport, can go in a particular period of time.

Example: The accompanying graph shows the distance that is travelled by a car over a certain period of time. From the graph the speed of the vehicle can be worked out.

The speed can be calculated by dividing the distance travelled by the time taken. (This gives the same equation as the gradient of the graph.)

In this case, the speed of the vehicle

= 20 km ÷ 45 minutes (that is, 0·75 hr)

= 26·67 km per hr.

axis (plur. **axes**) a straight line of reference, as in the horizontal and vertical axes of a graph.

Real numbers can be represented geometrically by a line (axis) marked off from the origin (0) using some numerical scale.

Any point in a plane can be similarly represented by the pair of numbers that correspond to its respective distances from two such axes, as shown in the accompanying time/distance graph; these numbers are the coordinates (see below) of the point.

coordinate any of two or more magnitudes used to define the position of a point on a graph.

Coordinates are known as an ordered pair of numbers as they are always given in the same form (x, y).

The x value is always given first, followed by the y value.

Example: The curve representing the function $y = x^2$ is the set of the pairs (x,y) of real numbers for which y is the square of x; thus, for example, (2,4), (–1,1), (–2,4), ($\sqrt{2}$,2), etc., are all in the graph of the function.

This system of coordinates is named after the French philosopher and mathematician René Descartes (or des Cartes, hence the adjective Cartesian).

function a relationship between two quantities or 'variables', whereby the values of one (the dependent variable) are uniquely determined by values of the other (the independent variable); see also the introduction (above).

gradient the rate of ascent or descent of a line on a graph.

Gradients may be either positive or negative depending upon which direction the line slopes. See also positive gradient and negative gradient.

The gradient of a straight line can be worked out by dividing the change in the upward distance by the change in distance to the right horizontally.

intercept the x-intercept is the coordinate at which a line or curve crosses the x-axis; the tan y-intercept is defined similarly for the y-axis.

negative gradient a gradient on a graph in which the line slopes downwards from left to right. See also gradient.

ordered pair (of numbers) see coordinates.

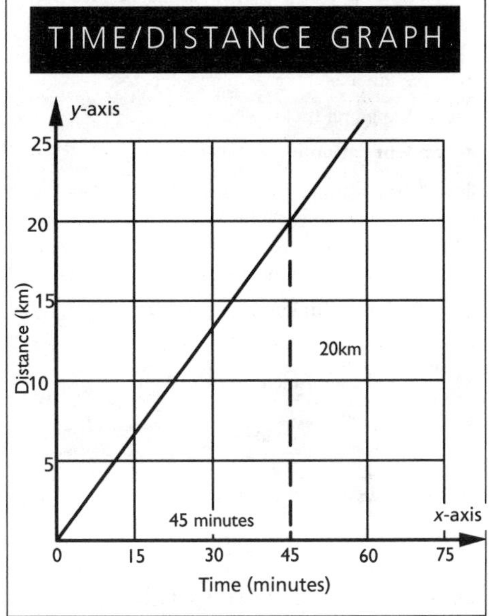

origin the point at which the axes of a graph cross. The origin has often, but has by no means always, the coordinates 0,0.

plane a two-dimensional area.

positive gradient a gradient on a graph in which the line slopes upwards from left to right. See also gradient.

straight line equation the equation $y = mx + c$ represents a straight line on a graph, for which m is the value of the gradient and c is the intercept.

Example: $y = 4x+5$ represents a straight line of gradient 4 through the point (0,5).

table of values a chart or table of values from the equation of a line, or of a curve, from which the graph of a line, or of a curve, may be plotted.

x-axis the horizontal axis of a graph. The x value is always given first.

y-axis the vertical axis of a graph. The y value is always given secondly, that is following the x value.

CALCULUS

Calculus is the branch of mathematics that studies continuous change in terms of the mathematical properties of the functions that represent it, and these results can be interpreted in geometric terms relating to the graph of the function.

Calculus was developed independently by Newton and Leibniz in the late 17th century. Because their presentation involved paradoxical references to infinitesimals, many scientists rejected their 'infidel mathematics', but at the same time there was considerable dispute about who should have the credit for its discovery.

coefficient a number or symbol which is used as a multiplier.

coordinate any of two or more magnitudes used to define the position of a point.

The real numbers can be represented geometrically by a line (an axis) on a graph. (See p. 245)

curve see graph (below).

dependent variable see function.

derivative the instantaneous rate of change of one variable in relation to another variable.

differential calculus the branch of mathematics concerned with differentiation.

differential coefficient of a product if

$$y = uv$$

where u and v are functions of x, then

$$\frac{dy}{dx} = u\frac{dv}{dx} + v\frac{du}{dx}$$

differential coefficient of a quotient if

$$y = \frac{u}{v}$$

where u and v are functions of x, then

$$\frac{dy}{dx} = \frac{v\dfrac{du}{dx} - u\dfrac{dv}{dx}}{v^2}$$

differentiation the process of finding the derivative of a function. This process can also be interpreted as geometry. However, it is not always necessary to work out a derivative by means of a graph. Instead, certain general principles apply.

The derivative of a function can itself be differentiated: for example, acceleration is the rate of change of velocity, and the derivative of the velocity function with respect to time can be worked out. This is the second derivative of the displacement function.

If y is any function of x, and Δy, Δx are corresponding increments of y and x, then the differential coefficient of y with respect to x (written $^{dy}/_{dx}$) is defined as

$$\underset{\Delta x \to 0}{\text{Lt}} \frac{[f(x - \Delta x) - f(x)]}{\Delta x}$$

$^{dy}/_{dx}$ gives the gradient of the curve, i.e. it measures the rate of change of one variable with respect to another.

Thus since velocity is the rate of change of displacement with respect to time, it may be expressed in calculus terms.

$$\frac{ds}{dt}$$

where s is the displacement of a body from a fixed point and the equation of motion of the body is of the form $s = f(t)$.

function a relationship between two quantities or 'variables' whereby the values of one (the dependent variable) are uniquely determined by the values of the other (the independent variable).

Suppose we go for a cycle ride and keep up a speed of 15 km/h. Then our distance from home is determined by how long we have been travelling. For example, after half an hour we will have travelled 7·5 km; after an hour 15 km; after 2 hours 30 km, and so on. We can express this relationship by saying that the distance is a function of the time we have been travelling.

Here the two quantities, time and distance, might be represented by the variables t and d, and the mathematical relationship between them means that for any number of units of time, t, we can work out the number of units of distance travelled, d, by multiplying t by 15.

In general, the notation for a function is $y = f(x)$, which indicates that the value of y depends upon the values of x; in that case, y is called the *dependent variable* and x is called the *independent variable*. The variables are thought of as running through a range of values – for example, if our journey takes a total of 3 hours, the domain of t is the interval (0,3), and the range of d is the interval (0,45).

Because a function associates elements of one set with those of another, it defines the set of all pairs of elements, (x,y), in which x is the value of the independent variable and y is the value of the function for the argument x. Another way of expressing this is that any point that satisfies the function $y = f(x)$ can be represented by the point $(x,f(x))$.

Since a function must be a many-one relation, every such pair has a different first element, so the pairs can be listed in a unique order. The function can be thought of as moving through the values of the independent variable as the value of the independent variable increases.

graph (short for **graphic formula**) a diagram that shows the relationship between certain sets of numbers. Mathematicians tend to use the term graph for the set of values of variables and call the diagram a curve. Since this way of representing change and dependency is equivalent to the function itself, curves provide us with a way of visualizing processes of change. See also p. 245.

increment the amount of increase.

independent variable see function.

infinitesimal an infinitely small quantity.

interval see function.

MECHANICS

Mechanics is that branch of physics which is concerned with the motion of bodies and the action of forces on bodies. This section deals with the mathematics of mechanics.

circular motion (where a body is moving in a circle with uniform speed) may be represented by the following equation: $vr\omega$, where v = linear velocity, r = the radius of the circle, and ω = the angular velocity.

The body will nevertheless have an acceleration (since a force is acting on it to make it move in a circle) but this will be directed towards the centre. The acceleration will be: $r\omega^2$, the force will be: $mr\omega^2$, where m is the mass of the body.

force changes an object's motion, thus making it move more or less quickly and/or causing it to change direction. A force F causes a mass m to accelerate at a rate a according to the equation: $F = ma$.

The effect of a force F in a direction at an angle θ to the direction in which the force is applied is called its component in that direction and is given by: $F\cos\theta$

impact of elastic bodies if the bodies are smooth and only the forces between the bodies are considered, the equations determining the velocities and directions of the bodies after impact will be found under momentum and the velocity of separation.

kinetic energy (symbol KE) of a particle of mass m moving with velocity v is:

$$\tfrac{1}{2}v^2$$

momentum the product of a mass and its velocity. The conservation of momentum principle states that the total momentum of bodies in any given direction is the same before and after impact. The following equation can be given:

$$m_1v_1 + m_2v_2 = m_1u_1\cos\alpha + m_2v_2\cos\beta$$

See velocity of separation for an explanation of the terms used in the above equation.

potential energy (symbol PE) gained by a mass m as it is raised through a height h is mgh.

projectiles formulae for calculations include the following. For simple cases in which air resistance is neglected and the vertical velocity is subject only to the acceleration of gravity, the results below may be derived from the fundamental equations of motion (where u = velocity and H = height):

The time of flight

$$T = \frac{2u\, sin q}{g}$$

The time to the greatest height

$$= \frac{T}{2} = \frac{u\, sin q}{g}$$

The greatest height obtained

$$H = \frac{u^2\, sin^2\, q}{2g}$$

The range on a horizontal plane

$$R = \frac{u^2\, sin^2\, q}{g}$$

For a given velocity of projection u there are, in general, two possible angles of projection to obtain a given horizontal range.

These directions will make equal angles with the vertical and horizontal respectively. For maximum range the angle makes 45° with the horizontal.

relative velocity may be calculated in the following manner. To find the velocity of a body A relative to a body B, combine with the velocity of A a velocity equal and opposite to that of B.

simple harmonic motion occurs when a particle moves so that its acceleration is directed towards a fixed point in its path, and is proportional to its distance from that point. The fundamental equation is:

$$\frac{d^2x}{dt^2} = -w^2x$$

By integrating the corresponding equation

$$v\frac{dv}{dx} + w^2x = 0$$

the velocity at any displacement of x is given by:

$$v = w\sqrt{a^2 - x^2}$$

where a is the maximum value of x. The displacement at time t is given by
$x = a \sin \omega t$ if timed from the centre, or
$x = a \cos \omega t$ if timed from the maximum displacement.

uniform acceleration equations include the following. If a particle accelerates at a constant rate (a) from a velocity u to a velocity v over a displacement s and during time t, then its motion is governed by the equations:

$$v = u + at$$

$$v^2 = u^2 + 2as$$

$$s = ut + \tfrac{1}{2}at^2$$

$$s = \tfrac{1}{2}(u + v)t$$

vector either a physical quantity with magnitude and direction (such as velocity or force) or a line that represents such a quantity.

velocity of separation is equal to the velocity of approach (also measured along the line of centres) multiplied by the coefficient of elasticity between the two bodies.

If the impact is oblique (and the bodies are smooth) the velocities at right angles to the line of centres is unchanged.

If u_1 and u_2, m_1 and m_2 are the initial velocities and masses of the two spheres, and α and β are the angles these velocities make with the line of centres, and v_1 and v_2 are the components of velocities along the line of centres after impact, the above statements may be represented by the following equation:

$$v_2 \pm v_1 = e(u_1\cos\alpha - u_2\cos\beta)$$

work done by a force F acting on a body as it covers a displacement s is Fs.

STATISTICS

Statistics is sometimes treated as a branch of mathematics, but it can also be regarded as a separate science – the science that is concerned with the collection, study and analysis of numerical data.

The data studied can be the result of surveys, forms, questionnaires or censuses, or may derive from systematic experiments and the recording of results or from observation and the recording of information. Governments have statistical departments recording and predicting finance, trade, population figures, industrial and agricultural production, and so on.

Data has to be sorted into a form that is useful. Different categories have to be identified so that the data can be presented in a form that is meaningful. At its simplest, this is achieved by means of frequency distribution tables and tally charts.

When data has been processed – into a frequency distribution table, for example, it can then be presented visually in a diagram. The forms most commonly used are the pictogram, the bar chart, the pie chart and the histogram.

bar chart a popular method of displaying statistical data. It is also, probably, the easiest of the methods considered here.

A bar chart consists of columns that are arranged either vertically or horizontally. (When the columns are arranged vertically a bar chart is sometimes referred to as a column graph.)

Each bar is the same width and, where there are spaces between them, those spaces are uniform. The length (in a horizontal bar chart) or the height (in a vertical bar chart) depends upon the size of the section of the data that it represents.

Example: The bar chart on page 537 shows the gross domestic products (GDPs) of the world's leading economic powers. (The GDP of a country is the money value of the total amount of goods and services that are produced by a country over a period of one year.)

The bar chart shows far more dramatically than a table of figures just how dominant the US economy is worldwide. It graphically reveals the challenge of Japan in second place, the large gap between the size of the Japanese and German economies, and the greater size of the German economy compared with the economies of the other leading European states – France, Italy, the UK and Spain.

column graph see bar chart.

frequency distribution table a table derived from information shown on the final column on a tally chart.

grouped data see tally chart.

histogram a visual method of showing data which resembles a vertical bar chart. It differs, however, in that it is the area rather than the height of each bar that represents the data. In a histogram – which is often but not always drawn on squared graph paper – there are no gaps between the bars.

ideograph another name for a pictogram.

pictograph another name for a pictogram.

pictogram (or **pictograph** or **ideograph**) a simple method of showing frequencies by means of symbols or small pictures. In a pictogram all the symbols are drawn the same size and are placed regularly in appropriate columns or blocks. Data of less than the scale size is shown by a part of the symbol, for example one half or one quarter of the symbol.

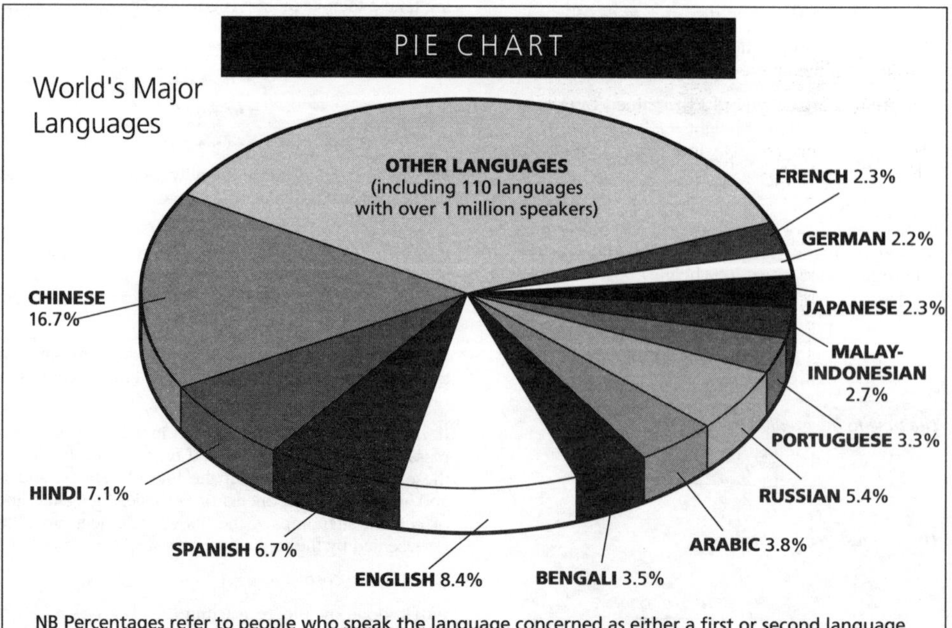

NB Percentages refer to people who speak the language concerned as either a first or second language

pie chart (or **pie graph**) a visual method of showing data in which a circle is drawn and divided into slices of a 'pie' to show the different shares of the total. The size of each slice depends upon the size of each item of data. A pie chart can only be used to show the sizes of parts of a known total.

Example: If a pie chart were to be drawn showing the world's major religions as a percentage of the total world population, in the chart 33·5% of the total might be shown as Christian.

The entire pie chart has an angle of 360° at the centre. Therefore the slice represented by 33·5% of the total will be 360 ÷ 100 = 3·6 × 33·5 = 120·6°. Similarly the percentage of the world's population following Islam is 18·2%; this would be represented by a slice whose angle at the centre of the circle is 65·5° (that is, 18·2 × 3·6°).

tally chart a table in which data is sorted into meaningful categories.

Example: In the cricket Test match between New Zealand and Pakistan held at Hamilton, in New Zealand, on 2, 3, 4, 5 January 1993 all of the batsmen in both sides batted in both innings. Pakistan scored 216 (including 8 extras) in the first innings and 174 (including 4 extras) in the second innings; New Zealand scored 264 runs in the first innings (including 33 extras) and only 93 in the second innings (including 22 extras).

The number of runs scored by each batsman was as follows:

4 0 0 92 14 23 27 32 13 2 1 133 43 2 2 14 6 12 16 0 3
0 8 0 11 12 0 75 15 33 4 10 2 4 8 9 19 0 9 9 4 13 0 0 0.

In this form it is not easy to make very much use of these figures, but if a tally chart such as the one shown here is drawn up then the information becomes more meaningful.

TALLY CHART

Number of runs scored by individual batsmen in the New Zealand v. Pakistan Test Match (January 1993)

Number of runs	Tallies
under 10	~~IIII~~ ~~IIII~~ ~~IIII~~ ~~IIII~~ ~~IIII~~ II
11-20	~~IIII~~ ~~IIII~~
21-30	II
31-40	II
41-50	I
51-60	
61-70	
71-80	I
81-90	I
91-100	
101-110	
111-120	
121-130	
131-140	I

From the list of scores one stroke is marked on the tally chart each time a score occurs within one of the chosen categories. Every fifth score is drawn across the previous four, giving handy blocks of five.

In this case the cricket scores are shown on the tally chart in categories, because it would be totally unwieldy to have a separate line for every line between 0 (the lowest score) and 133 (the highest score). Because it has been necessary to use these groups, the chart shows what is called grouped data.

(In the case of a tally chart showing, for example, the marks out ten for a French test taken by a class there would be no need to group the scores achieved – a separate line could be used for each mark between 0 and 10. Such a tally chart would show ungrouped data.)

A final column can be added to the above example to record the frequency with which scores fall into each category. It would appear as follows.

By omitting the central column – tallies – a frequency distribution table can be drawn up.

ungrouped data see tally chart.

NB: The figures used in the pie chart examples are given for mathematical purposes only. The most up-to-date figures for speakers of major languages and followers of major religions will be found in the chapters Language and Literature and Beliefs and Ideas.

TALLY CHART WITH FREQUENCY CHART

Number of runs scored by individual batsmen in the New Zealand v. Pakistan Test Match (January 1993)

Number of runs	Tallies	Frequency
under 10	IIII/ IIII/ IIII/ IIII/ IIII/ II	27
11–20	IIII/ IIII/	10
21–30	II	2
31–40	II	2
41–50	I	1
51–60		0
61–70		0
71–80	I	1
81–90	I	1
91–100		0
101–110		0
111–120		0
121–130		0
131–140	I	1

GEOMETRY AND TRIGONOMETRY

Geometry is that branch of mathematics which deals with the properties of lines, points, surfaces and solids. The rules of geometry – which have been discovered not invented – are used to derive angles, areas, distances, etc., which may be not otherwise be measured directly. A simple example of a mathematical model is the representation of a portion of the Earth's surface by a set of interlocking triangles, from the measurement of which maps may be constructed. Geometry establishes that two triangles each have angles of the same sizes if, and only if, corresponding pairs of sides are in the same proportions.

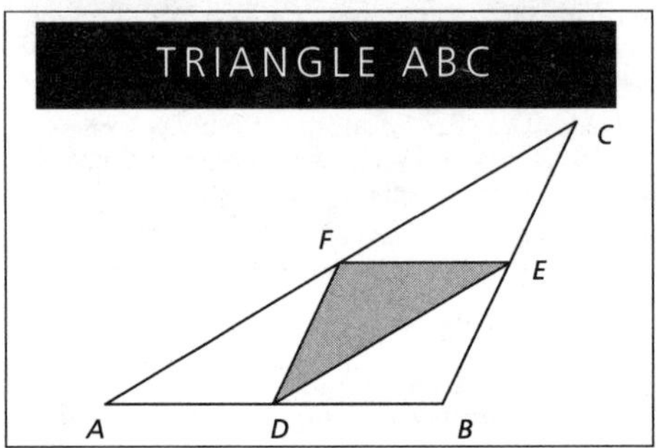

Here *D*, *E* and *F* are the centre-points of sides *AB*, *BC* and *CA* respectively. So, *DE* is half the length of *AC*, *EF* is half the length of *AB*, and *FD* is half the length of *BC*. Thus, the shaded triangle, and the angles at *D*, *E* and *F*, are respectively equal to those at *C*, *A* and *B*. Furthermore, the triangles *ADF*, *FEC*, *DBE* and *EFD* are all congruent, that is identical in shape and size, and are thus all similar to triangle *ABC*.

acute angle an angle of less than 90°.

cos see cosine.

cosine of an angle (shortened to **cos**) the ratio of the side adjacent to the given angle to the hypotenuse. In the diagram for Pythagoras' theorem (see p. 252), cos θ is AB/AC. (See also sine and tangent.)

hypotenuse the side of a right-angled triangle that is opposite the right angle.

line symmetry see symmetry.

plane figure a figure that lies entirely on one plane, i.e. they are two-dimensional. They includes polygons, quadrilaterals, triangles, circles and conic sections.

reflection (of a figure) the movement of a figure into a mirror image of its previous position. The size and shape of the figure remain unchanged.

rotation (of a figure) the movement of a figure in position in which one point of the plane – known as the centre of rotation – remains static. The size and shape of the figure remains unchanged.

rotational symmetry see symmetry.

sin see sine.

sine of an angle (shortened to **sin**) the ratio of the side opposite the given angle to the hypotenuse. The Greek letters θ and Ø are usually used to denote the angles, thus in the diagram for Pythagoras' theorem (see p. 252) we say that the sine of θ, usually written as sin θ, is BC/AC. (See also cosine and tangent.)

symmetry the correspondence of opposite parts in size, shape and position. There are two types of symmetry – line symmetry and rotational symmetry. If the triangle shown in the first column of this page were to be folded along the line *BF*, the two halves of the triangle would fit exactly one on top of the other. The whole shape that is the triangle is therefore said to be symmetrical and the fold line *BF* is known as the line of symmetry. Rotational symmetry occurs when a shape is rotated about its centre point and at some position during the rotation the shape appears not to have moved. The letters N and S have rotational symmetry. The letter H and the figure 8 have both line and rotational symmetry.

tan see tangent.

tangent of an angle (shortened to **tan**) the ratio of the opposite to the adjacent side; in the example for Pythagoras' theorem (p. 252) this is BC/AB. In this figure it easy to see that tan θ must always equal sinθ/cosθ. (See also cosine and sine.)

translation (of a figure) the movement of a figure from one position to another maintaining the same image.

triangulation the determining of the distance between two points on the Earth's surface by dividing an area into connected triangles.

trigonometry the branch of mathematics that deals with the relations between the angles or the sides of triangles.

Trigonometry relies on the recognition that in a right-angled triangle the ratio of the lengths of pairs of sides depends only on the sizes of the two acute angles of the triangle. These ratios are given names – sine, cosine and tangent.

values for sin, cos and tan of 30°, 45°, and 60° can be established using Pythagoras' theorem (see p. 252).

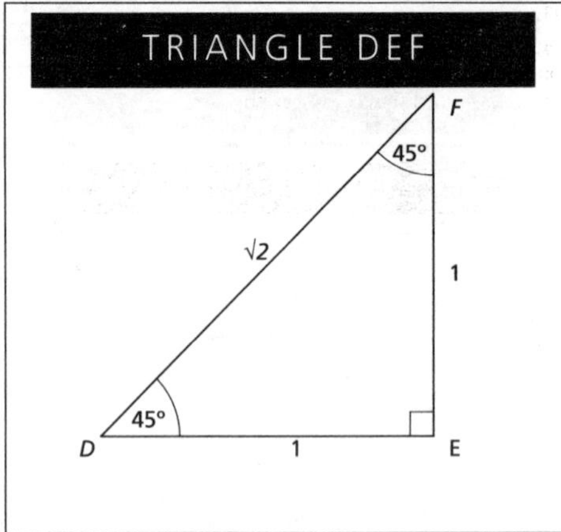

In triangle *DEF*, *DE* = *EF* = 1, so the angles at *D* and *F* are equal, that is they are each 45° (the internal angles of a triangle add up to 180°). Using Pythagoras' theorem,

$$DF^2 = 1^2 + 1^2 = 2$$

so

$$DF = \sqrt{2}$$

POLYGONS

A polygon is a closed plane figure with three or more straight sides that meet at the same number of vertices and do not intersect other than at those vertices. (A vertex is the point at which two sides of a polygon meet.) Although we tend to think of a polygon as being a many-sided figure, it can have as few sides as three (a triangle). The sum of the interior angles =

$$\frac{(2n-4)\times 90^\circ}{n}$$

where n = the number of sides.

The sum of the exterior angles of any polygon = 360°, regardless of the number of sides. (An exterior angle of a polygon is the angle between one side extended and the adjacent side.)

decagon a polygon with ten sides.

dodecagon a polygon with 12 sides.

heptagon a polygon with seven sides.

hexagon a polygon with six sides.

nonagon a polygon with nine sides.

octagon a polygon with eight sides.

parallelogram a quadrilateral whose opposite sides are equal in length and parallel. It has no lines of symmetry, unless it is also a rectangle, but it does have rotational symmetry about its centre, the point where the diagonals meet.

If one angle of a parallelogram is a right angle, then all the angles are right angles, and it is a rectangle. Any parallelogram can be dissected into a rectangle by cutting a right-angled triangle off one end, and sliding it to the opposite end.

The dissection changes neither the area of the parallelogram nor the length of the sides – the area of any parallelogram is equal to the area of a rectangle with same base and the same length.

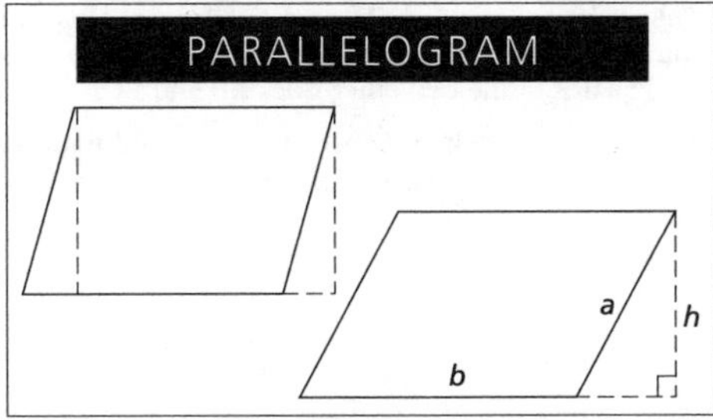

Area = bh Perimeter = 2 (a + b)

pentagon a polygon with five sides.

quadrilateral a polygon with four sides. A quadrilateral may be a rectangle, a square, a parallelogram, a rhombus or a trapezium (or trapezoid), or none of these.

rectangle a quadrilateral in which all the angles are right angles, thus the opposite sides are parallel in pairs. A rectangle may be a square (see below). A rectangle that is not a square has two lines of symmetry.

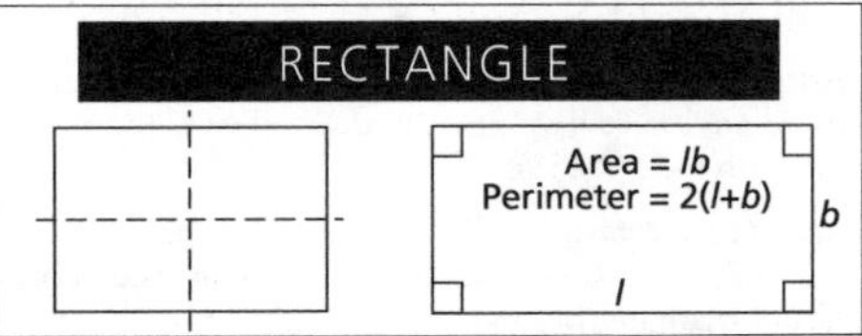

rhombus a parallelogram whose sides are all equal in length. Its diagonals are both lines of symmetry, and therefore bisect each other at right angles.

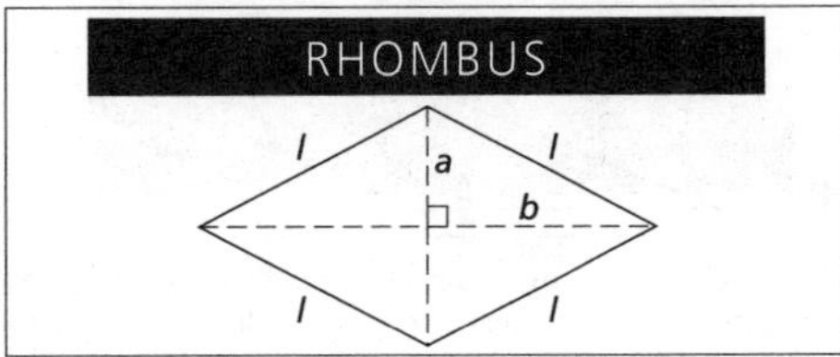

Area = ½ (2a) (2b) Perimeter = 4l

square a rectangle whose sides are equal . It has four lines of symmetry – both diagonals and the two lines joining the middle points of pairs of opposite sides.

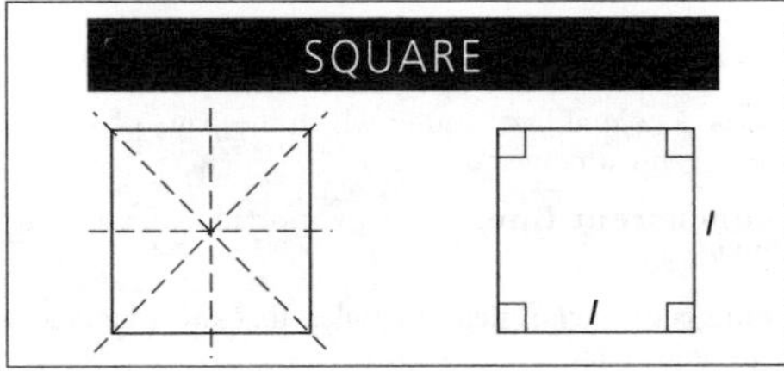

Area = l^2 Perimeter = 4l

trapezium a quadrilateral with two parallel sides of unequal length. (In North America – where such a plane figure is described as a trapezoid – a trapezium is a quadrilateral with no sides parallel.)

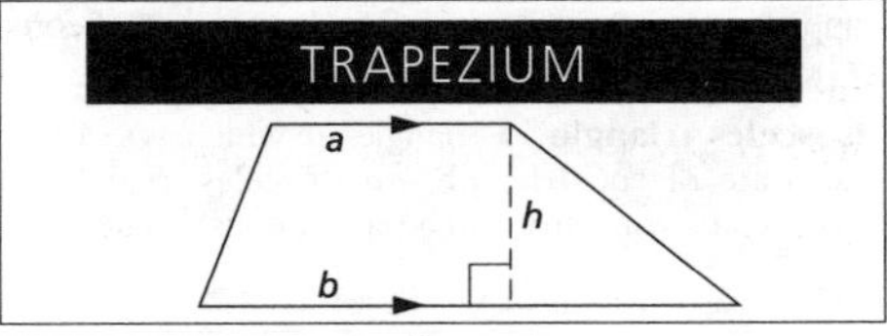

Area = $\frac{1}{2}(a+b)h$

To find the area three measurements have to be taken – the height between the pair of parallel sides and the length of both of the parallel sides. The area of a trapezium is equal to the height multiplied by the average length of the parallel sides; i.e. = 1/2 (the sum of the parallel sides) x the perpendicular distance between them.

trapezoid (North American usage) a trapezium.

triangle a polygon with three sides. See p. 252.

vertex the point where two sides of an angle intersect or the corner point of a square, cube or triangle.

TRIANGLES

A triangle is a plane figure which has three sides and three angles. It may also be defined as a three-sided polygon (see p. 251).

area (of a triangle) is one half of a parallelogram with the same base and the same height (see properties of triangles; below).

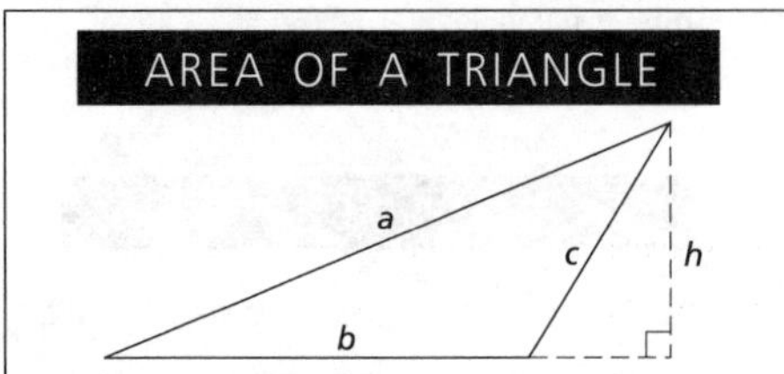

The area of a triangle can also be calculated from the lengths of its sides, using a formula discovered by the Greek mathematician Archimedes. If half the sum of the sides is s, then:

$$\text{Area} = \sqrt{s(s-a)(s-b)(s-c)},$$

where a, b, and c are the three sides and

$$s = \frac{a+b+c}{2}$$

axis a central line around which the parts of a figure are evenly arranged.

concurrent lines see properties of triangles (below).

congruent triangles triangles that are identical in size and shape.

diagonal a straight line between the opposite corners of a rectangle.

equilateral triangle a triangle which has all its sides equal. All the angles of an equilateral triangle are equal to 60°.

hypotenuse the side of a right-angled triangle that is opposite to the right angle (see Pythagoras' theorem – below).

isosceles triangle a triangle in which two of the sides are of equal length. An isosceles triangle has one axis of symmetry and a pair of equal angles.

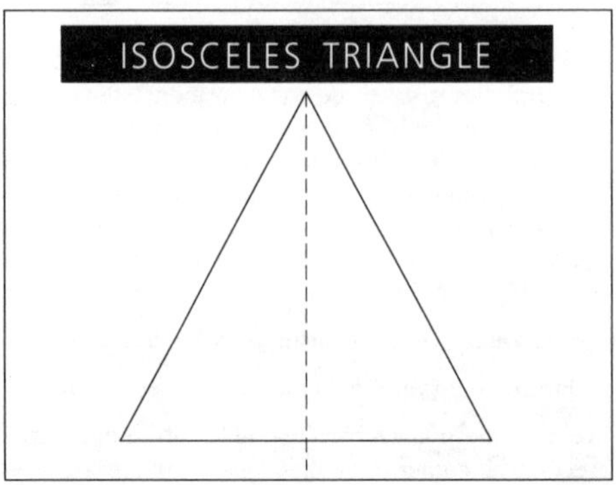

medians see properties of triangles (below).

properties (of triangles) include the following curious qualities.

The three lines that join the vertices of a triangle to the middle point of the opposite sides, called the medians, meet at a point – they are said to be concurrent.

The three lines that bisect the sides of a triangle at right angles also meet. The point at which they meet is the centre of the circle through the vertices of the triangle (see below).

Any triangle can be thought of as one half of a parallelogram that has been divided in two by one of its diagonals.

Pythagoras' theorem the most-proved theorem in geometry, indeed in the whole of mathematics. (E. S. Loomis published in 1940 a collection of more than 370 different proofs of Pythagoras' theorem, and more have been discovered since.)

Pythagoras is the probable discoverer of the geometrical theorem that is named after him. (He did not, however, discover the theorem in its Euclidean form.)

The theorem states that the area of the square drawn on the hypotenuse of a right-angled triangle is equal to the sum of the squares drawn on the other two sides. (It is, however, also true that the area of any shape drawn on the hypotenuse is equal to the sum of equivalent shapes drawn on the other two sides.)

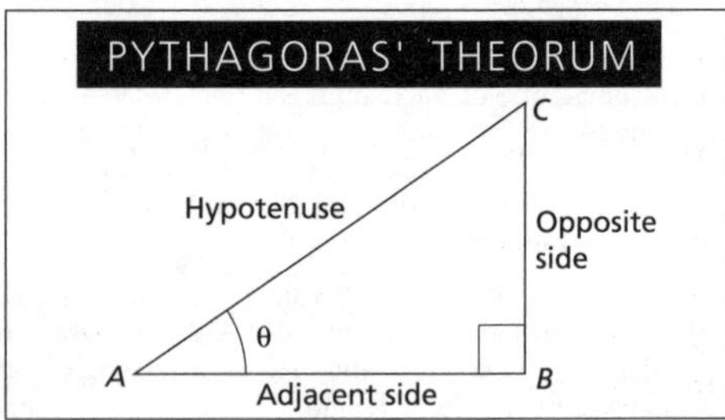

Thus, above, in the right-angled triangle ABC, the square of the hypotenuse AC is equal to the sum of the squares of the two other sides AB and BC.

There are an infinite number of right-angled triangles whose sides are integers. Four of the smallest have the sides:

3,	4,	5
5,	12,	13
8,	15,	17
7,	24,	25.

Such whole-number sets are sometimes called Pythagorean triples.

scalene triangle a triangle which has sides of three different lengths, and has no axes of symmetry.

symmetry the correspondence of opposite parts in size, shape and position.

triples (Pythagorean) see Pythagoras' theorem.

vertex (plural **vertices**) the point where two sides of an angle intersect or the corner point of a triangle.

CIRCLES AND OTHER CONIC SECTIONS

A circle is the path of a point that moves at a constant distance – the radius – from a fixed point (the centre of a circle). The circle is a special case of an ellipse (see below).

General equation (centre at *-g, -f*)

$$x^2 + y^2 + 2gx + 2fy + c = 0$$

Basic equation (centre at origin)

$$x^2 + y^2 = r^2$$

The area of a circle = πr^2

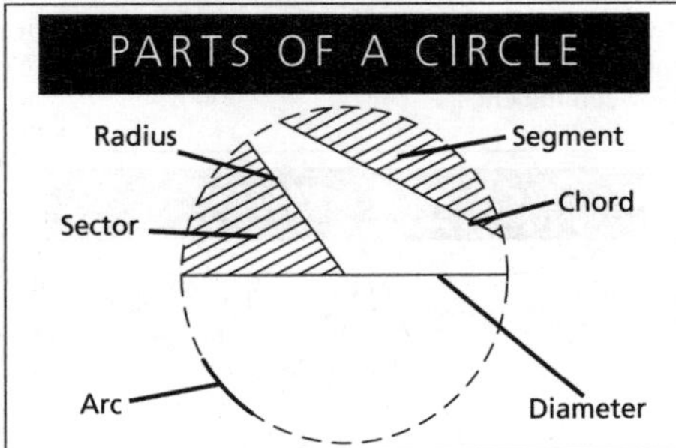

arc any part of the perimeter or circumference of a circle.

chord a straight line that joins two points that are on the circumference of a circle.

circle theorems include the following:

A diameter of a circle forms a right-angle at the circumference of the circle.

A tangent to a circle is always at right angles to the radius at the point of contact.

circumference the line that forms the perimeter of a circle. The circumference of a circle = $2\pi r$ or πd where r = radius, and d = diameter.

conic section curves that are formed by the intersection of a plane and a cone. An ellipse, a parabola, a hyperbola and a circle are all conic sections.

diameter a straight line that passes through the centre of a circle (or a sphere) from one side to the other. The term diameter is also used for the length of such a line.

ellipse a closed conic section with the appearance of a flattened circle. It is formed by an inclined plane that does not intersect the base of the cone. An ellipse

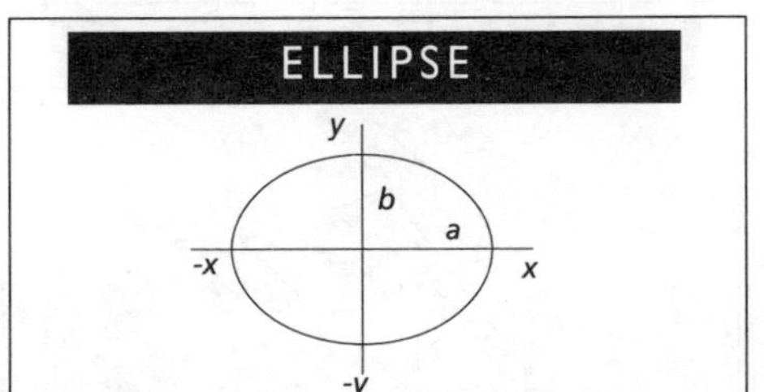

can also be thought of as a circle that has been stretched in one direction. The orbital path of each of the planets round the Sun is approximately an ellipse.

There are many ways to draw an ellipse. One of the simplest is to stretch a loop of thread round two pins, and hold it taut with a pencil. The path of the pencil would be an ellipse.

The area of an ellipse = πab.

Basic equation (centre at the origin)

$$\left(\frac{x_2}{a_2} + \frac{y_2}{b_2}\right) = 1$$

hemisphere one half of a sphere.

hyperbola a conic section that is formed by a plane that cuts a cone making a larger angle with the base than the angle made by the side of the cone.

Basic equation (centre at the origin)

$$\left(\frac{x^2}{a^2} - \frac{y^2}{b^2}\right) = 1$$

parabola a conic section that is formed by the intersection of a cone by a plane parallel to its sides.

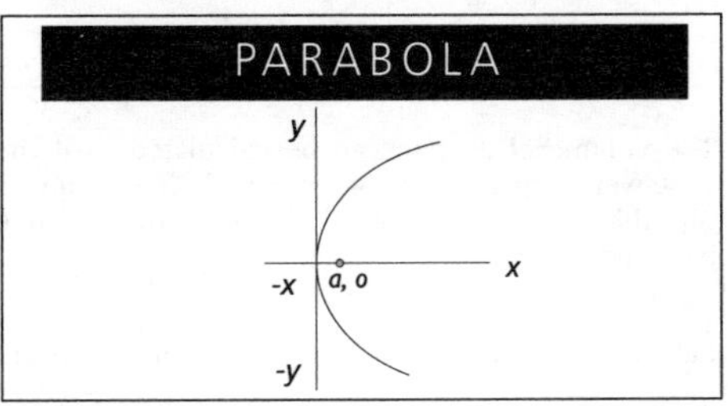

If you were to throw a ball up in the air then the path of the ball will be approximately a parabola with its axis vertical.

Basic equation (symmetrical about the x-axis with the focus at a,O) $y^2 = 4ax$

perimeter (of a circle) the circumference.

pi (which is indicated by the Greek letter π) the ratio of the circumference of a circle to its diameter (approximately 3·1411592...).

Pi was proved to be an irrational number – that is a number that cannot be written as an exact value – by Johann Heinrich Lambert (1728–77). In 1989 pi was worked out to 1,073,740,000 decimal places.

plane a surface that wholly contains a straight line connecting any two points lying on it.

radius (plural **radii**) a straight line between the perimeter or circumference of a circle and its centre.

sector a part of a circle that is included by two radii and an arc.

segment any part of a circle (or of a sphere) that is cut off by a line (or a plane) that is not necessarily a radius, in other words a chord .

tangent a line touching but not intersecting a curve or surface at one point only.

SOLIDS: AREAS AND VOLUMES

Solids are three dimensional figures, i.e. they have length, breadth and depth. Solids include rectangular blocks, prisms, pyramids, tetrahedrons, cylinders, cones and spheres.

The volume of any prism is always equal to the area of the base x the perpendicular height. The volume of any pyramid is one third the base area multiplied by the perpendicular height.

apex the highest point of a triangle.

circular prism see cylinder (below).

cone a solid figure with a circular plane base, narrowing to a point or apex. If the slant height of the cone is *l*, the area of the curved surface of a cone = πrl.

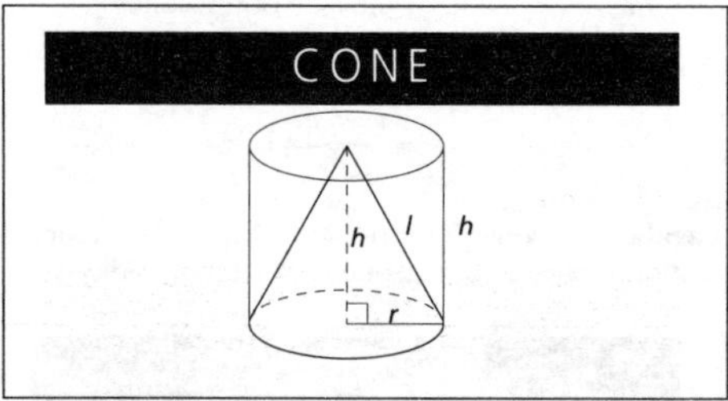

The volume of a cone can be calculated as if the cone were a special case of a pyramid. The volume is one third the volume of a cylinder with the same base and height.

The volume of a cone = $\frac{1}{3} p r^2 h$

cuboid a solid figure, all the faces of which are rectangles.

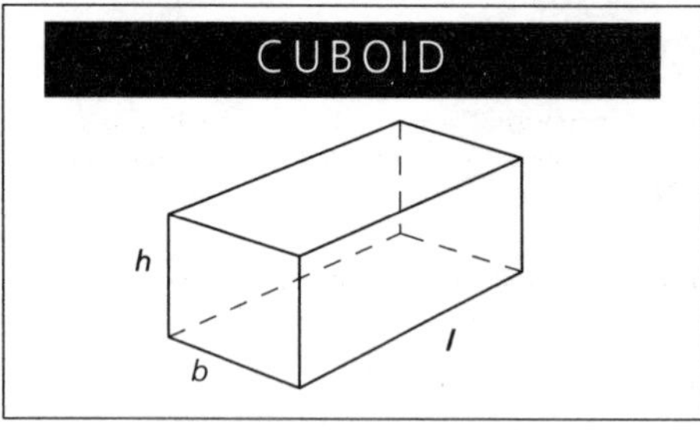

Surface area = $2(lb + bh + hl)$
Volume = lbh

cylinder a solid figure with straight sides and a circular section.

The area of the curved surface of a cylinder = $2\pi rh$

If the circles at both ends are included, then the total surface area =

$$2\pi rh + 2\pi r^2$$

The volume of a cylinder can be found by thinking of it as a special case of a prism. The volume equals the area of the base, multiplied by the height. The volume of a cylinder =

$$\pi r^2 h$$

prism a solid figure whose ends are identical polygons and whose sides are parallelograms (which could be rectangular).

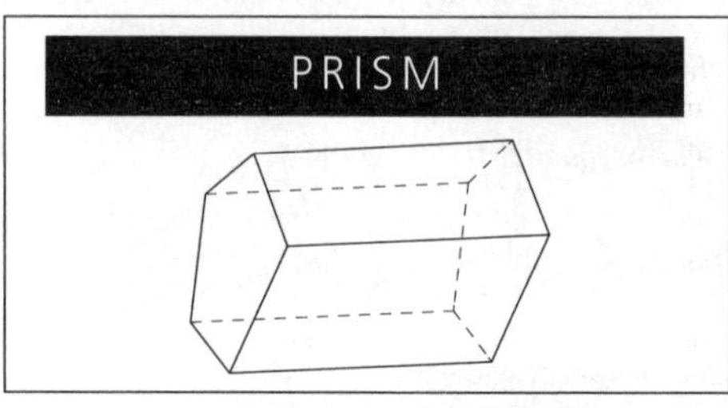

The volume of a prism equals the area of either of the ends, multiplied by the perpendicular distance between the ends.

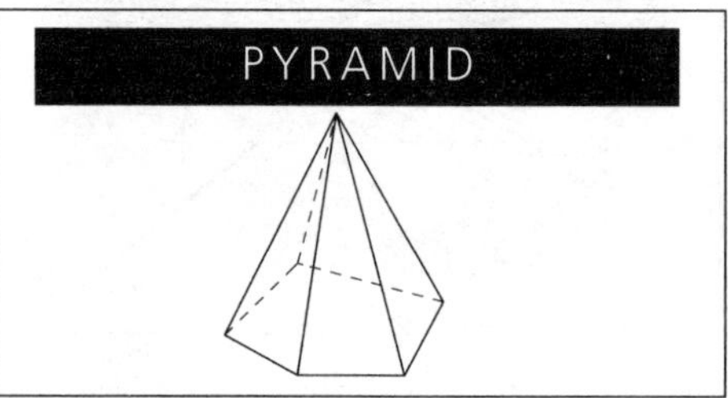

pyramid a solid figure whose base is a polygon, and whose special vertex – the apex – is joined to each vertex of the base. Therefore all its faces, apart from the base, are triangles.

Any pyramid can be fitted inside a prism so that the base of the pyramid is one end of the prism, and the apex of the pyramid is on the other end of the prism.

The volume of a pyramid on a rectangular base =

$$\frac{1}{3}(lbh)$$

rectangular block see cuboid (above).

sphere a solid figure every point of whose surface is equidistant from its centre,

Surface area = $4\pi r^2$ Volume = $\frac{4}{3} p r^3$

tetrahedron a pyramid whose base is a triangle. Any of the faces of a tetrahedron can be thought of as its base.

The volume of a tetrahedron = ⅓ (the area of the triangular base x the height).

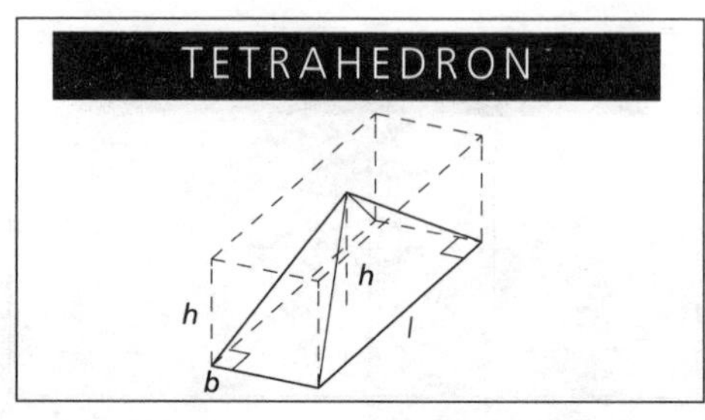

POLYHEDRA

A polyhedron is a solid shape with all plane faces. The faces of a regular polyhedron, or regular solid, are all identical regular polygons.

There are just five regular polyhedra – the regular tetrahedron, the cube, the regular octahedron, the regular dodecahedron and the regular icosahedron. The cube and the octahedron are dual polyhedra. The cube has six faces and eight vertices, while the octahedron has six vertices but eight faces. The regular dodecahedron and regular icosahedron are also dual polyhedra.

There are many more irregular polyhedra. The simplest to visualize have faces that are mixtures of two kinds of regular polygons. For example, the faces of the cuboctahedron are equilateral triangles and squares.

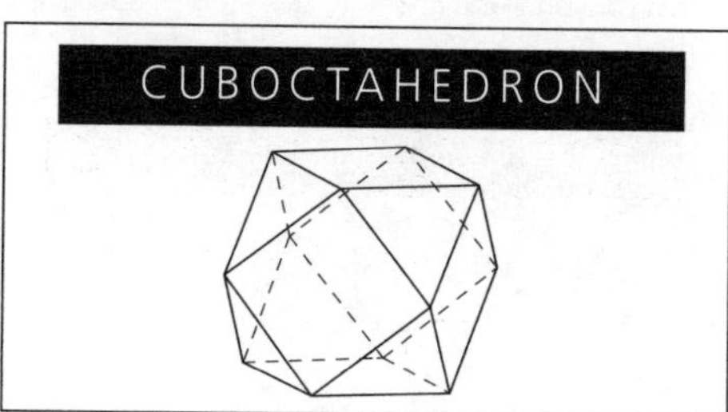

The mathematician Euler made an interesting discovery about the relationship between the number of faces (F), vertices (V) and edges (E) of polyhedra.

The equation F + V – E = 2 is true for all polyhedra.

The same relationship is true for an area divided into any number of regions (R) by boundaries or arcs (A) that join at nodes (N).

Thus R + N – A = 2.

If in a given example of regions:

R = 8 (the surrounding space counts as a region)
N = 12
A = 18

Thus R + N – A
= 8 + 12 – 18
= 2.

(It is interesting to note that for such a region, or indeed any map, no more than four colours are necessary so that no two adjoining regions have the same colour.)

cube a polyhedron which has:
6 faces which are all squares;
8 vertices; and
12 edges.

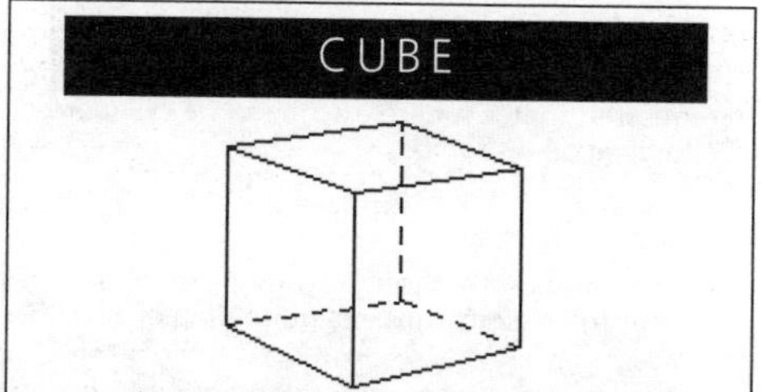

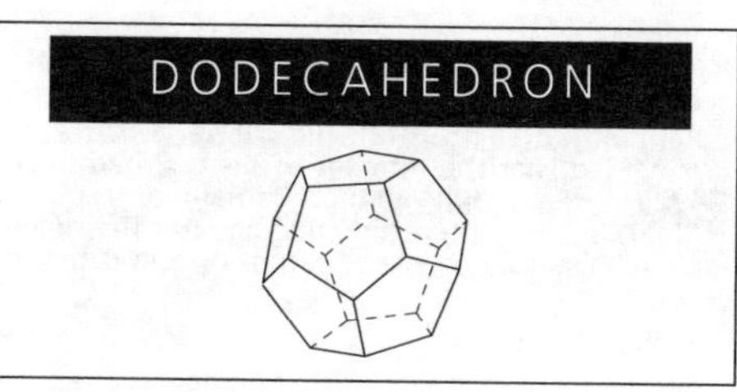

dodecahedron see regular dodecahedron (below).

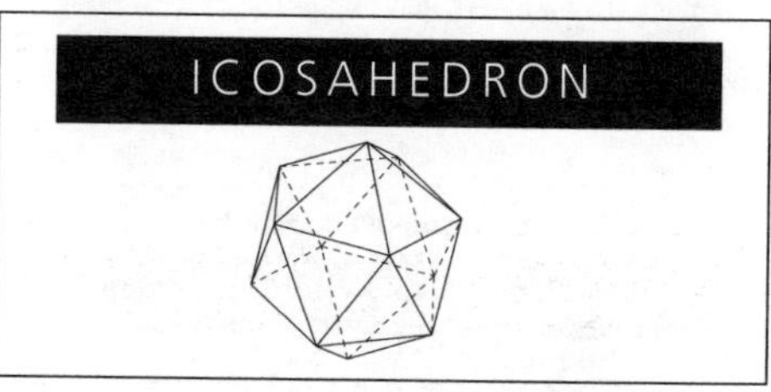

icosahedron see regular icosahedron (below).

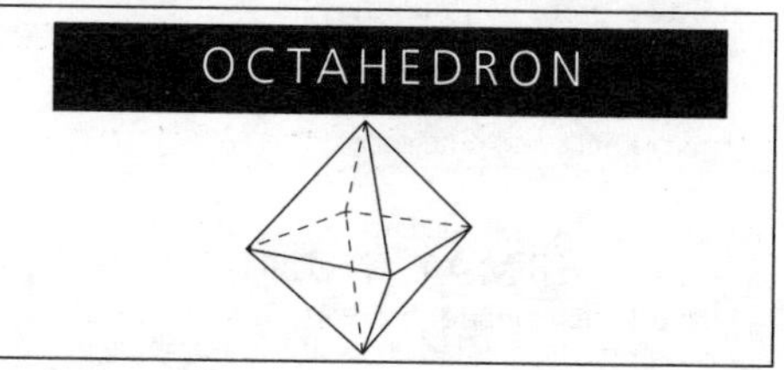

octahedron see regular octahedron (below).

regular dodecahedron a polyhedron which has:
12 faces which are all regular pentagons;
20 vertices; and
30 edges.

regular icosahadron a polyhedron which has:
20 faces which are all equilateral triangles;
12 vertices; and
30 edges.

regular octahedron a polyhedron which has:
8 faces all of which are equilateral triangles;
6 vertices; and
12 edges.

regular tetrahedron a polyhedron which has:
4 faces which are all equilateral triangles;
4 vertices; and
4 edges.

tetrahedron see regular tetrahedron (above).

vertex (plural **vertices**) a corner point of a triangle, cube or polyhedron, etc.

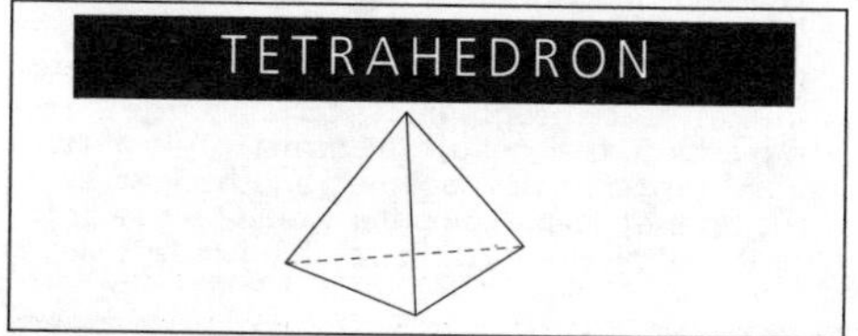

FASCINATION OF NUMBERS

Visiting the great Indian mathematician Srinivasa Ramanujan in hospital, his friend G.H. Hardy remarked that the number of his taxi had been 1729, surely a dull number. Ramanujan replied, 'No, it is a very interesting number. It is the smallest number expressible as a sum of two cubes in two different ways.'

$1729 = 10^3 + 9^3 = 12^3 + 1^3$

Ramanujan was fascinated by numbers, and it is no surprise that he found some weird approximations for π. You can check the following example easily with an electronic calculator.

π is the fourth root of $9^2 + 19^2/22$

FIBONACCI NUMBERS

Fibonacci numbers were named in the 19th century after Leonardo Fibonacci of Pisa, who introduced the Arabic figures 1 to 9 plus 0 to Europe in his *Liber abaci* in 1202. He earned the title of *Stupor Mundi* (wonder of the world) from the Holy Roman Emperor. In 1225 he published a recursive sequence of his Arabic numbers 1, 1, 2, 3, 5, 8, 13, 21, 34, 55, etc., in which each number is the sum of the two preceding numbers. In the 19th century this sequence was found to occur in nature – in the arrangement of leaf buds on a stem, animal horns, the genealogy of the male bee, and spirals in sunflower heads and pine cones.

FERMAT NUMBERS

Pierre Fermat made one very famous mistake in his career. He claimed that all the numbers in this sequence, called the Fermat numbers, were prime:

$F_0 = 2^1 + 1 = 3$; $F_1 = 2^2 + 1 = 5$; $F_2 = 2^4 + 1 = 17$;
$F_3 = 2^8 + 1 = 257$; $F_4 = 2^{16} + 1 = 65{,}537$.....

Unfortunately, only the first five are known to be prime. Euler showed in 1732 that $F_5 = 4{,}294{,}967{,}297 = 641 \times 6{,}700{,}417$, and every Fermat number tested since then has proved to be composite.

Actually finding the factors of a large number, even when you know that it is not prime, is very difficult. Only in 1990 did Mark Manasse and Arjen Lenstra manage to find the factors of F_9, a number of 155 digits, using a Connection machine, a massive parallel supercomputer at Florida State University. It has three prime factors, of 7, 49, and 99 digits.

PRIME NUMBERS

It is not known whether or not there are infinitely many *twin primes*. These are pairs of successive odd numbers that are both prime, like 5 and 7, 11 and 13, or 29 and 31.

Another famous conjecture about prime numbers is that of Christian Goldbach (1690–1764), who postulated that every even number is the sum of two prime numbers. It is not known whether this is true or false.

Prime numbers have recently become of great interest to cryptographers: certain codes are based on the result of multiplying two very large primes together, and because even the fastest possible computer would take years to factorize this product, the resulting code is virtually unbreakable.

RUSSIAN MULTIPLICATION

One of the most puzzling methods of doing long multiplication is said to have been invented centuries ago by Russian peasants. The method involves division and multiplication by two.

Example: 27 x 39.

Method:

Put one of the numbers to be multiplied in one column and the other number in a second column.	27	39
Divide the first column by 2 and ignore any remainders. Multiply the second column by 2.	13	78
Continue dividing the figures in the first column – and doubling the figures in the second column – until 1 is reached in the first column.	6 3 1	156 312 624
List all numbers in the *second* column that are on the same line as an *odd* number in the first column.	39 78 312 624	
Add together these numbers.	39 78 312 + 624 = 1053	
	27 x 39 =	1053

NINE

The number nine displays interesting properties in the nine times table. All the digits in every total add up to nine.

1 x 9 = 9	9 + 0 = 9
2 x 9 = 18	1 + 8 = 9
3 x 9 = 27	2 + 7 = 9
4 x 9 = 36	3 + 6 = 9
5 x 9 = 45	4 + 5 = 9
6 x 9 = 54	5 + 4 = 9
7 x 9 = 63	6 + 3 = 9
8 x 9 = 72	7 + 2 = 9
9 x 9 = 81	8 + 1 = 9
238 x 9 = 2142	2 + 1 + 4 + 2 = 9
44349 x 9 = 399141	3+9+9+1+4+1=27
	2 + 7 = 9

THE SPHERE

A little-known and interesting fact about the sphere is that the area of any zone of its curved surface lying between two parallel planes is exactly equal to the curved surface of the surrounding cylinder between the same two planes.

This fact was discovered by Archimedes, who requested that a sphere inscribed in a cylinder be engraved on his tomb.

This applies to any belt of the sphere, or to a cap or to the whole sphere.

It thus makes the calculation of what might appear to be a difficult area quite simple.

Famous Scientists

Abegg, Richard (1869–1910), German chemist whose 'rule of eight', concerning the electric basis of linkages between atoms, was a major contribution in the development of the modern valency theory.

Adrian, Lord (Edgar Douglas Adrian) (1889–1977), English physiologist who, with Sir Charles Sherrington, studied the nerve cell. They discovered the mechanism by which nerves carry messages to and from the brain.

Agassiz, Jean Louis (1807–73), Swiss-born US naturalist who made an important contribution to the study of glaciation, proving the existence of ice ages.

Aiken, Howard H. (1900–73), US mathematician who is credited with designing a forerunner to the digital computer.

Albert the Great, St (c. 1200–80), German bishop and philosopher who undertook 'to make intelligible' Aristotle's *Physica*.

Alcmaeon (c. 520 BC), Greek physician who is the first recorded practitioner of anatomical dissection.

Alvarez, Luis (1911–), US physicist who discovered resonance particles.

Amontons, Guillaume (1663–1705), French physicist who discovered that the temperature and pressure of gases are related.

Ampère, André Marie (1775–1836), French physicist who founded the branch of physics that he named electrodynamics and which is now known as electromagnetism. Ampère established a mathematical and physical description of the magnetic force between two electric currents. He formulated a law of electromagnetism – *Ampère's Law* – and pioneered techniques in measuring electricity.

Anderson, Carl David (1905–91), US physicist who discovered the positron, the first known particle of antimatter. He also discovered the first meson (1935).

Andrews, Thomas (1813–85), Irish chemist who discovered the critical temperature of gases.

Angström, Anders Jonas (1814–74), Swedish physicist who pioneered the science of spectroscopy. He undertook major research in heat conduction.

Apollonius (3rd century BC), Greek mathematician who is remembered for his treatise *Conic Sections* in which he described geometrical concepts of the cone.

Archimedes (c. 287–212 BC), Greek mathematician, philosopher and engineer. His extensions of the work of Euclid especially concerned the surface and volume of the sphere and the study of other solid shapes. His methods anticipated the fundamentals of integral calculus. Archimedes gave the first systematic account of determining centres of gravity. He founded the science of hydrostatics and discovered the principle now known as *Archimedes' Principle*.

Argand, Jean Robert (1768–1822), Swiss mathematician who revived a geometrical method of representing complex numbers. He developed what are now known as *Argand diagrams*, which have wide applications in mechanics and electricity.

Aristotle (c. 384–322 BC), Greek philosopher and scientist who reviewed the entire field of human knowledge that was known in his time. Aristotle travelled the Hellenic world founding academies. He tutored Alexander the Great before settling in Athens in 335 BC. His theory of causality stated that every event has four causes: material cause, the matter involved; formal cause, the way it is placed; efficient cause, which triggers the action or change; and final cause, what the event leads to.

Arrhenius, Svante August (1859–1927), Swedish chemist who developed the ionic theory of electrodes.

Astbury, William Thomas (1889–1961), English chemist who pioneered research on protein fibres.

Avery, Oswald Theodore (1877–1955), Canadian-born US bacteriologist whose studies of pneumococci had important implications for later DNA research.

Avicenna (Abu-Ali al-Husayn ibn-Sina; 980–1037), Uzbek-born Persian philosopher who was both a pioneer physician and an outstanding compiler of an encyclopedia covering medicine, mathematics and the natural sciences.

Avogadro, Amadeo (1776–1856), Italian physicist. *Avogadro's Law* states that under the same conditions of pressure and temperature, equal volumes of different gases contain an equal number of molecules.

Babbage, Charles (1792–1871), English mathematician who is regarded as the inventor of the modern computer. His complex 'analytical machine', which was intended to make any type of calculation, was not constructed until modern times.

Babinet, Jacques (1794–1872), French physicist who standardized light measurement.

Bacon, Roger (c. 1214–92), English Franciscan, philosopher and scientist whose scientific contributions included pioneering work on the magnifying glass and advocacy of the primacy of mathematical proof in science.

Balmer, Johann Jakob (1825–98), Swiss physicist who discovered the first mathematical formula to describe the wavelengths of spectral lines. This formula is basic to the development of atomic theory.

Barr, Murray Llewellyn (1908–), Canadian geneticist who discovered what are now called *Barr bodies* – densely staining nuclear bodies present in the somatic cells of female mammals.

Bartholin, Thomas (1616–80), Danish physician and mathematician who described the human lymphatic system.

Bateson, William (1861–1926), English biologist who named the science 'genetics'. His experiments concerning plant inheritance provided evidence that was fundamental to modern studies of heredity.

Beadle, George Wells (1903–89), US biochemist who proposed that specific genes control the production of specific enzymes.

Beckmann, Ernst Otto (1853–1923), German chemist who devised apparatus for determining freezing and boiling points, and the sensitive thermometer that is named after him.

Becquerel, Antoine Henri (1852–1908), French physicist who discovered radioactivity. He found a previously unknown type of radiation being emitted from uranium atoms within fluorescent uranium salts. His colleague Marie Curie later named this phenomenon radioactivity.

Beilstein, Friedrich Konrad (1838–1906), Russian-born German chemist whose *Handbook of Organic Chemistry* (1881) was a landmark in that field.

Bell, Alexander Graham (1847–1922), Scottish-born US inventor and physicist who invented the world's first telephone (1876).

Bell, John Stuart (1928–90), Northern Irish physicist whose *On the Einstein Podolsky Rosen Paradox* (1964) was one of the most influential papers in theoretical physics of modern times.

Berg, Paul (1926–), US molecular biologist who identified the first adaptor (1956) and devised a way of inserting 'foreign' genes into bacteria.

Bernal, John Desmond (1901–71), Irish crystallographer and pioneer of molecular biology.

Bernard, Claude (1813–78), French physiologist who made important discoveries concerning the part played by the pancreas in digestion, the glycogenic role of the liver and the way in which vasomotor nerves regulate the blood supply.

Bernoulli, Daniel (1700–82), Swiss physician and mathematician who described the theory of statics and the motion of fluids in his *Hydrodynamica*.

Bernoulli, Jakob (1654–1705), Swiss mathematician who laid down the foundations of the calculus of variations.

Berthelot, Marcellin (1827–1907), French chemist who discovered the detonation wave.

Berthollet, Count Claude Louis (1748–1822), French chemist who was the first to discover that the completeness of chemical reactions depends, in part, upon the masses of the reacting substances.

Berzelius, Jöns (1779–1848), Swedish chemist who prepared the first accurate list of atomic weights.

Bessel, Friedrich W(ilhelm) (1784–1846), German astronomer and mathematician whose solutions of certain differential equations are now known as *Bessel Functions*.

Bessemer, Sir Henry (1813–98), English metallurgist who decarbonized iron (1856), thus allowing the large-scale manufacture of steel.

Black, Joseph (1728–99), Scottish physicist who rediscovered 'fixed air' (carbon dioxide). He also developed the concepts of latent and specific heat.

Blackett, Patrick (Baron Blackett; 1897–1974), English physicist who discovered the positron.

Bloch, Felix (1905–83), Swiss-born US physicist. The *Bloch bands* are sets of discrete, closely adjacent energy levels that arise from quantum states when a nondegenerate gas condenses to a solid.

Bohm, David Joseph (1917–), US physicist whose *Quantum Theory* (1951) was a landmark in that field.

Bohr, Niels (1885–1962), Danish physicist who played a major role in the development of nuclear physics. In his classic paper *On the Constitution of Atoms and Molecules* (1913), the *Bohr theory* of the atom – combining Rutherford's model with Planck's quantum theory of radiation – was able to account for the known patterns of atomic radiation seen in spectra. Bohr's theory had an important impact on the development of quantum mechanics.

Boltzmann, Ludwig (1844–1906), Austrian theoretical physicist who made important advances in the theory of radiation and in statistical treatment of the behaviour of molecules in gases.

Bolyai, Janos (1802–60), Hungarian mathematician who investigated Euclid's parallel postulate. Bolyai eventually developed a non-Euclidean geometry, only to discover that Gauss had anticipated his work.

Boole, George (1815–64), English mathematician who laid the foundations of *Boolean algebra*, which was fundamental to the development of the digital electronic computer.

Borelli, Giovanni (1608–79), Italian physicist and physiologist – the first person to explain muscular movement.

Born, Max (1882–1970), German physicist whose work on crystals led to the development of the *Born-Haber cycle*, a theoretical cycle of reactions and changes by which the lattice energy of ionic crystals may be calculated. Born is, however, best known for his work on quantum physics.

Bosch, Carl (1874–1940), German chemist who devised the *Bosch process*, by which hydrogen is obtained from water gas and superheated steam.

Bose, Sir Jagadis Chandra (1858–1937), Indian physicist and botanist who is best known for his studies of electric waves.

Bose, Salyendranath (1894–1974), Indian physicist, chemist and mathematician who developed *Bose statistics*, the forerunner of modern quantum theory.

Bothe, Walther (1891–1957), German atomic physicist who devised the coincidence method of detecting the emission of electrons by X-rays.

Boyle, Robert (1627–91), Anglo-Irish physicist and chemist who formulated the law concerning the behaviour of gases that now bears his name. *Boyle's law* states that, at a given temperature, the pressure of a gas is proportional to its volume. Boyle pioneered the concept of elements in his suggestion of a corpuscular view of matter. He also distinguished between elements and compounds.

Boys, Sir Charles Vernon (1855–1944), English physicist who determined the gravitational constant.

Bragg, Sir William (1862–1942), English physicist who pioneered work in solid-state physics.

Brahe, Tycho (1546–1601), Danish mathematician and astronomer who was one of the most successful observers of celestial bodies before the use of telescopes.

Brattain, Walter (1902–87) US co-inventor of the transistor.

Brewster, Sir David (1781–1868), Scottish physicist – best known for his research on polarization of light.

Bronsted, Johannes Nicolaus (1879–1947), Danish physical chemist who devised the *Bronsted-Lowry definition*, which defines an acid as a substance with a tendency to lose a proton and a base as a substance that tends to gain a proton.

Brown, Robert (1773–1858), Scottish physician and botanist, who discovered the nucleus in cells but is best known for his observation under the microscope of what came to be known as *Brownian Motion*, the agitation of small suspended particles.

Bunsen, Robert (1811–99), German chemist who developed the *Bunsen burner* and laid the foundations for the field of spectrum analysis.

Candolle, Augustin Pyrame de (1778–1841), Swiss botanist who was the first to use the word taxonomy for a classification of plants by morphology (forms) rather than by their physiology (functions).

Cannizzaro, Stanislao (1826–1910), Italian chemist who is best known for his studies of atomic weights.

Cantor, George (1845–1918), Russian-born mathematician whose most important work was on finite and infinite sets. He founded set theory.

Cardano, Geronimo (1501–76), Italian physician and mathematician whose *Ars Magna* played a major role in the foundation of modern algebra.

Carnot, Nicholas Léonard Sadi (1796–1832), French physicist who virtually founded the science of thermodynamics. His researches led him to an early form of the second law of thermodynamics.

Cartan, Elie (1869–1951), French mathematician who contributed to the development of differential geometry and differential calculus.

Cauchy, Baron Augustin-Louis (1789–1857), French mathematician and physicist who developed the modern treatment of calculus and also the theory of functions.

Cavendish, Henry (1731–1810), English chemist and physicist whose discoveries included the properties of hydrogen, the composition of air, the composition of water and various properties of electricity.

Celsius, Anders (1701–44), Swedish astronomer who suggested the scale for measuring temperature that now bears his name.

Chadwick, Sir James (1891–1974), English physicist who discovered the neutron.

Chain, Ernst (1906–79), German-born British chemist who isolated and purified penicillin.

Chapman, Sydney (1888–1970), English mathematician and physicist who developed the theory of thermal diffusion.

Charles, Jacques (1746–1823), French physicist who developed *Charles's Law* which relates the expansion of gas with a rise in temperature.

Chladni, Ernst (1756–1827), German physicist who is regarded as one of the founders of the science of acoustics.

Claisen, Ludwig (1851–1930), German chemist who developed the condensation reactions that bear his name, the *Claisen-Schmidt condensation.*

Claude, Georges (1870–1960), French chemist and engineer who developed a process of separating the constituent gases of air by distillation of liquefied air.

Clausius, Rudolph (1822–88), German physicist who formulated the second law of thermodynamics.

Cockcroft, Sir John Douglas (1897–1967), English physicist who, with Walton, split the atom (1932).

Cohn, Ferdinand Julius (1828–98), German botanist who laid the foundations of modern bacteriology.

Conway, John Horton (1938–), English mathematician who is famous for his serious studies of mathematical recreations.

Copernicus, Nicolaus (Mikolaj Kopernik; 1473–1543), Polish astronomer who proposed that the Earth was in daily motion about its axis and in yearly motion about a stationary Sun.

Corey, Elias James (1928–), US synthetic chemist who is responsible for over 100 first syntheses.

Coriolis, Gustave-Gaspard (1792–1843), French mathematician and engineer who formulated laws to describe moving bodies – the *Coriolis force.*

Coulomb, Charles-Augustin de (1736–1806), French physicist who developed *Coulomb's law* which states that the force between two electrical charges is proportional to the product of the charges and inversely proportional to the square of the distance between them.

Crick, Francis (1916–), English biophysicist who – with James Watson and Maurice Wilkins – determined the molecular structure of DNA.

Crookes, Sir William (1832–1919), English chemist and physicist who invented a cathode-ray tube.

Curie, Marie Sklodowska (1867–1934), Polish-born French chemist who – with her husband Pierre – pioneered research into radioactivity. Following Becquerel's discovery of radioactivity – which Marie Curie named – she and Pierre studied pitchblende (uranium ore) to establish whether it owed much of its radioactivity to tiny quantities of highly active impurities. The Curies discovered the elements polonium and radium. The great radioactivity of the latter confirmed the immense possibilities of the energy that could be won from atomic processes.

Curie, Pierre (1859–1906), French physicist who researched the relationship between magnetism and heat. He discovered that, above a certain critical point (now known as the *Curie point*), ferromagnetic substances lose their magnetism. He formulated *Curie's law* which related how easy it is to magnetize a substance to its temperature. With his wife Marie, he studied radioactivity.

Cuvier, Baron Georges (1769–1832), French naturalist who classified animals according to principles of comparative anatomy.

d'Alembert, Jean Le Rond (1717–83), French philosopher and mathematician who formulated the *d'Alembert principle* – a generalization of Newton's third law of motion.

Dalton, John (1766–1844), English chemist and physicist who developed the atomic theory of matter defining the atom as the smallest particle of substance that can take part in a chemical reaction. His early studies on gases led to the formulation of *Dalton's law* which states that the total pressure of a mixture of gases is equal to the sum of the partial pressures of the individual component gases.

Dam, Carl Peter Henrik (1895–1976), Danish biochemist who isolated vitamin K.

Darwin, Charles Robert (1809–82), English naturalist who proposed the modern theory of evolution in his *On the Origin of Species by Means of Natural Selection* (1859). This was based upon observations made on a five-year expedition in South America and the Pacific region, in particular the Galapagos Islands. He proposed that species evolve by means of a process of natural selection involving the survival of the fittest and a gradual adaptation of animals to survive in changed circumstances or habitats. In *The Descent of Man* (1871) Darwin proposed the evolution of man from a primitive animal that was also the ancestor of the apes. His theories were highly controversial and had a profound effect upon both scientific and religious opinion.

Davy, Sir Humphry (1778–1829), English chemist who investigated the electrolysis of molten salts leading to the discovery of the metallic elements sodium, potassium, calcium, barium and magnesium and the isolation of strontium. He later discovered boron. No individual discovered more elements. Davy became well-known to the public for his invention of the miner's safety lamp.

Dawkins, Richard (1941–), English ethologist who – in *The Selfish Gene* (1976) – identified the apparently altruistic behaviour of some animals as the 'selfish gene' ensuring the survival of the species.

de Broglie, Prince Louis Victor (1892–1987), French physicist who is best known for his theory that – just as waves can behave like particles – particles can have wave-like properties. He stated that an electron can behave as if it were a wave motion – now known as a *de Broglie wave*.

Debye, Peter (1884–1966), Dutch-born US physicist and chemist who is best known for the *Debye-Hückel theory* of electrolytes.

Dehmelt, Hans Georg (1922–), German-born US physicist who isolated a single electron (1973).

Delbruck, Max (1907–81), German-born US pioneer in modern molecular genetics.

Desargues, Girard (1591–1661), French engineer, architect and geometrician who invented modern projective geometry.

Descartes, René (1596–1650), French philosopher, mathematician and military scientist who created analytical geometry, which allows geometrical problems to be solved by algebra.

de Sitter, Willem (1872–1934), Dutch mathematician and astronomer who proposed what came to be known as the *de Sitter universe*.

de Vries, Hugo (1848–1935), Dutch geneticist and plant physiologist who studied heredity in plants.

d'Herelle, Felix (1873–1949), Canadian bacteriologist who discovered the bacteriophage.

Diophantus of Alexandria (3rd century AD), Greek mathematician – a pioneer in algebra.

Dirac, Paul (1902–84), English mathematician and physicist who developed a general formulism for quantum mechanics (1926). His relativistic theory describes the properties of the electron.

Dobzhansky, Theodosius (1900–75), Ukrainian-born US geneticist whose studies of the fruit fly demonstrated that genetic variations within populations are far greater than had been imagined.

Doppler, Christian Johann (1803–53), Austrian physicist and mathematician who discovered the wave effect that now bears his name.

Draper, John William (1811–82), Anglo-US chemist who founded the science of photo-chemistry.

Dulbecco, Renato (1914–), Italian-born US molecular biologist and physician who introduced the concept of cell transformation in biology.

Dumas, Jean-Baptiste André (1800–84), French chemist who produced the substitution theory in chemistry.

Edeleman, Gerald Maurice (1929–), US biochemist whose work elucidates the chemical structure of antibodies.

Ehrlich, Paul (1854–1915), German bacteriologist who pioneered developments in haematology and immunology, and who founded the science of chemotherapy.

Einstein, Albert (1879–1955), German-born US physicist who revolutionized physics by developing the special and general theories of relativity. His international impact upon physics began in 1905 when he published four research papers, each one containing a major discovery in the subject: the special theory of relativity (which he proposed to account for the constant speed of light); the theory of Brownian movement; the photon theory of light and the equation relating mass and energy. His general theory of relativity was presented in 1916 and verified in 1919. Einstein spent much of his life applying the general theory to cosmological problems. Einstein became concerned to formulate a single theory that would cover both gravitation and electrodynamics.

Engler, Adolf (1844–1930), German botanist who – in his monumental *The Natural Plant Families* – developed a system of plant classification.

Eötvös, Baron Roland von (1848–1919), Hungarian physicist who introduced the *Eötvös law*, an equation that relates surface tension, temperature, density, and the relative molecular mass of a liquid.

Erlanger, Joseph (1874–1965), US neurophysicist who studied the differentiated functions of nerve fibres.

Esaki, Leo (1925–), Japanese physicist who has discovered a mechanical effect he named 'tunneling'.

Euclid (c. 3rd century BC), Greek mathematician who devised the first axiomatic treatment of geometry and studied irrational numbers. Until recent times, most elementary geometry textbooks were little more than versions of Euclid's great book *The Elements*.

Eudoxus (408–347 BC), Greek mathematician who is known for his theory of proportion.

Euler, Leonhard (1707–83), Swiss-born mathematician who was famed for being able to perform complex calculations in his head, and so was able to go on working after he went blind. Euler made particular contributions to analytical geometry, trigonometry and calculus. Euler was responsible for much of modern mathematical notation.

Everett, Hugo (1930–82), US physicist whose *Relative State Formulation of Quantum Mechanics* (1957) was one of the most influential works in quantum mechanics.

Fahrenheit, Gabriel Daniel (1686–1736), German-born physicist of Dutch ancestry who was the first person to use mercury in a thermometer. He devised for his thermometer a scale which bears his name.

Fairbank, William (1917–89), US physicist who announced in 1979 that he had isolated the quark – no-one has managed to reproduce his experiments.

Faraday, Michael (1791–1867), English physicist and chemist who made many important advances in electromagnetism. Faraday became an assistant to Davy who recognized his potential and taught him. Having discovered electro-magnetic induction in 1821, Faraday built a primitive model. He demonstrated the continuous production of current from a conductor moving in a field – in effect, a primitive dynamo. Faraday also liquefied chlorine and isolated benzene. In 1833 he formulated quantitative laws to express magnitudes of electrolytic effects – these are now known as *Faraday's laws of electrolysis*. In 1831 he made observations that led to the formulation of the law of induction which now bears his name.

Fermat, Pierre de (1601–65), French lawyer who studied mathematics as a hobby. He contributed to the development of calculus, analytic geometry, and the study of probability. Fermat is regarded as the creator of the modern theory of numbers. He is most famous for his last theorem, which he claimed to have solved, without recording his proof.

Fermi, Enrico (1901–54), Italian-born US physicist who established the theory of beta decay in the 1930s. He discovered statistical laws obeyed by particles such as the electron. He researched means of producing controlled and self-sustaining nuclear fission reaction. The result – the first nuclear reactor – was built and tested in Chicago in 1942. In 1943 Fermi helped to test the first atomic bomb.

Ferraris, Galileo (1847–97), Italian physicist and electrical engineer who discovered the principle of rotary magnetic field.

Feynman, Richard Phillips (1918–88), US physicist who developed the quantum approach to electromagnetic theory.

Fibonacci, Leonardo (also known as Leonardo Pisano) (c. 1170–1230), Italian mathematician who popularized the Hindu system of counting in Europe.

Fischer, Emil (1852–1919), German chemist and biochemist whose work on sugars and peptides did much to establish biochemistry as a separate science.

Fizeau, Armand-Hippolyte-Louis (1819–96), French physicist who achieved fame for his experiments determining the speed of light.

Fleischmann, Martin (1927–), Czech-born British chemist who announced in 1989 that he and Stanley Pons had achieved nuclear fusion by an electrolytic method under laboratory conditions.

Fleming, Sir Alexander (1881–1955), Scottish bacteriologist who accidentally discovered that the fungus Penicillium notatum was able to kill bacteria (1928).

Flerov, Georgii (1913–), Russian physicist who synthesized elements 102, 103, 104, 105, 106 and 107.

Florey, Paul John (1910–85), US chemist whose major work was on nonlinear polymers.

Foucault, Jean-Bernard-Léon (1819–68), French physicist who devised a way of measuring absolute velocity of light to within 1% of its true value.

Fourier, Jean-Baptiste (1768–1830), French mathematician and physicist who showed how the conduction of heat in solid bodies could be analysed in terms of infinite mathematical series, now known as *Fourier Series*.

Frankland, Sir Edward (1825–99), English chemist who was a pioneer in structural chemistry.

Franklin, Benjamin (1706–90), US inventor, diplomat, printer and publisher. As a scientist his most important work was in studying electricity.

Franklin, Rosalind (1920–58), English crystallographer who played an important part in the discovery of the structure of DNA. Her X-ray photograph of hydrated DNA was recognized by Watson as a helix. She worked independently of Crick and Watson and was producing a paper on the double-chain helix of DNA when they published.

Frege, Gottlob (1848–1925), German philosopher who gave a formal definition of a cardinal number.

Fresenius, Carl (1818–97), German analytical chemist who wrote works on qualitative and quantitative analysis that became standards.

Fresnel, Augustine Jean (1788–1827), French physicist who worked on the theory that light is a transverse wave motion.

Frisch, Otto Robert (1904–79), Austrian-born British physicist who worked with his aunt, Lise Meitner, on the discovery of nuclear fission.

Gabor, Dennis (1900–79), Hungarian-born British physicist who pioneered holography.

Galen (c. 131–200), Greek physician whose writing on anatomy was the standard text for 1500 years.

Galileo, Galilei (1564–1642), Italian astronomer, physicist and mathematician who was a pioneer in developing scientific methods of testing by systematic experimentation. The popular story concerning dropping weights from the famous Leaning Tower of Pisa is unsupported by evidence. Most of his work was concerned with the study of mechanics; Galileo was the first to apply mathematics in this field. Galileo was convicted of heresy for his support for Copernicus and obliged to recant.

Gallo, Robert (1937–), US physician who was one of the first people to identify HIV, the virus responsible for AIDS.

Gauss, Friedrich Carl (1777–1855), German mathematician who developed the theory of complex numbers.

Gay-Lussac, Joseph (1778–1850), French chemist and physicist who pioneered investigations into the behaviour of gases. He formulated the law of combining volumes.

Geiger, Hans (1882–1945), German physicist who assisted Rutherford. In 1913 he developed the *Geiger counter* for detecting atomic particles.

Gerhardt, Charles (1816–56), French chemist who formulated a theory of types to classify organic chemical compounds.

Gibbs, Josiah Willard (1839–1903), US founder of the science of chemical thermodynamics.

Glashow, Sheldon Lee (1932–), US physicist who is best known for an explanation of the forces that hold together elementary particles of matter.

Gödel, Kurt (1906–78), Austrian-born US mathematician who stunned the mathematical world in the 1930s by showing that Hilbert's dream of a general method of proving any mathematical theorem could not be realized.

Golgi, Camillo (1843–1926), Italian cytologist who discovered the organelles *Golgi bodies*.

Graham, Thomas (1805–69), Scottish chemist who defined diffusion. He is held to be the founder of colloid chemistry.

Grassman, Hermann (1809–77), German mathematician who discovered the calculus of extension, which may be regarded as an 'algebra' of geometry.

Haber, Fritz (1868–1934), German chemist who is best known for his discovery of an industrial process for synthesizing ammonia from nitrogen and hydrogen.

Haeckel, Ernst (1834–1919), German biologist who was an important supporter of Darwinism.

Hahn, Otto (1879–1968), German chemist who – with Fritz Strassmann – discovered nuclear fission. He worked with Lise Meitner mainly studying the application of radioactive methods to solve chemical problems; during this period Hahn and Meitner discovered the element protactinium. After Meitner fled from Germany (1938), Hahn continued his studies with Strassmann. They proved that when uranium was bombarded with neutrons, one of the products formed was a much lighter radiocative form of barium. This indicated that the uranium atom had divided into two lighter atoms. Hahn sent his results abroad to Meitner. She developed an explanation for what had happened and named the process nuclear fission.

Haldane, J(ohn) B(urdon) S(anderson) (1892–1964), Scottish biologist who explored new fields of research in genetics and evolution.

Hall, Marshall (1790–1857), English physiologist who suggested a scientific theory to explain reflex action.

Haller, Albrecht von (1708–77), Swiss physiologist, botanist, anatomist and poet who is regarded as the founder of experimental physiology.

Halley, Edmund (1656–1742), English astronomer and physicist who formulated the mathematical law relating pressure and height. Halley is, however, best known for his work in astronomy.

Harvey, William (1578–1657), English physician who discovered the nature of the circulation of blood in the body and the function of the heart as a pump.

Hawking, Stephen (1942–), English physicist who is best known for his theory of exploding black holes which draws upon both quantum mechanics and relativity theory. Hawking's *Brief History of Time* was a hugely popular exploration of space-time problems.

Haworth, Sir Walter (1883–1950), English chemist who was the first person to synthesize a vitamin.

Heisenberg, Werner von (1901–76), German physicist who discovered how to formulate quantum mechanics in terms of matrices.

Helmholtz, Hermann von (1821–94), German scientist, mathematician and philosopher who made important discoveries in acoustics, optics, physiology and meteorology. He is best known for his statement of the law of conservation of energy, the first law of thermodynamics.

Henry, Joseph (1797–1878), US scientist who discovered a number of important electrical properties, including self-induction.

Henry, William (1775–1836), English chemist and physician who formulated the gas law which now bears his name.

Hero of Alexandria (7th century AD), Greek mathematician who is best known for his formula for the area of a triangle and for his method of finding a square root.

Hershey, Alfred Day (1908–), US biologist who who is best known for an experiment in 1952 which appears to show that DNA is more involved than protein in the replication of genes.

Hertz, Gustav (1887–1975), German physicist who – with James Franck – proved that energy can be absorbed by an atom only in definite amounts.

Hertz, Heinrich (1857–94), German physicist who discovered radio waves. Hertz established that heat and light are electromagnetic radiations.

Hilbert, David (1862–1943), German mathematician who, in 1901, listed 23 major unsolved problems in mathematics – many of which still remain unsolved.

Hill, A(rchibald) V(ivian) (1886–1977), English biophysicist and physiologist whose main work concerned the production of heat in muscles.

Hipparchus (2nd century BC), Greek astronomer who was a pioneer in trigonometry.

Hittorf, Johann Wilhelm (1824–1914), German chemist and physicist who showed how the relative speeds of ions can be calculated.

Hodgkin, Dorothy (1910–94), English chemist who is best known for her work on the structures of penicillin and vitamins.

Hooke, Robert (1635–1703), English physicist and chemist who discovered the law of elasticity that is now known by his name. Hooke worked as an assistant to Boyle and put forward the first rational theory of combustion.

Hopkins, Sir Frederick Gowland (1861–1947), English biochemist who discovered growth stimulating vitamins.

Huxley, Hugh Esmor (1924–), English biologist who – with Jean Hanson – proposed the sliding filament theory of muscle contraction.

Huxley, Sir Julian (1887–1975), English biologist and educator whose studies included projects in embryology, behaviour and evolution.

Huxley, T(homas) H(enry) (1825–95), English biologist who advanced Darwin's theory of evolution but who suggested that change could be 'step-like' rather than gradual.

Huygens, Christiaan (1629–95), Dutch mathematician, physicist and astronomer who formulated the wave theory of light.

Ipatieff, Vladimir (1867–1952), Russian-born US chemist who pioneered research in high-pressure catalytic reactions of hydrocarbons.

Jabir, ibn Hayyan (or **Haijan**; c. 721–815), Arabian alchemist and writer (from what is now Iran) who is regarded as one of the founders of chemistry.

Jeans, Sir James (1877–1946), English astronomer, mathematician and physicist who was the first person to suggest that matter is continuously created throughout the universe.

Jenner, Edward (1749–1823), English physician who developed vaccination against smallpox.

Joliot-Curie, Frédéric (Frédéric Joliot; 1900–58), French physicist who – with his wife Irène (q.v.) – discovered artificial radioactivity.

Joliot-Curie, Irène (Irène Curie; 1896–1956), French physicist who was the daughter of Pierre and Marie Curie and the wife of Frédéric Joliot. Irène and Frédéric discovered radioactive elements that had been created artificially.

Joule, James Prescott (1818–89), English physicist who determined the relationship between heat and mechanical energy. He established that the different forms of energy – heat, mechanical energy and electrical energy – are basically the same.

Kamerlingh-Onnes, Helke (1853–1926), Dutch physicist who worked in low-temperature physics. He discovered superconductivity.

Kant, Immanuel (1724–1804), German philosopher who addressed the challenge of Newtonian mechanics. He proposed two basic forces: the attractive or gravitational force and the repulsive or elastic force.

Kelvin of Largs, Baron (William Thomson; 1824–1907), Scottish engineer, physicist and mathematician who was a major influence on scientific developments in his day. He played an important role in the development of the conservation law of energy, the mathematical analysis of electricity and magnetism, and researched in hydrodynamics. He is best known for his work on the absolute scale of temperature, which is now given in degrees Kelvin.

Kepler, Johannes (1571–1630), German astronomer who was the first to prove that the Earth orbits the Sun rather than the other way round.

Khorana, Har Gobind (1922–), Indian-born US biochemist who has studied the genetic composition of the cell nucleus.

al Khwarizmi (Muhammad ibn Musa al Khwarizmi; c. 825), Arabian mathematician whose book on algebra was influential in Europe when translated into Latin in the 12th century.

Kirchhoff, Gustav Robert (1824–87), German physicist who is remembered for *Kirchhoff's laws* which describe the currents and electric forces in electrical networks.

Klein, Felix (1849–1925), German mathematician who introduced a programme for the classification of geometry in terms of group theory.

Krebs, Sir Hans Adolf (1900–81), German-born British biochemist who is remembered for his discovery of the *Krebs cycle.*

Kurchatov, Igor (1903–60), Russian physicist who led the team that exploded the first Soviet atomic bomb.

Lagrange, Count Joseph Louis (1736–1813), Italian-born French physicist and mathematician who summarized research in mechanics since Newton. His work laid the foundations of the metric system.

Lamarck, Jean-Baptiste (1744–1829), French naturalist who defined vertebrates and invertebrates.

Lambert, Johann Heinrich (1728–77), German mathematician who was the first to show that pi (π) is not a rational number.

Landau, Lev (1908–68), Azeri physicist who was the first to describe ferromagnetism.

Landsteiner, Karl (1868–1943), Austrian pathologist who identified the blood types A, AB, B and O.

Langevin, Paul (1872–1946), French physicist who developed what is now known as sonar.

Laplace, Marquis Pierre-Simon de (1749–1827), French mathematician, astronomer and physicist who established probability theory on a rigorous basis.

Lavoisier, Antoine-Laurent (1743–94), French chemist whose work and discoveries laid the basis for much of modern chemistry. His researches concerned the gain or loss of weight of substances that are burned or reduced with charcoal. He ascribed these differences to the absorption or loss of a substance that he later called oxygen. He described the composition of water, combustion and the chemistry of many compounds.

Lawrence, Ernest Orlando (1901–58), US physicist who invented the cyclotron.

Le Bel, Joseph Achille (1847–1930), French chemist who devised the graphic conventions for drawing chemical formulae.

Le Châtelier, Henry-Louis (1850–1936), French chemist who developed what is now known as the *Le Châtelier principle.*

Lederberg, Joshua (1925–), US geneticist who demonstrated that bacteria possess genetic and behaviour systems.

Leeuwenhoek, Anton van (1632–1723), Dutch biologist whose observations using a microscope have been cited as the first steps in microbiology.

Leibniz, Gottfried Wilhelm (1646–1716), German mathematician, philosopher, logician, linguist, lawyer and diplomat who invented calculus independently of Newton. Leibniz's notation was, however, superior. He was the first, in 1671, to build a calculating machine that could multiply.

Lenz, H(einrich) F(riedrich) E(mil) (1804–65), Russian physicist whose research on induced electric current led him to formulate what is now known as *Lenz's law.*

Leonardo da Vinci (1452–1519), Italian Renaissance polymath whose contributions to art, architecture and science were prodigious. In science his influence was not as great as early as he deserved because his notebooks were not published until the 19th century.

Levene, Phoebus Aaron Theodor (1869–1940), Russian-born US biochemist who established that nucleic acids are genuine molecules independent of proteins.

Levi-Civita, Tullio (1873–1941), Italian mathematician who – with Ricci – developed absolute differential calculus.

Liebig, Baron Justus von (1803–73), German chemist whose application of chemistry to biology pioneered biochemistry.

Linde, Carl von (1842–1934), German engineer whose research on a continuous process for liquefying gases on a large scale led to refrigeration.

Linnaeus, Carolus (Carl Linné; 1707–78), Swedish botanist who systematically arranged an animal, plant and mineral kingdom. Linnaeus defined classes of plants on the basis of the number and arrangement of their stamens. Although his classification has been overtaken by dramatic advances in biology his binomial nomenclature of plants remains the basic pattern for the naming of all living systems with a generic name and a specific name.

Lorentz, Hendrick Antoon (1853–1928), Dutch physicist who developed the theory of electromagnetic radiation.

Lowry, Thomas (1874–1936), English chemist who confirmed that optical activity depends upon the wavelength of light.

Lucretius (c. 95–55 BC), Roman philosopher whose recognition of the struggle for existence anticipated Darwin by nearly 2000 years.

McClintock, Barbara (1902–93), US geneticist who, working on Drosophila (fruit fly), showed that gene action was connected with chromosomes.

Mach, Ernst (1838–1916), Austrian physicist whose most important work was in wave theory, optics and mechanics.

Maiman, Theodore Harold (1927–), US physicist who is best known for his pioneering work with laser beams.

Malpighi, Marcello (1628–94), Italian physiologist who showed how blood reaches tissues through tiny tubes, capillaries. Malpighi is thought to be the first to use microscopy to study animal and plant tissues.

Mandelbrot, Benoit (1924–), Polish-Lithuanian-born US mathematician who is best known for the *Mandelbrot set,* which is constructed from simple mapping by marking dots on a complex plane.

Marconi, Giuseppe (1874–1937), Italian physicist who invented the first successful system of telegraphy.

Martin, A(rcher) J(ohn) P(orter) (1910–), English biochemist who – with Synge – pioneered partition chromatography.

Maupertius, Pierre-Louis de (1698–1759), French mathematician and astronomer who formulated the principle of least action.

Maxwell, James Clerk (1831–79), Scottish physicist whose formulation of the electromagnetic theory of light revolutionized physics. He suggested that light is an electromagnetic vibration – this was later proved by Hertz. Maxwell also researched colour sensation and the kinetic theory of gases.

Mayer, Maria Goeppert (1906–72), German-born US physicist who independently developed a theory of the structure of atomic nuclei.

Maynard Smith, John (1920–), English biologist who is best known for his influential *Theory of Evolution* (1958).

Meitner, Lise (1878–1968), Austrian-born Swedish physicist whose research, with Otto Hahn and Fritz Strassmann, led to the discovery of nuclear fission. Meitner researched with Hahn for 30 years. Together they discovered protactium, studied beta decay and the results of the nuclear bombardment of uranium. Because she was Jewish, Meitner left Nazi Germany for Sweden in 1938. Hahn and Strassmann continued to involve her in their research at a distance. She correctly described – and named – the nuclear fission achieved by Hahn and Strassmann in 1938–39.

Mendel, Gregor (1822–84), Austrian monk and botanist whose experiments with plants with the garden pea led him to discover the basic principles of heredity. This, in turn, led him to lay the mathematical foundations of the science of genetics. Mendel formulated two basic laws – the law of segregation and the law of independent assortment.

Mendeleyev, Dmitri (1834–1907), Russian chemist who discovered that, by arranging the chemical elements in order of increasing atomic weight, a curious repetition of chemical properties at regular intervals was revealed. Recognizing the underlying order this implied, Mendeleyev discovered the Periodic Table.

Meselson, Matthew Stanley (1930–), US molecular biologist who demonstrated the semiconservative nature of DNA replication.

Metchnikoff, Elie (Ilya Mechnikov; 1845–1916), Russian microbiologist and zoologist who discovered in animals amoeba-like cells that engulf bacteria.

Meyer, Lothar (1830–95), German chemist who is best known for *Meyer's curves,* which show the periodicity of chemical elements.

Meyer, Viktor (1848–97), German chemist who devised a way of measuring the density of gases and vapours.

Michelson, A(lbert) A(braham) (1852–1931), German-born US physicist who established the speed of light as a fundamental constant.

Miescher, Johann Friedrich (1844–95), Swiss physiologist who discovered nucleic acids (1869).

Miller, Stanley (1930–73), US biochemist who synthesized amino acids.

Millikan, Robert Andrews (1868–1953), US physicist who determined the charge on the electron (1912) and studied the photoelectric effect.

Minkowski, Hermann (1864–1909), Lithuanian-born German mathematician who contributed to geometry and to the theories of numbers and of relativity. Einstein said that without the contribution of Minkowski, the general theory of relativity would not have been possible.

Monge, Gaspard (1746–1818), French mathematician who invented descriptive geometry.

Monod, Jacques (1910–76), French biochemist whose research led him to postulate the existence of messenger-RNA.

Morgan, Thomas Hunt (1866–1945), US geneticist who established the chromosome theory of heredity.

Mössbauer, Rudolph Ludwig (1929–), German physicist who discovered the effect that now bears his name and which is also known as recoil-free gamma-ray resonance.

Müller, Johannes (1801–58), German physiologist who correctly described the nature of sensory nerves.

Müller, Paul (1899–1965), Swiss chemist who developed DDT (dichlorodiphenyltrichloroethane).

Mulliken, Robert Sanderson (1896–1986), US physicist and chemist who, with Hund, developed the molecular-orbital theory of chemical bonding.

Musschenbroek, Pieter van (1692–1761), Dutch physicist who developed a device capable of storing and (under control) releasing electricity.

Nägeli, Karl Wilhelm von (1817–91), Swiss botanist whose pioneering work on plant cells made an important contribution to the subject.

Nambu, Yoichipo (1921–), Japanese physicist who has made important discoveries concerning the nature of quarks.

Napier, John (1550–1617), Scottish mathematician and theologian who devised logarithms as an aid to calculation.

Nernst, Walter Hermann (1864–1941), German chemist who is regarded as one of the founders of modern physical chemistry. He formulated the third law of thermodynamics.

Newlands, John (1838–98), English chemist who – before Mendeleyev – noticed that by arranging the chemical elements in order of increasing atomic weight a curious repetition of physical properties emerged.

Newton, Sir Isaac (1642–1727), English mathematician and physicist who could be regarded as the founder of modern physics. By 1666, at the age of 24, he had made important discoveries in mathematics (the binomial theorem and differential calculus, which he called fluxions), optics (the theory of colours) and medicine. In 1687 he published his *Philosophiae Naturalis Principia Mathematica,* generally known as the *Principia*. Through careful analysis of the available experimental data and the application of his theory he was able to explain many previously inexplicable phenomena, such as the tides and the precession of equinoxes. Using a prism, he split sunlight into the spectrum. He is chiefly remembered for his laws of motion and gravity. *Newton's laws of motion* state: that a body will remain at rest or travelling in a straight line at constant speed unless it is acted upon by an external force; that the resultant force exerted on a body is directly proportional to the acceleration produced by the force; and that to every action there is an equal and opposite reaction. *Newton's law of gravitation* states that every particle in the universe attracts every other particle with a force that is directly proportional to the product of their masses and inversely proportional to the square of the distance between them.

Noether, Emily (Amalie Noether; 1882–1935), German mathematician who was described as the 'most creative abstract algebraist of modern times'. Initially she had difficulty obtaining a lectureship because she was a woman. In 1933 Noether was dismissed from her post because she was Jewish. She emigrated to the USA.

Oersted, Hans Christiaan (1777–1851), Danish physicist who in 1819 discovered the magnetic effect produced by an electric current after noticing that the needle of a compass, which was close to a wire that was carrying a current, swung erratically and then came to rest at a right angle to the wire. This made Oersted realize that there was a magnetic field around the wire.

Ohm, Georg Simon (1787–1854), German physicist who discovered the law that is now named after him. *Ohm's law* states that the current flow through a conductor is directly proportional to the potential difference (voltage) and inversely proportional to the resistance.

Oppenheimer, J(ulius) Robert (1904–67), US physicist who directed the Los Alamos laboratory during the development of the atomic bomb (1943–45).

Ostwald, Wilhelm Friedrich (1853–1932), Latvian-born German chemist who pioneered the development of physical chemistry as a separate branch of chemistry.

Pappus of Alexandria (4th century AD), Greek mathematician whose *Synagoge* is a systematic study of ancient Greek mathematics. He is best known as a geometer.

Paracelsus (Philippus Bombast von Hohenheim; 1493–1541), Swiss doctor and alchemist who is sometimes called the Father of Chemistry.

Pardee, Arthur Beck (1921–), US biochemist who – with François Jacob and Jacques Monod – formulated the concept of a repressor molecule.

Pascal, Blaise (1623–62), French mathematician and physicist who discovered what became known as *Pascal's theorem* at the age of 16, when he was writing a book on conic sections. At the age of 19, he invented the first calculating machines, which performed addition and subtraction. He also investigated what became known as *Pascal's triangle*, and helped to develop the theory of probability before abandoning mathematics in favour of theology. In physics, Pascal is remembered for the principle (or law) which bears his name and which states that in a fluid at rest in a closed container a pressure change in one part is transmitted without loss to every portion of the fluid and to the walls of the container.

Pasteur, Louis (1822–95), French chemist and microbiologist who proved that living microorganisms cause disease and fermentation. Pasteur also laid the foundations of modern vaccine theory. In the 1870s, while studying anthrax, he inoculated chickens with a culture of chicken cholera. The birds survived and proved immune to subsequent inoculations of the same virus. Unwittingly, Pasteur had attenuated the virus, that is, he had weakened it to such a degree that the body's own natural defences could defeat it.

Pauli, Wolfgang (1900–58), Austrian-born US-Swiss physicist who discovered the exclusion principle, which states that in an atom no two electrons can have the same set of quantum numbers.

Pauling, Linus (1901–94), US chemist who applied the principles of quantum mechanics to his studies of chemical bonding. In 1939 he collected his work together in a book called *The Nature of the Chemical Bond* which was possibly the most influential chemical text of this century. In 1951 he announced that he had solved an important general structure of proteins, now known as the alpha-helix, which inspired Crick and Watson in their successful attempt to find the structure of DNA.

Pavlov, Ivan (1849–1936), Russian physiologist who is best known for developing the concept of the conditioned reflex. (Pavlov's dogs)

Peano, Giuseppe (1858–1932), Italian mathematician who is best known for his work on the mathematical development of logic.

Pearson, Karl (1857–1936), English biometrician who introduced many concepts to mathematics including standard deviation and chi-square.

Peltier, Jean-Charles (1785–1845), French physicist who discovered the effect that now bears his name, *Peltier's effect* – whereby at the junction of two different metals an electric current will produce either heat or cold.

Penrose, Roger (1931–), English mathematician who is also an influential theoretical physicist (in particular in the field of black holes). Penrose has developed a new cosmology based on complex geometry.

Penzias, Arno Allan (1933–), German-born US astrophysicist who – with Robert Wilson – discovered cosmic microwave background radiation.

Perrin, Jean (1870–1942), French physicist whose studies of the Brownian motion of suspended minute particles confirmed the atomic nature of matter.

Planck, Max (1858–1949), German physicist who discovered the quantum theory of radiation, which states that energy from an oscillating particle is emitted not continuously but rather in discrete packets of energy called quanta. Planck is generally regarded, with Einstein, as the co-founder of 20th-century physics. He expressed the relationship between energy emitted or absorbed by a body and the frequency of radiation mathematically as $E = nhv$, where E is the energy, n is the number, v is the frequency and h is the constant of proportionality, now known as the *Planck constant.*

Plato (c. 428–347 BC), Greek philosopher whose influence on religion, education, politics, ethics and philosophy was profound. Plato also made important contributions to science – he questioned what accounted for the 'uniform and orderly motions' of the planets and he established the principle of the mathematical analysis of nature.

Pliny (the Elder) (AD 23–79), Roman philosopher who recognized that the Earth is round. His *Natural History* increased interest in the natural world.

Poincaré, Henri (1854–1912), French mathematician, philosopher and astronomer – a major influence in cosmology, relativity and topology.

Poynting, John Henry (1852–1914), English physicist who is best known for *Poynting's vector* – he showed that the flow of energy at a point can be expressed by a simple formula in terms of electric and magnetic forces.

Priestley, Joseph (1733–1804), English cleric, political theorist and scientist who was one of the discoverers of oxygen.

Proust, Joseph Louis (1754–1826), French chemist whose law of definite proportions states that all compounds contain elements in definite proportions.

Pythagoras (c. 582–500 BC), Greek philosopher and mathematician who is popularly remembered today for *Pythagoras' theorem* although there is no evidence that he was the originator of it.

Rabi, Isidor Isaac (1899–1988), Austrian-born US physicist who pioneered atomic exploration.

Raman, Chandrasekhara Venkata (1888–1970), Indian physicist who discovered that when light traverses a material, some of that light changes in wavelength. This is now known as the *Raman effect.*

Ramanujan, Srinivasa Aaiyangar (1887–1920), Indian mathematician who had an astonishing intuition for the correct results, although many were not proved until later.

Ramsay, Sir William (1852–1916), Scottish chemist who discovered the noble gases neon, argon, krypton and xenon.

Rayleigh, Lord (John William Strutt; 1843–1919), English physicist whose discoveries in acoustics and optics are fundamental to the theory of wave propagation in fluids.

Réamur, René-Antoine de (1683–1757), French physicist and entomologist who devised the Réamur temperature scale, isolated gastric juice and made a major contribution to the early study of insects.

Regiomontanus (Johann Müller; 1436–76), German mathematician who was the leading practitioner of trigonometry in medieval Europe.

Ricci-Curbastro, Gregorio (1853–1925), Italian mathematician who played a leading role in the discovery of the absolute differential calculus.

Richter, Burton (1931–), US physicist who, with his colleagues, created and detected a heavy elementary particle which they called the psi.

Roberts, Richard (1943–), English molecular biologist who discovered the phenomenon of split genes.

Romer, Ole (1644–1710), Danish astronomer who demonstrated conclusively – from his observations of Jupiter's moons – that light travels at finite speed.

Röntgen, Wilhelm Conrad (1845–1923), German physicist who discovered X-rays. (The true nature of X-rays was not, however, established until 1912.)

Rumford, Count (Sir Benjamin Thompson; 1753–1814), US-born British physicist who was the first to suggest that heat is a form of energy.

Rutherford, Ernest (Baron Rutherford; 1871–1937), New Zealand physicist who is acknowledged as the founder of modern atomic theory. His theory of the scattering of alpha particles (1910) led him to suggest that the atom consists of a positively charged nucleus which is surrounded by orbiting planetary electrons. This model is known as the *Rutherford electron*. Rutherford was the first person to split the atom.

Rydberg, Johannes Robert (1854–1919), Swedish physicist who explained the atomic spectrum of hydrogen by means of a simple formula, which includes the *Rydberg constant* and two variables whose values are positive integers.

Sabin, Albert (1906–94), Polish-born US microbiologist who developed oral polio vaccine.

Sachs, Julius von (1832–97), German botanist whose researches into transpiration and photosynthesis greatly advanced the knowledge of plant physiology.

Sakharov, Andrei (1921–89), Russian physicist who made a major contribution to the development of Soviet nuclear weapons and who offered evidence for the existence of quarks. He is best known, however, as a campaigner for civil rights in the former Soviet Union.

Salk, Jonas Edward (1914–), US physician who developed a vaccine for polio.

Scheele, Karl Wilhelm (1742–86), Swedish chemist who discovered oxygen (1771) and chlorine (1774). As Scheele did not publish his results until 1777, Priestley – who had discovered oxygen in the meantime – was credited with the discovery.

Schrödinger, Edwin (1887–1961), Austrian theoretical physicist who – with Paul Dirac – made an important contribution to the wave theory of matter.

Schuster, Sir Arthur (1851–1934), German-born British physicist who was the first to show that an electric current is conducted by ions.

Schwann, Theodor (1810–82), German physiologist who was one of the first to propose the cell theory in biology.

Seaborg, Glenn Theodore (1912–), US nuclear chemist who is associated with the discovery or first isolation of elements 93–98, 101 and 102.

Seki, Kowa (1642–1708), Japanese mathematician who invented a form of calculus, and who used determinants before Liebniz.

Sharp, Phillip (1944–), US molecular biologist who – with Roberts – discovered split genes.

Sherrington, Sir Charles (1861–1952), English neurologist who – with Adrian – researched into the integrated nervous system (the motor-nerve system) of higher animals.

Siemens, Werner von (1816–92), German electrical engineer who was one of the founders of telegraphy.

Smith, Michael (1932–), English-born Canadian biochemist who introduced the concept of site specific mutagenesis into molecular biology.

Snell, Willebrord (1591–1626), Dutch mathematician and physicist who is best known for *Snell's law* in optics, which formulates the relationship between the path taken by a ray of light in crossing the boundary of separation between two contacting surfaces and the refractive index of each.

Spallanzani, Lazzaro (1729–99), Italian biologist who studied animal reproduction, mammalian bodily functions and microscopic life in nutrient cultures.

Starling, Ernest Henry (1866–1927), English physiologist who researched the mechanical controls on heart functions. He also studied digestion and coined the word 'hormone'.

Stephenson, George (1781–1848), English engineer who developed the first successful steam engines.

Stern, Otto (1888–1969), German-born US physicist who developed the molecular beam as a tool for studying the characteristics of molecules.

Stevin, Simon (1548–1620), Flemish mathematician who was influential in establishing the use of decimal fractions.

Stokes, Sir George Gabriel (1819–1903), Anglo-Irish physicist and mathematician who is best known for *Stokes's law*, which gives the force resisting motion of a spherical body through a viscous fluid.

Stoney, George Johnstone (1826–1911), Irish physicist who introduced the term 'electron'.

Sturgeon, William (1783–1850), English physicist who devised the first electromagnet.

Svedberg, Theodor (1884–1971), Swedish chemist who introduced the ultracentrifuge to investigate the molecular weights of very large molecules.

Swammerdam, Jan (1637–80), Dutch entomologist whose pioneering studies of insects under the microscope resulted in the first detailed descriptions of many species.

Sylvester, James Joseph (1814–97), English mathematician who developed the theory of algebraic invariants.

Szilard, Leo (1898–1964), Hungarian-born US physicist who was one of the first people to realize the significance of nuclear fission.

Tatum, Edward L(awrie) (1909–75), US biochemist who pioneered work in molecular genetics.

Teller, Edward (1908–), Hungarian-born US physicist who was the main scientific force behind the development of the US hydrogen bomb.

Tesla, Nikola (1856–1943), Croat-born US electrical engineer who discovered the rotating magnetic field, which became the basis of most AC machinery.

Thomson, Sir George Paget (1892–1975), English physicist who demonstrated that electrons undergo diffraction.

Thomson, Sir Joseph John (1856–1940), English physicist whose discovery of the electron revolutionized understanding of atomic structure.

Tomonaga, Shin'ichiro (1906–79), Japanese physicist who developed changes that made the quantum theory of mechanics fully consistent with the quantum theory of relativity.

Torricelli, Evangelista (1608–47), Italian mathematician and physicist who invented the barometer.

Turing, Alan (1912–54), English mathematician who pioneered computer theory. Turing discovered that it is impossible in general to predict if or when the *Turing machine* – a universal automatic machine capable of mathematical problem-solving which he designed – would stop.

Tyndall, John (1820–93), Anglo-Irish physicist who described the *Tyndall effect*, the scattering of light by particles of matter in its path.

Urey, Harold Clayton (1893–1981), US chemist who discovered deuterium (heavy hydrogen).

Van de Graaff, Robert Jemison (1901–67), US physicist who developed the *Van de Graaff generator* and the *Van de Graaff accelerator.*

van der Waals, Johannes Diderik (1837–1923), Dutch physicist who formulated the *van der Waals equation*, describing the behaviour of real gases.

Van't Hoff, Jacobus Henricus (1852–1911), Dutch chemist who created stereochemistry, the study of the three-dimensional structure of organic compounds.

Varmus, Harold (1939–), US microbiologist whose major research has been into oncogenes (genes with a cancer-causing capacity).

Veblen, Oswald (1880–1960), US mathematician whose contributions to differential equations and topology had implications in atomic physics.

Vesalius, Andrea (Andreas van Wesel; 1514–64), Flemish physician who was one of the first to dissect human corpses.

Volta, Count Alessandro (1745–1827), Italian physicist who invented the battery cell – the 'voltaic pile' made from copper and zinc discs which were separated by cardboard soaked in salt solution. He also discovered methane gas.

von Braun, Wernher (1912–77), German-born US rocket engineer who developed the V-2 and who played a major role in US space exploration.

von Karman, Theodore (1881–1963), Hungarian-born US aerodynamicist who discovered *Karman vortices*, the alternating vortices found behind obstacles placed in moving fluids.

Waksman, Selman (1888–1973), Ukrainian-born US microbiologist who isolated antibiotics – a word that he coined – from micro-organisms.

Wallace, Alfred Russell (1823–1913), Welsh naturalist who is best known for developing a theory of evolution independently of Darwin. He coined the phrase 'survival of the fittest'.

Watson, James (1928–), US geneticist who – with Francis Crick – discovered the molecular structure of DNA.

Watson-Watt, Sir Robert Alexander (1892–1973), Scottish physicist who played a major role in the development of radar.

Watt, James (1736–1819), Scottish inventor who is best known for his steam engine.

Weber, Wilhelm Eduard (1804–91), German physicist who investigated magnetism. In 1833 he devised the electromagnetic telegraph.

Weierstrass, Karl (1815–97), German mathematician who was a pioneer in the modern theory of functions.

Weismann, August (1834–1914), German biologist who made a major contribution to modern genetic theory by his 'germ plasm' theory.

Werner, Alfred (1866–1919), Swiss chemist who is known for his influential *New Ideas on Inorganic Chemistry.*

White, Gilbert (1720–93), English cleric and naturalist whose *Natural History of Selborne* (1789) was a landmark in nature study.

Whitehead, Alfred (1861–1947), English mathematician who collaborated with Russell on *Principia Mathematica* (1910–14).

Wiener, Norbert (1894–1964), US mathematician who founded the science of cybernetics.

Wilkins, Maurice (1916–), New Zealand-born British biophysicist who researched the molecular model of DNA with Francis Crick and James Watson.

Wilson, Kenneth (1936–), US physicist who developed a theory that explains the behaviour of different substances under pressure and temperature.

Witten, Edward (1951–), US physicist who has developed string theory, which attempts to unify general relativity with quantum mechanics.

Wöhler, Friedrich (1800–82), German chemist who was the first person to synthesize an organic chemical compound (urea) from an inorganic chemical compound (1828).

Woodward, R(obert) B(urns) (1917–79), US chemist who synthesized complex organic substances including quinine, cholesterol and vitamin B.

Young, Thomas (1773–1829), English physicist who established the principle of interference of light and thus confirmed the wave theory of light.

Yukawa, Hideki (1907–81), Japanese physicist who predicted the existence of the meson.

Zernike, Frits (1888–1966), Dutch physicist who invented the phase-contrast microscope.

Industry

IRON AND STEEL

Iron is extracted industrially from naturally occurring ores. The two most important of these are iron oxides – hematite (Fe_2O_3) and magnetite (Fe_3O_4). Mixed with carbon and heated to 1500 °C (2730 °F), iron oxides are reduced to metallic iron, the carbon combining with the oxygen to form carbon dioxide. This process is called *smelting*. In the Middle Ages charcoal was used to provide the carbon, but in 1709 Abraham Darby (1677–1717) of Coalbrookdale in Shropshire, England, succeeded in smelting iron with coke, which could readily be produced from coal. This made possible a huge increase in iron production during the Industrial Revolution.

The first link in the production of iron is the *blast furnace*, in which iron ore is reduced to iron. The biggest modern blast furnaces are huge constructions up to 30 m (100 ft) tall, with walls more than 3 m (10 ft) thick, and capable of making more than 10,000 tonnes (tons) of iron a day. The iron produced in the blast furnace is still contaminated with some residual impurities. Depending on the ore, it usually contains some 3 to 5% carbon, 1% manganese and 3% silicon.

From iron to steel

The iron tapped from a blast furnace is a raw material, not a finished product. To be useful, it must be converted either into cast iron or into steel. *Cast iron* is produced by remelting pig iron (iron that has been cast into moulds and allowed to cool) and carefully adjusting the proportions of carbon, silicon and other alloying elements. Strong and resistant to wear, cast iron can be machined and is easily cast into quite complex shapes. The moulds into which it is cast are made of sand contained in moulding boxes. The shape to be cast is impressed into the sand, and the molten iron poured into it. When solid, the casting is removed.

The great bulk of the iron produced in a blast furnace is converted into steel, by greatly reducing the carbon content. A way of removing carbon economically from pig iron was discovered in 1857 by the English engineer Henry Bessemer (1813–98). In the *Bessemer process*, air blown through the molten iron combined with some of the carbon, carrying it away as carbon monoxide and carbon dioxide. It also oxidized some of the iron, which then combined with the silicon and manganese to form a slag. After just 15 minutes, several hundred tonnes (tons) of iron had been converted into steel. The entire converter rotated on an axle like a cement mixer to pour out the molten steel.

A much slower and more controllable process was invented in the 1860s by a number of engineers – the *open-hearth process*. In this process, gas from low-grade coal was used to heat pig iron in a shallow furnace. The chemical changes were the same as in the Bessemer converter, but the process had the advantage that scrap steel could be added to the mixture. The process took up to 12 hours to produce steel, allowing very careful control of the final composition. Both the Bessemer and the open-hearth processes have been superseded in most countries by a process that combines the merits of both. In the *L-D process* (short for Linz-Donawitz), a jet of almost pure oxygen is blown through a lance onto the surface of molten iron. The process is quick and can absorb up to 20% scrap, while producing steel of very high quality. The addition of lime to the oxygen enables iron of higher phosphorus content to be converted, and in this form the process is known as the *basic oxygen furnace*.

For the more expensive steels, including alloy and stainless steels, *electric-arc furnaces* are used. Heat is provided by three carbon electrodes, which are lowered into a mixture of scrap and alloying additions. Silicon, manganese and phosphorus are removed as slag, and carbon is removed by adding some iron ore, which reacts just as in the blast furnace. The fact that an electric-arc furnace can melt a charge consisting entirely of scrap is a big advantage in developed countries, where recycled steel makes up a large proportion of total production.

Steel

Steel is sold in the form of cast slabs, or rolled into plates, strips, rods (for nails, screws and wire) or beams (for buildings, bridges and other constructional uses). To make it suitable for a particular use, the characteristics of a steel can be altered by a number of processes, including heat treatment and alloying.

The most important factor in any steel is the carbon content. High-carbon steels are harder and stronger, but they are also more brittle and cannot be welded. For adequate weldability, carbon contents below 0·2% are needed. The precise characteristics of any steel also depend on heat treatment, which determines the microstructure of the steel. Steel can be hardened by heating it to red heat – around 850 °C (1560 °F) – and then quenching it in water, but such a steel is also brittle. The hardness can largely be retained and the brittleness reduced by a second heating to a lower temperature – to around 250 °C (480 °F). The steel is then allowed to cool in air. Such steel is said to be *tempered*.

Alloying steel with other elements in addition to carbon is also important. A steel containing 3% nickel, for example, is immensely tough, and is used for gears and shafts that have to take a lot of strain. Steels containing up to 13% manganese have very hard edges, and are used for items such as rock-breaking machinery. The metal molybdenum is added to alloy steels to reduce brittleness. *Stainless steels*, containing around 14% chromium and sometimes nickel as well, do not rust because of the formation of an impermeable oxide layer on their surface. Such steels are now widely used for cutlery, kitchen sinks and the cladding of buildings.

Types of steel

Mild steel with 0·08% carbon content is used in car bodies, tin cans; with 0·2% carbon content used in buildings, bridges and ships.

Medium-carbon steel with 0·25–1·5% carbon content, is used in gunbarrels and railway wheels.

High-carbon steel with 0·45–1·5% carbon content is used in tools, scissors, and cutlery.

Cast iron with 2·5–4·5% carbon content is used in machine tools, engine blocks, ironmongery.

BUILDING CONSTRUCTION

The part of a building above ground level is called the *superstructure*; the part falling below ground level is referred to as the *substructure*. The stability of a building depends on its load-bearing components. There are three kinds of load: *dead* (resulting from the weight of the building itself); *live* (the result of furnishing, equipment and bodies); and *lateral* the result of sideways pressure, typically due to wind.

In a typical house, the load is borne principally by load-bearing walls. Internal dividing walls or partitions may or may not carry loads. Larger buildings may also use columns, arches and domes to support loads. The load-bearing substructure is known as the *foundations*, or *footings*, and for a house this is usually concrete supports for the load-bearing walls. Where the ground is soft, *raft foundations* may be used, which distribute the load evenly over the area occupied by the building. For larger buildings, *piles* may be driven through the ground to connect the substructure with ground of sufficient strength to support the building.

An alternative to load-bearing walls is *skeleton construction*, in which a structural frame carries the load, and the walls (*curtain walls*) are used simply to enclose space. In most conditions, load-bearing walls are not suitable for structures of more than four floors.

Materials

Over the long history of building construction, there has been a steady substitution of man-made materials for natural ones. Brick, concrete and steel have largely replaced natural stone, such as granite and sandstone, as the latter require expensive skilled labour both in preparation and in assembly. In the same way, thatch and slate have given way to tile for roofing and cladding. Although wood is still widely used for construction purposes, it too is increasingly being replaced by cheaper composite materials such as plywood (glued layers of wood) and particle board (wood and resin). Concrete and steel are now used for many building purposes, while synthetic materials such as PVC are becoming ever more common in non-structural applications.

New technology

In recent years building innovation has centred around the use of new materials and the potential for saving energy by means of refined insulation and ventilation techniques. The *dome* has also been resurrected as a means of covering the greatest area at the least cost. The stressed-skin dome, in which thin aluminium is stretched over a ribbed framework to form a combined curtain wall and roof, has been successful in specialized uses. In a refined version known as the geodesic dome, the somewhat heavy ribs are replaced by metal tubing in the form of linked hexagons and triangles. Another trend is towards the development of *tensile structures*, in which the roof is supported by means of cables stretched from pylons. This frees the space beneath the roof from any supporting structure, thereby increasing the usable area. The most notable application is in new sports stadiums, such as the Munich Olympic Stadium.

CIVIL ENGINEERING

Civil engineering embraces the design and building of major structures and systems

Modern roads have rigid pavements, in which the top layer was concrete, 15 to 30 cm (6 to 12 in) thick, laid on a prepared bed. Nowadays steel bars are laid within the concrete. The demands of heavy traffic led to the concept of high-speed, long-distance road. The US Bronx River Parkway of 1925 was followed by several variants – Mussolini's autostradas, Hitler's autobahns, and the Pan American Highway. Such roads were the predecessors of today's motorways.

Suspension bridges have a deck supported by suspenders that drop from one or more overhead cables. It requires strong anchorage at each end to resist the inward tension of the cables, and the deck is strengthened to control distortion by moving loads or high winds. Such bridges are nevertheless light-weight, and therefore the most suitable for very long spans.

Cantilever bridges exploit the potential of steel construction to produce a wide clearwater space. The spans have a central supporting pier and meet in midstream. The downward thrust where the spans meet is countered by firm anchorage of the spans at their other ends. Although the suspension bridge can span a wider gap, the cantilever offers better stability, which was important for 19th-century railway-builders.

In the 20th century, new forms of construction have been facilitated by the use of prestressed concrete – concrete surrounding tensioned steel cables that counter the stresses that occur under load. The box girder – a massive hollow box-shaped girder, which is both strong and light – has become a key component of concrete bridges.

Tunnel-building was developed in the 18th century to enable canals to penetrate hills, and the same techniques were exploited by the 19th-century railway-builders. Tunnels through hard rock could be unlined, but in soft or moist ground millions of bricks were used as lining.

Dams Crescent (horizontally arched) dams enable a much greater weight of water to be held than was possible with earlier constructions. Correct judgement of underlying rock strata is as important as good design. Concrete is now the preferred material for dam-construction, but earth, rock, stone and brick have been used.

CIVIL ENGINEERING RECORDS

Longest motorable road The Pan-American Highway from northwest Alaska to Santiago, Chile, thence eastward to Buenos Aires, (Argentina) and ending in Brasilia, Brazil at 24,140 km (15,000 mi).

Longest suspension bridge Humber Estuary Bridge, England (1980) at 1410 m (4626 ft).

Longest rail tunnel Seikan railway tunnel, Japan (1985) at 54 km (33 mi).

Longest tunnel of any kind is the New York City West Delaware water-supply tunnel (built 1937–44), which is 169 km (105 mi) long.

MINING

The Earth's crust, a thin layer that accounts for only about 0·6% of the planet's total volume, provides the fuels, metals and minerals upon which developed societies depend. The quantities of most metals in the crust are small – only iron, aluminium and magnesium are really plentiful. We are able to extract them only because they are not evenly distributed but occur in local concentrations where mining is economically possible. There are far greater concentrations of some metals, such as iron and nickel, in the Earth's mantle and core, but for the moment they are beyond our reach.

Mining methods

There are basically two kinds of mine – underground mines and opencast (or surface) mines. In an *underground mine*, horizontal tunnels several kilometres long are cut to get at a seam containing the desired mineral. Various techniques are then used to remove the mined material from the seam. In room-and-pillar mining, a common technique in coal mines in the USA, the coal is broken up by means of explosives and drills, and then removed to form large underground caverns, with the roof supported by pillars of unmined material. Longwall mining is more suitable for deeper deposits, such as those generally found in Europe. A working face of 100m (320 ft) or more is cut by huge machines, and the coal is transported back along roadways by automatic conveyors. Powered roof supports are used to prevent falls of rock at the working face. Some deep mines are very deep indeed: gold is mined in South Africa at depths of more than 3500m (11,500 ft), where the temperature of the rock may reach 49 °C (120 °F).

In *opencast mining*, the desired material is first exposed by removing any overlying material (the overburden) by means of scrapers, excavators, or draglines (huge buckets pulled along by steel cables). Relatively soft materials, such as coal, may then be removed by draglines, while for harder minerals the rock must first be broken up by blasting. In deep surface mines, such as the copper mines of Chile and Bingham Canyon in the USA, the ore is dug out in a series of terraces, or 'benches', that gradually expand and enlarge the pit. Roadways spiralling to the surface are provided for trucks to carry away the ore.

Alluvial mining, often used to recover tin and gold, makes use of the erosion of ores by water. Carried down by the flow of water, the ores (or native metal in the case of gold) can be recovered from the bottom of lakes and rivers by dredging or suction. The most primitive version of this is the panning technique used by gold prospectors. In Malaysia, huge dredges are used to pick up the tin-bearing gravels from the bottom of lakes.

An unusual method is used for mining sulphur, an element vital to the chemical industry. Developed by the American engineer Herman Frasch (1851–1914) at the end of the 19th century, the system uses three tubes of different diameters, one inside another, that are drilled down into reserves of naturally occurring sulphur. Water under pressure and at a temperature of 160 °C (320 °F) is pumped down the outer pipe, melting the sulphur. Compressed air is then pumped down the centre tube, driving the molten sulphur up through the middle tube. Sulphur obtained in this way is 99% pure. Today a considerable proportion of the world's sulphur is produced as a by-product of the purification of natural gas.

Common salt (sodium chloride) is found as salt deposits and in sea water. The salt deposits can be mined, while salt is recovered from sea water by evaporation in shallow pools. Magnesium chloride is also found in sea water in small but consistent amounts, and is extracted by reacting the sea water with lime, causing the magnesium to be deposited as a precipitate.

Types of mines

The mining method chosen to extract coal or other minerals depends principally on the depth of the seam or deposit:

Shaft mines are built to reach deep deposits. The mineral is reached by a shaft descending vertically into the ground.

Drift mines are used where seams appear as an outcrop at the surface, usually on the side of a hill. The seam can be entered and mined directly.

Slope mines are used for deposits at moderate depths. It enables the mineral to be hauled up an inclined tunnel in wagons.

Opencast mines are used where a mineral lies close to the surface. Layers of overlying soil and rock are removed to expose the mineral.

Discovering minerals

Fortunately for mankind, metals and minerals occur unevenly. Copper, tin, nickel, zinc, lead, mercury, silver and gold – all vital to our industrial society – are in fact extremely rare. Copper makes up only 100 parts per million of the Earth's crust, and lead only 20 parts per million. But the availability of metals does not depend so much on their abundance as on how easy it is to find and exploit their ores.

Sometimes bodies of ore advertise their presence by appearing at the surface, perhaps where erosion has scoured the rocks on a cliff face. Hidden reserves can be found by magnetic or gravimetric surveys – a mountain rich in iron ore will affect the Earth's magnetic field and the force of gravity in the immediate vicinity. Seismic and satellite surveying and knowledge of the local geology may also indicate the likelihood of a particular ore occurring.

MINE RECORDS

Gold The deepest gold mine – and the deepest mine of any kind in the world – is Western Deep Levels, Carletonville (Rand), South Africa at 3777 m (12,391 ft). The most productive gold mine may be Muruntau, Kyzyl Kum, Uzbekistan with an estimated 80 tonnes per year.

Coal The deepest coal mine is an exploratory shaft 2042m (6700 ft) deep in the Donbas field in Ukraine.

Quarry The largest quarry in the world is at Bingham Canyon, Utah, USA (see main text). It is 7·21 km^2 (2·81 sq mi) in area and represents 3355 million tonnes extracted.

Oldest mine The world's oldest known mine is an ochre (clay and hydrated ferric oxide) mine in Belgium dating from 41,250 BC.

CHEMICALS

In the 1930s the first of the man-made fibres was created – *nylon*. Its inventor was the US chemist Wallace Carothers (1896–1937), who found that under the right conditions hexamethylenediamine and adipic acid would form a polymer that could be pumped out through holes and then stretched to form long glossy threads that could be woven like silk. Its first use was to make parachutes for the US armed forces in World War II. In the postwar years it completely replaced silk in the manufacture of stockings. Many other synthetic fibres joined nylon, including Orlon, Acrilan, and Terylene. Most garments are now made of a blend of natural fibres and man-made fibres that make fabrics easier to look after.

The chemical industry turns readily available raw materials into thousands of useful products. principally from coal, oil, natural gas, air, water, limestone, salt and sulphur, the industry manufactures drugs, fertilizers and pesticides, soap and detergents, cosmetics, plastics, acids and alkalis, dyes, solvents, paints, explosives and gases. Biotechnology also produces useful products, but by biological rather than chemical methods. Living organisms – or substances produced from them – are used to make drugs, to improve crops, to brew alcohols, and even to extract minerals. Some of its methods, such as fermentation, are ancient, while others are so new that they are barely out of the research laboratory.

The chemical industry

The modern chemical industry can be divided for convenience into three categories: the *heavy inorganic sector*, which includes fertilizers and other chemicals produced in large amounts; the *fine chemicals sector*, which includes drugs and dyes; and the *heavy organic sector*, which includes plastics, man-made fibres and paints. The term *'organic'* was originally used to designate any chemical found in living organisms, but today the term refers to any chemical containing carbon. Because of the facility with which carbon atoms link to form molecules, the variety of such compounds is enormous – literally millions of carbon compounds can be synthesized.

In the heavy inorganic sector, *sulphuric acid* is the largest single product. Nearly half is used to produce superphosphate, with the rest going to a variety of chemical processes, including the production of explosives and artificial fibres. In 1908, the German chemist Fritz Haber (1868–1934) developed a catalytic method for combining the nitrogen in air with hydrogen to form *ammonia*, which is chiefly used in the manufacture of explosives and nitrate fertilizers.

In the fine chemicals sector, chemical substances are produced in smaller quantities than is the case with (say) fertilizers, but higher prices are charged. *Dyes* are produced in a huge range of colours, originally from coal but now mostly from crude oil. Many *drugs* are also synthesized using the methods of organic chemistry; some are produced biochemically.

In the heavy organic sector, materials are produced in large quantities, usually as raw materials for further processing into plastics, fibres, films or paints. Typical examples are benzene, phenol, toluene, vinyl chloride and ethylene. The main raw material is crude oil, which contains a range of hydrocarbons – chemicals made up of carbon and hydrogen. From crude oil individual hydrocarbons can be extracted by distillation or catalytic cracking. Hydrocarbons thus obtained are used to build more complex molecules by polymerization.

Biotechnology

The technique of *fermentation*, in which microorganisms such as yeast convert raw materials into useful products, has been known since earliest times. By the middle of the 19th century, industrial alcohol was being produced by fermentation in much the same way as beer or wine. After the price of crude oil went up in the 1970s, alcohol produced in this way has been able to compete under some circumstances with petrol, and large fermentation plants have been built in the USA and Brazil to convert plant material such as maize into fuel.

A number of acids can also be produced by fermentation – vinegar (dilute acetic acid) being an important example. Citric acid, widely used in food and drinks, was originally produced from citrus fruits, but a fermentation process developed by the US Pfizer company in the 1920s soon dominated the market. Pfizer still produces half the 250,000 tonnes (tons) of citric acid used every year. Other chemicals that can be produced by fermentation include glycerol, acetone and propylene glycol. Fermentation has proved equally useful in the drug industry. Following the discovery of the antibiotic penicillin in 1928, large-scale fermentation methods were developed in the 1940s to produce the drug commercially. Today a large number of drugs are produced in this way, as well as other biochemicals such as enzymes (biochemical catalysts), alkaloids, peptides and proteins.

The technique of *genetic engineering* has greatly increased the range of possible products. By altering the genetic blueprint of a microorganism, it can be made to produce a protein quite unlike anything it would produce naturally. For example, if the short length of the genetic material DNA responsible for producing growth hormones in humans is inserted into cells of a certain bacterium, the bacterium will produce the human hormone as it grows. It can then be extracted and used to treat children who would otherwise not grow properly. The same methods can be used to produce insulin for diabetics, while sheep have been genetically engineered so that they produce a human blood-clotting agent in their milk.

Pollution

The damage done to the environment by the growth of the chemical industry is an issue of widespread concern. The first attempts at controlling pollution by legislation were made in the 19th century, but poisonous discharges into streams still occur, and there is little control of the dumping of toxic wastes. A longer-term hazard is posed by the use of fertilizers, such as nitrates, which can pollute lakes and streams, and by percolating through the soil can reach groundwater. There is also anxiety about the use of genetic engineering techniques. It is possible, for example, that an accident could produce super-resistant species of germs or pests.

RADIO, TELEVISION AND VIDEO

The media used to carry information are radio waves, which lie at the low-frequency end of the electromagnetic spectrum. Radio waves occur naturally in space, emitted by stars and galaxies, but for broadcasting purposes, they are generated by accelerating electrons inside an *aerial* (or *antenna*) – a device used both to emit and receive radio waves. Like all electromagnetic waves, radio waves travel at the speed of light – 300,000 km (186 000 mi) per second in a vacuum.

The idea of using radio waves to carry visual information dates back to the early days of radio, but became practical only in 1926. The basic principle is to break up the image into a series of dots, which are then transmitted and displayed on a screen so rapidly that the human eye perceives them as a complete picture.

A TV set is basically a *cathode-ray tube*, in which a 'gun' fires a beam of electrons at a luminescent screen. As they strike it, the screen lights up. To make up the whole picture the beam is scanned to and fro in a series of lines (625 in modern sets), covering the entire screen in $^1/_{25}$ of a second.

The principle for recording TV programmes on video (magnetic tape) is the same as that of an audio tape recorder but the technology is more complex. The signals are recorded as magnetic patterns on the tape.

MILESTONES IN RADIO, TELEVISION AND VIDEO

1861 James Clerk Maxwell, Scottish physicist and mathematician, predicted the existence of an invisible form of electromagnetic wave travelling at the speed of light.

1887 Heinrich Hertz, German physicist, demonstrated the reality of Maxwell's waves, by allowing a small spark to jump across an air gap, and detecting the waves at the other side of a room with a similar air gap.

1894 Guglielmo Marconi, a young Italian inventor, made a bell ring in the attic of his parents' house in Bologna by sending a radio message across the room.

1901 Marconi succeeded in sending a radio message in Morse Code across the Atlantic, from Cornwall to Newfoundland.

1906 Music and speech was broadcast for the first time, by the American physicist Reginald Fessenden. The sounds were carried on radio waves by 'modulating' them, superimposing the sound waves on to the radio waves. The amplitude of the radio wave was altered to carry the sound – giving rise to the term *amplitude modulation*, or AM.

1907 Lee De Forest, an American inventor, used a triode valve to amplify radio signals.

1917 Lucien Lévy, in France, and Edwin Armstrong, in the USA, devised 'superheterodyne' circuits that made tuning much easier, reduced power requirements and simplified the construction of receivers.

1921 The first radio station, KDKA, began broadcasting in Pittsburgh, USA. The British Broadcasting Company (BBC) began daily transmissions the following year.

1925 Using a mechanical scanning system, the Scot John Logie Baird transmitted the first recognizable pictures of human faces.

1931 Vladimir Zworykin, a Russian-born inventor living in the USA, demonstrated the first practical electronic television camera.

1933 Edwin Armstrong devised frequency modulation (FM), in which the frequency rather than the amplitude of the carrier wave is modulated by the signal. This reduced the problem of random noise caused by static.

1936 The BBC television service was inaugurated at Alexandra Palace in London. It utilized two systems: Logie Baird's mechanical system, and an electronic system developed by an EMI research team under Isaac Schoenberg.

1945 Arthur C. Clarke, British science-fiction writer, described in *Wireless World* the possible use of a satellite in geostationary orbit for broadcasting radio and TV signals.

1951 Regular television broadcasting in colour was begun by Columbia Broadcasting System in New York.

1952 The first transistor radio, small enough to carry in the pocket, was made by Sony in Japan.

1953 The Federal Communications Commission in the USA adopted the NTSC (National Television Systems Committee) system for colour broadcasting.

1956 Improved colour TV became available using a system called SECAM (*Sequential Couleur à Memoire*) developed in France.

1958 The first video recording device, in which TV signals were recorded on magnetic tape, was installed in a US TV studio by the Ampex Corporation. A key invention, by Alexander Poniatoff of Ampex, was the rotating playback head, which enabled more information to be packed on to the tape.

1962 A third colour TV System PAL (Phase Alternance Line) was developed in Germany. (All three colour systems are incompatible.)

1962 The first transatlantic pictures were carried live, bounced off the communications satellite Telstar.

1963 The first geostationary satellites, the Syncom series built by Hughes Aircraft Corporation, were placed in orbit.

1965 Intelsat-1, Early Bird, went into geostationary orbit. It had the capacity for a single TV channel between Europe and North America.

1967 A colour TV service began in Britain, using the PAL system.

1970s Rival Video Cassette Recorder (VCR) systems emerged from Philips, Sony and JVC. The JVC system, known as VHS (video home system) proved the most successful and by the mid-80s millions of VCRs were installed in homes.

1974 Information systems, using the spare lines on a 625-line TV system, were broadcast in Britain. The BBC version is called Ceefax, the ITV system Oracle.

1974 ATS-6, an experimental direct broadcasting satellite, was launched by NASA and used to broadcast to Indian villages equipped with a receiver dish.

1979 The first regular direct broadcasting system, beaming pictures directly to people's houses (rather than through a ground station), was launched in Canada. The ANIK-B, requiring only a small rooftop dish, was the forerunner of many direct broadcasting systems.

1989 Commercial satellite broadcasting began in Britain with Sky Television, followed in 1990 by British Satellite Broadcasting (now merged).

HI-FI

Today's record decks use fundamentally the same principles as the original gramophone. Sound vibrations are converted into a groove that runs in a spiral from the edge of the flat disc towards the centre. The sound vibrations are played by side-to-side movements of the needle inside the groove. In the 1920s, the introduction of electrical recording methods improved the quality of recordings. *Microphones* were used to convert sounds into electrical currents, which could then be used to drive cutting machines to create the grooves. In playback, the vibrations picked up by the stylus were used to generate an electrical current, which could be amplified by electronic circuits and played through loudspeakers that converted the electrical signals back into sound.

Long-playing records (LPs), made of vinyl plastic instead of the breakable shellac and rotating at 33 rpm (revolutions per minute) instead of 78 rpm, were first produced in 1946. They required much lighter stylus pressures to avoid grinding away the soft plastic; and because the grooves were narrower, the styluses needed finer points, usually provided by the use of diamond or sapphire.

Stereophonic recordings became widely available after 1958. In making a stereo recording, two microphones are set up at a distance from one another, and each of them records its own set of sound signals. The aim is to simulate the way in which we hear sounds: having two ears, we simultaneously hear two sounds, which are slightly different and come from slightly different directions. Two signals recorded on separate strips along a tape are played back through two speakers.

At the heart of any hi-fi system is the *amplifier*. An amplifier is essentially a set of electronic circuits that boost the signal from the stylus or tape deck to operate the loudspeakers. The circuits are made from transistors, and amplifiers are designed to produce the minimum distortion of the signal. *Loudspeakers* convert the electrical signal from the amplifier back into sound. The current from the amplifier flows around a coil of wire inside the field of a permanent magnet. Interaction between the field produced by the current flowing through the coil and that of the permanent magnet makes the coil vibrate. The coil is attached to a cone of stiff lightweight material that vibrates with it and creates the sounds.

Tape recording

The *telegraphone*, introduced in 1898, recorded sound by the alternating magnetization of a steel wire, replaced in the 1930s by steel tape. After 1935 strong plastic tape covered with iron-oxide powder made tape recording widely available, and domestic *tape recorders* appeared in the 1950s. Sounds are recorded by passing the tape in front of a recording head that consists of an electromagnet fed by electrical signals from a microphone. A magnetic pattern corresponding to the sounds is created on the tape as iron oxide fragments align themselves with the magnetic field. In playback, the tape passes in front of a second head, inducing an electrical current that is proportional to the magnetization of the tape. The current is then passed through an amplifier to loudspeakers. The most common type of tape is the *compact cassette*.

Digital recording

Sounds are now recorded digitally, as a series of binary digits, or *bits*. In a *digital system*, the sound is 'sampled' 40,000 times a second, and its amplitude and frequency (volume and pitch) are recorded as a binary number. Recordings made in this way can be turned into ordinary discs, but the advantages of low distortion and a good signal-to-noise ratio are better preserved in the form of digital ('compact') discs. *Compact discs*, which were launched commercially in 1982, record the bits as a series of minute pits or blank spaces in the surface of the disc. The pits are 'read' by a laser device that scans the record, picking up a series of signals that are the original binary digits of the recording. The signals are converted to analogue currents that can be amplified and fed to loudspeakers. *Digital compact cassettes* and *recordable compact discs* are being developed.

MILESTONES IN HI-FI

1877 Thomas Edison invented the phonograph, using a cylinder with grooves on the surface, to record and play sound.

1888 The gramophone demonstrated for the first time by Emile Berliner. It used flat discs made from vulcanized rubber.

1895 Shellac replaced vulcanized rubber in the production of records.

1898 Valdemar Poulsen invented the telegraphone: forerunner of the modern tape recorder.

1901 Black discs with spiral grooves introduced by Emile Berliner.

1925 Introduction of electrical recording, with sounds recorded by microphones, transformed into electric current and converted into mechanical form to cut the master disk.

1933 The British company EMI pioneered stereophonic sound. It recorded two sound tracks within a single groove which were replayed through one stylus in two separate amplifying systems.

1935 The German companies AEG Telefunken and IG Farben introduced Magnetophone, the first commercial tape recorder using new magnetized plastic tape covered with iron-oxide powder.

1946 Columbia Records introduced long-playing 12-inch vinylite disks rotating at 33⅓ rpm.

1949 RCA introduced 7-inch disks rotating at 45 rpm.

1950s Domestic tape recorders on sale.

1958 Introduction of standard system of two-channel stereo for LPs.

1960s Transistors replaced valves in amplifiers.

1963 Philips introduced compact cassettes (more convenient that the open reel tapes).

1967 RM Dolby introduced the Dolby system of sound recording, which eliminates background hiss and improves sound quality.

1971 Introduction of quadrophonic sound systems.

1980 Walkmans – small portable tape recorders –introduced by Sony in Japan.

1982 Development of the compact disc (digital audio discs) by Philips and Sony.

TEXTILES

The creation of textiles requires two processes: the spinning of yarn, and the weaving of cloth. The basic principles of these two crafts have not changed since the earliest times, although the materials used have been supplemented by man-made fibres.

Natural fibres

Natural fibres come from a variety of sources: *wool* from sheep, *cotton* from the seed pod of the cotton plant, *flax* from the stem of the flax plant, *silk* from the delicate webs spun by silkworms fattened on the leaves of the mulberry tree. Among the more specialized fibres, the Angora goat produces *mohair*, while *cashmere* comes from the Kashmir goat. Camel hair and the fleece of the vicuña, a relative of the llama, are used in rugs and overcoats. *Jute*, a plant fibre, is used for making sacks and carpet backings, while *hemp*, another plant fibre, is used in sailcloth and canvas.

In their natural state, none of these fibres is very long. Wool fibres may be up to 20 cm (8 in) long, and flax a metre or more, but cotton fibres are rarely more than a few centimetres and are often as short as 3 mm (0·1 in). In order to make a continuous strand or *yarn*, the fibres have to be laid out in parallel lines and twisted together in the process called *spinning*.

Spinning

Having first been cleaned, the fibres are carded (laid parallel) by rolling them between two surfaces faced with points. Then they are combed to remove short fibres, and rolled in machines that pull out the yarn and give it a twist, which helps to hold the fibres together.

Stronger yarns are created by twisting two or more yarns together, and mixtures are made by combining fibres from different sources, such as wool and polyester. Finally the finished yarn is dyed and wound on bobbins (spools) for dispatch. Continuous improvement in mechanization since the 18th century has led to modern machines that are capable of producing thousands of metres of yarn an hour.

Unlike natural fibres, man-made fibres like *nylon* are continous. In principle, therefore, they can be used without spinning to make items such as net curtains, nylon stockings or tights. For more substantial garments, however, several filaments are wound together to make a thicker yarn. Synthetic fibres may also be cut into shorter lengths, and then blended with natural fibres and spun into a combination yarn.

Weaving

Two techniques are available for turning yarn into fabric: *weaving* and *knitting*. Traditionally knitting has been used for hosiery (including nylon stockings), for sweaters, and for women's dresses. Weaving is used to create bolts (rolls) of cloth, both for clothing and for furnishing fabrics.

The pattern of the weave can be altered to produce different effects. *Satin* gets its glossy appearance because the warp threads are interwoven not with every weft thread, but with every fourth or fifth. In *damask*, the same technique is used, but places where the warp lies on top are alternated with places where the weft does, producing subtle variations of shading. *Twill weaves* are used to produce gaberdine, serge and whipcord, and *pile weaves* for corduroy, plush, velour and velvet. The pile in such fabrics is created by cutting some of the threads after weaving, so that they stand out vertically from the surface of the fabric.

Printed patterns

Not all fabric patterns are produced by weaving. Colour printing, using as many as 16 different colours, can also be used. This method originated in India, and today printing is done on a series of rollers, one for each colour that is to be applied. Each roller, engraved with a part of the pattern, picks up dye from a trough as it rotates. The pattern is transferred to the fabric as it passes between the rollers, care being taken to ensure that the fabric cannot slip – otherwise the pattern would get out of register. After coming off the final roller at speeds of up to 180m (590 ft) a minute, the fabric is dried in an oven.

Knitting

In knitting, the yarns are not interwoven with one another but knotted. The range of patterns is more limited, but with modern knitting machines far more ambitious designs can be achieved than had previously been possible. The use of modern combination fabrics in which wool is mixed with man-made fibres has also allowed garments to be knitted that are easier to look after and that keep their shape better.

WEAVE, FIBRES AND PRINTS

cashmere a fine wool from the coat of the Kashmir goat.

chintz fabric printed with patterns rather than woven, originally from the Hindi word 'tchint', meaning mottled.

damask form of satin weave in which areas where warp threads lie on top are alternated with areas where weft threads do, producing variations of shading.

hemp fibre from hemp plant, used for canvas and sailcloth.

jute plant fibre used for making sacks and carpet backings.

mohair luxury fibre produced from the hair of the Angora goat.

satin weave in which the warp threads are interwoven not with every weft thread but with every third or fourth. This means that they lie on top, producing a glossy finish.

twill form of weave used to produce gaberdine, serge and whipcord.

warp the set of threads running lengthwise along the loom, and hence along the length of the finished cloth.

weft the set of threads running across the loom, weaving in and out of the warp threads.

velvet a pile weave in which some of the threads are cut after weaving so that they stand up to produce a carpet-like effect. Corduroy, plush and velour are also pile weaves.

INVENTIONS

abacus c. 3000 BC; probably developed in the Middle East.

adding machine 1623; by Wilhelm Schickard (German); Blaise Pascal invented an adding machine using 10:1 gearing to represent decimal columns in 1642. The earliest commercial machine was devised by William Burroughs (US) in St Louis, Missouri (1885).

aeropile c. 60 AD; by Hero of Alexandria (Greek); a toy-like aeropile that may be considered to be the ancestor of the piston steam engine.

aircraft (*theory*) 1717; by Emmanuel Swedenborg (Swedish) who produced the first 'rational design' for a flying machine; (*practical*) 1890; by Clément Ader (French) whose steam-powered *Eole* made the first hop by a man-carrying aeroplane at Armainvilliers, France. The first controlled and sustained power-driven flight occurred at Kitty Hawk, North Carolina, USA, on 17 December 1903 when Orville and Wilbur Wright (US) flew their chain-driven *Flyer 1* for a distance of 36·5 m (120 ft) at an airspeed of 48 km/h (30 mph).

airship 1852; by Henri Giffard (French) whose steam-powered coal-gas airship made the first airship flight from Paris to Trappes, France. Airship (rigid frame) 1900; by Count Ferdinand von Zeppelin (German).

aquatinting 1768; by Jean Baptiste Le Prince (French).

autogyro 1923; by Juan de la Cierva (Spanish), whose first successful autogyro flew at Girona, Spain, in January 1923.

bakelite 1909; by Leo Baekeland (Belgian-born US).

ball-point pen 1888; by John J. Loud (US); the first practical and low cost writing pens were perfected by Lazlo and Georg Biro (Hungarian) in 1938.

barbed wire 1867; by Lucien B. Smith (US).

barometer 1644; by Evangelista Torricelli (Italian).

battery (electric) 1800; by Alessandro Volta (Italian); the battery was demonstrated to Napoleon I in 1801.

bicycle 1839-40; by Kirkpatrick Macmillan (Scottish), whose invention had pedal-driven cranks.

bicycle (first direct drive) 1861; by Ernest Michaux (French).

bicycle tyres (pneumatic) 1888; by John Boyd Dunlop (Scottish), although the principle was patented but not developed by Robert William Thomson (English) in 1845.

bifocal lens 1780; by Benjamin Franklin (US).

boats 8th millennium BC; reed and dugout boats used; boats (*sailing*) 3rd millennium BC; in ancient Egypt.

bridge (metal) 1779; at Ironbridge, Telford, Shropshire, England.

bronze c. 3700 BC; in pre-dynastic Egypt.

Bunsen burner 1855; by Robert Wilhelm von Bunsen (German); Michael Faraday (English) had previously designed an adjustable burner.

burglar alarm 1858; by Edwin T. Holmes (US); the first electric burglar alarm was installed at Boston, Massachusetts, USA.

calculator (advanced) 1822; by Charles Babbage (English), who set out to design a 'differential engine', an advanced form of calculator for application to the problems of navigation.

car (petrol-driven) 1885; by Karl Benz (German); the first successful run was in Mannheim (late 1885); the car was patented in January 1886.

car tyres (pneumatic) 1895; by André and Edouard Michelin (French).

carburettor 1876; by Gottlieb Daimler (German).

carburettor spray 1892; by Charles E. Duryea (US).

carpet sweeper 1876; by Melville R. Bissell (US) at Grand Rapids, Michigan, USA.

cash register 1879; by James Ritty (US); built in Dayton, Ohio, USA.

cassette (compact) 1963; by Philips (Dutch).

cellophane 1908; by Dr Jacques Brandenberger (Swiss); machine production did not begin until 1911.

cement (portland) 1824; by Joseph Aspdin (English) at Wakefield, West Yorkshire, England.

chronometer 1735; by John Harrison (English), who received (1772) a prize of £20,000 that had been on offer by the British government since 1714.

clock (*mechanical*) 725; by I-Hsing and Liang-Tsan (Chinese). Earliest escapement; (*pendulum*) 1656; by Christiaan Huygens (Dutch).

clockwork 80 BC; by the ancient Greeks.

colour printing 1719; by Jakob Le Bon (German), who devised a three-colour engraving process.

compact disc 1978; by Philips (Dutch) and Sony (Japanese); launched commercially in 1982.

computer (*programmable electronic*) 1943; by Prof. Max Newman (English) and built by T.H. Flowers; this device – the Colossus (see Computing section) was used to break the German code Enigma; (*store-programmed*) 1948; at Manchester University, England; (*integrated circuit*) 1952; by W.A. Dummer (US).

computer language 1666; by Gottfried Wilhelm Leibniz, who proposed the basis of a language that would allow logical statements to be dealt with mathematically. The essence was the use of digits 0 for FALSE and 1 for TRUE. Leibniz – who went on to develop binary arithmetic – thus laid the foundations of the first computer language long before the invention of the computer.

dental plate 1817; by Anthony A. Plantson (US).

dental plate (rubber) 1855; by Charles Goodyear (US).

diesel engine 1895; by Rudolph Diesel (German), whose first commercial success with his engine was at Augsburg two years later.

disc brake 1902; by Dr F. Lanchester (English); the brake was first used on aircraft in 1953.

dynamo 1832; by Hyppolite Pixii (French); (*rotative*) 1833; by Joseph Saxton (English).

electric blanket 1883; exhibited in Vienna at the Austria Exhibition.

electric flat iron 1882; by H. W. Seeley (US) in New York City.

electric lamp 1879; by Thomas Alva Edison (US); the first practical demonstration was at Menlo Park, New Jersey, USA.

electric lamp (carbon filament) 1860; pioneer work on carbon filaments by Sir Joseph Swan (English).

electric motor (*DC*) 1873; by Zénobe Gramme (Belgian); (*AC*) 1888; by Nikola Tesla (Serbian-born US).

electrolysis 1894; by means of the German Castner-Kellner process.

electromagnet 1824; by William Sturgeon (English).

fountain pen 1884; by Lewis E. Waterman (US), although a fountain pen was patented but not developed by D. Hyde (US) in 1830.

galvanometer 1834; by André-Marie Ampère; the first measurement of the flow of electricity with a free-moving needle.

gas lighting 1792; by William Murdoch (English); a private house in Cornwall was lit by gas in 1792, a factory in Birmingham in 1798 and London streets in 1807.

glass (blowing) c. 50 BC; in Sidon, Lebanon.

glass (stained) *ante* 850; the earliest complete window is at Augsburg, Germany, and dates from c. 1080.

glassware c. 2600 BC; in Mesopotamia (modern Iraq).

glider 1853; by Sir George Cayley (English); a flight took place near Brompton Hall, Yorkshire. Sketches of a glider (dated 1716) were made by Emmanuel Swedenborg (Swedish).

gramophone 1878; by Thomas Alva Edison (US).

gyro-compass 1911; by Elmer A. Sperry (US); tested on *USS Delaware*.

gyroscope 1852; by Jean Foucault (French).

helicopter (*theory*) c. 1500; by Leonardo da Vinci who proposed the idea of a helicopter-like craft, although it is now known that the French built 'helicopter' toys before this time; (*operational*) 1909; by Igor Sikorsky (Ukrainian-born US) who built an unsuccessful helicopter in Russia. (The first practical helicopter was the German Focke-Achgelis built in 1936.)

hot-air balloon 1709; by Father Bartolomeu de Gusmão (Brazilian-born Portuguese), whose model hot-air balloon – which made an indoor flight at Terreiro do Paço, Portugal – is the earliest known; (*full-size*) 1783; by Jacques and Joseph Montgolfier (French), who achieved both tethered and free flight in the autumn of 1783.

hovercraft 1953; by Sir Christopher Cockerell (English), although the first air-cushion vehicle patent was made in 1877 by J. I. Thornycroft (English).

ink 2nd century AD; in China.

integrated circuit 1952; by Geoffrey Dummer (English); the first practical circuit was perfected by Harwick Johnson (US), at Princeton, New York, in 1953.

internal combustion powered vehicle 1805; by Isaac de Rivaz (Swiss); a primitive vehicle comprising a carriage powered by de Rivaz's 'explosion' engine.

jet engine 1930; by Frank Whittle (English); it was a gas turbine for jet propulsion.

laser 1960; by Dr Charles H. Townes (US) and demonstrated at Hughes Research, Malibu, California,USA.

laser typesetting 1976; by Monotype.

lift 1852; by Elisha G. Otis (US); the first elevator was installed at Yonkers, New York, USA.

lightning conductor 1752; by Benjamin Franklin (US) at Philadelphia, Pennsylvania, USA.

linoleum 1860; by Frederick Walton (English).

lithography 1796; by Aloys Senefelder (German).

loudspeaker 1900; by Horace Short (English); a compressed air 'auxetophone', which was first used on the Eifel Tower, Paris, in the summer of 1900; (*outdoor electric public address system*) 1916; by Bell Telephone on Staten Island Island, New York, USA.

machine gun (Gatling gun) 1861; by Richard Gatling (US). An earlier gun that operated on a basic machine gun principle was invented by James Puckle in 1718.

mackintosh 1823; by Charles Macintosh (Scottish), who produced a waterproof coat made from a fabric that sandwiched a layer of rubber between two layers of cloth.

map c. 2250 BC; in Sumeria; clay tablets of the River Euphrates; (*printed*) 1477; in Bologna, Italy.

margarine 1869; by Hippolyte Mège-Mouries (French).

match 1816; by François Devosne (French); a phosphorus (unsafe) match; (*safety*) 1845; by Anton von Schrötter (Austrian).

measure (*weight*) c. 3800 BC; the beqaa – a unit of weight equivalent to between 188·7–211·2 gm (6·65–7.45 oz) – was in use in the Amratian period of the ancient Egyptian civilization; (*length*) c. 3500 BC; the unit of length now generally referred to as the megalithic yard was used by megalithic tomb builders in NW Europe. It was equivalent to c. 82·9 cm (c. 2·72 ft).

mezzotint process 1642; by Ludwig van Siegen (German) who introduced printing in graduated tones.

microcomputer 1968–70; by Gilbert Hyatt (US) at Micro Computer Inc, who devised a single chip microcomputer.

microphone 1876; by Alexander Graham Bell (US); the name was coined two years later.

microprocessor 1971; by Marcian E. Hoff (US); it was launched by the US company Intel in the same year.

microscope 1590; by Zacharias Janssen (Dutch), whose device had a compound convex-concave lens.

mobile (cordless) telephone 1967; in USA.

motor cycle 1885; by Gottlieb Daimler (German); the motor cycle was first riden by Paul Daimler on 10 November 1885 at Cannstatt, Germany.

moveable type c. 1450; by Johannes Gutenberg (German).

neon lamp 1910; by Georges Claude (French); the neon lamp was first installed at the 1910 Paris Motor Show.

nuclear power station 1951; the first nuclear power station producing electricity was the EBR-1 in the USA.

nylon 1930s; by Walter Carrothers (US).

paper 2nd century AD; in China, although papyrus was used in ancient Egypt.

parachute 1783; by Louis-Sébastien Lenormand (French) who used a quasi-parachute in a descent in Montpellier, France, although Faustus Verancsis (Hungarian) is reputed to have used a framed canopy for a descent in Hungary in 1617.

parking meter 1935; by Carlton C. Magee (US) and first used in Oklahoma City, USA.

photocopier 1937; by Chester Carlson (US), who developed the first practical dry photocopier.

pipeline 1863; at Oil Creek, Pennsylvania, USA, although the pipes were torn up by Luddites.

pocket calculator 1971; by Jack St Clair Kilby (US), James van Tassell (US) and Jerry D. Merryman (US); the 'Pocketronic' which was manufactured by Texas Instruments Inc., Dallas, USA.

polythene 1930s; by British chemists.

porcelain 851; (earliest known) in China.

potter's wheel c. 6500 BC; in Asia Minor.

pressure cooker 1679; by Denis Papin (French).

printing (blocks) 2nd century AD; in China where blocks with pictures or letters cut into them were developed.

printing (linotype) 1884; by Otto Mergenthaler (US).

printing (monotype) 1887; by Tolbert Lanston (US).

printing press c. 1450; by Johannes Gutenberg (German); (*rotary*) 1844; by William Hoe (US).

programmable device 1804; by J. M. Jacquard (French), a weaver who invented a loom in which changes of pattern or material could be programmed by feeding in a set of punched cards.

pyramid 2856 BC by Imhotop (Egyptian); the earliest pyramid was the Djoser step pyramid, at Sakkara, Egypt.

radar 1922; by Dr Albert H. Taylor (US) and Leo C. Young (US); radio reflection effect first noted. Radar was first harnessed by Dr Rudolph Kühnold (German) at Kiel, Germany, in 1934; *(pulse ranging)* 1925; by Gregory Breit (US) and Merle A. Tuve (US); measured the height of the ionosphere by bouncing radio pulses off the ionized layer.

radio echo device 1904; by Christian Hülsmeyer (German), who developed a primitive radar-like device.

rail transport 1550; at Leberthal, Alsace, France, where wagons ran on wooden rails at a mine.

railway (*electric*) 1879; by Werner von Siemens (German) whose oval metre gauge demonstration track was shown at the Berlin Trades Exhibition; (*steam locomotive*) 1803; by Richard Trevithick (English), who built a steam locomotive for a 914 mm (3 ft) gauge iron plateway, although there is no evidence that it ran. His second locomotive drew wagons in which men rode at Penydarren, Glamorgan, Wales, on 22 February 1804.

rayon 1883; by Sir Joseph Swan (English); produced commercially at Courtauld's Ltd, Coventry, England in 1905; the name rayon was not used until 1924.

razor (*electric*) 1931; by Col. Jacob Schick (US) and first manufactured at Stamford, Connecticut, USA; razor (*safety*) 1895; by King C. Gillette (US), who patented the first disposable blades.

record (*gramophone*) 1901; by Emile Berliner (German-born US); (*long-playing*) 1948; by Dr Peter Goldmark (US) at the CBS Research laboratories.

refrigerator 1850; by James Harrison (Australian) and Alexander Catlin Twining (US); simultaneous development at Rodey Point, Victoria, Australia, and in Cleveland, Ohio; the first domestic refrigerator was installed at Chicago, Illinois, USA in 1913.

rocket (war) 1042; in China; war rockets propelled by gun-powder (charcoal-saltpetre-sulphur) were described by Zeng Gongliang.

rubber (*latex foam*) 1928; by Dunlop Rubber Co (UK); (*vulcanized*) 1841; by Charles Goodyear (US).

safety pin 1849; by Walter Hunt (US); first manufactured in New York City, USA.

Scotch tape 1930; by Richard Drew (US).

screw propeller 1836; by Sir Francis Pettit Smith (English).

self-starter 1911; by Charles F. Kettering (US) at Dayton, Ohio, USA and sold to Cadillac.

sewing machine 1829; by Barthélemy Thimmonnier (French), although a patent was issued to Thomas Saint (English) in 1793 for a type of sewing machine that was apparently undeveloped.

ship (power-driven) 1801–02; by William Symington (Scottish) whose Charlotte Dundas was the first successful power-driven vessel. She was a stern paddle-steamer built for the Forth and Clyde Canal, Scotland.

silk manufacture c.50 BC; in China where reeling machines were devised. (There were silk mills in Italy c. 1250.)

skyscraper 1882; by William Le Baron Jenny (US) who constructed the Home Insurance Co. Building (Chicago, USA), which had 10 storeys (the top four with steel beams).

slide rule 1621; by William Oughtred (English); the earliest slide between a fixed stock was developed by Robert Bissaker in 1654.

spectacles (*convex*) c. 1286; in Pisa, Italy; (*concave*) c. 1450; by Nicholas of Cusa (Italian), who developed concave lens for myopia.

spinning frame 1769; by Sir Richard Arkwright (English).

spinning jenny 1764; by James Hargreaves (English).

spinning mule 1779; by Samuel Crompton (English).

steam engine 1698; by Thomas Savery (English); (*condenser*) 1769; by James Watt (Scottish); (*marine*) 1783; by Marquis Jouffroy d'Abbans, who ascended a reach of the River Saône, near Lyon, France in the 180 tonnes paddle steamer *Pyroscaphe*; (*piston*) 1712; by Thomas Newcomen (English). See railway.

steam-powered vehicle 1769; by Nicolas-Joseph Cugnot (French); a three-wheeled steam-driven military tractor; (*model*) 1668; by Father Ferdinand Verbiest (Belgian); (*passenger*) 1801; by Richard Trevithick (English); an eight-seater vehicle which operated in Camborne, Cornwall, England.

steel production 1855; by Henry Bessemer (English).

stereophonic sound 1933; pioneer work by the British company EMI.

stocking frame 1589; by William Lee (English).

submarine 1776; by David Bushnell (US), who developed a device with a hand-propelled screw and a one-man crew; the vessel was used in New York, USA.

submersible 1624; by Cornelius Drebbel (Dutch) who demonstrated a 12-man wooden and leather submersible in the River Thames, England.

tape recorder 1935; by the German companies AEG Telefunken and IG Farben who both introduced commercial tape recorders in 1935.

tank 1914; by Sir Ernest Swinton (English); a model was designed by William Tritton and tested in 1915.

telegraph (mechanical) 1787; by M. Lammond (French) who demonstrated a working model in Paris.

telegraph code 1837; by Samuel B.P. Morse (US), although a very major part was played by his assistant Alfred Vail who was the first to transmit a code.

telegraphone 1898; by Valdemar Poulsen (Danish), whose pioneer magnetic recorder was the ancestor of the tape recorder.

telephone (*theory*) 1849; by Antonio Meucci (Italian), who devised and produced an instrument that worked imperfectly by electrical impulses; (*practical*) 1876; by Alexander Graham Bell (US); the first telephone exchange was constructed as Boston, Massachusetts, USA in 1878.

telephone (automatic exchange) 1889; by Alfred Strowger (US), a US undertaker who suspected he was losing trade through the transfer of his calls to another undertaker by telephonists.

telescope (*refractor*) 1608; by Hans Lippershey (Dutch); (*reflecting*) 1668–69; by Isaac Newton (English).

television 1925; by John Logie Baird (Scottish), who transmitted the first recognizable pictures.

television camera 1931; by Vladimir Zworykin (Russian-born US), who developed the first practical electronic television camera.

terylene 1941; by J.R. Whinfield (English) at Accrington, Lancashire, England.

thermometer 1593; by Galileo Galilei (Italian) for clinical use; (*mercury*) c. 1615; by Santorio Santorio (Italian).

transistor 1948; by John Bardeen (US), William Shockley (US) and Walter Brattain (US) at Bell Telephone Laboratories, although the first application for a patent was by Dr Julius E. Lilienfeld (Canadian) in 1925; (*junction*) 1951; by R.L. Wallace (US), Morgan Sparks (US) and Dr William Bradford Shockley (US).

transistor radio 1952; by Sony (Japan).

turbine (ship) 1894; by Hon. Sir Charles Parsons, whose *Turbinia* was 30m (100 ft) long and had a displacement of 45·2 tonnes.

turbojet engine 1937; by Dr Hans Pabst von Ohain (German); the first flight by an aeroplane powered by a turbojet engine was made by the Heinkel He 178, piloted by Erich Warsitz at Marienehe, Germany in August 1939.

typewriter 1867; by Christopher Sholes (US); manufactured by the gunsmith Philo Remington in 1874.

tyres (rubber) 1846; by Thomas Hancock (English).

vehicle (gas-powered) 1826; by Samuel Brown (English); the first vehicle powered with an internal combustion engine was a gas-powered carriage on Shooter's Hill, Blackheath, London.

Walkman 1980; by Sony (Japan) who developed small portable tape recorders, launching them commercially in 1980.

washing machine 1907; by Hurley Machine Co (US); marketed under the name of 'Thor' in Chicago, Illinois, USA.

watch before 1462 when there was the earliest mention of a named watchmaker, Bartholomeo Manfredi (Italian), in a reference to an earlier unnamed watchmaker; (*wrist*) 1790; by Jacquet-Droz and Leschot of Geneva, Switzerland.

water closet 1589; by Sir John Harington (English) and installed at Kelston, near Bath, England.

weaving (flying shuttle) 1733; by John Kay (English).

welder (electric) 1877; by Elisha Thomson (US).

wheel c. 3580 BC; by the Sumerian civilization, at Uruk (modern Iraq). (A pottery cup depicting 3 four-wheeled wagons – and dating from c. 3500 BC – has been found at Brónócice, Poland.)

windmill c. 600; in Iran for corn grinding.

writing c. 3600 BC; in Sumeria; pictographs.

zip fastener 1891; by Whitcomb L. Judson (US), although the first practical zip fastener was developed by in the USA by Gideon Sundback (Swedish) in 1913.

Energy

In the industrialized world, the vast amount of power that we demand is most often provided by means of electricity – the most convenient and flexible medium in which to transfer power from its source to where it is needed. However, in deciding how best to generate electricity in ever-increasing quantities, we are confronted with an unenviable choice. On the one hand, there is the gradual but inevitable damage to the environment caused by burning coal and oil; on the other, the unlikely but potentially catastrophic risks associated with nuclear power. The environmentally friendly and safe sources of energy – wind, solar and geothermal – still account for very little of the world's energy.

Most of the developed world's electricity is generated by burning coal or oil or from nuclear fission. In each case the heat produced by the fuel is used to raise steam, which turns the blades of a steam turbine. The turbine rotor is connected to the shaft of an electrical generator. In most developed countries and increasingly in the Third World, the power output is fed into a national grid system. Most developed countries have extensive and complex supply networks. Power stations are interlinked and centrally controlled, allowing power to be channelled to where it is required and extra stations to be started up to meet peaks in demand.

Producers of electricity

	Production in 1991 (in kW-hr)
USA	3,079,090,000,000
Russia	1,068,000,000,000
Japan	888,090,000,000
China	677,550,000,000
Germany	573,750,000,000
Canada	507,910,000,000
France	454,700,000,000
United Kingdom	322,130,000,000
India	309,370,000,000
Ukraine	279,000,000,000
Brazil	234,370,000,000
Italy	222,040,000,000
South Africa	169,650,000,000
Australia	156,880,000,000
Spain	155,700,000,000
Sweden	147,730,000,000
Poland	134,700,000,000
South Korea	132,230,000,000
Mexico	126,380,000,000
Norway	110,950,000,000
Taiwan	89,640,000,000
Kazakhstan	86,130,000,000
Netherlands	74,250,000,000
Belgium	71,950,000,000
Czech Republic	60,540,000,000
Turkey	60,340,000,000
Finland	58,140,000,000
Switzerland	57,800,000,000
Uzbekistan	57,400,000,000
Venezuela	57,150,000,000
Argentina	54,050,000,000
North Korea	53,500,000,000
Thailand	52,490,000,000
Austria	51,480,000,000

OIL

Oil and natural gas are hydrocarbons – organic compounds built from just two elements, hydrogen and carbon. Hydrocarbons range from light gases like methane (CH_4) to heavy solids like asphalt. Crude oil is a mixture of hydrocarbons – some light, some heavy – and is often found in conjunction with natural gas.

Three types of rock are needed to form an oil reserve: the sedimentary rocks in which the hydrocarbons form; porous rocks that can store the oil and gas like a sponge; and an impervious layer of rock over the top, ideally in the form of a dome, to form a trap.

When a likely area of oil has been identified, exploratory drilling begins. If economic amounts of oil are found, production wells are drilled. From a single derrick, many holes can be drilled, fanning outwards to reach all corners of the reserve. This is done with a tool called the *whipstock*, which forces the flexible drillstring to bend slightly. A large field may be drilled from several different platforms. Each hole is lined with steel casing embedded in concrete, and explosives are used to punch holes through the casing, to allow the oil to get into the hollow casing from the surrounding rock.

Once the well has been drilled, an arrangement of pipework and valves – called a 'christmas tree' because of its shape – is installed at the surface to control the flow. The pressure of the oil may be enough to drive it to the surface, but pumps can also be used. As pressure falls, it may be artificially increased by pumping water down other holes. Even with such techniques no more than 30 to 40% of the oil in place can be recovered.

To turn crude oil into useful products it must be refined. Two basic processes are used. *Fractional distillation* allows lighter fractions to be separated from heavier ones. *Catalytic cracking* uses heat, pressure, and certain catalysts to convert or 'split' some of the heavier fractions obtained by distillation into lighter, more useful ones.

Today the most valuable product is petrol (gasoline), used to drive the world's cars, so a growing proportion of each barrel is converted into that. The main producers and consumers of crude petroleum are listed below

Producers of crude petroleum

	Production (in barrels) in 1992*
Russia	3,313,000,000
Saudi Arabia	2,965,000,000
USA	2,617,000,000
Iran	1,251,000,000
China	1,011,000,000
Mexico	975,000,000
United Arab Emirates	842,000,000
Venezuela	771,000,000
United Kingdom	656,000,000
Norway	622,000,000
Canada	567,000,000
Indonesia	532,000,000
Libya	526,000,000
Egypt	334,000,000

Algeria	290,000,000
Qatar	249,000,000
Brazil	229,000,000
Malaysia	229,000,000
India	212,000,000
Syria	203,000,000
Australia	200,000,000
Kazakhstan	194,000,000
Argentina	181,000,000
Angola	180,000,000
Colombia	157,000,000
Gabon	133,000,000
Ecuador	107,000,000
Iraq	99,000,000
Azerbaijan	86,000,000
Yemen	68,000,000
Kuwait	61,000,000
Cameroon	61,000,000
Romania	59,000,000
Congo	55,000,000
Denmark	54,000,000
Brunei	53,000,000

* one barrel averages 159 litres

Consumers of crude petroleum

	Consumption (in barrels) in 1991/92*
USA	4,921,000,000
Russia	3,700,000,000
Japan	1,432,000,000
China	905,000,000
Germany	667,000,000
United Kingdom	591,000,000
France	555,000,000
Saudi Arabia	534,000,000
Italy	533,000,000
Canada	486,000,000
Mexico	471,000,000
Brazil	410,000,000
India	405,000,000
Venezuela	357,000,000
Netherlands	355,000,000
Singapore	326,000,000
Iran	310,000,000
Indonesia	299,000,000

* one barrel averages 159 litres

Oil reserves

The following figures relate to proved reserves of petroleum that are generally considered to be recoverable using current technology.

	Estimated reserves (in million barrels) in 1993
Saudi Arabia	259,000
Russia	156,000
Iraq	100,000
Kuwait	92,500
United Arab Emirates	64,750
Venezuela	63,300
Iran	61,300
Mexico	51,300
Libya	38,200
China	29,600
USA	22,800
Nigeria	18,200
Norway	16,800
Algeria	10,400
Indonesia	8400

GAS

Natural gas is often found together with oil, because it is formed in the same way and collects in the same kind of geological formations (see above).

The development of long-distance pipelines and ships that carry liquefied natural gas has greatly increased the market for gas, which is both an excellent fuel and a useful raw material for the chemical industry. Gas flows more readily than crude oil, so as much as 80% of the gas in place may be recovered.

The processing of gas involves separating it from any liquids and 'sweetening' it by removing gases such as hydrogen sulphide and carbon dioxide. The end product consists mostly of methane (more than 80%) combined with smaller amounts of ethane, propane and butane. The main producers of natural gas are listed below.

Producers of natural gas

	Production (in cubic metres) in 1992
Russia	643,000,000,000
USA	503,300,000,000
Canada	111,200,000,000
Netherlands	90,000,000,000
Turkmenistan	84,300,000,000
United Kingdom	53,900,000,000
Algeria	43,300,000,000
Mexico	42,000,000,000
Uzbekistan	41,600,000,000
Indonesia	40,500,000,000
Iran	35,100,000,000
Saudi Arabia	31,800,000,000
Argentina	30,800,000,000
Romania	28,300,000,000
Australia	21,500,000,000
Ukraine	20,900,000,000
Norway	19,900,000,000
Venezuela	17,700,000,000
Italy	16,900,000,000
Germany	16,100,000,000
India	13,800,000,000
Malaysia	12,800,000,000
Pakistan	12,300,000,000
Azerbaijan	11,700,000,000
Libya	10,200,000,000
Brunei	8,700,000,000
Qatar	8,200,000,000
Kazakhstan	7,900,000,000
Egypt	7,800,000,000
Trinidad and Tobago	7,300,000,000
New Zealand	6,900,000,000
Bahrain	6,300,000,000
Colombia	5,600,000,000
Thailand	5,500,000,000

Natural gas reserves

The following figures relate to proved reserves of natural gas that are generally considered to be recoverable using current technology.

	Estimated reserves (in cubic metres) in 1993
Russia	48,677,000,000,000
Iran	17,273,000,000,000
United Arab Emirates	5,448,000,000,000
Saudi Arabia	5,135,000,000,000
Qatar	4,672,000,000,000
USA	4,665,000,000,000
Venezuela	3,651,000,000,000
Algeria	3,650,000,000,000
Nigeria	3,451,000,000,000
Iraq	3,095,000,000,000
Norway	2,756,000,000,000
Canada	2,665,000,000,000
Australia	2,093,000,000,000
Mexico	1,983,000,000,000
Netherlands	1,929,000,000,000
Malaysia	1,895,000,000,000
Indonesia	1,374,000,000,000
Kuwait	1,347,000,000,000
China	1,274,000,000,000
Libya	1,233,000,000,000
Bangladesh	719,000,000,000
India	677,000,000,000
Argentina	674,000,000,000
Pakistan	671,000,000,000

Consumers of natural gas

	Consumption (in cubic metres) in 1991/92
Russia	643,000,000,000
USA	606,230,000,000
Germany	88,410,000,000
Canada	66,760,000,000
United Kingdom	57,470,000,000
Japan	56,760,000,000
Italy	52,070,000,000
Netherlands	49,850,000,000
Uzbekistan	37,800,000,000
Saudi Arabia	37,220,000,000
France	33,730,000,000
Romania	32,040,000,000

COAL

Coal is a carbon-based mineral that formed over many millions of years as a result of the gradual compacting of partially decomposed plant matter. Three basic types of coal are found: lignite, bituminous coal and anthracite.

Lignite (brown coal) has the lowest heat value, since it was formed more recently and contains less carbon and more water than the other varieties. About half the coal mined is used for generating electricity, with another quarter going to the steel industry as coking coal. The remainder is used in other industries or for home heating.

The burning of fossil fuels such as coal in power stations leads to the emission of several by-products that are potentially damaging to the environment. *Fly ash*, which results from burning pulverized coal, is effectively removed by passing the flue (or waste) gases from the furnace through an *electrostatis precipitator* - a series of electrically charged plates that hold back the tiny particles of ash.

However, other by-products pass straight out of the chimney and into the atmosphere, including sulphur dioxide and nitrogen oxides, major causes of acid rain, and carbon dioxide, which contributes to the greenhouse effect. Major coal-fired stations are likely to include desulphurization equipment. The major producers and consumers of coal are listed below.

Producers of coal (bituminous)

	Production (tonnes)
China	1,080,000,000
USA	907,400,000
Russia	353,300,000
India	229,000,000
Poland	215,000,000
Australia	214,000,000
Germany*	183,500,000
South Africa	176,200,000
Ukraine	133,600,000
Kazakhstan	130,300,000
United Kingdom**	89,000,000
Czech Republic	78,300,000
Canada	71,100,000
North Korea	67,000,000
Greece	51,900,000
Turkey	42,900,000
Yugoslavia (Serbia/Montenegro)	40,000,000
Romania	38,200,000
Spain	33,600,000
Bulgaria	30,300,000

*Germany is also the world's greatest producer of lignite (brown coal). Its annual output of 385,350,000 tonnes is over one third of the world's total annual production. ** c. 40,000,000 tonnes in 1994.

Consumers of coal

	Consumption (in tonnes) in 1991/92
China	1,058,210,000
USA	806,480,000
Germany	469,100,000
Russia	395,000,000
India	227,920,000
Poland	168,780,000
South Africa	133,500,000
Japan	117,940,000
United Kingdom	108,250,000
Australia	98,880,000
North Korea	91,100,000
Turkey	57,500,000
Greece	52,740,000
Canada	50,620,000

NUCLEAR ENERGY

In terms of electricity generation, the only difference between nuclear power stations and conventional stations is the means of raising steam to drive the turbines: the coal- or oil-burning furnace is simply replaced by a nuclear reactor. However, this entails a whole industry of its own.

Uranium-235 (U-235) is the form (or *isotope*) of the element uranium used as the fuel in most nuclear reactors. However, it is only present in tiny quantities - less than 1% - in mined uranium. The rest is made up of uranium-238. For many reactors, the proportion of U-235 has to be increased by a complex and very costly process known as *enrichment*. The fuel - enriched or natural uranium as required - is packed into fuel rods, which are placed in the core of a nuclear reactor.

The nuclei of U-235 atoms sometimes break apart when struck by neutrons, in a process known as *nuclear fission*. As the nucleus splits, two or three more neutrons are released. These go on to bombard other nuclei and may cause them to split, thus setting off a chain reaction. The reaction is essentially a controlled version of what happens when an atomic bomb explodes. To increase their chance of fissioning U-235 (rather than being captured without fission by U-238), the neutrons are slowed down using a *moderator* such as graphite. So much energy is released as the fuel is fissioned that a single tonne (ton) of uranium is equivalent of 25,000 tonnes of coal.

The vessel in which the fuel rods are placed is filled with a *coolant*. As nuclei split, energetic fragments fly off and are brought to rest in the surrounding coolant, so causing its temperature to rise. The coolant is constantly circulated through the core, so preventing the core from overheating and at the same time acting as the medium by which heat is channelled away from the core to raise steam.

The nuclear reaction can be slowed down or stopped altogether if control rods containing a material that absorbs neutrons, such as boron, are lowered into the reactor core.

Types of nuclear reactors

The first commercial nuclear power station, opened in 1956 at Calder Hall in Cumbria, England, was a *magnox reactor*. Magnox reactors are so called because their fuel – natural (unenriched) uranium – is clad in an alloy of magnesium and aluminium called magnox. They are cooled by carbon dioxide gas. In the 1970s a new generation of much bigger gas-cooled reactors was developed in Britain – the *advanced gas-cooled reactors* or AGRs. In an AGR, the heat exchangers are located within the pressure vessel itself. The carbon-dioxide coolant is pressurized and heated up to 600 °C (1112 °F) or more as it is pumped through the core, which is made up of fuel rods filled with enriched uranium dioxide.

Meanwhile, the Canadians have developed reactors that use 'heavy water' (deuterium oxide). Because heavy water (unlike ordinary water) absorbs few neutrons itself, reactors using it as moderator and coolant can operate with unenriched (and thus cheaper) fuel. The economy in fuel costs is offset, however, by the additional expenditure involved in producing heavy water.

Today, the most widespread nuclear power plants are *light-water reactors*. The coolant and moderator - ordinary ('light') water – is readily available and cheap, but the uranium fuel has to be highly enriched. In the case of *boiling-water reactors* (BWRs), the water is allowed to boil to make steam, which is less efficient at cooling and moderating the reactor, and so must be prevented from building up in the reactor core. In *pressurized-water reactors* or PWRs, the water must remain at even higher pressure than is required in a BWR, so that it can reach useful temperatures without boiling.

The world's reserves of uranium will not last for ever, but one sort of reactor could make them go a lot further – the *fast breeder reactor* or FBR. The drawback of fast reactors is that they require the reprocessing of spent nuclear fuel both to extract plutonium (its main fuel) in the first place and to recover it from the uranium blanket. Reprocessing is a highly complex and expensive operation – as well as being unpopular with environmentalists. Reservations about fast reactors have led some countries to halt FBR programmes and research.

The world's worst nuclear accident at Chernobyl in Ukraine in April 1986 highlighted the potential dangers of nuclear power. As a result of Chernobyl and another costly, though less serious, accident at a PWR on Three Mile Island in the USA many countries have slowed or halted their nuclear programmes.

Producers of nuclear power

	Production in 1991 (in kW-hr)
USA	612,740,000,000
France	331,500,000,000
Japan	213,100,000,000
Germany	162,900,000,000
Russia	106,800,000,000
Canada	85,300,000,000
Sweden	77,100,000,000
United Kingdom	66,100,000,000
South Korea	56,300,000,000
Spain	55,600,000,000
Belgium	42,900,000,000
Taiwan	33,900,000,000

ENERGY SOURCES

The respective contributions of fossil fuels (coal, oil, etc), hydroelectric power and nuclear power to the power requirements of selected countries are given as percentages in the following table.

	Fossil fuels	HEP	Nuclear power
Argentina	55.2	30.4	14.4
Australia*	89.7	10.3	—
Belgium	39.1	1.3	59.6
Brazil	6.5	92.9	0.6
Canada	22.5	60.7	16.8
China	81.5	18.5	—
Denmark*	97.8	0.1	—
France	13.5	13.6	72.9
Germany	67.9	3.7	28.4
Iceland*	0.2	93.5	—
India	76.4	21.8	1.8
Italy*	78.0	20.5	—
Japan	63.9	11.9	24.0
Korea, South	53.6	3.8	42.8
Mexico*	74.2	19.2	—
Netherlands	95.3	0.2	4.5
Nigeria	77.7	22.3	—
Norway	0.4	99.6	—
Pakistan	60.5	38.7	0.8
Poland	97.5	2.5	—
Russia	73.7	15.4	10.9
Saudi Arabia	100.0	—	—
Spain	46.1	18.2	35.3
Sweden	4.7	43.1	52.2
Taiwan	56.1	6.1	37.8
UK	76.2	1.9	21.9
USA	70.1	9.4	19.9

*The remaining contribution to national energy requirements is made by geothermally generated electricity.

HYDROELECTRIC POWER

In some countries, hydroelectric power (or hydropower) is the most important source of energy. Hydropower provides 8% of Western Europe's energy, and worldwide it provides roughly as much energy as nuclear power.

In a typical hydroelectric power plant, a river is dammed to create a reservoir that can provide a steady and controllable supply of running water. Water from the reservoir is channelled downstream to the power plant, where it causes a turbine to rotate. The turbine, in turn, drives an electric generator.

The electricity generated is then stepped up, by transformers at a substation, to the high voltages suitable for transmission. In areas where there are considerable fluctuations in electricity demand, pumped-storage plants may be installed. The surplus power available at off-peak periods is used to pump water to a separate reservoir. At peak times, the stored water is released to generate extra electrical power.

Major projects can be controversial as they may involve flooding environmentally sensitive areas. However, the latest design of low-head water turbines has reduced the necessary height difference (the 'head') between the turbine and the surface of the reservoir, making it possible to build smaller barrages or to place turbines directly into river beds.

The world's largest HEP plant is the Itaipu Dam on the Paraná River on the border of Brazil and Paraguay. It has a capacity of 12,600 MW and a planned capacity of 13,320 MW. The Turukhansk (Lower Tunguska) plant, which is under construction in Russia, will have a capacity of 20,000 MW.

Producers of hydroelectric power

	Production in 1991 (in kW-hr)
Canada	308,300,000,000
USA	289,400,000,000
Brazil	217,730,000,000
China	185,350,000,000
Russia	164,400,000,000
Norway	110,500,000,000
Japan	105,680,000,000
France	81,840,000,000
India	67,440,000,000
Sweden	63,670,000,000
Italy	45,500,000,000
Venezuela	34,300,000,000
Switzerland	33,400,000,000
Austria	32,740,000,000
North Korea	31,700,000,000
Paraguay	29,780,000,000
Spain	28,330,000,000
Colombia	27,790,000,000
Mexico	24,200,000,000
Turkey	22,750,000,000
New Zealand	21,840,000,000
Germany	21,200,000,000
Pakistan	17,370,000,000
Argentina	16,430,000,000
Australia	16,160,000,000
Romania	14,200,000,000
Kazakhstan	13,200,000,000
Finland	13,100,000,000

WIND POWER

The traditional windmill has tapped the energy of the winds for centuries. Its modern counterpart is far more sophisticated. The biggest ones have blades resembling giant aircraft propellers up to 60m (200 ft) across, and can generate 3 MW of electricity.

Two such machines provide a significant proportion of the electricity of the Orkney Islands, Scotland, and several large 'wind farms' have been built at coastal sites both in Europe and in the USA.

Another approach, pioneered in Britain, is a wind turbine with blades like a giant letter H, which rotate around a vertical axis. The mechanism of this tilts the blade tips inwards in high winds, thus regulating the supply.

SOLAR POWER

Direct solar energy is one of the simplest sources of power. Building designs, old and new, take advantage of the Sun for heating and lighting. Today, more active designs are becoming widespread. Each square metre (11⅝ sq ft) of a solar collector in northern Europe receives roughly 1000 kilowatt-hours of solar energy in the course of a year, and can use about half of this energy to heat water. A similar collector in California receives twice as much energy as this.

GEOTHERMAL POWER

Just 30 km (19 mi) beneath our feet, the rock has a temperature of around 900 °C (1650 °F). This heat comes primarily from the gradual radioactive decay of elements within the Earth. This source of power is not renewable, but it is immense. There is enough heat in the top 10 km (6 mi) of the Earth's crust, at depths accessible with current drilling techniques, to supply all our energy needs for hundreds of years.

In some parts of the world – for example, Iceland – the amount of geothermal heat reaching the surface is considerably greater than elsewhere, and can be used directly as a means of domestic heating. In other countries, blocks of flats are heated by hot water from wells 2 to 3 km (1.25 to 1.8 mi) deep.

The biggest reserves of geothermal heat, however, are to be found deeper still, at 6 km (3.75 mi) or so. As the rocks at this depth are dry, it is harder and more costly to get the heat out, because it is necessary to pump down water in order to bring the heat up. In an experimental project in Cornwall, England, three boreholes drilled to a depth of 2 km have been interconnected with a system of cracks, allowing water to be pumped from one borehole to another.

There are plans to drill holes to three times this depth, but even at current depths the water returns to the surface hot enough to produce steam to drive turbines.

Some estimates suggest that in Cornwall and other areas where the rocks are hotter at shallower depths, schemes of this kind could ultimately yield energy for Britain equivalent to 10 billion tonnes (tons) of coal.

Transport

AIRCRAFT

The term 'aircraft' includes every man-made device that flies in the atmosphere. The most important group of aircraft, called *aerodynes*, are not naturally buoyant but heavier than air. Aerodynes obtain their lift in a variety of ways: by jet thrust; by means of rotating blades; or by means of fixed wings, with a separate propulsion system to make the wings move through the air. A smaller group is the *aerostats*, which are naturally buoyant (lighter than air). Those without power are called balloons (gas-filled or hot-air), while those with propulsion and some means of steering are called airships or dirigibles.

The principle of flight

When the *weight* of an aircraft (due to the force of gravity) is exceeded by the *lift* (the upward force created by the wings or by hot air or lighter-than-air gases), the aircraft will rise in the air. In the case of aeroplanes and gliders, lift is produced as a result of the characteristic profile – the *aerofoil section* – of the wing. The wing is rounded and thicker at the front (the *leading edge*), and tapers away to a sharp edge at the back (the *trailing edge*).

Lift is created as the wings move through the air at speed and relies on the fact that air pressure drops as air speed increases. As air passes over the wing, it has to move further, and thus faster, over the more curved upper surface than the lower surface. This causes a considerable reduction in pressure above the wing, especially at the front, where the wing is thickest and the upper surface most sharply curved. Lift can be increased both by increasing the speed of airflow over the wing and by increasing the curvature of the upper wing surface.

Any aircraft with propulsion also experiences *thrust* – the resultant force pulling or pushing it through the air; and *drag* – the equal and opposite force caused by the resistance of the air to the frontal surfaces of the aircraft. Drag is effectively wasted energy, so the aim of aircraft designers is to reduce drag without sacrificing lift. Gliders, lacking an independent source of propulsion, have to fly downhill from the moment they are cast off after take-off. The pilot thus seeks columns of rising warmer air (*thermals*). Modern gliders are so efficient that they have climbed to nearly 15,000 m (49,200 ft) and flown 1460 km (907 mi).

Aircraft stability

In the absence of other forces, an aircraft's centre of gravity would have to be at the same point as its centre of lift for the craft to remain in equilibrium. In practice, however, because of thrust and drag, nearly all aeroplanes are designed to be naturally stable in the longitudinal plane, but with the centre of gravity ahead of the centre of lift. This causes a downward movement of the nose, which is counteracted by a constant download on the horizontal tail. Any disturbance tending to tilt the aircraft nose-up or nose-down is countered automatically by the change in the angle of the wings and of the horizontal tail. Today, thanks to extremely fast computers, fighter planes can be deliberately made naturally unstable. This has two advantages: instead of a download the tailplane imparts an upload, thus helping the wing instead of fighting it; and as the fighter is always trying to depart from straight flight (restrained by computers that apply restoring forces 40 or more times per second), the aircraft can be made exceptionally agile.

Aircraft controls

Aeroplanes and gliders are controlled in the longitudinal (*pitch*) axis by *elevators* on the tailplane, or by having a fully powered pivoted tailplane. A few modern designs have a foreplane instead of a tailplane, and a very few have both. Directional control is provided by a vertical *rudder*, which is usually located on the tailplane as well. The rudder is also an important control surface if a multi-engined aircraft should suffer failure of an engine mounted far out on a wing. Lateral (*roll*) control was formerly provided only by *ailerons* – pivoted portions of the trailing edge near the tips of the wings – but today roll control can be effected by asymmetric use of the tailplanes or by asymmetric deflection of *spoilers*. The spoilers are door-like surfaces hinged along the top of the wing. Differentially they control roll, and symmetrically they serve as airbrakes by increasing drag. Spoilers can also be used in *direct lift control* to enable the aircraft trajectory to be varied up or down without changing the attitude of the fuselage. On landing, spoilers act as 'lift dumpers', instantly killing wing lift and thus increasing the weight on the wheels and the effectiveness of the brakes.

All early aircraft used cables in tension or push/pull pivoted rods to convey pilot commands to the control surfaces. From about 1950 powered controls were widely introduced, in which the surfaces were moved by hydraulic actuators, the pilot's controls being provided with some form of artificial 'feel' so that he could sense what was happening. By 1970 *fly by wire* was rapidly becoming common, in which the pilot's controls send out small electrical signals, which are carried through multiple wires to the surface power units. Today *fly by light* is being introduced: pilot signals are conveyed as variable light output along optical fibres, thus offering colossal bandwidth and data-handling capacity.

The high-lift system

An aircraft has to work hardest during take-off and landing, when airspeed is at its lowest and yet maximum lift is required. To facilitate these manoeuvres, most aircraft have a *high-lift system*, brought into action for the approach and landing, and usually also for take-off. Along the leading edge of the wing there may be *slats*, slender portions of the wing moved out and away on parallel arms, or alternatively *Krüger flaps*, which swing down and around from underneath the leading edge. These full-span devices greatly increase the available lift, especially from a thin wing suitable for fast jets. Along the trailing edge are fitted *flaps*. These again come in many forms, but all swing back and down from the wing. When selected to a take-off setting, such as 15°, they increase lift and slightly increase drag; when fully down, at the landing setting of perhaps 40°, they increase lift even more but also greatly increase drag.

Aircraft propulsion

Until 1939 virtually all aeroplanes were powered by piston engines driving a *propeller*, which provides thrust by accelerating air through aerodynamic rotating blades. Almost all modern propellers are of the variable-pitch type - the angle at which the blades attack the air can be altered. The blades are set to fine pitch for take-off to match high engine speed with low aircraft speed, and then automatically adjusted to coarse pitch for cruising flight, to match economical low engine speed to high forward speed. After landing, some propellers can be set to reverse pitch to help brake the aircraft.

During and after World War II, the propeller gave way to the turbojet for most purposes. The turbojet itself was largely eclipsed by the turbofan, which offers better fuel economy and reduced noise levels.

MILESTONES IN AVIATION

1783 First manned balloon flight by the Montgolfier brothers in hot-air balloon in Paris.

1783 First hydrogen-balloon flight by the French physicist Jacques A.C. Charles. He travelled 26 km (16 miles), beginning in Paris.

1852 Henri Giffard of France manned the first flight of a mechanically-propelled airship – a *dirigible*. It measured 43m (144 ft) long and 12m (39 ft) wide.

1891 Otto Lilienthal of Germany began his controlled glider flight experiments.

1900 Count Ferdinand von Zeppelin of Germany flew the first of his rigid-frame airships. With an internal combustion engine and aluminium frame, it reached a speed of 29 kph (18 mph).

1903 The first successful flight by a 'heavier-than-air machine' by Orville and Wilbur Wright near Kitty Hawk, North Carolina, USA. During a later flight that day Wilbur Wright sustained flight for 59 seconds.

1907 Paul Cornu of France manned the first free vertical flight of a twin-rotor helicopter.

1908 The first cross-country flight of a 'heavier-than-air machine' by Henry Farman, from Mourmelons to Reims in France, in a machine using ailerons.

1909 Louis Blériot made the first cross-Channel flight, from Calais to Dover in 37 minutes.

1910 The Zeppelin airship entered commercial service in Germany.

1912 Construction of the monocoque introduced for the Deperdussin racer. The leading woman aviator of the day, Harriet Quimby, became the first woman to fly across the Channel.

1915 Start of the Zeppelin bomb raids over Great Britain. The first all-metal cantilever-wing aircraft, the German Junker J1, was built.

1919 John Alcock (English) and Arthur Brown (Scottish) made the first direct non-stop transatlantic crossing in 16 hours 27 minutes.

1923 The Spanish aviator Juan de la Cierva designed and flew the first autogyro.

1927 The American Charles Lindbergh made the first solo transatlantic flight, from New York to Paris.

1930 The jet engine was patented by Frank Whittle in Britain. It used a gas turbine for jet propulsion.

1935 The Douglas DC-3 'Dakota' – conceived as an airliner – made its maiden flight.

1936 The first entirely successful helicopter, Heinrich Focke's Fa-61, made its maiden flight.

1937 The world's largest airship, the *Hindenburg*, burst into flames in New Jersey, USA, ending the age of airship travel. The first flight of the US Lockheed XC-35, the first fully pressurized aircraft.

1939 The German Heinkel He-178 was the first aircraft to fly solely on the power of a turbojet engine. Igor Sikorsky designed the prototype modern helicopter, with a single main rotor and a small tail rotor.

1947 The American Bell X-1 exceeded the speed of sound in level flight.

1949 The De Havilland Comet became the first jet airliner. It entered service in 1952.

1954 The first experimental flight of vertical take-off aircraft.

1958 The first US jet airliner - the Boeing 707 – entered commercial service.

1964 First flight by the USAF Lockheed SR-71, reconnaissance aircraft which is the world's fastest jet. (It achieved an airspeed record of 3529·5 km/h – 2193·17 mph – on 28 July 1976.)

1967 Computer guidance systems were fitted into aircraft for the first time. The Autoland blind landing system was introduced into service in Britain.

1968 The first flight of the Soviet supersonic airliner, the Tupolev Tu-144.

1969 The Anglo-French supersonic airliner, Concorde, made its maiden flight. The first operational V/STOL (vertical/short take-off and landing) aircraft – the Harrier ('jump jet') – entered service with the Royal Air Force.

1970 The Boeing 747 became the first wide-bodied 'jumbo' jet to enter service.

1973 The MB-E1, the first electrically propelled aircraft, made its maiden flight.

1976 The supersonic airliner Concorde entered commercial service.

1977 The US *Gossamer Condor* became the first successful heavier-than-air human-powered aircraft.

1979 The first man-powered flight across the Channel is made by *Gossamer Albatross*.

1981 At the average speed of 48 kph (30 mph), Stephen Ptacek flew the *Solar Challenger* across the Channel, powered only by solar cells.

1989 The Bell-Boeing V-22 Osprey flew for the first time. Its tilt rotor concept combines the advantages of the aeroplane with those of the helicopter.

1991 The Stealth bomber used in the Gulf War. The low flat design of the aircraft has been successful in avoiding detection by radar.

MAIN COMMERCIAL AIRCRAFT IN AIRLINE SERVICE

Name of aircraft*	Nationality	Wingspan	Length	Max. cruising speed	Range with max. payload	Max. takeoff weight	Max. seating capacity
Boeing 737 (300)	USA	28.88 m *(94 ft 9 in)*	33.40 m *(109 ft 7 in)*	908 kph *(491 knots)*	4973 km *(2685 naut miles)*	62,882 kg *(138,500 lb)*	128
Boeing 727	USA	32.92 m *(108 ft 0 in)*	46.69 m *(153 ft 2 in)*	964 kph *(520 knots)*	3966 km *(2140 naut miles)*	92,025 kg *(209,500 lb)*	189
McDonnell Douglas MD-80	USA	32.87 m *(107ft 10 in)*	45.06 m *(147 ft 10 in)*	855 kph *(478 knots)*	2896 kph1 *(1563 naut miles)*	63,500 kg *(140,000 lb)*	172
Boeing 747 (300 and 400)	USA	64.31 m *(211 ft 0 in)*	70.66 m *(231 ft 10 in)*	985 kph *(532 knots)*	13,528 km[2] *(7300 naut miles)*	394,625 kg *(870,000 lb)*	660
McDonnell Douglas DC-9 (Series 40 and 50)	USA	28.47 m *(93 ft 5 in)*	36.37 m *(119 ft 3 in)*	929 kph *(501 knots)*	3326 km *(1796 naut miles)*	54,885 kg *(121,000 lb)*	139
Boeing 757	USA	38.05 m *(124 ft 10 in)*	47.32 m *(155 ft 3 in)*	914 kph *(493 knots)*	5150 km[3] *(2780 naut miles)*	115,670 kg *(255,000 lb)*	239
Boeing 767 (300)	USA	45.57 m *(156 ft 1 in)*	54.94 m *(180 ft 3 in)*	900 kph *(486 knots)*	7415 km *(4000 naut miles)*	159,210 kg *(351,000 lb)*	290
Fokker F27 Friendship	Netherlands	29.00 m *(95 ft 2 in)*	23.56 m *(77 ft 3 in)*	480 kph *(259 knots)*	2070 km *(1285 naut miles)*	20,410 kg *(45,000 lb)*	44
Airbus A320	International	34.09 m *(111 ft 9 in)*	37.57 m *(123 ft 3 in)*	903 kph *(487 knots)*	5430 km[4] *(2930 naut miles)*	73,500 kg *(162,040 lb)*	179
McDonnell Douglas DC-10	USA	50.40 m *(165 ft 4 in)*	55.50 m *(182 ft 1 in)*	908 kph *(490 knots)*	7413 km *(4000 naut miles)*	259,450 kg *(572,000 lb)*	380
Airbus A300	International	44.84 m *(147 ft 1 in)*	54.08 m *(177 ft 5 in)*	897 kph *(484 knots)*	9450 km[5] *(5100 naut miles)*	171,700 kg *(378,535 lb)*	375
De Havilland DHC-8 (300)	Canada	27.43 m *(90 ft 0 in)*	25.68 m *(84 ft 3 in)*	528 kph *(285 knots)*	1482 km[6] *(800 naut miles)*	19,505 kg *(43,000 lb)*	56
Boeing 707	USA	44.42 m *(145 ft 9 in)*	46.61 m *(152 ft 11 in)*	973 kph *(525 knots)*	9265 km[7] *(5000 naut miles)*	151,315 kg *(333,600 lb)*	219
McDonnell Douglas DC-8	USA	45.23 m *(148 ft 5 in)*	57.12 m *(187 ft 5 in)*	887 kph *(479 knots)*	8950 km *(4830 naut miles)*	161,025 kg *(355,000 lb)*	269
BAC One-eleven	UK	28.50 m *(93 ft 6 in)*	32.61 m *(107 ft 0in)*	871 kph *(470 knots)*	2744 km *(1480 naut miles)*	47,400 kg *(104,500 lb)*	119
BAC Aérospatiale Concorde	International	25.56 m *(83 ft 10 in)*	62.10 m *(203 ft 9 in)*	2179 kph *(1176 knots)*	6230 km *(3360 naut miles)*	185,065 kg *(408,000 lb)*	128

*Scheduled and non-circulated services including all-freight. Specifications apply to version in brackets.
Includes following number of passengers: 1115, 2412, 3186, 4150, 5269, 650, 7147, 78147.

WORLD'S MAJOR AIRPORTS

Airport name and location	*Terminal passengers (000)*	*International passengers (000)*	*Air transport movements (000)*	*Cargo (000 tonnes)*
O'Hare International, Chicago, USA	64,441*	5224*	822·5	846·4*
Dallas/Fort Worth Regional, USA	51,944*	2876*	747·9*	430·0*
Los Angeles International, USA	46,965*	11,456*	600·4*	1090·0*
Heathrow Airport, London, UK	44,968	38,257	388·2	754·8
Tokyo International (Haneda), Japan	42,639	n.a.	n.a.	489·7
Hartsfield International, Atlanta, USA	42,033	n.a.	595·9	464·0
San Francisco International, USA	31,789*	4,214*	385·4*	438·2*
Stapleton International, Denver, USA	30,877	n.a.	471·7	n.a.
Frankfurt International, Germany	30,085	23,711	324·6	1053·9
John F. Kennedy International, NY, USA	27,761*	15,110*	304·1*	1203·3*
Miami International, USA	26,484*	11,514*	405·6*	941·3*
Orly, Paris, France	25,009	9923	205·9	275·3
Charles de Gaulle, Paris, France	24,770	22,444	289·8	612·2
Newark International, NY, USA	24,287*	3316*	389·1*	523·1*
Osaka International, Japan	23,457	n.a.	n.a.	434·9
Logan International, Boston, USA	22,989*	3571*	451·4*	316·2*
Minneapolis–St Paul International, USA	22,907	n.a.	354·5	n.a.
Metropolitan, Detroit, USA	22,841*	1856*	373·3*	156·4*
Hong Kong International	22,061	22,061	121·4	956·9
Honolulu International, Oahu, USA	21,290*	5454*	261·3*	338·2
Kimpo International, Korea Republic	21,231	9800	145·7	959·7
Lambert International, St Louis, USA	20,985	n.a.	382·3	n.a.
New Tokyo International (Narita), Japan	19,996	19,022	119·2	1301·4
Gatwick, London, UK	19,841	18,690	175.5	190·2
La Guardia Airport, NY, USA	19,663*	1183*	308·6*	57·4*
Fiumicino, Rome, Italy	18,734*	9873*	188·9*	231·0*†
Schiphol, Amsterdam, Netherlands	18,714	18,609	238·8	695·0
Barajas, Madrid, Spain	18,097	8477	181·7	188·4
Seattle-Tacoma, USA	17,962*	1500*	336·9*	282·8*
Toronto International (Lester Pearson), Canada	17,911	9553	304·8	299·9
Changi, Singapore	16,882	16,882	125·5	719·0
Philadelphia International, USA	15,987*	1133*	331·2*	290·8*
Bangkok International, Thailand	14,857	11,281	128·1	438·4
Kingsford International, Sydney, Australia	14,252*	4,500*	198·5*	282·6*
Benito Juarez, Mexico City	14,168*	3,888*	192·6*	141·5
Arlanda, Stockholm, Sweden	12,881	6376	220·0	87·3
Zürich, Switzerland	12,717	12,007	191·5	271·5
Kastrup, Copenhagen, Denmark	12,148*	9,699*	208·3*	146·1*
Düsseldorf, Germany	12,076	9098	144·5	47·4

The figures given (for 1992) are the latest available. * Provisional/estimate figures; † 1991 figures

Most air cargo

Airports in the following sovereign states have the greatest amount of air cargo per annum.

	Air cargo (in tonnes)
USA	18,597,000,000
Japan	13,233,000,000
France	6,687,000,000
Canada	5,210,000,000
Germany	4,473,000,000
Taiwan	4,275,000,000
Russia	4,022,000,000
South Korea	2,664,000,000
Brazil	2,525,000,000
United Kingdom	2,389,000,000
Singapore	2,306,000,000
Netherlands	2,303,000,000
Australia	2,065,000,000
Italy	1,953,000,000
Mexico	1,726,000,000
China	1,350,000,000
Slovenia	1,216,000,000
Switzerland	1,063,000,000
Colombia	945,000,000
Thailand	926,000,000
Luxembourg	886,000,000
Israel	831,000,000
Norway	783,000,000
Malaysia	740,000,000
India	663,000,000
Spain	621,000,000
Chile	529,000,000
Belgium	486,000,000
Indonesia	460,000,000

MAJOR WORLD AIRLINES

Airline	*Passenger km* (000)	*Aircraft km* (000)	*Passengers carried*	*Total no. of aircraft*
American Airlines, USA	156,736,645	1,397,521	86,007,078	672
United Airlines, USA	148,841,416	1,116,941	66,596,466	536
Delta Air Lines, USA	129,541,081	1,196,203	83,117,228	554
Aeroflot, Russia	116,346,800	n.a.	62,088,700	108
Northwest Airlines, USA	94,345,003	748,349	43,541,885	372
British Airways, UK	72,491,376	400,260	25,377,732	226
Continental Airlines, USA	69,317,377	658,960	38,358,109	328
USAir, USA	56,482,045	760,863	54,654,575	438
Japan Airlines, (JAL), Japan	55,089,930	257,515	24,005,310	103
Lufthansa, Germany	48,660,520	419,204	26,918,512	219
Trans World Airlines (TWA), USA	46,689,405	363,859	22,454,914	168
All Nippon Airways, (ANA), Japan	38,310,188	173,576	35,129,234	103
Singapore Airlines, Singapore	37,104,900	160,534	8,512,000	54
Air France, France	37,034,221	283,711	13,753,604	139
KLM, Netherlands	31,054,024	189,605	8,250,111	63
Qantas Airways, Australia	30,843,158	145,532	4,850,446	50
Cathay Pacific, Hong Kong	27,465,906	118,830	8,338,911	48
Alitalia, Italy	27,389,846	214,445	19,687,941	135
Iberia, Spain	23,857,384	195,115	15,411,440	116
Korean Air Lines, South Korea	21,995,412	97,910	15,066,224	85
Air Canada, Canada	21,453,559	209,880	9,463,226	102
Thai Airways, Thailand	20,426,790	114,656	8,546,792	61

The figures given (for 1992) are the latest available.

Most airports

The following sovereign states have the greatest number of airports with scheduled flights

	Number of airports
USA	834
Australia	441
Indonesia	118
Brazil	110
Canada	106
Papua New Guinea	101
India	98
China	86
Japan	71
France	64
Colombia	63
Russia	58
Mexico	54
United Kingdom	53
Madagascar	50
Argentina	49

The following sovereign states do not have an airport receiving scheduled flights:

Andorra, Liechtenstein, San Marino, and the Vatican City. In early 1995, none of the airports in either Somalia or Bosnia-Herzegovina received any scheduled flights

Most air passengers

Airports in the following sovereign states have the greatest number of air passenger-km on scheduled flights per annum.

	Number of pasenger-km
USA	765,132,000,000
Russia	153,000,000,000
Germany	101,082,000,000
Japan	95,383,000,000
United Kingdom	87,208,000,000
Canada	47,413,000,000
China	39,900,000,000
Singapore	37,105,000,000
Australia	37,045,000,000
Taiwan	33,645,000,000
France	32,567,000,000
Brazil	27,832,000,000
Netherlands	27,576,000,000
Spain	27,240,000,000
Italy	21,697,000,000
Thailand	20,498,000,000
South Korea	19,957,000,000
Mexico	17,444,000,000
India	16,518,000,000
Switzerland	16,154,000,000
Saudi Arabia	16,068,000,000
Malaysia	14,929,000,000
Indonesia	14,919,000,000
Philippines	12,891,000,000
Kazakhstan	12,600,000,000
New Zealand	10,632,000,000

DISTANCE IN KILOMETRES BETWEEN AIRPORTS

	Athens	Bahrain	Bangkok	Bombay	Buenos Aires	Cairo	Chicago	Copenhagen	Frankfurt	Hong Kong	Johannesburg	Karachi	Lagos	Lima	London	Madrid	Manila	Mexico City	Montreal	Moscow	Nairobi	New York	Paris	Peking (Beijing)	Rio de Janeiro	Rome	San Francisco	Singapore	Sydney	Tehran	Tokyo	Vancouver
Athens		2829	7916	5164	11699	1117	8758	2136	1807	8541	7131	4320	4043	11762	2414	2359	9637	11274	7616	2251	4564	7914	2093	7617	9704	1047	10918	9053	15315	2458	9543	9792
Bahrain	2829		5358	2411	13293	1929		4461	4437	6389	6297	1661	5457	14333	5090	5185	7364	13963		3467	3399	10614	4822	6182	11460	3862		6326	12504	1048	8314	
Bangkok	7916	5358		3008	16877	7249		8601	8963	1719	8989	3701	10604	19676	9540	10157	2199	15717	13378	7069	7207	13912	9433	3296	16073	8814	12730	1443	7538	5457	4642	11782
Bombay	5164	2411	3008		14935	4339	12934		6564	4298		876	7617		7207	7512	5132		12069	5047	4529	12523	6999	4763		6160		3917	10152	2803	6782	
Buenos Aires	11699	13293	16877	14935		11844	9043	12086	11494	18443	8109	14716	7932	3151	11129	10079	11745	7391	9051	13488	10411	8528	11062	19277	1996	11170	10395	15867	11760	13781	18285	11297
Cairo	1117	1929	7249	4339	11844		9866	3197	2922	8123	6258	3556	3927	12435	3531	3349	9162	12363	8722	2913	3540	9009	3204	7530	9893	2125	11994	8255	14395	1955	9588	10835
Chicago	8758			12934	9043	9866		6849	6966		14009				6343		13062	2718	1198	7968		1187	6665	10554		7734		15039	14857		10067	2828
Copenhagen	2136	4461	8601		12086	3197	6849		678	8662	9204	5537	5511	11086	982	2058	9780	9507	5799	1539	6699	6184	1035	7191	10178	1535	8801	9959	16031	3657	8706	7657
Frankfurt	1807	4437	8963	6564	11494	2922	6966	678		9165	8684	5690	4853	10717	654	1420	10290	9545	5851	2021	6312	6185	471	7783	9560	966	9142	10270	16484	3765	9360	8057
Hong Kong	8541	6389	1719	4298	18443	8123		8662	9165		10694	4775	11835	18344	9640	10519	1125	14122	12425	7149	8750	12956	9627	1985	17687	9271	11097	2576	7374	6186	2936	10245
Johannesburg	7131	6297	8989		8109	6258	14009	9204	8684	10694		7041	4522	10901	9068	8097	10975	14588	12962	9164	2910	12822	8707	11699	7146	7718	16966	8649	11019	7283	13513	
Karachi	4320	1661	3701	876	14716	3556		5537	5690	4775	7041				6334	6658	5716		11241	4202	4367	11675	6128	4862	13004	5303	12983	4736	11003	1930	6969	11706
Lagos	4043	5457	10604	7617	7932	3927		5511	4853	11835	4522				5209	3827			8498	6251	3828	8440	4685	11455	6022	4018		11160		5850	13506	11938
Lima	11762	14333	19676		3151	12435		11086	10717	18344	10901				10143	9520		4241	6419	12620		5861	10248	16605	3776	10834	7255	18812			15413	8154
London	2414	5090	9540	7207	11129	3531	6343	982	654	9640	9068	6334	5000	10143		1244	10759	8901	5213	2506	6830	5536	365	8148	9245	1460	8610	10873	17008	4411	9585	7574
Madrid	2359	5185	10157	7512	10079	3349		2058	1420	10519	8097	6658	3827	9520	1244		11644	9063	5550	3418	6189	5758	1031	9199	8140	1360		11373	17661	4753	10764	8422
Manila	9637	7364	2199	5132	11745	9162	13062	9780	10290	1125	10975	5716			10759	11644		14218		8273	9401	13686	10752	2873	18107	10390	11221	2373	6258	7247	2993	
Mexico City	11274	13963	15717		7391	12363	2718	9507	9545	14122	14588			4241	8901	9063	14218		3712	10683		3366	9195	12427	7661		3027	16587	12978		11247	3940
Montreal	7616		13378	12069	9051	8722	1198	5799	5851	12425	12962	11241	8498	6419	5213	5550		3712		7036	11701	536	5523	10440	8189	6605	4072	14794	16011	9433	10384	3679
Moscow	2251	3467	7069	5047	13488	2913	7968	1539	2021	7149	9164	4202	6251	12620	2506	3418	8273	10683	7036		6366	7477	2479	5802	11526	2397		8443	6313	2486	7502	8180
Nairobi	4564	3399	7207	4529	10411	3540		6699	6312	8750	2910	4367	3828		6830	6189	9401		11701	6366		11828	6475	9219	8937	5380	15446	7456	12128	4374	11296	
New York	7914	10614	13912	12523	8528	9009	1187	6184	6185	12956	12822	11675	8440	5861	5536	5758	13686	3366	536	7477	11828		5829	10971	7723	6886	4149	15329	16002	9839	10824	3926
Paris	2093	4822	9433	6999	11062	3204	6665	1035	471	9627	8707	6128	4685	10248	365	1031	10752	9195	5523	2479	6475	5829		8214	9144	1100	8971	10728	16954	4198	9736	7938
Peking (Beijing)	7617	6182	3296	4763	19277	7530	10554	7191	7783	1985	11699	4862	11455	16605	8148	9199	2873	12427	10440	5802	9219	10971	8214		17302	8120		4486		5617	2132	8487
Rio de Janeiro	9704	11460	16073		1996	9893		10178	9560	17687	7146	13004	6022	3776	9245	8140	18107	7661	8189	11526	8937	7723	9144	17302		9186	10633	15738	13516		18519	11206
Rome	1047	3862	8814	6160	11170	2125	7734	1535	966	9271	7718	5303	4018	10834	1460	1360	10390		6605	2397	5380	6886	1100	8120	9186		10052	10010	16302	3396	9880	9007
San Francisco	10918		12730		10395	11994		8801	9142	11097	16966	12983		7255	8610		11221	3027	4072		15446	4149	8971		10633	10052		13579	11941	11829	8222	1286
Singapore	9053	6326	1443	3917	15867	8255	15039	9959	10270	2576	8649	4736	11160	18812	10873	11373	2373	16587	14794	8443	7455	15329	10728	4486	15738	10010	13579		6296	6615	5361	12811
Sydney	15315	12504	7538	10152	11760	14395	14857	16031	16484	7374	11019	11003			17008	17661	6258	12978	16011	6313	12128	16022	16954		13516	16302	11941	6296		12909	7826	12492
Tehran	2458	1048	5457	2803	13781	1955		3657	3765	6186	7283	1930	5850		4411	4753	7247		9433	2486	4374	9839	4198	5617		3396	11829	6615	12909		7713	10556
Tokyo	9543	8314	4642	6782	18285	9588	10067	8706	9360	2936	13513	6969	13506	15413	9585	10764	2993	11247	10384	7502	11296	10824	9736	2132	18519	9880	8222	5361	7826	7713		7500
Vancouver	9792		11782		11297	10835	2828	7657	8057	10245		11706	11938	8154	7574	8422		3940	3679	8180		3926	7938	8487	11206	9007	1286	12811	12492	10556	7500	

MOTOR VEHICLES

The engine is the power unit of a car, providing the motion that is ultimately transmitted to the driven wheels. However, a series of interconnected mechanisms, including the clutch, the gearbox and the differential, is required to transmit the power of the engine to the wheels in a usable form. At the same time, a number of subsidiary systems, including steering and brakes, are necessary in order to give adequate control over the movement of the car.

Most cars today are fitted with an overhead-valve, four-stroke petrol engine, with four or six cylinders linked to the crankshaft. The crankshaft also drives a camshaft, which opens and closes the valves at the top of each cylinder in the correct sequence. The four cylinders fire in turn so there is a power stroke for every half-revolution of the crankshaft.

Although the primary function of the engine is to spin the flywheel – the first link in the chain that transmits the engine's power to the wheels – the rotary motion of the crankshaft is also used to turn the *alternator*, which generates the current for the car's electrical systems. At the same time, the rotation of the camshaft drives both the oil pump and the distributor.

The ignition system

The purpose of the ignition system is to produce a spark of sufficient strength to ignite the petrol-air mixture at the exact moment when each piston in turn is nearly at the top of the compression stroke. The spark is produced as an electric current jumps (arcs) between the two electrodes of a spark plug; however, the voltage supplied by the battery is insufficient for this purpose.

The voltage from the battery is first boosted by the *coil* to around 15,000 volts before passing to the *distributor*, in which a spinning rotor (driven by the camshaft) directs the current to each spark plug in turn.

The fuel system

For efficient and economical combustion within the engine, the precise proportions of petrol and air in the fuel mixture entering the cylinders must be carefully regulated. This is generally achieved by a *carburettor*. Although different types of carburettor exist, nearly all are in the form of a tube into which air is drawn by the downward movement of the pistons on their successive induction strokes. As the air accelerates through the narrowed middle section of the carburettor, its pressure falls, so causing a jet of fuel to be drawn through a nozzle from a reservoir, which is itself fed by a pump from the petrol tank.

Within the carburettor, on the engine-side of the fuel jet, a circular flap (known as a butterfly valve) is actuated by the accelerator pedal in such a way as to control the volume of air-fuel mixture drawn into the engine, thus regulating engine speed. In most designs, a similar valve (the *choke*) on the air-intake side of the fuel jet regulates the amount of air entering the carburettor and thus the richness of the fuel mix.

Increasingly, direct *fuel-injection* is being used in place of the carburettor. This is more efficient and economical than the carburettor, since accurately metered and appropriate amounts of fuel can be delivered to each cylinder's combustion chamber. There are several systems – both mechanical and electrical – but the basic principle is that fuel is injected at high pressure into the combustion chamber from a point behind the inlet valve.

Transmission

The term 'transmission' embraces all the components that are responsible for transferring the engine's power from the flywheel to the driven wheels. The spinning motion of the flywheel is transmitted to the *gearbox* via the *clutch* (see diagram). When the clutch pedal is depressed, the spinning flywheel is disconnected from the shaft transmitting power to the gearbox, so allowing the car to move off gently and smooth gear-changes to be made.

A gearbox is necessary because – unlike (say) an electric motor – most internal-combustion engines develop their full power and torque (turning effort) within a relatively narrow band of engine speeds (usually between 3000 and 5000 revolutions per minute). By means of the gearbox (and partly by the differential; see below), the engine speed is kept within these limits while allowing the car to operate at widely varying speeds and in a wide range of driving conditions.

For example, a steep hill requires a low gear, because it is only at high engine speeds that the engine is able to deliver enough torque to keep the wheels turning. On the other hand, where little torque is required, as when travelling at speed on a level road, a high gear may be used, thus matching high road speed with (relatively) low engine speed. In this way engine life is prolonged, passenger comfort enhanced and fuel consumption kept to a minimum.

After passing through the gearbox-and-clutch assembly, the drive is transferred to the *differential*. In front-wheel-drive cars, transmission from gearbox to differential is direct; in rear-wheel-drive cars, if the engine is mounted at the front of the car, the differential is driven by a crown wheel and pinion at the end of a propeller shaft. The rotation rate of the shaft from the gearbox is further stepped down by the differential (normally to about a quarter of the gearbox speed). However, the differential's distinctive function is to allow power to be divided between the driven wheels in whatever proportion is required. Such a mechanism is necessary when cornering, because the outside driven wheel needs to be turned more rapidly than the inside wheel.

MOTORING MILESTONES

1885 Karl Benz produced the prototype of the automobile using an internal combustion motor.

1885–1886 Gottlieb Daimler patented his gas engine, using it first on a motorcycle and then on a four-wheeled vehicle.

1895 Pneumatic tyres – invented in 1888 – were adapted for use on motor vehicles.

The first motor car race was held, from Paris to Bordeaux and back.

1896 Henry Ford built his first car.

Clutch-and-gearbox assembly. The clutch consists of the flywheel (driven round by the crankshaft), a clutch (or friction) plate and a pressure plate. When the clutch is engaged (i.e. with the pedal released), powerful springs force the clutch plate against the flywheel, thereby linking the flywheel to the shaft transmitting power to the gearbox. When the clutch is disengaged, levers work against the springs to separate the clutch plate from the flywheel, so disconnecting the transmission. The friction linings on the clutch plate allow the plate to slip before becoming fully engaged, so preventing a shuddering jerk on starting.

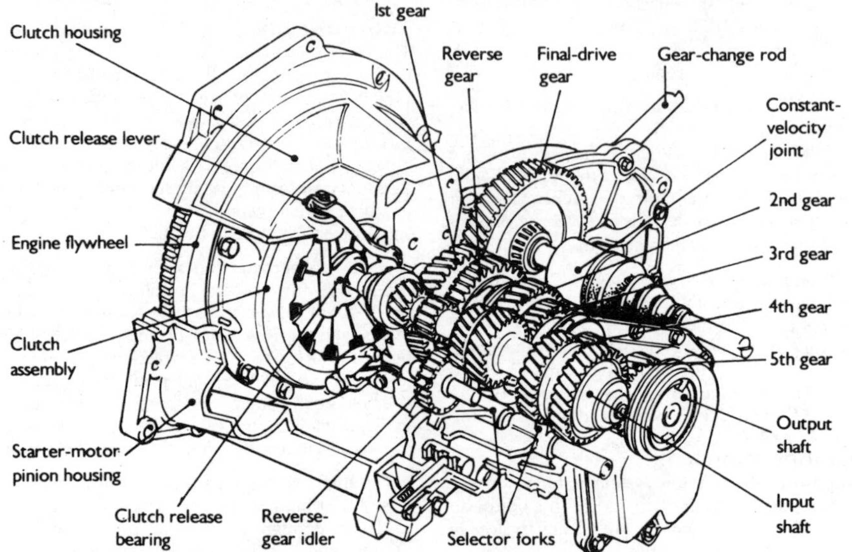

The gearbox allows optimum (i.e. high) engine speed to be matched to a wide variety of driving conditions. By means of selector forks actuated by the gearstick, different-sized gears linked to the input shaft can be engaged with different-sized gears on the shaft transmitting power to the differential. A (relatively) small gear on the input shaft engaged with a large gear on the transmission shaft produces low speed but high power; high speed and low power are achieved by reversing the gear ratios on the input and output shafts. In top gear, no gears are engaged and transmission passes directly through the gearbox to the differential.

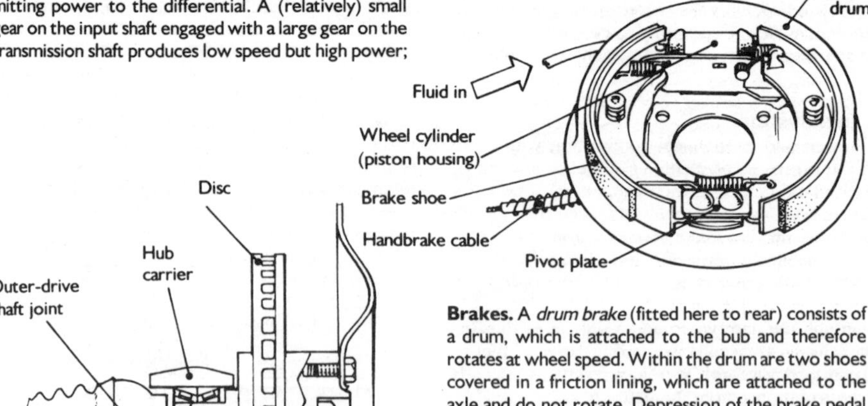

Brakes. A *drum brake* (fitted here to rear) consists of a drum, which is attached to the bub and therefore rotates at wheel speed. Within the drum are two shoes covered in a friction lining, which are attached to the axle and do not rotate. Depression of the brake pedal operates a hydraulic system that actuates a piston, which forces the shoes outwards and thus against the inner surface of the drum.

A *disc brake* (fitted here to front) consists of a steel disc, which is attached to the wheel and rotates at wheel speed. A hydraulic system operated by the brake pedal actuates a piston housed in a stationary calliper that straddles the disc, causing two brake pads to be forced onto each side of the disc. As with the drum brake, the resulting friction causes the car to slow down.

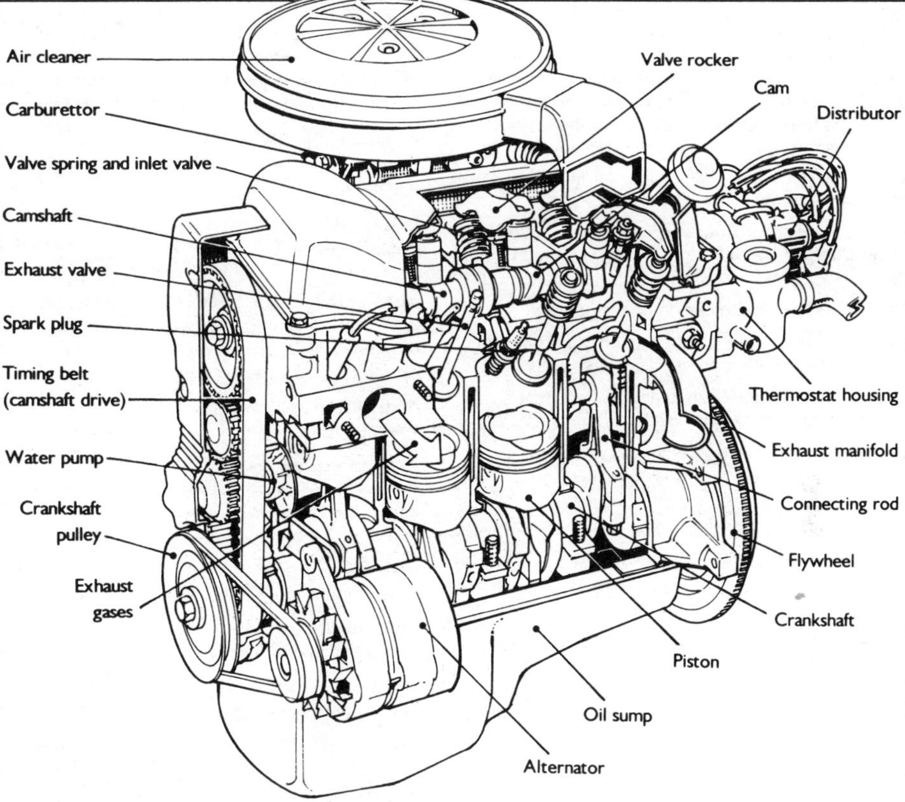

Engine. Four pistons fit tightly in four cylinders bored into the cylinder block. Each piston is driven downwards in a fixed sequence on the power stroke of the four-stroke cycle. A *connecting rod* from each cylinder is attached to a cranked (dog-legged) shaft (*the crankshaft*), which is turned a half-revolution by each successive power stroke. To one end of the crankshaft is bolted a heavy disc called *the flywheel*, which provides the drive to the gearbox via the clutch; at the other end, a belt-and-pulley system causes *the camshaft* to rotate at half the speed of the crankshaft. Pear-shaped lobes (*cams*) along the length of the camshaft act on a series of rocker mechanisms that cause the inlet and exhaust valves on each cylinder to open and close in exact timing with the four strokes of the piston.

Rack-and-pinion steering is a simple and effective system used in many cars. A toothed pinion at the base of the steering column acts on a toothed rack, moving it to left or right and thus converting the rotary motion of the steering wheel into linear motion. At each end of the rack, track rods act on pivoted steering arms, so altering the angle of the front wheels.

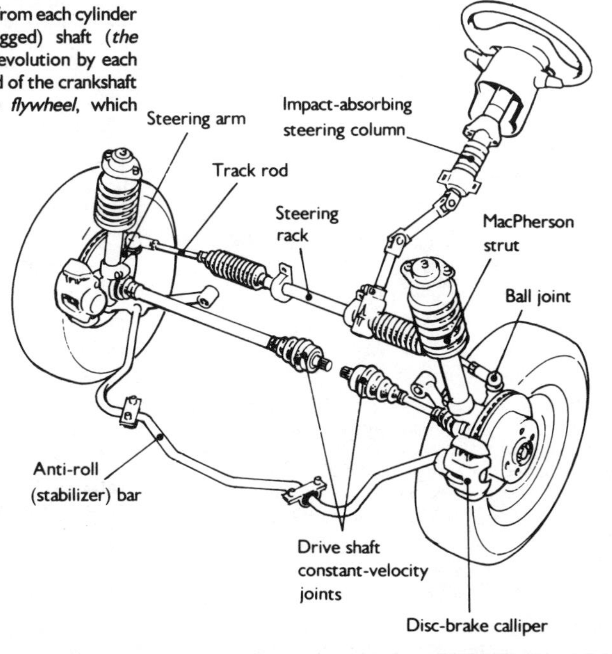

1903 The Ford Motor Company was founded by Henry Ford.

1906 Rolls-Royce began the production of the 'Silver Ghost'. A seven-litre, six-cylinder luxury tourer, it was capable of travelling considerable distances with complete reliability.

1908 The Ford Motor Company introduced the first production-line car – the Model T Ford.

1922 Independent front suspension was introduced in the Lambda, but was not in general use until after 1945.

1920s Mercedes pioneered supercharging.

1934 Citroën made the first car with front-wheel drive and independent front-wheel suspension.

1936 The first diesel-engined production car, the Mercedes-Benz 260D, was launched.

1940 The Jeep, the first vehicle to realize the potential of four-wheel drive, was launched.

1959 Austin Morris launched the Mini Minor, which profoundly influenced the design of all subsequent small cars.

1966 Electronic fuel-injection systems were developed in Britain.

1980 The Audi Quattro, the first mass-produced saloon car with four-wheel drive, was launched.

1980s Many countries introduced legislation to enforce or encourage the use of catalytic converters in cars to detoxify some of the harmful substances in the exhaust gases.

CAR GLOSSARY

air cleaner a filter, usually of paper, to remove dust from the air and to protect the engine.

anti-lock braking a system of braking which incorporates electronic (or other) means to stop a wheel from locking up and sliding under heavy braking. A major cause of accidents in slippery conditions is due to wheel lock-up.

alternator a device that generates electricity to recharge the battery.

anti-roll bar a device to limit roll on cornering.

cam an eccentric shape on the camshaft which operates rockers as the shaft rotates.

camshaft the shaft which operates valves through a series of cams along its length.

carburettor a device for mixing air and fuel in correct proportions.

catalytic converter a device which is installed in the exhaust system containing a catalyst (benign chemical). Exhaust emissions passing over the catalyst are converted into water, carbon dioxide and nitrogen (see exhaust emissions, below). Catalytic converters can only work with cars that are using unleaded fuel.

chassis the term used to describe the complete car except the body.

choke the device that regulates the amount of air entering the carburettor and thus the richness of the fuel mixture, which allows for easier starting in cold weather.

connecting rod a link which transmits the force of the burning fuel from the piston to the crankshaft.

constant-velocity joints joints which are used on front-wheel-drive cars to provide smooth power when cornering.

crankshaft a shaft with one or more cranks. Reciprocal motion of the pistons is converted to rotary motion through cranks (dog-legs) on the shaft.

differential an assembly of gears within the driving axle which allows one powered wheel to travel at a different speed from the other powered wheel, for example when a car goes around a bend.

distributor a device for directing high voltage to spark plugs.

exhaust emissions pollutants that are released with exhaust gas from a car. The most environmentally damaging are hydrocarbons, carbon monoxide, and oxides of nitrogen.

exhaust manifold tubes which gather exhaust from the cylinders and direct it into the exhaust pipe.

fan belt the belt that drives a cooling fan together with a dynamo or alternator in the car engine.

flywheel a wheel whose action smooths out the uneven operation of the engine.

four-wheel drive a type of vehicle designed to transmit engine power to the road via all four wheels instead of the more usual two wheels.

front-wheel drive a type of vehicle designed to transmit engine power to the road via the front wheels.

fuel-injection an efficient method of injecting the fuel mixture into the engine instead of causing it to be drawn in, as with a carburettor.

oil sump the reservoir of oil which flows through main bearings.

piston a cylindrical part or a disc that slides to and fro inside a hollow cylinder. In a car, the piston fits tight in the cylinder and transmits pressure of burning fuel mixture.

spark plug the source of the spark which ignites the fuel mixture inside the cylinder.

thermostat a device which closes off the radiator of the car when the engine is cold, to reduce the warming-up time.

timing belt the link between the crankshaft and the camshaft. The timing belt ensures that the valves open at right moment.

valve rocker a lever arrangement for transmitting force from the camshaft to the valves.

valve spring a spring which is used to close the valve through which fuel enters the engine, or exhaust gases leave it.

water pump a pump which circulates cooling water through the radiator and cylinder block.

ROAD TRANSPORT

All countries, no matter how small, have a road system, although only the states of the developed world have motorways and similar multi-lane highways. In the developing world, the greater part of the road system is not paved.

Longest road lengths

	Total road length	
	km	*mi*
USA	6,243,163	3,879,322
India	2,037,000	1,266,000
Brazil	1,670,148	1,037,780
Japan	1,115,609	693,206
China	1,041,136	646,931
Russia	884,000	549,000
Canada	825,743	513,092
Australia	810,264	503,474
France	810,000	503,300
Germany	621,267	386,037
Turkey	367,608	228,421
Poland	365,365	227,027
United Kingdom	358,034	222,472
Spain	331,961	206,271
Italy	303,906	188,838
Indonesia	266,326	165.487
Mexico	242,294	150,554
Argentina	211,369	131,338
Bangladesh	193,283	120,100
South Africa	182,329	113,294
Ukraine	168,979	104,998
Kazakhstan	164,900	102,500
Philippines	160,560	99,767
Romania	153,014	95,099
Iran	151,488	94,130

Shortest road lengths

Sovereign countries only

	Total road length	
	km	*mi*
Vatican City	>2	<1
Tuvalu	8	5
Nauru	16	10
Monaco	50	31
Micronesia	226	140
San Marino	237	147

Percentage of paved roads

Sovereign countries with the lowest percentage of paved roads.

	Percentage of paved roads
Chad	1
Central African Republic	2
North Korea	2
Mongolia	2
Bangladesh	4
Bolivia	4
Guinea	4
Tanzania	4
Kiribati	5
Papua New Guinea	6
Cameroon	7
Côte d'Ivoire	7
Rwanda	7
Colombia	8
Mali	8
Niger	8
Solomon Islands	8

In Austria, the Czech Republic, Denmark, Israel, Italy, Jordan, Kuwait, Liechtenstein, Monaco, Nauru, the Vatican City, and the United Kingdom all roads are classed as 'paved'.

Number of cars

Sovereign countries with the highest number of cars.

	Number of cars
USA	142,956,000
Japan	37,076,000
Germany	35,512,000
Italy	28,200,000
France	23,810,000
United Kingdom	19,742,000
Canada	12,811,000
Spain	12,537,000
Brazil	12,128,000
Russia	8,964,000
Australia	7,734,000
Mexico	6,819,000
Poland	6,112,000
Netherlands	5,658,000
Argentina	4,088,000
Belgium	3,970,000
Sweden	3,589,000
South Africa	3,404,000
Austria	3,101,000
Switzerland	3,086,000
Taiwan	3,034,000
Ukraine	2,920,000
South Korea	2,728,000
Czech Republic	2,436,000
India	2,391,000
Saudi Arabia	2,350,000
Hungary	2,016,000
Malaysia	2,000,000

Sovereign countries with the lowest number of cars.

	Number of cars
Kiribati	300
Tuvalu	under 500
Maldives	600
Marshall Islands	800
Tonga	1000
Solomon Islands	1400
São Tomé and Principe	1800
Western Samoa	2500
Bhutan	2600

Sovereign countries in which citizens have the greatest access to cars.

	Number of persons per car
San Marino	1.0
USA	1.3
Andorra	1.4
Monaco	1.4
Liechtenstein	1.5
Canada	1.6
Australia	1.8

Luxembourg	1.8
Iceland	1.9
Italy	1.9
New Zealand	1.9
Brunei	2.0
France	2.0
Switzerland	2.0
Cyprus	2.1
Germany	2.1
Japan	2.1
Norway	2.1
Belgium	2.2
Sweden	2.2
Austria	2.3
Finland	2.3
Netherlands	2.4
United Kingdom	2.5
Spain	2.6
Denmark	2.7
Qatar	2.9

Sovereign countries in which citizens have the least access to cars.

	Number of persons per car
Nepal	2259
Ethiopia	984
Bangladesh	850
Cambodia	737
Rwanda	697
Togo	658
Myanmar (Burma)	611
Chad	396
Burkina Faso	360
Bhutan	348
Uganda	326
Mali	267
Guinea	258
Afghanistan	257
Malawi	254
Tanzania	244
India	225
Liberia	209
Zaïre	203
Mozambique	202

Number of commercial vehicles

Sovereign countries with the highest number of buses, coaches, trucks and vans.

	Number of commercial vehicles
USA	45,416,000
Japan	22,936,000
France	5,192,000
China	4,209,000
Canada	3,458,000
Mexico	3,063,000
United Kingdom	2,861,000
Germany	2,764,000
Spain	2,615,000
Italy	2,521,000
Saudi Arabia	2,150,000
Australia	1,915,000
Thailand	1,903,000
Indonesia	1,533,000
South Korea	1,520,000
Argentina	1,512,000
South Africa	1,498,000
India	1,396,000
Poland	1,330,000

Road haulage

In Western Europe and North America, road transport has gradually taken the place of the railways in road haulage. Many 'freight only' branch railway lines have been axed even though the resulting increase in large lorries - popularly known as juggernauts - is widely regarded as an environmental disaster. In many developing countries, railways - where they exist - tend to play a greater role in road haulage. The following table - based upon 1992 data - records the total tonnage of goods transported by road.

Country	*Tonnes of goods transported by road pa (tonnes)*
USA	1,182,620,000
China	335,810,000
Russia	299,360,000
Japan	274,440,000
Brazil	260,400,000
India	210,000,000
Germany	171,460,000
Italy	157,400,000
Spain	150,000,000
France	147,700,000
United Kingdom	136,200,000
Mexico	108,880,000
Australia	85,530,000
Ukraine	78,500,000
Iran	68,250,000
Turkey	61,970,000
Poland	49,000,000
Kazakhstan	44,780,000
Canada	42,400,000

DRIVING ON THE LEFT

In the majority of sovereign states and dependent territories, it is the custom to drive on the right. In the UK it is believed that left-hand driving is a legacy of passing an approaching horseman or carriage right side to right side to facilitate right-armed defence against sudden attack. On the Continent postillions were mounted on the rear-most left horse in a team and thus preferred to pass left side to left side.

Left-hand driving is practised in the following sovereign states: Antigua and Barbuda, Australia, Bahamas, Bangladesh, Barbados, Bhutan, Botswana, Brunei, Cyprus, Dominica, Fiji, Grenada, Guyana, India, Indonesia, Ireland (Republic of), Jamaica, Japan, Kenya, Kiribati, Lesotho, Malaysia, Malawi, Malta, Mauritius, Mozambique, Namibia, Nepal, New Zealand, Pakistan, Papua New Guinea, St Christopher-Nevis, St Lucia, St Vincent and the Grenadines, Seychelles, Singapore, Solomon Islands, Somalia, South Africa, Sri Lanka, Suriname, Swaziland, Tanzania, Thailand, Tonga, Trinidad and Tobago, Tuvalu, Uganda, United Kingdom, Zambia, and Zimbabwe.

Left-hand driving is also practised in the following dependent territories: Anguilla, Bermuda, Cook Islands, Falkland Islands, Guernsey and its dependencies, Hong Kong, Jersey, Isle of Man, Montserrat, Norfolk Island, Turks and Caicos Islands, and Virgin Islands (British).

INTERNATIONAL VEHICLE REGISTRATION LETTERS

A	Austria
AFG	Afghanistan
AL	Albania
AND	Andorra
AUS	Australia
B	Belgium
BD	Bangladesh
BDS	Barbados
BER*	Belarus
BG	Bulgaria
BH	Belize
BR	Brazil
BRN	Bahrain
BRU	Brunei
BS	Bahamas
BUR	Burma (Myanmar)
C	Cuba
CDN	Canada
CH	Switzerland
CI	Côte d'Ivoire (Ivory Coast)
CL	Sri Lanka
CO	Colombia
CR	Costa Rica
CRO*	Croatia
CS	Czech Republic
CY	Cyprus
D	Germany
DK	Denmark
DOM	Dominican Republic
DY	Benin
DZ	Algeria
E	Spain
EAK	Kenya
EAT	Tanzania
EAU	Ugandas
EAZ	Zanzibar (Tanzania)
EC	Ecuador
ES	El Salvador
ET	Egypt
ETH	Ethiopia
EW*	Estonia
F	France and territories
FJI	Fiji
FL	Liechtenstein
FR	Faeroe Islands
GB	United Kingdom
GBA	Alderney
GBG	Guernsey
GBJ	Jersey
GBM	Isle of Man
GBZ	Gibraltar
GCA	Guatemala
GH	Ghana
GR	Greece
GRU*	Georgia
GUY	Guyana
H	Hungary
HK	Hong Kong
HKJ	Jordan
I	Italy
IL	Israel
IND	India
IR	Iran
IRL	Republic of Ireland
IRQ	Iraq
IS	Iceland
J	Japan
JA	Jamaica
K	Cambodia
KWT	Kuwait
L	Luxembourg
LAO	Laos
LAR	Libya
LB	Liberia
LR*	Latvia
LS	Lesotho
LT	Lithuania
M	Malta
MA	Morocco
MAL	Malaysia
MC	Monaco
MEX	Mexico
MOL*	Moldova
MS	Mauritius
MW	Malawi
N	Norway
NA	Netherlands Antilles
NIC	Nicaragua
NL	Netherlands
NZ	New Zealand
P	Portugal
PA	Panama
PAK	Pakistan
PE	Peru
PL	Poland
PNG	Papua New Guinea
PY	Paraguay
RA	Argentina
RB	Botswana
RC	Taiwan
RCA	Central African Republic
RCB	Congo
RCH	Chile
RH	Haiti
RI	Indonesia
RIM	Mauritania
RL	Lebanon
RM	Madagascar
RMM	Malis
RN	Niger
RO*	Russia
RO	Romania
ROK	Korea
ROU	Uruguay
RP	Philippines
RSM	San Marino
RU	Burundi
RWA	Rwanda
S	Sweden
SD	Swaziland
SF	Finland
SGP	Singapore
SLO*	Slovenia
SME	Suriname
SN	Senegal
SQ*	Slovakia
SWA	Namibia
SY	Seychelles
SYR	Syria
T	Thailand
TG	Togo
TN	Tunisia
TR	Turkey
TT	Trinidad and Tobago
UKR*	Ukraine
USA	United States of America
V	Vatican City
VN	Vietnam
WAG	Gambia
WAL	Sierra Leone
WAN	Nigeria
WD	Dominica
WG	Grenada
WL	St Lucia
WS	Western Samoa
WV	St Vincent and the Grenadines
YU	Yugoslavia
YV	Venezuela
Z	Zambia
ZA	South Africa
ZRE	Zaïre
ZW	Zimbabwe

* indicates a registration that is in use but has not been officially accepted.

Other countries either do not have registration letters or use letters that are not internationally recognized.

WORLDWIDE VEHICLE* MANUFACTURERS

Manufacturer	*Country of origin*	*Total vehicles manufactured (1993)*	*Principal makes (production 1993)*
General Motors	USA	7,785,000	Astra 734,544, Chevrolet full-size pickup 623,561, Corsa 371,817, Chevrolet Cavalier 353,921 Saturn 242,540, Pontiac Grand Am 236,618
Ford Motor Co.	USA	5,277,597	Escort/Orion 801,282, F-Series Pickup 684,206,Taurus 388,907, Ranger 354,441, Explorer 287,986,Econoline (van) 212,491, Aerostar 201,038
Toyota Motor Corp.	Japan	4,450,000	Corolla 605,000, Mark II 226,000, Corona170,000,Starlet 162,000, Previa/Estima 158,000, Tercel 150,000
Volkswagen AG	Germany	3,018,650	Golf 795,060, Passat 255,002, Vento 222,211, Audi 80 214,194, Polo 176,327, Audi 100 109,057
Nissan Motor Co.	Japan	2,817,795	Sunny 491,125, March/Micra 284,274, Bluebird 247,690, Datsun Pickup 205,694, Primera 179,992, Pulsar 174,580
Chrysler Corp.	USA	2,348,030	Dodge Shadow 126,166, Plymouth Sundance 101,336,Dodge Intrepid 90,458, Chrysler Concorde 79,874, Dodge Spirit 64,731, Plymouth Acclaim 52,467
Mitsubishi Motors Corp.	Japan	1,954,000	Mirage/Lancer 449,649, Minica Series 307,513, Delica Series 194,324, Pajero 167,389,Galant/Eterna/Emeraude 139,625
Fiat Group	Italy	1,786,600	Uno 344,848, Tipo 162,969, Cinquecento 151,039,Tempra123,018, Punto 65,876
Honda Motor Co.	Japan	1,762,197	Civic 638,559, Accord 521,756, Integra 136,739,Acty 118,388, Today 88,403, Prelude 56,995
Renault SA	France	1,761,306	Clio 443,838, Renault 19 373,633, Twingo 174,259,Renault 21 127,089, Renault 9 114,116, Safrane 65,925
Peugeot-Citroën PSA	France	1,751,650	Peugeot 106 274,500, Peugeot 306 256,900,Peugeot 405 237,100, Citroën ZX 226,800, Citroën Xantia 184,500, Citroën AX 179,100
Mazda Motor Corp.	Japan	1,093,679	Mazda 323 438,517, Mazda 626/MX-6 189,463, Mazda 929 67,735, Mazda MX-3 62,798, Mazda MPV 58,456, Mazda MX-5 57,297

*Principal makes are 1992 production figures for Japan only

WORLDWIDE VEHICLE* PRODUCTION AND ASSEMBLY

	United Kingdom	USA	Worldwide
1984	1,133,731	10,924,077	42,159,635
1985	1,311,256	11,671,475	44,690,081
1986	1,202,661	11,372,865	45,156,013
1987	1,388,772	10,975,334	46,384,697
1988	1,544,848	11,009,762	47,670,728
1989	1,625,672	11,124,945	48,080,447
1990	1,565,957	9,888,036	50,375,116
1991	1,454,041	8,883,767	47,441,562
1992	1,540,333	9,777,899	49,442,510
1993	1,496,066	10,890,082	48,428,359

*Includes cars, trucks, buses, tractors and commercial vehicles

RAILWAYS

Being both a stimulus and a result of the Industrial Revolution, railways have had an enormous social and economic impact over the last 175 years. Although railways have provided a public service for most of their history, it was in fact from old horse-drawn industrial lines used in the British coalfields that the modern railway developed. They enabled industries to be located far from their fuel sources and to enjoy nationwide markets for their products. People could choose from a wider range of commodities and easily travel outside their own district for business and pleasure. The cheap mass movement of people and commodities that was now possible caught the popular imagination and encouraged new enterprise, thus changing static agrarian communities and nations into dynamic industrialized societies.

Steam railways

In 1812 steam locomotives began regular service in England on the industrial Middleton Railway near Leeds, and in 1814 the English engineer George Stephenson introduced his first steam locomotive at the Killingworth Colliery, near Newcastle-upon-Tyne (see Milestones). Stephenson went on to complete the Stockton & Darlington Railway, the first public steam line, in 1825. In 1830 the first intercity railway, the Liverpool & Manchester, was opened, and in the same year the initial length of the first US public steam line, the Baltimore & Ohio Railroad, was completed.

Many continental European countries built their first railways in the 1830s, often using Stephenson locomotives. Canada built a line in the same decade, but more distant parts of the British Empire waited longer, with Australia's first line opening in 1854, South Africa's in 1860, and New Zealand's in 1863. In Europe and North America the great period of railway building was the second half of the 19th century. The peak British mileage of 32,908 km (20,449 mi) was reached in 1931, but 90% of that had been built before 1900. The US peak mileage was reached in 1916, at 408,762 km (254,000 mi). In developed countries competition from road transport has since caused many lines to close, but elsewhere in the world new railways are still being built.

Technical progress

Nineteenth-century innovations included automatic train brakes controlled from the locomotive and, in passenger service, corridor trains with toilet and dining facilities, steam heating, and electric lighting. Luxury trains, including sleeping cars with a high degree of personal service, have been successfully operated, mainly by the Pullman company in the USA and Wagons-Lits in Europe.

In the 20th century the steam locomotive was gradually replaced by electric and diesel traction. Electrification enabled trains to run more cheaply, more cleanly and, in practice, more often, while the greater power of electric locomotives allowed heavier trains and higher speeds. Diesel traction was particularly advantageous on lines where traffic was not heavy enough to justify the cost of electrification. To keep up with the image created by aircraft and racing cars, railways introduced streamlined trains – or 'streamliners' – in the 1930s, with trains such as the Silver Jubilee in England averaging 112 km/h (70 mph) or more. In the USA many of the streamliners were diesel-powered.

In some countries, including Britain, but not the USA, freight traffic has diminished since the 1920s. Freight trains tended to become faster and more specialized. 'Piggyback' (road trailers carried on flat cars) and removeable containers were widely used from the 1950s to combine the long-haul advantage of the train with the door-to-door advantage of the motor vehicle.

In 1964 high-speed trains, running on special track, appeared in Japan. The French TGV service between Paris and Lyon began in 1981, and has running speeds of up to 270 km/h (168 mph). In Britain the 200 km/h (125 mph) High-Speed Train (HST) differs from the Japanese and French examples in that it is diesel, not electric, and runs on existing track. Maglev (magnetic levitation) trains, which dispense with the steel rail and flanged wheel, became technically feasible in the 1970s, but seem unlikely (at least in the short term) to prove economic except for specialized short-haul transit.

Gauges

The gauge of a railway track – the distance between the two rails – is partly a matter of convention but can also be varied to suit particular purposes. The gauge used by Stephenson – 1435 mm (4 ft 8´ in) – became known as standard gauge, and has been used for more than half of the railway track ever laid. The advantage of narrow gauge is that it is cheaper to build, especially in hilly terrain, and allows the use of smaller and lighter rolling stock, which is cheaper to operate. Broad gauge, on the other hand, is suitable for larger rolling stock and generally allows higher running speeds, because of greater lateral stability. The inconvenience of different gauges is exemplified by Australia, where Victoria and South Australia chose 1600 mm (5 ft 3 in), Western Australia and Queensland 1067 mm (3 ft 6 in), and New South Wales standard gauge. These gauges are still in use, but the mainland state capitals now have standard-gauge connections. Sometimes, to accommodate trains of different gauges, a third rail is laid to create mixed gauge.

MILESTONES IN RAILWAYS

1500s Tramways – wooden tracks along which trolleys ran – were used in mines.

1804 Richard Trevithick (1771–1833) successfully operated his steam locomotive in South Wales.

1812 Matthew Murray (1765–1826) brought his steam cog locomotives into service at Middleton Colliery, West Yorkshire.

1813 William Hedley (1779–1843) and Timothy Hackworth (1786-1850) built a smooth-wheeled steam locomotive for Wylam Colliery, Northumberland.

1814 George Stephenson (1781–1848) built the *Blücher*, his first locomotive.

1825 George Stephenson opened the Stockton & Darlington Railway, the first public railway to use steam locomotives.

1827 Hackworth's *Royal George* was the first locomotive with six coupled wheels (to increase wheel-to-rail adhesion), and the first with cylinders driving direct to the wheels.

1829 At the Rainhill locomotive trials the *Rocket*, designed by Robert Stephenson (1803–59) and his father George, impressed the Liverpool & Manchester Railway management.

1830 The first intercity railway, the Liverpool and Manchester Line was opened. The first scheduled service in North America began when the South Carolina Railroad opened.

1835 Germany's first steam locomotive, built by Stephenson, went into service.

1836 First Russian locomotive, built by Stephenson, went into service.

1848 First railway in South America: Georgetown to Plaisance, Guyana (closed 1972).

1853 First railway in India, Bombay to Thana.

1854 First public railway service in Australia, from Melbourne to Port Melbourne, Victoria.

1856 Train services began on the first railway in Africa: Alexandria to Cairo in Egypt.

1859 First sleeping car built, desgined by George Pullman.

1863 The world's first underground railway opened in London.

1869 The first US transcontinental, the Union Pacific-Central Pacific Line stretched from Nebraska to California.

1872 First railway in Japan opened, from Yokohama to Shinagawa (to Tokyo later that year).

1879 Werner von Siemens demonstrated the first electric train in Berlin (Germany).

1880 First permanent railway in China.

1881 First public electric railway in the world opened near Berlin (Germany).

1883 Charles Lartique pioneered the first successful monorail in Ireland.

1887 Canada's first transcontinental service opened, running from Montréal to Vancouver.

1890 The first electric underground railway opened in London.

1897 The German Wilhelm Schmidt (1858–1924) introduced the first successful superheater, enhancing steam locomotive performance.

1900 Electrification of the Paris-Orléans line (France) began.

1901 Opening of the Trans-Siberian Railway from Moscow to Vladivostok (9336 km / 5801 mi), the longest railway in the world.

1913 The first diesel locomotive was built in Germany. A diesel-electric railcar began running successfully in Sweden.

1915 The Hungarian Kalman Kando built the first electric locomotive using high-frequency current.

1917 Trans-Australian railway opened: its 1693 km (1052 mi) between Kalgoorlie and Port Augusta traversed the Nullarbor Plain for 478 km (297 mi) without a curve, the world's longest straight stretch of railway.

1924 First diesel trains introduced in the USA.

1932 The record-breaking diesel train *Flying Hamburger* began running between Berlin and Hamburg (Germany).

1934 The *Burlington Zephyr*, the first diesel-electric streamliner, covered the 1626 km (1010 mi) from Denver to Chicago (USA) at an average speed of 125 km/h (77·6 mph).

1938 The British streamlined locomotive *Mallard* won the all-time steam speed record by reaching 203 km/h (126 mph).

1947 Nationalization of railways in Britain.

1958 A French electric locomotive reached 331 km/h (206 mph).

1960 Regular mainline steam traction ended in the USA. First electronic speed and braking control system introduced on St Petersburg subway.

1965 The Japanese Shinkansen high-speed trains entered service.

1968 Regular mainline steam traction ended in Britain.

1970 The National Railroad Passenger Corporation (Amtrak) was formed in the USA. It took over the passenger services of 22 leading railroads in the USA.

1973 British Rail's High Speed Train (HST) set a diesel rail speed record of 229 km/h (143 mph).

1977 Testing of Japan's National Railways' maglev (magnetic levitation), reaching speeds of 517 km/h (321 mph).

1981 The French TGV reached 270 km/h (168 mph) in its regular passenger service between Paris and Lyon.

1983 The French TGV cut the scheduled time for the 425 km (264 mi) journey from Paris to Lyon to 2 hours exactly.

1988 A new world speed record of 406.9 km/h (252 mph) was made by DB on the Fulda to Würzburg line in Germany.

Construction of steam locomotives ended at the Datong works, China, the last large steam locomotive works in the world.

The 53.85 km (33 mi 809 yards) Seikan Tunnel, between the islands of Honshu and Hokkaido in Japan was opened for passenger services.

1989 A new world speed record of 482.4 km/h (300 mph) by the French TGV-Atlantique.

1993 New Zealand railways were privatized. The Railways Bill, for privatizing railways, became law in the United Kingdom.

1994 Services began on the Folkestone (Kent) to Sangatte (Nord-Pas de Calais) Channel Tunnel. Eurostar passenger services link London (Waterloo) with Paris and Brussels; Le Shuttle vehicle-carrying trains link Folkestone with Sangatte.

PRINCIPAL RAILWAY SYSTEMS OF THE WORLD

Railway system	*Year of first railway*	*Gauge mm*	*ft in*	*Route length km*	*miles*	*Ownership*
USA	1830*	1435	4 8½	261,124	162,254	private, except Alaska RR
	Class I RRs			202,739	125,976	846 km (526 mi), state-owned
	Class II and III		53,916	33,502		
	Commuter RRs		4469	2777		
Russia	1837	1524	5 0	86,300	53,624	state-owned
Canada	1836	1435	4 8½	63,549	39,487	private, except: Canadian National 34,347 km (21,342 mi) British Columbia R 1953 km (1213 mi) owned by BC
India	1853			61,976	38,510	state-owned
		1676	5 6	33,831	21,021	
		1000	3 3⅜	23,898	14,849	
		610 and 762	2 0 and 2 6	4247	2639	
China	1880	1435	4 8½	c.54,000	c.33,500	state-owned
Germany	1835			41,039	25,500	state-owned
		1 435	4 8½	40,764	25,329	
			narrow	275	171	
Australia	1854			38,803	24,111	owned by separate states except
		1600	5 3	6642	4127	Australian National, 7315 km
		1435	4 8½	16,259	10,103	(4545 mi) of three gauges, owned
		1067	3 6	15,902	9881	by the Commonwealth
France	1832	1435	4 8½	34,680	21,549	state-owned
Argentina	1857			c.34,500	c.21,400	to be privatized
		1676	5 6	c.20,500	c.12,700	
		1435	4 8½	c.3000	c.1860	
		1000	3 3⅜	c.11,000	c.6840	
Poland	1845			27,137	16,862	state-owned
		1435	4 8½	24,287	15,091	
			narrow	2357	1465	
		1524	5 0	493	306	
South Africa	1860			23,619	14,676	state-owned
		1065	3 5⅞	23,259	14,452	
		610	2 0	360	224	
Ukraine	1866	1524†	5 0	22,760	14,142	state-owned
Brazil	1854			22,417	13,929	state-owned
		1600	5 3	1740	1081	
		1000	3 3⅜	20,664	12,840	
		760	2 6	13	8	
Japan	1872			20,984	13,038	all privatized
		1067	3 6	18,950	11,775	
		1435	4 8½	2034	1263	
Mexico	1850			20,306	12,618	state-owned
		1435	4 8½	20,216	12,562	
		914	3 0	90	56	
UK	1825			16,915	10,510	state-owned
British Rail		1435	4 8½	16,583	10,304	
N. Ireland Railways Co Ltd		1600	5 3	332	206	
Italy	1839	1435	4 8½	15,982	9931	state-owned
also in Sicily		950	3 1⅜	71	44	
Kazakhstan	1897	1524†	5 0	14,550	9041	state-owned
Spain	1848	1668	5 5⅝	12,691	7886	state-owned

MAJOR 'METRO' AND RAPID TRANSIT SYSTEMS

'Metros' systems are partly or wholly underground; rapid transit systems are generally partly or wholly overground.

City	System begun	Total length of route		Number of lines	Number of stations
London (UK)	1863	408 km	254 mi	10	273
New York (USA)	1868	398 km	247 mi	23	466
Paris (France)	1900	307 km	191 mi	18	430
Moscow (Russia)	1935	239 km	148 mi	9	148
Tokyo (Japan)	1927	217 km	135 mi	10	192
Berlin (Germany)	1902	212 km	132 mi	8	134
Mexico City (Mexico)	1969	158 km	98 mi	9	135
Chicago (USA)	1892	158 km	97 mi	6	143
Copenhagen (Denmark)	1934	135 km	84 mi	7	61
Washington DC (USA)	1976	131 km	81 mi	5	70
Boston (USA)	1897	127 km	78 mi	3	145
Seoul (South Korea)	1974	118 km	73 mi	4	105
San Francisco (USA)	1972	115 km	71 mi	1	34
Madrid (Spain)	1919	113 km	70 mi	10	155
Stockholm (Sweden)	1950	110 km	68 mi	3	99
Osaka (Japan)	1933	104 km	64 mi	7	84
Hamburg (Germany)	1912	96 km	59 mi	3	84
St Petersburg (Russia)	1955	83 km	51 mi	4	45
Barcelona (Spain)	1924	71 km	44 mi	5	98
Nagoya (Japan)	1957	69 km	43 mi	5	66
Milan (Italy)	1964	66 km	41 mi	3	81
Montréal (Canada)	1966	65 km	40 mi	4	65
Toronto (Canada)	1954	64 km	40 mi	3	65
Philadelphia (USA)	1907	63 km	39 mi	3	68
Bucharest (Romania)	1979	60 km	38 mi	2	21

OTHER 'METRO' AND RAPID TRANSIT SYSTEMS

(with the year in which the first metro section was opened)

* rapid transport systems that are wholly, or almost wholly, above ground

Amsterdam, Netherlands (1977); Antwerp*, Belgium; Athens, Greece (1925); Atlanta, USA (1979); Baku, Azerbaijan (1967); Baltimore, USA (1983); Beijing (Peking), China (1969); Belo Horizonte, Brazil (1986), Brussels; Belgium (1976); Budapest, Hungary (1896); Buenos Aires, Argentina (1913); Buffalo, USA (1984); Cairo, Egypt (1984); Calcutta, India (1984); Caracas, Venezuela (1983); Charleroi*, Belgium; Cleveland, USA (1955); Cologne, Germany; Detroit, USA (1986); Dneipropetrovsk, Ukraine (1984); Dublin*, Ireland; Edmonton*, Canada; Essen, Germany; Frankfurt, Germany (1968); Fukuoka, Japan (1981); Glasgow, UK (1896; reopened 1980); Gothenburg, Sweden; Grenoble*, France; Guadalajara*, Mexico; Haifa, Israel (1959); Hannover*, Germany; Helsinki, Finland (1982); Hong Kong (1979); Jakarta*, Indonesia; Karlsruhe*, Germany; Kharkov, Ukraine (1975); Kiev, Ukraine (1960); Kobe, Japan (1977); Kyoto, Japan (1981); Lille, France (1983); Lisbon, Portugal (1959); Los Angeles, USA (1993); Lyon, France (1978); Manchester*, UK; Manila*, Philippines; Marseille, France (1978); Melbourne*, Australia; Miami, USA (1984); Minsk, Belarus (1984); Munich, Germany (1971); Naples, Italy (1987); Newcastle-upon-Tyne*, UK; Nizhny Novgorod (formerly Gorky), Russia (1985); Novosibirsk, Russia (1985); Nürnberg, Germany (1972); Oslo, Norway (1966); Prague, Czech Republic (1974); Pusan, South Korea (1985); Pyongyang, North Korea (1973); Rio de Janeiro, Brazil (1979); Rome, Italy (1955); Rotterdam, Netherlands (1968); Samara (formerly Kubyshev), Russia (1987); Santiago, Chile (1975); São Paulo, Brazil (1975); Sapporo, Japan (1971); Sendai, Japan (1987); Sheffield*, UK; Singapore (1986); Stuttgart*, Germany; Tashkent, Uzbekistan (1977); Tbilisi, Georgia (1966); Tianjin, China (1980); Toulouse*, France; Tunis*, Tunisia; Vancouver*, Canada; Vienna, Austria (1976); Wuppertal*, Germany; Yerevan, Armenia (1981); and Yokohama, Japan (1972).

'Metros' or rapid transit systems are under construction in the following cities: Algiers, Algeria; Ankara, Turkey; Bangkok, Thailand; Belgrade*, Yugoslavia (Serbia-Montenegro); Bilbao, Spain; Birmingham*, UK; Bogotá*, Colombia; Dallas*, USA; Denver*, USA; Dortmund*, Germany; Duisburg*, Germany; Kuala Lumpur*, Malaysia; Leeds*, UK; Medellín, Colombia; Sofia, Bulgaria; Taipei*, Taiwan; Tehran, Iran; Valencia, Spain; Warsaw, Poland; and Yekaterinburg (formerly Sverdlovsk), Russia.

Metros or rapid transit systems are also planned for Baghdad, Iraq; Bologna*, Italy; Bordeaux*, France; Chongqing, China; Croydon*, UK; Guangzhou (Canton), China; Harbin, China; Nottingham*, UK; Shanghai, China; Shenyang, China; Turin*, Italy; and Wuhan, China.

SHIPPING

Over the last 50 years the design of commercial and naval ships has undergone radical changes both as a result of advances in technology and as a response to changing economic pressures and military threats. In all types of ship, automation has helped to reduce crew size and the cost of construction and operation. In spite of competition from the air, ships still carry the great majority of cargoes; and although the great transatlantic liners have disappeared, cruise ships and ferries flourish. In the military field, the need to cope with high-speed missiles – both in attack and defence – has meant that modern warships are now equipped with complex electronic and computer systems.

Passenger shipping

The growth of relatively cheap air travel has meant that virtually all long-distance passenger transport is now by air. The few liners that were built after World War II were either scrapped or converted to cruise ships or floating hotels. However, on shorter sea crossings, car and passenger ferries have expanded their activities to cope with the growth of demand for holidays abroad. Partly for economic reasons and partly in order to win customers, ferries have grown in size and speed, with particular attention being paid to on-board amenities and provision for fast boarding and unloading. The roll-on/roll-off design is now common. On some routes, the greater speed of the hovercraft has made it attractive to travellers.

With increasing leisure time, a demand has grown for sea cruises. Initially converted liners were used, but now most ships are specifically designed for the cruising trade. Visits are made to a number of ports where passengers can disembark for excursions to places of interest. Larger cruise liners can carry some 3000 people in relative luxury and with all facilities – such as swimming pools and dance halls – on board.

Cargo shipping

The rapid growth in demand for energy has meant that large volumes of oil need to be shipped around the world. To keep the price per tonne (ton) of oil as low as possible, the size of tankers has grown dramatically. Whereas before 1956 there were no tankers larger than 50,000 tonnes, ships of 100,000 tonnes were built in the 1960s. There are now Very Large Crude Carriers (VLCC) of between 200,000 to 400,000 tonnes and Ultra Large Crude Carriers (ULCC) of more than 400,000 tonnes. To transport natural gas to where it is needed has led to the development of the Liquefied Natural Gas (LNG) carrier.

Whilst the extraction of gas and oil from shallow-water off-shore sites had long been carried out, the need for more oil caused oil companies to look further afield to deeper, more exposed areas, such as the North Sea. In order to remain stationary while drilling, drilling ships with dynamic position control systems were required, as were saturated diving systems, production rigs and supply vessels of specialized design.

Bulk carriage of grain and metal ores was influenced by the need to keep transport as cheap as possible, with minimum manpower and minimum time in port. Bulk carriers therefore grew in the same way as tankers, and like them had machinery and accommodation aft with holds or tanks forward. Some large ships are designed to be able to take different cargoes (say oil or ore) on different occasions. Load distribution is then important to ensure that the strength limits of the hull are not exceeded.

Warship defences

The design of warships is dictated both by the need to carry out certain types of operation and by the need to counter the threat posed by an enemy. During World War II the pace of change accelerated and has continued to do so since. With developments in materials, electronics and computers, the growing complexity of the threats posed has been matched by the sophisticated means used to combat them.

One example is the threat posed by mines. World War II saw the appearance of *influence mines*, which are triggered by the magnetic, acoustic and/or pressure 'signature' of the target. The result of the development of mines and homing weapons (such as missiles and torpedoes which use similar devices) is that great emphasis has been placed on reducing the ship's signatures, thus their susceptibility to attack. The radar reflection of modern warships is reduced in a variety of ways: special materials are used, and much attention is paid to shaping and to minimizing the above-water profile. The magnetic signature of a ship can be significantly reduced by *degaussing*, a process in which special equipment is used to produce an opposing magnetic field. The acoustic signature can be reduced by specially designed propulsion units and by isolating noise sources within the ship. Finally, the susceptibility to infrared detection can be decreased by reducing hot spots within the ship.

Ships must be robust enough to withstand some damage and still remain effective fighting units. Various means of reducing vulnerability include protective plating against splinters, duplication of important systems, subdivisions of the ship, and limiting the area of the ship over which a hit can put any particular system out of action.

MILESTONES IN SHIPBUILDING

8th millennium BC Reed boats and dugout boats were used.

3rd millennium BC Sailing boats were used on the Nile in Egypt.

c. 1200 BC The Phoenicians developed ocean-going 'roundships'.

5th century BC The Greek trireme, the fastest of the Mediterranean galleys, was widely used.

8th century AD The Vikings of Scandinavia developed the longship with a hinged sternpost rudder and mast. It was sturdy enough to enable the Vikings to cross the Atlantic.

15th–16th centuries The Mediterranean *carrack* – with as many as four masts – became the standard large ship. The smaller version of the carrack, the *caravel*, was widely used by the Spanish and Portuguese for the voyages of discovery.

16th century The galleon became the standard fighting ship in western Europe.

18th century The ships of the line evolved from galleons. They had heavier timbers to allow bigger and more numerous guns to be carried.

18th–19th centuries Clipper cargo ships developed. The clipper sacrificed cargo space for a more streamlined design, increasing speed.

1802 The launch of the first commercially successful paddle-steamer, the *Charlotte Dundas*, in Scotland. (A small paddle-steamer had briefly sailed in 1783 in France but had proved impractical.)

1816 A steam-paddle service ran across the English Channel.

1821 The Royal Navy ordered its first paddle steamers for auxiliary missions (such as towing ships of the line over short distances). The first iron-hulled merchant ship, the *Aaron Manby*, was launched.

1836 The Swedish-American John Ericsson and Englishman Francis Pettit-Smith developed the screw propeller.

1838 The *Great Western* (designed by Brunel) and the *Sirius* crossed the Atlantic, proving that steam power was suitable for long voyages.

1840 The Royal Navy ordered its first screw steamer, HMS *Rattler*. Brunel redesigned the passenger liner SS *Great Britain* for screw propulsion.

1858–59 Construction began on the first ironclad, the French *Gloire*, a wooden warship covered with armoured plate. However, the British HMS *Warrior*, which had an iron hull and armoured plate, was the first ironclad to be launched (1859). The *Great Eastern*, five times as large as the largest ship then afloat, was launched. Of revolutionary length (to give it greater speed), the ship was divided into 22 compartments to make it more resistant to damage.

1886 The first custom-built oil tanker, the German ship *Gluckauf*, was launched.

1890s Battleships were designed to an all-metal (steel) construction.

1897 The first turbine-driven steamship, the *Turbinia*, was built by C. Parsons.

1898 The Italian Enrico Forlanini developed the first true hydrofoil.

1902 The first marine diesel engine was installed, on a French canal boat.

1905 The Royal Navy adopted the steam-turbine for the revolutionary battleship HMS *Dreadnought*.

1902–14 The diesel engine was widely adopted as a cheap propulsion unit for merchant ships and minor naval craft.

1920–39 The heyday of ocean liners. Their ever-increasing size, speed and standards of comfort culminated in the *Queen Mary* and the *Queen Elizabeth*.

1957–58 The first nuclear-powered ship, the Soviet naval icebreaker *Lenin*, was launched. The American merchant ship *Savannah* was the first commercial nuclear-powered ship.

1960s Container ships – carrying standardized containers for transporting cargo – were increasingly used by the world's merchant navies. Roll-on, roll-off vessels were developed from the design of naval landing-ships for ferry traffic.

1970s Larger oil tankers were launched, such as the Japanese Universe class of 326,000 tonnes (tons) deadweight. Hydrofoils entered commercial service as passenger ferries.

SHIPPING TONNAGES

Tonnage is the capacity of a ship expressed in terms of tonnes (tons). In the UK, the four tonnage systems are in use. *Gross registered tonnage* (GRT) is used for merchant shipping. It is the sum in cubic feet of all the enclosed spaces divided by 100, i.e. 1 grt=100 ft^3 of enclosed space. *Net registered tonnage* (NRT) is also used for merchant shipping. It is the gross registered tonnage (see above) less deductions for crew spaces, engine rooms and ballast, which cannot be utilized for paying passengers or cargo. *Deadweight tonnage* (DWT) is used mainly for tramp ships and oil tankers. It is the number of UK long tons (2240 lb; 1.016 tonnes) of cargo, stores, bunkers and passengers that is required to bring down a ship from her height line to her load-water line, i.e. the carrying capacity of a ship. *Displacement tonnage* is used for warships and US merchant shipping. It is the number of tons (tonnes) of sea water displaced by a vessel charged to its load-water line, i.e. the weight of the vessel and its contents in tons.

LARGEST SHIPS

The largest passenger vessel ever launched was the liner *Queen Elizabeth* (UK), which was 314m (1031 ft) long and had a gross tonnage of 82,998 tons (tonnes). She was retired in 1968 and sold for conversion as a seagoing college, Seawise University, which was destroyed by fire in Hong Kong in 1972. The largest active liner is the *Norway*, which was built as the *France* and served on the transatlantic route from 1961 to 1975. In 1979 she was bought by a Norwegian, renamed *Norway*, and recommissioned as a cruise ship in August 1979. *Norway* is 70,202.19 GRT and 315.66m (1035 ft 7 in) in length. The 77,000 tonne *Sun Princess*, under construction at the Fincantieri Yard in Italy, is scheduled to enter service with P & O in December 1995.

The largest battleships ever commissioned were the Japanese vessels *Yamato* and *Musashi* (both completed and sunk during World War II). Both ships had a full load displacement of 73,977 tonnes, an overall length of 263m (863 ft), a beam of 38.7m (127 ft) and a full load draught of 10.8m (35.5 ft). The largest battleship in active service is the USS Missouri, which is 270m (887 ft) long and has a beam of 32.9m (108 ft) with a full load displacement of 58,000 tonnes. The ship can attain a maximum speed of over 35 knots (64.75 mph).

The largest ship of any kind is the oil tanker *Jahre Viking* (formerly the *Happy Giant* and *Seawise Giant*), at 564,763 tonnes deadweight. The tanker is 485.45m (1504 ft) long overall, has a beam of 68.8m (226 ft) and a draught of 24.61m (80 ft). Declared a total loss after being disabled by severe bombardment in 1987-88 during the Iran-Iraq war, the tanker underwent extensive renovation - costing 60 million US dollars - and was relaunched under its new name in November 1991.

MAJOR PORTS

The figures in this list of the world's busiest ports are in tonnes of goods handled per year (1991).

Port	Tonnes
Rotterdam (Netherlands)	287,700,000
New Orleans (USA)	189,300,000
Singapore (Singapore)	187,800,000
Kobe (Japan)	171,500,000
Shanghai (China)	133,000,000
Houston (USA)	131,200,000
Nagoya (Japan)	128,900,000
New York (USA)	126,200,000
Yokohama (Japan)	123,900,000
Antwerp (Belgium)	102,000,000
Valdez (USA)	99,600,000
Osaka (Japan)	97,400,000
Kitakyushu (Japan)	95,200,000
Marseille (France)	90,300,000
Hong Kong (Hong Kong)	89,000,000

LAND-LOCKED STATES

The majority of countries have coastlines, although some have only very short littorals. Although the following sovereign countries are entirely land-locked, some of them have registered merchant fleets - mostly for use on rivers and lakes.

In Europe
Andorra, Austria, Belarus, the Czech Republic, Hungary, Liechtenstein, Luxembourg, Macedonia, Moldova, San Marino, Slovakia, Switzerland, and the Vatican City are land-locked.

Of these countries, the following have registered merchant fleets: Austria, the Czech Republic, Hungary, Luxembourg, and Switzerland.

In Africa
Botswana, Burkina Faso, Burundi, the Central African Republic, Chad, Ethiopia, Lesotho, Malawi, Mali, Niger, Rwanda, Swaziland, Uganda, Zambia, and Zimbabwe are land-locked.

Of these countries, Burundi, Ethiopia, Malawi and Uganda have registered merchant fleets.

In Asia
Afghanistan, Armenia, Azerbaijan, Bhutan, Kazakhstan, Kyrgyzstan, Laos, Mongolia, Nepal, Tajikistan, Turkmenistan, and Uzbekistan are land-locked. Although Azerbaijan, Kazakhstan and Turkmenistan have coasts on the Caspian Sea, and Kazakhstan and Uzbekistan have coasts on the Aral Sea, these 'seas' are, in fact, regarded as lakes and the countries concerned may be said to be land-locked.

Of these countries, Azerbaijan, Laos and Turkmenistan have registered merchant fleets.

In South America
Bolivia and Paraguay are land-locked, but both of these countries have registered merchant fleets.

MERCHANT SHIPPING

Merchant shipping may be defined as shipping that is engaged in commerce.

Flags of convenience

A large proportion of the world's merchant shipping flies flags of convenience. Ships are registered by their owners in other countries that offer financial, legal or other incentives to fly their flag. The first countries to offer such advantages were Liberia and Panama, which now have the world's largest registered merchant fleets, although almost all of the vessels involved are owned by European and North American companies.

In 1993, the largest merchant fleets in terms of registered tonnage were those of:

Country	*Registered tonnage*
Liberia	55,100,000
Panama	49,600,000
Greece	24,400,000
Japan	21,100,000
Norway	20,200,000
Cyprus	20,100,000
Bahamas	19,400,000
USA*	15,400,000
China	12,600,000
Malta	10,600,000
Russia	10,300,000
Singapore	9,500,000
Philippines	8,000,000
Hong Kong	7,100,000

* The US Reserve Fleet is included in the figure.

In 1993, the largest merchant fleets in terms of the number of registered vessels were those of:

Country	*Number of vessels*
Panama	3170
Liberia	1570
Russia	1360
Cyprus	1250
China	1230
Japan	910
Greece	900
Bahamas	820
Malta	750
Norway	740
USA	600
Poland	530
Spain	490
Japan	470
St Vincent and the Grenadines	430
Germany	420
South Korea	420

INLAND WATERWAYS

The following table lists the total length of inland waterways – canals, canalized rivers and lakes – of major countries.

Country	*Length of navigable inland waterways*	
	km	*mi*
China	138,600	86,100
Russia	85,000	53,000
Brazil	50,000	31,100
USA	41,010	25,480
Indonesia	21,580	13,400
Vietnam	17,700	11,000
India	16,180	10,050
Zaïre	15,000	9300
France	14,930	9280
Colombia	14,300	8900
Myanmar (Burma)	12,800	7950
Argentina	11,000	6800
Papua New Guinea	10,940	6790

MAJOR SHIP CANALS

The following canals can be used by ocean-going shipping.

Canal	*Route*	*Year opened*	*Length*
St Lawrence Seaway[1] (Canada – USA)	Montreal to Lake Ontario	1959	304 km1 (189 mi)
Main-Danube Canal (Germany)	Main River (Bamberg) to Danube River (Kelheim)	1992	171 km (106 mi)
Suez Canal (Egypt)	Mediterranean Sea to Red Sea	1869	162 km (101 mi)
Albert Canal (Belgium)	River Meuse (Maes) to River Scheld	1939	129 km (80 mi)
Kiel Canal (Germany)	North Sea to Baltic Sea	1895	99 km (62 mi)
Alfonso XIII Canal (Spain)	Seville to Gulf of Cadiz	1926	85 km (53 mi)
Panama Canal (Panama)	Pacific Ocean to Caribbean Sea	1914	81 km (50 mi)
Sabine-Neches Waterway (USA)[2]	Beaumont to Gulf of Mexico	1916	72 km (45 mi)
Houston Ship Canal (USA)[2]	Houston to Gulf of Mexico	1914	69 km (43 mi)
Manchester Ship Canal (UK)	Manchester to the Mersey estuary	1894	58 km (36 mi)
Welland Canal (Canada)	Lake Ontario to Lake Erie	1933	44 km (28 mi)
North Sea Canal (Noordzeekanaal) (Netherlands)	Amsterdam to Ijmuiden on the North Sea	1876	27 km (17 mi)
Chesapeake and Delaware Canal[3] (USA)	Chesapeake Bay to Delaware River	1829	22 km (14 mi)

1 The canalized section of the St Lawrence Seaway that enables shipping to sail 3769 km (2342 mi) from the North Atlantic up the St Lawrence estuary and through the Great Lakes to Duluth, Minnesota.

2 Part of a series of artificial and natural channels providing a discontinuous navigation, linking the Texan Gulf coast ports with the Mississippi Delta and Florida. Total length: 1770 km (1100 mi).

3 Part of the Atlantic Intracoastal Waterway, a series of artificial and natural channels providing a discontinuous navigation of 1900 km (3057 mi) between Massachusetts and Florida.

Other major navigation canals

The following canals are suitable for barges rather than for ocean-going shipping.

Canal	*Route*	*Year opened*	*Length*
Volga-Baltic Waterway (Russia)	Astrakhan to St Petersburg	1965	2300 km (1850 mi)
Grand Canal (China)	Beijing (Peking) to Harchon	540 BC – AD 1327	1781 km (1107 mi)
Karakumsky Canal (Turkmenistan)	Amu-Dar'ya (Oxus) to Khrebet Kopet Dag	1980	1069 km (664 mi)
New York State Barge Canal (USA)	Hudson River to Lake Erie	1918	837 km (520 mi)
Rajasthan Canal (India)	Bamgarh to Western Haryana	1955	649 km (403 mi)
Irtysh-Karaganda Canal (Kazakhstan)	Karaganda to River Irtysh	1971	451 km (280 mi)
Trent Canal (Canada)	Lake Huron to Lake Ontario	1833 – 1918	443 km (275 mi)

Computing

COMPUTERS

Computers are machines that carry out programmed sequences of instructions to manipulate coded data. The more common digital computers – the type described here – use number codes to represent data such as letters of the alphabet, numbers, visible images, sounds and other material.

The number system used is the binary system, by which all numbers (and hence number codes) can be represented by sequences of 0s and 1s (binary digits or *bits*), which on a computer can be represented by electric current being turned off and on respectively.

Each particle of data is represented by an 8-digit binary number, a *byte*. The ASCII – American Standard Code for Information Interchange (pronounced 'ass-key') – code is used for letters of the alphabet, digits 0 to 9 and punctuation marks and other signs. Other data can be coded in ways that may be specific to a type of computer or to a program and may not be easily interchangeable. Data size is measured in bytes, kilobytes (K; 1K = 2^{10} bytes) and megabytes (Mb; 1Mb = 2^{20} bytes).

Hardware and software

The electronic and mechanical components of a computer are called the *hardware*. The hardware of a computer contains the *processor*, which can carry out actions of arithmetic and comparison on binary digits. The bytes of information are stored in memory, allowing the processor to process them as fast as it can read them and deal with them.

Circuits called *ports* deal with the input of new data and the output of processed data (to a screen, printer or disk, for example).

All of these processes are carried out under the control of a *program*, which is another set of bytes in code. The program and the data – in other words the procedures required for computer operation – are called the *software* of the system. Computers are classified as:

Microcomputers which use a microprocessor, which is formed on one tiny chip of silicon.

Minicomputers which are computers (often used for small office networks) that are intermediate in capacity between a microcomputer and a mainframe computer.

Mainframes which are the most powerful general-purpose computers.

Supercomputers which are designed specifically for speed.

Minicomputers, large mainframe computers and supercomputers use sets of separate chips.

The processor and storage

The *processor* must be able to read bytes from the memory in sequence, and the bytes must be available in the correct order.

Data is stored inside the computer in memory and externally in *backing stores*. Each unit of memory is a tiny semiconductor switch storing one bit of information. A memory consists of a set of such units, organized into bytes and with each set accessible by using an address number, applied in binary signal form to the chip(s). The two fundamental types of memory are ROM and RAM.

ROM is Read-Only Memory. Each byte can be read when its address number is supplied (from the microprocessor) but the contents of the memory cannot be changed nor erased.

RAM is Random-Access Memory. RAM can be read or written and is usually volatile – its contents are lost when power is cut off. CMOS (complementary metal-oxide semiconductor) RAM will retain data either with battery back-up or even without any power supply and is used for retaining small amounts of permanent data.

Backing stores are used for long-term retention. Most read-write backing stores use magnetic storage on disk or tape and it is now possible to store 1.44 Mb on a disk whose diameter is about 90 mm (3.5 in).

Another form of backing store is the *CD-ROM* type, which stores data in read-only form using an optical disk (like an audio compact disk); read-write versions of this are being developed.

Another form is the *WORM* (Write Once Read Many) disk, which can be written by signals of higher-than-normal size and from then on used like the CD-ROM disk.

Programs

Originally, programmers worked in binary code using sets of switches in place of a keyboard. This *machine-code programming* (*first-generation language*) is feasible only for very short programs, and has been replaced by *assembly-language programming* (*second-generation language*), which uses brief instruction words like ADD. A program called an *assembler* then reads the words and associated numbers and converts them into machine code, but such programming demands that the programmer should have a very detailed knowledge of how the hardware works.

The writing of reliable large programs is a major problem. Such programs have to be divided and each programmer writes a section. The problems start when the sections are made to work together. The development of programming has aimed to make cooperation easier and reduce errors.

The *operating system* is an important aid. This is a program that attends to all the simple needs of the system, such as controlling the memory, keyboard, disk system, screen and other inputs and outputs. It also provides a set of standard routines that writers of programs can use with confidence. The other main aid is the use of *higher-level programming languages*, including third- or fourth-generation languages.

Computer languages

A *third-generation language* uses intelligible commands that allow the program to be read more easily. In addition, good languages are *portable* – the same commands can be used for programming any type of computer.

The differences between computers are dealt with by using different versions of the language program. Early third-generation languages (FORTRAN, ALGOL and COBOL) were each developed for specific needs. The popular BASIC language was first developed as a way of learning FORTRAN. More modern third-generation languages include Pascal, C and Prolog. All these languages are procedural, meaning that the programmer must write the sequence of instructions to be used on the data.

Object-oriented program languages are adaptations of familiar languages that allow for better organization when work is split among many writers.

Fourth-generation languages (4GL) can be described as programs that write programs. The programmer writes only descriptions of the types of data and how they are to be manipulated. Most 4GLs are specialized, creating one type of program only. Typical modern 4GLs for small computers include Matrix Layout, DataBoss and SkyMaster.

Speed and performance

The 'power' of a computer is measured in terms of its processing speed, memory capacity, and backing store size.

Modern microcomputers operate with four-byte units, running the timing clock at around 16 MHz, using 1Mb of memory and a backing store of 32 Mb to 640 Mb. Microcomputers can be connected together into networks to share a common backing store and printer(s). The speed of micros is determined mainly by the speed of moving data to and from the memory and backing stores. This can be improved by using *memory caches* – small pieces of fast-acting memory. Since the same data is often needed several times, it can be reached more quickly from fast memory than from main memory or backing stores.

Larger machines can use memory that operates much faster but which requires much more space and also needs cooling. *Supercomputers* are used for fast real-time processing (missile tracking, weather forecasting, analysing fast reactions) and are built in circular or spherical form to minimize the length of connectors between units. The speed of electric current in cables limits such computers, and it seems likely that the use of lasers, fibre optics and light-operated switches will result in even faster machines in the late 1990s.

Recent development has concentrated on desktop and laptop machines. Desktop machines now use faster processes, have larger memory capacity, and use much larger hard disk capacity than before – all at lower prices.

Laptop machines are now expected to match the performance of a desktop machine, and use high-resolution LCD screens, some in colour. Laptop machines are still handicapped by the limited performance of existing batteries, particularly rechargeable cells.

By 1992, the entry-level PC machine used the 80486 chip, with a specification which was the highest attainable in PC machines only two years earlier. Networked PC machines, or PCs networked to a mini-computer, are now more commonly used than a mainframe.

MILESTONES IN COMPUTING

3000 BC The abacus, using rods and beads for counting, probably developed in the Middle East and was widely used in Mediterranean countries.

1614 The Scot John Napier's logarithms allowed multiplication and division to be carried out by adding and subtracting. A device called 'Napier's bones' led to the invention of the slide rule.

1642 Blaise Pascal invented a mechanical adding machine using 10:1 gearing to represent decimal columns. The computing language Pascal is named after this pioneer of computation.

1666 Gottfried Wilhelm Leibniz proposed the basis of a language that would allow logical statements to be dealt with mathematically. The essence was the use of digits 0 for FALSE and 1 for TRUE. Leibniz went on to develop binary arithmetic.

1673 Leibniz improved Pascal's calculator by adding a method of shifting columns that allowed it to multiply and divide as well as add and subtract.

1804 The French weaver J.M. Jacquard invented a loom in which changes of pattern or material could be programmed by feeding in a set of punched cards.

The Jacquard loom was the first programmable device to be perfected.

1822 Charles Babbage, with support from the British Admiralty, set out to design a '*differential engine*', an advanced form of calculator for application to navigation problems. He was helped by Ada, Countess Lovelace (Byron's daughter), who pursued the idea that the analytical engine could be made programmable, and devised some programs. (The programming language ADA was named after her.)

Escalating costs prevented Babbage's machine being built, but another version is now being constructed.

1847 The English mathematician George Boole – working on Leibniz's ideas – developed a mathematical system for dealing with logical problems, Boolean algebra – now used for designing control systems and incorporated into computer systems.

1890 Herman Hollerith in the USA combined the ideas of the Jacquard loom and the *differential engine* to construct an analyser, the *tabulator*, which used data in the form of punched cards. The device was commissioned for processing the 1890 census, which was achieved in six weeks rather than the six years it would have taken manually.

The Hollerith Tabulator Corporation eventually became International Business Machines (IBM).

1898 The Dane Valdemar Poulsen devised the *telegraphone*, a magnetic recorder using steel wire – the ancestor of all modern magnetic disk devices.

1907 Lee de Forest in the USA devised the *triode thermionic valve* (vacuum tube). This allowed an electric current between two connectors to be controlled by a voltage at a third connector and paved the way for fast computers in the 1950s.

1930 Vannevar Bush, working in the USA at Massachusetts Institute of Technology (MIT), devised a form of *analogue computer*, a machine in which sizes of quantities are represented by electrical voltage size and actions, for example addition and multiplication, are represented by alterations of the voltage levels.

This machine – *the differential analyser* – used the principles of calculus in electrical form and allowed differential equations such as those governing missiles, flow of liquid in pipes, and flow of air over wings to be solved much more rapidly than by using pencil and paper. The machine was only partly electrical and required mechanical gearing to be changed at frequent intervals.

1936 The mathematician Alan Turing in the UK suggested that many apparently insoluble problems might become soluble if a 'universal computer' could be built which could be completely controlled by program instructions.

He also devised the *'Turing test'* to determine if a computer could think for itself. This was based on the principle that if a human could communicate with such a device without seeing it and never know that the device was a computer, then the device would have true intelligence.

1941 The German mathematician Konrad Zuse developed a digital computer using binary code to solve problems connected with rocket ballistics. The storage of bits during calculation was by electromagnetic relays, but the machine had no memory.

1943 Howard Aitken working at Harvard, USA, developed the Mark I computer, using relays as bit stores and with switches to input data in binary form. The machine stood 2·5m (8 ft) high and 15·5m (51 ft) wide and was used to solve the ballistics problems of large naval guns.

Under Turing's guidance, the decoding station at Bletchley Park (Buckinghamshire, UK) developed the Colossus computer to break the German Enigma codes, which were thought to be unbreakable. In some cases the information that was decoded could not be used for fear of revealing that the code was being cracked. Colossus was the first machine to use electronic devices (*thermionic valves*) in place of mechanical or electromechanical (relay) devices, allowing much faster processing and greater reliability. The sheer size of the machine and number of valves meant that the time between failures was short. Neither Mark I nor Colossus had a memory, so they could not be reprogrammed by using software.

1946 The ENIAC (Electronics Number Indicator and Calculator) machine was completed in the USA. This was the first really large and fast digital computer that used thermionic valves (vacuum tubes) as storage elements. ENIAC was 5·5m (18 ft) high, 24m (80 ft) long and weighed 30 tons, but it worked a thousand times faster than the Harvard Mark I. Nowadays even this machine could be outperformed by a modest laptop computer. ENIAC was initially used to carry out the calculations on the feasibility of the hydrogen bomb, although it was not its original purpose. Reprogramming the machine for other purposes had to be done by reconnecting wires, because, at that time, there was no provision for using software to control a digital computer.

1948 Manchester University demonstrated a computer that used thermionic valves and had a small and simple form of memory. This allowed for some software, for easier reprogramming and for more complex calculations in which intermediate results had to be held in the memory. The huge number of valves meant low reliability – one valve had to be replaced for every eight minutes of working time.

1949 Shockley, Brittain and Bardeen, working at Bell Laboratories (USA), invented the *transistor*, and the *switching device*. These were eventually able to replace thermionic valves in computers. The transistor was small, consumed very little electrical power and could be manufactured by automated methods. Initial samples measured 13 mm (0·5 in) long, but by the time transistors could be manufactured in quantity, in 1951, much smaller sizes were achieved. The semiconductor material used was germanium, but by 1956 silicon was being used to make superior devices.

Konrad Zuse constructed and marketed *digital computers* in Germany. These were developments of his Z4 design and used thermionic valves.

Wilkes and Renwick at Cambridge University demonstrated the EDSAC (Electronic Delay Storage Automatic Calculator) machine. This was said to achieve a calculating speed 15,000 times faster than the human brain.

Lyons, the British catering firm, developed LEO (Lyons Electronic Office), the first computer intended for commercial data processing as distinct from scientific and military engineering work. LEO was used for accounting and stock control. A later LEO MARK III was one of the first computers to use transistors in place of valves.

1951 The EDVAC (Electronic Digital Vacuum-tube Analysing Computer) was developed in the USA. Using thermionic valves, it was the first computer to use binary codes and to be programmed to create its own machine code using an assembler program.

1952 A computer was used for the first time in the USA to analyse voting patterns in a national election. It correctly predicted the outcome.

1954 IBM began the mass-production of computers. The IBM 7000 series were the first commercially obtainable computers that used transistors.

1956 The term *artificial intelligence* was coined.

1958 The first computer dating agency was set up.

1959 The *microchip* – or *integrated circuit* (IC) – was developed by Robert Noyce in the USA. A silicon transistor was manufactured on a surface of 6·45 mm^2 (0·1 in^2). It soon became possible to make ten transistors, and the electrical connections between them, in the same space. The microchip allowed circuits to be constructed using vastly greater numbers of transistors. This immensely improved reliability because failures arise mainly from interconnections and the use of chips greatly reduces the need for interconnections.

1965 Digital Equipment Corporation (DEC) – making use of transistor and IC techniques – produced the first widely-marketed minicomputer, leading to the famous PDP11 and VAX machines. By this time several hundred transistors and their connections could be made on a single chip.

In Germany, print was typeset by computer for the first time. The PROLOG language was devised to develop programs for artificial intelligence (AI) work. The IBM 360 computers made extensive use of ICs.

1971 The microprocessor, containing several thousand transistors on one chip, was developed by Ted Hoff at Intel. This device, the 4004, worked with 4-bit units and provided all the processing needed for a simple computer in one chip, to which a manufacturer needed only to add memory and input/output ports.

A coin-operated Hewlett-Packard computer was installed in a California public library, the first instance of easy access to a computer for the public.

1975 The first kit for constructing a personal computer became available.

1977 Steve Wozniak and Steve Jobs – working from the garage at Jobs' home and with a capital of $1300 – developed the Apple-1 computer, the first home computer. This was soon followed by the much more advanced Apple-2.

Reports began of health problems connected to the intensive use of VDUs, including eyestrain, back and shoulder problems, head and neck strains, and arm, wrist and leg pains.

1978 The first case of computer-related fraud by 'hacking' was reported. A hacker was charged with defrauding a Los Angeles bank of $10 ·2 million.

1979 Visicalc, the first spreadsheet program, was demonstrated on the Apple-2. This caused the demand for the machine to increase enormously and created a business – rather than academic – market for microcomputers.

Loughborough University (UK) published its VDU manual, which has been widely used for its recommendations on the best use of VDUs so as to avoid medical problems.

1980 The UK Post Office telephone service began its Prestel service using large mainframe computers to provide information to subscribers (such as travel agents) over telephone lines. The system later allowed electronic mail (e-mail) messages to be sent between subscribers.

New models of microcomputers proliferated worldwide, but most of the machines were incompatible with each other, had a limited range of uses, and were short-lived.

1981 IBM launched the IBM-PC microcomputer. Though the first models were less powerful than other contemporary designs, the use of an advanced form of Intel chip allowed IBM to develop the machine into a powerful unit (the PC-XT) that made the use of microcomputers acceptable for business purposes and imposed some standards on a chaotic industry.

Software developed for the PC was aimed at business users rather than at computer enthusiasts, and included the famous Lotus 1-2-3 spreadsheet and Word Perfect word processor. The MS-DOS operating system developed for the IBM PC was made available to users wishing to develop machines that will run IBM software.

Germany introduced regulations on the design and use of VDUs in an attempt to reduce medical problems.

1983 The IBM PC-XT was introduced, standardizing the 5.25 in floppy disk format for years to come. This machine could also be fitted with a hard disk.

1984 IBM introduced the PC-AT, a vastly faster and more advanced machine that could run the same software as their earlier models. This compatibility has been a feature of the IBM machines, allowing users to change machines without the need to scrap all of their software. The PC-AT used the Intel 80286 chip with 1Mb of memory and a 1.2Mb floppy disk drive along with a 20Mb hard disk.

The Apple Macintosh was introduced, using Motorola microprocessor chips (incompatible with Intel types) and pioneering WIMP (Window, Ikon, Mouse Programming) techniques. These ideas – first developed by Xerox – allowed computers to be used more easily. The *mouse* is a small hand-held device that can be pushed around a desk and which causes an arrow marker to move on the VDU screen. Buttons on the mouse are used to confirm selection of whatever the arrow on-screen is pointing to. Selections of menus appear in separate windows on-screen. The mouse is now available on all microcomputers.

1985 The Transputer – a form of microprocessor that can be linked to other identical units – was developed by Iain Barron in the UK. This allowed *parallel-processing* – in which several actions can be carried out simultaneously – as distinct from the *serial* (one item at a time) action of conventional processors. When *conventional processors* appear to be carrying out several tasks at once – *multi-tasking* – they are, in fact, timesharing the tasks by carrying out portions from each task in sequence.

1986 Machines of very similar construction to IBM machines – and able to run the same software – were suddenly reduced in price, particularly after the introduction of the Amstrad PC 1512.

The availability of low-cost computers, along with the development of a vast library of software for the PC, led to a huge surge in the use of the PC type of machine. The Data Protection Act was introduced in the UK.

1987 IBM and other manufacturers introduced a machine using the Intel 80386 chip. This allowed older software to be run at very high speeds, and also permitted multi-tasking, so that several programs could seem to be running together.

New standards for VDU construction and use appeared from the BSI (British Standards Institute).

Laser printers, using the principle of the Xerox copier, became available, allowing the rapid printing of very high-quality material. Laser printers are extensively used along with DTP (desktop publishing) software to revolutionize the production of documents. Laptop computers started to appear in large numbers.

1988 Acorn (UK) developed their RISC (Reduced Instruction Set Computer) microprocessor, which operates at a very high speed by using only the most common and simplest instruction steps. This led to the development of the advanced, fast Archimedes computer, which is sold extensively to UK educational institutes.

ICL and Tender Electronic Industries jointly designed an improved laser-read optical-disk system for computers. Wang's Freestyle computer was developed. This can work with handwritten data (using an electronic pen) and with spoken messages.

Steve Jobs announced the NEXT computer.

1989 Low-price clones of the fast 80386 computers became easily available, making this type of machine a standard for business. Intel released the 80496 chip, a development of the 80386 that includes some on-chip memory and avoids the need for a set of supporting chips.

Intel also produced their first RISC chip, the i860.

British Telecom developed light-operated computer circuits that promise much faster operation and the ability to be linked over large distances by optical fibres.

The Science Museum, London, started a fund-raising campaign to construct Babbage's difference engine (see above).

1990 IBM and others announced computers using the 80686 Intel chip. The price of clone machines - using the older chips – fell sharply, particularly those using 80386 chips. IBM also announced a machine that runs both MS-DOS (for older software) and the UNIX operating system (for software that runs on mainframe and mini computers).

Several firms announced multimedia systems, combining computing and video techniques. NEC announced the first laptop machine with a full-colour screen.

1991 The Windows 3.0 software provided the IBM PC type of machine with the ease of use of the Apple Macintosh, but at lower prices, stimulating a boom in software and faster machines to use it.

High-capacity storage devices using rewritable optical disks became available.

Small ink-jet printers became available for portable computers.

1992 Windows 3.1 launched. Its software dominated PC desktop computing, with both desktop and laptop machines requiring larger disk and memory capacity, while newer operating systems were developed.

Nickel hydride batteries were being developed to overcome problems with portables.

Dye-transfer colour printers became available at comparatively low prices.

Amstrad launched an A4 sized laptop using older technology – useful particularly for its built-in word-processor.

Networking became almost universal.

COMPUTING GLOSSARY

ADA a language developed for the US Defense Department to allow programming of missile-detection and similar systems with the minimum of flaws (or bugs).

addressing selecting memory by using a number unique to a unit memory applied in binary form along address lines.

ALGOL a third-generation language. ALGOL was the first to concentrate on logical as distinct from mathematical processing needs.

ALU abbreviation for arithmetic and logic unit, the central part of any microprocessor.

analogue (analog) computer a computer that deals with data having physical quantity and which is constantly changing. These changes are represented by changes in voltages. The output – which may be graphed instantly by a plotting pen – can in turn drive another device.

Analogue computers operate in real-time, as events occur, rather than handling previously stored and coded data as a digital computer does.

archive data stored in a form intended for long-term retention.

artificial intelligence (AI) the field of computing science involving the development of computer programs intended to simulate human learning and decision-making abilities. (See also Turing test.)

ASCII acronym for American Standard Code for Information Interchange in which each text character, number or punctuation mark has a value of 7-bits assigned to it, there being 128 (2^7 = 128) possible values. For example the letter A has value 65 (= binary 100001).

assembly language a low-level programming language that uses abbreviated commands that can easily be translated, using a program, into machine code.

backing store a storage system that is non-volatile (usually magnetic). This will retain large quantities of data when the computer is switched off.

BASIC acronym for Beginners All-Purpose Symbolic Instruction Code, a language developed originally for teaching FORTRAN but now recognized in its own right. Lack of standardization is the main drawback to use of BASIC.

baud a measure of the rate at which a digital transmission is sent, the units being bits per second.

binary code the representation of symbols or characters by patterns of 0s and 1s, which on a computer can be represented by electric current being turned off and on.

bit (from BInary digiT) the smallest unit of inform ation (a 0 or a 1) that can be recognized by a computer.

bug a fault in a program. This may be minor (requiring a key to be pressed twice) or major (causing a program to 'crash').

bulletin board a computer-linked database for holding messages and information.

byte a unit of measurement for computer memory capacity. A byte usually contains eight bits. Each byte corresponds to one character of data: a single letter, number or symbol.

C a third-generation language of great power and flexibility. An object-orientated version called C++ is also available.

Criticized on the grounds of obscurity ('a read-only language'), C is widely used for writing other programs.

cache a small element of memory (see RAM) immediately available to the central processor which operates at a higher speed than main memory.

CD-ROM a CD-type of disk that can be read by a conventional laser reader. It contains digital data from computers as distinct from digital representation of sound.

character any symbol (including numbers, letters, punctuation marks, mathematical symbols, etc.) capable of being stored and processed by a computer.

chip or **microchip** a small piece of crystal (usually silicon or other semiconductor material) printed and etched in a pattern to form a logical circuit (an integrated circuit).

circuit the complete path of an electrical current.

CISC see RISC.

clock an electronic circuit that provides electrical pulses at regular intervals to produce timing for the microprocessor actions. Clock rates of 16 MHz (16 million pulses per second) are common.

clone a close copy of a machine that will run the same software. Only the PC type of machine has been extensively cloned.

COBOL acronym for Common Business Orientated Language, the first (and main) language intended for writing data-processing programs for business use.

compiler a program that will convert the statements (commands) of a programming language into machine code that can be run in one step.

conductor a substance (such as a metal) that enables the passage of electricity.

crash a total program failure. This may result in the loss of all data held in memory.

cursor a small block or arrow on the computer screen to show the position of where the next keyed instruction will be implemented.

data raw material such as characters or symbols stored in a computer from which 'information' is derived after processing.

database a structured collection of data that can be analysed and interrogated on computer to retrieve items (or combinations of items) that match selected criteria.

desktop publishing (DTP) a system which permits book quality typesetting, with the addition of graphics and illustrations to made-up pages, to be achieved in a small office environment.

It owes its success largely to the advent of the IBM PC and AppleMacintosh, to the number of software packages available for word-processing, graphics manipulation and page make-up and to compact, high performance laser printers.

digital computer a computer that deals with data in binary-coded number form as distinct from the variable-voltage signals used in analogue computers.

disk a magnetic disk for storing data. See floppy disk, hard disk.

dot-matrix the method of representing characters by a set of dots either on the VDU screen or on paper when a dot-matrix printer is used.

DRAM acronym for Dynamic RAM. A widely used form of memory which is cheaper but slower than SRAM.

The charge on a capacitor determines whether a 1 or a 0 is stored at a particular memory location. The charge slowly leaks and has to be regularly refreshed. In SRAM, two transistors are so arranged that they lock onto the value stored at the memory location in question.

electronic mail (e-mail) information directed to specific users' screens or held in 'computer mailboxes' for access by users who type in codes. Information held on a bulletin board (see above) can be accessed by any user.

fibre optics the use of thin glass fibres to carry light signals. This is now replacing the use of copper cable carrying electronic signals.

Digital computers can use any medium that represents on and off signals; light is faster than electric current, and fibre optic cables can carry a far greater density of signals than can the equivalent size of electric cable.

fifth-generation language a computer language that involves the ability to make decisions and to learn. A computer using a fifth-generation language is addressed in normal language rather than in a programming language.

floppy disk a magnetic data-storage disk that is removable from the medium. Early disks were contained in cardboard envelopes and were floppy, but later versions use rigid plastic containers. Floppy disks operate at lower speeds and can handle less data than hard disks.

FORTRAN acronym for Formula Translation, one of the first programming languages for scientific and engineering uses.

fourth-generation language a computer language that requires no description of procedures, only a list of data and what is needed to be processed.

The output of a 4GL is generally a set of commands in a third-generation language, usually Pascal or C.

Gigabyte (Gb) one thousand megabytes, more accurately 2^{30} bytes (1073.741824 Mb).

GUI an acronym for Graphical User Interface, an arrangement on screen for simplifying computer operations in which files, directories, and applications are represented pictorially by icons arranged in windows. The icons can be selected or moved using a pointing device or mouse.

hacker (originally) a skilled mender of faulty programs. The term now refers to a person who gains illegal access to other computers either mischievously or for criminal intent.

hard disk a magnetic data-storage disk that is not removable from the medium (except on mainframe machines). It operates at much higher speeds and with much greater amounts of data than the removable (floppy) disks.

hardware all the electronics and mechanical parts of the computer as distinct from the programs and data (the software).

hard-wired restricted functioning of a computer, limited by soldered connections and not responsive to varying software commands.

icon a screen picture that represents a standard computer function. A typical example would be an onscreen 'wastebasket' to which a user can point to delete a file.

ink-jet a form of printer mechanism in which ink is squirted from a matrix or tiny jets on to the paper.

integrated circuit see chip.

interface an electronic circuit that converts electronic signals from one form to another or organizes the signals differently.

An interface is needed to allow the computer to be connected to any other piece of equipment, including the disk system and the screen.

interpreter a program that allows the statements of a programming language to be run line-by-line.

K symbol for kilobyte.

keying in typing at a computer keyboard.

kilobyte (K) loosely one thousand bytes, although strictly 1 K = 2^{10} = 1024 bytes.

laptop a portable computer that can be battery-operated and is light enough to be used on the lap while travelling.

laser disk a disk - like an audio CD - capable of storing vast quantities of archive files in a minute area. It is prepared by focusing a narrow beam of light on to it.

Its main use is archive storage of data (CD-ROM), but it can be used interactively (CDI).

machine-code the most elementary way of programming a computer by using binary codes directly.

mainframe a large computer whose stored data may be accessed by 100 or more terminals.

megabyte (Mb) loosely one million bytes, although strictly 1 Mb = 2^{20}.

memory usually refers to the currently accessible store (RAM). The term is sometimes used to refer to disk storage capabilities.

microchip see chip.

microprocessor a device capable of holding memory and instructions. A microprocessor is a basic unit of a microcomputer.

microcomputer a low-cost, independent computer unit based on the microprocessor. It requires low power and, unless linked to a network, has a limited memory.

minicomputer a small computer whose capabilities in speed, power and data handling are between those of a microcomputer and a mainframe.

Minicomputers were developed during the American space research programme to meet the need for a small computer that could be moved on site.

MIPS a measure of the average speed of a processor in Millions of Insructions Per Second.

modem a circuit that converts between digital signals and tone signals. It is used when computers need to communicate along telephone lines or radio links.

monitor see screen.

mouse a hand-held device that rolls across a table or board, its position reflecting the position of the cursor on the screen. It is used as an alternative to the computer keyboard to access a screen.

MS-DOS see operating system.

network a system of computers connected to each other through cables, by telephone, data communication technology or even by radio.

OCCAM a language developed specially for programming parallel-processing computers.

operating system a program that attends to all the routine tasks of running a computer, allowing other programs (applications programs) to make use of the disks, screen and keyboard, etc., without needing to write their own code for such operations.

PC machines all use the MS-DOS operating system; many minicomputers use a system called UNIX (which requires vast amounts of memory). Mainframe machines normally use operating systems that are provided by the manufacturer.

parallel-processor a microprocessor that can be run in conjunction with another, sharing memory and other parts of a computer system.

One common example is the use of a mathematical co-processor along with the main processor in PC machines. A more complex type is the transputer.

PASCAL a programming language originally designed for academic uses by Niklaus Wirth, but now widely used for systems programming, particularly in the form of Turbo-pascal from Borland International.

port a form of interface used to connect a computer to other units such as the keyboard, printer or modem.

portable language any programming language for which a program can be written that will work on all computers for which a compiler or interpreter is available without modification to the program.

processor the central unit of a computer that carries out the actions of arithmetic and comparison. It controls all of the other units under the command of a program.

program a set of instructions that a system follows to carry out tasks.

Prestel the British Telecom videotext information service, designed to be received on home television sets and computers. The communications are carried on public telephone lines.

PROM Programmable Read-Only Memory. A chip that can be written by larger-than-normal signals and then used as a ROM, retaining its data.

Data is erased by, for example, exposing the chip to ultra-violet light.

RAM Random Access Memory, memory available for current work. This is lost when the computer is switched off unless work is transferred out of the RAM on to permanent store such as a disk.

register a temporary store used in a processor to hold data while it is being used in arithmetic, logical or comparison actions.

relay switches switches controlled electromagnetically. They are typically used in analogue computers.

resistor a substance impeding the flow of a current.

RISC (Reduced Instruction Set Computer). A processor which responds to a smaller range of instructions (but those which are most frequently encountered) than the more traditional CISC (Complex Instruction Set Computer). It is consequently simpler and cheaper to make and runs more quickly.

ROM Read-Only Memory, a non-volatile memory (i.e. a memory that is not erased when the power is switched off) that must be present in any computer in order to make the machine usable.

The ROM normally contains the commands that allow the machine to make use of its disk system so that further commands (of an operating system) can be read in.

scanner a device that transforms an image into digitally coded signals that can be stored on computer and redisplayed.

Using scanners, printed text can be stored directly on to the disk without having to be keyed in.

screen the display device on a computer - also called a monitor, VDU (visual display unit) or VDT (visual display terminal).

Screens basically use cathode-ray tube technology of television to create an image.

SCSII acronym for Small Computer System Interface (pronounced 'scuzzy') a general purpose link between a computer and one or more external devices.

semiconductor a material, such as silicon, whose pure form has very low electrical conductivity but whose conductivity is enormously changed when traces of other elements are added – a process called *doping.*

The movement of particles within the semiconductor allows its electrical conduction to be controlled by electrical signals, making it an electrically-operated switch.

silicon chip see chip, semiconductor.

software the programs that give instructions to, or run on, a computer, as opposed to the electronics and mechanical parts of a computer (the hardware).

spreadsheet a form of data-analysing program that can be used for a very wide range of applications ranging from word tables to the analysis of complex mathematical relationships. In this latter use, altering one item of data on the screen will result in the recalculation of all the other items that depend on that item.

Spreadsheets are widely used for financial data and particularly in forecasting work.

SRAM static RAM, see DRAM.

terminal a device linked to a computer, comprising a keyboard or a screen, or both.

thermionic valve a device that uses metal plates to control the flow of electrons in a vacuum inside an evacuated tube. The electrons are emitted from a hot surface – the cathode – and the current between the cathode and the opposite surface – the anode – is controlled by the voltage on an intermediate grid.

Thermionic valves were formerly used for electronics circuits before the invention of transistors.

transistor a device that transfers current across a resistor.

transputer a large, fast and powerful chip. When paired with another chip it enables a computer to carry out two tasks simultaneously.

Turing test a test for successful artificial intelligence that depends on a human not knowing that he or she is communicating with a computer. No computer has ever passed the Turing test. See p. 315.

UNIX see operating system.

user-friendly (of computer products) simple and easy-to-use.

vacuum tube the American name for the thermionic valve.

VDT see screen.

VDU see screen.

voice recognition a computer's ability to respond to spoken words.

volatile (of memory) losing all data when the power is disconnected. RAM in computers is generally volatile, making it important to save data to a backing store.

window a portion of a screen that is used as if it were an independent separate screen.

workstation the equipment used by a computer operator and, increasingly, the associated furniture, lighting and working environment.

WORM acronym for Write Once Read Many times - a form of optical disk that can be written as well as read by the computer using it.

ARTIFICIAL INTELLIGENCE

A computer simply carries out orders and cannot think for itself. In the 1940s and 1950s computer scientists pioneered Artificial Intelligence (AI) with the aim of creating a thinking machine. So far they have failed, but in the process they have taught us much about the way that humans think. The British mathematician Alan Turing designed an experiment to test whether a machine shows intelligence. In Turing's experiment a human conducts a dialogue, by means of a computer terminal, with both a machine and another human, hidden behind a screen. Both respondents must answer every question put to them. Turing argued that if the questioner could not decide which of the two respondents was the machine, then the machine would have demonstrated intelligence. AI researchers have adopted two very different approaches to building intelligent machines. Some have tried to build machines that use the same principles as biological intelligence; others have chosen examples of intelligent behaviour (such as chess playing or language) and tried to build machines that copy it. AI scientists have attacked a wide range of problems. These include problem solving, natural language and vision. The first attempts to tackle problem solving (often used as a measure of intelligence) produced the Logic Theorem program in the 1950s. As its name suggests, it was capable of proving theorems. Later came a more advanced program called the General Problem Solver, which was able to tackle more complex mathematical problems. Since then computer scientists have made great strides in improving the problem-solving abilities of computers, but these are still confined to those problems that lie within the realms of logic.

A major goal of AI research is to enable humans to interact with computers using natural language – language that is written and spoken by humans, as distinct from computer-program languages. To understand and interpret such language, much more knowledge is needed than was once thought. Computers have to be able to work out the context in which a word is uttered in order to interpret what is being said; for example, there is a huge difference between 'close the door' and 'stay close to me'. To this end AI researchers have made use of the ideas of the linguist Noam Chomsky who suggested that language obeys a set of rules that can be expressed in mathematical terms.

Running parallel with this work on natural language, research has been undertaken into speech recognition. Speech-recognition systems use information about the structure and components of speech and are typically 'trained' in on one person's voice. The challenge is to develop a machine that can recognize what any one of a variety of speakers is saying – even if their voice is affected by, for instance, a cold – and distinguish speech from background noise.

Expert systems

The most tangible and practical result of AI research has been in the area of expert systems. These are designed to help humans make decisions, typically in solving problems where it would otherwise be necessary to call in an expert in a particular area. Many early expert systems tackled medical diagnosis, but industry and commerce have now begun to take them seriously. An expert system has three components: a *knowledge base*, in which the knowledge and experience of an expert are summarized in the form of rules; an *inference engine*, which is a program that searches the knowledge base for the best possible answer to a question; and a *user interface*, which allows the user to 'talk' to the system. Experts often find it difficult to explain to a computer engineer exactly how they reach their decisions, and translating the mechanics of these decisions – which may rely heavily on experience and intuition – into the exact mathematical logic required by a computer is a complex task. In fact expert systems are of no use where intuition or common sense is necessary – they can only be used where the decision-making process follows a simple, well-defined logic path. But such systems are very valuable where experts are scarce, or as a means of preserving knowledge and transferring it to others as individuals retire or change jobs.

Neural computing

The most promising approach to the creation of artificial intelligence has used the structure of the brain as the basis for computer architecture. *Neural networks* are connected microprocessors that mimic the complex network of interlinking neurones in the brain. The idea of neural networks has been around since the 1940s, but only since the early 1980s has interest been rekindled. Neural networks offer big advantages over conventional computers in searching large databases for close matches, or storing and accessing data. They consist of a large number of processors (*nodes*) – the points at which the information is processed – linked by communication channels. Neural computers learn by example; they are not programmed like conventional computers, which means that they are not simply given a series of instructions to carry out. They use the concept of *feedback* – where part of the output of a node is returned as input for another process, for self-correction – and hence they can interact with their environment. However, they are still a long way from a thinking machine.

Robotics

Another major branch of AI is robotics. While robots are used on the production lines of most car-manufacturing plants – for assembly and simple spot welding – they are very primitive. They inhabit a 'perfect' world, and have no sense of touch or vision to adapt to their environment, such as dealing with misplaced, faulty or missing components. Three-dimensional vision is crucial to developing practical systems. A wide range of techniques is being developed for extracting the salient features of an image; this would allow a robot to recognize and pick up an object from the production line, for example, even if the object were not in its correct position.

The thinking machine

The road to the thinking machine is proving longer and more difficult than the AI pioneers of the 1940s and 1950s believed. There is still much debate in the AI community about whether computers will ever be able to think, or to display the traits normally considered essential for intelligence. While the debate continues, research into AI is bringing a better understanding of brain function and our own intelligence, and an insight into such things as speech disorders and learning problems.

Digital Communications

A principal form of human communication involves the transmission of sound waves. Beyond earshot, the assistance of some kind of telecommunications arrangement is required in which a transmitter is linked by wire, cable or radio to a receiver where the original sounds are recreated. There are two main approaches to achieving this – *analogue* or *digital.*

In a telephone, for example, the signal sent along the cable is a continuous electrical replica or *analogue* of the original sound wave. The concept of analogue communication is, and has been, exceedingly important. The LP recordings of former times provided another example of this process: they contained a continuous impression of the original sound waves in the form of the variations in the groove – a kind of 'frozen' analogue. Similarly the variations of the magnetization of the iron oxide coating of an audio cassette tape form a replica of the original sound waves. As the compact cassette began to supplant the black vinyl of the LP so a new medium made its appearance in the form of the *compact disc* or *CD.* This works on an entirely different principle involving the *digital* storage, and transmission of information.

What is digital communication ?

In essence, this involves sending, or storing information, by numbers. Instead of creating an analogue replica of the original sound wave it is converted into a string of numbers which describe it as fully as possible and from which, at the receiver, it may be reconstructed. The key to this process is the use of *binary notation* to represent the numbers involved.

In binary notation only two different digits are required, namely 0 and 1 in contradistinction to the everyday system – the *decimal* or *denery* system which requires ten different digits – 0 to 9. Thus the decimal number 109 corresponds to binary 1101101:

$$\mathbf{1} \times 10^2 + \mathbf{0} \times 10^1 + \mathbf{9} \times 10^0 = \mathbf{109}$$

$$\mathbf{1} \times 2^6 + \mathbf{1} \times 2^5 + \mathbf{0} \times 2^4 + \mathbf{1} \times 2^3 + \mathbf{1} \times 2^2 + \mathbf{0} \times 2^1 + \mathbf{1} \times 2^0 = \mathbf{109}$$

Why digital ?

The importance of this idea in telecommunications and in computing is that a '1' may be represented electrically by, for example, a switch that is on, by a lamp that is lit or by a current flowing in a circuit. A '0' on the other hand would correspond to an open switch, an unlit lamp or the absence of a current flow. The *strength* of the current or the *brightness* of the lamp is, within fairly wide limits, *not critical.*

These *two-state* devices are therefore inherently more reliable, being less affected by power fluctuations or signal variations and so equipment using them is more stable. Audio circuits yield much higher fidelity with reduction in distortion; in digital computing great accuracy in the execution of programs and processing of data may be confidently expected – unlike the earlier analogue computers.

Communication to, and the storage and manipulation of, data in the digital computer takes place in the form of *bi*nary digi*ts* (abbreviated to *bits).* So that a computer can handle the numbers, characters of the alphabet and punctuation marks, an agreed code, the *American Standard Code for Information Interchange* (*ASCII*), gives numerical values for these. It has the capacity for 128 items, each being represented by 7 bits (2^7 = 128) In our earlier example the lower case letter 'm' is designated in the ASCII code by decimal 109 which is binary 1101101. An eighth bit is often added to provide an extended character set which can then include special symbols and accents in, for example, a word processing application.

The transistor and the 'chip'

The two-state device (in essence, an on-off switch) lies at the heart of digital computing circuits. In early *first generation* computers these came in the form of *thermionic valves.* Since each valve contained an electrical heater, together they consumed a considerable amount of power, there being a great number of such valves employed. A breakthrough in computing was the invention of the *transistor* by John Bardeen, William Shockley and Walter Brattain in 1948 and used in *second generation* computers This replaced the thermionic valve and consumed only a minute fraction of the power required by its predecessor. Unlike valves they work at comparatively low voltages and are also very much smaller; not unimportant where a large number of such devices are needed.

The next main development was that of the *integrated circuit* (*IC*) or 'chip', an invention credited to Geoffrey Dummer in 1952 and realized by Jack Kilby of Texas Instruments Inc in 1959. These formed the basis of *third generation* computers and in them the transistors are manufactured along with the other circuit componenents in a single unit on a wafer base made usually of semiconducting silicon. Nowadays 'very large scale integration' (*VLSI*) chips, the basis of *fourth generation* computers, contain millions of transistors so that an entire microprocessor can be contained within a single chip. The high density of components means that the signals being processed have less distance to travel resulting faster computing.

Networks

Computers are not only required to communicate with their human masters but also with each other. When a number of computers are connected together they form a *network.* The immediate connections between them are made typically by *coaxial cable* (similar to that used to connect a television set to its aerial). A network occupying the same geographical site and typically connected directly by some type of cable is called a *local area network* (*LAN*). LANs in turn may be connected using a device called a *router* to form a *wide area network* or *WAN* The links between WANs can be provided in many ways: by telephone , by special cables, radio link or satellite:

Telephone lines Being already physically in place these form a convenient link. But they have the disadvantage of generally being able to accept only analogue signals, so a modem is required. (See ISDN)

The telehone network is also used for the fast growing *fax* (*facsimile transmission*) service in which copy (typed or drawn) is scanned, converted to a digital signal, and sent via a modem to a fax machine at the other end where the process is reversed and a hard copy of the original is produced. Again telephone lines are used in the transfer of money electronically: *EFT (electronic funds transfer)* enables a customer's bank account to be automatically debited and funds transferred to that of a store without any cash being handled and with a great economy in paperwork.

Fibre-optic cable This consists of many thin flexible glass or plastic fibres to carry the signal, each surrounded by a glass cladding of lower refractive index to guide the light through the central core. The overall diameter is 125μm, about two and a half times the thickness of a human hair. The digital signal from the computer is translated into pulses of light by a laser or light emitting diode at one end and back into a digital signal at the other by a photodiode.

The idea of using glass fibre for transmitting signals goes back to 1966. It has now been developed into an important communications link. It is light, easy to install, smaller than its copper alternative, is free from the effects of electromagnetic interference and, above all, permits very high transmission speeds. It is expected in future that speeds of more than a gigabit (1000 megabits) per second will be achieved.

Satellite communication Communications satellites extend the range of high frequency radio links from country to country. Several of these have been put into orbit since the launch of *Early Bird,* the first, in 1965. The satellite transponder receives the signals from the ground station and retransmits them back to a receiving station, quite often in a different country. The positioning of an artificial satellite in a geostationary orbit (about 36,000 km or 22,250 miles above the Earth's Equator and rotating with the same angular veleocity as the Earth) means that it will always appear to be overhead.

The Internet

Often described as the largest computer network in the world, the Internet is composed of a vast number of private, public, corporate and academic networks linked globally and providing its users with an enormous range of information resources and potential.

The Internet had its origins in 1969 with a small number of computers belonging to the United States Department of Defense. This network, called ARPANET (Advanced Research Project Agency Network), was to be constructed in such a way that it would continue to work even if some of the cables connecting it were broken. The solution resulted in the development of software which enabled each computer to be connected to a few of its neighbours and for information to go by the shortest route and not to follow a prescribed fixed path. These considerations formed the basis of the present Internet and the important TCP/IP protocols *Transmission Control Protocol/Internet Protocol,* which underpin its working to this day. Those engaged on Defense contracts saw its possibilities and academics and commercial interests joined them in connecting to it, increasingly using the public telephone system to do so.

Now there are thought to be in excess of 10,000 networks invoved with more than 30 million estimated users and 75 countries with full Internet connections.

Connecting to the Internet A typical way of making a connection is by telephone, using a modem or

THE INTERNATIONAL INFORMATION HIGHWAY

Countries on Internet Algeria, Andorra, Argentina, Australia, Austria, Bahamas, Belgium, Brazil, Brunei, Bulgaria, Canada, Chile, China, China (Taiwan), Colombia, Costa Rica, Croatia, Cyprus, Czech Republic, Denmark, Ecuador, Egypt, Estonia, Finland, France, Germany, Greece, Hungary, Iceland, India, Indonesia, Ireland, Israel, Italy, Jamaica, Japan, Korea (South), Latvia, Liechtenstein, Lithuania, Luxembourg, Malaysia, Malta, Mexico, Monaco, the Netherlands, New Zealand, Nicaragua, Norway, Panama, Peru, Philippines, Poland, Portugal, Romania, Russia, Singapore, Slovakia, Slovenia, South Africa, Spain, Sweden, Switzerland, Thailand, Trinidad and Tobago, Tunisia, Turkey, Ukraine, the United Kingdom, the USA, Uruguay, the Vatican, and Venezuela.

Countries on Binet (but not Internet) Azerbaijan, Bahrain, Belarus, Iran, Kuwait, and Saudi Arabia.

Countries that are only able to send and receive e-mail Antigua, Armenia, Barbados, Belize, Bolivia, Bosnia-Herzegovina, Botswana, Burkina Faso, Cameroon, Congo, Côte d'Ivoire, Cuba, Dominica, Dominican Republic, Eritrea, Ethiopia, Fiji, Gambia, Georgia, Ghana, Grenada, Guatemala, Kazakhstan, Kenya, Kyrgyzstan, Lesotho, Macedonia, Madagascar, Malawi, Mali, Mauritius, Moldova, Mozambique, Namibia, Nepal, Niger, Nigeria, Pakistan, Papua New Guinea, Paraguay, Saint Christopher and Nevis, Saint Lucia, Saint Vincent and the Grenadines, San Marino, Senegal, Sri Lanka, Suriname, Swaziland, Tajikistan, Tanzania, Togo, Turkmenistan, Uganda, Uzbekistan, Vietnam, Yugoslavia (Serbia only), Zambia, and Zimbabwe.

Countries that are not yet on the Information Highway Afghanistan, Albania, Angola, Bangladesh, Benin, Bhutan, Burundi, Cambodia, Cape Verde, Central African Republic, Chad, Comoros, Djibouti, El Salvador, Equatorial Guinea, Gabon, Guinea, Guinea-Bissau, Guyana, Haiti, Honduras, Iraq, Jordan, Kiribati, Korea (North), Laos, Lebanon, Liberia, Libya, Maldives, Marshall Islands, Mauritania, Micronesia, Mongolia, Morocco, Myanmar (Burma), Nauru, Oman, Palau, Qatar, Rwanda, São Tomé e Principe, Seychelles, Sierra Leone, Solomon Islands, Somalia, Sudan, Syria, Tonga, Tuvalu, United Arab Emirates, Vanuatu, Western Samoa, Yemen, and Zaïre.

The details relating to Internet, Binet and e-mail record the situation in November 1994. Countries are continuously being added to each network.

by ISDN to an agreed Internet host. This might be one of the companies who provide commercial access to the Internet.

Internet addresses Internet addresses are unique and always take the same form:

userid@domain

The *userid,* the same as the *login,* is the name by which the user is identified to the particular computer, or is the account name for charging purposes. The *domain* after the '@' sign consists of a number of elements called *sub-domains* joined by full points and with no spaces. The rightmost sub-domain is called the *top-level domain* and is the most general The sub-domains to the left become increasingly more specific. Examples of top-level domains are:

.edu *educational institution*
.au *Australia*
.uk *United Kingdom*

The other sub-domains will typically include the name of the computer being used. Thus the editor of this book, if on the Internet, might have an address:

clive@ref2.gpl.com.uk

The userid is Clive and he is working at a computer named *ref2.gpl.com.uk* ie in the United Kingdom, in a commercial organization called *gpl. Ref2* is the most specific sub-domain. Note that only lowercase letters are generally used in Internet addresses, although capital letters may be used, on their own or mixed with lowercase letters.

Internet resources *e-mail* One of the most widely used applications on the Internet is the *mailing* facility. This enables users to send messages – usually text but pictures or sounds may be sent as well – without communicating *directly* with each other. Messages left at the host computer in the recipient's mailbox can be read later. Once read it can then be deleted, replied to, saved for future reference or forwarded to a third party. A message may be sent or copied simultaneously to more than one user with the option of including blind copies. The delivery of mail is controlled by a system called *SMTP, Simple Mail Transfer Protocol* which is part of the TCP/IP set of protocols. A program on each Internet computer called a *transport agent* runs in the background and is based on SMTP. The individual e-mail user runs a program called a *user agent* which interfaces with Internet mail system and there are several such programs available.

Telnet To connect directly to another Internet computer a Telnet program is used. This enables the operator, at the *local* computer to *login* directly to the *remote* computer and use it as his own. Telnet software, as in so many Internet applications, works on a client/server basis.

FTP If it is required to copy files from a remote computer having logged on to it, then a service called FTP, *File Transfer Protocal,* is used. This applies to larger and possibly more complex files than would be handled by e-mail. Authorization in the form of a userid and a password are often required when using FTP but a considerable amount of information is freely available on a wide range of topics in *anonymous FTP files.* To use this facility a userid of 'anonymous' is entered with the user's address as password. Again FTP employs a client/server system of operation.

One of the problems presented by such a wealth of information emanating from so many diverse sources is that of finding the particular item being sought, or even knowing if it exists. To assist in overcoming this, there are a number of tools available. Database software called *Archie* (from *Internet Archives Database,* originally developed at McGill University, Montréal, Canada) gives details and the full directory paths of files held on known Anonymous FTP hosts. This software is held at Archie server sites around the world. and is at present keeping track of over two million files at over 1500 Anonymous FTP hosts. Information from an Archie server can be obtained by telnetting using an Archie client, or by sending a request via e-mail. Another tool is *Gopher* which provides a particularly simple and consistent way of locating a file. A Gopher client program connects to a Gopher server and displays a menu of the information available which leads to further menus to be investigated, or ultimately to a particular file. To do all this the Gopher client program itself may have to set up a telnet or FTP connection. Most Gopher servers, and there are several thousand on the Internet, are available freely to the public.

The *World Wide Web,* also called *the Web, WWW* or *W3* is particularly easy to use and is an attempt to make Internet resources available in a particularly uniform way. It is based on the idea of *hypertext* in which the text of a document is flagged with *links.* When a link is selected a further relevant document or menu is called up, itself containing further links. and so allowing the browsing process to continue. Establishing these links may well involve the program using many different kinds of Internet resource – telnet, Gopher, etc. When the link involves video, picture or sound files the process is referred to as *hypermedia.* The client program is known as a browser and there are several such available. A popular example, *Mosaic,* is especially easy to use, the links being in colour.

Usenet is a large collection of topic-centred discussion groups called *newsgroups.* Each Usenet site, of which there are many thousands, is locally run and is organized by a *news administrator.* Not all Usenet computers are on the Internet, belonging to some other system such as UUCP for example, used by Unix computers. There is no central authority and groups are freely formed whenever users decide. Articles which make up the *news* are sent from one news server to another, a process called *news feed.* Some servers act as clearing houses providing simultaneous feed for many other servers and this greatly speeds up the process of news transmisson. The local administrator is responsible for deciding the expiry date of news items, normally within a few days to a fortnight, and the server program deletes them. On the Internet the *NNTP (Network News Transfer Protocol)* governs the transmission of such articles. A client program called a *newsreader* is employed to interface with Usenet. There are many such different programs and they allow a choice of groups to which to *subscribe* and select articles from these groups. Articles, once read, may be saved, copied to someone else, printed out or responded to with a follow-up article. The group with its local interest builds up with time a list of those questions which are asked most often of the group. A member of the group assembles these questions with their answers and makes them available on the server. It is considered etiquette for those contacting to the group to read this list of most *Frequently Asked Questions – FAQs* before making futher enquiries.

GLOSSARY

binary data data which is not text (or ASCII) data. A file which stores a picture for example, contains data in binary form.

Bitnet an international network, independent of the Internet, founded in 1981 at the City University of New York as network for IBM mainframe computers mainly in research establishments and universities. The link between Usenet and Bitnet is performed by *Bitnet/Usenet gateway* computers of which there are several. Bitnet is governed by the IBM protocols, *RSCS* (*Remote Spooling Communications Subsystem*) and *NJE* (*Network Job Entry*). These correspond to the TCP/IP protocols of the Internet.

bulletin board system (BBS) a service, often topic-centred, where information is available for access. Frequently run by an organization or single person

client a program that requests services on a network, frequently from a computer running a server program in a *client-server* arrangement.

CompuServe Compuserve Information Services, based in the US and with nodes around the world, is the largest BBS and offers a wide range of services including access to the Internet.

DAB (Digital audio broadcasting) Tests are being conducted in the UK by the BBC in the 217.5–230 MHz VHF band with broadcasts planned for 1995. DAB will provide CD quality reception with a wide dynamic range, virtually free from background noise and with a modest aerial installation. A new receiver will be required to take advantage of the system.

FidoNet an international telephone network of PCs linked to the Internet via a gateway.

gateway a computer specifically designed to link one network to another of a different kind, especially where different protocols are involved.

host on Internet each individual computer is known as a *host*; also a large mainframe or 'midi' computer can act as *host* to a number of *terminals* linked to it in a multiuser or time-sharing environment.

ISDN (Integrated Services Digital Network) is a digital link provided by the public telephone service which is available wherever the local exchange is digital. ISDN provides a complete, dial-up digital connection, operating at speeds many times that of a standard modem.

MIME (Multipurpose Internet Mail Extension) is a protocol which permits files containing binary data to be sent by the Internet mail system. In this case a user agent that supports MIME is employed.

modem from *mo*dulate-*dem*odulate, a device for converting a digital signal into a continuous, analog signal (modulation) for transmission along, typically, a telephone line and which reverses the process at the other end (demodulation) so restoring the original digital signal. The speed at which a modem operates is measured in bits per second.

NNTP (Network News Transfer Protocol) Part of the *TCP/IP* family of protocols governing the transmission of *Usenet* articles

node a single computer or device attached to network which can transmit or receive data, frequently both, and which is identified by a node ID

packet in networking, data is sent around a network in packets. These are collections of binary digital pulses typically containing data together with network information such as the address of the particular packet and its sequence in the transmission.

POP (Post Office Protocol) an *e-mail* protocol which can be used between a host (Unix) mail server and a PC or MAC client on a *LAN*.

PPP (point-to-point protocol) set of programs which enable a computer to link to the Internet conforming to the TCP/IP protocols and supplanting SLIP.

router a computer specifically designed to link one network to another. A router is used to link *LANs* to form a *WAN*, or indeed to connect WANS to form even larger WANs

server a program that provides services on a network, frequently to a computer running a client program in a *client-server* arrangement. It is also used, particularly in smaller networks (LANs), to refer to the machine running the program which is often described as a fileserver.

SLIP *serial line internet protocol,* a set of programs which enable a computer to link to the Internet conforming to the TCP/IP protocols.

SMTP (Simple Mail Transfer Protocol) Part of the TCP/IP family of protocols governing the transmission of mail messages.

TCP/IP (Transmission Control Protocol/Internet Protocol) the essential protocols upon which the Internet is founded and have their roots in the Unix operating system. Essentially, TCP organises the data into addressed packets, adds a sequence number to them with information for error detection; IP is responsible for routing the packets through the system, from computer to computer.

text file as distinct from a binary file, one which contains alphabet characters, numbers and punctuation, commonly represented by the *ASCII* code.

Unix a computer operating system developed in 1969 at the AT&T® Bell Telephone Laboratories in the US. It is important for Internet users: many of the computers on the Internet run under Unix and it forms the basis for creating and manipulating data files. Composing messages frequently involves the use of a Unix text editing program.

UUCP (Unix to Unix copy protocol)..a system for networking Unix based computers.

Wais (Wide Area Information Service) a generalized search facility. The Wais client program is instructed which *data source* to search and which *keywords* are required. The Wais server carries out a full text search, responds to the client which displays a list of the appropriate articles on the screen When a particular article is chosen, the client relays the request to the server which sends it back for display, one screen at a time, by the client

BELIEFS AND IDEAS

Philosophy

The word 'philosophy' is derived from the Greek, meaning 'love of wisdom'. Broadly speaking, 'philosophy' can be taken to mean any questioning of or reflection upon those principles underlying all knowledge and existence.

Philosophy differs from religion since its quest for underlying causes and principles does not depend on dogma and faith; and it differs from science, since it does not depend solely on fact. Its interrelation with both science and religion can be seen in the large number of philosophers who were also either theologians or scientists, and the few, such as Blaise Pascal and Roger Bacon, who were all three. Philosophy developed from religion, but became distinct when thinkers sought truth independent of theological considerations.

Until the 19th century the term 'philosophy' was used to include what we now distinguish as 'science' (from the Latin for 'knowledge'), and this terminology persists in some university courses such as 'natural philosophy' for physics and 'moral sciences' for what we now call philosophy. Eventually all the branches of science, from physics to psychology, broke away – psychology being the last to do so in the 20th century.

CLASSICAL PHILOSOPHY

Classical philosophy may be divided into three broad fields: ethics, metaphysics and epistemology:

Ethics

Ethics is the study of how we decide how people ought to live and act. Philosophers' opinions about ethics tend to resolve into an opposition between two main schools: the Idealists and the Utilitarians.

The Idealists consider that the goodness or badness of a course of action must be judged by standards derived from outside the everyday world: from God, or heaven, or perhaps from a human higher self. The Utilitarians hold that the effects that a course of action produces in this world are all that is relevant to its ethical value. The Utilitarians are more directly concerned than the Idealists with earthly welfare. The earliest Western philosopher of this tradition was Epicurus.

Metaphysics

Metaphysics originated as the title of one of Aristotle's treatises. It probably meant only that he wrote it after his treatise Physics, but the term is usually employed to describe speculation as to the ultimate nature of reality.

Epistemology

Epistemology is the study of the nature, grounds and validity of human knowledge – how we come to know; how far we can rely on different kinds of belief; how science can be separated from superstition; and how conflicts between rival scientific theories can be resolved.

The epistemologists who are usually called Rationalists assert that knowledge is born in the individual and has only to be drawn forth. The other point of view – Empiricism – is that at birth the mind is a passive blank sheet on which knowledge is then imprinted.

PHILOSOPHICAL SCHOOLS AND THEORIES

Since the days of the early Greeks, philosophers have been divided into different schools and have advanced opposing theories.

Modern philosophy is represented by three main movements: Hegelianism, analytical philosophy and phenomenology. These three movements – which are described below – would regard the classical description of philosophy into the three fields of metaphysics, ethics and epistemology as outmoded.

Among the many basic philosophical outlooks and theories are the following:

altruism the principle of living and acting in the interest of others rather than for oneself.

analytical philosophy a movement founded at the beginning of the 20th century by Bertrand Russell, building on the work of the mathematician Gottlob Frege. Analytical philosophy – which is no less critical of philosophical tradition – is based on the idea that authentic philosophy is essentially the study of logic, that is to say of formal patterns of reasoning abstracted from their metaphysical, ethical, epistemological or historical contexts.

asceticism the belief that withdrawal from the physical world into the inner world of the spirit is the highest good attainable.

atomism the belief that the entire universe is ultimately composed of interchangeable indivisible units.

critical theory a philosophical version of Marxism associated with the *Frankfurt School* (founded 1921).

criticism the theory that the path to knowledge lies midway between dogmatism and scepticism.

determinism the belief that the universe and everything in it (including individual lives) follows a fixed or pre-determined pattern. This belief has often been used to deny free will.

dialectical materialism the theory – often attributed to Marx – that reality is strictly material and is based on an economic struggle between opposing forces, with occasional interludes of harmony.

dogmatism the assertion of a belief without arguments in its support.

dualism the belief that the world consists of two radically independent and absolute elements, e.g. good and evil, or (especially) spirit and matter.

egoism the belief that the serving of one's own interests is the highest end.

empiricism the doctrine that there is no knowledge except that which is derived from experience. Empiricism holds that, at birth, the mind is a passive blank sheet on which knowledge is then imprinted. The classic representative of Empiricism was John Locke, a 17th-century English philosopher.

Epicurean is often used to describe one who indulges in excessive pleasure, but the usage is not just. Epicurus did not condone excesses. On the contrary, he said that pleasure was only good when moderate and calm.

existentialism the doctrine that the human self and human values are fictions, but inevitable ones, and that it is bad faith to deny one's own free will, even in a deterministic universe.

fatalism the doctrine that what will happen will happen and nothing we do will make any difference.

hedonism the doctrine that pleasure is the highest good.

Hegelianism the modern philosophy proposed by Hegel. At the beginning of the 19th century, Georg Wilhelm Friedrich Hegel criticized all previous conceptions of philosophy as being lifeless, one-sided and unhistorical. Hegel proposed that philosophy must always be rooted in history, but at the same time always striving for a conception of reality as a single developing whole, every part of which is animated by all the others.

humanism any system that regards human interests and the human mind as paramount in the universe.

idealism any system that regards thought or the idea as the basis either of knowledge or existence. Idealists consider that the goodness or badness of a course of action must be judged by standards derived from outside the everyday world: from God, or heaven, or perhaps from a human higher self. The Idealist school began with the Greek philosopher Plato.

interactionism the theory that physical events can cause mental events, and vice versa.

materialism the doctrine that asserts the existence of only one substance – matter – thus denying the existence of spirit.

monism a belief in only one ultimate reality, whatever its nature.

naturalism a position that seeks to explain all phenomena by means of strictly natural (as opposed to supernatural) categories.

nominalism the doctrine that general terms are, in effect, nothing more than words. (Compare realism.)

operationalism the doctrine that scientific concepts are tools for prediction rather than descriptions of hidden realities.

pantheism the belief that God is identical with the universe.

personalism the theory that ultimate reality consists of a plurality of spiritual beings or independent persons.

phenomenology a movement founded at the same time as analytic philosophy. It has come to dominate 20th-century European philosophy just as the analytic school has dominated philosophy in the English-speaking world. This movement claims that philosophers always tend to miss the one fundamental question – why our experience should be framed in terms of a distinction between an objective world and our subjective experience of it. Heidegger and Derrida have developed this line of thought by arguing that, so far from trying to build on past philosophy, we should attempt to 'destroy' or 'deconstruct' it.

pluralism the belief that there are more than two irreducible kinds of reality.

positivism the doctrine that man can have no knowledge outside science.

pragmatism a philosophical method that makes practical consequences the test of truth.

predestination the doctrine that the events of a human's life are determined beforehand.

rationalism the theory that reason alone, without the aid of experience, can arrive at the basic reality of the universe.

realism the doctrine that general terms have a real existence.

relativism the rejection of the concept of absolute and invariable truths.

scepticism the doctrine that nothing can be known with certainty.

sensationalism the theory that sensations are the ultimate and real components of the world.

stoicism a philosophical school that believed that reason (God) was the basis of the universe and that humanity should live in harmony with nature.

structuralism the doctrine that language is essentially a system of rules; or the extension of this idea to culture as a whole.

theism the belief in a God.

transcendentalism the belief in an ultimate reality that transcends human experience.

utilitarianism the belief that the effects that a course of action produces in this world are all that is relevant to its ethical value.

voluntarism the theory that will is a determining factor in the universe.

PHILOSOPHICAL TERMS

a posteriori knowledge knowledge that comes from experience.

a priori knowledge knowledge that can be derived from pure reasoning, without reference to experience, i.e. by reasoning (as in mathematics and logic).

aesthetics the study of the nature of beauty and taste, especially in art.

analytic truths truths that can be proved by analysing the concepts they involve.

axiom a necessary and self-evident proposition requiring no proof.

causality the relationship between a cause and its effect.

deduction reaching a conclusion by purely *a priori* means.

dialectic literally, debate; by extension, the technique of proceeding from a thesis, through its negation or antithesis, to a synthesis in which both are reconciled on a higher level.

empirical knowledge knowledge derived from experience rather than reason.

epistemology a branch of philosophy that attempts to answer questions about the nature of knowledge and especially the nature of science.

ethics a branch of inquiry that attempts to answer questions about right and wrong, good and evil; and how we decide how human life should be lived.

induction the process of drawing general conclusions from particular instances.

logic the study of the structure or form of valid arguments, disregarding their content.

metaphysics a branch of philosophy concerned with systems of ideas that attempt to explain the nature of reality.

paradox a statement whose truth implies its falsehood, e.g. the Cretan philosopher Epimenides said 'All Cretans are liars'. As he was Cretan himself, is his statement true or false?

sophistry a fallacious argument.

synthesis the outcome of the confrontation of two arguments by which a truth is discovered.

teleology the practice of explaining processes in terms of what they achieve rather than what preceded them.

MAJOR PHILOSOPHERS

Abelard, Peter (1079–1142), French theologian and philosopher. Abelard's nominalism caused him to be declared a heretic by the Church.

Adorno, Theodor (1903–69), German philosopher who combined Marxism with avant-garde aesthetics.

Anaximander of Miletus (611–547 BC), Greek philosopher. Anaximander continued Thales' quest for universal substance, but reasoned that universal substance need not resemble any known substances.

Anselm (1033–1109), Italian Augustinian and realist. Anselm is famous for his examination of the proof of God's existence.

Antisthenes (c. 450–c. 360 BC), Classical Greek philosopher. The chief of the group known as the Cynics, Antisthenes stressed discipline and work as the essential good.

Aquinas, St Thomas (1225–74), Italian scholastic philosopher. Aquinas evolved a compromise between Aristotle and Scripture, based on the belief that faith and reason are in agreement. His philosophical system is known as Thomism.

Aristotle (384–322 BC), Greek philosopher and scientist, whose works have influenced the whole of Western philosophy. Aristotle taught that there are four factors in causation: form; matter; motive cause, which produces change; and the end, for which a process of change occurs. Aristotle was a pupil of Plato. He thought of the good as divine, but his ethics had a more 'practical' bent. He equated happiness with the good and was responsible for the doctrine of the golden mean. This stated that every virtue is a middle-point between prodigality and stinginess.

Augustine of Hippo (AD 354–430), Greek philosopher who was an exponent of optimism. One of the greatest influences on medieval Christian thought, Augustine believed that God transcends human comprehension.

Averroës (1126–98), great philosopher of Muslim Spain, and a leading commentator on Aristotle. Averroës regarded religion as allegory for the common man and philosophy as the path to truth.

Avicenna (980–1037), Arabic follower of Aristotle and Neo-Platonism. Avicenna's works revived interest in Aristotle in 13th-century Europe.

Ayer, Alfred J. (1910–89), English philosopher. Ayer was the principal advocate of logical positivism, developed from Russell.

Bacon, Francis (1561–1626), English statesman and philosopher of science. In his major work, *Novum Organum*, Bacon sought to revive the inductive system of deductive logic in interpreting nature.

Beauvoir, Simone de (1908–86), French existentialist. The founder of modern feminist philosophy.

Bentham, Jeremy (1748–1832), English utilitarian. Bentham believed, like Kant, that the interests of the individual are at one with those of society. He regarded pleasure and pain rather than basic principle as the motivation for right action.

Bergson, Henri (1859–1941), French evolutionist. Bergson asserted the existence of a 'vital impulse' that carries the universe forward, with no fixed beginning and no fixed end. He believed that the future is determined by the choice of alternatives made in the present.

Berkeley, George (1685–1753), Anglo-Irish idealist and theist who taught that things exist only in being perceived and that the very idea of matter is contradictory.

Berlin, Sir Isaiah (1909–90), Latvian-born British moral and political philosopher and historian. Berlin argued against determinist philosophies of history. He emphasized the importance of moral values, and the necessity of rejecting determinism if the ideas of human responsibility and freedom are to be retained.

Boethius (c. AD 480–524), late Roman statesman. In *The Consolations of Philosophy* Boethius proposed that virtue alone is constant.

Comte, Auguste (1798–1857), French philosopher. Comte was the founder of positivism, a system which denied transcendent metaphysics and stated that the Divinity and man were one, that altruism is man's highest duty, and that scientific principles explain all phenomena.

Croce, Benedetto (1866–1952), Italian philosopher. Croce was noted for his role in the revival of historical realism.

Davidson, Donald (1917–), US philosopher. A leading philosopher of language, and follower of Quine.

Democritus of Abdera (460–370 BC), Greek philosopher who began the tradition in Western thought of explaining the universe in mechanistic terms.

Derrida, Jacques (1930–), French philosopher. The founder of deconstruction, a development of

Heidegger's technique of interpreting traditional philosophers with great care in order to reveal their constant incoherence.

Descartes, René (1596–1650), French dualist, rationalist and theist. The Cartesian system of Descartes is at the base of all modern philosophy. Descartes evolved a theory of knowledge that underlies modern science and philosophy based on the certainty of the proposition 'I think, therefore I am'.

Dewey, John (1859–1952), US pragmatist who developed a system known as instrumentalism. He saw man as continuous with, but distinct from, nature.

Empedocles of Acragas (c. 495–435 BC). Greek philosopher who believed that there were four irreducible substances (water, fire, earth and air) and two forces (love and hate).

Epicurus (341–270 BC), Greek philosopher. A proponent of atomism and hedonism, Epicurus taught that the test of truth is in sensation.

Erasmus, Desiderius (1466–1536), Dutch philosopher. The greatest of the humanists, Erasmus helped spread the ideas of the Renaissance throughout northern Europe.

Feuerbach, Ludwig (1804–72), German philosopher who argued that religion was no more than a projection of human nature. He was an important influence on Marx.

Fichte, Johann Gottlieb (1762–1814), German philosopher who formulated a philosophy of absolute idealism based on Kant's ethical concepts.

Frege, Gottlob (1848–1925), German mathematician who revolutionized formal logic and thus paved the way for analytic philosophy.

Habermas, Jurgen (1929–). German philosopher. Habermas is a critical Marxist with strong Kantian and liberal affinities.

Hegel, Georg Wilhelm Friedrich (1770–1831). German philosopher. Hegel's metaphysical system was rationalist and absolutist, based on the belief that thought and being are one, and nature is the manifestation of an Absolute Idea.

Heidegger, Martin (1889–1976), German student of Husser who furthered the development of phenomenology and greatly influenced atheistic existentialists.

Heraclitus of Ephesus (533–475 BC), Greek philosopher who opposed the concept of a single ultimate reality and held that the only permanent thing is change.

Hobbes, Thomas (1588–1679), English materialist who believed the natural state of man is war. In *Leviathan* Hobbes outlined a theory of human government whereby the state and man's subordination to it form the sole solution to human selfishness.

Hume, David (1711–76), Scottish empiricist, philosopher and historian. Hume developed the ideas of Locke into a system of scepticism according to which human knowledge is limited to the experience of ideas and sensations whose truth cannot be verified.

Husserl, Edmund (1859–1938), German philosopher who developed a system called phenomenology, which sought to ground knowledge in pure experience without presuppositions.

James, William (1842–1910), US psychologist and pragmatist who held that reality is always in the making and that each man should choose the philosophy best suited to him.

Kant, Immanuel (1724–1804), German founder of critical philosophy. At first influenced by Leibniz, then by Hume, Kant sought to find an alternative approach to the rationalism of the former and the scepticism of the latter. In ethics, he formulated the *Categorical Imperative*, which states that what applies to oneself must apply to everyone else unconditionally. This is the most famous part of Kant's ethics and is connected with the following phrase – before acting a certain way, a person must ask himself: 'Would I be happy if everyone behaved like that?'.

Kierkegaard, Soren (1813–55), Danish religious existentialist. Kierkegaard's thought is the basis of modern (atheistic) existentialism. He taught that only existence has reality, and the individual has a unique value.

Leibniz, Gottfried Wilhelm von (1646–1716), German idealist and absolutist. Leibniz's optimistic view was ridiculed by Voltaire in *Candide*. Leibniz held that reality consisted of units of force called monads.

Lévi-Strauss, Claude (1908–), French anthropologist and proponent of structuralism. His writings investigate the relationship between culture (exclusively an attribute of humanity) and nature, based on the distinguishing characteristics of man – the ability to communicate in a language.

Locke, John (1632–1704), English empiricist. Locke's influence in political, religious, educational and philosophical thought was wide and deep. In his great *Essay Concerning Human Understanding* he sought to refute the rationalist view that knowledge derives from first principles.

Machiavelli, Niccolò (1469–1527), Italian philosopher who placed the state as the paramount power in human affairs. His book *The Prince* brought him a reputation for amoral cynicism.

Maimonides (1135–1204), Jewish student of Aristotle. Maimonides sought to combine Aristotelian teaching with that of the Bible.

Marcel, Gabriel (1889–1973), French philosopher. Initially a student of the English-speaking idealists, Marcel was preoccupied with the Cartesian problem of the relation of mind and matter.

Marcuse, Herbert (1898–1979), German-born US philosopher who attempted to combine existentialism and psychoanalysis with a libertarian Marxism which was critical of Communism.

Marx, Karl (1818–83), German revolutionary thinker who, with Friedrich Engels, was the founder of modern Communism. Marx was a critical follower of Hegel.

Merleau-Ponty, Maurice (1907–61), French phenomenologist who was famous for insisting on the role of the human body in our experience of the world.

Mill, John Stuart (1806–73), English exponent of utilitarianism. Mill differed from Bentham by recognizing differences in quality as well as quantity in pleasure. His most famous work is *On Liberty* (1859).

Moore, George Edward (1873–1958), English moral philosopher who developed the doctrine of ideal utilitarianism in *Principia Ethica* (1903).

Nietzsche, Friedrich Wilhelm (1844–1900), German philosopher who held that the 'will to power' is basic in life and that the spontaneous is to be preferred to the orderly. He attacked Christianity as a system that fostered the weak, whereas the function of evolution is to evolve 'supermen'.

Parmenides of Elea (c. 495 BC), Greek philosopher. A member of the Eleatic school, Parmenides formulated the basic doctrine of idealism.

Pascal, Blaise (1623–62), French theist who held that sense and reason are mutually deceptive, that truth lies between dogmatism and scepticism.

Peirce, Charles S. (1839–1914), US physicist, mathematician and founder of the philosophical school called pragmatism. Peirce regarded logic as the basis of philosophy and taught that the test of an idea is whether it works.

Plato (c. 428–347 BC), Greek philosopher. The founder of the Academy at Athens, Plato developed the idealism of his teacher Socrates and was the teacher of Aristotle. The Idealist School began with Plato, who, in a series of dialogues, depicted his former teacher Socrates discussing the problems of philosophy. In the dialogues, Socrates' procedure is to draw out wisdom from those with whom he is discussing the question. In these dialogues, Plato developed a system of ethics that is essentially idealistic. Socrates argues that the good comes from the realm of 'ideas' or 'forms'. This is a perfect world of which the world of ordinary experience is only a pale replica.

Plotinus (AD 205–270), Greek philosopher who was the chief exponent of Neo-Platonism, a combination of the teachings of Plato and Oriental concepts.

Popper, Sir Karl (1902–94), Austrian-born British critical rationalist. He held that scientific laws can never be proved to be true and that the most that can be claimed is that they have survived attempts to disprove them.

Protagoras of Abdera (481–411 BC), Greek philosopher. An early relativist and humanist who doubted human ability to attain absolute truth.

Pyrrho of Elis (c. 365–275 BC), Greek philosopher. Pyrrho – who initiated the Sceptical school of philosophy – believed that man could not know anything for certain.

Quine, Willard van Orman (1908–), US philosopher who combined pragmatism with logical positivism and destroyed many of the dogmas of early analytic philosophy.

Rousseau, Jean-Jacques (1712–78), French social and political philosopher. Rousseau advocated a 'return to nature' to counteract the inequality among men brought about by civilized society.

Russell, Bertrand (1872–1970), English agnostic. Russell adhered to many systems of philosophy before becoming a major expounder of logical positivism – the view that scientific knowledge is the only factual knowledge.

Ryle, Gilbert (1900–76), English philosopher who studied the nature of philosophy and the concept of mind as well as the nature of meaning and the philosophy of logic.

Sartre, Jean-Paul (1905–80), French philosopher. An influential philosopher who developed the existentialist thought of Heidegger. An atheistic supporter of a subjective, irrational human existence, he was opposed to an orderly overall reality. His slogan was 'existence before essence'.

Schopenhauer, Arthur (1788–1860), German idealist who gave the will a leading place in his metaphysics. The foremost expounder of pessimism, expressed in *The World as Will and Idea*, he rejected absolute idealism as wishful thinking, and taught that the only tenable attitude lay in utter indifference to an irrational world. He held that the highest ideal was nothingness.

Socrates (c. 470–399 BC), Greek philosopher who developed the Socratic method of enquiry. Socrates was the teacher of Plato, through whose writings his idealistic philosophy was disseminated. Socrates taught that virtue was based on knowledge. He was accused of impiety and corruption of youth and was condemned to death. Socrates died by drinking hemlock.

Spencer, Herbert (1820–1903), English evolutionist. Spencer's 'synthetic philosophy' interpreted all phenomena according to the principle of evolutionary progress.

Spinoza, Benedict de (1632–77), Dutch rationalist metaphysician who developed the ideas of Descartes while rejecting his dualism.

Thales of Miletus (624–550 BC), Greek philosopher. Thales – an exponent of monism – is regarded as the first Western philosopher.

Whitehead, Alfred North (1861–1947), English evolutionist and mathematician who held that reality must not be interpreted in atomistic terms, but in terms of events. He held that God is intimately present in the universe, yet distinct from it – a view called pantheism.

Wittgenstein, Ludwig (1889–1951), Austrian philosopher. The most influential philosopher of the 20th century, Wittgenstein developed two highly original but incompatible systems of philosophy, both dominated by a concern with the relations between language and the world. Wittgenstein's *Tractatus Logico – Philosophicus* (1921) explores the relationship of language to the world.

Zeno of Citium (c. 335–263 BC), Greek philosopher. Chief of the Stoics – so called because they met in the *Stoa Poikile* or Painted Porch at Athens – Zeno taught that man's role is to accept nature and all it offers, good or bad.

Zeno of Elea (c. 495–430 BC), Greek philosopher. who argued that plurality and change are appearances, not realities.

Religion

Religion is one of the most universal activities known to humankind, being practised across virtually all cultures, and from the very earliest times to the present day. Religion appears to have arisen from the human desire to find an ultimate meaning and purpose in life, and this is usually centred around belief in a supernatural being (or beings). In most religions the devotees attempt to honour and/or to influence their god or gods – commonly through such practices as prayer, sacrifice or right behaviour.

THE MAJOR RELIGIONS OF THE WORLD

It is difficult to obtain figures for the number of adherents – either practising or nominal – of the world's major religions.

The estimates given below relate to 1993 and refer to religious 'affiliation', that is some formal or nominal connection with a religion.

In most cases the numbers of people practising a religion on a regular basis are much lower.

Religious affiliation	*Number of adherents (1993 est)*	*% of world's population*
1. **Christianity**	1,870,000,000	33.5%
Roman Catholic	*1,043,000,000*	*18.7%*
Protestant (excluding Anglican)	*382,000,000*	*6.9%*
Orthodox	*174,000,000*	*3.1%*
Anglican	*76,000,000*	*1.4%*
Other Christians	*196,000,000*	*3.5%*
2. **Islam**	1,014,000,000	18.2%
Sunni Islam	*842,000,000*	*15.1%*
Shia Islam	*162,000,000*	*2.9%*
Other Muslims	*10,000,000*	*0.2%*
3. **Hinduism**	751,000,000	13.5%
Vaishnavites	*526,000,000*	*10.5%*
Shaivites	*188,000,000*	*3.7%*
New and reformed Hindus	*15,000,000*	*0.3%*
4. **Buddhism**	334,000,000	6.3%
Mahayana	*187,000,000*	*3.7%*
Theravada	*127,000,000*	*2.2%*
Tantrayana (Lamaism)	*20,000,000*	*0.4%*
5. **Chinese folk religions** including Daoism	141,000,000	2.5%
6. **Shintoism**	109,000,000	2.0%
(This figure applies to those attached to the Shinto culture. Many Japanese practise both Buddhism and Shintoism. Those practising only Shintoism are thought to number under 4,000,000.)		
7. **African, Asian and other primal religions**	100,000,000	1.9%
8. **Sikhism**	20,000,000	0.4%
9. **Judaism**	18,000,000	0.3%
10. **Shamanism**	11,000,000	0.2%
11. **Confucianism**	6,200,000	0.1%
12. **Baha'ism**	5,800,000	< 0.1%
13. **Chondogyo**	4,200,000	< 0.1%
14. **Jainism**	4,000,000	< 0.1%
15. **Cao Dai**	2,500,000	< 0.1%
Other religions	110,000,000	2.0%
Nonreligious and atheists	1,155,000,000	20.7%

NB. The percentages do not add up to 100 as adherents of some religions, particularly Shintoism, may follow a second religion.

CHRISTIANITY

The Western calendar, shaped and determined by Christianity, sees the birth of Jesus of Nazareth, known as the Christ, as the turning point of history. In dating the modern era from the supposed date of his birth (it seems likely Jesus was actually born c. 4 BC), Christianity was making a profound statement about the significance of Jesus Christ. Jesus means the Saviour, taken from the Hebrew root '*yasha*', to save; Christ means the anointed one, from the Greek verb *chrio*, to anoint. For Christians, the Jewish child born in Bethlehem was no ordinary human. He was and is both human and divine, the Son of God. While it is possible to say that a historical person named Jesus lived between c. 4 BC and c. AD 29, it is only faith that can claim that he was the Christ, the anointed one of God, the long-awaited Messiah of the Jews.

The Nature of God

Christians believe that God is the creator of the universe and all life. They believe that Jesus Christ is the only Son of God, who has existed with God the Father from before time began. Jesus was incarnated (given human form), when by the power of the Holy Spirit, his human mother, Mary, gave birth to him. (The subsequent husband of the Virgin Mary – Joseph of Nazareth – was 27 generations descended from King David.) Christians believe that the purpose of Christ's incarnation was to reconcile humanity with God, as human sinfulness had broken the relationship with God. Through the death of Jesus upon the Cross at Calvary, God broke the power of sin and evil, and through the Resurrection (the rising) of Jesus from the dead on the third day God showed the triumph of life over death, and gave the promise of everlasting life to those who believe in Jesus.

In the doctrine of the Trinity, Christians believe that God is one but has three co-equal 'persons' – God the Father, God the Son (Jesus Christ) and the Holy Spirit.

Christian Teaching

The life and teaching of Christ are recorded in the four Gospels and in several quotations and stories found in other books of the New Testament of the Bible. These were all written by Christians who believed Jesus to be in some way both human and divine. Our knowledge of Jesus therefore comes from the pens of believers. Jesus taught that God is like a father who cares for every person on Earth. He taught that through repentance and forgiveness, God calls all humanity to him in love and seeks every individual to do his will on Earth. Jesus taught that through living as God wishes, the Kingdom of God – justice, love, mercy and peace – could come upon Earth, either in individual lives or possibly to the world as a whole.

The Apostles and the Church

The Church holds that through the 12 key disciples of Jesus, the apostles, authority on Earth was given to the Church, which is seen to be the body of Christ on Earth. The Church is therefore held to be essential to salvation – to being freed from sin and to the possibility of everlasting life. Jesus appointed 12 disciples. The following are common to the lists in the books of Matthew, Mark, Luke and the Acts.

Peter (martyred in Rome c. AD 64). A fisherman from Galilee called to be a disciple by Jesus at the beginning of his ministry, St Peter was recognized in the early Church as the leader of the disciples and is recognized by the Roman Catholic Church as the first of the popes. Peter, originally called Simon, was the brother of Andrew.

Andrew (said to have been crucified at Patras in Greece c. AD 65). The brother of Peter, St Andrew was a fisherman called by Jesus to be a fisher of men. He was previously a disciple of John the Baptist.

James the son of Zebedee (beheaded in the Holy Land c. AD 44). St James the Great, like his brother John and the apostles Peter and Andrew, was a fisherman, and was one of the first disciples to be called by Jesus.

John the Apostle (fate unknown). St John the Apostle (also known as St John the Divine) was a fisherman and the brother of James. He wrote the Gospel according to St John, the Revelation and three letters in the New Testament.

Philip (fate unknown). St Philip came from Bethsaida and was called at the same time as Bartholomew.

Bartholomew (said to have been martyred by the Babylonians). St Bartholomew is thought to have been called Nathaniel, the disciple whose calling is mentioned in St John. (Bartholomew is a family name, meaning son of Tolmai, not a given name.)

Thomas (said to have died in India). Known as 'Doubting Thomas', St Thomas was the apostle who requested physical proof of the Resurrection.

Matthew (fate unknown) St Matthew, who is believed to have been a tax collector, is traditionally said to have been the author of the first Gospel.

James the son of Alphaeus (fate unknown, although traditionally said to have been martyred in Persia). Also known as St James the Less.

Simon the Canaanite (or Simon Zelotes) (fate unknown). St Simon is thought to have been a member of the Jewish nationalist group, the Zealots.

Thaddeus (or **Jude**) (fate unknown). Called Judas (not Iscariot) in St Luke and Thaddeus in St Mark and St Matthew, this apostle is believed to have been a Zealot. He is better known as St Jude, patron of the desperate.

Judas Iscariot (traditionally said to have hanged himself after the Crucifixion.) The treasurer of the apostles, Judas betrayed Jesus to the chief priests for 30 pieces of silver. The name Iscariot is thought to derive from the Latin word *sicrius*, meaning murderer. Matthias was elected by the apostles to take the place of Judas.

Forms of Christianity

Christianity has three major forms: Roman Catholic, with the pope as head of the Church; Orthodox, with the patriarch of Constantinople (Istanbul) as the first amongst equals of the various patriarchs of the different Orthodox Churches, such as the Russian Church; and the Protestant movement, made up of denominations such as the Lutheran, Methodist, Baptist and Anglican Churches, and so on (see pp. 329–38).

THE BIBLE

The Old Testament

The 24 books of the Hebrew Bible are grouped into three divisions – *Torah* (The Law), *Nevi'im* (Prophets) and *Ketuvim* (Writings). The Torah was traditionally ascribed to Moses. Known to Christians as the Pentateuch, it has five books – Genesis, Exodus, Leviticus, Numbers and Deuteronomy. The Nevi'im has eight books – Joshua, Judges, Samuel, Kings, Isaiah, Jeremiah, Ezekiel, and the Book of the Twelve (the Minor Prophets). The Ketuvim comprises religious poetry and 'wisdom literature'. It has 11 books – Psalms, Proverbs, Job, the Song of Songs, Ruth, Lamentations, Ecclesiastes, Esther, Daniel, Ezra-Nehemiah, and Chronicles.

The Christian Church received these 24 books from Greek-speaking Jews. This version contained additional books, and parts of books, not found in Hebrew. These writings, which later became known as the *Apocrypha*, are regarded as Holy Scripture by the Roman Catholic Church, but at the Reformation they were denied this status by Protestants. The Old Testament reorders and divides some of the books of the Hebrew Bible. Samuel, Kings and Chronicles are divided into two, while Ezra and Nehemiah and each of the 12 Minor Prophets are counted as separate books.

The New Testament

The New Testament is called 'New' because it is believed by Christians to represent a new covenant of God with his people. It is based principally on the person and work of Jesus Christ. The 27 books of the New Testament are grouped into four divisions – the Gospels, the Acts of the Apostles, the Epistles and the Revelation (or Apocalypse). The four Gospels are traditionally ascribed to Matthew, Mark, Luke and John. Acts is a single book, traditionally ascribed to Luke. The Epistles are 21 books written to early churches or Christian individuals to teach the meaning and implications of the faith. Revelation (the Apocalypse) is a single book.

BOOKS OF THE BIBLE

Book	Number of Chapters	Notes
Genesis	50	The Creation and the Fall; the Flood; lives of Abraham, Isaac, Jacob and Joseph.
Exodus	40	The Liberation from Egypt; the Covenant; building the Sanctuary.
Leviticus	27	Priestly laws and rituals.
Numbers	36	Israel's wanderings in Sinai and the desert; the Passover.
Deuteronomy	34	Discourses by Moses before Israel entered the Promised Land.
Joshua	24	Conquest of the Promised Land; the tribes of Israel; Joshua.
Judges	21	Israel from the death of Joshua to the rise of the monarchy; David.
Ruth	4	Ruth, a story of family loyalty.
1 Samuel	31	Life of Samuel; Samuel and Saul; Saul and David.
2 Samuel	24	Reign of David.
1 Kings	22	Death of David; Solomon; division of the monarchy; Elijah
2 Kings	25	Elisha; the two kingdoms; the fall of Israel; the last years of Judah.
1 Chronicles	29	Genealogy of Israel from Adam; history of David.
2 Chronicles	36	History of Israel from Solomon to the end of the monarchy.
Ezra	10	The return from Exile; rebuilding the Temple; Ezra and Nehemiah.
Nehemiah	13	Reconstruction of Jerusalem; Nehemiah.
Tobit (only in the RC canon)	14	The story of Tobit in Exile.
Judith (only in the RC canon)	16	The story of Judith.
Esther	10*	The story of Mordecai and Esther. (* additional 91 verses in RC Bibles)
1 Maccabees (only in the RC canon)	16	Israel's fight for independence from the Hellenistic world.
2 Maccabees (only in the RC canon)	15	Heroism of the Jews in the fight for independence; divine protection.
Job	42	Story of Job's suffering – a (mainly poetic) dialogue between Job and God.
Psalms	150*	Poems and hymns from different period's of Israel's history.(* In the RC Vulgate and in Greek Bibles Psalm 11 is part of Psalm 10 and Psalms 12 to 146 are numbered 11 to 145. Psalm 147 is divided into Psalms 146 and 147 in the Vulgate and Greek Bibles.)
Proverbs	31	Wisdom poems; poems of Solomon; sayings of the wise.
Ecclesiastes	12	A collection of wisdom literature and personal observations about life.
Song of Solomon (or Song of Songs)	8	A collection of love lyrics.
Book of Wisdom (only in the RC canon)	19	A summary of the nature and value of wisdom.
Ecclesiasticus (only in the RC canon)	51	A collection of maxims on themes of morality.
Isaiah	66	The words and prophecies of Isaiah and second Isaiah; the Servant Songs.

Jeremiah	52	Oracles, biographical stories and narratives from various periods of Israel's history; not in chronological order.
Lamentations	5	Five poems – laments for Judah and Jerusalem.
Baruch (only in the RC canon)	6	Prayer of the exiles; the prerogative of Israel; complaints and hopes of Jerusalem; letter of Jeremiah.
Ezekiel	48	Ezekiel's visions and prophecies; the siege of Jerusalem; the Torah of Ezekiel.
Daniel	12*	Life and allegorical visions of Daniel; (*14 in RC Bibles – includes Prayer of Azariah, the song of the three young men, Susanna, and the story of Bel and the Dragon).
Hosea	14	Hosea's marriage and its symbolism; the crimes, punishment, repentance and reconciliation of Israel.
Joel	3*	The prophecies of Joel; (*4 in RC Bibles).
Amos	9	The prophecies of Amos.
Obadiah	1	Prophecy of Obadiah.
Jonah	4	Prophecy of Jonah – a light satire.
Micah	7	The prophecies of Micah.
Nahum	3	A short, alphabetical poem.
Habakkuk	3	Prophecy of Habakkuk.
Zephaniah	3	Prophecy of Zephaniah, centred on the Day of the Lord.
Haggai	2	Prophecy of encouragement after the Exile.
Zechariah	14	Visions of Zechariah; later writings of messianic hope.
Malachi	4	The Day of Yahweh; the purity of observance.
Matthew	28	Life and works of Jesus Christ with an emphasis on Jesus as King and the Kingdom of Heaven.
Mark	16	Life and works of Jesus Christ concentrating not on Jesus' teaching but on the mystery of his person. Probably the earliest of the four Gospels.
Luke	24	Life and works of Jesus Christ, concentrating on Jesus' mercy and forgiveness and the call to the poor and underprivileged.
John	21	Life and works of Jesus Christ but written on much broader lines than the other Gospels.
Acts of the Apostles	28	Describes the spread of the Christian faith from Jerusalem across the eastern Mediterranean to Rome.
Romans	16	The letter of Paul to the Church in Rome.
1 Corinthians	16	The first letter of Paul to the Church at Corinth.
2 Corinthians	13	The second letter of Paul to the Church at Corinth.
Galatians	6	The letter of Paul to the Church in Galatia.
Ephesians	6	The letter of Paul to the Church at Ephesus.
Philippians	4	The letter of Paul to the Church at Philippi.
Colossians	4	The letter of Paul to the Church at Colossae.
1 Thessalonians	5	The first letter of Paul to the Church at Thessalonica (Thessaloniki).
2 Thessalonians	3	The second letter of Paul to the Church at Thessalonica (Thessaloniki).
1 Timothy	6	The first letter from Paul to Timothy.
2 Timothy	4	The second letter from Paul to Timothy.
Titus	3	The letter from Paul to Titus.
Philemon	1	The letter from Paul to Philemon.
Hebrews	13	An anonymous letter to the Hebrews.
James	5	More a sermon than a letter – the letter of James to all Christians.
1 Peter	5	The first letter of Peter to all Christians.
2 Peter	3	The second letter of Peter to all Christians.
1 John	5	The first letter of John to all Christians.
2 John	1	The second letter of John to all Christians; this letter has only 11 verses.
3 John	1	The third letter of John to all Christians.
Jude	1	The letter of Jude to all Christians.
Revelation to John	22	A prophetic description of the end of the world and the return of Christ.

ROMAN CATHOLICISM

Rome was the only Western Church founded by an apostle (St Peter). From Ireland to the Carpathians, Christians came to acknowledge the bishop of Rome as Pope, and used Latin for worship, scripture-reading and theology. Roman Catholics recognize the pope as the lawful successor of St Peter, who was appointed head of the Church by Christ. In the 16th century most of north Europe broke with Rome to form reformed Protestant Churches. Catholic Christianity was extended to the Americas and parts of Asia and Africa. Since the Second Vatican Council (1962–66) Latin has largely given way to local languages. The Roman Catholic Church claims catholicity inasmuch as it was charged (*de jure*) by Christ to 'teach all nations' and *de facto* as it is the largest Christian Church. It claims infallibility in interpreting both the written and unwritten word of God. The Pope has delegated certain administrative powers to the Curia, the work of which is done by 11 permanent departments or congregations.

POPES

The Pope, the bishop of Rome, is considered by Catholics to be the Vicar of Christ on Earth and the successor of St Peter, the first bishop of Rome. He is elected by the College of Cardinals, meeting in secret conclave. At the end of 1994 there were 166 cardinals of whom 120 were under the age of 80 and therefore qualified as electors. There have been over 30 antipopes, rivals to the papacy elected in opposition to the one who has been chosen canonically.

St Peter c. 33–67
St Linus 67–76
St Cletus (also called Anacletus) 76–88
St Clement I 88–97
St Evaristus 97–105
St Alexander I 105–15
St Sixtus I 115–25
St Telesphorus 125–36
St Hyginus 136–40
St Pius I 140–55
St Anicetus 155–66
St Soterus 166–75
St Eleutherius 175–89
St Victor I 189–99
St Zephyrinus 199–217
St Callistus I 217–22
St Urban I 222–30
St Pontian 230–35
St Anterus 235–36
St Fabian I 236–50
St Cornelius 251–53
St Lucius I 253–54
St Stephen I 254–57
St Sixtus II 257–58
St Dionysius 259–68
St Felix I 269–74
St Eutychianus 275–83
St Caius 283–96
St Marcellinus 296–304
St Marcellus I 308–09
St Eusebius 309–10
St Miltiades 311–14
St Silvester I 314–35
St Mark 336–37
St Julius I 337–52
Liberius 352–66
St Damasus 366–84
St Siricius 384–99
St Anastasius I 399–401
St Innocent I 401–17
St Zosimus 417–18
St Boniface I 418–22
St Celestine I 422–432
St Sixtus III 432–40
St Leo I 440–61
St Hilary 461–68
St Simplicius 468–83
St Felix II 483–92
St Gelasius I 492–96
St Anastasius II 496–98
St Symmachus 498–514
St Hormisdas 514–23
St John I 523–26
St Felix III 526–30
Boniface II 530–32
John II (Mercurius) 533–35
St Agapetus I 535–36
St Silverius 536–37
Vigilius 537–55
Pelagius I 556–61
John III 561–74
Benedict I 575–79
Pelagius II 579–90
St Gregory I 590–604
Sabinianus 604–06
Boniface III 607
St Boniface IV 608–15
St Deusdedit I 615–18
Boniface V 619–25
Honorius I 625–38
Severinus 638–40
John IV 640–42
Theodore I 642–49
St Martin I 649–55
St Eugenius I 654–57
St Vitalian 657–72
Deusdedit II 672–76
Donus 676–78
St Agatho 678–81
St Leo II 681–83
St Benedict II 683–85
John V 685–86
Conon 686–87
St Sergius I 687–701
John VI 701–05
John VII 705–07
Sisinnius 707
Constantine 708–15
St Gregory II 715–31
St Gregory III 731–41
Saint Zacharias 741–52
Stephen 'II' 752 (died before he could be enthroned)
Stephen II or III 752–57
St Paul I 757–67
Stephen III or IV 768–72
Adrian I 772–95
St Leo III 795–816
Stephen IV or V 816–17
St Paschal I 817–24
Eugenius II 824–27
Valentine 827
Gregory IV 827–44
Sergius II 844–47
St Leo IV 847–55
Benedict III 855–58
St Nicholas I 858–67
Adrian II 867–72
John VIII 872–82
Marinus I 882–84
Adrian III 884–85
Stephen V or VI 885–91
Formosus 891–96
Boniface VI 896
Stephen VI or VII 896–97
Romanus 897
Theodore II 897

John IX 898–900
Benedict IV 900–03
Leo V 903
Sergius III 904–11
Anastasius III 911–13
Lando 913–14
John X 914–28
Leo VI 928
Stephen VII or VIII 928–31
John XI 931–35
Leo VII 936–39
Stephen VIII or IX 939–42
Marinus II 942–46
Agapetus II 946–55
John XII 955–64
Leo VIII 963–65
Benedict V 964–65
John XIII 965–72
Benedict VI 973–74
Benedict VII 974–83
John XIV (Pietro Canepanova) 983–84
John XV 985–96
Gregory V (Bruno of Carinthia) 996–99
Silvester II (Gerbert) 999–1003
John XVII (Sicco) 1003
John XVIII (Fasino) 1003–09
Sergius IV (Pietro Buccaporci) 1009–12
Benedict VIII 1012–24
John XIX 1024–32
Benedict IX 1032–44
Silvester III 1045
Benedict IX (restored) 1045
Gregory VI 1045–46
Clement II 1046–47
Benedict IX (restored) 1047–48
Damasus II (Poppo) 1048
St Leo IX 1048–54
Victor II 1055–57
Stephen IX or X 1057–58
Nicholas II 1058–61
Alexander II 1061–73
St Gregory VII (Hildebrand de Soana) 1064–85
Victor III (Desiderius, Prince of Benevento) 1086–87
Urban II (Odon de Lagery) 1088–99
Paschal II (Ranieri) 1099–1118
Gelasius II (Giovanni Gaetani) 1118–19
Callistus II (Gui de Bourgogne) 1119–24
Honorius II (Lamberto Scannabecchi) 1124–30
Innocent II (Gregorio Papareschi) 1130–43
Celestine II (Guido di Castello) 1143–44
Lucius II (Gerardo Caccianemici) 1144–45
Eugenius III (Bernardo Paganelli) 1145–53
Anastasius IV (Corrado) 1153–54
Adrian IV (Nicholas Breakspeare*) 1154–59
Alexander III (Rolando Bandinelli) 1159–81
Lucius III (Ubaldo Allucingoli) 1181–85
Urban III (Uberto Crivelli) 1185–87
Gregory VIII (Alberto di Morra) 1187
Clement III (Paolo Scolari) 1187–91
Celestine III (Giacinto Buboni) 1191–98
Innocent III (Lothario, Count of Segni) 1198–1216
Honorius III (Cencio Savelli) 1216–27
Gregory IX (Ugolino, Count of Segni) 1227–41
Celestine IV (Goffredo Castiglioni) 1241
Innocent IV (Sinibaldo Fieschi) 1243–54
Alexander IV (Rainaldo, Count of Segni) 1254–61
Urban IV (Jacques Pantaléon) 1261–64
Clement IV (Gui Faucois) 1265–68
Gregory X (Theobaldo Visconti) 1271–76
Innocent V (Pierre de Tarentaise) 1276
Adrian V (Ottobono dei Fieschi) 1276
John XXI (Pedro Juliani) 1276–77
Nicholas III (Giovanni Gaetano Orsini) 1277–80
Martin IV (Simon de Brion) 1281–85
Honorius IV (Giacomo Savelli) 1285–87
Nicholas IV (Girolamo Moschi) 1288–92
St Celestine V (Pietro del Morrone) 1294
Boniface VIII (Benedetto Gaetani) 1294–1303
Benedict XI (Nicola Boccasini) 1303–04
Clement V (Bertrand de Got) 1305–14
John XXII (Jacques Duèse) 1316–34
Benedict XII (Jacques Fournier) 1334–42
Clement VI (Pierre Roger) 1342–52
Innocent VI (Etienne Aubert) 1352–62
Urban V (Guillaume Grimoard) 1362–70
Gregory XI (Pierre Roger de Beaufort) 1370–78
Urban VI (Bartolommeo Prignano) 1378–89
Boniface IX (Pietro Tomacelli) 1389–1404
Innocent VII (Cosimo dei Migliorati) 1404–06
Gregory XII (Angelo Corrari) 1406–15
Martin V (Odo Colonna) 1417–31
Eugenius IV (Gabriele Condolmieri) 1431–47
Nicholas V (Tommaso Parentucelli) 1447–55
Callistus III (Alonso Borgia) 1455–58
Pius II (Aeneas Piccolomini) 1458–64
Paul II (Pietro Barbo) 1464–71
Sixtus IV (Francesco della Rovere) 1471–84
Innocent VIII (Giovanni Battista) 1484–92
Alexander VI (Roderigo Borgia) 1492–1503
Pius III (Francesco Todeschini) 1503
Julius II (Giuliano della Rovere) 1503–13
Leo X (Giovanni de Medici) 1513–21
Adrian VI (Adrian Florensz Boeyens**) 1522–23
Clement VII (Giulio de Medici) 1523–34
Paul III (Alessandro Farnese) 1534–49
Julius III (Giovanni Maria Ciocchi del Monte) 1550–55
Marcellus II (Marcello Cervini) 1555
Paul IV (Giovanni Pietro Carafa) 1555–59
Pius IV (Gianangelo de Medici) 1559–65
St Pius V (Antonio Michele Ghislieri) 1566–72
Gregory XIII (Ugo Buoncompagni) 1572–85
Sixtus V (Felice Perretti) 1585–90
Urban VII (Giovanni Battista Castagna) 1590
Gregory XIV (Niccolo Sfondrati) 1590–91
Innocent IX (Giovanni Antonio Facchinetti) 1591
Clement VIII (Ipollito Aldobrandini) 1592–1605
Leo XI (Alessandro Ottaviano de Medici) 1605
Paul V (Camillo Borghese) 1605–21
Gregory XV (Alessandro Ludovisi) 1621–23
Urban VIII (Maffeo Barberini) 1623–44
Innocent X (Giovanni Battista Pamfili) 1644–55
Alexander VII (Fabio Chigi) 1655–67
Clement IX (Giulio Rospigliosi) 1667–69
Clement X (Emilio Altieri) 1670–76
Innocent XI (Benedetto Odescalchi) 1676–89
Alexander VIII (Pietro Ottoboni) 1689–91
Innocent XII (Antonio Pignatelli) 1691–1700
Clement XI (Gianfrancesco Albani) 1700–21
Innocent XIII (Michelangelo de Conti) 1721–24
Benedict XIII (Pietro Francesco Orsini) 1724–30
Clement XII (Lorenzo Corsini) 1730–40
Benedict XIV (Prospero Lambertini) 1740–58
Clement XIII (Carlo della Torre Rezzonico) 1758–69
Clement XIV (Giovanni Ganganelli) 1769–74
Pius VI (Giovanni Angelo Braschi) 1775–99
Pius VII (Barnabo Chiaramonti) 1800–23
Leo XII (Annibale della Genga) 1823–29
Pius VIII (Francesco Xaverio Castiglioni) 1829–30
Gregory XVI (Bartolomeo Cappellari) 1831–46
Pius IX (Giovanni Maria Mastai-Ferretti) 1846–78
Leo XIII (Vincenzo Gioacchino Pecci) 1878–1903
St Pius X (Giuseppe Sarto) 1903–14
Benedict XV (Giacomo della Chiesa) 1914–22
Pius XI (Achille Ratti) 1922–39
Pius XII (Eugenio Pacelli) 1939–58
John XXIII (Angelo Giuseppe Roncalli) 1958–63
Paul VI (Giovanni Battista Montini) 1963–78
John Paul I (Albino Luciani) 1978
John Paul II (Karol Wojtyla) 1978–

Key: * Adrian IV was the only English Pope.

** Dutch, last non-Italian to be elected to the papacy until the Pole, Karol Wojtyla, was elected in 1978.

The Pope: HH John Paul II (b. Karol Wojtyla at Wadowice, near Krakow, Poland, 18 May 1920), Archbishop of Krakow 1964–78, created Cardinal 1967, elected Pope 16 October 1978, inaugurated 22 October 1978.

The Church is served by about 1,500,000 full-time professional staff (bishops, priests, nuns, monks, other religious and lay people). Roman Catholics represent almost 19% of humanity (see p.325). Local authority is exercised by bishops and archbishops in some 2360 dioceses throughout the world. Bishops gather in local, national or regional conferences to discuss local policies and visit Rome every five years to report direct to the Pope.

The largest Roman Catholic populations are to be found in the following countries:

Country	*Number of persons affiliated to the Roman Catholic Church (1993)*
Brazil	118,900,000
Mexico	80,680,000
USA	67,710,000
Philippines	54,630,000
Italy	47,560,000
France	44,080,000
Spain	37,730,000
Poland	36,520,000
Colombia	31,480,000
Argentina	30,710,000
Germany	28,690,000
Peru	21,090,000
Zaïre	20,560,000
Venezuela	18,040,000
Canada	13,330,000
Nigeria	11,080,000
Chile	10,930,000
Ecuador	10,210,000
India	10,000,000

The Roman Catholic Church is the largest religious denomination in the following countries:

Andorra, Angola, Argentina, Australia, Austria, Belgium, Belize, Bolivia, Brazil, Burundi, Cameroon, Canada, Cape Verde, Chile, Colombia, Congo, Costa Rica, Croatia, Cuba, Czech Republic, Dominica, Dominican Republic, Ecuador, El Salvador, France, Gabon, Grenada, Guatemala, Haiti, Honduras, Hungary, Ireland, Italy, Kenya, Lesotho, Liechtenstein, Lithuania, Luxembourg, Malta, Mexico, Micronesia, Monaco, Netherlands, Nicaragua, Palau, Panama, Paraguay, Peru, Philippines, Poland, Portugal, Rwanda, St Lucia, San Marino, São Tomé and Principe, Seychelles, Slovakia, Slovenia, Spain, Switzerland, Trinidad and Tobago, Uganda, USA, Uruguay, Venezuela, and Zaïre. The Vatican, the headquarters of the Church, is itself a self-governing city-state.

Uniat Churches

Some smaller non-Latin Churches also owe allegiance to the Pope. These eight organizations are called the Uniat Churches. Although these Churches are in full communion with the Roman Catholic Church, they retain their own organization and liturgies. Most Uniat rites are headed by a patriarch.

Apart from the Jacobite Church in southern India, most of the Uniat Churches are based in the Middle East. However, the largest of these Churches is the Ukrainian Uniat Church.

The (Roman) Catholic Christians of the Uniat Churches belong to the following rites:

The Armenian rite patriarchate of Cilicia was originally based in Cilicia (now in Turkey). The patriarch (or Catholicos) is now based in Antelias in Lebanon. The Armenian rite has about 1,000,000 adherents mainly in Lebanon and Syria, but also in Cyprus, Greece, Iran, the UAE, the USA, and Canada.

The Chaldean rite patriarch of Babylon is based in Baghdad, Iraq. The rite comprises 21 dioceses and archdioceses mainly in Iraq, Egypt, Iran, Syria and Lebanon. It is also represented in the USA and Turkey. Most of the rite's 600,000 adherents are in Iraq.

The Coptic rite patriarch of Alexandria is based in Cairo, Egypt. The rite comprises six dioceses and has about 200,000 adherents, most of whom are in Egypt.

The Jacobite rite, which is more correctly known as the Malankara Orthodox Syrian Church, is confined to southern India. The rite is based in Kottayam, Kerala state, and has about 1,600,000 adherents.

The Maronite rite patriarch of Antioch is based in Bkerke, Lebanon. The rite is the largest Christian Church in Lebanon and has over 1,250,000 adherents. It is also represented in other countries of the Middle East and in North America.

The Melkite rite patriarch of Antioch is based in Damascus, Syria. There are about 1,500,000 Melkites worldwide, with the majority being in Syria and Lebanon. The rite is also represented in the USA, Jordan, Brazil, Australia, Canada and Mexico.

The Syrian rite patriarch of Antioch is based in Beirut, Lebanon. There are about 150,000 adherents in the Middle East, mainly in Syria and Lebanon.

The Ukrainian Catholic (Uniat) Church is based in Lvov, western Ukraine. The Church was founded in Poland in 1596 to enable Orthodox clergy who transferred their allegiance to the Pope to retain their Eastern rite. In 1946 the Soviet authorities forcibly incorporated the Uniats into the Russian Orthodox Church, but clergy owing allegiance to the Pope continued to function as an 'underground' Church, which was recognized by the Soviet authorities in 1990. The Church is now of the three major Christian bodies of Ukraine. Its head is the Archbishop of Lvov. There are about 8,000,000 Ukrainian Uniat Catholics worldwide with over 5,000,000 in Ukraine (mainly in western Ukraine) and another 2,000,000 in Canada and the USA. Other Ukrainian Uniats are to be found in the UK, Australia, France, Russia, Poland and Belarus.

PATRON SAINTS

Patron saints of groups, professions and countries – and their feast days according to the Roman calendar – include those given below. (*Note: Not all of these saints are recorded in the Anglican calendar and some of those that are recorded appear on different dates.*)

academics St Albert the Great, 15 November.
accountants St Matthew, 21 September.
actors St Genesius, 26 August.
advertising executives St Bernardine of Siena, 20 May.
air pilots St Joseph of Copertino, 18 September.
announcers St John Chrysostom, 13 September.
archers St Sebastian, 20 January.
architects St Benedict, 21 March, and St Thomas, 21 December.
Argentina St Faith, 6 October.
artillerymen St Barbara, 4 December.
Austria St Leopold, 15 November, and St Florian, 14 December.
bakers St Michael, 29 September, and St Honorius of Amiens, 16 May.
bankers St Matthew, 21 September.
basket makers St Paul the Hermit, 25 January.
Belgium St Joseph, 19 March, and St Charles the Good, 2 March.
bellfounders St Agatha, 5 February.
biologists St Albert the Great, 15 November.
blind people St Clair, 2 January.
boatmen St Nicholas, 6 December.
boilermakers St Maurus, 15 January.
bookbinders St Celestine the Fifth, 19 May, and St John of God, 8 March.
booksellers St John of the Latin Gate, 6 May.
Brazil St Faith, 6 October.
Bulgaria St Cyril and Methodius, 24 May (Orthodox) or 14 February (Roman Catholic).
business executives St Expeditus, 19 April.
butchers St Nicholas, 6 December.
Canada St Joseph, 19 March; St Anne, 26 July; and St René Goupil, 18 October.
carpenters St Joseph, 19 March.
cavalrymen St George, 23 April.
charity St Vincent de Paul, 19 July, and St Louise de Marillac, 15 March.
chemists St Albert the Great, 15 November.
children St Nicholas, 6 December.
Chile St Faith, 6 October.
choirboys St Nicholas, 6 December.
circus performers St Julian the Hospitaller, 29 January.
clockmakers St Eligius, 1 December.
cooks St Martha, 29 July.
coopers St John the Baptist, 24 June, and St Michael, 29 September.
customs officers St Matthew, 21 September.
cutlers St John the Baptist, 24 June.
Czech Republic St Wenceslaus, 28 September, and St Ludmilla, 16 September.
deaf people St Francis de Sales, 29 January.
delicatessens St Anthony, 17 January.
Denmark St Canute, 19 January and 10 June.
dentists St Appollonia, 9 February.
diplomats St Gabriel, 24 March.
disabled ex-servicemen St Raphael, 24 October.
disabled people St Giles, 1 September.
doctors St Luke, 18 October, and St Pantaleon, 27 July.
domestic staff St Zita, 5 July.
down-and-outs St Alexis, 17 July, and St Giles, 1 September.
drinkers St Bibiana, 2 December.
drivers St Christopher, 25 July, and St Frances of Rome, 9 March.
dry cleaners/dyers St Maurice, 22 September.
editors St John Bosco, 31 January.
electricians St Lucy, 13 December.
emigrants St Frances Cabrini, 22 December.
engineers St Dominic La Caussade, 12 May.
England St George, 23 April.
Europe St Benedict 11 July and St Cyril and St Methodius (Roman Catholic feast day 14 February).
farmers St Benedict, 21 March.
farm workers St Isidore the Labourer, 15 May.
ferrymen St Julian the Hospitaller, 29 January.
Finland St Henry of Uppsala, 19 January.
fireman St Lawrence, 10 August.
fishermen St Peter, 29 June.
forestry workers St Hubert, 3 November.
France St Joan of Arc, 30 May; St Martin of Tours, 11 November; and St Michael the Archangel, 29 September.
furnishers St Louis of France, 25 August.
gardeners St Fiacre, 30 August, and St Dorothy, 2 February.
Germany St Boniface, 5 June.
glassworkers St Clair, 2 January.
glaziers St Luke, 18 October.
glove makers St Mary Magdalene, 22 July.
gravediggers St Maurus, 15 December.
hairdressers St Louis of France, 25 August.
hatters St James the Less, 1 May.
hermits St Anthony the Hermit, 17 January.
hired hands St Notburga, 13 September.
hospital staff St John of God, 8 March.
housekeepers St Martha, 29 July.
Hungary St Stephen of Hungary, 2 September, and St Stanislas Kostka, 15 August.
hunters St Hubert, 3 November.
immigrants St Frances Cabrini, 22 December.
innkeepers St Julian, 29 January, and St Vincent, 28 January.
insurance agents St Yves, 19 May.
interior decorators St Genevieve, 3 January.
Ireland St Patrick, 17 March, and St Brigit, 2 February.
Italy St Catherine of Siena, 24 April, and St Francis of Assisi, 4 October.
jewellers St Eligius, 1 December.
joiners St Joseph, 19 March.
journalists St Francis de Sales, 29 January, and St Bernardine of Siena, 20 May.
labourers St Isidore the Labourer, 10 May.
lacemakers St Anne, 26 July.
laundry workers St Clare, 12 August.
lawyers St Yves, 19 May, and St Raymund of Penafort, 23 January.
learner drivers St Expeditus, 19 April.
leatherworkers St Bartholomew, 24 August, and St Crispin and St Crispinian, 25 October.
Lithuania St Casimir, 4 March.
locksmiths St Peter, 29 April.
lost objects St Anthony of Padua, 13 June.

lovers St Valentine, 14 February.
machine workers St Benedict, 21 March.
Malta St Paul, 29 June.
managers St Thomas, 21 December.
market gardeners St Phocas, 22 September, and St Fiacre, 30 August.
merchants St Nicholas, 6 December.
messengers St Adrian, 8 September.
metalworkers St Stephen, 26 December.
Mexico Our Lady of Guadalupe, 12 October.
midwives St Raymund Nonnatus, 31 August.
millers St Blaise, 3 February, and St Winnoc, 6 November.
miners St Barbara, 4 December.
missionaries St Teresa of Avila, 3 October, and St Francis Xavier, 3 December.
musicians St Cecilia, 22 November, St Blaise, 3 February, and St Dunstan, 19 May.
naturalists St Albert the Great, 15 November.
navigators St Nicholas of Bari, 7 May, St Cuthbert, 20 March, and St Elmo, 2 June.
needlewomen St Clare, 12 August.
Nigeria St Patrick, 17 March.
Norway St Olaf, 29 July.
nurses St Camillus, 14 July.
opticians St Clair, 2 January.
orphans St Jerome Emiliani, 8 February.
painters St Luke, 18 October.
parachutists St Michael, 29 September.
pawnbrokers St Nicholas, 6 December.
pedestrians St Martin of Tours, 11 November.
people in desperate straits St Jude, 28 October.
perfumers St Mary Magdalene, 22 July.
Peru St Rose of Lima, 23 August, and St Joseph, 19 March.
pharmacists St James the Great, 25 July.
Philippines St Rose of Lima, 23 August.
philosophers St Catherine, 25 July.
photographers St Veronica, 6 August.
physicians St Luke, 18 October, and St Cosmas and St Damian, 27 September.
physicists St Albert the Great, 15 November.
pilgrims St James the Great, 25 July.
plumbers St Eligius, 1 December.
Poland St Casimir, 4 March, and St Stanislas, 7 May.
police St Genevieve, 3 January, and St Sebastian, 20 January.
poor people St Lawrence, 10 August.
porters St Christopher, 25 July.
Portugal St Anthony of Padua, 13 January.
potholers St Benedict, 21 March.
preachers St John Chrysostom, 13 September.
pregnant women St Anne, 26 July.
priests St John Vianney, 4 August.
printers St Augustine, 28 August.
prisoners St Leonard, 6 November.
prison officers St Hippolytus, 13 August.
quarry workers St Rock, 16 August.
race relations St Martin de Porres, 3 November.
radiologists St Michael, 29 September.
radio workers St Gabriel, 24 March.
refugees St Benedict Labre, 16 April.
Romania St Cyril and St Methodius, 7 July (Orthodox) and 14 February (Roman Catholic).
roofers St Vincent Ferrer, 5 April.
ropemakers St Paul, 29 June.
Russia St Nicholas, 6 December.
sacristans St Guy, 12 June.
sailors St Nicholas of Bari, 7 May.
Scotland St Andrew, 30 November, and St Margaret, 16 June (general) or 20 July (CofE only).
scouts St George, 23 April.
sculptors St Luke, 18 October.
secretaries St John Cassian, 23 July.
servants St Blandina, 2 June.
shepherdesses St Genevieve, 3 January.
shepherds St Germaine of Pibrac, 19 January.
shipwrights St Julian the Hospitaller, 29 January.
shoemakers/repairers St Crispin and St Crispinian, 25 October.
shopkeepers St Francis of Assisi, 4 October.
sick people St Camillus, 14 July.
Slovenia St Mary, Mother of God, 25 March.
soldiers St Maurice, 22 September, St Martin of Tours, 11 November, and St George, 23 April.
Spain St James the Great, 25 July, and St Ferdinand, 30 May.
spokesmen/women St John Chrysostom, 13 September.
students St Catherine, 11 November.
surgeons St Luke, 18 October.
Sweden (Lutheran) St Bridget of Sweden, 8 October; (Roman Catholic) St Eric, 18 May.
Switzerland St Gall, 16 October, and St Nicholas von Flüe, 25 September.
tanners St Bartholomew, 24 August.
tax collectors St Matthew, 21 September.
taxi drivers St Fiacre, 30 August, and St Christopher, 25 July.
teachers St Cassian of Imola, 13 August.
television workers St Gabriel, 24 March, and St Clare, 12 August.
tourists St Christopher, 25 July.
tour operators St Francis Xavier, 3 December.
tradesmen St Francis of Assisi, 4 October.
translators St Jerome, 30 September.
travellers St Julian the Hospitaller, 29 January, and St Christopher, 25 July.
Turkey St George, 23 April; St Andrew 30 November; and St John the Evangelist, 27 December.
underwriters St Yves, 19 May.
university academics St Thomas Aquinas, 28 July.
upholsterers St Genevieve, 3 January.
virgins St Maria Goretti, 6 July.
Ukraine St Vladimir, 15 July.
USA (Roman Catholic) Virgin Mary, 8 December – feast day of the Roman Catholic festival of Mary conceived without sin.
Venezuela St Faith, 6 October.
Wales St David, 1 March
weavers St Blaise, 3 February, and St Barnabas, 11 June.
wine growers St Vincent, 22 January, and St John of the Latin Gate, 6 May.
wine merchants St Nicholas, 6 December.
workers St Joseph, 19 March.
writers St Francis de Sales, 29 January.
young people St Casimir, 4 March, and St Louis Gonzaga, 21 July.
Venezuela St Faith, 6 October.

THE ORTHODOX CHURCHES

The countries with the largest Orthodox populations are the following:

Country	*Church*	*Number of adherents*
Russia	Russian Orthodox Church (about 10,000,000 Russians joined or rejoined the Russian Orthodox Church between 1990 and 1994)	50,000,000
Ethiopia	Ethiopian Orthodox Church, sometimes referred to as a Coptic Church	26,300,000
Ukraine	Ukrainian Orthodox Church, which still owes allegiance to the Moscow Patriarchate, and the Ukrainian Autocephalous Orthodox Church – also known as the Ukrainian Orthodox Church-Kiev patriarchate – which has seceded from the Russian Orthodox Church)	c. 20,000,000
Romania	Romanian Orthodox Church	19,800,000
Greece	Greek Orthodox Church	10,000,000
Belarus	Belarussian Orthodox Church	8,700,000
Bulgaria	Bulgarian Orthodox Church	7,400,000
Yugoslavia – Serbia and Montenegro	Serbian Orthodox Church	6,900,000
Georgia	Georgian Orthodox Church	3,600,000
Armenia	Armenian Apostolic Orthodox Church	2,800,000
Moldova	Russian Moldovan Orthodox Church	2,800,000
Bosnia-Herzegovina	Serbian Orthodox Church – see Yugoslavia, above	1,400,000
Macedonia	Macedonian Orthodox Church	1,200,000
USA	Greek Orthodox Archdiocese of North and South America, see Greece	800,000
Poland	Polish Autocephalous Orthodox Church	600,000
Cyprus (Greek Orthodox, see Greece above)		550,000
Australia (Greek Orthodox, see Greece above)		480,000

Most of the Churches called Orthodox derived from the ancient Greek Christianity of the Eastern Mediterranean.

The direct link with Churches founded by apostles and the memory of a Christian Roman Empire (the Byzantine Empire) that lasted until 1453 heighten the importance of tradition as a guide of the Church. Tradition includes the scriptures, the first seven Church councils and the writings of the Church fathers (the early medieval writers on Christian doctrine), the liturgy and the veneration of holy pictures (icons).

The Orthodox Church maintains that it is the 'one true Church of Christ which is not and has not been divided' and it regards the Roman Catholic Church as schismatic. The Ecumenical Patriarch of Constantinople (Istanbul) is the senior figure, but each autonomous Church has its own patriarch and is self-governing.

Ecumenical Patriarch of Constantinople: Patriarch Bartholomew I.

Apart from those shown in the table, Orthodox Churches include the Orthodox Church of Finland and the Orthodox Church of the Czech Republic and Slovakia. There are Russian Orthodox minorities in the Baltic States (Estonia, Latvia and Lithuania), Kazakhstan, Uzbekistan and other former Soviet republics and in the West (particularly in France and the USA), and Greek Orthodox minorities in many countries of the New World and in Western Europe (for example in the United Kingdom).

The collapse of Communism in the countries of the former Soviet Union and in Eastern Europe has resulted in a remarkable revitalization of the Churches in those states. In some cases, for example in Russia itself, the Orthodox Church has been the principal beneficiary of this growth, but other Christian Churches, particularly Baptists and various new movements, have also seen dramatic expansion in numbers.

ECUMENICISM

One characteristic of Christianity today is the increased understanding and co-operation both between Christians in different parts of the world and between Christians of different traditions and backgrounds. The word ecumenical is used to describe such spirit and action. Though sometimes used in a narrower sense to refer to the movement associated with the World Council of Churches, the word simply means 'worldwide' (from the Greek *oikumene*, 'inhabited world').

The World Council of Churches

The World Council of Churches (founded in 1948) has its headquarters in Geneva, Switzerland. The Council – whose membership includes most of the main Christian Churches, except the Roman Catholic – promotes ecumenical Christian action and study. There are similar organizations in many countries, for example Churches Together in England.

National Councils of Churches were founded in France, Finland, Japan, Korea, Mexico, the Netherlands, Nigeria, Sierra Leone and Sri Lanka during the first three decades of this century. Similar councils now exist in nearly 65 other countries.

PROTESTANTISM (including ANGLICANISM)

In 16th-century Europe, movements to reform the Church accompanied fresh interpretations of the Bible and the use of everyday language in place of Latin. These movements rejected Roman authority and established reformed national forms of Christianity in the various states of northern Europe, such as Lutheranism in Sweden and parts of Germany, Calvinism in Switzerland and Scotland, and Anglicanism in England. This process is known as the *Reformation*. The majority Protestant movement aimed to reform the Church within each state while keeping the idea that the Church embraced the whole community. The Radical (or Anabaptist) movement insisted that the Church consisted only of those who made a commitment to Christ, and broke the link with the state. A minority in Europe, this movement produced the dominant Christian forms in North America.

The 18th century saw movements for spiritual reform in Protestant countries. These brought the majority and radical streams closer together. European emigration brought all the Protestant traditions to America, Canada and Australia. In the USA they took new life and new shapes in a huge community – largely Christian, but multi-ethnic and with no national Church. Some completely new forms of Christianity also arose, such as Pentecostalism. Today the American scene is characterized by a large number of denominations. New expressions of Christianity are also appearing in the southern continents as Christians there meet situations not encountered in the West.

The Anglican Communion

Henry VIII renounced the supremacy of the pope in 1534, founding the Church of England with the monarch as its head. Protestant reforms were instituted during the reign of Edward VI (1547–53). After the reign of the Catholic Mary I, the independent Church of England was re-established in 1558. The Church of England retains the episcopal form of government and has preserved many of the Catholic traditions of liturgy. However, it holds most of the basic tenets of the reformed faith of Protestantism. Its doctrine is based upon the Thirty-Nine Articles; its liturgy is based upon *The Book of Common Prayer* (1549 and 1662) and its successors. The 18th-century Evangelical Movement emphasized the Protestant tradition, while the 19th-century Oxford Movement emphasized the Catholic tradition. These two movements continue in the Church of England as the Low Church and the High Church.

Each of the Churches of the Anglican Communion is self-governing. The archbishop of Canterbury is recognized as first among equals by the leaders of the provinces of the Anglican Communion.

The following countries have the largest Anglican populations:

Country and Church	*Number of Anglicans (1993)*
United Kingdom (Church of England, plus the Church in Wales and the Scottish Episcopal Church)	32,900,000 (nominal members; 1,400,000 practising)
Nigeria (Church of the Province of Nigeria)	10,000,000
Uganda (Church of the Province of Uganda)	4,700,000
USA (Episcopal Church in the USA)	4,470,000 (nominal members)
Australia (Anglican Church of Australia)	4,200,000 (nominal members; under 3,000,000 practising)
Canada (Anglican Church of Canada)	2,800,000 (nominal members; 800,000 practising)
Kenya (Church of the Province of Kenya)	2,000,000
South Africa (Church of the Province of Southern Africa)	1,300,000
New Zealand (Church of the Province of Aotearoa, New Zealand and Polynesia)	730,000 members

Other Anglican provinces include the Anglican Church of Papua New Guinea, the Anglican Church of the Southern Cone of America (Argentina, Chile, etc.), the Church in Wales, the Church of Ireland, the Church of the Province of Burundi, the Church of the Province of Central Africa, the Church of the Province of the Indian Ocean, the Church of the Province of Kenya, the Church of the Province of Melanesia, the Church of the Province of Myanmar, the Church of the Province of Rwanda, the Church of the Province of the Sudan, the Church of the Province of Tanzania, the Church of the Province of West Africa, the Church of the Province of the West Indies, the Church of the Province of Zaïre, the Episcopal Church in Jerusalem and the Middle East, the Episcopal Anglican Church of Brazil, the Holy Catholic Church in Japan, the Philippine Episcopal Church and the Scottish Episcopal Church.

Baptists

Baptist Churches, which take their name from the practice of baptism by immersion of adult believers, developed within the English and American Puritan movements in the 17th century. Individual Baptist churches are self-governing. There are more than 35,000,000 Baptists, the majority of whom live in the USA. The principal Baptist Churches include:

Southern Baptist Convention (USA) 15,400,000 members.
National Baptist Convention (USA) 7,000,000.
American Baptist Churches in the USA 1,500,000.
Nigerian Baptist Convention 500,000.
Euro-Asiatic Federation of the Unions of Evangelical Christians – Baptists (Russia and other former Soviet republics) 500,000.
Myanmar Baptist Convention 500,000.
Samavesam of Telegu Baptist Church (India) 425,000.
Conservative Baptist Association of America 250,000.
General Association of Regular Baptist Churches (USA) 185,000.
American Baptist Association 160,000.
Baptist Union of Great Britain 160,000.

Congregationalists

The liberal Protestant Congregationalist churches developed from the Independents in England in the 16th and 17th centuries. Each congregation is independent in the organization of its own affairs. In

England, Australia, Canada, India and the USA the majority of Congregationalist churches have joined United Churches (see below).

Christian Scientists

The Church of Christ, Scientist, is a liberal Protestant denomination founded in the USA by Mary Baker Eddy in 1879. Christian Scientists – who deny the deity but not the divinity of Jesus – emphasize the practice of spiritual healing. Christian Scientists claim their own sources of knowledge supplementary to the Scriptures.

The Church claims to have 2500 congregations worldwide, with a majority in North America.

Disciples of Christ

The Disciples of Christ were founded during a period of religious revival on the American frontier in the first half of the 19th century. They attempted to unite the divisions of Protestantism through a return to New Testament practice. The Principal Church of the Disciples is the Christian Church (Disciples of Christ; USA) with 1,000,000 disciples.

Independent African Churches

Dissatisfaction with Western forms of worship has encouraged the emergence of a number of African Churches. The Kimbanguist Church of Zaïre began in the 1920s when followers were attracted by the preaching and miraculous healings of Simon Kimbangui, a Baptist catechist.

Various Zion Churches in South Africa emphasize adult baptism by immersion, divine healing and preparation for a Second Coming. Aladura ('Owners of Prayer') Churches in West Africa emphasize prophets and divine healing. The incorporation of traditional African beliefs and values is a feature of a number of Churches.

The principal African Churches are:

Church of Jesus Christ on Earth through the Prophet Simon Kimbangui (Zaïre) 5,000,000 members.
Zion Christian Church (South Africa) 4,000,000.
Church of the Lord – Aladura (Nigeria) 1,100,000.
African Israel Nineveh Church (Kenya) 350,000.

Lutherans

The beliefs of the Lutheran Churches are derived from the teaching of the German Martin Luther (1483–1546) and were formulated in the Augsburg Confession of 1530. Luther taught that redemption could only be achieved through faith in Christ (justification by faith), and that Scripture is the sole rule of faith. Over 55,000,000 people belong to Lutheran Churches, whose greatest influence is in Germany and in Scandinavia.

The principal Lutheran Churches include:
United Churches (Germany) 13,500,000 members.
United Lutheran Protestant Church of Germany 10,000,000.
Evangelical Lutheran Church in Sweden 7,420,000.
Evangelical Lutheran Church in America 5,200,000.
Evangelical Lutheran Church of Denmark 4,550,000.
Evangelical Lutheran Church of Finland 4,400,000.
Evangelical Lutheran Church of Norway 3,800,000.
Lutheran Church – Missouri Synod (USA) 2,600,000.
United Evangelical Lutheran Churches in India 1,300,000.
Evangelical Church of the Lutheran Confession in Brazil 900,000.

Methodism

Methodism developed out of the religious revival within the Church of England led by John Wesley (1703–91) and his brother Charles (1707–88). The differences between the early Methodists and contemporary Anglicans were largely of emphasis rather than doctrine. All Methodist Churches have a strong central authority, and those of the American tradition are episcopal. Over 55,000,000 people belong to Methodist Churches, whose greatest influence is in the USA and southern and western Africa.

The principal Methodist Churches are:
United Methodist Church (USA) 9,800,000 members.
African Methodist Episcopal Church (USA) 3,500,000.
African Methodist Episcopal Zion Church (USA) 1,200,000.
Korean Methodist Church 1,300,000.
Methodist Church of Southern Africa 760,000.
Methodist Church Nigeria 490,000.
Methodist Church in India 470,000.
Methodist Church (UK) 410,000.

Old Catholics

The Old Catholics comprise congregations that have separated from the Roman Catholic Church since the 18th century. The Dutch Church of Utrecht was formed in 1724 in support of Jansenism, a movement based on the teachings of Cornelius Jansen, who held that the efficacy of the sacraments depended upon the state of grace of the recipient. Various Central European Old Catholic congregations seceded because of their opposition to the doctrine of papal infallability. There are 16,000 Old Catholics in Switzerland, and 28,000 in Germany.

Pentecostalists

Pentecostalism grew out of the revivalist movement in some Protestant Churches in the USA during the later part of 19th century, but its beginning as a Church is often traced to the work of Charles Parham in Kansas and Illinois in 1900. Pentecostalists emphasize 'baptism by the Holy Spirit', a post-conversion religious experience, which may be accompanied by divine healing and 'speaking in tongues'. In 1990 there were worldwide about 128,000,000 members of various Pentecostalist Churches.

Plymouth Brethren

The Plymouth Brethren were founded in 1831 by J.N. Darby in Plymouth (England). They have no clergy and no formal creed, and emphasize biblical prophecy and an imminent Second Coming.

Reformed Christians and Presbyterians

The Reformed Churches are Calvinistic rather than Lutheran in doctrine. They trace their origins to the teaching of the French Protestant John Calvin (1509–64), a leader of the Reformation in France and Switzerland. While believing that faith is dependent upon Scripture alone, Calvinists insist that, as man lacks free will, only the elect are predestined to be saved. The Reformed Churches include the Presbyterians, whose name is derived from their form of government by lay leaders – known as presbyters or elders – and by pastors.

The established Church of Scotland is Presbyterian in constitution. It is presided over by a Moderator who is chosen annually by the elected General Assembly, at which the British sovereign (as head of the Church) is represented by a Lord High Commissioner. Scotland is divided into 12 synods for administrative purposes.

The principal Reformed and Presbyterian Churches are:

Presbyterian Church (USA) 3,800,000 members.
Federation of Swiss Protestant Churches (comprising 18 reformed Churches) 2,900,000.
Netherlands Reformed Church 2,700,000.
Protestant Church in Indonesia 2,300,000.
Reformed Church in Hungary 2,000,000.
Church of Jesus Christ (Madagascar) 2,000,000.
Presbyterian Church of Korea 1,900,000.
Dutch Reformed Church (South Africa) 1,000,000.
United Church of Zambia 1,000,000.
Church of Scotland 840,000.
Reformed Churches in the Netherlands 770,000.
Reformed (Calvinist) Church (Romania) 700,000.

Seventh-day Adventists

Adventist Churches emphasize the imminence of the Second Coming. The Seventh-day Adventist Church was established in the 19th century in the USA, where there are 730,000 members (41,000 in Canada).

Society of Friends (Quakers)

The Society of Friends was founded in the 17th century by the English Puritan George Fox. Quakerism emphasizes the immediate application of Christ's teaching to everyday life, while rejecting the need for formalized services, creeds or clergy. Worship is spontaneous. Friends' meetings wait in silence for the 'inward light'. Quakers are pacifists. In the UK there are 18,000 members.

Unitarians

Unitarians deny the doctrine of the Trinity. The belief that God is one person was held by some in the early Church (Arianism), but modern Unitarianism dates in Europe from the 16th century, and in the English-speaking world from 1774, when Theophilus Lindsey founded a Unitarian chapel in London.

United Churches

The ecumenical movement among Christian Churches has resulted in the union of a number of Protestant Churches.

The pressure for unity has been particularly strong in countries without a Christian tradition where the historic differences between denominations appear meaningless.

The principal United Churches are:

Church of South India (formed 1947 with the union of Anglican, Congregational, Methodist, Presbyterian and Reformed Churches) 2,200,000 members.
United Church of Christ (USA; formed 1957 from the union of Congregational, Evangelical and Reformed Churches) 1,700,000.
Uniting Church in Australia (formed 1977 with the union of Congregational, Methodist and Presbyterian Churches) 1,300,000.
Church of North India (formed 1970 with the union of Anglican, Baptist, Congregational, Methodist and Presbyterian Churches) 1,000,000.
United Church of Canada (formed 1925 with the union of Congregational, Methodist and Presbyterian Churches. The Evangelical United Bretheren of Canada joined in 1968) 790,000.

MARGINAL GROUPS

Various movements related to Christianity stand apart from the forms mentioned above by not giving ultimate significance to Christ.

Western examples include some forms of Unitarianism (which deny Christ's divinity); the Watchtower Movement or Jehovah's Witnesses (who also deny Christ's divinity) and Mormonism (which claims its own supplementary literature to the Scriptures.)

Jehovah's Witnesses

The Jehovah's Witnesses – or the Watchtower Movement as they are officially known – grew out of the International Bible Studies Association, founded in Pittsburgh, Pennsylvania (USA) by Charles Taze Russell (1872).

The Jehovah's Witnesses movement is known for its literal interpretation of the Bible and its concern with Armageddon, the imminent final battle in which Witnesses will be saved. Although Witnesses deny Christ's divinity, they recognize Jesus as God's agent. They believe that the Theocracy (God's Kingdom) will be established on Earth after Armageddon and the Second Coming.

The Witnesses have faced persecution in a number of countries because they refuse to acknowledge many of the claims made on the individual by secular governments. They are renowned for not accepting blood transfusions.

Mormons

The Mormons – or the Church of Jesus Christ of Latter-Day Saints as they are officially known – are active missionaries. They were founded in the USA in 1830 by Joseph Smith. Smith claimed to have received from an angel the Book of Mormon, which is accepted by the Latter-Day Saints as an addition to Scripture.

Mormons hold the belief that God evolved from man and that man himself has the potential to attain deity. Mormonism denies the Trinity in favour of a polytheistic belief in three independent persons. It teaches that after death there is a full resurrection of the body and a reuniting of families. Dead relatives can be baptized or married in the faith to ensure their salvation.

The Mormons were led to their current centre in Salt Lake City, Utah, by Brigham Young. There are over 6,000,000 Mormons, the majority (4.2 million) in North America.

Unification Church

Sometimes known as 'the Moonies', the Unification Church was founded in the 1950s by a Korean, Sun Myung Moon. It is thought to have over 2,000,000 members, the majority in South Korea and Japan.

The Church teaches the 'Divine Principle' which holds that, following humanity's fall from grace, a restoration to perfection can be achieved through the first messiah, Jesus, and the second, the Reverend Moon. Love of creation and family life are of central importance to members.

ISLAM

Islam is the world's second largest religion. The Arabic term *islam* means 'the act of resignation' to God. It is derived from the root letters *slm*, from which come the noun *salam* (which means 'peace') and the verb *aslama* (which means 'he submitted'). Islam emphasizes an uncompromising monotheism and a strict adherence to religious practices. Muslims believe that Islam is the religion that brings peace to mankind when man commits himself to God and submits himself to His will, and that God's will was made known through the Qur'an (Koran), the book revealed to his messenger, the Prophet Muhammad (570–632).

Muhammad was a member of the Quraysh tribe, which guarded the sacred shrine known as the Kaaba in the Arab trading city of Mecca (Makka). In 610 Muhammad received his first revelations, which commissioned him to preach against the idolatry and polytheism of the Arab tribes. In 622, he led his followers to Medina (al-Madina), where political power was added to his spiritual authority. Before Muhammad died in 632, the whole of Arabia had embraced Islam or entered into a peace treaty with the Prophet.

Muslims believe that – over a period of 20 years – Muhammad received revelations from God (Allah) via the Archangel Gabriel. These revelations form the Qur'an (literally 'The Recitation'), Islam's scripture. Muhammad also accepted the inspiration of the Jewish and Christian scriptures. The collections of Muhammad's sayings and doings – the *Hadith* – are next in importance, for the Prophet is regarded as the best model of obedience to God's will. Muslims teach that Islam was the religion of Adam and the main prophet sent by God to call man back to his path. Muslims revere Abraham, Moses and Jesus amongst other prophets, but Muhammad is the final prophet, because the Qur'an completed and superseded earlier revelations.

The Pillars of Faith

Certain essential religious duties, described as the 'Five Pillars', are intended to develop the spirit of submission to God. They are:

Profession of the faith The basic belief of Islam is expressed in the *Shahada*, the Muslim confession of faith: 'There is no God but Allah and Muhammad is his Prophet!' From this fundamental belief are derived beliefs in angels (particularly Gabriel), the revealed Books (of the Jewish and Christian faiths in addition to the Qur'an), a series of prophets, and the Last Day, the Day of Judgement.

Prayer The act of worship is performed five times a day – at dawn, midday, mid-afternoon, sunset and before going to bed. After washing themselves, Muslims face in the direction of Mecca and pray communally at the mosque or individually in any place that is ritually clean, often using a prayer rug. Each prayer consists of a set number of 'bowings', for example two at dawn, four at midday. The 'bowing' is composed of a prescribed succession of movements, in which the worshipper stands, bows, kneels with forehead to the ground, and sits back on the haunches. Recitations in Arabic, mostly words of praise and verses from the Qur'an, accompany each movement. Attendance at the mosque is not compulsory, but men are required to go to the special congregational prayers held every Friday at noon. (The mosque also has an educational role and teaching ranges from advanced theology to religious instruction for children.)

Almsgiving An offering, known as *zakat*, is given by Muslims with sufficient means as an annual charitable donation.

Fasting Muslims fast from shortly before sunrise until sunset every day during the Islamic month of Ramadan, the month in which they believe the Qur'an was first revealed. The person fasting may not eat, drink or smoke. However, the sick, the elderly and children are exempt from fasting.

Pilgrimage Pilgrimage to Mecca (the *hajj*) is to be undertaken at least once in a lifetime by every Muslim who can afford it. The pilgrimage takes place during the Islamic month of Dhu'l-Hijja.

Jihad Jihad is sometimes regarded as another pillar of the faith. It means 'striving' and is commonly used to describe the duty of waging 'holy wars' to spread Islam and to defend Islamic lands.

Sects of Islam

Sunnism and Shiism (or Shiah Islam) are the two main forms of Islam. Although the majority of Muslims are Sunnis, the Shiites are dominant in Iran, which is about 93 per cent Shiite. The main difference between Sunni and Shiah Islam lies in the latter's belief that the charisma of the Prophet was inherited by his descendants, in whom they invest supreme spiritual and political authority. The Sunnis believe that orthodoxy is determined by the consensus of the community. Sunni caliphs exercised political but not spiritual authority – the historic caliphate ceased to exist in 1924 in Turkey.

Sunni Islam has four branches:

Hanafi which is dominant in Afghanistan, Bangladesh, Djibouti, Egypt, Jordan, Kazakhstan, Kyrgyzstan, Lebanon, Pakistan, Palestine, Syria, Tajikistan, Turkey, Turkmenistan, and Uzbekistan. In Egypt, Hanafi, Maliki and Shafi Islam are all significant.

Hanbali which is largely confined to Qatar and Saudi Arabia.

Maliki in Algeria, Chad, Egypt (see also Hanafi, above), Gambia, Guinea, Kuwait, Libya, Mali, Mauritania, Morocco, Niger, Senegal, Sudan, and Tunisia.

Shafi in the Brunei, Comoros, Egypt (see above), Indonesia, Malaysia, the Maldives, Somalia, and the United Arab Emirates.

Shiism has produced a variety of sects, including the Ismailis and Zaidis, though the majority are known as 'Twelvers' (*Ithna 'Ashariyya*). They believe that the 12th Imam or successor to Muhammad in linear descent disappeared and is now the Hidden Imam, who will return as the Mahdi before the end of the world. Senior religious lawyers, known as *mujtahids*, interpret the Hidden Imam and share his infallibility. The Ayatollah (literally 'sign of God') Khomeini was regarded, in Iran, as such a mujtahid. Other Shiites revere living Imams, such as the Aga Khan Khojas, whose leader (the Aga Khan) claims to be a descendant of the Prophet Muhammad through Ismail, the 7th Imam.

Shiite branches include: *Ithna 'Ashariyya* which is dominant in Azerbaijan, Bahrain, Ran and Iraq, *Zaidi* which is dominant in Yemen, and *Ibadi,* which is often regarded as belonging to neither the Sunni nor Shiite traditions, is dominant in Oman.

Islam's mystical or Sufi tradition has both Sunni and Shiite adherents. Many of its orders or circles have appointed or hereditary *pirs* (spiritual guides) and venerate their predecessors as saints. Sufi missionaries played an important role in Islam's expansion into Africa and Asia.

The small exclusive *Druze* sect, in Syria and Lebanon, has an eclectic system of doctrines.

Though the sheer variety of races and cultures embraced by Islam has produced differences, all segments of Muslim society are bound by a common faith and a sense of belonging to a single community. With the loss of political power during the period of Western colonialism in the 19th and early 20th centuries, the concept of the Islamic community, instead of weakening, became stronger.

This, in harness with the discovery of immense oil reserves, helped various Muslim peoples in their struggle to gain political freedom and sovereignty in the mid-20th century.

Islam as a total way of life is a missionary religion committed to bringing all men into the Household of Faith (*Dar-al-Islam*). However, it affords special status to followers of its sister faiths, Judaism and Christianity, which have existed as protected minority communities in many Muslim lands.

Adherents to Islam

The largest Islamic populations are to be found in the following countries:

Country	*Number of adherents (1993)*	*Sunni*	*Shia*
Indonesia	164,140,000	164,140,000	–
Pakistan	123,870,000	123,870,000	–
Bangladesh	99,710,000	99,710,000	–
India	99,000,000	99,000,000	–
Iran	59,740,000	4,740,000	55,000,000
Turkey	59,390,000	59,390,000	–
Egypt	51,400,000	51,400,000	–
Nigeria	41,200,000	41,200,000	–
China	28,000,000	28,000,000	–
Algeria	26,890,000	26,890,000	–
Morocco	26,120,000	26,120,000	–
Afghanistan	20,070,000	17,030,000	3,040,000
Iraq	18,860,000	6,710,000	12,150,000
Sudan	18,250,000	18,250,000	–
Saudi Arabia	17,210,000	17,210,000	–
Ethiopia	15,200,000	15,200,000	–

Islam is the largest religious denomination in the following countries:

Afghanistan, Albania, Algeria, Azerbaijan, Bahrain, Bangladesh, Bosnia-Herzegovina, Brunei, Chad, Comoros, Côte d'Ivoire, Djibouti, Egypt, Gambia, Guinea, Indonesia, Iran, Iraq, Jordan, Kazakhstan, Kuwait, Kyrgyzstan, Lebanon, Libya, Malaysia, Maldives, Mali, Mauritania, Morocco, Niger, Nigeria, Oman, Pakistan, Qatar, Saudi Arabia, Senegal, Somalia, Sudan, Syria, Tajikistan, Tanzania, Tunisia, Turkey, Turkmenistan, United Arab Emirates, Uzbekistan, and Yemen.

The largest Islamic minorities in predominantly Christian countries include:

Country	*Number of adherents of Islam (1993)*
Ethiopia	15,200,000
Russia	6,000,000
USA	4,910,000
Cameroon	2,860,000
Philippines	2,790,000
Yugoslavia (Serbia and Montenegro)	2,010,000
France	1,730,000
Germany	1,730,000
Eritrea	1,700,000
Kenya	1,690,000
Uganda	1,170,000
Bulgaria	890,000
United Kingdom	810,000

Islamic Law

The Shari'ah - the Islamic legal system and courts which regulate the lives of those who profess Islam – is in force in may countries of the Islamic world.

Countries in which only Islamic law, based on the Shari'ah, is in force:

Afghanistan, Djibouti, Jordan, Iran, Kuwait, Libya, the Maldives, Mauritania, Oman, Pakistan, Saudi Arabia, the United Arab Emirates, and Yemen. Sudan is in transition to Islamic law only.

(Gambling and alcohol are forbidden in Afghanistan, Algeria, Bangladesh, Brunei, Djibouti, Iran, Kuwait, Libya, Mauritania, Oman, Pakistan, Qatar, Saudi Arabia, the United Arab Emirates, and Yemen.)

Countries in which a combination of Islamic and secular law is in force:

Algeria, Bangladesh, the Comoros, Egypt, Iraq, Mali, Morocco, Qatar, Somalia, and Syria. In Brunei secular law and Islamic law exist side by side.

Countries of the Islamic world in which only secular law is in force:

Albania, Azerbaijan, Bahrain, Bosnia-Herzegovina, Chad, Gambia, Guinea, Indonesia, Kazakhstan, Kyrgyzstan, Malaysia, Niger, Senegal, Tajikistan, Turkey, Turkmenistan, and Uzbekistan.

Islam is the state religion established by law in the following countries:

Algeria, Bahrain, Bangladesh, Brunei, Comoros, Iran, Iraq, Jordan, Kuwait, Libya, Malaysia, Maldives, Mauritania, Morocco, Oman, Pakistan, Qatar, Saudi Arabia, Tunisia, and United Arab Emirates.

(In Lebanon Islam is one of two recognized state religions. In Indonesia Islam is recognized as a state religion alongside five other faiths.)

The following Islamic countries limit the freedom of other religions:

Afghanistan, Iran, Iraq, Libya, Malaysia, Pakistan, Saudi Arabia, Sudan, Turkey, and Yemen.

HINDUISM

The word Hindu was first used by Arab invaders in the 8th century AD to describe those who lived beyond the Sind or Indus Valley. The term Hinduism is now used to describe the religion and social institutions of the great majority of the people of India, though strictly speaking it is an English word. The origins of Hinduism (or *Sanatan-Dharma*, meaning 'ancient way of life') lie in the *Arya-Dharma* (Aryan way of life) of the Indo-Europeans who invaded the Indus Valley from Asia Minor and Iran c. 1500 BC. They wrote the *Vedas* (Rig-Veda, Yajur-Veda, Sama-Veda, Atharva-Veda), which are collections of prayers, hymns and formulas for worship. The Aryans worshipped nature-deities, including *Agni* (fire) and *Surya* (Sun).

The Aryans absorbed some of the traditions of the indigenous inhabitants. This process of assimilation resulted in the great epic poems composed between 200 BC and AD 200, the *Ramayana* and the *Mahabharata*, which includes the famous *Bhagavadgita*.

Three deities dominate these epics: Brahma, Vishnu and Shiva, representing creation, preservation and destruction. There are other gods and demi-gods, and also important *avatars* (incarnations), such as Krishna (a form of Vishnu). Some gods (e.g. the goddess of smallpox) are renowned for particular activities; others are local deities operating only in a particular area.

Philosophical Hinduism developed in the 5th century BC with a core of 18 *Upanishads* (philosophical scriptures). The laws of Manu (written during the first two centuries AD) contain the concept that God created distinct orders of men; priests (*Brahmans*); soldiers and rulers (*Kshatriyas*); farmers and traders (*Vaisyas*); and artisans and labourers (*Sudras*). The so-called caste system thus developed.

Hinduism tolerates a great variety of beliefs and practices and there is absolute freedom with regard to the choice and mode of one's philosophy. The Brahmans recognize six schools as orthodox. The best known are yoga, sankhya and vedanta, of which the great philosopher Shankara (Sankara; AD 788–820) was an exponent. The Brahmans regard Buddhism and Jainism as heterodox. The aim of Hindus is to be reunited with the absolute and thus escape the wheel of existence (*Samsara*), which is determined by *Karma* (literally 'deeds' or 'actions'). *Moksa* (release) may be gained through yoga, through *Jnana* (knowledge) or through *Bhakti* (devotion to one's God).

Hinduism traditionally divides life into four ideal periods: *Brahmacharya* (celibate period), *Grihastha* (householder), *Vanaprastha* (retired stage), and *Sannyasa* (renunciation). Hinduism embraces many local as well as national traditions and has numerous pilgrim centres, temples, ashrams (religious retreats) and orders of monks.

A Hindu temple (*mandir*) may be a huge, ornate building dedicated to the worship of a major deity – visited particularly during festivals and pilgrimages – or it may be a small shrine at the roadside at which offerings to a local spirit are made. The concept of the spiritual teacher, or guru, is important, and many contemporary gurus attract European as well as Indian devotees. The largest populations of Hindus are to be found in the following countries:

Country	*Number of adherents (1993)*
India	719,000,000
Nepal	17,200,000
Bangladesh	14,000,000
Sri Lanka	2,700,000
Pakistan	1,900,000
Malaysia	1,300,000
Mauritius	600,000

Hare Krishna

The International Society for Krishna Consciousness began in 1966 in the USA by an Indian monk or *sannyasi*, Bhaktivedanta Swami, known to his Western and Indian followers as 'Prabhupada'. It is a neo-Hindu movement based on a philosophy from northern India that focuses on love of the God *Krishna*. Service to God and humanity takes the form of temple worship, chanting and singing God's name.

HINDU GODS

Gods of the Vedas

Indra Thunder god, god of battle.
Varuna Guardian of order; divine overseer.
Agni God of fire.
Surya God associated with the sun.

Major gods of Hinduism

Brahma The creator; linked with the goddess Saraswati.
Vishnu The preserver; with Shiva, one of Hinduism's greatest gods. Vishnu has ten incarnations or avatars, and is married to Lakshmi.
Shiva A great god, associated with destruction. In Hindu mythology, Shiva is married to Parvati and is the father of Ganesh.
Ganesh The elephant-headed god, worshipped as the remover of obstacles and god of good luck.
Hanuman The monkey warrior-god associated with the god Rana.

Vishnu's ten avatars (incarnations)

Matsya The fish.
Kurma The tortoise.
Varaha The boar.
Narasimha The man-lion.
Vamana The dwarf.
Ramachandra or *Rama* The god of the *Ramayana* epic, identified by his bow and quiver of arrows.
Parasurama Rama bearing an axe.
Krishna The important god featured in the *Bhagavadgita*. He is worshipped particularly as a baby and as a flute-playing cowherd.
The Buddha The great teacher from the 6th–5th centuries BC and founder of Buddhism.
Kalki 'The one to come'; a future *avatar*.

Major goddesses of Hinduism

The goddesses are manifestations of the great creative spirit or *Shakti*. The most popular are:
Parvati Wife of Shiva; also known as *Uma*.
Durga All-powerful warrior goddess, also known as *Amba*, and linked with Shiva.
Kali Goddess associated with destruction.
Lakshmi Goddess of beauty, wealth and good fortune; wife of Vishnu.
Sarawati Goddess of learning, arts and music; wife of Brahma.

BUDDHISM

Buddhism is based on the teaching of Siddhartha Gautama (c. 563–483 BC) of the Gautama clan of the Sakyas in India. He was later named the Buddha, meaning 'the enlightened one'. After an early life of pleasure, Gautama became deeply dissatisfied, and he experimented with asceticism and yoga before experiencing *bodhi* or awakening during a long period of meditation under a tree. For the rest of his long life, Gautama taught about the impermanence and suffering of human life and the way to escape such suffering. The Buddha is said to have taught the four noble truths. These are:

- all forms of existence are subject to suffering (*dukkha*);
- the origin of suffering is craving;
- the cure for suffering is the cessation of craving;
- there is a 'Way' to end suffering. The 'Way' differs with the type of Buddhism. Zen Buddhists rely upon meditation; Therevada Buddhists believe that craving ceases by means of the *Eightfold Path* of right view, right thought, right speech, right action, right livelihood, right effort, right mindfulness and right concentration. This is represented in the Wheel of Law (*dharma chakra*), which has eight spokes for the eight steps towards enlightenment (*nirvana*).

The Buddha taught that since impermanence (*anicca*) is an unalterable fact of life, we can be truly happy only by becoming detached from the delusive notions of 'me' and 'mine'. This detachment is called the not-self (*anatta*). His teaching made no provision for God or the soul. He taught the law (*dharma*) of cause and effect, and encouraged his disciples to take refuge in the *sangha*, the monastic way of celibacy, non-violence, poverty and vegetarianism.

Buddhism is separated into three broad schools:

Therevada Buddhism. ('the school of the elders') is practised in Sri Lanka, Burma (Myanmar) and Thailand. It is said to have been the original Buddhism of India. This school remains non-theistic and emphasizes the importance of the celibate life to gain *nirvana*. In 1956, over 4,000,000 of India's untouchables converted to Therevada Buddhism.

Mahayana Buddhism. ('Greater Vehicle') is practised in Vietnam, Cambodia, Laos, China and Japan. Its subdivisions include Zen and Pure Land Buddhism. In Mahayana, the concept of the *Bodhisattva* ('one bound for enlightenment who delays entry into nirvana in order to help others') developed to include many such heavenly beings alongside, but subordinate to, the Buddha, who was regarded as having three bodies (*kaya*), the historical body, the bliss body, and the absolute body.

Tantrayama Buddhism developed in Tibet. This makes much use of *mantras* (sacred chants) and of images, which depict the Bodhisattvas as very active in the world, opposing evil. The male quality of compassion is often united with the female quality of wisdom.

In the West, Buddhism in all forms has attracted a significant following. The Friends of the Western Buddhist Order was formed in 1969 and seeks to find forms of expression amenable to the West, which some call *Navayana* (a 'New Vehicle').

CHINESE FOLK RELIGIONS AND DAOISM (TAOISM)

Chinese folk religions are now mainly practised by members of the 64 officially recognized minority peoples in the People's Republic of China. Traditional beliefs are most commonly encountered in remoter areas, but remnants of folk religion survive elsewhere in China and are widely practised in association with Daoism both in rural areas and in the cities.

These ancient traditional beliefs focus upon a constant interplay between the spirit world and the present physical world. There is a belief in demons and in divination. Demons – the *kuei-shen* – are manifested in all aspects of the natural world but, in particular, in mountains, rivers and rocks. As well as these spirits Chinese folk religion includes a belief in a panoply of ghosts, fairies and other supernatural beings with whom man must contend. As these spirits shun the light, firecrackers, bonfires and torches – as well as various charms – are used to scare the kuei away.

The centre of Chinese folk religion is, however, ancestor worship. The ancestor cult is deeply rooted in the Chinese regard for the family or kin group. Respect for the elderly and concern for the family have always been emphasized in Chinese society. The family unit is perceived as comprising the living members of the family group as well as the dead members of the family. The outward aspects of the ancestor cult include devotional acts at temples to the larger clan groups as well as reverence in the home, at temples and at the graves of family members. Funeral rites and pilgrimages to family graves are important.

The practice of Daoism is almost inseparable from these traditional folk religions.

Daoism, the Chinese teachings of the Way or Dao, is grounded in the works of Lao Tzu (6th–5th century BC) and Chuang-Tzu (4th century BC). It teaches that the Dao is the source of all things. The Dao works within the world, bringing about harmonious development. It acts as a model for rulers and for leaders who allow their people to live spontaneously according to their own conditions and needs. The Dao is symbolized by water and by female imagery rather than male imagery.

The goal of the Way is immortality which can only be achieved by the return to a properly balanced body composed of *yin* (the quiescent, feminine side) and *yang* (the active, male side).

Unlike Confucianism, Daoism advocates spontaneity and naturalness, abandoning oneself to the current of the Dao. Everything, good or bad, is the sublime operation of the Dao and should not be interfered with. Daoists naturally tend to solitude, meditation and simple living. Their techniques of quiet contemplation are similar to Buddhist meditation.

Daoism developed many schools and texts until the 16th century, and continued to have some impact on popular religion after that time in synthesis with other philosophical ideas and religious practices. The aspects of Daoism most well-known in the West are yin and yang, the book of divination the *I Ching* and a meditative form of exercise, *T'ai Chi*.

SHINTOISM

Shinto ('the way of the gods') is the native religion of Japan.

The religion gained the name Shinto during the 6th century AD to distinguish it from Buddhism, which was then reaching Japan from the Chinese mainland. The earliest surviving Shinto texts include semi-mythological genealogies of the emperors, tracing their divine descent from Amaterasu, the sun-goddess.

Early Shinto consisted of ritual practices directed at agriculture rather than philosophical or moral beliefs. The help of the sacred power (*kami*) was sought for the physical and spiritual needs of the people, and there was great stress laid upon purification by Shinto priests, and upon offerings and prayer. *Kami* is usually translated as 'god' or 'divinity' and – in so doing – the polytheistic nature of Shintoism is often overemphasized. The truthfulness of the *kami* can be recognized in every being at every moment.

The more important national shrines were dedicated to well-known national figures, but other shrines were set up for the worship of deities of mountain and forest.

Throughout its history Shintoism has been influenced by outside influences, especially Buddhism, Daoism and Confucianism. In the 19th century, the Shinto religion was divided into Shrine Shinto (*jinja*) and Sect Shinto (*kyoha*). A number of denominations were formed and these were dependent on private support for their teaching and organization. Different denominations had very little in common and varied widely in belief and practice. Some adhered to the traditional Shinto deities while others did not. Of the 13 denominations, *Tenrikyo* is the best known.

Unlike the other traditional religions that arose thousands of years ago, Shintoism is distinguished by its possession of a written rather than an oral sacred literature.

In 1871, Shinto became the Japanese national religion. State Shinto taught that a citizen's religious duty was obedience to the divine emperor. Shinto's perceived close links with extreme nationalism damaged its standing in postwar Japan. In 1946 Emperor Hirohito renounced all claims to divinity, and the new postwar constitution safeguards religious freedom and prohibits any association between religion and state.

Estimates of the number of practising adherents of Shinto range between 3,400,000 and nearly 110,000,000. Because the practice of Shinto and its traditions became the traditions of the Japanese nation, the majority of Japanese may be said to belong to the Shinto 'community'. Thus, about 109,000,000 people have some allegiance to Shintoism. However, most also practice some form of Buddhism and few have any active participation in the religion. Under 4,000,000 Japanese practice Shinto as their only religious observance. However, interest in Shinto is increasing and in 1990 Emperor Akihito was enthroned according to Shinto rites.

Shintoism has neither sought nor attracted non-Japanese followers.

PRIMAL RELIGIONS OF AFRICA AND ASIA

The word 'primal' is used to convey the idea that these religions came first in human history, and underlie all the major religions of the world. It is wrong to think of these religions as primitive. They often contain beliefs and ideas about the world that achieve high levels of sophistication. The primal religions that survive today are the religions of non-literate, usually tribal societies.

Unlike the universal religions such as Christianity, Islam, Hinduism and Buddhism – which have a wealth of written records and scriptures – the primal religions have no written sources. This does not mean, however, that primal religions are without history or are in some way 'fossilized' remnants of a past age. Like the universal religions, they have long and complex histories.

Christianity and Islam are popular in Africa, but there are also many traditional religions practised there by different tribal groups, such as the Nuer, Dinka, Dogon, Yoruba, Zande and Shona. These religions developed in pre-literate communities and environments that were often independent of one another and far apart. In African traditional religions – as in most primal religions – there is a conception of a supreme being, sometimes prominent in religious life, sometimes remote and uninterested in human affairs.

The Ashanti of Ghana call their god Nyame, and other West African peoples have similar names for their deity. The supreme god of the Yoruba people of Nigeria is known as Olorun, 'Owner of the Sky'. He is the creator of all things, the giver of life and breath, and the final judge of all people. In many parts of Africa the supreme being is considered so great and so remote that he is not worshipped. Divinities and ancestors, who act as intermediaries between people and the supreme god, are worshipped instead. Only in times of extreme distress is the god directly approached by the people.

Divinities are powerful named spirits, each with their own specific characteristics. Most African peoples believe in a multitude of divinities other than the supreme god. Common themes in African primal religions include divination, cults of affliction and possession, ancestor veneration, and secret societies.

In the Americas, Asia and Oceania, there is widespread belief in many deities. As well as powerful divinities and ancestor spirits, most primal peoples believe in numerous minor spirits, who may be good, malevolent or capricious. They may be the souls of the forgotten dead, who haunt the living, or the spirits of places such as rivers, mountains, bridges, rocks or trees.

In Oceania and in some other societies *mana* is a spiritual power or life force that is believed to permeate the universe. Originally a Melanesian word, it is now applied by anthropologists to spiritual power in other primal religions. Mana is not a spirit, and it has no will or purpose – it is impersonal and flows from one thing to another, and can be manipulated to achieve certain ends. Charms, amulets and medicines contain this power for the benefit of the wearer and user.

SIKHISM

Sikhism originated in the Punjab (India), where it is still the majority religion. It was founded by Guru Nanak (1479–1539), who taught how to lead a good life and seek final union with God.

Sikhism is based on the concept of the guru: that God is the true Guru; the Sikh spiritual teachers were called gurus; and the scriptures, the *Granth* are said to be the guru. Sikhs believe in the existence of only one true God and that through worship and meditation the most devoted Sikhs can experience and know him. They believe that each person is trapped in his own failings and weaknesses, and that the only hope is found in the mercy of the true Guru.

The Ten Gurus

Sikhism was developed under Nanak and the nine successive Sikh orthodox gurus, each chosen by his predecessor on the basis of his spiritual enlightenment

The succession of gurus is as follows:

Nanak 1469–1539; Angad 1504–52; Amar Das 1479–1534; Ram Das 1534–81; Arjan 1563–1606; Har Govind 1595–1644; Har Rai 1630–61; Har Krishan 1656–64; Tegh Bahadur 1621–75; Gobind Singh 1666–1708.

The Five Ks

The first five gurus developed the majority of the Sikh doctrines. The final guru, Gobind Singh, established the Sikh community with its shared symbols and the names 'Singh' and 'Kaur' for men and women respectively. The shared symbols are the so-called *five Ks*:

Kesh uncut hair worn in a turban and uncut beard;

Kangha a comb, to keep the hair clean;

Kara a metal bracelet;

Kaccha knee-length undershorts;

Kirpan a dagger.

Worship and Society

The holy scripture, the *Guru Granth*, is the central document for all Sikh rituals and ceremonies. It contains the teachings of the first five gurus. The Sikhs worship in temples known as *gurdwara* (the guru's door). The most important temple is the Golden Temple at Amritsar, which was built in the 16th century. There are no priests to conduct the services – anyone can lead the worship, although some are specially trained to read the *Granth*.

The Sikh community in the Punjab has called for the establishment of a separate Sikh homeland, *Khalistan*, and in the 1980s, a minority of extremist Sikhs began a campaign of terrorism to achieve this aim.

Sikhism has spread outside the Punjab during the 20th century to the United Kingdom, the USA, Canada and also to parts of southern and eastern Africa. It is an ethnic religion in that it attempts to keep the community intact and does not aim to convert members from outside. It does not deny the existence of other faiths but strives for its members to be devoted to God.

JUDAISM

The biblical account of the origin of the Jewish religion traces its history back to the revolt by Abraham against the idol-worship of his native Mesopotamia (now Iraq), when he smashed his father's idols and fled to Canaan (present-day Israel). Judaism is the oldest monotheistic religion. The word Jew is derived from the Latin *Judaeus*, that in turn is derived from the Hebrew *Yehudhi*, signifying a descendant of Jacob, Abraham's grandson.

The observance of the Passover (*Pesach*) from Egypt makes every believing Jew a participant in the event that delivered their ancestors from bondage and established a special relationship between themselves and God. The special relationship with the One God consists of an undertaking by the Jewish people to keep God's laws faithfully. Although Judaism expects non-Jews to observe certain basic ethical laws, it does not regard Jewish ritual as obligatory and does not seek converts. In fact, God promises the righteous of all people a place in the world to come, and the eventual re-establishment of the royal house of David; the *Messiah* (meaning the 'anointed') will inaugurate an age of universal peace and security.

Jewish scripture comprises the same books as the Christian Old Testament (see above). The *Torah* is the Hebrew name for the Law of Moses (the Pentateuch) which was divinely revealed to Moses on Mount Sinai, soon after the Exodus. The Hebrew scriptures also contain the books of the prophets, the wisdom literature (e.g. Solomon) and the historical writings (e.g. Kings). The *Talmud* contains civic and religious laws and is a collection of originally oral traditions. The *Mishnah* is the oral law dating from between the 1st century BC to the 3rd century AD.

The fall of Jerusalem (AD 70) resulted in the diaspora, which led to Jews settling throughout Europe, Africa and Asia Minor, often under severe discrimination and disabilities. Jewish emancipation began with Jewish enfranchisement in France in 1791. The new climate stimulated the growth of the Reform movement, which accepted for Judaism the status of a religious sect within the European nations, loyal to their countries of adoption. Orthodox Judaism regards all religious authority as deriving from the Torah, and the beliefs of Orthodox Judaism were codified as the Thirteen Principles of Faith by Rabbi Moses Maimonides (1135–1204). Conservative Judaism, which is strongest in the USA, stands midway between Orthodoxy and Reformed Judaism. It teaches that the faith must find its place in the contemporary world. There are also Liberal and Progressive Jews who reject the divinity of the Torah and rabbinic authority, and believe, to varying degrees, that Jewish practice must adapt to changing circumstances. They have introduced changes such as holding services partly in the vernacular (rather than Hebrew).

Ritual and Worship

Jewish law lays down a complex set of laws of *kashrut*, which distinguishes permitted (*kosher*) from prohibited (*treifa*) foods. Only cloven hoofed mammals that chew the cud, such as cows and sheep, are permitted as food, and they must be killed by a skilled *shochet* in a way that minimizes pain to the animal and drains as much blood as possible. Fish must have scales and fins (eels and sturgeon are forbidden); shellfish and birds of prey are prohibited. Milk and meat and their derivatives must be strictly separated and must not be cooked or prepared together, nor eaten at the same meal.

The Jewish day starts at sunset, and the week on Sunday, so that the *Shabbat*, the day of rest ordained by the Torah, is observed from dusk on Friday to nightfall on Saturday. This day of rest derives from the account of the creation in the Bible, where God rested on the seventh day. During Shabbat (the Sabbath) productive work is prohibited; other prohibitions include carrying, writing, cooking and travelling (except short distances by foot).

Synagogues were first built to serve as temporary places of worship after the destruction of the Temple in Jerusalem by the Babylonians (586 BC), but although the Jews did rebuild the Temple, the local houses of prayer continued. The second Temple was also destroyed and not rebuilt. To this day the synagogue service is modelled upon, and refers to, the Temple service. Many synagogues incorporate such ancient Jewish symbols as the Star of David, the *Menorah* (the seven-branched Temple candlestick), and the two tablets containing the Ten Commandments in their decoration. The congregation usually faces the Ark, a cupboard containing the Torah scrolls, which are handwritten on parchment. Above the Ark (usually in the wall facing Jerusalem) a light is kept burning as a sign of God's eternal presence. Services – held in the evening, morning and afternoon – centre on a period of silent prayer. For a formal service to take place, a quorum of ten men – a *minyan* – must be present, otherwise the Torah cannot be read. Any of the minyan can read the Torah or lead prayers. The rabbi is a teacher and interpreter of the Law.

Judaism as a total way of life revolves around the family as its main institution. Jews cannot surrender their religion. You are a Jew if your mother was Jewish. A boy becomes a man for religious purposes at his bar mitzvah at the age of 13, but is circumcised eight days after birth.

The majority of Jews still live in the diaspora, but the state of Israel (although officially secular) is important to most Jews as a symbol of the hope and pride that sustained their faith during centuries of persecution. Different groups from the diaspora preserve their distinctive traditions – including the Sephardim (from Portuguese, Spanish and North African communities), the Ashkenazim (from Central Europe), and most recently the Falasha (from Ethiopia). The largest Jewish populations are in the following countries:

Country	*Number of Jews (1993)*
USA	4,620,000
Israel	4,240,000
France	640,000
Russia	420,000
Canada	350,000
Ukraine	345,000
South Africa	115,000
Belarus	115,000

SHAMANISM

Shamanism consists of a wide range of traditional beliefs and folk religions that are usually closely related to the land. Shamanistic religions have survived mainly in remote areas

Shamanism is characterized by a whole range of religious specialists, including the medicine men of North America and the shamans of Siberia and the Arctic. Shamanism is generally found in hunting and gathering societies among peoples living in scattered, often migratory, groups. It is the dominant religious element among the Inuit (Eskimo) from Greenland to Alaska, and among the reindeer herders and fishers of northeastern Asia.

The shaman is a religious specialist – either a man or a woman – who, in times of trouble, mediates with the spirit world on behalf of his people. The shaman's power lies in his ability to enter an ecstatic trance. During ecstasy he sends out his soul to communicate with the spirit world, to ensure a favourable result for the hunt or to diagnose or cure disease.

CONFUCIANISM

Confucianism is an approach to life and way of thinking based on the teachings of Kongfuzi (Confucius; 551–479 BC). Kongfuzi was not the sole founder of Confucianism, but was rather a member of the founding group of *Ju* or meek ones. He was a scholar-official, a keeper of accounts from the province of Lu in China.

Kongfuzi taught that the main ethic is *jen* (benevolence), and that truth involves the knowledge of one's own faults. He believed in altruism and restraint, and insisted on filial piety. He believed that people could be led by example, and encouraged the rulers of his own time to imitate those in former periods whose leadership had brought about prosperity. Kongfuzi hoped for a true king (*wang*) who would rule by moral example rather than constraint. He stressed *li*, the rules of proper conduct in ritual, etiquette and social behaviour.

Kongfuzi himself is considered to represent the Confucian 'Ideal Person', a model of sincerity, modesty and rightmindedness. Gradually, through diligent training and study ('self-cultivation'), he was able to remould his own character to conform to the Will of Heaven.

Confucianism is better described as a philosophy or code of social behaviour than a religion. It has no church or clergy and is not a formal institution.

Kongfuzi's teachings were developed by Mengzi (Mencius; 372–289 BC) and became the basis of Chinese ethics and behaviour, in which there is an emphasis on the preservation of the family and the state, and the performance of proper rites for the ancestors. As its object was to emphasize the development of human nature and the person, Confucianism had a great hold over Chinese education for many years. During the early 19th century a good deal of Confucian teaching remained alongside other aspects of Chinese philosophy and practice. Confucianism has even survived the onslaught of Communist ideology.

OTHER RELIGIONS INCLUDE:

BAHA'ISM

Baha'ism evolved from the teachings of two 19th-century Persian visionaries – Mirza Ali Muhammad (1820–50), who called himself the Bab ('gateway'); and Mirza Husain Ali (1817–92), who called himself Baha'ullah ('Glory of God').

In 1863 Baha'ullah announced that he was the manifestation of God sent to redeem the world, as earlier prophesied by the Bab. He was imprisoned and exiled many times. He developed his teachings into a religion based on a new scripture, the *Kitab Akdas*.

After his death the followers of this faith grew in number until, today, it is present in over 70 countries but predominantly in southwest Asia. About two-thirds of its followers are converts from Islam or their descendants. The remainder are mostly west Europeans and Americans.

Baha'ullah's followers see him as a divine healer, relieving human suffering and uniting mankind. The Baha'i faith does not predict an end to this world, or any intervention by God, but declares that there will be a change within humanity and society by which the world will return to peace and recover from the deterioration of moral values.

Baha'ism is not a minor sect but a universal religion that emphasizes the value of all religion and the spiritual unity of all humanity. The Baha'i faith has been persecuted in Iran since 1979 and all Baha'i institutions were banned in that country in 1983.

CANDOMBLÉ

In Brazil, African and Amerindian influences interwove with spiritism and Roman Catholicism to produce Candomblé, a religion that combines African divinities, a belief in Jesus Christ and the Christian saints. Complex rituals include devotion to Christ, the saints and African deities and a quest for spiritual and physical healing and divination. Candomblé has been strongly condemned by the Roman Catholic Church, but many of the millions of participants in these practices consider themselves still to be Catholics.

CAO DAI

Cao Dai is largely confined to the former South Vietnam and, to a far lesser extent, to parts of the former North Vietnam. Altogether about 2,500,000 people follow Cao Dai in Vietnam. It is also practised by some small communities of Vietnamese in North America.

Ngo Van Chieu (1878–1932), a Vietnamese intellectual, founded Cao Dai amid great publicity in 1926. The religion is a combination of elements of other faiths, although its roots are probably Daoist.

The name Cao Dai means 'high tower', which is the Daoist symbol for the Supreme Being. Elements of Confucianism, traditional beliefs, Buddhism, Islam and Christianity are interwoven. Its founder sought the unity of all religions but Cao Dai developed as a religion on its own. Christianity, for example, is represented by a copy of the organization of Roman Catholic Church. The head of Cao Dai is a Pope, under whom are cardinals, archbishops, bishops, priests, etc.

Religious practice owes much to Daoism and Confucianism as well as Roman Catholicism.

There is considerable emphasis upon spirits and spiritualism. Although Cao Dai recognizes a single Supreme Being, reverence is also shown to a panoply of other spirits. Seven spirits are of particular importance: the prime figures of four major world faiths and three other persons, one a major 20th-century political figure of the Far East plus two figures from the history and culture of France (the colonial power in Vietnam). They are:

- Jesus Christ;
- Muhammad;
- the Buddha;
- Confucius;
- the Chinese nationalist leader Sun Yat-sen;
- Joan of Arc; and
- Victor Hugo.

Spiritual contact with these figures is important – indeed, the duty of one Cao Dai official was to take dictation of further novels from Hugo.

CHONDOGYO

Chondogyo was founded in 1860 in Korea, to which – apart from some small communities of Koreans in Japan and the USA – it is still confined. Its founder, Ch'oe Suun (1824–64), called the new religion the Tonghak movement, literally 'the Eastern Learning' – in contrast to the Western learning represented by Christianity. The result is a faith that teaches the existence of one God and which combines traditional Korean motifs (Confucian and Daoist) with some aspects of Christian practice. Its practice has been compared with Quakerism.

Ch'oe Suun claimed to have had a revelation from God. Shortly after the revelation he was martyred by the Korean royal government because his ideas were considered subversive to the dynasty. In time, Tonghak became known as Chondogyo (meaning 'the religion of the Heavenly Way').

Chondogyo was persecuted during the Japanese occupation of Korea, mainly because it played an important role in the revolt against Japanese rule in 1919. However, the egalitarian nature of Chondogyo has meant that the religion has been tolerated in North Korea, although its leaders have not acquiesced in Communism.

The main tenets of the faith are that God pervades the entire world and is present in individuals. This is summarized in the belief 'The human being is God'. Followers of Chondogyo believe that this oneness with God can be achieved through an honest practice of the faith and they are called upon to treat others as God.

The foundations of Chondogyo are faith, sincerity, steadfastness, and simplicity.

The writings of Ch'oe Suun, and his two successors as leaders of the movement, form the scripture of the religion. Religious practice includes prayer (including an invitation to the Almighty to enter oneself), scripture reading and an emphasis on silent meditation.

Five practises are recommended to followers:

- a formula chanted every evening at nine o'clock;
- prayers including the silent heart address or simgo;
- a service of worship on Sunday;
- the symbolic use of water as a symbol of purity;
- regular offerings of rice at the church.

Leaders of Chondogyo:

Ch'oe Suun 1860–64

Ch'oe Haewol 1864–98

Sohn Uiam 1898–1922

JAINISM

Jainism (from Hindi *jaina*, meaning 'saint') is an ancient religion that probably evolved during the first millennium BC. It spread from east to west across India, but, with the rise of Hinduism, Jainism declined and became restricted to two different regions of India, where it still exists today – Gujarat and Rajasthan in western India, and the Deccan in southern India.

Jainism has its own scriptures passed down orally from Mahavira (born c. 540 BC), one of the religion's great teachers. Jainism holds that the material world is eternal, moving on in a never-ending series of vast cycles. Like all Indian religions, it upholds the universal law of *karma*, which states that all actions, thoughts and words produce results that affect future deeds, forming a chain of cause and effect.

Jains do not believe in God – or gods – but in the perfectibility of the individual soul. In practice, the faith of Jainism seems very pessimistic as it sees the world as full of misery. However, prayer and worship can lead to liberation and salvation (*moksha*), when the individual soul is freed from matter and the suffering it brings. Jains practise non-violence (*ahimsa*), respect for all creatures, and vegetarianism.

NEW AGE RELIGIONS

The New Age movement is a 'child of the Sixties' when a spirit of openness to various belief systems – including oriental religions, the occult and paganism – led many young people to declare an 'Age of Aquarius'.

No single New Age religion exists. There is instead a syncretistic movement drawing upon various spiritual traditions in opposition to the Western Judeo-Christian tradition.

PARSIISM (ZOROASTRIANISM)

The origins of Zoroastrianism are attributed to the Persian (Iranian) prophet Zoroaster or Zarathustra (c.1200 BC). It was the Persian state religion from the 6th century BC to the 6th century AD. Following the expansion of Islam to Iran, the Zoroastrians were persecuted and retreated to the cities of Yadz and Kerman. In the 10th century AD, some fled to India. Bombay has become the centre of these Zoroastrians, known as Parsis.

Zoroastrianism acknowledges the existence of a good god, Ahura Mazda, and an evil spirit, Angra Mainyu. Ahura Mazda is assisted by angelic beings and it is believed that through their efforts good will finally triumph.

The main scripture is the *Avesta,* which stresses the importance of worship based on fire. Zoroastrians are also known for the towers of silence (daxma) they use for the disposal of the dead.

In the 19th century Parsi religious reforms led many Parsis, under the influence of Western education, to reject many aspects of traditional Zoroastrianism. The reformists advocated a pure monotheism. Zoroastrianism is a small religion – probably numbering no more than 120,000 – with a majority in either Bombay or the USA, but its followers are spread throughout the world. Intermarriage and conversion are not encouraged.

RASTAFARIANISM

The Rastafari movement had its origins in the United Negro Improvement Association, founded in 1914 by the Jamaican leader Marcus Garvey (1887–1940). The 1930s saw deep unrest and poverty among Black West Indians. This coincided with the publicity attracted by the coronation in 1930 of the Ethiopian emperor Haile Selassie (originally called Ras Tafari), who became a symbol to Garvey. Ethiopia came to be regarded as paradise to which exiled Blacks would return. Haile Selassie was regarded as a living god.

Followers, largely Black Jamaicans, believed Whites to be inferior to Blacks and saw their residence in the West Indies as a form of punishment. They looked for a 'return' to Ethiopia and a day when Blacks would rule over Whites. These beliefs have modified with time and the role ascribed to Haile Selassie diminished after his deposition (1974) and murder (1975).

The Rastafarians have acquired several well-known external characteristics – dreadlocks in the hair, a distinctive music style and the custom of smoking marijuana.

SCIENTOLOGY

The Church of Scientology was founded in 1955 by the American L. Ron Hubbard, a science fiction writer. It derived from dianetics, a form of psychotherapy developed by Hubbard. Followers aim to 'clear' or free the mind from past painful experiences or 'engrams'.

Scientologists believe in a highly structured spiritual world, the thetan (soul) and reincarnation. Scientology has attracted criticism concerning its claims and the cost of its courses.

SPIRITUALISM

Spiritualism is a religious belief in the ability of the spirits of the dead to communicate with the living – a belief common to most primal religions.

Modern practices date from the experiences in 1848 of the American Fox sisters who heard strange tapping sounds in their house and devised a similar code to communicate with the (deceased) intelligence that they claimed was making these noises. Spiritualism relies upon mediums who use telepathy to communicate with the spirit world.

THEOSOPHY

Theosophy is a religious philosophy whose name is derived from the Greek *theos* (meaning 'god') and *sophia* (meaning 'wisdom'). The term is used in a general sense to imply a particular type of mysticism that is based on knowledge of God through spiritual ecstasy.

Modern theosophy derives from the Theosophical Society, which was founded by the Russian Helena Blavatsky and the English Col. H.S. Olcott in 1875. Modern theosophy – which denies a personal god – teaches an intricate system of psychology and cosmology.

Theosophists believe in the transmigration of souls and a brotherhood of all humanity that ignores differences of creed and race.

Rudolf Steiner developed anthroposophy from similar principals (see p. 179).

TRANSCENDENTAL MEDITATION

Transcendental meditation (TM) was founded in India in 1958 by the Indian Maharishi Mahesh Yogi, whose teachings became very popular among young people in the West in the 1960s. The Maharishi developed a system of meditation that uses a mantra – a word or phrase in Sanskrit – which is mentally repeated to bring an individual into a deeper, quieter sense of consciousness. Followers are trained and receive a personal mantra. There are about 3,000,000 practitioners world-wide, mainly in the USA and India.

ANCIENT RELIGIONS

The majority of ancient religions were polytheistic. Most ancient peoples, whose religion had evolved beyond the primal stage, believed in a panoply of gods and goddesses. Elaborate ritual, with an emphasis upon sacrifice and divination, and an elite caste of priests were characteristics of ancient religions.

ANCIENT GREEK AND ROMAN RELIGION

Written evidence about religion in Europe begins with the Linear B texts of the Mycenaean civilization in Greece (c. 1450 BC). These show the importance of Poseidon the sea god and of 'the Lady' of various locations (presumably a mother goddess). Some other divine names occur, including Zeus and Hera, which later appear in the epic poetry of Homer.

Homer's gods lived ageless and immortal on Mount Olympus, but acted like humans – and not the best-behaved humans. They could change shape, intervene in human life, and might respond to gifts and prayers to change human destiny, but they did not change human nature.

By the 6th century BC the Olympian gods were part of the official worship of the Greek city-states. But ancient Greek religion had little to do with morality, and the moral, metaphysical and scientific concerns of the Athenian philosophers of the 5th and 4th centuries led to very different ideas of God. These ideas challenged popular religion, and in 399 BC the philosopher Socrates was condemned for atheism and corrupting youth by undermining the gods of the state.

Two forms of religious expression developed in early Rome. Domestic piety recognized household gods (*lares* and *penates*), while the state cult ensured corporate well-being. As Rome encountered Greek culture, the state deities were identified with Olympian equivalents.

As the Roman Empire expanded, its armies brought back foreign cults and religious ideas. The most important of these cults – until Christianity became the state religion in the 4th century AD – was Mithraism, a male-only mystery cult based on the worship of Mithras, the Persian god of light, truth and justice.

The Twelve Olympian Gods

Zeus the overlord of the Olympian gods; the God of the sky and its properties (Roman: Jupiter).

Hera the protector of women and marriage, and goddess of the sky; wife of Zeus (Roman: Juno).

Poseidon the god of the sea and earthquakes (Roman: Neptune).

Demeter the goddess of the harvest (Roman: Ceres).

Apollo the god of prophecy, music and medicine (there was no direct Roman equivalent).

Artemis the goddess of chastity, childbirth and the young (Roman: Diana).

Ares the god of war (Roman: Mars).

Aphrodite the goddess of love and beauty (Roman: Venus).

Hermes the god of trade and travellers (Roman: Mercury).

Athene (or **Athena**) the goddess of prudence and wise council; the protectress of Athens (Roman: Minerva).

Hephaestus the god of fire and metalcraft (Roman: Vulcan).

Hestia the goddess of fire (Roman: Vesta).

Other important deities

Adonis the god of vegetation and rebirth.

Aeolus the god of the winds.

Alphito the barley goddess of Argos.

Arethusa the goddess of springs and of fountains.

Asclepius the god of healing.

Atlas a Titan who carries the Earth.

Attis the god of vegetation.

Boreas the god of the northern wind.

Cronus the father of the god Zeus.

Cybele the goddess of the Earth.

Dionysus the god of wine and the 'good life' (Roman: Bacchus).

Eos the goddess of the dawn (Roman: Aurora).

Erebus the god of darkness.

Eros the god of love (Roman: Cupid).

Gaia (or **Gaea**) the goddess of the Earth.

Ganymede the beautiful youth who became cup-bearer to Zeus.

Hades see Pluto.

Hebe the goddess of youth.

Hecate the goddess of witchcraft, of magic and of the Moon.

Helios the god of the Sun (Roman: Sol).

Hygiea the goddess of health (Roman: Salus).

Hypnos the god of sleep (Roman: Somnus).

Irene the goddess of peace (Roman: Pax).

Iris the goddess of the rainbow.

Morpheus the god of sleep and of dreams.

Nemesis the god of retribution.

Nereus the god of the sea.

Nike the goddess of victory (Roman: Victoria).

Oceanus the Titan with divinity of the rivers and the seas.

Pan the god of flocks and of herds (and also associated with fertility) (Roman: Sylvanus).

Persephone the goddess of the underworld and of corn (Roman: Proserpina).

Pluto (or **Hades**) the god of the underworld.

Prometheus the Titan who was the god of fire and of the creation of man.

Rhea a Titaness; the mother of many gods, and the wife of Cronus.

Selene the goddess of the moon (Roman: Luna).

Thanatos goddess of night and death (Roman: Mors).

Triton a merman; the sea god.

Uranus the sky god who was responsible for the sun and rain.

ANCIENT EGYPTIAN RELIGION

The pharaohs of ancient Egypt were regarded as divine, and were called 'Horus' or 'Son of Re'. The autocratic rule of the pharaohs was legitimized by the mythology of Re as the Sun god and ruler of the gods; as 'Son of Re' the pharaoh embodied the life-giving power of the sun. Horus was the son of Isis, the Divine Mother, and of Osiris, the god of inundation, vegetation and the dead. As Horus, the pharaoh embodied the periodic renewal of life and fertility borne on the annual flooding of the land by the River Nile.

Local deities were often linked with national ones. The most significant was Amun, the god of invisibility, one of the characteristic elements of chaos out of which the Earth emerged. From c. 2000 BC he was combined with Amun to become Amun-Re, whose temple at Thebes was to become the most powerful and wealthiest in Egypt.

Gods and Goddesses of Ancient Egypt

Amun the god of Thebes; often represented as a man, sometimes with an erect penis.

Anubis the jackal-headed god of the necropolis; patron of the embalmers.

Aten the creator god manifest in the sun disc.

Atum the original sun god of Heliopolis.

Bastet the cat goddess.

Bes the domestic god, usually depicted as a dwarf.

Edjo the cobra goddess who appears as the pharaoh's protector on the royal diadem.

Geb the god of the Earth; the physical support of the world.

Hathor often represented as a cow, a cow-headed woman, or a woman with a cow's headdress. Hathor was recognized as the suckler of the pharaoh.

Horus the falcon god who was identified with the pharaoh during his reign. The son of Osiris and Isis, Horus grew up to avenge his father's murder by Seth.

Imhotep the architect of the Step Pyramid, and the chief minister of Djoser (c. 2700 BC). He was later venerated as the god of learning and of medicine.

Isis the wife of Osiris and mother of Horus.

Khepri the scarab-beetle god who was identified with the sun god Re as creator god.

Maat the goddess of truth, justice and order; usually depicted as a woman with an ostrich feather on her head.

Min the god of fertility and of the harvest; the protector of desert travellers and the god of the road.

Mut the vulture goddess of Thebes; a mighty divine mother.

Nekhbet the vulture goddess, who sometimes appears beside Edjo on the royal diadem.

Nephthys the sister of Isis.

Nut the goddess of the sky.

Osiris the god of the dead. He was identified with the dead king and depicted as a mummified king. Osiris was also the god of the inundation of the Nile and of vegetation.

Ptah the creator god of Memphis and the patron of craftsmen. He was represented as a mummified man.

Ptah-Soker-Osiris the god combining the principal gods of creation, death and the afterlife. He was represented as a mummified king.

Re or Ra the sun god of Heliopolis and the supreme judge. Other gods aspiring to universal recognition would often link their name to his, for example Amun-Re.

Re-Harakhti the falcon god, incorporating the characteristics of Re and Horus.

Sebek a protector of reptiles and patron of kings.

Sekhmet the lion-headed goddess, the wife of Ptah, venerated in the area of Memphis. She was regarded as the bringer of sickness and destruction to the enemies of Re.

Seth the god of violence and storms. Brother and murderer of Osiris, he was represented as an animal of unidentified type.

Shu the god of light and air.

Sobek the crocodile god.

Thoth the ibis-headed god of Hermopolis; the scribe to the gods and inventor of writing.

Thoueris the hippopotamus goddess, the patron of women in childbirth.

GERMANIC (NORSE) RELIGION

The religions of the Germanic peoples survived into the Middle Ages: Denmark, Norway and Iceland did not become Christian until the 10th and 11th centuries, and Sweden not until the 12th century. Germanic religion had many deities.

In early times, Odin, Tyr and Thor (see below) in particular were worshipped. There was no supreme deity, only a chaos of divine energy. The worshipper chose the divinity thought most likely to serve him.

People and Places in Norse Religion

Aesir the race of gods including Odin and Thor; defeated the Vanir.

Asgard the home of the gods.

Balder 'the Beautiful', son of Odin, slain by Loki.

Fenrir 'Great Wolf', son of Loki; bound up by Tyr, but will break free at Ragnarok.

Frey the fertility god, one of the Vanir.

Freya Frey's sister, consort of Odin.

Frigg Odin's wife. Her name is preserved in 'Friday'.

Hel the kingdom of the dead; also personified as Loki's daughter.

Loki the trickster god of Asgard. Imprisoned in a cave for the murder of Balder, he will break loose at Ragnarok.

Midgard the world of men. It is held by a coiled serpent, who will show himself at Ragnarok.

Njord father of Frey and Freya, associated with ships and sailing.

Norns three maidens who rule the fates of men and daily water the world tree Yggdrasil.

Odin (old Germanic **Wotan**; Anglo-Saxon **Woden**) the chief of the Aesir; the god of battle, poetry and death.

Ragnarok (German **Götterdämmerung**) 'the twilight of the gods', the coming day of destruction for Asgard and Midgard and their inhabitants in a battle with the forces of evil.

Thor the god of thunder.

Tyr (Old Germanic **Tiwaz**) a war god who has bound Fenrir.

Valhalla Odin's great hall for warriors.

Valkyries the spirit maidens who guide in battle and conduct the chosen slain to Valhalla.

Vanir a race of gods associated with fertility; they were defeated by the Aesir.

Yggdrasil the self-renewing world tree, which forms the centre of the worlds of gods, giants and men.

CELTIC RELIGION

Little is known about the Celtic deities owing to a lack of written material.

Celtic religious beliefs were centred on the relationship between the divine spirit world with the land and the waters. Hills, rocks, springs, rivers and many other features were thought to be the homes of guardian spirits. Trees were also inhabited by spirits and certain species had a ritualistic role.

The druids – the priest-poets of the Celts – took their name from an ancient Indo-European word meaning 'knowing the oak'.

Celtic Gods and Festivals

Belenus the god of war.

Beltane the festival of Bel's fire (May 1); marks the beginning of hunting and wooing.

The Brigits three Irish mother goddesses who presided over poetry, metalwork and healing. Celtic goddesses frequently manifested themselves in 'trinities'.

Cernunnos the stag-horned Lord of the Animals; appears on many surviving artifacts.

Cernunnos was a shamanistic figure who was also referred to as the Lord of the Animals.

Imbolc the festival of springtime (February 1).

Lug the sun god; also the patron of music. Lug was also the master of crafts.

Lugnasag the festival of harvest and the marriage of Lug.

Macha known in Britain as Rhiannon, Macha was the mare goddess. In Gaul Macha was known as Epona. Macha was one of the most powerful Celtic deities. Macha was a symbol of fertility.

Manannan the god of the oceans.

Morrigan the powerful crow goddess associated with death and battle. Morrigan personified both death and rebirth. She was known as the 'Great Queen'.

Samain the festival of the dead (November 1) and the end of summer.

AZTEC AND INCA RELIGION

Aztec religion was a combination of the beliefs of other Central American peoples. The Aztec religion and calendar were closely linked and important dates were marked by elaborate rituals performed by priests. The gods were appeased by constant sacrifices including human sacrifice and blood letting.

Inca religion combined animism with nature worship and fetishism (a belief in objects having magical powers). The cult of Viracocha (see below) was highly organized and, as the state religion of the Inca Empire, was compulsory. However, the cults of conquered peoples were also tolerated. Religious practice was elaborate and was characterized by divination and by both human and animal sacrifice.

Aztec Gods

Aztec gods included:

Centeotl the maize god.

Centzon Totochtin the '400 rabbits' – fertility gods.

Chalchiuhtlícue the wife of Quetzacóatl; the freshwater goddess.

Cihuacóatl the snake-woman goddess.

Ehécatl the wind god.

Huehuetéotl the god of fire.

Huixtocihuatl god of the sea.

Nanahuatzin a small ulcer-covered god who sacrificed himself in a sacred fire to become the Sun.

Omecihuatlt Lady of the Duality; one half of the Supreme Couple.

Ometecuhtli Lord of the Duality; one half of the Supreme Couple.

Quetzalcóatl the plumed serpent, he was the god of the morning and evening stars; Quetzalcóatl was patron of the priests. His worship demanded human sacrifice.

Tecciztécatl a bejewelled god who sacrificed himself in a sacred fire to become the Moon.

Teteoinnan the goddess of fecundity and mother of all gods.

Tezcatlipoca the god of the night sky; the protector of warriors.

Tlaloc the god of rain, thunder and lightning.

The Tlaloques the rain gods.

Tlazoltéotl the goddess of love and forgiveness.

Xipe Totec the god of spring and of plant growth.

Xochipilli the god of flowers.

Xolotl the twin of Quetzacóatl; the dog-headed god.

Inca Gods

Inca gods included:

Apu Illapu the rain god; god of farmers.

Inti the sun god; he was said to be the divine ancestor of the Sapa Incas.

Mama-Kilya the wife of Inti; the moon goddess.

Mama-Qoca the Sea Mother.

Paca-Mama Mother Earth.

Viracocha the supreme god; the creator of the Incas, and also of Earth, of humanity and of all living creatures. Viracocha had many titles including the Old Man of the Sky and the Ancient One. His cult was the official state religion of the Inca Empire.

Several constellations of stars had religious importance – Lyra (which was said to be shaped like a llama) was invoked for protection; the Pleiades were called the Little Mothers and festivals marked their reappearance.

LANGUAGE AND LITERATURE

Language

No one is certain how many living languages there are in the world, but it is likely that the number exceeds 5000. Each language is unique in that it has its own system of sounds, words and structures, and yet almost all are related either closely or distantly to other languages found in the same part of the world.

LANGUAGE FAMILIES

Languages are classed in families containing related tongues. The main language families are:

Altaic including Mongolian, Turkish and many of the languages of Central Asia.

Amerindian the languages of the native North Americans.

Austronesian the languages of the west Pacific.

Bantu the languages of sub-Saharan Africa, for example Xhosa and Zulu.

Dravidian languages of central and southern India and Sri Lanka, including Tamil and Telegu.

Finno-Ugrian Finnish, Estonian, Magyar (Hungarian), Lappish and some minorities in Russia.

Indo-Chinese languages of China, including Mandarin, Cantonese, Wu and Tibetan.

Indo-European the largest family. The Indo-European languages are spoken by about one half of the world's population. Based in South Asia and Europe, these languages have been taken to many parts of the world by European colonists. The group includes all the languages of Europe (except Basque, Finnish, Estonian, Lappish, and Magyar) as well as the Iranian group of languages and the Indic languages, including Hindi, Gujarati, Marathi, Urdu, Bengali, Sindhi, Sinhalese, and Punjabi.

Japanese only the Japanese language, which is unrelated to any other language.

THE WORLD'S PRINCIPAL LANGUAGES

Language	*Number of speakers as a first language (1993 est)*	*Notes*
1. **Mandarin** (Chinese)	830,000,000	The official language of China. Mandarin – also known as Putonghua – is standardized northern Chinese. Spoken in China and by Chinese communities throughout Southeast Asia. An additional 90,000,000 people speak Mandarin as a second language.
2. **Hindi**	330,000,000	One of the official languages of India. Spoken in north and central India. An additional 65,000,000 people speak Hindi as a second language.
3. **Spanish** (Castilian)	325,000,000	Spoken as a first language in Spain (except in Catalonia, Galicia and the Basque Country) and in Latin America (except Brazil). An official language in 21 countries. An additional 45,000,000 people speak Spanish as a second language.
4. **English**	320,000,000	The first language in Australia, Canada, Caribbean Commonwealth countries, Ireland, New Zealand, the UK and the USA, and widely spoken in Commonwealth and former Commonwealth countries including India, Kenya, Malaysia, Nigeria, Pakistan, South Africa, Tanzania, and Zimbabwe. An official language in 47 countries. An additional 140,000,000 people speak English as a second language.
5. **Bengali**	185,000,000	The official language of Bangladesh and the Indian state of West Bengal, and one of the official languages of India. An additional 9,000,000 people speak Bengali as a second language.
6. **Arabic**	175,000,000	Spoken throughout North Africa and southwestern Asia. An official language in 22 countries. An additional 30,000,000 people speak Arabic as a second language.
7. **Russian** (Great Russian)	170,000,000	The official language of the Russian Federation. Also spoken by a substantial minority of people in all of the former republics of the USSR. An additional 120,000,000 people speak Russian as a second language.
8. **Portuguese**	165,000,000	The official language of Portugal, Brazil and former Portuguese colonies in Africa – a total of seven countries. An additional 13,000,000 people speak Portuguese as a second language.
9. **Japanese**	125,000,000	Japanese is confined to Japan and Japanese communities abroad. An additional 1,000,000 people speak Japanese as a second language.
10. **German**	98,000,000	German is an official language of Germany, Austria, Switzerland, Luxembourg and Liechtenstein, and is also spoken by minorities throughout Central and Eastern Europe. An additional 21,000,000 people speak German as a second language.
12. **Urdu**	96,000,000	Urdu is the national language of Pakistan and is one of the official languages of India.
13. **Punjabi**	90,000,000	Spoken in the Indian state of Punjab and in adjoining areas of Pakistan. One of the official languages of India.

14. **Korean**	72,000,000	The official language of North and South Korea. Also spoken by Korean minorities in Central Asia and eastern Russia. An additional 1,000,000 people speak Korean as a second language.
15= **French**	71,000,000	Spoken in France, Québec, southern Belgium, western Switzerland and in French dependencies (for example in the Caribbean), and widely understood in former French colonies in Africa. An official language in 29 countries. An additional 53,000,000 people speak French as a second language.
15= **Telegu**	71,000,000	Spoken in Andhra Pradesh and adjoining areas of south India. One of the official languages of India.
17= **Tamil**	67,000,000	Spoken in the Indian state of Tamil Nadu and in parts of Sri Lanka and Malaysia. One of the official languages of India.
17= **Marathi**	67,000,000	Spoken mainly in the Indian state of Maharashtra. One of the official languages of India.
19. **Cantonese**	66,000,000	Spoken in Guangdong province, China, and in Hong Kong.
20. **Wu**	65,000,000	Spoken in eastern central China.
21= **Javanese**	61,000,000	Javanese is the first language of Java and parts of Sumatra and is spoken by minorities throughout the rest of Indonesia.
21= **Vietnamese**	61,000,000	Spoken in Vietnam and parts of adjoining states.
23. **Italian**	59,000,000	Spoken in Italy and the Swiss canton of Ticino and by Italian communities in the New World. An additional 4,000,000 speak Italian as a second language.
24. **Turkish**	54,000,000	Spoken in Turkey and in parts of neighbouring countries (particularly Bulgaria). An additional 6,000,000 people speak Turkish as a second language.
25. **Min**	50,000,000	Spoken in southeastern China and Taiwan.
26. **Thai**	49,000,000	Spoken in Thailand and in some adjoining areas.
27. **Malay-Indonesian**	48,000,000	Spoken in Malaysia, Indonesia (where it is known as Bahasa), and parts of southern Thailand. An additional 100,000,000 people (mainly in Indonesia) speak Malay-Indonesian as a second language.
28= **Kannada**	43,000,000	Spoken in southern India. One of the official languages of India.
28= **Tagalog-Pilipino**	43,000,000	The official language of the Philippines.
30. **Polish**	42,000,000	Spoken in Poland and in parts of Ukraine and Lithuania.
31. **Ukrainian**	41,000,000	Spoken in Ukraine, and in parts of Russia, Belarus and other former Soviet republics. An additional 5,000,000 people speak Ukrainian as a second language.
32. **Gujarati**	39,000,000	Spoken in the Indian state of Gujarat. One of the official languages of India.
33. **Hakka**	36,000,000	Spoken in southeastern China.
34. **Malayalam**	35,000,000	Spoken in Kerala in southern India.
35. **Farsi** (Persian)	34,000,000	The official language of Iran.
36= **Burmese**	31,000,000	The official language of Myanmar (Burma).
36= **Oriya**	31,000,000	Spoken in central and eastern India. One of the official languages of India.
38. **Romanian**	26,000,000	Spoken in Romania and Moldova.
39. **Sundanese**	25,000,000	Spoken in the Sunda region of Indonesia.
40. **Assamese**	23,000,000	Spoken in the Assam region of India. One of the official languages of India.
41= **Dutch-Flemish**	21,000,000	Spoken in the Netherlands and Belgium.
41= **Pushto**	21,000,000	Spoken in Afghanistan and Pakistan.
43. **Yoroba**	19,000,000	Spoken in southwestern Nigeria and Benin.
44. **Amharic**	18,000,000	Spoken in central Ethiopia.
45= **Ibo**	17,000,000	Spoken in southern Nigeria.
45= **Sindhi**	17,000,000	Spoken in Sind (Pakistan) and in neighbouring areas of India. One of the official languages of India.
47. **Serbo-Croat**	16,000,000	Spoken in Serbia, Montenegro, Croatia, and Bosnia-Herzegovina, and by minorities in Macedonia and Slovenia. An additional 4,000,000 people speak Serbo-Croat as a second language.
48= **Azeri**	15,000,000	Spoken in Azerbaijan and northwestern Iran.
48= **Zhuang**	15,000,000	Spoken in Guangxi Zhuang province, China.
49= **Nepali**	14,000,000	Spoken in Nepal and Bhutan.
49= **Magyar** (Hungarian)	14,000,000	Spoken in Hungary and in parts of Romania, Slovakia, Ukraine and Serbia.

Alphabets

THE GREEK ALPHABET

The Greek alphabet is the oldest surviving alphabet in Europe and is still widely understood outside the Greek-speaking world because its letters are used for a variety of scientific purposes. This alphabet is the ancestor of both the Roman and Cyrillic alphabets.

In the 9th century BC, the Phoenicians, who inhabited what is now Lebanon, introduced their alphabet to the Greeks. The order of the Phoenician symbols was retained by the Greeks, who modified both the forms and the names of certain characters. Thus the Phoenician aleph (meaning ox), beth (house), gimel (camel), for example, became the Greek alpha, beta, gamma. Unlike their Phoenician counterparts, however, the Greek letter-names have no meaning.

More importantly, the Greeks had no equivalent sound for some of the Phoenician consonantal symbols. However, instead of discarding them they adopted them for vowels, thus creating the first true alphabet. They also added five new symbols: omega, upsilon, phi, chi, and psi.

Upper case symbols (capitals) and lower case symbols (miniscules) were also introduced.

Several local alphabets developed in the Hellenic world, but two became dominant:

Ionic or **Ionian** (which is also known as the eastern Greek script); and

Chalcidean (or the western Greek script).

In 403 BC, the eastern variant, Ionian, was adopted as the official Athenian alphabet; and during the course of the next century this script spread throughout Greece, replacing its principal rival, the widespread Chalcidean alphabet.

From this Ionian (now usually referred to as Classical Greek) the capitals of the modern 24-letter alphabet of seven vowels and 17 consonants have descended virtually unchanged.

The early Greek alphabet was, like its Phoenician 'parent', written from right to left, but by about 500 BC the language was written from left to right, as now.

Three different scripts that were more suited to handwriting developed from the Classical Greek alphabet.

These three scripts were:

uncial an adaptation of the capitals of the Classical Greek alphabet, but adapted in a manner that is easier to write on paper than the Classical capitals, which were, initially, normally carved upon stone. Uncial, which may be described as being similar to hand printed capitals, was widely used, but this script disappeared at some point in the 9th century AD.

cursive is a flowing written script with an appearance that is similar to handwriting. This script includes many variations of shape of the letters from the capitals.

miniscule is also a flowing written script similar, in some respects, in appearance, to the cursive script (see above). Miniscule, which was developed around the 8th century AD, eventually replaced the letters of the uncial script. The modern letters used in Greek handwriting were developed from the letters of the minsicule script.

In the table of letters of the modern Greek alphabet (below), the standard capital versions of the letters are given on the first line of each entry. The middle line of each entry lists the name of each letter and the sound represented by that letter. The final line gives the miniscule version of each letter.

Α	Β	Γ	Δ	Ε	Ζ
alpha a	beta b	gamma g	delta d	epsilon e (short)	zeta dz
α	β	γ	δ	ε	ζ
Η	Θ	Ι	Κ	Λ	Μ
eta e	theta th	iota i	kappa k	lambda l	mu m
η	θ	ι	κ	λ	μ
Ν	Ξ	Ο	Π	Ρ	Σ
nu n	xi ks	omicron o (short)	pi	prho r	sigma s
ν	ξ	ο	π	ρ	σ
Τ	Υ	Φ	Χ	Ψ	Ω
tau t	upsilon u	phi ph	khi kh	psi ps	omega o
τ	υ	φ	χ	ψ	ω

THE CYRILLIC ALPHABET

Cyrillic is the second most widespread alphabet after the Roman alphabet. Its invention is attributed to the Greek missionaries St Cyril and his brother St Methodius in the 9th century. The Slavonic languages are very rich in sounds and therefore required a large number of characters in order to represent them. Originally of 43 letters adapted from the Greek alphabet and the Hebrew alphabet, the Russian Cyrillic alphabet was reformed after the 1917 Russian revolution when it was reduced to 33 letters.

Cyrillic is used to write Russian, Belarussian (also known as Belorussian), Bulgarian, Macedonian, Serb, Ukrainian and many other languages, most them Slavonic.

Some of these languages, such as Serb and Bulgarian, have introduced additional letters that apply only to these languages. At the same time, certain letters have been dropped from the various versions of the Cyrillic alphabet, although those letters that have been judged to be superfluous are not the same in all of the Slavonic languages. The major languages using the Cyrillic language, therefore, now have different numbers of letters:

Modern Russian has 32 letters (with one variant; see below); Belarussian has 32 letters; Ukrainian has 33 letters; Bulgarian has 30 letters; and Serbian has 30 letters.

The Central Asian languages, including Kazakh, Uzbek and Turkmen, were formerly written in Cyrillic. The Roman alphabet has been, or is being, introduced for most of these Central Asian languages, although Arabic is to be used for the Tajik language.

In the table of letters of the Russian Cyrillic alphabet (below), the standard capital versions of the letters are given on the first line of each entry.

The middle line of each entry lists the name of each letter and the sound represented by that letter.

The final line of each entry gives the miniscule version of the character.

А	**Б**	**В**	**Г**	**Д**	**Е**
a	b	v	g,gh	d	e
а	б	в	в	д	е
Ё	**Ж**	**З**	**И**	**Й**	**К**
e	j	z	i	i	k
ё	ж	з	и	й	к
Я	**М**	**Н**	**О**	**П**	**Р**
l	m	n	o	p	r
я	м	н	о	п	р
С	**Т**	**У**	**Ф**	**Х**	**Ц**
s, ss	t	ou	f	kh	ts
с	т	у	ф	х	ц
Ч	**Ш**	**Щ**	**Ъ**	**Ы**	**Ь**
tch	ch	chtch	hard symbol	y	mute
ч	ш	щ	ъ	ы	ь
Э	**Ю**	**Я**			
e	iou	ia			
э	Ю	я			

THE ARABIC ALPHABET

Arabic is the third most widespread alphabet after Roman and Cyrillic. It evolved from Aramaic around the 4th century.

Arabic – which is written from right to left – consists of 28 consonant letters, with vowels indicated by marks above or below. With the exception of elementary school books and editions of the Qur'an (Koran), vowel marks are usually omitted. An unusual feature is that each letter is written differently according to its position: whether it is at the beginning of a word, in the middle, or at the end, or even on its own.

Two forms developed: Kuffic and Naskhi.

Kuffic dates from the 7th century. Kuffic is the form in which the Qur'an was originally written. This upright, decorative script for inscriptions on metal or stone is now rarely used.

Nashki dates from the 10th century. From this cursive form come the numerous Arabic scripts in use today, among them those adapted for writing Persian (Farsi), Kurdish, Sindhi, Urdu, some African languages including Swahili, and the languages of Indonesia and Malaysia.

ARABIC ALPHABET

LETTER	NAME	TRANSLITERATION	LETTER	NAME	TRANSLITERATION
ا ـا ـا ا	alif	'	ض ـض ـضـ ضـ	ḍād	ḍ *(emphatic)*
ب ـب ـبـ بـ	bā'	b	ط ـط ـطـ طـ	ṭā'	ṭ *(emphatic)*
ت ـت ـتـ تـ	tā'	t	ظ ـظ ـظـ ظـ	ẓā'	ẓ
ث ـث ـثـ ثـ	thā'	th	ع ـع ـعـ عـ	'ayn	'
ج ـج ـجـ جـ	jīm	j	غ ـغ ـغـ غـ	ghayn	gh
ح ـح ـحـ حـ	ḥā'	ḥ	ف ـف ـفـ فـ	fā'	f
خ ـخ ـخـ خـ	khā'	kh	ق ـق ـقـ قـ	qāf	q
د ـد ـد د	dāl	d	ك ـك ـكـ كـ	kāf	k
ذ ـذ ـذ ذ	dhāl	dh	ل ـل ـلـ لـ	lām	l
ر ـر ـر ر	rā'	r *(rolled)*	م ـم ـمـ مـ	mīm	m
ز ـز ـز ز	zāy	z	ن ـن ـنـ نـ	nūn	n
س ـس ـسـ سـ	sīn	s	ه ـه ـهـ هـ	hā'	h
ش ـش ـشـ شـ	shīn	sh	و ـو ـو و	wāw	w
ص ـص ـصـ صـ	ṣād	ṣ *(emphatic)*	ي ـي ـيـ يـ	yā'	y

Isolated shape, Final shape, Median shape, Initial shape

INTERNATIONAL CODE OF SIGNALS

The International Code of Signals took its present form in 1887 and was adopted by all maritime nations in 1901. The International Code was revised in 1931 and again in 1969. It is communicated by visual signals and by radiotelegraphy. In its most usual visual form, the code comprises flags to denote all the letters of the alphabet. The full code allows 26 one-hoist signals, 650 with two, 15,600 with three, and 358,800 four-flag signals, making in all a possible 375,076 permutations. Each signal has a complete meaning and is published in a single volume, which has text in English, French, German, Greek, Italian, Japanese, Norwegian, Russian, and Spanish. No translation is necessary: with the code book, the officers of any merchant vessel can understand messages received. The International Code of Signals also uses a phonetic alphabet (see below), which is used not only at sea but by air controls, international telegraphy, short-wave radio users (such as the police and taxi firms), etc.

The phonetic alphabet

A Alpha (single-letter signal – I have a diver down; keep well clear at slow speed)
B Bravo (single-letter signal – I am taking in, or discharging, or carrying dangerous goods)
C Charlie (single-letter signal – Yes)
D Delta (single-letter signal – Keep clear of me; I am manoeuvring with difficulty)
E Echo (single-letter signal – I am altering my course to starboard)
F Foxtrot (single-letter signal – I am disabled; communicate with me)
G Golf (single-letter signal – I require a pilot)
H Hotel (single-letter signal – I have a pilot on board)
I India (single-letter signal – I am altering my course to port)
J Juliett (single-letter signal – I am on fire and have dangerous cargo on board; keep well clear)
K Kilo (single-letter signal – I wish to communicate with you)
L Lima (single-letter signal – You should stop your vessel immediately)
M Mike (single-letter signal – My vessel is stopped and making no way through the water)
N November (single-letter signal – No)
O Oscar (single-letter signal – Man overboard)
P Papa (single-letter signal – [in harbour] All persons should report aboard as the vessel is about to proceed to sea)
Q Quebec (single-letter signal – My vessel is healthy, and I request free pratique)
R Romeo (single-letter signal – no meaning assigned in the International Code, but used by vessels at anchor to warn of danger of collision in fog)
S Sierra (single-letter signal – My engines are going astern)
T Tango (single-letter signal – Keep clear of me: I am engaged in pair trawling)
U Uniform (single-letter signal – You are running into danger)
V Victor (single-letter signal – I require assistance)
W Whiskey (single-letter signal – I require medical assistance)
X X-ray (single-letter signal – Stop carrying out your intentions and watch for my signals)
Y Yankee (single-letter signal – I am dragging my anchor)
Z Zulu (single-letter signal – I require a tug)

THE INTERNATIONAL MORSE CODE

The International Morse Code is named after its American inventor Samuel Finley Breese Morse (1791–1872). He first exhibited his electric 'telegraph' machine in 1837, and demonstrated it with the first message in Morse at Morristown, New Jersey, USA on 6 January 1838. Morse was not the first to invent an electric telegraph. However, what distinguished Morse was the 'alphabet' code he invented around 1835. The first commercial use of the Morse system was a wire strung between the US Supreme Court in Washington DC and Mount Claire Station in Baltimore (May 1844). By 1851 lines linked all major American cities. By 1861 the network included California. The system was widely adopted elsewhere. A cross-Channel telegraph cable was laid between England and France in 1850. A trans-Atlantic telegraph cable was laid between Ireland and Newfoundland in 1858.

INTERNATIONAL MORSE CODE

A	● –	N	– ●
B	– ● ● ●	O	– – –
C	– ● – ●	P	● – – ●
D	– ● ●	Q	– – ● –
E	●	R	● – ●
F	● ● – ●	S	● ● ●
G	– – ●	T	–
H	● ● ● ●	U	● ● –
I	● ●	V	● ● ● –
J	● – – –	W	● – –
K	– ● –	X	– ● ● –
L	● – ● ●	Y	– ● – –
M	– –	Z	– – ● ●
1	● – – – –	6	– ● ● ● ●
2	● ● – – –	7	– – ● ● ●
3	● ● ● – –	8	– – – ● ●
4	● ● ● ● –	9	– – – – ●
5	● ● ● ● ●	0	– – – – –

THE SEMAPHORE CODE

In 1801, a former French artillery officer named Depillon devised a means of ship-to-shore communications using the movement of three arms pivoted on a mast. Depillon's invention, which he called sémaphore, was quickly adapted for coastal shipping. Depillon's system was modified by Sir Home Popham in 1816. Popham's two-arm system was replaced by Charles William Pasley's simpler semaphore in 1826. Semaphore machines were introduced, but, in 1880, a simpler more reliable semaphore, using two small hand-held flags, was introduced to supplement the semaphore machine. In this method of signalling, based on the circular movement of the two hands of a

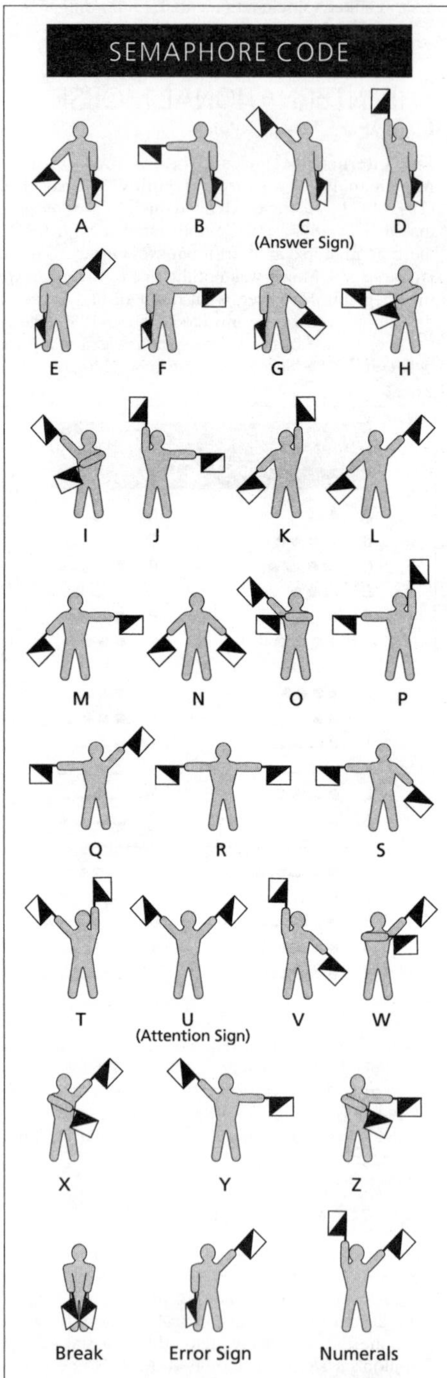

clock, the operator moves his or her arms through various positions to represent letters, numbers and special signs. The two flags are divided diagonally red and yellow (similar in design to Oscar, the International Code flag for the letter O).

BRAILLE

Louis Braille (1809–52) damaged his sight at the age of three when playing with an awl from the workbench of his father, a saddler. Blindness in both eyes followed shortly afterwards. As a child at a school for the blind, he learned to read using embossed letters. He also came across a method devised by Charles Barbier, an artillery officer, for sending messages to his soldiers at night. Composed of holes punched in cardboard, the messages could be deciphered solely by touch. Barbier's invention was primitive and, for anything more than the simplest messages, impractical. Nevertheless, the system sparked an idea in Braille. He began to experiment, and in 1824 at the age of 15, introduced his own system: a small 'cell' consisting of two vertical rows of three embossed dots arranged and numbered 1, 2, 3, down the left and 4, 5, 6, down the right.

This gave 63 possible combinations. From these, Braille worked out the letters of the alphabet (originally excluding W which is rarely used in French), punctuation marks, numerals, mathematical signs, and a number of common words such as 'and', 'for', 'of', 'with', 'the'. Braille looks complicated, but to a blind person with normal finger sensitivity, it is not so very different from deciphering the graphic symbols that form our written words. To read it, both hands are used: the right picks up the message as the left feels for the beginning of the next line. In this way, a skilled reader can understand up to 150 words a minute, about half the speed of a sighted person.

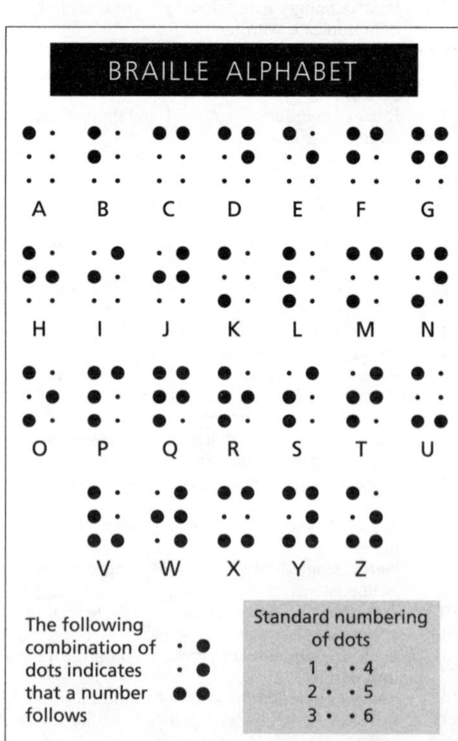

Literature

LITERARY FORMS AND TERMS

acrostic a number of lines of writing, e.g. a poem, in which certain letters, especially the first letters of each line, make a word or words.

act a major division of a dramatic work.

alexandrine a line of verse with six iambic feet.

allegory a poem, novel, drama, etc., in which the events and characters symbolize a deeper meaning beyond their apparent literal meaning.

alliteration a figure of speech in which the same consonant or vowel is repeated at the beginning of each or some of the words or stressed syllables in a line of poetry (e.g. the stuttering rifle's rapid rattle).

anagram a word made from another word by changing the order of the letters (e.g. god – dog).

anecdote a short amusing story about a person or event.

antonym a word that means the opposite of another word.

aphorism a short statement expressing a general truth in witty fashion (e.g. necessity is the mother of invention).

assonance the repetition of the same vowel sound in a line of verse.

autobiography an account of a person's life written by himself or herself.

ballad a song or poem that tells a story.

ballade a verse form consisting of three stanzas and an envoi, each ending with the same line.

biography an account of a person's life written by someone else.

blank verse unrhymed verse, often in iambic pentameters.

canto a division of a long poem.

clerihew a comic poem consisting of two couplets each with an irregular meter.

cliché an expression that has lost its force by being used too much (e.g. time flies).

colloquialism a word or phrase used in everyday informal speech rather than in a formal or literary context.

couplet two successive lines of poetry, usually rhyming and having the same meter.

dialogue speech of the characters in a novel or play.

doggerel comic verse of poor quality, usually with an irregular meter.

drama a work to be performed on stage, radio or television by actors.

dramatis personae (a list of) all the characters in a play or story.

eclogue a short pastoral poem in the form of a conversation or soliloquy.

elegy a serious meditative poem, esp. a lament for the dead.

envoi a brief dedicatory stanza at the end of certain forms of poetry, esp. ballads.

epic a long narrative poem recounting in an elevated style the deeds of a legendary hero.

epigram a short witty statement in verse or prose.

epithet a descriptive word or phrase added to or substituted for a person's name (e.g. Charles the Bold).

euphemism an inoffensive word or phrase substituted for an unpleasant or hurtful one.

fable a short tale in prose or verse that points to a moral.

farce a humorous play characterized by absurd or improbable situations.

fiction literary works invented by the imagination, such as novels and short stories.

foot a metrical division or unit of verse, consisting of two or more syllables, one of which has a strong stress, the other or others a weak stress (e.g. for mén/may cóme/ and mén/ may gó).

free verse unrhymed verse without a regular rhythm.

heroic couplet two lines of rhyming verse in iambic pentameters.

hyperbole deliberate use of exaggeration for emphasis.

iambic pentameter a line of verse consisting of five feet, each of which consists of a short syllable followed by a long one.

idiom an expression or group of words whose meaning cannot be worked out from the literal meaning of its constituent words.

idyll a work in verse or prose describing an idealized country life.

legend a popular story passed down from earlier times, the truth of which has not been established.

limerick a short humorous poem five lines in length.

litotes ironic understatement, especially the use of a negative to express the contrary (e.g. I won't be sorry when it's over = I will be extremely glad when it's over).

lyric poetry verse expressing the personal thoughts and feelings of the writer.

maxim a short phrase or statement expressing a general truth or principle or rule of conduct.

melodrama a dramatic work characterized by exciting and sensational events and usually having a happy ending.

metaphor a figure of speech in which one person or thing is described in terms of another (e.g. he is a cunning fox).

metonym a word used in metonymy (e.g. the bottle used to stand for alcoholic drink).

metonymy a figure of speech in which the name of an attribute or adjunct is substituted for that of the thing that is being referred to (e.g. crown used to refer to a monarch).

meter the rhythmic arrangement of syllables in poetry, according to the number and type of feet in a line.

monologue a long speech for a single performer in a drama.

myth a story about superhuman beings, regarded by ancient societies as being a true explanation of certain natural phenomena, how the world came into existence, etc.

novel an extended prose narrative recounting the story of fictional characters within a recognizable social context.

novella a short novel.

octave group of eight lines of verse.

ode a lyric poem in which the poet directly addresses the subject, with lines of differing lengths and a complex rhythm.

onomatopoeia formation of words whose sound imitates the sound of the noise or action described (e.g. bang, buzz, hiss).

oxymoron a figure of speech in which apparently contradictory terms are used together to achieve an epigrammatic effect (e.g. precious bane).

paradox a statement that appears to be self-contradictory, but on closer examination can be seen to contain a truth.

parody a literary work which imitates the style of a particular writer in a humorous or satirical way.

plot the story line of a novel or play.

poem a literary work in verse, characterized by concentrated or striking language used for its suggestive power as well as its literal meaning and often making use of rhyme, meter, alliteration, etc.

prose written language as in ordinary usage, as distinct from poetry.

pun the humorous use of a word to suggest different meanings, or of words of the same sound with different meanings; a play on words.

quatrain group of four lines of verse, often with alternate rhymes.

rhyme identity or similarity of sound between the endings of words or lines of verse.

rhyme royal verse form consisting of stanzas of seven lines of iambic pentameters with a complex rhyme scheme.

rondeau verse form consisting of ten or 13 lines using only two rhymes throughout and repeating the opening words twice as a refrain.

saga a long story recounting heroic deeds, especially a medieval tale of Scandinavian heroes; or a series of connected books about several generations of a family or other social group.

satire a literary work using ridicule, irony or sarcasm to expose folly or vice.

scene a subdivision of a play, smaller than an act, in which the action is continuous.

sestet a group of six lines of verse.

short story a prose narrative of shorter length than a novel.

soliloquy a speech in a drama in which a character expresses his or her thoughts aloud without addressing a particular person.

sonnet a poem consisting of 14 lines of iambic pentameters with rhymes arranged according to a fixed scheme, and divided into an octave and a sestet (a Petrarchan sonnet), or three quatrains and a couplet (an Elizabethan sonnet).

stanza a group of lines in a poem, arranged in a particular metrical pattern.

synecdoche a figure of speech in which a part is used to indicate a whole, or a whole used to indicate a part.

synonym a word identical or similar in meaning to another one.

tautology the use of words that repeat a meaning that has already been conveyed.

tercet group of three lines of verse.

tragedy a drama in which the protagonist, usually a man or woman of outstanding personal qualities, falls from grace through a combination of personal failing and circumstances that he or she cannot control; any dramatic or literary work dealing with sad or serious events and ending in disaster.

verse written language with a metrical structure; poetry.

villanelle a verse form usually consisting of five stanzas of three lines (tercets) and one stanza of four lines (quatrain), using only two rhymes throughout according to a fixed scheme.

POETS LAUREATE

The title of poet laureate has been bestowed upon a contemporary poet by the British monarch since the reign of Charles II. The laureate writes commemorative verses to celebrate major public occasions.

Holders of the post have been:

John Dryden (1631–1700; laureate 1668–88)

Thomas Shadwell (1642?–92; laureate 1688–92)

Nahum Tate (1652–1715; laureate 1692–1715)

Nicholas Rowe (1674–1718); laureate 1715–18)

Laurence Eusden (1688–1730; laureate 1718–30)

Colley Cibber (1671–1757; laureate 1730–57)

William Whitehead (1715–85; laureate 1757–85; appointed after Thomas Gray declined the offer)

Thomas Warton (1728–90; laureate 1785–90)

Henry James Pye (1745–1813; laureate 1790–1813)

Robert Southey (1774–1843; laureate 1813–43)

William Wordsworth (1770–1850; laureate 1843–50)

Alfred, Lord Tennyson (1809–92; laureate 1850–92; appointed after Samuel Rogers declined the offer)

Alfred Austin (1835–1913; laureate 1896–1913)

Robert Bridges (1844–1930; laureate 1913–30)

John Masefield (1878–1967; laureate 1930–67)

Cecil Day-Lewis (1904–72; laureate 1968–72)

Sir John Betjeman (1906–84; laureate 1972–84)

Ted Hughes (b. 1930; laureate 1984–)

LITERARY STYLES AND PERIODS

Classical literature

Western literature began with the literature of Greece and Rome, and the literatures of Europe have constantly imitated, adapted, reacted against and returned to this inescapable Classical inheritance. The 1500 years from Homer to the early Middle Ages saw the birth of almost all the major forms of prose and poetry, and the very concept of literature itself as a separate activity first made its appearance. The term 'Classical literature' may give the impression of order and a uniformity of style, but on closer inspection the literatures of Greece and Rome present a more varied scene.

Early Greek literature began with the epics of Homer. The first personal poetry appeared in the middle of the 7th century BC, while philosophical and historical writing in the 6th century BC marked the beginning of Greek literary prose. Tragedy – which is thought to have its roots in primitive rituals – began with the plays of Aeschylus, while comedy first appeared about the same time in the works of Aristophanes. The 4th century BC was an age of prose, but the chief writers of this Hellenistic age – Plato and Aristotle – worked in a genre (philosophy) sometimes now excluded from the category of literature.

From its beginning early Roman literature was heavily influenced by Greek, and it was not until the middle years of the 1st century BC that Latin really began to rival Greek for literary creativity. The greatest period of Roman literature was under the emperor Augustus, when Virgil and Horace flourished. Later genres range from imperial histories and elegant love poems to satire and low comedy.

Asian literature

The diverse cultures of the Middle East, India, China, and Japan produced bodies of writing which, while relatively unknown in the wider world, nonetheless offer a richness and scope equal to any other.

Literature written in Arabic owes much of its inspiration to the emergence of Islam. Persia possessed a literature more varied in its forms and content than that written in classical Arabic, and was to enrich the Arabic literary tradition with new genres such as the epic poem. Indian literature appeared extensively only in the 16th century when classical Sanskrit literature (c. 200 BC–AD c. 1100) became popular. Key Sanskrit texts include the epic poems *Ramayana* and *Mahabharata* (from the 3rd century BC). Popular prose in all Indian languages appeared in the 19th century and there is now a large literature in English.

China's literary heritage is particularly distinguished by its poetry, which was generally sung to musical accompaniment. The earliest and most famous work to survive is the *Shi jing* (Book of Songs), which includes love songs, folk songs, ritual hymns, and political songs. Chinese literature exerted a major influence on that of Japan, which, despite its briefer history, boasts high achievement in poetry, drama (particularly the *No* plays) and the novel. The haiku – a 17-syllable verse usually in lines of seven, five and seven syllables – is the best known of the characteristic forms of Japanese poem.

Medieval literature

Epic and Romance are loose terms used to describe the narrative literature of medieval Western Europe, most of which was in the form of long poems about mythical heroes. In Epic and Romance, national languages replaced the old universal literary language, Latin. This literature retains its vividness and immediacy and continues to spawn new creations in all the arts.

Perhaps the chief glory of medieval European literature lies in its stories, which were composed in poetry or prose for reciting, or in the form of plays for acting. They covered the known world, both its past and its present. Stories were the main source of popular and aristocratic entertainment and education. Since few people outside the Church and the nobility could read and write, the stories that have survived were written down and preserved within religious or noble communities. The most famous European collections of stories are Boccaccio's *Decameron* and Chaucer's *Canterbury Tales*. However, the chief subject of medieval literature was religion, alliterative religious poetry and mystery plays (based on the Christian story from the Creation to the Last Judgement) being among the most prominent genres. In the 15th century dramatized sermons called moralities first appeared, and throughout the medieval period fables (short tales or poems with a moral) were popular.

Renaissance literature

The Renaissance drama of the 16th century is a secular theatre of human activity rather than the religious drama of the Middle Ages. The stage no longer represents Heaven and Hell, but the world of history and the material present. In the 16th century a flowering of the professional theatre in England produced the plays of Marlowe, Kyd and Shakespeare. Their plays are largely dramatic reworkings of traditional stories. Ben Jonson, however, dealt with bourgeois characters in a contemporary English setting. The late 16th and early 17th centuries were also a 'golden age' for Spanish drama. Lope de Vega and Calderon achieved popularity through their prolific output of dramas. The English Jacobean theatre was dominated by revenge tragedies and court entertainments comprising expensive and elaborate masques.

Renaissance poetry, while less often celebrated than Renaissance painting, sculpture, architecture, or drama, flourished from the late-15th to the mid-17th century throughout Western Europe. The period saw a reawakening of interest in Classical learning that is reflected in the work of poets who showed a deep and imaginative interest in antiquity, its civilizations and especially its literature. Renaissance poetry is richly diverse in form and style and includes romantic epic, narrative verse and varieties of lyric (of which the most celebrated form was the sonnet).

Classicism in literature

Knowledge of and interest in the works of ancient Greek and Roman authors was a key aspect of the Renaissance. After that explosive fusion of old and new ideas came a period when Neoclassical writers tried to imitate in modern languages what they thought was the spirit and style of the classics. Neoclassicism was especially strong in the French theatre during the 17th century and in England from the Restoration of 1660 to the end of the 18th century.

In poetry, a taste for natural description and meditation became popular in the 18th century. Pastoral verse began with Pope and achieved perfection with Gray.

The beginnings of the novel

One of the most dramatic shifts in literary fashion occurred in the early 18th century, when a relatively new form, the novel – an extended prose narrative treating in a realistic manner the story of fictional individuals within a recognizable social context – achieved popularity with a wide audience. The novel soon came to be seen as a vehicle for serious literary expression.

Up to the 16th century the dominant literary form had been verse. There had been earlier examples of prose fiction, notably the *Satyricon* of Petronius, and *The Golden Ass* of Apuleius. The Italian novella – a type of short story of a humorous nature (found in Boccaccio's *Decameron*) – lent its name to the extended prose fictions of Defoe, Richardson and others. A number of important strands can be seen in the early novel. Some novels had a strong emphasis on realism – the representation of life as it is. The use of the first person narrative was often used to increase the realism. The epistolary novel written in the form of letters was also common. The picaresque novel – from the Spanish word *picaro,* meaning a wily rogue – enjoyed a vogue in the 17th century and is probably best represented by Don Quixote.

Romanticism

The word 'Romantic' was first used to describe a genre of literature around 1800 by the brothers Schlegel, August Wilhelm (1767–1845) and Friedrich (1772–1829). These German intellectuals idealized the era of classical antiquity, especially the culture of ancient Greece, and then contrasted it with the literature of the Christian era from the Middle Ages up to their own time. This second era they called modern – as distinct from ancient – and defined as Romantic.

Romanticism in British literature emerged, in the 1780s, in parallel with the revolutionary struggles of the French people. In a reaction against the rigidity of Classicism the Romantics believed in imagination, nature and the free expression of emotion. These traits are evident in the works of the English 'Lake poets' – Wordsworth, Coleridge and Southey.

Whereas in Europe Romanticism tended to seek a home in the novel and the drama, in Britain the movement was largely a poetic one; but it also manifested itself in certain types of prose. Among these were Gothic novels, tales of the macabre and the fantastic set in wild landscapes of rugged mountains, and ruined castles.

Later 19th-century literature

The novel became the dominant literary form in 19th-century Britain. At its best it is both popular and literary. The world that most 19th-century British novelists were writing about was one characterized by increasing urbanization and industrialization – a world dominated by the owners of capital.

In the 19th century American literature took on a specifically national character in its treatment of certain themes and ideas. Uncontaminated by history or tradition, the New World presented exciting possibilities for the creative writer. The writing of a native literature was a key factor in this process. Torn apart by the Civil War there was an even deeper need for literature to unite the nation and re-establish a national consciousness.

Realism The term Realism is commonly used to describe works of art that appear to represent the world as it is, not as it might or should be. It can be applied to literature from almost any period but is especially associated with those 19th-century novelists and dramatists who claimed to be giving detailed, accurate and objective descriptions of life, in sharp contrast to what they saw as the idealizing of their 18th-century predecessors.

Naturalism Towards the end of the 19th century prose fiction assumed a new focus with the appearance of Naturalism, a specialized form of Realism based on the philosophical doctrines of materialism and determinism. For the novelist it amounts to a belief that everything in the world – including human behaviour – has observable physical causes; and that the individual is therefore shaped by society.

Modern literature

The literary movements of the late-19th and early-20th century – Symbolism, Aestheticism and Modernism – shared a belief in the absolute value of art, reinforced by various forms of contempt for the everyday world, and especially for people who served its interests. There resulted a rift between writers and the public at large, who were seen as 'bourgeois' in a disparaging sense. Artists lived for their art alone, sometimes flaunting their difference from the rest of society by affected or deliberately shocking behaviour.

Towards the end of the 19th century and in the early years of the 20th, the great Realist consensus on the modern novel began to exhibit signs of strain, and finally broke up altogether. This development did not, of course, happen overnight, though there are signs of its origin in the later writings of Hardy, Conrad, James, Dostoevski, and even in those of the Realist novelist par excellence, Tolstoy himself.

Modern drama in Britain and America is distinctive for its concern with issues. These may, amongst other things, relate to politics, morality, racism, and/or religion. Equally, the main concerns of modern theatre may be to do with theatre itself – how it works; what it means; the nature of its conventions, and the kind of language it uses. The ideas explored in modern drama may be those specifically associated with Modernism. Foremost among these are the workings of time and memory; the problems surrounding communication, and a sense that life is meaningless. European theatre of the 20th century witnessed enormous expansion in experiment and innovation. Radical developments fundamentally challenged the basic relationship between performers and spectators established in the 19th century. Movements such as German Expressionism, Epic Theatre, the Theatre of Cruelty and the Theatre of the Absurd were designed to break away from the dominant theatrical convention of Naturalism.

Modern poetry includes both 'difficult' poetry and poetry that is more directly accessible to the reader. The difficult poetry is obscure and highly allusive in the Modernist manner exemplified by T.S. Eliot's *The Waste Land* and Ezra Pound's *Cantos*. The more accessible poetry – though not necessarily easy to understand – belongs to a tradition which does not break so abruptly with previous poetry.

FAMOUS WRITERS

Representative works, or the well-known works are given for most of the following selection of important writers.

Abu Nuwas (c. AD 762–c. 813), major Arabo-Iranian court poet.

Aeschylus (c. 525–456 BC), Greek tragic poet and dramatist: *Oresteia,* a trilogy of plays.

Alain-Fournier (Henri-Alban Fournier; 1886-1914), French novelist: *Le Grand Meaulnes* (1913).

Albee, Edward (1928–), US dramatist: *Who's Afraid of Virginia Woolf?* (1962).

Alcaeus (7th–6th centuries BC), Greek lyric poet.

Alcott, Louisa May (1832–88), US novelist: *Little Women* (1868).

Amis, Kingsley (1922–), English novelist and poet: *Lucky Jim* (1954).

Andersen, Hans Christian (1805–75), Danish novelist, dramatist and fairy tale writer: *The Ugly Duckling, The Snow Queen* and *The Little Mermaid.*

Anouilh, Jean (1910–75), French dramatist: *Antigone* (1944) and *Ring Round the Moon* (1947).

Apollinaire, Guillaume (1880–1918), French poet and prose writer: the collections *Alcools* (1913) and *Calligrammes* (1918).

Apuleius (active AD 155), Roman philosopher and author: *The Golden Ass,* a romance.

Archilochus (mid-7th century BC), Greek soldier-poet.

Arden, John (1930–), English dramatist: *Serjeant Musgrave's Dance* (1959).

Ariosto, Lodovico (1474–1533), Italian epic poet: *Orlando Furioso.*

Aristophanes (c. 445–385 BC), Greek comic dramatist: *Peace* (421 BC) and *Lysistrata* (411 BC).

Aristotle (384–322 BC), Greek philosopher: treatises on logic, metaphysics, politics, biology, etc.

Arnold, Matthew (1822–88), English poet, essayist and critic: *The Forsaken Merman, Dover Beach,* and *Essays in Criticism.*

Arrabal, Fernando (1932–), Spanish-born French dramatist and novelist: *Baal Babylon* (1959).

Asimov, Isaac (1920–92), US science fiction novelist: *I, Robot* (1950).

Attar, Farid ad-Din (d. c. 1229), Iranian mystic poet: *Conference of the Birds.*

Auden, W(ystan) H(ugh) (1907–73), US poet, dramatist and critic: *On the Frontier* (1938), *New Year Letter* (1941), *The Age of Anxiety* (1948), *Nones* (1951), and *About the House* (1965).

Austen, Jane (1775–1817), English novelist: *Sense and Sensibility* (1811), *Pride and Prejudice* (1813), *Mansfield Park* (1814), *Emma* (1815), and *Persuasion* (1818).

Ayckbourn, Alan (1939–), English playwright: *Relatively Speaking* (1967), *Absurd Person Singular* (1973), and *The Norman Conquests* (1974).

Ba Jin (1904–), Chinese novelist, essayist and short-story writer: *Jia (Family,* 1931).

Bacchylides (6th–5th centuries BC), Greek lyric poet of choral songs for victorious athletes.

Baldwin, James (1924–87), US novelist: *Go Tell it on the Mountain* (1954).

Balzac, Honoré de (1799–1850), French novelist: *La Comédie Humaine,* a sequence of 94 novels, including *Old Goriot* (1835) and *Lost Illusions* (1837–43).

Barrie, James (1860–1937), Scottish novelist, dramatist and children's story writer: *Peter Pan* (1904).

Baudelaire, Charles (1821–67), French poet: *Les Fleurs du mal* (1857; *The Flowers of Evil).*

Baum, L. Frank (1856–1919), US novelist and children's story writer: *The Wonderful Wizard of Oz* (1900).

Beaumarchais, Pierre-Augustin Caron de (1732–99), French comic dramatist: *Le Barbier de Seville* (1775) and *The Marriage of Figaro* (1784).

Beaumont, Francis (1584–1616), English dramatist who wrote romantic tragi-comedies in collaboration with Fletcher.

Beauvoir, Simone de (1908–86), French feminist writer: *The Second Sex* (1949).

Beckett, Samuel (1906–89), Irish dramatist and novelist: the plays *Waiting for Godot* (1952), *Endgame* (1957) and *Happy Days* (1961), and the novel *Malone Dies* (1951).

Behan, Brendan (1923–64), Irish novelist: *Borstal Boy* (1958) and *The Hostage* (1958).

Belloc, Hilaire (1870–1955), French-born English poet, essayist, historian and writer of verse for children: *The Bad Child's Book of Beasts* (1896) and *Cautionary Tales* (1907).

Bellow, Saul (1915–); US novelist: *Henderson the Rain King* (1959) and *Herzog* (1964).

Bembo, Pietro (1470–1547), Italian humanist, cleric and poet: *Gl'Asolami* (1505).

Bennett, Arnold (1867–1931), English novelist and critic: the trilogy *Clayhanger, Hilda Lessways,* and *These Twain* (1910–15).

Berryman, John (1914–72), US poet: *Homage to Mistress Bradstreet* (1956).

Betjeman, John (1906–84), English poet: *Collected Poems* (1968).

Bhattacharya, Bhabhani (1906–), Indian writer of social novels in English.

Blake, William (1757–1827), English poet: *Songs of Innocence* (1789) and *Songs of Experience* (1794).

Blok, Aleksandr (1880–1921), Russian Symbolist poet and dramatist: the poetry cycle *The Terrible World* (1907–16).

Boccaccio, Giovanni (1313–75), Italian poet and storyteller: *Decameron,* a collection of a hundred often earthy tales.

Boileau, Nicolas (1636–1711), French poet and critic: *L'Art Poétique,* a statement of classical aesthetics.

Boll, Heinrich (1917–85), German novelist: *Billiards at half-past Nine* (1959) and *Group Portrait with Lady* (1971).

Bond, Edward (1934–), English dramatist: *Saved* (1965).

Borges, Jorge Luis (1899–1986), Argentinian poet and short-story writer: *Fictions* (1944).

Brecht, Bertolt (1898–1956), German dramatist: *The Threepenny Opera* (1928), a musical drama, and the plays *Mother Courage* (1941), *The Good Woman of Setzuan* and *The Caucasian Chalk Circle.*

Brontë, Anne (1820–49), English novelist: *The Tenant of Wildfell Hall* (1847).

Brontë, Charlotte (1816–55), English novelist: *Jane Eyre* (1847), *Shirley* (1849) and *Villette* (1853).

Brontë, Emily (1818–48), English novelist: *Wuthering Heights* (1847).

Brooke, Rupert (1887–1915), English war poet: the sonnet *The Soldier* (1915).

Browning, Elizabeth Barrett (1806–61), English poet: *Sonnets from the Portuguese* (1847) and *Aurora Leigh* (1857).

Browning, Robert (1812–89), English poet: the poems *The Pied Piper of Hamelin* (1842) and *Home Thoughts from Abroad* (1845), the play *Pippa Passes* and *The Ring and the Book* (1868–69), a long poem in the form of a series of dramatic monologues.

Buchan, John (1875–1940), English adventure novelist: *The Thirty-Nine Steps.*

Büchner, Georg (1813–37), German dramatist: *Danton's Death* (1835) and *Woyzeck* (1837).

Buck, Pearl (1892-1973), US novelist: *The Good Earth* (1931).

Burgess, Anthony (1917–), English novelist and critic: *Clockwork Orange* (1962) and *Earthly Powers* (1980).

Burnett, Frances Hodgson (1849–1924), Anglo-US children's story writer: *Little Lord Fauntleroy* (1885) and *The Secret Garden* (1911).

Burns, Robert (1759–96), Scottish poet: notable for his use of the Scottish dialect: *'Tam o'Shanter'.*

Byatt, A(ntonia) S. (1936–), English novelist: *Possession* (1990).

Byron, Lord (George Gordon Byron; 1788–1824) English poet: *Childe Harold's Pilgrimage* (1812–18), and *Don Juan* (1819–24), a satirical epic.

Calderon de la Barca, Pedro (1600–81), Spanish dramatist: *El Alcalde de Zalamea.*

Callimachus (c. 310–240 BC), Greek poet and epigrammatist.

Camoëns, Luis de (1524–80), Portuguese poet: *The Lusiads* (1572), an epic of Portuguese exploration.

Camus, Albert (1913–60), French novelist, dramatist and essayist: the novels *The Outsider* (1942) and *The Plague* (1947), and the essay *The Myth of Sisyphus.*

Canetti, Elias (1905–), Bulgarian-born German writer: *Auto da fe* (1935) and *Crowds and Power* (1960) and his three volume memoirs.

Cao Zhan (1715–63), Chinese novelist: *The Dream of the Red Chamber.*

Cardenal, Ernesto (1925-), Nicaraguan revolutionary poet.

Carroll, Lewis (Charles Lutwidge Dodgson; 1832–98), English mathematician and children's story writer: *Alice's Adventures in Wonderland* (1865) and *Through the Looking-Glass* (1872).

Catullus (c. 84–c. 55 BC), Roman love poet.

Cervantes, Miguel de (1547–1616), Spanish poet and prose writer: *Don Quixote* (1615), a parody of chivalric literature – regarded by many as the first true novel.

Chandler, Raymond (1888–1969), US detective novelist: *The Big Step* (1939) and *The Long Goodbye* (1953).

Chateaubriand, François René de (1768–1848), French novelist and prose-writer: *Le Génie du Christianisme* (1802), *Atala* (1801) and *René* (1805).

Chatterjee, Bankim Chandra (1838–94), Indian nationalist writer: *Anandamath* (1882).

Chatterton, Thomas (1752–70), English poet.

Chatwin, Bruce (1940–89), English novelist: *Utz* (1988).

Chaucer, Geoffrey (?1343–1400), English poet: *Canterbury Tales,* an unfinished collection of 24 stories in verse and prose, and *Troilus and Criseyde.*

Chekhov, Anton (1860–1904), Russian dramatist: *Uncle Vanya* (1899), *The Three Sisters* (1901), and *The Cherry Orchard* (1904).

Christie, Agatha (1890–1976), English detective novelist, the creator of the detectives Hercule Poirot and Miss Marple.

Cicero (106–43 BC), Roman orator, statesman and writer.

Clarke, Arthur C. (1917–), English science fiction novelist: *2001: A Space Odyssey.*

Cocteau, Jean (1889–1963): French poet, novelist and dramatist: *Les Enfants terribles* (1929) and the play *La Machine Infernale* (1934).

Coleridge, Samuel Taylor (1772–1834), English poet: *Lyrical Ballads* (see Wordsworth), including *The Rime of the Ancient Mariner* and *Kubla Khan.*

Collins, William Wilkie (1824–89), novelist: the mystery novels *The Woman in White* (1860) and *The Moonstone* (1868).

Collodi, C. (Carlo Lorenzini; 1826–90), Italian novelist, journalist and writer of children's stories: *Pinocchio* (1880).

Conan Doyle, Sir Arthur (1859–1930), English detective novelist: *The Memoirs of Sherlock Holmes* (1894) and *The Hound of the Baskervilles* (1902).

Congreve, William (1670–1729), English comic dramatist: *The Way of the World* (1700) and *Love for Love* (1695), Restoration comedies.

Conrad, Joseph (Teodor Jozef Konrad Korzeniowski; 1857–1924), Polish-born English writer: *Lord Jim* (1900), *Heart of Darkness* (1902), *Nostromo* (1904), and *The Secret Agent* (1907).

Cooper, James Fenimore (1789–1851), US novelist: *The Spy* (1821), *The Last of the Mohicans* (1826), and *The Pathfinder* (1840).

Corneille, Pierre (1606–84), French classical tragic dramatist: *Le Cid* (1637), *Horace* (1640), *Cinna* (1640), *Polyeucte* (1643) and *Le Menteur* (1643).

Coward, Noel (1899–1973), English comic dramatist: *Private Lives* (1930) and *Blithe Spirit* (1941).

Dahl, Roald (1916–91), English novelist and children's story writer: *Charlie and the Chocolate Factory* (1964).

Dante Alighieri (1265–1321), Italian poet: *Divine Comedy.*

Daudet, Alphonse (1840–97), French novelist: *Lettres de mon moulin* (1869).

Davies, John (1596–1626), English poet: *Orchestra* (1596).

De Quincey, Thomas (1785–1859), English essayist: *Confessions of an English Opium Eater* (1821).

Defoe, Daniel (1660–1731), English novelist: *Robinson Crusoe* (1719) and *Moll Flanders* (1722).

Deledda, Grazia (1871–1936), Italian novelist: *The Woman and The Prince* (1900).

Demosthenes (384–322 BC), Greek orator and statesman.

Dickens, Charles (1812–70), English novelist: *Oliver Twist* (1838), *Nicholas Nickleby* (1839), *The Old Curiosity Shop* (1841), *Barnaby Rudge* (1841), *David Copperfield* (1850), *Bleak House* (1853), *Hard Times* (1854), *Little Dorrit* (1857), *A Tale of Two Cities* (1859), *Great Expectations* (1861), and *Our Mutual Friend* (1864–65).

Dickinson, Emily (1830–86), US poet.

Diderot, Denis (1713-84), French philosopher and writer: editor of the *Encyclopedie*.

Ding Ling (1904–86), Chinese novelist and short-story writer.

Disraeli, Benjamin (1804–81), English novelist and politician: the trilogy *Coningsby* (1844), *Sybil* (1845) and *Tancred* (1847).

Donne, John (1572–1631), English metaphysical poet: *Divine Sonnets*.

Dostoevski, Fyodor (1821–81), Russian novelist: *Crime and Punishment* (1866) and *The Brothers Karamazov* (1880).

Drabble, Margaret (1939-), English novelist.

Dreiser, Theodore (1871–1945), US novelist: *An American Tragedy* (1925).

Dryden, John (1631–1700), English satirical poet and tragic dramatist: *All for Love* (1677; a reworking of Shakespeare's Antony and Cleopatra) and *Absalom and Achitophel,* an allegorical poem.

Du Bartas, Guillaume (1544–1590), French religious poet: *La Semaine*.

Du Bellay, Joachim (?1522–1560), French poet.

Du Fu (Tu Fu; 712–770), Chinese poet whose works commented on social conditions: *The Army Carts*.

Dumas, Alexandre (1802–70), French novelist: *The Three Musketeers* (1844).

Duras, Marguerite (1914–), French novelist: *Le Vice-Consul* (1966) and *Emily L.* (1989).

Durrenmatt, Friedrich (1921–), Swiss dramatist: *The Physicist* (1962).

Eliot, George (Mary Ann Evans; 1819–80), novelist: *Adam Bede* (1859), *The Mill on the Floss* (1860), *Silas Marner* (1861) and *Middlemarch* (1871–2).

Eliot, T(homas) S(tearns) (1888–1965), English poet, dramatist and critic: *The Waste Land* (1922), *Four Quartets* (1943), and the plays *Murder in the Cathedral* (1935) and *The Cocktail Party* (1950).

Emerson, Ralph Waldo (1803–82), US poet and essayist.

Ennius (239–169 BC), Roman poet: the *Annals,* an historical epic.

Eschenbach, Wolfram von (?1170–1220), German poet: *Parzival*.

Euripides (c. 485–406 BC), Greek tragic dramatist: *Medea* (431).

Farquhar, George (1678–1707), English comic dramatist: *The Beaux' Stratagem* (1707).

Faulkner, William (1897–1962), US novelist: *The Sound and the Fury* (1929).

Fichte, Johann Gottfried (1762–1814), German philosopher: *Wissenschaftslehre* (1794).

Fielding, Henry (1707–54), English novelist and dramatist: *Joseph Andrews* (1742), *Shamela* (1741; a parody of Richardson's *Pamela*), *Jonathan Wild* and *Tom Jones* (1749).

Firdausi (933–1031), Iranian epic poet: *Book of Kings*.

Fitzgerald, F. Scott (1896–1940), US novelist: *The Beautiful and Damned* (1922), *The Great Gatsby* (1925), and *Tender is the Night* (1934).

Flaubert, Gustave (1821–80), French novelist: *Madame Bovary* (1857) and *Sentimental Education* (1869).

Fleming, Ian (1908–64), English suspense novelist, creator of James Bond: *Casino Royale* (1953) and *Diamonds are Forever* (1956).

Fletcher, John (1579–1625), English dramatist who wrote romantic tragi-comedies, in collaboration with Beaumont.

Fo, Dario (1926–), Italian dramatist: *Can't Pay, Won't Pay!* (1974).

Ford, John (1586–?1639), English dramatist: *'Tis Pity She's a Whore*.

Forster, E(dward) M(organ) (1879–1970), English novelist: *A Room with a View* (1908), *Howard's End* (1910) and *A Passage to India* (1924).

Forsyth, Frederick (1938–), English adventure novelist: *The Day of the Jackal* (1971) and *The Fourth Protocol* (1984).

Fowles, John (1926–), English novelist: *The Magus* (1966) and *The French Lieutenant's Woman* (1969).

France, Anatole (1844–1922), French novelist: *Les Dieux ont soif* (1912).

Frisch, Max (1911–), Swiss dramatist: *When the War is Over* (1949) and *Andorra* (1962).

Frost, Robert (1874–1963), US poet: *North of Boston* (1914) and *New Hampshire* (1923).

Fry, Christopher (1907–), English dramatist: *The Lady's Not for Burning* (1948), a verse drama.

Fuentes, Carlos (1928–), Mexican novelist: *When the Air is Clear* (1958).

Galsworthy, John (1867–1933), English novelist: *The Forsyte Saga* (1922–28).

Gaskel, Elizabeth (1810–65), English novelist: *Mary Barton* (1848), *Ruth* (1853), and *Cranford* (1853).

Gautier, Theophile (1811–72), French novelist and poet.

Geoffrey of Monmouth (d. 1155), Welsh chronicler: *History of the Kings of Britain* and *Vita Merlini*.

Ghazali (1058–1111), Iranian theologian and Islamic philosopher: *Restoration of the Sciences of Religion*.

Gide, André (1869–1951), French novelist: *The Immoralist* (1902), *Strait is the Gate* (1909), and *The Vatican Cellars* (1914).

Ginzburg, Natalia (1916–), Italian novelist: *The Advertisement* (1968).

Goethe, Johann Wolfgang von (1749–1832), German poet, dramatist, and novelist: the Romantic novella, *Die Leiden des jungen Werthers* (1774), the classical verse dramas *Iphigenia* (1787) and *Torquato Tasso* (1790) and his masterpiece *Faust* (1808).

Gogol, Nikolai (1809–52), Russian novelist and dramatist: *Dead Souls* (1842), a novel, and *The Government Inspector* (1836), a comic drama.

Golding, William (1911–93), English novelist: *Lord of the Flies* (1954), *Pincher Martin* (1956), and *The Spire* (1964).

Goldsmith, Oliver (?1730–74), Irish poet, dramatist and novelist: *The Deserted Village* (1771), a poem, *The Vicar of Wakefield* (1766), a novel, and *She Stoops to Conquer* (1773), a comedy.

Gordimer, Nadine (1923-), South African novelist: *The Conservationist* (1974).

Gorki, Maxim (1868–1936), Russian novelist: *Mother* and an autobiographical trilogy (1913–23).

Gower, John (?1330–1408), English poet: *Confessio Amantis* (*'The Lover's Confession'*).

Grahame, Kenneth (1859–1932), Scottish children's story writer: *The Wind in the Willows* (1908).

Grass, Günter (1927–), German novelist: *The Tin Drum* (1959) and *Dog Years* (1965).

Graves, Robert (1895–1985), English poet and novelist: *Goodbye to all that* (1929), his World War I autobiography, and *I, Claudius* (1934), a historical novel.

Gray, Thomas (1716–71), English poet: *Ode on a Distant Prospect of Eton College* and *Elegy Written in a Country Churchyard* (1751).

Greene, Graham (1904–91), English novelist: *Brighton Rock* (1938), *The Power and the Glory* (1940), *The Heart of the Matter* (1948), *Our Man in Havana* (1958) and *The Honorary Consul* (1973).

Grimm, Jakob (1785–1863), German philologist and, with his brother Wilhelm, collector of German folktales.

Grimm, Wilhelm (1786–1859), German philologist and collector of folktales.

Grimmelshausen, J.J.C. von (c. 1621–76), German novelist: *Simplicissimus* (1669), a picaresque novel set during the Thirty Years War.

Hafiz (1325–89), Iranian classical poet: *Diwan*.

Hammett, Dashiell (1894–1961), US detective novelist: *The Maltese Falcon* (1930).

Hardy, Thomas (1840–1928), English novelist and poet: *Far from the Madding Crowd* (1874), *The Return of the Native* (1878), *The Mayor of Casterbridge* (1886), *The Woodlanders* (1887), *Tess of the D'Urbervilles* (1891), and *Jude the Obscure* (1895) – all set in Dorset (part of Hardy's fictional 'Wessex').

Hariri, Abu Muhammad al-Kasim al- (1054–1122), Arabic writer of tales (from modern Iraq): *The Assemblies of al-Hariri*.

Hauptmann, Gerhard (1862–1946), German poet, dramatist and novelist: *Before Dawn* (1889) and *The Weavers* (1892).

Havel, Vaclav (1936–), Czech politician and dramatist: *The Garden Party* (1963) and *Largo Desolato* (1985).

Hawthorne, Nathaniel (1804–64), US novelist and short-story writer: *The Scarlet Letter* (1850), *The Blithedale Romance* (1852) and *The Marble Faun* (1860).

Heaney, Seamus (1939–), Irish poet: *North* (1975), *Field Work* (1979), and *Station Island* (1984).

Hebbel, Friedrich (1813–63), German novelist and darmatist: *Judith* (1840).

Heine, Heinrich (1797–1856), German poet and essayist: *Reisebilder* (1826) and *Das Buch der Lieder* (1827).

Hemingway, Ernest (1899–1961), US novelist: *A Farewell to Arms* (1929) and *For Whom the Bell Tolls* (1940).

Herbert, George (1593–1633), English metaphysical poet: *The Temple.*

Herder, Johann Gottfried (1744–1803), German philosopher, critic and collector of folk song.

Hergé, (Georges Rémi) (1907–83), Belgian illustrator and children's story writer, the creator of Tintin.

Herodotus (c. 490–c. 425 BC), Greek historian and prose writer, known as the 'father of history'.

Hesiod (?8th–7th centuries BC), Greek epic poet: *Theogony.*

Hesse, Herman (1877–1962), German-born Swiss novelist: *Siddhartha* (1922) and *Steppenwolf* (1927).

Hofmannsthal, Hugo von (1874–1929), Austrian poet and dramatist: *Elektra* (1903) and *Der Rosenkavalier* (1911).

Holderlin, Friedrich (1770–1843), German novelist and poet: the novel *Hyperion* (1797–99).

Homer (?8th century BC), Greek epic poet: *Iliad* and *Odyssey* (These may not in fact be the work of the same man.)

Hopkins, Gerard Manley (1844–89), English poet: the poems *Pied Beauty* and *The Windhover* (1918).

Horace (65–8 BC), poet: *Odes*, *Satires* and *Epistles.*

Hughes, Ted (1930–), English poet: *The Hawk in the Rain* (1975) and *Crow* (1970).

Hughes, Thomas (1822–96), English politician, novelist and children's story writer: *Tom Brown's Schooldays* (1857).

Hugo, Victor (1802–85), French poet, dramatist and novelist: the verse collections *Autumn Leaves* (1831) and *Les Contemplations* (1856), and the novels *The Hunchback of Nôtre Dame* (1831) and *Les Misérables* (1862).

Huxley, Aldous (1894–1963), English novelist: *Brave New World* (1932).

Huysmans, Joris-Karl (1848–1907), French novelist: *Against Nature* (1884).

Ibsen, Henrik (1828–1906), Norwegian dramatist: *Ghosts* (1881), *Hedda Gabler* (1890), and *The Master Builder* (1892).

Ihara Saikaku (1642–93), Japanese novelist: *The Life of an Amorous Man* (1682).

Ionescu, Eugène (1912–94), Romanian–born French dramatist: the absurd dramas *The Bald Prima Donna* and *The Rhinoceros.*

Irving, Washington (1783–1859), US essayist and short-story writer: *Sketch Book of Geoffrey Crayon* (1820), including the stories *Rip Van Winkle* and *The Legend of the Sleepy Hollow.*

Isherwood, Christopher (1904–87), English novelist and dramatist: *Mr Norris Changes Trains* (1935) and *Goodbye to Berlin* (1939).

Isocrates (436–338 BC), Greek orator and speechwriter.

Jalal ed-Din Rumi (d. 1273), Iranian classical poet.

James, Henry (1843–1916), US novelist: *The Wings of the Dove* (1902), *The Ambassadors* (1903), and *The Golden Bowl* (1904).

Jayadeva (12th century), Indian poet: *Gitagovinda.*

Johnson, Samuel (Dr Johnson; 1709–84), English lexicographer and writer: his famous *Dictionary* (1755), the poem *London* (1738), *A Journey to the Western Islands of Scotland* (1775) and *The Lives of the English Poets* (1779–81).

Jonson, Ben (1572–1637), English dramatist and poet: *Volpone* (1606), *The Alchemist* (1610) and *Bartholomew Fair* (1614).

Joyce, James (1882–1941), Irish writer: *Dubliners* (1914), a collection of short stories, and the novels *Portrait of the Artist as a Young Man* (1914–15), *Ulysses* (1922), and *Finnegan's Wake* (1939).

Juvenal (?AD 60–?140), Roman satirical poet.

Kafka, Franz (1883–1924), Czech novelist writing in German: *The Trial* (1925) and *The Castle* (1926).

Kaiser, Georg (1878–1945), German Expressionist dramatist: *Die Burger von Calais* (1914).

Kalidsa (?c. 4–5th centuries), Indian Sanskrit poet and dramatist: *Meghadula* and *Sakuntala and the Token of Recognition.*

Kästner, Erich (1899–1974), German novelist, poet and children's story writer: *Emil and the Detectives* (1929).

Kawabata Yasunari (1899–1972), Japanese novelist.

Keats, John (1795–1821), English poet: *Odes* (*To a Nightingale, On a Grecian Urn,* and *To Autumn*).

Kingsley, Charles (1819–75), English novelist: *Westward Ho!* (1855) and *The Water Babies* (1863), a children's story.

Kipling, Rudyard (1865–1936), English novelist, poet and short-story writer: *Plain Tales from the Hills* (1888), *Kim* (1902), and the children's stories *Jungle Book* (1894), and *Just So Stories* (1902).

Kleist, Ewald Christian von (1715–59), German lyric poet.

Kleist, Heinrich von (1777–1811), German dramatist: *Prinz Heinrich von Homburg.*

Kundera, Milan (1929–), Czech novelist: *The Joke* (1967).

Kyd, Thomas (1558–94), English dramatist: *The Spanish Tragedy* (1592), a revenge tragedy.

la Fayette, Madame de (Marie-Madeleine, Countess de la Fayette; 1634–93), French novelist: *The Princess of Cleves* (1678).

Laclos, Choderlos de (1741–1803), French novelist: *Dangerous Liaisons* (1782).

Laforgue, Jules (1860–87), French poet: *Les Complaintes* (1885).

Lagerlöf, Selma (1858–1940), Swedish novelist: *The Wonderful Adventures of Nils* (1907).

Lamartine, Alphonse de (1790–1869), French poet: *Méditations poétiques* (1820).

Langland, William (c. 1330–c. 1386), English alliterative poet: *Piers Plowman.*

Lao She (1899–1966), Chinese novelist and playwright.

Larkin, Philip (1922–85), English poet: *The North Ship* (1945), *The Less Deceived* (1955) and *The Whitsun Weddings* (1964).

Lawrence, D(avid) H(erbert) (1885–1930), English novelist, short-story writer and poet: *Sons and Lovers* (1913), *The Rainbow* (1915), *Women in Love,* and *Lady Chatterley's Lover* (1928).

Laxness, Halldor (1902–), Icelandic novelist.

Le Carré, John (1931–), English spy novelist: *The Spy Who Came in from the Cold* (1963) and *Tinker, Tailor, Soldier, Spy* (1974).

Lear, Edward (1812–88), English artist, poet and writer of children's verse: *The Book of Nonsense* (1846).

Leopardi, Giacomo (1798–1837), Italian lyric poet: *I Canti* (1816–36).

Lermontov, Mikhail (1814–41), Russian poet and novelist: the poems *The Angel* (1832) and *The Demon* (1841) and the novel *A Hero of Our Time* (1840).

Lessing, Doris (1919–), English novelist: *The Golden Notebook* (1962) and *The Good Terrorist* (1985).

Lessing, Gotthold Ephraim (1728–81), German dramatist and critic: *Miss Sara Sampson* (1755), *Minna von Barnhelm* (1767) and *Nathan the Wise* (1779).

Lewis, C(live) S(taples) (1898–1963), English scholar, science fiction novelist and children's story writer: *The Lion, the Witch and the Wardrobe* (1950) and *The Last Battle* (1956).

Li Bo (Li Po; 701–762), widely regarded as the greatest Chinese poet.

Lindsay, Sir David (c. 1486–1555), Scottish poet: *Ane Pleasant Satyre of the Thrie Estaitis.*

Livy (59 BC–AD 17), Roman historian: *History of Rome.*

Lope de Vega, Felix (1562–1635), prolific Spanish playwright and poet, who claimed to have written 1500 plays, of which only 500 survive.

Lorris, Guillaume de (d. 1237), French poet: *Roman de la Rose* (the first 4058 lines of the poem).

Lowell, Robert (1917–77), US poet: *Lord Weary's Castle* (1946) and *For the Union Dead* (1964).

Lu Xun (1881–1936), Chinese essayist and short-story writer.

Lucan (AD 39–65), Roman epic poet: *Pharsalia.*

Lucretius (c. 98–c. 55 BC), Roman poet and philosopher.

Luo Guan-zhong (active 14th century), Chinese novelist: *The Water Margin.*

MacDiarmid, Hugh (1892–1978), Scottish poet: *A Drunk Man Looks at the Thistle* (1926).

Maclean, Alistair (1922–87), Scottish adventure novelist: *HMS Ulysses* (1955), *The Guns of Navarone* (1957) and *Where Eagles Dare* (1967).

MacNeice, Louis (1907–63), Irish poet: *Blind Fireworks* (1929) and *Autumn Journal* (1939).

Maeterlinck, Maurice (1862–1949), Belgian dramatist.

Mailer, Norman (1923–), US novelist: *The Naked and the Dead* (1948).

Mallarmé, Stéphane (1842–98), French poet: *L'après-midi d'un faune* (1876; *The Afternoon of a Faun*) and *Vers et Prose.*

Malory, Sir Thomas (d. 1471), English writer of Arthurian romance in prose: *Morte D'Arthur.*

Mamet, David (1947–), US dramatist: *Glengarry Glen Ross* (1984).

Mann, Thomas (1875–1955), German novelist: *Death in Venice* (1912), a short story, and the novels *Buddenbrooks* (1900), *The Magic Mountain* (1924), and *Doctor Faustus* (1947).

Mao Dun (1896–1985), Chinese short-story writer and novelist: *Zi ye* (*Midnight*, 1933).

Mare, Walter de la (1873–1956), English poet: *Songs for Childhood* (1902) and the collection *The Listeners and Other Poems* (1912).

Marinetti, Filippo Tommaso (1876–1944), Italian dramatist, novelist and poet.

Marivaux, Pierre (1688–1763), French comic dramatist and novelist: *The Game of Love and Chance* (1730), *The Life of Marianne* (1731–41), *The Fortunate Peasant* (1735) and *The False Confidences* (1737).

Marlowe, Christopher (1564–93), English dramatist and poet: *Tamburlaine the Great* (c. 1587), *Dr Faustus* (c. 1588), *The Jew of Malta* (1589), and *Edward II* (c. 1592).

Marquez, Gabriel Garcia (1928–), Colombian novelist: *One Hundred Years of Solitude* (1967).

Marryat, Captain (Frederick Marryat; 1792–1848), English novelist and children's story writer: *The Children of the New Forest* (1847).

Martial (c. AD 40–104), Roman epigrammatist.

Marvell, Andrew (1621–78), English poet and satirist: *Miscellaneous Poems* (published posthumously).

Masudi (d. 956), Arab historian, geographer and philosopher (from modern Iraq).

Matsuo Basho (1644–94), Japanese haiku poet: *The Narrow Road to the Deep North* (1694).

Maugham, W. Somerset (1874–1965), English novelist and short–story writer: *Of Human Bondage* (1915), *The Moon and Sixpence* (1919), *Cakes and Ale* (1930) and the play *The Circle* (1921).

Maupassant, Guy de (1850–93), French novelist and short-story writer: *Boule de suif* (1881), a short story, and *Bel-Ami* (1885).

Mauriac, François (1885–1970), French novelist, poet and dramatist: *The Desert of Love* (1945).

Melville, Herman (1819–91), US short-story writer and novelist: *Moby Dick* (1851) and *Billy Budd* (1924).

Menander (342–292 BC), Greek comic dramatist.

Meun, Jean de (?1250–?1305), French poet: *Roman de la Rose* (the last 17,722 lines; see Guillaume de Lorris).

Mickiewicz, Adam (1798–1855), Polish poet: *Konrad Wallenrod* (1828).

Middleton, Thomas (1580–1627), English tragic dramatist: *Women Beware Women* (1621) and *The Changeling* (1622; with William Rowley).

Miller, Arthur (1915–), US dramatist: *Death of a Salesman* (1949) and *The Crucible* (1952).

Milne, A(lan) A(lexander) (1882–1956), English novelist, dramatist and children's story writer: *Winnie the Pooh* (1926) and *The House at Pooh Corner* (1928).

Milton, John (1608–74), English poet: the Christian epics *Paradise Lost* (1667) and *Paradise Regained (1677)*.

Mishima Yukio (1925–70), Japanese novelist: *The Temple of the Golden Pavilion* (1956) and *The Sea of Fertility* (1965–70).

Molière (Jean-Baptiste Poquelin; 1622–73), French actor and classical dramatist of comedy: *Le Bourgeois Gentilhomme* (1660), *Tartuffe* (1664), *Don Juan* (1665), *Le Misanthrope* (1666), *L'Avare* (1668; *'The Miser'*), and *Le Malade imaginaire* (1673).

Morante, Elsa (1913-), Italian novelist and poet: *House of Liars* (1948), *Arturo's Island* (1957) and *History: A Novel* (1977).

Moravia, Alberto (Alberto Pincherle; 1907–90), Italian novelist: *The Time of Indifference* (1929) and *The Conformist* (1952).

Morris, William (1834–96), English novelist, poet, and artist: *News from Nowhere* (1891).

Muir, Edward (1887–1944), Scottish poet and novelist: *First poems* (1925).

Murasaki Shikibu (973–1014), Japanese novelist: *The Tale of Genji.*

Murdoch, Iris (1919–), English novelist: *The Bell* (1958), *A World Child* (1975) and *The Sea, the Sea* (1978).

Musset, Alfred de (1810–57), French poet and dramatist: *Les Nuits* (1835–37), a collection of lyric poems, and *Lorenzaccio* (1834), a drama.

Mutanabbi (915–965), a leading classical Arab poet (form modern Iraq).

Nabokov, Vladimir (1899–1977), Russian-born US writer: *Lolita* (1958) and *Pale Fire* (1962).

Naguib Mahfouz (1911–), Egyptian novelist and short-story writer: *Midaq Alley* and *Miramar.*

Naipaul, V(idiadhar) S. (1932–), Trinidadian novelist: *In a Free State* (1971).

Narayan, R.K. (1906–), Indian novelist writing in English: *The Financial Expert* (1952), *The Vendor of Sweets* (1967), and *Malgudi Days* (1982).

Neruda, Pablo (1904–71), Chilean poet.

Nerval, Gerard de (1808–55), French poet: the sonnet sequence *Les Chimères* (1854).

Nesbit, E(dith) (1858–1924), English children's story writer: *The Railway Children* (1906).

Nizami (1140–1202), Iranian epic poet: *Five Treasures.*

Novalis (Friedrich Leopold von Hardenberg; 1772–1801), German poet and novelist: the poem: *Hymns to the Night* (1800).

Oe, Kenzaburo (1913–), Japanese novelist: *The Catch* (1958) and *A Personal Matter* (1964).

Omar Khayyám (?1048–?1122), Iranian poet: *Rubáiyát,* well known in the West through its translation by Edward Fitzgerald.

O'Neill, Eugene (1888–1953): US dramatist: *The Iceman Cometh* (1946) and *A Long Day's Journey Into Night* (1956).

Orton, Joe (1934–67), English dramatist: *Loot* (1965) and *What the Butler Saw* (1969).

Orwell, George (1903–50), English novelist and essayist: *Animal Farm* (1945), a political allegory, and *Nineteen Eighty-Four* (1949), a nightmarish fable of the future.

Osborne, John (1929–94), English dramatist: *Look Back in Anger* (1956).

Ovid (43 BC–AD 17), Roman poet: *Art of Love.*

Owen, Wilfred (1893–1918), English war poet: the poems *Anthem for Doomed Youth* and *Strange Meeting*.

Pasternak, Boris (1890–1960), Russian novelist: *Dr Zhivago* (1957).

Pater, Walter Horatio (1839–94), English critic: *Marius the Epicurean* (1885).

Pavese, Cesare (1908–50), Italian poet and novelist: *The Moon and the Bonfires* (1950).

Petrarch, Francesco (1304–74), Italian sonnet writer.

Petronius (d. AD 65), Roman satirical writer: *Satyricon*, comic novel.

Pindar (c. 520–445 BC), Greek lyric poet: *Epinician Odes*.

Pinter, Harold (1930–), English playwright: *The Birthday Party* (1958) and *The Caretaker* (1960).

Pirandello, Luigi (1867–1936), Italian dramatist: *Six Characters in Search of an Author* (1921).

Plath, Sylvia (1932–63), US poet: the verse collections *The Colossus* (1960) and *Ariel* (1965), and the novel *The Bell Jar* (1971).

Plato (c. 428–347 BC), Greek philosopher: *The Republic and The Laws*.

Plautus (c. 250–184 BC), Roman comic dramatist and writer.

Pliny the Younger (AD ?62–c.113), Roman orator and statesman, remembered for his letters.

Plutarch (c. AD 46–120), Greek biographer: *Parallel Lives*, a biography of 50 lives of famous Greeks and Romans.

Poe, Edgar Allan (1809–49), US poet, critic and short-story writer: *Tales of the Grotesque and Arabesque* (1840), including the macabre tale *The Fall of the House of Usher*.

Pope, Alexander (1688–1744), English satirical poet: *The Rape of the Lock* (1714), *The Dunciad* (1728–43), *Epistle to Arbuthnot* (1735) and *An Essay on Man* (1733–34).

Potter, Beatrix (1866–1943), English illustrator and children's story writer: *The Tale of Peter Rabbit* (1900).

Pound, Ezra (1885–1972), US poet: *Cantos* (1925–69).

Prévost, Antoine-François (L'Abbé Prévost; 1697–1763), French novelist: *Manon Lescaut* (1731).

Priestley, J(ohn) B(oynton) (1894–1984), English novelist and dramatist: the novel *The Good Companions* (1929) and the play *Laburnum Grove*.

Propertius (c. 50–after 16 BC), Roman elegiac poet.

Proust, Marcel (1871–1922), French novelist: the novel in seven sections *A la recherche du temps perdu* (*Remembrance of Things Past*; 1913–27).

Pushkin, Alexander (1799–1837), Russian poet and novelist: *Eugene Onegin* (1833), a verse novel.

Pynchon, Thomas (1937–), US novelist: *V* (1963) and *Gravity's Rainbow* (1973).

Qu Yuan (4th–3rd century BC), Chinese allegorical poet.

Rabelais, François (c. 1494–c. 1553), French humanist and physician: *Gargantua and Pantagruel*, a comic prose satire.

Racine, Jean (1639–99), French classical tragic dramatist: *Andromaque* (1667), *Britannicus* (1669), *Bérénice* (1670), *Bajazet* (1672), *Mithridate* (1673) and *Phèdre* (1677).

Radcliffe, Mrs (Ann) (1764–1823), English Gothic novelist: *The Mysteries of Udolpho* (1794).

Ransome, Arthur (1884–1967), English journalist and children's story writer: *Swallows and Amazons* (1931).

Rao, Raja (1909–), Indian novelist writing in English: *Kanthapura* and *The Serpent and the Rope*.

Richardson, Samuel (1689–1761), English novelist: *Pamela* (1740–41) and *Clarissa* (1747–48), epistolary novels.

Rifbjerg, Klaus (1931–), Danish poet, novelist and dramatist: *Findings About Myself* (1956).

Rilke, Rainer Maria (1875–1926), Austrian poet: *Duino Elegies* (1922) and *Sonnets to Orpheus* (1923).

Rimbaud, Arthur (1854–91), French poet: the collections *Illuminations* and *Une Saison en enfer*.

Robbe-Grillet, Alain (1922–), French novelist: *The Voyeur* (1955) and *Jealousy* (1957).

Robbins, Harold (1912–), US novelist: *The Carpetbaggers* (1961).

Ronsard, Pierre de (?1524–1585), French poet: *Sonnets pour Hélène*.

Rosenberg, Isaac (1890–1918), English war poet: the poem *Dead Man's Dump*.

Rousseau, Jean-Jacques (1712–78), French philosopher and novelist: *Discourses on the Origin of Inequality* (1755), *Emile* (1762), *Social Contract* (1762), and autobiographical *Confessions* (published posthumously).

Rudaki (d. 940–41), Iranian poet.

Rushdie, Salman (1947–), Indian-born British novelist: *Midnight's Children* (1981) and *Satanic Verses* (1988).

Sa'di (c. 1213–1291), Iranian classical poet: *Gulistan* and *Bustan*.

Sachs, Hans (1494–1576), German comic poet and dramatist.

Saint Pierre, Bernardin de (1737–1814), French novelist: *Paul and Virginie* (1787).

Saint-Exupéry, Antoine de (1900–44), French aviator, novelist and children's story writer: *Le Petit Prince* (1943).

Sallust (86–35 BC), Roman historian.

Sand, George (Amandine Aurore Lucie Dupin; 1804–76), French novelist: *The Haunted Pool* (1841) and *Fanchon the Cricket* (1850).

Sappho (b. mid-7th century BC), Greek lyric poetess, the pioneer of the brief subjective love poem.

Sartre, Jean-Paul (1905–80), French philosopher, dramatist and novelist: the novel *Nausea* (1937), the philosophical essay *Being and Nothingness* (1943), and the trilogy *Les Chemins de la liberté* (1945–49).

Sassoon, Siegfried (1886–1967), English war poet.

Sayers, Dorothy L. (1893–1957), English detective novelist: *The Nine Tailors* (1934) and *Gaudy Night* (1935).

Schiller, Friedrich (1759–1805), German dramatist and poet: *The Robbers* (1781), *Intrigue and Love*

(1784), *Don Carlos* (1787), the historical dramas *Wallenstein* (1798–9) and *Maria Stuart* (1800), *The Maid of Orleans* (1801) and *William Tell* (1803).

Scott, Sir Walter (1771–1832), Scottish novelist and poet: *Minstrelsy of the Scottish Border* (1802–3), a collection of ballads, *Ivanhoe* (1819), and *The Heart of Midlothian* (1818).

Sei Shonagon (966/7–1013), Japanese prose writer: *The Pillow Book.*

Seneca (AD 4–65), Roman philosopher–playwright and essayist.

Shakespeare, William (1564–1616), English poet-dramatist. His 37 plays – written between 1594 and 1611 – include comedies, history plays, tragedies and tragi-comedies: the tragedies *Titus Andronicus, Romeo and Juliet, Hamlet, King Lear, Othello, Macbeth, and Timon of Athens*; the histories *Henry VI, Richard II, Richard III, Henry IV, Henry V,* and *King John*; the comedies *The Taming of the Shrew, Love's Labour's Lost, A Midsummer Night's Dream, The Merchant of Venice, Much Ado About Nothing, Sir John Falstaff and the Merry Wives of Windsor, The Two Gentleman of Verona, The Comedy of Errors, As You Like It,* and *Twelfth Night;* the tragi-comedies *Pericles, Prince of Tyre, Troilus and Cressida, Measure for Measure, All's Well That Ends Well, Cymbelline, The Winter's Tale, The Tempest* and *Henry VIII*; the Roman plays *Julius Caesar, Antony and Cleopatra* and *Coriolanus*; the poems the *Sonnets* (1609).

Shaw, George Bernard (1856–1950), Irish dramatist and critic: *Arms and the Man* (1894), *Man and Superman* (1903), *John Bull's Other Island* (1904), *Major Barbara* (1905), *Pygmalion* (1913) and *Saint Joan* (1923).

Shawqi, Ahmad (1868–1932), Egyptian neoclassical poet.

Shelley, Mary Wollstonecraft (1797–1851), English Gothic novelist: *Frankenstein* (1818).

Shelley, Percy Bysshe (1792–1822), English poet: *Queen Mab*, a poem, *The Cenci* and *Prometheus Unbound,* (1820), verse dramas, *Adonais* (1821), an elegy on the death of Keats, and *The Mask of Anarchy* (1832).

Sheridan, Richard (1751–1816), English dramatist; *The Rivals* (1775) and *School for Scandal* (1777).

Sholokhov, Mikhail (1905–84), Russian novelist: *And Quiet Flows the Don* (1934).

Sidney, Sir Philip (1554–86), English pastoral poet: *Arcadia* (1590).

Simenon, Georges (1903–89), Belgian detective novelist, creator of the detective Maigret.

Sinclair, Upton (1878–1968), US novelist: *The Jungle* (1906).

Sitwell, Edith (1887–1965), English poet: *Façade* (1922).

Skelton, John (c. 1460–1529): English colloquial poet.

Smollett, Tobias (1721–71), Scottish novelist: *The Expedition of Humphry Clinker* (1741).

Solzhenitsyn, Alexander (1918–), Russian novelist: *One Day in the Life of Ivan Denisovitch* (1962), *First Circle* (1964), and *Cancer Ward* (1966).

Sophocles (c. 497–405 BC), Greek dramatist and tragic poet: *Oedipus Rex* (c. 430 BC), *Antigone* (441 BC).

Sorensen, Villy (1929-), Danish writer of short stories: *Guardian Stories* (1964).

Southey, Robert (1774–1843), English poet: the narrative poem *Thalaba* (1801) and his *Life of Nelson.*

Spender, Sir Stephen (1909–), English poet and critic: *The Pylons* (1933).

Spenser, Edmund (1552–99), English poet: *The Faerie Queene* (1590 and 1596), a moral allegory.

Steinbeck, John (1902–68), US novelist: *Of Mice and Men* (1937) and *Grapes of Wrath* (1939).

Stendhal (Marie Henri Beyle; 1783–1842), French novelist: *Scarlet and Black* (1830) and *The Charterhouse of Parma* (1839).

Sterne, Laurence (1713–68), Irish-born English novelist: *The Life and Opinions of Tristam Shandy* (1759–68).

Stevens, Wallace (1879–1955), US poet: *Harmonium* (1923) and *The Man with the Blue Guitar* (1937).

Stevenson, Robert Louis (1850–94), Scottish novelist: *Treasure Island* (1883) and *The Strange Case of Dr Jekyll and Mr Hyde* (1886).

Stoppard, Tom (1937–), Czech-born English dramatist: *Rosencrantz and Guildenstern are Dead* (1966) and *Arcadia* (1993).

Strassburg, Gottfried von (active 1210), German poet: *Tristan and Isolde.*

Strindberg, August (1849–1912), Swedish dramatist: *To Damascus* (1898–1901), *Miss Julie* (1888), *The Dance of Death* (1901) and *The Ghost Sonata* (1907).

Sutcliff, Rosemary (1920–92), English novelist and writer of historical novels for children: *Warrior Scarlet* (1958).

Swift, Jonathan (1667–1745), Anglo-Irish satirist: *Gulliver's Travels* (1726), a satirical fantasy.

Swinburne, Algernon Charles (1837–1909), English poet: *Songs before Sunset* (1871) and *Tristram of Lyonesse* (1882).

Synge, J(ohn) M(illington) (1871–1909), Irish dramatist: *Playboy of the Western World* (1907).

Tacitus (c. AD 56–117), Roman historian.

Tagore, Rabindranath (1861–1941), poet, novelist, playwright and essayist: *Gitanjali* (1912).

Tasso, Torquato (1544–95), major Italian epic poet: *Aminta* (1573) and *Jerusalem Delivered* (1575).

Tate, Allen (1899–1979), US poet: *Poems* (1928-1931).

Tawfiq al-Hakim (1898?–1987), Egyptian novelist and playwright: *The Return of the Spirit* (1933), *People of the Cave* (1933), and *Sheherazade* (1934).

Tennyson, Alfred, Lord (1809–92), English poet: the poems *The Lady of Shalott* (1832) and *The Lotus Eaters* (1833), the collections *In Memoriam* (1850) and *Idylls of the King* (1855).

Terrence (c. 190 or 180–159 BC), Roman dramatist and comic poet.

Theroux, Paul (1941–), US novelist and travel writer.

Thackeray, William Makepeace (1811–63), English novelist: *Vanity Fair* (1846–8) and *Pendennis* (1848–50).

Theocritus (c. 3rd century BC), Greek pastoral poet: *Idylls.*

Thomas, Dylan (1914–53), Welsh poet: *Deaths and Entrances* (1946), and the play for voices *Under Milk Wood* (1954).

Thomas, Edward (1878–1917), English poet: *Collected Poems*, including the poem *Adlestrop*.

Thoreau, Henry David (1817–62), US writer and essayist: *A Life in the Woods* (1854) and the influential essay *Civil Disobedience* (1849).

Thucydides (c. 455–399 BC), Athenian historian.

Tolkien, J(ohn) R(onald) R(euel) (1892–1973), English novelist: *The Hobbit* and *The Lord of the Rings*.

Tolstoy, Leo (1828–1910), Russian novelist: *War and Peace* (1869) and *Anna Karenina* (1877).

Trollope, Anthony (1815–82), English novelist: Barsetshire Chronicles (1857–67), a sequence of six novels, including *The Warden* and *Barchester Towers*.

Troyes, Chrétien de (active 1170–90), French poet: *Erec et Enide*, *Cligès* and *Perceval*.

Turgenev, Ivan (1818–83), Russian novelist, short-story writer and dramatist: *A Month in the Country* (1850), a play, and *Fathers and Sons* (1861), a novel.

Twain, Mark (Samuel Langhorne Clemens; 1835–1910), US novelist and short-story writer: *The Adventures of Tom Sawyer* (1876), *Life on the Mississippi* (1883), and *The Adventures of Huckleberry Finn* (1884).

Ueda Akinari (1734–1809), Japanese novelist: *Tales of Rain and Moon* (1776).

Updike, John (1932–), US novelist: *Rabbit, Run* (1960) and *Couples* (1968).

Vargas Llosa, Mario (1936–), Peruvian novelist: *The City and the Dogs* (1963).

Valery, Paul (1871–1945), French poet: *La Jeune Parque* (1917) and *Charmes* (1922).

Vanbrugh, Sir John (1664–1726), English comic dramatist: *The Relapse* (1696) and *The Provoked Wife* (1697), Restoration comedies.

Vega, Lope de (1562–1635), Spanish poet and dramatist: the epic *La Dragentea* (1598).

Verga, Giovanni (1840–1922), Italian novelist, dramatist and short story writer: the novel *I Malavoglia* (1828).

Verlaine, Paul (1844–96), French poet: *Romances sans paroles* (1874) and *Sagesse* (1881).

Vigny, Alfred de (1797–1863), French poet: the novel *Cinq-Mars* (1826) and the play *Chatterton* (1835).

Villon, François (b. 1431), French poet: *Le Lais* and *Le Testament*.

Virgil (70–19 BC), Roman poet: *Eclogues*, *Georgics* and the *Aeneid* (a national epic).

Vittorini, Elio (1908–1966), Italian novelist and dramatist: *The Red Carnation* (1948) and *Conversation in Sicily* (1941).

Voltaire (François-Marie Arouet; 1694–1778), French philosopher, dramatist and prose-writer: the epic poem *Le Henriade* (1723), the politico-philosophical *Lettres philosophiques* (1734), and *Zadig* (1747) and *Candide* (1759), philosophical tales.

Voznesensky, Andrei (1933–), Russian poet: *Goya* (1960).

Wace (b. c. 1100), Anglo-Norman poet: *Roman de Brut* and *Roman de Rou*.

Walpole, Horace (1717–97), English Gothic novelist: *The Castle of Otranto* (1765).

Wang Shifu (c. 1250–?1337), Chinese dramatist: *Romance of the Western Chamber*.

Waugh, Evelyn (1903–66), English novelist: *Decline and Fall* (1928), *A Handful of Dust* (1934), and *Brideshead Revisited* (1945).

Webster, John (c. 1578–c. 1632), English tragic dramatist: *The White Devil* (1612) and *The Duchess of Malfi* (1613–14).

Wedekind, Frank (1864–1918), German actor and dramatist: *The Awakening of Spring* (1909).

Wells, H(erbert) G(eorge) (1866–1946), novelist: the science-fiction stories *The Time Machine* (1895) and *War of the Worlds* (1898), *The Invisible Man* (1897), and the humorous novel *Kipps* (1904).

Wesker, Arnold (1932–), English dramatist: *Chicken Soup with Barley*, *Roots* and *I'm Talking About Jerusalem* (1958–60).

Wheatley, Dennis (1897–1977), English horror novelist.

White, Patrick (1912–1990), Australian novelist: *The Tree of Man* (1955), *Voss* (1957) and *Riders in the Chariot*.

Wieland, Christoph Martin (1733–1813), German poet and romantic writer.

Wiess, Peter (1916-1982), German dramatist and novelist: *Exile* (1962).

Wilde, Oscar (Fingal O'Flahertie Wills; 1854–1900), Irish dramatist, poet and novelist, famous for his witty epigrams: *The Picture of Dorian Gray* (1891), a novel, *The Importance of Being Earnest* (1895), a play, and *The Ballad of Reading Gaol* (1898), a poem.

Wilder, Thornton (1897-1975), US dramatist: *The Match Maker* (1954).

Williams, Tennessee (1911–83), US dramatist: *The Glass Menagerie* (1944), *A Streetcar Named Desire* (1947), and *Cat On A Hot Tin Roof* (1955).

Williams, William Carlos (1883–1963), US poet: the epic *Paterson* (1946–58).

Wodehouse, P(elham) G(renville) (1881–1975), English comic novelist: the Psmith and Jeeves novels.

Woolf, Virginia (1882–1941), English novelist: *Mrs Dalloway* (1925) and *To the Lighthouse* (1927).

Wordsworth, William (1770–1850), English poet: *Lyrical Ballads* (1798; a collection of poems written with Coleridge) and *The Prelude* (1798–1805).

Wycherley, William (1641–1715), English comic dramatist: *The Country Wife* (1675), a Restoration comedy.

Wyss, Johann Rudolph (1782–1830), Swiss novelist: *Swiss Family Robinson* (1827).

Yeats, W(illiam) B(utler) (1865–1939), Irish poet and dramatist: the poems *Sailing to Byzantium*, *Among School Children*, and *Lapis Lazuli*.

Yourcenar, Marguerite (1903-88), French novelist: *Memoirs of Hadrian* (1951) and *The Abyss* (1963).

Zola, Émile (1840–1902), French novelist: *The Dram Shop* (1877), *Nana* (1880), the novel cycle *The Rougon-Macquart*, including *Germinal* (1885) and *La Débâcle* (1892), and *J'accuse*, a letter criticizing the accusers of Dreyfus.

Zuckmayer, Carl (1896-1977), German dramatist: *The Happy Vineyard* (1925), *The Captain of Kopenick* (1931) and *The Devil's General* (1946).

NOBEL PRIZEWINNERS IN LITERATURE

1901 Sully-Prudhomme, French poet, noted for his later philosophical poetry.

1902 Theodor Mommsen, German historian: *History of Rome* (1854–56, 1885).

1903 Bjornstjerne Bjornsen, Norwegian novelist, poet and dramatist: helped revive Norwegian as a literary language.

1904 Frédéric Mistral, French poet: promoted Provençal as a literary language; and Juan Echegaray, Spanish dramatist: *The World and his Wife* (1881).

1905 Henryk Sienkiewicz, Polish novelist: *Quo Vadis?* (1895).

1906 Giosue Carducci, Italian Classical poet.

1907 Rudyard Kipling, British novelist and poet.

1908 Rudolf Eucken, German Idealist philosopher.

1909 Selma Lagerlöf, Swedish novelist: well-known for novels based on legends and sagas.

1910 Paul von Heyse, German poet, novelist and dramatist.

1911 Maurice Maeterlinck, Belgian Symbolist poet and dramatist: *Pelléas et Mélisande* (1892) and *The Blue Bird* (1908).

1912 Gerhart Hauptmann, German dramatist, novelist and poet: introduced naturalism to German theatre.

1913 R. Tagore, Indian playwright and poet.

1914 No award.

1915 Romain Rolland, French novelist and biographer: the 10-volume *Jean-Christophe* (1904–12).

1916 Verner von Heidenstam, Swedish lyric poet.

1917 Karl Gjellerup, Danish novelist; and Henrik Pontoppidan, Danish novelist: *Lucky Peter* (1898–1904).

1918 No award.

1919 Carl Spitteler, Swiss poet and novelist: *The Olympic Spring* (1900–05).

1920 Knut Hamsun, Norwegian novelist: *Pan* (1894) and *The Growth of the Soil* (1917).

1921 Anatole France, French novelist; his work is noted for its elegance and scepticism.

1922 Jacinto Benavente y Martinez, Spanish dramatist of social satires.

1923 William Butler Yeats, Irish poet.

1924 Wladyslaw Stanislaw Reymont, Polish novelist: *The Promised Land* (1895) and *The Peasants* (1904–05).

1925 George Bernard Shaw, Irish dramatist.

1926 Grazia Deledda, Italian Naturalist novelist.

1927 Henri Bergson, French dualist philosopher.

1928 Sigrid Undset, Norwegian novelist; her novels are about women and religion.

1929 Thomas Mann, German novelist.

1930 Sinclair Lewis, US satirical novelist: *Babbitt* (1922).

1931 Erik Axel Karlfeldt, Swedish lyric poet; wrote about love, nature and peasant life.

1932 John Galsworthy, British novelist and dramatist: *The Forsyte Saga* (1906–28).

1933 Ivan Bunin, Russian émigré novelist, best known for his short stories.

1934 Luigi Pirandello, Italian dramatist.

1935 No award.

1936 Eugene O'Neill, US dramatist.

1937 Roger Martin du Gard, French novelist: *Les Thibaults* (1922–40).

1938 Pearl Buck, US novelist; famous for her novels about China.

1939 Frans Eemil Sillanpää, Finnish novelist: *Meek Heritage* (1919) and *People of the Summer Night* (1934).

1940–43 No award.

1944 Johannes V. Jensen, Danish writer of essays and travel books.

1945 Gabriela Mistral, Chilean lyric poet.

1946 Hermann Hesse, German-born Swiss novelist.

1947 André Gide, French novelist and essayist.

1948 T.S. Eliot, US-born English poet.

1949 William Faulkner, US novelist.

1950 Bertrand Russell, English philosopher and mathematician.

1951 Pär Lagerkvist, Swedish novelist whose work was concerned with good and evil and man's search for God.

1952 François Mauriac, French poet, novelist and dramatist, well known for his Catholic novels.

1953 Sir Winston Churchill, English statesman, historian and orator.

1954 Ernest Hemingway, American novelist.

1955 Halldór Laxness, Icelandic novelist who wrote about Icelandic life in the style of the sagas.

1956 Juan Ramón Jiménez, Spanish lyric poet.

1957 Albert Camus, French novelist and dramatist.

1958 Boris Pasternak, Russian novelist and poet; declined award.

1959 Salvatore Quasimodo, Italian poet.

1960 Saint-John Perse, French lyric poet.

1961 Ivo Andri´c Yugoslav (Bosnian) novelist; best known for his Bosnian historical trilogy.

1962 John Steinbeck, US novelist.

1963 George Seferis, Greek poet and essayist; introduced Symbolism to Greek literature.

1964 Jean-Paul Sartre, French philosopher-writer; declined award.

1965 Mikhail Sholokhov, Russian novelist.

1966 Shmuel Yosef Agnon, Israeli novelist, considered the leading writer in Hebrew; and Nelly Sachs, German-born Swedish Jewish poet; her works concentrate on the persecution of Jews.

1967 Miguel Angel Asturias, Guatemalan novelist and poet, his work ranges from Guatemalan legends to international politics.

1968 Kawabata Yasunari, Japanese novelist.

1969 Samuel Beckett, Irish novelist and dramatist.

1970 Aleksandr Solzhenitsyn, Russian novelist.

1971 Pablo Neruda, Chilean poet who champions the cause of the working class.

1972 Heinrich Böll, German novelist, critical of Germany's political past.

1973 Patrick White, Australian novelist.

1974 Eyvind Johnson, Swedish novelist, well known for his four autobiographical novels; and Harry Martinson, Swedish novelist and poet: the poem *Aniara* (1956) and the novel *The Road* (1948).

1975 Eugenio Montale, Italian poet, well known for his complexity and pessimism.

1976 Saul Bellow, US novelist.

1977 Vicente Aleixandre, Spanish lyric poet, whose work sympathized with the Republican cause.

1978 Isaac Bashevis Singer, US author who wrote in Yiddish: described Jewish life in Poland.

1979 Odysseus Elytis, Greek poet: distinguished by his joyful and sensuous poetry.

1980 Czeslaw Milosz, Polish-US poet and novelist: *The Captive Mind* (1953).

1981 Elias Canetti, Bulgarian-born German writer: *Auto da fé* (1935) and *Crowds and Power* (1960).

1982 Gabriel García Márquez, Colombian novelist.

1983 William Golding, English novelist.

1984 Jaroslav Seifert, Czech poet: *Switch off the Lights* (1938).

1985 Claude Simon, French novelist; exponent of the *nouveau Roman.*

1986 Wole Soyinka, Nigerian playwright and poet whose work merges Nigerian and Western traditions.

1987 Joseph Brodsky, American (Russian émigré) poet and essayist; much of his work deals with loss and exile.

1988 Naguib Mahfouz, Egyptian novelist.

1989 Camilo José Cela, Spanish novelist, well-known for his brutally realistic novels.

1990 Octavio Paz, Mexican poet, exponent of Magic Realism, noted for his international perspective.

1991 Nadine Gordimer, South African novelist, whose work highlights relations between the races in contemporary South Africa.

1992 Derek Walcott, Saint Lucian poet, whose work reflects a historical vision of the West Indies.

1993 Toni Morrison, US novelist; for her depiction of Black America.

1994 Kenzaburo Oe, Japanese novelist.

OTHER PRIZEWINNERS

Booker Prize

The Booker McConnell Prize is an annual award for a novel by a citizen of the United Kingdom, a Commonwealth country, the Republic of Ireland or South Africa and first published in Britain. It was established in 1968 by the trading company Booker McConnell in collaboration with the Publishers' Association.

1969 P.H. Newby, *Something to Answer For*
1970 Bernice Rubens, *The Elected Member*
1971 V.S. Naipaul, *In a Free State*
1972 John Berger, *G*
1973 J.G. Farrell, *The Siege of Krishnapur*
1974 (joint prizewinners)
Nadine Gordimer, *The Conservationist*
Stanley Middleton, *Holiday*
1975 Ruth Prawer Jhabvala, *Heat and Dust*
1976 David Storey, *Saville*
1977 Paul Scott, *Staying On*
1978 Iris Murdoch, *The Sea, the Sea*
1979 Penelope Fitzgerald, *Offshore*
1980 William Golding, *Rites of Passage*
1981 Salman Rushdie, *Midnight's Children*
1982 Thomas Keneally, *Schindler's Ark*
1983 J.M. Coetzee, *Life and Times of Michael K.*
1984 Anita Brookner, *Hôtel du Lac*
1985 Keri Hulme, *The Bone People*
1986 Kingsley Amis, *The Old Devils*
1987 Penelope Lively, *Moon Tiger*
1988 Peter Carey, *Oscar and Lucinda*
1989 Kazuo Ishiguro, *The Remains of the Day*
1990 A.S. Byatt, *Possession*
1991 Ben Okri, *The Famished Road*
1992 (joint prizewinners)
Michael Ondaatje, *The English Patient*
Barry Unsworth, *Sacred Hunger*
1993 Roddy Doyle, *Paddy Clarke Ha Ha Ha*
1994 James Kelman, *How Late It Was, How Late*

Pulitzer fiction award-winners

The Pulitzer prizes are annual awards endowed by the American publisher Joseph Pulitzer in 1917. They are given for achievements in American journalism and literature. Awards are made for the best reporting of national news and of international news, the most distinguished editorial, the best local reporting and the best news photograph as well as for achievement in fiction.

1918 Ernest Poole, *His Family*
1919 Booth Tarkington, *The Magnificent Ambersons*
1920 No award
1921 Edith Wharton, *The Age of Innocence*
1922 Booth Tarkington, *Alice Adams*
1923 Willa Cather, *One of Ours*
1924 Margaret Wilson, *The Able McLaughlins*
1925 Edna Ferber, *So Big*
1926 Sinclair Lewis, *Arrowsmith*
1927 Louis Bromfield, *Early Autumn*
1928 Thornton Wilder, *The Bridge at San Luis Rey*
1929 Julia Peterkin, *Scarlet Sister Mary*
1930 Oliver LaFarge, *Laughing Boy*
1931 Margaret Ayer Barnes, *Years of Grace*
1932 Pearl S. Buck, *The Good Earth*
1933 T.S. Stribling, *The Store*

1934 Caroline Miller, *Lamb in His Bosom*
1935 Josephine Winslow Johnson, *Now in November*
1936 Harold L. Davis, *Honey in the Horn*
1937 Margaret Mitchell, *Gone With the Wind*
1938 John Phillips Marquand, *The Late George Apley*
1939 Marjorie Kinnan Rawlings, *The Yearling*
1940 John Steinbeck, *The Grapes of Wrath*
1941 No award
1942 Ellen Glasgow, *In This Our Life*
1943 Upton Sinclair, *Dragon's Teeth*
1944 Martin Flavin, *Journey in the Dark*
1945 John Hersey, *A Bell for Adano*
1946 No award
1947 Robert Penn Warren, *All the King's Men*
1948 James A. Michener, *Tales of the South Pacific*
1949 James Gould Cozzens, *Guard of Honor*
1950 A.B. Guthrie, Jr, *The Way West*
1951 Conrad Richter, *The Town*
1952 Herman Wouk, *The Caine Mutiny*
1953 Ernest Hemingway, *The Old Man and the Sea*
1954 No award
1955 William Faulkner, *A Fable*
1956 Mackinley Kantor, *Andersonville*
1957 No award
1958 James Agee, *A Death in the Family*
1959 Robert Lewis Taylor, *The Travels of Jamie McPheeters*
1960 Allen Drury, *Advise and Consent*
1961 Harper Lee, *To Kill a Mockingbird*
1962 Edwin O'Connor, *The Edge of Sadness*
1963 William Faulkner, *The Reivers*
1964 No award
1965 Shirley Ann Grau, *The Keepers of the House*
1966 Katherine Anne Porter, *The Collected Stories of Katherine Anne Porter*
1967 Bernard Malamud, *The Fixer*
1968 William Styron, *The Confessions of Nat Turner*
1969 N. Scott Momaday, *House Made of Dawn*
1970 Jean Stafford, *Collected Stories*
1971 No award
1972 Wallace Stegner, *Angle of Repose*
1973 Eudora Welty, *The Optimist's Daughter*
1974 No award
1975 Michael Shaara, *The Killer Angels*
1976 Saul Bellow, *Humboldt's Gift*
1977 No award
1978 James Alan McPherson, *Elbow Room*
1979 John Cheever, *The Stories of John Cheever*
1980 Norman Mailer, *The Executioner's Song*
1981 John Kennedy Toole, *A Confederacy of Dunces*
1982 John Updike, *Rabbit is Rich*
1983 Alice Walker, *The Color Purple*
1984 William Kennedy, *Ironweed*
1985 Alison Lurie, *Foreign Affairs*
1986 Larry McMurtry, *Lonesome Dove*
1987 Peter Taylor, *A Summons to Memphis*
1988 Toni Morrison, *Beloved*
1989 Anne Tyler, *Breathing Lessons*
1990 Oscar Hijuelos, *The Mambo Kings Play Songs of Love*
1991 John Updike, *Rabbit at Rest*
1992 Jane Simley, *A Thousand Acres*
1993 Robert Olen Butler, *A Good Scent from a Strange Mountain*
1994 E. Annie Proulx, *The Shipping News*

The Goncourt Prize

The Goncourt Prize – Prix Goncourt – is the most prestigious French literary prize. Founded in 1903, it is awarded annually by the Académie Goncourt for the best French novel of the year. The prize money, however, is nominal at 50 F. Notable winners of the Goncourt Prize include:

1919 Marcel Proust, *A l'Ombre des jeunes filles en Fleurs*
1933 André Malraux, *La Condition humaine*
1948 Maurice Druon, *Les Grandes Familles*
1954 Simone de Beauvoir, *Les Mandarins*
1968 Bernard Clavel, *Les Fruits d'hiver*
1975 Emile Ajar, *La Vie devant soi*

Prix Femina

The Prix Femina, founded in 1904 by the French magazine *Vie heureuse*, the forerunner of the magazine *Femina* and the Prix Interallié, founded in 1930. Notable winners of the Femina Prize include:

1931 Antoine de Saint-Exupéry, *Vol de nuit*
1968 Marguerite Yourcenar, *L'Oeuvre au noir*
1977 Régis Debray, *La Neige brûle*

The Whitbread Literary Awards

The Whitbread Literary Awards are given annually in six classes: novel, first novel, children's novel, poetry, biography and book of the year. Recent winners of the Whitbread Book of the Year have been:

1985 Douglas Dunn, *Elegies* (Poetry)
1986 Kazuo Ishiguro, *An Artist of the Floating World* (Novel)
1987 Christopher Nolan, *Under the Eye of the Clock* (Biography)
1988 Paul Sayer, *The Comforts of Madness* (First Novel)
1989 Richard Holmes, *Coleridge: Early Visions* (Biography)
1990 Nicholas Mosley, *Hopeful Monsters* (Novel)
1991 John Richardson, *A Life of Picasso* (Biography)
1992 Jeff Torrington, *Swing Hammer Swing* (First Novel)
1993 Joan Brady, *Theory of War* (Novel)
1994 William Trevor, *Felicia's Journey* (Novel)

OTHER PRIZES

Germany

Founded in 1927, the Goethe Prize is the most eminent German annual literary prize.

Notable winners of the Goethe Prize include:

1928 Albert Schweitzer
1930 Sigmund Freud
1946 Herman Hesse
1949 Thomas Mann
1976 Ingmar Bergman

Italy

Major literary prizes in Italy include the Bagutta Prize (founded in 1927), the Bancarella Prize (founded in 1952), the Campiello Prize (founded in 1963) and the Antonio Feltrenelli International Prize.

Russia

In 1992 the committee in charge of the Booker Prize established a Russian Booker Prize for a novel in the Russian language. The first prizewinner was Mark Kharitonov for *Lines of Fate*.

Common Abbreviations

AA Alcoholics Anonymous; anti-aircraft; Automobile Association
AAA Amateur Athletic Association
AB Alberta
ABA Amateur Boxing Association
ABC American Broadcasting Companies; Australian Broadcasting Company
ABTA Association of British Travel Agents
ac alternating current
a/c account
AC *Ante Christum* (Before Christ)
ACAS Advisory, Conciliation and Arbitration Service
ACT Australian Capital Territory
ACTT Association of Cinematograph, Television and Allied Technicians
ACTU Australian Council of Trade Unions
AD *anno Domini* (in the year of Our Lord)
ADC Aide-de-Camp
adj adjective
Adj Adjutant
ab lib *ab libitum* (at pleasure)
Adm Admiral
adv adverb; advocate
AEA Atomic Energy Authority (UK)
AEC Atomic Energy Commission (USA)
AEEU Amalgamated Engineering and Electrical Union
AERE Atomic Energy Research Establishment
AFC Air Force Cross; American Football Conference; Association Football Club
AFL/CIO American Federation of Labor/Congress of Industrial Organizations
AFM Air Force Medal
AFP *Agence France Presse*
AFRC Agricultural and Food Research Council
AFV Armoured fighting vehicle
AG Adjutant-General; Attorney-General
AGM air-to-ground missile; annual general meeting
AGR advanced gas-cooled reactor
AH *Anno Hegirae* (in the year of the Hegira)
AI artificial insemination; artificial intelligence
AIDS Acquired Immune Deficiency Syndrome
AK Alaska
AL Alabama
ALADI *Asociación Latino-americano de Integración* (Latin American Integration Association)
alt altitude
am *ante meridiem* (before noon)
AM amplitude modulation; *Anno mundi* (in the year of the world)
AMA American Medical Association
amp ampere; amplifier
amu atomic mass unit
AN *Alleanza Nazionale* (National Alliance – Italy)
ANC African National Congress (South Africa)
anon anonymous(ly)
ANSI American National Standards Institute
ANZAC Australian and New Zealand Army Corps
ANZUS Australia, New Zealand and the United States (defence pact)
AO Air Officer; Officer of the Order of Australia
AOC Air Officer Commanding
AONB Area of Outstanding Natural Beauty
AP Associated Press
APEX Association of Professional, Executive, Clerical and Computer Staff
APL a programming language (computing)
APR annual percentage rate
AR Arkansas; aspect ratio
ARF Association of South East Asian Nations Regional Forum
AS Anglo-Saxon
ASA Advertising Standards Authority; Amateur Swimming Association; American Standards Association
ASB *Alternative Service Book* (Church of England)
ASCIE American Standards Code for Information Exchange
ASEAN Association of South East Asian Nations
ASH Action on Smoking and Health
ASL American Sign Language
ASLEF Associated Society of Locomotive Engineers and Firemen
ASM air-to-surface missiles
ASPCA American Society for the Prevention of Cruelty to Animals
ATC Air Training Corps
AU astronomical unit
AUT Association of University Teachers
AV audio-visual; Authorized Version (Bible)
AVR Army Volunteer Reserve
AWACS Airborne Warning and Control System
AWOL absent without leave
AWU Australian Workers' Union
AZ Arizona

b born; bowled
BA Bachelor of Arts
BAA British Airports Authority; British Astronomical Association
BAFTA British Academy of Film and Television Arts
BAOR British Army of the Rhine
Bart Baronet
BAS Bachelor in Agricultural Science; British Antarctic Survey
BASIC Beginners' All-purpose Symbolic Instruction Code (computing)
BBC British Broadcasting Corporation
BC before Christ; British Columbia
BCG bacillus Calmette Guérin
B Ch (D) Bachelor of (Dental) Surgery
BCL Bachelor of Civil Law
B Com Bachelor of Commerce
BD Bachelor of Divinity
BDA British Dental Association
B Ed Bachelor of Education
Beds Bedfordshire
BEM British Empire Medal
B Eng Bachelor of Engineering
Berks Berkshire
BFI British Film Institute
BFPO British Forces Post Office
BIM British Institute of Management
BIOT British Indian Ocean Territory
BIS Bank for International Settlements
B Litt Bachelor of Letters; Bachelor of Literature
BM Bachelor of Medicine; British Museum
BMA British Medical Association
B Mus Bachelor of Music
Bp Bishop
B Pharm Bachelor of Pharmacy
B Phil Bachelor of Philosophy
Br British
BR British Rail
BRCS British Red Cross Society
Brig Brigadier
BSc Bachelor of Science
BSC British Steel Corporation
BSE bovine spongiform encephalopathy
BSI British Standards Institution
BST British Summer Time
Bt Baronet
BTEC Business and Technician Education Council
B Th Bachelor of Theology
Bucks Buckinghamshire
BVM Blessed Virgin Mary
BVMS Bachelor of Veterinary Medicine and Surgery

c *circa* (about)
C Celsius; Centigrade; Conservative
CA California; Chartered Accountant (Scotland)
CAA Civil Aviation Authority
CAB Citizens' Advice Bureau
CACM Central American Common Market
CAD computer-aided design
CAM computer-aided manufacture
Cambs Cambridgeshire
CAP Common Agricultural Policy
Capt Captain
CARICOM Caribbean Community and Common Market
CB citizens' band (radio); Companion of the Order of the Bath
CBC Canadian Broadcasting Corporation
CBE Commander of the British Empire
CBI Confederation of British Industry
CBS Columbia Broadcasting System (USA)
CC Chamber of Commerce; City Council; County Council
CCC County Cricket Club
C Chem Chartered Chemist

CCR camera cassette recorder
CCTV closed circuit television
CD Civil Defence; compact disc; *Corps Diplomatique*
CDA *Christen-Democratisch Appel* (Christian Democratic Appeal – Netherlands)
Cdr Commander
Cdre Commodore
CDROM compact disc read only memory
CDS Chief of the Defence Staff
CDU *Christlich-Demokratische Union Deutschlands* (Christian Democratic Union – Germany)
CE Civil Engineer
CEFTA Central European Free Trade Agreement
C Eng Chartered Engineer
CERN *Organisation Européene pour la Recherche Nucléaire* (European Organization for Nuclear Research)
CET Central European Time
cf compare
CFA *Communauté Financiere Africaine*
CFE College of Further Education
CGLI City and Guilds of London Institute
CGT capital gains tax; *Confédération Générale du Travail*
CH Companion of Honour
ChB Bachelor of Surgery
CHE College of Higher Education
Ches Cheshire
ChM Master of Surgery
CI Channel Islands
CIA Central Intelligence Agency
CID Criminal Intelligence Department
CIE *Corás Iompair Eireann* (Irish Transport Company)
cif cost, insurance, and freight
C-in-C Commander-in-Chief
CIPFA Chartered Institute of Public Finance and Accountancy
CIS Commonwealth of Independent States
C Lit Companion of Literature
CM Congregation of the Mission; Master of Surgery
CMG Companion of the Order of St Michael and St George
CND Campaign for Nuclear Disarmament
CNS central nervous system
CO Colorado; commanding officer
c/o care of
COBOL Common Business Oriented Language
Col Colonel
Con Conservative
cos cosine
CP *Centerpartiet* (Centre Party – Sweden)
CPI Consumer Price Index
Cpl Corporal
CPRE Council for the Preservation of Rural England
CPU central processing unit
CPVE Certificate of Pre-Vocational Education
CRE Council for Racial Equality
CSCE Conference on Security and Cooperation in Europe
CSE Certificate of Secondary Education
CSU *Christlich-Soziale Union Deutschlands* (Christian Social Union of Germany)
CT Connecticut
CTT capital transfer tax
CVO Commander of the Royal Victorian Order
CVP *Christelijke Volkspartij* (Flemish Christian Democrat Party – Belgium)

DA District Attorney
D-A digital-to-analog
DALR dry adiabatic lapse rate
DBE Dame of the British Empire
DBMS database management system
dc direct current
DC District of Columbia; District Council
D Ch Doctor of Surgery
DCL Doctor of Civil Law
DCM Distinguished Conduct Medal
DCMG Dame Commander of the Order of St Michael and St George
DCS Distinguished Service Cross
DCVO Dame Commander of the Royal Victorian Order
DD Doctor of Divinity
DDR *Deutsche Demokratische Republik* (East Germany)
DDS Doctor of Dental Surgery
DDT dichloro-diphenyl-trichloroethane
DE Delaware
Dem Democrat
Derbys Derbyshire
DES Department of Education and Science
DFC Distinguished Flying Cross
DFM Distinguished Flying Medal
DH Department of Health
DHA District Health Authority
DIA Defense Intelligence Agency (USA)
Dip Ed Diploma in Education
Dip HE Diploma in Higher Education
Dip Tech Diploma in Technology
DIY do-it-yourself
DJ disc jockey
D Litt Doctor of Letters; Doctor of Literature
DM Deutschmark
D Mus Doctor of Music
DnA *Det norsk Arbeiderparti* (Norwegian Labour Party)
DNA deoxyribonucleic acid
do *ditto* (the same)
DoE Department of the Environment
DOS disk operating system
DoT Department of Transport
DP data processing
D Phil Doctor of Philosophy
DPP Director of Public Prosecutions
Dr Doctor
D66 *Democraten 66* (Democracy 66 – Netherlands)
DSc Doctor of Science
DSC Distinguished Service Cross
DSM Distinguished Service Medal
DSN deep space network
DSO Distinguished Service Order (Companion of)
DSS Department of Social Security
DTI Department of Trade and Industry
DTP desktop publishing
DUP Democratic Ulster Unionist
DV *Deus volente* (God willing)

E East
EAC European Atomic Commission
EBRD European Bank of Reconstruction and Development
EBU European Boxing Union; European Broadcasting Union
EC European Community
ECA European Commission on Agriculture
ECG electrocardiogram
ECO Economic Cooperation Organization
ECOSOC United Nations Economic and Social Council
ECOWAS Economic Community of West African States
ECSC European Coal and Steel Community
ECT electroconvulsive therapy
ECU European Currency Unit
EDF European Development Fund
EDVAC electronic discrete variable automatic computer
EEA European Economic Area
EEC European Economic Community
EEG electroencephalogram
EFTA European Free Trade Area
e.g. *exempli gratia* (for example)
emf electromotive force
EMS European Monetary System
emu electromagnetic units
ENEA European Nuclear Energy Agency
EOC Equal Opportunities Commission
ER East Riding; *Elizabeth Regina* (Queen Elizabeth)
ERM Exchange Rate Mechanism
ERNIE Electronic random number indicator equipment
ESA European Space Agency
ESP extra-sensory perception
ESRC Economic and Social Research Council
ETA *Euzkadi ta Askatasuna* (Basque Homeland and Liberty – separatist organization)
et al *et alibi* (and elsewhere), *et alii* (and others)
etc. *et cetera* (and so forth)
et seq *et sequentia* (and the following)
EU European Union
EURATOM European Atomic Energy Commission

f *forte* (loud)
F Fahrenheit; Fellow of
FA Football Association
FAA Federal Aviation Administration (USA)

FAO Food and Agriculture Organization of the United Nations
FBI Federal Bureau of Investigation (USA)
FC football club
FCC Federal Communications Commission (USA)
FDIC Federal Deposit Insurance Corporation (USA)
FDF *Freie Demokratische Partei* (Free Democratic Party – Germany)
fec *fecit* (he/she made this)
ff *fecerunt* (they made this); *fortissimo* (very loud)
FF Fianna Fáil
FG Fine Gael
FIFA *Fédération Internationale de Football Association*
FIMBRA Financial Intermediaries, Managers and Brokers Regulatory Association
FL Florida
fm frequency modulation
FM Field Marshal
FO Flying Officer
fol folio
FORTRAN Formula Translation
FP *Folkpartiet liberalerna* (Liberal Party – Sweden)
FRELIMO *Frente de Libertaçao de Moçambique* (Front for the Liberation of Mozambique)
FTC Federal Trade Commission (USA)

GA Georgia (US state)
GATT General Agreement on Tariffs and Trade
GB Great Britain
GBE Knight/Dame Grand Cross of the Order of the British Empire
GC George Cross
GCB Knight/Dame Grand Cross of the Order of the Bath
GCC Cooperation Council for the Arab States of the Gulf
GCE General Certificate of Education
GCHQ Government Communications Headquarters
GCMG Knight/Dame Grand Cross of the Order of St Michael and St George
GCSE General Certificate of Secondary Education
GCVO Knight/Dame Grand Cross of the Royal Victorian Order
GDI gross domestic income
GDP gross domestic product
GDR German Democratic Republic
Gen General
Glos Gloucestershire
GM George Medal
GMB General, Municipal, Boilermakers and Allied Trades Union
GMC General Medical Council
GMPU Graphical, Paper and Media Union
GMT Greenwich Mean Time
GNP gross national product
GOC General Officer Commanding
GP general practitioner
Gp Capt Group Captain
G7 Group of Seven
GSO General Staff Officer

H *Hoyre* (Norwegian Conservative Party)
Hants Hampshire
HCF highest common factor
HE His/Her Excellency; His Eminence
HEH His Eminent Highness
HEP hydro-electric power
Herts Hertfordshire
HF high frequency
HGV heavy goods vehicle
HH His/Her Highness; His Holiness (Pope); His/Her Honour
HI Hawaii
HIH His/Her Imperial Highness
HIM His/Her Imperial Majesty
HIV human immunodeficiency virus
HJS *hic jacet sepultus* (here lies buried)
HM His/Her Majesty
HMC Headmasters' Conference
HMI His/Her Majesty's Inspector
HMS His/Her Majesty's Ship
HMSO His/Her Majesty's Stationery Office
HNC Higher National Certificate
HND Higher National Diploma
Hon Honorary; Honourable
hp horsepower
HP hire purchase
HQ headquarters
HSE Health and Safety Executive
HSH His/Her Serene Highness
HRH His/Her Royal Highness
ht height
HTR high-temperature reactor
Hunts Huntingdonshire
HWM high-water mark

IA Iowa
IAAS Incorporated Association of Architects and Surveyors
IAEA International Atomic Energy Association
IATA International Air Transport Association
IBA Independent Broadcasting Authority
Ibid *ibidem* (in the same place)
ICAO International Civil Aviation Organization
ICFTU International Confederation of Free Trade Unions
ICJ International Court of Justice
ICRC International Committee of the Red Cross
Id *idem* (the same)
ID Idaho
IDA International Development Association
ie *id est* (that is)
IEA International Energy Agency
IFAD International Fund for Agricultural Development
IFC International Finance Corporation
IHS *Iesus Hominum Salvator* (Jesus, Saviour of Mankind)
IL Illinois
ILO International Labour Organization
ILR Independent local radio
IMF International Monetary Fund
IMO International Maritime Organization
IN Indiana
Inc Incorporated
incog *incognito* (unknown)
in loc *in loco* (in its place)
INRI *Iesus Nazarenus Rex Iudaeorum* (Jesus of Nazareth, King of the Jews)
inst instant (the current month)
INTELSAT International Telecommunications Satellite Consortium
INTERPOL International Criminal Police Organization
IOC International Olympic Committee
IOM Isle of Man
IOU I owe you
IOW Isle of Wight
IQ intelligence quotient
IR infrared
IRA Irish Republican Army
IRC International Red Cross
ISBN International Standard Book Number
ISO International Organization for Standardization
ita International Teaching Alphabet
ITCZ intertropical convergence zone
ITN Independent Television News
ITU International Telecommunications Union
ITV Independent Television
IUPAC International Union of Pure and Applied Chemistry
IUPAP International Union of Pure and Applied Physics
IVF in vitro fertilization
IVR International Vehicle Registration

JP Justice of the Peace
JET Joint European Torus

K Köchel numeration (of Mozart's works)
KANU Kenya African Democratic Union
KB Knight Bachelor; Knight of the Bath
KBE Knight Commander of the Order of the British Empire
KC King's Counsel
KCB Knight Commander of the Bath
KCMG Knight Commander Grand Cross of the Order of St Michael and St George
KCVO Knight Commander of the Royal Victorian Order
Kesk *Suomen Keskusta* (Finnish Centre Party)
KF *Konservative Folkeparti* (Conservative Party – Denmark)
KG Knight of the Order of the Garter
KGB *Komitet Gosudarstvennoye Bezhopaznosti* (Soviet Committee of State Security)
KKK Ku Klux Klan
KMT *Kuomintang* (Taiwan)
ko knock-out
Kok *Kansallinen Kokoomus* (Finnish National Coalition Party)
kpc kiloparsec
KS Kansas
KStJ Knight of the Order of St John

Kt Knight
KT Knight of the Thistle
KV kilovolt
KW kilowatt
KY Kentucky
L Liberal
LA Louisiana
Lab Labour
Lancs Lancashire
Lat latitude
LAUTRO Life Assurance and Unit Trust Companies
LB London Borough
lbw leg before wicket
lc lower case
LCC London Chamber of Commerce
LCD liquid crystal display
LCJ Lord Chief Justice
LDC less developed country
LEA local education authority
Leics Leicestershire
LIFFE London International Financial Futures Exchange
Lincs Lincolnshire
Litt D Doctor of Letters
LLB Bachelor of Laws
LLD Doctor of Laws
LLM Master of Laws
LN *Lega Nord* (Northern League – Italy)
loc cit *loco citato* (in the place cited)
log logarithm
Long longitude
Lsd *Librae, solidi, denari* (pounds, shillings, pence)
LSD lysergic acid diethylamide
Ltd Limited
LU London Underground
LVO Lieutenant of the Royal Victorian Order
LW Long wave

M Member of; *Monsieur*
MA Massachusetts; Master of Arts
MAFF Ministry of Agriculture, Fisheries and Food
Maj Major
max maximum
MB Bachelor of Medicine; Manitoba
MBA Master of Business Administration
MBC Metropolitan Borough Council
MBE Member of the Order of the British Empire
MBS Mutual Broadcasting System (USA)
MC Master of Ceremonies; Military Cross
MCC Marylebone Cricket Club
MCh(D) Master of Surgery (Dentistry)
MD managing director; Maryland; Doctor of Medicine
MDS Master of Dental Surgery
ME Maine; Middle English; myalgic encephalomyelitis
MERCOSUR *Mercado del Sur* (Market of the South – trade pact)
MEd Master of Education
MEP Member of the European Parliament
Mgr Monsignor
MH Medal of Honour
MHF Master of Fox Hounds
MI Michigan; Military Intelligence
Middx Middlesex
min minimum
MIRAS Mortgage Interest Relief at Source
MIRV multiple independently targeted re-entry vehicle
Mlle *Mademoiselle*
MLR Minimum Lending Rate
MM Military Medal
Mme *Madame*
MN Merchant Navy; Minnesota
MO Medical Officer; Medical Orderly; Missouri
MoD Ministry of Defence
MOH Medal of Honour
MoT Ministry of Transport
MP Member of Parliament; Military Police
Mpc megaparsec
mph miles per hour
MR Master of the Rolls
MRA Moral Rearmament
MRC Medical Research Council
MS manuscript; Master of Surgery; Mississippi; *Moderata Samlingspartiet* (Moderate Party – Sweden); multiple sclerosis
MSc Master of Science
MSG monosodium glutamate
MSS manuscripts
MT Montana
MTh Master of Theology
Mus B Bachelor of Music
Mus D Doctor of Music
MV Merchant Vessel; Motor Vessel
MVO Member of the Royal Victorian Order
MW Medium wave

N North
n/a not applicable; not available
NAACP National Association for the Advancement of Colored People (USA)
NAAFI Navy, Army, and Air Force Institutes
NAFTA North American Trade Agreement
NALGO National and Local Government Officers' Association
NASA National Aeronautics and Space Administration
NAS/UWT National Association of Schoolmasters/Union of Women Teachers
NATO North American Treaty Organization
NB New Brunswick; *Nota bene* (note well)
NBC National Broadcasting Company (USA)
NC North Carolina
NCO non-commissioned officer
ND *Nea Demokratia* (New Democracy – Greece); North Dakota
NE Nebraska; northeast
NEB New English Bible
Nem con *Nemine contradicente* (no one contradicting)
NERC Natural Environment Research Council
NF Newfoundland
NFC National Football Conference (USA)
NFU National Farmers' Union
NGA National Graphical Association
NH New Hampshire
NHK *Nippon Hoso Kyokai* (Japan Broadcasting Corporation)
NHL National Hockey League
NHS National Health Service
NI National Insurance; Northern Ireland
NIMBY Not-in-my-backyard
NJ New Jersey
NLRB National Labor Relations Board (USA)
NM New Mexico
No *numero* (number)
non seq *non sequitur* (it does not follow)
Northants Northamptonshire
Northd Northumberland
Notts Nottinghamshire
NR North Riding
NRA National Rifle Association
NRAO National Radio Astronomy Observatory
NS New Style (calendar); Nova Scotia
NSPCC National Society for the Prevention of Cruelty to Children
NSW New South Wales
NT National Theatre; New Testament; Northern Territory; Northwest Territories
NUCPS National Union of Civil and Public Servants
NUJ National Union of Journalists
NUM National Union of Mineworkers
NUR National Union of Railwaymen
NUS National Union of Seamen; National Union of Students
NUT National Union of Teachers
NV Nevada
NVQ National Vocational Qualification
NW northwest
NY New York
NZ New Zealand

OAPEC Organization of Arab Petroleum Exporting Countries
OAS Organization of American States
OAU Organization of African Unity
Ob *obit* (died)
OC Officer commanding
OCarm Carmelite Order
OCart Carthusian Order
OE Old English; omissions excepted
OECD Organization for Economic Cooperation and Development
Ofgas Office of Gas Supply
OFM Friars Minor (Franciscans)
OFS Orange Free State
Oftel Office of Telecommunications
OH Ohio
OHMS On His/Her Majesty's Service
OIC Organization of the Islamic Conference
OK Oklahoma
OLJC Our Lord Jesus Christ
OM Order of Merit
ON Ontario
ONC Ordinary National Certificate
OND Ordinary National Diploma

ono or near offer
OP Order of Preachers (Dominicans)
op cit *opus citato* (in the work cited)
OPCS Office of Population Censuses and Surveys
OPEC Organization of Petroleum Exporting Countries
OR Oregon
OS Old Style (calendar); Ordnance Survey
OSA Augustinian Order
OSB Benedictine Order
OStJ Officer of the Order of St John of Jerusalem
OTC Officers' Training Corps
OU Open University
OXFAM Oxford Committee for Famine Relief
Oxon Oxfordshire

p page
p *piano* (softly)
pa *per annum*
PA Pennsylvania; personal assistant; Press Association
PASOK Pan-Hellenic Socialist Party
PAYE Pay as You Earn
pc parsec; *per centum* (per cent)
PC personal computer; Police Constable; politically correct; Poor Clares; Privy Counsellor
PCF *Parti Communiste Français*
PDS *Partei des Demokratischen Sozialismus* (Party of Democratic Socialism – Germany); *Partito Democratico della Sinistra* (Democratic Party of the Left – Italy)
PdvA *Partij van de Arbeid* (Dutch Labour Party)
PE physical education; Prince Edward Island
PEN International Association of Poets, Playwrights, Editors, Essayists and Novelists
PEP personal equity plan
PFP Partnership for Peace (NATO)
PGA Professional Golfers' Association
PH Purple Heart
PhD Doctor of Philosophy
PIN personal identification number
pl plural
PLA People's Liberation Army
plc public limited company
PLO Palestine Liberation Organization
pm *post meridiem* (after noon)
PM Prime Minister
PM of F Presidential Medal of Freedom
PMT pre-menstrual tension
PO Petty Officer; Pilot Officer; Post Office; postal order
POW prisoner of war
pp pages; *per procurationem* (by proxy); pianissimo
PP *Partido Popular* (Popular Party – Spain)
PPS Parliamentary Private Secretary
PQ Québec (province)
PR proportional representation; public relations
PRI *Partido Revolucionario Institucional* (Institutional Revolutionary Party – Mexico)
PRO Public Record Office; public relations officer
Ps Psalm
PS *Parti Socialiste* (Socialist Party – France); *Parti Socialiste* (Walloon Socialist Party – Belgium); *Partido Socialista* (Socialist Party – Portugal); *Post scriptum* (postscript)
PSBR public sector borrowing requirement
PSD *Partido Social Democratica* (Social Democratic Party – Portugal)
PSOE *Partido Socialista Obrero Español* (Spanish Socialist Workers' Party)
PSV public service vehicle
PT physical training
PTA parent teacher association
Pte Private
PTO please turn over
PVA polyvinyl acetate
PVC polyvinyl chloride
PVV *Partij voor Vrijheid en Vooruitgang* (Flemish Liberal Party – Belgium)
PYO pick-your-own

QB Queen's Bench
QC Queen's Counsel
QED *quod erat demonstrandum* (which was to be proved)
QGM Queen's Gallantry Medal
Qld Queensland
QPM Queen's Police Medal
QS Quarter Sessions
QSO quasi-stellar object (quasar); Queen's Service Order
quango quasi-autonomous non-governmental organization
qv *quod vide* (which see)

R *Regina* (Queen); *Rex* (King)
RA Royal Academy; Royal Academician; Royal Artillery
RAC Royal Armoured Corps; Royal Automobile Club
RADA Royal Academy of Dramatic Art
RAeS Royal Aeronautical Society
RAF Royal Air Force
RAI *Radiotelevisione Italiana*
RAM Random-access memory
RAMC Royal Army Medical Corps
RAN Royal Australian Navy
RBA Royal Society of British Artists
RBL Royal British Legion
RBS Royal Society of British Sculptors
RC Red Cross; Roman Catholic
RCM Royal College of Music
RD Royal Navy and Royal Marines Forces Reserve Decoration; Rural Dean
RE religious education; Royal Engineers
REM rapid eye movement
REME Royal Electrical and Mechanical Engineers
Rep Representative; Republican
Rev(d) Reverend
RGN Registered General Nurse
RGS Royal Geographical Society
RHA Regional Health Authority
RHS Royal Horticultural Society; Royal Humane Society
RI Rhode Island; Royal Institute of Painters in Watercolours; Royal Institution
RIBA Royal Institute of British Architects
RIP *Requiem in pace* (rest in peace)
RL Rugby League
RM Registered Midwife; Royal Marines
RMN Registered Mental Nurse
RMT National Union of Rail, Maritime and Transport Workers
RN Royal Navy
RNA ribonucleic acid
RNIB Royal National Institute for the Blind
RNID Royal National Institute for the Deaf
RNLI Royal National Lifeboat Institution
RNR Royal Naval Reserve
RNVR Royal Naval Volunteer Reserve
RNXS Royal Naval Auxiliary Service
RNZN Royal New Zealand Navy
Ro *Recto* (on the right-hand page)
ROC Royal Observer Corps
ROM read-only memory
Ro-Ro roll-on roll-off (ferry)
RoSPA Royal Society for the Prevention of Accidents
RP Royal Society of Portrait Painters
rpm revolutions per minute
RPR *Rassemblement pour la République* (Rally for the Republic – France)
RSA Republic of South Africa; Royal Scottish Academician; Royal Society of Arts
RSM Regimental Sergeant Major
RSPB Royal Society for the Protection of Birds
RSC Royal Shakespeare Company
RSPCA Royal Society for the Prevention of Cruelty to Animals
RSV Revised Standard Version (Bible)
RSVP *Répondez, s'il vous plaît* (Please reply)
RTE *Radio Telefís Eireann* (Irish Radio and Television)
RTPI Royal Town Planning Institute
RU Rugby Union
RUC Royal Ulster Constabulary
RV Revised Version (Bible)
RVM Royal Victorian Medal
RWS Royal Water Colour Society
RYS Royal Yacht Squadron

s second
S Saint; South
SA Salvation Army; South Africa; South Australia; *Sturm Abteilung* (Storm Troopers)
SAARC South Asian Association for Economic Cooperation
SADC Southern Africa Development Community
SADCC see SADC
SAE stamped addressed envelope
Salop Shropshire
SALR saturated adiabatic lapse rate
SALT Strategic Arms Limitation Talks
SAS Special Air Service Regiment
SBS Special Boat Squadron

SBN Standard Book Number
SC South Carolina
ScD Doctor of Science
SD *Socialdemokratiet* (Social Democratic Party – Denmark); South Dakota
SDAP *Sveriges Socialdemokratiska Arbetarepartiet* (Swedish Social Democratic Labour Party)
SDLP Social Democratic and Labour Party (Northern Ireland)
SDP Social Democratic Party; *Sozialdemokratische Partei Deutschlands* (Social Democratic Party), *Suomen Sosialidemokraattinen Puolue* (Finnish Social Democratic Party)
SDR special drawing rights
SE southeast
SEAQ Stock Exchange Automated Quotations
SEATO South East Asia Treaty Organization
SECAM *Séquence Electronique Couleur avec Mémoire* (Electronic Colour Sequence with Memory)
SERPS State Earnings Related Pension Scheme
SHAEF Supreme Headquarters Allied Expeditionary Force
SHAPE Supreme Headquarters Allied Powers, Europe
SI *Système Internationale*
sin sine
SJ Society of Jesus (Jesuits)
SK Saskatchewan
SOE Special Operations Executive
Som Somerset
SONAR sound navigation and ranging
SP starting price
SNP Scottish National Party
SP *Senterpartiet* (Centre Party – Norway); *Socialistische Partij* (Flemish Socialist Party – Belgium)
SPEC South Pacific Bureau for Economic Cooperation
SS Saints; *Schutzstaffel* (Protective Squad)
SSP statutory sick pay
SSR Soviet Socialist Republic
SSSI Site of Special Scientific Interest
St Saint
Staffs Staffordshire
START Strategic Arms Reduction Talks
stet let it stand
STD Professor of Sacred Theology; subscriber trunk dialling; sexually transmitted disease
STOL short take-off and landing
Sub Lt Sub Lieutenant
SVQ Scottish Vocational Qualification
SW southwest
SWAPO South West African People's Organization
SWET Society of West End Theatres

TA Territorial Army
tbsp tablespoon (measure)
tan tangent
Tas Tasmania
TB tuberculosis
TCCB Test and County Cricket Board
TD *Teach Dáil* (Member of the House – Ireland); Territorial Efficiency Decoration
TEFL teaching English as a foreign language
temp temperature; temporary staff
TESL teaching English as a second language
TGWU Transport and General Workers Union
TM Their Majesties
TN Tennessee
TNT trinitrotoluene
TRH Their Royal Highnesses
trs transpose
tsp teaspoon (measure)
TT teetotal; tuberculin tested
TUC Trades Union Congress
TV television
TVA Tennessee Valley Authority
TX Texas

UAE United Arab Emirates
uc upper case
UCAS Universities and Colleges Admissions System
UDA Ulster Defence Association
UDF *Union pour la Démocratie Française* (Union for French Democracy)
UDI unilateral declaration of independence
UDR Ulster Defence Regiment
UEFA Union of European Football Associations
UFF Ulster Freedom Fighters
UFO unidentified flying object
UHF ultrahigh frequency
UHT ultra-heat treated
UK United Kingdom
UKAEA United Kingdom Atomic Energy Authority
ult ultimately
UN United Nations
UNDP United Nations Development Programme
UNESCO United Nations Educational, Scientific and Cultural Organization
UNFPA United Nations Population Fund
UNHCR United Nations High Commissioner for Refugees
UNICEF United Nations International Children's Emergency Fund
UNIDO United Nations Industrial Development Organization
UNITA National Union for the Total Independence of Angola
UNRWA United Nations Relief and Works Agency
UP Uttar Pradesh
UPU Universal Postal Union
URC United Reformed Church
USA United States of America
USDAW Union of Shop, Distributive and Allied Workers
USSR Union of Soviet Socialist Republics
UT Utah
UU Ulster Unionist
UVF Ulster Volunteer Force

v *versus* (against)
VA Veterans' Association; Vicar Apostolic; Victoria and Albert Order; Virginia
VAT value added tax
VC Victoria Cross
VCR video cassette recorder
VD venereal disease
VDU visual display unit
Ven Venerable
Vic Victoria (Australia)
VHF very high frequency
VIP very important person
VLF very low frequency
Vo *Verso* (on the left-hand page)
VSO Voluntary Service Overseas
VT Vermont
VTOL vertical take-off and landing
VTR video tape recorder
VVD *Volkspartij voor Vryheid en Democratie* (People's Party for Freedom and Democracy – Netherlands)

W West
WA Washington (state); Western Australia
WAAC Women's Auxiliary Army Corps
WAAF Women's Auxiliary Air Force
WAC Women's Army Corps
WASP White Anglo-Saxon Protestant
WBA World Boxing Association
WBC World Boxing Council
WCC World Council of Churches
WEA Workers' Educational Association
WEU West European Union
WFTU World Federation of Trade Unions
WHO World Health Organization
WI West Indies; Wisconsin; Women's Institute
WIPO World Intellectual Property Organization
WMO World Meteorological Organization
WO Warrant Officer
Worcs Worcestershire
WR West Riding
WRAC Women's Royal Army Corps
WRAF Women's Royal Air Force
WRNS Women's Royal Naval Service
WRVS Women's Royal Voluntary Service
WVS Women's Voluntary Service
WTO World Trade Organization
WV West Virginia
WWF World Wildlife Fund
WY Wyoming

YHA Youth Hostels Association
YMCA Young Men's Christian Association
Yorks Yorkshire
YT Yukon Territory
YWCA Young Women's Christian Association

ZANU Zimbabwe African National Union

Media

Australia

Because of the great distances between Australia's five main cities, Australian newspapers are mainly regional. There are only two major national dailies: *The Australian* (153,000 copies) and *The Australian Financial Review*. Principal titles include:

Sunday Telegraph (Sunday), Sydney, 1,800,000 copies;

Sun-Herald (weekly), Sydney, 617,000 copies;

Herald-Sun News Pictorial (daily), Melbourne, 600,000 copies;

Sunday Mail (Sunday), Brisbane, 556,000 copies;

Sunday Times (Sunday), Perth, 335,000 copies;

Sunday Mail (Sunday), Adelaide, 309,000 copies;

The Sydney Morning Herald (daily), Sydney, 266,000 copies (400,000 Saturday edition);

The West Australian (daily), Perth, 263,00 copies;

Courier-Mail (daily), Brisbane, 251,000 copies (331,000 on Saturday).

The majority of periodicals are published in Melbourne or Sydney and distributed nationally. The periodicals with the largest circulations are:

The Open Road (six a year), motoring, 1,500,000 copies;

Australian Women's Weekly (which despite its name is monthly) 1,202,000 copies;

Woman's Day (weekly), 1,125,000 copies (including New Zealand);

TV Week (weekly), TV listings guide, 700,000 copies;

Reader's Digest (monthly), 473,000 copies.

The government-funded Australian Broadcasting Corporation (ABC) operates nationally providing one TV network and five radio networks. Commercial TV and radio operate under licences granted by the Australian Broadcasting Tribunal. There were 45 TV and 149 radio stations in 1992.

Austria

The six daily papers published in Vienna form the Austrian national press. Best-selling daily titles are:

Neue-Kronen Zeitung, Vienna, 577,000 copies (777,000 Sunday edition);

Kurier, Vienna, 391,000 copies (606,000 Sunday edition);

Kleine Zeitung, Graz, 268,000 copies.

The best-selling magazines are:

Auto Touring (monthly), motoring, 937,000 copies;

Niederosterreichische Nachrichten (weekly), local interest, 184,000 copies;

Neue Wochenschau (weekly), current affairs, 129,00 copies.

Belgium

The Belgian press is divided on linguistic grounds with 18 French-language and 15 Flemish-language dailies. Some papers are published in several regional editions under different names. They include:

De Standaard/Nieuwsblad/De Gentenaar, Brussels and Ghent, 370,000 copies;

Het Laatste Nieuws/De Nieuwe Gazet, Brussels, 296,000 copies;

Gazet van Antwerpen/Gazet van Mechelen, Antwerp and Malines, 185,000 copies;

Le Soir (evening), Brussels, 185,000 copies.

The principal periodicals include:

De Bond (weekly), general interest, 339,000 copies;

Vrouw & Wereld (monthly), women's interest, 297,000 copies;

Humo (weekly), general interest and TV listings, 264,000 copies.

Brazil

The size of Brazil – and the rivalry between São Paulo and Rio de Janeiro – has prevented the emergence of a national press. Readership of papers is small in comparison to the size of the population and most people rely upon radio and television for news. There are about 355 daily papers. Principal titles include:

Fôlha de São Paulo (daily), São Paulo, 375,000 copies (Sunday edition 610,000);

O Globo (daily), Rio de Janeiro, 350,000 copies (Sunday edition 520,000);

O Estado de São Paulo (daily), São Paulo, 242,000 copies (Sunday edition 460,000);

The principal periodicals include:

Veja (weekly), general interest, 800,000 copies;

Claudia (monthly), women's magazine, 460,000 copies;

Manequim (monthly), fashion magazine, 300,000 copies.

There are six main TV networks which operate 256 television stations. Most are under governmental control although privatization has begun. There are nearly 3000 radio stations, almost all under state control.

Canada

Satellite transmission has enabled the Toronto-based *Globe and Mail* and the *Financial Post* (76,000 copies; 166,000 Saturday edition) to achieve national circulations, but the Canadian press remains regional. There are 108 daily newspapers with those in Québec province published mainly in French. Principal titles include:

Toronto Star (daily), 550,000 copies (Saturday edition 758,000);

The Globe and Mail (daily), published in Toronto, 311,000 copies;

Le Journal de Montréal (daily), 294,000 copies (weekend edition 343,000);

Toronto Sun (daily), 256,000 copies (Sunday edition 453,000);

The Vancouver Sun (daily), 203,000 copies.

Some of the large circulation Canadian magazines are published in English and French editions. Principal magazines include:

Reader's Digest/Sélection (monthly), general interest, combined circulation of French and English editions, 1,682,000;

Chatelaine (monthly), women's magazine, combined circulation of English and French editions, 1,104,000;

TV Guide (weekly), 810,000 copies;

Canadian Living (monthly), general interest, 593,000 copies;

Leisure Ways (six a year), general interest, 586,000 copies;

Maclean's Canada's Weekly Newsmagazine (weekly), general interest, 580,000 copies.

The Canadian Broadcasting Corporation (CBC) is a public corporation; it operates both TV and radio channels. There are many privately owned TV and radio stations most of which have affiliations with CBC. The four main private networks are CTV, TVA, Quatre Saisons and Global. Satellite and cable TV are received by over 75% of households. US channels are popular.

China

The large circulation figures of the daily press reflect the enormous population of mainland China. In 1993 there were about 1750 newspapers. Each province publishes its own daily paper. The press is entirely state-controlled. The principal titles include:

Sichuan Ribao (Sichian Daily), Chengdu, 8,000,000 copies;

Guangming Ribao (Guangming Daily), Beijing, 6,000,000 copies;

Renmin Ribao (People's Daily), the official organ of the Communist Party of China, Beijing, 3,000,000 copies;

Qingdao Ribao (Qingdao Daily), Qingdao, 2,600,000 copies;

Gongren Ribao (Workers' Daily), trade union paper, Beijing, 2,500,000 copies;

Wenhui Bao (daily), Shanghai, 1,700,000 copies.

The periodicals with the largest circulations include:

Ban Yue Tan, (fortnightly review), 6,000,000 copies;

Nongmin Wenzhai (Peasants Digest) (weekly), 3,540,000 copies;

Jiating (Family) (weekly), 1,890,000 copies;

Shichang Zhoubao (Market Weekly), economic and financial, 1,000,000 copies.

The Ministry for Radio, TV and Films censors all broadcasts. There are 590 local television stations and the China Central Television Station operates three channels nationwide. A cable network covers some 30,000,000 households. There are two national radio stations and over 800 local stations, some broadcasting in local languages.

Denmark

Danish papers have a high circulation per head of the population. Best-selling daily titles are:

Ekstra Bladet (evening), Copenhagen, 203,000 copies (198,000 Sunday edition);

B.T., Copenhagen, 195,000 copies (226,000 Sunday edition);

Jyllands-Posten Morgenavisen, Viby, 114,000 copies (242,000 Sunday edition).

The magazines with the biggest readership are:

Samvirke (monthly), consumer affairs, 800,000 copies;

Helse-Familiens Laegemagasin (monthly), family health, 340,000 copies;

Se og Hor (weekly), news and TV listings, 306,000 copies.

Finland

The Finnish press is characterized by the independent ownership of its principal dailies. These include:

Helsingin Sanomat, Helsinki, 481,000 copies (572,000 Sunday edition);

Ilta-Sanomat, Helsinki, 209,000 copies (263,000 Sunday edition);

Aamulehti, Tampere, 135,000 copies (142,000 Sunday edition).

Given the small population of Finland, several magazines enjoy high circulations. They include:

Valitut Palat (Reader's Digest) (monthly), 342,000 copies;

Me (10 a year), family magazine, 340,000 copies;

Aku Ankka (weekly), children's magazine, 120,000 copies.

France

Although 23 daily newspapers are published in Paris, France has a regional rather than a national press. The 70 provincial daily papers dominate sales outside Paris. There are only two Sunday papers in Paris – instead, weekly news magazines are characteristic of the French press. The main newspaper titles include:

Ouest-France (daily), Rennes, 789,000 copies;

France-Dimanche (Sunday), Paris, 640,000 copies;

Le Figaro (daily), Paris, 434,000 copies;

Le Parisien (daily), Paris, 400,000 copies;

Sud-Ouest (daily), Bordeaux, 386,000 copies;

La Voix du Nord (daily), Lille, 370,000 copies;

L'Humanité-Dimanche (Sunday edition of the organ of the French Communist Party), Paris, 360,000 copies;

L'Equipe (daily sports), Paris, 320,000 copies;

Le Monde (daily), Paris, 307,000 copies;

France-Soir (daily evening), Paris, 302,000 copies.

The periodicals with the largest circulations include:

Télé 7 Jours (weekly), TV listings, 3,335,000 copies;

Télé-Poche (weekly), TV listings, 1,800,000 copies;

Modes et travaux (monthly), fashion magazine, 1,500,000 copies;

Sélection du Reader's Digest (monthly), general interest, 1,072,000 copies;

Nous Deux (monthly), women's illustrated stories, 823,000 copies;

Paris-Match (weekly), news magazine, 690,000 copies;

L'Express (weekly), news magazine, 669,000 copies;

Marie-Claire (monthly), women's magazine, 600,000 copies.

Radio France broadcasts seven main channels through 47 local radio stations. There are over 1700 local commercial radio stations and three national commercial stations. The two state-run TV channels (France2 and France3) compete with the three independent TV channels. Over 1,000,000 households subscribe to cable television.

Germany

Nearly 400 daily newspapers are published in Germany, most of them confined to small regional circulations. For historic reasons there is no national press although *Frankfurter Allgemeine Zeitung, Berliner Zeitung* and *Süddeutsche Zeitung* enjoy national circulations and prestige. 'Tabloid' papers such as *Bild-Zeitung* and *Super!* have increased in popularity. There are six principal newspaper groups – three based in Hamburg. Principal papers include:

Bild-Zeitung (daily), Hamburg and printed in 15 provincial centres, 4,900,000 copies;

Bild am Sonntag (Sunday), Hamburg, 2,400,000 copies;

Westdeutsche Allgemeine Zeitung (daily), Essen, 1,210,000 copies;

Freie Presse (daily), Chemnitz, 560,000 copies;

Mitteldeutsche Zeitung (daily), Halle, 510,000 copies;

Sächsische Zeitung (daily), Dresden, 450,000 copies;

Die Zeit (weekly), Hamburg, 491,000 copies;

Welt am Sonntag (Sunday), Hamburg, 430,000 copies;

Frankfurter Allgemeine Zeitung (daily), Frankfurt, 392,000 copies;

Süddeutsche Zeitung (daily), Munich, 390,000 copies;

Rheinische Post (daily), Düsseldorf, 390,000 copies.

Periodicals – by contrast – are mainly national rather than regional. Those with the largest circulations include:

Hörzu (weekly), TV listings guide, 3,857,000 copies;

TV Hören + Sehen (weekly), TV listings guide, 2,863,000 copies;

burda moden (monthly), fashion and cookery magazine, 2,300,000 copies;

Funk Uhr (weekly), TV listings guide, 2,013,000 copies;

Neue Post (weekly), general interest, 1,729,000 copies;

Das Beste aus Readers Digest (monthly), general interest, 1,600,000 copies;

Stern (weekly), current affairs and general interest, 1,479,000 copies;

Der Spiegel (weekly), current affairs, 1,400,000 copies;

Brigitte (fortnightly), women's magazine, 1,300,000 copies;

Bravo (weekly), young people's magazine, 1,218,000 copies.

ARD is the coordinating body for radio and TV networks in Germany. Five radio channels operate throughout the country. There are 15 regional broadcasting organizations. There are three television channels – one produced by ARD, one controlled by a public corporation and a third educational channel.

Greece

Greece has over 130 daily newspapers, most of which have only small regional circulations. A particular feature of the Greek press is afternoon papers which enjoy a higher circulation than morning titles. Best-selling papers include:

Eleftheros Typos (afternoon), Athens, 165,000 copies;

Ta Nea (afternoon), Athens, 135,000 copies;

Eleftherotypia (afternoon), Athens, 110,000 copies.

Greek periodicals have a much lower circulation than their West European counterparts. They include:

Tilerama (weekly), TV listings, 190,000 copies;

To Vima (weekly), current affairs, 165,000 copies;

Radiotilerash (weekly), TV listings, 135,000 copies.

India

The size of the country and its many social, religious and linguistic barriers have prevented the development of a national press. However, a small number of English-language newspapers – the *Times of India*, the *Indian Express*, the *Statesman* and *The Hindu* – enjoy nationwide circulations. These papers have largely metropolitan readerships and cover international issues as well as Indian events. Newspapers published in Indian languages have mainly rural readerships and tend to be more parochial. Most papers publish separate editions in a number of centres within the relevant linguistic region. The papers with the largest circulations include:

Malayala Manorama (Malayalam; daily), Kottayam and four other centres, 692,000 copies;

The Times of India (English; daily), Delhi, Bombay, Bangalore etc., 632,000 copies;

Punjab Kesari (Punjabi; daily), Jalandhar, Delhi and Ambala, 595,000 copies (892,000 Sunday edition);

Dainik Jagran (Hindi; daily), Kanpur and eight other centres, 580,000 copies;

Indian Express (English; daily), Delhi, Vijayawada, Madras, Bombay etc., 551,000 copies;

Gujarat Samachar (Gujarati; daily), Ahmedabad and three other centres, 550,000 copies;

Aj (Hindi; daily), Varanasi and 10 other centres, 507,000 copies.

The magazines with the largest circulations include:

India Today (English, Tamil, Hindi; fortnightly), general interest, 743,000 combined circulation;

Employment News (English, Hindi, Urdu; weekly), official publication, 425,000 combined circulation;

Grih Shobha (Hindi, Marathi, Gujarati; monthly), women's magazine, 400,000 combined circulation;

Competition Success Review (English; monthly), 240,000 copies.

All India Radio (AIR) runs 148 radio stations, operating in 72 languages. Doordarshan India (Television India) runs 18 TV stations. Both organizations are government-financed and controlled. Satellite TV has recently become both popular and influential.

Ireland

Seven daily papers are published in the Republic of Ireland (and British newspapers are also available in the country). The best-selling titles are:

Irish Independent, Dublin, 150,000 copies;

Evening Press, Dublin, 102,000 copies;

Evening Herald, Dublin, 95,000 copies;

Irish Times, Dublin, 95,000 copies.

The wide distribution of British magazines in Ireland means that the Republic has relatively few magazines. Those with the highest sales are:

RTE Guide (weekly), TV listings, 170,000 copies;

Irish Farmers Journal (weekly), 71,000 copies;

Woman's Way (weekly), 67,000 copies.

Italy

The Italian press is characterized by the small number of daily papers published – only 80 – and by their low circulations. The press is concentrated in Milan and Rome. There is no national press but *Corriere della Sera*, *La Repubblica* and *La Stampa* enjoy national circulations and prestige. Principal titles include:

La Gazetta dello Sport (daily sports), Milan, 830,000 copies;

La Repubblica (daily), Rome, 726,000 copies;

Corriere della Sera (daily evening), Milan, 660,000 copies;

Corriere dello Sport (daily sports), Rome with a dozen regional editions, 622,000 copies;

La Stampa (daily), Turin, 403,000 copies;

Il Messaggero (daily), Rome, 390,000 copies.

There are over 9000 periodicals – most with small circulations. However, a few motoring, women's and general interest magazines attract circulations that compare with the top magazines in major Western countries. The periodicals with the largest readerships are:

L'Automobile (monthly), motoring magazine, 1,500,000 copies;

Gente (weekly), political and current affairs, 901,000 copies.

Quattroroute (monthly), motoring magazine, 700,000 copies;

Oggi (weekly), topical and literary, 696,000 copies;

Panorama (weekly), current affairs, 504,000 copies;

Intimità (weekly), women's magazine, 468,000 copies.

Italy has nearly 2000 local commercial TV stations, seven of which are broadcast nationwide, as well as RAI (Radiotelevisione Italiana) – the national network which runs three channels – and a Catholic network. RAI broadcasts national radio channels; there are over 1000 local commercial radio stations.

Japan

Japanese papers enjoy some of the highest circulations in the world. There are over 100 principal daily newspapers in Japan where 580 copies of papers are printed for every 1000 people. The press is concentrated in Tokyo, whose papers form a national press. There are also important regional papers in Osaka, Nagoya and other major cities. Most Japanese newspapers publish both morning and evening editions. The principal titles include:

Asahi Shimbun (daily), Tokyo; copies – 8,200,000 (morning), 4,700,000 (evening);

Yomiuri Shimbun (daily), Tokyo; copies – 5,800,000 (morning), 2,900,000 (evening);

Nihon Keizai Shimbun (daily), Tokyo; copies – 2,920,000 (morning), 1,720,000 (evening);

Yomiuri Shimbun (daily), Osaka; copies – 2,400,000 (morning), 1,400,000 (evening);

Asahi Shimbun (daily), Osaka; copies – 2,300,000 (morning), 1,400,000 (evening);

Chunichi Shimbun (daily), Nagoya; copies – 2,200,000 (morning), 817,000 (evening).

By contrast, periodicals have low circulations and – because of the great number of TV stations – TV listings guides are largely absent. The periodicals with the highest circulations include the following:

Ie-no-Hikari (monthly), countryside magazine, 1,112,000 copies;

Lettuce Club (fortnightly), cookery, 800,000 copies;

Bungei-Shunju (monthly), general interest, 656,000 copies;

Hot-Dog Press (fortnightly), men's magazine, 650,000 copies;

Popeye (fortnightly), teenage magazine, 600,000 copies.

Croissant (fortnightly), women's and domestic magazine, 600,000 copies.

NHK – a non-commercial public corporation – runs two TV and three radio stations. There are nearly 400 commercial radio stations and over 6800 commercial television stations.

Mexico

The Mexican press is characterized by a large number of provincial daily titles. The best-selling newspapers include:

Esto (daily), Mexico City, 400,000 copies (450,000 Monday);

La Prensa (daily), Mexico City, 300,000 copies;

Ovaciones (daily), Mexico City, 205,000 copies (220,000 copies evening).

The best-selling periodicals include:

Tele-Guia (weekly), TV listings guide, 750,000 copies;

Fama (fortnightly), show business, 250,000 copies;

Ultima Moda (fortnightly), fashion magazine, 230,000 copies.

Netherlands

The national Dutch press comprises eight newspapers printd in Amsterdam, Rotterdam and the Hague. In addition there are over 70 provincial papers. The best-selling titles are:

De Telegraaf (daily), Amsterdam, 743,000 copies;

Algemeen Dagblad (daily), Rotterdam, 413,000 copies;

De Volkskrant (daily), Amsterdam, 354,000 copies.

The Dutch periodicals with the largest circulations are:

Veronica (weekly), radio and TV listings guide, 1,250,000 copies;

AVRO bode (weekly), TV listings guide, 921,000 copies;

Libelle (weekly), women's magazine, 758,000 copies.

Portugal

There are 30 daily papers but circulation figures are very low by EU standards. Best-selling titles are:

Correio da Manha (daily), Lisbon, 85,000 copies;

Publica (daily), Lisbon, 75,000 copies;

Jornal de Noticias (daily), Oporto, 70,000 copies.

The sales of periodicals are much larger. Magazines include:

Maria (weekly), women's interest, 392,000 copies;

Seleccoes do Reader's Digest (monthly), 294,000 copies;

TV Guia (weekly), TV listings, 257,000 copies.

Russia

The press in Russia is still undergoing drastic restructuring and the new 'freedom of the press' has been seen to have some restrictions. By 1993 there were nearly 5000 registered newspapers, including 200 national papers. The high circulation papers of the former Communist Party organs – *Izvestia* ('News'), *Pravda* ('Truth') and *Trud* ('Labour') – shrank as new, innovative papers, such as *Argumenty y Fakty*, appeared. Shortages of materials mean that some 'daily' newspapers are now published intermittently. Major titles (all published in Moscow) include:

Trud, 3,060,000 copies;

Argumenty y Fakty (weekly), 1,500,000 copies;

Selskaya Zhizn, 1,350,000 copies;

Izvestia, 1,000,000 copies;

Pravda, 610,000 copies.

Periodicals used to be published by various Communist Party bodies. The vast majority were of an educational and 'improving' nature, and carried propaganda. Some of these titles are still published – in much smaller numbers – by successor bodies, although they have changed greatly in style.

Veselye Kartinki (Merry Pictures) (monthly), pre-school children's magazine, 9,000,000 copies;

Murzilka (monthly), young children's magazine, 3,000,000 copies;

Yuny Naturalist (Young Naturalist), 1,500,000 copies;

Yuny Teknik (Young Technologist), 1,095,000 copies.

There are now two main broadcasting companies supplying radio and television companies.

Spain

Strong historic regional identities and the lack of a single national language have prevented the emergence of a national press in Spain. Only *ABC*, *Ya* and *El País* circulate thoughout most of the country. *El País* – published in Madrid, Barcelona, Valencia and Seville – is the nearest thing to a national newspaper. Circulation figures for Spain's 120 daily papers are low. The greatest circulations are enjoyed by:

El País (daily), see above, 407,000 combined circulation (1,122,000 Sunday edition);

ABC (daily), Madrid and Seville, 392,000 combined circulation (766,000 Sunday edition);

Marca (daily sports), Madrid, 310,000 copies;

La Vanguardia (daily), Barcelona, 195,000 copies (316,000 Sunday edition);

El Periódico (daily), Barcelona, 190,000 copies (380,000 Sunday edition);

La Opinión de Murcia (daily), Murcia, 180,000 copies.

Diario 16 (daily evening), Madrid, 180,000 copies (210,000 Sunday edition).

Current affairs, women's and general interest magazines and TV listings guides outsell newspapers in Spain. The periodicals with the largest sales are:

TP Teleprogramma (weekly), TV listings guide, 1,400,000 copies;

Pronto (weekly), general interest, 925,000 copies;

Tele Indiscreta (weekly), TV listings guide, 700,000 copies;

Hola! (weekly), general interest, 583,000 copies;

Hogar y Moda (weekly), women's magazine, 550,000 copies;

Interviú (weekly), general interest, 495,000 copies;

Panorama Internacional (weekly), general interest, 494,000 copies.

RTVE is a public corporation that controls and coordinates TV and radio. There are seven regional television companies including those broadcasting in Basque, Catalan and Galician. RNE runs 17 regional radio channels; three regional stations broadcast in Basque, Catalan and Galician. There are over 300 other local radio stations.

Sweden

Although there are nearly 60 regional daily newspapers in Sweden, the most influential titles are those published in Stockholm. The best-selling titles are:

Expressen (daily), Stockholm, 502,000 copies;

Dagens Nyheter (daily), Stockholm, 384,000 copies (434,000 Sunday);

Aftonbladet (evening daily), Stockholm, 343,000 copies.

Swedish magazines enjoy a wide circulation – family and domestic titles are the most popular. Best-selling titles include:

Var Bostad (11 a year), house and home, 990,000 copies;

ICA Kuriren (weekly), house and home, 509,000 copies;

Aret Runt (weekly), family magazine, 303,000 copies.

Switzerland

Four national languages and a strong local identity in individual cantons have encouraged many (107) daily newspapers. Best-selling titles include:

Blick (daily), Zurich, 382,000 copies;

Tages Anzeiger Zurich (daily), Zurich, 274,000 copies;

Neue Zuricher Zeitung (daily), Zurich, 152,000 copies;

Le Matin (daily), Lausanne, 152,000 copies.

French, German and Italian magazines circulate in Switzerland. Nevertheless, there are many Swiss magazines including:

Touring (fortnightly), travel/tourism magazine, combined circulation for German-, French- and Italian-language editions 1,240,000;

Der Schweizerische Beobachter (two a month), general interest magazine, 408,000 copies;

Trente jours (monthly), general interest, 400,000 copies.

United Kingdom

The UK has the highest circulation of newspapers in the EU. The tabloids, in particular, enjoy a very large readership. The UK has 26 national papers (daily, Sunday and weekly), plus 88 regional daily papers. The national press is centred in London, but the Scottish, Welsh and Northern Irish daily titles may be regarded as national within their own countries. The daily papers listed below are all published in London except where indicated. Those with the highest circulations are:

The Sun, 4,184,000 copies;

Daily Mirror, 2,536,000 copies;

Daily Mail, 1,764,000 copies;

Daily Express, 1,320,000 copies;

The Daily Telegraph, 1,092,000 copies;

Daily Record, Glasgow, 782,000 copies;

Daily Star, 759,000 copies;

Today, 657,000 copies;

The Times, 598,000 copies;

Evening Standard, 465,000 copies;

The Guardian, 379,000 copies;

Daily Sport, 300,000 copies;

The Independent, 289,000 copies;

Financial Times, 272,000 copies;

Manchester Evening News, Manchester, 221,000 copies;

Birmingham Evening Mail, Birmingham, 208,000 copies;

Sunday newspapers have a wider readership. Those with the highest circulation figures include:

News of the World, 4,866,000 copies;

Sunday Mirror, 2,574,000 copies;

The People, 2,051,000 copies;

The Mail on Sunday, 1,905,000 copies;

Sunday Express, 1,489,000 copies;

The Sunday Times, 1,165,000 copies.

Leisure, TV listings and women's interest magazines are the most successful of the UK's 7500 periodicals in terms of circulation. They include:

TV Weekly, 2,719,000 copies;

Sky TV Guide (monthly), 2,700,000 copies;

TV First (weekly), 2,098,000 copies;

Reader's Digest (monthly), general interest, 1,785,000 copies;

TV Week, 1,769,000 copies;

What's On TV? (weekly), 1,652,000 copies;

Take A Break (weekly), women's interest, 1,505,000 copies;

Radio Times (weekly), 1,441,000 copies;

Bella (weekly), women's interest, 1,000,000 copies.

The BBC (British Broadcasting Corporation) is a public corporation. It runs five national radio services, plus national regional services in Wales, Scotland and Northern Ireland. There are over 50 BBC local radio stations. There are three national and 80 local independent radio stations. There are four national television channels – BBC1, BBC2, ITV (Channel 3; an independent commercial station made up of regional programme contractors) and Channel 4 (which is replaced by S4C in Wales). British Sky Broadcasting offers sport, film, music, news and other satellite channels.

USA

In the USA there are almost 600 daily morning newspapers – 43 of which have a circulation of over 250,000 – and over 1000 evening and other daily papers. American daily papers place great emphasis on local news because of the strong interest in state, as opposed to national, news. The size of the USA has prevented the emergence of a national press, although the *Wall Street Journal* and the *New York Times* (both of which are printed at several locations) and the *Washington Post,* the *Los Angeles Times* and the (Boston) *Christian Science Monitor* enjoy national readerships. There are nine major newspaper groups. The papers with the biggest circulations include:

Wall Street Journal (daily), New York, 1,795,000 copies;

USA Today (daily), Arlington (Greater Washington DC), 1,429,000 copies;

Los Angeles Times (daily), 1,243,000 copies (1,576,000 Sunday edition);

New York Times (daily), 1,146,000 copies (1,762,000 Sunday edition);

Washington Post (daily), 839,000 copies (1,116,000 Sunday edition);

New York Daily News (daily), 782,0000 copies (983,000 Sunday edition);

Newsday (daily), published in New York, 758,000 copies (875,000 Sunday edition);

Chicago Tribune (daily), 734,000 copies (1,133,000 Sunday edition);

Detroit Free Press (daily), 622,000 copies (1,215,000 Sunday edition);

San Francisco Chronicle (daily), 570,000 copies (704,000 Sunday edition);

Chicago Sun-Times (daily), 538,000 copies (559,000 Sunday edition);

Atlanta Journal-Constitution (daily), 519,000 copies (704,000 Sunday edition);

Boston Globe (daily), 517,000 copies (798,000 Sunday edition);

Philadelphia Inquirer (daily), 516,000 copies (983,000 Sunday edition).

The periodicals enjoying the highest circulations in the USA include:

TV Guide (weekly), 16,330,000 copies;

Reader's Digest (monthly), 16,265,000 copies;

National Geographic Magazine (monthly), 9,921,000 copies;

Better Homes and Gardens (monthly), 7,600,000 copies;

Family Circle (every three weeks), general interest, 5,213,000 copies;

Good Housekeeping (monthly), 5,153,000 copies;

McCall's Magazine (monthly), women's magazine, 5,089,000 copies;

Ladies' Home Journal (monthly), 5,002,000 copies;

National Enquirer (weekly), general interest, 4,381,000 copies;

Time (weekly), current affairs, 4,095,000 copies;

Consumer Reports (monthly), 4,000,000 copies;

Playboy (monthly), men's magazine, 3,403,000 copies;

Redbook Magazine (monthly), women's magazine, 3,300,000 copies;

Sports Illustrated (weekly), 3,220,000 copies;

Newsweek (weekly), current affairs, 3,210,000 copies.

There are over 1500 commercial TV stations and 325 educational TV stations. There are about 10,000 commercial and educational radio stations. Cable television is widespread.

Painting and Sculpture

DRAWING

Drawing is the process of artistic depiction of objects or abstractions on a two-dimensional surface by linear (and sometimes tonal) means. The result may be a cartoon – a full size preparatory drawing for a painting or a work in another medium – or a finished work.

Drawing tools and media include:

chalk including black chalk (black stone) and red chalk (mineral) was used extensively from the 16th century for preparatory drawings. Chalk was also, and still is, used for finished works.

charcoal is charred wood. It was used extensively from the 16th century in preparatory drawings.

ink a liquid for drawing or painting. Generally the colours are a suspension or are present in a dye. Sometimes, as with Indian ink or white ink, there may be opaque pigments in suspension. Ink may be applied with a pen or a brush for a preparatory drawing or a finished work.

pencil the graphite pencil – developed in the 17th century – which replaced the silverpoint in preparing the surface to be painted on. Pencils are manufactured in varying degrees of softness and darkness. The graphite pencil is not only used to produce preliminary sketches but also for finished works.

silverpoint a metal point used mainly in the 15th century on prepared paper to make rough outlines that will be covered over by other media or to achieve a delicate effect through the tiny (and eventually tarnished) particles of silver left behind.

PAINTING

Painting is the visual and aesthetic expression of ideas and emotions primarily in two dimensions, using colour, line, shapes, texture and tones.

The great variety of painting techniques reflects the range of surfaces that are painted on; for instance, tempera technique is used for painting on wood panels, and fresco technique for painting on walls. Oil painting is done mainly on canvas, while acrylic, watercolour, gouache and pastels can all be used to paint on paper.

The earliest paintings known are some 15,000 years old, found in the caves of Lascaux in France and Altamira in Spain. The pigments used in these prehistoric sites include burnt wood, bone, chalk and earth colours.

Painting tools and media include:

airbrush technique a system of spraying colour with an airbrush, an implement that resembles a fountain pen. It has a small container near the nozzle. Air pressure is applied via a mechanical compressor and can be controlled to create fine, delicate lines or a wide sweep.

acrylic an opaque, water-soluble quick-drying paint. It can be applied with heavy knife-laid impasto (see below) or diluted with water to wash-like consistency. Acrylic paint is manufactured from pigment bound in a synthetic resin, normally acrylic or PVA. It is a 20th-century development, initially used in wall painting. The colour, unlike that of oil paint, does not alter with time.

fresco (Italian, 'fresh') a wall-painting technique in which powdered pigments are mixed in water and applied to a wet lime-plaster. The colours fuse with the plaster, forming a permanent waterproof surface. Best suited to a warm climate, it was widely used in Italian medieval and Renaissance painting, and also in Classical Roman times.

gouache a painting technique, similar to watercolour, in which the binding medium is glue. White pigment is added to give some opacity. Used by French painters since the 18th century, gouache is widely used in commercial illustration.

impasto the laying on of paint so thickly on a canvas that it protrudes from the surface.

oils the most widely used painting technique. Oil paint is based on a mixture of dry pigment and vegetable oil, commonly linseed, poppy or walnut oil. It is slow drying, so the artist is able to make revisions and build up layers of colour. The composition is built up in layers of thicker or thinner paint, and variety in brushwork can have significant visual effect.

Oil-painting techniques were first used widely in 15th-century Netherlandish painting, above all by Jan van Eyck, who developed an oil technique which produced a highly refined glass-like finish.

The composition is outlined with charcoal or transferred from a squared drawing onto the ground. Variety in brushwork can have significant visual effect. Paint can be thickly applied with a loaded brush or palette knife, but brushstrokes are imperceptible if paint is thinned to a runny consistency. Surface textures are achieved by *scumbling* (applying thin layers of lighter colours over darker underpainting), *stippling* (applying paint in light dabs) and *frottage* (taking a rubbing from a rough surface such as wood and applying paint on the resulting textured surface).

pastels sticks of pigment made by mixing powdered pigment with gum or resin binder. Pastels give soft colours which retain their freshness.

pigments colours derived from earths, natural dyes and minerals or chemically synthesized. The earliest pigments, used by prehistoric man, included burnt wood, bone, chalk and earth colours. In addition to these, medieval painters used:

verdigris (copper resinate; green),

ultramarine (lapis lazuli; blue),

white lead,

azurite (copper carbonate; blue),

madder (red),

lead-tin yellow, and

vermilion (cinnabar; red).

Later came *Prussian blue* (1705) and *Naples yellow*, but during the 19th century the range of colours expanded to include new chemical colours.

tempera a technique – used for painting on wood panels – based on a mixture of a water-based liquid with an oily or waxy medium. Traditionally egg white and egg yolk are used together with an oil such as linseed oil, but egg (which acts as a binder) may also be used with water alone. Its quick-drying properties and luminosity of colour account for the attraction of tempera.

watercolour painting a technique in which pigment is bound in a gum arabic medium and thinned with water for use. It was used as a paint in Egyptian painting, but most fully exploited by 18th- and 19th-century British landscape artists. Distinguished by its translucent quality, watercolour is extremely versatile.

Some watercolours are *monochrome* – painted in only one colour.

SCULPTURE

Sculpture describes the processes of carving, engraving, modelling, casting or assembling so as to produce representations or abstractions of an artistic nature in relief, in intaglio, or in the round.

The two main sculpture techniques are *carving* and *modelling*.

carving a carved image, created by cutting unwanted material away from a block of hard material, usually stone or wood.

Stone carving can be done from granite, limestone, sandstone, alabaster and a variety of marbles. Other materials that have been commonly carved for small-scale sculpture include ivory, amber and semi-precious stones.

modelling involves manipulating some soft and yielding material such as wax, clay or plaster until the desired image is achieved. A three-dimensional shape is built up around an *armature* (framework) in metal or wood. Models are generally turned into a more lasting form, either by heating, as with clay, or by *casting* them in bronze or some other metal.

The two principal techniques of casting are the *lost-wax process* and *sand casting*.

assemblage is the term used for all works of art constructed from everyday objects. It refers to works of three-dimensional and planar construction, including collage.

PRINTMAKING

Images were first printed from engraved wooden blocks onto parchment some 3000 to 4000 years ago. In the West, the development of printing coincided with the invention of movable type in the 15th century.

Since then, a great variety of different printing techniques have evolved, including *relief techniques*, *intaglio techniques* (where the image is printed from lines cut into a metal plate) and *planographic techniques* (which are characterized by surface-printing methods).

The principal techniques employed in printmaking include:

aquatint an intaglio technique used to imitate the effect of watercolours. A copper plate is coated with powdered resin. Repeated immersions in an acid bath produce a tonal effect as small areas of copper between the particles of dust are exposed.

engraving an intaglio technique that originated from the carving of gems and armour. A zinc or copper plate is engraved with a sharp tool. The plate is then inked with a tacky ink and all the uncut surfaces are wiped clean – leaving the ink only in the recessed furrows.

etching an intaglio technique used during the 17th and 18th centuries and revived in the late 19th century by James Whistler (1834–1903).

The design is etched onto a copper plate coated in a blackened acid-resistant material, using a steel needle, which exposes the metal. Before being inked and printed – using the same method as for engraving – the plate is immersed in acid, which bites into the exposed lines. To accentuate areas of light and shade, parts of the plate are protected with a varnish, and the plate is then re-immersed in the acid.

linocuts a relief technique using the floor-covering material linoleum, a cheap and easily carved surface. Although it does not allow great subtlety of detail, it was favoured by artists in the 1920s, including Picasso.

lithography a planographic technique depending upon the mutual incompatibility of water and grease.

A design is drawn or painted onto a grained alloy plate – originally a thin limestone slab – using a greasy material such as crayon or lithographic ink. A solution of nitric acid and gum arabic is applied to the unmarked areas which repels the lithographic ink wiped onto the plate before printing. The drawn surfaces attract the ink and the moist surfaces repel it. The method was invented by the Bavarian Aloys Senefelder in 1776.

mezzotint an intaglio technique used for reproductions after oil paintings in the 18th and 19th centuries.

A serrated rocker is passed over the plate, leaving a varying number of indentations in which ink will collect and produce tonal effects. The tone engraving is then produced by scraping away for darker tones and burnishing for highlights.

screen printing a 20th-century planographic method where a screen of silk or gauze is tautly stretched over a wooden or metal frame.

The design is applied to the screen in the form of a stencil so that areas not to be coloured are blocked out. Ink is wiped across the screen and forced through the mesh onto paper.

woodcuts a relief technique used as early as the 14th century and used extensively by Albrecht Dürer (1471–1528).

The design is drawn onto wood and cut away – along the grain – leaving only the raised lines of the image ready to be inked. The woodcut is printed by laying paper onto the inked block.

wood engraving a relief technique – thought to have been invented by Thomas Bewick (1753-1828) – that differs from woodcutting in that normally a hard, fine-grained wood is cut into across the grain. The resulting image is usually much finer than a woodcut. The technique was commonly used for fine book illustrations during the 19th century.

HISTORY OF ART

Prehistoric art

The world's most ancient works of art date from 30,000 BC. This is vastly earlier than the first written records and means that the greater part of art history is, in fact, prehistoric. It was during the prehistoric period that virtually all the major artistic media evolved, including drawing, painting, sculpture, ceramics and, arguably, architecture.

Palaeolithic art flourished from 30,000 BC. Figurines shaped out of clay, bone, stone, wood and ivory have been found scattered over a wide area from Spain to Siberia. They depict both animals and humans. Painting, engraving and relief on the walls of caves began later than figurine sculpture, and flourished after 15,000 BC. The hunters who created cave art were inspired by the animals around them, particularly by large mammals such as deer, horses, wild cattle, bison, woolly rhinoceroses and mammoths.

Neolithic art began as farming and settled village life spread across Europe (c. 6500–4000 BC). This encouraged both the use of pottery and the development of architecture. Shaped and decorated vessels were produced almost everywhere, but the most inventive and prolific potters lived in Eastern Europe. The Vinca culture produced thousands of fired-clay figurines, including some dramatically stylized heads found at Predionica in Serbia. Related cultures produced pots shaped like human figures, animals or even houses.

Bronze and Iron Age art dates from the 2nd millennium BC with the development of metalwork. In Eastern Europe, early cast bronze weapons and jewellery were delicately engraved with curved-line designs. Similar decoration appears on Scandinavian metalwork. During the 1st millennium BC many more bronze figures were cast, notably in Scandinavia, central Europe and Sardinia. Engraving remained common, but the beating or embossing of metalwork grew in importance. The early Celts decorated weapons, vessels and pieces of jewellery in such a fluid style that it is often impossible to separate the stylized Celtic heads and animals from the surrounding plant-like ornament.

Art of the ancient Near East and Egypt

Mesopotamian art flourished from 6000 to 3600 BC. Covering Sumeria, Assyria and Babylon, Mesopotamian art is represented by many styles, although most incorporate figures, animals (both real and mythical) and plants. It is now seen mainly in the sculptural works on palaces and on tiles.

Egyptian art flourished from 3100 to 341 BC. It is essentially a decorative tomb art, based on the notion of immortality; the deceased were recorded and equipped for the afterlife in writing (hieroglyphs), pictures and material wealth and goods.

Greek and Roman art

The art of Greece and Rome was characterized by a sense of proportion, harmony and balance. In general, Classical form has exerted a largely civilizing influence over the past two and a half millennia.

Greek art flourished from 2000 to 27 BC. Minoan and Mycenaean art (2000–1100 BC) consists mainly of sculptured engravings, decorated pottery and some frescos. The Archaic period (800–500 BC) saw the development of sculpture, especially human figures. This tendency was developed in the Classical period (500–323 BC), where the body was glorified and drapery carved to imitate movement. The Hellenistic period (323–27 BC) was characterized by greater emotional expression, and is notable for its portraits.

Roman art (100 BC to AD 400) excelled in copying Greek sculpture and relief carving to a very high quality. Portrait busts were popular, and Roman painting was mainly executed in fresco in a naturalistic style. Mosaic floors were also highly decorative. The Greeks and Romans themselves tended rather to appreciate highly wrought works in gold and silver. Since articles of precious metal were the first to be seized or melted down in times of war or hardship, such works have virtually all vanished, but contemporary accounts of shrines and individuals speak of great amounts of sculpture and vases made of gold and silver.

Islamic art (7th to 17th century)

Geographically, Islamic art extends from Indonesia in the east to Morocco and Spain in the west. The word 'Islamic' reflects a culture and society united by Islam. Islamic art developed from existing Byzantine, Persian and later Indian styles that prevailed when the conquering Muslim armies arrived. Originally based on superb Koranic calligraphy, it is a highly decorative art form which reaches its apotheosis in the miniature painting, the ceramic tile, and carpetmaking, in which floral and geometric motives reach a high peak of formal perfection. Although by no means absolute, traditionally there is a ban on the representation of living figures in a religious context, which accounts for the often semi-abstract nature of Islamic ornament and for the virtual absence of sculpture.

South Asian art

India's earliest civilization flourished in the Indus Valley between 2300–1700 BC, centred on the cities of Harappa and Mohenjo-Daro. Its architecture was utilitarian, but some fine statues in sandstone and slate were produced. Little survives between the time of the Harappa civilization and that of the Mauryas (321–185 BC), during whose rule Persian and Greek influences are apparent, notably in architecture. Essentially traditional and religious, Buddhist and Hindu works of art are symbols and manifestations of gods. One of the most distinctive Buddhist architectural forms is the *stupa*, an ornate burial mound. Temples for both religions became increasingly ornate and complex. In the 7th century fresco painting and rock sculpture in India had reached a peak and by the 13th century erotic carvings had become popular.

Chinese and Japanese art

Chinese art represents the longest surviving civilization in the world, with an art history stretching back at least 4000 years. The distinctiveness of Chinese art has been complemented by very high technical skills, and for many centuries ceramics, bronzes, jade carvings, silk and lacquer were produced to standards surpassing those of all other cultures. The advent of Buddhism (1st century AD) encouraged religious art in

China, in particular sculptures of Buddha. Landscape painting became popular under the Tang Dynasty (618–907) and Chinese pottery reached perfection under the Sung (960–1279), becoming much more elaborate under the Ming (1368–1644).

Japanese art was heavily influenced by Chinese art, but later indigenous Japanese art forms include *netsuke* (miniature sculptures), painted screens, and *Ukiyo-e* woodblock colour prints.

Australasian and Oceanic art
Pottery and metalwork were unknown in Australasia and Oceania before the arrival of Europeans. However, other art forms were flourishing. Cave paintings – both representational and abstract – and tree bark paintings have been found in Australia. Melanesia boasts highly decorated tools and utensils, bark drawings and statues. The art of bark painting, plaiting, weaving, tattooing, wood carving and personal adornment reached a degree of perfection in Polynesia, particularly New Zealand and Samoa.

Native American art
The greatest architecture and stone sculpture of the Americas is divided between the ancient civilizations of Mesoamerica and the Central Andes. Before and after the arrival of Europeans, tribal North America excelled in wooden sculpture, textiles and pottery.

African art
The finest African art, excluding the products of Egypt and the Muslim north, is largely concentrated in the rain forests and savannah woodland of central western Africa. Far to the north and south lies the ancient rock art of the Sahara and southern Africa. The earliest known sculptural tradition of sub-Saharan Africa emerged c. 500 BC in northern Nigeria. Superb metalworkers, the Benin Kingdom (1500–1700) produced plaques decorated in high and low relief with scenes of warriors, chiefs and Portuguese traders. African art is probably best known for its carved wooden masks and sculptures.

Early medieval art
The period between the Classical Age and the Renaissance formed an essential artistic bridgehead, when new approaches to pictorial form were worked out and deeper spiritual values attached to works of art. The major patron became the Christian Church, and most of the greatest monuments are related to churches and monasteries.

Byzantine art was, at first, an admixture of Hellenic, Roman, Middle Eastern and Oriental styles. It dates from and has its first centre in the establishment of Constantinople as capital of the Roman Empire in the East. The First Golden Age was in the 6th century. The Second Golden Age occurred between 1051 and 1185, when Western Europe was influenced by the severe, spiritually uplifted style of the Byzantines. These two Ages are dominated by the use of mosaic work, but by the Third Golden Age (1261–1450) this medium was being replaced by fresco painting.

Romanesque art flourished in western European in the 11th and 12th centuries. Mainly architectural, it was distinguished by the use of rounded arches. Sculpture is mainly church work intended to inspire awe of the divine power. Illuminated manuscripts of high quality survive.

Gothic art
Gothic painting and sculpture flourished alongside architecture. The Romanesque world of fantastic beasts is largely left behind and a new emphasis is placed on nature and humanity's place within its hierarchy. Gothic sculpture is narrative and realistic, particularly the friezes. In painting the style evolved more slowly and is seen in manuscript illumination and frescos.

International Gothic is a later mixture of styles of painting and sculpture in Europe. The main influences were northern France, the Netherlands and Italy, and its main features are rich and decorative colouring and detail, and flowing line.

Art of the early Renaissance
The term *renaissance* ('rebirth') was first coined in the 19th century to describe a period of intellectual and artistic renewal that lasted from about 1350 to about 1550. The dominant theme of this period is the revival of interest in classical literature and art by 14th- and 15th-century humanists and the rediscovery by artists of their cultural past. Florence was the first centre of such rediscovery, with Padua, Venice and finally Rome rivalling Florence in the pursuit of antiquarian learning and artistic excellence. After 1500, the movement spread to northern Europe. Architecture, painting and sculpture, deriving from Greek and Roman models and using classical motifs, moved into unparalleled prominence. Advances were made in the realistic depiction of figures. Other artistic inventions included perspective and painting with oil.

Netherlandish and German art of the period from around 1400 to 1570 is often described under the blanket term 'Northern Renaissance'. As in Italy, Flemish and German painters moved towards more realistic figure work, and their experimentations led to the development of portraiture, nudes, meticulously accurate details, distant landscapes, spatial illusionism and careful depiction of light and shadow. Oil painting was introduced and woodcuts and engravings achieved a new depth of expression.

Art of the High Renaissance and Mannerism
The focus of artistic activity in Italy shifted during the early 16th century from Florence to Rome. One of the most concentrated groups of artistic genius ever known was gathered in the papal city. At the same time, the artistic innovations of the Italian Renaissance began to spread to northern Europe. Artistic innovation later led to the superficial elegance of Mannerism. A style that became popular all over Catholic Europe, Mannerism displayed exaggerated sophistication and virtuosity – sometimes combined with a heightened emotionalism and religiosity. However, the Counter-Reformation brought in restrictions on subject matter and treatment in religious art, and by the end of the 16th century Mannerism had lost much of its vigour.

Art of Classicism and the Baroque
Classicism and the Baroque were the two dominant trends in the visual arts of the 17th century, particularly in Catholic countries and most importantly in Italy and France. Although frequently divergent and opposed, they both originated in the reaction in Italy against the

aridity of Late Mannerism. A return to the naturalism, harmonious equilibrium and compositional coherence of the High Renaissance was combined with a new physical realism, emotional immediacy and dynamic vigour. The Baroque style combined the dramatic effects of energetic movement, vivid colour and decorative detail with expressive originality and freedom. Classicism deployed more restrained qualities of directness and precision to enliven traditional ideas of balance and decorum.

Art of the Dutch School

In the 17th century a sudden flowering of the art of painting in the Netherlands coincided with the overthrow of Spanish rule and Dutch mercantile success throughout the world. Dutch artists concentrated on the types of painting in which they had long specialized – still life, scenes of everyday life, landscape and portraiture.

Rococo and Neo-Classical art

The synthesis in later 17th-century Italy of Classicist idealization and Baroque vigour was taken up in France and spread throughout Europe as the accepted courtly 'Grand Manner'. It was soon diluted by the 18th-century desire for the informal and undemanding, which found its artistic expression in the style known as Rococo. For perhaps the first time the prime function of art was perceived as decorative rather than illustrative or didactic. Rococo was not fully accepted in England, where Baroque licence had already been challenged early in the new century by the more 'rational' concept of *Palladianism*. By the 1750s a reaction to the still freer and more exotic forms of the Rococo appeared not only in England but in France, cradle of the style. Archaeological discoveries in Italy and Greece prompted a re-examination of the origins of European civilization. French intellectualism developed this into international Neo-Classicism.

Romanticism

The Romantic Movement in art emerged in the late 18th century, and flourished until the middle of the 19th. The movement was a reaction both against the aesthetic and ethical values of Classical and Neo-Classical art, and against the ugliness and materialism of the Industrial Revolution. The influence of Romantic writers was particularly important in providing both subject matter and a philosophy for the Romantic painters. The values of the wider Romantic movement are central to an understanding of the visual art of the period. Indeed it is the *content* of Romantic painting and the attitude of the artists themselves that give the movement coherence, as there are enormous variations in style and technique.

Realism

Realism was a movement that flourished between 1840 and 1880, originating in France, and soon spreading throughout Europe and to America. The Realists reacted against the subjectivity, individualism and historical obsessions of many of the Romantics, adopting instead a naturalistic style of art based on truth to nature. The grand, heroic subject matter of the Romantic movement was replaced by simple views of everyday life, and Romantic emotionalism was abandoned in favour of detached, objective observation. The term 'Realism' applies to both style and subject matter. Usually Realists avoided the vivid, dramatic brushstrokes favoured by Romantic artists, preferring to make their paintings distinct and precise, with straight forward subjects.

The Barbizon School takes its name from the village of Barbizon, near Fontainebleau (France), which, during the 1840s, became the centre for a group of French landscape painters. They began the direct study of nature, aiming to create a naturalistic depiction of landscape without the restrictions of academic conventions. Their work encouraged the emergence of Impressionism.

The Pre-Raphaelite Brotherhood refers to a brotherhood of seven London artists (1848–56) formed to make a return to the style of Italian painting before Raphael (hence the name) as a protest against the frivolity of the prevailing English School of the day. They included Holman Hunt, Millais and Rossetti. Their subject matter was often drawn from religion and legend, and their style minutely detailed.

The Arts and Crafts Movement (c. 1870–1900) was based on the revival of interest in the medieval craft system. Led by William Morris, the aims of the movement were to fuse the functional and the decorative, and to restore the worth of handmade crafts in the face of the growing mass-produced wares of the late 19th century.

Impressionism and Neo-Impressionism

Impressionism was neither a school nor a movement with a clearly defined programme. It was an ill-defined association of artists who joined together to mount independent group exhibitions, rather than compromise their art in order to be included in the Paris Salon, the official state-sponsored exhibition. There were eight Impressionist exhibitions, held from 1874 to 1886. Their work shared some techniques and certain subjects. Their approach was naturalistic, and their two main subjects were landscape and modern (often city) life. Often painted in the open air, their paintings show a concern with capturing the fleeting moment, particularly the effects of light, which they attempted to capture with a free handling of paint. At the final Impressionist exhibition, Seurat, Signac and Pissarro showed (Neo-Impressionist) canvases using the latest *divisionist* (or *pointillist*) techniques. This involved the use of pure colours applied in such small patches (often dots) that they appeared to fuse to form an intermediary tone when viewed from an appropriate distance. Hence grass might be composed of touches of blue alongside areas of yellow. These ideas were not new, but had been used in a much less systematic way by the Impressionist painters.

Post-Impressionism and Fauvism

Just as the Impressionists reacted against the established art of their day, a succession of artists later reacted against Impressionism itself. The *Post-Impressionists*, as they became known, were active mainly in France from 1880 to 1905. They included artists who painted in a wide variety of styles but who shared a desire to go beyond pure naturalism and to give more emphasis to colour, emotions and imagination. From these individuals the major art movements of the 20th century emerged. *Fauvism* (c. 1905–7) was a short-lived but highly influential

French movement of artists surrounding Matisse. It is summarized by the daring and spontaneous handling of paint in bold, brilliant and sometimes non-representational colour.

Symbolism, Secession and Expressionism

The *Symbolist* movement emerged in the 1880s as a reaction against the naturalist movement (the idea that art was an imitation of nature) and against modern industrialism and materialistic values. The Symbolists sought to escape into the past or into the world of fantasy, including dreams. They believed that art existed alongside, not in direct relation to, the real world, and that it had its own rules. Symbolism foreshadowed Surrealism. Anti-naturalism was also shared by many of the German and Austrian *Secessions* of the 1890s – breakaway groups who revolted against the academicism of conventional painting. Similarly, a diverse group of later artists, known as the *Expressionists,* wished to emphasize – often through unnaturalistic distortion – the importance of emotion and the artist's inner vision. A group of German Expressionist artists, known as *Die Brücke* ('The Bridge'), aimed to integrate art and life by using art as a means of communication. Another independent German Expressionist group was *Der Blaue Reiter* ('The Blue Rider'). Rather than promoting one particular tendency, its aim was for each artist to achieve an individual style. They did, however, share a use of bold colours and a tendency towards abstraction.

Abstraction

In the first half of the 20th century a revolution occurred in the practice of art. From 1910 artists in different countries began to produce abstract or non-figurative art, sometimes abstracting from a landscape or still life until the subject disappeared.

Cubism began around 1907 when artists such as Picasso and Braque began to analyse objects, breaking them down into geometrical shapes and restructuring them in order to show each form's many facets in a single image.

Futurism was founded in Italy in 1909 by the poet Filippo Marinetti. He urged artists to turn their backs on the art of the past and to seek inspiration from industrial society and the dynamism of modern life. Futurism aimed to incorporate the thrust of modern technology (particularly the sense of speed) into art. *Vorticism* in Britain and *Rayonism* in Russia shared some of the aims of Futurism.

De Stijl is a slightly later Dutch movement, which restricted itself to pure geometrical abstraction.

Dada and Surrealism

Dada and Surrealism grew out of the crisis of faith in a society whose intellectual and moral values were held responsible for the appalling destruction of World War I. Although they were essentially different in purpose and character, some common ground existed, and a number of Dada artists later joined the Surrealist movement.

Dada first emerged in 1916. It was an international movement that rejected existing social values and its art. Instead it aimed to be anarchic, anti-aesthetic and anti-rational; simultaneously art and anti-art.

Surrealism was founded in 1924. It was a French avant-garde movement of literary origin inspired by Dada, and greatly influenced by Freud's theories of psychoanalysis. Irrational association, spontaneous techniques and an elimination of premeditation to free the workings of the unconscious mind, as well as an interest in dreams, were the main motivations of its practitioners.

Movements in art since 1945

The postwar period has been characterized by extremely varied approaches to the problems of art.

Abstract Expressionism emerged in New York soon after World War II. It places emphasis on spontaneous personal expression, rejecting contemporary, social and aesthetic values. It was the first movement in the USA to develop independently of and actually influence Europe.

Action Painting was a technique used by some of the Abstract Expressionists. It involved spattering the canvas in a semi-random fashion, so recording the action of the painter at the moment of painting as well as his emotional state.

Conceptual Art grew partly out of Minimal Art as artists started to make works of a temporary character utilizing different types of process and system, e.g. inscribing imaginary geometric patterns on the landscape, and working with photographs and texts.

Environmental Art is an art movement in which the artist aims to create not just an object but an entire environment. In order to involve all the senses of the spectator it can include sight and sound effects combined with painted or sculptured work.

Kinetic Art is all art that incorporates movement – real or apparent – generated by motors, artificial light or optical illusion.

Minimal Art emerged in the mid-1960s from the rejection of the aesthetic qualities of art in favour of the physical reality of the art object. The material used is important, as are their strictly geometrical formats and placings within settings.

Neo-Expressionism is a mainly German movement of the 1980s. Paintings are executed with great vigour in styles. It marks a return to myths, religion and mysterious symbolism as subjects.

Op Art (optical art) is an abstract art form based on creating optical effects which appear to move on a flat surface. It reached its peak in the 1960s.

Pop Art was an almost simultaneous reaction against Abstract Expressionism in the UK and USA in the late 1950s. It uses the images of mass media, advertising and pop culture, presenting the common, everyday object as art.

Performance Art (also known as *Happenings*) began in the late 1950s, and involves the artist in directing and/or performing an entertainment (intended to be spontaneous) that involves a strong visual element and that may also include theatre, music, film, and the participation of the audience.

Photo-Realism is a mainly American movement, beginning in the late 1960s, in which the artist meticulously copies from a photograph.

MAJOR ARTISTS

Altdorfer, Albrecht (c. 1480–1538), German painter and engraver, distinguished by his development of the landscape genre: *The Battle of Alexander and Darius on the Issus* (1529).

Ando Hiroshige (1797–1858), Japanese painter and colour-print artist: *Fifty-three Stages of the Tokaido Highway* (1833).

Arp, Jean (Hans) (1887–1966), French Dadaist artist, celebrated for his rounded abstract sculptures.

Bacon, Francis (1909–92), Irish-born British painter, noted for the disturbing quality of his twisted figures: *Three Studies at the Base of a Crucifixion* (1944) and *Study after Velazquez*, a series of portraits of Pope Innocent X.

Balla, Giacomo (1871–1958), Italian Futurist painter and sculptor: the painting *Dynamism of a Dog on a Leash* (1912).

Beardsley, Aubrey (1872–98), English Symbolist artist and illustrator, noted for his decadent illustrations.

Beckman, Max (1884–1950), German Expressionist painter: *The Night* (1918–19).

Bellini, Giovanni (c. 1430–1516), member of a notable artistic early Renaissance Venetian family: the altarpieces of the Frari (1488), San Zaccaria (c. 1505) and other mythological scenes.

Bernini, Gianlorenzo (1598–1680), Italian High Baroque sculptor and painter: the sculptures *Apollo and Daphne* (1625) and *Ecstasy of Saint Theresa* (1645–52).

Beuys, Joseph (1921–86), influential German Performance artist: *Coyote* (1974), a week-long dialogue with a live coyote.

Boccioni, Umberto (1882–1916), Italian Futurist painter and sculptor: the sculpture *Unique Forms of Continuity in Space* (1913).

Bonnard, Pierre (1864–1947), French painter, noted for his middle-class interiors and nudes.

Bosch, Hieronymus (active 1480/1–1516), Flemish painter, celebrated for his fantastic and grotesque imagery: *Garden of Earthly Delights* (c. 1505–10).

Botticelli, Sandro (c. 1445–1510), early Renaissance Florentine painter: *Primavera* ('Spring'; 1477–78) and *Birth of Venus.*

Boucher, François (1703–70), French Rococo painter: *The Rising of the Sun, The Setting of the Sun* (1753), and *Reclining Girl* (1751), a famous female nude.

Boudin, Eugène (1824–98), French painter of seascapes and beach scenes: *Women on the Beach at Trouville* (1872).

Bouts, Dierick (active 1448–75), early Flemish painter, distinguished by his calm, reflective and elongated figures.

Brancusi, Constantin (1876–1957), highly influential Romanian-born French abstract sculptor, famous for his concentration of form and the qualities of his materials: *Endless Column* (1937).

Braque, Georges (1882–1963), French painter and co-founder of Cubism: *Grand Nu* ('Great Nude'; 1907–08) and the *Atelier* series (1948 onwards).

Bronzino, Agnolo (1507–72), Florentine Mannerist painter, well known for his portraits: *Venus, Cupid, Folly* and *Time.*

Brouwer, Adriaen (1605/6–38), Dutch painter specializing in scenes of peasant revelry: *The Smokers* (c. 1637).

Bruegel, Pieter (the Elder) (c. 1525–69), foremost of a Flemish family of painters: *Peasant Wedding Dance* (1566), a series of landscape paintings depicting the months of the year such as *Hunters in the Snow* (1565) and the proverb series including *The Blind Leading the Blind* (1568).

Burne-Jones, Edward (1833–98), English Symbolist painter, illustrator, and designer. Strongly influenced by the Pre-Raphaelites, he is noted for his ethereal aesthetic and dreamlike style.

Calder, Alexander (1898–1976), US Kinetic sculptor, best known for his metal mobiles.

Canaletto, Antonio (1697–1768), Venetian view painter of the period, noted for the topographical quality in his art.

Canova, Antonio (1757–1822), Italian Neo-Classical sculptor: *Daedulus and Icarus* (1779).

Caravaggio, Michelangelo Merisis da (1573–1610), early Italian Baroque painter notable for the dramatic use of light and shade: *The Beheading of St John the Baptist.*

Carra, Carlo (1881–1966), Italian Futurist painter.

Carracci, Annibale (1560–1609), member of a notable family of Italian painters: decoration of the gallery ceiling in the Farnese Palace, Rome.

Cassatt, Mary (1844–1926), US Impressionist painter, noted for her paintings of mothers and children and her graphics based on Japanese prints.

César (1921–), French sculptor, notable for his use of plastics and used materials: *The Yellow Buick* made from crushed car bodies.

Cézanne, Paul (1839–1906), French painter, briefly painted with the Impressionist group. Many of his works had a crucial influence on the Cubists.

Chagall, Marc (1887–1985), Russian-born French painter; although not a Surrealist his work has a dreamlike style with irrational juxtapositions: *I and the Village* (c. 1911).

Chirico, Giorgio de (1888–1928), Italian painter and forerunner of the Surrealists, notable for his haunting city-scapes.

Christo (1935–), Bulgarian-born Belgian artist, who has embarked on such projects as wrapping up sections of the Australian coastline in plastic.

Christus, Petrus (active 1444–72/3), Flemish painter: noted for the use of geometric perspective in *Lamentation* (c. 1448) and *St Eligius and Two Lovers* (1449).

Cimabue (active 1272–1302), Florentine painter who introduced more realistic painting: *The S. Trinità Madonna.*

Claude Lorraine (1600–82), French Classical landscape painter, notable for his rendering of light and atmosphere in his paintings.

Constable, John (1776–1837), English Romantic landscape painter: *The Hay Wain* (1821).

Corot, Camille (1796–1875), French landscape and figure painter, an important precursor of the Impressionists: *The Studio* (1870), *Ponte de Mantes* (1870), and *Sens Cathedral* (1874).

Correggio, Antonio (c. 1495–1534), influential Italian High Renaissance painter: *Jupiter and Io*.

Cortona, Pietro da (1596–1669), Italian Baroque painter: *Allegory of Divine Providence and Barberini Power* (1633–39), a ceiling fresco.

Courbet, Gustav (1819–77), French painter and foremost Realist artist: *The Peasants of Flagey*, *The Stonebreakers* and *A Burial at Ornans*.

Cuyp, Aelbert (1620–91), Dutch landscape painter, noted for his views of rivers and towns in evening and morning light: *View of the Dordrecht*.

Dali, Salvador (1904–89), Spanish Surrealist artist, famous for his hallucinatory paintings (and Surrealist film-making): *The Persistence of Memory* (1931).

Daubigny, Charles-François (1817–78), French landscape painter of the Barbizon school.

Daumier, Honoré (1808–79), French caricaturist, whose works contain bitter satires on political and social subjects.

David, Jacques-Louis (1748–1825), French Neo-Classical painter: *Death of Marat* (1793), *View of the Luxembourg Gardens* (1794), and *Mme de Verninac* (1799).

Degas, Edgar (1834–1917), French Impressionist painter and sculptor, whose favourite subjects were dancers and race horses: the bronze *The Little Dancer of Fourteen* (1880–81), *The Rehearsal* (1882), and *Two Laundresses* (1882).

Delacroix, Eugène (1798–1863), French Romantic painter: *The Massacre at Chios* (1823) and *The Death of Sardanapalus* (1827).

Delaunay, Robert (1885–1941), French painter, influenced by Cubism: *Circular Forms* (from 1912).

Derain, André (1880–1954), French painter, one of the founders of Fauvism.

de Stäel, Nicolas (1914–55), French-Russian abstract painter, whose works are characterized by broad patches of paint: *The Roofs* (1952).

Domenichino (1581–1641), Bolognese painter, noted for his landscapes.

Donatello (c. 1386–1466), highly influential early Renaissance Florentine sculptor: equestrian statue of *Gattemalata* (1443–47) and the high altar for the church of St Anthony.

Duccio di Buoninsegna (active 1278–1319), Sienese painter; influential in his introduction of two-dimensional decorative surface art in Siena.

Duchamp, Marcel (1887–1968), highly influential French Dadaist artist: *The Bride Stripped Bare by her Bachelors, Even* (1915–23).

Dufy, Raoul (1877–1953), French painter. Briefly connected with the Fauves but celebrated for his colourful scenes of racecourses and the seaside.

Dürer, Albrecht (1471–1528), German painter, engraver and theoretician: *Knight, Death and the Devil*, *St Jerome in his Cell*, and *Melancholia*.

Eakins, Thomas (1844–1916), US Realist painter: *The Biglen Brothers Racing* (1873) and *The Writing Master* (1881).

Ensor, James (1860–1949), Belgian painter, a major influence on Expressionism and Surrealism: *Entry of Christ into Brussels* (1880).

Epstein, Jacob (1880–1959), US-born English sculptor. Early Vorticist works include *The Rock-Drill* (1913–14); later work was more representational.

Ernst, Max (1891–1976), German Dadaist painter, sculptor and collagist, initially a Dadaist, then a Surrealist: *Here Everything is Still Floating* (1920).

Fra Angelico (c. 1399–1455), early Renaissance Florentine religious painter: cycle of frescos in San Marco, Florence.

Fra Bartolommeo (c. 1474–c. 1517), Florentine High Renaissance painter: *Last Judgement* in the Santa Maria Nuova.

Francesca, Piero della (c. 1420–92), early Renaissance Italian painter: *The Flagellation of Christ* (c. 1456) and the cycle *The Story of the True Cross* at the Church of San Francesco, Arezzo (1452–66).

Fragonard, Jean-Honoré (1732–1806), French Rococo painter: four *Progress of Love* paintings (1771–73) and *The Swing* (1769).

Frink, Elisabeth (1930–93), English sculptor who was best known for her monumental figurative bronzes.

Friedrich, Caspar David (1774–1840), German Romantic landscape painter, noted for his evocative scenes of mountain peaks and moonlit shores.

Frith, William Powell (1819–1909), English narrative painter: *Derby Day* (1858) and *The Railway Station* (1862).

Fuseli, Henry (1741–1825), Swiss Romantic painter living in England, notable for his explorations of the darker side of human nature: *The Nightmare* (1782).

Gabo, Naum (1890–1977), Russian sculptor and co-founder of Constructivism.

Gainsborough, Thomas (1727–88), English portrait and landscape painter: *Mr and Mrs Andrews* (c.1750), *The Blue Boy* (c. 1770), and *The Harvest Wagon* (c. 1770).

Gaudier-Brzeska, Henri (1891–1915), influential French Vorticist sculptor.

Gauguin, Paul (1848–1903), French painter, sculptor and printmaker, celebrated for his brightly coloured, mystical paintings of Brittany and the South Seas: *Where Do We Come From? What Are We? Where Are We Going?* (1897).

Gentile da Fabriano (c. 1370–1427), Italian painter of the International Gothic style: *Adoration of the Magi* (1423).

Géricault, Théodore (1791–1824), French Romantic painter and one of the founders of Romanticism: *Charging Chasseur* and *The Raft of the Medusa* (1819).

Ghiberti, Lorenzo (1378–1455), early Renaissance Florentine sculptor and goldsmith: bronze doors for the Florence Baptistery, the second set, so-called 'Gates of Paradise', includes highly sophisticated representations of space and form.

Giambologna (1529–1608), Flemish Mannerist sculptor: the influential sculpture *The Rape of the Sabines* (1579–83).

Giacometti, Alberto (1901–66), Swiss sculptor, well known for his elongated bronze human figures.

Gilbert and George (Gilbert Proesch, 1943– , and George Passmore, 1942–), English avant-garde artists involved in various art forms, including Performance Art; noted for the presentation of themselves as works of art.

Giorgione (c. 1476/8–1510), Venetian painter who introduced pastoral subjects to paintings.

Giotto di Bondone (c. 1267–1337), influential Florentine painter, who introduced a new naturalism: *Ognissanti Madonna* (c. 1310–15).

Goes, Hugo van der (active 1467–82), Flemish painter: Portinari altarpiece (c. 1474–76) and Monforte altarpiece (c. 1472).

Goncharova, Natalia (1881–1962), Russian Rayonist painter.

Goujon, Jean (active 1540–62), French Mannerist sculptor and architect: *Fountain of the Innocents* (1547–49) and the *Tribune of Caryatids*.

Goya y Lucientes, Francisco de (1746–1848), Spanish Romantic painter and etcher: *Maja Nude* and *Maja Clothed* (1797–1800), *The Third of May* (1814), and *The Disasters of War* (etchings, 1810–20).

Greco, El (Domenikos Theotocopoulos; 1541–1614), Greek Mannerist painter and sculptor (working in Spain): *The Burial of Count Orgaz* (1586) and *Christ Stripped of his Garments* (1577–79).

Grien, Hans Baldung (1484/5–1545), German religious and mythological painter: *Death and the Maiden*.

Gris, Juan (1887–1955), Spanish painter, noted for his development of the Cubist style: *Homage to Picasso* (1911–12).

Grosz, George (1893–1959), German illustrator, painter and satirical caricaturist.

Grünewal, Mathias (c. 1470–1528), German religious painter: crucifixion of Christ on the Isenheim altarpiece.

Guardi, Francesco (1712–93), member of a family of notable Venetian painters; celebrated for his view paintings and architectural scenes.

Gu Kaizhi (Ku K'ai-Chih; c. 345–405), a leading Chinese painter, considered to be the founder of landscape painting.

Hals, Frans (1580/85–1666), Dutch genre and portrait painter: *The Merry Drinker*, *The Laughing Cavalier*, *The Governors of the Almshouse*, and *Lady Regents of the Almshouse*.

Hamilton, Richard (1922–), English Pop artist, his work reflects his interest in marketing styles: *$he* (1958–61).

Hausmann, Raoul (1886–1971), Austrian Dadaist, well known for his photomontages.

Heartfield, John (Helmut Herzfelde; 1891–1968), German artist, notable for his political photomontages: *Hurrah, the Butter is Finished* (1935).

Heckel, Erich (1883–1970), German Expressionist painter, graphic artist and co-founder of *Die Brücke*.

Hepworth, Barbara (1903–75), English abstract sculptress.

Hobbema, Meindert (1638–1709), Dutch landscape painter: *Avenue at Middelharnis* (1689).

Hockney, David (1937–), English painter and draughtsman, initially prominent in Pop Art, but notable for his innovations in many styles: *A Bigger Splash*.

Holbein, Hans (the Younger) (1497/8–1543), German portrait and religious painter: *Dead Christ* (1521) and *Erasmus* (1517).

Holman Hunt, William (1827–1910), English painter and one of the founders of the Pre-Raphaelite Brotherhood, noted for the detail and symbolism in his paintings: *The Awakening Conscience* (1853–54).

Homer, Winslow (1836–1910), US landscape, seascape and genre painter: *The Northeaster*, *Cannon Rock* (1895), and *Saguenay River* (1899).

Honthorst, Gerard von (1590–1656), Dutch painter specializing in portraits and genre painting: *The Merry Fiddler* (1623).

Hooch, Pieter de (1629–84), Dutch genre painter celebrated for his use of light in garden and courtyard scenes: *Courtyard in Delft* (1658).

Hui Zong (1082–1135), a Chinese emperor and major painter of the flower-and-bird category of painting.

Huang Gong-Wang (1269–1354), major Chinese landscape painter of his time, celebrated for the introduction of dry ink and slanting brush technique.

Ingres, Jean Auguste Dominique (1780–1867), French Neo-Classical painter: known for his *Odalisque* series of female nudes.

Jawlensky, Alexej (1864–1941), Russian painter loosely associated with *Der Blaue Reiter*: *Head of a Young Girl* and *Night* (1933).

Johns, Jasper (1930–), US painter, printmaker and sculptor, best known as the founder of Pop Art: *Target* and *Flags* paintings.

Judd, Donald (1928–), US Minimalist sculptor. His work concentrates on rows of geometric units (often boxes).

Kalf, Willem (1619–93), Dutch still-life painter: *Still Life with a Nautilus Cup* (1642–46).

Kandinsky, Wassily (1866–1944), Russian-born painter, pioneer of abstract art and member of *Der Blaue Reiter*.

Katsushika Hokusai (1760–1849), Japanese painter, draughtsman and wood engraver (a major *Ukiyo-e* print designer): *Mangwa* (1814–78) and *Views of Mt Fuji*.

Kiefer, Anselm (1945–), German Neo-Expressionist painter, his work concentrates on German history.

Kirchner, Ernst Ludwig (1880–1938), German Expressionist painter, graphic artist and co-founder of *Die Brücke*.

Kitagawa Utamaro (1753–1806), Japanese colour-print artist (*Ukiyo-e* school): *Insects* (1788).

Klee, Paul (1879–1940), Swiss painter, graphic artist and an influential 20th-century artist. His works range from Symbolist to Abstract.

Klimt, Gustave (1863–1918), Austrian painter, and founder of the Vienna Secession, distinguished by his highly decorative paintings: *The Kiss* (1908).

Kline, Franz (1910–62), US abstract Expressionist painter, distinguished by his black strokes on white backgrounds.

Kneller, Godfrey (1646–1723), German-born British portrait painter.

Kokoschka, Oskar (1886–1980), Austrian Expressionist painter: *The Tempest* (1914).

Kooning, Willem de (1904–), US abstract Expressionist: *Woman* series.

Léger, Fernand (1881–1955), French painter, famous for his distinctive semi-abstract monumental style, often depicting people and machines.

Lely, Peter (Pieter van der Faes; 1618–80), Dutch Baroque portrait painter.

Le Nain, a family of French painters – the attribution of many of the paintings of the brothers Antoine (1588–1648), Louis (1593–1648), and Mathieu (1607–77) is not clear.

Leonardo da Vinci (1452–1519), one of the greatest Italian painters and sculptors (also architect, musician, engineer, and scientist): the unfinished *Adoration of the Magi*, *Madonna of the Rocks* (two versions: 1483–c. 1486 and 1483–1508), *The Last Supper* (c. 1495–98), and *Mona Lisa* (c. 1503).

Lewis, Wyndham (1882–1957), Canadian-born British painter, writer and leader of the Vorticists: *Workshop* (1914).

LeWitt, Sol (1928–), US Minimalist sculptor, noted for his displays of white and black cubes.

Leyden, Lucas van (c. 1489–1533), Dutch painter and engraver of historical and domestic scenes: *Last Judgement* (1526–27).

Lichtenstein, Roy (1923–), US Pop artist, best known for his enlarged paintings of comic strip images: *Whaam!* (1963).

Liebermann, Max (1847–1935), German painter and founder of the Berlin Secession.

Limbourg, Herman (d. c. 1416), Franco-Flemish manuscript illuminator: *Très Riches Heures*.

Limbourg, Jean (d. c. 1416), Franco-Flemish manuscript illuminator: *Très Riches Heures*.

Limbourg, Paul (d. c. 1416), Franco-Flemish manuscript illuminator: *Très Riches Heures*.

Lippi, Fra Filippo (c. 1406–69), early Renaissance Florentine painter: fresco paintings of the lives of St Stephen and St John the Baptist, Prato Cathedral (1452–65).

Lorenzetti, Ambrogio (active c. 1319–48), Sienese sculptor and painter known for his early realistic landscapes.

Lorenzetti, Pietro (active c. 1319–48), Sienese sculptor and painter known for his *Descent from the Cross*.

Lorraine, Claude see Claude.

Macke, Auguste (1887–1914), German painter, founder of *Der Blaue Reiter*.

Madox Brown, Ford (1821–93), English painter, whose style was similar to that of the Pre-Raphaelites: his social beliefs were reflected in his famous painting *Work* (1852–65).

Magritte, René (1898–1967), Belgian Surrealist, famous for his conventional paintings made bizarre by the unexpected juxtaposition of objects: *The Key of Dreams* (1930) and *Time Transfixed* (1938).

Malevich, Kasimir (1878–1935), Russian painter, founder of Suprematism: *White on White* series (c. 1918).

Manet, Edouard (1832–83), French painter, considered the father of modern painting: *Déjeuner sur l'herbe* ('Picnic on the grass'; 1863) and *Olympia* (1863).

Mantegna, Andrea (c. 1431–1506), northern Italian early Renaissance painter, celebrated for his perfectionist work on perspective.

Marc, Franz (1880–1916), German Expressionist painter, member of *Der Blaue Reiter*: *The Blue Horse* (1911) and *Fighting Forms* (1913).

Marquet, Albert (1875–1947), French painter, noted for his bright Fauve colours in his early paintings.

Martin, John (1789–1854), English painter and engraver, noted for his sensationalist apocalyptic scenes: *The Deluge* (1834).

Masaccio (1401–c. 1428), influential early Renaissance Florentine painter: *Trinity* fresco (1428), in Santa Maria Novella, Florence, and the fresco paintings in the Brancacci Chapel, Florence (c. 1425–28).

Masson, André (1896–1987), French Surrealist painter, notable for his spontaneous drawings undertaken while in a trance.

Massys, Quentin (1464/5–1530), Flemish painter: portrait of *Erasmus* (1517).

Matisse, Henri (1869–1954), influential 20th-century artist and founder of Fauvism: *Dance* and *Music* (1909–10), and the series of *Odalisques*.

Memling, Hans (c. 1435–94), German-born Flemish painter known for his religious subjects and portraits: *Adoration of the Magi* (1479).

Michelangelo Buonarroti (1475–1564), foremost Italian sculptor, painter, and architect: the sculpture *David* (1501–4), the ceiling of the Sistine Chapel (1508–12), statues *Moses and the Slaves* (1513–16) and the fresco *Last Judgement* (Sistine Chapel; 1536–41).

Millais, Sir John Everett (1829–96), English portrait, genre, landscape and history painter and co-founder of the Pre-Raphaelite Brotherhood. Best-known for *Bubbles* (1886), which was subsequently used in a soap advertisement.

Millet, Jean-François (1814–75), French Realist painter, celebrated for his dignified depiction of French peasants: *The Gleaners* (1857) and *The Angelus* (1859).

Miró, Joan (1893–1983), Spanish Surrealist painter: best known for his *Still Life with an Old Shoe* and *Dog Barking at the Moon.*

Modigliani, Amedeo (1884–1920), Italian painter and sculptor, famous for his elongated figures and erotic nudes: *Reclining Nude* (c. 1919).

Monaco, Lorenzo (c. 1370/2–1422/5), Sienese International Gothic painter and miniaturist: *Adoration* (c. 1424).

Mondrian, Piet (1872–1944), Dutch painter who developed from Symbolism to the pure abstraction of De Stijl: *Composition with Red, Yellow and Blue* (1939–42).

Monet, Claude (1840–1926), French Impressionist painter, particularly of landscapes: *Women in the Garden* (1867) and the series *Waterlilies* (1899–1926).

Moore, Henry (1898–1986), English sculptor, draughtsman and graphic artist, well known for his rounded forms: *Two Forms* (1934) and *Reclining Figure* (1938).

Moreau, Gustave (1826–98), French painter and one of the leading Symbolists, noted for his *femme fatale* paintings: *The Apparition* (1876) and *Sâlomé Dancing* (1876).

Morisot, Berthe (1841–95), French painter notable for her paintings of women and children.

Motherwell, Robert (1915–), US abstract Expressionist painter, also notable for his collages.

Munch, Edvard (1863–1944), Norwegian painter, a forerunner of Expressionism: *The Scream* (1893).

Murillo, Bartolome Esteban (1618–82), Spanish painter who is best known for his sentimental paintings of the Immaculate Conception.

Nash, Paul (1889–1946), English painter, whose visionary landscapes and war paintings show Surrealist influences.

Newman, Barnett (1905–70), US abstract Expressionist painter, noted for his large, coloured canvases broken by 'zips' (bands) of colour.

Nicholson, Ben (1894–1982), English abstract painter, some of whose works involve carved relief.

Nolde, Emil (1867–1956), German Expressionist and member of *Die Brücke*, well known for his landscapes and religious pictures.

Palmer, Samuel (1805–81), English Romantic painter and etcher of pastoral scenes.

Parmigianino (1503–40), Italian Mannerist painter and etcher: *The Vision of St Jerome* and *Madonna of the Long Neck* (c. 1535).

Patenir, Joachim (c. 1480–1524), Flemish landscape and religious painter: *Flight into Egypt.*

Pevsner, Antoine (1886–1962), Russian-born French painter, abstract sculptor and co-founder of Constructivism.

Picabia, Francis (1879–1953), French painter of the Dada school: *I see again in memory my dear Udnie* (1914).

Picasso, Pablo (1881–1973), Spanish painter, sculptor, graphic artist, founder of Cubism and the most outstanding artist of the 20th century: *The Old Guitarist* (1904), the Cubist *Les Demoiselles d'Avignon* (1907), and *Guernica* (1937).

Pisanello, Antonio (c. 1395–1455/6), Veronese painter: *St George and the Princess* and *Vision of St Eustace* (1435–38).

Pisano, Giovanni (active 1265–1314), Pisan sculptor: the pulpit in S Andrea, Pistoia (1301), particularly the panel of the *Massacre of the Innocents.*

Pissarro, Camille (1831–1903), French Impressionist painter, briefly flirted with pointillism during the 1880s.

Pollock, Jackson (1912–56), US abstract Expressionist painter, a notable exponent of Action Painting.

Pontormo, Jacopo da (1494–1556), Florentine painter, one of the creators of Mannerism: *Deposition* (c. 1526).

Poussin, Nicolas (1594–1665), French Classical painter, notable for the mathematical precision of his landscapes: *Landscape with Diogenes.*

Raphael (1483–1520), highly successful Italian painter: wall paintings in the Vatican, including *School of Athens, Triumph of Religion, The Miracle of Bolsena* and *The Deliverance of St Peter.*

Rauschenberg, Robert (1925–), US artist best known for his combination of Pop Art and Abstract Expressionism: *Combine* paintings and *Monogram* (1959).

Ray, Man (Emanuel Rabinovitch; 1890–1976), US painter, photographer and film-maker, involved both with Dada and Surrealism, and famous for his technical experimentation (see also Photography).

Redon, Odilon (1840–1916), French Symbolist painter and lithographer: *The Cyclops* (1898).

Rembrandt van Rijn (1606–69), Dutch painter, etcher and draughtsman, particularly celebrated for his portraits: *The Anatomy Lesson* (1632), *The Night Watch* (1642), and his series of self-portraits.

Reni, Guido (1575–1642), Italian Classical painter: ceiling fresco *Aurora* (1613).

Renoir, Auguste (1841–1919), French Impressionist painter: *Umbrellas* (1883), *The Bathers* (1884–87), and *The Theatre Box* (1874).

Reynolds, Joshua (1723–92), English portrait painter: *Mrs Siddons as the Tragic Muse* (1784).

Riley, Bridget (1931–), foremost English Op artist: *Fall* (1963).

Romano, Giulio (1492–1546), Italian painter, architect, decorator and one of the founders of Mannerism: the decoration of the Palazzo del Tè.

Romney, George (1734–1802), English portrait painter.

Rosa, Salvator (1615–73), Italian Baroque painter and etcher noted for his tempestuous landscapes.

Rossetti, Dante Gabriel (1828–82), English painter, poet and co-founder of the Pre-Raphaelite Brotherhood. He later worked in watercolours before returning to oils.

Rothko, Mark (1903–70), US abstract Expressionist, noted for his vast expanses of colour that fill the canvas.

Rouault, George (1871–1958), French painter, noted for his expressionist religious work.

Rousseau, Henri (1844–1910), French painter, noted for his naive, stylized jungle paintings (1900–10).

Rousseau, Théodore (1812–67), French landscape painter of the Barbizon School: *Descent of the Cattle* (1835).

Rubens, Peter Paul (1577–1640), foremost Flemish painter, celebrated for the epic grandeur of his work: *The Raising of the Cross* (1610–11) and *Descent from the Cross* (1611–14; Antwerp Cathedral).

Ruisdael, Jacob van (1628/9–82), Dutch landscape painter and etcher, distinguished by his dramatic scenes: *Jewish Cemetery* (c. 1660).

Saenredam, Pieter (1597–1665), Dutch painter of church interiors: *View in the Nieuwe Kert at Haarlem* (1652).

Sarto, Andrea del (1486–1530), Italian High Renaissance painter of frescos and altarpieces: *The Madonna of the Harpies* (1517).

Schiele, Egon (1890–1918), Austrian Expressionist draughtsman and painter, famous for his explicit and angular nudes.

Schongauer, Martin (active 1469–91), early German engraver: celebrated for his subtle description of light and texture.

Schwitters, Kurt (1887–1948), German Dadaist painter and sculptor, famous for his Merz pieces (haphazard combinations of materials).

Seurat, Georges (1859–91), French painter, founder and leading exponent of Neo-Impressionism: *Bathers at Asnières* (1884).

Sickert, Walter (1860–1942), English painter who concentrated on paintings of lower-class London life: *Ennui* (c. 1913).

Signac, Paul (1863–1935), French Neo-Impressionist painter, theoretician of Neo-Impressionism.

Sisley, Alfred (1839–99), French Impressionist painter born of English parents, well known for his landscapes.

Sluter, Claus (active c. 1380–d. 1405/6), Flemish International Gothic sculptor: monumental figures at Chartreuse de Champmol, Dijon (1390s–1403).

Steen, Jan (1626–79), prolific Dutch genre painter, notable for his scenes of merry-making: *St Nicholas' Feast.*

Stubbs, George (1724–1806), English painter known for his portraits of horses.

Sutherland, Graham (1903–80), English painter whose early landscapes had a dream-like Surreal quality; his later works include well-known portraits.

Suzuki Harunobu (1725–70), Japanese colour-print artist.

Teniers, Daniel (the Younger) (1610–90), a member of a family of Flemish painters: known for his scenes of peasant life.

Terborch, Gerard (1617–81), Dutch portrait and genre painter of genteel interiors: *Parental Admonition* (c. 1654/55).

Terbrugghen, Hendrick (1588–1629), Dutch painter specializing in genre painting: *The Flute Player* (1621).

Tiepolo, Giambattista (1696–1770), Italian Rococo painter: noted for the ceiling paintings and frescos in the Labia Palace and Palacio Real, Madrid.

Tinguely, Jean (1925–91), Swiss Kinetic artist, celebrated for his machines: *Homage to New York* (1960), a machine from assorted junk materials that blew itself up before an audience.

Tintoretto, Jacopo (1518–94), Venetian Mannerist painter: *Last Judgement.*

Titian (Tiziano Vecellio; c. 1487/90–1576), Venetian Renaissance painter, notable for his dream-like pastorals, colour, and free handling of paint: *Venus and Adonis* (1554) and the altarpiece of the *Assumption of the Virgin* (Church of Santa Maria Gloriosa dei Frari, Venice).

Toshusai Sharaku (d. 1801), Japanese *Ukiyo-e* printer. Unpopular in his day, but his work is now highly prized in the West.

Toulouse-Lautrec, Henri de (1864–1901), French painter and draughtsman, famous for his lithographs and posters of dance halls and cabarets: *Le Moulin Rouge* (1891).

Turner, Joseph Mallord William (1775–1851), foremost English Romantic landscape painter: *The Fighting Téméraire* (1838), and *Rain, Steam and Speed* (1844).

Uccello, Paolo (c. 1397–1475), early Renaissance Florentine painter: fresco *Deluge* and the panels depicting the *Rout of Romano*, which experiment with perspectives.

van Dongen, Kees (1877–1968), Dutch painter. His work developed along Fauvist lines, but his later works were principally of Parisian society.

van Dyck, Anthony (1599–1641), Flemish painter and etcher, known for his elegant portraits.

van Eyck, Hubert (active 1422–41), Flemish painter (brother of Jan).

van Eyck, Jan (active 1422–41), Flemish painter, celebrated for the realistic detail of his portraits: the Ghent altarpiece (1432; in collaboration with his brother Hubert).

van Gogh, Vincent (1853–90), Dutch painter, a major influence on 20th-century art: *The Potato Eaters*

THE WORLD'S MOST VALUABLE PAINTINGS AT AUCTION

The following are the highest prices paid at auction (up to 1 January 1995) for works of art by the following major artists. More than one work by several of the artists listed below have reached in excess of £10,000,000: at least four works by van Gogh and five works by Picasso have passed this figure.

van Gogh (see pp. 396–97): £44,378,696 for *Portrait du Dr. Gachet* at Christie's, New York (May 1990).

Renoir (see p. 395): £42,011,832 for *Au Moulin de la Galette* at Sotheby's, New York (May 1990).

Picasso (see p. 395): £33,123,028 for *Les noces de Pierrette* at Binoche and Godeau, Paris (Nov 1989).

Cézanne (see p. 391): £16,993,464 for *Nature morte - les grosses pommes* at Sotheby's, New York (May 1993).

Manet (see p. 394): £15,483,872 for *La rue Mosnier aux drapeaux* at Christie's, New York (Nov 1989).

Gauguin (see p. 392): £13,496,934 for *Mata Mua, in olden times* at Sotheby's, New York (May 1989).

Monet (see p. 395): £13,000,000 for *Dans la prairie* at Sotheby's, London (Jun 1988).

Kooning (see p. 394): £11,898,735 for *Interchange* at Sotheby's, New York (Nov 1989).

Kandinsky (see p. 393): £11,242,604 for *Fugue* at Sotheby's, New York (May 1990).

Constable (see p. 392): £9,800,000 for *The lock* at Sotheby's, London (Nov 1990).

Canaletto (see p. 391): £9,200,000 for *The Old Horse Guards, London, from St James's Park, with figures parading* at Christie's, London (Apr 1992).

Matisse (see p. 394): £8,741,723 for *Harmonie jaune* at Christie's, New York (Nov 1992).

Toulouse-Lautrec (see p. 396): £6,982,249 for *Fille à la fourrure, Mademoiselle Jeanne Fontaine* at Christie's, New York (May 1990).

Titian (see p. 396): £6,800,000 for *Venus and Adonis* at Christie's, London (Dec 1991).

Turner (see p. 396): £6,700,000 for *Seascape, Folkestone* at Sotheby's, London (Jul 1984).

Rembrandt (see p. 395): £6,600,000 for *Portrait of a girl, wearing a gold-trimmed cloak* at Sotheby's, London (Dec 1986).

Goya (see p. 393): £4,500,000 for *Bullfight: Suerte de Varas* at Sotheby's, London (Dec 1992).

Leonardo da Vinci (see p. 394): £3,364,879 for *Etude de draperie: personnage agenouille, tourne vers la gauche* at Sotheby's, Monaco (Dec 1989).

Rubens (see p. 396): £3,000,000 for *Forest at dawn with deer hunt* at Christie's, London (Dec 1989).

Velásquez (see p. 396): £2,310,000 for *Portrait of Juan de Pareja* at Christie's, London (Nov 1970).

Warhol (see p. 397): £2,251,656 for *Marilyn X* at Sotheby's, New York (Nov 1992).

(1885), *Les Souliers, A Cornfield of Cypresses, The Yellow Chair* and *Sunflowers* (1888–89).

Vasarély, Victor (1908–), Hungarian-born French painter: considered the pioneer of Op art, he is well known for his grid-like compositions.

Velásquez, Diego (1599–1660), Spanish painter: *Las Meninas* (1656), *Pope Innocent X* (1650), and *The Surrender of Breda* (1634–35).

Vermeer, Jan (1632–75), Dutch genre painter noted for his domestic interiors with subtle lighting and geometrical shapes: *Allegory of the Faith* (1669–70), *Allegory of Painting* (c. 1665), and *Girl with a Pearl Earring.*

Veronese, Paolo (1528–88), Venetian painter: frescos in the Villa Maser near Treviso, a series of religious feast scenes, including *Marriage at Cana* (1562) and *The Feast in the House of Levi* (1573).

Vlaminck, Maurice de (1876–1958), French Fauvist painter: *The Bridge at Chatou* (1906).

Vuillard, Edouard (1868–1940), French painter, noted for his domestic paintings: *Mother and Sister of the Artist* (c. 1893).

Warhol, Andy (1928–87), US painter and graphic designer, celebrated as one of the foremost Pop artists: prints of Campbell soup cans, Coca-cola bottles and Marilyn Monroe.

Watteau, Antoine (1684–1721), French Rococo painter who introduced romantic figures in a park or garden setting to the Rococo style: *Embarkation for Cythera* (1717).

Weyden, Rogier van der (c.1399–1464), influential Flemish painter: *The Deposition* (pre-1443) and the altarpiece of the *Last Judgement* (c. 1450).

Whistler, James McNeill (1834–1903), US painter and graphic artist, who worked in England. Briefly with the Realist school, his later, more Impressionist work became abstract: *Nocturne* series.

Winterhalter, Franz Xavier (1805–73), German portrait painter who enjoyed the patronage of European royalty.

Zurbaran, Francisco de (1598–1664), Spanish painter whose religious works are characterized by a powerful but austere style.

Photography

When Louis Daguerre announced his discovery of a process for making photographic images (or *daguerreotypes*) in 1839, the French painter Paul Delaroche declared, 'From today painting is dead!' Delaroche voiced the expectations of many: that the camera's ability to capture in an instant every detail of the real world would spell the end of painting and drawing, and that photography was the art form of the future.

An equally vocal opposing camp claimed that photography was a science, not an art – a purely mechanical process that could never rival in feeling or in expression the sensitive hand of the painter or draughtsman. (See Photography as art; below.)

Since 1839, photography has assumed a vast range of forms and uses – in science and medicine, in geographic exploration, anthropology, journalism and advertising – but its close relationship with art has continued throughout.

PHOTOGRAPHY: the technology

A *camera* is essentially a box that is lightproof except where the optical component, the *lens,* projects the image onto a sheet of material (*film*) inside the camera.

Film is coated with an emulsion whose chemical properties are changed by exposure to light, and which – after appropriate processing – can reproduce the image. The *emulsion* is made of silver halide grains (often silver bromide or iodide), suspended in gelatin.

After exposure to light and chemical processing (*development*), the grains become black metallic silver. When the unexposed silver halide in the parts wholly or partially untouched by light is dissolved away, the picture becomes permanent, or *fixed.* It is, however, a reversed, or *negative,* image, with the original light areas reproduced as dark areas, and vice versa. The conversion of the negative to a true, or positive, picture was a problem until a negative/positive technique was evolved, which brought the bonus that an unlimited number of positive prints could be produced from a single negative.

Flashbulbs were introduced in 1925 to allow photographs to be taken in circumstances in which the light would not otherwise have been adequate. The modern electronic, or speed, flash was introduced in 1940.

The first successful *colour film,* Kodakchrome, was introduced in 1935. This utilized three emulsion layers of differing colour response and was introduced for the production of postive transparencies.

The Polaroid-Land 'instant picture' camera (popularly known as the *Polaroid*) was first demonstrated in 1947. Processing agents were incorporated in the film and activated within the camera after exposure.

'Instant print' colour films were introduced in 1963 and in 1982 Polaroid introduced still-transparency films that can processed rapidly outside the camera.

The first commercial *video camera,* the Sony Mavica, was demonstrated in 1981.

PHOTOGRAPHY AS ART

One of photography's first uses was as an aid to artists: painters accustomed to painting from life found photographs an invaluable source of reference for detail and composition. Many early photographers attempted to gain status and approval by self-consciously adopting the high moral themes – and even copying the forms of – 19th-century painters; others favoured the deep tones and soft focus that suggested the delicate sweep of brushstrokes. Despite this, and with gradual improvements in photographic technology, photographers came to respect the photograph for its unique immediacy, its ability to capture a real sense of life.

Photography began to gain new status as an independent medium in the early-20th century. Early modernist photographers advocated 'pure' photograph, with aesthetic value beyond its descriptive or utilitarian function.

Many photographers now regarded as great masters would never have regarded themselves as artists at all, but they detected surreal qualities in everyday life. They documented the life they saw around them, and so fit into a broad documentary approach that encompasses a vast span of attitudes and subject matter.

Photographers continued to innovate and to find new ground. Photomontage – the technique of combining several photographs into one photograph – became popular, while some photographers experimented with new 'objectivity' and Pop Art. Since the 1950s photography and art have become more closely aligned. At the same time in the USA, a new, seemingly informal approach to urban or 'street' photography evolved. As photography has become ubiquitous in recent years, so its audience is now increasingly sophisticated in its reception of photographic images and less inclined to accept simple notions of photographic objectivity or 'truth'.

FAMOUS PHOTOGRAPHERS AND PHOTOGRAPHIC PIONEERS

Arbus, Diane (1923–71), US photographer, well-known for her intense portraits of American social outcasts.

Atget, Eugene (1857–1927), French photographer, recording the streets and scenes of old Paris; his unusual images of the commonplace inspired the Surrealists.

Brandt, Bill (1904–83), English photographer who mixed grim realism with the surreal, creating an evocative record of the British social scene.

Brassai (Gyula Halasz; 1899–1984), Hungarian-born French photographer. His pictures of bohemian Paris and his eye for the bizarre and the taboo was much appreciated by the Surrealists.

Cameron, Julia Margaret (1815–79), British photographer; pioneer of portrait photography.

Cartier-Bresson, Henri (1908–), French photographer; combined an artist's genius for perfect composition with a photojournalist's insistence on capturing the 'decisive moment'.

Daguerre, Louis-Jacques (1789–1851), French painter and physicist who produced the first successful silver image on copper plate (1835). He discovered that there was a second ('latent') image that could be developed with mercury powder. In 1837 Daguerre made permanent pictures using a salt 'fixer'. Positive and permanent, his Daguerreotype was the first popular photographic system.

Eastman, George (1854–1932), US manufacturer who introduced the Kodak camera, a roll-film box camera, which brought photography to the masses.

Evans, Walker (1903–75), US photographer; produced a powerful record of the faces, homes and lives of America's 1930s rural poor.

Fenton, Roger (1819–69), English pioneer war photographer, noted for his Crimean War pictures.

Fox Talbot, William Henry (1800–77), English chemist, linguist and photographer who in 1839 invented the photographic negative. In 1841 he patented his 'Calotype' process, using a paper-base negative image from which unlimited numbers of positive prints could be made. The use of gallic acid reduced his average exposure time to five minutes. In 1851 he took the first high-speed flash photograph, using the spark discharge of a battery. Fox Talbot was reluctant to share his knowledge. However, in 1854 he lost his legal claim to sole rights to the wet-plate process, after which photography progressed rapidly.

Heartfield, John (1891–1968), German pioneer of the photomontage. (See also Famous Artists.)

Hine, Lewis (1874–1940), US photographer, noted for his campaigning pictures of New York's poor and immigrant population from the turn of the century.

Kertesz, Andre (1894–1985), Hungarian-born US photographer, noted for his pioneering use of the small hand-held camera, the well-observed social scene, the surreal figure study, still life, and later the fashion image.

Le Gray, Gustave (1820–68), French inventor who, in 1851, introduced the waxed-paper process, which produced a negative almost as good as a glass plate.

Lumière, Auguste (1862–1954), French inventor and photographic pioneer; brother of Louis (see below).

Lumière, Louis (1864–1948), French inventor and photographic pioneer; brother of Auguste (see above). (In 1895, the Lumière brothers introduced a cinematograph for moving pictures.) In 1904, they marketed colour plates with an outer coating of green, red and blue starch grains. The developed image was re-exposed and developed ('reversed') to produce a positive colour transparency.

Maddox, Richard (1816–1902), English photographic pioneer who, in 1871, devised a method of producing dry photographic plates.

Maxwell, James Clerk (1831–79), Scottish physicist who is best known for the formulation of the electromagnetic theory of light. In 1861 he demonstrated the possibility of producing colour pictures by superimposing red, green and blue negatives of the same subject (the 'additive' process). Each negative was exposed through the corresponding colour filter. Practical application was delayed by the lack of red-sensitive emulsions.

Muybridge, Eadweard (Edward James Muggeridge; 1830–1904), English photographer, famous for his early experiments in capturing motion in photographic images, and for his landscape photographs of the American West.

Nagy, Laszlo Moholy (1894–1946), Hungarian-born US photographer, celebrated for his constructivist-inspired, semi-abstract images, and his inspiring teaching at the Bauhaus.

Niepce, Nicephore (1765–1833), French inventor who was the first to make a permanent photographic image. In his first successful picture the image was projected by a lens on to a metal plate covered with bitumen of judea, which hardens under the influence of light. Washing away the unhardened parts produced a printed plate. In 1847 Niepce made a binder for silver iodide from white of egg (albumen).

Ray, Man (Emanuel Rabinovitch; 1890–1976), US photographer who produced poetic and bizarre surreal images. (See also Famous Artists.)

Rodchenko, Aleksandr (1891–1956), Russian photographer and photomontagist; introduced 'New Photography' to post-revolutionary Russia.

Salomon, Erich (1886–1944), German photojournalist. Master of the candid shot, he caught politicians and celebrities off guard for the new magazines of the 1920s.

Sander, August (1876–1964), German photographer; celebrated for his ambitious project *Man of the Twentieth Century*, a picture of a society – the doomed Weimar Republic – through the faces of its people.

Smith, Eugene (1918–78), US photojournalist, notable for his impassioned documentary photographs from around the world (seen mostly in *Life* magazine in the 1940s and 50s).

Stieglitz, Alfred (1864–1946), US photographer, publisher and gallery owner whose work turned from pictorialism to a search for abstract form and a specifically photographic way of seeing.

Strand, Paul (1890–1976), US photographer who abandoned pictorialism for a pure, objective photographic approach to his subjects.

Warhol, Andy (1928–87), US Pop artist who used photographic images from the media. (See also Famous Artists.)

Weston, Edward (1886–1958), US photographer. His precise photographs of natural and human forms combine a formal beauty with the reality of the object.

Winogrand, Garry (1928–84), US photographer who created a highly influential brand of urban street photography, fusing the 'snapshot' approach with a sense of energy and crowded events in his images.

Zeiss, Carl (1816–88), German industrialist who became internationally known for the high quality of his optical equipment. In 1890, his famous factory at Jena (Thuringia, Germany) introduced the 'Protar' lens which utilized a wide range of different barium glasses to reduce distortion.

Architecture

Architecture is the art and science of designing and erecting buildings that are both suitable for an intended purpose and aesthetically pleasing. The design of a particular building will depend upon many factors, including the technology and materials available, the cost of those materials, the function of the building, and the taste of the building's architect, its owner and its users.

PERIODS AND STYLES OF ARCHITECTURE

Egyptian architecture

The appearance of Egyptian buildings was influenced by climatic features such as fierce heat and bright sunshine – which meant only small windows were required – and by a plentiful local supply of building stone. The pyramids developed from *mastabas* or tomb houses – small, flat-topped buildings with sloping sides. Later, monolithic buildings were increasingly replaced by a system of construction consisting of series of stone columns and horizontal beams. The most imposing buildings were tombs and temples, which were vast sprawling complexes of courtyards, halls and avenues built of stone. Stone was used only sparingly for secular buildings.

Near Eastern architecture

The use of mud-brick rather than stone and the increasing importance of vast palace complexes characterize Near Eastern architecture, which made use of elaborately niched and buttressed façades. Temples display a monumentality only paralleled by *ziggurats*, stepped pyramid-shaped temple towers. Enormous palaces were raised on platforms of mud-bricks and reached by broad stairs and ramps. Planned around inner courtyards, with numerous rooms connected by corridors, they were faced with stone and decorated with bas-reliefs of sculptured monsters, painting on plaster, and coloured glazed bricks. Structurally the buildings were quite sophisticated with some use of arches, vaults and domes. Persian architecture made greater use of stone and wooden columns, flat roofs and halls of tall columns.

Greek architecture

Buildings of the Early Greek period are characterized by the distinct appearance of the masonry wall in their construction. There are three types: *cyclopean*, which is constructed of large stone piles, the gaps between which are filled with smaller stones held together by clay; *stone blocks* laid in a regular course with joints that are not always vertical; and *polygonal*, where many-sided blocks are worked together to form a strong structure. The architecture of the later (Hellenic) period is distinguished by the use of the column. Columns gave Classical Greek buildings an uncomplicated appearance. The three *orders* of column were Doric (c. 640–c. 300 BC), Ionic (c. 560–c. 200 BC) and Corinthian (c. 420–c. 100 BC). An order is the design of an entire column consisting of base, shaft and capital with an entablature over the top as the horizontal element. The Doric order is the simplest of the three orders, the capital being a simple flattened cushion of stone. The more slender and ornamental columns of the Ionic order are topped by a capital that is ornamented with four spiral motifs called *volutes*. The Corinthian order is the lightest and least-used of the three Greek orders. The capital displays acanthus-leaf decoration combined with volutes that are smaller and more open than the Ionic.

Roman architecture

The Romans adopted the central concept of Greek architecture – the three orders – but changed the manner in which the orders were expressed through adopting arches and vaults, both Etruscan technical innovations not used by the Greeks. The Romans also added two new orders – the rarely used Tuscan (which is similar to the Doric but with a plain entablature) and the Composite (which displays Ionic volutes and Corinthian leaves). Roman architects used a wider variety of building materials than the Greeks. The introduction by the Romans of tufa, limestone, brick and especially concrete allowed structural innovations that were employed most successfully in vast structures. The major public buildings of Imperial Rome were characterized by flamboyant luxury, but only the husks of a few great buildings remain.

Byzantine architecture

Byzantine architecture is characterized by the construction of domes over square bases. The Romans had always built domes over cylindrical or polygonal bases, but the Byzantines effected the transition of the circular dome to the square base, usually composed of four arches, by inserting *pendentives*. The advantage of a square base over a circular or polygonal base was that vaulted aisles, semi-domed apses and other domes could be easily erected adjacent to a central dome.

Russian architecture initially followed the Byzantine pattern, but a distinct Russian personality soon emerged. The wide Byzantine windows were narrowed and roofs steepened to cope with the heavy snow of Russian winters, and in time domes were constructed in the bulbous shape that became a distinguishing feature of Russian architecture.

Early medieval architecture

Anglo-Saxon architecture flourished in England from the 6th century until the Norman Conquest of 1066. Most building was timber-framed. Surviving stone buildings reflect this in the application of long strips of stone, called *'long-and-short work'*, to wall-surfaces as non-structural decoration. Ecclesiastical and private buildings were generally small in scale, with small spaces or rooms opening into one another through narrow doorways.

Carolingian architecture developed initially at the court of Charlemagne at Aachen (Germany). It closely follows late Roman prototypes. Its massive sturdy piers are typical of the solidity of all Carolingian architecture.

Romanesque architecture emerged in the decades following the year 1000. A huge increase in church building took place: the typical Romanesque church grew from the simple groundplan of a Roman basilica – the addition of *transepts*, a *chancel* and an *apse* at the east end produced the cross-shaped groundplan followed with innumerable variations throughout the Middle Ages. The *nave* was often of considerable height. The interior elevations of the nave were often divided into two or three storeys with the *clerestory* at the top, *arcades* of columns at the bottom (opening into aisles parallel to but lower than the nave) and a *triforium* in the middle storey opening into the roof-space of the aisles. High towers were often built over the *crossing* of transepts and nave, and at the west end. These innovations were made possible by the development of simple stone vaulting systems. In earlier buildings vaults were usually either *barrel vaults* or *groin vaults*. The Romanesque style was disseminated throughout Europe quickly because of the network of related monasteries. Typically Romanesque architecture is massive and simple. Piers are large and where there are attached columns or mouldings these are large in scale. Local variations – or schools – are most noticeable in building materials and decoration. In Romanesque buildings in England and France special attention was paid to the embellishment of capitals surmounting columns and to doorways – the *tympanum* was usually elaborately carved.

Gothic architecture

The Gothic style emerged in the 12th century and survived in some areas of northern Europe until the 16th. In Gothic architecture a transcendental quality is evoked by pointed arches, vaulted ceilings and an emphasis on light through large pointed windows. Although pointed arches and windows are perhaps the most obvious features of Gothic building, what characterizes Gothic architecture is a method of building and a sense of structure and space that pervades the whole building, rather than any specific design feature. Rib-vaulting was begun by Romanesque builders, but the idea of building 'skeletons of stone' was not fully developed until Gothic buildings were designed. Walls became just infill between supporting piers and big windows for stained glass. The thick walls with passages typical of Romanesque were replaced with thin walls. Tracery gradually became lighter and more complex and decorative, leaving even larger areas of stained glass.

The interiors of Gothic cathedrals became increasingly vast, with naves of great height. The interior surfaces are articulated by ribs beginning at the ceiling vaults of the nave and running down the piers of the clerestory, triforium and nave arcades. This vertical thrust emphasizes the great height of the buildings, and as the clusters of ribs become increasingly narrow in diameter the whole interior seems lighter. The divisions between the aisles, nave, transepts, apse and chapels are less emphatic, creating a sense of spaces flowing into one another. Although the walls of great Gothic churches were lighter they still required support and *buttresses* – and sometimes *flying buttresses* – were added to the exterior of the building to carry the structural thrust from the vaults.

Gothic architecture is found, with various regional variations, throughout western and central Europe. Buildings of the *Early English* style have simple pointed *lancet* windows without tracery. In the *Decorated* style (c. 1250–1360) the vaults have additional ribs, the main piers are made up of clusters of small columns, and window tracery is used in a variety of flowing patterns. Decorated style is characterized by the *ogee arch* and decorated wall surfaces. During this period the tracery changed from geometric to flowing. The *Perpendicular* style (c. 1360–c. 1550), as its name implies, emphasized vertical features. Perpendicular tracery is made up of many geometrically arranged narrow stone bars, and arches and vaults are much flatter. Whereas the Decorated style added extra ribs to the vaulting, the Perpendicular was distinguished by many subordinate ribs in the vaults curving round to form a fan shape, often with additional carved decoration.

A particular feature of German Gothic is the *hall church*. In Italy the Classical, Romanesque and Byzantine traditions persisted much longer than in northern Europe and Italian Gothic has none of the structural and spatial daring of northern Gothic. Roofs are often flat or open timber with an absence of pinnacles and flying buttresses.

Renaissance architecture

The Renaissance, a period of intellectual and artistic renewal that lasted from c. 1350 to c. 1550, began in Italy because the physical remains of Classical Rome were more plentiful there than elsewhere in Europe.

The Early Renaissance style is found in various forms throughout Italy. High Renaissance buildings are generally bolder than Early Renaissance ones, reflecting the architects' greater familiarity with the Classical precedents, and the variety of uses to which they could put the orders of columns and pilasters. The Renaissance in France and England developed principally in palaces and large country houses rather than in church architecture. It also differed in character from Italian Renaissance architecture because the Gothic had flourished in northern Europe much longer.

In English and French Renaissance architecture, Classical features such as columns, pilasters and pediments were mixed with Gothic features and decoration to form picturesque buildings. In France, Renaissance features first appeared there before the end of the 15th century, but Renaissance architecture did not appear in England until the 16th century. English Renaissance houses have symmetrical façades and Renaissance details such as pilasters and balustrades, but the rooms are frequently distributed asymmetrically throughout the groundplan and the houses retain such medieval features as the great hall.

Mannerism followed hard on the heels of the High Renaissance in Italy. When Italian architects had thoroughly studied the way Classical architects used the basic elements of columns, pilasters and entablatures, they felt able to use these elements in new ways, for example greatly exaggerating the proportion of one element or adding features such as *consoles* for decoration rather than support. Although Mannerist features are found elsewhere in Europe, it is a particularly Italian phenomenon.

Early Palladian architecture stems from a different kind of Mannerism practised by Andrea Palladio, who followed the Mannerist practice of using Classical elements in ways that the Romans would never have done. However, he always followed a strict system of proportional rules, and the effect is always harmonious. The Palladian style became highly influential in England.

Baroque and Rococo

Baroque (one of the dominant trends in the visual arts in the 17th century) has been described as work that utilized movement, whether actual (e.g. curving walls) or implied (e.g. figures portrayed in vigorous action). It produced striking visual effects in buildings and decoration, although it could occasionally be over-ornate and theatrical. Although the Baroque style began in Italy (with Bernini, Borromini and Maderna), it was in Spain, Germany and Austria that Baroque architecture attained and exceeded the exuberance of Italian Baroque.

In England – where the chief proponents of the style were Wren and Vanbrugh – and also in France, Baroque exteriors are much more restrained and traditionally Classical.

Rococo developed in the 18th century from the desire for the informal in architecture. Highly decorative Rococo rooms became wholly or partly elliptical and decoration was derived from foliage, grotesques and shells. In Germany and Austria Rococo became even more lavish, and an emphasis on whimsical decoration and oval and circular spaces created a sense of fluidity.

Palladianism and Neo-Classicism

The influence of Palladio was not reflected in British architecture until around 1710. In Spain and Italy the Baroque persisted well into the 18th century. In France a grander classicism, more decorative and 'muscular' than Palladio's, prevailed. Around the middle of the 18th century British architecture became more consciously 'Antiquarian' or Neo-Classical in character.

The term 'Neo-Classical' meant 'Neo-Roman', for Greece was, in the 18th century, still a wild and little-known country. A Greek Revival reached its height in Britain between 1805 and 1830.

Contrasting with the purism of the Greek Revival is the *Picturesque* movement, which affected all the arts, including architecture. The architect John Nash – whose celebrated works are Neo-Classical – was equally at home designing 'picturesque' buildings mixing exotic styles such as Indian and Chinese. Although the Greek Revival remained strong in Scotland and in Germany until the 1850s, it was past its peak in England by about 1830 when the Gothic Revival began.

Gothic Revival architecture

Architects had used Gothic details sporadically throughout the 18th century, usually in Picturesque buildings. As scholars studied medieval buildings and began to classify the different Gothic styles, so architects became more serious about building in a consistent and authentic manner. By the 1830s and 1840s, the Gothic had been appropriated as a particularly British style. Pugin, along with the art critic John Ruskin, did not see the Gothic as just another style to be adopted and adapted – they believed that the Gothic was the only Christian style (Classical buildings being 'pagan'). From the late 1840s Gothic Revival buildings appeared all over Britain, and to a lesser extent Europe and the English-speaking world.

The Arts and Crafts movement in Britain is often seen as a secular and domestic equivalent to the Gothic Revival. It was begun in the late 1850s by William Morris, who hated the mechanical quality of machine-made goods and wished to revive traditional craftsmanship. Arts and Crafts is reflected in architecture in the revived use of traditional British building techniques and styles such as tile-hung walls, windows with small panes, and half-timbering.

Art Nouveau a style that appeared at the end of the 19th century. It is characterized by undulating curves and extreme forms of decoration derived from burgeoning vegetation.

Twentieth-century architecture

New building materials and new building types were developed during the 19th century. The most important technological advance was the use of iron for construction. Iron could be used with glass to create great new structures or with more conventional brick or stone supports for such purposes as roofing railway stations. It also began to be used structurally for buildings which would otherwise have been built only of stone or brick but the full potential of this system was not realized until the 20th century.

International Modernism owes its development to structural advances such as steel framing, which have revolutionized architectural design in the 20th century. Buildings supported by a steel frame can be built much higher than those relying upon a traditional load-bearing wall. The steel frame also allows the construction of buildings whose walls are little more than a skin of steel and glass. When concrete came into general use this principle was further extended by the use of cantilevers, where floors can be internally supported by columns, thus making the outer walls a separate structural element.

Gropius founded the *Bauhaus* school, where architects and designers were taught to be aware of the needs of modern-day living and to design functionally according to this understanding. Le Corbusier popularized the use of reinforced concrete (concrete with steel frame set within it for strength), flat roofs and buildings raised on stilts ('pilotis'). The style of buildings popularized by the Bauhaus, Le Corbusier and others is known as International Modernism, for the simple reason that the simplicity of the designs meant that similar buildings were found throughout the world. It remained the principal style for large-scale projects until the 1960s, when *High-Tech* architecture appeared.

High-tech began as student drawing-board exercises in the 1960s, and is a logical extension of the Modernist thesis that a building's structure should be evident from its appearance. High-Tech buildings express a building's machine-like functionalism by having its heating, electrical and water piping, and air conditioning, on the exterior.

Post-Modernism literally means any style of architecture that is not Modernist but has been used since the advent of Modernism. It has been particularly associated with architecture that uses such Classical details as columns and pediments in a decorative manner. The use of bright colours, simplified details, plastics, reflective glass and other shiny materials such as chromium is typical of Post-Modernism.

GLOSSARY OF ARCHITECTURAL TERMS

abacus the flat upper part of the capital of a column.

apse a semicircular termination or recess at the end of a chapel or the chancel of a church.

arcade a set of arches and its supporting columns.

architrave a beam extending across the top of the columns in Classical architecture.

baptistry a building used for baptisms; sometimes merely a bay or chapel reserved for baptisms.

barrel vault a continuous vault, either semicircular or pointed in section; also called tunnel vault.

bay a compartment or unit of division of an interior or of a façade – usually between one window or pillar and the next.

belvedere an open-sided structure designed to offer extensive views, usually in a formal garden.

boss a projection, usually carved, at the intersection of stone ribs of Gothic vaults and ceilings.

buttress a vertical mass of masonry built against a wall to strengthen it and to resist the outward pressure of a vault.

campanile a bell tower.

capital the top of a column, usually carved.

caryatid a sculptured female figure serving as a supporting column.

chancel that part of a church containing the altar, sanctuary and choir.

clerestory a row of windows in the upper part of the wall of a church.

console an ornamental Classical bracket supporting part of a wall.

cornice the projecting upper part of the entablature in Classical architecture; also decorative plasterwork between the wall and ceiling.

crossing the intersection of the nave and transepts in a church.

dado the lower part of an interior wall when panelled or painted separately from the main part.

drum the cylindrical lower part of a dome or cupola.

entablature in Classical architecture, the beam-like division above the columns, comprising architrave, frieze and cornice.

flying buttress an arch conveying the thrust of a vault towards an isolated buttress.

frieze the decorated central division of an entablature, between the architrave and the cornice.

groin vault (also called a **cross vault**) the intersection of two barrel vaults. Where barrel vaults require support along both edges, a groin vault only requires support at its four corners, thus allowing windows to be inserted between the supports.

hall church a church where the aisles are more or less the same height as the nave.

keystone the central, wedge-shaped stone of an arch, so called because the arch cannot stand up until it is in position.

lancet window a window with a single, sharply pointed arch. The style is associated with the Early English period of Gothic architecture.

mezzanine a low storey introduced between two loftier ones, usually the ground and first floors.

nave the main body of a church.

ogee arch a pointed arch with an S-shaped curve on both sides.

order any of several Classical styles of architecture. Each order is distinguished by its design of column. (See Greek Architecture, above.)

oriel a bay window on an upper floor, supported by projecting stonework.

pediment in Classical architecture, the low-pitched gable above the entablature, usually filled with sculpture.

pendentive a triangular section of vaulting with concave sides supporting a circular dome over a square or polygonal base.

pier the vertical masonry support for a wall arch.

rustication heavy stonework with the surface left rough, or with deeply channelled joints, used principally on Renaissance buildings.

spandrel a triangular space between the curves of two adjacent arches and the horizontal moulding above them.

tracery ornamental stonework dividing Gothic windows into smaller areas of glass.

triforium an arcade of arches, forming a gallery, above the arches of the nave or chancel of a church.

tympanum the triangular space bounded by the mouldings of a pediment; also, the semicircular space, often carved, between the lintel and arch of a Gothic doorway.

vault an arched structure – usually of stone, brick or concrete – forming a roof or ceiling.

THE SEVEN WONDERS OF THE WORLD

In the 2nd century BC the writer Antipater of Sidon described the following seven buildings as the pre-eminent sights of the ancient world:

The Pyramids of Giza (Egypt): the only one of the seven wonders still in existence.

The Hanging Gardens of Babylon: a series of landscaped terraces, probably 7th century BC.

The Statue of Zeus at Olympia: a large figure of Zeus enthroned, c. 420 BC.

The Temple of Artemis at Ephesus: a structure famous for its great size.

The Mausoleum of Halicarnassus: the huge tomb of the Anatolian king, Mausolus.

The Colossus of Rhodes: a vast bronze statue commemorating the siege of Rhodes (305–04 BC).

The Pharos of Alexandria: a huge lighthouse constructed c. 280 BC.

FAMOUS ARCHITECTS

Aalto, Alvar (1898–1976), Finnish architect, city planner and furniture designer: Säynätsalo Town Hall, Finland.

Adam, Robert (1728–92), Scottish Palladian architect and furniture and interior designer: Kedleston Hall, Derbyshire (England), and Syon House, London.

Alberti, Leon Battista (1404–72), Italian architect, writer and principal founder of Renaissance architectural theory: Palazzo Rucellai, Florence (Italy).

Aleijadhino (Antonio Francisco Lisboa; 1738–1814), Brazilian Baroque architect.

Apollodorus of Damascus (fl. first century AD), Greek engineer and architect: Trajan's Forum, Rome.

Archer, Thomas (1668–1743), English Baroque architect: Anglican cathedral, Birmingham (England).

Aronco, Raimondo d' (1857–1932), Italian Art Nouveau architect.

Arup, Sir Ove (1895–1988), English engineer.

Asam, Cosmas Damian (1686–1739), German Baroque architect – partner of his brother (see below).

Asam, Egid Quirin (1692–1750), German Baroque architect: St Johann Nepomuk church, Munich (Germany).

Asplund, Erik Gunnar (1885–1940), Swedish Modernist architect: Stockholm City Library.

Baillie Scott, Mackay Hugh (1865–1945), English architect of small country houses.

Baker, Sir Herbert (1862–1946), English 'Colonial' architect: New Delhi legislative buildings, India.

Barragán, Luis (1902–88), Mexican architect.

Barry, Sir Charles (1795–1860), English Neo-Classical architect: Houses of Parliament, London.

Bennisch, Günter (1922–), German architect: Olympic Park, Munich (Germany).

Behrens, Peter (1868–1940), German architect who played a major role in the evolution of German Modernism.

Bentley, John Francis (1839–1902), English Gothic Revival architect: Westminster RC Cathedral, London.

Berg, Max (1870–1947), German Expressionist architect: Breslau Centenary Hall (now Wroclaw, Poland).

Berlage, Hendrik Petrus (1856–1934), leading modern Dutch architect: Amsterdam stock exchange.

Bernini, Giovanni Lorenzo (1598–1680), Italian Baroque architect and sculptor: Piazza of St Peter's, Rome.

Bijvoet, Bernard (1889–1979), radical Dutch modernist architect.

Bindesboll, Michael (1800–56), Danish architect: Thorvaldsen Museum, Copenhagen.

Boffrand, Gabriel Germain (1667–1754), French Rococo court architect.

Bogardus, James (1800–74), US architect who played a major role in the development of the skyscraper.

Böhm, Göttfried (1922–), German modern architect whose buildings are known for their breathtaking internal spaces.

Borromini, Francesco (1599–1667), Italian Baroque architect: the church of S. Carlo alle Quattro Fontane, Rome.

Boullée, Etienne-Louis (1723–96), French architect, teacher and co-founder of the Neo-Classical movement.

Bramante, Donato (1444–1514), Italian Renaissance architect: Tempietto of S. Pietro in Montorio, Rome (one of the finest High Renaissance buildings although it is only 4.5m (15 ft) in diameter).

Breuer, Marcel (1902–81), Hungarian-born US Bauhaus architect: UNESCO building, Paris.

Brown, Lancelot ('Capability') (1716–83), English gardener, architect and landscape architect.

Brunelleschi, Filippo (1377–1446), Italian Renaissance architect and engineer: the dome of Florence Cathedral, a double shell of brickwork supported on ribs.

Burges, William (1827–84), English Gothic Revival architect: St Finbar's Cathedral, Cork (Ireland).

Burlington, Earl of (Richard Boyle; 1694–1753), English architect and patron of Palladian architecture: Chiswick House, west London (with William Kent).

Burton, Decimus (1800–81), English Neo-Classical architect: Palm House, Kew Gardens, London.

Butterfield, William (1814–1900), English architect of Gothic Revival churches characterized by their horizontal lines and strong use of colour: Keble College, Oxford.

Campbell, Colen (1676–1729), Scottish architect who is regarded as the founder of Palladianism in England.

Candela, Felix (1910–), Spanish-born Mexican architect whose buildings are characterized by their light weight concrete roof construction.

Chalgrin, Jean-François-Thérèse (1739–1811), French Neo-Classical architect: arc de Triomphe, Paris.

Chambers, Sir William (1723–96), Scottish pioneer Neo-Classical architect: Somerset House, London.

Chermayeff, Serge Ivan (1900–), Russian-born US architect: De La Warr Pavilion (with Eric Mendelsohn), Bexhill, East Sussex (England).

Churriguera, José de (1665–1725), member of a prominent family of architects who developed a distinctly Spanish Baroque.

Coates, Wells Wintemute (1895–1958), Canadian Modernist architect.

Cockerell, Charles Robert (1788–1863), English Classical architect: Taylorian Institute, Oxford.

Correa, Charles (1930–), Indian architect.

Costa, Lucio (1902–), Brazilian architect: masterplan of Brasilia, the new capital of Brazil.

Cuypers, Petrus (1827–1921), leading Dutch architect: Amsterdam Central Station.

Dance, George (1741–1825), English Neo-Classical architect: London Guildhall.

Deane, Thomas (1828–99), Irish architect.

Delorme, Philibert (1510–70), French Renaissance architect: châteaux of Anet and St. Germain-en-Laye and the palace of Fontainebleau, France.

Doesburg, Theo van (1883–1931), Dutch founder of De Stijl.

Doshi, B. V. (1927–), Indian architect whose modern buildings reflect traditional Indian styles.

Dudok, Willem Marinus (1884–1974), Dutch architect and town planner: Hilversum Town Hall, Netherlands.

Duiker, Johannes (1890–1935), radical Dutch Modernist architect.

Eames, Charles Ormand (1907–78), US architect, designer and film-maker.

Eiermann, Egon (1904–70), German architect: new Kaiser Wilhelm Memorial Church, Berlin.

Eiffel, Alexandre Gustave (1832–1923), French engineer: Eiffel Tower, Paris.

Engel, Carl Ludwig (1778–1840), German architect: Lutheran Cathedral, Helsinki.

Erskine, Ralph (1912–), Anglo-Swedish architect known for his housing projects.

Fischer, Johann Michael (1692–1766), German architect of late Baroque and Rococo churches.

Fischer von Erlach, Johann (1656–1723), Austrian Baroque and Rococo architect and influential architectural historian: Karlskirche, Vienna.

Fisker, Kay (1893–1965), Danish architect of housing projects.

Foster, Sir Norman (1938–), English High-Tech architect: Sainsbury Centre for the Visual Arts, Norwich (England).

Fry, Maxwell (1899–1987), English Modern Movement architect.

Fuller, Richard Buckminster (1895–1983), US architect and engineer who developed the geodesic dome: US pavilion at Expo 67, Montréal, Canada.

Gabriel, Ange-Jacques (1698–1782), French Neo-Classical architect: Le Petit Trianon, Versailles (France).

Garnier, Charles (1825–98), French creator of the 'Style Napoléon III': Paris Opera House.

Gaudi, Antoni (1852–1926), Spanish (Catalan) architect of extraordinary organic-looking facades, which rise up to an undulating roofline: church of the Sagrada Familia, Barcelona (Spain).

Gibberd, Sir Frederick (1908–84), English architect and town planner: RC cathedral, Liverpool (England).

Gibbs, James (1682–1754), English church architect: St Martin-in-the-Fields, London.

Gilbert, Cass (1859–1934), US architect of skyscrapers: Woolworth Building, New York.

Gilly, Friedrich (1772–1800), German pioneer of Neo-Classicism.

Giulio Romano (Giuliano Pippi; 1499–1546), Italian architect and principal founder of the Mannerist style: Palazzo del Tè, Mantua (Italy).

Goff, Bruce (1904–82), US Organic architect.

Griffin, Walter Burley (1876–1937), US architect and town planner: plans for Canberra, Australia.

Gropius, Walter (1883–1969), German architect, architectural theorist, teacher and founder of the Bauhaus, who aimed to make architecture reflect social needs: Fagus Factory, Alfeld (Germany).

Guimard, Hector (1867–1942), French architect: Art Nouveau stations on the Paris Metro.

Hardouin-Mansart, Jules (1646–1708), leading French Baroque architect: Place Vendôme, Paris.

Harrison, William K. (1895–1981), US architect: UN complex, New York.

Haussmann, Baron Georges Eugène (1809–91), French architect who planned the boulevards of Paris.

Hawksmoor, Nicholas (1661–1736), English Baroque architect, famous for his London churches: Castle Howard (with Vanbrugh), North Yorkshire (England).

Hoffmann, Josef (1870–1925), Austrian architect whose designs are famous for their simplicity.

Holland, Henry (1745–1806), English architect.

Horta, Baron Victor (1861–1947), Belgian Art Nouveau architect: town houses including the Hôtel Tassel, Brussels, with its sinuous iron that flows down from the ceiling to form bannisters.

Hunt, Richard Morris (1827–95), US architect: US Military Academy, West Point, New York.

Inwood, Henry William (1794–1843), English architect of Greek Revival churches.

Isozaki, Arata (1931–), leading Japanese modern architect: Museum of Contemporary Art, Los Angeles, California (USA).

Jacobsen, Arne (1902–71), Danish architect and interior and furniture designer whose designs were charcterized by their severe modernity: SAS Building, Copenhagen, and St Catherine's College, Oxford.

Johnson, Philip (1906–), prolific modern US architect: Glass House, New Canaan (Conn., USA) and Seagram Building, New York.

Jones, Inigo (1573–1652), English Palladian architect and designer: the Queen's Hose, Greenwich, London.

Juvarra, Filippo (1678–1736), leading 18th-century Italian architect: La Superga, Turin (Italy).

Kahn, Louis (1901–74), Estonian-born influential US architect: Salk Institute, La Jolla, California (USA).

Kent, William (1685–1748), English Palladian architect and pioneer of the English informal garden: Horse Guards Building, Whitehall, London.

Klenze, Leo von (1784–1864), German Neo-Classical architect: many Greek Revival public buildings in Munich, including Glyptothek.

Krier, Léon (1946–), Luxembourgeois-born US architect who is known for his detailed city centre and housing redevelopments.

Kurokawa, Kisho (1934–), influential Japanese architect: Municipal Museum of Art, Nagoya (Japan).

Latrobe, Benjamin Henry (1764–1820), English-born US Greek Revival architect: US Capitol, Washington DC.

Le Corbusier (Charles-Edouard Jeanneret; 1887–1965), Swiss-born French Internationalist Modernist architect and town planner whose contribution to architecture is generally recognized as the most important of the 20th century: Notre-Dame-du-Haut, Ronchamp, France, and Chandigarh, a new administrative town in India. He used pure geometrical forms in an innovative manner and was noted for an imaginative application of technical advances.

Le Vau, Louis (1612–70), French Baroque architect: the plan of Versailles (France).

Ledoux, Claude Nicholas (1736–1806), French architect and co-founder of the Revolutionary Neo-Classical movement.

L'Enfant, Pierre Charles (1754–1825), French-born US architect.

Leonidov, Ivan (1902–59), leading Russian architect who was forced into obscurity owing to his opposition to the constraints of the Soviet system.

Lescot, Pierre (c. 1515–78), French architect: rebuilding of the Louvre, Paris.

Lewerenitz, Sigurd (1885–1975), highly original Swedish architect: Chapel of the Resurrection, Woodland Cemetery, Stockholm.

Loos, Adolf (1870–1933), Austrian architect.

Lubetkin, Berthold (1901–90), Georgian-born British architect: Penguin Pool, London Zoo.

Lutyens, Sir Edwin (1869–1944), English architect of country houses (in partnership with Gertrude Jekyll, who designed the gardens) and town planner: Castle Drogo, Devon (England), and many principal buildings of New Delhi, India.

Mackintosh, Charles Rennie (1868–1928), Scottish Art Nouveau architect whose designs had a sparseness and economy: Glasgow School of Art.

Maderno, Carlo (1556–1629), Italian architect who largely determined the style of early Baroque: St Peter's, Rome (main facade and nave).

Maillart, Robert (1872–1940), Swiss architect of bridges.

Mansart, François (1598–1666), French Baroque architect who replaced the traditional steep pitch roof with the lower-angled form of the mansard roof.

May, Ernst (1886–1970), German-born British Functionalist architect and town planner.

Melnikov, Konstantin (1890–1974), Russian avant-garde Modernist architect.

Mendelsohn, Erich (1887–1953), German-born British architect: Einstein Tower, Potsdam, Germany, and De La Warr Pavilion (with Chermayeff), Bexhill, East Sussex (England).

Michaelangelo Buonarroti (1475–1564), Italian sculptor, artist and architect – see Major Artists.

Mies van der Rohe, Ludwig (1886–1969), German-born US architect who popularized the rectilinear forms of International Modernism: Seagram Building, New York.

Moser, Karl (1860–1936), influential Swiss architect.

Nash, John (1752–1835), English Neo-Classical town planner and architect: Regent's Park and Regent's Street, London.

Nervi, Pier Luigi (1891–1979), Italian architect and influential engineer in reinforced concrete.

Neumann, Johann Balthasar (1687–1753), German Baroque and Rococo architect: The Residenz, Wurzburg (Germany).

Niemeyer, Oscar (1907–), Brazilian Modernist architect: Government Buildings, Brasilia.

Olmstead, Frederick Law (1822–1903), US architect and writer who inspired the National Parks Movement in the USA: Central Park, New York.

Otto, Frei (1925–), German architect who was responsible for bringing 'tent' structures into modern architecture: Olympic Stadium, Munich (Germany).

Palladio, Andrea (1508–80), Italian architect and founder of the Palladian style: the Palazzo Chiericati and the Villa Capra (Rotonda), Vicenza (Italy).

Paxton, Sir Joseph (1801–65), English landscape gardener and architect: Great Conservatory, Chatsworth House, Derbyshire (England).

Pei, Ieoh Ming (1917–), Chinese-born US architect: National Gallery of Art, Washington DC.

Pelli, Cesar (1926–), Argentine architect: Canary Wharf, London.

Perret, Auguste (1874–1954), Belgian architect who was the first to exploit reinforced concrete architecturally.

Piano, Renzo (1937–), Italian architect whose work is characterized by technical innovations: Centre Beaubourg, Paris (with Rogers and Rice).

Piranesi, Giovanni Battista (1720–78), Italian architect, artist and draughtsman whose prints of Classical Rome were an important influence on the early Neo-Classical Movement.

Poelzig, Hans (1869–1936), major German architect: Grosses Schauspielhaus, Berlin.

Ponti, Gio (1891–1979), important modern Italian architect: Pirelli Tower, Milan (Italy).

Pugin, Augustus Welby Northmore (1812–52), leading Gothic Revival church architect: Birmingham and Nottingham RC cathedrals (England) and Cheadle RC church, Staffordshire (England).

Rainaldi, Carlo (1611–91), Italian Baroque architect.

Reidy, Alfonso Eduardo (1909–64), French-born Brazilian Modernist architect.

Repton, Humphry (1752–1818), English landscape gardener.

Richardson, H(enry) H(obson) (1838–86), innovative US architect: Holy Trinity church, Boston (USA).

Rietveld, Gerrit Thomas (1888–1964), important Dutch architect of the De Stilj School.

Rogers, Richard (1933–), English architect of major High-Tech buildings: Centre Beaubourg, Paris (with Rice and Piano) and Lloyds Building, London.

Saarinen, Eero (1910–61), Finnish-born US architect (son of Eliel). He experimented in various modern styles: Dulles Airport, Washington DC, and the chapel at Massachusetts Institute of Technology, Boston (USA).

Saarinen, Eliel (1873–1950), Finnish-born US Art Nouveau architect: Helsinki railway station. He had a profound influence upon modern American architecture, in particular skyscrapers and churches: *Chicago Tribune* office tower and the Tabernacle Church of Christ, Columbus, Indiana (USA).

Scamozzi, Vincenzo (1548 or 1550–1616), late Renaissance Italian architect and theatre designer.

Scharoun, Hans (1893–1972), German Modernist architect: Philharmonie concert hall, Berlin.

Schinkel, Karl Friedrich (1781–1841), the leading north German Neo-Classical architect and state architect of Prussia: the Altes Museum, Berlin.

Scott, Sir Giles Gilbert (1880–1960), influential English architect: Anglican cathedral, Liverpool (England).

Semper, Gottfried (1803–79), German Neo-Renaissance architect: Court Theatre, Dresden (Germany).

Sert, Josep Lluis (1902–83), major Spanish Modernist architect.

Shaw, Richard Norman (1831–1913), English architect: New Scotland Yard, London.

Sinan (1489–1588), leading Turkish architect: mosque of Sultan Suleyman, Istanbul.

Soane, Sir John (1753–1837), highly original English Neo-Classical architect: Bank of England, London.

Soleri, Paolo (1919–), Italian architect who has combined architecture and ecology in 'arcology'.

Soufflot, Jacques (1713–80), leading French Neo-Classical architect, the Pantheon, Paris.

Spence, Sir Basil (1907–76), English architect: Coventry cathedral, West Midlands (England).

Stirling, James (1926–), Scottish architect.

Street, George Edmund (1824–81), English Gothic Revival architect: Royal Courts of Justice, Strand, London.

Sullivan, Louis (1856–1924), US architect and pioneer of skyscrapers: Wainwright Building, St Louis, Missouri (USA).

Tange, Kenzo (1913–), major Japanese architect who mixes Modernist and more traditional styles: City Hall, Tokyo.

Taut, Bruno (1880–1938), influential pioneering German avant-garde architect.

Terry, Quinlan (1937–), English Post-Modernist architect whose Classical buildings have won public rather than professional acclaim: Brentwood RC cathedral, Essex (England).

Tessin, Nicodemus (the Elder) (1615–81), influential Swedish Baroque architect: Drottningholm Palace, Stockholm.

Unwin, Sir Raymond (1863–1940), English architect and town planner.

Utzon, Jørn (1918–), influential Danish architect: Sydney Opera House, Australia.

Vanbrugh, Sir John (1664–1726), English architect who developed a particularly personal and English Baroque: Blenheim Palace, Oxfordshire, and Castle Howard, North Yorkshire (England).

Vauban, Sébastien (1633–1707), French military architect and town planner.

Van Der Velde, Henry (1863–1957), Belgian architect who developed a unique Flemish Arts and Crafts style.

Venturi, Robert (1925–), leading US Post-Modernist architect.

Viollet-Le-Duc, Eugène Emmanuel (1814–1879), the leading French Gothic Revival architect.

Vitruvius (fl. first century BC), Roman architect, engineer and writer: *De architectura,* 10 volumes covering building materials, city planning and the design and construction of public and private buildings.

Voysey, C(harles) F(rancis) A(nnesley) (1857–1941), English domestic architect.

Wagner, Otto (1841–1918), influential Austrian architect whose writings gave rise to the Wagner Schools: Post Office Savings Bank, Vienna.

Wahlman, Lars (1870–1952), Swedish architect whose buldings echo Arts and Crafts: Engelbrekt Church, Stockholm.

Waterhouse, Alfred (1830–1905), English architect: Manchester Town Hall.

Wilkins, William (1778–1839), English architect who pioneered Greek Revival buildings: Downing College, Cambridge.

Wren, Sir Christopher (1632–1723), English Baroque architect: St Paul's Cathedral and many other London churches.

Wright, Frank Lloyd (1867–1959), probably the most influential US architect of the 20th century: Guggenheim Museum, New York, and the famous house Falling Water, Bear Run, Pennsylvania (USA).

Wyatt, James (1746–1813), fashionable English Neo-Classical architect: Radcliffe Observatory, Oxford.

Wyattville, Sir Jeffrey (1766–1840), English architect best known for his remodelling of Windsor Castle, Berkshire (England).

Yamasaki, Minoru (1912–), innovative Japanese architect.

Zakharov, Andreyan (1761–1811), leading Russian Classical architect: Admiralty complex, St Petersburg.

THE PERFORMING ARTS

Music

THE ORIGINS OF MUSIC

In its most primitive form, music may evoke the sound of the elements – earth, air, fire, water. Since humans have always been imitative animals, it seems natural that nature itself should have provided the scope for the earliest music and the materials for the earliest musical instruments.

Where these materials – sticks, stones, bones, bells, reed pipes or whatever – were not available, the human voice was a more than adequate substitute, relieving loneliness, making contact with other people, reflecting the rhythms of manual labour or simply of walking, celebrating victories, or paying tribute to primitive deities – often in combination with dancing.

The sophisticated evolution of music – even the notes of a simple scale or chord – took place over a period of centuries. There was certainly a rich musical tradition in the years before Christ – for example in India, China, Egypt and Greece, much of it tantalizing because it was passed on orally, not written down. Even today, in Asia particularly, this tradition persists, because music is regarded as improvisatory and contemplative, ceaselessly changing, rather than something perfected and fixed on paper.

In Europe, much of what we today call music emerged through the spread of Christianity and of Judaism, particularly through medieval *plainsong* chants, which were single lines of notated vocal melody in free rhythm (i.e. not divided into bar lengths) sung in churches, and through *Gregorian chant*, named after Pope Gregory I, in whose time (around AD 600) it was systematized. This still forms part of Roman Catholic musical ritual. However, its *modes* (or 'scales') gradually gave way to the modern scale.

THE COMPONENTS OF MUSIC

A musical *note* is more than just a 'noise'. It is a single sound of definite pitch and duration, which can be identified in writing. The *pitch* of a note is its height or depth in relation to other notes, or in relation to an absolute pitch. This absolute pitch has internationally been set at A = 440 Hz (hertz); that is, the A above middle C has a frequency of 440 cycles or vibrations per second.

A *scale* is a progression of notes in ascending or descending order, while a *melody* (or tune) assembles a series of notes into a recognizable musical shape. However, to suggest, as some people do, that modern music lacks 'melody' may merely mean that the listener has failed to identify, or come to terms with, the melodies it contains – even Beethoven and Verdi, to some ears, once seemed unmelodic.

A melody usually, though not necessarily, possesses *rhythm*, which listeners often assume to mean *beat*. In fact, the beat of a piece of music is simply its regular pulse, determined by the *bar lines* by which music is metrically divided (two beats in the bar and so forth).

Rhythm can be an infinitely more complex arrangement of notes into a mixture of short and long durations within a single bar or across a series of bars. The *time* in which a piece of music (or section of a piece) is written is identified by a *time signature* at the beginning of the piece or section. Thus 3/4 time (three-four time), which is waltz time, represents three crotchets to the bar. This means that the main beat comes every three crotchets: *1* 2 3, *1* 2 3, etc.; 4/4 time, which is march time, has four crotchets: *1* 2 3 4, *1* 2 3 4, etc.; 3/8 and 6/8 represent three and six quavers, respectively. There are also many more complex time signatures.

A melody may have *harmony*. This means that it is accompanied by *chords*, which are combinations of notes, simultaneously sounded. It may also have *counterpoint*, whereby another melody, or succession of notes with musical shape, is simultaneously combined with it.

'Rules' of harmony and counterpoint, stating which notes could be acceptably combined and which could not, have been matters of concern to scholars, teachers and pupils in the course of musical history. But as with any other grammar, progressive composers have known when to break or bend the rules to the benefit of their own music.

TONALITY

The old modes, or scales, employed in the Middle Ages gradually gave way in the 17th century to a modern *tonality* – scales laid out in 12 major and minor *keys*, each consisting of a sequence of seven notes, divided into tones and semitones.

Each of the 12 major and minor scales starts on one of the 12 semitones into which an octave is divided. Melodies in a specific key use the notes of that scale, and the order in which the notes are used determines the nature of the melody. On a piano the scale of C major consists entirely of white notes, starting on C.

The notes from C to the next C, either above or below, form an *octave*. A note and another note an octave above sound 'the same' because the higher note has double the frequency. For example, the A above middle C is 440 cycles per second, and the A above that is 880 cycles. From C to D (the first 'white' note above) represents an interval of a tone, from C to C sharp (the first 'black' note) an interval of a semitone, so called because it represents half a tone. But from E to F, and from B to C, also forms a semitone (on a piano there is no black note between them). A scale therefore consists of a mixture of tone and semitone intervals.

A *chromatic scale*, on the other hand, employs nothing but semitones, and thus requires all 12 of the white and black notes to be used. The *whole-tone scale* – used, for example, by Debussy – moves entirely in tones. Starting on C, it would consist of the notes C-D-E-F sharp–G sharp–A sharp.

In musical terminology, a sharp indicates a semitone rise in pitch, and a flat a semitone fall. A natural is a note that is neither sharp nor flat, though the indication sign needs only to be used in special circumstances.

The first note of a scale is known as the *tonic*, or 'keynote'. The tonic of the scale of C is therefore the note C. All other scales require one or more black notes to be played in order to produce the same sequence of intervals.

It is important to remember that scales are conventions – conventions to which our ears are attuned through familiarity. The modes of ancient Greece and medieval

PROLIFIC COMPOSERS

The most prolific of the classical composers was Wolfgang Amadeus Mozart (1756–91), who wrote about 1000 operas, operettas, symphonies, violin sonatas, divertimenti, serenades, motets, concertoes, string quartets, other chamber music, masses and litanies before he died aged 35.

Probably the most prolific of all composers was the German composer and organist Georg Philipp Telemann (1681–1767) who is believed to have written:

100 concerti
135 orchestral suites
c. 400 chamber works
c. 200 instrumental solos
c. 130 songs
c. 100 secular vocal pieces
c. 30 operas
c. 150 passions, oratorios, masses
c. 1270 cantatas

Telemann's work is known for his skilled use of counterpoint but is often said to be greater in extent than in depth.

Most Operas
The most prolific composers of operas were the Austrian composer and conductor Wenzel Müller (1767–1835) who composed c. 250 operas and similar works, Joaquin Casimiro (1808–86), who composed 209 (including musical plays) and Manuel Fernandez Caballero (1835–1906), who composed c. 200 Zarzuelas (Spanish operas). Müller's work attained widespread popularity in his day, but is now seldom played.

Among well-known composers, the most prolific composers of operas include:

Scarlatti 115
Offenbach 101
Vivaldi 94 (of which 45 survive)
Cimarosa 86
Albinoni 81
Donizetti 67
Salieri 42
Handel 42
Telemann c. 40
Rossini 38

Symphonies
A number of great composers have written nine symphonies. This exclusive club is formed by Ludwig van Beethoven (1770–1827), Anton Bruckner (1824–96), Dvořák, Glazunov, Schubert, and Vaughan Williams.

Among the most well-known composers, those with the greatest number of symphonies to their credit include:

Haydn 104
Hovhaness 63
Stamitz (JW) 58
Stamitz (K) 52
Mozart 41
Boccherini 30

Concertos
Probably the most prolific composers of concertos were Johann Joachim Quantz (1697–1773), who wrote 300 concertoes for the flute and Antonio Vivaldi (1678–1741), who wrote more than 460 concertoes, including the famous *Four Seasons*.

Among the most well-known composers, those with the greatest number of concertoes to their credit include:

Vivaldi 460 (plus)
Quantz 300
Tartini 135
Telemann 100
Albinoni 59
Mozart 52
Bach (JS) 49
Handel 44

Antonín Dvořák (1841–1904), Alexander Glazunov (1865–1936), Franz Schubert (1797–1828), and Ralph Vaughan Williams (1872–1958).

Europe employed different sequences of tones and semitones, and the scales used in Indian music and some modern jazz, for example, may use quarter tones.

The development of tonality was celebrated by Johann Sebastian Bach (1685–1750) in 24 keyboard preludes and fugues, one in each key, known as the *Well-tempered Clavier*. These displayed the advantages of the (at the time) novel system of *equal temperament*, whereby all of the notes of a keyboard instrument were 'tempered' to be precisely a semitone apart. The notes C sharp and D flat thus became identical, which was not (and still is not) the case with other instruments.

On a string instrument, where the notes are not pre-set, C sharp and D flat are slightly different from each other – imperceptibly so to the ears of most listeners.

In the course of a piece of music, a composer may often *modulate*, or change key, in order to avoid monotony. In Bach's time, an established and logical change was to the key based on the fifth note of the scale, known as the *dominant*. But modulations to harmonically more 'distant' keys were found to be a source of dramatic effects, as also was the sudden contrast between a minor key and a major, exploited by composers such as Beethoven with increasing freedom.

By the time Wagner composed *Tristan and Isolde* (1865), modulation had become so fluid that it was only a step away from *atonality*, or the composition of music in no fixed key at all.

Atonality was systematized by Schoenberg in what he described as *dodecaphonic* or 'twelve-note' music. In this method of composition, one of the major influences on 20th-century music, the twelve notes within an octave were employed in such a way that there was no home key and no reliance on modulation in the old sense, though key relationships did often remain implied, even if not specifically stated.

MUSICAL FORMS, STRUCTURES AND TERMS

absolute music music in which no extra-musical (i.e. descriptive) element is intended or should be inferred.

a cappella term to describe a vocal work without instrumental accompaniment.

aleatory music music in which each performance is dictated by chance elements.

anthem a short sacred vocal work.

aria a sung solo in opera or oratorio.

arietta a short aria.

atonal (of music) using all 12 notes of the scale.

aubade or **alborda** a morning song.

barcarolle a piece suggesting the song of a Venetian gondolier.

Baroque a period of music, c. 1650 to the death of Bach (1750).

boléro a Spanish dance in three-time.

bourrée an old French dance in common time (4/4).

cadence musical phrase used for ending phrases, sections or complete works.

cadenza a solo virtuoso piece before the final cadence in an aria, or at appropriate places in a concerto.

canon a work or section in which successive entries of the same melody overlap.

cantata a vocal work – sacred or secular – for one or more voices with instruments, sometimes short and light, sometimes extensive and with large forces, but always in several movements.

capriccio or **caprice** a fanciful work in free style.

cassation a divertimento-like work, probably intended for performance in the street.

catch a witty vocal piece for several voices in which the singers 'catch up' each other's words, often making puns with scatalogical or obscene results.

chaconne a graceful Spanish dance in three-time, its melody varied over a repeated bass phrase. Originally it was always in a major key.

chord a group of notes played simultaneously.

chromatic scale a scale including semitones so that all 12 notes within the octave are sounded.

classical strictly: a musical period of c. 1750 to c. 1800; loosely: 'serious' music as opposed to pop, jazz and light.

clef ('key') an indication of the 'register' in which the piece is to be performed. It takes the form of a medieval letter (C, F, or G) placed upon the relevant line of the stave. C = middle C; G = the fifth above; F = the fifth below.

coda ('tail') an ending piece designed to close a composition.

concertino a small concerto; also, the soloists in a concerto grosso.

concerto a work, usually in three movements, for one or more solo instruments with orchestra.

concerto grosso a Baroque form in which several soloists (the concertino) play against an orchestra; *cf* the later symphonie concertante.

concertstück ('concert piece') piece for soloist(s) and orchestra, usually in one movement.

continuo (often preceded by 'basso'), up to c. 1800, a keyboard instrument together with viol/double bass/cello/bassoon/archlute (in various combinations). Both instruments 'continued' the sound, i.e. they 'filled in' any missing harmonies not actually written down by the composer.

contrapuntal using counterpoint.

counterpoint two or more tunes played simultaneously without violating the rules of harmony.

descriptive music see programme music.

development see sonata form.

diatonic relating to the notes of the given key.

divertimento a multi-movement work of a diverting nature.

dodecaphony another term for twelve-note music.

dominant the keynote a fifth above the tonic.

duet a piece for two musicians.

ecossaise a piece in 'Scottish style'.

electronic music music consisting entirely of electronically produced sounds.

elegy a piece of a sad or funereal nature.

ensemble a group of musicians, smaller than an orchestra.

étude or **study** an exercise.

exposition see sonata form.

fantasia a piece whose imaginative course follows no formal rules.

finale the last movement of a multi-movement work; also, the ending of a movement.

fugato in fugal style. See fugue.

fugue a polyphonic composition in which the first statement of a tune is in the tonic; the second statement overlaps the first, and is in the dominant; and so on.

gavotte a lively dance in two-time.

gigue a jig, a sprightly dance in 6/8 or 12/8 time.

glee an 18th-century English piece for three or more voices unaccompanied.

harmony the art of combining notes into chords according to strict rules in a way that is pleasing.

hymn a song of praise to God.

impromptu a form originated by Chopin, supposedly extemporized.

incidental music music for a stage work.

intermezzo ('in the middle') a piece lying between two sections, whether in a piece of music, a play or an opera, etc.

introduction a piece which begins a work, often with material unrelated to the main work.

libretto ('little book') the text of an oratorio or opera. The 'big book' is the musical score.

lied a type of German Romantic song introduced in the late 18th century.

madrigal a secular song for several voices unaccompanied.

mass the Roman Catholic sung service of communion.

minimalism a modern American style of composition involving the extensive repetition of the simplest of melodies or rhythms, sometimes over slowly changing harmonies.

minuet an 18th-century dance in three-time.

modern a musical period from c. 1900 to the present day.

motet a part song, usually sacred in nature and usually unaccompanied.

movement a division of a musical work. The term derives from the various dance movements of the original suite.

musique concrète a French invention in which recorded sounds (usually from everyday life) are manipulated on tape into a composition.

nocturne a night piece.

obligato or **obbligato** ('obligatory' meaning 'indispensable') a vocal or instrumental part which plays an important, but not necessarily solo, role.

occasional music music written for a specific occasion.

opera drama set to music, in which most, or all, of the words are sung.

operetta light opera, often with spoken dialogue.

opus ('work') an individual work or group of works of a composer; each opus is given a number either by the composer or by a subsequent cataloguer. Opus numbers do not always reflect the chronology of composition.

oratorio the religious equivalent of opera but without action, costumes or scenery.

ornaments embellishments of a note or phrase, such as a *trill* (a rapid alternation of a written note with the one above or below), a *gracenote* (a subsidiary note appended to a written note), a *mordent* (a quick touching of the note below during the playing of a written note), etc.

overture the orchestral introduction to an opera or oratorio. A concert overture has no connection with a staged work.

passacaglia ('passing along the street') a form akin to the chaconne, but originally always in a minor key.

pentatonic scale a scale only using five notes (such as the black notes on a piano); often used in folk music.

pitch the precise height or depth of a note, according to its vibrations (cycles) per second. Today, A above middle C = 440 cycles per second.

polka a lively dance of Bohemian or Polish origin in three-time.

polonaise a slow or moderately-paced Polish dance in three-time.

polyphony ('many voiced') a style combining independent but interconnected melodic lines, i.e. using counterpoint.

prelude or **praeludium** an introductory movement.

programme music music which describes a place, event, person, etc. Compare absolute music.

recapitulation see sonata form.

recitative a vocal linking passage in an opera or oratorio imitating speech patterns; often declamatory, and less florid than an aria.

register the compass (lowest to highest notes) of a voice or instrument.

requiem a mass for the dead.

rhapsody a multi-sectioned piece akin to the capriccio, often with a nationalistic content.

ricercare ('research'), a learned piece written in the 16th and 17th centuries to explore obscure avenues of polyphony.

romance a vocal piece which sets a lyric tale to music; also, an instrumental work or movement in a graceful vein with a more agitated central section.

Romantic a period of music, c. 1800-c. 1900.

rondo a work in which the main section alternates with different sections ('episodes').

saltarello an Italian dance, quick, exciting, and involving jumping steps.

sarabande a stately Spanish dance in three-time.

scherzo ('joke') usually a rapid and light-hearted piece.

serenade a work for evening performance.

serial music music in which a sequence of notes are used equally and in strict rotation; the usual form is twelve-note music (see below).

siciliano a graceful dance in three-time, originating in Sicily.

singspiel a play with alternating musical pieces.

solo a work for one musician. In the 18th century solos were often accompanied.

sonata a (usually) multi-movement chamber work for one to four instrumentalists.

sonata form an 18th-century invention in which the first part ('exposition') states the musical material, modulating from tonic to dominant, the second part ('development') develops it (or other material), and the third part ('recapitulation') repeats it often with modifications in the tonic key. There is sometimes a coda.

song a sung melody, with or without accompaniment.

study see étude.

suite a work comprising several separate sections, or 'movements'; each section was originally a different dance.

symphonic poem or **tone poem** a 19th-century orchestral form, descriptive or evocative in character.

symphonie concertante a showy French invention (often wrongly termed 'sinfonia concertante') in which several soloists play against an orchestra; *cf* the earlier concerto grosso.

symphony a major orchestral work, usually of four movements.

tempo the pace at which a work is performed.

toccata a fantasia-like piece requiring brilliant execution.

tone poem see symphonic poem.

tonic term relating to the first degree of a minor or major scale.

trio a piece for three musicians. Larger groupings are equally self-explanatory: quartet, quintet, sextet, septet, octet, nonet, dectet.

trio sonata a Baroque and Classical chamber work for two melody instruments and continuo.

twelve-note music system of musical composition devised by Arnold Schoenberg (1874–1951) in which all 12 notes of the scale are used in sequence and in strict rotation.

variations a work which subjects a theme to a series of variations.

MUSICAL DIRECTIONS

accelerando becoming faster.

adagietto the diminutive of adagio, i.e. slightly quicker than adagio.

adagio ('at ease') a slow, comfortable pace.

allegretto the diminutive of allegro, i.e. a little slower than allegro.

allegro ('cheerful' or 'sprightly') a lively but not too fast a pace.

andante ('walking pace') moving along unhurriedly but regularly.

andantino the diminutive of andante. Originally this meant a little slower but today is taken to mean a little faster than andante.

arpeggio notes of a chord played upward or downward in quick succession, in imitation of a harp.

crescendo getting louder.

diminuendo getting quieter.

forte loudly.

fortissimo very loudly.

largo ('spacious') a broad, slow tempo.

lento slow.

mezza voce ('middle voice'), a subdued tone, between piano and forte.

mezzo moderately.

moderato moderate pace. Often used in conjunction with allegro, andante, etc, to moderate that pace.

pianissimo very quietly.

piano quietly.

pizzicato plucking the strings of a bowed instrument.

prestissimo very fast.

presto fast.

ralentando, ritardando or **ritenuto** getting slower.

sotto voce ('under the voice' or 'secretly') between forte and piano but nearer the latter.

vibrato rapid alteration of pitch or intensity of a note intended to impart 'expression'.

vivace lively. In old music, brightly but not too fast.

MUSIC SYMBOLS

Clefs

Clef symbols denote the register in which a work is to be performed.

Treble: 𝄞 = **G clef.** A representation of a medieval letter G, the focal point of which indicates the line G.

Bass: 𝄢 = **F clef.** A relic of the medieval letter F, centred on the F line.

Indications of Pitch

♭ = **Flat.** This sign flattens all the notes of the pitch indicated which follow it in the bar.

♯ = **Sharp.** This sign sharpens all the notes of the pitch indicated which follow it in the bar.

♮ = **Natural.** This sign indicates that a previously flattened or sharpened note is to return to its natural pitch.

Repeat Signs

Repeat (or da capo). Two vertical lines preceded by a colon instruct the player(s) to return to the beginning of the movement or piece, or to the previous repeat sign.

Note Lengths

Early notation employed four note lengths: double long, long, short ('breve'), and half-short ('semibreve'). Today, the longest note used – the breve – equals the early 'short', but it is uncommon.

Note	Names	Meaning
𝅝	semibreve (whole note)	half-short
𝅗𝅥	minim (half-note)	shortest (i.e. minimum)
♩	crotchet (quarter-note)	hook or crook (from its old appearance)
♪	quaver (eighth-note)	to trill, or quaver (quiver) in very short notes
𝅘𝅥𝅯	semiquaver (sixteenth-note)	half-quaver
𝅘𝅥𝅰	demisemiquaver (thirty-second-note)	half of half a quaver

Time Signatures

Examples of time signatures:

3/4 = three quarter-notes (crotchets) to the bar

3/8 = three eighth-notes (quavers) to the bar

POPULAR INSTRUMENTS

The following list of popular instruments includes a number that are now relatively uncommon but which play an important role in a few well-known pieces. Others, such as the hurdy-gurdy, were used to a greater extent in the past.

accordion was invented in Germany in 1822. It is box-like, with studs and, sometimes, a keyboard for note selection. See also concertina.

bongos small single-headed paired drums played with the hands; popular in Latin American music.

concertina resembles the accordion (see above). An English invention of 1829, it is hexagonal and never boasts a keyboard.

guitar a six-stringed development of the lute, possibly Moorish. It became the dominant instrument in Spanish music as early as the 8th century. The earliest surviving printed music for the guitar dates from 1546, while the first concerto for guitar dates from 1808.

harmonica see mouth organ.

hurdy-gurdy a European import from the East in the 9th century. It is roughly violin-shaped. The strings are activated by a resined wheel turned by a crank, and a keyboard stops the strings. The first 'art' use of the instrument was in 1733.

Jew's harp a metal frame holding a metal tongue which is plucked with the finger. The resulting vibrations are amplified by the player's mouth cavity. The first concerto was written for the instrument c. 1750. Sophisticated multi-instrument versions appeared later.

kazoo a membrane-vibrating instrument popular with children. The player hums through the instrument, modifying the voice with a hand over the membrane. It was first made in America c. 1850, probably based on ethnic African models.

keyboards a generic term for keyboard instruments. The tone is often extensively varied electronically. See also Keyboard instruments (Instruments of the concert orchestra; below).

mirliton another name for kazoo.

mouth organ or **harmonica** was invented in Germany in 1821, but the first concerto was not written for the instrument until 1951. Different notes are produced according to whether the instrument is blown or sucked; the chromatic version can reach four octaves by the use of a slide.

ocarina (Italian 'little goose') a goose-egg-shaped wind instrument, originally clay but now made from plastic. It originated in Egypt c. 3000 BC.

synthesizer an electronic sound-generator, created c. 1950 to imitate natural instruments, although it also creates its own tones. It is now common in popular music and commercialized jazz, where it is often attached to a keyboard.

tom tom a Western imitation of African drums, used since the 1920s in dance and jazz bands. The first 'art' use of the instrument was in 1943.

ukelele (Hawaiian 'jumping flea') was developed in Hawaii from a version of the Portuguese machada in the 1870s. It is popular in America, and has been widely used in jazz and light music.

zither a horizontal stringed instrument associated with Central Europe but widespread elsewhere in different varieties. The strings are plucked.

INSTRUMENTS OF THE CONCERT ORCHESTRA

The following instruments are those most usually found in a concert orchestra. The number of each of the most common of these instruments is to be found in the diagram on the next page.

Woodwind instruments

The following woodwind instruments are arranged in order of octaves. The piccolo, the first listed, lies an octave above the flute.

piccolo or **octave flute** *Earliest concerto:* c. 1735, by Vivaldi. *Earliest orchestral use:* 1717, Handel's *Water Music. History:* The name 'piccolo' (Italian 'small') dates from 1856, but the instrument goes back to prehistory with the flute and sopranino recorder as its more immediate parents.

flute (transverse or cross-blown) *Earliest concerto:* 1725, A. Scarlatti. *Earliest orchestral use:* 1681, Lully. *History:* Prehistoric (c. 18,000 BC); the modern Boehm flute dates from 1832.

oboe *Earliest concerto:* 1708, Marcheselli. *Earliest orchestral use:* 1657, Lully's *L'amour malade. History:* The oboe – the name comes from French *hautbois*, 'high wood' (1511) – originated in the Middle Ages from the schalmey family.

cor anglais *Earliest extant concerto:* 1817, Donizetti. *Earliest orchestral use:* 1722, Volckmar cantata. *History:* Purcell wrote for 'tenor oboe' c. 1690; this may have become the English horn. Alternatively, the name may come from 'angled horn', referring to its crooked shape.

clarinet *Earliest concerto:* c. 1740?, Vivaldi (concerto for two clarinets); c. 1747, Molter (concerto for one clarinet). *Earliest orchestral use:* 1726, Faber's Mass. *History:* The clarinet was developed by J. C. Denner (1655–1707) from the recorder and the schalmey families.

bass clarinet *Earliest orchestral use:* 1838, Meyerbeer's *Les Huguenots. History:* The prototype was made in 1772 by Gilles Lot of Paris; the modern Boehm form originated in 1838.

bassoon *Earliest concerto:* c. 1730?, Vivaldi. *Earliest orchestral use:* c. 1619. *History:* The bassoon was introduced in Italy c. 1540 as the lowest of the double-reed group.

double bassoon *Earliest orchestral use:* c. 1730, Handel. *History:* The instrument was 'borrowed' from military bands for elemental effects, particularly in opera.

saxophone *Earliest concerto:* 1903, Debussy's *Rhapsody. Earliest orchestral use:* 1844, Kastner's *Last King of Judah.* History: The saxophone was invented by Adolphe Sax, c. 1840.

Brass instruments

trumpet *Earliest concerto:* before 1700, Torelli; 1796, Haydn (keyed trumpet). *Earliest orchestral use:* c. 1800, keyed; 1835 valved, in Halévy's *La Juive. History:* The natural trumpet is of prehistoric origin: it formed the basis of the earliest orchestras.

horn *Earliest concerto:* 1717–21, Bach or Vivaldi (two horns); before 1721, Telemann (one horn). *Earliest*

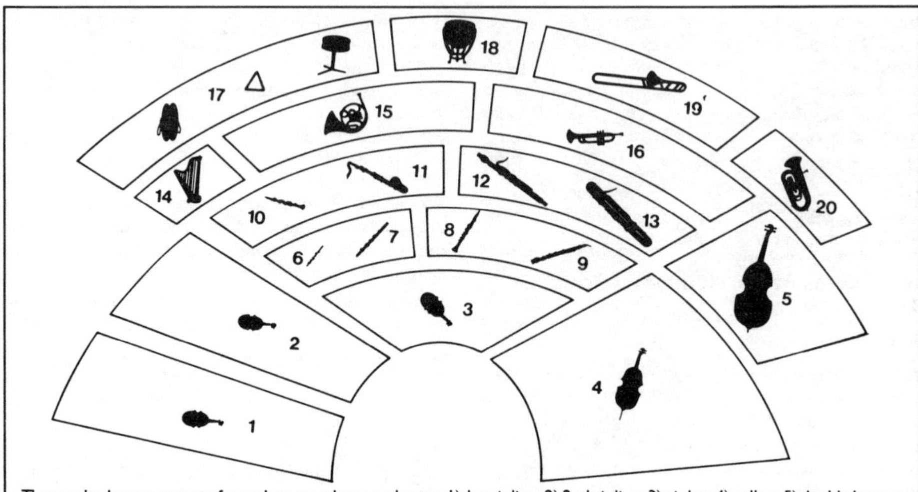

The standard arrangement of a modern symphony orchestra: 1) 1st violins; 2) 2nd violins; 3) violas; 4) cellos; 5) double basses; 6) piccolos; 7) flutes; 8) oboes; 9) cor anglais; 10) clarinets; 11) bass clarinets; 12 bassoons; 13) double bassoons; 14) harps; 15) horns; 16) trumpets; 17/18) percussions; 19) trombones; 20) tubas.

orchestral use: 1639, Cavalli. *History:* The horn was originally a prehistoric hunting instrument, and was, quite literally, the horn of an animal. The earliest music horns were the German helical horns of the mid-16th century; the rotary valve horn was patented in 1832.

trombone *Earliest concerto:* c. 1760, Wagenseil. *Earliest orchestral use:* c. 1600, as part of bass-line. *History:* The Roman *buccina* or slide-trumpet developed into the medieval sackbut, which became the modern trombone c. 1500.

tuba *Earliest concerto:* 1954, Vaughan Williams. *Earliest orchestral use:* 1830, Berlioz's *Symphonie Fantastique. History:* The tuba was patented by W. Wieprecht and Moritz, in Berlin in 1835.

Percussion instruments

The following list of percussion instruments includes a number that are relatively uncommon but which play an important role in a few well-known pieces.

anvil *History:* The anvil, which was originally a blacksmith's tool, has been used for musical effect since 1528.

bass drum *Earliest Western use:* 1680, Freschi's opera *Berenice vendicativa. Earliest orchestral use:* 1725, Finger's *Concerto alla Turchesa. History:* The bass drum is believed to have originated in the ancient Orient.

bells *History:* Bells have been used since ancient Egypt c. 3500 BC, but were first used in 'art' music in a funeral cantata by G. M. Hoffman, c. 1730.

castanets *History:* Castanets were known to the Egyptians by 730 BC. The name comes from the material from which they were made – chestnut wood (Spanish *castaña*).

Chinese blocks or **temple blocks** *Earliest orchestral use:* 1923, Walton's *Façade. History:* Chinese blocks originated in the ancient Far East where they were used in temple ceremonial. Chinese blocks entered European music via jazz bands, c. 1920.

cymbals *Earliest orchestral use:* 1680, Strungk's *Esther. History:* Cymbals originated in Ottoman Turkish military bands.

gong or **tam tam** *Earliest orchestral use:* 1791, Gossec's *Funeral March. History:* The gong originated in Indonesia by or before 300 BC.

kettle drum see timpani.

marimba *Earliest orchestral use:* before 1914, Grainger's *In a Nutshell. History:* The marimba developed as an African form of the xylophone (see below).

side or **snare drum** *Earliest orchestral use:* 1749, Handel's *Fireworks Music. History:* The small drums of prehistory were the direct ancestor of the medieval tabor, which developed into its modern form in the 18th century.

snare drum see side drum.

tambourine *Earliest orchestral use:* 1820. *History:* The tambourine was used by the Arabs in the Middle Ages, but the prototype of the modern instrument came from either ancient Assyria or ancient Egypt. The first known usage of the word 'tambourine' was in 1579.

tam tam see gong.

temple blocks see Chinese blocks.

tenor drum *Earliest orchestral use:* 1842. *History:* The modern tenor drum was originally developed for military use.

timpani or **kettle drum** *Earliest concerto:* c. 1780, J.C.C. Fischer. *Earliest orchestral use:* in an anonymous intermedia of 1565. *History:* The kettle drum originated in the ancient Orient.

triangle *Earliest orchestral use:* 1774, Glantz's *Turkish Symphony*, but it was used in opera from about 1680. *History:* The first known use of the triangle was in Ottoman Turkish military bands.

vibraphone a percussion instrument which consists of a set of metal bars placed over tubular metal resonators, which are caused to vibrate electronically. It is most commonly used in jazz bands. *Earliest orchestral use:* 1932. *History:* The instrument was first used in dance bands in the 1920s.

xylophone *Earliest orchestral use:* 1852, Kastner's *Livre-Partition. History:* The xylophone dates back to ancient times, probably originating in Africa. The earliest known use in Western music was in 1511.

Instruments of the strings section

cello see violoncello.

fiddle see violin.

violin *Earliest concerto:* 1698, Torelli. *Earliest orchestral use:* c. 1600. *History:* The violin family is descended from the lyre, although its more direct ancestors were the 6th-century crwth, rebec and fiddle. The first modern instruments, of Lombardic (North Italian) origin, appeared c. 1545. The words 'violin' and 'fiddle' both derive ultimately from the Latin *vitulari* (which means 'to skip like a calf').

viola *Earliest concerto:* before 1721, Telemann. *Earliest orchestral use:* c. 1600. *History:* See the violin, above.

violoncello or **cello** *Earliest concerto:* 1701, Jacchini. *Earliest orchestral use:* c. 1600. *History:* See the violin, above.

double bass *Earliest extant concerto:* c. 1765, Vanhal. *Earliest orchestral use:* c. 1600. *History:* The modern double bass developed alongside the violin family, but it is a closer relative to the bass viol or violone.

harp *Earliest concerto:* 1738, Handel. *Earliest orchestral use:* c. 1600. *History:* The harp is possibly prehistoric in origin, but it did not attain its modern form until 1792.

Keyboard instruments

The following list of keyboard instruments includes a number that are relatively uncommon in modern orchestras but which played an important role in many compositions in the past.

celesta an instrument invented by Mustel in Paris, in 1880; it was first used by an orchestra in Widor's ballet *Der Korrigane*, in the same year. Instead of strings, as in the piano (see below), the celesta's hammers strike metal plates to give a bell-like effect. See also glockenspiel (below).

clavichord an instrument which dates from the Middle Ages, but is little heard today. It has an exceedingly intimate voice, making it ideal for domestic use. In the clavichord, metal tangents (blades) strike upward to activate the string part-way along its length and to 'stop' (damp) the rest. Therefore, one string may serve for many notes but not simultaneously.

glockenspiel (German 'bell-play') an instrument related to the celesta (see above). The glockenspiel is sometimes equipped with a keyboard but more usually the plates are struck by hand-held hammers.

harmonium a portable reed-organ, which was invented by Grenié in Paris, c. 1835. In modern times it is not a common instrument, and it is now most usually heard as accompaniment for hymns in church. The first 'art' use of the harmonium was by César Franck about 1858.

harpsichord a keyboard instrument, which evolved from the psaltery during the 14th century – the earliest surviving example is dated 1521. The harpsichord usually has two manuals which control sets of strings that are plucked by plectra. Mainly a domestic instrument, the harpsichord also supported the bass line in early orchestras. The first solo concerto for the harpsichord was written c. 1720, but by c. 1800 the instrument had been eclipsed by the piano (pianoforte; see below).

Since about 1903, the harpsichord has been reintroduced and it has recently regained popularity with the revival of interest in ancient music.

organ a keyboard instrument which ultimately derives from the antique panpipes, but subsequent developments have made it the biggest and most powerful of all instruments. The first organ concerto was by Handel, c. 1730, while Saint-Saëns first used it in a symphony in 1886.

pianoforte or **piano** the most widely used modern keyboard instrument.

The first piano was built by Bartolomeo Cristofori in Florence shortly before 1700, working on the dulcimer principle of hammers hitting strings, and seeking a keyboard instrument which, unlike the harpsichord (see above), could play both loud and soft (hence, its early name, 'fortepiano'). Cristofori announced his perfected model in 1709 and examples exist from the 1720s. These early pianos display most of the principles of the modern piano, although three centuries of improvements to the instrument have refined the instrument enormously.

The earliest known printed music for the piano was by Giustini (1732). The first concerto composed for the piano was probably one by J. B. Schmidt in 1763.

The instrument attained its current name about 1776 and its modern iron-framed form about 1850. The upright 'parlour piano' is usually considered to be typical of the Victorian age, but the first were made in Germany during the 1770s.

The composer and pianist Muzio Clementi developed the techniques of the early piano to such a degree that he is often referred to as 'the father of the piano'. He developed both the techniques of piano playing and the instrument itself.

spinet a keyboard instrument which is the same shape as a harpsichord (see above), but which is smaller. The name may come from the Latin *spina* ('spines' or 'quills' – the plucking agent). It developed early in the 15th century.

virginals a table harpsichord (see above). The virginals are rectangular in shape. The first printed music in England for the instrument was *Parthenia*, published in London in 1611.

MUSICAL GENRES: A HISTORY OF MUSIC

Plainsong and Polyphony

Two of the crucial developments in the early history of Western music were *plainsong* and *polyphony*, both of which came about through the spread of the Christian religion, and whose musical foundations lay partly in Jewish chant, partly in Greece and Rome, and almost anywhere else where Christianity had taken root.

Plainsong consists of a single line of vocal melody in 'free' rhythm (i.e. not divided into metred bar lengths). Polyphony gained ground during the early years of Christianity and reached its peak in Gregorian chant, still used in the Roman Catholic Church today. Other parts of Europe produced their own ritual music of similar type. In *antiphons*, two separate bodies of singers performed plainsong chants in response to one another.

Plainsong, being confined to a single line of unaccompanied melody, falls into the category of *monophonic* music – Greek for 'single sound', implying absence of harmonic support or other melodies performed simultaneously with the original.

Polyphony conversely, means 'many sounds', and indicates the simultaneous sounding of two or more independent melodic lines to produce a coherent musical texture. The melodies in polyphony are described as being in *counterpoint* to each other, and the resulting music as *contrapuntal*. The art of polyphony began to emerge in Europe in the 12th and 13th centuries.

Ars Antiqua flourished at the most influential centre of musical activity in the 12th and 13th centuries, the church of Notre Dame in Paris. Here there developed a musical style based on plainsong and *organum*, an early form of polyphony involving the addition of parts to a plainsong melody. Such music was described by writers of the early 14th century as 'Ars Antiqua' (Latin for 'old art') to distinguish it from its successor 'Ars Nova' (Latin for 'new art')

Ars Nova flourished in France and Italy in the 14th century. It incorporated significant innovations in the areas of rhythm and harmony. The polyphonic setting of poetry to music began in this period in the form of the *ballade*, *rondeau* and *virelai*, collectively known as *chansons*. In France the *troubadours* – itinerant poet-musicians, often of aristocratic birth – were active in Provence in the 11th and 12th centuries. Their German equivalents were the *Minnesinger* (German 'love singers'), whose successors, the guilds of *Meistersinger* ('Mastersingers'), established themselves in some German cities in the 15th and 16th centuries.

The Renaissance

Generally, the beginning of the Renaissance in music is reckoned to be found in the increasing secularization of music that took place at the court of Burgundy in the early years of the 15th century. During this period significant developments occurred both in religious and secular musical forms.

In the domain of religious music, composers concentrated their efforts on the forms of the mass and the motet. Different types of mass setting developed, especially where the Reformation had established Protestant worship. In Germany the Lutheran chorale (later to exercise a deep influence on the music of J.S. Bach) took root, while in England the anthem (the Protestant equivalent of the Latin motet) took its place in the liturgy of the Church of England. But as the 16th century progressed, it was Italy that emerged as the crucially important musical centre. The polyphonic mass reached its apogee in the work of three great composers: Palestrina, Victoria and Lassus.

The art of the madrigal – a secular polyphonic composition for several voices, usually based on poems of some literary merit – had its roots in Italy, where early forms of the madrigal first appeared in the 14th century. Early madrigal composers were Flemish composers resident in Italy, and their madrigals were written for three or four voices. A larger number of voices and a more consistently polyphonic style became the norm as the century progressed.

Madrigals began to appear in England in the late 16th century. A native English tradition of madrigal composition incorporating features of the secular song, as exemplified by Byrd and Gibbons, was quickly established by composers such as Morley and Weelkes.

In the Middle Ages instruments were principally used to double voices in vocal polyphony or to provide music for dancing. A burgeoning of instrumental music took place in the 16th century when dance forms such as the stately *pavane* and vigorous *galliard* emerged. Non-dance forms of instrumental music included the *canzona*, the *ricercare* and the *fantasia*. Instrumental music in the 16th century was performed principally on the lute, the organ, the virginal and other stringed keyboard instruments, and by ensembles of viols and other instruments.

Music of the Baroque

Baroque, *Classical* and *Romantic* are the categories to which most music performed in the concert hall or opera house are assigned. But the boundaries of each are hazy, and the word Baroque is particularly difficult to define. A word of obscure origin, by the 17th and 18th centuries Baroque had become a term for the ornate, particularly ecclesiastical, architecture of the period. Other than defining a particular period between 1650 and 1750, Baroque has little meaning in application to music, though in its suggestion of ornateness of style it is obviously descriptive of certain types of 17th- and 18th-century composition.

A distinction is generally made between composers of the 'early Baroque' (such as Monteverdi, Frescobaldi and Schütz) and those of the 'late Baroque' (most notably Bach and Handel).

The vocabulary and techniques of instrumental and vocal composition underwent a massive expansion in the 17th century. Revolutionary change took place also in the formal organization of music: the medieval modes that had been the basis of polyphonic composition in the 16th century giving way during the 17th century to a system involving the exclusive use of modern scales.

In addition, innovations such as the *concertato* style – in which specific instrumental or vocal parts were accompanied by a *basso continuo*, or 'thorough bass' (involving a low-pitched instrument such as a cello or bass viol combined with a harpsichord, organ or lute) – distinguish the Baroque from the Renaissance that preceded it. The development of the two major new instrumental genres of the Baroque – the sonata and the concerto – was largely the work of Italian composers. As well as providing the emerging vocal genres of opera, cantata and oratorio, Italy was the principal source of instrumental ensemble music throughout the 17th century.

In France, as in England and Germany, composers were strongly influenced by Italian models of instrumental music. However, the greatest achievements of the French Baroque were in the domain of harpsichord music and opera. The overtures and dance movements from Lully's operas enjoyed a flourishing life outside the operatic context. So-called French overtures on the Lullian model were used by Handel in some of his operas and oratorios, and became an integral part of the Baroque orchestral suite.

Opera is the Italian word for 'work'. but as an abbreviation of *opera in musica* (a 'musical work'), it began to be used in 17th-century Italy for music dramas in which singers in costume enacted a story with instrumental accompaniment. The first true masterpieces in the form were by the Venetian composer Monteverdi, and many of the most prominent opera composers of the late 17th century and early 18th century came from Naples, giving rise to the term the *Neapolitan School.* The greatest operas of the early 18th century were written in England by Handel.

The Classical period

If the music of J.S. Bach represents the summit of the Baroque era, that of his sons, particularly Carl Philip Emanuel and Johann Christian, provides a link with the period loosely known as Classical. It was a time of new developments in the art of the symphony and concerto, of the birth of the string quartet and piano sonata, and of the humanizing of opera.

Vienna, the capital of the Austrian Habsburg Empire, now became the centre of musical progress, with Haydn, Mozart, and, before long, Beethoven as its principal representatives.

In the next generation Schubert was to sustain Vienna's musical pre-eminence. Both Beethoven and Schubert were to extend the Classical forms and infuse them with a Romantic sensibility. All four composers collectively became known as the First Viennese School. Classicism, in musical terms, has been defined as a style accepting certain basic conventions of form and structure (notably the sonata form; see under Musical Forms, Structures and Terms, above), and using these as a natural framework for the expression of ideas. Unlike Romantic music (see below), which developed out of Classicism, it saw no need to break the set boundaries, although in a discreet way its greatest practitioners did so more often than not.

Music of the Romantics

Romanticism in music was not necessarily born in 1800. But the first year of the 19th century, when Beethoven had just produced the first of his nine symphonies, is as good a time as any by which to commemorate the establishment of composers as individual artists – rather than as servants of rich patrons, which had been the case throughout the Baroque and Classical periods.

Beethoven, in his third symphony, the *Eroica* (1803–4), finally shattered the bounds of Classicism. It was not only the biggest symphony ever written until that time (though Beethoven himself was to surpass it in his ninth), it was also recognized to be a personal testament in music, the first of its kind, symbolizing Beethoven's battle with the growing deafness that was to destroy his career as a public performer, but which intensified his inspiration as a composer. The crucial role played by Beethoven in the progress of symphonic form, and of the art of the string quartet and piano sonata, was something no later composer could ignore. In his last quartets in particular, Beethoven explored the most profound emotional and spiritual tensions with a musical daring not seen again for another century.

The composer as artist was attracted to representational or *programme music* – music that evokes pictorial scenes or finds some way to tell a story in purely musical terms. Berlioz, Mendelssohn and Liszt were notable proponents of this genre. Liszt coined the term 'symphonic poem' for his descriptive orchestral works.

In opera, Wagner expanded and transformed the art of opera into what he preferred to describe as 'music drama'. In Italy, Verdi followed a parallel if more cautious path.

The rise of nationalist feeling all over Europe inspired many composers. Although Liszt's Hungarian Rhapsodies lacked Hungarian authenticity (in that Liszt mistook gypsy music for Hungarian folk music), nationalism in music was becoming a major force. Folk rhythms, folk dances, folk songs, folk legends and folk harmonies served as important sources of inspiration to such composers as Smetana, Dvořák, Grieg and Tchaikovsky.

Modernists and New Music

The years around 1900 marked the beginnings of Modernism. Wagner's *Tristan and Isolde* (1865) – see above – was the German figurehead, with Debussy's *Pelléas and Mélisande* (1902) as its French counterpart. From these two operas, the major trends in 20th-century music all flowed.

Modernism in music – as in the visual arts and literature – involved a radical break with existing conventions. It also involved what often appears as a greater distancing between the composer and the audience – audiences have tended to find Modernist works 'difficult'. However, although Modernism has been in the intellectual forefront of music in the 20th century, many composers have followed more accessible paths.

Music since 1945 has evolved in many different ways. For many composers – especially in the 1950s – the once revolutionary twelve-note technique of Schoenberg became the new orthodoxy, while the avant-garde of the 1960s and 1970s enthusiastically embraced the novel sound possibilities offered by the development of electronic music.

FAMOUS COMPOSERS

Albéniz, Isaac (1860–1909), Spanish composer whose works are characterized by traditional Spanish rhythms: *Iberia* (1906–09).

Albinoni, Tommaso (1671–1751), Italian composer who wrote prodigious amounts of instrumental and vocal music, including 81 operas.

Allegri, Gregorio (1582–1652), Italian composer: *Miserere.*

Auber, Daniel (1782–1871), French composer of 42 operas: *La Muette de Portici* (1828).

Bach, Carl Philipp Emmanuel (1714–88), German composer of over 200 sonatas and 13 symphonies – 3rd son of Johann Sebastian.

Bach, Johann Christian ('The English Bach'; 1735–82), German composer of concertos, symphonies, sacred music and 13 operas – 11th (youngest) son of Johann Sebastian (see below).

Bach, Johann Christoph Friedrich ('Buckeburg Bach'; 1732–95), German composer of oratorios, 14 symphonies and concertos – 9th son of Johann Sebastian (see below).

Bach, Johann Michael (1648–94), German composer of motets and choral works – brother of Johann Sebastian (see below).

Bach, Johann Sebastian (1685–1750), German composer of concertos, sonatas, over 250 cantatas and keyboard music. He is held by many to be the greatest of all Baroque composers: *Brandenburg Concertos* (1721), a collection of 48 preludes and fugues *The Well-Tempered Clavier* (1722–44), *St John Passion* (1723), *St Matthew Passion* (1729), the *Mass in B minor* (1733–38), and the *Goldberg Variations* (1742).

Bach, Wilhelm Friedemann ('Halle Bach'; 1710–84), German organist and composer – eldest son of Johann Sebastian (see above).

Balakirev, Mily (1837–1910), Russian composer who made an important contribution to the national school of Russian music.

Barber, Samuel (1910–81), US composer: *Adagio for Strings* (1938), the opera *Vanessa* (1957).

Bartók, Béla (1881–1945), Hungarian composer of fiercely modernist music based on folk music: *Music for Strings, Percussion and Celesta* (1936) and *Concerto for Orchestra* (1943).

Bax, Sir Arnold (1883–1953), English composer of romantic works: the tone poem *Tintagel* (1917).

Beethoven, Ludwig van (1770–1827), German composer of chamber music, 9 symphonies, 5 piano concertos, violin concerto, triple concertos, 32 piano sonatas, 16 string quartets and over 200 song settings: the opera *Fidelio* (1805), the symphonies *Eroica* (No. 3; 1803-04), *Pastoral* (No. 6; 1807–08) and *Choral* (No. 9; 1817–23), the piano sonatas *Pathétique* (1799), *Moonlight* (1800–01) and *Hammerklavier* (1817–18), the *Emperor* piano concerto (1809), and the *Missa Solemnis* (1819–22).

Bellini, Vincenzo (1801–35), Italian composer: the opera *Norma* (1831).

Benda, Jiri (1722–95), Czech composer who pioneered melodrama: *Ariadne auf Naxos* (1774).

Berg, Alban (1885–1935), Austrian composer: the operas *Wozzeck* (1914–22) and *Lulu* (1929–35), and the *Lyric Suite* (1928).

Berio, Luciano (1925–), Italian composer of electronic and other modern music.

Berlioz, Hector (1803–69), French composer: the symphonies *Symphonie Fantastique* (1830) and *Harold in Italy* (1834), the choral symphony *Roméo et Juliette* (1839), the operas *Benvenuto Cellini* (1834–37) and *Les Troyens* (*The Trojans*; 1856–58), and the cantata *La Damnation de Faust* (1846).

Berwald, Franz (1796–1868), Swedish composer of operas, concertos and four symphonies.

Binchois, Gilles (c. 1400–60), Franco-Flemish composer active at the Burgundian court.

Birtwhistle, Harrison (1934–), English composer: the opera *Punch and Judy* (1966–67).

Bizet, Georges (1838–75), French composer: the opera *Carmen* (1873–74).

Bloch, Ernst (1880–1959), Swiss composer who became a naturalized US citizen: *Israel Symphony* (1912–16).

Boccherini, Luigi (1743–1805), Italian composer of operas, 20 symphonies and 91 string quartets.

Boulez, Pierre (1925–), French composer of works using the twelve-note technique: *Le Marteau sans maître* (1953–55) and *Pli selon pli* (1957–62).

Brahms, Johannes (1833–97), German composer of symphonies, choral works and a large canon of chamber music: the choral works: *A German Requiem* (1868) and *Alto Rhapsody* (1869).

Britten, Benjamin (1913–76), English composer: operas: *Peter Grimes* (1945), *Billy Budd* (1951), *The Turn of the Screw* (1954) and *Death in Venice* (1973).

Bruckner, Anton (1824–96), Austrian composer: *Te Deum* (1881–84) and nine symphonies.

Bull, John (c. 1562–1628), English composer of keyboard music, especially for the virginals.

Busoni, Ferruccio (1866–1924), Italian composer: the piano piece *Fantasia contrappuntistica* (1910–12).

Byrd, William (1543–1623), English composer of sacred music, in particular for the Roman liturgy, and of fantasias for viol consort.

Cage, John (1912–92), US composer: the percussion and electronic pieces *Imaginary Landscapes* (1939–52).

Carter, Elliott (1908–), US composer: *Symphony of Three Orchestras* (1977).

Charpentier, Marc-Antoine (1634–1704), French composer of oratorios and motets: *Te Deum (c. 1690).*

Cherubini, Luigi (1760–1842), Italian composer of masses and 30 operas: the operas *Médée* (1797) and *les Deux Journées* (adapted in English as *The Water Carrier*, 1800).

Chopin, Frédéric (1810–49), Polish composer of nocturnes, ballades, mazurkas, polonaises, studies, waltzes and scherzos, all for the piano.

Cimarosa, Domenico (1749–1801), Italian composer of comic operas and of harpsichord sonatas.

Clementi, Muzio (1752–1832), Italian-born British composer and pianist who contributed to the development of piano techniques: a series of piano soanatas.

Copland, Aaron (1900–90), US composer of works based on American folk idioms: the ballets *Billy the Kid* (1938) and *Appalachian Spring* (1944).

Corelli, Arcangelo (1653–1713), Italian pioneer composer of concertos and sonatas: the 12 *Concerti Grossi* (1714) established the form of the concerto grosso.

Couperin, François ('Le Grand'; 1668–1733), French composer – nephew of Louis (see below). He composed in a wider range of genres than his uncle, but is best known for his elegant harpsichord pieces.

Couperin, Louis (c. 1626–61), French composer of harpsichord and organ music.

Cowell, Henry (1897–1965), US composer of 21 symphonies, chamber music and an opera.

Dallapiccola, Luigi (1902–75), Italian composer whose works were the first in Italy to use the twelve-note method.

Debussy, Claude (1862–1918), French composer whose works are characterized by a 'dream-like' quality sometimes called 'musical impressionism': numerous works for piano, the orchestral pieces *Prélude à l'après-midi d'une faune* (1892–94), *Nocturnes* (1897–99) and *La Mer* (1903–05), and the opera *Pelléas et Mélisande* (1902).

Delibes, Léo (1836–91), French composer: the opera *Lakmé* (1883) and the ballet *Coppélia* (1870).

Delius, Frederick (1862–1934), English composer: the orchestral piece *On hearing the first cuckoo in spring* (1911–13).

Denisov, Edison (1929–), Russian composer of highly original music which draws upon electronic techniques and folk music.

Desprès, Josquin (1440–1521), Flemish composer of masses, motets and chansons.

D'Indy, Vincent (1851–1931), French composer: *Symphonie Cévenole* (1886).

Donizetti, Gaetano (1797–1848), Italian composer: the operas *Maria Stuarda* (1835) and *Lucia di Lammermoor* (1835).

Dowland, John (1563–1626), English composer of songs with lute accompaniment.

Dufay, Guillaume (c. 1400–74), Franco-Flemish composer active at the Burgundian court.

Dunstable, John (c. 1385–1453), English composer active in France.

Dvořák, Antonín (1841–1904), Czech composer: *Slavonic Dances* (1878–86) and the symphony *From the New World* (No. 9; 1893).

Elgar, Edward (1857–1934), English composer: *Enigma Variations* (1898–99), the oratorio *The Dream of Gerontius* (1899–1900) and *Cello Concerto* (1919).

Falla, Manuel de (1876–1946), Spanish composer whose works echo Andalusian folk music: the ballet *The Three-Cornered Hat* (1917–19).

Fauré, Gabriel (1845–1924), French composer: the opera *Pénélope* (1913) and the *Requiem* (1877–90).

Franck, César (1822–90), Belgian composer: *Symphonic Variations* (1885).

Frescobaldi, Girolamo (1583–1643), Italian organist and composer of toccatas, fugues and capriccios.

Gabrieli, Andrea (c. 1510–86), Venetian composer in a flamboyant polychoral (multi-choir) style.

Gabrieli, Giovanni (?1557–1612), Venetian composer of motets featuring a rich instrumental accompaniment. He was the nephew and pupil of Andrea Gabrieli (see above).

Gesualdo, Carlo (c. 1560–1613), Italian composer of madrigals.

Gibbons, Orlando (1583–1625), English composer of sacred and secular music, including anthems.

Glass, Philip (1937–), US minimalist composer of avant-garde operas.

Glazunov, Alexander (1865–1936), Russian composer: the ballet *The Seasons* (1899).

Glinka, Mikhail (1804–57), Russian composer: the operas *A Life for the Tsar* (1836) and *Ruslan and Ludmilla* (1842).

Gluck, Christoph Willibald von (1714–87), German composer who made opera more genuinely dramatic: the operas *Orpheus and Eurydice* (1762) and *Alceste* (1767).

Górecki, Henryk (1933–), Polish composer: *Symphony No. 3* (1976).

Gounod, Charles François (1818–93), French composer: the opera *Faust* (1859).

Grainger, Percy (1882–1961), Australian-born US composer: folk songs and lighter works often based upon traditional tunes.

Granados, Enrique (1867–1916), Spanish composer of operas and piano music: *Goyescas* (1914–15).

Grieg, Edvard Hagerup (1843–1907), Norwegian composer: the incidental music for the play *Peer Gynt* (1875).

Handel, George Frideric (1685–1759), German-born British composer, impresario, musical director, virtuoso keyboard player and teacher. In his operas, oratorios, concertos and suites, he created a highly individual style of writing, best seen in: *Water Music* (1717), *Music for the Royal Fireworks* (1749), 42 operas, anthems including *Zadok the Priest* (1727), the *Concerti Grossi* (1734–40) and numerous oratorios, including *Saul* and *Israel in Egypt* (1739), *Messiah* (1741), *Solomon* (1748) and *Jephtha* (1752).

Haydn, Franz Joseph (1732–1809), Austrian composer of piano sonatas and trios, concertos, operas, masses, string quartets (a form he established) and

104 symphonies: the *London Symphonies* (Nos. 92–104; 1789–95), and the oratorios *The Creation* (1798) and *The Seasons* (1801).

Henze, Hans Werner (1926–), German composer: the oratorio *The Raft of Medusa* (1968) and the war opera *We Come to the River* (1976).

Hindemith, Paul (1895–1963), German composer who is associated with the term 'utility music': the opera *Mathis der Maler* (1933–35).

Holst, Gustav (1874–1934), English composer: the suite *The Planets* (1914–16) and *Egdon Heath* (1927).

Honegger, Arthur (1892–1955), Swiss composer: the orchestral piece *Pacific 231* (1923) and the oratario *Jeanne d'Arc au bûcher* (1934–35).

Hovhaness, Alan (1911–), US composer of 63 symphonies, 10 operas and choral works.

Humperdinck, Engelbert (1854–1921), German composer: the opera *Hansel und Gretel* (1893).

Ibert, Jacques (1890–1962), French composer: the orchestral piece *Divertissement* (1930).

Ireland, John (1879–1962), English composer of chamber music and songs.

Ives, Charles (1874–1954), US composer of highly individualistic works: the orchestral set *Three Places in New England* (1903–14).

Janácek, Leos (1854–1928), Czech composer of operas: *Jenufa* (1903), *Katya Kabanova* (1921), *The Cunning Little Vixen* (1923), *The Makropoulos Case* (1925) and *From the House of the Dead* (1928).

Khachaturian, Aram (1903–1978), Armenian composer: the ballet *Spartacus* (1954).

Kodály, Zoltán (1882–1967), Hungarian composer whose works are characterized by a strong national flavour: the opera *Háry János* (1925–26).

Krenek, Ernst (1900–91), Austrian-born US composer: the opera *Jonny spielt auf* (1925–26).

Lassus, Roland de (1532–94), Flemish composer of nearly 2000 works.

Lehár, Franz (1870–1948), Hungarian composer of operetta: *The Merry Widow* (1905).

Leoncavallo, Ruggero (1857–1919), Italian composer: the opera *Pagliacci* (1892).

Ligeti, Gyorgy (1923–), Hungarian composer: *Requiem* (1965) and the opera *Le Grand Macabre* (1975).

Liszt, (Ferencz) Franz (1811–86), Hungarian composer of a series of 13 descriptive orchestral works ('symphonic poems') and of piano pieces: the symphonies *Faust* (1854–57) and *Dante* (1856), the symphonic poem *Les Préludes* (1856), and the piano piece *Liebesträume* (1850).

Lully, Jean-Baptiste (1632–87), Italian-born French composer who established the form of the French opera, which was to reach its peak in the operas of Rameau.

Lutoslawski, Witold (1913–94), Polish composer of works incorporating modern techniques: *String Quartet* (1964).

Machaut, Guillaume de (c. 1300–77), French composer who championed isorhythms, whereby rhythm and melody followed strictly repeated patterns that were not in synchronization, and was a pioneer of chansons.

Mahler, Gustav (1860–1911), Austrian composer of nine large-scale symphonies: the symphonies *Resurrection* (No. 2; 1884–94) and *Symphony of a Thousand* (No. 8; 1906–07).

Marenzio, Luca (c. 1553–99), Italian composer of madrigals.

Martin, Frank (1890–1974), Swiss composer: *Petite Symphonie Concertante* (1946).

Mascagni, Pietro (1863–1945), Italian composer: the opera *Cavalleria rusticana* (1888).

Massenet, Jules (1842–1912), French composer: the operas *Manon* (1882–84) and *Don Quichotte* (1909).

Maxwell Davies, Peter (1934–), English composer: the opera *Taverner* (1970), the theatre pieces *Vesalii Icones* (1969) and *Eight Songs for a Mad King* (1969).

Mendelssohn, Felix (1809–47), German composer: the overtures *A Midsummer Night's Dream* (1826) and *Hebrides* (or *Fingal's Cave*; 1830), and the oratorios *St Paul* (1836) and *Elijah* (1846).

Messiaen, Olivier (1908–92), French composer of organ, piano and religious works: the piano work *Catalogue d'oiseaux* (1956–58).

Milhaud, Darius (1892–1974), French composer whose works are characterized by polytonality.

Monteverdi, Claudio (1567–1643), Italian composer of three innovative operas and the *Vespro della Beata Vergine* ('Vespers of the Blessed Virgin'; 1610), which runs the entire gamut of contemporary types of sacred music.

Morley, Thomas (1557–c. 1602), English organist and composer of madrigals.

Mozart, Wolfgang Amadeus (1756–91), Austrian composer of 41 symphonies, over 40 concertos, 26 string quartets, 21 operas, 7 string quintets and sonatas: the operas *Le nozze di Figaro* (*The Marriage of Figaro*; 1786), *Don Giovanni* (1787), *Così fan tutte* (1789) and *Die Zauberflöte* (*The Magic Flute*; 1791), the symphonies *Paris* (1778), *Prague* (1786) and *Jupiter* (1788), and the orchestral piece *Eine kleine Nachtmusik* (1787).

Mussorgsky, Modest (1839–81), Russian composer: the opera *Boris Godunov* (1868–72) and the piano piece *Pictures at an Exhibition* (1874).

Nielsen, Carl (1865–1931), Danish composer whose work is characterized by 'progressive tonality': six symphonies including *The Inextinguishable* (No. 4; 1915–16).

Nono, Luigi (1924–90), Italian composer of works characterized by their uncompromising severity: the opera *Intolleranza* (1960–61).

Ockeghem, Johannes (c. 1410–c. 1495), Flemish composer of sacred and secular music.

Offenbach, Jacques (1819–80), French composer of operetta: the opera *The Tales of Hoffmann* (1881).

Orff, Carl (1895–1982), German composer: the oratorio *Carmina Burana* (1935–36).

Pachelbel, Johann (1653–1706), German composer of canons, airs and 78 choral preludes.

Paganini, Niccolò (1782–1840), Italian virtuoso violinist and composer of violin concertos and caprices.

Palestrina, Giovanni (c. 1525–84), Italian composer of over 100 masses and 250 motets.

Parry, Hubert (1848–1918), English composer of songs and choral music: *Songs of Farewell* (1916) and *Jerusalem* (1916).

Pärt, Arvo (1935–), Estonian composer: three symphonies and *St John Passion* (1982).

Penderecki, Krzysztof (1933–), Polish composer of works characterized by the use of sensational effects: *Threnody for the Victims of Hiroshima* (1960) and the opera *The Devils of Loudon* (1969).

Pérotin (c. 1160–1225), French choirmaster of Notre Dame in Paris.

Poulenc, Francis (1899–1963), French composer: the ballet *Les Biches* (1923), four operas, piano pieces, choral works and songs.

Prokofiev, Sergey (1891–1953), Russian composer: the ballet *Romeo and Juliet* (1936), the operas *The Love for Three Oranges* (1919) and *War and Peace* (1941–52), and the piece for orchestra and narrator *Peter and the Wolf* (1936).

Puccini, Giacomo (1858–1924), Italian composer of operas: *La Bohème* (1895), *Tosca* (1899), and *Madama Butterfly* (1901–04).

Purcell, Henry (1659–95), English composer of theatre music, church music, string fantasias and sonatas: the miniature opera *Dido and Aeneas* (1683 or 4), the incidental music for *The Fairy Queen* (1692) and *Queen Mary's Funeral Music* (1695).

Quantz, Johann Joachim (1697–1773), German composer of 312 concertos for the flute.

Rakhmaninov, Sergey (1873–1943), Russian composer whose works – notably for piano – are characterized by Romantic nostalgia.

Rameau, Jean-Philippe (1683–1764), French composer of operas: *Hippolyte et Aricie* (1733) and *Castor et Pollux* (1737).

Ravel, Maurice (1875–1937), French composer: the orchestral pieces *Rapsodie espagnole* (1907), *Pavane pour une infante défunte* (1910) and *La Valse* (1919–20), and the ballet score *Boléro* (1928).

Resphigi, Ottorino (1879–1936), Italian composer: the ballet *The Fantastic Toyshop* (1919) and the orchestral suites *Fountains of Rome* (1914–16), *Old Airs and Dances for Lute* (1917) and *Pines of Rome* (1924).

Riley, Terry (1935–), US composer of minimalist music characterized by the extensive repetition of simple melodies in changing harmonies.

Rimsky-Korsakov, Nikolay (1844–1908), Russian composer of operas, including *The Snow Maiden* (1880–81) and *The Golden Cockerel* (1906–07), and of orchestral pieces, including *Sheherazade* (1888).

Rodrigo, Joaquín (1901–), Spanish composer of music for guitar and orchestra in a traditional Spanish style: *Concierto de Aranjuez* (1939).

Rossini, Gioacchino (1792–1868), Italian composer of 38 operas: *Tancredi* (1812), *The Barber of Seville* (1816), *La Cenerentola* (*Cinderella*; 1816), *La gazza ladra* (*The Thieving Magpie*; 1817) and *William Tell* (1829).

Saint-Saëns, Camille (1835–1921), French composer: the opera *Samson et Dalila* (1867–77) and the orchestral pieces *Danse macabre* (1874) and *Carnaval des animaux* (1886).

Salieri, Antonio (1750–1825), Italian composer of over 40 operas. His hostility to Mozart led to (groundless) rumours that he poisoned Mozart.

Sammartini, Giovanni Battista (c. 1698–75), Italian composer of about 2000 works in many genres.

Satie, Erik (1866–1925), French composer for piano: the ballet *Parade* (1917), and the piano pieces *Trois Gymnopédies* (1888) and *Trois morceaux en forme de poire* (1903).

Scarlatti, Alessandro (1660–1725), Neapolitan composer of operas (of which 115 survive). One of Scarlatti's important innovations was the three-movement form of the Italian opera overture or sinfonia, regarded by many as being the earliest forerunner of the Classical symphony.

Scarlatti, Domenico (1685–1757), Neapolitan composer – son of Alessandro (see above). His 550 single-movement sonatas for harpsichord considerably extended the technical and musical possibilities of keyboard writing.

Schoenberg, Arnold (1874–1951), Austrian composer whose later works are characterized by atonality, particularly the twelve-note system which he devised: the string sextet *Verklarte Nacht* (1899), the orchestral piece for soprano and five instruments *Pierrot Lunaire* (1912), and the opera *Moses und Aron* (1932–51).

Schubert, Franz (1797–1828), Austrian composer of 9 symphonies, string quartets, piano sonatas and 600 Lieder: the symphonies *Unfinished* (No. 8; 1822) and *Great* (No. 9; 1825), the piano quintet *Die Forelle* (*The Trout*; 1819), a string quartet in C major (1828), the piano sonata *Grand Duo* (1824), the song cycles *Die schöne Müllerin* (1823) and *Winterreise* (1827), and the song settings *Erlkönig* (1815) and *Die Forelle* (*The Trout*; 1817).

Schumann, Clara (Clara Josephine Wieck; 1819–96), German pianist and composer; wife of Robert (see below): works for orchestra and piano pieces.

Schumann, Robert (1810–56), German composer of songs, piano music and symphonies: the song cycles *Dichterliebe* (*Poet's Love*; 1840) and *Frauen-liebe und Leben* (1840).

Schütz, Heinrich (1585–1672), German composer of choral music whose style was to prove an influence on German composers up until the time of Bach.

Shnitke, Alfred (1934–), Russian composer of works that often include a humorous element.

Shostakovitch, Dmitri (1906–75), Russian composer of 15 symphonies and string quartets: the opera *The Lady Macbeth of the Mtsensk District* (1930–32).

Sibelius, Jean (1865–1951), Finnish composer: seven symphonies, the symphonic poems *Kullervo* (1892) and *Finlandia* (1899), and the suite *Karelia* (1893).

Skryabin, Alexander (1872–1915), Russian composer of symphonies and piano sonatas: the symphony *Prometheus* (No. 5; 1908–10).

Smetana, Bedrich (1824–84), Czech composer of operas, chamber music and symphonic poems: the opera *The Bartered Bride* (1866).

Stamitz, Johann (1717–57), German composer of the Mannheim School, whose works are characterized by 'Mannheim rockets' (brilliant scale passages).

Stamitz, Karl (1745–1801), German composer of the Mannheim School – son of Johann (see above).

Stanford, Charles Villiers (1852–1924), Irish composer: *Irish Symphony* (No. 3; 1887) and *Songs of the Sea* (1904).

Stockhausen, Karlheinz (1928–), German composer: the seven-part opera cycle *Licht* (1984–), the piece for three orchestras *Gruppen* (1957).

Strauss, Johann the elder (1804–49), Austrian composer of waltz music and *Radetzky March* (1848).

Strauss, Johann the younger (1825–99), Austrian composer: the operetta *Die Fledermaus* (1874), and the waltzes *An der schönen blauen Donau* (*Blue Danube*) and *Kaiser-Walzer* (*Emperor Waltz*).

Strauss, Richard (1864–1949), German composer of operas and symphonic poems: the operas *Salome* (1905), *Elektra* (1908) and *Der Rosenkavalier* (1910).

Stravinsky, Igor (1882–1971), Russian-born composer: the ballets *The Firebird* (1910), *Petrushka* (1911) and *The Rite of Spring* (1913).

Sullivan, Sir Arthur (1842–1900), English composer of operetta and oratorios, the former to libretti by W.S. Gilbert.

Szymanowski, Karol (1882–1937), Polish composer: the ballet *Harnasie* (1923–31).

Tallis, Thomas (c. 1505–85), English composer who introduced the European polyphonic tradition to England: masses, two settings of the *Magnificat,* and the extraordinary 40-part motet, *Spem in alium.*

Tartini, Giuseppe (1692–1770), Italian violinist and prolific composer: 135 violin concertoes and *Devil's Trill* sonata (after 1745).

Taverner, John (1944–), English composer whose music has a profound religious spirit: *The Protecting Veil* (1987).

Tchaikovsky, Pyotr Ilyich (1840–93), Russian composer: the symphony *Pathétique* (1893), the opera *Eugène Onegin* (1877–78), and the ballets *Swan Lake* (1875–76), *The Sleeping Beauty* (1888–89) and *Nutcracker* (1891–92).

Telemann, Georg Philipp (1681–1767), German composer of concertos and orchestral suites who, in his lifetime, enjoyed a greater reputation than his friends Bach and Handel.

Tippett, Michael (1905–), English composer: the operas *The Midsummer Marriage* (1952), *The Knot Garden* (1970) and *New Year* (1988).

Tomkins, Thomas (1572–1656), Welsh composer of polyphonic madrigals.

Torelli, Giuseppe (1658–1709), Italian composer of concertos.

Varèse, Edgard (1883–1965), French-born US composer, who made early experiments in electronic music.

Vaughan Williams, Ralph (1872–1958), English composer: *Sea Symphony* (1903–09), the opera *The Pilgrim's Progress* (1951) and songs based upon folk-songs.

Verdi, Giuseppe (1813–1901), Italian composer of opera: *Nabucco* (1841), *Il Trovatore* (1852), *La Traviata* (1853), *Aida* (1870), *Otello* (1886) and *Falstaff* (1892).

Victoria, Luis de (c. 1548–1611), Spanish composer of church music characterized by intense dramatic feeling.

Villa-Lobos, Heitor (1887–1959), Brazilian composer: the orchestral works *Bachianas Brasileiras* (1930–44).

Vivaldi, Antonio (1678–1741), Italian priest, violinist and composer: sacred music, 94 operas (of which 45 survive), sonatas, cantatas and more than 460 concertos, including *The Four Seasons* (1725).

Wagner, Richard (1813–83), German composer of opera: *The Flying Dutchman* (1841), *Tannhäuser* (1845), *Lohengrin* (1846–48), *Tristan and Isolde* (1857–59), *The Mastersingers of Nuremberg* (1862–67), *Parsifal* (1878–82) and the opera cycle *The Ring* (*Das Rheingold, Die Walküre, Siegfried* and *Götterdämmerung;* 1853–74).

Walton, William (1902–83), English composer: *Façade* (1921) and the cantata *Belshazzar's Feast* (1931).

Weber, Carl Maria von (1786–1826), German composer of operas, symphonies, chamber and piano music: the operas *Der Freischütz* (1821) and *Oberon* (1826).

Webern, Anton (1883–1945), Austrian composer whose works are characterized by serialism: chamber symphony (1924) and chamber concerto (1934).

Weelkes, Thomas (c. 1576–1623), English organist and composer of madrigals.

Weill, Kurt (1900–50), German composer: *Die Dreigroschenoper* (*The Threepenny Opera*; 1928).

Wilbye, John (1574–1638), English composer of madrigals.

Wolf, Hugo (1860–1903), Austrian composer, notably of songs: *Italian Serenade* (1892).

Xenakis, Iannis (1922–), Romanian-born Greek composer of works scored for conventional instruments but often written with the aid of a computer.

NICKNAMES OF PIECES OF CLASSICAL MUSIC

Alla Rustica Vivaldi's Concerto in G for strings (RV151); written in a 'rustic' style.

Alleluja Haydn's Symphony No 30 in C; features the Gregorian Alleluja theme.

American Dvořák's String Quartet in F, Op 96; written in Iowa, it uses Black American themes.

Antar Rimsky-Korsakov's Symphony No 2, Op 9; named for the early Russian poet Antar.

Antarctica Vaughan Williams' Symphony No 7; developed from the composer's film music for *Scott of the Antarctic.*

Appassionata Beethoven's Piano Sonata in F minor, Op 57; because of the passionate nature of the work.

Archduke Beethoven's Piano Trio in B flat; dedicated to Archduke Rudolf of Austria.

Babi Yar Shostakovich's Symphony No 13; named for the Babi Yar Jewish cemetery, Kiev.

Bear Haydn's Symphony No 82 in C; the finale begins with a 'growling' sound.

Bell Khachaturian's Symphony No 2; begins with a bell-like sound.

Bells of Zlonice Dvořák's Symphony No 1 in C minor, Op 3; said to incorporate the motifs of the bells of Zlonice, Dvořák's home.

Bird Haydn's String Quartet in C, Op 33; features birdsong impressions.

Chasse Haydn's Symphony No 73 in D; the finale was the overture to an opera featuring hunting.

Choral Beethoven's Symphony No 9 in D minor; has a choral finale.

Classical Prokofiev's Symphony No 1 in D, Op 25; written in the classical style.

Clock Haydn's Symphony No 101 in D; features a 'tick-tock' sound.

Coronation Mozart's Piano Concerto in D (K537); reputedly played at the coronation celebrations of Leopold II of Austria.

Death and the Maiden Schubert's String Quartet in D minor (D810); uses the theme of the song of that name.

Dissonance Mozart's String Quartet in C (K456); the first movement features harsh dissonances.

Dream Haydn's String Quartet in F, Op 50; the second movement has a dream-like quality.

Drum Roll Haydn's Symphony No 103 in E flat; begins with a drum roll.

Ebony Stravinsky's Clarinet Concerto; written for Woody Herman's ebony clarinet.

Eco in Lontano Vivaldi's Two-Violin Concerto in A (RV552); features an echo (Ital. *eco in lontano*, echo in the distance).

Emperor Beethoven's Piano Concerto No 5 in E flat; nickname used only in English – origin unknown.

Emperor Haydn's String Quartet in C, Op 76, No 3; from the slow theme of the third movement, said to have been inspired by *God Save the King.*

Eroica Beethoven's Symphony No 3 in E flat; named 'after a hero' (Napoleon I).

Fantasia Haydn's String Quartet in E flat, Op 76, No 6; after the slow movement, a fantasia.

Farewell Haydn's Symphony No 45 in F sharp minor; famous for the instrumentalists' departures during the finale, this symphony is said to commemorate the wish of the members of Haydn's orchestra to take a long overdue holiday.

Festive Smetana's Symphony in E; the finale features Haydn's 'Emperor Hymn'.

Fiery Angel Prokofiev's Symphony No 3 in C minor; based upon themes from the opera of the same name.

Fire Haydn's Symphony No 59 in A; was played between the acts of the opera *The Burning House.*

Four Temperaments Nielsen's Symphony No 2; based upon the medieval 'four humours'.

From the New World Dvořák's Symphony No 9 in E minor; written while the composer was in the USA.

Ghost Beethoven's Piano Trio in D, Op 70, No 1; the second movement has an eerie character.

Great Schubert's Symphony No 9 in C major; called Great to distinguish it from Schubert's Little Symphony, also in C major.

Haffner Mozart's Symphony No 35 in D, K 385; written for the Haffner family of Salzburg.

Hallelujah Handel's Organ Concerto in B flat, Op 7, No 3; features a motif from Handel's Hallelujah Chorus (from the *Messiah*).

Hammerklavier Beethoven's Piano Sonata in B flat, Op 106; written to be played on a hammered klavier.

Harmonious Blacksmith Handel's Harpsichord Suite No 5 in E; Handel is supposed to have been inspired while watching a blacksmith at Stanmore, near London.

Harp Beethoven's String Quartet in E flat, Op 74; features pizzicato passages in the first movement.

Hen Haydn's Symphony No 83 in G minor; features a 'clucking' sound.

Hoffmeister Mozart's String Quartet in D, K 499; published by Hoffmeister of Vienna.

Hornsignal Haydn's Symphony No 31 in D; features hunting horns.

Hunt Mozart's String Quartet in B flat, K 458; the finale suggests a hunting scene.

Hymn of Praise Mendelssohn's Symphony No 2 in B flat; there is choral finale resembling a hymn of praise.

Imperial Haydn's Symphony No 53 in D; the first movement has a ceremonial character.

Inextinguishable Nielsen's Symphony No 4; the work is said to express the inextinguishable human spirit.

Italian Bach's Solo Harpsichord Concerto; written in the Italian manner with three movements.

Italian Mendelssohn's Symphony No 4 in A; reflects the composer's impressions of his visit to Italy.

Joke Haydn's String Quartet in E flat, Op 33, No 3; the final movement has several false endings.

Jupiter Mozart's Symphony No 41 in C, K 551; may have been named Jupiter because of the impressive stature of the piece.

Kegelstadt Mozart's Trio in E flat, K 498; the 'skittle alley trio' was said to have been devised by Mozart while playing skittles.

Kreutzer Beethoven's Violin Sonata in A, Op 47; dedicated to the composer of the same name.

Lamentatione Haydn's Symphony No 26 in D minor; the work has a deep religious intensity.

Lark Haydn's String Quartet in D, Op 64, No 5; the ascent of the violin at the start is said to resemble a lark.

Leningrad Shostakovich's Symphony No 7 in C; written in Leningrad during the World War II siege.

Linz Mozart's Symphony No 36 in C, K 425; written in Linz.

Little Schubert's Symphony No 6 in C major; called Little to distinguish it from Schubert's Great.

Little Russian Tchaikovsky's Symphony No 2 in C minor; features the Little Russian folk song *The Crane*.

London Haydn's Symphony No 104 in D; written in London.

Matin Haydn's Symphony No 6 in D; one of three symphonies representing different times of day.

May Day Shostakovich's Symphony No 3 in E flat; commemorates the May Day workers' holiday.

Mercury Haydn's Symphony No 43 in E flat; thought to refer to the mercurial passagework in the first and final movements.

Midi Haydn's Symphony No 7 in C; one of three symphonies representing different times of day.

Military Haydn's Symphony No 100 in G; features Turkish military instruments.

Miracle Haydn's Symphony No 96 in D; said to be named after a performance during which a chandelier fell, miraculously causing no injuries. (The event happened, but during a performance of Symphony No 102.)

Moonlight Beethoven's Piano Sonata in C sharp minor; a name that reflects the mood of the piece.

1905 Shostakovich's Symphony No 11 in G minor; commemorates the abortive 1905 Russian Revolution.

1917 Shostakovich's Symphony No 12 in D minor; commemorates the 1917 Russian Revolution.

October Shostakovich's Symphony No 2 in C; commemorates the October Revolution.

Organ Saint-Saëns' Symphony No 3 in C minor; features an organ.

Oxford Haydn's Symphony No 92 in G; performed in Oxford when Haydn received an honorary doctorate.

Paris Mozart's Symphony No 31 in D, K 297; written for performance in Paris.

Pastoral Beethoven's Symphony No 6 in F; written in a rural temper, which was fashionable at the time.

Pathètique Beethoven's Piano Sonata in C minor, Op 13; refers to the sad nature of the piece.

Pathètique Tchaikovsky's Symphony No 6 in B minor; the composer's sad farewell piece.

Philosopher Haydn's Symphony No 22 in E flat; the first movement has a brooding character.

Polish Tchaikovsky's Symphony No 3 in D; the final movement features the rhythm of a polacca.

Post-Horn Mozart's Serenade in D, K 320; the sixth movement features a solo post-horn.

Prague Mozart's Symphony No 38 in D, K 504; written for performance in Prague.

Prodigal Son Prokofiev's Symphony No 4 in C; partly based on the ballet of that name.

Reformation Mendelssohn's Symphony No 5 in D minor; written for the 300th anniversary of the Augsburg Confession.

Rhenish Schumann's Symphony No 3 in E flat; reflects the composer's impressions of the Rhineland.

Romantic Bruckner's Symphony No 4 in E flat; originally contained a programme in the romantic manner.

Schoolmaster Haydn's Symphony No 55 in E flat; the adagio is said to suggest the slow pace of an aged teacher.

Scottish Mendelssohn's Symphony No 3 in A minor; reflects the composer's impressions of his visit to Scotland.

Sea Vaughan Williams' Symphony No 1; based on Walt Whitman's sea poems.

Simple Britten's Symphony; written for young people.

Soir Haydn's Symphony No 8 in G; one of three symphonies representing different times of day.

Sorrowful Songs Gorecki's Symphony No 3; features settings of Polish prayers and a folk song.

Study Bruckner's Symphony in F minor; originally intended as an exercise.

Sunrise Haydn's String Quartet in B flat, Op 76, No 4; the gradual emergence of the first violin from the harmonies is said to resemble the sun rising from mist.

Surprise Haydn's Symphony No 94 in G; named after the heavy chord that follows a quiet opening.

Tempest Beethoven's Piano Sonata in D minor, Op 31, No 1; describes the nature of the piece.

Titan Mahler's Symphony No 1 in D; named by the composer after the novel by Jean Paul.

Tragic Schubert's Symphony No 4 in C minor, D 417; describes the mood of the piece.

Trout Schubert's Piano Quintet in A, D 667; the fourth movement is a variation on his song *The Trout*.

Unfinished Schubert's Symphony No 8 in B minor, D 759; once thought to be incomplete, the final movement is now believed to have been lost.

Wagner Bruckner's Symphony No 3 in D minor; dedicated to the composer.

Waldstein Beethoven's Piano Sonata in C, Op 53; dedicated to Count Waldstein.

Wanderer Schubert's Fantasia in C, D 760; the second movement is based on the song of that name.

JAZZ

The roots of jazz lie in the music that began to develop in the Black communities of the Southern States of the USA towards the end of the 19th century. Particularly in New Orleans, the fusion of Black and European cultures enabled jazz to formulate and gain its own identity, at first in saloon bars and brothels but also in the street parades that were part of New Orleans life. Street bands playing slow marches for funeral processions, and fast ones for celebrating the memory of the deceased as the mourners returned home, were thus one of the original elements of jazz.

Ragtime – an early form of jazz – was characterized by witty syncopation of simple tunes. Ragtime was particularly associated with solo piano performance. In the early days the form and harmony of jazz were simple; the complexity came from the way the performers improvised collectively upon the simple melodies, and from their command of syncopation. Jazz music inevitably soon swept northwards to Chicago and other cities, before spreading abroad. The improvisation on the harmonic sequence of tunes rather than the melodies themselves was a development of immense importance. By the 1940s some jazz performances never stated the original melody, which was merely implied by its underlying harmonies.

Though jazz in the early days was predominantly the music of Black Americans, White musicians proved that it was not exclusively a Black preserve. As the popularity of jazz began to spread, so the bands, which had tended to comprise five, six or seven players, began to grow larger. During what became known as the 'swing' era, which dominated jazz just before World War II, bands consisting of brass and reed sections blowing against each other over a solid beat, grew fashionable. The major jazz watershed occurred, significantly, in 1945, at the end of World War II, when 'traditional' jazz, with its simple harmonies, gave way to the complexity, tension, abrasiveness and virtuosity of 'modern' jazz. Whether identified as 'cool' jazz, or as 'bop', 'bebop' or 'rebop', modern jazz gains much of its intensity of expression from the contrast between a steady beat and a convoluted solo line.

Jazz Singers and Performers

Armstrong, Louis 'Satchmo' (1900–71), US jazz trumpeter, bandleader and singer, who was known for his remarkable ability to improvise.

Basie, Count (William Basie; 1904–84), US jazz pianist and bandleader who was famous for his 'big band' style.

Bechet, Sidney (1897–1959), US jazz clarinetist and soprano saxophonist.

Beiderbecke, Bix (Leon Beiderbecke; 1903–31), US jazz cornetist, pianist and composer: the piano piece *In a Mist.*

Bolden, Buddy (Charles Bolden; 1878–1931), US jazz cornetist.

Brown, Charles (1920–), US jazz guitarist.

Brubeck, Dave (1920–), US jazz pianist.

Charles, Ray (1932–), US jazz singer, pianist and composer.

Cole, Nat King (Nathanial Coles; 1919–65), US jazz pianist and singer.

Coleman, Ornette (1930–), US jazz alto saxophonist.

Coltrane, John (1926–67), US jazz saxophonist.

Davis, Miles (1926–91), US jazz composer/trumpeter.

Domino, Fats (Antoine Domino; 1928–), US jazz and blues pianist, singer and composer

Dorsey, Jimmy (James Dorsey; 1904–57), US jazz alto saxophonist, clarinetist and bandleader.

Dorsey, Tommy (Thomas Dorsey; 1905–56), US jazz trombonist and bandleader.

Ellington, Duke (Edward Kennedy Ellington; 1899–1974), US jazz composer, bandleader and pianist: the song *Mood Indigo* was one of over 900 compositions. His band was one of the most influential in the development of jazz.

Evans, Gil (1912–88), US jazz pianist and composer.

Fitzgerald, Ella (1918–), US jazz singer.

Garner, Erroll (1923–), US jazz pianist.

Gillespie, Dizzy (John Birks Gillespie; 1917–93), US jazz trumpeter.

Goodman, Benny (Benjamin David Goodman; 1909–86), US jazz clarinetist/bandleader (known as the 'King of Swing'); his style began a new jazz era.

Grappelli, Stéphane (1908–), French jazz violinist and pianist.

Handy, William Christopher (1873–1958), US blues musician and songwriter: the song *St Louis Blues.*

Herman, Woody (Woodrow Herman; 1913–87), US clarinetist and bandleader.

Hines, Earl (1905–83), US jazz pianist, composer and bandleader.

Holiday, Billie (1915–59), US blues singer.

Miller, Glenn (1904–44), US jazz trombonist, composer and bandleader: the songs *Moonlight Serenade* and *In the Mood.*

Monk, Theolonius (1917–82), US jazz pianist.

Morton, 'Jelly Roll' (Ferdinand la Menthe Morton; 1885–1941), US jazz pianist, singer and songwriter.

Oliver, Joe 'King' (1885–1938), US jazz cornetist.

Parker, Charlie 'Bird' (Christopher Parker; 1920–55), US jazz saxophonist who became a leader of the 'bebop' movement.

Perkins, Carl (1928–58), US jazz pianist.

Peterson, Oscar (1925–), US jazz pianist.

Reinhardt, Django (1910–53), Belgian jazz guitarist.

Roach, Max (1925–), US jazz drummer.

Shaw, Artie (Arthus Arshewsky; 1910–), US jazz clarinetist and bandleader.

Smith, Bessie (1898–1937), US blues singer.

Tatum, Art (Arthur Tatum; 1910–56), US jazz pianist.

Vaughan, Sarah (1924–90), US jazz singer.

GRAMMY AWARDS

The Grammy Awards are organized by The National Academy of Recording Arts & Sciences in America. The Academy was founded in 1957 by recording artists, composers and recording workers to advance the arts and technology of recording. Grammy winners are selected in over 80 categories by voting members of the Academy, who number over 7000.

Grammy Record of the Year

1958 *Nel Blu Dipinto Di Blu (Volare)*, Domenico Modugno
1959 *Mack The Knife*, Bobby Darin
1960 *Theme From A Summer Place*, Percy Faith
1961 *Moon River*, Henry Mancini
1962 *I Left My Heart In San Francisco*, Tony Bennett
1963 *The Days Of Wine And Roses*, Henry Mancini
1964 *The Girl From Ipanema*, Stan Getz and Astrid Gilberto
1965 *A Taste Of Honey*, Herb Alpert and the Tijuana Brass
1966 *Strangers In The Night*, Frank Sinatra
1967 *Up, Up And Away*, 5th Dimension
1968 *Mrs Robinson*, Simon and Garfunkel
1969 *Aquarius/Let The Sun Shine In*, 5th Dimension
1970 *Bridge Over Troubled Water*, Simon and Garfunkel
1971 *It's Too Late*, Carole King
1972 *The First Time Ever I Saw Your Face*, Roberta Flack
1973 *Killing Me Softly With His Song*, Roberta Flack
1974 *I Honestly Love You*, Olivia Newton-John
1975 *Love Will Keep Us Together*, Captain & Tennille
1976 *This Masquerade*, George Benson
1977 *Hotel California*, Eagles
1978 *Just The Way You Are*, Billy Joel
1979 *What A Fool Believes*, The Doobie Brothers
1980 *Sailing*, Christopher Cross
1981 *Bette Davis Eyes*, Kim Carnes
1982 *Rosanna*, Toto
1983 *Beat It*, Michael Jackson
1984 *What's Love Got To Do With It*, Tina Turner
1985 *We Are the World*, USA For Africa
1986 *Higher Love*, Steve Winwood
1987 *Graceland*, Paul Simon
1988 *Don't Worry Be Happy*, Bobby McFerrin
1989 *Wind Beneath My Wings*, Bette Midler
1990 *Another Day In Paradise*, Phil Collins
1991 *Unforgettable*, Natalie Cole
1992 *Tears In Heaven*, Eric Clapton
1993 *I Will Always Love You*, Whitney Houston
1994 *All I Wanna Do*, Sheryl Crow

Grammy Song of the Year (Songwriter)

1958 *Nel Blu Dipinto Di Blu (Volare)*, Domenico Modugno
1959 *The Battle Of New Orleans*, Jimmy Driftwood
1960 *Theme From Exodus*, Ernest Gold
1961 *Moon River*, Henry Mancini and Johnny Mercer
1962 *What Kind of Fool Am I?*, Leslie Bricuse and Anthony Newley
1963 *The Days Of Wine And Roses*, Henry Mancini and Johnny Mercer
1964 *Hello, Dolly!*, Jerry Harman
1965 *The Shadow Of Your Smile* (love theme from *The Sandpiper*), Paul Francis Webster and Johnny Mandel
1966 *Michelle*, John Lennon and Paul McCartney
1967 *Up, Up And Away*, Jim Webb
1968 *Little Green Apples*, Bobby Russell
1969 *Games People Play*, Joe South
1970 *Bridge Over Troubled Water*, Paul Simon
1971 *You've Got A Friend*, Carole King
1972 *The First Time Ever I Saw Your Face*, Ewan McColl
1973 *Killing Me Softly With His Song*, Norman Gimbel and Charles Fox
1974 *The Way We Were*, Marilyn and Alan Bergman, and Marvin Hamlisch
1975 *Send In The Clowns*, Stephen Sondheim
1976 *I Write The Songs*, Bruce Johnston
1977 *Evergreen* (love theme from *A Star is Born*), Barbra Streisand and Paul Williams
You Light Up My Life, Joe Brooks
1978 *Just The Way You Are*, Billy Joel
1979 *What A Fool Believes*, Kenny Loggins and Michael McDonald
1980 *Sailing*, Christopher Cross
1981 *Bette Davis Eyes*, Donna Weiss and Jackie De Shannon
1982 *Always On My Mind*, Johnny Christopher, Mark James and Wayne Carson
1983 *Every Breath You Take*, Sting
1984 *What's Love Got To Do With It?*, Graham Lyle and Terry Britten
1985 *We Are The World*, Michael Jackson and Lionel Ritchie
1986 *That's What Friends Are For*, Dionne and friends
1987 *Somewhere Out There*, Linda Ronstadt and James Ingram
1988 *Don't Worry Be Happy*, Bobby McFerrin
1989 *Wind Beneath My Wings*, Larry Henley and Jeff Silbar
1990 *From A Distance*, Bette Midler
1991 *Unforgettable*, Irving Gordon
1992 *Tears In Heaven*, Eric Clapton and Will Jennings
1993 *A Whole New World* (theme from *Aladdin*), Alan Menken and Tim Rice
1994 *Streets Of Philadelphia*, Bruce Springsteen.

Best Pop Female Vocal Performance

1958 *Ella Fitzgerald Sings The Irving Berlin Story*, Ella Fitzgerald
1959 *But Not For Me*, Ella Fitzgerald
1960 *Mack The Knife*, Ella Fitzgerald
1961 *Judy At Carnegie Hall* (album), Judy Garland
1962 *Ella Swings Brightly With Nelson Riddle*, Ella Fitzgerald
1963 *The Barbra Streisand Album*, Barbra Streisand
1964 *People* (single), Barbra Streisand
1965 *My Name Is Barbra* (album), Barbra Streisand
1966 *If He Walked Into My Life* (single), Eydie Gormé
1967 *Ode To Billie Joe* (single), Bobbie Gentrie
1968 *Do You Know The Way To San José?* (single), Dionne Warwick
1969 *Is That All There Is?* (single), Peggy Lee
1970 *I'll Never Fall In Love Again* (album), Dionne Warwick
1971 *Tapestry* (album), Carole King
1972 *I Am Woman* (single), Helen Reddy
1973 *Killing Me Softly With His Song* (single), Roberta Flack
1974 *I Honestly Love You* (single), Olivia Newton-John
1975 *At Seventeen* (single), Janis Ian
1976 *Hasten Down The Wind* (album), Linda Ronstadt
1977 *Evergreen* (love theme from *A Star is Born*; single), Barbra Streisand
1978 *You Need Me* (single), Anne Murray
1979 *I'll Never Love This Way Again* (single), Dionne Warwick
1980 *The Rose* (single), Bette Midler
1981 *Lena Horne: The Lady And Her Music Live On Broadway* (album), Lena Horne

1982 *You Should Hear How She Talks About You* (single), Melissa Manchester
1983 *Flashdance What A Feeling* (single), Irene Cara
1984 *What's Love Got To Do With It?* (single), Tina Turner
1985 *Saving All My Love For You* (single), Whitney Houston
1986 *The Broadway Album* (album), Barbra Streisand
1987 *I Wanna Dance with Somebody (Who Loves Me)* (single), Whitney Houston
1988 *Fast Car* (single), Tracy Chapman
1989 *Nick Of Time* (track), Bonnie Raitt
1990 *Vision Of Love* (single), Mariah Carey
1991 *Something To Talk About* (single), Bonnie Raitt
1992 *Constant Craving* (single), k.d. lang
1993 *I Will Always Love You* (single), Whitney Houston
1994 *All I Wanna Do*, Sheryl Crow

Best Pop Male Vocal Performance

1958 *Catch A Falling Star*, Perry Como
1959 *Come Dance With Me*, Frank Sinatra
1960 *Georgia On My Mind*, Ray Charles
1961 *Lollipops And Roses* (single), Jack Jones
1962 *I Left My Heart In San Francisco* (album), Tony Bennett
1963 *Wives And Lovers* (single), Jack Jones
1964 *Hello, Dolly!* (single), Louis Armstrong
1965 *It Was A Very Good Year* (single), Frank Sinatra
1966 *Strangers In The Night* (single), Frank Sinatra
1967 *By The Time I Get To Phoenix* (single), Glen Campbell
1968 *Light My Fire* (single), José Feliciano
1969 *Everybody's Talkin'* (single), Nilsson
1970 *Everything Is Beautiful* (single), Ray Stevens
1971 *You've Got A Friend* (single), James Taylor
1972 *Without You* (single), Nilsson
1973 *You Are The Sunshine Of My Life* (single), Stevie Wonder
1974 *Fulfillingness' First Finale* (album), Stevie Wonder
1975 *Still Crazy After All These Years* (album), Paul Simon
1976 *Songs In The Key of Life* (album), Stevie Wonder
1977 *Handy Man* (single), James Taylor
1978 *Copacabana (At The Copa)* (single), Barry Manilow
1979 *52nd Street* (album), Billy Joel
1980 *This Is It* (track), Kenny Loggins
1981 *Breakin' Away* (album), Al Jarreau
1982 *Truly* (single), Lionel Richie
1983 *Thriller* (album), Michael Jackson
1984 *Against All Odds (Take A Look At Me Now)* (single), Phil Collins
1985 *No Jacket Required* (album), Phil Collins
1986 *Higher Love* (single), Steve Winwood
1987 *Bring on the Night* (album), Sting
1988 *Don't Worry Be Happy* (single), Bobby McFerrin
1989 *How Am I Supposed To Live Without You?* (single), Michael Bolton
1990 *Oh Pretty Woman* (single), Roy Orbison
1991 *When A Man Loves A Woman* (single), Michael Bolton
1992 *Tears In Heaven* (single), Eric Clapton
1993 *If I Ever Lose My Faith In You* (single), Sting
1994 *Streets Of Philadelphia*, Bruce Springsteen

EUROVISION SONG CONTEST

The Eurovision Song Contest has been held annually since 1956. Since the entry of the former Communist states of Central and Eastern Europe to the European Broadcasting Union (1992–93), not all members of the EBU have been able to participate in the Contest and a system of 'promotion and relegation' has been in operation. The 1995 Eurovision Song Contest will be the fortieth. Winners since 1956 have been:

1956 *Refrain*, sung by Lys Assia (Switzerland)
1957 *Net Als Toen*, Corry Brokken (Netherlands)
1958 *Dors Mon Amour*, André Claveau (France)
1959 *Een Beetje*, Teddy Scholten (Netherlands)
1960 *Tom Pilibi*, Jacqueline Boyer (France)
1961 *Nous, Les Amoureux*, Jean-Claude Pascal (Luxembourg)
1962 *Un Premier Amour*, Isabelle Aubret (France)
1963 *Dansevise*, Grethe and Jorgen Ingmann (Denmark)
1964 *Non Ho L'Età Per Amati*, Gigliola Cinquetti (Italy)
1965 *Poupée de Cire, Poupée de Son*, France Gall (Luxembourg)
1966 *Merci Chérie*, Udo Jürgens (Austria)
1967 *Puppet On A String*, Sandie Shaw (UK)
1968 *La, La, La*, Massiel (Spain)
1969 *Un Jour, Un Enfant*, Frida Boccara (France)
De Troubador, Lennie Kuhr (Netherlands)
Vivo Cantando, Salome (Spain)
Boom Bang-A-Bang, Lulu (UK)
1970 *All Kinds Of Everything*, Dana (Ireland)
1971 *Un Banc, Un Arbre, Une Rue*, Severine (Monaco)
1972 *Après Toi*, Vicky Leandros (Luxembourg)
1973 *Tu Te Reconnaîtras*, Anne-Marie David (Luxembourg)
1974 *Waterloo*, Abba (Sweden)
1975 *Ding-Dinge-Dong*, Teach-In (Netherlands)
1976 *Save Your Kisses For Me*, Brotherhood of Man (UK)
1977 *L'Oiseau Et L'Enfant*, Marie Myriam (France)
1978 *A-Ba-Ni-Bi*, Izhar Cohen and Alphabeta (Israel)
1979 *Hallelujah*, Gali Atari and Milk and Honey (Israel)
1980 *What's Another Year*, Johnny Logan (Ireland)
1981 *Making Your Mind Up*, Bucks Fizz (UK)
1982 *Ein bisschen Frieden*, Nicole (Germany)
1983 *Si La Vie Est Cadeau*, Corinne Hermes (Luxembourg)
1984 *Diggi-Loo, Diggy-Ley*, Herrey's (Sweden)
1985 *La Det Swinge*, Bobbysocks (Norway)
1986 *J'Aime La Vie*, Sandra Kim (Belgium)
1987 *Hold Me Now*, Johnny Logan (Ireland)
1988 *Ne Partez Pas Sans Moi*, Céline Dion (Switzerland)
1989 *Rock Me*, Riva (Yugoslavia)
1990 *Insieme: 1992*, Toto Cotugno (Italy)
1991 *Fangad Av En Stormvind*, Carola (Sweden)
1992 *Why Me?*, Linda Martin (Ireland)
1993 *In Your Eyes*, Niamh Kavanagh (Ireland)
1994 *Rock'n'Roll Kids*, Paul Harrington and Charlie McGettigan (Ireland)
1995 *Nocturne*, Secret Garden (Norway)

Number of wins:

Ireland 6 times; France and Luxembourg 5 times each; Netherlands and United Kingdom 4 times each; Sweden 3 times; Israel, Italy, Norway, Spain, and Switzerland twice each; Austria, Belgium, Denmark, Germany, Monaco, and Yugoslavia once each.

The following countries have also competed in the Song Contest but without success: Bosnia-Herzegovina, Croatia, Cyprus, Estonia, Finland, Greece, Hungary, Iceland, Lithuania, Malta, Morocco, Poland, Portugal, Russia, Slovakia, Slovenia, Turkey.

POPULAR MUSIC

Jazz has exerted a powerful influence on more obviously popular music. 'Rhythm and blues', an offshoot of the blues, featured an ensemble rather than a solo voice, and produced its own Negro-spiritual-inspired offshoot known as 'soul music'. 'Reggae', an Afro-Jamaican hybrid, originated in the 1960s and employs topical lyrics. 'Country and western' is America's modern equivalent of the European country dances of previous centuries. But above all jazz has inspired rock, a hybrid of American popular forms, both Black and White: blues, rhythm and blues, gospel, and country-and-western music. Since the advent of 'rock 'n' roll' in the 1950s, rock music – usually performed by groups using electronically amplified instruments – has established itself as the major force of present-day popular music.

In the 1950s Black artists such as the guitarist Chuck Berry vied for popularity with Whites such as Buddy Holly and most notably Elvis Presley, whose blend of physicality and tremulous baritone delivery in such numbers as 'Heartbreak Hotel' inspired an almost religious devotion in his fans.

The most significant developments in rock music in the 1960s took place in Britain, where the Beatles introduced more sophisticated lyricism to the genre, and the Rolling Stones brought an overt sexuality to their vigorous and pungent dance numbers. The 'Mersey Sound', associated with the Beatles in the 1960s, was not only a skilful brew of British and American trends of the period, but also combined genuine melodic flair with words (the best of them by John Lennon) of real literary merit. Nor did the talents of the Beatles suffer from the short-windedness of some pop music. Their LP album, *Sergeant Pepper's Lonely Hearts Club Band* (1967), was the pop equivalent of an integrated classical song cycle, a milestone in the progress of popular music. A similar literary distinction has stamped the songs of the American Bob Dylan, who achieved a synthesis of elements of rock 'n' roll and folk in his songs of protest. Other 1960s rock trends were the drug-influenced *acid rock* of such performers as the US guitarist Jimi Hendrix, and the highly amplified, rhythmic style of rock 'n' roll, known as *hard rock*, practised by such bands as The Who. A significant development in the late 1960s was the use of rock music in stage works or 'rock operas', such as *Hair*, *Jesus Christ Superstar* and The Who's *Tommy*.

In the early 1970s the *progressive rock* of British bands such as Pink Floyd and Genesis involved longer tracks, more advanced harmonies, and more complicated instrumental solo passages. It was partly in response to what some perceived as the artistic pretensions and pompous self-indulgence of such music that *punk rock* exploded onto the scene in the mid-1970s. In common with certain songs of the Rolling Stones, punk rock gave vivid and sometimes anarchic expression to working-class discontent, most notably in the abrasive and nihilistic anthems of its most notorious practitioners, the Sex Pistols. The 1980s and early 1990s saw an increasing divergence of styles and a growing use of electronic equipment. Production teams have played an increasingly influential role in the creation of rock music.

LEADING POP ARTISTS

Group members are listed alphabetically except where the lead appears in the group name. Singles are in single quotes; albums are in italics.

Abba Swedish pop group: Benny Andersson (b. Goran Benny Andersson), Agnetha Faltskog, Annifrid Lyngstad, Bjorn Ulvaeus. 'Dancing Queen'; *Voulez-Vous*.

Adams, Bryan Canadian rock singer (b. 5.11.1959). '(Everything I Do) I Do It For You'; *Waking Up The Neighbours*.

Animals English pop group: Eric Burdon, Chas Chandler, Alan Price, John Steel, Hilton Valentine. 'The House Of The Rising Sun'; *Animalization*.

Beach Boys US pop group: Al Jardine, Mike Love, Brian Wilson, Carl Wilson, Dennis Wilson. 'I Get Around'; 'California Girls'.

Beatles English pop group: George Harrison, John Lennon*, Paul McCartney*, Ringo Starr (b. Richard Starkey). 'Love Me Do'; 'Hard Day's Night'; *Sgt. Pepper's Lonely Heart's Club Band*.

Bee Gees English pop group: Barry Gibb, Maurice Gibb, Robin Gibb. 'Jive Talking'; *Saturday Night Fever*.

Berry, Chuck US rock and roll singer (b. 18.10.1926). 'My Ding-A-Ling'.

Blondie US pop group: Clem Burke, Jimmy Destri, Nigel Harrison, Debbie Harry, Chris Stein. 'Sunday Girl'; *Parallel Lines*.

Bon Jovi US rock group: Jon Bon Jovi (b. John Bongiovi Jr), David Bryan (b. David Rashbaum), Ritchie Sambora, Alec John Such, Tico Torres. 'Livin' On A Prayer'; *Slippery When Wet*.

Boone, Pat US pop singer (b. Charles Boone, 1.6.1934). 'Ain't That A Shame'; 'I'll Be Home'.

Bowie, David English pop singer (b. David Jones, 8.1.1947). 'Space Oddity'; *The Rise And Fall Of Ziggy Stardust And The Spiders From Mars*.

Brown, James US soul singer (b. 3.5.1928). 'Papa's Got A Brand New Bag'; 'Get Up I Feel Like Being A Sex Machine'.

Bush, Kate English pop singer (b. 30.7.1958). 'Wuthering Heights'; *Running Up That Hill*.

Byrds US rock group: Gene Clark, Michael Clarke, David Crosby, Chris Hillman, Jim McGuinn. 'Mr. Tambourine Man'.

Carpenters US pop duo: Karen Carpenter (b. 2.3.1950, d. 4.2.1983), Richard Carpenter (b. 15.10.1946). '(They Long To Be) Close To You', 'Top Of The World'.

Charles, Ray US singer and pianist (b. Ray Charles Robinson, 1930). 'Georgia On My Mind', 'This Little Girl Of Mine'; 'Drown In My Own Tears'.

Cher US pop singer (b. Cherilyn La Pier, 20.5.1946). 'Gypsies, Tramps And Thieves', 'I Found Someone'.

Clapton, Eric English singer/guitarist (b. Eric Clapp, 30.4.1945). 'Layla', *Slowhand*. See also CREAM

Clash English punk group: Nicky 'Topper' Headon, Mick Jones, Paul Simonon, Joe Strummer. 'Should I Stay Or Should I Go'; *Combat Rock*.

Cochran, Eddie US rock 'n' roll singer (b. 1938, d. 1960). 'Summertime Blues'; 'C'mon Everybody'.

Cole, Nat 'King' US pop singer (b. 17.3.1919, d. 15.2.1965). 'Pretend', 'When I Fall In Love'.

Collins, Phil English pop singer (b. 31.1.1951). 'You Can't Hurry Love', *Hello, I Must Be Going*. See also GENESIS.

Como, Perry US pop singer (b. Pierino Como, 18.5.1912). 'Magic Moments'.

Cooke, Sam US soul singer (b. 22.1.1931, d. 11.12.1964). 'Twistin The Night Away'.

Costello, Elvis English pop singer (b. Declan McManus, 25.8.1955). 'Oliver's Army'; *Trust*.

Cream English/Scottish rock group: Ginger Baker, Jack Bruce, Eric Clapton (b. Eric Clapp)*. *Disraeli Gears*; *Wheels Of Fire*.

Crosby, Stills, Nash and Young US/Canadian/English rock group: David Crosby, Stephen Stills, Graham Nash, Neil Young. *Four Way Street*; *American Dream*.

Deep Purple English rock group: Ritchie Blackmore, Roger Glover, Jon Lord, Ian Paice. 'Smoke On The Water'; *Made In Japan*.

Depeche mode English pop group: Andy Fletcher, Dave Gahan, Martin Gore, Alan Wilder. 'Master And Servant'; *A Broken Frame*.

Diamond, Neil US pop singer (b. 24.1.1941). 'I Am . . . I Said'; 'Forever In Blue Jeans'.

Dire Straits English rock group: Alan Clark, John Illsley, Mark Knopfler, Terry Williams. 'Sultans Of Swing'; *Brothers In Arms*.

Doors US rock group: John Densmore, Robbie Krieger, Ray Manzarek, Jim Morrison. 'Riders On The Storm'; *Morrison Hotel*.

Drifters US pop group: Clyde McPhatter, Bill Pinckney, Andrew Thrasher, Gerhart Thrasher. 'Save The Last Dance For Me'; 'Come On Over To My Place'.

Duran Duran English pop group: Simon Le Bon, Nick Rhodes, Andy Taylor, John Taylor, Roger Taylor. 'Girls On Film'; *Rio*.

Dylan, Bob US pop singer (b. Robert Zimmerman, 24.5.1941). 'Like A Rolling Stone'; *Blonde On Blonde*.

Eagles US rock group: Glenn Frey, Don Henley, Bernie Leadon, Randy Meisner. 'Hotel California'; *On The Border*.

Eurythmics Scottish/English pop duo: Annie Lennox (b. 25.1.1954), Dave Stewart (b. 9.9.1952). 'Sweet Dreams (Are Made Of This)'; *Be Yourself Tonight*.

Everly Brothers US pop duo: Don Everly (b. 1.2.1937), Phil Everly (b. 19.1.1939). 'All I Have To Do Is Dream', 'Cathy's Clown'.

Flack, Roberta US singer (b. 10.2.1937). 'The First Time Ever I Saw Your Face'; 'Killing Me Softly With His Song'.

Fleetwood Mac US/English rock group: Lindsey Buckingham, Mick Fleetwood, Christine McVie, John McVie, Stevie Nicks. *Rumours*; *Albatross*.

Four Seasons US pop group: Tommy DeVito, Bob Gaudio, Nick Massi, Franki Valli. 'Big Girls Don't Cry'; 'December 1963 (Oh What A Night)'.

Four Tops US pop group: Renaldo 'Obie' Benson, Abdul 'Duke' Fatir, Lawrence Peyton, Levi Stubbs. 'Reach Out I'll Be There'; 'Walk Away Renee'.

Francis, Connie US pop singer (b. Concetta Franconero, 12.12.1938).'Stupid Cupid'; 'Lipstick On Your Collar'.

Franklin, Aretha US soul singer (b. 25.3.1942). 'Respect'; 'I Say A Little Prayer'.

Fury, Billy English rock 'n' roll singer (b. Ronald Wycherly, 17.3.1941, d. 28.1.1983). 'Halfway To Paradise'; 'It's Only Make Believe'.

Gaye, Marvin US soul singer (b. 2.4.1939, d. 1.4.1984). 'I Heard It Through The Grapevine'; '(Sexual) Healing'

Genesis English rock group: Tony Banks, Phil Collins*, Mike Rutherford. *The Lamb Lies Down On Broadway*; *We Can't Dance*

Grateful Dead US rock group: Jerry Garcia, Bill Kreutzmann, Phil Lesh, Ron 'Pigpen' McKernan, Bob Weir. *Anthem Of The Sun*; *In The Dark*

Guns n' Roses US rock group: Steven Adler, Duff McKagan, Axl Rose (b. William Bailey), Slash (b. Saul Hudson), Izzy Stradlin (b. Jeffrey Isbell). 'Sweet Child O' Mine'; *Appetite For Destruction*

Bill Haley and his Comets US rock 'n' roll group: Bill Haley, Frank Beecher, Johny Grande, Ralph Jones, Rudy Pompilli, Al Rex, Billy Williamson. 'Rock Around The Clock'.

Hendrix, Jimi US singer/guitarist (b. Johnny Hendrix, 27.11.1942, d. 18.9.1970). 'Purple Haze'; *Are You Experienced?*

Buddy Holly and the Crickets US rock 'n' roll group: Buddy Holly (b. Charles Holley), Jerry Allison, Sonny Curtis, Joe B. Maudlin. 'Peggy Sue'; 'It Doesn't Matter Anymore'.

Houston, Whitney US pop singer (b. 9.8.1963). 'Saving All My Love For You'; 'I Will Always Love You'.

Jackson, Michael US pop singer (b. 29.9.1958). 'Billie Jean'; *Thriller*, *Bad*.

Joel, Billy US pop singer (b. 9.5.1949). 'Uptown Girl'; *An Innocent Man*.

John, Elton English pop singer (b. Reginald Dwight, 25.4.1947).'Rocket Man'; *Reg Strikes Back*.

Jones, Tom Welsh pop singer (b. 7.6.1940). 'It's Not Unusual'; 'Delilah'.

King, Carole US singer (b. Carole Klein, 1942). 'It's Too Late'; *Tapestry*.

Kinks English pop group: Mick Avory, Dave Davies, Ray Davies, Pete Quaife. 'Lola'; 'Sunny Afternoon'.

Led Zeppelin English rock group: John Bonham, John Paul Jones (b. John Baldwin), Jimmy Page, Robert Plant. 'Stairway To Heaven'; *Led Zeppelin*.

Lennon, John English pop singer (b. 9.10.1940, d. 8.12.1980). 'Imagine', 'Woman'; *Double Fantasy*. See also BEATLES.

Little Richard US rock 'n' roll singer (b. Richard Penniman, 5.12.1935). 'Long Tall Sally'; 'Tutti Frutti'.

Madonna US pop singer (b. Madonna Ciccone, 16.8.1958). 'Like A Virgin'; 'Vogue'.

Bob Marley and the Wailers Jamaican reggae group: Bob Marley, Aston Barrett, Carlton Barrett, Peter Tosh, Bunny Wailer. 'No Woman No Cry'; *Exodus*.

Paul McCartney English pop singer (b. 18.6.1942). 'Mull of Kintyre' (with Wings); 'Pipes Of Peace'. See also BEATLES.

Michael, George English pop singer (b. Georgios Panayiotou 25.6.63). 'Careless Whisper'; *Faith.*

Minogue, Kylie Australian pop singer (b. 28.5.68). 'I Should Be So Lucky'; 'Better The Devil You Know'.

Mitchell, Joni US folk singer (b. Roberta Joan Anderson, 1943). 'California'; *The Hissing Of Summer Lawns.*

Monkees US/English pop group: Mickey Dolenz, Davy Jones, Peter Tork, Mike Nesmith. 'I'm A Believer'; 'Daydream Believer'.

Morrison, Van Irish singer (b. George Ivan Morrison, 31.8.1945). *Astral Weeks*; *No Guru, No Method, No Teacher.*

Orbison, Roy US pop singer (b. 23.4.1936, d. 7.12.1988). 'Only The Lonely'; 'Oh Pretty Woman'.

Pet Shop Boys English pop duo: Chris Lowe (b. 4.10.59), Neil Tennant (b. 10.7.1954). 'West End Girls'; 'Go West'.

Pink Floyd English rock group: Dave Gilmour, Nick Mason, Roger Waters, Rick Wright. *Dark Side Of The Moon*; *The Wall.*

Police English/US pop group: Stewart Copeland, Sting (b. Gordon Sumner)*, Andy Summers. 'Message In A Bottle'; 'Every Breath You Take'.

Presley, Elvis US rock 'n' roll singer (b. 8.1.1935, d. 16.8.1977). 'Jailhouse Rock'; 'Heartbreak Hotel'.

Pretenders US/English pop group: Martin Chambers, Pete Farndon, Jim Honeyman-Scott, Chrissie Hynde. 'Brass In Pocket'; 'I Go To Sleep'.

Prince US pop singer (b. Prince Rogers Nelson, 7.6.1958). '1999', *Purple Rain.*

Queen English pop group: John Deacon, Brian May, Freddie Mercury (b. Frederick Bulsara), Roger Taylor (b. Roger Meddows-Taylor). 'Bohemian Rhapsody'; 'Radio Ga Ga'.

REM US pop group: Bill Berry, Peter Buck, Mike Mills, Michael Stipe. *Out of Time*; *Automatic For The People.*

Richard, Cliff English pop singer (b. Harry Webb, 14.10.1940). 'Summer Holiday'; 'We Don't Talk Anymore'.

Richie, Lionel US pop singer (b. 20.6.1949). 'Hello'; *Can't Slow Down.*

Rolling Stones English rock group: Mick Jagger, Keith Richard, Charlie Watts, Ron Wood, Bill Wyman. 'Get Off Of My Cloud'; *Sticky Fingers.*

Ross, Diana US pop singer (b. Diane Ross, 26.3.1944). 'Touch Me In The Morning'; 'Chain Reaction'.

Roxy Music English pop group: Brian Eno, Bryan Ferry, Andy Mackay, Phil Manzanera. 'Love Is The Drug'; *Avalon.*

Sex Pistols English punk group: Paul Cook, Steve Jones, Johnny Rotten (b. John Lydon), Sid Vicious (b. John Ritchie). 'Pretty Vacant'; *Never Mind The Bollocks – Here's The Sex Pistols.*

Shadows English pop group: Brian Bennet, Hank Marvin, Bruce Welch. 'Apache'; 'Dance On'.

Simon and Garfunkel US pop duo: Paul Simon (b. 5.11.41), Art Garfunkel (b. 13.10.1942). 'Mrs Robinson'; *Bridge Over Troubled Water.*

Sinatra, Frank US singer (b. 12.12.1915). 'My Way'.

Springfield, Dusty English pop singer (b. Mary O'Brien, 16.4.1939). 'I Only Want To Be With You'.

Springsteen, Bruce US rock singer (b. 23.9.1949). 'Born In The USA'.

Status Quo English rock group: John Coghlan, Alan Lancaster, Rick Parfitt, Francis Rossi. 'Down Down'; *Just Supposin'.*

Stewart, Rod English pop singer (10.1.1945). 'Maggie May'; 'Sailing'.

Sting English pop singer (b. Gordon Sumner, 2.10.51). 'Russians', *Ten Summoner's Tales.* See also POLICE.

Streisand, Barbra US singer (b. 24.4.1942). 'Evergreen'; *Guilty.*

Summer, Donna US pop singer (b. Adrian Donna Gaines, 31.12.1948). 'Love to Love You Baby'.

Supremes US pop group: Florence Ballard, Diana Ross (b. Diane Ross)*, Mary Wilson. 'Baby Love'; 'Stop! In The Name Of Love'.

Take That English pop group: Gary Barlow, Howard Donald, Jason Orange, Mark Owen, Robbie Williams. 'Pray'; 'Relight My Fire'.

Talking Heads English pop group: David Byrne, Chris Frantz, Jerry Harrison, Tina Weymouth. 'Road To Nowhere'; *Stop Making Sense.*

Temptations US pop group: Melvin Franklin, Eddie Kendricks, David Ruffin, Otis Williams, Paul Williams. 'My Girl'; 'Papa Was A Rolling Stone'.

10 cc English pop group: Lol Creme, Kevin Godley, Graham Gouldman, Eric Stewart. 'Rubber Bullets'; 'I'm Not In Love'.

T. Rex English pop group: Marc Bolan (b. Marc Feld, 30.7.1947, d. 16.9.77), Steve 'Peregrine' Took (b. 28.7.1949). 'Ride A White Swan'; 'Get It On'.

Turner, Tina US pop singer (b. Anna Mae Bullock, 26.11.1938). 'What's Love Got To Do With It?; *Private Dancer.*

UB40 English pop group: Astro (b. Terence Williams), Jim Brown, Ali Campbell, Robin Campbell, Earl Falconer, Norman Hassan, Brian Travers, Mickey Virtue. 'Red Red Wine'; *Signing Off.*

U2 Irish rock group: Bono (b. Paul Hewson), Adam Clayton, The Edge (b. David Evans), Larry Mullen Jr. *The Unforgettable Fire*; *Achtung Baby.*

Velvet Underground US pop group: John Cale, Sterling Morrison, Nico, Lou Reed (b. Louis Firbank), Maureen Tucker. *The Velvet Underground And Nico.*

Wet Wet Wet Scottish pop group: Graeme Clark, Tom Cunningham, Neil Mitchell, Marti Pellow (b. Mark McLoughlin). 'Goodnight Girl'; 'Love Is All Around'.

Who English pop group: Roger Daltrey, John Entwistle, Keith Moon, Pete Townshend. 'My Generation'; 'I Can See For Miles'.

Warwick, Dionne US pop singer (b. Marie Dionne Warrick, 12.12.1940). 'Walk On By'; 'Do You Know The Way To San José?'

Wonder, Stevie US pop singer (b. Steveland Judkins, 13.5.1950). 'Superstition', 'I Just Called To Say I Love You'.

Yardbirds English pop group: Jeff Beck, Chris Dreja, Jim McCarty, Keith Relf, Paul Samwell-Smith. 'Shapes Of Things', *Yardbirds.*

* see individual entry.

Dance

Forms of dance vary from those that employ the whole body in free and open movement to those in which movement is restricted to certain parts (just the eyes in the case of one Samoan courtship dance).

Dance is usually rhythmic, often with an element of repetition, and forms a pattern in both time and space. Dance can be a simple expression of pleasure in movement of the body or an art form of complex patterns and significant gestures.

DANCES

Popular Western dances include:

allemande (French 'from Germany') a 15th-century stately processional dance.

barn dance a traditional American form of dancing associated with festivities held on the completion of a new barn.

black bottom a type of jerky athletic foxtrot first mentioned in the *New York Times* in 1926.

bossa nova a variation of the samba, originating in Brazil.

Boston a slow 20th-century dance derived from the waltz.

bourée a lively 17th-century dance starting on the upbeat.

branle a 15th-century English clog dance with circular figures.

break dancing a modern dance in which dancers perform acrobatic feats. It was introduced c. 1980.

cakewalk a graceful walking dance which takes its name from the cakes offered as prizes for competitive performances held in the southern states of the USA from c. 1872. It was introduced into ballrooms from c. 1900.

cha cha cha a variation of the mambo in which couples dance with lightly linked hands. It was introduced in 1954.

chaconne a graceful dance introduced into Spain from Peru c. 1580 and then spread through western Europe.

Charleston one of the most popular dances of the 1920s, named after a Mack and Johnson song of 1923 about the town Charleston, South Carolina. The dance is characterized by a side kick from the knee.

conga a single-file dance developed in 1935 from the rumba and African dances.

contredanse a 17th-century dance for opposing groups. A mistranslation of 'country dance', contredanse developed in France and was reintroduced into England.

cotillion (French 'petticoat') a 17th-century dance for two groups of four pairs each. The quadrille developed from the cotillion in the 19th century.

courante (Italian 'current', that is 'running'), a stately 15th-century Italian dance which included the elegant bending of the knees.

disco dancing a flamboyant freestyle modern dance accompanied by exaggerated hand movement. It was popularized by the film *Saturday Night Fever* (1977).

foxtrot a dance in quadruple time, alternating long and short steps. There are both slow and quick variations. It was introduced in 1912 in the USA and was, allegedly, named after Harry Fox. The slow foxtrot evolved c. 1927 into the 'blues dance'.

galliard a sprightly medieval jigging dance from Italy. Its name implies 'gaiety'.

gavotte (Provençal dialect *gavoto*, 'a native of the Alps') a lively 17th-century dance in which each couple had the chance to dance on their own. It reached its greatest popularity at the court of the French king Louis XIV.

gigue a lively 17th-century dance based on the traditional English jig.

go-go a repetitious dance of verve, usually exhibitionist. It dates from 1965.

jitterbug a fast American dance to jazz accompaniment. It gained great popularity during World War II.

jive a jerky improvised variation of the jitterbug (see above).

the lancers a quadrille for eight or 16 couples.

Ländler (German 'small country') a traditional Austrian dance in which the partners turned in each other's arms with a hop and a step.

mambo an off-beat rumba of Cuban origin. It was introduced into the USA in 1948.

matelot a 17th-century Dutch sailor's clog dance.

mazurka a 17th-century Polish round dance for eight couples with the second beat accentuated.

minuet (from the French *pas menu*, 'small steps') a favourite at the French court, this delicate dance was often followed by the boisterous gavotte as a contrast. It was recorded by Lully in 1663.

morisca (Spanish 'Moorish') a Spanish dance derived from dances of Moorish Spain and first recorded in 1446 in Burgos.

one-step an early 20th-century dance characterized by long quick steps. It was a precursor of the foxtrot.

pasodoble a 20th-century Spanish-style two-step.

passacaglia a popular Italian 17th-century dance, resembling the chaconne, but in a minor key.

Paul Jones a 19th-century group dance in which partners are exchanged.

pavane a stately medieval processional dance, derived from instrumental music in Padua, and possibly the first stylized dance.

pogo a dance invented by punk rockers in 1976. Dancers jump vertically from the ground in imitation of a pogo stick.

polka a bouncing dance which was introduced to Paris in 1843. It developed from a Bohemian courtship dance.

quadrille a 19th-century French derivation of the 17th-century contredanse. It comprises a series of five 'figure' dances for four couples.

quickstep a dance in rapid quadruple time. It was invented in the USA in 1900 and reached a peak of popularity in the 1920s.

reggae a dance introduced from Jamaica in 1969. It is characterized by the strong accentuation of the upbeat.

rigaudon a lively French 17th-century dance, known in England as the rigadoon.

robotics a modern style of dance in which dancers imitate clockwork dolls with rigid limb movements.

rock'n'roll an energetic free dance, in part evolved from the jive and in part improvised. Characterized by a heavy beat and simple melody, it was introduced by Bill Haley and his Comets in 1953.

rumba a Cuban dance popularized in 1923.

samba a lively Latin American dance in double time. It originated in Brazil c. 1885 and was introduced to ballrooms c. 1920 as the maxixe. The name 'samba' was resumed c. 1940.

sarabande a slow and graceful dance, involving advances and retreats and couples passing between rows of dancers. It was introduced to Spain probably from Morocco c. 1588.

tango a lively syncopated 20th-century Latin American dance characterized by gliding steps and dramatic pauses. It was introduced to the USA from Argentina, but its origins may have been the Cuban *habañera.*

turkey trot a ragtime variation of the one-step. It gained considerable popularity during World War I.

twist a lively dance – characterized by body torsion and knee-flexing – in which partners rarely touch. It was introduced in 1961.

volta (Italian 'vault') a twirling 15th-century dance in which the woman is lifted from the floor and bounced upon the man's knees.

waltz an Austrian dance that developed from the Ländler (see above) in the 19th century.

BALLET

Ballet is a theatrical form of dance based upon a set of positions, steps and expressive gestures that demand considerable skill and training.

Balletic entertainments were first developed in the French court in the 16th century, but ballet companies in many countries have created their own distinctive national styles.

There are several ways in which ballet differs from other forms of dance. Most obvious is the 90° 'turned-out' position of the feet, which permits a remarkable degree of balance in all positions.

Ballet also requires a tension and arching of the foot and Achilles tendon to provide a powerful jump and to cushion landing.

BALLET TERMS

Among the ballet terms most commonly encountered are the following:

à terre steps which do not entail high jumps. They include the *glissade, pas balloné* and *pas brisé.*

battement ballet exercises.

batterie or **battu** a jump during which a dancer beats the calves sharply together.

corps de ballet a group of dancers supporting the principal dancers.

divertissement a self-contained dance within a ballet, which is designed purely as an entertainment or to show off a dancer's technique.

elevation any high jump in ballet. Elevations include the *entrechat, rivoltade, pas de chat,* and *cabriole.*

enchaînement a sequence of steps linked to make a harmonious whole.

entrechat a vertical jump during which the dancer changes the position of the legs after beating the calves together.

fouetté a spectacular pirouette in which the dancer throws his raised leg to the front and side in order to achieve momentum for another turn.

jeté a jump from one leg to the other, basic to many ballet steps.

These include the *grand jeté en avant,* in which the dancer leaps forward as if clearing an obstacle, and the *jeté fouetté* where the dancer performs a complete turn in mid-air.

pas a basic ballet step in which weight is transferred from one leg to another.

The term is also used in combination to indicate the number of performers in a dance; a *pas seul* is a solo and a *pas de deux* a dance for two dancers.

pirouette a complete turn on one leg, performed either on the ball of the foot or on the toes.

plié bending the legs from a standing position.

Demi-plié involves bending the knees as far as possible while keeping the heels on the floor.

relevé bending the body from the waist to one side or the other during a turn or a pirouette.

rivoltade or **revoltade** a step in which a dancer raises one leg in front, jumps from the other and turns in the air, landing in the original position but facing the other way.

saut a plain jump in the air without embellishment.

soutenu a movement executed at a slower tempo than usual.

sur les pointes on the toes.

variation a solo by a male ballet dancer in a *pas de deux.*

MAJOR CHOREOGRAPHERS AND DANCERS

Ailey, Alvin (1931–), US modern and contemporary choreographer.

Ashton, Frederick (1904–88), English classical choreographer.

Balanchine, George (1904–83), Russian classical choreographer: founder-choreographer of the New York City Ballet.

Baryshnikov, Mikhail (1948–), Latvian-born classical dancer based in North America.

Beauchamps, Pierre (1636–?1705), French choreographer and theorist who is credited with inventing the 'five positions'.

Bejart, Maurice (1927–), French choreographer of dance theatre.

Bintley, David (1957–), English classical choreographer.

Bolm, Adolph (1884–1951), Russian classical choreographer.

Bournonville, Auguste (1805–79), Danish choreographer who developed a free, more lyrical technique.

Bruhn, Erik (1928–), Danish classical choreographer.

Camargo, Marie (Marie-Anne de Cupis; 1710–70), Belgian dancer – *La Camargo* – acclaimed for her jumps, especially the entrechat.

Cerrito, Fanny (1817–1909), Neapolitan dancer.

Clark, Michael (1962–), English innovative contemporary dancer.

Cohan, Robert (1925–), US contemporary choreographer.

Cranko, John (1927–73), South African classical choreographer.

Cunningham, Merce (1919–), US post-modern pioneer.

Cullberg, Birgit (1908–), Swedish classical and modern choreographer.

Danilova, Alexandra (1903–), Russian classical dancer and teacher.

Delsarte, François (1811–71), French ballet theorist and choreographer who influenced Dalcroze and Shawn.

Didelot, Charles-Louis (1767–1837), Swedish choreographer and ballet master at St Petersburg.

Dolin, Anton (Sydney Healey-Kay; 1904–83), English classical dancer who danced with the Ballets Russes.

Duncan, Isadora (1877–1927), US pioneer of modern dance.

Dupond, Patrick (1959–), French classical and modern dancer (and pop singer).

Esler, Fanny (1818–84), Austrian dancer.

Farrell, Suzanne (1945–), US classical dancer.

Fokine, Michel (1880–1942), Russian classical choreographer.

Fonteyn, Margot (Margaret Hookham; 1918–91), English classical dancer who is widely recognized as the greatest British dancer. Her career was reinvigorated through her celebrated partnership with Rudolph Nureyev (see below).

Genee, Adeline (Anita Jensen; 1878–1970), Danish dancer who was influential in maintaining standards of British dancing.

Graham, Martha (1894–91), US founder of a distinctive style of modern dance.

Grigorovich, Yuri (1927–), Russian classical choreographer whose work is characterized by its spectacular quality.

Grisi, Carlotta (1819–99), Italian dancer.

Guillem, Sylvie (1966–), French classical dancer.

Helpmann, Robert (1909–1986), Australian classical and modern dancer and actor.

Hightower, Rosella (1920–), US classical dancer.

Humphrey, Doris (1895–1958), US modern choreographer.

Ivanov, Lev (1834–1901), Russian classical choreographer who worked with Petipa: *Nutcracker*.

Jacques-Dalcroze, Emile (Jacob Dalkes; 1865–1950), Austrian ballet theorist who trained Rambert.

Johansson, Christian (1817–1903), Danish teacher who was influential in the flowering of Russian ballet in the second half of the 19th century.

Joos, Kurt (1901–79), German classical and modern choreographer.

Karsavina, Tamara (1885–1978), Russian classical dancer.

Kirkland, Gelsey (1952–), US classical dancer.

Kylian, Jiri (1947–), Czech classical choreographer.

Laban, Rudolph von (1879–1958), Polish ballet theorist and notator.

Lavrovsky, Leonid (1905–67), Russian classical choreographer.

Lifar, Serge (1905–67), Russian classical choreographer.

Limon, José (1908–72), Mexican modern choreographer.

Lopokov, Fyodor (1886–1973), Russian classical choreographer.

MacMillan, Kenneth (1929–), Scottish classical and modern choreographer.

Makarova, Natalia (1940–), Russian classical dancer.

Markova, Alicia (Lilian Alicia Marks; 1910–), English classical dancer.

Martins, Peter (1946–), Danish classical dancer.

Massine, Leonide (1895–1979), Russian classical choreographer.

Mille, Agnes de (1909–), US classical and modern choreographer.

Morris, Mark (1956–), US classical and post-modern choreographer.

Neumeier, John (1942–), US classical choreographer.

Nijinska, Bronislav (1891–1972), Russian choreographer for Diaghilev's Ballets Russes.

Nijinsky, Vaslav (?1888–1950), Russian classical dancer who was a member of Diaghilev's Ballets Russes. The ballets *Petrushka* and *Scheherazade* were created for him.

Nikolais, Alwin (1912–), US modern choreographer.

Noverre, Jean-Georges (1727–1810), French choreographer: the inventor of the 'ballet d'action'.

Nureyev, Rudolph (1938–93), Russian classical dancer acclaimed for the power and athleticism of his dancing.

Pavlova, Anna (1881–1931), Russian classical dancer who was a member of Diaghilev's Ballets Russes: She created the chief role of *Les Sylphides*.

Perot, Jules (1810–92), French Romantic choreographer.

Petipa, Marius (1818–1910), French choreographer and ballet master at St Petersburg: the founder of the Russian classical style.

Petit, Roland (1924–), French dramatic classical choreographer.

Plisetskaya, Maya (1925–), Russian classical dancer who gained acclaim for her ability to integrate acting and dancing.

Robbins, Jerome (1918–), US classical and contemporary choreography.

Sainte-Leon, Arthur (1821–70), French Romantic choreographer: *Coppelia*.

Sallé, Marie (1707–56), French choreographer who placed emphasis on plot and interpretation.

Schaufuss, Peter (1949–), Danish classical dancer.

Schlemmer, Oskar (1888–1943), German choreographer who pioneered the Bauhaus style.

Seymour, Lynn (1939–), Canadian classical dancer.

Sibley, Antoinette (1939–), English classical dancer.

Sleep, Wayne (1948–), English classical, modern and show dancer.

Sokolow, Anna (1915–), US pioneer of modern dance.

Spessivtseva, Olga (1895–1991), Russian classical dancer.

Taglioni, Filippo (1777–1871), Italian Romantic choreographer.

Taglioni, Marie (1804–84), Italian dancer whose dancing typified the early Romantic ballet.

Tallchief, Margorie (1927–), US classical dancer – sister of Maria.

Tallchief, Maria (1925–), US classical dancer.

Taylor, Paul (1930–), US contemporary choreographer.

Tharp, Twyla (1941–), US choreographer in a variety of genres.

Tetley, Glen (1926–), US modern choreographer.

Tudor, Anthony (1908–87), English modern choreographer.

Ulanova, Galina (1910–), Russian classical dancer.

Vestris, Auguste (1760–1842), French dancer who developed the execution of ballet technique.

Vigagno, Salvatore (1769–1821), Neapolitan classical choreographer.

Weaver, John (1673–1760), English choreographer of 'pantomime-ballets'.

Wigman, Mary (1886–1973), German modern choreographer.

Zucchi, Virginia (1849–1930), Italian dancer who performed mainly in Russia.

MAJOR DANCE COMPANIES

Australia *Australian Ballet*, Victoria, formed 1962 by Peggy van Praagh.

Canada *National Ballet of Canada*, Toronto, formed 1951 by Celia France.

Cuba *Ballet Nacional de Cuba*, Havana, formed in 1948 as the Ballet Alicia Alonso.

Denmark *Royal Danish Ballet*, Copenhagen. One of the oldest companies in the world.

France *Ballets de l'Opéra*, Paris, Palais Garnier and Opéra Bastille, formed 1669 by Louis XIV.

Germany *Stuttgart Ballet*, Wurttemberg State Theatre Ballet, formed 1759. It rose to prominence when the influential choreographer John Cranko became director in 1961. *Tanztheater Wuppertal*, led by the noted choreographer Pina Bausch.

Netherlands *Netherlands Dance Theatre*, The Hague, formed 1959. It is noted for both classical and modern work.

Russia *Bolshoi Ballet*, Moscow, formed 1776 by Michael Maddox and Prince Urusov. *Maryinsky Ballet*, formerly Kirov, St Petersburg, formed 1738 as St Petersburg School of Ballet by Landé and Empress Anna Ivanova. The impresario Diaghilev used dancers from this company to start his Ballets Russes.

UK *Birmingham Royal Ballet*, formed in London in 1946 as the Sadlers Wells Opera Ballet (gained its present name upon moving to Birmingham in 1990). *English National Ballet*, London-based touring company, founded in 1950 as the Festival Ballet.

USA *American Ballet Theatre*, New York. Formed 1940 as the Ballet Theatre, it is a leading classical company. *Dance Theatre of Harlem*, New York. Formed 1969 by Arthur Mitchell, it was originally a classical company for black dancers. *Joffrey Ballet*, New York and Los Angeles. Formed 1956 by Robert Joffrey, it is noted for its modern and experimental work. *Mark Morris Dance Group*, a classical post-modern company formed by Mark Morris. *Martha Graham Dance Company*, New York. Founded 1929 by Martha Graham, one of the most important originators of modern dance. *Merce Cunningham Dance Company*, New York. Formed 1953 by contemporary dance pioneer Merce Cunningham. *New York City Ballet*, formed 1948 from the Ballet Society. It is dominated by the work and vision of its founding choreographer Balanchine. *San Francisco Ballet*. Formed 1933 by Adolf Bolm as the San Francisco Opera Ballet.

Stage and Screen

20TH-CENTURY ACTORS AND DIRECTORS

Allen, Woody (Allen Stewart Konigsberg; 1935–), US actor and director: *What's New Pussycat* (1965), *Annie Hall* (1977; **AA**, director), *Hannah and Her Sisters* (1986), *Crimes and Misdemeanours* (1990).

Altman, Robert (1925–), US director: *M*A*S*H* (1970), *Short Cuts* (1994).

Anderson, Judith (1898–), Australian-born actress.

Anderson, Lindsay (1923–94), English film director: *This Sporting Life* (1963).

Andrews, Julie (Julia Wells; 1934–), English actress: *Mary Poppins* (1964; **AA**), *The Sound of Music* (1965).

Antoine, André (1858–1943), French actor, director, critic and film producer.

Artaud, Antonin (1896–1949), French actor and director.

Ashcroft, Peggy (Edith Margaret Ashcroft; 1907–91), English stage and film actress. She was an outstanding Juliet in Gielgud's *Romeo and Juliet* in 1935.

Astaire, Fred (1899–87), US actor and dancer: *Top Hat* (1935), *Funny Face* (1957).

Attenborough, Richard (1923–), English actor, producer and director: *Gandhi* (1982).

Babenco, Hector (1946–), Brazilian director: *Kiss of the Spider Woman* (1985).

Bacall, Lauren (Betty Jean Perske; 1924–), US actress: *To Have and Have Not* (1944), *The Big Sleep* (1946), *Key Largo* (1948).

Bancroft, Anne (Anna Maria Italiano; 1931–), US film and stage actress: *The Miracle Worker* (1962; **AA**).

Bardot, Brigitte (Camille Javal; 1933–), French film actress: *And God Created Woman* (1956), *En Cas de Malheur* (1957), *Babette Goes to War* (1959), *Vie Privée* (1961), *Viva Maria* (1965), *The Novices* (1970).

Barker, Harley Granville (1877–1946), English-born director and producer who worked mainly in France.

Barrymore, Ethel (Ethel Blythe; 1878–1959), US stage and film actress.

Barrymore, John (1882–1942), US actor who played romantic leading men and Shakespearean roles.

Barrymore, Lionel (1878–1954), US character actor and director.

Bates, Alan (1934–), English actor: *The Fixer* (1968).

Baylis, Lillian (1874–1937), English theatre manager who founded the Old Vic.

Beatty, Warren (1937–), US film actor: *Splendour in the Grass* (1961), *Bonnie and Clyde* (1967), *Shampoo* (1975), *Reds* (1981), *Dick Tracy* (1990)

Beck, Julian (1925–85), US producer, director and actor.

Bene, Carmelo (1937–), Italian actor, director and dramatist.

Bergman, Ingmar (1918–), Swedish film writer, producer and director: *The Seventh Seal* (1957), *Through a Glass Darkly* (1961) and *Cries and Whispers* (1972).

Bergman, Ingrid (1915–1982), Swedish film actress: *Intermezzo* (1936), *Casablanca* (1943), *For Whom the Bell Tolls* (1943), *Gaslight* (1944; **AA**), *Spellbound* (1945), *Joan of Arc* (1948), *Anastasia* (1956; **AA**), *The Inn of the Sixth Happiness* (1958).

Berkeley, Busby (William Berkeley Enos; 1895–1976), US film director whose films were characterized by spectacular dancing sequences: *Gold Diggers of 1933* (1933).

Berkoff, Steven (1937–), English stage and film actor.

Bernhardt, Sarah (1844–1923), French actress who gained international acclaim for her tragic roles in *Phèdre*, *La Dame aux camélias* and *L'Aiglon*.

Berri, Claude (1954–), French film director: *Jean de Florette* and *Manon des Sources* (1986).

Bertolucci, Bernardo (1940–), Italian film director: *Last Tango in Paris* (1972) and *The Last Emperor* (1988).

Blin, Roger (1907–84), French actor.

Bogarde, Dirk (Derek Van Den Bogaerd; 1921–), English film actor: *Doctor in the House* (1953), *A Tale of Two Cities* (1958), *The Servant* (1963), *The Damned* (1969), *Death in Venice* (1970).

Bogart, Humphrey (1899–1957), US film actor: *A Devil With Women* (1930), *The Maltese Falcon* (1941), *Casablanca* (1942), *To Have and Have Not* (1943), *The Big Sleep* (1946), *Key Largo* (1948), *The African Queen* (1951; **AA**), *The Caine Mutiny* (1954).

Bondarchuk, Sergei (1920–), Russian film director: *Boris Godunov* (1986).

Borgnine, Ernest (1917–), US film actor: *Marty* (1955; **AA**).

Bow, Clara (1905–1965), US film actress: *Mantrap* (1926), *It* (1927), *Wings* (1927).

Branagh, Kenneth (1961–), Irish-born British actor-director: *Henry V* (1989).

Brando, Marlon (1924–), US film actor: *A Streetcar Named Desire* (1951), *The Wild One* (1953), *On the Waterfront* (1954; **AA**), *The Teahouse of the August Moon* (1956), *The Young Lions* (1958), *The Godfather* (1972; **AA**), *Last Tango in Paris* (1972).

Bresson, Robert (1907–), French film director: *Les Anges du péché* (1943) and *Un condamné à mort s'est echappé* (1956).

Brook, Peter (1925–), English stage director, noted for innovative productions of international theatre.

Brynner, Yul (Youl Bryner; 1915–1985), Russian-born film and stage actor: *The King and I* (1956; **AA**), *The Brothers Karamazov* (1958), *The Magnificent Seven* (1960), *Invitation to a Gunfighter* (1964)

Buñuel, Luis (1900–83), Spanish film director who collaborated with Salvador Dali in the first surreal films: *Un Chien Andalou* (1928), and notable later films including *Belle de jour* (1966) and *The Discreet Charm of the Bourgeoisie* (1972).

Burton, Richard (Richard Jenkins; 1925–1984), Welsh film and stage actor: *Look Back in Anger* (1959), *Cleopatra* (1962), *The VIPs* (1963), *Becket* (1964), *The Night of the Iguana* (1964), *Who's Afraid of Virginia Woolf?* (1966), *Anne of a Thousand Days* (1970).

Cacoyannis, Michael (1922–), Greek film director: *Stella* (1955) and *Electra* (1961).

Cagney, James (1899–1986), US film actor: *The Public Enemy* (1931), *Angels With Dirty Faces* (1938), *Yankee Doodle Dandy* (1942; **AA**).

Caine, Michael (Maurice Micklewhite; 1933–), English film actor: *Zulu* (1963), *Ipcress File* (1965), *Educating Rita* (1983), *Hannah and Her Sisters* (1985).

Campbell, Mrs Patrick (Beatrice Stella Tanner; 1865–1940), English actress.

Campion, Jane (1954–), New Zealand director: *An Angel at My Table* (1990), *The Piano* (1993).

Capra, Frank (1897–1991), US film director of gently satirical comedy films: *It Happened One Night* (1934), *Mr Deeds Goes To Town* (1936), *You Can't Take It with You* (1938), *It's a Wonderful Life* (1946).

Carné, Marcel (1909–), French film director: *Le Jour se Lève* (1939) and *Les Enfants du Paradis* (1945).

Chabrol, Claude (1930–), French film director: *Le Boucher* (1969).

Chaney, Lon (Alonzo Chaney; 1883–1930), US film actor: *The Hunchback of Notre Dame* (1923), *The Phantom of the Opera* (1925).

Chaplin, Sir Charles (1889–1977), English-born film actor and director: *The Tramp* (1915), *The Kid* (1920), *The Gold Rush* (1924), *The Circus* (1928), *City Lights* (1931), *Modern Times* (1936), *The Great Dictator* (1940), *Limelight* (1952).

Chen Kaige (1952–), Chinese director: *Yellow Earth* (1984), *Farewell My Concubine* (1993).

Chevalier, Maurice (1888–1972), French actor and singer: *Love Me Tonight* (1932), *Gigi* (1958), *Fanny* (1961).

Christie, Julie (1940–), English film actress: *Darling* (1965; **AA**), *Doctor Zhivago* (1965), *The Go-Between* (1971), *Heat and Dust* (1983).

Chukrai, Grigori (1921–), Russian film director: *The Forty-First* (1956).

Cimino, Michael (1943–), US director: *The Deer Hunter* (1978), *Heaven's Gate* (1980).

Clair, René (1898–1981), French film director: early comedies, including *An Italian Straw Hat* (1927), films experimenting with sound, including *Sous les toits de Paris* (1930) and notable later films, including *Les Belles de Nuit* (1952).

Clift, Montgomery (1920–66), US film actor: *Red River* (1948), *A Place in the Sun* (1951), *From Here to Eternity* (1953), *The Misfits* (1960) *Freud* (1963).

Close, Glenn (1947–), US stage and film actress: *Jagged Edge* (1985), *Dangerous Liaisons* (1988).

Cocteau, Jean (1889–1963), French writer, critic and film director who experimented with film as a serious art form: *Blood of a Poet* (1930).

Colbert, Claudette (Lily Claudette Chauchoin; 1905–), French film actress: *It Happened One Night* (1934; **AA**), *I Met Him in Paris* (1937), *Three Came Home* (1950).

Colman, Ronald (1891–1958), English film actor: *Raffles* (1930), *A Tale of Two Cities* (1935), *The Prisoner of Zenda* (1937), *Random Harvest* (1942), *A Double Life* (1948; **AA**).

Connery, Sean (Thomas Connery; 1929–), Scottish film actor: *Doctor No* (1962), *From Russia With Love* (1963), *Goldfinger* (1964), *The Untouchables* (1987; **AA**).

Cooper, Gary (Frank J. Cooper; 1901–61), US film actor: *Mr Deeds Goes to Town* (1936), *Sergeant York* (1941; **AA**), *For Whom the Bell Tolls* (1943), *High Noon* (1952; **AA**), *Vera Cruz* (1954).

Coppola, Francis Ford (1939–), US film director: *The Godfather* (1972) and *Apocalypse Now* (1979).

Costner, Kevin (1955–), US film actor and director: *Dances with Wolves* (1990; **AA**, director).

Coward, Sir Noel (1899–1973), English actor, writer and director: *In Which We Serve* (1941) *Our Man in Havana* (1959).

Crawford, Joan (Lucille le Sueur; 1906–77), US film actress: *Grand Hotel* (1932), *The Women* (1939), *Mildred Pierce* (1945; **AA**), *Whatever Happened to Baby Jane?* (1962).

Cronyn, Hume (1911–), US actor.

Crosby, Bing (Harry Lillis Crosby; 1901–77), US film actor and singer: *Road to Singapore* (1940), *Going My Way* (1944; **AA**), *The Bells of St Mary's* (1945), *White Christmas* (1954).

Cruise, Tom (1962–), US film actor: *Top Gun* (1985), *Rain Man* (1988), *Born on the Fourth of July* (1989).

Cukor, George (1899–83), US film director: *Little Women* (1933), *A Star Is Born* (1954) and *My Fair Lady* (1964).

Curtis, Tony (Bernard Schwarz; 1925–), US film actor: *Some Like it Hot* (1959), *Spartacus* (1960).

Cusack, Cyril (1910–94), Irish actor, dramatist and director: *Odd Man Out* (actor; 1947).

Dassin, Jules (1911–), US film director: *Never on Sunday* (1959).

Davis, Bette (Ruth Elizabeth Davis; 1908–89), US film actress: *Dangerous* (1935; **AA**), *The Private Lives of Elizabeth and Essex* (1939), *The Little Foxes* (1941), *All About Eve* (1950), *Whatever Happened to Baby Jane?* (1962).

Day, Doris (Doris Kappelhoff; 1924–), US film actress and singer: *Calamity Jane* (1953), *The Pyjama Game* (1957), *Pillow Talk* (1959).

Day-Lewis, Daniel (1958–), English actor: *My Beautiful Laundrette* (1985), *The Unbearable Lightness of Being* (1988), *My Left Foot* (1989).

Dean, James (1931–55), US film actor: *East of Eden* (1955), *Rebel Without a Cause* (1955).

De Mille, Cecil B. (1881–1959), US film producer and director: *The Ten Commandments* (1923), *King of Kings* (1927) and *The Greatest Show on Earth* (1952).

Dench, Judi (Judith Dench; 1935–), English stage actress and director.

Deneuve, Catherine (Catherine Dorleac; 1943–), French film actress: *Les Parapluies de Cherbourg* (1964), *Belle de Jour* (1967), *Mayerling* (1968).

De Niro, Robert (1943–), US film actor: *The Godfather Part Two* (1974; **AA**), *The Deer Hunter* (1978), *Raging Bull* (1980; **AA**), *The Mission* (1986).

Depardieu, Gerard (1948–), French film actor and director: *Le Dernier Metro* (1980), *Jean de Florette* (1985), *Trop Belle Pour Toi* (1989), *Cyrano de Bergerac* (1991).

De Sica, Vittorio (1902–74), Italian director: *Bicycle Thieves* (1948).

Dietrich, Marlene (Maria Magdalena von Losch; 1901–92), German film actress: *The Blue Angel* (1930), *Shanghai Express* (1932), *Destry Rides Again* (1939), *A Foreign Affair* (1948).

Disney, Walt (1901–66), US film producer and director who created the cartoon characters Mickey Mouse and Donald Duck.

Dmytryk, Edward (1908–), US film director: *Crossfire* (1947).

Donat, Robert (1905–58), English actor: *The Thirty-Nine Steps* (1935), *The Citadel* (1938), *Goodbye Mr Chips* (1939; **AA**), *The Winslow Boy* (1948).

Douglas, Kirk (Issur Danielovitch Demsky; 1916–), US film actor: *Gunfight at the OK Corral* (1957), *Paths of Glory* (1957), *Spartacus* (1960), *Lonely Are the Brave* (1962).

Douglas, Michael (1944–), son of Kirk, US film actor and producer: *Wall Street* (1987; **AA**), *Falling Down* (1992).

Dunaway, Faye (1941–), US film actress: *Bonnie and Clyde* (1967), *Network* (1976; **AA**).

Eastwood, Clint (1930–), US film actor and director: *A Fistful of Dollars* (1964), *For a Few Dollars More* (1965), *The Good The Bad and The Ugly* (1966), *Dirty Harry* (1971), *Every Which Way But Loose* (1978), *Unforgiven* (1993; **AA**, director).

Eisenstein, Sergei (1898–1948), Russian director who used symbols to reinforce ideas and edited shots to make a 'collision' of images: *Battleship Potemkin* (1925).

Eldridge, Florence (1901–88), US stage actress.

Espert, Nuria (1936–), Spanish actress.

Evans, Edith (1888–1976), English actress: *The Importance of Being Earnest* (1952).

Fairbanks, Douglas (Douglas Ullman; 1883–1939), US film: *The Mark of Zorro* (1920), *The Three Musketeers* (1921), *Robin Hood* (1921), *The Thief of Baghdad* (1923), *Don Q Son of Zorro* (1925).

Fassbinder, Rainer Werner (1946–82), German film director: *Despair* (1977).

Fellini, Federico (1920–), Italian film director: *La Strada* (1954), *La Dolce Vita* (1959).

Fields, W.C. (Claude Dukinfield; 1879–1946), US film actor: *David Copperfield* (1934), *My Little Chickadee* (1940), *The Bank Dick* (1940).

Finch, Peter (William Mitchell; 1916–77), English actor: *A Town Like Alice* (1956), *The Trials of Oscar Wilde* (1960), *Sunday Bloody Sunday* (1971), *Network* (1976; **AA**).

Finney, Albert (1936–), English stage and film actor: *The Dresser* (1983).

Flynn, Errol (1909–59), Irish-born US actor: *Captain Blood* (1935), *The Adventures of Robin Hood* (1938), *The Sea Hawk* (1940), *They Died With Their Boots On* (1941), *Too Much Too Soon* (1958).

Fo, Dario (1926–), Italian actor, writer and director of popular political theatre.

Fonda, Henry (1905–82), US actor: *Young Mr Lincoln* (1939), *The Grapes of Wrath* (1940), *Twelve Angry Men* (1957), *On Golden Pond* (1981; **AA**).

Fonda, Jane (1937–), daughter of Henry, US film actress: *They Shoot Horses Don't They?* (1969), *Klute* (1971; **AA**), *Coming Home* (1978; **AA**), *On Golden Pond* (1981).

Fontanne, Lyn (Lillie Louise Fontanne; 1887–1983), English-born US actress who usually played opposite her husband Alfred Lunt.

Ford, Harrison (1942–), US film actor: *Star Wars* (1977), *Raiders of the Lost Ark* (1981), *Indiana Jones and the Temple of Doom* (1984), *The Witness* (1985).

Ford, John (Sean O'Feeney; 1895–1973), US film director: *The Grapes of Wrath* (1940), *How Green Was My Valley* (1941), *The Quiet Man* (1952), and Western films, including *Stagecoach* (1939).

Forman, Miloš (1932–), Czech film director: *The Fireman's Ball* (1967). *One Flew Over the Cuckoo's Nest* (1975; **AA**), *Amadeus* (1984; **AA**).

Forsyth, Bill (1947–), Scottish film director: *Gregory's Girl* (1980) and *Local Hero* (1983).

Fosse, Bob (1925–88), US film director: *All That Jazz* (1979).

Gabin, Jean (Alexis Moncourge; 1904–76), French stage and film actor: *Pepe le Moko* (1937), *La Grande Illusion* (1937), *La Bete Humaine* (1938), *Le Jour se Leve* (1939), *Le Chat* (1972).

Gable, Clark (1901–60), US film actor: *It Happened One Night* (1934; **AA**), *Mutiny On the Bounty* (1935), *Gone With the Wind* (1939), *The Misfits* (1961).

Gambon, Michael (1940–), English stage and film actor: *The Cook, The Thief, His Wife and Her Lover* (1989).

Gance, Abel (1899–1981), French film director: the epic *Napoléon* (1927), which used a wide screen with three overlapping images.

Garbo, Greta (Greta Gustafson; 1905–90), Swedish film actress: *Grand Hotel* (1932), *Queen Christina* (1933), *Anna Karenina* (1935), *Camille* (1936), *Ninotchka* (1939).

Gardner, Ava (1922–90), US film actress: *Show Boat* (1951), *The Barefoot Contessa* (1954), *The Night of the Iguana* (1964).

Garland, Judy (Frances Gumm; 1922–69), US film actress and singer: *The Wizard of Oz* (1939), *Meet Me in St Louis* (1944), *A Star is Born* (1954).

Gassman, Vittorio (1922–), Italian actor-director: *A Wedding* (1978).

Gere, Richard (1949–), US film actor: *Yanks* (1979), *An Officer and a Gentleman* (1982), *Pretty Woman* (1990).

Gibson, Mel (1956–), US-born Australian actor: *Mad Max Beyond the Thunderdome* (1985), *Lethal Weapon* (1987).

Gielgud, John Sir (1904–), English stage actor known for classical and modern roles. He played *Hamlet* over 500 times.

Gish, Lillian (Lillian de Guiche; 1896–93), US film actress: *Birth of a Nation* (1914), *Intolerance* (1916), *The Wind* (1928), *A Wedding* (1978), *The Whales of August* (1987).

Godard, Jean-Luc (1930–), French film director: *A Bout de Souffle* (1960).

Goddard, Paulette (Marion Levee; 1905–90), US film actress: *Modern Times* (1936), *The Great Dictator* (1940).

Gordon, Ruth (1896–1985), US actress: *Harold and Maude* (1971), *Rosemary's Baby* (1968).

Grant, Cary (Archibald Leach; 1904–86), English-born US actor: *She Done Him Wrong* (1933), *Bringing Up Baby* (1938), *The Philadelphia Story* (1940), *Arsenic and Old Lace* (1944), *North by Northwest* (1959), *Charade* (1963).

Greenaway, Peter (1942–), English director: *The Draughtsman Contract* (1982), *Drowning By Numbers* (1988), *The Cook, The Thief, His Wife and Her Lover* (1989).

Griffith, D.W. (1875–1948), US director: *The Birth of a Nation* (1915), *Intolerance* (1916).

Grotowski, Jerzy (1933–), Polish director of the innovative Lab Theatre.

Guinness, Sir Alec (1914–), English stage and film actor: *Oliver Twist* (1948), *Kind Hearts and Coronets* (1949), *The Lavender Hill Mob* (1951), *The Bridge on the River Kwai* (1957; **AA**), *Tunes of Glory* (1960), *Lawrence of Arabia* (1962).

Güney, Yilmaz (1937–84), Turkish film director: *Yol* (1981).

Guthrie, Tyrone (1900–71), Anglo-Irish director.

Hackman, Gene (1930–), US film actor: *Bonnie and Clyde* (1967), *The French Connection* (1971; **AA**), *Mississippi Burning* (1989).

Hall, Peter (1930–), English director. Founder of the Royal Shakespeare Company.

Hanks, Tom (1956–), US actor: *Big* (1988), *Philadelphia* (1993).

Hardy, Oliver (1892–1957), US comedy film actor and **Laurel, Stan** (Arthur Stanley Jefferson; 1890–1965), English-born US comedy film actor: *The Music Box* (1932), *Sons of the Desert* (1933), *Way Out West* (1936), *A Chump at Oxford* (1940).

Harlow, Jean (Harlean Carpentier; 1911–37), US film actress: *Hell's Angels* (1930).

Harrison, Rex (Reginald Carey; 1908–90), English stage and film actor: *Blithe Spirit* (1945), *My Fair Lady* (1964; **AA**), *The Yellow Rolls-Royce* (1964), *Doctor Dolittle* (1967).

Havilland, Olivia de (1916–), US film actress: *Gone With the Wind* (1939), *To Each His Own* (1946; **AA**), *The Heiress* (1949; **AA**).

Hayes, Helen (Helen Brown; 1900–93), US stage and film actress: *Sin of Madelon Claudet* (1932; **AA**), *Airport* (1970; **AA**).

Hayworth, Rita (Margarita Carmen Cansino; 1918–87), US film actress: *The Strawberry Blonde* (1941), *Cover Girl* (1944), *Gilda* (1946), *Miss Sadie Thompson* (1953), *Pal Joey* (1957).

Hepburn, Audrey (Audrey Hepburn-Ruston; 1929–93), Belgian-born US film actress: *Roman Holiday* (1953; **AA**), *The Nun's Story* (1959), *Breakfast at Tiffany's* (1961), *Charade* (1963).

Hepburn, Katharine (1907–), US film actress: *Morning Glory* (1933; **AA**), *Little Women* (1933), *The Philadelphia Story* (1940), *The African Queen* (1951), *Guess Who's Coming to Dinner?* (1967; **AA**), *The Lion in Winter* (1968; **AA**), *On Golden Pond* (1981; **AA**).

Hepworth, Cecil (1874–1956), English film-maker: *Rescued by Rover* (1905), an early film shot on outside location.

Hertzog, Werner (1942–), German film director: *Aguirre, Wrath of God* (1973) and *Fitzcarraldo* (1982).

Heston, Charlton (John Charlton Carter; 1924–), US film actor: *The Ten Commandments* (1956), *Ben Hur* (1959; **AA**), *El Cid* (1961), *55 Days at Peking* (1963), *The Agony and the Ecstasy* (1965), *Khartoum* (1966).

Hitchcock, Alfred (1899–1980), English film director who worked in Hollywood from 1939: *Rebecca* (1940), *Psycho* (1960) and *The Birds* (1963).

Hoffman, Dustin (1937–), US film actor: *The Graduate* (1967), *Midnight Cowboy* (1969), *All the President's Men* (1976), *Kramer vs Kramer* (1979; **AA**), *Tootsie* (1983), *Rain Man* (1988; **AA**).

Holden, William (1918–81), US film actor: *Sunset Boulevard* (1950), *Stalag 17* (1953; **AA**), *The Bridge on the River Kwai* (1957), *The Wild Bunch* (1969).

Holm, Ian (1931–), English stage and film actor.

Hope, Bob (Leslie Townes Hope; 1903–), English-born US film actor: *Thanks For the Memory* (1938), *Road to Singapore* (1940), *Road to Morocco* (1942).

Hopkins, Anthony (1937–), Welsh stage and film actor: *The Silence of the Lambs* (1991; **AA**).

Hopper, Dennis (1936–), US actor: *Easy Rider* (1969; actor and director), *The American Friend* (1975), *Blue Velvet* (1986).

Horniman, Annie (1860–1937), English theatre manager who started the repertory theatre movement in the UK.

Howard, Alan (1937–), English stage actor.

Howard, Leslie (Leslie Stainer; 1890–1943), English actor: *The Scarlet Pimpernel* (1935), *Pygmalion* (1938), *Gone With the Wind* (1939).

Howard, Trevor (1916–88), English actor: *Brief Encounter* (1946), *The Third Man* (1949), *Mutiny on the Bounty* (1962), *The Charge of the Light Brigade* (1968).

Hudson, Rock (1925–85), US film actor: *Magnificent Obsession* (1954), *Pillow Talk* (1959).

Huston, John (1906–87), US film director: *The Maltese Falcon* (1941), *The African Queen* (1951) and *The Night of the Iguana* (1964).

Jackson, Glenda (1937–), English stage and film actress and MP: *Women in Love* (1970; **AA**), *Sunday Bloody Sunday* (1971), *A Touch of Class* (1973; **AA**).

Jacobi, Derek (1938–), English stage and film actor: *Henry V* (1989).

Janscó, Miklós (1921–), Hungarian director: *The Round-Up* (1966), *The Confrontation* (1969).

Jarman, Derek (1942–94), English director: *Sebastiane* (1976), *Caravaggio* (1986).

Jolson, Al (Asa Yoelson; 1886–1950), Lithuanian-born US film actor: *The Jazz Singer* (1927), *The Singing Fool* (1928), *Sonny Boy* (1929).

Jouvet, Louis (1887–1951), French actor, director and designer who had a great influence on 20th-century French theatre.

Karloff, Boris (William Henry Pratt; 1887–1969), English actor: *Frankenstein* (1931), *The Mask of Fu Manchu* (1932).

Kaye, Danny (David Daniel Kaminsky; 1913–87), US film actor: *The Secret Life of Walter Mitty* (1947), *Hans Christian Andersen* (1952).

Kazan, Elia (Elia Kazanjoglou; 1909–), Greek-born US film director: *A Streetcar Named Desire* (1951) and *On the Waterfront* (1954).

Keaton, Buster (1895–1966), US comedy film actor: *The Butcher Boy* (1917), *The Paleface* (1922).

Kelly, Gene (Eugene Curran Kelly; 1912–), US film actor and dancer: *For Me and My Gal* (1942), *An American in Paris* (1951), *Singin' in the Rain* (1952), *Invitation to the Dance* (1956).

Kelly, Grace (from 1956 HSH Princess Grace of Monaco; 1928–82), US actress: *The Country Girl* (1954; **AA**), *Rear Window* (1954), *High Society* (1956).

Kerr, Deborah (Deborah Kerr-Trimmer; 1921–), Scottish actress: *Love on the Dole* (1941), *From Here to Eternity* (1953), *The King and I* (1956), *The Sundowners* (1960).

Kline, Kevin (1947–), US stage and film actor: *A Fish Called Wanda* (1988).

Knipper, Olga (1868–1959), Russian actress who gained great acclaim in leading roles in the plays of her husband, Chekhov.

Kobayashi, Masaki (1916–), Japanese film director: *The Human Condition* (1959–61).

Korda, Alexander (1893–1956), Hungarian-born director: *The Private Life of Henry VIII* (1932).

Kozintsev, Grigori (1905–73), Russian film director: *Hamlet* (1964).

Kramer, Stanley (1913–), US director: *The Defiant Ones* (1958), *Guess Who's Coming To Dinner? (1967)*.

Kubrick, Stanley (1928–), US film director and writer: *Paths of Glory* (1957), *Lolita* (1962), *2001: A Space Odyssey* (1968) and *A Clockwork Orange* (1971).

Kurosawa, Akira (1910–), Japanese film director: *Seven Samurai* (1954) and *Ran* (1986).

Ladd, Alan (1913–64), US film actor: *This Gun For Hire* (1942), *The Great Gatsby* (1949), *Shane* (1953).

Lamour, Dorothy (Dorothy Kaumeyer; 1914–), US film actress: *Road to Singapore* (1940), *Road to Morocco* (1942).

Lancaster, Burt (1913–94), US film actor: *Elmer Gantry* (1960; **AA**), *Birdman of Alcatraz* (1962).

Lang, Fritz (1890–1976), Austrian film director: *Metropolis* (1931).

Laughton, Charles (1899–1962), English film and stage actor: *The Private Life of Henry VIII* (1933; **AA**), *Mutiny on the Bounty* (1935), *The Hunchback of Notre Dame* (1939), *Hobson's Choice* (1954).

Laurel, Stan, see Hardy, Oliver.

Leachman, Cloris (1926–), US actress: *The Last Picture Show* (1971; **AA**).

Lean, David (1908–91), English film director: *Oliver Twist* (1948), *The Bridge on the River Kwai* (1957) and *Lawrence of Arabia* (1962).

Leigh, Vivien (Vivien Hartley; 1913–67), English film and stage actress: *Gone With The Wind* (1939; **AA**), *Lady Hamilton* (1941), *A Streetcar Named Desire* (1951; **AA**).

Lemmon, Jack (1925–), US film actor: *Mister Roberts* (1955; **AA**), *Some Like it Hot* (1959), *Irma La Douce* (1963), *The Odd Couple* (1968), *Save the Tiger* (1973; **AA**).

Leone, Sergio (1921–89), Italian-American director of spaghetti Westerns: *A Fistful of Dollars* (1964), *The Good The Bad and the Ugly* (1967).

Littlewood, Joan (1914–), innovative English stage director.

Loach, Ken (1936–), English film director: *Kes* (1970), *Riff-Raff* (1990).

Lollobrigida, Gina (1927–), Italian film actress: *Belles de Nuit* (1952), *Solomon and Sheba* (1959).

Loren, Sophia (Sophia Scicoloni; 1934-), Italian film actress: *Boy on a Dolphin* (1957), *Two Women* (1961; **AA**), *The Millionairess* (1961).

Losey, Joseph (1909–84), US film director who worked mainly in Britain: *The Servant* (1963) and *The Go-Between* (1971).

Loy, Myrna (Myrna Williams; 1905–), US film actress: *The Jazz Singer* (1927), *The Mask of Fu Manchu* (1932), *The Rains Came* (1939), *The Best Years of our Lives* (1946).

Lubitsch, Ernst (1892–1947), German-born US director of comedies: *Heaven Can Wait* (1943).

Lunt, Alfred (1892–1977), US actor-director who was particularly associated with the plays of Noel Coward – see also Lyn Fontanne, above.

Lynch, David (1946–), US director *The Elephant Man* (1980), *Blue Velvet* (1986).

Maclaine, Shirley (Shirley Maclean Beaty; 1934–), US stage and film actress: *Irma La Douce* (1963), *Sweet Charity* (1968), *Terms of Endearment (*1983; **AA**).

MacLiammóir, Michaél (1898–1978), Irish stage actor-director.

Magnani, Anna (1908–73), Italian stage actress.

Malina, Judith (1926–), German-born US stage producer and director.

Malkovich, John (1953–), US stage and film actor: *Dangerous Liaisons* (1988).

Malle, Louis (1932–), French film director: *Les Amants* (1958) and *Au revoir les enfants* (1987).

March, Fredric (1897–1975), US stage actor.

Marvin, Lee (1924–87), US film actor: *Cat Ballou* (1965; **AA**).

Mason, James (1909–84), English film and stage actor: *The Wicked Lady* (1946), *The Desert Fox* (1951), *A Star is Born* (1954), *The Shooting Party* (1984).

Mastroianni, Marcello (1923–), Italian film actor: *La Dolce Vita* (1959), *Divorce Italian Style* (1962).

Matthau, Walter (Walther Matasschanskayasky; 1920–), US film actor: *The Fortune Cookie* (1966; **AA**), *The Odd Couple* (1968), *Hello Dolly* (1969), *The Sunshine Boys* (1975).

McKellen, Ian (1939–), English stage actor.

McQueen, Steve (1930–80), US film actor: *The Magnificent Seven* (1956), *The Great Escape* (1963), *The Cincinnati Kid* (1965), *Bullitt* (1968).

Méliès, Georges (1861–1938), French impresario who turned his theatre into a cinema and developed trick photography through the use of stop action and double exposure: the fantasy film *Voyage to the Moon* (1902).

Meyerhold, Vsevolod Emilievich (1874–1940), Russian actor, director and producer who experimented in 'nonrealistic' theatre.

Milland, Ray (Reginald Truscott-Jones; 1905–86), US film actor: *The Lost Weekend* (1945; **AA**).

Miller, Jonathan (1934–), English director of plays for stage and television, and of opera.

Mills, Sir John (1908–), English stage and film actor: *Waterloo Road* (1944), *Great Expectations* (1946), *Hobson's Choice* (1954), *Tunes of Glory* (1960), *Ryan's Daughter* (1971; **AA**).

Minnelli, Liza (1946–), US film actress: *Cabaret* (1972; **AA**).

Mirren, Helen (1946–), English stage and film actress.

Mitchum, Robert (1917–), US film actor: *Night of the Hunter* (1955), *The Sundowners* (1960), *Ryan's Daughter* (1971).

Monroe, Marilyn (Norma Jean Baker; 1926–62), US film actress: *All About Eve* (1950), *Gentlemen Prefer Blondes* (1953), *The Seven Year Itch* (1955), *Some Like it Hot* (1959), *The Misfits* (1961).

Moreau, Jeanne (1928–), French actress: *The Lovers* (1959), *Jules et Jim* (1961), *Diary of a Chambermaid* (1964).

Moskvin, Ivan Mikhailovich (1874–1946), Russian actor.

Murnau, F.W. (1888–1931), German film-maker: *Nosferatu* (1921), an early Dracula film.

Neagle, Anna (Marjorie Robertson; 1904–86), English stage and film actress: *Nell Gwyn* (1934), *Victoria the Great* (1937), *Nurse Edith Cavell* (1939).

Nemirovich-Danchenko, Vladimir (1858–1943), Russian director, drama teacher and co-founder of the Moscow Art Theatre.

Neville, John (1925–), English actor and director, who has been particularly associated with the Stratford Festival in Ontario, Canada.

Newman, Paul (1925–), US film actor: *The Hustler* (1961), *Butch Cassidy and the Sundance Kid* (1969), *The Colour of Money* (1986).

Nichols, Mike (1931–), US director: *Who's Afraid of Virginia Woolf?* (1966), *The Graduate* (1967).

Nicholson, Jack (1937–), US film actor: *Easy Rider* (1969), *Five Easy Pieces* (1970), *One Flew Over the Cuckoo's Nest* (1975; **AA**), *Terms of Endearment* (1983; **AA**), *Prizzi's Honor* (1985).

Niven, David (1909–83), Scottish actor: *Raffles* (1940), *Around the World in Eighty Days* (1956), *Separate Tables* (1958; **AA**).

Nunn, Trevor (1940–), English director – particularly associated with the Royal Shakespeare Company.

O'Neill, James (1846–1920), Irish-born US actor.

O'Toole, Peter (1932–), Irish film actor: *Lawrence of Arabia* (1962), *Becket* (1964), *The Lion in Winter* (1968), *Goodbye Mr Chips* (1969).

Oberon, Merle (Estelle O'Brien Merle Thompson; 1911–79), English film actress: *The Scarlet Pimpernel* (1934), *Wuthering Heights* (1939).

Olivier, Laurence (Lord Olivier; 1907–89), English stage and film actor and director: *Wuthering Heights* (1939), *Pride and Prejudice* (1940), *Henry V* (1944; special **AA**), *Hamlet* (1948; **AA**), *Richard III* (1956), *The Entertainer* (1960).

Pabst, Georg (1887–1967), German film director: *Pandora's Box* (1928).

Pacino, Al (Alfredo Pacino; 1939–), US film actor: *The Godfather* (1972), *Scent of a Woman* (1993; **AA**).

Page, Geraldine (1924–87), US stage actress.

Pasolini, Pier Paolo (1922–75), Italian film director: *Gospel According to St Matthew* (1963).

Paxinou, Katina (1900–74), Greek stage and film actress.

Peck, Gregory (1916–), US film actor: *The Gunfighter* (1950), *The Big Country* (1958), *Beloved Infidel* (1959), *To Kill a Mockingbird* (1962; **AA**).

Peckinpah, Sam (1926–84), US director of Western films: *The Wild Bunch* (1969).

Pickford, Mary (Gladys Smith; 1893–1979), Canadian film actress: *Pollyanna* (1919), *Little Lord Fauntleroy* (1921), *Coquette* (1929; **AA**).

Pidgeon, Walter (1897–1984), Canadian film actor: *How Green Was My Valley* (1941), *Mrs Miniver* (1942).

Piscator, Erwin (1893–1966), German producer and director, who, with Brecht, developed 'epic theatre'.

Planchon, Roger (1931–), French director of the Theatre National Populaire since 1972.

Poitier, Sidney (1924–), US film actor: *The Blackboard Jungle* (1955), *Porgy and Bess* (1959), *Lilies of the Field* (1963; **AA**), *In the Heat of the Night* (1967), *Guess Who's Coming to Dinner?* (1967).

Polanski, Roman (1933–) Polish director: *Rosemary's Baby* (1968), *Chinatown* (1974).

Porter, Edwin (1869–1941), pioneer US film-maker: the 12-minute *The Great Train Robbery* (1903), which was shot on outside locations.

Porter, Eric (1928– 95), English stage actor.

Powell, Michael (1905–90), English director who worked in collaboration with Emeric Pressburger: *Black Narcissus* (1947), *The Red Shoes* (1948), *Peeping Tom* (1960).

Preminger, Otto (1906–86), Austrian-born US film director: *Anatomy of a Murder* (1959), *Exodus* (1961).

Pressburger, Emeric (1902–88), Hungarian director who worked in collaboration with Michael Powell: *The Black Narcissus* (1947), *The Red Shoes* (1948).

Quinn, Anthony (1915–), US film actor: *Viva Zapata* (1952; **AA**), *Lust for Life* (1956; **AA**), *Zorba the Greek* (1964).

Ray, Satyajit (1921–92), Indian film director: *Pather Panchali* (1955).

Redford, Robert (1936–), US film actor and director: *Butch Cassidy and the Sundance Kid* (1969), *The Candidate* (1972), *The Sting* (1973), *All the President's Men* (1976).

Redgrave, Michael (1908–85), English stage actor.

Redgrave, Vanessa (1937–), English film and stage actress; daughter of Michael: *Camelot* (1967), *Isadora* (1968), *Julia* (1977; **AA**), *The Ballad of the Sad Cafe* (1991).

Reed, Carol (1906–76), English film director: *The Third Man* (1949), *Oliver!* (1968; **AA**).

Reinhardt, Max (Max Goldman; 1873–1943), Austrian director who was instrumental in the foundation of the Salzburg Festival.

Reisz, Karel (1926–), Czech-born British film director: *Saturday Night and Sunday Morning* (1960) and *The French Lieutenant's Woman* (1984).

Réjane (Gabrielle Réju; 1856–1920), French actress.

Renoir, Jean (1894–1979), French film director: *La Grande Illusion* (1937) and *La Règle du Jeu* (1939).

Resnais, Alain (1922–), French film director: *Hiroshima Mon Amour* (1959).

Richardson, Ralph (1902–83), English stage actor, known for his classical and modern roles.

Riefenstahl, Leni (1902–94), German film director: the propagandist films *Triumph of the Will* (1934) and *Olympia* (1938).

Robeson, Paul (1898–1976), US actor and singer.

Robinson, Edward G. (Emanuel Goldenberg; 1893–1973), Romanian-born US film actor: *Little Caesar* (1930), *Double Indemnity* (1944), *Key Largo* (1948).

Robson, Flora (1902–84), English stage and film actress: *Saratoga Trunk* (1945).

Roeg, Nicholas (1928–), English director: *Performance* (1970) and *Bad Timing* (1980).

Rogers, Ginger (Virginia McMath; 1911–95), US film actress and dancer: *Flying Down to Rio* (1933), *Top Hat* (1935), *Follow the Fleet* (1936), *Kitty Foyle* (1940; **AA**).

Rohmer, Eric (1920–), French director: *Ma Nuit Chez Maud* (1969).

Rooney, Mickey (Joe Yule Jnr; 1920–), US film actor: *Boys' Town* (1938; special **AA**), *Babes in Arms* (1939), *The Bold and the Brave* (1956).

Rossellini, Roberto (1906–77), Italian film director: *Rome, Open City* (1945).

Russell, Jane (1921–), US film actress: *The Paleface* (1948), *Gentleman Prefer Blondes* (1953).

Russell, Ken (1927–), English film director: *Women in Love* (1969) and *Tommy* (1975).

Rutherford, Margaret (1892–1972), English stage and film actress: *The VIPs* (1963).

Sanders, George (1906–72), US film actor: *The Moon and Sixpence* (1942), *The Picture of Dorian Gray* (1944), *All About Eve* (1950; **AA**).

Schlesinger, John (1926–), English film director: *Midnight Cowboy* (1969).

Schwarzenegger, Arnold (1947–), US actor: *Conan the Barbarian* (1982), *The Terminator* (1984), *True Lies* (1994).

Scofield, Paul (1922–), English Shakespearean actor.

Scorsese, Martin (1942–), US director: *Mean Streets* (1973), *Taxi Driver* (1976), *Raging Bull* (1980).

Scott, George C. (1927–), US stage and film actor and director: *Patton* (1970).

Segal, George (1934–), US film actor: *The Owl and the Pussycat* (1970), *A Touch of Class* (1973).

Sellers, Peter (1925–80), English film actor: *I'm All Right Jack* (1959), *Only Two Can Play* (1962), *The Pink Panther* (1963), *Dr Strangelove* (1963), *Being There* (1979).

Sennett, Mack (1884–1960), US director of slapstick comedy films: the cleverly edited and speeded-up antics of the Keystone Cops, and films featuring such actors as Roscoe 'Fatty' Arbuckle, Charlie Chaplin and Buster Keaton.

Sher, Anthony (1949–), South African-born British stage actor.

Signoret, Simone (1921–85), French actress: *Room at the Top* (1959; **AA**).

Simmons, Jean (1929–), English actress: *Great Expectations* (1946), *Black Narcissus* (1946), *Elmer Gantry* (1960).

Sinatra, Frank (1915–), US singer and actor: *From Here to Eternity* (1953; **AA**), *The Man With the Golden Arm* (1956), *High Society* (1956), *Pal Joey* (1957), *The Manchurian Candidate* (1962).

Smith, Maggie (1934–), English stage and film actress: *The VIPs* (1963), *The Prime of Miss Jean Brodie* (1969; **AA**), *California Suite* (1978; **AA**).

Spielberg, Steven (1947–), US film director and producer: *E.T.* (1982), *The Color Purple* (1986), *Schindler's List* (1993; **AA**).

Stallone, Sylvester (1946–), US film actor: *Rocky* (1976), *Rambo* (1985).

Stanislavsky, Constantin (1863–1938), Russian actor and director who developed the Stanislavsky method of acting, better known as 'the method'.

Stanwyck, Barbara (1907–90), US film actress: *Stella Dallas* (1937), *The Lady Eve* (1941), *Double Indemnity* (1944).

Steiger, Rod (1925–), US film actor: *On the Waterfront* (1954), *Al Capone* (1958), *In the Heat of the Night* (1967; **AA**).

Sternberg, Josef von (1894–1969), Austrian-born US film director: *Blue Angel* (1930).

Stewart, James (1908–), US film actor: *Mr Smith Goes to Washington* (1939), *Destry Rides Again* (1939), *The Philadelphia Story* (1940; **AA**), *It's a Wonderful Life* (1946), *Harvey* (1950).

Stone, Oliver (1946–), US director: *Platoon* (1986), *Born on the Fourth of July* (1989).

Streep, Meryl (Mary Louise Streep; 1951–), US film and stage actress: *The Deer Hunter* (1978), *Kramer vs Kramer* (1979; **AA**), *The French Lieutenant's Woman* (1981), *Sophie's Choice* (1982; **AA**), *Silkwood* (1983), *Out of Africa* (1986).

Streisand, Barbra (1942–), US singer and actress: *Funny Girl* (1968), *Hello Dolly* (1969), *Funny Lady* (1975), *A Star is Born* (1976).

Sutherland, Donald (1935–), Canadian film actor: *M*A*S*H* (1970), *Kelly's Heroes* (1970), *Klute* (1971).

Swanson, Gloria (G. Svensson; 1897–1983), US film actress: *Sadie Thompson* (1928), *Queen Kelly* (1928), *Sunset Boulevard* (1950).

Szabó, István (1938–), Hungarian director: *Mephisto* (1981).

Tarantino, Quentin, US director: *Reservoir Dogs* (1993), *Pulp Fiction* (1994).

Tarkovsky, Andrei (1932–88), Russian film director: *Andrei Rublev* (1966) and *Solaris* (1971).

Tati, Jacques (1908–82), French actor and director of comedy films: *Monsieur Hulot's Holiday* (1951).

Taylor, Elizabeth (1932–), British-born US film actress: *National Velvet* (1944), *Cat on a Hot Tin Roof* (1958), *Butterfield 8* (1960; **AA**), *Cleopatra* (1962), *Who's Afraid of Virginia Woolf?* (1966; **AA**).

Temple, Shirley (1928–), US child film actress *Bright Eyes* (1934; **AA**).

Terry, Ellen (1847–1928), English actress – leading lady in many of Irving's productions. Both Ibsen and Shaw created roles for her.

Thompson, Emma (1959–), English stage and film actress; wife of Kenneth Branagh: *Howard's End* (1993; **AA**).

Thorndyke, Sybil (1882–1976), English Shakespearean actress who created the title role in Shaw's *Saint Joan*.

Tracy, Spencer (1900–67), US film actor: *The Power and the Glory* (1933), *Captains Courageous* (1937; **AA**), *Northwest Passage* (1940), *Pat and Mike* (1952), *Guess Who's Coming to Dinner?* (1967).

Tree, Herbert Beerbohm (1853–1917), English actor-manager.

Truffaut, François (1932–84), French film director: *Les Quatre-cent Coups* (1959) and *Day for Night* (1973).

Tutin, Dorothy (1931–), English stage and film actress.

Ustinov, Peter (1921–), English film and stage actor and dramatist. *Topkapi* (1964).

Valentino, Rudolph (Rodolpho d'Antonguolla; 1895–1926), Italian-born film actor: *The Four Horsemen of the Apocalypse* (1921), *The Sheik* (1921), *Blood and Sand* (1922), *Son of the Sheik* (1926).

Vidor, King (1894–1982), American film director and producer: *The Big Parade* (1925), *Hallelujah!* (1929) and *The Citadel* (1938).

Visconti, Luchino (1906–76), Italian film director: *Ossessione* (1942) and *Death in Venice* (1970).

Wajda, Andrzej (1926–), Polish film director: *Ashes and Diamonds* (1958).

Warner, Jack (1882–1978), US film producer who founded – with his brothers **Harry** (1881–1958), **Albert** (1884–1967), and **Samuel** (1888–1927) – the Warner Brothers studios.

Wayne, John (Marion Morrison; 1907–79), US actor: *Stagecoach* (1939), *The Searchers* (1956).

Weigel, Helen (1900–72), German stage actress.

Weine, Robert (1881–1938), German film director: *Cabinet of Dr Cagliari* (1919), a film using expressionist settings.

Weir, Peter (1944–), Australian film director: *Picnic at Hanging Rock* (1975) and *Dead Poets Society* (1989).

Welles, Orson (1915–85), US film director and stage and film actor: *Citizen Kane* (1940), *The Third Man* (1949), *The Trial* (1962).

Wenders, Wim (1945–), German director: *Paris, Texas* (1984), *Wings of Desire* (1987).

Wilder, Billy (Samuel Wilder; 1906–), Austrian-born US film director: *Double Indemnity* (1944) and *Sunset Boulevard* (1950).

Williams, Emlyn (1905–87), Welsh actor-dramatist.

Williamson, Nicol (1938–), Scottish stage actor.

Wolfit, Donald (1902–68), English actor-manager.

Wood, Natalie (Natasha Gurdin; 1938–81), US film actress: *Rebel Without a Cause* (1955), *West Side Story* (1961), *Bob and Carol and Ted and Alice* (1969).

Worth, Irene (1916–), American actress.

Wyler, William (1902–81), US film director: *The Best Years of Our Lives* (1946).

Zeffirelli, Franco (Franco Zeffirelli Corsi; 1923–), Italian stage and film director and designer: *Romeo and Juliet* (1968).

Zinneman, Fred (1907–), Austrian-born US film director: *High Noon* (1952), *A Man For All Seasons* (1966) and *The Day of the Jackal* (1973).

Zhang Yimou (1950–), Chinese director: *Ju Dou* (1989), *Raise the Red Lantern* (1991).

Zukor, Adolphe (1873–1976), Hungarian-born US film-maker and founder of the Famous Players-Paramount studios *The Count of Monte Cristo* and *The Prisoner of Zenda*.

AA = Academy Award

MOTION PICTURE ACADEMY AWARDS (OSCARS)

1928
Actor: Emil Jannings, *The Way of All Flesh.*
Actress: Janet Gaynor, *Seventh Heaven.*
Director: Frank Borzage, *Seventh Heaven*; Lewis Milestone, *Two Arabian Knights* (tie).
Picture: *Wings*.

1929
Actor: Warner Baxter, *In Old Arizona.*
Actress: Mary Pickford, *Coquette.*
Director: Frank Lloyd, *The Divine Lady.*
Picture: *Broadway Melody.*

1930
Actor: George Arliss, *Disraeli.*
Actress: Norma Shearer, *The Divorcee.*
Director: Lewis Milestone, *All Quiet on the Western Front.*
Picture: *All Quiet on the Western Front.*

1931
Actor: Lionel Barrymore, *Free Soul*
Actress: Marie Dressler, *Min and Bill*
Director: Norman Taurog, *Skippy*
Picture: *Cimarron.*

1932
Actor: Fredric March, *Dr Jekyll and Mr Hyde*;
Wallace Beery, *The Champ* (tie).
Actress: Helen Hayes, *Sin of Madelon Claudet.*
Director: Frank Borzage, *Bad Girl.*
Picture: *Grand Hotel.*
Special: Walt Disney, *Mickey Mouse.*

1933
Actor: Charles Laughton, *Private Life of Henry VIII.*
Actress: Katharine Hepburn, *Morning Glory.*
Director: Frank Lloyd, *Cavalcade.*
Picture: *Cavalcade.*

1934
Actor: Clark Gable, *It Happened One Night.*
Actress: Claudette Colbert, *It Happened One Night.*
Director: Frank Capra, *It Happened One Night.*
Picture: *It Happened One Night.*

1935
Actor: Victor McLaglen, *The Informer.*
Actress: Bette Davis, *Dangerous.*
Director: John Ford, *The Informer.*
Picture: *Mutiny on the Bounty.*

1936
Actor: Paul Muni, *Story of Louis Pasteur.*
Actress: Luise Rainer, *The Great Ziegfeld.*
Sup. Actor: Walter Brennan, *Come and Get It.*
Sup. Actress: Gale Sondergaard, *Anthony Adverse.*
Director: Frank Capra, *Mr Deeds Goes to Town.*
Picture: *The Great Ziegfeld.*

1937
Actor: Spencer Tracy, *Captains Courageous.*
Actress: Luise Rainer, *The Good Earth.*
Sup. Actor: Joseph Schildkraut, *Life of Emile Zola*
Sup. Actress: Alice Brady, *In Old Chicago.*
Director: Leo McCarey, *The Awful Truth.*
Picture: *Life of Emile Zola.*

1938
Actor: Spencer Tracy, *Boys Town.*
Actress: Bette Davis, *Jezebel.*
Sup. Actor: Walter Brennan, *Kentucky.*
Sup. Actress: Fay Bainter, *Jezebel.*
Director: Frank Capra, *You Can't Take It With You.*
Picture: *You Can't Take It With You.*

1939
Actor: Robert Donat, *Goodbye, Mr Chips.*
Actress: Vivien Leigh, *Gone With the Wind.*
Sup. Actor: Thomas Mitchell, *Stage Coach.*
Sup. Actress: Hattie McDaniel, *Gone With the Wind.*
Director: Victor Fleming, *Gone With the Wind.*
Picture: *Gone With the Wind.*

1940
Actor: James Stewart, *The Philadelphia Story.*
Actress: Ginger Rogers, *Kitty Foyle.*
Sup. Actor: Walter Brennan, *The Westerner.*
Sup. Actress: Jane Darwell, *The Grapes of Wrath.*
Director: John Ford, *The Grapes of Wrath.*
Picture: *Rebecca.*

1941
Actor: Gary Cooper, *Sergeant York.*
Actress: Joan Fontaine, *Suspicion.*
Sup. Actor: Donald Crisp, *How Green Was My Valley.*
Sup. Actress: Mary Astor, *The Great Lie.*
Director: John Ford, *How Green Was My Valley.*
Picture: *How Green Was My Valley.*

1942
Actor: James Cagney, *Yankee Doodle Dandy.*
Actress: Greer Garson, *Mrs Miniver.*
Sup. Actor: Van Heflin, *Johnny Eager.*
Sup. Actress: Teresa Wright, *Mrs Miniver.*
Director: William Wyler, *Mrs Miniver.*
Picture: *Mrs Miniver.*

1943
Actor: Paul Lukas, *Watch on the Rhine.*
Actress: Jennifer Jones, *The Song of Bernadette.*
Sup. Actor: Charles Coburn, *The More the Merrier.*
Sup. Actress: Katina Paxinou, *For Whom the Bell Tolls.*
Director: Michael Curtiz, *Casablanca.*
Picture: *Casablanca.*

1944
Actor: Bing Crosby, *Going My Way.*
Actress: Ingrid Bergman, *Gaslight.*
Sup. Actor: Barry Fitzgerald, *Going My Way.*
Sup. Actress: Ethel Barrymore, *None But the Lonely Heart.*
Director: Leo McCarey, *Going My Way.*
Picture: *Going My Way.*

1945
Actor: Ray Milland: *The Lost Weekend.*
Actress: Joan Crawford, *Mildred Pierce.*
Sup. Actor: James Dunn, *A Tree Grows in Brooklyn.*
Sup. Actress: Anne Revere, *National Velvet.*
Director: Billy Wilder, *The Lost Weekend.*
Picture: *The Lost Weekend.*

1946
Actor: Frederic March, *The Best Years of Our Lives.*
Actress: Olivia de Havilland, *To Each His Own.*
Sup. Actor: Harold Russell, *The Best Years of Our Lives.*

Sup. Actress: Anne Baxter, *The Razor's Edge.*
Director: William Wyler, *The Best Years of Our Lives.*
Picture: *The Best Years of Our Lives.*

1947
Actor: Ronald Colman, *A Double Life.*
Actress: Loretta Young, *The Farmer's Daughter.*
Sup. Actor: Edmund Gwenn, *Miracle on 34th Street.*
Sup. Actress: Celeste Holm, *Gentleman's Agreement.*
Director: Elia Kazan, *Gentleman's Agreement.*
Picture: *Gentleman's Agreement.*

1948
Actor: Laurence Olivier, *Hamlet.*
Actress: Jane Wyman, *Johnny Belinda.*
Sup. Actor: Walter Huston, *Treasure of Sierra Madre.*
Sup. Actress: Claire Trevor, *Key Largo.*
Director: John Huston, *Treasure of Sierra Madre.*
Picture: *Hamlet.*

1949
Actor: Broderick Crawford, *All the King's Men.*
Actress: Olivia de Havilland, *The Heiress.*
Sup. Actor: Dean Jagger, *Twelve O'Clock High.*
Sup. Actress: Mercedes McCambridge, *All the King's Men.*
Director: Joseph L. Mankiewicz, *Letter to Three Wives.*
Picture: *All the King's Men.*

1950
Actor: José Ferrer, *Cyrano de Bergerac.*
Actress: Judy Holliday, *Born Yesterday.*
Sup. Actor: George Sanders, *All About Eve.*
Sup. Actress: Josephine Hull, *Harvey.*
Director: Joseph L. Mankiewicz, *All About Eve.*
Picture: *All About Eve.*

1951
Actor: Humphrey Bogart, *The African Queen.*
Actress: Vivien Leigh, *A Streetcar Named Desire.*
Sup. Actor: Karl Malden, *A Streetcar Named Desire.*
Sup. Actress: Kim Hunter, *A Streetcar Named Desire.*
Director: George Stevens, *A Place in the Sun.*
Picture: *An American in Paris.*

1952
Actor: Gary Cooper, *High Noon.*
Actress: Shirley Booth, *Come Back, Little Sheba.*
Sup. Actor: Anthony Quinn, *Viva Zapata!*
Sup. Actress: Gloria Grahame, *The Bad and the Beautiful.*
Director: John Ford, *The Quiet Man.*
Picture: *Greatest Show on Earth.*

1953
Actor: William Holden, *Stalag 17.*
Actress: Audrey Hepburn, *Roman Holiday.*
Sup. Actor: Frank Sinatra, *From Here to Eternity.*
Sup. Actress: Donna Reed, *From Here to Eternity.*
Director: Fred Zinnemann, *From Here to Eternity.*
Picture: *From Here to Eternity.*

1954
Actor: Marlon Brando, *On the Waterfront.*
Actress: Grace Kelly, *The Country Girl.*
Sup. Actor: Edmond O'Brien, *The Barefoot Contessa.*
Sup. Actress: Eve Marie Saint, *On the Waterfront.*
Director: Elia Kazan, *On the Waterfront.*
Picture: *On the Waterfront.*

1955
Actor: Ernest Borgnine, *Marty.*
Actress: Anna Magnani, *The Rose Tattoo.*
Sup. Actor: Jack Lemmon, *Mister Roberts.*
Sup. Actress: Jo Van Fleet, *East of Eden.*
Director: Delbert Mann, *Marty.*
Picture: *Marty.*

1956
Actor: Yul Brynner, *The King and I.*
Actress: Ingrid Bergman, *Anastasia.*
Sup. Actor: Anthony Quinn, *Lust for Life.*
Sup. Actress: Dorothy Malone, *Written on the Wind.*
Director: George Stevens, *Giant*
Picture: *Around the World in 80 Days.*

1957
Actor: Alec Guinness, *The Bridge on the River Kwai.*
Actress: Joanne Woodward, *The Three Faces of Eve.*
Sup. Actor: Red Buttons, *Sayonara.*
Sup. Actress: Miyoshi Umeki, *Sayonara.*
Director: David Lean, *The Bridge on the River Kwai.*
Picture: *The Bridge on the River Kwai.*

1958
Actor: David Niven, *Separate Tables.*
Actress: Susan Hayward, *I Want to Live.*
Sup. Actor: Burl Ives, *The Big Country.*
Sup. Actress: Wendy Hiller, *Separate Tables.*
Director: Vincente Minnelli, *Gigi.*
Picture: *Gigi.*

1959
Actor: Charlton Heston, *Ben Hur.*
Actress: Simone Signoret, *Room at the Top.*
Sup. Actor: Hugh Griffith, *Ben Hur.*
Sup. Actress: Shelley Winters, *Diary of Anne Frank.*
Director: William Wyler, *Ben Hur.*
Picture: *Ben Hur.*

1960
Actor: Burt Lancaster, *Elmer Gantry.*
Actress: Elizabeth Taylor, *Butterfield 8.*
Sup. Actor: Peter Ustinov, *Spartacus.*
Sup. Actress: Shirley Jones, *Elmer Gantry.*
Director: Billy Wilder, *The Apartment.*
Picture: *The Apartment.*

1961
Actor: Maximilian Schell, *Judgement at Nuremberg.*
Actress: Sophia Loren, *Two Women.*
Sup. Actor: George Chakiris, *West Side Story.*
Sup. Actress: Rita Moreno, *West Side Story.*
Director: Jerome Robbins, Robert Wise, *West Side Story.*
Picture: *West Side Story.*

1962
Actor: Gregory Peck, *To Kill a Mockingbird.*
Actress: Anne Bancroft, *The Miracle Worker.*
Sup. Actor: Ed Begley, *Sweet Bird of Youth.*
Sup. Actress: Patty Duke, *The Miracle Worker.*
Director: David Lean, *Lawrence of Arabia.*
Picture: *Lawrence of Arabia.*

1963
Actor: Sidney Poitier, *Lilies of the Field.*
Actress: Patricia Neal, *Hud.*
Sup. Actor: Melvyn Douglas, *Hud.*
Sup. Actress: Margaret Rutherford, *The VIPs.*

Director: Tony Richardson, *Tom Jones.*
Picture: *Tom Jones.*

1964
Actor: Rex Harrison, *My Fair Lady.*
Actress: Julie Andrews, *Mary Poppins.*
Sup. Actor: Peter Ustinov, *Topkapi.*
Sup. Actress: Lila Kedrova, *Zorba the Greek.*
Director: George Cukor, *My Fair Lady.*
Picture: *My Fair Lady.*

1965
Actor: Lee Marvin, *Cat Ballou.*
Actress: Julie Christie, *Darling.*
Sup. Actor: Martin Balsam, *A Thousand Clowns.*
Sup. Actress: Shelley Winters, *A Patch of Blue.*
Director: Robert Wise, *The Sound of Music.*
Picture: *The Sound of Music.*

1966
Actor: Paul Scofield, *A Man for All Seasons.*
Actress: Elizabeth Taylor, *Who's Afraid of Virginia Woolf?*
Sup. Actor: Walter Matthau, *The Fortune Cookie.*
Sup. Actress: Sandy Dennis, *Who's Afraid of Virginia Woolf?*
Director: Fred Zinnemann, *A Man for All Seasons.*
Picture: *A Man for All Seasons.*

1967
Actor: Rod Steiger, *In the Heat of the Night.*
Actress: Katharine Hepburn, *Guess Who's Coming to Dinner*
Sup. Actor: George Kennedy, *Cool Hand Luke.*
Sup Actress: Estelle Parsons, *Bonnie and Clyde.*
Director: Mike Nichols, *The Graduate.*
Picture: *In the Heat of the Night.*

1968
Actor: Cliff Robertson, *Charly.*
Actress: Katharine Hepburn, *The Lion in Winter;* Barbra Streisand, *Funny Girl* (tie).
Sup. Actor: Jack Albertson, *The Subject Was Roses.*
Sup. Actress: Ruth Gordon, *Rosemary's Baby.*
Director: Sir Carol Reed, *Oliver!*
Picture: *Oliver!*.

1969
Actor: John Wayne, *True Grit.*
Actress: Maggie Smith, *The Prime of Miss Jean Brodie.*
Sup. Actor: Gig Young, *They Shoot Horses Don't They?*
Sup. Actress: Goldie Hawn, *Cactus Flower.*
Director: John Schlesinger, *Midnight Cowboy.*
Picture: *Midnight Cowboy.*

1970
Actor: George C. Scott, *Patton.* (refused)
Actress: Glenda Jackson, *Women in Love.*
Sup. Actor: John Mills, *Ryan's Daughter.*
Sup. Actress: Helen Hayes, *Airport.*
Director: Franklin Schaffner, *Patton.*
Picture: *Patton.*

1971
Actor: Gene Hackman, *The French Connection.*
Actress: Jane Fonda, *Klute.*
Sup. Actor: Ben Johnson, *The Last Picture Show.*
Sup. Actress: Cloris Leachman, *The Last Picture Show.*
Director: William Friedkin, *The French Connection.*
Picture: *The French Connection.*

1972
Actor: Marlon Brando, *The Godfather.*
Actress: Liza Minnelli, *Cabaret.*
Sup. Actor: Joel Grey, *Cabaret.*
Sup. Actress: Eileen Heckart, *Butterflies Are Free.*
Director: Bob Fosse, *Cabaret.*
Picture: *The Godfather.*

1973
Actor: Jack Lemmon, *Save the Tiger.*
Actress: Glenda Jackson, *A Touch of Class.*
Sup. Actor: John Houseman, *The Paper Chase.*
Sup. Actress: Tatum O'Neal, *Paper Moon.*
Director: George Roy Hill, *The Sting.*
Picture: *The Sting.*

1974
Actor: Art Carney, *Harry and Tonto.*
Actress: Ellen Burstyn, *Alice Doesn't Live Here Anymore.*
Sup. Actor: Robert De Niro, *The Godfather, Part II*
Sup. Actress: Ingrid Bergman, *Murder on the Orient Express.*
Director: Francis Ford Coppola, *The Godfather, Part II*
Picture: *The Godfather, Part II.*

1975
Actor: Jack Nicholson, *One Flew Over the Cuckoo's Nest.*
Actress: Louise Fletcher, *One Flew Over the Cuckoo's Nest.*
Sup. Actor: George Burns, *The Sunshine Boys.*
Sup. Actress; Lee Grant, *Shampoo.*
Director: Milos Forman, *One Flew Over the Cuckoo's Nest.*
Picture: *One Flew Over the Cuckoo's Nest.*

1976
Actor: Peter Finch, *Network.*
Actress: Faye Dunaway, *Network.*
Sup. Actor: Jason Robards, *All the President's Men.*
Sup. Actress: Beatrice Straight, *Network.*
Director: John G. Avildsen, *Rocky.*
Picture: *Rocky.*

1977
Actor: Richard Dreyfuss, *The Goodbye Girl.*
Actress: Diane Keaton, *Annie Hall.*
Sup. Actor: Jason Robards, *Julia.*
Sup. Actress: Vanessa Redgrave, *Julia.*
Director: Woody Allen, *Annie Hall.*
Picture: *Annie Hall.*

1978
Actor: John Voight, *Coming Home.*
Actress: Jane Fonda, *Coming Home.*
Sup. Actor: Christopher Walken, *The Deer Hunter.*
Sup. Actress: Maggie Smith, *California Suite.*
Director: Michael Cimino, *The Deer Hunter.*
Picture: *The Deer Hunter.*

1979
Actor: Dustin Hoffman, *Kramer vs Kramer.*
Actress: Sally Field, *Norma Rae.*
Sup. Actor: Melvyn Douglas, *Being There.*
Sup. Actress: Meryl Streep, *Kramer vs Kramer.*
Director: Robert Benton, *Kramer vs Kramer.*
Picture: *Kramer vs Kramer.*

1980
Actor: Robert De Niro, *Raging Bull.*
Actress: Sissy Spacek, *Coal Miner's Daughter.*
Sup. Actor: Timothy Hutton, *Ordinary People.*
Sup. Actress: Mary Steenburgen, *Melvin and Howard.*
Director: Robert Redford, *Ordinary People.*
Picture: *Ordinary People.*

1981
Actor: Henry Fonda, *On Golden Pond.*
Actress: Katharine Hepburn, *On Golden Pond.*
Sup. Actor: John Gielgud, *Arthur.*
Sup. Actress: Maureen Stepleton, *Reds.*
Director: Warren Beatty, *Reds.*
Picture: *Chariots of Fire.*

1982
Actor: Ben Kingsley, *Gandhi.*
Actress: Meryl Streep, *Sophie's Choice.*
Sup. Actor: Louis Gossett, Jr, *An Officer and a Gentleman.*
Sup. Actress: Jessica Lange, *Tootsie.*
Director: Richard Attenborough, *Gandhi.*
Picture: *Gandhi.*

1983
Actor: Robert Duvall, *Tender Mercies.*
Actress: Shirley MacLaine, *Terms of Endearment.*
Sup. Actor: Jack Nicholson, *Terms of Endearment.*
Sup. Actress: Linda Hunt, *The Year of Living Dangerously.*
Director: James L. Brooks, *Terms of Endearment.*
Picture: *Terms of Endearment.*

1984
Actor: F. Murray Abraham, *Amadeus.*
Actress: Sally Field, *Places in the Heart.*
Sup. Actor: Haing S. Ngor, *The Killing Fields.*
Sup. Actress: Peggy Ashcroft, *A Passage to India.*
Director: Milos Forman, *Amadeus.*
Picture: *Amadeus.*

1985
Actor: William Hurt, *Kiss of the Spider Woman.*
Actress: Geraldine Page, *The Trip to Bountiful.*
Sup. Actor: Don Ameche, *Cocoon.*
Sup. Actress: Anjelica Huston, *Prizzi's Honor.*
Director: Sydney Pollack, *Out of Africa.*
Picture: *Out of Africa.*

1986
Actor: Paul Newman, *The Color of Money.*
Actress: Marlee Matlin, *Children of a Lesser God.*
Sup. Actor: Michael Caine, *Hannah and Her Sisters.*
Sup. Actress: Dianne Wiest, *Hannah and Her Sisters.*
Director: Oliver Stone, *Platoon.*
Picture: *Platoon.*

1987
Actor: Michael Douglas, *Wall Street.*
Actress: Cher, *Moonstruck.*
Sup. Actor: Sean Connery, *The Untouchables.*
Sup. Actress: Olympia Dukakis, *Moonstruck.*
Director: Bernardo Bertolucci, *The Last Emperor.*
Picture: *The Last Emperor,* Herndale, Columbia.

1988
Actor: Dustin Hoffman, *Rain Man.*
Actress: Jodie Foster, *The Accused.*
Sup. Actor: Kevin Kline, *A Fish Called Wanda.*
Sup. Actress: Geena Davis, *The Accidental Tourist.*
Director: Barry Levinson, *Rain Man.*
Picture: *Rain Man.*

1989
Actor: Daniel Day-Lewis, *My Left Foot.*
Actress: Jessica Tandy, *Driving Miss Daisy.*
Sup. Actor: Denzel Washington, *Glory.*
Sup. Actress: Brenda Fricker, *My Left Foot.*
Director: Oliver Stone, *Born on the Fourth of July.*
Picture: *Driving Miss Daisy.*

1990
Actor: Jeremy Irons, *Reversal of Fortune.*
Actress: Kathy Bates, *Misery.*
Sup. Actor: Joe Pesci, *Goodfellas.*
Sup. Actress: Whoopi Goldberg, *Ghosts.*
Director: Kevin Costner, *Dances with Wolves.*
Picture: *Dances with Wolves.*

1991
Actor: Anthony Hopkins, *The Silence of the Lambs.*
Actress: Jodie Foster, *The Silence of the Lambs.*
Sup. Actor: Jack Palance, *City Slickers.*
Sup. Actress: Mercedes Ruehl, *The Fisher King.*
Director: Jonathan Demme, *The Silence of the Lambs.*
Picture: *The Silence of the Lambs.*

1992
Actor: Al Pacino, *Scent of a Woman.*
Actress: Emma Thompson, *Howard's End.*
Sup. Actor: Gene Hackman, *Unforgiven.*
Sup. Actress: Marisa Tomei, *My Cousin Vinny.*
Picture: *Unforgiven.*

1993
Actor: Tom Hanks, *Philadelphia.*
Actress: Holly Hunter, *The Piano.*
Sup. Actor: Tommy Lee Jones, *The Fugitive.*
Sup. Actress: Anna Paquin, *The Piano.*
Director: Steven Spielberg, *Schindler's List.*
Picture: *Schindler's List.*

1994
Actor: Tom Hanks, *Forrest Gump.*
Actress: Jessica Lange, *Blue Sky.*
Sup. Actor: Martin Landau, *Ed Wood.*
Sup. Actress: Diane Wiest, *Bullits Over Broadway.*
Director: Robert Zemeckis, *Forrest Gump.*
Picture: *Forrest Gump.*

Among the above list of Oscar winners, some names are notably absent. Peter O'Toole has been nominated seven times but has never won an Oscar. Richard Burton was also nominated seven times without winning, while Deborah Kerr was nominated six times without winning. Alfred Hitchcock never won an Oscar and the following actors have won Oscars for directing but not for acting: Richard Attenborough, Warren Beatty, Kevin Costner, Clint Eastwood and Robert Redford. Famous films that did not win an Oscar include: *The Maltese Falcon, High Society* and *Double Indemnity.*

Film Festivals

THE BERLIN FILM FESTIVAL

The Berlin Film Festival was founded in 1951. From 1952 to 1955 the award for best film was voted for by the audience. From 1956 the Golden Bear for Best Picture was introduced. Winners of the best film award have been:

1952 *She Danced for the Summer* (Sweden)
1953 *The Wages of Fear* (France)
1954 *Hobson's Choice* (UK)
1955 *The Rats* (Germany)
1956 *Invitation to the Dance* (UK)
1957 *Twelve Angry Men* (USA)
1958 *The End of the Day* (Sweden)
1959 *The Cousins* (France)
1960 *Lazarillo de Tormes* (Spain)
1961 *La Notte* (Italy)
1962 *A Kind of Loving* (UK)
1963 *Oath of Obedience* (Germany)
The Devil (Italy)
1964 *Dry Summer* (Turkey)
1965 *Alphaville* (France)
1966 *Cul de Sac* (UK)
1967 *Le Départ* (Belgium)
1968 *Ole Dole Doff* (Sweden)
1969 *Early Years* (Yugoslavia)
1970 No award
1971 *The Garden of the Finzi-Continis* (Italy)
1972 *The Canterbury Tales* (Italy)
1973 *Distant Thunder* (India)
1974 *The Apprenticeship of Duddy Kravitz* (Canada)
1975 *Orkobefogadas* (Hungary)
1976 *Buffalo Bill and the Indians* (USA) – declined award
1977 *The Ascent* (USSR)
1978 *The Trouts* (Spain)
The Words of Max (Spain)
1979 *David* (Germany)
1980 *Heartland* (USA)
Palermo oder Wolfsburg (Germany)
1981 *Di Presa Di Presa* (Spain)
1982 *Die Sehnsucht der Veronica Voss* (Germany)
1983 *Ascendancy* (UK)
The Beehive (Spain)
1984 *Love Streams* (USA)
1985 *Wetherby* (UK)
Die Frau und der Fremde (Germany)
1986 *Stammheim* (Germany)
1987 *The Theme* (USSR)
1988 *Red Sorghum* (China)
1989 *Rain Man* (USA)
1990 *Music Box* (USA)
Larks on a String (Czechoslovakia)
1991 *House of Smiles* (Italy)
1992 *Grand Canyon* (USA)
1993 *The Woman from the Lake of Scented Souls* (China)
The Wedding Banquet (Taiwan/USA)
1994 *In the Name of the Father* (UK)

THE CANNES FILM FESTIVAL

The Cannes Film Festival, which was first held in 1946, was established by the French government. The Palme d'Or is awarded annually for the best film. Winners of the best film award have been:

1946 *La Bataille du Rail* (France)
1947 *Antoine et Antoinette* (France)
1948 No festival
1949 *The Third Man* (UK)
1950 No festival
1951 *Miracle in Milan* (Italy)
Miss Julie (Sweden)
1952 *Othello* (Morocco)
Two Cents Worth of Hope (Italy)
1953 *Wages of Fear* (France)
1954 *Gate of Hell* (Japan)
1955 *Marty* (USA)
1956 *World of Silence* (France)
1957 *Friendly Persuasion* (USA)
1958 *The Cranes are Flying* (USSR)
1959 *Black Orpheus* (France)
1960 *La Dolce Vita* (Italy)
1961 *Viridiana* (Spain)
Une aussi Longue Absence (France)
1962 *The Given Word* (Brazil)
1963 *The Leopard* (Italy)
1964 *The Umbrellas of Cherbourg* (France)
1965 *The Knack* (UK)
1966 *A Man and a Woman* (France)
Signore e Signori (Italy)
1967 *Blow-Up* (UK)
1968 Festival disrupted – no awards
1969 *If* (UK)
1970 *M*A*S*H* (USA)
1971 *The Go-Between* (UK)
1972 *The Working Class Goes To Paradise* (Italy)
The Mattei Affair (Italy)
1973 *Scarecrow* (USA)
The Hireling (UK)
1974 *The Conversation* (USA)
1975 *Chronicle of the Burning Years* (Algeria)
1976 *Taxi Driver* (USA)
1977 *Padre Padrone* (Italy)
1978 *L'Albero Degli Zoccoli* (Italy)
1979 *The Tin Drum* (Germany)
Apocalypse Now (USA)
1980 *All That Jazz* (USA)
Kagemusha (Japan)
1981 *Man of Iron* (Poland)
1982 *Missing* (USA)
Yol (Turkey)
1983 *The Ballad of Narayama* (Japan)
1984 *Paris, Texas* (Germany)
1985 *When Father Was Away on Business* (Yugoslavia)
1986 *The Mission* (UK)
1987 *Under the Sun of Satan* (France)
1988 *Pelle the Conqueror* (Denmark)
1989 *Sex, Lies and Videotape* (USA)
1990 *Wild at Heart* (USA)
1991 *Barton Fink* (USA)
1992 *Best Intentions* (Sweden)
1993 *Farewell My Concubine* (China)
The Piano (Australia)
1994 *Pulp Fiction* (USA)

TONY AWARDS

The Tony Awards, named in honour of actress Antoinette Perry, are given annually for 'distinguished achievement' in the theatre in the USA by the League of New York Theatres.

Tony Awards are made in the following categories: best play, leading actor (in a play), leading actress (in a play), featured actor (in a play), featured actress (in a play), direction (of a play), book (of a musical), original score (of a musical), leading actor (in a musical), leading actress (in a musical), featured actor (in a musical), featured actress (in a musical), direction (of a musical), best scenic design, best choreography, best costume design, best lighting design, best revival, and special awards.

Tony Best Play (since 1983)

1983 *Torch Song Trilogy* by Harvey Fierstein
1984 *The Real Thing* by Tom Stoppard
1985 *Biloxi Blues* by Neil Simon
1986 *I'm Not Rappaport* by Herb Gardner
1987 *M. Butterfly* by David Henry Hwang
1988 *The Heidi Chronicles* by Wendy Wasserstein
1990 *The Grapes of Wrath* by Frank Galati
1991 *Lost in Yonkers* by Neil Simon
1992 *Dancing at Lughnasa* by Brian Friel
1993 *Angels in America: Millennium Approaches* by Tony Kushner

Tony Leading Actor in a Play (since 1983)

1983 Harvey Fierstein for *Torch Song Trilogy*
1984 Jeremy Irons for *The Real Thing*
1985 Derek Jacobi for *Much Ado About Nothing*
1986 Judd Hirsch for *I'm Not Rappaport*
1987 James Earl Jones for *Fences*
1988 Ron Silver for *Speed-The-Plow*
1989 Philip Bosco for *Lend Me A Tenor*
1990 Robert Morse for *Tru*
1991 Nigel Hawthorne for *Shadowlands*
1992 Judd Hirsch for *Conversations With My Father*
1993 Ron Leibman for *Angels in America: Millennium Approaches*

Tony Leading Actress in a Play (since 1983)

1983 Jessica Tandy for *Foxfire*
1984 Glenn Close for *The Real Thing*
1985 Stockard Channing for *Joe Egg*
1986 Lily Tomlin for *The Search for Signs of Intelligent Life in the Universe*
1987 Linda Lavin for *Broadway Bound*
1988 Joan Allen for *Burn This*
1989 Pauline Collins for *Shirley Valentine*
1990 Maggie Smith for *Lettice and Lovage*
1991 Mercedes Roehl for *Lost in Yonkers*
1992 Glenn Close for *Death and the Maiden*
1993 Madeline Kahn for *The Sisters Rosenzweig*

Tony Featured Actor in a Play (since 1983)

1983 Matthew Broderick for *Brighton Beach Memoirs*
1984 Joe Mantegna for *Glengarry Glen Ross*
1985 Barry Miller for *Biloxi Blues*
1986 John Mahoney for *The House of Blue Leaves*
1987 John Randolph for *Broadway Bound*
1988 B. D. Wong for *M. Butterfly*
1989 Boyd Gaines for *The Heidi Chronicles*
1990 Charles Durning for *Cat on a Hot Tin Roof*
1991 Kevin Spacey for *Lost in Yonkers*
1992 Larry Fishburne for *Two Trains Running*
1993 Stephen Spinella for *Angels in America: Millennium Approaches*

Tony Featured Actress in a Play (since 1983)

1983 Judith Ivey for *Steaming*
1984 Christine Baranski for *The Real Thing*
1985 Judith Ivey for *Hurlyburly*
1986 Swoosie Kurtz for *The House of Blue Leaves*
1987 Mary Alice for *Fences*
1988 L. Scott Caldwell for *Joe Turner's Come and Gone*
1989 Christine Baranski for *Rumors*
1990 Margaret Tyzack for *Lettice and Lovage*
1991 Irene Worth for *Lost in Yonkers*
1992 Brid Brennan for *Dancing at Lughnasa*
1993 Debra Monk for *Redwood Curtain*

Tony Best Direction in a Play (since 1983)

1983 Gene Saks for *Brighton Beach Memoirs*
1984 Mike Nichols for *The Real Thing*
1985 Gene Saks for *Biloxi Blues*
1986 Jerry Zaks for *The House of Blue Leaves*
1987 Lloyd Richards for *Fences*
1988 John Dexter for *M. Butterfly*
1989 Jerry Zaks for *Lend Me a Tenor*
1990 Frank Galati for *The Grapes of Wrath*
1991 Jerry Zaks for *Six Degrees of Separation*
1992 Patrick Mason for *Dancing at Lughnasa*
1993 George C. Wolfe for *Angels in America: Millennium Approaches*

Tony Best Musical (Book) (since 1983)

1983 *Cats* by T. S. Eliot
1984 *La Cage aux Folles* by Harvey Fierstein
1985 *Big River* by William Hauptman
1986 *The Mystery of Edwin Drood* by Rupert Holmes
1987 *Les Misérables* by Alain Bourbil and Claude-Michel Schönberg
1988 *Into the Woods* by James Lupine
1989 No award
1990 *City of Angels* by Larry Gelbert
1991 *The Secret Garden* by Marsha Norman
1992 *Falsettos* by William Finn and James Lapine
1993 *Kiss of the Spider Woman – The Musical* by Livent Us Inc

Tony Best Musical (Score) (since 1983)

1983 *Cats*
1984 *La Cage aux Folles*
1985 *Big River*
1986 *The Mystery of Edwin Drood*
1987 *Me and My Girl*
1988 *Into the Woods*
1989 No award
1990 *City of Angels*
1991 *The Will Rogers Follies*
1992 *Falsettos*
1993 *Kiss of the Spider Woman – The Musical*
The Who's Tommy

BAFTA AWARDS

The British Academy of Film and Television Arts Awards, known as BAFTA, are presented annually.

BAFTA Best Film

1947 *The Best Years of Our Lives* (USA)
1948 *Hamlet* (UK)
1949 *Bicycle Thieves* (Italy)
1950 *All About Eve* (USA)
1951 *La Ronde* (France)
1952 *The Sound Barrier* (UK)
1953 *Jeux Interdits* (France)
1954 *Le Salaire de la Peur* (France)
1955 *Richard III* (UK)
1956 *Gervaise* (France)
1957 *The Bridge on the River Kwai* (UK)
1958 *Room at the Top* (UK)
1959 *Ben Hur* (USA)
1960 *The Apartment* (USA)
1961 *Ballad of a Soldier* (USSR); *The Hustler* (USA)
1962 *Lawrence of Arabia* (UK)
1963 *Tom Jones* (UK)
1964 *Dr Strangelove* (UK)
1965 *My Fair Lady* (UK)
1966 *Who's Afraid of Virginia Wolf?* (USA)
1967 *A Man For All Seasons* (UK)
1968 *The Graduate* (USA)
1969 *Midnight Cowboy* (USA)
1970 *Butch Cassidy and the Sundance Kid* (USA)
1971 *Sunday, Bloody Sunday* (UK)
1972 *Cabaret* (USA)
1973 *Day For Night* (France)
1974 *Lacombe Lucien* (France)
1975 *Alice Doesn't Live Here Anymore* (USA)
1976 *One Flew Over the Cuckoo's Nest* (USA)
1977 *Annie Hall* (USA)
1978 *Julia* (USA)
1979 *Manhattan* (USA)
1980 *The Elephant Man* (UK)
1981 *Chariots of Fire* (UK)
1982 *Gandhi* (UK)
1983 *Educating Rita* (UK)
1984 *The Killing Fields* (UK)
1985 *The Purple Rose of Cairo* (USA)
1986 *A Room With a View* (UK)
1987 *Jean de Florette* (France)
1988 *The Last Emperor* (Italy/UK/China)
1989 *Dead Poets Society* (USA)
1990 *Goodfellas* (USA)
1991 *The Commitments* (UK/USA)
1992 *Howards End* (UK)
1993 *Schindler's List* (USA)
1994 *Four Weddings and a Funeral* (UK)

BAFTA Leading Actor

1968 Spencer Tracey, *Guess Who's Coming to Dinner*
1969 Dustin Hoffman, *Midnight Cowboy* and *John and Mary*
1970 Robert Redford, *Butch Cassidy and the Sundance Kid, Tell Them Willie Boy is Here* and *Downhill Racer*
1971 Peter Finch, *Sunday, Bloody Sunday*
1972 Gene Hackman, *The French Connection* and *The Poseidon Adventure*
1973 Walter Matthau, *Pete'n'Tillie* and *Charley Varrick*
1974 Jack Nicholson for *The Last Detail* and *Chinatown*
1975 Al Pacino, *The Godfather Part II* and *Dog Day Afternoon*
1976 Jack Nicholson, *One Flew Over the Cuckoo's Nest*
1977 Peter Finch, *Network*
1978 Richard Dreyfuss, *The Goodbye Girl*
1979 Jack Lemmon, *The China Syndrome*
1980 John Hurt, *The Elephant Man*
1981 Burt Lancaster, *Atlantic City USA*
1982 Ben Kingsley, *Gandhi*
1983 Michael Caine, *Educating Rita*
Dustin Hoffman, *Tootsie*
1984 Dr Haing S. Ngor, *The Killing Fields*
1985 William Hurt, *Kiss of the Spider Woman*
1986 Bob Hoskins, *Mona Lisa*
1987 Sean Connery, *The Name of the Rose*
1988 John Cleese, *A Fish Called Wanda*
1989 Daniel Day-Lewis, *My Left Foot*
1990 Philippe Noiret, *Cinema Paradiso*
1991 Anthony Hopkins, *The Silence of the Lambs*
1992 Robert Downey Jr, *Chaplin*
1993 Anthony Hopkins, *The Remains of the Day*
1994 Hugh Grant, *Four Weddings and a Funeral*

BAFTA Leading Actress

1968 Katharine Hepburn, *Guess Who's Coming to Dinner* and *The Lion in Winter*
1969 Maggie Smith, *The Prime of Miss Jean Brodie*
1970 Katharine Ross, *Tell Them Willie Boy is Here* and *Butch Cassidy and the Sundance Kid*
1971 Glenda Jackson, *Sunday, Bloody Sunday*
1972 Liza Minelli, *Cabaret*
1973 Stephane Audret, *The Discreet Charm of the Bourgeoisie* and *Just Before Nightfall*
1974 Joanne Woodward, *Summer Wishes, Winter Dreams*
1975 Ellen Burstyn, *Alice Doesn't Live Here Anymore*
1976 Louise Fletcher, *One Flew Over the Cuckoo's Nest*
1977 Diane Keaton, *Annie Hall*
1978 Jane Fonda, *Julia*
1979 Jane Fonda, *The China Syndrome*
1980 Judy Davis, *My Brilliant Career*
1981 Meryl Streep, *The French Lieutenant's Woman*
1982 Katharine Hepburn, *On Golden Pond*
1983 Julie Walters, *Educating Rita*
1984 Maggie Smith, *A Private Function*
1985 Peggy Ashcroft, *A Passage to India*
1986 Maggie Smith, *A Room with a View*
1987 Ann Bancroft, *84 Charing Cross Road*
1988 Maggie Smith, *The Lonely Passion of Judith Hearne*
1989 Pauline Collins, *Shirley Valentine*
1990 Jessica Tandy, *Driving Miss Daisy*
1991 Jodie Foster, *The Silence of the Lambs*
1992 Emma Thompson, *Howards End*
1993 Holly Hunter, *The Piano*
1994 Susan Sarandon, *The Client*

BAFTA Best Film not in the English Language

1982 *Christ Stopped at Eboli* (Italy)
1983 *Danton* (France/Poland)
1984 *Carmen* (Spain)
1985 *Colonel Redl* (Hungary/Germany/Austria)
1986 *Ran* (Japan)
1987 *The Sacrifice* (Sweden)
1988 *Babette's Feast* (Denmark)
1989 *Life and Nothing But* (France)
1990 *Cinema Paradiso* (Italy/France)
1991 *The Nasty Girl* (Germany)
1992 *Raise the Red Lantern* (Hong Kong)
1993 *Farewell My Concubine* (China)
1994 *To Live* (Russia)

A – Z of Sports

British sporting champions are in the UK chapter.

AMERICAN FOOTBALL

American football evolved in US universities in the late 19th century from soccer and rugby. The first professional game was played in 1895 at Latrobe (Pa.). The American Professional Football Association was formed in 1920 and 12 teams contested the first league season. The association became the National Football League (NFL) in 1922. The American Football League (AFL) was formed in 1960. The two leagues merged in 1970, and were reorganized into the National Football Conference (NFC) and the American Football Conference (AFC). The major trophy is the Super Bowl, held annually since 1967, initially between the NFL and AFL champions, and since 1970 the champions of the NFC and AFC. The game is 11-a-side (12-a-side in Canada) with substitutes freely used. Pitch dimensions (NFL): 109·7 × 47·8 m (360 × 160 ft). Ball length 280–286 mm (11–11¼ in), weighing 397–425 g (14–15 oz).

Super Bowl winners

1967–68	Green Bay Packers
1969	New York Jets
1970	Kansas City Chiefs
1971	Baltimore Colts
1972	Dallas Cowboys
1973–74	Miami Dolphins
1975–76	Pittsburgh Steelers
1977	Oakland Raiders
1978	Dallas Cowboys
1979–80	Pittsburgh Steelers
1981	Oakland Raiders
1982	San Francisco 49ers
1983	Washington Redskins
1984	Los Angeles Raiders
1985	San Francisco 49ers
1986	Chicago Bears
1987	New York Giants
1988	Washington Redskins
1989–90	San Francisco 49ers
1991	New York Giants
1992	Washington Redskins
1993–94	Dallas Cowboys
1995	San Francisco 49ers

ARCHERY

Archery became an organized sport in the 3rd century AD and is portrayed in Mesolithic cave paintings. It became firmly established as an international sport in 1931 with the founding of the governing body, *Fédération Internationale de Tir à l'Arc* (FITA). The most popular form of archery is termed target archery. Other forms are field archery, shooting at animal figures, and flight shooting, which has the sole object of achieving distance. The World Target Championships, first held in Poland in 1931, have been biennial since 1957. The sport was included in the Olympic Games from 1900 to 1908, again in 1920 (the Belgian style of shooting) and was re-introduced in 1972. In 1992 a new format was introduced for Olympic competition with archers initially tackling a FITA round of 36 arrows each at 90m, 70m, 50m and 30m for men; and at 70m, 60m, 50m and 30m for women. The top 32 then met in a head-to-head knock-out competition. The 1992 Olympic champions were: (men) *individual* Sébastien Flute (France), *team* Spain; (women) *individual* Cho Youn-jeong (South Korea), *team* South Korea.

ATHLETICS (TRACK AND FIELD)

Organized athletics is usually dated to the ancient Olympic Games c. 1370 BC. The earliest known Olympiad was in July 776 BC, when Coroibos of Elis is recorded as winning the foot race over a distance of about 180–185m (164–169 yd).

Today, the sport is administered internationally by the International Amateur Athletic Federation (IAAF), formed in 1912, initially with 17 members. It ratified the first list of world records in 1914. The IAAF now has 206 nations affiliated to it, more than any other international organization, sporting or otherwise.

The major championships are the quadrennial Olympic Games and the World Championships. The modern Olympics were revived in 1896 and separate World Championships were introduced in 1983, initially quadrennially and now biennally. World Championships have been held at Helsinki, Finland (1983), Rome, Italy (1987), Tokyo, Japan (1991), Stuttgart, Germany (1993), and Gothenburg (Göteborg), Sweden (1995).

Marathon events, held since 1896, commemorate the legendary run of an unknown Greek courier, probably Pheidippides, who in 490 BC ran some 38·6 km (24 miles) from the Plain of Marathon to Athens with news of a Greek victory over the numerically superior Persian army. Since 1908 the distance has been standardized as 42,195m (26 miles 385 yd).

Dimensions in field events:

Shot (men) – weight 7·26 kg (16 lb), diameter 110–130 mm
Shot (women) – weight 4 kg, diameter 95–110 mm
Discus (men) – weight 2 kg, diameter 219–221 mm
Discus (women) – weight 1 kg, diameter 180–182 mm
Hammer (men) – weight 7·26 kg (16 lb), length 117·5–121·5 cm, diameter of head 110–130 mm
Hammer (women) – weight 4 kg, length 116–119·5 cm, diameter of head 95–110 mm
Javelin (men) – weight 800 g, length 260–270 cm
Javelin (women) – weight 600 g, length 220–230 cm

Track & field athletics world records

Men	*min:sec*	
100m	9·85	Leroy Burrell (US) 1994
200m	19·72	Pietro Mennea (Italy) 1979
400m	43·29	Butch Reynolds (USA) 1988
800m	1:41·73	Sebastian Coe (UK) 1981
1000m	2:12·18	Sebastian Coe (UK) 1981
1500m	3:44·39	Noureddine Morceli (Alg) 1993
2000m	4:50·81	Saïd Aouita (Morocco) 1987
3000m	7:25·11	Noureddine Morceli (Alg) 1994
5000m	12:56·96	Haile Gebrselassie (Eth) 1994
10,000m	26:52·23	William Sigei (Ken) 1994
20 km	56:55·6	Arturo Barrios (Mex) 1991
1 hour	21,101 m	Arturo Barrios (Mex) 1991
25,000m	1hr 13:55·8	Toshihiko Seko (Jap) 1981
30,000m	1hr 29:18·8	Toshihiko Seko (Jap) 1981

Marathon	2hr 06:50	Belayneh Dinsamo (Eth) 1988
3000m steeple	8:02·08	Moses Kiptanui (Ken) 1992
110m hurdles	12·91	Colin Jackson (UK) 1993
400m hurdles	46·78	Kevin Young (USA) 1992
4 × 100m relay	37·4	USA 1992
4 × 400m relay	2:54·29	USA 1993

	metres	
High jump	2·45	Javier Sotomayor (Cuba) 1993
Pole vault	6·14	Sergey Bubka (Ukraine) 1994
Long jump	8·95	Mike Powell (USA) 1991
Triple jump	18·17	Mike Conley (US) 1992
Shot	23·12	Randy Barnes (USA) 1990
Discus	74·08	Jürgen Schult (GDR) 1986
Hammer	86·74	Yuriy Sedykh (USSR) 1986
Javelin	95·66	Jan Zelezný (Czech Rep) 1993
Decathlon	8891 pts	Dan O'Brien (USA) 1992

Track walking	*min:sec*	
20 km	1hr 17·25	Bernardo Segura (Mex) 1994
50 km	3hr 41:38·4	Raúl González (Mex) 1979

Road walking – fastest recorded time		
50 km	3hr 37:41	Andrey Perlov (USSR) 1989

* Ben Johnson's 9·83 in 1987 was nullified as a record following his admission of drug taking, as was his 9·79 in 1988.

Women	*min:sec*	
100m	10·49	Florence Griffith-Joyner (USA) 1988
200m	21·34	Florence Griffith-Joyner (USA) 1988
400m	47·6	Marita Koch (GDR) 1985
800m	1:53·28	Jarmila Kratochvilová (Czech)
1000m	2:30·67	Christine Wachtel (GDR) 1990
1500m	3:50·46	Qu Yunxia (China) 1993
1 mile	4:15·61	Paula Ivan (Rom) 1989
2000m	5:25·36	Sonia O'Sullivan (Ire) 1986
3000m	8:06·11	Wang Junxia (China) 1993
5000m	14:37·33	Ingrid Kristiansen (Nor) 1986
10,000m	29:31·78	Wang Junxia (China) 1993
Marathon	2hr 21:06	Ingrid Kristiansen (Nor) 1985
100m hurdles	12·21	Yordanka Donkova (Bulg) 1988
400m hurdles	52·74	Sally Gunnell (UK) 1993
4 × 100m	41·37	GDR 1985
4 × 400m	3:15·17	USSR 1988

	metres	
High jump	2·09	Stefka Kostadinova (Bulg) 1986
Pole vault	4·06	Sun Caiyun (China) 1995
Long jump	7·52	Galina Chistyakova (USSR) 1988
Triple Jump	15·09	Anna Biryukova (Russia) 1993
Shot	22·63	Natalya Lisovskaya (USSR) 1987
Discus	76·8	Gabrielle Reinsch (GDR) 1988
Hammer	66 86	Mihaela Melinte (Rom) 1995
Javelin	80.0	Petra Felke (GDR) 1988
Heptathlon	7291 pts	Jackie Joyner-Kersee (USA) 1988

Track walking	*min:sec*	
5000m	20:07 52	Beate Anders (GDR) 1990
10 km	41:56 23	Nadezhda Ryashkina (USSR) 1990

Road walking – fastest recorded time		
10 km	41:3	Kerry Saxby (Austral) 1988
	41·3	Ileana Salvador (Italy) 1993

1992 Olympic champions

Men	*min:sec*	
100m	9·96	Linford Christie (UK)
200m	20·01	Michael Marsh (USA)
400m	43·5	Quincy Watts (USA)
800m	1:43·66	William Tanui (Ken)
1500m	3:40·12	Fermin Cacho (Spain)
5000m	13:12·52	Dieter Baumann (Germany)
10,000m	27:46·7	Khalid Skah (Morocco)
Marathon	2hr 13:23	Hwang Young-cho (S Korea)
3000m steeple	8:08·94	Matthew Birir (Ken)
110m hurdles	13·12	Mark McKoy (Canada)
400m hurdles	46·78	Kevin Young (USA)
4 × 100m	37·4	USA
4 × 400m	2:55·74	USA
20 km walk	1hr 21:45	Daniel Plaza (Spain)
50 km walk	3hr 50:13	Andrey Perlov (Russia)

	metres	
High jump	2·34	Javier Sotomayor (Cuba)
Pole vault	5·8	Maksim Tarasov (Russia)
Long jump	8·67	Carl Lewis (USA)
Triple jump	18·17	Mike Conley (USA)
Shot	21·7	Mike Stulce (USA)
Discus	65·12	Romas Ubartas (Lithuania)
Hammer	82·54	Andrey Abduvaliyev (Tajik)
Javelin	89·66	Jan Zelezný (Czech)
Decathlon	8611 pts	Robert Zmelík (Czech)

Women	*min:sec*	
100m	10·82	Gail Devers (USA)
200m	21·81	Gwen Torrence (USA)
400m	48·83	Marie-José Pérec (France)
800m	1:55·54	Ellen van Langen (Neths)
1500m	3:55·3	Hassiba Boulmerka (Alg)
3000m	8:46·04	Yelena Romanova (Russia)
10,000m	31:06·02	Derartu Tulu (Eth)
Marathon	2hr 32:41	Valentina Yegorova (Russia)
100 m hurdles	12·64	Paraskevi Patoulidou (Greece)
400 m hurdles	53·23	Sally Gunnell (UK)
4 × 100m	42·11	USA
4 × 400m	3:20·2	United team (12 out of 15 former Soviet republics).

	metres	
High jump	2·02	Heike Henkel (Germany)
Long jump	7·14	Heike Drechsler (Germany)
Shot	21·06	Svetlana Krivelyova (Russia)
Discus	70·06	Maritza Martén (Cuba)
Javelin	68·34	Silke Renk (Germany)
Heptathlon	7044 pts	Jackie Joyner-Kersee (USA)

European Championships

European Championships, held every four years, were first staged for men in 1934 and (separately) for women in 1938. Men's and women's events were combined at one venue from 1946.

1994 European champions

Men	*min:sec*	
100m	10·14	Linford Christie (UK)
200m	20·3	Geir Moen (Nor)
400m	45·09	Du'aine Ladejo (UK)
800m	1:46·12	Andrea Benvenuti (Italy)
1500m	3:35·27	Fermin Cacho (Spain)
5000m	13:36·93	Dieter Baumann (Germany)
10,000m	28:06·03	Abel Antón (Spain)

Marathon	2:10·31	Martin Fíz (Spain)
3000m steeple	8:22·4	Alessandro Lambruschini (Italy)
110m hurdles	13·08	Colin Jackson (UK)
400m hurdles	48·06	Oleg Tverdokhleb (Ukr)
4 x 100m relay	38·57	France
4 x 400m relay	2:59·13	UK
20 km walk	1:18·45	Mikhail Shchennikov (Russia)
50 km walk	3:41·07	Valeriy Spitsyn (Russia)
	metres	
High jump	2·35	Steinar Hoen (Nor)
Pole vault	6·0	Rodion Gataullin (Russia)
Long jump	8·09	Ivailo Mladenov (Bulg)
Triple jump	17·62	Denis Kapustin (Russia)
Shot	20·78	Aleksandr Klimenko (Ukr)
Discus	64·78	Vladimir Dubrovshchik (Belarus)
Hammer	81·1	Vasiliy Sidorenko (Russia)
Javelin	85·2	Steve Backley (UK)
Decathlon	8453 pts	Alain Blondel (France)

Women

	min:sec	
100m	11·02	Irina Privalova (Russia)
200m	22·32	Irina Privalova (Russia)
400m	50·33	Marie-José Pérec (France)
800m	1:58·55	Lyubov Gurina (Russia)
1500m	4:18·93	Lyudmila Rogachova (Russia)
3000m	8:31·84	Sonia O'Sullivan (Ire)
10,000m	31:08·75	Fernanda Ribeiro (Port)
Marathon	2:29·54	Manuela Machado (Port)
100m hurdles	12·72	Svetla Dimitrova (Bulg)
400m hurdles	53·33	Sally Gunnell (UK)
4 x 100m relay	42·9	Germany
4 x 400m relay	3:22·34	France
10 km walk	42:37	Sari Essayah (Fin)
High jump	2·0	Britta Bilac (Slovenia)
Long jump	7·14	Heike Drechsler (Germany)
Triple Jump	14·89	Ana Biryukova (Russia)
Shot	19·61	Viktoriya Pavlysh (Ukr)
Discus	68·72	Ilke Wyludda (Germany)
Javelin	68·0	Trine Hattestad (Nor)
Heptathlon	6419 pts	Sabine Braun (Germany)

AUSTRALIAN FOOTBALL

Originally a hybrid of soccer, Gaelic football and rugby, Australian football laws were codified in 1866, with the oval (rather than round) ball in use by 1867. In 1877 the Victorian Football Association was founded, from which eight clubs broke away to form the Victorian Football League (VFL). Four more teams were admitted by 1925, and in 1987 teams from Queensland and Western Australia joined the league which became the Australian Football League. The AFL (formerly the VFL) Grand Final is played annually at the Melbourne Cricket Ground. Teams are 18-a-side. Pitch dimensions are: width 110–155m (120–170 yd), length 135–185m (150–200 yd), encompassing an oval boundary line. The oval ball measures 736 mm (29½ in) in length, 572 mm (22½ in) in diameter and weighs 452–482 g (16–17 oz).

BADMINTON

The modern game is believed to have evolved from Badminton Hall (Glos), England, c. 1870, or from a game played in India at about the same time. Modern rules were first codified in Poona, India, in 1876. A similar game was played in China 2000 years earlier. The International Badminton Federation was founded in 1934, and now has over 100 member nations. The main centres of the sport are Canada, China, Denmark, India, Indonesia, Japan, Malaysia, New Zealand, South Korea, USA, and the UK. The World Championships, instituted in 1977 and initially held every three years, are now staged biennially, as are the international team competitions – the Thomas Cup (for men; first held 1949) and the Uber Cup (for women; first held 1957). China won both competitions in 1986, 1988 and 1990. In 1992 Malaysia won the Thomas Cup and China won the Uber Cup and in 1994 Indonesia won both. The major tournament prior to the introduction of World Championships was the annual All England Championships, initially held in 1899. Badminton was played as a demonstration sport at the Olympic Games in 1972 and 1988, and it became a medal sport in 1992, when the winners were: men's singles: Alan Budi Kusuma (Indonesia); women's singles: Susi Susanti (Indonesia); men's doubles: Kim Moon-soo and Park Joo-bong (S Korea); women's doubles: Hwang Hye-young and Chung So-young (S Korea).

Court dimensions: 13·41 × 6·1m (44 × 20 ft; singles game 3ft narrower). The net is 1·5m (5 ft) high at the centre; two or four players.

BASEBALL

The modern, or Cartwright, rules, were introduced in New Jersey in 1846, although a game of the same name had been played in England prior to 1700. Baseball is mainly played in America, where there are two leagues, the National (NL) and the American (AL), founded in 1876 and 1901 respectively. It is also very popular in Japan. The winners of each US league meet annually in a best of seven series of games – the World Series – established permanently in 1905. Baseball was added to the Olympic programme in 1992, when the gold medal was won by Cuba.

Recent World Series winners

1980	Philadelphia Phillies (NL)
1981	Los Angeles Dodgers (NL)
1982	St Louis Cardinals (NL)
1983	Baltimore Orioles (AL)
1984	Detroit Tigers (AL)
1985	Kansas City Royals (AL)
1986	New York Mets (NL)
1987	Minnesota Twins (AL)
1988	Los Angeles Dodgers (NL)
1989	Oakland Athletics (AL)
1990	Cincinnati Reds (NL)
1991	Minnesota Twins (AL)
1992–93	Toronto Blue Jays (AL)
1994	Cancelled due to players' strike

The game is 9-a-side. A standard ball weighs 148 g (5–5¼ oz) and is 23 cm (9–9½ in) in circumference. Bats are up to 7 cm (2¾ in) in diameter and up to 1·07m (42 in) in length.

BASKETBALL

A game resembling basketball was played by the Olmecs in Mexico, but the modern game was devised by (Canadian-born) Dr James Naismith in Massachusetts, in 1891. The governing body is the *Fédération Internationale de Basketball Amateur* (FIBA), formed in 1932. By 1992, 193 national federations were members of FIBA. It has been an Olympic sport for men since 1936, and for women since 1976.

World championships, first held for men in 1950 and for women in 1953, are held every four years. Teams are 5-a-side, with seven substitutes allowed. The rectangular court is 26m (85 ft) in length, and 14m (46 ft) wide, and the ball is 75–78 cm (30 in) in circumference and weighs 600–650 g (21–23 oz).

Olympic champions

Men

USA: 1936, 1948, 1952, 1956, 1960, 1964, 1968, 1976, 1984, 1992
USSR: 1972, 1988
Yugoslavia: 1980

Women

USSR: 1976, 1980
USA: 1984, 1988
Unified team (a combined team representing 12 of the 15 former Soviet republics): 1992

World champions

Men

Argentina: 1950
USA: 1954, 1986, 1994
Brazil: 1959, 1963
USSR: 1967, 1974, 1982
Yugoslavia: 1970, 1978, 1990

Women

USA: 1953, 1957, 1979, 1986, 1990
USSR: 1959, 1964, 1967, 1971, 1975, 1983
Brazil: 1994

BIATHLON

A combination of cross-country skiing and rifle shooting, in which competitors ski over prepared courses carrying a small-bore rifle, the biathlon has been an Olympic event for men since 1960 and women since 1992.

Men compete individually over 10 km or 20 km. There are two shooting competitions at a target 50m away over the 10 km distance and four (both prone and standing) over the 20 km distance. The relay event is four by 7·5 km, each member shooting once prone and once standing. Penalties are imposed for missing the target. The women's equivalent distances are 7·5 km, 15 km and three by 7·5 km relay. The governing body, *L'Union Internationale de Pentathlon Moderne et Biatholon* (UIPMB), has administered the sport since 1957, and staged the first World Championships in 1958.

BILLIARDS

Probably deriving from the old French word *billiard* (a stick with a curved end), a reference from 1429 suggests the game was originally played on grass. Louis XI of France is believed to be the first to have played billiards on a table. Rubber cushions were introduced in 1835, and slate beds in 1836. The World Professional and Amateur Championships have been held since 1870 and 1926 respectively. Dimensions of table: 3·66 × 1·87m (12 × 6 ft).

BOARDSAILING (WINDSURFING)

Following a High Court decision, Peter Chilvers has been credited with devising the prototype boardsail in 1958. As a sport, it was pioneered by Henry Hoyle Schweitzer and Jim Drake in California in 1968. The World Championships were first held in 1973 and boardsailing was added to the Olympic Games in 1984.

BOBSLEIGH AND TOBOGGANING

Although the first known sledge dates back to c. 6500 BC in Finland, organized bobsleighing began in Davos, Switzerland, in 1889. The International Federation of Bobsleigh and Tobogganing was formed in 1923, followed by the International Bobsleigh Federation in 1957. The World and Olympic Championships began in 1924, and competition is for crews of two or four. The driver steers while the rear man operates brakes and corrects skidding. With the four-man, the middle two riders alter weight transference for cornering. The oldest tobogganing club is the St Moritz in Switzerland, founded in 1887, and home of the Cresta Run, which dates from 1884. The course is 1212·25m (3977 ft) long with a drop of 157m (514 ft). Solo speeds reach 145 km/h (90 mph). In lugeing, the rider sits or lies back, as opposed to lying face down in tobogganing.

BOWLING (TEN-PIN)

The ancient German game of nine-pins was banned in Connecticut in 1847, and subsequently in other US states. Ten-pin bowling was introduced to beat the ban. Rules were first standardized by the American Bowling Congress (ABC), formed in 1895. Concentrated in the USA, the game is also very popular in Japan and Europe. The World Championships were introduced for men in 1954 and women in 1963, under the *Fédération Internationale des Quilleurs* (FIQ), which governs a number of bowling games. The ten pins are placed in a triangle at the end of a lane of total length 19·16m (62 ft 10¾ in) and width 1·06m (42 in).

BOWLS

Outdoor bowls goes back at least as far as the 13th century in England, but it was forbidden by Edward III because its popularity threatened the practice of archery. The modern rules were framed in 1848–9 in Scotland by William Mitchell. There are two types of greens, the crown and the level, the former being played almost exclusively in northern and Midland England. Lawn bowls is played mostly in the UK and Commonwealth countries. The International Bowling Board was formed in 1905. The Men's and Women's World Championships are held every four years, with singles, pairs, triples and fours events. The World Championships for Indoor Bowls were introduced in 1979 and are staged annually.

BOXING

Competitively, boxing began in ancient Greece as one of the first Olympic sports. Boxing with gloves was first depicted on a fresco from the isle of Thera, c. 1520 BC. Prize-fighting rules were formed in England in 1743 by Jack Broughton, but modern day boxing was regularized in 1867 when the 8th Marquess of Queensberry gave his name to the new rules. Boxing only became a legal sport in 1901. Professional boxing has several world governing bodies, the two oldest being the World Boxing Council (WBC) and the World Boxing Association (WBA). Neither body has been able to agree on fight regulations, and the situation has been further complicated by the formation of the International Boxing Federation (IBF) in the USA in 1983, the World Boxing Organization (WBO) in 1988 and other bodies since then. Recognized weight categories are:

Limit in lb (kg)	*Weight category*
105 (48)	strawweight (WBC), mini-flyweight (WBA, IBF, WBO)
108 (49)	light-flyweight (WBC), junior flyweight (WBA, IBF, WBO)
112 (51)	flyweight
115 (52)	super-flyweight (WBC), junior bantamweight (WBA, IBF, WBO)
118 (54)	bantamweight
122 (55)	super bantamweight (WBC), junior featherweight (WBA,IBF, WBO)
126 (57)	featherweight
130 (59)	super featherweight (WBC), junior lightweight (WBA, IBF, WBO)
135 (61)	lightweight
140 (64)	super lightweight (WBC), junior welterweight (WBA, IBF, WBO)
147 (67)	welterweight
154 (70)	super lightweight (WBC), junior middleweight (WBA, IBF, WBO)
160 (73)	middleweight
168 (76)	super middleweight
175 (79)	light heavyweight
190 (86)	junior heavyweight (WBO), cruiser-weight (WBC, WBA, IBF)
190 (86)+	heavyweight

Weight categories in amateur boxing are:

Limit in kg (lb)	*Weight category*
48 (106)	light flyweight
51 (112)	flyweight
54 (119)	bantamweight
57 (126)	featherweight
60 (132)	lightweight
63·5 (140)	light welterweight
67 (148)	welterweight
71 (157)	light middleweight
75 (165)	middleweight
81 (179)	light heavyweight
91 (201)	heavyweight
91 (201)+	super heavyweight

CANOEING

Modern canoes and kayaks originated among the Indians and Inuit (Eskimos) of North America, but canoeing as a sport is attributed to an English barrister, James MacGregor, who founded the Royal Canoe Club in 1866. With a kayak, the paddler sits in a forward-facing position and uses a double-bladed paddle, whereas in a canoe the paddler kneels in a forward-facing position and propels with a single-bladed paddle. An Olympic sport since 1936, competitions for Olympic titles are now held at flat water in nine events for men at 500m and 1000m, and three for women each at 500m. In 1992 slalom events were reintroduced with three men's events and one women's event.

CHESS

Derived from the Persian word *Shah* (king or ruler), the game originated in India under the name *Caturanga* (literally 'four corps'). The earliest surviving chessmen are an ivory set found in Russia, dated c. AD 200. By the 10th century, chess was played in most of Europe. There are now some 40 million enthusiasts in Russia and the former Soviet republics. The governing body is the *Fédération Internationale des Echecs* (FIDE; founded 1922), which has been responsible for the World Chess Championship competitions since 1946, although official champions date from 1886 and there were unofficial champions before then. Players are graded by FIDE according to competitive results on the ELO scoring system, with results issued twice yearly. Grandmaster level is 2500, a rating currently attained by about 100 players. The highest rating ever achieved is 2805 by the current world champion Gary Kasparov, reached in 1992, having surpassed Bobby Fischer's previous best of 2785 (1991). The highest rated woman player is Judit Polgar (Hungary) at 2595. She became, at 15, the youngest ever Grandmaster on 20 December 1991.

World champions

1851–58	Adolf Anderssen (Germany)
1858–62	Paul Morphy (USA)
1862–66	Adolf Anderssen (Germany)
1866–94	Wilhelm Steinitz (Austria)
1894–1921	Emanuel Lasker (Germany)
1921–27	José Capablanca (Cuba)
1927–35	Alexandre Alekhine (France)
1935–37	Max Euwe (Neths)
1937–46	Alexandre Alekhine (France)
1948–57	Mikhail Botvinnik (USSR)
1957–58	Vasiliy Smyslov (USSR)
1958–60	Mikhail Botvinnik (USSR)
1960–61	Mikhail Tal (USSR)
1961–63	Mikhail Botvinnik (USSR)
1963–69	Tigran Petrosian (USSR)
1969–72	Boris Spassky (USSR)
1972–75	Bobby Fischer (USA)
1975–85	Anatoliy Karpov (USSR)
1985–	Gary Kasparov (USSR/Russia)

In 1993, Kasparov and Nigel Short (UK) were due to contest the world title, but decided to form the Professional Chess Association and to play their championship matches outside the auspices of FIDE, who declared that a contest between Anatoliy Karpov and Jan Timman (Neths), who were beaten by Short in the Challengers' Tournament, was to be for the world title. Karpov won 12·5 to 8·5.

Women's world champions

1927–44	Vera Menchik* (UK)
1950–53	Lyudmila Rudenko (USSR)
1953–56	Yelizaveta Bykova (USSR)
1956–58	Olga Rubtsova (USSR)
1958–62	Yelizaveta Bykova (USSR)
1962–78	Nona Gaprindashvili (USSR)
1978–91	Maya Chiburdanidze (USSR)
1991–	Xie Jun (China)

* The reorganization of the sport after 1946, and the death of Menchik in 1944 left chess without a women's champion.

CRICKET

A drawing dated c. 1250 shows a bat and ball game resembling cricket, although the formal origins are early 18th century. The formation of the MCC

(Marylebone Cricket Club) in 1787 resulted in codified laws by 1835. The International (Imperial until 1965) Cricket Conference (ICC), was formed by England, Australia and South Africa in 1909. India, New Zealand and West Indies joined in 1926, Pakistan (1953), Sri Lanka (1981), and Zimbabwe (1992). South Africa ceased to be a member in 1961, but was readmitted in 1992. Other, non-Test playing nations have been admitted: 19 as associate members and five as affiliated members. The World Cup, the international one-day tournament, is held every four years, with the Test-playing countries plus the winner of the ICC Trophy, which is competed for by non-Test playing countries.

World Cup winners

1975 West Indies
1979 West Indies
1983 India
1987 Australia
1991 Pakistan

The first Women's World Cup was held in 1973. *Winners:* 1973 England, 1978 Australia, 1982 Australia, 1988 Australia, 1993 England.

Dimensions: Ball circumference 20·79–22·8 cm ($8\frac{3}{16}$–9 in), weight 155–163 g (5½–5¾ oz); pitch 20·11m (22 yd) from stump to stump.

In the UK, the first-class counties (now 18) have competed in the county championship, or preceding inter-county matches, since 1864. See the UK chapter.

In Australia, the annual first-class inter-state competition has been contested for the Sheffield Shield from 1891–92. Sheffield Shield winners have been New South Wales (42 times), Victoria (25), South Australia (12), Western Australia (11), and Queensland (1). Tasmania has never won the Shield. Recent winners:

1982 South Australia
1983 New South Wales
1984 Western Australia
1985–86 New South Wales
1987–89 Western Australia
1990 New South Wales
1991 Victoria
1992 Western Australia
1993–94 New South Wales
1995 Queensland

In India, the annual first-class inter-state championship is the Ranji Trophy, instituted in 1934. Bombay has won the Trophy on a record 32 occasions. Recent winners have been:

1983 Karnataka
1984–85 Bombay
1986 Delhi
1987 Hyderabad
1988 Tamil Nadu
1989 Delhi
1990 Bengal
1991 Haryana
1992 Delhi
1993 Punjab
1994–95 Bombay

In New Zealand, the annual first-class competition was the Plunkett Shield from 1906 to 1974–75. Since 1974–75, the six first-class sides have competed in the Shell series. Recent winners have been:

1983 Wellington
1984 Canterbury
1985 Wellington
1986 Otago
1987 Central Districts
1988 Otago
1989 Auckland
1990 Wellington
1991 Auckland
1992 Central Districts and Northern Districts
1993 Northern Districts
1994 Canterbury

In Pakistan, the premier first-class competition is the Quaid-e-Azam Trophy (contested since 1954). Karachi has won the competition nine times. Recent winners have been:

1983 United Bank
1984 National Bank
1985 United Bank
1986 Karachi
1987 National Bank
1988 Habib Bank
1989 ADBP
1990 PIA

SUMMARY OF TEST MATCH RESULTS

To 1 May 1995

The first figure is number of wins by the team on the left over the team in that column, the second figure is number of draws. Thus in England v Australia Tests, England have won 90, Australia 111, with 84 Tests left drawn.

	A	E	I	NZ	P	SA	SL	WI	Z	Wins	Tests
Australia	-	111/84	24/17*	13/12	12/17	31/15	4/3	31/21*		226	550
England	90/84	-	31/36	34/37	14/31	47/39	3/1	25/38		244	712
India	8/17*	14/36	-	12/14	4/33	0/3	7/4	7/31	1/1	53	292
New Zealand	7/12	4/37	6/14	-	4/16	3/6	4/7	4/13	1/1	33	236
Pakistan	10/15	7/31	7/33	16/16	-	0/0	10/5	7/11	4/1	61	223
South Africa	13/15	19/39	1/3	11/6	1/0	-	1/2	0/0		46	193
Sri Lanka	0/3	1/1	1/6	2/7	1/5	0/2	-	0/0	0/3	5	62
West Indies	27/21*	46/38	27/31	9/13	12/11	1/0	1/0	-		123	313
Zimbabwe			0/1	0/1	1/1		0/3			1	13

* plus one tie. There have been two tied Tests:
9–14 Dec 1960 at Brisbane, Australia v West Indies, 18–22 Sep 1986 at Madras, Australia v India
Note this included the first 3 of the 4 Tests West Indies v Australia 1995
* plus one tie. There have been two tied Tests: Australia v West Indies 1960 and Australia v India 1986

1991–92 Karachi Whites
1993 Karachi
1994 Lahore

In South Africa, the annual first-class competition for the Currie Cup (now Castle Currie Cup) has been held since 1889–90. Transvaal has won the competition 28 times outright and four shared; Natal has won 22 times and three shared. Recent winners have been:

1983–5 Transvaal
1986 Western Province
1987–88 Transvaal
1989 Eastern Province
1990 Eastern Province and Western Province
1991 Western Province
1992 Eastern Province
1993–94 Orange Free State
1995 Natal

In the West Indies, the annual first-class competition is the Red Stripe Cup (preceded by the Shell Shield 1966 to 1987). Barbados has won the championship no fewer than 14 times. Recent winners have been:

1983 Guyana
1984 Barbados
1985 Trinidad and Tobago
1986 Barbados
1987 Guyana
1988–89 Jamaica
1990 Leeward Islands
1991 Barbados
1992 Jamaica
1993 Guyana
1994 Leeward Islands
1995 Barbados

CURLING

Similar to bowls on ice, curling dates from the 15th century, although organized administration of the sport only began in 1838 with the Grand (later Royal) Caledonian Curling Club in Edinburgh. The sport is most popular in Scotland and Canada. The International Curling Federation was formed in 1966, and curling was included in the 1988 and 1992 Olympic Games as a demonstration sport, as it had been in 1924, 1932, and 1964.

CYCLING

The first known cycling race was held over 2 km (1·2 mi) in Paris on 31 May 1868. The Road Record Association in Britain was formed in 1888, and F. T. Bidlake devised the time trial (1890) as a means of avoiding traffic congestion caused by ordinary mass road racing. Competitive racing, popular worldwide, is now conducted both on road and track. The Tour de France (founded 1903) is the longest-lasting non-motorized sporting event in the world, lasting 21 days annually. The yellow jersey, to distinguish the leading rider, was introduced in 1919. A range of road and track events are contested annually. There are separate amateur and professional categories for men's road racing, but for track events the categories were merged in 1993 and there has never been any distinction for women's events. World Championships were first held in 1893 at two events, the sprint and the motor-paced over 100 km.

Tour de France winners (from 1947)

1947 Jean Robic (France)
1948 Gino Bartali (Italy)
1949 Fausto Coppi (Italy)
1950 Ferdinand Kübler (Switz)
1951 Hugo Koblet (Switz)
1952 Fausto Coppi (Italy)
1953–55 Louison Bobet (France)
1956 Roger Walkowiak (France)
1957 Jacques Anquetil (France)
1958 Charly Gaul (Lux)
1959 Frederico Bahamontès (Spain)
1960 Gastone Nencini (Italy)
1961–64 Jacques Anquetil (France)
1965 Felice Gimondi (Italy)
1966 Lucien Aimar (France)
1967 Roger Pingeon (France)
1968 Jan Janssen (Neths)
1969–72 Eddy Merckx (Belgium)
1973 Luis Ocana (Spain)
1974 Eddy Merckx (Belgium)
1975 Bernard Thevenet (France)
1976 Lucien van Impe (Belgium)
1977 Bernard Thevenet (France)
1978–89 Bernard Hinault (France)
1980 Joop Zoetemelk (Neths)
1981–82 Bernard Hinault (France)
1983–84 Laurent Fignon (France)
1985 Bernard Hinault (France)
1986 Greg LeMond (USA)
1987 Stephen Roche (Ire)
1988 Pedro Delgado (Spain)
1989–90 Greg LeMond (USA)
1991–94 Miguel Induráin (Spain)

Cycling has been included in the modern Olympic Games since 1896. There are currently seven men's and two women's events on the Olympic programme.

1992 Olympic champions

Men
Sprint: Jens Fiedler (Germany)
1000m time trial: José Moreno (Spain) 1:03·342
4000m individual pursuit: Chris Boardman (UK)
50 km points race: Giovanni Lombardi (Italy)
Road race: Fabio Casartelli (Italy)
Team time trial: Germany
Team pursuit: Germany

Women
Sprint: Erika Salumyae (Estonia)
Road race: Kathryn Watt (Austral)
3000m individual pursuit: Petra Rossner (Germany).

DARTS

Brian Gamlin of Bury, England, is credited with devising the present numbering system on the dartboard, although in non-sporting form darts began with the heavily weighted throwing arrows used in Roman and Greek warfare. Very popular in the UK, where there are some 6,000,000 players, darts has spread in America and parts of Europe. The World championships were first held in 1978. Winners have been:

1978 Leighton Rees (Wales)
1979 John Lowe (England)
1980–81 Eric Bristow (England)
1982 Jocky Wilson (Scotland)

1983	Keith Deller (England)
1984–86	Eric Bristow (England)
1987	John Lowe (England)
1988	Bob Anderson (England)
1989	Jocky Wilson (Scotland)
1990	Phil Taylor (England)
1991	Dennis Priestley (England)
1992	Phil Taylor (England)
1993	John Lowe (England)
1994	John Part (Canada)
1995	Richie Burnett (Wales)

In 1992, dissatisfied with the WBO's organisation of the game, many of the world's top players formed the World Darts Council (WDC), and that organisation introduced its own World Championship at the end of 1993. Their champions have been: 1993–94 Dennis Priestley (England); 1994–95 Phil Taylor (England).

EQUESTRIANISM

Horse riding is some 5000 years old. Schools of horsemanship, or equitation, were established in the 16th century, primarily in Italy and France. The earliest known jumping competition was in Islington, London, in 1869. An Olympic event since 1912, events are held in dressage, show jumping and three-day event, with team and individual titles for each. Dressage (the French term for the training of horses) is a test of a rider's ability to control a horse through various manoeuvres within an area of 60 × 20m (66 × 22 yd). In show jumping, riders jump a set course of fences, incurring four faults for knocking a fence down or landing (one or more feet) in the water, three faults for a first refusal, six faults then elimination for 2nd and 3rd, and eight faults for a fall. The three-day event encompasses dressage, cross country and jumping. The governing body is the *Fédération Equestre Internationale*, founded in 1921.

1992 Olympic champions

Individual:
Show jumping: Ludger Beerbaum (Germany) on Classic Touch.
Three-day event: Matthew Kyan (Austral) on Kibah Tic Toc.
Dressage: Nicole Uphof (Germany) on Rembrandt.
Team:
Show jumping: Netherlands.
Three-day event: Australia.
Dressage: Germany.

FENCING

Fencing (fighting with single sticks) was practised as a sport, or a religious ceremony, in Egypt as early as 1360 BC. The modern sport developed from the duelling of the Middle Ages. There are three types of sword used today. With the foil (introduced in the 17th century), only the trunk of the body is acceptable as a target. The épée (a mid-19th century introduction) is marginally heavier and more rigid, and the whole body is a valid target. The sabre (a late 19th-century introduction) has cutting edges on both sides of the blade, and scores on the whole body from the waist upwards. Only with the sabre can points be scored with the edge of the blade rather than the tip. Women compete in foil only at the Olympic Games, but the women's épée was added to the annual World Championships from 1989. For men, there are individual and team events for each type of sword in the Olympics. The world governing body is the *Fédération Internationale d'Escrime*, founded in 1913.

1992 Olympic champions

Men

	Individual	*Teams*
Foil	Philippe Omnès (France)	Germany
Epée	Eric Srecki (France)	Germany
Sabre	Bence Szabó (Hungary)	Unified Team, a combined team representing 12 of the 15 former Soviet republics.

Women

Foil	Giovanna Trillini (Italy)	Italy

FIVES

Eton Fives originate from a handball game first recorded as being played against the buttress of Eton College Chapel in 1825. The rules were codified in 1877, and last amended in 1981. Rugby Fives, a variation, dates from c. 1850. Both are more or less confined to the UK.

FOOTBALL (Association)

A game resembling football, *Tsu-Chu-Tsu*, meaning 'to kick the ball with feet' was played in China around 400 BC. Calcio, closer to the modern game, existed in Italy in 1410. References in England date to Edward II's reign – he banned the game in 1314. Soccer rules were first formulated at Cambridge University in 1846. The Football Association (FA) was founded in England in 1863. Eleven per side became standard in 1870. The governing body, *the Fédération Internationale de Football Association* (FIFA), was founded in Paris in 1904 and football is now played throughout the world. Internationally, the World Cup has been held every four years since 1930 (except in 1942 and 1946). The European Championship (instituted 1958 as the Nations Cup) is held every four years. The European Champions Club Cup, instituted in 1955 as the European Cup, is contested annually by the league champions of the member countries of the Union of European Football Associations (UEFA). The European Cup Winners' Cup was instituted in 1960 for national cup winners (or runners-up if the winners are in the European Cup). The UEFA Cup was instituted in 1955 as the Inter-City Fairs Cup, and has been held annually since 1960. The European Super Cup (instituted in 1972) is played between the winners of the European Champions Club Cup and the Cup Winners' Cup; and the World Club Championship (instituted in 1960) is a contest between the winners of the European Cup and the Copa Libertadores (the South American equivalent). (See also the UK chapter.)

Football is an 11-a-side game; the ball's circumference is 68–71 cm (27–28 in) and weight 396–453 g (14–16 oz). Pitch length 91–120m (100–130 yd), width 45–91m (50–100 yd).

The World Cup

Year	*Winner*	*Venue*
1930	Uruguay	Uruguay
1934	Italy	Italy

1938	Italy	France
1950	Uruguay	Brazil
1954	Germany (W)	Switzerland
1958	Brazil	Sweden
1962	Brazil	Chile
1966	England	England
1970	Brazil	Mexico
1974	Germany (W)	Germany (W)
1978	Argentina	Argentina
1982	Italy	Spain
1986	Argentina	Mexico
1990	Germany (W)	Italy
1994	Brazil	USA

European Championships

Held every four years, the championship is played over a two-year period. Originally called the European Nations Cup, it took its present name in 1968.
Winners:

1960	USSR
1964	Spain
1968	Italy
1972	Germany (W)
1976	Czechoslovakia
1980	Germany (W)
1984	France
1988	Netherlands
1992	Denmark

African Nations Cup

First contested in 1957, and now held biennially.
Winners:

1957	Egypt	1978	Ghana
1959	Egypt	1980	Nigeria
1962	Ethiopia	1982	Ghana
1963	Ghana	1984	Cameroon
1965	Ghana	1986	Egypt
1968	Zaïre	1988	Cameroon
1970	Sudan	1990	Algeria
1972	Congo	1992	Ivory Coast
1974	Zaïre	1994	Nigeria
1976	Morocco		

South American Cup

First contested in 1960 as the South American Champion's Club Cup. Like the European Cup it was open to national league champions of countries affiliated to the South American Confederation. In 1965 league runners-up were also allowed to enter the competition and, that year, its name was changed to the Copa Libertadores de América.
Winners:

1960–61	Peñarol (Uru)
1962–63	Santos (Bra)
1964–65	Independiente (Arg)
1966	Peñarol (Uru)
1967	Racing Club (Arg)
1968–70	Estudiantes (Arg)
1971	Nacional Montevideo (Uru)
1972–75	Independiente (Arg)
1976	Cruzeiro (Bra)
1977–78	Boca Juniors (Arg)
1979	Olimpia (Par)
1980	Nacional Montevideo (Uru)
1981	Flamengo (Bra)
1982	Peñarol (Uru)
1983	Gremio (Bra)
1984	Independiente (Arg)
1985	Argentinos Juniors (Arg)
1986	River Plate (Arg)
1987	Peñarol (Uru)
1988	Nacional Montevideo (Uru)
1989	Nacional Medellín (Col)
1990	Olimpia (Par)
1991	Colo Colo (Chl)
1992–93	São Paulo (Bra)
1994	Velez Sarsfield (Arg)

European Champion Clubs Cup

1956–60	Real Madrid
1961–62	Benfica (Lisbon)
1963	AC Milan
1964–65	Internazionale Milan
1966	Real Madrid
1967	Glasgow Celtic
1968	Manchester United
1969	AC Milan
1970	Feyenoord (Rotterdam)
1971–73	Ajax Amsterdam
1974–76	Bayern Munich
1977–78	Liverpool
1979–80	Nottingham Forest
1981	Liverpool
1982	Aston Villa
1983	SV Hamburg
1984	Liverpool
1985	Juventus (Turin)
1986	Steaua Bucharest
1987	FC Porto
1988	PSV Eindhoven
1989–90	AC Milan
1991	Red Star Belgrade
1992	Barcelona
1993	Marseille
1994	AC Milan
1995	Ajax Amsterdam

European Super Cup

After Ajax won the European Cup for the second successive year (1972) the Dutch newspaper *De Telegraaf* suggested they play the winners of the Cup-winners Cup for a Super Cup. They played, and beat, Glasgow Rangers over two legs. UEFA did not recognize the event until 1974. There was no competition in 1981 and 1985. In 1984, 1986 and 1991 the cup was decided on one match.
Winners:

1972	Ajax	1984	Juventus
1973	Ajax	1986	Steaua Bucharest
1974	Bayern Munich	1987	FC Porto
1975	Dynamo Kiev	1988	KV Mechelen
1976	Anderlecht	1989	AC Milan
1977	Liverpool	1990	AC Milan
1978	Anderlecht	1991	Manchester United
1979	Nottingham Forest	1992	Barcelona
1980	Valencia	1994	Parma
1982	Aston Villa	1995	AC Milan
1983	Aberdeen		

European Cup Winners' Cup

1961	Fiorentina (Florence)
1962	Atletico Madrid
1963	Tottenham Hotspur
1964	Sporting Lisbon
1965	West Ham United
1966	Borussia Dortmund
1967	Bayern Munich

1968 AC Milan
1969 Slovan Bratislava
1970 Manchester City
1971 Chelsea
1972 Glasgow Rangers
1973 AC Milan
1974 FC Magdeburg
1975 Dynamo Kiev
1976 Anderlecht (Brussels)
1977 SV Hamburg
1978 Anderlecht (Brussels)
1979 Barcelona
1980 Valencia
1981 Dynamo Tbilisi
1982 Barcelona
1983 Aberdeen
1984 Juventus (Turin)
1985 Everton
1986 Dynamo Kiev
1987 Ajax Amsterdam
1988 Mechelen
1989 Barcelona
1990 Sampdoria (Genoa)
1991 Manchester United
1992 Werder Bremen
1993 Parma
1994 Arsenal
1995 Real Zaragoza

UEFA Cup

1958 Barcelona
1960 Barcelona
1961 AS Roma
1962–63 Valencia
1964 Real Zaragoza
1965 Ferencvaros (Budapest)
1966 Barcelona
1967 Dynamo Zagreb
1968 Leeds United
1969 Newcastle United
1970 Arsenal
1971 Leeds United
1972 Tottenham Hotspur
1973 Liverpool
1974 Feyenoord (Rotterdam)
1975 Borussia Mönchengladbach
1976 Liverpool
1977 Juventus (Turin)
1978 PSV Eindhoven
1979 Borussia Mönchengladbach
1980 Eintracht Frankfurt
1981 Ipswich Town
1982 IFK Göteborg
1983 Anderlecht (Brussels)
1984 Tottenham Hotspur
1985–86 Real Madrid
1987 IFK Göteborg
1988 Bayer Leverkusen
1989 Napoli
1990 Juventus (Turin)
1991 Internazionale Milan
1992 Ajax Amsterdam
1993 Juventus (Turin)
1994 Internazionale Milan
1995 Parma

GAELIC FOOTBALL

Gaelic football developed from a traditional Irish inter-parish 'football free for all' with no time limit, no defined playing area nor specific rules. The Gaelic Athletic Association established the game in its present form in 1884; teams are 15-a-side. Played throughout Ireland, the All-Ireland Championship, first held in 1887, is contested annually by Irish counties; the final is played at Croke Park, Dublin, each September.

GLIDING

The first authenticated man-carrying glider was designed by Sir George Cayley in 1853. In competitive terms, gliders contest various events – pure distance, distance to a declared goal, to a declared goal and back, height gain and absolute altitude. The World Championships, first held in 1937, have been biennial since 1948. Hang-gliding has flourished in recent years, boosted by the invention of the flexible 'wing' by Francis Rogallo in the early 1960s. The first official World Championships were held in 1976.

GOLF

A prohibiting law passed by the Scottish Parliament in 1457 declared 'goff be utterly cryit doune and not usit'. This is the earliest mention of golf, although games of similar principle date as far back as AD 400. Golf is played worldwide today. Competition is either 'match play', contested by individuals or pairs and decided by the number of holes won, or 'stroke play', decided by the total number of strokes for a round. The modern golf course measures an average total distance of between 5500 and 6400m, and is divided into 18 holes of varying lengths. Clubs are currently limited to a maximum of 14, comprising 'irons' Nos. 1–10 (with the face of the club at increasingly acute angles), and 'woods' for driving. Golf balls in the UK and North America have the minimum diameter of 42·62 mm (1·68 in). Professionally, the four major tournaments are the British Open, the US Open, the US Masters and the US Professional Golfers' Association (USPGA). The Ryder Cup has been contested every two years from 1927 (apart from during the War). The USA have been opposed by Great Britain 1927–71, Great Britain and Ireland 1973–77, and Europe from 1979. The current format is for four foursomes and four fourball matches on each of the first two days, and 12 singles on the third and final day. The USA have 23 wins to 5 (with two draws) to date, with Europe successful in 1985 and 1987, the 1989 match drawn, and the USA winning in 1991 and 1993. The Walker Cup has been contested every two years from 1927 (apart from during the War) between amateur US and British teams (British and Irish from 1981). The USA have 30 wins to 3 (with one draw) to date, with Great Britain winning in 1938, 1971 and 1989. The Curtis Cup is a biennial team competition between women's teams from the USA and Great Britain and Ireland, first held at Wentworth in 1932 and named after the American sisters Margaret and Harriet Curtis. The USA have 20 wins to 5 (with two draws including 1994) to date, with Great Britain and Ireland winning in 1952, 1956, 1986, 1988 and 1992.

The British Open Golf Championship

The oldest open championship in the world, 'The Open', was first held in October 1860 at the Prestwick Club (South Ayrshire), Scotland. It was then over 36 holes; since 1892 it has been over 72 holes of stroke play. Since 1920, the Royal and Ancient Golf Club has managed the event. Winners have been:

Winners (UK unless specified)	*Score*
1860 Willie Park, Sr	174
1861 Tom Morris, Sr	163
1862 Tom Morris, Sr	163
1863 Willie Park, Sr	168
1864 Tom Morris, Sr	167
1865 Andrew Strath	162
1866 Willie Park, Sr	169
1867 Tom Morris, Sr	170
1868 Tom Morris, Jr	170
1869 Tom Morris, Jr	154
1870 Tom Morris, Jr	149
1871 Not held	
1872 Tom Morris, Jr	166
1873 Tom Kidd	179
1874 Mungo Park	159
1875 Willie Park, Sr	166
1876 Robert Martin	176
1877 Jamie Anderson	160
1878 Jamie Anderson	170
1879 Jamie Anderson	170
1880 Robert Ferguson	162
1881 Robert Ferguson	170
1882 Robert Ferguson	171
1883 Willie Fernie	159
1884 Jack Simpson	160
1885 Bob Martin	171
1886 David Brown	157
1887 Willie Park, Jr	161
1888 Jack Burns	171
1889 Willie Park, Jr	155
1890 John Ball	164
1891 Hugh Kirkcaldy	169
1892 Harold Hilton	305
1893 William Auchterlonie	322
1894 John Taylor	326
1895 John Taylor	322
1896 Harry Vardon	316
1897 Harry Hilton	314
1898 Harry Vardon	307
1899 Harry Vardon	310
1900 John Taylor	309
1901 James Braid	309
1902 Alexander Herd	307
1903 Harry Vardon	300
1904 Jack White	296
1905 James Braid	318
1906 James Braid	300
1907 Arnaud Massy (France)	312
1908 James Braid	291
1909 John Taylor	295
1910 James Braid	299
1911 Harry Vardon	303
1912 Edward (Ted) Ray	295
1913 John Taylor	304
1914 Harry Vardon	306
1920 George Duncan	303
1921 Jock Hutchinson (USA)	296
1922 Walter Hagen (USA)	300
1923 Arthur Havers	295
1924 Walter Hagen (USA)	301
1925 James Barnes (USA)	300
1926 Robert T. Jones, Jr (USA)	291
1927 Robert T. Jones, Jr (USA)	285
1928 Walter Hagen (USA)	292
1929 Walter Hagen (USA)	292
1930 Robert T. Jones, Jr (USA)	291
1931 Tommy Armour (USA)	296
1932 Gene Sarazen (USA)	283
1933 Denny Shute (USA)	292
1934 Henry Cotton	283
1935 Alfred Perry	283
1936 Alfred Padgham	287
1937 Henry Cotton	283
1938 Reg Whitcombe	295
1939 Richard Burton	290
1946 Sam Snead (USA)	290
1947 Fred Daly	293
1948 Henry Cotton	284
1949 Bobby Locke (S Africa)	283
1950 Bobby Locke (S Africa)	279
1951 Max Faulkner	285
1952 Bobby Locke (S Africa)	287
1953 Ben Hogan (USA)	282
1954 Peter Thomson (Aus)	283
1955 Peter Thomson (Aus)	281
1956 Peter Thomson (Aus)	286
1957 Bobby Locke (S Africa)	279
1958 Peter Thomson (Aus)	278
1959 Gary Player (S Africa)	284
1960 Kel Nagle (Aus)	278
1961 Arnold Palmer (USA)	284
1962 Arnold Palmer (USA)	276
1963 Bob Charles (NZ)	277
1964 Tony Lema (USA)	279
1965 Peter Thomson (Aus)	285
1966 Jack Nicklaus (USA)	282
1967 Robert de Vicenzo (Argentina)	278
1968 Gary Player (S Africa)	299
1969 Tony Jacklin	280
1970 Jack Nicklaus (USA)	283
1971 Lee Trevino (USA)	278
1972 Lee Trevino (USA)	278
1973 Tom Weiskopf (USA)	276
1974 Gary Player (S Africa)	282
1975 Tom Watson (USA)	279
1976 Johnny Miller (USA)	279
1977 Tom Watson (USA)	268
1978 Jack Nicklaus (USA)	281
1979 Severiano Ballesteros (Spain)	283
1980 Tom Watson (USA)	271
1981 Bill Rogers (USA)	276
1982 Tom Watson (USA)	284
1983 Tom Watson (USA)	275
1984 Severiano Ballesteros (Spain)	276
1985 Sandy Lyle	282
1986 Greg Norman (Aus)	280
1987 Nick Faldo	279
1988 Severiano Ballesteros (Spain)	273
1989 Mark Calcavecchia (USA)	275
1990 Nick Faldo	270
1991 Ian Baker-Finch (Aus)	272
1992 Nick Faldo	272
1993 Greg Norman (Aus)	267
1994 Nick Price (Zimbabwe)	268

US Open

First played on a 9-hole course at Newport, Rhode Island, on 4 October 1895, and annually – over 72 holes of stroke play – at a variety of venues from 1898.

Winners (since 1946; US unless specified)	*Score*
1946 Lloyd Mangrum	284
1947 Lew Worsham	282
1948 Ben Hogan	287
1949 Cary Middlecoff	286
1950 Ben Hogan	287
1951 Ben Hogan	287
1952 Julius Boros	281
1953 Ben Hogan	283
1954 Ed Furgol	284
1955 Jack Fleck	287
1956 Cary Middlecoff	281
1957 Dick Mayer	282
1958 Tommy Bolt	283
1959 Billy Casper	282
1960 Arnold Palmer	280
1961 Gene Littler	281
1962 Jack Nicklaus	283
1963 Julius Boros	293
1964 Ken Venturi	278
1965 Gary Player (S Africa)	282
1966 Billy Casper	278
1967 Jack Nicklaus	275
1968 Lee Trevino	275
1969 Orville Moody	281
1970 Tony Jacklin (UK)	281
1971 Lee Trevino	280
1972 Jack Nicklaus	290
1973 Johnny Miller	279
1974 Hale Irwin	287
1975 Lou Graham	287
1976 Jerry Pate	277
1977 Hubert Green	278
1978 Andy North	285
1979 Hale Irwin	284
1980 Jack Nicklaus	272
1981 David Graham (Austral)	273
1982 Tom Watson	282
1983 Larry Nelson	280
1984 Fuzzy Zoeller	276
1985 Andy North	279
1986 Raymond Floyd	279
1987 Scott Simpson	277
1988 Curtis Strange	278
1989 Curtis Strange	278
1990 Hale Irwin	280
1991 Payne Stewart	283
1992 Tom Kite	285
1993 Lee Janzen	272
1994 Ernie Els (S Africa)	279

US Masters

Held annually at the Augusta National course in Georgia, the Masters was introduced in 1934. Both the course and the tournament were the idea of the legendary golfer Bobby Jones. Entry to the Masters is by invitation only and the eventual winner is presented with the coveted green jacket. It is contested over 72 holes of stroke play.

Winners (since 1946; US unless specified)

Year	Winner	Score
1946	Herman Keiser	282
1947	Jimmy Demaret	281
1948	Claude Harmon	279
1949	Sam Snead	282
1950	Jimmy Demaret	283
1951	Ben Hogan	280
1952	Sam Snead	286
1953	Ben Hogan	274
1954	Sam Snead	289
1955	Cary Middlecoff	279
1956	Jack Burke, Jr	289
1957	Doug Ford	282
1958	Arnold Palmer	284
1959	Art Wall, Jr	284
1960	Arnold Palmer	282
1961	Gary Player (S Africa)	280
1962	Arnold Palmer	280
1963	Jack Nicklaus	286
1964	Arnold Palmer	276
1965	Jack Nicklaus	271
1966	Jack Nicklaus	288
1967	Gay Brewer	280
1968	Bob Goalby	277
1969	George Archer	281
1970	Billy Casper	279
1971	Charles Coody	279
1972	Jack Nicklaus	286
1973	Tommy Aaron	283
1974	Gary Player (S Africa)	278
1975	Jack Nicklaus	276
1976	Raymond Floyd	271
1977	Tom Watson	276
1978	Gary Player (S Africa)	277
1979	Fuzzy Zoeller	280
1980	Severiano Ballesteros (Spain)	275
1981	Tom Watson	280
1982	Craig Stadler	284
1983	Severiano Ballesteros (Spain)	280
1984	Ben Crenshaw	277
1985	Bernhard Langer (Ger)	282
1986	Jack Nicklaus	279
1987	Larry Mize	285
1988	Sandy Lyle (UK)	281
1989	Nick Faldo (UK)	283
1990	Nick Faldo (UK)	278
1991	Ian Woosnam (UK)	277
1992	Fred Couples	275
1993	Bernhard Langer (Ger)	277
1994	José-Maria Olazábal (Spain)	279
1995	Ben Crenshaw	274

GREYHOUND RACING

Greyhounds were first used in sport at coursing (chasing of hares by pairs of dogs) and brought to England by the Normans in 1067. The use of mechanical devices was first practised in England, but the sport was popularized in the USA. The first regular track was opened at Emeryville, California, in 1919. Races are usually conducted over distances of between 210m (230 yd) for the sprint and 1096m (1200 yd) for the marathon. The Derby, the major race in Britain, was instituted in 1927.

GYMNASTICS

Tumbling and similar exercises were performed c. 2600 BC as religious rituals in China. The ancient Greeks coined the word gymnastics, which encompassed various athletic contests including boxing, weightlifting and wrestling. A primitive form was practised in the ancient Olympic Games, but the foundations of the modern sport were laid by the German Johann Friedrich Simon in 1776, and the first national federation was formed in Germany in 1860. The International Gymnastics Federation was founded in Belgium in 1881, and gymnastics was included in the first modern Olympic Games in 1896. Current events for men are: floor exercises, horse vaults, rings, pommel horse, parallel bars and horizontal bar. The events for women are: floor exercises, horse vault, asymmetrical bars and balance beam. Rhythmic gymnastics for women was introduced for the first time at the 1984 Los Angeles Games. Russia, Belarus, Ukraine, USA, Romania, China and Japan are now the strongest nations.

At the 1992 Olympics the Unified team – representing 12 of the 15 former Soviet republics – won both men's and women's team competitions. The men's all-round champion was Vitaliy Shcherbo of Belarus who won six gold medals in all (four individual golds and a team gold). He became the most bemedalled Olympian in 1992 at any sport. The women's all-round champion was Tatyana Gutsu (Ukraine).

1992 Individual Olympic champions

Men

Overall Vitaly Shcherbo (Belarus)
Floor exercises Li Xiaoshuang (China)
Parallel bars Vitaly Shcherbo (Belarus)
Pommel horse Vitaly Shcherbo (Belarus) and Pae Gil-su (N Korea)
Rings Vitaly Shcherbo (Belarus)
Horizontal bars Trent Dimas (USA)
Horse vault Vitaly Shcherbo (Belarus)

Women

Overall Tatyana Gutsu (Ukr)
Asymmetrical bars Li Lu (China)
Balance beam Tatyana Lysenko (Ukr)
Floor exercises Lavinia Milosovici (Rom)
Horse vault Lavinia Milosovici (Rom) and Henrietta Onodi (Hung)
Rhythmic gymnastics Alexandra Timoschenko (Ukr)

HANDBALL

Handball, similar to soccer only using the hands rather than the feet, emerged at the end of the 19th century. It is a growing sport; by 1992 there were 102 countries affiliated to the International Handball Federation. Handball was introduced into the Olympic Games in 1936 as an 11-a-side outdoor game, but on its reintroduction (1972), it was an indoor 7-a-side sport (the standard size of the team was reduced to its present level in 1952, although in Britain handball is often played with teams of five). The 1992 Olympic winners: the Unified Team, a combined team representing 12 of the 15 former Soviet republics (men) and South Korea (women).

HARNESS RACING

Trotting races were held in Valkenburg, in the Netherlands, in 1554, but harness racing was developed, and is most popular, in North America. The sulky, the lightweight vehicle, first appeared in 1829.

Horses may trot, moving their legs in diagonal pairs, or pace, moving fore and hind legs on one side simultaneously.

HOCKEY

Early Greek wall carvings c. 500 BC show hockey-like games, while curved-stick games appear on Egyptian tomb paintings c. 2050 BC. Hockey in its modern form, however, developed in England in the 19th century, with Teddington HC (formed 1871) standardizing the rules. The English Hockey Association was founded in 1886. The governing body, the *Fédération Internationale de Hockey* (FIH), was formed in 1924. Hockey was included in the 1908 and 1920 Olympic Games, with England the winners on both occasions. It has been held at every Games from 1928 and the tournaments were dominated by India, winners at all six Games 1928–1956, and also in 1964 and 1980, and by Pakistan, winners in 1960, 1968 and 1984. However, their supremacy has been successfully challenged by nations from Europe and Australasia in recent years. Women's hockey was introduced to the Olympics in 1980. The 1992 Olympic champions were Germany (men) and Spain (women). Dimensions: ball circumference 223–224 cm ($8^1/_5$–9½/ in) and weight 155–163 g (5½–5¾ oz); pitch length 91·44m (100 yd); width 50–55m (55–60 yd).

FIH (IHF) World Cup

First contested in 1971 for men and 1974 for women. *Winners:*

Men

Pakistan	1971, 1978, 1982, 1994
Netherlands	1973, 1990
India	1975
Australia	1986

Women

Netherlands	1974, 1978, 1983, 1986, 1990
Germany (W)	1976, 1981
Australia	1994

HORSE RACING

Early organized racing appears to have been confined to chariots – Roman riders had a foot on each of two horses. The first horse-back races were staged by the Greeks in the 33rd Ancient Olympiad in 648 BC. The first recognizable modern race meeting was held at Smithfield, London, in 1174, while the first known prize money was a purse of gold presented by the English king Richard I in 1195. Winners of the major British horse races are to be found in the United Kingdom chapter.

Prix de l'Arc de Triomphe

Europe's most prestigious race was first run in 1920. It is run over 2400m (c. 1 mile 4 furlongs) at Longchamp, Paris, on the first Sunday in October. Recent winners have been:

1980	Detroit (Pat Eddery)
1981	Gold River (Gary Moore)
1982	Akiyda (Yves Saint-Martin)
1983	All Along (Walter Swinburn)
1984	Sagace (Yves Saint-Martin)
1985	Rainbow Quest (Pat Eddery)
1986	Dancing Brave (Pat Eddery)
1987	Trempolino (Pat Eddery)
1988	Tony Bin (John Reid)
1989	Carroll House (Michael Kinane)
1990	Saumarez (Gerald Mossé)
1991	Suave Dancer (Cash Asmussen)
1992	Subotica (Thierry Jarnet)
1993	Urban Sea (Eric Saint-Martin)
1994	Carnegie (Thierry Jarnet)

HURLING

Hurling is an ancient game that has been played in Ireland since pre-Christian times, but has been standardized only since the founding of the Gaelic Athletic Association in 1884. The hurl, or stick, is similar to a hockey stick only flat on both sides. The All-Ireland Championship, first held in 1887, is contested annually by Irish counties; the final is played at Croke Park, Dublin, each September.

ICE HOCKEY

A game similar to hockey on ice was played in Holland in the early 16th century, but the birth of modern ice hockey took place in Canada, probably at Kingston, Ontario, in 1855. Rules were first formulated by students of McGill University in Montreal, who formed a club in 1880. The International Ice Hockey Federation was formed in 1908, and the World and Olympic Championships inaugurated in 1920. The USSR and the Unified team, a combined team representing 12 of the 15 former Soviet republics, have won eight of the last ten Olympic titles. The 1994 winners were Sweden. The major professional competition is the National Hockey League (NHL) in North America, founded in 1917, whose teams contest the Stanley Cup. Teams are 6-a-side; the ideal rink size is 61 m (200 ft) long and 26m (85 ft) wide.

ICE AND SAND YACHTING

Ice, sand and land yachting require, in basic form, a wheeled chassis beneath a sailing dinghy. Dutch ice yachts are thought to date back to 1768, but ice yachting today is mainly confined to North America. Land and sand yachts of Dutch construction go back even further to 1595. The sports are governed by the International Federation of Sand and Land Yacht which recognizes speed records. International championships were first staged in 1914.

ICE SKATING

Second-century Scandinavian literature refers to ice skating, although archaeological evidence points to origins ten centuries earlier. The first English reference is 1180; the first British club, the Edinburgh Skating Club, was formed around 1742. Steel blades, allowing precision skating, were invented in America in 1850. The International Skating Union was founded in 1892. Ice skating competition is divided into figure skating, speed skating and ice dancing. Figure skating has been an Olympic event since the Winter Games were first organized in 1924, but there were also events at the 1908 and 1920 Games. Ice dancing was not included until 1976. The first international speed skating competition was in Hamburg, Germany, in 1885, with World Championships officially dated from

1893. Speed skating for men was first included in the 1924 Olympics; women's events were included in 1960.

Recent Olympic figure skating champions

Singles

Men		Women
1980	Robin Cousins (UK)	Anett Pötzsch (GDR)
1984	Scott Hamilton (USA)	Katarina Witt (GDR)
1988	Brian Boitano (USA)	Katarina Witt (GDR)
1992	Viktor Petrenko (Ukr)	Kristi Yamaguchi (USA)
1994	Aleksey Urmanov (Rus)	Oksana Bayul (Ukr)

Pairs

1980 Irina Rodnina and Aleksandr Zaitsev (USSR)
1984 Yelena Valova and Oleg Vasilyev (USSR)
1988 Yekaterina Gordeyeva and Sergey Grinkov (USSR)
1992 Natalya Mishkutienok and Artur Dmitriyev (*Unified Team)
1994 Yekaterina Gordeyeva and Sergey Grinkov (Rus)

Ice Dance

1980 Natalya Linichuk and Gennadiy Karponosov (USSR)
1984 Jayne Torvill and Christopher Dean (UK)
1988 Natalya Bestemianova and Andrey Bukin (USSR)
1992 Marina Klimova and Sergey Ponomarenko (*Unified Team)
1994 Oksana Gritschuk/Yevgeniy Platov (Russia)

* a combined team representing 12 of the 15 former Soviet republics.

JUDO

Judo developed from Japanese fighting arts, the most popular of which was ju-jitsu, thought to be of ancient Chinese origin. 'Ju' means 'soft', i.e. the reliance on speed and skill as opposed to 'hard' brute force. Judo as a modern combat sport was devised in 1882 by Dr Jigoro Kano. Points are scored by throws, locks on joints, certain pressures on the neck, and immobilizations. Today, students are graded by belt colours from white to black, the 'master' belts. Grades of black belts are 'Dans', the highest attainable being Tenth Dan. The International Judo Federation was founded in 1951 and the World Championships were first held in 1956, with women competing from 1980. Judo has been included in the Olympics since 1964 (except 1968), and there are currently eight weight divisions. Women's judo became an Olympic sport in 1992.

1992 Olympic champions

Men

Weight	*Winner*
Over 95 kg	David Khakkaleichvili (Georgia)
95 kg	Antal Kovács (Hung)
86 kg	Waldemar Legien (Poland)
78 kg	Hidehiko Yoshida (Japan)
71 kg	Toshihiko Koga (Japan)
65 kg	Rogeno Sampalo (Brazil)
60 kg	Nazim Gusseinov (Azerbaijan)

Women

Weight	*Winner*
Over 75 kg	Zhuang Xiaoyan (China)
Up to 72 kg	Kim Mi-jung (S Korea)
66 kg	Odalis Reve (Cuba)
61 kg	Catherine Fleury (France)
56 kg	Miríam Blasco (Spain)
52 kg	Almudena Munoz (Spain)
48 kg	Cécile Nowak (France)

KARATE

Literally meaning 'empty hand' fighting, karate is based on techniques devised from the 6th-century Chinese art of Shaolin boxing (*Kempo*), and was developed by an unarmed populace in Okinawa as a weapon against Japanese forces c. 1500. Transported to Japan in the 1920s by Funakoshi Gichin, the sport was refined and organized with competitive rules. There are five major styles in Japan: shotokan, wado-ryu, goju-ryu, shito-ryu and kyokushinkai, each placing different emphases on speed and power. The military form of *taekwondo* is the Korean martial art. *Wu shu* is a comprehensive term embracing all Chinese martial arts. *Kung fu* is one aspect of these arts popularized by the cinema. Many forms of the martial arts have gained devotees in Europe and the Americas.

LACROSSE

North American Indians played the ancestor of the sport *baggataway*, and a French clergyman, likening the curved stick to a bishop's crozier, called it *la crosse*. The French may also have named it after their game *Chouler à la crosse*, known in 1381. Certainly in its recognizable form the game had reached Europe by the 1830s, and was introduced into Britain in 1867. The International Federation of Amateur Lacrosse (IFAL) was founded in 1928. The men's World Championships were held in 1967 and every four years from 1974, with the USA winning on each occasion to 1994, except against Canada in 1978. Lacrosse was played in the 1904 and 1908 Olympic Games, and as a demonstration sport in 1928, 1932 and 1948. The women's World Championships were held in 1969, 1974 and 1978, and a World Cup in 1982, 1986, 1989 and 1993, when the winners were the USA.

The game is 10-a-side (12-a-side for women at international level). Pitch dimensions: 100 × 64m (100 × 70 yd). Ball weight in England 142 g (5 oz), circumference 184–203·2 mm (7¼–8 in), colour yellow; in USA weight 142–149 g (5–5¼ oz), circumference 196·9–203·2 mm (7¾–8 in), colour orange or white.

MODERN PENTATHLON AND BIATHLON

In the ancient Olympic Games, the pentathlon was the most prestigious event. It then consisted of discus, javelin, running, jumping and wrestling. The modern pentathlon, introduced into the Olympics in 1912, consists of riding (an 800m course with 15 fences; riders do not choose their mounts); fencing (épée), shooting, swimming (300m freestyle) and finally a cross-country run of 4000m. Scaled points awarded for each activity. The sport's governing body is *L'Union Internationale de Pentathlon Moderne et Biathlon*, the UIPMB. It was founded in 1948 as the UIPM, taking on the administration of biathlon in 1957 (see Biathlon). Poland won the 1992 Olympic team title and provided the individual champion in Arkadiusz Skvzypaszrek. The World Championships have been held annually for men from 1949 and for women from 1981.

MOTORCYCLE RACING

The earliest motorcycle race, which also included motorcars, was held at Sheen House, Richmond (London), in 1897 over a 1·6 km (1 mile) oval course. The first international race for motorcycles only was held in 1905. The *Fédération Internationale des Clubs Motocyclystes* (FICM) organized the 1905 event, but it has since been succeeded as the governing body by the *Fédération Internationale Motocycliste* (FIM). The World Championships were started in 1949 by the FIM and competitors gain points from a series of grand prix races. Races are currently held for the following classes of bike: 50 cc, 125 cc, 250 cc, 500 cc and side-cars. In road racing the Isle of Man TT races (Auto-Cycle Union Tourist Trophy), first held in 1907, are the most important series. The 60·72 km (37·73 miles) 'Mountain' course, with 264 corners and curves, has been in use since 1911. In motocross, or scrambling, competitors race over rough country including steep climbs and drops, sharp turns, sand, mud and water.

MOTOR RACING

The first known race between automobiles was over 323 km (201 miles) in Wisconsin (USA) in 1878, but it is generally accepted that the first 'real' race was the Paris-Bordeaux-Paris run of 1178 km (732 miles) in 1895. Emile Levassor (Fra), the winner, averaged 24·15 kph (15·01 mph). The first closed circuit race was in Rhode Island (USA), 1896, while the oldest grand prix is the French, inaugurated in 1906. Competition at the highest level, the Formula One, is over the series of grand prix races (each usually about 656 km/200 miles in length) held worldwide, points scored according to placing. The first World Championships were held in 1950, with the Manufacturers' Championships starting in 1958. Formula Two and Three Championships are held for cars with lesser cubic capacities. Other forms of competition include the Le Mans circuit, a 24-hour race for touring cars; 'rallying over public roads through several thousands miles; and drag racing, a test of sheer acceleration, most firmly established in the USA. Indy Car racing and the Indianapolis 500 are major motor racing competitions in the USA.

World Driver Champions

1950	Giuseppe Farina (Italy)
1951	Juan Manuel Fangio (Argentina)
1952–53	Alberto Ascari (Italy)
1954–57	Juan Manuel Fangio (Argentina)
1958	Mike Hawthorn (UK)
1959–60	Jack Brabham (Austral)
1961	Phil Hill (USA)
1962	Graham Hill (UK)
1963	Jim Clark (UK)
1964	John Surtees (UK)
1965	Jim Clark (UK)
1966	Jack Brabham (Australia)
1967	Denny Hulme (NZ)
1968	Graham Hill (UK)
1969	Jackie Stewart (UK)
1970	Jochen Rindt (Austria)
1971	Jackie Stewart (UK)
1972	Emerson Fittipaldi (Brazil)
1973	Jackie Stewart (UK)
1974	Emerson Fittipaldi (Brazil)
1975	Niki Lauda (Austria)
1976	James Hunt (UK)
1977	Niki Lauda (Austria)
1978	Mario Andretti (USA)
1979	Jody Scheckter (S Africa)
1980	Alan Jones (Austral)
1981	Nelson Piquet (Brazil)
1982	Keke Rosberg (Fin)
1983	Nelson Piquet (Brazil)
1984	Niki Lauda (Austria)
1985–86	Alain Prost (France)
1987	Nelson Piquet (Brazil)
1988	Ayrton Senna (Brazil)
1989	Alain Prost (France)
1990–91	Ayrton Senna (Brazil)
1992	Nigel Mansell (UK)
1993	Alain Prost (France)
1994	Michael Schumacher (Germany)

NETBALL

Modern netball, which grew out of basketball, was invented in the USA in 1891. The use of rings instead of baskets dates from 1897, and the term netball was coined in 1901 in England, where the sport was introduced in 1895. National Associations date from 1924 and 1926 in New Zealand and England. The International Federation was formed in 1960. The World Championships have been held every four years, since 1963, with the most recent winners being Australia in 1983 and 1991, and New Zealand in 1987. Netball is a no-contact, 7-a-side sport played almost exclusively by females. The court measures 30·48 × 15·24m (100 × 50 ft); ball circumference 68–71 cm (27–28 in), weight 397–454 g (14–16 oz).

ORIENTEERING

'Orienteering' was first used to describe an event held in Oslo (Norway) in 1900, based on military exercises, but the founding of the modern sport is credited to a Swede, Major Ernst Killander, in 1918. Basically a combination of cross-country running and map-reading, the sport is very popular in Scandinavia and has a keen band of followers in Britain. The International Orienteering Federation was founded in 1961, and the World Championships have been held since 1966, largely dominated by Sweden and Norway.

PELOTA VASCA (Jaï Alaï)

The sport, which originated in Italy as *longue paume,* was introduced into France in the 13th century. Said to be the fastest of all ball games, various forms of pelota are played according to national character or local custom throughout the world. 'Gloves' and 'chisteras' (curved frames attached to a glove) are of varying sizes, and courts can be open or enclosed with wide differences in dimensions and detail. The *Federacion Internacional de Pelota Vasca* has staged the World Championships every four years since 1952. Pelota was a demonstration sport at the 1992 Olympics.

PÉTANQUE

Pétanque, or boules, originated in France from its parent game *jeu provençal.* Its origins go back over 2000 years, but it was not until 1945 that the *Fédération Française de Pétanque et Jeu Provençal* was formed, and subsequently the *Fédération Internationale* (FIPJP).

POLO

The game, played by teams of four on horseback, has its origins in Manipur, India, c. 3100 BC. It is also claimed to be of Persian origin, having been played as *Pulu* c. 525 BC. Polo was introduced to England from India in 1869, and now has a keen following in the USA and Argentina. Polo is played on the largest pitch of any game, with maximum length of 274m (300 yds) and width of 182m (200 yds) without boards, or 146m (160 yds) with boards. Polo games are often contested on a handicap basis, each player being awarded a handicap measured in goals up to a maximum of ten, attained by the world's best players.

POWERBOAT RACING

Steamboat races date from 1827, and petrol engines from 1865, but powerboat racing started in about 1900. International racing was largely established by the presentation of a Challenge Trophy in 1903, by Sir Alfred Harmsworth, which has been won most often by the USA. Races are also held for 'circuit' or shorter course competition, and offshore events began in 1958. Speed records are recognized in various categories by the various governing bodies.

RACKETBALL

Two versions of the game exist: (American) racquetball and (British) racketball. The original game was invented in 1949 by the American Joe Sobek when he sawed half the handle off a tennis racquet. In the USA the International Racquetball Association – founded in 1968 – changed its name in 1980 to the American Amateur Racquetball Association (AARA). The sport now has more than ten million players in the USA. The international governing body is the International Racquetball Federation (IRF). British racketball – introduced in 1976 – uses squash courts 9·75m by 6·4m (32 ft by 21 ft) and a less bouncy ball than that used in the larger American courts.

RACKETS

Rackets is an indoor racket and ball game for two or four players, derived – as other forms of handball – from games played in the Middle Ages. In England it was often played against walls of buildings, especially those of the Fleet Prison, London, in the 18th century. An inmate, Robert Mackay, claimed the first world title in 1920. The World Championship has been held since 1988 by James Male (UK), and is now determined on a challenge basis.

REAL TENNIS

Real tennis evolved from the game *jeu de paume* ('game of the palm') played in French monasteries in the 11th century, in which the hand, rather than a racket, was used. The long-handled racket was not invented until about 1500. The World Championship at real tennis is the oldest world championship of any sport, dating to approximately 1740. Today, real tennis is only played in five countries – England, Scotland, USA, France and Australia – and the total number of courts in use throughout the world has dwindled to approximately 30. Robert Fahey of Australia took the world men's title in 1994 and Sally Jones (UK) won the women's world title in 1993.

ROLLER SKATING

The first roller skate was devised by Jean-Joseph Merlin of Belgium in 1760, but proved disastrous in demonstration. The present four-wheeled type was patented by New Yorker James L. Plimpton in 1863. Competition is along similar lines to ice skating – speed, figure and dance.

ROWING

A literary reference to rowing is made by the Roman poet Virgil in the *Aeneid*. Regattas were held in Venice c. AD 300. The earliest established sculling race is the Doggett's Coat and Badge, first rowed in 1716 from London Bridge to Chelsea on the River Thames (London), and still contested annually. The governing body, the *Fédération Internationale de Sociétés d'Aviron*, was founded in 1892, and the first major international meeting, the European Championships, was held a year later. Olympic Championships were first held in 1900 for men and in 1976 for women. Current events are held for: (men) single, double and coxless quadruple sculls, coxless and coxed pairs, coxless and coxed fours and eights; (women) single and double sculls, coxless pairs, coxless quadruple sculls, coxless fours and eights. With sculling, the sculler has a smaller oar in each hand rather than pulling one oar with both hands.

The Oxford-Cambridge Boat Race was first held in 1829, from Hambledon Lock to Henley Bridge (River Thames), and won by Oxford. The current course, used continuously since 1864, is from Putney to Mortlake and measures 6·779 km (4 miles 374 yd). In the 141 races to 1995, Cambridge have won 72 times, Oxford 68 and a dead heat was declared in 1877.

RUGBY LEAGUE

The game originated as a breakaway from rugby union in 1895, on account of the English governing body forbidding northern rugby clubs paying players, who thus lost Saturday wages. Three years later full professionalism came into being. In 1906 the major change from 15-a-side to 13 was made, and the title 'rugby league' was adopted in 1922. Rugby league is played principally in Great Britain, Australia, New Zealand, France and Papua New Guinea. Australia won the World Cup in 1988 and 1992. (See also the UK chapter.) Dimensions: Pitch length maximum 100·58m (110 yd), width maximum 68·58m (75 yd). Ball length 27·3–29·2 cm (10¾–11½ in), circumference at widest point 584–610 mm (23–24 in).

RUGBY UNION

Rugby union was developed at Rugby School, England. A traditional yarn tells of William Webb Ellis illegally picking up the ball and running with it during a football game, although this may be apocryphal. Certainly the game was known to have been played at Cambridge University by 1839. The Rugby Football Union was formed in January 1871. The International Board consists of the eight major rugby-playing nations: Australia, England, France, Ireland, New Zealand, Scotland, South Africa, and Wales. (See the UK chapter for British champions.)

The game is 15-a-side. Dimensions: pitch of maximum 68·58m (75 yd) width, and 91·44m (100 yd) between goal lines. Ball length 27·9–28·5 cm (10¾–11½ in) and weight 382–439 g (13½–15½ oz).

Rugby World Cup

The first World Cup was contested by 16 national teams in Australia and New Zealand in 1987. In the final New Zealand beat France 29–9. The second World Cup was played in Britain and France in 1991, with Australia beating England 12–6 in the final at Twickenham. The third is in South Africa in 1995.

In New Zealand, the Ranfurly Shield, an inter-provincial championship, was first held in 1904. It is not a knock-out competition, but one in which the champion province puts its title up for a challenge. The title last changed hands in 1985 when Auckland defeated Canterbury. A national league championship began in 1976. Recent winners have been:

1983	Canterbury
1984-85	Auckland
1986	Wellington
1987–90	Auckland
1991	Otago
1992	Waikato
1993-94	Auckland

In South Africa, the inter-provincial tournament is the Currie Cup, first held in 1889. The Cup has most often been won by Western Province (29 times) and Northern Transvaal (18 times). Recent winners:

1983–86	Western Province
1987–88	Northern Transvaal
1989	Northern Transvaal and Western Province
1990	Natal
1991	Northern Transvaal
1992	Natal
1993–84	Transvaal

In Australia, the game is played chiefly in New South Wales and Queensland. The principal competition is the Sydney First Grade Premiership in which the most successful club is Randwick.

SHINTY

Shinty (from the Gaelic *sinteag*, a bound) goes back some 2000 years in Celtic history and legend, to the ancient game of *camanachd*, the sport of the curved stick. Having been introduced by the invading Irish Gaels it kept close associations with hurling but is essentially native to Scotland. The governing body, the Camanachd Association, was set up in 1893.

SHOOTING

The first recorded club for gun enthusiasts was the Lucerne Shooting Guild in Switzerland, dating from c. 1466, and the first known shooting match took place in Zürich in 1472. The National Rifle Association in Britain was founded in 1860. The Clay Pigeon Shooting Association developed from trap shooting in the USA. Skeet shooting is a form of clay pigeon designed to simulate a range of bird game and was invented in the USA in 1915. Pistol events, like air rifle, are judged by accuracy in scoring on a fixed target, from various distances and positions. Shooting events for men were held in the first modern Olympic Games in 1896, but the 1984 Games included two mixed events (men and women) for the first time. Only two other Olympic sports have mixed competition, equestrianism and yachting. At the 1992 Olympics there were seven men's, four women's and two mixed events.

SKIING

A well-preserved ski found in Sweden is thought to be 4500 years old, and various other evidence from Russia and Scandinavia chronicles primitive skiing. The modern sport dates from 1843 with a competition in Tromso, Norway. The first modern slalom was held at Murren, Switzerland, in 1922 and the International Ski Federation (FIS) was founded in 1924. Alpine skiing is racing on prepared slopes, against the clock, whereas Nordic skiing is either cross-country or ski jumping. The Alpine World Championships date from 1931, and Alpine skiing has been included in the Olympics since 1936 as a combination event. Events are now split into downhill, slalom, giant slalom, super giant slalom and Alpine combination (slalom and downhill). Nordic events were included in the Olympic Games from 1924 and comprise cross-country, ski jumping, and the combination of the two disciplines. The world's best skiers contest a series of events each winter for the World Cups in Alpine skiing and the Nordic events of cross-country and ski jumping.

Overall Alpine World Cup champions

Men

1967–68	Jean-Claude Killy (France)
1969–70	Karl Schranz (Austria)
1971–73	Gustavo Thoeni (Italy)
1974	Piero Gros (Italy)
1975	Gustavo Thoeni (Italy)
1976–78	Ingemar Stenmark (Sweden)
1979	Peter Lüscher (Switz)
1980	Andreas Wenzel (Liechtenstein)
1981–83	Phil Mahre (USA)
1984	Pirmin Zurbriggen (Switz)
1985–86	Marc Girardelli (Lux)
1987–88	Pirmin Zurbriggen (Switz)
1989	Marc Girardelli (Lux)
1990	Pirmin Zurbriggen (Switz)
1991	Marc Girardelli (Lux)
1992	Paul Accola (Switz)
1993	Marc Girardelli (Lux)
1994	Kjetil Andre Aamodt (Nor)
1995	Alberto Tomba (Italy)

Women

1967–68	Nancy Greene (Canada)
1969	Gertrud Gabi (Austria)
1970	Michèle Jacot (France)
1971–75	Annemarie Moser-Pröll (Austria)
1976	Rosi Mittermaier (Germany)
1977	Lise-Marie Morerod (Switz)
1978	Hanni Wenzel (Liechtenstein)
1979	Annemarie Moser-Pröll (Austria)
1980	Hanni Wenzel (Liechtenstein)
1981	Marie-Thérèse Nadig (Switz)
1982	Erika Hess (Switz)
1983	Tamara McKinney (USA)
1984	Erika Hess (Switz)
1985	Michela Figini (Switz)
1986–87	Maria Walliser (Switz)
1988	Michela Figini (Switz)
1989	Vreni Schneider (Switz)

1990–92 Petra Kronberger (Austria)
1993 Anita Wachter (Austria)
1994–95 Vreni Schneider (Switz)

SNOOKER

Colonel Sir Neville Chamberlain concocted the game of snooker as a cross between 'black pool', 'pyramids' and billiards, in 1875 at Madras, India. The term 'snooker' came from the nickname given to first-year cadets at the Royal Military Academy, Woolwich (London). The game reached England in 1885, when the world billiards champion, John Roberts, who had been introduced to snooker in India, demonstrated the new sport. Rules were codified in 1919, and the World Professional Championship was instituted in 1927. Since 1970 the professional game has been controlled by the World Professional Billiards and Snooker Association. A full size table measures 3·66 × 1·87m (12 × 6 ft); ball values are: red (1), yellow (2), green (3), brown (4), blue (5), pink (6) and black (7).

Recent world champions:
1970 Ray Reardon (Wales)
1971 John Spencer (England)
1972 Alex Higgins (Northern Ireland)
1973–76 Ray Reardon (Wales)
1977 John Spencer (England)
1978 Ray Reardon (Wales)
1979 Terry Griffiths (Wales)
1980 Cliff Thorburn (Canada)
1981 Steve Davis (England)
1982 Alex Higgins (Northern Ireland)
1983–84 Steve Davis (England)
1985 Dennis Taylor (Northern Ireland)
1986 Joe Johnson (England)
1987–89 Steve Davis (England)
1990 Stephen Hendry (Scotland)
1991 John Parrott (England)
1992–95 Stephen Hendry (Scotland)

SOFTBALL

Softball, the indoor derivative of baseball, was invented by George Hancock in Chicago, USA, in 1887, and rules were first codified in Minnesota in 1895. The name softball was adopted in 1930. A 9-a-side game (except in the USA), softball is played in Canada, Japan, the Philippines, most of Latin America, New Zealand and Australia. The ball is as hard as a baseball, but, unlike baseball, must be pitched underarm and released below hip level. The pitching distance is 14m (45 ft 11 in) for men, 11·11m (36 ft 5½ in) for women and 18·3m (60 ft) in between bases for both. 'Slow pitch' softball is a modern variation.

SPEEDWAY

Motorcycle racing on dust track surfaces has been traced back to 1902 in the USA, but the first 'short track' races were in Australia in 1923. Evolving in Britain in the 1920s, the National League was instituted in 1932. The first World Championships, for individual riders, was held at Wembley, London, in 1936. The team competition was introduced in 1960, and the pairs in 1970. The Long Track championship was inaugurated in 1971. Ice speedway world championships were instituted in 1966 with an individual competition; a team competition was added in 1979.

SQUASH

Squash developed at Harrow School, England, in 1817 from a game used for practising rackets but with a softer, 'squashy' ball. The first national championship was held in the USA in 1907. The British Open Championships, for women and men, were first contested in 1922 and 1930 respectively. The International Squash Rackets Federation (ISRF) was founded in 1967 and the Women's International Squash Rackets Federation in 1976. In 1992 the ISRF abandoned the name of rackets and reconstituted as the World Squash Federation (WSF). Court dimensions: 9·75m (31 ft 11¾ in) long and 6·40m (21 ft) wide, with front wall height 4·75m (15 ft 7 in) up to the boundary line. The 'tin' runs along the bottom of the front wall, above which the ball must be hit.

SURFING

Originating in Polynesia, the first reference to surfing on a board dates from 1779 in an account written in Hawaii. Revived in the early 20th century in Australia, hollow boards were introduced in 1929. The World Amateur Championships began in 1964.

SWIMMING

Competitive swimming dates from 36 BC in Japan, which was the first country to seriously adopt the sport. In Britain, organized competitive swimming was only introduced in 1837 when the National Swimming Society was formed. Australia led modern developments with an unofficial world 100 yd championship in 1858 at Melbourne. The first widely used technique (possibly excepting the 'doggy paddle') was the breaststroke. From this developed the side-stroke, a similar action performed sideways, last used by an Olympic champion, Emil Rausch (of Germany), to win the 1904 one-mile event. A style resembling the front crawl had been seen in various parts of the world by travellers in the mid-19th century. Backstroke developed as inverted breaststroke, which modified towards inverted crawl. Butterfly began as an exploitation of a loophole in the rules for breaststroke allowing the recovery of arms from the water, and was recognized as a separate stroke in 1952. The medley event, using all four strokes in turn, originated in the USA in the 1930s. The world-governing body for swimming, diving, water polo and synchronized swimming is the *Fédération Internationale de Natation Amateur* (FINA), founded in 1908. The World Championships in swimming were first held in 1973, and are now held quadrennially. Swimming has been an integral part of the Olympics since 1896, the first modern Olympic Games, with 100m, 400m, 1500m and 100m freestyle events for men. Women first competed in 1912. Diving was introduced in 1904 (1912 for women), and water polo in 1900. Synchronized swimming, a form of water ballet, was first recognized internationally in 1952 and was included in the first World Championships in 1973. It appeared in the Olympics for the first time in 1984.

Swimming world records

Men
50m freestyle: 21·81 Tom Jager (USA) 1990
100m freestyle: 48·21 Aleksandr Popov (Russia) 1994
200m freestyle: 1:46·69 Giorgio Lamberti (Italy) 1989

400m freestyle: 3:43·8 Kieren Perkins (Austral) 1994
800m freestyle: 7:46 Kieren Perkins (Austral) 1992
1500m freestyle: 14:41·6 Kieren Perkins (Austral) 1994
4 × 100m freestyle: 3:16·53 USA 1988
(Chris Jacobs, Troy Dalbey, Tom Jager, Matt Biondi)
4 × 200m freestyle: 7:11·95 (*Unified team) 1992
(Dmitriy Lepikov, Vladimir Pychnenko, Venyamin Tayanovich, Yevgeniy Sadoviy)
100m backstroke: 53·86 Jeff Rouse (USA) 1992
200m backstroke: 1:56·57 Martin Lopez-Zubero (Spain) 1991
100m breaststroke: 1:00·95 Karoly Guttler (Hung) 1993
200m breaststroke: 2:10·16 Mike Barrowman (USA) 1992
100m butterfly: 52·84 Pablo Morales (USA) 1986
200m butterfly: 1:55·69 Melvin Stewart (USA) 1991
200m individual medley: 1:58·16 Jani Sievinen (Fin) 1994
400m individual medley: 4:12·30 Tom Dolan (USA) 1994
4 × 100m medley: 3:36·93 USA 1988
(David Berkoff, Richard Schroeder, Matt Biondi, Chris Jacobs)

Women
50m freestyle: 24·51 Le Jingyi (China) 1994
100m freestyle: 54·01 Le Jingyi (China) 1994
200m freestyle: 1:56·78 Franziska van Almsick (Ger)
400m freestyle: 4:03·85 Janet Evans (USA) 1988
800m freestyle: 8:16·22 Janet Evans (USA) 1989
1500m freestyle: 15:52·10 Janet Evans (USA) 1988
4 × 100m freestyle: 3:37·91 China 1994 (Le Jingyi, Shan Ying, Le Ying, Lu Bin)
4 × 200m freestyle: 7:55·47 GDR 1987
(Manuela Stellmach, Astrid Strauss, Anke Möhring, Heike Friedrich)
100m backstroke: 1:00·16 He Cihong (China) 1994
200m backstroke: 2:06·62 Krizstina Egerszegi (Hung) 1991
100m breaststroke: 1:07·69 Samantha Riley (Aus) 1994
200m breaststroke: 2:24·76 Rebecca Brown (Aus) 1994
100m butterfly: 57·93 Mary T. Meagher (USA) 1981
200m butterfly: 2:05·96 Mary T. Meagher (USA) 1981
200m individual medley: 2:11·65 Li Lin (China) 1992
400m individual medley: 4:36·10 Petra Schneider (GDR) 1982
4 × 100m medley: 4:01·67 China 1994 (He Cihong, Dai Guohong, Liu Limin, Li Yingyi)

* a combined team representing 12 of the 15 former Soviet republics.

1992 Olympic swimming champions

Men
50m freestyle: 21·90 Aleksandr Popov (Russia)
100m freestyle: 49·02 Aleksandr Popov (Russia)
200m freestyle: 1:46·70 Yergeniy Sadovyi (Russia)
400m freestyle: 3:45 Yergeniy Sadovyi (Russia)
1500 m freestyle: 14:43·48 Keiren Perkins (Austral)
4 × 100m freestyle: 3:16·74 (USA)
4 × 200m freestyle: 7:11·95 (*Unified Team)
100m backstroke: 53·98 Mark Tewksbury (Canada)
200m backstroke: 1:58·47 Martin Lopez-Zubero (Spain)
100m breaststroke: 1:01·5 Nelson Diebel (USA)
200m breaststroke: 2:10·16 Mike Barrowman (USA)
100m butterfly: 53·32 Pablo Morales (USA)
200m butterfly: 1:56·26 Melvin Stewart (USA)
200m individual medley: 2:00·76 Tamás Darnyi (Hung)
400m individual medley: 4:14·23 Tamás Darnyi (Hung)
4 × 100m medley: 3:36·93 (USA)
Springboard diving: Mark Lenzi (USA)
Highboard diving: Sun Shuwei (China)

* a combined team representing 12 of the 15 former Soviet republics.

Women
50m freestyle: 24·79 Yang Wenyi (China)
100m freestyle: 54·64 Zhuang Yong (China)
200m freestyle: 1:57·65 Nicole Haislett (USA)
400m freestyle: 4:07·18 Dagmar Hase (Germany)
800m freestyle: 8:25·52 Janet Evans (USA)
4 × 100m freestyle: 3:39·46 (USA)
100m backstroke: 1:00·68 Krisztina Egerszegi (Hung)
200m backstroke: 2:07·06 Krisztina Egerszegi (Hung)
100m breaststroke: 1:08 Yelena Rudkovskaya (Belarus)
200m breaststroke: 2:26·65 Kyoko Iwasaki (Japan)
100m butterfly: 58·62 Qian Hong (China)
200m butterfly: 2:08·67 Summer Sanders (USA)
200m individual medley: 2:11·65 Li Lin (China)
400 m individual medley: 4:36·54 Krisztina Egerszegi (Hung)
4 × 100m medley: 4:02·54 (USA)
Springboard diving: Gao Min (China)
Highboard diving: Fu Mingxia (China)
Synchronized (solo): Kristen Babb-Sprague (USA)
Synchronized (duet): Karen and Sarah Josephson (USA)

World Championships
World Championships separate from the Olympic Games were first held in 1973, and are now staged every four years. 1994 winners were:

Men
50m freestyle: 22·17 Aleksandr Popov (Russia)
100m freestyle: 49·12 Aleksandr Popov (Russia)
200m freestyle: 1:47·32 Antti Kasvio (Fin)
400m freestyle: 3:43·8 Kieren Perkins (Austral)
1500m freestyle: 14:50·52 Kieren Perkins (Austral)
4 × 100m freestyle: 3:16·9 USA
4 × 200m freestyle relay: 7:17·7 Sweden
100m backstroke: 55·17 Martin López Zubero (Spain)
200m backstroke: 1:57·42 Vladimir Selkov (Russia)
100m breaststroke: 1:01·24 Norbert Rózsa (Hung)
200m breaststroke: 2:12·81 Norbert Rózsa (Hung)
100m butterfly: 53·51 Rafal Szukala (Poland)
200m butterfly: 1:56·54 Denis Pankratov (Russia)
200m individual medley: 1:58·16 Jani Sievinen (Fin)
400m individual medley: 4:12·30 Tom Dolan (USA)
4 × 100m medley relay: 3:37·74 USA
25 km river/sea swim: 5:35:25·56 Greg Steppel (Can)
1m Springboard diving : Evan Stewart (Zimbabwe)
3m Springboard diving: Yu Zhuocheng (China)
Highboard diving: Dmitriy Sautin (Russia)

Women
50m freestyle: 24·51 Le Jingyi (China)
100m freestyle: 54·01 Le Jingyi (China)
200m freestyle: 1:56·78 Franziska van Almsick (Ger)
400m freestyle: 4:09·64 Yang Aihua (China)
800m freestyle: 8:29·85 Janet Evans (USA)
4 x 100m freestyle: 3:37·91 China
4 x 200m freestyle relay: 7:57·96 China
100m backstroke: 1:00·57 He Cihong (China)
200m backstroke: 2:07·4 He Cihong (China)
100m breaststroke: 1:07·69 Samantha Riley (Austral)

200m breaststroke: 2:26·87 Samantha Riley (Austral)
100m butterfly: 58·98 Liu Limin (China)
200m butterfly: 2:07·25 Liu Limin (China)
200m individual medley: 2:12·34 Lu Bin (China)
400m individual medley: 4:39·14 Dai Guohong (China)
4 x 100 m medley relay: 4:01·67 China
25km river/sea swim: 5:48:25·04 Melissa Cunningham (Austral)
1m Springboard diving : Chen Lixia (China)
3m Springboard diving: Tan Shuping (China)
Highboard diving: Fu Mingxia (China)
Synchronized swimming solo: Becky Dyroen Lancer (USA)
Synchronized swimming duet: Becky Dyroen Lancer & Jill Sudduth (USA)
Synchronized swimming team: USA

TAEKWONDO

Taekwondo is a martial art developed over 20 centuries in Korea. All its activities are based on a defensive spirit and it was officially recognized as part of Korean tradition and culture in 1955. The sport has spread internationally and there are now an estimated 22 million practitioners in the 144 countries that are members of the World Taekwondo Federation. Taekwondo was a demonstration sport at the Olympic Games in 1988 and 1992.

TABLE TENNIS

The earliest evidence of a game resembling table tennis goes back to London sports goods manufacturers in the 1880s. Known as *gossima*, it was the introduction of the celluloid ball and the noise it made when hit that brought the name 'ping pong' and the Ping Pong Association in 1902. Interest declined until the use of attached rubber mats to the wooden bats (allowing spin) in the early 1920s. The International Table Tennis Association was founded in 1926, and the World Championships have been held since 1927. The Swaythling and Corbillon Cups are held as world team championships, instituted in 1927 and 1934 for men and women respectively. China won the Swaythling Cup on four successive occasions from 1981 and again in 1994, but Sweden won in 1989, 1991 and 1993, and China have dominated the Corbillon Cup with nine successive wins between 1975 and 1993, although the combined Korean team won in 1991 and Russia in 1994. Dimensions: ball diameter 37·2–38·2 mm (1·46–1·5 in), weight 2·4–2·53 g (0·08 oz), table length 2·74m (9 ft), 1·525m (5 ft) wide.

TENNIS

Lawn tennis evolved from the indoor game of real tennis (see above) and 'field tennis' is mentioned in a 1793 magazine. Major Harry Gem founded the first club in Leamington Spa, Warwickshire (UK), in 1872. The All England Croquet Club added Lawn Tennis to their title in 1877 when they held their first Championships. The United States Lawn Tennis Association (now USLTA) was founded in 1881; the English association was founded in 1888. The International (Lawn) Tennis Federation was formed in Paris in March 1913. The Wimbledon, or All England, Championships have been regarded since 1877 as the most important in the world, alongside the US, French and Australian Opens. Together these four make up the 'Grand Slam', the elusive distinction of holding all four titles at once. The US Open (instituted 1881) is now held at Flushing Meadows, New York, and the French at Roland Garros, Paris. The Australian Championships, now held at Flinders Park, Melbourne, were instituted in 1905. Men and women today compete in various 'circuits' in the second richest sport in the world after golf. 'Grand prix' tournaments are scaled according to a standard, with points accumulated to decide world rankings. The international team competition for men is the Davis Cup, won most times by the USA (30), Australia (Australasia 1907–19; 26), and Great Britain (9).

Davis Cup winners (since 1973)

1973	Australia	1984–85	Sweden
1974	South Africa	1986	Australia
1975	Sweden	1987	Sweden
1976	Italy	1988–89	Germany (W)
1977	Australia	1990	USA
1978–79	USA	1991	France
1980	Czechoslovakia	1992	USA
1981–82	USA	1993	Germany
1983	Australia	1994	Sweden

The women's international team competition for the Federation Cup (now the Fed Cup) has been held annually since 1963. The USA have a record 14 wins, including 1986 and 1989–90, with Australia achieving seven wins and the former Czechoslovakia five, including 1983–5 and 1988. Spain won in 1991, 1993 and 1994, and Germany in 1992.

Lawn tennis was included in the Olympic Games from 1896 to 1924 and as a demonstration sport in 1968 before being reintroduced as a medal sport in 1988. The 1992 Olympic winners were: men's singles, Marc Rosset (Switzerland); men's doubles, Boris Becker and Michael Stich (Germany); women's singles, Jennifer Capriati (USA); women's doubles, Gigi Fernandez and Mary Joe Fernandez (USA).

The Wimbledon Championships

Wimbledon, 'The All England Championships', dates back to 1877 when it comprised one event, the men's singles. Women's singles and men's doubles were introduced in 1884, with women's doubles and mixed doubles becoming full Championship events in 1913.

Men's Singles (since 1946)

1946	Yvon Petra (France)
1947	Jack Kramer (USA)
1948	Bob Falkenburg (USA)
1949	Ted Schroeder (USA)
1950	Budge Patty (USA)
1951	Dick Savitt (USA)
1952	Frank Sedgman (Austral)
1953	Vic Seixas (USA)
1954	Jaroslav Drobny (Czech)
1955	Tony Trabert (USA)
1956–57	Lew Hoad (Austral)
1958	Ashley Cooper (Austral)
1959	Alex Olmedo (USA)
1960	Neale Fraser (Austral)
1961–62	Rod Laver (Austral)
1963	Chuck McKinley (USA)
1964–65	Roy Emerson (Austral)
1966	Manuel Santana (Spain)
1967	John Newcombe (Austral)
1968–69	Rod Laver (Australa)

1970–71 John Newcombe (Austral)
1972 Stan Smith (USA)
1973 Jan Kodes (Czech)
1974 Jimmy Connors (USA)
1975 Arthur Ashe (USA)
1976–80 Bjorn Borg (Sweden)
1981 John McEnroe (USA)
1982 Jimmy Connors (USA)
1983–84 John McEnroe (USA)
1985–86 Boris Becker (Germany)
1987 Pat Cash (Austral)
1988 Stefan Edberg (Sweden)
1989 Boris Becker (Germany)
1990 Stefan Edberg (Sweden)
1991 Michael Stich (Germany)
1992 Andre Agassi (USA)
1993–94 Pete Sampras (USA)

Women's Singles (since 1946)

1946 Pauline Betz (USA)
1947 Margaret Osborne (USA)
1948–50 Louise Brough (USA)
1951 Doris Hart (USA)
1952–54 Maureen Connolly (USA)
1955 Louise Brough (USA)
1956 Shirley Fry (USA)
1957–58 Althea Gibson (USA)
1959–60 Maria Bueno (Brazil)
1961 Angela Mortimer (UK)
1962 Karen Susman (USA)
1963 Margaret Smith (Austral)
1964 Maria Bueno (Brazil)
1965 Margaret Smith (Austral)
1966–68 Billie Jean King née Moffitt (USA)
1969 Ann Jones (UK)
1970 Margaret Smith-Court (Austral)
1971 Evonne Goolagong (Austral)
1972–73 Billie Jean King (USA)
1974 Chris Evert (USA)
1975 Billie Jean King (USA)
1976 Chris Evert (USA)
1977 Virginia Wade (UK)
1978–79 Martina Navratilova (Czech)
1980 Evonne Goolagong-Cawley (Austral)
1981 Chris Evert-Lloyd (USA)
1982 Martina Navratilova (USA;formerly Czech)
1983–87 Martina Navratilova (USA)
1988–89 Steffi Graf (Germany)
1990 Martina Navratilova (USA)
1991–93 Steffi Graf (Germany
1994 Conchita Martinez (Spain)

Women's Doubles

1946 Louise Brough & Margaret Osborne (USA)
1947 Pat Todd & Doris Hart (USA)
1948–50 Louise Brough & Margaret Osborne-du Pont (USA)
1951–53 Doris Hart & Shirley Fry (USA)
1954 Louise Brough & Margaret Osborne-du Pont (USA)
1955 Angela Mortimer & Anne Shilcock (UK)
1956 Angela Buxton (UK) & Althea Gibson (USA)
1957 Althea Gibson & Darlene Hard (USA)
1958 Maria Bueno (Brazil) & Althea Gibson (USA)
1959 Jean Arth & Darlene Hard (USA)
1960 Maria Bueno (Brazil) & Darlene Hard (USA)
1961 Karen Hantze & Billie Jean Moffitt (USA)
1962 Karen Hantze-Susman & Billie Jean Moffitt (USA)
1963 Maria Bueno (Brazil) & Darlene Hard (USA)
1964 Margaret Smith & Lesley Turner (Austral)
1965 Maria Bueno (Brazil) & Billie Jean Moffitt (USA)
1966 Maria Bueno (Brazil) & Nancy Richey (USA)
1967 Rosemary Casals & Billie Jean King née Moffitt (USA)
1968 Billie Jean King & Rosemary Casals (USA)
1969 Margaret Smith-Court & Judy Tegart (Austral)
1970 Billie Jean King & Rosemary Casals (USA)
1972 Billie Jean King & Rosemary Casals (USA)
1972 Billie Jean King (USA) & Betty Stove (Neths)
1973 Billie Jean King & Rosemary Casals (USA)
1974 Evonne Goolagong (Austral) & Peggy Michel (USA)
1975 Ann Kiyomura (USA) & Kazuko Sawamatsu (Japan)
1976 Chris Evert (USA) & Martina Navratilova (Czech)
1977 Helen Cawley (Australia) & Joanne Russell (USA)
1978 Kerry Reid & Wendy Turnbull (Australia)
1979 Billie Jean King (USA) & Martina Navratilova (Czech)
1980 Kathy Jordan & Anne Smith (USA)
1981–84 Martina Navratilova (Czech) & Pam Shriver (USA)
1985 Kathy Jordan (USA) & Liz Smylie (Austral)
1986 Martina Navratilova & Pam Shriver (USA)
1987 Claudia Kohde-Kilsch (Germany) & Helena Sukova (Czech)
1988 Steffi Graf (Germany) & Gabriella Sabatini (Argentina)
1989–90 Jana Novotna and Helena Sukova (Czech)
1991 Larisa Savchenko and Natalya Zvereva (USSR)
1992–94 Gigi Fernandez (USA) & Natalya Zvereva (Belarus)

Men's Doubles

1946 Tom Brown & Jack Kramer (USA)
1947 Bob Falkenburg & Jack Kramer (USA)
1948 John Bromwich & Frank Sedgman (Austral)
1949 Ricardo Gonzales & Frank Parker (USA)
1950 John Bromwich & Adrian Quist (Austral)
1951–52 Ken McGregor & Frank Sedgman (Austral)
1953 Lew Hoad & Ken Rosewall (Austral)
1954 Rex Hartwig & Mervyn Rose (Austral)
1955 Rex Hartwig & Lew Hoad (Austral)
1956 Lew Hoad & Ken Rosewall (Austral)
1957 Budge Patty & Gardnar Mulloy (USA)
1958 Sven Davidson & Ulf Schmidt (Sweden)
1959 Roy Emerson & Neale Fraser (Austral)
1960 Rafael Osuna (Mex) & Dennis Ralston (USA)
1961 Roy Emerson & Neale Fraser (Austral)
1962 Bob Hewitt & Fred Stolle (Austral)
1963 Rafael Osuna & Antonio Palafox (Mex)
1964 Bob Hewitt & Fred Stolle (Austral)
1965 John Newcombe & Tony Roche (Austral)
1966 Ken Fletcher & John Newcombe (Austral)
1967 Bob Hewitt & Frew McMillan (S Africa)
1968–70 John Newcombe & Tony Roche (Austral)
1971 Roy Emerson & Rod Laver (Austral)
1972 Bob Hewitt & Frew McMillan (S Africa)
1973 Jimmy Connors (USA) & Ilie Nastase (Rom)
1974 John Newcombe & Tony Roche (Austral)
1975 Vitas Gerulaitis & Sandy Mayer (USA)

1976 Brian Gottfried (USA) & Raul Ramirez (Mex)
1977 Ross Case & Geoff Masters (Austral)
1978 Bob Hewitt & Frew McMillan (S Africa)
1979 John McEnroe & Peter Fleming (USA)
1980 Peter McNamara & Paul McNamee (Austral)
1981 John McEnroe & Peter Fleming (USA)
1982 Peter McNamara & Paul McNamee (Austral)
1983–84 John McEnroe & Peter Fleming (USA)
1985 Balazs Taroczy (Hung) & Heinz Gunthardt (Switz)
1986 Joachim Nystrom & Mats Wilander (Sweden)
1987–88 Ken Flach & Robert Seguso (USA)
1989 John Fitzgerald (Austral) & Anders Järryd (Sweden)
1990 Rick Leach & Jim Pugh (USA)
1991 John Fitzgerald (Austral) & Anders Järryd (Sweden)
1992 John McEnroe (USA) & Michael Stich (Germany)
1993–94 Todd Woodbridge & Mark Woodforde (Austral)

Mixed Doubles
1946 Tom Brown & Louise Brough (USA)
1947–48 Louise Brough (USA) & John Bromwich (Austral)
1949 Sheila Summers & Eric Sturgess (S Africa)
1950 Louise Brough (USA) & Eric Sturgess (S Africa)
1951–52 Doris Hart (USA) & Frank Sedgman (Austral)
1953–55 Doris Hart & Vic Seixas (USA)
1956 Shirley Fry & Vic Seixas (USA)
1957 Darlene Hard (USA) & Mervyn Rose (Austral)
1958 Lorraine Coghlan & Bob Howe (Austral)
1959–60 Darlene Hard (USA) & Rod Laver (Austral)
1961 Lesley Turner & Fred Stolle (Austral)
1962 Margaret Osborne-du Pont (USA) & Neale Fraser (Austral)
1963 Margaret Smith & Ken Fletcher (Austral)
1964 Lesley Turner & Fred Stolle (Austral)
1965–66 Margaret Smith & Ken Fletcher (Austral)
1967 Billie Jean King (USA) & Owen Davidson (Austral)
1968 Margaret Smith-Court & Ken Fletcher (Austral)
1969 Ann Jones (UK) & Fred Stolle (Austral)
1970 Rosemary Casals (USA) & Ilie Nastase (Rom)
1971 Billie Jean King (USA) & Owen Davidson (Austral)
1972 Rosemary Casals (USA) & Ilie Nastase (Romania)
1973–74 Billie Jean King (USA) & Owen Davidson (Australia)
1975 Margaret Smith-Court (Austral) & Marty Riessen (USA)
1976 Françoise Durr (France) & Tony Roche (Austral)
1977 Greer Stevens & Bob Hewitt (S Africa)
1978 Betty Stove (Neths) & Frew McMillan (S Afr)
1979 Greer Stevens & Bob Hewitt (S Afr)
1980 Tracey Austin & John Austin (USA)
1981 Betty Stove (Neths) & Frew McMillan (S Afr)
1982 Anne Smith (USA) & Kevin Curren (S Afr)
1983–84 Wendy Turnbull (Austral) & John Lloyd (UK)
1985 Martina Navratilova (USA) & Paul McNamee (Austral)
1986 Kathy Jordan & Ken Flach (USA)
1987 Jo Durie & Jeremy Bates (UK)
1988 Zina Garrison & Sherwood Stewart (USA)
1989 Jana Novotna (Czech) & Jim Pugh (USA)
1990 Zina Garrison & Rick Leach (USA)
1991 John Fitzgerald and Elizabeth Smylie (Austral)
1992 Cyril Suk (Czech) & Larisa Savchenko (Latvia)
1993 Mark Woodforde (Austral) & Martina Navratilova (USA)
1994 Todd Woodbridge (Austral) & Helena Sukova (Czech Rep)

Recent Winners of the US Open
Men's singles (US unless specified)
1979–81 John McEnroe
1982–83 Jimmy Connors
1984 John McEnroe
1985–87 Ivan Lendl (Czech)
1988 Mats Wilander (Sweden)
1989 Boris Becker (Germany)
1990 Pete Sampras
1991–92 Stefan Edberg (Sweden)
1993 Pete Sampras (USA)
1994 Andre Agassi (USA)

Women's singles (US unless specified)
1980 Chris Evert-Lloyd
1981 Tracy Austin
1982 Chris Evert-Lloyd
1983–84 Martina Navratilova
1985 Hana Mandlikova (Czech)
1986–87 Martina Navratilova
1988–89 Steffi Graf (Germany)
1990 Gabriela Sabatini (Argentina)
1991–92 Monica Seles (Yugo)
1993 Steffi Graf (Germany)
1994 Arantxa Sánchez Vicario (Spain)

Recent Winners of the French Open
Men's singles
1978–81 Bjorn Borg (Sweden)
1982 Mats Wilander (Sweden)
1983 Yannick Noah (France)
1984 Ivan Lendl (Czech)
1985 Mats Wilander (Sweden)
1986–87 Ivan Lendl (Czech)
1988 Mats Wilander (Sweden)
1989 Michael Chang (USA)
1990 Andrés Gómez (Ecuador)
1991–92 Jim Courier (USA)
1993–94 Sergi Bruguera (Spain)

Women's singles
1979–80 Chris Evert-Lloyd (USA)
1981 Hana Mandlikova (Czech)
1982 Martina Navratilova (USA)
1983 Chris Evert-Lloyd (USA)
1984 Martina Navratilova (USA)
1985–86 Chris Evert-Lloyd (USA)
1987–88 Steffi Graf (Germany)
1989 Arantxa Sánchez (Spain)
1990–92 Monica Seles (Yugo)
1993 Steffi Graf (Germany)
1994 Arantxa Sánchez Vicario (Spain)

Recent Winners of the Australian Open
Men's singles
1980 Brian Teacher (USA)
1981–82 Johan Kriek (S Africa)
1983–84 Mats Wilander (Sweden)

1985 Stefan Edberg (Sweden)
1986 No championship held.
1987 Stefan Edberg (Sweden)
1988 Mats Wilander (Sweden)
1989–90 Ivan Lendl (Czech)
1991 Boris Becker (Germany)
1992–93 Jim Courier (USA)
1994 Pete Sampras (USA)
1995 Andre Agassi (USA)

Women's singles
1980 Hana Mandlikova (Czech)
1981 Martina Navratilova (USA)
1982 Chris Evert-Lloyd (USA)
1983 Martina Navratilova (USA)
1984 Chris Evert-Lloyd (USA)
1985 Martina Navratilova (USA)
1987 Hana Mandlikova (Czech)
1988–90 Steffi Graf (Germany)
1991–93 Monica Seles (Yugo)
1994 Steffi Graf (Germany)
1995 Mary Pierce (France)

TRAMPOLINING

The word 'trampoline' originates from the Spanish *trampolin*, a springboard, and indeed springboards date to circus acrobats of the Middle Ages. The birth of the sport follows the invention of the prototype "T" trampoline by the American George Nissen in 1936. The World Championships, administered by the International Trampolining Association, were instituted in 1964 and held biennially since 1968.

VOLLEYBALL

The modern game was invented as minnonette in 1895 by William Morgan in Massachusetts, USA, as a game for those who found basketball too strenuous. The name volleyball came a year later. The game spread rapidly worldwide and reached Britain in 1914. The first international tournament was the European Championship in 1948, the year after the founding of the International Volleyball Federation. Volleyball was not included in the Olympics until 1964. The 1992 Olympic titles were won by Brazil (men) and Cuba (women). World Champions in 1994 were Italy (men) and Cuba (women). Court dimensions are 18 × 9m (89 ft × 29 ft 6⅜ in); ball circumference 65–67 cm (25½–26½ in), 250–260 g (8·85–9·9 oz) in weight. Net height is 2·43m (7 ft 11¾ in) for men and 2·24 m (7 ft 4¼ in) for women.

WALKING

Walking races have been included in the Olympics since 1906 but walking matches have been known since 1859. Walking as a sport is defined as 'progression by steps so that unbroken contact with the ground is maintained'. Road walking has become more prevalent than track walking. The Olympic distances are currently 20 km and 50 km for men and 10 km for women.

WATER SKIING

Water skiing as we now know it was pioneered by Ralph Samuelson (USA) on Lake Pepin, Minnesota, in 1922. Having tried and failed with snow skis, he gave exhibitions with pine board skis culminating in the first jump, off a greased ramp, in 1925. The *Union Internationale de Ski Nautique* was set up in 1946 and the British Water Ski Federation was formed in 1954. Competitively, the sport is divided into trick skiing, slalom and ski jumping. (Trick skiing, performed at lower speeds, involves gymnastic feats rewarded according to difficulty.) The World Championships, begun in 1947 and held biennially, include an overall title, which was won by the USA at all 17 championships 1957–89, but by Canada in 1991 and 1993. Skiing barefoot brought a new element to the sport and competitions are held for straight speed records.

WEIGHTLIFTING

In China during the Zhou dynasty, weightlifting became a compulsory military test. Competitions for lifting weights of stone were held in the ancient Olympic Games. The amateur sport, however, is modern with competitions dating from c. 1850. The first championships termed 'world' from 1891. The International Weightlifting Federation was established in 1920. Weightlifting was included in the first modern Olympics in 1896, and then from 1920. There are now ten weight divisions, from up to 54 kg (119 lbs) to over 108 kg (238 lbs). Competition is decided by the aggregate of two forms of lifting, the snatch and the clean and jerk. A third form, the press, was dropped in 1976 because of the difficulty in judging it. Eastern European countries, especially Russia and Bulgaria, have dominated the sport in which world records have recently been broken more frequently than in any other. Women's world championships, dominated by China, have been held bienially from 1987. *Powerlifting* involves different techniques which perhaps have greater emphasis on sheer strength rather than technique. The three basic lifts are the squat (or deep knee bend), bench press and dead lift. The International Powerlifting Federation was founded in 1972, with the USA generally dominant in the majority of the men's and women's weight categories.

WRESTLING

One of the oldest sports in the world, organized wrestling may date to c. 2750–2600 BC. It was the most popular sport in the ancient Olympic Games, and victors were recorded from 708 BC. Wrestling developed in varying forms in different countries, with the classical Greco-Roman style popular in Europe, and free style more to the liking of countries in the East and the Americas. The main distinction is that in Greco-Roman the wrestler cannot seize his opponent below the hips nor grip with the legs. The International Amateur Wrestling Federation (FILA) also recognizes sambo wrestling, akin to judo and popular in the former USSR. FILA was founded in 1912, although the sport was in the first modern Olympics in 1896. There are currently ten weight divisions in both free style and Greco-Roman events at the Games. *Sumo wrestling* is a traditional form in Japan dating to 23 BC. Conducted with ceremony and mysticism, weight and bulk are vital since the object is to force the opponent out of the circular ring, using any hold.

YACHTING

Yachting dates to the race for a £100 wager between Charles II and his brother James, Duke of York, on the Thames in 1661. The first recorded regatta was held in 1720 by the Cork Harbour Water Club (later Royal Cork Yacht Club), the oldest yacht club. The sport did not prosper until the seas became safe after the Napoleonic Wars in 1815. That year the Yacht Club (later the Royal Yacht Squadron) was formed and organized races at Cowes, Isle of Wight, the beginning of modern yacht racing. The International Yacht Racing Union (IYRU) was founded in 1907. There were seven classes of boat at the 1992 Olympic Games, one of which, the 470, had separate competitions for men and women. Other major competitions include the Admiral's Cup – a biennial inter-nation, Channel and inshore race from Cowes (Isle of Wight) to Fastnet Rock, Ireland, and back to Plymouth (Devon), England – and the quadrennial Whitbread Round the World Race, instituted in 1973. The America's Cup was originally won as an outright prize by the schooner *America* in 1851 at Cowes and later offered by the New York Yacht Club as a challenge trophy. Since 1870 the Cup has been challenged by the UK in 16 contests, by Canada and New Zealand in two, Australia eight and Italy, but the USA were undefeated until 1983, when *Australia II* defeated the American boat *Liberty*. Denis Conner in *Stars & Stripes* regained the Cup over *Kookaburra III* (Australia) in 1987 and defended it against New Zealand in 1988. In 1992 Bill Koch successfully defended the Cup for the USA against Italy. In 1995 the New Zealand yacht *Black Magic* beat the US boat *Young America*.

The Olympic Games

The ancient Olympic Games were staged every four years at Olympia, 120 miles west of Athens, Greece. The earliest celebration of which there is a certain record is that of July 776 BC, from which all subsequent Games are dated. However, earlier Games were certainly held, perhaps dating back to 1370 BC. The early Games had considerable religious significance. The Games grew in size and importance to the height of their fame in the 5th and 4th centuries BC. Events included running, jumping, wrestling, throwing the discus, boxing and chariot racing. As well as being sporting contests, the Olympics were great artistic festivals upholding the Greek ideal of perfection of mind and body. Winners were awarded a branch of wild olive, the Greeks' sacred tree. The final Olympic Games of the ancient era were held in AD 393 before the Roman Emperor, Theodosius I, decreed the prohibition of the Games, which were not favoured by the early Christians and which were then long past their great days. The first modern Games, in Athens in 1896, were at the instigation of Pierre de Fredi, Baron de Coubertin (1863–1937). A far cry from today's huge organization, just 311 competitors (from 13 countries) took part, of whom 230 were from Greece and others were foreign tourists. By contrast, 169 countries were represented by 9369 participating sports men and women at the 1992 Games in Barcelona, Spain.

Celebration of the Modern Olympic Games

	Year	Venue	Date	Countries	Competitors Male	Competitors Female
I	1896	Athens, Greece	6–15 Apr	13	311	–
II	1900	Paris, France	20 May–28 Oct	22	1319	11
III	1904	St Louis, USA	1 July–23 Nov	13[1]	617	8
*	1906	Athens, Greece	22 Apr–2 May	20	877	7
IV	1908	London, England	27 Apr–31 Oct	22	2013	43
V	1912	Stockholm, Sweden	5 May–22 July	28	2491	55
VI	1916	Berlin, Germany	Not held due to war	–	–	–
VII	1920	Antwerp, Belgium	20 Apr–12 Sept	29	2618	74
VIII	1924	Paris, France	4 May–27 July	44	2956	136
IX	1928	Amsterdam, Netherlands	17 May–12 Aug	46	2724	290
X	1932	Los Angeles, USA	30 July–14 Aug	37	1281	127
XI	1936	Berlin, Germany	1–16 Aug	49	3738	328
XII	1940	Tokyo, then Helsinki	Not held due to war	–	–	–
XIII	1944	London, England	Not held due to war	–	–	–
XIV	1948	London, England	29 July–14 Aug	59	3714	385
XV	1952	Helsinki, Finland	19 July–3 Aug	69	4407	518
XVI	1956[2]	Melbourne, Australia	22 Nov–8 Dec	67	2958	384
XVII	1960	Rome, Italy	25 Aug–11 Sept	83	4738	610
XVIII	1964	Tokyo, Japan	10–24 Oct	93	4457	683
XIX	1968	Mexico City, Mexico	12–27 Oct	112	4749	781
XX	1972	Munich, Germany	26 Aug–10 Sept	122	6086	1070
XXI	1976	Montreal, Canada	17 July–1 Aug	92	4834	1251
XXII	1980	Moscow, USSR	19 July–3 Aug	81	4238	1088
XXIII	1984	Los Angeles, USA	28 July–12 Aug	140	5458	1620
XXIV	1988	Seoul, South Korea	20 Sept–5 Oct	159	6279	2186
XXV	1992	Barcelona, Spain	25 July–8 Aug	169	6659	2710
XXVI	1996	Atlanta, USA	20 July–4 Aug			
XXVII	2000	Sydney, Australia				

* This celebration to mark the tenth anniversary of the Modern Games was officially intercalated but is not numbered.
[1] Including newly discovered French national.
[2] The equestrian events were held in Stockholm, Sweden, 10–17 June with 158 competitors from 29 countries.

Table of Olympic medal winners – Summer Games, 1896–1992*

		Gold	Silver	Bronze	Total
1	USA	789	603	518	1910
2	USSR/Unified team[6]	442	361	333	1136
3	Germany[1]	186	227	236	649
4	United Kingdom	177	224	218	619
5	France	161	175	191	527
6	Sweden	133	149	171	453
7	GDR[2]	154	131	126	411
8	Italy	153	126	131	410
9	Hungary	136	124	144	404
10	Finland	98	77	112	287
11	Japan	90	83	93	266
12	Australia	78	76	98	252
13	Romania	59	70	90	219
14	Poland	43	62	105	210
15	Canada	45	67	80	192
16	Netherlands	45	52	72	169
17	Switzerland	42	63	58	163
18	Bulgaria	38	69	55	162
19	Czechoslovakia	49	50	49	148
20	Denmark	26	51	53	130
21	Belgium	35	47	44	126
22	Norway	43	37	34	114
23	China	36	41	37	114
24	Greece	24	40	39	103
25	South Korea	31	27	41	99
26	Yugoslavia	26	30	30	86
27	Cuba	36	25	23	84
28	Austria	19	29	33	81
29	New Zealand	27	10	28	65
30	Turkey	26	15	12	53
31	South Africa[3]	16	17	20	53
32	Argentina	13	19	15	47
	(Russia[6]	17	16	12	47)
33	Spain	17	19	10	46
34	Mexico	9	13	18	40
35	Brazil	9	10	21	40
36	Kenya	13	13	13	39
37	Iran	4	12	17	33
38	Jamaica	4	13	9	26
39	Estonia[4]	7	6	10	23
40	North Korea[5]	6	5	10	21
	(Ukraine[6]	4	11	4	19)
41	Egypt	6	6	6	18
	(Belarus[6]	9	4	2	15)
42	Ireland	5	5	5	15
43	India	8	3	3	14
=44	Ethiopia	6	1	6	13
=44	Portugal	2	4	7	13
=44	Mongolia	0	5	8	13
45	Pakistan	3	3	4	10
=46	Morocco	4	2	3	9
=46	Uruguay	2	1	6	9
=47	Venezuela	1	2	5	8
=47	Chile	0	6	2	8
	=47 Nigeria	0	4	4	8
=47	Philippines	0	1	7	8
48	Trinidad	1	2	4	7
=49	Indonesia	2	3	1	6
=49	Latvia[4]	0	4	2	6
=49	Colombia	0	2	4	6
	(Georgia[6]	3	0	2	5)
=50	Uganda	1	3	1	5
=50	Tunisia	1	2	2	5
=50	Puerto Rico	0	1	4	5
	(Armenia[6]	3	1	0	4)
=51	Peru	1	3	0	4
=51	Algeria	1	0	3	4
=51	Lebanon	0	2	2	4
=51	Taipei (Taiwan)	0	2	2	4
=51	Ghana	0	1	3	4
=51	Thailand	0	1	3	4
	(Moldova[6]	1	1	1	3)
=52	Bahamas	1	0	2	3
=52	Croatia	0	1	2	3
=53	Luxembourg	1	1	0	2
=53	Lithuania	1	0	1	2
=53	Suriname	1	0	1	2
	(Azerbaijan[6]	1	0	1	2)
=53	Namibia	0	2	0	2
=53	Tanzania	0	2	0	2
	(Uzbekistan[6]	0	2	0	2)
=53	Cameroon	0	1	1	2
=53	Haiti	0	1	1	2
=53	Iceland	0	1	1	2
=53	Israel	0	1	1	2
=53	Panama	0	0	2	2
=53	Slovenia	0	0	2	2
	(Kazakhstan[6]	0	0	2	2)
	(Tajikistan[6]	1	0	0	1)
=54	Zimbabwe	1	0	0	1
=54	Côte d'Ivoire	0	1	0	1
=54	Singapore	0	1	0	1
=54	Sri Lanka	0	1	0	1
=54	Syria	0	1	0	1
=54	Costa Rica	0	1	0	1
=54	Netherlands Antilles	0	1	0	1
=54	Senegal	0	1	0	1
=54	Virgin Islands	0	1	0	1
=54	Barbados	0	0	1	1
=54	Bermuda	0	0	1	1
=54	Dominican Rep	0	0	1	1
=54	Guyana	0	0	1	1
=54	Iraq	0	0	1	1
=54	Niger	0	0	1	1
=54	Zambia	0	0	1	1
=54	Qatar	0	0	1	1
=54	Djibouti	0	0	1	1

*including 1909 [1]Germany 1896–1952 and 1992, Federal Republic of Germany (West) 1956–88. Medals won by the combined German teams of 1956, 1960 and 1964 have been allocated to FDR and the GDR according to the athlete's origins [2]GDR, East Germany, 1956-88 [3]South Africa, up to 1960 and from 1992 [4]Estonia and Latvia, up to 1936 and from 1992 [5]North Korea, from 1964 [6]the Unified Team was a combined team that took part in the 1992 Games representing 12 of the 15 former Soviet republics; in individual events athletes represented their individual republics which are shown above in brackets.

AFRICAN AND ASIAN GAMES

The Asian Games are multi-sport competitions open to athletes from Asian nations. The games have been held in: 1951 New Delhi, India; 1954 Manila, Philippines; 1958 Tokyo, Japan; 1962 Djakarta, Indonesia; 1966 Bangkok, Thailand; 1970 Bangkok, Thailand; 1974 Tehran, Iran; 1978 Bangkok, Thailand; 1982 New Delhi, India; 1986 Seoul, South Korea; 1990 Beijing (Peking), China; 1994 Hiroshima, Japan.

The All African Games are multi-sport competitions open to athletes from African nations. The Games have been held in: 1965 Brazzaville, Congo; 1973 Lagos, Nigeria; 1978 Algiers, Algeria; 1987 Nairobi, Kenya; 1991 Cairo, Egypt; 1995 Harare, Zimbabwe

Celebrations of the Winter Games

	Year	Venue	Date	Countries	Competitors Male	Competitors Female
I*	1924	Chamonix, France	25 Jan–4 Feb	16	281	13
II	1928	St Moritz, Switzerland	11–19 Feb	25	468	27
III	1932	Lake Placid, USA	4–15 Feb	17	274	32
IV	1936	Garmisch-Partenkirchen, Germ.	6–16 Feb	28	675	80
V	1948	St Moritz, Switzerland	30 Jan–8 Feb	28	636	77
VI	1952	Oslo, Norway	14–25 Feb	22	623	109
VII	1956	Cortina d'Ampezzo, Italy	26 Jan–5 Feb	32	687	132
VIII	1960	Squaw Valley, USA	18–28 Feb	30	521	144
IX	1964	Innsbruck, Austria	29 Jan–9 Feb	36	893	200
X	1968	Grenoble, France	6–18 Feb	37	1065	228
XI	1972	Sapporo, Japan	3–13 Feb	35	1015	217
XII	1976	Innsbruck, Austria	4–15 Feb	37	900	228
XIII	1980	Lake Placid, USA	13–24 Feb	37	833	234
XIV	1984	Sarajevo, Yugoslavia†	7–19 Feb	49	1287	223
XV	1988	Calgary, Canada	23 Feb–6 Mar	57	1113	315
XVI	1992	Albertville, France	8–23 Feb	64	1269	460
XVII	1994	Lillehammer, Norway	12–27 Feb	67	1302	542
XVIII	1998	Nagano, Japan				

*There were Winter Games events included in the Summer Games of 1908 (London) and 1920 (Antwerp) which attracted six countries, 14 males and seven females for the first, and 10 countries, 73 males and 12 females for the latter. † now in Bosnia-Herzegovina.

Table of Olympic medal winners – Winter Games, 1924–94

Nation	Gold	Silver	Bronze	Total
USSR/CIS	88	63	67	218
Norway	73	77	64	214
USA	53	55	39	147
Austria	36	48	44	128
Germany	45	43	37	125
Finland	36	45	42	123
GDR	39	36	35	110
Sweden	39	26	34	99
Switzerland	27	29	29	85
Italy	25	21	21	67
Canada	19	21	24	64
France	16	16	21	53
Netherlands	14	19	17	50
Czechoslovakia	2	8	16	26
Russia	11	8	4	23
United Kingdom	7	4	12	23
Japan	3	8	8	19
Liechtenstein	2	2	5	9
South Korea	6	2	2	8
China	-	4	2	6
Hungary	-	2	4	6
Poland	1	1	2	4
Belgium	1	1	2	4
Yugoslavia	-	3	1	4
Kazakhstan	1	2	-	3
Slovenia	-	-	3	3
Spain	1	-	1	2
Ukraine	1	-	1	2
Luxembourg	-	2	-	2
Belarus	-	2	-	2
North Korea	-	1	1	2
Uzbekistan	1	-	-	1
New Zealand	-	1	-	1
Romania	-	-	1	1
Bulgaria	-	-	1	1
Australia	-	-	1	1

COMMONWEALTH GAMES

The Commonwealth Games are multi-sport competitions held every four years and contested by representatives of the nations of the Commonwealth. They were first staged as the British Empire Games in 1930, when 11 nations competed. The Games became the British Empire and Commonwealth Games in 1954 and the British Commonwealth Games in 1970, although the word 'British' has now been dropped from the title. England, Northern Ireland, Scotland, Wales, the Isle of Man, Jersey and Guernsey are represented separately in the Games.

1930 Hamilton, Canada
1934 London, England
1938 Sydney, Australia
1950 Auckland, New Zealand
1954 Vancouver, Canada
1958 Cardiff, Wales
1962 Perth, Australia
1966 Kingston, Jamaica
1970 Edinburgh, Scotland
1974 Christchurch, New Zealand
1978 Edmonton, Canada
1982 Brisbane, Australia
1986 Edinburgh, Scotland
1990 Auckland, New Zealand
1994 Victoria, Canada

PAN-AMERICAN GAMES

The Pan-American Games are multi-sport competitions open to athletes from North, Central and South American and Caribbean nations. They have been held every four years since 1951.

1951 Buenos Aires, Argentina
1955 Mexico City, Mexico
1959 Chicago, USA
1963 São Paulo, Brazil
1967 Winnipeg, Canada
1971 Cali, Colombia
1975 Mexico City, Mexico
1979 San Juan, Puerto Rico
1983 Caracas, Venezuela
1987 Indianapolis, USA
1991 Havana, Cuba
1995 Mar del Plata, Argentina

HISTORY

Kings, Rulers and Statesmen

Heads of state and/or government for selected states.

ARGENTINA

Presidents (since 1946)
Gen. Juan Domingo Perón *Peronist* 1946–55
Gen. Eduardo Lonardi *military* 1955
Gen. Pedro Eugenio Aramburu *military* 1955–58
Arturo Frondizi *Radical* 1958–62
Dr José Maria Guido *np* 1962–63
Dr Arturo Umberto Illia *Radical* 1963–66
Gen. Juan Carlos Ongania *military* 1966–70
Gen. Roberto Levingston *military* 1970–71
Gen. Alejandro Agustin Lanusse *military* 1971–73
Héctor Cámpora *Peronist* 1973
Raúl Lastiri *Coalition* 1973
Gen. Juan Domingo Perón *Peronist* 1973–74
Maria Estela Martinez de Perón *Peronist* 1974–76 (the first woman president in the world)
Gen. Jorge Rafael Videla *military* 1976–81
Gen. Roberto Viola *military* 1981
Gen. Leopoldo Fortunato Galtieri *military* 1981–82
Gen. Reynaldo Bignone *military* 1982–83
Dr Raúl Alfonsin *Radical* 1983–88
Carlos Saul Menem *Peronist* 1988–
Key: *np* = non-party

AUSTRIA

Emperors (before 1804, see Holy Roman Empire)
Franz I 1804–35
Ferdinand I 1835–48
Franz Joseph I 1848–1916
Karl I 1916–18

Presidents
Dr Karl Seitz 1918–20
Dr Michael Hainisch 1920–28
Dr Wilhelm Miklas 1928–1938 when Austria was included within the German Reich
Dr Karl Renner 1945–50
Dr Theodor Körner 1951–57
Dr Adolf Schärf 1957–65
Dr Franz Jonas 1965–74
Dr Rudolf Kirchschläger 1974–86
Dr Kurt Waldheim 1986–92
Thomas Klestil 1992–

Chancellors (since 1945)
Dr Karl Renner *Coalition* 1945
Dr Leopold Figl *PP* 1945–53
Dr Julius Raab *PP* 1953–61
Dr Alfons Gorbach *PP* 1961–74
Dr Josef Klaus *PP* 1974–70
Dr Bruno Kreisky *Soc* 1970–83
Dr Fred Sinowatz *Soc-PP* 1983–86
Dr Franz Vranitzky *Soc-PP* 1986–
Key: *PP* = People's Party (conservative); *Soc* = Social Democrat

AUSTRALIA

Prime Ministers
Sir Edmund Barton *Coalition* 1901–03
Alfred Deakin *Lib-Lab* 1903–04
John Christian Watson *Lab* 1904
Sir George Houston Reid *Coalition* 1904–05
Alfred Deakin *Lib-Lab* 1905–08
Andrew Fisher *Lab* 1908–09
Alfred Deakin *Lib-Con* 1909–10
Andrew Fisher *Lab* 1910–13
Sir Joseph Cook *Lib* 1913–14
Andrew Fisher *Lab* 1914–15
William Morris Hughes *Lab-Nat* 1915–23
Stanley Melbourne Bruce *Nat-Co* 1923–29
James Henry Scullin *Lab* 1929–32
Joseph Aloysius Lyons *UA* 1932–39
Sir Earle Christmas Grafton Page *Co-UA* 1939
Sir Robert Gordon Menzies *UA-Co* 1939–41
Sir Arthur William Fadden *Co-UA* 1941
John Joseph Curtin *Lab* 1941–45
Francis Michael Forde *Lab* 1945
Joseph Benedict Chifley *Lab* 1945–49
Sir Robert Gordon Menzies *Lib-Co* 1949–66
Harold Edward Holt *Lib-Co* 1966–67
Sir John McEwen *Lib-Co* 1967–68
John Grey Gorton *Lib-Co* 1968–71
William McMahon *Lib-Co* 1971–72
Edward Gough Whitlam *Lab* 1972–75
John Malcolm Fraser *Lib-Co* 1975–83
Robert (Bob) James Lee Hawke *Lab* 1983–91
Paul Keating *Lab* 1991–
Key: *Co* = Country Party (now National Party); *Lab* = Labor Party; *Lib* = Liberal Party; *Nat* = Nationalist (after 1931, United Australia Party); *UA* = United Australia Party (after 1944, Liberal Party)

BELGIUM

Kings
Léopold I 1831–65
Léopold II 1865–1909
Albert I 1909–34
Léopold III 1934–51
Baudouin I 1951–93
Albert II 1993–

Prime Ministers (since 1958)
Gaston Eyskens *SC* 1958–61
Théo Lefèvre *SC* 1961–65
Pierre Harmel *SC* 1965–66
Paul vanden Boeynants *SC* 1966–68
Gaston Eyskens *SC* 1968–72
Edmond Leburton *Soc* 1972–74
Léo Tindemans *SC* 1974–78
Paul vanden Boeynants *SC* 1978–79
Wilfried Martens *SC* 1979–81
Mark Eyskens *SC* 1981
Wilfried Martens *SC* 1981–92
Jean-Luc Dehaene *SC* 1992–
Key: *SC* = Social Christian (conservative); *Soc* = Socialist

BRAZIL

Presidents (since 1930)
Dr Getúlio Dornelles Vargas *New State* 1930–45
Chief Justice Dr José Linhares *caretaker* 1945–46
Marshal Eurico Gaspar Dutra *military* 1946–51
Dr Getúlio Dornelles Vargas *PTB* 1951–54
Dr João Café Filho *PTB* 1954–55
Carlos Coimbra de Luz *caretaker* 1955
Nereu de Oliveira Ramos *caretaker* 1955–56
Juscelino Kubitschek de Oliveira *Coalition* 1956–61
Jãnio de Silva Quadros *np-UDN* 1961
Pascoal Ranieri Mazzilli *caretaker* 1961
João Belchior Goulart *PTB* 1961-64
Pascoal Ranieri Mazzilli *caretaker* 1964

Marshal Humberto de Alencar Castelo *military* 1964–67
Marshal Artur da Costa e Silva *military* 1967–69
Gen. Emilio Garrastazu Medici *military* 1969–74
Gen. Ernesto Geisel *military* 1974–79
Gen. João Baptista de Oliveira Figueiredo *military* 1979–85
Tancredo Neves *PFL* 1985
José Sarney *PFL* 1985–90
Fernando Collor de Mellor *PRN* 1990–92
Itamar Franco *PRN* 1992–95
Fernando Henrique Cardoso *PSDB* 1995–
Key: *np* = non-party; *PFL* = Liberal Front; *PRN* = National Reconstruction Party; *PSDB* = Social Democratic Party of Brazil; *PTB* = Brazilian Labour Party; *UDN* = National Democratic Union

BULGARIA

Princes
Alexander I 1879–86
Ferdinand I 1886–1908 when he became king

Kings
Ferdinand I 1908–1918
Boris III 1918–43
Simeon II 1943–46

Presidents
Vassil Kolarov *Comm* 1946–47
Mintso Neitsev *Comm* 1947–50
Georgi Damyanov *Comm* 1950–58
Dimiter Ganev *Comm* 1958–64
Georgi Traikov *Comm* 1964–71
Todor Zhivkov *Comm* 1971–89
Petar Mladenov *Comm* 1989–90
Zhelo Zhelev *UDF* 1990–
Key: *Comm* = Communist; *UDF* = Union of Democratic Forces

CANADA

Prime Ministers
Sir John Alexander MacDonald *Lib-Con* 1867–73
Alexander MacKenzie *Lib* 1873–78
Sir John Alexander MacDonald *Lib-Con* 1878–91
Sir John Joseph Caldwell Abbott *Lib-Con* 1891–92
Sir John Sparrow David Thompson *Lib-Con* 1892–94
Sir Mackenzie Bowell *Lib-Con* 1894–96
Sir Charles Tupper *Lib-Con* 1896
Sir Wilfred Laurier *Lib* 1896–1911
Sir Robert Laird Borden *Con* 1911–20
Arthur Meighen *Con* 1920–21
William Lyon MacKenzie King *Lib* 1921–26
Arthur Meighen *Con* 1926
William Lyon MacKenzie King *Lib* 1926–30
Richard Bedford Bennett *Con* 1930–35
William Lyon Mackenzie King *Lib* 1935–48
Louis Stephen St Laurent *Lib* 1948–57
John George Diefenbaker *PCon* 1957–63
Lester Bowles Pearson *Lib* 1963–68
Pierre Elliott Trudeau *Lib* 1968–79
Charles Joseph Clark *PCon* 1979–80
Pierre Elliot Trudeau *Lib* 1980–84
John Napier Turner *Lib* 1984
Brian Mulroney *PCon* 1984–93
Kim Campbell *PCon* 1993
Jean Chrétien *Lib* 1993–
Key: *Con/PCon* = Conservative; *Lib* = Liberal

CHILE

Presidents (since 1946)
Juan Antonio Rios *Radical* 1942–46
Alfredo Duhalde *interim* 1946
Admiral Vicente Merino Bielech *interim* 1946
Gabriel González Videla *Radical* 1946–52
Carlos Ibáñez del Campo *Coalition* 1952–58
Jorge Alessandri *Con-Lib* 1958–64
Eduardo Frei *Christian Democrat* 1964–70
Salvador Allende *Marxist* 1970–73 (killed)
Gen. Augusto Pinochet *military* 1973–90
Patricio Aylwin *Christian Democrat* 1990–94
Eduardo Frei *Christian Democrat* 1994–

CHINA

Manchu Emperors
Shun-Chih 1644–61
Kangxi 1661–1722
Yangzheng 1722–35
Qian-long 1735–96
Jiajiang 1796–1820
Daoguang 1821–50
Xian Feng 1851–61
Tongzhi 1862–75
Guangxu 1875–1908
Xuan Zong (personal name *Puyi*) 1908–12

Presidents (Republic of China)
In all there were 15 presidents, or claimants to the presidency of China, between 1912 and 1949; the more notable included: Sun Yixian (*Sun Yat-sen*) 1912, 1917–25; Gen. Yuan Shikai 1912–16; Jiang Jie Shi (*Chiang Kai-shek*) 1928–31, 1943–49.

Presidents (People's Republic)
Mao Zedong 1949–58
Marshal Zhu De 1958–59
Liu Shaoqui 1959–68
Dung Pi Wu 1968–75
(No president 1975–83)
Li Xiannian* 1983–88
Yang Shangkun 1988–93
Jiang Zemin 1993–

Prime Ministers (since 1949)
Zhou Enlai 1949–76
Hua Guofeng* 1976–80
Zhao Ziyang 1980–87
Li Peng 1987–

Leaders of the Communist Party
Mao Zedong 1949–76
Hua Guofeng* 1976–81
Hu Yaobang 1981–87
Zhao Ziyang 1987–89
Jiang Zemin 1989–
Key: * Since 1977 Deng Xiaoping has been the effective ruler of China although he has not held any of the three major offices of state.

CHINA, REPUBLIC OF (TAIWAN)

Presidents
Gen. Li Tsung-jen *KMT* 1949–50
Chiang Kai-shek (*Jiang Jie Shi*) *KMT* 1950–75
Dr Yen Chia-kan *KMT* 1975–78
Chiang Ching-kuo *KMT*1978–88
Lee Teng-hui *KMT* 1988–
Key: *KMT* = Kuomintang

CZECHOSLOVAKIA

Presidents
Tomás Garrigue Masaryk 1918–35
Edvard Benes 1935–38

Gen. Jan Sirovy 1938
Dr Emil Hacha 1938–39
(German occupation 1939–45)
Edvard Benes *np* 1940–45 (in exile); 1945–48
Klemens Gottwald *Comm* 1945–53
Antonín Zapotocky *Comm* 1953–57
Antonín Novotny *Comm* 1957–68
Gen. Ludvik Svoboda *Comm* 1968–75
Dr Gustáv Husák *Comm* 1975–89
Vaclav Havel *CF* 1989–92

Prime Ministers* (1946–92)
Klemens Gottwald *Comm* 1946–48
Antonín Zapotocky *Comm* 1948–53
Viliam Siroky *Comm* 1953–63
Josef Lenart *Comm* 1963–68
Oldrich Cernik *Comm* 1968–70
Lubomir Strougal *Comm* 1970–88
Ladislav Adamec *Comm* 1988–89
Marian Calfa *CF-PAV coalition* 1989–92
Vaclav Klaus *CDU* 1992
Key: *CDU* = Civic Democratic Union; *CF* = Civic Forum; *Comm* = Communist; *np* = non-party; *PAV* = Public Against Violence. *From 1948 to 1989 the effective ruler of Czechoslovakia was the leader of the Communist Party; the more notable included: Rudolf Slánsky 1948–52; Antonín Novotny 1953–68; Alexander Dubcek 1968–69; Gustáv Husák 1969–87.

CZECH REPUBLIC

Presidents of the Czech Republic
Vaclav Havel 1993–

Prime Ministers of the Czech Republic
Vaclav Klaus *CDU* 1993–
Key: *CDU* = Civic Democratic Union

DENMARK

Kings and Queens (since 1448)
Christian I 1448–81
Hans 1481–1513
Christian II 1513–23
Frederik I 1523–33
Christian III 1533–59
Frederik II 1559–88
Christian IV 1588–1648
Frederik III 1648–70
Christian V 1670–99
Frederik IV 1699–1730
Christian VI 1730–46
Frederik V 1746–66
Christian VII 1766–1808
Frederik VI 1808–39
Christian VIII 1839–48
Frederik VII 1848–63
Christian IX 1863–1906
Frederik VIII 1906–1912
Christian X 1912–47
Frederik IX 1947–72
Margrethe II 1972–

Prime Ministers (since 1945)
Vilhelm Buhl *Coalition* 1945
Knud Kristensen *Lib* 1945–47
Hans Hedtoft *Soc Dem* 1947–50
Erik Eriksen *Lib-Con* 1950–53
Hans Hedtoft *Soc Dem* 1953–55
Hans Christian Hansen *Soc Dem* 1955–60
Viggo Kampmann *Soc Dem* 1960
Jens Otto Krag *Soc Dem* 1960–68
Hilmar Baunsgaard *Radical* 1968–71
Jens Otto Krag *Soc Dem* 1971–72
Anker Jorgensen *Soc Dem* 1972–73
Poul Hartling *Lib* 1973–75
Anker Jorgensen *Soc Dem* 1975–82
Poul Schlüter *Lib-Con* 1982–93
Poul Nyrup Rasmussen *Soc Dem* 1993–
Key: *Con* = Conservative; *Lib* = Liberal; *Soc Dem* = Social Democrat

EGYPT (Modern)

Kings
Fuad I 1922–36
Faruq 1936–1952
Fuad II 1952–53

Presidents
Gen. Muhammad Neguib *military* 1952–54
Col. Gamal Abdel Nasser *military* 1954–70
Anwar Sadat *NDP* 1970–81 (assassinated)
Gen. Muhammad Hosni Mubarak *NDP* 1981–
Key: *NDP* = National Democratic Party

FINLAND

Presidents
Dr Kaarlo Juho Stahlberg *NPP* 1919–25
Lauri Relander *AP* 1925–31
Dr Pehr Svinhufvud *Coalition* 1931–37
Kyösti Kallio *Coalition* 1937–40
Risto Ryti *Coalition* 1940–44
Marshal Carl Gustav Mannerheim *Coalition* 1944–46
Juhi Kusti Paasikiva *Coalition* 1946–56
Dr Urho Kaleva Kekkonen *AP* 1956–82
Mauno Henrik Koïvisto *Soc Dem* 1982–94
Martti Ahtisaari Soc Dem 1994–
Key: *AP* = Rural Party; *NPP* = National Progressive Party; *Soc Dem* = Social Democrat

FRANCE

Kings (since 987)
Hugues 987–996
Robert II 996–1031
Henri I 1031–60
Philippe I 1060–1108
Louis VI 1108–37
Louis VII 1137–80
Philippe II 1180–1223
Louis VIII 1223–26
Louis IX (St Louis) 1226–70
Philippe III 1270–85
Philippe IV 1285–1314
Louis X 1314–16
Jean I 1316
Philippe V 1316–22
Charles IV 1322–28
Philippe VI 1328–50
Jean II 1350–64
Charles V 1364–80
Charles VI 1380–1422
Charles VII 1422–61
Louis XI 1461–83
Charles VIII 1483–98
Louis XII 1498–1515
François I 1515–47
Henri II 1547–59

François II 1559–60
Charles IX 1560–74
Henri III 1574–89
Henri IV 1589–1610
Louis XIII 1610–43
Louis XIV 1643–1715
Louis XV 1715–74
Louis XVI 1774–92
(Louis XVII nominally 1793–95)

First Republic
The Convention 1792–1795
Directorate 1795–99
Consulate (three consuls) 1799–1804

Emperor (First Empire)
Napoleon I (Bonaparte) 1804–14

King
Louis XVIII 1814–15

Emperors (First Empire)
Napoleon I (restored) 1815
(Napoleon II nominally 1815, for 16 days)

Kings
Louis XVIII (restored) 1815–24
Charles X 1824–30
(Louis XIX nominally 1830, for 1 day)
(Henri V nominally 1830, for 8 days)
Louis–Philippe 1830–48

President of Second Republic
Louis–Napoleon Bonaparte 1848–52

Emperor (Second Empire)
Napoleon III (Louis–Napoleon Bonaparte) 1852–70

Presidents of Third Republic
Adolphe Thiers 1871–73
Patrice Mac–Mahon, duc de Magenta 1873–79
Jules Grévy 1879–87
Sadi Carnot 1887–94 (assassinated)
Jean Casimir–Périer 1894–95
Félix Faure 1895–99
Emile Loubet 1899–1906
Armand Fallières 1906–13
Raymond Poincaré 1913–20
Paul Deschanel 1920
Alexandre Millerand 1920–24
Gaston Doumergue 1924–31
Paul Doumer 1931–32 (assassinated)
Albert Lebrun 1932–40

French State (at Vichy)
Philippe Pétain 1940–44

Heads of Provisional Government
General Charles de Gaulle 1944–46
Félix Gouin 1946
Georges Bidault 1946
Vincent Auriol 1946
Léon Blum 1946–47

Presidents of Fourth Republic
Vincent Auriol 1947–54
René Coty 1954–58

Presidents of Fifth Republic
General Charles de Gaulle 1959–69
Georges Pompidou 1969–74
Valéry Giscard d'Estaing 1974–81
François Mitterand 1981–95
Jacques Chirac 1995–

Prime Ministers of Third Republic
In all there were 88 PMs of the Third Republic; the more notable included: Léon Gambetta 1881–82; Georges Clemenceau 1906–09, 1917–20; Aristide Briand 1909–11, 1913, 1915–17, 1921–22, 1925–26, 1929; Raymond Poincaré 1912–13, 1922–24, 1926–29; Edouard Herriot 1924–25, 1926, 1932; Pierre Laval 1931–32, 1935–36; Edouard Daladier 1933, 1934, 1938–40; Léon Blum 1936–37, 1938.

Prime Ministers of Fourth Republic
In all there were 24 PMs of the Fourth Republic; the more notable included: Robert Schuman 1947–1948; 1948; Pierre Mendès–France 1954–55; General Charles de Gaulle 1958–59.

Prime Ministers of Fifth Republic
Michel Debré *Gaullist* 1959–62
Georges Pompidou *Gaullist* 1962–68
Maurice Couve de Murville *Gaullist* 1968–69
Jacques Chaban–Delmas *Gaullist* 1969–72
Pierre Messmer *Gaullist* 1972–74
Jacques Chirac *Gaullist* 1974–76
Raymond Barre *np* 1976–81
Pierre Mauroy *Soc* 1981–84
Laurent Fabius *Soc* 1984–86
Jacques Chirac *Gaullist* 1986–88
Michel Rocard *Soc* 1988–91
Edith Cresson *Soc* 1991–92
Pierre Bérégovoy *Soc* 1992–93
Edouard Balladur *Gaullist* 1993–95
Alain Juppé *Gaullist* 1995–
Key: *np* = non–party; *Soc* = Socialist

GERMANY

Kings of Prussia
Friedrich I 1701–13
Friedrich Wilhelm I 1713–40
Friedrich II (*Frederick the Great*) 1740–86
Friedrich Wilhelm II 1786–97
Friedrich Wilhelm III 1797–1840
Friedrich Wilhelm IV 1840–61
Wilhelm I 1861–71 when he also became Emperor of Germany

Emperors of Germany
Wilhelm I 1871–88
Friedrich III 1888
Wilhelm II 1888–1918

Provisional Government
Six–man ruling council 1918–19

Presidents
Friedrich Ebert 1919–25
Marshal Paul von Beneckendorff und von Hindenburg 1925–34

Leaders of the Third German Reich
Adolf Hitler 1934–45
Admiral Karl Dönitz 1945 (6 days)

Allied occupation 1945–49

Presidents of the Federal Republic
Prof. Theodor Heuss 1949–59
Dr Heinrich Lübke 1959–69
Dr Gustav Heinemann 1969–74
Walter Scheel 1974–79
Karl Carstens 1979–84
Richard von Weizsacker 1984–94
Roman Herzog 1994–

Chancellors of the German Empire
Otto, Prince von Bismarck-Schönhausen 1871–90
Count Leo von Caprivi 1890–94
Prince Chlodwig von Hohenlohe-Schillingsfürst 1894–1900
Prince Bernhard von Bülow 1900–09
Theobald von Bethmann-Hollweg 1909–17
Dr George Michaelis 1917
Count Georg von Hertling 1917
Prince Maximilian of Baden 1918
Friedrich Ebert 1918

Chancellors of the Republic
Six-man ruling council 1918–19
Philipp Scheidemann *SPD* 1919
Gustav Bauer *SPD* 1919–20
Hermann Müller *SPD* 1920
Konstantin Fehrenbach *Centre-Cath* 1920–21
Dr Joseph Wirth *Centre* 1921–22
Dr Wilhelm Cuno *np* 1922–23
Dr Gustav Stresemann *DVolk* 1923
Dr Wilhelm Marx *Centre* 1923–25
Dr Hans Luther *np* 1925–26
Dr Wilhelm Marx *Centre* 1926–28
Hermann Müller *SPD* 1928–30
Dr Heinrich Brüning *Centre* 1930–32
Franz von Papen *Nat* 1932
General Curt von Schleider *np* 1932–33
Adolf Hitler *Nazi* 1933–34

The Third German Reich 1934–45 (see above)

Allied occupation 1945–49 (see above)

Federal German Chancellors
Konrad Adenauer *CDU* 1949–63
Prof Ludwig Erhard *CDU* 1963–1966
Dr Kurt Georg Kiesinger *CDU* 1966–1969
Dr Willy Brandt *SPD* 1969–1974
Walter Scheel *FDP* 1974
Helmut Schmidt *SPD* 1974–82
Helmut Kohl *CDU* 1982–
Key: *Cath* = Catholic; *CDU* = Christian Democrat (conservative); *DVolk* = German People's Party; *Nat* = National Party; *np* = non–party; *SPD* = Social Democrat; *FDP* = Free Democratic Party

East Germany
The German Democratic Republic (East Germany), which was established in the Soviet zone of occupation in 1949, united with the Federal Republic of Germany in October 1990. Effective power was held by the leader of the Socialist Unity Party (the Communist Party); the more notable included: Walter Ulbricht 1950–71; Erich Honecker 1971–89.

GREECE

Kings
Othon 1832–62
Giorgios I 1863–1913
Konstantinos I 1913–17
Alexandros 1917–20
Konstantinos I (restored) 1920–22
Giorgios II 1922–24

Presidents of the Hellenic Republic
Admiral Pavlos Kondoriotis 1924–26
Gen. Theodoros Pangalos 1926
Admiral Pavlos Kondoriotis 1926–29
Alexandros Zaimis 1929–35

Kings
Giorgios II (restored) 1935–47
Pavlos 1947–64
Konstantinos II 1964–73

Presidents of the Hellenic Republic
Giorgios Papadopoulos 1973
Gen Phaedon Gizikis 1973–74
Mikael Stassinopoulos 1974–75
Konstantinos Tsatos 1975–85
Christos Sartzetakis 1985–90
Konstantinos Karamanlis 1990–95
Kostis Stephanopoulos 1995–

Prime Ministers of Greece (since 1967)
Giorgios Papadopoulos *military* 1967–73
Spyros Markezinis *military* 1973
Adamantios Androutsopoulos *military* 1973–74
Konstantinos Karamanlis *NDP* 1974–80
Giorgios Rallis *NDP* 1980–84
Andreas Papandreou *PASOK* 1984–89
Tzannis Tzannetakis *caretaker* 1989
Yannis Grivas *caretaker* 1989–90
Xenefon Zolotas *caretaker* 1990
Konstantinos Mitsotakis *NDP* 1990–93
Andreas Papandreou *PASOK* 1993–
Key: *NDP* = New Democracy Party (conservative); *PASOK* = Panhellenic Socialist Movement

HOLY ROMAN EMPIRE

Emperors
Karl I (*Charlemagne*) 800–814
Ludwig I (*Louis I*) 814–40
Lothar I 840–55
Ludwig II (*Louis II*) 855–75
Karl II (*Charles II*) 875–77
Karl III (*Charles III*) 877–87
Arnulf 887–98
Ludwig III (*Louis III*) 899–911
Konrad I* 911–18
Heinrich I* (*Henry I*) 919–36
Otto I 936–73
Otto II 973–83
Otto III 983–1002
Heinrich II (*Henry II*) 1002–34
Konrad II 1024–39
Heinrich III (*Henry III*) 1039–56
Heinrich IV (*Henry IV*) 1056–1105
Heinrich V (*Henry V*) 1105–25
Lothar II 1125–37
Konrad III* 1138–52
Friedrich I (*Frederick Barbarossa*) 1152–90
Heinrich VI (*Henry VI*) 1190–97
Philipp* 1198–1208
Otto IV 1198–1215
Friedrich II (*Frederick II*) 1215–50
Konrad IV* 1250–54
Konrad V 1254 (claimant)
Richard* 1257
Alfons* 1267
Rudolf I* 1273–91
Adolf* 1292–98
Albrecht I (*Albert I*) 1298–1308
Heinrich VII (*Henry VII*) 1308–13
Ludwig IV (*Louis IV*) 1314–47
Karl IV (*Charles IV*) 1347–78
Wenzel 1378–1400
Rupprecht Klem* 1400–1410

Sigismund 1410–37
Albrecht II* (*Albert II*) 1438–39
Friedrich III (*Frederick III*) 1440–93
Maximilian I 1493–1519
Karl V (*Charles V*) 1519–55
Ferdinand I 1556–64
Rudolf II 1576–1612
Matthias 1612–19
Ferdinand II 1619–37
Ferdinand III 1637–57
Leopold I 1658–1705
Joseph I 1705–11
Karl VI (*Charles VI*) 1711–40
Karl VII (*Charles VII*) 1742–45
Franz I Stephan (*Francis I*) 1745–65
Joseph II 1765–90
Leopold II 1790–92
Franz II (*Francis II*) 1792–1806, when he abdicated and abolished the Holy Roman Empire (see Austria).
* = emperor-elect

HUNGARY

Presidents
Zoltan Tildy *SP* 1946–48
Arpad Szakasits *Comm* 1948–50
Sándor Rónai *Comm* 1950–52
István Dobi *Comm* 1952–67
Pál Losonczi *Comm* 1967–87
Károly Németh *Comm* 1987–88
Bruno Straub *Comm* 1988–89
Mátyás Szuros *caretaker* 1989–90
Arpad Gongz *AFD* 1990–

Prime Ministers* (since 1948)
István Dobi *Comm* 1948–52
Mátyás Rákosi *Comm* 1952–53
Imre Nagy *Comm* 1953–55
Andras Hegedus *Comm* 1955–56
Imre Nagy *Comm* 1956
Janos Kadar *Comm* 1956–58
Dr Ferenc Münnich *Comm* 1958–61
Janos Kadar *Comm* 1961–65
Gyula Kallai *Comm* 1965–67
Jenö Fock *Comm* 1967–75
György Lázár *Comm* 1975–87
Károly Grocz *Comm* 1987–88
Miklos Németh *Comm* 1988–90
Joszef Antall *DF* 1990–93
Peter Boross DF 1993–94
Gyula Horn Soc 1994–
Key: *AFD* = Alliance of Free Democrats (liberal); *Comm* = Communist; *DF* = Democratic Forum (conservative); Soc = Socialist Party; *SP* = Smallholders' Party *From 1948 to 1989 the effective ruler of Hungary was the leader of Socialist Workers' (Communist) Party; they included: Mátyás Rákosi 1949–53 and 1953–56; Janos Kadar 1956–88

INDIA

Presidents
Dr Rajendra Prasad 1949–62
Dr Sarvapalli Radhakrishnan 1962–67
Dr Zahir Hussain 1967–69
Varahgiri Venkata Giri 1969–74
Fakhruddin Ali Ahmed 1974–77
Basappa Danappa Jatti 1977
Neelam Sanjiva Reddy 1977–82
Giani Zail Singh 1982–87
Ramaswamy Venkataraman 1987–92
Shankar Dayal Sharma 1992–

Prime Ministers
Jawaharlal Nehru *Congress* 1949–64
Gulzarilal Nanda *Congress* 1964
Lal Bahadur Shastri *Congress* 1964–66
Gulzarilal Nanda *Congress* 1966
Indira Gandhi *Congress (I)* 1966–77
Morarji Desai *Janata* 1977–79
Charan Singh *Janata* 1979–80
Indira Gandhi *Congress (I)* 1980–84 (assassinated)
Rajiv Gandhi *Congress (I)* 1984–89
Vishwanath Pratap Singh *Coalition* 1989–90
Chandra Shekhar *Coalition* 1990–91
P.V. Narasimha Rao *Congress (I)* 1991–

INDONESIA

Presidents
Dr Muhammad Achmed Sukarno *np* 1949–67
Gen. T.N.I. Suharto *Golkar* 1967–
Key: *np* = non–party

IRAN

Shahs (from 1796)
Agha Muhammad Khan 1796–97 (assassinated)
Fath 'Ali Shah 1797–1834
Muhammad Shah 1834–48
Naser od–Din Shah 1848–96 (assassinated)
Mozaffar od-Din Shah 1896–1907
Muhammad 'Ali Shah 1907–09
Ahmed Mirza Shah 1909–25
Reza Shah Pahlavi 1925–41
Muhammad Reza Shah Pahlavi 1941–79

Presidents
Islamic Council 1979–80
Abdolhasan Bani-Sadr 1980
Presidential Council 1980–81
Muhammad Ali Rajai 1981
Ali Khamenei 1981–89
Ali Akbar Hashemi Rafsanjani 1989–

IRAQ

Kings
Faysal I 1923–33
Ghazi I 1933–39 (killed accidentally)
Faysal II 1939–58 (assassinated)
Presidents
Gen Muhammad Najib Rubai 1958–63
Col Abdul Salam Mohammed Aref 1963–66
Maj-Gen Abdul Rahman Aref 1966–68
Maj-Gen Ahmed Hassan Bakr 1968–79
Saddam Hussein 1979–

IRELAND

Presidents
Dr Douglas Hyde 1938–45
Sean Thomas O'Kelly 1945–59
Eamon de Valera 1959–73
Erskine Childers 1973–74
Cearbhall O'Dalaigh 1974–76
Dr Patrick Hillery 1976–90
Mary Robinson 1990–

Heads of Government (before 1937 Executive President; since 1937 Taoiseach)
Arthur Griffith *Rep* 1922

Michael Collins *Rep* 1922
William Thomas Cosgrave *FG* 1922–32
Eamon de Valera *FF* 1932–48
John Costello *FG* 1948–51
Eamon de Valera *FF* 1951–54
John Costello *FG* 1954–57
Eamon de Valera *FF* 1957–59
Sean Lemass *FF* 1959–66
John Mary (Jack) Lynch *FF* 1966–73
Liam Cosgrave *FG–Lab* 1973–77
John Mary (Jack) Lynch *FF* 1977–79
Charles Haughey *FF* 1979–81
Garret Fitzgerald *FG–Lab* 1981–82
Charles Haughey *FF* 1982
Garret Fitzgerald *FG–Lab* 1982–87
Charles Haughey *FF* 1987–92
Albert Reynolds *FF–Lab* 1992–94
John Bruton *FG–Lab* 1994–
Key: *FF* = Fianna Fail; *FG* = Fine Gael; *Lab* = Labour; *Rep* = Republican.

ISRAEL

Prime Ministers
David Ben Gurion *Mapai* 1948–53
Moshe Sharett *Mapai* 1953–55
David Ben Gurion *Mapai* 1955–63
Levi Eshkol *Mapai* 1963–69
Gen. Yigal Allon *Lab* 1969
Golda Meir *Lab* 1969–74
Yitzhak *Lab* 1974–77
Menahem Begin *Likud* 1977–83
Yitzhak Shamir *Likud* 1983–84
Shimon Peres *Coalition* 1984–86
Yitzhak Shamir *Coalition** 1986–92
Yitzhak Rabin *Lab* 1992–
Key: *Lab* = Labour (formed from Mapai in 1968); * from 1990 *Likud*.

ITALY

Kings
Vittorio Emanuele II 1861–78
Umberto I 1878–1900 (assassinated)
Vittorio Emanuele III 1900–46
Umberto II 1946

Presidents
Alcide de Gasperi 1946
Enrico de Nicola 1946–48
Luigi Einaudi 1948–55
Giovanni Gronchi 1955–62
Antonio Segni 1962–64
Giuseppe Saragat 1964–71
Giovanni Leone 1971–78
Amintore Fanfani (acting) 1978
Alessandro Pertini 1978–85
Francesco Cossiga 1985–92
Oscar Luigi Scalfaro 1992–

Prime Ministers of the Kingdom of Italy
In all there were 42 PMs of the Kingdom of Italy; the more notable included: Camillo Benso, Count Cavour 1861; Francesco Crispi 1879–81, 1893–96; Giovanni Giolitti 1892–93, 1903–05, 1911–14, 1920–21; Francesco Nitti 1919–20; Benito Mussolini 1922–43; Marshal Pietro Badoglio 1943–44; Alcide de Gasperi 1945–46.

Prime Ministers of the Republic
Alcide de Gasperi *CD Coalition* 1946–53
Giuseppe Pella *CD Coalition* 1953–54
Amintore Fanfani *CD Coalition* 1954
Mario Scelba *CD Coalition* 1954–55
Antonio Segni *CD Coalition* 1955–57
Adone Zoli *CD Coalition* 1957–58
Amintore Fanfani *CD Coalition* 1958–59
Antonio Segni *CD Coalition* 1959–60
Fernando Tambroni *CD Coalition* 1960
Amintore Fanfani *CD Coalition* 1960–63
Giovanni Leone *CD Coalition* 1963
Aldo Moro *CD Coalition* 1963–68
Giovanni Leone *CD Coalition* 1968
Mariano Rumor *CD Coalition* 1968–70
Emilio Colombo *CD Coalition* 1970–72
Giulio Andreotti *CD Coalition* 1972–73
Mariano Rumor *CD Coalition* 1973–74
Aldo Moro *CD Coalition* 1974–76
Giulio Andreotti *CD Coalition* 1976–79
Ugo La Malfa *Rep Coalition* 1979
Giulio Andreotti *CD Coalition* 1979
Francesco Cossiga *CD Coalition* 1979–80
Arnaldo Forlani *CD Coalition* 1980–81
Giovanni Spaldolini *Coalition* 1981–82
Amintore Fanfani *CD Coalition* 1982–83
Bettino Craxi *Soc Coalition* 1983–87
Amintore Fanfani *CD Coalition* 1987
Giovanni Goria *CD Coalition* 1987–88
Ciriaco De Mita *CD Coalition* 1988–90
Giulio Andreotti *CD Coalition* 1990–92
Giuliano Amato *Soc Coalition* 1992–93
Carlo Azeglio Ciampi *non-party* 1993–
Silvio Berlusconi *Forza Italia Coalition* 1993–95
Lamberto Dini *non–party* 1995–
Key: *CD* = Christian Democrat; *Coalition* = some of the periods indicated as government by coalition included more than one coalition; *Rep* = Republican; *Soc* = Socialist

JAPAN

Emperors (since 1763)
Gosakuramachi 1763–71
Gomomozono 1771–79
Kokaku 1779–1817
Ninko 1817–46
Komei (*personal name* Osahito) 1846–66
Meiji (*personal name* Mutsuhito) 1867–1912
Taisho (*personal name* Yoshihito) 1912–26
Showa (*personal name* Hirohito) 1926–89
Heisei (*personal name* Akihito) 1989–

Prime Ministers of Japan (since 1945)
Kijuro Shidehara *np* 1945–46
Ichiro Hatayma *Lib* 1946
Shigeru Yoshida *np* 1946–47
Tetsu Katayama *Soc* 1947–48
Hitoshi Ashida *Coalition* 1948
Shigeru Yoshida *Lib* 1948–55
Ichiro Hatoyama *Lib-Dem* 1955–56
Tanzan Ishibashi *Lib-Dem* 1956–1957
Nobusuke Kishi *Lib-Dem* 1957–60
Hayeto Ikeda *Lib-Dem* 1960–64
Eisaku Sato *Lib-Dem* 1964–72
Kakeui Tanaka *Lib-Dem* 1972–74
Takeo Miki *Lib-Dem* 1974–76
Takeo Fukuda *Lib-Dem* 1976–78
Masayoshi Ohira *Lib-Dem* 1978–80
Zenko Suzuki *Lib-Dem* 1980–82
Yasuhiro Nakasone *Lib-Dem* 1982–87

Noboru Takeshita *Lib-Dem* 1987–89
Sosuke Uno *Lib-Dem* 1989
Toshiki Kaifu *Lib-Dem* 1989–91
Kiichi Miyazawa *Lib-Dem* 1991–93
Morihiro Hosoakawa *Coalition* 1993–94
Tsutomu Hata *Coalition* 1994
Tomiichi Murayama *Soc* 1994–
Key: *Lib* = Liberal; *Lib-Dem* = Liberal Democrat; *np* = non-party; *Soc* = Socialist.

KOREA

Presidents of South Korea
Dr Syngman Rhee *Lib* 1948–60
Huh Chung *acting* 1960
Yun Po Sun *Dem* 1960–62
Gen. Park Chung Hi *military-DRP* 1962–1980 (assassinated)
Choi Kyu Hah *DRP* 1980
Gen. Chun Doo Hwan *military-DJP* 1980–87
Roh Tae Woo *DJP/DLP* 1987–93
Kim Young Sam *DLP* 1993–
Key: *Lib* = Liberal; *DJP* = Democratic Justice Party; *DLP* = Democratic Liberal Party; *DRP* = Democratic Reunification Party; *Dem* = Democrat.

LUXEMBOURG

Grand Dukes and Grand Duchesses
Guillaume I 1815–40
Guillaume II 1840–49
Guillaume III 1849–90
Adolphe I 1890–1905
Guillaume IV 1905–1912
Marie-Adélaide 1912–19
Charlotte 1919–64
Jean I (*John*) 1964–

Prime Ministers (since 1945)
Pierre Dupong *Christian Social* 1945–53
Joseph Bech *Christian Social* 1953–58
Pierre Frieden *Christian Social* 1958–59
Pierre Werner *Christian Social* 1959–74
Gaston Thorn *Democrat* 1974–79
Pierre Werner *Christian Social* 1979–84
Jacques Santer *Christian Social* 1984–95
Jean-Claude Juncker *Christian Social* 1995–

MALAYSIA

Prime Ministers
Tuanku Abdul Rahman 1963–70
Tuanku Abdul Razak 1970–76
Datuk Hussein bin Onn 1976–81
Mohammad Mahathir 1981–

MEXICO

Presidents
There have been over 80 presidents of Mexico; the more notable before 1924 included: Gen. Antonio López de Santa Anna 1833–35, 1839, 1842, 1843, 1844; Gen. Benito Juárez 1858, 1859–61, 1867–72; Gen. Porfirio Diáz 1877–80, 1884–1911.

Presidents since 1924
Gen. Plutarco Elías Calles *PRI* 1924–28
Emilio Portes Gil *PRI* 1928–30
Pascual Ortiz Rubio *PRI* 1930–32
Gen. Abelardo Rodríguez *PRI* 1932–34
Gen. Lázardo Cárdenas *PRI* 1934–40
Gen. Manuel ávila Camacho *PRI* 1940–46
Miguel Alemán Valdès *PRI* 1946–52
Adolfo Ruiz Cortines *PRI* 1952–58
Adolfo López Mateos *PRI* 1958–64
Dr Gustavo Díaz Ordaz *PRI* 1964–70
Luis Echeverría Alvárez *PRI* 1970–76
José López Portillo *PRI* 1976–82
Miguel de la Madrid Hurtado *PRI* 1982–88
Carlos Salinas de Gortari *PRI* 1988–94
Ernesto Zedillo *PRI* 1994–
Key: *PRI* = Institutional Revolutionary Party (so–named since 1929)

NETHERLANDS

Kings and Queens
Willem I 1815–40
Willem II 1840–49
Willem III 1849–90
Wilhelmina 1890–1948
Juliana 1948–80
Beatrix 1980–

Prime Ministers (since 1945)
Prof. Willem Schermerhorn *Lab-Cath* 1945–46
Dr Louis Beel *Cath-Lab* 1946–48
Dr Willem Drees *Lab-Cath* 1948–58
Dr Louis Beel *Cath-led coalition* 1958–59
Prof. Jan de Quay *Cath-led coalition* 1959
Dr Louis Beel *Cath-led coalition* 1959
Prof. Jan de Quay *Cath-led coalition* 1959–63
Dr Victor Marijnen *Cath-led coalition* 1963–65
Dr Joseph Cals *Cath-led coalition* 1965–66
Prof. Jelle Zijstra *Cath-led coalition* 1966–67
Petrus de Jong *Cath-led coalition* 1967–71
Barend Biesheuvel *Cath-led coalition* 1971–73
Dr Johannes den Uyl *Lab-led coalition* 1973–77
Andreas van Agt *CDA-led coalition* 1977–82
Rudolph Lubbers *CDA-led coalition* 1982–94
Willem (Wim) Kok *Lab-led coalition* 1994–
Key: *Cath* = Catholic (merged with another confessional party to form Christian Democratic Appeal in 1980); *CD* = Christian Democratic Appeal; *Lab* = Labour.

NEW ZEALAND

Prime Ministers of the Dominion
Sir Joseph Ward *Lib* 1907–12
William Fergusson Massey *Ref* 1912–25
Sir Francis Bell *Ref* 1925
Joseph Gordon Coates *Ref* 1925–28
Sir Joseph Ward *UP* 1928–30
George Forbes *Ref-UP* 1930–35
Michael Joseph Savage *Lab* 1935–40
Peter Fraser *Lab* 1940–49
Sir Sidney George Holland *Nat* 1949–57
Sir Keith Jacka Holyoake *Nat* 1957
Sir Walter Nash *Lab* 1957–60
Sir Keith Jacka Holyoake *Lab* 1960–72
Sir John Ross Marshall *Nat* 1972
Norman Eric Kirk *Lab* 1972–74
Hugh Watt (acting PM) *Lab* 1974
Wallace Rowling *Lab* 1974–75
Sir Robert David Muldoon *Nat* 1975–84
David Lange *Lab* 1984–89
Geoffrey Palmer *Lab* 1989–90
Michael Moore *Lab* 1990
Jim Bolger *Nat* 1990–

Key: *Lab* = Labour; *Lib* = Liberal (succeeded by the United Party in 1927); *Nat* = National Party (formed from a merger of the Reform Party and the United Party in 1936); *Ref* = Reform Party; *UP* = United Party.

NIGERIA

Presidents

Dr Nnamdi Azikiwe 1963–66
Dr Nwafor Orizu *caretaker* 1966
Gen Johnson Aguiyi-Ironsi *military* 1966 (assassinated)
Gen Yakubu Gowon *military* 1966–75
Brig Murtala Ramat Muhammad *military* 1975–76 (assassinated)
Lieut-Gen Olusegun Obasanjo *military* 1976–79
Alhaji Shehu Shagari 1979–83
Gen Muhammadu Buhari *military* 1983–85
Gen Ibrahim Babangida *military* 1985–93
Chief Ernest Adegunle Shonekan *caretaker* 1993
Gen Sani Abacha *military* 1993–

NORWAY

Kings (since independence restored)

Haakon VII 1905–51
Olav V 1951–91
Harald V 1991–

Prime Ministers (since 1945)

Einar Gerhardsen *Lab* 1945–51
Oscar Torp *Lab* 1951–55
Einar Gerhardsen *Lab* 1955–63
Johan Lyng *Lib-CP-CPP* 1963
Einar Gerhardsen *Lab* 1963–65
Per Borten *CP-led coalition* 1965–71
Trygve Bratteli *Lab* 1971–72
Lars Korvald *Coalition* 1972–73
Trygve Bratteli *Lab* 1973–76
Odvar Nordli *Lab* 1976–81
Gro Harlem Bruntland *Lab* 1981
Kare Willoch *Con (from 1983 coalition)* 1981–86
Gro Harlem Bruntland *Lab* 1986–89
Jan Syse *Con-led coalition* 1989–90
Gro Harlem Brundtland *Lab* 1990–

Key: *CP* = Centre Party; *CPP* = Christian People's Party; *Lab* = Labour; *Lib* = Liberal; *Con* = Conservative

PAKISTAN

Presidents

Maj. Gen. Iskander Mirza 1956–58
Gen. Muhammad Ayub Khan 1958–69
Gen. Agha Muhammad Yahya Khan 1969–71
Zulfiqar Ali Bhutto 1971–73
Fazal Elahi Chaudhri 1973–78
Gen. Muhammad Zia ul–Haq 1978–88
Ghulam Ishaq Khan 1988–93
Wassim Sajjad 1993
Farooq Ahmed Leghari 1993–

Prime Ministers

Liaquat Ali Khan *ML* 1947–51
Khwaja Nazimuddin *ML* 1951–53
Mohammed Ali *ML* 1953–55
Chaudhri Muhammad Ali *ML* 1955–56
Hussein Shaheed Suhrawardy *AL* 1956–57
Ismael Ibrahim Chundrigar *AL* 1957
Malik Firoz Khan Noon *AL* 1957–58
Gen. Muhammad Ayub Khan *military* 1958–69
Gen. Agha Muhammad Yahya Khan *military* 1969–71
Nural Amin *caretaker* 1971
Zulfiqar Ali Bhutto *PPP* 1971–77
Gen. Muhammad Zia ul-Haq *military* 1977–85
Muhammad Khan Junejo *ML* 1985–88
Gen. Muhammad Zia ul-Haq *military* 1988
(Period without a PM 1988)
Benazir Bhutto *PPP* 1988–90
Ghulam Mustafa Jatoi *IDA* 1990
Nawaz Sharif *IDA* 1990–93
Balkh Sher Mazari *caretaker* 1993
Moeen Qureshi *caretaker* 1993
Benazir Bhutto *PPP* 1993–

Key: *AL* = Awami League; *IDA* = Islamic Democratic Alliance; *ML* = Muslim League; *PPP* = Pakistan People's Party.

PHILIPPINES

Presidents

Manuel Roxas *Lib* 1946–48
Elphino Quirino *Lib* 1948–53
Rámon Magsaysay *Nat* 1953–57
Carlos Polestico Garcia *Nat* 1957–61
Diosdado Macapagal *Lib* 1961–65
Ferdinand Marcos *Nat* 1965–86
Corazón Aquino *UNIDO* 1986–92
Gen. Fidel Ramos *PPP* 1992–

Key: *Lib* = Liberal; *Nat* = Nacionalista; *PPP* = People Power Party.

POLAND

Presidents†

Marshal Jósef Pilsudski* *PPS* 1918–22
Gabriel Narutowicz *caretaker* 1922
Stanislaw Wojciechowski *np* 1922–26
Prof Ignacy Móscicki *np* 1926–39
(Poland under German occupation 1939–44)
Boleslaw Bierut *Comm* 1944–52
Aleksander Zawadski *Comm* 1952–64
Edward Ochab *Comm* 1964–68
Marshal Marian Spychalski *Comm* 1968–70
Józef Cyrankiewicz *Comm* 1970–72
Prof Henryk Jablonski *Comm* 1972–85
Gen. Wojciech Jaruzelski *Comm* 1985–1990
Lech Walesa *first Solidarity/then non-party* 1990–

Prime Ministers (since 1949)

Józef Cyrankiewicz *Comm* 1949–52
Boleslaw Bierut *Comm* 1952–54
Józef Cyrankiewicz *Comm* 1954–70
Piotr Jaroszewicz *Comm* 1970–80
Edward Babiuch *Comm* 1980
Józef Pinkowski *Comm* 1980–81
Gen. Wojciech Jaruzelski *Comm* 1981–85
Prof. Zbigniew Messner *Comm* 1985–88
Dr Mieczyslaw Rakowski *Comm* 1988–89
Tadeusz Mazowiecki *Solidarity* 1989–91
Jan Krzysztof Bielecki *Solidarity* 1991
Jan Olszewski *Centre Alliance* 1991–92
Waldemar Pawlak *PPP* 1992
Hannah Suchocka *Dem U* 1992–93
Waldemar Pawlak *PPP Coalition* 1993–95
Jozef Oleksy *Dem Left Coalition* 1995–

Key: *Comm* = Communist; *Dem Left* = Democratic Left (former Communist); *Dem U* = Democratic Union; *np* = non–party; *PPP* = Polish Peasant Party; *PPS* = Polish Socialist Party; * Pilsudski was military dictator of Poland 1926–35. †From 1945 to 1989 the effective ruler of Poland was the leader of the

Communist Party; the more notable included: Boleslaw Bierut 1945–56; Wladyslaw Gomulka 1956–70; Edward Gierek 1970–89

PORTUGAL

Presidents

Dr Téofilo Braga 1910–11
Dr Manuel da Arriaga 1911–15
Dr Téofilo Braga 1915
Dr Bernardino Luis Machado 1915–17
Major Cardoso da Silva Pais 1917–18
Admiral João da Canto e Castro 1918–19
Dr Antonio José de Almeida 1919–23
Manoel Teixeira Gomes 1923–25
Dr Bernardino Luis Machado 1925–26
Commander José Mendes Cabecadas 1926
Gen. Manoel Gomes de Costa 1926
Gen. Oscar de Carmona 1926–51
Marshal Francisco Craveiro Lopés 1951–58
Admiral Américo Tomás 1958–74
Gen. Antonio de Spinola 1974
Gen. Francisco da Costa Gomes 1974–76
Gen. Antonio Ramalho Eanes 1976–86
Dr Mário Lopés Soares 1986–

Prime Ministers (since 1932)

Dr Antonio de Oliveira Salazar *NU* 1932–68
Prof. Marcelo Caetano *NU* 1968–74
Gen. Antônio de Spinola *MFA* 1974
Prof. Adelino da Palma Carlos *MFA-Soc-Comm* 1974
Col. Vasco dos Santos Goncalves *Soc-Comm* 1974–75
Admiral José Pinheiro de Azevedo *Soc-Comm* 1975–1976
Commander Vasco Almeida e Costa *Coalition* 1976
Dr Mário Lopés Soares *Soc* 1976–78
Prof. Carlos Mota Pinto *Coalition* 1978–79
Dr Maria de Lourdes Pintasilgo *caretaker* 1979–80
Dr Francisco sá Carneiro *AD* 1980
Dr Francisco Pinto Balsemão *AD* 1980–82
Prof. Diogo Freitas do Amaral *Coalition* 1982–83
Dr Mário Lopés Soares *Soc* 1983–85
Anibal Cavaco Silva *PSD* 1985–

Key: *AD* = Democratic Alliance; *Comm* = Communist; *MFA* = Armed Forces Movement; *NU* = National Union; *PSD* = Social Democrat; *Soc* = Socialist.

ROMAN EMPERORS

Claudian Emperors

Augustus (Octavianus) 27 BC–AD 14
Tiberius AD 14–37
Gaius Caesar (better known as Caligula) 37–41 (assassinated)
Claudius I 41–54
Nero 54–68

Later Claudian Emperors

Galba 68–69 (assassinated)
Otho 69
Vitellius 69 (assassinated)

Flavian Emperors

Vespasianus 69–79
Titus 79–81
Domitianus 81–96 (assassinated)

Antonine Emperors

Nerva 96–98
Trajanus 98–117
Hadrianus 117–38
Antoninus Pius 138–61
Lucius Verus 161–69
Marcus Aurelius 169–180
Commodus 180–192 (assassinated)

Emperors of African and Asian origin (including co–emperors)

Pertinax 193 (assassinated)
Didius Julianus 193 (assassinated)
Septimus Severus 193–211
Marcus Aurelius Antoninus I (better known as Caracalla) 211–217 (assassinated)
Geta 209–12 (assassinated)
Macrinus 217–19 (assassinated)
Marcus Aurelius Antoninus II (better known as Elagabalus) 218–22 (assassinated)
Severus Alexander 222–35 (assassinated)
Maximinus 235–38 (assassinated)
Gordianus I 238
Gordianus II 238 (assassinated)
Pupienus Maximus 238 (assassinated)
Balbinus 238 (assassinated)
Gordianus III 238–44 (assassinated)
Philippus 244–49 (assassinated)
Decius 249–51 (assassinated)
Gallius 251–53 (assassinated)
Hostilianus 251
Aemilianus 253 (assassinated)
Valerianus 253–60
Gallienus 260–68 (assassinated)

Illyrian Emperors

Claudius II 268–70
Quintillus 270
Aurelianus 270–75 (assassinated)
Ulpia Severina (Empress) 275
Tacitus 275–76 (assassinated)
Florianus 276 (assassinated)
Probus 276–82 (assassinated)
Carus 282–83
Carinus 283–85
Numerianus 283–84 (assassinated)

Collegiate Emperors

(More than one emperor ruled at a time in a 'collegiate' system.)

Diocletianus 284–305
Maximianus 286–305
Constantius I (better known as Chlorus) 305–06
Galerius 305–11
Severus 306–07
Maximianus (restored) 307–08
Maximinus Daia 308–13
Constantinus I (Constantine the Great) 312–37
Maxentius 306–12 (assassinated)
Licinius 308–24
Constantinus II 337–40
Constans I 337–50 (assassinated)
Constantius II 337–61
Magnus Magnentius 350–53
Julianus (Julian the Apostate) 361–63
Jovianus 363–64

Collegiate Emperors (ruling part of the Empire)

Valentinianus I 364–75 (Emperor in the West)
Gratianus 367–83 (Emperor in the West; assassinated)
Valens 364–78 (Emperor in the East)
Procopius 365–66 (Emperor in the East)

Valentinianus II 375–85 (Emperor in the West)
Magnus Maximus 383–88 (Emperor in the West)
Flavius Victor 386–88 (Emperor in the West)
Theodosius I 379–95 (Emperor in the East 379–88; in the East and in the West 388–95)
Valentinianus II (restored) 388–92 (Emperor in the West)
Eugenius 392–94 (Emperor in the West)
Honorius 393–95 (Emperor in the West; in 395 he became emperor of the Western Roman Empire)

Emperors of the Western Empire
Honorius 395–423
Constantius III 421
Valentinianus III 425–55 (assassinated)
Petronius Maximus 455 (assassinated)
Avitus 455–56
Majorianus 457–61
Libius Severus 461–65
Anthemius 467–72
Olybrius 472
Glycerius 473–74
Julius Nepos 474–75
Romulus Augustus 475–76 when expelled from Rome.

ROMANIA

Kings
Carol I 1881–1914
Ferdinand I 1914–27
Mihai I 1927–30
Carol II 1930–40
Mihai I (restored) 1940–47

Presidents
Prof. Constantin Parhon *Comm* 1948–52
Dr Petru Groza *Comm* 1952–58
Ion Gheorghe Maurer *Comm* 1958–61
Gheorghe Gheorghiu–Dej *Comm* 1961–65
Chivu Stoica *Comm* 1965–67
Nicolae Ceausescu *Comm* 1967–89
Ion Iliescu *NSF* 1989–
Key: *Comm* = Communist; *NSF* = National Salvation Front.

RUSSIA

Tsars (from 1533; after 1721 the tsar was officially styled emperor)
Ivan IV (*Ivan the Terrible*) 1533–84
Fyodor I (*Theodore I*) 1584–98
Irina 1584 (11 days)
Boris (*Boris Godunov*) 1598–1605
Fyodor II (*Theodore II*) 1605
Dmitri 1605–06
Vasily IV 1606–10
Mikhail (*Michael*) 1613–45
Aleksey (*Alexei*) 1645–76
Fyodor III (*Theodore III*) 1676–82
Ivan V (co–Tsar) 1682–96
Piotr I (*Peter I; the Great*) 1682–1725
Ekaterina I (*Catherine I*) 1725–27
Piotr II (*Peter II*) 1727–30
Anna 1730–40
Ivan VI 1740–41
Elisaveta (*Elizabeth*) 1741–62
Piotr III (*Peter III*) 1762
Ekaterina II (*Catherine II; the Great*) 1762–96
Pavel (*Paul*) 1796–1801
Aleksandr I (*Alexander I*) 1801–25
Nikolai I (*Nicholas I*) 1825–55
Aleksandr II (*Alexander II*) 1855–81
Aleksandr III (*Alexander III*) 1881–94
Nikolai II (*Nicholas II*) 1894–1917

Presidents of the Russian Federation
Yakov Sverdlov 1917–19
Mikhail Kalinin 1919–22

Presidents of the USSR
Mikhail Kalinin 1922–46
Nikolai Shvernik 1946–53
Marshal Kliment Voroshilov 1953–60
Leonid Ilich Brezhnev 1960–64
Anastas Mikoyan 1964–65
Nikolai Podgorny 1965–77
Leonid Ilich Brezhnev 1977–82
Vassili Kuznetsov (acting President) 1982–83
Yuri Andropov 1983–84
Konstantin Chernenko 1984–85
Andrei Gromyko 1985–88
Mikhail Gorbachov 1988–91

Prime Ministers (1917–92)
Vladymir Ilich Lenin (*b. Ulyanov*) 1917–24
Aleksey Rykov 1924–30
Genrikh Yagoda 1930–31
Vyacheslav Molotov 1931–41
Marshal Josif Djugashvili Stalin 1941–53
Georgy Malenkov 1953–55
Marshal Nikolai Bulganin 1955–58
Nikita Khruschev 1958–64
Alexei Kosygin 1964–80
Nikolai Tikhonov 1980–85
Nikolai Ryzhkov 1985–1990
Valentin Pavlov 1990–91

USSR Communist Party leaders
Marshal Josif Djugashvili Stalin 1922–53
Nikita Khruschev 1953–64
Leonid Brezhnev 1964–82
Yuri Andropov 1982–84
Konstantin Chernenko 1984–85
Mikhail Gorbachov 1985–91

Presidents of the Russian Federation
Boris Yeltsin 1991–

Premiers of the Russian Federation
Ygor Gaidar (acting PM) 1992
Victor Chernomyrdin 1992–

SAUDI ARABIA

Kings
Abdul Aziz (better known as *ibn Saud*) 1932–53
Saud 1953–64
Faisal 1964–75 (assassinated)
Khaled 1975–82
Fahd 1982–

SLOVAKIA

Presidents
Michal Kovac 1993–

Prime MInisters
Vladimir Meciar *Movement for Dem Slovakia* 1993–94
Jozef Moravcik *Coalition* 1994
Vladimir Meciar *Movement for Dem Slovakia* 1994–

SOUTH AFRICA

Presidents
Charles Robberts Swart *Nat* 1961–67
Jozua François Naudé *Nat* 1967–68

Jacobus Johannes Fouché *Nat* 1968–75
Dr Nicolaas Diederich *Nat* 1975–78
Balthazar John Vorster *Nat* 1978–79
Marais Viljoen *Nat* 1979–84
Pieter Willem Botha *Nat* 1984–89
Frederick Willem de Klerk *Nat* 1989–94
Nelson Mandela ANC 1994–

Prime Ministers (the post was abolished in 1984)
Gen Louis Botha *SA* 1910–19
Field Marshal Jan Christiaan Smuts *SA* 1919–24
Gen James Barry Munnik Hertzog *Nat* 1924–39
Field Marshal Jan Christiaan Smuts *UP* 1939–48
Daniel François Malan *Nat* 1948–54
Johannes Gerhardhus Strijdom *Nat* 1954–58
Charles Robberts Swart *Nat* 1958
Hendrik Verwoerd *Nat* 1958–66 (assassinated)
Balthazar John Vorster *Nat* 1966–78
Pieter Willem Botha *Nat* 1978–84
Key: *ANC* = African National Congress; *Nat* = Nationalist Party; *SA* = South African Party; *UP* = United Party.

SPAIN

Kings and Queens*
Fernando V (*Ferdinand V*) 1474–1516
Isabel I (*Isabella I*) 1474–1504
Juana 1504–55
Felipe I (*Philip I*) 1504–06
Carlos I (*Emperor Charles V*) 1516–56
Felipe II (*Philip II*) 1556–98
Felipe III (*Philip III*) 1598–1621
Felipe IV (*Philip IV*) 1621–65
Carlos II (*Charles II*) 1665–1700
Felipe V (*Philip V*) 1700–24
Luis 1724
Felipe V (restored) 1724–46
Fernando VI (*Ferdinand VI*) 1746–59
Carlos III (*Charles III*) 1759–88
Carlos IV (*Charles IV*) 1788–1808
Fernando VII (*Ferdinand VII*) 1808
Carlos IV (restored) 1808
José (*Joseph Bonaparte*) 1808–13
Fernando VII (restored) 1813–33
Isabel II (*Isabella II*) 1833–68
(Regency 1868–70)
Amadeo 1870–73

Presidents of the First Republic
Estanislao Figueras y Moragas 1873
Francisco José Pi y Margall 1873
Nicolás Salmerón 1873
Emilio Castelar y Ripoli 1873–74
Marshal Francisco Serrano y Domínguez 1874

Kings and Queens
Alfonso XII 1874–85
Maria Cristina 1885–86
Alfonso XIII 1886–1931

Presidents of the Second Republic
Niceto Alcalá Zamora y Torres 1931–36
Manuel Azaña y Diaz 1936

Leader (Caudillo) of the Spanish State
Gen. Francisco Franco y Bahamonde 1936–75

King
Juan Carlos I 1975–

Prime Ministers (since 1936)
Gen. Francisco Franco y Bahamonde (Head of government) *Falange* 1936–73
Admiral Luis Carrero Blanco *Falange* 1973
Carlos Arias Navarro *np* 1973–75
Adolfo Suárez González *UCD* 1975–81
Leopoldo Calvo Sotelo *UCD* 1981–82
Felipe González *PSOE* 1982–
Key: *np* = non–party; *PSOE* = Socialist Workers' Party; *UCD* = Centre Democrat. *including joint sovereigns

SWEDEN

Kings and Queens (since 1523)
Gustaf I Adolf 1523–60
Eric XIV 1560–68
Johan III 1568–92
Sigismund 1592–99
Carl IX 1599–1611
Gustaf II Adolf (*Gustavus Adolphus*) 1611–32
Christina 1632–54
Carl X Gustaf 1654–60
Carl XI 1660–97
Carl XII 1697–1718
Ulrika Eleonora 1718–26
Fredrik 1726–51
Adolf Fredrik 1751–71
Gustaf III 1771–92 (assassinated)
Gusfaf IV Adolf 1792–1809
Carl XIII 1809–18
Carl XIV Johan 1818–44
Oscar I 1844–59
Carl XV 1859–72
Oscar II 1872–1907
Gustaf V 1907–50
Gustaf VI Adolf 1950–73
Carl XVI Gustaf 1973–

Prime Ministers (since 1932)
Per Albin Hansson *Soc Dem* 1932–46
Tage Erlander *Soc Dem* 1946–69
Olof Palme *Soc Dem* 1969–76
Nils Olof Thorbjörn Fälldin *Centre* 1976–78
Ola Ullsten *Lib* 1978–79
Nils Olof Thorbjörn Fälldin *Centre* 1979–82
Olof Palme *Soc Dem* 1982–86 (assassinated)
Ingvar Carlsson *Soc Dem* 1986–91
Carl Bildt *Mod* 1991–94
Ingvar Carlsson *Soc Dem* 1994–
Key: *Lib* = Liberal; *Soc Dem* = Social Democrat; *Mod* = Moderate Party.

THAILAND

Kings (since 1782)
Rama I 1782–1809
Rama II 1809–24
Rama III (*Nang Klao*) 1824–51
Mongkut (*Rama IV*) 1851–68
Chulalongkorn (*Rama V*) 1868–1910
Vijiravudh (*Rama VI*) 1910–25
Prajadhipok (*Rama VII*) 1925–35
Ananda Mahidol (*Rama VIII*) 1935–46
Bhumipol (*Rama IX*) 1946–

Prime Ministers (since 1958)
Field Marshal Sarit Thanarat *military* 1958–63
Gen Thanom Kittikachorn *military* 1963–73
Dr Sanya Thammasak *interim* 1973–75

Seni Pramoj *Democratic Party* 1975
Kukrit Pramoj *Social Action* 1975–76
Seni Pramoj *Democratic Party* 1976
Admiral Sa'ngad Chaloryoo *military* 1976
Thanin Kraivichien *interim* 1976–77
Gen. Kriangsak Chomanan *military* 1977–80
Gen. Prem Tinsulanonda *milit/Social Action* 1980–88
Gen. Chatichai Choonhavan *Coalition* 1988–91
Anand Panyarachun *interim* 1991–92
Narong Wongwan *Coalition* 1992
Gen. Suchinda Kraprayoon *military* 1992
Anand Panyarachun *Coalition* 1992–
Chuan Leekpai *Coalition* 1992–

TURKEY

Presidents
Kemal Atatürk (*b. Mustafa Kemal*) *RPP* 1923–38
Gen Ismet Inönü *RPP* 1938–50
Gen Celal Bayer *DP* 1950–60
Gen Cemal Gürsel *military* 1960–66
Gen Cevdet Sunay *np* 1966–73
Admiral Fahri Korutürk *np* 1973–80
Gen Kenan Evren *military* 1980–89
Turgat Ozal *MP* 1989–93
Hussmettin Cindoruk *(acting)* 1993
Suleyman Demirel *True Path* 1993–
Prime Ministers (since 1950)
Adnan Menderes (executed) 1950–60
Gen Cemal Gürsel 1960–61
Gen Ismet Inönü 1961–65
Suleyman Demirel 1965–71
Nihat Erim 1971–72
Ferit Melen 1972–73
Naim Talu 1973–74
Bulent Ecevit 1974
Sadi Irmak 1974–75
Bulent Ecevit 1975–77
Suleyman Demirel 1977–78
Bulent Ecevit 1978–79
Suleyman Demirel 1979–80
Adm. Bulent Ulusu 1980–83
Turgat Ozal 1983–89
Yildirim Akbulut 1989–91
Mesut Yilmaz 1991
Suleyman Demirel 1991–93
Erdal Inonu 1993
Tansu Ciller 1993–
Key: *DP* = Democrat; *MP* = Motherland Party; *np* = non–party; *RPP* = Republican People's Party

UKRAINE

Presidents
Leonid Kravchuk 1991–94
Leonid Kuchma 1994–

Prime Ministers
Vitold Fokin 1991–92
Valentyn Symonenko 1992
Leonid Kuchma 1992–93
Yefim Zvagilsky 1993
Leonid Kravchuk (acting) 1993–94
Vitaly Masol 1994–

UNITED KINGDOM

See UK Chapter

UNITED STATES OF AMERICA

Presidents
George Washington *Fed* 1789–97
John Adams *Fed* 1797–1801
Thomas Jefferson *Dem Rep* 1801–09
James Madison *Dem Rep* 1809–17
James Monroe *Dem Rep* 1817–25
John Quincy Adams *Dem Rep* 1825–29
Andrew Jackson *Dem* 1829–37
Martin Van Buren *Dem* 1837–41
William H. Harrison *Whig* 1841
John Tyler *Whig* 1841–45
James K. Polk *Dem* 1845–49
Zachary Taylor *Whig* 1849–50
Millard Fillmore *Whig* 1850–53
Franklin Pierce *Dem* 1853–57
James Buchanan *Dem* 1857–61
Abraham Lincoln *Rep* 1861–65 (assassinated)
Andrew Johnson *Dem U* 1865–69
Ulysses Simpson Grant (*b. Hiram Grant*) *Rep* 1869–77
Rutherford B. Hayes *Rep* 1877–81
James A. Garfield *Rep* 1881 (assassinated)
Chester A. Arthur *Rep* 1881–85
Grover Cleveland *Dem* 1885–89
Benjamin Harrison *Rep* 1889–93
Grover Cleveland *Dem* 1893–97
William McKinley *Rep* 1897–1901 (assassinated)
Theodore Roosevelt *Rep* 1901–09
William H. Taft *Rep* 1909–13
Woodrow Wilson *Dem* 1913–21
Warren Gamaliel Harding *Rep* 1921–23
Calvin Coolidge *Rep* 1923–29
Herbert C. Hoover *Rep* 1929–33
Franklin Delano Roosevelt *Dem* 1933–45
Harry S. Truman *Dem* 1945–53
Dwight D. Eisenhower *Rep* 1953–61
John Fitzgerald Kennedy *Dem* 1961–63 (assassinated)
Lyndon B. Johnson *Dem* 1963–69
Richard M. Nixon *Rep* 1969–74
Gerald R. Ford (*b. Leslie Lynch King*) *Rep* 1974–77
Jimmy Carter *Dem* 1977–81
Ronald Reagan *Rep* 1981–89
George Bush *Rep* 1989–93
William J. (Bill) Clinton *Dem* 1993–
Key: *Dem* = Democrat; *Dem Rep* = Democratic Republican; *Dem U* = Democrat (Union); *Fed* = Federalist; *Rep* = Republican

VIETNAM

Presidents (of North Vietnam 1945–76; of united Vietnam since 1976)
Ho Chi Minh 1945–69
Ton Duc Thang 1969–80
Troung Chinh 1981–87
Vo Chi Cong 1987–

YUGOSLAVIA

Kings
Peter I 1918–21
Alexander I 1921–34 (assassinated)
Peter II 1934–41(-45 in exile)
Presidents
Dr Ivan Ribar 1945–53
Marshal Josip Broz Tito 1953–80
Collective presidency after 1980 – Yugoslavia disintegrated 1991

Time Charts

PREHISTORY TO 3000 BC

c. 70 million	First primates appear.
c. 6–4 million	*Australopithecus* genus appears in southern and eastern Africa with perfect erect posture.
c. 2·5 million	Probable appearance of *Homo habilis* and first tools in Africa.
c. 1·7 million	First structured habitat is built by *Homo habilis* in southern and eastern Africa.
c. 1·6 million	Emergence of *Homo erectus* in eastern Africa.
c. 1·5 million	More sophisticated Acheulian bifacial tools are in use in Africa.
c. 1 million	Beginning of lower Palaeolithic Culture in Europe and the Near East. *Homo erectus* controls fire.
c. 700,000	Acheulian bifacial tools are used in Europe.
c. 300,000	*Homo erectus* develops strategies for hunting large mammals.
c. 250,000	Development of the Levalloisian method of cutting stone; flakes of a predetermined form are produced.
c. 200,000	Emergence of *Homo sapiens*.
c. 100,000	Rise of stone flake industries; beginning of Middle Palaeolithic Culture in Europe and the Near East.
c. 130,000	*Homo sapiens* splits into two lines, *Homo sapiens neanderthalensis* and *Homo sapiens sapiens* (modern humans) in Africa and possibly the Near East.
c. 80,000	Appearance of *Homo sapiens sapiens* in western Asia and Near East. First burials and religious thought.
c. 40,000	Probable arrival of *Homo sapiens sapiens* (modern humans) in Australia.
c. 35,000	*Homo sapiens sapiens* (modern man) in Europe.
c. 30,000	Beginning of Upper Palaeolithic Age. Appearance of figurative art. Neanderthals extinct.
c. 23,000	Modern humans probably arrive in America.
c. 18,000	Development of arrowhead industry influenced by Eastern cultures. Height of Palaeolithic art.
c. 15,500–10,000	Development of cave art and more sophisticated mural art.
c. 15,000	Cave wall paintings at Lascaux. Cave art begins in South America.
c. 14,000–11,000	Free standing round cabins are built for the first time.
c. 11,000	First permanent settlements in Middle East. Systematic gathering, storing of wild cereal and hunting.
c. 9000–4000	Beginning of the Neolithic period.
c. 8500–8000	Wheat and barley – the first cereals – grown in Jordan.
c. 8000	First systematic harvesting of pulses in France.
c. 8000–7000	Beginning of art in northern Europe.
c. 7600	First agriculture in southwest Asia.
c. 7500–7000	The domestication of goats and sheep in Near East.
c. 6000	The first farming communities of southeast Europe appear.
c. 5000	Domestication of llamas in South America and some agricultural development in Mexico.
c. 4500	Megalithic menhirs in Brittany and Portugal.
c. 4000	Rice cultivation in China.
c. 4000–3000	Development of the world's first known cities in Mesopotamia.
c. 3000–2500	Gradual progression to Bronze Age in central-western Asia, Europe, Egypt and China.

THE ANCIENT WORLD

Europe

c. 3000 BC Development of the Minoan civilization in Crete: foundation of Knossos and Phaestus.

c. 2500–2400 Simple henges erected in England.

c. 2200–1450 Middle Minoan Age: control of the sea ensures Minoan prosperity.

c. 2000 Stone circles of Carnac (Brittany) erected.

---

c. 1700 Bronze Age in Western Europe.

c. 1600 Linear B script in use in Minoan civilization.

1500–1150 Mycenaean civilization begins its domination in mainland Greece.

c. 1500 Beginning of Urnfield cultures in Hungary and Romania.

c. 1450 The Minoan city of Knossos falls to invaders (possibly Mycenaeans).

c. 1300 First Celts appear in the Upper Danube area.

c. 1200 Sack of Troy (possibly by Mycenaeans).

1200–1100 Dorians overthrow the Mycenaean civilization and usher in period of Greek 'Dark Ages'.

1000 A village settlement existed on the site of Rome.

900–500 Celtic Hallstatt culture (iron-using) supersedes Urnfield cultures.

850 Foundation of Carthage by Phoenicians from Tyre.

c. 800 Emergence of polis – Greek city-states.

753 Traditional date of foundation of Rome.

750 Greeks settle southern Italy.

c. 750–600 Increase in the number of city-states; the political rights of the citizen restricts the power of the aristocracy.

594 Solon introduces reforms in Athens.

509 Last Roman king expelled; establishment of Republic.

499–479 Greek–Persian Wars: Greek city-states revolt against Persian rule; Persians eventually routed and Athens and Sparta emerge as the dominant forces in Greece.

c. 450 Celtic La Tène culture: Celtic, Greek and Etruscan civilizations come into contact; culture characterized by abstract and figurative patterned art and ironwork with Greek influences.

Egypt

c. 3100–2700 BC Menes conquers the Delta, unites Upper and Lower Egypt and becomes pharaoh of the first unified dynasty; foundation of Memphis.

c. 3000 Hieroglyphic and Elamite pictographic scripts in use.

c. 2575–2134 Old Kingdom. Building of Great Pyramids at Giza.

c. 2134–2040 First Intermediate Period: era of anarchy and political fragmentation.

c. 2040 Unity of Egypt is restored under Mentuhotep of Thebes: start of the Middle Kingdom: administrative reforms, co-regencies and the conquest of Nubia.

---

c. 1640–1550 Hyksos invade and rule Egypt; Thebans remain independent; Hebrews enter Egypt.

c. 1550 Ahmose, Prince of Thebes, expels Hyksos and reunites Egypt.

1540–1479 Tutmosis begins period of Egyptian expansion: foundation of empire in Palestine and Syria extending to the Euphrates.

1360 Amenhotep IV (Akhenaton) rejects all gods except Aton, the Sun disc; imperial neglect leads to loss of Asian empire.

c. 1300 Oppression of Jews under Rameses II; Jewish exodus from Egypt.

1200–1100 Attempts by the Sea People to invade Egypt thwarted by Rameses III.

1070–1000 Egypt divided: priesthood of Amun rule in Thebes, while pharaohs rule in Tanis.

---

814 Traditional date of the foundation of Carthage.

750 Nubians conquer Egypt.

525 Egyptian attempt to regain independence fails; Persians take control.

332 Egypt conquered by Alexander the Great; on his death (305) Ptolemy (Alexander's general) founds the Hellenistic Kingdom of Egypt.

THE ANCIENT WORLD

Near East

c. 3000 BC Beginnings of the Sumerian civilization;foundation of city states Uruk, Eridu and Ur.

c. 2334–2279 Sargon the Great founds Akkad and Akkadian Empire; conquers all Mesopotamia.

c. 2200 Guti tribesmen from Iran destroy Akkadian Empire.

c. 2113 Third dynasty of Ur founded by Ur-Nammu; a period of prosperity follows.

c. 2006 Sack of Ur by Elamites (a people of ancient Iran).

c. 1792–1750 Hammurabi of Babylon reunites Mesopotamia.

c. 1650 Foundation of Hittite Old Kingdom by King Mursilis.

c. 1500 Migration of Phrygians into Asia Minor: establishment of Phrygia.

1380–1350 Hittite Empire reaches greatest extent under Suppiluliumas I.

1313–1283 Unsuccessful Hittite invasions of Egypt.

c. 1230 Jews occupy Israel.

c. 1200 Overthrow of Hittite Empire by Phrygians and allied tribes.

1200–1100 'Sea People' raid Syria and Palestine.

c. 1100 Assyrian Empire set up in Mesopotamia.

c. 1000 Israelite Kingdom founded by Saul and David.

911–824 Period of Assyrian expansion.

c. 935 Israelite Kingdom divided into Israel and Judah.

c. 850 Chaldea (now Armenia) attacked by Assyrians.

722 Palestine annexed by Assyrians; many Jews exiled to Babylon.

670 Assyrians destroy Memphis and Thebes but fail to hold Egypt.

626 Nabopolassar establishes the Chaldean dynasty of Babylon.

612 Medes, Babylonians and Scythians bring down Assyrian Empire.

600 Assyrian Empire divided amongst its conquerors.

605–562 Nebuchadnezzar II of Babylon extends the empire to include Syria and Palestine; extensive building programme (including the Hanging Gardens).

539 Cyrus the Great conquers Babylonian Empire and founds Achaemenid Persian Empire that dominates the Middle East.

536 Return of Jews from Babylon to Judah.

Southern and Eastern Asia

2850 BC Legendary Golden Age of China begins.

c. 2300 Indus Valley civilization: development of the cities of Harappa and Mohenjo-daro.

c. 2000 Neolithic farming spread to southern India.

c. 1500 Aryan invasion of India: fall of Indus Civilization; intermingling of Aryan and indigenous Dravidian cultures produces Hinduism. Rice farming established in Indochina.

c. 1500–1050 Shang dynasty in China; Bronze Age in China; first evidence of Chinese script.

1500–400 Ganges civilization in India.

1122–256 Zhou dynasty in China.

c. 800 Hindu Iron Age culture established in the Ganges basin.

c. 800–700 Growth of Chinese cities and merchant class; iron industry develops; flourishing of literature and philosophy: Kongfuzi (Confucius), Mengzi (Mencius) and Taoism.

771 Nomad attacks on China cause removal of capital to Luoyang: start of Later Zhou period: imperial power diminished.

c. 500 Emergence of Buddhist and Jain religions. Indian agriculturalists colonize Sir Lanka.

c. 481–221 'Warring States' in China – a period of anarchy during which power devolved to smaller states.

326 Alexander the Great conquers the Indus Valley.

c. 300 Sir Lanka converted to Buddhism.

CLASSICAL WORLD (to fall of Rome)

Hellenic World

499 BC Ionian Greeks revolt against Persian rule: beginning of the Greek-Persian wars.

490 Battle of Marathon: defeat of the Persians by the Greeks.

480 Battle of Salamis: Greeks defeat Persian fleet.

479 Greek army defeat Persians at Plataca and Mycale and liberate Greece.

478 Athenian empire; Athens assumes leadership of the Delian League.

462–429 Pericles dominates Athens as the city-state's leading politician.

431 Outbreak of Peloponnesian War between Athens and Sparta.

413 Athenian fleet destroyed.

404 Athenian surrender to Sparta: beginning of Spartan domination of Greece.

399 Execution of Socrates.

378–377 Athens founds the Aegean Confederacy.

371 Thebans defeat Spartans and begin Theban hegemony in Greece.

338 Philip II of Macedon conquers Greek city-states (at Battle of Chaeronea).

336 Philip II assassinated: accession of Alexander (the Great).

334–326 Alexander's invasion and conquer of the Persian Empire: Granikos (334), Issos (333), Gaugamela (332) and Hydapses (326).

326–323 Spread of Greek Civilization: Alexander occupies Egypt, Syria and invades the Punjab.

323 Alexander the Great dies at Babylon: the Hellenistic Age in Middle East and Eastern Mediterranean begins.

323–301 Power-struggle between Alexander's generals for control of the empire. By 301 BC Ptolemy gains Egypt, Seleucus most of the Asiatic provinces (the Seleucid Empire).

c. 240 Greece dominated by two federations of city-states: Aetolia and Achaea.

238 Foundation of kingdom of Pergamon.

c. 211–167 Macedonian Wars: Rome finally defeats Macedonia which becomes a Roman province.

148–146 Rome annexes Greece.

133 Attalos III of Pergamon bequeaths his kingdom to Rome.

64 Seleucid Empire falls to Rome.

AD 324–337 Constantine I (the Great) reunited Roman Empire but moved the capital to Constantinople (formerly Byzantium).

395 Division of Roman Empire into East (Byzan tine Empire) and West.

Roman World

509 BC Foundation of Roman republic.

390 Rome sacked by Celts.

290 End of Third Samnite War; Rome dominates central Italy.

275 Rome completes conquest of peninsular Italy after the defeat of Pyrrhus and southern Italian Greek cities.

264–241 First Punic War between Rome and Carthage: Sicily becomes first Roman province.

218–202 Second Punic War: Hannibal initially inflicts crushing blows on Roman forces but is finally defeated at Zama. Rome gains Carthaginian provinces in Spain.

149–146 Third Punic War: Carthage destroyed and Africa becomes a Roman province.

133–96 Expansion of Roman Empire to include Asia (W. Turkey; 133), southern Gaul (121), Cilicia (101) and Cyrenaica (96).

91 Social War: Italian cities revolt against Rome. Roman franchise granted to most Italians.

73 Spartacus leads Third Servile War (suppressed 71).

60 First Triumvirate: Pompey, Caesar and Crassus.

58 Caesar begins his conquest of Gaul.

49 Caesar at war with Pompey and Senate.

48 Caesar takes Rome and becomes dictator.

44 Caesar assassinated by Brutus and Cassius.

43–42 Second Triumvirate: Antony and Octavian effectively divide Roman Empire.

31 Octavian defeats Antony and Cleopatra at Actium, annexes Egypt and becomes dictator of Rome.

27 Octavian is proclaimed emperor – 'Augustus'.

AD 43 Roman invasion of Britain.

66 First Jewish revolt.

68–69 Anarchy following death of Nero; order restored by Vespasian.

70 Titus destroys Jerusalem.

98–180 Period of peace and prosperity under Antonine emperors.

122–126 Construction of Hadrian's Wall.

193–197 Civil war in Rome; order restored by Severus.

212 All free inhabitants of Empire gain Roman citizenship.

260 Persians overrun Syria and capture Emperor Valerian.

284–305 Diocletian reforms Roman Empire; establishes 'college' of emperors.

313 Edict of Milan: Christianity tolerated in Roman Empire.

395 Empire divided into East and West.

410 Visigoths sack Rome; Romans withdraw from Britain.

476 Final Western Roman Empire overthrown: fall of the Roman Empire.

AFRICA (c. 900 to the Colonial Age)

Northern and Eastern Africa

973–1171 Fatimid dynasty in Egypt.

1050–1140 Almoravid Empire flourishes in Morocco.

1147–1269 Almohad Empire controls coast of North Africa from western Sahara to Egyptian border.

1171–1250 Ayyubid dynasty in Egypt.

c. 1200 Christian kingdoms in the Sudan fall to Muslim invaders.

1250–1517 Mamelukes rule Egypt.

1448 First European fort on African coast established by the Portuguese at Arguin (Mauritania).

c. 1450 Sultanate of Agadès (in modern Niger) becomes powerful in southern Sahara.

1498–c. 1600 Portuguese active on Kenyan coast.

1516 Corsair (pirate) cities of North African coast accept authority of Ottoman Empire.

1517 Egypt comes under Ottoman rule.

1553 Beginning of Sharifian dynasties in Morocco.

1591 Songhay Empire (modern Mali) destroyed by Morocco.

c. 1600–c. 1800 Kingdom of Gondar flourishes in Ethiopia.

1798–1801 French invasion of Egypt.

1805–1840 Reign of Mehemet Ali in Egypt.

1820 Mehemet Ali takes northern Sudan.

1830 French invasion of Algeria.

1841 Egypt achieves virtual independence from Ottoman Empire.

1850–1868 Emperor Theodore consolidates independent Ethiopia.

1861 Zanzibar becomes independent from Oman.

1862 France acquires Djibouti.

1867 British expedition to Ethiopia.

1869 Suez Canal opens.

1881 France establishes a protectorate over Tunisia.

1882 Britain occupies Egypt.

1885 The Mahdists take Khartoum, kill General Gordon and create a theocratic state in the Sudan.

1890 Germany colonizes modern Rwanda, Burundi and mainland Tanzania. Zanzibar becomes a British protectorate.

1894 British protectorate established in Uganda.

1896 Ethiopia successfully counters attempted invasion by Italian forces.

1899 Joint Anglo-Egyptian rule established in the Sudan. Southern Somalia becomes an Italian colony.

1904 French and Spanish rule established in Morocco.

1905–1906 First Moroccan Crisis: French interests in Morocco disputed by Germany.

Southern and Western Africa

c. 800–1000 Takrur state controls modern Senegal.

c. 1000 Rise of the Kanem Empire (northern Nigeria).

c. 1200–1400 Great Zimbabwe Empire.

c. 1400 Kanem-Borno Empire powerful in northern Nigeria and Chad.

c. 1400 Rise to power of Mossi states in modern Burkina Faso.

1441 Portuguese arrive in Guinea-Bissau.

1482 Portuguese establish trading base on Gold Coast (Ghana).

c. 1450–1550 Powerful Kongo and Ndongo kingdoms in Angola and Zaïre.

c. 1500 Portuguese slaving bases established along West coast of Africa.

1531 Portuguese establish trading posts in Mozambique.

1638 The Dutch take Mauritius. France establishes fort of Saint-Louis in Senegal.

1652 Cape settlement established by Dutch East India Company.

c. 1700–1830 Kingdom of Dahomey (modern Benin) flourishes as one of the principal slave trading states.

c. 1700 Rise of Asante kingdom to power in modern Ghana.

1713 Britain becomes dominant in Nigerian slave trade.

1798 Britain occupies the Cape.

1813 British missionaries become active in Bechuanaland (modern Botswana).

1821–1822 American Colonization Society establishes Liberia for freed slaves.

1835–1837 The Great Trek: Boers leave the Cape to found the republics of the Transvaal and Orange Free State.

1843 Britain annexes the Gambia and Natal.

1847 Liberia becomes independent.

1850 Britain ousts Danes from Gold Coast (Ghana).

1861 Britain acquires Lagos (Nigeria).

1880s Brazza establishes French protectorate over the Congo.

1884 German protectorates of Kamerun (Cameroon) and South West Africa (Namibia) proclaimed.

1885 Congo Free State (Zaïre) becomes a personal possession of King Léopold II of the Belgians. British colonization of Nigeria.

1889–1890 French rule in Central Africa and Chad begins.

1890s French take Mossi kingdom (modern Burkina Faso). British South Africa Company establishes control in modern Zambia and Zimbabwe.

1896 French take Madagascar, overthrowing the Merina monarchy.

1899 Beginning of Boer War in South Africa.

THE EARLY MIDDLE AGES

Britain and Northern Europe

400-500 Saxons, Jutes and Angles (Germanic tribes) invade and settle in Britain.

519 Kingdom of Wessex founded.

c. 595 Kingdom of Mercia founded.

407 Withdrawal of the last Roman troops from Britain.

---

654 Kingdom of Northumbria formed.

---

787 Viking raids on Britain begin: pillage of Lindisfarne.

757–796 Construction of Offa's Dyke separates England and Wales during the reign of Offa of Mercia.

795 Norwegians settle in Ireland.

800s Viking settlements made in Ireland.

844 Kenneth MacAlpin becomes king of Picts and Scots: forms Kingdom of Alban, unifying Scotland.

866 Danes conquer Northumbria, East Anglia and Mercia.

874 Danes and Norwegians settle Iceland.

---

937 Battle of Brunanburh: Athelstan of Wessex defeats north Welsh, Scots and Norse.

954 England united by Wessex.

991 Renewed Viking raids on England.

1013 The Dane Swegn overthrows King Aethelred and becomes King of England.

1016 Cnut, son of Swegn, becomes king of England after succession dispute with Aethelred.

1027 Cnut becomes king of Norway.

1035 Death of Cnut: division of the Danish Empire (Denmark, England and Norway).

1042 Edward the Confessor succeeds Cnut's son Harthacnut to the English throne.

1066 Harold, Earl of Wessex succeeds Edward; William of Normandy challenges succession and defeats Harold at the Battle of Hastings.

1070 Rebellion in northern England crushed by William the Conqueror.

Byzantine Empire

527 Accession of Justinian I to Byzantine throne: beginning of military expansion and administrative reform.

534 Byzantines under General Belisarius conquer Vandal kingdom in North Africa.

551 Belisarius recovers Italy from Ostrogoths.

---

c. 650 Byzantine empire overrun by Persians, Slavs, Bulgars and Arabs: Constantinople besieged by Arabs in 673–77 and 718.

---

726 Emperor Leo III introduces Iconoclastic Decree banning use of religious images: leads to religious disunity.

c. 750 The Byzantine Empire retains only Greece and Asia Minor.

751 Foundation of Carolingian dynasty ends Byzantine power in the west.

---

811 Bulgars defeat Byzantines.

843 Restoration of images as an aid to worship; end of period of religious disunity.

867–886 Revival of Byzantine Empire under Basil I.

---

961 Byzantines recover Crete.

965 Byzantines recover Cyprus.

971 Eastern Bulgaria conquered by Byzantines.

976–1025 Basil II's reign over Byzantine Empire.

1018 Byzantines finally conquer the Bulgarians under Basil II ('the Bulgar-Slayer').

1048 Seljuk Turks begin expansion into Byzantine Empire and attack Armenia.

1055 Seljuk Turks take Baghdad.

1060 Normans invade and annex Sicily.

c. 1070 Byzantines lose southern Italy to the Normans.

1071 Byzantine army destroyed by Seljuk Turks at Manzikert: Turks overrun Anatolia (present-day Asian Turkey).

1081 Revival of Byzantine power under Alexius I Comnenus.

THE EARLY MIDDLE AGES

Western Europe

c. 486 Clovis defeats last Roman governor in Western Europe and founds the Frankish kingdom and the Merovingian dynasty.

c. 496 Franks acquire Rhineland.

c. 500 Franks conquer Visigoths and extend their empire to the Pyrenees.

---

638 Death of King Dagobert I: power passes to 'mayors of the palace'.

---

711 Successful Muslim invasion of Spain.

718 Foundation of Christian kingdom of Asturias in northern Spain.

732 Battle of Poitiers: Arabs defeated by Franks under Charles Martel.

751 Pepin I founds Carolingian dynasty after usurping the Merovingian throne.

771 Charlemagne (Carolingian king) begins military campaign of conquest: Saxony (772), Lombard Kingdom (773), Bavaria (788), Avar Kingdom (795–96).

792–793 Revolts in Benevento and Saxony against Carolingian rule; attacks by Muslims; famine.

---

800 Charlemagne crowned Emperor of what became known as Holy Roman Empire.

c. 840 Viking raids on Carolingian Empire begin.

843 Treaty of Verdun divides Carolingian Empire.

845 Viking attack on Paris.

846 Arabs attack Rome.

884–887 Temporary reunion of Carolingian Empire under Charles the Fat.

885–886 Viking siege of Paris.

---

929 Umayyad caliphatē established in Córdoba, Spain.

955 Battle of Lechfeld: Germans halt westward expansion of Magyars.

962 Coronation of Emperor Otto: Holy Roman Empire becomes largely German.

987 Hugh Capet, King of France, founds Capetian dynasty.

1031 Fragmentation of Muslim Spain: northern Spain dominates Iberian Peninsula.

1032 Kingdom of Burgundy becomes part of German Empire.

1092 Almoravids dominate most of Muslim Spain.

1094 Christian soldier, El Cid, takes Valencia.

The Church

563 Foundation of Iona monastery by St Columba: Celtic Christianity established in northern Britain.

590 Gregory the Great becomes pope.

597 St Augustine of Canterbury travels to Kent to convert English to Christianity; becomes first Archbishop of Canterbury. Conversion of King Ethelbert.

---

653 Lombards convert to Christianity.

663 Synod of Whitby establishes the domination of Roman Christianity over Celtic Christianity.

---

726 Beginning of the Iconoclast Movement (the abolition of the veneration of icons).

754 Pope gains temporal powers in central Italy.

c. 750 Boniface evangelized Germany.

---

843 Restoration of the veneration of icons in the Eastern Christian Church.

864–865 Bulgars and Serbs converted to Orthodox Christianity.

---

910 Abbey of Cluny founded in France: spreads monastic reforms.

955 Magyars accept Christianity.

965–966 Danish and Polish sovereigns accept Christianity.

970s Christianity spread to Bohemia.

988 Orthodox Christianity established in Kiev Rus.

1053 Pope defeated and captured by the Normans at Melfi.

1054 East-West Schism: Eastern (Orthodox) Church and Western (Roman) Church finally split.

1059 Pope Nicholas II decrees that only cardinals have the right to elect the pope.

1073 Gregory VII becomes pope and enforces papal authority and Church discipline.

1099 Godfrey of Bouillon leads First Crusade: takes Jerusalem.

THE LATER MIDDLE AGES

British Isles

1100 William Rufus killed in New Forest.

1135 Stephen of Blois seizes English throne.

1138–1146 Civil war between adherents of Stephen and Matilda.

1141 Matilda becomes 'Lady of England' for 7 months.

1144 Geoffrey Plantagenet, Count of Anjou, conquers Normandy.

1152 Henry Plantagenet, Duke of Normandy and Count of Anjou, marries Eleanor, Duchess of Aquitaine: gains half of France.

1154 Henry Plantagenet inherits English throne and establishes Plantagenet empire in England and France.

1169 Beginning of the Anglo-Norman invasion of Ireland.

1171 Henry II invades Ireland and claims sovereignty.

1179 Grand Assize: judicial reform.

1204 King John loses Normandy to France.

1215 King John forced to concede Magna Carta (charter of rights for Clergy, Barons and Commoners).

1258 Simon de Montfort forces reforms on Henry III.

1277–1283 Conquest of Wales by Edward I.

1290 Scottish throne disputed by 13 claimants. Jews expelled from England.

1296 Annexation of Scotland by Edward I.

1298 Scottish hero, William Wallace, defeated by Edward I.

1298 Robert Bruce continues struggle for Scottish independence.

1306 Robert Bruce crowned King Robert I of Scotland.

1314 Battle of Bannockburn: Edward II of England disastrously defeated by Robert the Bruce and his army: ensures Scottish independence.

1337 Beginning of the Hundred Years War: series of Anglo-French conflicts originating from English claims on the French throne.

1340 Battle of Sluys: English gain control of the English Channel in the Hundred Years War.

1346 English victory at Battle of Crécy. Scottish King captured at Battle of Neville's Cross.

Northern and Eastern Europe

1081–1118 Revival of Byzantine power under Alexius Comnenus.

1138 Beginning of Hohenstaufen dynasty (Holy Roman Emperors). Poland fragments into independent principalities.

1139 Division of Russian state into independent principalities.

1174 Coast of Finland settled by Swedes.

1176 Byzantine Emperor suffers major defeat by the Seljuk Turks: end of Byzantine revival.

1177 Peace of Venice between Pope and Emperor.

1198 Bohemia becomes a kingdom.

1223 Byzantines recover Salonika.

1227 Danes defeated by Germans: cede Holstein to German Empire.

1237 Volga Bulgars conquered by Mongols.

1238 Mongols conquer principality of Vladimir, the Georgians and the Cumans.

1240 Kiev falls to Mongols.

1241 Mongols invade Poland and Hungary but withdraw shortly after.

1261 Restoration of the Byzantine Empire in Constantinople.

1291 The Swiss cantons of Uri, Schwyz and Unterwalden declare themselves independent of the Habsburgs.

1300 Foundation of the Islamic Ottoman Empire in northern Anatolia by Osman I.

1316–1341 Creation of the Lithuanian Empire by Gediminas.

1320 Golden Horde (Mongols) lose Kiev to Lithuanians.

1336 Ottomans take Bergama.

1346 Estonia is sold to Teutonic Knights by Danes. The Black Death enters Europe and spreads to western and southern Europe.

THE LATER MIDDLE AGES

Western and Southern Europe

1110 Saragossa (last independent emirate of Muslim Spain) taken over by the Almoravid Berber dynasty.

1118 King of Aragon captures Saragossa.

1137 Union of Catalonia and Aragon through marriage.

1138–1139 Foundation of the Kingdom of Portugal.

1144 Alfonso of Portugal annexes Lisbon.

---

c. 1150–1200 Rise of the early Italian city-states.

1155 Frederick Barbarossa, a bitter rival of Pope Alexander III, becomes Emperor.

1158 Imperial authority in northern Italy is restored by Frederick Barbarossa.

1160 Henry the Lion, Duke of Saxony and Bavaria, conquers the Wends of the Lower Elbe.

1180 Frederick Barbarossa banishes Henry the Lion.

1191 Richard I of England captures Cyprus.

---

after 1204 Great expansion of Venetian territory and commerce in the eastern Mediterranean.

1209–1228 Simon de Montfort leads crusades against the Albigensian sect (European followers of the Cathar heresy).

1212 Christian kings defeat Almohades in southern Spain.

1218 Frederick II succeeds Otto IV and becomes master of the Empire and Kingdom of Sicily.

1229 Albigensian heretics crushed; territory ceded to France and Inquisition established in Toulouse.

1248 Moors lose Seville to Ferdinand III of Castile.

1249 Moors expelled from Portugal.

1250 Death of Emperor Frederick II.

1256–1273 Interregnum in Holy Roman Empire: period of political anarchy in Germany.

1266 Angevin French gain control of Sicily.

1266–1268 Charles of Anjou takes Sicilian crown and defeats Conradin of the Hohenstaufen.

1282 'Sicilian Vespers': rule of Charles of Anjou overthrown in successful Sicilian rebellion.

1302 Matins of Bruges, popular revolt in Flanders.

1306 Jews expelled from France.

1328 Extinction of Capetian dynasty in France; Philip VI (Valois) challenged by Edward III of England.

1330 Moors reconquer Gibraltar.

1347 Calais is taken by Edward III. Popular revolt in Rome led by Cola di Rienzi.

The Church

1100 Foundation of the Latin Kingdom of Jerusalem: becomes a Crusader state along with Antioch and Edessa.

1109 Capture of Tripoli by Crusaders: becomes fourth Crusader state.

1122 Concordat of Worms: reaffirms papal spiritual, and imperial temporal, power over bishops.

1147 Second Crusade: prompted by the fall of Edessa.

1170 Murder of Thomas Becket, Archbishop of Canterbury: later canonized by Pope.

1184 Creation of the Inquisition.

1189–1192 Third Crusade prompted by Saladin's capture of Jerusalem: led by Richard Lionheart, Frederick Barbarossa and Philip Augustus of France; only Acre retained.

1199 Foundation of the Order of Teutonic Knights by Emperor Frederick II to overcome and convert pagans in the north-east of Europe.

1202-4 Fourth Crusade: sack of Constantinople.

1209 St Francis of Assisi founds Franciscan Order.

1215 Fourth Lateran Council – major pastoral reforms; foundation of the Dominican friars.

1217–1221 Fifth Crusade: Damietta, Egypt taken.

1221 Crusades surrender Damietta on assurances of safe conduct from Egypt.

1228 Crusade of Frederick II: by negotiation adds Jerusalem to the Kingdom of Acre.

1229 Teutonic Knights begin conversions in Prussia.

1244 Jerusalem falls to band of fugitive Turks.

1248 Seventh Crusade led by Louis IX of France takes Damietta, Egypt.

1270 Eighth Crusade; Louis IX dies on Crusade against Tunis.

1274 Death of Thomas Aquinas.

1291 Fall of Acre: end of Crusades in Holy Land.

1307–1314 Destruction of the Order of Knights Templar.

1309 Teutonic Knights take Danzig. Papal court moves to Avignon and is dominated by French interests.

THE LATER MIDDLE AGES

British Isles

1360 Treaty of Brétigny temporarily halted the Hundred Years War: England renounces claim to French throne and gains Aquitaine, Calais and Ponthieu.

1369 Renewal of Hundred Years War.

1375 Truce in Hundred Years War.

1381 Peasants' Revolt against the Poll Tax led by Wat Tyler and John Ball.

1399 Richard II deposed in England; the House of Lancaster usurps the throne.

1400–1408 National Welsh rebellion led by Owen Glendower fails.

1406 Prince James of Scotland captured by the English.

1415 Henry V again claims the French throne; invades France and wins battle of Agincourt.

1420 Henry V marries daughter of Charles VI and becomes heir to French throne.

1424 James I of Scotland finally released by English.

1455 Beginning of War of the Roses (civil war): House of York (white rose), and House of Lancaster (red rose) go to war over the succession to the throne.

1460 Yorkist victory in Battle of Northampton, but Richard of York is later killed at Wakefield.

1461 Yorkists defeated at Battle of St Albans, but son of Richard of York crowned Edward IV.

1469 Orkney and Shetland incorporated into Scotland.

1470 Lancastrian invasion restores Henry VI to throne.

1471 Edward regains throne after Battles of Barnet and Tewkesbury.

1485 Henry Tudor finally defeats Richard III at Bosworth field; his marriage to Edward IV's eldest daughter ends war: beginning of Tudor dynasty.

Northern and Eastern Europe

1354 Ottomans take Ankara.

1356 Ottoman Turks enter Europe.

1361 Ottomans capture of Adrianople, which becomes their European capital.

1363 Ottomans defeat Bosnians, Serbs and Hungarians.

1380 Supremacy of Ottoman Sultan recognized by Byzantine Emperor John Palaeologus. Union of Norway and Denmark.

1386 Union of the crowns of Poland and Lithuania.

1389–1393 Ottoman annexation of Serbia, the Turkish emirates in Anatolia and Bulgaria.

1393 Ottoman annexation of Bulgaria and last emirate of Anatolia.

1395 Tamerlane defeats the Golden Horde.

1397 Norway, Sweden and Denmark come under one sovereign: Eric of Pomerania.

1399 Lithuanians defeated by Golden Horde.

By 1400 All territories surrounding Constantinople have been conquered by the Ottoman Turks.

1404 Four sons of Beyazit, Ottoman Sultan, fight for the succession to the Ottoman Empire.

1417 Followers of John Huss begin Hussite movement in Bohemia.

1410 Battle of Tannenberg - the Teutonic Order is defeated by the Poles and Lithuanians.

1419 Hussites reject Emperor Sigismund's claim to Bohemian crown: beginning of Hussite War (till 1436).

1439 End of Scandinavian Union.

1453 Constantinople falls to Ottoman Turks; end of Byzantine Empire.

1460 The Ottoman Turks capture Morea (the Peloponnese).

1466 Restoration of western Prussia to Poland by Teutonic Knights.

1475–1477 War between Swiss and Charles the Bold of Burgundy: Charles defeated and killed at Nancy.

1477 Habsburg Emperor Frederick III driven out of Austria by King of Hungary.

1478 Hungary gains Lusatia, Moravia and Silesia through treaty with the Bohemians.

1480 Ivan III of Moscow defeats the Mongols.

THE LATER MIDDLE AGES

Western and Southern Europe

1356 Black Prince of England captures French King John at Poitiers.

1358 Jacquerie French peasant uprising: ends with the massacre of peasants at Meaux.

1366–1367 War in Castile: the Black Prince invades and restores King Pedro to the throne.

1369 Renewal of Hundred Years War.

1383 Establishment of the House of Avis in Portugal.

1384 Philip of Burgundy gains Flanders through marriage: beginning of Burgundian Empire.

1385 Portuguese defeat of Castile ensures Portuguese independence.

1396 Peace of Paris: 28-year truce in the Hundred Years War.

1410 France weakened by Civil War between Burgundy and Orléans.

1411 Sigismund of Hungary is elected German Emperor.

1417 Normandy falls to Henry V.

1419 Anglo-Burgundian alliance.

1422 Death of Henry V and Charles VI: France divided between English Duke of Bedford and French Charles VII.

1428 English lay siege to Orléans.

1429 French inspired to retake Orléans by Joan of Arc: Charles VII crowned King of France.

1430 Joan of Arc captured by Burgundians and burnt at stake (1431).

1434 Cosimo di Medici dominates Florence and begins Medici dynasty.

1435 Burgundians abandon alliance with England and ally with Charles VII (who recaptures Paris in 1436).

1442 All of southern Italy comes under Spanish rule.

1454 Peace of Lodi ends Italian wars.

1450–1453 France regains Normandy (1450), Guienne (1451) and Bordeaux (1453) from English.

1453 England ceases attempts to conquer France (retains only Calais): end of Hundred Years War.

1469 Marriage of Ferdinand II (king of Aragon after 1479) to Isabella I (queen of Castile after 1474) led to the unification of Spain.

1477 Burgundy is annexed by French crown.

1492 Granada, the last Muslim state in Spain, falls to Ferdinand and Isabella.

1494–1495 French invasion of Italy.

The Church

1377 Papacy returns to Rome.

1378 Death of Pope Gregory XI: The Great Schism: two Popes elected; Pope Urban VI in Rome recognized by England, Italy and Germany, and Clement VII in Avignon recognized by France, Scotland, Spain and Sicily; the split reflects the political split of the Hundred Years War.

1387 Lithuania accepts Christianity.

late 14th century Lollard heresy in England.

1409 Attempt by General Council of Pisa to end Schism fails.

1412 John Huss excommunicated for speaking out against sale of indulgences.

1414–1417 Council of Constance finally ends Great Schism; election of new Pope, Martin V. John Huss burnt at stake.

1478 Establishment of the Spanish Inquisition.

1492 Jews expelled from Spain.

RENAISSANCE AND THE REFORMATION

Spanish possessions	Britain and Ireland	France
1492 Granada, the last Muslim emirate in Iberia, falls to Spain. Jews are expelled from Spain. **1494** Treaty of Tordesillas: Spain and Portugal agree to divide the New World.	**1494** Irish Parliament made subservient to English Parliament (Poynings' Laws).	**1491** Charles VIII of France acquires Brittany through marriage. **1494** Charles VIII invades Italy to claim the crown of Naples: start of Franco-Italian wars.
1516 Charles I of Spain (Emperor Charles V) succeeds. **1518–1523** Revolt in Spain by comunero movement.	**1513** Battle of Flodden: English defeat Scots and kill James IV. **1514** Anglo-French alliance. **1515** Thomas Wolsey becomes a cardinal and Lord Chancellor of England.	**1513** France invaded by English forces under Henry VIII. **1515** Francis I invades Italy and defeats the Swiss and Milanese. **1520** Abortive Anglo-French alliance: Field of the Cloth of Gold.
1550 Duke of Alba sent to restore order in rebellious Spanish Netherlands.	**1533** Henry VIII divorces Catherine of Aragon and breaks with Rome to become Supreme Head of the English Church: beginning of the English Reformation. **1535** Sir Thomas More and John Fisher executed for refusing to accept Succession Oath. **1536–1539** Dissolution of the monasteries by Henry VIII. **1536** Union of England and Wales.	**1529** Peace of Cambrai between France and Spain temporarily halts the Habsburg-Valois Wars. **1536** Emperor Charles V invades Provence.
1556 Charles V abdicates: hands Spain, Netherlands and Naples to his son, Philip II.	**1552** Cranmer's Prayer Book: Protestant in character. **1553** England becomes Catholic again under Queen Mary: persecution of Protestants. **1558** Elizabeth I comes to the throne. **1559–1563** Protestantism re-established in England by Acts of Supremacy and Uniformity, and the 39 Articles.	**1552** Annexation of Metz, Toul and Verdun by King Henry II of France. **1558** France gains Calais, England's last possession in France. **1559** Treaty of Cateau: Cambrésis ends Franco-Italian wars. **1559–1598** French Wars of Religion between Huguenots (Protestants) and the Catholic League.
1567 Protestant Dutch revolt against Spanish Habsburg rule begins. **1576** Sack of Antwerp by Spanish soldiers. **1579** Dutch northern provinces form Union of Utrecht.	**1560s** Beginning of Anglo-Spanish maritime feud. **1567** Mary Queen of Scots forced to abdicate. **1568** Flight of Mary Queen of Scots to England, where she is imprisoned by Elizabeth I.	**1560–1574** Regency of Catherine de Medici. **1572** Massacre of St Bartholomew: slaughter of Huguenots.
1580 Philip II of Spain takes throne of Portugal. **1581** United Provinces – the northern Protestant Netherlands – proclaim independence from Spain. **By 1600** The Spanish Empire comprises the Iberian Peninsula, most of Latin America, parts of Italy and the Netherlands and the East Indies.	**1587** Execution of Mary Queen of Scots after implication in plot to assassinate Elizabeth I. **1588** Defeat of Spanish Armada by English fleet. **1594** Irish rebellion against English rule led by Earl of Tyrone.	**1589** Henry, King of Navarre, becomes Henry IV of France and converts to Catholicism. **1598** Edict of Nantes guarantees freedom of worship for Protestants; end of French Wars of Religion.

RENAISSANCE AND THE REFORMATION

The Empire and Eastern Europe	Italy	The Church
1496 Philip of Habsburg marries Joan (the Mad), heiress to Castile and Aragon.	**1494** French forces drive the Medici out of Florence and invade Rome. **1495** French retreat from Italy.	**1478** Establishment of Spanish Inquisition. **1492** Rodrigo Borgia becomes Pope Alexander VI.
1504 Philip of Habsburg becomes King of Castile, as Philip I. **1519** Charles I of Spain inherits Austrian Habsburg lands; elected Holy Roman Emperor as Charles V.	**1501** France and Spain agree to divide the Kingdom of Naples between them. **1503** Ferdinand V of Spain becomes King of Naples. **1512** France expelled from Italy by joint Venetian, Spanish and Papal forces.	**1517** Martin Luther nails his 95 Theses criticizing the Church to the Wittenberg Church door: beginning of the Reformation. **1519** Luther renounces papal supremacy. **1520** Luther declared a heretic: accepts the protection of the Elector of Saxony.
1522 Charles V divides his dominions between Austrian and Spanish Habsburgs: his brother Ferdinand I succeeds to Austria. **1524–1525** Peasants' War in Germany. **1526** Ferdinand I gains Hungarian and Bohemian crowns through marriage. Hungary defeated by Ottoman Turks at Battle of Mohács.	**1527** Italy falls under the control of Charles V. Expulsion of the Medici. **1530** The Medici family return to Florence. **1531** Alessandro de Medici becomes duke of Tuscany. **1535** Death of the last Sforza ruler of Milan. **1540** Milan becomes Spanish.	**1523** Ulrich Zwingli presents his Theses in Zurich: precipitates the spread of Protestantism in Switzerland. **1525–1527** Spread of Lutheranism: Teutonic Knights (1525), Sweden (1527) and parts of Switzerland. **1529** Luther and Zwingli divided on the nature of the Eucharist.
1547 Ivan the Terrible becomes Tsar. **1555** Peace of Augsburg: every prince of the Empire allowed to choose the faith of his territory. **1556** Charles V abdicates: his brother Ferdinand I becomes emperor.	**1545** Beginning of Farnese dynasty in Parma. **1556** Charles V abdicates: Naples in favour of his son, Philip II as successor.	**1533–1535** The English Reformation begins. **1536** Denmark becomes Lutheran. **1541–1563** Council of Trent: the Roman Catholic Church reforms in a response to the Reformation: Counter-Reformation. **1551–1552** Council of Trent rejects Lutheran and Zwinglian beliefs. **1559** Church of England re-established on the basis of the 39 Articles.
1564 Ivan the Terrible embarks on reign of terror. **1571** Battle of Lepanto between Ottoman Turks and Holy League (forces of Venice, Spain, Genoa and Papacy): Ottomans defeated.		**1562–1563** Council of Trent ends any hope of reconciliation with the Protestants.
1584 Death of Ivan the Terrible: his successor, Theodore I, is challenged by the aristocratic boyar families.	**1580** Carlo Emmanuele I begins territorial expansion of duchy of Savoy. **1597** Death of last Este duke of Ferrara.	**1582** Pope Gregory XIII introduces Gregorian Calendar. **1596** Catholic influence in Poland and the Ukraine extended by the Union of Brest-Litovsk. **1598** Edict of Nantes recognizes the rights of Protestant Huguenots in France.

ASIA: 500 BC TO THE COLONIAL AGE

China

1122–256 BC Zhou dynasty.

800–300 China beset by warring states.

551–479 Development of Confucian social thought.

481–221 'Warring states' in China.

221 The State of Qin unites China: abolition of feudalism and the building of the Great Wall.

206 BC–220 AD Han dynasty assumes power: conquest of Korea (107 BC), invention of paper and the introduction of Buddhism.

220–280 North China succumbs to warlordism and invasions from non-Chinese people.

265–316 Jin dynasty.

589–618 Sui dynasty: reunites China and undertakes major government reforms. Expensive military ventures contribute to the empire's collapse.

618–907 Tang dynasty: empire extended; invention of printing and gunpowder and increase in international trade.

755 Abortive rebellion of An Lushan: nomad invasions and revolts further weaken the empire.

907 Last Tang emperor abdicates: China fragments; period of military dictators and warfare.

960 Sung dynasty reunites much of northern China and restores peace.

1127 Northern invasion by Jin horsemen forces the removal of the Sung dynasty to the south.

1279 Mongols conquer all of China: beginning of harsh Mongol rule under Kublai Khan.

1275–1292/5 Marco Polo enters the service of Kublai Khan and travels widely within the empire.

1368 Overthrow of the Mongols in China by the native Ming dynasty.

1403–1424 Emperor Yongle extends empire, moves capital to Beijing and encourages Confucianism.

1424 Death of Yongle; expansionist policies abandoned; 150 years of relative peace.

1517 European traders and missionaries given limited access to the empire.

1592 Unsuccessful Japanese incursions into China.

1644 Ming dynasty collapses after rebellions and attacks by the Manchus; foundation of Qing dynasty.

1683 Taiwan is incorporated into China.

1693 Kangxi leads invasion of Mongolia.

1692 Catholic missionaries are allowed to make conversions.

1715 Christianity banned.

1735–1795 Expansion of Empire into Turkistan, Annam (Vietnam), Burma and Nepal.

1757 Foreign traders are restricted to Guangzhou.

1793 British delegations denied diplomatic relations.

c. 1800–1900 Western involvement in China increases; imperial power diminished.

Japan

c. 400 BC Rice farming reaches Japan from Korea.

2nd century AD Civil war in Japan.

c. 400 AD The Yamamoto clan dominate their rivals, establishing imperial rule.

594–622 Under Prince Shotoku Taishi the study of Buddhism and Chinese writing is encouraged; the Chinese administrative system and calendar is copied.

710–784 Chinese-style imperial court establised at Nara.

c. 800–900 Imperial power is undermined by the Fujiwara family. Decline in Chinese influence.

c. 1000–1100 The Fujiwara effectively hold power. Development of a military class – the Samurai – in the provinces.

1100–1192 Civil war between military rivals.

1192 Samurai Minamoto Yaritomo conquers rivals; establishes first shogunate (military government), usurping the power of the emperor.

1192–1333 Under the Kamakura Shogunate Zen Buddhism becomes popular. Feudalism is introduced.

1333 Takanju Ashikaya defeats the Hojos (regents), overthrows the emperor and installs Koyo on throne.

1339 Emperor Koyo appoints Ashikaya as Shogun.

1339–1400 Fighting between daimyo (feudal lords) and their Samurai armies leads to political chaos.

1542 Portuguese introduce muskets into Japan.

1573 The Japanese warrior, Oda Nobunaga ousts the Shogun from Kyoto and establishes firm rule.

1582 Oda Nobunaga is assassinated; his successor, Hideyoshi continues to unify country.

1591 Hideyoshi breaks power of daimyo and disarms peasants.

1592 Invasion of Korea; Seoul is captured but the Chinese armies force a retreat.

1603 Hideyoshi dies. Establishment of Tokugawa shogunate; further curbs on the freedom of daimyo.

1630s Christianity and travel abroad is proscribed and foreigners discouraged: Japan becomes isolated from the rest of the world.

1650–1800 Period of economic growth: emergence of merchant class and rising educational standards.

c. 1750 Tokyo becomes world's largest city.

589–618 Sui dynasty: reunites China and undertakes major government reforms. Expensive military ventures contribute to the Empire's collapse.

1853–1854 US commodore Perry enters two Japanese ports: US trade and technology ends Japanese isolation.

1868 Popular support for the Tokugawa shogunate declines and imperial power (Meiji restoration) is restored.

ASIA: 500 BC TO THE COLONIAL AGE

India

c. 500–400 BC Emergence of Buddhism and Jainism: leads to a succession of Hindu and later Buddhist dynasties.

321–185 BC The Maurya dynasty becomes the first all India Hindu empire (excluding the southern tip).

185 BC–320 AD Disintegration of Maurya Dynasty: India dissolves into small kingdoms with local power struggles.

320–540 AD Northern India is reunited by the Gupta dynasty.

600–650 Harsha dynasty: Buddhist empire in the north.

c. 700–800 First Muslim invasion of India; Sind (southern Pakistan) is made a province of the Caliphate.

c. 900 Tamils from southern India begin to settle in Sri Lanka.

1000–1200 Beginning of the main Muslim invasions from Afghanistan; collapse of Hindu kingdoms.

14th century Muslim conquest of northern India complete.

1526 Mogul invasions; Mogul Empire established by Babur.

1530 Humayun succeeds Babur as Mogul Emperor.

1540 Unable to assert his authority, Hamayun is exiled to Persia.

1554–1555 Hamayun recovers the throne: Persian cul ture influences the administration, architecture and court language.

1555 Akbar, the greatest Mogul ruler, succeeds. Military conquest of Rajasthan, Gujarat, Bengal, Kashmir and North Deccan; introduction of centralized administration and religious tolerance.

1605–1627 Encouragement of the arts under the rule of Jahangir.

1628–1656 Reign of Shah Jahan: building of the Taj Mahal.

1657 Shah Jahan falls ill; struggle for succession by his four sons; Aurangzeb kills his brothers, imprisons his father and becomes emperor.

1659–1707 Aurangzeb continues expansionist policies and by 1700 covers all of India except the far south. He ends religious tolerance which increases opposition to Mogul rule.

1674 Sivaji defeats Moguls; Maratha kingdom established in west central India.

c. 1700 British East India Company secures the important ports in India.

1707–1761 Aurangzeb dies: regional dynasties assert their independence leading to a power vaccum.

1761 Battle of Panipat: Maratha defeated in their attempt to dominate all India.

c. 1760s British East India Company has become the dominant force in India.

Southeast Asia

c. 400–500 AD The Mon Kingdom in Burma established.

c. 800 Arrival of the Burmans from China; hostilities break out with indigenous people.

c. 800 Jayavarman II expells Javanese invaders from Khmer (Cambodia), re-unites country and founds Khmer Kingdom: introduction of cult of god-king and foundation of Angkor.

c. 800–900 Migration of people from southern China: foundation of Lao people.

c. 849–1287 Burma unified by the people of Pagan; revolts by Mon and Shan people; spread of Buddhism.

c.900–1000 People of south and western China migrate to and settle Siam (Thailand).

939 Annamese (of central Vietnam) overthrow Chinese and set up independent kingdom.

1220–1296 Overthrow of Khmer control in Siam: the kingdoms of Sukhothai and Chiangmai dominate.

1287–1301 Pagan falls to Mongols.

1350–1400 The Ayuthia succeeds the Sukhothai kingdom; Siamese devastate declining Khmer kingdom and unite Siam.

1354 Foundation of kingdom of Lanxang in Laos.

1431 Khmer rulers abandon Angkor for Phnom Penh: decline of Khmer empire.

1471 Annamese conquer the Champa (part of Vietnam).

1539 Burma reunited under the Toungoo.

1550–1700 Siamese-Burmese Wars.

1558 Rebellion in Annam: kingdom divides into two.

1701 Kingdom of Lanxang divides into two.

1752 Toungoo dynasty falls in Burma.

1757 The Burmese dynasty of Konbaung is established; series of wars with Siam begins.

1767 Burma overthrows Ayuthia Kingdom and occupies Siam.

1770 Burma repels a Chinese invasion.

1777 Burmese expelled from Siam under leadership of General Taksin.

1784 Burma conquers kingdom of Arakan bringing Burmese territory to the border of British India.

c. 1800–1850 Laos fragments into several states.

1802 Reunion of Annam under Nguyen Anh (with French assistance).

1824–1851 General Chakri of Siam (later Rana I) founds new dynasty; Bangkok becomes new capital and Thai empire extended into Laos and northern Malaya.

1864 Cambodia becomes a French protectorate.

THE AMERICAS TO THE COLONIAL AGE

Caribbean and North America

10,000 BC Temporary landbridge during Ice Age connects Asia and Alaska: a few Siberian families reach North America. Population spreads from Alaska over North America; their descendants become American Indian hunters.

c. 8000 BC Ciboney (hunter-gatherer-fishing people) of South America reach Hispaniola.

c. 5000 BC First centres of population in Mexico.

5000–4000 BC Arrival of Inuit (Eskimo) in North America.

c. 1500–400 BC Olmec culture in Mesoamerica (Mexico and Northern Central America).

c. 100 BC Development of first true city, Teotihuacán; dominates central Mexico for 600 years.

AD 200–1000 Migration of Arawak Indians from NE South America to Caribbean.

AD 300 Rise of Maya civilization in Central America (Mexico, Guatemala and Yucatán peninsula).

AD 500 Beginning of maize cultivation in North America.

AD 500–1600 American Indians in the Mississippi Basin, become farmers with small settlements.

c. 900 Toltecs establish a military state in Tula, Northern Mexico, and by 985 control Mexico.

c. 1000 Arawak culture in the Caribbean destroyed by migrating Caribs from South America.

c. 1180 Toltec state overrun by nomadic tribes.

c. 1200–1250 Migration of Aztec people into North Mexico; foundation of Aztec Empire.

c. 1200–1450 Mayapán becomes a powerful city.

1400–1500 Expansion of Aztec Empire to cover most of modern Mexico.

1441 Sack of Mayapán by rival cities; several smaller Maya states are formed.

1519 The Spaniard Cortés reaches the Aztec Empire; Montezuma welcomes him believing him to be a demi-god.

1520 Aztec revolt; Montezuma is killed.

1521 Aztec Empire defeated by Spaniards.

Andean America

9000 BC South America settled from Central America.

2500 BC Development of agriculture in Indian communities.

1000–200 BC Chavin culture flourishes on Peruvian coast; improved agriculture (maize) and metallurgy.

AD 600–1000 Rise of Ayamará Indians in Bolivia.

AD 1000 Chimú state formed on north coast of Peru.

c. 1200 Foundation of Inca dynasty by Manco Capac; foundation of capital, Cuzco.

1438 Emperor Pachacuti rebuilds Cuzco and embarks on period of expansion.

1471–1474 Emperor Topa Inca extends empire (Tahuantinsuyu) into southern Peru; begins road-building programme.

1476 Chimú state (Ecuador) conquered by Topa Inca.

1480 Bolivia succumbs to Inca rule.

1484 North and central Chile and north-west Argentina conquered by Incas.

1493 Huayna Capac becomes Inca emperor; founds second capital, Quito.

1498 Inca territory extends to Colombia.

1525 Disputed Inca succession leads to civil war: empire partitioned between the brothers Huascar and Atahuallpa.

1532 Spaniards, under Pizarro reach the coast and Atahuallpa is taken prisoner.

1533 Spanish execute Atahuallpa and taken Cuzco.

1535 Inca Empire completely dominated by the Spanish.

COLONIAL AMERICA TO 1850

North America

1497 Cabot discovers Newfoundland.

1605 French settle Nova Scotia.

1607 Jamestown, Virginia, is founded by the English.

1620 English Pilgrim Fathers settle Plymouth, Massachusetts.

1650s Colonization of Canada by the French.

1664 English gain New York, from the Dutch.

1670 Foundation of Hudson's Bay Company.

1699–1702 French colonization of Louisiana.

1744–1754 Britain and France go to war over control of North America.

1763 France ousted from Canada by British.

1765 British impose the Stamp Act on American colonies.

1773 Boston Tea Party.

1774 Continental Congress issues Declaration of Rights.

1775 War of American Independence breaks out at Lexington.

1776 US Declaration of Independence.

1778 France, Holland and Spain (1779) join war against Britain.

1781 British surrender at Yorktown; American loyalists emigrate to Canada.

1787 US Constitution.

1803 Louisiana Purchase: Mississippi Valley sold to US by France.

1819 USA gains Florida from Spain.

1837 Papineau and McKenzie Rebellions in Canada.

Caribbean

1492 Columbus discovers Bahamas, Cuba and Hispaniola.

1493 Hispaniola settled by Spanish. Columbus discovers Jamaica and Puerto Rico.

1498 Columbus discovers Trinidad.

1505 Discovery of Bermuda by Juan Bermudez. First black slaves brought to Hispaniola. Puerto Rico conquered by Spanish.

1536–1609 Beginning of French and British penetration into Spanish Caribbean.

1612 English colonization of Bermuda.

1630–1640 First English and French claims to West Indian islands.

1655 English capture Jamaica from Spanish and begin colonization.

1697 Spain loses Haiti (half of Hispaniola) to the French.

1761 British dominate the West Indies.

1763 Britain gains Grenada from France.

1791 Toussaint L'Ouverture leads successful Black slave revolt in Haiti.

1796 British capture Guyana.

1801 Haiti becomes a republic.

1833–1880 Abolition of slavery in colonies by Britain 1833; France 1848; Holland 1863; Spain (Puerto Rico) 1873, (Cuba) 1880.

Latin America

1494 Spain and Portugal agree to divide New World colonies.

1498 Third journey by Columbus; discovers Venezuela.

1500 Pedro Alvares Cabral lands in Brazil and claims territory for Portugal.

1501 Portuguese exploration of Brazil.

1502 Columbus explores Central American coastline.

1519 Cortez begins expedition to Mexico.

1520 Last emperor of Aztecs surrenders to Cortez; foundation of Spanish Mexico.

c. 1520 Missionaries arrive inSpanish colonies: forced conversions begin.

1523–1535 Spanish conquest of Central America.

1532 Portuguese begin to settle Brazil.

1532–1533 Pizarro conquers Incas in Peru.

c. 1549 Silver found in Peru and Mexico: wealth sent to Spain.

1717 Spanish reorganization of South American colonies.

1780–1781 Peruvian Indians revolt against Spanish rule.

1808–1820 Nationalist uprisings in Spanish colonies; Simon Bolivár emerges as nationalist leader.

1811–1830 Full independence in South American colonies: Paraguay and Venezuela (1811), Argentina (1816), Chile (1818), Colombia (1819), Mexico, Central America and Peru (1821), Brazil (1822), Uruguay (1828).

THE 17TH CENTURY

Britain and Ireland

1600 Irish Rebellion ends when Earl Tyrone surrenders to English Governor.

1603 James VI of Scotland succeeds to English throne as James I, uniting the two crowns.

1605 Failure of Catholic Gunpowder Plot to blow up Parliament; conspirators executed (1606).

1629 Charles I begins personal rule.

1638–1639 First Bishops' War: Charles unsuccessfully attempts to impose Anglicanism on Scots.

1640 Second Bishops' War: Charles defeated by Scots; forced to call Long Parliament.

1642 Outbreak of Civil War between supporters of the King (Cavaliers) and Parliamentarians (Roundheads); King flees London.

1644 Battle of Marston Moor: a decisive victory for the Roundheads and Scots.

1645 Formation of the Roundhead New Model Army; Oliver Cromwell becomes second in Command; victory in Battle of Naseby.

1646–1647 Scots sell Charles to Parliament.

1649 Charles executed; England becomes a Commonwealth.

1649–1650 Irish and Scottish rebels defeated by Cromwell.

1653 Cromwell becomes Lord Protector and effective dictator.

1660 Richard Cromwell loses political control and retires; Restoration of Charles II (after agreeing to an amnesty and religious toleration).

1665 Great Plague of London; 60,000 killed.

1666 Great Fire of London.

1677 Mary, daughter of Duke of York and eventual heir to the throne, marries the Dutch William III of Orange.

1678 'Popish Plot': wave of anti-Catholicism.

1679 Exclusion Crisis: Parliament attempts to prevent the succession of Catholic James, Duke of York.

1685 Death of Charles II; Catholic James II succeeds; countrywide revolts.

1688 'Glorious Revolution': William III of Orange arrives in England to take throne (with Parliamentary backing); James II flees to France.

1689 William III and Mary become joint sovereigns; Bill of Rights establishes a constitutional monarchy.

1690 Battle of the Boyne (in Ireland): William III defeats James and retains crown.

1694 Death of Queen Mary: William III becomes sole sovereign.

France

1610 Marie de Medici becomes Regent for the child Louis XIII.

1627–1628 La Rochelle, a Huguenot port, is attacked and besieged by Chief Minister Richelieu; Huguenots surrender and lose political power.

1635 France declares war on Spain, entering the Thirty Years War.

1643 French defeat Spanish at Rocroi. Louis XIV, 'The Sun King', succeeds to French throne.

1648 Fronde (a period of civil disorder) begins with riots in Paris.

1652 France paralysed by Fronde; Dunkirk falls to Spain.

1658 Battle of the Dunes: French and British defeat Spanish; England regains Dunkirk.

1659 Treaty of Pyrenees ends Franco-Spanish War; France replaces Spain as major western European power.

1661 Louis XIV takes control of government.

1662 Charles II sells Dunkirk to Louis XIV.

1665 Colbert becomes Controller-General of Finance: heralds period of economic prosperity.

1669 Protestant worship further restricted.

1672 France declares war on Dutch who are joined by the Holy Roman Empire, Brandenburg and finally Spain and Lorraine. Third Anglo-Dutch War (1672–74).

1678 Treaty of Nijmegen ends war between France and the Netherlands (and Spain); Peace of Nijmegen (1679) ends war between France and Empire.

1683 Death of Colbert: end of economic prosperity.

1685 Edict of Nantes revoked: Protestantism banned; thousands of Huguenots flee France.

1688 France invades Rhineland; precipitates Nine Years War (or War of the Grand Alliance).

1689 Formation of the Grand Alliance of England, the United Provinces, Austria, Spain and Savoy against France.

1697 France finally defeated by Grand Alliance: Peace of Ryswick.

THE 17TH CENTURY

Spain

1604 General Spinola of Spain captures Ostend.

1607 Spanish fleet defeated by Dutch.

1609 Spain agrees to a nine-year truce in the war with the Netherlands.

1621–1648 Spain wages an unsuccessful war against the United Provinces.

1635 Spain at war with France, entering the Thirty Years War.

1640 Catalans and Portuguese rebel against Spanish rule.

1643 Spain defeated by French at Rocroi.

1659 Treaty of Pyrenees ends Franco-Spanish War; Spain loses its place as principal western European power to France.

1665 Spanish defeated by British and Portuguese forces: Portugal regains independence.

1668 Spain recognizes independence of Portugal in Treaty of Lisbon.

1692 Spanish crown declares bankruptcy.

1698 Spanish Empire partitioned. Charles II of Spain leaves territories to infant Elector Prince of Bavaria in his will.

1699 Death of infant Elector Prince of Bavaria; re-opens question of Spanish Succession.

1700 Philip of Anjou, grandson of Louis XII becomes heir.

Rest of Europe

1600 Failure of coup against Geneva by Carlo Emmanuele I (of Savoy).

1613 Beginning of Romanov Dynasty in Russia.

1618 Protestant Bohemian revolt against future Habsburg Emperor Ferdinand II sparks off Thirty Years War.

1625 Protestant Danes renew war against the Catholic Habsburg Emperor, Ferdinand II.

1629 Danes suffer a series of defeats and withdraw from war; Swedes – led by Gustavus Adolphus – declare war on Habsburg Emperor.

1632 Gustavus Adolphus defeats Habsburgs at Lützen but is killed in battle.

1635 France goes to war with Habsburgs in alliance with Sweden and United Provinces.

1648 Treaty of Westphalia settles most of the issues of the Thirty Years War except the Franco-Spanish War; full Dutch independence.

1649 Establishment of serfdom in Russia.

1652–1654 Anglo-Dutch sea war; Dutch finally recog nize English Navigation Acts.

1654 Abdication of Queen Christina of Sweden.

1658 Danes finally expelled from southern Sweden: Peace of Roskilde.

1665–1667 Second Anglo-Dutch Naval War.

1667 Truce of Andrusovo ends 13-year war between Russia and Poland; Kiev ceded to Russia.

1671 Turks declare war on Poland.

1672 Poland invaded by Turks and Cossacks; Poles surrender Podolia and Ukraine.

1673 Battle of Khorzim: Turks defeated by Poles led by Jan Sobieski.

1674 Jan Sobieski elected King of Poland.

1681 Treaty of Radzin: Russia gains most of Ukraine from Turkey.

1682 Accession of Peter the Great in Russia.

1683 Sobieski expels Turks from Vienna.

THE 18TH CENTURY

Britain	Western and Southern Europe	Northern and Eastern Europe
1701 Act of Settlement excludes Roman Catholic Stuarts from throne and recognizes the Hanoverian claim. **1707** Act of Union unites Scotland and England. **1712** Last execution for witchcraft in Britain. **1714** George the Elector of Hanover becomes George I. **1715** First Jacobite uprising in Scotland defeated.	**1701** War of the Spanish Succession begins. **1704** British defeat French at Blenheim; British fleet captures Gibraltar from Spain. **1713** Treaty of Utrecht: end of War of Spanish Succession. **1715** Death of Louis XIV. **1719** France declares war on Spain.	**1700** Great Northern War breaks out between Sweden and Russia, Denmark and Poland over supremacy in the Baltic. **1701** Charles XII of Sweden invades Poland. **1703–1712** Hungarian revolt against Austria. **1706** Sweden imposes Stanislaus on the Polish throne. **1708** Sweden invades Russia. **1709** Peter (the Great) of Russia defeats Charles XII of Sweden at Battle of Poltava. **1711** Turkey declares war on Russia.
1720 South Sea Bubble: failure of South Sea Company causes financial panic. **1721** Walpole becomes first Prime Minister.	**1720** 'Mississippi Bubble' in France. Treaty of Hague ends hostilities between Spain and Quadruple Alliance (Britain, France, Holy Roman Empire and the Netherlands). **1725** Treaty of Vienna: alliance between Spanish Bourbons and Austrian Habsburgs. **1727–1729** War between Britain and Spain and France: Spain besieges Gibraltar (until 1728).	**1720** Treaty of Nystadt ends Great Northern War: Sweden loses an empire and Russia becomes a major Baltic power. **1725** Death of Peter the Great.
1730 Methodists founded by John and Charles Wesley. Introduction of four-year crop rotation by Lord Townshend. **1736** Porteous riots in Edinburgh.	**1739** Britain and Spain at war over British trade with South American colonies; merges with War of the Austrian Succession in 1740.	**1733–1735** War of the Polish Succession: France and Spain fight Austria and Russia. **1734–1735** War between Turkey and Persia.
742 Fall of Walpole. **1745–1746** Last Jacobite rebellion in Britain fails.	**1740** War of the Austrian Succession: Maria Theresa succeeds to the thrones of Austria, Bohemia and Hungary: Frederick the Great seizes Silesia for Prussia. **1744–1748** Britain and France at war over the colonies in North America. **1748** End of the War of the Austrian Succession.	**c. 1740s** Danubian principalities (Moldavia and Walachia) increasingly independent under Greek 'princes'.
c. 1750 Development of manufacturing industry; beginning of the Industrial Revolution. **1750** Britain joins Austro-Russian alliance against Prussia. **1755** Joint French and Indian War against Britain in North America. **1756** Outbreak of the Seven Years War.	**1753** France faces national bankruptcy. **1755** Lisbon destroyed by earthquake. **1756** Diplomatic revolution: alliance between Britain and Prussia and alliance between France and Austria. Beginning of Seven Years War sparked off by British and French colonial rivalry and European struggle between Prussia and Austria.	**1756** Outbreak of the Seven Years War. **1757** Sweden joins Seven Years War against Britain and Prussia.

THE 18TH CENTURY

Britain

1760 Enclosure Act changes farming practice: beginning of the Agricultural Revolution.

1762 Britain declares war on Spain.

1763 End of Seven Years War. MP and journalist John Wilkes is imprisoned for attacking the government in his paper.

1764 Wilkes is expelled from the House of Commons.

1765 Stamp Act imposes a tax on the American colonies: anti-British feeling increases campaign for independence.

1771 Richard Arkwright establishes first factory system for cotton spinning.

1775 War of American Independence breaks out at Lexington.

1776 American Declaration of Independence.

1780 Anti-Catholic riots in London.

1781 British troops surrender in America: end of War of Independence.

1782 Irish Parliament made independent of British parliament.

1791 Birmingham riots: fear of the spread of revolution in France leads to repressive rule.

1793 Britain joins continental powers against Revolutionary France.

Western and Southern Europe

1761 Influenza epidemic spreads across Europe.

1763 Peace of Paris: end of Seven Years War.

1770 Smallpox epidemic in Europe.

1778 Holland and France join American colonies in War of Independence.

1779–1783 Spain enters War of Independence against Britain and lays siege to Gibraltar.

1781 Joseph I of Austria introduces religious toleration and abolishes serfdom.

1789 French Revolution: overthrow of Bourbon monarchy; abolition of feudal rights and privileges.

1792 France declares war on Austria and Prussia; beginning of Revolutionary Wars; National Convention formed to rule France; France becomes a Republic.

1793 Louis XVI executed; Reign of Terror begins under Robespierre.

1794 Robespierre executed: end of Reign of Terror.

1795 Napoleon leads army into renewed Revolutionary Wars.

1799 Napoleon seizes power in France.

Northern and Eastern Europe

1762 Accession of Catherine II (the Great); Russia changes sides in Seven Years War and allies with Prussia against Austria. Russian noblemen gain economic and social rights that free them from service obligations.

1766 Catherine II grants freedom of worship in Russia.

1772 First partition of Poland between Russia, Prussia and Austria.

1773–1774 The Cossack leader Pugachev leads popular revolt against rule of Catherine II: uprising crushed.

1775 Reforms of provincial government carried out by Catherine II.

1784 Convention of Constantinople: Turkey accepts Russian annexation of Crimea.

1787 Russia and Turkey at war.

1788 Famine in Hungary.

1793 Second partition of Poland.

1795 Third partition of Poland.

THE 19TH CENTURY

Britain and Ireland

1801 Act of Union joins Britain and Ireland, abolishing Irish Parliament.

1805 British fleet defeats the French and Spanish at Battle of Trafalgar; Nelson mortally wounded.

1807 Slave trade abolished in British Empire.

1810 Durham miners strike.

1811 Prince of Wales becomes regent (future George IV), owing to insanity of George III.

1812 Assassination of PM Spencer Percival. Anglo-American War (until 1814).

1815 Britain gains the Cape, Mauritius, Ascension Island, Heligoland, Ceylon, Trinidad, Tobago, St Lucia in postwar settlement.

1819 Peterloo Massacre of peaceful radical demonstrators in Manchester.

1820 Cato Street conspiracy: plot to assassinate Cabinet uncovered.

1828 Nonconformists allowed to hold office.

1829 Catholic Emancipation Act: Catholics can hold office.

1832 First Reform Bill extends vote.

1833 Slavery abolished in British Empire.

1834 Tamworth Manifesto.

1836 Chartist Movement begins.

1838 Foundation of the Anti-Corn Law League.

1839 First Chartist Petition.

Western Europe

1802 Peace of Amiens ends war between Britain and France.

1803 Britain declares war on France in renewal of Napoleonic Wars.

1804 Napoleon becomes Emperor; Code Napoleon adopted in France.

1805 Nelson defeats the French and Spanish fleets at Trafalgar. Napoleon defeats Austro-Russian forces at Austerlitz.

1806 Napoleon abolishes Holy Roman Empire; creation of the Confederation of the Rhine; beginning of economic warfare between France and Britain.

1810 Napoleon marries Marie Louise of Austria.

1813 Napoleon defeated at Battle of Leipzig.

1814 Napoleon abdicates and is exiled to Elba; Congress of Vienna.

1815 Napoleon's 100 Days end in defeat at Waterloo; Congress of Vienna resumes; Confederation of Germany formed.

1822 End of Congress System of diplomatic alliances. Civil war in Spain.

1823 Spanish Liberals defeated in civil war with help of French troops.

1830 July Revolution in France – Bourbons overthrown and Liberal Orleans monarchy established. Revolution in Belgium leads to independence.

1830–1831 Successful Belgian revolt against Dutch rule.

Southern and Eastern Europe

1801 France defeats Turks at Heliopolis, Egypt. Assassination of Tsar Paul of Russia; accession of Alexander I.

1804 Persia and Russia at war over Russian annexation of Georgia.

1804–1813 Serbian revolt against Turkish Ottoman rule.

1805 Napoleon crowns himself king of Italy.

1807 Peninsular War sparked off by Napoleon's invasion of Portugal.

1811 French finally driven out of Portugal.

1812 Napoleon invades Russia and defeats Russian forces at Battle of Borodino, but retreats from Moscow in the severest winter conditions.

1813 Battle of Vittoria: French driven from Spain by Wellington's forces: ends Peninsular War.

1815 Kingdom of Poland re-established (under Russian rule). UK gains the Ionian Islands at Congress of Vienna.

1817 Revolt of Greeks against Turkish rule.

1820–1832 Greek war of independence against Turks.

1825 Decembrist uprising in Russia leads to repressive rule by Tsar Nicholas I.

1826 Russia and Persia at war.

1827 Russians win war and annex Armenia.

1830 Polish uprising against Russia. Revolution in northern Italy against Austrian occupation.

1831 Italian nationalist movement founded by Mazzini.

1832 Poland becomes a Russian province.

THE 19TH CENTURY

The Americas

1803 USA makes 'Louisiana Purchase' from France.

1804 Haiti proclaims its independence from France.

1807 Colombian independence movement begins.

1808 Uprisings in Spain's South American colonies.

1810 Simon Bolivár becomes popular nationalist leader in South America.

1812–1814 Anglo-American War.

1810–1820 Independence for Paraguay and Venezuela (1811), Argentina (1816), Chile (1818), Colombia (1819).

1813 USA seizes West Florida from Spain.

1817 Independent government of Venezuela formed by Bolivár.

1819 Spain cedes Florida to USA.

1820 Missouri Compromise: slave-owning states allowed to join union.

1820–1830 Independence for Mexico and Peru (1821), Brazil (1822), Uruguay (1828).

1823 Monroe Doctrine warns European powers against further New World colonization.

1830 Large-scale removal of Indians to reservations begins. Ecuador becomes independent of Colombia.

1836 Battles of the Alamo and San Jacinto; Texas gains independence from Mexico.

1837 Papineau and Mackenzie Rebellions in Canada.

1838 Foundation of Central American republics.

Africa and Middle East

1801 Third Xhosa War between the Xhosa people and colonial forces.

1805 Mehemet Ali becomes Pasha of Egypt and begins to modernize Egypt.

1806 Britain seizes Cape Colony from Dutch.

1807 Sierra Leone and Gambia become British colonies.

1809 Ecuador becomes part of Colombia.

1810 Mauritius and Seychelles annexed by Britain.

1811 Fourth Xhosa War (see 1801).

1815 UK gains the Cape at Congress of Vienna.

1818 Zulu Kingdom formed by Shaka.

1818–1819 Fifth Xhosa War (see 1801).

1820 Gold Coast becomes a British colony.

1821–1822 Foundation of Liberia.

1824–1831 First Ashanti War in the Gold Coast.

1830 Algeria becomes a French colony.

1834–1835 Sixth Xhosa War: Chief Hintsa shot while in British custody (see 1801).

1836 Great Trek begins: Boers settle Orange Free State and Transvaal.

1838 Massacre of Zulus at Battle of Blood River.

Asia and Australasia

1803–1805 First Maratha War in India.

1804 Castle Hill Rising of convicts in New South Wales.

1806 Sepoy mutiny against British at Vellore, India.

1808 Overthrow of Governor Bligh in Rum Rebellion, Australia.

1811 British occupy Java; restored to Dutch in 1819. Russians fail to force Japan to open trade with West.

1814 Missionary work in New Zealand.

1815 UK gains Ceylon; revolt against British rule (1817) repressed.

1819 Singapore is founded as British colony.

1824 Britain gains Assam. First Anglo-Burmese War (until 1826).

1825–1830 Java War: Dutch defeat Javanese anti-colonial forces.

1828 Western Australia founded.

1834 South Australia founded.

1837 Colonization of New Zealand begins.

1838–1842 First Anglo-Afghan War.

1839 First Opium War between Britain and China.

THE 19TH CENTURY

Britain and Ireland

1843 Agitation in Ireland for repeal of Act of Union.

1846 Repeal of Corn Laws. Potato famine in Ireland.

1847 Young Ireland Movement founded.

1850 Palmerston intervenes in Don Pacifico Affair.

1851 Great Exhibition of London.

1853 Gladstone's first Budget.

1867 Second major Reform Act doubles the electorate. Trade Unions declared illegal.

1868 First Trades Union Congress. Disraeli becomes PM.

1869 Disestablishment of Church of Ireland.

1870 Gladstone's Irish Land Act.

1871 Trade Unions declared legal.

1872 Ballot Act introduces secret ballot in elections.

1877 Parnell leads Irish Nationalist MPs in policy of obstruction in House of Commons.

1881–82 Parnell imprisoned.

1882 Phoenix Park Murders spark off Anglo-Irish Crisis.

1884 Third Reform Act.

1886 First Irish Home Rule Bill fails.

1890 Divorce scandal ends Parnell's political career.

1891 Keir Hardie becomes first Independent Labour Party MP.

1893 Second Irish Home Rule Bill fails.

Western Europe

1848 Revolutions in Paris and Berlin suppressed by 1849; universal suffrage introduced in France.

1848 Second French Republic established; Louis Philippe abdicates.

1850 France abolishes universal suffrage.

1851 Fall of Second Republic in France; Louis Napoleon becomes Emperor Napoleon III.

1862 Bismarck becomes Chancellor of Prussia. Prussia gains Schleswig Holstein after war with Denmark (1864).

1866 Austro-Prussian War. Prussia defeats Austria at Könninggrätz and ends Austrian influence in Germany; Prussia annexes Hanover, Nassau and Hesse-Cassel.

1867 Formation of North German Confederation. Austro-Hungarian 'Dual Monarchy' founded.

1871 France defeated in Franco-Prussian War: Alsace ceded to Germany; German unification under Kaiser Wilhelm I: Bismarck becomes Chancellor of Germany. Paris Commune is crushed.

1882 Italy, Germany and Austria form the Triple Alliance.

1884 Berlin Conference intensifies 'Scramble for Africa' – race by European powers for African colonies.

1890 Fall of Bismarck. Anglo-German agreement over colonies.

1894 Dreyfus Affair begins in France; splits nation.

1897 First Zionist Congress meets in Basel, Switzerland.

Southern and Eastern Europe

1841 Straits Convention closes the Dardanelles to non-Ottoman warships.

1848 Revolution against Austrian Empire in Italian states, Prague and Budapest suppressed by 1849.

1854 Crimean War starts: France, Britain, Austria and Turkey against Russia.

1856 End of Crimean War: Treaty of Paris guarantees Turkey's integrity.

1861 Italian unification led by Garibaldi and Cavour. Emancipation of Russian serfs.

1863 Polish and Lithuanian revolt against Russian rule.

1868 Liberal uprising in Spain: Isabella II deposed.

1869 Carlist uprising in Spain crushed.

1870 Italy annexes Rome.

1873 First Spanish Republic.

1877 Massacre of Bulgarians by Turks: Russo-Turkish War.

1878 End of Russo-Turkish War; Romania, Serbia and Montenegro independent.

1887 Renewal of Russo-German Reinsurance Treaty and Triple Alliance.

1891 Launch of the Young Turk Movement.

1894 and **1896** Massacres of Armenians by Turks.

THE 19TH CENTURY

The Americas	Africa and Middle East	Asia and Australasia
1840 Act of Union joins Upper and Lower Canada. **1845** US-Mexican War starts. **1847** Mormons settle Salt Lake City. **1848** End of US-Mexican War. USA gains California and New Mexico. Californian gold rush.	**1841** Mehemet Ali recognized as hereditary ruler of Egypt. **1846–1853** Xhosa War: Xhosa resist expansion of Dutch and British colonists in Cape Colony.	**1840** New Zealand becomes a British colony. **1841** Britain occupies Hong Kong. **1842** Massacre in Khyber Pass as British retreat from Afghanistan. **1845** Maori rising against British in New Zealand. **1845–1849** Sikh Wars: British annexation of the Punjab.
1850 Compromise over slavery in new US states. **1850–1890** Indian wars on the western US plains.	**1851** British occupy Lagos. End of slave trade. **1854** Livingstone begins exploration of central Africa.	**1850** Taiping Rebellion starts in China. **1856–1860** Second Opium War. **1857–1858** Indian Mutiny suppressed; Crown government of India begins.
1860–1861 Southern US states secede to form Confederacy. **1861** American Civil War begins. **1863** Emancipation of slaves in USA. **1865** Confederacy surrenders; Lincoln assassinated. **1866** Civil Rights Bill for US Blacks passed. **1867** USA purchases Alaska from Russia.	**1866** Livingstone's third expedition in Africa. **1868** Britain annexes Basutoland. **1869** Opening of Suez Canal.	**c. 1860s** Gold rushes in New Zealand. **1860** Second Maori War in New Zealand. Chinese ports forced to trade with West. **1864** Qing Dynasty finally crushes Taiping Rebellion; 20 million dead. **1867** End of transportation of convicts to Australia. **1867–1869** Tokugawa shogunate toppled in Japan; Meiji reforms begin.
1876 Battle of Little Big Horn Custer's US cavalry wiped out by Sioux. **1879** War of the Pacific: Chile defeats Peru and Bolivia; Bolivia loses Pacific coast.	**1873** Second Ashanti War. **1875–1900** The 'Scramble for Africa' – intensifies after the 1884 Berlin Conference. **1877** Britain annexes the Transvaal. **1879** Britain and France gain control of Egypt. Zulu Wars.	**1877** Queen Victoria becomes Empress of India. **1878** Second Anglo-Afghan War.
1889 Panama Canal Scandal. Brazil becomes a republic. North and South Dakota, Washington, Montana join USA.	**1881** First Boer War. Nationalist revolt in Egypt. **1883** Kruger becomes President of the Transvaal. **1885** Khartoum falls to Mahdi: death of General Gordon.	**1882** French capture Hanoi. Chinese assert suzerainty over Annam. **1885** Indian National Congress meets for first time. Britain and Germany annex New Guinea.
1890 Battle of Wounded Knee: final defeat of Sioux. **1893** USA overthrows Hawaiian government. **1898** Spanish-American War: Spain cedes Puerto Rico, Guam, Philippines and Cuba to USA.	**1890** Establishment of Rhodesia by Cecil Rhodes. **1895** Rhodes resigns after Jameson Raid. **1896** Italy fails to take Ethiopia. **1898** Fashoda Incident. **1899** Second Boer War starts.	**1894** War between China and Japan begins. **1895** End of war between China and Japan: Japan gains Formosa (Taiwan) and Korea.

THE 20TH CENTURY TO 1939

Britain and Ireland

1900 Labour Representative Committee formed.

1901 Death of Queen Victoria.

1902 End of Boer War.

1906 British Labour Party founded after election.

1909 Lloyd George's 'People's Budget' introduces social security measures: leads to constitutional crisis (1910–11).

1911 Parliament Act reduces powers of House of Lords.

1913 House of Lords rejects Third Irish Home Rule Bill. Militant suffragette demonstrations held in London.

1914 Britain declares war on Germany: outbreak of World War I.

1915 Coalition government formed.

1916 Easter Rising in Ireland suppressed.

1918 Civil war in Ireland.

1921 Irish Free State established in Southern Ireland: civil war continues (until 1923).

1924 First Labour Government.

1926 General Strike.

1929 Hunger march from Glasgow to London.

1931 Dominion states gain full independence. National government formed after fall of Labour government.

1932 Great Hunger March.

1936 Abdication of Edward VIII.

1937 PM Chamberlain adopts policy of appeasement of Germany.

1939 Britain declares war on Germany: outbreak of World War II.

Western Europe

1904 Entente Cordiale between Britain and France established.

1905 Norway becomes independent from Sweden.

1906 End of Dreyfus affair.

1907 Germany opposes arms limitations at the Hague Peace Conference. Triple Entente of France, Britain and Russia formed.

1908 Austria annexes Bosnia and Herzegovina.

1914 Austrian heir Archduke Franz Ferdinand assassinated: Austria declares war on Serbia; Germany declares war on Russia and France: outbreak of WWI.

1914 Beginning of trench warfare on Western Front.

1916 One million dead at Battle of the Somme.

1918 Austria-Hungary and Germany surrender.

1919 Treaty of Versailles; Spartacist Rising in Berlin crushed.

1920 Weimar Republic established in Germany.

1923 Kapp Putsch fails: Hitler arrested.

1923–1925 Franco-Belgian occupation of Ruhr when Germany defaults on reparations.

1927 German economy collapses on Black Friday.

1930 107 Nazis are elected to Reichstag.

1933 Hitler becomes Chancellor of Germany.

1935 Anti-semitism is legalized in Germany by Nuremberg laws.

1936 Rome-Berlin Axis formed.

1936 Germany and Japan sign Anti-Comintern Pact.

1938 German annexation of Austria – *Anschluss* – and Czech Sudetenland.

1939 Germany signs non-aggression pact with USSR; invades Czechoslovakia and Poland: outbreak of WWII.

Southern and Eastern Europe

1900 Assassination of Umberto I, King of Italy.

1903 Formation of Bolshevik Party in Russia.

1905 'Bloody Sunday' Revolution in Russia: Duma (Parliament) set up with limited powers.

1908 Assassination of Carlos, King of Portugal.

1910 Portugal becomes a republic.

1915 Italy joins Allies and Bulgaria joins Central Powers.

1916 Portugal and Romania join war against Germany.

1917 October Revolution: Bolsheviks take control.

1918 Russia withdraws from war; Russian Civil War.

1919 End of Habsburg Empire: independence for Czechoslovakia, Poland, Yugoslavia and Hungary.

1921 Greece and Turkey at war.

1921 End of Russian Civil War.

1922 Fascists march on Rome: Mussolini becomes PM.

1924 Death of Lenin: Stalin emerges as successor.

1925 Mussolini establishes dictatorship.

1929 Lateran Treaties recognize sovereignty of Vatican City.

1930 Beginning of the extermination of Kulaks (wealthy peasants) in USSR.

1933 Stalinist purges begin.

1935 Soviet 'Show Trials' of ex-Party members.

1936 Outbreak of Spanish Civil War.

1937 Italy joins Anti-Comintern Pact.

1939 Nationalists win Spanish Civil War. German-Soviet pact assigns Baltic States to USSR. USSR invades Finland.

THE 20TH CENTURY TO 1939

The Americas	Africa and Middle East	Asia and Australasia
1901 US President McKinley assassinated: T. Roosevelt succeeds him. **1902** Cuba becomes fully independent. **1903** USA gains control of Panama Canal zone. Panama secedes from Colombia.	**1900** North and South Nigeria become British protectorates. **1902** End of Boer War. **1904** Massacres of Herero rebels by Germans in South West Africa. **1906** Revolution in Iran forces the establishment of a constitution. **1907** Belgian government takes over control of Congo from Léopold III following atrocities. **1910** South Africa becomes independent dominion.	**1900** Anti-Western Boxer Rebellion in China ends after foreign intervention. **1901** Australian Commonwealth established. **1904** Russo-Japanese War. **1907** New Zealand becomes an independent dominion.
1910 Mexican Civil War begins. **1914** Canada enters war against Central Powers. **1915** *Lusitania* sunk by German U-boat. **1916** US troops occupy Dominican Republic. **1917** USA declares war on Germany. **1919** US President Wilson instrumental in the establishment of the League of Nations.	**1911** Agadir Crisis: Germany sends gunboat to Morocco to force territorial concessions from France. **1914** South Africa enters the war against the Central Powers. **1917** Britain supports idea of Jewish state in Palestine in Balfour Declaration. **1919** Ottoman Empire dismantled: Britain gains mandate over Palestine and Iraq; France gains mandate over Syria.	**1911–1912** Revolution in China ends imperial rule: republic established. **1914** Australia and New Zealand enter the war against the Central Powers; German territories in the Pacific occupied – Western Samoa by New Zealand, Nauru by Australia, Micronesia and the Marshall Islands by Japan. **1919** Punjab riots; Amritsar Massacre by British troops fuels Indian nationalist sentiment.
1920 USA enters period of isolation after Senate votes against membership of the League of Nations. Beginning of Prohibition in USA. **1921** US women are given the vote. **1928** Outbreak of Chaco War between Paraguay and Bolivia. **1929** Wall St Crash precipitates Great Depression worldwide.	**1920** Kenya becomes a British colony. **1921** Reza Khan seizes power in Iran (becomes Shah in 1925). **1922** British protectorate over Egypt ends. **1923** Turkish republic formed with Mustapha Kemal as president. **1929** Arab-Jewish clashes and anti-British riots in Palestine.	**1921** Gandhi begins civil disobedience campaign in India. Chinese Communist Party formed. **1923** Sun Yat-sen establishes Nationalist Chinese government. **1927–1928** Civil War in China: Nationalists defeat Communists and form government.
1930 Vargas comes to power in Brazil. **1930s** Order restored in Mexico by Institutional Revolutionary Party – redistribution of land (1934–39). **1933** President F.D. Roosevelt launches New Deal policy to counter effects of Depression. End of Prohibition. **1935–1939** US Neutrality Acts prevent US involvement in non-American wars.	**1930** Haile Selassie crowned emperor of Ethiopia. **1930s** Growth of Afrikaner nationalism in South Africa. **1932** Saudi Arabia established. **1935–1936** Italians invade and occupy Ethiopia.	**1931** Mukden Incident: Japan seizes Manchuria. **1932** Indian Congress is declared illegal: Gandhi is arrested. **1934–1935** 'Long March' by defeated Chinese Communists. **1935** Burma separated from India. **1937** Japan invades China. **1938** Japan gains effective control over China.

THE 20TH CENTURY SINCE 1939

Britain and Ireland	Western Europe	Southern and Eastern Europe
1940 National government formed under Churchill following Dunkirk evacuation. Battle of Britain. **1940–1941** London Blitz. **1945** Labour government comes to power: establishment of welfare state. **1948** British Citizenship Act: all Commonwealth citizens qualify for British passports. **1949** Irish Republic leaves Commonwealth.	**1940** Germany invades France. **1941** First extermination camps set up in Germany. **1944** D-Day Allied landings. **1945** Germany surrenders; Germany and Austria occupied; United Nations founded. **1945–1946** Nuremburg Trials. **1948** Communists blockade Berlin: Allied Berlin Airlift. **1949** NATO is formed. Germany is divided into East and West Germany.	**1940** Italy joins war against Allies. **1941** Germany invades Yugoslavia, Greece and USSR. **1941** Bulgaria and Romania join the Axis Powers. **1943** Invasion of Sicily by Allies; Italy surrenders. **1944** Soviet offensive in East. **1945–1948** Communist takeover in eastern Europe. **1946** Civil War in Greece.
1956 Suez Crisis leads to resignation of PM Eden. **1958** Race riots in London and Nottingham.	**1952** End of Allied occupation of West Germany. **1957** Treaty of Rome establishes the European Economic Community (EEC; later EC). **1958** Fifth Republic of France established under Charles De Gaulle. **1959** EFTA founded.	**1952–1957** Campaign by Greek Cypriots to end British rule. **1953** Death of Stalin; Khrushchev comes to power. **1955** Warsaw Pact formed. **1956** De-Stalinization in Eastern Europe; Soviet troops crush anti-Soviet uprising in Hungary.
1963 France vetoes Britain's application to join EEC. **1968** Britain withdraws from East of Suez. Immigration control introduced. **1969** Troops sent to Northern Ireland to restore order.	**1961** Berlin Wall is built. **1968** Anti-government student demonstrations and strikes in France. **1969** Beginning of Ostpolitik in West Germany. French president De Gaulle resigns.	**1964** Clashes between Greeks and Turks break out in Cyprus. **1964** Brezhnev comes to power, insists USSR has right to intervene in the affairs of Communist states. **1967** Military coup in Greece. **1968** 'Prague Spring' in Czechoslovakia; reform ended when Soviet troops invade.
1972 Direct rule introduced in Northern Ireland. **1973** Britain and Ireland join EC. **1974** Power-sharing experiment in Northern Ireland abandoned. **1979** Winter of industrial action. Right-wing Conservative premiership of Margaret Thatcher begins.	**1971** Women gain the vote in Switzerland. **1973** East and West Germany establish diplomatic relations. **1973** Denmark joins EC.	**1970** Unrest in Poland; riots in Gdansk. **1974** Overthrow of Portuguese dictatorship. Turkish invasion of Cyprus leads to partition. Demo cracy restored in Greece. **1975** Death of Franco: restoration of democracy in Spain.
1982 Falklands War. **1984–1985** Year-long miners strike. **1985** Anglo-Irish Accord on Northern Ireland. **1987** Third Thatcher government formed. **1990** Thatcher resigns; John Major becomes PM. **1992** Conservatives win fourth consecutive term of office.	**1981** Mitterrand, first socialist president of French Fifth Republic. **1986** Spain and Portugal join EC. **1989** Berlin Wall opened. **1990** German reunification. **1992** Single European market established. **1995** Austria, Finland and Sweden join EC/EU.	**1981** Greece joins EC. **1985** Gorbachov comes to power: begins policy of reform. **1989–1990** Fall of Communist regimes in Eastern Europe: free elections. **1990** German reunification. **1991** Break up of USSR into 15 independent republics; Gorbachov resigns. **1992** Civil war leads to break up of Yugoslavia.

THE 20TH CENTURY SINCE 1939

The Americas

1941 Lend Lease Act passed. USA enters war on Allied side.

1942 US troops arrive in Europe, North Africa and the Pacific.

1946–1955 Juan Perón in power in Argentina.

1947 Truman Doctrine: containment of Communism.

1948 Marshall Plan adopted to provide US aid to Europe.

1949 Escalation of Cold War between USA and USSR after explosion of first Soviet atomic bomb.

1950–1954 McCarthy witch-hunt of suspected Communists in USA.

1956–1958 Cuban Civil War: Fidel Castro comes to power.

1957 US Civil Rights Act passed; race riots in southern states.

1960 Bay of Pigs: attempt by US-backed exiles to invade Cuba fails.

1961 Cuban Missile Crisis.

1963 President Kennedy is assassinated; Martin Luther King leads Civil Rights Campaign.

1967 Race riots in the USA.

1968 Martin Luther King and Robert Kennedy assassinated. Growing opposition to US role in Vietnam.

1972 Civil War breaks out in El Salvador.

1973 Peace of Paris: US troops withdraw from Vietnam. Left-wing Allende government overthrown in Chile by General Pinochet with indirect US help.

1974 Watergate scandal forces Nixon to resign.

1979 Somoza overthrown by Sandinistas in Nicaragua.

1980 Cold War heats up following invasion of Afghanistan.

1986 'Iran-gate' scandal.

1987 INF Treaty signed by USA and USSR.

1990 Chile and Brazil hold free elections: return to civilian government.

Africa and Middle East

1941 War extends to North Africa.

1942 Montgomery defeats German-Italian forces at El Alamein.

1943 Germans and Italians withdraw from North Africa.

1948 State of Israel established; first Arab-Israeli War.

1948 Nationalists in power in South Africa: policy of apartheid begins.

1952 Moroccan uprising against French; Mau Mau rebellion starts in Kenya.

1954 Nasser takes full control of Egypt. Beginning of Algerian War of Independence.

1956 Suez Crisis. Independence for Morocco, Sudan and Tunisia.

1957–1975 Decolonization in Black Africa.

1962 Algeria achieves independence after bitter struggle.

1965 White Rhodesian government unilaterally declares independence: guerrilla fighting follows.

1967 Six Day Arab-Israeli War; Israel defeats Arabs and captures Sinai, the West Bank, Gaza and Golan: PLO formed.

1970 Jordanian civil war; Palestinians expelled.

1973 Third Arab-Israeli War; Arab oil embargo on the West.

1974–1975 Portuguese African colonies gain independence.

1975 Lebanese civil war begins.

1977 Crackdown on anti-apartheid activity in South Africa.

1979 Islamic Revolution in Iran.

1980 Rhodesia becomes independent; renamed Zimbabwe.

1980–1988 Iran-Iraq War.

1982 Israel invades Lebanon.

1986 Palestinians intensify violent anti-Israeli campaign.

1990 South Africa begins to dismantle apartheid. Iraq invades Kuwait.

1991 Gulf War: US led coalition defeats Iraq.

1994 Majority rule in South Africa.

Asia and Australasia

1941 Japan bombs Pearl Harbor: Britain and USA declare war on Japan.

1940–1942 Japan invades Indochina (1940), the Philippines (1941), Malaya, Singapore, East Indies and Burma (1942).

1945 US atomic bombs dropped on Hiroshima and Nagasaki; Japan surrenders.

1946–1949 Nationalists defeated in Chinese Civil War: Mao Zedong and Communists come to power.

1947 India gains independence; Pakistan becomes separate state.

1948 Gandhi assassinated.

1950–1953 Korean War.

1950–1951 Chinese invasion of Tibet.

1954 Vietnam gains independence from French; divided into Communist North and Western-backed South Vietnam.

1962 A US military command is set up in South Vietnam.

1965 US marines sent to Vietnam. Chinese Cultural Revolution begins.

1968 Tet Offensive by North Vietnamese forces.

1969 USA begins talks with North Vietnamese.

1971 Bangladesh becomes an independent state.

1973 US troops leave Vietnam.

1975 South Vietnam surrenders: end of Vietnam War.

1976 Mao Zedong dies: end of era in Chinese history.

1979 Soviet forces back coup in Afghanistan: civil war breaks out. Vietnam invades Cambodia.

1986 Overthrow of President Marcos of the Philippines.

1988 Vietnamese forces withdraw from Cambodia.

1989 Soviet troops are gradually withdrawn from Afghanistan. Peaceful pro-democracy demonstrations are violently crushed in Tiananmen Square, China.

Battles

100 MAJOR BATTLES

The following list outlines 100 battles that were either important turning points in the history of the world or have otherwise achieved lasting fame.

Marathon 490 BC Greco-Persian Wars: Under Miltiades and Callimachus, the Athenians defeated a Persian seaborne invasion of Attica (Greece). By tradition, Pheidippides ran to bring news of the victory to Athens, giving the name 'marathon' to the long-distance race.

Thermopylae 480 BC Greco-Persian Wars: the Greek advance guard – consisting of 300 Spartans under Leonidas, Helots (semi-slaves) and others – defended the pass against Xerxes' invading army. Even when surrounded, cut off and facing certain death, the Greek advance guard fought on in an act of epic heroism.

Salamis 480 BC Greco-Persian Wars: following Themistocles' strategy, the Greeks were able to outmanoeuvre and defeat the Persian fleet. The Persians were forced to abandon the Peloponnese (southern Greece), checking their conquest of Greece.

Plataea 479 BC Greco-Persian Wars: victory of the Greek infantry forces led by Pausanias the Spartan, over the Persian forces of Xerxes I, at Plataea. The battle forced the Persians to abandon their attempt to conquer Greece and ended the Greco-Persian Wars.

Aegosopotami 405 BC Peloponnesian War (Athens against Sparta): the Athenian fleet was taken by surprise and destroyed by the Spartans under Lysander. The siege and surrender of Athens followed, making Sparta the dominant power in Greece.

Leuctra 371 BC Epaminondas led the Thebans to victory over the Spartans, making Thebes the dominant power in Greece.

Chaeronea 338 BC Philip II of Macedon defeated the Greek allies (mainly Thebans and Athenians) ensuring Macedonian domination of Greece.

Issus 333 BC Conquests of Alexander the Great: Alexander led the Macedonian army to victory against the Persians under King Darius. The conquest added Syria and Egypt to his sphere of domination.

Gaugamela 331 BC Conquests of Alexander the Great: despite being outnumbered, Alexander led the Macedonian army to victory against the Persians under King Darius. He conquered Mesopotamia (modern Iraq) and Persia (modern Iran), ending the Persian empire.

Hydaspes 326 BC Conquests of Alexander the Great: Alexander and the Macedonian army defeated the forces of King Porus, but the troops demanded a return home.

Cannae 216 BC Second Punic War (Rome against Carthage): at Cannae in southern Italy, Rome suffered its worst military defeat when Hannibal's Carthaginian army surrounded and annihilated the Roman forces, with estimates of Roman losses from c. 50,000 to 70,000 men. However, Hannibal was unable to follow up his victory.

Metaurus 207 BC Second Punic War: Hasdrubal led a Carthaginian force to bring reinforcements to his brother Hannibal, but was defeated and destroyed by the Romans at Metaurus in northern Italy. The defeat helped force Hannibal to withdraw from Italy.

Zama 202 BC Second Punic War: Hannibal was defeated at Zama (in modern Tunisia) by Scipio Africanus in northern Africa, forcing Carthage to concede defeat and ending the Second Punic War. Rome became the dominant power in the western Mediterranean.

Pydna 168 BC Rome against Macedon: the Romans showed the superiority of their tactics when they defeated the Macedonian phalanx led by King Perseus. The victory at Pydna (central Greece) gave Rome effective control of Greece.

Carrhae 53 BC Crassus' expedition against the Parthians: Crassus' Roman army was defeated by the Parthian horse-archers and heavy cavalry when they attempted to capture Ctesiphon, the capital of the Parthian Empire. The defeat checked Roman eastward expansion.

Actium 31 BC Mark Antony and Cleopatra's Egyptian fleet was defeated by Octavian, the nephew of Julius Caesar, at Actium (western Greece). It brought to an end the civil wars that had plagued the Roman world for the last 50 years. Octavian became the first emperor (Augustus).

Teutoburger Wald AD 9 In their attempt to conquer Germany, three Roman legions led by Quintilius Varus were defeated and killed by the Germans under Arminius. The defeat fixed the Roman frontier at the Rhine.

Milvian Bridge AD 312 In the power struggle following the breakdown of the Tetrarchy system for running the Roman Empire, Constantine defeated his rival Maxentius. Having had a dream in which he saw the 'Chi-rho' symbol and words 'In hoc signo vinces' ('in this sign you will conquer'), Constantine became a Christian and the first Christian emperor.

Adrianople AD 378 In an attempt to escape the Huns, the Goths settled in the Roman Empire. However, they were treated so badly that they rebelled, and defeated the Romans, killing the Emperor Valens. They went on to sack Rome in AD 410, eventually establishing a kingdom in Spain.

Catalaunian Fields AD 451 Attila and the Huns were defeated by a combined force of Romans and Visigoths under Aetius and Theodoric. Attila retreated into central Europe.

Yarmuk AD 636 Arab conquests: at Yarmuk in Palestine the Arabs defeated the forces of the Byzantine emperor and conquered Syria and Palestine (including the Holy Places). It allowed them to go on to conquer Egypt and North Africa.

Quadisiya AD 636 Arab conquests: the Arabs defeated the Persians and conquered Iraq. The defeat enabled them to go on and conquer Persia the following year.

Poitiers AD 732 Arab conquests: the Franks, led by Charles Martel, defeated an Arab invasion of France, limiting the Arab conquests in Europe to Spain and Portugal.

Ethandune AD 878 Viking battles: Alfred of Wessex defeated the 'Great Army' of Danish Vikings, and forced them to make peace at Wedmore. The defeat prevented the total conquest of England by Vikings, and allowed Alfred's successors to reconquer and unite the country.

Lechfeld AD 955 Magyar (Hungarian) conquests: at Lechfeld in southern Germany, the Emperor Otto I inflicted a crushing and fatal defeat on the Hungarians, who then adopted Christianity and settled down as a bulwark against attacks on Europe from the East during the rest of the Middle Ages.

Hastings 1066 Norman Conquest: an army of Norman and French soldiers led by Duke William of Normandy defeated the Saxon army of King Harold (who died in battle). William was subsequently crowned king of England.

Manzikert 1071 At Manzikert (in modern Turkey), the Seljuk Turks, under their sultan Alp Arslan, defeated a large Byzantine army led by Emperor Romanus Diogenes (who was captured). The Byzantine Empire was severely weakened by the permanent loss of control of the interior of Asia Minor.

Hattin 1187 The Crusades: Saladin led the Arab forces in victory against the army of the Latin (Christian) kingdom of Jerusalem at Hattin in Palestine, and were able to conquer almost all of Palestine.

Las Navas de Tolosa 1212 La Reconquista: The Christian Spaniards defeated the Muslim Almoravids of North Africa, recovering the impetus in their reconquest of Spain from the Muslims. The success of the Reconquista was now assured.

Muret 1213 Albigensian Crusade: Northern French forces under Simon de Montfort defeated the forces of Count Raymond of Toulouse and King Peter of Aragon. Most of Languedoc fell under de Montfort's control, marking the beginning of the end of both Languedoc's independence and the Cathar heresy.

Ain Jalut 1260 Mongol conquests: at Ain Jalut in Palestine, the Egyptian Mamluks led by Sultan Qutuz defeated the Mongols and repelled their invasion of Syria. The Mamluks became the chief power in the eastern Mediterranean.

Courtrai 1302 The communal militias of Flanders showed that infantry, if determined enough, could repel armoured knights. They defeated the army of the king of France when the French knights embarked on a rash charge.

Bannockburn 1314 Anglo-Scottish Wars: Robert the Bruce's Scottish forces defeated the English under Edward II who had employed poor tactics. The victory helped secure Scottish independence.

Morgarten 1315 Swiss Wars of Independence: the Swiss combined missile and halberd attacks with an ambush to defeat a superior Austrian army, ensuring the eventual independence of the Swiss Confederation.

Crécy 1346 Hundred Years War: a smaller English army, led by Edward III, used its archers to shoot to pieces the ill-coordinated assaults of the poorly led French.

Poitiers 1356 Hundred Years War: the French, led by John II, dismounted most of their fully armoured men, to avoid a repetition of Crécy, but were outmanoeuvred and defeated by the Black Prince (son of Edward III of England). King John and most of the great nobles were captured.

Kosovo 1389 Ottoman conquests: Turkish forces destroyed the Serbian army, gaining control over much of the western Balkans, as the Serbian Empire collapsed.

Nicopolis 1396 Ottoman conquests: a Crusading force, intending to bring help to Byzantium, was outmanoeuvred at Nicopolis (in modern Bulgaria) and forced to surrender by the Turks under Sultan Bayezit. Subsequent Turkish conquests continued unchecked.

Agincourt 1415 Hundred Years War: after a long period of French dominance, Henry V of England invaded France and, although outnumbered three to one, defeated the over-confident French. Much of France subsequently fell under English control.

Orléans 1429 Hundred Years War: inspired by Joan of Arc, the French defeated the English and raised the siege of Orléans. The defeat led to the eventual expulsion of the English from France.

Castillon 1454 Hundred Years War: the English attempt to recover lost territory in France came to an end with their defeat at the hands of a reorganized French army. Cannon played a part in the French victory.

Nancy 1477 Swiss-Burgundian War: Swiss pikemen defeated the army of Charles the Bold, Duke of Burgundy, whose dreams of creating a powerful state between France and Germany died with him on the battlefield. Swiss mercenaries became the most sought-after troops in Europe.

Bosworth 1485 Wars of the Roses: Henry Tudor's Lancastrian army defeated the army of King Richard III (the Yorkist claimant). Richard was killed, and Henry became King Henry VII, founding the Tudor dynasty.

Marignano 1515 Italian Wars: French and Venetian forces under King Francis I defeated the forces of the Holy Roman Empire (Swiss mercenaries), shattering the myth of Swiss invincibility.

Pavia 1525 Italian Wars: Francis I of France was defeated and captured by the forces of the Holy Roman Empire, who recaptured control of Italy from the French.

Panipat 1526 An Indian (Hindu) army was defeated and destroyed by the Muslim forces of Zahir-ud-din (Babur) at Panipat in northern India. He went on to found the Mogul Empire, which later dominated most of India.

Mohács 1526 Turkish forces led by Suleiman 'the Magnificent' defeated the Hungarians. Hungary was incorporated into the Ottoman Empire, and the Turks went on to besiege Vienna (1529), but failed to take it.

Malta 1565 Turkish forces led by Dragut and Piali attacked Malta, which was defended by the Knights of St John under Grand Master La Valette. The Turkish failure to capture the island put a limit on their westward expansion.

Lepanto 1571 In a major sea battle off the coast of central Greece, the Ottoman fleet was destroyed by the fleet of the Holy League organized by Pope Pius V and led by Don John of Austria. It was the first major Turkish defeat by the Christian powers.

Gravelines 1588 The Spanish Armada fleet sent by Philip II of Spain to conquer England was attacked at anchor and defeated by the English fleet led by Lord Howard of Effingham. Invasion plans were abandoned and the fleet suffered severe losses on the way home round the north and west of the British Isles.

Ivry 1590 French Wars of Religion: Huguenot (French Protestant) forces under Henry of Navarre (later Henry IV of France) defeated the forces of the Catholic League. The wars came to an end when Henry became a Catholic and introduced religious toleration.

White Mountain 1620 Thirty Years War: the army of the Catholic League, commanded by Tilly, defeated the Bohemian rebels near Prague, and the authority of the Habsburg family was restored in Bohemia. However, the campaign against Frederick of the Palatinate, who had been named as king by the rebels, led to the spread of war throughout the Holy Roman Empire and the involvement of many countries.

Breitenfeld 1631 Thirty Years War: the Swedes under King Gustavus Adolphus defeated the army of the Catholic League, commanded by Tilly, in southern Germany. This checked Habsburg attempts to increase their control over the Holy Roman Empire and strengthen Catholicism.

Lützen 1632 Thirty Years War: the Swedes again defeated the Habsburg forces under Wallenstein, and achieved a dominant position in Germany. However, Gustavus Adolphus was killed in this battle in southern Germany.

Nordlingen 1634 Thirty Years War: the combined forces of the Austrian and Spanish Habsburgs inflicted a severe defeat on the Swedes at Nordlingen in Bavaria. This led France (Sweden's ally) to take a direct part in the war, which prevented the Peace of Prague (1635) from taking effect.

Rocroi 1643 Thirty Years War: the French under Prince de Condé defeated the Spanish, shattering the myth of Spanish invincibility, and beginning an era of French military superiority.

Marston Moor 1644 English Civil War: Parliamentary forces under the command of Sir Thomas Fairfax, David Leslie and Oliver Cromwell, defeated the Royalist forces led by Prince Rupert of the Rhine, nephew of King Charles I. The king lost control of virtually all of the north of England.

Naseby 1645 English Civil War: the reorganized forces of Parliament – the New Model Army – under Oliver Cromwell inflicted a crushing defeat on the army of King Charles I. The battle decided the outcome of the war and the king surrendered to the Scots in 1646.

Boyne 1690 War of the English Succession: north of Dublin, the army of William of Orange (King William III) defeated the Irish and French forces of King James II, who abandoned the struggle to regain his throne and returned to France.

Zenta 1697 War of the Holy League: the Turks had been in retreat since the failure of the siege of Vienna, and this defeat by the Austrians forced them to make peace at Carlowitz, and cede the whole of Hungary to Austria. This marked the beginning of decline of the Ottoman Empire.

Blenheim 1704 War of the Spanish Succession: English and Dutch troops under John Churchill, later Duke of Marlborough, marched across Germany to defeat a Franco-Bavarian force at Blenheim in Bavaria and save Vienna. This prevented France from gaining a major advantage in the first years of the war, and marked England's re-emergence as a military power.

Ramillies 1706 War of the Spanish Succession: the Anglo-Dutch army under Marlborough defeated the French. However, they were unable to break through the French ring of fortresses that defended the north-eastern frontier.

Oudenarde 1708 War of the Spanish Succession: Marlborough's army again defeated the French, but without any conclusive result.

Poltava 1709 Great Northern War: Charles XII of Sweden turned his forces on his Russian enemy, Peter 'the Great' of Russia. However, his invasion failed when he was surrounded during an extremely hard winter and defeated at Poltava (in modern Ukraine). Although the war contined until 1721, Sweden never really recovered and her days of empire were over.

Peterwardein 1716 Austro-Turkish War: Eugene of Savoy, the colleague of Marlborough, led the Austrian forces to its greatest victory over the Turks. By the Peace of Passarowitz the Turks handed Serbia to Austria.

Dettingen 1744 War of the Austrian Succession: Allied forces – British, Dutch and German – under George II of England defeated the French. This was the last time a British sovereign commanded his troops in battle.

Culloden 1746 Jacobite Rebellions: the British army under the Duke of Cumberland defeated the Scottish Highland clans – led by Prince Charles Edward (Bonnie Prince Charlie) – who were supporting the Stuart claim to the throne. It marked the end of Jacobite Rebellions.

Plassey 1757 Seven Years War: the forces of the British East India Company under Robert Clive defeated a much larger army under the Rajah of Bengal, partly by bribing an ally of the Rajah. The victory – at Plassey, north of Calcutta – allowed the company (and therefore Britain) to begin its control over India.

Heights of Abraham 1759 Seven Years War: British forces led by General Wolfe captured Québec when they defeated French forces under Montcalm. Canada fell under British control as a result.

Wandewash 1760 Seven Years War: the French under Lally Tollendal were defeated by British forces led by Sir Eyre Coote at Wandewash, south of Madras. This ended any French challenge to British dominance in India.

Bunker Hill 1775 American War of Independence: the British redcoats defeated the American rebels, despite their stiff resistance, in the first major battle of the war, but at the cost of 1000 British casualties.

Saratoga 1777 American War of Independence: a British attack, led by 'Gentleman Johnny' Burgoyne, on New England through the Hudson Valley ended in failure when he was surrounded and forced to surrender at Saratoga.

Yorktown 1781 American War of Independence: the British under Cornwallis were penned into a corner by the Americans, led by George Washington, and the French fleet. The British were forced to surrender and accept American independence.

Valmy 1792 French Revolutionary Wars: an Austro-Prussian army under the Duke of Brunswick, which had invaded France to restore the monarchy, was defeated by the French. This safeguarded the Revolution.

Trafalgar 1805 Napoleonic Wars: after a failed attempt to invade England, the combined fleets of France and Spain were defeated by the British fleet under Horatio Nelson. The victory – off the southern coast of Spain – heralded the era of total British command of the sea, despite Nelson's death.

Austerlitz 1805 Napoleonic Wars: abandoning his invasion of England, Napoleon turned on his continental enemies and – at Austerlitz, near Brno – defeated the Austrians and Russians, who both soon made peace.

Jena 1806 Napoleonic Wars: the Prussians challenged Napoleon and were routed at Jena in five weeks. It left Napoleon supreme in Europe, and led to massive reforms in Prussia which enabled her to become dominant in Germany later.

Leipzig 1813 Napoleonic Wars: following his disastrous Russian campaign, Napoleon was attacked by a large coalition of Austrian, Prussian, Russian and Swedish forces under Schwarzenberg and Blücher. Napoleon was defeated and had to abandon Germany to his enemies. The defeat contributed to the collapse of the Napoleonic empire (Napoleon abdicated in 1814).

Waterloo 1815 Napoleonic Wars: escaping from exile in Elba, Napoleon returned to France, only to be defeated by the British army under Arthur Wellesley, the Duke of Wellington. He returned to exile in St Helena, and Europe enjoyed a long period of peace.

Gettysburg 1863 American Civil War: the Confederate (Southern) invasion of the North under Lee failed with heavy losses. The repeating rifles of the Union army inflicted massive casualties on the attackers.

Königgratz (Sadowa) 1866 Austro-Prussian War: Moltke's Prussian forces defeated the Austro-Hungarian army under Benedek at Sadowa (in the modern Czech Republic). Austria was forced to accept Prussian dominance in Germany.

Sedan 1870 Franco-Prussian War: the French forces under Marshal MacMahon and Emperor Napoleon III were defeated by the Prussians under Moltke and forced to surrender. It led ultimately to the overthrow of the Second Empire and the unification of Germany.

Ondurman 1898 Second Sudanese Campaign: the British and Egyptian forces under Kitchener defeated the Sudanese thanks to their repeating rifles. It was the first battle in which a fully automatic machine-gun (the Maxim gun) was used.

Tsushima 1905 Russo-Japanese War: the Russian Baltic fleet had been sent to support the Russian campaign in Korea, but was completely defeated by the Japanese, who went on to win the war. Japan emerged as a major power and Russia experienced an unsuccessful revolution.

Marne 1914 World War I: the German invasion of France via Belgium was stopped by French counterattacks on the line of the River Marne. The Germans fell back to the River Aisne and 'dug in', setting the pattern of trench warfare.

Tannenberg 1914 World War I: two Russian armies advancing towards Königsberg (modern Kaliningrad, Russia) were respectively defeated and forced to retreat by Generals von Hindenburg and Ludendorff. Russia never again entered Germany during the war.

Verdun 1916 World War I: in an attempt to inflict massive casualties on the French, the German commander Falkenhayn attacked the symbolic fortress of Verdun with massive firepower. The French, commanded by Pétain, held the fort, but at a cost of 700,000 lives on each side.

Somme 1916 World War I: the British Army under Haig attacked in their first major offensive of the war. Allied casualties were high, 600,000 men, and the gains, a few kilometres of mud, very limited.

Jutland 1916 World War I: in the war's only major sea battle, the Germans inflicted more damage to the British fleet than they suffered, but the Germans retired into harbour for the rest of the war, leaving Britain's vital control of the sea secure.

Passchendaele 1917 World War I: a British offensive under Haig to relieve the pressure on the mutinous French army and capture German submarine bases on the Belgian coast failed as a result of atrocious conditions. The sea of mud made advance impossible, but 300,000 British casualties were suffered after persistent frontal assaults.

Cambrai 1917 World War I: the first use of tanks on a large scale (381 British tanks) made a serious gap in the German defences. Unfortunately, the initial success was not exploited.

Meggido 1918 World War I: the Battle of Meggido, fought on the traditional site of Armageddon (Palestine), saw the British under Allenby defeat the Turks and go on to occupy Damascus and the rest of Syria, effectively ending the Ottoman Empire.

Battle of Britain 1940 World War II: during the first air battle the German Air Force (Luftwaffe) attempted to gain control of the air to neutralize the British Navy and allow an invasion of Britain. After early successes, the switch to attacking London gave the hard-pressed RAF time to recover as German losses mounted. Soon the Germans abandoned day bombing attacks, and postponed the invasion plans. The use of radar for the first time made a significant contribution to the British effort.

El Alamein 1942 World War II: the British 8th Army under Montgomery defeated the German and Italian forces under Rommel, removing the threat to Egypt and the Suez Canal and beginning a continuous advance that cleared North Africa by 1943. It is often seen as the turning point in British fortunes in the war.

Stalingrad 1942 World War II: following a successful offensive in the second year of the Russian campaign, the German Sixth Army was surrounded and cut off by the Russians in Stalingrad (now Volgograd). Hitler refused to allow them to retreat, and 100,000 German troops were captured.

Coral Sea 1942 World War II: Japanese and American carrier-borne aircraft clashed and although losses were about even, the Japanese plans for an attack on New Guinea were stopped.

Midway 1942 World War II: in a naval battle dominated by carrier-borne aircraft, the Japanese attack on the Hawaiian Islands was defeated. This marked the end of the Japanese advance in the Pacific.

Philippine Sea 1944 World War II: the biggest carrier battle of all time was a crushing American victory. Japanese losses of carriers and planes were so heavy that the Japanese Navy lost its capability to launch airborne operations.

Leyte Gulf 1944 World War II: in the last major naval battle of the war, the Japanese fleet lost three battleships, four carriers, ten cruisers and eleven destroyers in clashes with American forces at Leyte Gulf in the Philippines.

Imphal/Kohima 1944 World War II: after the Japanese conquest of Malaya and Burma, their attempted invasion of India was checked by General Slim's 14th Army at Imphal and Kohima. Supported by the American-led Chinese in the northeast, the British and Commonwealth forces began an offensive that liberated all of Burma (Myanmar) by summer 1945.

Dien Bien Phu 1954 The French attempt to keep control of their former colony Vietnam ended when their fortified base at Dien Bien Phu was overrun by the Vietminh guerrillas led by General Giap. It led to the establishment of the Communist state of North Vietnam and the non-Communist state of South Vietnam.

ECONOMY AND SOCIETY

Economics

ECONOMIC TERMS

accelerator the impetus to increase new investment in an economy as rising demand puts pressure on existing supply capacities.

advertising the use of the media (commercials, television, newspapers, posters) to promote the sales of products and services.

aggregate demand the total amount of spending on goods and services in an economy.

aggregate supply the total amount of goods and services produced by an economy.

agricultural policy a policy aimed at improving the efficiency of the farm sector and protecting farmers' incomes by the use of grants and price and income support.

appreciation an increase in the price of an asset, or value (exchange rate) of a country's currency that makes imports cheaper and exports more expensive. (See depreciation, and floating exchange rate.)

arbitrage the buying and selling of products, etc., between separate markets (e.g. two countries) in order to take advantage of any price differences in these markets.

asset an item of property (a house, shares, etc.) that has a money value.

balance of payments the balance of a country's imports and exports; a financial statement of a country's transactions with other countries in goods and services ('the current account') and capital flows (investment, loans, etc.).

balance of trade a financial statement of a country's transactions with other countries in goods.

balance sheet a financial statement of a firm's assets and liabilities on the last day of a trading period.

bank a financial institution that accepts deposits from persons and businesses, and provides them with various facilities (money transmission via cheques, loans and overdrafts, etc.).

bank deposit a sum of money held on deposit with a bank either as a 'current account' (withdrawable on demand) or a 'deposit account' (from which withdrawals can be made, subject to notice being given).

barriers to entry obstacles in the way of new firms attempting to enter a market, such as customer brand loyalty to established firm's products.

barter the exchange of one product for another product. (See money.)

base rate the lowest or 'floor' interest rate charged by the banks on loans and overdrafts. This usually applies only to their most creditworthy customers, others being charged higher rates.

bill of exchange a financial security representing an amount of credit extended by one firm to another, usually for three months.

black economy economic activities that go 'unrecorded', in particular, work performed by people who wish to avoid disclosing their income to the tax authorities.

black market an 'unofficial' market in a product which is either prohibited by law (e.g. narcotics) or which is in short supply.

bond a financial security issued by a company or the government as a means of raising long-term loan finance.

budget (government) a financial statement of a government's receipts (from taxes, etc.) and expenditures (social security, etc.).

budget deficit an excess of expenditure over receipts in a government's budget.

budget surplus an excess of receipts over expenditures in a government's budget.

building society a financial institution that accepts deposits from persons and businesses and makes mortgages available for house purchase (and limited banking facilities).

business cycle the tendency for industrial production to swing upwards ('recovery' to 'boom') and downwards ('recession' to 'slump') as demand in the economy rises and falls.

capital physical assets, such as factories used to produce products, and financial assets, such as shares used to finance physical investment.

capital formation additions to the capital stock of an economy.

capital goods products such as machinery and equipment that are purchased by businesses as opposed to consumers. (See consumer goods.)

capital stock a country's accumulated stock of productive assets such as factories, machinery and equipment.

cartel a group of producers (e.g. the OPEC oil cartel) who act together to fix uniform prices, limit production, etc.

central bank the premier bank of a country (usually owned by the state). It is responsible for regulating the state's internal and external monetary affairs. (See monetary policy, and exchange rate.)

centrally-planned economy an economy in which all or most of the country's productive assets are owned by the state as opposed to individuals and firms. (See nationalization and command economy.)

cheque a written order drawn upon a bank. It is a means of purchasing products or withdrawing cash from a bank deposit.

collusion a market situation where suppliers act together to suppress competition. (See cartel.)

command economy an economic system in which economic decision-making is centralized in the hands of the state. Another name for a centrally-planned economy.

commodity market a market that is engaged in the buying and selling of commodities such as tin, copper, wheat, cattle, etc., and the determination of market prices for these products.

common market a group of countries that have entered a formal agreement to provide for the free movement of products, capital and labour across national boundaries.

comparative advantage the advantage possessed by a country engaged in international trade if it can produce a given good at a lower resource cost than other countries.

competition a market situation where suppliers compete against one another in terms of price, quality, advertising, etc.

competition policy a policy aimed at improving market efficiency and protecting consumers by controlling monopolies, mergers, cartels and anti-competitive practices such as refusals to supply, exclusive dealing, etc.

concentration a measure of the extent to which the supply of a particular product is controlled by the leading suppliers.

consumer goods products such as toys, bread, etc., which are purchased by consumers as opposed to businesses. (See capital goods.)

consumption the proportion of current income that is used to purchase goods and services. (See savings.)

convertibility the ability to exchange one foreign currency for another currency.

corporation tax a levy by the government on the income (profits) earned by businesses.

cost the payment (wages, materials, etc.) incurred by a firm in producing its products.

cost of living the general level of prices in an economy as measured by a price index. (See retail price index.)

credit an amount of money made available in the form of a loan, overdraft, mortgage, etc., to persons or businesses.

currency bank notes and coins issued by the monetary authorities of a country. They form part of a country's money supply.

debt an amount of money owing to a person or business that has advanced credit in the form of a loan, overdraft, or mortgage.

deflation a reduction in the level of demand and a fall in the rate of growth of the general price level (disinflation). (See inflation.)

deindustrialization a relative decline in the industrial sector of the economy compared to other sectors, particularly services.

demand the want, need or desire for a product backed by the money to purchase it.

demand curve a line depicting the total amount of a product that buyers are prepared to purchase over a range of prices. (See equilibrium market price.)

depreciation a fall in the value of an asset due to wear and tear, or in the value (exchange rate) of a country's currency; the latter makes imports more expensive and exports cheaper. (See appreciation and floating exchange rate.)

devaluation an administered reduction in the value (exchange rate) of a country's currency under a fixed exchange rate system; this makes imports more expensive and exports cheaper. (See revaluation.)

discount market a market engaged in the buying and selling of bills of exchange and Treasury bills.

disposable income the income remaining to households after the payment of all taxes on income.

diversification the combination in one firm of a number of unrelated productive activities, e.g. brewing and publishing.

dividend income received from the ownership of shares.

dumping the sale of a product in an export market at a price that is *lower* than its domestic price.

economic growth an increase in the amount of goods and services produced in an economy over time.

economics the study of the allocation of *limited* resources of capital, labour, etc., to meet the (*unlimited*) demands of society for goods and services.

economies of scale a fall in the average cost of producing a product as the volume of output is increased.

ECU a unit of account, based upon a basket of European currencies, used as a reserve asset in the European Monetary System, the system that enables member states of the EC to coordinate their exchange rates through the Exchange Rate Mechanism (ERM). ECU is an abbreviation for European Currency Unit.

elasticity of demand the extent to which the demand for a product is affected by changes in its *own* price, consumer's income and the prices of *other* products.

embargo a ban on international trade with a particular country or in particular products.

equilibrium market the price at which the total demand for a product is exactly equal to the total quantity supplied so that the market price 'stabilizes' for the present. (See excess demand, and excess supply.)

eurocurrency a currency that is used to finance trade and investment outside its country of origin, in Western Europe.

European Community (EC) or **European Union** an alliance of 15 European countries that seeks to establish free trade between members (the 'Common Market').

European Currency Unit see ECU.

European Monetary System (EMS) the mechanism that coordinates the exchange rates of member countries of the European Community and facilitates the settlement of payments imbalances. (See European Currency Unit and fixed exchange rates.)

ERM see ECU.

EU European Union (see p. 557).

excess demand demand for a product that is greater than supply at the prevailing price which causes the price to rise. (See equilibrium market price.)

excess supply supply of a product that is greater than demand at the prevailing price. Excess supply causes the price to fall. (See equilibrium market price.)

exchange rate the price of one foreign currency expressed in terms of another. Exchange rates between currencies may be left to 'float' upwards or downwards day-by-day according to market forces, or the authorities may intervene to stabilize or 'fix' the exchange rate at a particular value. (For the exchange rates of all currencies against the US$, see currencies listing p. 539.)

export a product (or asset) that is sold in an overseas market. (See balance of payments.)

factors of production natural resources (tin, wheat, etc.), labour and capital that are used as inputs in the production of goods and services.

fiscal policy the manipulation by the government of taxes, tax rates and government expenditure as a means of controlling the level of spending in the economy.

fixed exchange rate an exchange rate for a currency that is 'pegged' at a particular value by the authorities as opposed to being allowed to 'float' according to market forces.

floating exchange rate an exchange rate for a currency that is free to fluctuate according to market forces as opposed to being 'fixed' by the authorities.

foreign exchange market a market that is engaged in the buying and selling of foreign currencies and the determination of exchange rates between currencies.

free trade international trade that takes place without barriers such as tariffs being placed on the free movement of products between countries. (See common market.)

futures market a market in which financial securities and commodities are transacted for delivery at some specified future date. (See spot market.)

General Agreement on Tariffs and Trade (GATT) a negotiating forum for the removal of tariffs and other obstacles to free trade.

gross domestic product (GDP) the money value of the total amount of goods and services produced by an economy over a one-year period.

gross national product (GNP) GDP plus net property income (profits, interest, dividends) from abroad.

hedging the buying and selling of commodities and financial securities on the futures market in order to counteract price fluctuations.

horizontal integration the specialization by a firm in a *particular* line (or 'stage') of production.

import a product (or asset) that is bought from an overseas supplier. (See balance of payments.)

income wages, profits, interest, rents, etc., that are received for performing work, or supplying an asset.

income tax a levy by the government on the income received by individuals.

index-linking the linking of incomes (wages, pensions, etc.) and assets to the general price level so that their values are not eroded by inflation.

industrial policy a policy aimed at improving market efficiency by supporting innovation and promoting rationalization schemes to remove excess capacity.

inflation a persistent tendency for the general price level of goods to rise over a period of time.

insurance company a financial institution that specializes in collecting premiums from policy holders, to provide them with cover against various risks, including loss of life, fire and theft.

interest income received from lending out money in the form of loans, mortgages, etc.

interest rate the (percentage) rate at which charges are made for borrowing money in the form of loans, overdrafts, mortgages, etc.

International Monetary Fund (IMF) an institution that oversees the exchange-rate policies of member countries and provides financial support for countries in balance-of-payments difficulties.

international trade the import and export of goods and services between countries. (See free trade, and comparative advantage.)

investment the creation of *physical* assets such as factories and the acquisition of *financial* assets such as stocks and shares.

investment trust company a financial institution that issues shares and uses its capital to invest in other companies' stocks and shares.

invisible trade imports and exports of *services*, transfers of interest, profit etc. as opposed to goods. (See visible trade, and balance of payments.)

legal tender that part of the money supply which is issued by the government (typically, notes and coins).

loan a sum of money advanced by a lender (creditor) to a borrower (debtor). (See interest rate.)

M0 a UK money supply definition comprising bank notes and coins plus banks' till money and operational balances at the Bank of England.

M3 a UK money supply definition comprising M0 (see above) plus private sector bank deposits and public sector sterling deposits.

macroeconomics is concerned with how the economy as a whole 'works'. It seeks to identify determinants of the levels of national income, output and spending, employment and prices, and the balance of payments.

market an exchange mechanism that brings together the buyers and sellers of a product, thereby establishing product prices. (See equilibrium market price.)

market economy (or **private enterprise**) an economic system in which the means of production are privately held by individuals and businesses.

merger a combination of two or more firms by the mutual agreement of the firm's management and shareholders. (See takeover.)

microeconomics is concerned with how resources that are scarce are allocated to produce a multitude of goods and services to meet the demands of consumers for these products.

mixed economy an economy in which a country's productive resources are owned both by the state (the public sector) and by individuals and firms (the private sector).

monetarism an economic doctrine that emphasizes the influence of money on the functioning of the economy, in particular its role in causing inflation.

monetary policy the manipulation by the government of the money supply, credit and interest rates as a means of controlling the level of spending in the economy.

money a financial asset such as notes and coins issued by the government, which is generally acceptable as a 'medium of exchange' and can be used to pay for goods and services.

money market a market dealing in the short-run lending and borrowing of money to finance bills of exchange and Treasury bills.

money supply the total amount of money (principally, notes, coins, and bank deposits) in an economy that can be used to finance the purchase of goods, services and assets.

Monopolies and Mergers Commission a UK body that investigates monopolies, mergers and takeovers to determine whether they are in 'the public interest'.

monopoly a market situation where one producer controls the entire supply of a good or service.

mortgage a sum of money advanced by a lender (e.g. a building society) to a borrower, usually as a means of financing the purchase of an asset (a house, or a factory).

multinational company a business that owns productive assets (factories, offices, etc.) in a number of countries.

multiplier the process whereby some initial increase in income in an economy leads to further increases in income as that income is spent and re-spent.

national debt the money owed by the government to domestic and overseas lenders arising from accumulated budget deficits.

national income the total money value of the income resulting from a country's economic activities over a one-year period.

nationalization the taking into public ownership of a business or resource previously in the private sector.

Office of Fair Trading the UK body charged with administering British competition policy.

oligopoly a market situation where the supply of a product is controlled by a few large producers.

option the right to sell or buy a commodity or financial asset at an agreed price on the futures market.

overdraft a facility provided by a bank, etc., that enables a customer to take out more money than they have deposited with the bank up to a specified limit.

pension fund a financial institution that specializes in collecting superannuation contributions from members during their working lives, and providing them with a pension income when they retire.

price the money value of a product or asset.

price level the general level of prices in an economy as measured by a price index. (See retail price index.)

prices and incomes policy the control of prices and incomes (particularly wages) in order to stop or slow inflation in an economy.

price system an allocative mechanism in which the interaction of buyers and sellers in markets establishes product prices and determines which and how many products are required.

private enterprise economy an economy in which all or most of a country's productive assets are owned by individuals and firms as opposed to the state.

privatization the sale of a nationalized (publicly owned) business, etc., to the private sector by issuing share capital.

productivity a measure of the efficiency of a given resource input (labour, capital) in producing output.

profit the income received from selling a product or asset at a price higher than it cost to produce or buy.

protectionism the erection of barriers to trade, such as tariffs, to protect domestic producers from the competition of low-priced imports.

public sector borrowing requirement (PSBR) the money borrowed by the government to cover a budget deficit.

quantity theory of money the proposition that inflation is caused by an 'excessive' increase in the money supply.

quota a limitation on the production of, or trade in, a product. Quotas are imposed by suppliers or by the government.

regional policy a policy aimed at removing regional imbalances in income and unemployment levels by e.g. providing financial support to firms located in 'depressed' areas.

rent income received from the ownership of property.

Restrictive Practices Court a UK body that investigates trade practices such as price-fixing agreements between firms to determine whether they are in 'the public interest'.

retail price index (RPI) a measure of the average prices of a 'basket' of goods and services bought by consumers over time. (See inflation.)

revaluation an administered increase in the value of an asset, or value (exchange rate) of a country's currency under a fixed exchange-rate system.

savings that proportion of current income that is not immediately spent, but is invested and used to finance future consumption.

share a financial security issued by a joint-stock company as a means of raising capital, which in the case of an ordinary share carries voting and dividend rights.

specialization a form of division of labour whereby each individual or business concentrates their productive efforts on a single or limited number of activities.

speculation the buying and selling of a commodity or financial asset in order to make a capital gain.

spot market a market in which financial securities, commodities, etc., are transacted for *immediate* delivery. (See futures market.)

standard of living the general level of economic prosperity in an economy.

stock a fixed-interest financial security issued by a company or government as a means of raising capital.

stock exchange or **capital market** a market engaged in the buying and selling of existing stocks and shares and in raising capital by the issue of new securities.

supply the amount of a product offered for sale by suppliers.

supply curve a line depicting the total amount of a product that producers are prepared to supply over a range of prices. (See equilibrium market price.)

takeover the acquisition by one firm of another firm by purchasing its share capital. (See merger.)

tariff a tax levied by the government on imported goods, often as a means of protecting domestic producers from foreign competition.

tax a levy by the government on the income of individuals and businesses (e.g. income tax and corporation tax), spending (e.g. value added tax), wealth (e.g. inheritance tax), imported goods (e.g. customs duty), etc.

terms of trade an index of the relative prices of a country's imports and exports, indicating that if export prices go up faster than import prices the country is better off.

Treasury bill a British financial security (with a life of three months) issued by the government as a means of borrowing money.

unemployment rate the percentage of the available labour force in an economy currently out of work.

unit trust a financial institution that sells 'units' to savers, using the moneys received to invest in stocks and shares, etc.

value added tax (VAT) a levy by the government on the value added to a good or service at each separate 'stage' in its production.

vertical integration the combination in one firm of a number of sequentially linked activities in the production of a good or service, e.g. oil extraction, refining and petrol retailing.

visible trade imports and exports of *goods* that are recorded by the customs authorities as they enter or leave a country. (See invisible trade, and balance of payments.)

wage income received by persons for undertaking employment.

wealth the stock of assets owned by an individual or a country.

wealth tax a tax (called an inheritance tax in the UK) levied on a person's assets when those assets are transferred to others.

NOBEL ECONOMICS PRIZE

1969 Ragnar Frisch, Norwegian, Jan Tinbergen, Dutch: work in econometrics.

1970 Paul A. Samuelson, US: scientific analysis of economic theory.

1971 Simon Kuznets, US: research on the economic growth of nations.

1972 Sir John Hicks, English, Kenneth J. Arrow, US: general economic equilibrium theory.

1973 Wassily Leontief, US: work on input analysis.

1974 Gunnar Myrdal, Swedish, Friedrich von Hayek, British: analysis of the interdependence of economic, social and institutional phenomna.

1975 Leonid V. Kantorovich, Russian, Tjalling C. Koopmans, US: contributions to the theory of optimum allocation of resources.

1976 Milton Friedman, US: consumption analysis, monetary theory and economic stabilization.

1977 Bertil Ohlin, Swedish, James Meade, English: contributions to theory of international trade.

1978 Herbert A. Simon, US: decision-making processes in economic organization.

1979 W. Arthur Lewis, English, Theodore W. Schultz, US: economic processes in developing nations.

1980 Lawrence R. Klein, US: development and analysis of empirical models of business fluctuations.

1981 James Tobin, US: empirical macroeconomic theories.

1982 George Stigler, US: work on the economic effects of governmental regulation.

1983 Gerard Debrau, US: mathematical proof of supply and demand theory.

1984 Sir Richard Stone, English: the development of a national income accounting system.

1985 Franco Modigliani, US: analysis of household savings and financial markets.

1986 James McGill Buchanan, US: political theories advocating limited government role in the economy.

1987 Robert M. Solow, US: contributions to the theory of economic growth.

1988 Maurice Allais, French: contributions to the theory of markets and efficient use of resources.

1989 Trygve Haavelmo, Norwegian: testing fundamental econometric theories.

1990 Harry Markowitz, Merton Miller, William Sharpe, US: pioneering theories on managing investment portfolios and corporate finances.

1991 Ronald H. Coase (British-born) US: work on the value and social problems of companies.

1992 Gary S. Becker, US: work linking economic theory to aspects of human behaviour, drawing on other social sciences.

1993 Robert W. Fogel, Douglas C. North, US: economic history research.

1994 John F. Nash, John C. Harsanyi, US, Reinhard Selten, German: game theory.

NATIONAL ECONOMIES

The gross national product (GNP) and the gross national product per head of the population are given for each sovereign state. (GNP is gross domestic product, or GDP, plus net property income, such as profits, interest and dividends, from abroad. GDP may be defined as the money value of the total amount of goods and services produced by a national economy over a one-year period.)

Figures (in US $) are also given for total imports and total exports. For the currency of each state see the following section.

Afghanistan *GNP ($ million):* 3100 (1988); *per head:* $220. *Imports ($ million):* 737 (1991). *Exports ($ million):* 243 (1991). *Main imports*: machinery and transport equipment 37.7% (1989/90), basic manufacture 18.3% (1989/90). *Main exports*: dried fruit and nuts 42.7% (1990), carpets and rugs 16.5% (1990). *Principal trading partner*: Russia.

Albania *GNP ($ million):* 1167 (1993); *per head:* $340. *Imports ($ million):* 147 (1991). *Exports ($ million):* 80 (1991). *Main imports*: machinery and transport equipment 30.9% (1990), fuels, minerals and metals 24.5% (1990). *Main exports*: fuels, minerals and metals 46.8% (1990), food 22.1% (1990). *Principal trading partners*: Italy, Germany, Czech Republic.

Algeria *GNP ($ million):* 44,000 (1994 est); *per head:* $1700. *Imports ($ million):* 7770 (1993). *Exports ($ million):* 10,230 (1993). *Main imports*: electrical and non-electrical machinery 30.4% (1990), food and beverages 19.4% (1990). *Main exports*: petroleum and natural gas 96.9% (1990). *Principal trading partners*: France, Italy, USA, Germany.

Andorra *GNP ($ million):* 930 (1992 est); *per head:* $16,600. *Imports ($ million):* 700.4 (1987). *Exports ($ million):* 24.6 (1987). *Main imports*: electrical and electronic equipment 11.9% (1990), transport equipment 9.8% (1990). *Main exports*: wearing apparel 52.1% (1990), mineral water 15.9% (1990). *Principal trading partners*: France, Spain.

Angola *GNP ($ million):* 8300 (1991); *per head:* $950. *Imports ($ million):* 443 (1987). *Exports ($ million):* 2147 (1987). *Main imports*: raw materials 50.2% (1991). *Main exports*: mineral fuels 89.8% (1991), diamonds 5.5% (1991). *Principal trading partners*: USA, Portugal.

Antigua and Barbuda *GNP ($ million):* 425 (1993); *per head:* $6390. *Imports ($ million):* 215 (1991). *Exports ($ million):* 32 (1991). *Main imports*: basic manufacture 64.4% (1990). *Main exports*: manufactures 69.3% (1990). *Principal trading partners*: USA, UK, Germany.

Argentina *GNP ($ million):* 300,200 (1994 est); *per head:* $8960. *Imports ($ million):* 16,784 (1993). *Exports ($ million):* 13,118 (1993). *Main imports*: machinery and transport equipment 34.4% (1991), chemical products 22.1% (1991). *Main exports*: food products and live animals 39.1% (1991), petroleum products 21.1% (1991). *Principal trading partners*: USA, Brazil, Netherlands, Germany.

Armenia *GNP ($ million):* 2471 (1993 est); *per head:* $660. *Imports ($ million):* 85 (1993 est). *Exports ($ million):* 29 (1993 est). *Main imports*: food products; coal and natural gas. *Main exports*: processed food, chemicals. *Principal trading partners*: Georgia, Russia.

Australia *GNP ($ million):* 316,700 (1994 est); *per head:* $17,970. *Imports ($ million):* 45,577 (1993). *Exports ($ million):* 42,723 (1993). *Main imports*: machinery 28.8% (1991/92), basic manufacturers 15.5% (1991/92). *Main exports*: crude materials 24.7% (1991/92), mineral fuels and lubricants 19.7% (1991/92). *Principal trading partners*: Japan, USA, New Zealand, Germany, UK.

Austria *GNP ($ million):* 195,100 (1992 est); *per head:* $24,970. *Imports ($ million):* 48,578 (1993). *Exports ($ million):* 40,174 (1993). *Main imports*: machinery and transport equipment 39.1% (1991), chemicals and related products 9.1% (1991). *Main exports*: machinery and transport equipment 38.3% (1991), chemicals 8.9% (1991). *Principal trading partners*: Germany, Italy, Switzerland, France.

Azerbaijan *GNP ($ million):* 5424 (1993 est); *per head:* $730. *Imports ($ million):* 241 (1993 est). *Exports ($ million):* 351 (1993 est). *Main imports*: food and live animals. *Main exports*: petroleum and petroleum products. *Principal trading partners*: Russia, Turkey.

Bahamas *GNP ($ million):* 3059 (1993); *per head:* $11,500. *Imports ($ million):* 1801 (1991). *Exports ($ million):* 1517 (1991). *Main imports*: crude petroleum 52.2% (1990). *Main exports*: crude petroleum 58.8% (1990), chemicals 17.5% (1990). *Principal trading partners*: USA, Saudi Arabia.

Bahrain *GNP ($ million):* 4283 (1993); *per head:* $7870. *Imports ($ million):* 3825 (1993). *Exports ($ million):* 3689 (1993). *Main imports*: crude-petroleum products 41.7% (1991), non-petroleum products 58.3% (1991). *Main exports*: petroleum products 77.6% (1991), aluminium products 11.3% (1991). *Principal trading partners*: Saudi Arabia, USA, United Arab Emirates.

Bangladesh *GNP ($ million):* 25,382 (1993); *per head:* $220. *Imports ($ million):* 3987 (1993). *Exports ($ million):* 2272 (1993). *Main imports*: textile, yarn, fabrics and made-up articles 19.8% (1991/92), machinery and transport equipment 8.8% (1991/92). *Main exports*: ready-made garments 54.6% (1991/92), jute manufactures 15.2% (1991/92). *Principal trading partners*: USA, Japan, Germany, South Korea, India.

Barbados *GNP ($ million):* 1620 (1993); *per head:* $6240. *Imports ($ million):* 574 (1993). *Exports ($ million):* 179 (1993). *Main imports*: machinery 16.7% (1991), food and beverages 16.1% (1991). *Main exports*: sugar 13.1% (1991), chemicals 10.0% (1991). *Principal trading partners*: USA, UK, Trinidad.

Belarus *GNP ($ million):* 29,290 (1993 est); *per head:* $2840. *Imports ($ million):* 747 (1993 est). *Exports ($ million):* 715 (1993 est). *Main imports*: food transport equipment and vehicles, industrial raw materials.

Main exports: food and live animals, vehicles. *Principal trading partners*: Russia, Ukraine, Germany.

Belgium *GNP ($ million)*: 227,600 (1994 est); *per head*: $22,710. *Imports ($ million)*: 125,047 (1992). *Exports ($ million)*: 123,132 (1992). *Main imports*: machinery and transport equipment 26.0% (1991), chemicals and chemical products 11.5% (1991). *Main exports*: machinery and transport equipment 26.0% (1991), chemicals and chemical products 11.5% (1991). *Principal trading partners*: Germany, Netherlands, France, UK, Italy.

Belize *GNP ($ million)*: 499 (1993); *per head*: $2440. *Imports ($ million)*: 281 (1993). *Exports ($ million)*: 115 (1993). *Main imports*: machinery and transport equipment 23.1% (1991), manufactured goods 17.5% (1991). *Main exports*: sugar 27.0% (1991), orange concentrate 14.8% (1991). *Principal trading partners*: USA, UK, Mexico.

Benin *GNP ($ million)*: 2189 (1993); *per head*: $420. *Imports ($ million)*: 207 (1989). *Exports ($ million)*: 97 (1989). *Main imports*: manufactured articles 30.7% (1989), fuel products 15.3% (1989). *Main exports*: raw cotton 60.0% (1989), fuels 21.3% (1989). *Principal trading partners*: France, Portugal, USA, Netherlands.

Bhutan *GNP ($ million)*: 253 (1993); *per head*: $170. *Imports ($ million)*: 102 (1991). *Exports ($ million)*: 72 (1991). *Main imports*: petroleum products 8.5% (1989), rice 5.8% (1989). *Main exports*: electricity 28.4% (1989), minerals 18.5% (1989). *Principal trading partner*: India.

Bolivia *GNP ($ million)*: 5472 (1993); *per head*: $770. *Imports ($ million)*: 1206 (1993). *Exports ($ million)*: 728 (1993). *Main imports*: raw materials for industry 36.9% (1992), capital goods for industry 19.2% (1992). *Main exports*: zinc 22.3% (1992), natural gas 22.2% (1992). *Principal trading partners*: USA, Argentina, UK, Brazil.

Bosnia-Herzegovina No figures available.

Botswana *GNP ($ million)*: 3630 (1993); *per head*: $2590. *Imports ($ million)*: 1776 (1993). *Exports ($ million)*: 1725 (1993). *Main imports*: transport equipment 19.2% (1990), machinery and electrical goods 18.5% (1990). *Main exports*: diamonds 78.8% (1992); copper-nickel matte 5.9% (1992). *Principal trading partners*: South Africa, UK.

Brazil *GNP ($ million)*: 636,800 (1994 est); *per head*: $4070. *Imports ($ million)*: 27,740 (1993). *Exports ($ million)*: 38,783 (1993). *Main imports*: crude petroleum 16.0% (1991), non-electrical machinery 14.9% (1991). *Main exports*: non-electrical machinery and equipment 8.2% (1991), iron ore 8.2% (1991). *Principal trading partners*: USA, Germany, Japan, Netherlands, Argentina.

Brunei *GNP ($ million)*: 3500 (1991); *per head*: $13,890. *Imports ($ million)*: 1176 (1992). *Exports ($ million)*: 2370 (1992). *Main imports*: machinery and transport equipment 32.8% (1988), manufactured goods 23.7% (1988). *Main exports*: crude petroleum 46.9% (1991), natural gas 44.6% (1991). *Principal trading partners*: Japan, Singapore, South Korea.

Bulgaria *GNP ($ million)*: 10,400 (1994 est); *per head*: $1230. *Imports ($ million)*: 4239 (1992). *Exports ($ million)*: 4071 (1992). *Main imports*: machinery and equipment 38.9% (1991), fuels, minerals, raw materials and metals 15.8% (1991). *Main exports*: machinery and equipment 30.6% (1991), consumer goods 22.3% (1991). *Principal trading partners*: Russia, Germany, Italy.

Burkina Faso *GNP ($ million)*: 2928 (1993); *per head*: $300. *Imports ($ million)*: 533 (1991). *Exports ($ million)*: 106 (1991). *Main imports*: manufactured goods 26.6% (1990), machinery and transport equipment 24.1% (1990). *Main exports*: raw cotton 56.7% (1990), manufactured goods 23.2% (1990). *Principal trading partners*: France, Côte d'Ivoire, Taiwan.

Burundi *GNP ($ million)*: 1102 (1993); *per head*: $180. *Imports ($ million)*: 204 (1993). *Exports ($ million)*: 68 (1993). *Main imports*: machinery and transport equipment 34.9% (1991); food and food products 11.6% (1991). *Main exports*: coffee 81.0% (1991), tea 9.1% (1991). *Principal trading partners*: Belgium, Germany.

Cambodia *GNP ($ million)*: 1725 (1991); *per head*: $200. *Imports ($ million)*: 215 (1989 est). *Exports ($ million)*: 25 (1989 est). *Main imports*: machinery and transport equipment 36.9% (1985), petroleum and petroleum products 30.2% (1985). *Main exports*: rubber 82.9% (1985), basic manufactures 5.1% (1985). *Principal trading partners*: Thailand, Singapore, Russia.

Cameroon *GNP ($ million)*: 9663 (1993); *per head*: $770. *Imports ($ million)*: 1175 (1992). *Exports ($ million)*: 1815 (1992). *Main imports*: machinery and transport equipment 30.8% (1990), basic maufactures 23% (1990). *Main exports*: crude petroleum 54.2% (1990), cocoa 10.5% (1990). *Principal trading partners*: France, Netherlands, USA, Germany.

Canada *GNP ($ million)*: 576,100 (1994 est); *per head*: $20,470. *Imports ($ million)*: 138,684 (1993). *Exports ($ million)*: 144,693 (1993). *Main imports*: road motor vehicles and parts 19.5% (1991), chemicals 6.7% (1991). *Main exports*: road motor vehicles and parts 21.0% (1991), crude materials 12.1% (1991). *Principal trading partners*: USA, Japan, UK, Germany, France.

Cape Verde *GNP ($ million)*: 347 (1993); *per head*: $870. *Imports ($ million)*: 180 (1992). *Exports ($ million)*: 5 (1992). *Main imports*: food and live animals 25.2% (1989), machinery and transport equipment 25.0% (1989). *Main exports*: petroleum products 60.0% (1989), food and live animals 27.5% (1989). *Principal trading partners*: Portugal, Spain, Netherlands.

Central African Republic *GNP ($ million)*: 1263 (1993); *per head*: $390. *Imports ($ million)*: 165 (1992). *Exports ($ million)*: 124 (1992). *Main imports*: food products 18.7% (1991), transportation equipment 13.3% (1991). *Main exports*: diamonds 51.1% (1991), cotton 18.9% (1991). *Principal trading partners*: Belgium, France, Germany.

Chad *GNP ($ million)*: 1248 (1993); *per head*: $200. *Imports ($ million)*: 297 (1991). *Exports ($ million)*:

194 (1991). *Main imports*: petroleum products 16.8% (1983), cereal products 16.8% (1983). *Main exports*: raw cotton 91.1% (1983), live cattle and frozen meat 1.8% (1983). *Principal trading partners*: France, Portugal, USA, Nigeria.

Chile *GNP ($ million)*: 47,500 (1994 est); *per head*: $3510. *Imports ($ million)*: 11,125 (1993). *Exports ($ million)*: 9202 (1993). *Main imports*: intermediate goods 57.8% (1991), capital goods 23.9% (1991). *Total exports*: mining 48.7% (1991), industrial products 36.6% (1991). *Principal trading partners*: USA, Japan, Brazil, Germany.

China *GNP ($ million)*: 418,500 (1994 est); *per head*: $360. *Imports ($ million)*: 103,088 (1993). *Exports ($ million)*: 90,970 (1993). *Main imports*: machinery and transport equipment 30.8% (1991), products of textile industries, rubber and metal products 16.5% (1991). *Main exports*: products of textile industries, rubber and metal products 20.1% (1991), food and live animals 10.0% (1991). *Principal trading partners*: Hong Kong, Japan, USA, Germany, Singapore.

China (Taiwan) *GNP ($ million)*: 252,200 (1994 est); *per head*: $12,050. *Imports ($ million)*: 77,099 (1993). *Exports ($ million)*: 84,678 (1993). *Main imports*: electronic machinery 17.5% (1992), non-electrical machinery 13.5% (1992). *Main exports*: non-electrical machinery 19.6% (1992), electronic machinery 16.9% (1992). *Principal trading partners*: Japan, USA, Hong Kong, Germany.

Colombia *GNP ($ million)*: 70,100 (1994 est); *per head*: $2230. *Imports ($ million)*: 6516 (1992). *Exports ($ million)*: 6917 (1992). *Main imports*: machinery 25.3% (1991), chemicals 11.0% (1991). *Main exports*: petroleum and petroleum products 28.8% (1991), coffee 18.2% (1991). *Principal trading partners*: USA, Germany, Japan, Venezuela, Netherlands.

Comoros *GNP ($ million)*: 272 (1993); *per head*: $520. *Imports ($ million)*: 69 (1992). *Exports ($ million)*: 22 (1992). *Main imports*: rice 11.9% (1992), vehicles 10.7% (1992). *Main exports*: vanilla 70.4% (1992), ylang-ylang 19.5% (1992). *Principal trading partners*: France, USA, Italy.

Congo *GNP ($ million)*: 2318 (1993); *per head*: $920. *Imports ($ million)*: 472 (1991). *Exports ($ million)*: 1029 (1991). *Main imports*: machinery 22.4% (1988), food, beverages and tobacco 21.3% (1988). *Main exports*: petroleum and products 76.7% (1988), wood and wood products 15.6% (1988). *Principal trading partners*: France, USA, Spain.

Costa Rica *GNP ($ million)*: 7041 (1993); *per head*: $2160. *Imports ($ million)*: 2907 (1993). *Exports ($ million)*: 2085 (1993). *Main imports*: basic manufactures for industry 38.0% (1991), non-durable consumer goods 12.3% (1991). *Main exports*: garments 26.4% (1991), bananas 25.1% (1991). *Principal trading partners*: USA, Germany, Japan.

Côte d'Ivoire (Ivory Coast) *GNP ($ million)*: 8397 (1993); *per head*: $630. *Imports ($ million)*: 5347 (1992). *Exports ($ million)*: 6220 (1992). *Main imports*: Crude and refined petroleum 22.5% (1992), machinery and transport equipment 21.2% (1992). *Main exports*: cocoa beans and products 33.8% (1992), coffee beans and products 7.3% (1992). *Principal trading partners*: France, Nigeria, Netherlands.

Croatia *GNP ($ million)*: 24,400 (1991); *per head*: $5110. *Imports ($ million)*: 4667 (1993 est). *Exports ($ million)*: 3903 (1993 est). *Main imports*: petroleum and petroleum products, food. *Main exports*: aluminium products, food and live animals. *Principal trading partners*: Italy, Germany.

Cuba *GNP ($ million)*: 17,000 (1991); *per head*: $1580. *Imports ($ million)*: 3690 (1991). *Exports ($ million)*: 3585 (1991). *Main imports*: minerals, fuels and lubricants 32.4% (1989), machinery and transport equipment 31.2% (1989). *Main exports*: sugar 73.2% (1989), minerals and concentrates 9.2% (1989). *Principal trading partners*: Russia, Germany, China.

Cyprus *GNP ($ million)*: 7539 (1993); *per head*: $10,380. *Imports ($ million)*: 2590 (1993). *Exports ($ million)*: 867 (1993). *Main imports*: consumer goods 25.6% (1992), transport equipment 15.7% (1992). *Main exports*: clothing 14.2% (1992), potatoes 4.8% (1992). *Principal trading partners*: UK, Lebanon, Japan, Italy.

Czech Republic *GNP ($ million)*: 37,400 (1994 est); *per head*: $3630. *Imports ($ million)*: 12,567 (1993 est). *Exports ($ million)*: 12,936 (1993 est). *Main imports*: machinery and transport equipment, minerals, fuels and lubricants. *Main exports*: machinery and transport equipment, basic manufactures. *Principal trading partners*: Germany, Austria, Slovakia, UK, Russia.

Denmark *GNP ($ million)*: 148,800 (1994 est); *per head*: $28,830. *Imports ($ million)*: 30,498 (1993). *Exports ($ million)*: 37,034 (1993). *Main imports*: intermediate goods for industry 44.6% (1993), machinery 10.5% (1993). *Main exports*: non-electrical and electrical machinery 23.3% (1992), chemical products 10.0% (1992). *Principal trading partners*: Germany, Sweden, UK, USA, Netherlands.

Djibouti *GNP ($ million)*: 448 (1993); *per head*: $780. *Imports ($ million)*: 245 (1991). *Exports ($ million)*: 17 (1991). *Main imports*: food, tobacco and beverages 32.7% (1991), textiles and footwear 11.7% (1991). *Main exports*: live animals 15.5% (1991), food and food products 12.8% (1991). *Principal trading partners*: France, Yemen, Ethiopia.

Dominica *GNP ($ million)*: 193 (1993); *per head*: $2680. *Imports ($ million)*: 111 (1992). *Exports ($ million)*: 56 (1992). *Main imports*: machinery and transport equipment 26.1% (1990), basic manufactures 24.5% (1990). *Main exports ($ million)*: bananas 55.8% (1990), coconut-based soaps 20.5% (1990). *Principal trading partners*: UK, USA, Jamaica.

Dominican Republic *GNP ($ million)*: 8039 (1993); *per head*: $1080. *Imports ($ million)*: 2443 (1993). *Exports ($ million)*: 555 (1993). *Main imports*: crude petroleum and petroleum products 25.3% (1991), agricultural products 19.3% (1991). *Main exports*: ferronickel 33.5% (1991), raw sugar 20.1% (1991). *Principal trading partners*: USA, Netherlands, Venezuela, Japan, Mexico.

Ecuador *GNP ($ million):* 13,217 (1993); *per head:* $1170. *Imports ($ million):* 2562 (1993). *Exports ($ million):* 2904 (1993). *Main imports*: industrial raw materials 41.2% (1991), industrial capital goods 22.1% (1991). *Main exports*: crude petroleum 37.1% (1991), bananas 25.1% (1991). *Principal trading partners*: USA, Japan, Germany, Brazil.

Egypt *GNP ($ million):* 53,300 (1994 est); *per head:* $930. *Imports ($ million):* 8184 (1993). *Exports ($ million):* 2244 (1993). *Main imports*: machinery and transport equipment 23.5% (1992), foodstuffs 19% (1992). *Main exports*: petroleum and petroleum products 45.4% (1992), cotton yarn, textiles and fabrics 15.5% (1992). *Principal trading partners*: USA, Germany, France, Italy.

El Salvador *GNP ($ million):* 7233 (1993); *per head:* $1320. *Imports ($ million):* 1912 (1993). *Exports ($ million):* 732 (1993). *Main imports*: chemical products 15.1% (1991), crude petroleum 9.0% (1991). *Main exports*: coffee 37.8% (1991), raw sugar 5.5% (1991). *Principal trading partners*: USA, Guatemala, Germany, Mexico.

Equatorial Guinea *GNP ($ million):* 161 (1993); *per head:* $360. *Imports ($ million):* 92 (1992). *Exports ($ million):* 41 (1992). *Main imports*: machinery and transport equipment 58.2% (1990), petroleum and petroleum products 7.7% (1990). *Main exports*: ships and boats 38.7% (1990), textile fibres and waste 11.5% (1990). *Principal trading partners*: Netherlands, Spain, France.

Eritrea *GNP ($ million):* 400 (1992 est); *per head:* $110 (1992 est). *Imports ($ million):* n/a. *Exports ($ million):* n/a. *Main imports*: machinery, petroleum and petroleum products. *Main exports*: textiles, hides. *Principal trading partners*: USA, Italy.

Estonia *GNP ($ million):* 2400 (1994 est); *per head:* $1560. *Imports ($ million):* 438 (1992). *Exports ($ million):* 473 (1992). *Main imports*: mineral products 27.2% (1992), machinery 18.3% (1992). *Main exports*: textiles and textile articles 14.0% (1992), base metals and articles 11.3% (1992). *Principal trading partners*: Russia, Finland, Sweden, Germany.

Ethiopia *GNP ($ million):* 6206 (1992); *per head:* $110. *Imports ($ million):* 799 (1992). *Exports ($ million):* 169 (1992). *Main imports*: machinery 16.7% (1992), petroleum and petroleum products 12.3% (1992). *Main exports*: coffee 55.0% (1992), hides 18.1% (1992). *Principal trading partners*: USA, Germany, Japan.

Fiji *GNP ($ million):* 1626 (1993); *per head:* $2140. *Imports ($ million):* 634 (1993). *Exports ($ million):* 405 (1993). *Main imports*: durable manufactures 24.9% (1992), machinery and transport equipment 24.7% (1992). *Main exports*: sugar 40.9% (1992), gold 11.2% (1992). *Principal trading partners*: Australia, UK, New Zealand, Japan.

Finland *GNP ($ million):* 101,800 (1994 est); *per head:* $20,240. *Imports ($ million):* 18,032 (1993). *Exports ($ million):* 23,466 (1993). *Main imports*: raw materials 52.1% (1992), consumer goods 21.9% (1992). *Main exports*: metal products and machinery 33.3% (1992), paper, paper products and graphic arts 30.3% (1992). *Principal trading partners*: Germany, Sweden, UK, France, Russia.

France *GNP ($ million):* 1,329,400 (1994 est); *per head:* $23,140. *Imports ($ million):* 201,838 (1993). *Exports ($ million):* 209,349 (1993). *Main imports*: machinery 24.5% (1992), agricultural products 11.7% (1992). *Main exports*: machinery 27.2% (1992), agricultural products 16.1% (1992). *Principal trading partners*: Germany, Italy, UK, Belgium, USA, Netherlands.

Gabon *GNP ($ million):* 5004 (1993); *per head:* $4050. *Imports ($ million):* 884 (1991). *Exports ($ million):* 2273 (1991). *Main imports*: machinery and mechanical equipment 29.2% (1989), food and agricultural products 14.6% (1989). *Main exports*: crude petroleum and petroleum products 80.0% (1992), wood 9.0% (1992). *Principal trading partners*: France, USA, Germany, Spain.

Gambia *GNP ($ million):* 372 (1993); *per head:* $360. *Imports ($ million):* 222 (1991). *Exports ($ million):* 42 (1991). *Main imports*: food 30.4% (1991), basic manufactures 18.1% (1991). *Main exports*: peanuts 12.4% (1991), fish and fish preparations 9.1% (1991). *Principal trading partners*: Belgium, UK, New Zealand.

Georgia *GNP ($ million):* 3071 (1993 est); *per head:* $560. *Imports ($ million):* n/a. *Exports ($ million):* n/a. *Main imports*: food and live animals. *Main exports*: food and live animals. *Principal trading partners*: Russia, Azerbaijan.

Germany *GNP ($ million):* 2,050,800 (1994 est); *per head:* $25,100. *Imports ($ million):* 326,981 (1993). *Exports ($ million):* 362,064 (1993). *Main imports*: machinery and transport equipment 34.6% (1992), chemicals and chemical products 8.6% (1992). *Main exports*: transport equipment 16.6% (1992), chemicals and chemical products 12.6% (1992). *Principal trading partners*: France, Netherlands, Italy, UK, Belgium, USA, Japan.

Ghana *GNP ($ million):* 7036 (1993); *per head:* $430. *Imports ($ million):* 1275 (1991). *Exports ($ million):* 1024 (1991). *Main imports*: machinery and transport equipment 28.1% (1987), mineral fuels and lubricants 14.1% (1987). *Main exports*: cocoa 53.9% (1987), logs and sawn timber 17.9% (1987). *Principal trading partners*: UK, USA, Netherlands, Germany, Nigeria.

Greece *GNP ($ million):* 85,400 (1994 est); *per head:* $8320. *Imports ($ million):* 23,220 (1992). *Exports ($ million):* 9509 (1992). *Main imports*: machinery and transport equipment 34.1% (1992), food, beverages and tobacco 11.7% (1992). *Main exports*: food, beverages and tobacco 27.8% (1992), clothing 21.5%. (1992). *Principal trading partners*: Germany, Italy, France, Netherlands, UK, Japan.

Grenada *GNP ($ million):* 219 (1993); *per head:* $2410. *Imports ($ million):* 107 (1992). *Exports ($ million):* 20 (1992). *Main imports*: machinery and transport equipment 24.2% (1991), food 23.9% (1991). *Main exports*: bananas 19.0% (1991), nutmeg 17.6% (1991). *Principal trading partners*: USA, UK, Trinidad and Tobago.

Guatemala *GNP ($ million):* 11,092 (1993); *per head:* $1110. *Imports ($ million):* 2599 (1993). *Exports ($ million):* 1340 (1993). *Main imports*: primary and intermediate materials for industry 39.5% (1991), capital goods 19.0% (1991). *Main exports*: coffee 22.7% (1991), sugar 11.4% (1991). *Principal trading partners*: USA, El Salvador, Mexico, Japan.

Guinea *GNP ($ million)*: 3170 (1993); *per head*: $510. *Imports ($ million)*: 693 (1990). *Exports ($ million)*: 788 (1990). *Main imports*: intermediate goods 33.7% (1988), capital goods 13.1% (1988). *Main exports*: bauxite 56.9% (1990), alumina 20.7% (1990). *Principal trading partners*: France, USA, Belgium.

Guinea-Bissau *GNP ($ million)*: 233 (1993); *per head*: $220. *Imports ($ million)*: 62 (1993). *Exports ($ million)*: 16 (1993). *Main imports*: transport equipment 28.7% (1988), building materials 17.9% (1988). *Main exports*: cashews 52.8% (1988), peanuts 11.3% (1988). *Principal trading partners*: Portugal, Italy, Spain.

Guyana *GNP ($ million)*: 285 (1993); *per head*: $350. *Imports ($ million)*: 382 (1992). *Exports ($ million)*: 423 (1992). *Main imports*: capital goods 40.6% (1991), fuels and lubricants 21.9% (1991). *Main exports*: sugar 35.3% (1991), bauxite 30.2% (1991). *Principal trading partners*: UK, USA, Trinidad.

Haiti *GNP ($ million)*: 2471 (1991); *per head*: $370. *Imports ($ million)*: 278 (1992). *Exports ($ million)*: 78 (1992). *Main imports*: food and live animals 28.6% (1992), mineral fuels 21.4% (1992). *Main exports*: local manufactures 62.5% (1992), coffee 12.4% (1992). *Principal trading partners*: USA, France, Italy, Belgium.

Honduras *GNP ($ million)*: 3220 (1993); *per head*: $580. *Imports ($ million)*: 1130 (1993). *Exports ($ million)*: 814 (1993). *Main imports*: machinery and transport equipment 25.9% (1991), mineral fuels 18.8% (1991). *Main exports*: bananas 42.3% (1991), coffee 19.2% (1991). *Principal trading partners*: USA, Japan, Germany.

Hungary *GNP ($ million)*: 40,700 (1994 est); *per head*: $3950. *Imports ($ million)*: 12,570 (1993). *Exports ($ million)*: 8886 (1993). *Main imports*: industrial consumer goods 22.2% (1992), machinery and transport equipment 20.7% (1992). *Main exports*: industrial consumer goods 26.2% (1992), food and live animals 24.0% (1992). *Principal trading partners*: Germany, Austria, Italy, Czech Republic, Russia.

Iceland *GNP ($ million)*: 6236 (1993); *per head*: $23,620. *Imports ($ million)*: 1349 (1993). *Exports ($ million)*: 1399 (1993). *Main imports*: consumer goods 21.7% (1992), capital goods 18.4% (1992). *Main exports*: frozen cod fillets 18.2% (1992), salted fish 9.6% (1992). *Principal trading partners*: UK, Germany, Norway, USA.

India *GNP ($ million)*: 265,300 (1994 est); *per head*: $300. *Imports ($ million)*: 22,761 (1993). *Exports ($ million)*: 21,553 (1993). *Main imports*: mineral fuels and lubricants 27.5% (1992), machinery, transport equipment and fabricated metals 21.7% (1992). *Main exports*: cut and polished diamonds 14.0% (1992), ready-made garments 12.3% (1992). *Principal trading partners*: USA, Japan, Germany, UK, Saudi Arabia, Belgium.

Indonesia *GNP ($ million)*: 156,100 (1994 est); *per head*: $830. *Imports ($ million)*: 27,311 (1992). *Exports ($ million)*: 33,861 (1992). *Main imports*: machinery and transport equipment 45.0% (1991), chemicals 13.3% (1991). *Main exports*: crude petroleum 19.5% (1991), natural gas 14.3% (1991). *Principal trading partners*: Japan, USA, Singapore, Germany.

Iran *GNP ($ million)*: 30,300 (1994 est); *per head*: $500. *Imports ($ million)*: 30,662 (1992). *Exports ($ million)*: 18,415 (1992). *Main imports*: motor vehicles and machinery 28.5% (1992), iron and steel 15.0% (1992). *Main exports*: petroleum and products 95.8% (1992), carpets 6.1% (1992). *Principal trading partners*: Germany, Japan, France, Turkey.

Iraq *GNP ($ million)*: 20,000 (1994 est); *per head*: $1030. *Imports ($ million)*: 4834 (1990). *Exports ($ million)*: n/a. *Main imports*: machinery and transport equipment 30.3% (1990), food and live animals 27.9% (1990). *Main exports*: fuels and other energy 99.5% (1989), food and agricultural raw materials 0.5% (1989). (The export of petroleum and petroleum products ceased in 1990 under the terms of UN sanctions.) *Principal trading partners*: Jordan, Turkey, Germany.

Ireland *GNP ($ million)*: 52,000 (1994 est); *per head*: $14,760. *Imports ($ million)*: 21,853 (1993). *Exports ($ million)*: 29,014 (1993). *Main imports*: machinery and transport equipment 34.7% (1991), chemicals 13.3% (1991). *Main exports*: machinery and transport equipment 29.4% (1991), food 20.0% (1991). *Principal trading partners*: UK, USA, Germany, France, Netherlands.

Israel *GNP ($ million)*: 74,600 (1994 est); *per head*: $13,690. *Imports ($ million)*: 22,619 (1992). *Exports ($ million)*: 14,770 (1992). *Main imports*: investment goods 17.2% (1992), diamonds 16.3% (1992). *Main exports*: machinery 30.7% (1992), diamonds 24.5% (1992). *Principal trading partners*: USA, Belgium, Germany, UK, Japan.

Italy *GNP ($ million)*: 1,034,500 (1994 est); *per head*: $18,120. *Imports ($ million)*: 188,451 (1992). *Exports ($ million)*: 178,155 (1992). *Main imports*: machinery and transport equipment 33.2% (1991), chemicals and chemical products 14.8% (1991). *Main exports*: machinery and transport equipment 41.9% (1991), chemicals and chemical products 9.9% (1991). *Principal trading partners*: Germany, France, USA, UK, Switzerland, Netherlands.

Jamaica *GNP ($ million)*: 3362 (1993); *per head*: $1390. *Imports ($ million)*: 2097 (1993). *Exports ($ million)*: 1069 (1993). *Main imports*: fuels 17.3% (1991), consumer goods 17.1% (1991). *Main exports*: alumina 44.7% (1992), bauxite 8.4% (1992). *Principal trading partners*: USA, UK, Germany.

Japan *GNP ($ million)*: 4,686,600 (1994 est); *per head*: $37,590. *Imports ($ million)*: 241,624 (1993). *Exports ($ million)*: 362,244 (1993). *Main imports*: food, beverages and tobacco 16.0% (1992), petroleum and petroleum products 15.6% (1990). *Main exports*: motor vehicles 17.8% (1991), office machinery 7.5% (1990). *Principal trading partners*: USA, China, Germany, Taiwan, South Korea, Australia.

Jordan *GNP ($ million)*: 5000 (1994 est); *per head*: $1520. *Imports ($ million)*: 3539 (1993). *Exports ($ million)*: 1232 (1993). *Main imports*: food and live animals 18.8% (1992), machinery and appliances 12.4% (1992). *Main exports*: phosphate fertilizers 19.3% (1992), potash 13.6% (1992). *Principal trading partners*: India, Iraq, USA, Saudi Arabia, Germany.

Kazakhstan *GNP ($ million):* 24,200 (1994 est); *per head:* $1410. *Imports ($ million):* 358 (1993 est). *Exports ($ million):* 1271 (1993 est). *Main imports:* food and live animals. *Main exports:* natural gas, food and live animals. *Principal trading partners:* Russia, Uzbekistan.

Kenya *GNP ($ million):* 6743 (1993); *per head:* $270. *Imports ($ million):* 1711 (1993). *Exports ($ million):* 1336 (1993). *Main imports:* machinery and transport equipment 42.2% (1990), crude petroleum 14.7% (1990). *Main exports:* tea 25.9% (1990), coffee 18.4% (1990). *Principal trading partners:* UK, Germany, Japan, USA.

Kiribati *GNP ($ million):* 54 (1993); *per head:* $710. *Imports ($ million):* 37 (1992). *Exports ($ million):* 5 (1992). *Main imports:*, machinery and transport equipment 47.3% (1992), food 21.1% (1992). *Main exports:* copra 66.8% (1992), fish and fish preparations 11.3% (1992). *Principal trading partners:* Australia, Japan, USA.

Korea (North) *GNP ($ million):* 22,900 (1991); *per head:* $1040. *Imports ($ million):* 2280 (1991). *Exports ($ million):* 1240 (1991). *Main imports:* crude petroleum, coal and coke. *Main exports:* minerals and metallurgical products. *Principal trading partners:* Russia, Japan, China.

Korea (South) *GNP ($ million):* 400,400 (1994 est); *per head:* $9090. *Imports ($ million):* 83,800 (1993). *Exports ($ million):* 82,236 (1993). *Main imports:* machinery and transport equipment 34.5% (1992), mineral fuels and lubricants 17.9% (1992). *Main exports:* machinery and transport equipment 42.5% (1992), manufactured goods 24.1% (1992). *Principal trading partners:* Japan, USA, Hong Kong, Germany, Australia, Canada.

Kuwait *GNP ($ million):* 34,120 (1993); *per head:* $23,350. *Imports ($ million):* 6580 (1993). *Exports ($ million):* 10,536 (1993). *Main imports:* machinery and transport equipment 29.5% (1989), manufactured articles 22.1% (1989). *Main exports:* petroleum and products 92.2% (1989). *Principal trading partners:* Japan, Netherlands, USA, Germany.

Kyrgyzstan *GNP ($ million):* 3752 (1993 est); *per head:* $830. *Imports ($ million):* 112 (1993 est). *Exports ($ million):* 112 (1993 est). *Main imports:* food, coal. *Main exports:* food and live animals. *Principal trading partners:* Russia, Kazakhstan.

Laos *GNP ($ million):* 1295 (1993); *per head:* $290. *Imports ($ million):* 240 (1990). *Exports ($ million):* 72 (1990). *Main imports:* cereals and food products. *Main exports:* wood 33.3% (1989), electricity 23.8% (1989). *Principal trading partners:* Thailand, Japan, China.

Latvia *GNP ($ million):* 4700 (1994 est); *per head:* $1810. *Imports ($ million):* 1088 (1993 est). *Exports ($ million):* 1179 (1993 est). *Main imports:* fuel 38.9% (1993), machinery and equipment 19.2% (1993). *Main exports:* machinery and equipment 19.7% (1993), agricultural products and foodstuffs 14.9% (1993). *Principal trading partners:* Russia, Germany.

Lebanon *GNP ($ million):* 3100 (1994 est); *per head:* $1120. *Imports ($ million):* 3748 (1991). *Exports ($ million):* 490 (1991). *Main imports:* consumer goods, machinery and transport equipment. *Main exports:* jewellery, clothing. *Principal trading partners:* Italy, Saudi Arabia, Turkey, France.

Lesotho *GNP ($ million):* 1254 (1993); *per head:* $660. *Imports ($ million):* 699 (1990). *Exports ($ million):* 59 (1990). *Main imports:* manufactured goods 44.1% (1985), food and live animals 18.2% (1985). *Main exports:* manufactured goods 83.1% (1991), food and live animals 11.6% (1991). *Principal trading partners:* South Africa, UK.

Liberia *GNP ($ million):* 984 (1989); *per head:* $390. *Imports ($ million):* 394 (1989). *Exports ($ million):* 460 (1989). *Main imports:* machinery and transport equipment 31.1% (1988), petroleum and products 22.7% (1988). *Main exports:* iron ore 55.1% (1988), rubber 28.0% (1988). *Principal trading partners:* Germany, USA, Italy, France, Netherlands.

Libya *GNP ($ million):* 28,900 (1990); *per head:* $6800. *Imports ($ million):* 5361 (1991). *Exports ($ million):* 11,235 (1991). *Main imports:* foodstuffs 42.3% (1989), agricultural goods 18.5% (1989). *Main exports:* crude petroleum 96.8% (1989). *Principal trading partners:* Italy, Germany, Spain, France.

Liechtenstein *GNP ($ million):* 1100 (1994 est); *per head:* $36,800. *Imports ($ million):* 626 (1991). *Exports ($ million):* 1200 (1991). *Main imports:* machinery and transport equipment 29.2% (1991), limestone, cement and building materials 13.7% (1991). *Main exports:* machinery and transport equipment 47.3% (1991), metal products 18.0% (1991). *Principal trading partners:* Switzerland, Austria.

Lithuania *GNP ($ million):* 8500 (1994 est); *per head:* $2260. *Imports ($ million):* 515 (1993 est). *Exports ($ million):* 700 (1993 est). *Main imports:* petroleum and gas 48.9% (1992). *Main exports:* machinery 29.2% (1992). *Principal trading partners:* Russia, Ukraine, Poland.

Luxembourg *GNP ($ million):* 14,233 (1993); *per head:* $35,850. *Imports ($ million):* 8115 (1991). *Exports ($ million):* 6277 (1991). *Main imports:* metal products, machinery and transport equipment 48.7% (1991), mineral products 11.9% (1991). *Main exports:* metal products, machinery and transport equipment 56.9% (1991), plastic materials and rubber manufactures 12.6% (1991). *Principal trading partners:* Belgium, Germany, France.

Macedonia *GNP ($ million):* 1709 (1993 est); *per head:* $780. *Imports ($ million):* 1199 (1993 est). *Exports ($ million):* 1055 (1993 est). *Main imports:* fuel, machinery and transport equipment. *Main exports:* agricultural products. *Principal trading partner:* Bulgaria. Before the imposition of UN sanctions in May 1992, over 60% of Macedonia's trade was with Yugoslavia (Serbia and Montenegro.)

Madagascar *GNP ($ million):* 3039 (1993); *per head:* $240. *Imports ($ million):* 452 (1992). *Exports ($ million):* 268 (1992). *Main imports:* mineral products 20.0% (1992), chemical products 13.7% (1992). *Main exports:* vanilla 19.1% (1992), shrimps 14.1% (1992). *Principal trading partners:* France, USA, Japan, Germany.

Malawi *GNP ($ million):* 2034 (1993); *per head:* $220. *Imports ($ million):* 546 (1993). *Exports ($ million):*

320 (1993). *Main imports*: basic manufactures 40.6% (1989), machinery and equipment 14.9% (1989). *Main exports*: tobacco 75.6% (1991), tea 8.0% (1991). *Principal trading partners*: South Africa, UK, USA, Germany.

Malaysia *GNP ($ million)*: 65,600 (1994 est); *per head*: $3440. *Imports ($ million)*: 45,657 (1993). *Exports ($ million)*: 47,178 (1993). *Main imports*: machinery and transport equipment 53.9% (1993), manufactured goods 15.9% (1993). *Main exports*: machinery and transport equipment 41.2% (1991), mineral fuels 15.7% (1991). *Principal trading partners*: Japan, Singapore, USA, UK, Germany.

Maldives *GNP ($ million)*: 194 (1993); *per head*: $820. *Imports ($ million)*: 191 (1993). *Exports ($ million)*: 35 (1993). *Main imports*: food, beverages and tobacco 28.9% (1990), basic manufactures 24.5% (1990). *Main exports*: apparel and clothing 27.6% (1990), frozen skipjack tuna 26.3% (1990). *Principal trading partners*: USA, UK, Thailand, Sri Lanka.

Mali *GNP ($ million)*: 2744 (1993); *per head*: $300. *Imports ($ million)*: 500 (1990). *Exports ($ million)*: 354 (1991). *Main imports*: machinery, appliances and transport equipment 29.3% (1990), food products 12.7% (1990). *Main exports*: raw cotton and cotton products 44.9% (1990), live animals 24.0% (1990). *Principal trading partners*: France, Côte d'Ivoire, Algeria.

Malta *GNP ($ million)*: 2606 (1992); *per head*: $6850. *Imports ($ million)*: 2172 (1993). *Exports ($ million)*: 1352 (1993). *Main imports*: machinery and transport equipment 47.0% (1991), semi-manufactured goods 18.2% (1991). *Main exports*: machinery and transport equipment 29.4% (1991), clothing and footwear 13.2% (1991). *Principal trading partners*: Italy, Germany, UK, France.

Marshall Islands *GNP ($ million)*: 76 (1991); *per head*: $1577. *Imports ($ million)*: 56 (1991). *Exports ($ million)*: 3 (1991). *Main imports*: food and live animals 24.3% (1991), machinery and transport equipment 16.2% (1991). *Main exports*: crude coconut oil 48.3% (1991), frozen fish 27.0% (1991). *Principal trading partner*: USA.

Mauritania *GNP ($ million)*: 1087 (1993); *per head*: $510. *Imports ($ million)*: 639 (1990). *Exports ($ million)*: 469 (1990). *Main imports*: food 30.6% (1988). *Main exports*: fish 58.6% (1989), iron ore 31.3% (1989). *Principal trading partners*: France, Japan, Italy, Spain.

Mauritius *GNP ($ million)*: 3309 (1993); *per head*: $2980. *Imports ($ million)*: 1715 (1993). *Exports ($ million)*: 1299 (1993). *Main imports*: manufactured goods - material 35.3% (1992), machinery and transport equipment 24.9% (1992). *Main exports*: clothing and textiles 52.8% (1992), sugar 28.1% (1992). *Principal trading partners*: UK, France, South Africa, USA.

Mexico *GNP ($ million)*: 386,500 (1994 est); *per head*: $4300. *Imports ($ million)*: 50,147 (1993). *Exports ($ million)*: 30,241 (1993). *Main imports*: metallic products, machinery and equipment 52.9% (1991), chemical products 8.1% (1991). *Main exports*: metallic products, machinery and equipment 28.0% (1991), crude petroleum 26.1% (1991). *Principal trading partners*: USA, Japan, Germany, Spain, Canada.

Micronesia *GNP ($ million)*: 99 (1989); *per head*: $980. *Imports ($ million)*: 73 (1989). *Exports ($ million)*: 7 (1989). *Main imports*: food, beverages and tobacco 34.0% (1989), manufactured goods 26.2% (1989). *Main exports*: copra 25.6% (1988), manufactured goods 12.8% (1988). *Principal trading partners*: Japan, USA.

Moldova *GNP ($ million)*: 5160 (1993 est); *per head*: $1180. *Imports ($ million)*: 181 (1993 est). *Exports ($ million)*: 174 (1993 est). *Main imports*: coal, natural gas. *Main exports*: food and agricultural products. *Principal trading partners*: Ukraine, Romania.

Monaco *GNP ($ million)*: 390 (1994 est); *per head*: $13,050. *Imports ($ million)*: n/a. *Exports ($ million)*: n/a. *Principal trading partners*: France, Italy. No separate figures are available for Monaco whose imports and exports are included in the French total.

Mongolia *GNP ($ million)*: 943 (1993); *per head*: $400. *Imports ($ million)*: 829 (1990). *Exports ($ million)*: 593 (1990). *Main imports*: machinery and transport equipment 31.1% (1990), fuels, minerals and metals 27.2% (1990). *Main exports*: minerals and metals 48.1% (1990), raw materials and food products 27.9% (1990). *Principal trading partners*: China, Russia, Japan.

Morocco *GNP ($ million)*: 27,645 (1993); *per head*: $1030. *Imports ($ million)*: 6760 (1993). *Exports ($ million)*: 3991 (1993). *Main imports*: capital goods 26.9% (1991), crude oil 14.3% (1991). *Main exports*: food 27.9% (1990), consumer goods 26.0% (1991). *Principal trading partners*: France, Spain, USA, Germany, Italy.

Mozambique *GNP ($ million)*: 1375 (1993); *per head*: $80. *Imports ($ million)*: 955 (1993). *Exports ($ million)*: 132 (1993). *Main imports*: foodstuffs 30.0% (1992), capital goods 22.9% (1992). *Main exports*: shrimps 46.3% (1992), cashew nuts 12.6% (1992). *Principal trading partners*: South Africa, Spain, USA, Japan.

Myanmar (Burma) *GNP ($ million)*: 22,200 (1991) *per head*: $530. *Imports ($ million)*: 814 (1993). *Exports ($ million)*: 583 (1993). *Main imports*: machinery and equipment 51.4% (1989), raw materials for industry 31.4% (1989). *Main exports*: agricultural products 31.5% (1989), forest products 23.8% (1989). *Principal trading partners*: Singapore, Japan, China, Thailand.

Namibia *GNP ($ million)*: 2594 (1993); *per head*: $1660. *Imports ($ million)*: 1165 (1991). *Exports ($ million)*: 1305 (1991). *Main imports*: chemical and petroleum products 21.5% (1988), food and agricultural products 17.1% (1988). *Main exports*: minerals 75.9% (1991), agricultural products 11.0% (1991). *Principal trading partners*: South Africa, UK.

Nauru *GNP ($ million)*: 102 (1993 est); *per head*: $10,160. *Imports ($ million)*: 14 (1988). *Exports ($ million)*: 74 (1988). *Main exports*: phosphates 99%. *Principal trading partners*: Australia, New Zealand.

Nepal *GNP ($ million)*: 3170 (1993); *per head*: $160. *Imports ($ million)*: 792 (1992). *Exports ($ million)*: 374 (1992). *Main imports*: basic manufactured goods 26.0% (1991), machinery and transport equipment

25.1% (1991). *Main exports*: basic manufactures 57.3% (1991), food and live animals 14.7% (1991). *Principal trading partners*: India, USA, Germany.

Netherlands *GNP ($ million):* 321,200 (1994 est); *per head:* $20,990. *Imports ($ million):* 126,557 (1993). *Exports ($ million):* 139,075 (1993). *Main imports*: machinery and transport equipment 32.8% (1991), foodstuffs, beverages and tobacco 12.0% (1991). *Main exports:* machinery and transport equipment 24.7% (1991), foodstuffs, beverages and tobacco 20.6% (1991). *Principal trading partners*: Germany, Belgium, France, UK, USA, Italy.

New Zealand *GNP ($ million):* 50,400 (1994 est); *per head:* $14,670. *Imports ($ million):* 9636 (1993). *Exports ($ million):* 10,537 (1993). *Main imports*: machinery 24.8% (1993), minerals, chemicals and plastics 23.1% (1993). *Main exports*: food and live animals 48.1% (1993), basic manufactures 24.1% (1993). *Principal trading partners*: Australia, USA, Japan, UK, South Korea.

Nicaragua *GNP ($ million):* 1421 (1993); *per head:* $360. *Imports ($ million):* 892 (1992). *Exports ($ million):* 218 (1992). *Main imports*: non-durable consumer goods 23.2% (1990), petroleum products 16.4% (1990). *Main exports*: coffee 21.0% (1990), meat 20.0% (1990). *Principal trading partners*: USA, Germany, Japan.

Niger *GNP ($ million):* 2313 (1993); *per head:* $270. *Imports ($ million):* 355 (1991). *Exports ($ million):* 312 (1991). *Main imports*: raw materials and machinery 42.5% (1989), consumer goods 36.6% (1989). *Main exports*: uranium 71.5% (1989), live animals 10.5% (1989). *Principal trading partners*: France, Nigeria, Côte d'Ivoire.

Nigeria *GNP ($ million):* 64,200 (1994 est); *per head:* $720. *Imports ($ million):* 8119 (1992). *Exports ($ million):* 11,886 (1990). *Main imports*: machinery and transport equipment 43.2% (1992), manufactured goods 27.8% (1992). *Main exports*: crude petroleum 97.9% (1992). *Principal trading partners*: USA, Germany, Spain, UK, France.

Norway *GNP ($ million):* 111,400 (1994 est); *per head:* $26,060. *Imports ($ million):* 23,956 (1993). *Exports ($ million):* 31,853 (1993). *Main imports*: machinery and transport equipment 37.8% (1992), metals and metal products 9.6% (1992). *Main exports*: crude petroleum 37.9% (1992), machinery and transport equipment 14.8% (1992). *Principal trading partners*: UK, Sweden, Germany, France, Denmark.

Oman *GNP ($ million):* 9631 (1993); *per head:* $5600. *Imports ($ million):* 4114 (1993). *Exports ($ million):* 5299 (1993). *Main imports*: machinery and transport equipment 41.9% (1991), manufactured goods 17.5% (1991). *Main exports*: petroleum 86.1% (1991). *Principal trading partners*: Japan, South Korea, United Arab Emirates.

Pakistan *GNP ($ million):* 54,500 (1994 est); *per head:* $430. *Imports ($ million):* 9500 (1993). *Exports ($ million):* 6688 (1993). *Main imports*: petroleum products 15.0% (1992), specialized machinery 14.0% (1992). *Main exports*: textile fabrics 48.7% (1992), ready-made garments 19.7% (1992). *Principal trading partners*: Japan, USA, Germany, Hong Kong, UK.

Palau *GNP ($ million):* n/a. *Imports:* greatly exceed exports. *Main imports*: food, machinery and transport equipment. *Main exports*: shells, copra and handicrafts. *Principal trading partner*: USA.

Panama *GNP ($ million):* 6621 (1993); *per head:* $2580. *Imports ($ million):* 2188 (1993). *Exports ($ million):* 553 (1993). *Main imports*: mineral fuels 15.2% (1991), machinery and apparatus 13.8% (1991). *Main exports*: bananas 43.5% (1991), shrimps 11.1% (1991). *Principal trading partners*: USA, Germany, Japan, Ecuador.

Papua New Guinea *GNP ($ million):* 4637 (1993); *per head:* $1120. *Imports ($ million):* 1299 (1993). *Exports ($ million):* 2491 (1993). *Main imports*: machinery and transport equipment 41.6% (1989), basic manufactures 20.1% (1989). *Main exports*: gold 43.1% (1992), copper ore and concentrates 18.1% (1992). *Principal trading partners*: Australia, Japan, Germany, USA.

Paraguay *GNP ($ million):* 6995 (1993); *per head:* $1500. *Imports ($ million):* 1689 (1993). *Exports ($ million):* 657 (1992). *Main imports*: machinery and transport equipment 21.0% (1992), fuels and lubricants 11.7% (1992). *Main exports*: cotton fibres 31.9% (1992), soybean flour 20.9% (1992). *Principal trading partners*: Brazil, Netherlands, Argentina, USA, Japan.

Peru *GNP ($ million):* 34,040 (1993); *per head:* $1490. *Imports ($ million):* 4901 (1993). *Exports ($ million):* 3463 (1993). *Main imports*: raw and intermediate materials 44.0% (1992), machinery and transport equipment 27.6% (1992). *Main exports*: copper 23.1% (1992), fish products 12.6% (1992). *Principal trading partners*: USA, Japan, Colombia, Germany, Brazil.

Philippines *GNP ($ million):* 63,200 (1994 est); *per head:* $970. *Imports ($ million):* 18,757 (1993). *Exports ($ million):* 11,089 (1993). *Main imports*: machinery and transport equipment 25.2% (1991), mineral fuels and lubricants 14.9% (1991). *Main exports*: food and live animals 13.9% (1991), machinery and transport equipment 13.9% (1991). *Principal trading partners*: USA, Japan, Taiwan, Germany.

Poland *GNP ($ million):* 96,400 (1994 est); *per head:* $2520. *Imports ($ million):* 18,834 (1993). *Exports ($ million):* 14,143 (1993). *Main imports*: machinery and transport equipment 37.6% (1991), fuel and power 18.8% (1991). *Main exports*: machinery and transport equipment 22.4% (1991), iron and steel products 15.9% (1991). *Principal trading partners*: Germany, Russia, UK, Austria, Switzerland.

Portugal *GNP ($ million):* 67,300 (1992); *per head:* $6460. *Imports ($ million):* 24,337 (1993). *Exports ($ million):* 15,429 (1993). *Main imports*: machinery and transport equipment 36.5% (1992), chemicals and chemical products 8.9% (1992). *Main exports*: textiles and clothing 29.4% (1992), machinery and transport equipment 19.9% (1992). *Principal trading partners*: Germany, Spain, France, Italy, UK.

Qatar *GNP ($ million):* 7871 (1993); *per head:* $15,140. *Imports ($ million):* 1720 (1991). *Exports ($ million):* 3107 (1991). *Main imports*: machinery and transport equipment 42.4% (1991), manufactured goods 19.0%

(1991). *Main exports*: crude petroleum and products 86.9% (1991). *Principal trading partners*: Japan, UK, USA.

Romania *GNP ($ million):* 31,200 (1994 est); *per head:* $1370. *Imports ($ million):* 6522 (1993). *Exports ($ million):* 4892 (1993). *Main imports*: raw materials 47.6% (1990), machinery 23.7% (1990). *Main exports*: raw materials and mineral fuels 33.7% (1989), machinery and transport equipment 30.8% (1990). *Principal trading partners*: Russia, Germany, Italy.

Russia *GNP ($ million):* 330,000 (1994 est); *per head:* $2230. *Imports ($ million):* 26,807 (1993 est). *Exports ($ million):* 44,297 (1993 est). *Main imports*: Food and food products. *Main exports*: Food, coal, natural gas. *Principal trading partners*: Germany, Ukraine, Kazakhstan, Poland, Bulgaria.

Rwanda *GNP ($ million):* 1499 (1993); *per head:* $200. *Imports ($ million):* 288 (1992). *Exports ($ million):* 68 (1992). *Main imports*: machinery and transport equipment 14.5% (1991), mineral fuels and lubricants 12.8% (1991). *Main exports*: coffee 60.2% (1991), tea 23.4% (1991). *Principal trading partners*: Germany, Belgium, Kenya, Japan.

St Christopher and Nevis *GNP ($ million):* 185 (1993); *per head:* $4470. *Imports ($ million):* 111 (1990). *Exports ($ million):* 28 (1990). *Main imports*: food and live animals 15.6% (1988), non-electrical machinery 13.1% (1988). *Main exports*: sugar and molasses 34.0% (1990), garments 20.0% (1990). *Principal trading partners*: USA, UK, Trinidad.

St Lucia *GNP ($ million):* 480 (1993); *per head:* $3040. *Imports ($ million):* 313 (1992). *Exports ($ million):* 123 (1992). *Main imports*: machinery and transport equipment 21.4% (1990), food and live animals 19.4% (1990). *Main exports*: bananas 58.1% (1990), clothing 15.3% (1990). *Principal trading partners*: UK, USA, Trinidad.

St Vincent and the Grenadines *GNP ($ million):* 233 (1993); *per head:* $2130. *Imports ($ million):* 135 (1992). *Exports ($ million):* 83 (1992). *Main imports*: basic manufactures 23.9% (1990), food products 21.7% (1990). *Main exports*: bananas 53.9% (1990). *Principal trading partners*: USA, UK, Trinidad.

San Marino *GNP ($ million):* 220 (1994 est); *per head:* $10,200. *Imports ($ million):* n/a. *Exports ($ million):* n/a. *Main imports:* food, machinery and transport equipment. *Main exports:* wine, woollen goods, building stone. No other figures are available. *Principal trading partner*: Italy.

São Tomé e Principé *GNP ($ million):* 41 (1993); *per head:* $330. *Imports ($ million):* 21 (1990). *Exports ($ million):* 4 (1990). *Main imports*: capital goods 30.8% (1992), food and live animals 14.0% (1992). *Main exports*: cocoa 60.0% (1992). *Principal trading partners*: Portugal, Germany, Netherlands.

Saudi Arabia *GNP ($ million):* 125,100 (1994 est); *per head:* $8190. *Imports ($ million):* 29,079 (1991). *Exports ($ million):* 47,797 (1991). *Main imports*: transport equipment 21.0% (1991), machinery and appliances 19.4% (1991). *Main exports*: crude petroleum 78.1% (1991), refined petroleum 13.2% (1991). *Principal trading partners*: USA, Japan, UK, Germany, Netherlands.

Senegal *GNP ($ million):* 5867 (1993); *per head:* $730. *Imports ($ million):* 1292 (1990). *Exports ($ million):* 741 (1990). *Main imports*: machinery and transport equipment 21.3% (1990), petroleum products 16.0% (1990). *Main exports*: peanut oil 16.6% (1990), petroleum products 12.4% (1990). *Principal trading partners*: France, India, Nigeria, Italy.

Seychelles *GNP ($ million):* 444 (1993); *per head:* $6522. *Imports ($ million):* 189 (1993). *Exports ($ million):* 51 (1993). *Main imports*: manufactured goods 30.8% (1992), machinery and transport equipment 20.7% (1992). *Main exports*: petroleum products 53.3% (1992), canned tuna 29.8% (1992). *Principal trading partners*: France, UK, Singapore, Bahrain.

Sierra Leone *GNP ($ million):* 647 (1993); *per head:* $140. *Imports ($ million):* 149 (1993). *Exports ($ million):* 115 (1993). *Main imports*: food and live animals 34.3% (1992), machinery and transport equipment 18.9% (1992). *Main exports*: rutile 43.9% (1992), bauxite 25.9% (1992). *Principal trading partners*: USA, UK, Nigeria, Belgium.

Singapore *GNP ($ million):* 68,900 (1994 est); *per head:* $23,960. *Imports ($ million):* 85,234 (1993). *Exports ($ million):* 74,012 (1993). *Main imports*: crude petroleum 8.8% (1992), office machines 7.8% (1992). *Main exports*: office machines 20.4% (1992), petroleum products 10.7% (1992). *Principal trading partners*: USA, Japan, Malaysia, Thailand, Hong Kong.

Slovakia *GNP ($ million):* 11,900 (1994 est); *per head:* $2250. *Imports ($ million):* 6245 (1993 est). *Exports ($ million):* 5394 (1993 est). *Main imports*: petroleum and petroleum products, natural gas. *Main exports:* metals and finished engineering products. *main trading partners*: Czech Republic, Ukraine, Poland, Germany.

Slovenia *GNP ($ million):* 12,566 (1993 est); *per head:* $6310. *Imports ($ million):* 6488 (1993 est). *Exports ($ million):* 6088 (1993 est). *Main imports*: machinery and transport equipment 30.3% (1993), basic manufactures 17.7% (1993). *Main exports*: machinery and transport equipment 27.4% (1993), basic manufactures 26.1% (1993). *Principal trading partners*: Italy, Austria, Croatia, Germany.

Solomon Islands *GNP ($ million):* 261 (1993); *per head:* $750. *Imports ($ million):* 110 (1991). *Exports ($ million):* 102 (1991). *Main imports*: machinery and transport equipment 32.5% (1991), manufactured goods 22.8% (1991). *Main exports*: fish products 47.0% (1991), timber products 23.6% (1991). *Principal trading partners*: Japan, Australia, UK.

Somalia *GNP ($ million):* 946 (1990); *per head:* $150. *Imports ($ million):* 403 (1990). *Exports ($ million):* 81 (1990). *Main imports*: petroleum 33.1% (1988), agricultural inputs 20.9% (1988). *Main exports*: live animals 56.7% (1991), bananas 26.7% (1991). *Principal trading partners*: Italy, Saudi Arabia, Yemen.

South Africa *GNP ($ million):* 118,500 (1994 est); *per head:* $2910. *Imports ($ million):* 20,017 (1993). *Exports ($ million):* 24,261 (1993). *Main imports*: machinery and apparatus 14.9% (1991), transport equipment 14.1% (1991). *Main exports*: gold 29.4% (1991), metals and products 14.4% (1991). *Principal trading partners*: Germany, USA, UK, Japan, Netherlands.

Spain *GNP ($ million):* 482,800 (1994 est); *per head:* $12,080. *Imports ($ million):* 78,626 (1993). *Exports ($ million):* 59,585 (1993). *Main imports*: machinery 12.4% (1992), agricultural products 10.1% (1992). *Main exports*: transport equipment 21.4% (1992), agricultural products 13.6% (1992). *Principal trading partners*: France, Germany, Italy, UK, USA, Netherlands.

Sri Lanka *GNP ($ million):* 10,658 (1993); *per head:* $600. *Imports ($ million):* 3991 (1993). *Exports ($ million):* 2859 (1993). *Main imports*: machinery and transport equipment 26.5% (1991), basic manufactures 24.0% (1991). *Main exports*: basic manufactures 50.9% (1991), food and live animals 34.5% (1991). *Principal trading partners*: USA, Japan, UK.

Sudan *GNP ($ million):* 12,100 (1993); *per head:* $450. *Imports ($ million):* 1400 (1991). *Exports ($ million):* 325 (1991). *Main imports*: basic manufactures 23.1% (1991), machinery 17.1% (1991). *Main exports*: cotton 44.6% (1989), sesame seeds 11.0% (1989). *Principal trading partners*: Thailand, Saudi Arabia, UK, Japan.

Suriname *GNP ($ million):* 488 (1993); *per head:* $1210. *Imports ($ million):* 470 (1991). *Exports ($ million):* 420 (1991). *Main imports*: semi-manufactured goods 41.0% (1991), machinery and transport equipment 19.1% (1991). *Main exports*: alumina 73.9% (1990), aluminium 8.2% (1990). *Principal trading partners*: USA, Norway, Netherlands.

Swaziland *GNP ($ million):* 933 (1993); *per head:* $1050. *Imports ($ million):* 901 (1992). *Exports ($ million):* 550 (1990). *Main imports*: machinery and transport equipment 23.9% (1991), minerals, fuels and lubricants 15.9% (1991). *Main exports*: sugar 33.5% (1991), wood and products 11.5% (1991). *Principal trading partners*: South Africa, Canada, UK.

Sweden *GNP ($ million):* 201,900 (1994 est); *per head:* $23,360. *Imports ($ million):* 42,681 (1993). *Exports ($ million):* 49,857 (1993). *Main imports*: machinery and transport equipment 36.0% (1992), chemicals 10.6% (1992). *Main exports*: machinery and transport equipment 42.7% (1992), paper products 11.1% (1992). *Principal trading partners*: Germany, UK, USA, Norway, Denmark.

Switzerland *GNP ($ million):* 252,700 (1994); *per head:* $36,780. *Imports ($ million):* 56,716 (1993). *Exports ($ million):* 58,687 (1993). *Main imports*: machinery and electronics 19.7% (1992), chemical products 12.4% (1992). *Main exports*: machinery and electronics 27.6% (1992), chemical products 23.1% (1992). *Principal trading partners*: Germany, France, Italy, USA, UK.

Syria *GNP ($ million):* 14,607 (1993); *per head:* $1170. *Imports ($ million):* 4140 (1993). *Exports ($ million):* 3146 (1993). *Main imports*: machinery and equipment 17.8% (1992), transport equipment 13.1% (1992). *Main exports*: crude petroleum 60.0% (1992), vegetables and fruit 7.6% (1992). *Principal trading partners*: France, Italy, Germany, Saudi Arabia.

Tajikistan *GNP ($ million):* 2686 (1993 est); *per head:* $470. *Imports ($ million):* 374 (1993 est). *Exports ($ million):* 263 (1993 est). *Main imports*: food and food products. *Main export*: food products, electricity. *Principal trading partners*: Uzbekistan, Russia.

Tanzania *GNP ($ million):* 2521 (1993); *per head:* $100. *Imports ($ million):* 1127 (1993). *Exports ($ million):* 349 (1993). *Main imports*: machinery and transport equipment 34.9% (1988), basic manufactures 16.3% (1988). *Main exports*: coffee 20.3% (1990), cotton 18.7% (1990). *Principal trading partners*: Germany, UK, Japan, Italy.

Thailand *GNP ($ million):* 145,200 (1994 est); *per head:* $2510. *Imports ($ million):* 46,058 (1993). *Exports ($ million):* 36,800 (1993). *Main imports*: electrical power equipment and machinery 33.5% (1991), mineral fuels and lubricants 9.2% (1991). *Main exports*: electrical power equipment and machinery 22.9% (1991), textiles and apparel 13.1% (1991). *Principal trading partners*: Japan, USA, Singapore, Germany.

Togo *GNP ($ million):* 1325 (1993); *per head:* $330. *Imports ($ million):* 491 (1991). *Exports ($ million):* 253 (1991). *Main imports*: machinery and transport equipment 25.0% (1989), food products 18.5% (1989). *Main exports*: calcium phosphates 53.2% (1989), cotton 15.8% (1989). *Principal trading partners*: France, Canada, Netherlands, Germany.

Tonga *GNP ($ million):* 150 (1993); *per head:* $1610. *Imports ($ million):* 61 (1993). *Exports ($ million):* 16 (1993). *Main imports*: food and live animals 25.4% (1992), basic manufactures 20.4% (1992). *Main exports*: squash 50.3% (1992), vanilla beans 12.1% (1992). *Principal trading partners*: Japan, Australia, New Zealand, USA.

Trinidad and Tobago *GNP ($ million):* 4776 (1993); *per head:* $3730. *Imports ($ million):* 1448 (1993). *Exports ($ million):* 1612 (1993). *Main imports*: capital goods 16.8% (1991), mineral fuels and lubricants 14.7% (1991). *Main exports*: petroleum products 33.1% (1991), crude petroleum 30.7% (1991). *Principal trading partners*: USA, Venezuela, UK.

Tunisia *GNP ($ million):* 15,332 (1993); *per head:* $1780. *Imports ($ million):* 6215 (1993). *Exports ($ million):* 3804 (1993). *Main imports*: textiles 10.9% (1992), chemical products 2.8% (1992). *Main exports*: clothing and accessories 30.0% (1992), petroleum and products 13.3% (1992). *Principal trading partners*: France, Italy, Germany.

Turkey *GNP ($ million):* 120,900 (1994 est); *per head:* $2020. *Imports ($ million):* 29,174 (1993). *Exports ($ million):* 15,343 (1993). *Main imports*: non-electrical machinery 19.2% (1992), crude petroleum 12.5% (1992). *Main exports*: textiles 36.1% (1992), agricultural products 15.4% (1992). *Principal trading partners*: Germany, Italy, USA, Saudi Arabia, France.

Turkmenistan *GNP ($ million):* 4895 (1993 est); *per head:* $1270. *Imports ($ million):* 501 (1993 est). *Exports ($ million):* 1049 (1993 est). *Main imports*: food and food products. *Main exports*: natural gas, food products. *Principal trading partners*: Russia, Uzbekistan, Iran.

Tuvalu *GNP ($ million):* 4.6 (1990); *per head:* $530. *Imports ($ million):* 4 (1989). *Exports ($ million):* 0.06 (1989). *Main imports*: food 29.3% (1989),

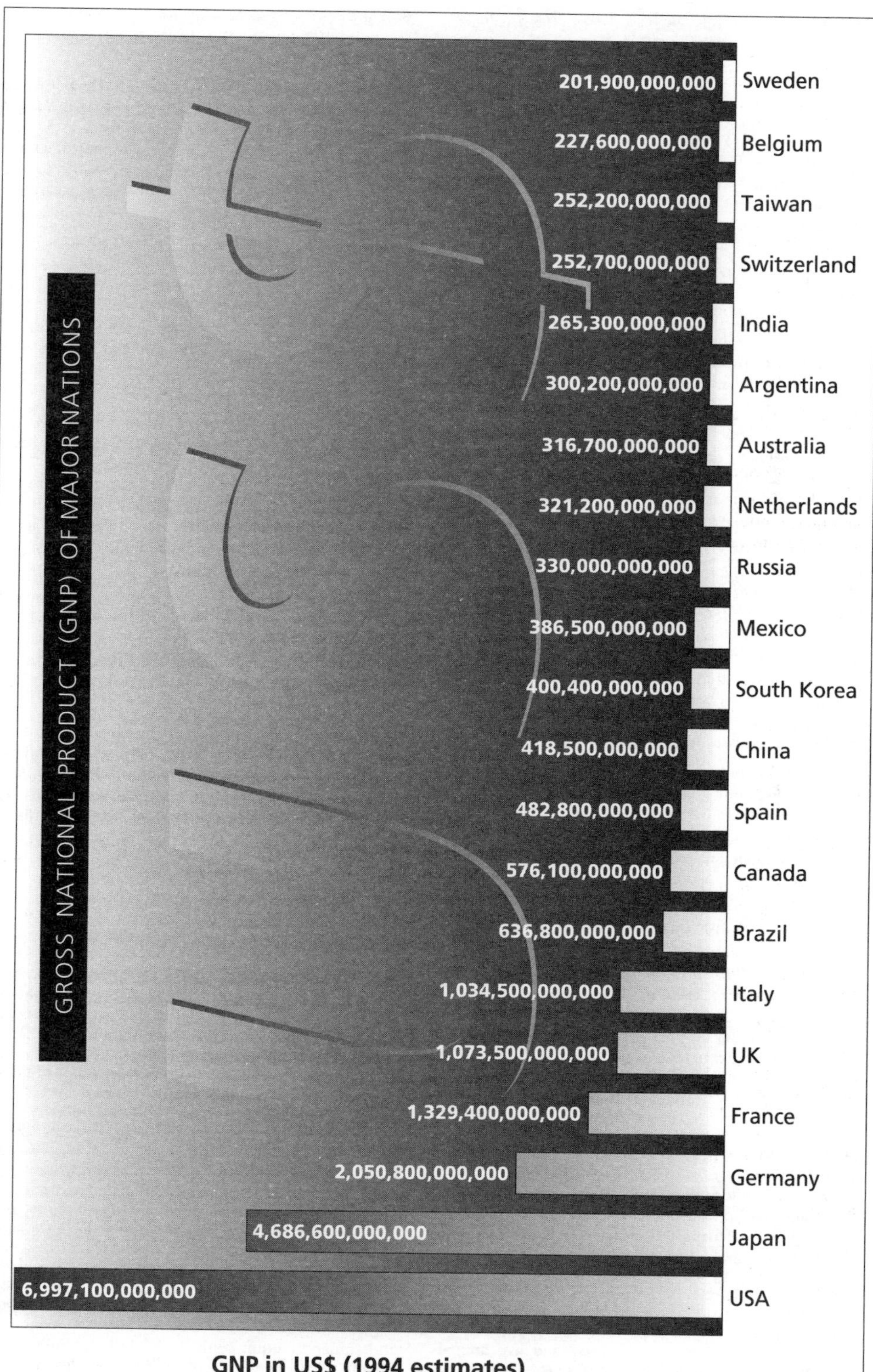
GROSS NATIONAL PRODUCT (GNP) OF MAJOR NATIONS
201,900,000,000 Sweden
227,600,000,000 Belgium
252,200,000,000 Taiwan
252,700,000,000 Switzerland
265,300,000,000 India
300,200,000,000 Argentina
316,700,000,000 Australia
321,200,000,000 Netherlands
330,000,000,000 Russia
386,500,000,000 Mexico
400,400,000,000 South Korea
418,500,000,000 China
482,800,000,000 Spain
576,100,000,000 Canada
636,800,000,000 Brazil
1,034,500,000,000 Italy
1,073,500,000,000 UK
1,329,400,000,000 France
2,050,800,000,000 Germany
4,686,600,000,000 Japan
6,997,100,000,000 USA

GNP in US$ (1994 estimates)

manufactured goods 28.2% (1989). *Main exports*: clothing and footwear 29.5% (1989), copra 21.5% (1989). *Principal trading partners*: Australia, New Zealand.

Uganda *GNP ($ million)*: 3486 (1993); *per head*: $190. *Imports ($ million)*: 439 (1992). *Exports ($ million)*: 179 (1993). *Main imports*: sugar 16.0% (1984), motor vehicles 10.8% (1984). *Main exports*: unroasted coffee 79.6% (1990), cotton 3.3% (1990). *Principal trading partners*: Kenya, Netherlands, France, UK.

Ukraine *GNP ($ million)*: 30,000 (1994 est); *per head*: $570. *Imports ($ million)*: 2431 (1993 est). *Exports ($ million)*: 3116 (1993 est). *Main imports*: food products, natural gas and petroleum. *Main exports*: food products, coal. *Principal trading partners*: Russia, Poland, Germany, Iran.

United Arab Emirates *GNP ($ million)*: 38,720 (1993); *per head*: $22,470. *Imports ($ million)*: 19,520 (1993). *Exports ($ million)*: 15,837 (1990). *Main imports*: machinery and transport equipment 30.5% (1987), basic manufactures 16.8% (1987). *Main exports*: crude petroleum 65.6% (1989). *Principal trading partners*: Japan, UK, USA, France.

UK *GNP ($ million)*: 1,073,500 (1994 est); *per head*: $18,480. *Imports ($ million)*: 205,390 (1993). *Exports ($ million)*: 180,180 (1993). *Main imports*: machinery and transport equipment 37.6% (1992), chemicals and chemical products 9.2% (1992). *Main exports*: machinery and transport equipment 40.8% (1992), chemicals and chemical products 13.8% (1992). *Principal trading partners*: Germany, USA, France, Netherlands, Japan, Italy, Belgium.

USA *GNP ($ million)*: 6,997,100 (1994 est); *per head*: $27,270. *Imports ($ million)*: 603,438 (1993). *Exports ($ million)*: 464,773 (1993). *Main imports*: machinery and transport equipment 43.4% (1992), basic and miscellaneous manufactures 29.2% (1992). *Main exports*: machinery and transport 44.8% (1992), basic and miscellaneous manufactures 18.8% (1992). *Principal trading partners*: Canada, Japan, Mexico, Germany, UK, Taiwan.

Uruguay *GNP ($ million)*: 12,314 (1993); *per head*: $3910. *Imports ($ million)*: 2289 (1993). *Exports ($ million)*: 1647 (1993). *Main imports*: machinery and appliances 20.2% (1992), transport equipment 15.8% (1992). *Main exports*: textiles and products 27.1% (1992), live animals and products 22.5% (1992). *Principal trading partners*: Brazil, Argentina, USA, Germany.

Uzbekistan *GNP ($ million)*: 21,100 (1993 est); *per head*: $960. *Imports ($ million)*: 947 (1993 est). *Exports ($ million)*: 707 (1993 est). *Main imports*: food and food products. *Main exports*: food products, natural gas. *Principal trading partners*: Russia, Kazakhstan, Turkmenistan.

Vanuatu *GNP ($ million)*: 198 (1993); *per head*: $1230. *Imports ($ million)*: 82 (1992). *Exports ($ million)*: 24 (1992). *Main imports*: machinery and transport equipment 27.5% (1992), food and live animals 17.4% (1992). *Main exports*: copra 32.8% (1992), beef and veal 13.3% (1992). *Principal trading partners*: Japan, Australia, New Zealand.

Vatican City no figures available. The Holy See does not have an 'economy' in the accepted sense of the term.

Venezuela *GNP ($ million)*: 62,000 (1994 est); *per head*: $3000. *Imports ($ million)*: 12,200 (1993). *Exports ($ million)*: 14,066 (1993). *Main imports*: machinery and transport equipment 33.3% (1990), chemicals 14.3% (1990). *Main exports*: crude petroleum and products 79.7% (1990). *Principal trading partners*: USA, Germany, Japan, Italy, Colombia.

Vietnam *GNP ($ million)*: 13,200 (1994 est); *per head*: $190. *Imports ($ million)*: 2194 (1991). *Exports ($ million)*: 1970 (1991). *Main imports*: machinery and transport equipment 26.0% (1991), fuel and lubricants 22.9% (1991). *Main exports*: fuels and lubricants 35.6% (1991), food and live animals 34.3% (1991). *Principal trading partners*: Hong Kong, Japan, Singapore, France.

Western Samoa *GNP ($ million)*: 159 (1993); *per head*: $980. *Imports ($ million)*: 105 (1993). *Exports ($ million)*: 6 (1993). *Main imports*: food 21.3% (1983), machinery 21.0% (1983). *Main exports*: taro 37.5% (1991), coconut cream 28.8% (1991). *Principal trading partners*: New Zealand, Australia, USA, Japan.

Yemen *GNP ($ million)*: 6746 (1991); *per head*: $540. *Imports ($ million)*: 1572 (1990). *Exports ($ million)*: 693 (1990). *Main imports*: food and live animals 39.6% (1990), basic manufactured goods 20.0% (1990). *Main exports*: petroleum and petroleum products 91.1% (1990), food and live animals. *Principal trading partners*: Japan, Saudi Arabia, USA, Italy, France.

Yugoslavia (Serbia and Montenegro) *GNP ($ million)*: 28,400 (1990); *per head*: $2729; hyper-inflation has greatly reduced this figure. *Imports ($ million)*: n/a. *Exports ($ million)*: n/a. *Main imports*: machinery and transport equipment 22.7% (1991), mineral fuels and lubricants 19.0% (1991). *Main exports*: manufactured goods 49.9% (1991), machinery and transport equipment 19.6% (1991). *Principal trading partners*: Russia, Italy, Germany. **NB** Since the imposition of UN sanctions in May 1992 trade has been interrupted, except for foodstuffs and medicines.

Zaïre *GNP ($ million)*: 8123 (1991); *per head*: $220. *Imports ($ million)*: 401 (1992). *Exports ($ million)*: 416 (1992). *Main imports*: machinery and transport equipment 31.7% (1991), basic manufactures 21.1% (1991). *Main exports*: copper 47.6% (1990), diamonds 11.4% (1990). *Principal trading partners*: Belgium, USA, France, Germany, China.

Zambia *GNP ($ million)*: 3152 (1993); *per head*: $370. *Imports ($ million)*: 870 (1992). *Exports ($ million)*: 870 (1992). *Main imports*: machinery and transport equipment 38.3% (1988), basic manufactures 19.8% (1988). *Main exports*: copper 85.2% (1988), cobalt 6.1% (1988). *Principal trading partners*: South Africa, UK, USA, Japan.

Zimbabwe *GNP ($ million)*: 5400 (1994 est); *per head*: $510. *Imports ($ million)*: 2055 (1991). *Exports ($ million)*: 1532 (1991). *Main imports*: machinery and transport equipment 37.3% (1990), fuels 15.6% (1990). *Main exports*: tobacco 17.0% (1990), gold 13.8% (1990). *Principal trading partners*: South Africa, UK, Germany, USA, Japan.

COUNTRIES WITH THE HIGHEST GNP PER CAPITA

Japan	US$37,590 per capita (1994 est)
Liechtenstein	US$36,800 per capita (1994 est)
Switzerland	US$36,780 per capita (1994 est)
Luxembourg	US$35,800 per capita (1993 est)
Denmark	US$28,830 per capita (1994 est)
USA	US$27,270 per capita (1994 est)
Norway	US$26,060 per capita (1994 est)
Germany	US$25,100 per capita (1994 est0
Austria	US$24,970 per capita (1994 est)
Singapore	US$23,960 per capita (1994 est)
Iceland	US$23,620 per capita (1993)
Sweden	US$23,360 per capita (1994 est)
Kuwait	US$23,350 per capita (1993)
France	US$23,140 per capita (1994 est)
Belgium	US$22,710 per capita (1994 est)
UAE	US$22,470 per capita (1993)
Netherlands	US$20,990 per capita (1994 est)
Canada	US$20,470 per capita (1994 est)
Finland	US$20,240 per capita (1994 est)
UK	US$18,480 per capita (1994 est)
Italy	US$18,120 per capita (1994 est)
Australia	US$17,970 per capita (1994 est)
Andorra	US$16,600 per capita (1992 est)
Qatar	US$15,140 per capita (1993)
Ireland	US$14,760 per capita (1994 est)
New Zealand	US$14,670 per capita (1994 est)
Brunei	US$13,890 per capita (1991)
Israel	US$13,690 per capita (1994 est)
Monaco	US$13,020 per capita (1994 est)
Spain	US$12,080 per capita (1994 est)
Taiwan	US$12,050 per capita (1994 est)
Bahamas	US$11,500 per capita (1993)
Cyprus	US$10,380 per capita (1993)
San Marino	US$10,200 per capita (1994 est)
Nauru	US$10,160 per capita (1994 est)

COUNTRIES WITH THE LOWEST GNP PER CAPITA

Mozambique	US$80 per capita (1993)
Tanzania	US$100 per capita (1993)
Eritrea	US$110 per capita (1992)
Sierra Leone	US$140 per capita (1993)
Somalia	US$150 per capita (1993)
Nepal	US$160 per capita (1993)
Bhutan	US$170 per capita (1993)
Burundi	US$180 per capita (1993)
Uganda	US$190 per capita (1993)
Vietnam	US$190 per capita (1994 est)
Cambodia	US$200 per capita (1991)
Chad	US$200 per capita (1993)
Rwanda	US$200 per capita (1993)
Afghanistan	US$220 per capita (1988)
Bangladesh	US$220 per capita (1993)
Guinea-Bissau	US$220 per capita (1993)
Malawi	US$220 per capita (1993)
Zaire	US$220 per capita (1993)
Madagascar	US$240 per capita (1993)
Kenya	US$270 per capita (1993)
Niger	US$270 per capita (1993)
Laos	US$290 per capita (1993)
Burkina Faso	US$300 per capita (1993)
India	US$300 per capita (1994 est)
Mali	US$300 per capita (1993)

CURRENCIES OF THE WORLD

At April 1995

On the financial markets, currencies are most commonly quoted in US dollars, as given here.

Afghanistan 1 afghani = 100 puls (puli); 1$US = 3463.03 Afghanis.

Albania 1 new lek = 100 qindarka (qintars); 1$US = 100.49 leks.

Algeria 1 dinar = 100 centimes; 1$US = 43.38 Algerian dinars.

Andorra uses French and Spanish currency.

Angola 1 new kwanza = 100 lwei; 1$US = 597,151.0 new kwanza. The lwei is now valueless and no longer circulates.

Antigua and Barbuda 1 East Caribbean dollar[1] = 100 cents; 1$US = 2.7 East Caribbean dollars.

Argentina 1 peso = 100 centavos; 1$US = 0.99 Argentine pesos.

Armenia dram; 1US$ = 400 Armenian drams.

Australia 1 Australian dollar = 100 cents; 1US$ = 1.37 Australian dollars.

The Australian dollar also circulates in Australian external territories.

Austria 1 Schilling = 100 Groschen; 1$US = 9.94 Austrian Schillings.

Azerbaijan manat; 1US$ = 4410 Azeri manats.

Bahamas 1 Bahamian dollar = 100 cents; 1$US = 1 Bahamian dollar.

Bahrain 1 Bahrain dinar = 1000 fils; 1$US = 0.38 Bahrain dinars.

Bangladesh 1 taka = 100 poisha; 1$US = 39.65 takas.

Barbados 1 Barbados dollar = 100 cents; 1$US = 2.01 Barbadian dollars.

Belarus 1 Belarussian rouble = 100 kopeks; 1US$ = 11,600 Belarussian roubles. The Belarussian rouble is to be replaced by the Russian rouble when the agreed monetary union between Russia and Belarus takes effect.

Belgium 1 Belgian franc (frank) = 100 centimes (centiemen); 1$US = 29.14 Belgian francs.

Belize 1 Belizean dollar = 100 cents; 1$US = 2 Belizean dollars.

Benin 1 CFA franc[2] = 100 centimes; 1$US = 497.08 CFA francs.

Bhutan 1 ngultrum = 100 chetrums; 1$US = 31.61 ngultrums. The ngultrum is fixed at a par with the Indian rupee which is also legal tender in Bhutan.

Bolivia 1 boliviano = 100 centavos; 1$US = 4.75 bolivianos.

Bosnia-Herzegovina The Croatian and Serbian/Yugoslav currencies are in use.

Botswana 1 pula = 100 thebe; 1$US = 2.72 pulas.

Brazil 1 real = 100 centavos; 1$US = 0.91 reals.

Brunei 1 Brunei dollar = 100 cents; 1$US = 1.42 Brunei dollars.

Bulgaria 1 lev = 100 stotinki (stotinka); 1$US = 24.6053.

Burkina Faso 1 CFA franc[2] = 100 centimes; 1$US = 497.08 CFA francs.

Burundi 1 Burundi franc = 100 centimes; 1$US = 236.2 Burundi francs.

Cambodia 1 new riel = 100 sen; 1$US = 2625 new riels.

Cameroon 1 CFA franc[2] = 100 centimes; 1$US = 497.08 CFA francs.

Canada 1 Canadian dollar = 100 cents; 1$US = 1.40 Canadian dollars.

Cape Verde 1 Cape Verde escudo = 100 centavos; 1$US = 82.97 Cape Verde escudos.

Central African Republic 1 CFA franc[2] = 100 centimes; 1$US = 497.08 CFA francs.

Chad 1 CFA franc[2] = 100 centimes; 1$US = 497.08 CFA francs.

Chile 1 Chilean peso = 100 centavos; 1$US = Ch$ 409.3 Chilean pesos.

China, People's Republic 1 yuan (or renminbiao) = 10 jiao (chiao) = 100 fen; 1$US = 8.43 yuan.

China (Taiwan) 1 new Taiwan dollar = 100 cents; 1$US = 25.99 new Taiwan dollars.

Colombia 1 Colombian peso = 100 centavos; 1$US = 869.05 Colombian pesos.

Comoros 1 Comorian franc = 100 centimes; 1$US = 372.44 Comorian francs.

Congo 1 CFA franc[2] = 100 centimes; 1$US = 497.08 CFA francs.

Costa Rica 1 Costa Rican colón = 100 céntimos; 1$US = 171.41 Costa Rican colóns.

Côte d'Ivoire 1 CFA franc[2] = 100 centimes; 1$US = 497.08 CFA francs.

Croatia 1 kuna = 100 para; 1$US = 5.088 kunas.

Cuba 1 Cuban peso = 100 centavos; 1$US = 1 Cuban peso (official rate).

Cyprus 1 Cyprus pound = 100 cents; 1$US = 0.45 Cyprus pounds.

Turkish currency is used in northern Cyprus.

Czech Republic 1 Czech koruna = 100 haléř; 1$US = 26.19 Czech korunas.

Denmark 1 Danish krone = 100 ore; 1$US = 5.61 Danish krone.

Danish currency is also used in the Faeroe Islands and Greenland.

Djibouti 1 Djibouti franc = 100 centimes; 1$US = 177.72 Djibouti francs.

Dominica 1 East Caribbean dollar[1] = 100 cents; 1$US = 2.7 East Caribbean dollars.

Dominican Republic 1 Dominican peso = 100 centavos; 1$US = 13.72 Domincan pesos.

Ecuador 1 sucre = 100 centavos; 1$US = 2435 sucres.

Egypt 1 Egyptian pound = 100 piastres = 1000 millièmes; 1$US = 3.41 Egyptian pounds.

El Salvador 1 Salvadorian colón = 100 centavos; 1$US = 8.76 Salvadorean colóns.

Equatorial Guinea 1 CFA franc[2] = 100 centimes; 1$US = 497.08 CFA francs.

Eritrea uses Ethiopian currency.

Estonia 1 kroon = 100 cents; 1$US = 11.25 kroons.

Ethiopia 1 birr = 100 cents; 1$US = 5.8 birrs.

Fiji 1 Fiji dollar = 100 cents; 1$US = 1.40 Fijian dollars.

Finland 1 markka (Finnmark) = 100 penniä (penni); 1$US = 4.41 markka.

France 1 French franc = 100 centimes; 1$US = 4.97 francs.

French currency is also used in overseas départements and collectivités territoriales – Guadeloupe, Guyane, Martinique, Réunion, Mayotte, and St Pierre et Miquelon.

The French overseas territories of French Polynesia, New Caledonia, and the Wallis and Futuna Islands use the CFP franc. 1 CFP franc = 100 centimes; 1$US = 90.29 CFP francs.

Gabon 1 CFA franc[2] = 100 centimes; 1$US = 497.08 francs.

Gambia 1 dalasi = 100 butut; 1$US = 9.55 dalasi.

Georgia uses Russian currency and the Georgian coupon (which was not quoted on the international exchanges in April 1995). The Georgian coupon is to be replaced by the Lary.

Germany 1 Deutschmark = 100 Pfennige; 1$US = 1.41 DM.

Ghana 1 new cedi = 100 pesewas; 1$US = 1080 cedis.

Greece 1 drachma (which is nominally divided into 100 leptae (lepta), although these no longer circulate); 1$US = 231.5 drachmae.

Grenada 1 East Caribbean dollar[1] = 100 cents; 1$US = 2.7 East Caribbean dollars.

Guatemala 1 quetzal = 100 centavos; 1$US = 5.67 quetzals.

Guinea 1 Guinean franc = 100 centimes; 1$US = 1014.54 Guinean francs.

Guinea-Bissau 1 Guinea peso = 100 centavos; 1$US = 15,369 Guinea pesos.

Guyana 1 Guyanese dollar = 100 cents; 1$US = 142.8 Guyanese dollars.

Haiti 1 gourde = 100 centimes; 1$US = 19 gourdes.

Honduras 1 lempira = 100 centavos; 1$US = 9 lempiras.

Hungary 1 forint = 100 fillér; 1$US = 119.8 forints.

Iceland 1 new Icelandic krona = 100 aurar (eyrir); 1$US = 64.15 Icelandic kronas.

India 1 Indian rupee = 100 paisa (paise); 1$US = 31.61 Indian rupees.

Indonesia 1 rupiah = 100 sen; 1$US = 2232 rupiahs.

Iran 1 Iranian rial = 100 dinars; 1$US = 1749 Iranian rials.

Iraq 1 Iraqi dinar = 5 riyals = 20 dirhams = 1000 fils; 1$US = 0.6 Iraqi dinars (official rate).

Ireland 1 Irish pound (punt) = 100 pence; 1$US = 0.63 punts.

Israel 1 new Israel shekel = 100 agorot (agora); 1$US = 2.99 new Israeli shekels.

Italy Italian lira (lire), which was nominally subdivided into 100 centesimi; 1$US = 1720 lire.

Jamaica 1 Jamaican dollar = 100 cents; 1$US = 32.3 Jamaican dollars.

Japan yen; 1$US = 88.73 yen.

Jordan 1 Jordanian dinar = 1000 fils; 1$US = 0.69 Jordanian dinars.

Kazakhstan tenge (which was not quoted on the international exchanges in April 1995). Kazakhstan also uses Russian currency.

Kenya 1 Kenya shilling = 100 cents; 1$US = 43.93 Kenya shillings.

Kiribati uses Australian currency.

Korea, Democratic People's Republic (North Korea) 1 won = 100 chon (jun); 1$US = 2.15 North Korean won (official rate).

Korea, Republic of (South Korea) 1 won = 10 hwan = 100 chun (jeon); 1$US = 770.75 South Korean won.

Kuwait 1 Kuwaiti dinar = 1000 fils; 1$US = 0.29 Kuwaiti dinars.

Kyrgyzstan som (which was not quoted on the international exchanges in April 1995). Kyrgyzstan also uses Russian currency.

Laos 1 new kip = 100 at; 1$US = 729 new kip.

Latvia 1 Lats = 100 cents; 1US$ = 0.52 Lats.

Lebanon 1 Lebanese pound = 100 piastres; 1$US = 1635.5 Lebanese pounds.

Lesotho 1 loti (maloti) = 100 lisente; 1$US = 3.61 maloti. The Lesothan loti is kept on a par with the South African rand.

Liberia 1 Liberian dollar = 100 cents; 1$US = 1 Liberian dollar (official rate). The Liberian dollar is fixed on a par with the US dollar which is also legal tender in Liberia.

Libya 1 Libyan dinar = 1000 dirhams; 1$US = 0.36 Libyan dinars.

Liechtenstein uses Swiss currency.

Lithuania 1 Litas = 100 cents; 1US$ = 4 Litas.

Luxembourg 1 Luxembourg franc = 100 centimes; 1$US = 29.14 Luxembourg francs. The Luxembourg franc is fixed on a par with the Belgian franc which is also legal tender in Luxembourg.

Macedonia (Former Yugoslav Republic of) 1 Macedonian denar = 100 para (which was not quoted on the international exchanges in April 1995).

Madagascar 1 Malagasy franc (franc malgache) = 100 centimes; 1$US = 3972 Malagasy francs.

Malawi 1 Malawi kwacha = 100 tambala; 1$US = 15.25 Malawi kwachas.

Malaysia 1 ringgit or Malaysian dollar = 100 sen; 1$US = 2.55 ringgits.

Maldives 1 rufiyaa (Maldivian rupee) = 100 laaris (larees); 1$US = 11.77 Maldivian rupees.

Mali 1 CFA franc[2] = 100 centimes; 1$US = 497.08 CFA francs.

Malta 1 Maltese lira (Maltese pound) = 100 cents = 1000 mils; 1$US = 0.35 Maltese lira.

Marshall Islands uses US currency.

Mauritania 1 ouguiya = 5 khoums; 1$US = 126.85 ougiya.

Mauritius 1 Mauritian rupee = 100 cents; 1$US = 17.38 Mauritian rupees.

Mexico 1 Mexican peso = 100 centavos; 1$US = 6.87 Mexican pesos.

Micronesia uses US currency.

Moldova 1 Moldovan leu = 100 bani; 1US$ = 4.42 Moldovan leu.

Monaco uses French currency.

Mongolia 1 tugrik = 100 möngös; 1$US = 415.57 tugriks.

Morocco 1 Moroccan dirham = 100 francs (centimes); 1$US = 8.44 Moroccan dirhams.

Mozambique 1 metical (meticais) = 100 centavos; 1$US = 7337 meticais.

Myanmar (Burma) 1 kyat = 100 pyas; 1$US = 5.48 kyats.

Namibia uses South African currency.

Nauru uses Australian currency.

Nepal 1 Nepalese rupee = 100 paisa; 1$US = 49.4 Nepalese rupees.

Netherlands 1 Netherlands gulden (known in English as the guilder) or florin = 100 cents; 1$US = 1.58 Netherlands gulden. The Netherlands overseas dependencies have their own currencies.

In Aruba, 1 Aruban florin = 100 cents; 1$US = 1.79 Aruban florins.

In the Netherlands Antilles, 1 Antillean guilder = 100 cents; 1$US = 1.79 Netherlands Antilles guilders.

New Zealand 1 New Zealand dollar = 100 cents; 1$US = 1.54 New Zealand dollars.

Nicaragua 1 Córdoba oro = 100 centavos; 1$US = 7.30 Córdobas oro.

Niger 1 CFA franc[2] = 100 centimes; 1$US = 497.08 CFA francs.

Nigeria 1 naira = 100 kobo; 1$US = 75 nairas.

Norway 1 Norwegian krone (kroner) = 100 ore; 1$US = 6.29 Norwegian kroner.

Oman 1 rial Omani = 1000 baiza; 1$US = 0.38 rials Omani.

Pakistan 1 Pakistani rupee = 100 paisa; 1$US = 30.85 Pakistani rupees.

Palau uses US currency.

Panama 1 balboa = 100 centésimos; 1$US = 1 balboa. The Panamanian balboa is kept on a par with the US dollar which is also legal tender in Panama. The only notes circulating in Panama are in US denominations; Panamanian currency circulates in coins.

Papua New Guinea 1 kina = 100 toea; 1$US = 1.19 kinas.

Paraguay 1 guaraní = 100 céntimos; 1$US = 1960 guaranís.

Peru 1 new sol = 100 céntimos; 1$US = 2.26 new sols.

Philippines 1 Philippine peso = 100 centavos; 1$US = 25.9 Philippine pesos.

Poland 1 zloty = 100 groszy; 1$US = 2.36 zlotys.

Portugal 1 Portuguese escudo = 100 centavos; 1$US = 148.69 Portuguese escudos.

The Portuguese overseas territory of Macau has its own currency, the pataca. 1 pataca = 100 avos; 1$US = 7.99 patacas.

Qatar 1 Qatar riyal = 100 dirhams; 1$US = 3.64 Qatar riyals.

Romania 1 leu (lei) = 100 bani; 1$US = 1841 lei.

Russia 1 rouble = 100 kopeks; 1$US = 4867.5 roubles.

Rwanda 1 Rwandese franc = 100 centimes; 1$US = 134.9 Rwandese francs.

St Christopher and Nevis 1 East Caribbean dollar[1] = 100 cents; 1$US = 2.7 East Caribbean dollars.

St Lucia 1 East Caribbean dollar[1] = 100 cents; 1$US = 2.7 East Caribbean dollars.

St Vincent and the Grenadines 1 East Caribbean dollar[1] = 100 cents; 1$US = 2.7 East Caribbean dollars.

San Marino uses Italian currency.

São Tomé and Princípe 1 dobra = 100 centimes; 1$US = 1610.05 dobras.

Saudi Arabia 1 Saudi riyal = 100 halalah; 1$US = 3.75 Saudi riyals.

Senegal 1 CFA franc[2] = 100 centimes; 1$US = 497.08 CFA francs.

Seychelles 1 Seychelles rupee = 100 cents; 1$US = 4.67 Seychelles rupee.

Sierra Leone 1 leone = 100 cents; 1$US = 595 leones.

Singapore 1 Singaporean dollar = 100 cents; 1$US = 1.42 Singaporean dollars.

Slovakia 1 koruna = 100 haléru (halér); 1$US = 29.3 Slovakian korunas.

Slovenia 1 tolar = 100 cents; 1$US = 113.98 tolars.

Solomon Islands 1 Solomon Islands dollar = 100 cents; 1$US = 3.32 Solomon Islands dollars.

Somalia 1 Somali shilling = 100 cents; 1$US = 2620 Somali shillings.

South Africa 1 rand = 100 cents; 1$US = 3.61 rands.

Spain 1 Spanish peseta = 100 céntimos; 1$US = 129.75 Spanish pesetas.

Sri Lanka 1 Sri Lanka rupee = 100 cents; 1$US = 49.37 Sri Lankan rupees.

Sudan 1 Sudanese dinar = 100 piastres; 1$US = 41.66 Sudanese dinars.

Suriname 1 Suriname gulden (guilder) or florin = 100 cents; 1$US = 419 Suriname gulden.

Swaziland 1 lilangeni (emalangeni) = 100 cents; South African (qv); 1$US = E 3.1685. The Swazi lilangeni is kept on a par with the South African rand.

Sweden 1 Swedish krona (kronor) = 100 öre; 1$US = 7.32 Swedish kronor.

Switzerland 1 Swiss franc (Schweizer Franken) = 100 Rappen (centimes); 1$US = 1.17 Swiss francs.

Syria 1 Syrian pound = 100 piastres; 1$US = 42 Syrian pounds.

Tajikistan uses Russian currency.

Tanzania 1 Tanzanian shilling = 100 cents; 1$US = 552.5 Tanzanian shillings.

Thailand 1 baht = 100 satangs; 1$US = 24.7 bahts.

Togo 1 CFA franc[2] = 100 centimes; 1$US = 497.08 CFA francs.

Tonga 1 pa'anga = 100 seniti; 1$US = 1.37 pa'anga. The Tongan pa'anga is kept on a par with the Australian dollar.

Trinidad and Tobago 1 Trinidad and Tobago dollar = 100 cents; 1$US = 5.7 Trinidad and Tobago dollars.

Tunisia 1 Tunisian dinar = 1000 millimes; 1$US = 0.96 Tunisian dollars.

Turkey 1 Turkish lira = 100 kurus; 1$US = 42,132 Turkish lira.

Turkmenistan manat (which was not quoted on the international exchanges in April 1995). Turkmenistan also uses Russian currency.

Tuvalu uses Australian currency.

Uganda 1 Uganda new shilling = 100 cents; 1$US = 922 Uganda shillings.

Ukraine karbovanets (no subdivisions); 1 US$ = 129,520.0 karbovanets.

United Arab Emirates 1 United Arab Emirates dirham = 100 fils; 1$US = 3.67 UAE dirhams.

United Kingdom 1 pound sterling = 100 new pence (pennies); 1$US = 0.627 pounds sterling. (Banks in Scotland issue their own notes.)

The Channel Islands, Gibraltar and the Isle of Man use British currency. These territories also issue their own notes.

A number of other British dependencies and overseas territories have their own currencies.

Anguilla and Montserrat use the East Caribbean dollar.

In Bermuda, 1 Bermuda dollar = 100 cents; 1$US = 1 Bermuda dollar. The Bermuda dollar is kept on a par with the US dollar.

In the Cayman Islands, 1 Cayman Islands dollar = 100 cents; 1$US = 0.83 Cayman Islands dollars.

In Hong Kong, 1 Hong Kong dollar = 100 cents; 1$US = 7.73 Hong Kong dollars.

The pound sterling and the US dollar are legal tender in the British Indian Ocean Territory.

The US dollar is legal tender in the British Virgin Islands and the Turks and Caicos Islands.

The Falkland Islands pound and the St Helena pound are both kept on a par with the pound sterling.

USA 1 US dollar = 100 cents.

US currency is also used in American Samoa, Guam, North Mariana Islands, Puerto Rico, and the US Virgin Islands. (See also Liberia, Marshall Islands, Micronesia, Palau and Panama.)

Uruguay 1 Uruguayan new peso = 100 centésimos; 1$US = 5.975 new Uruguayan pesos.

Uzbekistan som (which was not quoted on the international exchanges in April 1995). Uzbekistan also Russian currency.

Vanuatu vatu; 1$US = 110.2 vatu.

Vatican City uses Italian currency.

Venezuela 1 bolívar = 100 céntimos; 1$US = 169.79 bolívars.

Vietnam 1 dông = 10 hào = 100 xu; 1$US = 11,213 dong.

Western Samoa 1 tala = 100 sene; 1$US = 2.47 talas.

Yemen is unique in having two official national currencies.

In the former Yemen Arab Republic (the former North Yemen), 1 Yemeni riyal = 100 fils; 1$US = 12 rials. In the former People's Democratic Republic of Yemen (the former South Yemen), 1 Yemeni riyal or dinar = 100 fils is in circulation; 1$US = 84 Yemeni riyals.

Yugoslavia (Serbia and Montenegro) 1 new dinar = 100 para; in April 1995, the new dinar was not quoted on the international exchange markets.

Zaïre 1 Zaïre = 100 makuta (likuta) = 10,000 sengi; 1$US = 3719.5 zaïres.

Zambia 1 Zambian Kwancha = 100 ngwee; 1$US = 792.92 Zambian Kwanchas.

Zimbabwe 1 Zimbabwe dollar = 100 cents; 1$US = 8.39 Zimbabwe dollars.

[1] *The East Caribbean dollar* is the common currency of Anguilla, Antigua and Barbuda, Dominica, Grenada, Montserrat, St Christopher and Nevis, St Lucia, and St Vincent and the Grenadines.

[2] *The CFA Franc* is the common currency of Benin, Burkina Faso, Cameroon, Central African Republic, Chad, Congo, Equatorial Guinea, Gabon, Ivory Coast, Mali, Niger, Senegal, and Togo.

WORLD'S MAJOR COMPANIES

In the 1980s and 1990s, the trend has been towards a more integrated world economy and the growth of multinational companies. The top 100 multinational companies are thought to account for almost one fifth of the world's productive assets and a greater proportion of world trade. Many of the larger multinational firms are based in the USA or Japan, but a growing number are based in Western Europe, and a few are South Korean or Latin American.

In the following list of the world's major non-banking and/or insurance or other financial companies, individual companies are ranked according to their total assets.

The figures concerning assets given below (in US$ million) are for the year-end of 1993, except for: NKK (where the figure relates to the financial year ending 31 March 1993); Proctor and Gamble (where the figure relates to the financial year ending 30 June 1993); for Hanson and for Siemens (where the figures relate to the financial year ending 30 September 1993); and Fujitsu, Hitachi, Honda Motor, Matsushita Electric Industrial, Mitsubishi Electric, Mitsubishi Heavy Industries, NEC, Nippon Oil, Nippon Steel, Nissan Motor, Sony and Toshiba (where the figures relate to the financial year ending 31 March 1994).

1. General Electric Co.
Status: an American multinational company. *Principal interests:* Electronics and electrical equipment. *Total assets:* US$ (million) 251,506.0.

2. Ford Motor Co.
Status: an American multinational company. *Principal interests:* Manufacture of motor vehicles and parts. *Total assets:* US$ (million) 198,938.0.

3. General Motors Corporation
Status: an American multinational company. *Principal interests:* Manufacture of motor vehicles and parts. *Total assets:* US$ (million) 188,200.9.

4. Royal Dutch/Shell Group
Status: a jointly-owned British-Dutch multinational company. *Principal interests:* Petroleum refining. *Total assets:* US$ (million) 99,664.6.

5. Toyota Motor Corporation
Status: a Japanese multinational company. *Principal interests:* Manufacture of motor vehicles and parts. *Total assets:* US$ (million) 88,150.0.

6. Hitachi Ltd.
Status: a Japanese multinational company. *Principal interests:* Electronics and electrical equipment. *Total assets:* US$ (million) 87,217.7.

7. Exxon Corporation
Status: an American multinational company. *Principal interests:* Petroleum refining. *Total assets:* US$ (million) 84,145.0.

8. International Business Machines Corporation (IBM)
Status: an American multinational company. *Principal interests:* Communications. *Total assets:* US$ (million) 81,113.0

9. Matsushita Electric Industrial Co.
Status: a Japanese multinational company. *Principal interests:* Electronics and electrical equipment. *Total assets:* US$ (million) 80,006.2.

10. Nissan Motor Co. Ltd.
Status: a Japanese multinational company. *Principal interests:* Manufacture of motor vehicles and parts. *Total assets:* US$ (million) 71,564.0.

11. Daimler-Benz AG
Status: a German multinational company. *Principal interests:* Manufacture of motor vehicles and parts. *Total assets:* US$ (million) 52,271.3.

12. Toshiba Corporation
Status: a Japanese multinational company. *Principal interests:* Communications. *Total assets:* US$ (million) 52,252.8.

13. ENI (Ente Nazionale Idrocarburi)
Status: an Italian state-owned multinational company. (Many state-owned enterprises in Italy are being privatized. At the beginning of 1995, there were no plans for the privatization of ENI.) *Principal interests:* Petroleum refining. *Total assets:* US$ (million) 51,912.7.

14. Philip Morris Cos. Ltd.
Status: an American multinational company. *Principal interests:* Food industry. *Total assets:* US$ (million) 51,205.0.

15. Samsung
Status: a South Korean multinational company. *Principal interests:* Electronics and electrical equipment. *Total assets:* US$ (million) 50,492.4.

16. Pemex (Petróleos Mexicanos)
Status: Mexican state-owned multinational. (Early in 1995, there was a possibility that Pemex would be privatized in order to help the Mexican government tackle the economic crisis facing that country.) *Principal interests:* Petroleum refining. *Total assets:* US$ (million) 49,294.0.

17. Fiat SpA
Status: an Italian multinational company. *Principal interests:* Manufacture of motor vehicles and parts. *Total assets:* US$ (million) 48,898.4.

18. Siemens AG
Status: a German multinational company. *Principal interests:* Petroleum refining. *Total assets:* US$ (million) 46,194.6.

19. British Petroleum Co. plc
Status: a British multinational company. *Principal interests:* Petroleum refining. *Total assets:* US$ (million) 45,828.9.

20. Volkswagen AG
Status: a German multinational company. *Principal interests:* Manufacture of motor vehicles and parts. *Total assets:* US$ (million) 45,586.7.

21. Elf Aquitaine
Status: a French multinational company. *Principal interests:* Petroleum refining. *Total assets:* US$ (million) 45,455.5.

22. Daewoo
Status: a South Korean multinational company. *Principal interests:* Electronics and electrical equipment. *Total assets:* US$ (million) 44,352.1.

23. Alcatel Alsthom
Status: a French multinational company. *Principal interests:* Telecommunications. *Total assets:* US$ (million) 43,938.3.

24. Chrysler Corporation
Status: an American multinational company. *Principal interests:* Manufacture of motor vehicles and parts. *Total assets:* US$ (million) 43,830.0.

25. Nippon Steel
Status: a Japanese multinational company. *Principal interests:* Metals. *Total assets:* US$ (million) 42,444.2.

26. Sony Corporation
Status: a Japanese multinational company. *Principal interests:* Electronics and electrical equipment. *Total assets:* US$ (million) 41,698.1.

27. Mobil
Status: an American multinational company. *Principal interests:* Petroleum refining. *Total assets:* US$ (million) 40,585.0.

28. NEC Corporation
Status: a Japanese multinational company. *Principal interests:* Electronics and electrical equipment. *Total assets:* US$ (million) 39,451.3.

29. Mitsubishi Heavy Industries
Status: a Japanese multinational company. *Principal interests:* Industrial equipment. *Total assets:* US$ (million) 39,229.4.

30. Xerox
Status: an American multinational company. *Principal interests:* Chemical industry. *Total assets:* US$ (million) 37,053.0.

31. E.I. Du Pont de Nemours & Co.
Status: an American multinational company. *Principal interests:* Manufacture of motor vehicles and parts. *Total assets:* US$ (million) 43,830.0.

32. Hanson
Status: a British multinational company. *Principal interests:* Widely diversified interests. *Total assets:* US$ (million) 35,991.9.

33. Renault SA
Status: a French state-owned multinational company. (Many state-owned enterprises in France are being privatized. At the beginning of 1995, there were no plans for the privatization of Renault SA.) *Principal interests:* Manufacture of motor vehicles and parts. *Total assets:* US$ (million) 35,920.1.

34. Fujitsu
Status: a Japanese multinational company. *Principal interests:* Communications refining. *Total assets:* US$ (million) 35,104.9.

35. Chevron Corporation
Status: an American multinational company. *Principal interests:* Petroleum refining. *Total assets:* US$ (million) 34,736.0.

36. PDVSA
Status: a Venezuelan state-owned multinational company. *Principal interests:* Petroleum refining. *Total assets:* US$ (million) 34,120.0.

37. INI
Status: a Spanish multinational group of companies (some companies within the multinational are state-owned; others are in private hands). *Principal interests:* Industrial equipment. *Total assets:* US$ (million) 33,230.9.

38. Mitsubishi Electric
Status: a Japanese multinational company. *Principal interests:* Electronics and electrical equipment. *Total assets:* US$ (million) 32,764.5.

39. RJR Nabisco Holdings
Status: an American multinational company. *Principal interests:* Tobacco products. *Total assets:* US$ (million) 31,295.0.

40. Nestlé SA
Status: a Swiss multinational company. *Principal interests:* Food industry. *Total assets:* US$ (million) 30,233.9.

41. Honda Motor Co. Ltd.
Status: a Japanese multinational company. *Principal interests:* Manufacture of motor vehicles and parts. *Total assets:* US$ (million) 28,526.2.

42. Amoco
Status: an American multinational company. *Principal interests:* Petroleum refining. *Total assets:* US$ (million) 28,486.0.

43. NKK
Status: a Japanese multinational company. *Principal interests:* Metals. *Total assets:* US$ (million) 28,453.6.

44. Texaco Inc.
Status: an American multinational company. *Principal interests:* Petroleum refining. *Total assets:* US$ (million) 26,626.0.

45. Nippon Oil
Status: a Japanese multinational company. *Principal interests:* Petroleum refining. *Total assets:* US$ (million) 26,062.8.

46. Dow Chemical
Status: an American multinational company. *Principal interests:* Chemical industry. *Total assets:* US$ (million) 25,505.0.

47. Proctor & Gamble Co.
Status: an American multinational company. *Principal interests:* Health and household goods manufacture. *Total assets:* US$ (million) 24,935.0.

48. ABB Asea Brown Boveri
Status: a Swiss multinational company. *Principal interests:* Electronics and electrical engineering. *Total assets:* US$ (million) 24,904.0.

49. Unilever Group
Status: a joint British/Dutch multinational company. *Principal interests:* Food industry. *Total assets:* US$ (million) 24,735.5.

50. CEA-Industrie
Status: a French state-owned multinational company. (Many state-owned enterprises in France are being privatized. At the beginning of 1995, there were no plans for the privatization of CEA-Industrie.) *Principal interests:* Chemicals industry. *Total assets:* US$ (million) 23,909.3.

MAJOR STOCK EXCHANGES

Country	*Principal stock exchange*	*Principal indices**
Argentina	Buenos Aires	General Index
Australia	Sydney	All Ordinaries, All Mining
Austria	Vienna	Credit Aktien, Traded Index
Belgium	Brussels	BEL20
Brazil	São Paulo	Bovespa
Canada	Toronto	Metals and Minerals, Composite Index, Portfolio, TSE 300
Chile	Santiago	IPGA General
China	Beijing	-
Denmark	Copenhagen	Copenhagen SE
Finland	Helsinki	HEX General
France	Paris	SBF 250, CAC 40
Germany	Frankfurt	FAZ Aktien, Commerzbank, DAX
Greece	Athens	Athens SE
Hong Kong	Hong Kong	Hang Seng
India	Bombay	BSE Sens
Indonesia	Jakarta	Jakarta Composite
Ireland	Dublin	ISEQ Overall
Italy	Milan	Banca Commerciale Italiana, MIB General
Japan	Tokyo	Nikkei 225, Nikkei 300, Topix, 2nd Selection
Malaysia	Kuala Lumpur	KLSE Composite
Mexico	Mexico City	IPC
Netherlands	Amsterdam	CBS Ttl Rtn General, CBS All Share
New Zealand	Wellington	Cap. 40
Norway	Oslo	Oslo SE
Pakistan	Karachi	KSE 100
Philippines	Manila	Manila Composite
Portugal	Lisbon	BTA
Singapore	Singapore	Singapore SES All-Singapore
South Africa	Johannesburg	JSE Gold, JSE Indl.
South Korea	Seoul	Korea Composite Ex
Spain	Madrid	Madrid SE
Sweden	Stockholm	Affarsvardn General
Switzerland	Zürich	Swiss Bank Ind., SBC General
Taiwan	Taipei	Weighted Pr.
Thailand	Bangkok	Bangkok SET
Turkey	Istanbul	Istanbul Composite
United Kingdom	London	FT-SE 100, FT-SE Mid 250, FT-SE All Share Prices, FT-SE 350
USA	New York (Wall Street)	Dow Jones Industrials, Dow Jones Home Bonds, Dow Jones Transport, Dow Jones Utilities, Standard and Poors Composite, Standard and Poors Industries, Standard and Poors Financial, NYSE Composite, Amex Market Val., NASDAQ Composite

* Share indices indicate the relative price of selected securities and share issues on the world's major stock exchanges.

Production figures

Most of the annual production figures given in this section are for 1992. In some cases the latest comparable production figures available were for 1990, which are indicated by *.

MAJOR MINERAL ORES

Bauxite

Country	*Production (in tonnes)*
Australia	39,980,000 p.a.
Guinea	17,800,000 p.a.
Brazil	10,800,000 p.a.
Russia	5,800,000 p.a.
India	4,840,000 p.a.
Jamaica	4,130,000 p.a.
Suriname	3,140,000 p.a.
China	2,500,000 p.a.

Chromium ore

Country	*Production (in tonnes)*
South Africa	4,200,000 p.a.
Kazakhstan	3,620,000 p.a.
India	960,000 p.a.
Albania	610,000 p.a.

Copper ore

Country	*Production (in tonnes)*
Chile	1,920,000 p.a.
USA	,630,000 p.a.
Canada	745,000 p.a.
China	560,000 p.a.
Russia*	550,000 p.a.
Zambia	385,000 p.a.
Poland	380,000 p.a.
Peru	370,000 p.a.

Diamonds

Country	*Production (in carats)*
Australia	35,000,000 p.a.
Botswana	16,000,000 p.a.
Zaïre	15,000,000 p.a.
Russia*	15,000,000 p.a
South Africa	10,150,000 p.a.
Brazil	1,500,000 p.a.

Gold

Country	*Production (in tonnes)*
South Africa	600 p.a.
USA	300 p.a.
Australia	240 p.a.
Russia	240 p.a.
Canada	240 p.a.

Iron ore

Country	*Production (in tonnes)*
China	170,000,000 p.a.
Brazil	150,000,000 p.a.
Australia	115,000,000 p.a.
Russia	97,300,000 p.a.
Ukraine	75,700,000 p.a.
USA	55,500,000 p.a.
India	37,000,000 p.a.
Canada	32,700,000 p.a.
South Africa	28,900,000 p.a.
Kazakhstan	22,000,000 p.a.
Venezuela	20,000,000 p.a.
Sweden	12,600,000 p.a.
Mauritania	11,550,000 p.a.

Silver

Country	*Production (in tonnes)*
Mexico	2290 p.a.
USA	1850 p.a.
Peru	1770 p.a.
Russia*	1500 p.a.
Canada	1340 p.a.

Tin ore

Country	*Production (in tonnes)*
Brazil	30,000 p.a.
Indonesia	29,400 p.a.
China	26,000 p.a.
Malaysia	20,500 p.a.
Thailand	11,500 p.a.
Bolivia	7700 p.a.

Uranium

Country	*Production (tonnes)*
Canada	9250 p.a.
Russia	8200 p.a.
Australia	3750 p.a.
Niger	3000 p.a.
France	2100 p.a.
South Africa	1750 p.a.
USA	1750 p.a.
Namibia	1500 p.a.

Zinc ore

Country	*Production (tonnes)*
Canada	1,195,000 p.a.
Australia	1,020,000 p.a.
Russia	940,000 p.a.
China	710,000 p.a.
Peru	605,000 p.a.
USA	545,000 p.a.

MAJOR CROPS

Apples

Country	*Production (in tonnes)*
China	4,820,000 p.a.
USA	4,400,000 p.a.
Germany	2,660,000 p.a.
France	2,330,000 p.a.

Bananas

Country	*Production (in tonnes)*
India	6,400,000 p.a.
Brazil	5,650,000 p.a.
Philippines	3,900,000 p.a.
Ecuador	3,600,000 p.a.
Indonesia*	2,350,000 p.a.

Barley

Country	*Production (in tonnes)*
Russia	22,100,000 p.a.
Germany	14,450,000 p.a.
Ukraine	14,000,000 p.a.

Canada	10,900,000 p.a.
France	10,470,000 p.a.
USA	10,110,000 p.a.
Turkey	7,800,000 p.a.
United Kingdom	7,390,000 p.a.
Spain	6,000,000 p.a.

Maize (Corn)

Country	*Production (in tonnes)*
USA	190,000,000 p.a.
China	93,350,000 p.a.
Brazil	30,600,000 p.a.
France	14,600,000 p.a.
Mexico	13,630,000 p.a.
Kazakhstan	13,270,000 p.a.
Argentina	10,700,000 p.a.
Romania	10,490,000 p.a.
South Africa*	9,200,000 p.a.
India	8,200,000 p.a.

Millet

Country	*Production (in tonnes)*
India	9,000,000 p.a.
China	4,500,000 p.a.
Nigeria	3,200,000 p.a.
Kazakhstan	3,100,000 p.a.
Niger	1,790,000 p.a.

Rice

Country	*Production (in tonnes)*
China	187,450,000 p.a.
India	110,945,000 p.a.
Indonesia	47,770,000 p.a.
Bangladesh	27,400,000 p.a.
Vietnam	21,500,000 p.a.
Thailand	18,500,000 p.a.
Burma (Myanmar)	13,770,000 p.a.
Japan	13,250,000 p.a.
Brazil	9,960,000 p.a.
Philippines	9,200,000 p.a.
South Korea	7,480,000 p.a.
USA	7,100,000 p.a.

Cocoa beans

Country	*Production (in tonnes)*
Côte d'Ivoire	700,000 p.a.
Brazil	345,000 p.a.
Ghana	280,000 p.a.
Malaysia	225,000 p.a.
Indonesia	215,000 p.a.
Nigeria*	170,000 p.a.
Cameroon	95,000 p.a.

Coffee

Country	*Production (in tonnes)*
Brazil	1,300,000 p.a.
Colombia	1,050,000 p.a.
Indonesia	405,000 p.a.
Mexico	300,000 p.a.
Côte d'Ivoire	240,000 p.a.
Ethiopia	215,000 p.a.
Guatemala	195,000 p.a.
Uganda	180,000 p.a.
Costa Rica	170,000 p.a.

Cotton lint

Country	*Production (in tonnes)*
China	5,700,000 p.a.
Uzbekistan	4,000,000 p.a.
USA	3,800,000 p.a.
Pakistan	2,100,000 p.a.
Brazil	1,880,000 p.a.
India	1,700,000 p.a.
Tajikistan	820,000 p.a.
Turkey	615,000 p.a.

Potatoes

Country	*Production (in tonnes)*
Russia	34,330,000 p.a.
China	33,350,000 p.a.
Poland	23,400,000 p.a.
Ukraine	20,400,000 p.a.
USA	18,970,000 p.a.
India	15,250,000 p.a.
Germany	10,230,000 p.a.
Belarus	8,000,000 p.a.
United Kingdom	7,880,000 p.a.
Netherlands	7,600,000 p.a.
France	6,500,000 p.a.

Rubber

Country	*Production (in tonnes)*
Thailand	1,400,000 p.a.
Indonesia	1,295,000 p.a.
Malaysia	1,250,000 p.a.
India*	290,000 p.a.

Sugar beet

Country	*Production (in tonnes)*
France	31,330,000 p.a.
Ukraine	28,600,000 p.a.
Germany	25,725,000 p.a.
USA	25,265,000 p.a.
Russia	24,300,000 p.a.
China	16,240,000 p.a.
Turkey	15,100,000 p.a.
Italy	14,960,000 p.a.
Poland	11,100,000 p.a.
United Kingdom	8,500,000 p.a.

Sugar cane

Country	*Production (in tonnes)*
Brazil	270,670,000 p.a.
India	240,290,000 p.a.
China	73,105,000 p.a.
Cuba	58,000,000 p.a.
Thailand	46,805,000 p.a.
Pakistan	35,660,000 p.a.
Mexico	35,330,000 p.a.
Colombia	28,930,000 p.a.

Tea

Country	*Production (in tonnes)*
India	730,000 p.a.
China	565,000 p.a.
Kenya	190,000 p.a.
Sri Lanka	180,000 p.a.
Indonesia*	165,000 p.a.

Tobacco

Country	*Production (in tonnes)*
China	3,120,000 p.a.
USA	750,000 p.a.
Brazil	585,000 p.a.
India	560,000 p.a.
Turkey	245,000 p.a.

Wheat

Country	*Production (in tonnes)*
China	95,005,000 p.a.
India	54,520,000 p.a.
USA	53,915,000 p.a.
Russia	38,900,000 p.a.
France	32,600,000 p.a.
Canada	29,870,000 p.a.
Turkey	20,400,000 p.a.
Ukraine	19,500,000 p.a.
Kazakhstan	18,500,000 p.a.
Germany	15,800,000 p.a.
Australia	15,700,000 p.a.
Pakistan	14,640,000 p.a.
Argentina	9,400,000 p.a.

LIVESTOCK

Cattle

Country	*Number*
India	198,400,000
Brazil	153,000,000
USA	99,560,000
China	81,410,000
Sudan	67,000,000
Russia	54,700,000
Argentina	50,020,000
Mexico	32,420,000
Ethiopia	31,000,000
Colombia	24,770,000
Bangladesh	23,700,000
France	20,930,000
Germany	18,500,000
Pakistan	17,790,000

Sheep

Country	*Number*
Australia	148,205,000
China	112,820,000
New Zealand	52,570,000
India	55,740,000
Russia	52,200,000
Iran	45,000,000
Turkey	40,550,000
Kazakhstan	34,500,000
South Africa*	32,600,000
Pakistan	30,160,000
United Kingdom	28,930,000
Uruguay	25,700,000
Spain	24,630,000
Ethiopia	23,200,000
Sudan	21,600,000

Pigs

Country	*Number*
China	364,000,000
USA	57,685,000
Russia	35,400,000
Brazil	33,050,000
Poland	22,100,000
Spain	17,240,000
Netherlands	14,160,000
Mexico	13,840,000
Romania	12,000,000
Germany	10,400,000

AGRICULTURAL AND ALLIED PRODUCTS

Beef and veal

Country	*Production (in tonnes)*
USA	10,530,000 p.a.
Russia	8,200,000 p.a.
Brazil	2,8000,000 p.a.
Argentina	2,640,000 p.a.
Germany	2,180,000 p.a.
Mexico	2,005,000 p.a.
France	1,715,000 p.a.
Australia	1,490,000 p.a.
Italy	1,160,000 p.a.
Canada	990,000 p.a.

Beer

Country	*Production (in hectolitres)*
USA	230,000,000 p.a.
Germany	113,000,000 p.a.
China	64,000,000 p.a.
Japan	63,000,000 p.a.
Russia	60,200,000 p.a.
United Kingdom	54,900,000 p.a.
Brazil	34,000,000 p.a.
Mexico	31,500,000 p.a.

Butter and ghee

Country	*Production (in tonnes)*
Russia	1,570,000 p.a.
India	1,040,000 p.a.
Germany	650,000 p.a.
USA	635,000 p.a.
France	540,000 p.a.

Cow's milk

Country	*Production (in tonnes)*
USA	67,375,000 p.a.
Russia	58,700,000 p.a.
Germany	29,300,000 p.a.
India	27,000,000 p.a.
France	26,600,000 p.a.

Eggs

Country	*Production (in tonnes)*
China	6,845,000 p.a.
USA	4,005,000 p.a.
Japan	2,465,000 p.a.
Russia	2,230,000 p.a.

Fishing catch (maritime and freshwater)

Country	*Production (in tonnes)*
China	12,095,000 p.a.
Japan	9,310,000 p.a.
Russia	6,965,000 p.a.

Peru	6,945,000 p.a.
Chile	6,165,000 p.a.
USA	5,855,000 p.a.
India	3,620,000 p.a.
Indonesia	3,190,000 p.a.
Thailand	3,065,000 p.a.
South Korea	2,985,000 p.a.
Norway	2,390,000 p.a.
Denmark*	1,970,000 p.a.
Iceland	1,760,000 p.a.
Canada	1,530,000 p.a.
Spain	1,350,000 p.a.

Paper (and paperboard)

Country	*Production (in tonnes)*
USA	72,700,000 p.a.
Japan	29,100,000 p.a.
China	18,500,000 p.a.
Canada	16,600,000 p.a.
Germany	13,500,000 p.a.
Finland	8,500,000 p.a.

Roundwood

Country	*Production (in tonnes)*
USA	495,000,000 p.a.
India	279,800,000 p.a.
China	277,000,000 p.a.
Brazil	264,600,000 p.a.
Canada	178,000,000 p.a.
Indonesia	172,990,000 p.a.
Nigeria	111,600,000 p.a.
Russia	65,800,000 p.a.

Sheep meat

Country	*Production (in tonnes)*
Australia	649,000 p.a.
China	570,000 p.a.
New Zealand	550,000 p.a.
Russia	420,000 p.a.
United Kingdom	382,000 p.a.

Sugar

Country	*Production (in tonnes)*
India	12,530,000 p.a.
Brazil	8,675,000 p.a.
China	7,835,000 p.a.
Cuba	7,625,000 p.a.
USA	6,530,000 p.a.

Wine

Country	*Production (in tonnes)*
France	6,200,000 p.a.
Italy	5,915,000 p.a.
Spain	3,105,000 p.a.
USA	1,490,000 p.a.
Argentina	1,465,000 p.a.
Germany	1,015,000 p.a.

Wool

Country	*Production (in tonnes)*
Australia	548,000 p.a.
New Zealand	226,000 p.a.
China	123,000 p.a.
Argentina	67,000 p.a.
Uruguay	64,000 p.a.

MANUFACTURED GOODS

Aluminium

Country	*Production (in tonnes)*
USA	6,460,000 p.a.
Canada	1,900,000 p.a.
Australia	1,265,000 p.a.
Germany	1,230,000 p.a.
Brazil	1,140,000 p.a.
Japan	1,130,000 p.a.

Cars

Country	*Number*
Japan	7,450,000 p.a.
USA	5,400,000 p.a.
Germany	4,270,000 p.a.
France	3,215,000 p.a.
Spain	1,830,000 p.a.
South Korea	1,300,000 p.a.
United Kingdom	1,200,000 p.a.
Belgium	1,065,000 p.a.
Russia*	1,030,000 p.a.
Italy	775,000 p.a.

Cement

Country	*Production (in tonnes)*
China	305,000,000 p.a.
Japan	89,565,000 p.a.
Russia	77,500,000 p.a.
USA	65,050,000 p.a.
India	51,660,000 p.a.
South Korea	43,270,000 p.a.
Italy	40,320,000 p.a.
Germany*	40,000,000 p.a.

Crude steel

Country	*Production (in tonnes)*
Japan	109,650,000 p.a.
USA	91,600,000 p.a.
China	82,000,000 p.a.
Russia	77,100,000 p.a.
Ukraine	45,000,000 p.a.
Germany	38,875,000 p.a.
South Korea	27,800,000 p.a.
Canada	25,990,000 p.a.
Italy	25,100,000 p.a.
Brazil	23,900,000 p.a.
France	18,000,000 p.a.

Colour television sets

Country	*Number*
South Korea	16,175,000 p.a.
USA	14,720,000 p.a.
China	13,150,000 p.a.
Japan	9,755,000 p.a.
Russia	4,400,000 p.a.

Shipping (merchant)

Country	*Launched (in tonnes)*
Japan	5,245,000 p.a.
South Korea	2,420,000 p.a.
Romania	1,035,000 p.a.
Germany	780,000 p.a.
Taiwan	740,000 p.a.

ENERGY

See p. 281.

Population and Social Trends

WORLD POPULATION

Somewhere between 24 June and 11 July 1987, the human population of the planet Earth reached five billion. Yet, two hundred years before that, when the world's population was barely more than one billion, political economists such as Thomas Malthus and David Ricardo were already predicting that the human species would breed itself into starvation. Nevertheless, despite their predictions, the human population keeps increasing – but so too does the food supply.

Two contending views have emerged concerning the extent to which burgeoning populations affect food supply. The first is that population must be controlled if persistent malnutrition and starvation are not to become the inevitable lot for a substantial portion of the globe. The second is that, even with a projected global population of 10 billion by the year 2060, there is sufficient food to feed everyone.

Population increase

In 1995, every day, the population of the world increases by an estimated 243,000 people – that is nearly an additional 89,000,000 people in one year. The rate of increase varies from an average of 0·32% per annum in Europe to 2·73% in Africa.

LIFE EXPECTANCY

Highest	
Japan	79
Macau	79
Hong Kong	78
Iceland	78
Martinique	78
Sweden	78
Switzerland	78
Australia	77
Canada	77
France	77
Greece	77
Guadeloupe	77
Italy	77
Netherlands	77
Norway	77
Spain	77
Lowest	
Afghanistan	42
Uganda	42
Guinea	43
Sierra Leone	43
Guinea-Bissau	44
Central African Republic	44
Malawi	44
Zambia	44
Gambia	45
Mali	45
Angola	46
Benin	46
Haiti	46
Niger	47
Mozambique	47
Somalia	47

Non-sovereign territories are shown in italics.

Population Growth

Period	*World population*
Neolithic period	under 10,000,000
4000 BC	c. 50,000,000
AD 500	c. 100,000,000
AD 800	c. 200,000,000
c. 1550	c. 500,000,000
1805	1,000,000,000
1926	2,000,000,000
1960	3,000,000,000
1974	4,000,000,000
1987	5,000,000,000
1998 (projected)	6,000,000,000
2010 (projected)	7,000,000,000
2023 (projected)	8,000,000,000
2039 (projected)	9,000,000,000
2060 (projected)	10,000,000,000

FERTILITY

In the following tables the crude birth rate measures the number of births per year per thousand. In the table listing territories with the highest crude birth rates, the figures given refer to the period 1985–90 (except for Mali where an earlier estimate is given).

Crude live birth rates

Highest	*Births per 1000*	***Lowest***	*Births per 1000*
Rwanda	52·1	Ukraine	9·6 (1992)
Yemen	52·0	Bulgaria	9·9 (1992)
Niger	51·7	Italy	9·9 (1991)
Angola	51·3	Japan	9·9 (1991)
Guinea	51·0	Slovenia	9·9 (1992)
Uganda	50·5	Spain	9·9 (1991)
Somalia	50·4	Germany	10·0 (1992)
Ivory Coast	49·9	Greece	10·0 (1991)
Ethiopia	49·5	San Marino	10·1 (1989)
Afghanistan	49·3	*Norfolk Island*	10·8 (1981)
Benin	49·1	Portugal	11·4 (1992)
Mali	48·7	Romania	11·4 (1992)
Zambia	48·6	Andorra	11·7 (1991)
Comoros	48·5	Belgium	11·7 (1992)
Nigeria	48·5	*Hong Kong*	11·9 (1991)
Sierra Leone	48·2	Hungary	11·9 (1992)
Tanzania	47·9	Austria	12·0 (1991)
Zaïre	47·8	*Guernsey*	12·0 (1992)
Liberia	47·3		

Non-sovereign territories are shown in italics.

POPULATION DENSITY

The least densely-populated territories are to be found in high latitudes (e.g. Greenland and the Falkland Islands), in the major desert areas (e.g. Mongolia, Western Sahara, Mauritania and Namibia), or in parts of the world where tropical rain forests still remain the dominant vegetation type. The most densely-populated territories are mostly very small states or former colonial trading outposts with the character of city-states, or relatively small islands with diverse economies. Among the most populous states in the table is one low-income country that is heavily dependent on the productivity of its rich soils

(Bangladesh), one middle-income country now rapidly industrializing (South Korea), and one major high-income country (The Netherlands).

Population density

Greatest	Pop. per km² (1992)	Least	Pop. per km² (1990)
Macau	*20,778*	*Greenland*	*0·03*
Monaco	18,792	*Falkland Islands*	*0·16*
Hong Kong	*5407*	*Western Sahara*	*0·94*
Gibraltar	*5167*	*Guyane (French Guiana)*	*1·16*
Singapore	4560	Mongolia	1·47
Vatican	2273	Namibia	1·86
Bermuda	*1170*	Mauritania	2·09
Malta	1136	Australia	2·27
Bangladesh	828	Botswana	2·40
Bahrain	786	Iceland	2·52
Channel Islands	*733*	Suriname	2·68
Barbados	602	Canada	2·74
Mauritius	531	Libya	2·77
Nauru	476	Guyana	3·76
Tuvalu	462	Gabon	4·62
South Korea	440	Chad	4·64
Puerto Rico	*404*	Central African Republic	5·09
San Marino	393	Niger	6·10
The Netherlands	372	Mali	6·58

Non-sovereign territories are shown in italics

POPULATION BY AGE

Third World countries with high birth rates tend to have young populations, whereas developed countries with low birth rates tend to have more elderly populations.

Population

Youngest	% of pop. under 15 (1992)	Oldest	% of pop. over 65 (1992)
Gaza	*60*	Sweden	18
Yemen	51	Denmark	16
West Bank	*50*	Norway	16
Ethiopia	49	United Kingdom	16
Kenya	49	Austria	15
Niger	49	Belgium	15
Togo	49	France	15
Botswana	48	Germany	15
Burkina Faso	48	Italy	15
Comoros	48	Switzerland	15
Iraq	48	Bulgaria	14
Malawi	48	Finland	14
Rwanda	48	Greece	14
Syria	48	Hungary	14
Zambia	48	Japan	14
Zimbabwe	48	San Marino	14
		Spain	14

Non-sovereign territories are shown in italics

POPULATION OF MAJOR WORLD REGIONS (millions)

	1900	*1950*	*1995*	*2025 est*	*2100 est*
World	1622	2518	5692	8121	10,958
Asia*	1070	1558	3667	5091	6525
Africa	110	222	719	1431	2643
Latin America	64	166	475	686	883
North America	81	166	295	362	384
Europe	290	393	507	514	478
Oceania	7	13	29	38	45

* includes the populations of the states of the former USSR.

POPULATION GROWTH: SELECTED COUNTRIES (thousands)

	1900	*1950*	*1995 est*	*2025 est*
China	453,000	554,760	1,119,332	1,471,282
India	240,000	357,561	934,228	1,370,028
USA	**76,000**	**152,271**	**263,119**	**322,675**
Indonesia	38,000	79,538	192,543	265,111
Brazil	18,000	53,444	161,374	223,734
Japan	**45,000**	**83,625**	**125,213**	**124,294**
Bangladesh	29,000	42,484	121,110	182,313
Nigeria	13,600	32,935	111,273	216,900
Pakistan	16,000	40,031	129,704	242,811
Mexico	13,500	27,376	90,464	135,610
Vietnam	11,500	29,954	74,109	116,830
Canada	**5,250**	**13,737**	**28,130**	**34,208**
Germany	**43,000**	**68,376**	**81,109**	**74,964**
Italy	**47,000**	**46,789**	**57,867**	**54,209**
United Kingdom	**38,325**	**50,616**	**58,288**	**60,562**
France	**41,000**	**41,736**	**58,125**	**62,555**
USSR	124,500	180,075		
Russian Federation			148,940	153,498

G7 countries are shown in bold.

URBANIZATION

Urbanization – the increased migration of rural dwellers into cities – has been a particular feature of the second half of the 20th century. In 1950 under 30% of the population of the world lived in urban regions, but by 1990 almost 44% lived in cities, towns or their suburbs.

The greatest proportion of urban dwellers is to be found in countries of the developed world. Some 96% of the population of Belgium, for example, is urban.

Urban population

The definitions of 'urban' vary from country to country, often quite markedly, and these variations influence the positions of countries within the tables.

Rapid urbanization is characteristic of the Third World. Conversely, in developed countries of the Western world, there is little scope for further growth in the level of urbanization. Indeed, in developed states the pattern of net population movement from country to town has been succeeded in the last few decades by a net movement from town to country ('counterurbanization').

Percentage of urban population

Highest		Lowest	
Gaza	100·0	Burundi	5·0
Macau	100·0	Bhutan	6·0
Monaco	100·0	Rwanda	6·0
Singapore	100·0	Uganda	11·3
Vatican City	100·0	Nepal	12·1
Belgium	96·0	Ethiopia	14·7
Kuwait	96·0	Malawi	16·5
Andorra	94·3	Bangladesh	18·0
Hong Kong	94·0	Laos	20·0
Israel	92·0	Vietnam	20·6
Iceland	90·6	Burkina Faso	21·0
San Marino	90·4	Guinea-Bissau	21·0
Uruguay	89·4	Lesotho	21·0
United Kingdom	89·0	Niger	21·0
Netherlands	88·7	Mali	22·0
		Sri Lanka	22·0

Non-sovereign territories are shown in italics

MARRIAGE RATES (selected countries)

	Marriages per 1000 population	Year
Bangladesh	11·3	1988
Brazil	5·2	1990
Canada	7·1	1990
France	4·8	1992
Germany	6·2	1991
Italy	5·3	1991
Jamaica	5·3	1992
Japan	6·0	1991
Maldives	18·1	1991
Sweden	4·3	1992
United Kingdom	6·5	1990
USA	9·3	1992

DIVORCE RATES (selected countries)

	Divorces per 1000 population	Year
Canada	3·0	1990
Cuba	4·2	1992
Egypt	1·4	1992
Iran	0·7	1991
Italy	0·5	1990
Russia	4·0	1991
Sweden	2·3	1991
UK	2·9	1990

MALE-FEMALE RATIO

In 1990, the world population was 50·3% male. Higher figures than this are found in territories that attract a male labour force from abroad, and in countries where a preference for sons leads to a higher death rate for girl than for boy infants. High female-to-male ratios are found in territories which have large elderly populations, in the territories of origin of male migrant labourers, and in countries still suffering the effects of heavy wartime military losses. The latter is a factor in Russia, although Russia also suffers high death rates among men of middle age.

The countries with the highest percentage of males are as follows:

	% of males
Qatar	67·2
Bahrain	57·5
Kuwait	56·5
Pitcairn	*55·8*
Andorra	53·3
Vanuatu	52·2
India	51·8
Papua New Guinea	51·7
China	51·5
Iran	51·1
Libya	51·1
New Caledonia	*51·1*

The countries with the highest percentage of females are as follows:

	% of females
Russia	55·1
Belarus	53·2
Estonia	53·2
Botswana	52·2
Isle of Man	*52·1*
Austria	51·9
Burkina Faso	51·9
Germany	51·8
Vietnam	51·4
France	51·3
USA	51·2
Tanzania	51·1

Non-sovereign territories are shown in italics.

THE WORLD'S MAJOR CITIES

Almost one half of the world's population lives in cities. At the end of the 19th century only one tenth were city dwellers. But by the year 2025 over 75% of humanity will live in cities. This change represents one of the greatest revolutions in social history.

By 1995 there were 300 cities with a population of over 1,000,000. Of these cities, 138 are in Asia, 53 in Europe, 52 in North and Central America, 25 in South America, 27 in Africa and 5 in Australasia/Oceania. Over the past decade, the growth of the largest cities has been very impressive, particularly those in the Third World.

The population figures given below relate to the agglomeration or urban area of each major city: that is the city, its immediate suburbs and the surrounding built-up area rather than for local government districts. By using this definition for the urban area of every city listed below, a more accurate comparison of size has been possible. The list also reveals that some very large cities, for example Tokyo and Bombay, have satellite 'millionaire' cities within their urban areas.

City	*Country*	*(Population of city, as defined for local government purposes)*	*Date of census or estimate*	*Population of urban area (the city and its suburbs)*
Tokyo	Japan	(city 11,610,000; Yokohama 3,251,000, Kawasaki 1,168,000, Chiba 834,000; Sagamihara 545,000; Funabashi 529,000)	(1992 est)	**25,000,000**
New York	USA	(city 7,323,000; Newark 275,000)	(1990 census)	**18,087,000**
São Paulo	Brazil	(city 9,394,000)	(1991 est)	**18,100,000**
Mexico City	Mexico	(city 8,237,000; Nezahualcóyotl 1,260,000)	(1990 census)	**15,050,000**
Los Angeles	USA	(city 3,485,000; Long Beach 429,000; Anaheim 266,000)	(1990 census)	**14,532,000**
Shanghai	China	(city 13,400,000)	(1992 est)	**13,400,000**
Cairo	Egypt	(city 6,663,000; El-Giza 2,096,000; Shubra El-Kheima 812,000)	(1991 est)	**13,300,000**
Bombay	India	(city 9,926,000; Kalyan 1,014,000)	(1991 census)	**12,596,000**
Buenos Aires	Argentina	(city 9,927,000)	(1991 census)	**12,582,000**
Rio de Janeiro	Brazil	(city 5,474,000; Nova Iguaçu 1,512,000)	(1991 est)	**11,141,000**
Calcutta	India	(city 4,388,000)	(1991 census)	**11,022,000**
Seoul	South Korea	(city 10,613,000)	(1990 census)	**11,000,000**
Beijing (Peking)	China	(city 10,940,000)	(1992 est)	**10,940,000**
Tianjin (Tientsin)	China	(city 9,090,000)	(1992 est)	**9,090,000**
Paris	France	(city 2,175,000)	(1990 census)	**9,063,000**
Moscow	Russia	(city 8,769,000)	(1989 est)	**8,967,000**
Osaka	Japan	(city 2,495,000; Kobe 1,468,000; Sakai 799,000, Higashiosaka 496,000)	(1992 est)	**8,735,000**
Delhi	India	(city 7,207,000)	(1991 census)	**8,419,000**
Jakarta	Indonesia	(city 8,223,000)	(1990 census)	**8,223,000**
Karachi	Pakistan	(city 8,070,000)	(1995 est)	**8,070,000**
Chicago	USA	(city 2,784,000)	(1990 census)	**8,066,000**

By contrast, it is interesting to note that in 1900 only 16 cities (including suburbs) had over 1,000,000 inhabitants.

London	(United Kingdom)	6,400,000
New York	(USA)	4,200,000
Paris	(France)	3,900,000
Berlin	(Germany)	2,400,000
Chicago	(USA)	1,700,000
Vienna	(Austria)	1,600,000
Tokyo	(Japan)	1,400,000
St Petersburg	(Russia)	1,400,000
Philadelphia	(USA)	1,400,000
Manchester	(United Kingdom)	1,200,000
Birmingham	(United Kingdom)	1,200,000
Moscow	(Russia)	1,200,000
Peking now referred to as **Beijing**	(China)	1,100,000
Calcutta	(India)	1,000,000
Boston	(USA)	1,000,000
Glasgow	United Kingdom)	1,000,000

In time, the term 'millionaire city' came to be used for a city with over 1,000,000 inhabitants.

INTERNATIONAL WORLD

International Organizations

THE UNITED NATIONS

At the United Nations Conference in San Francisco, USA, in April 1945, 50 countries signed the United Nations Charter, which came into effect in October 1945. The UN was founded as 'a general organization...for the maintenance of international peace and security'. Of the world's sovereign states, only Taiwan (Republic of China), Switzerland, the Vatican City, Kiribati, Nauru, Palau, Tonga and Tuvalu are not UN members. (However, Switzerland and the Vatican City have observer status at the UN.)

Members of the UN

Original members (1945): Argentina, Australia, Belarus (although not independent until 1991), Belgium, Bolivia, Brazil, Canada, Chile, China (represented by the Republic of China, which after 1949 was confined to Taiwan; in 1971, the UN withdrew recognition from Taiwan in favour of the People's Republic of China), Colombia, Costa Rica, Cuba, Czechoslovakia (held since 1993 by the Czech Republic), Denmark, Dominican Republic, Ecuador, Egypt, El Salvador, Ethiopia, France, Greece, Guatemala, Haiti, Honduras, India (although not independent until 1947), Iran, Iraq, Lebanon, Liberia, Luxembourg, Mexico, the Netherlands, New Zealand, Nicaragua, Norway, Panama, Paraguay, Peru, the Philippines, Poland, Saudi Arabia, South Africa, Syria, Turkey, Ukraine (although not independent until 1991), the USSR (held since 1991 by Russia), the United Kingdom, the USA, Uruguay, Venezuela, Yugoslavia (suspended 1992).

Elected in 1946: Afghanistan, Iceland, Sweden, Thailand.

Elected in 1947: Pakistan, Yemen.

Elected in 1948: Burma (Myanmar since 1989).

Elected in 1949: Israel.

Elected in 1950: Indonesia.

Elected in 1955: Albania, Austria, Bulgaria, Cambodia, Finland, Hungary, Ireland, Italy, Jordan, Laos, Libya, Nepal, Portugal, Romania, Spain, Sri Lanka (elected as Ceylon).

Elected in 1956: Japan, Morocco, Sudan, Tunisia.

Elected in 1957: Ghana, Malaysia (elected as Malaya).

Elected in 1958: Guinea.

Elected in 1960: Benin (elected as Dahomey), Burkina Faso (elected as Upper Volta), Cameroon, the Central African Republic, Chad, Congo, Côte d'Ivoire (elected as Ivory Coast), Cyprus, Gabon, Madagascar, Mali, Niger, Nigeria, Senegal, Somalia, Togo, Zaïre (elected as the Congolese Republic).

Elected in 1961: Mauritania, Mongolia, Sierra Leone, Tanzania (elected as Tanganyika).

Elected in 1962: Algeria, Burundi, Jamaica, Rwanda, Trinidad and Tobago, Uganda.

Elected in 1963: Kenya, Kuwait, Zanzibar (ceased membership 1964 upon its merger with Tanganyika).

Elected in 1964: Malawi, Malta, Zambia.

Elected in 1965: Gambia, Maldives, Singapore.

Elected in 1966: Barbados, Botswana, Guyana, Lesotho.

Elected in 1967: South Yemen (ceased membership 1990 upon its merger with Yemen).

Elected in 1968: Equatorial Guinea, Mauritius, Swaziland.

Elected in 1970: Fiji.

Elected in 1971: Bahrain, Bhutan, Oman, Qatar, the United Arab Emirates.

Elected in 1973: Bahamas, Germany (Federal Republic of), German Democratic Republic (East Germany; ceased membership upon its reunification with the Federal Republic of Germany in 1990).

Elected in 1974: Bangladesh, Grenada, Guinea-Bissau.

Elected in 1975: Cape Verde, Comoros, Mozambique, Papua New Guinea, São Tomé e Principe, Suriname.

Elected in 1976: Angola, Seychelles, Western Samoa.

Elected in 1977: Djibouti, Vietnam.

Elected in 1978: Dominica, Solomon Islands.

Elected in 1979: St Lucia.

Elected in 1980: St Vincent and the Grenadines, Zimbabwe.

Elected in 1981: Antigua and Barbuda, Belize, Vanuatu.

Elected in 1983: St Christopher and Nevis.

Elected in 1984: Brunei.

Elected in 1990: Liechtenstein, Namibia.

Elected in 1991: Estonia, Korea (People's Democratic Republic of - North Korea), Korea (Republic of - South Korea), Latvia, Lithuania, Marshall Islands, Federated States of Micronesia.

Elected in 1992: Armenia, Azerbaijan, Bosnia-Herzegovina, Croatia, Georgia, Kazakhstan, Kyrgyzstan, Moldova, San Marino, Slovenia, Tajikistan, Turkmenistan, Uzbekistan.

Elected in 1993: Andorra, Eritrea, Macedonia (elected as The Former Yugoslav Republic of Macedonia), Monaco, Slovakia.

The Organs of the UN

The UN has five principal organs (see below). All are based at New York (USA), except the World Court, which is based at The Hague (Netherlands).

The official languages of the UN are: Arabic, Chinese, English, French, Spanish and Russian.

The General Assembly is composed of all the member-states. It can discuss anything within the scope of the Charter. Each member-state has up to five delegates but only one vote. A President is elected by the General Assembly each September for a term of one year. Decisions of the General Assembly are made by a qualified majority (two thirds) of those present on 'important' question, and by a simple majority on other issues.

The Security Council is the main organ for maintaining peace and security. It has five permanent members: China, France, Russia (this seat was held by the USSR from 1945 to 1991), the United Kingdom and the USA. (There are suggestions that Japan and Germany should also become permanent members.) In addition to the five existing permanent members, 10 other members are elected by the General Assembly for a term of two years. Decisions of the Security Council are reached by a majority vote of at least nine of the 15 members. However, any of the five existing permanent members can exercise its right of veto.

The Economic and Social Council acts as a coordinating body for the numerous specialized agencies created by the UN. The Council (which has 54 members elected for a term of three years) aims to promote international cooperation in economic, social and related fields.

The International Court of Justice (the **World Court**) offers legal rulings on any case brought before it by UN members. In the event of a party failing to adhere to a judgement of the Court, the other party may have recourse to the Security Council. The World Court comprises 15 judges elected by the Security Council and the General Assembly for a term of nine years.

The Secretariat performs the role of a civil servce for the UN. Its head is the Secretary-General, who combines the task of administrative officer of the organization with that of international mediator.

The Secretaries-General of the UN have been:

Trygve Lie (Norway) 1946-53
Dag Hammarskjöld (Sweden) 1953-61
U Thant (Burma) 1961-72
Kurt Waldheim (Austria) 1972-81
Javier Perez de Cuellar (Peru) 1982-92
Boutros Boutros Ghali (Egypt) 1992-

The Trusteeship Council was established to oversee the progress to independence of former German, Japanese and Italian colonies. As its work has been completed, it has ceased to exist.

Specialized agencies of the UN

FAO (Food and Agriculture Organization of the United Nations) aims to improve levels of nutrition and standards of living and the production and distribution of food and all agricultural products, and, in so doing, to eliminate hunger. *HQ:* Rome (Italy).

GATT (General Agreement on Tariffs and Trade) ceased to exist in 1995; see WTO (below).

IAEA (International Atomic Energy Agency) aims to encourage the use of atomic energy for peaceful purposes. *HQ:* Vienna (Austria).

ICAO (International Civil Aviation Organization) encourages safety measures and coordinates facilities for international flight. *HQ:* Montréal (Canada).

IDA (International Development Association) assists less developed countries by providing credits on special terms. It is an affiliate of the World Bank.

IFAD (International Fund for Agricultural Development) generates grants or loans to increase food production in developing countries. *HQ:* Rome (Italy).

IFC (International Finance Corporation) promotes the flow of private capital internationally and stimulates the capital markets. The IFC is an affiliate of the World Bank (see below).

ILO (International Labour Organization) aims to establish international labour standards and to improve social and economic well-being. *HQ:* Geneva (Switzerland).

IMF (International Monetary Fund) promotes international monetary cooperation. *HQ:* Washington DC (USA).

IMO (International Maritime Organization) coordinates safety at sea. *HQ:* London (UK).

ITU (International Telecommunications Union) allocates telecommunications frequencies and standardizes telecommunications practices. *HQ:* Geneva (Switzerland).

UNESCO (United Nations Educational, Scientific and Cultural Organization) stimulates popular education and the spread of culture. *HQ:* Paris (France).

UNIDO (United Nations Industrial Development Organization) promotes industrialization in developing countries. *HQ:* Vienna (Austria).

UPU (Universal Postal Union) aims to unite members in a single postal territory. *HQ:* Berne (Switzerland).

WHO (World Health Organization) promotes the attainment by all peoples of the highest possible standards of health. *HQ:* Geneva (Switzerland).

WIPO (World Intellectual Property Organization) promotes protection of intellectual property (inventions, copyright). *HQ:* Geneva (Switzerland).

WMO (World Meteorological Organization) standardizes meteorological observations and applies the information to the greatest international benefit of shipping, agriculture, etc. *HQ:* Geneva (Switzerland).

World Bank (International Bank for Reconstruction and Development) encourages development through capital investment (in particular, investment in poorer nations). *HQ:* Washington DC (USA).

WTO (World Trade Organization) lays down a common code of practice in international trade, encourages tariff cuts and other measures to achieve world free trade. It replaced GATT in 1995. *HQ:* Geneva (Switzerland).

Sudsidiary organs of the UN

The subsidiary organs of the UN are programmes or funds that are devoted to achieving economic and social progress in developing countries. They include:

UNDP (United Nations Development Programme) the funding source of the technical assistance provided through the UN system. *HQ:* New York (USA).

UNFPA (United Nations Population Fund) responds to needs in population and family planning. *HQ:* New York (USA).

UNHCR (United Nations High Commissioner for Refugees) provides international protection for refugees. *HQ:* Geneva (Switzerland).

UNICEF (United Nations International Children's Emergency Fund) aims to meet the needs of children, particularly those in developing countries. *HQ:* New York (USA).

UNRWA (United Nations Relief and Works Agency) provides relief and welfare services for Palestinian refugees. *HQ:* Vienna (Austria).

UN contributions

Country	*% of UN budget contributed (1994)*
USA	25·0
Japan	12·45
Russia	9·4
Germany	8·93
France	6·0
United Kingdom	5·02
Italy	4·29
Canada	3·11
Spain	1·98
Ukraine	1·87
Brazil	1·59
Australia	1·51
Netherlands	1·5
Sweden	1·11
Belgium	1·06

UN peacekeeping forces

Peacekeeping forces have been established by the UN Security Council to act as observers, to provide assistance, maintain ceasefires and prevent or contain conflicts. Currently over 78,000 personnel (contingents provided by UN members) are deployed. The majority of UN troops have traditionally come from non-aligned nations. The UN forces deployed in 1995 are:

***MINURSO** in the Western Sahara
ONUMOZ in Mozambique
***ONUSAL** in El Salvador
***UNAMIR** in Rwanda
***UNAVEM** in Angola
***UNDOF** in the Golan Heights
UNFICYP in Cyprus
UNIFIL in Lebanon
***UNIKOM** on Kuwaiti-Iraqi border
***UNMOGIP** in Kashmir (India and Pakistan)
+**UNPROFOR** in Bosnia-Herzegovina, and Macedonia
+**UNCRO** in Croatia
***UNOMIG** in Georgia
UNOMIH in Haiti
***UNOMIL** in Liberia
***UNOMUR** on the Ugandan-Rwandese border
***UNTSO** in Israel
ONUSOM deployed in Somalia; withdrew in 1995.

* Observer or Assistance Missions only
\+ Protection Mission

OTHER WORLD BODIES

The Bank for International Settlements (BIS)

The BIS is the central banks' bank. It was founded in 1930, originally to settle German reparations due after World War I. It aims to encourage cooperation between the central banks of different countries and and to protect the facilities for international financial settlements and operations. The Board of Directors comprises two delegates from the central banks of Belgium, France, Germany, Italy, the United Kingdom and nine other countries elected by the total membership. The USA has also has the right to permanent representation but does not exercise this right.

Chairman of the Board of Directors: Dr W.F. Duisenberg (The Netherlands).

Headquarters: Basel (Switzerland).

Membership: nearly 90 central banks.

The Commonwealth

The Commonwealth may be said to have its foundations in the 1926 Imperial Conference, which defined the position of the dominions as 'freely associated...members of the British Commonwealth of Nations'. The modern Commonwealth dates from 1949 when India became a republic but remained a member of the Commonwealth, recognizing the British sovereign as 'the symbol of the free association of...independent member states.' The majority of members are republics and some have their own sovereign, but all recognize the British sovereign as Head of the Commonwealth. The Commonwealth is an informal grouping of the UK and the majority of its former dependencies. It has no written constitution. It aims to encourage international, scientific and technical, educational and economic cooperation between members.

Secretary-General: Chief Emeka Anyaoku (Nigeria).

Headquarters: London (UK).

Membership: (dates of Commonwealth membership are in brackets) Antigua and Barbuda (1981), Australia (founder member), Bahamas (1973), Bangladesh (1972), Barbados (1966), Belize (1981), Botswana (1966), Brunei (1981), Canada (founder member), Cyprus (1961), Dominica (1978), Gambia (1965), Ghana (1957), Grenada (1974), Guyana (1966), India (founder member), Jamaica (1962), Kenya (1963), Kiribati (1979), Lesotho (1966), Malawi (1964), Maldives (1982), Malta (1964), Mauritius (1968), Namibia (1990), Nauru (special member; 1968), New Zealand (founder member), Nigeria (1960), Pakistan (founder member; withdrew 1972, readmitted 1989), Papua New Guinea (1975), St Christopher and Nevis (1983), St Lucia (1979), St Vincent and the Grenadines (1979), Seychelles (1976), Sierra Leone (1961), Singapore (1965), Solomon Islands (1978), South Africa (founder member; withdrew 1960; readmitted 1994), Sri Lanka (founder member as Ceylon), Swaziland (1968), Tanzania (joined as Tanganyika; 1961), Tonga (1970), Trinidad and Tobago (1962), Tuvalu (special member; 1978), Uganda (1962), United Kingdom (founder member),

Vanuatu (1980), Western Samoa (1970), Zambia (1964), Zimbabwe (1980). Special members do not participate in Commonwealth ministerial meetings.

Group of Seven (G7)

G7 is an informal grouping of the leading Western economic powers. Since 1975, the heads of government of these states have met for annual summits concerning major economic, monetary and political problems. The Group of Seven, which was originally the Group of Five but was expanded when Canada and Italy joined, has neither a constitution nor secretariat.

Membership: Canada, France, Germany, Italy, Japan, the United Kingdom, the USA. The EU/EC has observer status; Russia has also been invited as an observer to recent G7 summits.

International Criminal Police Organization (Interpol)

Interpol was established in 1923 as the International Criminal Police Commission and was restructured and renamed in 1956. It aims to promote mutual assistance between criminal police authorities. The policy-making body of Interpol, the General Assembly, meets annually.

Secretary-General: William O'Neil (Canada).

Headquarters: Lyon (France).

Membership: over 175 states.

International Energy Agency (IEA)

The IEA is an autonomous agency of OECD (see below). Founded in 1974, the Agency aims to improve energy supplies and to develop alternative sources of energy.

Executive Director: Helga Steeg (Germany).

Headquarters: Paris (France).

Membership: Australia, Austria, Belgium Canada, Denmark, Finland, France, Germany, Greece, Iceland, Ireland, Italy, Japan, Luxembourg, Netherlands, Norway, Portugal, Spain, Sweden, Switzerland, Turkey, the United Kingdom, the USA.

International Olympic Committee (IOC)

The first Olympic Games of the modern era took place in Athens (Greece) in 1896. The International Olympic Committee was formed in 1894.

Headquarters: Lausanne (Switzerland).

Membership: A record 169 countries took part in the 1992 Summer Olympic Games.

The International Red Cross and Red Crescent

The International Red Cross and Red Crescent movement is a neutral organization founded to negotiate between warring parties, to protect casualties of armed conflict, to develop the activities of individual societies, to protect prisoners of war (under the terms of the Geneva Convention), and to coordinate relief for the victims of natural and other disasters. The Conference of the International Red Cross and Red Crescent meets every four years.

Headquarters: Geneva (Switzerland).

Membership: The Red Cross or Red Crescent societies of over 165 countries.

The Non-Aligned Movement

The Non-Aligned Movement is not a formal organization but a conference that usually meets every three years. The aims of the movement are to promote world peace, to reject any system of world power blocs, and to help bring about a more even distribution of the world's wealth. The end of the Cold War has reduced both the influence and the impetus of the movement.

Membership: Over 100 countries have attended the last two conferences.

Organization of Petroleum Exporting Countries (OPEC)

OPEC was founded in Baghdad (Iraq) in 1960. It aims to coordinate the petroleum-producing and petroleum-exporting policies of members.

Secretary-General: Dr Subroto (Indonesia).

Headquarters: Vienna (Austria).

Membership: Algeria, Gabon, Indonesia, Iran, Iraq, Kuwait, Libya, Nigeria, Qatar, Saudi Arabia, the United Arab Emirates, Venezuela.

The Organization of Economic Cooperation and Development (OECD)

OECD was founded in 1961 to replace the Organization for European Economic Co-operation, which had been established in connection with the Marshall Aid Plan in 1948. It aims to encourage and develop economic and social welfare in member nations and to stimulate aid to developing countries.

Secretary-General: Jean-Claude Paye (France).

Headquarters: Paris (France).

Membership: (Membership is by invitation rather than application.) Australia, Austria, Belgium, Canada, Denmark, Finland, France, Germany, Greece, Iceland, Ireland, Italy, Japan, Luxembourg, Mexico, Netherlands, Norway, Portugal, Spain, Sweden, Switzerland, Turkey, the United Kingdom, the USA.

Hungary, the Czech Republic and South Korea are expected to become members in the near future. Poland and Slovakia may also become members.

The World Council of Churches

The World Council of Churches was established in 1948 in Amsterdam (Netherlands). It unites Protestant (including Anglican), Orthodox and Old Catholic Churches. Its governing body is the Assembly, which comprises delegates from members and which meets every seven or eight years. Its activities are categorized under four main headings: unity and renewal; life, education and mission; justice, peace and creation; and sharing and service.

General Secretary: Dr Konrad Raiser (Germany).

Headquarters: Geneva (Switzerland).

Membership: over 330 Churches from over 110 countries.

REGIONAL ORGANIZATIONS

Andean Pact

The Andean Pact was founded in 1992 to establish a free-trade area, with a common external tariff, in northern and western South America.

Headquarters: Lima (Peru).
Members: Bolivia, Colombia, Ecuador, Peru, Venezuela.

ANZUS

ANZUS was founded in 1951 to form a collective defence policy for the preservation of peace in the Pacific region.

Headquarters: Canberra (Australia).
Members: Australia, New Zealand, the USA.

Asia-Pacific Economic Co-operation (Apec)

Apec was founded in 1993 to encourage trade between the countries bordering the Pacific Ocean. Its 18 members have 38% of the world's population, are responsible for 50% of the world's economic production, and 41% of the world's trade. Trade barriers are to be removed between industrial members by 2010 and developing nations by 2020.

Members: Australia, Brunei, Canada, Chile, China, Indonesia, Japan, (South) Korea, Malaysia, Mexico, New Zealand, Papua New Guinea, Philippines, Singapore, Taiwan, Thailand, the USA. Hong Kong is also a member.

Association of South East Asian Nations (ASEAN)

ASEAN was founded in 1967 to accelerate the economic, social and cultural development of members, to maintain stability in the region and to encourage cooperation between members.

Secretary-General: Dato' Ajit Singh (Malaysia).
Headquarters: Jakarta (Indonesia).
Members: Brunei, Indonesia, Malaysia, Philippines, Singapore, Thailand. Laos and Vietnam are observers.

Association of South East Asian Nations Regional Forum (ARF)

ARF was founded in 1994 as an informal conference to bring together the main economic and military powers of the Far East and Southeast Asia.

Headquarters: Jakarta (Indonesia).
Members: Australia, Brunei, Cambodia, China, Indonesia, Japan, (South) Korea, Laos, Malaysia, New Zealand, Papua New Guinea, Philippines, Russia, Singapore, Thailand, the USA, Vietnam.

Black Sea Economic Co-operation Zone

Founded in 1992, the Black Sea Economic Co-operation Zone aims to promote trade and economic cooperation between members and to control pollution in the Black Sea.

Members: Armenia, Azerbaijan, Bulgaria, Georgia, Moldova, Romania, Russia, Turkey, Ukraine.

Caribbean Common Market (CARICOM)

CARICOM was founded in 1973 at the same time as its sister organization, the Caribbean Community (see below). CARICOM aims to promote economic cooperation between members, and shares its organization with the Caribbean Comunity.

Secretary-General: Edwin Carrington (Guyana).
Headquarters: Georgetown (Guyana).
Members: Antigua and Barbuda, Bahamas, Barbados, Belize, Dominica, Dominican Republic*, Grenada, Guyana, Haiti*, Jamaica, St Christopher and Nevis, St Lucia, St Vincent and the Grenadines, Trinidad and Tobago, Suriname*, Venezuela*. Three non-sovereign territories are also members: British Virgin Islands, Montserrat, Turks and Caicos Islands. * associates.

Caribbean Community

The Caribbean Community was founded in 1973 at the same time as CARICOM (see above). The Community and CARICOM share a single administrative organization and common membership. The Community aims to promote cooperation in health, cultural, scientific and technological matters, and to coordinate the foreign policies of members..

Central American Common Market (CACM)

The CACM was founded in 1960, but lapsed in 1969. The organization was revived (1992-93) and began the establishment of a free-trade area in Central America in 1995. CACM has a small Secretariat.

Secretary-General: Rafael Rodriguez Loucel (Guatemala).
Headquarters: Guatemala City (Guatemala).
Members: Costa Rica, El Salvador, Guatemala, Honduras, Nicaragua.

Central European Free Trade Area (CEFTA)

CEFTA was founded in 1992 to establish a free-trade area. This objective is now expected to be reached by 1998. Slovenia has signed free-trade agreements with the CEFTA countries, but is not yet a member of the organization. The CEFTA states are often referred to as the *Visegrad Group*.

Members: Czech Republic, Hungary, Poland, Slovakia.

Colombo Plan

The Colombo Plan for Co-operative Economic and Social Development was founded in 1950 to promote economic and social development within the region. and to encourage training programmes, capital and technical cooperation.

Headquarters: Colombia (Sri Lanka).
Members: Afghanistan, Australia, Bangladesh, Bhutan, Cambodia, Canada, Fiji, Indonesia, Iran, Japan, (South) Korea, Laos, Malaysia, Maldives, Myanmar (Burma), Nepal, New Zealand, Pakistan, Papua New Guinea, Philippines, Singapore, Sri Lanka, Thailand, the United Kingdom, the USA,

Commonwealth of Independent States (CIS)

Following the dissolution of the USSR in December 1991, Belarus, Russia and Ukraine concluded an agreement to found an organization that is, in some limited respects, the successor to the USSR in economic, military and political cooperation. All former Soviet states, except the three Baltic republics, have now joined. The principal objective of the CIS is to provide unitary control of strategic armed forces (including nuclear weapons) that formerly belonged to the USSR. The aim to create a 'single economic space' has largely been abandoned as individual members have adopted their own economic policies and agreements as well their own currencies. CIS peacekeeping forces have been in operation in Moldova, Azerbaijan and Tajikistan. In 1993, some members established a defence alliance, an economic coordination committee and a Commonwealth bank. The affairs of the CIS are largely dealt with on a direct inter-state basis rather than by central institutions. The chairmanship rotates between member states; in 1995, the chair is held by Tajikistan.

Headquarters: Minsk (Belarus).
Members: Armenia, Azerbaijan, Belarus, Georgia, Kazakhstan, Kyrgyzstan, Moldova, Russia, Tajikistan, Turkmenistan, Ukraine, Uzbekistan.

Communauté Financière Africaine (CFA)

The CFA is a monetary union founded to supply a common currency for former French African possessions. The CFA franc is pegged to the French franc.

Headquarters: Paris (France).
Members: Benin, Burkina Faso, Cameroon, Central African Republic, Chad, Congo, Côte d'Ivoire, Equatorial Guinea, Gabon, Mali, Niger, Senegal, Togo.

Co-operation Council for the Arab States of the Gulf (GCC)

The GCC was established in 1981 to promote economic, cultural and social co-operation between the Arab states of the Gulf. It has since also taken on a security role, notably during the Gulf War of 1991. In March 1991, the members of the GCC concluded economic and defence agreements with Egypt and Syria, although the latter are not members of the Council.

Headquarters: Riyadh (Saudi Arabia).
Members: Bahrain, Kuwait, Oman, Qatar, Saudi Arabia, the United Arab Emirates.

Council of Europe

The Council was founded in 1949 to achieve greater European unity, to safeguard members' common European heritage and to facilitate economic and social progress. Membership is restricted to European democracies. The Council of Ministers (foreign ministers of members) meets twice a year. Agreements are formalized as European Conventions or recommendations to governments. The Parliamentary Assembly of the Council (which meets three times a year) comprises delegations from member states. Delegations range in size from 18 members (Italy, France, Germany, the United Kingdom) to two (San Marino, Liechtenstein). The Council has achieved over 140 conventions and agreements including the European Convention of Human Rights (1950).

Headquarters: Strasbourg (France).
Members: Andorra, Austria, Belgium, Bulgaria, Cyprus, Czech Republic, Denmark, Estonia, Finland, France, Germany, Greece, Hungary, Iceland, Ireland, Italy, Liechtenstein, Lithuania, Luxembourg, Malta, Netherlands, Norway, Poland, Portugal, Romania, San Marino, Slovakia, Slovenia, Spain, Sweden, Switzerland, Turkey, the United Kingdom. The following are 'guest' members: Albania, Belarus, Bosnia-Herzegovina, Croatia, Latvia, Macedonia, Moldova, Russia, Ukraine.

Economic Community of West African States (ECOWAS)

ECOWAS was founded in 1975 to promote trade and co-operation between members and to increase self-reliance within West Africa. Its most public achievement to date was the dispatch of an ECOWAS force to intervene in the Liberian civil war in 1990. The ECOWAS Assembly comprises heads of state/heads of government of members. The Assembly meets once a year and is chaired by each member in turn.

Headquarters: Abuja (Nigeria).
Members: Benin, Burkina Faso, Cape Verde, Gambia, Ghana, Guinea, Guinea-Bissau, Liberia, Mali, Mauritania, Niger, Nigeria, Senegal, Sierra Leone, Togo.

Economic Co-operation Organization (ECO)

The ECO was founded in 1965 to promote trade in southwest Asia. The organization lapsed but was revived and expanded in 1992 to aid the development of Central Asia.

Members: Azerbaijan, Iran, Kyrgyzstan, Pakistan, Tajikistan, Turkmenistan, Turkey, Uzbekistan.

European Economic Area (EEA)

The EEA is a free-trade alliance between the members of the EU/EC and three other West European states. It aims to extend the EU's four 'single market freedoms' in the movement of goods, of services, of capital and of labour to create a unified market that includes all of Western Europe except Switzerland. All non-EU members have adopted the harmonization measures that have been implemented by the EU under the Single European Act (1986).

Members: EU states, Iceland, Liechtenstein, Norway.

European Union (EU)

See pp. 562–63.

Group of Three

The Group of Three was set up in 1995 to achieve a a common market by 2005.

Members: Colombia, Mexico, Venezuela.

Latin American Integration Association (ALADI)

ALADI (Asociación Latinoamericano de Integración) was founded in 1980 as a replacement for the Latin American Free Trade Area (founded 1961). It aims to encourage trade and to remove tariffs between members. ALADI maintains a small secretariat.

Secretary-General: Jorge Luis Ordonez (Colombia).
Headquarters: Montevideo (Uruguay).
Members: Argentina, Bolivia, Brazil, Chile, Colombia, Ecuador, Mexico, Paraguay, Peru, Uruguay, Venezuela. The following have observer status: Costa Rica, Cuba, Dominican Republic, El Salvador, Guatemala, Honduras, Italy, Nicaragua, Panama, Portugal, Spain.

League of Arab States (Arab League)

The League was founded in 1945 to protect the independence and sovereignty of members, to strengthen ties between them, and to encourage coordination of their social, economic, political, cultural and legal policies. The League comprises a Council (on which each state has one vote), special committees, over 20 specialized agencies and a Secretariat.

Secretary-General: Dr Ahmad al-Meguid (Egypt).
Headquarters: Cairo (Egypt).
Members: Algeria, Bahrain, Djibouti, Egypt, Iraq, Jordan, Kuwait, Lebanon, Libya, Mauritania, Morocco, Oman, Qatar, Saudi Arabia, Somalia, Sudan, Syria, Tunisia, the United Arab Emirates, Yemen. The Palestine Liberation Organization (currently governing Gaza-Jericho) is also in membership.

Mercosur (Mercado del Sur)

Mercado del Sur (the Market of the South), which originated in a free-trade agreement between Argentina and Brazil in 1988, is scheduled to become a free market in goods, services and labour. The first tariff reductions were made at the beginning of 1995.
Members: Argentina, Brazil, Paraguay, Uruguay.

North American Free Trade Agreement (NAFTA)

NAFTA's origins lie in the free-trade agreement signed by the USA and Canada in 1989. It was extended in 1994 to include Mexico. NAFTA aims to eliminate tariffs, quotas and import licences between states of the North American continent. The Agreement has no formal secretariat.

Members: Canada, Mexico, the USA.

North Atlantic Treaty Organization (NATO)

NATO, which was founded in 1949, is a collective defence organization whose members agree to treat an attack on any one of them as an attack against all. The North Atlantic Council, the highest authority of the alliance, comprises 16 permanent representatives (one from each member), plus observers from the signatories of NATO's Partnership for Peace (see below). The Council is chaired by the Secretary-General of NATO. The foreign ministers of NATO meet at least twice a year. The defence of the NATO area is the responsibility of the Defence Planning Committee (DPC). Neither France nor the signatories of the Partnership for Peace are members of the DPC, which meets regularly at ambassadorial level.

NATO's Partnership for Peace (PFP), adopted in 1994, aims to provide former Warsaw Pact countries, CIS members and neutral states with an agreement that will bring them closer to NATO without formal membership. Through PFP some members will eventually move to full NATO membership. PFP is flexible, offering each partner a different relationship with NATO. Partners open up their defence plans to NATO scrutiny and advice, and share training with NATO.

Secretary-General: Willy Claes (Belgium).
Headquarters: Brussels (Belgium).
Members: Belgium, Canada, Denmark, France, Germany, Greece, Iceland, Italy, Luxembourg, Netherlands, Norway, Portugal, Spain, Turkey, the United Kingdom, the USA.
Partners for Peace: Albania, Armenia, Azerbaijan, Belarus, Bulgaria, Czech Republic, Finland, Georgia, Hungary, Kazakhstan, Kyrgyzstan, Latvia, Lithuania, Moldova, Poland, Romania, Slovakia, Slovenia, Sweden, Ukraine. Russia agreed to sign a long-delayed partnership agreement in 1995.

Organization of African Unity (OAU)

The OAU was founded in 1963 to promote African unity and collaboration in economic, social, cultural, political, defence, scientific, health and other matters, and to eliminate colonialism from Africa. The OAU Assembly of heads of state/government meets annually and is presided over by a chairman, who is elected annually by the Assembly. The main administrative body of the OAU is the Secretariat.

Secretary-General: Salim Ahmed Salim (Tanzania).
Headquarters: Addis Ababa, (Ethiopia).
Members: Algeria, Angola, Benin, Botswana, Burkina Faso, Burundi, Cameroon, Cape Verde, Central African Republic, Chad, Comoros, Congo, Côte d'Ivoire, Djibouti, Egypt, Equatorial Guinea, Eritrea, Ethiopia, Gabon, Gambia, Ghana, Guinea, Guinea-Bissau, Kenya, Lesotho, Liberia, Libya, Madagascar, Malawi, Mali, Mauritania, Mauritius, Mozambique, Namibia, Niger, Nigeria, Rwanda, São Tomé e Principe, Senegal, Seychelles, Sierra Leone, Somalia, South Africa, Sudan, Swaziland, Tanzania, Togo, Tunisia, Uganda, Zaïre, Zambia, Zimbabwe. In 1982, the Sahrawi Democratic Republic (Western Sahara) was admitted to membership; Morocco, which claims Western Sahara, withdrew in protest.)

Organization of Arab Petroleum Exporting Countries (OAPEC)

OAPEC was founded in 1968 to encourage cooperation in economic activities, to ensure the flow of oil to consumer markets, and to promote a favourable climate for the investment of capital and expertise. The oil ministers of members form a Ministerial Council, which meets twice a year. The General Secretariat is the organ of OAPEC.

Headquarters: Cairo (Egypt).
Members: Algeria, Bahrain, Egypt, Iraq, Kuwait, Libya, Qatar, Saudi Arabia, Syria, the United Arab Emirates.

Organization of American States (OAS)

The OAS, founded in 1948 as the successor to the Pan American Union, aims to maintain the independence and territorial integrity of members, to achieve peace and justice on the continent, and to encourage collaboration and inter-American solidarity.

Secretary-General: Dr Cesar Gaviria Trujillo (Colombia).
Headquarters: Washington DC (USA).
Members: Antigua and Barbuda, Argentina, Bahamas, Barbados, Belize, Bolivia, Brazil, Canada, Chile, Colombia, Costa Rica, Dominica, Dominican Republic, Ecuador, El Salvador, Grenada, Guatemala, Guyana, Haiti, Honduras, Jamaica, Mexico, Nicaragua, Panama, Paraguay, Peru, St Christopher and Nevis, St Lucia, St Vincent and the Grenadines, Suriname, Trinidad and Tobago, the USA, Uruguay, Venezuela. Cuba is a member but has been suspended since 1962.

Organization of the Islamic Conference (OIC)

OIC was founded in 1971 to promote Islamic solidarity, consolidate economic, social and cultural co-operation between members, and safeguard the Holy Places of Islam and independence of Muslim people.

Headquarters: Jeddah (Saudi Arabia).
Members: Afghanistan, Algeria, Bahrain, Bangladesh, Benin, Brunei, Burkina Faso, Cameroon, Chad, Comoros, Djibouti, Egypt, Gabon, Gambia, Guinea, Guinea-Bissau, Indonesia, Iran, Iraq, Jordan, Kuwait, Lebanon, Libya, Malaysia, Maldives, Mali, Mauritania, Morocco, Niger, Nigeria, Oman, Pakistan, Qatar, Saudi Arabia, Senegal, Sierra Leone, Somalia, Sudan, Syria, Tunisia, Turkey, Uganda, the United Arab Emirates, Yemen. The Palestine Liberation Organization (currently governing Gaza-Jericho) is also in membership; Mozambique is an associate.

Organization on Security and Cooperation in Europe (OSCE)

The OSCE was founded as the Conference on Security and Cooperation in Europe (CSCE), which grew out of a security conference held in Helsinki (Finland) in 1975. The aims of the OSCE were formulated by the Charter of Paris (1990), which has been described as the formal end of the Cold War. Members affirm an adherence to democracy and human rights, and a commitment to settle disputes by peaceful means. OSCE foreign ministers meet at least once a year.

Secretary-General: Wilhelm Hoynck (Germany).
Headquarters of the Secretariat (and Forum for Security Cooperation): Vienna (Austria).
Office for Democratic Institutions and Human Rights: Warsaw (Poland).
Office of the High Commission on National Minorities: The Hague (Netherlands).
Members: Albania, Armenia, Austria, Azerbaijan, Belarus, Belgium, Bulgaria, Canada, Croatia, Cyprus, Czech Republic, Denmark, Estonia, Finland, France, Georgia, Germany, Greece, Hungary, Iceland, Ireland, Italy, Kazakhstan, Kyrgyzstan, Latvia, Liechtenstein, Lithuania, Luxembourg, Malta, Moldova, Monaco, Netherlands, Norway, Poland, Portugal, Romania, Russia, San Marino, Slovakia, Slovenia, Spain, Sweden, Switzerland, Tajikistan, Turkey, Turkmenistan, Ukraine, Uzbekistan, the United Kingdom, the USA, Vatican City. The Former Yugoslav Republic of Macedonia is an observer; Yugoslavia has been suspended.

Southern Africa Development Community (SADC or SADCC)

The SADC, or SADCC, was founded by neighbours of South Africa to lessen the influence of that country upon their economies. Since the advent of majority rule to South Africa, SADC works to promote regional trade and development among the countries of Southern Africa, including South Africa.

Headquarters: Gaborone (Botswana).
Members: Angola, Botswana, Lesotho, Malawi, Mozambique, Namibia, South Africa, Swaziland, Tanzania, Zambia, Zimbabwe.

South Asian Association for Economic Cooperation (SAARC)

The Association was founded in 1985 to encourage trade and economic development in South Asia.

Headquarters: Delhi (India).
Members: Bangladesh, Bhutan, India, Maldives, Nepal, Pakistan, Sri Lanka.

South Pacific Bureau for Economic Cooperation (SPEC)

The SPEC was founded in 1973 to encourage regional trade, economic development and the expansion of transport links between members. The administration of the Bureau is shared with that of the South Pacific Forum (see below).

Headquarters: Suva (Fiji).
Members: The same as the South Pacific Forum.

South Pacific Forum

The South Pacific Forum, which has no formal constitution, was founded in 1971 to further cooperation between members in a wide range of issues of mutual interest from environmental to social, and from scientific to international. A particular concern is the status and development of those Pacific territories remaining under colonial administration. The Forum has a small Secretariat, which is headed by a Secretary-General.

Secretary-General: Ati George Sokomanu (*Vanuatu*).
Headquarters: Suva (Fiji).
Members: Australia, Fiji, Kiribati, Marshall Islands, Micronesia, Nauru, New Zealand, Palau, Papua New Guinea, Solomon Islands, Tonga, Tuvalu, Vanuatu, Western Samoa. The Cook Islands and Niue, self-governing territories of New Zealand, are members. Other dependent territories are associates.

West European Union (WEU)

The WEU, founded in 1955, seeks to harmonize the security and defence of the countries of Western Europe. The WEU was reactivated in 1984 to strengthen NATO and has virtually taken on the role of the EU/EC's putative defence arm.

A Council of Ministers (the foreign and defence ministers of members) meets twice a year under a rotating presidency (each member holds the presidency for six months). The Permanent Council of the WEU (the members' ambassadors in Brussels) meets on a regular basis; representatives of the associate and observer members also participate.

The Assembly of the WEU, which meets twice a year, comprises 108 members of the national parliaments of full members.

Secretary-General: Dr Willem van Eekelen (Netherlands).
Headquarters: Brussels (Belgium).
Parliamentary headquarters: Paris (France).
Members: Belgium, France, Germany, Greece, Italy, Luxembourg, Netherlands, Portugal, Spain, the United Kingdom. The associate and observer members are: Austria, Bulgaria, Czech Republic, Denmark, Estonia, Finland, Hungary, Iceland, Ireland, Latvia, Lithuania, Norway, Poland, Romania, Slovakia, Sweden, Turkey.

THE EUROPEAN UNION

In 1950, the governments of Belgium, France, the Federal Republic of Germany (West Germany), Italy, Luxembourg and Italy began negotiations to integrate their interests in specific fields. The result was the Treaty of Paris (1951) under which the European Coal and Steel Community (ECSC) was set up. In 1957 under the terms of the Treaty of Rome, the European Economic Community (EEC) and the European Atomic Energy Commission (Euratom) were established, with memberships identical to the ECSC.

The three Communities were distinct entities until 1967 when, for all practical purposes, they merged their executives and decision-making bodies into a single *European Community* (EC). The Community has since been enlarged as indicated below.

ENLARGEMENT OF THE EC/EU

1957: Belgium, France, Germany (Federal Republic), Italy, Luxembourg, Netherlands.
1973: Denmark, Ireland, United Kingdom.
1981: Greece.
1986: Portugal, Spain.
1995: Austria, Finland, Sweden.
By special arrangement, Andorra, Monaco and San Marino are included within the EU.
Associates:. Cyprus, Malta, Hungary, Poland (who have applied for full membership), plus Czech Republic, Slovakia, Romania, Bulgaria, Estonia, Latvia, Lithuania and Slovenia.

Community finance

After 1975 the EC had its own revenue independent of national contributions. The general budget covers all the expenditure of the Community. Member states are required to supply funds appropriate to these needs.

There are three main institutions of the Community: the Commission, the Council of Ministers and the European Parliament.

The European Commission

The European Commission consists of 20 members appointed by their national governments for a term of four years. The Commissioners appoint from their number a President and six Vice-Presidents. The Commission, which acts independently of national

EU or EC?

A new European body, the European Union (EU), came into being on 1 November 1993 following the ratification of the Maastricht Treaty. The European Union expressed 'an ever closer union among the people of Europe'. The governments of the member states agreed to a series of objectives that include (eventually) a single currency, and a commitment that the European Union should 'assert its identity on the international scene'. The European Union has not replaced the European Community. The EC, its bodies and structures now form one of the three 'pillars' (see Maastricht Treaty) that comprise the European Union. In most of its dealings the Commission acts as the Commission of the European Community *not* of the EU, although there are circumstances in which the Commissioners are called to act for the EU rather than the EC.

The Union implies no additional obligations upon members or their citizens. It does, however, mean some additional rights for citizens of EU countries. Every citizen of the 15 states is now, also, a citizen of the European Union. Every EU citizen has the right to vote or stand for election in elections for local and regional government authorities in any country of the Union.

Also every EU citizen may vote or stand for election for the European Parliament in any EU state. Also, any EU citizen who finds him or herself in difficulty in any country which is outside the Union may apply to the embassy or consulate of any EU state for assistance.

THE MAASTRICHT TREATY

The Maastricht Treaty was drawn up by the 12 members of the EC in 1991. The Treaty marks a decisive step from a 'common market' to a much closer and deeper unification of the economic, political and social systems of member countries.

The three main areas of concern in the Treaty may be summarized as: monetary union, subsidiarity, and the 'pillars' of the European Union (EU).

Monetary union is a central feature of the Treaty. It was hoped that this could be established by a three-stage plan for the irrevocable change to a single currency, the *European Currency Unit* (ECU). In the first stage, all countries were to participate in the *European Exchange Mechanism* (ERM), which requires members to keep the exchange value of their currencies to a 'fixed' rate against other members' currencies. Speculative pressures on the British pound and the Italian lira forced the withdrawal of these currencies from the system in 1992, and further pressure on other currencies in 1993 forced EC governments to effectively suspend the ERM by allowing member currencies to move by 15% on either side of their central rates. This enabled members to pursue their own exchange policies but at the cost of at least postponing monetary union.

Subsidiarity became a 'buzz' word for politicians following Maastricht. The Treaty affirms that, wherever possible, decisions should be 'taken as closely as posible to the citizens'. This principle, referred to as subsidiarity (Article 3b of the Treaty), requires that the Community confines itself to doing what cannot be sufficiently achieved by member states acting alone and can, therefore, be better achieved at Community level.

The 'pillars' of the European Union (see above) were defined by the Treaty. Under Maastricht, cooperation in certain fields is to be channelled through new inter-governmental bodies rather than through existing bodies of the European Community. Maastricht defined a European Union resting on three 'pillars'. The first pillar is the EC, which is schedueld to assume additional monetary responsibilities. The second pillar, concerning foreign and security matters, and the third pillar, concerning co-operation in a wide variety of areas such as immigration, political asylum and law enforcement, were defined as inter-governmental bodies representing the member states.

With the (probable) postponement of monetary union, the Maastricht Treaty implies a considerable widening of cooperation between members at governmental level, without adding substantially to the powers of the Commission.

governments, makes proposals to the Council of Ministers (see below) and executes the decisions of the Council.

Headquarters: Brussels (Belgium).

THE COMMISSIONERS

Jacques Santer (Luxembourg) President of the Commission.
Martin Bangemann (Germany) Industrial policy.
Rita Bjørregaard (Denmark) Environment.
Emma Bonino (Italy) Fishing and consumer affairs.
Sir Leon Brittan (UK) Trade, Asia, North America.
Hans van den Broek (Netherlands) Foreign policy, Eastern Europe.
Edith Cresson (France) Research, Training.
Joâo de Deus Pinheiro (Portugal) Africa, Caribbean, Pacific.
Franz Fischler (Austria) Agriculture.
Padraig Flynn (Ireland) Social policy.
Anita Gradin (Sweden) Immigration and interior policy.
Neil Kinnock (UK) Transport.
Erkki Liikanen (Finland) Budget.
Manuel Marin (Spain) Mediterranean, Latin America.
Mario Monti (Italy) Internal market.
Marcelino Oreja (Spain) Institutional affairs.
Christos Papoutsis (Greece) Energy.
Yves-Thibaut de Silguy (France) Economic and monetary matters.
Karel Van Miert (Belgium) Competition policy.
Monika Wulf-Mathies (Germany) Regional policy.

The Council of Ministers

The Council of Ministers is the main decision-making body of the EU. It consists of the foreign ministers of each of the 15 members. Specialist councils, for example the 15 ministers of agriculture, also meet, while heads of government meet three times a year as the *European Council.* Ministers represent national interests. The decisions of the Council are normally unanimous although there is provision for majority voting in certain areas. The *Presidency of the Council of Ministers* rotates (see box), with each member state taking the chair for a period of six months. Council meetings are normally held in the country that currently holds the Presidency, but are also held in Brussels.

The European Parliament

The European Parliament consists of 626 members directly elected for five years by universal adult suffrage according to local practice in each member state. (All members except the United Kingdom use proportional representation.) Members (MEPs) have the right to be consulted on legislative proposals submitted by the Council of Ministers or the Commission and the power to reject or amend the budget of the EC. The Parliament also has the authority to dismiss the Commission in a vote of censure.

COUNCIL PRESIDENCY

January–June 1995	France
July–December 1995	Spain
January–June 1996	Italy
July–December 1996	Ireland
January–June 1997	Netherlands
July–December 1997	Luxembourg
January–June 1998	United Kingdom
July–December 1998	Austria
January–June 1999	Germany
July–December 1999	Finland
January–June 2000	Portugal
July–December 2000	France
January–June 2001	Sweden
July–December 2001	Belgium
January–June 2002	Spain
July–December 2002	Denmark

MEPs BY NATION

Austria	21 seats
Belgium	25 seats
Denmark	16 seats
Finland	16 seats
France	87 seats
Germany	99 seats
Greece	25 seats
Ireland	15 seats
Italy	87 seats
Luxembourg	6 seats
Netherlands	31 seats
Portugal	25 seats
Spain	64 seats
Sweden	22 seats
United Kingdom	87 seats

Headquarters: Strasbourg (France), although there is also a parliamentary building used for meetings in Brussels (Belgium), where committees of the European Parliament also meet. The Secretariat of the Parliament is based in Luxembourg City.

There are 19 parliamentary Standing Committees specializing in matters ranging from foreign affairs and security to women's rights. Parliament is run by a bureau consisting of a President and 14 Vice-Presidents, elected by MEPs from their number.

MEPs sit in multi-national political groupings. A grouping with members from one country only must have at least 26 MEPs to gain recognition; a grouping from two countries requires 21 MEPs for recognition; a grouping from three requires 16 MEPs; and a grouping from four or more requires only 13 MEPs.

The largest political groupings are the Party of European Socialists (led by Pauline Green, United Kingdom), the (conservative) European People's Party (which includes British Conservative MEPs), the European Liberal Democratic and Reformist Group (which includes British Liberal Democrats), the (largely former Communist) Confederal Group of the European United Left, and the Green Group.

The Court of Justice of the European Communities (The European Court)

The European Court consists of 13 judges and six advocates appointed for six years by the governments of member states acting in concert, with at least one representative from each country. The Court is responsible for deciding upon the legality of the decisions of the Council of Ministers and the Commission, and for adjudicating between states in the event of disputes.

Headquarters: Luxembourg City.

The Court of Auditors of the European Commission

The Court (which was established in 1977) is responsible for the external audit of the resources managed governments, makes proposals to the Council of Ministers (see below) and executes the decisions of the Council.

Headquarters: Brussels (Belgium).

The Council of Ministers

The Council of Ministers is the main decision-making body of the EU. It consists of the foreign ministers of each of the 15 members. Specialist councils, for example the 15 ministers of agriculture, also meet, while heads of government meet three times a year as the *European Council.* Ministers represent national interests. The decisions of the Council are normally unanimous although there is provision for majority voting in certain areas. The *Presidency of the Council of Ministers* rotates (see box), with each member state taking the chair for a period of six months. Council meetings are normally held in the country that currently holds the Presidency, but are also held in Brussels.

The European Parliament

The European Parliament consists of 626 members directly elected for five years by universal adult suffrage according to local practice in each member state. (All members except the United Kingdom use proportional representation.) Members (MEPs) have the right to be consulted on legislative proposals submitted by the Council of Ministers or the Commission and the power to reject or amend the budget of the EC. The Parliament also has the authority to dismiss the Commission in a vote of censure.

Headquarters: Strasbourg (France), although there is also a parliamentary building used for meetings in Brussels (Belgium), where committees of the European Parliament also meet. The Secretariat of the Parliament is based in Luxembourg City.

There are 19 parliamentary Standing Committees specializing in matters ranging from foreign affairs and security to women's rights. Parliament is run by a bureau consisting of a President and 14 Vice-Presidents, elected by MEPs from their number.

MEPs sit in multi-national political groupings. A grouping with members from one country only must have at least 26 MEPs to gain recognition; a grouping from two countries requires 21 MEPs for recognition; a grouping from three requires 16 MEPs; and a grouping from four or more requires only 13 MEPs.

The largest political groupings are the Party of European Socialists (led by Pauline Green, United Kingdom), the (conservative) European People's Party (which includes British Conservative MEPs), the European Liberal Democratic and Reformist Group (which includes British Liberal Democrats), the (largely former Communist) Confederal Group of the European United Left, and the Green Group.

The Court of Justice of the European Communities (The European Court)

The European Court consists of 13 judges and six advocates appointed for six years by the governments of member states acting in concert, with at least one representative from each country. The Court is responsible for deciding upon the legality of the decisions of the Council of Ministers and the Commission, and for adjudicating between states in the event of disputes.

Headquarters: Luxembourg City.

SINGLE EUROPEAN MARKET

A key objective of the Community is to secure the economic benefits of free trade through the creation of a 'common market' providing for the unrestricted movement of goods, services, capital and labour.

Under the founding legislation of the EC, the Treaty of Rome, attention centred on the elimination of various visible restrictions on inter-state trade such as tariffs, quotas and cartels. More recently, under the Single European Act (1986) and the Masstricht Treaty (1991), the intent has been to create a more unified EU/EC bloc providing not only greater opportunities, but also paving the way for a deeper integration of the member states of the Union economically, politically, monetarily and socially.

The Single European Act itself is concerned specifically with sweeping away a large number of less visible obstacles to trade arising from historical differences in the policies and practices of individual member states. The intention was to end the fragmentation of the Community into national markets and to create a 'level playing field' so that businesses can produce and sell their products throughout the Union.

The Single European Act committed members to remove various impediments to the movement of goods, services, capital and people through the progressive introduction of various practices and regulations. Hitherto, trade has been obstructed and costs and prices increased in many ways: by different national bureaucratic requirements and technical standards, different national taxation structures, and restrictive government procurement practices and subsidies given to local firms.

The Act was introduced in 1992 at a time when intra-Community trade already accounted for over 50% of members' total external trade and it has helped boost that total up to well over 60%. The immediate benefits of the single market are primarily economic. Consumers benefit from a wider choice of goods and services, and from lower prices owing to increased competition. EU citizens also benefit from the ability to live and work anywhere in the Union.

This free trade area has been expanded into the European Economic Area (EEA) as Norway, Iceland and Liechtenstein have also applied the provisions of the single market.

The Court of Auditors of the European Commission

The Court (which was established in 1977) is responsible for the external audit of the resources managed by the EU/EC. It consist of 15 members (one from each country) elected for six years by the Council of Ministers.

Headquarters: Luxembourg City

The European Investment Bank

The Bank, which works on a non-profit making basis, makes or guarantees loans for investment projects in member states. Priority is given to regional development.

Headquarters: Luxembourg City

Consultative bodies of the EU/EC

Defence

The existence of nuclear weapons of proven capability has deterred direct conflict between the major powers since the end of World War II. The collapse of Communism in Eastern Europe has effectively ended the confrontation between East and West. The signature of the Charter of Paris in November 1990 formally ended the Cold War, but large nuclear stockpiles remain. However, fear of superpower imbalance has been replaced by fear of 'proliferation' – the spread of nuclear capability to powers outside the major blocs. Until 1989-90 the greatest danger of conflict seemed to lie in Europe. Soviet forces have withdrawn from Hungary, the Czech Republic, Slovakia, Poland and the former East Germany. A number of US and British bases in Western Europe have also closed. Local or regional conflicts in other parts of the world are now seen as a greater threat, for example the Iraqi invasion of Kuwait in August 1990, although the civil wars in former Yugoslavia have greatly increased tension in Europe in 1992–93.

For details of the main defence pacts see International Organizations.

MAJOR ARMED FORCES

The strength of major armed forces is most commonly compared in terms of nuclear capacity or total manpower. Other important factors include the numbers of combat aircraft, the size of navies and the proportion of GDP (Gross Domestic Product) devoted to defence. In the following lists, the armed forces of major countries are compared in terms of these five categories.

Manpower

Country	*Total excluding reserves*
China	3,030,000
Russia	2,720,000
USA	1,913,750
India	1,265,000
North Korea	1,132,000
Vietnam	857,000
South Korea	633,000
Pakistan	580,000
Turkey	560,000
Iran	528,000
Germany	447,000
France	431,000
Egypt	410,000
Syria	408,000
Iraq	382,000

Nuclear warheads

The US and Russian totals given below are subject to the Strategic Arms Reduction (START) agreements and are in the process of being reduced.

In addition to the eight countries listed below there are other countries with nuclear stockpiles, but their existence is not proven. They are thought to include Israel, India and North Korea.

In 1993, South Africa admitted that it had had a nuclear capability but had destroyed its weapons. Iran, Iraq and Pakistan all have ambitions to acquire nuclear weapons.

Country	*Number of nuclear warheads*
USA	5921
Russia	2968
France	426
Ukraine*	176
United Kingdom	144
Kazakhstan*	104
China	80
Belarus*	54

* The warheads indicated for these countries are under the control of the Commonwealth of Independent States (CIS; see International Organizations) and are, therefore, unlikely to be used unilaterally.

Combat aircraft

Country	*Number of combat aircraft*
China	4970
Russia	3700
USA	3485
Ukraine	1100
France	808
North Korea	732
India	674
Israel	662
Germany	653
Syria	639
Turkey	573
Belarus	502
Sweden	499
Egypt	492
Romania	486

Navies

Country	*Vessels including submarines*
Russia	1722
China	1301
USA	576
North Korea	569
Taiwan	197
Germany	172
Japan	159
Turkey	151
United Kingdom	150
France	148
Romania	141
India	131
Spain	106
Sweden	104
Indonesia	103

Percentage of GDP spent on defence

Country	*Percentage of GDP*
Ukraine	49·57%
Saudi Arabia	33·75%
Kuwait	33·20%
North Korea	26·70%
Georgia	25·56%
Belarus	23·74%
Ethiopia	21·62%
Iraq	21·10%
Moldova	18·42%
Angola	17·21%
Oman	15·92%
United Arab Emirates	14·55%
Israel	13·20%
Syria	13·02%
Jordan	12·75%

WARS IN THE 1990s

The conflicts listed below (chronologically) started or continued in the 1990s.

Kashmir (1947–49, 1965, intermittent): Kashmir is the principal bone of contention between India and Pakistan since the partition of the sub-continent. Tension over the state has led to war twice and the problem of Kashmir, part of which (Azad Kashmir) is occupied by Pakistan, remains unresolved. Fighting between Indian and Pakistani forces continues intermittently along the far-northern end of the ceasefire line, and, since 1989, Kashmiri separatist guerrillas are active in parts of the state.

Ethiopia/Eritrea (1961–1991): Rebel forces in Eritrea and Tigray fought government forces for independence. Eritrea effectively seceded in 1991 and assumed full sovereignty in May 1993; spasmodic fighting continues in Ethiopia, especially in the Tigray and Oromo districts.

Chad (1965–): Civil wars between the Muslim Arab North and the Christian and animist Black African South. Idriss Deby successfully led rebel forces against the government (1989). Unrest, and Libyan interference, continues in the north.

Northern Ireland (1969–94): Sectarian conflict between Protestant extremists intent on remaining part of the UK and Catholic extremists intent on reuniting Ireland. British troops – initially deployed in a peacekeeping role – were opposed by paramilitary groups such as the (loyalist) Ulster Defence Association (UDA) and the (nationalist) Provisional Irish Republican Army (IRA). A ceasefire was declared by the IRA in 1994, but British troops are still deployed.

Western Sahara (1972–91): The Polisario liberation movement began its fight against Spanish rule in the territory in 1972. Spain withdrew, dividing the Western Sahara between Morocco and Mauritania (1976). Morocco absorbed the Mauritanian sector when Mauritania withdrew (1979). In 1976, the Polisario declared independence and conducted a guerrilla campaign against Moroccan rule until 1991 when a UN-brokered ceasefire was agreed. Sporadic fighting continues.

Lebanon (1975–91): Civil war between Christian and Muslim forces reduced Lebanon to ungovernable chaos. Syria and Israel intervened and a Syrian-backed government imposed a semblance of order (1991), but spasmodic fighting in the south between Hizbollah fundamentalists and Israeli-backed forces continues.

Mozambique (1975–94): Mozambique virtually disintegrated in civil war between the Front for Liberation of Mozambique (FRELIMO) government and the Mozambique National Resistance Organization (RENAMO). Peace moves were made in 1993-94 and the civil war officially ended in 1994, although spasmodic fighting continues.

Sri Lanka (1975–): Indian intervention (1987-90) led to a bitter counter-insurgency operation of the civil war between the ruling Sinhalese and the ethnic-Indian Tamils (particularly the Tamil Tigers), who are fighting for an independent Tamil state. After a brief ceasefire in 1995 fighting resumed.

East Timor (1975–): Indonesia seized the former Portuguese colony of East Timor in 1975, despite the territory's declaration of independence and the opposition of the UN. Rebel Timorese activity continues.

Angola (1976–): UNITA (National Union for the Total Independence of Angola) forces – initially aided by South Africa – fought the left-wing MPLA (People's Movement for the Liberation of Angola) government. The MPLA won the civil war of 1975-76, but continued to be opposed by UNITA rebels. A UN-supervised ceasefire (1991) was breached and the civil war resumed in 1992 when UNITA refused to accept the result of multi-party elections. A further ceasefire in 1995 followed heavy UNITA losses in 1994-95, but spasmodic fighting continues.

Afghanistan (1979–): Civil war was triggered by the Soviet invasion (1979). Mujahaddin guerrillas (Muslim fundamentalists) fought government forces even after the Soviet withdrawal (1989). In 1992 fundamentalists took Kabul and formed a provisional government, but factional – largely ethnic – fighting continues.

Cambodia (1979–1991): The 1991 ceasefire ended civil war between the Vietnamese-backed government and Pol Pot's Khmer Rouge. Free elections were held and the monarchy restored, but spasmodic fighting continues as the Khmer Rouge withdrew from the peace process.

El Salvador (1980–91): A UN-supervised peace agreement ended civil war between the government and left-wing Farabundo Marti National Liberation Front (FMLN) guerrillas.

Peru (1980–): Revolutionary activities of the Maoist Sendero Luminoso ('Shining Path') group triggered a counter-insurgency campaign by the government. Guerrilla activity has decreased since the capture of the Sendero Luminoso leader.

Philippines (1982–): Communist insurgency increased in 1982, but, by 1993, the problem had been contained, although sporadic fighting continues.

Sudan (1983–): Civil war continues between Islamic government forces and the Christian and animist guerrillas of the Sudan People's Liberation Army (SPLA). The latter is subject to violent internal fighting. Western humanitarian aid has been disrupted. By 1995, government forces had gained the advantage.

Palestinian Intifada (1987–): The Palestinian uprising in the West Bank and Gaza Strip against Israeli occupying forces has been characterized by riots and shootings. Unrest continues despite a peace agreement between the Israelis and the PLO (Palestine Liberation Organization) granting limited Palestinian autonomy in Gaza and Jericho.

Myanmar (Burma; 1988–): Military rule since 1988 has been opposed by a variety of political and nationalist groups. Non-Burman minorities have joined forces to fight against the military. However, by 1995 government forces had contained most of the minorities.

Somalia (1988–): An Ethiopian-backed uprising in northern Somalia (1988) began armed opposition to President Barre, who fled (1991) after guerrillas attacked the capital, Mogadishu. The rebels have since fought among themselves and Somalia has descended into chaos. US Marines intervened (1992) to deliver humanitarian aid, but to little effect, and the UN presence ceased in 1995.

Liberia (1989–): ECOWAS deployed a peacekeeping force (1990) to end a civil war initially between the National Patriotic Front of Liberia (NLFL) and government forces, but fighting flared up between NLFL and rival rebel groups (1992) and is still continuing.

Bougainville (Papua New Guinea; 1989–91): Secessionist guerillas were active on the mineral-rich island of Bougainville until 1991 when government forces contained the situation.

Kuwait (1990–91): Iraqi troops invaded Kuwait in 1990. A US-led multi-national force – under the auspices of the UN – used air attacks on Iraq and a 100-hour ground campaign to liberate Kuwait in 1991. Since then, the UN has monitored the border and the USA has initiated air strikes to deter Iraqi aggression.

Rwanda (1990–94): In 1990, the Front patriotique rwandais (FPR), an army of Tutsi refugees, invaded Rwanda, occupying much of the north. After a plane carrying President Habyarimana was shot down (1994), government (Hutu) forces went on the rampage. In the ensuing ethnic violence, between 500,000 and 1,000,000 Tutsis were massacred by Hutus and over 2,000,000 refugees fled the country. Hutu forces continue spasmodic border activity against the new FPR government.

Sierra Leone (1991–): The rebel Revolutionary United Front, a product of the civil war in Liberia, began activities against the central government in 1991. By May 1995, the RUF controlled the greater part of the country.

Iraq (1991–): After the Gulf War (see Kuwait), Saddam Hussein faced uprisings by Shi'ite Muslims in the south and Kurds in the north. Allied 'no-fly' zones in these areas (and threats of intervention) have restrained Iraq, but small-scale attacks on the Shi'ites continue.

Georgia (1991–92): A civil war between supporters and opponents of President Gamsakhurdia was followed by continuing secessionist wars (see below).

Georgia-Abkhazia (1992–93): Muslim secessionist forces were aided by Russians in 1993. By September 1993, Abkhazian forces had gained control of almost the entire region. A Russian-brokered ceasefire came into force in December 1993, but unrest continues and the Georgian authorities have lost control of the area.

Georgia-South Ossetia (1992): Muslim secessionists in South Ossetia fought an intermittent campaign to unite with North Ossetian co-nationals in Russia. A peace force established a buffer zone in June 1992.

Bosnia-Herzegovina (1991–): After Bosnia-Herzegovina received international recognition as a sovereign state in 1992, Bosnian Serbs fought against Croats and Muslims (although the latter also fought each other) for control of what was central Yugoslavia. The Serbs occupied about 70% of Bosnia, killing or expelling Muslims and Croats in a campaign of 'ethnic cleansing'. A UN force was deployed in 1992 to supervise the delivery of humanitarian aid. The Serbs set up an internationally-unrecognized republic based at Pale. Peace negotiations continue, but the fighting persists. Several ceasefires have been agreed and, subsequently, collapsed.

Croatia (1991–): War between Croats and ethnic Serbs in Krajina and parts of Slavonia followed the break-up of Yugoslavia. A ceasefire was negotiated in early 1992 and a UN force deployed, but fighting resumed in 1993. Further uneasy ceasefires followed, but, in 1995, Croat forces retook Serb-occupied western Slavonia.

Moldova (1992): Civil war broke out in 1992 when Russian and Ukrainian minorities, fearing a reunion of Moldova with Romania, proclaimed the republic of Transdnestria. The intervention of CIS (mainly Russian) forces brought an uneasy peace, but the Moldovan authorities no longer control Transdnestria.

Armenia-Azerbaijan (Nagorno-Karabakh region; 1992–): Azeri and Armenian forces are fighting for control of Nagorno Karabakh, an enclave of Orthodox Christian Armenians surrounded by the Shi'ite Muslim Azeris. A Russian-brokered ceasefire has been attempted.

Tajikistan (1992–): The ex-Communist rulers of this former Soviet republic have effectively defeated Islamic fundamentalists in the north, but fighting continues intermittently in the south along the Afghan frontier.

Zaïre (1992–): Spasmodic fighting occurs in the two Kasai provinces and in Shaba (the former Katanga) as secessionists have taken advantage of the collapse of law and order in much of the country.

Mexico (1994-): An uprising by Zapatista guerrillas in Chiapas province (southern Mexico) has led to a counter-insurgency campaign which still continues.

Yemen (1994): The uneasy union between former (traditionalist) North Yemen and former (Communist) South Yemen, negotiated in 1990, proved more apparent than real in many respects. Regional stresses, and resentment in the South, resulted in civil war in 1994. The South declared independence but was defeated within one month.

Haiti (1994): US forces intervened in Haiti to replace a repressive military regime and to ensure that the results of a presidential election were enforced. Some troops (as well as UN forces) remain in Haiti.

Chechenya (1994–): Intervention by Russian forces to prevent the secession of Chechenya from the Russian Federation led to heavy fighting, particularly for the Chechen capital, Grozny. Russian victory was still elusive in mid-1995 as spasmodic fighting continued in the mountains.

Peru-Ecuador (1995): Border disputes between Peru and Ecuador led to some fighting early in 1995. A ceasefire was negotiated quickly.

Countries of the World

This section describes the 192 sovereign states of the world; their dependent territories plus disputed and other territories are to be found beginning on page 729.

AFGHANISTAN

Official name: Jamhuria Afghanistan (Republic of Afghanistan).
Member of: UN.
Area: 652,225 km² (251,824 sq mi).
Population: 20,270,000 (1993 est).
Capital: Kabul 2,000,000 (including suburbs; 1993 est).
Other major cities: Kandahar (Qandahar) 226,000, Herat 177,000, Mazar-i-Sharif 131,000 (1988 est).
Languages: Pushto (52%), Dari (Persian; 30%) – both official.
Religion: Sunni Islam (74%), Shia Islam (25%).
Education: is compulsory, in theory, between the ages of seven and 15. *Adult literacy:* 29%. *Universities:* five.
Defence: Owing to civil war, there are no recognizable national forces. *Conscription:* four years, in theory, but not operating in practice.

Government

The constitution provides for a two-chamber National Assembly to be elected for four years by universal adult suffrage. The Loya Jirgha (the supreme state body, which consists of the National Assembly and the Cabinet, and provincial, legal and tribal representatives) elects the President, who appoints a Prime Minister and the Council of Ministers.
Local government: 31 provinces.
President: (provisional) Burhanuddin Rabbani.
Prime Minister: to be appointed.

Geography

The central highlands, dominated by the Hindu Kush, cover over 75% of the country and contain several peaks over 6400 m (21,000 ft). North of the highlands are plains, an important agricultural region, while the southwest of the country is desert and semidesert.
Principal rivers: Helmand, Amu Darya (Oxus).
Highest point: Noshaq 7499m (24,581 ft).

Climate: The central highlands have very cold winters and short cool summers, while the desert regions have cold winters and hot summers. Except in parts of the highlands, it is dry.

Economy

Most of the usable land is pasture, mainly for sheep, but cereal crops, particularly wheat and maize, are also important. Principal exports include fresh and dried fruit, wool, cotton and natural gas. The economy has been damaged by civil war, and much of the infrastructure has been destroyed. ***Currency:*** Afghani.

Recent History

In the 19th century, rivalry between Russia and Britain, who regarded Afghanistan as the key to India, led to instability. Britain attempted to assert control in two disastrous wars (1839–42 and 1878–81). Independence was only achieved in 1921 after a third war with the British. A period of unrest followed until a more stable monarchy was established in 1933. A coup in 1973 overthrew the monarchy. A close relationship with the USSR resulted from the 1978 Saur Revolution, but the Soviet invasion (1979) led to civil war. In 1989 the Soviets withdrew, leaving the cities in the hands of the government and Muslim fundamentalist guerrillas controlling the countryside. In 1992 fundamentalists took Kabul and formed a provisional government, but factional – largely ethnic – fighting continues. By 1995 the government had lost control of much of the country.

ALBANIA

Official name: Republika e Shqipërisë (Republic of Albania).
Member of: UN, OSCE.
Area: 28,748 km² (11,100 sq mi).
Population: 3,422,000 (1993 est).
Capital: Tirana (Tiranë) 244,000 (1990 est).
Other major cities: Durrës 85,000, Elbasan 83,000, Shkodër 82,000, Vlorë 74,000 (1990 est).
Languages: Albanian (Gheg and Tosk dialects) – Tosk is the official language.
Religion: Sunni Islam (20%) – practising religion was banned from 1967 to 1990.

Education: is compulsory between the ages of seven and 15. *Adult literacy:* 92%. *Universities:* three.
Defence: (1993 figures) *Army:* 60,000 personnel. *Air force:* 11,000. *Navy:* 2000. *Conscription:* 15 months.

Government

A President and a 140-member People's Assembly are elected under a system of proportional representation by universal adult suffrage for four years. The Assembly elects a Prime Minister and a Council of Ministers.
Largest parties: (centre) Democratic Party, (former Communist) Socialist Party, Social Democratic Party.
Local government: 27 districts (to be reorganized into 12 prefectures).
President: Sali Berisha (Democratic Party).
Prime Minister: Aleksandr Meksi (Democratic Party).

Geography

Coastal lowlands support most of the country's agriculture. Mountain ranges cover the greater part of Albania.
Principal rivers: Semani, Drini. ***Highest point:*** Mount Korab 2751m (9025 ft).
Climate: The Mediterranean coastal areas experience hot, dry summers and mild, wet winters. The mountainous interior has equally hot summers but very cold winters.

Economy

Albania is poor by European standards. The economy relies on agriculture and the export of chromium. In 1990 Albania ended its self-imposed economic isolation and sought foreign financial, technical and humanitarian assistance. Nevertheless, the country has experienced continuing emigration and a collapse in industrial output. Most state-owned cooperative land has been redistributed into private hands and an agency to privatize state-owned industry has been established. ***Currency:*** Lek.

Recent History

The Ottoman Turks invaded Albania in the 14th century. By 1900, Ottoman enfeeblement encouraged Albanian nationalism, and in 1912, independence was declared. The country was occupied in both the Balkan Wars and World War I, and the formation of a stable government within recognized frontiers did not occur until the 1920s. Interwar Albania was dominated by Ahmed Zogu (1895–1961), who made himself king (as Zog I) in 1928. He fled when Mussolini invaded in 1939. Communist-led partisans took power when the Germans withdrew (1944). Under Enver Hoxha (1908–85), the regime pursued rapid modernization on Stalinist lines, allied, in turn, to Yugoslavia, the USSR and China, before opting (in 1978) for self-sufficiency and isolation. The liberal wing of the Communist Party won a power struggle (1990), instituted social and economic reforms, and held multi-party elections (1991). The Socialists (former Communists) were defeated in 1992. Albania faces severe economic problems and the threat of disorders in the neighbouring Serbian province of Kosovo, where ethnic Albanians (who make up 90% of the population) are denied civil rights by the minority Serb community.

ALGERIA

Official name: El Djemhouria El Djazaïria Demokratia Echaabia (the Democratic and Popular Republic of Algeria).
Member of: UN, OAU, Arab League, OPEC.

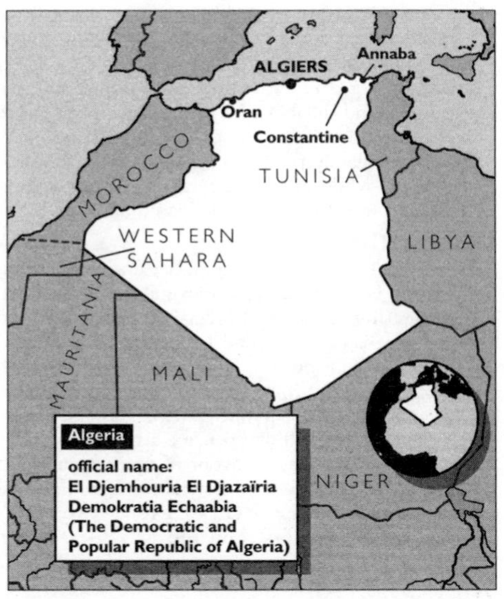

Area: 2,38,741 km² (919,595 sq mi).
Population: 27,030,000 (1993 est).
Capital: Algiers (El Djazaïr or Alger) 1,722,000 (1989 est; including suburbs).
Other major cities: Oran (Ouahran) 664,000, Constantine (Qacentina) 449,000, Annaba 348,000, Blida (El-Boulaida) 191,000 (1989 est; including suburbs).
Languages: Arabic (official; 83%), French, Berber (17%).
Religion: Sunni Islam (official; over 99%).
Education: is compulsory between the ages of six and 15. *Adult literacy:* 57%. *Universities:* 10 plus seven university centres.
Defence: (1993 figures) *Army:* 105,000 personnel. *Air force:* 10,000. *Navy:* 6700. *Conscription:* 18 months.

Government

The constitution provides for the election of a President, who is head of state and of government, and a 296-member National People's Assembly by universal adult suffrage every five years. In 1992 the constitution was suspended and a military council was appointed.
Largest parties: (banned fundamentalist) Islamic Salvation Front (FIS), (socialist) National Liberation Front (FLN).
Local government: 48 departments (or wilayat).
President: Lamine Zeroual (non-party).
Prime Minister: Mokdad Sifi (non-party).

Geography

Over 85% of Algeria is covered by the Sahara Desert. To the north lie the Atlas Mountains, which enclose a dry plateau. In the southeast are the Hoggar mountains. Along the Mediterranean coast are plains and lower mountain ranges. ***Highest point:*** Mount Tahat 3003m (9852 ft). ***Principal river:*** Chelif.
Climate: The Mediterranean climate along the coastline is characterized by hot summers, mild winters and adequate rainfall. In the Sahara, it is hot and arid.

Economy

Petroleum and natural gas are the main exports and

important industries are based on oil and gas. Civil strife is adding to severe economic problems, which include high unemployment. Farmers and farm workers account for over 20% of the adult population, but lack of rain and suitable land mean that Algeria has to import two thirds of its food. The small amount of arable land mainly produces wheat, barley, fruit and vegetables, while arid pasturelands support sheep, goats and cattle. ***Currency:*** Algerian dinar.

Recent History

During the 18th century, Algeria became a centre for piracy and in 1830 the French invaded on the pretext of protecting trade. Colonization followed, and coastal Algeria was attached to metropolitan France. By 1860 much of the best land was in French hands. Nationalist riots in Sétif were ruthlessly suppressed in 1945, and in 1954 the Front de Libération Nationale (FLN) initiated a revolt that became a bitter war. A rising by French settlers, in favour of the integration of Algeria with France, led to the crisis that returned de Gaulle to power in France (1958). Despite two further risings by the settlers, and the activities of the colonists' terrorist organization, the OAS, Algeria gained independence in 1962. The first president, Ahmed Ben Bella (1916–), was overthrown in 1965 by Houari Boumédienne (1932–78), who established a one-party socialist state under the FLN. After his successor, Chadli Benjedid (1929–), introduced multi-party democracy (1990), Islamic fundamentalism became a political force. In 1992 the second round of multi-party elections was cancelled when fundamentalists gained a large lead in the first round. The military took power and suspended political activity. In 1994 the struggle between the military and fundamentalists became more violent. Thousands of people were killed in the unrest in which intellectuals and foreigners working in Algeria were assassinated by fundamentalists.

ANDORRA

Official name: Principat d'Andorrà (The Principality of Andorra).
Member of: UN.
Area: 468 km² (181 sq mi).
Population: 62,000 (1993 est).
Capital: Andorra la Vella 35,600 (town 22,400; 1990 est).
Other main towns: Ordino 13,200, Encamp 11,800 (1990 est).
Languages: Catalan (30%; official), Spanish (59%), French (6%).
Religion: Roman Catholic (90%).

Education: is compulsory between the ages of six and 14. *Adult literacy:* virtually 100%. *Universities:* none.
Defence: Andorra has no armed forces.

Government

Andorra has joint heads of state (co-princes) – the president of France and the Spanish bishop of Urgel – who delegate their powers to permanent representatives who retain certain rights of veto under the 1993 constitution. The 28-member General Council, which is elected for four years by universal adult suffrage, comprises 14 members elected by constituencies and 14 members elected on a national list. The General Council chooses an Executive Council (government).
Largest party: (centre right) National Democratic Group (AND). (Most members of Parliament are independents.)
Local government: seven parishes.
Senior co-prince: Dr Juan Marti Alansis, Bishop of Urgel.
Prime Minister: Marc Forne Molne (ind).

Geography

In the eastern Pyrenees, Andorra is surrounded by mountains up to 3000 m (9840 ft) high. ***Principal river:*** Valira. ***Highest point:*** Pla del'Estany 3011m (9678 ft).
Climate: Andorra is mild in spring and summer, but cold for six months, with snow in the winter.

Economy

Tourism has been encouraged by the development of ski resorts and by the duty-free status of consumer goods. ***Currency:*** French and Spanish currency.

Recent History

Andorra's joint allegiance to Spanish and French 'co-princes' dates directly from an agreement made in 1278 between the Spanish bishop of Urgel and the count of Foix, an ancestor of the Bourbon kings of France. The reforms of 1993 included a new constitution, the legalization of trade unions and political parties, a separate judiciary, independent diplomatic representation and UN membership. Andorra is included within the EU/EC by special agreement.

ANGOLA

Official name: A República de Angola (The Republic of Angola).
Member of: UN, OAU.
Area: 1,246,700 km² (481,351 sq mi).
Population: 10,916,000 (1993 est).
Capital: Luanda 1,200,000 (1988 est).
Other major cities: Huambo 203,000, Benguela 155,000 Lobito 150,000 (1983 est).
Languages: Portuguese (official), Umbundu (38%), Kimbundu (27%), Lunda (13%), Kikongo (12%).
Religions: Roman Catholic (60%), animist (20%).
Education: is compulsory, in theory, between the ages of seven and 15. *Adult literacy:* 42%. *Universities:* one.
Defence: (1993 figures) *Army:* 120,000 personnel. *Air force:* 6000. *Navy:* 1500. *Conscription:* none.

Government

A 220-member National Assembly is elected by universal adult suffrage for three years and a President for six years. The President appoints a Prime Minister and a Council of Ministers.

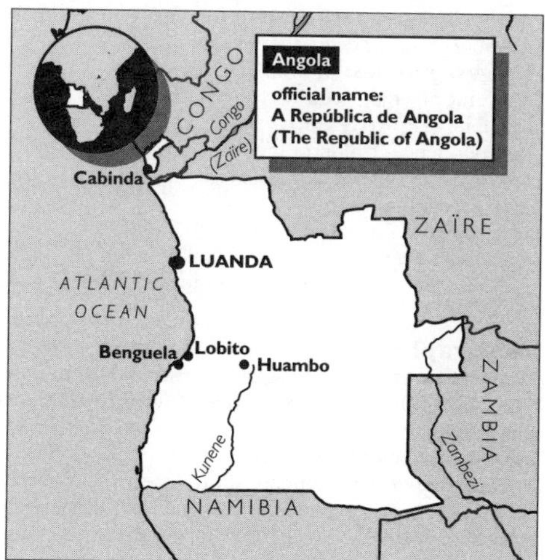

Largest parties: (former Marxist) People's Liberation Movement of Angola (MPLA), National Union for the Total Independence of Angola (UNITA).
Local government: 18 provinces.
President: José Eduardo dos Santos (MPLA).
Prime Minister: Marcolino José Carlos Moco (MPLA).

Geography

Plateaux, over 1000 m (3300 ft), cover 90% of Angola. In the west is a narrow coastal plain and in the southwest is desert. ***Principal rivers:*** Kunene (Cunene), Kwanza, Congo (Zaïre). ***Highest point:*** Serra Mòco 2620m (8596 ft).
Climate: Angola is tropical, with slightly lower temperatures in the uplands. October to May is the rainy season, but the southwest is dry all year.

Economy

Angola's economy has been wrecked by war. The country is, however, rich in minerals, particularly diamonds, iron ore and petroleum. Although less than 5% of the land is arable, over half the adult population is engaged in agriculture. The main export crop is coffee. ***Currency:*** New Kwanza.

Recent History

The Portuguese arrived in the late 15th century and developed a major slave trade. In the 20th century, forced labour, heavy taxation and discrimination from white settlers helped to stimulate nationalism. Portugal's repression of all political protest led to the outbreak of guerrilla wars in 1961. When independence was finally conceded (1975), three rival guerrilla movements fought for control of Angola. With Soviet and Cuban support, the (Marxist-Leninist) MPLA, under Dr Agostinho Neto (1922–79), gained the upper hand and repulsed an invasion from South Africa. In the 1980s, Cuban troops continued to support the MPLA government against the South African-aided UNITA movement in the south. Foreign involvement in the civil war ended in 1990. Following a ceasefire (1991), multi-party elections were held in 1992. UNITA forces resumed the conflict after rejecting the election results, but a new ceasefire and power-sharing agreement was signed in 1994.

ANTIGUA AND BARBUDA

Member of: UN, CARICOM, Commonwealth, OAS.
Area: 442 km² (170.5 sq mi).
Population: 66,000 (1993 est).
Capital: St John's 36,000 (1986 est).
Language: English (official).
Religions: Anglican (44%), Moravian.
Education: is compulsory between the ages of six and 15. *Adult literacy:* 90%. *Universities:* one university centre.
Defence: (1993 figures) *Defence force:* about 100 personnel.

Government

The 17-member House of Representatives is elected by universal adult suffrage for five years. The 17-member Senate is appointed. A Prime Minister and Cabinet of Ministers, commanding a majority in the lower house, are appointed by the Governor General, the representative of the British Queen as sovereign of Antigua.
Largest parties: Antigua Labour Party, United National Democratic Party.
Local government: six community councils on Antigua and one island council on Barbuda.
Prime Minister: Lester Bird (Antigua Labour Party).

Geography

Antigua is a low limestone island. Barbuda – 45 km / 25 mi to the north – is a flat wooded coral island. Redonda is a rocky outcrop. ***Principal rivers:*** none. ***Highest point:*** Boggy Peak 402m (1319 ft).
Climate: The tropical climate is moderated by sea breezes. Rainfall is low for the West Indies, and Antigua island suffers from drought.

Economy

Tourism is the mainstay of the country. In an attempt to diversify the economy, the government has encouraged agriculture, but the lack of water on Antigua island is a problem. ***Currency:*** East Caribbean dollar.

Recent History

Antigua was colonized by English settlers in 1632. Black slaves were imported to work the sugar plantations. Barbuda was colonized from Antigua (1661) and run as a private estate by the Codrington family until it was annexed to Antigua in 1860. Britain granted Antigua complete internal self-government in 1967 and independence in 1981.

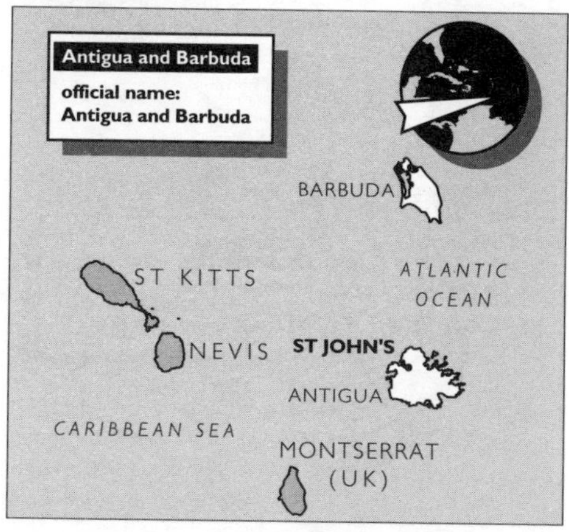

ARGENTINA

Official name: República Argentina (the Argentine Republic).
Member of: UN, OAS, ALADI, Mercosur.
Area: 2,766,889 km^2 (1,068,302 sq mi), excluding territories claimed by Argentina: the Falkland Islands (Islas Malvinas), South Georgia, South Sandwich Islands, and parts of the Antarctic.
Population: 33,500,000 (1993 est).
Capital: Buenos Aires 12,582,000 (city 9,927,000; 1991 census).
Other major cities: Córdoba 1,179,000 (city 982,000), Rosario 1,096,000 (city 955,000), Mendoza 729,000 (city 597,000), La Plata 644,000 (city 560,000), (San Miguel de) Tucumán 626,000 (city 497,000), Mar del Plata 523,000 (city 407,000) (1991 census).
Languages: Spanish (95%; official), Guarani (3%).
Religion: Roman Catholic (92%).
Education: is compulsory between the ages of six and 14. *Adult literacy:* 95%. *Universities:* 52 (29 state and 23 private).
Defence: (1993 figures) *Army:* 35,000 personnel. *Air force:* 16,000. *Navy:* 20,000. *Paramilitary:* 17,000. *Conscription:* 6–12 months army, 12 months air force, 14 months navy.

Government

Under the terms of a revised constitution, the President and Vice-President are elected for a maximum of two terms of four years by direct universal adult suffrage. The lower house of Congress (the Chamber of Deputies) has 259 members elected by universal suffrage for four years, with one half of its members retiring every two years. The 48 members of the upper house (the Senate) are chosen by provincial legislatures to serve for nine years, with 16 members retiring every three years.
Largest parties: (Peronist) Justicialista National Movement (PJ), (centre left) Radical Civil Union (UCR), (rightist) Movement for Dignity and Independence, Union of the Democratic Centre.
Local government: 22 provinces, one federal district and a federal territory.
President: Carlos Saul Menem (PJ).
External territory: Chile claims sovereignty over part of Antarctica. See Other Territories (beginning on p. 729).

Geography

The Andes extend as a rugged barrier along the border with Chile. South of the Colorado River is Patagonia, an important pastureland – although much of it is semidesert. Nearly 80% of the population lives in the pampas, whose prairies form one of the world's most productive agricultural regions. The subtropical plains of northeast Argentina contain part of the Gran Chaco prairie and rain forests. ***Principal rivers:*** Paraná, Colorado, Negro, Salado, Chubut. ***Highest point:*** Cerro Aconcagua 6960m (22,834 ft).
Climate: Most of Argentina has a mild temperate climate, although the south is cooler and the northeast is subtropical. The higher parts of the Andes have a subpolar climate. Rainfall is heavy in the Andes and the far northeast, but generally decreases towards the south and southwest, which are dry.

Economy

Argentina is one of the world's leading producers of beef, wool, mutton, wheat and wine. The pampas produce cereals, while fruit and vines are important in the northwest. Pasturelands cover over 50% of Argentina – for beef cattle in the pampas and for sheep in Patagonia. However, manufacturing (including chemicals, steel, cement, paper, pulp and textiles) now makes the greatest contribution to the economy. The country is rich in natural resources including petroleum, natural gas, iron ore and precious metals, and has great potential for hydroelectric power. Argentina's status as an economic power declined between the 1930s and 1980s, but financial reforms greatly improved prospects in the 1990s. ***Currency:*** Peso.

Recent History

From 1880, large-scale European immigration and British investment helped Argentina to develop a flourishing economy. Prosperity was ended by the Depression, and, in 1930, constitutional rule was interrupted by a military coup. In 1946, a populist leader, Juan Perón (1895–1974), came to power with the support of the unions. His wife Eva was a powerful and popular figure, and after her death (1952), Perón was deposed (1955) because of his unsuccessful economic policies. Succeeding civilian governments were unable to conquer rampant inflation, and the military took power again (1966–73). An unstable period of civilian rule (1973–76) included Perón's brief second presidency. In the early 1970s, urban terrorism grew and the economic crisis deepened, prompting another coup. The military junta that seized control in 1976 received international condemnation when thousands of opponents of the regime were arrested or disappeared. In April 1982, President Galtieri ordered the invasion of the Falkland Islands and its dependencies, which had long been claimed by Argentina. A British task force recaptured the islands in June 1982, and Galtieri resigned. Constitutional rule was restored in 1983. Argentina's economic prospects have greatly improved since 1989 under President Carlos Menem.

ARMENIA

Official name: Hayastani Hanrapetut'yun (Republic of Armenia).
Member of: UN, CIS, OSCE.
Area: 29,800 km^2 (11,506 sq mi).
Population: 3,550,000 (1993 est).
Capital: Yerevan 1,283,000 (1991 est).
Other major city: Kumayri (Gyumri; formerly Leninakan) 163,000 (1991 est).
Languages: Armenian (official; 93%), Azeri (3%).
Religion: Armenian Apostolic (Orthodox) majority.
Education: is compulsory between the ages of six and 15. *Adult literacy:* no figures available. *Universities:* two.
Defence: (1993 figures) *Army:* 50,000. (There are also 23,000 Russian troops in Armenia.) *Conscription:* two years.

Government

A 185-member State Council and an executive President are elected by universal adult suffrage for four years. The President appoints a Prime Minister and a Cabinet.
Largest parties: Pan-Armenian National Movement (HHSh), Armenian National Movement, (ultra-nationalist) Union for National Self-Determination.
Local government: 37 districts.
President: Levon Ter-Petrosyan (HHSh).
Prime Minister: Hrant Bagratian (HHSh).

Geography

All of Armenia is mountainous – only 10% of the country is under 1000 m (3300 ft). ***Principal rivers:*** Araks, Zanga. ***Highest point:*** Mt Aragats 4090m (13,418 ft).
Climate: Armenia has a dry continental climate with considerable local variations owing to altitude and aspect.

Economy

The industrial sector includes chemicals, metallurgy, textiles, precision goods and food processing. Major projects have provided hydroelectric power and irrigation water for agriculture. Privatization has begun. The war against Azerbaijan has devastated the economy and resulted in a severe energy shortage. ***Currency:*** Dram.

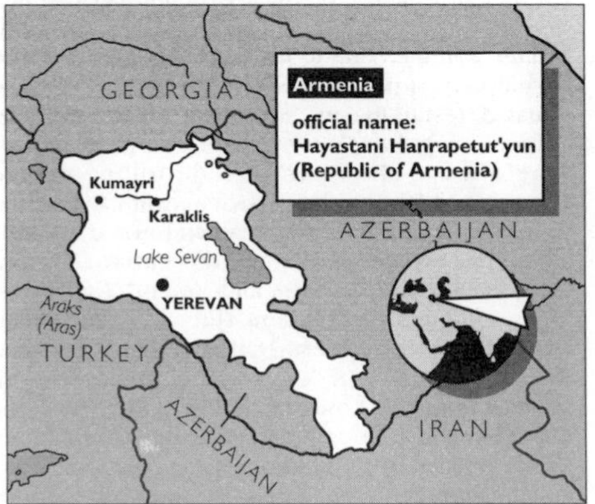

Recent History

Russia annexed eastern Armenia between 1813 and 1828. The western Armenians under Ottoman rule suffered persecution and, in 1896 and in 1915, large-scale massacres. During World War I Turkey deported nearly 2,000,000 Armenians (suspected of pro-Russian sympathies) to Syria and Mesopotamia. The survivors contributed to an Armenian diaspora in Europe and the USA. Following the collapse of Tsarist Russia, an independent Armenian state emerged briefly (1918–22), but faced territorial wars with all its neighbours. Armenia was annexed by the Soviet Union in 1922 and became a separate Union Republic within the USSR in 1936. After the abortive coup by Communist hardliners in Moscow, Armenia declared independence and received international recognition when the USSR was dissolved (1991). From 1990 to 1994 Azeri and Armenian forces were involved in a violent dispute concerning the status of Nagorno Karabakh, an enclave of Orthodox Christian Armenians surrounded by the Shiite Muslim Azeris. In 1994, after Armenia had overrun 20% of Azerbaijan, a Russian-brokered ceasefire was signed.

AUSTRALIA

Official name: The Commonwealth of Australia.
Member of: UN, Commonwealth, ANZUS, OECD, Apec.
Area: 7,682,300 km^2 (2,966,136 sq mi).
Population: 17,729,000 (1993 est).
Capital: Canberra 310,000 (including suburbs; 1991 census).
Other major cities: Sydney 3,699,000, Melbourne 3,154,000, Brisbane 1,327,000, Perth 1,193,000, Adelaide 1,050,000, Newcastle 433,000, Gold Coast 274,000, Wollongong 240,000, Hobart 184,000, Geelong 151,000, Townsville 114,000, Sunshine Coast 110,000, Launceston 89,000, Cairns 86,000, Darwin 78,000, Ballarat 75,000, Rockhampton 64,000, Bendigo 62,000 (all including suburbs; 1991 census).
Language: English (official).
Religions: Anglican (26%), Roman Catholic (26%), Uniting Church in Australia (8%), Orthodox.
Education: is compulsory between the ages of six and 15 (six and 16 in Tasmania). *Adult literacy:* over 99%. *Universities:* 38.
Defence: (1993 figures) *Army:* 28,600 personnel. *Air force:* 19,300. *Navy:* 15,300. *Conscription:* none.

Government

The Federal Parliament consists of two chambers elected by compulsory universal adult suffrage. The Senate has 76 members elected by proportional representation – 12 senators elected from each state for six years, 2 from both territories elected for three years. The House of Representatives has 148 members elected for three years. A Prime Minister, who commands a majority in the House of Representatives, is appointed by the Governor General, who is the representative of the British Queen as sovereign of Australia. The Prime Minister chairs the Federal Executive Council (or Cabinet), which is responsible to Parliament. Each state has its own government.

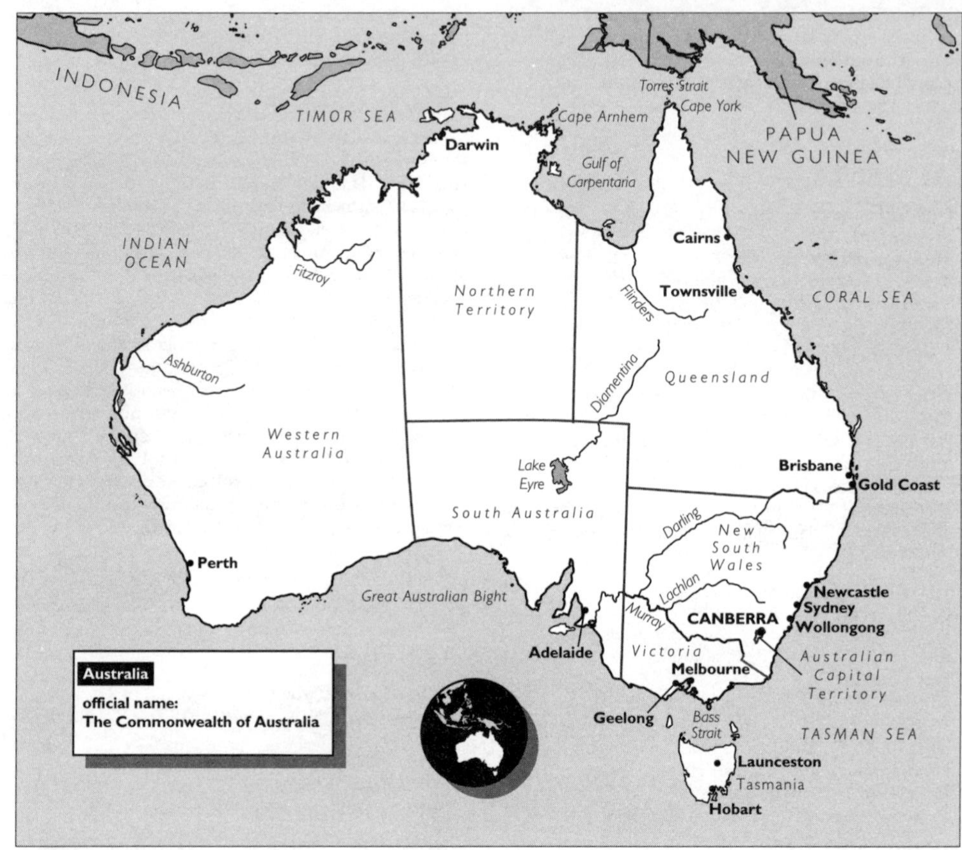

Largest parties: Australian Labor Party (ALP), (conservative) Liberal Party of Australia, (conservative) National Party of Australia.
Local government: six states and two territories.
Prime Minister: Paul Keating (ALP).

States and Territories

New South Wales *Area:* 801,600 km² (309,500 sq mi). *Population:* 6,000,000 (1993 est). *Capital:* Sydney.
Queensland *Area:* 1,727,200 km² (666,875 sq mi). *Population:* 3,095,000 (1993 est). *Capital:* Brisbane.
South Australia *Area:* 984,000 km² (379,925 sq mi). *Population:* 1,460,000 (1993 est). *Capital:* Adelaide.
Tasmania *Area:* 67,800 km² (26,175 sq mi). *Population:* 472,000 (1993 est). *Capital:* Hobart.
Victoria *Area:* 227,600 km² (87,875 sq mi). *Population:* 4,461,000 (1993 est). *Capital:* Melbourne.
Western Australia *Area:* 2,525,500 km² (975,100 sq mi). *Population:* 1,673,000 (1993 est). *Capital:* Perth.
Australian Capital Territory *Area:* 2400 km² (925 sq mi). *Population:* 298,000 (1993 est). *Capital:* Canberra.
Northern Territory *Area:* 1,346,200 km² (519,750 sq mi). *Population:* 168,000 (1993 est). *Capital:* Darwin.
External territories: Ashmore and Cartier Islands, Australian Antarctic Territory, Christmas Island, Cocos (Keeling) Islands, Coral Sea Islands Territory, Heard and MacDonald Islands, Norfolk Island. See Other Territories (beginning on p. 729).

Geography

Vast areas of desert cover most of central and western Australia, a region of plateaux between 400 and 600 m (1300–2000 ft) with occasional higher regions, such as the Kimberley Plateau. In contrast to this scarcely populated area – which covers more than 50% of the country – are the narrow coastal plains of the fertile, well-watered east coast, where the majority of Australians live. Behind the plains (which range from temperate forest in the south, through subtropical woodland to tropical rain forest in the north) rise the Eastern Uplands, or Great Dividing Range, a line of ridges and plateaux, stretching from Cape York Peninsula in the north to the island of Tasmania. The Australian Alps rise to Mt Kosciusko (see below). The Great Artesian Basin extends from the Gulf of Carpentaria to the Murray River and Eyre Basins. Landforms in the basin include rolling plains, plateaux, salt lakes and river valleys, while the natural vegetation ranges from savannah and mixed forest to arid steppe and desert. Between the Murray River and Eyre Basins are the Flinders and Mount Lofty Ranges. Many of Australia's rivers flow intermittently.
Principal rivers: Murray, Darling, Lachlan, Flinders. 837 km (520 mi).
Highest point: Mt Kosciusko 2230m (7316 ft).
Climate: The north is tropical with wet summers (January to March) and dry winters. The Timor Sea coast is subject to summer monsoons. The

Queensland coast experiences tropical cyclones and has the heaviest rainfall, over 2500 mm (100 in) near Cairns. The interior is extremely hot and dry – over 30% of Australia has less than 255 mm (10 in) of rain a year. The coastal fringes in the south are either temperate or subtropical, with winter rainfall, hot or warm summers and mild winters. Winter snowfall occurs in the southeast and Tasmanian highlands.

Economy

Since World War II, Australia's economy has been dominated by mining. Minerals now account for over 30% of the country's exports. Australia has major reserves of coal, petroleum, natural gas, uranium, iron ore, copper, nickel, bauxite, gold and diamonds. Manufacturing and processing based upon these resources include iron and steel, construction, oil refining and petrochemicals, vehicle manufacturing and engineering. Food-processing and textile industries are also prominent. Australia's reliance on agriculture has decreased, although the country is still the world's leading producer of wool. Major interests include sheep, cattle, cereals (in particular wheat), sugar (in Queensland) and fruit. Severe drought affected large areas in the early 1990s. A strong commercial sector, with banks and finance houses, adds to the diversity of the economy. ***Currency:*** Australian dollar.

Recent History

In 1901, the Commonwealth of Australia was founded. Fear of invasion from Asia or German New Guinea, and the desire to achieve free trade between the six British colonies, encouraged federation. Australia made an important contribution in World War I – one fifth of its servicemen were killed in action. The heroic landing at Gallipoli in the Dardanelles is a national day of remembrance in Australia. The Depression hit the country badly, but the interwar years did see international recognition of Australia's independence. World War II, during which the north was threatened by Japan, strengthened links with America. Australian troops fought in Vietnam and important trading partnerships have been formed with Asian countries. Since 1945, migrants from all over Europe and many parts of Asia have gained assisted passage to Australia, further diluting the British connection and encouraging the growth of republicanism.

AUSTRIA

Official name: Republik Österreich (Republic of Austria).
Member of: UN, EU/EC, OSCE, OECD.
Area: 83 859 km² (32,378 sq mi).
Population: 7,940,000 (1993 est).
Capital: Vienna (Wien) 2,045,000 (city 1,540,000; 1991 census).
Other major cities: Linz 434,000 (city 203,000), Graz 395,000 (city 238,000), Salzburg 267,000 (city 144,000), Innsbruck 235,000 (city 118,000), Klagenfurt 89,000, Villach 53,000, Wels 53,000, Sankt Pölten 41,000 (1991 census).
Language: German (official; 96%).
Religion: Roman Catholic (84%).
Education: is compulsory between the ages of six and 15. *Adult literacy:* virtually 100%. *Universities:* six plus 14 institutes of university status.

Defence: (1993 figures) *Army:* 46,000 personnel. *Air force* 6000. *Conscription:* six months, plus 60–90 days reserve training.

Government

Executive power is shared by the Federal President (who is elected by universal adult suffrage for a six-year term) and the Council of Ministers, led by the Federal Chancellor. The President appoints a Chancellor who commands a majority in the Federal Assembly's lower chamber, the Nationalrat, whose 183 members are elected by universal adult suffrage according to proportional representation for a term of four years. The 64 members of the upper chamber – the Bundesrat – are elected by the assemblies of the nine provinces of the Federal Republic.
Largest parties: Social Democratic Party (SPO), (conservative) People's Party (OVP), (right-wing) Freedom Party (FPO), Liberal Forum.
Local government: nine provinces.
President: Thomas Klestil (OVP).
Federal Chancellor: Dr Franz Vranitzky (OVP).

Provinces

Burgenland *Area:* 3965 km² (1531 sq mi). *Population:* 271,000 (1991 census). *Capital:* Eisenstadt.
Carinthia (Kärnten) *Area:* 9533 km² (3681 sq mi). *Population:* 548,000 (1991 census). *Capital:* Klagenfurt.
Lower Austria (Niederösterreich) *Area:* 19,174 km² (7403 sq mi). *Population:* 1,474,000 (1991 census). *Capital:* Sankt Pölten.
Salzburg *Area:* 7154 km² (2762 sq mi). *Population:* 482,000 (1991 census). *Capital:* Salzburg.
Styria (Steiermark) *Area:* 16,388 km² (6327 sq mi). *Population:* 1,185,000 (1991 census). *Capital:* Graz.
Tirol *Area:* 12,648 km² (4883 sq mi). *Population:* 631,000 (1991 census). *Capital:* Innsbruck.
Upper Austria (Oberösterreich) *Area:* 11,980 km² (4626 sq mi). *Population:* 1,333,000 (1991 census). *Capital:* Linz.
Vienna (Wien) *Area:* 415 km² (160 sq mi). *Population:* 1,540,000 (1991 census). *Capital:* Vienna.
Vorarlberg *Area:* 2601 km² (1004 sq mi). *Population:* 331,000 (1991 census). *Capital:* Bregenz.

Geography

The Alps – much of which are covered by pastures and forests – occupy nearly two thirds of Austria. Lowland Austria, in the east, consists of low hills, the Vienna Basin and a flat marshy area beside the Neusiedler See on the Hungarian border. Along the Czech border is a forested massif rising to 1200 m (4000 ft). ***Principal rivers:*** Danube (Donau), Inn. ***Highest point:*** Grossglockner 3797 m (12,457 ft).
Climate: There are many local variations in climate owing to altitude and aspect. The east is drier than the west, and is, in general, colder than the Alpine region in the winter and hotter, but more humid, in the summer. Areas over 3000 m (10,000 ft) are snow-covered all year.

Economy

Although Austria produces about 90% of its own food requirements, farming employs only 7% of the labour force. The arable land in the east has fertile soils producing good yields of cereals and grapes for wine. Dairy produce is an important export from the pasturelands in the east and in the Alps. The mainstay of the economy is manufacturing industry, including machinery and transport equipment, iron and steel products, refined petroleum products, cement and paper. Natural resources include hydroelectric power potential and extensive forests. The Alps attract winter and summer visitors, making tourism a major foreign-currency earner. ***Currency:*** Schilling.

Recent History

Defeat in the Austro-Prussian War (1866) excluded Austrian influence from Germany, and the Austro-Hungarian Habsburg Empire was left to dominate unstable south-central Europe. In 1914, a Serb assassinated the heir to the Austro-Hungarian throne – an event which precipitated World War I. In 1918–19, the Habsburg empire was dismembered. A separate Austrian republic was established despite considerable support for union with Germany. Unstable throughout the 1920s and 1930s, Austria was annexed by Germany in 1938 (the Anschluss). Austria was liberated in 1945, but Allied occupation forces remained until 1955 when the independence of a neutral republic was recognized. The collapse of Communism in Eastern Europe (1989–91) allowed Austria to renew traditional links with Hungary and the Czechs. Austria joined the EU/EC in 1995.

AZERBAIJAN

Official name: Azarbayjan Respublikasy (Republic of Azerbaijan).
Member of: UN, CIS, OSCE.
Area: 86,600 km² (33,400 sq mi).
Population: 7,283,000 (1993 est).
Capital: Baku 1,757,000 (1989 est).
Other major cities: Gyanzha (Ganca; formerly Kirovabad) 270,000, Sumgait 236,000 (1989 est).
Languages: Azeri (83%), Russian (6%), Armenian (2%).
Religion: Shia Islam majority.
Education: is compulsory between the ages of six and 15. *Adult literacy:* no figures available. *Universities:* two.
Defence: (1993 figures) *Army:* 30,000 personnel. *Paramilitary:* 20,000. *Conscription:* none.

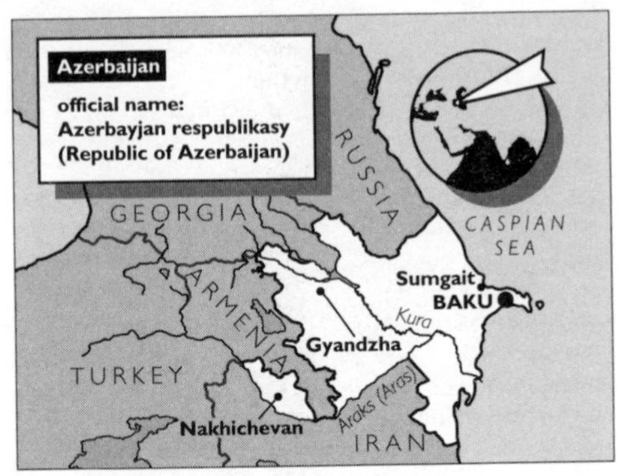

Government

An executive President and a 50-member Assembly (Milli Majlis) are elected by universal adult suffrage for four years. The President appoints a Prime Minister and a Cabinet.
Largest parties: New Azerbaijan, Popular Front of Azerbaijan, Party of National Independence.
Local government: two autonomous republics, nine cities, 54 districts.
President: Geidar Aliyev (New Azerbaijan).
Prime Minister: Fuad Quliyev.

Autonomous republics

Nagorno Karabakh *Area:* 4400 km² (1700 sq mi). *Population:* 193,000 (1991 est). *Capital:* Stepanakert.
Nakhichevan *Area:* 5500 km² (2100 sq mi). *Population:* 306,000 (1991 est). *Capital:* Nakhichevan.

Geography

Azerbaijan comprises lowlands beside the Caspian Sea, part of the Caucasus Mountains in the north and the Little Caucasus in the southwest. The republic includes the Nakhichevan enclave to the west of Armenia. ***Principal rivers:*** Kura, Araks. ***Highest point:*** Bazar-Dyuzi 4466m (14,652 ft).
Climate: A wide climatic range includes dry and humid subtropical conditions beside the Caspian Sea and continental conditions in the mountains.

Economy

Important reserves of oil and natural gas are the mainstay of the economy and the basis of heavy industries. Although industry dominates the economy, agriculture contributes a variety of exports, including cotton and tobacco. Sturgeon are caught in the Caspian Sea for the important caviar industry. The war with Armenia has damaged the economy and Azerbaijan suffers very high inflation. ***Currency:*** Manat.

Recent History

Russia took northern Azerbaijan in 1813, and Nakhichevan and the rest of the present state in 1828. However, the greater part of the land of the Azeris remained under Persian rule. During World War I, a nationalist Azeri movement became allied with the Turks. An independent Azeri state was founded with Turkish assistance (1918), but was invaded by the Soviet Red Army in 1920. Azerbaijan became part of the Soviet Union in 1922 and a separate Union Republic within the USSR in 1936. Independence was declared following the abortive coup in Moscow by Communist hardliners and was internationally recognized when the USSR was dissolved (1991).

Independent Azerbaijan has been politically unstable. From 1990 to 1994 Azeri and Armenian forces were involved in a violent dispute concerning the status of Nagorno Karabakh, an enclave of Orthodox Christian Armenians surrounded by the Shiite Muslim Azeris. After Armenian forces had occupied 20% of Azerbaijan, a Russian-brokered ceasefire was agreed in 1994.

BAHAMAS

Official name: The Commonwealth of the Bahamas.
Member of: UN, Commonwealth, OAS, CARICOM.
Area: 13,939 km² (5382 sq mi).
Population: 266 000 (1993 est).
Capital: Nassau 169,000 (1990 census).
Other major city: Freeport 25,000 (1990 census).
Language: English (official).
Religions: Baptist (29%), Roman Catholic (26%).
Education: is compulsory between the ages of five and 14. *Adult literacy:* 95%. *Universities:* one university college.
Defence: (1993 figures) *Paramilitary:* 850 personnel.

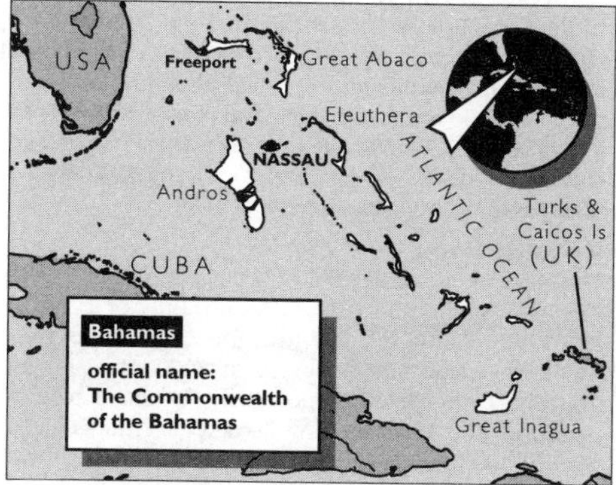

Government

The Senate (the upper house of Parliament) has 16 appointed members. The House of Assembly (the lower house) has 49 members elected by universal adult suffrage for five years. A Prime Minister, who commands a majority in the House, is appointed by the Governor General, who is the representative of the British Queen as sovereign of the Bahamas. The Prime Minister chairs the Cabinet, which is responsible to the House.
Largest parties: (centre) Free National Movement (FNM), (centre-right) Progressive Liberal Party (PLP).
Local government: 20 districts.
Prime Minister: Hubert A. Ingraham (FNM).

Geography

The Bahamas comprises some 700 long, flat, narrow islands, and over 2000 barren rocky islets. ***Principal rivers:*** none. ***Highest point:*** Mount Alvernia 63m (206 ft).
Climate: The climate is mild and subtropical, with no great seasonal variation in temperature. Rainfall averages just over 1000 mm (40 in). The islands are liable to hurricanes.

Economy

Tourism – mainly from the USA – is the major source of income, and, with related industries, it employs the majority of the labour force. The islands have become a tax haven and financial centre. ***Currency:*** Bahamian dollar.

Recent History

Although the first representative assembly of the Britsh colony met in 1729, internal self-government was not achieved until 1964. Independence was granted in 1973.

BAHRAIN

Official name: Daulat al-Bahrain (The State of Bahrain).
Member of: UN, Arab League, OPEC, GCC.
Area: 691 km² (267 sq mi).
Population: 516,000 (1991 est).
Capital: Manama 152,000 (1988 est).
Other major city: al-Muharraq 78,000 (1988 est).
Language: Arabic (official).
Religion: Sunni Islam (33%), Shia Islam (60%).
Education: is not compulsory. *Adult literacy:* 70%. *Universities:* two.
Defence: (1993 figures) *Army:* 6000 personnel. Air force: 700. Navy: 500. *Conscription:* none.

Government

Bahrain is ruled directly by an Amir (a hereditary monarch), who appoints a Council of Ministers and a 30-member Consultative Council.
Largest parties: There are no political parties.
Local government: nine regions and two towns.
Sovereign: HH Shaikh Isa II bin Salman Al-Khalifa, Amir of Bahrain (succeeded upon the death of his father, 2 November 1961).
Prime Minister: Shaikh Khalifa bin Sulman Al-Khalifa.

Geography

Bahrain comprises an archipelago of 35 small islands. Bahrain Island, the largest, consists mainly of sandy plains and salt marshes, and is linked to Saudi Arabia by causeway. ***Principal rivers:*** none. ***Highest point:*** Jabal al-Dukhan 134m (440 ft).
Climate: The climate is very hot. The annual average rainfall is 75 mm (3 in).

Economy

The wealth of Bahrain is due to its petroleum and natural gas resources, and the oil-refining industry. As reserves began to wane in the 1970s, the government encouraged diversification. As a result, Bahrain is now one of the Gulf's major banking and communication centres. ***Currency:*** Bahraini dinar.

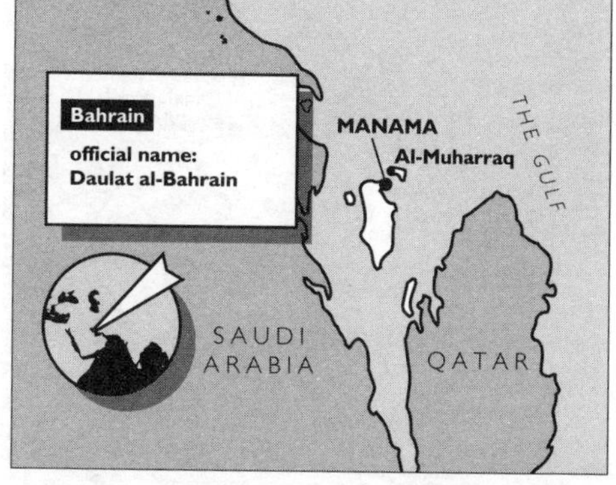

Recent History

Rule by the Sunni al-Khalifa family began in 1783. In the 19th century, Bahrain signed a series of treaties under which it became a British protectorate. Bahrain was the first Gulf state to develop its petroleum industry (from 1932). Since independence in 1971, there has been tension between the Sunni and Shiite communities. This increased following the suspension of the Assembly and the constitution in 1975, and in 1994 Shiite discontent resulted in rioting. Bahrain joined the coalition forces against Iraq after the invasion of Kuwait (1990–91).

BANGLADESH

Official name: Gana Praja Tantri Bangla Desh (People's Republic of Bangladesh).
Member of: UN, Commonwealth.
Area: 143,998 km² (55,598 sq mi).
Population: 115,075,000 (1993 est).
Capital: Dhaka 6,105,000 (city 3,397,000; Narayaganj 269,000; 1991 census).
Other major cities: Chittagong 2,133,000 (city 1,566,000),Khulna 1,029,000 (city 601,000), Rajshahi 517,000 (city 325,000), Mymensingh 186,000, Barisal 180,000 (1991 census).
Language: Bengali (official; 97%).
Religions: Sunni Islam (over 85%; official), Hindu (12%).
Education: is compulsory between the ages of five and 10. *Adult literacy:* 35%. *Universities:* nine.
Defence: (1993 figures) *Army:* 93,000 personnel. *Air force:* 6500. *Navy:* 7500. *Paramilitary:* 55,000. *Conscription:* none.

Government

The Parliament (Jatiya Sangsad) comprises 300 members elected for five years by universal adult suffrage and 30 women chosen by the elected members. Parliament elects a President – who serves for five years – and a Prime Minister, who appoints a Council of Ministers.
Largest parties: (centre right) Bangladesh National Party (BNP), (social democrat) Bangladesh Awami League, (left-wing) Jatiya Party, (Islamic fundamentalist) Jamit-i-Islami.
Local government: 64 districts.
President: Abdur Rahman Biswas.
Prime Minister: Begum Khaleda Zia (BNP).

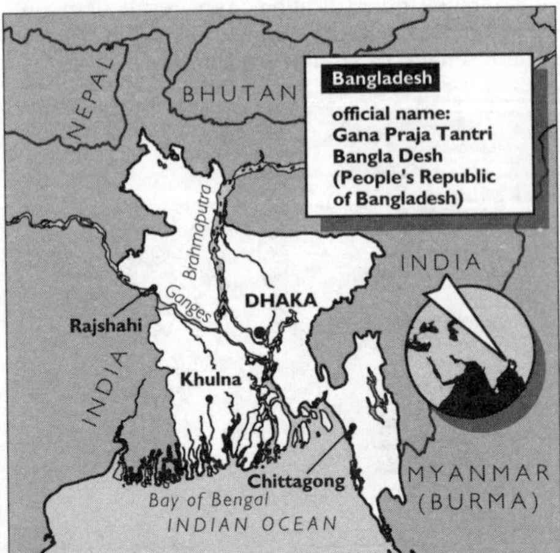

Geography

Most of Bangladesh is alluvial plains in the deltas of the rivers Ganges and Brahmaputra which combine as the Padma. The swampy plains, generally less than 9 m (30 ft) above sea level, are dissected by rivers dividing into numerous distributaries with raised banks. The south and southeast coastal regions contain mangrove forests (the Sundarbans). The only uplands are the Sylhet Hills in the northeast and the Chittagong hill country in the east. ***Principal rivers:*** Ganges, Brahmaputra (Jumuna). ***Highest point:*** Keokradong 1230m (4034 ft).
Climate: The climate is tropical with the highest temperatures between April and September. Most of the country's rainfall comes during the annual monsoon (June to October), when intense storms accompanied by high winds bring serious flooding. Rainfall totals range from 1000 mm (40 in) in the west to 5000 mm (200 in) in the Sylhet Hills.

Economy

With a rapidly increasing population, Bangladesh is among the world's poorest countries and is heavily dependent on foreign aid. Over 70% of the labour force is involved in agriculture. Rice is produced on over 75% of the cultivated land, but although the land is fertile, crops are subject to floods and cyclones. A major Flood Action Plan, started in 1992, will alter the course of rivers and raise embankments. The main cash crops are jute and tea. Industries include those processing agricultural products – jute, cotton and sugar. There are reserves of natural gas. ***Currency:*** Taka.

Recent History

The area came under British rule within India after 1757. On partition in 1947, as the majority of its inhabitants were Muslim, the area became the eastern province of Pakistan. Separated by 1600 km (1000 mi) from the Urdu-speaking, politically dominant western province, East Pakistan saw itself as a victim of economic and ethnic injustice. Resentment led to civil war in 1971 when Indian aid to Bengali irregulars gave birth to an independent People's Republic of Bangladesh ('Free Bengal') under Sheik Mujib-ur-Rahman. Mujib's assassination in 1975 led eventually to a takeover by General Zia-ur-Rahman, who amended the constitution to create an 'Islamic state'. Zia in turn was assassinated in 1981 and General Ershad took power in 1982. After Ershad was deposed (1990), a parliamentary system was reintroduced.

BARBADOS

Member of: UN, Commonwealth, OAS, CARICOM.
Area: 430 km² (166 sq mi).
Population: 260,000 (1993 est).
Capital: Bridgetown 102,000 (city 7500; 1990 census). (There are no other settlements that can be recognized as towns.)
Language: English.
Religions: Anglican (40%), Methodist, Pentecostalist.
Education: is compulsory between the ages of five and 16. *Adult literacy:* 98%. *Universities:* one university centre.
Defence: (1993 figures) *Defence force:* 155 personnel.

Government

The 21 members of the Senate are appointed; the 28 members of the House of Assembly are elected by

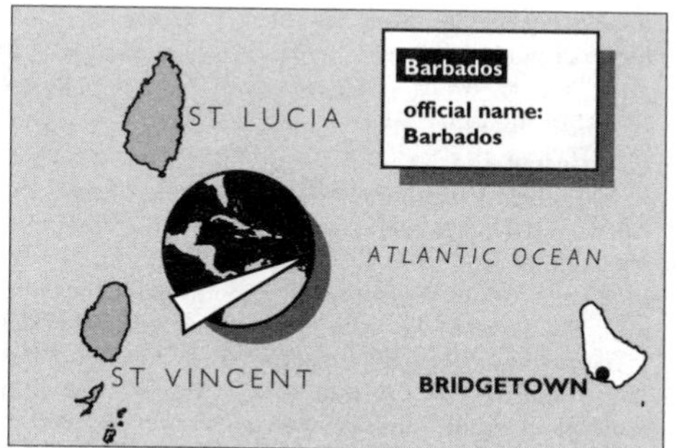

universal adult suffrage for five years. The Governor General, the representative of the British Queen as sovereign of Barbados, appoints a Prime Minister who commands a majority in the House. The PM appoints a Cabinet responsible to the House.

Largest parties: (social democratic) Barbados Labour Party (BLP), (social democratic) Democratic Labour Party (DLP).

Local government: 11 parishes, with no administrative role.

Prime Minister: Owen Arthur (BLP).

Geography

Barbados is generally flat and low, except in the north. ***Principal rivers:*** no major rivers. ***Highest point:*** Mount Hillaby 340m (1115 ft).

Climate: Barbados has a tropical climate. Rainfall is heavy, with totals everywhere above 1000 mm (40 in). The island is subject to hurricanes.

Economy

Tourism (the main source of income) employs about one third of the labour force. The government has encouraged diversification and there has been growth in banking and insurance. Sugar – once the mainstay of Barbados – remains the main crop. ***Currency:*** Barbados dollar.

Recent History

Economic and political power in the British colony of Barbados remained with a small white minority. In the 1930s, economic and social conditions for black Barbadians were miserable. Riots in 1937 led to reforms and also greatly increased black political consciousness. As a result, Barbadians, such as Grantley Adams and Errol Barrow, became prominent in Caribbean politics. Barbados became independent in 1966.

BELARUS

Official name: Respublika Belarus (Republic of Belarus). Formerly known as Byelorussia.

Member of: UN, CIS, OSCE.

Area: 207,600 km^2 (80,200 sq mi).

Population: 10,353,000 (1993 est).

Capital: Minsk (Mensk) 1,643,000 (including suburbs; 1991 est)

Other major cities: Gomel (Homel) 503,000, Vitebsk (Vitsyebsk) 369,000, Mogilev (Mahilyou) 363,000, Grodno (Hrodno) 277,000, Brest 269,000 (1991 est)

Languages: Belarussian (official; 79%), Russian (official; 13%), Polish (4%).

Religions: Belarussian Orthodox majority; Roman Catholic minority.

Education: is compulsory between the ages of seven and 17. *Adult literacy*: no figures available. *Universities:* three and four polytechnics of university status.

Defence: (1993 figures) *Army:* 50,500 personnel. *Air force:* 14,100. *Air defence:* 15,600. *Border guards:* 8000. *Conscription:* 18 months.

Government

A 160-member Assembly (Sejm) and a President – who appoints a Prime Minister and a Council of Ministers – are elected by universal adult suffrage for four years.

Largest parties/groups: former Communist group, the (socialist) Agrarians, (socialist) Belarus for Democracy, and independents.

Local government: six regions.

President: Aleksandr Lukashenko (non-party).

Prime Minister: Mikhail Chigir.

Geography

Belarus comprises lowlands covered with glacial debris in the north, fertile well-drained tablelands and ridges in the centre, and the low-lying Pripet Marshes in the south and east. Much of the country is flat.

Principal rivers: Dnepr, Pripyat (Pripet), Neman, Dvina. ***Highest point:*** Dzyarzhynskaya Mountain 346m (1135 ft).

Climate: The continental climate is moderated by the proximity of the Baltic Sea. Belarussian winters are considerably milder than those experienced in European Russia to the east.

Economy

Although Belarus has few natural resources, its economy is overwhelmingly industrial. Major heavy engineering, chemical, fertilizer, oil refining and synthetic fibre industries were established as part of the centrally planned Soviet economy, but output has declined since 1991. Belarus is dependent upon trade with other former Soviet republics, from which it imports the raw materials for its industries and upon which it relies as a market for its industrial goods. Almost no progress has been made towards establishing a market economy. Severe economic problems include high inflation and contamination from Chernobyl (see below). Agriculture is dominated by raising fodder crops for beef cattle, pigs and poultry. Flax is grown for export and the local linen industry. Extensive forests supply important woodworking and paper industries. ***Currency:*** Belarussian rouble.

Recent History

The Belarussians came under Russian rule as a result of the three partitions of Poland (1772, 1793 and 1795). The region suffered some of the fiercest fighting between Russia and Germany during World War I. Following the Russian Revolution, a Byelorussian Soviet republic was proclaimed (1919). The republic was invaded by the Poles in the same year and divided between Poland and the USSR in 1921. Byelorussia was devastated during World War II. In 1945 the Belarussians were reunited in a single Soviet republic. A perceived lack of Soviet concern for the republic at the time of the accident at the Chernobyl nuclear power station (just over the Ukrainian border) strengthened a reawakening Belarussian national identity. Contamination from Chernobyl affected about 20% of the republic, causing some areas to be sealed off and necessitating the eventual resettlement of up to 2,000,000 people. Byelorussia declared independence following the abortive coup by Communist hardliners in Moscow and – as Belarus – received international recognition when the USSR was dissolved (1991). In 1995 Belarus voted in favour of close economic union with Russia.

BELGIUM

Official names: Royaume de Belgique and Koninkrijk België (Kingdom of Belgium).
Member of: UN, NATO, EU/EC, OSCE, WEU, OECD.
Area: 30,519 km² (11,783 sq mi).
Population: 10,072,000 (1993 est).
Capital: Brussels (Bruxelles or Brussel) 1,331,000 (city 951,000; 1992 est).
Other major cities: Antwerp (Antwerpen or Anvers) 668,000 (city 465,000), Liège (Luik) 485,000 (city 197,000), Charleroi 295,000 (city 207,000), Ghent (Gent or Gand) 251,000 (city 230,000), Bruges (Brugge) 117,000, Namur (Namen) 104,000, Louvain (Leuven) 86,000, La Louvière 77,000 (1992 est).
Languages: Flemish (58% as a first language), French (42% as a first language), small German minority.
Religion: Roman Catholic (86%).
Education: is compulsory between the ages of six and 16. *Adult literacy:* virtually 100%. *Universities:* seven universities and 11 other institutes of university status.
Defence: (1993 figures) *Army:* 54,000 personnel. *Air force:* 17,300. *Navy:* 4400. *Others:* 5000. *Conscription:* was abolished in 1994.

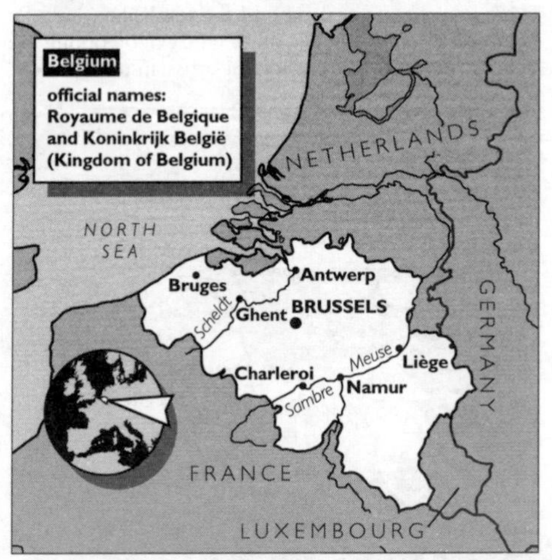

Government

Belgium is a constitutional monarchy. The Chamber of Deputies (the lower house of Parliament) comprises 150 members elected by universal adult suffrage for four years under a system of proportional representation. The Senate (the upper house) has 182 members: 106 directly elected, 50 chosen by provincial councils, 25 co-opted, plus the heir to the throne. The King appoints a Prime Minister who commands a majority in the Chamber, and, upon the PM's advice, other members of the Cabinet. The directly elected regional councils of Flanders, Wallonia and Brussels have very considerable powers.
Largest parties: (conservative Flemish) Christian Democrats (CVP). (conservative Francophone) Christian Democrats (PSC), (Flemish) Socialist Party (SP), (Francophone) Socialist Party (PS), (Flemish) Liberal Freedom and Progress Party (PVV), (Francophone) Liberal Reform Party (PRL), (right-wing Flemish nationalist) Vlaams Blok, (right-wing Flemish nationalist) Volksunie.
Local government: three autonomous regions and nine provinces.
Sovereign: HM Albert II, King of the Belgians (succeeded 9 August 1993, following the death of his brother 31 July 1993).
Prime Minister: Jean-Luc Dehaene (CVP).

Regions

Brussels (Bruxelles/Brussel) *Area:* 162 km² (62 sq mi). *Population:* 951,000 (1992 est). *Capital:* Brussels.
Flanders (Vlaanderen) *Area:* 13,511 km² (5217 sq mi). *Population:* 5,769,000 (1991 census). *Capital:* Ghent.
Wallonia (Wallonie) *Area:* 16,845 km² (6504 sq mi). *Population:* 3,256,000 (1991 census). *Capital:* Liège.

Geography

The forested Ardennes plateau occupies the southeast. The plains of central Belgium, an important agricultural region, are covered in fertile loess. The flat, low-lying north contains the sandy Kempenland plateau in the east and the plain of Flanders in the west. Enclosed by dykes behind coastal sand dunes are polders, former marshes reclaimed from the sea.
Principal rivers: Scheldt (Schelde or Escaut), Meuse (Maes), Sambre. ***Highest point:*** Mount Botrange 694m (2277 ft).
Climate: Belgium experiences relatively cool summers and mild winters, with ample rainfall throughout the year. Summers are hotter and winters colder inland.

Economy

Belgium is a small, densely populated industrial country with few natural resources. In the centre and the north, soils are generally fertile and the climate encourages high yields of wheat, sugar beet, grass and fodder crops. Metalworking – originally based on small mineral deposits in the Ardennes – is the most important industry. Textiles, chemicals, ceramics, glass and rubber are also important, but, apart from coal, most raw materials required by industry now have to be imported. Economic problems since the 1970s have mirrored Belgium's linguistic divide, with high unemployment largely confined to the French-speaking (Walloon) south, while industry in the Flemish north has prospered. Banking, commerce and administration employ increasing numbers, and Brussels has benefited from its role as the unofficial 'capital' of the EU/EC. ***Currency:*** Belgian franc.

Recent History

In 1830 the Belgians rebelled against Dutch rule and proclaimed their independence. Belgian neutrality was recognized by the Congress of London (1831) and the crown was offered to Leopold of Saxe-Coburg Gotha, Queen Victoria's uncle. Belgium's neutrality was broken by the German invasion in 1914 (which led to Britain's declaration of war under the 1831 treaty). The brave resistance of King Albert I in 1914–18 earned international admiration; the capitulation of Leopold III when Belgium was again occupied by Germany (1940–45) was severely criticized. The Belgian Congo (Zaïre), acquired as a personal possession by Leopold II (1879), was relinquished amidst scenes of chaos in 1960. Belgium is now the main centre of administration of the EU/EC and of NATO, but it is troubled by acute rivalry between its Flemish and French speakers and has adopted a federal system based upon linguistic regions.

BELIZE

Member of: UN, Commonwealth, CARICOM, OAS.
Area: 22,965 km² (8867 sq mi).
Population: 204,000 (1993 est).
Capital: Belmopan 4000 (1992 est).
Other major towns and cities: Belize City 45,000, Orange Walk 11,700, Corozal 7100 (1992 est).
Languages: English (majority; official), Creole (33%), Spanish (32%).
Religion: Roman Catholic (62%).
Education: is compulsory between the ages of five and 14. *Adult literacy:* 93%. *Universities:* one university and one university centre.
Defence: (1993 figures) *Army:* 640 personnel. *Air force:* 20. *Navy:* 50. *Paramilitary:* 500. (There are 1500 British troops in Belize.)

Government

The eight members of the Senate are appointed by the Governor General, the representative of the British Queen as sovereign of Belize. The 28 members of the House of Representatives are elected by universal adult suffrage for five years. The Governor General appoints a Prime Minister who commands a majority in the House, and, on the PM's advice, a Cabinet, which is responsible to the House.
Largest parties: (conservative) United Democratic Party (UDP), (centre) People's United Party (PUP).
Local government: seven districts.
Prime Minister: Manuel Esquivel (UDP).

Geography

Tropical jungle covers much of Belize. The south contains the Maya Mountains. The north is mainly swampy lowlands. ***Principal rivers:*** Belize, Hondo, New River. ***Highest point:*** Victoria Peak 1122m (3681 ft).
Climate: The subtropical climate is tempered by trade winds. Rainfall is heavy, but there is a dry season between February and May.

Economy

The production of sugar, bananas and citrus fruit for export dominates the economy. ***Currency:*** Belize dollar.

Recent History

English pirates and loggers settled in the area in the 17th century. Black slaves were imported to cut timber. In 1862 the area formally became the colony of British Honduras. The colony gained independence – as Belize – in 1981, but Guatemala continued to claim it as part of her territory until 1991.

BENIN

Official name: La République du Bénin (Republic of Benin).
Member of: UN, OAU, ECOWAS.
Area: 112,622 km² (43,484 sq mi).
Population: 5,090,000 (1993 est).
Capital: Porto-Novo 208,000 (1983 est).
Other major cities: Cotonou 487,000, Parakou 66,000 (1983 est).
Languages: French (official), Fon (47%), Adja (12%).
Religions: animist (61%), Sunni Islam (16%).
Education: is compulsory, in theory, between the ages of six and 12. *Adult literacy:* 23%. *Universities:* one.
Defence: (1993 figures) *Army:* 12,000 personnel. *Conscription:* none.

Government

A President is elected by universal adult suffrage for five years and a 64-member National Assembly for four years. The President appoints a Cabinet.
Largest parties: (former monopoly) Union for the

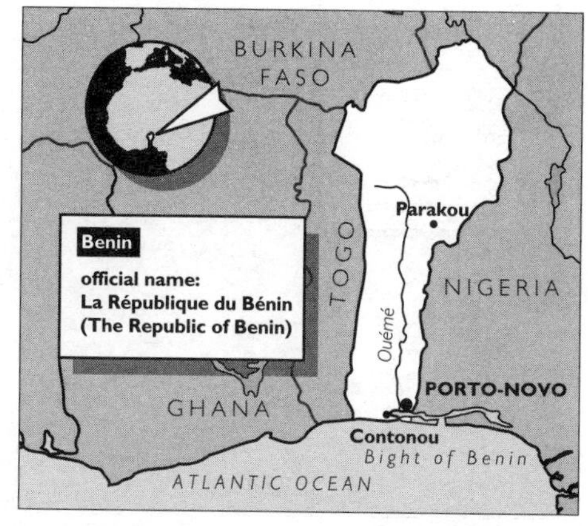

Triumph of the Return of Democracy (UTRD), (coalition) National Convention for Forces for Change (CNFC).
Local government: six provinces.
President: Nicephore Soglo (UTRD).

Geography
The Atacora Massif occupies the northwest; in the northeast, plains slope down to the Niger Valley. The plateaux of central Benin fall in the south to a low fertile region. A narrow coastal plain is backed by lagoons. ***Principal rivers:*** Ouémé, Niger. ***Highest point:*** Atacora Massif 641m (2103 ft)
Climate: The north is tropical; the south is equatorial.

Economy
The economy is based on agriculture, which occupies the majority of the labour force. The main food crops are cassava (manioc), yams and maize; the principal cash crop is palm oil. In the late 1980s, central planning was abandoned in favour of a market economy.
Currency: CFA franc.

Recent History
Benin was called Dahomey until 1975. In the 1890s, Dahomey was conquered by the French. Political turmoil followed independence in 1960, and five coups took place between 1963 and 1972, when a Marxist-Leninist government came to power. A multi-party system was restored in 1991.

BHUTAN

Official name: Druk-yul (Realm of the Dragon/Bhutan).
Member of: UN.
Area: 46,500 km² (17,954 sq mi).
Population: 1,442,000 (1990 UN est; in 1993 the Bhutanese government estimated the population to be 642,000).
Capital: Thimphu 30,000 (1993 est.)
Other main towns: Puntsholing 10,000, Paro 8000 (1990 est).
Languages: Dzongkha (Tibetan; official; 70%); Nepali (30%).
Religions: Buddhist (70%), Hindu (25%).
Education: is not compulsory. *Adult literacy:* 18%. *Universities:* one college of university status.
Defence: (1993 figures) *Army:* 5000 personnel. *Conscription:* none.

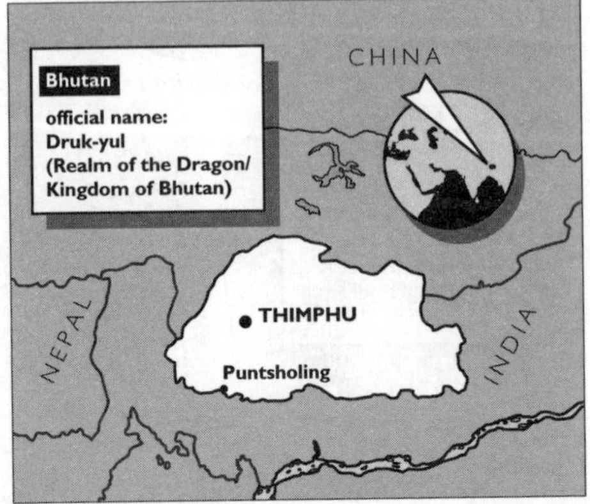

Government
Bhutan is a hereditary monarchy in which the King shares power with a Council of Ministers, the Buddhist Head Abbot and a 151-member National Assembly, comprising 106 members directly elected by universal adult suffrage for three years and other appointed members.
Largest parties: There are no political parties.
Local government: 20 districts.
Sovereign: HM, the Druk Gyalpo, Jigme Singhye Wangchuk, King of Bhutan (succeeded 24 July 1972 on the death of his father).
Prime Minister: The King.

Geography
The Himalaya cover most of Bhutan. The valleys of central Bhutan are wide and fertile. The Duars Plain, a subtropical jungle, lies along the Indian border. ***Principal rivers:*** Amo-chu, Wang-chu. ***Highest point:*** Khula Kangri 7554m (24,784 ft).
Climate: The climate is tropical and very wet in the Duars Plain. Temperatures get progressively lower with altitude, resulting in permanent snow cover in the north. Precipitation is heavy.

Economy
Bhutan is one of the poorest and least developed countries in the world. Over 90% of the labour force is involved in producing food crops. ***Currency:*** Ngultrum.

Recent History
Contact with British-dominated India led to border friction and partial annexation in 1865. In 1949 India returned this territory but assumed influence over Bhutan's external affairs. In 1907 the governor of Tongsa became Bhutan's first king. In the 1990s there has been discrimination against the Nepali minority.

BOLIVIA

Official name: Républica de Bolivia (Republic of Bolivia).
Member of: UN, OAS, ALADI, Andean Pact.
Area: 1,098,581 km² (424,164 sq mi).
Population: 7,715,000 (1993 est).
Capital: La Paz (administrative capital) 1,050,000, Sucre (legal capital) 96,000 (1988 est).
Other major cities: Santa Cruz 615,000, Cochabamba 377,000, Oruro 195,000 (1988 est).

Languages: Spanish (55%), Aymara (22%), Quéchua (5%) – all official.
Religion: Roman Catholic (official; 95%).
Education: is compulsory, in theory, between the ages of six and 14. *Adult literacy:* 78%. *Universities:* 10 (including two private universities).
Defence: (1993 figures) *Army:* 25,000 personnel. *Air force:* 4000. *Navy:* 4500. *Conscription:* selective; 12 months.

Government

The President (who appoints a Cabinet), the 27-member Senate and the 130-member Chamber of Deputies are elected for four-year terms by universal adult suffrage.
Largest parties: (right-wing) National Revolutionary Movement (MNR), (centrist) Patriotic Accord (AP), (centrist) Civic Solidarity Union (UCS), (centre-left) Conscience of the Fatherland (Condepa).
Local government: nine departments.
President: Gonzalo Sanchez de Lozada (MNR).

Geography

The Andes divide into two parallel chains between which is an extensive undulating depression (the Altiplano), containing Lake Titicaca, the highest navigable lake in the world. The lowlands in the east and northeast include tropical rain forests (the Llanos), subtropical plains and semiarid grasslands (the Chaco). ***Principal rivers:*** Beni, Mamoré, Pilcomayo, Paraguay. ***Highest point:*** Sajama 6542m (21,463 ft).
Climate: Rainfall is negligible in the southwest, and heavy in the northeast. Temperature varies with altitude from the cold Andean summits and cool, windy Altiplano to the tropical northeast.

Economy

Bolivia is relatively poor, despite being rich in natural resources such as petroleum and tin. Lack of investment, past political instability and high mining costs have retarded development. Agriculture is labour intensive, producing domestic foodstuffs (potatoes and maize), and export crops (sugar cane and cotton). The illegal cultivation of coca (for cocaine) is causing concern. ***Currency:*** Boliviano.

Recent History

A revolt against Spanish rule (1809) led to a power struggle between loyalists and nationalists, ending in independence in 1825. The remainder of the 19th century was characterized by political instability. In three devastating wars – the War of the Pacific (1879–83), alongside Peru against Chile, and the Chaco Wars (1928–30 and 1933–35) against Paraguay – Bolivia sustained great human and territorial losses. After 1935, political instability continued with a succession of military and civilian governments. Since 1982, however, Bolivia has had democratically elected governments.

BOSNIA-HERZEGOVINA

Official name: Bosna i Hercegovina (Bosnia-Herzegovina).
Member of: UN, OSCE.
Area: 51,129 km² (19,741 sq mi).
Population: 4,365,000 (1991 census); c. 3,500,000 (late 1993 est; many refugees left Bosnia in 1992–94 and over 200,000 people have been killed in the war).
Capital: Sarajevo 526,000 (city 416,000; 1991 census); by 1994 the population of Sarajevo was c. 300,000.

Other major cities: Tuzla 130,000 (1991 census; over 230,000 by 1994), Banja Luka 143,000 (1991 census).
Languages: Serbo-Croat – a single language with two written forms.
Religions: (pre-1992) Sunni Islam (44%), Serbian Orthodox (33%), Roman Catholic (17%).
Education: is compulsory between the ages of seven and 15. *Adult literacy:* 86%. *Universities:* four.
Defence: (1993 figures) *Army:* 60,000 personnel. (Croat forces: 50,000; Serb forces: 80,000).

Government

Two separate assemblies – largely representing the previous national Assembly divided upon religio-linguistic grounds – have evolved: the (internationally-recognized) government of the Federation of Bosnia and Herzegovina (largely Muslim and Croat) based in Sarajevo and the (Bosnian Serb) government of the self-styled Republika Srpska based in Pale.
Largest parties: The party system has broken down in Bosnia.
Local government: Before the Bosnian war there were 100 districts.
President: Alija Izetbegovic.
Prime Minister: Haris Silajdzic.

Geography

Ridges of the Dinaric Mountains, rising to over 1800 m (6000 ft), occupy the greater part of the country and in places form arid karst limestone plateaux. The north comprises restricted lowlands in the valley of the River Sava. The tiny coastline on the Adriatic is less than 20 km (13 mi) long. ***Principal rivers:*** Sava, Bosna, Drina. ***Highest point:*** Maglic 2387m (7831 ft).
Climate: Bosnia (the north) has cold winters and warm summers; Herzegovina (the south) enjoys milder winters and warmer summers.

Economy

The economy has been devastated by war since 1992. Central and east Bosnia is forested. Agriculture is a major employer and sheep, maize, olives, grapes and citrous fruit are important. Bosnia has little industry.
Currency: Bosnia uses Yugoslav and Croatian currency.

Recent History

During the 19th century, several revolts against Turkish rule were put down with ferocity. A major revolt (1875–76) attracted international concern, but the great powers overrode Bosnia's pan-Slavic aspirations at the Congress of Berlin (1877–78) and assigned Bosnia-Herzegovina to Habsburg Austro-Hungarian rule. In Sarajevo in 1914, Gavrilo Princip, a Bosnian Serb student, assassinated Archduke Franz Ferdinand, the heir to the Austro-Hungarian Empire – an event that helped precipitate World War I. In 1918, Bosnia became part of the new Kingdom of Serbs, Croats and Slovenes, which was renamed Yugoslavia in 1929. Following the German invasion (1941), Bosnia was included in the Axis-controlled puppet state of Croatia. In 1945, when Yugoslavia was reorganized by Marshal Tito on Soviet lines, Bosnia-Herzegovina became a republic within the Communist federation. After the secession of Slovenia and Croatia and the beginning of the Yugoslav wars (1991), tension grew between Serbs and Croats in Bosnia. The Muslim Bosnians reasserted their separate identity. In 1992, a referendum, which was boycotted by the Serbs, gave a majority in favour of Bosnian independence.

International recognition of Bosnia-Herzegovina was gained in 1992, but Bosnian Serbs, encouraged by Serbia, seized 70% of the country, killing or expelling Muslims and Croats in a campaign of 'ethnic cleansing'. Areas of Herzegovina inhabited by ethnic Croats were effectively brought within the orbit of Croatia. International peace and humanitarian efforts were attempted and the UN declared certain enclaves to be 'safe havens' for Bosnian Muslims. In 1994 the Bosnian Croats and Muslims agreed to form a federation, but the Bosnian Serbs, despite pressure from the Serb (Yugoslav) government in Belgrade, refused to accept various international peace plans. In 1995, the situation deteriorated after Bosnian Serbs took UN personnel as hostages.

BOTSWANA

Official name: The Republic of Botswana.
Member of: UN, OAU, Commonwealth.
Area: 581,730 km² (224,606 sq mi).
Population: 1,406,000 (1993 est).
Capital: Gaborone 138,000 (1991 est).
Other main town: Francistown 56,000 (1991 est).
Languages: English (official), Setswana (majority; national).
Religions: animist (over 50%), various Protestant Churches.
Education: is not compulsory. *Adult literacy:* 74%. *Universities:* one.
Defence: (1993 figures) *Army:* 6000 personnel. *Air force:* 100. *Conscription:* none.

Government

Thirty of the 36 members of the National Assembly are elected by universal adult suffrage for five years. Of the remainder, four are nominated by the President; the Speaker and Attorney General are non-voting members. The President, who chairs and appoints a Cabinet, is elected for five years by the Assembly. There is also a 15-member advisory House of Chiefs.
Largest parties: (centre) Botswana Democratic Party (BDP), (socialist) Botswana National Front (BNF).
Local government: nine districts and four towns.
President: Dr Quett Masire (BDP).

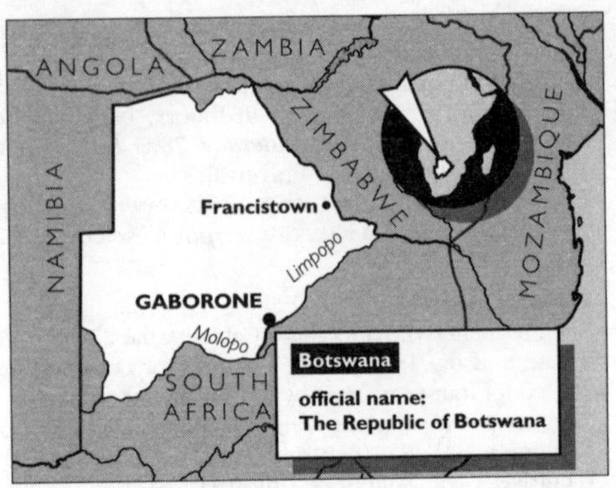

Geography

A central plateau divides a flat near-desert in the east of Botswana from the Kalahari Desert and Okavango Swamps in the west. ***Principal rivers:*** Okavango, Limpopo, Chobe, Shashi. ***Highest point:*** Mount Otse 1489m (4885 ft)
Climate: The climate is subtropical with extremes of heat and occasionally temperatures below freezing. Much of Botswana suffers drought.

Economy

Nomadic cattle herding and the cultivation of subsistence crops occupies the majority of the labour force. The mainstay of the economy is mining for diamonds, copper-nickel and coal. ***Currency:*** Pula.

Recent History

British missionaries had been active since 1813 in the area, which became the British protectorate of Bechuanaland in 1885. Development was slow, and many Africans had to seek work in South Africa. Nationalism was late to develop, and independence – as Botswana – was granted without a struggle in 1966. Under the first president, Sir Seretse Khama, and his successor, Botswana has succeeded in remaining a democracy.

BRAZIL

Official name: A República Federativa do Brasil (the Federative Republic of Brazil).
Member of: UN, OAS, ALADI, Mercosur.
Area: 8,511,996 km² (3,286,482 sq mi).
Population: 156,493,000 (1993 est).
Capital: Brasília 1,864,000 (city 1,841,000; 1991 est).
Other major cities: São Paulo 18,100,000 (city 9,394,000), Rio de Janeiro 11,140,000 (city 5,474,000, Nova Iguacu 1,512,000), Belo Horizonte 3,462,000 (city 1,530,000), Pôrto Alegre 3,016,000 (city 1,237,000), Recife 2,860,000 (city 1,297,000), Salvador 2,472,000 (city 2,070,000), Fortaleza 2,169,000 (city 1,709,000), Curitiba 1,926,000 (city 1,248,000), Belém 1,334,000 (city 1,246,000), Goiânia 1,268,000 (city 912,000), Manaus 1,164,000 (city 1,005,000), Campinas 846,000 (city 748,000) (1991 est).
Language: Portuguese (official).
Religions: Roman Catholic (89%), Protestant Churches (nearly 7%).
Education: is compulsory between the ages of seven and 14. *Adult literacy:* 81%. *Universities:* 95 (including 55 state universities).

Defence: (1993 figures) *Army:* 196,000 personnel. *Air force:* 50,700. *Navy:* 50,000. *Conscription:* 12 months.

Government

The President – who appoints a Cabinet – is elected for a five-year term by universal adult suffrage. The lower house of the National Congress (the Chamber of Deputies) has 503 members elected for four years by compulsory universal adult suffrage. The 91 members of the upper house (the Federal Senate) are elected directly for an eight-year term – one third and two thirds of the senators retiring alternately every four years. Each of the 26 states has its own legislature.

Largest parties: (centre-left) Brazilian Democratic Movement (PMDB), (centrist) Liberal Front (PFL), (leftist) Democratic Labour Party (PDT), (conservative) National Reconstruction Party (PRN), Social Democratic Party (PDS), Social Democratic Party of Brazil (PSDB), (socialist) Workers' Party of Brazil (PTB), Christian Democratic Party (PCD).

Local government: 26 states, one federal district, one federal territory.

President: Fernando Enrique Cardoso (PSDB).

States and Territories

Acre *Area:* 153,698 km² (59,343 sq mi). *Population:* 417,000 (1991 census). *Capital:* Rio Branco.

Alagoas *Area:* 29,107 km² (11,238 sq mi). *Population:* 2,513,000 (1991 census). *Capital:* Maceió.

Amapá *Area:* 142,359 km² (54,965 sq mi). *Population:* 289,000 (1991 census). *Capital:* Macapá

Amazonas *Area:* 1,567,954 km² (605,390 sq mi). *Population:* 2,089,000 (1991 census). *Capital:* Manaus.

Bahia *Area:* 566,979 km² (218,912 sq mi). *Population:* 11,802,000 (1991 census). *Capital:* Salvador.

Ceará *Area:* 145,694 km² (56,253 sq mi). *Population:* 6,353,000 (1991 census). *Capital:* Fortaleza.

Espírito Santo *Area:* 45,733 km² (17,658 sq mi). *Population:* 2,598,000 (1991 census). *Capital:* Vitória.

Goiás *Area:* 340,166 km² (131,339 sq mi). *Population:* 4,025,000 (1991 census). *Capital:* Goiânia.

Maranhão *Area:* 329,556 km² (127,242 sq mi). *Population:* 4,922,000 (1991 census). *Capital:* São Luís.

Mato Grosso *Area:* 901,421 km² (348,040 sq mi). *Population:* 2,021,000 (1991 census). *Capital:* Cuiabá.

Mato Grosso do Sul *Area:* 357,472 km² (138,021 sq mi). *Population:* 1,778,000 (1991 census). *Capital:* Campo Grande.

Minas Gerais *Area:* 586,624 km² (226,497 sq mi). *Population:* 15,746,000 (1991 census). *Capital:* Belo Horizonte.

Pará *Area:* 1,246,833 km² (481,405 sq mi). *Population:* 5,085,000 (1991 census). *Capital:* Belém.

Paraiba *Area:* 53,958 km² (20,833 sq mi). *Population:*

3,201,000 (1991 census). *Capital:* João Pessoa.
Paraná *Area:* 199,324 km² (76,959 sq mi). *Population:* 8,416,000 (1991 census). *Capital:* Curitiba.
Pernambuco *Area:* 101,023 km² (39,005 sq mi). *Population:* 7,110,000 (1991 census). *Capital:* Recife.
Piauí *Area:* 251,273 km² (97,017 sq mi). *Population:* 2,581,000 (1991 census). *Capital:* Teresina.
Rio de Janeiro *Area:* 43,653 km² (16,855 sq mi). *Population:* 12,584,000 (1991 census). *Capital:* Rio de Janeiro.
Rio Grande do Norte *Area:* 53,167 km² (20,528 sq mi). *Population:* 2,414,000 (1991 census). *Capital:* Natal.
Rio Grande do Sul *Area:* 280,674 km² (108,369 sq mi). *Population:* 9,128,000 (1991 census). *Capital:* Pôrto Alegre.
Rondônia *Area:* 238,379 km² (92,039 sq mi). *Population:* 1,130,000 (1991 census). *Capital:* Pôrto Velho.
Roraima *Area:* 225,017 km² (86,880 sq mi). *Population:* 216,000 (1991 census). *Capital:* Boa Vista.
Santa Catarina *Area:* 95,318 km² (36,803 sq mi). *Population:* 4,536,000 (1991 census). *Capital:* Florianópolis.
São Paulo *Area:* 248,256 km² (95,852 sq mi). *Population:* 31,193,000 (1991 census). *Capital:* São Paulo.
Sergipe *Area:* 21,863 km² (8441 sq mi). *Population:* 1,492,000 (1991 census). *Capital:* Aracaju.
Tocantins *Area:* 277,322 km² (107,075 sq mi). *Population:* 920,000 (1991 census). *Capital:* Palmas.
Federal District (Distrito Federal) *Area:* 5794 km² (2237 sq mi). *Population:* 1,596,000 (1991 census). *Capital:* Brasília.
Fernando de Noronha *Area:* 26 km² (10 sq mi). *Population:* 1300 (1991 census). *Capital:* No capital; this island federal territory is administered from the mainland.

Geography

Nearly one half of Brazil is drained by the world's largest river system, the Amazon, whose low-lying basin is still largely covered by tropical rain forest, although pressure on land has encouraged deforestation. North of the Amazon Basin, the Guiana Highlands contain Brazil's highest peak – Pico da Neblina. A central plateau of savannah grasslands lies south of the Basin. In the east and south, a densely populated coastal plain adjoins the Brazilian Highlands, a vast plateau divided by fertile valleys and mountain ranges. ***Principal rivers:*** Amazon, Paraná, São Francisco, Negro, Branco, Purus, Jurua, Tocantins, Madeira. ***Highest point:*** Pico da Neblina 3014m (9888 ft).

Climate: The Amazon Basin and the southeast coast are tropical with heavy rainfall. The rest of Brazil is either subtropical or temperate (in the savannah). Only the northeast has inadequate rainfall.

Economy

Agriculture employs about one quarter of the labour force. The principal agricultural exports include coffee, sugar cane, soyabeans, oranges, beef cattle and cocoa. Timber was important, but environmental concern is restricting its trade. Rapid industrialization since 1945 has made Brazil a major manufacturing country. While textiles, clothing and food processing are still the biggest industries, the iron and steel, chemical, petroleum-refining, cement, electrical, motor-vehicle and fertilizer industries have all attained international stature. Brazil has enormous – and, in part, unexploited – natural resources, including iron ore, phosphates, uranium, copper, manganese, bauxite, coal and vast hydroelectric power potential. In the last two decades, rampant inflation has hindered development. ***Currency:*** Real.

Recent History

The long reign of Pedro II (reigned 1840-89) brought stability and economic growth to Brazil. Opposition from landowners (angered by the abolition of slavery in 1888) and the military (who were excluded from political power) led to a coup and the end of the monarchy in 1889. The republic was initially stable, but social unrest mounted and, in 1930, Getúlio Vargas seized power. Vargas attempted to model Brazil on Mussolini's Italy, but was overthrown by the military in 1945. Vargas was elected president again (1950), but he committed suicide to avoid impeachment (1954). Short-lived civilian governments preceded a further period of military rule (1964–85), during which the economy expanded rapidly, but political and social rights were restricted. Civilian rule was restored in 1985 and in 1990 Brazilians were able for vote for a president for the first time in 29 years.

BRUNEI

Official name: Negara Brunei Darussalam (Sultanate of Brunei).
Member of: UN, Commonwealth, ASEAN, Apec.
Area: 5765 km² (2226 sq mi).
Population: 275,000 (1993 est).
Capital: Bandar Seri Begawan 52,000 (1988 est).
Other main towns: Seria 21,000, Kuala Belait 21,000 (1988 est).
Languages: Malay (official; over 50%), Chinese (26%), English.
Religions: Sunni Islam (official; 66%), Buddhist (12%).
Education: is compulsory between the ages of five and 14. *Adult literacy:* 85%. *Universities:* one.
Defence: (1993 figures) *Army:* 3600 personnel. *Air force:* 300. *Navy:* 550. *Conscription:* none.

Government

The Sultan, a hereditary monarch, rules by decree, assisted by a Council of Ministers and a 21-member advisory council, both of which he appoints.

Largest parties: There are no political parties.
Local government: four districts.
Sovereign: HM Haji Hassanal Bolkiah, Sultan of Brunei (succeeded upon the abdication of his father, 5 October 1967).
Prime Minister: The Sultan.

Geography

Brunei consists of two coastal enclaves. The (larger) western part is hilly; the eastern enclave is more mountainous and forested. ***Principal rivers:*** Belait, Brunei, Temburong. ***Highest point:*** Bukit Pagon 1850m (6070 ft).
Climate: Brunei has a tropical monsoon climate with rainfall totals in excess of 2500 mm (100 in).

Economy

Exploitation of substantial deposits of petroleum and natural gas has given Brunei one of the world's highest per capita incomes. Most of the country's food has to be imported. ***Currency:*** Brunei dollar.

Recent History

By the 19th century the sultans of Brunei held a reduced territory that had become a pirates' paradise. The British restored order and established a protectorate from 1888 to 1971. Oil was discovered in 1929. Independence was restored in 1984 under the absolute rule of Sultan Hassanal Bolkiah, allegedly the world's richest man.

BULGARIA

Official name: Republika Bulgariya (Republic of Bulgaria).
Member of: UN, OSCE.
Area: 110,994 km² (42,855 sq mi).
Population: 8,473,000 (1992 census).
Capital: Sofia (Sofiya) 1,221,000 (city 1,141,000; 1990 est).
Other major cities: Plovdiv 379,000, Varna 315,000, Burgas 205,000, Ruse 192,000, Stara Zagora 165,000, Pleven 138,000, Dobrich 116,000, Sliven 112,000, Shumen 111,000 (1990 est).
Languages: Bulgarian (official; 89%), Turkish (9%).
Religions: Orthodox (80%), Sunni Islam (8%).
Education: is compulsory between the ages of six and 16. *Adult literacy:* 96%. *Universities:* five (including a technical university), plus 18 other institutes of university status.
Defence: (1993 figures) *Army:* 52,000 personnel. *Air force:* 21,800. *Navy:* 3000. *Others:* 22,600. *Conscription:* 18 months.

Government

The 240-member National Assembly is elected under a system of proportional representation every five years by universal adult suffrage. The President – who is directly elected for five years – appoints a Prime Minister who commands a majority in the Assembly. The PM, in turn, chooses a Council of Ministers
Largest parties: (former Communist) Bulgarian Socialist Party (BSP), (centre-liberal) Union of Democratic Forces (UDF), (mainly ethnic Turkish) Movement for Rights and Freedom (MRF), New Union for Democracy (NUD).
Local government: nine regions.
President: Zhelo Zhelev (UDF).
Prime Minister: Zhan Videnov (BSP).

Geography

The Balkan Mountains run from east to west across central Bulgaria. To the north, low-lying hills slope down to the River Danube. To the south, a belt of lowland separates the Balkan Mountains from a high, rugged massif. ***Principal rivers:*** Danube, Maritsa. ***Highest point:*** Musala 2925m (9596 ft).
Climate: The continental north has warm summers and cold winters, while the southeast has a more Mediterranean climate.

Economy

With fertile soils, and few other natural resources, Bulgaria's economy has a strong agricultural base specializing in cereals (wheat, maize, barley), fruit (grapes) and, increasingly, tobacco. For nearly half a century, production was centred on large-scale, mechanized cooperatives, but privatization of land began in 1990. Agricultural products are the basis of the food processing, wine and tobacco industries. Other major industries include engineering, fertilizers and chemicals. Tourism is increasingly important. Bulgaria's trading patterns and economy were disrupted by the collapse of the Communist East European trading bloc in 1990–91. Industrial production has declined, and the country has experienced high rates of emigration, unemployment and inflation. State-run industries are being privatized. ***Currency:*** Lev.

Recent History

Five centuries of Turkish rule reduced Bulgarians to illiterate peasantry, but folk memories of past glories remained. Most Bulgarians remained Christian, and a 19th-century national revival sought to restore an independent Church as the first step towards the restoration of nationhood. Russian intervention produced both a Bulgarian Church (1870) and state (1878). The latter was an autonomous principality until 1908, and an independent kingdom until 1946. However, the boundaries, established at the Congress of Berlin (1878), failed to satisfy the Bulgarians, who waged five wars to win the lands they had been promised in the earlier Treaty of San Stefano (1877). Victorious in the first two wars (1885 and 1912), Bulgaria was on the losing side in the final Balkan War (1913) and in World Wars I and II (1915–18 and 1941–44), and forfeited territory. After the Red Army invaded (1944), a Communist regime, tied closely to the USSR, was established and the king was exiled (1946). Following popular demonstrations in 1989, the hardline leader Todor Zhivkov (1911–) was replaced by reformers who renounced the Communist Party's leading role. Free elections were held in 1990, since when short-lived coalitions have attempted to tackle Bulgaria's severe economic problems.

BURKINA FASO

Official name: Burkina Faso or République de Burkina (Republic of Burkina) (previously known as Upper Volta).
Member of: UN, OAS, ECOWAS.
Area: 274,400 km^2 (105,946 sq mi).
Population: 9,780,000 (1993 est).
Capital: Ouagadougou 442,000 (1985 est).
Other major cities: Bobo-Dioulasso 229,000, Koudougou 52,000 (1985 est).
Languages: French (official), Mossi (48%), Fulani (10%).
Religions: animist (49%), Sunni Islam (40%).
Education: is compulsory, in theory, between the ages of seven and 14. *Adult literacy:* 18%. *Universities:* one.
Defence: (1993 figures) *Army:* 7000 personnel. *Air force:* 200. *Others:* 1500. *Conscription:* none.

Government

Elections by universal adult suffrage are held every five years for a 107-member Assembly and every seven years for a President.
Largest parties: (leftist) Organization for Popular Democracy Labour Movement (ODF-MT), National Convention of Progressive Patriots-Social Democratic Party (CNPP-PSD).
Local government: 30 provinces.
President: Captain Blaise Campoare (ODF-MT).
Prime Minister: Youssouf Ouedraogo (ODF-MT).

Geography

The country consists of plateaux about 500 m (1640 ft) high. ***Principal rivers:*** Black Volta, White Volta.
Highest point: Mount Tema 747m (2451 ft).
Climate: The country is hot and dry, with adequate rainfall – 1000 mm (40 in) – only in the savannah of the south. The north is semidesert.

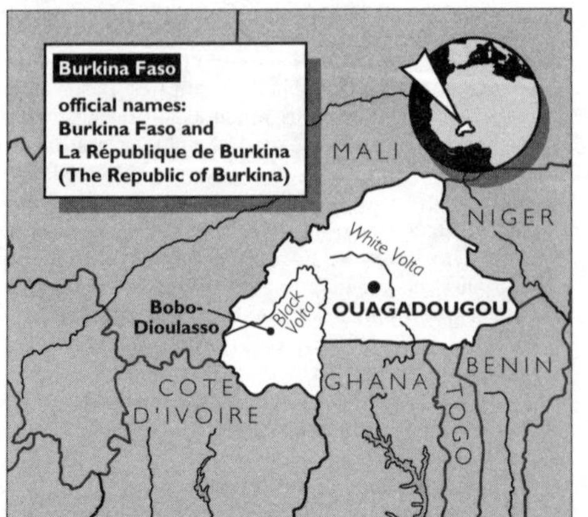

Economy

Burkina Faso, one of the world's poorest states, has been severely stricken by drought in the last two decades. Nomadic herdsmen and subsistence farmers – producing mainly sorghum, sugar cane and millet – form the bulk of the population. Cotton, manganese and zinc are exported. ***Currency:*** CFA franc.

Recent History

Mossi kingdoms dominated the area for centuries before French rule began in the 1890s. In the colonial era, the country was a labour reservoir for more developed colonies to the south. Since independence in 1960, the country – which kept the name Upper Volta until 1984 – has had a turbulent political history, with a succession of military coups. Multi-party rule was restored in 1992.

BURMA see MYANMAR

BURUNDI

Official names: La République du Burundi/ Republika y'Uburundi (The Republic of Burundi).
Member of: UN, OAU.
Area: 27,834 km^2 (10,747 sq mi).
Population: 5,600,000 (1993 est).
Capital: Bujumbura 227,000 (1990 est).
Other main city: Gitega 21,000 (1990 est).
Languages: Kirundi (majority) and French – both official; Kiswahili.
Religion: Roman Catholic (65%).
Education: is not compulsory. *Adult literacy:* 74%. *Universities:* one.
Defence: (1993 figures) *Army:* 5500 personnel. *Air force:* 150. *Paramilitary:* 1500. *Conscription:* none.

Government

A President is elected by universal adult suffrage for five years and an 81-member Assembly is directly elected for four years. The President appoints a Prime Minister and a Cabinet.
Largest parties: Front for Democracy in Burundi (Frodebu), (former monopoly) Union for National Progress (Uprona).
Local government: 15 provinces.
President: Sylvestre Ntibantunganya (Frodebu).
Prime Minister: Antoine Nduwayo (Uprona).

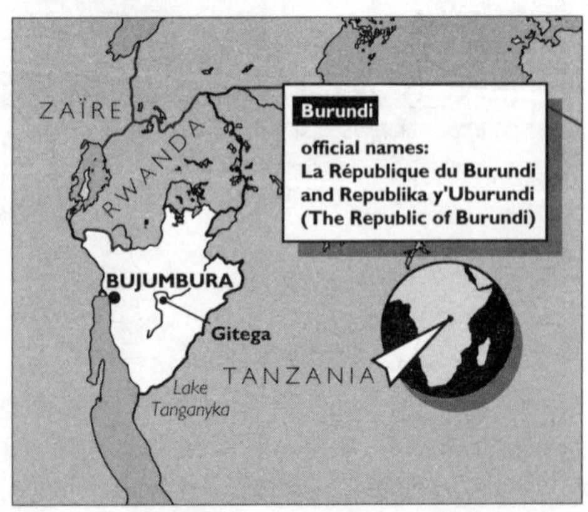

Geography

Burundi is a high plateau, rising from Lake Tanganyika in the west. ***Principal rivers:*** Kagera, Ruzizi, Ruvubu. ***Highest point:*** Mont Hela 2685m (8809 ft).

Climate: The lowlands are hot and humid. Temperatures are cooler in the mountains.

Economy

Over 92% of the labour force is involved in agriculture, producing both subsistence crops and crops for export, such as coffee. The economy has been damaged by recurring tribal conflict. ***Currency:*** Burundi franc.

Recent History

Burundi was a kingdom in which the minority Tutsi people dominated the Hutu majority. Colonized by Germany in 1890, it was taken over by Belgium after World War I. Independence came in 1962, after much ethnic conflict. Following a military coup in 1966, a republic was established. The killing of the deposed king in 1972 led to a massacre of the Hutu. There have since been further coups and unrest, including a wave of ethnic murders following the assassination of the democratically elected (Hutu) president by (Tutsi) army officers in 1993. Tension between Burundi's Hutus and Tutsis increased after the massacre of Tutsis by Hutus in neighbouring Rwanda (1994).

CAMBODIA

Official name: Preah Reach Ana Pak Kampuchea (Kingdom of Cambodia).
Member of: UN.
Area: 181,035 km² (69,898 sq mi).
Population: 9,280,000 (1993 est).
Capital: Phnom-Penh 900,000 (1991 est).
Other major city: Battambang (Batdambang) 45,000 (1987 est).
Languages: Khmer (official), French.
Religion: Buddhist (official; majority).
Education: is compulsory, in theory, between the ages of six and 12. *Adult literacy:* 74%. *Universities:* one.
Defence: (1993 figures) *Army:* 50,000 personnel. *Air force:* 1000. *Navy:* 1000. *Local paramilitary:* 50,000. *Conscription:* none.

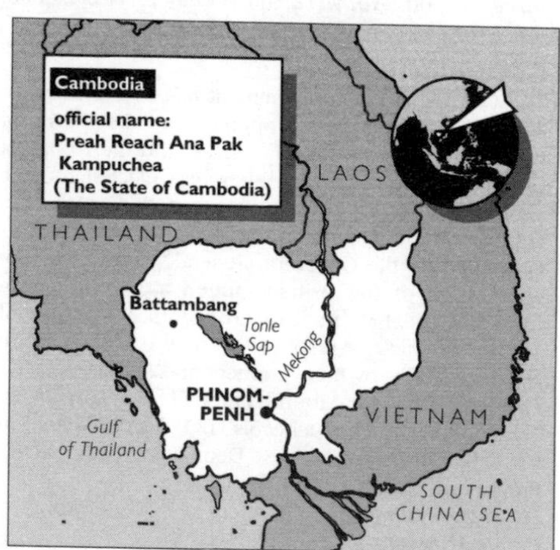

Government

The 120-member National Assembly is elected by universal adult suffrage for five years. The monarchy was restored in 1993. The King appoints a Prime Minister who enjoys a majority in the Assembly. The PM, in turn, appoints a Council of Ministers.
Largest parties: (monarchist-centrist) United National Front for an Independent, Neutral, Peaceful and Cooperative Cambodia (FUNCINPEC), (former Communist) Cambodian People's Party (CPP), (Buddhist) Liberal Democratic Party.
Local government: 22 provinces.
Sovereign: HM Norodom Sihanouk, King of Cambodia (who was restored to the throne on 24 September 1993, having abdicated 2 March 1955. He originally came to the throne on 16 April 1941).
Prime Minister: HRH Prince Norodom Ranariddh (FUNCINPEC).

Geography

Central Cambodia consists of fertile plains in the Mekong River valley and surrounding the Tonle Sap (Great Lake). To the north and east are plateaux covered by forests and savannah. The mountains occupy the south ***Principal river:*** Mekong. ***Highest point:*** Phnum Aural 1813m (5947 ft).
Climate: Cambodia is tropical and humid. The monsoon season (June–November) brings heavy rain to the whole country, with annual totals as high as 5000 mm (200 in) in the mountains.

Economy

Invasion, civil wars, massacres of the civilian population (1976–79) and the (temporary) abolition of currency (in 1978) all but destroyed the economy. Aided by the Vietnamese from 1979 to 1989, agriculture and, to a lesser extent, industry were slowly reconstructed. The rebuilding of Cambodia's infrastructure increased in the 1990s but the country remains one of the world's poorest nations. Rice yields – formerly exported – still fall short of Cambodia's own basic needs. ***Currency:*** Riel.

Recent History

A French protectorate was established in 1863 and continued, apart from Japanese occupation during World War II, until independence in 1953. Throughout this period, the monarchy remained in nominal control. In 1955, King Norodom Sihanouk abdicated to lead a broad coalition government, but he could not prevent Cambodia's involvement in the Vietnam War or allay US fears of his sympathies for the Communists. In 1970 he was overthrown by a pro-USA military junta, which, in turn, was attacked by Communist Khmer Rouge guerrillas, who sought to create a self-sufficient workers' utopia. The Khmer Rouge were finally victorious in 1975. Under Pol Pot, they forcibly evacuated the towns and massacred over one million of their compatriots. In 1978 Vietnam – Cambodia's traditional foe – invaded, overthrowing the Khmer Rouge. The hostility between the two countries was sharpened by the Sino-Soviet split in which they took different sides. After Vietnamese troops withdrew (1989), forces of the exiled government coalition invaded. In 1991, the country's warring factions agreed a peace plan that included free elections and UN supervision and participation in the administration of Cambodia. Although the Khmer Rouge withdrew from the plan, multi-party elections were held in 1993 and the monarchy was restored. The Khmer Rouge remain active in parts of the country.

CAMEROON

Official name: La République unie du Cameroun (The United Republic of Cameroon).
Member of: UN, OAU.
Area: 475,442 km² (183,569 sq mi).
Population: 13,100,000 (1993 est).
Capital: Yaoundé 712,000 (1987 est).
Other major cities: Douala 1,117,000, Garoua 142,000, Maroua 123,000, Bafoussam 113,000, Nkongsamba 112,000 (1987 est).
Languages: French and English (both official).
Religions: animist (40%), Sunni Islam (20%), Roman Catholic (20%).
Education: is compulsory, in theory, between the ages of six and 12 in East Cameroon, and six and 13 in West Cameroon. *Adult literacy:* 54%. *Universities:* one.
Defence: (1993 figures) *Army:* 6600 personnel. *Air force:* 300. *Navy:* 1200. *Paramilitary:* 4000. *Conscription:* none.

Government

The 180 members of the National Assembly are elected for a five-year term by universal adult suffrage. The President – who is also directly elected for a five-year term – appoints a Prime Minister and a Council of Ministers.
Largest parties: (former monopoly) Cameroon People's Democratic Movement (RDPC) and its allies – National Union for Democracy and Progress (UNDP), Union for the Peoples of Cameroon (UPC), Movement for the Defence of the Republic (MDR); (opposition coalition) Union for Change (UC).
Local government: 10 provinces.
President: Paul Biya (RDPC).
Prime Minister: Simon Achidi Achu (RDPC).

Geography

In the west, a chain of highlands rises to the volcanic Mount Cameroon. In the north, savannah plains dip towards Lake Chad. The coastal plains and plateaux in the south and the centre are covered with tropical forest. ***Principal rivers:*** Bénoué, Sanaga. ***Highest point:*** Mount Cameroon 4069m (13,353 ft).
Climate: Cameroon is tropical, with hot, rainy conditions on the coast, but drier inland.

Economy

Cameroon is a major producer of cocoa, and other export crops include bananas, coffee, cotton, rubber and palm oil. The diversity of Cameroon's agriculture, and the rapid development of the petroleum industry, have given Cameroon one of the highest living standards in tropical Africa. ***Currency:*** CFA franc.

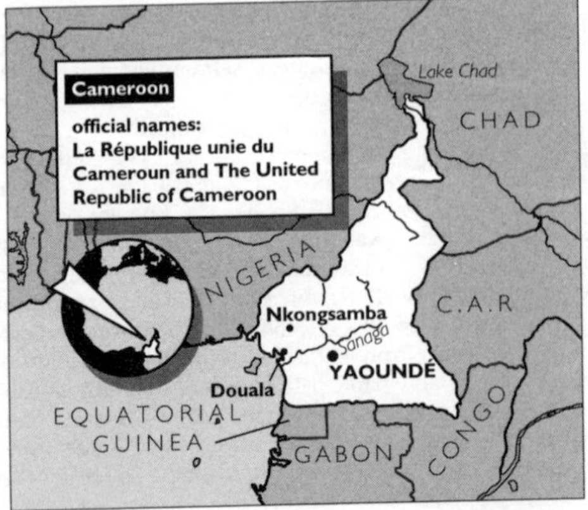

Recent History

Germany declared a protectorate over Kamerun in 1884. After World War I, Cameroon was divided between the UK and France. The French Cameroons became independent in 1960. Following a plebiscite (1961), the north of the British Cameroons merged with Nigeria; the south federated with the former French territory. A single-party state was established in 1966 and a unitary system replaced the federation in 1972. Political pluralism returned in 1992, but multi-party elections in 1993 were alleged to be fraudulent by the opposition.

CANADA

Member of: UN, Commonwealth, OAS, NATO, NAFTA, OSCE, G7, Apec.
Area: 9,970,610 km² (3,849,674 sq mi).
Population: 28,149,000 (1993 est).
Capital: Ottawa 921,000 (city 314,000; 1991 census).
Other major cities: Toronto 3,893,000 (city 636,000), Montréal 3,127,000 (city 1,018,000), Vancouver 1,603,000 (city 472,000), Edmonton 840,000 (city 617,000), Calgary 754,000 (city 711,000), Winnipeg 652,000 (city 617,000), Québec 646,000 (city 168,000), Hamilton 600,000 (city 318,000), St Catharine's-Niagara 365,000 (St Catharine's city 129,000), Halifax 321,000 (city 114,000), Victoria 288,000 (city 71,000), Windsor 262,000 (city 191,000), Oshawa 240,000 (city 129,000), Saskatoon 210,000 (city 186,000), Regina 192,000 (city 179,000), St John's 172,000 (city 96,000), Chicoutimi-Jonquière 161,000 (Chicoutimi 63,000), Sudbury 158,000 (city 93,000) (1991 census).
Languages: English (62% as a first language; official), French (25% as a first language; official); bilingual 16%.
Religions: Roman Catholic (45%), United Church of Canada (15%), Anglican (10%).
Education: is compulsory in all provinces between the ages of five or six and 15 or 16. *Adult literacy:* 97%. *Universities:* 69.
Defence: (1993 figures) *Army:* 20,000 personnel. *Air force:* 20,600. *Navy:* 12,500. *Other forces:* 25,000. *Conscription:* none.

Government

The Canadian Federal Parliament has two houses – a Senate of 112 members appointed by the Governor General to represent the provinces, and the House of Commons, whose 295 members are elected for five years by universal adult suffrage. A Prime Minister, commanding a majority in the House of Commons, is appointed by the Governor General, who is the representative of the British Queen as sovereign of Canada. The PM, in turn, appoints a Cabinet of Ministers which is responsible to the House. Each province has its own government and legislature.
Largest parties: Liberal Party (Lib), (nationalist Francophone) Bloc Québecois (BQ), (radical) Reform Party, (social democrat) New Democratic Party (NDP), Progressive Conservative Party (PC).
Local government: 10 provinces and two territories.
Prime Minister: Jean Chrétien (Lib).

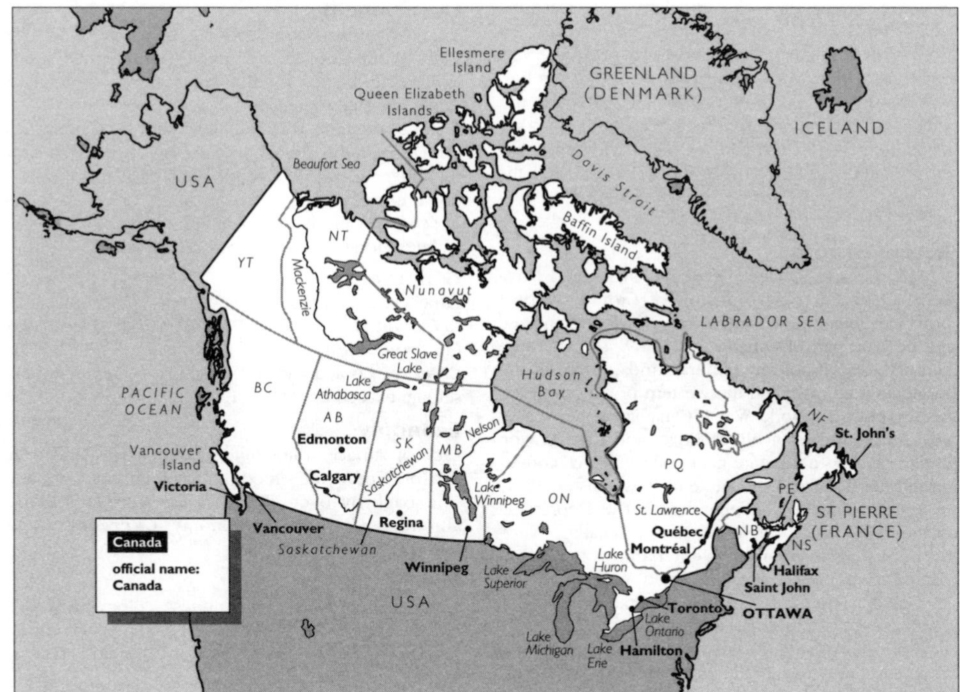

Provinces and territories

Alberta *Area:* 661,199 km² (255,285 sq mi). *Population:* 2,628,000 (1992 est). *Capital:* Edmonton.

British Columbia *Area:* 948,596 km² (366,255 sq mi). *Population:* 3,448,000 (1992 est). *Capital:* Victoria.

Manitoba *Area:* 650,087 km² (250,947 sq mi). *Population:* 1,112,000 (1992 est). *Capital:* Winnipeg.

New Brunswick *Area:* 73,437 km² (28,354 sq mi). *Population:* 749,000 (1992 est). *Capital:* Fredericton.

Newfoundland and Labrador *Area:* 404,517 km² (156,185 sq mi). *Population:* 581,000 (1992 est). *Capital:* St John's.

Nova Scotia *Area:* 55,490 km² (21,425 sq mi). *Population:* 921,000 (1992 est). *Capital:* Halifax.

Ontario *Area:* 1,068,582 km² (412,582 sq mi). *Population:* 10,593,000 (1992 est). *Capital:* Toronto.

Prince Edward Island *Area:* 5657 km² (2184 sq mi). *Population:* 130,000 (1992 est). *Capital:* Charlotte town.

Québec *Area:* 1,540,680 km² (594,860 sq mi). *Population:* 7,143,000 (1992 est). *Capital:* Québec.

Saskatchewan *Area:* 652,330 km² (251,866 sq mi). *Population:* 1,004,000 (1992 est). *Capital:* Regina.

Northwest Territories Area: 3,379,285 km² (1,304,903 sq mi). *Population:* 58,000 (1992 est). *Capital:* Yellowknife. Northwest Territories are to be divided into Northwest Territories (probably renamed Denedeh) and Nunavut.

(**Northwest Territories** or **Denedeh** *Area:* 1,178,000 km² (454,900 sq mi). *Population:* 36,000 (1992 est). *Capital:* Yellowknife.)

(**Nunavut** *Area:* 2,201,400 km² (850,000 sq mi). *Population:* 22,000. *Capital:* Iqaluit.)

Yukon Territory *Area:* 482,515 km² (186,299 sq mi). *Population:* 28,000 (1992 est). *Capital:* Whitehorse.

Geography

Nearly one half of Canada is covered by the Laurentian (or Canadian) Shield, a relatively flat region of hard rocks stretching round Hudson's Bay. Inland, the Shield ends in a scarp that is pronounced in the east, beside the lowlands around the St Lawrence River and the Great Lakes. To the west, a line of major lakes (including Lake Winnipeg) marks the boundary with the interior plains, the Prairies. A broad belt of mountains – over 800 km (500 mi) wide – lies west of the plains. This western cordillera comprises the Rocky, Mackenzie, Coast and St Elias Mountains, which include Canada's highest point, Mount Logan. A lower, discontinuous, chain of highlands borders the east of Canada, running from Baffin Island to Nova Scotia. ***Principal rivers:*** Mackenzie-Slave, Peace, St Lawrence, Yukon-Nisutlin, Nelson, Saskatchewan. ***Highest point:*** Mount Logan 5951m (19,524 ft).

Climate: Much of Canada experiences extreme temperatures, with mild summers and long, cold winters. The climate in the far north is polar. Average winter temperatures only remain above freezing point on the Pacific coast. Precipitation is heavy in the west. In the rest of the country, rainfall totals are moderate or light. Most of Canada experiences heavy winter snowfalls.

Economy

Canada enjoys one of the highest standards of living in the world, due, in part, to great mineral resources. There are substantial deposits of zinc, nickel, gold, silver, iron ore, uranium, copper, cobalt and lead, as well as major reserves of petroleum and natural gas, and enormous hydroelectric-power potential. These resources are the basis of such industries as petroleum refining, motor vehicles, metal refining, chemicals and iron and steel. Canada is one of the world's leading exporters of cereals – in particular, wheat from the Prairie provinces. Other agricultural interests include fruit (mainly apples), beef cattle and potatoes. Vast coniferous forests have given rise to large lumber, wood-pulp and paper industries. Rich Atlantic and Pacific fishing grounds have made Canada the world's leading exporter of fish and seafood. The country has an important banking and insurance sector, and the economy is closely linked with that of the USA within NAFTA. ***Currency:*** Canadian dollar.

Recent History

In 1867 Ontario, Québec, New Brunswick and Nova Scotia formed the Dominion of Canada. Other provinces joined (1870–1905), but Newfoundland did not become part of Canada until 1949. The late 19th century saw important mineral finds, such as the Klondike gold rush, and the western provinces developed rapidly. In World War I, Canadian forces distinguished themselves at Vimy Ridge, and Canada won itself a place as a separate nation at the peace conferences after the war. The Statute of Westminster (1931) recognized Canadian independence. The Depression of the 1930s had a severe impact on Canada – Newfoundland, for example, went bankrupt. Canada played an important role in World War II and the Korean War, and was a founder member of NATO. Since the 1970s there has been friction over the use and status of the French language. Since constitutional amendments recognizing Québec's special status were rejected in 1990, separatist pressure has increased in the province.

CAPE VERDE

Official name: A República de Cabo Verde (The Republic of Cape Verde).
Member of: UN, OAU, ECOWAS.
Area: 4033 km² (1557 sq mi).
Population: 350,000 (1993 est).
Capital: Praia 62,000 (1990 est).
Other major city: Mindelo 47,000 (1990 est).
Languages: Portuguese (official), Crioulu (Creole; majority).
Religion: Roman Catholic (over 92%).
Education: is compulsory between the ages of six and 13. *Adult literacy:* 47%. *Universities:* none.
Defence: (1993 figures) *Army:* 1000 personnel. *Air force:* 100. *Conscription:* none.

Government

The 79-member National Assembly is elected for five years by universal adult suffrage. The Assembly elects a President – also for five years – who appoints a Prime Minister and a Council of Ministers.
Largest parties: (centre) Movement for Democracy (MPD), (socialist former monopoly) African Party for the Independence of Cape Verde (PAICV).
Local government: 14 districts.
President: Antonio Mascarenhas (MPD).
Prime Minister: Carlos Veiga (MPD).

Geography

Cape Verde consists of ten volcanic, semiarid islands. ***Principal rivers:*** none. ***Highest point:*** Monte Fogo (an active volcano) 2829m (9281 ft).
Climate: Cooled by northeast winds, temperatures seldom exceed 27 °C (80 °F). Rainfall is low.

Economy

Lack of surface water hinders agriculture, and over 90% of Cape Verde's food has to be imported. Money sent back by over 700 000 Cape Verdeans living abroad is vital to the economy. ***Currency:*** Cape Verde escudo.

Recent History

Cape Verde, a former Portuguese colony, achieved independence in 1975 under a Marxist-Leninist regime. A free-market economy and a multi-party system were introduced in 1990.

CENTRAL AFRICAN REPUBLIC

Official name: La République centrafricaine (The Central African Republic).
Member of: UN, OAU.
Area: 622,436 km² (240,323 sq mi).
Population: 2,999,000 (1993 est).
Capital: Bangui 598,000 (1988 est).
Other major cities: Bambari 52,000, Berbérati 42,000 (1987 est).
Languages: French (official), Sangho (national).
Religions: various Protestant Churches (48%), Roman Catholic (32%), animist (under 20%).
Education: is compulsory, in theory, between the ages of six and 14. *Adult literacy:* 34%. *Universities:* one.
Defence: (1993 figures) *Army:* 3500 personnel. *Air force:* 300. *Paramilitary:* 2700. *Conscription:* none.

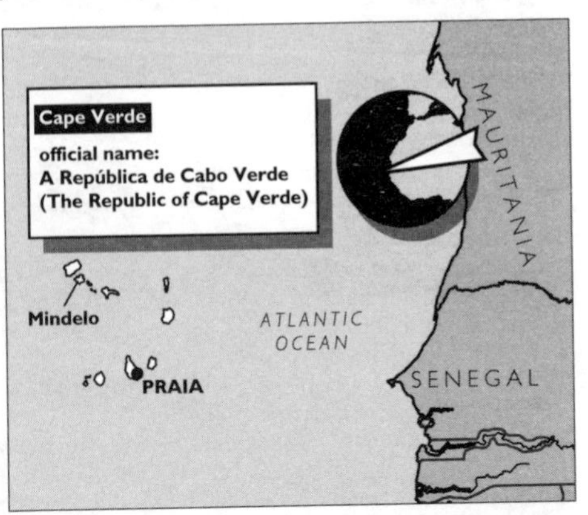

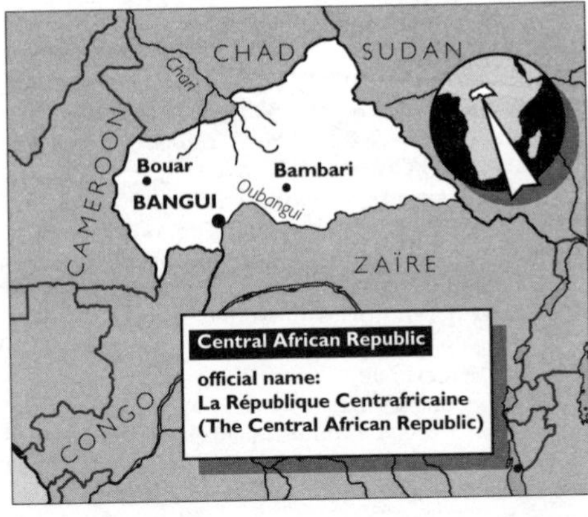

Government

The President – who appoints a Council of Ministers – is elected for a six-year term by universal adult suffrage. The 85-member National Assembly is elected directly for a five-year term. An appointed Economic and Regional Council has some of the functions of an upper house.
Largest parties: Central African People's Liberation Party (MPLC), (former monopoly) Central African Democratic Rally (RDC), Patriotic Front for Progress (FPP), Liberal Democratic Party (PDL), Alliance for Democracy and Progress (ADP), David Dacko Movement (MDD).
Local government: 16 prefectures.
President: Ange-Félix Patasse (MPLC).
Prime Minister: Jean-Luc Mandaba (MPLC).

Geography

The country is a low plateau, rising along the border with Sudan to the Bongos Mountains and in the west to the Monts Karre. ***Principal rivers:*** Oubangui, Chari, Zaire. ***Highest point:*** Mont Gaou 1420m (4659 ft).
Climate: The north is savannah, with little rain between November and March. The south is equatorial with high temperatures and heavy rainfall.

Economy

Subsistence farming dominates, although cotton and coffee are grown for export. Diamonds contribute over 30% of the state's foreign earnings. The country is poor, and – largely owing to mismanagement under Bokassa – its economy has declined since independence. ***Currency:*** CFA franc.

Recent History

French influence began in 1889, and the region became the French colony of Oubangi-Chari in 1903. It suffered greatly from the activities of companies that were granted exclusive rights to large areas of the colony. Independence – as the Central African Republic – was gained in 1960. Jean-Bédel Bokassa took power in a coup in 1965. In 1976 he declared himself emperor and was crowned in an extravagantly expensive ceremony. Revolts by students and schoolchildren helped to end his murderous regime in 1979. Multi-party elections were held in 1993.

CHAD

Official name: La République du Tchad (The Republic of Chad).
Member of: UN, OAU.
Area: 1,284,000 km² (495,752 sq mi).
Population: 6,118,000 (1993 est).
Capital: N'Djamena 688,000 (1992 est).
Other major cities: Sarh 130,000, Moundou 118,000 (1992 est).
Languages: French and Arabic (both official); over 100 local languages.
Religions: Sunni Islam (50%), animist (25%).
Education: is compulsory, in theory, between the ages of six and 14. *Adult literacy:* 30%. *Universities:* one.
Defence: (1993 figures) *Army:* 25,000 personnel. *Air force:* 200. *Paramilitary:* 4500. *Conscription:* none.

Government

Following a military coup in 1991, a transitional government system was introduced in 1993 when a national conference chose a 57-member Higher Transitional Council.

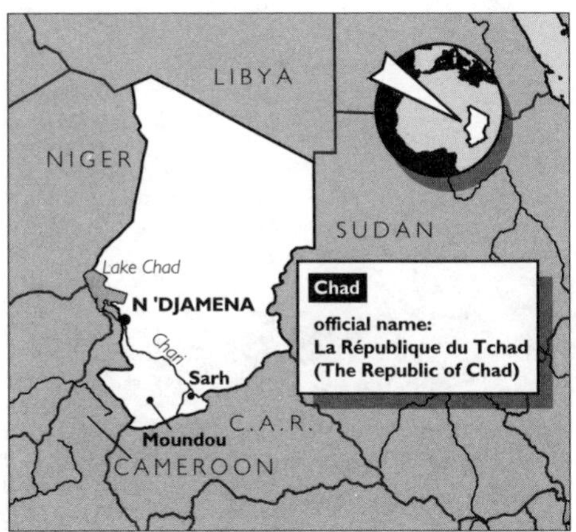

Largest parties: Patriotic Salvation Movement (MPS); about 30 other political parties have been registered for the forthcoming multi-party elections.
Local government: 14 prefectures.
President: Idriss Deby (MPS).
Prime Minister: Delwa Kassire Koumakoye (MPS).

Geography

Deserts in the north include the Tibesti Mountains. Savannah and semidesert in the centre slope down to Lake Chad. The Oubangui Plateau in the south is covered by tropical rain forest. ***Principal rivers:*** Chari, Logone. ***Highest point:*** Emi Koussi 3415m (11,204 ft).
Climate: Chad is hot and dry in the north, and tropical in the south.

Economy

Chad – one of the poorest countries in the world – has been wracked by civil war and drought. With few natural resources, it relies on subsistence farming, exports of cotton and on foreign aid. ***Currency:*** CFA franc.

Recent History

The area around Lake Chad became French in the late 19th century. The French conquest of the north was not completed until 1916. Since independence in 1960, Chad has been torn apart by a bitter civil war between the Muslim Arab north and the Christian and animist Black African south. Libya and France intervened forcefully on several occasions, but neither was able to achieve its aims. In 1987, an uneasy ceasefire was declared, but, following another civil war, military regimes took power in 1990 and 1991 and unrest continues.

CHILE

Official name: República de Chile (The Republic of Chile).
Member of: UN, OAS, ALADI, Apec.
Area: 756,626 km² (292,135 sq mi).
Population: 13,542,000 (1993 est).
Capital: Santiago 5,181,000 (city 4,628,000; 1993 est). (The legislature meets at Valparaiso.)
Other major cities: Viña del Mar 319,000, Concepción 318,000, Valparaiso 302,000, Temuco 263,000, Talcahuano 258,000, Antofagasta 228,000 (1993 est).
Languages: Spanish (official; 95%), Araucanian (5%).
Religions: Roman Catholic (79%), various Protestant Churches (6%).

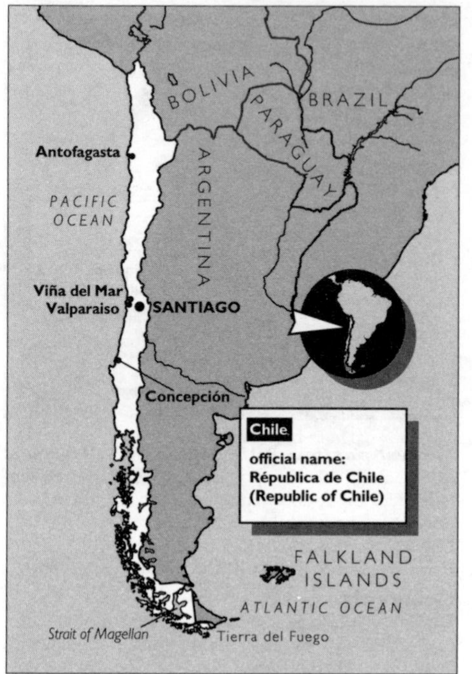

Education: is compulsory between the ages of six or seven and 13 or 14. *Adult literacy:* 93%. *Universities:* 27 (including institutes of university status).

Defence: (1993 figures) *Army:* 54,000 personnel. *Air force:* 12,800. *Navy:* 25,000. *Paramilitary:* 31,000. *Conscription:* two years.

Government

Executive power is held by the President, who appoints a Cabinet of Ministers. The President is elected by universal adult suffrage for four years. The National Congress has an upper chamber of 39 senators directly elected for eight years and eight senators appointed by the President, and a lower chamber of 120 deputies elected for four years by universal adult suffrage.

Largest parties: (conservative) Christian Democrat Party (PDC), Socialist Party (PAIS), (right-wing) National Renovation Party (RN), (right-wing) Independent Democratic Union (UDI).

Local government: 12 regions and one metropolitan area.

President: Eduardo Frei (PDC).

External territory: Chile claims sovereignty over part of Antarctica. See Other Territories (beginning on p. 729).

Geography

For almost 4000 km (2500 mi), the Andes form the eastern boundary of Chile. Parallel to the Andes is a depression, in which lies the Atacama Desert in the north and fertile plains in the centre. A mountain chain runs between the depression and the coast, and, in the south, forms a string of islands. ***Principal rivers:*** Loa, Maule, Bio-Bio. ***Highest point:*** Ojos del Solado 6895m (22,588 ft).

Climate: The temperate climate is influenced by the cool Humboldt Current. Rainfall ranges from being negligible in the Atacama Desert in the north to heavy – over 2300 mm (90 in) – in the south.

Economy

The main agricultural region is the central plains, where cereals (mainly wheat and maize) and fruit (notably grapes) are important. Major fishing grounds yield one of the world's largest catches of fish. There are considerable mineral resources and great hydroelectric-power potential. Chile is a leading exporter of copper, and has major reserves of iron ore, coal, petroleum and natural gas. Industry includes food processing, timber industries and textiles. Chile has achieved high economic growth rates in the 1990s and has developed important trading links with other Pacific Rim countries. ***Currency:*** Chilean peso.

Recent History

In 1817, troops led by José de San Martín crossed from Argentina to aid O'Higgins, who led Chile to independence from Spain in 1818. O'Higgins offended the powerful landowners and was exiled in 1823. For the next century – during which Chile gained territory in two wars against Peru and Bolivia – conservative landowners held power. Between the late 1920s and the 1940s, Chile was governed by liberal and radical regimes, but social and economic change was slow. The election of the Christian Democrats (1964) brought some reforms, but not until Salvador Allende's Marxist government was elected in 1970 were major changes – including land reform – realized. Chile was polarized between right and left, and political chaos resulted in a US-backed military coup led by General Augusto Pinochet in 1973. Tens of thousands of leftists were killed, imprisoned or exiled by the junta. Pinochet reversed Allende's reforms, restructuring the economy in favour of landowners and exporters. Pressure on the dictatorship from within Chile and abroad brought the return of democratic rule in 1990.

CHINA

Official name: Zhonghua Renmin Gongheguo (The People's Republic of China).

Member of: UN, Apec.

Area: 9,571,900 km² (3,695,710 sq mi).

Population: 1,179,470,000 (1993 est).

Capital: Beijing (Peking) 10,940,000 (including suburbs; 1992 est).

Other major cities: Shanghai 13,400,000, Tianjin (Tientsin) 9,090,000 (both 1992 est), Shenyang 4,450,000, Wuhan 3,750,000, Guangzhou (Canton) 3,580,000, Chongqing 2,980,000, Harbin 2,930,000, Chengdu 2,810,000, Xian 2,760,000, Nanjing (Nanking) 2,500,000, Zibo 2,460,000, Dalian (Darien) 2,400,000, Jinan 2,290,000, Changchun 2,070,000, Qingdao 2,040,000, Shenzhen 2,000,000, Taiyuan 1,900,000, Zhengzhou 1,660,000, Kunming 1,500,000, Guiyang (Kweiyang) 1,490,000, Tangshan 1,490,000, Lanzhou (Lanchow) 1,480,000, Anshan 1,370,000, Qiqihar (Tsitsihar) 1,370,000, Fushun 1,330,000, Hangzhou 1,330,000, Nanchang 1,330,000, Changsha 1,300,000, Shijiazhuang (Shihkiachwang) 1,300,000, Fuzhou (Fushu) 1,270,000, Jilin (Kirin) 1,250,000, Baotou (Paotow) 1,180,000, Huainan 1,170,000, Luoyang 1,160,000, Urümqi 1,110,000, Datong

1,090,000, Handan 1,090,000, Ningbo 1,070,000, Nanning 1,050,000 (1991 est).

Languages: Chinese (Guoyo or 'Mandarin' dialect in the majority, with local dialects in south and south-east, e.g. Cantonese and Wu), small Mongol, Tibetan and other minorities.

Religions: Officially atheist but those religions and philosophies practised include traditional Chinese folk religions, Confucianism and Daoism (over 20% together), Buddhism (c. 15%).

Education: is compulsory between the ages of seven and 12. *Adult literacy:* 78%. *Universities:* 79 state universities, several private universities, plus 45 other institutes of university status.

Defence: (1993 figures) *Army:* 2,300,000 personnel. *Air force:* 470,000. *Navy:* 260,000. *Paramilitary:* 1,200,000. *Conscription:* is selective; three years in the army and the marines, four years in the navy and air force.

Government

The 2921 deputies of the National People's Congress are elected for a five-year term by the People's Congresses of the provinces, and by the army. The Congress elects a Standing Committee, a President (for a five-year term), a Prime Minister and a State Council (or Cabinet) – all of whom are responsible to the Congress.

Political party: The only legal party is the Chinese Communist Party, which holds a Congress every five years. The Party Congress elects a Central Committee, which in turn elects a Politburo, and it is these two bodies that hold effective power.

Local government: 22 provinces, five autonomous provinces and three municipal provinces.

President: Jiang Zemin.

General Secretary of the Communist Party: Jiang Zemin.

Prime Minister: Li Peng.

Provinces

Anhui *Area:* 139,900 km^2 (54,000 sq mi). *Population:* 57,610,000 (1992 est). *Capital:* Hefei..

Beijing (Peking) (municipal province) *Area:* 16,800 km^2 (6500 sq mi). *Population:* 10,940,000 (1992 est). *Capital:* Beijing.

Fujian *Area:* 123,100 km^2 (47,500 sq mi). *Population:* 30,790,000 (1992 est). *Capital:* Fuzhou.

Gansu *Area:* 366,500 km^2 (141,500 sq mi). *Population:* 22,850,000 (1992 est). *Capital:* Lanzhou.

Guangdong *Area:* 197,100 km^2 (76,100 sq mi). *Population:* 64,390,000 (1992 est). *Capital:* Guangzhou (Canton).

Guangxi Zhuang (autonomous province) *Area:* 220,400 km^2 (85,100 sq mi). *Population:* 43,240,000 (1992 est). *Capital:* Nanning.

Guizhou *Area:* 174,000 km^2 (67,200 sq mi). *Population:* 33,150,000 (1992 est). *Capital:* Guiyang.
Hainan *Area:* 34,300 km^2 (13,200 sq mi). *Population:* 6,740,000 (1992 est). *Capital:* Haikou.
Hebei *Area:* 202,700 km^2 (78,200 sq mi). *Population:* 62,200,000 (1992 est). *Capital:* Shijiazhuang.
Heilongjiang *Area:* 463,600 km^2 (179,000 sq mi). *Population:* 35,750,000 (1992 est). *Capital:* Harbin.
Henan *Area:* 167,000 km^2 (64,500 sq mi). *Population:* 87,630,000 (1992 est). *Capital:* Zhengzhou.
Hubei *Area:* 187,500 km^2 (72,400 sq mi). *Population:* 55,120,000 (1992 est). *Capital:* Wuhan.
Hunan *Area:* 210,500 km^2 (81,300 sq mi). *Population:* 62,090,000 (1992 est). *Capital:* Changsha.
Jiangsu *Area:* 102,600 km^2 (39,600 sq mi). *Population:* 68,440,000 (1992 est). *Capital:* Nanjing.
Jiangxi *Area:* 164,800 km^2 (63,600 sq mi). *Population:* 38,650,000 (1992 est). *Capital:* Nanchang.
Jilin *Area:* 187,000 km^2 (72,200 sq mi). *Population:* 25,090,000 (1992 est). *Capital:* Changchun.
Liaoning *Area:* 151,000 km^2 (58,300 sq mi). *Population:* 39,900,000 (1992 est). *Capital:* Shenyang.
Nei Monggol (Inner Mongolia) (autonomous province) *Area:* 1,177,500 km^2 (454,600 sq mi). *Population:* 21,840,000 (1992 est). *Capital:* Hohhot.
Ningxia Hui (autonomous province) *Area:* 66,400 km^2 (25,600 sq mi). *Population:* 4,800,000 (1992 est). *Capital:* Yinchuan.
Qinghai *Area:* 721,000 km^2 (278,400 sq mi). *Population:* 4,540,000 (1992 est). *Capital:* Xining.
Shaanxi *Area:* 195,800 km^2 (75,600 sq mi). *Population:* 33,630,000 (1992 est). *Capital:* Xian.
Shandong *Area:* 153,300 km^2 (59,200 sq mi). *Population:* 85,700,000 (1992 est). *Capital:* Jinan.
Shanghai (municipal province) *Area:* 6200 km^2 (2400 sq mi). *Population:* 13,400,000 (1992 est). *Capital:* Shanghai.
Shanxi *Area:* 157,100 km^2 (60,700 sq mi). *Population:* 29,420,000 (1992 est). *Capital:* Taiyuan.
Sichuan *Area:* 569,000 km^2 (219,700 sq mi). *Population:* 108,970,000 (1992 est). *Capital:* Chengdu.
Tianjin (Tientsin) (municipal province) Area: 11,300 km^2 (4400 sq mi). *Population:* 9,090,000 (1992 est). *Capital:* Tianjin.
Xinjiang Uygur (Sinkiang) (autonomous province) *Area:* 1,646,900 km^2 (635,900 sq mi). *Population:* 15,550,000 (1992 est). *Capital:* Urümqi.
Xizang (Tibet) (autonomous province) *Area:* 1,221,600 km^2 (471,700 sq mi). *Population:* 2,260,000 (1992 est). *Capital:* Lhasa.
Yunnan *Area:* 436,200 km^2 (168,400 sq mi). *Population:* 37,820,000 (1992 est). *Capital:* Kunming.
Zhejiang *Area:* 101,800 km^2 (39,300 sq mi). *Population:* 42,020,000 (1992 est). *Capital:* Hangzhou.

Geography

China is the third largest country in the world in area and the largest in population. Almost half of China comprises mountain chains, mainly in the west, including the Altaï and Tien Shan Mountains in Xinjiang Uygur, and the Kun Lun Mountains to the north of Tibet. The Tibetan Plateau – at an altitude of 3000 m (10,000 ft) – is arid. In the south of Tibet is the Himalaya, containing 40 peaks over 7000 m (23,000 ft). In the far south, the Yunnan Plateau rises to nearly 3700 m (12,000 ft), while in the far northeast, ranges of hills and mountains almost enclose the Northeast Plain, formerly known as Manchuria. The Nan Ling Range of hills and mountains crosses central China and separates the basins of the Yellow (Huang He) and Yangtze (Chang Jiang). In east and central China, three great lowlands support intensive agriculture and dense populations – the plains of central China, the Sichuan Basin and the North China Plain. A vast loess plateau, deeply dissected by ravines, lies between the Mongolian Plateau – which contains the Gobi Desert – and the deserts of the Tarim and Dzungarian Basins in the northwest. ***Principal rivers:*** Yangtze (Chang Jiang), Huang He (Yellow River), Xijiang (Sikiang), Heilongjiang (Amur), Wu, Xi Jiang, Dadu. ***Highest point:*** Mt Everest 8863m (29,078 ft).
Climate: In general, temperatures increase from north to south, and rainfall increases from northwest to southeast. Northeast China has a continental climate with warm and humid summers, long cold winters, and rainfall under 750 mm (30 in). The central lowlands contain the hottest areas of China, and have 750 to 1100 mm (30 to 40 in) of rainfall. The south is wetter, while the extreme subtropical south experiences the monsoon. The continental loess plateau is cold in the winter, warm in summer and has under 500 mm (20 in) of rain. The northwest is arid, continental and experiences cold winters. The west – Tibet, Xinjiang Uygur, Gansu and Nei Monggol – experiences an extreme climate owing to its altitude and distance from the sea; rainfall is low and most of Tibet has ten months of frost.

Economy

Agriculture occupies 60% of the labour force. All large-scale production is on collective farms, but traditional and inefficient practices remain. Almost half the arable land is irrigated, and China is the world's largest producer of rice. Other major crops include wheat, maize, sweet potatoes, sugar cane and soyabeans. Livestock, fruit, vegetables and fishing are also important, but China is unable to supply all its own food. Mineral and fuel resources are considerable and, for the most part, underdeveloped. They include coal, petroleum, natural gas, iron ore, bauxite, tin and antimony in major reserves, as well as huge hydroelectric power potential. The economy is centrally planned, with all industrial plant owned by the state. Petrochemical products account for nearly one quarter of China's exports. Other major industries include iron and steel, cement, vehicles, fertilizers, food processing, clothing and textiles. Recent reforms have promoted an 'open-door' policy under which joint ventures with other countries and foreign loans have been encouraged, together with a degree of small-scale private enterprise. Special Economic Zones and 'open cities' were designated in the south and central coastal areas to encourage industrial links with the West. Although foreign investment temporarily diminished after the 1989 pro-democracy movement was suppressed, sustained economic progress has been achieved particularly in the Shanghai area and in southern China, where Guangdong province is the centre of major industrial development. Very high growth rates have been achieved during the past decade. ***Currency:*** Renminbi (or Yuan).

Recent History

At the beginning of the 20th century, China was in turmoil. The authority of the emperor had been weakened in the 19th century by outside powers greedy for trade and by huge rebellions, which had left large areas of the country beyond the control of the central government. In 1911, a revolution, led by the Guomintang (Kuomintang or Nationalists) under

Sun Zhong Shan (Sun Yat-sen; 1866–1925), overthrew the last of the Manchu emperors. Strong in the south, where Sun had established a republic in 1916, the Nationalists faced problems in the north, which was ruled by independent warlords. Sun's successor, Jiang Jie Shi (Chiang Kai-shek; 1887–1976), made some inroads in the north, only to be undermined by the emergent Communist Party. After a series of disasterous urban risings, the Communist Mao Zedong (Mao Tse-tung; 1893–1976) concentrated on rural areas. After being forced to retreat from Jiangxi in 1934, Mao led his followers for 12 months on a 9000 km (5600 mi) trek, the 'Long March', to the remote province of Shaanxi. In 1931, the Japanese seized Manchuria and established a puppet regime. After the Japanese seized Beijing (Peking) and most of coastal China in 1937, Jiang and Mao combined against the invaders but were able to achieve little against superior forces.

After World War II, the Soviets tried to ensure that Mao's Communists took over China. In 1946, Mao marched ino Manchuria, beginning a civil war that lasted until 1949, when Mao declared a People's Republic in Beijing and Jiang fled to the offshore island of Taiwan, where a Nationalist government was set up (see Taiwan, below). In 1950, Chinese forces invaded Tibet, an independent state since 1916. Repressive Communist rule alienated the Tibetans, who, loyal to their religious leader, the Dalai Lama, unsuccessfully rose in revolt in 1959. Since then, Chinese settlement in Tibet has threatened to swamp Tibetan culture. Chinese 'volunteers' were active in the Korean War (1950–53) on behalf of the Communist North Koreans. China has been involved in a number of border disputes and conflicts, including clashes with the USSR in the 1950s, with India in 1962, and with Vietnam in 1979. Relations with the USSR deteriorated in the 1950s, triggered by ideological clashes over the true nature of Communism. The Sino-Soviet split led to the acceleration of Chinese research into atomic weapons – the first Chinese bomb was tested in 1964 – and a rapprochement with the USA in the early 1970s.

The 'Great Leap Forward', an ambitious programme of radicalization in the 1950s, largely failed. In the 1960s, Mao tried again to spread more revolutionary ideas in the so-called Cultural Revolution. Militant students formed groups of Red Guards to attack the existing hierarchy. Thousands died as the students went out of control, and the army had to restore order. After Mao's death (1976), China was effectively under the leadership of Deng Xiaoping (1904–), although he held none of the major state or party offices. A more careful path has been followed at home and abroad; a rapprochement with the USSR was agreed in 1989, and agreement was reached with the UK for the return of Hong Kong to Chinese rule in 1997. China was opened up to foreign technology and investment, together with a degree of free enterprise, but this led to internal pressures for political change, culminating in massive pro-democracy demonstrations by workers and students in 1989. These were brutally suppressed in the massacre of students in Tiananmen Square, Beijing, and hardline leaders gained in influence. Economic progress has been the priority in the 1990s and standards of living have improved. However, an ageing political leadership has continued to deny many basic human rights.

CHINA, REPUBLIC OF (TAIWAN)

Official name: Chung-hua Min Kuo (also transliterated as Zhonghua Minguo) (The Republic of China).
Member of: Apec.
Area: 35,981 km² (13,893 sq mi).
Population: 20,926,000 (1993 est).
Capital: Taipei 2,720,000 (1993 est).
Other major cities: Kaohsiung 1,406,000, Taichung 802,000, Tainan 695,000, Panchiao 544,000 (1993 est).
Language: Chinese (northern or Amoy dialect, popularly known as Mandarin).
Religions: various Chinese folk religions (over 48%; includes Daoism), Buddhist (over 40%).
Education: is compulsory between the ages of six and 15. *Adult literacy:* 93%. *Universities:* 16 plus 11 other institutes of university status.
Defence: (1993 figures) *Army:* 312,000 personnel. *Air force:* 70,000. *Navy:* 60,000. *Paramilitary:* 25,800. *Conscription:* two years.

Government

The 161-member Parliament (the Legislative Yuan) comprises 125 members elected by universal adult suffrage for six years and additional indirectly elected members. The 325-member National Assembly – also directly elected for four years – has no legislative powers, other than to amend the constitution. The President, who from 1996 will be directly elected for six years, appoints a Prime Minister and a Council of Ministers.

Largest parties: (Nationalist Chinese) Guomintang (Kuomintang; KMT), (mainly Taiwanese) Democratic People's Party (DPP).
Local government: 16 counties and seven municipalities.
President: Lee Teng-hui (KMT).
Prime Minister: Lien Chan (KMT).

Geography

Taiwan is an island 160 km (100 mi) off the southeast coast of China. Its mountainous interior rises in the south to Yu Shan. Most of the inhabitants live on the coastal plain in the west. ***Principal rivers:*** Hsia-tanshui, Chosui. ***Highest point:*** Yu Shan 3997m (13,113 ft).
Climate: Taiwan – which is subtropical in the north, and tropical in the south – has rainy summers and mild winters. Tropical cyclones (typhoons) may occur between July and September.

Economy

Despite Taiwan's diplomatic isolation, the island is a major international trading nation, exporting machinery, electronics, and textiles. Mineral resources include coal, marble, gold, petroleum and natural gas. Taiwan has achieved a GDP over one half that of its giant neighbour, mainland China. Despite the fertility of the soil, agriculture has declined in relative importance. ***Currency:*** New Taiwan dollar.

Recent History

A Japanese takeover (1895) of the Chinese island of Taiwan began the modernization of agriculture, transport and education. In 1949, the Nationalist forces of Jiang Jie Shi (Chiang Kai-shek) were driven onto Taiwan by the Communist victory on the mainland. Under US protection, the resulting authoritarian regime on Taiwan declared itself the Republic of China, and claimed to be the legitimate government of all China. America's rapprochement with the mainland People's Republic of China lost Taiwan its UN seat in 1971 and US recognition in 1978. In 1991 Taiwan effectively recognized Communist China, but the island's international status remains problematic. By the late 1980s Taiwan was moving cautiously towards democracy, and in 1988 a native Taiwanese was elected President. A new constitution in 1991 marked the transition to a more Taiwanese, less Chinese, identity.

COLOMBIA

Official name: La República de Colombia (The Republic of Colombia).
Member of: UN, OAS, ALADI, Andean Pact.
Area: 1,141,748 km² (440,831 sq mi).
Population: 33,952,000 (1993 est).
Capital: (Santa Fé de) Bogotá 5,026,000 (including suburbs; 1993 est).
Other major cities: Medellín 2,121,000 (city 1,595,000), Cali 1,657,000, Barranquilla 1,034,000, Cartagena 707,000 (city 688,000), Cúcuta 460,000, Bucaramanga 350,000 (all including suburbs; 1992 est).
Languages: Spanish (official; 99%), over 150 Indian languages.
Religion: Roman Catholic (official; 93%).
Education: is compulsory for five years taken between the ages of six and 14. *Adult literacy:* 87%. *Universities:* 25 state and 24 private universities.
Defence: (1993 figures) *Army:* 120,000 personnel. *Air force:* 7000. *Navy:* 13,000. *Paramilitary:* 8500. *Conscription:* one to two years.

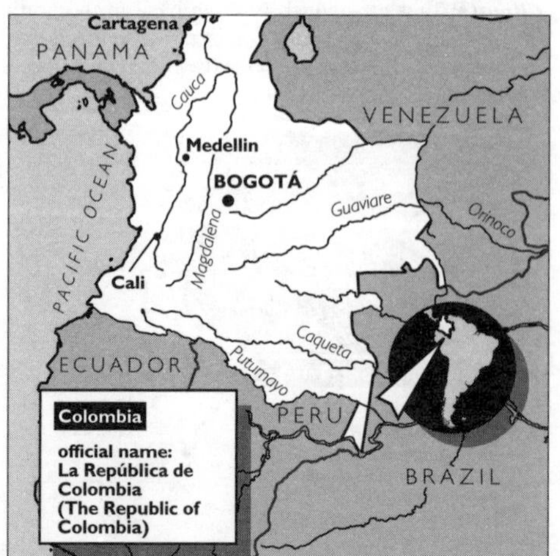

Government

A President (who appoints a Cabinet of 13 members), a Senate of 102 members and a House of Representatives of 161 members are elected for a four-year term by universal adult suffrage.
Largest parties: Liberal Party (PL), Social Conservative Party (PSC), (leftist) April 19th Movement (ADM-19).
Local government: 32 departments and the capital territory.
President: Ernesto Samper (PL).

Geography

The Andes run north to south through Colombia. The greater part of Colombia lies east of the Andes in the mainly treeless grassland plains of the Llanos and the tropical Amazonian rain forest. A coastal plain lies to the west of the mountains. ***Principal rivers:*** Magdalena, Cauca, Amazon. ***Highest point:*** Pico Cristóbal Colón 5775m (18,947 ft).
Climate: The lower Andes are temperate; the mountains over 4000 m (13,100 ft) experience perpetual snow. The rest of the country is tropical. The coasts and the Amazonian Basin are hot and humid, with heavy rainfall. The Llanos have a savannah climate.

Economy

Colombian coffee is the backbone of the country's exports; other cash crops include bananas, sugar cane, flowers and tobacco. However, profits from the illegal cultivation and export of marijuana and cocaine probably produce the greatest revenue. Mineral resources include iron ore, silver, coal, petroleum and natural gas. The main industries are food processing, petroleum refining, fertilizers, cement, textiles, clothing, and iron and steel. ***Currency:*** Colombian peso.

Recent History

The struggle for independence from Spain (1809–19) was fierce and bloody. Almost from that time, the centralizing pro-clerical Conservatives and the federalizing anti-clerical Liberals have struggled for control leading to civil wars (1899–1902 and 1948–57) in which 400,000 people died. From 1957 to 1974 there were agreements between the Liberals and Conservatives to protect a fragile democracy threatened by left-wing guerrillas and right-wing death squads. In the early 1990s, a combination of security measures and amnesties curbed the activities of powerful drug-trafficking cartels, and left-wing guerrillas abandoned their armed struggle in favour of legitimate political activity. Although the infamous Medellín drugs cartel was curtailed in the early 1990s, a new drugs cartel has risen to take its place in Cali.

COMOROS

Official name: La République fédérale islamique des Comores (The Federal Islamic Republic of the Comoros).
Member of: UN, OAU.
Area: 1862 km² (719 sq mi) (excluding Mayotte, which is administered by France).

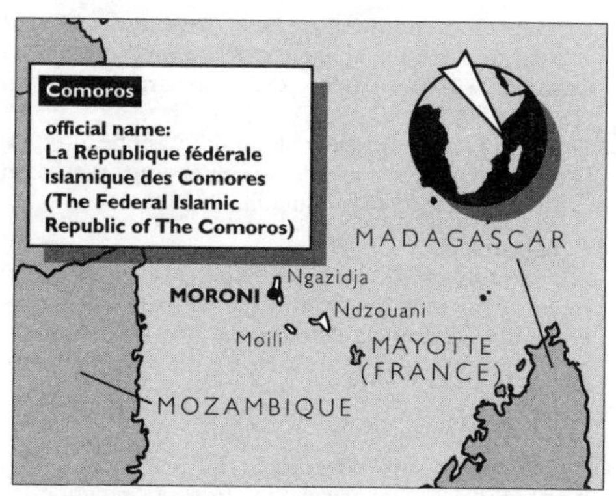

Population: 497,000 (1991 est; excluding Mayotte).
Capital: Moroni 60,000 (city 22,000; 1988 est).
Other main town: Mutsamudu 14,000 (1988 est).
Languages: French and Arabic – both official; Comoran (a blend of Swahili and Arabic).
Religion: Sunni Islam (official; 99%).
Education: is compulsory between the ages of seven and 16. *Adult literacy:* 50%. *Universities:* none.
Defence: (1993 figures) *Army:* 800 personnel. *Conscription:* none.

Government

The President – who is elected for a five-year term by universal adult suffrage – appoints a Council of Ministers. The 42 members of the Federal Assembly are directly elected for five years.
Largest parties: Rally of Democrats for the Republic (RDR), National Union for Democracy for the Comoros (UNDC), (former monopoly) Udzima.
Local government: three island governates.
President: Siad Mohamed Djohar (RDR).
Prime Minister: Halifa Houmadi (RDR).

Islands

Moili *Area:* 290 km² (112 sq mi). *Population:* 25,000 (1991 est). *Capital:* Fomboni.
Ndzouani *Area:* 424 km² (164 sq mi). *Population:* 198,000 (1991 est). *Capital:* Mutsamudu.
Ngazidja *Area:* 1148 km² (443 sq mi). *Population:* 256,000 (1991 est). *Capital:* Moroni.

Geography

Ngazidja (Grande Comore), the largest island, is dry and rocky, rising to an active volcano, Mount Kartala. Ndzouani (Anjouan) is a heavily-eroded volcanic massif. Moili (Mohéli) is a forested plateau with fertile valleys.
Principal rivers: no significant rivers. ***Highest point:*** Mount Kartala 2361m (7746 ft).
Climate: The tropical climate of the Comoros is dry from May to October, but with heavy rain for the rest of the year.

Economy

Poor and eroded soils, overpopulation and few resources combine to make these underdeveloped islands one of the world's poorest countries. Subsistence farming occupies the majority of the population, although vanilla, cloves and ylang-ylang are produced for export. ***Currency:*** Comoran franc.

Recent History

The four Comoran islands became a French colony in 1912. In a referendum in 1974, three islands voted to become independent, which they declared themselves without French agreement. The fourth island, Mayotte, voted against independence, and remains under French rule. From 1978 to 1990, when free elections were held, the republic was an Islamic single-party state.

CONGO

Official name: La République du Congo (The Republic of the Congo).
Member of: UN, OAU.
Area: 342,000 km² (132,047 sq mi).
Population: 2,772,000 (1993 est).
Capital: Brazzaville 940,000 (1992 est).
Other major cities: Pointe-Noire 576,000, Loubomo 84,000 (1992 est).
Languages: French (official), Lingala patois (50%), Monokutuba patois (over 40%), Kongo (45%), Teke (20%).
Religions: Roman Catholic (53%), animist (25%).
Education: is compulsory, in theory, between the ages of six and 16. *Adult literacy:* 57%. *Universities:* one.
Defence: (1993 figures) *Army:* 10,000 personnel. *Air force:* 500. *Navy:* 350. *Paramilitary:* 6100. *Conscription:* none.

Government

The 125-member National Assembly and the President are elected for five years by universal adult suffrage. The 60-member Senate is directly elected for six years. The President appoints a Premier and a Council of Ministers.
Largest parties: Pan-African Union for Social Democracy (UPADS), Union for Democratic Renewal (UDR), (former monopoly, former Communist) Congolese Party of Labour (PCT), Rally for Democratic Social Progress (RDPS), Rally for Democracy and Development (RDD).
Local government: 13 regions.
President: Pascal Lissouba (UPADS).
Prime Minister: Gen. Jacques-Joachim Yhombi-Opango (RDD).

Geography

Behind a narrow coastal plain, the plateaux of the interior are covered by tropical rain forests and rise

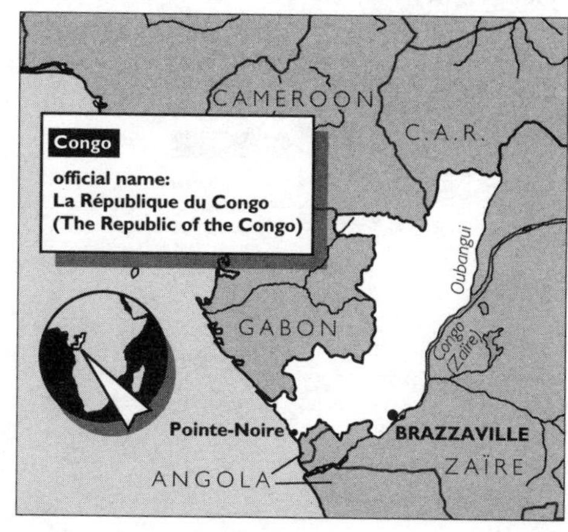

over 700 m (2300 ft). ***Principal river:*** Zaïre (Congo), Oubangui, Niara. ***Highest point:*** Mont de la Lékéti 1040m (3412 ft).
Climate: The Congo's tropical climate is hot and humid. Rainfall exceeds 1200 mm (47 in) a year.

Economy

Petroleum and timber are the mainstays of the economy, which was centrally planned until 1991. Congo is crippled by external debt. Subsistence agriculture – chiefly for cassava – occupies over 30% of the labour force. ***Currency:*** CFA franc.

Recent History

In the 1880s, the explorer Brazza placed the kingdom of the Teke people under French protection, and in 1905 the region became the colony of Moyen-Congo. Independence was gained in 1960. A Marxist-Leninist state was established in 1963, but a multi-party system was restored in 1991.

COSTA RICA

Official name: República de Costa Rica (The Republic of Costa Rica).
Member of: UN, OAS, CACM.
Area: 51,000 km² (19,730 sq mi).
Population: 3,200,000 (1993 est).
Capital: San José 1,040,000 (city 303,000; 1991 est).
Other major cities: Alajuela 158,000, Cartago 109,000, Puntarenas 92,000. Limon 68,000 (1991 est).
Language: Spanish (official).
Religion: Roman Catholic (official).
Education: is compulsory between the ages of six and 15. *Adult literacy:* 93%. *Universities:* six.
Defence: (1993 figures) No armed forces, but 7500 paramilitary Civil Guards.

Government

Executive power is vested in the President, who appoints a Cabinet of Ministers. The President and the 57-member Legislative Assembly are elected for four-year terms by compulsory universal adult suffrage.
Largest parties: (centre-left) National Liberation Party (PLN), (conservative) Social Christian Unity Party (PUSC).
Local government: seven provinces.
President: José Maria Figueres (PLN).

Geography

Between a narrow plain on the Pacific coast and a wider plain along the Caribbean coast rise a central plateau and mountain ranges. ***Principal river:*** Rio Grande. ***Highest point:*** Chirripó Grande 3819m (12,529 ft).
Climate: Rainfall is heavy along the Caribbean coast, but the Pacific coast is drier. Temperatures are warm in the lowlands, cooler in the highlands.

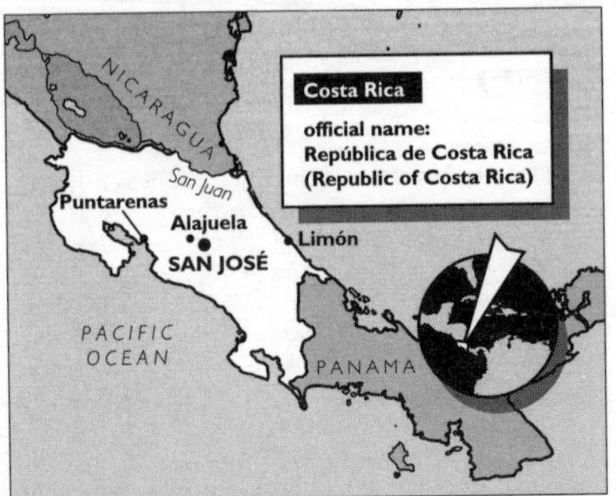

Economy

Coffee is Costa Rica's major export. Bananas, sugar cane, beef cattle, cocoa and timber are also important. ***Currency:*** Costa Rican colon.

Recent History

The area was under Spanish rule – as part of Guatemala – until 1821. Although it was part of the Central American Federation (1823–38), Costa Rica developed largely in isolation from its neighbours. Dominated by small farms, Costa Rica prospered, attracted European immigrants and developed a stable democracy. Following a brief civil war in 1948, the army was disbanded. Costa Rica has since adopted the role of peacemaker in Central America.

COTE D'IVOIRE

Official name: La République de la Côte d'Ivoire (The Republic of the Ivory Coast). Since 1986 Côte d'Ivoire has been the only official name.
Member of: UN, OAU, ECOWAS.
Area: 322,462 km² (124,503 sq mi).
Population: 13,460,000 (1993 est).
Capitals: Yamoussoukro (capital *de jure* and administrative capital) 120,000, Abidjan (legislative capital) 2,535,000 (including suburbs; 1987 est).
Other major cities: Bouaké 390,000, Daloa 102,000 (1987 est).
Languages: French (official), Bete (20%), Senufo (14%).
Religions: animist (60%), Christian (mainly Roman Catholic; 20%), Sunni Islam (20%).
Education: is compulsory, in theory, between the ages of seven and 13. *Adult literacy:* 54%. *Universities:* one.
Defence: (1993 figures) *Army:* 5500 personnel. *Air force:* 900. *Navy:* 700. *Paramilitary:* 7800. *Conscription:* none.

Government

The President – who is elected for a five-year term by universal adult suffrage – appoints a Prime Minister and a Council of Ministers. The 175-member National Assembly is also directly elected for five years.
Largest parties: (former monopoly) Democratic Party (PD), Ivorian Popular Front (FPI), Workers' Party (PIT).
Local government: 13 regions.
President: Henri Konan-Bédié (PD).
Prime Minister: Daniel Kablan Duncan (PD).

Geography

The north is a savannah-covered plateau. In the south, tropical rain forest, increasingly cleared for plantations, ends at the narrow coastal plain.
Principal rivers: Sassandra, Bandama, Komoé.
Highest point: Mount Nimba 1752m (5748 ft).
Climate: The south is equatorial with high temperatures and heavy rainfall; the north has similar temperatures but is drier.

Economy

The country depends on exports of cocoa, coffee and timber, and has suffered since the 1980s when prices for these commodities fell. Natural resources include petroleum, natural gas and iron ore. Political stability has helped economic growth. ***Currency:*** CFA franc.

Recent History

Colonized by France in the 19th century, the Ivory Coast became a relatively prosperous part of French West Africa. Independence was achieved in 1960 under the presidency of Félix Houphouët-Boigny (1905–94), who kept close links with France in return for aid and military assistance. After over a decade of single-party rule, multi-party elections were held in 1990, but the opposition claimed electoral fraud.

CROATIA

Official name: Republika Hrvatska (The Republic of Croatia).
Member of: UN, OSCE.
Area: 56,538 km² (21,829 sq mi), including the area (about 20%) that is controlled by Serb forces.
Population: 4,820,000 (1993 est).
Capital: Zagreb 934,000 (city 707,000; 1991 census).
Other major cities: Split 207,000 (city 189,000), Rijeka 206,000 (city 168,000), Osijek 105,000, Zadar 76,000, Pula 62,000, Karlovac 60,000 (1991 census).
Languages: Croat (75%) – the form of Serbo-Croat written in the Latin alphabet; Serbian (24%).
Religions: Roman Catholic majority, Orthodox minority.
Education: is compulsory between the ages of six and 15. *Adult literacy:* 97%. *Universities:* six.
Defence: (1993 figures) *Army:* 95,000 personnel. *Air force:* 300. *Navy:* 4000. *Paramilitary:* 40,000. *Conscription:* 10 months.

Government

The Assembly (Sabor) comprises a 138-member Chamber of Representatives (the lower house) elected by universal adult suffrage for four years and a 63-member Chamber of Municipalities (the upper house), comprising three members from each of the 21 counties into which the republic is divided. An executive President is directly elected for five years.

The President appoints a Prime Minister and a Council of Ministers who enjoy a majority in the lower house.
Largest parties: (nationalist) Croatian Democratic Union (CDU), Croatian Social-Liberal Party (CSLP), (former Communist) Social Democratic Party-Party of Democratic Reform (SDP-PDRC), Croatian People's Party (CPP).
Local government: 21 counties.
President: Franjo Tudjman (CDU).
Prime Minister: Nikica Valentic (CDU).

Geography

Croatia comprises plains in the east (Slavonia), hills around Zagreb, and barren limestone ranges running parallel to the Dalmatian coast. The area around Dubrovnik is detached from the rest of Croatia.
Principal rivers: Sava, Danube, Drava. ***Highest point:*** Troglav 1913m (6275 ft).
Climate: The interior is colder and drier than the Mediterranean coast.

Economy

Manufacturing (aluminium, textiles and chemicals), mining (bauxite) and oil dominate the economy. Slavonia grows cereals, potatoes and sugar beet. The economy has been damaged by the Yugoslav wars since 1991, and the lucrative Dalmatian tourist industry has collapsed. ***Currency:*** Kuna.

Recent History

The Croats strove to preserve their identity within the Habsburg Austro-Hungarian Empire. By 1900 a Croat national revival looked increasingly to independent Serbia to create a South ('Yugo') Slav state. After World War I when the Habsburg Empire was dissolved (1918), the Croats joined the Serbs, Slovenes and Montenegrins in the state that was to become Yugoslavia in 1929. However, the Croats soon resented the highly centralized Serb-dominated kingdom. Following the German invasion (1941), the occupying Axis powers set up an 'independent' Croat puppet state that adopted anti-Serb policies. In 1945 Croatia was reintegrated into a federal Communist Yugoslav state by Marshal Tito, but after Tito's death (1980), the Yugoslav experiment faltered in economic and nationalist crises. Separatists came to power in Croatia in free elections (1990) and declared independence (1991). Serb insurgents, backed by the Yugoslav federal army, occupied 30% of Croatia, including those areas with an ethnic Serb majority – Krajina and parts of Slavonia. The fierce Serbo-Croat war came to an uneasy halt in 1992 after Croatian independence had gained widespread diplomatic recognition and a UN monitoring force was agreed. In 1995 Croatia retook western Slavonia from the Serbs.

CUBA

Official name: La República de Cuba (The Republic of Cuba).
Member of: UN, OAS (suspended).
Area: 110,860 km^2 (42,803 sq mi).
Population: 10,890,000 (1993 est).
Capital: Havana (La Habana) 2,096,000 (including suburbs; 1990 est).
Other major cities: Santiago de Cuba 405,000, Camagüey 283,000, Holguín 228,000, Guantánamo 200,000, Santa Clara 194,000, Bayamo 125,000, Cienfuegos 124,000 (1990 est).
Language: Spanish.
Religion: Roman Catholic (39%), non-religious (over 40%).
Education: is compulsory between the ages of six and 17. *Adult literacy:* 96%. *Universities:* five (including a university college).
Defence: (1993 figures) *Army:* 145,000 personnel. *Air force:* 15,000. *Navy:* 13,500. *Paramilitary:* 19,000. *Conscription:* two years.

Government

The 589-member National Assembly is directly elected for five years by citizens aged 16 and over. The Assembly elects 31 of its members to form the Council of State, whose President – as head of state and government – appoints a Council of Ministers.
Political party: The Communist Party is the only legal political party.
Local government: 14 provinces plus one special municipality.
President: Fidel Castro Ruz.

Geography

Three ranges of hills and mountains run east to west across Cuba. ***Principal river:*** Cauto. ***Highest point:*** Pico Turquino 1974m (6476 ft).
Climate: The climate is semitropical. Temperatures average 26 °C (78 °F), and rainfall is heavy. The island is subject to hurricanes.

Cuba
official name:
La República de Cuba
(The Republic of Cuba)

Economy

Sugar (the leading export), tobacco and coffee are the main crops. State-controlled farms occupy most of the land but are unable to meet Cuba's food needs. Rationing is in force. Nickel is Cuba's second most important export. The end of the Communist trade bloc and of Soviet subsidies brought the Cuban economy to the verge of collapse. The value of the currency is plummeting in real terms and severe fuel shortages have hit both transport and industry. ***Currency:*** Cuban peso.

Recent History

The first war for independence from Spain (1868–78) was unsuccessful. The USA intervened in a second uprising (1895–98), forcing Spain to relinquish the island, but independence was not confirmed until after two periods of American administration (1899–1901 and 1906–09). Under a succession of corrupt governments, the majority of Cubans suffered abject poverty. In 1959, the dictatorship of Fulgencio Batista was overthrown by the guerrilla leader Fidel Castro (1926–), whose revolutionary movement merged with the Communist Party to remodel Cuba on Soviet lines. In 1961, US-backed Cuban exiles attempted to invade at the Bay of Pigs, and relations with America deteriorated further in 1962 when the installation of Soviet missiles on Cuba almost led to world war. Castro encouraged revolutionary movements throughout Latin America, and his troops bolstered Marxist governments in Africa. The upheavals in the USSR and Eastern Europe (1989–91) left Cuba increasingly isolated as a hardline Marxist state. In 1994, a flood of refugees from Cuba to the USA raised tension between the two countries.

CYPRUS

Official name: Kypriaki Dimokratia (in Greek) or Kibris Cumhuriyeti (in Turkish) (The Republic of Cyprus).
Member of: UN, Commonwealth, OSCE.
Area: 9251 km^2 (3572 sq mi) – of which 3355 km^2 (1295 sq mi) are in the Turkish-controlled zone.
Population: 756,000 (1992 est) – of which 186,000 are in the Turkish-controlled zone.
Capital: Nicosia (Lefkosia) 217,000 (including 40,000 in the Turkish-controlled zone) (1992 est).
Other major cities: Limassol (Lemesos) 137,000, Larnaca (Larnax) 69,000, Paphos (Pafos) 31,000 (1992 est).
Languages: Greek (74%), Turkish (24%; including settlers from the Turkish mainland).
Religions: Greek Orthodox (75%), Sunni Islam (over 20%, including settlers from the Turkish mainland).
Education: is compulsory between the ages of five and a half and 15. (In the Turkish zone, education is compulsory between the ages of seven and 15.) *Adult literacy:* 95%. *Universities:* one (plus one university and several university colleges in the Turkish zone).
Defence: (1993 figures) *Army:* 10,000 personnel (including 1300 seconded from the Greek army). (In the Turkish zone, there is an army of 4000, plus some 30,000 troops from Turkey.) *Conscription:* 26 months.

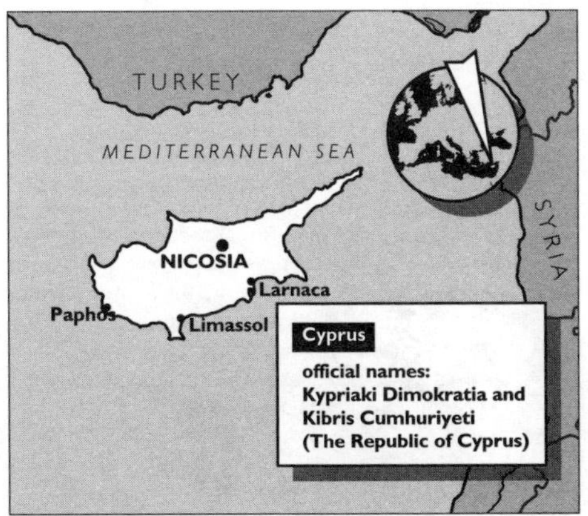

Government

A 56-member House of Representatives is elected by universal adult suffrage in the Greek Cypriot community for five years – an additional 24 seats for the Turkish Cypriot community remain unfilled. The President – who appoints a Council of Ministers – is elected from the Greek Cypriot community by universal adult suffrage for a five-year term. There is provision in the constitution for a Vice President to be similarly elected from the Turkish Cypriot community. In 1975, the administration of the Turkish Cypriot community unilaterally established the 'Turkish Republic of Northern Cyprus', which is unrecognized internationally except by Turkey.
Largest parties: (conservative) Democratic Rally (DISY), (Communist) Progressive Party of Working People (AKEL), (centre-right) Democratic Party (DIKO), Socialist Party (EDEK). (In the Turkish zone, the main political party is the National Unity Party.)
Local government: five districts.
President: Glafcos Clerides (DISY).

Geography

The south of the island is covered by the Troodos Mountains. Running east to west across the centre of Cyprus is a fertile plain, north of which are the Kyrenian Mountains and the Karpas Peninsula. ***Principal rivers:*** Pedieos, Karyota. ***Highest point:*** Mount Olympus 1951m (6401 ft)
Climate: Cyprus has a Mediterranean climate with hot dry summers and mild, variable winters.

Economy

Potatoes, fruit, wine, clothing and textiles are exported from the Greek Cypriot area, in which ports, resorts and an international airport have been constructed to replace facilities lost since partition. The Turkish Cypriot area – which exports fruit, potatoes and tobacco – relies heavily on aid from Turkey. Tourism is important in both zones. ***Currency:*** Cyprus pound; Turkish currency is used in the Turkish-controlled zone.

Recent History

The Ottoman Turks ceded Cyprus to British administration in 1878. During the 1950s, Greek Cypriots, led by Archbishop (later President) Makarios III (1913–77), campaigned for Enosis (union with Greece). The Turkish Cypriots advocated partition, but following a terrorist campaign by the Greek Cypriot EOKA movement, a compromise was agreed. In 1960, Cyprus became an independent republic. Power was shared by the two communities, but the agreement broke down in 1963. UN forces intervened to stop intercommunal fighting. The Turkish Cypriots set up their own administration. When pro-Enosis officers staged a coup (1974), Turkey invaded the north. Cyprus was effectively partitioned. Over 200,000 Greek Cypriots were displaced from the north, into which settlers arrived from Turkey. Since then, UN forces have manned the 'Attila Line' between the Greek south and Turkish north. Attempts have been made to reunite Cyprus as a federal state. Cyprus is an associate member of the EU/EC and has applied for full membership.

CZECH REPUBLIC

Official name: Ceská Republika (Czech Republic).
Member of: UN, OSCE, CEFTA.
Area: 78,864 km² (30,450 sq mi).
Population: 10,340,000 (1993 est).
Capital: Prague (Praha) 1,214,000 (1991 census).
Other major cities: Brno 388,000, Ostrava 328,000, Plzen 173,000, Olomouc 104,000, Liberec 101,000, Hradec Králové 100,000, Ceské Budejovice 97,000, Pardubice 95,000, Zlin 83,000 (1991 census).
Language: Czech.
Religions: Roman Catholic (39%), various Protestant Churches (4%).
Education: is compulsory between the ages of six and 16. *Adult literacy:* virtually 100%. *Universities:* 14.
Defence: (1993 figures) *Army:* 41,900 personnel. *Air force:* 35,600. *Conscription:* 12 months.

Government

The 200-member Chamber of Deputies (lower house) is elected by universal adult suffrage under a system of proportional representation for four years. The 81-member Senate is directly elected for six years. A President, whose role is largely ceremonial, is elected for a four-year term by an electoral college comprising both houses of Parliament. The President appoints a Prime Minister and Council of Ministers, who are responsible to the Assembly.
Largest parties: Christian Democratic Party (ODS), Christian Democratic Union-Czech People's Party

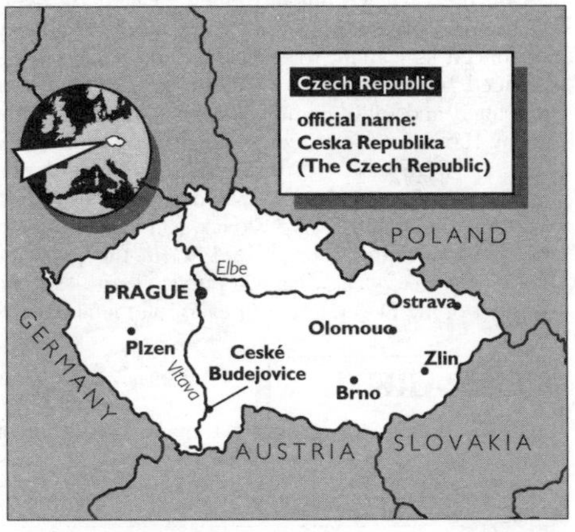

(KDU-CSL), Civic Democratic Alliance (ODA), Christian Democratic Party (KDS), (coalition) Left Bloc, Social Democratic Party (CDDS), Liberal Social Union (LSU).
Local government: eight regions and 75 districts.
President: Vaclav Havel (non-party).
Prime Minister: Vaclav Klaus (ODS).

Geography

In the west (Bohemia), the Elbe basin is ringed on three sides by uplands: the Bohemian Forest in the south and west, the Ore Mountains and the Giant Mountains in the north and the Bohemian-Moravian Highlands in the east. The Moravian plain lies to the east of Bohemia. ***Principal rivers:*** Elbe (Labe), Vlatava. ***Highest point:*** Snezka 1602m (5256 ft).
Climate: The climate is continental with cold winters and warm summers.

Economy

Apart from coal, there are few mineral resources, but the country is heavily industrialized and some areas have suffered heavy pollution. Manufactures include industrial machinery, motor vehicles and consumer goods. Much of industry has been privatized. The Czech Republic has attracted considerable foreign investment (80% German) and its economy is increasingly linked to that of Germany. The timber industry is important. The main crops include wheat, maize, potatoes, barley and sugar beet. Tourism, particularly to Prague, is becoming important. ***Currency:*** Czech Koruna.

Recent History

Nationalism in the Habsburg Czech lands grew in the 19th century, and on the collapse of the Austro-Hungarian Empire, the Czechs and Slovaks united in an independent state (1918) – largely due to the efforts of Thomas Masaryk, who became Czechoslovakia's first president. In 1938, Hitler demanded that Germany be granted the Sudetenland, where ethnic Germans predominated. Lacking allies, Czechoslovakia was dismembered. The Nazi occupation included the massacre of the inhabitants of Lidice (1942). Following liberation (1945), a coalition government was formed, but the Communists staged a takeover in 1948. In 1968, moves by Party Secretary Alexander Dubček to introduce political reforms met with Soviet disapproval, and invasion by Czechoslovakia's Warsaw Pact allies. In 1989, student demonstrations developed into a peaceful revolution led by the Civic Forum movement. Faced by overwhelming public opposition, the Communist Party renounced its leading role and hardline leaders were replaced by reformers. A coalition government was appointed and Civic Forum's leader – the playwright Vaclav Havel – was elected president. Free multi-party elections were held (1990), Soviet forces withdrawn (1991) and Czechoslovakia strengthened ties with Western Europe. Increased Slovak nationalism led to the division of the country in 1993 in the peaceful 'Velvet Divorce'. The Czech Republic is an associate member of the EU/EC and aspires to full membership.

DENMARK

Official name: Kongeriget Danmark (Kingdom of Denmark).
Member of: UN, EU/EC, NATO, OSCE, OECD, WEU (observer).

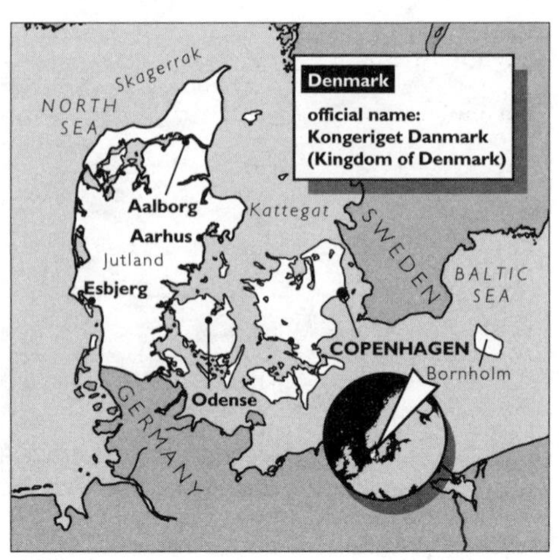

Area: 43,094 km² (16,639 sq mi) – 'metropolitan' Denmark, excluding dependencies.
Population: 5,187,000 – 'metropolitan' Denmark, excluding dependencies (1993 est).
Capital: Copenhagen (København) 1,337,000 (city 466,000; Frederiksberg 87,000; 1993 est).
Other major cities: Aarhus (Århus) 271,000, Odense 181,000, Aalborg (Ålborg) 157,000, Esbjerg 82,000, Randers 61,000, Kolding 58,000, Herning 57,000, Helsingor 57,000, Horsens 55,000, Vejle 52,000, Roskilde 51,000 (all including suburbs; 1992 est).
Language: Danish (99%; official).
Religion: Evangelical Lutheran (89%; official).
Education: is compulsory between the ages of six and 16. *Adult literacy:* virtually 100%. *Universities:* seven institutes of university status (universities, technical universities and university centres).
Defence: (1993 figures) *Army:* 16,900 personnel. *Air force:* 6300. *Navy:* 4500. *Conscription:* nine to 12 months.

Government

Denmark is a constitutional monarchy. The 179-member Parliament (Folketing) is elected by universal adult suffrage under a system of proportional representation for a four-year term. Two members are elected from both of the autonomous dependencies. The Monarch appoints a Prime Minister, who commands a majority in the Folketing. The PM appoints a State Council (Cabinet), which is responsible to the Folketing.
Largest parties: Social Democratic Party (SDP), Conservative People's Party (KF), Liberal Party (Venstre), Socialist People's Party (SFP), (anti-tax, anti-state bureaucracy) Progress Party (FP), Centre Democrats (CD), Radical Liberals (RV), (left-wing) Unity List.
Local government: 14 counties (amtskommuner), one city and one borough.
Sovereign: HM Margrethe II, Queen of Denmark (succeeded upon the death of her father, 14 January 1972).
Prime Minister: Poul Nyrup Rasmussen (SDP).
Danish autonomous dependencies: Faeroe Islands and Greenland. See Other Territories (beginning on p. 729).

Counties

Aarhus (Århus) *Area:* 4561 km² (1781 sq mi). *Population:* 610,000 (1993 est). *Capital:* Aarhus.
Bornholm *Area:* 588 km² (227 sq mi). *Population:* 45,000 (1993 est). *Capital:* Ronne.
Copenhagen (Kobenhavn) (city) *Area:* 88 km² (34 sq mi). *Population:* 466,000 (1993 est). *Capital:* Copenhagen.
Copenhagen (Kobenhavn) (county)*Area:* 526 km² (203 sq mi). *Population:* 604,000 (1993 est). *Capital:* Copenhagen.
Frederiksberg (borough) *Area:* 9 km² (3 sq mi). *Population:* 87,000 (1993 est). *Capital:* Frederiksberg.
Frederiksborg *Area:* 1347 km² (520 sq mi). *Population:* 346,000 (1993 est). *Capital:* Hillerod.
Fyn *Area:* 3486 km² (1346 sq mi). *Population:* 465,000 (1993 est). *Capital:* Odense.
North Jutland (Nordjylland) *Area:* 6173 km² (2383 sq mi). *Population:* 487,000 (1993 est). *Capital:* Aalborg (Ålborg).
Ribe *Area:* 3131 km² (1209 sq mi). *Population:* 221,000 (1993 est). *Capital:* Ribe.
Ringkobing *Area:* 4853 km² (1874 sq mi). *Population:* 269,000 (1993 est). *Capital:* Ringkobing.
Roskilde *Area:* 891 km² (344 sq mi). *Population:* 221,000 (1993 est). *Capital:* Roskilde.
South Jutland (Sonderjylland) *Area:* 3938 km² (1520 sq mi). *Population:* 251,000 (1993 est). *Capital:* Aabenraa (Åbenrå).
Storstrom *Area:* 3398 km² (1312 sq mi). *Population:* 257,000 (1993 est). *Capital:* Nykobing Falster.
Vejle Area: 2997 km² (1157 sq mi). *Population:* 334,000 (1993 est). *Capital:* Vejle.
Viborg *Area:* 4122 km² (1592 sq mi). *Population:* 230,000 (1993 est). *Capital:* Viborg.
West Zealand (Vestsjaelland) *Area:* 2984 km² (1152 sq mi). *Population:* 286,000 (1993 est). *Capital:* Soro.

Geography

Denmark is a lowland of glacial moraine – only Bornholm, in the Baltic, has ancient hard surface rocks. The highest point is on the Jutland Peninsula, which occupies about two thirds of Denmark. Over 400 islands, of which 97 are inhabited, lie to the east of Jutland. The largest islands are Zealand (Sjaelland), Fyn and Lolland. ***Principal river:*** Gudená. ***Highest point:*** Yding Skovhøj 173m (568 ft).
Climate: The climate is temperate and moist, with mild summers and cold winters. Bornholm – to the east – is more extreme.

Economy

Denmark has a high standard of living, but few natural resources. Agriculture is organized on a cooperative basis, and produces cheese and other dairy products, bacon and beef – all mainly for export. About 20% of the labour force is involved in manufacturing, with iron and metal working, food processing, brewing, engineering and chemicals as the major industries. Petroleum and natural gas from the North Sea have reduced the costly burden of fuel imports. ***Currency:*** Danish krone.

Recent History

In the 20th century, Denmark's last colonial possessions were either sold (Virgin Islands) or given independence (Iceland) or autonomy (Greenland). The country was occupied by Nazi Germany (1940–45), and has since been a member of the Western Alliance. From the 1960s, Denmark's economic and political ties have increasingly been with Germany and the UK, rather than the traditional links with Norway and Sweden. Thus, in 1973, Denmark joined the EC, but the political consequence of joining the Common Market has been a further fragmentation of the country's political parties.

DJIBOUTI

Official name: Jumhuriya Jibuti (The Republic of Djibouti).
Member of: UN, OAU, Arab League.
Area: 23,200 km² (8950 sq mi).
Population: 565,000 (1993 est), plus over 130,000 refugees from Somalia.
Capital: Djibouti 450,000 (1989 est).
Other main town: Ali Sabih 4000 (1989 est).
Languages: Arabic and French (both official); Somali (Issa; 37%).
Religion: Sunni Islam (96%; official).
Education: is not compulsory. *Adult literacy:* 34%. *Universities:* none.
Defence: (1993 figures) *Army:* 3900 personnel. *Paramilitary:* 900. (There are 4000 French troops in Djibouti.) *Conscription:* none.

Government

The 65-member Chamber of Deputies and a President are elected by universal adult suffrage – respectively for five and six years. The President appoints a Prime Minister and Council of Ministers, who are responsible to him.
Largest parties: (former monopoly) Popular Rally for Progress (RPP), New Democratic Party (PND).
Local government: five districts.
President: Hassan Gouled Aptidon (RPP).
Prime Minister: Barkat Gourad Hamadou (RPP).

Geography

Djibouti is a low-lying desert below sea level in two basins but rising to hills in the north. ***Principal rivers:*** There are no all-year rivers. ***Highest point:*** Musa Ali Terara 2062m (6768 ft).
Climate: Djibouti is extremely hot and dry, with rainfall under 125 mm (5 in) on the coast.

Economy

Lack of water largely restricts agriculture to grazing sheep and goats. The economy depends on the expanding seaport and railway, which both serve Ethiopia. ***Currency:*** Djibouti franc.

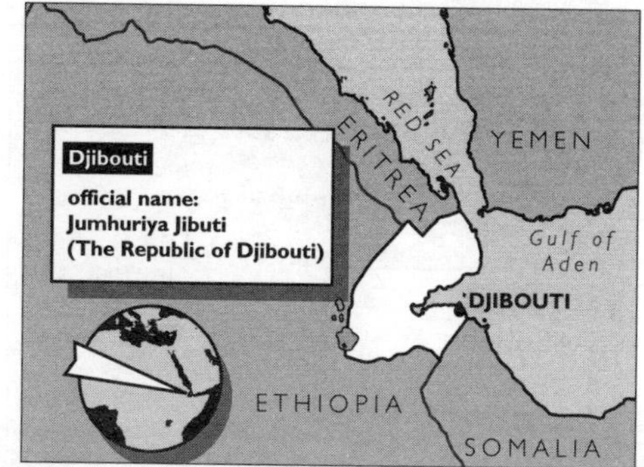

Recent History

France acquired a port in 1862 and established the colony of French Somaliland in 1888. In the 1950s and 1970s, the Afar tribe and Europeans voted to remain French, while the Issas (Somalis) opted for independence. In 1977, the territory became the Republic of Djibouti, but the new state has suffered ethnic unrest and drought. From 1981 to 1992 Djibouti was a one-party state.

DOMINICA

Official name: Commonwealth of Dominica.
Member of: UN, Commonwealth, OAS, CARICOM.
Area: 750 km² (290 sq mi).
Population: 71,200 (1990 census).
Capital: Roseau 16,000 (city 8000; 1990 census).
Languages: English (official), French patois.
Religion: Roman Catholic (77%).
Education: is compulsory between the ages of five and 15. *Adult literacy:* 94%. *Universities:* two university centres.
Defence: There are no defence forces.

Government

Every five years, 21 members of the House of Assembly are elected by universal adult suffrage and nine are appointed by the President, who is elected for a five-year term by the House. The President appoints a Prime Minister and Cabinet.
Largest parties: (conservative) Dominica Freedom Party (DFP), (centre) Dominican United Workers' Party (DUWP), (left-wing) Dominica Labour Party.
Local government: 10 parishes.
President: Crispin Sorhaindo.
Prime Minister: Eugenia Charles (DFP).

Geography

Dominica is surrounded by steep cliffs. Its forested interior is mountainous. ***Principal rivers:*** Layou, Castle Bruce. ***Highest point:*** Morne Diablotin 1447m (4747 ft).
Climate: Dominica has a tropical climate with little seasonal variation and very heavy rainfall.

Economy

Dominica is a poor island. It produces bananas, timber and coconuts, and exports water to drier neighbours. Tourism is increasing in importance. ***Currency:*** East Caribbean dollar.

Recent History

A British colony after 1783, Dominica was a member of the West Indies Federation (1958–62), gained autonomy in 1967 and independence in 1978.

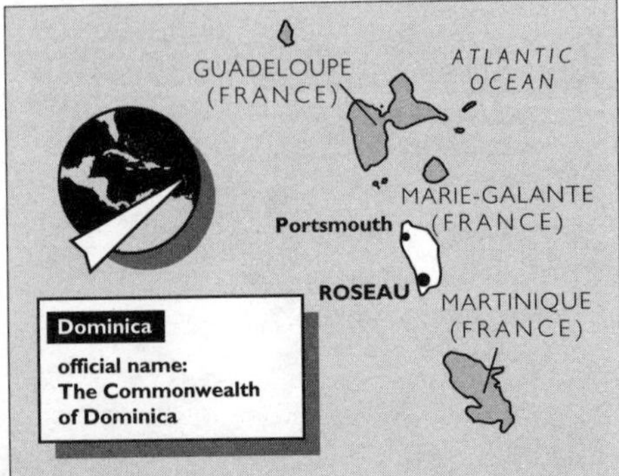

DOMINICAN REPUBLIC

Official name: República Dominicana (The Dominican Republic).
Member of: UN, OAS, CARICOM.
Area: 48,443 km² (18,704 sq mi).
Population: 7,635,000 (1993 est).
Capital: Santo Domingo 2,200,000 (including suburbs; 1989 est).
Other major cities: Santiago de los Caballeros 467,000, La Romana 92,000 (including suburbs; 1989 est).
Language: Spanish (official).
Religion: Roman Catholic (over 90%).
Education: is compulsory between the ages of seven and 14. *Adult literacy:* 83%. *Universities:* eight.
Defence: (1993 figures) *Army* 15,000 personnel. *Air force:* 4200. *Navy:* 4000. *Paramilitary:* 15,000. *Conscription:* none.

Government

The President and the National Congress – a 30-member Senate and a 120-member Chamber of Deputies – are elected for four years by universal adult suffrage. The President appoints a Cabinet of Secretaries of State.
Largest parties: (conservative) Social Christian Reform Party (PRSC), (left-wing) Dominican Revolution Party (PLD).
Local government: 29 provinces plus a national district.
President: Joaquin Balaguer (PRSC).

Geography

The republic is the eastern two thirds of the island of Hispaniola. The fertile Cibao Valley in the north is an important agricultural region. Most of the rest of the country is mountainous. ***Principal rivers:*** Yaque del Norte, Yaque del Sur. ***Highest point:*** Pico Duarte 3175m (10,417 ft).
Climate: The climate is largely subtropical, but it is cooler in the mountains. Rainfall is heavy, but the west and southwest are arid. Hurricanes are a hazard.

Economy

Sugar is the traditional mainstay of the economy, but nickel and iron ore have become the principal exports. Tourism is now the greatest foreign-currency earner. ***Currency:*** Peso oro.

Recent History

The 19th century witnessed a succession of tyrants, and by 1900 the republic was bankrupt and in chaos. The USA intervened (1916–24). Rafael Trujillo

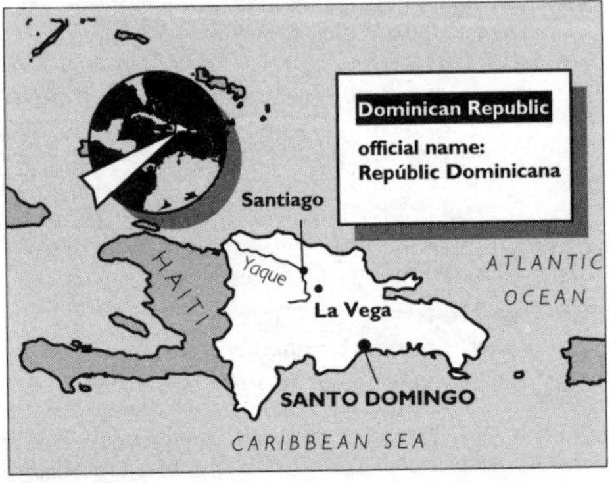

(1891–1961) became president in 1930 and ruthlessly suppressed opposition. He was assassinated in 1961. Civil war in 1965 ended after intervention by US and Latin American troops. Since then, an infant democracy has faced grave economic problems.

ECUADOR

Official name: República del Ecuador (The Republic of Ecuador).
Member of: UN, OAS, ALADI, Andean Pact.
Area: 272,045 km² (105,037 sq mi).
Population: 10,986,000 (1993 est).
Capital: Quito 1,388,000 (city 1,001,000; 1990 census).
Other major cities: Guayaquil 1,764,000 (city 1,508,000), Cuenca 272,000 (city 195,000), Machala 144,000, Portoviejo 133,000 (1990 census).
Language: Spanish (official; 93%), Quéchua.
Religion: Roman Catholic (93%).
Education: is compulsory for six years to be taken between the ages of six and 14. *Adult literacy:* 88%. *Universities:* 25 universities and polytechnics of university status.
Defence: (1993 figures) *Army:* 50,000 personnel. *Air force:* 3500. *Navy:* 4500. *Conscription:* one year; selective.

Government

The President is elected by compulsory universal adult suffrage for a single term of four years. The 77-member Chamber of Representatives is also directly elected – 65 members for two years (on a provincial basis), 12 members for four years (on a national basis). The President appoints a Cabinet of Ministers.
Largest parties: (centre-right) Social Christian Party (PSC), (right-wing) Roldosist Party (PRE), (conservative coalition) Republican Unity Party (PUR), Conservative Party (PCE), Democratic Left (ID), Popular Democracy Party (DP), Popular Democracy Movement (MPD), Socialist Party (PSE).
Local government: 21 provinces.
President: Sixto Duran Ballen (PUR).

Geography

The Andes divide the Pacific coastal plain in the west from the Amazonian rain forest in the east. Ecuador includes the Galapagos Islands, comprising 16 main islands and associated islets, about 1000 km (600 mi) offshore. ***Principal rivers:*** Guayas, Napo, Pastaza, Curaray, Daule. ***Highest point:*** Chimborazo 6266m (20,556 ft).

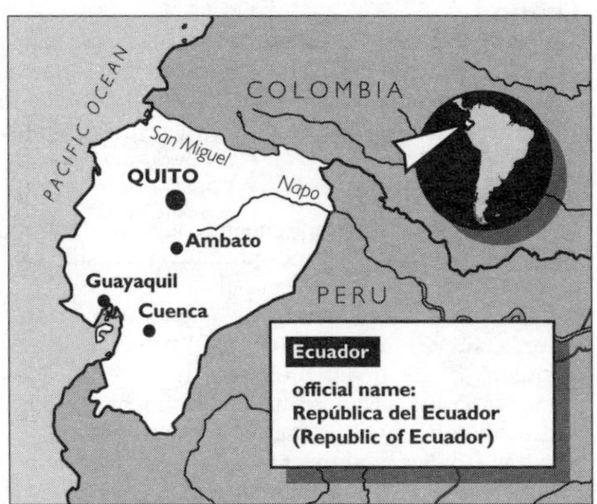

Climate: The Amazonian Basin has a wet tropical climate. The tropical coastal plain is humid in the north, arid in the south. The highland valleys are mild, but the highest peaks have permanent snow.

Economy

Agriculture is the biggest single employer, and major exports include cocoa, coffee and, in particular, bananas. Petroleum is the major foreign-currency earner. Problems include high inflation and foreign debt. ***Currency:*** Sucre.

Recent History

Initially federated with Colombia and Venezuela, Ecuador became completely independent in 1830. Throughout the 19th century there were struggles between liberals and conservatives. Since 1895 there have been long periods of military rule, but democratically elected governments have been in power since 1978. Relations with neighbouring Peru have long been tense – war broke out in 1941, when Ecuador lost most of its Amazonian region, and there were border skirmishes in 1981 and 1995.

EGYPT

Official name: Jumhuriyat Misr al-'Arabiya (Arab Republic of Egypt).
Member of: UN, OAU, Arab League.
Area: 997,739 km² (385,229 sq mi).
Population: 57,110,000 (1993 est).
Capital: Cairo (El-Qahira) 13,300,000 (city 6,663,000; El-Giza 2,096,000; Shubra El-Kheima 812,000; 1991 est)
Other major cities: Alexandria (El-Iskandariyah) 3,295,000, Port Said (Bur Sa'id) 449,000, El-Mahallah El-Kubra 400,000, Suez (El Suweis) 376,000, Tanta 372,000, El-Mansura 362,000 (1991 est).
Language: Arabic (official).
Religions: Sunni Islam (90%), Coptic Christian (7%).
Education: is compulsory, in theory, between the ages of six and 14. *Adult literacy:* 48%. *Universities:* 13.
Defence: (1993 figures) *Army:* 310,000 personnel. *Air force:* 30,000. *Navy:* 20,000. *Air defence:* 70,000. *Conscription:* three years; selective.

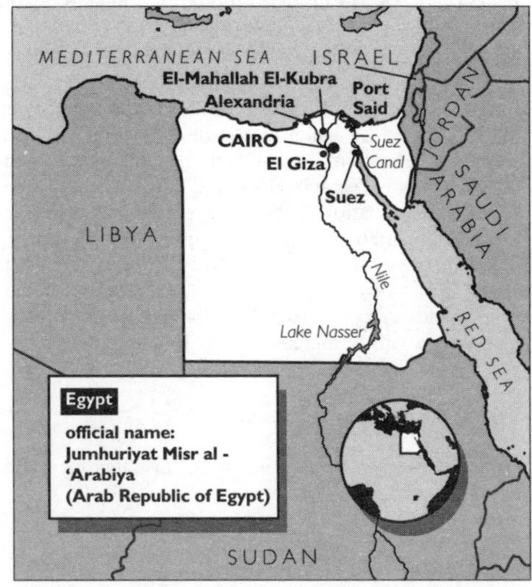

Government

Every five years, 454 members are elected by universal adult suffrage to the Majlis (People's Assembly); up to 10 additional members are appointed by the President, who is nominated by the Assembly and confirmed by referendum for a six-year term. The President appoints a Prime Minister and other Ministers.

Largest parties: (centrist) National Democratic Party (NDP), (traditional rightist) New Wafd Party (NWP), Socialist Labour Party (SLP), National Progressive Unionist Party (NPU).

Local government: 26 governates.

President: Mohammed Hosni Mubarak (NDP).

Prime Minister: Dr Atef Sedki (NDP).

Geography

Desert covers more than 90% of Egypt. The Western Desert, which stretches into Libya and Sudan, is low-lying. The Eastern Desert is divided by wadis and ends in the southeast in mountains beside the Red Sea. Most Egyptians live in the Nile River valley and delta, intensively cultivated lands that rely on irrigation by the annual flood of the Nile. East of the Suez Canal is the Sinai Peninsula. ***Principal river:*** Nile. ***Highest point:*** Mount Catherine (Jabal Katrina) 2642m (8668 ft).

Climate: Egyptian winters are mild and summers are hot and arid. Alexandria has the highest rainfall total – 200 mm (8 in) – while the area beside the Red Sea receives virtually no rain.

Economy

Over one third of the labour force is involved in agriculture, producing maize, wheat, rice and vegetables for the domestic market and cotton and dates mainly for export. Petroleum reserves (small by Middle Eastern standards), canal tolls and tourism are important foreign-currency earners. However, tourism has suffered a major decline since 1993 owing to the activities of militant Islamic fundamentalists. The economy is held back by rapid population growth and by the demands of a large public sector and food subsidies. ***Currency:*** Egyptian pound.

Recent History

The UK, a major creditor, occupied Egypt (1882) and established a protectorate (1914–22). The corrupt regime of King Farouk was toppled in a military coup (1952) and a republic was established (1953). The radical Gamal Abdel Nasser (1918–70) became president in 1954. He nationalized the Suez Canal and made Egypt the leader of Arab nationalism. Nasser was twice defeated by Israel in Middle East wars, but his successor, President Anwar Sadat, made peace with Israel and was ostracized by the Arab world. Since Sadat's assassination (1981), Egypt has regained its place in the Arab fold. The prominent role played by Egypt in the coalition against Saddam Hussein's Iraq (1991) confirmed Egypt as one of the leaders of the Arab world. In the 1990s rising violence has accompanied the growth of militant Islamic fundamentalism.

EL SALVADOR

Official name: La República de El Salvador (The Republic of El Salvador).

Member of: UN, OAS, CACM.

Area: 21,393 km² (8260 sq mi).

Population: 5,517,000 (1993 est).

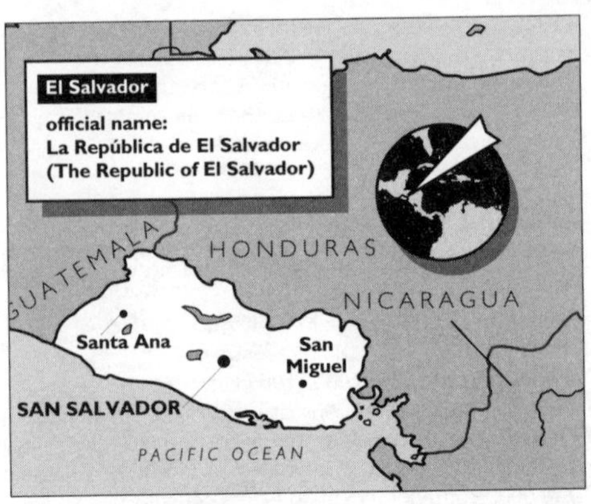

Capital: San Salvador 1,522,000 (city 423,000; Nueva San Salvador 117,000; 1992 est).

Other major cities: Santa Ana 202,000 (city 145,000), San Miguel 182,000 (1992 est).

Language: Spanish (official).

Religion: Roman Catholic (82%).

Education: is compulsory between the ages of seven and 16. *Adult literacy:* 73%. *Universities:* two state and several private universities.

Defence: (1993 figures) *Army:* 28,000 personnel. *Air force:* 2000. *Navy:* 5000. *Conscription:* two years; selective.

Government

The President – who appoints a Cabinet of Ministers – is elected by universal adult suffrage for a single five-year term. Every three years, direct elections are also held for the 84-member National Assembly.

Largest parties: (right-wing) Nationalist Republican Alliance (ARENA), Christian Democratic Party (PDC), (left-wing coalition) Democratic Convergence-Farabundo Marti Liberation Front (CD-FMLN), (right-wing) National Conciliation Party (PCN).

Local government: 14 departments.

President: Armando Caleron Sol (ARENA).

Geography

The country is mountainous, with ranges along the border with Honduras and a higher volcanic chain in the south. ***Principal river:*** Lempa. ***Highest point:*** Volcán de Santa Ana 2381m (7812 ft).

Climate: The tropical coast is hot and humid, while the interior is temperate.

Economy

Agricultural products, in particular coffee and sugar cane, account for nearly two thirds of the country's exports. The economy declined from the 1970s to 1992 owing to the state of near civil war. ***Currency:*** Colon.

Recent History

The country has suffered frequent coups and political violence. In 1932 a peasant uprising was harshly suppressed. El Salvador's overpopulation has been partially relieved by migration to neighbouring states. After a soccer match between El Salvador and Honduras in 1969, war broke out because of illegal immigration by Salvadoreans into Honduras. Political and economic power is concentrated into the hands of a few families, and this has led to social tension. A state of virtual civil war existed from the late 1970s to

1992 with the US-backed military, assisted by extreme right-wing death squads, combating left-wing guerrillas. The government and guerrillas signed a peace agreement, which came into effect in 1992, when constitutional multi-party rule was restored.

EQUATORIAL GUINEA

Official name: La República de Guinea Ecuatorial (The Republic of Equatorial Guinea).
Member of: UN, OAU.
Area: 28,051 km² (10,831 sq mi).
Population: 377,000 (1993 est).
Capital: Malabo 37,000 (1988 est).
Other major town: Bata 24,000 (1988 est).
Languages: Spanish (official), Fang, Bubi.
Religion: Roman Catholic majority.
Education: is compulsory, in theory, between the ages of six and 14. *Adult literacy:* 62%. *Universities:* two university centres.
Defence: (1993 figures) *Army:* 11,000 personnel. *Air force:* 100. *Navy:* 120. *Paramilitary:* 2000. *Conscription:* none.

Government

Elections are held by universal adult suffrage for a President to serve for seven years and an 80-member National Assembly for five years.
Largest parties: (former monopoly) Democratic Party of Equatorial Gunea (PDGE), People's Social Democratic Convention (CPDS), Social Democratic Union (UDS).
Local government: seven provinces.
President: Brig. Gen. Teodoro Obiang Nguema Msasogo (PDGE).

Geography

The republic consists of the fertile island of Bioko (formerly Fernando Póo), the much smaller islands of Pagalu (formerly Annobón) and the Corisco Group, and the district of Mbini (formerly Río Muni) on the African mainland. ***Principal river:*** Mbini. ***Highest point:*** Pico de Basilé 3008m (9868 ft).
Climate: The tropical climate is hot and humid with heavy rainfall.

Economy

Mbini exports coffee and timber; Bioko exports cocoa. The economy relies heavily on foreign aid. ***Currency:*** CFA franc.

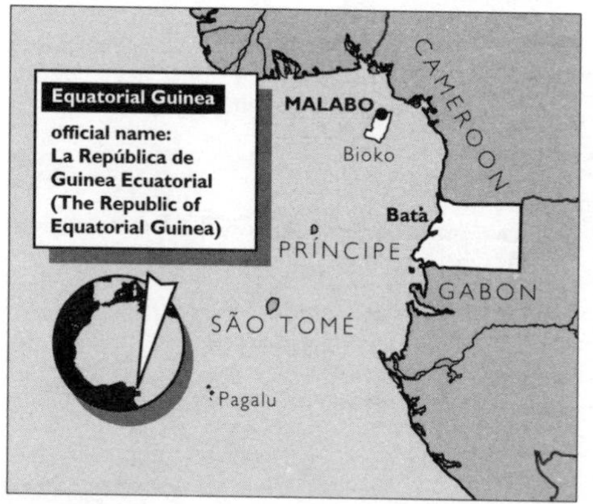

Recent History

The harsh plantation system practised during the Spanish colonial era attracted much international criticism. Independence in 1968 began under the dictatorship of Francisco Nguema, who was overthrown by a military coup in 1979. Severe economic decline has been experienced since the 1970s. Although political pluralism was restored in 1993, allegations of abuses of human rights continue and the 1993 elections were condemned by Western observers.

ERITREA

Official name: Eritrea.
Member of: UN, OAU.
Area: 117,400 km² (45,300 sq mi).
Population: 3,670,000 (1993 est).
Capital: Asmara (Asmera) 344,000 (1991 est).
Other major city: Massawa (Mitsiwa) 40,000 (1991 est).
Languages: Tigrinya (majority), Tigre, Arabic.
Religions: Sunni Islam (50%), Coptic Christian (under 50%), Roman Catholic minority.
Education: is not compulsory. *Adult literacy:* 20%. *Universities:* one.
Defence: (1993 figures) *Army:* 85,000 personnel. *Conscription:* 12–18 months (for men and women).

Government

The Provisional National Assembly comprises the Central Committee of the Eritrean People's Liberation Front (EPLF), 30 members chosen by the Central Committee and 30 members elected by provincial authorities. The Assembly elects a President, who appoints a State Council (Cabinet). The EPLF took control of Eritrea in 1991 and formed a provisional government for a period not exceeding four years. A new constitution and a multi-party system are scheduled to be introduced in 1995.
Largest party: The EPLF (see above) is currently the only major party.
Local government: 10 provinces.
President: Issaias Afewerki (EPLF).

Geography

Eritrea is physically an extension of the Ethiopian high plateau, although there are low coastal plains. The country includes the Dahlak Islands in the Red Sea. ***Principal river:*** Barka (seasonal). ***Highest point:*** Ramlo 2130m (6986 ft).
Climate: Eritrea has a dry tropical climate.

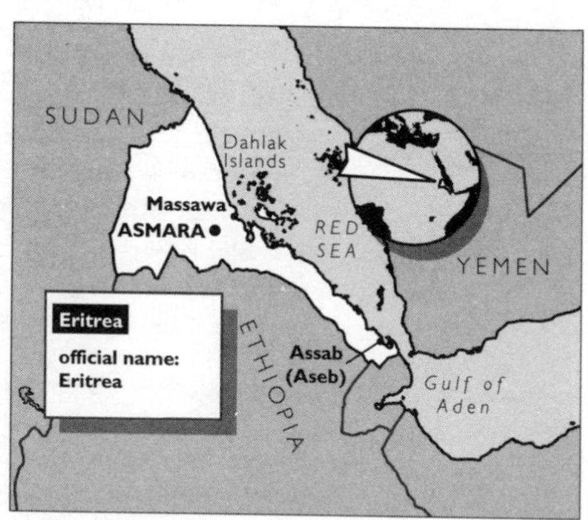

Economy
A 30-year war of secession has shattered the economy and substantial foreign aid will be needed for reconstruction. Most Eritreans are involved in agriculture, growing sorghum or keeping livestock for hides (the main export), but aridity is a major problem. Before the war of independence, Eritrea was one of the most industrialized areas of Africa and some industries, including footwear and textiles, remain. ***Currency:*** Ethiopian currency is used provisionally.

Recent History
After 1870 the region was disputed by Egypt and Ethiopia, but in 1889 a third player, Italy, arrived on the scene. The Italian colony of Eritrea was created in 1890. Used as a base for Italy's conquest of Ethiopia (1935–36), Eritrea came under British rule in 1941 when Italy was removed from East Africa. In 1952, the territory was federated as an autonomous state with Ethiopia, but its incorporation as an Ethiopian province in 1962 sparked a rebellion against Ethiopia that lasted until 1991. By 1977 the EPLF (see above) controlled most of the region. In 1991, after the EPLF was instrumental in toppling the Communist government in Ethiopia, Eritrea effectively seceded from Ethiopia. After a referendum produced an overwhelming majority in favour of independence, Eritrea gained internationally recognized statehood in 1993.

ESTONIA

Official name: Eesti Vabariik (Republic of Estonia).
Member of: UN, OSCE.
Area: 45,226 km² (17,462 sq mi).
Population: 1,536,000 (1993 est).
Capital: Tallinn 505,000 (city 498,000; 1993 est).
Other major cities: Tartu 114,000, Narva 87,000, Kohta-Järve 56,000, Parnu 52,000 (1993 est).
Languages: Estonian (63%), Russian (31%).
Religions: Lutheran (30%), Orthodox (10%).
Education: is compulsory between the ages of six and 15. *Adult literacy:* virtually 100%. *Universities:* six universities and institutes of university status.
Defence: (1993 figures) *Army:* 2500 personnel. *Navy:* 500. *Paramilitary:* 2000. *Conscription:* 12 months (to be introduced).

Government
A 101-member Assembly (Riigokogu) is elected by universal adult suffrage for four years. A President – who appoints a Prime Minister and a Council of Ministers who are responsible to the Assembly – is directly elected for five years.
Largest parties: (nationalist) Pro Patria/Isamaa (PPNCP), Centre Faction, Moderates, Rural Centre Party (ERCP), (former Communist) Union of the Coalition Party (UCP), (nationalist) Estonian National Independence Party (ENIP).
Local government: 15 counties and six towns.
President: Lennart Meri.
Prime Minister: Tiit Vahi (UCP).

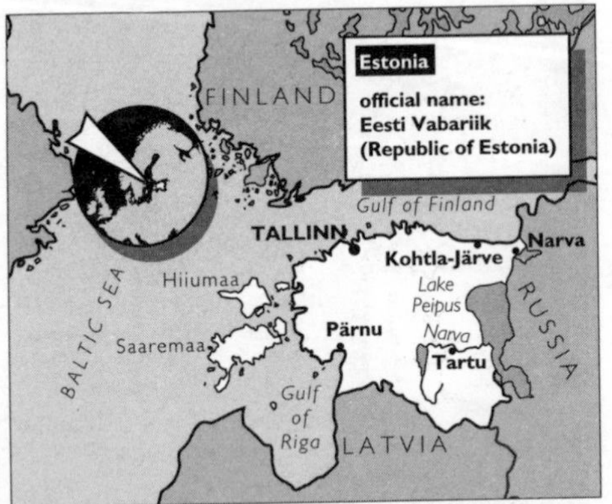

Geography
Estonia comprises a low-lying gently undulating mainland and two main islands. The only hilly country is in the southeast. ***Principal rivers:*** Narva, Parnu. ***Highest point:*** Mount Munamägi 318m (1042 ft). ***Climate:*** The moist temperate climate is characterized by mild summers and cold winters.

Economy
Major industries include engineering and food processing. Gas for heating and industry is extracted from bituminous shale. The important agricultural sector is dominated by dairying. After 1991, severe economic difficulties resulted from Estonia's heavy dependency upon trade with Russia. However, the adoption of a separate, stable Estonian currency increased trade with Scandinavian countries and the start of privatization halted the decline. ***Currency:*** Kroon.

Recent History
When the Communists took power in Russia (1917), Estonia (which had been Russian since 1712) seceded, but a German occupation and two Russian invasions delayed independence until 1919. Estonia's fragile democracy was replaced by a dictatorship in 1934. The Non-Aggression Pact (1939) between Hitler and Stalin assigned Estonia to the USSR, which invaded and annexed the republic (1940). Estonia was occupied by Nazi Germany (1941–44). When Soviet rule was reimposed (1945), large-scale Russian settlement replaced over 120,000 Estonians who had been killed or deported to Siberia. In 1988, reforms in the USSR allowed Estonian nationalists to operate openly. Nationalists won a majority in the republic's parliament and seceded following the failed coup by Communist hardliners in Moscow (1991). The USSR quickly recognized Estonia's independence. The introduction of strict Estonian citizenship laws (1992) that denied full rights to most ethnic Russians increased tension with Russia. Although the citizenship law was eased in 1993, relations with Russia remain difficult. In 1994–95 Estonia negotiated an associate agreement with the EU/EC.

ETHIOPIA

Official name: Ityopia (Ethiopia). Previously known as Abyssinia.
Member of: UN, OAU.
Area: 1,133,882 km² (437,794 sq mi).
Population: 51,831,000 (1993 est).
Capital: Addis Ababa 1,739,000 (1991 est).
Other major cities: Dire Dawa 122,000, Gondar 95,000, Nazret 91,000 (1991 est).
Languages: Amharic (official), Arabic, Oromo (40%).

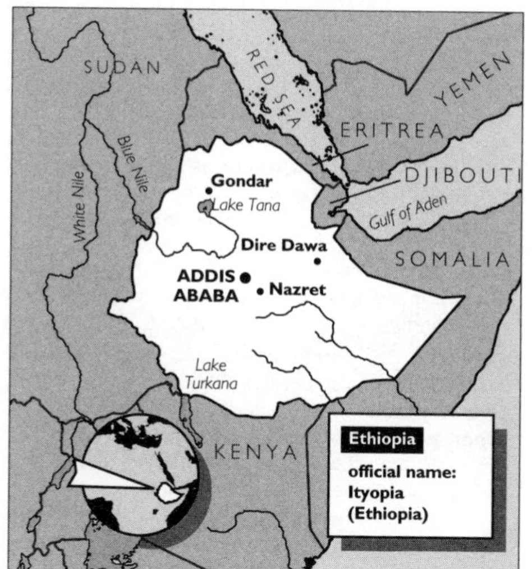

Religions: Ethiopian Orthodox (52%), Sunni Islam (45%).
Education: is not compulsory. *Adult literacy:* 5%. *Universities:* one.
Defence: (1993 figures) *Armed forces:* c. 100,000 personnel. *Conscription:* 12–18 months; selective.

Government

In 1991, an 87-member Council of Representatives was appointed. Elections were held in 1994 for a Constitutional Assembly, which will draft a new constitution.
Largest parties: (coalition) Ethiopian People's Democratic Movement (EPDM), various Oromo and other ethnic parties.
Local government: nine regions.
President: Meles Zenawi (EPDM).
Prime Minister: Tamirat Layne (EPDM).

Geography

The Western Highlands – including the Tigray Plateau and the Semien Mountains (rising to over 4000 m / 13,000 ft) – are separated from the lower Eastern Highlands by a wide rift valley. ***Principal rivers***: Blue Nile (Abay Wenz), Shebele, Awash, Omo. ***Highest point:*** Ras Dashen 4620m (15,157 ft).
Climate: Ethiopia is very hot and dry in the north and east. The highlands have a temperate climate.

Economy

Secessionist wars have damaged an impoverished, underdeveloped economy. Most Ethiopians are involved in subsistence farming, but drought and overgrazing have led to desertification. Coffee is the main foreign-currency earner. The end of finance from former Communist countries has increased Ethiopia's difficulties. Aid from international relief agencies is important. ***Currency:*** Ethiopian Birr.

Recent History

Ethiopia survived the European scramble for empire and defeated an Italian invasion (1896). However, the Italians occupied Ethiopia from 1936 to 1941. Emperor Haile Selassie (1892–1975) played a prominent part in African affairs, but – failing to modernize Ethiopia or overcome its extreme poverty – he was overthrown, and later murdered, in 1974. Allied to the USSR, a left-wing military regime instituted revolutionary change, but, even with Cuban help, it was unable to overcome secessionist guerrilla movements in Eritrea and Tigray. Drought, soil erosion and civil war brought severe famine in the 1980s and 1990s. The Marxist-Leninist regime was toppled by Tigrayan forces in 1991. The interim authorities recognized Eritrean independence in 1993.

FIJI

Official name: Matanitu Ko Viti (Sovereign Democratic Republic of Fiji).
Member of: UN.
Area: 18,333 km² (7078 sq mi).
Population: 762,000 (1993 est).
Capital: Suva 141,000 (city 72,000; 1986 census).
Other main town: Lautoka 29,000 (1986 census).
Languages: English (official), Fijian (50%), Hindi (45%).
Religions: Methodist (45%), Hindu (38%).
Education: is not compulsory. *Adult literacy:* 87%. *Universities:* one.
Defence: (1993 figures) *Army:* 3600 personnel. *Navy:* 300. *Conscription:* none.

Government

The 70-seat House of Representatives is elected by universal adult suffrage for five years to represent four ethnic voting lists – 37 members are elected by Fijians, 27 by Indians, 1 by Rotumans and 5 by others. The 80-member traditional Fijian Council of Chiefs elects the President and 24 of the 34 members of the appointed Senate. The President appoints a Prime Minister.
Largest parties: Fijian Political Party (FPP), (Indian) National Federation Party (NFP), (largely Indian) Fiji Labour Party (FLP), (multiracial) General Voters' Party (GUP).
Local government: 14 provinces.
President: Kamisese Mara (FPP).
Prime Minister: Sitiveni Rabuka (FPP).

Geography

The mountainous larger islands are volcanic in origin. The smaller islands are mainly coral reefs. ***Principal rivers:*** Nodi, Ba, Rewa. ***Highest point:*** Tomaniivi (formerly Mount Victoria) 1424m (4672 ft).

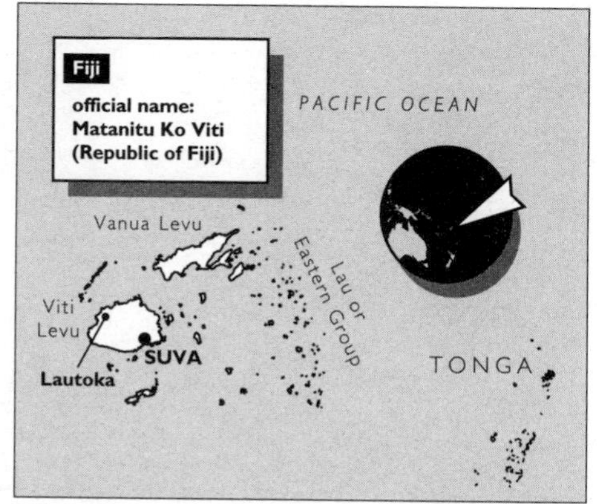

Climate: Fiji experiences high temperatures and heavy rainfall with local variations.

Economy

Fiji's economy depends on agriculture, with sugar cane as the main cash crop. Copra, ginger, fish and timber are also exported. Tourism is increasing in importance. ***Currency:*** Fiji dollar.

Recent History

During a period of great unrest, Chief Cakobau, who controlled the west, requested British assistance and ceded Fiji to Britain (1874). Indian labourers arrived to work on sugar plantations, reducing the Fijians, who retained ownership of most of the land, to a minority. Since independence (1970), racial tension and land disputes have brought instability. A military takeover in 1987 overthrew an Indian-led government and established a Fijian-dominated republic outside the Commonwealth. Recent emigration of Indians has resulted in the reemergence of a Fijian majority.

FINLAND

Official name: Suomen Tasavalta (Republic of Finland).
Member of: UN, EU/EC, OSCE, OECD.
Area: 338,145 km² (130,558 sq mi).
Population: 5,029,000 (1993 est).
Capital: Helsinki (Helsingfors) 1,014,000 (city 502,000; Espoo 179,000; Vantaa 159,000; 1993 est).
Other major cities: Turku (Åbo) 266,000 (city 160,000), Tampere (Tammerfors) 263,000 (city 175,000), Oulu (Uleaborg) 103,000, Lahti 94,000, Kuopio 82,000, Pori (Björneborg) 76,000, Jyväskylä 68,000, Kotka 56,000, Lappeenranta (Villmanstrand) 56,000, Vaasa (Vasa) 54,000 (1993 est).
Languages: Finnish (94%), Swedish (6%).
Religions: Lutheran (88%), Finnish Orthodox – both official.
Education: is compulsory between the ages of seven and 16. *Adult literacy:* virtually 100%. *Universities:* 21 universities and institutes of university status.
Defence: (1993 figures) *Army:* 27,300 personnel. *Air force:* 3000. *Navy:* 2500. *Conscription:* 11 months.

Government

The 200-member Parliament (Eduskunta) is elected for four years under a system of proportional representation by universal adult suffrage. Executive power is vested in a President elected for six years by direct popular vote. The President appoints a Council of State (Cabinet) – headed by a Prime Minister – responsible to the Parliament.
Largest parties: Centre Party (Kesk), Social Democratic Party (SDP), (conservative) National Coalition Party (Kok), Left-Wing Alliance (Vasemmistoliitto), Swedish People's Party (SFP), Green Union (VL), Finnish Christian Union (SKL), Rural Party (SMP).
Local government: 12 provinces, including the internally self-governing province of Aland.
President: Martti Ahtisaari.
Prime Minister: Paavo Lipponen (SDP).

Provinces

Aland Islands (Ahvenanmaa) (autonomous province) *Area:* 1527 km² (590 sq mi). *Population:* 25,000 (1993 est). *Capital:* Mariehamn (Maarianhamina).
Häme (Tavastehus) *Area:* 16,341 km² (6309 sq mi). *Population:* 688,000 (1993 est). *Capital:* Hämeenlinna.
Keski-Suomi (Mellersta Finland) *Area:* 16,251 km² (6275 sq mi). *Population:* 256,000 (1993 est). *Capital:* Jyväskylä.
Kuopio *Area:* 16,510 km² (6375 sq mi). *Population:* 259,000 (1993 est). *Capital:* Kuopio.
Kymi (Kymmene) *Area:* 10,783 km² (4163 sq mi). *Population:* 335,000 (1993 est). *Capital:* Kouvola.
Lappi (Lappland) *Area:* 93,057 km² (35,930 sq mi). *Population:* 202,000 (1993 est). *Capital:* Rovaniemi.
Mikkeli (St Michel) *Area:* 16,321 km² (6302 sq mi). *Population:* 208,000 (1993 est). *Capital:* Mikkeli.
Oulu (Uleaborg) *Area:* 56,868 km² (21,957 sq mi). *Population:* 446,000 (1993 est). *Capital:* Oulu.
Pohjois-Karjala (Norra Karelen) *Area:* 17,782 km² (6866 sq mi). *Population:* 178,000 (1993 est). *Capital:* Joensuu.
Turku-Pori (Abo-Bjorneborg) *Area:* 22,839 km² (8818 sq mi). *Population:* 732,000 (1993 est). *Capital:* Turku.
Uusimaa (Nyland) *Area:* 9898 km² (3822 sq mi). *Population:* 1,278,000 (1993 est). *Capital:* Helsinki.
Vaasa (Vasa) *Area:* 26,418 km² (10,200 sq mi). *Population:* 448,000 (1993 est). *Capital:* Vaasa.

Geography

Nearly one third of Finland lies north of the Arctic Circle and one tenth of the country is covered by lakes, some 50,000 in all. Saimaa – the largest lake – has an area of over 4400 km² (1700 sq mi). During the winter months the Gulfs of Bothnia (to the west) and of Finland (to the south) freeze. The land is glaciated, and except for mountains in the northwest most of the country is lowland. ***Principal rivers:*** Paatsjoki, Torniojoki, Kemijoki, Kokemäenjoki. ***Highest point:*** Haltiatunturi 1328m (4357 ft).
Climate: Finland has warm summers with long, extremely cold, winters, particularly in the north.

Economy

Forests cover about two thirds of the country and wood products provide 30% of Finland's foreign earnings. Metalworking and engineering (in particular shipbuilding) are among the main Finnish industries, which have a reputation for quality and good design. Apart from forests, copper and rivers suitable for hydroelectric power, there are few natural resources.

However, Finland enjoys a high standard of living, but the collapse of trade with Russia – traditionally a major trading partner – has created economic difficulties for Finland since 1991–92. The fishing industry is large and the agricultural sector produces enough dairy products for export. ***Currency:*** Markka.

Recent History

Throughout the 19th century Finland was a grand duchy ruled by the Russian emperor. Tension grew as Russia sought to strengthen its political and cultural leverage. In 1906, Finland was allowed to call its own Duma (Parliament), but repression followed again in 1910. After the Russian Revolution of 1917, civil war broke out in Finland. The pro-Russian party was defeated and an independent republican constitution (still in force today) was established (1919). Finland's territorial integrity lasted until the Soviet invasion in 1939, after which land was ceded to the USSR. The failure of a brief alliance with Germany led to further cession of territory to the Soviet Union in 1944. Finland has, since 1945, retained its neutrality and independence. Finland has achieved some influence through the careful exercise of its neutrality, for example hosting the first sessions of CSCE (now the OSCE; the 'Helsinki accords'). Following the collapse of the USSR (1991), Finland renegotiated its close relationship with Russia and in 1995 became a member of the EU/EC.

FRANCE

Official name: La République française (The French Republic).
Member of: UN, EU/EC, NATO, OSCE, G7, OECD, WEU.
Area: 543,965 km² (210,026 sq mi) – 'metropolitan' France, excluding overseas départements and collectivités territoriales (whose status is between that of an overseas département and an overseas territory).
Population: 57,456,000 (1993 est) – 'metropolitan' France.
Capital: Paris 9,063,000 (city 2,175,000; 1990 census).
Other major cities: Lyon 1,262,000 (city 422,000), Marseille 1,087,000 (city 808,000), Lille 950,000 (city 178,000), Bordeaux 686,000 (city 213,000), Toulouse 608,000 (city 366,000), Nantes 492,000 (city 252,000), Nice 476,000 (city 346,000), Toulon 438,000 (city 170,000), Grenoble 400,000 (city 154,000), Strasbourg 388,000 (city 256,000), Rouen 380,000 (city 105,000), Valenciennes 336,000 (town 39,000), Cannes 336,000 (city 69,000), Lens 323,000 (town 35,000), Saint-Etienne 313,000 (city 202,000), Nancy 311,000 (city 102,000), Tours 272,000 (city 133,000), Béthune 260,000 (town 26,000), Clermont-Ferrand 254,000 (city 140,000), Le Havre 254,000 (city 197,000), Rennes 245,000 (city 204,000), Orléans 243,000 (city 108,000),

Montpellier 235,000 (city 211,000), Dijon 226,000 (city 152,000), Mulhouse 224,000 (city 110,000), Reims 206,000 (city 185,000), Angers 206,000 (city 146,000), Brest 201,000 (city 153,000), Douai 200,000 (city 44,000), Dunkerque 193,000 (town 71,000), Metz 193,000 (city 124,000), Le Mans 189,000 (city 148,000), Caen 189,000 (city 116,000), Mantes-la-Jolie 189,000 (town 45,000), Avignon 181,000 (city 89,000), Limoges 170,000 (city 136,000) (1990 census).

Languages: French (official; over 93% as a first language), Arabic (over 2% as a first language), with German, Breton and Basque minorities.

Religions: Roman Catholic (74%), Sunni Islam (over 2%).

Education: is compulsory between the ages of six and 16. *Adult literacy:* 99%. *Universities:* 75 including polytechnics of university status.

Defence: (1993 figures) *Army:* 241,400 personnel. *Air force:* 91,600. *Navy:* 65,400. *Paramilitary:* 96,300. *Conscription:* 10 months.

Overseas départements and territories: Guadeloupe, Guyane (French Guiana), Martinique, Réunion, Mayotte, Saint-Pierre-et-Miquelon, French Polynesia, New Caledonia, Southern and Antarctic Territories, and Wallis and Futuna Islands. See Other Territories, beginning on p. 729.

Government

Executive power is vested in the President, who is elected for a 7-year term by universal adult suffrage. The President appoints a Prime Minister and a Council of Ministers – both responsible to Parliament – but it is the President, rather than the PM, who presides over the Council of Ministers. The Senate (the upper house) comprises 321 members – 296 of whom represent individual départements and 13 representing overseas départements and territories – elected by members of municipal, local and regional councils. The remaining 12 senators are elected by French citizens resident abroad. Senators serve for nine years, with one third of the Senate retiring every three years. The National Assembly (the lower house) comprises 577 deputies elected for a five-year term by universal adult suffrage from single-member constituencies, with a second ballot for the leading candidates if no candidate obtains an absolute majority in the first round.

Largest parties: (conservative Gaullist) Rally for the Republic (RPR), (centrist coalition) Union for French Democracy (UDF), Socialist Party (PS), Communist Party (PCF), (right-wing) National Front (FN).

Local government: 95 départements grouped into 22 regions.

President: Jacques Chirac (RPR).

Prime Minister: Alain Juppé (RPR).

Regions

Alsace *Area:* 8280 km² (3197 sq mi). *Population:* 1,640,000 (1992 est). *Administrative centre:* Strasbourg.

Aquitaine *Area:* 41,309 km² (15,950 sq mi). *Population:* 2,827,000 (1992 est). *Administrative centre:* Bordeaux.

Auvergne *Area:* 26,013 km² (10,044 sq mi). *Population:* 1,317,000 (1992 est). *Administrative centre:* Clermont-Ferrand.

Brittany (Bretagne) *Area:* 27,209 km² (10,506 sq mi). *Population:* 2,816,000 (1992 est). *Administrative centre:* Rennes.

Burgundy (Bourgogne) *Area:* 31,582 km² (12,194 sq mi). *Population:* 1,612,000 (1992 est). *Administrative centre:* Dijon.

Centre *Area:* 39,151 km² (15,116 sq mi). *Population:* 2,400,000 (1992 est). *Administrative centre:* Orléans.

Champagne-Ardenne *Area:* 25,606 km² (9886 sq mi). *Population:* 1,346,000 (1992 est). *Administrative centre:* Reims.

Corsica (Corse) *Area:* 8680 km² (3352 sq mi). *Population:* 251,000 (1992 est). *Administrative centre:* Ajaccio.

Franche-Comté *Area:* 16,202 km² (6256 sq mi). *Population:* 1,104,000 (1992 est). *Administrative centre:* Besançon.

Ile de France *Area:* 12,011 km² (4637 sq mi). *Population:* 10,836,000 (1992 est). *Administrative centre:* Paris.

Languedoc-Roussillon *Area:* 27,376 km² (10,570 sq mi). *Population:* 3,065,000 (1992 est). *Administrative centre:* Montpellier.

Limousin *Area:* 16,942 km² (6541 sq mi). *Population:* 719,000 (1992 est). *Administrative centre:* Limoges.

Lorraine *Area:* 23,547 km² (9092 sq mi). *Population:* 2,299,000 (1992 est). *Administrative centre:* Nancy.

Lower Normandy (Basse Normandie) *Area:* 17,589 km² (10,506 sq mi). *Population:* 1,398,000 (1992 est). *Administrative centre:* Caen.

Midi-Pyrénées *Area:* 45,349 km² (17,509 sq mi). *Population:* 2,461,000 (1992 est). *Administrative centre:* Toulouse.

Nord-Pas-de-Calais *Area:* 12,413 km² (4793 sq mi). *Population:* 3,969,000 (1992 est). *Administrative centre:* Lille.

Pays de la Loire *Area:* 32,082 km² (12,387 sq mi). *Population:* 3,087,000 (1992 est). *Administrative centre:* Nantes.

Picardy (Picardie) *Area:* 19,399 km² (7490 sq mi). *Population:* 1,827,000 (1992 est). *Administrative centre:* Amiens.

Poitou-Charentes *Area:* 25,809 km² (9965 sq mi). *Population:* 1,602,000 (1992 est). *Administrative centre:* Poitiers.

Provence-Alpes-Côte-d'Azur *Area:* 31,400 km² (12,123 sq mi). *Population:* 5,481,000 (1992 est). *Administrative centre:* Marseille.

Rhône-Alpes *Area:* 43,698 km² (16,871 sq mi). *Population:* 5,441,000 (1992 est). *Administrative centre:* Poitiers.

Upper Normandy (Haute Normandie) *Area:* 12,318 km² (4756 sq mi). *Population:* 1,753,000 (1992 est). *Administrative centre:* Rouen.

Geography

The Massif Central – a plateau of old hard rocks, rising to almost 2000 m (6500 ft) – occupies the middle of France. The Massif is surrounded by four major lowlands, which together make up over 60% of the total area of France. The Paris Basin – the largest of these lowlands – is divided by low ridges and fertile plains and plateaux, but is united by the river system of the Seine and its tributaries. To the east of the Massif Central is the narrow Rhône-Saône Valley, while to the west the Loire Valley stretches to the Atlantic. Southwest of the Massif Central lies the Aquitaine Basin, a large fertile region drained by the River Garonne and its tributaries. A discontinuous ring of uplands surrounds France. In the northwest the Armorican Massif (Brittany) rises to 411 m (1350 ft). In the southwest the Pyrenees form a high natural boundary with Spain. The Alps in the southeast divide France from Italy and contain Europe's highest peak, Mont Blanc (4807 m / 15,771 ft). The lower Jura – in the east – lie on the Swiss border, while the Vosges Mountains separate the Paris Basin from the Rhine Valley. In the northeast the Ardennes extend into Belgium. The Mediterranean island of Corsica is an ancient massif rising to 2710 m (8891 ft). ***Principal rivers:*** Rhine (Rhin), Loire, Rhône, Saône, Allier, Dordogne, Charente, Loir, Cher, Isère. ***Highest point:*** Mont Blanc 4807m (15,771 ft).

Climate: The Mediterranean south has warm summers and mild winters. The rest of France has a temperate climate, although the more continental east experiences warmer summers and colder winters. Rainfall is moderate, with highest falls in the mountains and lowest falls around Paris.

Economy

Nearly two thirds of France is farmed. The principal products include cereals (wheat, maize, barley), meat and dairy products, sugar beet and grapes for wine. France is remarkably self-sufficient in agriculture, with tropical fruit and animal feeds being the only major imports. However, the small size of land holdings remains a problem despite consolidation and the efforts of cooperatives. Reafforestation is helping to safeguard the future of the important timber industry. Natural resources include coal, iron ore, copper, bauxite and tungsten, as well as petroleum and natural gas, and plentiful sites for hydroelectric power plants. Major French industries include textiles, chemicals, steel, food processing, motor vehicles, aircraft, and mechanical and electrical engineering. Traditionally French firms have been small, but mergers have resulted in larger corporations able to compete internationally. France is the world's fourth industrial power after the USA, Japan and Germany. During the later 1980s many state-owned corporations were privatized. Over 50% of the labour force is involved in service industries, in particular administration, banking, finance, and tourism. ***Currency:*** French franc.

Recent History

In the 1890s the French colonial empire reached its greatest extent, in particular in Africa, Southeast Asia and the Pacific. The Third Republic also saw continuing conflict over France's own boundaries – Alsace-Lorraine was lost in 1870 but recovered in 1918 at the end of World War I, during which trench warfare in northern France claimed countless lives. In World War II, Germany rapidly defeated the French in 1940 and completely occupied the country in 1942. Marshal Philippe Pétain (1856–1951) led a collaborationist regime in the city of Vichy, while General Charles de Gaulle (1890–1970) headed the Free French in exile in London from 1940. After the war, the Fourth Republic (1946–58) was marked by instability, the Suez Crisis of 1956, and nationalist revolts in some of the colonies, notably Vietnam and Algeria. The troubles in Algeria – including the revolt of the French colonists and the campaign of their terrorist organization, the OAS – led to the end of the Fourth Republic and to the accession to power of General de Gaulle in 1959. As first president of the Fifth Republic, de Gaulle granted Algeria independence (1962). While the French colonial empire – with a few minor exceptions – was being disbanded, France's position within Western Europe was being strengthened, especially by vigorous participation in the European Community. At the same time, de Gaulle pursued a foreign policy independent of the USA, building up France's non-nuclear armaments and withdrawing French forces from NATO's integrated command structure. Although restoring political and economic stability to France, domestic dissatisfaction – including the student revolt of 1968 – led de Gaulle to resign in 1969. De Gaulle's policies were broadly pursued by his successors as president, Georges Pompidou (in office 1969–74) and Valéry Giscard d'Estaing (1974–81). The modernization of France continued apace under the country's first Socialist president, François Mitterrand (1981–95).

GABON

Official name: La République gabonaise (The Gabonese Republic).
Member of: UN, OAU, OPEC.
Area: 267,667 km² (103,347 sq mi).
Population: 1,280,000 (1993 est).
Capital: Libreville 352,000 (1988 est).
Other major cities: Port-Gentil 164,000, Masuku (formerly Franceville) 75,000 (1988 est).
Languages: French (official), Fang (30%).
Religions: Roman Catholic (71%), animist (28%).
Education: is compulsory, in theory, between the ages of six and 16. *Adult literacy:* 61%. *Universities:* two.
Defence: (1993 figures) *Army:* 3250 personnel. *Air force:* 1000. *Navy:* 500. *Paramilitary:* 4800. *Conscription:* none.

Government

The President – who is elected by universal adult suffrage for five years – appoints a Council of Ministers (over which he presides) and a Prime Minister. The National Assembly has 120 members directly elected for five years.
Largest parties: (former monopoly) Gabonese Democratic Party (PDG), Gabonese Progress Party (PGP), National Rally of Woodcutters (RNB).
Local government: nine provinces.
President: Omar Bongo (PDG).
Prime Minister: Casimir Oye-Mba (PDG).

Geography

Apart from the narrow coastal plain, low plateaux make up most of the country. The centre is occupied by the Massif du Chaillu. ***Principal rivers:*** Ogooué,

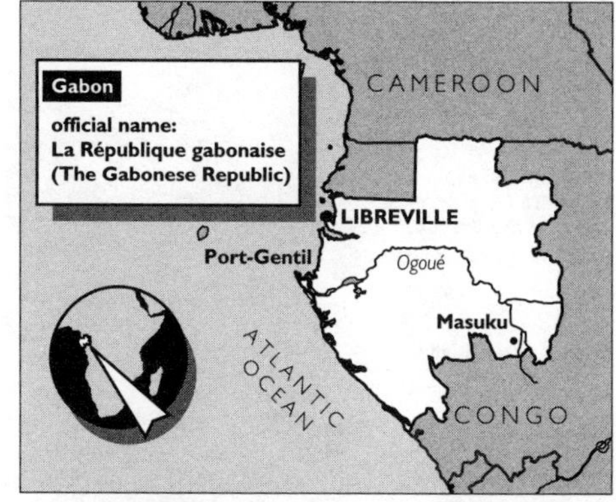

Woleu. ***Highest point:*** Mont Iboundji 3215m (980 ft). ***Climate:*** The equatorial climate is hot and humid with little seasonal variation.

Economy

Petroleum, natural gas, manganese, uranium and iron ore – and a relatively small population – make Gabon one of the richest Black African countries, although most Gabonese are subsistence farmers. ***Currency:*** CFA franc.

Recent History

The French colonized Gabon in the late 19th century. Pro-French Léon M'Ba (1902–67) led the country to independence in 1960. Deposed in a coup (1964), he was restored to power by French troops. Under his successor, Albert-Bernard Bongo, Gabon has continued its pro-Western policies. From 1968 to 1990 Gabon was a single-party state.

GAMBIA

Official name: The Republic of the Gambia.
Member of: UN, OAU, Commonwealth, ECOWAS.
Area: 10,689 km² (4127 sq mi).
Population: 1,033,000 (1993 est).
Capital: Banjul 171,000 (city 44,000; Serekunda 68,000; 1986 est).
Other main town: Brikama 24,000 (1986 est).
Language: English (official).
Religions: Sunni Islam (90%), various Protestant Churches (9%).
Education: is not compulsory. *Adult literacy:* 27%. *Universities:* one university-level college.
Defence: (1993 figures) *Army:* 800 personnel. *Conscription:* none.

Government

The constitution provides for a President and 36 of the 50 members of the House of Representatives to be elected by universal adult suffrage every five years; the remaining members are appointed. The President appoints a Vice-President – to lead the government in the House – and a Cabinet of Ministers. The constitution was suspended following a military coup in 1994.
Largest parties: (before the 1994 coup) (socialist) People's Progressive Party (PPP), National Convention Party (NCP), Gambia People's Party (GPP).
Local government: six divisions.
President: Lieut. Yayeh Jameh.

Geography

The Gambia is a narrow low-lying country on either bank of the River Gambia. ***Principal river:*** Gambia. ***Highest point:*** an unnamed point on the Senegalese border 43m (141 ft).
Climate: The climate is tropical, with a dry season from November to May.

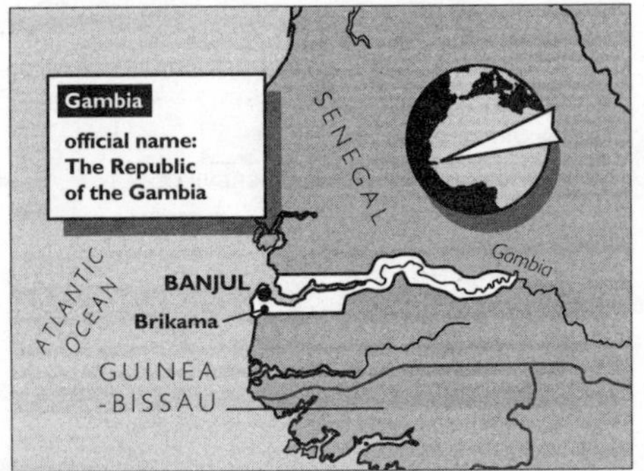

Economy

The economy is largely based on the cultivation of groundnuts and tourism – the latter was the major foreign-currency earner but has declined since the 1994 coup. ***Currency:*** Dalasi.

Recent History

A British colony was established in 1843. The Gambia achieved independence in 1965 under Sir Dawda K. Jawara. In 1981 an attempted coup against his rule encouraged efforts to merge with the neighbouring French-speaking country of Senegal, but the confederation was dissolved in 1989. After independence the country remained a democracy until the military took power in 1994.

GEORGIA

Official name: Sakartvelos Respublica (The Republic of Georgia).
Member of: UN, CIS, OSCE.
Area: 69,700 km² (26,900 sq mi).
Population: 5,493,000 (1993 est).
Capital: Tbilisi 1,283,000 (1991 est).
Other cities: Kutaisi 238,000, Rustavi 162,000, Batumi 137,000, Sukhumi 122,000 (1991 est).
Languages: Georgian (70%), Armenian (8%), Russian (6%), Azeri (3%), Ossetian (2%), Greek (2%).
Religion: Georgian Orthodox majority.
Education: is compulsory between the ages of seven and 17. *Adult literacy:* no figures available. *Universities:* three, plus a polytechnic of university status.
Defence: (1993 figures) *Army:* 15,000 personnel. *Conscription:* two years.

Government

The constitution provides for the election for four years by universal adult suffrage of a 235-member legislature and a President – who appoints a Council of Ministers. In 1993 the legislature dissolved itself, having granted emergency powers to the President.
Largest parties: Citizen's Union of Georgia (CUG),

(coalition nationalist) Round Table-Free Georgia.
Local government: two autonomous republics and over 10 regions.
President: Eduard Shevardnadze (CUP).
Prime Minister: Otar Patsatsia (CUP).

Autonomous republics

Abkhazia *Area:* 8600 km² (3300 sq mi). *Population:* 534,000 (1991 est). *Capital:* Sukhumi.
Adzharia *Area:* 3000 km² (1200 sq mi). *Population:* 382,000 (1991 est). *Capital:* Batumi.

Geography

The spine of the Caucasus Mountains forms the northern border of Georgia. A lower range, the Little Caucasus, occupies south Georgia. Central Georgia comprises the Kolkhida lowlands. ***Principal rivers:*** Inguri, Rioni, Kura, Kodori. ***Highest peak:*** Elbrus, 5642m (18,510 ft).
Climate: Coastal and central Georgia has a moist Mediterranean climate. The rest of Georgia is drier. Climate varies considerably with altitude and aspect.

Economy

Despite a shortage of cultivable land, Georgia has a diversified agricultural sector including tea, citrus fruit, tobacco, cereals, vines, livestock and vegetables. Natural resources include coal, manganese and plentiful hydroelectric power. Machine building, food processing and chemicals are major industries. The economy was damaged by civil war in 1991 and 1992. ***Currency:*** Georgian coupon. (The Russian rouble is also used.)

Recent History

Russia annexed Georgia by degrees (1801–78). Following the Russian Revolution (1918), a Georgian republic, allied to Germany, was proclaimed. A British occupation (1918–20) in favour of the White Russians failed to win local support, and Georgia was invaded by the Soviet Red Army (1921). Georgia became part of the Soviet Union in 1921 and a separate Union Republic of the USSR in 1936. Following the abortive coup by Communist hardliners in Moscow (1991), Georgia declared independence. Locked into a fierce civil war, Georgia temporarily remained outside the CIS when the USSR was dissolved. A state council – led by Eduard Shevardnadze, the former Soviet Foreign Minister – replaced a military council in 1992. War erupted in northern Georgia when Abkhazian Muslims attempted secession in 1992. A Russian-brokered ceasefire came into force in 1994.

GERMANY

Official name: Bundesrepublik Deutschland (The Federal Republic of Germany).
Member of: UN, EU/EC, NATO, G7, OECD, OSCE, WEU.
Area: 356,733 km² (137,735 sq mi).
Population: 79,754,000 (1993 est).
Capital: Berlin (capital in name only) 3,590,000 (city 3,446,000), Bonn (administrative capital) 542,000 (city 296,000) (1992 est).
Other major cities: Essen 4,700,000 (Essen-Ruhr agglomeration; city 627,000; Dortmund 601,000; Duisburg 537,000; Bochum 399,000; Gelsenkirchen 294,000; Oberhausen 225,000; Herne 179,000; Mülheim 177,000), Hamburg 1,924,000 (city 1,669,000), Munich (München) 1,465,000 (city 1,229,000), Cologne (Köln) 1,419,000 (city 960,000; Leverkusen 161,000), Frankfurt 1,268,000 (city 654,000), Stuttgart 1,091,000 (city 592,000), Düsseldorf 913,000 (city 578,000), Hannover 680,000 (city 518,000), Bremen 622,000 (city 546,000), Nuremberg (Nürnberg) 617,000 (city 498,000), Dresden 580,000 (city 485,000), Mannheim 539,000 (city 315,000; Ludwigshafen 165,000), Leipzig 532,000 (city 503,000), Wuppertal 485,000 (city 386,000), Solingen 357,000 (city 166,000), Mönchengladbach 341,000 (city 263,000), Bielefeld 322,000, Chemnitz 306,000 (city 288,000), Halle 303,000, Augsburg 281,000 (city 260,000), Karlsruhe 279,000, Magdeburg 275,000, Münster 264,000, Wiesbaden 264,000, Brunswick (Braunschweig) 259,000, Kiel 259,000 (city 247,000), Krefeld 246,000, Aachen 244,000, Rostock 244,000, Saarbrücken 236,000 (city 192,000), Lübeck 230,000 (city 216,000), Erfurt 205,000, Kassel 197,000, Freiburg 194,000, Mainz 183,000, Hamm 180,000, Osnabrück 165,000, Ulm 160,000 (city 112,000) (1992 est).
Language: German (official).
Religions: Lutheran and Churches of Lutheran tradition (43%), Roman Catholic (36%), Sunni Islam (2%).
Education: is compulsory between the ages of six and 16 (full-time) and at least part-time between the ages of 16 and 18. *Adult literacy:* virtually 100%. *Universities:* 85.
Defence (1993 figures) *Army:* 287,000 personnel. *Air force:* 90,000. *Navy:* 31,000. (There are 193,000 US, British and French toops in Germany.) *Conscription:* 12 months.

Government

Each of the 16 states (*Länder*, singular *Länd*) is represented in the 79-member upper house of Parliament – the Federal Council (Bundesrat) – by three, four or six members of the state government (depending on population) appointed for a limited period. The lower house – the Federal Assembly (Bundestag) – has 662 members elected for four years by universal adult suffrage under a mixed system of single-member constituencies and proportional representation. Executive power rests with the Federal Government, led by a Federal Chancellor – who is elected by the Bundestag. The President is elected for a five-year term by the Bundesrat and an equal number of representatives of the states. Each state has its own parliament and government.
Largest parties: (conservative) Christian Democratic Union (CDU) and (its Bavarian equivalent) Christian Social Union (CSU), Social Democratic Party (SPD), (liberal) Free Democratic Party (FDP), (former East German Communist) Party of Democratic Socialism (PDS), (Green) Die Grünen.
Local government: 16 states (Länder).
President: Roman Herzog (CDU).
Federal Chancellor (Prime Minister): Helmut Kohl (CDU).

States

Baden-Württemberg *Area:* 35,751 km² (13,804 sq mi). *Population:* 10,002,000 (1992 est). *Capital:* Stuttgart.
Bavaria (Bayern) *Area:* 70,554 km² (27,241 sq mi). *Population:* 11,596,000 (1992 est). *Capital:* Munich.
Berlin *Area:* 889 km² (343 sq mi). *Population:* 3,446,000 (1992 est). *Capital:* Berlin.
Brandenburg *Area:* 29,053 km² (11,219 sq mi). *Population:* 2,543,000 (1992 est). *Capital:* Potsdam.
Bremen *Area:* 404 km² (156 sq mi). *Population:*

684,000 (1992 est). *Capital:* Bremen.
Hamburg *Area:* 755 km^2 (292 sq mi). *Population:* 1,669,000 (1992 est). *Capital:* Hamburg.
Hesse (Hessen) *Area:* 21,114 km^2 (8152 sq mi). *Population:* 5,837,000 (1992 est). *Capital:* Wiesbaden.
Lower Saxony (Niedersachsen) *Area:* 47,364 km^2 (18,287 sq mi). *Population:* 7,476,000 (1992 est). *Capital:* Hannover.
Mecklenburg-West Pomerania (Mecklenburg-Vorpommern) *Area:* 23,598 km^2 (9111 sq mi). *Population:* 1,892,000 (1992 est). *Capital:* Schwerin.
North Rhine Westphalia (Nordrhein-Westfalen) *Area:* 34,070 km^2 (13,155 sq mi). *Population:* 17,510,000 (1992 est). *Capital:* Düsseldorf.
Rhineland Palatinate (Rheinland-Pfalz) *Area:* 19,846 km^2 (7664 sq mi). *Population:* 3,821,000 (1992 est). *Capital:* Mainz.
Saarland *Area:* 2570 km^2 (992 sq mi). *Population:* 1,077,000 (1992 est). *Capital:* Saarbrücken.
Saxony (Sachsen) *Area:* 18,338 km^2 (7080 sq mi). *Population:* 4,679,000 (1992 est). *Capital:* Dresden.
Saxony-Anhalt (Sachsen-Anhalt) *Area:* 20,443 km^2 (7893 sq mi). *Population:* 2,823,000 (1992 est). *Capital:* Magdeburg.
Schleswig-Holstein *Area:* 15,731 km^2 (6074 sq mi). *Population:* 2,649,000 (1992 est). *Capital:* Kiel.
Thuringia (Thüringen) *Area:* 16,251 km^2 (6275 sq mi). *Population:* 2,572,000 (1992 est). *Capital:* Erfurt.

Geography

The North German Plain, a region of fertile farmlands and sandy heaths, is drained by the Rivers Elbe, Weser and Oder. In the west, the plain merges with the North Rhine lowlands which contain the Ruhr coalfield and over 20% of the country's population. A belt of plateaux, formed of old hard rocks, crosses the country from east to west and includes the Hunsrück and Eifel highlands in the Rhineland and the Taunus and Westerwald uplands in Hesse, and extends into the Harz and Erz Mountains in Thuringia. The Rhine cuts through these central plateaux in a deep gorge. In southern Germany, the Black Forest (Schwarzwald) separates the Rhine valley from the fertile valleys and scarplands of Swabia. The forested edge of the Bohemian uplands marks the Czech border, while the Bavarian Alps form the frontier with Austria. ***Principal rivers:*** Rhine (Rhein), Elbe, Danube (Donau), Main, Weser, Oder, Moselle (Mosel), Havel, Neckar, Leine. ***Highest point:*** Zugspitze 2962m (9718 ft).
Climate: The climate is temperate, but with considerable variations between the generally mild north coastal plain and the Bavarian Alps in the south, which have cool summers and cold winters. The eastern part of the country has warm summers and cold winters.

Economy

Germany is the world's third economic power after the USA and Japan. The country's recovery after World War II has been called the 'German economic miracle'. The principal industries include mechanical and electrical engineering, chemicals, textiles, food processing and vehicles, with heavy industry and engineering concentrated in the Ruhr, chemicals in cities on the Rhine and motor vehicles in large provincial centres such as Stuttgart. From the 1980s, there has been a spectacular growth in high-technology industries. Apart from coal and brown coal, Germany has relatively few natural resources, and the country relies heavily upon imports. Labour has also been in short supply, and large numbers of 'guest workers' (*Gastarbeiter*) – particularly from Turkey and the former Yugoslavia – have been recruited. Since reunification in 1990 the labour shortage in the western part of the country has also been met by migration from the former GDR. Service industries employ almost twice as many people as manufacturing industry. Banking and finance are major foreign-currency earners and Frankfurt is one of the world's leading financial and business centres. Reunification has presented major problems and its costs led to an economic downturn. The GDR's economy had previously been the most successful in the Communist bloc, but, since reunification, many East German firms have been unable to compete with their Western counterparts. A trust (the *Treuhandanstalt*) was set up to oversee the privatization of the 8000 state-run firms in the east, but many have gone bankrupt and unemployment in the former GDR is high. The main German agricultural products include hops (for beer), grapes (for wine), sugar beet, wheat, barley, and dairy products. The collectivized farms of the former GDR were privatized in 1991. Forests cover almost 30% of Germany and support a flourishing timber industry. ***Currency:*** Deutsche Mark.

Recent History

From 1871 to 1918, an expansionist unified Germany attempted to extend its influence throughout Europe, engaged in naval and commercial rivalry with Britain, and built a colonial empire. Under the mercurial Emperor William II (reigned 1888–1918), Germany was a destabilizing force in world politics. Defeat in World War I (1914–18) led to the loss of much territory in Europe and the colonies overseas, the end of the German monarchies, the imposition of substantial reparations and the occupation of the Rhineland by Allied forces until 1930. The liberal Weimar republic (1919–33) could not bring economic or political stability. In the early 1930s the Nazi Party gained popularity, urging the establishment of a strong centralized government, an aggressive foreign policy, 'Germanic character' and the overturn of the postwar settlement. In 1933, Adolf Hitler (1889–1945) became Chancellor and in 1934 President. His Third Reich (empire) annexed Austria (1938), dismembered Czechoslovakia (1939) and embarked on the extermination of the Jews and others that the Nazis regarded as 'inferior'. Invading Poland (1939), he launched Germany into war, defeat, occupation and division.

In 1945, Germany lost substantial territories to Poland and was divided into four zones of occupation by the Allies – Britain, France, the USA and the USSR. Their intention was a united, disarmed Germany, but cooperation between the Allies rapidly broke down, and in 1948–49 the USSR blockaded West Berlin. The western zones of Germany were merged economically in 1948. After the merger of the western zones to form the Federal Republic of Germany, the German Democratic Republic was proclaimed in the Soviet zone (October 1949). The GDR's economic progress suffered by comparison with that of the Federal Republic. Food shortages and repressive Communist rule led to an abortive uprising in the GDR in 1953. West Germany gained sovereignty – as a member of the Western Alliance – in 1955. The division of Germany was only grudgingly accepted in West Germany. Chancellor Konrad Adenauer (1876–1967) refused to recognize East Germany as a separate state and relations with the Soviet Union remained uncertain. Major problems with the Eastern bloc included the undefined status of the areas taken over by Poland in 1945 and the difficult position of West Berlin – a part of the Federal Republic isolated within Communist East Germany.

Relations between East and West Germany were soured as large numbers of East Germans fled to the West, and this outflow was stemmed only when Walter Ulbricht (East German Communist Party leader 1950–71) ordered the building of the Berlin Wall. Adenauer strove to gain the acceptance of West Germany back into Western Europe through reconciliation with France and participation in the European Community. The economic revival of Germany begun by Adenauer continued under his Christian Democrat (conservative) successors as Chancellor – Ludwig Erhard (1963–66) and Georg Kiesinger (1966–69). Under Social Democrat Chancellors – Willy Brandt (1969–74) and Helmut Schmidt (1974–82) – treaties were signed with the USSR (1970) and Poland (recognizing the Oder-Neisse line as Poland's western frontier), and relations with the GDR were normalized (1972). Under Helmut Kohl (Christian Democrat Chancellor from 1982) West Germany continued its impressive economic growth and enthusiastic membership of the EC, and acted as an economic and cultural magnet for much of Eastern Europe.

The root causes of the GDR's problems resurfaced in the late 1980s. The ageing Communist leadership led by Erich Honecker proved unresponsive to the mood of greater freedom emanating from Gorbachov's USSR. In 1989 fresh floods of East Germans left the GDR for the West by way of Czechoslovakia and Hungary. Massive public demonstrations in favour of reform resulted in a change of leadership and the opening of the Berlin Wall (November 1989), allowing free movement between East and West. Demonstrations in favour of more radical change continued, and a coalition government was appointed in the GDR. When the GDR's economy collapsed, West Germany proposed monetary union and the call for German reunification became unstoppable. Despite the initial opposition of the USSR, the reunification of Germany as a full member of the EC and NATO took place in October 1990. Soviet troops withdrew from the former GDR in 1994.

GHANA

Official name: The Republic of Ghana.
Member of: UN, OAU, Commonwealth, ECOWAS.
Area: 238,533 km² (92,099 sq mi).
Population: 15,635,000 (1993 est).
Capital: Accra 1,580,000 (includes Tema 190,000) (1988 est).
Other major cities: Kumasi 490,000, Sekondi-Takoradi 175,000, Tamale 170,000 (1988 est).
Languages: English (official), Asante, Ewe, Ga.
Religions: Various Protestant Churches (30%), Roman Catholic (over 25%), Sunni Islam (20%), animist (17%).
Education: is compulsory, in theory, between the ages of six and 16. *Adult literacy:* 60%. *Universities:* five (including institutes of university status).
Defence: (1993 figures) *Army:* 5000 personnel. *Air force:* 1000. *Navy:* 900. *Paramilitary:* 5000. *Conscription:* none.

Government

The 200-member House of Parliament and a President are elected for four years by universal adult suffrage. The President appoints a 25-member Council of State, whose members include representatives of regional assemblies..
Largest parties: National Democratic Congress (NDC), (left-wing) National Convention Party (NCP), Independence Party (IP).
Local government: 10 regions.
President: Jerry Rawlings (NDC).

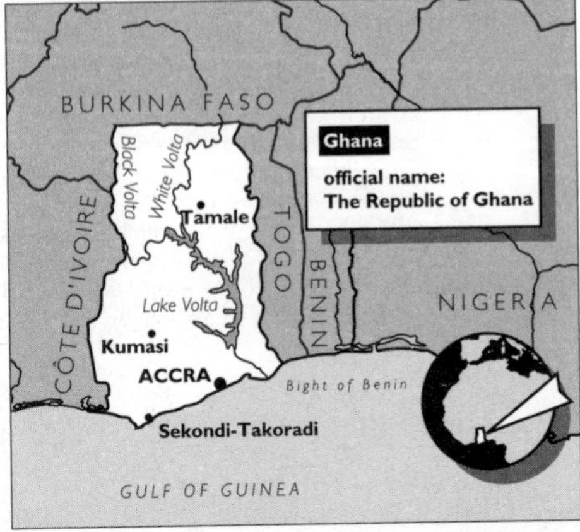

Geography

Most of the country is low-lying plains and plateaux. The central Volta Basin – which ends in steep escarpments – contains the large Lake Volta reservoir. ***Principal river:*** Volta (Black Volta and White Volta), Tano. ***Highest point:*** Afadjato 885m (2903 ft).
Climate: The climate is tropical with 2000 mm (80 in) of rainfall on the coast, decreasing markedly inland. The north is subject to the hot, dry Harmattan wind from the Sahara.

Economy

Political instability and mismanagement damaged the economy in the 1970s and 1980s. Nearly one half of the labour force is involved in farming. Cocoa is the main cash crop. Timber and mining for bauxite, gold and diamonds are important. ***Currency:*** Cedi.

Recent History

Britain established the Gold Coast colony in 1874. The great inland kingdom of Ashanti was not finally conquered until 1898. After World War II, the prosperity of the cocoa industry, increasing literacy and the dynamism of Dr Kwame Nkrumah (1909–72) helped the Gold Coast set the pace for decolonization in Black Africa. After independence in 1957 – as Ghana – Nkrumah's grandiose policies and increasingly dictatorial rule led to his overthrow in a military coup in 1966. Ghana has since struggled to overcome its economic and political problems. There were six coups in 20 years, including two by Flight Lieutenant Jerry Rawlings (1979 and 1982). A multi-party system was restored in 1992.

GREECE

Official name: Ellenikí Dimokrátia (Hellenic Republic) or Ellás (Greece).
Member of: UN, EU/EC, NATO, OSCE, OECD, WEU.
Area: 131,957 km² (50,949 sq mi).
Population: 10,310,000 (1993 est).
Capital: Athens (Athínai) 3,097,000 (includes Piraeus (Piraiévs) 196,000) (1991 census).
Other major cities: Thessaloníki (formerly Salonika) 706,000 (city 396,000), Patras (Pátrai) 154,000, Heraklion (Iráklion, formerly Candia) 115,000, Lárisa 113,000, Volos 76,000, Kavalla 58,000, Serres 50,000, Canea (Khania) 50,000 (1991 census).
Languages: Greek (official; over 96% as a first language), Macedonian (recognized by the Greek government as a dialect of Bulgarian; 1.5%), Vlach.
Religion: Orthodox (98%; official).
Education: is compulsory between the ages of six and 15. *Adult literacy:* 93%. *Universities:* 16.
Defence: (1993 figures) *Army:* 113,000 personnel. *Air force:* 26,800. *Navy:* 19,500. *Paramilitary:* 26,500. *Conscription:* 18–23 months.

Government

The 300-member Parliament is elected for four years by universal adult suffrage under a system of proportional representation. The President – who is elected for a five-year term by Parliament – appoints a Prime

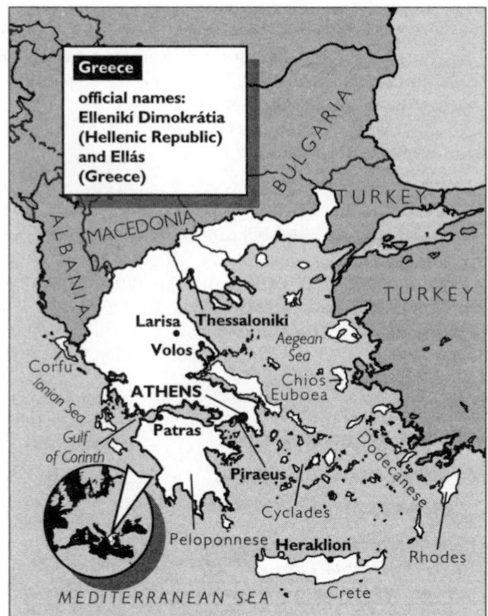

Minister (who commands a majority in Parliament) and other Ministers.

Largest parties: Pan-Hellenic Socialist Party (PASOK), (conservative) New Democracy Party (NDP), (centre-right) Political Spring, (Communist-led) Left Alliance (KKE).

Local government: 51 provinces grouped into 13 regions, plus the autonomous monks' republic of Mount Athos.

President: Kostis Stephanopoulos (ind).

Prime Minister: Andreas Papandreou (PASOK).

Regions

Attica (Attikí) *Area:* 3808 km^2 (1470 sq mi). *Population:* 3,523,000 (1991 census). *Capital:* Athens.

Central Greece (Stereá Ellás) *Area:* 15,549 km^2 (6004 sq mi). *Population:* 579,000 (1991 census). *Capital:* Lamia.

Central Macedonia (Kedrikí Makedhonía) *Area:* 18,811 km^2 (7263 sq mi) (excluding Mount Athos, see below). *Population:* 1,738,000 (1991 census). *Capital:* Thessaloníki.

Crete (Kríti) *Area:* 8336 km^2 (3218 sq mi). *Population:* 537,000 (1991 census). *Capital:* Heraklion.

Eastern Macedonia and Thrace (Anatolikí Makedhonía kaí Thráki) *Area:* 14,157 km^2 (5466 sq mi). *Population:* 570,000 (1991 census). *Capital:* Komotini.

Epirus (Ipiros) *Area:* 9203 km^2 (3553 sq mi). *Population:* 339,000 (1991 census). *Capital:* Ioannina.

Ionian Islands (Iónioi Nísoi) *Area:* 2307 km^2 (891 sq mi). *Population:* 191,000 (1991 census). *Capital:* Corfu (Kérkira).

North Aegean (Vóreion Aiyaíon) *Area:* 3836 km^2 (1481 sq mi). *Population:* 198,000 (1991 census). *Capital:* Mitilini.

Peloponnese (Pelopónnisos) *Area:* 15,490 km^2 (5981 sq mi). *Population:* 606,000 (1991 census). *Capital:* Tripolis.

South Aegean (Nótion Aiyaíon) *Area:* 5286 km^2 (2041 sq mi). *Population:* 258,000 (1991 census). *Capital:* Siros.

Thessaly (Thessalía) *Area:* 14,037 km^2 (5420 sq mi). *Population:* 731,000 (1991 census). *Capital:* Larisa.

Western Greece (Dhytikí Ellás) *Area:* 11,350 km^2 (4382 sq mi). *Population:* 702,000 (1991 census). *Capital:* Patras.

Western Macedonia (Dhytikí Makedhonía) *Area:* 9451 km^2 (3649 sq mi). *Population:* 293,000 (1991 census). *Capital:* Kozani.

Mount Athos (Ayion Oros) *Area:* 336 km^2 (130 sq mi). *Population:* 1400 (1991 est). *Capital:* Karyai.

Geography

Over 80% of Greece is mountainous. The mainland is dominated by the Pindus Mountains, which extend from Albania south into the Peloponnese Peninsula. The Rhodope Mountains lie along the Bulgarian border. Greece has some 2000 islands, of which only 154 are inhabited. ***Principal rivers:*** Vardar, Struma, Nestos, Aliákon, Piniós, Evrótas. ***Highest point:*** Mount Olympus (Olimbos) 2917m (9570 ft).

Climate: Greece has a Mediterranean climate with hot dry summers and mild wet winters. The north and the mountains are colder.

Economy

Agriculture involves 25% of the labour force. Much of the land is marginal – in particular the extensive sheep pastures. Greece is largely self-sufficient in wheat, barley, maize, sugar beet, fruit, vegetables, and cheese, and produces enough wine, olives (and olive oil) and tobacco for export. The industrial sector is expanding rapidly and includes processing local petroleum and natural gas, lignite, and bauxite. Tourism, a large merchant fleet, and money sent back by Greeks working abroad are major foreign-currency earners. Greece receives special economic aid from the EC. ***Currency:*** Drachma.

Recent History

Under a Danish prince – who became King George I in 1863 – Greece gained extra territory in 1863, 1881 and 1913, as Turkish power declined. The 20th century has been marked by great instability. Eleuthérios Venizélos (1864–1936) dominated Greek politics from 1910 to 1935, a period of rivalry between republicans and royalists. An attempt by his rival King Constantine I to seize Anatolia from Turkey (1921–22) ended in military defeat and the establishment of a republic in 1924. The monarchy was restored in 1935, but it depended upon a military leader, General Ioannis Metaxas (1871–1941), who, claiming the threat from Communism as justification, ruled as virtual dictator. The nation was deeply divided. The German invasion of 1941 was met by rival resistance groups of Communists and monarchists, and the subsequent civil war between these factions lasted from 1945 to 1949, when, with British and US aid, the monarchists emerged victorious. Continued instability in the 1960s led to a military coup in 1967. King Constantine II, who had not initially opposed the coup, unsuccessfully appealed for the overthrow of the junta and went into exile. The dictatorship of the colonels ended in 1974 when their encouragement of a Greek Cypriot coup brought Greece to the verge of war with Turkey. Civilian government was restored, and a new republican constitution was adopted in 1975. Greece has forged closer links with Western Europe, in particular through membership of the EC (1981). Greek opposition delayed international recognition of the former Yugoslav republic of Macedonia (1992–93) and in 1994 Greece defied the EC by imposing an economic blockade on Macedonia.

GRENADA

Official name: The State of Grenada.
Member of: UN, OAS, Commonwealth, CARICOM.
Area: 344 km² (133 sq mi).
Population: 91,000 (1991 census).
Capital: St George's 36,000 (city 4400; 1991 census).
Language: English (official); French-African patois.
Religions: Roman Catholic (82%), Anglican.
Education: is compulsory between the ages of six and 14. *Adult literacy:* 85%. *Universities:* one university centre.
Defence: There is a small paramilitary unit of the police force.

Government

The 13-member Senate is appointed. The 15-member House of Representatives is elected for five years by universal adult suffrage. The Governor General – the representative of the British Queen as sovereign of Grenada – appoints a Prime Minister (who commands a majority in the House) and a Cabinet.
Largest parties: (centre) National Democratic Congress (NDC), (right-wing) Grenada United Labour Party (GULP), the National Party (TNP), (centre) New National Party (NPP).
Local government: nine parishes and one town.
Prime Minister: Nicholas Braithwaite (NDC).

Geography

A forested mountain ridge covers much of this well-watered island. The island of Carriacou forms part of Grenada. ***Principal river:*** Great River. ***Highest point:*** Mount St Catherine 840m (2757 ft).
Climate: Grenada has a tropical maritime climate with a dry season from January to May.

Economy

The production of spices, in particular nutmeg, is the mainstay of a largely agricultural economy. Tourism is increasing in importance. ***Currency:*** East Caribbean dollar.

Recent History

Grenada was ceded to Britain in 1783. Independence was gained in 1974. The left-wing New Jewel Movement seized power in a coup in 1979. In 1983 the Premier Maurice Bishop was killed in a further coup in which more extreme members of the government seized power. Acting upon a request from East Caribbean islands to intervene, US and Caribbean forces landed in Grenada. After several days' fighting, the coup leaders were detained. Constitutional rule was restored in 1984.

ST VINCENT
CARIBBEAN SEA
THE GRENADINES
Carriacou
GRENADA
ST GEORGE'S
Grenada
official name:
The State of Grenada

GUATEMALA

Official name: República de Guatemala (Republic of Guatemala).
Member of: UN, OAS, CACM.
Area: 108,889 km² (42,042 sq mi).
Population: 9,713,000 (1993 est).
Capital: Guatemala City 2,074,000 (city 1,133,000; 1993 est)
Other major cities: Puerto Barrios 338,000 (city 39,000), Quezaltenango 246 000 (city 98,000), Escuintla 66,000 (1993 est).
Language: Spanish (official; about 55% as a first language), over 20 Mayan languages (45%).
Religions: Roman Catholic (official; 65%), various Protestant Evangelical Churches (35%).
Education: is compulsory in urban areas only between the ages of seven and 14. *Adult literacy:* 60%. *Universities:* five.
Defence: (1993 figures) *Army:* 42,000 personnel. *Air force:* 700. *Navy:* 1200. *Paramilitary:* 12,500. *Conscription:* 30 months.

Government

A President – who appoints a Cabinet – and the 116-member National Congress are elected for a four-year term by universal adult suffrage. The National Congress comprises 87 members elected by constituencies and 29 members elected under a system of proportional representation.
Largest parties: (centre-right) Union of National Centre, (right-wing) Christian Democratic Party (PDGC), (centre-right) Movement for Action and Solidarity (MAS).
Local government: 22 departments.
President: Ramiro de Leon Carpio (non-party).

Geography

A mountain chain – containing over 30 volcanoes – separates Pacific and Atlantic coastal lowlands. ***Principal rivers:*** Motagua, Sarstun, Polochic, Dulce, Usumacinta. ***Highest point:*** Tajumulco 4220m (13,845 ft).

Climate: The coastal plains have a tropical climate; the mountains are more temperate.

Economy

More than one half of the labour force is involved in agriculture. Coffee is the major export, while the other main crops include sugar cane and bananas. ***Currency:*** Quetzal.

Recent History

Until recent times, Guatemala has a history of being ruled by dictators allied to landowners. However, in the 1950s President Jacobo Arbenz expropriated large estates, dividing them among the peasantry. Accused of being a Communist, he was deposed by the army with US military aid (1954). For over 30 years, the left was suppressed, leading to the emergence of guerrilla armies. Thousands of dissidents were killed or disappeared. Civilian government was restored in 1986. In 1993, President Serrano was deposed after attempting to impose a dictatorship, and a government of national unity was formed.

GUINEA

Official name: La République de Guinée (The Republic of Guinea).

Member of: UN, OAU, ECOWAS.

Area: 245,857 km² (94,926 sq mi).

Population: 7,420,000 (1993 est).

Capital: Conakry 705,000 (1983 est).

Other major city: Kankan 89,000 (1983 est).

Languages: French (official), Fulani (40%), Soussou (11%).

Religion: Sunni Islam (85%).

Education: is compulsory, in theory, between the ages of seven and 13. *Adult literacy:* 24%. *Universities:* two.

Defence: (1993 figures) *Army:* 8500 personnel. *Air force:* 800. *Navy:* 400. *Paramilitary:* 9600. *Conscription:* two years.

Government

Power is exercised by the 15-member Military Committee for National Recovery, whose President is head of state and of government. Political parties are allowed but no date has been set for multi-party elections to a new unicameral parliament.

Largest parties: Party of Unity and Progress (PUP), Rally for Guinean People (RPG), Union of the New Republic (UNR).

Local government: 33 prefectures grouped into eight regions.

President: Gen. Lansana Conte (PUP).

Geography

Tropical rain forests cover the coastal plain. The interior highlands and plains are covered by grass and scrubland. The southwest mountains rise to Mount Nimba. ***Principal rivers:*** Niger, Milo, Bouka, Konkouré. ***Highest point:*** Mount Nimba 1752m (5747 ft).

Climate: The climate is tropical with heavy rainfall. Temperatures are cooler in the highlands.

Economy

Bauxite accounts for 80% of Guinea's exports. However, over 75% of the labour force is involved in agriculture, producing bananas, oil palm and citrus fruits for export, and maize, rice and cassava as subsistence crops. Despite mineral wealth, Guinea is one of the world's poorest states and relies heavily on aid. ***Currency:*** Guinean franc.

Recent History

Increasing French influence in the 19th century led to the establishment of the colony of French Guinea (1890). Unlike the rest of French Africa, Guinea voted for a complete separation from France in 1958, suffering severe French reprisals as a result. The authoritarian radical leader Sékou Touré (1922–84) isolated Guinea, but he became reconciled with France in 1978. The leaders of a military coup (1984) have achieved some economic reforms, but a return to constitutional rule has been postponed.

GUINEA-BISSAU

Official name: Republica da Guiné-Bissau (Republic of Guinea-Bissau).

Member of: UN, OAU, ECOWAS.

Area: 36,125 km² (13,948 sq mi).

Population: 1,035,000 (1993 est).

Capital: Bissau 125,000 (1988 est).

Other main town: Bafatá 13,500 (1980 est).

Languages: Portuguese (official), Crioulo (Creole dialect; majority).

Religions: animist (55%), Sunni Islam (40%).

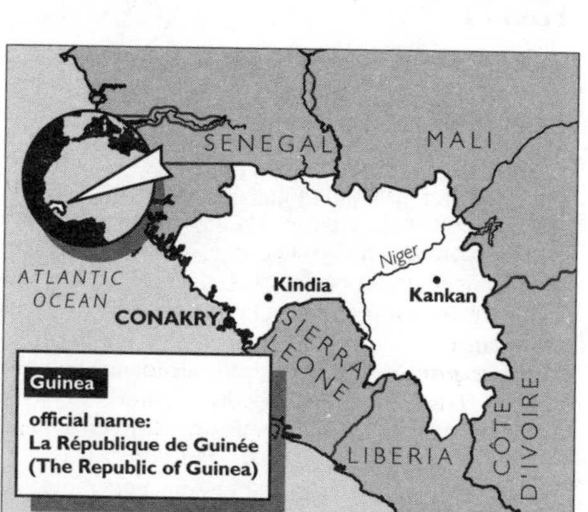

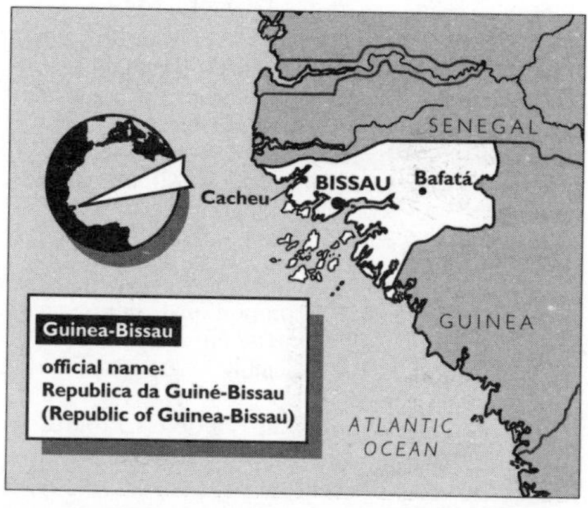

Education: is compulsory, in theory,, between the ages of seven and 12. *Adult literacy:* 37%. *Universities:* one.
Defence: (1993 figures) *Army:* 6800 personnel. *Air force:* 100. *Navy:* 300. *Paramilitary:* 2000. *Conscription:* none.

Government

The 150-member Assembly – which is elected by universal adult suffrage – elects a President, who appoints a Prime Minister and a Cabinet of Ministers.
Largest parties: (former monopoly socialist) African Party for the Independence of Guinea-Bissau and Cape Verde (PAIGC), Guinea-Bissau Resistance-Bafata Movement (RGB-MB), Party for Renovation and Development (PRD).
Local government: nine regions.
President: Gen. João Bernardo Vieira (PAIGC).
Prime Minister: Manuel Saturnino (PAIGC).

Geography

Most of the country is low-lying, with swampy coastal lowlands and a flat forested interior plain. The northeast is mountainous. ***Principal rivers:*** Corubal, Cacheu. ***Highest point:*** an unnamed point on the Fouta Djallon plateau 180m (591 ft).
Climate: The climate is tropical with a dry season from December to May.

Economy

The country has one of the lowest standards of living in the world. Its subsistence economy is based mainly on rice. Palm kernels and timber are exported.
Currency: Peso.

Recent History

The colony of Portuguese Guinea was created in 1879. Failing to secure reform by peaceful means, the PAIGC movement mounted a liberation war (1961–74). Independence was proclaimed in 1973 and recognized by Portugal in 1974. Multi-party politics were introduced in 1991.

GUYANA

Official name: The Cooperative Republic of Guyana.
Member of: UN, Commonwealth, OAS, CARICOM.
Area: 215,083 km² (83,044 sq mi).
Population: 730,000 (1993 est).
Capital: Georgetown 195,000 (including suburbs; 1986 est).
Other main town: Linden 30,000 (1986 est).
Languages: English (official), Hindu, Urdu.
Religions: Hinduism (34%), various Protestant Churches (34%), Roman Catholic (18%), Sunni Islam.
Education: is compulsory between the ages of six and 14. *Adult literacy:* 96%. *Universities:* one.
Defence: (1993 figures) *Army:* 1500 personnel. *Air force:* 100. *Navy:* 100. *Paramilitary:* 4500. *Conscription:* none.

Government

The 65-member National Assembly is elected for five years under a system of proportional representation by universal adult suffrage. The President – the leader of the majority in the Assembly – appoints a Prime Minister and Cabinet.
Largest parties: (left-wing) People's Progressive Party (PPP), (left-wing) People's National Congress (PNC), (left-wing) Forum for Democracy, (left-wing) Working People's Alliance (WPA), (conservative) United Force.
Local government: 10 regions.
President: Cheddi Jagan (PPP).
Prime Minister: Samuel Hinds (PPP).

Geography

A coastal plain is protected from the sea by dykes. Tropical rain forest and plateaux cover much of the interior. The Pakaraima range rises on the western border. ***Principal rivers:*** Courantyne, Berbice, Demerara, Essequibo. ***Highest point:*** Mount Roraima 2772m (9094 ft).
Climate: The interior is tropical, while the coastal plain is more moderate.

Economy

Guyana depends on mining bauxite and growing sugar cane and rice. Nationalization and emigration have caused economic problems. ***Currency:*** Guyana dollar.

Recent History

British Guiana was formed in 1831. From the 1840s large numbers of Indian and Chinese labourers were imported from Asia to work on sugar plantations. Racial tension between their descendants – now the majority – and the Black community (descended from imported African slaves) led to violence in 1964 and 1978. Guyana has been independent since 1966.

HAITI

Official name: La République d'Haïti (Republic of Haiti).
Member of: UN, OAS, CARICOM.
Area: 27,750 km² (10,714 sq mi).
Population: 6,903,000 (1993 est).
Capital: Port-au-Prince 1,402,000 (including suburbs; 1992 est).
Other major cities: Les Cayes 251,000, Jacmel 238,000, Gonaïves 175,000, Port de Paix 161,000, Cap Haïtien 157,000 (including suburbs; 1988 est).
Languages: Creole (90%), French – both official.
Religions: Roman Catholic (official; nominally 80%); voodoo (practised by the majority).
Education: is compulsory, in theory, between the ages of six and 12. *Adult literacy:* 53%. *Universities:* two.
Defence: (1993 figures) *Army:* 6000 personnel. *Air force:* 150. *Navy:* 250. *Conscription:* none.

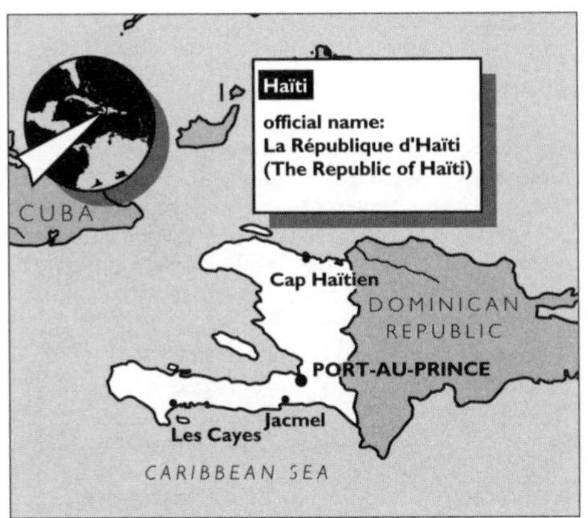

Government

The constitution provides for a President, 27-member Senate and 77-member Chamber of Deputies elected for five years.

Largest parties: (centre-left coalition) National Front for Change and Democracy (FNCD); many other small parties.

Local government: nine departments.

President: Fr. Jean-Bertrand Aristide (FNCD).

Prime Minister: Smarck Michel (FNCD).

Geography

Haiti is the western part of the island of Hispaniola. Mountain ranges – up to 2800m (8800 ft) – run from east to west, separated by densely populated valleys and plains. ***Principal rivers:*** Artibonite, Trois Rivières. ***Highest point:*** Pic La Selle 2674m (8793 ft).

Climate: Haiti's tropical climate is moderated by altitude and by the sea.

Economy

Over 65% of the labour force are involved in agriculture, mainly growing crops for local consumption. Coffee is the main cash crop. With few resources, overpopulated Haiti is the poorest country in the western hemisphere. ***Currency:*** Gourde.

Recent History

Coups, instability and tension between Blacks and mulattos wracked Haiti until the US intervened (1915–35). President François Duvalier ('Papa Doc'; in office 1956–71) and his son Jean-Claude (1971–86) cowed the country into submission by means of their infamous private militia, the Tontons Macoutes. Several coups have followed the violent end to the Duvalier era. A free multi-party election – the first in Haiti's history – took place in 1991, but constitutional government was suspended following a military coup nine months later when President Aristide was deposed. International sanctions and US intervention restored Aristide to power in 1994. Many thousands of Haitians attempt to enter the USA illegally every year.

HONDURAS

Official name: La República de Honduras (Republic of Honduras).

Member of: UN, OAS, CACM.

Area: 112,088 km^2 (43,277 sq mi).

Population: 5,150,000 (1993 est).

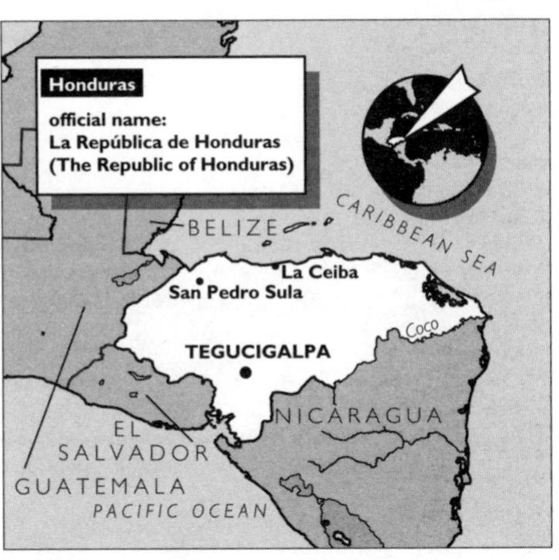

Capital: Tegucigalpa 679,000 (including suburbs; 1988 census).

Other major cities: San Pedro Sula 461,000, La Ceiba 72,000 (including suburbs; 1988 census).

Language: Spanish (official).

Religion: Roman Catholic (85%); various Protestant Evangelical Churches.

Education: is compulsory, in theory, between the ages of seven and 13. *Adult literacy:* 73%. *Universities:* four.

Defence: (1993 figures) *Army:* 14,000 personnel. *Air force:* 1800. *Navy:* 1000. *Conscription:* eight months.

Government

The President and the 128-member National Assembly are elected by universal adult suffrage for four years.

Largest parties: Liberal Party of Honduras (PLH), (right-wing) National Party of Honduras (PNH).

Local government: 18 departments and one central district.

President: Carlos Roberto Reina (PLH).

Geography

Over three quarters of Honduras is mountainous. There are small coastal plains. ***Principal rivers:*** Patuca, Ulúa. ***Highest point:*** Cerro Selaque 2849m (9347 ft).

Climate: The tropical lowlands experience high rainfall (1500–2000 mm / 60–80 in). The more temperate highlands are drier.

Economy

Over 40% of Hondurans work in agriculture, but despite agrarian reform, living standards remain low. Bananas and coffee are the leading exports. There are few natural resources. ***Currency:*** Lempira.

Recent History

Between independence from Spain and the early 20th century, Honduras experienced constant political upheaval and wars with neighbouring countries. US influence was immense, largely owing to the substantial investments of the powerful United Fruit Company in banana production. After a short civil war in 1925, a succession of military dictators governed Honduras until 1980. Since then the country has had democratically elected pro-US centre-right civilian governments.

HUNGARY

Official name: Magyar Köztársásag (The Hungarian Republic) or Magyarország (Hungary).
Member of: UN, OSCE, CEFTA.
Area: 93,033 km^2 (35,920 sq mi).
Population: 10,296,000 (1993 est).
Capital: Budapest 1,992,000 (1993 est).
Other major cities: Debrecen 215,000, Miskolc 192,000, Szeged 178,000, Pécs 169,000, Györ 130,000, Nyíragyháza 115,000, Székesfehérvár 110,000, Kecskemét 105,000 (1992 est).
Language: Magyar (Hungarian; official; 97%).
Religions: Roman Catholic (56%), Calvinist and Lutheran Churches (22%).
Education: is compulsory between the ages of six and 14. *Adult literacy:* 99%. *Universities:* 20 (including 10 technical universities).
Defence: (1993 figures) *Army:* 60,500 personnel. *Air force:* 17,500. *Paramilitary:* 9000. *Conscription:* 12 months.

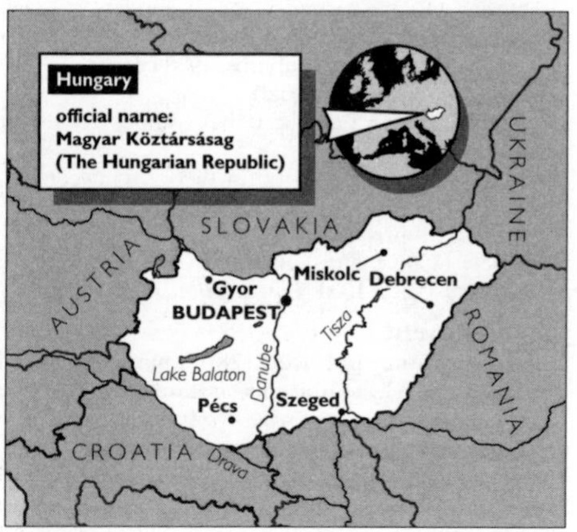

Government

The 386-member National Assembly is elected by universal adult suffrage, with 58 members elected from a national list, 152 elected on a county basis and 176 elected from single-member constituencies. The President – who is elected by the Assembly – appoints a Prime Minister and Cabinet from the majority in the Assembly.
Largest parties: (former Communist) Hungarian Socialist Party (MSzP), (liberal) Alliance of Free Democrats (SzDSz), (centre-right) Hungarian Democratic Forum (MDF), Independent Smallholders' Party (FKgP), Christian Democratic People's Rally (KDNP), (centre-right) Federation of Young Democrats (FIDESz).
Local government: 19 counties plus the capital.
President: Arpad Goncz (SzDSz).
Prime Minister: Gyula Horn (MSzP).

Geography

Hungary west of the River Danube is an undulating lowland. The thickly wooded highlands of the northeast contain the highest point, Kékes. The centre and east is a large expanse of flat plain, the Great Alfold.
Principal rivers: Danube (Duna), Tisza, Rába, Drava. ***Highest point:*** Kékes 1015m (3330 ft).
Climate: The climate is continental with long, hot and dry summers, and cold winters.

Economy

Nearly one seventh of the labour force is involved in agriculture. Major crops include cereals (maize, wheat and barley), sugar beet, fruit, and grapes for wine. Despite large reserves of coal, Hungary imports over 50% of its energy needs. The steel, chemical fertilizer, pharmaceutical, machinery and vehicle industries are important. Since the early 1980s, private enterprise and foreign investment have been encouraged, and most large state enterprises have been privatized.
Currency: Forint.

Recent History

In 1867, Austria granted Hungary considerable autonomy in the Dual Monarchy – the Austro-Hungarian Empire. Defeat in World War I led to a brief period of Communist rule under Béla Kun (1919), then occupation by Romania. In the postwar settlement, Hungary lost two thirds of its territory. The Regent Admiral Miklás Horthy (1868–1957) cooperated with Hitler during World War II in an attempt to regain territory, but defeat in 1945 resulted in occupation by the Red Army, and a Communist People's Republic was established in 1949. The Hungarian Uprising in 1956 was a heroic attempt to overthrow Communist rule, but was quickly suppressed by Soviet forces, and its leader, Imre Nagy, was executed. János Kadar – Party Secretary 1956–88 – tried to win support with economic progress. However, in the late 1980s reformers in the Communist Party gained the upper hand, and established a fully democratic, multi-party state. Soviet troops left Hungary in 1990. The country has taken rapid steps to establish a free-market economy. Hungary has become an associate, and has applied for full membership, of the EU/EC. The status of 3,000,000 ethnic Hungarians in neighbouring states has become an issue.

ICELAND

Official name: Lýdveldid Island (The Republic of Iceland).
Member of: UN, NATO, OSCE.
Area: 102,819 km^2 (39,699 sq mi).
Population: 264,000 (1993 est).
Capital: Reykjavik 154,000 (city 101,000; Kópavogur 17,000; Hafnarfjördhur 16,000; 1992 est).
Other major towns: Akureyri 15,000, Keflavik 7500 (1992 est).
Language: Icelandic (official; 100%).
Religion: Evangelical Lutheran (93%).
Education: is compulsory between the ages of six and 15. *Adult literacy:* virtually 100%. *Universities:* one.
Defence: (1993 figures) *Coastguards:* 130.

Government

The 63-member Althing (Parliament) is elected under a system of proportional representation by universal adult suffrage for a four-year term and meets as an Upper House of 20 members and a Lower House of 43 members. The President – who is also directly elected for four years – appoints a Prime Minister and a Cabinet who are responsible to the Althing.
Largest parties: (conservative) Independence Party (IP), Progressive Party (PP), Social Democratic Party (SDP), (socialist) People's Alliance (PA), Women's Alliance (WA).

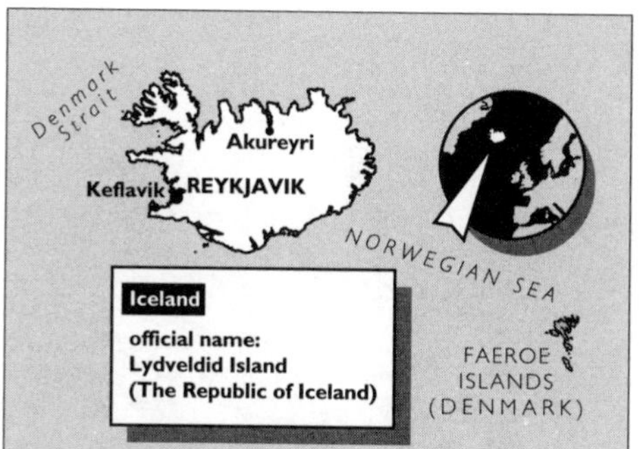

Local government: seven districts.
President: Vigdis Finnbogadottir.
Prime Minister: David Oddson (IP).

Geography

The greater part of Iceland has a volcanic landscape with hot springs, geysers and some 200 volcanoes – some of them active. Much of the country is tundra. The south and centre are covered by glacial icefields, the largest of which contains the country's highest peak. ***Principal rivers:*** Thjórsa, Hvita, Skjalfanda. ***Highest point:*** Hvannadalshnúkur 2119m (6950 ft). ***Climate:*** The cool temperate climate is warmed by the Gulf Stream, which keeps Iceland milder than most places at the same latitude.

Economy

The fishing industry provides the majority of Iceland's exports. Hydroelectric power is used to smelt aluminium; geothermal power warms extensive greenhouses. Ample grazing land makes Iceland self-sufficient in meat and dairy products. ***Currency:*** Krona.

Recent History

Nationalism grew in the 19th century, and in 1918 Iceland gained independence, linked to Denmark only by their shared monarchy. In World War II the Danish link was severed and a republic was declared (1944). Disputes over fishing rights in Icelandic territorial waters led to clashes with British naval vessels in the 1950s and 1970s.

INDIA

Official name: Bharat (Republic of India).
Member of: UN, Commonwealth.
Area: 3,287,263 km² (1,269,219 sq mi) – including 121,667 km² (44,976 sq mi) of Jammu and Kashmir claimed by India but occupied by Pakistan and China.
Population: 896,570,000 (1993 est).
Capital: Delhi 8,419,000 (city 7,207,000; 1991 census).
Other major cities: Bombay 12,596,000 (city 9,926,000; Kalyan 1,014,000; Thane 797,000), Calcutta 11,022,000 (city 4,388,000; Hoara 946,000), Madras 5,422,000 (city 3,841,000), Hyderabad 4,254,000 (city 3,146,000), Bangalore 4,130,000 (city 3,303,000), Ahmedabad 3,298,000 (city 2,873,000), Poona (Pune) 2,485,000 (city 1,560,000), Kanpur 2,111,000 (city 1,958,000), Nagpur 1,661,000 (city 1,622,000), Lucknow 1,642,000 (city 1,592,000), Surat 1,517,000 (1,497,000), Jaipur 1,514,000 (city 1,455,000), Kochi (formerly Cochin) 1,140,000 (city 564,000), Coimbatore 1,136,000 (city 853,000), Vadodara (formerly Baroda) 1,115,000 (city 1,021,000), Indore 1,104,000 (city 1,087,000), Patna 1,099,000 (city 917,000), Madurai 1,094,000 (city 952,000), Bhopal 1,064,000, Visakhapatnam 1,052,000 (city 750,000), Varanasi (formerly Banares or Benares) 1,026,000, Ludhiana 1,012,000, Agra 956,000 (city 899,000), Jabalpur 887,000 (city 740,000), Allahabad 858,000 (city 806,000), Meerut 847,000 (city 752,000), Vijaywada 845,000 (city 701,000), Jamshedpur 835,000 (city 461,000), Thiruvananthapuram (formerly Trivandrum) 826,000 (city 524,000), Dhanbad 818,000, Kozhikode (formerly Calicut) 801,000 (city 420,000) (1991 census).
Languages: Hindi (30%; official), English (official), Bengali (8%), Telugu (8%), Marathi (8%), Tamil (7%), Urdu (5%), Gujarati (5%); over 1600 other languages.
Religions: Hindu (83%), Sunni Islam (11%), Christian (mainly Roman Catholic) (nearly 3%).
Education: is compulsory, in theory, between the ages of six and 14. *Adult literacy:* 48%. *Universities:* 180 universities and institutes of university status.
Defence: (1993 figures) *Army:* 1,100,000 personnel. *Air force:* 110,000. *Navy:* 55,000. *Conscription:* may occur only in the event of an emergency.

Government

The upper house of the federal parliament – the 245-member Council of States (Rajya Sabha) – consists of 12 members nominated by the President and 233 members elected by state assemblies. One third of the Council retires every two years. The lower house – the House of the People (Lok Sabha) – consists of 542 members elected for a five-year term by universal adult suffrage, plus two nominated members. The President – who serves for five years – is elected by the federal parliament and the state assemblies. The President appoints a Prime Minister – who has a majority in the House – and a Council of Ministers, who are responsible to the House. Each of the 25 states has its own legislature. ***Largest parties:*** Congress (I) Party, Janata Dal (People's Party; JD), (right-wing Hindu) Bharatiya Janata Party (Indian People's Party; NJP), Communist Party of India – Marxist (CPIM), Communist Party of India (CPI), All India Anna Dravida Munnetra Kazagan (AIADMK), Telegu Desam (TD), Revolutionary Socialist Party (RSP).
Local government: 25 states and seven Union territories.
President: Shankar Dayal Sharma.
Prime Minister: P.V. Narasimha Rao (Congress I).

States and Union Territories

Andhra Pradesh *Area:* 275,068 km² (106,204 sq mi). *Population:* 66,508,000 (1991 census). *Capital:* Hyderabad.
Arunachal Pradesh *Area:* 83,743 km² (32,333 sq mi). *Population:* 865,000 (1991 census). *Capital:* Itanagar.
Assam *Area:* 78,438 km² (30,285 sq mi). *Population:* 22,414,000 (1991 census). *Capital:* Dispur.
Bihar *Area:* 173,877 km² (67,134 sq mi). *Population:* 86,374,000 (1991 census). *Capital:* Patna.
Goa *Area:* 3702 km² (1429 sq mi). *Population:* 1,170,000 (1991 census). *Capital:* Panaji.
Gujarat *Area:* 196,024 km² (75,685 sq mi). *Population:* 41,310,000 (1991 census). *Capital:* Gandhinagar.
Haryana *Area:* 44,212 km² (17,070 sq mi). *Population:* 16,464,000 (1991 census). *Capital:* Chandigarh (see Union territories, below).

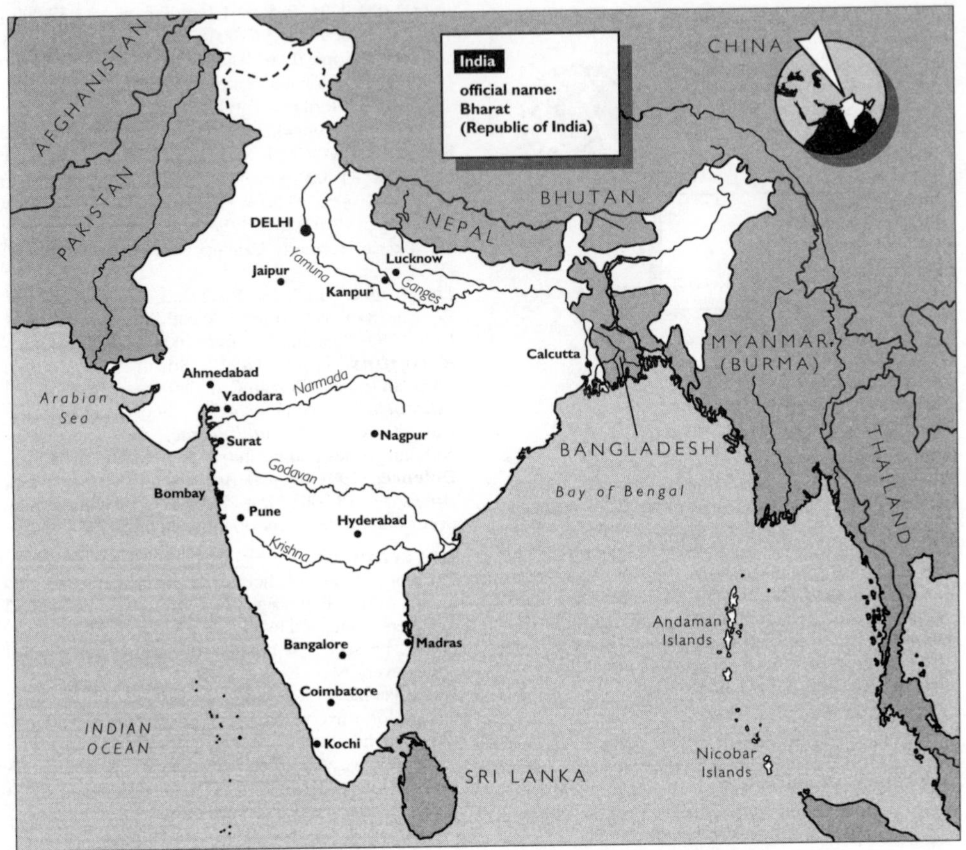

Himachal Pradesh *Area:* 55,673 km² (21,495 sq mi). *Population:* 5,171,000 (1991 census). *Capital:* Shimla.

Jammu and Kashmir *Area:* 222,236 km² (85,805 sq mi) – part of Jammu and Kashmir is occupied by Pakistan and by China; see Area (of India), above. *Population:* 7,719,000 (area under Indian administration only; 1991 census). *Capital:* Srinagar.

Karnataka *Area:* 191,791 km² (74,051 sq mi). *Population:* 44,977,000 (1991 census). *Capital:* Bangalore.

Kerala *Area:* 38,863 km² (15,005 sq mi). *Population:* 29,099,000 (1991 census). *Capital:* Thiruvananthapuram (Trivandrum).

Madhya Pradesh *Area:* 443,446 km² (171,215 sq mi). *Population:* 66,181,000 (1991 census). *Capital:* Bhopal.

Maharashtra *Area:* 307,690 km² (118,800 sq mi). *Population:* 78,937,000 (1991 census). *Capital:* Bombay.

Manipur *Area:* 22,327 km² (8621 sq mi). *Population:* 1,837,000 (1991 census). *Capital:* Imphal.

Meghalaya *Area:* 22,429 km² (8660 sq mi). *Population:* 1,775,000 (1991 census). *Capital:* Shillong.

Mizoram *Area:* 21,081 km² (8140 sq mi). *Population:* 690,000 (1991 census). *Capital:* Aizawl.

Nagaland *Area:* 16,579 km² (6401 sq mi). *Population:* 1,210,000 (1991 census). *Capital:* Kohima.

Orissa *Area:* 155,707 km² (60,119 sq mi). *Population:* 31,660,000 (1991 census). *Capital:* Bhubaneshwar.

Punjab *Area:* 50,362 km² (19,445 sq mi). *Population:* 20,282,000 (1991 census). *Capital:* Chandigarh (see Union territories, below).

Rajasthan *Area:* 342,239 km² (132,140 sq mi). *Population:* 44,006,000 (1991 census). *Capital:* Jaipur.

Sikkim *Area:* 7096 km² (2740 sq mi). *Population:* 406,000 (1991 census). *Capital:* Gangtok.

Tamil Nadu *Area:* 130,058 km² (50,216 sq mi). *Population:* 55,859,000 (1991 census). *Capital:* Madras.

Tripura *Area:* 10,486 km² (4049 sq mi). *Population:* 2,757,000 (1991 census). *Capital:* Agartala.

Uttar Pradesh *Area:* 294,411 km² (113,673 sq mi). *Population:* 139,112,000 (1991 census). *Capital:* Lucknow.

West Bengal *Area:* 88,752 km² (34,267 sq mi). *Population:* 68,078,000 (1991 census). *Capital:* Calcutta.

Andaman and Nicobar Islands (Union Territory) *Area:* 8249 km² (3185 sq mi). *Population:* 281,000 (1991 census). *Capital:* Port Blair.

Chandigarh (Union Territory) *Area:* 114 km² (44 sq mi). *Population:* 642,000 (1991 census). *Capital:* Chandigarh.

Dadra and Nagar Haveli (Union Territory) *Area:* 491 km² (190 sq mi). *Population:* 138,000 (1991 census). *Capital:* Silvassa.

Daman and Diu (Union Territory) *Area:* 112 km^2 (43 sq mi). *Population:* 102,000 (1991 census). *Capital:* Daman.

Delhi (Union Territory) *Area:* 1483 km^2 (572 sq mi). *Population:* 9,421,000 (1991 census). *Capital:* Delhi.

Lakshadweep (Union Territory) *Area:* 32 km^2 (12 sq mi). *Population:* 52,000 (1991 census). *Capital:* Kavaratti.

Pondicherry (Union Territory) *Area:* 492 km^2 (190 sq mi). *Population:* 808,000 (1991 census). *Capital:* Pondicherry.

Geography

The Himalaya cut the Indian subcontinent off from the rest of Asia. Several Himalayan peaks within India rise to over 7000 m (23,000 ft). South of the Himalaya, the basins of the Rivers Ganges and Brahmaputra and their tributaries are intensively farmed and densely populated. The Thar Desert is along the border with Pakistan. In south India, the Deccan – a large plateau of hard rocks – is bordered in the east and west by the Ghats, discontinuous ranges of hills descending to coastal plains. Natural vegetation ranges from tropical rain forest on the west coast and monsoon forest in the northeast and far south, through dry tropical scrub and thorn forest in the Deccan to Alpine and temperate vegetation in the Himalaya. ***Principal rivers:*** Ganges (Ganga), Brahmaputra, Sutlej, Narmada, Krishna, Yamuna. ***Highest point:*** (in Indian controlled territory) Kangchenjunga 8598m (28,208 ft). (K2, which has a height of 8610m/28,250 ft, is in the Pakistani-occupied part of Jammu and Kashmir.)

Climate: India has three distinct seasons: a hot season from March to June, a wet season (when the southwest monsoon brings heavy rain) from June to October, and a cooler drier season from November to March. Temperatures range from the cool of the Himalaya to the tropical heat in the south.

Economy

Two thirds of the labour force are involved in subsistence farming, with rice and wheat as the principal crops. Cash crops tend to come from large plantations and include tea, cotton, jute and sugar cane – all grown for export. The monsoon rains and irrigation make cultivation possible in many areas, but drought and floods are common. India is a major industrial power. Major coal reserves provide the power base for industry. Other mineral deposits include diamonds, bauxite, and titanium, copper and iron ore, as well as substantial reserves of natural gas and petroleum. The textile, vehicle, iron and steel, pharmaceutical and electrical industries make important contributions to the economy, but India has balance-of-payment difficulties and relies upon foreign aid for development. Over one third of the population is below the official poverty line. Privatization of some state enterprises began in the early 1990s. ***Currency:*** Rupee.

Recent History

The British Indian Empire included present-day Pakistan and Bangladesh, and comprised the Crown Territories of British India and over 620 Indian protected states. The latter covered about 40% of India, and enjoyed varying degrees of autonomy under their traditional princes. From the middle of the 19th century the British cautiously encouraged Indian participation in the administration of British India. British institutions, the railways and the English language – all imposed upon India by a modernizing imperial power – fostered the growth of an Indian sense of identity beyond the divisions of caste and language. However, ultimately the divisions of religion proved stronger. The Indian National Congress – the forerunner of the Congress Party – was first convened in 1885, and the Muslim League first met in 1906. Nationalist demands grew after British troops fired without warning on a nationalist protest meeting – the Amritsar Massacre (1919). The India Acts (1919 and 1935) granted limited autonomy and created an Indian federation, but the pace of reform did not satisfy Indian expectations. In 1920, Congress – led by Mohandas (Mahatma) Gandhi (1869–1948) – began a campaign of non-violence and non-cooperation with the British authorities. However relations between Hindus and Muslims steadily deteriorated. By 1940 the Muslim League was demanding a separate sovereign state.

By 1945, war-weary Britain had accepted the inevitability of Indian independence. However, religious discord forced the partition of the subcontinent in 1947 into predominantly Hindu India – under Jawaharlal (Pandit) Nehru (1889–1964) of the Congress Party – and Muslim Pakistan (including what is now Bangladesh) – under Mohammad Ali Jinnah (1876–1948) of the Muslim League. Over 70 million Hindus and Muslims became refugees and crossed the new boundaries, and thousands were killed in communal violence. The frontiers remained disputed. India and Pakistan fought border wars in 1947–49, 1965 (over Kashmir) and again in 1971 – when Bangladesh gained independence from Pakistan with Indian assistance. Kashmir is still divided along a cease-fire line. There were also border clashes with China in 1962. Under Nehru – PM 1947–64 – India became one of the leaders of the nonaligned movement of Third World states. Under the premiership (1966–77 and 1980–84) of his daughter Indira Gandhi (1917–84) India continued to assert itself as the dominant regional power. Although India remained the world's largest democracy – despite Mrs Gandhi's brief imposition of emergency rule – local separatism and communal unrest have threatened unity. The Sikhs have conducted an often violent campaign for an independent homeland – Khalistan – in the Punjab. In 1984 Mrs Gandhi ordered the storming of the Golden Temple of Amritsar, a Sikh holy place that extremists had turned into an arsenal. In the same year Mrs Gandhi was assassinated by her Sikh bodyguard. Her son Rajiv Gandhi (PM 1984–89) was assassinated in the 1991 election campaign. Tension and violence between Hindus and Muslims has increased since a campaign (1990–) to build a Hindu temple on the site of a mosque in the holy city of Ayodhya. The once dominant Congress Party has split and a range of smaller parties, some regional in character, has flourished. Coalition government is now the norm in India.

INDONESIA

Official name: Republik Indonesia (Republic of Indonesia).

Member of: UN, ASEAN, OPEC, Apec.

Area: 1,919,317 km^2 (741,052 sq mi) – including East Timor which has an area of 14,874 km^2 (5743 sq mi), see Other Territories (beginning on p. 729) – or 1,904,443 km^2 (735,309 sq mi) excluding East Timor.

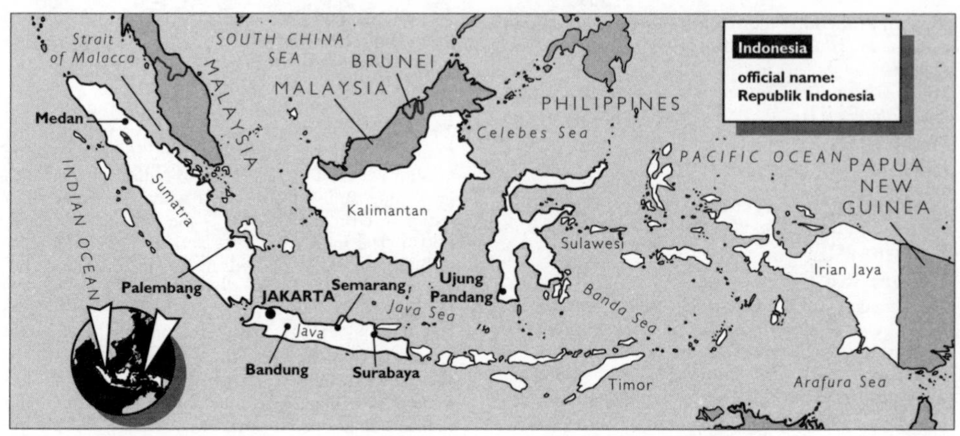

Population: 188,216,000 (1993 est) – including East Timor which has a population of 7488,000 (1990 census).
Capital: Jakarta 8,223,000 (1990 est).
Other major cities: Surabaya 2,473,000, Bandung 2,057,000, Medan 1,730,000, Semarang 1,249,000, Palembang 1,141,000, Ujung Pandang (Makasar) 944,000 (all including suburbs; 1990 est).
Languages: Bahasa Indonesia (official), Javanese (34%), Sundanese (14%); Madurese (6%).
Religions: Sunni Islam (80%), Roman Catholic (3%), other Christians (7%), Hindu (2%).
Education: is compulsory, in theory, between the ages of seven and 15. *Adult literacy:* 78%. *Universities:* 49 state and many private universities.
Defence: (1993 figures) *Army:* 202,900 personnel. *Air force:* 24,000. *Navy:* 44,000. *Paramilitary:* 215,000. *Conscription:* two years; selective.

Government

Every five years elections are held by universal adult suffrage for 400 members of the House of Representatives; 100 additional members are chosen by the President. The People's Consultative Assembly – which comprises the House of Representatives plus 500 representatives of provincial governments, occupational and special interests – meets every five years to oversee principles of state policy and to elect the President, who appoints a Cabinet.
Largest parties: (alliance) Golkar, (Islamic) United Development Party (PPP), (mainly Christian and nationalist) Indonesian Democratic Party (PDI).
Local government: 24 provinces (including East Timor), a metropolitan and two autonomous districts.
President: Gen. T.N.I. Suharto (Golkar).

Geography

Indonesia consists of nearly 3700 islands of which about 3000 are inhabited. The southern chain of mountainous, volcanic islands comprises Sumatra, Java with Madura, Bali and the Lesser Sunda Islands. Java and Madura are fertile and densely populated, containing nearly 65% of Indonesians. The northern chain comprises Kalimantan, the irregular mountainous island of Sulawesi (Celebes), the Moluccas group and Irian Jaya (western New Guinea). Over 50% of the country is covered by tropical rain forests.
Principal rivers: Kapuas, Barito, Digul, Mamberamo.
Highest point: Ngga Pulu 5030m (16,503 ft)
Climate: The climate is tropical with heavy rainfall throughout the year.

Economy

Indonesia has great mineral wealth – petroleum, natural gas, tin, nickel and bauxite – but is relatively poor because of its great population. Over 50% of Indonesians are subsistence farmers with rice being the major crop, but both estate and peasant farmers produce important quantities of rubber, tea, coffee and spices for export. Industry – largely concerned with processing mineral and agricultural products – is expanding and Indonesia achieved high economic growth rates in the 1980s and early 1990s. ***Currency:*** Rupiah.

Recent History

The East Indies were the major and most profitable part of the Dutch Empire. The Netherlands retained control until 1942, when the Japanese invaded and were welcomed by most Indonesians as liberators from colonial rule. Upon Japan's surrender in 1945, Achmed Sukarno (1901–70) – the founder of the nationalist party in 1927 – declared the Dutch East Indies to be the independent republic of Indonesia. Under international pressure, the Dutch accepted Indonesian independence (1949) after four years of intermittent but brutal fighting. Sukarno's rule became increasingly authoritarian. In 1962 he seized Netherlands New Guinea, which was formally annexed as Irian Jaya in 1969, although a separatist movement persists. Between 1963 and 1966 Sukarno tried to destabilize the newly created Federation of Malaysia by armed incursions into North Borneo. General Suharto's suppression of a Communist uprising in 1965–66 enabled him to reverse Sukarno's anti-Americanism and eventually to displace him with the support of both the students and the army. Around 80,000 members of the Communist Party were killed in this period. The annexation of Portuguese East Timor by Indonesia in 1976 is unrecognized by the international community, and guerrilla action by local nationalists continues. International protests followed the killing of unarmed Timorese demonstrators by Indonesian troops in 1991. An ambitious programme of resettlement has been attempted to relieve overcrowded Java, but the Javanese settlers have been resented in the outlying, underdeveloped islands.

IRAN

Official name: Jomhori-e-Islami-e-Irân (Islamic Republic of Iran). Known as Persia until 1935.
Member of: UN, OPEC.
Area: 1,638,057 km² (632,457 sq mi).

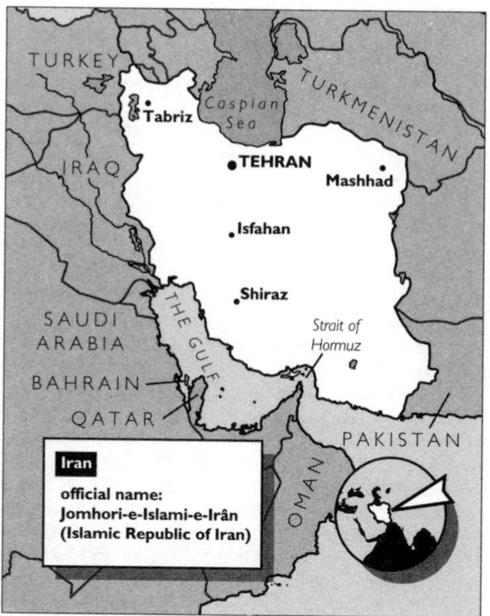

Population: 60,770,000 (1993 est).
Capital: Tehran 7,100,000 (including suburbs; 1991 est).
Other major cities: Mashhad 1,464,000, Isfahan 987,000, Tabriz 971,000, Shiraz 848,000, Ahwaz 580,000 (including suburbs; 1986 census).
Languages: Farsi or Persian (official; 45%), Azeri (26%); Kurdish, Luri and Baluchi minorities.
Religion: Shia Islam (official; 98%).
Education: is compulsory, in theory, between the ages of six and 10. *Adult literacy:* 54%. *Universities:* 29.
Defence: (1993 figures) *Army:* 320,000 personnel. *Air force:* 15,000. *Navy:* 18,000. *Revolutionary Guards:* 120,000. *Conscription:* two years.

Government

A Council of Experts – 83 Shiite clerics – is elected by universal adult suffrage to appoint the Wali Faqih (religious leader), who exercises supreme authority over the executive, legislature, judiciary and military. The 270-member Islamic Consultative Assembly (Majlis) and the President are directly elected for four years. The President appoints a Prime Minister and Cabinet who are responsible to the Majlis.
Largest parties: Iran is effectively a non-party state.
Local government: 24 provinces.
Wali Faqih (Supreme religious leader and Commander-in-Chief of the Armed Forces): Ayatollah Mohammed Ali Hoseini Khamenei.
President: Hojatolislam Ali Akbar Hashemi Rafsanjani.

Geography

Apart from restricted lowlands along the Gulf, the Caspian Sea and the Iraqi border, Iran is a high plateau, surrounded by mountains. The Elburz Mountains in the north include the country's highest peak, Demavend; the Zagros Mountains form a barrier running parallel to the Gulf. In the east, lower areas of the plateau are covered by salt deserts. ***Principal rivers:*** Karun, Safid, Atrak, Karkheh. ***Highest point:*** Demavend 5604m (18,386 ft);
Climate: Iran has an extreme climate ranging from very hot on the Gulf to sub-zero temperatures in winter in the northwest. The Caspian Sea coast has a subtropical climate with adequate rainfall. Most of Iran, however, is arid.

Economy

Petroleum is Iran's main source of foreign currency. The principal industries are petrochemicals, carpet-weaving, textiles, vehicles and cement. The war with Iraq (see below) and the country's international isolation have severely interrupted trade and Iran suffers a lack of investment. Over a quarter of the labour force is involved in agriculture, mainly producing cereals (wheat, maize and barley) and keeping livestock, but lack of water, land ownership problems and manpower shortages have restricted yields. ***Currency:*** Rial.

Recent History

In the 19th century, Russia and Britain became rivals for influence in the region. In 1921, an Iranian Cossack officer, Reza Khan Pahlavi (1877–1944), took power. Deposing the Qajar dynasty in 1925, he became Shah (emperor) himself as Reza I and modernized and secularized Iran. However, because of his pro-German sentiments, he was forced to abdicate by Britain and the USSR (1941) and was replaced by his son Mohammed Reza (1919–80). The radical nationalist PM Muhammad Mussadiq briefly toppled the monarchy (1953). Regaining his throne, the Shah tightened his grip through oppression and sought popularity through land reform and rapid development with US backing. However, Westernization offended the clergy, and an alliance of students, the bourgeoisie and religious leaders eventually combined against him, overthrowing the monarchy in 1979 and replacing it with a fundamentalist Islamic Republic inspired by the Ayatollah Ruhollah Khomeini (1900–89). The Western-educated classes fled Iran as the clergy tightened control. Radical anti-Western students seized the US embassy and held 66 American hostages (1979–81). In 1980, Iraq invaded Iran, beginning a bitter war that lasted until 1988. Following the death of Khomeini in 1989, economic necessity brought a less militant phase of the Islamic revolution. The new president, Rafsanjani, emphasized pragmatic rather than radical policies and attempted to heal the diplomatic rift with Western powers. President Saddam Hussein of Iraq returned occupied Iranian territory following the invasion of Kuwait (1990). Iran continues to sponsor militant Islam abroad but tensions inside the regime have increased as economic discontent grows.

IRAQ

Official name: Al-Jumhuriya al-'Iraqiya (The Republic of Iraq).
Member of: UN, Arab League, OPEC.
Area: 438,574 km² (169,335 sq mi).
Population: 19,435,000 (1993 est).
Capital: Baghdad 5,348,000 (city 3,845,000; 1988 est).
Other major cities: Basrah 617,000, Mosul 571,000, Kirkuk 570,000, Irbil 334,000 (1985 est).
Languages: Arabic (official; 80%), Kurdish (19%).
Religions: Sunni Islam (41%), Shia Islam (51%), various Christian minorities.
Education: is compulsory between the ages of six and 12. *Adult literacy:* 60%. *Universities:* eight.
Defence: (1993 figures) *Army:* 350,000 personnel. *Air force:* 30,000. *Navy:* 2000. *Conscription:* 18–24 months.

Government
The 250-member National Assembly is elected for four years by universal adult suffrage. The non-elected Revolutionary Command Council appoints the President, who appoints a Council of Ministers.
Largest parties: The Arab Ba'ath Socialist Party is the only effective legal party.
Local government: 18 governates; the Kurdish provinces of northern Iraq have *de facto* self-government.
President: Saddam Hussein (Ba'ath).
Prime Minister: Saddam Hussein (Ba'ath).

Autonomous Kurdish region
Area: 38,650 km^2 (14,923 sq mi). *Population:* 2,362,000 (1991 est). *Capital:* Irbil.

Geography
The basins of the Rivers Tigris and Euphrates contain most of the arable land and most of the population. Desert in the southwest occupies nearly one half of Iraq. The northeast is occupied by the highlands of Kurdistan. ***Principal rivers:*** Tigris (Dijlah), Euphrates (al Furat). ***Highest point:*** Rawanduz 3658m (12,001 ft).
Climate: Summers are hot and dry with temperatures over 40 °C (104 °F). Most of the rainfall – ranging from 100 mm (4 in) in the desert to 1000 mm (40 in) in the mountains – comes in winter.

Economy
Irrigated land in the Tigris and Euphrates basins produces cereals, fruit and vegetables for domestic consumption, and dates for export. Iraq depends upon its substantial reserves of petroleum but exports have been halted by international sanctions and the Gulf War (1991), during which the economy was devastated. Iraq faces economic collapse. Inflation is rampant and there is a shortage of many basic commodities. ***Currency:*** Iraqi dinar.

Recent History
At the beginning of the 20th century, Iraq was called Mesopotamia and had been part of the Turkish Ottoman Empire for over 350 years. In World War I the British occupied the area, but Iraqi nationalists were disappointed when Iraq became a monarchy under a British Mandate (1920). In 1932 Iraq became fully independent. Following a military coup that brought pro-German officers to power in 1941, the British occupied Iraq until 1945. The royal family and the premier were murdered in the 'Free Officers' coup in 1958. A reign of terror against the left followed a further coup in 1963. In 1968 Ba'athist (pan-Arab nationalist) officers carried out another coup. Embittered by the Arabs' humiliation in the 1967 war and by US support for the Israelis, the regime turned to the Soviets. In 1980 President Saddam Hussein attacked a weakened Iran, responding to Iran's threat to export Islamic revolution. What had been intended as a quick victory became a costly war (1980–88) with many casualties. In an attempt to restore Iraq's economic fortunes Saddam invaded and annexed oil-rich Kuwait (1990). Following Iraq's failure to respond to repeated UN demands to withdraw, the UN authorized armed action by a US-led coalition. Kuwait was liberated in the short Gulf War (1991). After the war, Saddam suppressed revolts by Shiites in the south and Kurds in the north. International efforts established refugee camps for Kurds in a 'safe zone' and the Iraqi authorities lost control of the Kurdish areas. Despite being forced to accept UN inspection of Iraq's chemical and biological weapons and nuclear capacity, Saddam continued to defy UN demands concerning Iraqi disarmament and in 1994 threatened Kuwait again. Faced with the prospect of a renewed coalition, Saddam recognized Kuwaiti independence.

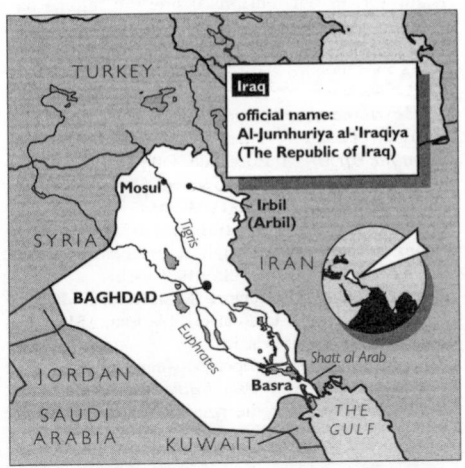

Iraq
official name:
Al-Jumhuriya al-'Iraqiya
(The Republic of Iraq)

IRELAND
Official name: Poblacht na h'Éireann (Republic of Ireland).
Member of: UN, EU/EC, OSCE, OECD, WEU (observer).
Area: 70,285 km^2 (27,137 sq mi).
Population: 3,516,000 (1993 est).
Capital: Dublin 921,000 (city 478,000; Dún Laoghaire 55,000; 1991 census).
Other major cities: Cork 174,000 (city 127,000), Limerick 77,000 (city 52,000), Galway 51,000, Waterford 41,000, Dundalk 29,000 (town 27,000), Bray 25,000, Drogheda 24,000, Sligo 18,000 (1991 census).
Languages: Irish (official; 5% as a first language), English (over 94% as a first language).
Religion: Roman Catholic (93%).
Education: is compulsory between the ages of six and 15. *Adult literacy:* virtually 100%. *Universities:* seven universities and university colleges.
Defence: (1993 figures) *Army:* 11,200 personnel. *Air force:* 800. *Navy:* 1000. *Conscription:* none.

Government
The Seanad (Senate) comprises 60 members – 11 nominated by the Taoiseach (Prime Minister), the rest indirectly elected for a five-year term to represent vocational and special interests. The Dáil (House) comprises 166 members elected for five years by universal adult suffrage under a system of proportional representation. The President – whose role is largely ceremonial – is directly elected for a seven-year term. The Taoiseach and a Cabinet of Ministers are appointed by the President upon the nomination of the Dáil, to whom they are responsible.
Largest parties: (centre-right) Fianna Fáil (FF), (centre-right) Fine Gael (FG), (social democratic) Labour Party (Lab), (centre-right) Progressive Democrats, (left-wing) Democratic Left.

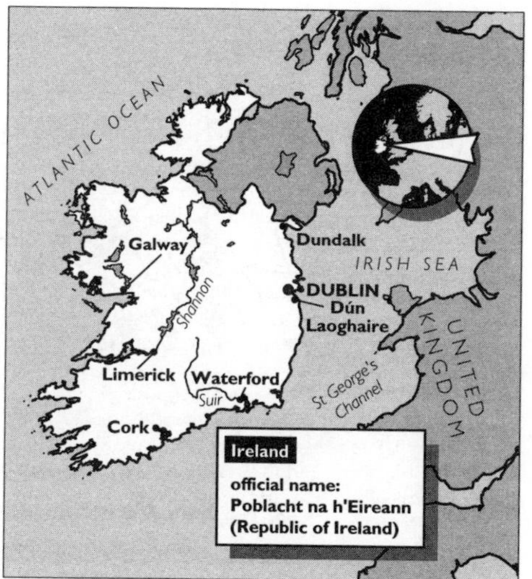

Local government: 26 counties (one of which is divided into two for administrative purposes) and five county boroughs.
President: Mary Robinson.
Taoiseach (Prime Minister): John Bruton (FG).

Counties

Carlow *Area:* 896 km^2 (346 sq mi). *Population:* 41,000 (1991 census). *County town:* Carlow.
Cavan *Area:* 1891 km^2 (730 sq mi). *Population:* 53,000 (1991 census). *County town:* Cavan.
Clare *Area:* 3188 km^2 (1231 sq mi). *Population:* 91,000 (1991 census). *County town:* Ennis.
Cork *Area:* 7460 km^2 (2880 sq mi). *Population:* 410,000 (1991 census). *County town:* Cork.
Donegal *Area:* 4830 km^2 (1865 sq mi). *Population:* 128,000 (1991 census). *County town:* Lifford.
Dublin *Area:* 922 km^2 (356 sq mi). *Population:* 1,024,000 (1991 census). *County town:* Dublin.
Galway *Area:* 5940 km^2 (2293 sq mi). *Population:* 180,000 (1991 census). *County town:* Galway.
Kerry *Area:* 4701 km^2 (1815 sq mi). *Population:* 122,000 (1991 census). *County town:* Tralee.
Kildare *Area:* 1694 km^2 (654 sq mi). *Population:* 123,000 (1991 census). *County town:* Naas.
Kilkenny *Area:* 2062 km^2 (796 sq mi). *Population:* 74,000 (1991 census). *County town:* Kilkenny.
Laoighis *Area:* 1719 km^2 (664 sq mi). *Population:* 52,000 (1991 census). *County town:* Portlaoise.
Leitrim *Area:* 1525 km^2 (581 sq mi). *Population:* 25,000 (1991 census). *County town:* Carrick-on-Shannon.
Limerick *Area:* 2686 km^2 (1037 sq mi). *Population:* 162,000 (1991 census). *County town:* Limerick.
Longford *Area:* 1044 km^2 (403 sq mi). *Population:* 30,000 (1991 census). *County town:* Longford.
Louth *Area:* 823 km^2 (318 sq mi). *Population:* 91,000 (1991 census). *County town:* Dundalk.
Mayo *Area:* 5398 km^2 (2084 sq mi). *Population:* 111,000 (1991 census). *County town:* Castlebar.
Meath *Area:* 2336 km^2 (902 sq mi). *Population:* 106,000 (1991 census). *County town:* Navan.
Monaghan *Area:* 1291 km^2 (498 sq mi). *Population:* 51,000 (1991 census). *County town:* Monaghan.
Offaly *Area:* 1998 km^2 (771 sq mi). *Population:* 58,000 (1991 census). *County town:* Tullamore.
Roscommon *Area:* 2463 km^2 (951 sq mi). *Population:* 52,000 (1991 census). *County town:* Roscommon.
Sligo *Area:* 1796 km^2 (693 sq mi). *Population:* 55,000 (1991 census). *County town:* Sligo.
Tipperary *Area:* 4254 km^2 (1643 sq mi). (North Riding 1996 km^2 (771 sq mi); South Riding 2258 km^2 (872 sq mi).) *Population:* 133,000 (North Riding 58,000; South Riding 75,000.) (1991 census). *County towns:* Nenagh (North Riding); Clonmel (South Riding).
Waterford *Area:* 1838 km^2 (710 sq mi). *Population:* 92,000 (1991 census). *County town:* Waterford.
Westmeath *Area:* 1763 km^2 (681 sq mi). *Population:* 62,000 (1991 census). *County town:* Mullingar.
Wexford *Area:* 2351 km^2 (908 sq mi). *Population:* 102,000 (1991 census). *County town:* Wexford.
Wicklow *Area:* 2025 km^2 (782 sq mi). *Population:* 97,000 (1991 census). *County town:* Wicklow.

Geography

Central Ireland is a lowland crossed by slight ridges and broad valleys, bogs and large lakes, including Loughs Derg and Ree. Except on the east coast north of Dublin, the lowland is surrounded by coastal hills and mountains, including the Wicklow Mountains, the Ox Mountains and the hills of Connemara and Donegal in the west. The highest uplands in Ireland are the Macgillicuddy's Reeks in Kerry (the southwest). The rugged Atlantic Coast is highly indented. ***Principal rivers:*** Shannon, Barrow, Suir, Blackwater, Boyne. ***Highest point:*** Carrauntuohill 1041m (3414 ft) ***Climate:*** Ireland has a mild temperate climate. Rainfall is high, ranging from over 2500 mm (100 in) in the west and southwest to 750 mm (30 in) in the east.

Economy

Manufactured goods – in particular machinery, metals and engineering, electronics and chemical products – now account for over 80% of Ireland's exports. Agriculture – the traditional mainstay of the economy – concentrates upon the production of livestock, meat and dairy products. Food processing and brewing are major industries. Natural resources include lead-zinc, offshore petroleum and natural gas, and HEP sites. Ireland suffers high rates of unemployment and emigration. ***Currency:*** Punt (Irish pound).

Recent History

In the 1840s thousands died in the Irish potato famine. Many more were evicted by Anglo-Irish landowners and joined a mass emigration, especially to the USA – between 1845 and 1851 Ireland's population declined by almost 3,000,000. Daniel O'Connell (1775–1847) led a movement seeking to repeal the Union with Britain, and to gain land and civil rights for the Roman Catholic majority. His campaign helped lead to Catholic Emancipation (1829), after which Irish Catholics were able to become MPs in the British Parliament. However, relations between the Protestant and Catholic communities deteriorated, in part owing to increasingly violent actions by nationalist Fenians whose goal was Irish independence. English policy on Ireland vacillated between conciliation and coercion. Gladstone, recognizing the need for reform, disestablished the (Anglican) Church of Ireland and granted greater security of tenure to peasant farmers. In the

1880s Charles Stewart Parnell (1846–91) led a sizeable bloc of Irish MPs in a campaign to secure Irish Home Rule (i.e. self-government). Home Rule Bills were introduced in 1883 and 1893, but after their rejection by Parliament, more revolutionary nationalist groups gained support in Ireland.

Fearing Catholic domination, Protestant Unionists in Ulster opposed the Third Home Rule Bill in 1912. Nationalists declared an independent Irish state in the Dublin Easter Rising of 1916, which was put down by the British. After World War I, Irish nationalist MPs formed a provisional government in Dublin led by Eamon de Valera (later PM and President; 1882–1975). Except in the northeast, British administration in Ireland crumbled and most of the Irish police resigned to be replaced by English officers – the 'Black and Tans'. Fighting broke out between nationalists and British troops and police, and by 1919 Ireland had collapsed into violence. The British response in 1920 was to offer Ireland two Parliaments – one in Protestant Ulster, another in the Catholic south. Partition was initially rejected by the south, but by the Anglo-Irish Treaty (1921) dominion status was granted, although six (mainly Protestant) counties in Ulster – Northern Ireland – opted to remain British. The Irish Free State was proclaimed in 1922 but de Valera and the Republicans refused to accept it. Civil war broke out between the provisional government – led by Arthur Griffith and Michael Collins – and the Republicans. The fighting ended in 1923, but de Valera's campaign for a republic continued and in 1937 the Free State became the Republic of Eire. The country remained neutral in World War II and left the Commonwealth – as the Republic of Ireland – in 1949. Relations between south and north – and between the Republic and the UK – were often tense during the 'troubles' in Northern Ireland that lasted from 1968 until the ceasefire by terrorist groups in 1994. The Anglo-Irish Agreement (1985) provided for the participation of the Republic in political, legal and security matters in Northern Ireland, and the government of the Republic is taking an active role in the Northern Ireland peace process.

ISRAEL

Official name: Medinat Israel (The State of Israel).
Member of: UN.
Area: 20,770 km² (8019 sq mi) including East Jerusalem, or 20,700 km² (7992 sq mi) excluding East Jerusalem.
Population: 5,451,000 (1993 est) including East Jerusalem.
Capital: Jerusalem (not recognized internationally as capital) 544,000 (including East Jerusalem; 1992 est).
Other major cities: Tel-Aviv 1,132,000 (city 353,000, Holon 162,000, Petach-Tikva 149,000, Bat-Yam 146,000, Rishon LeZiyyon 140,000), Haifa 400,000 (city 246,000), Netanya 140,000, Beersheba (Be'er Sheva) 128,000, Ramat Gan 123,000 (1992 est).
Languages: Hebrew (official; 85%), Arabic (15%).
Religions: Judaism (official; 85%), Sunni Islam (13%), various Christian denominations.
Education: is compulsory between the ages of six and 13. *Adult literacy:* 92%. *Universities:* six plus two institutes of university status.
Defence: (1993 figures) *Army:* 134,000 personnel. *Air force:* 32,000. *Navy:* 10,000. *Conscription:* 36 months for men, 24 months for women.

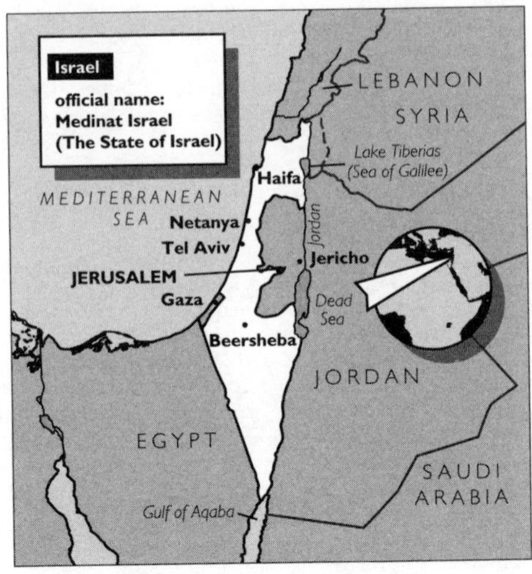

Government

The 120-member Assembly (Knesset) is elected by proportional representation for four years by universal adult suffrage. A Prime Minister and Cabinet take office after receiving a vote of confidence from the Knesset. The President is elected for a five-year term by the Knesset.
Largest parties: (centre-left) Labour Party (Lab), (right-wing) Likud, Meretz Party, (right-wing) Tzomet Party, (ultra-orthodox) Shas Party, National Religious Party, United Tora Judaism Party.
Local government: six districts, 31 towns and 49 regions.
President: Ezer Weizman.
Prime Minister: Yitzhak Rabin (Lab).
Self-governing Palestinian entity: Gaza and Jericho. See Other Territories (beginning on p. 729).
Israeli-occupied territories: Golan and West Bank. See Other Territories (beginning on p. 729).

Geography

Israel – within the boundaries established by the 1949 cease-fire line – consists of a fertile thin coastal plain beside the Mediterranean, parts of the arid mountains of Judaea in the centre, the Negev Desert in the south and part of the Jordan Valley in the northeast. ***Principal river:*** Jordan. ***Highest point:*** (in Israel proper) Jebel Jarmaq 1208m (3963 ft).
Climate: Israel's climate is Mediterranean with hot, dry summers and mild, wetter winters. The greater part of Israel receives less than 200 mm (8 in) of rain a year.

Economy

Severe economic problems stem, in part, from Israel's large defence budget and political circumstances, which have until recently prevented trade with neighbouring countries. Israel is a major producer and exporter of citrus fruit. Much land is irrigated and over 75% of Israel's arable land is farmed by collectives (kibbutzim) and cooperatives. Mineral resources are few, but processing imported diamonds is a major source of foreign currency. Tourism – to biblical sites – is important. ***Currency:*** Shekel.

Recent History

The Turkish Ottoman Empire ruled the area from the early 16th century until 1917–18, when Palestine was captured by British forces. The Zionists had hoped to establish a Jewish state, and this hope was intensified following the Balfour Declaration in favour of a homeland (1917). However, Palestine came under British administration and it was not until 1948–49 – after the murder of some 6,000,000 Jews in concentration camps by the Nazis – that an explicitly Jewish state emerged. The establishment of a Jewish state met with hostility from Israel's neighbours, leading to a series of Arab-Israeli wars.

In 1956, while the UK and France were in conflict with Egypt over the Suez Canal, Israel attacked Gaza and Sinai, but later withdew. In 1967, in six days, a coalition of Egypt, Jordan and Syria was defeated and Israel occupied Sinai, Gaza, the West Bank and the Golan Heights. In 1973, Egypt attacked Israel, but a ceasefire was arranged within three days. Egypt and Israel made peace in 1979, and Israel began to withdraw from Sinai in stages. Iraeli forces invaded Lebanon in 1982, intent on destroying bases of the Palestine Liberation Organization (PLO). Israel withdrew from most of Lebanon in 1985. In 1987, the *intifada* (Palestinian uprising) against continued Israeli rule in Gaza and the West Bank began.

Israeli politics in the 1980s and 1990s have been characterized by political instability owing to the system of proportional representation and the large number of very small parties. The large-scale influx of Soviet Jews into Israel after 1990 gave extra impetus to the *intifada*. Having come under increased international pressure to achieve a Middle East settlement, Israel reached an agreement with the PLO, led by Yasser Arafat, in 1993 for limited Palestinian self-rule in the Gaza Strip and Jericho and an Israeli military withdrawal from these territories. Further peace talks are scheduled but are threatened by Arab opposition to Arafat and the peace process, and by continued expansion of Israeli settlement in the West Bank in defiance of the 1993 agreement.

ITALY

Official name: Repubblica Italiana (Republic of Italy).
Member of: UN, EU/EC, NATO, G7, OECD, OSCE, WEU.
Area: 301,277 km^2 (116,324 sq mi).
Population: 57,235,000 (1993 est).
Capital: Rome (Roma) 2,985,000 (city 2,791,000; 1990 census).
Other major cities: Milan (Milano) 3,670,000 (city 1,432,000), Naples (Napoli) 2,905,000 (city 1,206,000),

Turin (Torino) 1,114,000 (city 992,000), Genoa (Genova) 786,000 (city 701,000), Palermo 755,000 (city 734,000), Florence (Firenze) 433,000 (city 408,000), Bologna 412,000, Catania 384,000 (city 364,000), Bari 373,000 (city 353,000), Venice (Venezia) 321,000, Messina 275,000, Verona 257,000, Trieste 252,000 (city 230,000), Taranto 244,000, Padua (Padova) 218,000, Cagliari 212,000, Salerno 206,000 (city 151,000), Brescia 202,000 (city 196,000), Reggio di Calabria 179,000, Modena 178,000, Parma 173,000, Livorno 171,000, Prato 166,000, Foggia 159,000, Perugia 151,000, Ferrara 141,000 (1991 census).

Languages: Italian (official; over 94% as a first language), small Sardinian-, Rhaetic-, Slovene-, German-, French- and Albanian-speaking minorities.

Religion: Roman Catholic (83%).

Education: is compulsory between the ages of six and 13. *Adult literacy:* 97%. *Universities:* 55 (including private universities).

Defence: (1993 figures) *Army:* 223,300 personnel. *Air force:* 77,700. *Navy:* 43,600. *Conscription:* 12 months.

Government

The two houses of Parliament are elected for a five-year term by universal adult suffrage. The Senate (upper house) has 315 members elected by citizens aged 25 and over to represent the regions, plus former Presidents and five life senators, chosen by the President. The Chamber of Deputies has 630 members elected by citizens aged 18 and over. Three quarters of the members of both houses are now elected by the first-past-the-post system; the remaining one quarter are elected under a system of proportional representation. The President is elected for a seven-year term by Parliament and 58 regional representatives. The President appoints a Prime Minister – who commands a majority in Parliament – and a Council of Ministers (Cabinet) who are responsible to Parliament.

Largest parties: (conservative) Forza Italia Party (Forza), (right-wing) National Alliance (which includes the former neo-Fascists; AN), (former Communist) Democratic Party of the Left (PDS), (northern federalist) Northern League (Lega), (southern anti-Mafia) La Rete, (conservative) Popular Party (PP), the Greens, (Marxist) Communist Party Refoundation (RC), Socialist Party (PSI).

Local government: 95 provinces grouped into 20 regions, five of which (Sicily, Sardinia, Trentino-Alto Adige, Valle d'Aosta and Friuli Venezia Giulia) have a greater degree of autonomy.

President: Oscar Luigi Scalfaro.

Prime Minister: Lamberto Dini (non-party).

Regions

Abruzzi *Area:* 10,794 km^2 (4168 sq mi). *Population:* 1,249,000 (1991 census). *Capital:* L'Aquila. (Pescara shares some of the functions of capital with L'Aquila.)

Basilicata *Area:* 9992 km^2 (3858 sq mi). *Population:* 592,000 (1991 census). *Capital:* Potenza.

Calabria *Area:* 15,080 km^2 (5823 sq mi). *Population:* 2,010,000 (1991 census). *Capital:* Catanzaro.

Campania *Area:* 13,595 km^2 (5249 sq mi). *Population:* 5,626,000 (1991 census). *Capital:* Naples.

Emilia Romagna *Area:* 22,123 km^2 (8542 sq mi). *Population:* 3,984,000 (1991 census). *Capital:* Bologna.

Friuli-Venezia Giulia *Area:* 7845 km^2 (3029 sq mi). *Population:* 1,216,000 (1991 census). *Capital:* Trieste.

Lazio *Area:* 17,203 km^2 (6642 sq mi). *Population:* 5,146,000 (1991 census). *Capital:* Rome.

Liguria *Area:* 5418 km^2 (2092 sq mi). *Population:* 1,702,000 (1991 census). *Capital:* Genoa.

Lombardy (Lombardia) *Area:* 23,857 km^2 (9211 sq mi). *Population:* 8,941,000 (1991 census). *Capital:* Milan.

Marche *Area:* 9693 km^2 (3743 sq mi). *Population:* 1,447,000 (1991 census). *Capital:* Ancona.

Molise *Area:* 4438 km^2 (1713 sq mi). *Population:* 321,000 (1991 census). *Capital:* Campobasso.

Piedmont (Piemonte) *Area:* 25,399 km^2 (9807 sq mi). *Population:* 4,338,000 (1991 census). *Capital:* Turin.

Puglia *Area:* 19,348 km^2 (7470 sq mi). *Population:* 3,971,000 (1991 census). *Capital:* Bari.

Sardinia (Sardegna) *Area:* 24,090 km^2 (9301 sq mi). *Population:* 1,645,000 (1991 census). *Capital:* Cagliari.

Sicily (Sicilia) *Area:* 25,709 km^2 (9926 sq mi). *Population:* 4,990,000 (1991 census). *Capital:* Palermo.

Trentino-Alto Adige *Area:* 13,618 km^2 (5258 sq mi). *Population:* 935,000 (1991 census). *Capitals:* Bolzano (Bozen) and Trento. (The two provinces of Bozen and Trento have a degree of autonomy.)

Tuscany (Toscana) *Area:* 22,992 km^2 (8877 sq mi). *Population:* 3,599,000 (1991 census). *Capital:* Florence.

Umbria *Area:* 8456 km^2 (3265 sq mi). *Population:* 823,000 (1991 census). *Capital:* Perugia.

Valle d'Aosta *Area:* 3262 km^2 (1259 sq mi). *Population:* 117,000 (1991 census). *Capital:* Aosta.

Veneto *Area:* 18,364 km^2 (7090 sq mi). *Population:* 4,453,000 (1991 census). *Capital:* Venice.

Geography

The Alps form a natural boundary between Italy and its western and northern neighbours. A string of lakes – where the mountains meet the foothills – include Lakes Maggiore, Lugano and Como. The fertile Po Valley – the great lowland of north Italy – lies between the Alpine foothills in the north, the Apennine Mountains in the south, the Alps in the west and the Adriatic Sea in the east. The narrow ridge of the Ligurian Alps joins the Maritime Alps to the Apennines, which form a backbone down the entire length of the Italian peninsula. The Italian coastal lowlands are few and relatively restricted, but include the Arno Basin in Tuscany, the Tiber Basin around Rome, the Campania lowlands around Naples, and plains beside the Gulf of Taranto and in Puglia. The islands of Sardinia and Sicily are both largely mountainous. Much of Italy is liable to earthquakes. Italy has four active volcanoes, including Etna on Sicily and Vesuvius near Naples. ***Principal rivers:*** Po, Tiber (Tevere), Arno, Volturno, Adige, Piave, Adda. ***Highest point:*** 4760m (15,616 ft), just below the summit of Mt Blanc (Monte Bianco).

Climate: Italy enjoys a Mediterranean climate with warm, dry summers and mild winters. Sicily and Sardinia tend to be warmer and drier than the mainland. The Alps and the Po Valley have colder, wetter winters.

Economy

Northern Italy, with its easy access to the rest of Europe, is the main centre of Italian industry. The south, in contrast, remains mainly agricultural, producing grapes, sugar beet, wheat, maize and tomatoes. Most farms are small – and many farmers in the south are resistant to change – thus average incomes in southern Italy (the 'Mezzogiorno') are much lower than in the north. Farming in the north is more mechanized and major crops include wheat, maize, rice, grapes (for the important wine industry), fruit and fodder crops for dairy herds. Industrialization in the south is being actively promoted. The industries of the north are well developed and include electrical and electronic goods, motor vehicles and bicycles, textiles, clothing, leather goods, cement, glass and china. The north is also an important financial and banking area, and Milan is the commercial capital of Italy. Apart from marble and Alpine rivers that have been harnessed for HEP, Italy has few natural resources. Tourism and money sent back by Italians living abroad are important sources of foreign currency. A crippling public deficit has added to Italy's growing economic problems. ***Currency:*** Lira.

Recent History

Political development after unification (1860) was unsteady. Overseas ventures – such as the attempt to annex parts of Ethiopia (1895–96) – were often frustrated. Parliament was held in low esteem and the end of the 19th century saw a series of assassinations, including King Umberto I in 1900. Italy entered World War I on the Allied side in the expectation of territorial gains from Austria. However, Italy won far less territory than anticipated in the peace treaties after the war, when fear of Communist revolution led to an upsurge of Fascism. Benito Mussolini (1883–1945) became Prime Minister in 1922 with a programme of extensive domestic modernization and an aggressive foreign policy. In 1936 Italy allied with Germany in the Rome-Berlin Axis, and in 1940 war was declared on Britain and France. When Italy was invaded by Allied troops in 1943, Mussolini was dismissed by the king and Italy joined the Allies.

In 1946 a republic was proclaimed. Communist influence increased, both at local and national level. However, the dominance of the (conservative) Christian Democrats kept the Communists out of the succeeding coalitions that ruled Italy and after 1989–90 the Communists declined as a political force. Particularly in the 1970s, terrorist movements – of both the left and the right – were active, kidnapping and assassinating senior political and industrial figures. Attempts have been made to effect a true unification of the country by encouraging the economic development of the south. However, the political structure of Italy remains unstable, with a succession of short-lived coalitions, and in the 1990s public disillusion with state institutions grew. Italy was weakened by corruption, the activities of the Mafia and the growth of regional separatism in the north. The traditional political parties collapsed and, after constitutional reform (1993), new political movements – including the (populist) Forza Italia, the (regional separatist) Northern League, the (right-wing) National Alliance and (former Communist) Democratic Party of the Left – dominated the first elections of the 'Second Republic' in 1994. However, instability remained and the right-wing coalition government lasted less than one year.

IVORY COAST

see COTE D'IVOIRE

JAMAICA

Member of: UN, Commonwealth, OAS, CARICOM.
Area: 10,991 km² (4244 sq mi).
Population: 2,472,000 (1993 est).

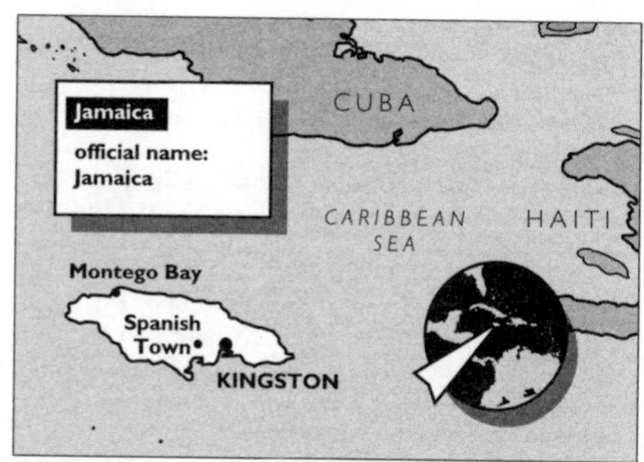

Capital: Kingston 662,000 (city 104,000; 1991 est).
Other major cities: Spanish Town 92,000, Montego Bay 83,000 (1991 est).
Language: English.
Religions: Church of God (17%), Anglican (10%).
Education: is compulsory in most districts between the ages of six and 13. *Adult literacy:* 98%. *Universities:* one.
Defence: (1993 figures) *Army:* 3000 personnel. *Air force:* 170. *Coastguards:* 150. Conscription: none.

Government

The 60-member House of Representatives is elected for five years by universal suffrage. The 21-member Senate is appointed on the advice of the PM and the Leader of the Opposition. The Governor General – the representative of the British Queen as sovereign of Jamaica – appoints a Prime Minister who commands a majority in the House. The PM appoints a Cabinet of Ministers.
Largest parties: (social democratic) People's National Party (PNP), (centre) Jamaica Labour Party (JLP).
Local government: 14 parishes.
Prime Minister: Percival J. Patterson (PNP).

Geography

Coastal lowlands surround the interior limestone plateaux (the 'Cockpit Country') and mountains. The latter include the Blue Mountains. ***Principal rivers:*** Black River, Great River. ***Highest point***: Blue Mountain Peak 2256m (7402 ft).
Climate: The lowlands are tropical and rainy; the highlands are cooler and wetter.

Economy

Agriculture is the mainstay of the economy, with sugar cane and bananas as the main crops. Jamaica is a leading exporter of bauxite. Tourism is a major foreign currency earner. ***Currency:*** Jamaican dollar.

Recent History

By the 1930s, severe social and economic problems led to rioting and the birth of political awareness in the British colony of Jamaica. Since independence in 1962, power has alternated between the radical People's National Party – led until 1992 by Michael Manley – and the more conservative Jamaican Labour Party.

JAPAN

Official name: Nihon ('The Land of the Rising Sun'/Japan).
Member of: UN, G7, OECD, Apec.
Area: 377,835 km² (145,883 sq mi).

Population: 124,670,000 (1993 est).
Capital: Tokyo 25,000,000 (city 11,610,000; Yokohama 3,251,000; Kawasaki 1,168,000; Chiba 834,000; Sagamihara 545,000; Funabashi 529,000; 1992 est).
Other major cities: Osaka 8,735,000 (city 2,495,000; Kobe 1,468,000; Sakai 799,000; Higashiosaka 496,000), Kyoto 2,606,000 (city 1,345,000), Nagoya 2,095,000, Sapporo 1,704,000, Fukuoka 1,214,000, Hiroshima 1,072,000, Kitakyushu 1,015,000, Sendai 920,000, Kumamoto 625,000, Okayama 595,000, Hamamatsu 548,000, Kagoshima 532,000 (1992 est).
Language: Japanese (official).
Religions: Shintoism (about 40%) overlaps with Buddhism (74%), Christian denominations (4%). (The percentage of those following the Shinto tradition, as opposed to the Shinto religion, is much higher.)
Education: is compulsory between the ages of six and 15. *Adult literacy:* virtually 100%. *Universities:* 523.
Defence: (1993 figures) *Army:* 149,900 personnel. *Air force:* 44,700. *Navy:* 43,100. *Conscription:* none.

Government

The Emperor is head of state but has no executive power. The 252-member House of Councillors – the upper house of the Diet – is elected for six years by universal adult suffrage. One half of the councillors retire every three years. A system of proportional representation is used to elect 50 of the councillors. The 500-member House of Representatives is directly elected for 4 years – 300 members are elected by the first-past-the-post system and 200 members are elected under a system of proportional representation. The Diet chooses a Prime Minister who commands a majority in the lower house. The PM, in turn, appoints a Cabinet of Ministers, who are responsible to the Diet.
Largest parties: (centre-right) Liberal Democratic Party (Jiminto or LDP), (reformist centre-right coalition) New Frontier Party (NFP), Social Democratic Party (Shakaito or SDP), (reformist) New Harbinger Party (Sakigake), Communist Party.
Local government: 47 prefectures grouped into nine regions.
Sovereign: HIM the Heisei Emperor (known outside

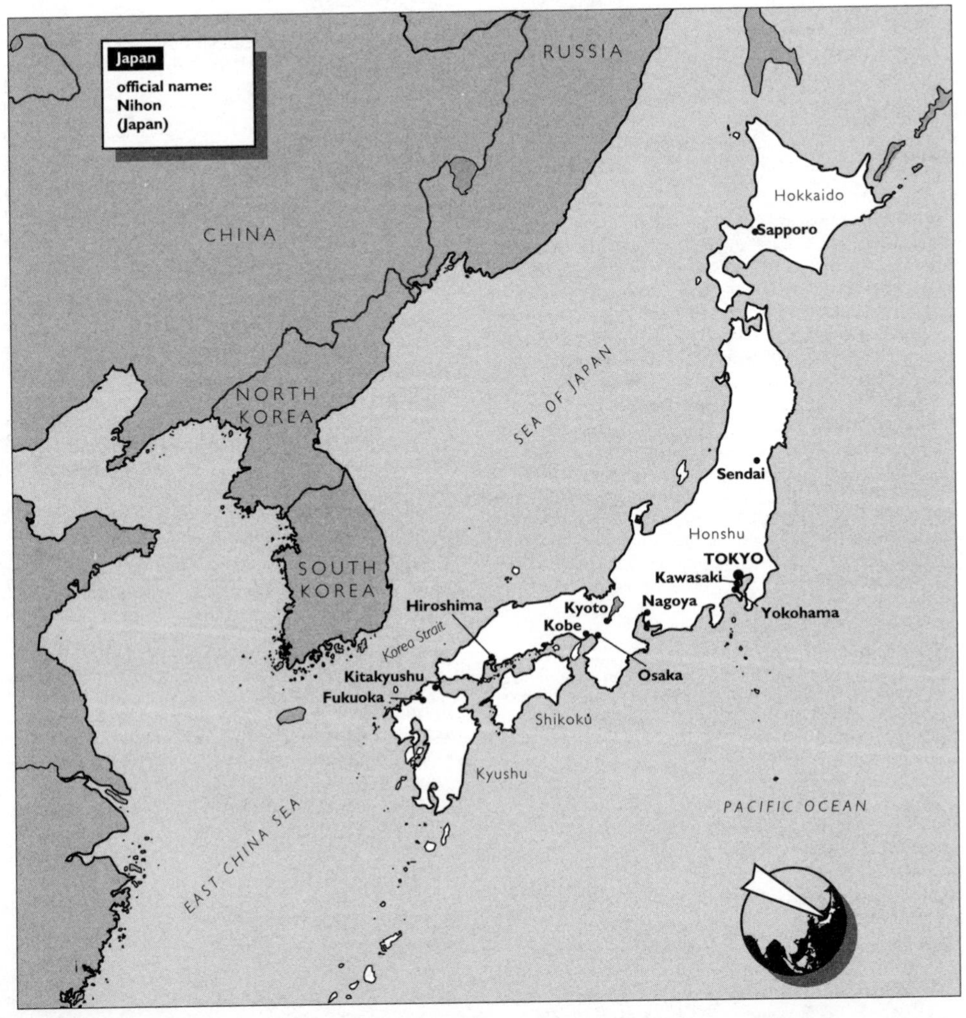

Japan as Emperor Akihito) (succeeded upon the death of his father, 7 January 1989).
Prime Minister: Tomiichi Murayama (SDP).

Regions

(There are no regional administrations or capitals.)
Chubu *Area:* 66,777 km^2 (25,783 sq mi). *Population:* 21,162,000 (1992 est).
Chugoku *Area:* 31,887 km^2 (12,311 sq mi). *Population:* 7,754,000 (1992 est).
Hokkaido *Area:* 83,520 km^2 (32,247 sq mi). *Population:* 5,659,000 (1992 est).
Kanto *Area:* 32,383 km^2 (12,503 sq mi). *Population:* 39,047,000 (1992 est).
Kinki *Area:* 33,074 km^2 (12,770 sq mi). *Population:* 22,343,000 (1992 est).
Kyushu *Area:* 42,162 km^2 (16,278 sq mi). *Population:* 13,314,000 (1992 est).
Ryukyu *Area:* 2255 km^2 (871 sq mi). *Population:* 1,238,000 (1992 est).
Shikoku *Area:* 18,808 km^2 (7262 sq mi). *Population:* 4,182,000 (1992 est).
Tohoku *Area:* 66,972 km^2 (25,857 sq mi). *Population:* 9,752,000 (1992 est).

Geography

Japan consists of over 3900 islands, of which Hokkaido in the north occupies 22% of the total land area, and Shikoku and Kyushu in the south respectively occupy 5% and 11% of the area. The central island of Honshu occupies 61% of the area and contains 80% of the population. To the south of these main islands, the Ryukyu Islands – including Okinawa – stretch almost to Taiwan. Nearly 75% of Japan is mountainous. The population is concentrated into small coastal plains. The principal lowlands are Kanto (around Tokyo), Nobi (around Nagoya) and the Sendai Plain in the north of Honshu. There are also over 60 active volcanoes, and the country is prone to severe earthquakes. ***Principal rivers:*** Tone, Ishikari, Kitakami, Shinano, Kiso. ***Highest point:*** Fujiyama 3776m (12,388 ft), an extinct volcano.
Climate: Japan experiences great variations in climate. Although the whole country is temperate, the north has long cold snowy winters, while the south has hot summers and mild winters. Rainfall totals are high, with heavy rain and typhoons being common in the summer months.

Economy

Despite the generally crowded living conditions in the cities, the Japanese enjoy a high standard of living. The country has the second largest industrial economy in the world, despite having very few natural resources. Japanese industry is heavily dependent on imported raw materials – about 90% of Japan's energy requirements are imported and petroleum is the single largest import. Japan's economic success is based on manufacturing industry, which – with construction – employs 30% of the labour force. Japan is the world's leading manufacturer of motor vehicles, and one of the major producers of ships, steel, synthetic fibres, chemicals, cement, electrical goods and electronic equipment. Rapid advances in Japanese research and technology have helped the expanding export-led economy. The banking and financial sectors have prospered, and Tokyo is one of the world's main stock exchanges and commercial centres. Agriculture is labour intensive. Although Japan is self-sufficient in rice, agriculture is not a priority and a high percentage of its food requirements – particularly cereals and fodder crops – have to be imported. The traditional Japanese diet is sea-based and the fishing industry is a large one. ***Currency:*** Yen.

Recent History

At the end of the 19th century, the Meiji Emperor overthrew the last shogun and restored power to the throne. He encouraged Western institutions and a Western-style economy, so that by the beginning of the 20th century Japan was rapidly industrializing and on the brink of becoming a world power. By the end of the Meiji era (1912), Japan had established an empire. Japan had defeated China (1894–95) – taking Port Arthur and Taiwan – and startled Europe by beating Russia (1904–05) by land and at sea. Korea was annexed in 1910. Allied with Britain from 1902, Japan entered World War I against Germany in 1914, in part to gain acceptance as an imperial world power. However, Japan gained little except some of the German island territories in the Pacific and became disillusioned that the country did not seem to be treated as an equal by the Great Powers. The rise of militarism and collapse of world trade led to the rise of totalitarianism and a phase of aggressive Japanese expansion. Japan became allied to Nazi Germany and in 1941 Japanese aircraft struck Pearl Harbor in Hawaii, bringing the USA into World War II. An initial rapid Japanese military expansion across Southeast Asia and the Pacific was halted, and the war ended for Japan in disastrous defeat and the horrors of atomic warfare.

Emperor Hirohito (reigned 1926–89) surrendered in 1945. Shintoism – which had come to be identified with aggressive nationalism – ceased to be the state religion, and in 1946 the emperor renounced his divinity. The Allied occupation (1945–52) democratized politics and began an astonishing economic recovery based on an aggressive export policy. The economy was jolted by major rises in petroleum prices in 1973 and 1979, but Japan maintained its advance to become a technological front-runner and, after the USA, the world's second largest economy. However, Japan's protectionism has led to accusations of unfair trading practices. By 1988 Japan surpassed the USA as the world's largest aid-donor. The Japanese political world was dominated by the Liberal Democrats, who held office from 1955 to 1993 despite a number of financial scandals. Since then a number of coalitions have held power.

JORDAN

Official name: Al-Mamlaka al-Urduniya al-Hashemiyah (The Hashemite Kingdom of Jordan).
Member of: UN, Arab League.
Area: 88,946 km^2 (34,342 sq mi).
Population: 3,765,000 (1993 est).
Capital: Amman 1,270,000 (1992 est).
Other major cities: Zarqa 359,000, Irbid 216,000, Salt 134,000 (1992 est).
Language: Arabic (official).
Religions: Sunni Islam (over 80%), Shia Islam and various Christian minorities.
Education: is compulsory between the ages of six and 15. *Adult literacy:* 80%. *Universities:* nine.
Defence: (1993 figures) *Army:* 90,000 personnel. *Air force:* 10,000. *Navy:* 600. *Paramilitary:* 200,000. *Conscription:* two years; selective.

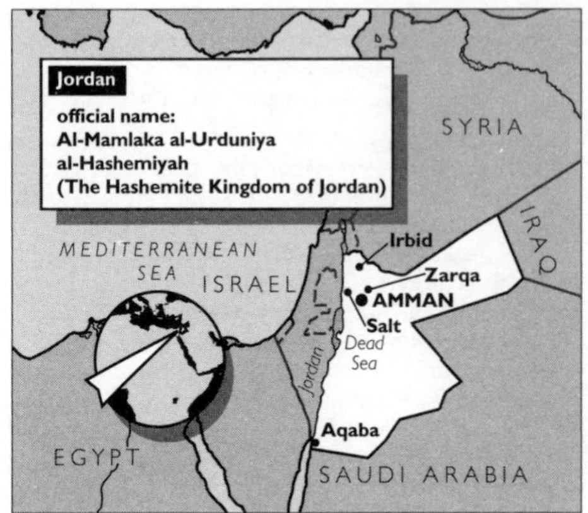

Government

Jordan is a constitutional monarchy. The King appoints the 30 members of the Senate for eight years. The 80-member House of Representatives is elected for four years by universal adult suffrage.

Largest parties: Islamic Action Front, (leftist) Jordanian Arab Democratic Party. Most members sit as independent centrists or independent Islamists.

Local government: five provinces.

Sovereign: HM Hussein I, King of Jordan (succeeded upon the deposition of his father, on grounds of illness, 11 August 1952).

Prime Minister: Sharif Zeid bin Shaker (non-party).

Geography

The steep escarpment of the East Bank Uplands borders the Jordan Valley and the Dead Sea. Deserts cover over 80% of the country. ***Principal river:*** Jordan (Urdun). ***Highest point:*** Jabal Ramm 1754m (5754 ft).

Climate: The summers are hot and dry; the winters are cooler and wetter, although much of Jordan experiences very low rainfall.

Economy

Apart from potash – the main export – Jordan has few resources. Arable land accounts for only 5% of the total area. Foreign aid and money sent back by Jordanians working abroad are major sources of foreign currency. ***Currency:*** Jordanian dinar.

Recent History

In World War I the British aided an Arab revolt against (Turkish) Ottoman rule. The League of Nations awarded the area east of the River Jordan – Transjordan – to Britain as part of Palestine (1920), but in 1923 Transjordan became a separate emirate. In 1946 the country gained complete independence as the Kingdom of Jordan with Amir Abdullah (1880–1951) as its sovereign. The Jordanian army fought with distinction in the 1948 Arab-Israeli War, and occupied the West Bank territories, which were formally incorporated into Jordan in 1950. In 1951 Abdullah was assassinated. His grandson King Hussein (reigned 1952–) was initially threatened by radicals encouraged by Egypt's President Nasser. In the 1967 Arab-Israeli War, Jordan lost the West Bank, including Arab Jerusalem, to the Israelis. In the 1970s, the power of the Palestinian guerrillas in Jordan challenged the very existence of the Jordanian state. After a short bloody civil war in 1979 the Palestinian leadership fled abroad. King Hussein renounced all responsibility for the West Bank in 1988. A ban on party politics ended in 1991. There has since been a growth in support for Islamic fundamentalism. In 1994 Jordan signed a peace treaty with Israel.

KAZAKHSTAN

Official name: Qazaqstan Respublikasi (The Republic of Kazakhstan).

Member of: UN, CIS, OSCE.

Area: 2,717,300 km² (1,049,200 sq mi).

Population: 17,170,000 (1993 est).

Capital: Alma-Ata (Almaty) 1,156,000 (1991 est).

Other major cities: Karaganda (Qaraghandy) 609,000, Chimkent (Shymkent) 439,000, Semipalatinsk (Semey), Pavlodar 343,000 (1991 est).

Languages: Kazakh (40%), Russian (38%), German.

Religions: Sunni Islam majority, Russian Orthodox.

Education: is compulsory between the ages of seven and 17. *Adult literacy:* no figures available. *Universities:* three, plus two polytechnics of university status.

Defence: (1993 figures) *Army:* 44,000 personnel. *Conscription:* none.

Government

An executive President and 135 members of the 177-member Parliament (Kenges) are elected for four years by universal adult suffrage. The remaining 42 members of the Kenges are elected from a 'state list' by national and regional government officials (who are state appointees). The President appoints a Prime Minister and a Cabinet of Ministers.

Largest parties: Congress of People's Unity of Kazakhstan (SNEK), Trades Union Federation, (progressive coalition) People's Congress of Kazakhstan, Socialist Party.

Local government: 19 regions and two cities.

President: Nursultan Nazarbayev (SNEK).

Prime Minister: Akezhan Kazhegeldin (SNEK).

Geography

Kazakhstan comprises a vast expanse of low tablelands (steppes) in Central Asia. In the west, plains descend below sea level beside the Caspian Sea. Uplands include ranges of hills in the north and

mountain chains, including the Tien Shan, in the south and east. Kazakhstan has several salt lakes, including the Aral Sea, which is shrinking because of excessive extraction of irrigation water from its tributaries. Deserts include the Kyzylkum in the south, the Kara Kum in the centre, and the Barsuki in the north. ***Principal rivers:*** Syrdarya, Irtysh, Ishim, Ural, Chu. ***Highest point:*** Khan Tengri 6995m (22,949 ft). ***Climate:*** The Kazakh climate is characterized by bitterly cold winters and hot summers. Rainfall is low, ranging from 200 mm (8 in) in the north to 500 mm (20 in) or more in the southeast, and negligible in the deserts.

Economy

Kazakhstan is a major supplier of food and raw materials for industry to other former Soviet republics, particularly Russia. The transition to a market economy was begun in earnest in 1994. Agriculture employs almost 50% of the labour force. Large collective farms on the steppes in the north contributed one third of the cereal crop of the former USSR. Other major farming interests include sheep, fodder crops, fruit, vegetables and rice. Kazakhstan is rich in natural resources, including coal, tin, copper, lead, zinc, gold, chromite, oil and natural gas. Kazakhstan has attracted Western investment to exploit its mineral wealth. Industry is represented by iron and steel (in the Karaganda coalfield), pharmaceuticals, food processing and cement. ***Currency:*** Tenge.

Recent History

In the 18th century the Russians began to penetrate the Kazakh steppes. During the Tsarist period there was large-scale Russian peasant settlement on the steppes, but Russian rule was resented and there was a major Kazakh revolt during World War I. After the Russian revolution, Kazakh nationalists formed a local government and demanded autonomy (1917). The Soviet Red Army invaded in 1920. Kazakhstan did not become a full Union Republic within the USSR until 1936. Widespread immigration from other parts of the USSR became a flood in 1954–56, when the 'Virgin Lands' of north Kazakhstan were opened up for farming. By the time Kazakhstan declared independence – following the abortive coup by Communist hardliners in Moscow (September 1991) – the Kazakhs formed a minority within their own republic. When the USSR was dissolved (December 1991), Kazakhstan was internationally recognized as an independent republic. In 1995 President Nazarbayev dissolved parliament to rule by decree.

KENYA

Official names: Jamhuri ya Kenya and Republic of Kenya.
Member of: UN, OAU, Commonwealth.
Area: 582,646 km² (224,961 sq mi).
Population: 28,110,000 (1993 est).
Capital: Nairobi 1,505,000 (including suburbs; 1990 est).
Other major cities: Mombasa 426,000, Kisumu 167,000, Nakuru 102,000 (1985 est).
Languages: Swahili (official), English, Kikuyu (21%), Luhya (14%), Luo (11%), with over 200 tribal languages.
Religions: Roman Catholic (27%), Independent African Churches (27%), various Protestant Churches (19%), animist (19%).

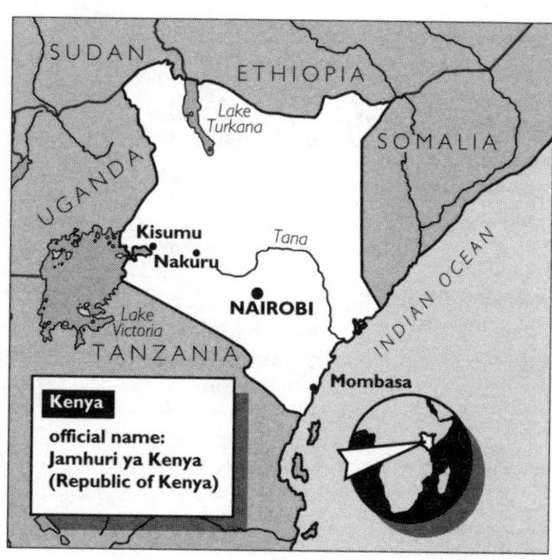

Education: is not compulsory. *Adult literacy:* 59%. *Universities:* four.
Defence: (1993 figures) *Army:* 20,500 personnel. *Air force:* 1400. *Navy:* 2500. *Paramilitary:* 5000. *Conscription:* none.

Government

The President and 188 members of the 200-member National Assembly are elected by universal adult suffrage every five years. The remaining Assembly members, the Vice President and the Cabinet of Ministers are appointed by the President.
Largest parties: (former monopoly) Kenya African National Union (KANU), Forum for the Restoration of Democracy-Kenya (FORD-K), Forum for the Restoration of Democracy-Asili (FORD-A), Democratic Party (DP).
Local government: seven provinces, plus the capital.
President: Daniel arap Moi (KANU).

Geography

The steep-sided Rift Valley divides the highlands that run from north to south through central Kenya.Plateaux extend in the west to Lake Victoria and in the east to coastal lowlands. ***Principal rivers:*** Tana, Umba, Kerio, Turkwel. ***Highest peak:*** Mount Kenya 5199m (17,058 ft).
Climate: The coastal areas have a hot and humid equatorial climate. The highlands – which are cooler – experience high rainfall. The north is very hot and arid.

Economy

Over 75% of the labour force is involved in agriculture. Major crops include wheat and maize for domestic consumption, and coffee, tea, sisal and sugar cane for export. Large numbers of beef cattle are reared, and Kenya is one of the few states in black Africa to have a major dairy industry. Tourism is an important source of foreign currency. ***Currency:*** Kenya shilling.

Recent History

The varied black African peoples of the area were brought forcibly under British rule in 1895 in the East African Protectorate, which became the colony of Kenya in 1920. White settlement in the highlands was bitterly resented by the Africans – particularly the Kikuyu – whose land was taken. Racial discrimination and attacks on African customs also created discontent.

Black protest movements emerged in the 1920s and, after 1945, developed into nationalism, led by Jomo Kenyatta (c. 1893–1978), who in 1947 became the first president of the Kenya African Union. When the violent Mau Mau rising – which involved mainly Kikuyu people – broke out (1952–56), Kenyatta was held responsible and was imprisoned on doubtful evidence (1953–61). After the British had crushed the Mau Mau revolt in a bloody campaign, they negotiated with Kenyatta and the other nationalists. Independence, under Kenyatta's KANU party, followed in 1963. His moderate leadership and pro-capitalist policies were continued by his successor, Daniel arap Moi. Considerable restrictions on political activity followed an attempted military coup (1982). From 1969 to 1991, KANU was the only legal political party, but multi-party elections were held in 1993.

KIRIBATI

Official name: Republic of Kiribati.
Member of: Commonwealth.
Area: 811 km² (313 sq mi).
Population: 77,000 (1993 est).
Capital: Bairiki (on Tarawa) 25,000 (1990 census).
Languages: English (official), I-Kiribati.
Religions: Roman Catholic (over 50%), Kiribati Protestant (Congregational; over 40%).
Education: is compulsory between the ages of six and 14. *Adult literacy:* 90%. Universities: one university centre.
Defence: There are no armed forces.

Government

The President and 39 members of the Assembly are elected by universal adult suffrage every four years. A member for Banaba, and an additional member, are appointed to the Assembly. The President appoints a Cabinet, which is responsible to the Assembly.
Largest parties: All members of the Assembly are independents.
Local government: three island groups.
President: Teburoro Tito (non-party).

Geography

With the exception of the island of Banaba – which is composed of phosphate rock – Kiribati comprises three groups of small coral atolls.
Climate: Kiribati has a maritime equatorial climate with high rainfall.

Economy

Most islanders are involved in subsistence farming and fishing. Copra is almost the only export.
Currency: Kiribati uses Australian currency.

Recent History

The Gilbert Islands – which became British in 1892 – were occupied by Japan (1942–43). British nuclear weapons were tested on Christmas Island (1957–64). In 1979, the Gilbert Islands gained independence as Kiribati (pronounced Kiri-bass).

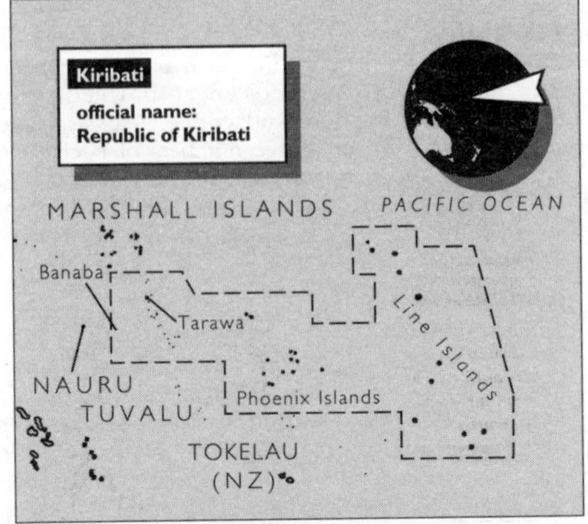

KOREA DPR
(North Korea)

Official name: Chosun Minchu-chui Inmin Konghwa-guk (Democratic People's Republic of Korea). Popularly known as North Korea.
Member of: UN.
Area: 122,762 km² (47,398 sq mi).
Population: 22,645,000 (1993 est).
Capital: Pyongyang 2,640,000 (1986 est).
Other major cities: Hamhung 775,000, Chongjin 755,000, Nampo 691,000, Sinuiju 500,000 (1986 est).
Language: Korean.
Religions: Daoism and Confucianism (14%), Chondogyo (14%).
Education: is compulsory between the ages of five and 16. *Adult literacy:* 99%. *Universities:* one.
Defence: (1993 figures) *Army:* 1,000,000 personnel. *Air force:* 82,000. *Navy:* 45,000. *Conscription:* five to eight years in the army; three to four years in the air force; five to ten years in the navy.

Government

The Party Congress of the (Communist) Korean Worker's Party elects a Central Committee, which, in turn, elects a Politburo, the seat of effective power. Unopposed elections are held every four years for the 615-member Supreme People's Assembly. The Assembly elects the President, Prime Minister and

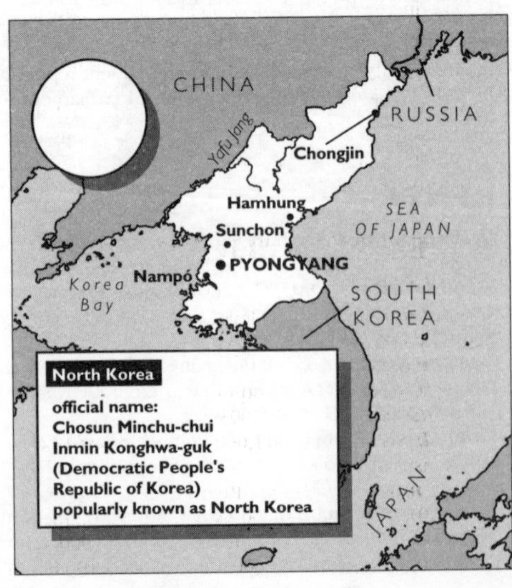

Central People's Committee, which nominates Ministers.
Largest parties: The (Communist) Korean Worker's Party is the only political party allowed.
Local government: nine provinces and two cities.
President: Kim Jong-Il. (At the time of going to press, Kim Jong-Il was *de facto* President, although he had not formally assumed the office.)
Prime Minister: Kang Song San.

Geography

Over three quarters of the country consists of mountains, which rise in the northeast to the volcanic peak Mount Paek-tu. ***Principal rivers:*** Imjin, Chongchon, Yalu (Yafu Jiang). ***Highest point:*** Mount Paek-tu 2744m (9003 ft).
Climate: The country has long cold dry winters and hot wet summers.

Economy

Over 30% of the labour force work on cooperative farms, mainly growing rice. Natural resources include coal, zinc, magnetite and iron ore. Great emphasis has been placed on industrial development, notably metallurgy and machine-building. The end of barter deals with the former USSR (1990–91) brought a sharp economic decline. Money sent home by North Koreans working in Japan and Russia is the main foreign-currency earner. ***Currency:*** Won.

Recent History

Korea – a Japanese possession from 1910 to 1945 – was divided into zones of occupation in 1945. The USSR established a Communist republic in their zone north of the 38th parallel (1948). North Korea launched a surprise attack on the South in June 1950, hoping to achieve reunification by force. The Korean War (1950–53) devastated the peninsula. At the cease-fire in 1953 the frontier was re-established close to the 38th parallel. North Korea has the world's first Communist dynasty, whose personality cult has surpassed even that of Stalin. President Kim Il-Sung (1912–94) and his son and successor Kim Jong-Il have rejected any reform of the country's Communist system. Since the collapse of Communism in the former USSR and Eastern Europe, North Korea has become increasingly isolated. The country's refusal to allow international inspection of suspected nuclear weapons installations increased tension in 1994. However, agreement was reached with the USA by which America will supply light-water reactors – which could not be used for nuclear weapons – in return for North Korea dismantling its nuclear development programme.

KOREA, REPUBLIC OF
(South Korea)

Official name: Daehan-Minkuk (Republic of Korea). Popularly known as South Korea.
Member of: UN, Apec.
Area: 99,263 km² (38,326 sq mi).
Population: 44,042,000 (1993 est).
Capital: Seoul (Soul) 11,000,000 (city 10,613,000; 1990 census).
Other major cities: Pusan 3,825,000 (city 3,798,000), Taegu 2,248,000 (city 2,229,000), Inchon 1,817,000 (city 1,682,000), Kwangju 1,206,000 (city 1,139,000), Taejon 1,062,000 (city 1,049,000), Ulsan 682,000, Suwon 644,000 (1990 census).
Language: Korean (official).
Religions: Buddhist (24%), various Protestant Churches (16%), Roman Catholic (5%).
Education: is compulsory between the ages of six and 12. *Adult literacy:* 96%. *Universities:* 127 universities and institutes of university status.
Defence: (1993 figures) *Army:* 520,000 personnel. *Air force:* 53,000. *Navy:* 60,000. *Conscription:* 26 months in the army; 30 months in the navy and the air force.

Government

The 299-member National Assembly is elected by universal adult suffrage every four years – 237 members are directly elected to represent constituencies; the remaining 62 members are chosen under a system of proportional representation. The President – who appoints a State Council (Cabinet) and a Prime Minister – is directly elected for a single five-year term.
Largest parties: Democratic Liberal Party (DLP), Democratic Party (DP), United People's Party (UPP).
Local government: nine provinces and six cities.
President: Kim Young Sam (DLP).
Prime Minister: Lee Hong Koo (DLP).

Geography

Apart from restricted coastal lowlands and the densely populated Han and Naktong basins, most of the country is mountainous. ***Principal rivers:*** Naktong, Han.
Highest point: Halla-san 1950m (6398 ft), an extinct volcano on Cheju island.
Climate: Korea experiences cold dry winters and hot summers during which the monsoon brings heavy rainfall.

Economy

One fifth of the labour force is involved in farming. The principal crops are rice and barley. South Korean industry is dominated by a small number of large family conglomerates. The important textile industry was the original manufacturing base. South Korea is now the world's leading producer of ships and footwear and a major producer of electronic equipment, electrical goods, steel, petrochemicals and motor vehicles. Banking and finance are expanding. The country experienced high economic growth rates in the 1980s and early 1990s. ***Currency:*** Won.

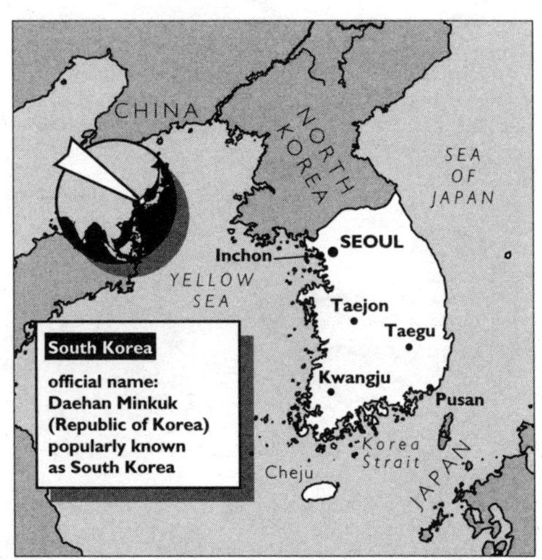

Recent History

From the 17th century, Korea became the 'Hermit Kingdom', cutting itself off from the outside world. In 1910 Korea fell victim to a harsh Japanese colonial rule. After World War II, the peninsula was divided into Soviet and US zones of occupation. In 1948 the Republic of Korea was established in the American (southern) zone. The surprise invasion of the South by the Communist North precipitated the Korean War (1950–53). The war cost a million lives and ended in stalemate with the division of Korea confirmed. Closely allied to the US, an astonishing economic transformation took place in South Korea. However, the country has experienced long periods of authoritarian rule, including the presidencies of Syngman Rhee and Park Chung-Hee, but the election of ex-General Roh Tae Woo (1987) introduced a more open regime. Much prestige was gained through the successful Seoul Olympic Games. The establishment of trading and diplomatic contacts with China and former Communist countries has further isolated North Korea.

KUWAIT

Official name: Daulat al-Kuwait (State of Kuwait).
Member of: UN, Arab League, OPEC, GCC.
Area: 17,818 km² (6880 sq mi).
Population: 1,430,000 (1993 est).
Capital: Kuwait City 1,375,000 (including agglomeration; 1993 unofficial est).
Language: Arabic (official).
Religion: Sunni Islam (official; 70%), Shia Islam (30%).
Education: is compulsory between the ages of six and 14. *Adult literacy:* 80%. *Universities:* two.
Defence: (1993 figures) *Army:* 9000 personnel. *Air force:* 2500. *Navy:* 1200. *Paramilitary:* 5000. *Others:* 1000. *Conscription:* two years.

Government

Kuwait is a monarchy ruled by an Amir, who appoints a Prime Minister and a Cabinet. A 50-member National Assembly is elected for four years by literate male Kuwaiti nationals whose families fulfil stringent residence qualifications.
Largest parties: There are unofficial groups rather than political parties.
Local government: five governates.
Sovereign: HH Shaikh Jabir III bin Ahmad as-Sabah, Amir of Kuwait (succeeded upon the death of his cousin, 31 December 1977).
Prime Minister: HH Shaikh Saad al-Abdullah as-Sabah, Crown Prince of Kuwait.

Geography

Most of Kuwait is desert, relatively flat and low lying. ***Principal rivers***: none. ***Highest point:*** Ash Shaqaya 289m (951 ft).
Climate: Kuwait experiences extremes of heat in summer. Almost all the annual rainfall of 100 mm (4 in) comes during the cooler winter.

Economy

The economy was devastated by the Iraqi invasion and Gulf War (1991), but reconstruction followed rapidly. Large reserves of petroleum and natural gas are the mainstay of the economy. Owing to lack of water, little agriculture is possible. ***Currency:*** Kuwait dinar.

Recent History

In 1760 the Sabah family created the emirate that has lasted to today, although from 1899 to 1961 Kuwait was a British-protected state. Oil was discovered in 1938 and was produced commercially from 1946. In August 1990 Iraq invaded and annexed Kuwait. When Iraq failed to respond to repeated UN demands to withdraw, the UN authorized armed action. Kuwait was liberated by a US-led coalition early in 1991 in the short Gulf War. After liberation, pressure for constitutional change grew and the constitution (suspended since 1968) was restored. Before 1990, Kuwait had a large population of foreign workers, mainly Palestinians, who were perceived to have favoured the Iraqi occupation forces. Since 1991, most of the non-Kuwaiti Arab workers have fled or been deported, to be replaced by migrants from the Indian subcontinent on short-term contracts. Iraq made further threats against Kuwait in 1994 but was forced to climb down – and formally recognize Kuwaiti independence – after international pressure.

KYRGYZSTAN

Official name: Kyrgyzstan Respublikasy (Republic of Kyrgyzstan). Formerly known as Kirghizia.
Member of: UN, CIS, OSCE.
Area: 198,500 km² (76,600 sq mi).
Population: 4,525,000 (1993 est).
Capital: Bishkek (formerly Frunze) 642,000 (1991 est).
Other major cities: Osh 219,000, Dzhalal-Abad 74,000 (1991 est).
Languages: Kyryz (53%), Russian (21%), Uzbek (13%).
Religion: Sunni Islam majority.

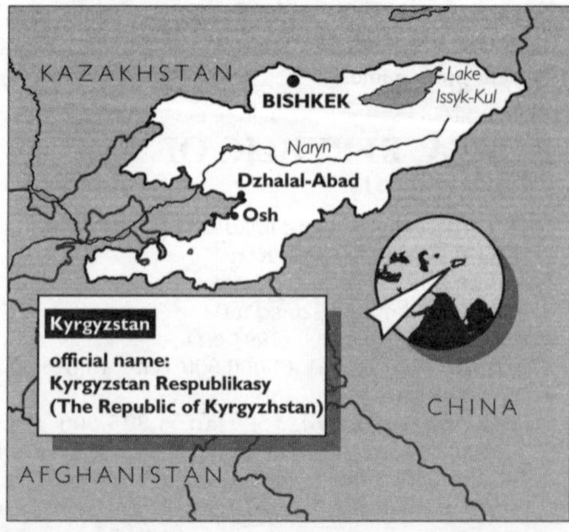

Education: is compulsory between the ages of six and 14. *Adult literacy:* no figures available. *Universities:* two.
Defence: (1993 figures) *Army:* 12,000 personnel. *Conscription:* 18 months.

Government

A 105-member legislature and an executive President are elected for five years by universal adult suffrage. The parliament divides into a 35-member house that is in permanent session and a 70-member house that meets occasionally. The President appoints a Prime Minister and a Council of Ministers.
Largest parties: Kyrgyzstan Democratic Movement (KDM), Communist Party, Kyrgyz Social Democratic Party.
Local government: six regions, plus the capital.
President: Askar Akayev (KDM).
Prime Minister: to be appointed.

Geography

Most of Kyrgyzstan lies within the Tien Shan mountains. Restricted lowlands – including the Chu valley and part of the Fergana valley – contain most of the population. **Principal rivers:** Sarydzhaz, Naryn, Kyzylsu. **Highest point:** Pik Pobedy 7439m (24,406 ft). **Climate:** The country's altitude and position deep within the interior of Asia combine to produce an extreme continental climate with low precipitation.

Economy

Agriculture is dominated by large (still mainly collectivized) farms that specialize in growing fodder crops for sheep and goats, and cotton under irrigation. Natural resources include coal, lead, zinc and great HEP potential. Food processing and light industry are expanding and privatization has begun. Problems include a lack of investment and a 'brain drain' of qualified Russians. **Currency:** Som.

Recent History

The nomadic Kyrgyz retained their independence until after 1850, when the area was annexed by Russia. Opposition to the Russians (who were given most of the best land) was expressed in a major revolt in 1916 and continuing guerrilla activity after the Russian Revolution. A Soviet Republic was founded in 1926 and Kirghizia became a full Union Republic within the USSR in 1936. After the abortive coup by Communist hardliners, Kirghizia declared independence and – under its new name, Kyrgyzstan – received international recognition when the Soviet Union was dissolved (1991).

LAOS

Official name: Saathiaranagroat Prachhathippatay Prachhachhon Lao (The Lao People's Democratic Republic).
Member of: UN.
Area: 236,800 km² (91,429 sq mi).
Population: 4,533,000 (1991 est).
Capital: Vientiane (Viengchane) 422,000 (1990 est).
Other major cities: Savannakhet 97,000. Luang Prabang (Louangphrabang) 68,000, Pakse 47,000 (1985 est).
Language: Lao (official; 96%).
Religion: Buddhism (57%), traditional local religions.
Education: is compulsory, in theory, between the ages of seven and 15. *Adult literacy:* 84%. *Universities:* one.
Defence: (1993 figures) *Army:* 33,000 personnel. *Air force:* 3500. *Navy:* 500. *Conscription:* 18 months.

Government

There is constitutional provision for a 79-member Supreme People's Assembly elected for five years by universal adult suffrage. The President, Prime Minister and Council of Ministers are effectively responsible to the Central Committee of the (Communist) Lao People's Revolutionary Party. A new constitution is to be drafted.
Largest parties: The (Communist) Lao People's Revolutionary Party is the only legal party.
Local government: 16 provinces plus the capital.
President: Nouhak Phoumsavan.
Prime Minister: Gen. Khamtai Siphandon.

Geography

Except for the Plain of Jars in the north and the Mekong Valley and low plateaux in the south, Laos is mountainous. **Principal rivers:** Mekong, Ou, Ngum, Kong. **Highest point:** Phou Bia 2819m (9248 ft). **Climate:** Laos has a tropical climate with heavy monsoon rains between May and October.

Economy

Laos is one of the poorest countries in the world. Most Laotians work on collective farms, mainly growing rice. Western investment has been encouraged since 1990. **Currency:** Kip.

Recent History

A French protectorate was established in 1893. Japanese occupation in World War II led to a declaration of independence which the French finally accepted in 1954. However, the kingdom was wracked by civil war, with royalist forces fighting Communist Pathet Lao. The Viet Cong used Laos as a supply route in the Vietnam War, and US withdrawal from Vietnam allowed the Pathet Lao to take over Laos (1975). Since 1990 the government has begun to introduce reforms, but there is no suggestion that a multi-party system will be tolerated.

LATVIA

Official name: Latvijas Republika (Republic of Latvia).
Member of: UN, OSCE.
Area: 64,610 km² (24,946 sq mi).
Population: 2,595,000 (1993 est).

Capital: Riga 874,000 (1993 est).
Other major cities: Daugavpils 124,000, Liepaja 108,000, Jelgava 72,000, Jūrmala 60,000 (1993 est).
Languages: Lettish (over 53%), Russian (34%).
Religions: Lutheran (22%), Roman Catholic (7%).
Education: is compulsory between the ages of seven and 17. *Adult literacy:* 98%. *Universities:* two.
Defence: (1993 figures) *Army:* 1650 personnel. *Border guards:* 4140. *Air force:* 180. *Navy:* 630. *Conscription:* 18 months.

Government

A 100-member Assembly (Saeima) is elected by universal adult suffrage for three years. The President – who appoints a Prime Minister and a Cabinet – is elected by the Assembly, also for three years.
Climate: (centre-right) Latvia's Way (LC), (radical nationalist) Latvian National Independence Movement (LNNK), Harmony for Latvia (SL), Farmers' Union (LZS), (former Communist) Equality Party, (centre-right) Christian Democratic Union (LKDS), Democratic Centre Party (DCP).
Local government: 26 districts and seven towns.
President: Guntis Ulmanis (LZS).
Prime Minister: Maris Gailis (LC).

Geography

Latvia comprises an undulating plain, lower in the west (Courland) than in the east (Livonia). ***Principal rivers:*** Dvina (Daugava or Western Dvina), Aiviekste, Lielupe. ***Highest point:*** Osveyskoye 311m (1020 ft).
Climate: Latvia has a moist, temperate climate with mild summers and cold winters.

Economy

Engineering dominates a heavily industrialized economy. Latvia has relied on Russian trade and faces severe difficulties as it introduces a free market. Agriculture specializes in dairying and meat production. ***Currency:*** Lat.

Recent History

Latvia was annexed by Russia in the 18th century. Latvian national consciousness grew throughout the 19th century. Following the Communist takeover in Russia (1917), Latvian nationalists declared independence (1918). A democratic system lasted until 1936 when General Ulmanis established a dictatorship. The Non-Aggression Pact (1939) between Hitler and Stalin assigned Latvia to the USSR, which invaded and annexed the republic (1940). After occupation by Nazi Germany (1941–44), Soviet rule was reimposed. Large-scale Russian settlement replaced over 200,000 Latvians, who were killed or deported to Siberia. In 1988, reforms in the USSR allowed Latvian nationalists to operate openly. Nationalists won a majority in Latvia's parliament and seceded following the failed coup by Communist hardliners in Moscow (1991). The USSR recognized Latvia's independence in September 1991. Tension remains over the large Russian minority in Latvia. In 1994–95, Latvia negotiated an associate agreement with the EU/EC.

LEBANON

Official name: Al-Lubnan (The Lebanon).
Member of: UN, Arab League.
Area: 10,230 km² (3950 sq mi).
Population: 2,910,000 (1993 est).
Capital: Beirut 1,500,000 (including suburbs; 1990 est).
Other major cities: Tripoli (Tarabulus) 240,000, Zahleh 200,000, Sidon (Saida) 100,000 (all including suburbs; 1990 est).
Language: Arabic (official).
Religions: Islam – Shia (31%) and Sunni (27%), Druze minority; Maronite Christian (22%), other Christian Churches (16%; Armenian, Greek Orthodox, Syrian).
Education: is not compulsory. *Adult literacy:* 80%. *Universities:* five.
Defence: (1993 figures) *Army:* 40,000 personnel. *Air force:* 800. *Navy:* 500. *Paramilitary:* 9000. (There are also 30,000 Syrian troops in Lebanon.) *Conscription:* none.

Government

A 128-member National Assembly – comprising 64 deputies elected by Muslims, 64 by Christians – is elected by universal adult suffrage for four years, using a system of proportional representation. The Assembly elects a (Maronite) President, who appoints a (Sunni Muslim) Prime Minister, who, in turn, appoints a Council of Ministers (six Christians and five Muslims).
Largest parties: (Shia Islamic) Amal, (Islamic fundamentalist) Hizbollah, (Maronite) Phalangist Party, (mainly Druze) Progressive Socialist Party.
Local government: six governates.
President: Elias Hrawi.
Prime Minister: Rafik al-Hariri.

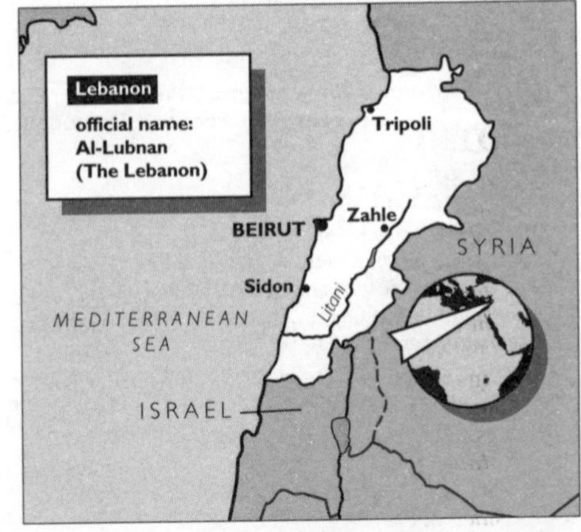

Geography

Behind a narrow coastal plain, the mountains of Lebanon rise. Beyond the fertile Beka'a Valley, to the east, are the Anti-Lebanese range and Hermon Mountains. ***Principal rivers:*** Litani, Orontes (Nahr al-Asi), Kabir. ***Highest point:*** Qurnat as-Sawda 3088 m (10,131 ft).

Climate: The lowlands have a Mediterranean climate. The cooler highlands receive heavy winter snowfall.

Economy

Reconstruction of an economy devastated by civil war began in 1991. The principal agricultural crops are citrus fruit (grown mainly for export), wheat, barley and olives. The illegal cultivation of opium poppies is economically significant. The textile and chemical industries and the financial sector are important. ***Currency:*** Lebanese Pound.

Recent History

Under the Ottoman (Turkish) Empire, Lebanon was administered as part of Syria, although Druze princes enjoyed considerable autonomy. Intercommunal friction was never far from the surface. A massacre of thousands of Maronites by the Druzes (1860) brought French intervention. After World War I, France received Syria as a League of Nations mandate, and created a separate Lebanese territory to protect Christian interests. The constitution under which Lebanon became independent in 1943 enshrined power-sharing between Christians and Muslims. The relative toleration between the various religious groups in Lebanon began to break down in the late 1950s when Muslim numerical superiority failed to be matched by corresponding constitutional changes. Radical Muslim supporters of the union of Syria and Egypt in 1958 clashed with the pro-Western party of Camille Chamoun (President 1952–58). Civil war ensued, and US marines landed in Beirut to restore order. The 1967 Arab-Israeli war and the exile of the Palestinian leadership to Beirut (1970–71) destabilized Lebanon. Civil war broke out in 1975, with subsequent Syrian and Israeli interventions. The war plunged the country into ungovernable chaos. In 1990 the defeat of Christian militia by Syrian troops allowed the Lebanese government to reassert its authority over the whole of Beirut. Most Lebanese sectarian militias were disarmed in 1991, when the civil war seemed to be over. However, Israeli-sponsored forces continue to occupy the south and the (Islamic fundamentalist) Hizbollah forces control the Beka'a Valley. The continued presence of Syrian troops on Lebanese soil has permitted a reconstruction of the Lebanese state.

LESOTHO

Official name: The Kingdom of Lesotho.
Member of: UN, Commonwealth, OAU.
Area: 30,355 km² (11,720 sq mi).
Population: 1,903,000 (1993 est).
Capital: Maseru 130,000 (city 110,000; 1988 est).
Other main towns: Teyateyaneng 14,000, Mafeteng 13,000 (1988 est).
Languages: Sesotho and English – both official.
Religions: Roman Catholic (44%), various Protestant Churches (49%).
Education: is compulsory, in theory, between the ages of seven and 13. *Adult literacy*: 74%. *Universities:* one.

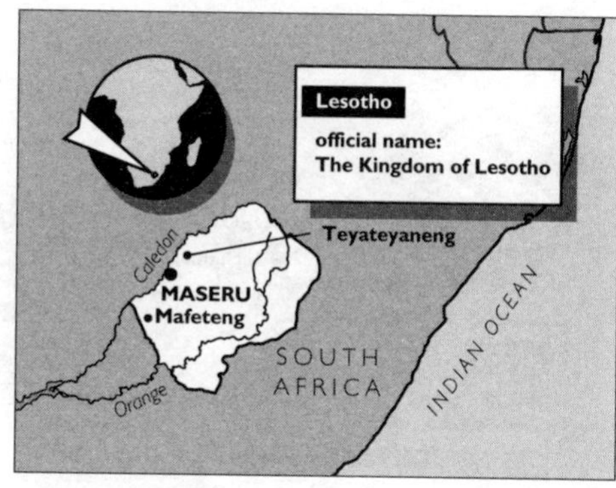

Defence: (1993 figures) *Army:* 2000. *Conscription:* none.

Government

Lesotho is a constitutional monarchy in which the King is the ceremonial head of state. A 65-member National Assembly is elected by universal adult suffrage for five years. A Prime Minister and a Cabinet of Ministers are responsible to the Assembly. The Senate (upper house) consists of eight nominated members and traditional chiefs.
Largest parties: Basotho Congress Party (BCP), Basotho National Party (BNP).
Local government: 10 districts.
Sovereign: HM Moshoeshoe II, King of Lesotho (restored 25 January 1995).
Prime Minister: Ntsu Mokhehle (BCP).

Geography

Most of Lesotho is mountainous, with the highest peaks in the Drakensberg Mountains. ***Principal rivers:*** Orange, Caledon. ***Highest point:*** Thabana Ntlenyana 3482m (11,425 ft).

Climate: Lesotho has a mild subtropical climate with lower temperatures in the highlands.

Economy

Livestock – cattle, sheep and goats (for mohair) – are the mainstay of the economy. Natural resources include diamonds. Abundant water is exported to South Africa. About one third of Lesotho's adult male labour force is employed in South Africa. ***Currency:*** Loti (plural Maloti).

Recent History

The kingdom escaped incorporation in South Africa by becoming a British protectorate (known as Basutoland) in 1868. Since independence (1966), land-locked Lesotho remains dependent on South Africa. Chief Jonathan (PM 1966–86) attempted to limit South African influence but was deposed in a coup. Further political instability followed. King Moshoeshoe II was deposed by the military (1990), replaced by his son (Letsie III), and eventually restored (1995) after Letsie attempted to dismiss the elected government.

LIBERIA

Official name: The Republic of Liberia.
Member of: UN, OAU, ECOWAS.
Area: 99,067 km² (38,250 sq mi).
Population: 2,885,000 (1993 est); in 1994 up to 800,000 of this total were refugees in neighbouring countries.

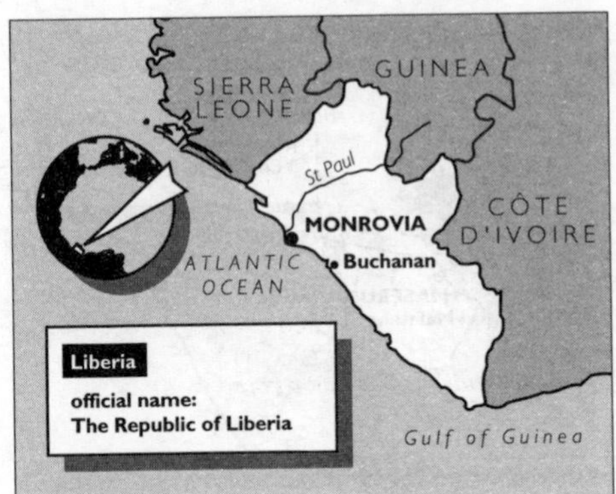

Capital: Monrovia 465,000 (1987 est).
Other main town: Buchanan 24,000 (1987 est).
Language: English (official).
Religions: animist (50%), Sunni Islam (26%), Christian Churches (24%).
Education: is compulsory, in theory, between the ages of seven and 16. *Adult literacy:* 40%. *Universities:* one university; one university college.
Defence: (1993 figures) *Armed forces:* c. 2000 personnel under the control of the provisional authorities. (There are about 12,000 ECOWAS troops in Liberia.)

Government

The constitution provides for a President, a 26-member Senate and a 64-member House of Representatives to be elected for six years by universal adult suffrage. The President appoints a Cabinet of Ministers. The Liberian political system broke down in 1990 owing to civil war. A provisional Council of State has been formed and a return to constitutional rule has been agreed to take effect in 1996.
Largest parties: The Liberian political system broke down in 1990 owing to civil war.
Local goverment: 11 counties and four towns.
Provisional head of state (Chairman of the Council of State): David Kpormakpor.

Geography

A low swampy coastal belt borders a higher zone of tropical forest. Further inland, plateaux rise to a mountainous region on the Guinean border. ***Principal rivers:*** Mano, Morro, Lofa, St Paul, St John. ***Highest point:*** Mount Nimba 1372m (4500 ft).
Climate: Liberia has a tropical climate with a wet season in the summer and a dry season in winter.

Economy

Over 70% of the labour force is involved in agriculture, producing cassava and rice as subsistence crops and rubber, coffee and cocoa for export. Liberia is a major exporter of iron ore. The economy has been disrupted by a civil war since 1990. ***Currency:*** Liberian dollar (US currency is also in circulation).

Recent History

Founded by the American Colonization Society in 1821–22 as a settlement for freed slaves, Liberia was declared a republic in 1847. Black American settlers dominated the local Africans and extended their control inland. From 1878 to 1980 power was held by presidents from the True Whig Party, including William Tubman (President 1944–71). Samuel Doe, the first Liberian of local ancestry to rule, took power in a military coup (1980), but was overthrown in a civil war (1990). Despite the presence of an ECOWAS peace-keeping force civil war continued until 1994 when all seven warring factions agreed to a ceasefire.

LIBYA

Official name: Daulat Libiya al-'Arabiya al-Ishtrakiya al-Jumhuriya (The Great Socialist People's Libyan Arab Jamahiriya).
Member of: UN, Arab League, OPEC.
Area: 1,757,000 km² (678,380 sq mi).
Population: 4,573,000 (1993 est).
Capital: Tripoli (Tarabulus) 591,000 (1988 est). In 1988 government functions were decentralized to Sirte (Surt) and Al Jofrah as well as Tripoli and Benghazi.
Other major cities: Benghazi (Banghazi) 446,000, Misurata (Misratah) 122,000, az-Zawiyah 89,000 (1988 est).
Language: Arabic (official).
Religion: Sunni Islam (over 97%).
Education: is compulsory between the ages of six and 15. *Adult literacy:* 64%. *Universities:* four.
Defence: (1993 figures) *Combined forces:* 70,000 personnel. *Conscription:* two years; selective.

Government

Over 1110 delegates from directly elected local Basic People's Congresses, trade unions, 'popular committees' and professional organizations meet as the Great People's Congress, which chooses a Revolutionary Leader – head of state – and the General People's Committee (which is equivalent to a Council of Ministers). The appointed General Secretariat assists the Congress.
Largest parties: There are no political parties.
Local government: 10 governates.
Head of state (Leader of the Revolution): Moamar al Gaddafi.
Head of government (Secretary-General of the General People's Committee): Mohammed al-Zanati.

Geography

The Sahara Desert covers most of Libya. In the north-

west (Tripolitania) coastal oases and a low plain support farming. In the northeast (Cyrenaica) a coastal plain and mountains support Mediterranean vegetation. The Tibesti Mountains lie along the border with Chad. ***Principal rivers:*** There are no perennial rivers. ***Highest point:*** Bette 2286m (7500 ft).
Climate: Libya is hot and dry, with lower temperatures and higher rainfall near the coast.

Economy
Libya is one of the world's largest producers of petroleum. Liquefied gas is also exported. Coastal oases produce wheat, barley, nuts, dates and grapes. Libya is overdependent upon a single commodity and the imposition of UN sanctions on Libya has damaged the economy. ***Currency:*** Libyan dinar.

Recent History
In 1911 the Italians took Libya from the (Turkish) Ottoman Empire. The British Eighth Army defeated the Italians at El Alamein in the Libyan Desert (1942), and after World War II the country was divided between British and French administrations. Libya became independent in 1951 under King Idris, formerly Amir of Cyrenaica. Although oil revenues made Libya prosperous, the pro-Western monarchy became increasingly unpopular. In 1969 junior army officers led by Moamar al Gaddafi (1942–) took power. Gaddafi nationalized the oil industry, but his various attempts to federate with other Arab countries proved abortive. In the 1970s he began a cultural revolution, dismantled formal government, collectivized economic activity, limited personal wealth and suppressed opposition. Libya's alleged support of terrorism provoked US air raids on Tripoli and Benghazi in 1986, and UN sanctions in 1992.

LIECHTENSTEIN
Official name: Fürstentum Liechtenstein (The Principality of Liechtenstein).
Member of: UN, OSCE.
Area: 160 km² (62 sq mi).
Population: 30,100 (1993 est).
Capital: Vaduz 4900 (1991 est).
Other main town: Schaan 5000 (1991 est).
Language: German (official).
Religions: Roman Catholic (87%), Lutheran (8%).
Education: is compulsory between the ages of seven and 16. *Adult literacy:* 100%. *Universities:* none.
Defence: There are no armed forces.

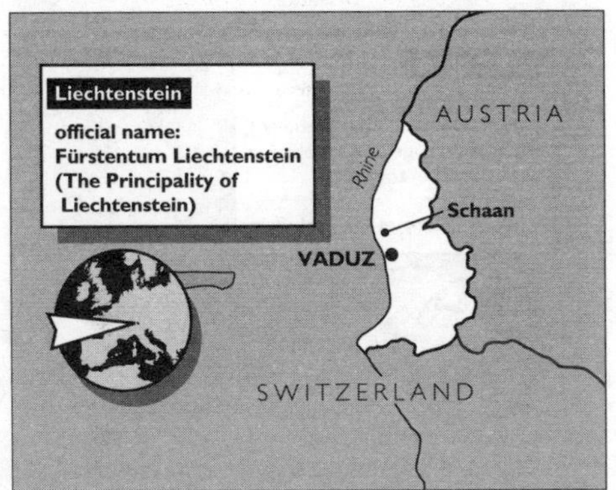

Government
The country is a monarchy ruled by a Prince. The 25-member Landstag is elected under a system of proportional representation by universal adult suffrage for four years. The Landstag elects a 5-member Cabinet, including a Prime Minister.
Largest parties: Fatherland Union (VU), Progressive Citizens' Party (FBP), (Green) Free List.
Local government: 11 communes.
Sovereign: HSH Hans Adam II, Sovereign Prince of Liechtenstein (succeeded upon the death of his father, 13 November 1989).
Prime Minister: Dr Mario Frick (VU).

Geography
The Alps in the east of the principality rise to the Austrian border. The west comprises the floodplain of the Rhine. ***Principal river:*** Rhine (Rhein). ***Highest point***: Grauspitze 2599m (8326 ft).
Climate: The country has a mild Alpine climate.

Economy
Liechtenstein has one of the highest standards of living in the world. Tourism, banking and manufacturing (precision goods) are all important. ***Currency:*** Liechtenstein uses Swiss currency.

Recent History
Separated from Germany by Austrian territory, Liechtenstein was the only German principality not to join the German Empire in 1871. Since 1924 the country has enjoyed a customs and monetary union with Switzerland, although since 1989 the principality has taken a more active role internationally, for instance joining the UN.

LITHUANIA
Official name: Lietuvos Respublika (Lithuania).
Member of: UN, OSCE.
Area: 65,301 km² (25,213 sq mi).
Population: 3,760,000 (1993 est).
Capital: Vilnius 590,000 (1993 est).
Other major cities: Kaunas 429,000, Klaipeda 206,000, Siauliai 148,000, Panevezys 132,000 (1993 est).
Languages: Lithuanian (81%), Russian (10%), Polish (7%).
Religions: Roman Catholic (80%), Lutheran and Russian Orthodox minorities.

Education: is compulsory between the ages of six and 16. *Adult literacy*: no figures available. *Universities:* six.
Defence: (1993 figures) *Army:* 4300 personnel. *Border guards:* 5000. *Air force:* 250. *Navy:* 250. *Conscription:* 12 months.

Government

The 141-member Parliament (Seimas) is elected by universal adult suffrage for four years. The President, who is directly elected for five years, chooses the Prime Minister, who, in turn, appoints a Cabinet of Ministers.
Largest parties: (former Communist) Lithuanian Democratic Labour Party (LDLP), (nationalist) Citizens' Charter of Lithuania Movement (Sajudis), Christian Democratic Party (CDP), Social Democratic Party (SDP), Polish Union (PU).
Local government: 66 districts.
President: Algirdas Mykolas Brazauskas (LDLP).
Prime Minister: Adolfas Slezevicius (LDLP).

Geography

Lithuania comprises a low-lying plain dotted with lakes and crossed by ridges of glacial moraine that rise to their greatest height in the southeast. A 100 km (60 mi) sandspit separates a large lagoon from the Baltic Sea.
Principal rivers: Neman (Nemunas), Merkys, Neris, Nevezis. ***Highest point:*** Juozapine 294m (964 ft).
Climate: Lithuania has a transitional climate between the milder temperate areas to the west and the more extreme continental areas to the east.

Economy

About 15% of the labour force is engaged in farming, mainly cattle rearing and dairying. Much of Lithuania is heavily forested. The engineering, timber, cement and food-processing industries are important, but Lithuania faces an uncertain future as it dismantles state control and breaks away from the former Soviet trade system. About one third of the economy had been privatized by 1994. An agreement of association with the EU/EC was negotiated in 1994–95.
Currency: Litas.

Recent History

Lithuania was annexed by Russia in 1795. Lithuanian national consciousness increased throughout the 19th century and Lithuanians rose with the Poles against Russian rule in 1830–31 and 1863. German forces invaded in 1915 and encouraged the establishment of a Lithuanian state. After World War I, the new republic faced invasions by the Red Army from the east and the Polish army from the west (1919–20). Internationally recognized boundaries were not established until 1923. The dictatorship of Augustinas Voldemaras (1926–29) was followed by that of Antonas Smetona (1929–40). The Non-Aggression Pact (1939) between Hitler and Stalin assigned Lithuania to the USSR, which invaded and annexed the republic (1940). Lithuania was occupied by Nazi Germany (1941–44). When Soviet rule was reimposed (1945), large-scale Russian settlement replaced over 250,000 Lithuanians who had been killed or deported to Siberia. In 1988, reforms in the USSR allowed Lithuanian nationalists to operate openly. Nationalists won a majority in the republic's parliament, but their declaration of independence (1990) brought a crackdown by Soviet forces in Lithuania. Following the failed coup by Communist hardliners in Moscow (August 1991), the USSR recognized Lithuania's independence.

LUXEMBOURG

Official names: Groussherzogtum Letzeburg (in Letzeburgish), Grand-Duché de Luxembourg (French), and Grossherzogtum Luxemburg (German) (Grand Duchy of Luxembourg).
Member of: UN, EU/EC, NATO, OSCE, OECD.
Area: 2586 km² (999 sq mi).
Population: 392,000 (1993 est).
Capital: Luxembourg 117,000 (city 78,000; 1991 census).
Other major towns: Esch-sur-Alzette 24,000, Differdange 16,000, Dudelange 15,000, Pétange 12,000, Sanem 12,000 (1991 census).
Languages: Letzeburgish (national; 72% as a first language); French (6% as a first language, but universally understood) and German (10% as a first language) – both official; Portuguese (9% as a first language).
Religion: Roman Catholic (95%).
Education: is compulsory between the ages of six and 15. *Adult literacy:* virtually 100%. *Universities:* one university centre.
Defence: (1993 figures) *Army:* 10,400 personnel. *Air force:* 50. *Conscription:* none.

Government

Luxembourg is a monarchy with a Grand Duke or Duchess as sovereign. The 60-member Chamber of Deputies is elected under a system of proportional representation by universal adult suffrage for five years. A Council of Ministers and a Premier – commanding a majority in the Chamber – are appointed by the sovereign.
Largest parties: (centre-right) Social Christian Party (PCS), Socialist Party (POSL), (liberal) Democratic Party (PD), Green Alternative and Green Ecologists, (pensioners' rights) 5/6 Action Committee.
Local government: 12 cantons.
Sovereign: HRH Jean I, Grand Duke of Luxembourg (succeeded upon the abdication of his mother, 12 November 1964).
Prime Minister: Jean-Claude Juncker (PCS).

Geography

The Oesling, in the north, is a wooded plateau. The Gutland, in the south, is a lowland region of valleys and ridges. ***Principal rivers:*** Moselle, Alzette, Our, Sûre. ***Highest point:*** Huldange 559m (1835 ft).
Climate: Luxembourg has relatively cool summers and mild winters.

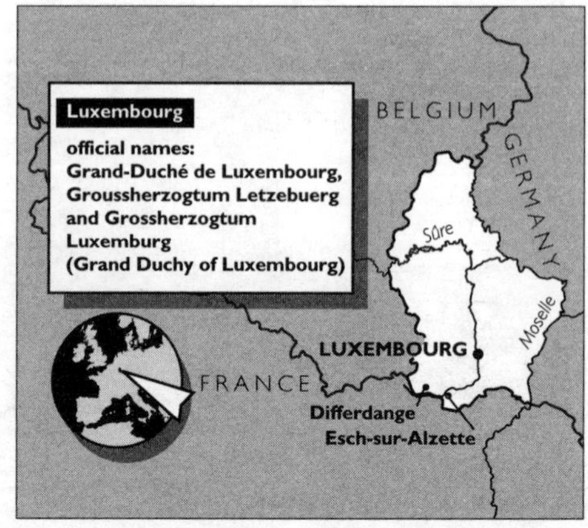

Economy
The iron and steel industry – originally based on local ore – is important. Luxembourg has become a major banking centre. The north grows potatoes and fodder crops; the south produces wheat and fruit, including grapes. ***Currency:*** Luxembourgeois franc.

Recent History
In 1815 Luxembourg became a Grand Duchy with the Dutch king as sovereign, but in 1890 it was inherited by a junior branch of the House of Orange. In 1831 the western (French-speaking) part of the state became part of Belgium. Occupied by the Germans during both World Wars, Luxembourg concluded an economic union with Belgium in 1922 and has enthusiastically supported European unity. Luxembourg City is one of EU/EC's three centres of administration.

MACEDONIA
Official names: (internal) Republika Makedonija (Republic of Macedonia) and (international) The Former Yugoslav Republic of Macedonia.
Member of: UN, OSCE (observer).
Area: 25,713 km^2 (9928 sq mi).
Population: 1,937,000 (1994 census).
Capital: Skopje 563,000 (city 408,000; 1991 census).
Other major cities: Bitolj (Bitola) 79,000, Kumanovo 61,000, Tetovo 47,000 (1991 census).
Languages: Macedonian (67%), Albanian (23%), Turkish (4%).
Religions: Macedonian Orthodox (over 60%), Sunni Islam (nearly 25%).
Education: is compulsory between the ages of seven and 15. *Adult literacy:* 89%. *Universities:* two.
Defence: (1993 figures) *Army:* 10,400 personnel. *Air force:* 50. *Conscription:* nine months.

Government
The 120-member Assembly is elected for four years by universal adult suffrage. A President – who appoints a Cabinet and a Prime Minister – is elected by the Assembly.
Largest parties: (nationalist) Internal Macedonian Revolutionary Organization-Democratic Party for Macedonian National Unity (IMRO), (former Communist) Social Democratic Alliance of Macedonia (SDSM), (mainly ethnic Albanian) Party of Democratic Prosperity-National Democratic Party (PDP), Alliance of Reform Forces-Liberal Party (ALF-LP).
Local government: 34 communes.
President: Kiro Gligorov.
Prime Minister: Branko Crvenkovski (SDSM).

Geography
Macedonia is a plateau about 760m (2500 ft) high, bordered by mountains including the Sar range. The central Vardar valley is the only major lowland. ***Principal rivers:*** Vardar, Strumica. ***Highest point:*** Korab 2753m (9032 ft).
Climate: The climate tends towards continental with cold, snowy winters and warm summers.

Economy
Macedonia was one of the least developed regions of Yugoslavia. The republic is largely agricultural, raising sheep and cattle and growing cereals and tobacco. Steel, chemical and textile industries rely, in part, upon local resources that include iron ore, lead and zinc. The economy has been severely damaged by intermittent Greek trade blockades and the disruption of trade with Serbia (owing to international sanctions against that country). ***Currency:*** Macedonian denar.

Recent History
When (Turkish) Ottoman power declined in the 19th century, Bulgaria, Serbia and Greece all claimed the region on an ethnic, religious or historical basis. Macedonia remained under Turkish rule until the First Balkan War (1912), after which those areas with a Greek-speaking majority were assigned to Greece and the remainder was partitioned between Bulgaria and Serbia, the latter gaining the area comprising the present republic. Bulgaria continued to claim all Macedonia and occupied the region during World War I. In 1918 Serbian Macedonia was incorporated within the new kingdom of Serbs, Croats and Slovenes, which was renamed Yugoslavia in 1929. When Yugoslavia was reorganized on Soviet lines by Marshal Tito in 1945 a separate Macedonian republic was formed within the Communist federation. After Tito's death (1980), the Yugoslav experiment faltered and local nationalist movements arose. Following the secession of Slovenia and Croatia and the outbreak of the Yugoslav civil war (1991), Macedonia declared its own sovereignty. Despite initial opposition from Greece, which denied the existence of a 'Macedonian' people, the republic gained international recognition in 1992. However, in 1994 Greece imposed a total trade embargo on Macedonia (with the exception of food imports and medical supplies). This move, which devastated the Macedonian economy, was condemned by all of Greece's EU partners. The nationalist aspirations of some of Macedonia's Albanian minority have increased tension.

MADAGASCAR
Official name: Repoblika Demokratika n'i Madagaskar (The Democratic Republic of Madagascar).
Member of: UN, OAU.
Area: 587,041 km^2 (226,658 sq mi).
Population: 13,355,000 (1993 est).
Capital: Antananarivo (Tananarive) 802,000 (1990 est).
Other major cities: Toamasina 145,000, Fianarantsoa

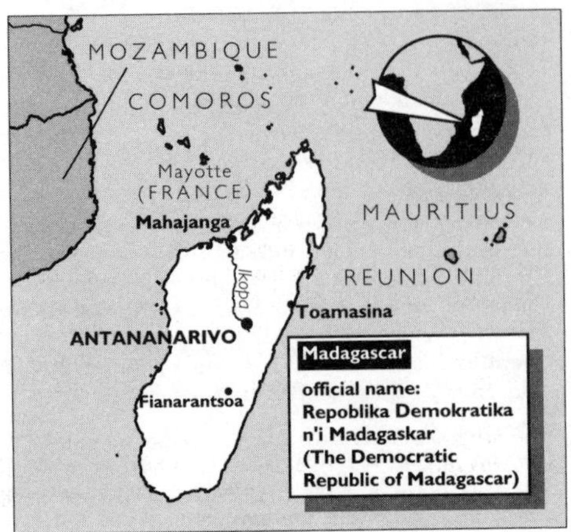

125,000, Mahajanga 122,000 (1990 est).
Languages: Malagasy and French (both official).
Religions: animist (47%), Roman Catholic (28%), Protestant Church of Jesus Christ in Madagascar (22%).
Education: is compulsory for five years, taken between the ages of six and 13. *Adult literacy:* 80%. *Universities:* six (including five university centres).
Defence: (1993 figures) *Army:* 20,000 personnel. *Air force:* 500. *Navy:* 500. *Paramilitary:* 7500. *Conscription:* none.

Government

A President – who appoints a Prime Minister and a Cabinet – is elected by universal adult suffrage for seven years. A 138-member National Assembly (lower house) is directly elected by a system of proportional representation for four years. The Senate (upper house) comprises delegates appointed by the President and chosen by an electoral college for four years.
Largest parties: Rasalama Active Forces Committee (FVCR), National Union for Democracy and Development (UNDD), (former monopoly) Advanced Guard of the Malagasy Republic (AREMA).
Local government: six provinces.
President: Albert Zafy (UNDD).
Prime Minister: Francisque Ravony (UNDD).

Geography

Massifs form a spine running from north to south through the island. To the east is a narrow coastal plain; to the west are fertile plains and low plateaux. ***Principal rivers:*** Onilahy, Mangoky, Tsiribihina, Betsiboka. ***Highest point:*** Tsaratanana peak 2876m (9436 ft).
Climate: The climate is tropical, although the highlands are cooler. The north receives monsoon rains, but the south is dry.

Economy

Over three quarters of the labour force are involved in agriculture. The main crops are coffee and vanilla for export, and rice and cassava for domestic consumption. The island is an important producer of chromite. ***Currency:*** CFA franc.

Recent History

In the early 19th century, the island was united by the Merina kingdom. Merina sovereigns attempted to modernize Madagascar, but the island was annexed by France in 1896, although resistance continued until 1904. Strong nationalist feeling found expression in a major rising (1947–48) that was suppressed with heavy loss of life. Independence was finally achieved in 1960. After a military coup in 1972, Madagascar had left-wing governments. Political and economic reforms began in 1990 and multi-party elections in 1993 resulted in a change of power.

MALAWI

Official name: The Republic of Malawi.
Member of: UN, Commonwealth, OAU.
Area: 118,484 km^2 (45,747 sq mi).
Population: 10,580,000 (1993 est).
Capital: Lilongwe 234,000 (1987 census).
Other major cities: Blantyre 331,000, Mzuzu 44,000, Zomba 43,000 (1987 census).
Languages: English and Chichewa (over 50%) – both official.
Religions: various Protestant Churches (34%; mainly Presbyterian and Anglican), Roman Catholic (28%), animist (20%), Sunni Islam (16%).
Education: is compulsory, in theory, between the ages of six and 13. *Adult literacy:* 42%. *Universities:* one.
Defence: (1993 figures) *Army:* 10,000 personnel. *Paramilitary:* 1500. *Conscription:* none.

Government

An executive President – who appoints a Cabinet – and the 177-member National Assembly are elected for five years.
Largest parties: United Democratic Front (UDF), (former monopoly) Malawi Congress Party (MCP), Aliance for Democracy (Aford).
Local government: three administrative regions.
President: Bakili Muluzi (UDF).

Geography

Plateaux cover the north and centre. The Rift Valley contains Lake Nyasa (Lake Malawi) and the Shire Valley. The Shire Highlands run along the Mozambican border in the southeast. ***Principal rivers:*** Shire, Rukuru. ***Highest point:*** Mount Sapitawa 3002m (9849 ft).
Climate: Malawi has an equatorial climate with heavy rainfall from November to April.

Economy

Agriculture is the mainstay of the economy, providing most of Malawi's exports. Tobacco, tea and sugar

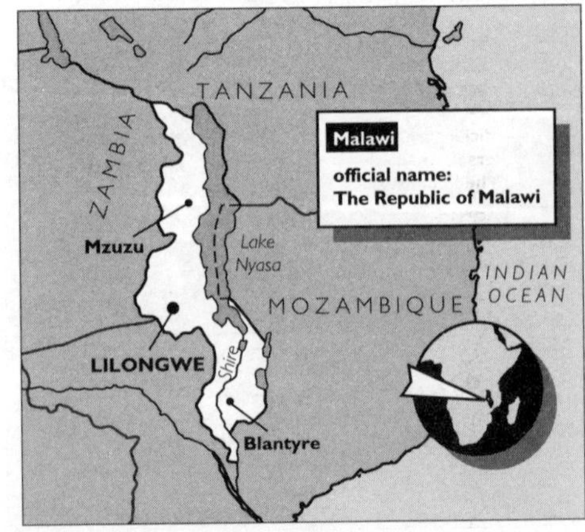

cane are the main crops. Malawi is one of the world's poorest nations. ***Currency:*** Kwacha.

Recent History

David Livingstone and other British missionaries became active in the area from the 1860s. A British protectorate, later called Nyasaland, was declared in 1891. In 1915 the Rev. John Chilembwe led a violent rising in the fertile south, where Africans had lost much land to white settlers. Federation with the white-dominated Central African Federation (1953–63) was resented. The nationalist leader – later President – Dr Hastings Kamuzu Banda (c. 1902–) helped to break the Federation. From independence as Malawi in 1964 until 1994, Banda provided strong rule and – despite criticism – maintained close relations with South Africa. The one-party state, established in 1966, was abandoned after pressure for political reforms grew in 1992–93. Banda was defeated in multi-party elections in 1994.

MALAYSIA

Official name: Persekutuan Tanah Melaysiu (The Federation of Malaysia).
Member of: UN, Commonwealth, ASEAN, Apec.
Area: 330,442 km² (127,584 sq mi).
Population: 19,077,000 (1993 est).
Capital: Kuala Lumpur 1,233,000 (including suburbs; 1991 census).
Other major cities: Ipoh 383,000, Johor Baharu 329,000, Malacca (Melaka) 296,000, Petaling Jaya 255,000, Tawau 245,000, Klang (Kelang) 244,000, Kuala Trengganu (Kuala Terengganu) 229,000, Sandakan 223,000, Kota Bahru (Kota Baharu) 220,000, George Town 219,000, Kota Kinabalu 208,000, Kuantan 198,000 (1991 est).
Languages: Bahasa Malaysia (Malay; official; 58%), English, Chinese (32%), Tamil.
Religions: Sunni Islam (official; over 55%), Buddhist, Daoist and various Christian minorities.
Education: is compulsory between the ages of six and 14. *Adult literacy:* 78%. *Universities:* seven.
Defence: (1993 figures) *Army:* 90,000 personnel. *Air force:* 12,500. *Navy:* 12,000. *Paramilitary:* 18,000. *Conscription:* none.

Government

The Yang di-Pertuan Agong (the King of Malaysia) holds office for five years. He is elected – from their own number – by the hereditary sultans who reign in nine of the 13 states. The 70-member Senate (upper house) comprises 40 members appointed by the King and two members elected by each of the state and territorial assemblies for a three-year term. The 192-member House of Representatives is elected by universal adult suffrage for five years. The King appoints a Prime Minister and a Cabinet commanding a majority in the House. The states have their own governments.
Largest parties: Barisan Nasional (National Front, a coalition of parties including the United Malays National Organization; BN), (social democrat) Democratic Action Party (DAP), Sabah United Party (PBS), Spirit of 46 Party.
Local government: 13 states and two territories.
Sovereign: HM Ja'afar ibni Al-Marhum, the Yang di-Pertuan Agong (King of Malaysia), Sultan of Negeri Sembilan (inaugurated 26 April 1994).
Prime Minister: Dato' Dr Mahathir bin Mohamed (BN).

States and territories

Johore (Johor) (sultanate) *Area:* 18,986 km² (7331 sq mi). *Population:* 2,074,000 (1991 census). *Capital:* Johore Bahru (Johor Baharu).
Kedah (sultanate) *Area:* 9426 km² (3639 sq mi). *Population:* 1,305,000 (1991 census). *Capital:* Alor Star (Alor Setar).
Kelantan (sultanate) *Area:* 14,943 km² (5769 sq mi). *Population:* 1,182,000 (1991 census). *Capital:* Kota Bahru (Kota Baharu).
Malacca (Melaka) (state) *Area:* 1650 km² (637 sq mi). *Population:* 505,000 (1991 census). *Capital:* Malacca (Melaka).
Negeri Sembilan (sultanate) *Area:* 6643 km² (2565 sq mi). *Population:* 691,000 (1991 census). *Capital:* Seremban.
Pahang (sultanate) *Area:* 35,965 km² (13,886 sq mi). *Population:* 1,037,000 (1991 census). *Capital:* Kuantan.
Perak (sultanate) *Area:* 21,005 km² (8110 sq mi). *Population:* 1,880,000 (1991 census). *Capital:* Ipoh.
Perlis (sultanate) *Area:* 795 km² (307 sq mi). *Population:* 184,000 (1991 census). *Capital:* Kangar.
Penang (Pulau Pinang) (state) *Area:* 1031 km² (398 sq mi). *Population:* 1,065,000 (1991 census). *Capital:* George Town.
Sabah (state) *Area:* 73,620 km² (28,425 sq mi). *Population:* 1,737,000 (1991 census). *Capital:* Kota Kinabalu.
Sarawak (state) *Area:* 124,449 km² (48,050 sq mi). *Population:* 1,648,000 (1991 census). *Capital:* Kuching.
Selangor (sultanate) *Area:* 7956 km² (3072 sq mi). *Population:* 2,289,000 (1991 census). *Capital:* Shah Alam.
Trengganu (Terengganu) (sultanate) *Area:* 12,955 km² (5002 sq mi). *Population:* 771,000 (1991 census). *Capital:* Kuala Trengganu (Kuala Terengganu).
Kuala Lumpur (territory) *Area:* 243 km² (94 sq mi). *Population:* 1,145,000 (1991 census). *Capital:* Kuala Lumpur.
Labuan (territory) *Area:* 91 km² (35 sq mi). *Population:* 54,000 (1991 census). *Capital:* Victoria.

Geography

Western (Peninsular) Malaysia consists of mountain ranges – including the Trengganu and Cameron Highlands – running north to south and bordered by

densely populated coastal lowlands. Tropical rainforest covers the hills and mountains of Eastern Malaysia (Sabah and Sarawak, the northern part of the island of Borneo). ***Principal rivers:*** Rajang, Baram, Pahang, Kelantan, Perak. ***Highest point:*** Kinabalu (in Sabah) 4101m (13,455 ft).
Climate: Malaysia has a tropical climate with heavy rainfall (up to 2500 mm / 100 in in the west). There is more seasonal variation in precipitation than temperature, with the northeast monsoon (from October to February) and the southwest monsoon (from May to September) bringing increased rainfall, particularly to Peninsular Malaysia.

Economy

Rubber, petroleum and tin are the traditional mainstays of the Malaysian economy, but all three suffered drops in price on the world market in the 1980s. Pepper (mainly from Sarawak), cocoa and timber are also important. One third of the labour force is involved in agriculture. Large numbers of Malays grow rice as a subsistence crop. Manufacturing industry is now the largest exporter; major industries include rubber, tin, timber, textiles, machinery and cement. The government has greatly encouraged industrialization, investment and a more active role for the ethnic Malay population in industry, which – with commerce and finance – has been largely the preserve of Chinese Malaysians. Malaysia has experienced high economic growth rates since the early 1980s. The tourist industry is being promoted. ***Currency:*** Ringgit.

Recent History

In 1867, the British established an administration for the Straits Settlements – Malacca, Penang and Singapore. Ignoring Thai claims to overlordship in the peninsula, the British took over the small sultanates as protected states. The British suppressed piracy, developed tin mining with Chinese labour and rubber plantations with Indian workers. Sarawak became a separate state under Sir James Brooke – the 'White Raja' – and his family from 1841, and was ceded to the British Crown in 1946. Sabah became British – as British North Borneo – in 1881. The Japanese occupied the whole of Malaysia during World War II. A Federation of Malaya – the peninsula – was established in 1948, but was threatened by Communist insurgency until 1960. Malaya became independent in 1957 with a constitution protecting the interests of the Malays, who were fearful of the energy and acumen of the Chinese. Sabah, Sarawak and Singapore joined the Federation – renamed Malaysia – in 1963. Singapore left in 1965, but the unity of the Federation was maintained, with British armed support, in the face of an Indonesian 'confrontation' in Borneo (1965–66). Tension between Chinese and Malays led to riots and the suspension of parliamentary government (1969–71), but scarcely hindered the rapid development of a resource-rich economy. During the 1980s, the growth of Islamic fundamentalism led to a defensive re-assertion of Islamic values and practices among the Muslim Malay ruling elite.

THE MALDIVES

Official name: Dhivehi Jumhuriya (Republic of Maldives).
Member of: UN, Commonwealth.
Area: 298 km² (115 sq mi).
Population: 237,000 (1993 est).
Capital: Malé 55,000 (1990 census).
Language: Dhivehi (Maldivian; official).

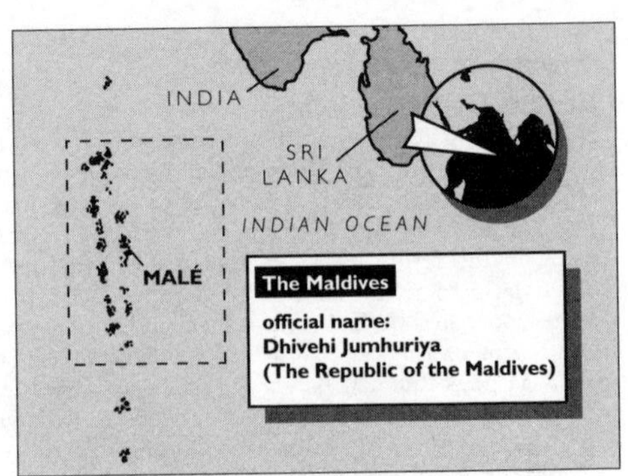

Religion: Sunni Islam (official; almost 100%).
Education: is not compulsory. *Adult literacy:* 90%. *Universities:* none.
Defence: There are no armed forces.

Government

The Majilis (Assembly) consists of eight members appointed by the President, and 40 elected by universal adult suffrage for five years. The President – who is directly elected for five years – appoints a Cabinet.
Largest parties: There are no political parties.
Local government: 20 districts.
President: Maumoon Abdul Gayoom.

Geography

The country is a chain of over 1190 small low-lying coral islands, of which 203 are inhabited. ***Principal rivers:*** none. ***Highest point:*** 3m (10 ft).
Climate: The climate is tropical with heavy rainfall brought by the monsoon between May and August.

Economy

The tourist industry has displaced fishing as the mainstay of the economy. However, 35% of Maldivians subsist on fish and coconuts. The greatest problem facing the low-lying Maldives is flooding from tropical monsoons and tidal waves. ***Currency:*** Rufiyaa.

Recent History

From 1887 until independence in 1965 the Maldives were a British protectorate, but the ad-Din sultanate, established in the 14th century, was only abolished in 1968.

MALI

Official name: La République du Mali (The Republic of Mali).
Member of: UN, OAU, ECOWAS.
Area: 1,248,574 km² (482,075 sq mi).
Population: 8,645,000 (1993 est).
Capital: Bamako 658,000 (1987 census).
Other major cities: Ségou 89,000, Mopti 74,000, Sikasso 73,000 (1987 census).
Languages: French (official), Bambara (60%).
Religions: Sunni Islam (90%), animist (9%).
Education: is compulsory, in theory, between the ages of seven and 16. *Adult literacy:* 32%. *Universities:* none.
Defence: (1993 figures) *Army:* 6900 personnel. *Air force:* 400. *Navy:* 50. *Paramilitary:* 7800. *Conscription:* two years; selective.

Government

A President is elected by universal adult suffrage for five years and the 129-member National Assembly is directly

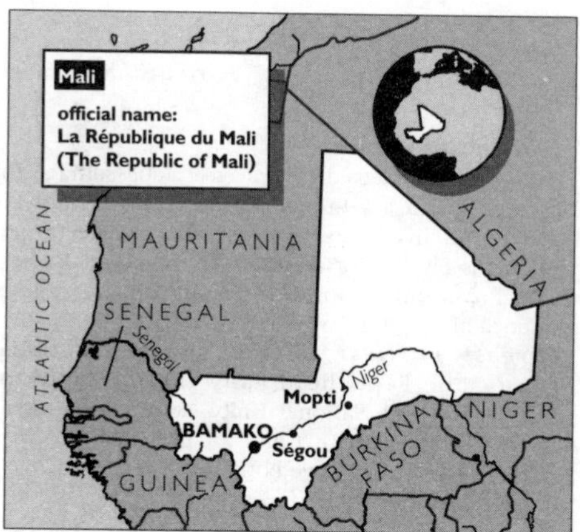

elected for three years. (Thirteen of the 129 seats are reserved for representatives of Malians living abroad.) The President appoints a Premier and a Cabinet.
Largest parties: Alliance for Democracy in Mali (ADEMA), Union for Democracy and Development, Sudanese Union-African Democratic Rally (US-RDA), National Council for Democracy (CNID), Asembly for Democracy and Progress (RDP).
Local government: eight administrative regions and one district (the capital).
President: Alpha Oumar Konare (ADEMA).
Prime Minister: Ibrahim Boubacar Keita. (ADEMA).

Geography

The low-lying flat plateaux and plains of Mali rise towards the Adrar des Iforas range in the northeast. The south is savannah; the Sahara Desert is in the north. ***Principal rivers:*** Niger, Bani, Senegal. ***Highest point:*** Hombori Tondo 1155m (3789 ft).
Climate: Mali is hot and largely dry, although the south has a wet season from June to October.

Economy

Drought in the 1970s and 1980s devastated Mali's livestock herds. Only one fifth of Mali can be cultivated, producing mainly rice, millet and sorghum for domestic use, and cotton for export. ***Currency:*** CFA franc.

Recent History

Mali is named after an empire in the area (12th–14th centuries). Conquered by France (1880–95), it became the French Sudan. Mali became independent in 1960. After an army coup in 1968, military governments ruled Mali until multi-party politics were restored in 1992.

MALTA

Official names: Repubblika Ta'Malta and Republic of Malta.
Member of: UN, Commonwealth, OSCE.
Area: 316 km² (122 sq mi).
Population: 363,000 (1993 est).
Capital: Valletta 205,000 (city 9200; Birkirkara 21,000; Qormi 20,000; Hamrun 14,000; Sliema 14,000; Zabbar 13,000; 1992 est for the combined Inner Harbour and Outer Harbour regions).
Languages: Maltese and English – both official.
Religion: Roman Catholic (official; 98%).

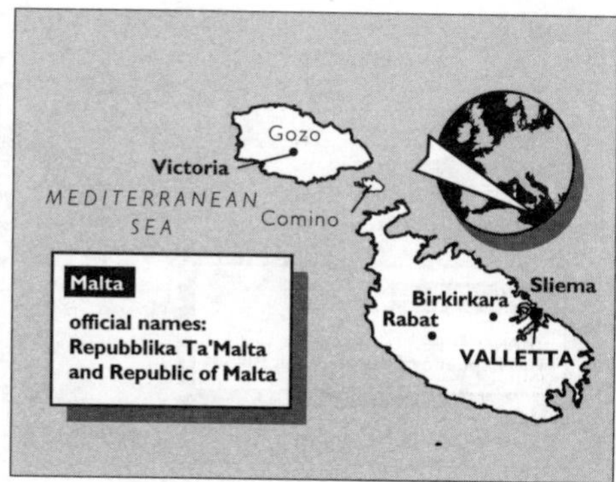

Education: is compulsory between the ages of five and 16. *Adult literacy:* 96%. *Universities:* one.
Defence: (1993 figures) *Army:* 1650 personnel. *Conscription:* none.

Government

The 65-member House of Representatives is elected by universal adult suffrage under a system of proportional representation for five years. The President, whose role is ceremonial, is elected for five years by the House. The President appoints a Premier and a Cabinet who command a majority in the House.
Largest parties: (conservative) National Party (PN), (social democratic) Labour Party (MLP).
Local government: 67 local councils are to be established.
President: Ugo Mifsud Bonicci.
Prime Minister: Eddie Fenech Adami (PN).

Geography

The islands of Malta, Gozo and Comino consist of low limestone plateaux with little surface water. ***Principal rivers:*** none. ***Highest point:*** an unnamed point 249m (816 ft).
Climate: The climate is Mediterranean with hot dry summers, and cooler wetter winters.

Economy

The main industries are footwear and clothing, food processing and ship repairing. Tourism is the principal foreign-currency earner. Malta is virtually self-sufficient in agricultural products. ***Currency:*** Maltese Lira.

Recent History

As a British colony (from 1814), Malta became a vital naval base, and the island received the George Cross for its valour in World War II. Malta gained independence in 1964. Maltese political life has polarized between the National Party and the Maltese Labour Party. Malta now has associate membership of the EU/EC.

MARSHALL ISLANDS

Official name: The Republic of the Marshall Islands.
Member of: UN.
Area: 181 km² (70 sq mi).
Population: 52,000 (1993 est).
Capital: Dalap-Uliga-Darrit (on Majuro) 14,600 (1990 census).
Languages: Marshallese and English (both official).
Religions: various Protestant Churches (over 90%),

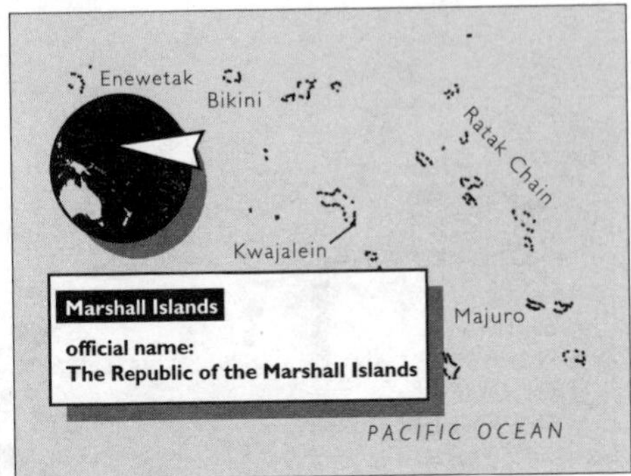

Roman Catholic minority.
Education: is compulsory between the ages of six and 14. *Adult literacy:* 91%. *Universities:* one university centre.
Defence: There are no armed forces. The USA is responsible for the islands' defence.

Government

The 33-member Nitijela (Parliament) is elected by universal adult suffrage for four years. The members elect a President from their own number. The traditional 12-member Council of Chiefs has advisory and consultative powers only.
Largest parties: The only party (Ralik Ratak Democratic Party) is in opposition The other members sit as independents.
Local government: 25 districts.
President: Amata Kabua.

Geography

The Marshall Islands comprise over 1150 small coral atolls and islands below 6 m (20 ft) high. ***Principal rivers:*** none. ***Highest point:*** an unnamed point 6m (20 ft).
Climate: The tropical climate is characterized by heavy rainfall.

Economy

With practically no resources, the islands depend on subsistence farming, tourism and US grants. ***Currency:*** The Marshall Islands use US currency.

Recent History

The islands were under Spanish (1875–85), German (1885–1914), and Japanese (1914–45) administration before becoming part of the US Pacific Islands Trust Territory. In 1986, US administration was terminated, but the USA retains responsibility for the islands' defence. The islands' independence was recognized when the UN terminated the trusteeship in 1990.

MAURITANIA

Official name: Jumhuriyat Muritaniya al-Islamiya (Islamic Republic of Mauritania).
Member of: UN, OAU, Arab League.
Area: 1,030,700 km^2 (397,950 sq mi).
Population: 2,170,000 (1993 est).
Capital: Nouakchott 393,000 (1988 census).
Other main towns: Kaédi 30,000, Kiffa 29,000, Rosso 28,000 (1988 census).
Languages: Arabic (official; 81%), French.
Religion: Sunni Islam (official; 99%).
Education: is not compulsory. *Adult literacy:* 34%. *Universities:* one.
Defence: (1993 figures) *Army:* 15,000 personnel. *Air force:* 150. *Navy:* 500. *Paramilitary:* 5000. *Conscription:* two years.

Government

A President is elected by universal adult suffrage for six years and a 79-member National Assembly is elected for five years. A 56-member Senate (upper house) is elected for six years by municipal leaders. The President appoints a Prime Minister and a Council of Ministers.
Largest parties: (former monopoly) Social Democratic Republican Party (PRDS), Rally for Democracy and National Unity (RDUN), Mauritian Renewal Party (PMR), Union of Democratic Forces (UFD). Other parties have boycotted recent elections.
Local government: 13 provinces.
President: Col. Maaouiya Sidi Mohammed Ould Taya (PRDS).
Prime Minister: to be appointed.

Geography

Isolated peaks rise above the plateaux of the Sahara Desert that cover most of Mauritania, which is remarkably flat. ***Principal river:*** Sénégal. ***Highest point:*** Kediet Ijill 915m (3002 ft).
Climate: The climate is hot and dry, with adequate rainfall only in the south.

Economy

Persistent drought has devastated the nomads' herds of cattle and sheep. Fish from the Atlantic and iron ore are virtually the only exports. ***Currency:*** Ouguiya.

Recent History

The French arrived on the coast in the 17th century, but did not annex the Arab emirates inland until 1903. Mauritania became independent in 1960. When Spain withdrew from the Western Sahara (1976), Morocco and Mauritania divided the territory between them, but Mauritania could not defeat the Polisario guerrillas fighting for Sahrawi independence and gave up its claim (1979). Tension between the dominant Arab north and Black African south led to violence in 1989. Military rulers held power from 1979. In 1992 free elections were held, but the opposition boycotted the poll.

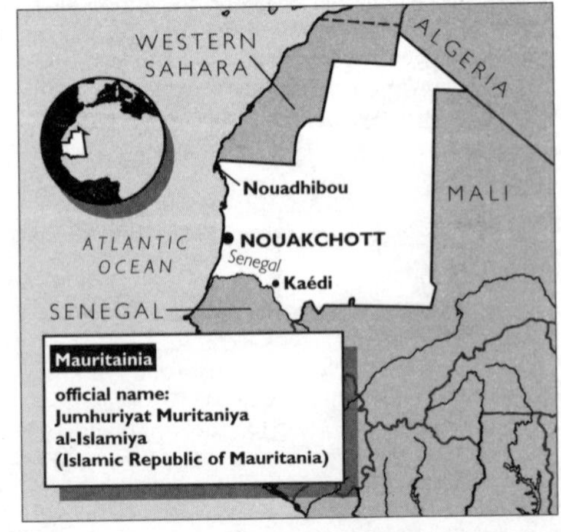

MAURITIUS

Official name: The Republic of Mauritius.
Member of: UN, OAU, Commonwealth.
Area: 2040 km^2 (788 sq mi).
Population: 1,105,000 (1993 est).
Capital: Port Louis 143,000 (1992 est).
Other major towns: Beau Bassin-Rose Hill 94,000, Vacoas-Phoenix 92,000 (1992 est).
Languages: English (official), Creole (French; nearly 30%), Hindi (over 20%), Bhojpuri.
Religions: Hindu (51%), Roman Catholic (25%), Sunni Islam (17%), with Protestant minorities.
Education: is compulsory between the ages of five and 11. *Adult literacy:* 82%. *Universities:* one.
Defence: (1993 figures) *Paramilitary:* 1300 personnel. *Conscription:* none.

Government

Elections are held by universal adult suffrage every five years for 62 members of the Assembly; up to 8 additional members may be appointed. The President, whose role is ceremonial, is elected by the Assembly. The President appoints a Prime Minister who commands a majority in the Assembly. The PM, in turn, appoints a Cabinet responsible to the Assembly.
Largest parties: Mauritian Socialist Party (MSM), Mauritian Militant Movement (MMM), Organization for the People of Rodrigues (OPR), Movement of Democratic Workers (MTD), Mauritius Labour Party (MLP), Mauritian Social Democratic Party (PMSD).
Local government: five municipalities and four districts.
President: Cassam Uteem.
Prime Minister: Aneerood Jugnauth (MSM).

Geography

The central plateau of Mauritius is surrounded by mountains. Other islands in the group include Rodrigues and the Agalega Islands. ***Principal rivers:*** Grand River South, Grand River North West. ***Highest point:*** Piton de la Rivière Noire 826m (2711 ft).
Climate: The climate is subtropical, although it can be very hot from December to April. Rainfall is high in the uplands.

Economy

Tourism (the major foreign-currency earner) and the export of sugar cane dominate the economy. Diversification is being encouraged, and the clothing industry is of increasing importance. ***Currency:*** Mauritius rupee.

Recent History

In 1814 Mauritius became British. Black slaves were imported, followed in the 19th century by Indian labourers whose descendants are the majority community. Independence was gained in 1968 and a republic was declared in 1992.

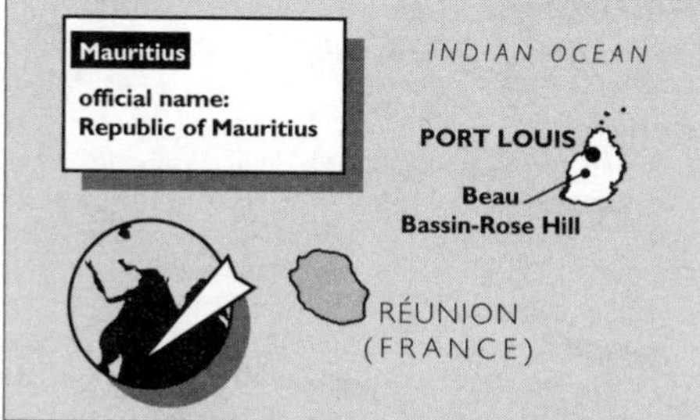

MEXICO

Official name: Estados Unidos Mexicanos (United Mexican States).
Member of: UN, OAS, NAFTA, ALADI, OECD, Apec.
Area: 1,958,201 km^2 (756,066 sq mi).
Population: 89,960,000 (1993 est).
Capital: Mexico City 15,050,000 (city 8,237,000; Nezahualcóyotl 1,260,000; 1990 census).
Other major cities: Guadalajara 1,650,000 (city 1,629,000), Monterrey 1,069,000 (city 1,064,000), Puebla 1,055,000 (city 1,007,000), León 872,000 (city 758,000), Ciudad Juarez 798,000, Tijuana 753,000 (city 699,000), Mexicali 602,000, Culiacán 602,000, Acapulco 592,000 (city 515,000), Mérida 557,000 (city 523,000), Chihuahua 531,000 (city 516,000), San Luis Potosí 526,000 (city 489,000), Aguascalientes 506,000 (1990 census).
Languages: Spanish (92%; official), various Indian languages.
Religion: Roman Catholic (91%).
Education: is compulsory between the ages of six and 12. *Adult literacy:* 87%. *Universities:* 82.
Defence: (1993 figures) *Army:* 130,000 personnel. *Air force:* 8000. *Navy:* 37,000. *Conscription:* one year; decided by lottery; part-time.

Government

The 64-member Senate and the President – who may serve only once – are elected by universal adult suffrage for six years. The 500-member Chamber of Deputies is directly elected for three years – 200 of the members are elected under a system of proportional representation; the remaining 300 represent single-member constituencies. The President appoints a Cabinet.
Largest parties: (centrist) Institutional Revolutionary Party (PRI), (centre-right reformist) National Action Party (PAN), (left-wing reformist) Democratic Revolutionary Party (PRD), (Marxist) Cardenista Front of National Reconstriuction.
Local government: 31 states and one federal district.
President: Ernesto Zedillo (PRI).

States

Aguascalientes *Area:* 5471 km^2 (2112 sq mi). *Population:* 719,000 (1990 census). *Capital:* Aguascalientes.
Baja California Norte *Area:* 69,921 km^2 (26,997 sq mi). *Population:* 1,661,000 (1990 census). *Capital:* Mexicali.
Baja California Sur *Area:* 73,475 km^2 (28,369 sq mi). *Population:* 318,000 (1990 census). *Capital:* La Paz.
Campeche *Area:* 50,812 km^2 (19,619 sq mi). *Population:* 535,000 (1990 census). *Capital:* Campeche.
Chiapas *Area:* 74,211 km^2 (28,653 sq mi). *Population:* 3,210,000 (1990 census). *Capital:* Tuxtla Gutiérrez.
Chihuahua *Area:* 244,938 km^2 (94,571 sq mi). *Population:* 2,442,000 (1990 census). *Capital:* Chihuahua.
Coahuila *Area:* 149,982 km^2 (57,908 sq mi). *Population:* 1,972,000 (1990 census). *Capital:* Saltillo.
Colima *Area:* 5191 km^2 (2004 sq mi). *Population:* 429,000 (1990 census). *Capital:* Colima.

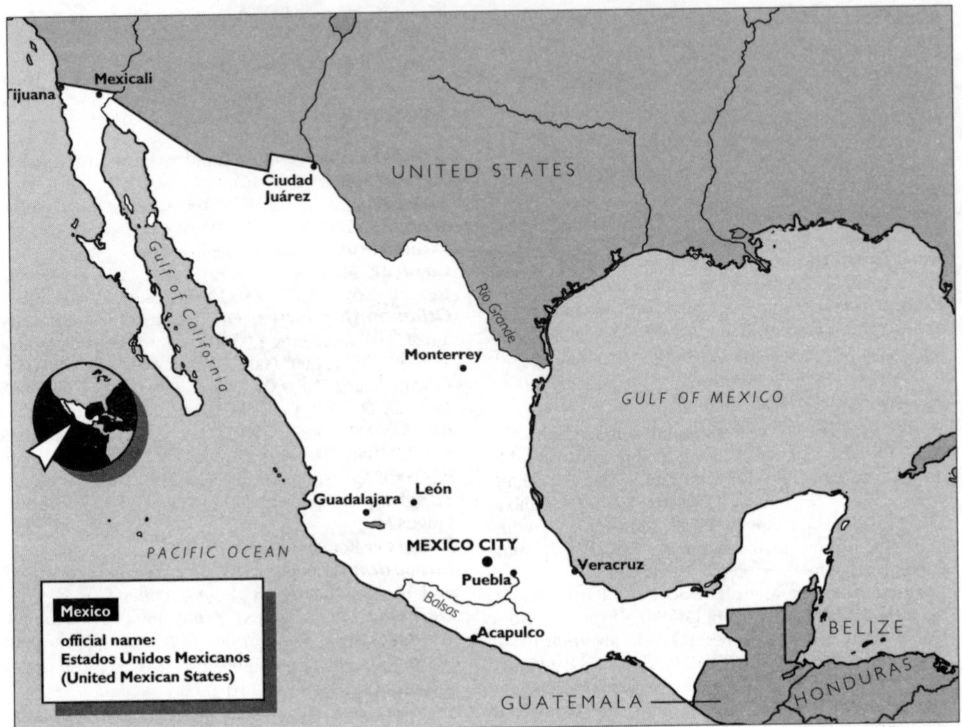

Durango *Area:* 123,181 km² (47,560 sq mi). *Population:* 1,349,000 (1990 census). *Capital:* Durango.

Guanajuato *Area:* 30,491 km² (11,773 sq mi). *Population:* 3,983,000 (1990 census). *Capital:* Guanajuato.

Guerrero *Area:* 64,281 km² (24,819 sq mi). *Population:* 2,621,000 (1990 census). *Capital:* Chilpancingo.

Hidalgo *Area:* 20,813 km² (8036 sq mi). *Population:* 1,888,000 (1990 census). *Capital:* Pachuca.

Jalisco *Area:* 80,836 km² (31,211 sq mi). *Population:* 5,303,000 (1990 census). *Capital:* Guadalajara.

México *Area:* 21,355 km² (8245 sq mi). *Population:* 9,816,000 (1990 census). *Capital:* Toluca.

Michoacán *Area:* 59,928 km² (23,138 sq mi). *Population:* 3,548,000 (1990 census). *Capital:* Morelia.

Morelos *Area:* 4950 km² (1911 sq mi). *Population:* 1,195,000 (1990 census). *Capital:* Cuernavaca.

Nayarit *Area:* 26,979 km² (10,417 sq mi). *Population:* 825,000 (1990 census). *Capital:* Tepic.

Nuevo León *Area:* 64,924 km² (25,067 sq mi). *Population:* 3,099,000 (1990 census). *Capital:* Monterrey.

Oaxaca *Area:* 93,952 km² (36,275 sq mi). *Population:* 3,020,000 (1990 census). *Capital:* Oaxaca.

Puebla *Area:* 33,902 km² (13,090 sq mi). *Population:* 4,126,000 (1990 census). *Capital:* Puebla.

Querétaro *Area:* 11,449 km² (4420 sq mi). *Population:* 1,051,000 (1990 census). *Capital:* Querétaro.

Quintana Roo *Area:* 50,212 km² (19,387 sq mi). *Population:* 493,000 (1990 census). *Capital:* Chetumal.

San Luis Potosí *Area:* 63,068 km² (24,351 sq mi). *Population:* 2,003,000 (1990 census). *Capital:* San Luis Potosí.

Sinaloa *Area:* 58,328 km² (22,521 sq mi). *Population:* 2,204,000 (1990 census). *Capital:* Culiacán.

Sonora *Area:* 182,052 km² (70,291 sq mi). *Population:* 1,824,000 (1990 census). *Capital:* Hermosillo.

Tabasco *Area:* 25,267 km² (9756 sq mi). *Population:* 1,502,000 (1990 census). *Capital:* Villahermosa.

Tamaulipas *Area:* 79,384 km² (30,650 sq mi). *Population:* 2,250,000 (1990 census). *Capital:* Ciudad Victoria.

Tlaxcala *Area:* 4016 km² (1551 sq mi). *Population:* 761,000 (1990 census). *Capital:* Tlaxcala.

Veracruz *Area:* 71,699 km² (27,683 sq mi). *Population:* 6,228,000 (1990 census). *Capital:* Jalapa.

Yucatán *Area:* 38,402 km² (14,827 sq mi). *Population:* 1,363,000 (1990 census). *Capital:* Mérida.

Zacatecas *Area:* 73,252 km² (28,283 sq mi). *Population:* 1,276,000 (1990 census). *Capital:* Zacatecas.

Federal District (Distrito Federal) *Area:* 1479 km² (571 sq mi). *Population:* 8,237,000 (1990 census). *Capital:* Mexico City.

Geography

Between the Sierra Madre Oriental mountains in the east and the Sierra Madre Occidental in the west is a large high central plateau. Volcanoes include Volcán Citlaltepetl (Pico de Orizaba). The coastal plains are generally narrow in the west, but wider in the east. The Yucatán Peninsula in the southeast is a broad limestone lowland; Baja California in the northwest is a long narrow mountainous peninsula. ***Principal rivers:*** Rio

Bravo de Norte (Rio Grande), Río Conchos, Grijalva, Usumacinta, Papaloapan, Río Balsas. ***Highest point:*** Volcán Citlaltepetl (Pico de Orizaba) 5610m (18,405 ft). ***Climate:*** There is considerable climatic variation, in part reflecting the complexity of the relief. In general, the south and the coastal lowlands are tropical; the central plateau and the mountains are cooler and drier.

Economy

Over 20% of the labour force is involved in agriculture and many Mexicans are still subsistence farmers growing maize, wheat, kidney beans and rice. Coffee, cotton, fruit and vegetables are major export crops. Mexico is the world's leading producer of silver. The exploitation of large reserves of natural gas and petroleum enabled Mexico's spectacular economic development since the 1970s, but social and economic reforms did not keep up with this growth. An expanding industrial base includes important petrochemical, textile, motor-vehicle and food-processing industries. In the early 1990s low labour costs and the new NAFTA trade agreement encouraged major US companies to set up plant in Mexico. However, economic problems remain, and high unemployment has stimulated immigration – often illegal – to the US. A major crisis of confidence in 1995 sent the peso into steep decline and Mexico required a US rescue package. ***Currency:*** Peso.

Recent History

In 1836 Texas rebelled against Mexico, declaring independence. When the USA annexed Texas in 1845, war broke out, resulting in the loss of half Mexico's territory – Texas, New Mexico and California. A period of reform began in 1857, with a new liberal constitution. A civil war (1858–61) between reformists and conservatives was won by the reformists under Benito Juárez (1806–72), but the economy was shattered. After Mexico failed to repay debts, Spain, Britain and France invaded in 1863. Although Spain and Britain soon withdrew, France remained, appointing Archduke Maximilian of Austria (1832–67) as Emperor (1864). Under US pressure and Mexican resistance, the French withdrew in 1867. Maximilian remained in Mexico City and was captured and executed. Juárez re-established the republic. The authoritarian rule of General Porfirio Díaz (President 1876–80 and 1888–1910) brought peace, but wealth was concentrated into a few hands. Revolution against the power of the landowners erupted in 1910. The reformist policies of President Francisco Madero (1873–1913) were supported by the outlaw Pancho Villa (1877–1923), but revolutionary violence continued, and in 1916–17 a US expeditionary force was sent against Villa. From 1924 the revolution became anticlerical and the Church was persecuted. Order was restored when the Institutional Revolutionary Party came to power in 1929. In the 1930s the large estates were divided and much of the economy was nationalized. Political opposition was tolerated, although the ruling party is virtually guaranteed perpetual power. A more liberal economic and political climate emerged in the 1990s, but Mexico's 'coming of age' – marked by membership of NAFTA and OECD – has been marred by political assassinations (1994), a peasant uprising in the state of Chiapas (since 1994) and a major economic crisis (1995).

MICRONESIA

Official name: The Federated States of Micronesia.
Member of: UN.
Area: 702 km^2 (271 sq mi).
Population: 103,000 (1993 est).
Capital: Palikir (on Pohnpei) 2000 (1990 est).
Other major towns: Wenn (formerly Moen) 10,400, Tol 6700, Kolonia 6300 (1990 est).
Languages: English, Trukese, Ponapean, Yapese, Kosraean.
Religions: various Protestant Churches (majority), Roman Catholic (minority).
Education: is compulsory between the ages of six and 14. *Adult literacy:* 77%. *Universities:* none.
Defence: There are no armed forces. The USA is responsible for the islands' defence.

Government

The President (who serves for four years) and the 14-member National Congress are elected by universal adult suffrage. Congress comprises one senator elected from each of the four states for four years, and ten senators elected by constituencies for two years.
Largest parties: There are no political parties.
Local government: four states.
President: Bailey Olter.

States

Chuuk (Truk) *Area:* 127 km^2 (49 sq mi). *Population:* 54,000 (1992 est). *Capital:* Wenn (Moen).
Kosrae *Area:* 110 km^2 (42 sq mi). *Population:* 7200 (1992 est). *Capital:* Kosrae.
Pohnpei (formerly Ponape) *Area:* 345 km^2 (133 sq mi). *Population:* 33,000 (1992 est). *Capital:* Kolonia.
Yap *Area:* 119 km^2 (46 sq mi). *Population:* 14,000 (1992 est). *Capital:* Colonia.

Geography

The Micronesian islands comprise over 600 islands in two main groups. The majority of the islands are low coral atolls, but Kosrae and Pohnpei are mountainous. ***Principal rivers:*** no significant rivers. ***Highest point:*** Mt Totolom 791m (2595 ft).
Climate: The climate is tropical with heavy rainfall.

Economy

Apart from phosphate, the islands have practically no resources and depend upon subsistence agriculture, fishing and US grants. ***Currency:*** Micronesia uses US currency.

Recent History

The islands were under Spanish (1874–99), German (1899–1914), and Japanese (1914–45) administration before becoming part of the US Pacific Trust Territory. In 1986, US administration was terminated,

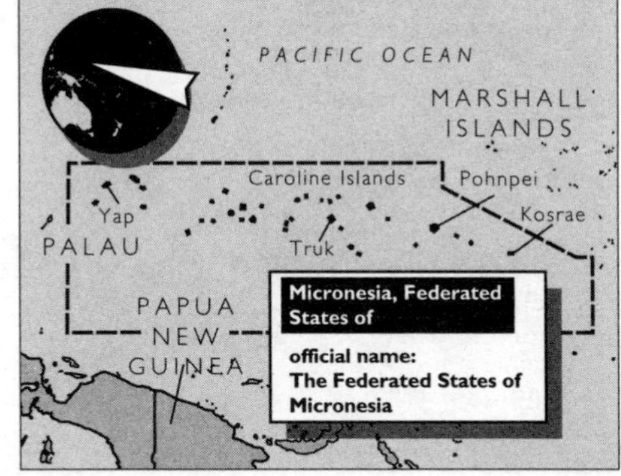

although the USA retains responsibility for the islands' defence. The Federated States' independence was recognized when the UN terminated the trusteeship in 1990.

MOLDOVA

Official name: Republica Moldoveneasca (Republic of Moldova). Formerly known as Moldavia.
Member of: UN, CIS, OSCE.
Area: 33,702 km² (13,012 sq mi).
Population: 4,362,000 (1993 est).
Capital: Chisinau (formerly Kishinev) 754,000 (city 676,000; 1991 est).
Other major cities: Tiraspol 186,000, Balti 165,000, Tighina (formerly Bendery) 142,000 (1990 est).
Languages: Moldovan (Romanian; 67%), Ukrainian (13%), Russian (13%), Gagauz (4%).
Religion: Orthodox majority – both Romanian and Russian.
Education: is compulsory between the ages of seven and 17. *Adult literacy:* no figures available. *Universities:* one.
Defence: (1993 figures) *Army:* 9300 personnel. *Paramilitary:* 2500. (There are Russian troops stationed in Transdnestria.) *Conscription:* 18 months.

Government

A President and a 104-member Parliament are elected for four years by universal adult suffrage. The President appoints a Premier and a Cabinet.
Largest parties: (nationalist centre) Agrarian Democratic Party (ADP), (former Communist) Socialist Party, (pro-Russian) Yedinstvo (Unity) Party, (pro-Romanian) Peasants and Intellectuals Bloc, Christian Democratic People's Front.
Local government: 40 districts and 10 cities. (There is constitutional provision for two autonomous regions: Transdnestria and Gaugazia.)
President: Mircea Snegur (ADP).
Prime Minister: Andrei Sangheli (ADP).

Geography

Most of Moldova comprises a plain between the River Prut and the Dnestr valley. In the centre of the republic, the Kodry Hills form the highest ground in Moldova. ***Principal rivers:*** Prut, Dnestr. ***Highest point:*** Mount Balaneshty 430m (1409 ft).
Climate: The country experiences a mild, slightly continental climate.

Economy

Collective farms grow fruit (particularly grapes for wine), vegetables, wheat, maize and tobacco. Little progress has been made to privatize agriculture or industry, which includes food processing and engineering. The collapse of the Soviet trade system and the war in Trans-Dnestr have damaged the economy.
Currency: Moldovan leu.

Recent History

Known as Bessarabia, the region was ceded to the Russians in 1812. Briefly restored to the Romanian principality of Moldavia (1856–78), Bessarabia remained Russian until World War I. An autonomous Bessarabian republic was proclaimed in 1917, but was suppressed by a Russian Bolshevik invasion (1918). The Russians were removed by Romanian forces and Bessarabia became part of the kingdom of Romania (1918). When Romania entered World War II as a German ally, the USSR reoccupied Bessarabia, which was reorganized as the Moldavian Soviet Republic in 1944. Following the abortive coup by Communist hardliners in Moscow (1991), Moldavia declared independence. As Moldova, the republic received international recognition when the Soviet Union was dissolved. Civil war broke out in 1992 when Russian and Ukrainian minorities – fearing an eventual reunion of Moldova with Romania – proclaimed the breakaway republic of Transdnestria. The intervention of CIS (mainly Russian) forces brought an uneasy peace, but Moldovan authorities no longer control Transdnestria. In a 1994 referendum Moldova rejected union with Romania.

MONACO

Official name: Principauté de Monaco (Principality of Monaco).
Member of: UN, OSCE.
Area: 2.21 km² (0.85 sq mi).
Population: 29,900 (1990 est).
Capital: Monaco 1200 (1990 est).
Other main town: Monte-Carlo 13,200 (1990 est).
Languages: French (official), Monegasque.
Religion: Roman Catholic (90%).
Education: is compulsory between the ages of six and 16. *Adult literacy:* virtually 100%. *Universities:* none.
Defence: Except for the palace guard, there are no armed forces.

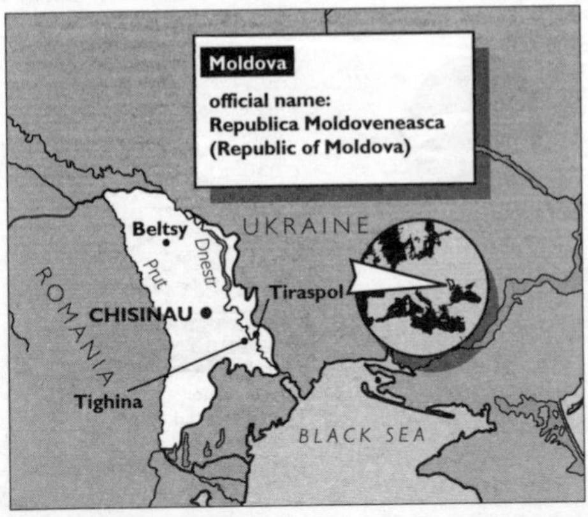

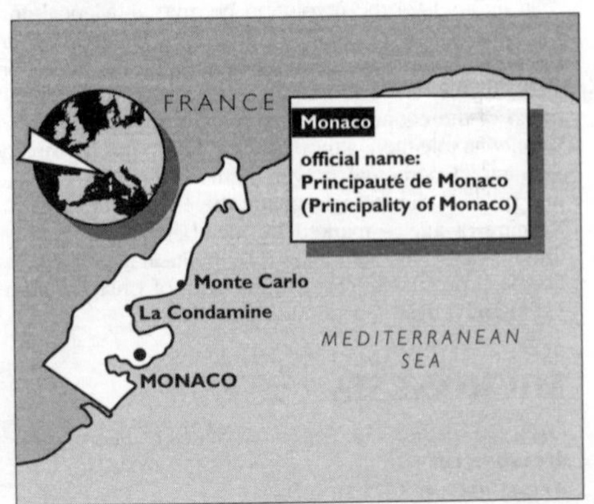

Government

Monaco is a constitutional monarchy. Legislative power is jointly held by the Prince and the 18-member National Council, which is elected by universal adult suffrage for five years. Executive power is held by the Prince, who appoints a four-member Council of Government and a French civil servant – the Minister of State – to head it.

Largest parties: There are no formal political parties but political groups include Liste Campora and Liste Médecin.

Local government: three communes.

Sovereign: HSH Rainier III, Sovereign Prince of Monaco (succeeded upon the death of his grandfather, 9 May 1949).

Minister of State: Jacques Dupont.

Geography

Monaco comprises a rocky peninsula and a narrow stretch of coast. Since 1958 Monaco's area has increased by 20% through reclamation of land from the sea. ***Principal river:*** Vésubie. ***Highest point:*** an unnamed point 162m (533 ft).

Climate: Monaco has a Mediterranean climate.

Economy

Monaco depends upon real estate, banking, insurance, light industry and tourism. ***Currency:*** Monaco uses French currency.

Recent History

The greater part of the principality was lost – and eventually annexed by France – in 1848. Since 1861 Monaco has been under French protection. Prince Rainier III granted a liberal constitution in 1962. By special agreement, Monaco is included within the EU/EC.

MONGOLIA

Official name: Mongol Uls (Mongolian Republic).

Member of: UN.

Area: 1,566,500 km^2 (604,800 sq mi).

Population: 2,255,000 (1993 est).

Capital: Ulan Bator (Ulaan Baatar) 619,000 (1993 est).

Other major city: Darhan 80,000, Erdenet 49,000 (1991 est).

Languages: Khalkh Mongolian (official; 78%), Kazakh.

Religion: Religion was suppressed from 1924 to 1990. Buddhism – the traditional religion – is now being encouraged.

Education: is compulsory between the ages of six and 16. *Adult literacy:* 98%. *Universities:* four, plus five institutes of university status.

Defence: (1993 figures) *Army:* 20,000 personnel. *Air force:* 1250. *Paramilitary:* 10,000. *Conscription:* two years.

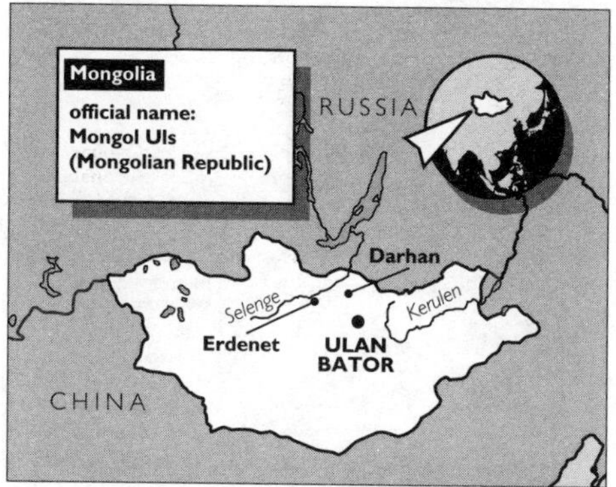

Government

The 76-member Great Hural and a President are elected by universal adult suffrage for four years. The President appoints a Prime Minister and a Council of Ministers.

Largest parties: (former Communist) Mongolian People's Revolutionary Party (BDY), Mongolian National Democratic Party (DG).

Local government: 21 provinces plus the capital.

President: Punsalmaagiyn Ochirbat (DG).

Prime Minister: Puntsagiyn Jasray (BDY).

Geography

Mongolia comprises mountains in the north, a series of basins in the centre, and the Gobi Desert and Altai Mountains in the south. ***Principal rivers:*** Onon, Selenge (Selenga), Hovd. ***Highest point:*** Nayramdal Uul (Hüyten Orgil) 4362m (14,350 ft).

Climate: Mongolia has a dry climate with generally mild summers and severely cold winters.

Economy

Mongolia depends on collectivized animal herding (cattle, sheep, goats and camels). Cereals (including fodder crops) are grown on a large scale on state farms. The industrial sector is dominated by food processing, hides and wool. Copper is a major export. The former USSR was Mongolia's principal trading partner and Soviet grants represented one third of Mongolia's GNP. The end of aid from Russia and the disruption of trade since 1991 have led to severe economic difficulties. ***Currency:*** Tugrik.

Recent History

In the 17th century, Mongolia was annexed by China, but 'Outer' Mongolia – the north – retained autonomy as a Buddhist monarchy. In 1921, Outer Mongolia broke away from China with Soviet assistance and in 1924 the Mongolian People's Republic was established. Pro-democracy demonstrations led to a liberalization of the regime in 1990. The Communists won the first multi-party elections.

MOROCCO

Official name: Al-Mamlaka al-Maghribiya (The Kingdom of Morocco).

Member of: UN, Arab League.

Area: 458,730 km^2 (177,115 sq mi), excluding the disputed Western Sahara (or 710,850 km^2 (274,461 sq mi) with the Western Sahara).

Population: 26,494,000 (1993 est), excluding Western Sahara, which had 195,000 inhabitants in 1993.

Capital: Rabat 1,545,000 (includes Salé; 1992 est).

Other major cities: Casablanca (Dar el Beida) 3,311,000 (city 1,069,000), Marrakech 745,000, Meknès 660,000, Oujda 635,000, Kénitra 610,000, Fez (Fès) 605,000 (1992 est).

Languages: Arabic (official; 75% as a first language but universally understood), Berber (about 25%), French.

Religion: Sunni Islam (official; 98%).

Education: is compulsory for six years, to be taken

between the ages of seven and 16. *Adult literacy:* 50%. *Universities:* 11.

Defence: (1993 figures) *Army:* 175,000 personnel. *Air force:* 13,500. *Navy:* 7000. *Paramilitary:* 10,000. *Conscription:* 18 months.

Government

Morocco is a constitutional monarchy. The 333-member Chamber of Representatives consists of 222 members elected by universal adult suffrage for six years and 111 members chosen by an electoral college representing municipal authorities and professional bodies. The King appoints a Prime Minister and Cabinet.

Largest parties: Constitutional Union (UC), Popular Movement (MP), National Popular Movement (MNP), National Democratic Party (PND), Socialist Union of Popular Forces (USFP), Istiqal Party (PI), Organization of Democratic and Popular Change (OADP), National Rally of Independents.

Local government: officially, 49 provinces and prefectures, including four provinces which are in the disputed Western Sahara.

Sovereign: HM Hassan II, King of Morocco (succeeded upon the death of his father, 26 February 1961).

Prime Minister: Abdellatif Filali.

Disputed territory: Western Sahara. See Other Territories (beginning on p. 729).

Geography

Over one third of Morocco is mountainous. The principal uplands are the Grand, Middle and Anti Atlas Mountains in the west and north and a plateau in the east. Much of Morocco – and all of the Western Sahara – is desert. ***Principal rivers:*** Moulouya, Sebou, Oum er-Rbia. ***Highest point:*** Jebel Toubkal 4165m (13,665 ft).

Climate: The north has a Mediterranean climate with hot dry summers and warm wetter winters. The south and much of the interior have semiarid and tropical desert climates.

Economy

Over 40% of the labour force is involved in farming, producing mainly citrus fruits, grapes (for wine) and vegetables for export, and wheat and barley for local consumption. Morocco is the world's leading exporter of phosphates. Other resources include iron ore, lead and zinc. Many important industries and services are in state ownership. Tourism is growing. ***Currency:*** Dirham.

Recent History

In the 19th century Spain confirmed control of several long-claimed coastal settlements. In the 'Moroccan Crises' (1905–06 and 1911), French interests in Morocco were disputed by Germany. Under the Treaty of Fez in 1912 France established a protectorate over Morocco, although the Spanish enclaves remained. The 1925 Rif rebellion stirred nationalist feelings, but independence was not gained until 1956. King Hassan II (reigned 1961–) has survived left-wing challenges through strong rule and vigorous nationalism – as in his 1975 'Green March' of unarmed peasants into the then-Spanish (Western) Sahara. Morocco still holds Western Sahara despite international pressure and the activities of the Algerian-backed Polisario guerrillas fighting for the territory's independence. A ceasefire was agreed in 1991, but a scheduled UN-sponsored referendum on Western Sahara has yet to be held.

MOZAMBIQUE

Official name: A República de Moçambique (Republic of Mozambique).

Member of: UN, OAU.

Area: 799,380 km² (308,641 sq mi).

Population: 15,650,000 (1993 est).

Capital: Maputo 1,070,000 (1989 est).

Other major cities: Beira 292,000, Nampula 197,000 (1989 est).

Languages: Portuguese (official), Makua-Lomwe (52%).

Religions: animist (60%), Roman Catholic (15%), Sunni Islam (15%).

Education: is compulsory, in theory, between the ages of seven and 14. *Adult literacy:* 33%. *Universities:* one.

Defence: (1993 figures) *Army:* 45,000 personnel. *Air force:* 4000. *Navy:* 1000. (There are about 6000 UN troops in Mozambique.) *Conscription:* none.

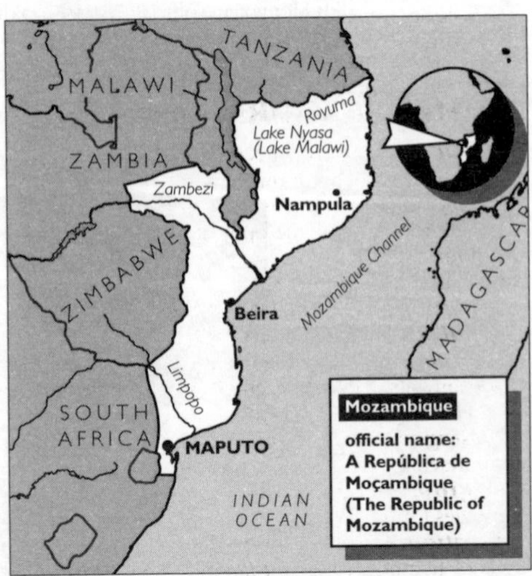

Government

The constitution provides for elections by universal adult suffrage for a 250-member Assembly and a President for five years. The President appoints a Prime Minister and Council of Ministers.

Largest parties: (former Marxist) Front for the Liberation of Mozambique (Frelimo), (centre-right) National Mozambican Resistance (Renamo), National Mozambican Union.

Local government: 10 provinces, plus the capital.

President: Joaquim Aberto Chissano (Frelimo).

Prime Minister: Mario da Graca Machungo (Frelimo).

Geography

The Zambezi River separates high plateaux in northern Mozambique from lowlands in the south. Much of Mozambique comprises the largest coastal plain in southern Africa. ***Principal rivers:*** Limpopo, Zambezi (Zambèze), Rovuma, Shire. ***Highest point:*** Mount Bingo 2436m (7992 ft).

Climate: Mozambique has a tropical climate, with maximum rainfall and temperatures from November to March.

Economy

Over 80% of the labour force is involved in farming, mainly growing cassava and maize. Fishing is a major employer – prawns and shrimps make up nearly 50% of Mozambique's exports. The economy has been devastated by civil war and drought, and famine is widespread. Mozambique is usually stated to be the poorest country in the world (in terms of GDP per head). ***Currency:*** Metical.

Recent History

The Portuguese founded coastal trading posts from 1531, but only gained control of the interior at the end of the 19th century. Forced labour and minimal development fuelled nationalist feelings, and in 1964 the Frelimo movement launched a guerrilla war against Portuguese rule. Independence was gained in 1975, and a Marxist-Leninist state was established. The pressures of poverty and the destabilization of the country by South Africa – through support for the Renamo guerrilla movement – led to renewed ties with the West. Marxism was abandoned by Frelimo in 1989. A ceasefire – and a UN presence in Mozambique – were agreed in 1992 and multi-party elections were held in 1994.

MYANMAR (BURMA)

Official name: Myanma Naingngandaw (The Union of Myanmar). The name Burma was officially dropped in 1989, but is still in widespread use internationally and by the opposition in the country.

Member of: UN.

Area: 676,577 km² (261,228 sq mi).

Population: 44,615,000 (1991 est).

Capital: Rangoon (Yangon) 2,880,000 (1990 est).

Other major cities: Mandalay 533,000, Moulmein (Mawlamyine) 230,000, Pegu (Bago) 151,000, Bassein (Pathein) 144,000 (1983 census).

Languages: Burmese (official; 80%), Karen, Mon, Shan, Kachin.

Religion: Buddhist (88%), various Christian Churches (5%).

Education: is compulsory, in theory, between the ages of five and 10. *Adult literacy:* 79%. *Universities:* five.

Defence: (1993 figures) *Army:* 265,000 personnel. *Air force:* 9000. *Navy:* 12,500. *Paramilitary:* 50,000. *Conscription:* none.

Government

Power is held by a 19-member State Law-and-Order Restoration Council. There is constitutional provision for a 489-member Assembly elected by universal adult suffrage, a Council of Ministers and a Council of State, whose Chairman is head of state.

Largest parties: (military-backed) National Unity Party, (coalition opposition) Democratic Alliance of Burma.

Local government: seven divisions and seven states. (The states are, in theory, autonomous.)

Chair of the State Law and Order Restoration Council and Prime Minister: Gen. Than Shwe.

States

Chin *Area:* 36,019 km² (13,907 sq mi). *Population:* 369,000 (1983 census). *Capital:* Hakha.

Kachin *Area:* 89,041 km² (34,379 sq mi). *Population:* 905,000 (1983 census). *Capital:* Myitkyina.

Karen *Area:* 30,383 km² (11,731 sq mi). *Population:* 1,055,000 (1983 census). *Capital:* Pa-an.

Kayah *Area:* 11,733 km² (4530 sq mi). *Population:* 168,000 (1983 census). *Capital:* Loi-kaw.

Mon *Area:* 12,297 km² (4748 sq mi). *Population:* 1,680,000 (1983 census). *Capital:* Moulmein.

Rakhine (formerly **Arakan**) *Area:* 36,778 km² (14,200 sq mi). *Population:* 2,046,000 (1983 census). *Capital:* Sittwe (formerly Akyab).

Shan *Area:* 155,801 km² (60,155 sq mi). *Population:* 3,717,000 (1983 census). *Capital:* Taunggyi.

Geography

The north and west of Burma are mountainous. In the east, is the Shan Plateau along the Thai border. Central and south Burma consists of tropical lowlands. ***Principal rivers:*** Irrawaddy, Salween, Chindwin, Sittang, Mekong. ***Highest point:*** Hkakado

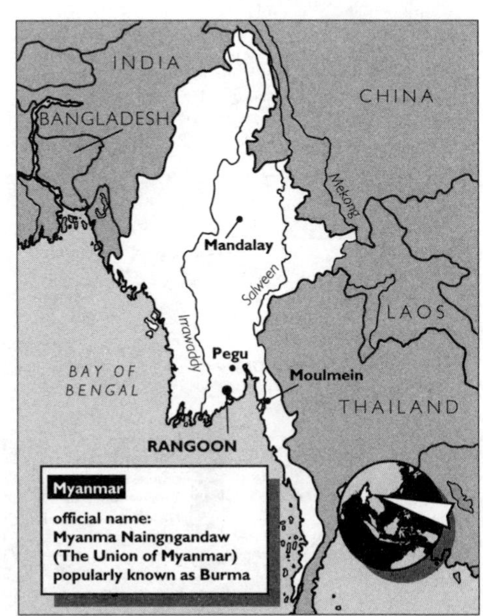

Razi 5881m (19,296 ft).
Climate: Burma is tropical, experiencing monsoon rains – up to 5000 mm (200 in) in the south – from May to October.

Economy

Burma is rich in agriculture, timber, and minerals, but because of poor communications, self-imposed isolation, lack of development and rebellions by a number of ethnic minorities, the country has been unable to realize its potential. Subsistence farming involves about 80% of the labour force. ***Currency:*** Kyat.

Recent History

British expansion from India led to total annexation (1826–85). Separated from British India in 1937, Burma became a battleground for British and Japanese forces in World War II. In 1948, Burma left the Commonwealth as an independent republic, keeping outside contacts to a minimum, particularly following the coup of General Ne Win in 1962. Continuing armed attempts to gain autonomy by non-Burman minorities strengthened the role of the army. The military retained power following multi-party elections in 1990 and detained leaders of the winning party (including Aung San Suu Kyi, who was awarded the 1991 Nobel Peace Prize). The government has come under strong international pressure to introduce reforms, but it has continued to exert military pressure on minorities, including the Karen and Muslims. By 1995 most of the ethnic rebellions had been either put down, contained or ended by truces.

NAMIBIA

Official name: Republic of Namibia.
Member of: UN, OAU, Commonwealth.
Area: 824,292 km² (318,261 sq mi).
Population: 1,402,000 (1993 est).
Capital: Windhoek 115,000 (1988 est).
Other major cities: Walvis Bay 21,000, Swakopmund 16,000 (1988 est).
Languages: English (official), Afrikaans, German, local languages.
Religions: Lutheran (30%), Roman Catholic (20%), other Christian Churches (30%).
Education: is compulsory between the ages of seven and 16. *Adult literacy:* 73%. *Universities:* one.

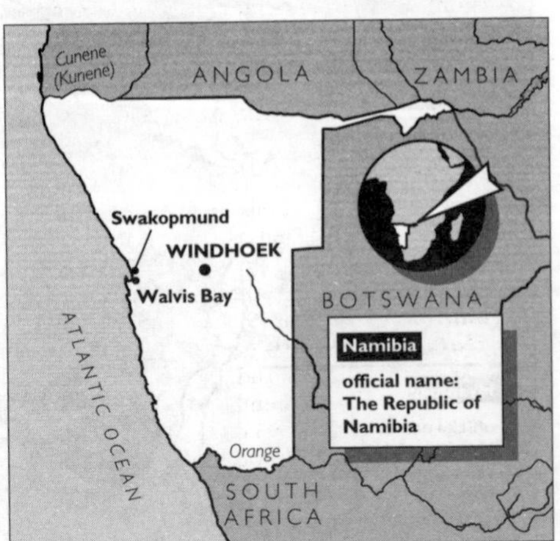

Defence: (1993 figures) *Army:* 8000 personnel. *Navy:* 100. *Conscription:* none.

Government

A 72-member Assembly is elected by universal adult suffrage for five years. The President, who is elected by the Assembly, appoints a Cabinet of Ministers.
Largest parties: South West African People's Organization (SWAPO), (centre) Democratic Turnhalle Aliance (DTA).
Local government: 13 regions.
President: Sam Nujoma (SWAPO).
Prime Minister: Hage Geingob (SWAPO).

Geography

The coastal Namib Desert stretches up to 160 km (100 mi) inland and contains the highest point, the Brandberg. Beyond the Central Plateau, the Kalahari Desert occupies the eastern part of the country.
Principal rivers: Kunene, Orange, Okavango.
Highest point: Brandberg 2579m (8461 ft).
Climate: Namibia has a hot dry tropical climate. Average coastal rainfall is under 100 mm (4 in).

Economy

Over 30% of the labour force is involved in farming, mainly raising cattle and sheep, but Namibia is prone to drought. The economy depends upon exports of diamonds and uranium, and is closely tied to South Africa. ***Currency:*** Namibia uses South African currency.

Recent History

A German protectorate of South West Africa – excluding Walvis Bay, which had been British since 1878 – was declared in 1884. Seeking land for white settlement, the Germans established their rule after great bloodshed – over three quarters of the Herero people were killed in 1903–04. South Africa conquered the territory during World War I, and (after 1919) administered it under a League of Nations mandate. In 1966, the UN cancelled the mandate, but South Africa – which had refused to grant the territory independence – ignored the ruling. The main nationalist movement, SWAPO, began guerrilla warfare to free Namibia, the name adopted by the UN for the state. South Africa unsuccessfully attempted to exclude SWAPO's influence. After a ceasefire agreement in 1989, UN-supervised elections were held in 1989 for a constituent assembly. Independence, under the presidency of SWAPO leader Sam Nujoma, was achieved in 1990. South Africa ceded Walvis Bay to Namibia in 1994.

NAURU

Official name: The Republic of Nauru.
Member of: Commonwealth (special member).
Area: 21 km² (8 sq mi).

Population: 9400 (1990 est).
Capital: no official capital; Yaren (no population figure available) is capital *de facto*.
Languages: Nauruan (official), English.
Religions: Nauruan Protestant Church, Roman Catholic.
Education: is compulsory between the ages of six and 16. *Adult literacy:* virtually 100%. *Universities:* one university centre.
Defence: There are no armed forces. Australia is responsible for Nauru's defence.

Government

The 18-member Parliament – which is elected by universal adult suffrage for three years – elects a President, who appoints a Cabinet of Ministers.
Largest parties: The only party is the (opposition) Democratic Party of Nauru; the other members sit as independents.
Local government: 14 districts.
President: Bernard Dowiyogo.

Geography

Nauru is a low-lying coral atoll. ***Principal rivers:*** none. ***Highest point:*** an unnamed point 68m (225 ft).
Climate: Nauru has a tropical climate with heavy rainfall, particularly between November and February.

Economy

Nauru depends almost entirely upon the export of phosphate rock, stocks of which are expected to run out after 2010. Shipping and air services and 'tax haven' facilities are planned to provide revenue when the phosphate is exhausted. ***Currency:*** Nauru uses Australian currency.

Recent History

Germany annexed Nauru in 1888 after a request from German settlers on Nauru for protection during unrest between rival clans. Australia captured Nauru in 1914 and administered it – except for a period of Japanese occupation (1942–45) – until independence in 1968.

NEPAL

Official name: Nepal Adhirajya (Kingdom of Nepal).
Member of: UN.
Area: 147,181 km² (56,827 sq mi).
Population: 19,265,000 (1993 est).
Capital: Kathmandu 420,000 (city 235,000; 1987 est).
Other major cities: Biratnagar 130,000, Patan (also known as Lalitpur) 117,000 (1987 est).

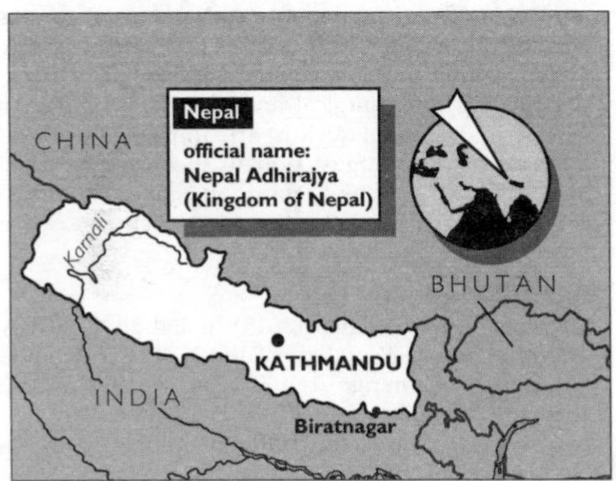

Languages: Nepali (official; 58%), Bihari (19%).
Religions: Hindu (official; 90%), Buddhist (5%).
Education: is compulsory, in theory, between the ages of six and 11. *Adult literacy:* 38%. *Universities:* two.
Defence: (1993 figures) *Army:* 34,800 personnel. *Air force:* 200. *Conscription:* none.

Government

Nepal is a constitutional monarchy. The 205-member House of Representatives (lower house) is elected for five years by universal adult suffrage. The House elects a Prime Minister and other Ministers. The National Council (upper house) consists of 60 appointed and indirectly elected members chosen for a six-year term.
Largest parties: Communist Party of Nepal (United Marxist Leninist) (UML), (centrist) Nepali Congress Party (NCP), (right-wing) National Democratic Party (NDP).
Local government: 14 zones.
Sovereign: HM King Birendra of Nepal (succeeded upon the death of his father, 31 January 1972).
Prime Minister: Man Mohan Adhikary (UML).

Geography

In the south are densely populated subtropical lowlands. A hilly central belt is divided by fertile valleys. The Himalaya dominate the north, and include Mount Everest on the Chinese border. ***Principal rivers:*** Kosi, Gandak, Karnali. ***Highest point:*** Mount Everest 8863m (29,078 ft).
Climate: The climate varies between the subtropical south and the glacial Himalayan peaks. All of Nepal experiences the monsoon.

Economy

Nepal is one of the least developed countries in the world. Most of the labour force is involved in subsistence farming, mainly growing rice, barley and maize. Forestry is important, but increased farming has led to deforestation. ***Currency:*** Nepalese rupee.

Recent History

From 1846 to 1950 the Rana family held sway as hereditary chief ministers of a powerless monarchy. Their isolationist policy preserved Nepal's independence at the expense of its development. A brief experiment with democracy was followed by a reassertion of royal autocracy (1960). Violent pro-democracy demonstrations (1990) forced the king to concede a democratic constitution. Multi-party elections were held in 1991 and 1994.

THE NETHERLANDS

Official name: Koninkrijk der Nederlanden (The Kingdom of the Netherlands).
Member of: UN, EU/EC, NATO, OECD, OSCE.
Area: 41,863 km² (16,163 sq mi).
Population: 15,302,000 (1993 est).
Capital: Amsterdam – capital in name only – 1,091,000 (city 720,000), The Hague ('s Gravenhage) – the seat of government and administration – 694,000 (city 445,000) (1993 est).
Other major cities: Rotterdam 1,091,000 (city 596,000), Utrecht 543,000 (city 234,000), Eindhoven 391,000 (city 195,000), Arnhem 308,000 (city 133,000), Heerlen-Kerkrade 269,000 (Heerlen city 95,000),

Enschede 254,000 (city 147,000), Nijmegen 247,000 (city 147,000), Tilburg 236,000 (city 162,000), Haarlem 214,000 (city 149,000), Dordrecht 212,000 (city 113,000), Groningen 209,000 (city 170,000), 's Hertogenbosch 196,000 (city 94,000), Leiden 192,000 (city 114,000), Geleen-Sittard 184,000 (Sittard town 47,000), Breda 165,000 (city 128,000), Maastricht 164,000 (118,000) (1993 est).

Language: Dutch (official).

Religions: Roman Catholic (36%), Netherlands Reformed and Calvinist (27%).

Education: is compulsory between the ages of five and 16. *Adult literacy:* virtually 100%. *Universities:* 13 universities plus nine other institutes of university status.

Defence: (1993 figures) *Army:* 43,300 personnel. *Air force:* 12,000. *Navy:* 14,900. *Conscription:* nine months (to be abolished by 1998).

Government

The Netherlands is a constitutional monarchy. The 75-member First Chamber of the States-General is elected for six years term by the 12 provincial councils – with one half of the members retiring every three years. The 150-member Second Chamber is elected for four years by universal adult suffrage under a system of proportional representation. The monarch appoints a Prime Minister who commands a majority in the Second Chamber. The PM, in turn, appoints a Council of Ministers who are responsible to the Chamber.

Largest parties: (conservative) Christian Democratic Appeal Party (CDA), (social democratic) Labour Party (PvdA), (liberal) People's Party of Freedom and Democracy (VVD), (reformist) Democracy 66 (D66), (Calvinist) Political Reformed Party (SGP), Reformed Political Federation (PPR), (Calvinist) Evangelical Political Federation (RPF), the Association for the Elderly, (centre-right) Centre Democrats, Green Left, Socialist Party (PS).

Local government: 12 provinces.

Sovereign: HM Queen Beatrix of the Netherlands (succeeded upon the abdication of her mother, 30 April 1980).

Prime Minister: Willem (Wim) Kok (PvdA).

Dependencies of the Netherlands: Aruba and Netherlands Antilles. See Other Territories (beginning on p. 729).

Provinces

The areas of the provinces, below, do not include 7926 km^2 (3060 sq mi) of inland water.

Drenthe *Area:* 2654 km^2 (1025 sq mi). *Population:* 446,000 (1992 est). *Capital:* Assen.

Flevoland *Area:* 1422 km^2 (549 sq mi). *Population:* 233,000 (1992 est). *Capital:* Lelystad.

Friesland *Area:* 3353 km^2 (1295 sq mi). *Population:* 602,000 (1992 est). *Capital:* Leeuwarden.

Gelderland *Area:* 5011 km^2 (1935 sq mi). *Population:* 1,829,000 (1992 est). *Capital:* Arnhem.

Groningen *Area:* 2346 km^2 (906 sq mi). *Population:* 555,000 (1992 est). *Capital:* Groningen.

Limburg *Area:* 2170 km^2 (838 sq mi). *Population:* 1,116,000 (1992 est). *Capital:* Maastricht.

North Brabant (Noord Brabant) *Area:* 4946 km^2 (1910 sq mi). *Population:* 2,225,000 (1992 est). *Capital:* 's Hertogenbosch.

North Holland (Noord Holland) *Area:* 2665 km^2 (1029 sq mi). *Population:* 2,422,000 (1992 est). *Capital:* Haarlem.

Overijssel *Area:* 3339 km^2 (1289 sq mi). *Population:* 1,032,000 (1992 est). *Capital:* Zwolle.

South Holland (Zuid Holland) *Area:* 2908 km^2 (1123 sq mi). *Population:* 3,272,000 (1992 est). *Capital:* The Hague.

Utrecht *Area:* 1331 km^2 (514 sq mi). *Population:* 1,037,000 (1992 est). *Capital:* Utrecht.

Zeeland *Area:* 1792 km^2 (692 sq mi). *Population:* 359,000 (1992 est). *Capital:* Middelburg.

Geography

Over one quarter of the Netherlands – one of the world's most densely populated countries – lies below sea level. A network of canals and canalized rivers cross the west of the country where sand dunes and man-made dykes protect low-lying areas and polders (land reclaimed from the sea). The coast has been straightened by sea walls protecting Zeeland in the southwest and enclosing a freshwater lake, the IJsselmeer, in the north. The east comprises low sandy plains. ***Principal rivers:*** Rhine (Rijn) – which divides into branches including the Lek, Waal and Oude Rijn; IJssel, Maas (Meuse), Schelde (Scheldt).

Highest point: Vaalserberg 321m (1050 ft).

Climate: The country has a maritime temperate climate, with cool summers and mild winters.

Economy

Despite having few natural resources – except natural gas – the country has a high standard of living. Agriculture and horticulture are highly mechanized and concentrate on dairying and glasshouse crops, particularly flowers. Food processing is a major industry, and the country is a leading exporter of cheese. Manufacturing includes chemical, machinery, petroleum refining, metallurgical and electrical engineering industries. Raw materials are imported through Rotterdam – the largest port in the world – which serves much of Western Europe. Banking and finance are well developed. ***Currency:*** Gulden (known in English as the guilder).

Recent History

The Congress of Vienna (1815) united all three Low Countries in the Kingdom of the Netherlands under the House of Orange, but Belgium broke away in 1830 and Luxembourg in 1890. The Dutch were neutral in World War I, but suffered occupation by the Germans from 1940–45. Following a bitter colonial war, the Dutch accepted that they could not reassert control over Indonesia after World War II. The Dutch have shown enthusiasm for European unity, and, with the other Low Countries, founded Benelux, the core of the EC. Dutch politics is characterized by a large number of small parties, some of a confessional nature, and a system of proportional representation has prevented any of these parties attaining a parliamentary majority. The formation of a new governent after each general election has been difficult and time-consuming.

NEW ZEALAND

Official names: New Zealand and Aotearoa.
Member of: UN, Commonwealth, ANZUS, Apec.
Area: 270,534 km² (104,454 sq mi).
Population: 3,520,000 (1993 est).
Capital: Wellington 327,000 (1993 est) (city 150,000; 1991 census).
Other major cities: Auckland 910,000 (city 316,000; Manukau 227,000; North Shore 151,000), Christchurch 313,000 (city 293,000), Hamilton 152,000 (city 101,000), Napier with Hastings 111,000 (Napier city 52,000), Dunedin 111,000, Palmerston North 74,000 (city 71,000), Tauranga 74,000 (city 67,000), Rotorua 54,000, Invercargill 52,000*, New Plymouth 48,000*, Nelson 47,000 (city 38,000), Whangarei 44,000, Wanganui 41,000* (urban areas 1993 est; cities 1991 census). (* urban area figures; the local government district is larger, but includes countryside.)
Languages: English (official), Maori.
Religions: Anglican (24%), Presbyterian (18%), Roman Catholic (15%).
Education: is compulsory between the ages of six and 16. *Adult literacy:* virtually 100%. *Universities:* seven.
Defence: (1993 figures) *Army:* 4800 personnel. *Air force:* 3700. *Navy:* 4300. *Conscription:* none.

Government

The 99-member House of Representatives is elected by universal adult suffrage for three years under a system of proportional representation. Four constituencies have a Maori electorate. The Governor General – the representative of the British Queen as sovereign of New Zealand – appoints a Prime Minister who commands a majority in the House. The PM, in turn, appoints a Cabinet, which is responsible to the House.

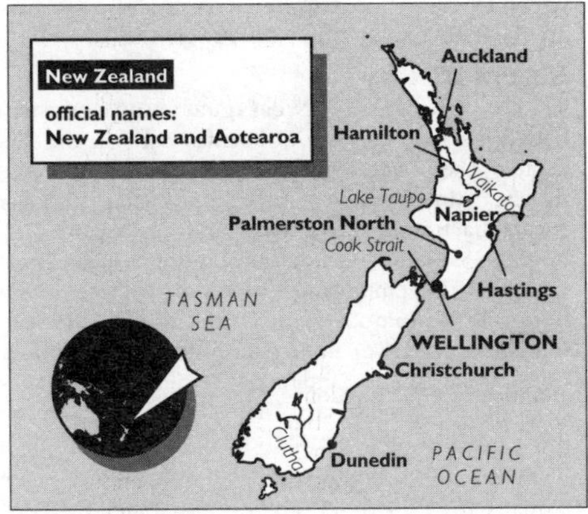

Largest parties: (conservative) National Party (NP), (social democratic) Labour Party, Alliance Party, New Zealand First.
Local government: 16 regions, one island group, one island territory.
Prime Minister: Jim Bolger (NP).
Dependent Territories and Associated Territories: Ross Dependency, Cook Islands and Niue. See Other Territories (beginning on p. 729). For Tokelau, see below.

Regions

Auckland *Area:* 5132 km² (1981 sq mi). *Population:* 954,000 (1991 census). *Capital:* Auckland.
Bay of Plenty *Area:* 12,473 km² (4816 sq mi). *Population:* 208,000 (1991 census). *Capital:* Whakatane.
Canterbury *Area:* 45,346 km² (17,508 sq mi). *Population:* 442,000 (1991 census). *Capital:* Christchurch.
Gisborne *Area:* 8352 km² (3225 sq mi). *Population:* 44,000 (1991 census). *Capital:* Gisborne.
Hawke's Bay *Area:* 14,164 km² (5469 sq mi). *Population:* 140,000 (1991 census). *Capital:* Napier.
Manuwatu-Wanganui *Area:* 22,215 km² (8577 sq mi). *Population:* 227,000 (1991 census). *Capital:* Palmerston North.
Marlborough *Area:* 10,520 km² (4062 sq mi). *Population:* 37,000 (1991 census). *Capital:* Blenheim,
Nelson *Area:* 442 km² (171 sq mi). *Population:* 47,000 (1991 census). *Capital:* Nelson.
Northland *Area:* 12,829 km² (4953 sq mi). *Population:* 132,000 (1991 census). *Capital:* Whangarei.
Otago *Area:* 31,991 km² (12,352 sq mi). *Population:* 186,000 (1991 census). *Capital:* Dunedin.
Southland *Area:* 32,676 km² (12,616 sq mi). *Population:* 103,000 (1991 census). *Capital:* Invercargill.
Taranaki *Area:* 7257 km² (2802 sq mi). *Population:* 107,000 (1991 census). *Capital:* New Plymouth.
Tasman *Area:* 10,458 km² (4038 sq mi). *Population:* 30,000 (1991 census). *Capital:* Westport.
Waikato *Area:* 24,653 km² (9519 sq mi). *Population:* 339,000 (1991 census). *Capital:* Hamilton.
Wellington *Area:* 8125 km² (3137 sq mi). *Population:* 403,000 (1991 census). *Capital:* Wellington.
West Coast *Area:* 23,336 km² (9010 sq mi). *Population:* 35,000 (1991 census). *Capital:* Greymouth.
Chatham Islands (island group; not included in any region) *Area:* 963 km² (372 sq mi). *Population:* 800 (1991 census). *Capital:* Waitangi.
Tokelau (autonomous island territory) *Area:* 13 km² (5 sq mi). *Population:* 1700 (1991 census). *Capital:* There is no capital; each atoll has its own administrative centre.

Geography

Mountains run from north to south through South Island, and in the southwest reach the sea in the deeply indented coast of Fjordland. The Canterbury Plains lie to the east of the mountains. North Island is mainly hilly with isolated mountains, including volcanoes – two of which are active. Lowlands on North Island are largely restricted to coastal areas and the Waikato Valley. ***Principal rivers:*** Waikato, Clutha, Wanganui, Manawatu, Waihou, Rangitaiki, Mokau. ***Highest point:*** Mount Cook, which, since a major

rock fall in 1991, rises to 3754m (12,315 ft).
Climate: The climate is temperate, although the north is warmer. Rainfall is abundant almost everywhere, but totals vary considerably with altitude and aspect, rising to over 6350 mm (250 in) on the west coast of South Island.

Economy

The majority of New Zealand's export earnings come from agriculture, in particular meat, wool and dairy products. Forestry is expanding and supports an important pulp and paper industry. Apart from coal, lignite, natural gas and gold, the country has few natural resources, although its considerable hydroelectric-power potential has been exploited to produce plentiful cheap electricity – an important basis of New Zealand's manufacturing industry. Natural gas – from the Kapuni Field on North Island and the Maui Field off the Taranaki coast – is converted to liquid fuel. Despite its small domestic market and being remote from the world's major industrial powers, New Zealand has a high standard of living. ***Currency:*** New Zealand dollar.

Recent History

The Maori Wars (1860-70) retarded the European settlement of North Island, while – in the last quarter of the 19th century – the discovery of gold and the introduction of refrigerated ships to export meat and dairy products greatly stimulated the colonization and economy of South Island. However, by the beginning of the 20th century, North Island was dominant again, and by 1911 migrants from Britain had boosted the country's population to one million. Subsequent immigration has remained overwhelmingly British, although there are sizeable communities of Samoans, Cook Islanders and Croats. Liberal governments (1891–1912) pioneered many reforms and social measures, including votes for women (1893) and the world's first old-age pensions (1898). British colonial status ended when New Zealand became a dominion in 1907, although the country did not formally acknowledge its independent status until 1947.

In World War I, New Zealand fought as a British ally in Europe, achieving distinction in the disastrous Allied expedition to the Gallipoli peninsula during the campaign against Turkey (1915). When Japan entered World War II in 1941, New Zealand's more immediate security was threatened. The major role played by the USA in the Pacific War led to New Zealand's postwar alliance with Australia and America in the ANZUS pact, and the country sent troops to support the Americans in Vietnam. The entry of Britain into the EC in 1973 restricted the access of New Zealand's agricultural products to what had been their principal market. Since then New Zealand has been forced to seek new markets, particularly in the Far and Middle East. Under Labour governments (1972–75 and 1984–90), the country adopted an independent foreign and defence policy. Since 1990 the National (conservative) government has sharply restricted the welfare state.

NICARAGUA

Official name: República de Nicaragua (Republic of Nicaragua).
Member of: UN, OAS, CACM.
Area: 131,779 km² (50,880 sq mi).
Population: 4,265,000 (1993 est).
Capital: Managua 1,108,000 (city 682,000; 1988 est).
Other major cities: León 101,000, Granada 89,000 (1988 est).

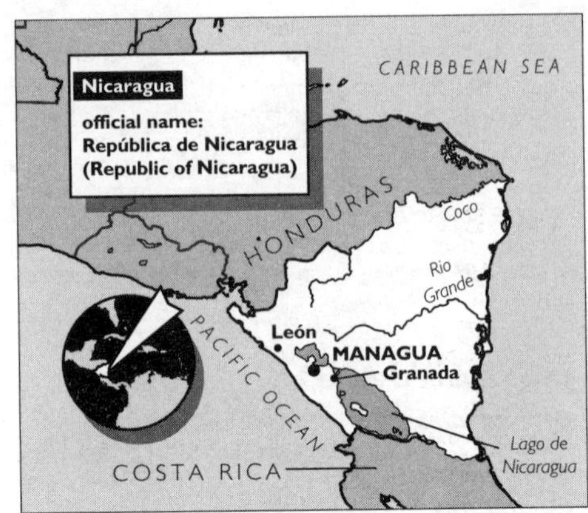

Languages: Spanish (official), Miskito.
Religion: Roman Catholic (90%).
Education: is compulsory between the ages of seven and 13. *Adult literacy:* 74%. *Universities:* four.
Defence: (1993 figures) *Army:* 13,500 personnel. *Air force:* 1200. *Navy:* 500. *Conscription:* was abolished in 1990.

Government

The 92-member National Assembly is elected by proportional representation by universal adult suffrage for six years. The President, who is also directly elected for six years, appoints a Cabinet.
Largest parties: (left-wing) Sandinista National Liberation Front (FSLN), (coalition) Popular Opposition Alliance (APO; formerly UNO).
Local government: 16 departments.
President: Violeta Chamorro (APO).

Geography

Most Nicaraguans live on a fertile plain on the Pacific coast. Mountain ranges in the west and centre rise to Pico Mogotón. Tropical jungle covers the Atlantic coastal plain. ***Principal rivers:*** Coco, Grande, Escondido. ***Highest point:*** Pico Mogotón 2107m (6913 ft).
Climate: The climate is tropical and humid with a rainy season from May to October.

Economy

The largely agricultural economy was damaged in the 1980s by guerrilla warfare, a US trade embargo and hurricanes. Privatization and strict austerity programmes are in force. Coffee, cotton and sugar cane are the main export crops. ***Currency:*** Cordoba.

Recent History

In the 19th century, Nicaragua witnessed strife between conservatives and liberals. Early in the 20th century, the political situation deteriorated, provoking American intervention – US marines were based in Nicaragua from 1912 to 1925, and again from 1927 until 1933. General Anastasio Somoza became president in 1937. Employing dictatorial methods, members of the Somoza family, or their supporters, remained in power until overthrown by a popular uprising led by the Sandinista guerrilla army in 1979. Accusing the Sandinistas of introducing Communism, the USA imposed a trade embargo on Nicaragua, making it increasingly dependent on Cuba and the USSR. Right-wing Contra guerrillas, financed by the

USA, fought the Sandinistas from bases in Honduras. A ceasefire between the Contras and Sandinistas was agreed in 1989. In free presidential elections in 1990, the Sandinista incumbent Daniel Ortega was defeated by Violeta Chamorro.

NIGER

Official name: La République du Niger (The Republic of Niger).
Member of: UN, OAU, ECOWAS.
Area: 1,186,408 km² (458,075 sq mi).
Population: 8,515,000 (1993 est).
Capital: Niamey 398,000 (1988 census).
Other major cities: Zinder 121,000, Maradi 113,000 (1988 census).
Languages: French (official), Hausa (85%).
Religion: Sunni Islam (85%).
Education: is compulsory, in theory, between the ages of seven and 15. *Adult literacy:* 11%. *Universities:* two.
Defence: (1993 figures) *Army:* 5200 personnel. *Air force:* 100. *Paramilitary:* 5400. *Conscription:* two years; selective.

Government

An 83-member National Assembly is elected by universal adult suffrage for five years. The President – who appoints a Prime Minister – is also directly elected for a maximum of two five-year terms.
Largest parties: (former monopoly) National Movement for Social Development (MNSD), (coalition) Alliance of Forces for Change (AFC).
Local government: eight departments.
President: Mahamane Ouamane (AFC).
Prime Minister: Amadou Hama.

Geography

Most of Niger lies in the Sahara Desert; the south and the Niger Valley are savannah. The central Aïr Mountains run from north to south in a series of mountainous 'islands'. ***Principal river:*** Niger.
Highest point: Mont Gréboun 1944m (6379 ft).
Climate: Niger is dry and hot. The south has a rainy season from June to October.

Economy

Livestock herds and harvests of subsistence crops – millet, sorghum, cassava and rice – have been reduced by desertification, and the country is one of the poorest in West Africa. Uranium is mined.
Currency: CFA franc.

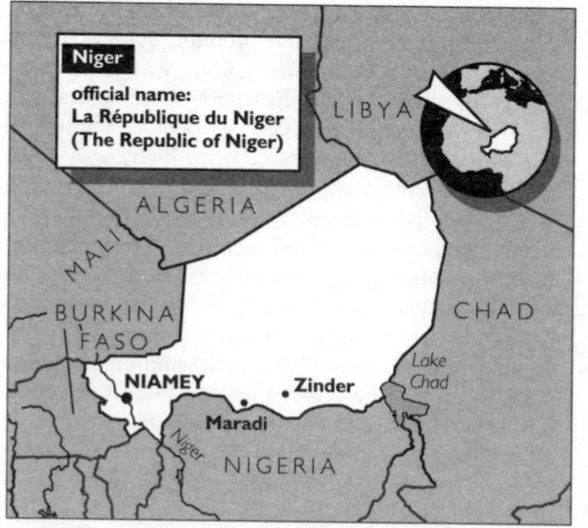

Recent History

The French territory of Niger was proclaimed in 1901, but much of the country was not pacified until 1920. Independence was gained in 1960. After the economy was wracked by a prolonged drought, the military took power in a coup (1974). Multi-party politics were restored in 1992 and in free elections in 1993 and 1995 power changed hands peacefully.

NIGERIA

Official name: The Federal Republic of Nigeria.
Member of: UN, OAU, OPEC, ECOWAS, Commonwealth.
Area: 923,768 km² (356,669 sq mi).
Population: 91,550,000 (1993 est).
Capital: Abuja 379,000 (1991 census).
Other major cities: Lagos 5,686,000 (city 1,347,000), Ibadan 1,295,000, Kano 700,000, Ogbomosho 661,000, Oshogbo 442,000, Ilorin 431,000, Abeokuta 387,000, Port Harcourt 371,000, Zaria 345,000, Ilesha 343,000, Onitsha 336,000, Iwo 335,000, Ado-Ekiti 325,000, Kaduna 310,000 (1991 census).
Languages: English (official), with over 150 local languages including Hausa, Yoruba and Ibo.
Religions: Sunni Islam (48%), various Protestant Churches (17%), Roman Catholic (17%).
Education: is compulsory, in theory, between the ages of six and 15. *Adult literacy:* 51%. *Universities:* 31.
Defence: (1993 figures) *Army:* 62,000 personnel. *Air force:* 9500. *Navy:* 7300. *Conscription:* none.

Government

A constitutional assembly was summoned in 1994. The Forces Ruling Council, whose President is head of state and of government, holds power following a coup in 1993. The 30 state administrations, the 450-member Federal Assembly and the two officially-sanctioned political parties were suspended in 1993.

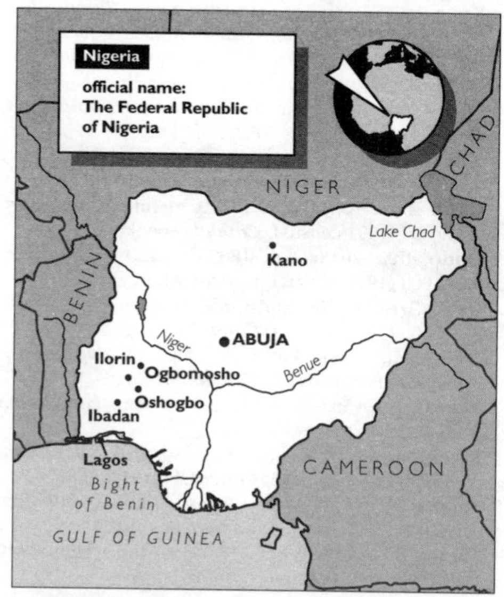

Largest parties: The two officially-sanctioned political parties were suspended in 1993.
Local government: 30 states and one federal capital territory.
President: Gen. Sani Abacha.

States

The areas of the states are estimates.

Abia *Area:* 4300 km^2 (1650 sq mi). *Population:* 2,298,000 (1991 census). *Capital:* Umuahia.
Adamawa *Area:* 44,800 km^2 (17,300 sq mi). *Population:* 2,124,000 (1991 census). *Capital:* Yola.
Akwa *Area:* 5100 km^2 (2000 sq mi). *Population:* 2,360,000 (1991 census). *Capital:* Uyo.
Anambra *Area:* 9700 km^2 (3750 sq mi). *Population:* 2,768,000 (1991 census). *Capital:* Akwa.
Bauchi *Area:* 64,600 km^2 (24,950 sq mi). *Population:* 4,294,000 (1991 census). *Capital:* Bauchi.
Benue *Area:* 33,900 km^2 (13,100 sq mi). *Population:* 2,780,000 (1991 census). *Capital:* Makurdi.
Borno *Area:* 32,500 km^2 (12,500 sq mi). *Population:* 2,597,000 (1991 census). *Capital:* Maiduguri.
Cross River *Area:* 12,600 km^2 (4900 sq mi). *Population:* 1,866,000 (1991 census). *Capital:* Calabar.
Delta *Area:* 9600 km^2 (3700 sq mi). *Population:* 2,570,000 (1991 census). *Capital:* Asaba.
Edo *Area:* 25,600 km^2 (9900 sq mi). *Population:* 2,160,000 (1991 census). *Capital:* Benin City.
Enugu *Area:* 5300 km^2 (2050 sq mi). *Population:* 3,161,000 (1991 census). *Capital:* Enugu.
Imo *Area:* 11,850 km^2 (4600 sq mi). *Population:* 2,486,000 (1991 census). *Capital:* Owerri.
Jigawa *Area:* 20,400 km^2 (7900 sq mi). *Population:* 2,830,000 (1991 census). *Capital:* Dutse.
Kaduna *Area:* 46,350 km^2 (17,900 sq mi). *Population:* 3,969,000 (1991 census). *Capital:* Kaduna.
Kano *Area:* 22,900 km^2 (8850 sq mi). *Population:* 5,632,000 (1991 census). *Capital:* Kano.
Katsina *Area:* 23,900 km^2 (9250 sq mi). *Population:* 3,678,000 (1991 census). *Capital:* Katsina.
Kebbi *Area:* 37,900 km^2 (14,600 sq mi). *Population:* 2,062,000 (1991 census). *Capital:* Birnin Kebbi.
Kogi *Area:* 10,300 km^2 (4000 sq mi). *Population:* 1,566,000 (1991 census). *Capital:* Ilorin.
Kwara *Area:* 66,900 km^2 (25,800 sq mi). *Population:* 2,099,000 (1991 census). *Capital:* Lokoja.
Lagos *Area:* 3345 km^2 (1292 sq mi). *Population:* 5,686,000 (1991 census). *Capital:* Ikeja.
Niger *Area:* 65,040 km^2 (25,110 sq mi). *Population:* 2,482,000 (1991 census). *Capital:* Minna.
Ogun *Area:* 16,760 km^2 (6470 sq mi). *Population:* 2,339,000 (1991 census). *Capital:* Abeokuta.
Ondo *Area:* 20,960 km^2 (8090 sq mi). *Population:* 3,884,000 (1991 census). *Capital:* Akure.
Osun *Area:* 15,100 km^2 (5830 sq mi). *Population:* 2,203,000 (1991 census). *Capital:* Oshogbo.
Oyo *Area:* 22,600 km^2 (8730 sq mi). *Population:* 3,489,000 (1991 census). *Capital:* Ibadan.
Plateau *Area:* 58,030 km^2 (22,400 sq mi). *Population:* 3,284,000 (1991 census). *Capital:* Jos.
Rivers *Area:* 21,850 km^2 (8440 sq mi). *Population:* 3,984,000 (1991 census). *Capital:* Port Harcourt.
Sokoto *Area:* 64,600 km^2 (24,900 sq mi). *Population:* 4,392,000 (1991 census). *Capital:* Sokoto.
Taraba *Area:* 46,600 km^2 (18,000 sq mi). *Population:* 1,481,000 (1991 census). *Capital:* Jalingo.
Yobe *Area:* 83,900 km^2 (32,600 sq mi). *Population:* 1,411,000 (1991 census). *Capital:* Damaturu.
Federal Capital Territory *Area:* 7315 km^2 (2824 sq mi). *Population:* 379,000 (1991 census). *Capital:* Abuja.

Geography

Inland from the swampy forest and tropical jungles of the coastal plains, Nigeria comprises a series of plateaux covered – for the most part – by open woodland or savannah. The far north is semi-desert. Isolated ranges of hills rise above the plateaux, the highest of which are the central Jos Plateau and the Biu Plateau in the northeast. ***Principal rivers:*** Niger, Benue, Sokoto, Kaduna, Gongola, Cross River, Yobe, Osse. ***Highest point:*** Vogel Peak (Dimlang) 2042m (6700 ft).
Climate: The coastal areas are very humid and hot, with an average temperature of 32 °C (90 °F). Rainfall is heavy on the coast but decreases gradually inland – although there is a rainy season from April to October. The dry far north experiences the Harmattan, a hot wind blowing out of the Sahara.

Economy

Nigeria is the major economic power in West Africa. The country depends upon revenue from petroleum exports, but a combination of falling petroleum prices and OPEC quotas has resulted in major economic problems, although it has encouraged diversification. Natural gas is to be exported in liquid form to Europe. Major industries include petrochemicals, textiles and food processing. Over 50% of the labour force is involved in agriculture, mainly producing maize, sorghum, cassava, yams and rice as subsistence crops. Cocoa is an important export. *Currency:* Naira.

Recent History

In 1861, Lagos was acquired by Britain, and in 1885 a British protectorate was established on the coast. In the scramble for empire, the commercial Royal Niger Company colonized the interior from 1886, and in 1900 its territories were surrendered to the British Crown as the protectorate of Northern Nigeria. In 1914 the coast and the interior were united to form Britain's largest African colony. An unwieldy federal structure introduced in 1954 was unable to contain regional rivalries after independence (1960). In 1966, the first PM, Sir Abubakar Tafawa Balewa (1912–66), and other prominent politicians were assassinated in a military coup. After a counter-coup brought General Yakubu Gowon to power, a bitter civil war took place (1967–70) when the Eastern Region – the homeland of the Ibo – attempted to secede as Biafra. Although the East was quickly re-integrated once Biafra was defeated, Nigeria remained politically unstable. The number of states has been gradually increased from three to 30 in an attempt to prevent any one state becoming dominant. A military coup overthrew Gowon in 1975, and an attempt at civilian rule (1979–83) also ended in a coup. Another coup brought General Ibrahim Babangida to power in 1985. Following unrest, limited civilian rule was introduced in 1993 but a further military coup took place in the same year. Presidential elections were annulled and the presumed winner of those elections was detained in 1994, after having declared himself president.

NORWAY

Official name: Kongeriket Norge (Kingdom of Norway).
Member of: UN, NATO, OSCE, OECD.
Area: 323,878 km² (125,050 sq mi), or 386,958 km² (149,469 sq mi) including the Arctic island territories of Svalbard (formerly known as Spitsbergen) – 62,924 km² (24,295 sq mi) – and Jan Mayen – 380 km² (147 sq mi).
Population: 4,310,000 (1993 est).
Capital: Oslo 467,000 (1992 est).
Other major cities: Bergen 213,000, Trondheim 138,000, Stavanger 98,000, Kristiansand 66,000, Drammen 52,000, Tromso 51,000 (1991 est).
Languages: two official forms of Norwegian – Bokmaal (80%), Nynorsk (or Landsmaal; 20%); Lappish.
Religion: Lutheran (official; 88%).
Education: is compulsory between the ages of seven and 16. *Adult literacy:* virtually 100%. *Universities:* 14, including university centres and colleges of university status.
Defence: (1993 figures) *Army:* 12,900 personnel. *Air force:* 8200. *Navy:* 8300. *Conscription:* 12 months in the army and air force; 15 months in the navy.

Government

Norway is a constitutional monarchy. The 165-member Parliament (Storting) is elected under a system of proportional representation by universal adult suffrage for a four-year term. In order to legislate, the Storting divides itself into two houses – the Lagting (containing one quarter of the members) and the Odelsting (containing the remaining three quarters of the members). The King appoints a Prime Minister who commands a majority in the Storting. The PM, in turn, appoints a Council of Ministers who are responsible to the Storting.
Largest parties: (social democratic) Labour Party (DnA), Centre Party (SP), Conservative Party (H), Christian Democratic Party (KrF), Socialist Left Party (SVP), Progress Party (FP), Liberal Party.
Local government: 19 counties plus the dependencies of Svalbard and Jan Mayen (see above).
Sovereign: HM Harald V, King of Norway (succeeded upon the death of his father, 17 January 1991).
Prime Minister: Gro Harlem Brundtland (DnA).
Norwegian Antarctic Territories: Bouvet Island, Peter I Island, Queen Maud Land. See Other Territories (beginning on p. 729).

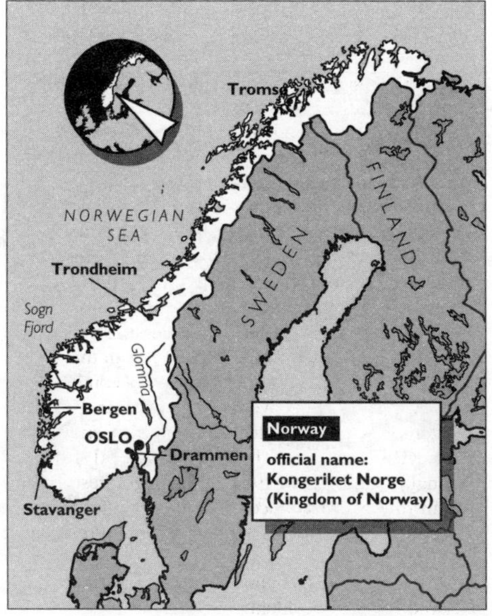

Geography

Norway's coastline is characterized by fjords, a series of long narrow inlets formed by glacial action. The greater part of Norway comprises highlands of hard rock. The principal lowlands are along the Skagerrak coast and around Oslofjord and Trondheimsfjord. Svalbard is a bleak archipelago in the Arctic. Jan Mayen is an active volcanic island between Norway and Greenland. ***Principal rivers:*** Glomma (Glama), Namsen, Lågen, Otra, Tanaelv. ***Highest point:*** Galdhopiggen 2469m (8098 ft).
Climate: Norway's temperate climate is the result of the warming Gulf Stream. Summers are remarkably mild for the latitude, while winters are long and very cold. Precipitation is heavy – over 2000 mm (80 in) in the west, with marked rain shadows inland.

Economy

Norway enjoys a high standard of living. Agriculture is heavily subsidized and only a small proportion of the land can be cultivated – chiefly for fodder crops for dairy cattle. Timber is a major export for Norway, over 50% of which is forested. Fishing is an important foreign-currency earner, and fish farming – which has been encouraged by government development schemes – is taking the place of whaling and deep-sea fishing. Manufacturing – which has traditionally been concerned with processing fish, timber and iron ore – is now dominated by petrochemicals and allied industries, based upon large reserves of petroleum and natural gas in Norway's sector of the North Sea. Petroleum and natural gas supply over one third of the country's export earnings. The development of industries such as electrical engineering has been helped by cheap hydroelectric power. There is some economic uncertainty after Norway's rejection of EU membership (1994). ***Currency:*** Norwegian krone.

Recent History

At the end of the Napoleonic Wars, Danish-ruled Norway attempted to regain autonomy, but the country came under the rule of the kings of Sweden, although a separate Norwegian Parliament was allowed a considerable degree of independence. Growing nationalism in Norway placed great strains upon the union with Sweden, and in 1905 – following a vote by the Norwegians to repeal the union – King Oscar II of Sweden gave up his claims to the Norwegian crown to allow a peaceful separation of the two countries. After a Swedish prince declined the Norwegian throne, Prince Carl of Denmark was confirmed as King of Norway – as Haakon VII – by a plebiscite. Norway was neutral in World War I, and declared neutrality in World War II, but was occupied by German forces (1940) who set up a puppet government under Vidkun Quisling. After the war, Norway joined NATO. In 1972, and again in 1994, Norway agreed to enter the EC, but a national referendum rejected membership on both occasions, leaving Norway increasingly isolated outside Western Europe's economic, political and defence organizations.

OMAN

Official name: Sultanat 'Uman (Sultanate of Oman).
Member of: UN, Arab League, GCC.
Area: 306,000 km² (118,150 sq mi).
Population: 1,700,000 (1993 est).
Capital: Muscat 380,000 (city 85,000; 1990 est).
Other main towns: Sohar 92,000, Rustaq 66,000 (1990 est).
Languages: Arabic (official).
Religion: Ibadi Islam (75%), Sunni Islam (25%).
Education: is not compulsory. *Adult literacy:* 41%. *Universities:* one.
Defence: (1993 figures) *Army:* 20,000 personnel. *Air force:* 3500. *Navy:* 3500. *Others:* 9000. *Conscription:* none.

Government

Oman is a monarchy ruled by a Sultan who appoints a Cabinet. He also chooses two of the four members elected from each of the 40 provinces to form an 80-member Majlis (an embryonic legislature).
Largest parties: There are no political parties.
Local government: eight governates.
Sovereign: HM Qaboos bin Said, Sultan of Oman (succeeded upon the deposition of his father, 23 July 1970).
Prime Minister: The Sultan.

Geography

A barren range of hills rises sharply behind a narrow coastal plain. Desert extends inland into the Rub' al Khali ('The Empty Quarter'). A small detached portion of Oman lies north of the United Arab Emirates. ***Principal rivers:*** There are no permanent streams. ***Highest point:*** Jabal al-Akhdar 3107m (10,194 ft).
Climate: Oman is very hot in the summer, but milder in winter and the mountains. The state is extremely arid with an average annual rainfall of 50 to 100 mm (2–4 in).

Economy

Oman depends almost entirely upon exports of petroleum and natural gas. Owing to aridity, less than 1% of Oman is cultivated. The oil industry and much of the state's modern commercial infrastructure depends upon foreign workers. ***Currency:*** Omani rial.

Recent History

A British presence was established in the 19th century and Oman did not regain complete independence until 1951. Sultan Qaboos – who came to power in a palace coup in 1970 – has modernized and developed Oman. In the 1970s South Yemen supported left-wing separatist guerrillas in the southern province of Dhofar, but the revolt was suppressed with military assistance from the UK.

PAKISTAN

Official name: Islami Jamhuria-e-Pakistan (Islamic Republic of Pakistan).
Member of: UN, Commonwealth.
Area: 796,095 km² (307,374 sq mi), excluding Pakistani-held areas of Kashmir (known as Azad Kashmir) and the disputed Northern Areas (Gilgit, Baltistan and Diamir) – these Pakistani-occupied territories comprise 83,716 km² (33,323 sq mi).
Population: 127,960,000 (1993 est; excluding Pakistani-held areas of Kashmir (known as Azad Kashmir) and the disputed Northern Areas (Gilgit, Baltistan and Diamir) – these Pakistani-occupied territories had an estimated population of 3,330,000 in 1990.
Capital: Islamabad 320,000 (including suburbs; 1995 est).
Other major cities: Karachi 8,070,000, Lahore 4,590,000, Faisalabad 1,710,000, Rawalpindi 1,310,000, Hyderabad 1,240,000, Multan 1,190,000, Gujranwala 1,085,000, Peshawar 920,000, Sialkot 500,000 (all including suburbs; 1995 est).
Languages: Urdu (national; 20%), Punjabi (60%), Sindhi (12%), English, Pushto, Baluchi.
Religions: Sunni Islam (official; 92%), Shia Islam (5%), with Ismaili Muslim, Ahmadi and Christian minorities.
Education: is not compulsory. *Adult literacy:* 26%. *Universities:* 22.
Defence: (1993 figures) *Army:* 510,000 personnel. *Air force:* 45,000. *Navy:* 22,000. *Paramilitary:* 273,000. *Conscription:* none.

Government

The 87-member Senate (the upper house) comprises 19 senators elected for six years by each of the four

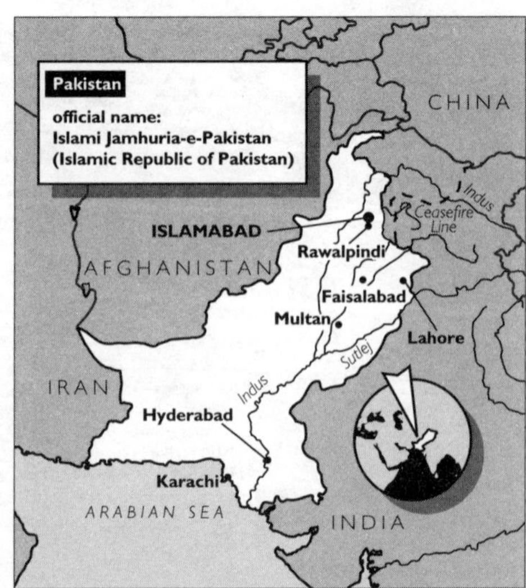

provinces, plus 8 senators elected from the federally administered Tribal Areas and 3 senators chosen to represent the federal capital. The 217-member National Assembly is elected by universal adult suffrage for five years. Ten of these members are elected to represent non-Islamic minorities. The President – who is chosen by the Federal Legislature to serve for five years – appoints a Prime Minister who commands a majority in the National Assembly. The PM, in turn, appoints a Cabinet of Ministers, responsible to the Assembly. The four provinces have their own legislatures.

Largest parties: Pakistan People's Party (PPP), Pakistan Muslim League (Nawaz Group; PML-Nawaz), Pakistan Muslim League (Junejo Group; PML-Junejo), Awami National Party (ANP), Islami Jamhoori Mahaz (IJM), Pakhtoon Khwa Milli Awami Party, Pakistan Islami Front.

Local government: four provinces, centrally-administered Tribal Areas and one federal territory. (The disputed territories under Pakistani control are organized as Azad Kashmir and three Northern Areas.)

President: Farooq Ahmad Khan Leghari.

Prime Minister: Benazir Bhutto (PPP).

Provinces

Baluchistan (Balochistan) *Area:* 347,190 km^2 (134,051 sq mi). *Population:* 6,200,000 (1992 est). *Capital:* Quetta.

North-West Frontier *Area:* 74,521 km^2 (28,773 sq mi). *Population:* 15,800,000 (1992 est). *Capital:* Peshawar.

Punjab *Area:* 205,344 km^2 (79,284 sq mi). *Population:* 68,600,000 (1992 est). *Capital:* Lahore.

Sind (Sindh) *Area:* 140,914 km^2 (54,407 sq mi). *Population:* 27,600,000 (1992 est). *Capital:* Karachi.

Tribal Areas *Area:* 27,220 km^2 (10,509 sq mi). *Population:* 3,100,000 (1992 est). *Capital:* administered from Islamabad.

Federal Capital Territory *Area:* 906 km^2 (350 sq mi). *Population:* 320,000 (1995 est). *Capital:* Islamabad.

Geography

The Indus Valley divides Pakistan into a highland region in the west and a lowland region in the east. In Baluchistan – in the south – the highlands consist of ridges of hills and low mountains running northeast to southwest. In the north – in the North-West Frontier Province and the disputed territories – the mountain chains rise to over 7000 m (21,300 ft) and include the Karakoram, parts of the Himalaya and the Hindu Kush. The Indus Valley – and the valleys of its tributaries – form a major agricultural region and contain the majority of Pakistan's population. A continuation of the Indian Thar Desert occupies the east. ***Principal rivers:*** Indus, Sutlej, Chenab, Jhelum, Kech. ***Highest point:*** Tirich Mir 7700m (25,263 ft). K2 (Mount Godwin Austen), at 8607 m (28,238 ft) the second highest peak in the world, is in the disputed territories.

Climate: The north and west of Pakistan are arid; the south and much of the east experience a form of the tropical monsoon. Temperatures vary dramatically by season and with altitude, from the hot tropical coast to the cold mountains of the far north.

Economy

More than one half of the labour force is involved in subsistence farming, with wheat and rice as the main crops. Cotton is the main foreign-currency earner. The government is encouraging irrigation schemes, but over one half of the cultivated land is subject to either waterlogging or salinity. Although there is a wide range of mineral reserves – including coal, gold and copper – these resources have not been extensively developed. Manufacturing is dominated by food processing, textiles and consumer goods. Unemployment and underemployment are major problems, and the country relies heavily upon foreign aid and money sent back by Pakistanis working abroad. ***Currency:*** Pakistan rupee.

Recent History

From the 18th century the region came under British rule. Pakistan as a nation was born in August 1947 when British India was partitioned as a result of demands by the Muslim League for an Islamic state in which Hindus would not be in a majority. Large numbers of Muslims moved to the new state and up to one million people died in the bloodshed that accompanied partition. Pakistan had two 'wings' – West Pakistan (the present country) and East Pakistan (now Bangladesh) – separated by 1600 km (1000 mi) of Indian territory. A number of areas were disputed with India. Kashmir – the principal bone of contention – was effectively partitioned between the two nations, and in 1947–49 and 1965 tension over Kashmir led to war between India and Pakistan. The problem of Kashmir is unsolved with fighting continuing intermittently along parts of the ceasefire line.

The Muslim League leader Muhammad Ali Jinnah (1876–1949) was the first Governor General, but Jinnah, who was regarded as 'father of the nation', died soon after independence. Pakistan – which became a republic in 1956 – suffered political instability and periods of military rule, including the administrations of General Muhammad Ayub Khan (from 1958 to 1969) and General Muhammad Yahya Khan (from 1969 to 1971). Although East Pakistan contained the majority of the population, from the beginning West Pakistan held political and military dominance. In elections in 1970, Shaikh Mujibur Rahman's Awami League won an overwhelming majority in East Pakistan, while the Pakistan People's Party (PPP) won most of the seats in West Pakistan. Mujibur Rahman seemed less interested in leading a new Pakistani government than in winning autonomy for the East. In 1971, after abortive negotiations, the Pakistani army was sent from the West to East Pakistan, which promptly declared its independence as Bangladesh. Civil war broke out and India supported the new state, forcing the Pakistani army to surrender by the end of the year.

The leader of the PPP, Zulfiqar Ali Bhutto (PM 1972–77), was deposed in a military coup led by the Army Chief of Staff, Muhammad Zia al-Haq. Bhutto was imprisoned (1977) for allegedly ordering the murder of the father of a former political opponent, sentenced to death (1978) and, despite international protests, hanged (1979). In 1985 Zia lifted martial law and began to return Pakistan to civilian life. Zia was killed in a plane crash (1988). Following elections in 1988, Bhutto's daughter and the PPP's new leader, Benazir, became the first woman Prime Minister of an Islamic state. Since then – although both Benazir Bhutto and and her successor were dismissed by the President – constitutional rule has been in force. Benazir Bhutto returned to power in 1993.

PALAU

Official name: The Republic of Palau.
Member of: Palau has not yet joined any major international organizations.
Area: 508 km² (196 sq mi).
Population: 15,500 (1991 est).
Capital: Koror 9500 (1990 census).
Languages: Palauan (official; majority), Sonsorolese, English.
Religions: Roman Catholic (majority); various Evangelical and Pentecostal Churches.
Education: is compulsory between the ages of six and 14. *Adult literacy:* no figures available. *Universities:* none.
Defence: There are no armed forces. The USA is responsible for the islands' defence.

Government

A President and Congress are elected by universal adult suffrage for four years. The Congress comprises a 14-member Senate and a 16-member House of Delegates. The 16-member Council of Chiefs has advisory powers only.
Largest parties: Coalition for Open, Honest and Just Government, Ta Belau Party.
Local government: 16 districts.
President: Kuniwo Nakamura (Ta Belau).

Geography

Palau comprises the volcanic, hilly, tropical island of Babelthuap, about 20 other small hilly islands and nearly 330 small atolls. ***Principal rivers:*** Babelthuap has many unnnamed streams. ***Highest point:*** Makelulu (on Babelthuap) 218m (715 ft).
Climate: Palau has a tropical maritime climate with heavy rainfall and little seasonal variation.

Economy

Most Palauans are involved in subsistence farming and fishing. Tourism and the sale of fishing rights to foreign fleets are the main sources of foreign currency. ***Currency:*** Palau uses US currency.

Recent History

Spain – which had claimed the area since 1543 – sold the islands to Germany in 1899. Occupied by Japanese forces in 1914, Palau remained under Japanese rule until taken by the USA in 1944. In 1947 Palau became part of the UN Pacific Islands Trust Territory under US administration. Palau became an autonomous republic in 1981 but, between 1983 and 1994 Palauans repeatedly rejected a Compact of Free Association with the USA, because the Compact would have entitled the USA to base nuclear weapons in the islands or its territorial waters. Palau eventually assumed complete independence in October 1994.

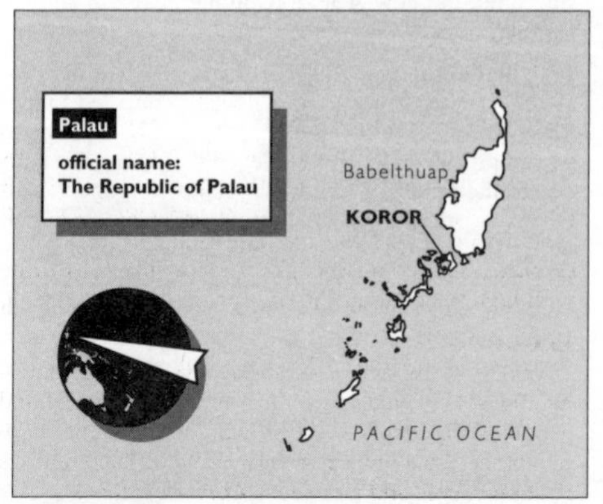

PANAMA

Official name: La República de Panamá (The Republic of Panama).
Member of: UN, OAS.
Area: 75,517 km² (29,157 sq mi).
Population: 2,563,000 (1993 est).
Capital: Panama City 828,000 (city 585,000; San Miguelito 243,000; 1990 census).
Other major cities: Colón 141,000, David 103,000 (1990 census).
Language: Spanish (official).
Religion: Roman Catholic (85%).
Education: is compulsory for six years, taken between the ages of six and 15. *Adult literacy:* 88%. *Universities:* three.
Defence: (1993 figures) *Paramilitary:* 11,000 personnel. *Air force:* 400. *Navy:* 400. *Conscription:* none.

Government

A 72-member Legislative Assembly and a President – who appoints a Cabinet of Ministers – are elected by universal adult suffrage for five years.
Largest parties: (nationalist) Democratic Revolutionary Party (PRD), (right-wing) Arnulfist Party (PA), (centre-right) Papa Egoro Movement (MPE), (centre-right) Nationalist Republican Liberal Movement (MORELINA).
Local government: nine provinces.
President: Ernesto Perez Balladares (PRD).

Geography

Panama is a heavily forested mountainous isthmus joining Central America to South America. ***Principal rivers:*** Chucunaque, Tuira, Balsas. ***Highest point:*** Baru 3475m (11,401 ft), an extinct volcano.
Climate: Panama has a tropical climate with little seasonal change in temperature.

Economy

Income from the Panama Canal is a major foreign-currency earner. Panama – which has a higher standard of living than its neighbours – has become an important 'offshore' banking centre. Major exports include bananas and shrimps. ***Currency:*** Balboa.

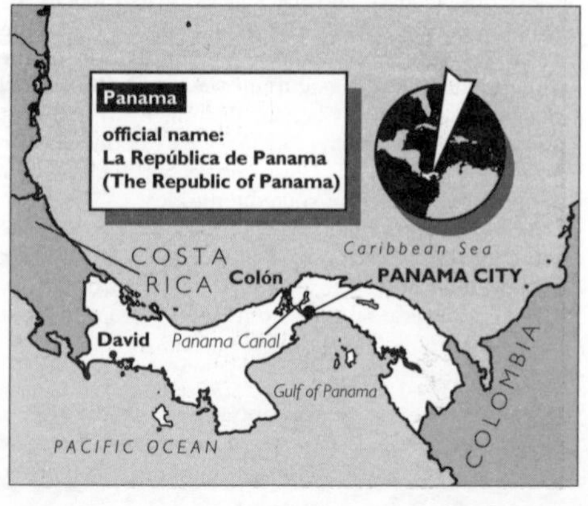

Recent History

In the 1880s, a French attempt to construct a canal linking the Atlantic and Pacific Oceans through Panama (then part of Colombia) proved unsuccessful. After Colombia rejected US proposals for completing the canal, Panama became independent (1903), sponsored by the USA. The canal eventually opened in 1914. From 1903 to 1979 the USA controlled land extending 8 km (5 mi) on either side of the canal – the Canal Zone. Panama will gain complete control of the canal itself in 2000. From 1983 to 1989 effective power was in the hands of General Manuel Noriega, who was deposed by a US invasion and taken to stand trial in the USA, where he was found guilty of criminal activities. The first completely free elections in Panama's history were held in 1994.

PAPUA NEW GUINEA

Official names: The Independent State of Papua New Guinea and Papua Niugini.
Member of: UN, Commonwealth, Apec.
Area: 462,840 km^2 (178,704 sq mi).
Population: 3,920,000 (1993 est).
Capital: Port Moresby 193,000 (1990 census).
Other major cities: Lae 81,000, Madang 27,000, Wewak 23,000 (1990 census).
Languages: English (official), Pidgin English, Motu and over 700 local languages.
Religions: Roman Catholic (33%), various Protestant Churches (nearly 60%).
Education: is not compulsory. *Adult literacy:* 52%. *Universities:* two.
Defence: (1993 figures) *Army:* 3200 personnel. *Air force:* 100. *Navy:* 500. *Paramilitary:* 4600. *Conscription:* none.

Government

A 109-member Parliament is elected for five years by universal adult suffrage. The Governor General – the representative of the British Queen as sovereign of Papua New Guinea – appoints a Prime Minister who commands a majority in Parliament. The PM, in turn, appoints a Cabinet, which is responsible to Parliament.
Largest parties: Pangu Party, People's Democratic Movement (PDM), People's Action Party (PAP), People's Progress Party (PPP), (socialist) Melanesian Alliance (MA).
Local government: 19 provinces, plus the national capital district.

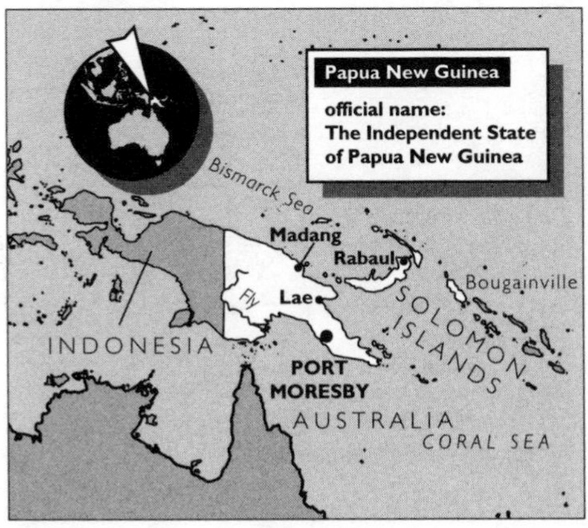

Prime Minister: Julius Chan (PPP).

Provinces

Central *Area:* 29,500 km^2 (11,400 sq mi). *Population:* 141,000 (1991 census). *Capital:* Port Moresby (the National Capital District, see below).
Eastern Highlands *Area:* 11,200 km^2 (4300 sq mi). *Population:* 300,000 (1991 census). *Capital:* Goroka.
East New Britain *Area:* 15,500 km^2 (6000 sq mi). *Population:* 184,000 (1991 census). *Capital:* Rabaul.
East Sepik *Area:* 42,800 km^2 (16,550 sq mi). *Population:* 248,000 (1991 census). *Capital:* Wewak.
Enga *Area:* 12,800 km^2 (4950 sq mi). *Population:* 239,000 (1991 census). *Capital:* Wabag.
Gulf *Area:* 34,500 km^2 (13,300 sq mi). *Population:* 68,000 (1991 census). *Capital:* Kerema.
Madang *Area:* 29,000 km^2 (11,200 sq mi). *Population:* 270,000 (1991 census). *Capital:* Madang.
Manus *Area:* 2100 km^2 (800 sq mi). *Population:* 33,000 (1991 census). *Capital:* Lorengau.
Milne Bay *Area:* 14,000 km^2 (5400 sq mi). *Population:* 157,000 (1991 census). *Capital:* Alotau (Samara).
Morobe *Area:* 34,500 km^2 (13,300 sq mi). *Population:* 364,000 (1991 census). *Capital:* Lae.
New Ireland *Area:* 9600 km^2 (3700 sq mi). *Population:* 87,000 (1991 census). *Capital:* Kavieng.
North Solomons (formerly **Bougainville**) *Area:* 9300 km^2 (3600 sq mi). *Population:* 160,000 (1991 census). *Capital:* Arawa (Buka).
Oro (formerly **Northern**) *Area:* 22,800 km^2 (8800 sq mi). *Population:* 97,000 (1991 census). *Capital:* Popondetta.
Sandaun (formerly **West Sepik**) *Area:* 36,300 km^2 (14,000 sq mi). *Population:* 135,000 (1991 census). *Capital:* Vanimo.
Simbu (formerly **Chimbu**) *Area:* 6100 km^2 (2350 sq mi). *Population:* 184,000 (1991 census). *Capital:* Kundiawa.
Southern Highlands *Area:* 23,800 km^2 (9200 sq mi). *Population:* 303,000 (1991 census). *Capital:* Mendi.
Western *Area:* 99,300 km^2 (38,350 sq mi). *Population:* 109,000 (1991 census). *Capital:* Daru.
Western Highlands *Area:* 8500 km^2 (3300 sq mi). *Population:* 291,000 (1991 census). *Capital:* Mount Hagen.
West New Britain *Area:* 21,000 km^2 (8100 sq mi). *Population:* 128,000 (1991 census). *Capital:* Kimbo.
National Capital District *Area:* 240 km^2 (100 sq mi). *Population:* 193,000 (1991 census). *Capital:* Port Moresby.

Geography

Broad swampy plains surround Papua New Guinea's mountainous interior. Over 15% of the total land area comprises outlying islands, of which the largest are Bougainville, New Britain and New Island. ***Principal rivers:*** Sepik, Strickland, Fly River. ***Highest point:*** Mount Wilhelm 4509m (14,493 ft).
Climate: The country experiences a tropical climate with high temperatures and heavy monsoonal rainfall.

Economy

Over 80% of the labour force is involved in agriculture – mainly subsistence farming – although agricultural exports include coffee, cocoa and coconuts. The mainstay of the economy is minerals, including large reserves of copper, gold and petroleum. ***Currency:*** Kina.

Recent History

A British protectorate, established in the southeast in 1884, was transferred to Australia (1906) and renamed Papua. Northeast New Guinea came under German administration in 1884, but was occupied by Australian forces in 1914. From 1942 to 1945 Japanese forces occupied New Guinea and part of Papua. In 1949 Australia combined the administration of the territories, which achieved independence as Papua New Guinea in 1975. Bougainville island, a major source of copper, attempted to secede (1990–92). Fighting on the island decreased in 1992 and peace talks began, but the dispute continues.

PARAGUAY

Official name: La República del Paraguay (The Republic of Paraguay).
Member of: UN, OAS, Mercosur, ALADI.
Area: 406,752 km² (157,048 sq mi).
Population: 4,613,000 (1993 est).
Capital: Asunción 945,000 (city 608,000; San Lorenzo 124,000; Lambaré 100,000; Fernando de la Mora 95,000; 1992 census).
Other major cities: Ciudad del Este 134,000, Pedro Juan Caballero 80,000, Concepción 63,000 (1992 census).
Languages: Spanish (7% as a first language; official), Guaraní (48% as a first language); bilingual Spanish-Guaraní (40%).
Religion: Roman Catholic (official; 96%).
Education: is compulsory between the ages of seven and 13. *Adult literacy:* 90%. *Universities:* two.
Defence: (1993 figures) *Army:* 12,500 personnel. *Air force:* 1000. *Navy:* 3000. *Paramilitary:* 8000. *Conscription:* 12 months in the army and air force; 18 months in the navy.

Government

A President (who may not serve for consecutive terms), an 80-member Chamber of Deputies (lower house) and a 45-member Senate (upper house) are elected by universal adult suffrage for five years.
Largest parties: (conservative) Colorado Party (PC), (centre-left) Authentic Radical Liberal Party (PLRA), (coalition) National Encounter.
Local government: 17 departments.
President: Juan Carlos Wasmosy (PC).

Geography

The country west of the Paraguay River – the Chaco – is a flat semiarid plain. The region east of the river is a partly forested undulating plateau. ***Principal rivers:*** Paraguay, Paraná, Picomayo, Apa. ***Highest point:*** Cerro San Rafael 850m (2789 ft).
Climate: The climate is subtropical with considerable variation in rainfall between the wet southeast and the dry west.

Economy

Agriculture – the main economic activity – is dominated by cattle ranching, cotton and soyabeans. Cheap hydroelectric power from installations on the Paraná, including the Yacyreta-Agipe dam (the world's largest), has stimulated industry. ***Currency:*** Guarani.

Recent History

Since independence in 1811, Paraguay has suffered many dictators, including General José Francia, who totally isolated Paraguay (1814–40). War against Argentina, Brazil and Uruguay (1865–70) cost Paraguay over one half of its population and much territory. Wars with Bolivia (1929-35) further weakened Paraguay. General Alfredo Stroessner gained power in 1954, ruling with increasing disregard for human rights until his overthrow in a military coup in 1989. Free elections were held in 1992.

PERU

Official name: República del Perú (Republic of Peru).
Member of: UN, OAS, Andean Pact, ALADI.
Area: 1,285,216 km² (496,225 sq mi).
Population: 22,915,000 (1993 est).
Capital: Lima 6,415,000 (city 5,760,000; Callao 638,000; 1990 est).
Other major cities: Arequipa 685,000, Trujillo 532,000, Chiclayo 426,000, Piura 325,000, Chimbote 297,000, Cuzco 275,000, Iquitos 270,000 (1990 est).
Languages: Spanish (68% as a first language), Quechua (27%), Aymara (3%) – all official.
Religion: Roman Catholic (official; 91%).
Education: is compulsory between the ages of six and 12. *Adult literacy:* 89%. *Universities:* 27 state and 19 private universities.
Defence: (1993 figures) *Army:* 75,000 personnel. *Air force:* 15,000. *Navy:* 25,000. *Paramilitary:* 60,000. *Conscription:* two years.

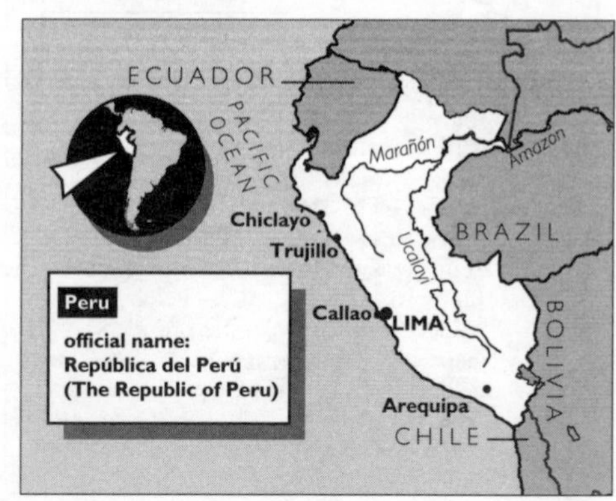

Government

The President and the 120-member National Congress are elected by universal adult suffrage for five years. Former presidents serve as additional life members of the Senate. The President appoints a Council of Ministers headed by a Prime Minister.

Largest parties: Cambio 90, (left-wing) American Popular Revolutionary Alliance (APRA), Popular Christian Party (PPC), Independent Moral Front, (liberal) Popular Action (AP), Renovation, Democratic Movement of the Left (MDI).

Local government: 25 departments.

President: Alberto Fujimori (Cambio).

Prime Minister: Efrain Goldenberg Schrieber.

Geography

The coastal plain is narrow and arid. The Andes – which are prone to earthquakes – run in three high parallel ridges from north to south. Nearly two thirds of Peru is tropical forest (the Selva) in the Amazon Basin. ***Principal rivers:*** Amazon-Ucayali, Tumbes, Ene, Marañón, Urubamba, Napo. ***Highest point***: Huascarán 6768m (22,205 ft).

Climate: A wide climatic variety includes semitropical desert – cooled by the Humboldt Current – on the coast, the very cold Alpine High Andes and the tropical Selva with a heavy rainfall.

Economy

About one third of the labour force is involved in agriculture. Subsistence farming dominates in the interior; crops for export are more important near the coast. Major crops include coffee, sugarcane, cotton and potatoes, as well as coca for cocaine. Sheep, llamas, vicuñas and alpacas are kept for wool. Rich natural resources include silver, copper, coal, gold, iron ore, petroleum and phosphates. The fishing industry – once the world's largest – has declined since 1971. A combination of natural disasters, a very high birth rate, guerrilla warfare and the declining value of exports has severely damaged the economy. ***Currency:*** New Sol.

Recent History

Independence was proclaimed in 1821 after the Argentine San Martín took Lima, but Spanish forces did not leave until 1824. Independent Peru saw political domination by large landowners. Progress was made under General Ramon Castilla (1844–62) and civilian constitutional governments at the beginning of the 20th century, but instability and military coups have been common. War (1879–83) in alliance with Bolivia against Chile resulted in the loss of nitrate deposits in the south, while victory against Ecuador (1941) added Amazonian territory. From 1968 a reformist military government instituted land reform, attempting to benefit workers and the Indians, but faced with mounting economic problems the military swung to the right in 1975. In 1980 elections were held, but owing to the economic crisis and the growth of an extreme left-wing guerrilla movement – the Sendero Luminoso ('Shining Path') – Peru's democracy remained under threat. In 1992, the president effected a coup, suspending the constitution and detaining opposition leaders. Subsequent elections were boycotted by the principal opposition parties. Guerrilla activity lessened after the capture of the leader of Sendero Luminoso, Abimael Guzman, in 1992.

THE PHILIPPINES

Official name: Repúblika ñg Pilipinas (Republic of the Philippines).

Member of: UN, ASEAN, Apec.

Area: 300,076 km² (115,860 sq mi).

Population: 64,955,000 (1993 est).

Capital: Manila 7,832,000 (city 1,599,000; Quezon City 1,667,000; Caloocan City 761,000, Pasay City 368,000; 1990 census).

Other major cities: Davao City 850,000, Cebu City 610,000, Zamboanga City 442,000, Bacolod City 364,000 (1990 census).

Languages: Pilipino (based on Tagalog; national; 55%), Tagalog (over 20%), Cebuano (24%), Ilocano (11%), English, Spanish and many local languages.

Religions: Roman Catholic (84%), Aglipayan Church (4%), Sunni Islam (5%).

Education: is compulsory between the ages of seven and 13. *Adult literacy:* 89%. *Universities:* 55.

Defence: (1993 figures) *Army:* 68,000 personnel. *Air force:* 15,500. *Navy:* 23,000. *Paramilitary:* 60,000. *Conscription:* none.

Government

The President and the 24-member Senate – the upper House of Congress – are elected by universal adult suffrage for six years. The House of Representatives comprises 201 directly elected members and no more than 50 members appointed by the President from minority groups. The President appoints a Cabinet of Secretaries. Part of Mindanao island and the Sulu Archipelago form an autonomous region (see below).

Largest parties: Democratic Filipino Struggle (DFS), National Union of Christian Democrats (NUCD), (right-wing) National People's Coalition, Liberal Party (LP).

Local government: 76 provinces grouped into 15 regions (one of which is autonomous).

President: Fidel Ramos (independent).

Autonomous Region

Muslim Mindanao *Area:* 13,122 km² (5698 sq mi). *Population:* 1,830,000 (1990 est). *Capital:* Cotabato City.

Geography

Some 2770 of the Philippines' 7000 islands are named. The two largest islands, Luzon and Mindanao, make up over two thirds of the country's area. Most

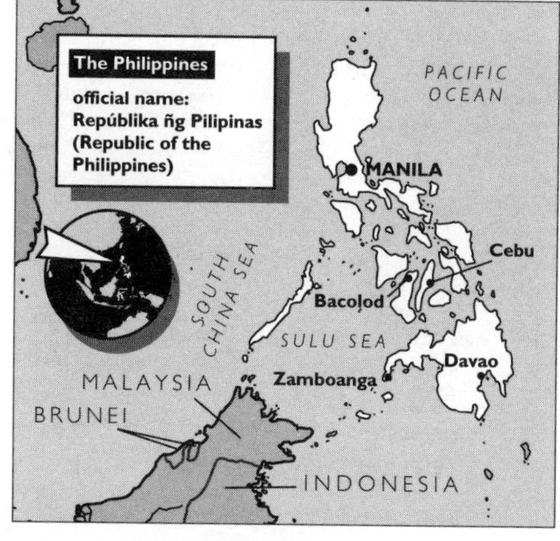

of the archipelago is mountainous with restricted coastal plains, although Luzon has a large, densely populated central plain. ***Principal rivers:*** Mindanao, Cagayan, Agno, Pampanga, Pasig. ***Highest point:*** Mount Apo, on Mindanao, 2954m (9692 ft).
Climate: The climate is tropical maritime with high humidity, high temperatures and heavy rainfall. Typhoons are frequent.

Economy

Almost one half of the labour force is involved in agriculture. Rice and maize are the principal subsistence crops, while coconuts, sugar cane, pineapples and bananas are grown for export. Deforestation is a problem as land is cleared for cultivation. Major industries include textiles, food processing, chemicals and electrical engineering. Mineral resources include copper (a major export), gold, petroleum and nickel. Money sent back by Filipinos working abroad is an important source of foreign currency. ***Currency:*** Philippine peso.

Recent History

In 1896, a combination of rising nationalism and resentment at economic injustice led to an unsuccessful revolt against Spanish rule. The islands were ceded to the USA after the Spanish-American War (1898), but American rule had to be imposed by force and resistance continued until 1906. A powerful American presence had a profound effect on Filipino society, which bears the triple imprint of Asian culture, Spanish Catholicism and American capitalism. US policy in the Philippines wavered between accelerating and delaying Filipino self-rule. In 1935 the nationalist leader Manuel Quezon became president of the semi-independent 'Commonwealth' of the Philippines. The surprise Japanese invasion of 1941 traumatized the islands' American and Filipino defenders. Japan set up a puppet 'Philippine Republic', but, after the American recapture of the archipelago, a fully independent Republic of the Philippines was established in 1946.

Between 1953 and 1957 President Ramon Magsaysay crushed and conciliated Communist-dominated Hukbalahap guerrillas, but his death ended a programme of land reforms. Coming to power in 1965, Ferdinand Marcos (1917–89) inaugurated flamboyant development projects, but his administration presided over large-scale corruption. Marcos used the continuing guerrilla activity as a justification for his increasingly repressive rule. When he attempted to rig the result of presidential elections in 1986, Marcos was overthrown in a popular revolution in favour of Corazon Aquino, the widow of a leading opposition politician who had allegedly been murdered on Marcos' orders. Her government faced several attempted coups, but she was succeeded by the democratically elected President Fidel Ramos in 1992. Insurgency by groups including Communists and Islamic nationalists remains a problem.

POLAND

Official name: Polska Rzecpospolita (Republic of Poland).
Member of: UN, CEFTA, OSCE.
Area: 312,683 km^2 (120,727 sq mi).
Population: 38,520,000 (1993 est).
Capital: Warsaw (Warszawa) 1,656,000 (1990 est).

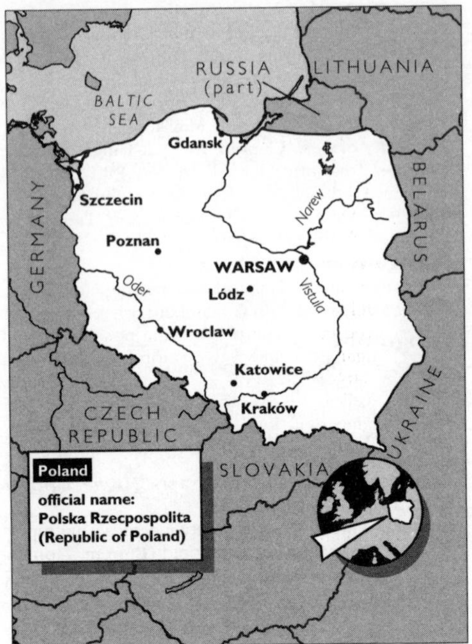

Other major cities: Katowice 1,604,000 (city 367,000; Sosnowiec 260,000; Bytom 230,000; Gliwice 222,000; Zabrze 202,000, Tychy 190,000, Chorzów 132,000); Lódz 848,000, Gdansk 768,000 (city 465,000; Gydnia 252,000), Kraków 751,000, Wroclaw 643,000, Poznan 590,000, Szczecin 413,000, Bydgoszcz 382,000, Lublin 351,000, Bialystok 271,000, Czestochowa 258,000, Radom 226,000, Kielce 213,000 (1990 est).
Language: Polish (official).
Religion: Roman Catholic (93%).
Education: is compulsory between the ages of seven and 14. *Adult literacy:* 99%. *Universities:* 31 (including technical unversities and institutes of university status).
Defence: (1993 figures) *Army:* 162,400 personnel. *Air force:* 79,800. *Navy:* 19,200. *Conscription:* 18 months.

Government

The 100-member Senate (upper house) and the 460-member Sejm (lower house) are elected for four years by universal adult suffrage. In the Sejm 391 seats are contested in constituencies and the remaining 69 are elected according to a system of proportional representation on party lists. The President – who is also directly elected – appoints a Prime Minister who commands a majority in the Sejm. The PM, in turn, appoints a Council of Ministers.
Largest parties: (former Communist) Democratic Left Alliance (SLD), (centre-left) Polish Peasant Party (PSL), (centre) Democratic Union (UD), (former Solidarity) Union of Labour (UP), (conservative) Confederation for an Independent Poland (KPN), (independent) Non-Party Block to Support Reform (BBWR).
Local government: 49 provinces.
President: Lech Walesa.
Prime Minister: Jozef Oleksy (SLD).

Geography

Most of Poland consists of lowlands. In the north are the Baltic lowlands and the Pomeranian and Mazurian lake districts. Central Poland is a region of plains. In the south are the hills of Little Poland and the Tatra Mountains. ***Principal river:*** Vistula (Wisla), Oder (Odra), Wieprz, Warta, Prosna. ***Highest point:*** Rysys 2499m (8199 ft).

Climate: Poland's climate tends towards continental with short warm summers and longer cold winters.

Economy

Polish agriculture remains predominantly small-scale and privately owned. Over 25% of the labour force is still involved in agriculture, growing potatoes, wheat, barley, sugar beet and fodder crops. The industrial sector is large-scale. Poland has major deposits of coal, as well as reserves of natural gas, copper and silver. Engineering, food processing, and the chemical, metallurgical and paper industries are important, but the economic situation has steadily deteriorated since the 1960s. However, since privatization was accelerated after 1991, Poland has made impressive economic reforms and achieved higher growth rates than other East European countries. Living standards have, however, decreased. Poland is an associate of the EU/EC. ***Currency:*** Zloty.

Recent History

In the 19th century the greater part of Poland was within Imperial Russia, against which the Poles revolted unsuccessfully in 1830, 1848 and 1863. National feeling also grew in the areas ruled by Austria and Prussia. After World War I, Poland was restored to statehood (1919), but the country was unstable. Marshal Józef Pilsudski (1867–1935) staged a coup in 1926, and became a virtual dictator. During the 1930s relations with Hitler's Germany became strained. An alliance with Britain was not enough to deter Hitler from attacking Poland, and thus precipitating World War II (1939). Poland was partitioned once again, this time between Nazi Germany and the USSR. Occupied Poland lost one sixth of its population, including almost all the Jews, and casualties were high after the ill-fated Warsaw Rising (1944). Poland was liberated by the Red Army (1945), and a Communist state was established. The new Poland lost almost one half its territory in the east to the USSR, but was compensated in the north and west at the expense of Germany.

A political crisis in 1956 led to the emergence of a Communist leader who enjoyed a measure of popular support, Wladyslaw Gomulka. In 1980, following the downfall of Gomulka's successor, Edward Gierek, a period of unrest led to the birth of the independent trade union Solidarity (*Solidarnosc*), led by Lech Walesa (1943–). Martial law was declared by General Wojciech Jaruzelski in 1981 in an attempt to restore Communist authority. Solidarity was banned and its leaders were detained, but public unrest and economic difficulties continued. In 1989 Solidarity was legalized and agreement was reached on political reform. Solidarity won free elections to the new Senate, and with the support of former allies of the Communists won enough seats to gain a majority in the Sejm, and to form a government. Solidarity leader Lech Walesa became President in 1990. Since multi-party elections for the Sejm were held in 1991, Solidarity has split and several short-lived coalition governments have held office.

PORTUGAL

Official name: A República Portuguesa (The Portuguese Republic).

Member of: UN, EU/EC, NATO, WEU, OSCE.

Area: 92,389 km² (35,672 sq mi), including Madeira and the Azores.

Population: 10,421,000 (1993 est).

Capital: Lisbon (Lisboa) 2,131,000 (city 950,000; Amadora 100,000; Barreiro 55,000; Almada 45,000; Queluz 45,000; 1990 est).

Other major cities: Oporto (Porto) 1,695,000 (city 450,000; Vila Nova de Gaia 65,000), Setúbal 80,000, Coímbra 75,000, Braga 67,000, Funchal 47,000, Evora 35,000 (1990 est).

Language: Portuguese (official; 100%).

Religion: Roman Catholic (94%).

Education: is compulsory between the ages of six and 15. *Adult literacy:* 87%. *Universities:* 19.

Defence: (1993 figures) *Army:* 27,200 personnel. *Air force:* 11,000. *Navy:* 12,500. *Paramilitary:* 40,000. *Conscription:* four to eight months in the army; four to 18 months in the navy and air force.

Government

An executive President is elected for a five-year term by universal adult suffrage. The 230-member Assembly is directly elected for four years. The President appoints a Prime Minister who commands a majority in the Assembly. The PM, in turn, appoints a Council of Ministers (Cabinet), responsible to the Assembly. Madeira and the Azores have their own autonomous governments.

Largest parties: (centre) Social Democratic Party (PSD), Socialist Party (PS), Communist Alliance (CDU), (centre) Centre Democratic Party (CDS).

Local government: 18 districts and two autonomous regions.

President: Mario Alberto Soares (PSD).

Prime Minister: Annibal Cavaço Silva (PSD).

Overseas territory: Macau. See Other Territories (beginning on p. 729).

Districts and autonomous regions

Aveiro *Area:* 2808 km² (1084 sq mi). *Population:* 656,000 (1991 census). *Capital:* Aveiro.

Azores (Açores) (autonomous region) *Area:* 2247 km² (868 sq mi). *Population:* 237,000 (1991 census). *Capital:* Ponta Delgada.

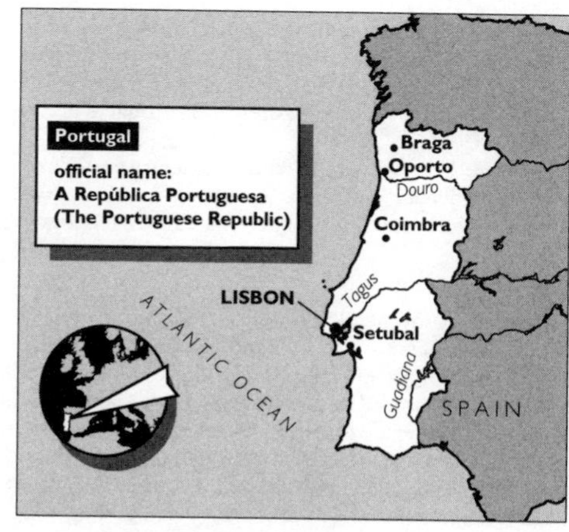

Beja *Area:* 10,225 km² (3948 sq mi). *Population:* 168,000 (1991 census). *Capital:* Beja.
Braga *Area:* 2673 km² (1032 sq mi). *Population:* 746,000 (1991 census). *Capital:* Braga.
Bragança *Area:* 6608 km² (2551 sq mi). *Population:* 158,000 (1991 census). *Capital:* Bragança.
Castelo Branco *Area:* 6675 km² (2577 sq mi). *Population:* 215,000 (1991 census). *Capital:* Castelo Branco.
Coimbra *Area:* 3947 km² (1524 sq mi). *Population:* 428,000 (1991 census). *Capital:* Coimbra.
Evora *Area:* 7393 km² (2854 sq mi). *Population:* 174,000 (1991 census). *Capital:* Evora.
Faro *Area:* 4960 km² (1915 sq mi). *Population:* 340,000 (1991 census). *Capital:* Faro.
Guarda *Area:* 5518 km² (2131 sq mi). *Population:* 188,000 (1991 census). *Capital:* Guarda.
Leiria *Area:* 3515 km² (1357 sq mi). *Population:* 428,000 (1991 census). *Capital:* Leiria.
Lisbon (Lisboa) *Area:* 2761 km² (1066 sq mi). *Population:* 2,064,000 (1991 census). *Capital:* Lisbon.
Madeira (autonomous region) *Area:* 794 km² (306 sq mi). *Population:* 253,000 (1991 census). *Capital:* Funchal.
Oporto (Porto) *Area:* 2395 km² (925 sq mi). *Population:* 1,622,000 (1991 census). *Capital:* Oporto.
Portalegre *Area:* 6065 km² (2342 sq mi). *Population:* 134,000 (1991 census). *Capital:* Portalegre.
Santarém *Area:* 6747 km² (2605 sq mi). *Population:* 443,000 (1991 census). *Capital:* Santarém.
Setúbal *Area:* 5064 km² (1955 sq mi). *Population:* 714,000 (1991 census). *Capital:* Setúbal.
Viana do Castelo *Area:* 2255 km² (871 sq mi). *Population:* 249,000 (1991 census). *Capital:* Viana do Castelo.
Vila Real *Area:* 4328 km² (1671 sq mi). *Population:* 237,000 (1991 census). *Capital:* Vila Real.
Viseu *Area:* 5007 km² (1933 sq mi). *Population:* 401,000 (1991 census). *Capital:* Viseu.

Geography

Behind a coastal plain, Portugal north of the River Tagus is a highland region at the centre of which is the mainland's principal mountain range, the Serra da Estrela. A wide plateau in the northeast is a continuation of the Spanish Meseta. Portugal south of the Tagus is mainly an undulating lowland. The Atlantic islands of Madeira and the Azores are respectively nearly 1000 km (620 mi) and 1200 km (745 mi) southwest of the mainland. ***Principal river:*** Tagus (Rio Tejo), Guadiana, Douro, Minho, Zézere. ***Highest point:*** (mainland) Estrela 1993m (6539 ft). At 2315m (7713 ft), Pico in the Azores is Portugal's highest peak.

Climate: Portugal has a mild and temperate climate which is wetter and more Atlantic in the north, and drier, hotter and more Mediterranean inland and in the south.

Economy

Agriculture involves 15% of the labour force, but lacks investment following land reforms in the 1970s, since when production has fallen. Major crops include wheat and maize, grapes (for wines such as port and Madeira), tomatoes, potatoes and cork trees. Portugal lacks natural resources. Manufacturing industry includes textiles and clothing (both of which are major exports), footwear, food processing, cork products, and, increasingly, electrical appliances and petrochemicals. Tourism and money sent back by Portuguese working abroad are major foreign-currency earners. Despite impressive recent economic development Portugal remains Western Europe's poorest country. ***Currency:*** Escudo.

Recent History

Instability wracked Portugal for much of the 19th century. Portugal's African empire was confirmed, although the country lacked the power to gain more territory in the scramble for Africa. The monarchy was overthrown in 1910, but the Portuguese republic proved unstable and the military took power in 1926. From 1932 to 1968, under the dictatorship of Premier Antonio Salazar (1889–1970), stability was achieved but at great cost. Portugal became a one-party state, and expensive colonial wars dragged on as Portugal attempted to check independence movements in Angola and Mozambique. In 1974 there was a left-wing military coup whose leaders granted independence to the African colonies (1974–75), and initially attempted to impose Marxism on the country. However, elections in 1976 decisively rejected the far left. Civilian rule was restored as Portugal effected a transition from dictatorship to democracy, and simultaneously – through the loss of empire and membership of the EC – became more closely integrated with the rest of Europe.

QATAR

Official name: Dawlat Qatar (State of Qatar).
Member of: UN, Arab League, OPEC, GCC.
Area: 11,427 km² (4412 sq mi).
Population: 521,000 (1993 est).
Capital: Doha 272,000 (city 217,000; ar-Rayyanim 42,000; al-Wakrah 13,000; 1986 est).
Other main town: Umm Sa'id 6000 (1986 est).
Language: Arabic.
Religion: Wahhabi Sunni Islam (official; 98%).
Education: is not compulsory. *Adult literacy:* 76%. *Universities:* one.
Defence: (1993 figures) *Army:* 8000 personnel. *Air force:* 800. Navy: 700. *Conscription:* none.

Government

Qatar is an absolute monarchy. The Amir – who is head of state and of government – appoints a Council of Ministers and a 35-member Advisory Council.
Largest parties: There are no political parties.

Local government: nine municipalities.
Sovereign: HH Shaikh Khalifah bin Hamad Al-Thani, Amir of Qatar (succeeded upon the deposition of his cousin, 22 February 1972).
Prime Minister: The Amir.

Geography

Qatar is a low barren peninsula projecting into the Gulf. ***Principal rivers:*** none. ***Highest point:*** Dukhan Heights 73m (240 ft).
Climate: Qatar is very hot in summer, but milder in winter. Rainfall averages 50 to 75 mm (2 to 3 in).

Economy

The export of petroleum and natural gas gives Qatar a high standard of living. The steel and cement industries have been developed in an attempt to diversify. ***Currency:*** Qatari riyal.

Recent History

In the 1860s Britain intervened in a dispute between Qatar and its Bahraini rulers, installing a member of the Qatari ath-Thani family as ruler. Qatar was part of the (Turkish) Ottoman Empire from 1872 until 1915. Its ruler signed protection treaties with Britain in 1916 and 1934, and did not regain complete independence until 1971.

ROMANIA

Official name: Rômania.
Member of: UN, OSCE,
Area: 237,500 km² (91,699 sq mi).
Population: 22,789,000 (1993 est).
Capital: Bucharest (Bucuresti) 2,351,000 (1992 census).
Other major cities: Constanta 351,000, Iasi 343,000, Timisoara 334,000, Cluj-Napoca 328,000, Galati 326,000, Brasov 324,000, Craiova 304,000, Ploesti 252,000, Braila 235,000, Oradea 221,000, Bacau 205,000 (1992 census).
Languages: Romanian (official; 89%), Hungarian (10%), German.
Religions: Romanian Orthodox (70%), Greek Catholic, Roman Catholic and Calvinist minorities.
Education: is compulsory between the ages of six and sixteen. *Adult literacy:* 96%. *Universities:* 17 (including four technical universities).
Defence: (1993 figures) *Army:* 161,000 personnel.

Air force: 23,100. *Navy:* 19,000. *Paramilitary:* 22,000. *Conscription:* 12 months in the army and air force; 18 months in the navy.

Government

The President is elected by universal adult suffrage for four years. The 341-member National Assembly and 143-member Senate are directly elected under a modified system of proportional representation for four years. In both houses, seats are reserved for ethnic minorities. The President appoints a Prime Minister who, in turn, appoints a Council of Ministers.
Largest parties: (socialist) Party of Social Democracy of Romania (PSDR), (socialist) National Salvation Front (NSF), (right-wing) Romanian National Unity Party, (ethnic Hungarian) Democratic Union of Romania, (right-wing) Greater Romanian Party, (former Communist) Socialist Labour Party, (centrist) Democratic Convention of Romania – an electoral alliance of Christian Democratic National Peasants' Party, New Liberal Party, Romanian Social Democratic Party and Romanian Ecology Party.
Local government: 40 counties plus the capital.
President: Ion Iliescu (PSDR).
Prime Minister: Nicolae Vacaroiu (PSDR).

Geography

The Carpathian Mountains run through the north, east and centre of Romania. Moldavia is the plateau east of the Carpathians; Walachia is the plain south of these mountains. To the west of the Carpathians is the tableland of Transylvania and the Banat lowland. In the south the Danube Plain ends in a delta on the Black Sea. ***Principal rivers:*** Danube (Dunăria), Prut, Mures, Olt, Siret, Ialomita. ***Highest point:*** Moldoveanu 2544m (8346 ft).
Climate: Romania experiences cold snowy winters and hot summers. Rainfall is moderate in the lowlands but heavier in the Carpathians.

Economy

State-owned industry – which employs nearly 40% of the labour force – includes mining, metallurgy, mechanical engineering and chemicals. Natural resources include petroleum and natural gas. Large forests support a timber and furniture industry. Major crops include maize, sugar beet, wheat, potatoes and grapes for wine, but agriculture has been neglected, and food supplies have fallen short of Romania's needs. Most farming land has been privatized. Economic mismanagement under Ceausescu decreased low living standards, and Romania faces severe economic difficulties. Much of industry remains unprivatized. ***Currency:*** Leu.

Recent History

Romanian unity was achieved when Alexander Cuza was elected prince of both Walachia and Moldavia (1859). A German dynasty was chosen in 1866, and Romania's independence was internationally recognized in 1878. When both the Russian and Austro-Hungarian Empires collapsed at the end of World War I, Romania won additional territory with substantial Romanian populations from both. 'Greater Romania' was beset with deep social and ethnic divisions, which found expression in the rise of the Fascist Iron Guard in the 1930s. King Carol II suppressed the Guard and substituted his own dictatorship, but he was forced by Germany to cede lands back to Hungary (1940), while the USSR retook considerable territories, including the present Moldova. Carol fled and Romania – under Marshal Ion Antonescu – joined the Axis powers (1941), fighting the USSR to regain lost territories. King Michael dismissed Antonescu and declared war on Germany as the Red Army invaded (1944), and a Soviet-dominated government was installed (1945). The monarchy was abolished in 1947. From 1952, under Gheorghe Gheorghiu-Dej (1901–65) and then under Nicolae Ceausescu (1918–89), Romania distanced itself from Soviet foreign policy while maintaining strict Communist orthodoxy at home. Ceausescu – and his wife Elena – impoverished Romania by their harsh, corrupt and nepotistic rule. When the secret police put down demonstrations in Timisoara (1989), the leaders of an anti-Ceauscescu conspiracy within the army and the Communist Party took power, executing Nicolae and Elena Ceausescu on charges of genocide and corruption. A National Salvation Front (NSF) was formed and the Communist Party was dissolved. An international team of monitors judged multi-party elections in 1990 to be 'flawed' but not fraudulent. The NSF split and its larger offshoot, the Party of Social Democracy, has formed the government since 1992. Power remains largely in the hands of former Communists.

RUSSIA

Official name: Rossiyskaya Federativnaya Respublika (Republic of the Russian Federation) or Rossiya (Russia).

Member of: UN, CIS, OSCE.

Area: 17,075,400 km^2 (6,592,800 sq mi).

Population: 148,000,000 (1993 est).

Capital: Moscow (Moskva) 8,967,000 (city 8,769,000; 1989 est).

Other major cities: St Petersburg (Sankt-Peterburg; formerly Leningrad) 5,020,000 (city 4,456,000), Nizhny Novgorod (formerly Gorky) 1,438,000, Novosibirsk 1,436,000, Yekaterinburg (formerly Sverdlovsk) 1,367,000, Samara (formerly Kuybyshev) 1,257,000, Omsk 1,148,000, Chelyabinsk 1,143,000, Kazan 1,094,000, Perm 1,091,000, Ufa 1,083,000, Rostov 1,020,000, Volgograd 999,000, Krasnoyarsk 912,000, Saratov 905,000, Voronezh 887,000, Vladivostok 648,000, Izhevsk (formerly Ustinov) 635,000, Yaroslavl 633,000 (1989 est).

Languages: Russian (83%), Tatar (4%), Ukrainian (3%), Chuvash (1%), Bashkir (1%), Belarussian (1%), Chechen (1%), plus more than 100 other languages. Over 0.5% of the population speak one of the following languages as a first language: German, Udmurt, Mordovian, Mari, Kazakh, Avar and Armenian.

Religions: Orthodox (27%), with Sunni Islam, Jewish, Baptist and other minorities.

Education: is compulsory between the ages of seven and 17. *Adult literacy:* no figures available. *Universities:* 42 universities, 32 polytechnics of university status and over 100 other institutes offering degree-level courses.

Defence: (1993 figures) *Army:* 1,000,000 personnel. *Border guards:* 100,000. *Air force:* 170,000. *Navy:* 300,000. *Paramilitary:* 220,000. *Others:* 240,000. *Conscription:* 18 months in the army and air force; 24 months in the navy. (Conscription is compulsory in theory, but avoidance of conscription has become widespread.)

Government

Russia is a federation of republics and other regions, which exercise varying degrees of self-government. An executive President, who appoints a Council of Ministers including a Prime Minister, is directly elected for a maximum of two five-year terms. The bicameral Federal Assemby is elected by universal adult suffrage for four years. The lower house (the State Duma) comprises 450 members, of whom 225 are elected by single member constituencies and 225 are elected from party lists under a system of proportional representation. The upper house, the Federal Council, comprises two members elected from each of the 89 republics and regions that comprise the Federation.

Largest parties: (liberal reformist) Russia's Choice, (right-wing ultra-nationalist) Liberal Democratic Party, Communist Party, (left-wing nationalist) Agrarian Party, (liberal reformist) Yabloko, (liberal reformist) Party of Unity and Accord, (corporatist) Women of Russia Movement. A large number of members sit as independents.

Local government: 22 republics, one of which (Russia) is divided into 68 other regions, which have similar powers to the republics.

President: Boris Yeltsin (non-party).

Prime Minister: Victor Chernomyrdin (non-party).

Republics

Adygea *Area:* 7600 km^2 (2900 sq mi). *Population:* 442,000 (1992 est). *Capital:* Maykop.

Bashkortostan formerly **Bashkiria** *Area:* 143,600 km^2 (55,400 sq mi). *Population:* 4,008,000 (1992 est). *Capital:* Ufa.

Buryatia *Area:* 351,300 km^2 (135,600 sq mi). *Population:* 1,059,000 (1992 est). *Capital:* Ulan-Ude.

Chechenya *Area:* 14,300 km^2 (5500 sq mi). *Population:* 900,000 (1992 est). *Capital:* Grozny.

Chuvashia *Area:* 18,300 km^2 (7100 sq mi). *Population:* 1,353,000 (1992 est). *Capital:* Cheboksary.

Dagestan *Area:* 50,300 km^2 (19,400 sq mi). *Population:* 1,890,000 (1992 est). *Capital:* Makhachkala.

Gorno-Altay *Area:* 92,600 km^2 (35,700 sq mi). *Population:* 198,000 (1992 est). *Capital:* Gorno-Altaisk.

Ingushetia *Area:* 5000 km^2 (2000 sq mi). *Population:* 410,000 (1992 est). *Capital:* Nazran.

Kalmykia or **Khalmg Tangch** *Area:* 76,100 km^2 (29,400 sq mi). *Population:* 327,000 (1992 est). *Capital:* Elista.

Karbardino-Balkaria *Area:* 12,500 km^2 (4800 sq mi). *Population:* 784,000 (1992 est). *Capital:* Nalchik.

Karachay-Cherkessia *Area:* 14,100 km^2 (5400 sq mi). *Population:* 431,000 (1992 est). *Capital:* Cherkess.

Karelia *Area:* 172,400 km^2 (66,600 sq mi). *Population:* 800,000 (1992 est). *Capital:* Petrozavodsk.

Khakassia *Area:* 61,900 km^2 (23,900 sq mi). *Population:* 581,000 (1992 est). *Capital:* Abakan.

Komi *Area:* 415,900 km^2 (160,600 sq mi). *Population:* 1,255,000 (1992 est). *Capital:* Syktyvkar.

Mari El *Area:* 23,200 km^2 (9000 sq mi). *Population:* 762,000 (1992 est). *Capital:* Ioshkar-Ola.

Mordvinia formerly **Mordova** *Area:* 26,200 km^2 (10,100 sq mi). *Population:* 964,000 (1992 est).

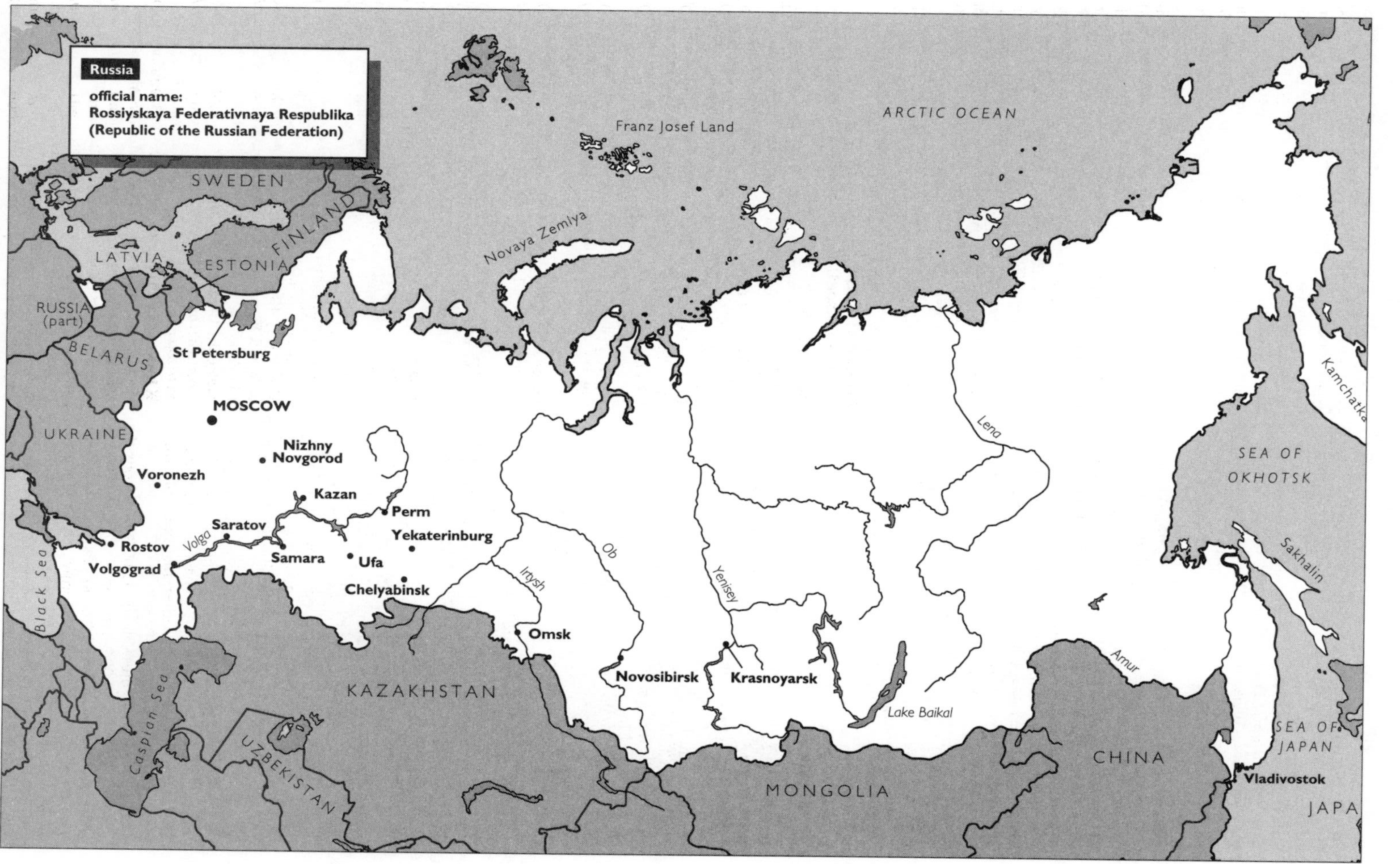
Russia
official name:
Rossiyskaya Federativnaya Respublika
(Republic of the Russian Federation)
ARCTIC OCEAN
Franz Josef Land
Novaya Zemlya
SWEDEN
FINLAND
LATVIA
ESTONIA
RUSSIA (part)
BELARUS
UKRAINE
St Petersburg
MOSCOW
Nizhny Novgorod
Voronezh
Kazan
Perm
Saratov
Yekaterinburg
Rostov
Volga
Samara
Ufa
Volgograd
Chelyabinsk
Black Sea
Caspian Sea
KAZAKHSTAN
UZBEKISTAN
Irtysh
Omsk
Ob
Novosibirsk
Yenisey
Krasnoyarsk
Lake Baikal
Lena
Amur
MONGOLIA
CHINA
Kamchatka
SEA OF OKHOTSK
Sakhalin
SEA OF JAPAN
Vladivostok

Capital: Saransk.

North Ossetia (Severo-Osetiya) *Area:* 8000 km^2 (3100 sq mi). *Population:* 695,000 (1992 est). *Capital:* Vladikavkaz.

Russia (Rossiya) *Area:* 12,198,300 km^2 (4,709,800 sq mi). *Population:* 125,115,000 (1992 est). *Capital:* Moscow. Russia, unlike the other 21 republics, has no government of its own; it is divided into 68 regions, autonomous regions, territories and autonomous districts.

Sakha formerly **Yakutia** *Area:* 3,103,200 km^2 (1,198,200 sq mi). *Population:* 1,093,000 (1992 est). *Capital:* Yakutsk.

Tatarstan *Area:* 68,000 km^2 (26,300 sq mi). *Population:* 3,696,000 (1992 est). *Capital:* Kazan.

Tuva or **Tyva** *Area:* 170,500 km^2 (65,800 sq mi). *Population:* 306,000 (1992 est). *Capital:* Kyzyl-Orda.

Udmurtia *Area:* 42,100 km^2 (16,300 sq mi). *Population:* 1,637,000 (1992 est). *Capital:* Izhevsk.

Geography

Russia is the largest country in the world and covers over 10% of the total land area of the globe. Most of the land between the Baltic and the Ural Mountains is covered by the North European Plain, south of which the relatively low-lying Central Russian Uplands stretch from the Ukrainian border to north of Moscow. To the east of the Urals is the vast West Siberian Lowland, the greater part of which is occupied by the basin of the River Ob and its tributaries. The Central Siberian Plateau – between the Rivers Yenisey and Lena – rises to around 1700m (5500 ft). Beyond the Lena are the mountains of east Siberia, including the Chersky Mountains and the Kamchatka Peninsula. Much of the south of Siberia is mountainous. The Yablonovy and Stanovoy Mountains rise inland from the Amur Basin, which drains to the Pacific coast. The Altai Mountains lie south of Lake Baikal and along the border with Mongolia. Between the Black and Caspian Seas are the high Caucasus Mountains on the Georgian border. The Kaliningrad enclave between Poland and Lithuania on the Baltic is a detached part of Russia. ***Principal rivers:*** Yenisey-Angara-Selanga, Ob-Irtysh, Lena-Kirenga, Amur-Argun, Volga, Tungaska, Northern Dvina, Pechora, Vitim, Vilyuy, Olenek, Amga, Kolyma. ***Highest point:*** Elbrus 5642m (18,510 ft) on the Georgian border.

Climate: Russia has a wide range of climatic types, but most of the country is continental and experiences extremes of temperature. The Arctic north is a severe tundra region in which the subsoil is nearly always frozen. The forested taiga zone, to the south, has long hard winters and short summers. The steppes and the Central Russian Uplands have cold winters, but hot, dry summers. Between the Black and Caspian seas, conditions become almost Mediterranean. The Kaliningrad enclave has a more temperate climate than the rest of western Russia.

Economy

Russia is one of the largest producers of coal, iron ore, steel, petroleum and cement. However, its economy is in crisis. The economic reforms (1985–91) of Mikhail Gorbachov introduced decentralization to a centrally-planned economy. Since 1991, reform has been accelerated through the introduction of free market prices and the encouragement of private enterprise. However, lack of motivation in the labour force affects many sectors of the economy and poor distribution has resulted in shortages of many basic goods. Inflation became rampant after 1991, but Russia's economic decline slowed in 1994. Manufacturing involves one third of the labour force and includes the steel, chemical, textile and heavy machinery industries. The production of consumer goods is not highly developed. Agriculture is large-scale and organized either into state-owned farms or collective farms, although the right to own and farm land privately has been introduced. Despite mechanization and the world's largest fertilizer industry, Russia cannot produce enough grain for its needs, in part because of poor harvests, and poor storage and transport facilities. Major Russian crops include wheat, barley, oats, potatoes, sugar beet and fruit. Natural resources include the world's largest reserves of coal, nearly one third of the world's natural gas reserves, one third of the world's forests, major deposits of manganese, gold, potash, bauxite, nickel, lead, zinc and copper, as well as plentiful sites for hydroelectric power installations. Machinery, petroleum and petroleum products are Russia's major exports and the republic is self-sufficient in energy. Russia has a large trade surplus with the other former Soviet republics. ***Currency:*** Rouble.

Recent History

Under Nicholas II (reigned 1894–1917), Russia saw rapid industrialization, rising prosperity, and (after 1906) limited constitutional reform, but his reign was cut short by World War I and the revolutions of February 1917. In November 1917, the Bolsheviks (Communists), led by Vladimir Ilich Lenin (1870-1924), overthrew the provisional government in a coup. Russia withdrew from the war, ceded Poland to Germany and Austria and recognized the independence of the Baltic states, Finland and Ukraine. Other parts of the former empire soon declared independence, including the states of Transcaucasia and Central Asia. A civil war between the Bolsheviks and the White Russians (led by former Tsarists) lasted until 1922. The Communists reconquered most of the former Russian empire and in December 1922 formed the Union of Soviet Socialist Republics (USSR). The economy was reorganized under central control, but shortages and famine were soon experienced. After Lenin's death (1924), a power struggle took place between the supporters of Joseph Stalin (1879-1953) and Leon Trotsky (1879-1940). Stalin expelled Trotsky's supporters from the Communist Party and exiled him. The rapid industrialization of the country began. In 1929-30, Stalin, liquidated the kulaks (richer peasants). Severe repression continued until his death: opponents were subject to 'show trials', and millions died as a result of starvation or political execution.

In World War II – in which up to 20 million Soviet citizens may have died – the USSR at first concluded a pact with Hitler (1939), and invaded Poland, Finland, Romania and the Baltic states, annexing considerable territory. However, in 1941 the Germans invaded the USSR. In victory the Soviet Union was confirmed as a world power, controlling a cordon of satellite states in Eastern Europe and challenging the West in the Cold War. However, the economy stagnated and the country was drained by the burdens of an impoverished and overstretched empire. Leonid Brezhnev (leader 1964–82) reversed the brief thaw that had been experienced under Nikita Khrushchev (leader 1956–64), and far-reaching reform had to await the policies of Mikhail Gorbachov (1931–) after 1985.

Faced with severe economic reforms, Gorbachov attempted to introduce reconstruction (*perestroika*) and greater openness (*glasnost*) by implementing social, economic and industrial reforms. The state of the economy also influenced the desire to reduce military spending by reaching agreements on arms reduction with the West. Dissent was tolerated, a major reform of the constitution led to more open elections, and the Communist Party gave up its leading role. Many hardliners in the Communist Party were defeated by reformers (many of them non-Communists) in elections in 1989. The abandonment of the Brezhnev Doctrine – the right of the USSR to intervene in the affairs of Warsaw Pact countries (as it had done militarily in Hungary in 1956 and Czechoslovakia in 1968) – prompted rapid change in Eastern Europe, where one after another the satellite states renounced Communism and began to implement multi-party rule.

From 1989 there were increased nationalistic stirrings within the USSR, particularly in the Baltic republics and the Caucasus. In August 1991, an attempt by a group of Communist hardliners to depose Gorbachov was defeated by the resistance of Russian President Boris Yeltsin (1931–) and by the refusal of the army to take action against unarmed civilian protesters. The opposition of Yeltsin and the Russian parliament to the coup greatly enhanced the status and powers of Russia and the 14 other Union Republics. Fourteen of the 15 republics declared independence and the secession of the three Baltic republics was recognized internationally. The remaining republics began to renegotiate their relationship. Gorbachov suspended the Communist Party and – with Yeltsin – initiated far-reaching political and economic reforms. However, it was too late to save the Soviet Union, whose fate was sealed by the refusal of Ukraine, the second most important of the republics, to participate in the new looser Union proposed by Gorbachov. By the end of 1991 the initiative had passed from Gorbachov to Yeltsin, who was instrumental in establishing the Commonwealth of Independent States (CIS), a military and economic grouping of sovereign states that eventually included all the former Union republics except the Baltic states.

After Gorbachov resigned and the Soviet Union was dissolved (December 1991). Russia took over the international responsibilities of the USSR, but faced a severe economic crisis and a constitutional crisis as Communist hardliners in the Congress disputed power with President Yeltsin. The constitutional dispute came to a head in 1993, when a core of Communist and nationalist hardliners organized an armed uprising in the parliament building in Moscow. After the parliamentary uprising was put down by army intervention, Yeltsin introduced a new constitution which concentrates power in the president's hands. However, extreme right-wing nationalists and hardline Communists gained considerable support in multi-party elections to the new Federal Assembly in 1993. Support for Yeltsin further decreased when, against Russian public and parliamentary opinion, the Russian army crushed the bid of the rebel Caucasian republic of Chechenya to secede from the Russian Federation (1995). Russia has, however, regained much influence with CIS members and has organized cease-fires in Nagorno Karabkh (which is disputed between Armenia and Azerbaijan) and in the Abkhazian region of Georgia, maintained peace-keeping troops in Tajikistan and the Trans-Dnestr region of Moldova, and concluded an economic and monetary union with Belarus.

RWANDA

Official name: La République rwandaise (French) or Republika y'u Rwanda (Kinyarwanda) (Republic of Rwanda).
Member of: UN, OAU.
Area: 26,338 km^2 (10,169 sq mi).
Population: 5,500,000 (1994 est), after massacres and the flight of refugees
Capital: Kigali 300,000 (1991 est); the population was reduced by at least 50% in 1994.
Other main towns: Ruhengeri 30,000, Butare 29,000 (1991 est).
Languages: French (12%; official), Kinyarwanda (85%; official)
Religions: Roman Catholic (63%), animist (21%)
Education: is compulsory, in theory, between the ages of seven and 15. *Adult literacy:* 50%. *Universities:* one.
Defence: No figures available.

Government

The constitution provides for the election of a President – who appoints a Council of Ministers – and a 70-member Assembly for five years by universal adult suffrage.
Largest parties: Since 1994 there have been no effective political parties in Rwanda apart from the Rwandese Patriotic Front (FPR).
Local government: 11 prefectures.
President: Pasteur Bizimungu (FPR).
Prime Minister: Faustin Twagiramungu (FPR).

Geography

Rwanda is a mountainous country. Most of the western boundary is formed by Lake Kivu. ***Principal rivers:*** Kagera, Ruzizi. ***Highest point:*** Mount Karisimbi 4507m (14,787 ft).
Climate: The climate is tropical with cooler temperatures in the mountains.

Economy

The economy was devastated by civil war and genocide in 1994. Most Rwandans are subsistence farmers. Coffee and tin are the main exports. There are major (unexploited) reserves of natural gas under Lake Kivu. ***Currency:*** Rwanda franc.

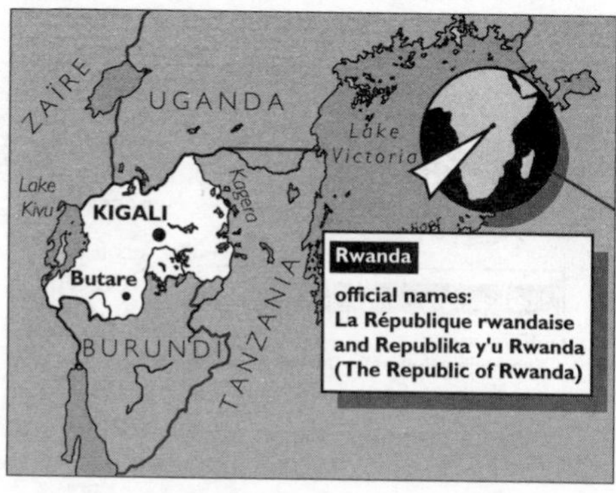

Recent History
The kingdom of Rwanda – whose Tutsi minority dominated the majority Hutu tribe – was a German possession from 1890 to 1916 and then under Belgian rule until independence in 1962. The Tutsi monarchy was overthrown by the Hutu in 1961 and many Tutsis fled into exile. From 1978 to 1991 Rwanda was a single-party state. Tribal violence followed a Tutsi attempt to regain power in 1983 and in 1990–91 the FPR, an army of Tutsi refugees, occupied much of the north. After a plane carrying President Habyarimana was shot down in 1994, government forces went on the rampage. In the ensuing ethnic violence Hutu militias massacred over 500,000 Tutsis and over 2,000,000 (mainly Hutu) refugees fled the country as the FPR took power. The UN sanctioned a (largely French) peace-keeping mission and international aid programmes are bringing relief to refugees at camps in Zaïre and Tanzania.

SAINT CHRISTOPHER AND NEVIS

Official name: The Federation of Saint Christopher and Nevis. St Christopher is popularly known as St Kitts.
Member of: UN, Commonwealth, OAS, CARICOM.
Area: 262 km² (101 sq mi).
Population: 41,800 (1991 census).
Capital: Basseterre 15,000 (1991 census).
Other main town: Charlestown 1200 (1991 census).
Language: English (official).
Religions: Anglican (36%), Methodist (32%).
Education: is compulsory between the ages of five and 17. *Adult literacy:* 98%. *Universities:* one university centre.
Defence: There is a small paramilitary unit in the police force.

Government
The National Assembly consists of 11 members elected by universal adult suffrage for five years and three or four appointed members. The Governor General – the representative of the British Queen as sovereign of St Kitts – appoints a Prime Minister who commands a majority in the Assembly. The PM appoints a Cabinet responsible to the Assembly.
Largest parties: People's Action Movement (PAM), St Kitts Labour Party (SKLP), Nevis Reformation Party (NRP), (Nevis-based) Concerned Citizens' Movement.
Local government: There are no administrative districts on St Kitts; Nevis has its own legislature.
Prime Minister: Kennedy Simmonds (PAM).

Autonomous island
Nevis *Area:* 93 km² (36 sq mi). *Population:* 9100 (1991 census). *Capital:* Charlestown.

Geography
St Kitts and Nevis are two well-watered mountainous islands, set 3 km (2 mi) apart. ***Principal rivers:*** There are many streams, most unnamed. ***Highest point:*** Mount Misery 1156m (3792 ft).
Climate: The moist tropical climate is cooled by sea breezes.

Economy
The economy is based on agriculture (mainly sugar cane) and tourism. ***Currency:*** East Caribbean dollar.

Recent History
In 1882, St Kitts was united with Nevis and the more distant small island of Anguilla in a single British colony, which gained internal self-government in 1967. When Anguilla – a reluctant partner – proclaimed independence, the British intervened, eventually restoring Anguilla to colonial rule, while St Kitts-Nevis progressed to independence in 1983.

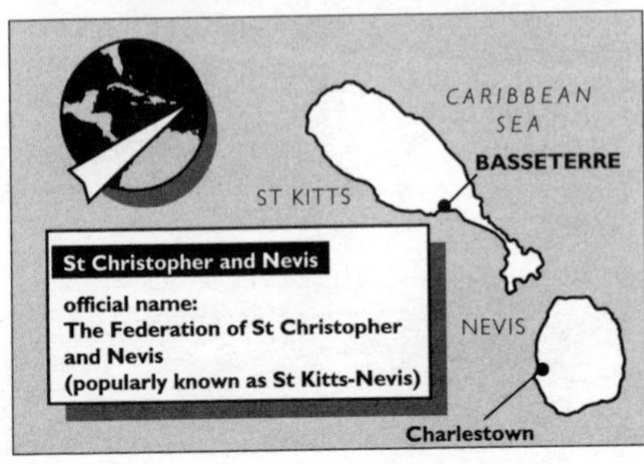

SAINT LUCIA

Member of: UN, Commonwealth, OAS, CARICOM.
Area: 616 km² (238 sq mi).
Population: 136,000 (1993 est).
Capital: Castries 57,000 (city 11,000; 1990 census).
Other main town: Vieux Fort 23,000 (1990 census).
Languages: English (official), French patois (majority).
Religion: Roman Catholic (over 80%).
Education: is compulsory between the ages of five and 15. *Adult literacy:* 85%. *Universities:* one university centre.
Defence: There is a small paramilitary unit in the police force.

Government
The 11-member Senate is appointed. The 17-member House of Assembly is elected by universal adult suffrage for five years. The Governor General – as representative of the British Queen as sovereign of St Lucia – appoints a Prime Minister who commands a majority in the House. The PM, in turn, appoints a Cabinet which is responsible to the House.
Largest parties: United Workers' Party (UWP), Labour Party (SLP).
Local government: eight administrative districts.
Prime Minister: John Compton (UWP).

Geography
St Lucia is a forested mountainous island. ***Principal rivers:*** There are many streams, most unnamed.
Highest point: Mount Gimie 959m (3145 ft).
Climate: St Lucia has a wet tropical climate. There is a dry season from January to April.

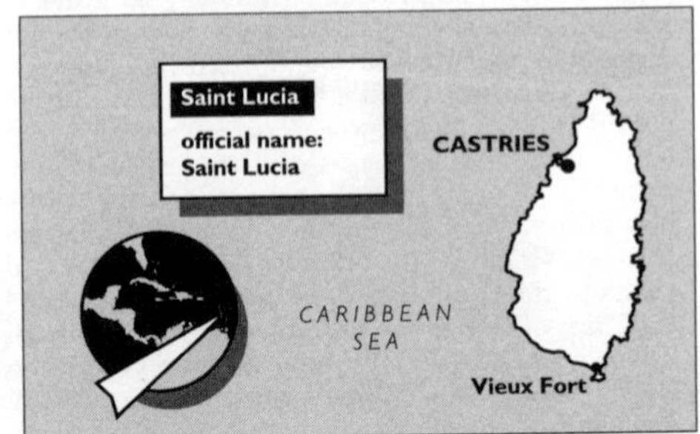

Economy
The economy depends on agriculture, with bananas and coconuts as the main crops. Tourism is the largest single employer on the island. ***Currency:*** East Caribbean dollar.

Recent History
St Lucia was finally confirmed as a British colony in 1814. Internal self-government was achieved in 1967 and independence in 1979.

SAINT VINCENT AND THE GRENADINES

Member of: UN, OAS, Commonwealth, CARICOM.
Area: 389 km² (150 sq mi).
Population: 109,000 (1993 est).
Capital: Kingstown 26,000 (city 15,500; 1991 census).
Language: English (official).
Religions: Anglican (42%), Methodist (21%).
Education: is not compulsory. *Adult literacy:* 85%. *Universities:* none.
Defence: There is a small paramilitary unit in the police force.

Government
The single-chamber House of Assembly consists of six nominated senators and 15 representatives elected for five years by universal adult suffrage. The Governor General – who is the representative of the British Queen as sovereign of St Vincent – appoints a Prime Minister who commands a majority of the representatives. The PM in turn appoints a Cabinet responsible to the House.
Largest parties: New Democratic Party (NDP), Unity Labour Party (ULP).
Local government: five parishes on St Vincent; two districts in the Grenadines.
Prime Minister: James P. Mitchell (NDP).

Geography
The mountainous wooded island of St Vincent rises to Mount Soufrière – an active volcano – at 1234 m (4048 ft). The Grenadines – which include Bequia and Mustique – are a chain of small islands to the south of St Vincent. ***Principal rivers:*** There are many streams, most unnamed. ***Highest point:*** Mount Soufrière 1234m (4048 ft).
Climate: The country experiences a tropical climate with heavy rainfall in the mountains.

Economy
Bananas and arrowroot are the main crops of a largely agricultural economy. Upmarket tourism is being promoted in the Grenadines. ***Currency:*** East Caribbean dollar.

Recent History
The island became a British colony in 1763, gained internal self-government in 1969, and achieved independence in 1979.

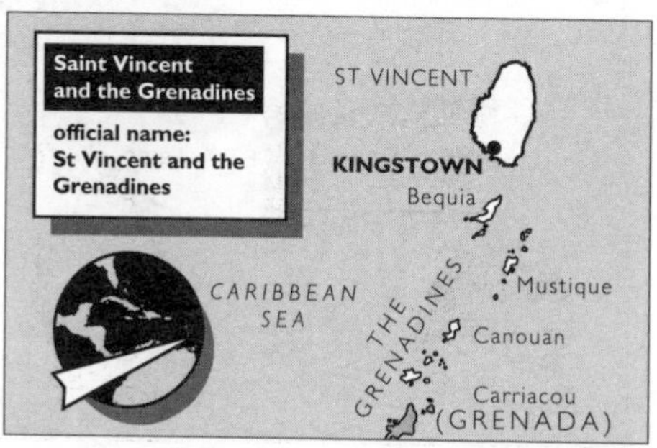

SAN MARINO

Official name: Serenissima Reppublica di San Marino (Most Serene Republic of San Marino).
Member of: UN, OSCE.
Area: 61 km² (23 sq mi).
Population: 24,100 (1993 est).
Capital: San Marino 9000 (city 4200; 1991 est).
Other main town: Serravalle 7300 (1991 est).
Language: Italian (official).
Religion: Roman Catholic (official; 95%).
Education: is compulsory between the ages of six and 13. *Adult literacy:* 98%. *Universities:* none.
Defence: There is a 50-member public security force.

Government
The 60-member Great and General Council is elected by universal adult suffrage for five years. The Council elects two of its members to be Captains-Regent, who jointly hold office as heads of state and of government for six months. The Captains-Regent preside over a 10-member Congress of State – the equivalent of a Cabinet – which is elected by the Council for five years.
Largest parties: (conservative) Christian Democratic Party (PDCS), Socialist Party (PSS), (former Communist) Democratic Progressive Party (PDP), Popular Democratic Alliance (PDA), Democratic Movement (MD), Reformed Communist Party (RC).
Local government: nine districts.
Heads of state: The Captains Regent (see above).

Geography
The country is dominated by the triple limestone peaks of Monte Titano. ***Principal rivers:*** San Marino, Ausa. ***Highest point:*** Monte Titano 739m (2424 ft).
Climate: San Marino has a mild Mediterranean climate.

Economy
Manufacturing and tourism – in particular visitors on excursions – are the mainstays of the economy. ***Currency:*** San Marino uses Italian currency.

Recent History
San Marino retained its autonomy because of its isolation and by playing off powerful neighbours against each other. Its independence was recognized by Napoleon Bonaparte (1797), the Congress of Vienna (1815) and the new Kingdom of Italy (1862). In 1957 a

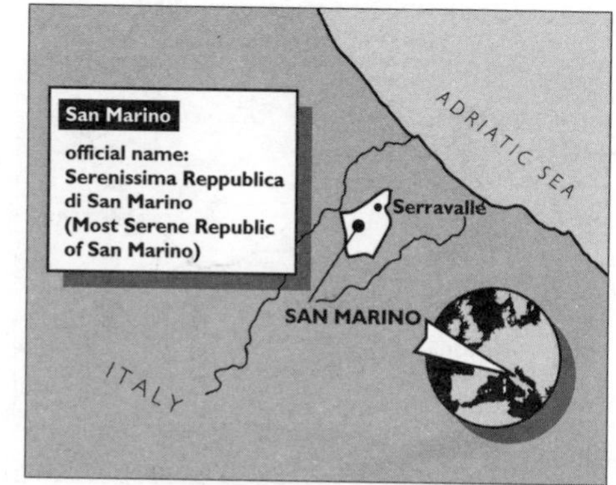

bloodless 'revolution' replaced the Communist-Socialist administration that had been in power since 1945. San Marino is included in the EU/EC by special agreement.

SÃO TOMÉ E PRÍNCIPE

Official name: A República de São Tomé e Príncipe (Republic of São Tomé and Príncipe).
Member of: UN, OAU.
Area: 964 km² (372 sq mi).
Population: 125,000 (1993 est).
Capital: São Tomé 43,000 (1993 est).
Other main town: Trindade 11,400 (1993 est).
Languages: Portuguese (official); Fang (90%).
Religion: Roman Catholic (50%).
Education: is compulsory for four years, to be taken between the ages of seven and 14. *Adult literacy:* 54%. *Universities:* none.
Defence: (1993 figures) *Paramilitary:* 900 personnel.

Government

The 55-member National Assembly is elected by universal adult suffrage for four years. The President – who appoints a Prime Minister and Council of Ministers – is also directly elected for five years.
Largest parties: (moderate) Democratic Convergence Party (PCD), (left-wing former monopoly) Movement or the Liberation of São Tomé and Príncipe (MLSTP), (centrist) Democratic Convergence Party.
Local government: seven districts; Príncipe has autonomy.
President: Miguel Trovoada (PCD).
Prime Minister: Carlos da Graca (PCD).

Autonomous island

Príncipe *Area:* 142 km² (55 sq mi). *Population:* 5600 (1991 census). *Capital:* Santo António.

Geography

The republic consists of two mountainous islands about 144 km (90 mi) apart. ***Principal rivers:*** There are many unnamed streams. ***Highest point:*** Pico de São Tomé 2024m (6640 ft).
Climate: The climate is tropical. A wet season – with heavy rainfall – lasts from October to May.

Economy

Cocoa is the mainstay of a largely agricultural economy. Most of the land is nationalized. ***Currency:*** Dobra.

Recent History

Early in the 20th century, the islands' plantations were notorious for forced labour. Independence from Portugal was gained in 1975 as a one-party socialist state. The Marxist system was abandoned in 1990, and multi-party elections were held in 1991.

SAUDI ARABIA

Official name: Al-Mamlaka al-'Arabiya as-Sa'udiya (The Kingdom of Saudi Arabia).
Member of: UN, Arab League, OPEC, GCC.
Area: 2,240,000 km² (864,869 sq mi).
Population: 17,420,000 (1993 est).
Capital: Riyadh (Ar Riyad) 2,000,000 (including suburbs; 1986 est).
Other major cities: Jeddah (Jiddah) 1,400,000, Mecca (Makkah) 620,000, Medina (Al-Madinah) 500,000, Taif 205,000, Buraida 185,000, Abha 155,000 (all including suburbs; 1986 est).
Language: Arabic (official).
Religion: Islam (official) – Sunni (mainly Wahhabi) 92%, Shia 8%.
Education: is not compulsory. *Adult literacy:* 62%. *Universities:* seven.
Defence: (1993 figures) *Army:* 72,000 personnel. *Air force:* 18,000. *Navy:* 11,000. *Paramilitary:* 5700. *Conscription:* none.

Government

Saudi Arabia is an absolute monarchy. . The King appoints a Council of Ministers and a 60-member consultative Council to hold office for four years.
Largest parties: There are no political parties.
Local government: 13 provinces.
Sovereign: HM King Fahd ibn Abdul Aziz Al Saud (succeeded upon the death of his brother, 13 May 1982). (In Saudi Arabia, the formal title of the King is 'Custodian of the Two Holy Mosques'.)
Prime Minister: The King.

Geography

Over 95% of the country is desert, including the Rub 'al-Khali ('The Empty Quarter') – the largest expanse of sand in the world. The Arabian plateau ends in the west in a steep escarpment overlooking a coastal plain beside the Red Sea. ***Principal rivers:*** There are no permanent streams. ***Highest point:*** Jebel Razikh 3658m (12,002).
Climate: The country is very hot – with temperatures up to 54 °C (129 °F). The average rainfall is 100 mm (4 in), but many areas receive far less and may not experience any precipitation for years.

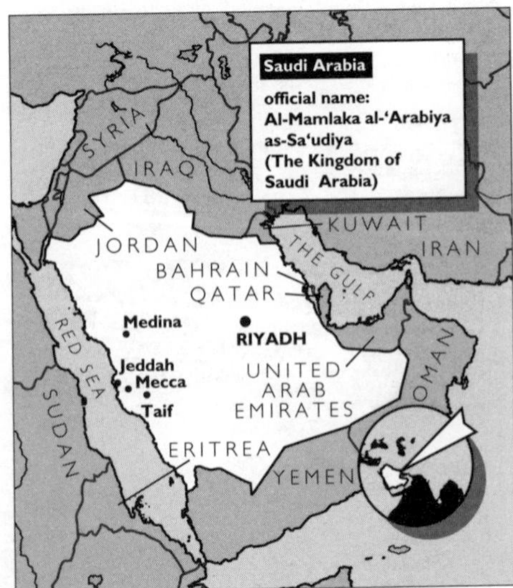

Economy

Saudi Arabia's spectacular development and present prosperity are based almost entirely upon exploiting vast reserves of petroleum and natural gas. Industries include petroleum refining, petrochemicals and fertilizers. The country has developed major banking and commercial interests. Less than 1% of the land can be cultivated. ***Currency:*** Rial.

Recent History

In 1744 a Muslim preacher – Muhammad ibn abd al-Wahhab – and the ancestor of the country's present rulers, the Saudis, formed an alliance that was to spearhead the Wahhabi political-religious campaign. In the 20th century the Wahhabis united most of Arabia under Ibn Saud (1882–1953). In 1902 Ibn Saud took Riyadh and in 1906 defeated his rivals to control central Arabia (Nejd). Between 1912 and 1927 he added the east, the southwest (Asir) and the area around Mecca (Hejaz). In 1932 these lands became the kingdom of Saudi Arabia. Although the country has been pro-Western, after the 1973 Arab-Israeli War, Saudi Arabia put pressure on the USA to encourage Israel to withdraw from the occupied territories of Palestine by cutting oil production. Saudi Arabia has not escaped problems caused by religious fundamentalism and the rivalry between Sunni and Shia Islam. Saudi Arabia found itself bound to support Iraq in its war with Shiite Iran (1980), but played a major role in the coalition against Iraq in the Gulf War (1991). In the early 1990s fundamentalist and liberal opposition to the Saudi government increased.

SENEGAL

Official name: La République du Sénégal (The Republic of Senegal).
Member of: UN, OAU, ECOWAS.
Area: 196,722 km² (75,954 sq mi).
Population: 7,900,000 (1993 est).
Capital: Dakar 1,730,000 (1992 est).
Other major cities: Thiès 201,000, Kaolack 180,000, St Louis 180,000, Ziguinchor 150,000 (1988 est).
Languages: French (official), Wolof (36%), Serer (19%).
Religions: Sunni Islam (94%), Roman Catholic.
Education: is compulsory, in theory, between the ages of seven and 13. *Adult literacy:* 29%. *Universities:* two.
Defence: (1993 figures) *Army:* 8500 personnel. *Air force:* 600. *Navy:* 700. *Conscription:* two years; selective.

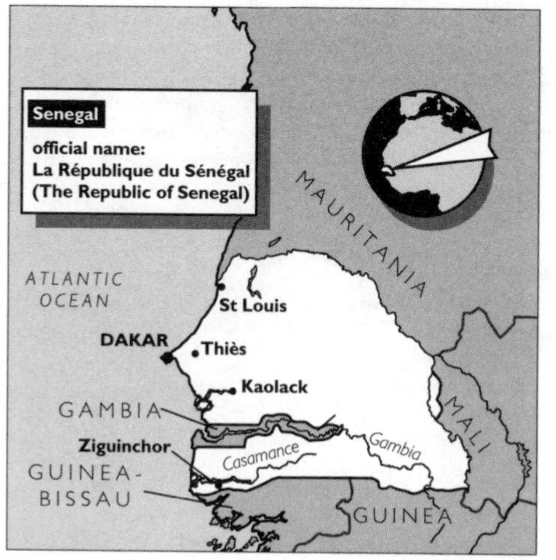

Government

Every five years the 120-member National Assembly is elected by universal adult suffrage. The Assembly comprises 60 members elected from single member constituencies and 60 members elected nationally by proportional representation. The President, who is directly elected for a maximum of two seven-year terms, appoints and leads a Cabinet which includes a Prime Minister.

Largest parties: Socialist Party (PS), (liberal) Democratic Party (PDS), (coalition) Jappoo Liggeenyal, Democratic League and Movement for the Labour Party.
Local government: 10 regions.
President: Abdou Diouf (PS).
Prime Minister: Habib Thiam (PS).

Geography

Senegal is mostly low-lying and covered by savannah. The Fouta Djallon mountains occupy the south. The Gambia forms a long finger of territory that almost divides Senegal in two. ***Principal river:*** Sénégal, gambia (Gambie), Saloum, Casamance. ***Highest point:*** Fouta Djallon 500m (1640 ft.).
Climate: Senegal has a tropical climate with a dry season from October to June.

Economy

Agriculture involves over 75% of the labour force. Groundnuts and cotton are grown as cash crops, and rice, maize, millet and sorghum as subsistence crops. The manufacturing sector is one of the largest in West Africa, but unemployment is a major problem. ***Currency:*** CFA franc.

Recent History

A national political awareness developed in the French colony of Senegal in the early 20th century, and the country contributed substantially to the nationalist awakening in French Africa. After independence in 1960, under the poet Léopold Sedar Senghor (1906–), Senegal maintained close relations with France, and received substantial aid. Attempted federations with Mali (1959–60) and Gambia (1981–89) were unsuccessful. Senghor retired in 1980, having re-introduced party politics.

SEYCHELLES

Official name: The Republic of Seychelles.
Member of: UN, OAU, Commonwealth.
Area: 455 km² (176 sq mi).
Population: 71,000 (1993 est).
Capital: Victoria 24,000 (1987 est).
Languages: Creole (95%), English, French – all official.
Religions: Roman Catholic (92%), Anglican.
Education: is compulsory between the ages of six and 15. *Adult literacy:* 84%. *Universities:* one polytechnic.
Defence: (1993 figures) *Army:* 1100 personnel. *Paramilitary:* 1000. *Conscription:* two years.

Government

The President – who appoints a Council of Ministers – and the 33-member National Assembly are elected for five years by universal adult suffrage. The National Assembly comprises 22 members elected

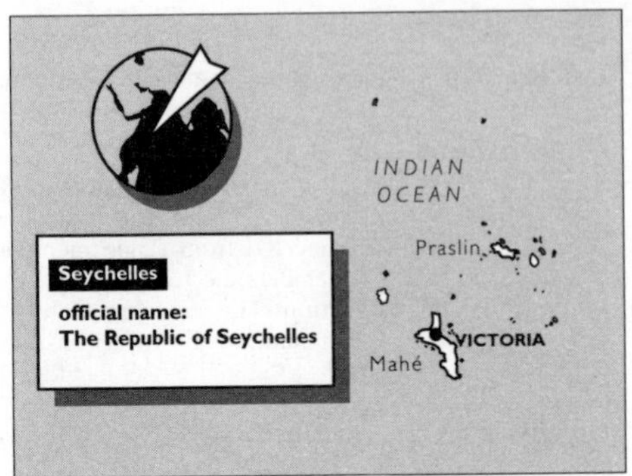

from constituencies and 11 members elected nationally under a system of proportional representation.
Largest parties: (former monopoly socialist) Seychelles People's Progressive Party (SPPP), (conservative) Democratic Party (DPS), (coalition) United Opposition.
Local government: five island groups (but these do not have elected councils).
President: France Albert René (SPPP).

Geography

The Seychelles consist of 40 mountainous granitic islands and just over 50 smaller coral islands. ***Principal rivers:*** There are no significant rivers. ***Highest point:*** Morne Seychellois 906m (2972 ft). ***Climate:*** The islands have a pleasant tropical maritime climate with heavy rainfall.

Economy

The economy depends heavily on tourism, which employs about one third of the labour force. Fishing has expanded, and tuna and prawns are major exports. ***Currency:*** Seychelles rupee.

Recent History

The islands were a Brtish colony before independence in 1976. The PM – France Albert René – led a coup against President James Mancham in 1977, and established a one-party socialist state. Attempts to overthrow René, including one involving South African mercenaries (1981), were unsuccessful. Multiparty elections were held in 1992.

SIERRA LEONE

Official name: The Republic of Sierra Leone.
Member of: UN, OAU, Commonwealth, ECOWAS.

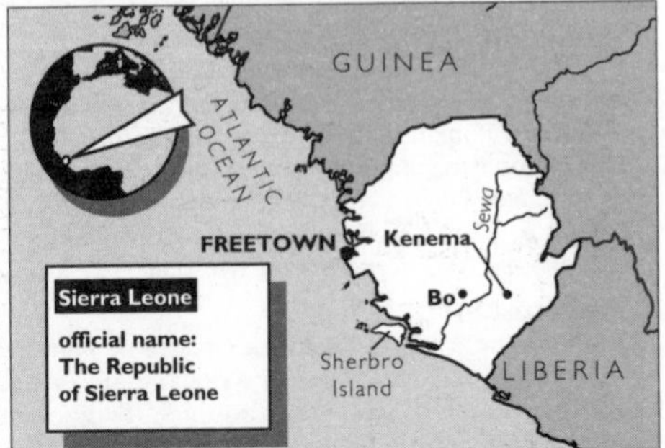

Area: 71,740 km² (27,699 sq mi).
Population: 4,490,000 (1993 est).
Capital: Freetown 550,000 (city 470,000; Koidu 80,000; 1985 census).
Other main city: Bo 26,000 (1985 census).
Languages: English (official), Krio, Mende (34%), Temne (31%).
Religions: animist (52%), Sunni Islam (39%).
Education: is not compulsory. *Adult literacy:* 21%. *Universities:* one.
Defence: (1993 figures) *Army:* 6000 personnel. *Navy:* 150. *Conscription:* none.

Government

There is constitutional provision for a President – who appoints a Cabinet – to be elected for seven years by universal adult suffrage and for a 124-member House of Representatives to be directly elected for five years. Power is currently exercised by a military council.
Largest parties: Although a return to multi-party rule has been agreed, in principal, no parties are currently operating.
Local government: four regions divided into 12 districts.
Head of state (Chairman of the National Provisional Ruling Council): Capt. Valentine Strasser.

Geography

The savannah interior comprises plateaux and mountain ranges rising to Bintimani Peak. The swampy coastal plain is forested. ***Principal rivers:*** Great Scarcies, Little Scarcies, Rokel, Wanje, Moa, Sewa. ***Highest point:*** Bintimani Peak 1948m (6390 ft). ***Climate:*** The climate is tropical with a dry season from November to June.

Economy

Subsistence farming – mainly rice – involves the majority of the labour force. Rutile, bauxite and cocoa are major exports. Unrest and the decline of diamond mining have added to severe economic problems, and by 1995 much of the infrastructure of the country had been destroyed. ***Currency:*** Leone.

Recent History

Freetown, a settlement for former slaves, became a British colony in 1808. The interior was added in 1896. Independence was gained in 1961. A disputed election led to army intervention (1967), and Dr Siaka Stevens – who came to power in a coup in 1968 – introduced a one-party state. A military junta seized power in 1992, but the country gradually collapsed into anarchy. By 1995, a guerrilla movement controlled part of the south and east, and law-and-order had broken down in much of the country.

SINGAPORE

Official name: Hsing-chia p'o Kung-ho Kuo (Chinese) or Republik Singapura (Malay) or Republic of Singapore.
Member of: UN, ASEAN, Commonwealth, Apec.
Area: 639 km² (247 sq mi).
Population: 2,876,000 (1993 est).
Capital: Singapore 2,876,000 (1993 est).
Languages: Chinese (77%), Malay (14%), Tamil (5%), English – all official.
Religions: Buddhist and Daoist (54%), Sunni Islam

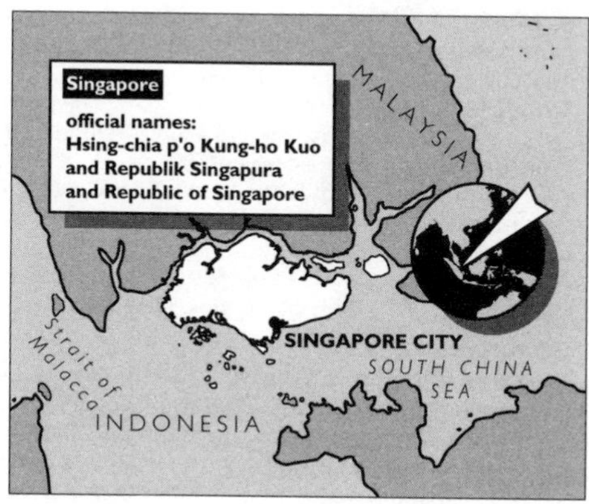

(15%), various Christian Churches (13%), Hinduism.
Education: is compulsory between the ages of six and 16. *Adult literacy:* 91%. *Universities:* two.
Defence: (1993 figures) *Army:* 45,000 personnel. *Air force:* 6000. *Navy:* 4500. *Paramilitary:* 11,600. *Conscription:* two years.

Government

The 81 members of Parliament are elected from single- and multi-member constituencies by universal adult suffrage for five years. The President – who is elected by Parliament for four years – appoints a Prime Minister who commands a parliamentary majority. The PM, in turn, appoints a Cabinet which is responsible to Parliament. The constitution is to be revised in 1995 to create an executive presidency.
Largest parties: People's Action Party (PAP), Singapore Democratic Party (SDP), Workers' Party (WP).
Local government: There are no administrative divisions.
President: Ong Teng Cheong (PAP).
Prime Minister: Goh Chok Tong (PAP).

Geography

Singapore is a low-lying island – with 56 islets – joined to the Malay peninsula by causeway. ***Principal rivers:*** Seletar, Kalang. ***Highest point:*** Bukit Timah 177m (581 ft).
Climate: The climate is tropical with monsoon rains from December to March.

Economy

Singapore relies on imports for its flourishing manufacturing industries (electronics, oil refining, rubber processing, food processing) and entrepôt trade. Finance and tourism are important. Singapore has the second highest standard of living in Asia. ***Currency:*** Singaporean dollar.

Recent History

The city of Singapore was revived by Sir Stamford Raffles for the British East India Company (1819), and developed rapidly as a port for shipping Malaya's tin and rubber. It acquired a cosmopolitan population and became a strategic British base. Occupied by the Japanese (1942–45), it achieved self-government (1959), and joined (1963) and left (1965) the Federation of Malaysia. After independence it became wealthy under the strong rule of Prime Minister Lee Kuan Yew (1923– ; PM 1965–91).

SLOVAKIA

Official name: Republika Slovenská (Slovak Republic).
Member of: UN, CEFTA, OSCE.
Area: 49,036 km² (18,933 sq mi).
Population: 5,330,000 (1993 est).
Capital: Bratislava 447,000 (including suburbs; 1992 est).
Other major cities: Kosice 237,000, Nitra 91,000, Presov 90,000, Banská Bystrica 86,000, Zilina 85,000 (including suburbs; 1992 est).
Languages: Slovak (87%), Hungarian (12%).
Religions: Roman Catholic (60%), Evangelical Churches (6%).
Education: is compulsory between the ages of six and 15. *Adult literacy:* virtually 100%. *Universities:* three, plus seven other institutions of university status.
Defence: (1993 figures) *Army:* 33,000 personnel. *Air force:* 14,000. *Paramilitary:* 4000. *Conscription:* 12 months.

Government

The 150-member Assembly is elected under a system of proportional representation by universal adult suffrage for four years. The Assembly elects a President for a five-year term. The President appoints a Prime Minister and a Council of Ministers, responsible to the Assembly.
Largest parties: (socialist nationalist) Movement for a Democratic Slovakia (HZDS), (former Communist) Party of the Democratic Left (SDL), (centre) Christian Democratic Movement (KDH), (left-wing) Union of Slovak Workers (ZRS), National Democratic Party (NDS), (reformist) Democratic Union (DU), (right-wing) Slovak National Party (SNS), MKDH-ESWS (an electoral alliance of ethnic Hungarian parties).
Local government: 38 districts grouped into three regions and the capital.
President: Michal Kovac (HZDS).
Prime Minister: Vladimir Meciar (HZDS).

Geography

Slovakia mainly comprises mountain ranges, including the Tatra Mountainson the Polish border. The only significant lowlands are in the south adjoining the River Danube. ***Principal rivers:*** Danube, Vah, Hron, Nitra. ***Highest point:*** Gerlachovka 2655m (8711 ft).
Climate: The climate is continental with warm, relatively dry, summers and cold winters.

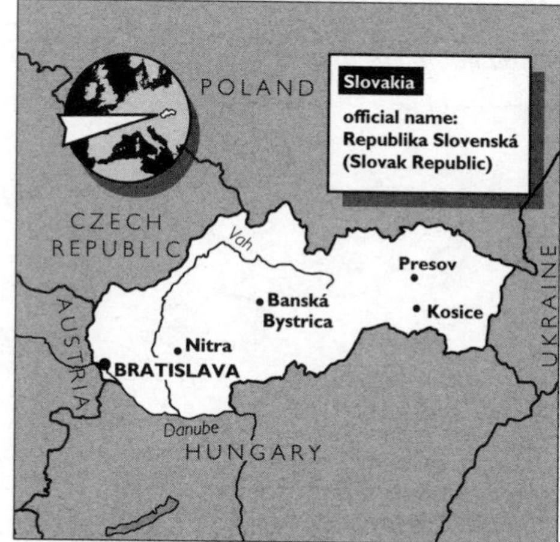

Economy

Slovakia has a mainly agricultural economy into which heavy industry – particularly steel and chemicals – was introduced when the country was part of Communist Czechoslovakia. Wheat, maize, potatoes, barley and sheep are important. Varied natural resources include iron ore and brown coal. At the dissolution of Czechoslovakia about two-thirds of Slovak industry was privatized, but independent Slovakia has slowed the privatization of its uncompetitive out-of-date factories. ***Currency:*** Slovakian koruna.

Recent History

Slovak nationalism grew in the 19th century and increased Magyarization under the Austro-Hungarian Dual Monarchy (1867–1918) was greatly resented. On the collapse of the Habsburg Empire (1918), the Slovaks joined the Czechs to form Czechoslovakia. When Hitler's Germany dismembered Czechoslovakia in 1938, Slovakia became an Axis puppet state. A popular revolt against German rule (the Slovak Uprising) took place in 1944. Following liberation (1945) Czechoslovakia was re-established. After the Communist takeover in 1948, heavy industry was introduced into rural Slovakia. In 1968, moves by Party Secretary Alexander Dubcek (a Slovak) to introduce political reforms met with Soviet disapproval, and invasion by Czechoslovakia's Warsaw Pact allies. The conservative wing of the Communist party regained control until 1989, when student demonstrations developed into a peaceful revolution. The Communist Party renounced its leading role. A new government, in which Communists were in a minority, was appointed. In 1990 free multi-party elections were held, Soviet troops were withdrawn and the foundations of a market economy were laid, but the pace of economic reform brought distress to Slovakia, whose old-fashioned industries were ill-equipped to face competition. Increased Slovak separatism led to the division of the country in 1993. Independent Slovakia faces possible tension concerning a large Hungarian minority. Slovakia has achieved associate status of the EU/EC and aspires to full membership.

SLOVENIA

Official name: Republika Slovenija (The Republic of Slovenia).
Member of: UN, OSCE.
Area: 20,256 km² (7821 sq mi).
Population: 1,997,000 (1993 est).

Capital: Ljubljana 323,000 (city 28,900; 1991 census).
Other major cities: Maribor 153,000 (city 104,000), Celj 41,000, Kranj 36,000 (1991 census).
Languages: Slovene (91% as a first language; official), with Serb, Croat, Italian and Magyar minorities.
Religion: Roman Catholic (over 60%).
Education: is compulsory between the ages of seven and 15. *Adult literacy:* over 99%. *Universities:* two, plus a university institute.
Defence: (1993 figures) *Army:* 15,000 personnel. *Paramilitary:* 4500. *Conscription:* seven months.

Government

The 90-member National Assembly and a President – who appoints a Prime Minister and Cabinet – are directly elected by universal adult suffrage for four years. The Assembly comprises 38 members elected by single-member constituencies, 50 members elected nationally under a system of proportional representation and one member elected by each of the national minorities (Italian and Hungarian).
Largest parties: (centrist) Liberal Democratic Party (LDS), Slovenian Christian Democrats (SKD), Associated List of Social Democrats (ZLSD), (agrarian) Slovenian People's Party, (centrist) Democratic Party, (right-wing) Slovenian National Party (SNS), Independent SNS Deputy Group, Greens (Eco), Social Democratic Party of Slovenia (SDSS).
Local government: 38 districts.
President: Milan Kucan.
Prime Minister: Dr Janez Drnovsek (LDS).

Geography

Most of Slovenia comprises mountains, including the Karawanken and Julian Alps in the northwest and the Dinaric Alps in the west. In the east, hill country adjoins the Drava valley; in the southwest, Slovenia has a very short Adriatic coastline. ***Principal rivers:*** Drava, Mura, Savinja, Sava. ***Highest point:*** Triglav 2864m (9396 ft),
Climate: The south and west have a Mediterranean climate; the north and east are more continental. Rainfall is heavy in the mountains.

Economy

With a standard of living approaching that of West European countries, Slovenia was the most industrialized and economically developed part of Yugoslavia. Industries include iron and steel, textiles and coal mining. Agriculture specializes in livestock and fodder crops. Forestry is important. Privatization of agriculture and industry was completed by 1995. Slovenia has not suffered the severe economic decline that has characterized other former Yugoslav republics. ***Currency:*** Tolar.

Recent History

Slovenia was under (Austrian) Habsburg rule almost continuously for 600 years until 1918, but retained their national identity. The 19th century saw a Slovene national revival, and, when the Habsburg Empire collapsed (1918), the Slovenes joined the Serbs, Croats and Montenegrins in the new state that was renamed Yugoslavia in 1929. When Yugoslavia became a Communist federal state in 1945, the Slovene lands were reorganized as the republic of Slovenia. After the death of Yugoslav President Tito (1980), the federation faltered in nationalist crises. Slovenia, the wealthiest part of Yugoslavia, edged towards democracy. In free elections in 1990, nationalists gained a majority in the

Slovene Assembly, which declared independence in June 1991. Following reverses in a short campaign, Yugoslav federal forces were withdrawn from Slovenia, whose independence gained international recognition in 1992. Slovenia has become an associate member of the EU/EC.

SOLOMON ISLANDS

Official name: Solomon Islands.
Member of: UN, Commonwealth.
Area: 28,370 km² (10,954 sq mi).
Population: 349,000 (1993 est).
Capital: Honiara 37,000 (1991 est).
Other main town: Gizo 3700 (1991 est).
Languages: English (official), Pidgin English, over 85 local (mainly Melanesian) languages.
Religions: Anglican (34%), Roman Catholic (19%), other Christian Churches.
Education: is not compulsory. *Adult literacy:* 54%. *Universities:* one university centre.
Defence: There are no armed forces.

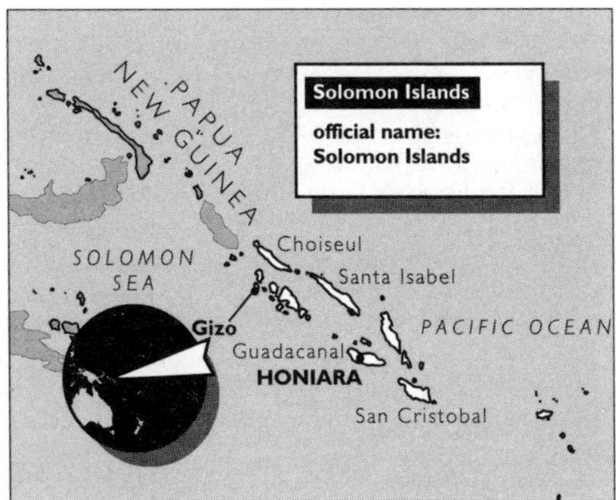

Government

The 47-member National Parliament – which is elected by universal adult suffrage for four years – elects a Prime Minister who appoints a Cabinet. A Governor General is the representative of the British Queen as sovereign of the islands. A federal republican constitution is to be adopted.
Largest parties: Group for National Unity (GNUR), People's Alliance Party (PAP), National Action Party (NAP), Labour Party, United Party (UP), Christian Fellowship Group, National Front for Progress.
Prime Minister: Francis Billy Hilly (non-party).

Geography

The principal islands of mountainous volcanic Solomons form a parallel double chain of islands. The smaller islands are atolls. ***Principal rivers:*** There are many streams, most of which are unnamed. ***Highest point:*** Mount Makarakomburu 2447m (8028 ft).
Climate: The climate is tropical with temperature and rainfall maximums from November to April.

Economy

Most of the labour force is involved in subsistence farming, although copra and cocoa are exported. Fishing is a major industry. ***Currency:*** Solomon Islands dollar.

Recent History

The islanders were exploited as a workforce for plantations in other Pacific islands before Britain established a protectorate in 1893. Occupied by the Japanese (1942–45), the Solomons were the scene of fierce fighting, including a major battle for Guadalcanal (see p. 445). Independence was gained in 1978.

SOMALIA

Official name: Soomaaliya (Somalia).
Member of: UN, Arab League, OAU.
Area: 637,657 km² (246,201 sq mi).
Population: 8,050,000 (1991 est); up to 1,000,000 Somalis are refugees in surrounding countries.
Capital: Mogadishu 1,000,000 (1986 est).
Other major cities: Hargeisa 400,000, Baidoa 300,000, Burao 300,000 (1986 est).
Languages: Somali (national), Arabic (official).
Religion: Sunni Islam (official).
Education: is compulsory, in theory, between the ages of six and 14. *Adult literacy:* 24%. *Universities:* one (closed since 1991).
Defence: Since 1991 there have been no national armed forces.

Government

The most recent constitution provides for the election of a 171-member Assembly and a President by universal adult suffrage. Since 1991 there has been no effective government.
Largest parties: There are currently no political parties, but many factions compete for power.
Local government: (in theory) 16 regions.
Head of state: none.

Geography

Somalia occupies the 'Horn of Africa'. Low-lying plains cover most of the south, while semi-arid mountains occupy the north. ***Principal rivers:*** Juba, Shebelle (Shebeli). ***Highest point:*** Surud Ad 2408m (7900 ft).
Climate: Somalia is hot and largely dry with rainfall totals in the north as low as 330 mm (13 in).

Economy

Nearly two thirds of the labour force are nomadic herdsmen or subsistence farmers. Bananas are grown for export in the south, but much of the country suffers drought. As a result of the civil war since 1991,

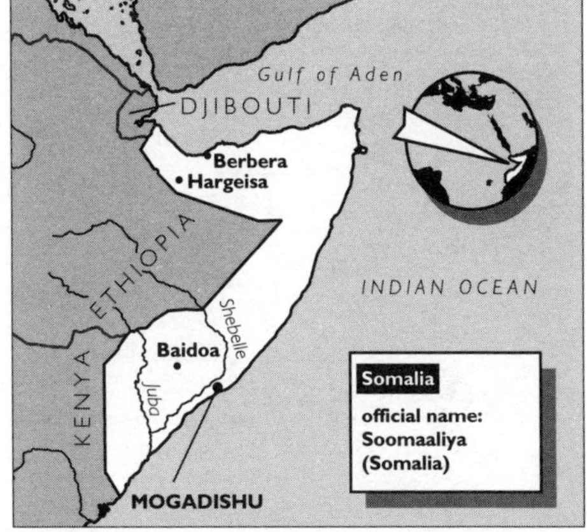

much of the economic infrastructure of the country has been destroyed and widespread famine has occurred. ***Currency:*** Somali shilling.

Recent History

In 1886 Britain established a protectorate in the north of the region, while the Italians took the south. In World War II the Italians briefly occupied British Somaliland. In 1960 the British and Italian territories were united as an independent Somalia. In 1969 the president was assassinated and the army – under Major-General Muhammad Siad Barre – seized control. Barre's socialist Islamic Somalia became an ally of the USSR. In 1977 Somali guerrillas, with Somali military support, drove the Ethiopians out of the largely Somali-inhabited Ogaden. Somalia's Soviet alliance was ended when the USSR supported Ethiopia to regain the Ogaden. Barre was overthrown in 1991. Since 1991 the infrastructure of Somalia has collapsed in bitter civil war between several factions and the former British north has attempted to secede. In 1992, a US-led UN force intervened to relieve famine victims, but UN involvement ended in 1995 with the conflict between various Somali clans and warlords no nearer solution.

SOUTH AFRICA

Official names: Republic of South Africa and Republiek van Suid-Afrika.
Member of: UN, OAU, Commonwealth.
Area: 1,223,201 km² (433,246 sq mi).
Population: 40,716,000 (1993 est).
Capital: Pretoria (administrative capital) 1,000,000 (1993 est) (city 443,000; 1985 census), Cape Town (legislative capital) 2,320,000 (1993 est) (city 777,000; 1985 census)
Other major cities: Johannesburg 4,000,000 (city proper 632,000; 'Greater Johannesburg' 1,609,000; Soweto 1,000,000, Sasolburg 540,000; Vereeniging 540,000), Durban 1,190,000 (city 634,000), Port Elizabeth 790,000 (city 273,000), Bloemfontein (judicial capital) 250,000 (city 104,000) (agglomerations 1993 est; cities 1985 census).

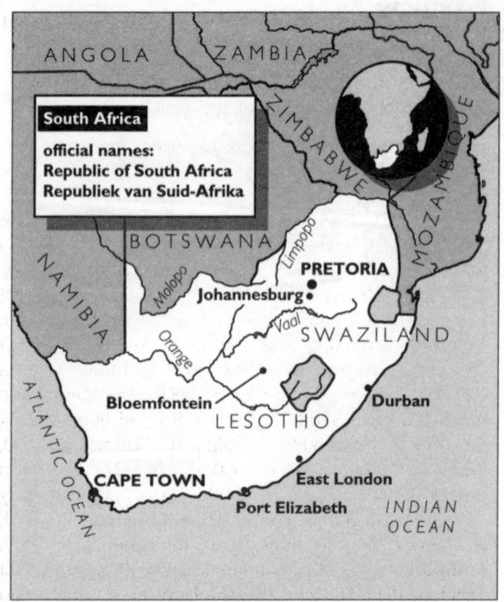

Languages: Xhosa (21%), Zulu (16%), English, Afrikaans, Sesotho, North Sotho, Tswana, Swazi, Ndebele, Venda, Tsonga – all official.
Religions: independent Black Churches (22%), Afrikaans Reformed (12%), Roman Catholic (8%), Methodist (6%), with Anglican, Hindu and Sunni Islam minorities.
Education: is compulsory between the ages of seven and 16. *Adult literacy:* 77%. *Universities:* 21.
Defence: (1993 figures) *Army:* 47,000 personnel. *Air force:* 10,000. *Navy:* 4500. *Others:* 6000. *Conscription:* none.

Government

The Constitutional Assembly – which is scheduled to draft and agree a final constitution within two years – comprises a Senate (upper house) and a National Assembly (lower house). The 90-member Senate comprises ten senators appointed from each of the nine provinces in proportion to the number of votes each party receives in that province. The 400-member National Assembly comprises 200 members elected by universal adult suffrage from constituencies and 200 members elected according to a system of proportional representation from the nine provinces. A President and two Vice-Presidents are elected by the Assembly. A Cabinet of National Unity is responsible to the Assembly.
Largest parties: African National Congress (ANC), (conservative, formerly white) National Party (NP), (mainly Zulu) Inkatha Freedom Party (IFP), (white right-wing) Freedom Front (FF), (liberal) Democratic Party (DP), (nationalist) Pan African Congress, African Christian Democratic Front.
Local government: nine provinces form a quasi-federal system.
President : Nelson Mandela (ANC).

Provinces

Eastern Cape *Area:* 170,616 km² (65,875 sq mi). *Population:* 6,665,000 (1993 est). *Capital:* King William's Town.
Eastern Transvaal *Area:* 81,816 km² (39,736 sq mi). *Population:* 2,838,000 (1993 est). *Capital:* Nelspruit.
Gauteng (formerly Pretoria-Witwatersrand Area) *Area:* 18,760 km² (7243 sq mi). *Population:* 6,847,000 (1993 est). *Capital:* Johannesburg (Pretoria is co-capital).
Kwazulu/Natal *Area:* 91,481 km² (35,321 sq mi). *Population:* 8,549,000 (1993 est). *Capital:* Pietermaritzburg. (Ulundi is co-capital).
Northern Cape *Area:* 363,389 km² (140,305 sq mi). *Population:* 764,000 (1993 est). *Capital:* Kimberley.
Northern Transvaal *Area:* 119,606 km² (46,180 sq mi). *Population:* 5,121,000 (1993 est). *Capital:* Pietersburg.
North West Province *Area:* 118,710 km² (45,834 sq mi). *Population:* 3,507,000 (1993 est). *Capital:* Mmbatho.
Orange Free State *Area:* 129,437 km² (49,976 sq mi). *Population:* 2,805,000 (1993 est). *Capital:* Bloemfontein.
Western Cape *Area:* 129,386 km² (49,956 sq mi). *Population:* 3,620,000 (1993 est). *Capital:* Cape Town.

Geography

The Great Escarpment rises behind a discontinuous coastal plain and includes the Drakensberg Mountains. A vast plateau occupies the interior, undulating in the

west and rising to over 2400m (about 8000 ft) in the east. Much of the west is semi-desert, while the east is predominantly savannah grassland (veld). ***Principal rivers:*** Orange (Oranje), Limpopo, Vaal, Caledon, Olifants, Marico, Sand. ***Highest point:*** Injasuti 3408m (11,182 ft).
Climate: South Africa has a subtropical climate with considerable regional variations. The hottest period is between December and February. Rainfall is highest on the east coast, but much of the country is dry.

Economy

The country is the world's leading exporter of gold – which normally forms about 40% of South African exports – and a major producer of uranium, diamonds, chromite, antimony, platinum and coal (which meets three quarters of the country's energy needs). Industry includes chemicals, food processing, textiles, motor vehicles and electrical engineering. Agriculture supplies one third of South Africa's exports, including fruit, wine, wool and maize. The highest standard of living in Africa is very unevenly distributed between Whites and Non-whites. The withdrawal of some foreign investors in the 1970s and 1980s increased the drive towards self-sufficiency. The new South Africa is experiencing an economic recovery. ***Currency:*** Rand.

Recent History

Britain acquired the Cape (1814), abolished slavery (1833), and annexed Natal (1843). The Boers (or Afrikaners) – of Dutch and French Huguenot descent – moved inland on the Great Trek (1835–37) to found the republics of the Transvaal and Orange Free State. After the discovery of diamonds (1867) and gold (1886), the Boers – led by Paul Kruger (1825–1904), president of the Transvaal – resisted British attempts to annex their republics in which British settlers were denied political rights. This culminated in the Boer War (1899–1902). Despite their military superiority, the British initially suffered defeats and were beseiged in a number of towns, including Mafeking and Ladysmith. In 1900 the Boers were beaten in the field but began guerrilla action. The British responded by interning the families of the guerrillas, and more than 20,000 Boer women and children died of disease in internment camps. Although they lost the war, the Afrikaners were politically dominant when the Union of South Africa was formed (1910). The creation of the African National Congress (ANC) in 1912 was a protest against White supremacy, and by the 1920s Black industrial protest was widespread. South Africa entered World War I as a British ally, taking German South West Africa (Namibia) after a short campaign (1914–15) – after the war, the territory came under South African administration. Despite strong Afrikaner opposition, South Africa – under General Jan Christiaan Smuts (1870–1950; PM 1919–24 and 1939–48) – joined the Allied cause in World War II.

After the Afrikaner National Party came to power (1948), racial segregation was increased by the policy of apartheid ('separate development'), which deprived Blacks of civil rights, segregated facilities (such as schools and hospitals) and areas of residence by race, and confined black political rights to restricted homelands ('Bantustans'). Black opposition was crushed following a massacre of demonstrators at Sharpeville, and the ANC was banned (1960) by the government of Hendrik Verwoerd (1901–66; PM 1958–66, when he was assassinated). International pressure against apartheid increased. In 1961 South Africa left the Commonwealth, the majority of whose members continue to press for economic sanctions against South Africa. In 1966 the UN cancelled South Africa's trusteeship of South West Africa (Namibia), but South Africa continued to block the territory's progress to independence.

Black opposition revived in the 1970s and 1980s and found expression in strikes, the Soweto uprising of 1976, sabotage and the rise of the Black consciousness movement. South African troops intervened in the civil war in Angola against the Marxist-Leninist government (1981) and were active in Namibia against SWAPO nationalist guerrillas. P.W. Botha (1916– ; PM 1978–1984 and president 1984–89) granted political rights to the Coloured and Indian communities, and implemented minor reforms for Blacks. However, in 1986 – in the face of continuing unrest – Botha introduced a state of emergency, under which the press was strictly censored, the meetings of many organizations were banned and the number of political detainees – including children – rose sharply. His successor F.W. de Klerk released some ANC prisoners, promised further reforms and agreed to UN-supervised elections in Namibia leading to independence for that territory.

In 1990 de Klerk lifted the ban on the ANC and released its imprisoned leader Nelson Mandela (1918–). In 1990–91, negotiations between the government and Black leaders led to the dismantling of the legal structures of apartheid. Fighting between (mainly Xhosa) ANC and (mainly Zulu) Inkatha supporters in Black townships caused concern, but a new constitution was agreed and the 'homelands' were reabsorbed into South Africa. The first multi-racial elections in South Africa were held in March 1994. Mandela was elected President and a multi-party multi-racial Cabinet of National Unity was formed. South Africa has since joined the OAU and rejoined the Commonwealth.

SPAIN

Official name: Reino de España (Kingdom of Spain).
Member of: UN, NATO, EU/EC, OECD, OSCE, WEU.
Area: 504,782 km² (194,897 sq mi) including the Canary Islands, Ceuta and Melilla.
Population: 39,952,000 (1991 census).
Capital: Madrid 4,846,000 (city 3,121,000; Móstoles 193,000; Leganés 173,000; Alcalá de Henares 159,000; Fuenlabrada 145,000; Alcorcon 140,000, Getafe 139,000; 1991 census).
Other major cities: Barcelona 3,400,000 (city 1,707,000; L'Hospitalet 269,000; Badalona 206,000; Sabadell 184,000; Santa Coloma de Gramanet 132,000), Valencia 1,060,000 (city 777,000), Seville (Sevilla) 754,000 (city 684,000), Zaragoza 614,000, Málaga 525,000, Bilbao 477,000 (city 372,000), Las Palmas (de Gran Canaria) 348,000, Valladolid 345,000, Murcia 329,000, Córdoba 309,000, Palma de Mallorca 309,000, Granada 287,000, Vigo 277,000, Alicante 271,000, Gijón 260,000, La Coruña 251,000, Cádiz 240,000 (city 157,000), Vitoria (Gasteiz) 209,000, Oviedo 203,000, Santander 194,000, Santa Cruz de Tenerife 192,000, Pamplona 191,000, Salamanca 186,000, Jérez de la Frontera 184,000, Elche 181,000, Donostia-San Sebastián

174,000, Cartagena 172,000, Burgos 169,000, Tarrasa 154,000, Alméria 153,000, León 144,000, Huelva 141,000 (all including suburbs; 1991 census).

Languages: Spanish or Castilian (official; as a first language over 70%), Catalan (as a first language over 20%), Basque (3%), Galician (4%).

Religion: Roman Catholic (95%).

Education: is compulsory between the ages of six and 16. *Adult literacy:* 86%. *Universities:* 37 institutions of university status.

Defence: (1993 figures) *Army:* 138,900 personnel. *Air force:* 29,800. *Navy:* 32,000. *Paramilitary:* 66,300. *Conscription:* nine months.

Government

Spain is a constitutional monarchy. The Cortes (Parliament) comprises a Senate (Upper House) and a Chamber of Deputies (Lower House). The Senate consists of 208 senators – 4 from each province, 5 from the Balearic Islands, 6 from the Canary Islands and 2 each from Ceuta and Melilla – elected by universal adult suffrage for four years, plus 47 senators indirectly elected by the autonomous communities. The Congress of Deputies has 350 members directly elected for four years under a system of proportional representation. The King appoints a Prime Minister (President of the Council) who commands a majority in the Cortes. The PM, in turn, appoints a Council of Ministers (Cabinet) responsible to the Chamber of Deputies.

Largest parties: Socialist Workers' Party (PSOE), (conservative) Popular Party (PP), (left-wing coalition) United Left (includes the Communist Party; UI), (Catalan) CIU (an electoral allianc of two Catalan nationalist parties), Basque Nationalist Party (PNV).

Local government: 17 autonomous communities (regions) plus two (North African) presidios.

Sovereign: HM Juan Carlos I, King of Spain (succeeded upon the restoration of the monarchy, 22 November 1975).

Prime Minister: Felipe González (PSOE).

Autonomous communities

Andalusia (Andalucia) *Area:* 87,268 km² (33,694 sq mi). *Population:* 6,984,000 (1992 est). *Capital:* Seville.

Aragón *Area:* 47,650 km² (18,398 sq mi). *Population:* 1,207,000 (1992 est). *Capital:* Zaragoza.

Asturias *Area:* 10,565 km² (4079 sq mi). *Population:* 1,119,000 (1992 est). *Capital:* Oviedo.

Balearic Islands (Islas Baleares) *Area:* 5014 km² (1936 sq mi). *Population:* 686,000 (1992 est). *Capital:* Palma de Mallorca.

Basque Country (Euskadi or **Pais Vasco)** *Area:* 7261 km² (2803 sq mi). *Population:* 2,130,000 (1992 est). *Capital:* Vitoria (Gasteiz).

Canary Islands (Islas Canarias) *Area:* 7242 km² (2796 sq mi). *Population:* 1,502,000 (1992 est). *Capitals:* Santa Cruz de Tenerife. and Las Palmas (alternate and equal capitals).

Cantabria *Area:* 5289 km² (2042 sq mi). *Population:* 526,000 (1992 est). *Capital:* Santander.

Castile-La Mancha (Castilla-La Mancha) *Area:* 79,230 km² (30,591 sq mi). *Population:* 1,717,000 (1992 est). *Capital:* Toledo.

Castile and León (Castilla y León) *Area:* 94,193 km² (36,368 sq mi). *Population:* 2,618,000 (1992 est). *Capital:* Valladolid.

Catalonia (Catalunya or **Cataluña)** *Area:* 31,930 km² (12,328 sq mi). *Population:* 6,018,000 (1992 est). *Capital:* Barcelona.

Extremadura *Area:* 41,602 km² (16,063 sq mi). *Population:* 1,131,000 (1992 est). *Capital:* Mérida.

Galicia (Galiza) *Area:* 29,434 km² (11,365 sq mi). *Population:* 2,793,000 (1992 est). *Capital:* Santiago de Compostela.

Madrid *Area:* 7995 km² (3087 sq mi). *Population:* 4,910,000 (1992 est). *Capital:* Madrid.

Murcia *Area:* 11,317 km² (4370 sq mi). *Population:* 1,038,000 (1992 est). *Capital:* Murcia.

Navarre (Navarra) *Area:* 10,421 km² (4023 sq mi). *Population:* 522,000 (1992 est). *Capital:* Pamplona.

La Rioja *Area:* 5034 km² (1944 sq mi). *Population:* 260,000 (1992 est). *Capital:* Logroño.

Valencia *Area:* 23,308 km² (8998 sq mi). *Population:* 3,798,000 (1992 est). *Capital:* Valencia.

Ceuta (North African enclave) *Area:* 19 km² (7 sq mi). *Population:* 71,000 (1992 est). *Capital:* Ceuta.

Melilla (North African enclave) *Area:* 14 km² (5 sq mi). *Population:* 56,000 (1992 est). *Capital:* Melilla.

Geography

In the north of Spain a mountainous region stretches from the Pyrenees – dividing Spain from France – through the Cantabrian mountains to Galicia on the Atlantic coast. Much of the country is occupied by the central plateau, the Meseta. This is around 600 m (2000 ft) high, but rises to the higher Sistema Central in Castile, and ends in the south at the Sierra Morena. The Sierra Nevada range in Andalusia in the south contains Mulhacén, mainland Spain's highest peak. The principal lowlands include the Ebro Valley in the northeast, a coastal plain around Valencia in the east, and the valley of the Guadalquivir River in the south. The Balearic Islands in the Mediterranean comprise four main islands – Mallorca (Majorca), Menorca (Minorca), Ibiza and Formentera – with seven much smaller islands. The Canary Islands, off the coast of Morocco and the Western Sahara, comprise five large islands – Tenerife, Fuerteventura, Gran Canaria, Lanzarote and La Palma – plus two smaller islands and

six islets. The cities of Ceuta and Melilla are enclaves on the north coast of Morocco. ***Principal rivers:*** Tagus (Tajo), Ebro, Guadalquivir, Douro (Duero), Guadiana Júcar, Segura. ***Highest point:*** Pico del Tiede (in the Canaries) 3718m (12,198 ft). Mulhacén is mainland Spain's highest peak at 3478m (11,411 ft).
Climate: The southeast has a Mediterranean climate with hot summers and mild winters. The dry interior is continental with warm summers and cold winters. The high Pyrenees have a cold Alpine climate, while the northwest (Galicia) has a wet Atlantic climate with cool summers.

Economy

Over 10% of the labour force is involved in agriculture. The principal crops include barley, wheat, sugar beet, citrus fruit and grapes (for wine). Pastures for livestock occupy some 20% of the land. Manufacturing developed rapidly from the 1960s, and there are now major motor-vehicle, textile, plastics, metallurgical, shipbuilding, chemical and engineering industries. Foreign investors have been encouraged to promote new industry, but unemployment remains high. Banking and commerce are important, and tourism is a major foreign-currency earner. Over 53,000,000 foreign tourists a year visit Spain, mainly staying at beach resorts on the Mediterranean, Balearic Islands and the Canaries. ***Currency:*** Peseta.

Recent History

In the last decades of the 19th century, the political situation became increasingly unstable, with the turmoil of labour disturbances, pressure for provincial autonomy, and growing anti-clericalism. As a result of the Spanish-American War of 1898 the last significant colonial possessions – Cuba, the Philippines, Guam and Puerto Rico – were lost. The end of Spain's empire inflicted a severe wound to Spanish pride and led to doubts as to whether the constitutional monarchy of Alfonso XIII (1886–1941) was capable of delivering the dynamic leadership that Spain was thought to require.

Spain remained neutral in World War I, during which social tensions increased. A growing disillusionment with parliamentary government and political parties led to a military coup in 1923 led by General Miguel Primo de Rivera (1870–1930). Primo was initially supported by Alfonso XIII, but in 1930 the King withdrew that support. However, the range of forces arrayed against the monarchy and the threat of civil war led Alfonso to abdicate (1931). The peace of the succeeding republic was short-lived. Neither of the political extremes – left nor right – was prepared to tolerate the perceived inefficiency and lack of authority of the Second Spanish Republic. In 1936, the army generals rose against a newly elected republican government. Nationalists – led by General Francisco Franco (1892–1975) and supported by Germany and Italy – fought the republicans in the bitter Spanish Civil War (see p. 443). Franco triumphed in 1939 to become ruler – Caudillo – of the neo-Fascist Spanish State. Political expression was restricted, and from 1942 to 1967 the Cortes (Parliament) was not directly elected. Spain remained neutral in World War II, although it was beholden to Germany. After 1945, Franco emphasized Spain's anti-Communism – a policy that brought his regime some international acceptance from the West during the Cold War.

In 1969, Franco named Alfonso XIII's grandson Juan Carlos (1938–) as his successor. The monarchy was restored on Franco's death (1975) and the King eased the transition to democracy through the establishment of a liberal constitution in 1978. In 1981 Juan Carlos played an important role in putting down an attempted army coup. In 1982 Spain joined NATO and elected a socialist government. Since 1986 the country has been a member of the EC. Despite the granting of regional autonomy (1978), Spain continues to be troubled by campaigns for provincial independence, for example in Catalonia, and by the violence of the Basque separatist movement ETA.

SRI LANKA

Official name: Sri Lanka Prajatantrika Samajawadi Janarajaya (Democratic Socialist Republic of Sri Lanka).
Member of: UN, Commonwealth.
Area: 65,610 km² (25,332 sq mi).
Population: 17,615,000 (1993 est).
Capital: Colombo – administrative capital – 1,935,000 (city 615,000; Sri Jayewardenepura Kotte, usually known as Kotte – legislative capital and the national capital designate – 109,000; Dehiwala-Mt Lavinia 191,000; Moratuwa 170,000; 1990 est).
Other major cities: Jaffna 143,000, Kandy 102,000, Galle 84,000 (1990 est).
Languages: Sinhala (72%), Tamil (21%), English – all official.
Religions: Buddhist (69%), Hindu (15%), Sunni Islam (8%), Christian (mainly Roman Catholic; 7%).
Education: is compulsory, in theory, between the ages of five and 15. *Adult literacy:* 84%. *Universities:* nine.
Defence: (1993 figures) *Army:* 90,000 personnel. *Air force:* 10,700. *Navy:* 10,100. *Paramilitary:* 71,000. *Conscription:* none.

Government

The 225-member Parliament is elected for six years under a system of proportional representation by universal adult suffrage. The President – who is also directly elected for six years – appoints a Cabinet and a Prime Minister who are responsible to Parliament. Constitutional changes scheduled for 1995 include the return of a parliamentary (rather than a presidential) system of government.
Largest parties: (socialist) Sri Lanka Freedom Party (SLFP), (social democratic) United Nationalist Party

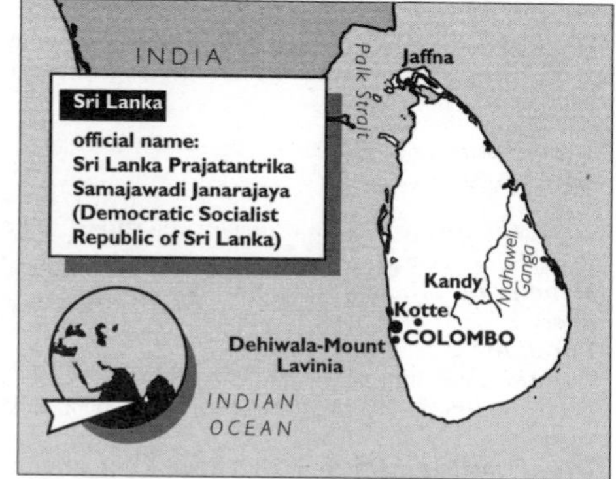

(UNP), (Tamil) Eelavar Democratic Front (EDF), (coalition) Tamil United Liberation Front (TULF), Sri Lankan Muslim Congress, (Buddhist) Mahajana Eksath Peramuna, (Communist) United Socialist Alliance.
Local government: nine provinces.
President: Chandrika Bandaranaike Kumaratunga (SLFP).
Prime Minister: Sirimavo Bandaranaike (SLFP).

Geography

The relief of the island is dominated by a massif in the southern central region. Most of the rest of the island consists of forested lowlands which in the north are flat and fertile. ***Principal rivers:*** Mahaweli, Aruvi Aru. ***Highest point:*** Pidurutalagala 2524m (8281 ft).
Climate: The island has a tropical climate modified by the monsoon. Rainfall totals vary between 5000 mm (20 in) in the southwest and 1000 mm (40 in) in the northeast.

Economy

About one half of the labour force is involved in agriculture, growing rice for domestic consumption, and tea, rubber and coconuts for export. Major irrigation and hydroelectric installations on the Mahaweli River are being constructed. Industries include food processing and textiles, but the economy – in particular tourism – has been damaged by separatist guerrilla activity. ***Currency:*** Sri Lankan rupee.

Recent History

Sri Lanka was known as Ceylon before 1972. From 1796 British rule replaced the Dutch, uniting the entire island for the first time. Nationalist feeling grew from the beginning of the 20th century, leading to independence in 1948, and a republican constitution in 1972. The country has been bedevilled by Tamil-Sinhalese ethnic rivalry, which led to major disorders in 1958, 1961 and since 1977. In 1971 a Marxist rebellion was crushed after heavy fighting. Sri Lanka elected the world's first woman Prime Minister, Sirimavo Bandaranaike (1916– ; PM 1960–65, 1970–77 and 1994–). Since the 1980s separatist Tamil guerrillas have fought for an independent homeland (Eelam). Fighting between rival Tamil guerrilla groups, Sinhalese extremists and government forces reduced the northeast to near civil war. An Indian 'peacekeeping' force intervened (1987), but this aggravated an already complex situation. Indian forces withdrew in 1990, and Tamil guerrilla activity continued in the northeast. Tension increased in 1993 after the assassination of President Premasada by a Tamil. Elections in 1993 brought to power the (socialist) Sri Lanka Freedom Party, which is prepared to grant autonomy to a Tamil region. A ceasefire was agreed, and peace talks proposed, in 1995.

SUDAN

Official name: Al Jumhuriyat as-Sûdân (The Republic of Sudan).
Member of: UN, Arab League, OAU.
Area: 2,505,813 km² (967,500 sq mi).
Population: 25,000,000 (1993 est).
Capital: Khartoum 2,300,000 (1990 est) (city 476,000, Omdurman 526,000, Khartoum North 341,000; 1983 census).
Other major cities: Port Sudan (Bûr Sûdân)

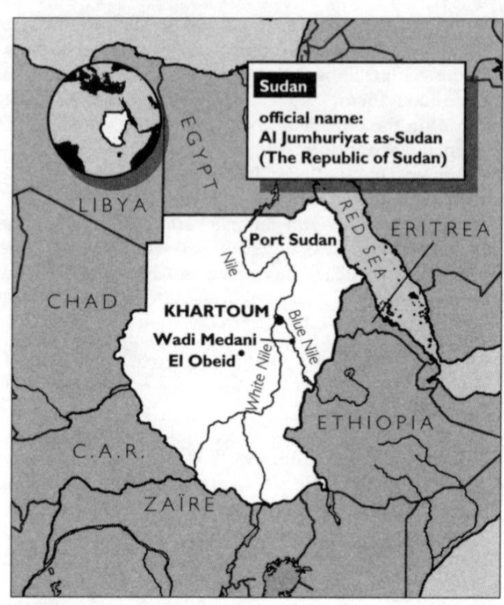

207,000, Wadi Medani 145,000, Al-Obeid 138,000 (1983 est).
Language: Arabic (over 50%; official).
Religions: Sunni Islam (70%), animist (22%), various Christian Churches (8%).
Education: is not compulsory. *Adult literacy:* 27%. *Universities:* six.
Defence: (1993 figures) *Army:* 68,000 personnel. *Air force:* 3000. *Navy:* 1800. *Paramilitary:* 41,000. *Conscription:* three years; conscription is only effective in the north.

Government

Since the military coup in 1989, Sudan has been ruled by the 15-member Command Council of the Revolution of National Salvation, whose chairman is head of state and of government. A 300-member Transitional National Assembly was appointed in 1992. It is envisaged that in future the Assembly will comprise representatives from provincial councils, which, in turn, will consist of delegates from directly elected popular committees.
Largest parties: Political activity is suspended.
Local government: 26 states.
Head of state and of government: Lt-Gen. Omar Hassan Ahmed al-Bashir.

Geography

The Sahara Desert covers much of the north and west, but is crossed by the fertile Nile Valley. The southern plains are swampy. Highlands are confined to hills beside the Red Sea and mountains on the Ugandan border. ***Principal rivers:*** Nile (Blue Nile or Bahr al-Azraq and White Nile or Bahr al-Jabal), Bahr al-Ghazal, Sobat. ***Highest point:*** Kinyeti 3187m (10,456 ft).
Climate: The south is equatorial, but the north is dry with some areas receiving negligible rainfall.

Economy

Over 65% of the labour force is involved in agriculture, growing cotton for export and sorghum and millet for domestic consumption. Since the early 1980s Sudan has been severely affected by drought, civil war and famine. ***Currency:*** Dinar.

Recent History

In 1820–21 Sudan was conquered by the Egyptians, who were challenged in the 1880s by an Islamic leader who claimed to be the Mahdi. The Mahdists took Khartoum, killed Sudan's Egyptian-appointed governor, General Charles George Gordon (1885), and created a theocratic state. Britain intervened, and from 1899 Sudan was administered jointly by Britain and Egypt. Nationalism developed strongly after World War I, but independence was only gained in 1956. Sudan remains politically unstable, alternating between civilian and military regimes. The civil war between the Muslim north and the animist-Christian south that began in 1955 remains unresolved. The military regime that came to power in 1989 has intensified the offensive against Christian rebels in the south, has encouraged Islamic fundamentalism and has led Sudan into international isolation through its backing for Iraq and Libya.

SURINAME

Official name: Republiek Suriname (Republic of Suriname).
Member of: UN, OAS.
Area: 163,265 km^2 (63,037 sq mi).
Population: 405,000 (1993 est).
Capital: Paramaribo 246,000 (city 68,000; 1988 est).
Other main town: Nieuw Amsterdam 6000 (1988 est).
Languages: Dutch (official; 30%), Sranang Togo (Creole; 31% as a first language), Hindi (30% as a first language), Javanese (15% as a first language), Chinese, English (official), Spanish (official – designate).
Religions: Hinduism (28%), Roman Catholic (22%), Sunni Islam (20%), Moravian (15%).
Education: is compulsory between the ages of six and 12. *Adult literacy:* 95%. *Universities:* one.
Defence: (1993 figures) *Army:* 1400 personnel. *Air force:* 150. *Navy:* 240. *Conscription:* Abolished in 1993.

Government

The 51-member National Assembly is elected for five years by universal adult suffrage. A President and a Vice-President – who is also the Prime Minister – are elected by the Assembly. The President appoints a Cabinet.
Largest parties: (coalition of socialist and ethnic parties) New Front for Democracy and Development (NFDD), (coalition anti-military) New Democracy Party (NDP), (coalition anti-military) Democratic Alternative '91.
Local government: nine districts.
President: Ronald Venetiaan (NFDD).
Prime Minister: Jules R. Ajodhia (NFDD).

Geography

Suriname comprises a swampy coastal plain, a forested central plateau, and mountains in the south. ***Principal rivers:*** Courantyne, Nickerie, Coppename, Saramacca, Suriname, Maroni. ***Highest point:*** Juliana Top 1230m (4035 ft).
Climate: Suriname has a tropical climate with heavy rainfall.

Economy

The extraction and refining of bauxite is the mainstay of the economy. Other exports include shrimps, sugar and oranges. The economy has been hampered by instability and emigration. ***Currency:*** Suriname guilder.

Recent History

Suriname has a mixed population, including American Indians, and the descendants of African slaves and of Javanese, Chinese and Indian plantation workers. Since independence from the Netherlands in 1975, racial tension has contributed to instability and there have been several coups.

SWAZILAND

Official name: Umbuso Weswatini (The Kingdom of Swaziland).
Member of: UN, Commonwealth, OAU.
Area: 17,363 km^2 (6704 sq mi).
Population: 814,000 (1993 est).
Capitals: Mbabane – administrative capital – 39,000, Lobamba – legislative capital – 6000 (1986 census).
Other major city: Manzini 52,000 (1986 census).
Languages: siSwati and English (both official).
Religions: various Protestant Churches (37%), independent African Churches (28%), animist (21%), Roman Catholic (11%).
Education: is not compulsory. *Adult literacy:* 67%. *Universities:* one.
Defence: (1993 figures) *Army:* 2700 personnel. *Conscription:* two years; selective.

Government

Swaziland is a monarchy in which the King appoints a Prime Minister and Cabinet. The King is advised by the 30-member Senate and the 65-member House of Assembly, and appoints 10 members to the House

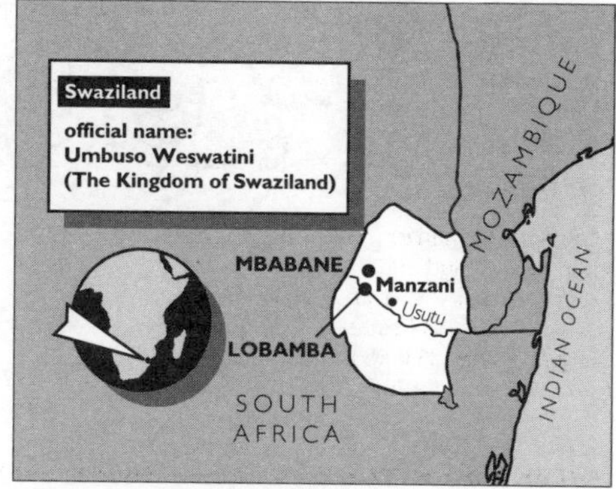

and 20 to the Senate. The 45 other members of the House are elected by universal adult suffrage; the 10 other members of the Senate are appointed by the House.
Largest parties: There are no political parties.
Local government: 55 districts.
Sovereign: HM Mswati III, King of Swaziland (succeeded upon the abdication of his mother as Queen Regent, 25 April 1986).
Prime Minister: Prince Jameson Mbilini Dlamini.

Geography

From the mountains of the west – which rise to 1869 m (6100 ft) – Swaziland descends in steps of savannah (veld) towards hill country in the east. ***Principal rivers:*** Lomati, Komati, Usutu, Umbeluzi, Mkhondvo.
Highest point: Emlembe 1863m (6113 ft).
Climate: The veld is subtropical, while the highlands are temperate.

Economy

The majority of Swazis are subsistence farmers. Cash crops include sugar cane (the main export).
Currency: Lilangeni (plural emalangeni).

Recent History

The Swazi kingdom was formed early in the 19th century, and came under British rule in 1904. The country resisted annexation by the Boers in the 1890s and by South Africa during the colonial period. Following independence (1968), King Sobhuza II suspended the constitution in 1973 and restored much of the traditional royal authority. A bitter power struggle after his death (1982) lasted until King Mswati III was invested in 1986.

SWEDEN

Official name: Konungariket Sverige (Kingdom of Sweden).
Member of: UN, EU/EC, OECD, OSCE.
Area: 449,964 km² (173,732 sq mi).

Population: 8,727,000 (1993 est).
Capital: Stockholm 1,471,000 (city 679,000; 1990 census).
Other major cities: Göteborg (Gothenburg) 720,000 (city 432,000), Malmö 466,000 (city 235,000; Lund 90,000), Uppsala 171,000 (city 168,000), Linköping 124,000, Orebro 122,000, Norrköping 121,000, Vasteras 120,000, Jönköping 112,000, Helsingborg 110,000, Boras 102,000, Sundsvall 94,000 (1990 census).
Languages: Swedish (official; nearly 100%), small Lappish minority.
Religion: Evangelical Lutheran Church of Sweden (over 85%).
Education: is compulsory between the ages of six and 15 or seven and 16. *Adult literacy:* virtually 100%. *Universities:* 20 institutions of university status.
Defence: (1993 figures) *Army:* 43,500 personnel. *Air force:* 11,500. *Navy:* 9800. *Conscription:* seven to 15 months in the army and air force; eight to 12 months in the navy.

Government

Sweden is a constitutional monarchy in which the King is ceremonial and representative head of state without any executive role. The 349-member Riksdag (Parliament) is elected for three years by universal adult suffrage under a system of proportional representation. The Speaker of the Riksdag nominates a Prime Minister who commands a parliamentary majority. The PM, in turn, appoints a Cabinet of Ministers who are responsible to the Riksdag.
Largest parties: Social Democratic Labour Party (SDAP), (conservative) Moderate Party (MS), Liberal Party (FP), Centre Party (CP), Christian Democratic Party (KdS), (right-wing) New Democracy Party, (former Communist) Left Party (VP).
Local government: 24 counties (lan).
Sovereign: HM Carl XVI Gustaf, King of Sweden (succeeded upon the death of his grandfather, 15 September 1973).
Prime Minister: Ingvar Carlsson (SDAP).

Counties

Alvsborg *Area:* 11,395 km² (4400 sq mi). *Population:* 446,000 (1991 est). *Capital:* Vänersborg.
Blekinge *Area:* 2941 km² (1136 sq mi). *Population:* 151,000 (1991 est). *Capital:* Karlskrona.
Gävleborg *Area:* 18,191 km² (7024 sq mi). *Population:* 289,000 (1991 est). *Capital:* Gävle.
Gothenburg and Bohus (Göteborg och Bohus) *Area:* 5141 km² (1985 sq mi). *Population:* 748,000 (1991 est). *Capital:* Gothenburg.
Gotland *Area:* 3140 km² (1212 sq mi). *Population:* 58,000 (1991 est). *Capital:* Visby.
Halland *Area:* 5454 km² (2106 sq mi). *Population:* 261,000 (1991 est). *Capital:* Halmstad.
Jämtland *Area:* 49,443 km² (19,090 sq mi). *Population:* 136,000 (1991 est). *Capital:* Ostersund.
Jönköping *Area:* 9944 km² (3839 sq mi). *Population:* 310,000 (1991 est). *Capital:* Jönköping.
Kalmar *Area:* 11,170 km² (4313 sq mi). *Population:* 242,000 (1991 est). *Capital:* Kalmar.
Kopparberg *Area:* 28,194 km² (10,886 sq mi). *Population:* 290,000 (1991 est). *Capital:* Falun.
Kristianstad *Area:* 6087 km² (2350 sq mi). *Population:* 293,000 (1991 est). *Capital:* Kristianstad.
Kronoberg *Area:* 8458 km² (3266 sq mi). *Population:* 179,000 (1991 est). *Capital:* Växjö.

Malmöhus *Area:* 4938 km² (1907 sq mi). *Population:* 794,000 (1991 est). *Capital:* Malmo.
Norrbotten *Area:* 98,913 km² (38,191 sq mi). *Population:* 266,000 (1991 est). *Capital:* Lulea.
Orebro *Area:* 8519 km² (3289 sq mi). *Population:* 274,000 (1991 est). *Capital:* Orebro.
Ostergötland *Area:* 10,562 km² (4078 sq mi). *Population:* 408,000 (1991 est). *Capital:* Linköping.
Skaraborg *Area:* 7937 km² (3065 sq mi). *Population:* 279,000 (1991 est). *Capital:* Mariestad.
Södermanland *Area:* 6060 km² (2340 sq mi). *Population:* 258,000 (1991 est). *Capital:* Nyköping.
Stockholm *Area:* 6488 km² (2505 sq mi). *Population:* 1,670,000 (1991 est). *Capital:* Stockholm.
Uppsala *Area:* 6989 km² (2698 sq mi). *Population:* 279,000 (1991 est). *Capital:* Uppsala.
Värmland *Area:* 17,584 km² (6789 sq mi). *Population:* 285,000 (1991 est). *Capital:* Karlstad.
Västerbotten *Area:* 55,401 km² (21,390 sq mi). *Population:* 256,000 (1991 est). *Capital:* Umea.
Västernorrland *Area:* 21,678 km² (8370 sq mi). *Population:* 261,000 (1991 est). *Capital:* Härnösand.
Västmanland *Area:* 6302 km² (2433 sq mi). *Population:* 260,000 (1991 est). *Capital:* Västeras.

Geography

The mountains of Norrland – along the border with Norway and in the north of Sweden – cover two thirds of the country. Svealand – in the centre – is characterized by a large number of lakes. In the south are the low Smaland Highlands and the fertile lowland of Skane. ***Principal rivers:*** Göta, Ume, Torne, Angerman, Klr, Dal. ***Highest point:*** Kebnekaise 2111m (6926 ft)

Climate: Sweden experiences long cold winters and warm summers, although the north – where snow remains on the mountains for eight months – is more severe than the south, where Skane has a relatively mild winter.

Economy

Sweden's high standard of living has been based upon its neutrality in the two World Wars, its cheap and plentiful hydroelectric power and its mineral riches. The country has about 15% of the world's uranium deposits, and large reserves of iron ore that provide the basis of domestic heavy industry and important exports to Western Europe. Agriculture – like the bulk of the population – is concentrated in the south. The principal products include dairy produce, meat, barley, sugar beet and potatoes. Vast coniferous forests are the basis of the paper, board and furniture industries, and large exports of timber. Heavy industries include motor vehicles (Saab and Volvo), aerospace and machinery, although the large shipbuilding industry has ceased to exist. Rising labour costs, high inflation and labour unrest added to growing economic problems, and Sweden was badly hit by recession in the early 1990s. As a result, the state has reduced its activities and a programme of privatization was implemented. ***Currency:*** Krona.

Recent History

In 1814 Sweden lost Finland and the last possessions south of the Baltic, but gained Norway from Denmark in compensation. The union of Norway and Sweden was dissolved in 1905 when King Oscar II (reigned 1872–1907) gave up the Norwegian throne upon Norway's vote for separation. In the 20th century neutral Sweden developed a comprehensive welfare state under social democratic governments. The country assumed a moral leadership on world issues but was jolted by the (unclaimed) assassination of PM Olof Palme (1986). In the 1990s economic necessity has obliged Sweden to dismantle aspects of the welfare system. The country became a member of the EU/EC in 1995.

SWITZERLAND

Official names: Confederaziun Helvetica (Romansch), Schweizerische Eidgenossenschaft (German), Confédération suisse (French) and Confederazione Svizzera (Italian) (Swiss Confederation).
Member of: OECD, OSCE.
Area: 41,293 km² (15,943 sq mi).
Population: 6,996,000 (1993 est).
Capital: Berne (Bern) 299,000 (city 134,000; 1990 est).
Other major cities: Zürich 839,000 (city 343,000), Geneva (Genève) 389,000 (city 165,000), Basel 359,000 (city 170,000), Lausanne 263,000 (city 123,000), Luzern 161,000 (city 59,000), St Gallen 126,000 (city 73,000), Winterthur 108,000 (city 86,000), Biel/Bienne 83,000 (city 53,000), Thun 78,000 (city 38,000), Lugano 69,000 (city 25,000), Neuchâtel 66,000 (city 33,000), Fribourg (Freiburg) 57,000 (city 34,000) (1990 est).
Languages: German (65% as a first language), French 18% (first language), Italian (10% first language), Romansch (under 1%) – all official.
Religions: Roman Catholic (47%), various Reformed Protestant Churches (43%).
Education: is compulsory between the ages of seven and 15. *Adult literacy:* virtually 100%. *Universities:* seven universities, plus three other institutions of university status.
Defence: (1993 figures) There are no standing forces. The armed forces comprise 400,000 personnel when mobilized. *Conscription:* 17 weeks at the age of 20; refresher courses between the ages of 21 and 32; 39 days between the ages of 33 and 42 for the Landwehr (militia); a further 13 days between the ages of 43 and 50 for the Landsturm (home guard).

Government

Switzerland is a federal republic in which each of the 20 cantons and 6 half-cantons has its own government with very considerable powers. Federal matters are entrusted to the Federal Assembly comprising the 46-member Council of States and the 200-member National Council. The Council of States is directly elected for three or four years with two members from each canton and one from each half-canton. The National Council is elected for four years by universal adult suffrage under a system of proportional representation. The Federal Assembly elects a seven-member Federal Council – the equivalent of a Cabinet – for four years. The Federal Council appoints one of its members to be President for one year. All constitutional amendments must be approved by a referendum.

Largest parties: (liberal) Radical Democratic Party (FDP), Social Democratic Party (SP), (conservative) Christian Democratic Party (CVP), (centre) Swiss People's Party (SVP), Environmentalists (GPS), Liberal Democrats (LPS), Independent Alliance (LDU), Automobile Party (APS), (right-wing) Swiss Democrats, Ticino League, (former Communist) Workers' Party.

Local government: 20 cantons and 6 half-cantons

President: (for 1995) Kaspar Villiger (FDP); (for 1996) Jean-Pascal Delamuraz.

Cantons and half-cantons

Aargau *Area:* 1404 km^2 (542 sq mi). *Population:* 505,000 (1992 est). *Capital:* Aarau.

Appenzell Ausser-Rhoden (half-canton) *Area:* 243 km^2 (94 sq mi). *Population:* 52,000 (1992 est). *Capital:* Herisau.

Appenzell Inner-Rhoden (half-canton) *Area:* 173 km^2 (67 sq mi). *Population:* 14,000 (1992 est). *Capital:* Appenzell.

Basel-Land (Basel-Landschaft) (half-canton) *Area:* 428 km^2 (165 sq mi). *Population:* 231,000 (1992 est). *Capital:* Liestal.

Basel Stadt *Area:* 37 km^2 (14 sq mi). *Population:* 196,000 (1992 est). *Capital:* Basel.

Bern (Berne) *Area:* 6051 km^2 (2336 sq mi). *Population:* 953,000 (1992 est). *Capital:* Bern.

Fribourg (Freiburg) *Area:* 1671 km^2 (645 sq mi). *Population:* 212,000 (1992 est). *Capital:* Fribourg.

Geneva (Genève) *Area:* 282 km^2 (109 sq mi). *Population:* 379,000 (1992 est). *Capital:* Geneva.

Glarus *Area:* 685 km^2 (265 sq mi). *Population:* 38,000 (1992 est). *Capital:* Glarus.

Graubünden (Grisons) *Area:* 7105 km^2 (2743 sq mi). *Population:* 173,000 (1992 est). *Capital:* Chur.

Jura *Area:* 836 km^2 (323 sq mi). *Population:* 66,000 (1992 est). *Capital:* Delémont.

Lucerne (Luzern) *Area:* 1493 km^2 (576 sq mi). *Population:* 324,000 (1992 est). *Capital:* Lucerne.

Neuchâtel *Area:* 803 km^2 (310 sq mi). *Population:* 162,000 (1992 est). *Capital:* Neuchâtel.

Nidwalden (half-canton) *Area:* 276 km^2 (107 sq mi). *Population:* 33,000 (1992 est). *Capital:* Stans.

Obwalden (half-canton) *Area:* 491 km^2 (189 sq mi). *Population:* 29,000 (1992 est). *Capital:* Sarnen.

St Gallen (Sankt Gallen) *Area:* 2026 km^2 (782 sq mi). *Population:* 427,000 (1992 est). *Capital:* St Gallen.

Schaffhausen *Area:* 298 km^2 (115 sq mi). *Population:* 72,000 (1992 est). *Capital:* Schaffhausen.

Schwyz *Area:* 908 km^2 (351 sq mi). *Population:* 113,000 (1992 est). *Capital:* Schwyz.

Solothurn *Area:* 791 km^2 (305 sq mi). *Population:* 230,000 (1992 est). *Capital:* Solothurn.

Thurgau *Area:* 991 km^2 (383 sq mi). *Population:* 210,000 (1992 est). *Capital:* Frauenfeld.

Ticino *Area:* 2812 km^2 (1086 sq mi). *Population:* 290,000 (1992 est). *Capital:* Bellinzona.

Uri *Area:* 1077 km^2 (416 sq mi). *Population:* 34,000 (1992 est). *Capital:* Altdorf.

Valais (Wallis) *Area:* 5224 km^2 (2017 sq mi). *Population:* 254,000 (1992 est). *Capital:* Sion.

Vaud *Area:* 3211 km^2 (1240 sq mi). *Population:* 593,000 (1992 est). *Capital:* Lausanne.

Zug *Area:* 239 km^2 (92 sq mi). *Population:* 86,000 (1992 est). *Capital:* Zug.

Zürich *Area:* 1729 km^2 (668 sq mi). *Population:* 1,159,000 (1992 est). *Capital:* Zürich.

Geography

The parallel ridges of the Jura Mountains lie in the northwest on the French border. The south of the country is occupied by the Alps. Between the two mountain ranges is a central plateau that contains the greater part of Switzerland's population, agriculture and industry. ***Principal rivers:*** Rhine (Rhein), Rhône, Reuss, Ticino, Inn, Aare. ***Highest point:*** Dufourspitze (Monte Rosa) 4634m (15,203 ft).

Climate: Altitude and aspect modify Switzerland's temperate climate. Considerable differences in temperature and rainfall are experienced over relatively short distances; for instance, the cold Alpine climate around the St Gotthard Pass is only 50 km (just over 30 miles) from the Mediterranean climate of Lugano.

Economy

Nearly two centuries of neutrality have allowed Switzerland to build a reputation as a secure financial centre. Zürich is one of the world's leading banking and commercial cities. The country enjoys one of the highest standards of living in the world. Industry – in part based upon cheap hydroelectric power – includes engineering (from turbines to watches), textiles, food processing (including cheese and chocolate), pharmaceuticals and chemicals. Dairying, grapes (for wine) and fodder crops are important in agriculture, and there is a significant timber industry. Tourism and the international organizations based in Switzerland are major foreign-currency earners. Foreign workers – in particular Italians – help alleviate the country's labour shortage. ***Currency:*** Swiss franc.

Recent History

Switzerland occupies a strategic position, but the Swiss have used their remarkable position to withdraw from, rather than participate in, European power politics. Tensions in the early 19th century saw attempts by some cantons to secede and set up a new federation, but the compromises of a new constitution in 1848 – which is still the basis of Swiss government – balanced cantonal and central power. As a neutral country Switzerland proved the ideal base for the Red Cross (1863), the League of Nations (1920) and other world organizations, but Switzerland has avoided membership of any body it considers might compromise its neutrality. In national referenda the Swiss have voted against membership of the UN and of the EEA (the trade agreement that links EC countries and those West European countries that have not joined the Common Market).

SYRIA

Official name: Al-Jumhuriya al-'Arabiya as-Suriya (The Syrian Arab Republic).
Member of: UN, Arab League.
Area: 185,180 km² (71,498 sq mi) – including the Israeli-occupied Golan Heights.
Population: 13,400,000 (1993 est).
Capital: Damascus (Dimashq) 1,451,000 (1992 est).
Other major cities: Halab (formerly Aleppo) 1,445,000, Homs 518,000, Latakia (Ladhiqiyah) 284,000 (1992 est).
Languages: Arabic (89%; official); Kurdish (6%).
Religions: Islam (official; Sunni 90%, Shia and Druze minorities), with various Orthodox and Roman Catholic minorities (9%).
Education: is compulsory between the ages of six and 12. *Adult literacy:* 65%. *Universities:* four.
Defence: (1993 figures) *Army:* 300,000 personnel. *Air force:* 40,000. *Air defence:* 60,000. *Navy:* 8000. *Conscription:* 30 months.

Government

The 250-member National People's Assembly is elected by universal adult suffrage for four years. The President – who is directly elected for seven years – appoints a Prime Minister (to assist him in government) and a Council of Ministers.
Largest parties: The National Progressive Front – including the ruling Ba'ath Party – has a leading role. The Front also includes the Arab Socialist Union Party, Syrian Arab Socialist Party, Arab Socialist Party, and Communist Party.
Local government: 14 districts.
President: Hafez al-Assad (Ba'ath).
Prime Minister: Mahmoud Zubi (Ba'ath).

Geography

Behind a well-watered coastal plain, mountains run from north to south, rising to Jabal ash Shaik (Mount Hermon). Inland, much of the country is occupied by the Syrian Desert. ***Principal rivers:*** Euphrates (Al Furat), Orontes. ***Highest point:*** Jabal ash Shaik (Mount Hermon) 2814m (9232 ft).
Climate: The coast has a Mediterranean climate. The arid interior has hot summers and cool winters.

Economy

Petroleum is the main export, although Syria's petroleum reserves are small by Middle East standards. Agriculture involves 25% of the labour force, with farming concentrated in the coastal plain and irrigated land in the Euphrates Valley. Major crops include cotton, wheat and barley. ***Currency:*** Syrian pound.

Recent History

Syria was part of the (Turkish) Ottoman Empire for 400 years. Ottoman rule was not ended until 1917, when a combined British-Arab army was led into Damascus. In 1920, independence was declared, but the victors of World War I handed Syria to France (1920) as a trust territory. From independence in 1946 until 1970 Syria suffered political instability. The pan-Arab, secular, socialist Ba'ath Party engineered Syria's unsuccessful union with Egypt (1958–61). Syria fought wars with Israel in 1948–49, 1967 and 1973 (see pp. 454–55), and in the 1967 Arab-Israeli War Israel captured the strategic Golan Heights from Syria. A pragmatic Ba'athist leader Hafiz Assad came to power in 1970 and allied Syria to the USSR. Assad's popularity has been challenged by Syria's increasing involvement in Lebanon since 1976 and by Shiite fundamentalism. After 1989–90, economic pressures lessened Syria's dependence upon the USSR and the collapse of the Soviet Union in 1990 brought a more pragmatic phase to Syria's foreign relations. Syria's participation in the coalition against Iraq (1990–91) gained greater international acceptance for Syria, which had attracted criticism for sympathizing with terrorist groups.

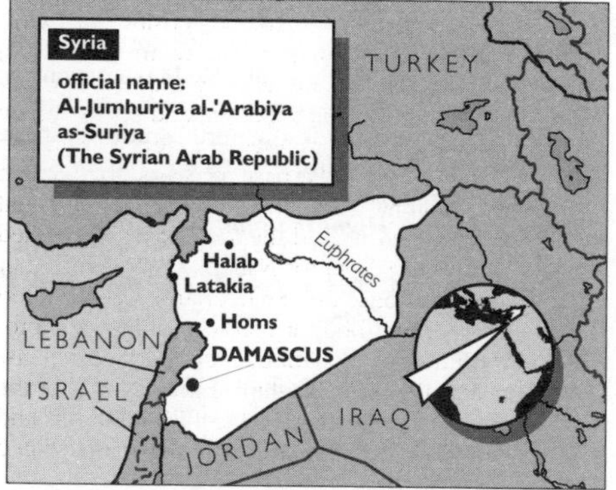

TAJIKISTAN

Official name: Jumhurii Tojikiston (Republic of Tajikistan).
Member of: UN, CIS, OSCE.
Area: 143,100 km² (55,300 sq mi).
Population: 5,705,000 (1993 est).
Capital: Dushanbe 592,000 (1991 census).
Other major cities: Khodzhent (Khujand; formerly Leninabad) 165,000, Kulyab 79,000 (1991 census).
Language: Tajik (official; 59%), Uzbek (23%), Russian (10%).
Religion: Sunni Islam majority.
Education: is compulsory between the ages of seven and 17. *Adult literacy:* No figures available. *Universities:* two.
Defence: (1993 figures) *Army:* 3000 personnel. (There are also over 25,000 CIS troops, mainly Russian, in Tajikistan.) *Conscription:* none.

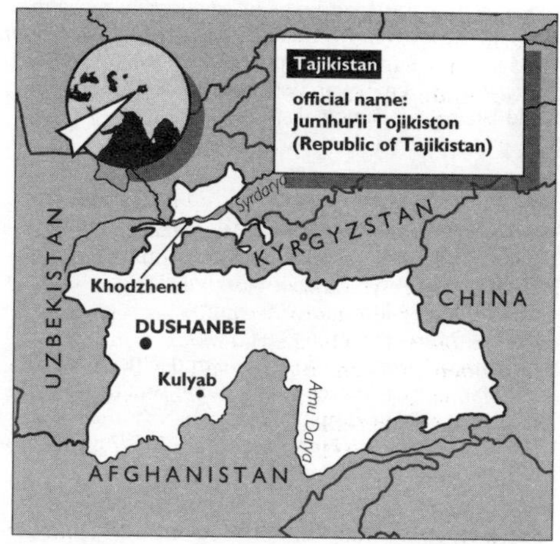

Government
The constitution provides for the election of an 80-member Majlis (legislature) and a President for four years.
Largest parties: (pro-Communist) People's Party, (former) Communist Party. (The anti-Communist parties were banned in 1993.)
Local government: three regions, plus the capital city and one autonomous republic.
President: Imamali Rakmanov (former Communist).
Prime Minister: Jamshed Karimov (former Communist).

Autonomous republic
Badakhshan *Area:* 63,700 km² (24,600 sq mi). *Population:* 167,000 (1992 est). *Capital:* Khorog.

Geography
The mountainous republic of Tajikistan lies within the Tien Shan range and part of the Pamirs. The most important lowland is the Fergana valley. ***Principal rivers:*** Syrdarya, Amu Darya, Vakhsh. ***Highest point:*** Mount Garmo, which was known as Pik Kommunizma (Communism Peak) when it was the highest mountain in the USSR, 7495m (24,590 ft).
Climate: High altitude and the country's position deep in the interior of Asia combine to give most of Tajikistan a harsh continental climate. The Fergana valley has a subtropical climate.

Economy
Cotton is the mainstay of the economy. Other agricultural interests include fruit, vegetables and raising cattle. Major natural resources include coal, natural gas, iron ore, oil, lead, zinc and hydroelectric-power potential. Industries include textiles and carpet-making. The economy, which remains centrally planned and largely state-owned, has been devastated by civil war. Tajikistan remains economically dependent upon Russia. ***Currency:*** Tajikistan uses Russian currency.

Recent History
In the 19th century most of the Tajiks owed allegiance to the (Uzbek) khan of Bukhara. The area was annexed by Tsarist Russia (1860–68). After the Russian Revolution, the area was reoccupied by the Soviet Red Army (1920), but Tajik revolts simmered from 1922 to 1931. Tajikistan became a Union Republic within the USSR in 1929, declared independence after the abortive coup by Communist hardliners in Moscow (September 1991), and was internationally recognized when the Soviet Union was dissolved (December 1991). Since independence the country has been wracked by civil war between former Communists and Islamic fundamentalists.

TANZANIA
Official names: Jamhuri ya Muungano wa Tanzania (Swahili) or The United Republic of Tanzania.
Member of: UN, Commonwealth, OAU.
Area: 945,087 km² (364,900 sq mi).
Population: 26,540,000 (1993 est).
Capitals: Dodoma – legislative and official capital – 204,000, Dar es Salaam – joint administrative capital – 1,361,000 (1988 census).
Other major cities: Mwanza 223,000, Tanga 187,000, Zanzibar 158,000 (1988 census).
Languages: English (official), Swahili (90%; 9% as a first language), 120 local languages.

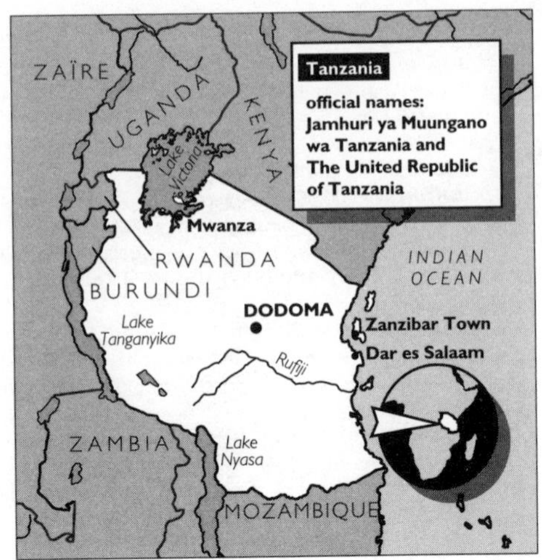

Religions: animist (40%), Sunni Islam (33%), Roman Catholic (20%).
Education: is not compulsory. *Adult literacy:* 46%. *Universities:* two.
Defence: (1993 figures) *Army:* 45,000 personnel. *Air force* 3500. *Navy:* 1000. *Paramilitary:* 1400. *Conscription:* none.

Government
The President is elected by universal adult suffrage for a maximum of two five-year terms. The President appoints a Cabinet of Ministers and two Vice Presidents – one is the President of Zanzibar, the other concurrently Prime Minister. The 244-member National Assembly comprises 119 members directly elected from the mainland, 50 members directly elected from Zanzibar, plus appointed and indirectly elected members. Zanzibar has its own legislature.
Largest parties: (former monopoly) Revolutionary Party/Chama Cha Mapinduzi (CCM), National Convention for Reconstruction and Reform, Republic Party, (Zanzibar-based) Bismallah Party, (Zanzibar-based) Movement for Democratic Alternative.
Local government: 20 regions (mainland Tanzania), plus three regions in the autonomous state of Zanzibar.
President: Ali Hassan Mwinyi (CCM).
Prime Minister: Cleopa David Msuya (CCM).

Autonomous island
Zanzibar *Area:* 1554 km² (601 sq mi). *Population:* 376,000 (1988 census). *Capital:* Zanzibar.

Geography
Zanzibar comprises three small islands. The mainland – formerly Tanganyika – comprises savannah plateaux divided by rift valleys and a north-south mountain chain rising to Kilimanjaro, the highest point in Africa. ***Principal rivers***: Rufiji, Pangani, Wami, Ruvu, Ruvuma, Kagera. ***Highest point:*** Kilimanjaro 5894m (19,340 ft).
Climate: Tanzania has a tropical climate, although the mountains are cooler.

Economy
Subsistence farming involves over 80% of the labour force. Cash crops include coffee and cotton. Mineral resources include diamonds and gold. ***Currency:*** Tanzanian shilling.

Recent History

Zanzibar was an Omani possession from the 18th century, became an independent sultanate in 1856 and then a British protectorate (1890–1963). After independence in 1963 the sultan of Zanzibar was deposed in a radical left-wing coup. The mainland became the colony of German East Africa in 1884, the British trust territory of Tanganyika in 1919 and an independent state in 1961. President Julius Nyerere's policies of self-reliance and egalitarian socialism were widely admired, but proved difficult to implement and were largely abandoned by the time he retired as President in 1985. In 1964 Tanganyika and Zanzibar united to form Tanzania. The country was effectively a one-party state from 1965 until 1992, when the principle of political pluralism was conceded.

THAILAND

Official name: Prathet Thai (Kingdom of Thailand).
Member of: UN, ASEAN, Apec.
Area: 513,115 km² (198,115 sq mi).
Population: 57,830,000 (1993 est).
Capital: Bangkok 5,876,000 (including suburbs; 1990 census). (The Thai government has approved the site of a new capital near Chachoengsao, which is located 120 km (75 mi) east of Bangkok. The new city is expected to be constructed by 2010.)
Other major cities: Nakhon Ratchasima (Khorat) 278,000, Songkhla 243,000, Nonthaburi 233,000, Khon Kaen 206,000 (1990 census).
Language: Thai (official).
Religions: Buddhism (95%), Sunni Islam (4%).
Education: is compulsory for six years, to be taken between the ages of seven and 15. *Adult literacy:* 89%. *Universities:* 16 state and 19 private universities.

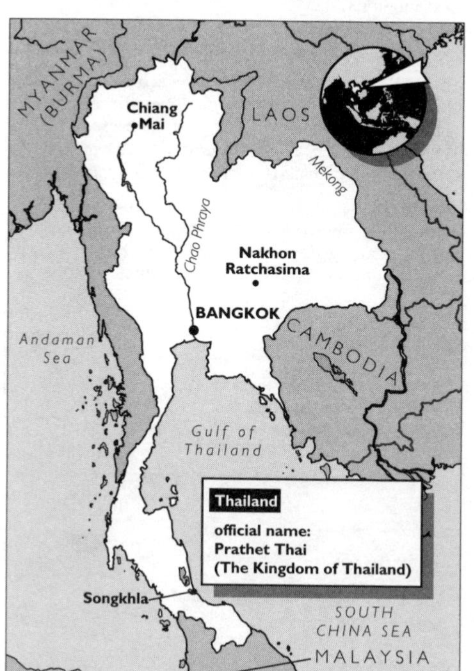

Defence: (1993 figures) *Army:* 180,000 personnel. *Air force:* 43,000. *Navy:* 62,000. *Paramilitary:* 141,700. *Conscription:* two years.

Government

Thailand is a constitutional monarchy. The National Assembly comprises a non-political Senate whose 270 members are appointed and a 360-member House of Representatives elected by universal adult suffrage for four years. The King appoints a Prime Minister who commands a majority in the House. The PM appoints a Cabinet of Ministers responsible to the House.
Largest parties: (liberal) Democrat Party (DP), (conservative) Thai Nation Party (TNP), (right-wing) National Development Party (NDP), (reformist) New Aspiration Party (NAP), Palang Dharma/Righteous Party, (reformist) Solidarity Party (SP).
Local government: 76 provinces.
Sovereign: HM Bhumibol Adulyadej (Rama IX), King of Thailand (succeeded upon the death of his brother, 9 June 1946).
Prime Minister: Chuan Leekpai (DP).

Geography

Central Thailand is a densely populated fertile plain. The north comprises rugged ranges of fold mountains. The infertile Khorat Plateau occupies the northeast, while the mountainous Isthmus of Kra joins southern Thailand to Malaysia. ***Principal rivers:*** Mekong, Mun, Chi, Chao Phraya (Ping, Wang, Yom, Nan). ***Highest point:*** Doi Inthanon 2595m (8514 ft).
Climate: Thailand has a subtropical climate with heavy monsoon rains from June to October, a cool season from October to March and a hot season from March to June.

Economy

Agriculture involves over two thirds of the labour force, mainly growing rice (a major export), tapioca and rubber. Tin and natural gas are the main natural resources. Manufacturing – based on cheap labour – is expanding and includes textiles, clothes, electrical and electronic engineering. Thailand achieved high economic growth rates throughout the 1980s and early 1990s. Tourism is a major foreign-currency earner.
Currency: Baht.

Recent History

Before 1939 Thailand was known as Siam. The adroit diplomacy of its rulers enabled it to remain free of European colonization. Rama I (reigned 1782–1809), founder of the present dynasty, moved the capital to Bangkok. His successors were forced to cede their claims over neighbouring lands to Britain and France.
A constitutional monarchy was established by a bloodless coup (1932), whose Westernized leaders (Pibul Songgram and Pridi Phanomyang) struggled for political dominance for the next quarter of a century. During World War II Thailand was forced into an alliance with Japan. Since then Thailand has made a decisive commitment to the US political camp, which has brought major benefits in military and technical aid. Despite continuing army interventions in politics, Thailand has prospered. However, the stability of the country was compromised by the wars in Vietnam and by the continuing Cambodian conflict (until 1991), as Cambodian refugees and guerrillas remained in Thai border regions.

TOGO

Official name: La République togolaise (The Togolese Republic).
Member of: UN, OAU, ECOWAS.
Area: 56,785 km^2 (21,925 sq mi).
Population: 3,810,000 (1993 est).
Capital: Lomé 366,000 (1983 est).
Other main towns: Sokodé 34,000, Kpalimé 26,000 (1983 est).
Languages: French, Ewe (47%), Kabiye (22%) – all official.
Religions: animist (50%), Roman Catholic (26%), Sunni Islam (15%).
Education: is compulsory, in theory, between the ages of six and 12. *Adult literacy:* 43%. *Universities:* one.
Defence: (1993 figures) *Army:* 4800 personnel. *Air force:* 250. *Navy:* 200. *Paramilitary:* 750. *Conscription:* two years; selective.

Government

The President – who appoints a Prime Minister and a Council of Ministers – is elected by universal adult suffrage for five years. The 81-member National Assembly is also directly elected for five years.
Largest parties: Action Committee for Renewal (CAR), Union of Justice and Democracy (UTD), (former monopoly) Rally for the Togolese People (RPT).
Local government: five regions.
President: Gen. Gnassingbe Eyadema (RPT).
Prime Minister: Edem Kodjo (RPT).

Geography

Inland from a narrow coastal plain is a series of plateaux rising in the north to the Chaine du Togo. ***Principal rivers:*** Mono, Oti, Ogou. ***Highest point:*** Mont Agou (formerly Pic Baumann) 986m (3235 ft).
Climate: Togo has a hot and humid tropical climate, although the north is drier.

Economy

The majority of the labour force is involved in subsistence farming, with yams and millet as the principal crops. Phosphates are the main export. ***Currency:*** CFA franc.

Recent History

Colonized by Germany in 1884, Togoland was occupied by Franco-British forces in World War I, after which it was divided between them as trust territories. British Togoland became part of Ghana; the French section gained independence as Togo in 1960, and subsequently relations with Ghana have been strained. Togo has experienced great political instability and several coups. A multi-party system was restored in the 1990s, but civil unrest has persisted owing to continued military intervention in political life.

BURKINA FASO
Togo
official name:
La République togolaise
(The Togolese Republic)
GHANA
BENIN
Sokodé
Kpalimé
NIGERIA
LOMÉ
GULF OF GUINEA

TONGA

Official name: Pule'anga Fakatu'i'o Tonga (The Kingdom of Tonga).
Member of: Commonwealth.
Area: 780 km^2 (301 sq mi).
Population: 99,000 (1993 est).
Capital: Nuku'alofa 29,000 (1986 est).
Other main town: Mu'a 4000 (1986 est).
Languages: Tongan and English (both official).
Religions: Methodist (43%; official), Roman Catholic (16%).
Education: is compulsory between the ages of five and 14. *Adult literacy:* 93%. *Universities:* one university centre.
Defence: (1993 figures) *Paramilitary:* (part of the police force) 300 pesonnel. *Conscription:* none.

Government

Tonga is a constitutional monarchy. The King appoints a Prime Minister and other Ministers to the Privy Council, which acts as a Cabinet. The 31-member Legislative Assembly comprises the King, the Privy Council, 9 hereditary nobles (chosen by their peers) and 9 representatives of the people elected for three years by universal adult suffrage.
Largest parties: There are no political parties.
Local government: five districts.
Sovereign: HM Taufa'ahau Tupou IV, King of Tonga (succeeded upon the death of his mother, 15 December 1965).
Prime Minister: Baron Vaea.

Geography

The 172 Tongan islands – 36 of which are inhabited – comprise a low limestone chain in the east and a higher volcanic chain in the west. ***Principal rivers:*** There are no rivers. ***Highest point:*** Kao 1030m (3380 ft).
Climate: The climate is warm with heavy rainfall.

Economy

Agriculture involves most Tongans. Yams, cassava and taro are grown as subsistence crops. Coconut products are the main exports. *Currency:* Pa'anga.

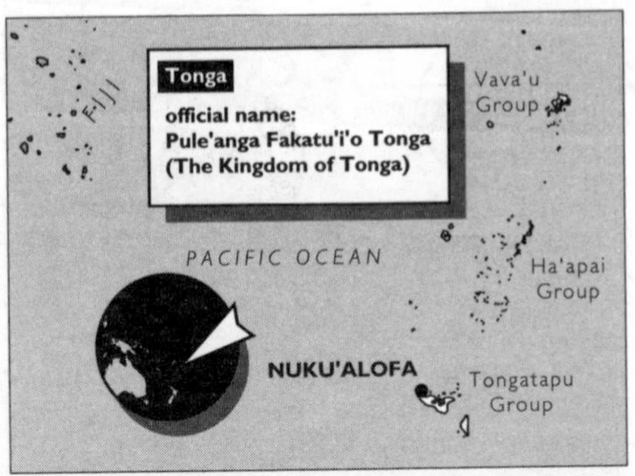

Recent History

European intervention began when Captain Cook visited Tonga (1773–77). Civil war in the first half of the 19th century was ended by King George Tupou I (reigned 1845–93), who reunited Tonga, preserved its independence and gave it a modern constitution. From 1900 to 1970 Tonga was a British protectorate. Since 1987 pressure for constitutional reform has increased.

TRINIDAD AND TOBAGO

Official name: Republic of Trinidad and Tobago.
Member of: UN, Commonwealth, CARICOM, OAS.
Area: 5128 km² (1980 sq mi).
Population: 1,249,000 (1993 est).
Capital: Port of Spain 496,000 (city 51,000; 1990 census).
Other major towns: Chaguanas 58,000, San Fernando 30,000, Arima 30,000 (1990 census).
Languages: English (official), Hindu (25%).
Religions: Roman Catholic (34%), Hinduism (25%), Anglican (15%), Sunni Islam (6%).
Education: is compulsory between the ages of five and 11. *Adult literacy:* 96%. *Universities:* one.
Defence: (1993 figures) *Army:* 2000 personnel. *Paramilitary:* 4800. *Coastguards:* 550. *Conscription:* none.

Government

The 31-member Senate – the Upper House of Parliament – is appointed by the President, who is elected by a joint sitting of Parliament. The 36-member House of Representatives is elected for five years by universal adult suffrage. The President appoints a Prime Minister who commands a majority in the House. The PM, in turn, appoints a Cabinet, which is responsible to the House. Tobago has full internal self-government.
Largest parties: (centre) People's National Movement (PNM), (socialist) United National Congress (UNC), (Tobago-based) National Alliance for Reconstruction.
Local government: four counties, two cities, three boroughs and an autonomous unitary state (Tobago).
President: Noor Mohammed Hassanali.
Prime Minister: Patrick Manning (PNM).

Unitary state

Tobago *Area:* 300 km² (116 sq mi). *Population:* 50,000 (1990 census). *Capital:* Scarborough.

Geography

Trinidad is generally low-lying and undulating, although it risesv to hills in the Northern Range. Tobago is more mountainous. ***Principal rivers:*** Caroni, Orotoire, Oropuche. ***Highest point:*** Cerro del Aripo 940m (3085 ft).
Climate: Trinidad has a humid tropical climate, with a dry season from January to May.

Economy

Petroleum and petrochemicals are the mainstay of the economy. Trinidad also has important reserves of natural gas and asphalt. Tourism is a major foreign-currency earner. ***Currency:*** Trinidad and Tobago dollar.

Recent History

The islands merged as a single British colony in 1899 and gained independence in 1962 under Dr Eric Williams. His moderate policies brought economic benefits but provoked a Black Power revolt and an army mutiny in 1970. The country has been a republic since 1976. In 1990 a small group of Islamic fundamentalists attempted a coup.

TUNISIA

Official name: Al-Jumhuriya at-Tunisiya (Republic of Tunisia).
Member of: UN, Arab League, OAU.
Area: 164,150 km² (63,378 sq mi).
Population: 8,530,000 (1993 est).
Capital: Tunis 1,420,000 (city 620,000; Aryanah 131,000; 1989 est).
Other major cities: Sfax (Safaqis) 222,000, Sousse (Susah) 102,000 (1989 est).
Languages: Arabic (official), Berber minority.
Religion: Sunni Islam (official; 99%).
Education: is compulsory, in theory, between the ages of six and 16. *Adult literacy:* 65%. *Universities:* four.
Defence: (1993 figures) *Army:* 27,000 personnel. *Air force:* 3500. *Navy:* 5000. *Paramilitary:* 13,000. *Conscription:* one year; selective.

Government

The President and the 163-member National Assembly are elected by universal adult suffrage for a five-year term. Nineteen seats are reserved for opposition members. The President appoints a Cabinet, headed by a Prime Minister.

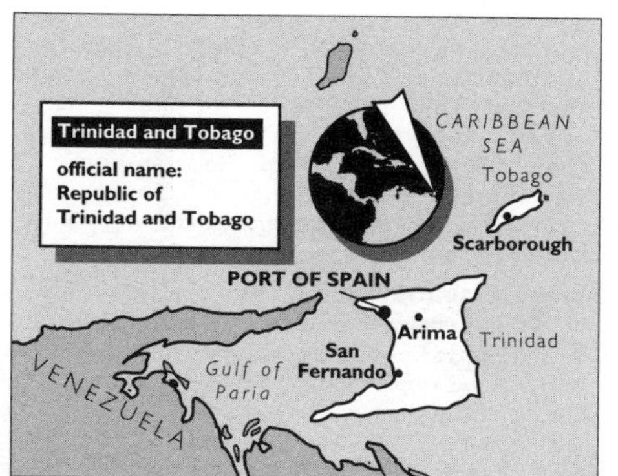

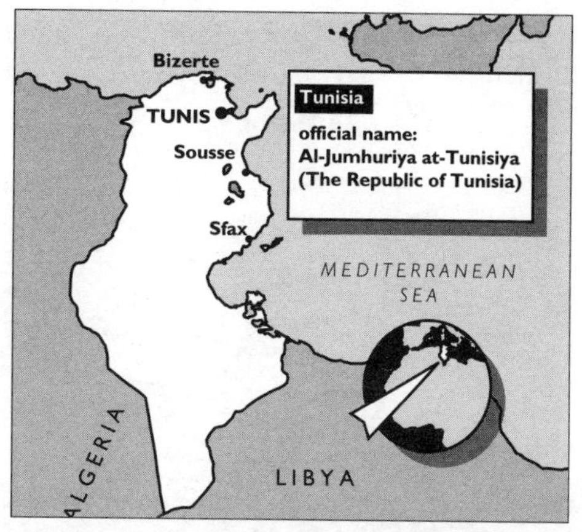

Largest parties: (former monopoly) Democratic Constitutional Rally (RCD; formerly known as the Destour Socialist Rally), Movement of Democratic Socialists (MDS), (former Communist) Renovation Movement (MR), (banned Islamic) Renaissance Party/al-Nahda.
Local government: 23 governates.
President: Zine el-Abidine Ben Ali (RCD).
Prime Minister: Hamed Karoui (RCD).

Geography

The Northern Tell and the High Tell mountains occupy the north and northwest. Wide plateaux cover central Tunisia. The Sahara Desert lies south of a zone of shallow salt lakes. ***Principal river:*** Majardah. ***Highest point:*** Jabal ash-Shanabi 1544m (5066 ft). ***Climate:*** The north has a Mediterranean climate with adequate rainfall. The south has a hot dry climate.

Economy

Phosphates and petroleum are the mainstay of the economy. The main crops are wheat, barley and vegetables, plus olives and citrus fruit for export. Tourism is a major foreign-currency earner. Unemployment is a major problem and many Tunisians seek work in Europe. ***Currency:*** Tunisian dinar.

Recent History

In 1881 France established a protectorate, although the bey (monarch) remained the nominal ruler. Nationalist sentiments grew in the 20th century. Tunisia was occupied by the Germans (1942–43). Independence was gained under Habib Bourguiba (1903–) in 1956 and the monarchy was abolished (1957). In the late 1980s the regime became increasingly unpopular and intolerant of opposition. Since Bourguiba was deposed by his PM (1988) – because of 'incapacity' – multi-party politics have been permitted.

TURKEY

Official name: Türkiye Cumhuriyeti (Republic of Turkey).
Member of: UN, NATO, OECD, OSCE.
Area: 779,452 km² (300,948 sq mi).
Population: 59,870,000 (1993 est).
Capital: Ankara 3,022,000 (city 2,560,000; 1990 census).
Other major cities: Istanbul 6,620,000 (city 6,293,000), Izmir 2,665,000 (city 2,319,000), Adana 1,430,000 (city 972,000), Bursa 1,031,000 (city 775,000), Konya 1,015,000 (city 543,000), Gaziantep 760,000 (city 574,000), Icel (Mersin) 701,000 (city 414,000), Kayseri 588,000 (city 461,000), Diyarbakir 560,000 (city 371,000), Manisa 557,000 (city 158,000), Sanliurfa 521,000 (city 240,000), Antalya 514,000 (city 353,000) (1990 census).
Languages: Turkish (86%; official); Kurdish (under 15%). There is no agreement regarding the size of the Kurdish population in Turkey; some sources claim that 20% of Turkey's population is Kurdish.
Religions: Sunni Islam (67%), Shia Islam (30%), various Christian Churches (3%).
Education: is compulsory for five years, to be taken between the ages of six and 14. *Adult literacy:* 81%. *Universities:* 57.
Defence: (1993 figures) *Army:* 370,000 personnel. *Air force:* 60,000. *Navy:* 50,000. *Paramilitary:* 70,000. *Conscription:* 18 months.

Government

The 450-member National Assembly is elected by universal adult suffrage for five years. The President – who is elected by the Assembly for seven years – appoints a Prime Minister and a Cabinet commanding a majority in the Assembly.
Largest parties: True Path Party (DYP) which is to merge with the Social Democratic Populist Party (SHP), (conservative) Motherland Party (ANAP), (conservative Islamic) Refah/Welfare Party (RP), (right-wing) National Movement Party, Democratic Left (DSP).
Local government: 76 provinces.
President: Suleyman Demirel (DYP).
Prime Minister: Dr Tansu Ciller (DYP).

Geography

Turkey west of the Dardanelles – 5% of the total area – is part of Europe. Asiatic Turkey consists of the central Anatolian Plateau and its basins, bordered to the north by the Pontic Mountains, to the south by the Taurus Mountains, and to the east by high ranges rising to Agridagi (Mount Ararat). ***Principal rivers:*** Euphrates (Firat), Tigris (Dicle), Kizil Irmak, Sakarya, Yesil Irmak, Göksu, Susurluk, Gediz, Büyükmenderes (Maeander), Seyhan, Ceyhan. ***Highest point:*** Agridagi (Mount Ararat) 5137m (16,853 ft).
Climate: The coastal regions have a Mediterranean climate. The interior is continental with hot, dry summers and cold, snowy winters.

Economy

Agriculture involves one half of the labour force. Major crops include wheat, rice, tobacco, and cotton. Both tobacco and cotton have given rise to important processing industries, and textiles are Turkey's main export. Manufacturing – in particular the chemical and steel industries – has grown rapidly. Natural resources include copper and coal. Unemployment is severe. Money sent back by the large number of Turks working in Western Europe is a major source of foreign currency. Tourism is increasingly important. ***Currency:*** Turkish lira.

Recent History

In the 19th century, the (Turkish) Ottoman Empire came to be regarded as 'the sick man of Europe', and the future of the empire and its Balkan territories troubled Europe as 'the Eastern Question'. In 1908 the Young Turks revolt attempted to stop the decline, but defeat in the Balkan Wars (1912–13) virtually expelled Turkey from Europe. Alliance with Germany in World War I ended in defeat and the loss of all non-Turkish areas. The future of Turkey in Asia itself seemed in doubt when Greece took the area around Izmir and the Allies defined zones of influence. General Mustafa Kemal (1881–1938) – later known as Atatürk ('father of the Turks') – led forces of resistance in a civil war and went on to defeat Greece. Turkey's present boundaries were established in 1923 by the Treaty of Lausanne. With the abolition of the sultanate (1922) Turkey became a republic, which Atatürk transformed into a secular Westernized state. Islam was disestablished, Arabic script was replaced by the Latin alphabet, the Turkish language was revived, and women's veils were banned.

Soviet claims on Turkish territory in 1945 encouraged a pro-Western outlook, and in 1952 Turkey joined NATO. PM Adnan Menderes was overthrown by a military coup in 1960 and hanged on charges of corruption and unconstitutional rule. Civilian government was restored in 1961, but a pattern of violence and ineffective government led to a further army takeover in 1980. In 1974, after President Makarios was overthrown in Cyprus by a Greek-sponsored coup, Turkey invaded the island and set up a Turkish administration in the north (1975). Differences with Greece over Cyprus have damaged the country's attempts to join the EC, as has the country's record on human rights. In 1983 civilian rule replaced the military government. Since then Turkey has drawn as close as possible to Western Europe, although the emergence of Islamic fundamentalism since the late 1980s has raised doubts concerning Turkey's European identity. Following the exodus of Iraqi Kurdish refugees into Turkey (1991), unrest among Turkey's ethnic Kurds intensified. A Kurdish terrorist movement has been active not only in Turkey but also in Europe, where Turkish diplomatic and other offices have been targets. In 1995, Turkey intervened in northern Iraq to attack Kurdish bases. This action attracted international criticism.

TURKMENISTAN

Official name: Tiurkmenostan (Turkmenistan).
Member of: UN, CIS, OSCE.
Area: 488,100 km² (188,500 sq mi).
Population: 4,295,000 (1993 est).
Capital: Ashkhabad (Ashgabat) 416,000 (1991 est).
Other major city: Chardzhou (Charjew) 166,000 (1991 est).

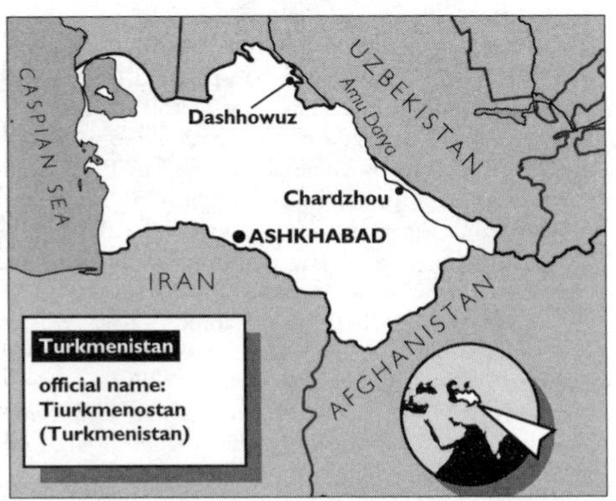

Languages: Turkmen (72%), Russian (9%), Uzbek (9%).
Religion: Sunni Islam majority.
Education: is compulsory between the ages of seven and 15. *Adult literacy:* No figures are available. *Universities:* one university; one polytechnic.
Defence: (1993 figures) *Army:* 28,000 personnel. *Conscription:* 18 months; selective in practice.

Government

A 50-member legislature (Majlis) and a President are elected by universal adult suffrage for five years. The President appoints a Prime Minister and a Cabinet.
Largest party: (former Communist) Democratic Party (DP). There is no effective opposition.
Local government: four provinces, plus the capital city.
President: Saparmuryad Niyazov (DP).
Prime Minister: Saparmuryad Niyazov (DP).

Geography

The sandy Kara-Kum Desert occupies the centre of the republic, over 90% of which is desert. The Kopet Dag mountains form the border with Iran. ***Principal rivers:*** Amu Darya (Oxus), Tedzhen, Murgab, Atrek.
Highest point: Firyuza 2942m (9652 ft).
Climate: Turkmenistan has a continental climate characterized by hot summers, freezing winters and very low precipitation.

Economy

Turkmenistan is rich in oil and natural gas. Industries include engineering, metal processing and textiles. Collective farms grow cotton under irrigation and raise sheep, camels and horses. The economy remains largely state-owned and centrally planned, although reforms began in 1993. ***Currency:*** Manat.

Recent History

The region came under Russian rule between 1869 and 1881. The Turkmens fiercely resisted the Russians and rose in revolt in 1916. An autonomous Transcaspian government was formed after the Russian Revolution, and the area was not brought under Soviet control until the Red Army invaded in 1919. The Turkmen territories were reorganized and eventually admitted as a full Union Republic of the USSR in 1925. Independence was declared following the abortive coup by Communist hardliners in Moscow, and the republic received international recognition when the USSR was dissolved (1991). Since independence, opposition has been curtailed and President Niyazov has been the object of a growing personality cult.

TUVALU

Official name: Tuvalu.
Member of: Commonwealth (special member).
Area: 24 km² (9 sq mi).
Population: 9500 (1993 est).
Capital: Fongafale on Funafuti atoll 3400 (1990 est).
Languages: Tuvaluan and English.
Religion: Protestant Church of Tuvalu (98%).
Education: is compulsory, in theory, between the ages of six and 12. *Adult literacy:* 45%. *Universities:* one university centre.
Defence: There are no armed forces.

Government

The 12-member Parliament – which is elected by

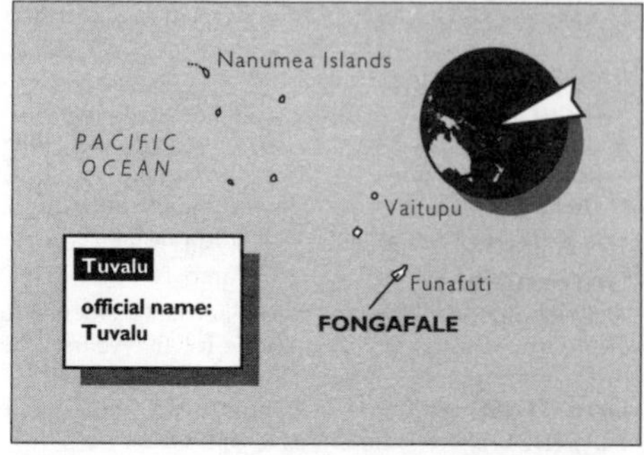

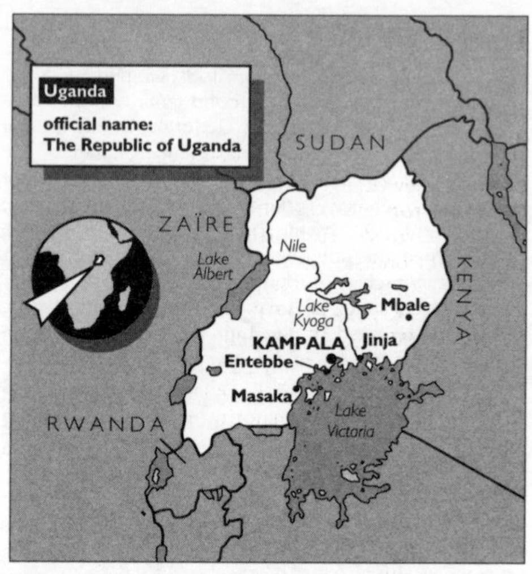

universal adult suffrage for four years – chooses a Prime Minister who appoints other Ministers. A Governor General represents the British Queen as sovereign of Tuvalu.

Largest parties: There are no political parties.

Local government: eight island councils.

Prime Minister: Kamuta Latasi.

Geography

Tuvalu comprises nine small atolls. ***Principal rivers:*** There are no rivers. ***Highest point:*** an unnamed point, 6m (20 ft) above sea level.

Climate: Tuvalu experiences high temperatures and heavy rainfall – 3000–4000 mm (120–160 in).

Economy

Subsistence farming – based on coconuts, pigs and poultry – involves most of the labour force. The only export is copra from coconuts. ***Currency:*** Tuvalu dollar.

Recent History

Claimed for Britain in 1892 as the Ellice Islands, the territory became linked administratively with the Gilbert Islands. A referendum in 1974 showed a majority of Polynesians in the Ellice Islands in favour of separation from the Micronesians of the Gilbert Islands (Kiribati). Independence was achieved as Tuvalu in 1978.

UGANDA

Official name: The Republic of Uganda.

Member of: UN, Commonwealth, OAU.

Area: 241,139 km^2 (93,104 sq mi).

Population: 16,583,000 (1991 census).

Capital: Kampala 773,000 (1991 census).

Other major cities: Jinja 61,000, Mbale 54,000, Masaka 49,000, Gulu 43,000, Entebbe 42,000 (1991 census).

Languages: English and Swahili (both official), with local languages including Luganda.

Religions: Roman Catholic (45%), animist (32%), various Protestant Churches (17%), Sunni Islam (6%).

Education: is not compulsory. *Adult literacy:* 48%. *Universities:* three.

Defence: (1993 figures) *Army:* 60,000 personnel. *Conscription:* none.

Government

Elections were held in 1994 for a 288-member (constituent) Assembly comprising 214 members elected by universal adult suffrage, 10 members nominated by the President, 56 members nominated by special interest groups (trade unions, women's organizations, etc.) and eight members nominated by the four principal political parties in operation before parties were banned in 1988. The President, who is elected by the Assembly for five years, appoints a Prime Minister and other Ministers.

Largest parties: Multi-party politics have been suspended.

Local government: 38 districts.

President: Yoweri Museveni.

Prime Minister: Kintu Musoke.

Geography

Most of Uganda is a plateau. This ends in the west at the Great Rift Valley and the Ruwenzori Mountains. Lake Victoria covers southeast Uganda. ***Principal rivers:*** Nile, Aswa, Dopeth-Okok, Kafu, Katonga. ***Highest point:*** Ngaliema (formerly Margherita Peak) 5118m (16,763 ft)

Climate: Uganda's tropical climate is moderated by its altitude.

Economy

Agriculture involves over 75% of the labour force; coffee accounts for 90% of Uganda's exports. Subsistence crops include plantains, cassava and sweet potatoes. Instability has damaged the economy. ***Currency:*** Uganda shilling.

Recent History

The British protectorate of Uganda – established in 1894 – was built around the powerful African kingdom of Buganda, whose continuing special status contributed to the disunity that has plagued the country since independence in 1962. Dr Milton Obote, who suppressed the Buganda monarchy in 1966, was overthrown in a coup by General Idi Amin in 1971. Amin earned international criticism when political and human rights were curtailed, opponents of the regime were murdered and the Asian population was expelled. The army took over in 1979, supported by Tanzanian troops. Obote was restored but was ousted in a military coup in 1985, since when instability and guerrilla action have continued. In 1994, a constituent assembly was called and the traditional kingdoms, including Buganda, were revived. In some rural areas, AIDS has devastated the population.

UKRAINE

Official name: Ukraina (The Ukraine).
Member of: UN, CIS, OSCE.
Area: 603,700 km² (233,100 sq mi).
Population: 52,345,000 (1993 est).
Capital: Kiev (Kyiv) 2,616,000 (1990 est).
Other major cities: Kharkov (Kharkiv) 1,618,000, Dnepropetrovsk (Dnipropetrovske) 1,187,000, Donetsk (Donetske) 1,117,000, Odessa 1,106,000, Zaporozhye (Zaporizhia) 891,000, Lvov (Lviv) 798,000, Krivoi Rog (Kryvyi Rih) 717,000, Mariupol 520,000, Nikolayev (Mikolaiv) 508,000, Lugansk (Luhansk) 501,000 (1990 est).
Languages: Ukrainian (74%), Russian (22%).
Religions: Orthodox majority – Ukrainian Autocephalous and Russian; Ukrainian Uniat (Roman Catholic; largest denomination).
Education: is compulsory between the ages of seven and 15. *Adult literacy:* No figures available. *Universities:* 11 universities and eight polytechnics of university status.
Defence: (1993 figures) *Army:* 217,000 personnel. *Air force:* 171,000. *Navy:* 3000. *Paramilitary:* 72,000. *Conscription:* 18 months.

Government

A 450-member legislature is elected for four years by universal adult suffrage. Voting is conducted in three rounds and to be successful, in either of the first two rounds, candidates must have an overall majority. The President – who appoints a Prime Minister and a Council of Ministers – is directly elected for five years. ***Largest parties:*** Communist Party (CP), Socialist Party (SP), (nationalist) Rukh, (centrist) Labour Party. The largest group of members sit as independents. ***Local government:*** 24 regions, one metropolitan area (Kiev) and one autonomous republic (Crimea). ***President:*** Leonid Kuchma (non-party). ***Prime Minister:*** Vitaly Masol (non-party).

Autonomous republic

Crimea (Krym) *Area:* 27,000 km² (10,400 sq mi). *Population:* 2,596,000 (1991 est). *Capital:* Simferopol.

Geography

Most of Ukraine – after Russia, the largest country in Europe – comprises plains (steppes), interrupted by low plateaux and basins. The north includes part of the Pripet Marshes; the south is a coastal lowland beside the Black Sea and the Sea of Azov. Central Ukraine comprises the Dnepr Lowland and the Dnepr Plateau, the most extensive upland in the republic. Eastern Ukraine comprises the Don Valley and part of the Central Russian Upland. The most diverse scenery is in the west, where the Carpathian Mountains form a barrier before a lowland, which stretches into Hungary. The Crimean Peninsula consists of parallel mountain ridges and fertile valleys. ***Principal rivers:*** Dnepr (Dnepro), Bug (Boh), Tisa (Tysa), Dnestr (Dnister), Danube, Donets. ***Highest point:*** Hoverla 2061m (6762 ft).
Climate: The Crimean Peninsula has a Mediterranean climate. The rest of Ukraine is temperate. Winters are milder and summers are cooler in the west. Snowfall is heaviest in the north and the Carpathians. Rainfall is moderate, usually with a summer maximum.

Economy

Ukraine was known as the bread basket of the USSR. Large collectivized farms on the steppes grow cereals, fodder crops and vegetables. Potatoes and flax are important in the north; fruit farming (including grapes and market gardening) is widespread, particularly in the Crimea. Natural resources include iron ore, oil, manganese and rock salt, but the vast Donets coalfield is the principal base of Ukraine's industries. The Ukrainian iron and steel industry was almost as large as that of Russia. Other major industries include consumer goods, heavy engineering (railway locomotives, shipbuilding, generators), food processing, and chemicals and chemical equipment. Within the USSR, Ukraine had surpluses of electricity, cereals and many industrial goods. The economy has been almost untouched by reform since the break-up of the USSR. Production has fallen; the country faces a huge energy deficit, rampant inflation and declining industries and standards of living. ***Currency:*** Karbovanets.

Recent History

Tsarist Russia united most of Ukraine under Russian rule (1793) in the second partition of Poland. In 1876 Russia banned the use of the Ukrainian language in schools and in print. However, the Ukrainian nationalist movement continued in the more liberal atmosphere of Galicia in the west, which had been annexed by Austria in the first partition of Poland (1772). The Ukrainians in Russia took the opportunity afforded by World War I and the Russian Revolution to proclaim independence (1918), but a Ukrainian Soviet government was established in Kharkov. Ukraine united with Galicia when the Austro-Hungarian Empire collapsed. The new state was invaded by Poland in pursuit of territorial claims and by the Soviet Red Army in support of the Kharkov Soviet. The Red Army prevailed and in 1922 Ukraine became one of the founding republics of the USSR, but the Lvov district of Galicia remained in Polish hands.

From 1928, Soviet leader Joseph Stalin instituted purges in Ukraine and a new programme of Russification. After World War II – when Ukraine was occupied by Nazi Germany – Soviet Ukraine was enlarged by the addition of Lvov (from Poland), Bukovina (from Romania), and Ruthenia (from Czechoslovakia), and finally, in 1954, Crimea (from Russia). Ukrainian nationalism was spurred by the perceived Soviet indifference to Ukraine at the time of the nuclear accident at Chernobyl, north of Kiev, in 1986. Ukrainian politicians responded to the restructuring of the USSR in the late 1980s by seeking increased autonomy. The decision of the republic to declare independence following the abortive coup by Communist hardliners in Moscow (September 1991) hastened the demise of the USSR. Ukraine gained international recognition in December 1991 when the Soviet Union was dissolved, but tension remained between Moscow and Kiev concerning the allegiance of Soviet forces in Ukraine, and the status of Crimea and the Black Sea fleet. Ukraine's economic collapse since independence increased the separatist feelings of the Russian majority in eastern Ukraine and in Crimea.

UNITED ARAB EMIRATES

Official name: Al-Imarat Al'Arabiya Al-Muttahida (The United Arab Emirates).
Member of: UN, Arab League, OPEC, GCC.
Area: 83,600 km² (32,280 sq mi).
Population: 1,990,000 (1993 est).
Capital: Abu Dhabi 363,000 (1989 est).
Other major cities: Dubai 585,000, al'Ayn 176,000, Sharjah 125,000 (1989 est).
Languages: Arabic (official; 20–25%); English (commercial); various languages of the Indian subcontinent (70%); Iranian.
Religion: Sunni Islam (official; majority).
Education: is compulsory between the ages of six and 12. *Adult literacy:* 73%. *Universities:* one.
Defence: (1993 figures) *Army:* 53,000 personnel. *Air force:* 2500. *Navy:* 2000. *Conscription:* none.

Government

The hereditary absolute rulers of the seven emirates form the Supreme Council of Rulers. The Supreme Council elects one of its members as President, who appoints a Prime Minister and Council of Ministers. The Supreme Council also appoints a 40-member advisory Federal National Council for two years. ***Climate:*** There are no political parties.
Local government: seven emirates.
President: HH Shaikh Zayid bin Sultan Al Nihayyan.
Prime Minister: HH Shaikh Maktum bin Rashid Al Maktum.

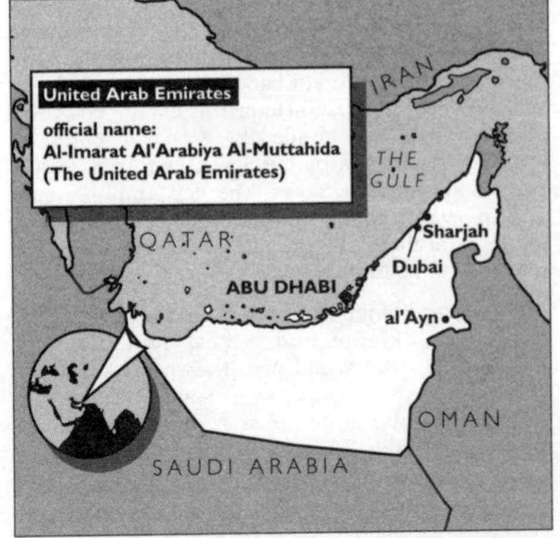

Emirates

Abu Dhabi *Area:* 73,000 km² (28,210 sq mi). *Population:* 798,000 (1991 est). *Capital:* Abu Dhabi.
Ajman *Area:* 260 km² (100 sq mi). *Population:* 76,000 (1991 est). *Capital:* Ajman.
Dubai *Area:* 3900 km² (1510 sq mi). *Population:* 501,000 (1991 est). *Capital:* Dubai.
Fujairah *Area:* 1300 km² (500 sq mi). *Population:* 63,000 (1991 est). *Capital:* Fujairah.
Ras al-Khaimah *Area:* 1700 km² (660 sq mi). *Population:* 130,000 (1991 est). *Capital:* Ras al-Khaimah.
Sharjah *Area:* 2600 km² (1000 sq mi). *Population:* 314,000 (1991 est). *Capital:* Sharjah.
Umm al-Qaiwain *Area:* 780 km² (300 sq mi). *Population:* 27,000 (1991 est). *Capital:* Umm al-Qaiwain.

Geography

Most of the country is a low-lying desert. The only other major relief features are the Hajar Mountains in the east and the Buraymi oasis (around al'Ayn) on the Omani border. ***Principal rivers:*** There are no rivers.
Highest point: Al-Hajar 1189m (3901 ft).
Climate: Summer temperatures exceed 40 °C (104 °F); winter temperatures are milder. Rainfall is very low.

Economy

Based upon the export of offshore and onshore reserves of petroleum and natural gas, the country has one of the highest standards of living in the world. Dry docks, fertilizer factories, commercial banking interests, international airports and an entrepôt trade have been developed. Immigrants from the Indian subcontinent and Iran form the majority of the labour force. Agriculture is confined to oases and a few coastal sites irrigated by desalinated water.
Currency: Dirham.

Recent History

A political vacuum in the mid-18th century was filled by the British, who saw the region as a link in the trade route to India. Treaties ('truces') were signed with local rulers during the 19th century, bringing the Trucial States under British protection. In 1958 oil was discovered in Abu Dhabi. When the British withdrew in 1971 the Trucial States formed the United Arab Emirates.

UNITED KINGDOM

Official name: The United Kingdom of Great Britain and Northern Ireland.
Member of: UN, EU/EC, NATO, G7, OECD, OSCE, WEU, Commonwealth.
Area: 244,088 km² (94,242 sq mi).
Population: 58,080,000 (1993 est).
Capital: London (see below).
Languages: English (over 98% as a first language), various languages of the Indian subcontinent (under 2% as a first language), Welsh (0.05%), Gaelic (0.014%).
Religions: Anglican (55% nominal; 4% practising), Roman Catholic (9%), Presbyterian (3%, including Church of Scotland), Methodist (2%), various other Christian Churches (4%), Sunni Islam (2%).
Education: is compulsory between the ages of five and 16. *Adult literacy:* virtually 100%. *Universities:* 94 (including the autonomous colleges of the University of Wales).

Defence: (1993 figures) *Army:* 134,600 personnel. *Air force:* 80,900. *Navy:* 59,300. *Conscription:* none.

England

Area: 130,439 km^2 (50,363 sq mi).
Population: 47,837,300 (1992 est).
Capital: London 7,926,000 (London Urban Area; Greater London 6,803,000; 1992 est).
Other major cities: Birmingham 2,360,000 (West Midlands Urban Area; city 1,009,000; Dudley 305,000; Walsall 263,000; Wolverhampton 248,000; Solihull 201,000), Manchester 2,337,000 (Greater Manchester Urban Area; city 435,000; Stockport 289,000; Bolton 264,000; Salford 230,000; Oldham 220,000; Rochdale 206,000), Leeds-Bradford 1,581,000 (West Yorkshire Urban Area; Leeds 772,000, Bradford 478,000), Newcastle-upon-Tyne 797,000 (Tyneside Urban Area; city 282,000; Gateshead 203,000), Liverpool 690,000 (Urban Area; city 479,000), Sheffield 673,000 (Urban Area; city 531,000), Nottingham 631,000 (Urban Area; city 283,000), Bristol 568,000 (Urban Area; city 397,000), Brighton 495,000 (Brighton-Worthing Urban Area; Brighton town 155,000), Portsmouth 476,000 (Urban Area; city 190,000), Leicester 423,000 (Urban Area; city 285,000), Stoke-on-Trent 389,000 (The Potteries Urban Area; city 253,000), Middlesbrough 380,000 (Teesside Urban Area; town 146,000),

Bournemouth 376,000 (Urban Area; town 159,000), Coventry 348,000 (Urban Area; city 305,000), Hull 331,000 (Kingston-upon-Hull Urban Area; city 269,000), Southampton 322,000 (Southampton-Eastleigh Urban Area; city 208,000), Preston 320,000 (Urban Area; town 131,000), Southend 299,000 (Urban Area; town 165,000), Blackpool 293,000 (Urban Area; town 152,000), Birkenhead 279,000 (Wirral Urban Area; town 99,000), Plymouth 258,000 (Urban Area and city), Rochester 247,000 (Medway Towns Urban Area; city 148,000) (figures are for urban areas – cities and their agglomerations – not for local government areas; 1992 est).

Northern Ireland

Area: 14,122 km^2 (5453 sq mi) of which 13,483 km^2 (5205 sq mi) is land.

Population: 1,610,000 (1992 est).

Capital: Belfast 437,000 (Urban Area; city 288,000; Newtownabbey 75,000; Castlereagh 62,000; 1992 est).

Other major towns and cities: Derry/Londonderry 96,000, Craigavon-Portadown-Lisburn 77,000, Bangor 35,000 (figures are for urban areas – towns and their agglomerations – not for local government areas; 1992 est).

Scotland

Area: 78,759 km^2 (30,409 sq mi).

Population: 5,111,000 (1992 est).

Capital: Edinburgh 527,000 (Urban Area; city 439,000; 1992 est).

Other major towns and cities: Glasgow 1,648,000 (Central Clydeside Urban Area; city 684,000; Motherwell 144,000; Paisley 84,000; Hamilton 52,000), Aberdeen 231,000 (Urban Area; city 217,000), Dundee 172,000 (Urban Area and city), Greenock 91,000 (Urban Area; town 58,000), Falkirk 74,000 (Urban Area; town 36,000), Ayr 62,000 (Urban Area; town 52,000) (figures are for urban areas – towns and their agglomerations – not for local government areas; 1992 est).

Wales

Area: 20,768 km^2 (8019 sq mi).

Population: 2,899,000 (1992 est).

Capital: Cardiff 326,000 (Urban Area; city 296,000; 1992 est).

Other major towns and cities: Swansea 289,000 (Urban Area; city 188,000), Newport 137,000 (Urban Area and town), Rhondda-Pontypridd 128,000 (Urban Area; Rhondda 79,000), Wrexham 80,000 (Urban Area; town 40,000), Merthyr Tydfil 60,000 (Urban Area and town), Aberdare 55,000 (Urban Area; town 32,000), Pontypool 50,000 (Urban Area; town 30,000), Bridgend 50,000 (Urban Area; town 31,000) (figures are for urban areas – towns and their agglomerations – not for local government areas; 1992 est).

Government

The UK is a constitutional monarchy without a written constitution. The House of Lords – the Upper (non-elected) House of Parliament – comprises over 750 hereditary peers and peeresses, over 20 Lords of Appeal (non-hereditary peers), over 370 life peers, and 2 archbishops and 24 bishops of the Church of England. The House of Commons consists of 651 members elected for five years by universal adult suffrage. The sovereign appoints a Prime Minister who commands a majority in the Commons.

Largest parties: Conservative Party (Con), Labour Party (Lab), Liberal Democrats (Lib Dem), Ulster Unionist Party (UU), (Welsh Nationalist) Plaid Cymru (PC), (Northern Irish) Social Democratic and Labour Party (SDLP), Scottish National Party (SNP), Democratic Unionist Party (DUP).

Local government: English local government is being reformed: there are proposals for 46 counties (not all of which will have county councils) and over 110 unitary authorities (including Greater London and metropolitan boroughs). Northern Ireland is divided into 26 all-purpose districts. Scotland is divided into 32 all-purpose districts. Wales is divided into 22 all-purpose districts.

Sovereign: HM Queen Elizabeth II of the United Kingdom of Great Britain and Northern Ireland (succeeded upon the death of her father, 6 February 1952).

Prime Minister: John Major (Con).

Crown Dependencies: (associated with but not part of the UK) Guernsey and Dependencies (Alderney and Sark), Isle of Man, Jersey. See Other Territories (beginning on p. 729).

Dependencies: Anguilla, Bermuda, British Antarctic Territory, British Indian Ocean Territory, British Virgin Islands, Cayman Islands, Falkland Islands, Gibraltar, Hong Kong, Montserrat,Pitcairn Islands, St Helena and Dependencies (Ascension and Tristan da Cunha), South Georgia and South Sandwich Islands, and Turks and Caicos Islands. See Other Territories (beginning on p. 729).

Geography

The UK comprises the island of Great Britain, the northeast part of Ireland plus over 4000 other islands. Lowland Britain occupies the south, east and centre of England. Clay valleys and river basins – including those of the Thames and the Trent – separate relatively low ridges of hills, including the limestone Cotswolds and Cleveland Hills, and the chalk North and South Downs and the Yorkshire and Lincolnshire Wolds. In the east, low-lying Fenland is largely reclaimed marshland. The flat landscape of East Anglia is covered by glacial soils. The northwest coastal plain of Lancashire and Cheshire is the only other major lowland in England. A peninsula in the southwest – Devon and Cornwall – contains granitic uplands, including Dartmoor and Exmoor. The limestone Pennines form a moorland backbone running through northern England. The Lake District (Cumbria) is a mountainous dome rising to Scafell Pike, the highest point in England at 978m (3210 ft).

Wales is a highland block, formed by a series of plateaux above which rise the Brecon Beacons in the south, Cader Idris and the Berwyn range in the centre, and Snowdonia in the north, where Snowdon reaches 1085m (3560 ft).

In Scotland, the Highlands in the north and the Southern Uplands are separated by the rift valley of the Central Lowlands, where the majority of Scotland's population, agriculture and industry are to be found. The Highlands are divided by the Great Glen in which lies Loch Ness. Although Ben Nevis is the highest point at 1392m (4406 ft), the most prominent range of the Highlands is the Cairngorm Mountains. The Southern Uplands lie below 853m (2800 ft). Scottish lowlands include Buchan in the northeast, Caithness in the north and a coastal plain around the Moray Firth. To the west of Scotland are the many islands of the Inner and Outer Hebrides, while to the north are the Orkney and Shetland Islands.

Uplands in Northern Ireland include the Sperrin Mountains in the northwest, the uplands in County Antrim, and the Mourne Mountains rising to Slieve Donard at 852m (2796 ft). Lough Neagh – at the centre of Northern Ireland – is the UK's largest lake.

Principal rivers: Severn, Thames (with Churn), Trent-Humber, Aire (with Yorkshire Ouse), Bedford Ouse, Wye, Tay, Nene. ***Highest point:*** Ben Nevis 1392m (4406 ft).

Climate: The temperate climate of the UK is warmed by the North Atlantic Drift. There is considerable local variety, particularly in rainfall totals, which range from just over 500 mm (20 in) in the southeast to 5000 mm (200 in) in northwest Scotland.

Economy

About one sixth of the British labour force is involved in manufacturing. The principal industries include iron and steel, motor vehicles, electronics and electrical engineering, textiles and clothing, and consumer goods. British industry relies heavily upon imports of raw materials. The UK is self-sufficient in petroleum (from the North Sea) and has important reserves of natural gas. The coal industry declined as seams became uneconomic. As Britain is a major trading nation, London is one of the world's leading banking, financial and insurance centres, and the 'invisible earnings' from these services make an important contribution to exports. Tourism is another major foreign-currency earner. Agriculture involves about 1% of the labour force and is principally concerned with raising sheep and cattle. Arable farming is widespread in the east, where the main crops are barley, wheat, potatoes and sugar beet. Economic problems have included repeated crises of confidence in the value of the pound, credit squeezes and high rates of unemployment. Since 1980 most major nationalized industries have been privatized. ***Currency:*** Pound sterling.

Recent History

The reign of Queen Victoria (1837–1901) witnessed the height of British power. Britain – the first country to undergo an industrial revolution – dominated world trade. British statesmen – including PMs Sir Robert Peel (1788–1850), Lord Palmerston (1784–1865), William Ewart Gladstone (1809–98) and Benjamin Disraeli (1804–81) – dominated the world stage. The British Empire included much of Africa, the Indian subcontinent and Australasia. Parliamentary democracy increased with the gradual extension of the right to vote, starting with the Reform Act of 1832. Representative government was granted to distant colonies, beginning with Canada and Australia, but was denied to Ireland, where nationalist sentiment was stirring. By 1900 Britain's economic dominance was being challenged by the USA and, more particularly, by Germany. Rivalry with Imperial Germany was but one factor contributing to the causes of World War I. PM Herbert Asquith (1852–1928) led a reforming Liberal Government from 1908 to 1916 but – after criticism of his conduct of the war – he was replaced by David Lloyd George (1863–1945), who as Chancellor of the Exchequer had introduced health and unemployment insurance.

The 'old dominions' – Canada, Australia, New Zealand and South Africa – emerged from the war as autonomous countries, and their independent status was confirmed by the Statute of Westminster (1931). The Easter Rising in Ireland (1916) led to the partition of the island in 1922. Only Northern Ireland – the area with a Protestant majority – stayed within the United Kingdom, but from 1968 to 1994 bitter conflict resurfaced in the province as Roman Catholic republicans – seeking unity with the Republic of Ireland – clashed with Protestant Loyalists intent upon preserving the link with Britain. British troops were stationed in Northern Ireland to keep order and to defeat the terrorist violence of the IRA and Loyalist illegal organizations. In 1994 the terrorist organizations declared a ceasefire and the Northern Ireland peace process began.

In World War II, Britain – led by PM Sir Winston Churchill (1874–1965), who had strenuously opposed appeasement in the 1930s – played a major role in the defeat of the Axis powers, and from 1940 to 1941 the UK stood alone against an apparently invincible Germany. Following the war, the Labour government of Clement Attlee (1883–1967) established the 'welfare state'. At the same time, the British Empire began its transformation into a Commonwealth of some 50 independent states, starting with the independence of India in 1947. By the late 1980s Britain was no longer a world power, although a British nuclear deterrent was retained.

By the 1970s the UK was involved in restructuring its domestic economy and, consequently, its welfare state – from 1979 to 1990 under the Conservative premiership of Margaret Thatcher (1925–). The country has also joined (1973) and has attempted to come to terms with the EU/EC. Britain has resisted European federalism, in particular moves to introduce a common currency and the Social Charter. In 1994–95, the question of devolution of government to Scotland and Wales, which had been a major issue of the later 1970s, resurfaced.

UNITED STATES OF AMERICA

Official name: The United States of America.
Member of: UN, NATO, OAS, OECD, NAFTA, OSCE, G7, ANZUS, Apec.
Area: 9,529,063 km^2 (3,679,192 sq mi).
Population: 256,561,000 (1993 est).
Capital: Washington D.C. 3,924,000 (city 598,000; 1990 census).
Other major cities: New York 18,087,000 (city 7,323,000, Newark 275,000), Los Angeles 14,532,000 (city 3,485,000, Long Beach 429,000, Anaheim 266,000), Chicago 8,066,000 (city 2,784,000), San Francisco 6,253,000 (city 724,000, San Jose 782,000, Oakland 372,000), Philadelphia 5,899,000 (city 1,586,000), Detroit 4,665,000 (city 1,028,000), Boston 4,172,000 (city 574,000), Dallas 3,885,000 (city 1,007,000, Fort Worth 478,000), Houston 3,711,000 (city 1,631,000), Miami 3,193,000 (city 359,000), Atlanta 2,834,000 (city 394,000), Cleveland 2,760,000 (city 506,000), Seattle 2,559,000 (city 516,000), San Diego 2,498,000 (city 1,111,000), Minneapolis-St Paul 2,464,000 (city 368,000, St Paul 272,000), St Louis 2,444,000 (city 397,000), Baltimore 2,382,000 (city 736,000), Pittsburgh 2,243,000 (city 370,000), Phoenix 2,122,000 (city 983,000), Tampa 2,068,000 (city 280,000), Denver 1,848,000 (city 468,000), Cincinnati 1,744,000 (city 364,000), Milwaukee 1,607,000 (city 628,000), Kansas City 1,566,000 (city 435,000),

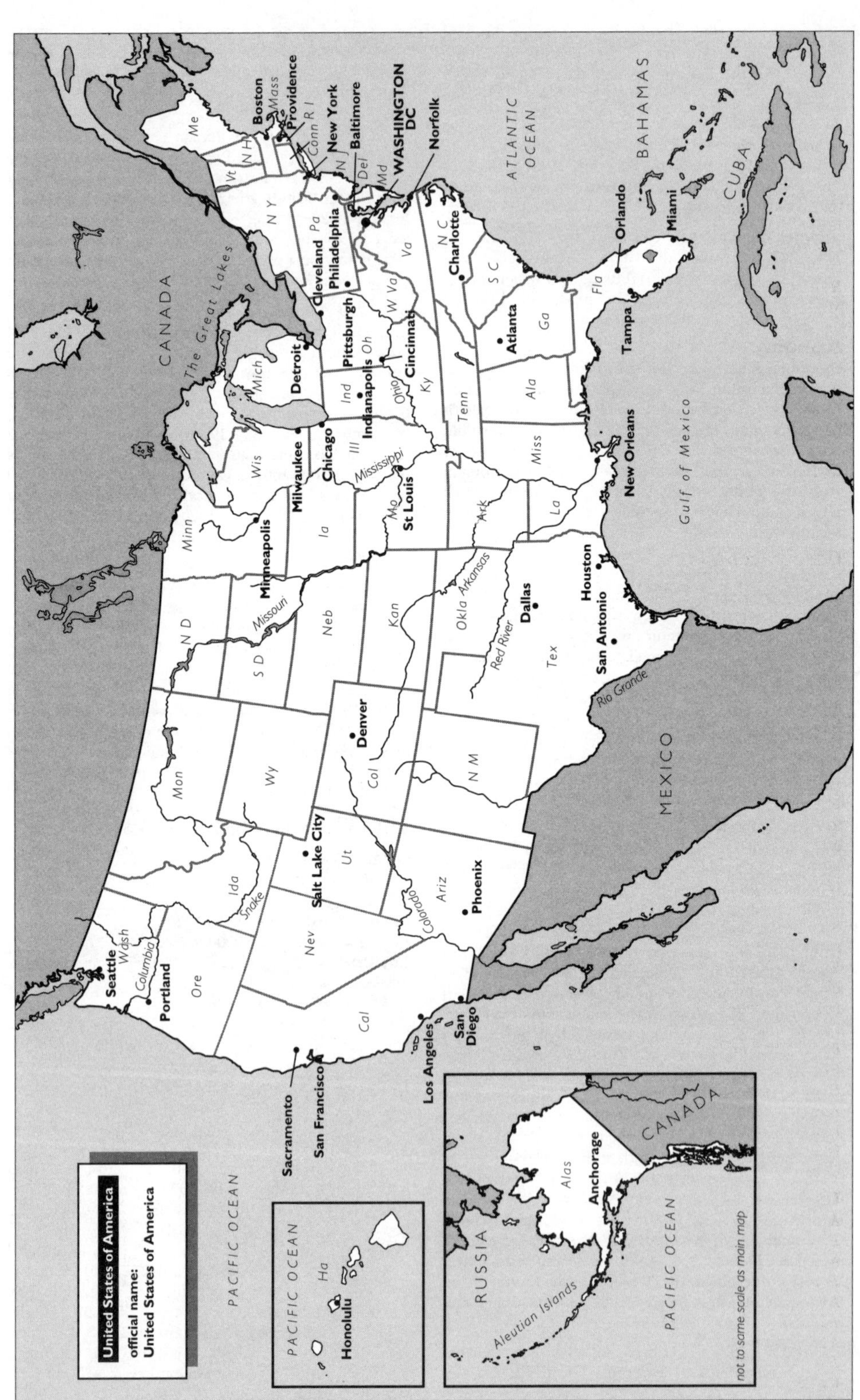
United States of America
official name:
United States of America
CANADA
The Great Lakes
ATLANTIC OCEAN
BAHAMAS
CUBA
Gulf of Mexico
MEXICO
PACIFIC OCEAN
Me
Boston
Mass
Providence
R I
Conn
New York
Baltimore
WASHINGTON DC
Norfolk
N H
Vt
N Y
N J
Del
Md
Pa
Philadelphia
Cleveland
Pittsburgh
Va
W Va
N C
Charlotte
S C
Atlanta
Ga
Fla
Orlando
Miami
Tampa
Mich
Detroit
Oh
Cincinnati
Ind
Indianapolis
Ohio
Ky
Tenn
Ala
Miss
New Orleans
Wis
Milwaukee
Chicago
Ill
Mississippi
St Louis
Mo
Ark
La
Minn
Minneapolis
Ia
N D
S D
Missouri
Neb
Kan
Okla
Arkansas
Red River
Dallas
Houston
San Antonio
Tex
Rio Grande
Mon
Wy
Denver
Col
N M
Ida
Snake
Salt Lake City
Ut
Ariz
Phoenix
Colorado
Nev
Wash
Seattle
Columbia
Portland
Ore
Cal
Sacramento
San Francisco
Los Angeles
San Diego
PACIFIC OCEAN
Ha
Honolulu
RUSSIA
Alas
Anchorage
CANADA
Aleutian Islands
PACIFIC OCEAN
not to same scale as main map

Sacramento 1,481,000 (city 369,000), Portland 1,478,000 (city 437,000), Norfolk 1,396,000 (city 261,000), Columbus 1,377,000 (city 633,000), San Antonio 1,302,000 (city 936,000), Indianapolis 1,250,000 (city 742,000), New Orleans 1,239,000 (city 497,000), Buffalo 1,189,000 (city 328,000), Charlotte 1,162,000 (city 396,000), Providence 1,142,000 (city 161,000), Hartford 1,086,000 (city 140,000), Orlando 1,073,000 (city 165,000), Salt Lake City 1,072,000 (city 160,000), Rochester 1,002,000 (city 232,000) (1990 census).

Languages: English (official), Spanish (6%, as a first language).

Religions: Roman Catholic (23%), Baptist (10%), Methodist (5%), Lutheran (3%), Judaism (2%), Orthodox (2%), Presbyterian (2%), Mormons (2%).

Education: is compulsory in all states. The years of compulsory schooling vary from state to state, but seven to 16 is the average. *Adult literacy:* over 85%. *Universities:* 658 universities and 980 other colleges of university status, plus over 1900 other institutions that offer degree-level courses.

Defence: (1993 figures) *Army:* 586,200 personnel. *Air force:* 449,900. *Navy:* 510,000. *Marine corps:* 183,000. *Conscription:* none, although there is a selective call-up in time of war.

Government

Congress comprises the Senate (the Upper House) and the House of Representatives (the Lower House). The Senate has 100 members – two from each state – elected by universal adult suffrage for six years, with one third of the senators retiring every two years. The 435-member House of Representatives is directly elected for a two-year term from single-member constituencies. Additional non-voting members of the House are returned by the District of Columbia, Guam, Puerto Rico, United States Virgin Islands and American Samoa. Executive federal power is vested in the President, who serves a maximum of two four-year terms. The President and Vice President are elected by an electoral college of delegates pledged to support individual presidential candidates – the college itself is elected by universal adult suffrage. Upon the approval of the Senate, the President appoints a Cabinet of Secretaries. Each of the 50 states has a separate constitution and legislature with wide-ranging powers. Executive power in each state is held by a directly elected Governor.

Largest parties: Democratic Party (Dem), Republican Party (Rep).

Local government: 50 states and one federal district.

President: Bill (William Jefferson) Clinton (Dem).

Dependencies: North Mariana Islands, Puerto Rico, American Samoa,Guam, United States Virgin Islands, Johnston Atoll, Kingman Reef, Midway Islands, Wake Island, and Howland, Baker and Jarvis Islands. See Other Territories (beginning on p. 729).

US States

Alabama *Area:* 133,915 km² (51,705 sq mi). *Population:* 4,187,000 (1993 est). *Capital:* Montgomery.

Alaska *Area:* 1,530,693 km² (591,004 sq mi). *Population:* 599,000 (1993 est). *Capital:* Juneau.

Arizona *Area:* 295,259 km² (114,000 sq mi). *Population:* 3,936,000 (1993 est). *Capital:* Phoenix.

Arkansas *Area:* 137,754 km² (53,187 sq mi). *Population:* 2,424,000 (1993 est). *Capital:* Little Rock.

California *Area:* 411,047 km² (158,706 sq mi). *Population:* 31,211,000 (1993 est). *Capital:* Sacramento.

Colorado *Area:* 269,594 km² (104,091 sq mi). *Population:* 3,566,000 (1993 est). *Capital:* Denver.

Connecticut *Area:* 12,997 km² (5018 sq mi). *Population:* 3,277,000 (1993 est). *Capital:* Hartford.

Delaware *Area:* 5294 km² (2045 sq mi). *Population:* 700,000 (1993 est). *Capital:* Dover.

Florida *Area:* 151,939 km² (58,664 sq mi). *Population:* 13,679,000 (1993 est). *Capital:* Tallahassee.

Georgia *Area:* 152,576 km² (58,910 sq mi). *Population:* 6,917,000 (1993 est). *Capital:* Atlanta.

Hawaii *Area:* 16,760 km² (6471 sq mi). *Population:* 1,172,000 (1993 est). *Capital:* Honolulu.

Idaho *Area:* 216,430 km² (83,564 sq mi). *Population:* 1,099,000 (1993 est). *Capital:* Boise.

Illinois *Area:* 149,885 km² (57,871 sq mi). *Population:* 11,697,000 (1993 est). *Capital:* Springfield.

Indiana *Area:* 94,309 km² (36,413 sq mi). *Population:* 5,713,000 (1993 est). *Capital:* Indianapolis.

Iowa *Area:* 145,752 km² (56,275 sq mi). *Population:* 2,814,000 (1993 est). *Capital:* Des Moines.

Kansas *Area:* 213,096 km² (82,277 sq mi). *Population:* 2,531,000 (1993 est). *Capital:* Topeka.

Kentucky *Area:* 104,659 km² (40,410 sq mi). *Population:* 3,789,000 (1993 est). *Capital:* Frankfort.

Louisiana *Area:* 123,677 km² (47,752 sq mi). *Population:* 4,295,000 (1993 est). *Capital:* Baton Rouge.

Maine *Area:* 86,156 km² (33,265 sq mi). *Population:* 1,239,000 (1993 est). *Capital:* Augusta.

Maryland *Area:* 27,091 km² (10,460 sq mi). *Population:* 4,965,000 (1993 est). *Capital:* Annapolis.

Massachusetts *Area:* 21,455 km² (8284 sq mi). *Population:* 6,012,000 (1993 est). *Capital:* Boston.

Michigan *Area:* 251,493 km² (97,102 sq mi). *Population:* 9,476,000 (1993 est). *Capital:* Lansing.

Minnesota *Area:* 224,329 km² (86,614 sq mi). *Population:* 4,517,000 (1993 est). *Capital:* St Paul.

Mississippi *Area:* 123,514 km² (47,689 sq mi). *Population:* 2,643,000 (1993 est). *Capital:* Jackson.

Missouri *Area:* 180,514 km² (69,697 sq mi). *Population:* 5,234,000 (1993 est). *Capital:* Jefferson City.

Montana *Area:* 380,847 km² (147,046 sq mi). *Population:* 839,000 (1993 est). *Capital:* Helena.

Nebraska *Area:* 200,349 km² (77,355 sq mi). *Population:* 1,607,000 (1993 est). *Capital:* Lincoln.

Nevada *Area:* 286,352 km² (110,561 sq mi). *Population:* 1 ,389,000 (1993 est). *Capital:* Carson City.

New Hampshire *Area:* 24,032 km² (9279 sq mi). *Population:* 1,125,000 (1993 est). *Capital:* Concord.

New Jersey *Area:* 20,168 km² (7787 sq mi). *Population:* 7,879,000 (1993 est). *Capital:* Trenton.

New Mexico *Area:* 314,924 km² (121,593 sq mi). *Population:* 1,616,000 (1993 est). *Capital:* Santa Fe.

New York *Area:* 136,583 km² (52,735 sq mi). *Population:* 18,197,000 (1993 est). *Capital:* Albany.

North Carolina *Area:* 136,412 km² (52,669 sq mi). *Population:* 6,945,000 (1993 est). *Capital:* Rayleigh.

North Dakota *Area:* 183,117 km² (70,702 sq mi). *Population:* 635,000 (1993 est). *Capital:* Bismarck.

Ohio *Area:* 115,998 km² (44,787 sq mi). *Population:* 11,091,000 (1993 est). *Capital:* Columbus.

Oklahoma *Area:* 181,185 km² (69,956 sq mi). *Population:* 3,231,000 (1993 est). *Capital:* Oklahoma City.

Oregon *Area:* 251,418 km² (97,073 sq mi). *Population:* 3,032,000 (1993 est). *Capital:* Salem.

Pennsylvania *Area:* 119,251 km² (46,043 sq mi). *Population:* 12,048,000 (1993 est). *Capital:* Harrisburg.

Rhode Island *Area:* 3139 km² (1212 sq mi). *Population:* 1,000,000 (1993 est). *Capital:* Providence.
South Carolina *Area:* 80,582 km² (31,113 sq mi). *Population:* 3,643,000 (1993 est). *Capital:* Columbia.
South Dakota *Area:* 199,730 km² (77,116 sq mi). *Population:* 715,000 (1993 est). *Capital:* Pierre.
Tennessee *Area:* 109,152 km² (42,144 sq mi). *Population:* 5,099,000 (1993 est). *Capital:* Nashville.
Texas *Area:* 691,027 km² (266,807 sq mi). *Population:* 18,031,000 (1993 est). *Capital:* Austin.
Utah *Area:* 219,887 km² (84,899 sq mi). *Population:* 1,860,000 (1993 est). *Capital:* Salt Lake City.
Vermont *Area:* 24,900 km² (9614 sq mi). *Population:* 576,000 (1993 est). *Capital:* Montpelier.
Virginia *Area:* 105,586 km² (40,767 sq mi). *Population:* 6,491,000 (1993 est). *Capital:* Richmond.
Washington *Area:* 176,479 km² (68,139 sq mi). *Population:* 5,255,000 (1993 est). *Capital:* Olympia.
West Virginia *Area:* 62,758 km² (24,323 sq mi). *Population:* 1,820,000 (1993 est). *Capital:* Charleston.
Wisconsin *Area:* 171,496 km² (66,215 sq mi). *Population:* 5,038,000 (1993 est). *Capital:* Madison.
Wyoming *Area:* 253,324 km² (97,809 sq mi). *Population:* 470,000 (1993 est). *Capital:* Cheyenne.
District of Columbia *Area:* 179 km² (69 sq mi). *Population:* 578,000 (1993 est). *Capital:* Washington.

Geography

The Atlantic coastal plain stretches along the entire east coast, including the lowland peninsula of Florida, and along the coast of the Gulf of Mexico, where it reaches up to 800 km (500 mi) inland. The Blue Ridge escarpment rises sharply to the west of the plain. This is the most easterly part of the forested Appalachian Mountains, which stretch for some 2400 km (1500 mi) and reach 2037 m (6684 ft) at Mount Mitchell. The largest physical region of the USA is a vast interior plain drained by the Mississippi and major tributaries, including the Missouri, Arkansas, Nebraska, Ohio and Red River. This lowland stretches from the Great Lakes in the north to the coastal plain in the south, and from the Rocky Mountains in the west to the Appalachians in the east. The Central Lowlands – the eastern part of the lowland – comprise the Cotton Belt in the south and the Corn (maize) Belt in the north. The Great Plains – the drier western part of the lowland – begin some 480 km (300 mi) west of the Mississippi. The west of the USA is the country's highest region and includes the Rocky Mountains in the east and the Cascades, the Sierra Nevada and the Coastal Ranges in the west. The mountains continue north into Alaska. The western mountainous belt is prone to earthquakes, in particular along the line of the San Andreas Fault in California. Within the mountains are deserts – including the Mojave and the Arizona Deserts – and the large Intermontane Plateau containing the Great Basin, an area of internal drainage around the Great Salt Lake. The 20 islands of Hawaii are volcanic in origin and contain active volcanoes. The USA's natural vegetation ranges from tundra in Alaska to tropical vegetation in Hawaii, and includes coniferous forest in the northwest, Mediterranean scrub in south California, desert in the Intermontane Plateau, and prairie grasslands on the Great Plains. ***Principal rivers:*** Mississippi (with Missouri and Red Rock), Rio Grande, Yukon (with Nisutlin), Colorado, Pecos, Arkansas, Red River, Snake River, Ohio, Tennessee, Alabama, Hudson. ***Highest point:*** Mount McKinley 6194m (20,320 ft).
Climate: The mountains behind the Pacific northwest coast are the wettest region of the USA. Coastal California has a warm Mediterranean climate. Desert or semidesert conditions prevail in mountain basins. The continental Great Plains receive 250–750 mm (10–30 in) of rain a year, while the Central Lowlands to the east are generally wetter. Extremes of temperature are experienced in the north of the continental interior. The east is generally temperate. The Appalachians and the east coastal plain are humid, with temperatures rising in the south, where Florida is subtropical. Coastal Alaska has a cold maritime climate while the north and interior is polar. Hawaii has a Pacific climate with high temperatures and little seasonal variation.

Economy

The position of the USA as the world's leading economic power is threatened by Japan. The USA is self-sufficient in most products apart from petroleum, chemicals, certain metals and manufactured machinery, and newsprint. Agriculture is heavily mechanized and produces considerable surpluses for export. The main crops include maize, wheat, soyabeans, sugar cane, barley, cotton, potatoes and a wide variety of fruit (including citrus fruit in Florida and California). More than 25% of the USA is pastureland, and cattle and sheep are important in the Great Plains. Forests cover over 30% of the country and are the basis of the world's second largest timber industry. The USA has great natural resources, including coal (mainly in the Appalachians), iron ore, petroleum and natural gas (mainly in Texas, Alaska and California), copper, bauxite, lead and silver, and major rivers that have proved suitable for hydroelectric power plants. The industrial base of the USA is diverse. Principal industries include iron and steel, motor vehicles, electrical and electronic engineering, food processing, chemicals, cement, aluminium, aerospace industries, telecommunications, textiles and clothing, and consumer goods. Tourism is a major foreign-currency earner. Service industries involve over three quarters of the labour force. Finance, insurance and banking are important, and Wall Street (New York) is one the world's major stock exchanges. US economic policy exerts an influence throughout the world, thus a revival of pressure for trade protectionism since the late 1980s has caused international concern. ***Currency:*** US dollar.

Recent History

Between 1880 and 1900 the USA emerged as an industrial giant. At the same time, the population increased dramatically, as immigrants flocked to the New World, in particular from Germany, eastern Europe and Russia. Interest in world trade increased American involvement abroad. The Cuban revolt against Spanish rule led the USA into a war against Spain (1898) and brought US rule to the Philippines, Puerto Rico and Guam. American participation in World War I from 1917 hastened the Allied victory, but the idealistic principles favoured by President Woodrow Wilson (1856–1924) were compromised in the post-war settlement. After the war the USA retreated into isolationism and protectionism in trade. The imposition of Prohibition (1919–33) increased smuggling and the activities of criminal gangs, but the 1920s were prosperous until the Depression began in 1929 with the collapse of the stock market. Federal investment and intervention brought relief through the New Deal programme of President Franklin Roosevelt

(1882–1945). The Japanese attack on Pearl Harbor brought the USA into World War II. American involvement in the European and Pacific theatres of war was decisive and committed the USA to a world role as a superpower in 1945. US assistance was instrumental in rebuilding Europe (through the Marshall Plan) and Japan.

From the late 1940s to the end of the 1980s, the USA confronted the Soviet Union's perceived global threat in the Cold War. As the leader of the Western alliance, the USA established bases in Europe, the Far East and the Indian and Pacific Oceans, so encircling the Soviet bloc. The USA was involved in the Korean War (1950–53) against Chinese and North Korean forces, and in direct military intervention in Guatemala (1954), Lebanon (1958 and 1983–85), the Dominican Republic (1965), Panama (1968 and 1989) and Grenada (1983). The greatest commitment, however, was in Vietnam, where from 1964 to 1973 US forces attempted to hold back a Communist takeover of Indochina, but a growing disenchantment with the war forced an American withdrawal.

From the 1950s the civil rights movement – led by Martin Luther King (1929–68) – campaigned for full political rights for Blacks and for desegregation of schools, hospitals, buses, etc. In the early 1960s President John F. Kennedy (1917–63) made racial discrimination illegal. Kennedy supported the unsuccessful invasion of Cuba by right-wing exiles (1961) and was assassinated in 1963. Growing economic problems in the 1970s led to the election of a monetarist President, Ronald Reagan (1911–), in 1981. The USA continued to support movements and governments perceived as being in the Western interest – for example, backing Israel in the Middle East, providing weapons to the UNITA guerrillas in Angola and the Contra guerrillas in Nicaragua, and leading the coalition against Iraq (1990–91) after the latter's invasion of Kuwait. However, the increasing economic challenge from Japan, and the collapse of Communism in Eastern Europe (1989) and the USSR (1991), raised questions about the USA's future world role. From 1990–91 some overseas bases were closed and stocks of nuclear weapons were cut. In 1992, American forces led relief efforts in Somalia and in 1994 intervened in Haiti as part of an international effort to restore the deposed president. However, since 1993, under President Bill Clinton, domestic issues have taken priority over foreign affairs.

American political life is dominated by two parties – the Republicans and the Democrats. The Republican Party (formed in 1854) began as a party dedicated to national rather than states' rights. The older Democratic Party, which was traditionally anti-federalist, was the dominant force in US politics from 1800 to 1856. From the Civil War to the 1930s the Republicans were usually the dominant party. Both parties are coalitions of shifting interests. In the 1990s the Republicans have been characterized as anti-statist, in particular with regard to welfare, while the Democrats (who draw much of their support from liberals and minorities) have sought to extend the arm of government.

URUGUAY

Official name: La República Oriental del Uruguay (The Eastern Republic of Uruguay).
Member of: UN, OAS, ALADI, Mercosur.

Area: 176,215 km^2 (68,037 sq mi).
Population: 3,150,000 (1993 est).
Capital: Montevideo 1,370,000 (city 1,312,000; 1985 census).
Other major cities: Salto 80,000, Paysandú 76,000, Las Piedras 58,000, Rivera 57,000 (1985 census).
Language: Spanish (official).
Religions: Roman Catholic (58%), various Protestant Churches.
Education: is compulsory between the ages of six and 14. *Adult literacy:* 95%. *Universities:* two.
Defence: (1993 figures) *Army:* 17,200 personnel. *Air force:* 3000. *Navy:* 4500. *Paramilitary:* 1200. *Conscription:* none.

Government

The President and Congress – consisting of a 31-member Senate and a 99-member Chamber of Deputies – are elected for five years by universal adult suffrage. The President appoints a Council of Ministers.
Largest parties: (conservative) National Party (PN), (centre) Colorado Party (PC), (left-wing coalition) Broad Front (FA), (social democratic) New Space (EN).
Local government: 19 departments.
President: Julio Sanguinetti (PC).

Geography

Uruguay consists mainly of low plains and plateaux. The southeast contains hill country. The coastline is fringed by tidal lakes. ***Principal rivers:*** Río Negro, Uruguay, Santa Lucia. ***Highest point:*** Cerro de las Animas 500m (1643 ft).
Climate: Uruguay has a temperate climate with warm summers and mild winters. Rainfall averages around 900 mm (35 in).

Economy

Pastureland – for sheep and beef cattle – covers about 80% of the land. Meat, wool and hides are the leading exports. Despite a lack of natural resources, Uruguay has a high standard of living, but the demands of the welfare state have placed a burden on the economy.
Currency: Peso.

Recent History

Until 1903 Uruguay was ruled by dictators and wracked by civil war. However, prosperity from cattle and wool, and the presidencies of the reformer José Battle (1903–07 and 1911–15), turned Uruguay into a democracy and an advanced welfare state. A military dictatorship held power during the Depression. By the late 1960s economic problems had ushered in a period of social and political turmoil, and urban guerrillas became active. In 1973 a coup installed a military dictatorship that made Uruguay notorious for abuses of human rights. In 1985 the country returned to democratic rule.

UZBEKISTAN

Official name: Ozbekiston Jumhuriyati (Republic of Uzbekistan).
Member of: UN, CIS, OSCE.
Area: 447,400 km^2 (172,700 sq mi).
Population: 21,180,000 (1993 est).
Capital: Tashkent 2,120,000 (1992 est).
Other major cities: Samarkand (Samarqand) 372,000, Namangan 333,000, Andizhan 302,000, Bukhara 235,000 (1992 est).
Languages: Uzbek (official; 71%), Russian (8%), Tajik (4%).
Religion: Sunni Islam majority.
Education: is compulsory between the ages of six and 14. *Adult literacy:* No figures available. *Universities:* three universities, plus two polytechnics of university status.
Defence: (1993 figures) *Army:* 38,000 personnel. *Air force:* 2000. *Conscription:* 18 months.

Government

A 150-member Assembly (Majlis) is elected for four years by universal adult suffrage. The President is directly elected for five years.
Largest parties: (former Communist) Democratic Party (DP), (reformist) Fatherland Party (FP).
Local government: 12 regions and one autonomous republic.
President: Islam A. Karimov (DP).
Prime Minister: Abdulhashim Mutalov (DP).

Autonomous republic

Karakalpakstan *Area:* 164,900 km^2 (63,700 sq mi). *Population:* 1,311,000 (1992 est). *Capital:* Nukus.

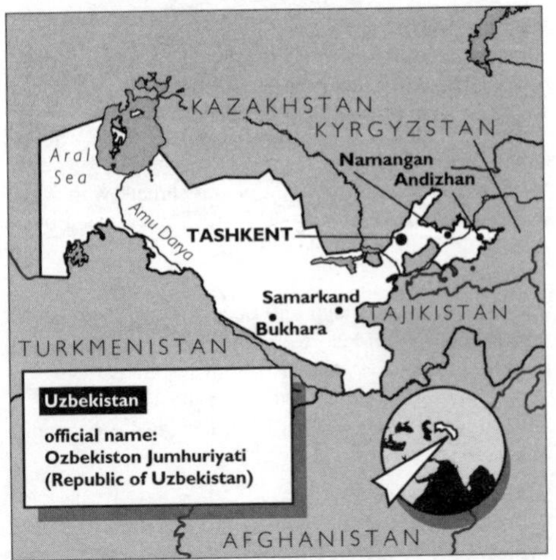

Geography

Western Uzbekistan is flat and mainly desert. The mountainous east includes ridges of the Tien Shan and part of the Fergana valley. ***Principal rivers:*** Amu Darya (Oxus), Syrdarya, Naryn, Zeravshan.
Highest point: Bannovka 4488m (14,724 ft).
Climate: Uzbekistan has a warm continental climate characterized by hot summers and low rainfall. Only the mountains receive over 500 mm (20 in) of rain a year.

Economy

Uzbekistan is one the world's leading producers of cotton, but the extraction of irrigation from the Amu Darya and its tributaries has contributed to the gradual shrinkage of the Aral Sea. The republic has important reserves of natural gas and major machine and heavy engineering industries. The economy is still mainly state-owned and centrally planned, and reforms have been slowed by the government.
Currency: Som.

Recent History

The Uzbeks did not finally come under Russian rule until the khans of Bukhara and Khiva became vassals of the Tsar (1868–73). After the Russian Revolution, the Basmachi revolt (1918–22) resisted Soviet rule, but the khans were eventually deposed (1920) and Soviet republics established (1923–24). Uzbekistan was created in 1924, when the boundaries of Soviet Central Asia were reorganized. Independence was declared after the abortive coup in Moscow by Communist hardliners and international recognition was achieved when the USSR was dissolved (1991). Alleged abuses of human rights in independent Uzbekistan have attracted international criticism.

VANUATU

Official names: The Republic of Vanuatu or La République de Vanuatu.
Member of: UN, Commonwealth.
Area: 12,189 km^2 (4706 sq mi).
Population: 160,000 (1993 est).
Capital: Port-Vila 19,000 (1991 est).
Other major town: Luganville 7000 (1989 est).
Languages: English (official; 60% as a second language), French (official; 40% as a second language), Bislama (national; 82% as a first language), 130 local dialects.
Religions: Presbyterian (33%), Anglican (30%), animist (20%), Roman Catholic (17%).

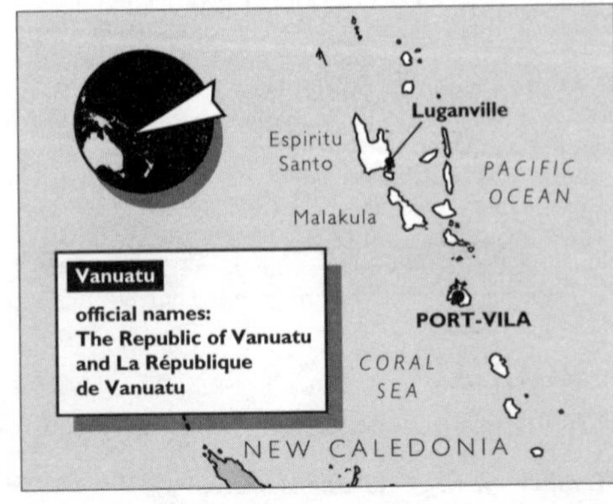

Education: is not compulsory. *Adult literacy:* 53%. *Universities:* one university centre.
Defence: (1993 figures) *Paramilitary:* 300 personnel. *Conscription:* none.

Government

The 46-member Parliament is elected for four years by universal adult suffrage. It elects a Prime Minister, who appoints a Council of Ministers. The President is elected for five years by Parliament and the Presidents of Regional Councils.
Largest parties: (centre-right) Union of Moderate Parties (UMP), (socialist) Vanuaaku Pati (VP), (centre-right) National United Party (NUP), Melanesian Progressive Party (MPP), (socialist) Our Land Party.
Local government: 11 regions.
President: Jean-Marie Leye (UMP).
Prime Minister: Maxime Carlot (UMP).

Geography

Vanuatu comprises over 75 islands, some of which are mountainous and include active volcanoes.
Principal rivers: There are many unnamed streams.
Highest point: Mont Tabwémasana 1879m (6165 ft).
Climate: Vanuatu's tropical climate is moderated by southeast trade winds from May to October.

Economy

Subsistence farming occupies the majority of the labour force. The main exports include copra, fish and cocoa. Tourism is increasingly important. ***Currency:*** Vatu.

Recent History

British and French commercial interests in the New Hebrides in the 19th century resulted in joint control over the islands and the establishment of a condominium in 1906. The islands gained independence as Vanuatu in 1980, but have been troubled by attempted secession and political unrest.

VATICAN CITY

Official name: Stato della Cittá del Vaticano (State of the Vatican City). Also known as the Holy See.
Member of: OSCE.
Area: 0.44 km^2 (0.17 sq mi).
Population: 750 (1989 est).
Languages: Italian and Latin (both official).
Religion: The Vatican is the headquarters of the Roman Catholic Church.
Education: There are five pontifical universities and 11 pontifical colleges.
Defence: There is a 100-member papal guard, the Swiss Guard.

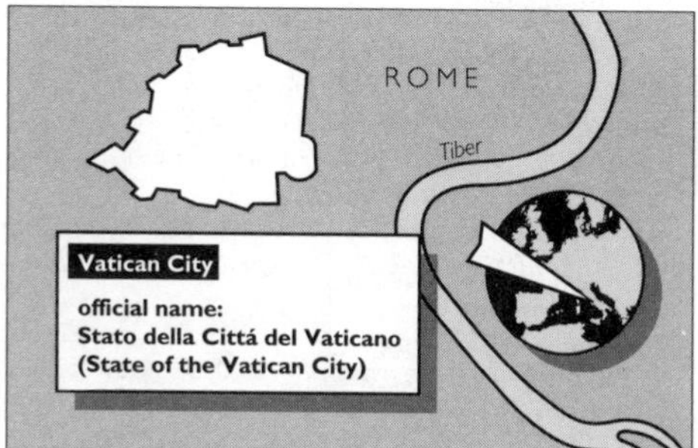

Government

The Pope is elected Bishop of Rome and head of the Roman Catholic Church for life by the Sacred College of Cardinals. The Vatican City is administered by a Pontifical Commission appointed by the Pope.
Pontiff: HH Pope John Paul II (born Karol Wojtlya) (elected 16 October 1978).

Geography

The state consists of the Vatican City, a walled enclave in Rome, plus a number of churches in Rome (including the cathedral of St John Lateran), the papal villa at Castelgandolfo and the Vatican Radio station at Santa Maria di Galeria.

Recent History

The tiny Vatican City state is all that remains of the once extensive Papal States. All except Rome and Latium were lost during Italian unification. When the French troops protecting the Pope were withdrawn in 1870, Italian forces entered Rome, which became the capital of the new kingdom of Italy. Pope Pius IX (reigned 1846–78) protested at the loss of his temporal power and retreated into the Vatican, from which no Pope emerged until 1929, when the Lateran Treaties provided for Italian recognition of the Vatican City as an independent state. Since the 1960s the Papacy has again played an important role in international diplomacy, particularly under Popes Paul VI (reigned 1963–78) and John Paul II (1978–).

VENEZUELA

Official name: La República de Venezuela (Republic of Venezuela).
Member of: UN, OAS, ALADI, Andean Pact.
Area: 912,050 km^2 (352,144 sq mi).
Population: 20,662,000 (1993 est).
Capital: Caracas 3,436,000 (city 1,290,000; 1990 est).
Other major cities: Maracaibo 1,401,000 (city 1,207,000), Valencia 1,274,000 (city 955,000), Maracay 957,000 (city 538,000), Barquisimeto 787,000 (city 724,000), Ciudad Guyana 542,000, Barcelona 455,000 (city 109,000) (1990 est).
Languages: Spanish (official; 98%), various Amerin-

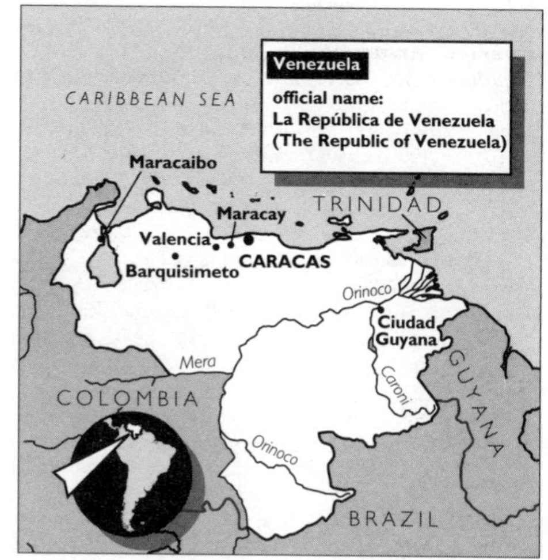

dian languages.
Religion: Roman Catholic (92%).
Education: is compulsory between the ages of five and 15. *Adult literacy:* 92%. *Universities:* 20 universities and two polytechnics of university status.
Defence: (1993 figures) *Army:* 34,000 personnel. *Air force:* 7000. *Navy:* 11,000. *Paramilitary:* 23,000. *Conscription:* 30 months; selective.

Government

The President and both Houses of the National Congress are elected for five years by universal adult suffrage. The Senate – the upper House – comprises 49 elected senators, plus former Presidents. The Chamber of the Deputies has 205 directly elected members. The President appoints a Council of Ministers.
Largest parties: (centre-left) Democratic Action (AD), Social Christian Party (COPEI), (centre-right) Convergence (Convergencia), (left-wing) Radical Cause Party (Causa R), Socialist Movement (MAS).
Local government: 22 states, one federal district and one federal dependency (comprising 75 islands).
President: Rafael Caldera (Convergencia).

States

Anzoátegui *Area:* 43,300 km^2 (16,700 sq mi). *Population:* 924,000 (1990 census). *Capital:* Barcelona.
Amazonas *Area:* 175,750 km^2 (67,900 sq mi). *Population:* 60,000 (1990 census). *Capital:* Puerto Ayacucho.
Apure *Area:* 76,500 km^2 (29,500 sq mi). *Population:* 305,000 (1990 census). *Capital:* San Francisco de Apure.
Aragua *Area:* 7014 km^2 (2700 sq mi). *Population:* 1,195,000 (1990 census). *Capital:* Maracay.
Barinas *Area:* 35,200 km^2 (13,600 sq mi). *Population:* 456,000 (1990 census). *Capital:* Barinas.
Bolívar *Area:* 238,000 km^2 (91,900 sq mi). *Population:* 969,000 (1990 census). *Capital:* Ciudad Bolívar.
Carabobo *Area:* 4650 km^2 (1795 sq mi). *Population:* 1,559,000 (1990 census). *Capital:* Valencia.
Cojedes *Area:* 14,800 km^2 (5700 sq mi). *Population:* 197,000 (1990 census). *Capital:* San Carlos.
Delta Amacuro *Area:* 40,200 km^2 (15,500 sq mi). *Population:* 91,000 (1990 census). *Capital:* Tucupita.
Falcón *Area:* 24,800 km^2 (9600 sq mi). *Population:* 633,000 (1990 census). *Capital:* Coro.
Guárico *Area:* 64,986 km^2 (25,091 sq mi). *Population:* 526,000 (1990 census). *Capital:* San Juan de los Morros.
Lara *Area:* 19,800 km^2 (7600 sq mi). *Population:* 1,270,000 (1990 census). *Capital:* Barquisimeto.
Mérida *Area:* 11,300 km^2 (4400 sq mi). *Population:* 616,000 (1990 census). *Capital:* Barcelona.
Miranda *Area:* 7950 km^2 (3070 sq mi). *Population:* 2,026,000 (1990 census). *Capital:* Los Teques.
Monagas *Area:* 28,900 km^2 (11,200 sq mi). *Population:* 503,000 (1990 census). *Capital:* Maturín.
Nueva Esparta *Area:* 1150 km^2 (440 sq mi). *Population:* 281,000 (1990 census). *Capital:* La Asunción.
Portuguesa *Area:* 15,200 km^2 (5900 sq mi). *Population:* 626,000 (1990 census). *Capital:* Guanare.
Sucre *Area:* 11,800 km^2 (4600 sq mi). *Population:* 723,000 (1990 census). *Capital:* Cumaná.
Táchira *Area:* 11,100 km^2 (4300 sq mi). *Population:* 860,000 (1990 census). *Capital:* San Cristóbal.
Trujillo *Area:* 7400 km^2 (2900 sq mi). *Population:* 520,000 (1990 census). *Capital:* Trujillo.
Yaracuy *Area:* 7100 km^2 (2700 sq mi). *Population:* 412,000 (1990 census). *Capital:* San Felipe.
Zulia *Area:* 63,100 km^2 (24,400 sq mi). *Population:* 2,387,000 (1990 census). *Capital:* Maracaibo.
Federal Dependencies (Dependencias Federales) *Area:* 120 km^2 (50 sq mi). *Population:* 2200 (1990 census). *Capital:* no capital; administered from the federal capital.
Federal District (Distrito Federal) *Area:* 1930 km^2 (745 sq mi). *Population:* 2,266,000 (1990 census). *Capital:* Caracas.

Geography

Mountains (which include part of the Andes) rise sharply behind the coastal plains of the north and northeast. In the northwest, the Maracaibo basin contains a large freshwater lake. Central Venezuela comprises low-lying grassland plains (the Llanos). The Guiana Highlands in the southeast include many high steep-sided plateaux. ***Principal rivers:*** Orinoco, Caroní, Caura, Aro, Ventuari, Meta. ***Highest point:*** Pico Bolívar 5007m (16,423 ft).
Climate: The tropical coast is arid. The cooler mountains and the tropical Llanos are wet, although the latter has a dry season from December to March.

Economy

As petroleum and natural gas account for 80% of export earnings, the fall in petroleum prices in the 1980s damaged Venezuela's economy. Agriculture is mainly concerned with raising beef cattle, and growing sugar cane and coffee for export; bananas, maize and rice are grown as subsistence crops. ***Currency:*** Bolivar.

Recent History

Independence from Spanish rule was followed by a series of military coups, revolts and dictators, including Juan Vicente Gómez, whose harsh rule lasted from 1909 to 1935. Since General Marcos Peréz Jiménez was overthrown (1958), Venezuela has been a civilian democracy. However, there have been two abortive coup attempts in the 1990s, partly as a result of economic uncertainty.

VIETNAM

Official name: Công hoa xâ hôi chu nghia Viêt Nam (The Socialist Republic of Vietnam).
Member of: UN.
Area: 331,033 km^2 (127,812 sq mi).
Population: 70,902,000 (1993 est).
Capital: Hanoi 2,095,000 (1992 est).
Other major cities: Ho Chi Minh City (formerly Saigon) 4,076,000, Haiphong 1,517,000, Da Nang 370,000, Can Tho 285,000 (1992 est).
Language: Vietnamese (official; 84%), Tay, Khmer.
Religions: Buddhist (55%), Roman Catholic (7%), Cao Dai (3%), Buddhist minority.
Education: is compulsory between the ages of six and 11. *Adult literacy:* 88%. *Universities:* seven universities.
Defence: (1993 figures) *Army:* 700,000 personnel. *Air force:* 15,000. *Air defence:* 150,000. *Navy:* 42,000. *Paramilitary:* over 4,000,000. *Conscription:* three years.

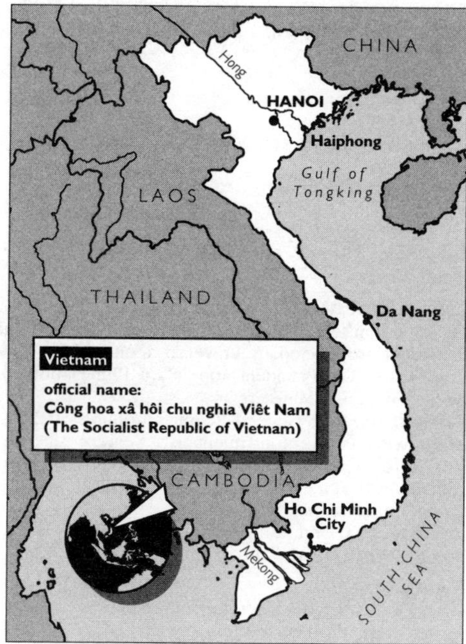

Government

The 395-member National Assembly is elected by universal adult suffrage for five years. The Assembly elects, from its own members, a Council of State – whose Chairman is head of state – and a Council of Ministers, headed by a Prime Minister.

Largest parties: Effective power is in the hands of the Communist Party, the only legal party.

Local government: 53 provinces and three cities.

President: Le Duc Anh.

Prime Minister: Vo Van Kiet.

Secretary General of the Communist Party: Do Muoi.

Geography

Plateaux, hill country and chains of mountains in Annam (central Vietnam) lie between the Mekong River delta in the south and the Red River (Hongha) delta in the north. ***Principal rivers:*** Mekong, Red River (Hong), Lo, Chay, Chu, Black (Da). ***Highest point:*** Fan si Pan 3142m (10,308 ft).

Climate: Vietnam has a hot humid climate, although winters are cool in the north. Heavy rainfall comes mainly during the monsoon season from April to October.

Economy

Over three quarters of the labour force is involved in agriculture, mainly cultivating rice. Other crops include cassava, maize and sweet potatoes for domestic consumption, and rubber, tea and coffee for export. Natural resources include coal, phosphates and tin, which are the basis of industries in the north. The wars in Vietnam, involvement in Cambodia and the loss of skilled workers through emigration have all had a serious effect on the economy. Despite aid from the USSR and the Eastern bloc up to the end of the 1980s, Vietnam remains underdeveloped. Attempts have been made to encourage Western investment since 1989–90. ***Currency:*** Dong.

Recent History

The French intervened in the area from the 1860s, established a protectorate in Vietnam in 1883 and formed the Union of Indochina – including Cambodia and Laos – in 1887. Revolts against colonial rule in the 1930s marked the start of a period of war and occupation that lasted for over 40 years. The Japanese occupied Vietnam in 1940 and eventually set up a puppet government under the Emperor Bao Din. In 1941, the Communist leader Ho Chi Minh etablished the Viet Minh as a nationalist guerrilla army to fight the Japanese. At the end of the war, the Viet Minh received US aid and, after the Japanese surrender, a republic was established in Hanoi with Ho as president. French rule was not reestablished until 1946, with Ho's state initially recognized as a 'free state' within French Indochina. After clashes between the Hanoi government and the French, Ho left Hanoi and began a guerrilla war against the French and the restored Emperor Bao Din. The Viet Minh gradually gained all of Tonkin and in 1954 forced the French to surrender at Dien Bien Phu after a siege of 55 days.

The Geneva Peace Agreement (1954) partitioned Vietnam between a Communist republic in the north and a zone ruled by Bao Din in the south. Elections for the whole country were scheduled for 1956 but the Communists refused to participate. In South Vietnam, Bao Din was deposed (1955) and Ngo Dinh Diem proclaimed a republic.. Diem's oppressive rule encouraged Communist guerrilla activity in the south and in 1960 the (Communist) Viet Cong was formed in the south to overthrow the pro-Western government. In 1961, US President John F. Kennedy sent American military advisers to help South Vietnam. By 1964, the 'advisers' had grown into an army of regular US troops and the Americans had begun regular aerial bombardment of the north. The 1968 (Communist) Tet offensive was withstood but the weakness of South Vietnam became evident. Opposition to the war increased in the USA. Although peace talks began in 1969, US forces were active in Cambodia and Laos by 1970. The war was formally ended by the Paris Peace Agreement (1973), but continued after the withdrwaal of US troops.

Since the Communist takeover of the south (1975) and the reunification of Vietnam, reconstruction has been hindered by a border war with China (1979) and the occupation of Cambodia (1979–89) by Vietnamese forces. Lack of Western aid and investment has hindered economic development, and this, combined with political repression, led to large numbers of refugees (the 'Boat People') fleeing Vietnam. Since 1989–90 more pragmatic policies have been adopted, but, although liberalizatin of the economy is being pursued, there is no indication that political reforms will follow.

WESTERN SAMOA

Official names: The Independent State of Western Samoa and Malo Sa'oloto Tuto'atasi o Samoa i Sisifo.

Member of: UN, Commonwealth.

Area: 2831 km^2 (1093 sq mi).

Population: 163,000 (1993 est).

Capital: Apia 33 000 (1991 census).

Languages: English and Samoan (official).

Religions: Congregational (47%), Roman Catholic (22%), Methodist.

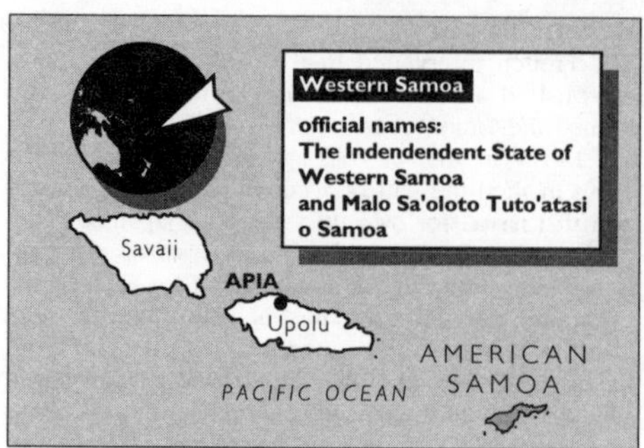

Education: is compulsory between the ages of six and 15. *Adult literacy:* virtually 100%. *Universities:* one.
Defence: There are no armed forces. Defence remains the responsibility of New Zealand.

Government

Forty-seven of the 49 members of the Assembly (Fono) are elected for five years by universal adult suffrage. Only members of the Matai (the elected clan leaders) are eligible to stand for election. The other two members of the Assembly are elected by non-Samoan residents. The current head of state is analogous to a constitutional monarch, but future heads of state will be elected for a five-year term by the Assembly. The head of state appoints a Prime Minister, who, in turn, appoints a Council of Ministers.
Largest parties: Human Rights Protection Party (HRPP), Samoan National Development Party (SNDP), Samoan Democracy Party (SDP).
Local government: 11 political districts.
Head of state: Malietoa Tanumafili II.
Prime Minister: Tofilau Eti Alesana (HRPP).

Geography

The country consists of seven small islands and two larger and higher volcanic islands. ***Principal rivers:*** There are many streams, mainly unnamed. ***Highest point:*** Silisili 1858m (6096 ft).
Climate: The islands have a tropical climate with high temperatures and very heavy rainfall.

Economy

The majority of Samoans are involved in subsistence agriculture. Copra (from coconuts), cocoa and bananas are the main exports. ***Currency:*** Tala.

Recent History

From the 1870s the USA, UK and Germany became active in Samoa. In 1899 the three rival powers divided the group, giving the western islands to Germany. New Zealand occupied the German islands in 1914, and administered Western Samoa until independence in 1962. A large proportion of the economically active population has emigrated to New Zealand.

YEMEN

Official name: Al-Jamhuriya al-Yamaniya (Republic of Yemen).
Member of: UN, Arab League.
Area: 472,099 km^2 (182,278 sq mi) *de facto* or 531,870 km^2 (205 356 sq mi) according to Yemeni territorial claims.
Population: 12,460,000 (1993 est).
Capital: Sana'a 427,000 (including suburbs; 1986 est).
Other major cities: Aden 318,000, Taiz 178,000, Hodeida (al-Hudaydah) 155,000, Mukalla (al-Mukalla) 154,000 (1986 est).
Language: Arabic (official).
Religion: Islam – Sunni Islam (54%), Zaidist Shia Islam (46%).
Education: is not compulsory. *Adult literacy:* 39%. *Universities:* two.
Defence: (1993 figures) *Army:* 60,000 personnel. *Air force:* 3000. *Navy:* 1500. *Paramilitary:* 20,000. *Conscription:* compulsory, in theory, for three years in former North Yemen and two years in former South Yemen.

Government

A 301-member House of Representatives and a President are elected by universal adult suffrage for four years. The President appoints a Prime Minister and a Council of Ministers.
Largest parties: General People's Congress (GPC), (right-wing Islamic fundamentalist) Yemeni Alliance for Reform (YAR), Islah Islamic Party, (former Communist) Yemeni Socialist Party (YSP).
Local government: 17 governates.
President: Lt. Gen. Ali Abdullah Saleh (GPC).
Prime Minister: Abd al-Aziz Abd al-Ghani.

Geography

The Yemen Highlands rise from a narrow coastal plain beside the Red Sea. An arid plateau in the east extends into the Arabian Desert. ***Principal rivers:*** There are no perennial rivers. ***Highest point:*** Hadur Shu'ayb 3760m (12,336 ft).
Climate: Most of the highlands have a temperate climate, but the rest of the country is hot and dry.

Economy

Cereal crops, coffee and citrus fruit are grown under irrigation in the fertile highlands. In the south, subsistence farming and fishing occupy the majority of the labour force. Money sent back by Yemenis working abroad is an important source of revenue. ***Currencies:*** The two official currencies are the (former North Yemeni) Riyal and the former (South Yemeni) Dinar.

Recent History

The Ottoman Turks were not finally expelled from the north until 1911, when Imam Yahya secured Yemen's independence. Britain took Aden as a staging post to India (1839) and gradually established a protectorate over the south. In 1963 an armed rebellion began against British rule in South Yemen (then known as South Arabia), which gained independence in 1967

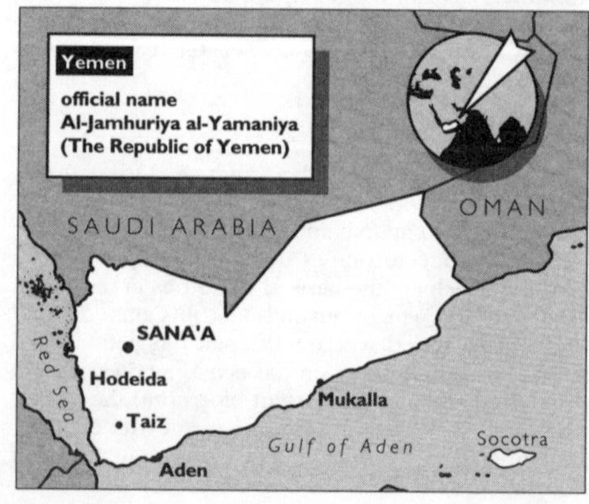

after a civil war between rival liberation movements. A republican revolution broke out in North Yemen in 1962, and from 1963 until 1970 a civil war was fought, with President Nasser's Egypt supporting the victorious republicans and Saudi Arabia supporting the royalists. Relations between North Yemen and (Marxist) South Yemen were difficult. The collapse of South Yemen's Communist trading partners (1989–90) undermined the country's weak economy, and the two countries merged in 1990. However, the union was uneasy: the economies of the two former states were not merged, and social and political differences between North and South Yemen were enormous. In 1994 the strains upon the union exploded in a short, bitter civil war as the South unsuccessfully attempted secession.

YUGOSLAVIA (SERBIA AND MONTENEGRO)

Official name: Federativna Republika Jugoslavija (The Federal Republic of Yugoslavia).
Member of: UN (suspended).
Area: 102,173 km^2 (39,449 sq mi).
Population: 10,561,000 (1991 est).
Capital: Belgrade (Beograd; see below).
Languages: Serb (the version of Serbo-Croat written in the Cyrillic alphabet; includes Montenegrin; 73%), Albanian (16%), Hungarian (under 4%).
Religions: Orthodox (over 75%), Sunni Islam (over 12%), small Roman Catholic minority.
Education: is compulsory between the ages of seven and 15. *Adult literacy:* 89%. *Universities:* six.
Defence: (1993 figures) *Army:* 100,000 personnel. *Air force:* 29,000. *Navy:* 7500. *Conscription:* 12 months.

Montenegro

Area: 13,812 km^2 (5333 sq mi).
Population: 615,000 (1991 census).
Capital: Podgorica (formerly Titograd) 130,000 (city 111,000; 1991 census).
Other main cities: Niksic 75,000, Bar 35,000 (1991 census).

Serbia

Area: 88,361 km^2 (34,116 sq mi).

Population: 9,791,000 (1991 census).
Capital: Belgrade (Beograd) 1,555,000 (city 1,500,000; 1991 census).
Other major cities: Novi Sad 260,000 (city 179,000), Niš 230,000 (city 176,000), Pristina 210,000 (city 108,000) (1991 census).

Government

Yugoslavia comprises two equal republics – Serbia and Montenegro. The Federal Assembly comprises a Chamber of Republics, which has 40 members (20 elected by each of the republican parliaments), and a 138-member Chamber of Citizens, which is elected by universal adult suffrage for four years. The Assembly elects a Federal President – who appoints a Premier and a Cabinet. The republics have their own legislatures and governments with very considerable powers and Serbia, in particular, has virtually assumed sovereign powers. The Serbian 250-member National Assembly and a President are elected by universal adult suffrage for four years. The 125-member Montenegrin Assembly and a President are also directly elected.
Largest parties: (former Communist) Socialist Party of Serbia (SPS), (right-wing) Serbian Radical Party (SRP), (centre) Serbian Democratic Movement, (Serbian) Democratic Party, (former Communist) Democratic Party of Socialists of Montenegro (DPS), (Montenegrin) Alliance of Reform Forces, New Socialist Party of Montenegro.
Local government: two republics (see above).
Federal President of Yugoslavia: Zoran Lilic (SPS).
Prime Minister of Yugoslavia: Radoje Kontic (SPS).
President of Serbia: Slobodan Milosevic (SPS).
President of Montenegro: Momir Bulatovic (DPS).

Geography

Ridges of mountains occupy the greater part of the country. The north (Vojvodina) is occupied by plains drained by the rivers Danube and Tisa. The Yugoslav coastline is now confined to a short stretch on the Adriatic in Montenegro. ***Principal rivers:*** Danube (Dunav), Morava, Sava, Ibar, Tisa, Drina. ***Highest point:*** Titov Vrh 2747m (9012 ft).
Climate: Coastal Montenegro has a Mediterranean climate; inland, in Serbia, there is a moderate continental climate.

Economy

Agriculture involves over one quarter of the labour force. Most of the land is privately owned. Major crops include maize, wheat, sugar beet, potatoes, citrus fruit and fodder crops for sheep. Industry – which is mainly concentrated around Belgrade – includes food processing, textiles, metallurgy, motor vehicles and consumer goods. The country's economy was severely damaged by the wars that began in 1991, by rampant inflation and an international embargo on trade with Serbia and Montenegro. ***Currency:*** Dinar.

Recent History

Both Serbia and Montenegro were recognized as independent in 1878. By the beginning of the 19th century the Slavs within the Austro-Hungarian Habsburg Empire looked increasingly to Serbia to create a South ('Yugo') Slav state. After Serbia gained Macedonia in the Balkan Wars (1912–13), Austria grew wary of Serb ambitions. The assassination of the Habsburg heir (1914) by a Bosnian Serb student provided Austria with an excuse to quash Serbian independence. This led directly to World War I and the dissolution of the Habsburg Empire, whose South Slav peoples united with Serbia and Montenegro in 1918.

The interwar Kingdom of Serbs, Croats and Slovenes – renamed Yugoslavia in 1929 – was run as a highly centralized 'Greater Serbia'. The country was wracked by nationalist tensions, and Croat separatists murdered King Alexander in 1934. Yugoslavia was attacked and dismembered by Hitler in 1941, and Yugoslavs fought the Nazis and each other. The Communist-led partisans of Josip Broz Tito (1892–1980) emerged victorious in 1945, and re-formed Yugoslavia on Soviet lines. Expelled by Stalin from the Soviet bloc in 1948 on account of their indiscipline, the Yugoslav Communists rejected the Soviet model, and pursued policies of decentralization, workers' self-management and non-alignment. However, after Tito's death in 1980, the Yugoslav experiment faltered in economic and nationalist crises.

In 1990, free elections were held throughout Yugoslavia. In 1991 Slovenia, Croatia and Macedonia declared independence. Following reverses in a short campaign, federal forces were withdrawn from Slovenia, but Serb insurgents, backed by Yugoslav federal forces, occupied one third of Croatia, including those areas with an ethnic Serb majority. In 1992, the fierce Serbo-Croat war came to an uneasy halt and a UN monitoring force was agreed. Croatia and Slovenia gained international recognition of their independence. When Bosnia-Herzegovina received similar recognition, Bosnian Serbs, encouraged by Serbia, seized 70% of Bosnia, killing or expelling Muslims and Croats in a campaign of 'ethnic cleansing'. Serbia was widely blamed for the continuation of the conflict and – with Montenegro – was subjected to UN sanctions. International efforts to end the conflict were attempted and humanitarian aid was supplied to Bosnian Muslims by the UN. Tension also rose in Kosovo province, where Serbia forcefully resisted the separatist aspirations of ethnic Albanians. Owing to Greek opposition, international recognition of Macedonia was delayed until 1993. Faced with economic disaster, the rump Yugoslavia has been anxious to have sanctions lifted, but Serbian pressure on the Bosnian Serbs to accept various peace plans has been largely ineffective.

ZAÏRE

Official name: La République du Zaïre (Republic of Zaïre).
Member of: UN, OAU.
Area: 2,344,885 km² (905,365 sq mi).
Population: 42,470,000 (1993 est).
Capital: Kinshasa 3,804,000 (1991 est).
Other major cities: Lubumbashi 740,000, Mbuji-Mayi 613,000, Bukavu 418,000, Kisangani 373,000, Kananga 372,000 (1991 est).
Languages: French (official); four national languages – Kiswahili, Tshiluba, Kikongo and Lingala; over 400 local languages.
Religions: Roman Catholic (48%), various Protestant churches (28%), Kimbanguists (17%).
Education: is compulsory, in theory, between the ages of six and 12. *Adult literacy:* 38%. *Universities:* four.
Defence: (1993 figures) *Army:* 25,000 personnel. *Air force:* 1800. *Navy:* 1300. *Paramilitary:* 21,000. *Conscription:* compulsory, in theory; the length of service varies.

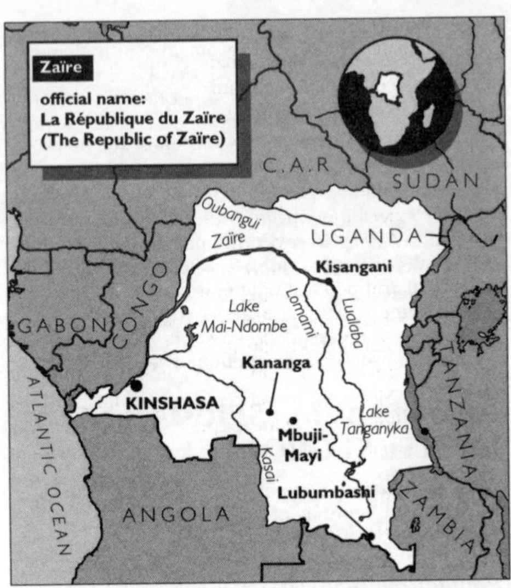

Government

The constitution provides for the election of a 222-member National Legislative Council by compulsory universal suffrage for five years. The President – who is directly elected for seven years – appoints a Prime Minister and a Cabinet of Ministers. The 443-member nominated High Council of the Republic-Transitional Parliament is a constituent assembly.
Largest parties: (former monopoly) Popular Movement of the Revolution (MPR), plus over 160 registered groups.
Local government: 10 regions, plus the capital city.
President: Marshal Mobutu Sese Seko (MPR).
Prime Minister: Léon Kengo wa Dondo (ind).

Geography

Over 60% of the country comprises a basin of tropical rain forest, drained by the River Zaïre (Congo) and its tributaries. Plateaux and mountain ranges surrounding the basin include the Ruwenzori Massif in the east. ***Principal rivers:*** Zaïre (Congo), Lomami, Aruwimi, Ubangi (Oubangui), Kasai. ***Highest point:*** Mount Ngaliema (formerly Margherita Peak) 5109m (16,763 ft)
Climate: Zaïre has a humid, tropical climate with little seasonal variation, although the north is drier from December to February.

Economy

Over 65% of the labour force is involved in agriculture. Although subsistence farming predominates, coffee, tea and palm products are exported. Minerals are the mainstay of the economy, with copper, cobalt, zinc and diamonds normally accounting for about 60% of Zaïre's exports. However, much of the country's infrastructure has broken down and Zaïre has one of the lowest standards of living in Africa. ***Currency:*** Zaïre.

Recent History

The region was ravaged by the slave trade, and in 1885 became the personal possession of King Leopold II of the Belgians. However, international outrage at the brutality of the regime in the Congo Free State forced the king to grant the region to Belgium as a colony in 1908. As the Belgian Congo, the colony became a major exporter of minerals. The provision of social services, especially primary education, was relatively advanced, but the administration curbed almost all African political activity. As a result, the country was inadequately prepared when Belgium suddenly decolonized the Congo in 1960. Within days of independence, the army mutinied and the richest region – Katanga, under Moïse Tshombe – attempted to secede. The Congo invited the United Nations to intervene, but the UN force was only partly successful in overcoming continuing civil wars. Colonel Mobutu twice intervened and in 1965 made himself head of state. He renamed the country Zaïre, gradually restored the authority of the central government, and introduced a one-party state (1967). Mobutu's strong rule attracted international criticism. Following growing popular pressure, he was obliged to concede political pluralism and a national conference to bring democracy to Zaïre (1991). In 1992–93 conflicts erupted between Mobutu and the conference (represented by the PM), and law-and-order broke down in parts of the country. Except in isolated pockets, Zaïre as a nation-state has practically ceased to exist and ethnic unrest is widespread.

ZAMBIA

Official name: The Republic of Zambia.
Member of: UN, Commonwealth, OAU.
Area: 752,614 km^2 (290,586 sq mi).
Population: 8,505,000 (1991 est).
Capital: Lusaka 982,000 (1992 est).
Other major cities: Ndola 376,000, Kitwe 338,000, Mufulira 153,000 (1992 est).
Languages: English, Tonga (16%), Kaonda, Lunda, Luvale – all official; Bemba (34%).
Religions: various Protestant Churches (50%), animist (25%), Roman Catholic (20%).
Education: is compulsory, in theory, between the ages of seven and 14. *Adult literacy:* 73%. *Universities:* two.
Defence: (1993 figures) *Army:* 20,000 personnel. *Air force:* 1600. *Paramilitary:* 1400. *Conscription:* none.

Government

A President and the 150-member National Assembly are elected by universal adult suffrage for five years. The President appoints a Prime Minister and a Cabinet. ***Largest parties:*** Movement for Multiparty Democracy (MMD), (former monopoly) United National Independence Party (UNIP), National Party (NP), Caucus for National Unity (CNU).
Local government: nine provinces.
President: Frederick Chiluba (MMD).

Geography

Zambia comprises plateaux some 1000 to 1500 m (3300 to 5000 ft) high, above which rise the Muchinga Mountains and the Mufinga Hills. ***Principal rivers:*** Zambezi, Kafue, Kabompo, Luangwa, Luapula. ***Highest point:*** an unnamed peak in the Muchinga escarpment 2164m (7100 ft).
Climate: Zambia has a tropical climate with a wet season from November to April.

Economy

Zambia's economy depends upon the mining and processing of copper, lead, zinc and cobalt. Agriculture is underdeveloped and many basic foodstuffs have to be imported. Maize and cassava are the main crops. ***Currency:*** Kwacha.

Recent History

The area was brought under the control of the British South Africa Company of Cecil Rhodes in the 1890s. In 1924 Britain took over the administration from the Company, but development of the colony (named Northern Rhodesia) was initially slow. Skilled mining jobs were reserved for white immigrants, and, fearing increased discrimination, Africans opposed inclusion in the Central African Federation, with Nyasaland (Malawi) and Southern Rhodesia (Zimbabwe), in 1953. Against strong opposition from white settlers, Kenneth Kaunda (1924–) led Northern Rhodesia, renamed Zambia, to independence in 1964. Zambia was a one-party state from 1973 to 1990. In elections in 1991 Kaunda was defeated in the first democratic change of government in English-speaking Black Africa. Zambia faces major economic and social problems, including an AIDS epidemic.

ZIMBABWE

Official name: The Republic of Zimbabwe.
Member of: UN, Commonwealth, OAU.
Area: 390,757 km^2 (150,872 sq mi).
Population: 10,687,000 (1993 est).
Capital: Harare (formerly Salisbury) 1,184,000 (1992 est).
Other major cities: Bulawayo 621,000, Chitungwiza 274,000, Mutare (Umtali) 132,000, Gweru

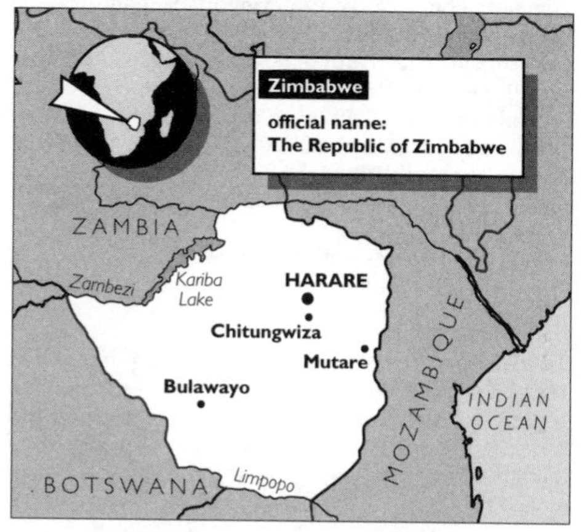

125,000 (1989 est).
Languages: English (official), Chishona, Sindebele.
Religions: Animist (42%), Anglican (30%), Roman Catholic (15%), Presbyterian.
Education: is compulsory between the ages of seven and 14. *Adult literacy:* 76%. *Universities:* two.
Defence: (1992 figures) *Army:* 47,000 personnel. *Air force:* 1200. *Paramilitary:* 4000. *Conscription:* one year; selective.

Government

The 150-member House of Assembly comprises 120 members elected by universal adult suffrage for six years, 12 nominated members, 10 traditional chiefs and eight appointed provincial governors. The President – who is elected by Parliament for six years – appoints a Cabinet which is responsible to the Assembly.
Largest parties: Zimbabwe African National Union (ZANU-PF), Zimbabwe Unity Movement (ZUM), Forum Party.
Local government: eight provinces.
President: Robert Mugabe (ZANU-PF).

Geography

Central Zimbabwe comprises the ridge of the Highveld, rising to between 1200 and 1500 m (about 4000 to 5000 ft). The Highveld is bounded on the southwest and northeast by the Middle Veld and the Lowveld plateaux. ***Principal rivers:*** Zambezi, Sabi, Limpopo. ***Highest point:*** Mount Inyangani 2592m (8503 ft).
Climate: The climate is tropical in the lowlands and subtropical at altitude. There is a pronounced dry season from June to September.

Economy

Agriculture involves over 65% of the labour force. Tobacco, sugar cane, cotton, wheat and maize are exported as well as being the basis of processing industries. Natural resources include coal, gold, asbestos and nickel. ***Currency:*** Zimbabwe dollar.

Recent History

The area was gradually penetrated by British and Boer hunters, missionaries and prospectors from the 1830s, and was occupied by the British South Africa Company of Cecil Rhodes in the 1890s. The highlands of what became Southern Rhodesia were settled by White farmers, who deprived Africans of land and reduced them to a cheap labour force. Britain took over the administration from the Company in 1923 and granted self-government to the White colonists. Immigration from Britain and South Africa increased after World War II, but the Whites remained outnumbered by the Africans by more than 20 to 1. Racial discrimination stimulated African nationalism, initially led by Joshua Nkomo (1917–). When the short-lived Central African Federation of South Rhodesia, North Rhodesia (Zambia) and Nyasaland (Malawi) was dissolved (1963), Britain refused the White South Rhodesian administration independence without progress to majority rule.

The White government led by Ian Smith (1919–) unilaterally declared independence in 1965, renaming the country Rhodesia. Internal opposition was crushed and international economic sanctions were overcome, but guerrilla wars, mounted by African nationalists during the 1970s, became increasingly effective. In 1979 Smith had to accept majority rule, but the constitution he introduced was unacceptable either to the Zimbabwe African People's Union (ZAPU) of Joshua Nkomo or to the Zimbabwe African National Union (ZANU) of Robert Mugabe (1928–). All parties agreed to the brief reimposition of British rule to achieve a settlement. ZANU under Mugabe took the country to independence in 1980. In 1987 ZANU and ZAPU finally agreed to unite, effectively introducing a virtual one-party state.

THE LARGEST AND SMALLEST COUNTRIES

Smallest sovereign states

	Country	km²	sq mi
1	Vatican City	0·44	0·17
2	Monaco	2·21	0·85
3	Nauru	21	8
4	Tuvalu	24	9
5	San Marino	61	23
6	Liechtenstein	160	62
7	Marshall Islands	181	70
8	St Christopher	262	101
9	Maldives	298	115
10	Malta	316	122
11	Grenada	344	133
12	St Vincent	389	150
13	Barbados	430	166
14	Antigua	442	171
15	Seychelles	455	176
16	Andorra	468	181
17	Palau	508	196
18	St Lucia	616	238
19	Singapore	639	247
20	Bahrain	691	267
21	Micronesia	702	271
22	Tonga	780	301
23	Dominica	751	290
24	Kiribati	811	313
25	Sao Tomé	964	372
26	Comoros	1862	719
27	Mauritius	2040	788

Largest sovereign states

	Country	km²	sq mi
1	Russia	17,075,400	6,592,800
2	Canada	9,970,610	3,849,674
3	China	9,571,900	3,695,710
4	USA	9,529,063	3,679,192
5	Brazil	8,511,996	3,286,482
6	Australia	7,682,300	2,966,136
7	India	3,287,263	1,269,219
8	Argentina	2,766,889	1,068,302
9	Kazakhstan	2,717,300	1,049,200
10	Sudan	2,505,813	967,500
11	Algeria	2,381,741	919,595
12	Zaire	2,344,885	905,365
13	Saudi Arabia	2,240,000	864,869
14	Mexico	1,958,201	756,066
15	Indonesia	1,919,317	741,052
16	Libya	1,757,000	678,380
17	Iran	1,638,057	632,457
18	Mongolia	1,566,500	604,800
19	Peru	1,285,216	496,225
20	Chad	1,284,000	495,752
21	Mali	1,248,574	482,075
22	Angola	1,246,700	481,351
23	South Africa	1,223,201	472,278
24	Niger	1,186,408	458,075
25	Colombia	1,141,748	440,831
26	Ethiopia	1,133,882	437,794
27	Bolivia	1,098,581	424,164

OTHER TERRITORIES

American Samoa

Status: an unincorporated United States external territory.
Area: 197 km^2 (96 sq mi).
Population: 46,800 (1990 census).
Capital: Fagatogo (in Pago Pago urban area).
Main town: Pago Pago 4000 (1990 census).
Geography: The territory, in the western Pacific, comprises six main rocky tropical islands (of which Tutuila is the largest), plus Swain's Island to the north.
Economy: The main employers are tuna-canning and tourism. Most islanders are engaged in subsistence farming. Lack of resources and a rapidly increasing population have forced many islanders to migrate to the USA.
Recent History: The USA established a naval base in Pago Pago in 1878. The local chiefs ceded the islands to the USA in 1904. The islands became an unicorporated territory of the USA in 1922 and received internal self-government in 1948.

Anguilla

Status: a British Dependent Territory.
Area: 96 km^2 (37 sq mi) – Anguilla 91 km^2 (35 sq mi), Sombrero 5 km^2 (2 sq mi).
Population: 9000 (1992 est); Sombrero has no permanent population.
Capital: The Valley 500 (1988 est).
Geography: Anguilla is a low-lying coral island in the eastern Caribbean. Sombrero is a rocky island 48 km (30 mi) to the north.
Economy: Tourism is the dominant industry. Expatriot Anguillans, in the US Virgin Islands and the UK, outnumber the island's resident population.
Recent History: British settlement began in the 17th century. After 1825, the island was administratively attached to St Kitts (St Christopher). Protests against this association began in the 19th century and culminated in a unilateral declaration of independence in 1967. British troops and police intervened in 1969 and the island reverted to direct British control in 1971, although Anguilla was not formally separated from St Kitts-Nevis until 1980.

Argentine Antarctic Territory

Status: an Argentine territorial claim – all territorial claims south of latitude 60°S are in abeyance under the terms of the Antarctic Treaty (1959).
Geography: Argentina claims that part of Antarctica between 74°W and 25°W, a claim that overlaps with the British territorial claim.

Aruba

Status: an autonomous part of the Kingdom of the Netherlands.
Area: 193 km^2 (75 sq mi).
Population: 68,900 (1991 est).
Capital: Oranjestad 20,000 (1991 est).
Geography: Aruba is a relatively flat island 24 km (15 mi) north of the Venezuelan coast.
Economy: Tourism is the major foreign-currency earner, and financial services and data processing are of growing importance. Lack of water restricts farming and most foodstuffs are imported.
Recent History: Aruba, claimed by the Dutch in 1634, remained inhabited only by Arawak Indians until the 19th century when Spanish, Dutch and other settlers arrived. Part of the Dutch West Indies (later known as the Netherlands Antilles) until 1986, Aruba is now a separate autonomous part of the Kingdom of the Netherlands. Independence is scheduled for 1997 or 1998.

Ashmore and Cartier Islands

Status: an Australian external territory.
Area: 5 km^2 (2 sq mi).
Population: uninhabited.
Geography: These tropical islands are sandy and coral reefs.
Recent History: The islands were annexed by Britain in 1878 (Ashmores) and 1931 (Cartier), and transferred to Australia in 1931. They became an Australian external territory in 1978.

Australian Antarctic Territory

Status: an Australian external territory – all territorial claims south of latitude 60°S are in abeyance under the terms of the Antarctic Treaty (1959).
Area: 6,043,700 km^2 (2,333,500 sq mi).
Geography: Argentina claims that part of Antarctica between 160°E and 142°E and that part between 136°E and 45°E.

Bermuda

Status: a British Crown colony.
Area: 54 km^2 (21 sq mi).
Population: 61,000 (1991 est).
Capital: Hamilton 6000 (1991 est).
Geography: Bermuda comprises over 100 small islands in the northwestern Atlantic. Seven islands are linked by causeways and bridges.
Economy: Tourism dominates the economy, supplying over 60% of foreign-currency earnings and accounting for 65% of employment, both directly and indirectly. There has been an important recent growth in 'offshore' financial services.
Recent History: A Crown colony since the 17th century, Bermuda received internal self-govenment in 1968. In the 1960s and 1970s, there was racial tension between the majority of African origin and the minority of European origin.

Bouvet Island

Status: a Norwegian Antarctic dependency. As Bouvet lies north of the area covered by the terms of the Antarctic Treaty (1959), Norway's claim to the island is uncontested.
Area: 59 km^2 (23 sq mi).
Population: no permanent population.
Geography: Bouvet Island is a bleak volcanic glaciated island 1600 km (1000 mi) north of the Antarctic mainland.

British Antarctic Territory

Status: a British territorial claim – all territorial claims south of latitude 60°S are in abeyance under the terms of the Antarctic Treaty (1959).
Area: 1,800,000 km^2 (700,000 sq mi).
Geography: Britain claims that part of Antarctica between 20°W and 80°W, extending to the South Pole. This claim overlaps with Chilean and Argentine claims.

British Indian Ocean Territory

Status: a British territory.
Area: 60 km^2 (23 sq mi).
Population: 2900 military personnel (1991 est).

Geography: The territory comprises five coral atolls of the Chagos Archipelago, northeast of Mauritius.
Recent History: The territory was created in 1965 to provide defence and communication facilities in the Indian Ocean for the UK and USA.

British Virgin Islands
Status: a British Crown colony.
Area: 153 km^2 (59 sq mi).
Population: 16,700 (1991 census).
Capital: Road Town 2500 (1991 census).
Geography: The colony comprises three main mountainous volcanic islands (Tortola, Virgin Gorda and Jost van Dyke), a flat coralline island (Anegada), and more than 60 small islands and cays. They form the eastern part of the Virgin Islands group in the Caribbean.
Economy: The British Virgin Islands are totally overshadowed by their larger neighbour, the US Virgin Islands. In fact, American currency is used in the British islands. Tourism and 'offshore' financial services dominate the economy, and money sent home by islanders working in the US Virgin Islands is of great importance.
Recent History: The islands became English in 1672 and were part of the Leeward Islands from 1872 to 1954, when they became a separate colony. Full internal self-government was granted in 1967.

Cayman Islands
Status: a British Crown colony.
Area: 259 km^2 (100 sq mi).
Population: 27,000 (1991 est).
Capital: George Town 12,900 (1989 census).
Geography: The three low-lying Cayman Islands are 290 km (180 mi) west of Jamaica.
Economy: The economy relies upon tourism, which employs nearly one third of the labour force, and upon financial services. Based upon its good communications with the nearby USA, its political stability and bank secrecy laws, the colony is the largest 'offshore' financial centre in the world. As a result, living standards are very high.
Recent History: The islands were a dependency of Jamaica until 1959, when they became a separate colony. Since then, Cayman Islanders have tried to restrict the electorate (to exclude immigrants) and to preserve the status quo, which is perceived to encourage 'offshore' finance.

Chilean Antarctic Territory
Status: a Chilean territorial claim – all territorial claims south of latitude 60°S are in abeyance under the terms of the Antarctic Treaty (1959).
Geography: Chile claims that part of Antarctica between 90°W and 53°W. This claim overlaps with British and Argentine claims.

Christmas Island
Status: an external territory of Australia..
Area: 135 km^2 (52 sq mi).
Population: 1275 (1991 census).
Capital: Flying Fish Cove.
Geography: Christmas Island is an isolated tropical mountain with abrupt cliffs rising from the sea. It lies 360 km (200 mi) south of Java.
Economy: The island depends upon phosphate workings.
Recent History: The island was claimed by Britain in 1888 and Malay and Chinese workers were imported to mine phosphate. After occupation by Japan (1942-45) during World War II, the island was ceded by the UK to Australia in 1958.

Cocos (Keeling) Islands
Status: an external territory of Australia.
Area: 14 km^2 (5 ·5 sq mi).
Population: 650 (1991 census).
Capital: Bantam Village 480 (1991 census).
Geography: Situated about 2225 km (1390 mi) southwest of Sri Lanka, the Cocos form two atolls comprising 27 small coral tropical islands.
Economy: Large stands of coconut palms produce copra, the only export.
Recent History: The Cocos were settled in the 1830s when John Clunies-Ross imported Malays to work the coconut palms. Britain annexed the Cocos (1857), granting them to the Clunies-Ross family, who ruled until 1978, when Australia bought out their interests. The islands were ceded by the UK to Australia in 1955.

Cook Islands
Status: a self-governing territory of New Zealand.
Area: 237 km^2 (92 sq mi).
Population: 19,000 (1991 est).
Capital: Avarua (on Rarotonga) 3000 (1991 est).
Geography: The 15 tropical Cook Islands comprise a northern group of mountainous volcanic islands and a southern group of coral atolls.
Economy: Papayas are the main export. Other sources of income include 'offshore' banking, postage stamps and money sent back by over 20,000 Cook Islanders working in New Zealand.
Recent History: The islands became British in 1888 and were ceded to New Zealand in 1901. In 1965 they became self-governing in free association with New Zealand and are empowered to gain independence unilaterally.

Coral Sea Islands Territory
Status: an external territory of Australia.
Area: 8 km^2 (5 sq mi).
Population: no permanent population.
Geography: The tiny widely-scattered islands are very low-lying outcrops of sand and coral.
Recent History: The groups of atolls were constituted as the Coral Sea Islands Territory in 1969.

East Timor
Status: disputed territory.
Area: 14,874 km^2 (5743 sq mi).
Population: 748,000 (1990 census).
Capital: Dili (Oekussi) 60,000 (1990 est).
Geography: East Timor comprises the mountainous eastern half of the tropical island of Timor (part of Indonesia), plus an enclave in the western part of the island.
Economy: The economy, which formerly depended upon coffee, has been devastated by violence associated with Indonesia's annexation of East Timor. Much of the population has been uprooted; many villages have been destroyed.
Recent History: East Timor – Portuguese since the 16th century – was proclaimed independent by the local nationalist movement Fretilin in 1975. Indonesian forces invaded immediately. In 1976, East Timor was annexed by Indonesia, but this action is not recognized by the UN. Up to 200,000 people have died

during Indonesia's conquest, and subsequent occupation, of the territory. International protests followed the killing of unarmed Timorese demonstrators by Indonesian troops in 1991.

Faeroe Islands

Status: an internally self-governing part of the Kingdom of Denmark.
Area: 1399 km^2 (540 sq mi).
Population: 48,400 (1991 est).
Capital: Tórshavn 16,200 (1991 est).
Geography: Lying between Scotland and Iceland, the Faeroes comprise 17 inhabited, one uninhabited island and many rocky islets, all with high cliffs.
Economy: Farming is dominated by sheep rearing. Fishing, the main industry, has contracted recently owing to declining stocks. The Faeroese economy depends heavily upon considerable subsidies from Denmark. The islands, although part of Denmark for most purposes, are not part of the EU/EC.
Recent History: The Faeroes, which were once part of Norway, have been represented in the Danish parliament since 1851. The islands have had their own local assembly since 1852 and have enjoyed internal self-government since 1948.

Falkland Islands

Status: a British Crown colony.
Area: 12,170 km^2 (4698 sq mi).
Population: 2120 (1991 census; excludes military personnel).
Capital: Port Stanley 1560 (1991 census).
Geography: The Falklands consist of two main and over 100 small bleak islands in the southern Atlantic, about 700 km (480 mi) northeast of Cape Horn.
Economy: The barren interior is used as pasture for sheep and wool, which is the only major export. Fishing is of growing importance.
Recent History: The islands were claimed and (briefly) settled by Britain in the 18th century. Argentina claimed and settled the uninhabited islands in 1820, but was expelled from the Falklands by the USA in 1831. Britain resumed its occupation in 1833 and a British community was established in the islands. Argentina continued to claim the islands, initially through diplomatic activity. Briatin maintained that ceding the islands to Argentina would be contrary to the principle of self-determination of the islands' inhabitants. In April 1982, Argentine troops invaded and occupied the Falklands, but they were defeated and expelled by British forces in June in the same year.

French Guiana (Guyane)

Status: an overseas French département, an integral part of the French Republic.
Area: 90,000 km^2 (34,750 sq mi).
Population: 115,000 (1990 census).
Capital: Cayenne 42,000 (1990 census).
Geography: The territory, which lies between Brazil and Suriname, is a tropical lowland, mainly covered in jungle.
Economy: The economy depends upon timber and upon subsidies from metropolitan France. Very little land is cultivated and mineral ores, including bauxite, are not widely exploited.
Recent History: The area finally became French in 1819 and, including the notorious Devil's Island, was used as a penal colony from 1798 to 1935. It became an overseas département of the French Republic in 1946.

French Polynesia

Status: an overseas French territory.
Area: 4167 km^2 (1609 sq mi).
Population: 199,000 (1991 est).
Capital: Papeete (on Tahiti) 79,000 (1988 est).
Geography: The territory has over 130 mainly mountainous tropical islands and coral atolls in five groups in the east Pacific: the Windward Islands (including Tahiti), the Leeward Islands, and the Tuamotu, Austral and Marquesas Islands. The territory also includes Clipperton Island to the south of Mexico.
Economy: Tourism is the main foreign-currency earner. Coconut oil and pearls are exported.
Recent History: The islands, which were annexed by France between 1791 and 1900, became an overseas territory of the French Republic in 1958.

French Southern and Antarctic Territories

Status: French dependencies (Kerguelen and the other islands) plus the French territorial claim in Antarctica (Adélie Land) – all territorial claims south of latitude 60°S are in abeyance under the terms of the Antarctic Treaty (1959).
Area: 439,797 km^2 (169,806 sq mi) – Adélie Land 432,000 km^2 (166,800 sq mi), Kerguelen archipelago 7215 km^2 (2786 sq mi), Crozet archipelago 515 km^2 (199 sq mi), Amsterdam Island 60 km^2 (23 sq mi), St Paul Island 7 km^2 (3 sq mi).
Population: no permanent population, although there is a long-established scientific settlement, Port-aux-Français, on Kerguelen.
'Capital': Port-aux-Français.
Geography: The territory comprises that part of of Antarctica between 136°E and 142°E (Adélie Land), plus two bleak archipelagos (Kerguelen and Crozet) and two small islands (Amsterdam and St Paul) in the extreme south of the Indian Ocean.

Gaza and Jericho (the Palestinian entity)

Status: internally self-governing entity from which Israeli forces have, mainly, withdrawn.
Area: 412 km^2 (159 sq mi) – Gaza 352 km^2 (136 sq mi), Jericho 60 km^2 (23 sq mi).
Population: 780,000 (1992 est) – Gaza 755,000, Jericho 25,000.
'Capital': Gaza City (Ghazza) 755,000 (city 60,000; 1992 est).
Geography: The area governed by the Palestinian authority comprises the arid low lying Gaza Strip, between Israel and Egypt, and the small enclave around Jericho, in the Jordan Valley.
Economy: The Gaza Strip has some agriculture, producing citrus fruit, wheat and vegetables, but the area is greatly overpopulated and unemployment is high. Many residents live in refugee camps and rely upon international charitable organizations. There is some industry including textiles and clothing. Jericho produces fruit and vegetables, but relies upon tourism as a major employer. Many Palestinians used to cross into Israel to work, and the closure of the border to most of these daily commuters (since 1994) has added to the economic distress.
Recent History: Gaza and Jericho were part of (Turkish) Ottoman-ruled Palestine until World War I and were then included in the British League of Nations mandate of Palestine. After 1948–49, Jericho was incorporated into Jordan and the Gaza Strip into

Egypt. Israel took both areas during the Arab-Israeli War of 1967. In 1964, the Palestine Liberation Organization (PLO) was formed by exiled Palestinians with the objective of overthrowing Israel. Beginning in 1988, an uprising (*intifada*) by Palestinians living in Gaza and the West Bank increased tensions in the area. International efforts to secure a Middle East peace accord accelerated in 1991 and a Norwegian-sponsored Israeli-PLO agreement (1993–94) secured limited Palestinian autonomy in Gaza and Jericho. The PLO leader, Yasser Arafat, has adopted some of the trappings of a state for the Palestinain entity, but he has been frustrated in attempts to continue the peace process by continuing Israeli settlement in the West Bank (which is contrary to the Oslo peace accord) and by continuing terrorist attacks on Israeli civilians and military by Palestinians rejecting the accord. A phased withdrawal of Israeli forces from Jericho and most of Gaza has been completed, but (in 1995) there was little prospect of further Israeli withdrawal from the occupied West Bank or of the holding of elections scheduled for the Palestinian Authority.

Gibraltar

Status: a British Crown colony.
Area: 6·5 km^2 (2 ·5 sq mi).
Population: 31,300 (1991 est).
Capital: Gibraltar 31,300 (1991 est).
Geography: Gibraltar is a small rocky peninsula connected to the south coast of Spain by a narrow isthmus. It commands the north side of the Atlantic entrance to the Mediterranean.
Economy: Gibraltar depends upon tourism, ship repairing, banking and finance – the Rock has become an 'offshore' banking centre – and the re-export trade. Owing to lack of space, there is no agriculture.
Recent History: The strategic importance of Gibralter – a British colony since 1713 – has greatly diminished with the decline of the British Empire since World War II. Spain continues to claim the Rock and blockaded Gibraltar from 1969 to 1982–84. Gibraltar has enjoyed internal self-government since 1964 and became part of the EC when the UK joined that organization in 1973.

Golan Heights

Status: Syrian territory under Israeli occupation and formally annexed by Israel in 1981.
Area: 378 km^2 (146 sq mi).
Population: 26,000 (1990 est).
Main town: al-Qunaytirah 5000 (1990 est).
Geography: The mountainous Golan Heights are fertile in the south. They form a strategic zone between Syria and Israel.
Economy: Golan has been settled by Israelis who have established kibbutzim and large vineyards.
Recent History: The Golan Heights were part of Syria until taken by Israeli forces during the Arab-Israeli War of 1967. A UN buffer zone between the Syrian and Israeli armistice lines was established in 1973. The annexation of Golan by Israel (1981) is not recognized by the international community. In 1994, the Israeli government indicated that it was willing to discuss Golan with Syria as part of an overall peace settlement. Informal contacts have taken place, but Syria demands the return of the entire area and there is widespread Israeli opposition to concessions over Golan.

Greenland

Status: an internally self-governing part of the Kingdom of Denmark.
Area: 2,175,600 km^2 (839,800 sq mi).
Population: 55,500 (1991 est).
Capital: Nuuk (formerly Godthab) 12,200 (1991 est).
Geography: Arctic Greenland, the largest island in the world, has a highly indented fjord coastline. Over four-fifths of the island are covered by a permanent ice cap. The ice-free land is largely mountainous with a tundra vegetation.
Economy: The economy is dominated by fishing and fish-processing. The harsh environment restricts agriculture to 1% of the island in the southwest, where hay and vegetables are grown and sheep are kept.
Recent History: Greenland – the site of a Norse settlement between the 10th and 15th centuries – became a Danish colony in 1721. In 1953, Greenland became part of Denmark. In 1979, the island received home rule, retaining its status as part of Denmark.

Guadeloupe

Status: a French overseas département, an integral part of the French Republic.
Area: 1705 km^2 (658 sq mi) – Basse-Terre 848 km^2 (327 sq mi), Grande-Terre 590 km^2 (228 sq mi), Marie-Galante 158 km^2 (61 sq mi), St Martin 54 km^2 (21 sq mi), St Barthélemy 21 km^2 (8 sq mi), La Désirade 20 km^2 (8 sq mi), Iles des Saintes 13 km^2 (5 sq mi).
Population: 378,000 (1990 census).
Capital: Basse-Terre (also capital of Basse-Terre) 14,000 (1990 census).
Other capitals: Pointe-à-Pitre (Grande-Terre) 89,000 (city 26,000), Grand-Bourg (Marie-Galante) 6000, Marigot (St Martin), Gustavia (St Barthélemy), Grande-Anse (La Désirade), Terre-de-Bas (Iles des Saintes) (1990 census).
Geography: Guadeloupe comprises a group of Caribbean islands: Grande-Terre and Basse-Terre, which lie between Antigua and Dominica, are separated by a narrow channel; Marie-Galante, La Désirade and Iles des Saintes are close by; St Martin is half of a north Caribbean island whose southern half is Dutch (Sint Maarten); St Barthélemy lies south of Sint Maarten.
Economy: Bananas and sugar cane are the main exports. Tourism is the principal foreign-currency earner.
Recent History: The islands have been French since the 17th century, although St Barthélemy was a Swedish colony until purchased by France in 1877. In 1946, Guadeloupe became an overseas French département.

Guam

Status: an unincorporated United States territory.
Area: 541 km^2 (209 sq mi).
Population: 133,000 (1990 census).
Capital: Agaña 4900 (city 1100; 1990 census).
Main town: Dededo 32,000 (1990 census).
Geography: Guam is a tropical island in the western Pacific. The north is a limestone plateau; the south comprises volcanic hills.
Economy: Guam, a duty-free port, atracts large numbers of Japanese tourists. US military bases are the major employers.
Recent History: After the Spanish-American War,

Guam was ceded by Spain to the USA (1898). Guam was occupied by the Japanese from 1941 to 1944, and became an unincorporated US territory in 1950.

Guernsey and dependencies

Status: an internally self-governing state associated with, but not part of, the UK.

Area: 78·5 km^2 (30 sq mi) – Guernsey 65 km^2 (25 sq mi), Alderney 8 km^2 (3 sq mi), Sark 5 ·5 km^2 (2 sq mi).

Population: 61,600 (1991 est) – Guernsey 58,900 (1991 census), Alderney 2100 (1991 est), Sark 550 (1991 est).

Capital: St Peter Port 19,000 (1986 est). The capital of Alderney is St Anne's (1800; 1986 est). Sark has no capital as settlement on the island is dispersed.

Geography: Guernsey, a plateau surrounded by coastal cliffs, is 48 km (30 mi) west of Normandy. Its smaller dependencies of Alderney and Sark are respectively north and east of Guernsey.

Economy: Guernsey's economy is dominated by tourism. Guernsey has become an 'offshore' banking centre, although it does not yet rival Jersey in this respect.

Recent History: Guernsey, along with the other Channel Islands, is the only remaining part of the Duchy of Normandy, attached to the British Crown. The islands were occupied by Germany from 1940 to 1945.

Heard and McDonald Islands

Status: an external territory of Australia.

Area: 417 km^2 (161 sq mi).

Population: no permanent population.

Geography: The islands, whch lie about 4000 km (2500 mi) southwest of Australia, are almost entirely covered in ice.

Hong Kong

Status: a British Crown colony, with adjoining areas, the New Territories, leased from China.

Area: 1076 km^2 (415 sq mi) – Hong Kong Island 80 km^2 (31 sq mi), Kowloon 43 km^2 (17 sq mi), New Territories 953 km^2 (368 sq mi).

Population: 6,019,000 (1993 est).

Capital: Victoria (part of the Hong Kong agglomeration).

Geography: Hong Kong comprises Hong Kong island, Kowloon peninsula and the hilly New Territories on the Chinese mainland, plus Lantau island and 234 smaller islands.

Economy: Hong Kong has emerged as one of the economic 'little dragons' of the Far East with an impressive GDP that is one third that of its giant neighbour, the People's Republic of China. The colony grew as a trading 'gateway' to China, and became the financial and banking centre for Communist China. Hong Kong is a leading industrial power, originally based upon cheap labour. Principal exports include clothing, textiles, electrical machinery, data-processing and telecommunications equipment, and sound equipment. The economy has been increasingly integrated with that of the neighbouring Chinese province of Guangdong, but confidence has been dented by disputes between China and Britain concerning the impending return of Hong Kong to China.

Recent History: China ceded Hong Kong island to Britain in 1842. Kowloon was added to the colony in 1860 and the UK acquired a lease on the New Territories in 1898. Japan occupied Hong Kong from 1941 to 1945. Hong Kong is to return to China on 1 July 1997, when the lease on the New Territories expires. Under the Basic Law (agreed by the UK and China), Hong Kong will become a Special Administrative Region of China, retaining its present laws and economic system and enjoying considerable autonomy. However, disputes between Britain and China concerning the construction of a new airport and the constitutional reforms introduced by the Governor, Chris Patten, have cast some doubts on the full implementation of the agreement.

Howland, Baker and Jarvis Islands

Status: unincorporated US territories.

Area: 5 km^2 (2 sq mi).

Population: uninhabited.

Geography: These three arid tropical islands are situated in the South Pacific.

Recent History: The islands were claimed by the USA in 1857. In 1936 they became unincorporated US territories.

Isle of Man

See Man, Isle of (below).

Jersey

Status: an internally self-governing state associated with, but not part of, the UK.

Area: 116·2 km^2 (44 ·8 sq mi).

Population: 84,000 (1991 census).

Capital: St Helier 32,000 (1991 census).

Geography: The island of Jersey, which is 19 km (12 mi) west of the French Cotentin peninsula, is surrounded by cliffs and is deeply incised by valleys.

Economy: The economy of Jersey is based upon tourism, farming (which concentrates upon dairying and the breeding of Jersey cattle for export, early potatoes and tomatoes), and, increasingly, upon 'offshore' banking.

Recent History: Jersey, along with the other Channel Islands, is the only remaining part of the Duchy of Normandy, attached to the British Crown. The islands were occupied by Germany from 1940 to 1945.

Johnston Atoll

Status: an unincorporated US territory.

Area: 1·3 km^2 (0 ·5 sq mi).

Population: no permanent population.

Geography: Johnston Atoll, a semi-circular reef, comprises four small tropical Pacific coral islands.

Recent History: The atoll was claimed by the USA in 1856 in order to exploit its guano. A US air base was established in 1941. The atoll has been used in association with nuclear-weapons testing.

Kingman Reef

Status: an unincorporated US territory.

Area: 0·03 km^2 (0 ·01 sq mi).

Population: uninhabited.

Geography: Only parts of Kingman Reef, a coral atoll in the Pacific, are permanently above sea level.

Recent History: The reef has been a US possession since 1922.

Macau

Status: a Special Territory of Portugal.

Area: 18 km^2 (6 ·9 sq mi).

Population: 378,000 (1993 est).

Capital: Macau 378,000 (1993 est).

Geography: The territory comprises the peninsula of Macau on the Chinese mainland and two small

adjoining islands.
Economy: Nearly one half of the labour force is involved in the manufacturing industry, in particular textiles and clothing, plastic goods, toys, furniture, electrical goods and electronics, and footwear. The growth of these industries was encouraged by Macau's free port status. Tourism, attracted by casinos, makes a major contribution to the economy.
Recent History: Macau, a Portuguese colony since 1557, has since 1974 been a Special Territory under Portuguese administration but, in which, China has a leading role. Negotiations between Portugal and China (1987) resulted in an agreement to transfer sovereignty of Macau to China in 1999, when the territory will become a Special Administrative Region of China.

Man, Isle of

Status: an internally self-governing state associated with, but not part of, the UK.
Area: 572 km^2 (221 sq mi).
Population: 69,800 (1991 census).
Capital: Douglas 30,700 (town 22,200; Onchan 8500; 1991 census).
Geography: The island, which has a rocky indented coast, lies in the Irish Sea between the northwest coast of England and Northern Ireland.
Economy: The economy largely depends upon tourism, although 'offshore' banking and other financial interests are growing in importance.
Recent History: The Isle of Man was held by a succession of English and Scottish overlords before being sold to the British Crown in 1765, when Man became a Crown Dependency but not part of the UK. In recent years, Man has exercised increasing independence from the UK.

Martinique

Status: a French overseas département, an integral part of the French Republic.
Area: 1128 km^2 (436 sq mi).
Population: 360,000 (1990 census).
Capital: Fort-de-France 102,000 (1990 census).
Geography: Martinique, which lies between St Lucia and Dominica, rises steeply from the sea to its mountainous interior.
Economy: Bananas and sugar cane (for rum) are the main exports. Tourism is increasingly important.
Recent History: The island, a French possession since 1635, became an overseas French département in 1946.

Mayotte

Status: a French territorial collectivity, an integral part of the French Republic.
Area: 376 km^2 (145 sq mi).
Population: 94,400 (1990 census).
Capital: Mamoudzou 12,000 (1990 census).
Geography: Mayotte is the most southeasterly island of the Comoros group.
Economy: Mayotte depends upon the export of vanilla and ylang-ylang.
Recent History: The Comoros became French in 1843. France has administered Mayotte separately since 1975, when the three western islands unilaterally declared independence.

Midway Islands

Status: an unincorporated US territory.
Area: 5 km^2 (2 sq mi).
Population: no permanent population. There is a US military establishment in the islands.
Geography: The subtropical Midway Islands, northwest of Hawaii, form a circular atoll.
Recent History: Midway – a US possession since 1867 – came under the control of the US Navy in 1903. The Battle of Midway (1942) was a turning point in World War II in the Pacific.

Montserrat

Status: a British Crown colony.
Area: 98 km^2 (38 sq mi).
Population: 12,400 (1989 est).
Capital: Plymouth 1500 (1989 est).
Geography: Montserrat is a small mountainous island in the Leeward group of the easten Caribbean.
Economy: The economy is dominated by tourism and services, particularly data-processing, and the island is a computer centre of regional significance.
Recent History: Montserrat, a British possession since 1632, did not become a separate colony until 1956. The island has enjoyed internal self-government since 1960, but resists independence.

Netherlands Antilles or Antilles of the Five

Status: an autonomous part of the Kingdom of the Netherlands.
Area: 800 km^2 (309 sq mi) – Curaçao 444 km^2 (171 sq mi), Bonaire 288 km^2 (111 sq mi), Sint Maarten 34 km^2 (13 sq mi), St Eustatius (also known as Statia) 21 km^2 (8 sq mi), Saba 13 km^2 (5 sq mi).
Population: 191,000 (1991 est) – Curaçao 144,000, Bonaire 11,100, Sint Maarten 33,500, St Eustatius 1100, Saba 1800.
Capital: Willemstad 125,000 (also capital of Curaçao) (city 50,000: 1985 est).
Other capitals: Philipsburg (Sint Maarten) 6000, Kralendijk (Bonaire) 1200, Oranjestad (St Eustatius), The Bottom (Saba).
Geography: Curaçao and Bonaire lie off the coast of Venezuela; Sint Maarten is the southern half of the island shared with France in the Leeward group; St Eustatius and Saba are two very small islands north of St Kitts.
Economy: Curaçao depends upon refining Venezuelan oil and ship repairing. Bonaire produces textiles and salt. Tourism is important in all the islands.
Recent History: All five islands were claimed by the Dutch in the 17th century. With Aruba, they formed the Dutch West Indies (known after 1845 as the Netherlands Antilles). Aruba seceded in 1986. The islands are now a separate autonomous part of the Kingdom of the Netherlands

New Caledonia

Status: a French overseas territory.
Area: 19,103 km^2 (7376 sq mi).
Population: 164,000 (1989 census).
Capital: Nouméa 65,000 (1989 census).
Geography: New Caledonia island is a long, narrow, mountainous semi-tropical island 1500 km (900 mi) east of Queensland. The Loyalty Islands, Isle of Pines and Chesterfield and Beleep Islands are all part of the territory.
Economy: Tourism and the production of nickel, the main foreign-currency earners, have been affected by political unrest since the 1980s.

Recent History: New Caledonia, which was annexed by France in 1853, became a French overseas territory in 1946. The Melanesian Kanaks, who form 43% of the population, increased pressure for independence in the 1980s, but were outvoted by people of European and Asian descent, who are concentrated around Nouméa. Rising political tension led to violence in 1984–85 and 1988. The territory was divided into three autonomous provinces in 1988. A referendum in 1987 rejected independence.

Niue

Status: a self-governing territory of New Zealand.
Area: 259 km^2 (100 sq mi).
Population: 2270 (1990 est).
Capital: Alofi 1000 (1989 est).
Geography: Sub-tropical Niue, east of Tonga, comprises a coral plateau ending in steep sea cliffs.
Economy: Niue lacks natural resources and has little water. Tourism is being developed. Over 12,000 Niueans have migrated to work in New Zealand.
Recent History: Britain annexed Niue in 1900, but in 1901 transferred the territory to New Zealand. In 1974 Niue became self-governing in free association with New Zealand and is empowered to gain independence unilaterally.

Norfolk Island

Status: an Australian external territory.
Area: 34·5 km^2 (13 ·3 sq mi).
Population: 1980 (1990 est).
Capital: Kingston 1980 (1990 est).
Geography: The island, which is fertile and hilly, lies about 1400 km (875 mi) east of Queensland.
Economy: The economy relies upon tourism and revenue from issuing postage stamps.
Recent History: After being a penal settlement in the early 19th century, Norfolk Island was resettled from Pitcairn Island in 1856. Britain ceded the colony to New South Wales in 1897, but it was transferred to Australia as an external territory in 1913.

North Mariana Islands

Status: a United States Commonwealth territory.
Area: 471 km^2 (184 sq mi).
Population: 43,300 (1990 census).
Capital: Chalan Kanoa (on Saipan) 39,000 (1990 census).
Geography: The islands are a chain of 16 mountainous tropical islands in the western Pacific.
Economy: Farming, mainly in smallholdings, produces subsistence crops and vegetables for export. Tourism now dominates the economy.
Recent History: The islands were sold by Spain to Germany in 1899. Japan took the group in 1914 during World War I and received them as a League of Nations trusteeship in 1921. The islands saw fierce fighting during World War II. The groups was included in the US United Nations Trust Territory of the Pacific Islands from 1947 to 1978, when they became a separate internally self-governing territory in free association with the USA.

Palestinian entity

See Gaza and Jericho (above).

Paracel Islands

Status: disputed territory.
Area: 160 km^2 (62 sq mi).
Population: no figures are available; Chinese forces are stationed in the islands.
Geography: The islands comprise over 130 small low-lying arid coral reefs in the South China Sea.
Recent History: The islands were annexed to French Indochina in 1932. By 1950, the islands were claimed by both North and South Vietnam, and by both Communist China and Taiwan. The discovery of oil in nearby waters prompted a Chinese occupation of the Paracels.

Peter I Island

Status: a Norwegian territorial claim – all territorial claims south of latitude 60°S are in abeyance under the terms of the Antarctic Treaty (1959).
Area: 180 km^2 (69 sq mi).
Population: no permanent population.
Geography: Peter I Island is an ice-covered island 450 km (280 mi) north of Antarctica.

Pitcairn Islands

Status: a British settlement.
Area: 44 km^2 (17 sq mi).
Population: 67 (1992 est).
Capital: Adamstown 67 (1992 est).
Geography: The group comprises four sub-tropical islands in the South Pacific about 4800 km (3000 mi) east of New Zealand. Pitcairn Island is volcanic in origin and rugged but fertile.
Economy: Pitcairn depends upon subsistence farming, fishing and the sale of postage stamps.
Recent History: Populated by nine mutineers from the Bounty and their consorts (1790), Pitcairn became overpopulated by the middle of the 19th century and some islanders were removed to Norfolk Island.

Puerto Rico

Status: a United States Commonwealth territory.
Area: 9104 km^2 (3515 sq mi).
Population: 3,612,000 (1993 est).
Capital: San Juan 1,230,000 (city 427,000; 1990 census).
Geography: Puerto Rico, the easternmost island of the Greater Antilles, is crossed from east to west by a mountainous chain. The islands of Vieques and Culebra are included in the Commonwealth.
Economy: Although Puerto Rico has no mineral resources, manufacturing industry dominates with pharmaceuticals, petrochemicals, electrical and electronic equipment, food processing and textiles as the major industries. The island is densely populated and there has been large-scale migration to the USA. US federal funds have developed the infrastructure and encouraged the service sector.
Recent History: Puerto Rico, a Spanish colony from 1509, was ceded to the USA in 1898 following the Spanish-American War. The island gained internal self-government in 1952 when it became a Commonwealth, and despite periodic debates concerning its status, Puerto Rico has, so far, rejected the options of independence or US statehood.

Queen Maud Land

Status: a Norwegian territorial claim – all territorial claims south of latitude 60°S are in abeyance under the terms of the Antarctic Treaty (1959).
Area: as no inland limit to the claim has been made, no estimate of the area can be given.
Geography: Norway claims that part of Antarctica between 20°W and 45°E.

Réunion

Status: a French overseas département, an integral

part of the French Republic.

Area: 2542 km^2 (982 sq mi) – Réunion 2512 km^2 (970 sq mi); the rest of the total is made by the following Indian Ocean islets: Iles Glorieuses, Juan de Nova, Tromelin, Bassas de India, Ile Europa.

Population: 598,000 (1990 census); the islets are unihabited.

Capital: St Denis 101,000 (1990 census).

Geography: Réunion is a rugged volcanic tropical island east of Madagascar.

Economy: The economy is dominated by sugar cane, which accounts for 90% of exports.

Recent History: Réunion became a French possession in 1638 and an overseas French département in 1974.

Ross Dependency

Status: a New Zealand dependency – all territorial claims south of latitude 60°S are in abeyance under the terms of the Antarctic Treaty (1959).

Area: 730,000 km^2 (282,000 sq mi).

Geography: New Zealand claims that part of Antarctica between 160°E and 150°E.

St Helena and Dependencies

Status: British Crown colony.

Area: 411 km^2 (159 sq mi) – St Helena 122 km^2 (47 sq mi), Ascension 88 km^2 (34 sq mi), Tristan da Cunha group 201 km^2 (78 sq mi).

Population: 7100 (1992 est) – St Helena 5700, Ascension 1100 (excluding service personnel), Tristan da Cunha 300.

Capital: Jamestown 1500 (on St Helena) (1992 est). The capital of Ascension is Georgetown; the capital of Tristan da Cunha is Edinburgh.

Geography: St Helena is a mountainous island in the South Atlantic. Ascension is a barren, rocky island 1130 km (700 mi) northwest of St Helena. The Tristan da Cunha group of six bleak, mountainous islands lies 2120 km (1320 mi) southwest of St Helena.

Economy: St Helena relies upon UK subsidies and fishing. Ascension is a communications base.

Recent History: St Helena became British in 1659; Ascension was annexed by Britain in 1815 when Napoleon I was exiled to St Helena. Tristan da Cunha was annexed in 1816, but evacuated from 1961 to 1963 after a volcanic eruption.

St Pierre and Miquelon

Status: a French territorial collectivity, an integral part of the French Republic.

Area: 242 km^2 (93 sq mi) – St Pierre group 26 km^2 (10 sq mi), Miquelon-Langlade 216 km^2 (83 sq mi).

Population: 6400 (1990 census).

Capital: St Pierre 5700 (1990 census).

Geography: The territory comprises two main islands and six islets 25 km (16 mi) off the southern coast of Newfoundland.

Economy: Fishing, fish-freezing and tourism are, apart from government service, almost the only sources of employment.

Recent History: The only remains of the once-large French possessions in North America, the islands were settled from France in the 17th century. During Prohibition in the USA (1920–33), the islands were involved in supplying illicit alcohol into America. Since 1976, St Pierre-Miquelon has been an integral part of the French Republic.

South Georgia and South Sandwich Islands

Status: British Territories.

Area: 4091 km^2 (1580 sq mi) – South Georgia 3755 km^2 (1450 sq mi); South Sandwich Islands 336 km^2 (130 sq mi).

Population: no permanent population; there is a small military garrison and a scientific station at Grytviken in South Georgia.

'Capital': Grytviken.

Geography: South Georgia is a bleak, mountainous island 1290 km (800 mi) east of the Falkland Islands. Much of the island is under permanent snow cover. The South Sandwich Islands, which are 760 km (470 mi) southeast of South Georgia, are active volcanoes which are covered by glaciers.

Recent History: Both groups of islands, which were annexed by Britain in 1775, are claimed by Argentina. In 1955, Argentina refused a British referral of the dispute to the International Court of Justice. Argentine personnel occupied some of the South Sandwich Islands in 1976 and Argentine forces invaded South Georgia in 1982. Britain retook both groups in 1982 and, in 1985, separated them from the Falkland Islands, to which they had been attached as dependencies since 1908.

Sovereign Military Order of Malta

Status: a sovereign Roman Catholic order occupying two buildings that enjoy extra-territorial status. (The Knights of Justice of this charitable monastic order live as a religious community. They elect for life one of their number to be Prince and Grand Master, who is recognized as a sovereign by over 40 countries. The military order, which issues its own currency and passports, has many of the trappings of a state, and is sometimes said to be the 'smallest country in the world'. Recognition is, however, largely confined to Roman Catholic countries.)

Area: 1·2 ha (2 acres).

Head of state: HEH (His Eminent Highness) Fra (Brother) Andrew Bartie, Prince and Grand Master.

Geography: The territory of the order comprises the Villa del Priorato di Malta (on the Aventine Hill in Rome) and 68 via Condotti (in the same city).

Recent History: The 'Knights of Malta' ruled Rhodes until 1523 and then Malta, until expelled by Napoleon I (1798). Since the 1830s, their territory has been confined to their properties in Rome.

Spratly Islands

Status: disputed territory.

Area: not defined.

Population: no permanent population.

Geography: The islands comprise a large number of very small, rocky islets in the South China Sea.

Recent History: The Spratly Islands, which are thought to contain valuable mineral resources, were claimed by France as part of French Indochina in the 1930s, and are now claimed (in all or in part) by Vietnam, China, Taiwan, Malaysia, the Philippines and Brunei. In 1995, tension between China and the Philippines rose concerning the dispute.

Turks and Caicos Islands

Status: a British Crown colony.

Area: 430 km^2 (166 sq mi).

Population: 12,400 (1990 census).

Capital: Cockburn Town 2500 (1990 census) on Grand Turk island.

Geography: The 30 Turks and Caicos Islands form two groups of low-lying islands to the southeast of the Bahamas.
Economy: The economy depends upon tourism and 'offshore' banking and finace.
Recent History: The islands, which finally became British in 1766, were linked administratively to Jamaica until 1956. They became a separate colony in 1962. The islands were rocked by scandal in 1985-86 when the Chief Minister, another minister and a member of the legislature were arrested, and later imprisoned in Florida, on charges involving illicit drugs. The next Chief Minister and two of his ministers were subsequently found guilty of malpractice.

Virgin Islands of the United States

Status: an unincorporated US external territory.
Area: 352 km^2 (136 sq mi).
Population: 102,000 (1990 census).
Capital: Charlotte Amalie 12,300 (1990 census).
Geography: The territory comprises three main islands (St Croix, St Thomas, and St John) and about 50 small cays. About 64 km (40 mi) east of Puerto Rico, the islands command the Anegada Passage, one of the principal routes from the Atlantic to the Caribbean.
Economy: The islands have no natural resources. Tourism, which dominates the economy, is encouraged by the climate and the fact that the whole territory enjoys free port status. St Croix has one of the world's largest oil refineries.
Recent History: Denmark acquired St John and St Thomas in 1671 and St Croix in 1733. The USA purchased the islands from Denmark in 1917 because of their strategic position guarding the shipping to the Panama canal. Since 1954, the islands have had a measure of internal self-government.

Wake Island

Status: an unincorporated US territory.
Area: 8 km^2 (3 sq mi).
Population: no permanent population; about 300 US service personnel in 1990.
Geography: Wake comprises three small arid tropical islands around a lagoon, west of Hawaii.
Recent History: The island was claimed by the USA in 1899. After a major battle (1941), Japanese forces took Wake Island, occupying it until 1945.

Wallis and Futuna Islands

Status: an overseas French territory.
Area: 274 km^2 (106 sq mi).
Population: 13,700 (1990 est).
Capital: Mata-Utu 810 (1990 est).
Geography: This Pacific territory comprises two tropical archipelagoes: Wallis (or the kingdom of Uvéa), a volcanic island, plus some coral reefs; and Futuna, two mountainous islands divided between the kingdoms of Sigave and Alo.
Economy: Large numbers of islanders have left owing to unemployment. The economy relies upon government employment and money sent back by islanders working abroad. Copra is the only export.
Recent History: France established a protectorate over Wallis in 1887 and Futuna in 1888. US forces took the islands from 1942 to 1946 during World War II. The islands became a French overseas territory in 1961.

West Bank

Status: under Israeli occupation.
Area: 5819 km^2 (2247 sq mi) – excluding East Jerusalem and Jericho.
Population: 930,000 (1990 est) – excluding East Jerusalem and Jericho.
Main towns: Nablus (Nabulus) 106,000, Hebron (Al-Khalil) 87,000 (1990 est).
Geography: The West Bank is a mountainous area between the Israeli border in the west and the Dead Sea and the flat valley of the River Jordan in the east. The enclave of Jericho has autonomy (see Gaza and Jericho, above).
Economy: The Jordan Valley supports farming, mainly for citrus fruit and vegetables. The West Bank is overpopulated and unemployment is high. Many residents live in refugee camps and rely upon international charitable organizations, other foreign (largely) Arab aid and money sent back by Palestinians working abroad.
Recent History: The West Bank was part of (Turkish) Ottoman-ruled Palestine until World War I and was then included in the British League of Nations mandate of Palestine. After 1948–49, the area was incorporated into Jordan, but was taken by Israel during the Arab-Israeli War of 1967. In 1964, the Palestine Liberation Organization (PLO) was formed by exiled Palestinians with the objective of overthrowing Israel. Beginning in 1988, an uprising (*intifada*) by Palestinians living in the West Bank increased tensions in the area. In 1988 Jordan severed all legal ties with the West Bank. International efforts to secure a Middle East peace accord accelerated in 1991 and a Norwegian-sponsored Israeli-PLO agreement (1993–94) secured limited Palestinian autonomy in Gaza and Jericho (see above). The extension of the peace accord to the rest of the West Bank has been frustrated by continuing Israeli settlement in the West Bank (which is contrary to the Oslo peace accord) and by continuing terrorist attacks on Israeli civilians and military by Palestinians rejecting the accord.

Western Sahara

Status: a disputed territory under Moroccan administration.
Area: 266,000 km^2 (102,676 sq mi).
Population: 195,000 (1993 est).
Capital: El-Aaiun (Laayoune) 97,000 (1982 est).
Geography: The Western Sahara is a low, flat desert region with no permanent streams.
Economy: The economy is dominated by the production of phosphate at Bu Craa, the largest phosphate deposit in the world.
Recent History: The area became Spanish in 1884. In 1972–73, the Polisario liberation movement's fight against Spanish rule began. Spain withdrew, dividing the territory between Morocco and Mauritania. Morocco absorbed the Mauritanian area when Mauritania withdrew (1979). In 1976, Polisario declared independence as the Sahrawi Arab Democratic Republic. A ceasefire, an agreement to hold a referendum on the territory's future and the deployment of a UN force were agreed in 1991, but the plebiscite has yet to be held.

World Political Leaders

Abacha, Sanni (various birthdates given) Nigerian military politician. Head of State (1994–). He overthrew General Babangida, under whom he had served previously.

Ahern, Bertie (1951–), Irish politician. Minister of Labour (1987–94). Leader of the Fianna Fail Party (1994–).

Ahtisaari, Martti (1937–). Finnish politician and diplomat. Minister for Foreign Affairs (1984–86), Undersecretary-General of the UN (1987–91), Secretary of State for Foreign Affairs (1991–94), President of Finland (1994–).

Akayev, Askar (1944–), Kyrgyz politician. President (1990–).

Akihito (1933–), Emperor of Japan (1990–). He is known in Japan as the *Heisei* emperor.

Albert II (1934–), King of the Belgians (1993–).

Aliyev, Geidar (1927–), Azeri (former Communist) politician. President of Azerbaijan (1993–).

Arafat, Yasser (1929–), Egyptian-Palestinian politician. Chairman of the Palestine Liberation Organization (PLO; 1969–). Despite challenges to his authority from radical Palestinian factions in the late 1980s and early 1990s, he was a signatory to the Israeli-Palestinian Peace Accord (1993).

Aristide, Jean-Bertrand (1953–), Haitian clergyman and politician. President of Haiti (1990–91 and since 1994). A left-wing Catholic priest, he was overthrown by a military coup in 1991, but reinstated after US intervention in 1994.

Assad, Hafez al- (1928–), Syrian air force officer and politician. Leader of the Baath Party. PM (1970–71), President of Syria (1971–). His 23 years of rule have been repressive. In the early 1990s he attempted to improve relations with the West, aligning Syria with the US-dominated coalition during the Gulf War (1991).

Aung San Suu Kyi (1945–), Burmese politician. With the National League for Democracy she won the 1990 elections but was kept under house arrest and prevented from taking up political office. She received the Nobel Peace Prize in 1991 for her stand against the military regime.

Aznar, Jose Maria (1953–), Spanish politician. Leader of the (conservative) People's Party.

Balaguer, Joaquin (1907–), Dominican politician of the Partido Reformista (PR). Minister of Foreign Affairs (1954–55), of Education and Arts (1955–57), Vice-President of Dominican Republic (1957–60), President (1960, 1966–78, and 1986–).

Balladur, Edouard (1929–), French Gaullist politician. Minister of the Economy, of Finance and Privatization (1986–88). PM (1993–95).

Bandaranaike, Sirimavo (1916–), Sri Lankan politician. President of Sri Lanka Freedom Party (1960–), PM, Minister of Defence and External Affairs (1960–65), PM, Minister of Defence and Foreign Affairs, Planning, Economic Affairs and Plan Implementation (1970–77), PM (1994-). In 1960, she was the world's first woman PM.

Bashir, Omar Hassan Ahmed al- Sudanese army officer. PM, Minister of Defence, Culture and Information (1989–). He came to power following a military coup in 1989.

Beatrix (1938–), Queen of the Netherlands (1980–).

Ben Ali, Zine el-Abidine (1936–), Tunisian politician of the Democratic Constitutional Rally (RCD). President of Tunisia (1987–). He came to power after forcing his predecessor, Habib Bourghiba, to resign.

Berisha, Sali (1945–), Albanian politician (Albanian Democratic Party). President (1992–). First non-Communist president since World War II.

Berlusconi, Silvio (1936–), Italian businessman and politician. Leader of Forza Italia Party (1993–). PM (1993-94).

Bhumipol (1927–), King of Thailand (1946–).

Bhutto, Benazir (1953–), Pakistani politician. Leader in exile of the Pakistan Peoples Party (PPP; 1984–86), leader of the PPP in Pakistan (1986–). PM (1988–90 and 1993-).

Bildt, Carl (1949–), Swedish politician. Leader of the Moderate Party (MS; 1986–), PM (1991–94).

Birendra (1945–), King of Nepal (1972–).

Biya, Paul (1933–), Cameroonian politician. Minister of State, Secretary-General to President (1968–75), PM (1975–82), President (1982–).

Blair, Tony (Anthony) (1953–), English Labour politician. Member of the Shadow Cabinet (1984–), leader of the British Labour Party (1994–).

Bolger, Jim (James) (1935–), New Zealand politician. Minister of Fisheries and Associated Minister of Agriculture (1977), Minister of Labour (1978–84), Minister of Immigration (1978–81), leader of the National Party (since 1990), PM (1990–).

Bongo, (Albert-Bernard) Omar (1935–), Gabonese politician (Gabonese Democratic Party; PDG). Vice-President (1966–67), President (1967–).

Boross, Peter (1928–), Hungarian Independent politician. Minister of State for the Office of Information and the Office of National Security (1990), Minister of Home Affairs (1990–93), PM (1993-94).

Bossi, Umberto (1941–), Italian politician. Leader of the Northern League (1987–).

Bouchard, Lucien (1938–), Canadian politician. Minister of the Environment (1988–90). In 1990 he established Bloc Québecois.

Bourassa, Robert (1933–), Canadian politician. Leader of Liberal Party of Quebec (1970–77 and 1983–), PM of Quebec (1970–76 and 1985–).

Boutros Ghali, Boutros (1922–), Egyptian politician and international civil servant. Minister of State for Foreign Affairs (1977–91). Secretary-General of the United Nations (1992–).

Brazauskas, Mykolas Algirdas (1932–), Lithuanian politician. First Secretary of the Lithuanian Communist Party (1988–90), leader of the Democratic Labour Party (1990–), deputy PM (1990–91), President of Lithuania (1993–).

Brinkman, Elco (1948–), Dutch politician. Minister for Welfare, Health and Cultural Affairs (1982–89), leader of the Christian Democrat Appeal Party (CDA; 1994–).

Brundtland, Gro Harlem (1939–), Norwegian politician. Environment Minister (1974–79), leader of the Labour Party (1981–) and PM (1981, 1986–89 and 1990–).

Bruton, John (1947–), Irish politician (Fine Gael). Minister of Finance (1981–82), Industry, Trade, Commerce, Tourism (1982–86), Finance (1986–87), leader of Fine Gael (1990–), PM (1994-).

Buthelezi, Mangosuthu Gatsha (1928–), South African Zulu leader and politician. PM of Kwazulu homeland (1972–94), leader of the Inkatha Movement (1989–), Minister of the Interior (1994–). Despite the factional fighting between Inkatha and ANC supporters, Chief Buthelezi participated in the 1994 elections and joined Nelson Mandela's cabinet.

Caldera, Rafael (1916–), Venezuelan politician of the Social Christian Party (COPEI). President of Venezuela (1969–74 and 1994–).

Cardoso, Fernando Enrique (1931–), Brazilian politician (Brazilian Social Democratic Party). Foreign Minister (1992-93), Finance Minister (1993-95). President (1995-).

Carl XVI Gustaf (1946–), King of Sweden (1973–).

Carlsson, Ingvar (1934–), Swedish politician. Minister of Education (1969–73), of Housing and Physical Planning (1973–79), Deputy PM (1982–86), leader of the Social Democratic Labour Party (SDAP; 1986–), Minister of the Environment (1985–86), PM (1986–91 and 1994-).

Castro (Ruz), Fidel (1927–), Cuban Communist politician. PM (1959–76), President (1976–). He led the revolutionary forces that ousted Fulgencio Batista and declared the Cuban revolution. Opposed by the USA, he increasingly established diplomatic, economic and military links with the USSR. His defeat of the abortive Bay of Pigs invasion (1961), and survival of the Cuban Missile Crisis (1962), increased his popularity. However, the collapse of the Soviet Union has left his regime isolated.

Cavaco Silva, Anibal (1939–), Portuguese politician. Minister of Finance and Planning (1980–81), leader of Social Democrat Party (PSD), PM (1985–).

Chamorro, Violeta Barrios de (c. 1939–), Nicaraguan politician of the National Opposition Union. President of Nicaragua (1990–). She beat Daniel Ortega in the presidential elections.

Chernomyrdin, Viktor (1938–), Russian politician. PM (1991–).

Chiluba, Frederick (1943–), Zambian politician of the Movement for Multiparty Democracy (MMD). President of Zambia (1991–). He defeated the longstanding president, Kenneth Kaunda in the first elections since 1973.

Chirac, Jacques (1932–), French Gaullist politician. Secretary of State for Employment Problems (1967–68), Secretary of State for Economy and Finance (1968–71), Minister for Parliamentary Relations (1971–72), for Agriculture and Rural Development (1972–74), of the Interior (1974), PM (1974–76 and 1986–88), President (1995-).

Chissano, Joaquim Alberto (1939–), Mozambican politician of FRELIMO. PM (1974–75), Minister of Foreign Affairs (1975–86), President of Mozambique (1986–).

Chrétien, Jean (1934–), Canadian politician. Secretary of State for External Affairs, deputy PM (1984), leader of the National Liberal Party (1990–), PM (1993–).

Christopher, Warren (1925–), US diplomat and Democrat politician. Deputy Secretary of State (under Jimmy Carter) (1977–81) and Secretary of State (1993–).

Ciller, Tansu (1946–), Turkish politician. Leader of the True Path Party (DYP) and PM (1993–).

Clark, Helen (1950–), New Zealand politician of the Labour Party. Minister of Housing and Minister of Conservation (1987–89), of Health (1989–90), of Labour (1989–90), deputy PM (1989–90), leader of the Labour Party (1994–).

Clarke, Kenneth (1940–), English Conservative politician. British Minister of Housing and Conservation (1988-89), Health (1989-90), Education and Science (1990-92), for the Home Office (1992-93), and Chancellor for the Exchequer (1993–).

Clerides, Glafcos (1920–), Greek Cypriot politician of the Democratic Rally. Minister of Justice (1959–60), Acting President (1974), President (1993–).

Clinton, Bill (William Jefferson) (1946–), US Democratic politician. Governor of Arkansas (1979–81 and 1983–93) and 42nd President of the USA (1993–). He won a liberal and progressive reputation as Governor of Arkansas and defeated George Bush to become the first Democrat in the White House for 13 years.

D'Alema, Massimo (1949-), Italian politician. Leader of the (former Communist) Party of the Democratic Left (1994-).

da Silva, Luis Inacio (Lula) (1946–), Brazilian trade unionist and politician. Leader of the Partido dos Trabalhadores (PT).

Dehaene, Jean-Luc (1940–), Belgian Christian Democrat politician. Minister of Social Affairs and Institutional Reforms (1981–88), Deputy PM and Minister of Communications and Institutional Reforms (1988–92), PM (1992–).

De Klerk, Frederik Willem (1936–), South African politician. President of South Africa (1989–94), Second Deputy President (1994–). He negotiated peace with the African National Congress, released Nelson Mandela from prison, and initiated constitutional negotiations for a non-racial 'New South Africa'.

Delors, Jacques (1925–), French Socialist politician and EC official. French Minister for the Economy and Finance (1981–83), for the Economy, Finance and Budget (1983–84), President of the European Commission (1985-95).

Demirel, Suleyman (1924–), Turkish politician of the True Path Party (DYP). PM (1965–71, 1975–77, 1979–80 and 1991–93), President (1993–).

Deng Xiaoping (1904–), Chinese Communist politician. General Secretary of the Chinese Communist Party (1956–67). Denounced during the Cultural Revolution (1967) and in 1976, he was rehabilitated both times. He remains effective leader of China although he holds no official post. Although he has encouraged modernization, he was responsible for the violent repression of the pro-democracy demonstration at Tiananmen Square in 1989.

Denktash, Rauf (1924–), Turkish Cypriot politician.

Dini, Lamberto (1931–), Italian financier. Non-party PM (1995–).

Diouf, Abdou (1935–), Senegalese politician of the Senegalese Progressive Union (UPS). Minister of Planning and Industry (1968–70), PM (1970–80), President of Senegal (1981–).

Dole, Robert (1923–), US Republican politician. Kansas senator (1968–). Effective leader of the opposition since the election of Bill Clinton.

dos Santos, Jose Eduardo (1942–), Angolan politician of the MPLA. Foreign Minister (1975), First Deputy PM, Minister of Planning and Head of National Planning (1978–79), President (1979–).

Duran Ballen, Sixto (1922–), Ecuadorian politician of the United Republican Party. President (1992–).

Ecevit, Bulent (1925–), Turkish politician. Minister of Labour (1961–65), PM (1974, 1977 and 1978–79), leader of the Democratic Left Party (1989–).

Elizabeth II (1926–), Queen of Great Britain and Northern Ireland (1952–).

Engholm, Björn (1939–), German politician. Minister for Education and Science (1981–82), State Premier of Schleswig-Holstein (1988–), Leader of the Social Democrat Party (SPD: 1990–93).

Fahd (1923–), King of Saudi Arabia (1982–). Minister of Education (1953), Minister of the Interior (1962–75), deputy PM (1975–82), PM (1982–).

Fenech Adami, Eddie (1934–), Maltese politician. Leader of the National Party (1977–), PM (1987–).

Fini, Gianfranco (1952–), Italian politician. Leader of the (former neo-fascist) National Alliance (1991–).

Finnbogadottir, Vigdis (1930–), Icelandic politician. President of Iceland (1980–).

Five, Kaci Kullman (1951–), Norwegian politician. Minister of Trade and Shipping (1989–90). Leader of the Conservative Party.

Frei Ruiz-Tagle, Eduardo (1943–), Chilean Christian Democrat politician. President (1994–). Son of the former president, Eduardo Frei Montalva.

Fujimori, Alberto (1938–), Peruvian politician and founder of the Change '90 Movement. President (1990–).

Gadaffi, Moamar al (1942–), Libyan politician. President of Libya (1971–). He led a military coup to overthrow King Idris I in 1969. Allegations of international terrorism have left him isolated and at odds with the USA.

Gaidar, Yegor (1956–), Russian politician. Deputy PM (1991–92), PM (1992), leader of the Democratic Choice of Russia party (1994–).

Gingrich, Newt (1943–), US (conservative) Republican politican. Speaker of the House of Representatives (1995–).

Gligorov, Kiro (1918–). Macedonian politician of the Social Democratic League (SDLM). President of Macedonia (1991–).

Goh Chok Tong (1941–), Singaporean politician. Minister of State for Finance (1977–79), Minister for Trade and Industry (1979–81), for Health and Second Minister for Defence (1981–82), for Defence and Second Minister for Health (1982–84), PM (1990–).

Goncz, Arpad (1922–), Hungarian politician. Acting President of Hungary (1989), President of Hungary (1990–).

Gonzalez, Felipe (1942–), Spanish politician. Leader of the Spanish Socialist Party (PSOE; 1980–), PM (1982–). He dismantled the last remnants of General Franco's system, took Spain into the EC and modernized the economy.

Gore, Al(bert) (1948–), US Democratic politician. Senator of Tennessee (1985–92) and Vice-President (1992–).

Haider, Joerg (1950–), Austrian politician and leader of the Freedom Party.

Hans Adam II (1945-), Prince of Liechtenstein (1989-).

Harald V (1937–), King of Norway (1990–).

Hassan II (1929–), King of Morocco (1961–). Minister of Defence (1960–61), deputy PM (1960–61), PM (1961–63 and 1965–67), Minister of Defence (1972–73).

Hassanal, Bolkiah (1946–), Sultan of Brunei (1967–), PM of Brunei (1984–), Minister of Finance and Home Affairs (1984–86), of Defence (1986–).

Hata, Tsutomu (1936–), Japanese politician. Deputy PM and Minister of Foreign Affairs (1993–94), PM (1994). A disaffected Liberal Democrat, he helped bring down the Miyazawa government, joined the coalition government under Hosakawa, and briefly became PM himself in 1994 with the Japanese Renewal Party (JRP).

Havel, Vaclav (1935–), Czech playwright, writer and politician. Founder and leader of Civic Forum (1989), President of Czechoslovakia (1989–93), President of Czech Republic (1993–). A human rights activist, he led peaceful demonstrations against the Communist regime in 1989.

Herzog, Roman (1934–), German Christian Democrat politician. President (1994–).

Horn, Gyula (1932–), Hungarian politician. (Communist) Minister of Foreign Affairs (1989–90), leader of the Hungarian Socialist Party (HSP; 1990–), PM (1994–).

Hosakawa, Morihiro (1938–), Japanese politician. Founder and leader of the Japan New Party (JNP; 1992–), PM (1993–94). A disaffected Liberal Democrat, he founded the new party and headed a coalition government.

Howard, John (1939–), Australian politician. Leader of the Conservative Party (1995–).

Hrawi, Elias (1930–), Lebanese politician. President of Lebanon (1989–).

Hurd, Douglas (1930–), English Conservative politician. British Secretary of State for Northern Ireland (1984–85), for the Home Office (1985–89), for Foreign and Commonwealth Affairs (1989–).

Hussein (1935–), King of Jordan (1952–). He has pursued moderate, pragmatic policies in the face of politicial upheavals within and outside his country.

Iliescu, Ion (1930–), Romanian politician. President of the National Salvation Front (1989–90), President of Provisional Council for National Unity (1990), President of Romania (1990–).

Isa II (1933-), Amir of Bahrain (1961-).

Izetbegovic, Alija (1925–), Bosnian politician of the Moslem Democratic Action. President of Bosnia-Herzegovina (1992–).

Jabir III (1928–), Amir of Kuwait. PM (1965–67), Crown Prince (1966–77), Amir (1978–). In 1986 he suspended the national assembly and resumed feudal rule. He fled to Saudi Arabia during the invasion of Kuwait (1990–91).

Jagan, Cheddi (1918–), Guyanese politician of the Progressive People's Party (PPP). Minister of Agriculture, Lands and Mines and Leader of the House of Assembly (1953), Minister of Trade and Industry (1957–61), PM (1957–64), Minister of Development and Planning (1961–64), Leader of the Opposition (1964–73), General Secretary of PPP (1970–), PM (1992–).

Jean I (1925–), Grand Duke of Luxembourg (1964–).

Jiang Zemin (1926–), Chinese Communist politician. General Secretary of the Chinese Communist Party (CCP; 1987–), President of China (1993–).

Jigme Singhye Wangchuk (1955-), King of Bhutan (1972-).

John Paul II (Karol Wojtyla; 1920–), Pope and head of the Pontifical Commission which administrates the Vatican City (1978–). He is the first non-Italian Pope since 1522.

Jospin, Lionel (1937-), French Socialist politician. First Secretary of the Socialist Party (1981-87), presidential candidate (1995).

Juan Carlos I (1938–), King of Spain (1975–). He succeeded when the monarchy was restored following the death of Franco. He played a major role in defeating the attempted coup in 1981.

Jugnauth, Aneerood (1930–), Mauritian politician of the Mouvement Socialiste Mauricien (MSM). PM of Mauritius (1982–).

Juncker, Jean-Claude (1954–), Luxembourgeois politician (Christian Social Party). Minister of Finance and Labour (1992–95), PM (1995–).

Juppé, Alain (1945–), French politician of the Rally for the Republic Party (RPR). Foreign Minister (1993–95), PM (1995–).

Karadzic, Radovan (various birthdates given) Montenegrin-born Bosnian politician of the Serbian Democratic Party. President of the self-proclaimed Republika Srpska.

Karimov, Islam (1938–), Uzbek politician. Head of the Communist Party in Uzbekistan (1990–), President of Uzbekistan (1991–).

Keating, Paul (1944–), Australian politician. Treasurer and deputy leader of the Australian Labor Party (1983–91) and PM (1991–). He has led the campaign to make Australia a republic.

Khalifa bin Hamad (1930), Amir of Qatar (1972-).

Khamenei, Ayatollah Mohammed Ali Hoseini (1940–), Iranian religious leader and politician. Wali Faqih (Religious Leader; 1989–). He succeeded on the death of Ayatollah Khomeini.

Khamtay Siphandon, General (1923–), Laotian Communist politician. PM (1993–).

Kim Jong Il (1942–), North Korean Communist politician. The eldest son of Kim Il-Sun, he took over after his father died in 1994, but, by mid-1995, had not formally become President of North Korea.

Kim Young Sam (1927–), South Korean politician. President of South Korea (1992–). In 1990 he merged the RDP with the ruling Democratic Justice Party and the New Democratic Republican Party to form the Democratic Liberal Party (DLP).

Kinkel, Klaus (1936–), German politician. Leader of the Free Democrats (1993–95). Foreign Minister (since 1992), Vice-Chancellor (1993–).

Klaus, Vaclav (1941–), Czech politician. Finance Minister (1989–92), deputy PM (1991–92), Chair of the Civic Democratic Party, PM (1992–).

Klestil, Thomas (1933–), Austrian diplomat. President of Austria (1992–).

Kohl, Helmut (1930–), German politician. Leader of the German Christian Democrat Party (CDU; 1973–), Leader of the Opposition in the Bundestag (1976–82), Chancellor of West Germany (1982–91), of a united Germany (1991–). Since reunification he has had to contend with problems arising from the integration of the formerly Communist East of the country into the West German market economy.

Kok, Wim (1938–), Dutch politician. Leader of the Labour Party (PvdA; 1986–), Deputy PM and Finance Minister (1989–94), PM (1994–).

Konan-Bedie, Henri (1934–), Ivorian politician. Minister of Finance (1966–77), President of Cote d'Ivoire (1993–).

Konare, Alpha Oumar (1946–), Malian politician. President (1992–).

Kono, Yohei (1937–), Japanese politician. Leader of the Liberal Democratic Party (1993–).

Kovac, Michal (1931–), Slovakian politician of the Movement for a Democratic Slovakia (HZDS). President of Slovakia (1993–).

Kozyrev, Andrei (1951–), Russian politician. Minister of Foreign Affairs (1990–).

Kravchuk, Leonid (1934–), Ukrainian Communist politician. President of Ukraine (1990–94).

Kucan, Milan (1941–), Slovenian politician. President (1990–).

Kuchma, Leonid (1938–), Ukrainian politician. PM (1992–93), President (1994–).

Kuncze, Gabor (1950–), Hungarian politician. Parliamentary leader of the Alliance of Free Democrats (AFD; 1993–).

Lacalle, Luis Alberto (1941–), Uruguayan politician (Blanco Party). President of Uruguay (1990–).

Le Duc Anh (1920–), Vietnamese Communist politician and general. President (1992–).

Le Pen, Jean-Marie (1928–), French right-wing politician. President of the National Front (1972–).

Lee Kuan Yew (1923–), Singaporean politician and founder of the People's Action Party (PAP). PM (1959–90). He has overseen a successful programme of economic development.

Lee Teng-hui (1923–), Taiwanese politician. Governor Taiwan Province (1981–84), Vice-President (1984–88), President (1988–).

Leghair, Farooq Ahmad Khan (1940–), Pakistani politician of the Pakistan People's Party (PPP). Minister of Water and Power (1989–90), Minister of Finance (1993), Minister for Foreign Affairs (1993), President (1993–).

Leon, Ramiro de (1942–), Guatemalan politician. President (1993–). A human-rights campaigner, he took over following a crisis over the presidential succession.

Li Peng (1928–), Chinese Communist politician. PM (1987–). He has maintained firm central and party control over the economy.

Lipponen, Paavo (1941–), Finnish politician. Leader of the Social Democratic party. PM (1995-).

Lukashenko, Alexander (1955–), Belarussian populist politician. President (1994–).

Major, John (1943–), English Conservative politician. British Chief Secretary to Treasury (1987–89), Secretary of State for Foreign and Commonweath Affairs (1989), Chancellor of Exchequer (1989–90). Leader of the Conservative Party and PM (1990–).

Mandela, Nelson (1918–), South African politician. President of the African National Congress (1991–). President of South Africa (1994–). An ANC activist from the 1940s, he became the symbolic leader of most Black South Africans during his imprisonment from 1962. He was freed by de Klerk in 1991 and headed ANC negotiations with the government before winning multi-racial elections to become President.

Manning, Patrick (1946–), Trinidadian politician. Minister of Information, and of Industry and Commerce (1981), of Energy (1981–86), leader of the People's National Movement Party (1987–), PM of Trinidad and Tobago (1991–).

Manning, Preston (1942–), Canadian politician. Founder and leader of the Reform Party (1987–).

Margrethe II (1940–), Queen of Denmark (1972–).

Masire, Quett (1925–), Botswanan politician for the Botswana Democratic Party (BDP). Deputy PM (1965–66), Vice-President and Minister of Finance (1966–80), Minister of Development Planning (1967–80), President (1980–).

Mazowiecki, Tadeusz (1927–), Polish politician and founder member of Solidarity. PM (1989–90).

McKinnon, Donald (1939–), New Zealand politician of the National Party. Minister of External Relations and Trade, Minister of Foreign Affairs, Deputy PM (1990–).

McLaughlin, Audrey (1936–), Canadian politician. Leader of the New Democratic Party (NDP; 1989–).

Mahathir bin Mohammad (1925–), Malaysian politician. Minister of Education (1974–77), Trade and Industry (1977–81), Defence (1981–86), Home Affairs (1986–87), Deputy PM (1976–81), PM (1981–).

Meciar, Vladimir (1931–), Slovakian politician of the Movement for a Democratic Slovakia (HZDS). PM (1992–94 and 1994-). He was influential in the campaign for Slovakian independence.

Meksi, Aleksandr (1939–), politician from the Albanian Democratic Party. PM (1992–).

Meles Zenawi (various birthdates given) Ethiopian politician of the Ethiopian People's Revolutionary Democratic Front (EPRDF). President of Ethiopia (1991–).

Menem, Carlos (1935–), Argentinian politician. President of the Peronist (Justice) Party in La Rioja (1968–), Governor of La Rioja (1983–89) and President of Argentina (1989–). He has introduced widespread privatization and public spending cuts.

Meri, Lennart (1929–), Estonian politician of the nationalist Fatherland Party and member of the Isamaa coalition. Minister of Foreign Affairs (1991–92), President of Estonia (1992–).

Mifsud Bonnici, Hugo (1932–), Maltese politician of the National Party. Minister of Education (1987–94), President of Malta (1994–).

Milosevic, Slobodan (1941–), Nationalist Serbian politician. President of Serbia (1988–), effective ruler of 'rump Yugoslavia' (1992–). An advocate of a 'Greater Serbia', he encouraged the secession of Serbs in Croatia and Bosnia, leading to civil wars.

Mitterrand, François (1916–), French Socialist politician. Minister for Ex-Servicemen, Minister of State (1947–54), Minister of the Interior (1954–55), Minister for State for Justice (1956–57), First Secretary of the Socialist Party (1971–81), President of France (1981–95).

Mobuto Sese Seko (1930–), Zairean politician. Secretary of State for National Defence (1960), President of Zaire (1965–), Minister of Foreign Affairs (1966–72). He seized power in a military coup at the end of the Congo Crisis, and maintained order by imposing harsh policies. Rebellions and allegations of corruption have undermined his rule.

Moi, Daniel arap (1924–), Kenyan politician and leader of KANU (Kenyan African National Union). Minister of Education (1961–62), of Local Government (1962–64), Home Affairs (1964–67), Vice-President of Kenya (1967–68), Minister of Home Affairs and President of Kenya (1978–). He has continued the pro-capitalist policies of his predecessor, Jomo Kenyatta, but imposed restrictions on political activities after an attempted to coup in 1990. In multiparty elections in 1993 he was returned to power.

Moshoeshoe II (1938–), King of Lesotho (1960–90 deposed and 1995–).

Mswati III (1968–), King of Swaziland (1986–). He has supreme powers as the 1968 constitution was suspended in 1973.

Mubarak, Mohammed Hosni (1928–), Egyptian politician. Leader of the National Democratic Party (NDP; 1982–), President of Egypt (1981–), PM (1981–82). He succeeded to the presidency on the assassination of Sadat, whose moderate policies he has continued.

Mugabe, Robert (1924–), Zimbabwean politician. PM of Zimbabwe (1980–88), President (1988–). As leader of the Zimbabwe African National Union (ZANU; 1963–), he fought with Joshua Nkomo's Zimbabwe African People's Union (ZAPU) against the white government of Rhodesia until independence (as Zimbabwe) in 1980. He won the fierce power struggle with Nkomo, and the two parties agreed an alliance in 1976 and finally merged in 1986.

Muluzi, Bakili (1943–), Malawian politician of the United Democratic Front (UDF). President of Malawi (1994–).

Murayama, Tomiichi (1924–), Japanese Socialist politician. PM (1994–).

Museveni, Yoweri (1944–), Ugandan politician. President of Uganda and Minister of Defence (1986–). He came to power following a military coup.

Narasimha Rao, P. V. (1921–), Indian politician of the Congress (I) Party. Chief Minister of Andhra Pradesh (1971–73), Minister of External Affairs (1980–85), of Defence and Acting Minister of Planning (1985), of Human Resources Development and Health and Family Welfare (1985–88), of External Affairs (1988–90). Leader of Congress (I) and PM (1991–). He took over the Party leadership after the assassination of Rajiv Gandhi, and went on to win the general election. During his time in office he has had to deal with the growth of the militant Hindu fundamentalism and ethnic fighting.

Nazarbayev, Nursultan (1940–), Kazakh politician. President of Kazakhstan (1990–). A Communist politician under the USSR, he retained power in Kazakhstan after independence.

Netanyahu, Benjamin (1949–), Israeli politician. Deputy Minister of Foreign Affairs (1988–92), Leader of the Likud Party (1993–).

Niyazov, Saparmuryad (1940–), Turkmen politician. PM (1985), Head of the Communist Party in Turkmenistan (1985–90), President of (independent) Turkmenistan (1990–).

Norodom Rannariddh, Prince (1944–), leader of the royalist Funcinpec (United National Front for an Independent, Neutral, Peaceful and Cooperative Cambodia), PM (1993–). Son of KIng Norodom Sihanouk.

Nuhayyan, Sheikh Sultan Zayid bin Al (1918–), Ruler of Emirate of Abu Dhabi. President of United Arab Emirates (1971–).

Nujoma, Sam (1929–), Namibian politician. President of SWAPO (1959–), President of Namibia (1990–). Nujoma was arrested in 1959 and forced into exile in 1960. He returned to Namibia in 1966 and took up the armed struggle against South Africa. On Namibian independence he became president.

Ochirbat, Punsalmaagiyn (1942–), Mongolian politician (originally Communist), Minister of Fuel and Power Industry and Geology (1976), Minister of External Economic Relations (1985), President of Mongolia (1990– ; from 1993 for the opposition party).

Oddsson, David (1948–), Icelandic politician. Leader of the Independence Party (1991–), PM and Minister for the Statistical Bureau (1991–).

Oleksy, Jozef (1946-), Polish politician (former Communist Democratic Left Party). PM (1995–).

Panyarachun, Anand (1932–), Thai politician. PM (1991–).

Papandreou, Andreas (1919–), Greek politician. Minister of Economic Co-ordination (1965), Leader of the Pan-Hellenic Socialist Party (PASOK; 1974–), Leader of Opposition (1977–81), PM (1981–89 and 1993–), Minister of Defence (1981–86).

Patterson, P (Percival). J. (1935–), Jamaican politician. Deputy PM and Minister of Development (1989–92), Finance Minister (1990–91), leader of the People's National Party (PNP) and PM (1992–).

Pawlak, Waldemar (1959–), Polish politician of the Polish Peasant Party. PM (1993–95).

Peres, Shimon (1923–), Israeli politician of the Labour Party. Minister for Economic Development in the Administered Areas and for Immigrant Absorption (1969–70), of Transport and Communications (1970–74), of Information (1974), of Defence (1974–77), Acting PM (1977), Leader of the Opposition (1974–84), PM (1984–86), Minister of the Interior and of Religious Affairs (1984–85), Deputy PM and Finance Minister (1988–90), Minister of Foreign Affairs (1992–).

Perez Balladres, Ernesto (1946–), Panamian politician. President (1994–).

Perry, William (1927–), US Democrat politician. Deputy Secretary of State for Defense (1993–94) and Secretary of State for Defense (1994–).

Peterson, Niels, Helveg (1939–), Danish politician of the Radical Liberal Party. Minister for Economic Affairs (1988–90), Foreign Minister (1993–).

Phoumsavanh, Nouhak (1914–), Laotian Communist politician. President of Laos (1992–).

Pol Pot (1925–). Cambodian Communist politician. Leader of the Khmer Rouge (1962–85), PM (1976–79). His attempt to create a self-sufficient workers' utopia resulted in the massacre of up to 2,000,000 of his compatriots. He was overthrown by the Vietnamese in 1978, and although no longer the military leader of the Khmer Rouge he remains an influential figure within the organization.

Prescott, John (1938–), English politician. Deputy leader of the British Labour Party (1994-).

Qaboos bin Said (1940–), Sultan of Oman, PM, Minister of Foreign Affairs, Defence and Finance (1970–).

Rabbini, Burhanuddin (1943–), Afghan politician. President of Afghanistan (1992–).

Rabin, Yitshak (1922–), Israeli Labour politician. Minister of Labour (1974), Leader of the Labour Party (1974–77), PM (1974–77 and 1992–). His second term of office saw the signing of the Israeli-Palestinian Peace Accord.

Rabuka, Sitiveni (1948–), Fijian army officer and politician. Head of State (1987), Minister of Home Affairs (1987–90), deputy PM and Minister of Home Affairs (1991–92), PM (1992–). Following the election of an Indian-dominated government in 1987, Rabuka staged two successive military coups. He helped introduce a new constitution in 1990 that guaranteed political power for the native Melanese population.

Rafsanjani, Ali Akbar Hashemi (1934–), Iranian politician. President of Iran (1989–).

Rainier III (1923–), Prince of Monaco (1949–).

Ramos, Fidel (1928–), Filippino politician and army officer. Secretary of National Defence (1988–92), President (1992–).

Rasmussen, Poul Nyrup (1944–), Danish politician. Leader of the Social Democratic Party (1992–), PM (1993–).

Rawlings, Flight Lt. Jerry (1947–), Ghanaian politician. Head of the Armed Forces Revolutionary Council (1979), Head of State (1982–), Chairman of the Provisional National Defence Council (1981–92), Chief of Defence (1982–). Rawlings took power in 1979 following his first coup but returned power to an elected government the same year. After his second coup in 1981, however, he remained head of a military government. In 1992 he was returned to power after multi-party elections.

Reno, Janet (1938–), US Democrat politician. State Attorney for Florida (1978-93), Attorney General of the USA (1993-).

Robinson, Mary (1944–), Irish politician. President of Ireland (1990–).

Rocard, Michel (1930–), French Socialist politician. Minister of State, Minister of Planning and Regional Development (1981–83), of Agriculture (1983–85), PM (1988–91).

Saddam Hussein (1937–), Iraqi politician of the Ba'ath Party. Vice-President of the Revolutionary

Command Council (1969–79), President of the Revolutionary Command Council (1979–), President of Iraq (1979–), PM (1994–). He has ruled repressively and embroiled his country in two disastrous wars, the Iran–Iraq War (1980–88) and the Gulf War, which followed the invasion of Kuwait (1991). Although still in power he faces rebellions from the Kurds in the north and economic UN sanctions.

Saleh, Ali Abdullah (c. 1942–), Yemeni politician and army officer. President of Yemen Arab Republic (North Yemen; 1978–90), of the Republic of Yemen (1990–).

Samper, Ernesto (1951–), Colombian politician of the Liberal Party. President (1994–).

Sanchez de Lozada, Gonzalo (1930–), Bolivian politician of the Revolutionary Nationalist Movement (MNR). President of Bolivia (1993–).

Santer, Jacques (1937–), Luxembourgeois politician of the Social Christian Party. Minister of Finance, of Labour and of Social Security (1979–84), PM (1984–95). President of the European Commission (1995–).

Savimbi, Jonas (1934–), Angolan military leader and politician. Initially associated with the FNLA Party, he broke away to form UNITA and fought first against the Portuguese for independence and then against the MPLA government. However, he refused to accept the results of the 1992 free elections and has resumed the military struggle.

Scalfaro, Oscar Luigi (1918–), Italian politician. Minister of Transport and Civil Aviation in the Moro, Leone and Andreotti governments of the 1960s and 1970s, Minister of Education (1976–79), and of the Interior (1983–87). President (1992–).

Scharping, Rudolf (1948–), German politician. State Premier of Rhineland-Palatinate (1991–), leader of the Social Democratic Party (SPD; 1993–).

Sedki, Atef (1930–), Egyptian politician of the National Democratic Party (NDP). PM (1986–).

Shamir, Yitzhak (1915–), Israeli politician of the Likud Party. Minister of Foreign Affairs (1980–83), PM (1983–84 and 1986–92), Minister of Foreign Affairs (1984–86), Acting Minister of the Interior (1987–88). While in office he refused to negotiate with the PLO.

Sharif, Nawaz (1949–), Pakistani politician of the Islamic Democratic Alliance. Chief Minister of Punjab (1988–90), PM of Pakistan (1990–93).

Sharma, Shankar Dayal (1918–), Indian politician. Chief Minister of Bhopal (1952–56), Minister of Communications (1974–77), Vice-President of India (1987–92), President of India (1992–).

Shevardnadze, Eduard (1928–), Georgian politician. Soviet Foreign Minister (1985–90), President of Georgia (1992–). As Foreign Minister under Gorbachov he revolutionized Soviet foreign policy. Relations with the West were improved, a number of arms reduction treaties agreed with the USA and its NATO allied, and the Soviet Union abandoned its commitment to intervene in the affairs of Warsaw Pact countries. In 1991 he resigned from the Communist Party and as Foreign Minister. The following year he became President of Georgia.

Sihanouk, Norodom (1922–), King of Cambodia (1941–55 abdicated, and since 1993), PM and Minister of Foreign Affairs (1955–60), Head of State (1960–70 and 1975–76), self-styled President of a National Government of Cambodia (while in exile) (1982–90), restored as King of Cambodia (1993–). After his abdication in 1955 he dominated Cambodian political life until 1970, when he was overthrown in a US-backed military coup. He was nominal head of state (1975–76) following the victory of the Khmer Rouge in the civil war, but was finally forced into exile. He returned to Cambodia in 1989 to help broker a UN-sponsored peace settlement. He regained the throne in 1993 following multi-party elections.

Snegur, Mireca (1940–), Moldavian politician. President of Moldava (1990–).

Soares, Mario (1924–), Portuguese Socialist politician. PM (1976–78 and 1983–85), President (1986–). He became Portugal's first civilian president for 60 years.

Soglo, Nicéphore (1934–), Beninese politician. PM of Benin (1990–91) and President (1991–).

Solana, Javier (1942–), Spanish politician. Minister of Education (1988–92), Minister of Foreign Affairs (1992–).

Spring, Dick (1950–), Irish politician. Leader of the Labour Party (1982–), Deputy PM (1982–87), Minister for the Environment (1982–83), for Energy (1983–87), Tánaiste (Deputy PM), Minister for Foreign Affairs (1993–).

Stephanopoulos, Kostis (1926–), Greek independent politician. President (1995–).

Strasser, Valentine (1965–), Sierra Leone politician. Head of State and Chairman of the National Ruling Council (NPRC) (1992–).

Suharto, T.N.I. (1921–), Indonesian army officer and politician. President (1967–). He came to power after the overthrow of his predecessor, Achmed Sukarno. During the coup tens of thousands of supposedly Communist sympathizers were killed. His invasion of East Timor in 1975 has been internationally condemned.

Taya, Maaouiya Ould (1943–), Mauritanian military officer and politician. PM and Minister of Defence (1981–84), Minister of Defence and President (1984–). Taya ruled as head of a military government until 1992 when he was returned to power in multiparty elections.

Ter-Petrosyan, Levon (1945–), Armenian politician and leader of the Armenian National Movement. President (1991–).

Than Shwe Burmese politician. Defence Chief (1992), Head of military junta of Myanmar (State Law and Order Restoration Council; SLORC) (1992–).

Tudjman, Franjo (1922–), Croatian politician of the Croat Democratic Union. President of Croatia (1990–).

Ulmanis, Guntis (1939–), Latvian politician (Communist 1965–89). President (1993–).

Vacaroiou, Nicolae (1943–), Romanian independent politician. PM (1992–).

Vahi, Tiit (1947–), Estonian politician. Leader of the (former Communist) Coalition Party. PM (1995-).

Videnov, Zhan (1960–), Bulgarian Socialist (former Communist) politician. PM (1995-).

Vranitzky, Franz (1937–), Austrian politician of the Social Democratic Party (SPL). Federal Minister of Finance (1984–86), Federal Chancellor (1986–).

Waigel, Theo (1939–), German politician. Leader of the Christian Social Union (CSU; 1988–), Minister of Finance (1989–).

Walesa, Lech (1943–), Polish politician. President of Poland (1990–). As an underground trade union organizer in Gdansk in the 1970s, he helped create the free trade union Solidarity. Imprisoned after the declaration of martial law in 1981, he negotiated the agreement that ended Communist rule in Poland (1989). He split from Solidarity in 1993.

Wasmosy, Juan Carlos (1939–), Paraguayan politician of the Colorado Party. President (1993–).

Weizman, Ezer (1924–), Israeli politician, originally of the Likud Party but later of the Labour Party. Minister of Transport (1969–70), of Defence (1977–80), of Communications (1984–88), of Science (1988–93), President (1993–).

Yeltsin, Boris (1931–), Russian politician. President of the Russian Federation (within the Soviet Union) (1990–91), President of the independent Russian Federation (1991–). The dominant statesman of post-Communist Russia, he led the opposition to the Soviet coup of August 1991 and was instrumental in the establishment of the Commonwealth of Independent States (CIS). He introduced deregulation and privatization to the independent economic problems but has faced political crises.

Zafy, Albert (1943–), Madagascan politician. President of Madagascar (1993–).

Zedillo, Ernesto (1951–), Mexican politician of the Institutional Revolutionary Party (PRI). Minister of Planning and Federal Budget (1988–92), Minister of Education (1992–93). President of Mexico (1994–).

Zhelev, Zhelo (1936–), Bulgarian politician of the Union of Democratic Forces. President (1990–).

Zhirinovsky, Vladimir (1947–), Russian nationalist politician. Leader of the Liberal Democratic Party.

Zia, Begum Khalida (1945–), Bangladeshi politician (widow of the former President General Ziaur Rahman). Leader of the Bangladesh Nationalist Party (BNP; 1982–), PM (1991–).

NOBEL PEACE PRIZE WINNERS

The Nobel Peace Prize is awarded annually by the Norwegian Nobel Committee, which is appointed by the Norwegian Parliament, the Storting.

The other Nobel Prizes, which were established under the terms of the will of Alfred Nobel (1833-96), a Swedish chemist, are awarded annually by specified Swedish organizations.

1901 Jean Henri Dunant, Swiss philanthropist:founder of the Red Cross.

Frédéric Passy, French economist: advocate of international arbitration and peace.

1902 Elie Ducommun, Swiss writer, and Charles Albert Gobat, Swiss: for their work for peace within the International Peace Bureau.

1903 Sir William Cremer, English trade unionist; an advocate of international arbitration.

1904 Institute of International Law (fd. 1873).

1905 Bertha von Suttner, Austrian novelist: for her influential peace novels.

1906 Theodore Roosevelt, US President: for mediation at the end of Russo-Japanese War (1904).

1907 Ernesto Teodoro Moneta, Italian journalist: founder of the International League for Peace, president of the International Peace Conference (1906).

Louis Renault, French jurist: for his international arbitration.

1908 Klas Pontus Arnoldson, Swedish politician: for mediating the dissolution of the Norwegian-Swedish Union.

Fredrik Bajer, Danish politician: for his work for female emancipation and the peace movement.

1909 Baron d'Estournelles de Constant, French diplomat.

Auguste Beernaert, Belgian politician: for work at the Hague Peace Conferences.

1910 International Peace Bureau (fd. 1891).

1911 Tobias Asser, Dutch jurist: for his part in forming the Permanent Court of Justice .

Alfred Fried, Austrian pacifist: co-founder of the German peace movement.

1912 Elihu Root, US politician: for his international arbitration.

1913 Henri Lafontaine, Belgian lawyer: president of International Peace Bureau.

1914–16 No awards.

1917 International Red Cross Committee.

1918 No award.

1919 Woodrow Wilson, US president: for his important role in the post-World War I international settlement.

1920 Léon Bourgeois, French politician: advocate of the League of Nations and international cooperation.

1921 Karl Branting, Swedish politician: for his conciliatory international diplomacy.

Christian Lous Lange, Norwegian peace advocate: for his work as secretary general of the Inter-Parliamentary Union.

1922 Fridtjof Nansen, Norwegian explorer and statesman: for relief work after World War I.

1923–24 No awards.

1925 Sir Austen Chamberlain, English politician: for work on the Locarno Pact (1925).

Charles G. Dawes, US politician: for reorganization of German reparation payments.

1926 Aristide Briand, French politician.

Gustav Stresemann, German politician: for his work for European reconciliation.

1927 Ferdinand Buisson, French educationalist: co-founder of League of Human Rights (1898).

Ludwig Quidde, German historian and politician: for his work for peace in Germany.

1928 No award.

1929 Frank B. Kellogg, US politician: for the Kellogg-Briand Pact (1928).

1930 Nathan Söderblom. Swedish Lutheran archbishop: for his efforts for peace through church unity.

1931 Jane Addams, US social reformer and pacifist: for her social work, support of women's suffrage, and peace,

Nicholas Murray Butler, US educationalist: for his work in forming the Carnegie Endowment for International Peace.

1932 No award.

1933 Sir Norman Angell, English economist: for his work on the economic futility of war.

1934 Arthur Henderson, English politician: for his work for disarmament.

1935 Carl von Ossietzky, German journalist who spoke out against Nazi rearmament.

1936 Carlos Saavedra Lamas, Argentinian jurist: for his efforts to end the Chaco War (1932-35).

1937 Viscount Cecil of Chelwood, English politician: drafting the League of Nations Covenant 1919.

1938 Nansen International Office for Refugees.

1939–1943 No awards.

1944 International Red Cross Committee.

1945 Cordell Hull, US politician: for his part in organizing the United Nations.

1946 Emily Greene Balch, US sociologist and political scientist: leader of the women's movement for peace.

John R. Mott, US Methodist evangelist: for work in international missionary movements.

1947 American Friends Service Committee, a US Quaker organization that promotes peace through programmes of social service and Friends Service Council, its British counterpart.

1948 No award.

1949 Lord Boyd-Orr, Scottish scientist: for his work on nutritional requirements.

1950 Ralph Bunche, US diplomat: for negotiating the Arab-Israeli truce in 1949.

1951 Léon Jouhaux, French trade unionist: co-founder of the International Confederation of Free Trade Unions.

1952 Albert Schweitzer, German missionary, doctor and philosopher: for his medical and other work in Africa.

1953 George C. Marshall, US politician: for the Marshall (European recovery) Plan.

1954 Office of the United Nations High Commissioner for Refugees.

1955–56 No award.

1957 Lester B. Pearson, Canadian politician: for his efforts to solve the Suez Crisis (1956).

1958 Dominique Georges Pire, Belgian cleric and educationalist: for his aid to displaced Europeans after World War II.

1959 Philip Noel-Baker, English politician: an advocate of world disarmament.

1960 Albert Lutuli, South African: for his non-violent struggle against apartheid.

1961 Dag Hammarskjöld, Swedish Secretary General of the UN (posthumously awarded).

1962 Linus Pauling, US chemist: for campaigns for the control of nuclear weapons and nuclear testing.

1963 International Red Cross Committee. and League of Red Cross Societies: for their relief work after natural disasters.

1964 Martin Luther King, Jr., US Black civil rights leader.

1965 United Nations Children's Fund.

1966–67 No award.

1968 René Cassin, French jurist: principal author of the UN Declaration of Human Rights.

1969 International Labour Organization.

1970 Norman E. Borlaug, US agricultural scientist: for agricultural technology.

1971 Willy Brandt, German politician: for reconciliation between West and East Germany.

1972 No award.

1973 Henry Kissinger, US politician, and Le Duc Tho, North Vietnamese politician: for the peace settlement of the Vietnam War. (Le Duc Tho declined the award.)

1974 Eisaku Sato, prime minister of Japan: for his anti-nuclear policies.

Sean MacBride, Irish statesman: for his campaign for human rights.

1975 Andrei D. Sakharov, Russian nuclear physicist: for his advocacy of human rights and disarmament.

1976 Mairead Corrigan, Northern Irish, and Betty Williams, Northern Irish: for campaigning to end sectarian strife in Northern Ireland.

1977 Amnesty International: for work to secure the release of political prisoners.

1978 Menachem Begin, Israeli prime minister, and Anwar el-Sadat, president of Egypt: for the Israel-Egypt peace treaty (1979).

1979 Mother Teresa of Calcutta, (ethnic Albanian) Macedonian-born Indian charity worker: for her charity for the destitute in India.

1980 Adolfo Pérez Esquivel, Argentinian sculptor and architect: for work for human rights in Latin America.

1981 United Nations High Commissioner for Refugees.

1982 Alva Myrdal, Swedish diplomat: for advocacy of nuclear disarmament,

Alfonso García Robles, Mexican diplomat: for advocacy of nuclear disarmament.

1983 Lech Walesa, Polish politician and trade unionist: for the Solidarity free trade union movement.

1984 Desmond Tutu, South African Anglican Archbishop of Johannesburg: for peaceful anti-apartheid campaigns.

1985 International Physicians for the Prevention of Nuclear War.

1986 Elie Wiesel, French writer and human rights activist.

1987 Oscar Arias Sánchez, president of Costa Rica: for promoting a peace in Central America.

1988 United Nations Peacekeeping Forces.

1989 The Dalai Lama, spiritual and exiled temporal leader of Tibet.

1990 Mikhail Gorbachov, Soviet president: for promoting greater openness in the Soviet Union, and helping to end the Cold War.

1991 Aung San Suu Kyi, Burmese politician: for her non-violent campaign for democracy in Myanmar (Burma).

1992 Rigoberta Menchu, Guatemalan Indian spokeswoman: for her campaign for indigenous people.

1993 Nelson Mandela, leader of the South African African National Congress (ANC), and F.W. de Klerk, president of South Africa: for their work to bring about an end to aprtheid in South Africa.

1994 Yasser Arafat, chairman of the Palestine Liberation Organization (PLO), Yitzhak Rabin, prime minister of Israel, and Shimon Peres, foreign secretary of Israel: for bringing about an accord on Palestinian self-rule.

Countries of the United Kingdom

The United Kingdom (UK) comprises the island of Great Britain – England, Wales and Scotland – and Northern Ireland.

Area: 244,088 km² (94,242 sq mi).

Population: 58,080,000 (1993 est).

ENGLAND

England is geographically the southern and larger part of the island of Great Britain. The islands off the English coast, such as the Isle of Wight and the Isles of Scilly, are administratively part of England. Politically and geographically England is that part of Great Britain governed by English law (which also pertains in Wales).

Area: 130,439 km² (50,363 sq mi).

Population: 47,837,300 (1991 est).

Capital: London.

Local government in England

A review of local government in England began in 1992 and was still in progress at the time of going to press. The initial proposals were for single-tier unitary authorities, but subsequent recommendations tended to retain the status quo over much of the country. However, the new administrative counties of Avon, Humberside, Cleveland, and Hereford and Worcester were abolished and elections were held for the successor unitary authorities (based upon existing district councils and mergers of district councils) in these areas in 1995. It was also proposed that the traditional counties of Rutland and Huntingdonshire be revived.

The following list of counties (and the unitary authorities that geographically fall within them) reflect the new system proposed by the Local Government Commission and/or approved by Parliament by May 1995.

The boundaries of the traditional English counties were redrawn for administrative purposes only in 1974. The reforms that began in 1995 are, in part, a return to those traditional counties.

Bedfordshire

Area: 1236 km² (477 sq mi).

Population: 536,600 (1992 est).

Bedfordshire will comprise the administrative county of Bedfordshire plus a single unitary authority. (See map; p. 750.)

Bedfordshire (administrative county):
Area: 1192 km² (460 sq mi). *Population:* 358,500. *Administrative HQ:* Bedford. The administrative county will be divided into three districts: Mid Bedfordshire (HQ: Ampthill), North Bedfordshire (HQ: Bedford), and South Bedfordshire (HQ: Leighton Buzzard).

Luton (unitary authority)
Area: 43 km² (17 sq mi). *Population:* 176,200. *Administrative HQ:* Luton. (Shown as B1 on p. 750.)

Berkshire

Area: 1262 km² (487 sq mi).

Population: 762,000 (1992 est).

Berkshire will comprise six unitary authorities; there will be no county council. (See map on p. 748.)

Bracknell Forest (unitary authority)
Area: 109 km² (42 sq mi). *Population:* 100,300. *Administrative HQ:* Bracknell. (Shown as BK6 on p. 748).

Newbury (unitary authority)
Area: 706 km² (273 sq mi). *Population:* 141,800. (Shown as BK1 on p. 748.)

Reading (unitary authority)
Area: 40 km² (16 sq mi). *Population:* 137,100. (Shown as BK2 on p. 748.)

DEFINITIONS OF BRITAIN

Various names are used for the islands geographically known as the British Isles. Geographical, political, legal and popular usages differ.

The British Isles
The British Isles is a convenient but purely geographical term to describe the group of islands lying off the north west coast of Europe that comprises the United Kingdom, the Republic of Ireland and the Crown dependencies of the Isle of Man and the Channel Islands.

Area: 314,798 km² (121,544 sq mi).

Great Britain
Great Britain is the geographical and political name of the main or principal island of the British Isles group. In a strict geographical sense, off-shore islands, for example the Isle of Wight, Anglesey or Shetland, are not part of Great Britain.

The name Great Britain – for the union of England and Wales with Scotland – came into popular (but unofficial) use when James VI of Scotland succeeded Queen Elizabeth I of England in 1603. With the Union of the parliaments of England and Scotland, on 1 May 1707, the style 'Great Britain' was formally adopted.

Area: (of the island of Great Britain) 218,041 km² (84,186 sq mi).

Area: (of the union of England and Wales with Scotland) 229,966 km² (88,791 sq mi).

Crown Dependencies of Jersey, Guernsey and the Isle of Man
The Crown dependencies are territories associated with the United KIngdom, but they are not part of the UK. The islands are not part of the EC, but enjoy a special relationship with it. For Guernsey see p. 733, for Jersey see p. 733 and for the Isle of Man see p.734.

Slough (unitary authority)
Area: 21 km² (8 sq mi). *Population:* 104,800. (Shown as BK3 on p. 748.)

Windsor and Maidenhead (unitary authority)
Area: 199 km² (77 sq mi). *Population:* 135,500. *Administrative HQ:* Maidenhead. (Shown BK4 on p. 748.)

Wokingham (unitary authority)
Area: 179 km² (69 sq mi). *Population:* 142,500. (Shown as BK5 on p. 748.)

Buckinghamshire

Area: 1876 km² (724 sq mi).

Population: 643,700 (1992 est).

Buckinghamshire will comprise the administrative county of Buckinghamshire plus a single unitary authority. (See map; p. 748.)

Buckinghamshire (administrative county):
Area: 1568 km² (606 sq mi). *Population:* 462,700. *Administrative HQ:* Aylesbury. The administrative county will be divided into four districts: Aylesbury Vale (HQ: Aylesbury), Chiltern (HQ: Amersham), South Buckinghamshire (HQ: Slough; i.e. outside the district), and Wycombe (HQ: High Wycombe).

Milton Keynes (unitary authority)
Area: 309 km² (119 sq mi). *Population:* 181,000. (Shown as B1 on p. 748.)

Cambridgeshire

Area: 2476 km² (956 sq mi). NB: It was proposed early in 1995 that the traditional county of Huntingdonshire should be revived. The statistics given here exclude Huntingdonshire (see below). If the proposal to revive the county is not adopted, Huntingdonshire will continue to be part of Cambridgeshire. (See map; p. 750.)

Population: 528,500 (1992 est).

It has been proposed that Cambridgeshire will comprise the administrative county of Cambridgeshire plus a single unitary authority.

Cambridgeshire (administrative county):
Area: 2142 km² (827 sq mi). *Population:* 358,500. *Administrative HQ:* Cambridge. It is proposed that

the administrative county will be divided into four districts: Cambridge, East Cambridgeshire (HQ: Ely), Fenland (HQ: Wisbech), and South Cambridgeshire (HQ: Cambridge)

Peterborough (unitary authority; proposed)
Area: 334 km² (129 sq mi). Population: 156,200. (Shown as C1 on p. 750.)

Cheshire

Area: 2328 km² (899 sq mi).

Population: 966,900 (1992 est).

It has been proposed that Cheshire will comprise the administrative county of Cheshire plus two unitary authorities. (See map; p. 752.)

Cheshire (administrative county)
Area: 2081 km² (803 sq mi). *Population:* 658,700 (1992 est). *Administrative HQ:* Chester. It is proposed that the administrative county will be divided into six districts: Chester, Congleton (HQ: Sandbach), Crewe and Nantwich (HQ: Crewe), Ellesmere Port and Neston (HQ: Ellesmere Port), Macclesfield, and Vale Royal (HQ: Frodsham).

Halton (unitary authority; proposed)
Area: 74 km² (29 sq mi). Population: 124,500. Administrative HQ: Widnes. (Shown as C2 on p. 752.)

Warrington (unitary authority; proposed)
Area: 176 km² (68 sq mi). Population: 183,700. (Shown as C1 on p. 752.)

Cornwall

Area: 3530 km² (1363 sq mi).

Population: 475,400 (1992 est).

Administrative HQ: Truro.

Cornwall comprises seven administrative districts: Caradon (HQ: Liskeard), Carrick (HQ: Truro), Kerrier (HQ: Camborne), North Cornwall (HQ: Bodmin), Penwith (HQ: Penzance), Restormel (HQ: St Austell), and the Isles of Scilly (HQ: Hugh Town). (See map; p. 751.)

Cumbria

Area: 6817 km² (2632 sq mi).

Population: 490,200 (1992 est).

Administrative HQ: Carlisle

Cumbria will comprise six administrative districts: Allerdale (HQs: Wigton and Workington), Barrow-in-Furness, Carlisle, Copeland (HQ: Whitehaven), Eden (HQ: Penrith), and South Lakeland (HQ: Kendal). (See map; p. 752.)

Derbyshire

Area: 2629 km² (1015 sq mi).

Population: 947,300 (1992 est)

Derbyshire will comprise the administrative county of Derbyshire plus a single unitary authority. (See map; p. 750.)

Derbyshire (administrative county)
Area: 2551 km² (985 sq mi). Population: 720,200. *Administrative HQ:* Matlock. The administrative county will comprise seven districts: Amber Valley (HQ: Ripley), Bolsover (HQ: Chesterfield), Chesterfield, Derbyshire Dales (HQ: Matlock), Erewash (HQ: Ilkeston), High Peak (HQ: Chapel-en-le-Frith), North East Derbyshire (HQ: Chesterfield), and South Derbyshire (HQ: Swadlincote).

Derby (unitary authority)
Area: 78 km² (30 sq mi). *Population:* 227,100. (Shown as D1 on p. 750.)

Devon

Area: 6698 km² (2586 sq mi).

Population: 1,045,100 (1992 est).

It has been proposed that Devon will comprise the administrative county of Devon plus two or three unitary authorities. (See map; p. 751.)

Comprises the administrative county of Devon plus two unitary authorities. (See map; p. 751.)

Devon (administrative county)
Area: 6517 km² (2516 sq mi). *Population:* 560,000. *Administrative HQ:* Exeter. It is proposed that the administrative county of Devon will comprise seven districts (eight if Exeter is not granted unitary status; see below): East Devon (HQ: Sidmouth), Mid Devon (HQ: Tiverton), North Devon (HQ: Barnstaple), South Hams (HQ: Totnes), Teignbridge (HQ: Newton Abbot), Torridge (HQ: Bideford), and West Devon (HQ: Tavistock).

Exeter (unitary authority; proposed)
Area: 44 km² (17 sq mi). *Population:* 106,500. (Shown as D3 on the map of Devon; p. 751.)

Plymouth (unitary authority)
Area: 74 km² (29 sq mi). *Population:* 257,500. (Shown as D1 on the map of Devon; p. 751.)

Torbay (unitary authority)
Area: 63 km² (24 sq mi). *Population:* 121,600. *Administrative HQ:* Torquay. (Shown on the map of Devon as D2; p. 751.)

Dorset

Area: 2653 km² (1024 sq mi).

Population: 664,200 (1992 est).

Dorset will comprise the administrative county of Dorset plus two unitary authorities. (See map; p. 751.)

Dorset (administrative county)
Area: 2492 km² (962 sq mi). *Population:* 327,000. *Administrative HQ:* Dorchester. The administrative county will comprise five districts: East Dorset (HQ: Wimborne), North Dorset (HQ: Blandford Forum), Purbeck (HQ: Wareham), West Dorset (HQ: Dorchester), and Weymouth and Portland (HQ: Weymouth).

Bournemouth and Christchurch (unitary authority)
Area: 97 km² (37 sq mi). *Population:* 200,900. *Administrative HQ:* Bournemouth. (Shown as D1 on the map of Dorset on p. 751.)

Poole (unitary authority)
Area: 65 km² (25 sq mi). *Population:* 136,300. (Shown as D2 on the map of Dorset on p. 751.)

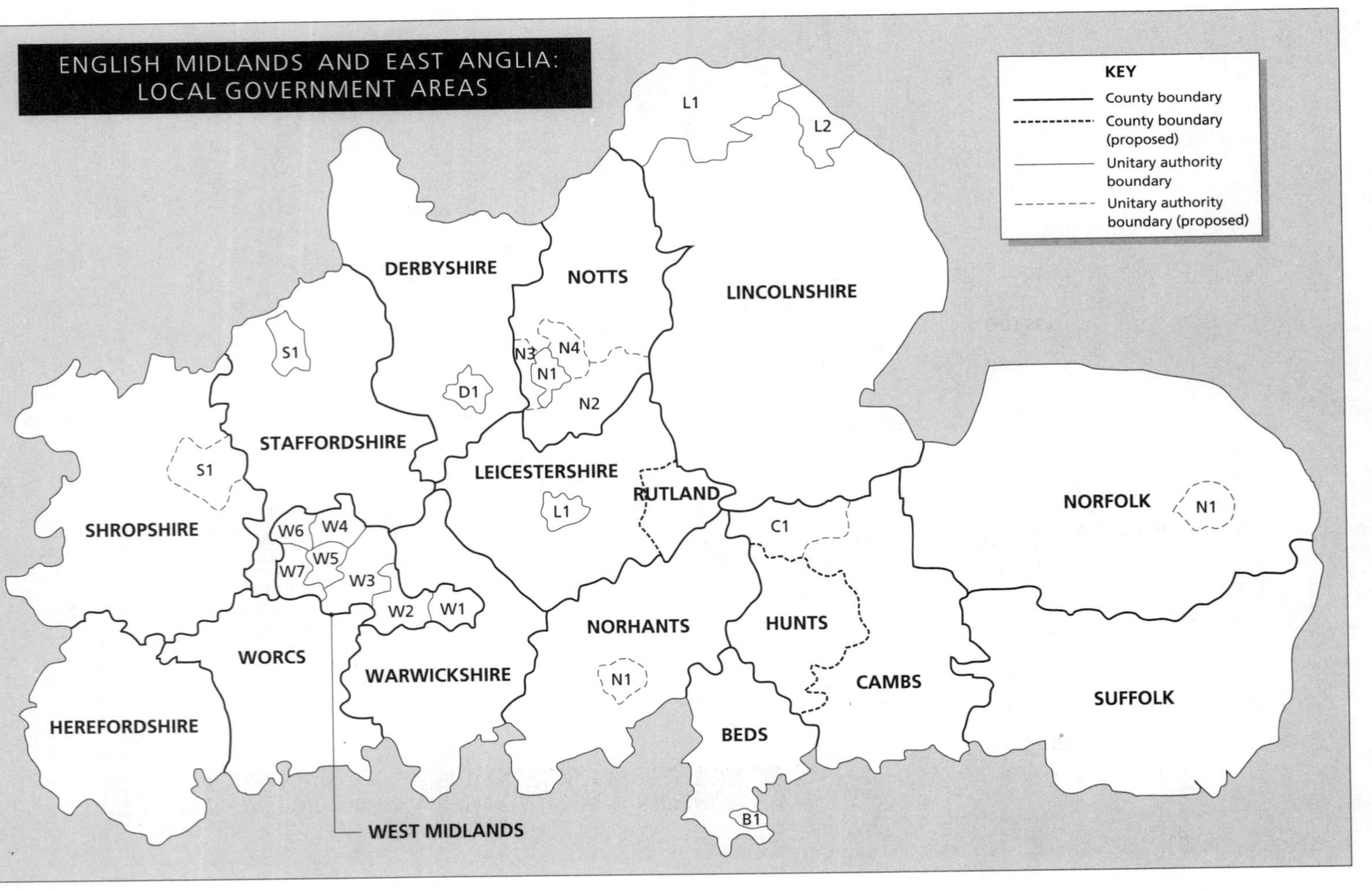
ENGLISH MIDLANDS AND EAST ANGLIA:
LOCAL GOVERNMENT AREAS
KEY
County boundary
County boundary (proposed)
Unitary authority boundary
Unitary authority boundary (proposed)
L1
L2
DERBYSHIRE
NOTTS
LINCOLNSHIRE
S1
N3
N4
N1
N2
D1
STAFFORDSHIRE
S1
LEICESTERSHIRE
RUTLAND
L1
NORFOLK
N1
SHROPSHIRE
W6
W4
W5
W7
W3
W2
W1
C1
NORHANTS
HUNTS
WORCS
WARWICKSHIRE
N1
CAMBS
SUFFOLK
HEREFORDSHIRE
BEDS
B1
WEST MIDLANDS

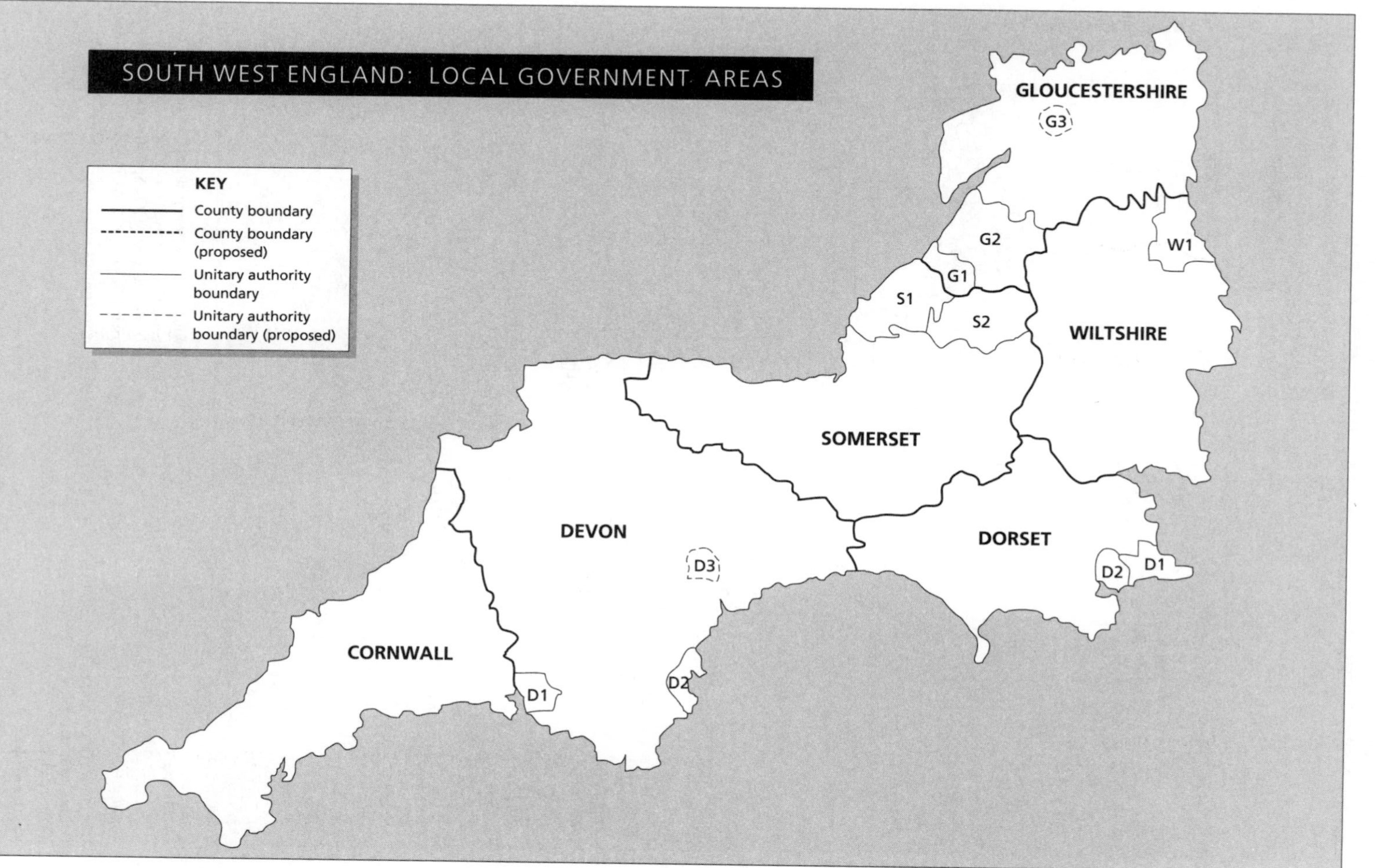
SOUTH WEST ENGLAND: LOCAL GOVERNMENT AREAS
KEY
County boundary
County boundary (proposed)
Unitary authority boundary
Unitary authority boundary (proposed)
GLOUCESTERSHIRE
G3
G2
G1
W1
S1
S2
WILTSHIRE
SOMERSET
DEVON
D3
DORSET
D2
D1
CORNWALL
D1
D2

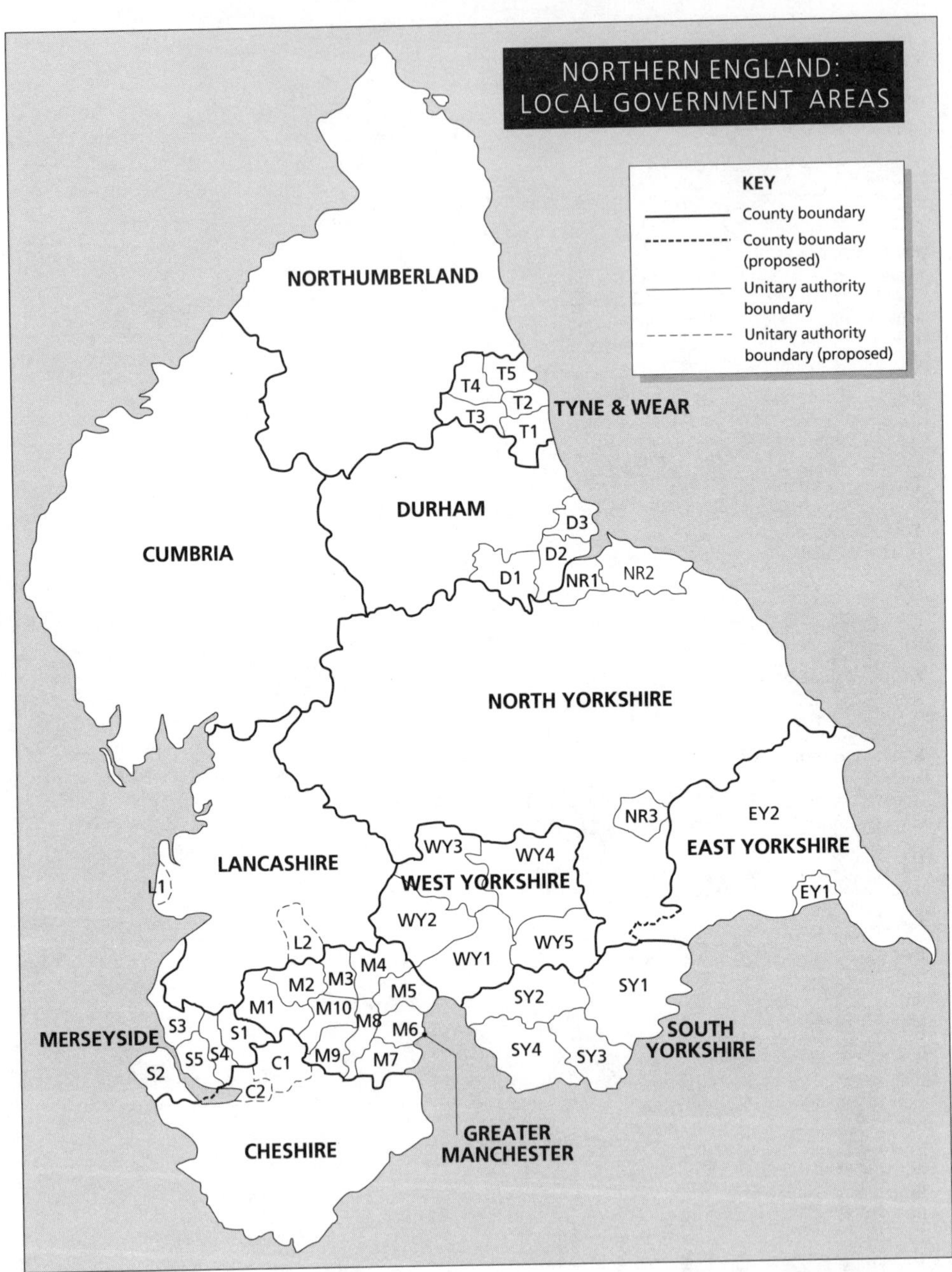

Durham

Area: 2726 km² (1053 sq mi).

Population: 875,600 (1992 est).

Durham will comprise the administrative county of County Durham plus three unitary authorities. (See map; p. 752.)

County Durham (administrative county)
Area: 2231 km² (861 sq mi). *Population:* 507,000. *Administrative HQ:* Durham. The administrative county will comprise seven districts: Chester-le-Street, Derwentside (HQ: Consett), Durham, Easington (HQ: Peterlee), Sedgefield (HQ: Spennymoor), Teesdale (HQ: Barnard Castle), and Wear Valley (HQ: Crook).

Darlington (unitary authority)
Area: 197 km² (76 sq mi). *Population:* 100,100. (Shown as D1 on p. 752.)

Hartlepool (unitary authority)
Area: 94 km² (36 sq mi). *Population:* 91,900. (Shown as D3 on p. 752.)

Stockton-on-Tees (unitary authority)
Area: 204 km² (79 sq mi). *Population:* 176,600. (Shown as D2 on p. 752.)

East Sussex

Area: 1794 km² (693 sq mi).

Population: 720,600 (1992 est).

East Sussex will comprise the administrative county of East Sussex plus one unitary authority. (See map; p. 748.)

East Sussex (administrative county)
Area: 1713 km² (662 sq mi). *Population:* 475,700. *Administrative HQ:* Lewes. The administrative county will comprise five districts: Eastbourne, Hastings, Lewes, Rother (HQ: Bexhill), and Wealden (HQs: Crowborough and Hailsham).

Brighton and Hove (unitary authority)
Area: 81 km² (31 sq mi). *Population:* 244,900. *Administrative HQ:* Brighton. (Shown as ES1 on p. 748.)

East Yorkshire

(which may be known as the **East Riding of Yorkshire**)
Area: 2703 km² (1044 sq mi).

Population: 585,300 (1992 est).

East Yorkshire will comprise two unitary authorities: there will be no county council.

East Riding of Yorkshire (unitary authority)
Area: 2631 km² (1016 sq mi). *Population:* 316,800. *Administrative HQ:* Beverley. (Shown on p. 752 as EY2.)

Kingston-upon-Hull (City and County of; unitary authority)
Area: 71 km² (28 sq mi). *Population:* 268,500. *Administrative HQ:* Hull. (Shown on p. 752 as EY1.)

Essex

Area: 3662 km² (1414 sq mi).

Population: 1,556,000 (1992 est).

It is proposed that Essex will comprise the administrative county of Essex plus at least one, and possibly three, unitary authorities. (See map; p. 748.)

Essex (administrative county)
Area: 3137 km² (1211 sq mi). *Population:* 935,000. *Administrative HQ:* Chelmsford. These statistics exclude Basildon and Thurrock which are likely to become unitary authorities (see below). It is proposed that the administrative county will have nine districts (11 if Basildon and Thurrock are included): Braintree, Brentwood, Chelmsford, Colchester, Epping Forest (HQ: Epping), Harlow, Maldon, Tendring (HQ: Clacton), and Uttlesford (HQ: Saffron Walden).

Basildon (proposed unitary authority)
Area: 110 km² (43 sq mi). *Population:* 161,800. (Shown as E2 on p. 748.)

Southend (unitary authority)
Area: 251 km² (97 sq mi). *Population:* 327,600. (Shown as E1 on p. 748.)

Thurrock (proposed unitary authority)
Area: 164 km² (63 sq mi). *Population:* 131,200. *Administrative HQ:* Grays Thurrock. (Shown as E1 on p. 748.)

Gloucestershire

Area: 3260 km² (1259 sq mi).

Population: 1,165,000 (1992 est).

It is proposed that Gloucestershire will comprise the administrative county of Gloucestershire plus two or three unitary authorities (depending on the status of the city of Gloucester). (See map; p. 751.)

Gloucestershire (administrative county)
Area: 2614 km² (1009 sq mi). *Population:* 435,900. *Administrative HQ:* Gloucester. These statistics exclude Gloucester which may become a unitary authority (see below). It is proposed that the administrative county will comprise five districts: Cheltenham, Cotswold (HQ: Cirencester), Forest of Dean (HQ: Coleford), Stroud, and Tewkesbury.

Bristol (City and County of; unitary authority)
Area: 110 km² (42 sq mi). *Population:* 396,600. (Shown as G1 on p. 751.)

Gloucester (proposed unitary authority)
Area: 41 km² (15 sq mi). *Population:* 105,400. (Shown as G3 on p. 751.)

South Gloucestershire (unitary authority)
Area: 497 km² (192 sq mi). *Population:* 226,900. *Administrative HQs:* Kingswood and Thornbury. (Shown as G2 on p. 751.)

Greater London

Area: 1578 km² (609 sq mi).

Population: 6,904,600 (1992 est).

Greater London was untouched by the local government review that began in 1992. Greater London has no county council; it comprises the following unitary authorities (London boroughs) plus the City of London. (See map; p. 748.)

Barking and Dagenham
Area: 34 km² (13 sq mi). *Population:* 146,200. *Administrative HQ:* Dagenham.

Barnet
Area: 89 km² (35 sq mi). *Population:* 302,200. *Administrative HQ:* Hendon.

Bexley
Area: 61 km² (23 sq mi). *Population:* 219,500. *Administrative HQ:* Bexleyheath.

Brent
Area: 44 km² (17 sq mi). *Population:* 247,000. *Administrative HQ:* Wembley.

Bromley
Area: 152 km² (59 sq mi). *Population:* 293,400.

City of London
Area: 2.7 km² (1 sq mi). *Population:* 3900.

Camden
Area: 22 km² (8 sq mi). *Population:* 180,800.

Croydon
Area: 87 km² (33 sq mi). *Population:* 320,700.

Ealing
Area: 55 km² (21 sq mi). *Population:* 283,700.

Enfield
Area: 81 km² (31 sq mi). *Population:* 262,600.

Greenwich
Area: 48 km² (18 sq mi). *Population:* 215,000. *Administrative HQ:* Woolwich.

Hackney
Area: 20 km² (8 sq mi). *Population:* 189,600.

Hammersmith and Fulham
Area: 16 km² (6 sq mi). *Population:* 156,000. *Administrative HQ:* Hammersmith.

Haringey
Area: 30 km² (12 sq mi). *Population:* 211,000. *Administrative HQ:* Wood Green.

Harrow
Area: 51 km² (20 sq mi). *Population:* 204,900.

Havering
Area: 117 km² (45 sq mi). *Population:* 231,300. *Administrative HQ:* Romford.

Hillingdon
Area: 110 km² (43 sq mi). *Population:* 237,600. *Administrative HQ:* Uxbridge.

Hounslow
Area: 58 km² (22 sq mi). *Population:* 206,800.

Islington
Area: 15 km² (6 sq mi). *Population:* 174,800.

Kensington and Chelsea
Area: 12 km² (5 sq mi). *Population:* 146,900. *Administrative HQ:* Kensington.

Kingston upon Thames
Area: 38 km² (14 sq mi). Population: 137,800.

Lambeth
Area: 27 km² (11 sq mi). *Population:* 258,800. *Administrative HQ:* Brixton.

Lewisham
Area: 35 km² (13 sq mi). *Population:* 239,900. *Administrative HQ:* Catford.

Merton
Area: 38 km² (15 sq mi). *Population:* 172,800. *Administrative HQ:* Morden.

Newham
Area: 36 km² (14 sq mi). *Population:* 223,700. *Administrative HQ:* East Ham.

Redbridge
Area: 56 km² (22 sq mi). *Population:* 232,000. *Administrative HQ:* Ilford.

Richmond upon Thames
Area: 55 km² (21 sq mi). *Population:* 165,000. *Administrative HQ:* Twickenham.

Southwark
Area: 29 km² (11 sq mi). *Population:* 227,400. *Administrative HQ:* Camberwell.

Sutton
Area: 43 km² (17 sq mi). *Population:* 171,900.

Tower Hamlets
Area: 20 km² (8 sq mi). *Population:* 168,500. *Administrative HQ:* Bethnal Green.

Waltham Forest
Area: 40 km² (15 sq mi). *Population:* 218,400. *Administrative HQ:* Walthamstow.

Wandsworth
Area: 35 km² (13 sq mi). *Population:* 265,900.

Westminster, City of
Area: 22 km² (8 sq mi). *Population:* 188,600.

Greater Manchester

Area: 1289 km² (497 sq mi).

Population: 2,573,500 (1992 est).

Greater Manchester was untouched by the local government review that began in 1992. There is no county council; Greater Manchester comprises the following unitary authorities (Metropolitan boroughs). (See map; p. 752.)

Bolton
Area: 140 km² (54 sq mi). *Population:* 263,800. (Shown as M2 on p. 752.)

Bury
Area: 99 km² (38 sq mi). *Population:* 180,600. (Shown as M3 on p. 752.)

Manchester
Area: 116 km² (45 sq mi). *Population:* 434,600. (Shown as M8 on p. 752.)

Oldham
Area: 141 km² (54 sq mi). *Population:* 220,200. (Shown as M5 on p. 752.)

Rochdale
Area: 160 km² (62 sq mi). *Population:* 205,700. (Shown as M4 on p. 752.)

Salford
Area: 97 km² (37 sq mi). *Population:* 230,300. (Shown as M10 on p. 752.)

Stockport
Area: 126 km² (49 sq mi). *Population:* 288,800. (Shown as M7 on p. 752.)

Tameside
Area: 103 km² (40 sq mi). *Population:* 221,000. *Administrative HQ:* Ashton-under-Lyne. (Shown as M6 on p. 752.)

Trafford
Area: 106 km² (41 sq mi). *Population:* 215,900. *Administrative HQ:* Stretford. (Shown as M9 on p. 752.)

Wigan
Area: 199 km² (77 sq mi). *Population:* 312,400. (Shown as M1 on p. 752.)

Hampshire

Area: 3775 km² (1458 sq mi).

Population: 1,585,500 (1992 est).

Hampshire will comprise the administrative county of Hampshire plus two unitary authorities. (See map; p. 748.)

Hampshire (administrative county)
Area: 3683 km² (1422 sq mi). *Population:* 1,187,900. *Administrative HQ:* Winchester. The administrative county of Hampshire will comprise 11 districts: Basingstoke and Deane (HQ: Basingstoke), East Hampshire (HQ: Petersfield), Eastleigh, Fareham,

Gosport, Hart (HQ: Fleet), Havant, New Forest (HQ: Lyndhurst), Rushmoor (HQ: Farnborough), Test Valley (HQ: Andover), and Winchester.

Portsmouth (unitary authority)
Area: 42 km² (16 sq mi). *Population:* 189,500. (Shown as H2 on p. 748.)

Southampton (unitary authority)
Area: 50 km² (19 sq mi). *Population:* 208,100. (Shown as H1 on p. 748.)

Herefordshire

Area: 2181 km² (842 sq mi).

Population: 170,000 (1992 est).

Administrative HQ: Hereford.

Herefordshire is to be a county and a unitary authority with no subdivisions. (See map; p. 750.)

Hertfordshire

Area: 1639 km² (633 sq mi).

Population: 994,300 (1992 est).

Administrative HQ: Hertford.

Hertfordshire comprises 10 administrative districts: Broxbourne (HQ: Cheshunt), Dacorum (HQ: Hemel Hempstead), East Hertfordshire (HQs: Hertford and Bishop's Stortford), Hertsmere (HQ: Borehamwood), North Hertfordshire (HQ: Letchworth), St Albans, Stevenage, Three Rivers (HQ: Rickmansworth), Watford, and Welwyn Hatfield (HQ: Welwyn Garden City). (See map; p. 748.)

Huntingdonshire

Area: 923 km² (356 sq mi).

Population: 149,200 (1992 est).

Administrative HQ: Huntingdon.

It is proposed that the traditional county of Huntingdonshire be revived as a unitary authority. If this proposal is not adopted, Huntingdonshire will continue to be a district of Cambridgeshire (see above). (See map; p. 750.)

Isle of Wight

Area: 380 km² (147 sq mi).

Population: 125,600 (1992 est).

Administrative HQ: Newport.

The Isle of Wight is a county and unitary authority without any subdivisions. (See p. 748.)

Kent

Area: 3728 km² (1440 sq mi).

Population: 1,539,300 (1992 est).

It is proposed that Kent will comprise the administrative county of Kent plus at least one unitary authority based upon the Medway Towns. Proposals for two other unitary authorities (Dartford and Gravesham) have been considered. (See map; p. 748.)

Kent (administrative county)
Area: 3537 km² (1366 sq mi). *Population:* 1,295,500. *Administrative HQ:* Maidstone. It is proposed that the administrative county of Kent will comprise 12 districts: Ashford, Canterbury, Dartford, Dover, Gravesham (HQ: Gravesend), Maidstone, Sevenoaks, Shepway (HQ: Folkestone), Swale (HQ: Sittingbourne), Thanet (HQ: Margate), Tonbridge and Malling (HQ: West Malling), and Tunbridge Wells.

Rochester-upon-Medway/Gillingham (proposed unitary authority; the name has not been decided)
Area: 191 km² (74 sq mi). *Population:* 243,800. *Administrative HQs:* Strood and Gillingham. (Shown as K1 on p. 748.)

Lancashire

Area: 3070 km² (1185 sq mi).

Population: 1,413,500 (1992 est).

It is proposed that Lancashire will comprise the administrative county of Lancashire plus two unitary authorities. (See map; p. 752.)

Lancashire (administrative county)
Area: 2898 km² (1119 sq mi). *Population:* 1,123,100. *Administrative HQ:* Preston. These statistics exclude the two proposed unitary authorities. It is proposed that the administrative county of Lancashire will comprise 12 districts: Burnley, Chorley, Fylde (HQ: St Anne's), Hyndburn (HQ: Accrington), Lancaster, Pendle (HQ: Nelson), Preston, Ribble Valley (HQ: Clitheroe), Rossendale (HQ: Rawtenstall), South Ribble (HQ: Leyland), West Lancashire (HQ: Ormskirk), and Wyre (HQ: Poulton-le-Fylde).

Blackburn (proposed unitary authority)
Area: 137 km² (53 sq mi). *Population:* 138,300. (Shown as L2 on p. 752.)

Blackpool (proposed unitary authority)
Area: 35 km² (14 sq mi). *Population:* 152,100. (Shown as L1 on p. 752.) It has been suggested that Wyre and Fylde districts (see above) might be included in the proposed unitary authority.

Leicestershire

Area: 2157 km² (833 sq mi).

Population: 868,900 (1992 est).

It is proposed that Leicestershire will comprise the administrative county of Leicestershire (minus the traditional county of Rutland) plus a single unitary authority. The statistics in this section exclude Rutland.

Leicestershire (administrative county)
Area: 2084 km² (805 sq mi). *Population:* 583,500. *Administrative HQ:* Glenfield, Leicester. It is proposed that the administrative county will comprise seven districts: Blaby (HQ: Narborough), Charnwood (HQ: Loughborough), Harborough (HQ: Market Harborough), Hinckley and Bosworth (HQ: Hinckley), Melton (HQ: Melton Mowbray), North West Leicestershire (HQ: Coalville), and Oadby and Wigston (HQ: Wigston).

Leicester (unitary authority)
Area: 73 km² (28 sq mi). *Population:* 285,400. (Shown as L1 on the map of Leicestershire on p. 750.)

Lincolnshire

Area: 6897 km² (2663 sq mi).

Population: 912,000 (1992 est).

Lincolnshire will comprise the administrative county of Lincolnshire plus two unitary authorities. (See map; p. 750.)

Lincolnshire (administrative county)
Area: 5921 km² (2286 sq mi). *Population:* 596,800. *Administrative HQ:* Lincoln. The administrative county comprises seven administrative districts: Boston, East Lindsey (HQ: Louth), Lincoln, North Kesteven (HQ: Sleaford), South Holland (HQ: Spalding), South Kesteven (HQ: Grantham), and West Lindsey (HQ: Gainsborough).

North East Lincolnshire (unitary authority)
Area: 192 km² (74 sq mi). *Population:* 161,500. *Administrative HQs:* Grimsby and/or Cleethorpes. (Shown as L2 on the map of Lincolnshire on p. 750.)

North Lincolnshire (unitary authority)
Area: 784 km² (303 sq mi). *Population:* 153,700. *Administrative HQs:* Scunthorpe and/or Brigg. (Shown as L1 on the map of Lincolnshire on p. 750.)

Merseyside

Area: 655 km² (253 sq mi).

Population: 1,445,700 (1992 est).

Merseyside was untouched by the local government review that began in 1992. Merseyside has no county council; it comprises the following unitary authorities (Metropolitan boroughs). (See map; p. 752.)

Knowsley
Area: 97 km² (38 sq mi). *Population:* 155,500. *Administrative HQ:* Kirkby. (Shown as S4 on p. 752.)

Liverpool
Area: 113 km² (44 sq mi). *Population:* 479,000. (Shown as S5 on p. 752.)

St Helens
Area: 133 km² (51 sq mi). *Population:* 180,900. (Shown as S1 on p. 752.)

Sefton
Area: 153 km² (59 sq mi). *Population:* 294,900. *Administrative HQ:* Bootle. (Shown as S3 on p. 752.)

Wirral
Area: 159 km² (63 sq mi). *Population:* 335,300. *Administrative HQ:* Wallasey. (Shown as S2 on p. 752.)

Norfolk

Area: 5385 km² (2079 sq mi).

Population: 762,900 (1992 est).

It is proposed that Norfolk will comprise the administrative county of Norfolk plus a single unitary authority. (See map; p. 750.)

Norfolk (administrative county)
Area: 5346 km² (2064 sq mi). *Population:* 635,200. *Administrative HQ:* Norwich. It is proposed that the administrative county will comprise six districts: Breckland (HQ: Attleborough), Broadland (HQ: Norwich), Great Yarmouth, King's Lynn and West Norfolk (HQ: King's Lynn), North Norfolk (HQ: Cromer), and South Norfolk (*HQ:* Long Stratton).

Norwich (proposed unitary authority)
Area: 39 km² (15 sq mi). *Population:* 127,700. (Shown as N1 on the map of Norfolk on p. 750.)

Northamptonshire

Area: 2367 km² (914 sq mi).

Population: 590,200 (1992 est).

It is proposed that Northamptonshire will comprise the administrative county of Northamptonshire plus a single unitary authority. (See map; p. 750.)

Northamptonshire (unitary authority)
Area: 2282 km² (881 sq mi). *Population:* 404,200. *Administrative HQ:* Northampton. It is proposed that the administrative county will comprise six districts: Corby, Daventry, East Northamptonshire (HQ: Thrapston), Kettering, South Northamptonshire (HQ: Towcester), and Wellingborough.

Northampton (proposed unitary authoriy)
Area: 81 km² (31 sq mi). *Population:* 186,000. (Shown as N1 on the map of Northamptonshire on p. 750.)

Northumberland

Area: 5026 km² (1941 sq mi).

Population: 307,200 (1992 est).

Administrative HQ: Morpeth.

Northumberland comprises six administrative districts: Alnwick, Berwick-upon-Tweed, Blyth Valley (HQ: Seaton Delaval), Castle Morpeth (HQ: Morpeth), Tynedale (HQ: Hexham), and Wansbeck (HQ: Ashington). (See map; p. 752.)

North Yorkshire

(which may be known as the **North Riding of Yorkshire**)

Area: 8608 km² (3324 sq mi).

Population: 1,104,600 (1992 est).

North Yorkshire will comprise the administrative county of North Yorkshire plus three unitary authorities. (See map; p. 752.)

North Yorkshire (administrative county)
Area: 8280 km² (3197 sq mi). *Population:* 619,300. *Administrative HQ:* Northallerton. The administrative county will comprise seven districts: Craven (HQ: Skipton), Hambleton (HQ: Northallerton), Harrogate, Richmondshire (HQ: Richmond), Ryedale (HQ: Malton), Scarborough, and Selby.

Middlesbrough (unitary authority)
Area: 54 km² (21 sq mi). *Population:* 145,700. (Shown as NR1 on p. 752.)

Redcar and Cleveland (unitary authority)
Area: 245 km² (4 sq mi). *Population:* 145,800. *Administrative HQ:* South Bank. (Shown as NR2 on p. 752.)

York (unitary authority)
Area: 29 km² (11 sq mi). *Population:* 103,800. (Shown as NR3 on p. 752.)

Nottinghamshire

Area: 2160 km² (834 sq mi).

Population: 1,025,300 (1992 est).

It is proposed that Nottinghamshire will comprise the administrative county of Nottinghamshire plus at least one, and possibly four, unitary authorities. The districts of Broxtowe (N3 on the map of Nottinghamshire; see p. 750), Gedling (N4) and Rushcliffe (N2) (see below) have been considered for unitary authority status or as part of a larger Nottingham unitary authority.

Nottinghamshire (administrative county)
Area: 2085 km² (805 sq mi). *Population:* 742,800. *Administrative HQs:* West Bridgford, Nottingham. These statistics include the districts of Broxtowe, Gedling and Rushcliffe (see above). It is proposed that the administrative county will comprise seven districts: Ashfield (HQ: Kirkby-in-Ashfield), Bassetlaw (HQ: Worksop), Broxtowe (HQ: Beeston), Gedling (HQ: Arnold), Mansfield, Newark and Sherwood (HQ: Kelham), and Rushcliffe (HQ: West Bridgford).

Nottingham (unitary authority)
Area: 75 km² (29 sq mi). *Population:* 282,500 (1992 est). (Shown as N1 on the map of Nottinghamshire on p. 750.)

Oxfordshire

Area: 2583 km² (997 sq mi).

Population: 587,100 (1992 est).

Administrative HQ: Oxford.

The administrative county of Oxfordshire comprises five districts: Cherwell (HQ: Bodicote), Oxford, South Oxfordshire (HQ: Crowmarsh Gifford), Vale of White Horse (HQ: Abingdon), and West Oxfordshire (HQ: Witney). (See map; p. 748.)

Rutland

Area: 394 km² (152 sq mi).

Population: 33,400 (1992 est).

Administrative HQ: Oakham.

It is proposed that the traditional county of Rutland be revived as a unitary authority. If this proposal is not adopted, Rutland will remain a district of Leicestershire (see above).

Shropshire

Area: 3488 km² (1347 sq mi).

Population: 412,800 (1992 est).

It is proposed that Shropshire will comprise the administrative county of Shropshire plus one unitary authority. (See map; p. 750.)

Shropshire (administrative county)
Area: 3197 km² (1235 sq mi). *Population:* 270,500. *Administrative HQ:* Shrewsbury. It is proposed that the administrative county will comprise five districts: Bridgnorth, North Shropshire (HQ: Wem), Oswestry, Shrewsbury and Atcham (HQ: Shrewsbury), and South Shropshire (HQ: Ludlow).

Wrekin or **Telford** (proposed unitary authority; the name had not been decided at the time of going to press)
Area: 290 km² (112 sq mi). *Population:* 142,300. *Administrative HQ:* Telford. (Shown as S1 on the map of Shropshire on p. 750.)

Somerset

Area: 4178 km² (1613 sq mi).

Population: 817,300 (1992 est).

Somerset will comprise the administrative county of Somerset plus two unitary authorities. (See map; p. 751.)

Somerset (administrative county)
Area: 3452 km² (1333 sq mi). *Population:* 472,500. *Administrative HQ:* Taunton. The administrative county of Somerset comprises five districts: Mendip (HQ: Shepton Mallet), Sedgemoor (HQ: Bridgwater), South Somerset/Yeovil (HQ: Yeovil), Taunton Deane (HQ: Taunton), and West Somerset (HQ: Williton).

Bath and North East Somerset (unitary authority)
Area: 351 km² (136 sq mi). *Population:* 164,500. *Administrative HQ:* Bath. (Shown as S2 on p. 751.)

North West Somerset (unitary authority)
Area: 375 km² (145 sq mi). *Population:* 180,400. *Administrative HQ:* Weston-super-Mare. (Shown as S1 on p. 751.)

South Yorkshire

Area: 1559 km² (602 sq mi).

Population: 1,304,300 (1992 est).

South Yorkshire was untouched by the local government review that began in 1992. There is no county council; South Yorkshire comprises the following unitary authorities (Metropolitan boroughs). (See map; p. 752.)

Barnsley
Area: 328 km² (127 sq mi). *Population:* 224,800. (Shown as SY2 on p. 752.)

Doncaster
Area: 581 km² (224 sq mi). *Population:* 292,500. (Shown as SY1 on p. 752.)

Rotherham
Area: 283 km² (109 sq mi). *Population:* 255,100. (Shown as SY3 on p. 752.)

Sheffield
Area: 367 km² (142 sq mi). *Population:* 531,000. (Shown as SY4 on p. 752.)

Staffordshire

Area: 2715 km² (1048 sq mi).

Population: 1,051,800 (1992 est).

Staffordshire will comprise the administrative county of Staffordshire plus a single unitary authority. (See map; p. 750.)

Staffordshire (administrative county)
Area: 2623 km² (1013 sq mi). *Population:* 798,900. *Administrative HQ:* Stafford. The administrative county will comprise eight districts: Cannock Chase (HQ: Cannock), East Staffordshire (HQ: Burton-upon-Trent), Lichfield, Newcastle-under-Lyme, South Staffordshire (HQ: Codsall), Stafford, Staffordshire Moorlands (HQ: Leek), and Tamworth.

Stoke-on-Trent (unitary authority)
Area: 93 km² (36 sq mi). *Population:* 252,900. (Shown as S1 on the map of Staffordshire on p. 750.)

Suffolk

Area: 3798 km² (1466 sq mi).

Population: 648,000 (1992 est).

Administrative HQ: Ipswich.

Suffolk comprises seven administrative districts: Babergh (HQ: Hadleigh), Forest Heath (HQ: Mildenhall), Ipswich, Mid Suffolk (HQ: Needham

Market), St Edmundsbury (HQ: Bury St Edmunds), Suffolk Coastal (HQ: Woodbridge), and Waveney (HQ: Lowestoft). (See map; p. 750.)

Surrey

Area: 1677 km² (648 sq mi).

Population: 1,036,700 (1992 est).

Administrative HQ: Kingston-upon-Thames (i.e. outside the county; the traditional county town is Guildford).

Surrey comprises 11 administrative districts: Elmbridge (HQ: Walton-on-Thames), Epsom and Ewell (HQ: Epsom), Guildford, Mole Valley (HQ: Dorking), Reigate and Banstead (HQ: Reigate), Runnymede (HQ: Addlestone), Spelthorne (HQ: Staines), Surrey Heath (HQ: Camberley), Tandridge (HQ: Oxted), Waverley (HQ: Godalming), and Woking. (See map; p. 748.)

Tyne and Wear

Area: 537 km² (207 sq mi).

Population: 1,134,400 (1992 est).

Tyne and Wear was untouched by the local government review that began in 1992. There is no county council; Tyne and Wear comprises the following unitary authorities (Metropolitan boroughs). (See map; p. 752.)

Gateshead

Area: 143 km² (55 sq mi). *Population:* 203,100. (Shown as T3 on p. 752.)

Newcastle upon Tyne

Area: 112 km² (43 sq mi). *Population:* 281,700. (Shown as T4 on p. 752.)

North Tyneside

Area: 84 km² (32 sq mi). *Population:* 195,200. *Administrative HQ:* North Shields. (Shown as T5 on p. 752.)

South Tyneside

Area: 63 km² (42 sq mi). *Population:* 157,300. *Administrative HQ:* South Shields. (Shown as T2 on p. 752.)

Sunderland

Area: 135 km² (52 sq mi). *Population:* 297,100. (Shown as T1 on p. 752.)

Warwickshire

Area: 1979 km² (764 sq mi).

Population: 491,900 (1992 est).

Administrative HQ: Warwick.

Warwickshire comprises five administrative districts: North Warwickshire (HQ: Atherstone), Nuneaton and Bedworth (HQ: Nuneaton), Rugby, Stratford-on-Avon, and Warwick (HQ: Leamington Spa.) (See map; p. 750.)

West Midlands

Area: 899 km² (347 sq mi).

Population: 2,630,500 (1992 est).

The West Midlands was untouched by the local government review that began in 1992. There is no county council; the West Midlands consist of the following unitary authorities (Metropolitan boroughs). (See map; p. 750.)

Birmingham

Area: 265 km² (102 sq mi). *Population:* 1,009,100. (Shown as W3 on p. 750.)

Coventry

Area: 97 km² (37 sq mi). *Population:* 304,600. (Shown as W1 on p. 750.)

Dudley

Area: 98 km² (38 sq mi). *Population:* 311,000. (Shown as W7 on p. 750.)

Sandwell

Area: 86 km² (33 sq mi). *Population:* 294,100. *Administrative HQ:* Oldbury. (Shown as W5 on p. 750.)

Solihull

Area: 179 km² (69 sq mi). *Population:* 200,900. (Shown as W2 on p. 750.)

Walsall

Area: 106 km² (41 sq mi). *Population:* 263,400. (Shown as W4 on p. 750.)

Wolverhampton

Area: 69 km² (27 sq mi). *Population:* 247,500. (Shown as W6 on p. 750.)

West Sussex

Area: 1969 km² (760 sq mi).

Population: 712,600 (1992 est).

Administrative HQ: Chichester.

The administrative county of West Sussex comprises seven districts: Adur (HQ: Shoreham), Arun (HQ: Littlehampton), Chichester, Crawley, Horsham, Mid Sussex (HQ: Haywards Heath), and Worthing. (See map; p. 748.)

West Yorkshire

Area: 2034 km² (785 sq mi).

Population: 2,093,500 (1992 est).

West Yorkshire was untouched by the local government review that began in 1992. There is no county council; West Yorkshire comprises the following unitary authorities (Metropolitan boroughs). (See map; p. 752.)

Bradford

Area: 366 km² (141 sq mi). *Population:* 477,500. (Shown as WY3 on p. 752.)

Calderdale

Area: 363 km² (140 sq mi). *Population:* 193,900. *Administrative HQ:* Halifax. (Shown as WY1 on p. 752.)

Kirklees

Area: 410 km² (158 sq mi). *Population:* 383,200. *Administrative HQ:* Huddersfield. (Shown as WY2 on p. 752.)

Leeds

Area: 562 km² (217 sq mi). *Population:* 721,800. (Shown as WY4 on p. 752.)

Wakefield

Area: 333 km² (129 sq mi). *Population:* 317,100. (Shown as WY5 on p. 752.)

Wiltshire

Area: 3476 km² (1342 sq mi).

Population: 579,400 (1992 est).

Wiltshire will comprise the administrative county of Wiltshire plus a single unitary authority. (See map; p. 751.)

Wiltshire (administrative county)
Area: 3246 km² (1252 sq mi). *Population:* 405,800. *Administrative HQ:* Trowbridge. The administrative county of Wiltshire will have four districts: Kennet (HQ: Devizes), North Wiltshire (HQ: Chippenham), Salisbury, and West Wiltshire (HQ: Trowbridge).

Swindon or **Thamesdown** (unitary authority; the name had not been decided at the time of going to press)
Area: 230 km² (89 sq mi). *Population:* 173,600. *Administrative HQ:* Swindon. (Shown as W1 on p. 751.)

Worcestershire

Area: 1742 km² (673 sq mi).

Population: 520,400 (1992 est).

Administrative HQ: Worcester.

Worcestershire will comprise six administrative districts: Bromsgrove, Malvern Hills (HQ: Malvern), Redditch, Worcester, Wychavon (HQ: Pershore), and Wyre Forest (HQ: Stourport-on-Severn).

ENGLISH CITIES

The title 'city' has been bestowed, or is in official use by traditional usage, in the following places in England. The civic head in each city is a mayor, except in the case of cities marked with an asterisk (*), in which the civic head is a lord mayor.

Bath (city status 1850), Birmingham* (1889), Bradford* (1897), Bristol* (1540), Cambridge (1951), Canterbury* (traditional), Carlisle (1158), Chester (traditional), Chichester (traditional), Coventry* (traditional), Derby (1977), Durham (traditional), Ely (traditional), Exeter (traditional), Gloucester (traditional), Hereford (traditional), Hull* (Kingston-upon-Hull; 1897), Lancaster (1937), Leeds* (1893), Leicester* (1919), Lichfield (traditional), Lincoln (traditional), Liverpool* (1880), London* (traditional), Manchester* (1847), Newcastle-upon-Tyne* (1882), Norwich* (traditional), Nottingham* (1897), Oxford* (1546), Peterborough (1894), Plymouth* (1928), Portsmouth* (1926), Ripon (1836), Rochester (traditional), St Albans (1887), Salford (1926), Salisbury (traditional), Sheffield* (1893), Southampton (1964), Stoke-on-Trent* (1910), Sunderland (1992), Truro (1877), Wakefield (1888), Wells (traditional), Westminster* (1965), Winchester (traditional), Worcester (traditional), and York* (traditional).

LOCAL COUNCILS IN GREAT BRITAIN

All councillors in the United Kingdom are elected for a period of four years. The majority of councils are elected under the 'whole council' pattern, that is an election every four years for the entire council in single-member wards (for district councils and unitary authority councils in England, Scotland, Wales and Northern Ireland) or electoral divisions (for county councils in England). Parish and community councils follow the 'whole council' pattern, but elections tend to be for multi-member areas. In the metropolitan districts, however, there are larger wards usually represented by three councillors and one seat for each ward comes up for election in rotation, so that there are elections for one third of the council in three years out of four. English non-metropolitan districts may opt for either the 'whole council' system or the 'thirds' system.

County councils (in England) provide major services such as roads, education, social services, the police and fire services, trading standards, and strategic planning.

Metropolitan district councils (in England) discharge the bulk of local government functions. However, a small number of parish councils (see below) exist within metropolitan districts. Also, the six metropolitan counties each have three Joint Boards, for police, fire and civil defence, and transport, comprising nominees from the district councils. All metropolitan authorities have either borough (or city) status, and the chair of the council is either the mayor (or lord mayor).

Unitary authority councils (in England) also discharge the bulk of local government functions. Parish councils (see below) operate within most unitary authorities. Arrangements have been made for unitary authorities to share certain provisions (such as police) with adjoining or surrounding counties. Some unitary authorities have borough (or city) status and the chair of the council is either the mayor (or lord mayor).

Greater London boroughs provide all local government functions except those that are either organized through joint or ad hoc arrangements between boroughs or those fire and civil defence matters provided by a Joint Board.

District councils (in England) provide local services such as housing, recreation, environmental health and waste collection. Some district councils have borough (or city) status and the chair of the council is either the mayor (or lord mayor). Town and parish councils operate within most district councils.

District councils (in Scotland) are unitary authorities that discharge all local functions except those (such as police) which are provided by residual bodies from the previous system of regions and island authorities. The chair of some districts is called the provost or, if the district has city status, lord provost. There are also elected community councils at local level (see below).

County councils and county borough councils (Wales) are unitary authorities with similar powers to Scottish districts. Councils are known as either county councils (where they cover an area similar to a former traditional county) or county borough councils (in urban or other areas). In those councils with borough (or city) status, the chair of the council is either the mayor (or lord mayor). There are also elected community councils at local level (see below).

Parish councils (in England) have responsibilities in matters such as recreation facilities, community halls, parks, allotments, and footpaths. All English parishes with over 200 electors have a council; smaller parishes hold biannual parish meetings. Some parishes have town status (see below).

Town councils (in England) have powers almost identical to those of Parish Councils (above). The chair of the council is called the mayor.

Community councils (in Wales) are the equivalent of the English parish councils (q.v.).

Community councils (in Scotland) are not, in fact, local authorities. These councils, which have no powers, are elected to represent the views of their local communities.

WALES, the Principality of

Wales was incorporated into England by Act of Parliament in 1536. The county boundaries between England and Wales expressly cannot be altered by the ordinary processes of local government reorganization.

Area: 20,768 km² (8019 sq mi).

Population: 2,881,000 (1991 est).

Capital: Cardiff.

Local government districts in Wales

The number in brackets after the name of each district refers to the map (opposite). Population figures are 1992 estimates. At the time of going to press, a final decision concerning the site of the administrative headquarters of some authorities (marked *) had not been taken. Elections for the new 22 councils took place in May 1995. The new all-purpose authorities will take office on 1 April 1996 when the former set-up of counties and districts is abolished.

Some of the new districts are coterminous with former districts or counties. The new districts are geographical and administrative units: some are called counties; others are county boroughs. Many people still refer to the former 13 counties (Anglesey, Brecknockshire, Caernarvonshire, Cardiganshire, Carmarthenshire, Denbighshire, Flintshire, Glamorgan, Merioneth, Monmouthshire, Montgomeryshire, Pembrokeshire, and Radnorshire) that were abolished as administrative units in 1974. (In 1974, these 13 traditional counties were replaced, for administrative purposes, by eight new counties: Clwyd, Dyfed, Gwent, Gwynedd, Mid-Glamorgan, Powys, South Glamorgan, and West Glamorgan.) The new counties of Flintshire, Denbighshire and Monmouthshire do not correspond to the former traditional counties bearing those names. However, the new districts of Anglesey, Cardiganshire, Carmarthenshire and Pembrokeshire do correspond to the former traditional counties.

Aberconwy and Colwyn (county borough)
(1) *Area:* 1130 km² (436 sq mi). *Population:* 109,000. *Administrative HQ*:* either Colwyn Bay or Llandudno.

Anglesey (county)
(2) *Area:* 719 km² (278 sq mi). *Population:* 69,000. *Administrative HQ:* Llangefni.

Blaenau Gwent (county borough)
(3) *Area:* 109 km² (42 sq mi). *Population:* 73,000. *Administrative HQ:* Ebbw Vale.

Bridgend (county borough)
(4) *Area:* 246 km² (95 sq mi). *Population:* 130,000. *Administrative HQ:* Bridgend.

Caernarfonshire and Merioneth (county)
(5) *Area:* 2548 km² (984 sq mi). *Population:* 116,000. *Administrative HQ*:* either Caernarfon or Bangor.

Caerphilly (county borough)
(6) *Area:* 279 km² (108 sq mi). *Population:* 171,000. *Administrative HQ*:* either Pontllanfraith or Ystrad Mynach.

Cardiff (City of) (county borough)
(7) *Area:* 139 km² (54 sq mi). *Population:* 302,000. *Administrative HQ:* Cardiff.

Cardiganshire (county)
(8) *Area:* 1797 km² (694 sq mi). *Population:* 68,000. *Administrative HQ:* Aberystwyth.

Carmarthenshire (county)
(9) *Area:* 2398 km² (926 sq mi). *Population:* 169,000. *Administrative HQ:* Carmarthen.

Denbighshire (county)
(10) *Area:* 844 km² (326 sq mi). *Population:* 91,000. *Administrative HQ:* Ruthin.

Flintshire (county)
(11) *Area:* 437 km² (169 sq mi). *Population:* 144,000. *Administrative HQ:* Mold.

Merthyr Tydfil (county borough)
(12) *Area:* 111 km² (43 sq mi). *Population:* 60,000. *Administrative HQ:* Merthyr Tydfil.

Monmouthshire (county)
(13) *Area:* 851 km² (329 sq mi). *Population:* 81,000. *Administrative HQ*:* either Pontypool or Cwmbran (both of which are outside the district).

Neath and Port Talbot (county borough)
(14) *Area:* 442 km² (171 sq mi). *Population:* 140,000. *Administrative HQ*:* either Neath or Port Talbot.

Newport (county borough)
(15) *Area:* 191 km² (74 sq mi). *Population:* 137,000. *Administrative HQ:* Newport.

Pembrokeshire (county)
(16) *Area:* 1590 km² (614 sq mi). *Population:* 114,000. *Administrative HQ:* Haverfordwest.

Powys (county)
(17) *Area:* 5204 km² (2009 sq mi). *Population:* 121,000. *Administrative HQ:* Llandrindod Wells.

Rhondda, Cynon, Taff (county borough)
(18) *Area:* 424 km² (164 sq mi). *Population:* 238,000. *Administrative HQ*:* either Aberdare, or Pentre or Pontypridd.

Swansea (City of) (county borough)
(19) *Area:* 378 km² (146 sq mi). *Population:* 232,000. *Administrative HQ:* Swansea.

Torfaen (county borough)
(20) *Area:* 126 km² (49 sq mi). *Population:* 91,000. *Administrative HQ:* Pontypool.

Vale of Glamorgan, The (county borough)
(21) *Area:* 337 km² (130 sq mi). *Population:* 119,000. *Administrative HQ:* Barry.

Wrexham (county borough)
(22) *Area:* 499 km² (193 sq mi). *Population:* 123,000. *Administrative HQ:* Wrexham.

CITIES IN WALES

Only three places in Wales may officially use the title 'city'. The civic heads of the two most recent Welsh cities are mayors, although the civic head of Cardiff is a lord mayor.

The Welsh cities are:

Cardiff (city status 1905), St David's (city status 1995), Swansea (city status 1969).

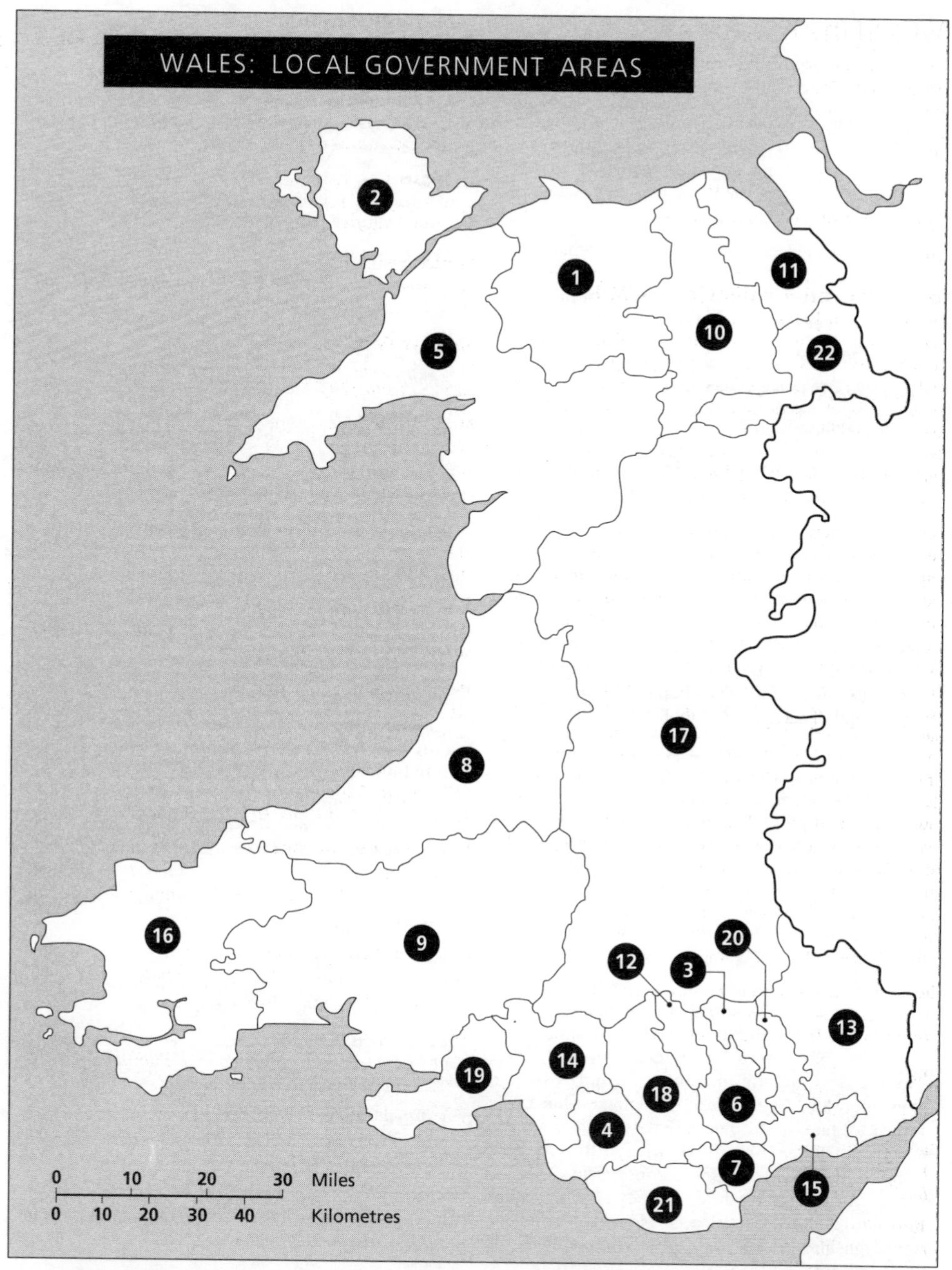

PLACE NAMES IN WELSH

Anglesey (Môn), Barry (Y Barri), Brecon (Aberhonddu), Bridgend (Pen-y-bont ar Ogwr), Caernarfonshire (Sir Caernarfon), Cardigan (Aberteifi), Cardiganshire (Ceredigion or Sir Aberteifi), Cardiff (Caerdydd), Carmarthenshire (Sir Caerfyrddin), Chepstow (Casgwent), Denbighshire (Sir Dinbych), Fishguard (Abergwaun), Flintshire (Sir y Fflint), Haverfordwest (Hwlffordd), Holyhead (Caergybi), Lampeter (Lanbedr Pont Steffan), Merioneth (Meirionydd), Mold (Yr Wyddgrug), Monmouth (Trefynwy), Monmouthshire (Sir Fynwy), Mountain Ash (Aberpennar), Neath (Castelnedd), Newport (Casnewydd), Pembroke (Penfro), Pembrokeshire (Sir Benfro), St David's (Tyddewi), Swansea (Abertawe), Vale of Glamorgan (Bro Morgannwg), Welshpool (y Trallwng), Wrexham (Wrecsam).

SCOTLAND

Scotland consists of the northern and smaller part of the island of Great Britain.

The Kingdom of Scotland effectively lost much of its independence in 1603 when King James VI of Scotland became King James I of England. From 1603 to 1707 Scotland remained (for part of the time only nominally) an independent nation.

Scotland and England continued to have separate parliaments until the Union of the Parliaments at Westminster on 1 May 1707. Scotland continues to have its own distinctive legal system.

Area: 78,759 km² (30,409 sq mi).

Population: 5,111,000 (1992 est).

Capital: Edinburgh.

Local government districts in Scotland

The number in brackets after the name of each district refers to the map (opposite). Population figures are 1993 estimates.

At the time of going to press, a final decision concerning the site of the administrative headquarters of some authorities (marked *) had not been taken. Elections for the new 32 district councils took place in April 1995. The new all-purpose authorities will take office on 1 April 1996 when the former set-up of regions and districts will be abolished.

Some of the new districts are identical to former districts or regions. The regions and island authorities were: Borders, Central, Dumfries and Galloway, Fife, Grampian, Highland, Lothian, Orkney (an island authority), Shetland (an island authority), Strathclyde, Tayside, and Western Isles (an island authority).

The new districts are geographical and administrative units, although many people still refer to the former 33 counties that were abolished as administrative units in 1973.

These traditional counties were: Aberdeenshire, Angus (or Forfarshire), Argyll (or Argyllshire), Ayrshire, Banffshire, Berwickshire, Buteshire, Caithness, Clackmannanshire, Dumfries-shire, Dunbartonshire, East Lothian (Haddingtonshire), Fife, Inverness-shire, Kincardineshire (or Mearns), Kinross-shire, (the Stewartry of) Kirkcudbrightshire, Lanarkshire, Midlothian (or Edinburghshire), Moray (or Elginshire), Nairnshire, Orkney, Peebles-shire, Perthshire, Renfrewshire, Ross and Cromarty, Roxburghshire, Selkirkshire, Shetland (or Zetland), Stirlingshire, Sutherland, West Lothian (or Linlithgowshire), and Wigtownshire.

The new districts of Aberdeenshire, Angus, Midlothian, Moray and Renfrewshire do not correspond to the former traditional counties bearing those names.

However, the new districts of Clackmannan, East Lothian, Fife, Orkney, Shetland and West Lothian do correspond to the former traditional counties bearing those names.

Aberdeen (City of)
(1) *Area:* 182 km² (70 sq mi). *Population:* 218,000. *Administrative HQ:* Aberdeen.

Aberdeenshire
(2) Area: 6317 km² (2439 sq mi). *Population:* 224,000. *Administrative HQ:* Aberdeen.

Angus
(3) *Area:* 2184 km² (843 sq mi). *Population:* 112,000. *Administrative HQ:* Forfar.

Argyll and Bute
(4) *Area:* 7023 km² (2712 sq mi). *Population:* 90,000. *Administrative HQ:* Lochgilphead.

Borders, The
(5) *Area:* 4727 km² (1825 sq mi). *Population:* 105,000. *Administrative HQ:* Newtown St Boswells.

Clackmannan
(6) *Area:* 158 km² (61 sq mi). *Population:* 49,000. *Administrative HQ:* Alloa.

Dumbarton and Clydebank
(7) *Area:* 176 km² (68 sq mi). *Population:* 98,000. *Administrative HQ**: either Dumbarton or Clydebank.

Dumfries and Galloway
(8) *Area:* 6446 km² (2489 sq mi). *Population:* 148,000. *Administrative HQ:* Dumfries.

Dundee (City of)
(9) *Area:* 55 km² (21 sq mi). *Population:* 153,000. *Administrative HQ:* Dundee.

East Ayrshire
(10) *Area:* 1275 km² (492 sq mi). *Population:* 124,000. *Administrative HQ:* Kilmarnock.

East Dunbartonshire
(11) *Area:* 176 km² (68 sq mi). *Population:* 110,000. *Administrative HQ**: either Milngavie or Kirkintilloch.

East Lothian
(12) *Area:* 666 km² (257 sq mi). *Population:* 86,000. *Administrative HQ:* Haddington.

East Renfrewshire
(13) *Area:* 168 km² (65 sq mi). *Population:* 84,000. *Administrative HQ:* Paisley (i.e outside the district).

Edinburgh (City of)
(14) *Area:* 260 km² (100 sq mi). *Population:* 442,000. *Administrative HQ:* Edinburgh.

Falkirk
(15) *Area:* 293 km² (113 sq mi). *Population:* 143,000. *Administrative HQ:* Falkirk.

Fife
(16) *Area:* 1340 km² (518 sq mi). *Population:* 351,000. *Administrative HQ:* Glenrothes.

Glasgow (City of)
(17) Area: 175 km² (67 sq mi). *Population:* 524,000. *Administrative HQ:* Glasgow.

Highland
(18) *Area:* 26,119 km² (10,085 sq mi). *Population:* 207,000. *Administrative HQ:* Inverness. (Although the council meets at Dingwall.)

Inverclyde
(19) *Area:* 167 km² (65 sq mi). *Population:* 90,000. *Administrative HQ:* Greenock.

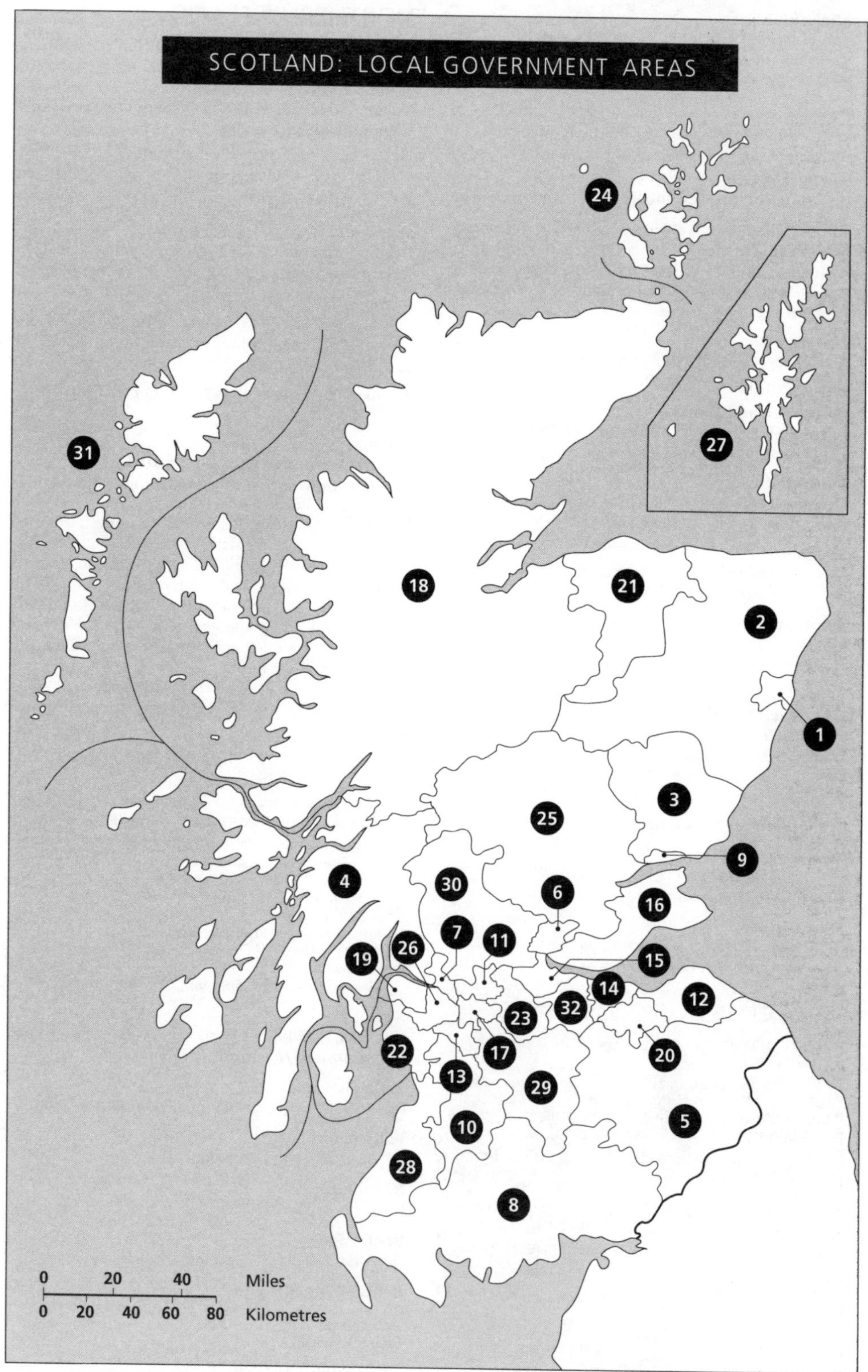
SCOTLAND: LOCAL GOVERNMENT AREAS
24
27
31
18
21
2
1
3
25
9
4
30
6
16
7
11
19
26
15
14
12
32
23
20
22
17
13
29
5
10
28
8
0 20 40 Miles
0 20 40 60 80 Kilometres

Midlothian
(20) *Area:* 350 km² (135 sq mi). *Population:* 80,000. *Administrative HQ:* Edinburgh (i.e. outside the district).

Moray
(21) *Area:* 2237 km² (864 sq mi). *Population:* 86,000. *Administrative HQ:* Elgin.

North Ayrshire
(22) *Area:* 888 km² (343 sq mi). *Population:* 139,000. *Administrative HQ:* Irvine.

North Lanarkshire
(23) *Area:* 476 km² (184 sq mi). *Population:* 327,000. *Administrative HQ*:* Cumbernauld, Coatbridge or Motherwell.

Orkney
(24) *Area:* 1025 km² (396 sq mi). *Population:* 20,000. *Administrative HQ:* Kirkwall.

Perthshire and Kinross
(25) *Area:* 5395 km² (2083 sq mi). *Population:* 131,000. *Administrative HQ:* Perth.

Renfrewshire
(26) *Area:* 262 km² (101 sq mi). *Population:* 178,000. *Administrative HQ:* Paisley.

Shetland
(27) *Area:* 1471 km² (568 sq mi). *Population:* 23,000. *Administrative HQ:* Lerwick.

South Ayrshire
(28) *Area:* 1230 km² (475 sq mi). *Population:* 114,000. *Administrative HQ:* Ayr.

South Lanarkshire
(29) *Area:* 1778 km² (686 sq mi). *Population:* 308,000. *Administrative HQ*:* East Kilbride, Hamilton or Lanark.

Stirling
(30) *Area:* 2243 km² (866 sq mi). *Population:* 82,000. *Administrative HQ:* Stirling.

Western Isles
(31) *Area:* 3070 km² (1185 sq mi). *Population:* 29,000. *Administrative HQ:* Stornoway.

West Lothian
(32) *Area:* 427 km² (165 sq mi). *Population:* 147,000. *Administrative HQ:* Linlithgow.

CITIES OF SCOTLAND

The title 'city' is officially used in Scotland by six towns.

This title has been acquired by traditional usage, rather than by royal prerogative or by royal charter, which is the case with many cities in England and all three cities in Wales.

The civic head of each of the six Scottish cities is the lord provost.

The cities of Scotland are:

Aberdeen	first charter 1179
Dundee	first charter c. 1179
Edinburgh	first charter c. 1124
Elgin	first charter 1234
Glasgow	first charter 1690
Perth	first charter 1210

NORTHERN IRELAND

Northern Ireland consists of six of the nine counties of the ancient Irish province of Ulster in the north-eastern corner of the island. From 1921 until 1973 Northern Ireland had a federal relationship with Westminster. The Northern Ireland Parliament - popularly known as Stormont - enjoyed autonomy. Stormont was abolished in 1973, although some legislative functions were transferred to the new Northern Ireland Assembly and Executive. However, after the collapse of the Executive in 1974, the British Secretary of State for Northern Ireland became responsible for the government of Northern Ireland. This measure was intended to be temporary but direct rule has continued.

Area: 14,122 km² (5453 sq mi), of which 13,483 km² (5205 sq mi) is land.

Population: 1,610,000 (1993 est).

Capital: Belfast.

Districts in Northern Ireland

For local government purposes, the province is divided into 26 districts, whose councils have responsibility for a range of local services including leisure, the environment and regulatory services. The six traditional counties of Northern Ireland - Antrim, Armagh, Down, Fermanagh, Londonderry and Tyrone - no longer exist as administrative units, although the Fermanagh district is identical with the former County Fermanagh. The number in brackets after the name of each district refers to the map (on p. 765). Population figures are 1992 estimates. The districts are named after their administrative headquarters except where indicated below.

Northern Ireland is also divided into five Education and Library Areas and four Health and Services Areas. The area boards are not directly elected, but one third of their members are district councillors, while the remainder are persons appointed by the appropriate UK minister. (Other functions, such as police, planning, water, fire services, roads and housing, are run centrally from Stormont.)

The districts of Northern Ireland are:

Antrim
(1) *Area:* 578 km² (223 sq mi). *Population:* 46,200.

Ards
(2) *Area:* 381 km² (147 sq mi). *Population:* 65,500. *Administrative HQ:* Newtownards.

Armagh
(3) *Area:* 671 km² (259 sq mi). *Population:* 52,400.

Ballymena
(4) *Area:* 632 km² (244 sq mi). *Population:* 57,000.

Ballymoney
(5) *Area:* 419 km² (162 sq mi). *Population:* 24,300.

Banbridge
(6) *Area:* 446 km² (172 sq mi). *Population:* 33,800..

Belfast (City of)
(7) *Area:* 115 km² (44 sq mi). *Population:* 288,700.

Carrickfergus
(8) *Area:* 82 km² (32 sq mi). *Population:* 33,600.

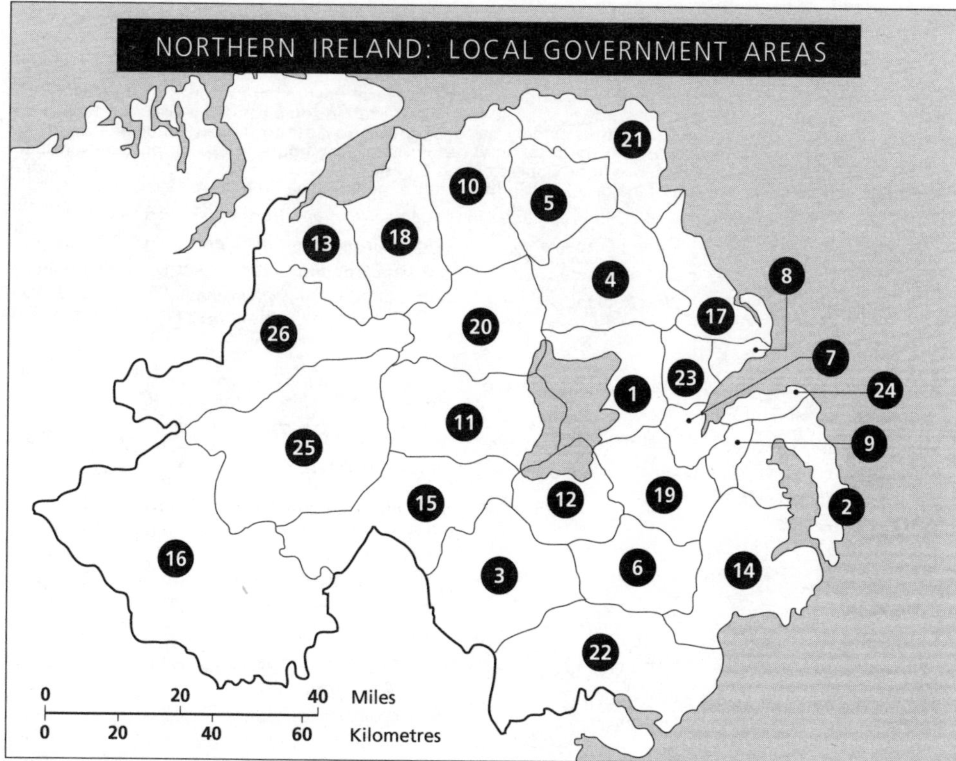

Castlereagh
(9) *Area:* 85 km² (33 sq mi). *Population:* 62,000. *Administrative HQ:* Belfast (i.e. outside the district).

Coleraine
(10) *Area:* 486 km² (187 sq mi). *Population:* 51,500.

Cookstown
(11) *Area:* 622 km² (240 sq mi). *Population:* 31,000.

Craigavon
(12) *Area:* 379 km² (146 sq mi). *Population:* 76,600. *Administrative HQ:* Portadown.

Derry
(13) *Area:* 387 km² (150 sq mi). *Population:* 98,500. *Administrative HQ:* Derry/Londonderry.

Down
(14) *Area:* 650 km² (251 sq mi). *Population:* 59,500. *Administrative HQ:* Downpatrick.

Dungannon
(15) *Area:* 783 km² (302 sq mi). *Population:* 45,700.

Fermanagh
(16) *Area:* 1877 km² (725 sq mi). *Population:* 55,300. *Administrative HQ:* Enniskillen.

Larne
(17) *Area:* 336 km² (130 sq mi). *Population:* 29,700.

Limavady
(18) *Area:* 586 km² (226 sq mi). *Population:* 30,000.

Lisburn
(19) *Area:* 446 km² (172 sq mi). *Population:* 103,100.

Magherafelt
(20) *Area:* 572 km² (221 sq mi). *Population:* 36,400.

Moyle
(21) *Area:* 494 km² (191 sq mi). *Population:* 14,700. *Administrative HQ:* Ballycastle.

Newry and Mourne
(22) *Area:* 909 km² (351 sq mi). *Population:* 84,200. *Administrative HQ:* Newry.

Newtownabbey
(23) *Area:* 151 km² (58 sq mi). *Population:* 75,300. *Administrative HQ:* Ballyclare.

North Down
(24) *Area:* 82 km² (31 sq mi). *Population:* 73,300. *Administrative HQ:* Bangor.

Omagh
(25) *Area:* 1130 km² (436 sq mi). *Population:* 46,300.

Strabane
(26) *Area:* 862 km² (333 sq mi). *Population:* 35,700.

NORTHERN IRISH CITIES

Three places in Northern Ireland may officially use the title 'city'. All three have acquired this status through either royal prerogative or royal charter. They are:

Armagh	city status 1995
Belfast	city status 1888
Derry/Londonderry	city status (as Londonderry) 1604.

URBAN AREAS OF THE UNITED KINGDOM

Recognizing the difficulty of defining the population of towns, the Office of Population Censuses and Surveys has defined a number of conurbations and urban areas. Many district councils - particularly those in Metropolitan areas and those created under the terms of the local government reforms of the 1990s - do not meet the ordinary concepts of a town, e,g, Kirklees and Wirral. In some cases, e.g Glasgow, Newcastle and Nottingham, the local government boundary has been drawn so close to the city centre that many of the suburbs have been excluded from the total. In yet other cases, the figures given for boroughs include large areas of countryside; eg. Canterbury, Doncaster and Carlisle. The urban areas listed here give a more accurate impression of the size of major centres in the United Kingdom. The figures are 1992 estimates.

See also p. 714 for more details of other urban areas in Scotland, Wales and Northern Ireland.

Name of place	*Name of urban area*	*Major local government area*	*Population*
London	Greater London	Greater London (county) 6,904,600	7,926,000
Birmingham	West Midlands	Birmingham (city) 1,009,000, Dudley 305,000, Walsall 263,000, Wolverhampton 248,000, Solihull 201,000	2,360,000
Manchester	Greater Manchester	Manchester (city) 435,000, Stockport 289,000, Bolton 264,000, Salford 230,000, Oldham 220,000, Rochdale 206,000	2,337,000
Glasgow	Central Clydesdale	Glasgow (city) 684,000, Motherwell 144,000, Paisley 84,000, Hamilton 52,000	1,648,000
Leeds	West Yorkshire	Leeds (city) 772,000, Bradford (city) 478,000	1,581,000
Newcastle-upon-Tyne	Tyneside	Newcastle (city) 203,000	797,000
Liverpool	Liverpool	Liverpool (city) 479,000	690,000
Sheffield	Sheffield	Sheffield (city) 531,000	673,000
Nottingham	Nottingham	Nottingham (city) 283,000	631,000
Bristol	Bristol	Bristol (city) 397,000	568,000
Edinburgh	Edinburgh	Edinburgh (city) 439,000	527,000
Brighton	Brighton-Worthing-Littlehampton	Brighton (town) 155,000	495,000
Portsmouth	Portsmouth	Portsmouth (city) 190,000	476,000
Belfast	Belfast	Belfast (city) 288,000	437,000
Leicester	Leicester	Leicester (city) 285,000	423,000
Stoke-on-Trent	The Potteries	Stoke-on-Trent (city) 253,000	389,000
Middlesbrough	Teesside	Middlesbrough (town) 146,000	380,000
Bournemouth	Bournemouth	Bournemouth (town) 159,000	376,000
Coventry	Coventry-Bedworth	Coventry (city) 305,000	348,000
Hull	Kingston-upon-Hull	Hull (city) 269,000	331,000
Cardiff	Cardiff	Cardiff (city) 296,000	326,000
Southampton	Southampton-Eastleigh	Southampton (city) 208,000	322,000
Preston	Preston	Preston (town) 131,000	320,000
Southend	Southend	Southend (town) 165,000	299,000
Blackpool	Blackpool	Blackpool (town) 152,000	293,000
Swansea	Swansea	Swansea (city) 188,000	289,000
Birkenhead	Birkenhead	Birkenhead (town) 99,000	279,000
Plymouth	Plymouth	Plymouth (city) 258,000	258,000
Rochester	The Medway Towns	Rochester-upon-Medway (city) 148,000	247,000
Aldershot	Aldershot	Aldershot with Farnborough (Rushmoor borough) 87,700	245,000
Aberdeen	Aberdeen	Aberdeen (city) 217,000	231,000
Luton	Luton-Dunstable	Luton (town) 176,000	228,000
Derby	Derby	Derby (city) 227,000	227,000
Reading	Reading	Reading (town) 137,000	220,000
Sunderland	Sunderland-Whitburn	part of Sunderland (city) 297,100	202,000
Norwich	Norwich	Norwich (city) 137,000	199,000
Northampton	Northampton	Northampton (town) 186,000	186,000

Physical Geography

HIGHEST PEAKS

In Scotland

Ben Nevis (Highland)	1392m (4406 ft)
Ben Macdhui (Aberdeenshire)	1310m (4300 ft)
Braeriach (Highland/Aberdeenshire)	1294m (4248 ft)
North Top (Ben Macdhui - above)	*1293m (4244 ft)*
Cairn Toul (Aberdeenshire)	1292m (4241 ft)
South Plateau (Braeriach -above)	*1264m (4149 ft)*
Sgor an Lochan Uaine (Cairn Toul)	*1254m (4116 ft)*
Coire Sputan Dearg (Ben Macdhui)	*1248m (4095 ft)*
Cairngorm (Highland/Moray)	1244m (4084 ft)
Aonach Beag (Highland)	1237m (4060 ft)
Coire an Lochain (Braeriach)	*1230m (4036 ft)*
Carn Mor Dearg (Highland)	1222m (4012 ft)
Aonach Mor (Highland)	1218m (3999 ft)

In Wales

(all in Caernarfonshire and Merioneth)

Snowdon (Yr Wyddfa)	1085m (3560 ft)
Garnedd Ugain (Snowdon)	*1065m (3493 ft)*
Carnedd Llewelyn	1062m (3484 ft)
Carnedd Dafydd	1044m (3426 ft)
Glyder Fawr	999m (3279 ft)
Glyder Fâch	994m (3262 ft)
Pen Yr Oleu-wen (Carnedd Dafydd)	*978m (3210 ft)*
Foel Grach (Carnedd Llewelyn)	*974m (3195 ft)*
Yr Elen (Carnedd Llewelyn)	*960m (3151 ft)*

In England

(all in Cumbria)

Scafell Pike	978m (3210 ft)
Sca Fell	963m (3162 ft)
Helvellyn	950m (3116 ft)
Broad Crag (Scafell Pike – above)	*930m (3054 ft)*
Skiddaw	930m (3053 ft)
Lower Man (Helvellyn)	*924m (3033 ft)*
Ill Crags (Scafell Pike)	*922m (3025 ft)*
Great End (Scafell Pike)	*909m (2984 ft)*
Bow Fell	902m (2960 ft)
Great Gable	898m (2949 ft)
Cross Fell	893m (2930 ft)

In Northern Ireland

Slieve Donard	852m (2796 ft)
Slieve Commedagh	767m (2516 ft)
Slieve Bearnagh	730m (2395 ft)
Slieve Mael Beg	704m (2310 ft)
Slieve Lamagan	703m (2306 ft)
Slieve Binnian	685m (2247 ft)
Slieve Mael Mor	682m (2238 ft)

Note: Secondary peaks are shown in italics.

Largest islands in the UK

Largest islands in England	km²	sq mi
Isle of Wight	381·0	147·1
*Sheppey (Kent)	94·0	36·3
*Hayling (Hampshire)	26·8	10·4
*Foulness (plus attendant linked islands) (Essex)	26·1	10·1
*Portsea (Hampshire)	24·3	9·4
*Canvey (Essex)	18·5	7·1
*Mersea (Kent)	18·0	7·0
*Walney (Cumbria)	13·0	5·0
*Wallasea (Essex)	10·7	4·1
St Mary's, Isles of Scilly	6·3	2·4
*Thorney (West Sussex)	5·0	1·9

** Islands bridged or otherwise linked to mainland.*

Largest islands in Scotland		
Lewis with Harris (Wn. Isles)	2225·3	859·2
*Skye (Highland)	1666·1	643·3
Mainland, Shetland	967·0	373·4
Mull (Argyll & Bute)	899·3	347·2
Islay (Argyll & Bute)	614·5	246·6
Mainland, Orkney	536·1	207·0
Arran (Argyll & Bute)	435·3	168·1
Jura (Argyll & Bute)	370·4	143·0
North Uist (Western Isles)	351·5	135·7
South Uist (Western Isles)	332·5	128·4
Yell, Shetland	214·2	82·7
Hoy, Orkney	136·9	52·8

Largest islands in Wales		
*Anglesey (Ynys Mon)	713·8	275·6
Holy I (Anglesey)	39·4	15·2
Skomer (Pembrokeshire)	2·9	1·1
Ramsey (Pembrokeshire)	2·6	1·0
Caldey (Pembrokeshire)	2·8	0·8
Bardsey (Caernarfonshire & Merioneth)	2·0	0·8

WATERFALLS

The highest British waterfalls are:

Waterfall	*Location*	*Height*
Eas A'Chual Aluinn	Highland	200m (658 ft)
Falls of Glomach	Highland	112m (370 ft)
Pistyll-y-Llyn	Powys/ Cardiganshire	c. 73m (c. 240 ft)
Pistyll Rhaeadr	Powys/ Denbighshire	73m (240 ft)
Foyers	Highland	62m (205 ft)
Falls of Clyde	South Lanarkshire	62m (204 ft)

The highest falls in England are Cauldron Snout (Cumbria) at 60m (200 ft).

LONGEST RIVERS OF THE UNITED KINGDOM

Name of watercourse	*Length*	*Remotest source*	*Mouth*
Severn (for 254 km)	354 km (220 mi)	Lake on E side of Plinlimmon, Powys	Bristol Channel
Thames (for 178 km)-Isis (69 km)-Churn	346 km (215 mi)	Seven Springs, Glos	North Sea
Trent (for 236 km)-Humber (61 km)	297 km (185 mi)	Biddulph Moor, Staffs	North Sea (Humber)
Aire (for 126 km)-(Yorkshire) Ouse (72 km)-Humber (61 km)	259 km (161 mi)	NW of North Yorkshire	North Sea (Humber)
Ouse (Great or Bedford)	230 km (143 mi)	nr Brackley, Northants	The Wash
Wye (or Gwy)	215 km (135 mi)	Plinlimmon, Powys	Into Severn S of Chepstow
Tay (for 150 km)-Tummel	188 km (117 mi)	(Tay) Beinn Oss (Perthshire and Kinross)	North Sea
Nene	161 km (100 mi)	nr Naseby, Northants	The Wash
Clyde (inc. Daer Water)	158 km (99 mi)	nr Earncraig Hill, South Lanarkshire	Firth of Clyde (measured to Port Glasgow)
Spey	158 km (98 mi)	Loch Spey, Highland	North Sea
Tweed	155 km (97 mi)	Tweed's Well, Borders	North Sea
Dee (Aberdeenshire)	137 km (85 mi)	W of Cairn Toul, Aberdeenshire	North Sea
Avon (Warwickshire)	137 km (85 mi)	nr Naseby, Northants	Into Severn at Tewkesbury
Don (Aberdeenshire)	130 km (81 mi)	Carn Cuilchathaidh, Aberdeenshire	North Sea
Tees	127 km (79 mi)	Cross Fell, Cumbria	North Sea
Bann (Upper Bann-Lough Neagh-Lower Bann)	122 km (76 mi)	Mountains of Mourne	Atlantic Ocean
Tyne (for 55 km)-North Tyne (63 km)	119 km (73 mi)	Cheviots, between Peel Fell and Carter Fell Northumberland	North Sea
Dee (Cheshire)	113 km (70 mi)	Bala Lake, Caernarfonshire & Merioneth	Irish Sea
Eden	111 km (69 mi)	Pennines, SE of Kirkby Stephen, Cumbria	Solway Firth, Irish Sea
Usk	105 km (65 mi)	Talsarn Mt, Powys	Bristol Channel
Wear	105 km (65 mi)	W of Wearhead, Northumberland	North Sea

MAJOR LOCHS AND LAKES

Name	*Area km²*	*Area sq mi*	*Max. length*	*Max. breadth*	*Max. depth*
Northern Ireland					
Lough Neagh	381·7	147·4	28 km/18 mi	17 km/11 mi	31m/102 ft
Lower Lough Erne	105	40·6	28 km/18 mi	8·8 km/5·5 mi	68m/226 ft
Scotland					
Loch Lomond	71·2	27·5	36·4 km/22·6 mi	8 km/5 mi	189m/623 ft
Loch Ness	56·6	21·9	36·6 km/22·8 mi	3·2 km/2 mi	228m/751 ft
Loch Awe	38·7	15·0	41·km/25·5 mi	3·2 km/2 mi	93m/307 ft
Loch Maree	28·4	11·0	21·7 km/13·5 mi	3·2 km/2 mi	111m/367 ft
Loch Morar	26·6	10·3	18·5 km/11·5 mi	2·4 km/1.5 mi	309m/1017 ft
Loch Tay	26·3	10·2	23·4 km/14·6 mi	1·7 km/1.1 mi	154m/508 ft
England					
Windermere	14·7	5·7	16·8 km/10·5 mi	1·5 km/0·9 mi	66m/219 ft
Ullswate	8·9	3·4	11·8 km/7·4 mi	1·0 km/0·6 mi	62m/205 ft
Bassenthwaite Water	5·3	2·1	6·1 km/3·8 mi	1·2 km/0·7 mi	21m/70 ft
Derwentwater	5·3	2·1	4·6 km/2·9 mi	1·9 km/1·2 mi	21m/72 ft
Wales					
Lake Vyrnwy (dammed)	8·2	3·2	7·5 km/4·7 mi	0·6 km/0·3	36m/120 ft
Bala Lake (Llyn Tegid)	4·3	1·7	6·1km/3·8 mi	0·5 km/0·3	38m/125 ft

Government

The UK is a constitutional monarchy without a written constitution. Parliament comprises two houses - the House of Lords (the upper house) and the House of Commons (the lower house).

The House of Lords

The Lords is made up of over 750 hereditary peers and peeresses, over 20 Lords of Appeal (the Law Lords; non-hereditary peers), over 370 life peers, and 2 archbishops and 24 bishops of the Church of England. All members of the Lords are non-elected.

The House of Commons

The House of Commons consists of 651 members elected for five years by universal adult suffrage. The House of Commons is, undoubtedly, the dominant element within Parliament today. Its 651 Members of Parliament are the basis of British parliamentary democracy. Finance remains at the centre of the Commons' power. The House has the sole right to deliberate issues of taxation without which government would be impossible.

The Prime Minister

The post of Prime Minister was not officially recognized until this century, but it had long been accepted that the monarch's treasurer had to be able to command a majority in the Commons. The power of the premier is still ill-defined, but ultimately it depends upon maintaining a majority in the Commons.

The Prime Minister can exercise the prerogative powers of the monarch, and choose, transfer and dismiss Cabinet ministers and junior members of the government. The Prime Minister is also the First Lord of the Treasury, the political head of the Civil Service. He chairs the Cabinet, and the major Cabinet committees.

The Cabinet

The Cabinet is the major policy-making body of the government. Members of the Cabinet are chosen by the Prime Minister from the Commons or Lords - in modern times overwhelmingly from the Commons. They attend Cabinet meetings either as heads of government departments or 'without portfolio' (without the responsibility of a department). Because modern governments have such a great workload, the Cabinet increasingly works through a system of committees. Some are permanent committees dealing with tasks such as managing the economy, while others are formed to deal with particular problems.

The Cabinet are collectively responsible to Parliament for the actions of the government, and if defeated in a motion of confidence must either resign or seek a dissolution of Parliament and a renewed mandate from the electorate. The Cabinet works under the convention of collective responsibility. This means that even if not all Cabinet ministers agree on a subject, the Cabinet must act unanimously.

The Privy Council

The main purpose of the Privy Council is to advise the sovereign on the approval of Orders in Council and on the issue of royal proclamations. All cabinet ministers must be Privy counsellors and are sworn in on first assuming office. Membership is for life and is awarded by the monarch, on the recommendation of the Prime Minister. It is also awarded to eminent citizens of the UK and of Commonwealth countries with independent monarchs.

The Speaker and Leader of the House

The Speaker, the Leader of the House and the party whips do much to ensure that matters on the floor of the House of Commons proceed smoothly.

The Speaker's function as spokesperson for the House remains important, but his or her duties to regulate debate, decide points of order and interpret the rules of the House, are vital day-to-day functions that require tact and the confidence of all parties in the selection of one of their number as Speaker. Once selected, the Speaker is extremely careful to betray no hint of his or her former party allegiance.

The working of the Commons is also facilitated by the work of the Leader of the House, who is chosen by the Prime Minister to organize government business going through the Commons. This entails working with the chief whips of the major parties to ensure that adequate scrutiny is given to measures, whilst preserving the government's legislative timetable.

The Opposition

The Commons has adapted itself over centuries to the changing conditions within which scrutiny of government must take place. The Opposition is now formalized under a Leader of the Opposition, who since 1937 has been paid by the Crown.

The *Leader of the Opposition* - the leader of the second biggest party in the House - creates a 'Shadow Cabinet', so the actions of all ministers can be effectively examined.

Committees

Perhaps the most effective scrutiny takes place not on the floor of the House but in committees. There are many types of committee. Select Committees usually report on specific matters, such as Public Accounts, Privileges and Members' Interests. In 1978 the select-committee system was reorganized to provide a committee to examine each of the government departments.

All bills before Parliament, many statutory instruments and EU/EC documents, must pass through a Standing, or Legislative Committee, appointed to examine their clauses in detail.

Similar committees exist in the House of Lords, and on some issues Joint Committees of both Houses are held.

The electoral system

The UK uses a 'first-past-the-post' system for electing Members of Parliament. Each constituency elects one MP, the person gaining the most votes being elected. In a contest between four parties, it would be possible for an MP to be elected with less than a third of the total vote.

At a national level, it is possible for the party that obtains the largest number of votes not to win the election. The British system tends to produce majority governments that do not have to rely on coalition partners to govern.

THE CABINET

The membership of the Government at 1 June 1995. Cabinet posts are indicated in bold.

Prime Minister, First Lord of the Treasury and Minister for the Civil Service: John Major.

Agriculture, Fisheries and Food, Minister of : William Waldegrave.

Defence, Secretary of State for: Malcolm Rifkind.

Education, Secretary of State for: Gillian Shephard.

Employment, Secretary of State for: Michael Portillo.

Environment, Secretary of State for the: John Selwyn Gummer.

Exchequer, Chancellor of the: Kenneth Clarke.

Foreign Secretary: Douglas Hurd.

Health, Secretary of State for: Virginia Bottomly.

Home Secretary: Michael Howard

Leader of the House of Commons (and Lord President of the Council): Tony Newton.

Leader of the House of Lords (and Lord Privy Seal): Viscount Cranborne.

Lord Chancellor: Lord Mackay of Clashfern.

National Heritage, Secretary of State for: Stephen Dorrell.

Northern Ireland, Secretary of State for: Sir Patrick Mayhew.

Public Service and Science, Minister of Public Service and Science (also Chancellor of the Duchy of Lancaster): David Hurd.

Scotland, Secretary of State for: Ian Lang.

Social Security, Secretary of State for: Peter Lilley.

Trade and Industry, Secretary of State for (and President of the Board of Trade): Michael Heseltine.

Transport, Secretary of State for: Dr Brian Mawhinney.

Chief Secretary to the Treasury: Jonathan Aitken.

Wales, Secretary of State for: John Redwood.

Minister without Portfolio (and Chairman of the Conservative Party): Jeremy Hanley.

THE SPEAKER

The Speaker of the House of Commons: Betty Boothroyd, MP for West Bromwich West, elected 1992.

THE ELECTORATE

Election	*Size of the electorate*
5 July 1945	33,240,391
23 Feb 1950	33,269,770
25 Oct 1951	34,465,573
25 May 1955	34,858,263
8 Oct 1959	35,397,080
15 Oct 1964	35,894,307
31 Mar 1966	35,965,127
18 June 1970	39,247,683
28 Feb 1974	39,752,317
10 Oct 1974	40,083,286
3 May 1979	41,093,262
9 June 1983	42,197,344
11 June 1987	43,181,321
9 April 1992	43,803,880

LEADER OF THE OPPOSITION

The Leader of the Opposition: Tony (Anthony) Blair, leader of the Labour Party since 1994; MP for Sedgefield (Durham).

THE RESULTS OF THE GENERAL ELECTIONS since 1945

Election and date	*Total seats*	*Result and share of poll* Conservatives	Labour	Liberals	*Others*	*% turn-out of electorate*
5 July 1945	640	213 (39·8)	**393** (47·8)	12 (9·0)	22 (2·8)	72·7%
23 Feb 1950	625	298 (43·5)	**315** (46·4)	9 (9·1)	3 (1·3)	84·0%
25 Oct 1951	625	**321** (48·0)	295 (48·7)	6 (2·5)	3 (0·7)	82·5%
25 May 1955	630	**344** (49·8)	277 (46·3)	6 (2·7)	3 (1·2)	76·7%
8 Oct 1959	630	**365** (49·4)	258 (43·8)	6 (5·9)	1 (0·9)	78·8%
15 Oct 1964	630	303 (43·4)	**317** (44·2)	9 (11·1)	1 (1·3)	77·1%
31 Mar 1966	630	253 (41·9)	**363** (47·9)	12 (8·5)	2 (1·7)	75·9%
18 June 1970	630	**330** (46·4)	288 (43·0)	6 (7·5)	6 (3·1)	72·0%
28 Feb 1974	635	297 (38·2)	**301** (37·2)	14 (19·3)	23 (5·3)	78·8%
10 Oct 1974	635	277 (35·8)	**319** (39·3)	13 (18·3)	26 (6·6)	72·8%
3 May 1979	635	**339** (43·9)	268 (36·9)	11 (13·8)	17 (5·4)	75·9%
9 June 1983	650	**397** (42.4)	209 (27·6)	17 (25·4) (Alliance)	21 (4·6)	72·7%
11 June 1987	650	**375** (42·3)	229 (30·8)	17 (12·8) (Lib. Dem)	24 (3·4)	75·4%
9 April 1992	651	**336** (41·9)	271 (34·4)	20 (17·8) (Lib. Dem)	24 (5·8)	78%

PRIME MINISTERS OF GREAT BRITAIN AND OF THE UK

The biographical detail for each of 52 prime ministers of Great Britain and the United Kingdom includes: final style as prime minister (with earlier or later styles); dates of birth and death; party affiliation and date or dates as prime minister; and membership of Parliament with the constituency and dates.

1.The Rt Hon., Sir Robert **WALPOLE**, KG (1726), 1st Earl of Orford (of the 2nd creation); b. 1676, d. 1745; Whig; ministries 3 Apr 1721–8 Feb 1742, (Walpole's absolute control of the Cabinet can only be said to have dated from 15 May 1730); MP (Whig) for Castle Rising (1701–2); King's Lynn (1702–42) (expelled from the House for a short period 1712–13).

2. The Rt Hon., the Hon. Sir Spencer Compton, 1st and last Earl of **WILMINGTON,** KG (1733), KB (1725, resigned 1733), (PC 1716), cr. Baron Wilmington 1728; cr. Earl 1730; b. 1673, d. 1743; Whig; ministry 16 Feb 1742–2 Jul 1743; MP for Eye (1698–1710; originally Tory until about 1704); East Grinstead (1713–15); Sussex (Whig) (1715–28); Speaker 1715–27.

3. The Rt Hon., the Hon. Henry **PELHAM**, (PC 1725); b. c. 1695, d. in office; Whig; ministry 27 Aug 1743–6 Mar 1754 (with an interval 10–12 Feb 1746); MP Seaford (1717–22); Sussex (1722–54).

4. The Rt Hon. Sir William Pulteney, 1st and last Earl of **BATH**, (cr. 1742) PC (1716) (struck off 1731); b. 1684, d. 1764; Whig; kissed hands 10 Feb 1746, resigned 12 Feb (unable to form a ministry); MP Hedon (or Heydon) 1705–34; Middlesex 1734–42.

5. His Grace the 1st Duke of **NEWCASTLE** upon Tyne and 1st Duke of Newcastle-under-Lyme (The Rt Hon., the Hon. Sir Thomas Pelham-Holles), Bt, KG (1718), (PC 1717); known as Lord Pelham of Laughton (1711–14); Earl of Claire (1714–15); cr. Duke of Newcastle upon Tyne 1715 and cr. Duke of Newcastle-under-Lyme 1756; b. 1698, d. 1768; ministries (a) 16 Mar 1754–26 Oct 1756, (b) 2 Jul 1757–25 Oct 1760, (c) 25 Oct 1760–25 May 1762.

6. His Grace the 4th Duke of **DEVONSHIRE**, (Sir William Cavendish), KG (1756), (PC 1751, but struck off roll 1762); known as Lord Cavendish of Hardwick until 1729 and Marquess of Hartington until 1755; b. 1720, d. 1764; Whig; ministry 16 Nov 1756–May 1757; MP (Whig) for Derbyshire (1741-51). Summoned to Lords (1751).

7. The Rt Hon. James **WALDEGRAVE**, 2nd Earl of Waldegrave from 1741, PC (1752), KG (1757); b. 1715, d. 1763; Tory; ministry, kissed hands 8 Jun 1757, resigned 12 Jun (unable to form a ministry); took seat in House of Lords in 1741.

8. The 3rd Earl of **BUTE**, (The Rt Hon., the Hon. Sir John Stuart, KG (1762), KT (1738, resigned 1762), (PC 1760)); until 1723 was The Hon. John Stuart; b. 1713, d. 1792; Tory; ministry 26 May 1762–8 Apr 1763.

9. The Rt Hon., the Hon. George **GRENVILLE**, (PC 1754); prior to 1749 was G. Grenville Esq; b. 1712, d. 1770; Whig; ministry 16 Apr 1763–10 Jul 1765; MP for Buckingham (1741–70).

10. The Most Hon. The 2nd Marquess of **ROCKINGHAM** (The Rt Hon. Lord Charles Watson-Wentworth), KG (1760), (PC 1765); known as Hon. Charles Watson-Wentworth until 1739; Viscount Higham (1739–46); Earl of Malton (1746–50); succeeded to Marquessate 1750; b. 1730, d. in office; Whig; ministries (a) 13 Jul 1765–Jul 1766, (b) 27 Mar–1 Jul 1782 (died in office). Took his seat in House of Lords 21 May 1751.

11. The 1st Earl of **CHATHAM**, (The Rt Hon. William Pitt (PC 1746); cr. Earl 4 Aug 1766; b. 1708, d. 1788; Whig; ministry 30 Jul 1766–14 Oct 1768 (his health in 1767 prevented his being PM in other than name); MP (Whig) Old Sarum (1735–47); Seaford (1747–54); Aldborough (1754–6); Okehampton (1756–7) (also Buckingham (1756), Bath (1757–66)).

12. His Grace the 3rd Duke of **GRAFTON**, (The Rt Hon. Sir Augustus Henry FitzRoy) KG (1769), (PC 1765); prior to 1747 known as the Hon. Augustus H. FitzRoy; 1747–57 as Earl of Euston; succeeded to dukedom in 1757; b. 1735, d. 1811; Whig; ministry 14 Oct 1768–28 Jan 1770 (he was virtually PM in 1767 when Lord Chatham's ministry broke down); MP (Whig) Bury St Edmunds (1756–7).

13. Lord **NORTH,** (The Rt Hon., the Hon. Sir Frederick North), KG (1772), (PC 1766); succ. (1790) as 2nd Earl of Guildford; b. 1732, d. 1792; Tory; ministry 28 Jan 1770–20 Mar 1782; MP (Tory) for Banbury (1754–90) (can be regarded as a Whig from 1783). Took his seat in the House of Lords 25 Nov 1790.

14. The 2nd Earl of **SHELBURNE**, (Rt Hon., the Hon. Sir William Petty, KG (1782) (PC 1763); formerly, until 1751, William Fitz-Maurice; Viscount Fitz-Maurice (1753–61); succeeded to Earldom 1761; cr. the 1st Marquess of Lansdowne (1784); b. 1737, d. 1805; Whig; ministry 4 Jul 1782–24 Feb 1783; MP Chipping Wycombe (1760–1). Took seat in House of Lords (as Baron Wycombe) 3 Nov 1761.

15. His Grace the 3rd Duke of **PORTLAND**, The Most Noble Sir William Henry Cavendish Bentinck, KG (1794) (PC 1765); assumed additional name of Bentinck in 1775; Marquess of Titchfield from birth until he succeeded to the dukedom 1762; b. 1738, d. 1809; Tory; ministries (a) 2 Apr–Dec 1783 (coalition), (b) 31 Mar 1807–Oct 1809 (Tory); MP (Whig) Weobley, Herefordshire (1761–2).

16. The Rt Hon., the Hon. William **PITT**, (PC 1782) prior to 1766 was William Pitt, Esq.; b. 1759, d. in office; Tory; ministry (a) 19 Dec 1783–14 Mar 1801, (b) 10 May 1804–23 Jan 1806 (died in office); MP (Tory) Appleby 1781–1806.

17. The Rt Hon. Henry **ADDINGTON** (PC 1789); cr. 1st Viscount Sidmouth 1805; b. 1757, d. 1844; Tory; ministry 17 Mar 1801–30 Apr 1804; MP Devizes (1783–1805). Speaker 1789–1801. As a peer he supported the Whigs in 1807 and 1812 administration.

18. The Rt Hon. the 1st Baron **GRENVILLE** of Wotton-under-Bernewood (William Wyndham Grenville (PC(I) 1782; PC 1783)); cr. Baron 1790; b. 1759, d. 1834; Whig; ministry 10 Feb 1806–Mar 1807; MP Buckingham (1782–4), Buckinghamshire (1784–90). Speaker Jan–Jun 1789.

19. The Rt Hon., the Hon. Spencer **PERCEVAL** (PC 1807), KC (1796); b. 1762, d. in office; Tory; ministry 4 Oct 1809–11 May 1812 (murdered in the lobby of the House); MP (Tory) Northampton (1796–7).

20. The Rt Hon. the 2nd Earl of **LIVERPOOL**, (Sir Robert Banks Jenkinson, KG (1814) (PC 1799)); R.B. Jenkinson, Esq. until 1786; from 1786–96 The Hon. R. B. Jenkinson; from 1796–1808 (when he succeeded to the earldom) Lord Hawkesbury; b. 1770, d. 1828; Tory; ministries (a) 8 Jun 1812–29 Jan 1820, (b) 29 Jan 1820–17 Feb 1827; summoned to House of Lords 1803; elected MP (Tory) for Appleby in 1790 but did not sit as he was under age; Rye (1796–1803).

21. The Rt Hon. George **CANNING** (PC 1800); b. 1770, d. in office; Tory; ministry 10 Apr–8 Aug 1827 (d. in office); MP (Tory) Newtown, IOW. (1793–6), Wendover (1796–1802), Tralee (1802–6), Newton (1806–7), Hastings (1807–12), Liverpool (1812–23), Harwich (1823–6), Newport (1826–7), and Seaford (1827).

22. The Viscount **GODERICH**, (Rt Hon., the Hon. Frederick John Robinson (PC 1812, PC (I) c. 1833); cr. Earl of Ripon 1833; b. 1782, d. 1859; Tory; ministry 31 Aug 1827–8 Jan 28; MP Carlow (1806–7); Ripon (1807–27).

23. His Grace The 1st Duke of **WELLINGTON**, (The Most Noble, The Hon. Sir Arthur Wellesley, KG (1813), GCB (1815), GCH (1816), (PC 1807, PC (I) 1807)); known as The Hon. Arthur Wesley until 1804; then as The Hon. Sir Arthur Wellesley, KB, until 1809 when cr. the Viscount Wellington; cr. Earl of Wellington February 1812;

Marquess of Wellington October 1812 and Duke May 1814; Field Marshal (1813); b. 1769, d. 1852; Tory; ministries (a) 22 Jan 1828–26 Jun 30, (b) 26 Jun–21 Nov 1830, (c) 17 Nov–9 Dec 1834; MP Rye (1806); St Michael (1807); Newport, IOW (1807–9). Took seat in House of Lords 1814.

24. The 2nd Earl **GREY,** (The Rt Hon., the Hon. Sir Charles Grey, Bt (1808), KG (1831), (PC 1806)); styled Viscount Howick 1806–7 and previously The Hon. Charles Grey; b. 1764, d. 1845; Whig; ministry 22 Nov 1830–Jul 1834; MP (Whig) Northumberland (17Ë86–1807); Appleby (1807); Tavistock (1807).

25. The 3rd Viscount **MELBOURNE**, (The Rt Hon., The Hon. Sir William Lamb, Bt (PC (UK & I) 1827)); b. 1779, d. 1848; Whig; ministries (a) 17 Jul–Nov 1834, (b) 18 Apr 1835–20 Jun 1837, (c) 20 Jun 1837–Aug 1841; MP (Whig) Leominster (1806); Haddington Burgh (1806–7); Portarlington (1807–12); Peterborough (1816–19); Hertfordshire (1819–26); Newport, IOW (1827); Bletchingley (1827–28). Took his seat in House of Lords 1 Feb 1829.

26. The Rt Hon. Sir Robert **PEEL,** Bt (PC 1812); until 1830 he was Robert Peel, Esq., MP, when he succeeded as 2nd Baronet; b. 1788, d. 1850; Conservative; ministries (a) 10 Dec 1834–8 Apr 1835, (b) 30 Aug 1841–29 Jun 1846; MP (Tory) Cashel (Tipperary) (1809–12); Chippenham (1812–17); Univ. of Oxford (1817–29); Westbury (1829–30); Tamworth (1830–50).

27.The Rt Hon. Lord John **RUSSELL** (PC 1830), and after 30 July 1861 1st Earl Russell, KG (1862), GCMG (1869); b. 1792, d. 1878; Liberal; ministries (a) 30 Jun 1846–Feb 1852 (Whig), (b) 29 Oct 1865–Jun 1866 (Liberal); MP (Whig) Tavistock (1813–17, 1818–20 and 1830–1); Hunts (1820–6); Bandon (1826–30); Devon (1831–2); S. Devon (1832–5); Stroud (1835–41); City of London (1841–61). Took seat in the House of Lords on 30 July 1861.

28.The 14th Earl of **DERBY,** Rt Hon. Sir Edward Geoffrey Smith-Stanley, Bt, KG (1859), GCMG (1869), PC 1830, PC (I) (1831); until 1834 known as the Hon. E. G. Stanley, MP; 1834–44 known as Lord Stanley MP; b. 1799, d. 1869; Tory; ministries (a) 23 Feb–18 Dec 1852, (b) 20 Feb 1858–11 Jun 1859, (c) 28 Jun 1866–26 Feb 1868; MP (Whig) Stockbridge (1822–6); Preston (1826–30); Windsor (1831–2); North Lancs (1832–44). Summoned 1844 to House of Lords as Lord Stanley (of Bickerstaffe); succeeded to Earldom 1851; became a Tory in 1835.

29.The Rt Hon. Sir George Hamilton Gordon, Bt, 4th Earl of **ABERDEEN**, KG (1855), KT (1808), (PC 1814); until 1791 known as the Hon. G. Gordon; known as Lord Haddo 1791–1801; assumed additional name of Hamilton November 1818; b. 1784, d. 1860; Peelite; ministry 19 Dec 1852–5 Feb 1855. Took seat in House of Lords 1814.

30.The Rt Hon. Sir Henry John Temple, 3rd and last Viscount **PALMERSTON** (a non-representative peer of Ireland), KG (1856), CGB (1832), (PC 1809); known as the Hon. H. J. Temple 1784–1802; b. 1784, d. 1865; Liberal; ministries (a) 6 Feb 1855–19 Feb 1858, (b) 12 Jun 1859–18 Oct 1865; MP (Tory) Newport, IoW (1807–11); Cambridge Univ. (1811–31); Bletchingley (1831–2); S. Hampshire (1832–4); Tiverton (1835–65); from 1829 a Whig and latterly a Liberal.

31.The Rt Hon. Benjamin **DISRAELI,** 1st and last Earl of Beaconsfield, KG (1878), (PC 1852); prior to 12 Aug 1876 Benjamin Disraeli; b. 1804, d. 1881; Conservative; ministries (a) 27 Feb–Nov 1868, (b) 20 Feb 1874–Apr 1880; MP (Con.) Maidstone (1837–41); Shrewsbury (1841–7); Buckinghamshire (1847–76), when he became a peer.

32.The Rt Hon. William Ewart **GLADSTONE** (PC 1841); b. 1809, d. 1898; Liberal; ministries (a) 3 Dec 1868–Feb 1874, (b) 23 Apr 1880–12 Jun 1885, (c) 1 Feb–20 Jul 1886, (d) 15 Aug 1892–3 Mar 1894; MP Tory, Newark (1832–45); Univ. of Oxford (1847–65) (Peelite to 1859, thereafter a Liberal); S. Lancashire (1865–8); Greenwich (1868–80); Midlothian (1880–95).

33. The Rt Hon. Robert Arthur Talbot Gascoyne-Cecil, the 3rd Marquess of **SALISBURY**, KG (1878), GCVO (1902), (PC 1866); known as Lord Robert Cecil till 1865; and as Viscount Cranbourne, MP, 1865–68; b. 1830, d. 1903; Conservative; ministries (a) 23 Jun 1885–28 Jan 1886, (b) 25 Jul 1886–Aug 1892, (c) 25 Jun 1895–22 Jan 1901, (d) 23 Jan 1901–11 Jul 1902; MP (Con.) for Stamford (1853–68).

34. The Rt Hon. Sir Archibald Philip Primrose, Bt, 5th Earl of **ROSEBERY**, KG (1892), KT (1895), VD (PC 1881); b. the Hon. A. P. Primrose; known as Lord Dalmeny 1851–68; Earl of Midlothian from 1911 although he did not adopt the style; b. 1847, d. 1929; Liberal; ministry 5 Mar 1894–21 Jun 1895.

35. The Rt Hon. Arthur James **BALFOUR** (PC 1885, PC (I) 1887); KG (1922), later (1922) the 1st Earl of Balfour, OM (1916); b. 1848, d. 1930; Conservative; ministry 12 Jul 1902–4 Dec 1905; MP (Con.) Hertford (1874–85); E. Manchester (1885–1906); City of London (1906–22).

36. The Rt Hon. Sir Henry **CAMPBELL-BANNERMAN,** GCB (1895), (PC 1884); known as Henry Campbell until 1872; b. 1836, d. 1908; Liberal; ministry 5 Dec 1905–5 Apr 1908; MP (Lib.) Stirling District (1868–1908).

37. The Rt Hon. Herbert Henry **ASQUITH** (PC 1892, PC (I) 1916); later (1925) 1st Earl of Oxford and Asquith, KG (1925); b. 1852, d. 1928; Liberal; ministries (a) 7 Apr 1908–7 May 1910, (b) 8 May 1910–5 Dec 16 (coalition from 25 May 1915); MP (Lib.) East Fife (1886–1918); Paisley (1920–4).

38. The Rt Hon. David **LLOYD GEORGE**, OM (1919), (PC 1905); later (1945) 1st Earl Lloyd-George of Dwyfor; b. 1863, d. 1945; Liberal; ministry 7 Dec 1916–19 Oct 1922 (Coalition); MP Caernarvon Boroughs (1890–1945) (Lib. 1890–1931 and 1935–45; Ind. Lib. 1931– 5).

39. The Rt Hon. (Andrew) Bonar **LAW** (PC 1911); b. 1858 (in Canada), d. 1923; Conservative; ministry 23 Oct 1922–20 May 1923; MP Bootle Div. of Lancashire (1911–18); Central Div. of Glasgow (1918–23).

40. The Rt Hon. Stanley **BALDWIN** (PC 1920, PC (Can.) 1927); later (1937) 1st Earl Baldwin of Bewdley, KG (1937); b. 1867, d. 1947; Conservative; ministries (a) 22 May 1923–22 Jan 1924 (Conservative), (b) 4 Nov 1924–4 Jun 1929 (Conservative), (c) 7 Jun 1935–20 Jan 1936 (Nat. Government), (d) 21 Jan–11 Dec 1936 (Nat. Government), (e) 12 Dec 1936–28 May 1937 (Nat. Government); MP (Con.) Bewdley Div. of Worcestershire (1908–37).

41. The Rt Hon. (James) Ramsay **MACDONALD** (PC 1924, PC (Can.) (1929); b. 1866, d. 1937; Labour; ministries (a) 22 Jan–4 Nov 1924, (b) 5 Jun 1929–7 Jun 1935 (from 1931 National Coalition); MP (Lab.) Leicester (1906–18); (Lab.) Aberavon (1922–9); (Lab.) Seaham Div. Co. Durham (1929–31); (Nat. Lab.) (1931–5); MP for Scottish Univs. (1936–7).

42. The Rt Hon. (Arthur) Neville **CHAMBERLAIN** (PC 1922); b. 1869, d. 1940; Conservative; ministry 28 May 1937–10 May 1940 (National Government); MP (Con.) Ladywood Div. of Birmingham (1918–29); Edgbaston Div. of Birmingham (1929–40).

43. The Rt Hon. Sir Winston (Leonard Spencer) **CHURCHILL**, KG (1953), OM (1946), CH (1922), TD (PC 1907); b. 1874, d. 1965; Conservative; ministries (a) 10 May 1940–26 Jul 1945 (Coalition but from 23 May 1945 Con.), (b) 26 Oct 1951–6 Feb 1952 (Con.), (c) 7 Feb 1952–5 Apr 1955 (Con.); MP (Con. until 1904, then Lib.) Oldham (1900–6); (Lib.) N.-W. Manchester (1906–8); Dundee (1908–18 as Lib. until 1922 as Coalition Lib.); Epping Div. of Essex (1924–45); Woodford Div. of Essex (1945–64).

44. The Rt Hon. Clement (Richard) **ATTLEE** CH (1945), (PC 1935); cr. 1955 1st Earl Attlee, KG (1956), OM (1951); b. 1883, d. 1967; Labour; ministry 26 Jul 1945–26 Oct 1951; MP Limehouse Div. of Stepney (1922–50); West Walthamstow (1950–5).

45. The Rt Hon. Sir (Robert) Anthony **EDEN,** KG (1954), MC (1917), (PC 1934); cr. 1961 1st Earl of Avon; b. 1897, d. 1977; Conservative; ministry 6 Apr 1955–9 Jan 1957; MP Warwick and Leamington (1923–57).

46. The Rt Hon. (Maurice) Harold **MACMILLAN**, OM (1976) (PC 1942); cr. 1984 1st Earl of Stockton; b. 1894, d. 1986; Conservative; ministry 10 Jan 1957–18 Oct 1963; MP Stockton-on-Tees (1924–9 and 1931–45); Bromley (1945–64).

47. The Rt Hon. Sir Alexander (Frederick) **DOUGLAS-HOME,** KT (1962) (PC 1951); known until 1918 as the Hon. A. F. Douglas-Home; thence until 11 July 1951 as Lord Dunglas; thence until his disclaimer of 23 Oct 1963 as the (14th) Earl of Home, Lord Home of the Hirsel; cr. 1974 Baron Home of the Hirsel (Life Peer); b. 1903; Conservative; ministry 19 Oct 1963–16 Oct 1964; MP South Lanark (1931–45); Lanark (1950–1); Kinross and West Perthshire (1963–74).

48. The Rt Hon. Sir (James) Harold **WILSON**, KG (1976), OBE (civ.) (1945), (PC 1947); cr. 1983 Baron Wilson of Rievaulx (Life Peer); b. 1916, d. 1995; Labour; ministries (a) 16 Oct 1964–30 Mar 1966, (b) 31 Mar 1966–17 Jun 1970, (c) 4 Mar–10 Oct 1974, (d) 10 Oct 1974–5 Apr 1976; Labour; MP Ormskirk (1945–50); Huyton (1950–83).

49. The Rt Hon. Sir Edward (Richard George) **HEATH,** KG (1992), MBE (mil.) (1946), (PC 1955); b. 1916; Conservative; ministry 18 Jun 1970–3 Mar 1974; MP Bexley (1950–74); Old Bexley-Sidcup (1974–).

50. The Rt Hon. Sir (Leonard) James **CALLAGHAN** KG (1987), (PC 1964); cr. 1987 Baron Callaghan of Cardiff (Life Peer); b. 1912; Labour; ministry 5 Apr 1976–4 May 1979; MP South Cardiff (1945–50); Southeast Cardiff (1950–83), Cardiff South and Penarth (1983–87).

51. The Rt Hon. Mrs Margaret (Hilda) **THATCHER** OM nee Roberts (from Nov 1990 Lady Thatcher although she did not use the style), cr. 1992 Baroness Thatcher of Kesteven (Life Peeress) (PC 1970); b. 1925; Conservative; ministries (a) 4 May 1979–9 Jun 83, (b) 10 Jun 1983–4 May 1987, (c) 12 Jun 1987–28 Nov 90; MP Finchley (1959–74); Barnet, Finchley (1974–92).

52. The Rt Hon. John **MAJOR** (PC 1987); b. 1943; Conservative; ministries (a) 28 Nov 1990–9 Apr 1992, (b) 11 Apr 1992-to date; MP for Huntingdon (1983–).

PARTY LEADERS (since 1955)

Conservative Party
1955–57 Sir Anthony Eden
1957–63 Harold Macmillan
1963–65 Sir Alexander Douglas-Hume
1965–75 Edward Heath
1975–90 Margaret Thatcher
1990– John Major

Labour Party
1955–63 Hugh Gaitskell
1963–76 Harold Wilson
1976–80 James Callaghan
1980–83 Michael Foot
1983–92 Neil Kinnock
1992–94 John Smith
1994– Tony Blair

Liberal Party (from 1988 **Liberal Democrats**)
1956–67 Joe Grimond
1967–76 Jeremy Thorpe
1976–88 David Steel
1988– J.J.D. (Paddy) Ashdown

The Royal Family

KINGS OF ALL ENGLAND

Athelstan eldest son of the eldest son of King Alfred of the West Saxons, acceded 924 or 925. The first to establish rule over all England (excluding Cumbria) in 927; d. 27 Oct 939 aged over 40 years.

Edmund younger half-brother of Athelstan; acceded 939 but did not regain control of all England until 944–45. Murdered 26 May 946 by Leofa at Pucklechurch, near Bristol (Glos).

Edred younger brother of Edmund; acceded May 946. Effectively king of all England 946–48, and from 954 to his death on 23 Nov 955. Also intermittently during the intervening period.

Edwy son of Edmund, b. c. 941; acceded November 955 (crowned at Kingston, Greater London); lost control of the Mercians and Northumbrians in 957; d. 1 Oct 959, aged about 18.

Edgar son of Edmund, b. 943; acceded October 959 as king of all England (crowned at Bath, 11 May 973); d. 8 July 975, aged c. 32.

Edward the Martyr son of Edgar by Aethelflaed, b. c. 962; acceded 975; d. 18 Mar 978 or 979, aged 16 or 17.

Ethelred the Unready (unraed, i.e. ill-counselled), second son of Edgar by Aelfthryth, b. ?968–69; acceded 978 or 979 (crowned at Kingston, 14 Apr 978 or 4 May 979); dispossessed by the Danish king, Swegn Forkbeard, 1013–14; d. 23 Apr 1016, aged c. 47 or 48.

Swegn (Forkbeard), king of Denmark 987–1014, acknowledged as king of all England from about September 1013 to his death on 3 Feb 1014.

Edmund Ironside probably the third son of Ethelred, b. c. 992; chosen as king in London, April 1016. In the summer of 1016 he made an agreement with Cnut whereby he retained dominion only over Wessex; d. 30 Nov 1016.

Cnut younger son of King Swegn Forkbeard of Denmark, b. c. 995. Secured Mercia and Danelaw in the summer 1016; assumed dominion over all England December 1016; king of Denmark 1019–35; king of Norway 1028–1035; overlord of the king of the Scots and probably ruler of the Norse-Irish kingdom of Dublin; d. 12 Nov 1035, aged c. 40 years.

Harold Harefoot natural son of Cnut by Aelfgifu of Northampton, b. ?c. 1016–17; chosen as regent for his half-brother, Harthacnut, late 1035 or early 1036; sole King 1037; d. 17 Mar 1040, aged c. 23 or 24 years.

Harthacnut son of Cnut by Emma, widow of King Ethelred (d. 1016) b. ?c. 1018; titular king of Denmark from 1028; effectively king of England from June 1040; d. 8 June 1042, aged c. 24 years.

Edward the Confessor elder half-brother of Harthacnut and son of King Ethelred and Emma, b. 1002–5; acceded 1042; crowned 3 Apr 1043; d. 5 Jan 1066, aged between 60 and 64. Declared a saint by the Church.

Harold Godwinson brother-in-law of Edward the Confessor and brother of his Queen Edith, son of Godwin, Earl of Wessex, b. ?c. 1020; acceded 6 Jan 1066; killed 14 Oct 1066.

Edgar Etheling grandson of Edmund Ironside; chosen by Londoners as king after the Battle of Hastings, October 1066, but apparently not crowned; he submitted to William I before 25 Dec 1066; believed to be still living c. 1125.

KINGS AND QUEENS OF ENGLAND, OF GREAT BRITAIN (after 1707) AND OF THE UNITED KINGDOM (after 1801)

William I (the Conqueror) illegitimate son of Robert I, 6th Duke of Normandy, and Herleva, d. of Fulbert the Tanner; m. 1050 or 1051 Matilda (d. 1083), dau of Baldwin V, Count of Flanders, issue 4s 5d; b. 1027/28; acceded 25 Dec 1066; d. 9 Sept 1087, aged 59 or 60, of an abdominal injury from his saddle pommel. He succeeded by right of conquest by winning the Battle of Hastings 1066.

William II third son of William I; b. between 1056 and 1060; unm.; acceded 26 Sept 1087; d. 2 Aug 1100 (according to tradition) of impalement by a stray arrow while hunting, aged 40–44.

Henry I fourth son of William I; b. 1068; m. (1) 1100 Eadgyth (known as Matilda; d. 1118), dau of Malcolm III, King of Scots, issue 1s 1d and a child who d. young; m. (2) 1121 Adela (d. 1151), dau of Godfrey VII, Count of Louvain, no issue; acceded 5 Aug 1100; d. 1 Dec 1135 aged 67.

Stephen third son of Stephen (sometimes called Henry), Count of Blois, and Adela, dau of William I; b. between 1096 and 1100; m. 1125 Matilda (d. 1151), dau of Eustace II, Count of Boulogne, issue 3s 2d; acceded 22 Dec 1135; d. 25 Oct 1154 aged 54–58. He usurped the throne from Henry's only surviving legitimate child, Matilda, who reigned in 1141.

Matilda only surviving legitimate child of Henry I; b. Feb 1102; m. (1) 1114 Henry V, Holy Roman Emperor (b. 1086; d. 1125), no issue; m. (2) 1130 Geoffrey V, Count of Anjou (b. 1113; d. 1151), issue 3s; reigned April–November 1141; d. 10 Sept 1167 aged 65.

Henry II eldest son of Geoffrey V, Count of Anjou (surnamed Plantagenet), and Matilda (see above); b. 5 Mar 1133; m. 1152 Eleanor (b. c.1122; d. 1204), dau of William X, Duke of Aquitaine, issue 5s 3d; acceded 19 Dec 1154; d. 6 July 1189 aged 56.

Richard I (the Lionheart) third son of Henry II; b. 8 Sept 1157; m. 1191 Berengaria (d. after 1230), dau of Sancho VI, King of Navarre, no issue; acceded 3 Sept 1189; d. 6 Apr 1199 from a mortal arrow wound, aged 41.

John fifth son of Henry II; b. 24 Dec 1167; m. (1) 1189 Isabel (also known as Avisa; d. 1217), dau of William, Earl of Gloucester, dissolved, no issue; m. (2) 1200 Isabella (d. 1246), dau of Aimir, Count of Angouleme, issue 2s 3d; acceded 27 May 1199; d. 18–19 Oct 1216 aged 48. John usurped the throne from his nephew, Arthur, the only son of Geoffrey, Duke of Brittany (second son of Henry II), and from his niece, Eleanor.

Henry III elder son of John and Isabella; b. 1 Oct 1207; m. 1236 Eleanor (d. 1291), dau of Raymond Berengar IV, Count of Provence, issue 2s 3d and at least 4 other children who d. in infancy; acceded 28 Oct 1216; d. 16 Nov 1272, aged 65.

Edward I eldest surviving son of Henry III; b. 17/18 June 1239; m. (1) 1254 Eleanor (d. 1290), dau of Ferdinand III, King of Castile, issue 4s 7d; m (2) 1299 Margaret (b. 1282; d. 1317), dau of Philip III, King of France, issue 2s 1d; acceded 20 Nov 1272; d. 7 July 1307, aged 68.

Edward II fourth and only surviving son of Edward I and Eleanor; b. 25 Apr 1284; m. 1308 Isabella (b. 1292; d. 1358), dau of Philip IV, King of France, issue 2s 2d; acceded 8 July 1307 (deposed 20 Jan 1327); murdered 21 Sept 1327, aged 43 (traditionally by disembowelling with red-hot iron). Edward II was deposed by Parliament, having been imprisoned on 16 Nov 1326).

Edward III elder son of Edward II; b. 13 Nov 1312; m. 1328 Philippa (b. c1314; d. 1369), dau of William I, Count of Holland; acceded 25 Jan 1327; d. 21 June 1377, aged 64.

Richard II eldest surviving son of Edward, the Black Prince (eldest son of Edward III); b. 6 Jan 1367; m. (1) 1382 Anne (b. 1366; d. 1394), dau of Charles IV, Holy Roman Emperor, no issue; m. (2) 1396 Isabelle (b. 1389; d. 1409), dau of Charles VI, King of France, no issue; acceded 22 June 1377 (deposed 30 Sept 1399); d. 14 Feb 1400, possibly murdered, aged 33. Richard's throne was usurped by Henry, Duke of Lancaster (later Henry IV), who had him imprisoned from 19 Aug 1399 until his death.

Henry IV eldest son of John of Gaunt (4th son of Edward III), and Blanche (great-great-grand-dau of Henry III); b. probably April 1366; m. (1) c.1380/81 Lady Mary de Bohun (b. c.1368/70; d. 1394), dau of Humphrey, Earl of Hereford, issue 5s 2d; m. (2) 1403 Joan (b. c.1370; d. 1437), dau of Charles II, King of Navarre, no issue; acceded 30 Sept 1399; d. 20 Mar 1413 aged 46 (probably). He usurped the throne of Richard II.

Henry V eldest surviving son of Henry IV and Mary; b. probably 16 Sept 1387; m. 1420 Catherine (b. 1401; d. 1437), dau of Charles VI, King of France, issue 1s; acceded 21 Mar 1413; d. 31 Aug/Sept 1422 aged 34.

Henry VI only son of Henry V; b. 6 Dec 1421; m. 1445 Margaret (b. 1430; d. 1482), dau of René, Duke of Anjou, issue 1s; acceded 1 Sept 1422; deposed by his third cousin Edward IV 4 March 1461; regained the throne 6 Oct 1470–11 Apr 1471, when he was again deposed by Edward IV; murdered by stabbing 21 May 1471 at the Tower of London, aged 49.

Edward IV eldest son of Richard, 3rd Duke of York (who was descended from two sons of Edward III); b. 28 Apr 1442; m. 1464 Elizabeth (b. c.1437; d. 1492), dau of Sir Richard Woodville, issue 3s 7d; acceded 4 Mar 1461; deposed in favour of Henry VI 6 Oct 1470; restored 11 Apr 1471; d. 9 Apr 1483 aged 40.

Edward V eldest son of Edward IV; b. 2 Nov 1470; unm.; acceded 9 Apr 1483 (deposed 25 June 1483); (traditionally) murdered, possibly in 1483 or in 1486, at the Tower of London. Edward was deposed when the throne was usurped by his uncle, Richard III (the only surviving brother of Edward IV).

Richard III only surviving brother of Edward IV (see above); b. 2 Oct 1452; m. 1472 Anne (b. 1456; d. 1485), dau of Richard Nevill, Earl of Warwick, issue 1s; acceded 26 June 1483; killed 22 Aug 1485 at the Battle of Bosworth Field, aged 32.

Henry VII only child of Edmund Tudor, 1st Earl of Richmond, and Margaret Beaufort, great-great-grand-daughter of Edward III; b. 27 Jan 1457; m. 1486 Elizabeth (b. 1466; d. 1503), dau of Edward IV, issue 3s 4d; acceded 22 Aug 1485; d. 21 Apr 1509 aged 52.

Henry VIII only surviving son of Henry VII; b. 28 June 1491; m. (1) 1509 Catherine (b. 1485; d. 1536), dau of Ferdinand II, King of Aragon and widow of Henry's elder brother Arthur, divorced, 2s 2d; m. (2) 1533 Anne (b. 1507; beheaded 1536), dau of Sir Thomas Boleyn, issue 1d; m. (3) 1536 Jane (d. 1537), dau of Sir John Seymour, issue 1s; m. (4) 1540 Anne (b. 1515; d. 1557), dau of John, Duke of Cleves, divorced, no issue; m. (5) 1540 Catherine (beheaded 1542), dau of Lord Edmund Howard, no issue; m. (6)

1543 Catherine (b. c1512; d. 1548), dau of Sir Thomas Parr, no issue; acceded 22 Apr 1509; d. 28 Jan 1547 aged 55.

Edward VI only surviving son of Henry VIII, by Jane Seymour; b. 12 Oct 1537; unm.; acceded 28 Jan 1547; d. 6 July 1553 aged 15.

Jane eldest daughter of Henry Grey, 3rd Marquess of Dorset, and Frances (dau of Mary Tudor, sister of Henry VIII); b. Oct 1537; m. 1553 Lord Guilford Dudley, son of John Dudley, Duke of Northumberland, no issue; acceded 6 July (proclaimed 10 July) 1553 (deposed 19 July); beheaded 12 Feb 1554 in the Tower of London, aged 16.

Mary I only surviving child of Henry VIII and Catherine of Aragon; b. 18 Feb 1516; m. 1554 Philip II, King of Spain (b. 1527; d. 1598), no issue; acceded 19 July 1553; d. 17 Nov 1558 aged 42. Mary's husband Philip was styled, but not crowned, king.

Elizabeth I daughter of Henry VIII and Anne Boleyn; b. 7 Sept 1533; unm.; acceded 17 Nov 1558; d. 24 Mar 1603 aged 69.

James I only son of Henry Stuart, Lord Darnley, and Mary, Queen of Scots (dau of James V of Scotland, son of Margaret Tudor, sister of Henry VIII); b. 19 June 1566; m. 1589 Anne (b. 1574; d. 1619), dau of Frederick II, King of Denmark, issue 3s 4d; acceded (to English throne) 26 Mar 1603 (to Scottish throne 24 July 1567); d. 27 Mar 1625 aged 58.

Charles I only surviving son of James I; b. 19 Nov 1600; m. 1625 Henrietta Maria (b. 1609; d. 1669), dau of Henry IV, King of France, issue 4s 5d; acceded 27 Mar 1625; beheaded 30 Jan 1649, aged 48. The kingship was *de facto* declared abolished 17 Mar 1649 with the victory of Parliamentarians in the English Civil War.

Charles II eldest surviving son of Charles I; b. 29 May 1630; m. 1662 Catherine (b. 1638; d. 1705), dau of John, Duke of Braganza, no issue; acceded 29 May 1660 (but *de jure* 30 Jan 1649); d. 6 Feb 1685 aged 54.

James II only surviving son of Charles I; b. 14 Oct 1633; m. (1) 1660 Anne (b. 1637; d. 1671), dau of Edward Hyde, issue 4s 4d; m. (2) Mary d'Este (b. 1658; d. 1718), dau of Alfonso IV, Duke of Modena, issue 2s 5d; acceded 6 Feb 1685 (his reign ended 11 Dec 1688 when he was deemed by legal fiction to have ended his reign by flight); d. 6 Sept 1701 aged 67.

William III only son of William II, Prince of Orange, and Mary (Stuart), daughter of Charles I; b. 4 Nov 1650; m. Mary II (see below); acceded 13 Feb 1689 (with Mary II); d. 8 Mar 1702 following a fracture of right collarbone, aged 51.

Mary II elder surviving dau of James II and Anne Hyde; b. 30 Apr 1662; m. 1677 William III (see above), no issue; acceded 13 Feb 1689 (with William II); d. 28 Dec 1694 aged 32.

Anne only surviving dau of James II and Anne Hyde; b. 6 Feb 1665; m. 1683 George (b. 1653; d. 1708), son of Frederick III, King of Denmark, 2s 3d – all d. young (and 12 other confinements); acceded 8 Mar 1702; d. 1 Aug 1714 aged 49.

George I eldest son of Ernest Augustus, Duke of Brunswick-Lüneburg and Elector of Hanover, and Princess Sophia, 5th and youngest dau of Elizabeth, Queen of Bohemia, eldest dau of James I; b. 28 May 1660; m. 1682 Sophia (b. 1666; d. 1726), dau of George William, Duke of Lüneburg-Celle, divorced, issue 1s 1d; acceded 1 Aug 1714; d. 11 June 1727 aged 67. George succeeded in the terms of the Act of Settlement (which excluded all Roman Catholics and their spouses).

George II only son of Geroge I; b. 30 Oct 1683; m. 1705 Caroline (b. 1683; d. 1737), dau of John Frederick, Margrave of Brandenburg-Ansbach, issue 3s 5d; acceded 11 June 1727; d. 25 Oct 1760 aged 76.

George III eldest son of Frederick Lewis, Prince of Wales, and grandson of George II; b. 24 May (O.S.) 1738; m. 1761 Charlotte (b. 1744; d. 1818), dau of Charles Louis Frederick, Duke of Mecklenburg-Strelitz, issue 9s 6d; acceded 25 Oct 1760; d. 29 Jan 1820, aged 81. George III's eldest son became Regent 5 Feb 1811 owing to his insanity.

George IV eldest son of George III; b. 12 Aug 1762; m. (1) 1785 (in a ceremony not recognized under English law) Maria Fitzherbert; m. (2) 1795 Caroline (b. 1768; d. 1821), dau of Charles, Duke of Brunswick-Wolfenbüttel, issue 1d; acceded 29 Jan 1820; d. 26 June 1830 aged 67.

William IV oldest surviving son of George III; b. 21 Aug 1765; m. 1818 Adelaide (b. 1792; d. 1849), dau of George, Duke of Saxe-Meiningen, issue 2d (d. young); acceded 26 June 1830; d. 20 June 1837 aged 71.

Victoria only child of Edward, Duke of Kent and Strathearn, 4th son of George III; b. 24 May 1819; m. 1840 Albert (b. 1819; d. 1861), son of Ernest I, Duke of Saxe-Coburg-Gotha, issue 4s 5d; acceded 20 June 1837; d. 22 Jan 1901, aged 81.

Edward VII elder surviving son of Victoria; b. 9 Nov 1841; m. 1863 Alexandra (b. 1844; d. 1925), dau of Christian IX, King of Denmark, issue 3s 3d; acceded 22 Jan 1901; d. 6 May 1910 aged 68.

George V only surviving son of Edward VII; b. 3 June 1865; m. 1893 Mary (b. 1867; d. 1953), dau of Francis, Duke of Teck, issue 5s 1d; acceded 6 May 1910; d. 20 Jan 1936 aged 70.

Edward VIII eldest son of George V; b. 23 June 1894; m. 1937 Wallis Simpson (nee Warfield), no issue; acceded 20 Jan 1936 (abdicated 11 Dec 1936); d. 28 May 1972 aged 77. Edward VIII abdicated for himself and his heirs in order to marry Wallis Simpson, an American divorcee.

George VI second son of George V; b. 14 Dec 1895; m. 1923 Lady Elizabeth Bowes-Lyon (b. 1900), dau of the 14th Earl of Strathmore, issue 2d; acceded 11 Dec 1936; d. 6 Feb 1952 aged 56.

Elizabeth II elder daughter of George VI; b. 21 Apr 1926; m. 1947 Philip (b. 1921), son of Prince Andrew of Greece and Denmark, acceded 6 Feb 1952.

KINGS OF SCOTLAND

The formation of Scotland began in 843 when Kenneth I (MacAlpin), King of Dalriada (the kingdom of the Scots), became King of Caledonia (the kingdom of the Picts).

Kings of Alba

Kenneth I (MacAlpin; 843–858/9), King of Dalriada from 841.

Donald I (858/9–862/3), brother of Kenneth I.

Constantine I (862/3–877), son of Kenneth I. Killed in battle by the Danes.

Aedh (877–78), son of Kenneth I. Murdered by King Giric of Strathclyde.

Eochaid (878–89), nephew of Aedh. Deposed by Donald II.

Donald II (889–900), son of Constantine I.

Constantine II (900–42), son of Aedh. Abdicated to become Abbot of St Andrews; d. 952.

Malcolm I (942–54), son of Donald II. Murdered.

Indulf (954–62), son of Constantine II. Killed by the Vikings.

Dubh (962–966/7), son of Malcolm I. Murdered.

Culen (966/7–971), son of Indulf. Murdered.

Kings of Scots

Kenneth II (971–95), son of Malcolm I. Took the title King of Scots – Alba was from this time known as Scotland. Received Lothian from King Edgar of England.

Constantine III (995–97), son of Culen. Killed by Kenneth III.

Kenneth III (997–1005), son of Dubh. Killed by Malcolm II.

Malcolm II (1005–34), b. c. 954; d. 25 Nov 1034, aged c. 80 years. Consolidated the kingdom of Scotland by annexing Strathclyde, c. 1016.

Duncan I (1034–40), son of Malcolm II's daughter, Bethoc.

Macbeth (1040–57), probably son of Malcolm II's daughter, Donada; d. aged c. 52 years.

Lulach (1057–8), stepson of Macbeth; d. aged c. 26.

Malcolm III (Canmore; 1058–93), son of Duncan I; d. aged c. 62.

Donald Bane (1093–4 and 1094–7), son of Duncan I, twice deposed.

Duncan II (May–Oct 1094), son of Malcolm III; d. aged c. 34.

Edgar (1097–1107), son of Malcolm III, half-brother of Duncan II; d. aged c. 33.

Alexander I (1107–24), son of Malcolm III and brother of Edgar; d. aged c. 47.

David I (1124–53), son of Malcolm III and brother of Edgar; d. aged c. 68.

Malcolm IV (1153–65), son of Henry, Earl of Northumberland, and grandson of David I; d. aged c. 24.

William I (the Lion; 1165–1214), brother of Malcolm IV; d. aged c.72 (from 1174 to 1189 the king of England was acknowledged as overlord of Scotland).

Alexander II (1214–49), son of William I; d. aged 48.

Alexander III (1249–86), son of Alexander II; d. aged 44.

Margaret (Maid of Norway; 1286–90), dau of Margaret (dau of Alexander III) by King Eric II of Norway. Queen Margaret never visited her realm; d. aged 7.

First Interregnum 1290–2.

John (Balliol; 1292–96), son of Dervorguilla, a great-great-granddau of David I. He was awarded the throne from 13 contestants by the adjudication of King Edward I of England. He was overthrown by an English invasion and abdicated; d. in 1313 aged 63.

Second Interregnum 1296–1306.

Robert I (the Bruce; 1306–29), grandson of Robert de Bruce (one of the 13 claimants to the Scottish throne in 1291) and a descendant of David I; d. aged c. 55.

David II (1329–71; deposed September–December 1332 and not in effective control of most of Scotland 1333–56), son of Robert I; d. aged 46.

Edward (1332 and 1333–56), son of John; he acknowledged Edward III of England as his overlord in 1333 and surrendered all claims to the Scottish crown to him in 1356; d. 1364 aged over 60.

Robert II (1371–90), founder of the Stewart dynasty, son of Walter the Steward and Marjorie Bruce (dau of Robert I); d. aged 74.

Robert III (1390–1406), legitimated natural son of Robert II; d. aged c. 69.

James I (1406–37), son of Robert III, captured by the English 13 days before his accession and kept prisoner in England till March 1424; d. aged 42.

James II (1437–60), son of James I; d. aged 29.

James III (1460–88), son of James II; d. aged 36.

James IV (1488–1513), son of James III and Margaret of Denmark, married Margaret Tudor; d. aged 40.

James V (1513–42), son of James IV and Margaret Tudor; d. aged 30.

Mary (Queen of Scots; 1542–67), daughter of James V and Mary of Lorraine, acceded aged 6 or 7 days, abdicated 24 July 1567 and was succeeded by her son, James VI (by her second husband, Henry Stuart, Lord Darnley). She was executed 8 Feb 1587, aged 44.

James VI (1567–1625), son of Mary and Lord Darnley (see above), succeeded to the English throne as James I on 24 Mar 1603, so effecting a personal union of the two realms; d. aged 58.

THE ORDER OF SUCCESSION

1 HRH The Prince CHARLES, The Prince of Wales, b. 14 Nov 1948. (He m. 29 Jul 1981 (separated 1992), Lady DIANA Spencer – HRH The Princess of Wales – who was b. 1 Jul 1961.) **2 HRH Prince WILLIAM** of Wales, b. 21 June 1982 – elder son of The Prince Charles. **3 HRH Prince HENRY of Wales**, b. 15 Sept 1984 – younger son of The Prince Charles. **4 HRH The Prince ANDREW**, The Duke of York, b. 19 Feb 1960 – second son of HM Queen Elizabeth II. (He m. 23 Jul 1986 (separated 1992), Miss SARAH Ferguson – HRH The Duchess of York – who was b. 15 Oct 1959.) **5 HRH Princess BEATRICE of York**, b. 8 Aug 1988 – elder dau of The Prince Andrew. **6 HRH Princess EUGENIE of York**, b. 23 Mar 1990 – younger dau of The Prince Andrew. **7 HRH The Prince EDWARD**, b. 10 Mar 1964 – youngest son of HM Queen Elizabeth II. **8 HRH The Princess ANNE**, The Princess Royal, b. 15 Aug 1950 – only dau of HM Queen Elizabeth II. (She m. (1) 14 Nov 1973 Captain MARK Phillips, divorced 1992; m. (2) 12 Dec 1992 Commander Timothy Laurence.) **9 PETER Phillips**, b. 15 Nov 1977 – son of The Princess Anne. **10 ZARA Phillips**, b. 15 May 1981 – dau of The Princess Anne. **11 HRH The Princess MARGARET**, The Countess of Snowdon, b. 21 Aug 1930 – younger dau of HM King George VI. (She m. 6 May 1960 ANTHONY Armstrong-Jones, created Earl of Snowdon; divorced 1978.) **12 DAVID Armstrong-Jones**, Viscount Linley, b. 3 Nov 1961 – son of The Princess Margaret. (He m. 8 Oct 1993 Hon. SERENA Stanhope.) **13 Lady SARAH Chatto**, b. 1 May 1964 – dau of The Princess Margaret. (She m. 14 Jul 1994 DANIEL Chatto.) **14 HRH Prince RICHARD**, the (2nd) Duke of Gloucester, b. 26 Aug 1944 – surviving son of HRH The Prince Henry, Duke of Gloucester, who was the third son of HM King George V. (He m. 8 Jul 1972 BIRGITTE van Deurs – HRH The Duchess of Gloucester.)

The Economy

The three basic sectors of an economy are the primary goods sector (raw materials and farming), the industrial goods or secondary sector (manufactures, construction, gas, electricity, etc.) and the service or tertiary sector (retailing, banking, tourism, etc.). The relative importance of each of these sectors tends to change as the economy grows and matures. The British economy has been characterized by a relative decline in their industrial goods sector and a corresponding increase in the importance of the service sector. Factors affecting a country's industrial structure include the level and pattern of demand, relative supply costs and prices, technological advance, governmental policies, and exposure to foreign competition. This latter factor has become more important in recent years.

GOVERNMENT EXPENDITURE (£ billion)

Function	*1983*	*1984*	*1985*	*1986*	*1987*	*1988*	*1989*	*1990*	*1991*	*1992*	*1993*
Defence	15·8	17·1	18·2	19·1	18·9	19·8	21·0	22·9	23·2	24·5	24·4
Public order/safety	5·3	5·8	6·2	6·8	7·5	8·4	9·4	10·9	12·9	13·8	15·0
Education	16·3	16·9	17·3	19·3	20·8	22·6	24·8	26·7	29·4	31·9	33·9
Health	15·9	16·8	17·9	19·2	20·9	22·9	25·2	27·8	31·2	34·9	36·9
Social security	39·3	42·2	46·2	49·9	52·1	54·2	57·3	62·9	73·8	84·5	93·2
Housing & community amenities	7·4	8·0	7·0	8·1	9·2	8·5	8·0	7·8	8·7	10·3	10·9
Recreation and cultural affairs	2·0	2·1	2·2	2·4	2·6	2·8	3·2	3·6	3·9	3·8	3·7
Fuel and energy	0·5	1·2	1·1	−1·2	−3·4	−3·0	−1·8	−3·0	−3·0	−0·6	0·9
Agriculture, forestry & fishing	2·3	2·5	2·6	2·1	2·3	2·5	2·0	2·6	2·7	2·9	3·9
Mining, manufacturing, mineral resources and construction	2·7	2·4	2·4	1·9	1·3	0·9	1·5	1·3	1·6	1·3	1·5
Transport and communication	5·1	3·5	4·1	3·7	4·0	4·5	7·1	9·4	6·7	6·4	6·8
General public services	5·1	5·5	6·0	6·3	6·5	7·6	9·3	10·6	11·5	12·8	12·6
Other economic affairs and services	3·3	4·2	4·3	4·1	3·7	3·6	5·1	6·7	4·4	4·6	5·0
Other expenditure	17·3	18·8	22·1	20·5	22·6	22·9	24·9	25·1	21·5	23·0	24·1

BALANCE OF PAYMENTS (£ million)

The balance of payments is a measure of Britain's trading position in relation to the rest of the world. Exports and imports ('visible' trade) in addition to 'invisibles' (including tourism, banking and insurance) are taken into account in determining the balance of payments. This balance illustrates whether the UK has a surplus of income over expenditure.

Year	*Visible Exports*	*Visible Imports*	*Visible Balance*	*Invisible Balance*	*Current Balance (– deficit/+ surplus)*
1965	4913	5173	–260	+183	–77
1970	8130	8141	–11	+835	+821
1975	19,185	22,441	–3256	+1731	–1524
1980	47,149	45,792	+1357	+1487	+2843
1981	50,668	47,416	+3252	+3496	+6748
1982	55,331	53,421	+1910	+2741	+4649
1983	60,700	62,237	–1537	+5066	+3529
1984	70,265	75,601	–5336	+6818	+1482
1985	77,991	81,336	–3345	+5583	+2238
1986	72,627	82,186	–9559	+8688	–871
1987	79,153	90,735	–11,582	+7099	–4482
1988	80,346	101,826	–21,480	+5302	–16,179
1989	92,154	116,837	–24,663	+2171	–22,512
1990	101,718	120,527	–18,809	–226	–19,035
1991	103,413	113,697	–10,284	+2108	–8176
1992	107,343	120,447	–13,104	+3273	–9831
1993	121,300	134,694	–13,394	+1594	–11,800
1994	135,200	145,727	–10,527	+10,359	–168

INFLATION: CONSUMER PRICE INDEX (1985 = 100)

	1982	1983	1984	1985	1986	1987	1988	1989	1990	1991	1992	1993	1994
UK	85·9	89·8	94·3	100·0	103·4	107·7	113·0	121·8	133·3	141·1	146·4	148·7	152·4
Germany*	92·5	95·6	97·9	100·0	99·9	100·1	101·4	104·2	107·0	110·7	115·1	119·9	123·5
France	80·3	88·0	94·6	100·0	102·5	105·9	108·7	112·7	116·5	120·2	123·0	125·6	127·8
Italy	72·1	82·6	91·6	100·0	105·8	110·9	116·5	123·8	131·8	140·0	147·3	153·6	160·0
Japan	94·1	95·8	98·0	100·0	100·6	100·7	101·4	103·7	106·9	110·4	112·3	113·8	114·5
USA	89·7	92·6	96·6	100·0	101·9	105·7	110·0	115·3	121·5	126·6	130·5	134·3	137·8

* Figures are for West Germany only up to 1993.

VALUE OF UK EXPORTS

Category	*£ millions*	*% of total*
Food and live animals (chiefly for food)	6258	4·7
Beverages and tobacco	3709	2·8
Beverages	*2830*	*2·1*
Crude materials, inedible (except fuel)	662	0·5
Mineral fuels, lubricants and related minerals	8916	6·7
Petroleum and related products	*8503*	*6·4*
Animal and vegetable oils and fats	171	0·1
Chemicals and related products	18,737	14·0
Manufactured goods (classified chiefly by material)†	19,512	14·6
Machinery and transport equipment	55,329	41·3
Road vehicles	*9409*	*7·0*
Miscellaneous manufactured articles	17,320	2·9
Others	1450	1·1
Total	**133,786**	

1994 figures; † including textiles, metals, iron and steel, leather and paper

VALUE OF UK IMPORTS

Category	*£ millions*	*% of total*
Food and live animals (chiefly for food)	12,252	8·2
Beverages and tobacco	2237	1·5
Beverages	*1857*	*1·2*
Crude materials, inedible (except fuel)	5620	3·8
Mineral fuels, lubricants and related minerals	5902	4·0
Petroleum and related products	*4598*	*3·1*
Animal and vegetable oils and fats	539	0·4
Chemicals and related products	14,481	9·8
Manufactured goods (classified chiefly by material)†	24,362	16·4
Machinery and transport equipment	60,370	40·7
Road vehicles	*16,219*	*10·9*
Miscellaneous manufactured articles	21,653	14·6
Others	982	0·7
Total	**148,371**	

1994 figures; † including textiles, metals, iron and steel, leather and paper

WORKFORCE

Agriculture, forestry and fishing	247,000
Production industries	
Coal, oil and natural gas	76,000
Electricity, gas and water supply	230,000
Manufacturing industries	4,227,000
Construction	864,000
Service industries	
Wholesale distribution and repairs	1,083,000
Retail distribution	2,275,000
Hotels and catering	1,205,000
Transport	849,000
Post and telecommunications	358,000
Banking, finance and insurance	2,666,000
Public administration	1,761,000
Education	1,848,000
Medical and other health, services, veterinary services	1,569,000
Other services	1,752,000

Total no. of men in employment
10,634,000

Total no. of women in employment
10,377,000

figures for Great Britain only (1994).

UNEMPLOYMENT

(seasonally adjusted)

Year	*Total*	*% rate*
1980	1,363,800	5·1
1981	2,171,500	8·1
1982	2,544,100	9·5
1983	2,787,200	10·4
1984	2,915,500	10·6
1985	3,027,000	10·9
1986	3,096,900	11·1
1987	2,804,900	10·0
1988	2,274,800	8·0
1989	1,782,100	6·2
1990	1,660,800	5·8
1991	2,286,100	8·0
1992	2,765,000	9·7
1993	2,900,600	10·3
1994	2,619,400	9·4

Unemployment figures for 1981-85 are annual averages. All figures relate to claimants over 18 years old.

UK EXPORTS: BY COUNTRY

Country	£ millions	% of total
Germany	17,658	13·2
USA	16,807	11·3
France	13,647	10·2
Netherlands	9750	7·3
Belgium and Luxembourg	7706	5·8
Italy	6949	5·2
Ireland	6711	5·0
Spain	5073	3·8
Sweden	3347	2·5
Japan	2992	2·2
Switzerland	2460	1·8
Hong Kong	2307	1·7
Norway	2011	1·5
Australia	1918	1·4
Canada	1914	1·4
Singapore	1838	1·4
Denmark	1766	1·3
Saudi Arabia	1516	1·1
Malaysia	1307	1·0
Finland	1305	1·0
Others	24,804	18·1
Total	**133,786**	

1994 figures

UK IMPORTS: BY COUNTRY

Country	£ millions	% of total
Germany	22,524	15·2
USA	17,682	11·9
France	15,553	10·5
Netherlands	10,075	6·8
Japan	8899	6·0
Italy	7301	4·9
Belgium and Luxembourg	7272	4·9
Ireland	5817	3·9
Switzerland	4819	3·2
Sweden	4159	2·8
Spain	3771	2·5
Norway	3710	2·5
Hong Kong	3084	2·1
Finland	2254	1·5
Denmark	2096	1·4
Singapore	1896	1·3
Canada	1880	1·3
Taiwan	1581	1·1
Portugal	1259	0·8
Malaysia	1204	0·8
Others	21,535	14·5
Total	**148,371**	

1994 figures

DURABLE GOODS OWNERSHIP : BY SOCIO-ECONOMIC GROUP (%)

Socio-economic categories by head of household. (Figures for Great Britain 1993)

	Professional	*Employers & managers*	*Non-manual-Inter-mediate*	*Junior*	*Skilled manual*	*Unskilled manual*	*Economically inactive*	*All households*
Deep freezer (includes fridge-freezer)	94	94	90	90	93	85	79	92
Washing machine	98	96	94	91	94	85	80	94
Tumble drier	65	68	60	51	58	43	34	59
Microwave oven	75	79	73	72	76	58	45	50
Dishwasher	39	40	25	13	15	5	7	23
Telephone	99	98	97	91	90	72	88	92
Television	98	99	98	98	99	98	99	98
Colour	97	98	96	97	98	93	94	97
B & W	1	1	2	1	1	5	5	1
Video	91	92	88	86	90	73	50	89
Home computer	51	41	38	26	29	17	9	33
CD player	62	58	36	20	49	33	18	52
Central heating	95	93	88	85	84	72	79	86
Car/van more than one	54	53	36	20	31	10	7	35

AVERAGE WEEKLY INCOME: 1965–1993 (in £)

	1965	*1970*	*1975*	*1980*	*1985*	*1988*	*1989*	*1990*	*1991*	*1992*	*1993*
Average gross household income	24·64	35·40	72·87	147·18	216·86	283·86	303·84	335·67	362·65	342·93	353·03
Average disposable household income	20·19	29·54	58·15	121·50	175·30	233·20	251·62	276·29	299·63	280·04	238·44

Defence

THE ARMY

The recommendations of the White Paper *Options for Change* will be implemented over the next five years extensively changing the make-up of the regular units of the Army. The following list includes all the principal regular units in May 1995.

Household Cavalry Life Guards; Blues and Royals (Royal Horse Guards and 1st Dragoons)

Royal Armoured Corps 1st Queen's Dragoon Guards; Royal Scots Dragoon Guards (Carabiniers and Greys); Royal Dragoon Guards; Queen's Royal Hussars (Queen's Own and Royal Irish); 9th/12th Royal Lancers (Prince of Wales's); King's Royal Hussars; Light Dragoons; Queen's Royal Lancers; Royal Tank Regiment (2 regiments).

Royal Regiment of Artillery

Royal Horse Artillery

Corps of Royal Engineers

Royal Corps of Signals

The Guards Division Grenadier Guards; Coldstream Guards; Scots Guards; Irish Guards; Welsh Guards.

The Scottish Division Royal Scots; Royal Highland Fusiliers; King's Own Scottish Borderers; Black Watch; The Highlanders (Gordons, Seaforth and Camerons); Argyll and Sutherland Highlanders

The Queen's Division Princess of Wales's Own Royal Regiment (2 battalions); Royal Regiment of Fusiliers (2 battalions); Royal Anglian Regiment (2 battalions)

The King's Division King's Own Royal Border Regiment; King's Regiment; Prince of Wales' Own Regiment of Yorkshire; Green Howards; Queen's Lancashire Regiment; Duke of Wellington's Regiment

The Prince of Wales' Division Devonshire and Dorset Regiment; 22nd (Cheshire) Regiment; Royal Welch Fusiliers; Royal Regiment of Wales; Royal Gloucestershire, Berkshire and Wiltshire Regiment; Worcestershire and Sherwood Foresters; Staffordshire Regiment.

The Light Division Light Infantry (2 battalions); Royal Green Jackets (2 battalions).

The Parachute Regiment (3 batallions)

The Brigade of Gurkhas Royal Gurkha Rifles (3 battalions); Queen's Gurkha Engineers; Queen's Gurkha Signals; Queen's Gurkha Transport Regiment.

Special Air Service Regiment

Army Air Corps

The Services inc. Royal Logistics Corps, Medical, Veterinary, Training, Electrical and other corps.

PRINCIPAL SERVICE BASES

Some of the following bases are due to close by 1997:

Army The Army is based at the following places in the UK: Aldermaston, Aldershot, Andover, Arborfield, Ballymena, Belfast, Benbecula, Blandford, Bordon, Beaconsfield, Ballykinler, Blackdown, Bulford, Camberley, Catterick, Chatham, Chattenden, Chichester, Chester, Colchester, Deepcut, Devizes, Edinburgh, Exeter, Glasgow, Hereford, Inverness (Fort George), Kirton, Larkhill, Lisburn, Lichfield, Liverpool, London, Londonderry, Lulworth, Lurgan, Middle Wallop, Ouston (Newcastle), Pirbright, Preston, Ripon, Royston, Shrewsbury, Shrivenham, South Cerney, Stirling, Strensall (York), Tern Hill, Thorney Island, Tidworth, Upavon, Warminster, Woolwich, Worthy Down, Winchester, York. Bases are also maintained abroad, mainly in Germany, the Falkland Islands and Cyprus.

Royal Navy/Royal Marines The Royal Navy and the Royal Marines are based at the following places in the UK: Coulport, Devonport, Dartmouth, Deal (RM), Faslane, Greenock, Greenwich, Gosport, Lympstone (RM), Portsmouth, Portland, Poole (RM), Rosyth, South Queensferry, Weymouth.

Royal Air Force The Royal Air Force is based at the following places in the UK: Abingdon, Aberporth, Aldergrove, Benson, Bentley Priory, Boddington, Binbrook, Bracknell, Brawdy, Buchan, Brize Norton, Cranwell, Cardington, Church Fenton, Coltishall, Coningsby, Cosford, Cottesmore, Culdrose, Digby, Dishforth, Fairford, Farnborough, Finningley, Hendon, Halton, High Wycombe, Honington, Kemble, Kinloss, Leeming, Lossiemouth, Llanbedr, Linton, Lyneham, Manston, Marham, Netheravon, Northolt, Newton (Notts), Odiham, Stanmore Park, Scampton, Swinderby, St. Mawgan, Waddington, Wattisham, Woodvale, West Drayton, Wittering, Valley, Yeovilton. Bases are also maintained abroad, mainly in Germany, the Falkland Islands and Cyprus

SHIPS OF THE LINE

Polaris/Trident SSBNs 3 (*Repulse, Renown, Vanguard*); Fleet submarines 3; Type 2400 submarines 4; Oberon class submarines 1; Type 42 guided missile destroyers 12; Type 23 frigates 5; Type 22 frigates 14; Type 21 frigates 5; Leander class frigates 1; ASW carriers 3 (*Ark Royal, Invincible, Illustrious*); Assault ships 1; plus 26 patrol and coastal combatants, 30 mine-counter-measure vessels, and 32 other vessels.

HM FORCES PERSONNEL (1995)

Regulars	
Royal Navy males	47,550
Royal Navy females	4500
Royal Marines	7250
Army males	127,000
Army females	7600
RAF males	74,100
RAF females	6800
Total regulars:	274,800
Regular reserves	
Royal Navy	27,500
Royal Marines	2700
Army	190,100
RAF	46,100
Total reserves:	349,300
Volunteer reserves/Auxiliary forces	
Royal Navy	5800
Royal Marines	1200
Territorial Army	68,500
Royal Irish Regiment (part-time)	5700

The Law

The law of England and Wales is divided into: *civil law,* disputes between individuals, and *criminal law,* acts harmful to the community.

Civil law governs rights and duties between citizens. As it includes the law of contract civil law deals with important business matters such as trade, credit and insurance, but also governs more commonplace agreements. In civil cases the person injured, known as 'the plaintiff', will use the law to bring an action against the defendant in a civil court, probably seeking damages (compensation). Another civil remedy is an injunction, where the plaintiff seeks a court order to stop the offending behaviour rather than damages.

Criminal law governs those situations where the accused person is said to have broken a law that has caused an injury not just to another individual, but also to the state. This law covers offences that range from murder, manslaughter, assault and sexual crimes, to offences against property such as theft, burglary and criminal damage. The purpose of the criminal law is quite different from that of civil law; the state prosecutes accused persons in a criminal court not for compensation, but to punish them. Serious criminal cases are tried on indictment by a judge and jury, but most cases – summary offences –can be decided by magistrates, or justices of the peace, who are not lawyers and are usually unpaid.

Except for some libel cases, a jury is never used in a civil case in Britain. In England and Wales a jury is composed of 12 impartial people, aged between 18 and 70. At the end of the case they decide if the accused is guilty or not guilty; a majority verdict, with up to two dissenters, is allowed. If the jury cannot agree, there may be a retrial.

SCOTTISH LAW

Scottish law is quite different from that in England and Wales. It is characterized by the system of public prosecution, independent of the police, and headed by the Lord Advocate. The Lord Advocate, through the Crown Office, is responsible for bringing prosecutions in the High Court, sheriff courts and district courts. The High Court of Justiciary is the senior court for criminal cases, and tries all serious crimes such as murder, rape, treason, etc. It is also the final appeal court for any indictment trial. District courts deal with minor summary offences and are administered by local government authorities. Prosecution is carried out by procurators-fiscals – lawyers and full-time civil servants – and presided over by lay justices (in Glasgow by stipendiary magistrates). Most civil cases are tried in the sheriff courts. Sheriffs principals head the six sheriffdoms of Scotland, which are divided into sheriff court districts and administered by sheriffs. Sheriffs principals and sheriffs have equal powers in criminal cases, and in serious cases they sit with a 15-member jury, who may return a third verdict of 'not proven'. An appeal from the decision of a sheriff court can be made to the Court of Session, in Edinburgh.

THE COURTS IN ENGLAND AND WALES

County Courts Most minor civil cases are dealt with in County Courts. Such cases include those where the sum in dispute is under £5000, cases where the two parties consent to County Court jurisdiction, uncontested divorces, and some bankruptcy proceedings (outside London). Civil cases pertaining to the family are dealt with in a Magistrates' Court.

High Court of Justice is the superior civil court. It is divided into three Divisions: the Chancery Division (dealing mainly with equity, bankruptcy and contentious probate business), the Queen's Bench (concerned with commercial and maritime law, civil cases not assigned to other courts, and appeals from the lower courts), and the Family Division (dealing with family law). High Court judges sit alone to hear cases at first instance.

Magistrates' Courts deal with most minor criminal offences. They usually consist of three lay magistrates (Justices of the Peace) sitting without a jury and advised by a legally qualified clerk of the justices. These courts also deal with the preliminary proceedings of some serious cases in order to decide whether or not evidence justifies a Crown Court trial.

Crown Courts deal with serious criminal offences, the sentencing of offenders from a Magistrates' Court in cases where its sentencing powers are inadequate, and appeals from the lower courts. Appeals upon a point of law, however, are made to the High Court, and may go on to the House of Lords. They are presided over by a High Court or Circuit judge, always sitting with a 12-member jury. The Crown Courts in England and Wales are organized into six circuits and three tiers. First tier courts are served by both High Court and Circuit judges, and are able to hear civil and criminal cases. Second tier courts are also served by both High Court and Circuit judges but hear only criminal cases. Third tier courts are served by Circuit judges and hear criminal cases. The six circuits are:

Midland and Oxford Circuit 1st tier courts: Birmingham, Lincoln, Nottingham, Oxford, Stafford, Warwick. 2nd tier courts: Leicester, Northampton, Shrewsbury, Worcester. 3rd tier courts: Coventry, Derby, Grimsby, Hereford, Peterborough, Stoke-on-Trent, Wolverhampton.

North Eastern Circuit 1st tier courts: Leeds, Newcastle-upon-Tyne, Sheffield, Teesside (Middlesbrough). 2nd tier court: York. 3rd tier courts: Bradford, Doncaster, Durham.

Northern Circuit 1st tier courts: Carlisle, Liverpool, Manchester, Preston. 3rd tier courts: Barrow-in-Furness, Bolton, Burnley, Lancaster.

South Eastern Circuit 1st courts: Chelmsford, Lewes, London (Royal Courts of Justice - High Court), Norwich. 2nd tier courts: Ipswich, London (Central Criminal Court), Luton, Maidstone, Reading, St Albans. 3rd tier courts: Aylesbury, Bury St Edmunds, Cambridge, Canterbury, Chichester, Guildford, King's Lynn, London (Croydon, Harrow, Inner London, Isleworth, Kingston-upon-Thames, Knightsbridge, Middlesex Guildhall, Snaresbrook, Southwark, Wood Green), Southend.

Wales and Chester Circuit 1st tier courts: Caernarfon, Cardiff, Chester, Mold, Swansea. 2nd tier courts: Carmarthen, Merthyr Tydfil, Newport, Welshpool. 3rd tier courts: Dolgellau, Haverfordwest, Knutsford, Warrington.

Western Circuit 1st tier courts: Bristol, Exeter, Truro, Winchester. 2nd tier courts: Dorchester, Gloucester, Plymouth. 3rd tier courts: Barnstaple, Bournemouth, Devizes, Newport (IOW), Portsmouth, Salisbury, Southampton, Swindon, Taunton.

The House of Lords is the supreme judicial court for the United Kingdom. It is the ultimate court of appeal for all courts, except the Scottish criminal courts.

Education

NUMBER OF SCHOOLS

	Maintained	Independent
England and Wales	31,860	2480
Scotland	3800	120
Northern Ireland	1320	18

NUMBER OF PUPILS

Primary school	4,998,000
Secondary/middle	3,458,000

PUPIL TEACHER RATIOS (Primary schools)

England	22·0
Wales	22·3
Scotland	19·5
Northern Ireland	22·6

THE NATIONAL CURRICULUM

A key element of the 1988 Education Act is the national curriculum, which should be fully implemented by 1997.

The national curriculum defines three core subjects: English (or Welsh in Wales), mathematics and science. Several foundation subjects were also defined: history, geography, music, art, technology, a modern language (at secondary level) and PE – to be studied by all pupils. State schools must follow the national curriculum. Independent schools need not do so, but many are choosing to follow it fairly closely.

The original intention was that national curriculum subjects should occupy 70% of the timetable, and the Department of Education and Science (DES) laid down percentages of the school timetable to be spent on each subject. Wider educational topics such as social education, political and economic awareness, and careers education were also to be studied. Religious education was to be compulsory and schools were to be free to offer additional subjects.

After protests the DES agreed the necessity for flexibility and asked schools to tailor courses according to pupils' needs. More room was also found for additional subjects including extra languages, business studies, classics and home economics. But making more timetable space for other subjects meant changing the original intention that all core and foundation subjects must be compulsory until the age of 16. Pupils will now study either art or music, and either history or geography (although neither of these is compulsory after 14), while technology (a compulsory subject until the age of 14 and encouraged thereafter) need not be studied to GCSE standard.

Education under the national curriculum divides a pupil's time into four key stages: 5–7 years old, 8–11, 12–14 and 15–16. Each key stage has standard assessment tasks and attainment targets, defining the knowledge and skills pupils should achieve at the end of each stage. Core subject assessment tests are taken at the ages of seven, 11 and 14.

UNIVERSITIES

The following alphabetical list of universities details each institution's year of foundation (as a university), location, and full-time student population as at 1994:

University of Aberdeen (1495), Aberdeen, Scotland AB9 1FX. Student nos: 9500.

University of Abertay Dundee (1994), Bell Street, Dundee, DD1 1HG. Student nos: 4100.

Anglia Polytechnic University (1992), Victoria Road South, Chelmsford, Essex, CM1 1LL. Student nos: 7900. Campuses at Chelmsford, Cambridge and Brentwood.

Aston University (1966), Aston Triangle, Birmingham, B4 7ET. Student nos: 4300.

University of Bath (1966), Claverton Down, Bath, BA2 7AY. Student nos: 5400.

The Queen's University of Belfast (1908), University Road, Belfast, Northern Ireland, BT7 1NN. Student nos: 10,600.

University of Birmingham (1900), PO Box 363, Birmingham B15 2TT. Student nos: 13,000.

University of Central England in Birmingham (1992), Perry Barr, Birmingham, B42 2SU. Student nos: 15,100.

Bournemouth University (1992), Poole House, Fern Barrow, Poole, Dorset, BH12 5BB. Student nos: 8000.

University of Bradford (1966), Richmond Road, Bradford, West Yorkshire, BD7 1DP. Student nos: 6700.

University of Brighton (1992), Lewes Road, Brighton, BN2 4AT. Student nos: 9800. Campuses in Brighton and Eastbourne.

University of Bristol (1909), Senate House, Bristol, BS8 1TH. Student nos: 10,300.

University of the West of England, Bristol (1992), Coldharbour Lane, Frenchay, Bristol, BS16 1QY. Student nos: 12,300.

Brunel, the University of West London (1966), Uxbridge, Middlesex, UB8 3PH. Student nos: 5300. Campuses at Uxbridge and Runnymede.

University of Buckingham (1976), Buckingham, MK18 1EG. Student nos: 1000. (Independent. Degree courses last two, rather than three, years.)

University of Cambridge (1284 – date of foundation of Peterhouse), Cambridge CB2 1QJ. Student nos: 14,000. *Colleges, Halls and Societies:* Peterhouse (1284), Clare (1326), Pembroke (1347), Gonville and Caius (1348), Trinity Hall (1350), Corpus Christi (1352), King's (1441), Queens' (1448), St Catharine's (1473), Jesus (1496), Christ's (1505), St John's (1511), Magdalene (1542), Trinity (1546), Emmanuel (1584), Sidney Sussex (1596), Downing (1800), Fitzwilliam (1869), Girton (1869), Newnham (1871), Selwyn (1882), Hughes Hall (1885), Homerton (1894), St Edmund's (1896), New Hall (1954), Churchill (1959), Wolfson (1965), Darwin (1964), Lucy Cavendish (1965), Clare Hall (1966), Fitzwilliam (1966), Robinson (1977).

City University (1966), Northampton Square, London, EC1V 0HB. Student nos: 5800.

Coventry University (1992), Priory Street, Coventry, CV1 5FB. Student nos: 14,900.

Cranfield University (1969), Cranfield, Bedford, MK43 1EG. Student nos: 2300. Campuses at Cranfield, Silsoe (Bedford) and Shrivenham (Wiltshire).

De Montfort University (1992), PO Box 143, Leicester, LE1 9BH. Student nos: 18,000. Campuses at Leicester, Milton Keynes, Bedford and Lincoln.

University of Derby (1993), Kedleston Road, Derby DE3 1GB. Student nos: 7500.

University of Dundee (1967), Dundee, Scotland, DD1 4HN. Student nos: 6700.

University of Durham (1832), Old Shire Hall, Durham DH1 3HP. Student nos: 7800. Joint University College of Teesside at Stockton is maintained with the University of Teesside.

University of East Anglia (1963), Norwich, NR4 7TJ. Student nos: 6600.

University of East London (1992), Romford Road, London, E15 4LZ. Student nos: 11,000. Main sites at Barking, Dagenham and Newham.

University of Edinburgh (1583), Old College, Edinburgh, Scotland EH8 9YL. Student nos: 15,600.

University of Essex (1964), Wivenhoe Park, Colchester, Essex, CO4 3SQ. Student nos: 5100.

University of Exeter (1955), The Queen's Drive, Exeter, EX4 4QJ. Student nos: 8300.

University of Glamorgan (1992), Pontypridd, Mid Glamorgan, CF37 1DL. Student nos: 9800.

Glasgow Caledonian University (1993), 70 Cowcaddens Road, Glasgow G4 OBA. Student nos: 10,500.

University of Glasgow (1451), Glasgow, Scotland G12 8QQ. Student nos: 13,500.

University of Greenwich (1992), Wellington Street, Woolwich, London, SE18 6PF. Student nos: 13,500. Campuses at Greenwich, Avery Hill and Dartford.

Heriot-Watt University (1966), Riccarton, Edinburgh, Scotland, EH14 4AS. Student nos: 8900.

University of Hertfordshire (1992), College Lane, Hatfield, Hertfordshire, AL10 9AB. Student nos: 12,100. Campuses at Hatfield, Watford and Hertford.

University of Huddersfield (1992), Queensgate, Huddersfield, HD1 3DH. Student nos: 10,000.

University of Hull (1954), Hull, HU6 7RX. Student nos: 9000.

University of Humberside (1992), Cottingham Road, Hull, HU6 7RT. Student nos: 9000. Campuses in Hull and Grimsby.

University of Keele (1962), Keele, Staffordshire, ST5 5BG. Student nos: 5200.

University of Kent at Canterbury (1965), Canterbury, Kent, CT2 7NZ. Student nos: 6500.

Kingston University (1992), Penrhyn Road, Kingston upon Thames, Surrey, KT1 2EE. Student nos: 11,000.

University of Central Lancashire (1992), Preston, Lancashire, PR1 2TQ. Student nos: 12,200.

University of Lancaster (1964), University House, Lancaster, LA1 4YW. Student nos: 7000.

University of Leeds (1904), Leeds, LS2 9JT. Student nos: 17,500.

Leeds Metropolitan University (1992), Calverley Street, Leeds, LS1 3HE. Student nos: 14,200.

University of Leicester (1957), University Road, Leicester, LE1 7RH. Student nos: 8200.

University of Liverpool (1903), PO Box 147, Liverpool, L69 3BX. Student nos: 12,000.

Liverpool John Moores University (1992), 70 Mount Pleasant, Liverpool, L3 5UX. Student nos: 19,000.

University of London (1836), Senate House, Malet Street, London WC1E 7HU. Student nos: 68,000. *Colleges and Schools:* Birkbeck College; Heythrop College; Goldsmith's College; Imperial College of Science, Technology and Medicine; King's College; London School of Economics and Political Science; Queen Mary and Westfield College; Royal Holloway; Royal Veterinary College; School of Oriental and African Studies; School of Pharmacy; University College; Wye College (based at a campus at Ashford, Kent). Plus *Medical Schools:* Charing Cross and Westminster Medical School, King's College of Medicine and Dentistry, London Hospital Medical School, Royal Free Hospital School of Medicine, St Bartholomew's Hospital Medical College, St George's Hospital Medical School, St Mary's Hospital Medical School, United Medical and Dental Schools of Guy's and St Thomas's Hospitals, University College and Middlesex School of Medicine, and three post-graduate medical institutions, 15 Senate institutions and five associated institutions.

London Guildhall University (1993), 117-119 Hounsditch, London EC3 7BU. Student nos: 8600.

Loughborough University of Technology (1966), Loughborough, Leicestershire, LE11 3TU. Student nos: 9400.

University of Luton (1993), Park Square, Luton, LU1 3JU. Student nos: 10,500.

University of Manchester (1851), Manchester M13 9PL. Student nos: 15,000.

University of Manchester Institute of Science and Technology (UMIST; 1824), PO Box 88, Manchester M60 1QD. Student nos: 6000.

Manchester Metropolitan University (1992), All Saints, Manchester, M15 6BH. Student nos: 23,000. Campuses in Manchester, Crewe and Alsager.

Middlesex University (1992), Bramley Road, Oakwood, Middlesex, N14 4XS. Student nos: 13,800. Campuses at Barnet, Hendon, Enfield and Trent Park.

Napier University (1992), 219 Colinton Road, Edinburgh EH14 1DJ. Student nos: 7700.

University of Newcastle upon Tyne (1852), Kensington Terrace, Newcastle upon Tyne, NE1 7RU. Student nos: 11,500.

University of North London (1992), Holloway Road, London, N7 8DB. Student nos: 9100.

University of Northumbria at Newcastle (1992), Ellison Road, Newcastle upon Tyne, NE1 8ST. Student nos: 11,300. There is also a site in Carlisle.

University of Nottingham (1948), University Park, Nottingham, NG7 2RD. Student nos: 11,400. There is one campus and a smaller site at Sutton Bonington.

Nottingham Trent University (1992), Burton Street, Nottingham, NG1 4BU. Student nos: 13,900.

The Open University (1969), Walton Hall, Milton Keynes, Buckinghamshire, MK7 6AA. Student nos: over 150,000 (The university is non-residential. Tuition is by correspondence and special radio, TV and video programmes, short residential schools and locally-based tutors.)

University of Oxford (1249 - date of foundation of University College), Oxford OX1 2JD. Student nos: 14,500. *Colleges, Halls and Societies:* University (1249), Balliol (1263), Merton (1264), St Edmund Hall (1278), Exeter (1314), Oriel (1326), Queen's (1341), New College (1379), Lincoln (1427), Magdalen (1428), All Souls (1438), Brasenose (1509), Corpus Christi (1517), Christ Church (1546), Trinity (1554), St John's (1555), Jesus (1571), Wadham (1610), Pembroke (1624), Worcester (1714), Hertford (1740), Manchester (1786), Regent's Park (1810), Keble (1870), Lady Margaret Hall (1878), Somerville (1879), Mansfield (1886), St Hugh's (1886), St Hilda's (1893), St Anne's (1893; 1952 present constitution), Campion Hall (1896), St Benet's (1897), Greyfriars (1910), Blackfriars (1921), St Peter's (1929), Nuffield (1937), St Antony's (1953), St Catherine's (1962), Linacre (1962), St Cross (1965), Wolfson (1965), Green (1979), Kellogg (1990).

Oxford Brookes University (1992), Headington, Oxford, OX3 0BP. Student nos: 10,800.

University of Paisley (1992), High Street, Paisley, Renfrewshire PA1 2BE. Student nos: 6200. Campuses at Paisley and Ayr.

University of Plymouth (1992), Drake Circus, Plymouth, PL4 8AA. Student nos: 9030. Campuses at Plymouth, Exmouth, Exeter and Newton Abbot.

University of Portsmouth (1992), University House, Winston Churchill Avenue, Portsmouth, PO1 2UP. Student nos: 11,300.

University of Reading (1926), PO Box 217, Reading, Berkshire, RG6 2AH. Student nos: 9300.

The Robert Gordon University (1992), Schoolhill, Aberdeen AB9 1FR. Student nos: 6000.

University of St Andrews (1411), College Gate, St Andrews, Scotland KY16 9AJ. Student nos: 5200.

University of Salford (1967), Salford, M5 3WT. Student nos: 7000.

University of Sheffield (1905), Western Bank, Sheffield, S10 2TN. Student nos: 14,000.

Sheffield Hallam University (1992), Pond Street, Sheffield, S1 1WB. Student nos: 16,900.

South Bank University (1992), Borough Road, London SE1 0AA. Student nos: 15,300.

University of Southampton (1952), Highfield, Southampton, SO9 5NH. Student nos: 10,000.

Staffordshire University (1992), College Road, Stoke-on-Trent, ST4 2DE. Student nos: 10,000. Campuses at Stoke and Stafford.

University of Stirling (1967), Stirling, Scotland, FK9 4LA. Student nos: 5200.

University of Strathclyde (1964), 16 Richmond Street, Glasgow, Scotland, G1 1XQ. Student nos: 13,200.

University of Sunderland (1992), Edinburgh Building, Chester Road, Sunderland SR1 3SD. Student nos: 12,100.

University of Surrey (1966), Guildford, Surrey, GU2 5XH. Student nos: 5700.

University of Sussex (1961), Sussex House, Falmer, Brighton, BN1 9RH. Student nos: 8200.

University of Teesside (1992), Borough Road, Middlesbrough, Cleveland, TS1 3BA. Student nos: 7000. (Joint University College on Teesside at Stockton maintained with the University of Durham.)

Thames Valley University (1992), St Mary's Road, London W5. Student nos: 15,000. Sites at Ealing, Slough, Chiswick and Westminster.

University of Ulster (1965), Coleraine, County Londonderry, Northern Ireland, BT52 1SA. Student nos: 11,700. Sites at Coleraine and Jordanstown.

University of Wales (1893), Cathays Park, Cardiff, CF1 3NS. Student nos: 26,000. Six colleges:

> **University College, Aberystwyth** (1872), King's Street, Aberystwyth SY23 2AX
>
> **University College of North Wales** (1884), Bangor, Gwynedd LL57 2DG.
>
> **University of Wales College of Cardiff** (1883), POB 68, Cardiff, CF1 3XA
>
> **St David's University College** (1822), Lampeter, Dyfed SA48 7ED
>
> **University College of Swansea** (1920), Singleton Park, Swansea, SA2 8PP
>
> **University of Wales College of Medicine** (1931), Heath Park, Cardiff CF4 4XN.

University of Warwick (1965), Coventry, CV4 7AL. Student nos: 12,700.

University of Westminster (1992), 309 Regent Street, London, W1R 8AL. Student nos: 7800. Sites in Westminster and Harrow.

University of Wolverhampton (1992), Wulfrana Street, Wolverhampton, WV1 1SB. Student nos: 17,000. Campuses in Wolverhampton, Dudley and Walsall.

University of York (1963), Heslington, York, YO1 5DD. Student nos: 5300.

Religion

THE ANGLICAN COMMUNION

About 55% of the population of the UK nominally belongs to the Churches of the Anglican Communion (the Church of England, the Church in Wales, the Episcopal Church in Scotland and the Church of Ireland). However, only 4% of the population are practising Anglicans. The Archbishop of Canterbury is Primate of All England.

ARCHBISHOPS OF CANTERBURY (since the Reformation)

Thomas Cranmer	1532–55
Reginald Pole*	1555–58
Matthew Parker	1559–75
Edmund Grindal	1575–83
John Whitgift	1583–1604
Richard Bancroft	1604–10
George Abbot	1611–33
William Laud	1633–45
Interregnum	
William Juxon	1660–63
Gilbert Sheldon	1663–77
William Sancroft	
John Tillotson	1691–94
Thomas Tenison	1694–1715
William Wake	1715–37
John Potter	1737–47
Thomas Herring	1747–57
Matthew Hutton	1757–58
Thomas Secker	1758–68
Frederick Cornwallis	1768–83
John Moore	1783–1805
Charles Manners Sutton	1805–28
William Howley	1828–48
John Bird Sumner	1848–62
Charles Thomas Longley	1862–68
Archibald Campbell Tait	1868–82
Edward White Benson	1883–96
Frederick Temple	1896–1902
Randall Thomas Davidson	1903–28
Cosmo Gordon Lang	1928–42
William Temple	1942–44
Geoffrey Francis Fisher	1945–61
(Arthur) Michael Ramsay	1961–74
(Frederick) Donald Coggan	1974–80
Robert Alexander Kennedy Runcie	1980–91
George Leonard Carey	1991–

*under whom allegiance to Rome was briefly restored

The Church of England

The Church of England has 105 bishops, over 10,800 full-time clergy (about 800 of whom are women) and about 16,100 churches. There are two provinces (Canterbury and York), each under an archbishop. The provinces are subdivided into dioceses: 30 in the province of Canterbury; 14 in York. The dioceses are:

Canterbury (archbishopric; Most Rev George Carey) covers E Kent; 195 clergy.

Bath and Wells (cathedral at Wells) covers Somerset; 255 clergy.

Birmingham covers Birmingham area; 230 clergy.

Bristol covers S Glos and N Wilts; 170 clergy.

Chelmsford covers Essex and E Grtr London; 470 clergy.

Chichester covers E and W Sussex; 355 clergy.

Coventry covers Warwicks and part of W Midlands; 170 clergy.

Derby covers Derbyshire (most of); 220 clergy.

Ely covers Cambs (most of), Hunts and part of Norfolk; 165 clergy.

Exeter covers Devon and part of Cornwall; 295 clergy.

Gloucester covers Glos (except S); 200 clergy.

Guildford covers W Surrey; 215 clergy.

Hereford covers Hereford and S Salop; 135 clergy.

Leicester covers Leics; 185 clergy.

Lichfield covers Staffs, N Salop and part of W Midlands; 410 clergy.

Lincoln covers Lincs; 250 clergy.

London covers N, NW and central Grtr London and part of Herts and Surrey; 605 clergy.

Norwich covers Norfolk (most of); 225 clergy.

Oxford covers Oxon, Berks and Bucks; 485 clergy.

Peterborough covers Norhants, Rutland and part of Cambs; 185 clergy.

Portsmouth covers SE Hants and IOW; 190 clergy.

Rochester covers E Kent and part of Grtr London; 245 clergy.

St Albans covers Herts (most of) and Beds; 330 clergy.

St Edmundsbury and Ipswich (cathedral at Bury St Edmunds) covers Suffolk; 200 clergy.

Salisbury covers S and central Wilts and Dorset (most of); 260 clergy.

Southwark covers E Surrey and S Grtr London; 430 clergy.

Truro covers Cornwall (most of); 140 clergy.

Winchester covers Hants (except SE), part of Dorset and Channel Isles; 260 clergy.

Worcester covers Worcs and part of W Midlands; 175 clergy.

(The province of Canterbury also includes the diocese of Gibraltar in Europe.)

York (archbishopric; Most Rev. David Hope) covers E Yorks and N Yorks (most of); 330 clergy.

Blackburn covers Lancs (most of) and part of Grtr Manchester; 280 clergy.

Bradford covers part of W Yorks and W part of N Yorks; 135 clergy.

Carlisle covers Cumbria; 175 clergy.

Chester covers Ches (most of), S Merseyside and S of Grtr Manchester; 310 clergy.

Durham covers Durham and S of Tyne and Wear; 280 clergy.

Liverpool covers Merseyside (except S) and parts of Lancs and Ches; 295 clergy.

Manchester covers central and E of Grtr Manchester; 355 clergy.

Newcastle covers Northd and N of Tyne and Wear; 180 clergy.

Ripon covers central N Yorks and part of W Yorks; 190 clergy.

Sheffield covers S Yorks and part of E Yorks and N Yorks; 240 clergy.

Sodor and Man (cathedral at Peel) covers IOM; 20 clergy.

Southwell covers Notts; 220 clergy.

Wakefield covers part of W Yorks; 205 clergy

THE CHURCH IN WALES

The Church in Wales is the Anglican Church in the Principality (established until 1920). It is headed by the Archbishop of Wales, who is at present elected by the six bishops from their own number. Future archbishops will also automatically hold the see of Llandaff. The current Archbishop of Wales is the Bishop of St Asaph (Most Rev. Alwyn Jones).

Bangor covers NW Wales; 70 clergy.

Llandaff covers S and central Glamorgan; 170 clergy.

Monmouth (cathedral at Newport) covers SE Wales; 110 clergy.

St Asaph covers NE Wales; 110 clergy.

St David's covers SW Wales; 130 clergy.

Swansea and Brecon (cathedral at Brecon) covers W Glamorgan and S Powys; 100 clergy.

THE EPISCOPAL CHURCH OF SCOTLAND

The Church of the Anglican tradition in Scotland was founded in 1690. It is headed by a Primus, elected by the seven bishops from their own number.

The current Primus is the Most Rev. Richard Holloway, Bishop of Edinburgh.

Aberdeen and Orkney (cathedral at Aberdeen) covers Aberdeenshire (most of), Orkney and Shetland; 15 clergy.

Argyll and the Isles (cathedral at Oban) covers Argyll and Bute; 10 clergy.

Brechin (cathedral at Dundee) covers Dundee and parts of Angus and Aberdeenshire; 15 clergy.

Edinburgh covers Stirling (part of), Falkirk, Edinburgh, the Lothians and Borders; 65 clergy.

Glasgow and Galloway (cathedral at Glasgow) covers SE Scotland; 45 clergy.

Moray, Ross and Caithness (cathedral at Inverness) covers Highland, Moray and Western Isles; 15 clergy.

St Andrews, Dunkeld and Dunblane (cathedral at Perth) covers Perthshire and Kinross, Fife, Clackmannan; 30 clergy.

THE ROMAN CATHOLIC CHURCH

In Great Britain, there are seven archbishops, 39 bishops, about 7200 priests, about 3300 priests and lay brothers in religious orders, over 12,500 nuns, over 3500 churches, and over 5,000,000 practising members. About 9% of the population of the UK belongs to the Roman Catholic Church. The head of the Church in England and Wales is the Archbishop of Westminster, and in Scotland, the Archbishop of St Andrews and Edinburgh.

Archbishops of Westminster

Cardinal Nicholas Wiseman	1850–65
Cardinal Henry Edward Manning	1865–92
Cardinal Herbert Vaughan	1892–1903
Cardinal Francis Bourne	1903–35
Cardinal Arthur Hinsley	1935–43
Cardinal Bernard William Griffin	1943–56
Cardinal William Godfrey	1956–63
Cardinal John Carmel Heenan	1963–76
Cardinal (George) Basil Hume	1976–

In England and Wales

There are five archdioceses and 17 other dioceses.

Westminster (archbishopric; HE Cardinal (George) Basil Hume, OSB) covers Central, W, N and NW Grtr London, Herts and part of Surrey; 830 clergy; **Brentwood** covers Essex and E part of Grtr London; 185 clergy; **East Anglia** (cathedral at Norwich) covers Cambs, Hunts, Norfolk, Suffolk; 130 clergy; **Northampton** covers Beds, Bucks, Northants, part of Berks; 160 clergy; **Nottingham** covers Derbys (most of), Leics, Lincs, Notts (most of) and Rutland; 225 clergy.

Birmingham (archbishopric) covers W Midlands, Staffs, Warwicks, Worcs, Oxons (N of Thames); 495 clergy; **Clifton** (cathedral at Bristol) covers Glos, Wilts and Somerset; 255 clergy; **Shrewsbury** covers Salop, Ches (most of), S Merseyside and parts of Grtr Manchester and Derbys; 220 clergy.

Cardiff (archbishopric) covers SE Wales and Hereford; 140 clergy.; **Menevia** (cathedral at Swansea) covers SW and mid Wales; 60 clergy; **Wrexham** covers N Wales; 95 clergy.

Liverpool (archbishopric) covers Merseyside (most of) and parts of Cheshire, Lancashire and Grtr Manchester; 555 clergy; **Hallam** (cathedral at Sheffield) covers S Yorks, N Notts and parts of Derbys; 100 clergy; **Hexham and Newcastle** (cathedral at Newcastle) covers Durham, Northd and Tyne and Wear; 290 clergy; **Lancaster** covers N Lancs and Cumbria; 250 clergy; **Leeds** covers W Yorks and parts of N Yorks; 250 clergy; **Middlesbrough** covers E Yorks and most of N Yorks; 195 clergy; **Salford** covers most of Grtr Manchester and SE Lancs; 405 clergy.

Southwark (archbishopric) covers Grtr London S of Thames and Kent; 555 clergy; **Arundel and Brighton** (cathedral at Arundel) covers E and W Sussex and most of Surrey; 325 clergy; **Plymouth** covers Devon, Cornwall and most of Dorset; 160 clergy; **Portsmouth** covers Hampshire, Berks S of the Thames, Oxon S of the Thames, part of Dorset and the Channel Isles; 270 clergy.

In Scotland
There are two archdioceses and six other dioceses.

Glasgow (archbishopric; HE Cardinal Thomas Winning) covers Glasgow and former county of Dunbartonshire; 335 clergy; **Motherwell** covers N and S Lanarkshire; 190 clergy; **Paisley** covers former county of Renfrewshire; 95 clergy.

St Andrews and Edinburgh (archbishopric; cathedral at Edinburgh) covers SE and E central Scotland and S of Fife; 210 clergy; **Aberdeen** covers N and NE Scotland plus Orkney and Shetland; 60 clergy; **Argyll and the Isles** (cathedral at Oban) covers Argyll and Bute, Western Isles and SW Highland; 35 clergy; **Dunkeld** (cathedral at Dundee) covers Angus, Dundee, Perthshire and Kinross, N Fife; 65 clergy; **Galloway** (cathedral at Ayr) covers N, E and S Ayrshire, and Dumfries and Galloway; 75 clergy.

ROMAN CATHOLIC CHURCH IN IRELAND

There are four archdioceses and 22 other dioceses in the hierachy, which covers the whole island of Ireland.

Armagh (archdiocese; HE Cardinal Cahal Daly) 270 clergy; *Ardagh and Clonmacnois* (cathedral at Longford) 105 clergy; *Clogher* (cathedral at Monaghan) 120 clergy; *Derry* (cathedral at Londonderry) 145 clergy; *Down and Connor* (cathedral at Belfast) 70 clergy; *Dromore* (cathedral at Newry); *Kilmore* (cathedral at Cavan) 50 clergy; *Meath* (cathedral at Mullingar) 270 clergy; *Raphoe* (cathedral at Letterkenny) 100 clergy.

Cashel and Emly (archdiocese; cathedral at Thurles) 120 clergy; *Cloyne* (cathedral at Cobh) 105 clergy; *Cork and Ross* (cathedral at Cork) 360 clergy); *Kerry* (cathedral at Killarney) 140 clergy; *Killaloe* (cathedral at Ennis) 185 clergy; *Limerick* 230 clergy.

Dublin (archdiocese) 990 clergy; *Ferns* (cathedral at Enniscorthy) 145 clergy; *Kildare and Leighlin* (cathedral at Carlow) 225 clergy; *Ossory* (cathedral at Kilkenny) 125 clergy; *Waterford and Lismore* (cathedral at Waterford) 205 clergy.

Tuam (archdiocese) 165 clergy; *Achonry* (cathedral at Ballaghdereen) 55 clergy; *Clonfert* (cathedral at Loughrea) 75 clergy; *Elphin* (cathedral at Sligo) 100 clergy; *Galway and Kilmacduagh* (cathedral at Galway) 200 clergy; *Killala* (cathedral at Ballina) 50 clergy.

PRESBYTERIAN CHURCHES

About 3% of the British population belongs to the Presbyterian Churches including the Church of Scotland (see below). Other major Presbyterian Churches in the UK include the Presbyterian Church of Wales (the only Church of Welsh origin, it has about 130 ministers and over 970 churches), and the Presbyterian Church in Ireland.

The Church of Scotland – the Established Church in Scotland – is governed by kirk sessions, presbyteries (of which there are 47 at district level), and the General Assembly. A kirk session consists of the minister and the elected elders of each parish. There are about 1700 churches. Churches are grouped into 46 presbyteries, which consist of all the ministers in the district, one elder from each congregation in the district plus members of the diaconate. The annual General Assembly is presided over by the Moderator, who holds office for one year.

Moderator of the General Assembly (1995): Rt. Rev. James Harkness.

METHODIST CHURCHES

Some 2% of the British population belongs to Methodist Churches. Most Methodist congregations in the UK belong to the Methodist Church in Great Britain, which was formed in 1932 from the union of the Wesleyan Methodist Church, the Primitive Methodist Church and the United Methodist Church. It is governed by the annual Conference, by district synods, and by local circuit meetings. Other Methodist Churches include the Independent Methodist Church (which is Congregationalist in character) and the Wesleyan Reform Union (which is Methodist in doctrine, Congregationalist in its organization). In 1994, there were about 3600 Methodist ministers and over 6900 Methodist churches in the United Kingdom.

OTHER CHRISTIAN GROUPS

Other major Christian organizations combined in the UK account for about 4% of the population. They include:

The Baptist Union of Great Britain, which in 1994, had about 1800 pastors and 2100 churches.There are also separate Baptist Unions in Ireland (with about 70 pastors and 100 churches) and Wales (with about 115 pastors and 540 churches). There is also a (smaller) Baptist Union in Scotland.

The Congregational Federation, which includes those congregations in England and Wales that did not join the United Reformed Church in 1972. In 1994, the Federation had over 115 ministers and 310 churches.

The Salvation Army - founded by William Booth in 1865 – is characterized by a military-style organization. It is administered locally by colonels and over larger areas by commissioners and territorial commissioners who elect the world leader of the Army, the General. In 1994, there were about 1800 active officers and nearly 1000 places of worship in the UK.

The United Reformed Church was formed by the union of the Congregational Church in England and Wales and the Presbyterian Church of England. It is divided into 12 provinces. In 1994, there were about 800 full-time ministers and 1800 churches

ISLAM

About 2% of the population follows Islam, overwhelmingly Sunni Islam. In 1995, there were about 315 mosques in the United Kingdom.

JUDAISM

Less than 1% of the population practises Judaism. The representative body of British Judaism is the Board of Deputies of British Jews, established in 1760, and the leader is the Chief Rabbi. The Court of Judgement (the Beth Din) is a rabbinic body that arbitrates and gives religious judgements, e.g. in matters of marriage and dietary laws.

Sport

Information on international sport is given in the chapter beginning on p. 450.

ATHLETICS

National athletics records

UK national records (at May 1995) that are also World, Commonwealth, or European records have been noted: *w* = World record; *c* = Commonwealth record; *e* = European record.

Track events - men

	min:sec	
100m	9·87	Linford Christie 1994 *c, e*
200m	*19·87	John Regis 1994
400m	44·47	David Grindley 1992
800m	1:41·73	Sebastian Coe 1981 *w, c, e*
1000m	2:12·18	Sebastian Coe 1981 *w, c, e*
1500m	3:29·67	Steve Cram 1985*c, e*
1 mile	3:46·32	Steve Cram 1985*c, e*
2000m	4:51·39	Steve Cram 1985*c, e*
3000m	7:32·79	David Moorcroft 1982 *e*
5000m	13:00·41	David Moorcroft 1982 *c, e*
10,000m	27:23·06	Eamonn Martin 1988
20,000m	57:28·7	Carl Thackery 1990*c*
25,000m	1 hr 15:22·6	Ronald Hill 1965*c*
30,000m	1 hr 31:30·4	James Alder 1970*c, e*
1 hour	20,855 m	Carl Thackeray 1990 *c*
110m hurdles	12·91	Colin Jackson 1992 *w, c, e*
400m hurdles	47·82	Kriss Akabusi 1991
3000m steeplechase	8:07·96	Mark Rowland 1988
4 x 100m	37·77	National Team: C. Jackson, A. Jarrett, J. Regis, L. Christie 1993
4 x 200m	1:21·29	National Team: M. Adam, A. Mafe, L. Christie, J. Regis 1989
4 x 400m	2:57·53	National Team: R. Black, D. Redmond, J. Regis, K. Akabusi 1991 *c, e*
4 x 800m	7:03·89	National Team: P. Elliot, G. Cook, S. Cram, S. Coe 1982 *w, c, e*
4 x 1500m	14:56·8	National Team: A. Mottershead, G. M. Cooper, S. Emson,R. Wood 1979

Field events – men

	metres	
High jump	2·37	Stephen Smith 1992 *c*
Pole vault	5·65	Keith Stock 1981
Long jump	8·23	Lynn Davies 1968
Triple jump	*17·57	Keith Connor 1982 *c*
Shot	21·68	Geoffrey Capes 1980*c*
Discus	†64·32	William Tancred 1974
Hammer	77·54	Martin Girvan 1984*c*
Javelin	91·46	Stephen Backley 1992 *c*
Decathlon	8847 pts	Daley Thompson 1984 *c, e*

* set at high altitude; records at low altitude:
200m: 19·94 John Regis 1993, triple jump: 17·44m Jonathon Edwards 1993

† Willam Tancred threw 64·94m in 1974 and Richard Slaney threw 65·16 m in 1985 but neither of these throws were ratified.

Track events – women

	min:sec	
100m	11·10	Kathryn Smallwood (now Cook) 1981
200m	22·10	Kathryn Cook (*née* Smallwood) 1984
400m	49·43	Kathryn Cook 1984 *c*
800m	1:57·42	Kirsty McDermott (now Wade) 1985 *c*
1000m	2:33·70	Kirsty McDermott 1985 *c*
1500m	3:59·96	Zola Budd (now Pieterse) 1985 *c*
1 mile	4:17·57	Zola Budd (now Pieterse) 1985 *c*
2000m	5:26·93	Yvonne Murray 1994 *c*
3000m	8:28·83	Zola Budd (now Pieterse) 1985 *c*
5000m	14:48·07	Zola Budd (now Pieterse) 1985 *c*
10,000m	30:57·07	Elizabeth McColgan (*née* Lynch) 1991 *c*
100m hurdles	12·82	Sally Gunnell 1988
400m hurdles	52·74	Sally Gunnell 1991 *w, c, e*
4 x 100m	42·43	National Team: H. Hunte (now Oakes), K. Smallwood (now Cook), B. Goddard (now Callender), S. Lannaman 1980 *c*
4 x 200m	1:31·57	National Team: D. Hartley (*née* Murray), V. Elder (*née* Bernard), S. Colyear (now Danville), S. Lannaman 1977 *c*
4 x 400m	3:22·01	National Team: Phyllis Smith (*née* Watt), L. Hanson, L. Keough, S. Gunnell 1991
4 x 800m	8:19·9	National Team: A. Williams, P. Fryer, Y. Murray, D. Edwards

Field events – women

	metres	
High jump	1·95	Diana Elliot 1982
Pole vault	3·65	Kate Staples 1994
Long jump	6·90	Beverly Kinch 1983 *c*
Triple jump	14·08	Michelle Griffith 1994 *c*
	14·22	(unratified) Ashia Hansen 1994
Shot	19·36	Judith Oakes 1988
Discus	67·48	Margaret Ritchie 1981 *c*
Hammer	60·56	Lorraine Shaw 1995
Javelin	77·44	Fatima Whitbread 1986 *c*
Heptathlon	6623 pts	Judy Simpson (*née* Livermore) 1986

ASSOCIATION FOOTBALL

Domestic competitions in England are dominated by the professional Premier League and the Football League championships. The Football League was formed in 1888 with 12 teams and now has 71 teams divided between three divisions. The 22-team Premier League was formed from the former First Division of the Football League for the season 1992/3.

'Non-League' or semi-professional football is also widespread in England and Wales with the semi-professional GM Vauxhall Conference as the major competition. Promotion and relegation operate between the Premier League and the Football League, between the Football League and the GM Vauxhall Conference, and between the GM Vauxhall Conference and three regional leagues – the Beazer Homes League (in the south and west of England, Wales and the Midlands), the Diadora League (in the south of England) and the Unibond League (in the north of England).

ENGLISH FOOTBALL CHAMPIONS

Winners of the Football League:

1888/9	Preston North End
1889/90	Preston North End
1890/1	Everton
1891/2	Sunderland
1892/3	Sunderland
1893/4	Aston Villa
1894/5	Sunderland
1895/6	Aston Villa
1896/7	Aston Villa
1897/8	Sheffield United
1898/9	Aston Villa
1899/1900	Aston Villa
1900/1	Liverpool
1901/2	Sunderland
1902/3	Sheffield Wednesday
1903/4	Sheffield Wednesday
1904/5	Newcastle United
1905/6	Liverpool
1906/7	Newcastle United
1907/8	Manchester United
1908/9	Newcastle United
1909/10	Aston Villa
1910/1	Manchester United
1911/2	Blackburn Rovers
1912/3	Sunderland
1913/4	Blackburn Rovers
1914/5	Everton
1919/20	West Bromwich Albion
1920/1	Burnley
1921/2	Liverpool
1922/3	Liverpool
1923/4	Huddersfield Town
1924/5	Huddersfield Town
1925/6	Huddersfield Town
1926/7	Newcastle United
1927/8	Everton
1928/9	Sheffield Wednesday
1929/30	Sheffield Wednesday
1930/1	Arsenal
1931/2	Everton
1932/3	Arsenal
1933/4	Arsenal
1934/5	Arsenal
1935/6	Sunderland
1936/7	Manchester City
1937/8	Arsenal
1938/9	Everton
1946/7	Liverpool
1947/8	Arsenal
1948/9	Portsmouth
1949/50	Portsmouth
1950/1	Tottenham Hotspur
1951/2	Manchester United
1952/3	Arsenal
1953/4	Wolverhampton Wanderers
1954/5	Chelsea
1955/6	Manchester United
1956/7	Manchester United
1957/8	Wolverhampton Wanderers
1958/9	Wolverhampton Wanderers
1959/60	Burnley
1960/1	Tottenham Hotspur
1961/2	Ipswich Town
1962/3	Everton
1963/4	Liverpool
1964/5	Manchester United
1965/6	Liverpool
1966/7	Manchester United
1967/8	Manchester City
1968/9	Leeds United
1969/70	Everton
1970/1	Arsenal
1971/2	Derby County
1972/3	Liverpool
1973/4	Leeds United
1974/5	Derby County
1975/6	Liverpool
1976/7	Liverpool
1977/8	Nottingham Forest
1978/9	Liverpool
1979/80	Liverpool
1980/1	Aston Villa
1981/2	Liverpool
1982/3	Liverpool
1983/4	Liverpool
1984/5	Everton
1985/6	Liverpool
1986/7	Everton
1987/8	Liverpool
1988/9	Arsenal
1989/90	Liverpool
1990/1	Arsenal
1991/2	Leeds United

Winners of the Premier League:

1992/3	Manchester United
1993/4	Manchester United
1994/5	Blackburn Rovers

FA CUP WINNERS

Year	Winner
1872–3	Wanderers
1874	Oxford University
1875	Royal Engineers
1876–8	Wanderers
1879	Old Etonians
1880	Clapham Rovers
1881	Old Carthusians
1882	Old Etonians
1883	Blackburn Olympic
1884–6	Blackburn Rovers
1887	Aston Villa
1888	West Bromwich Albion
1889	Preston North End
1890–1	Blackburn Rovers
1892	West Bromwich Albion
1893	Wolverhampton Wanderers
1894	Notts County
1895	Aston Villa
1896	Sheffield Wednesday
1897	Aston Villa
1898	Nottingham Forest
1899	Sheffield United
1900	Bury
1901	Tottenham Hotspur
1902	Sheffield United
1903	Bury
1904	Manchester City
1905	Aston Villa
1906	Everton
1907	Sheffield Wednesday
1908	Wolverhampton Wanderers
1909	Manchester United
1910	Newcastle United
1911	Bradford City
1912	Barnsley
1913	Aston Villa
1914	Burnley
1915	Sheffield United
1920	Aston Villa
1921	Tottenham Hotspur
1922	Huddersfield Town
1923	Bolton Wanderers
1924	Newcastle United
1925	Sheffield United
1926	Bolton Wanderers
1927	Cardiff City
1928	Blackburn Rovers
1929	Bolton Wanderers
1930	Arsenal
1931	West Bromwich Albion
1932	Newcastle United
1933	Everton
1934	Manchester City
1935	Sheffield Wednesday
1936	Arsenal
1937	Sunderland
1938	Preston North End
1939	Portsmouth
1946	Derby County
1947	Charlton Athletic
1948	Manchester United
1949	Wolverhampton Wanderers
1950	Arsenal
1951–2	Newcastle United
1953	Blackpool
1954	West Bromwich Albion
1955	Newcastle United
1956	Manchester City
1957	Aston Villa
1958	Bolton Wanderers
1959	Nottingham Forest
1960	Wolverhampton Wanderers
1961–2	Tottenham Hotspur
1963	Manchester United
1964	West Ham United
1965	Liverpool
1966	Everton
1967	Tottenham Hotspur
1968	West Bromwich Albiont
1969	Manchester City
1970	Chelsea
1971	Arsenal
1972	Leeds United
1973	Sunderland
1974	Liverpool
1975	West Ham United
1976	Southampton
1977	Manchester United
1978	Ipswich Town
1979	Arsenal
1980	West Ham United
1981–2	Tottenham Hotspur
1983	Manchester United
1984	Everton
1985	Manchester United
1986	Liverpool
1987	Coventry City
1988	Wimbledon
1989	Liverpool
1990	Manchester United
1991	Tottenham Hotspur
1992	Liverpool
1993	Arsenal
1994	Manchester United
1995	Everton

The FA Challenge Cup – which is open to all senior clubs in England and Wales – was introduced in 1871, 17 years before the birth of the Football League. The final has been played at Wembley Stadium since 1923. Winners are listed above.

The Coca Cola (previously League, Milk, Littlewoods) Cup is competed for by members of the Premier and Football leagues and was instituted in 1960. Winners since 1988 have been:

1988	Luton Town
1989–90	Nottingham Forest
1991	Sheffield Wednesday
1992	Manchester United
1993	Arsenal
1994	Aston Villa
1995	Liverpool

The Scottish League – now comprising 40 teams in four divisions – was founded in 1890. Entrance to the Scottish League is by election rather than promotion. Winners of the First Division (to 1974/5) and of the Premier Division (since that date) are listed in the accompanying box.

The Scottish Cup was started in 1873. The final has been held at Hampden Park since World War I (except for 1921 when it was played at Celtic Park and 1924 when it was played at Ibrox Park). Winners are listed in the accompanying box.

The FA Trophy is competed for by the semi-professional clubs in England and Wales. The FA Vase is open to other non-League clubs.

SCOTTISH LEAGUE CHAMPIONS

Champions of the First Division (1890/1–1974/5) and the Premier Division (since 1975/6) have been:

Aberdeen 1954/5, 1979/80, 1983/4, 1984/5

Dumbarton 1890/1 (shared), 1891/2

Celtic 1892/3, 1893/4, 1895/6, 1897/8, 1904/5, 1905/6, 1906/7, 1907/8, 1908/9, 1909/10, 1913/4, 1914/5, 1915/6, 1916/7, 1918/9, 1921/2, 1925/6, 1935/6, 1937/8, 1953/4, 1965/6, 1966/7, 1967/8, 1968/9, 1969/70, 1970/1, 1971/2, 1972/3, 1973/4, 1976/7, 1978/9, 1980/1, 1981/2, 1985/6, 1987/8

Dundee 1961/2

Dundee United 1982/3

Hearts 1894/5, 1896/7, 1957/8, 1959/60

Hibernian 1902/3, 1947/8, 1950/1, 1951/2

Kilmarnock 1964/5

Motherwell 1931/2

Rangers 1890/1 (shared), 1898/9, 1899/1900, 1900/1, 1901/2, 1910/1, 1911/2, 1912/3, 1917/8, 1919/20, 1920/1, 1922/3, 1923/4, 1924/5, 1926/7, 1927/8, 1928/9, 1929/30, 1930/1, 1932/3, 1933/4, 1934/5, 1936/7, 1938/9, 1946/7, 1948/9, 1949/50, 1952/3, 1955/6, 1956/7, 1958/9, 1960/1, 1962/3, 1963/4, 1974/5, 1975/6, 1977/8, 1986/7, 1988/9, 1989/90, 1990/1, 1991/2, 1992/3, 1993/4, 1994/5

Third Lanark 1903/4

SCOTTISH FA CUP WINNERS

Winners of the Scottish FA Cup since 1874 have been:

Aberdeen 1947, 1970, 1982, 1983, 1984, 1986, 1990
Airdrieonians 1924
Dumbarton 1883
Celtic 1892, 1899, 1900, 1904, 1907, 1908, 1909, 1911, 1912, 1914, 1923, 1925, 1927, 1931, 1933, 1937, 1951, 1954, 1955, 1965, 1967, 1969, 1971, 1972, 1974, 1975, 1977, 1980, 1985, 1988, 1989, 1995
Clyde 1939, 1958
Dundee 1910
Dundee United 1994
Dunfermline Athletic 1961, 1968
East Fife 1938
Falkirk 1913, 1957
Hearts 1891, 1896, 1901, 1906, 1956
Hibernian 1887, 1902
Kilmarnock 1920, 1929
Morton 1922
Motherwell 1952, 1991
Partick Thistle 1921
Queen's Park 1874, 1875, 1876, 1880, 1881, 1882, 1884, 1886, 1890, 1893
Rangers 1894, 1897, 1898, 1903, 1928, 1930, 1932, 1934, 1935, 1936, 1948, 1949, 1950, 1953, 1960, 1962, 1963, 1964, 1966, 1973, 1976, 1978, 1979, 1981, 1992, 1993
Renton 1885, 1888
St Bernard's 1895
St Mirren 1926, 1959, 1987
Third Lanark 1889, 1905
Vale of Leven 1877, 1878, 1879

CRICKET

There are four English domestic competitions. The County Championship, a league of the 18 first-class counties with matches over four days (from 1993); the one-day knockouts of the Nat. West (previously Gillette) Trophy of 60-over matches and the Benson & Hedges of 55; and the one-day Sunday League formerly sponsored by John Player (1969–86) and Refuge Assurance (1987–91); under a new sponsor (Axa Equity and Law games were increased from 40 to 50 overs per innings in 1993 but went back to 40 overs in 1994). Winners of these competitions are listed in the accompanying boxes.

SUNDAY LEAGUE WINNERS

Winners
Derbyshire 1990
Durham no wins
Essex 1981, 1984, 1985
Glamorgan 1973
Gloucestershire no wins
Hampshire 1975, 1978, 1986
Kent 1972, 1973, 1976
Lancashire 1969, 1970, 1989
Leicestershire 1974, 1977
Middlesex 1992
Northamptonshire no wins
Nottinghamshire 1991
Somerset 1979
Surrey no wins
Sussex 1982
Warwickshire 1980, 1994
Worcestershire no wins
Yorkshire 1983

COUNTY CHAMPIONS

From 1864, when eight counties took part in inter-county matches, to 1889, champion counties were proclaimed, principally on the basis of fewest points lost. It was not until 1890 that the county championship was officially recognized and a points system introduced.

Winners
Derbyshire 1936
Durham no wins
Essex 1979, 1983, 1984, 1986, 1991, 1992
Glamorgan 1948, 1969
Gloucestershire 1873=, 1874, 1876, 1877
Hampshire 1961, 1973
Kent 1906, 1909, 1910, 1913, 1970, 1977=, 1978
Lancashire 1879=, 1881, 1882=, 1889=, 1897, 1904, 1926, 1927, 1928, 1930, 1934, 1950=
Leicestershire 1975
Middlesex 1866, 1903, 1920, 1921, 1947, 1949=, 1976, 1977=, 1980, 1982, 1985, 1990, 1993
Northamptonshire no wins
Nottinghamshire 1865, 1868, 1869=, 1871, 1872, 1873=, 1875, 1879=, 1880, 1882=, 1883, 1884, 1885, 1886, 1889=, 1907, 1929, 1981, 1987
Somerset no wins
Surrey 1864, 1887, 1888, 1889=, 1890, 1891, 1892, 1894, 1895, 1899, 1914, 1950=, 1952, 1953, 1954, 1955, 1956, 1957, 1958, 1971
Sussex no wins
Warwickshire 1911, 1951, 1972, 1994
Worcestershire 1964, 1965, 1974, 1988, 1989
Yorkshire 1867, 1869=, 1870, 1893, 1896, 1898, 1900, 1901, 1902, 1905, 1908, 1912, 1919, 1922, 1923, 1924, 1925, 1931, 1932, 1933, 1935, 1937, 1938, 1939, 1946, 1949=, 1959, 1960, 1962, 1963, 1966, 1967, 1968

BENSON & HEDGES CUP WINNERS

Winners
Combined Universities no wins
Derbyshire 1993
Durham no wins
Essex 1979
Glamorgan no wins
Gloucestershire 1977
Hampshire 1988, 1992
Ireland no wins
Kent 1973, 1976, 1978
Lancashire 1984, 1990
Leicestershire 1972, 1975, 1985
Middlesex 1983, 1986, 1992
Minor Counties no wins
Northamptonshire 1980
Nottinghamshire 1989
Scotland no wins
Somerset 1981, 1982
Surrey 1974
Sussex no win
Warwickshire 1994
Worcestershire 1991
Yorkshire 1987

Matches involving Oxford and Cambridge Universities are also considered to be first class.

GILLETTE/NATWEST CUP WINNERS

Winners
Derbyshire 1981
Durham none
Essex 1985
Glamorgan none
Gloucestershire 1973
Hampshire 1991
Kent 1967, 1974
Lancashire 1970, 1971, 1972, 1975, 1990
Leicestershire none
Middlesex 1977, 1980, 1984, 1988
Northamptonshire 1976, 1992
Nottinghamshire 1987
Somerset 1979, 1983
Surrey 1982
Sussex 1963, 1964, 1978, 1986
Warwickshire 1966, 1968, 1989, 1993
Worcestershire 1994
Yorkshire 1965, 1969

GOLF

For a list of the winners of the British Open see the chapter on international sport beginning on p. 450.

HORSE RACING

In Britain the Jockey Club is now the governing body of flat racing, steeplechasing and hurdle racing, having merged with the National Hunt Committee in 1968. The flat racing season in Britain takes place between late March and early November. Thoroughbreds may not run until they are two years old. The five classic races are the Two Thousand Guineas and the One Thousand Guineas (held at Newmarket over 1600 m (1 mile), the Derby and the Oaks (held at Epsom over 2400 m (1½ miles) and the St Leger (held at Doncaster over 2800 m (1¾ miles).

Steeplechase and hurdle races are run over distances of 2 or more miles, with at least one ditch and six birch fences for every mile. The UK National Hunt season can last from early August to 1st June, and the two most important steeplechases are the Grand National, first run in 1839, at Aintree over a course of 7220 m (4 miles 856 yd) with 30 jumps, and the Gold Cup run over 5·2 km (3¼ miles) at Cheltenham.

The premier British hurdle race is the Champion Hurdle, held annually over 3·2 km (2 miles) at Cheltenham. Recent winners of major races are listed below. (The name of the jockey is given in brackets.)

The Derby (winners since 1980)
1980 Henbit (Willie Carson)
1981 Shergar (Walter Swinburn)
1982 Golden Fleece (Pat Eddery)
1983 Teenoso (Lester Piggott)
1984 Secreto (Christy Roche)
1985 Slip Anchor (Steve Cauthen)
1986 Shahrastani (Walter Swinburn)
1987 Reference Point (Steve Cauthen)
1988 Kahyasi (Ray Cochrane)
1989 Nashwan (Willie Carson)
1990 Quest for Fame (Pat Eddery)
1991 Generous (Alan Munro)

1992 Dr Devious (John Reid)
1993 Commander in Chief (Michael Kinane)
1994 Erhaab (Willie Carson)

Grand National (winners since 1980)
1980 Ben Nevis (Charlie Fenwick)
1981 Aldaniti (Bob Champion)
1982 Grittar (Dick Saunders)
1983 Corbiere (Ben De Haan)
1984 Hallo Dandy (Neale Doughty)
1985 Last Suspect (Hywel Davies)
1986 West Tip (Richard Dunwoody)
1987 Maori Venture (Steve Knight)
1988 Rhyme N'Reason (Brendan Powell)
1989 Little Polveir (Jimmy Frost)
1990 Mr Frisk (Marcus Armytage)
1991 Seagram (Nigel Hawke)
1992 Party Politics (Carl Llewellyn)
1993 race cancelled
1994 Miinnehoma (Richard Dunwoody)
1995 Royal Athlete (Jason Titley)

Cheltenham Gold Cup (winners since 1980)
1980 Master Smudge (Richard Hoare)
1981 Little Owl (Jim Wilson)
1982 Silver Buck (Robert Earnshaw)
1983 Bregawn (Graham Bradley)
1984 Burrough Hill Lad (Phil Tuck)
1985 Forgive 'N' Forget (Martin Dwyer)
1986 Dawn Run (Jonjo O'Neill)
1987 The Thinker (Ridley Lamb)
1988 Charter Party (Richard Dunwoody)
1989 Desert Orchid (Simon Sherwood)
1990 Norton's Coin (Graham McCourt)
1991 Garrison Savannah (Mark Pitman)
1992 Cool Ground (Adrian Maguire)
1993 Jodami (Mark Dwyer)
1994 The Fellow (Adam Kondrat)
1995 Master Oats (Norman Williamson)

RUGBY LEAGUE

RUGBY LEAGUE CHAMPIONS

Batley 1923/4
Bradford Northern 1979/80, 1980/1
Dewsbury 1972/3
Featherstone Rovers 1976/7
Halifax 1906/7, 1964/5, 1985/6
Huddersfield 1911/2, 1912/3, 1914/5, 1928/9, 1929/30, 1948/9, 1961/2
Hull 1919/20, 1920/1, 1935/6, 1955/6, 1957/8, 1982/3
Hull Kingston Rovers 1922/3, 1924/5, 1978/9, 1983/4, 1984/5
Hunslet 1907/8, 1937/8
Leeds 1960/1, 1968/9, 1971/2
Leigh 1905/6, 1981/2
Oldham 1909/10, 1910/1, 1956/7
St Helens 1931/2, 1952/3, 1958/9, 1965/6, 1969/70, 1970/1, 1974/5
Salford 1913/4, 1932/3, 1936/7, 1938/9, 1973/4, 1975/6
Wakefield Trinity 1966/7, 1967/8
Warrington 1947/8, 1953/4, 1954/5
Widnes 1987/8, 1988/9
Wigan 1908/9, 1921/2, 1925/6, 1933/4, 1945/6, 1946/7, 1949/50, 1951/2, 1959/60, 1986/7, 1987/8, 1989/90, 1990/1, 1991/2, 1992/3, 1993/4,1994/5
Workington Town 1950/1

The major domestic rugby league trophies are the Challenge Cup (instituted 1897), the League Championship (instituted 1907), the Premiership Trophy (instituted 1975) and the Regal Trophy (formerly John Player Trophy; instituted 1972).

Challenge Cup Winners (from 1980)
1980 Hull Kingston Rovers
1981 Widnes
1982 Hull
1983 Featherstone Rovers
1984 Widnes
1985 Wigan
1986 Castleford
1987 Halifax
1988–95 Wigan

RUGBY UNION

The International Rugby Football Board was formed in 1890. Teams representing the British Isles have toured Australia, New Zealand and South Africa since 1888, although they were not composed of players from all the Home Countries until 1924, when the term 'British Lions' was first coined.

The International Championship – between England, Ireland, Scotland, and Wales – was first held in 1884, with France included from 1910. Now also known as the Five Nations tournament, the 'Grand Slam' – winning all four matches – is prized. The 'Triple Crown' is achieved when a Home Country side defeats the other three.

International Championship
Winners (outright/shared wins)

Wales (22/11)	1893, 1900, 1902, 1905, 1906*, 1908–9, 1911, 1920*, 1922, 1931, 1932*, 1936, 1939*, 1947*, 1950, 1952, 1954*–5*, 1956, 1964*, 1965–6, 1969, 1970*, 1971, 1973*, 1975–6, 1978–9, 1988*, 1994
England (21/9)	1883–4, 1886*, 1890*, 1892, 1910, 1912*, 1913–4, 1921, 1923–4, 1928, 1930, 1932*, 1934, 1937, 1939*, 1947*, 1953, 1954*, 1957–8, 1960*, 1963, 1973*, 1980, 1991–2, 1995
Scotland (13/8)	1886*, 1887, 1890*, 1891, 1895, 1901, 1903–4, 1907, 1920*, 1925, 1926*–7*, 1929, 1933, 1938, 1964*, 1973*, 1984, 1986*, 1990
Ireland (10/8)	1894, 1896, 1899, 1906*, 1912*, 1926*–7*, 1932*, 1935, 1939*, 1948–9, 1951, 1973*, 1974, 1982, 1983*, 1985
France (10/8)	1954*, 1955*, 1959*, 1960*, 1961–2, 1967–8, 1970*, 1973*, 1977, 1981, 1983*, 1986*, 1987, 1988*, 1989, 1993

* denotes shared win (there was a quintuple tie in 1973)

The championships of 1885, 1888–9, 1897–8 and 1972 were not completed for various reasons.

Grand Slam

A Five Nations country has defeated the other four countries during one season as follows:

England (11)	1913–14, 1921, 1923–4, 1928, 1957,1980, 1991–2, 1995
Wales (8)	1908–9†, 1911, 1950, 1952, 1971, 1976, 1978
France (4)	1968, 1977, 1981, 1987
Scotland (3)	1925, 1984, 1990
Ireland (1)	1948

†not including France at that time

The majority of English clubs participate in the Courage Leagues, comprising five national leagues of 10 clubs, two regional leagues, and a pyramid of divisional and county leagues. Courage League champions have been:

1985/6	Gloucester	1990/1	Bath
1986/7	Bath	1991/2	Bath
1987/8	Leicester	1992/3	Bath
1988/9	Bath	1993/4	Bath
1989/90	Wasps	1994/5	Leicester

Since 1971/2 the major clubs and winners of county cup competitions have competed in the RFU Knockout Competition (known from 1971 to 1988 as the John Player Special Cup and since 1988 as the Pilkington Cup). Winners have been:

1972	Gloucester
1973–74	Coventry
1975	Bedford
1976–77	Newcastle Gosforth
1978	Gloucester
1979–81	Leicester
1982	Gloucester and Moseley (shared)
1983	Bristol
1984–87	Bath
1988	Harlequins
1989–90	Bath
1991	Harlequins
1992	Bath
1993	Leicester
1994–95	Bath

The premier competition in Scotland is the McEwans League which began in 1973/4. The eight divisions of the league stand at the top of a pyramid of local competitions. Winners have been:

1973/4	Hawick	1984/5	Hawick
1974/5	Hawick	1985/6	Hawick
1975/6	Hawick	1986/7	Hawick
1976/7	Hawick	1987/8	Kelso
1977/8	Hawick	1988/9	Kelso
1978/9	Heriot's Former Pupils	1989/90	Melrose
1979/80	Gala	1990/1	Boroughmuir
1980/1	Gala	1991/2	Melrose
1981/2	Hawick	1992/3	Melrose
1982/3	Gala	1993/4	Melrose
1983/4	Hawick	1994/5	Stirling County

The (knockout) Welsh Rugby Union Challenge Cup (formerly the Schweppes Cup, Swalec Cup from 1992/3) was first competed in 1971/2. Winners have been;

1971/2	Neath	1984/5	Llanelli
1972/3	Llanelli	1985/6	Cardiff
1973/4	Llanelli	1986/7	Cardiff
1975/6	Llanelli	1987/8	Llanelli
1976/7	Newport	1988/9	Neath
1977/8	Swansea	1989/90	Neath
1978/9	Bridgend	1990/1	Llanelli
1979/80	Bridgend	1991/2	Llanelli
1980/1	Cardiff	1992/3	Llanelli
1981/2	Cardiff	1993/4	Cardiff
1982/3	Pontypool	1994/5	Swansea
1983/4	Cardiff		

Since 1990/1 there has also been a league system in Wales with various local competitions feeding the national league. Champions have been:

1990/1	Neath	1993/4	Swansea
1991/2	Swansea	1994/5	Cardiff
1992/3	Llanelli		

TENNIS

For a list of Wimbledon champions see the chapter on international sport beginning on p. 450.

BRITISH NATIONAL SWIMMING RECORDS

MEN
Freestyle
min:sec
50 m; 22·43; Mark Foster 1992
100 m; 50·24; Michael Wenham Fibbens 1992
200 m; 1:48·84; Paul Palmer 1993
400 m; 3:48·14; Paul Palmer 1993
800 m; 8:0·63; Ian Wilson 1991
1500 m; 15:03·72; Ian Wilson 1991
4 × 100 m; 3:21·41; GB team (Michael Wenham Fibbens, Mark Andrew Foster, Paul Howe, Roland Lee) 1992
4 × 200 m; 7:22·57; GB team (Paul Palmer, Steven Mellor, Stephen Akers, Paul Howe) 1992
Breaststroke
100 m; 1:1·33; Nicholas Gillingham 1992
200 m; 2:11·29; Nicholas Gillingham 1992
Butterfly
100 m; 53·30; Andrew Jameson 1988
200 m; 2:0·21; Philip Hubble 1981
Backstroke
100 m; 55·0; Martin Harris 1995
200 m; 1:59·52; Adam Ruckwood at Sheffield 1995
Medley
200 m; 2:3·20; Neil Cochran 1988
400 m; 4:24·20; John Philip Davey 1987
4 × 100 m; 3:41·66; GB team (Martin Harris, Martin Gillingham, Mike Fibbens, Mark Foster) 1993

WOMEN
Freestyle
min:sec
50 m; 26·01; Caroline Woodcock 1989
100 m; 56·11; Karen Pickering 1992
200 m; 1:59·74; June Alexandra Croft 1982
400 m; 4:7·68; Sarah Hardcastle 1986
800 m; 8:24·77; Sarah Hardcastle 1986
1500 m; 16:39·46; Sarah Hardcastle 1994
4 × 100 m; 3:48·87; GB team (Karen Pickering, Sharron Davies, Caroline Woodcock, Joanne Coull) 1989
4 × 200 m; 8:3·7; England team (Annabelle Cripps, Sarah Hardcastle, Karen Marie Mellor, Zara Letitia Long) 1986
Breaststroke
100 m; 1:10·39; Susannah 'Suki' Brownsdon 1987
200 m; 2:30·63; Marie Hardiman 1994
Butterfly
100 m; 1:1·33; Madeleine Scarborough 1990
200 m; 2:11·97; Samantha Purvis 1984
Backstroke
100 metres; 1:3·49; Katherine Read 1992
200 m; 2:13·91; Katherine Read 1992
Medley
200 m; 2:17·21; Jean Cameron Hill 1986
400 m; 4:46·83; Sharron Davies 1980

INDEX

Emboldened figures indicate a main entry.

A

B

C

D

F

G

H

I

L

M

N

O

P

Q

R

S

T

U

Z